DICTIONARY OF AMERICAN BIOGRAPHY

AMERICAN
COUNCIL
★ OF ★
LEARNED
SOCIETIES

DICTIONARY
OF AMERICAN BIOGRAPHY

The *Dictionary of American Biography* was published originally in twenty volumes. Supplementary volumes were added in 1944 and 1958. This edition of the work combines all twenty-two volumes.

The present Volume I (Abbe–Brazer) contains Volumes I and II of the original edition, but these are now denominated "Part 1" and "Part 2" of the Volume. Volumes II through XI are arranged similarly, the Second Part in each instance representing a volume of the original series. For ease in reference, although the articles follow one another in strict alphabetical order, each Second Part is preceded by a half-title page which relates that Part to its place in the original numbering of the volumes.

The Errata list at the head of Volume I contains corrections of fact and additional data which have come to the attention of the Editors from the first publication of the work up to the present. Minor typographical corrections have been made in many instances directly on the plates.

PUBLISHED UNDER THE AUSPICES OF
THE AMERICAN COUNCIL OF LEARNED SOCIETIES

The American Council of Learned Societies, organized in 1919 for the purpose of advancing the study of the humanities and of the humanistic aspects of the social sciences, is a nonprofit federation comprising forty-five national scholarly groups. The Council represents the humanities in the United States in the International Union of Academies, provides fellowships and grants-in-aid, supports research-and-planning conferences and symposia, and sponsors special projects and scholarly publications.

MEMBER ORGANIZATIONS
AMERICAN PHILOSOPHICAL SOCIETY, 1743
AMERICAN ACADEMY OF ARTS AND SCIENCES, 1780
AMERICAN ANTIQUARIAN SOCIETY, 1812
AMERICAN ORIENTAL SOCIETY, 1842
AMERICAN NUMISMATIC SOCIETY, 1858
AMERICAN PHILOLOGICAL ASSOCIATION, 1869
ARCHAEOLOGICAL INSTITUTE OF AMERICA, 1879
SOCIETY OF BIBLICAL LITERATURE, 1880
MODERN LANGUAGE ASSOCIATION OF AMERICA, 1883
AMERICAN HISTORICAL ASSOCIATION, 1884
AMERICAN ECONOMIC ASSOCIATION, 1885
AMERICAN FOLKLORE SOCIETY, 1888
AMERICAN DIALECT SOCIETY, 1889
AMERICAN PSYCHOLOGICAL ASSOCIATION, 1892
ASSOCIATION OF AMERICAN LAW SCHOOLS, 1900
AMERICAN PHILOSOPHICAL ASSOCIATION, 1901
AMERICAN ANTHROPOLOGICAL ASSOCIATION, 1902
AMERICAN POLITICAL SCIENCE ASSOCIATION, 1903
BIBLIOGRAPHICAL SOCIETY OF AMERICA, 1904
ASSOCIATION OF AMERICAN GEOGRAPHERS, 1904
HISPANIC SOCIETY OF AMERICA, 1904
AMERICAN SOCIOLOGICAL ASSOCIATION, 1905
AMERICAN SOCIETY OF INTERNATIONAL LAW, 1906
ORGANIZATION OF AMERICAN HISTORIANS, 1907
AMERICAN ACADEMY OF RELIGION, 1909
COLLEGE ART ASSOCIATION OF AMERICA, 1912
HISTORY OF SCIENCE SOCIETY, 1924
LINGUISTIC SOCIETY OF AMERICA, 1924
MEDIAEVAL ACADEMY OF AMERICA, 1925
AMERICAN MUSICOLOGICAL SOCIETY, 1934
SOCIETY OF ARCHITECTURAL HISTORIANS, 1940
ECONOMIC HISTORY ASSOCIATION, 1940
ASSOCIATION FOR ASIAN STUDIES, 1941
AMERICAN SOCIETY FOR AESTHETICS, 1942
AMERICAN ASSOCIATION FOR THE ADVANCEMENT OF SLAVIC STUDIES, 1948
METAPHYSICAL SOCIETY OF AMERICA, 1950
AMERICAN STUDIES ASSOCIATION, 1950
RENAISSANCE SOCIETY OF AMERICA, 1954
SOCIETY FOR ETHNOMUSICOLOGY, 1955
AMERICAN SOCIETY FOR LEGAL HISTORY, 1956
AMERICAN SOCIETY FOR THEATRE RESEARCH, 1956
SOCIETY FOR THE HISTORY OF TECHNOLOGY, 1958
AMERICAN COMPARATIVE LITERATURE ASSOCIATION, 1960
AMERICAN SOCIETY FOR EIGHTEENTH-CENTURY STUDIES, 1969
ASSOCIATION FOR JEWISH STUDIES, 1969

DICTIONARY

OF

American Biography

VOLUME VII

MILLS - PLATNER

Edited by

DUMAS MALONE

Charles Scribner's Sons *New York*

Prompted solely by a desire for public service the New York Times Company and its President, Mr. Adolph S. Ochs, have made possible the preparation of the manuscript of the Dictionary of American Biography through a subvention of more than $500,000 and with the understanding that the entire responsibility for the contents of the volumes rests with the American Council of Learned Societies.

VOLUME VII, PART 1
MILLS - OGLESBY

(VOLUME XIII OF THE ORIGINAL EDITION)

CROSS REFERENCES FROM THIS VOL-
UME ARE MADE TO THE VOLUME
NUMBERS OF THE ORIGINAL EDITION.

CONTRIBUTORS
VOLUME VII, PART 1

Charles G. Abbot	C. G. A.	Sarah G. Bowerman	S. G. B.
Willis J. Abbot	W. J. A.	Walter Russell Bowie	W. R. B.
Thomas P. Abernethy	T. P. A.	Julian P. Boyd	J. P. B.
Adeline Adams	A. A.	William K. Boyd	W. K. B.
James Truslow Adams	J. T. A.	William L. Boyden	W. L. B.
Daniel Dulany Addison	D. D. A.	William Bridgwater	W. B—r.
Nelson F. Adkins	N. F. A.	Crane Brinton	C. B—n.
Cyrus Adler	C. A.	Ruth Lee Briscoe	R. L. B.
Robert Greenhalgh Albion	R. G. A.	Robert Bruce	R. B.
Carroll S. Alden	C. S. A.	Solon J. Buck	S. J. B.
John Lincoln Alger	J. L. A.	John W. Buckham	J. W. B.
Harold M. Anderson	H. M. A.	Charles W. Burr	C. W. B.
Neal L. Anderson	N. L. A.	Huntington Cairns	H. Ca—s.
John Clark Archer	J. C. A—h—r.	Robert G. Caldwell	R. G. C—l.
Percy M. Ashburn	P. M. A.	Earnest Elmo Calkins	E. E. Ca—s.
Astley P. C. Ashhurst	A. P. C. A.	Lester J. Cappon	L. J. C.
Clifford W. Ashley	C. W. A.	Harry J. Carman	H. J. C.
Frederick W. Ashley	F. W. A.	William S. Carpenter	W. S. C.
Albert W. Atwood	A. W. A.	Charles Joseph Chamberlain	C. J. C.
Warren O. Ault	W. O. A.	Charles E. Chapman	C. E. C.
Joseph Cullen Ayer	J. C. Ay—r.	Edward P. Cheyney	E. P. C.
William F. Bade	W. F. B.	Francis A. Christie	F. A. C.
Edward M. Bailey	E. M. B.	Robert C. Clark	R. C. C.
Roland H. Bainton	R. H. B.	Rudolf A. Clemen	R. A. C.
Horace B. Baker	H. B. B.	Ernest W. Clement	E. W. C.
Ray Palmer Baker	R. P. B.	Harry Clemons	H. Cl—s.
Hayes Baker-Crothers	H. B–C.	Oral Sumner Coad	O. S. C.
Thomas S. Barclay	T. S. B.	Collier Cobb	C. C.
Lewellys F. Barker	L. F. B.	Frederick W. Coburn	F. W. C.
Gilbert H. Barnes	G. H. B.	Robert P. Tristram Coffin	R. P. T. C.
Claribel R. Barnett	C. R. B.	Fannie L. Gwinner Cole	F. L. G. C.
Adriaan J. Barnouw	A. J. B—w.	Rossetter G. Cole	R. G. C—e.
Allen J. Barthold	A. J. B—d.	Christopher B. Coleman	C. B. C.
Clarence Bartlett	C. B—t.	John R. Commons	J. R. C.
George A. Barton	G. A. B.	Robert Spencer Cotterill	R. S. C.
Robert Duncan Bass	R. D. B.	George S. Cottman	G. S. C.
Frances Bates	F. B.	Theodore S. Cox	T. S. C.
William G. Bean	W. G. B.	Katharine Elizabeth Crane	K. E. C.
W. J. Bender	W. J. B.	Verner W. Crane	V. W. C.
Orval Bennett	O. B.	Abigail Curlee	A. C.
Adolph B. Benson	A. B. B.	Edward E. Curtis	E. E. Cu—s.
Percy W. Bidwell	P. W. B.	Robert E. Cushman	R. E. C.
Alan Rogers Blackmer	A. R. B.	Arthur B. Darling	A. B. D.
Helen C. Boatfield	H. C. B.	Donald Davidson	D. D.
Ernest Ludlow Bogart	E. L. B.	Arthur Powell Davis	A. P. D.
Charles K. Bolton	C. K. B.	Richard E. Day	R. E. D.
Milledge Louis Bonham, Jr.	M. L. B., Jr.	Charles A. Dinsmore	C. A. D.
Witt Bowden	W. B—n.	Roland B. Dixon	R. B. D.
George F. Bowerman	G. F. B.	Eleanor Robinette Dobson	E. R. D.

Contributors

WILLIAM HOWE DOWNES	W. H. D—s.	GURNEY C. GUE	G. C. G.
DONALD MARQUAND DOZER	D. M. D.	CHARLES BURTON GULICK	C. B. G.
STELLA M. DRUMM	S. M. D.	CHARLES W. HACKETT	C. W. H.
LOUISE B. DUNBAR	L. B. D.	LE ROY R. HAFEN	L. R. H.
WALDO H. DUNN	W. H. D—n	PHILIP M. HAMER	P. M. H.
LIONEL C. DUREL	L. C. D.	J. G. deR. HAMILTON	J. G. deR. H.
GEORGE B. DUTTON	G. B. D.	WILLIAM A. HAMMOND	W. A. H.
EDWARD DWIGHT EATON	E. D. E.	ALVIN F. HARLOW	A. F. H.
WALTER PRICHARD EATON	W. P. E.	GEORGE M. HARPER	G. M. H.
EDWIN FRANCIS EDGETT	E. F. E.	ALBERT BUSHNELL HART	A. B. H.
GRANVILLE D. EDWARDS	G. D. E.	FREEMAN H. HART	F. H. H.
MARTIN EGAN	M. E—n.	MARY BRONSON HARTT	M. B. H.
LUTHER P. EISENHART	L. P. E.	MARGARET HARWOOD	M. H.
THOMPSON C. ELLIOTT	T. C. E.	DANIEL C. HASKELL	D. C. H.
ELIZABETH BRECKENRIDGE ELLIS	E. B. E.	STEPHEN J. HERBEN	S. J. H.
MILTON ELLIS	M. E—s.	FREDERICK C. HICKS	F. C. H.
BARNETT A. ELZAS	B. A. E.	GRANVILLE HICKS	G. H.
JOHN NORRIS EVANS	J. N. E.	JOHN DONALD HICKS	J. D. H.
PAUL D. EVANS	P. D. E.	FREDERICK W. HODGE	F. W. H.
JOHN O. EVJEN	J. O. E.	RAYMOND HOLDEN	R. H.
CHARLES FAIRMAN	C. F.	JOHN HAYNES HOLMES	J. H. H.
PAUL PATTON FARIS	P. P. F.	OLIVER W. HOLMES	O. W. H.
HALLIE FARMER	H. F—r.	A. VAN DOREN HONEYMAN	A. V-D. H.
OSCAR W. FIRKINS	O. W. F.	STEPHEN HENRY HORGAN	S. H. H.
DANIEL MOORE FISK	D. M. F.	WALTER HOUGH	W. H.
EDWARD FITCH	E. F.	JOHN TASKER HOWARD	J. T. H.
JOHN E. FLITCROFT	J. E. F.	G. EVANS HUBBARD	G. E. H.
HENRY WILDER FOOTE	H. W. F.	ARTHUR W. HUMMEL	A. W. H.
ALLYN B. FORBES	A. B. F.	LOUIS C. HUNTER	L. C. H.
AMELIA C. FORD	A. C. F.	AUGUSTUS E. INGRAM	A. E. I.
HUGHELL E. W. FOSBROKE	H. E. W. F.	RAY W. IRWIN	R. W. I.
HAROLD N. FOWLER	H. N. F.	ASHER ISAACS	A. I.
L. WEBSTER FOX	L. W. F.	EDITH J. R. ISAACS	E. J. R. I.
PHILIP FRANKLIN	P. F.	JOSEPH JACKSON	J. J.
JOSEPH C. W. FRAZER	J. C. W. F.	ALFRED P. JAMES	A. P. J.
JOHN H. FREDERICK	J. H. F.	SMITH ELY JELLIFFE	S. E. J.
JOHN C. FRENCH	J. C. F.	HOWARD MUMFORD JONES	H. M. J.
HERBERT FRIEDMANN	H. F—n.	H. DONALDSON JORDAN	H. D. J.
CLAUDE M. FUESS	C. M. F.	JAMES R. JOY	J. R. J.
JOHN F. FULTON	J. F. F.	LOUIS C. KARPINSKI	L. C. K.
FRANKLIN DeR. FURMAN	F. DeR. F.	DELBERT KAY	D. K.
CAROLINE E. FURNESS	C. E. F.	LOUISE PHELPS KELLOGG	L. P. K.
HERBERT P. GALLINGER	H. P. G.	RAYNER W. KELSEY	R. W. K.
GILBERT J. GARRAGHAN	G. J. G.	ROLAND G. KENT	R. G. K.
CURTIS W. GARRISON	C. W. G.	JOHN KIERAN	J. K.
F. LYNWOOD GARRISON	F. L. G.	FISKE KIMBALL	F. K.
SAMUEL W. GEISER	S. W. G.	JOHN A. KROUT	J. A. K.
GEORGE HARVEY GENZMER	G. H. G.	L. B. KRUEGER	L. B. K.
W. J. GHENT	W. J. G.	LEONARD W. LABAREE	L. W. L.
GEORGE W. GOLER	G. W. G.	JOHN W. LANG	J. W. L.
CARDINAL GOODWIN	C. G.	HERBERT S. LANGFELD	H. S. L.
COLIN B. GOODYKOONTZ	C. B. G—z.	ALEXANDER S. LANGSDORF	A. S. L.
ARMISTEAD CHURCHILL GORDON, JR.	A. C. G., Jr	CONRAD H. LANZA	C. H. L.
KENNETH M. GOULD	K. M. G.	STEPHEN LEACOCK	S. L.
LOUIS H. GRAY	L. H. G.	MAX LERNER	M. L.
JOHN N. GREELY	J. N. G.	CHARLES LEE LEWIS	C. L. L.
EDWIN L. GREEN	E. L. G	FREDERIC THOMAS LEWIS	F. T. L.
		GEORGE M. LEWIS	G. M. L.

Contributors

W. Lee Lewis	W. L. L.	Leigh Page	L. P.
Arnold J. Lien	A. J. L.	Scott H. Paradise	S. H. P.
Anna Lane Lingelbach	A. L. L.	John I. Parcel	J. I. P.
Ella Lonn	E. L.	Stanley M. Pargellis	S. M. P.
Harry Miller Lydenberg	H. M. L.	John C. Parish	J. C. P.
Virginia MacAdam	V. M.	Charles W. Parker	C. W. P.
Helen McAfee	H. M.	Henry Bamford Parkes	H. B. P.
N. E. McClure	N. E. M.	John Jay Parry	J. J. P.
Roger P. McCutcheon	R. P. M.	Edward L. Parsons	E. L. P.
W. J. McGlothlin	W. J. M.	James W. Patton	J. W. P.
R. Tait McKenzie	R. T. M.	Charles O. Paullin	C. O. P.
John McNaugher	J. M.	Frederic Logan Paxson	F. L. P.
John H. T. McPherson	J. H. T. M.	C. C. Pearson	C. C. P.
James C. Malin	J. C. M.	James H. Peeling	J. H. P.
W. C. Mallalieu	W. C. M.	Dexter Perkins	D. P—s.
Arthur T. Mann	A. T. M.	Frederick T. Persons	F. T. P.
H. A. Marmer	H. A. M.	A. Everett Peterson	A. E. P.
Frederick H. Martens	F. H. M.	Robert H. Pfeiffer	R. H. P.
Lawrence Martin	L. M.	James M. Phalen	J. M. P.
Shailer Mathews	S. M—s.	David Philipson	D. P—n.
Robert Douthat Meade	R. D. M.	Paul Chrisler Phillips	P. C. P.
Albert B. Meredith	A. B. M—h.	David deSola Pool	D. deS. P.
Newton D. Mereness	N. D. M.	Arthur Pope	A. P.
Robert L. Meriwether	R. L. M.	Jermain G. Porter	J. G. P.
George P. Merrill	G. P. M.	Charles Shirley Potts	C. S. P.
Frank J. Metcalf	F. J. M.	Arthur Chilton Powell	A. C. P.
Perry Miller	P. M.	Edward Preble	E. P.
Edwin Mims, Jr.	E. M., Jr.	Herbert I. Priestley	H. I. P.
Broadus Mitchell	B. M.	Leon C. Prince	L. C. P.
Stewart Mitchell	S. M—l.	Richard J. Purcell	R. J. P.
Wilmot B. Mitchell	W. B. M.	Arthur Hobson Quinn	A. H. Q.
Carl W. Mitman	C. W. M.	Lowell Joseph Ragatz	L. J. R.
Conrad Henry Moehlman	C. H. M.	Charles W. Ramsdell	C. W. R.
E. V. Moffett	E. V. M.	George H. Ramsey	G. H. R.
John R. Mohler	J. R. M.	James G. Randall	J. G. R.
Raymond Moley	R. M.	Daniel S. Rankin	D. S. R.
Frank Monaghan	F. M—n.	Albert G. Rau	A. G. R.
Fulmer Mood	F. M-d.	P. O. Ray	P. O. R.
Robert E. Moody	R. E. M.	Thomas T. Read	T. T. R.
Albert B. Moore	A. B. M—e.	Herbert S. Reichle	H. S. R.
Austin L. Moore	A. L. M.	Charles Dudley Rhodes	C. D. R.
Charles Moore	C. M.	Leon B. Richardson	L. B. R.
Samuel Eliot Morison	S. E. M.	Robert E. Riegel	R. E. R.
Richard B. Morris	R. B. M.	James Alexander Robertson	J. A. R.
Jarvis M. Morse	J. M. M.	Burr Arthur Robinson	B. A. R.
Josiah Morse	J. M—e.	J. Magnus Rohne	J. M. R.
Donald H. Mugridge	D. H. M.	James H. Ropes	J. H. R.
David Saville Muzzey	D. S. M.	Lois K. M. Rosenberry	L. K. M. R.
H. Edward Nettles	H. E. N.	Victor Rosewater	V. R.
Allan Nevins	A. N.	Frank Edward Ross	F. E. R.
Lyman C. Newell	L. C. N.	Henry Kalloch Rowe	H. K. R.
A. R. Newsome	A. R. N.	Joseph L. Rubin	J. L. R.
Robert Hastings Nichols	R. H. N.	Durward V. Sandifer	D. V. S.
Joe L. Norris	J. L. N.	George Henry Sargent	G. H. S.
Alexander D. Noyes	A. D. N.	Max Savelle	M. S.
Hermon M. Noyes	H. M. N.	Joseph Schafer	J. S.
Ellis P. Oberholtzer	E. P. O.	Herbert W. Schneider	H. W. S—d—r.
John Chadwick Oliver	J. C. O.	H. W. Schoenberger	H. W. S—g—r.

Contributors

CARL F. SCHREIBER	C. F. S.	OLIN F. TOWER	O. F. T.
HAMILTON SCHUYLER	H. S.	MILTON HAIGHT TURK	M. H. T—k.
FRANKLIN D. SCOTT	F. D. S.	ALONZO H. TUTTLE	A. H. T.
ROY W. SELLARS	R. W. S.	ROLAND GREENE USHER	R. G. U.
ROBERT FRANCIS SEYBOLT	R. F. S.	GEORGE B. UTLEY	G. B. U.
GEORGE DUDLEY SEYMOUR	G. D. S.	WILLIAM T. UTTER	W. T. U.
ROBERT SHAFER	R. S.	IRENE VAN FOSSEN	I. V-F.
ROBERT K. SHAW	R. K. S.	S. C. VESTAL	S. C. V.
WILLIAM BRISTOL SHAW	W. B. S.	HENRY R. VIETS	H. R. V.
JAY J. SHERMAN	J. J. S.	HAROLD G. VILLARD	H. G. V.
GUY EMERY SHIPLER	G. E. S.	OSWALD GARRISON VILLARD	O. G. V.
FRED W. SHIPMAN	F. W. S.	EUGENE M. VIOLETTE	E. M. V.
LESTER B. SHIPPEE	L. B. S.	BUZ M. WALKER	B. M. W.
WILBUR H. SIEBERT	W. H. S—t.	ALEXANDER J. WALL	A. J. W.
FRANCIS BUTLER SIMKINS	F. B. S.	JAMES J. WALSH	J. J. W.
CHARLES P. SISSON	C. P. S.	FREDERIC A. WASHBURN	F. A. W.
CLARENCE R. SKINNER	C. R. S.	W. RANDALL WATERMAN	W. R. W.
DAVID EUGENE SMITH	D. E. S.	LUTHER ALLAN WEIGLE	L. A. W.
EDWARD CONRAD SMITH	E. C. S.	THEODORE H. WEISENBURG	T. H. W.
WILLIAM E. SMITH	W. E. S—h.	FRANCIS P. WEISENBURGER	F. P. W.
WILLIAM ROY SMITH	W. R. S.	ALLAN WESTCOTT	A. W.
HERBERT WEIR SMYTH	H. W. S—h.	ARTHUR P. WHITAKER	A. P. W.
W. E. SNYDER	W. E. S—r.	MELVIN J. WHITE	M. J. W.
M. E. SPALDING	M. E. S.	WILLIAM A. WHITE	W. A. W.
E. WILDER SPAULDING	E. W. S.	MARY T. WHITLEY	M. T. W.
THOMAS M. SPAULDING	T. M. S.	HENRY F. WICKHAM	H. F. W.
HARRIS ELWOOD STARR	H. E. S.	JEANNE ELIZABETH WIER	J. E. W.
BERTHA MONICA STEARNS	B. M. S.	CLARENCE RUSSELL WILLIAMS	C. R. W—s.
GEORGE W. STEPHENS	G. W. S.	MARY WILHELMINE WILLIAMS	M. W. W.
WENDELL H. STEPHENSON	W. H. S—n.	STANLEY T. WILLIAMS	S. T. W.
WAYNE E. STEVENS	W. E. S—s.	CHARLES C. WILLIAMSON	C. C. W.
WITMER STONE	W. S.	FRANCIS T. WILLIAMSON	F. T. W.
WILLIAM W. SWEET	W. W. S.	JAMES SOUTHALL WILSON	J. S. W.
HENRY O. SWINDLER	H. O. S.	HARRY A. WOLFSON	H. A. W.
CHARLES S. SYDNOR	C. S. S.	HELEN SUMNER WOODBURY	H. S. W.
C. R. WALTHER THOMAS	C. R. W. T.	MAUDE H. WOODFIN	M. H. W.
DAVID Y. THOMAS	D. Y. T.	CARL R. WOODWARD	C. R. W—d.
MILTON HALSEY THOMAS	M. H. T—s.	WALTER C. WOODWARD	W. C. W.
FREDERIC L. THOMPSON	F. L. T.	ROBERT H. WOODY	R. H. W
HERBERT THOMS	H. T.	HELEN WRIGHT	H. W.
IRVING L. THOMSON	I. L. T.	WALTER L. WRIGHT, JR.	W. L. W., Jr.
J. MONROE THORINGTON	J. M. T.	LAWRENCE C. WROTH	L. C. W.
EDWARD LAROCQUE TINKER	E. L. T.	DONOVAN YEUELL	D. Y.

DICTIONARY OF
AMERICAN BIOGRAPHY

—

Mills — Oglesby

MILLS, ANSON (Aug. 31, 1834–Nov. 5, 1924), soldier and inventor, was born on a farm near Thorntown, Ind., where his father, James P. Mills, a descendant of a Philadelphian of Penn's time, had taken up land about 1830. There he had married Sarah Kenworthy, also of Quaker ancestry, whose family came to North Carolina in the eighteenth century. Anson Mills's boyhood was spent on the farm, where he became a practical carpenter and weaver, as well as farmer. He entered West Point in 1855, but was unprepared to carry the course and was discharged early in 1857. His next four years were spent in Texas, where, during his work as a surveyor, he made the original plat of the city of El Paso and gave the place its name. When the Civil War broke out, he cast one of the two antisecession votes recorded in the county, and started for Washington. In June 1861 he received an antedated commission (May 14, 1861) as first lieutenant in a regular infantry regiment just organized.

His first battle was Shiloh, and until the end of the war he was in the field in the West, under Buell, Rosecrans, and Thomas, fighting in the Murfreesboro, Chickamauga, Atlanta, and Nashville campaigns. He was promoted to captain in 1863. On Oct. 13, 1868, he was married to Hannah Cassel, daughter of William C. Cassel, of Zanesville, Ohio. From 1865 to 1893 practically all of his service was on the frontier, involving much Indian fighting, notably the Rosebud campaign of 1876. He was transferred to the cavalry in 1871, was promoted to major in 1878, to lieutenant-colonel in 1890, and to colonel in 1892.

As early as 1866 he had patented a cartridge belt which was much more satisfactory than the regulation box. It had certain faults, however, which he hoped to obviate by weaving the whole belt in one piece, without sewing. For years he worked to perfect this invention. Later, in writing of his wife, he said: "I purchased foot-power lathes, drills, etc., to develop models of my various patents in belts and equipment. I installed them in one of her best rooms in each succeeding one of perhaps twenty posts, soiling the carpets with grease, filings and shavings, which would have driven most wives mad" (*My Story*, p. 126). All difficulties were finally overcome, and the belt was adopted by the United States Army, the requirements of which in those days, however, were small. The war with Spain caused Mills and his associates to expand their factory so as to produce a thousand belts a day, but the early termination of the war "put us in a practically bankrupt condition, a hundred thousand belts on hand and no market for them, and a large indebtedness" (*Ibid.*, p. 322). Some of the belts were disposed of by presenting them to two Canadian regiments preparing to leave for the war in South Africa, and by June 1901 orders were received for equipping three thousand British troops. The success of the belt was assured. Military and hunting equipment of all sorts is now manufactured under Mills's patents. Mills himself, however, sold out his interest in 1905, having seen his invention a success and having made a fortune in his old age.

In 1894 he was designated as the American member of the International Boundary Commission, charged with settling cases involving the boundary with Mexico. He continued as commissioner until 1914, although he had been appointed brigadier-general in 1897 and placed on the retired list. His autobiography, *My Story,*

I

was privately printed in 1918. He died in Washington, where he had made his home since 1894.

[In addition to the autobiography (in which the date of birth is apparently a misprint), see F. B. Heitman, *Hist. Reg. and Dict. U. S. Army* (1903), I, 713; *Who's Who in America,* 1924–25; *Washington Post,* Nov. 6, 1924, *Evening Star* (Washington), Nov. 5, 1924.]

T. M. S.

MILLS, BENJAMIN (Jan. 12, 1779–Dec. 6, 1831), Kentucky legislator and jurist, was born in Worcester County, Md., but when quite young he was taken by his family to Washington, Pa., where he spent his youth. After the usual elementary education he studied medicine but postponed its practice for teaching and was for a time at the head of Washington Academy (now Washington and Jefferson College). He removed with his father to Bourbon County, Ky., where, abandoning medicine, he studied law and began practice in Paris about 1805. He represented Bourbon County in the state House of Representatives for six terms, 1806, 1809, 1813, 1814, 1815, and 1816. His repeated election to the House indicated the unusual measure of public confidence that he enjoyed. During the later period he was a member of the committee on courts of justice. In 1816 he was a candidate before the legislature for the United States Senate but was defeated by a few votes. In 1817 he was appointed judge of the Montgomery circuit court and the next year was transferred to the Fayette circuit at the request of the Fayette bar.

In 1820 with his appointment as associate justice of the court of appeals, he entered on the most important phase of his career, a phase that was disastrous to his personal fortunes and popularity. The relief laws passed by the legislature to aid those who had suffered by the collapse of state banks were declared unconstitutional by the court in 1823, and this action resulted in the dissolution of the court by the angry legislature and the creation of a new court. There ensued in Kentucky the notorious "court contest" around which Kentucky politics centered for a decade. Mills and his two colleagues refused to give up their positions or to recognize the validity of the action of the legislature. Since the relief laws were popular in Kentucky he was severely denounced for his attitude. In the end the old court was sustained but he had worn himself out and had lost his usefulness as a jurist. In December 1828 he resigned. He was immediately reappointed by the governor, but the Senate refused to confirm him. He continued to reside in Frankfort, however, and devoted himself to the practice of law. He died of apoplexy. He was known for his extensive charities which were quite often beyond his means,

was a member of the Presbyterian Church, for a long time one of its elders, and was one of the founders of the American Bible Society. His grandson was Benjamin Fay Mills [*q.v.*].

[Shane MSS., II cc4, Wis. Hist. Lib.; Lewis and R. H. Collins, *Hist. of Ky.,* revised ed. (2 vols., 1874); H. Levin, *The Lawyers and Lawmakers of Ky.* (1897); W. H. Perrin, J. H. Battle, and G. C. Kniffin, *Kentucky* (1886); A. M. Stickles, *The Critical Court Struggle in Ky.* (1929); *Ky. Gazette* (Lexington), Dec. 8, 1831; *Focus* (Louisville), Dec. 8, 1831.]

R. S. C.

MILLS, BENJAMIN FAY (June 4, 1857–May 1, 1916), evangelist and liberal religious leader, was born at Rahway, N. J. His father, Thornton A. Mills, son of Benjamin Mills [*q.v.*] of Kentucky, was a Presbyterian minister who became moderator of the General Assembly of the Presbyterian Church in the United States of America; his mother, Anna (Cook) Mills, had been a missionary in India. He prepared for college at Phillips Academy, Andover, and was graduated with the degree of A.B. from Lake Forest University in 1879. Ordained to the Congregational ministry in 1878, he had brief pastorates in villages of Dakota and New York, and in 1884 became minister of the Congregational church at West Rutland, Vt. His pastorate here was characterized by a revival of religious interest which attracted the attention of neighboring ministers; as a result he was invited to conduct a two-week series of evangelistic meetings at Middlebury. The community and college were deeply stirred, and more than three hundred people professed conversion.

In May 1886 he resigned his pastorate to devote himself to itinerant, interdenominational evangelism. His culture and training caused him to be welcomed as an evangelist of a new type; and for ten years, in city after city, his work met with extraordinary success. Toward the end of this period, under the influence of Prof. George D. Herron [*q.v.*] of Grinnell College, he began to develop a social interpretation of the gospel which led him to question the worth of individual, personal evangelism. This attitude of mind appeared in his address before the World's Parliament of Religions at Chicago in 1893. In 1895 he accepted for one year a pastorate at Albany, N. Y., in order that he might study in the state library; thence he went to Boston and began to preach his new social gospel in Music Hall and the Hollis Street Theatre, under the auspices of a committee headed by Edward Everett Hale [*q.v.*]. In 1897 he definitely withdrew from the evangelical ministry and from evangelistic work. He said that he did this, "first, because I despaired of the possibility of a genuine, widespread awakening and inspiration of the church; second, because of a social vision, by which I came to conceive of Christ as the Saviour of the social organization rather than of individuals; and third, because of the universal viewpoint which came to me through my study of the great books of all ages and nations, through which the Bible ceased to be to me the exclusively inspired Word of God" (*Advance,* June 24, 1915, p. 1251).

After two years in Boston, Mills was for four years (1899-1903) minister of the First Unitarian Church of Oakland, Cal. He then removed to Los Angeles and devoted himself to lecturing on liberal religion and the conduct of life in a sort of itinerant ministry similar to that of his evangelistic period. He was founder and minister (1904-11) of the Los Angeles Fellowship; and founder and leader (1911-14) of the Chicago Fellowship. These were independent religious organizations based upon principles which he formulated thus: "Absolute Trust as the Fixed Attitude of Mind, and Perfect Love as the Unvarying Practice of the Life" (*Ibid.*). He chose as motto the comprehensive question, "What is the Loving Thing to Do?" the answer to which he believed would solve all practical questions. He finally came to feel that these principles, though true, fall short of a genuine gospel and give insufficient impulse to right living. In 1915 he experienced a reconversion to the Christian faith, and sought readmission to its ministry. He was received into the Chicago Presbytery and began again to conduct evangelistic meetings in various cities. He died at Grand Rapids, Mich., survived by his wife, Mary Russell (Hill) Mills, to whom he was married on Oct. 31, 1879, by three sons, and three daughters.

Mills published, in his evangelistic period, *Power from On High* (1890); *A Message to Mothers* (1892); *Victory Through Surrender* (1892); *God's World, and Other Sermons* (1893); and in his non-evangelical period, *Twentieth Century Religion* (copr. 1898, 1899), and *The Divine Adventure* (1905). He published a brief spiritual autobiography in a series of articles entitled, "Why I Return to the Church," which appeared in three numbers of *The Advance,* beginning June 24, 1915.

[Besides the series of articles mentioned above, see the following: "The Passing of B. Fay Mills," in *Advance,* May 11, 1916; *Congregationalist,* Aug. 19, 1915, May 25, 1916; *Christian Advocate,* Sept. 23, 1897; *North Shore Leader* (Chicago), May 5, 1916; J. J. Francis and C. B. Morrell, *Mills Meetings Memorial Vol.* (1892).]   L. A. W.

MILLS, CHARLES KARSNER (Dec. 4, 1845–May 28, 1931), neurologist, was born in Philadelphia, the son of James and Lavinia Ann (Fitzgerald) Mills. He graduated from Central High School in 1864, having served in the Union army during the Civil War. In a series of articles entitled "The Military History of the Falls of Schuylkill," published in the *Weekly Forecast,* a suburban paper, Mar. 13–Oct. 16, 1913, he gave a complete account of the emergency campaigns of 1862 and 1863 in which he took part. For several years after he finished his high-school course he was engaged in teaching. He then began the study of medicine, graduating from the medical department of the University of Pennsylvania in 1869. In 1871 he received the degree of Ph.D.

After a few years of general practice he became interested in nervous and mental diseases, in which he subsequently specialized. In 1874 he was made chief of the clinic for nervous diseases in the University Hospital, and in 1877 he was appointed neurologist to the Philadelphia Hospital. In the latter year he became lecturer on electrotherapeutics in the University of Pennsylvania, and was connected with that institution until his death, being successively lecturer in neuropsychiatry, professor of mental diseases, and professor of neurology in charge of the department. His work in this last position was so meritorious that the "Philadelphia school of neurology" which he created, was known all over the scientific world. In 1915 he was made emeritus professor of neurology. From 1883 to 1898 he was professor of nervous and mental diseases in the Philadelphia Polyclinic, of which he was one of the founders. In 1914 he organized a graduate course in the wards of the Philadelphia General Hospital, and later became professor of neurology in the Graduate Medical School of the University of Pennsylvania, which position he held until a few years before his death. He was also professor of nervous diseases in the Woman's Medical College of Pennsylvania (1891-1902), and was connected with many hospitals in both the city and the state. He took an active part in the proceedings of the American Neurological Association from its establishment until his death, was elected president in 1887, and again in 1924 on the fiftieth anniversary of its organization. In 1883 he founded the Philadelphia Neurological Society.

Mills wrote extensively on many subjects. His neurologic contributions alone number 345, his predominant interest being in cerebral localization and the philosophy of neurology. His bibliography covers such subjects as neurologic surgery, cerebral morphology, vasomotor and trophic diseases, hydrophobia, multiple neuritis, poliomyelitis, myotonia and athetoid spasm, surface thermometry, electrotherapeutics, problems in electrical potential, hypnotism, hysteria, neurasthenia, psychotherapeutics, mental overwork, Swedish movements and systemized therapeutic exercises, occupational neuroses, localization of tumors of the brain by Roentgen exploration, the treatment of aphasia by training, disorders of pantomime (a forerunner of subsequent work on apraxia), the symptomatology of lenticular lesions, intradural root anastomosis, insanity in children and adults, criminal lunacy and the medico-legal aspects of nervous diseases and insanity. In 1898 he published *The Nervous System and Its Diseases,* undoubtedly the most scholarly contribution on diseases of the brain and cranial nerves which had appeared up to that time in the American literature of the subject. He wrote a great deal on medical biography and history, and even produced some poetry in his younger days. Among his biographical sketches are *Benjamin Rush and American Psychiatry* (1886); *Isaac Ray, the Great Alienist* (1888), and a tribute to his friend of many years, Dr. S. Weir Mitchell. His historical papers include "History of Medical Jurisprudence in Philadelphia," in F. P. Henry's *The Standard History of the Medical Profession in Philadelphia* (1897); *Neurology in Philadelphia from 1874 to 1904* (1904); *Historical Memoranda Concerning the Philadelphia Hospital for the Insane* (1909); and *The Philadelphia Almshouse and the Philadelphia Hospital from 1854 to 1908* (1909). His longest poem, *The Schuylkill, a Centennial Poem by M. K. C.,* was published in book form in 1876. He was a witness in the Guiteau, Thaw, and other important cases, and was highly esteemed in the realm of medical jurisprudence. On Nov. 6, 1873, he married Clara Elizabeth, daughter of Charles Wilson and Harriet (Friel) Peale of Philadelphia. He was survived by a daughter and three sons.

[*Semi-centennial Vol. of the Am. Neurological Asso., 1875–1924* (1924) contains bibliog. of Mills publications; for further data see T. H. Weisenburg in *Archives of Neurology and Psychiatry,* July 1931; *Jour. Am. Medic. Asso.,* June 13, 1931; *Jour. of Nervous and Mental Disease,* Nov. 1931; *Who's Who in America,* 1930–31; *Public Ledger* (Phila.), May 28, 1931.]   T. H. W.

MILLS, CLARK (Dec. 13, 1810–Jan. 12, 1883), sculptor, pioneer bronze founder, was born in Onondaga County, N. Y. At the age of five, upon his father's death, he was placed with an uncle, from whom he ran away eight years later because of real or fancied ill-treatment. Thereafter he made his own way. He worked as a farmhand, at scant wages not always paid;

at times he attended school in winter. He hauled lumber in Syracuse, but when oxen were supplied instead of horses, he found life too slow and went to work on the canal. Later, while cutting cedar posts in a swamp, he froze his feet and for months could wear no shoes. Seeking lighter labor, he worked with a cabinet-maker, at first for instruction, afterward for board. He spent two years as millwright's apprentice, for a time was employed in plaster and cement mills, and then drifted to New Orleans, La. After a year there he passed to Charleston, S. C., where he worked in stucco until 1835. In that year he began modeling busts in clay. His experiences from 1828 to 1835 had developed all his native hardihood, versatility, and inventiveness. He next discovered a new method of taking casts from the living face, which gained him considerable work in portraiture, then he studied marble-cutting. In Carolina marble he carved a bust of John C. Calhoun. It was bought by the city council of Charleston and in 1846 won for Mills a gold medal, grandiloquently inscribed in Latin and in English. He was offered means for study abroad by certain well-to-do men of the city but he declined because of work offered at home. John S. Preston, who had befriended the sculptor Powers, invited him to Columbia, S. C., where he made ten busts, to be cut in marble after further study in art. William C. Preston suggested that before going abroad, Mills should see the statuary in Washington, D. C., and paid the expenses of the round trip; he also gave Mills orders for two busts, those of Webster and of Crittenden. On his travels Mills stopped at Richmond, Va., and there studied Houdon's "Washington," the first statue he had ever seen. As to Greenough's "Washington," in the guise of the Olympian Zeus, he pronounced the anatomy perfect, but the treatment lacking in historical truth. He resolved that should he himself have a statue to make, "the world should find fault for his giving too much truth, and not for want of it" (*Round Table,* May 14, 1864, p. 340).

His opportunity came in 1848, when Cave Johnson, president of the Jackson monument committee, proposed that before going to Europe the young man should make a design for an equestrian monument to General Jackson. Mills had never seen either Jackson or an equestrian statue and at first refused. Nevertheless, the thought took possession of him and after nine months of study he produced a small model in which the hind feet of the horse came well under the center of the group, thus giving a lifelike effect of perfect balance entirely satisfactory to the committee. A contract for twelve thousand dollars was made, the committee to furnish the bronze. After two years of strenuous labor, the full-size plaster model was finished; for the bronze, Congress appropriated cannon captured by Jackson. Then appeared the true magnitude of the task. The industry of bronze casting was almost unknown in the United States and never before had so large a piece been undertaken in the country. After seemingly insuperable difficulties had been overcome, largely through the resourcefulness and pertinacity of the sculptor, the pioneer equestrian statue emerged in bronze. Dedicated in January 1853, on the thirty-eighth anniversary of the battle of New Orleans, it still stands in Lafayette Square across from the White House in Washington, indulgently viewed by sophisticates who perceive its lack of sculptural dignity, but perhaps overlook its pioneer importance. Congress now voted to Mills an additional twenty thousand dollars, doubtless well earned; it also awarded him a fifty-thousand-dollar contract for an equestrian statue of Washington for the capital city and in 1860 commissioned him to cast in bronze Crawford's colossal "Liberty" for the Capitol dome. The city of New Orleans ordered a replica of the "Jackson." With these projects assured, Mills bought land three miles from Washington and there erected a suitable studio and foundry. A gale wrecked the studio, a fire destroyed the foundry, but both were soon rebuilt. The New Orleans replica was dedicated in 1856, the "Washington" in 1860, and the "Liberty" in 1863. The "Washington" lacks interest and is without even such unity of design as may be descried in the "Jackson," a third replica of which was erected in Nashville, Tenn., in 1880. Other works by Mills are numerous portrait busts; the Corcoran Gallery owns his "Calhoun" and his "Washington." His final undertaking was an enormous design for a Lincoln monument, to include thirty-six heroic figures, equestrian and pedestrian. The project fell into oblivion after his death at Washington in 1883. He was survived by a widow, two sons, and a step-daughter. One of his sons, Theodore Augustus, was a sculptor of talent who died in 1916.

[Lorado Taft, *The Hist. of Am. Sculpture* (1930); Chas. E. Fairman, *Art and Artists of the Capitol* (1927); "Mr. Clark Mills, the Sculptor," *Round Table*, May 14, 1864; "Sculpture at the Capital," *Ibid.*, Sept. 8, 1866; H. T. Tuckerman, *Book of the Artists* (1867); Leila Mechlin, "Art Life in Washington," *Records of the Columbia Hist. Soc., Wash., D. C.*, vol. XXIV (1922); W. O. Hart, "Clark Mills," *Ibid.*; *Am. Art Rev.*, vol. II (1881), p. 131; *Frank Leslie's Illustrated Newspaper*, Mar. 3, 1860; *Evening Star* (Wash., D. C.), Jan. 12, 1883; *Washington Post*, Jan. 13, 15, 1883.]
A. A.

MILLS, CYRUS TAGGART (May 4, 1819–Apr. 20, 1884), missionary, educator, and business man, was born in Paris, N. Y., youngest of the three sons of William and Mary Mills. He grew up in the midst of the poverty which was common among families on the frontier during the early part of the nineteenth century. Although he was inadequately prepared for college when he entered Williams, and was obliged to work his way through, he graduated in 1844, seventh in a class of thirty-three. The influence of Mark Hopkins [*q.v.*] was a force that Mills delighted to acknowledge throughout his life. From Williams College he went to the Union Theological Seminary, New York, worked his way through there, and graduated in 1847. At some time during his period of preparation he became interested in missionary work in India, and took up the study of Tamil while in the theological seminary. On Feb. 2, 1848, he was ordained by the Third Presbytery of New York and on Sept. 11 he married Susan Lincoln Tolman [see Mills, Susan Lincoln Tolman]. The two sailed almost immediately for India, under appointment of the American Board of Commissioners for Foreign Missions.

Full of enthusiasm, the young couple landed in Ceylon and Mills took charge of Batticotta Seminary, an institution devoted to training native teachers and preachers. His administration was successful and he established an enviable reputation among both his colleagues and the natives of the community; but the climate was enervating and the environment was unhealthful. A constitution none too rugged at any time was soon undermined by the diseases common to that section, and after six years of arduous labor he and his wife returned to the United States. Then followed four years of recuperation, agitation on behalf of foreign missionary work, pastoral labors in Berkshire, N. Y. (1856–58), business ventures, and, finally, determination to undertake again the work in foreign fields. This time he and his wife went to the Hawaiian Islands, and in 1860 took charge of Oahu College near Honolulu. He found the college dependent on the American Board for support, but put it on a self-supporting basis during the four years he remained in charge. Obviously his business acumen had not deserted him, though his body had not fully recuperated from the ravages of disease contracted in India. His health failed again and in 1864 he returned to the United States, spent a year at Ware, Mass., and in 1865 settled in California. From Mary Atkins he bought a school for young ladies at Benicia and devoted his energies to administering it. His missionary zeal was tinctured, however, with a penchant for business venture, and within a few years he acquired about sixty acres of land in what was then called Brooklyn, five miles south of Oakland and east of the southern end of San Francisco Bay. On this new site he erected a modern building with accommodations for about one hundred and twenty-five women, and in 1871 moved the school from Benicia, giving the name of Mills Seminary to the new institution.

The transfer brought heavy financial obligations. About one hundred and sixty thousand dollars had been spent, approximately eighty thousand of which remained unpaid. To the task of canceling this obligation he now turned his attention. He had invested in lands in the southern part of California, and while looking after his property there, a few years before his death, he was induced to make another venture. The country around Pomona interested him, the need for water attracted his attention, and in 1882, with M. L. Wicks, he formed a company to supply the town with water, which soon became the Pomona Land & Water Company, of which Mills was president until his death. From his various financial investments and from gifts he paid off the obligations with the exception of seven thousand dollars, about forty thousand dollars being contributed from his own private funds.

He was a hard worker, patient and persevering in the tasks he assigned himself, keenly interested in the development of the community in which he lived, and judicious in his financial investments. Recognizing his limitations in purely educational matters he wisely sought the advice of his wife, and frequently her decision could be seen behind his action in connection with campus administration. He died in Oakland, Cal.

[*In Memoriam: Rev. Cyrus Taggart Mills, D.D.* (n.d.), which appeared at the time of his death, gives the most complete account; see also *Reports of the Am. Board of Commissioners for Foreign Missions*, 1849–54, 1861–64; R. A. Keep, *Fourscore Years: A Hist. of Mills Coll.* (1931); *The Friend* (Honolulu), Nov. 1860, July 1864, June 1884; *Hawaiian Gazette*, June 1891; San Francisco *Morning Call* and San Francisco *Evening Bulletin*, Apr. 21, 1884; Oakland *Times*, Apr. 21 and 24, 1884; Oakland *Tribune*, Apr. 21, 23, 26, and 29, 1884.]   C.G.

MILLS, DARIUS OGDEN (Sept. 5, 1825–Jan. 3, 1910), merchant, banker, and philanthropist, was born in North Salem, Westchester County, N. Y., his parents being James and Hannah (Ogden) Mills. The Mills family was of North-of-England origin, and had come to America before the Revolution. Darius' father was unfortunate in local investments, and at the age of seventeen, after an elementary education at excellent private schools in the neighborhood of his home, the boy was obliged to go to work. As a clerk in New York City, he showed aptitude for the mercantile and banking business and in 1847, when he was but twenty-two years old, he became on invitation of a cousin, cashier of the Merchants' Bank of Erie County, Buffalo, N. Y., with a percentage share in the institution's profits.

Discovery of gold in California in 1848 started an exodus of young Eastern business men to the Pacific Coast. Two of Mills's brothers had equipped a sailing ship with merchandise and had embarked for San Francisco by the Cape Horn route. Mills himself hesitated long, but at the end of 1848 set forth for the same destination by way of the Isthmus. He went as a passenger, provided with the necessary money to engage in merchandising or banking, or both. Unable to obtain passage from Panama to San Francisco—previous north-bound vessels having been deserted by their crews in the "gold rush" from the California port and tied up in that harbor—Mills turned to the West coast of South America, and at Callao was able to charter a bark. Arriving at San Francisco in June 1849, he at once bought merchandise and proceeded to establish a trading business; first, temporarily, at Stockton; then, and permanently, at Sacramento.

His undertaking, which comprised not only buying of gold dust and selling of goods, but dealing in New York exchange, proved highly profitable. After a brief visit to the East at the end of 1849, he returned to Sacramento, establishing there in 1850 the Bank of D. O. Mills & Company, which thereafter led in the business activities of the city. During the following decade he accumulated a large fortune. In 1864 he was active in organizing the Bank of California at San Francisco, of which he was president until July 1873. Two years later, however, as a result of business conditions following the panic of 1873 and also of the rash policies of his successor in the institution's presidency, W. C. Ralston, the Bank of California was forced to suspend payments, and Mills was called back to his old office. Through his endeavors, barely a month after the bank had closed, it resumed business and entered on a career of prolonged prosperity. During his residence on the Pacific Coast, he had been an organizer and important benefactor of such Californian enterprises as the San Francisco Protestant Orphan Asylum, St. Luke's Hospital, and the University of California, of which he long acted as regent and treasurer. He also contributed largely to the Lick Observatory, of which he was trustee, and in behalf of which he personally equipped and sent to South America in 1903 an astronomical expedition to study solar phenomena. In March 1878 he definitely retired from active business on the Pacific Coast, though retaining large investments in that section.

Residing thereafter in New York City, he became investor and director in many of the large Eastern banking, railway, and industrial concerns. He was active in philanthropic enterprises, notably in the construction, during 1888 and afterward, of the "Mills hotels." These embodied a pioneer attempt to provide household accommodations at a low cost but with modern equipment, for people of small means. In them a bed in a private room was obtainable for twenty cents a night, and wholesome meals could be secured at prices ranging from five to fifteen cents. They were so carefully managed that, despite the small charges, they returned to the owner a slight surplus over interest, taxes, maintenance, and depreciation. Mills was connected with other enterprises for providing shelter and credit at low rates and with numerous public charities; he was also a generous contributor to the Metropolitan Museum of Art and the New York Botanical Garden.

Personally, he was a man of quick and positive decision on financial problems and of strong executive capacity. He never courted publicity, and was sometimes described as retiring in manner; but he possessed a quiet urbanity in social conversation, which displayed itself in his numerous visits to the country houses of well-known Englishmen, and in his contacts with British statesmen and royalty. During his later years he spent much time in foreign travel, increasing in his European visits his collections of books and paintings. He was married, Sept. 5, 1854, to Jane Templeton Cunningham, and was survived by two children.

[J. T. Scharf, *Hist. of Westchester County, N. Y.* (1886), II, 509–13; *Lick Observatory Bull., No. 173* (vol. V, 1908–10); Henry Clews, *Fifty Years in Wall Street* (1908); *Who's Who in America,* 1908–09; *Cosmopolitan,* July 1902; *Outlook,* Jan. 15, 1910; *N. Y. Tribune,* Jan. 5, 1910.]   A. D. N.

MILLS, ELIJAH HUNT (Dec. 1, 1776– May 5, 1829), congressman and lawyer, was born in Chesterfield, Hampshire County, Mass., the son of the Rev. Benjamin and Mary (Hunt) Mills. After the death of his mother in 1779 and of his father in 1785, he was adopted by his maternal uncle, Elijah Hunt of Northampton. Graduating from Williams College in 1797, he devoted himself to the study of law, in 1803 was admitted to the bar at Northampton, and became one of the most prominent lawyers in western Massachusetts. From 1804 to 1814 he occupied the position of town clerk and in the latter year was appointed advocate (district attorney) for Hampshire County. In 1823 he and Samuel Howe opened a law school in Northampton. The number of students is reported to have ranged from ten to fifteen, many of them coming from the South. The instruction was by lectures, recitations, moot courts, and discussion, written and oral, of legal questions. There is no record of the continuance of the school after 1830. Entering political life as a Federalist, Mills became one of the active leaders of this party in western Massachusetts. He was elected to the Massachusetts House of Representatives in 1811 and served through 1814. From 1815 to 1819 he served two terms in the United States House of Representatives. In 1819 he was elected to the Massachusetts House of Representatives of which body he was made speaker in May 1820. He had occupied this position less than two weeks when he was elected to the United States Senate for the remainder of the term of Prentiss Mellen (resigned) ending Mar. 3, 1821, and for the next full term. He failed of reëlection and was succeeded in 1827 by Webster. He returned to Northampton where he died on May 5, 1829, at the age of fifty-two, having suffered much from ill-health during the period of his service in the Senate.

Mills took an active part in the Federalist opposition to the War of 1812. He was one of the committee appointed by the Hampshire County Convention of 1809 to prepare an address protesting against the Embargo. In the convention of delegates from the towns of the three river counties of Massachusetts held in Northampton, July 1812, he was a member of the committee which prepared a memorial to President Madison urging the immediate negotiation of peace. He was author (*Hampshire Gazette,* May 13, 1829) of the "Address of the House of Representatives to the People of Massachusetts" (*Niles' Weekly Register,* Aug. 29, 1812), adopted June 26, 1812, a severe arraignment of the war which urged opposition to it by all constitutional means. A Fourth of July address delivered by Mills at Northampton in 1813 was less restrained: "The rights of commerce, and the constitutional privileges of New England must be ransomed from the grasp of usurpation; 'Peaceably if you can, forcibly if you must'" (*An Oration Pronounced at Northampton,* 1813, p. 23). As a member of Congress, however, his Federalism became more subdued and his career while inconspicuous was characterized by moderation and intelligence. Acquaintance with leading men in the opposite party led him to qualify earlier judgments. His legal training gave him a particular interest in constitutional questions and he occasionally took the floor in support of his views. He was a strong advocate of a national system of bankruptcy. In support of the commercial interest of Massachusetts he opposed the tariff of 1824. He was twice married: in 1802 to Sarah Hunt who died in the same year, and in 1804 to Harriette Blake. He had seven children by his second wife.

[Calvin Durfee, *Williams Biog. Annals* (1871); Solomon Clark, *Antiquities, Historicals and Grads. of Northampton* (1882); *Proc. of a Convention . . . Holden at Northampton, the 14th and 15th of July, 1812* (1812); *Columbian Centinel* (Boston), Sept. 1804, Jan.–June 1820, May 1829, May 13, 1829; *Hampshire Gazette* (Northampton, Mass.), Feb.–Nov. 1800, Jan. 1825, May 1829; letters in the possession of the Mass. Hist. Soc.]   L. C. H.

MILLS, HIRAM FRANCIS (Nov. 1, 1836–Oct. 4, 1921), hydraulic and sanitary engineer, was born at Bangor, Me., the son of Preserved Brayton and Jane (Lunt) Mills. In 1856 he was graduated from Rensselaer Polytechnic Institute. During the next twelve years, while he was serving an apprenticeship under several distinguished engineers, he assisted in the construction of the Bergen Tunnel and the Hoosac Tunnel; he erected dams on the Deerfield River and on the Penobscot River; and he conducted various studies in connection with water-power developments at Cohoes, N. Y., and North Billerica, Mass. In 1868 he opened his own office in Boston, where he soon attained a high place in his profession. Although he was consulted by many corporations and municipalities throughout the United States and Mexico, his principal work was done in Massachusetts, where he became chief engineer of the Essex Company, of Lawrence, and of the Locks and Canals Company, of Lowell.

At Lowell he undertook a series of experiments on the flow of water in natural and artificial channels which led to the perfection of the piezometer and advanced materially the development of the turbine. Owing to the pressure of other duties, however, he early abandoned his interest in this phase of hydraulics, and his conclusions were not systematized until the posthumous publication of *Flow of Water in Pipes* (1923). As consulting engineer to the Boston Metropolitan Water and Sewerage Board, he was chiefly responsible for the design of the water supply, drainage, and sewerage systems of the areas under its jurisdiction. Possibly because his father was a physician, he had always been interested in epidemiology. When the Massachusetts State Board of Health was organized in 1886, he therefore accepted the chairmanship of the committee on water supply and sewerage, a position which he held for twenty-eight years. Much of the success of the Board was due to his efforts, for he not only standardized methods of sampling and analysis but he also initiated far-reaching experiments on the purification of water and sewage. From these investigations emerged the great experiment station at Lawrence, which has long been recognized as the foremost in America, if not in the world. As a result of the studies completed under his direction, the death rate from typhoid throughout Massachusetts was reduced eight-ninths. Since Mills had always been skeptical of the theory of self-purification of streams by rapid flow which was popular in his day, he constructed at Lawrence a slow-sand filter which, because of its obvious efficiency, marked the beginning of a new era in municipal engineering. Absorbed as he was in his professional activities, he nevertheless wrote numerous articles, brochures, and memoirs in his special field. Among these, his contributions to the *Proceedings* (vol XIV, 1879) of the American Academy of Arts and Sciences, of which he was a fellow, the *Journal of the Franklin Institute* (February 1870), the *Transactions of the American Society of Civil Engineers* (April 1885, November 1893), and the *Journal of the New England Water Works Association* (March 1887, September 1894), are especially significant.

Although Mills, who was inclined to be a recluse and a mystic, shrank from publicity of any kind, he dedicated his life wholeheartedly to the welfare of the community. To the cause of education he devoted no inconsiderable share of his energy, serving on a number of local boards and on important committees at both the Lawrence Scientific School of Harvard University and the Massachusetts Institute of Technology. He was a successful man of affairs, director and president of several corporations; and he accumulated a fortune which enabled him to remember in his will the institutions to which he was especially devoted and to found, at Harvard University, the Elizabeth Worcester Mills Fund for cancer research in memory of his wife, Elizabeth Worcester, whom he married Oct. 8, 1873, and who died Mar. 23, 1917. His name is also perpetuated by foundations in Lawrence and Lowell. His death occurred in Hingham, Mass.

[H. B. Nason, *Biog. Record Officers and Grads. Rensselaer Polytechnic Inst.* (1887); R. A. Hale, in *Trans. Am. Soc. Civil Engineers*, vol. LXXXVII (1924); *Who's Who in America*, 1920–21; *Boston Herald*, Oct. 6, 1921; *Flow of Water in Pipes* (1923), mentioned above, which contains personal notes on Mills by J. R. Freeman.]   R. P. B.

MILLS, LAWRENCE HEYWORTH (1837–Jan. 29, 1918), Iranian scholar, was born in New York City, the son of Philo L. and Elizabeth Caroline (Kane) Mills. He was probably descended from Peter van der Meulen, of Amsterdam, who emigrated from Leyden to New England in the second half of the seventeenth century, settled in Windsor, Conn., and changed his name to Mills. Lawrence was educated at the University of the City of New York (A.B. 1858; A.M. 1863) and the Protestant Episcopal Theological Seminary in Virginia (B.D. 1861). He married Maria Bowen Swann, daughter of Robert Paige Swann of Leesburg, Va., and had three sons and one daughter. Ordered deacon in 1861 and priested in the following year, he was successively curate (1861–64) and rector (1864–67) of St. Ann's, Brooklyn, and then (1867–70) rector of St. John's, Hartford, Conn.

After 1872 he made his permanent residence outside the United States. From 1873 to 1877 he was associate rector of the American Episcopal Church in Florence, and then went to Germany, where he studied Vedic and Iranian under Rudolf von Roth and laid the foundation of his entire later career. By 1883 his studies of the Avesta had won such distinction that he was requested by F. Max Müller to complete the translation of the texts left unfinished at that time by James Darmesteter. This work appeared at Oxford in 1887 as Volume XXXI of *The Sacred Books of the East,* and in the same year Mills settled in Oxford. In 1897 a group of his English and Indian friends established for him a chair of "Zend Philology" at the University, the first full professorship of its kind. This he held until his death, when the position automatically ceased.

Mills was a prolific writer. His publications include more than a hundred papers and nearly a dozen books. The latter, besides the translation already mentioned, were: *A Study of the Five Zarathushtrian (Zoroastrian) Gâthâs, with Texts and Translations* (Leipzig, 1894); *The Ancient Manuscript of the Yasna with its Pahlavi Translation (A.D. 1323) Generally Quoted as J 2, Reproduced in Facsimile* (Oxford, 1893); *The Gâthâs of Zarathushtra (Zoroaster) in Metre and Rhythm* (Oxford, 1900); *Zarathstra, Philo, the Achaemenids, and Israel* (2 parts, Leipzig, 1905–06); *Avesta Eschatology Compared with the Books of Daniel and Revelations* [!] (Chicago, 1908); *The Yasna of the Avesta . . . A Study of Yasna I* (Leipzig, 1910); *Our Own Religion in Ancient Persia* (Chicago, 1913); *A Dictionary of the Gâthic Language of the Zend Avesta* (Leipzig, 1913); *An Expo-sition of the Lore of the Avesta in Catechetical Dialogue* (Bombay, 1916); *The Creed of Zarathushtra* (Bombay, 1916); and *The Fundamental and Dominant Presence of Zoroastrian Thought in the Jewish Exilic, Christian and Muhammadan Religions, and in the Greek and Gnostic Philosophies with Their Modern Successors* (Bombay, 1917).

Mills's work was practically restricted to that portion of the Avesta known as the Yasna, and especially to its Gāthās, a group of seventeen hymns in an archaic dialect traditionally ascribed to Zoroaster himself. He gives, in original and translation, both the Avesta text and its Oriental versions; and this is of value as a convenient assemblage of all the native material. The worth of his translations, on the other hand, is diminished by excessive reliance on Zoroastrian tradition, as is his exegesis. In his enthusiasm for the Gāthās he sought to find borrowings from Persia in the Old Testament that are by no means certain; and he was far from adequately equipped either in comparative linguistics or in comparative religion. To these shortcomings he added a style of curious involution and obscurity, so that it was not strange that his work excited little attention in circles of strict scholarship.

Mills was never attached to any of the Oxford Colleges, even as honorary fellow, and his life was rather isolated. He imagined himself, apparently quite without reason, the victim of jealousy on the part of Continental Iranists and of ingratitude on the part of some of his pupils. Theologically, as might be expected from his Virginia training, he was a pronounced Evangelical or Low Churchman, with tendencies toward the "Broad Church" point of view.

[*Biog. Cat. of the Chancellors, Professors and Graduates of the Dept. of Arts and Science of the Univ. of the City of New York* (1894); Paul Carus, "Professor Mills, the Zendavesta Scholar," *Open Court,* Aug. 1905; *Monist,* Apr. 1918; *Jour. Royal Asiatic Soc.,* Jan. 1919; *Who's Who* (British), 1917; *N. Y. Times,* Feb. 1, 1918; H. R. Stiles, *The Hist. and Geneals. of Ancient Windsor,* vol. II (1893); personal acquaintance.]   L. H. G.

MILLS, ROBERT (Aug. 12, 1781–Mar. 3, 1855), architect, engineer, was born in Charleston, S. C., the son of William Mills, a Scotchman, who came to America from Dundee in 1770 and married Anne Taylor, "a lady of ancient and honorable Carolina lineage." Robert received his early education at the College of Charleston and was unique among Americans at that early day in resolving to secure regular training for the career of a professional architect. Of the professionals then or previously active in the United States as architects, James Hoban, William Thornton, George Hadfield, and Benjamin H. Latrobe were British born; L'Enfant, Hallet, Mangin, and Godefroy were Frenchmen. James Hoban [q.v.], who had learned building and drawing as a boy in the school of the Dublin Society of Arts and had designed and built the South Carolina state capitol at Columbia, had won the competition for the President's House in Washington and had been established there since 1792. To him young Mills repaired in 1800 for his initiation. On his journey northward he saw the newly completed capitol at Richmond, modeled by Jefferson on the Maison Carrée. "The location of the building is on a high eminence and commands an extensive prospect," he wrote later; "I remember the impression it made on my mind when first I came in view of it coming from the South. It gave me an idea of the position and effect of those Greek temples which are the admiration of the world" (autobiographical fragment, Dimitry papers). From honest Hoban, who on occasion contracted for buildings as well as designed them, he learned the rudiments of construction, and of draftsmanship and rendering.

He was eager, however, to go beyond the somewhat obsolete academism of the Irish builder architect and found his opportunity when he came to the attention of Thomas Jefferson [q.v.], pioneer of the Roman revival and encourager of American talents. He was taken into Jefferson's family at "Monticello" in 1803. The house, which Jefferson had given its first Palladian impress before the Revolution, was then being remodeled on more classical lines, suggested in part by those of the Hôtel de Salm. Here Mills had the benefit of Jefferson's collection of architectural books, then unrivaled in America. During his stay he made an admirable tinted drawing in elevation of the front of the house as Jefferson's design of 1796 would bring it to completion—a drawing which has sometimes misled his biographers to consider Mills as the architect of a house begun before he was born and redesigned when he was but fifteen years of age. Mills also made a drawing from the design of Jefferson for a rebuilding of "Shadwell," never executed. This drawing (preserved like the other in the Coolidge Collection of the Massachusetts Historical Society, and bearing the inscription "T. Jefferson, Arch't. R. Mills, Del't, 1803") shows a version of Jefferson's favorite *villa rotonda* type, having a high central dome, with many other features to which he was attached, such as the oval salon, octagonal bows, and alcove bedrooms (F. Kimball, *Thomas Jefferson, Architect*, 1916).

Besides teaching Mills what he could, Jefferson recommended him to the others from whom he could best learn. To Charles Bulfinch [q.v.] who had seen the monuments of Paris under Jefferson's guidance and had followed his route in southern France, he had given Mills an introduction on the young student's tour of the northern states in 1802. He now advised him to attach himself to Benjamin H. Latrobe [q.v.], who had the fine foreign training of Cockerell and Smeaton. Latrobe, the first of the newcomers to succeed in establishing himself in professional architectural practise as it is known today, had been appointed by Jefferson as surveyor of the public buildings of the United States. From 1803 to 1808 Mills was in Latrobe's office as a draftsman and clerk. Some of his first experience was on the Chesapeake & Delaware Canal. In 1807 he was supervising for his employer the erection of the Bank of Philadelphia, a vaulted edifice in the Gothic style. From Latrobe, the father of the Greek revival in America, he imbibed not only his knowledge of Greek forms, but his principles of professional practice and his scientific engineering skill.

Early in the period of his training Mills began to make designs for buildings independently. In 1802, when only twenty-one, he submitted a plan for South Carolina College which secured a half share of the prize, the other half going to Edward Clark who become the contractor for the building, Rutledge College, since rebuilt. In 1804 he designed the Congregational Church in Charleston, the "Circular" church, in which he adopted for the first time in America the auditorium type of plan suited for the preaching service. A design for a penitentiary for South Carolina, from this period, did not come to execution.

In 1808 he established himself in independent practice in Philadelphia, where he remained until 1817. Among his first designs here was that for a row of houses still standing on Ninth Street between Locust and Walnut. In 1809 he also designed Washington Hall. In 1810 he submitted a design for the State House at Harrisburg, still preserved there, from which was erected, with some modifications, the building which stood until late in the nineteenth century. A semicircular portico of Ionic columns adorned the principal front, with balancing outbuildings. Over the center rose a tall drum surrounded by a peristyle and crowned by a low Roman dome (contemporary engraving by J. L. Frederick for *The Casket*). The Unitarian Church in Philadelphia, of octagonal form, was begun in 1811 and dedicated Feb. 14, 1813; and Dr. Stoughton's Church, circular, seating four thousand, was executed at the same period. In 1812 Mills rebuilt for municipal offices the wings of the old State House (Independence Hall), since restored to nearly their original aspect. In the same year he had a share in the design of the remarkable Upper Ferry Bridge (burned in 1838), a single timber arch of 360 feet span, much the longest in the world at that day. The Gothic house built by John Dorsey, one of Mills's principal patrons, is presumed to have been from his design, as is the picturesque Burlington County prison in New Jersey, still standing.

Commissions for a number of buildings in Richmond came to him after he won the competition for the Monumental Church which memorialized the victims of the theatre fire of Dec. 26, 1811. In this church, still standing, Mills again used the octagonal form, with a portico of Egyptian columns. The Wickham house (now the Valentine Museum), also from 1812, has a salon bowed toward the garden and a richly designed central circular staircase. In 1814 he gave a design for the Court House, with which Godefroy [q.v.] was also concerned. The building was destroyed many years ago. The Brockenbrough house, afterwards occupied by Jefferson Davis as the "White House of the Confederacy," and the lovely Archer house (recently demolished) were likewise from this time.

The citizens of Baltimore were the first to undertake an important public monument to Washington. A competition was instituted in 1814, in which many of the leading architects of the time took part. Joseph Ramée, later the designer of Union College in Schenectady, proposed a great Roman triumphal arch; Mills, a tall Greek column. The latter was chosen. The corner stone was laid in Mount Vernon Place, on July 4, 1815, and the monument, crowned by a figure of Washington by Causici, was completed in 1829. The design was the first of the colossal Greek Doric type, preceding the Wellington columns in London and Dublin. Other commissions in Baltimore followed, and Mills took up his residence there in 1817. During his stay of three years he designed the First Baptist Church ("Round Top"), a smaller model of the Roman Pantheon, with a portico of six columns, and St. John's Evangelical Episcopal Church, with three aisles (both buildings illustrated on the margins of the Poppleton plat of Baltimore). He was also made president and chief engineer of the water-works company.

The great prize of the profession in these years was the building for the Bank of the United States in Philadelphia, for which a competition was advertised in July 1818. Mills submitted two distinct sets of designs, with additional variants. All of his façades extended the full width of the plot, permitting a variety of effects: a long Doric colonnade with terminal masses; a six-column portico with flanking wings of the same order. For the central banking room Mills proposed a simple rotunda, or a square with flanking apses screened by columns. The design submitted by Latrobe was preferred, however, and executed, with some modifications, by Strickland.

In 1820 Mills returned to Charleston to become a member of the Board of Public Works of his native state. He is referred to in public documents of that period as "State Engineer and Architect," and as "Civil and Military Engineer of the State." South Carolina had entered on an extensive scheme of internal improvements, with annual appropriations exceeding $100,000, spent chiefly on roads and on river and canal development. To his interest in the latter subject Mills had already testified in his *Treatise on Inland Navigation*, published in 1820 before his departure from Baltimore. Extensive works were built under his direction on the Saluda, Broad, and Catawba rivers, with numerous locks, and the rivers and bays were connected by several canals. By 1826 he could write "We now have an inland navigation equal to 2,370 miles" (*Statistics of South Carolina*, p. 301). The Board of Public Works had charge also of the public buildings of the state and the districts, for which appropriations ranged from $50,000 to $80,000 annually. Those erected from 1820 to 1830 were on designs made by Mills or revised by him. They included, in 1822, the court houses at Kingstree, Newberry, Yorkville, and Greenville, the jails at Union, Spartanburg, Lancaster, and Yorkville. Among the buildings undertaken, one of the more notable was the fireproof Record Building in Charleston, begun in 1822. It is of great simplicity, with porticos of four Greek Doric columns on each front. Others in Charleston included a wing of the prison, planned on the principle of solitary confinement, and several powder magazines. The Baptist Church, of the temple type, was also his work. Special importance attaches to his designs, still preserved, for the State Hospital for the Insane at Columbia, of which the central portion was erected in 1822. At a period very early in the development of modern ideas in the care of the insane, this building was not a prison but a hospital: fireproof, with all its rooms and wards having southern exposure to a garden court, and with a roof garden over the whole structure. (The building is discussed in its institutional aspects by Dr. J. W. Babcock in the *Handbook of South Carolina*, 1st ed., 1907, and in vol. III, pp. 587-613, of *The Institutional Care of the Insane in the United States and Canada*, 1916, ed. by H. M. Hurd.) The facade showed a portico of six Greek Doric columns at the principal story.

Mills's manuscript designs reveal his authorship of certain houses in Columbia, both the first Ainslee Hall, about 1830 (now Chicora College for Women), and the second (now the center building of the Presbyterian Theological Seminary). At Camden, S. C., his work comprised the Presbyterian Church, the DeKalb monument—a squat obelisk on a pedestal—of which the corner stone was laid by Lafayette in 1825, and the Court House (1826), which was of the full hexastyle temple form. While in Charleston Mills issued a number of valuable publications relative to his native state: *Internal Improvement of South Carolina* (1822); a most accurate *Atlas of the State of South Carolina* (1825); and *Statistics of South Carolina, Including a View of Its . . . History* (1826).

In 1824 designs were invited for the Bunker Hill Monument, and Mills submitted one not unlike that for the monument in Baltimore, a great Greek Doric column, surmounted by a. tripod and banded with military trophies. He states in sketches of his life that he proposed an obelisk form, doubtless as an alternative, and considered that his idea had been adopted in the executed work. The simple obelisk actually erected was the work of Solomon Willard.

With the cessation of state appropriations for public works in 1830 Mills removed to Washington. A stanch Jacksonian as he had been a stanch Jeffersonian, he had hopes of federal employment, which were not to be disappointed. His first recorded project in the capital was one for a Potomac bridge, advocated by President Jackson (W. B. Bryan, *A History of the National Capital*, vol. II, 1916, p. 250). Soon he was receiving various governmental commissions, such as those for the custom houses at New Bedford, and Newburyport, Mass., New London, and Middletown, Conn.—buildings solid and of Tuscan simplicity. On July 6, 1836, he was appointed "Architect of Public Buildings," a position which he held for fifteen years. During his tenure of this office there fell to him three of the principal buildings of the nineteenth century in Washington: the Treasury, the Patent Office, and the Post Office. For the Treasury, of which he built the Fifteenth Street front (1836-

39), he adopted the motive of a long unbroken colonnade, in which he used the Ionic order of the Erechtheum. It is a façade of great impressiveness. Although the sandstone in which it was first executed suffered badly from exposure, the recent replacement with granite followed faithfully the original lines and still preserves the design of Mills. For the central feature of the front of the Patent Office (1836-40) he used his favorite portico of the Greek Doric, but this time with the eight columns and the proportions of the Parthenon, happily situated on a fine vista. For the old Post Office (begun 1839) which fronts it, he recurred to academic forms, with pilasters above a tall basement.

The crowning success of his life was his victory in competition for the design of the Washington Monument at the capital. This project, which antedated even the formation of the national government, was revived in 1833 by the formation of the Washington National Monument Association; funds were solicited by popular subscription, and designs were invited by advertisement in 1836. That of Mills, officially adopted, proposed an obelisk six hundred feet in height, surrounded at the base by a circular colonnaded building with a portico at the principal face, surmounted by the figure of Washington in a triumphal chariot. The order was to be a very massive Doric. Subscriptions came slowly, and the corner stone was not laid until 1848. After a good beginning the work languished for lack of funds and was suspended in 1855, the year of Mills's death, when the shaft had reached a height of 152 feet. In spite of the efforts of the Association it could not be resumed, and it was not until after many years and much controversy that, in 1878, Congress made possible the continuance of construction, and the obelisk itself was carried to completion in 1884 at a height of 555 feet. It was then the highest of human structures. In it the simplicity and grandeur of the form were matched with the character of the subject.

Much further work for the government and some for other clients fell to Mills as architect of public buildings. No less than eight of the Marine Hospitals were from his designs (some of which he published in 1837), as were the jail in Washington (1839), the court house in Alexandria (1838), and the Library at South Carolina College (1838). The chief work of his later incumbency was in remodeling the heating, ventilating, and lighting systems of the Capitol, and in correcting the acoustic defects of the old Hall of Representatives. In 1850 he was called on by the Senate Committee on Public Buildings for designs for the enlargement of the Capitol, and submitted plans for the north and south wings as well as for an enlargement of the dome, employing masonry construction (Glenn Brown, *History of the United States Capitol*, vol. II, 1902, plate 137). Although this scheme was reported favorably by the committee, a competition was instituted, and Mills was directed to prepare the working plans, "utilizing the four sets of drawings which had been submitted for what he might find them to be worth" (*Ibid.*, II, 117). He doubtless had but little stomach for this task, and being past seventy, soon relinquished it, retiring from public office in 1851. Thomas U. Walter [*q.v.*], who had been one of the competitors, was then chosen as the architect. During his years in Washington Mills had continued his activity in publication with *The American Pharos, or Lighthouse Guide* (1832), and a *Guide to the Capitol of the United States,* which first appeared in 1834 and was frequently reprinted. As late as 1853 he published a report on waterworks for the city of Washington.

Mills was a humanitarian, a reformer, a man of broad and prophetic vision. In matters of institutional care, whether of the insane, the criminal, or the poor, he was able by his profession to contribute to a more enlightened treatment. He saw clearly the hygienic, the social, and, in less degree, the economic problems of his native state, was an advocate of the drainage of its lowlands, and of the abolition of slavery through colonization of the blacks. He early urged the introduction of railroads and the advantages of trunk lines, including a transcontinental road, although he took no recorded part in the actual establishment of the railroads, his engineering work falling within the period of canal transportation. In architecture he stands as the first native-born professional, and as one of the chief exponents of the Greek revival. His works now appear a little stereotyped, a little arid, but very sober, very competent, very dignified—contributing to that austere tradition still so powerful in American architectural style.

He was married in 1808 to Eliza Barnwell Smith, daughter of General Smith of "Hackwood Park," Frederick County, Va. Of his four daughters, all of whom married, two left issue: Mary, wife of Alexander Dimitry [*q.v.*], an officer in the American diplomatic service, and Sarah, wife of Dr. John Evans. Mills was a member of the Society of Artists organized in Philadelphia in 1810, and its first secretary. According to an old Washington lady who knew him in her youth, he was "a man of strikingly strong features, of evidently studious hab-

its, with an air of deep absorption or abstraction; a man of unusual dignity and reserve, yet affable and kindly. He was of simple and correct taste in dress, and his presence was always an interesting one to everybody." She speaks of his regular attendance at the Presbyterian Church and of his one vice, the intemperate use of snuff (Gallagher memoranda). His portrait, drawn by St. Memin, has been several times reproduced.

[A number of drawings and other papers of Mills have been preserved among his descendants in New Orleans. A memorandum book and about eighty "Miscellaneous Papers" as well as certain documents in the Jefferson Papers, are in the MSS. Div. Lib. of Cong. Other documents are in the office of the Supt. of the U. S. Capitol, the archives of S. C., the Hist. Soc. of Pa., and the Mass. Hist. Soc. Autobiographical sketches by Mills, preserved in part in manuscript, formed the basis of the notice in Wm. Dunlap's *Hist. of the Rise and Progress of the Arts of Design in the U. S.* (1834), vol. II, upon which were based the accounts in *The Dict. of Architecture Issued by the Architectural Pub. Soc.* (1848–92), vol. IV, and in P. A. Planat's *Encyclopédie de l'Architecture* (1888–95), vol. V. The skilful wording of Mills's manuscript, itself not overstepping the truth, has given rise to exaggerated claims as to his share in certain enterprises. Some of these occur in an article by his grandson, C. P. Dimitry [*q.v.*], in the New Orleans *Daily Picayune*, May 26, 1895, which has been frequently used by later writers, notably Glenn Brown in the biographical sketch of Mills in his *Hist. of the U. S. Capitol*, vol. II (1902). This work, like the *Doc. Hist. of the U. S. Capitol* (1904), includes many official papers. A valuable notice by C. C. Wilson, *Robert Mills, Architect* (1919), corrects many misconceptions, and offers new material, particularly on his works in South Carolina. Extensive documentary research has been undertaken by Mrs. H. M. Pierce Gallagher, and is in part embodied in well-illustrated papers published in the *Architectural Record*, Apr., May, 1929. See also Montgomery Schuyler, "The Old Greek Revival," pt. 2, *Am. Architect*, Dec. 21, 1910, which is inaccurate in some details; and obituary in the *Daily National Intelligencer* (Washington), Mar. 5, 1855.]   F. K.

MILLS, ROBERT (Mar. 9, 1809–Apr. 13, 1888), merchant and planter, the fourth child of Adam and Janet (Graham) Mills, was born in Todd County, Ky. On May 15, 1826, he entered Cumberland College (now George Peabody College for Teachers), where he studied until the following May. When he was twenty-one he set out for Texas to join an elder brother, Andrew G. Mills, in merchandizing at Brazoria. Since Andrew was a sea-faring man, the management of the business devolved upon Robert. The firm supplied planters and other merchants of the Brazos and Colorado valleys with necessities bartered for pelts and cotton, and extended its trade area even across the Rio Grande. Trains of burros returned to Mexico laden with goods in exchange for specie and bars of Mexican silver, which Robert stacked like stovewood in the counting room. He and Andrew fought in the battle of Velasco against the Mexi-

Mills

Mills

cans on June 26, 1832. After Andrew's death in 1835, Robert and his younger brother, David G. Mills, conducted the firm, first as R. Mills & Company, later as R. & D. G. Mills. About 1849 Mills, realizing that the Brazos would never be navigable, removed to Galveston. The next year he became a partner of Mills, McDowell & Company of New York and of McDowell, Mills & Company of New Orleans. From 1850 till 1863 John William Jockusch, the Prussian consul at Galveston, was a third partner. Their ships and steamboats plied the rivers of Texas and the ocean, transporting cotton and sugar to the markets of the world. In 1852 Mills was president and director of the Galveston and Brazos navigation company that hoped to connect these two points by an intercoastal canal. From the beginning he performed the double function of merchant and banker, dealing in exchange and advancing credit to customers. In the absence of banks, R. & D. G. Mills countersigned the questionable notes of the Northern Bank of Mississippi at Holly Springs. Between twenty-five and five hundred thousand dollars of this money were reported to have circulated as readily as gold in Texas and in New Orleans. The suspension in 1852 of the affiliated houses in New York and New Orleans sent "Mills's money" below par for only one day in Galveston. In 1859 the supreme court of Texas decided that the partnership had violated no statute in reissuing these notes and remitted a fine of one hundred thousand dollars, assessed against the firm in 1857 by the district court of Galveston (23 *Texas Reports*, 295-309). While Robert was building up the commission and banking business in Texas, David was equally successful in operating their plantations. By 1860 the brothers had four sugar and cotton plantations, "Low Wood," "Bynum," "Palo Alto," and "Warren," embracing approximately 3,300 acres in cultivation and 100,000 acres of unimproved land. They owned another 100,000 acres scattered over the state. They were also the largest slaveholders in Texas; they emancipated about eight hundred slaves in 1865. Though reputed to have been worth between three and five million dollars before the Civil War, R. & D. G. Mills in 1873 were bankrupt. Thereupon Robert surrendered to his creditors his plate, carriages, and his mansion, though he might have claimed the protection of the homestead law. His declining years were embittered by inactivity, poverty, and dependence upon relatives. He died in Galveston, where he was buried from Trinity Church. He married Elizabeth McNeel, who died with their first-born child.

[Records of Brazoria County, Angleton, Tex.; tax assessor's rolls, Comptroller's Department, Austin; manuscript census of 1850 and 1860, Bureau of Census, Washington, D. C., and State Library, Austin; correspondence with Bruce R. Payne, Ballinger Mills, Julius W. Jockusch, and Henry A. Perry; J. H. Brown, *Hist. of Texas*, vol. I (copr. 1892), pp. 187, 228; W. M. Gouge, *The Fiscal Hist. of Texas* (1852); A. J. Strobel, *The Old Plantations and their Owners of Brazoria County* (1926); *Southwestern Hist. Quart.*, July 1923; *Democratic Telegraph and Texas Register* (Houston), Aug. 14, 1850; Jan. 17, 1851, Jan. 30, 1852, Mar. 26, 1853, Feb. 11, 25, Mar. 7, Oct. 28, Nov. 4, 11, 1857, Jan. 13, July 7, 1858; *Semi-Weekly Journal* (Galveston), Dec. 24, Mar. 22, 1850, Oct. 15, 1852; *State Gazette* (Austin), Feb. 7, 1852, Jan. 24, 31, 1857; *Galveston Tri-Weekly News* (Houston), June 1, 1864; *Washington American* (Tex.), Apr. 19, 1856; *Galveston Daily News*, Apr. 14, 15, 19, 22, 1888; *Austin Weekly Statesman*, Apr. 15, 19, 1888.]   A. C.

MILLS, ROGER QUARLES (Mar. 30, 1832–Sept. 2, 1911), representative and senator from Texas, was born in Todd County, Ky. His parents were Tabitha (Daniel) and Charles Henley Mills, a planter. His grandfather was Charles Mills of Hanover County, Va. At the age of seventeen he went to Palestine, Tex., where he studied law in the office of a brother-in-law, Reuben A. Reeves. Admitted to the bar in 1852 by act of legislature, he began practice in Corsicana. His marriage on Jan. 7, 1858, to Caroline R. Jones, the daughter of a large ranch owner, added substantially to his prestige in the community. In 1859 and 1860 he represented Navarro County in the state legislature, where he became known as an eloquent advocate of secession. He entered the Confederate army early in 1861 and remained in it to the end of the war. At Oak Hills, Mo., in August 1861 he fought as a private in the ranks of the 3rd Texas Cavalry. From 1862 to the end of the war, he was colonel of the 10th Texas Infantry and was called upon more than once to command the brigade with which it served. At Missionary Ridge and again at Atlanta he was severely wounded. The official records show that his reputation for courage was well earned (*War of the Rebellion: Official Records (Army)*, 1 ser., vol. XXXI, pt. 2, 1890, p. 750).

The years that followed the war were lean for the young lawyer at Corsicana, but in 1872, when the state Democratic convention met in his home town, he gained a nomination as congressman-at-large which at the time was equivalent to an election. Year after year he was returned by his admiring fellow citizens, serving in the House of Representatives from Mar. 4, 1873, until his resignation on Mar. 28, 1892. In 1877 he was one of the most outspoken opponents of the Electoral Commission, which he regarded as a device to steal a fairly won election. Nevertheless, he was a generous opponent and in 1884 came to the aid of McKinley whose seat was being contested, an act which the Ohio congressman never forgot. Mills belonged to the picturesque group, called at first in derision and, as the years went on, in growing affection, "The Confederate Brigadiers." Their political philosophy, like their manners, was old fashioned, and they usually favored economy and lower taxes. In 1887 he was in a strategic position to advocate his favorite views. Seniority had brought him the chairmanship of the ways and means committee at the moment when Cleveland had made a tariff for revenue the central theme of an exciting presidential contest. The Mills bill provided for the reduction of tariff on manufactured articles and placed lumber, wool, salt, and other raw materials on the free list. The bill, after a bitter debate, passed the Democratic House, but was, of course, promptly shelved by the Republican Senate. During the campaign of 1888 he was in great demand as a speaker. A speech in New York City on July 4, 1888, especially, aroused national attention (*Speeches of Hon. Thomas B. Reed . . . and Hon. Roger Q. Mills*, 1888; see *Nation*, July 12, 1888). Before a popular audience he was always at his best, earnest, simple, and eloquent; in running debate, especially under the stinging satire of opponents like Reed of Maine, he sometimes lost his temper, and his language was not always remarkable for moderation. In two essays printed in *Both Sides of the Tariff Question*, copr. 1889, he explained his point of view in a mood that was calmer though no less effective.

In 1891, largely on account of his opposition to free silver, he was defeated for the speakership by a younger man, Charles Frederick Crisp of Georgia, but his prestige in Texas was still sufficient to obtain his election to the Senate, where he served from March 1892 to March 1899. He was a close friend of President Cleveland and a supporter of his policies. His opposition to prohibition in 1887 and his dislike for free silver had already made him many enemies, among them the powerful ex-governor, James Hogg. The age of the Confederate brigadiers had passed, and in 1899, when Mills came up for reëlection, he was passed over in favor of Governor Culberson. He spent his remaining years in Corsicana. At the time of his death the discovery of oil had made the old senator a wealthy man.

[Unpublished thesis by Durell Carothers in the Lib. of Rice Institute; *War of the Rebellion: Official Records (Army)*, 1 ser., vols. XXII, pt. 1, XXIII, XXX, pt. 2; L. E. Daniell, *Personnel of the Texas State Government* (1892); *The Encyc. of the New West*, ed. by W. S. Speer and J. H. Brown (1881); *Biog. Dir. of Am. Cong.* (1928); *Dallas Morning News*, Sept. 3, 1911; *Galveston Daily News*, Sept. 3, 1911.]
R. G. C—l.

MILLS, SAMUEL JOHN (Apr. 21, 1783–June 16, 1818), Congregational clergyman, was the son of Samuel John and Esther (Robbins) Mills. His father was long pastor of the church at Torringford, Conn., in which town the younger Samuel was born. His original purpose was to be a farmer, but his religious experiences finally impelled him to enter the ministry. He became much concerned about his spiritual welfare in the revival of 1798, and for two years thereafter felt convinced that he would go to hell. In the autumn of 1801, however, his mother's piety enabled him to rejoice in God's perfections without considering his own future destiny, and he afterwards realized that this was his conversion. Immediately the idea came to him of going abroad to preach the gospel to the heathen, the first time probably that such an enterprise had been seriously considered in the United States.

Accordingly, in 1801, he sold a farm which had been bequeathed to him by his grandmother, and entered Morris Academy, Litchfield. In 1806 he became a student at Williams College, where, during his first year, he was a leader in a religious revival. He proposed to several of his friends that they should become foreign missionaries and secured from them a favorable response. Graduating in 1809, he spent a few months at Yale, in the hope of enlisting supporters of the missionary project there, but his stay was fruitless save for his discovery of Henry Obookiah, a native of the Sandwich Islands, who had recently found his way to New Haven. Early in 1810 he proceeded to Andover Theological Seminary taking Obookiah with him; Obookiah was converted soon afterwards, and his conversion resulted in the foundation a few years later of the Foreign Mission School at Cornwall, Mass. While in the seminary Mills talked about missions incessantly. In June 1810, he and three of his friends presented a paper to the General Association of Massachusetts, in which they declared their desire to go as missionaries to the heathen and asked for counsel. As a result the American Board of Commissioners for Foreign Missions was formed, which in 1812 sent out ten missionaries to Calcutta, and by 1820 had eighty-one missionaries under its charge.

On his graduation from Andover in 1812, Mills was licensed to preach and was sent by the Connecticut and Massachusetts Home Missionary societies on a tour of the country beyond the

Alleghanies, from Cincinnati to New Orleans, in company with John F. Schermerhorn; in 1814-15 he made a second and more extensive journey with Daniel Smith. They preached the gospel, distributed Bibles and tracts, promoted the formation of Bible societies, and collected information about the religious and moral condition of the inhabitants. They endured great hardships and were sometimes in danger of their lives from starvation, Indians, and flooded rivers. In collaboration with Schermerhorn he published in 1814 *A Correct View of That Part of the United States Which Lies West of the Allegany Mountains, with Regard to Religion and Morals,* and with Smith, in 1815, *Report of a Missionary Tour through That Part of the United States Which Lies West of the Allegany Mountains.* On June 21, 1815, Mills was ordained at Newburyport, Mass. During the next two years he resided at Albany, New York, Philadelphia, and Washington; and in these years he was the instigator and the chief organizer of the American Bible Society, of the United Foreign Missionary Society (formed by the Presbyterian and Dutch Reformed churches), and of a school for training negro preachers. He also spent some months visiting the poor in the city of New York, and distributing Bibles and tracts. He planned a missionary tour of South America, and hoped finally to accompany Obookiah to the Sandwich Islands.

He became particularly interested in the negroes, however, and when the American Colonization Society was formed in 1817 he at once offered his services. With Ebenezer Burgess he was dispatched to Africa to find suitable territory for purchase. They set out for England in November and were almost wrecked in a storm in which their ship was deserted by the captain, but finally made port at St. Malo. After consulting with the leaders of the English anti-slavery movement they sailed in February 1818 for Sierra Leone, where they spent three months negotiating with a number of native chiefs, and selecting territory for the future colony of Liberia. On the return voyage, begun May 22, 1818, Mills caught a chill, died of fever, and was buried at sea.

Few men with such slender natural endowments have accomplished more. He was quite undistinguished as a scholar, writer, or preacher; he was slow of tongue, inert in manner, and unimpressive in personality. Nevertheless, he was a good judge of men, and had considerable ability as an organizer. His unquenchable ardor and tireless energy made him the father of foreign missionary work in the United States, and the chief creator of four important philanthropic institutions.

[Samuel Orcutt, *Hist. of Torrington, Conn.* (1878); Calvin Durfee, *Williams Biog. Annals* (1871); *Gen. Cat. Theol. Sem., Andover, Mass., 1808-1908* (n.d.); Gardiner Spring, *Memoirs of the Rev. Samuel J. Mills* (1820); W. B. Sprague, *Annals Am. Pulpit,* vol. II (1857); E. G. Stryker, *Missionary Annals: A Story of One Short Life* (copr. 1888); T. C. Richards, *Samuel J. Mills, Missionary Pathfinder, Pioneer, and Promoter* (1906); *Conn. Courant* (Hartford), Sept. 8, 1818; *Conn. Jour.* (New Haven), Sept. 22, 1818.]

H.B.P.

MILLS, SUSAN LINCOLN TOLMAN (Nov. 18, 1826–Dec. 12, 1912), missionary and educator, was the third in a family of six children, five of whom were girls. On her father's side she was descended from Thomas Tolman, a native of England, who settled in Dorchester, Mass., in 1630. In 1835 her parents, John and Elizabeth (Nichols) Tolman, moved from Enosburg, Vt., her birthplace, to Ware, Mass., where she received her early education. She entered Mount Holyoke Seminary (now Mount Holyoke College) in 1842, and graduated in 1845. During the next three years she taught at that institution under the direction of Mary Lyon [*q.v.*] and on Sept. 11, 1848, she married Rev. Cyrus Taggart Mills [*q.v.*].

During the years from 1848 to 1884 she assisted her husband in missionary and educational work. Their first engagement was at Batticotta Seminary in Ceylon, India, an institution devoted to the education of native teachers and preachers. Besides helping in administering the affairs of the seminary, she also supervised the work of several day schools. After six years, which sorely taxed their health, they returned to the United States. With improvement in health came the old urge for foreign service, and in 1860 they went to the Hawaiian Islands. Cyrus Mills became president of Oahu College in Honolulu, and his wife taught English and natural sciences. During the four years of their sojourn she established an enviable reputation among the young people of the school and of the community by her wholesome advice and her cheerful disposition. Returning to the United States in 1864 they settled in California the following year, and purchased a young ladies' seminary from Mary Atkins at Benicia.

The acquisition of this school opened the field to which Mrs. Mills dedicated the remainder of her active life—the "Christian education" of young women. Benicia was not the most desirable place for such a school, however, and they acquired about sixty acres of land five miles south of Oakland and just east of the south end of San Francisco Bay, erected a comfortable building which would accommodate about one hundred and twenty-five students, and moved to the new site in 1871. Mills Seminary—for this was the name given to the school at that time—was favorably regarded from the very beginning. In 1877 the property was deeded to a board of trustees. When Cyrus Mills died in 1884, his wife was appointed to the board in his place and was practically in charge of the institution until Homer B. Sprague assumed the duties of president in the autumn of 1885. In the meantime a four years' college course was added to the curriculum, a college charter was secured from the state of California, and Mills Seminary became Mills College. In 1890 Mrs. Mills became president, and during the nineteen years she held the office she proved an efficient executive. In 1901 she transferred property to the trustees valued at about $200,000, which was to be administered by the board for the benefit of the college. Beginning in 1906, the seminary classes were eliminated, one each year, and the institution was devoted entirely to the higher education of young women. Mrs. Mills retired from the presidency in 1909, but as president emeritus she continued to exercise considerable influence over the administration of the college. The growth of the institution while under her charge, together with the addition of the college curriculum, is ample justification for recognizing her as the founder of Mills College. She died at Oakland, Cal.

[C. K. Wittenmyer, ed., *The Susan Lincoln Mills Memory Book* (1915); R. A. Keep, *Fourscore Years: A Hist. of Mills Coll.* (1931); *Who's Who in America*, 1912–13; *San Francisco Examiner*, Dec. 13, 1912.]

C. G.

MILLSPAUGH, CHARLES FREDERICK (June 20, 1854–Sept. 15, 1923), botanist, was born at Ithaca, N. Y., the son of John Hill Millspaugh, an artist, and Marion (Cornell) Millspaugh, sister of Ezra Cornell [*q.v.*]. At an early age he took great interest in sports and natural history. While still a boy he became acquainted with Louis Agassiz and began a long friendship which had much to do with shaping his subsequent career. On Sept. 19, 1877, he married Mary Louisa Spaulding, who died in 1907, and in 1910 he married Clara Isobel Mitchell.

He studied at Cornell University, 1871–73, then at the New York Homeopathic Medical College and Hospital, where he received the degree of M.D. in 1881. From 1881 to 1890 he practised medicine at Binghamton, N. Y., and then for one year at Waverly, N. Y. During this time he became interested in botany and made a special study of plants used in medicine,

preparing a monumental two-volume work, illustrated by himself with 180 colored plates, which was published in 1887 under the title, *American Medicinal Plants*. His skill as an artist, which he attributed to early instruction from his father, added to the value of this work, which brought him so prominently before the botanical fraternity that in 1891 he was called to the chair of botany in the University of West Virginia. Here he published a "Preliminary Catalogue of the Flora of West Virginia" (*Annual Report of the West Virginia Agricultural Experiment Station*, 1892, pp. 315–537), and began to specialize in the *Euphorbiaceae*, contributing a number of papers on this subject to various journals between 1890 and 1915.

After the World's Columbian Exposition (1893), he became curator of botany at the Field Museum of Natural History, Chicago, a position which he held until his death. He built up the herbarium, both by purchases and by his own collecting, until it became one of the largest and probably the most thoroughly catalogued and the most safely housed of all herbaria. He made many collecting trips to Mexico, Yucatan, the Bahamas, and the West Indies, besides expeditions in the United States and a journey around the world. Nearly forty papers were published as a result of these collections. As a museum curator he was particularly successful; he watched the visitors, noting which displays attracted most attention, then developed others along similar lines. His labels, striking and efficient, are models which other museums might well copy. Glass flowers, and plants made of a combination of glass and wax, formed an interesting and instructive part of the botanical exhibit. He was an excellent lecturer and in this capacity his services were in great demand and brought prestige to the Museum. He was a professorial lecturer in botany at the University of Chicago, professor of medical botany in the Chicago Homœopathic Medical College, a fellow of the American Association for the Advancement of Science, of the Faculdad de Medicina, Mexico, and of the Faculdad de Medicina, Brazil, and was president of the Wild Flower Preservation Society for several years.

In person, he was a man of unusually fine appearance. He was athletic, and a good tennis player even at an age when most men are too slow for such sport. Throughout his public career he was prominent socially. His distinguished appearance made a good first impression which improved with acquaintance. His extensive travels, wide information, and knowledge of the world developed contacts which brought invitations to yacht cruises among the Antilles, where so much of his collecting was done. A few years before his death he went to Santa Catalina Island to rest after a serious operation, but while there studied the flora of the island and, in collaboration with L. W. Nuttall, prepared an extensive paper.

Chief among his publications, in addition to those already mentioned, were the following: "Contribution to the Coastal and Plain Flora of Yucatan" (*Field Museum Publications, Botanical Series I*, 1895, 1896, 1898); "*Plantae Yucatanae*" (*Ibid., Series III*, 1903, 1904); "Flora of West Virginia" (*Ibid., Series I*, 1896), with L. W. Nuttall; "The Living Flora of West Virginia" (*West Virginia Geological Survey Reports*, 5A, 1913); "Flora of Santa Catalina Island" (*Field Museum Publications, Botanical Series V*, 1923), with Nuttall.

[E. E. Sherff, in *Bot. Gazette*, Apr. 1924; *Who's Who in America*, 1922–23; *Cornell Alumni News*, Oct. 11, 1923; *Chicago Daily Tribune*, Sept. 17, 1923; complete list of Millspaugh's publications at the Field Museum.]   C.J.C.

MILMORE, MARTIN (Sept. 14, 1844–July 21, 1883), sculptor, was born in Sligo, County Sligo, Ireland, of excellent Irish stock. After the death of his father, a schoolmaster, in 1851, the widowed mother with her four young sons came to the United States and settled in Boston. Martin and his brother Joseph were educated at the Brimmer School and the Latin School, while in addition Martin had art lessons at the Lowell Institute for seven years. Joseph, the eldest son, was early obliged to go to work. At first a cabinet-maker's assistant, he later became a proficient stone-cutter, with a recognized talent for sculpture. From this brother Martin, while still in school, received lessons in wood-carving, which determined him to become a sculptor. His earliest effort was a bust of himself, made by the aid of a mirror. Wishing to study modeling in clay, he presented himself at the newly built studio of Thomas Ball [q.v.], during the first hour after that sculptor had taken possession. Ball did not give lessons, but, touched by the lad's disappointment, gave him a work room and materials, in return for which the boy agreed to keep the studio clean and attend to the fires. The close association thus begun lasted from 1860 to 1864, when Milmore set up his own studio.

In the early sixties Ball was building up, bowlful by bowlful, the plaster model of his famous equestrian statue of Washington, and Milmore as observer and helper was initiated into many branches of the sculptor's craft. While still with Ball he produced a little figure called "Devotion," ordered for the Sanitary Fair of 1863, and a high relief, "Phosphor," of which he sold the original and two replicas. In 1864, through the purchaser of one of the replicas, he received a commission for three granite figures for the Boston Horticultural Hall: "Ceres," over twelve feet high, "Flora" and "Pomona," each eight feet high. The "Ceres" he modeled in plaster, after the manner of Ball in the Washington equestrian. He spent two years on these figures, his brother Joseph assisting him in the cutting. In 1865 came his much praised bust of Charles Sumner, presented by the Massachusetts legislature to George William Curtis and now in the Senate wing of the Capitol, Washington, D. C.

Milmore's growing fame was established in 1867 when the City of Boston accepted his design for the Roxbury Soldiers' Monument, Forest Hills Cemetery. An excellent piece of work for its day, it has as its chief feature the seven-foot bronze statue of a soldier resting on his gun and contemplating the graves of his fallen comrades. The success of this monument paved the way for the most significant undertaking of Milmore's career, the Soldiers' and Sailors' Monument erected on Boston Common in 1877, which became the prototype of numerous Civil War memorials throughout the land. In Milmore's design an extensive granite base, with bronze panels on its sides and symbolic bronze figures at four piers, supports at its center a high shaft crowned by a bronze figure of "Liberty." Now outmoded, the monument remains a sincere and dignified effort. To model the sculpture, he went to Rome, where he spent studious years from 1870 to 1875. During his stay he made portrait busts of Pope Pius IX, Wendell Phillips, and Ralph Waldo Emerson. "Milmore was a picturesque figure," wrote one of his contemporaries, "somewhat of the Edwin Booth type, with long dark hair and large dark eyes. He affected the artistic (as all of us artists used to, more or less), wearing a broad-brimmed soft black hat, and a cloak. His appearance was striking, and he knew it." (Daniel Chester French, to the writer of this sketch, Feb. 7, 1931.)

Other busts by Milmore are Lincoln, Grant, Daniel Webster, Cardinal McCloskey, and George Ticknor, the last-mentioned now owned by the Boston Public Library. At West Point, N. Y., is his bronze statue of Gen. Sylvanus Thayer. At Erie, Pa., Keene, N. H., Charlestown, Mass., and Fitchburg, Mass., are typical Civil War monuments from his hand. His brother Joseph, a sculptor of scarcely less talent than himself, was his constant collaborator; the great granite Sphinx commemorating the Union dead, at Mount Auburn Cemetery, Cambridge, Mass., is their joint work. Martin Milmore's monuments were among the best of their time, yet were not good enough to have a truly vitalizing influence on American monumental art. T. H. Bartlett, an informed if acrimonious critic, writ-. ing in the eighties, found them better in intention than in execution, while Lorado Taft (*post*, p. 255) writes: "Milmore stands for good workmanship rather than for poetic expression. Few, if any, of his productions seem inspired. . . . There is nothing epic in his grasp of war subjects, nothing lyric in his treatment of gentler themes. . . . But we find throughout good honest construction, adequate modelling, and, rarest of all, a sense of the monumental in line and mass."

Milmore died, unmarried, at Boston Highlands, aged thirty-eight. His grave in Forest Hills Cemetery, Roxbury, is marked by one of the most famous pieces of sculpture in the United States—"Death and the Young Sculptor," by Daniel Chester French.

[C. R. Post, "Martin Milmore," in *Art Studies, Medieval, Renaissance, and Modern* (1925), vol. III; H. T. Tuckerman, *Book of the Artists* (1867), incorrect as to place of birth; "New Monument in Boston," *Art Journal* (N. Y.), Oct. 1877; obituaries of Martin and Joseph Milmore in *Am. Architect and Building News*, Aug. 18, 1883, and Jan. 30, 1886; Justin Winsor, *The Memorial Hist. of Boston*, vol. III (1881); Lorado Taft, *The Hist. of Am. Sculpture* (rev. ed., 1930); C. E. Fairman, *Art and Artists of the Capitol of the U. S. A.* (1927); Thomas Ball, *My Threescore Years and Ten* (1891); *Boston Evening Transcript*, July 23, 1883.]
A. A.

MILNER, JOHN TURNER (Sept. 29, 1826–Aug. 18, 1898), civil engineer, industrialist, was born in Pike County, Ga., the son of Willis Jay and Elizabeth (Turner) Milner. His parents were pioneer settlers of Georgia, the Milners being Virginians and the Turners North Carolinians. John's early youth was spent on a farm which his father ran in addition to his activities as a railroad contractor, builder, and miner. The boy received a simple schooling and at the age of ten was working in his father's gold mines in Lumpkin County. In the years immediately following he gained from his father some practical insight into railroad construction. He matriculated at the University of Georgia in 1843 and made a brilliant record until ill health forced him to leave at the end of his third year.

Railroads were then new and construction work was in no small measure a matter of empiricism. What young Milner had learned by actual experience he combined with his scientific training and within two years became principal assistant in building the Macon & Western Railroad. This activity was pioneering of a sort, but far more alluring was the gold rush of 1849, which Milner joined, journeying to California by the overland route. After arriving he abandoned mining, however, to become city surveyor of San José, then the capital of the new territory. Returning to Georgia in 1854, he soon removed to Alabama, where he built the Montgomery & West Point Railroad. Meanwhile, a number of enterprising citizens who had tapped the coal and iron deposits of the state were proclaiming the urgent need of a railroad to make accessible the rich mineral resources north of the Black Belt. Persistent argument before a cotton-growing legislature finally resulted, in 1858, in an appropriation for a reconnoissance through the region, and Milner was appointed to undertake the survey. His *Report of the Chief Engineer . . . of the South & North Alabama Railroad Company* (1859) was far-reaching in its ultimate effects. Although construction was suspended during the Civil War, his proposals were eventually followed and his predictions substantiated. He projected the road from Decatur, Ga., to Elyton, Ala., through the richest coal and iron region. By analogy with the state-owned Western & Atlantic of Georgia, he showed how the iron industry would be stimulated to the advantage of the railroad and the state as a whole, and he discussed the value of slave labor, which he declared to be more reliable and cheaper than white. With aid from the Confederacy the railroad was built part way into the mineral region; Milner and Frank Gilmer, a partner, were also granted a subsidy to aid them in erecting the Oxmoor furnaces, in order to provide war materials.

When work on the South & North Alabama Railroad was resumed after the war, Milner made an agreement with the rival Alabama & Chattanooga Railroad concerning the location of the crossing of the two, so that both might benefit from the sale of land where a new city would presumably arise. A site near Village Creek was selected; and both roads were surveyed and located toward it. The Carpet-baggers, who controlled both the legislature and the Alabama & Chattanooga, broke the agreement, however, and diverted the direction of the road toward Elyton, on land in the vicinity of which they had taken sixty-day options, thereby hoping to ruin Milner, who had invested heavily in the district first chosen. Milner, however, by his tactics in surveying kept his opponents in such doubt as to where he would actually locate the crossing that they did not dare take up the options, and on the minute the sixty days expired the land was purchased by a Montgomery banker, Josiah Morris, for Milner and his friends. They formed the Elyton Land Company, which, in 1871, founded Birmingham. The following year the Louisville & Nashville Railroad took over the South & North, and Milner retired from railroading.

Subsequently, he organized the Newcastle Coal & Iron Company (1873) and was connected with the Experimental Coke & Iron Company, which was instrumental in producing the first coke pig iron in Birmingham in 1876. This same year he wrote a pamphlet, *Alabama: As It Was, As It Is, and As It Will Be,* setting forth somewhat enthusiastically the resources and industrial possibilities of the state. His Milner Coal & Railroad Company, established in 1879, he sold a decade later at a profit of over $200,000. On Dec. 30, 1855, he married Flora J. Caldwell of Greenville, Ala., by whom he had one son and three daughters. From 1888 to 1896 he served as state senator from Jefferson County. He was a member of the Presbyterian Church. He died at his Newcastle home from a paralytic stroke at the age of seventy-two.

[The best sketch of Milner is found in T. M. Owen, *Hist. of Ala. and Dict. of Ala. Biog.* (1921), vol. IV; an obituary is in *The Age-Herald* (Birmingham), Aug. 19, 1898; Ethel Armes, *The Story of Coal and Iron in Ala.* (1910), contains a detailed account of his work with the South & North Railroad and excerpts from his writings; contemporary and inaccurate sketch of his career, with special reference to the rise of Birmingham, is published in *Jefferson County and Birmingham, Ala., Hist. and Biog.* (1887), J. W. Du Bose, ed.]
                                L. J. C.

MILNER, MOSES EMBREE [See CALIFORNIA JOE, 1829–1876].

MILNER, THOMAS PICTON [See PICTON, THOMAS, 1822–1891].

MILROY, ROBÉRT HUSTON (June 11, 1816–Mar. 29, 1890), soldier and Indian agent, was born in Washington County, Ind., the son of Samuel and Martha (Huston) Milroy. He came of fighting stock being, it was claimed, a descendant of Robert Bruce through his great-grandfather, John McElroy, who fled from Scotland, changed his name to Milroy, and later settled near Carlisle, Pa. Robert Milroy's immediate ancestors were Indian fighters, and his father contributed stoutly to the upbuilding of the young state of Indiana. The son fully sustained the family reputation. The Milroys removed from Washington County to Carroll County, Ind., when he was ten years old. In 1840 he entered Norwich University in Vermont and graduated in 1843 with the degrees of Bachelor of Arts and Master of Military Science. In the Mexican War he raised a voluntary company in

Carroll County. Mustered into service on June 20, 1846, at New Albany, he was mustered out at New Orleans on June 16, 1847. On May 17, 1849, he was married to Mary Jane Armitage of Alexandria, Pa., who bore him seven children. He took a law course at the University of Indiana, where he received the degree of Bachelor of Laws in 1850, was admitted to the bar, and began practice at Delphi, Ind. In 1850 he was elected a delegate from Carroll County to the state's second constitutional convention as, by an interesting coincidence, his father had been sent to the first one. He was appointed to the bench of the 8th judicial circuit, but resigned, removed to Rensselaer, Ind., in 1854 and took up the practice of law.

In Indiana he is best known as a soldier of the Civil War. At the first call for troops he proceeded to raise a voluntary company in Rensselaer. Of this he was made captain but on Apr. 27, 1861, was mustered into the three months' service as colonel of the 9th Regiment of Indiana Volunteers. At the expiration of this term of service he reënlisted for the three years' service with the same rank, but on Sept. 3 of that year was promoted brigadier-general, and on Nov. 29, 1862, major-general of volunteers. Much of his field service was in western Virginia, where his measures to suppress guerrilla warfare were so drastic that the Confederates offered a large reward for him, dead or alive. As major-general he commanded the second division of the VIII Army Corps, being stationed at Winchester, Va., when Lee made his movement northward toward Pennsylvania. He engaged the Confederate army till driven back with losses so disastrous that they were afterward the subject of military investigation, but he was finally exonerated. He claimed that his retarding of Lee's forces enabled Meade to prepare for Gettysburg. He remained in the service till the end of the war.

After the war he occupied positions of trust and responsibility. He was one of the trustees of the Wabash and Erie Canal. In 1872 he became superintendent of Indian affairs in the state of Washington, and from 1875 to 1885 he was Indian agent with headquarters at Olympia, where he died. Twenty years later a bronze statue of heroic size was erected at his old home, Rensselaer, where it still perpetuates his memory. Personally, he was of fine, athletic appearance, fully six feet and two inches in height; he had piercing black eyes; and these, together with an aquiline nose and long silver hair, gained for him the sobriquet of the "Gray Eagle." Carl Schurz wrote that "he lived on a footing of very democratic comradeship with his men. The most extraordinary stories were told of his discussing with his subordinates what was to be done, of his permitting them to take amazing liberties with the orders to be executed. . . . But he did good service, was respected and liked by all" (*The Reminiscences of Carl Schurz*, II, 1907, p. 388).

[*Norwich University* (3 vols., 1911); T. A. Wylie, *Ind. University* (1890); F. B. Heitman, *Hist. Register and Dict. of the U. S. Army* (1903); *War of the Rebellion: Official Records (Army)*, 1 ser., XXI, 3 ser., II, III; 4 ser., II; T. B. Helm, *Hist. of Carroll County, Ind.* (1882); J. H. Stewart, *Recollections of the Early Settlement of Carroll County* (1872), pp. 38, 47, 170.]

G. S. C.

MILTON, JOHN (Apr. 20, 1807–Apr. 1, 1865), governor of Florida, was born in Jefferson County, Ga., the son of Elizabeth (Robinson) and Homer Virgil Milton, a planter and an officer in the War of 1812. His great-grandfather, John Milton, emigrated from England and, about 1730, settled in Halifax County, N. C., from which his grandfather, also John Milton, removed to Georgia, where as first secretary of state he saved the records from the British and in 1789 received two votes of the Georgia electors for the presidency. The boy was educated in the academy at Louisville, Ga. He studied law in the office of Roger L. Gamble of Louisville and after admission to the bar began the practice of his profession at that place. In two years he removed to Columbus, Ga., and a little later to Mobile, Ala. His law practice continued at this place and at New Orleans until 1846 with a two years' interruption, when he served as a captain of Mobile volunteers in the Seminole War. In 1846 he removed to Florida, settling down on his plantation near Marianna, in Jackson County, where he made his home until his death. He was a Democratic elector in 1848 and in 1849 was elected to the state Senate.

His claim to remembrance rests on his record as war governor of Florida. He was inaugurated governor in 1861 and began his term inauspiciously by denouncing the state secession convention for assuming legislative functions and by refusing to recognize the executive council that the convention had created to limit the governor's powers. During his term as governor his time was so taken up with military affairs that he had scant opportunity to show his ability in any other field. He was an earnest advocate of war-time prohibition both because he deplored drunkenness and because he wished corn to be conserved for other purposes. He approved, if he did not originate, the Florida law providing for the issue of paper money secured by the public land of the state. While not hesitating at times to assert the doctrine of state rights with such vigor as to cause Secretary Benjamin moments of acute distress, the records indicate that on the whole he gave the Confederacy a greater measure of cooperation than was usual among Southern governors. He resisted the recruiting of cavalry in the state on the ground that Florida topography was not suitable for cavalry activities. He differed from the Confederate military authorities in regard to the abandonment of certain Florida ports and the defense of others. Particularly he insisted on the defense of Apalachicola, and, unable to obtain Confederate cooperation to that end, he proposed to Alabama and Georgia a joint defense of the port. He constantly, though vainly, urged that the Confederacy give him charge of military affairs in Florida and more than once hinted to Davis that he would rather be a Confederate brigadier-general than a civilian governor. Failing in all these things, he did his utmost to raise troops for the Confederacy and to keep them supplied with clothing and hospital supplies. He met the Confederate requisitions for money promptly and, throughout the war, received Confederate money for taxes to the practical exclusion of the Florida paper itself. He was vigorous in the use of the militia for the defense of the state and is entitled to credit for the fact that Florida was the only Southern state whose capital remained uncaptured at the end of the war. It must be conceded, however, that the security of Florida during the war may have been due less to defensive measures than to its lack of importance. As the fortunes of the Confederacy ebbed the governor remained defiant, opposed all peace proposals that left the independence of the Confederacy unrecognized, and, upon the collapse of the Southern cause, his mind gave way and he destroyed his own life. He was married twice: first, on Dec. 9, 1826, to Susan Amanda Cobb, of Cobbham, Ga., and, after her death in 1840, to Caroline Howze of Marion, Ala.

[Papers in the supreme court library of the state house at Tallahassee; date of birth and other information from W. H. Milton, Marianna, Fla.; extract from Sarah L. Jones, *Life in the South* (1863), in *Fla. Hist. Soc. Quart.*, July 1909; *War of the Rebellion: Official Records (Army)*, esp. 1 ser. VI, LII, pt. 2; R. H. Rerick, *Memoirs of Fla.* (1902), vol. I; W. W. Davis, *The Civil War and Reconstruction in Fla.* (1913); *Makers of America* (1909, Fla. ed.), vol. I, pp. 148–153.]

R. S. C.

MINER, ALONZO AMES (Aug. 17, 1814–June 14, 1895), Universalist clergyman, president of Tufts College, was born in Lempster, a small village in Sullivan County, N. H., the sec ond of the five children of Benajah Ames and Amanda (Carey) Miner. He was a descendant of Thomas Miner (or Minor) who emigrated to Charlestown, Mass., in 1629, removed to Hingham in 1636, and later joined the younger Winthrop's colony at New London, Conn. Alonzo's parents had rebelled against the strict Calvinism of their time, thus becoming marked people in their community. The boy therefore grew up in the atmosphere of theological debate and early acquired an intense interest in all the issues of his day. His education was somewhat irregular and informal, due partly to the lack of advantages in the sparsely populated country, and more to the fact that a serious accident made him a semi-invalid in his early years. He attended schools in Lempster, Hopkinton, Lebanon, and Franklin, N. H., and in Cavendish, Vt. Much of his study, however, was carried on alone, with the advice and direction of clergymen.

At the age of twenty he was taken into partnership by the principal of the school at Chester, Vt., and a year later he was called to become head of the academy at Unity, N. Y., where he remained for four years. On Aug. 24, 1836, he married Maria S. Perley, whom he had known since childhood, and who now became preceptress at the academy. There were no children. Teaching, however, was only a stepping-stone to his chosen life work. When he was twenty-five years of age, he became a Universalist preacher, conducting services in various small rural communities in the neighborhood, and in 1839 he was ordained.

His first full-time pastorate was in Methuen, Mass., where he quickly earned a name for himself as a public defender of his faith by engaging in frequent debates with orthodox preachers. From Methuen, he was called to a pastorate in Lowell, Mass. Here he became a public man in the ordinary sense of the term, for he began championing public causes and soon found himself in the midst of great discussions and struggles. First, he became a passionate upholder of the temperance movement, taking the extreme stand of absolute abstinence, which in those days was unpopular, and pleading that the church should espouse the cause. Next, in 1843, he was drawn into the anti-slavery movement and threw himself with characteristic abandon into the effort to free the slaves. His love for the church, however, was so strong that he found a double battle on his hands, for he was also opposed to the extreme reformers such as Garrison who advocated "Come-Outism" to church members. His debates on this subject attracted large crowds and gave him a high reputation as a

good logician and fearless fighter. In 1848, he was called to the pastorate of the School Street Church, the Second Universalist Society of Boston, as an associate of Hosea Ballou, 1771–1852 [q.v.]. With this church he remained for forty-three years, rounding out a life of distinguished service in many fields.

In 1862, he became president of Tufts College, largely because the college was in financial difficulties, and because his administrative genius, it was believed, would be adequate to the need. He served without salary, devoting heroic efforts to raising money, teaching classes, and carrying on his work as minister of the church. Through his contacts with men of means and influence, he was able finally to pull the college through its crisis, not only adding largely to the endowment, but also increasing its equipment and faculty. He resigned from the presidency of the college in 1874, and resumed his full-time connection with the church, maintaining, however, his interest in educational institutions, serving as trustee of the college, and being active in promoting the development of Dean Academy in Massachusetts and Goddard Seminary in Vermont. He died in Boston, after a short illness, in his eighty-first year.

[L. L. Selleck, *One Branch of the Miner Family* (1928); G. H. Emerson, *Life of Alonzo Ames Miner* (1896); A. B. Start, *Hist. of Tufts Coll.* (1896); G. H. Emerson, in *Sketches of Successful New Hampshire Men* (1882), ed. by J. B. Clarke; *Boston Daily Advertiser,* June 15, 1895.]
C.R.S.

MINER, CHARLES (Feb. 1, 1780–Oct. 26, 1865), editor, congressman, the son of Seth and Anna (Charlton) Miner and a descendant of Thomas Miner (or Minor) who came to Massachusetts from Somersetshire about 1629, was born in Norwich, Conn. His father was a printer, and after attending the schools near his home Charles worked for some time at his father's trade in New London. During the winter of 1798–99 he studied surveying, and on Feb. 8, 1799, set out for the Wyoming Valley in Pennsylvania to take charge of preparing his father's lands, held under the Connecticut claim, for settlement. In 1802 he joined his brother Asher at Wilkes-Barre in publishing the *Luzerne Federalist and Susquehannah Intelligencer.*

In 1804 Charles Miner bought his brother's interest, becoming sole proprietor of the paper, which he published until 1809 and again in 1810–11. On Feb. 1, 1811, he began the publication of a new journal, the *Gleaner and Luzerne Intelligencer,* which gained a considerable reputation and became something of a political power. During these years he wrote a series of humorous sketches for the columns of his paper, later collected in book form under the title *Essays from the Desk of Poor Robert the Scribe* (1815). In one of them, "Who'll Turn Grindstone?", which appeared in the *Luzerne Federalist,* Sept. 7, 1810, he originated the phrase "to have an axe to grind," which has since come to have a very definite meaning in American speech. He also wrote and published "The Ballad of James Bird," which was circulated widely. In May 1806 he was chosen a member of the first borough council of Wilkes-Barre and in October 1807 was elected a member of the Pennsylvania House of Representatives in which he served till 1809. He was elected again in 1812.

In 1816 he sold the *Gleaner* and went to Philadelphia to become editor and part owner of the *True American,* a daily paper. The next year, unable to stand city life, he returned to Wilkes-Barre, and in July 1817 bought the *Chester and Delaware Federalist* at West Chester, Pa., to which place he removed his family. He soon changed this paper's name to the *Village Record,* under which title it was for years one of the best-known provincial weeklies in the United States. He was elected as a Federalist representative from Pennsylvania to the Nineteenth and Twentieth congresses (Mar. 4, 1825–Mar. 3, 1829) but was not a candidate for reëlection in 1828 because of increasing deafness and the need of his services at home. He resumed the post of editor and publisher of the *Village Record* but in 1832 sold the paper and returned to Wilkes-Barre, retiring to private life. During the next few years he spent a great deal of time and effort in writing his *History of Wyoming* (1845), a standard work dealing with the massacre of July 3, 1778, and the long-disputed land claims of Connecticut and Pennsylvania. It was based on original investigations and interviews with old residents.

While in Congress he became the close personal friend of the leading men of the times, including President Adams, Henry Clay, and others, who continued to correspond with him on political questions after his retirement. He was opposed to slavery, and on May 13, 1826, offered a series of resolutions in the House of Representatives in favor of its abolition in the District of Columbia and its eventual extinction in the United States. These were not favorably received by the House, but he persistently pressed the question throughout the term of his service. He endeavored to popularize silk-growing in the United States, was one of the first to plant mulberry trees and to undertake the raising of silk worms, and drew up and introduced into Congress the first resolutions on silk-culture. He

was an early promoter of the anthracite coal trade in Pennsylvania and of canals as a part of internal improvement. With three others he leased the Mauch Chunk mine from the Lehigh Coal Mine Company, and in 1814 was a member of the firm of Hillhouse, Miner & Cist which was responsible for sending the first boatload of anthracite down the Schuylkill River to Philadelphia. Although this first load was very hard to sell, Miner through his writings did much to introduce anthracite and popularize its use. He married Letitia Wright on Jan. 16, 1804, and was the father of ten children, of whom only three survived him. One of his daughters was the mother of Charlton T. Lewis [*q.v.*]. He died at his home, "The Retreat," near Wilkes-Barre, at the age of eighty-five. Although he was a man of varied activities his reputation rests upon the fact that he was one of the most original and influential of the Pennsylvania editors of the first part of the nineteenth century.

[C. F. and E. M. T. Richardson, *Charles Miner: A Pa. Pioneer* (1916); J. T. Sharf and Thompson Westcott, *Hist. of Phila.* (1884), I, 578; *Biog. Dir. Am. Cong.* (1928); O. J. Harvey, *A Hist. of Lodge No. 61, F. and A. M., Wilkesbarre, Pa.* (1897); *Proc. and Colls. Wyoming Hist. and Geol. Soc., 1922,* vol. XVIII (1923).]
J. H. F.

MINER, MYRTILLA (Mar. 4, 1815–Dec. 17, 1864), promoter of negro education, was born in Brookfield, N. Y., to which place her father's family had come from Norwich, Conn. That portion of New York State was then a wilderness, the Miners were very poor, and there were no educational opportunities for the children. Myrtilla, though physically frail, was possessed by a desire for learning. She disliked house and farm work and, after teaching herself to read, borrowed books, or purchased them with money earned by picking hops. She wrote naïvely and with no satisfactory result to Hon. William H. Seward, governor of New York, asking for advice about securing an education. At fifteen, she was teaching a country school, which she was soon obliged to leave because of "spinal trouble." Recovering partially, she secured admission to a school in Clinton, N. Y., promising to pay her expenses when she was able to teach. Often ill, she studied in bed and after a year secured a position in a public school of Rochester, N. Y. From there she went to a school in Providence, R. I., and then to Newton Institute, a school for planters' daughters at Whitesville, Miss. The milder climate benefited her health but her first sight of negro slavery shocked her profoundly. She came to believe that in education lay the salvation of the negro, and asked for permission to instruct the slaves on one of the plantations, but was told that it was a criminal offense in Mississippi to teach a slave to read. After two years there, she returned North, very ill again. During her illness she made a vow that if she recovered she would devote herself to the cause of the slaves.

When she regained a measure of health, without money or influence, she determined to start a normal school for colored girls in Washington, D. C., a stronghold of aristocratic, pro-slavery feeling, Frederick Douglass [q.v.], negro philanthropist, whom she consulted, knowing the difficulties, discouraged her. She begged money, paper, almost anything, and on Dec. 3, 1851, in a small apartment, opened her normal school for free colored girls. The school had six students at the start, fifteen after a month, forty after two months. With her teaching, she carried on a continuous campaign for funds. In 1853, through the kindness of Thomas Williamson and Samuel Rhoads of the Society of Friends of Philadelphia, who loaned $2,000 and consented to act as trustees, and of Harriet Beecher Stowe, who gave $1,000 of her earnings from *Uncle Tom's Cabin*, she was able to purchase for $4,000 three acres between N Street and New Hampshire Avenue, with a small house, barn, and orchard. In March 1854 the school was moved to this location, which was then on the outskirts of the city. The house was often attacked and threatened, but a high fence, a dog, and the sight of the mistress and her assistant practising with a revolver in the yard warned off intruders. By 1856 the school was placed under trustees, one of whom was Johns Hopkins [q.v.]. Printed solicitations for funds aroused public antagonism and Walter Lenox, a former mayor of Washington, wrote an article, which appeared in the *National Intelligencer* (May 6, 1857), attacking the school and all attempts at negro education as aids in the abolition movement. The institution was several times under other management, or temporarily closed, on account of Miss Miner's poor health.

In 1861 she went to California, where she supported herself by practising clairvoyance and magnetic healing. An accident in which she was thrown from a carriage was followed by symptoms of tuberculosis, to which she was probably always predisposed. She returned to Washington by steamer, arriving there only a few days before her death, which occurred at the home of her friend, Mrs. Nancy M. Johnson. Her funeral was conducted by Rev. William Henry Channing [q.v.] of the Unitarian Church and she was buried at Oak Hill Cemetery, Georgetown. Her work did not lapse, however; on

Mar. 3, 1863, Congress incorporated the Institution for the Education of Colored Youth in the District of Columbia. In 1871 it was joined with Howard University, but separated in 1876, and in 1879 as the Miner Normal School (now Miner Teachers' College) it became part of the public school system of the District.

[E. M. O'Connor, *Myrtilla Miner: A Memoir* (1885); G. S. Wormley, "Myrtilla Miner," in *Jour. of Negro Hist.*, Oct. 1920; *Washington Daily Times*, Dec. 20, 1864, Washington *Daily Morning Chronicle*, Dec. 19, 1864.]
         S. G. B.

MING, JOHN JOSEPH (Sept. 20, 1838–June 17, 1910), Roman Catholic priest and sociologist, was born in Gyswyl, Unterwalden, Switzerland. On completion of a classical course in the Benedictine College of Engelburg, he entered the Society of Jesus (Sept. 7, 1856) and passed through the various cycles of the novitiate, juniorate, teaching apprenticeship, and the study of theology in the Jesuit institutions of Aachen and Maria-Laach, Switzerland. On Sept. 13, 1868, he was ordained. Honored with a preachership at Kreuzberg, a center for pilgrimages, he was soon assigned, after completion of a rigid tertianship, to the chair of theology at the seminary of the prince-bishop of Görz in Austria. In 1872 when the German government expelled the Jesuits, Ming accompanied a number of his brethren to the United States—men whose scholarship incidentally improved the Society's institutions of higher learning in this country.

After two years of parochial work, Ming taught theology in the archdiocesan Seminary of St. Francis near Milwaukee. Soon the Society required his services, and he lectured in sociology and philosophy in various Jesuit institutions—Springhill College in Alabama, Canisius College in Buffalo, N. Y., Campion College at Prairie du Chien, Wis., and finally at St. Louis University, where he remained twenty-one years. An inspiring teacher of sound scholarship and conservative tone, he gained recognition especially in the Mid-West as a Catholic pioneer in the sociological field. A laborious writer, he found time to contribute a number of articles to *America,* the *Messenger of the Sacred Heart,* and the *Catholic Encyclopedia,* as well as to write a score of sound essays on economic and social subjects for the *American Catholic Quarterly Review,* which in Ming's day was probably the most erudite of Catholic publications. His brochure on *The Temporal Sovereignty of the Holy See* (1892) has been widely quoted. His scholarship is evinced in such volumes as *The Data of Modern Ethics Examined* (1894), *The Characteristics and the Religion of*

Modern Socialism (1908), and *Morality of Modern Socialism* (1909). At the time of his death, at Saint Stanislaus' Jesuit Home, Parma, Ohio, he was gathering material for a book on labor problems.

[*America*, July 2, 1910; *Am. Cath. Who's Who* (1911); *The Cath. Encyc. and Its Makers* (1917); *Cleveland Plain Dealer*, June 18, 1910; materials from the archives at Woodstock, Md.]   R. J. P.

MINOR, BENJAMIN BLAKE (Oct. 21, 1818–Aug. 1, 1905), editor, lawyer, educator, was born at Tappahannock, Essex County, Va., the eldest child of Dr. Hubbard Taylor and Jane (Blake) Minor. His grandfather, Thomas Minor, Jr., of Spotsylvania County, a substantial planter, served as an officer through the Revolution, while his great-grandfather, James Taylor, Jr., of Caroline County, fought in the French and Indian War, and was a distinguished member of the House of Burgesses, of the Virginia Conventions of 1775 and 1776, of the first Virginia Senate, and of the convention which ratified the federal Constitution. His mother's father was a successful plantation owner and merchant whose vessels traded as far as the West Indies.

Benjamin Minor received his early education in private schools in Essex County. At the age of twelve, he entered the classical academy of Thomas Hanson in Fredericksburg. He was admitted in 1834 to the junior class of Bristol College, a mechanical institution near Philadelphia, and in 1835 matriculated at the University of Virginia, which he attended until 1837, taking diplomas in several "schools," but no degree. In 1838–39 he attended the College of William and Mary, studying "moral philosophy and political economy" under President Thomas R. Dew [*q.v.*] and law under Judge N. Beverley Tucker. In 1839 he received the degree of LL.B. Too young to practise, he spent the next year in the office of the clerk of the circuit court of Fredericksburg and also visited sessions of the legislature in Richmond. He began the practice of law in Petersburg in October 1840, and took a part in the exciting presidential campaign of Harrison and Tyler. In the spring of the next year he opened his office in Richmond. On May 26, 1842, he was married, in Columbia, Tenn., to Virginia Maury Otey, daughter of James Hervey Otey, Protestant Episcopal Bishop of Tennessee.

His editorial career began the year after his marriage. Thomas W. White, proprietor of the *Southern Literary Messenger*, died Jan. 19, 1843, and in the *Messenger* for August of that year Minor was announced as the new editor and proprietor. From the beginning he conducted the magazine with vigor and definiteness of purpose. He had no experience as an editor and the somewhat amateurish air which had marked the *Messenger* under White's ownership was not discarded; but the journal now reflected a more positive and energetic personality. Minor determined from the beginning to identify it with Southern writers and Southern views, and though he continued to publish articles from other sections, his policy succeeded in making the magazine strongly provincial. He attempted to reopen relations with the *Messenger's* most distinguished editor and in April 1845 announced that "E. A. Poe, Esq.," would contribute "monthly a *critique raisonnée* of the most important forthcoming works"; but the only products of Poe's pen that appeared during Minor's editorship were a revised form of "The Raven" (March 1845) and "The Literary Life of Thingum Bob, Esq.," in December 1844. Perhaps the most noteworthy article printed in the *Messenger* in this period was "Paper on the Gulf Stream and Currents of the Sea," by Lieut. Matthew Fontaine Maury [*q.v.*], in July 1844. In November 1845, the editor announced the purchase from William Gilmore Simms [*q.v.*] of the *Southern and Western Monthly Magazine and Review,* which was merged with the *Messenger* in January 1846 under the title of the *Southern and Western Literary Messenger and Review.* The issue for October 1847 was the last to appear under Minor's editorship; in that year he sold the magazine to young John R. Thompson [*q.v.*] and accepted the principalship of the Virginia Female Institute of Staunton, Va.

After one session in this school he returned in 1848 to Richmond, where he resumed the practice of the law and founded the Home School for Young Ladies. On July 4, 1860, he was elected president of the University of Missouri and professor of moral and political science there. The institution was closed by the provisional government in March 1862, and President Minor, forced to retire, remained in Columbia until 1865, maintaining himself during the Civil War by teaching a boys' school and giving public lectures. In 1865 he opened a school for girls in St. Louis, but after four years disposed of it and engaged in life insurance and public lecturing until 1889 when he returned to Richmond to remain for the remainder of his life. He was one of the founders of the Richmond Male Orphan Asylum. While practising law he edited *Decisions of Cases in Virginia by the High Court of Chancery, by George Wythe, with a Memoir of the Author* (1852) and a new edition of Hening and Munford's *Virginia Reports*. He was the author of *The Southern Literary Messenger, 1834–1864* (1905). A deeply religious and patriotic man, he devoted much time in his latter years to the activities of historical and patriotic societies and the Episcopal church. He died in Richmond and was buried in Hollywood Cemetery.

["Sketch of Author" in Minor's *The So. Lit. Messenger, 1834–1864* (1905); L. G. Tyler, *Encyc. of Va. Biog.* (1915), vol. III; J. B. Minor, *The Minor Family of Va.* (1923); F. L. Mott, *A Hist. of Am. Mags.* (1930); *Times Dispatch* (Richmond), Aug. 2, 1905; *News Leader* (Richmond), Aug. 1, 1905; autobiog. article in *Evening Journal* (Richmond), Aug. 1, 1905.]

J. S. W.

MINOR, JOHN BARBEE (June 2, 1813–July 29, 1895), teacher of law and author of legal works, brother of Lucian Minor [*q.v.*], was the ninth and youngest child of Lancelot and Mary Overton (Tompkins) Minor, and a descendant of Maindort Doodes, a Dutch mariner, and his son Doodes Minor, who were naturalized in Virginia in 1673. He was born at "Minor's Folly," Louisa County, Va., and after attending local schools and spending a year at Kenyon College, Gambier, Ohio, in 1831 he entered the University of Virginia. Augmenting his slender resources by tutoring, he remained three years, received diplomas from several academic schools, and graduated in law. Admitted to the bar, he practised about six years in Buchanan, Botetourt County, demonstrating his industry, painstaking care, and veneration for the common law, qualities which were to distinguish him later.

Returning to Charlottesville, he continued practice until 1845, when, at thirty-two, despite strong opposition because of his youth and comparative obscurity, he was appointed professor of law in the University of Virginia, the fourth to occupy that chair. He immediately raised the law school's standards and made graduation more difficult; the enrollment steadily increased. Like his predecessors, he taught the law unaided, from 1845 to 1851 and again during the Civil War. His system of instruction was that of searching analysis, based on the methods of Hale and Blackstone. Exquisite in diction, remarkably clear in exposition, wealthy in illustration, rising almost to eloquence, his lectures aroused the enthusiasm of the most indifferent of his students and stimulated the dullest minds. His zealous and almost fanatical love for the common law led him to oppose every contemplated change therein—his only defect, perhaps, as a teacher and author. Preëminent in legal education, he established the high position of the law school of the University of Virginia among American law schools. Originally a Union man, deeming secession neither wise nor warranted under the Constitution, he supported Virginia's course, however, as "necessary revolution," her only possible self-respecting reply to Lincoln's call for troops. In March 1865 when Sheridan passed through Charlottesville from his devastating Valley campaign, Minor, aided by Prof. Socrates Maupin, secured safe-guards from the Union commanders, thereby saving the University from pillage and possible destruction. After Appomattox, again with Maupin, he borrowed money on his personal credit to prepare for the session of 1865–66. From 1870 until his death he conducted a private summer law class —an early experiment in summer instruction. In 1875 he began publication of the *Institutes of Common and Statute Law* (1875–95), a monumental contribution to American jurisprudence. An outgrowth of blackboard analyses of his courses in common and statute law, it went through many editions, was cited in all American courts, and still remains an authority. He was also the author of *The Virginia Report 1799–1800* (1850) and an *Exposition of the Law of Crimes and Punishments* (1894).

Despite honorary degrees he preferred to be called simply "Mr. Minor," abjuring even the title "Professor" because of its misuse. His energy was amazing and his industry untiring. Although he was strong-tempered and positive to dogmatism, his character was mellowed with gentleness. He was deeply religious, intolerantly hating moral obliquity but having compassion for the transgressor. Long a vestryman in the Episcopal church, he held family prayers daily, superintended an ante-bellum Sunday school for slaves, taught a students' Bible class, and powerfully championed the temperance movement. Six feet tall and well proportioned, he had a dignity of presence that was the embodiment of strength, wisdom, and virtue. He married: first, Martha Macon Davis; following her death, Anne Jacqueline Fisher Colston; and after the latter's death, Ellen Temple Hill. He had three children by his first wife, and five by the second, one of whom was Raleigh Colston Minor [*q.v.*]. On a bust presented by alumni to the University of Virginia a few weeks before he died, after fifty years of service, is inscribed: "He Taught the Law and the Reason Thereof."

[J. B. Minor, *The Minor Family of Va.* (1923); P. A. Bruce, *Hist. of the Univ. of Va. 1819–1919* (5 vols., 1920–22); P. B. Barringer and J. M. Garnett, eds., *Univ. of Va.* (1904), vol. I; *Va. Law Reg.*, Nov. 1895; *The Green Bag*, Sept. 1895; *Report of . . . Va. State Bar Asso.*, vol. IX (1896); *The Alumni Bull. of the*

Univ. of Va., July 1895, Feb. 1896; Univ. of Va. Mag., Nov. 1895; The Richmond Dispatch, July 30, 1895.]

T. S. C.

MINOR, LUCIAN (Apr. 24, 1802–July 8, 1858), temperance advocate, was born in Louisa County, Va., the son of Lancelot and Mary (Tompkins) Minor and the brother of John Barbee Minor [q.v.]. Plain Dutch ancestors, important and interesting Virginia family connections, and the simple atmosphere of a Piedmont farmer's home were his birthright. His earliest education was at the simple, rigorous school conducted by his father. Being poor in health as well as in purse the lad, for a while, drove the mail to Fredericksburg. Then he attended the Nelsons' classical school nearby and later taught school. A few months spent in studying law at the College of William and Mary enabled him to graduate in 1823. After a year or two in Alabama he settled as a lawyer in his home county. From 1828 to 1852 he was commonwealth's attorney for the county. The rough-and-tumble of law practice and of politics, however, did not appeal to him; he was modest, sternly moral, incapable of flattery or intrigue, and a poor judge of men; he liked to formulate his ideas independently and to state them with frankness in language suited to cultured ears. Accordingly in 1834 he toured New England on foot, making eager, keen, and unprejudiced observations and seeking the acquaintance of distinguished men, among whom Francis Wayland impressed him most favorably. In "Letters from New England" published in the Southern Literary Messenger (Nov. 1834–Apr. 1835) he set down his observations with literary skill and taste. Many years later parts of the journal on which the letters were based were printed by Lowell in the Atlantic Monthly ("A Virginian in New England Thirty-five Years Ago," Sept.–Dec. 1870, June 1871). He was impressed by New England's superiority in public spirit, social and civic organization, and comforts of living. In 1835 appeared also his Address of Education . . . before the Institute of Education at Hampden-Sidney College (also printed in Southern Literary Messenger, Dec. 1835) in which he frankly pointed out the pauperizing tendencies of the Virginia public school system.

In 1830 he had spoken before a local temperance society to advocate wine and beer as substitutes for ardent spirits; in 1834 at the Charlottesville convention of temperance advocates he spoke out for total abstinence, having become convinced that this was the necessary basis of any broad temperance reform movement. There-after the movement interested him most. In the extensive organization of the Sons of Temperance of the United States he was an enthusiastic officer, lecturer, and editorial supervisor; for it he wrote Reasons for Abolishing the Liquor Traffic (1853), 30,000 copies of which were distributed; and to him the order erected a monument in Williamsburg. Though he did not originate the Virginia prohibitory movement of the '40's and '50's, he prepared its legislative papers, served as chairman of its central committee, came nearest to effecting an organization of the counties behind it, and published in the Southern Literary Messenger of July 1850 "The Temperance Reformation in Virginia," a brief history of the movement. This activity was grounded on considerations of humanity and statesmanship rather than on religion, for until his latest years the practices of professed Christians deterred him from any examination of their principles. In 1855 he became professor of law in the College of William and Mary. Though his distinguished younger brother, John Barbee Minor [q.v.], believed him capable of rivaling Story and Tucker, his actual law writing was slight: an article on the civil duties of justices of the peace in John A. G. Davis' Treatise on Criminal Law (1838), a one-volume edition of Hening and Munford's Reports (1857), and an edition of the first three volumes of Call's Reports (1854). He was married on May 4, 1846, to Lavinia Callis Price. They had four children.

[J. R. Lowell, "A Virginian in New England," Atlantic Monthly, Aug. 1870, with autobiographical fragment and early journal; "Vita" in A. J. Morrison, Six Addresses on the State of Letters and Science in Va. (1917); Southern Literary Messenger, Sept. 1858; J. B. Minor, The Minor Family in Va. (copr. 1923); C. C. Pearson, unpublished manuscript "Liquor and Anti-Liquor in Va.," in possession of author; John B. Minor, Manuscript Sketch of Lucian Minor in private possession; information from Mrs. Farrell D. Minor, Beaumont, Texas.]

C. C. P.

MINOR, RALEIGH COLSTON (Jan. 24, 1869–June 14, 1923), author, publicist, teacher of law, was born at the University of Virginia, the son of John Barbee Minor [q.v.] and Anne Jacqueline Fisher (Colston). After studying under tutors and in private schools, he entered the University of Virginia in 1883 at the age of fourteen. He received his baccalaureate degree at eighteen, his master's degree one year later, and graduated in law in 1890. Following admission to the bar, he practised in Richmond for three years and then returned to the University of Virginia as assistant professor of law, being a colleague of his father. After the latter's death the son, in 1895, became adjunct professor and in 1899 was made professor. He taught for three decades, the overlapping teaching careers of father and son covering a period of seventy-eight years, a unique record of unbroken family service in the same school of the same university. His principal subjects were real property, constitutional law, conflict of laws, and international law. His book on *The Law of Real Property* appeared in 1908. Although based on the second volume of his father's *Institutes*, it was none the less an original work and became an outstanding authority in Virginia. In 1910, collaborating with Prof. John Wurts of Yale, he published a smaller edition dealing less with Virginia law and hence more suitable for use in other localities. He stands as one of America's three pioneers in the field of private international law or, as Justice Story named it, the conflict of laws. In 1901, at the age of thirty-two, he achieved international recognition by the publication of his *Conflict of Laws*, an American legal classic, which materially clarified the existing chaotic condition of that difficult branch of jurisprudence, and placed subsequent writers on the subject largely in his debt. For more than fifteen years, in addition to his classes in the University of Virginia, he delivered lectures on conflict of laws at Georgetown University. His last writing was *A Republic of Nations* (1918). Impressed by the tremendous failure of public opinion as a preventive of war and recognizing that any world tribunal would have jurisdiction over justiciable disputes only, whereas war results primarily from political questions, he deemed that the path to permanent peace lies in the formation of a union of nations to which its members would relinquish for joint administration their war-breeding political powers—the regulation of international commerce, the acquisition of territory, and the treatment of aliens. Written before the Armistice, his book was a thoughtful humanitarian's unequivocal and forward-looking contribution toward the solution of a baffling problem. Minor was also the author of *The Law of Tax Titles in Virginia* (1898) and *Notes on the Science of Government and the Relations of the States to the United States* (1913). A tranquil scholar and an imperturbable teacher, perhaps too calm and placid, he exacted a high standard of proficiency from his students, who respected him for his learning and loved him for his character. Courageous and happy in disposition, stanch and unyielding in principle, unworldly in viewpoint, he was an idealist as a writer, a teacher, and a man. An Episcopalian, he had a broad and tolerant religious outlook. He was modest to the extreme, although possessed of a marked yet unconscious

dignity. In 1897 he married Natalie Embra Venable, a daughter of Charles Scott Venable, a colonel in the Confederate army and professor of mathematics in the University of Virginia; two children were born to them. Devoted to the University, Minor labored actively for its advancement but steadfastly opposed co-education, coördination, and the general tendency to make it a standardized state university. The institution, indeed, was almost a part of him; there he was born and educated, there as childhood playmates he and his wife first met, there he spent his happy married life, there distinction came to him, there he died and is buried.

[J. B. Minor, *The Minor Family of Va.* (1923); P. A. Bruce, *Hist. of the Univ. of Va., 1819–1919*, vols. IV, V (1921–22); P. B. Barringer and J. M. Garnett, *Univ. of Va.* (1904), vol. II; *Univ. of Va. Alumni News*, June 1923; *Va. Law Rev.*, Dec. 1923, Feb. 1926; *Proc. ... Va. State Bar Asso.*, vol. XXXV (1923); *Richmond Times-Dispatch*, June 15, 1923.]   T. S. C.

MINOR, ROBERT CRANNELL (Apr. 30, 1839–Aug. 3, 1904), landscape painter, born in New York, the son of Israel and Charlotte (Crannell) Minor, was a descendant of Thomas Minor (or Miner) who came to New England in 1629. Upon leaving school Robert worked for his father, who was a coal dealer, but after a brief experience he found that he had no taste for business, and decided to take up painting. He studied for two years under Alfred C. Howland in New York, then went to Antwerp, where he continued his training under H. Boulanger and Joseph Van Luppen. From Antwerp he turned to Paris, and after three years of experimentation there, joined the artists' colony at Barbizon, where he was fortunate enough to become the disciple of that brilliant colorist, Narcisse Diaz. This relationship proved to be the turning-point in his career; it determined the direction in which his work was to develop, and he became an avowed Barbizon man. Before returning to the United States he spent two years painting landscapes in the south of England. He exhibited "The Silent Lake" at the Paris Salon of 1872, and several landscapes at the Royal Academy and the Grosvenor Gallery in London. Most of his English subjects were found in the Wold of Kent. So many of his works had appeared in the current exhibitions in America during his long absence that he found himself already well known when he returned and set up his easel in the old University Building, Washington Square, New York. In the exhibition of the Society of American Artists, 1878, he had several pictures, among them "The Studio of Corot," which was a delicate early-morning effect not wholly unlike the work of Corot himself. He was made a National Academician in 1897; and served as president of the Salmagundi Club in 1898. While a student in Antwerp he had been vice-president of the Société Artistique et Littéraire; and he was a member of several other artistic associations. His New York clubs were the Lotos and the National Arts. The Lotos Club purchased one of his paintings from the National Academy Exhibition of 1896.

One of his favorite sketching grounds for several seasons was Keene Valley in the Adirondacks, and other places in northern New York attracted him for a time, but his final choice was Waterford, Conn., not far from New London, where he did much of his best and ripest work, and where he died. He had married Isabel Smith in 1860, and a son and a daughter survived him. Soon after his death a collection of 109 of his pictures were exhibited and sold at the American Art Galleries, New York (1905), bringing a total of $35,190. Emerson McMillin bought nine works, including "The End of Summer," for which he paid $1,200. This noble composition, with its fine old trees and luminous sky, reminds the observer in a vague way of both Ruysdael and Rousseau. McMillin was also the owner of "Sunrise," while "Eventide" belongs to the Corcoran Gallery, Washington, D. C. No American landscapist, with the possible exception of George Inness, has drawn so much inspiration from the Fontainebleau group of French masters as Minor. His body of work forms a handsome memorial to the great tradition of French nineteenth-century landscape painting. He had thoroughly assimilated the ways and means of his master, Diaz, had much of the same instinctive sense of color, and composed with the same pictorial dignity and distinction.

[*Biog. Sketches of Am. Artists* (Mich. State Lib., 1924) ; *Am. Art Annual*, 1905–06 ; Wm. Cothren, *Hist. of Ancient Woodbury, Conn.* (1854), I ; *Who's Who in America*, 1903–05 ; Cat. of sale exhibit of R. C. Minor's works, 1905 ; *The Private Coll. of Foreign and Am. Paintings formed by E. McMillin* (1913) ; *Catalogue of the Thos. B. Clarke Coll. of Am. Pictures* (1891) ; *N. Y. Evening Mail*, Mar. 8, 1878 ; *N. Y. Times*, Aug. 4, 5, 1904.]   W. H. D—s.

MINOR, VIRGINIA LOUISA (Mar. 27, 1824–Aug. 14, 1894), woman suffragist, was born in Goochland County, Va., the daughter of Warner and Maria (Timberlake) Minor. Her father, a first cousin of Lucian and John B. Minor [*qq.v.*], was a descendant of Maindort Doodes, a Dutch mariner, and his son, Doodes Minor, who became naturalized citizens of Virginia in 1673. Except for a short period of study in the academy for young ladies at Charlottes-

ville, Va., the greater part of her education was received at home. She was noted in these early years, as she continued to be, for her personal charm and beauty. On Aug. 31, 1843, she was married to Francis Minor, a relative, who was a graduate of Princeton and the University of Virginia, and a lawyer by profession. For a year they lived in Mississippi and then moved to St. Louis. During the Civil War Mrs. Minor was actively engaged in welfare and relief work among the sick and wounded in the hospitals of the St. Louis area. To the depression and sorrow which the war brought to her, was added, in 1866, the grief occasioned by the accidental death of her only child, Francis Gilmer, then fourteen years of age.

She had long been keenly interested in politics and public affairs, and soon after the war she became active in the movement to raise the status of women in America. She was convinced that the extension of the suffrage to women was essential to the accomplishment of this object, which conviction was enthusiastically shared by her husband. In 1866 she launched the woman-suffrage movement in Missouri, and early in the following year she took a leading part in the organization of the Woman Suffrage Association of Missouri—the first organization in the world to make its exclusive aim that of enfranchising women—of which she was elected president. At the woman-suffrage convention held at St. Louis in 1869, she made a militant speech, urging women no longer to submit to their inferior condition. A set of resolutions, drafted by her husband, asserting the right of woman suffrage under the national Constitution was adopted. On Oct. 15, 1872, as "a native-born, free white citizen of the United States, and of the State of Missouri, . . . over the age of twenty-one years," she made her famous claim to the right to vote and presented herself for registration. Reese Happersett, the registrar of voters, refused to place her name on the list because "she was not a 'male' citizen, but a woman." In association with her husband (since the status of a woman under the common law made it impossible for her to bring suit independently of him), she sued for damages in the circuit court at St. Louis. The decision was against the plaintiffs. On appeal to the supreme court of Missouri, the court unanimously upheld the decision. The case was carried to the Supreme Court of the United States, and Francis Minor was one of the attorneys who presented arguments. In giving the unanimous opinion of the court in upholding the Missouri decisions, Chief Justice Waite centered his elaborate argument around two main propositions; first, that "if the courts can consider any question settled, this is one"; and second, that "the Constitution of the United States does not confer the right of suffrage upon any one" (21 *Wallace*, 177, 178). While the congenitally feeble legal case was lost, the publicity accompanying it no doubt contributed to the victory which came later. In 1889 she appeared before the Senate committee on woman suffrage to reiterate her stock arguments. Her last office was an honorary vice-presidency of the Interstate Woman Suffrage Convention, held at Kansas City in 1892. Two years later she was buried in Bellefontaine cemetery in St. Louis with religious solemnity but, of her own choice, without an officiating clergyman, since she had long regarded the clergy as hostile to the great mission of her life.

[E. C. Stanton, S. B. Anthony, and M. J. Gage, *Hist. of Woman Suffrage*, vol. II (1882); Wm. Hyde and H. L. Conard, *Encyc. of the Hist. of St. Louis* (1899), vol. IV; M. S. Scott, "Hist. of Woman Suffrage in Mo.," in *Mo. Hist. Rev.*, Apr.–July 1920; *Minor* vs. *Happersett*, 53 *Mo.*, 58, and 21 *Wallace*, 162 (1874); *The St. Louis Republic*, Aug. 16, 1894, p. 7; J. B. Minor, *The Minor Family of Va.* (copr. 1923); unpublished family genealogy by Minor Meriwether.]

.A. J. L.

MINOT, CHARLES SEDGWICK (Dec. 23, 1852–Nov. 19, 1914), biologist and educator, was the son of William Minot, "a well-to-do Boston lawyer," and Katharine Maria Sedgwick, grand-daughter of Theodore Sedgwick and a descendant of Jonathan Edwards. "He was born not merely a Bostonian, but a legendary Bostonian" (Porter, *post*, p. 467). Forsaking the legal traditions of his family, at the age of sixteen, he appeared before the Boston Society of Natural History with descriptions of new species of butterflies, and had elected to study at the Massachusetts Institute of Technology where entrance was easy and the curriculum congenial. With the Technology B.S. in 1872, he could enter the graduate school of Harvard College as a candidate for the S.D. degree in natural history. That degree he obtained in 1878 after six years of very independent studies. Part of this time was spent as the first research pupil of his lifelong friend, Henry P. Bowditch, in the physiological laboratory of the Harvard Medical School; and part abroad with Ludwig, Leuckart, and His at Leipzig, Semper at Würzburg, and Ranvier at Paris. Publications in British, French, and German journals, divided between reports of physiological experiments and studies of the miscroscopic structure of invertebrates, served as his doctor's thesis. He had acquired new insight into the aims of the naturalist and the method of science.

Two years later, minor appointments in the Harvard Medical School were "procured for him with some difficulty" (Eliot, *post*, p. 89), for he was not a doctor of medicine, and agreed with Semper that doctors are "spoilt zoologists." He remained on the Harvard faculty until his death. Medical education in America had reached its lowest ebb, but the tide was turning. Minot, eager for improvement, said of American schools, "there prevails the miserable delusion that they are good." He was a reformer. Though reserved and aristocratic, "he pursued his ends with clear-sighted intensity and indomitable persistence," often finding it "hard to see that his opponent had some reason on his side" (Eliot, *post*, p. 91). Limiting his investigations to human embryology, Minot published in 1892 a monumental *résumé* of that subject— *Human Embryology*, 815 pages—which soon appeared in German translation. Through his *Laboratory Text-book of Embryology* (1903; 2nd ed. 1910) he introduced the general use of pig embryos as the best laboratory substitute for those of man. He invented widely used forms of microtomes, and made a large and very methodical collection of prepared sections of embryos—the prototype of similar collections in other universities. His plan for a great embryological institute at Harvard led quite directly to the founding of the Carnegie Laboratory of Embryology in Baltimore. His prolonged studies comprehended in *The Problem of Age, Growth, and Death* (New York, 1908; Japanese translation, Tokyo, 1915) were a search into the fundamental nature of senility. His recognition of a special type of "sinusoidal" circulation, in which the blood bathes closely the glandular substance, proves to be of fundamental importance. "Not only by his original researches, by his masterly books and by his fine addresses and lectures, but in countless other ways he helped his fellow-workers in science" (Cattell, *post*, p. 59); and in recognition thereof he received a full professorship at Harvard (1892) and honorary doctorates from Yale, Oxford, Toronto, and St. Andrews. He was married, on June 1, 1889, to Lucy Fosdick of Groton, Mass. He died without issue. In Mall's critical judgment "Minot has done more than any other American to add dignity to the career of anatomy."

[Biographical sketches of Minot, by his associates, and minutes concerning him, include the following: Frederic T. Lewis, *Boston Medic. and Surgic. Jour.*, Dec. 10, 1914, pp. 911–14; Henry H. Donaldson, *Science*, Dec. 25, 1914, pp. 926–27; Minute by Prof. Cattell for the Am. Asso. for the Advancement of Science, *Science*, Jan. 8, 1915, p. 59; Minute by Professor Huntington for the Am. Asso. of Anatomists, *Anatomical Record*, Jan. 1915, pp. 42–43; C. Frank Allen, *Technology Rev.*, Jan. 1915, pp. 91–95; Henry H. Donaldson and Charles W. Eliot, Addresses before the Boston Soc. of Natural Hist., Mar. 17, 1915, in the *Proceedings*, vol. XXXV, pp. 79–93, portrait, President Eliot's address being also in *Science*, May 14, 1915, pp. 701–04; John L. Bremer, *Harvard Grads'. Mag.*, Mar. 1915, pp. 374–78; W. T. Porter, *Boston Medic. and Surgic. Jour.*, Apr. 1, 1915, pp. 467–70; Frederic T. Lewis, *Anatomical Record*, Jan. 1916, pp. 133–64, portrait and bibliography; W. T. Councilman, *Proc. Am. Acad. Arts and Sci.*, vol. LIII, Sept. 1918, pp. 840–47; Edward S. Morse, *Nat. Acad. Sci. Biog. Memoirs*, vol. IX (1920), pp. 263–85, portrait and bibliography.]   F. T. L.

MINOT, GEORGE RICHARDS (Dec. 22, 1758–Jan. 2, 1802), jurist and historian, was born in Boston, Mass., the youngest of the ten children of Stephen Minot, a Boston merchant, A. B. Harvard, 1730, and Sarah Clark, daughter of Jonas Clark, of Boston. The Minots were early associated with Dorchester, George Minot, son to Thomas Minot of Saffron Walden, in Essex, England, having emigrated to Massachusetts and been admitted freeman of the town in 1634. According to the Rev. James Freeman, who wrote a memoir of the historian, Minot's father was "educated" and his mother "affectionate," and the "intermediate ancestors were gentlemen of respectable characters." The chief influence on his youth seems to have been the good example of his brother, Francis, who died in 1774, at the age of twenty-eight. In 1767 Minot entered the South Latin School in Boston, where his diligence, discretion, and decorum soon made him the favorite pupil of his teacher, John Lovell. In July 1774 he matriculated at Harvard and attracted the attention of his tutor, John Wadsworth, by his amiable manners and his love of books. When Wadsworth died in 1777 at the early age of thirty-seven, Minot established a reputation as a public speaker with the funeral oration he was selected to deliver. As a consequence, he was chosen to pronounce the valedictory address at the time he took his "second-degree" (A.M.) in July 1781. Years later, Minot noted in his Journal for January 1800, on the occasion of his speech on the death of Washington: "A whole edition of my Eulogy sold in a day."

On receiving his degree of A.B. in July 1778, Minot entered the law office of William Tudor, through whose influence he was appointed in 1781 clerk of the Massachusetts House of Representatives in the first Great and General Court which met after the adoption of the new constitution in 1780. From Jan. 9 to Feb. 7, 1788, he served as secretary of the convention called to consider the ratification of the Federal Constitution. As a result of his conspicuous success in both these offices, he was appointed judge of probate for the County of Suffolk in January 1792. He had already made his mark as the historian of Shays's Rebellion. *The History of the Insurrection in Massachusetts in the Year Seventeen Hundred and Eighty-Six and the Rebellion Consequent Thereon* was first published in Worcester in 1788. A second edition was brought out in Boston in 1810. The reception of this volume encouraged Minot to begin a continuation of the history of Massachusetts from the point at which Thomas Hutchinson had left off. The first volume of his *Continuation of the History of the Province of Massachusetts Bay, from the Year 1748* was published at Boston in February 1798—four introductory chapters containing a survey of the period from 1630 to the Treaty of Aix-la-Chapelle. A second volume, carrying events through 1765, was published posthumously in June 1803. John Adams, who was "not satisfied with Hutchinson, though his work is valuable" (quoted, Freeman, *post*, p. 101), praised Minot's performance in a letter written from Philadelphia, Feb. 28, 1798. Just as he was completing his second volume, Minot died suddenly in Boston.

Besides being a member of the Amicable Fire Society and president of the Massachusetts Charitable Fire Society, Minot was one of the original ten members of the Massachusetts Historical Society, founded in 1791, and served the organization as librarian, 1793–95, and treasurer, 1796–99. Although his politics took color from his associates and circumstances, his history of Shays's Rebellion is by no means unreasonably hostile. His style was modeled on what already in college had become his favorite reading: Robertson, and Burke's contributions to the *Annual Register*. New methods of scholarship were to supplant his *Continuation* by the middle of the nineteenth century, and he did not live to cover that portion of the history of Massachusetts which he could have narrated at first hand. The reproduction of his portrait (*Proceedings of the Massachusetts Historical Society*, 1 ser., vol. I, 1879, facing p. 42) shows Minot to have been a man of distinguished, if not handsome, appearance, the only fault of whose character, according to a friend, was "a temper by nature irascible" (Freeman, *post*, p. 88). The eulogy John Quincy Adams delivered before the Massachusetts Charitable Fire Society, May 28, 1802, was long and enthusiastic. For ten years (1789–99) he was in almost constant correspondence with Fisher Ames. Minot married Mary Speakman, by whom he had one son, George Richards Minot, and a daughter.

[Jas. Freeman, "Character of the Hon. Geo. Richards Minot . . .," and notes and selections from Minot's journal, *Mass. Hist. Soc. Colls.*, 1 ser. VIII (1802); *New-Eng. Hist. and Geneal. Reg.*, Apr., July 1847; the

Mass. Gazette (Boston), Feb. 8, 1788; the *Polyanthos* (Boston), Mar. 1806; the *Boston Gazette*, Jan. 4, 7, 1802; the *Columbian Centinel and Mass. Federalist*, Jan. 6, 20, 1802.]
S. M—l.

MINTO, WALTER (Dec. 5, 1753–Oct. 21, 1796), mathematician, was born in Cowdenham, County Merse, Scotland. His family was of Spanish origin and had once had rank but his parents were very poor. He was given a sufficiently good schooling, however, and was attending the University of Edinburgh at the age of fifteen. Hume was then teaching there. At the wishes of his parents and friends he studied theology, living during this time with a Mr. Watson in Perthshire, and occupying his leisure time with writing verse and humorous articles for the magazines. He planned to go to Italy as a pilgrim, begging his way, but Hume recommended him as tutor to two boys, the sons of George Johnstone, formerly the governor of West Florida and member of the British Parliament, and Minto sailed for Italy with the boys. There they established themselves in the home of Giuseppe Slop, a professor of astronomy in the University of Pisa. On Mar. 13, 1781, William Herschel discovered the planet Uranus and Minto was in Pisa when the exciting discovery was announced in the papers of Florence. He reported that in May 1781 he and the Italian professor saw the planet "in an excellent reflecting telescope." Two years later Minto published his treatise, *Researches into Some Parts of the Theory of the Planets* (London, 1783), containing mathematical formulae dealing with the determination of astronomical magnitudes and also observational data concerning the new planet made by a number of observers. At the time the treatise was written the new planet had not been named Uranus and Minto suggested the name Minerva "because, being a telescopic star, it may be said to denote the modesty of the Goddess of Wisdom."

Following his return to Edinburgh he became a teacher of mathematics. He had considerable correspondence with the philosophers of England, wrote several papers on astronomy, and collaborated with D. S. Erskine, Earl of Buchan, in *An Account of the Life, Writings, and Inventions of John Napier of Merchiston* (Edinburgh, 1787), supporting Napier's claim as the inventor of logarithms. Having warmly supported the cause of American independence, in 1786 he sailed for America and soon afterward became the principal of Erasmus Hall at Flatbush, Long Island. In 1787 he was called to the College of New Jersey to succeed Ashbel Green [*q.v.*] as professor of mathematics and

natural philosophy. His fellow countryman, Dr. John Witherspoon, was president of the college and Minto had heard favorably of the institution. He was given a salary of £200 per year, including room and board in Nassau Hall. His inaugural oration, "On the Progress and Importance of the Mathematical Sciences," presented on the evening before the annual commencement in 1788, was subsequently published. Shortly after his arrival President Witherspoon wrote to the Earl of Buchan expressing his approval of Minto. He became treasurer of the college and wrote his textbook of mathematics, which was in manuscript at the time of his death. He was married to Mary Skelton of Princeton. They had no children. He died in October 1796, at the age of forty-two, and was buried in the Princeton cemetery.

[The principal source is the article, "Walter Minto, LL.D.," in the *Princeton Mag.*, Mar. 1850. See also V. L. Collins, *President Witherspoon, a Biog.* (1925), vol. II; and J. F. Hageman, *Hist. of Princeton and its Institutions* (2 vols., 1879).]
L. P. E.

MINTURN, ROBERT BOWNE (Nov. 16, 1805–Jan. 9, 1866), merchant, was born to the purple in New York social and commercial circles and went even farther in both fields, winning general respect for his philanthropic as well as his business success. His grandfather, the elder William Minturn, had moved a profitable business from Newport to New York. His father, William Minturn, Jr., who married Sarah Bowne, was a partner in the firm of Minturn, Champlin & Company, which was prominent until its failure at the close of the War of 1812. Robert was forced to go into business at thirteen upon the death of his father. In 1825 he became the partner of Charles Green, whom he had served as clerk, and in 1829 he entered the counting-house of Fish, Grinnell & Company, a connection probably traceable to the marriage of his sister Sarah to Henry Grinnell in 1822. This firm had been established about 1815 by Preserved Fish and Joseph Grinnell [*qq.v.*] from New Bedford. Starting as commission merchants for whale oil, the firm expanded into the management of transatlantic packets, shipowning, and general commerce. By 1832 the two original partners retired and the firm was reorganized as Grinnell, Minturn & Company, Minturn joining with Joseph Grinnell's younger brothers, Moses Hicks and Henry [*qq.v.*].

Under its new name the firm attained a secure position as one of the greatest of the New York commercial houses, ranking with the Griswolds, Howlands, and Lows. "All is fish that gets into their nets," wrote Scoville about 1860 (*post*, I,

p. 100). In Latin America they were behind the Howlands, though their Cuban business was so extensive that Minturn sent his son to Spain to learn the language. In China they competed successfully with the houses of Griswold and Low which virtually specialized in that trade. They did a great deal of business with England and extended their influence into almost all parts of the world. They seem to have shared with the Welds of Boston the honor of being the greatest American ship-owners of the day. Their blue and white or red and white swallowtail house flags flew over more than fifty vessels, including regular packet lines to Liverpool and London as well as some of the finest clippers of the day. They owned the *North Wind* and *Sea Serpent* and above all, the greatest of the clippers, Donald McKay's *Flying Cloud*.

Minturn's fortune was estimated at $200,000 as early as 1846. He and his partners were more public spirited than many of the other New York merchants of the day. He himself served as commissioner of emigration to improve the condition of the incoming foreigners and was instrumental in founding the Association for Improving the Condition of the Poor, and St. Luke's Hospital. His wife was Anna Mary Wendell, the daughter of John Lansing Wendell of Albany, whom he married on June 2, 1835. She has been credited with the idea of establishing Central Park and he supported her in the project. At first a Whig, Minturn was later a Republican and was first president of the Union League Club. He has been described, like others of his family, as dark, tall, and handsome. George William Curtis pictured him as "gentle, just and generous; modest, humane and sagacious; his sense of responsibility growing with his increasing fortune, until his devoted life was that of a humble almoner of the Divine bounty" (*Harper's Weekly*, Jan. 27, 1866). He died suddenly of paralysis at his New York home.

[The sources for Minturn's biography are fragmentary. See R. B. Minturn, Jr., *Memoir of Robert Bowne Minturn* (1871); J. A. Scoville, *The Old Merchants of N. Y. City* (4 vols., 1863–66); *The Diary of Philip Hone* (2 vols., 1927), ed. by Allan Nevins; Henry Hall, *America's Successful Men of Affairs*, vol. I (1895); L. H. Weeks, *Prominent Families of N. Y.*, vol. I (1897); F. G. Griswold, *The House Flags of the Merchants of N. Y., 1800–1860* (1926); O. T. Howe and F. C. Matthews, *Am. Clipper Ships* (2 vols., 1927); M. Y. Beach, *Wealth and Pedigree of the Wealthy Citizens of N. Y.* (1846); *N. Y. Times, N. Y. Tribune*, Jan. 10, 1866.]
           R. G. A.

MINTY, ROBERT HORATIO GEORGE (Dec. 4, 1831–Aug. 24, 1906), soldier, railroad official, was born in County Mayo, Ireland, son of a British officer. He served under his father as ensign in the British army (1849–53) in

Africa, Honduras, and the West Indies. In 1853 he emigrated to Michigan and upon the outbreak of the Civil War entered military service. Within a few months he had been commissioned major, 2nd Michigan Cavalry, lieutenant-colonel, 3rd Michigan Cavalry, and colonel, 4th Michigan Cavalry (July 31, 1862). During 1863–64 he brilliantly commanded a cavalry unit known as the Sabre Brigade (*Battles and Leaders of the Civil War*, vol. IV, 1888, p. 413) and led a division in General Kilpatrick's raid around the city of Atlanta, being promoted brigadier-general of volunteers in 1864. Subsequently, in Wilson's final raids through Alabama and Georgia, he commanded a division in the march upon Macon (*Ibid.*, p. 761). A noteworthy incident of his service during this period was his participation in the capture of President Jefferson Davis, and the latter's confinement at Fortress Monroe.

Minty received the brevets of brigadier-general and major-general of volunteers (Mar. 13, 1865) for gallant and meritorious services, and on two different occasions received the thanks of Congress. He declined proffer of a majority in the regular army and was mustered out of the military service, Aug. 15, 1865. Of his services and character, Gen. James H. Wilson wrote: "He was an educated soldier of great intelligence and enterprise. . . . He was in every respect a modest and obedient officer, an excellent disciplinarian, and as good a leader as Murat himself" (*Under the Old Flag*, 1912, II, pp. 171–72). After the close of the war he became general manager of the Elizabethtown and Paducah Railroad, making his home at Elizabethtown, Ky., and later was connected in various capacities with railroad administration in the West and Southwest. He passed away in 1906 at Jerome, Ariz., and was interred at Ogden, Utah. Twice married, he was survived by his second wife, Laura Abbott Minty, to whom he had been married at Maysville, Ky., on May 14, 1871, and by three children.

[See H. M. Cist, *The Army of the Cumberland* (1882); J. G. Vale, *Minty and the Cavalry* (1886); J. C. O'Connell, *The Irish in the Revolution and the Civil War* (1903); *Hist. Colls., Pioneer Soc. of the State of Mich.*, vol. XXVI (1896); *Detroit Free Press*, Oct. 9, 1896. Information as to certain facts was supplied by Minty's son, Courtney Abbott Minty, Tucson, Ariz.]
           C. D. R.

MINUIT, PETER (1580–1638), director-general of New Netherland and governor of New Sweden, was born at Wesel, then in the Duchy of Cleves. The spelling Minnewit reflects the Dutch pronunciation of his name. He himself gave it the sound of the French *minuit*, and he bore a bat, as an emblem of midnight, in his coat of arms (Memorandum book of Arend van Buchel, *Rijksarchief,* The Hague). Moreover, in the earliest Dutch record that refers to him, he is called not Peter but Pierre Minuit. He was therefore probably of French or Walloon descent, but in his letters he employed the Dutch language, which he wrote without fault except for occasional lapses into German orthography. According to the Rev. Jonas Michaëlius, Minuit served as a deacon in the Dutch Church at Wesel. In the civil records of Wesel it is recorded on Apr. 15, 1625, that he had left for foreign parts. The capture of Wesel by the Spaniards in the previous year had probably driven him to Holland. From there he sailed for the Dutch colony of New Netherland, perhaps on the same ship with Willem Verhulst, the Company's provisional director of the new settlement. He is mentioned in 1625 among the members of the Director's Council, but he must have returned to Holland before the end of the year, for he was on board *Het Meeuwtje* (The Little Gull), which sailed from The Texel on Jan. 9, 1626, and arrived at the mouth of the Hudson on May 4, 1626.

Minuit returned to Manhattan in a minor capacity, possibly that of supercargo. Verhulst, at that time, was still at the head of the colony. On Sept. 23, 1626, however, the latter was sent back to Holland, having been deposed by the Council of New Netherland, which appointed Peter Minuit his successor. Minuit had evidently not intended to stay in Manhattan, for he had left his wife in Holland; it was only after his appointment that he sent for her to join him. He was the first to be officially designated as director-general. One of his first acts in his new capacity was the purchase of Manhattan Island from the Indian sachems for trinkets valued at sixty gilders ($24). By this transaction the accomplished fact of occupation acquired a semblance of legality which the West India Company was eager to lend to its enterprise. Little is known about Minuit's administration, owing to the disappearance of the Company's records. When the fort was completed according to Crijn Fredericksen's plans, Minuit made New Amsterdam the rallying point of the isolated settlements north and south of Manhattan; he brought eight families down the river from Fort Orange, leaving a garrison there of sixteen men under Bastiaen Jansen Krol, and ordered Fort Nassau on the South River, near the present site of Gloucester, N. J., to be evacuated and the garrison to be transferred to New Amsterdam. When, in 1628, the Rev. Jonas Michaëlius began church services in the fort, Minuit and his brother-in-law Jan Huyghen, the Company's storekeeper, consented to serve as elders. In 1627 he started diplomatic relations with Governor Bradford and opened trade with the Plymouth colonists. The peaceful relations with his English neighbor lasted longer than those with the Dutch Reformed ministers, who, instead of trying to mediate in the quarrel between Minuit and the secretary, Johan van Remunde, stirred up the fire of discord.

In 1631 the Amsterdam Chamber of the West India Company recalled the director-general for examination. Minuit, together with Remunde, sailed in the *Eendracht* (Concord), a fitting conveyance for the pair. Minuit's examination lasted for several months and resulted in his dismissal from the Company's service, whereas Johan van Remunde was allowed to return to his post. In 1635 Minuit was living in Emmerich, in the Duchy of Cleves, as appears from a letter of Samuel Blommaert, a director of the West India Company, to the Swedish chancellor Axel Oxenstierna, recommending him as the very man to conduct successfully an expedition that was to plant a Swedish colony on Delaware Bay. In January 1637, at a meeting at The Hague between Blommaert, Minuit, and Spiering, a representative of Swedish interests in Holland, it was decided to establish a Swedish company for the purpose of trading to the American coast from Florida to Terra Nova and of establishing a colony there. The capital needed was fixed at 24,000 guilders, one-eighth of which was supplied by Minuit himself.

Late in the fall of 1637, Minuit sailed from Göteborg in the *Key of Calmar,* which was accompanied by the yacht *The Griffin.* In March 1638 they arrived at the mouth of the South River, or Delaware. They sailed up the Minquas Kill, concluded on Mar. 29 a contract with the chiefs of the Indians, who sold them a tract of land on the right bank of the Delaware, and Minuit, having erected the arms of the Queen of Sweden, in the presence of the sachems, gave the country the name of New Sweden. He christened the Minquas Kill the Elbe, and here he built Fort Christina, on the site of the present city of Wilmington. Willem Kieft, his successor at New Amsterdam, sent Minuit a protest which the latter ignored. As soon as Fort Christina was completed, Minuit left Måns Kling in charge of it and sailed in the *Key of Calmar* for the island of St. Christopher. Here he exchanged his cargo for tobacco. While he was paying a visit to the captain of *Het Vliegende Hert* (The Flying Stag), a Rotterdam merchantman, a hurricane swept the coast and the ship was lost in the storm. Thus Minuit's career came to a sudden end. If we must believe Michaëlius, he was "a slippery fellow who, under the painted mask of honesty, was a compound of all iniquity and wickedness." But in view of Blommaert's high opinion of his protégé, there is reason to believe that what the dominie took for a mask was the man's own face. He was, perhaps, not overscrupulous, and a man of coarser fiber than the scholarly preacher, but courage, self-reliance, determination, and shrewdness were not lacking in his nature.

[*Documents Relating to New Netherland, 1624–26, in the Henry E. Huntington Library* (1924) and *N. Y. State Lib. Van Rensselaer Bowier Manuscripts* (1908), trans. and ed. by A. J. F. van Laer; E. B. O'Callaghan, *Documents Relative to the Colonial Hist. of the State of N. Y.*, vol. I (1856); *Ecclesiastical Records: State of N. Y.*, vol. I (1901); *Narratives of New Netherland, 1609–64* (1909), ed. by J. Franklin Jameson; *Narratives of Early Pa., West N. J., and Del., 1630–1707* (1912), ed. by A. C. Myers; I. N. P. Stokes, *The Iconography of Manhattan Island* (6 vols., 1915–28); G. W. Kernkamp, "Brieven van Samuel Blommaert aan den Zweedschen Rijkskanselier Axel Oxenstierna, 1635–1641," *Bijdragen en Mededeelingen van het Historisch Genootschap*, vol. XXIX (1908); Albert Eekhof, *Jonas Michaëlius, Founder of the Church in New Netherland* (Leyden, 1926); L. P. Boer, "Peter Minuit," *N. Y. Geneal. and Biog. Record*, Jan. 1928; Friedrich Kapp, "Peter Minnewit aus Wesel," *Historische Zeitschrift*, vol. XV (1866); Amandus Johnson, *The Swedish Settlements on the Delaware* (1911), vol. I.]
A. J. B—w.

MIRÓ, ESTEBAN RODRÍGUEZ (1744–1795), Spanish governor of Louisiana, was born in Catalonia. He entered the Spanish army as a cadet at the age of sixteen and took part in the campaign of 1762 against Portugal. During the American Revolution he served in the West Florida campaigns as first aide-de-camp to Bernardo de Gálvez [*q.v.*], and was rewarded with promotion to the rank of colonel and command of the regular Louisiana regiment. When Gálvez left Louisiana in 1782, Miró was made acting governor. Upon Gálvez's promotion to viceroy of New Spain, Miró's appointment was made permanent by a commission dated Aug. 19, 1785. The commandants of Mobile and Pensacola and the governor of Natchez were subordinated to him. In 1789 he was promoted to the rank of brigadier-general. On the retirement of the intendant of Louisiana, Martin Navarro, the intendancy was combined with the governorship (May 10, 1788), and Miró discharged the duties of both offices until Dec. 30, 1791, when he was succeeded by the Baron de Carondelet [*q.v.*]. Returning to Spain, he defended himself successfully against various charges, one of which was that, under cover of the intrigue with James Wilkinson [*q.v.*], he had for several years made an annual profit of $2,000 by the purchase of Kentucky tobacco (Archivo Histórico Nacional, Madrid, *Consejo de Indias, residencia* of Miró). He was promoted to the rank of *mariscal de campo* shortly before his death, which occurred in Spain.

His administration was filled with alarms caused by disputes with the United States and its frontiersmen. His conduct with respect to these was not so aggressive, independent, or venal as it has sometimes been described. Toward the Southern Indians, whom he sought to control through Alexander McGillivray [*q.v.*] and Panton, Leslie & Company, his policy was purely defensive. In the Bourbon County episode (1785) and in his relations with the Georgia land companies (1790–91) he earnestly sought to avoid a rupture. His notorious intrigue with James Wilkinson was begun on the initiative of the latter and carried on (as were all his important affairs) under minute directions from Madrid. His encouragement of foreign immigration and partial opening of the Mississippi to the Western Americans was due not to bribery but to an explicit royal order of 1788. He gave Louisiana a mild and beneficent administration, encouraging commerce and agriculture, opposing the establishment of the Inquisition, and making every effort to restore New Orleans after the great fire of 1788. The construction of several notable public buildings was begun at this time.

His influence with the people of lower Louisiana was increased by his marriage to Céleste Eléonore Elizabeth Macarty, sprightly daughter of a wealthy creole family. In 1787 he asked that his salary of 4,000 pesos be increased, complaining that the high prices and lavish style of living at New Orleans had consumed most of her dowry of 16,000 pesos as well as his own savings. He spoke French and had some knowledge of English. It was rumored that his secretary did all his work for him, and in 1787 he thought it proper voluntarily to assure the colonial secretary that the rumor was unfounded. Vicente Folch, commandant of Mobile and Pensacola, was his nephew.

[Charles Gayarré, *Hist. of La.: The Spanish Domination* (1854), vol. III; Grace King, *Creole Families of New Orleans* (1921); *La. Hist. Quart.*, Jan., Oct. 1919; A. P. Whitaker, *The Spanish-American Frontier, 1783–1795* (1927); Alcée Fortier, *A Hist. of La.* (1904), vol. II; documents on Miró's relations to Spanish-American intrigues, in *Am. Hist. Rev.*, July 1904, Oct. 1909, Jan. 1910.]
A. P. W.

MITCHEL, JOHN (Nov. 3, 1815–Mar. 20, 1875), journalist, Irish nationalist, the son of the Rev. John and Mary (Haslett) Mitchel, was born at Camnish, County Londonderry, Ireland.

He is said to have graduated from Trinity College in 1834. After a brief period as a bank clerk he entered a solicitor's office and studied law. On Feb. 3, 1837, he married Jane Verner, and in 1840 he began to practise law in Newry. He did not become active in politics until 1845 when he joined the Young Ireland movement, a protest against O'Connell's policy of non-resistance. In the same year he became a member of the staff of the *Nation,* but in time he became dissatisfied, and when, in January 1847, the Irish Confederation was formed he founded the *United Irishmen* to advocate armed resistance to England and the repeal of the Union. He was arrested and in May 1848 a packed jury found him guilty of treason-felony and he was sentenced to fourteen years transportation. His remarkable speech from the dock was the culminating point in his career. After he had spent some months in Bermuda his failing health caused his transfer to Van Diemen's Land, from which he and his family, who had joined him in 1851, escaped in 1853. He was enthusiastically welcomed in San Francisco on Oct. 9, 1853, receiving a similar reception in New York on Nov. 29. Within two weeks he had conceived the plan of a newspaper. This was the *Citizen,* dedicated to the cause of Irish freedom, which began publication in New York on Jan. 7, 1854. The paper quickly attained a circulation of 50,000, but Mitchel's bluntness soon arrested its growth. In his controversy with Henry Ward Beecher [*q.v.*] he launched a bitter fight against the abolitionists and imprudently announced himself in favor of slavery. By writing against the temporal power of the pope he alienated a large group of Catholic readers and at the same time he antagonized the members of the Know-Nothing party. In the face of these disputes his enthusiasm for America sensibly diminished.

In 1854 he twice visited Virginia. His cordial receptions there determined him to settle in the South, and at the end of the year he gave up the *Citizen* and in the following spring settled on a farm at Tuckaleechee Cove, thirty-two miles from Knoxville, Tenn. He busied himself with farming and with extensive lecture tours. In the fall of 1856 he moved to Knoxville, where one year later he began to publish the *Southern Citizen,* an extremist paper devoted to the slavery interests. It survived almost two years; the second year it was published in Washington. In the midst of these labors Mitchel was still interested in Irish freedom, and when, in 1859, it appeared that France might declare war on Great Britain, he hastened to Paris. This was an idle quest, but in July 1860 he moved his family to

Paris and became the French correspondent for several papers, among them the *Charleston Standard.* Late in 1862 he returned to New York, succeeded in reaching Virginia, and there his three sons joined the Confederate army while he edited the *Richmond Enquirer* and served on the ambulance committee of the Confederate army. In the spring of 1864 he broke his connections with Jefferson Davis and became editor of the *Examiner.* Early in 1865 he went to New York as editor of the *Daily News,* a Democratic paper actively opposed to the Grant administration. For his violent writings he was imprisoned more than four months in Fortress Monroe; from this imprisonment he never recovered his mental or physical powers. He spent the winter of 1865–66 in Paris as a Fenian agent, returning to Richmond to engage in literary work. He again returned to New York as editor of the *Irish Citizen,* published from Oct. 19, 1867, to July 27, 1872. Here he fought Grant and criticized the Fenian movement, which diminished the paper's circulation. During the winter of 1872–73 he wrote a series of articles attacking J. A. Froude's views on the Irish. He returned to Ireland for the last time in 1875. There, as a last gesture of defiance to the British government, he accepted election to Parliament, shortly after which he died.

During the period of his exile from Ireland Mitchel confessed that he was "truly dead and a ghost"; following his conviction in 1848 he did not actively participate, with one small exception, in any important Irish movement. He had much love of Ireland, but a far greater hatred of England, and his desire for vengeance against England motivated him throughout his life. His intense nationalism prevented his feeling any spirit of kinship with other men working in similar causes; for liberty in the abstract and humanity at large he cared nothing; Socialists he termed "worse than wild beasts," and for Communists, "unhappy creatures," he recommended "grape and cannister." He was neither poet nor dreamer, merely a hard-headed patriot who sought to combat British force with Irish violence. His present influence in Ireland is explained by the eloquence of his writings, especially his *Jail Journal* (1854) and *The Crusade of the Period: and Last Conquest of Ireland (Perhaps)* (1873).

[The standard biography is Wm. Dillon, *Life of John Mitchel* (2 vols., 1888). Consult also: the biography and lengthy bibliography in the *Dict. Nat. Biog.;* Émile Montégut, *John Mitchel: A Study of Irish Nationalism* (English translation, Dublin, 1915); P. S. O'Hegarty, *John Mitchel, an Appreciation* (Dublin, 1915); Ida A. Taylor, *Revolutionary Types* (London, 1904); and the *Sun* (N. Y.), Mar. 22, 1875.] F. M—n.

Mitchel

MITCHEL, JOHN PURROY (July 19, 1879–July 6, 1918), lawyer, mayor of New York City, was born and reared in Fordham, N. Y. He came of fighting Irish stock. His paternal grandfather was John Mitchel [q.v.]; his father, James Mitchel, served on the staff of Stonewall Jackson, then after the war moved his family to New York, where he served the city as fire marshal. The family of his mother, Mary Purroy, were prominent in anti-Tammany circles. Mitchel was educated in the public schools, pursued academic studies at St. John's College, and graduated from Columbia in 1899, having achieved a distinguished record in oratory and debate. In 1901 he graduated with honors from the New York Law School. His brief career at the bar, begun in partnership with George V. Mullan, was merely a prelude to spectacular political achievements. He first attracted public attention in 1906 through an appointment by Corporation Counsel Ellison as special investigator of the office of Borough President of Manhattan, John F. Ahearn. A political admirer described him at this time as "a gosling with the fuzz on him—lean, lank, long-necked and embarrassed. . . . But you ought to have seen him pitch in!" (*Collier's*, Aug. 25, 1917, p. 41). "Young Torquemada," as he was soon called, was also empowered to investigate Borough President Louis Haffen of the Bronx. His work was reviewed by Governor Hughes, who removed both officials. In 1909, as running-mate of Gaynor, he was elected president of the Board of Aldermen and served as acting mayor of the city during the chief executive's prolonged illness. In recognition of the exceptional administrative talent which Mitchel had demonstrated, President Wilson in May 1913 appointed him collector of the Port of New York, but the anti-Tammany forces drafted him almost at once as their candidate for the mayoralty, and he received the public support of the President (*New York Times*, July 31, 1913). Running on the issue of civic reform as a Fusion party candidate against McCall, he was elected by a plurality of 121,209 votes (*Ibid.*, Nov. 6, 1913).

Entering office at the age of thirty-four, Mitchel was the youngest mayor in the history of the city. To this position he brought youthful vigor, nervous energy, practical idealism, and the manner and appearance of the cultivated gentleman in politics. He at once embarked upon a serious program of municipal reform and ignored party ties in making numerous appointments. He maintained that an administration must stand or fall on the record of the police department and selected for the post of police commissioner his friend, Arthur Woods, who performed the duties of the office with distinction. He promoted active executive control by employing to advantage the agencies of the chamberlain and the commissioner of accounts. A champion of home-rule, he fought to eliminate the inequalities of the state tax quotas and instituted a program of tax relief for the city. Opposing any increase in the huge funded debt of the city, he had the new commitments cut appreciably, and in the economic depression at the outbreak of the World War, he formed a citizens' committee, with Judge Gary as chairman, which studied the unemployment problem, raised a modest relief fund, and established workshops. Long before the United States was drawn into the war, he sought to lend all the weight of his official influence to promote military preparedness. He consistently opposed volunteer armies, condemned pacifism, and advocated universal military training. He served in the officers' training camp at Plattsburg during the summers of 1915 and 1916. During the summer of 1917 he officiated as host at the receptions to the numerous allied missions which came to the United States.

Despite an engaging personality, an unquestioned honesty of purpose, and a record of creditable achievement, Mitchel and his administration became increasingly unpopular. He was looked upon by many as undemocratic, the associate of captains of industry and the companion of wealthy society. "Too much Fifth Avenue, too little First Avenue," expressed a popular feeling. His administration was charged with inadequate supervision of real-estate purchases. Mitchel was personally responsible for the introduction by way of experiment in the public schools of the plan of vocational training and industrial education conducted in Gary, Ind. The crude manner with which the plan was introduced enflamed popular indignation, and the assumption by many of the people that it was a deliberate scheme to train the masses for menial labor aroused them against the system. But the most serious cause of Mitchel's subsequent defeat was the sensational "charities controversy." Charges were raised by Fusion reform officials against the secretary of the state board of charities, and an investigation by the Fusion charities' commissioner revealed that certain Catholic and Protestant institutions were being grossly mismanaged. Both Catholics and Protestants resented the investigation, and despite the fact that Mitchel was himself a Catholic, strong religious feeling was aroused. It was also discovered that the Fusion police department had been for some time tapping wires on private telephone conversations. Finally, in his campaign for reëlection against John F. Hylan, Mitchel wrapped himself in a mantle of patriotism and denounced his opponent as pro-German and possessing a "yellow streak" (*New York Times,* Oct. 28, 29, 1917). These insubstantial issues did not strengthen him with the German- and Irish-American voters.

Mitchel was defeated for the Republican nomination by W. M. Bennett with a bare majority of 224 votes in a bitterly fought contest (*New York Times,* Sept. 27, 1917), and in the November election, despite a huge campaign fund, he was crushed by the Tammany ticket. Although clearly disappointed, he lost no time in joining the aviation corps. He had virtually completed his training for service at the front, when, at Gerstner Field, Lake Charles, La., on July 6, 1918, he fell from a single-seater scout plane at a height of about five hundred feet. An investigation revealed that his safety belt had been unfastened at the time of the accident. He was survived by his widow, Olive Child Mitchel, the daughter of Franklin D. Child of New York, whom he had married on Apr. 3, 1909.

[Wm. Dillon, *Life of John Mitchel* (2 vols., 1888), for the Mitchel family background; H. L. McBain, "John Purroy Mitchel," *Nat. Municipal Rev.,* Sept. 1918; Chas. A. Beard, "John Purroy Mitchel," *Survey,* July 13, 1918; "John Purroy Mitchel: His Chief Contribution to City Government," *Survey,* Aug. 3, 1918; *John Purroy Mitchel, 1879–1918: In Memoriam* (1918), pub. by the Class of 1899, Columbia; D. F. Malone, "John Purroy Mitchel," *World's Work,* Feb. 1914; Julian Street, "New York's Fighting Mayor," *Collier's,* Aug. 25, 1917; O. G. Villard, "John Purroy Mitchel," *Nation,* July 13, 1918; Emanie M. Sachs, "Being Human: a Great Mayor and What Happened to Him," *Century,* Feb. 1926; *Speech made by Hon. John Purroy Mitchel, ... at the Dinner of the Committee of 107 at the Aldine Club, Monday, Apr. 12, 1915* (1915); *Speech of Hon. John Purroy Mitchel, at the Dinner of the Committee of 107 at the Hotel Asior, Tuesday, May 2, 1916* (1916); Eda Amberg and William H. Allen, *Civic Lessons from Mayor Mitchel's Defeat* (1921); *N. Y. Times,* Jan. 25, 30, Sept. 8, 1915; Jan. 22, 27, Mar. 4, June 28, 1916; and New York press for July 7, 1918.]   R. B. M.

MITCHEL, ORMSBY MacKNIGHT (July 28, 1809–Oct. 30, 1862), astronomer, Union soldier, was the son of John and Elizabeth (MacAlister) Mitchel, both of Scotch-Irish descent. Some five years before his birth his parents moved from Virginia to Union County, Ky., settling at what is now Morganfield. Here, in the rudest surroundings, Ormsby MacKnight, the youngest child of a large family, was born. Two or three years later the father died. After vainly trying to win a livelihood from the plantation, the widow moved with her children to Lebanon, Ohio, not far from Cincinnati.

It was in this center of education and trade that Mitchel received his early schooling. When about fourteen years of age he started to support himself, working as a clerk in Xenia. A little later, having seen a notice of a pending examination for entrance to the United States Military Academy, he determined to apply for an appointment, which through influential family friends in Washington he secured. Reporting for examination June 1, 1825, he was admitted, and graduated fifteenth in his class of forty-six, in 1829. His love for mathematics, derived from his father, resulted in such marked proficiency that upon graduation he was detailed as assistant professor at the Academy. There he met a young widow, Louisa (Clark) Trask, who was living with her father, Judge Clark, at Cornwall-on-the-Hudson. In the summer of 1831 they were married. After brief service at Fort Marion, St. Augustine, Fla., Mitchel resigned his commission in 1832, and moved to Cincinnati. While teaching at West Point he had studied law; he was now admitted to the bar and became the partner of E. D. Mansfield [*q.v.*]. Neither partner really cared for the law, however, and before long Mansfield became a journalist and Mitchel drifted back into teaching. The Cincinnati College, founded in 1819, was reëstablished in 1835, and the year following he was appointed to its faculty as professor of mathematics, philosophy, and astronomy. In 1836–37 he was also chief engineer of the Little Miami Railroad.

Thus began in the most casual way the career that was to give Mitchel a permanent place in the annals of American science. In his teaching of astronomy he became enthusiastic himself on the subject and aroused so great an interest in his students and their friends that he was persuaded to give a short course of public lectures. In his diary he wrote of this venture: "On the first evening my audience was respectable, on the second evening my house was filled, and on the third it was overflowing" (Mitchel, *post,* p. 51). On the platform he showed himself to be a gifted orator, and invitations to speak in several of the larger cities came to him. A member of one of his audiences wrote: "In New York the music hall is thronged night after night to hear his impassioned eloquence poured in an unbroken flow of 'thoughts that breathe and words that burn' on the excited thousands" (Porter, *post,* p. 8). This magical gift of oratory, together with indomitable energy and perseverance, enabled Mitchel to carry to completion a scheme which at first seemed chimerical. In 1825 John Quincy Adams had endeavored to persuade Congress to found a national observatory, but without avail. In 1843, however, Mitchel's lectures on celestial phenomena roused his audience to such a pitch of enthusiasm that they provided him with means to erect "the first astronomical establishment worthy of the name" in the United States (Clerke, *post*, p. 8). Moreover, his lectures in other parts of the country had no small part in stimulating the interest which resulted in the establishment, at very nearly the same time, of the Harvard Observatory and the Naval Observatory at Washington.

The Cincinnati Astronomical Society had been founded in 1842, and in 1845 there was erected on one of the hills outside the city the second largest telescope in the world, and by far the largest on the Western continent. In 1846 Mitchel began the publication of the *Sidereal Messenger,* which he conducted until October 1848—the first magazine ever devoted to a popular exposition of astronomy. In 1846, also, he was offered the Rumford professorship at Harvard, but declined it, since he felt obliged to direct the Cincinnati Observatory for at least ten years. During this period he took great interest in the establishment of the Dudley Observatory at Albany, and in fact furnished the plans for it; when, therefore, in 1859 he was asked to become its director, he accepted.

His astronomical work was practically ended, however. Soon after the outbreak of the Civil War the President appointed him a brigadier-general of volunteers (Aug. 9, 1861), and he was assigned to command the Department of the Ohio. Later the departments of the Ohio and the Cumberland were united, and Mitchel served under Gen. D. C. Buell [*q.v.*]. In April 1862 he made the memorable dash from Shelbyville, Tenn., to Huntsville, Ala., surprising and capturing the city without firing a gun, and thus getting control of the Memphis & Charleston Railroad. For this brilliant exploit the thanks of the War Department were telegraphed to him and he was promoted to be major-general of volunteers. His relations with Buell, who found his discipline lax and his control of his troops unsatisfactory, grew increasingly strained, however; and in the summer of 1862 he tendered his resignation. It was not accepted, but in the fall (Sept. 17) he was transferred to the command of the Department of the South and the X Army Corps, with headquarters at Hilton Head, S. C. Before he could organize the work there he was stricken with yellow fever, and died at Beaufort on Oct. 30. He was the author of two books published during his lifetime: *Planetary and Stellar Worlds* (1848) and *Popular Astronomy*

(1860). A posthumous volume, *The Astronomy of the Bible,* was copyrighted in 1863.

[F. A. Mitchel, *Ormsby MacKnight Mitchel, Astronomer and General* (1887), a biography by his son; J. G. Porter, *Hist. Sketch of the Cincinnati Observatory, 1843–93* (1893); G. W. Cullum, *Biog. Reg. Officers and Grads. U. S. Mil. Acad.* (3rd ed., 1891), Vol. I; *Proc. Cincinnati Astron. Soc. in Commemoration of Prof. Ormsby M. Mitchel* (1862); A. M. Clerke, *A Pop. Hist. of Astronomy during the Nineteenth Century* (1887); *Battles and Leaders of the Civil War* (4 vols., 1887–88), esp. vol. II; *War of the Rebellion: Official Records* (*Army*), 1 ser. IV, VII, X (pt. 1), XIV, XVI; *Evening Star* (Washington), Nov. 5, 1862.]   J.G.P.

MITCHELL, ALEXANDER (Oct. 18, 1817–Apr. 19, 1887), banker, financier, congressman, and railroad builder, was born in Ellon, Aberdeenshire, Scotland, and died in New York City. His parents were John and Margaret (Lendrum) Mitchell. The father, a well-to-do farmer, was the son of an emigrant from the north of England; the mother was of pure Scottish descent. At twenty-two, Alexander Mitchell came to America as secretary of the Wisconsin Marine & Fire Insurance Company, with headquarters at Milwaukee. The guiding spirit behind this organization was George Smith [*q.v.*], also a Scotchman, who had obtained the charter from the Wisconsin territorial legislature in February 1839, ostensibly to do an insurance business. Shortly after its organization, however, the company began doing a full-fledged banking business under a clause in its charter which authorized it to receive money on deposit and issue certificates therefor. Various efforts were made to repeal the charter, but were frustrated, largely through the strategy and astuteness of Alexander Mitchell, who maintained that a court at law, rather than the legislature, should determine whether or not the corporation was usurping powers not conferred upon it in the charter. Despite the hostile attitude of the legislature at almost every session, the institution continued to thrive and flourish during the forties. By Dec. 1, 1852, the certificates of deposit outstanding totaled $1,470,235, which went a long way toward meeting the currency needs of the Northwest.

Soon after Wisconsin was admitted as a state in 1848, the attorney-general commenced proceedings by *quo warranto* to test the legality of the charter. This was the correct legal procedure, and there is no question but that the charter would have been revoked had a truce not been declared. In 1852 Wisconsin passed its free-banking law, and it is generally understood that Mitchell had agreed that if the free-banking law were ratified by a vote of the people at the November election, the Wisconsin Marine &

Fire Insurance Company would be reorganized under the laws of the state. The law was approved by the people, and in January 1853 the Wisconsin Marine & Fire Insurance Company became a state bank, with Alexander Mitchell as president. In 1854, Mitchell bought Smith's holdings and became the principal owner. At the outbreak of the Civil War the free banks in Wisconsin faced financial ruin. In 1861 about two-thirds of the collateral placed in trust with the state treasurer to safeguard the interests of the noteholder were the bonds of seceding states. Alexander Mitchell is commonly credited with the execution of a scheme whereby approximately a million dollars' worth of Wisconsin war bonds were assigned to the solvent banks and substituted for the depreciated Southern bonds. As a result, more than two-thirds of the 110 banks in the state remained in good standing. He was the first president of the Wisconsin Bankers' Association.

It was as a railroad builder, however, that Mitchell rendered his greatest contribution to society. During the fifties, most of the railroads which now cross Wisconsin were substantially completed, but they were without tributary or connecting lines, and their revenues were insufficient to pay operating expenses. In 1863 the Milwaukee & St. Paul Railway Company was organized and got a continuous road from Milwaukee to La Crosse by welding together several hitherto unconnected lines. It failed to pay running expenses and the interest on the mortgage debt, and the bondholders were about to foreclose in the spring of 1865. Mitchell was the only director who opposed this policy and maintained that with proper management the road could be made to pay its way. He accepted the challenge to take the presidency and was elected to that office in 1865. Within a year the road was again on a paying basis. At that time it comprised in all about 270 miles. When Mitchell died in 1887, the corporation, whose name had been changed in 1874 to the Chicago, Milwaukee & St. Paul Railway Company, owned and operated over 5,000 miles of railway, covering Wisconsin, northern Illinois, Minnesota, Iowa, and South Dakota. Mitchell, South Dakota, was named in Mitchell's honor.

In politics he was originally a Whig; in the late fifties he became a Republican and a loyal supporter of Lincoln; later he championed the Reconstruction policies of Andrew Johnson and became a Democrat. An unsuccessful candidate in 1868, he was elected to Congress in 1870 and again in 1872. In 1877 he was nominated by the Wisconsin Democrats for governor, but re-

fused to run. He was married, Oct. 7, 1841, to Martha Reed. He left the bulk of his fortune to his only son, John L. Mitchell, who represented Wisconsin in the United States Senate from 1893 to 1899.

[J. J Knox, *A Hist. of Banking in the U. S.* (1900), pp. 740–46; A. M. Thomson, *A Political Hist. of Wis.* (1900), pp. 304–06; E. B. Usher, *Wisconsin, Its Story and Biog.* (1914), VII, 2012–19, III, 471–81; *Milwaukee Sentinel,* Apr. 20, 1887; *Chicago Tribune,* Apr. 24, 1887; J. D. Butler, "Alexander Mitchell," in *Wis. Hist. Soc. Colls.,* XI (1888), 442; *Proc. Am. Soc. Civil Engineers,* vol. XIII (1887); *Biog. Dir. Am. Cong.* (1928).]
L.B.K.

MITCHELL, DAVID BRYDIE (Oct. 22, 1766–Apr. 22, 1837), governor of Georgia and agent of the United States to the Creek Indians, was born near Muthill, Perthshire, Scotland, the son of John Mitchell. His uncle, David Brydie, a successful physician, served both as soldier and surgeon in the American Revolution, took part under General Screven in the skirmish near Midway, and, captured by the British after the fall of Savannah, died on a prison ship, leaving his estate to his nephew who in 1783 arrived in Savannah to claim it. The youth of seventeen was charmed with the new life. He made friends rapidly, studied law in the office of William Stephens, and in 1795 was elected attorney-general. He was sent to the state House of Representatives, opposed the fraudulent Yazoo scheme, and gained a popular favor that made him major-general of the Georgia militia about 1804 and governor of the state from 1809 to 1813 and again from 1815 to 1817. His messages and activities as governor show him as a liberal supporter of internal improvements, education, road building, and, especially frontier defense. He signed the first Georgia law against dueling though he himself had, at least once, been involved in such an affair. He foresaw the dangers of Indian attack and induced the General Assembly to devote $30,000 to a series of frontier forts and provision of arms. The necessity for such preparations was even more apparent when the Fort Mims massacre of 1813 vindicated his judgment as to the danger.

He resigned as governor on Nov. 4, 1817, to accept an appointment by President Monroe as Indian agent to the Creek nation. The Indian situation in Georgia at the time was most difficult. The white people were growing restless over the prospect of the erection of a permanent Indian territory covering a large part of the most desirable section of the state. Pressure brought to bear on the Indians produced a strained situation, which the War of 1812 enhanced. The president selected Mitchell for the delicate position of Indian agent on account of his skilful conduct of Indian relations while he was governor. He brought to conclusion on Jan. 22, 1818, a treaty in which the Creeks ceded to Georgia about 1,500,000 acres of land in two sections where the demand was greatest. His agency was terminated in 1821 by a charge brought by Gov. John Clark [q.v.] that he was concerned in the smuggling into the vicinity of a number of African slaves. He denied those charges and others concerning his administration of Indian affairs, but the president decided that the evidence was clearly against him (*Niles' Weekly Register,* Apr. 15, 1820, Apr. 21, 1821). He retired to Milledgeville, where he died. The state legislature provided for the erection of a marble tomb to his memory.

[A few letters in Lib. of Cong.; W. J. Northen, *Men of Mark in Ga.,* vol. II (1910); L. L. Knight, *Georgia's Landmarks* (2 vols. 1913–14); George White, *Hist. Colls. of Ga.* (1855); Clark Howell, *Hist. of Ga.* (1926), vol. I; *Daily Georgian* (Savannah), Apr. 28, 1837.]   J. H. T. M.

MITCHELL, DAVID DAWSON (July 31, 1806–May 23, 1861), fur-trader, soldier, superintendent of Indian Affairs, was born in Louisa County, Va. He was a man of culture as well as ability. Entering the fur trade at St. Louis in 1828 as a clerk in the employ of the American Fur Company, he was first assigned to the "Ioway Outfit" and in 1830 was transferred to the "Upper Missouri Outfit," with which he remained during the rest of his fur-trading career. He built Fort Mackenzie in 1832, amidst dangers and difficulties that appeared insurmountable. His battles with the Indians marked him as a leader of great courage and resource. As a tribute to his meritorious service the fort built by Leclerc in 1833 was named Fort Mitchell. In 1835 he became a partner in the establishment, but after his marriage in 1840 to Martha Eliza Berry—daughter of Maj. Taylor Berry, a retired army officer, landowner, and speculator —he settled down in St. Louis. Six children were born of this marriage. He was appointed superintendent of Indian Affairs, central division, in September 1841, and held this office, with one interval, almost continuously until 1853.

At the beginning of the Mexican War he entered the volunteer service as lieutenant-colonel of the 2nd Missouri Regiment, organized and commanded by Sterling Price [q.v.]. He afterwards served under Col. Alexander Doniphan [q.v.], and was conspicuous in the battles of Brazito and Sacramento; Doniphan's report

commended him for bravery. When money was needed to purchase army supplies for the campaign to open communication with General Wool, Mitchell, being a handsome and conspicuous officer, flattered the notorious gambling-house queen, Señora Tules, by escorting her to a fandango in Santa Fé, and borrowed from her a large sum of money for the use of the army. He led the advance in the subsequent campaign, taking Chihuahua and then marching on to join Zachary Taylor near Saltillo. On Feb. 10, 1847, shortly before the battle of Sacramento, Mitchell impressed into service some traders, their men, wagons, teams, and equipment. Although he was acting under orders from Colonel Doniphan, his superior officer, a final judgment of $95,000 was rendered against him after the war on account of this incident. Upon the recommendation of the Secretary of the Treasury, made Feb. 27, 1851, Congress voted to pay the judgment in his behalf.

Mitchell remained in the army for several years after the war, and was again made superintendent of Indian Affairs in 1851. Early in 1855 he promoted the organization of a corporation known as the Missouri and California Overland Mail and Transportation Company, which he served as president for several years. He was a second to Gov. Benjamin Gratz Brown [q.v.] in the famous Brown-Reynolds duel of 1856. In 1858 he supplied the United States government with a large number of mules for the Utah Military Expedition.

[Pierre Chouteau Maffitt Collection, Fort Tecumseh letter book (1830–32); Fort Union letter book, all MSS. in Mo. Hist. Soc.; U. S. Commissioner of Indian Affairs, *Ann. Reports,* 1842–53; W. E. Connelley, *Doniphan's Expedition and the Conquest of N. Mex. and Cal.* (1907); St. Louis city directories; Susan Shelby Magoffin, *Down the Santa Fé Trail* (1926) ed. by Stella M. Drumm; *Mo. and Cal. Overland Mail and Transportation Company, Charter, Memorial, Addresses,* etc. (1856); *Sen. Doc. 53,* 32 Cong., 1 Sess.; *House Doc. 281,* 37 Cong., 2 Sess.; H. M. Chittenden, *The Am. Fur Trade of the Far West* (1902); *Missouri Republican,* May 24 and 25, 1861; W. B. Stevens, *The Brown-Reynolds Duel* (1911).]   S. M. D.

MITCHELL, DONALD GRANT (Apr. 12, 1822–Dec. 15, 1908), agriculturist, landscape gardener, and author, better known as Ik Marvel, was born in Norwich, Conn., the son of the Rev. Alfred Mitchell, a Congregational minister, and Lucretia Mumford Woodbridge. He was the grandson of Stephen Mix Mitchell [q.v.]. His father died in 1831, his mother in 1839. A tubercular tendency inherited from the Woodbridges proved fatal to six of the nine children of his parents before 1846, and he himself overcame the disease only by good fortune. He prepared for college at John Hall's school, Ellington, Conn., then entered Yale, where in his last year he was an editor of the *Yale Literary Magazine*. As a student he was alert and independent. Graduating in 1841, he retired to an ancestral farm in Salem township, New London County, Conn., where, after the manner of his father, he indulged his love for rural things and continued his literary work. In 1843 the New York Agricultural Society awarded him a silver medal for plans of farm buildings. In the autumn of 1844 he went as clerk to Joel W. White, consul to Liverpool, and remained in the consular office until January 1845, when failing health necessitated retirement to the milder climate of the island of Jersey. After resting for two months on the sands of St. Aubin's Bay he traveled from March 1845 to August 1846 over the British Isles and the Continent, much of the time on foot. This outdoor life so far overcame his pulmonary weakness that he returned to America in September 1846 in comparatively good health.

From 1846 to 1855 Mitchell's life was unsettled. From Washington, D. C., he wrote for the *Morning Courier and New York Enquirer* over the signature Ik Marvel, a name by which he later came to be well known. In New York under the guidance of John Osborne Sargent [*q.v.*] he read law "after a fashion," but for the most part engaged in literary work. His first volume, *Fresh Gleanings* (1847), is a good record of his European travel. In June 1848 he went to Paris and wrote a series of thirty letters for the *Courier and Enquirer* on the progress of the revolution of that year. Upon his return to Sargent's office he wrote his second book, *The Battle Summer* (1850), which treats of aspects of the revolution prior to those described in his newspaper correspondence. A projected sequel was never written. During 1850 he edited the *Lorgnette,* a journal designed to satirize the follies of New York society. His *Reveries of a Bachelor* (1850) was immediately popular. Fourteen thousand copies were sold within a year. It was followed in 1851 by *Dream Life,* which sold almost as well. On May 31, 1853, he married Mary Frances Pringle, of Charleston, S. C., and went to Venice as United States consul. Resigning the Venetian consulate in February 1854 he resided in Paris until May 1855, when he returned to America.

In June 1855 he purchased a two-hundred-acre farm, later increased to 360 acres, near New Haven, Conn., and named it "Edgewood." His natural taste, cultivated by his residence abroad, recoiled from the ugliness of much in American life, and he set himself the task of arousing his countrymen to a sense of beauty in farming,

home building, and town planning. "Edgewood" became an object lesson to pilgrims from all over America, and his series of Edgewood books propagated his gospel. "We gratefully acknowledge that you have laid the foundation for scientific and beautiful park building throughout this country," said Christopher Clarke in 1904 when he presented a silver cup to Mitchell on behalf of the New England Association of Park Superintendents.

Mitchell was strikingly handsome and had a rare sense of humor. By temperament retiring and reserved, he was a delightful companion when once he gave his confidence. Calm and judicious, he was never an extremist. "Good example will do very much in way of reform," he once wrote, "more, in most instances, than any zeal of impeachment." He always maintained a modest and apologetic attitude toward his own literary efforts, although he made a place for himself in American letters. He used the English language in its purest forms, achieving his effects by sincerity and simplicity rather than by display. Occasionally he tried his hand at a bit of verse, such as in his "To Torquatus" in *Scribner's Magazine,* March 1891. He contributed to the leading American periodicals from 1842 to 1897. His books, in addition to those already named, are: *Fudge Doings* (1855); *My Farm of Edgewood* (1863); *Seven Stories* (1864); *Wet Days at Edgewood* (1865); *Doctor Johns* (1866); *Rural Studies* (1867, republished as *Out-of-Town Places,* 1884); *About Old Story Tellers* (1877); *Woodbridge Record* (1883); *Daniel Tyler* (1883); *Bound Together* (1884); *English Lands, Letters and Kings* (4 vols., 1889–97), and *American Lands and Letters* (2 vols., 1897–99). The Edgewood edition of his *Works* in fifteen volumes was published in 1907.

[The history of Mitchell's genealogy is given in his own *Woodbridge Record.* Waldo H. Dunn, *The Life of Donald G. Mitchell, Ik Marvel* (1922), is based upon original documents and contains an extensive bibliography.]   W. H. D—n.

MITCHELL, EDWARD CUSHING (Sept. 20, 1829–Feb. 27, 1900), college president, Old Testament scholar, grandson of Nahum Mitchell [*q.v.*], was descended from Experience Mitchell, one of the Pilgrim passengers on the ship *Anne* in 1623. His father, Silvanus Lazell Mitchell, a graduate of Harvard, married Lucia Whitman, and in the Old Colony village of East Bridgewater, Mass., Edward C. Mitchell was born. At the age of sixteen he matriculated at Waterville (later Colby) College in Maine, where he was graduated in the class of 1849. There he made lasting friendships which influenced his character; and during the same period a deepening religious feeling decided him to enter the ministry. He had qualities suited to that profession. He possessed the dignity and courtly presence of a gentleman of the old school, yet was approachable and friendly. His family had joined in the Unitarian secession from the old Puritanism, and were disappointed that he should enter the Baptist ministry, but his own conviction of duty was not moved. After college he went to the Newton Theological Institution, where he followed the three years' course, graduating in 1853, and remained a year for post-graduate study. He was ordained at Calais, Me., in 1854, and became minister of the Baptist church at that place, serving for two years. He then served brief pastorates at Brockport, N. Y., 1857–58, and Rockford, Ill., 1858–63.

For years he had been a diligent student of the Bible, and in 1863 he was invited to become professor of Biblical literature in Shurtleff College, Alton, Ill., where he remained until 1870. He then held the chair of Hebrew and Old Testament literature in the Baptist Union Theological Seminary, Chicago, from 1870 to 1877. While on leave of absence in Europe, 1876–77, he acted as professor of Hebrew in Regent's Park College, London, a Baptist institution, temporarily filling a vacancy created by the death of one of the faculty. He then crossed the Channel to Paris, where he was president of the Baptist Theological Seminary, 1878–82. Returning to Chicago, he was editor of the *Present Age*, 1883–84, then, in 1884–85, president of Roger Williams University, an institution for negroes, at Nashville, Tenn. In 1886–87 he supplied the pulpit of a Baptist church at Neponset, Mass., and in 1887 he found in New Orleans the work to which he gave the rest of his life—the presidency of Leland University, another school for the higher education of negroes. During his thirteen years in this position he enhanced the reputation of the institution in the South, made friends for the college and for himself, and exerted .a remarkable influence over the colored people in Louisiana.

In 1884, soon after his return from Europe, Mitchell gave a series of lectures on the Lowell Institute platform in Boston on "Biblical Science and Modern Discovery." During the same period he delivered lecture courses in Worcester and Brooklyn and at the School of Hebrew at Morgan Park, Ill. He had previously published the results of his diligent study in a *Critical Handbook of the New Testament* (1879; 2nd American edition 1895), and while in Paris had issued a French edition of this work under the title *Les Sources du Nouveau Testament* (1882). He also revised Benjamin Davies' *Compendious and Complete Hebrew and Chaldee Lexicon to the Old Testament* (1879), edited *Gesenius' Hebrew Grammar* (1880), and wrote *An Elementary Hebrew Grammar and Reading Book* (1884). He was married twice. By his first wife, Maria (Morton) Mitchell, he had two sons and a daughter. His second wife, Marcia (Savage) Mitchell, was "Lady Principal" of Leland University while he was president.

[*Watchman*, Mar. 15, 1900; alumni records, Newton Theol. Inst.; Nahum Mitchell, *Hist. of the Early Settlement of Bridgewater in Plymouth Colony, Mass.* (1897); *Daily Picayune* (New Orleans), Mar. 1, 1900; catalogues of institutions mentioned.]   H. K. R.

MITCHELL, EDWARD PAGE (Mar. 24, 1852–Jan. 22, 1927), editor, came from a family which in America traces to Experience Mitchell, a passenger in 1623 on the ship *Anne* from Leyden, the third vessel to bring settlers to Plymouth, and his wife Jane Cook. He was born in Bath, Me., son of Edward H. and his wife Frances A. Page Mitchell. His background was the New England of theologians, soldiers, teachers, sailors, merchants, farmers; his boyhood environment that of the rigid Sabbatarians of the time tempered by the sympathetic understanding of a father intellectually curious and naturally enterprising. He inherited a sturdy frame, tall stature, natural dignity of bearing; his mind was equipped for the most serious and the most whimsical exercises. Eight years after his birth the family moved from Bath to New York City, where Mitchell attended Grammar School 35 and George W. Clarke's Mount Washington Collegiate Institute, watched the troops pass on to the front in the Civil War, saw some of the most violent phases of the Draft Riots, and absorbed an understanding of the city which endured throughout his life. His earliest published writings were a series of letters descriptive of Southern life written at fourteen to the Bath (Maine) *Times* from the Gen. Bryan Grimes plantation on the Tar River, North Carolina, which his father leased in an unsuccessful cotton speculation. They reveal acute comprehension and unexpected power of observation; yet their author had no intention of making a literary career when, a conditioned sub-freshman, he entered Bowdoin College with the class of 1871. His purpose was to practise medicine. As a student he excelled in the humanities; he was the author of the college song "Phi Chi," still sung by all Bowdoin men; he taught school in the long vacation; he was suspended for participation in a hazing. But he was graduated A.B. and later became an Overseer of the college.

It was the necessity of earning money to pay for his education in medicine that took Mitchell to Edward Stanwood, assistant editor of the Boston *Advertiser,* from whom in 1871 he obtained work as a reporter. His career in Boston was cut short by an impairment of his sight, but he was with the *Advertiser* long enough to cover fires and horse races, to meet, among others, Edward Everett Hale, John Fiske, Oliver Wendell Holmes, John Boyle O'Reilly, and others of equal flavor, to get the smell of ink; and newspaper life engulfed him. He retired to Bath for treatment of his eyes, and there in the course of his recovery he wrote, when just past twenty, an imaginative tale, "The Tachypomp," in pseudo-scientific style. The story was published in *Scribner's Monthly* (March 1874) and it stood the test of time so well that forty years later (May 1913) the *Century* republished it as one of the "specimens of the characteristic fiction read by an earlier generation." Mitchell might have become an eminent fiction writer, but journalism claimed him, and when, in 1873, the Dingley brothers offered him, on probation, a place on their Lewiston, Maine, *Journal,* he accepted fifteen dollars a week and with skill and pleasure performed the arduous and multifarious tasks of a country newspaper man. Among his duties were those of exchange editor, and in this capacity he first became acquainted with the New York *Sun.* In 1874 his wage was increased to twenty dollars a week when he married (Oct. 29, 1874) Annie Sewall Welch; twenty-five dollars was later refused him. But his success in fiction emboldened him to submit manuscripts to the *Sun,* and Charles Anderson Dana recognized his talent. Thus on Oct. 1, 1875, at the latter's invitation, Mitchell joined the staff of the paper to work directly under Dana. From that day until his death, he lived for the *Sun,* and from the beginning of his service until the end he possessed the unquestioning confidence of the paper's successive proprietors.

For fifty-two years, in the anonymity of the newspaper, Mitchell used his well-stored mind, his genius for wit, his capacity for exposition, and his faculty for denunciation for the sustenance of policies he believed would best serve the interests of America, for the exposure of men and schemes he held to be fraudulent, and for the amusement of the readers of the newspaper. Men he appraised for himself; in the detection of shams and pretenders he was uncanny; and he was as tolerant of amiable weakness as he was relentless in the exposure of evil design. Newspaper purpose and policy never swerved his mind from the search for fact: in the *Sun's*

campaign against the Whiskey Ring the zeal which sought every incriminating circumstance was as energetically employed to detect and expose the false accuser; the pen that defined the attempt of Cleveland to reëstablish the monarchy in Hawaii as "this policy of infamy" was inked to praise unreservedly that Executive when he used the army to protect the mails in the railroad strikes of 1894 and when in the Venezuela crisis of 1895 he asserted the Monroe Doctrine. In the final and successful effort to make possible the Panama Canal his contribution to the contest drew forth from Philippe Bunau-Varilla, in his capacity of minister plenipotentiary from the Republic of Panama, a telegram (Feb. 24, 1904) reading: "The last battle is fought and the victory complete. I shall always remember that I owe it to the victory of 1902 in which you took the most eminent share" (*Memoirs, post,* p. 340). In the campaign to prevent the entrance of the United States into the League of Nations, Mitchell again demonstrated his skill in argumentation. His historical knowledge, his fertility of resource, his appraisal of public opinion, all were exercised with tremendous energy, and, in his opinion, the outcome of that struggle was a supreme victory for American institutions and independence. It was his last great battle and was fought by a man convinced of the justice of his cause.

From an ill-defined but authoritative official status perhaps best described as that of chief editorial writer, Mitchell became editor of the *Sun* on July 20, 1903, under the ownership of William M. Laffan. On Laffan's death, Nov. 19, 1909, at the latter's wish, he assumed the office of president of The Sun Printing and Publishing Association to hold it until the property was sold. When William C. Reick became owner and president, Dec. 17, 1911, Mitchell again gave all his time to the editorship. He was continued in this by Frank Munsey when Munsey became proprietor, June 30, 1916, and held that post under the Munsey management until 1920 when, to conserve his health, he sought less arduous duties, and by vote of the stockholders on motion of Munsey, was retained for life as a permanent member of the staff. On the death of Munsey, Dec. 22, 1925, his successor, William T. Dewart, induced Mitchell to accept a directorship of the *Sun* and the *Evening Telegram,* and his counsel and pen were thereafter used as occasion suggested in the product of the newspapers until his death; he was in consultation with his associates within a few days of his passing. Professional tribute to his place in journalism was paid at an Amen Corner dinner in

New York City given in his honor, Jan. 7, 1922, at which several hundred newspaper editors from all parts of the United States were present.

Annie Sewall Welch Mitchell died Dec. 13, 1909, having borne four sons. The family home was in Glen Ridge, N. J., a residential borough Mitchell did much to establish. On July 22, 1912, Mitchell married Ada M. Burroughs, of Brooklyn, by whom he had one son, Burroughs. After his second marriage he made his home at Watchapey Farm, Charlestown, R. I., where his property included part of the battlefield on which his ancestors fought King Philip. His death occurred in the Mohican Hotel, New London, Conn., and his body was interred in the family plot in Glen Ridge, Jan. 25, 1927. He was a member of no church and was independent in politics.

[The principal source of information concerning Mitchell is his *Memoirs of an Editor* (1924). Other sources include F. M. O'Brien, *The Story of The Sun* (ed. 1928); *Lit. Digest*, Feb. 12, 1927; *Outlook*, Feb. 2, 1927; *Who's Who in America*, 1926–27; and files and records of The Sun Printing and Publishing Association.]   H. M. A.

MITCHELL, ELISHA (Aug. 19, 1793–June 27, 1857), geologist, botanist, was born in Washington, Litchfield County, Conn., the son of Abner and Phoebe (Eliot) Mitchell. His father, a farmer, was descended from Matthew Mitchell who came to Massachusetts from Yorkshire in 1635 and two years later settled at Wethersfield, Conn.; his mother was a grand-daughter of the Rev. Jared Eliot [q.v.], a man distinguished in his day for the successful pursuit of knowledge in many branches of science. In Mitchell's commanding presence, great bodily vigor, quaint humor, and liberal philanthropy, he bore a marked resemblance to this great-grandfather. In boyhood he showed an insatiable desire for knowledge and a special interest in objective science, which were encouraged by his schoolmaster, the Rev. Azel Backus [q.v.], then head of a classical school in Litchfield County. At Yale, where he was a classmate of Denison Olmsted [q.v.], Mitchell was marked by the "dignity of his bearing, his handsome face, the originality of the views he set forth, the humor with which he enlivened his arguments, and the evident intimacy of his acquaintance with great English authors" (Phillips, "Sketch," *post*, pp. 9–10). He graduated at the head of his class in 1813. After a term or two as usher in the school of Dr. Eigenbrodt, Jamaica, Long Island, and about a year in charge of a girls' school at New London, Conn., he was appointed a tutor at Yale in 1816. During the following year, recommended by Rev. Sereno E. Dwight of New Haven,

chaplain of the United States Senate, to Judge William Gaston [q.v.], member of Congress from North Carolina and trustee of the University, Mitchell and Denison Olmsted were called to professorships in the University of North Carolina at Chapel Hill, Mitchell being chosen professor of mathematics and natural philosophy, and Olmsted, professor of chemistry, geology, and mineralogy. Mitchell studied for a short time at Andover Theological Seminary and on Dec. 30, 1817, received a license to preach, then removed to North Carolina, where he entered upon his professorial duties at Chapel Hill in January 1818. Here he continued for the remaining thirty-nine years of his life. He married Maria Sybil North, daughter of Dr. Elisha North [q.v.], of New London, Nov. 19, 1819, and had three sons and four daughters. In August 1821, at Hillsborough, N. C., he was ordained to the ministry by the Presbytery of Orange. Four years later, when Olmsted accepted a professorship at Yale, Mitchell succeeded him in the chair of chemistry, geology, and mineralogy.

Even while professor of mathematics, he had made frequent botanical excursions through the country around Chapel Hill; and after the change in his professorship he extended and multiplied the excursions, "so that when he died he was known in almost every part of North Carolina, and he left no one behind him better acquainted with its mountains, valleys, and plains; its birds, beasts, bugs, fishes, and shells; its trees, flowers, vines, and mosses; its rocks, stones, sands, clays, and marls" (*Memoir, post*, p. 8). He contributed accounts of his observations to Silliman's *American Journal of Science* and other periodicals, wrote "Agricultural Speculations" for *Papers on Agricultural Subjects . . . Published by Order of the Board of Agriculture of North Carolina* (vol. I, 1825); in 1827 published part III of the "Report on the Geology of North Carolina" (*Ibid.*, vol. III); and in 1842, *Elements of Geology*, accompanied by a geological map of North Carolina. Perhaps his best work was that printed privately for the use of his students— manuals of natural history, botany, zoölogy, and mineralogy. His chief claim to distinction, however, is that he was the first to measure the height of the mountain now called Mitchell's Peak or Mount Mitchell, the highest peak in the United States east of the Rockies. Accompanied by his daughter, he first explored the region in 1835, and visited it several times thereafter, revising his measurements. To settle a controversy with Thomas L. Clingman [q.v.] who had measured the peak in 1844 and claimed priority, asserting that Mitchell had measured not the highest, but a lesser peak, the latter made a fifth expedition to the mountains in 1857. Equipped with improved instruments and accompanied by his son, he set about his task in the middle of June. On the 27th, with the work half done, he started to cross the mountain alone to the home of former guides on the Caney River. Overtaken by a storm, he slipped down a steep bank, fell into a creek, and was drowned. His body was recovered ten days later from a pool at the place now called Mitchell's Falls. Buried at Asheville, it was removed in June of the following year and reinterred with formal ceremonies on the top of Mount Mitchell.

[Charles Phillips, *A Memoir of the Rev. Elisha Mitchell* (1858) and "Sketch of Elisha Mitchell" in *Jour. Elisha Mitchell Sci. Soc., 1883–84* (1884); *N. C. Univ. Mag.,* Mar. 1858; Wm. Cothren, *Hist. of Ancient Woodbury* (2 vols., 1854–72); Collier Cobb, in *Appleton's Pop. Sci. Mo.,* Oct. 1896; S. A. Ashe, *Biog. Hist. of N. C.,* vol. I (1905); K. P. Battle, *Hist. of the Univ. of N. C.* (2 vols., 1907–12); "Diary of a Geological Tour in 1827 and 1828," ed. by K. P. Battle, in *Univ. of N. C. James Sprunt Hist. Monograph No. 6* (1905); F. B. Dexter, *Biog. Sketches Grads. Yale Coll.,* vol. VI (1912); *Geneal. of the Descendants of John Eliot* (1905); *N. C. Standard* (Raleigh), July 15, 1857.]

C. C.

MITCHELL, GEORGE EDWARD (Mar. 3, 1781–June 28, 1832), physician, soldier, congressman, was born at Head of Elk (later called Elkton), Cecil County, Md., one of a family of eight children. His father, Dr. Abraham Mitchell, moved to Cecil County from Lancaster County, Pa., some time before 1767. His mother, Mary Thompson Mitchell, was the daughter of a physician. The son studied medicine in his father's office and afterward attended the University of Pennsylvania, where he graduated from the medical department in 1805. Back again in Elkton, in partnership with his father, he became interested in politics. He was elected to the Maryland House of Delegates, session of 1808–09, where he vigorously supported the Jefferson administration. He declined reëlection to the General Assembly but was elected a member of the state executive council, on which he served as president from 1809 to 1812.

In January 1809 he had declined a commission as captain of light dragoons in the regular army, but at the outbreak of the War of 1812 he resigned from the executive council and on May 1, 1812, was appointed major of the 3rd Maryland Artillery and recruited a company of volunteers in Cecil County. On Mar. 3, 1813, he was promoted to the rank of lieutenant-colonel. He was wounded at the capture of York, Canada, and also fought at Fort George, in the spring of 1813. During the summer and fall he was in command of Fort Niagara. His most brilliant exploit was at Fort Oswego, N. Y., in the following year. In April 1814, while on the march from Sacketts Harbor to Buffalo, he was met at Batavia by General J. J. Brown, who had ridden forty miles during the night to reach him, and was ordered to Fort Oswego, at the mouth of the Oswego River. Twelve miles up the river, at Great Falls (now Fulton), there was an important depot of naval stores, the loss of which would have seriously crippled the American forces on Lake Ontario. To defend this was his real object. Marching at the rate of fifty miles a day, Mitchell with about three hundred men reached Fort Oswego on Apr. 30, 1814. They found the walls of the fort rotting, and some of the cannon useless. Pitching all the tents available near the town of Oswego, across the river, to make a show of force, the little company withdrew into the fort, repairing its defenses as best they could. On the morning of May 5th eight British ships with 222 guns appeared in the harbor, saw the tents near the town, and attacked the fort. They were repulsed but the next day landed a party and were met in the open field by Mitchell's much smaller force. After two hours' fighting, the Americans retreated to a position farther up the river, determined to save the stores at all costs. On May 7th, however, the British withdrew. For his gallantry Mitchell was brevetted colonel, and during the closing months of the war commanded the center of the Army of the Niagara. After peace was declared, the Maryland General Assembly passed a series of resolutions in his honor and presented him with a sword. He was placed in charge of the 4th military department and retained his commission until June 1, 1821, when he retired to his estate, "Fair Hill," which he had inherited from his father.

In 1822 Mitchell was elected without opposition as a Democrat to the Eighteenth Congress and was reëlected in 1824. He wrote and introduced the resolution in January 1824 inviting Lafayette to America. When the latter arrived in Washington he proposed the resolution inviting him to a seat in Congress and was made chairman of the congressional reception committee. A friendship was established between Lafayette and Mitchell which lasted to the end of their lives. He was not a candidate for Congress in 1826, but was elected in 1828 and again in 1830. He was an unsuccessful candidate for governor of Maryland in 1829. He died at Washington, June 28, 1832, while attending Congress, and was buried in the Congressional Cemetery.

He had married, on May 28, 1816, Mary Hooper of Dorchester County, Md., by whom he had seven children.

[*Biog. Dir. Am. Cong.* (1928); Geo. Johnston, *Hist. of Cecil County, Md.* (1881); *Daily Nat. Intelligencer* (Wash., D. C.), June 30, 1832.]   I.L.T.

MITCHELL, HENRY (Sept. 16, 1830–Dec. 1, 1902), hydrographer, engineer, the son of William Mitchell, 1791–1869 [*q.v.*], and Lydia (Coleman) Mitchell, came of Quaker stock long settled in America. He was born and reared in Nantucket, Mass., at a time when whaling furnished the basis of the prosperity there and Nantucket whalers were ranging the seas from the Arctic to the Antarctic. The nature of its industry fostered in the island community the study of navigation, including mathematics and astronomy. Mitchell's education was obtained in private schools and also at home, where his immediate family furnished good examples and excellent instructors. His mother had been a teacher prior to her marriage; his sister, Maria Mitchell [*q.v.*], twelve years his senior, was busily engaged at home in her astronomical labors; while his father, a teacher and later a bank official and one of the overseers of Harvard College, was an able astronomer who enjoyed a wide acquaintance among American men of science.

In 1849 Mitchell entered the Coast Survey. At first assigned to triangulation, he was later transferred to hydrographic work, in which field his abilities soon became manifest. After serving several years in junior capacities, he was assigned to make tide and current investigations in various harbors of the North Atlantic states. The results of his researches are embodied in numerous papers which appeared principally in the annual reports of the Coast Survey between the years 1854 and 1888. In these investigations his attention was directed particularly to the study of the tidal régime as related to hydrographic features, and he was successful in elucidating the complex of forces and factors at work in maintaining or changing shore lines and channels. His principal publications are: *Tides and Tidal Phenomena* (1868); "On the Reclamation of Tide Lands and Its Relation to Navigation" (Coast Survey *Report*, 1869); "On a Physical Survey of the Delaware River in Front of Philadelphia" (*Ibid.*, 1878); "Physical Hydrography of the Gulf of Maine" (*Ibid.*, 1879); "On the Circulation of the Sea through New York Harbor" (*Ibid.*, 1886); *The Under-Run of the Hudson* (1888).

Recognized as the leading hydrographer in America, he was drafted into the service of vari-ous government commissions. In 1868 he was sent to Europe to report on hydrographic and engineering progress, and while there he made an inspection of the Suez Canal, his report, entitled "The Coast of Egypt and the Suez Canal," appearing in the *North American Review* for October 1869. He was consulting engineer for various harbors. In 1874 he was appointed a member of the commission on the construction of an interoceanic ship canal to make an inspection and investigation of proposed routes. That same year he was appointed by President Grant a member of the board of engineers to survey the mouth of the Mississippi River, and in 1879 President Hayes appointed him a member of the Mississippi River commission. His scientific attainments likewise received wide recognition. He was elected to membership in various scientific societies; in 1867 Harvard conferred upon him the degree of M.A., in 1869 he was appointed professor of physical hydrography at the Massachusetts Institute of Technology, and in 1875 was made a member of the National Academy of Sciences.

In 1888, after thirty-nine years' service, he resigned from the Coast Survey. The following year he was offered the superintendency of the Survey by President Harrison, but his health did not permit him to assume the burdens of the office. He thereafter lived a quiet, studious life, and with his wife and daughter spent his summers at Nantucket and his winters near Boston. During this period he wrote a biographical sketch of Maria Mitchell (*Proceedings of the American Academy of Arts and Sciences,* vol. XXV, 1890), and one of Ferdinand de Lesseps (*Ibid.,* vol. XXXI, 1896). Mitchell was married three times: first, to Mary Dawes of Boston, who died twelve years later; second, in 1873, to Margaret Hayward, who died in 1875, about five months after the birth of a daughter, his only child; and third, two years later, to his deceased wife's elder sister, Mary Hayward, who died in March 1902. Mitchell's death occurred about nine months thereafter, at the home of his daughter in New York City.

[*Vital Records of Nantucket, Mass. to the Year 1850,* vol. II (1926); *Who's Who in America,* 1901–02; *N. Y. Times,* Dec. 2, 1902; official records Coast and Geodetic Survey; family records.]   H.A.M.

MITCHELL, HINCKLEY GILBERT THOMAS (Feb. 22, 1846–May 19, 1920), Methodist Episcopal clergyman, scholar, was born in Lee, Oneida County, N. Y. His father, James, was the descendant of a colonial New England line; the ancestry of his mother, Sarah Gilbert (Thomas), was partly Welsh and partly

German. Until the age of sixteen he lived in the vicinity of his birthplace (after 1857 on a farm near Prospect), working on the farm and attending the district school, where his thirst for knowledge and his religious feelings were awakened. During the winter of 1862–63 he attended the Seminary at Falley where, in 1864, he joined the Methodist church in fulfilment of a vow. From 1867 to 1869, after finishing his preparation for college, he taught school and worked as a bookkeeper. In preparation for the ministry he entered Wesleyan University in 1869 (A.B. 1873), and Boston University School of Theology in 1873 (S.T.B. 1876). He then studied Semitic languages (chiefly Hebrew under Franz Delitzsch) at Leipzig, 1876–78, where he obtained the degree of Ph.D. in 1879. His dissertation, "Final Constructions in Biblical Hebrew," was later reprinted in the *Journal of Biblical Literature* (vol. XXXIV, 1915).

In the fall of 1879 he became pastor of the Methodist Church in Bearytown (or Fayette), N. Y.; during his incumbency of ten months he was married, June 29, 1880, at Springfield, Mass., to Alice Stanford of Alton, Ill., whom he had met at Leipzig. He taught Latin and Hebrew at Wesleyan University, 1880–83, and from 1883 to 1905 occupied the chair of Hebrew in Boston University School of Theology. From 1882 to 1888 he served as secretary of the Society of Biblical Literature and as editor of its *Journal*. He spent the months from March to September 1888 in Jerusalem and in 1891–92 studied in Leipzig and Paris. In 1901–02 he was director of the American School of Oriental Research in Jerusalem. In the meantime he had been championing in his classes the critical study of the Old Testament and in 1895 he was charged with "Unitarian" tendencies on account of his denial of the Mosaic authorship of the Pentateuch. During the next ten years he became a theological storm center in the Methodist Church. The Methodist bishops warned him in 1899; in 1905 they refused to confirm his reappointment in Boston University, and his chair was given to Prof. Albert C. Knudson. After devoting the years 1906–08 to literary work and the year 1909 to travel in Europe, he was appointed to the chair of Hebrew in Tufts College, which he held to the day of his death. After 1915 he also taught the New Testament.

He wrote the following books: *Hebrew Lessons* (1884); *Amos* (1893); *Isaiah 1–12* (1897); *The World before Abraham* (1901); *Genesis* (1909); *A Critical and Exegetical Commentary on Haggai and Zechariah* (1912); *The Ethics of the Old Testament* (1912). He translated Charles Piepenbring's *Theology of the Old Testament* (1893) and edited *Tales Told in Palestine* (1904), collected by J. E. Hanauer. He was a contributor to the *Harvard Theological Review*, the *American Journal of Theology*, the *Old Testament and Semitic Studies in Memory of William Rainey Harper* (2 vols., 1908), and the *Journal of Biblical Literature*. He left an unfinished autobiography, *For the Benefit of My Creditors* (1922), which was published after his death. As a scholar he was painstaking, accurate, and conscientious, though not brilliant; as a man he was devout and rigidly loyal to his ideals.

[The fullest source is Mitchell's autobiography, *For the Benefit of My Creditors* (1922); see also: *Who's Who in American Methodism* (1916); for his difficulty with the bishops see *Current Lit.*, Jan. 1906, *Outlook*, Dec. 16, 1905; *Independent*, Nov. 16, 1905; for obituaries, *Jour. of Biblical Lit.*, vol. XL (1921), pp. v–vi, and *Boston Evening Transcript*, May 20, 1920. Mitchell never used the "Thomas" in his name, although it appears in *Who's Who in America*, 1912–13–1920–21.]

R. H. P.

MITCHELL, ISAAC (*c*. 1759–Nov. 26, 1812), newspaper editor, and novelist, was born in the vicinity of Albany, N. Y. He first appears as editor of the *American Farmer and Dutchess County Advertiser*, a newspaper established at Poughkeepsie, Jan. 8, 1799, under his guidance. In November 1801 he transferred his services to a rival publication, the *Guardian*, in which he purchased an interest, and in June 1802 renamed it the *Political Barometer*. Four years later this paper again changed hands, and Mitchell became editor of the *Republican Crisis* in Albany. In 1812 he returned to Poughkeepsie, where he bought out the *Republican Herald* and began to issue the *Northern Politician*. After a few months, however, he contracted typhus fever, of which he died.

The distinction due him is derived from the bizarre specimen of early American fiction which he wrote and printed over his signature in weekly installments in the *Political Barometer,* beginning with the issue of June 5, 1804, and concluding with that of Oct. 30, 1804. In its original version Mitchell's story has the title, "Alonzo and Melissa, a Tale." On Dec. 2, 1810, a copyright for the publication of the story in book form was obtained in the name of Joseph Nelson "as proprietor" of the *Political Barometer*. That paper advertised, Sept. 25, 1811, "A New Novel, *The Asylum or Alonzo and Melissa,* will be ready for delivery to subscribers and others on Monday next," while on Oct. 2, 1811, the *Republican Herald* of Poughkeepsie advertised: "New Novel just published by Joseph Nelson ... *The Asylum or Alonzo and Melissa,* An American Tale founded on fact by I. Mitchell. In two volumes." The first book contains a preface, a lengthy dissertation on novel writing in general, and an episode with little bearing on the main story, which is unfolded in the second book. This edition of Mitchell's novel was never reprinted. (Copies are in the Library of Congress, the Harvard University Library, and the Poughkeepsie Public Library.)

In the same year, 1811, there appeared at Plattsburg, N. Y., an extraordinary example of plagiarism, a one-volume novel entitled *Alonzo and Melissa or The Unfeeling Father,* of which Daniel Jackson, Jr. (b. May 31, 1790), a teacher at Plattsburg Academy, claimed to be author and proprietor. Jackson's story, a continuous narrative without chapter divisions, is identical, except for a few verbal substitutions, with Isaac Mitchell's newspaper story in the *Political Barometer* of 1804. (Jackson, in one instance, substituted "permit" where Mitchell used "suffer.") The chief change Jackson made was in the title. Only one copy of Jackson's 1811 edition is now known to exist (in the possession of the Huntington Library in California), but from its second edition in 1824, the pirated novel became a "best seller." It enjoyed a period of phenomenal popularity extending to 1876, during which it was reprinted at least eleven times.

Why copyright claims were not brought against Daniel Jackson was an unsolved problem until the recent discovery of obituary notices in the *Northern Politician* of Poughkeepsie which show that Joseph Nelson, proprietor of the *Political Barometer* and of the copyright of Mitchell's novel, died Nov. 3, 1812 (*Northern Politician,* Nov. 11, 1812), and Isaac Mitchell himself, some three weeks later.

[Mitchell's obituary in the *Northern Politician,* Dec. 2, 1812; a group of controversial letters on the authorship of *Alonzo and Melissa* is in the *N. Y. Times Sat. Rev. of Books,* June 4, 11, Sept. 3, 17, 1904; Jan. 21, 28, Mar. 4, 1905. See also N. Y. *Evening Post,* Dec. 10, 31, 1904; Feb. 3, 1905; the *Nation* (N. Y.), Dec. 8, 1904; Feb. 2, 1905; Feb. 25, 1909; *Booknotes* (Providence, R. I.), Jan. 14, Feb. 11, Mar. 25, 1905. See also Edmund Platt, *The Eagle's Hist. of Poughkeepsie* (1905); Frank Hasbrouck, *The Hist. of Dutchess County, N. Y.* (1909). The Poughkeepsie Public Library has partial files of the *Political Barometer,* the *Northern Politician,* the *Poughkeepsie Journal,* the *Republican Herald.* For records of the marriage and death of Mitchell's daughter, Aurelia, see Helen W. Reynolds, *Notices of Marriages and Deaths 1778–1825* (Colls. Dutchess County Hist. Soc., 1930). L. D. Loshe, *The Early Am. Novel* (1907, repr. 1930), gives an outline of *Alonzo and Melissa* with a critical appraisal of its importance. E. L. Pearson, *Queer Books* (1928), has a picture of the title-page of Jackson's 1811 edition.]   D. S. R.

MITCHELL, JAMES TYNDALE (Nov. 9, 1834–July 4, 1915), jurist, was the son of Edward P. Mitchell, a merchant of St. Louis, and Elizabeth (Tyndale) Mitchell, member of a Philadelphia family. He was born on his grandfather's farm near Belleville, Ill. At seven he was sent to school in Philadelphia, whither his parents later moved. After attending the Zane Street Grammar School and Central High School in Philadelphia, he entered Harvard College and received the degree of A.B. in 1855. In 1860 he graduated from the law department of the University of Pennsylvania, having previously read law in the office of George W. Biddle and having already been admitted, in 1857, to the Philadelphia bar. His public career began in 1860, when he became assistant city solicitor of Philadelphia. In 1863 he became editor of the *American Law Register.* His editorial work for this journal (1863–88) and for the *Weekly Notes of Cases* (1875–99) covered more than a third of a century. From 1865 to 1873 he served as librarian of the Law Association of Philadelphia. On Dec. 4, 1871, he was elected judge of the district court of the city and county of Philadelphia. In January 1875, under the new state constitution, he became judge of common pleas of Court No. 2 of Philadelphia. He served in this capacity until elected an associate justice of the supreme court of Pennsylvania in 1888, and in this court he served as associate justice till 1903 and as chief justice from 1903 till the expiration of his term in 1910. He was then appointed prothonotary of the supreme court, and this post he held till his death in Philadelphia in 1915.

During his service on the supreme court Mitchell participated in 11,580 cases. He wrote 1,008 opinions, including thirty-four dissenting opinions. In initiating change and shaping policy, this vast amount of judicial work had little significance. Mitchell was once described as "a brake upon the wheels of progress," a man little inclined "to change the ancient ways of the law," imbued with "a tenacious love of the things which time had hallowed" (F. S. Brown, in *Legal Intelligencer,* Jan. 7, 1916, p. 12). His principal positive influence was in connection with legal procedure. In this field he was recognized as an authority and published *Motions and Rules at Common Law According to the Practice of the Courts of Philadelphia County* (1879). His opinions did much to clarify and to standardize the relations of the courts to each other, to juries, and to the bar. In addition to his editorial work for legal journals, he collaborated with Henry Flanders in editing and publishing under official auspices *The Statutes at Large of Pennsylvania from 1682 to 1801* (16 vols., 1896–1911). His ventures in the field of history included *The District Court of the City and County of Philadelphia* (1875). His interest in history was further attested by his active official connection with the Pennsylvania Historical Society for more than half a century, and by his extensive collection of autographs and manuscripts. He never married.

[The best biography is the laudatory but detailed account by H. L. Carson in *Pa. Mag. of Hist. and Biog.*, Jan. 1916. See also: *Pittsburg Legal Jour.*, July 17, 1909; J. H. Martin, *Martin's Bench and Bar of Phila.* (1883); *Pa. Bar Asso.: Reception and Banquet Tendered to James Tyndale Mitchell* . . . *Nov. 3, 1907* (1908); and S. W. Pennypacker, *The Autobiog. of a Pennsylvanian* (1918). Mitchell's judicial opinions are scattered through 124–226 *Pa. Reports*. Some of his letters are indexed in the collections of the Pa. Hist. Soc.; and the Society has thirty-four boxes of Mitchell papers.]   W. B—n.

MITCHELL, JOHN (d. 1768), physician, botanist, author, and maker of one map, was born probably in the British Isles, though one contemporary understood that he was a native of Virginia (Kalm, *post*, I, p. 384; Martin, in Miller, *post*, pp. 349–50). He could not have emigrated to Virginia until 1721 or 1725 at the earliest. He received his first instruction in botany from Dr. Charles Alston, of the University of Edinburgh (Thatcher, *post*, April 1931, p. 132; January 1932, p. 50), and perhaps held the degree of M.D., but whether from that institution or another is uncertain. He was the physician of the poor of Christ Church Parish in Middlesex County, Va., for some time following 1735, and received his compensation in tobacco; he was made justice of the peace in that county in 1738. He may have been a Quaker. He knew or corresponded with John Bartram, Benjamin Franklin, Cadwallader Colden, Carl von Linné (Linnæus), J. F. Grovenius, Peter Collinson, Pehr Kalm, John Clark, Alexander Munro, the Earl of Bute, and many others, including the Duke of Argyle with whom he traveled in Scotland in 1749. He lived at Urbanna, Va., and practised his profession successfully there and nearby for eleven years following 1735, yet he himself had to leave America in 1746 because of persistent ill health. On the voyage home his ship was attacked by a French privateer and he lost valuable botanical collections, diaries, and medical notes, some of which were irreparably damaged before being returned to him.

He resided chiefly in or near London after leaving Virginia. His versatility is indicated by his writings, which include, in addition to a number of professional letters, a discussion of the principles of botany and zoölogy, written in 1738 (*Acta Physico-Medica Academiæ Cæsareæ . . . Ephemerides . . . Germaniæ*, vol. VIII, Nürnberg, 1748; reprinted as *D. Johannis Mitchell Dissertatio Brevis de Principiis Botanicorum et Zoologorum*, 1769); an account of the opossum

(1745; *MS.* No. I 468, archives of the Royal Society, first printed in 1932, see *Virginia Magazine of History*, October 1932, pp. 338–46); "An Essay upon the Causes of the Different Colours of People in Different Climates" (*Philosophical Transactions of the Royal Society*, vol. XLIII, 1746); "An Account of the Preparation and Uses of the Various Kinds of Potash" (*Ibid.*, vol. XLV, 1750); "A Letter . . . Concerning the Force of Electrical Cohesion" (*Ibid.*, vol. LI, pt. 1, 1760); and "Remarks on the Journal of Batts and Fallam in their Discovery of the Western Parts of Virginia in 1671" (probably written between 1755 and 1760; first printed by Berthold Fernow in *The Ohio Valley in Colonial Days*, 1890, pp. 230–40). He is also generally credited with being the author of two anonymous books on contemporary problems: *The Contest in America between Great Britain and France* (1757), and *The Present State of Great Britain and North America* (1767). With less certainty, a work entitled *American Husbandry* (1775) has been attributed to him, and, with still less plausibility, *A New and Complete History of America*, of which three volumes appeared in 1756 (Carrier, *post*). His reputation in medicine is established because his method of treating yellow fever, as practised after his death by Dr. Benjamin Rush of Philadelphia, is thought to have saved more than six thousand lives in that city during the epidemic of 1793. Mitchell's letters to Cadwallader Colden and Benjamin Franklin describing this method, which was the result of experience in Virginia epidemics in 1737, 1741, and 1742, were published, wholly or in part, in the *Philadelphia Medical Museum* (vol. I, 1805), and the *American Medical and Philosophical Register* (October 1813 and January 1814). As a botanist Mitchell collected and described many plants and introduced many into the permanent flora of the British Isles, although not all the new genera and species which he proposed turned out to be really new. An American partridge berry, *Mitchella repens*, was named for him. In 1747 he was elected a fellow of the Royal Society. In 1751–53 he aspired to be postmaster general of the American Colonies.

His most important work, however, was the great map which he commenced to make in 1750 and published five years later. He was intimate with George Dunk, Earl of Halifax, in or before 1753. Through this intimacy he doubtless secured access to the great depot of American manuscript maps and geographical materials in the archives of the Board of Trade and obtained the opportunity to compile his *Map of the Brit-*

*ish and French Dominions in North America
with the Roads, Distances, Limits, and Extent of
the Settlements,* scale 1 : 2,000,000. It was published at London, under the auspices of the board,
shortly after Feb. 13, 1755. Twenty years later
the fourth English edition appeared, with the
title simplified by the substitution of the words
British Colonies for the words *British and French
Dominions.* In the intervening years the map
had been printed at least five times in England;
it was also translated and printed eight times in
France, twice in The Netherlands, and twice in
unacknowledged plagiarism by Antonio Zatta in
Italy. There was also a full-scale French reproduction of two parts of the map during the
American Revolution. Portions of the map were
copied twice in Spain. Its quality and timeliness
were attested further by more than a score of
small-scale, simplified plagiarisms published in
England between 1755 and 1782, including such
well-known maps as those of Jean Palairet;
none of these acknowledged indebtedness to
Mitchell. The whole map and different portions of it have since been reproduced in the publications of half a dozen historical and geographical societies in the United States and Canada,
and officially by the British Foreign Office, the
Province of Ontario, the Province of Quebec,
the Dominion of Canada (1910 and 1926), the
states of Maine, Massachusetts, Maryland, and
Virginia, and (at intervals from 1829 to 1933)
by the government of the United States of America.

The map is thought to have been in use in the
British House of Commons during the debate on
the Quebec Act of 1774; it is known to have hung
in the halls of Congress in 1802 and several
times subsequently. It was used in the peace
negotiations at the end of the American Revolution, in the discussion of British land grants in
the Ohio and Mississippi valleys, and in scores
of controversies involving the boundary lines
existing at the time of its publication. Great
Britain and the United States agreed to its official status in the Convention of Sept. 29, 1827;
the King of The Netherlands made one of his
conclusions, albeit an erroneous one, after using
it in 1831; it exerted substantial influence in the
negotiation and ratification of the Webster-
Ashburton treaty of 1842, and serious argument
was based upon it by Great Britain before the
Court of Arbitration at The Hague in 1910 in
connection with the North Atlantic Coast Fisheries Arbitration. It was submitted in evidence
before the Law Lords of the British Privy Council in 1926 in the appeal of Price Brothers &
Company, Limited, from a judgment of the su-

preme court of Canada, and in 1926–27 in the
Canada-Newfoundland (Labrador) boundary
case. It was used as evidence before the Supreme Court of the United States in 1926 in
the Wisconsin-Michigan boundary case, in
1926–27 in the Great Lakes level case, and in
1932 in the New Jersey-Delaware boundary case.
Without serious doubt Mitchell's is the most important map in American history.

[A. F. Pollard, in *Dict. Nat. Biog.,* XXXVIII
(1894), 70; Lyman Carrier, "Dr. John Mitchell, Naturalist, Cartographer, and Historian," *Ann. Report
Am. Hist. Asso.* for 1918, vol. I (1921), pp. 201–19,
and article in *Jour. Am. Soc. of Agronomy,* May 1919;
Lawrence Martin, "Mitchell's Map" in Hunter Miller,
Treaties and Other International Acts, III (1933),
328–51, "Mitchell's Map" (unpublished book), and
notes and articles in various publications of the Library
of Congress, 1926–33; Herbert Thatcher, "Dr. Mitchell,
M.D., F.R.S., of Virginia," chapters at irregular intervals in *Va. Mag. of Hist. and Biog.,* beginning Apr.
1931; biographical references in each of the works
cited above; see also Pehr Kalm, *En Resa til Norra
America,* I (1753), 384; Joseph Lucas, *Kalm's Account
of His Visit to England* (1892), pp. 31–32. Among the
famous, or important, or annotated copies of Mitchell's
map which have survived and been identified are the
"King George Map" and the "Record Office Map" (in
the British Museum and the Colonial Office at London,
respectively), John Jay's Mitchell (N. Y. Hist. Soc.),
the Steuben-Webster Mitchell, and the "Sheet which
contains the Bay of Passamaquoddy," sent by Benjamin Franklin to Thomas Jefferson when the latter was
secretary of state (both maps in Dept. of State, Washington, D. C.), and d'Aranda's transcription of the
Franklin red-line map (*Archivo Histórico Nacional,*
Madrid). The most comprehensive collection of original printed editions of Mitchell's map, together with
facsimiles, photostats of annotated copies, etc., is that
in the Lib. of Cong.]   L.M.

MITCHELL, JOHN (Feb. 4, 1870–Sept. 9,
1919), labor leader, was born in Braidwood, Ill.
His father, Robert Mitchell, was a Civil War
veteran and a coal miner. John's mother, Martha
(Halley) Mitchell, died when he was two and
a half years old. His father was killed when
John was six and he was brought up by his step-
mother, a devout Presbyterian. His early education was gained from a few weeks a season at
the district school. He went into the mines at
the age of twelve, although the state law put the
limit at thirteen. Faced by the industrial depression of 1886–87 he set out on two tramping trips
to Colorado and Wyoming mines but returned
to Illinois as penniless as he left. In 1885 he
joined the Knights of Labor, but in the strike of
1888 in Spring Valley, which lasted a year and
resulted in a twenty per cent. reduction in wages,
he learned the need of a separate miners' union.
Later, in 1890, when pressure from below
brought the Knights and the trade union together in this industry to form the United Mine
Workers of America, Mitchell joined the local
branch. On June 1, 1891, he was married to
Katherine O'Rourke, the daughter of a miner.

He joined in the many discussions with fellow workers on the remedies for unemployment and low wages, reading law for a year and studying social and economic problems.

In 1894 Mitchell was one of 125,000 men who obeyed the call of the weak national United Mine Workers of America to strike and was discharged at its end. Obtaining work in a near-by camp he was found by an old acquaintance who picked the youthful miner to be secretary-treasurer of the sub-district. Mitchell's willingness to serve at a time when the organization was still weak conduced to his advancement and in 1897 he became a member of the State Executive Board. That year he had an active part in the first victorious national strike called by the union. Elected a delegate to the national convention of the union, he was elected vice-president, and in September 1898, almost by accident, he stepped into the vacant presidency. In the anthracite coal fields of Pennsylvania in 1902 he brought together 150,000 English and non-English mine workers, who by a five months' strike won from the consolidated owners an advance of wages, a reduction of hours, and an arbitration agreement which was continued and strengthened after that time. He thus, at the age of thirty-two, became the leader of the first successful organization of immigrant labor from eastern and southern Europe, speaking more than a dozen languages and hitherto despised and exploited by the English-speaking laborers and their employers. He sought out the possible leaders of the many nationalities, trained them in the principles of united action, and won the support of public opinion, business men, and especially of Catholic priests. He himself in time accepted the Catholic faith.

Physically Mitchell was slight and wiry. He had a sober, thoughtful appearance which was enhanced by the long ministerial black coat he wore. He was recognized as distinctly conservative. In this position he was fortunately aided by the recovery of business prosperity, after 1898, and the resulting ability of employers to grant better terms of employment. It was the depression in the bituminous coal fields, after 1904, and the failure of several strikes against a falling market, that led to his defeat by the bituminous mine workers in 1907. Yet he retained the devotion of the anthracite workers. He was the least hurried of labor leaders. His ability to wait for his opponents to involve themselves in contradictions, and then his ability to state the issue in moderate but clear and convincing terms, so evident at the conference called by President Roosevelt, at which Mitchell was bitterly assailed by the employers who had refused to confer until national pressure was brought to bear, caused Roosevelt to say of him: "There was only one man in the room who behaved like a gentleman, and that man was not I." It was in 1902, when he had organized and conducted the anthracite strike, that he became a national figure and achieved the name, bestowed by his admirers, of "the greatest labor leader the country ever saw."

Mitchell's presidency of the union ended in 1908, after which he lectured on trade unionism. He then became head of the trade-agreement department of the National Civic Federation, from which he resigned in 1911 on account of a resolution of the United Mine Workers calling for his resignation either from the union or from the Civic Federation. In 1915 he was appointed chairman of the New York state industrial commission, a position which he held until his death in New York City in September 1919. He had published in 1903 *Organized Labor*, showing his interest in the reconciliation of the ideals of labor and capital through the recognition of the union. In 1913 he published *The Wage Earner and His Problems*, which gave in familiar terms the purposes of unions and the human needs they meet. This book had a part in creating and fashioning the forces of national thought and action on the labor problem.

[A complete bibliography is contained in Elsie Glück's excellent and complete study *John Mitchell, Miner— Labor's Bargain with the Gilded Age* (1929) which is based on study of original sources. See also an article by his secretary, Elizabeth C. Morris, "John Mitchell, the Leader and the Man," *Independent*, Dec. 25, 1902; W. E. Weyl, "John Mitchell, the Man the Miners Trust," *Outlook*, Mar. 24, 1906; *Who's Who in America*, 1918–19.]   J.R.C.

MITCHELL, JOHN AMES (Jan. 17, 1845– June 29, 1918), artist, novelist, and editor, was born in New York City, the son of Asa and Harriet (Ames) Mitchell. Early in life he showed an aptitude for drawing. He attended Phillips Exeter Academy and the Lawrence Scientific School at Harvard, aiming toward an architectural career. Later he studied architecture in Boston and from 1867 to 1870 at the École des Beaux-Arts in Paris. In 1876, after following the profession for a few years in Boston, he returned to Paris, this time to study painting at the Atelier Julien. Here he developed an interest in studies in black and white and succeeded so well that some of his etchings were published in *L'Art*. In 1880 he returned to New York to work as an illustrator. He believed that there ought to be some American medium for the publication of line work by Americans, a belief confirmed by the fact that a zinc process for the reproduction of black and white had recently been developed. With this much to go on, with a ten-thousand-dollar legacy as capital, and against the advice of friends, he founded *Life,* with Edward S. Martin as literary editor. The first issue appeared Jan. 4, 1883. At the outset the young founder had some difficulty finding enough illustrators to keep up with his ideas but he soon gathered about him a number of promising young men, among them Francis Gilbert Attwood of the *Harvard Lampoon,* Oliver Herford, and Charles Dana Gibson. The editor himself contributed cartoons and editorials.

As an editor Mitchell had very decided opinions and was not afraid to express them. He was an outspoken opponent of modern medicine and fought the use of serum in the cure of any disease. He contended that sanitation, not vaccination, had reduced the scourge of smallpox, and he was opposed to the use of dogs, which he loved, in medical vivisection. Owing to his outspoken policy he was frequently involving his magazine in libel suits, one of the chief being that brought by the theatrical producers, Klaw and Erlanger, who objected to a cartoon run in *Life* after the Iroquois Theatre fire in Chicago in 1903. In this as in many cases the jury returned a verdict in favor of the weekly. The success of *Life* was due largely to Mitchell's quick ability to divine and anticipate the trends in American popular thought and to give expression to them in the form of humor. His belief that humor should depend not upon old hackneyed jokes but upon topics of current interest led to an emphasis on politics. It was said that politicians of the nineties and early nineteen hundreds feared *Life's* cartoons more than its editorials. When Mitchell had well established his magazine he began writing novels. His best known were *Amos Judd* (1895) and *The Pines of Lory* (1901). His other works include: *The Summer School of Philosophy at Mt. Desert* (1881), illustrated by the author; *A Romance of the Moon* (1886); *The Last American* (1889); *Life's Fairy Tales* (1892); *That First Affair* (1896); *Gloria Victis* (1897); *The Villa Claudia* (1904); *The Silent War* (1906), and *Pandora's Box* (1911).

Although Mitchell was a great lover of dogs he was an even greater lover of children. It was this interest which prompted him to establish "Life's Fresh Air Fund," which made possible the establishment of summer camps for poor city children. Mitchell's last two campaigns were the result of the war: one a bitter anti-German battle resulting from the torpedoing of the *Lusitania* and the other a movement to raise funds for French war orphans. Through *Life* he collected more than two hundred thousand dollars for the latter purpose and in 1918 subscribers to the magazine were supporting 2,800 French children. Mitchell retained until his death a controlling interest in *Life* and had a hand in passing upon all material published in it. He died of apoplexy at his summer home in Ridgefield, Conn., survived by his wife, Mary Mott Mitchell. During his life he was a member of the National Institute of Arts and Letters.

[Jubilee number of *Life,* Jan. 1893; Sinclair Lewis, "John Ames Mitchell," *Book News Monthly,* Mar. 1912; E. S. Martin, "John Ames Mitchell, 1845–1918," *Harvard Grads.' Mag.,* Sept. 1918; *Am. Mag.,* June 1911; *Life,* July 18, 1918; *N. Y. Times,* June 30, 1918.]   R. H.

MITCHELL, JOHN HIPPLE (June 22, 1835–Dec. 8, 1905), lawyer, United States senator from Oregon, son of John Hipple and Jemima Mitchell, was born in Washington County, Pa. His father took him at the age of five to a farm in the neighboring Butler County where he attended a rural school. At seventeen he began teaching during the winter while in the other months of the year he studied at Butler Academy and afterward also at Witherspoon Institute. He then read law and was admitted to its practice in 1857 at Butler, Pa. In this period of his life he was married to Sadie Hoon whom he left behind with their two children when he went to California in 1860. He remained for only a short time in California, then went on to Portland, Ore., arriving in July 1860. Here, under the name of Mitchell, he took up the practice of law, during his first year was appointed city attorney, and in his second year was elected a member of the city council. With the outbreak of the Civil War he supported the Unionist cause, helped to defeat the movement to form at that time a "Pacific Coast Republic," and in 1862 was elected to the state Senate as a candidate of the Unionist party. Reëlected to that body in 1864, he was made its president and in 1866 came within one vote of being elected United States senator, an election won in 1872 against Henry W. Corbett. In the meantime, he had built up a lucrative law practice, associated, 1862–83, with Joseph N. Dolph and aided by his connection with Ben Holladay, who dominated river and railroad transportation in Oregon, and whose interests in the Oregon legislature Mitchell defended. During the senatorial campaign of 1872 the Corbett faction quoted him as having boasted: "Whatever is Ben Holladay's politics, is my politics, and whatever Ben Holladay wants, I want" (Joseph Gaston,

Portland, Its History and Builders, 1911, I, p. 561).

After his election as senator in 1872 the Democratic opposition brought up against him his Pennsylvania "past" in an effort to prevent him from taking his seat. In 1862 he had married Mattie Price of Oregon City without securing a divorce from his first wife. There were six children in his Oregon family. He was charged with having deserted his family in Pennsylvania, with financial dishonesty, with bigamy, and with living under an assumed name, charges which the Senate committee on privileges and elections decided (June 27, 1874) did not merit investigation. Mitchell, however, felt compelled to make reply to this attack in a public letter in which he protested his innocence (*Oregon State Journal*, June 7, 1873). He did, however, secure a divorce from his first wife and legalize the change in his name by an act of the Multnomah county court in 1874. The story of his private life continued to come up in succeeding campaigns, but more detrimental to his political success was the opposition of the Corbett group and of Harvey W. Scott, editor of the Portland *Morning Oregonian* and a rival for the leadership of the Republican party in the state, who came to oppose bitterly Mitchell's successive attempts to be reëlected United States senator. (For Scott's version of the beginning of this feud see the *Oregonian*, Dec. 14, 1905, p. 8.) The attacks in the *Oregonian* became more virulent after Mitchell had caused Scott's removal in 1876 as customs' collector at Portland. In 1878 a Democratic majority in the legislature brought about the election of James H. Slater to succeed him as senator, and in 1882, unable to secure his own election, he threw his vote to his law partner, Dolph, who was ultimately elected.

The regular legislative session of 1885 adjourned without the election of a senator, but at a called session Mitchell was a second time elected, Nov. 18, 1885. Seventeen Democrats voted for him after the *Oregonian* had printed facsimile letters written by Mitchell, showing marital infidelity, and charged that his conduct in the United States Senate had been "as grossly mercenary and corrupt" as his private life had been immoral (*Oregonian*, Nov. 16, 1885). Later it was charged that he had bought the votes necessary to his election with money furnished by the Southern Pacific Railroad (Joseph Gaston, *The Centennial History of Oregon*, 1912, I, pp. 665–68). He had, however, a large and devoted following and he was reëlected in 1891 without Republican opposition. He failed of reëlection in

1897 because his stand on the money question had satisfied neither gold nor silver men. In 1901 he was for the fourth time elected United States senator. In July 1905 he was convicted in the United States district court on an indictment of having received fees for expediting the land claims of clients before the United States Land Commissioner, a charge that the evidence, as presented by special prosecutor Francis J. Heney, seemed amply to sustain. (Full stenographic report of the trial, *Oregonian*, June–July, 1905.) His death came pending an appeal. The Senate departed from its usual custom in honoring a deceased member by refusing either to adjourn or to send a delegation to attend his funeral.

Mitchell was the most popular political leader of his generation in Oregon. Possessed of an impressive physical presence and considerable power as a public speaker, as well as being adept in the politician's art, he drew thousands of devoted followers. His friends were rewarded with office and he secured generous appropriations for light-houses, for the improvement of rivers and harbors, and for public buildings throughout Oregon. He was also adroit in championing the popular will on questions of public interest. He supported the interstate commerce, the Sherman silver purchase, and Chinese exclusion acts in the Senate; gave his approval to the "Oregon system" of initiative, referendum, and direct primary; supported woman's suffrage, and made capital of the opposition of the *Oregonian* by representing himself as the candidate of the people against the conservative and business interests.

[H. W. Scott, *Hist. of the Ore. Country* (1924), vols. I, IV, and V, and *Hist. of Portland* (1890); *Who's Who in America*, 1903–05; *Morning Oregonian*, Jan. 17, 1898, Dec. 9, 1905; *Oregon State Jour.*, Dec. 16, 1905.]

R. C. C.

MITCHELL, JOHN KEARSLEY (May 12, 1793–Apr. 4, 1858), physician, chemist, and physiologist, was born in Shepherdstown, Jefferson County, Va. (now in W. Va.). His father, Alexander, a Scotch physician belonging to an Ayrshire family of prosperous farming folk, had settled in America some years before and had married Elizabeth Kearsley, of a Pennsylvania family. He died when he was thirty-six years old. When eight years of age John, whose mother also had died, was sent to his father's people in Scotland, to receive his schooling at Ayr and his academic degree from the University of Edinburgh. He returned to Virginia, and in 1816 began the study of medicine, first under a preceptor in Jefferson County and then under Dr. Nathaniel Chapman in the University of Pennsylvania, where he was graduated M.D. in 1819. His health at this time was not good—he had had several hemorrhages from the lungs while a medical student—and he became a ship's surgeon. He continued in this position for three years, making voyages to Canton and Calcutta. In 1822 he began practice in Philadelphia and in the same year married Sarah Matilda Henry, daughter of Alexander Henry. He had nine children, of whom Silas Weir Mitchell [q.v.] was the third. In 1824 he lectured on the institutes of medicine and physiology in the Philadelphia Medical Institute, and later (1833–38), on chemistry in the Franklin Institute. In 1841 he was elected to the chair of theory and practice of medicine in the Jefferson Medical College, Philadelphia, which position he held till his death. He was also visiting physician to the Pennsylvania Hospital and to the city hospital. In 1856 he had an apoplexy which left him with a residual hemiplegia and a slight difficulty in articulation, but without mental defect. He died of pneumonia.

Mitchell wrote a great deal on medical subjects. He was strongly of the opinion that rheumatism was a disease of the spinal cord and had considerable success by local treatment of the spine. He was the first to describe the spinal arthropathies. He was an early writer on osmosis and on the liquefaction of carbonic acid gas. He was much interested in mesmerism and wrote about it. He described the cure of muscular cramps and spasm by the application of a tourniquet to the middle of the forearm, a procedure he had learned in Japan. In 1849 he published a volume containing six lectures, *On the Cryptogamous Origin of Malarious and Epidemical Fevers,* in which, on *a priori* grounds, he maintained the parasitic origin of these diseases. In addition to his scientific interests, he had a definite trend toward literature, and in 1839 published *Indecision, a Tale of the Far West, and Other Poems.* The book does not show great genius, but does prove the author had definite poetic instincts. He was very fond of music and had an excellent tenor voice. Weir Mitchell derived his literary and scientific genius from his father but did not possess his musical ability.

[S. H. Dickson, *The Late Prof. J. K. Mitchell; Inaugural Lecture, Jefferson Medic. Coll.* (1858); F. H. Garrison, *An Intro. to the Hist. of Medicine* (1929); *Trans. Medic. Soc., State of Pa.,* n.s. IV (1859); *Boston Medic. and Surgic. Jour.,* Aug. 8, 1849; *Charleston Medic. Jour.,* Jan. 1858; *Medic. and Surgic. Reporter,* May 1858; *North Am. Medico-Chirurgical Rev.,* May 1858; *Daily News* (Phila.), Apr. 5, 1858.] C. W. B.

MITCHELL, JONATHAN (1624–July 9, 1668), Congregational clergyman, the fifth son of Matthew and Susan (Butterfield) Mitchell, was born in the parish of Halifax, Yorkshire, England. He was brought by his parents to America in 1635, graduated from Harvard in 1647, and was ordained on Aug. 21, 1650. The year previous he had received a call to succeed Hooker at Hartford, but because of a prior commitment he became pastor of the church at Cambridge, Mass., as successor to Thomas Shepard, whose widow, Margaret (Boradel) Shepard, he married on Nov. 19, 1650. In May of the same year he became and continued for the rest of his life to be a fellow of Harvard. Cotton Mather says that "his *Sermons* ... were admirably *Well-studied. ...* And when he came to Utter what he had Prepared, his Utterance had had such a becoming *Tuneableness,* and *Vivacity,* to set it off, as was indeed Inimitable; though many of our Eminent Preachers, that were in his Time Students at the *Colledge,* did essay to Imitate him" (*Magnalia,* Bk. IV, ch. iv, §9). "Such *Holiness* and *Patience,* and sweet *Condescension,* were his *Incomparable* Abilities accompanied withal, that Good Men, who otherwise differed from him, would still speak of him with Reverence" (*Ibid.,* §14). In the course of his career he came to differ with Henry Dunster, the president of Harvard, under whom he had been trained, and who "was unaccountably fallen into the Briars of Antipædobaptism; and being briar'd in the Scruples of that Perswasion" (*Ibid.,* §10). A remonstrance cost Dunster the presidency of the college, but did not disturb the friendship of the two men.

Mitchell "*was a Circle, whereof the Center was at* Cambridge, *and the Circumference took in more than all* New England" (*Ibid.,* §13). His most outstanding achievement was the adoption by the Synod of 1662 of the "Half-Way Covenant," of which he was a leading advocate, an attempt to meet the problem which arose because of declining religious enthusiasm. The requisite for church membership in the earlier period had been a personal experience of religion, but many could not meet the test, so it was proposed to relax the standard half way. In accord with previous usage only the regenerate should be admitted to the Lord's Supper, but the children of those who did not dissent from the doctrine of the church, and were not scandalous in life, might be brought to baptism. Thus the good standing of the unregenerate parents received a partial recognition and there was a greater chance of retaining the children within the fold, for "The Lord hath not set up

Churches onley that *a few old Christians* may keep one another warm while they live, and then carry away the Church into the cold grave with them when they dye" (*A Defence of the Answer and Arguments of the Synod*, 1664, p. 45). The Half-Way Covenant was an incongruous combination of two conceptions of the church, as an ark of salvation comprising all in the parish, and as a community of the saints, composed only of the converted. The whole compromise was swept away by the revival of Jonathan Edwards.

Mitchell lived to be but forty-three or forty-four. In spite of exercise he could not free himself from "an ill Habit of Body. Of extream Lean he soon grew extream Fat; and in an *extream* hot Season a *Fever* arrested him" (Mather, *op. cit.*, §16). Several of his sermons were published after his death under the title: *A Discourse of the Glory to which God Hath Called Believers by Jesus Christ* (London, 1677).

[A brief biography with a complete bibliography is contained in J. L. Sibley, *Biog. Sketches of the Grads. of Harvard Univ.* (1873), I, 141–57. The primary source is the life by Cotton Mather, in *Magnalia Christi Americana* (1702). There is a sketch of his connection with the Half-Way Covenant in W. Walker, *The Creeds and Platforms of Congregationalism* (1893), ch. xi, together with the text of the "Preface to the Result of 1662," which is "probably from the pen of Jonathan Mitchell," pp. 301 ff. The theological aspects of Mitchell's relation to the Half-Way Covenant are more fully discussed by F. H. Foster in *A Genetic Hist. of the New England Theol.* (1907). For family genealogy and sketch of Mitchell see Wm. Cothren, *Hist. of Ancient Woodbury, Conn.*, vol. II (1872).]

R. H. B.

MITCHELL, LUCY MYERS WRIGHT (Mar. 20, 1845–Mar. 10, 1888), historian of ancient art, was born at Urumiah, Persia, the eldest child of the Rev. Austin Hazen Wright, M.D., and Catherine A. (Myers) Wright. Her paternal ancestors, of English stock, came to New England between 1630 and 1640 and were among the first settlers of Hartford, Vt., where her father was born. Her mother, of German and New England descent, went in 1843 to Urumiah to teach in the school of the mission of which Dr. Wright was in charge. There they were married in 1844, and there four daughters and a son were born and passed their early years. The father was a scholarly linguist, and the children constantly heard foreign languages spoken. In 1860 the family came to America, and a little later Lucy entered Mount Holyoke Seminary; but in 1864, at her own request, returned with her father to Persia. After his sudden death, in 1865, she came to America and in 1867 was married to Samuel S. Mitchell of Morristown, N. J. She and her husband went as missionaries to Syria, but the failure of his health forced them to leave that country, and the rest of her life was passed almost continuously in Europe. She spoke Syriac, Arabic, French, German, and Italian, and until 1873 was interested chiefly in philological researches. She prepared a dictionary of modern Syriac, which was not published; the manuscript became the property of Cambridge University, England.

In 1873 she began those studies in classical archeology which resulted in her becoming one of the foremost archeologists of her time. Her husband, who was a painter of considerable ability, rendered her valuable assistance with pen and pencil and discriminating criticism. In Rome (1876–78) she gave parlor lectures to ladies on Greek and Roman sculpture, taking her hearers also to the museums. Many of the leading archeologists of Europe aided and encouraged her in her work; she was granted special opportunities in museums and libraries; and in 1884 she was made a regular member of the Imperial German Archeological Institute, an honor which had been bestowed upon only one other woman. In Berlin (1884–86), as part of her preparation for a work on Greek vases and vase-paintings, she began the study of ancient and modern Greek and of the art of photography, making excellent progress in all these pursuits. In the winter of 1886–87, however, it became apparent that she was suffering from renal and cardiac disease, and after a long struggle for life at Montreux and Lausanne she died at Lausanne early in 1888.

Lucy Mitchell was tall and fair, with a cordial and responsive expression and manner which gained her friends at once. She was of an earnest and intense temperament, but modest and retiring, and was happiest when serving others. Her one book is *A History of Ancient Sculpture* with its accompanying volume of plates entitled *Selections from Ancient Sculpture* (1883). Without claiming great originality she made full use of the discoveries which had been made and published up to that time, and added sound observations of her own. The book was highly praised by competent critics, and, in spite of subsequent discoveries, remains a scholarly and eminently readable presentation of its subject, a work which will always be of value. Her other published writings comprise articles, for the most part on Greek art, in the *Century Magazine* and the *New York Times*.

[T. D. Seymour in the *Critic*, Apr. 14, 1888; *N. Y. Times*, Apr. 3, 1888; obituary notice of Prof. John Henry Wright in *Harvard Grads. Mag.*, Mar. 1909.]

H. N. F.

MITCHELL, MARGARET JULIA (June 14, 1837–Mar. 22, 1918), actress, affectionately known as "Maggie Mitchell" to play-goers of four decades, created in the title rôle of *Fanchon the Cricket* a dramatic miniature of such delicacy, faithfulness, charm, and subtle power, that it must rank among the finer traditions of the stage. She was born in New York City. Her elder half-sisters, Mary and Emma Mitchell, were early on the stage, and when she was twelve, Maggie herself became so ambitious to act that her mother placed her under the tutelage of a veteran English player. On June 2, 1851, she made her first appearance at Burton's Chambers Street Theatre as little Julia in *The Soldier's Daughter*. Her playing won her an engagement for the ensuing season at the Bowery Theatre, where she played boy parts, dancing between the acts. Here she scored her first real hit some months later as Oliver Twist. After winning favor in New York and Boston with the James M. Robinson company, she began to star. During nomad years she ranged principally up and down the Ohio and the Mississippi in such light plays as *A Middy Ashore, The Pet of the Petticoats, The Daughter of the Regiment,* and *Our Maggie.* She was a favorite everywhere, especially in the South, and in 1857 she was the principal attraction at Burton's Theatre, New York.

In 1860 she appeared in New Orleans in the title rôle of *Fanchon the Cricket,* a play adapted for her from George Sand's *La Petite Fadette,* which was to bring her wealth and a unique place in the hearts of the people. Until then she had been but one of many clever American comediennes. After appearing with brilliant success in the South and in Boston, where the play was given with an all-star cast, on the night of June 9, 1862, she opened at Laura Keene's little theatre, rechristened the New Olympic, in New York. It is said that after the last rousing curtain-call, she walked off the stage, famous. The play ran for six weeks, and during twenty succeeding years, never staled with the public. In temperament and physique she fitted the part, that of a sprite-like child, grand-daughter to a reputed witch, herself a trifle "touched by the moon." The actress was a little creature, winsome and piquant rather than beautiful, and animated with an electric energy which followed Fanchon through her lightning changes of mood. From skipping about the scene, laughing spontaneously, she dropped to sudden mysterious melancholy or flashed into elfin rages. It was "one of those perfect bits of acting before which even the chronic fault-finder is dumb" (Phelps, *post,* p. 402). The grace of her fantastic shadow-dances inspired verses

by Emerson. In later life she played with ability many other parts, notably Jane Eyre, which the poet Longfellow urged her to repeat in England, Pauline in *The Lady of Lyons,* Mignon, and Parthenia in *Ingomar.* But it is her Fanchon which will be remembered.

Maggie Mitchell was apparently married three times. Her first marriage, said to have taken place in the fifties, ended in divorce. On Oct. 15, 1868, she was happily married at Troy, N. Y., to her manager, Henry Paddock, of Cleveland, by whom she had two children, who survived her. In 1892 she left the stage, retiring to Elberon, N. J. Paddock having died, she married again before 1909, Charles Abbott, formerly her leading man, whose legal name seems to have been Mace, for she was buried as Margaret Julia Mace. After this marriage she made her home in New York, where she died of apoplexy in 1918.

[T. Allston Brown, *A Hist. of the N. Y. Stage* (1903), vols. I and III; J. N. Ireland, *Records of the N. Y. Stage from 1750 to 1860* (1867); J. B. Clapp and E. F. Edgett, *Players of the Present,* pt. 1 (1899), pt. 2 (1900); H. P. Phelps, *Players of a Century* (1880); F. E. McKay and C. E. L. Wingate, *Famous Am. Actors of Today* (1896); *Who's Who in America,* 1916–17; *Galaxy,* Aug. 1868; *Dramatic Mirror,* Apr. 6, 1918; *N. Y. Times, N. Y. Tribune,* Mar. 23, 1918.]
M. B. H.

MITCHELL, MARIA (Aug. 1, 1818–June 28 1889), astronomer and teacher, was the sister of Henry [*q.v.*] and the daughter of William Mitchell, 1791–1869 [*q.v.*], and Lydia (Coleman) Mitchell, both of Quaker ancestry. She was born on the island of Nantucket, which had been for more than a century the principal seat of the whaling industry. Its captains undertook long voyages on uncharted and perilous seas, and were perforce expert navigators and commanders of men. During their long absences their wives shouldered the family responsibilities alone and thus acquired an unusual freedom of action and independence of judgment, while their Quaker training made them simple and genuine. Born into such a community, Maria Mitchell was endowed with some of its finest traits, a keen intellect, a strong character, and a nature simple and truthful. Her father was deeply interested in astronomy and with plain equipment kept up continuous observations of the sky. He made a business of rating chronometers which were brought him by returning captains. He often called upon his children for assistance, and Maria, who was the third in a family of ten, began at an early age to be his special helper. She excelled in arithmetic and often worked out formulas which she did not understand. She also learned to use her father's instruments, at first to help him but later for her own pleasure. Her education was carried on in the schools of Nantucket where her teachers encouraged her love of mathematical studies, but before long she outstripped them and began working by herself.

While she was still young, an excellent opportunity came for her to cultivate her talent. She was appointed librarian of the town Atheneum, and as her hours were not confining she had abundant leisure for private study. She found the scientific shelves well stocked with books on mathematical subjects, and read such difficult works as Laplace's *Mécanique Céleste,* annotated by Bowditch, and Gauss's *Theoria Motus* in the original Latin. Having in addition to her intellectual tastes a strong interest in young people, she gladly acted as guide to their reading and often formed helpful friendships with them. Both she and her father, through their interest in astronomy, were brought into contact with eminent scientific men in Boston and the vicinity whose friendship proved most valuable.

Her free evenings were spent with the telescope exploring the sky, and she observed among other objects the positions of several comets and worked out their orbits. On one eventful evening in October 1847 she discovered a new comet. It was announced by her father to their friends in Boston who in turn communicated it to astronomers in Europe, then the distributing center for astronomical information. The discovery brought her a gold medal from the king of Denmark, offered several years earlier, in order to stimulate an interest in astronomy, to any one who should discover a comet previously unknown. This unusual and picturesque achievement brought her friendly recognition from other astronomers and scientific men. She was elected to membership in several learned societies, among them the American Academy of Arts and Sciences (honorary member, 1848; later fellow), was appointed a computer for the *American Ephemeris and Nautical Almanac,* and was presented with an excellent telescope by a group of American women, the use of which enlarged her observing program. Women of intellectual ambitions pointed to her work as an example of what a woman could accomplish as a scholar when given opportunity and encouragement. She was received everywhere as a person of distinction and ranked in the public eye with such progressive women as Julia Ward Howe, Lucy Stone, and Mary A. Livermore [*qq.v.*], in whose projects she was deeply interested. In 1857-58 she traveled

abroad with the purpose of visiting observatories and meeting scientific men, taking with her many letters of introduction. The resulting contacts greatly enriched her experience.

After the death of her mother in 1861 she and her father removed to Lynn, Mass. In succeeding years she followed with interest the plans and fortunes of Vassar College, the new enterprise for the advanced education of women which was announced to the world in 1861, but she was quite surprised when its founder, Matthew Vassar, invited her to become its first professor of astronomy. Since she had no experience as a teacher she hesitated to accept; but, encouraged by her father, she yielded and in 1865, at the age of forty-seven, took up the duties of a professor in a new and untried institution. She was the only member of the faculty widely known both at home and abroad, and her name at once inspired confidence in the college and indicated its purpose of maintaining a high standard of scholarship. Her uncompromising support of this ideal was of inestimable value in the early days of Vassar, when its inadequate endowment made it dependent for its existence upon the approval of a somewhat unsympathetic public. She had a powerful influence upon her students, not only in their intellectual development but in preparation for their later usefulness in society. She mingled in their social life and her simplicity and wit made her gatherings in the observatory ever memorable. Her strength of character, her genuineness, her kindly human interest made her an impressive personality. In 1869 her scientific attainments brought her election as a member of the American Philosophical Society, while her position as an educator was recognized by institutions other than Vassar, several of which conferred honorary degrees upon her. She died at Lynn, in her seventy-first year. In 1922 a bust of her was unveiled in the Hall of Fame of New York University.

[Phebe Mitchell Kendall, *Maria Mitchell: Life, Letters, and Journals* (1896); Mary W. Whitney, "Life and Work of Maria Mitchell," in *Papers Read before the Asso. for the Advancement of Women: 18th Women's Cong., Toronto, Can., Oct. 1890* (1891); "Maria Mitchell," in *Sidereal Messenger,* IX (1890), 49; Henry Mitchell, "Maria Mitchell," in *Proc. Am. Acad. Arts and Sci.,* vol. XXV (1890); M. K. Babbitt, *Maria Mitchell as Her Students Knew Her* (1912); *Boston Transcript,* June 28, 1889; J. M. Taylor and E. H. Haight, *Vassar* (1915); other references in accounts of the beginnings of Vassar College.]   C. E. F.

MITCHELL, NAHUM (Feb. 12, 1769–Aug. 1, 1853), jurist, author, composer, and congressman, was born at East Bridgewater, Mass. Through his father, Cushing Mitchell, who married Jennet Orr of East Bridgewater, he was fourth in descent from Experience Mitchell, of London, who arrived at Plymouth in the *Anne* in 1623. Nahum prepared for college under the Hon. Beza Hayward of Bridgewater, and entered Harvard in July 1785, receiving the degree of A.B. in 1789. In the meantime he had "kept" school at Weston, Bridgewater, and Plymouth. In the autumn of 1789 he began to read law with Judge John Davis, 1761-1847 [*q.v.*], then living at Plymouth. Admitted to the bar on Nov. 24, 1792, he began practice at East Bridgewater. Six years later he was first elected to the state House of Representatives, of which he remained a member until 1802. For one term (1803-05) he represented the Plymouth district in Congress as a Federalist, and subsequently served again in the state House of Representatives (1809-10, 1812-13). He was state senator from Plymouth County (1813-14), member of the governor's council (1814-21) and treasurer of Massachusetts (1821-26). From 1812 to 1821 he sat as a justice of the circuit court of common pleas, serving as chief justice during the last two years. He was on commissions to establish the boundaries with Rhode Island and Connecticut in 1801 and 1823, respectively. In 1827 he was chosen chairman of the commissioners in charge of the route for the Boston & Albany Railroad. In 1839-40, as a representative from Boston, he sat in the Massachusetts General Court for the last time.

In spite of his almost constant service to the commonwealth, Mitchell found time to build up an "honorable practice" at law. In his leisure he grew trees, studied music, and compiled facts of local history. He presided over the first temperance society of his native town, helped to found and endow there in 1799 the Plymouth County Academy, as a trustee of which he served for fifty-four years, and sponsored, as president, Bridgewater's first lyceum (1827). The variety and extent of his interests and his duties make the description of him as a man "exact and methodical in his habits; of untiring industry; and of a remarkably even temper" seem eminently fitting.

His interest in music led him to assist Bartholomew Brown and others in compiling *The Columbian and European Harmony: or Bridgewater Collection of Sacred Music* (1802). The third edition, 1810, carried the title: *Templi Carmina ... or The Bridgewater Collection of Sacred Music,* and later editions were generally known simply as "The Bridgewater Collection." It was widely used in New England churches and had no little influence in determining the character of church music in that field. Some of the compositions were the work of Mitchell himself.

Meanwhile, he had been carefully collecting material for his *History of the Early Settlement of Bridgewater, in Plymouth County, Massachusetts* (1840), an excellent work of its kind, on which he was engaged at intervals for over forty years. In its first form it was published as "A Description of Bridgewater" in the *Collections of the Massachusetts Historical Society* (2 ser., vol. VII, 1818), of which society he was elected a member the same year. From 1835 to 1836 he served as its librarian and from 1839 to 1844, as treasurer. A reprint in facsimile of the *History* was brought out at Bridgewater in 1897, and contains as a frontispiece a reproduction of the portrait of Mitchell painted in 1837 by Bass Otis of Boston. According to a fellow member of the Massachusetts Historical Society, Ellis Ames, Mitchell's "antiquarian and genealogical knowledge was copious and exact" (*Proceedings,* April 1854, p. 561).

"Economical and unassuming in manner," Mitchell, with his "genial face, his tall, erect, dignified person and elastic step," was a familiar sight about Plymouth County for years. On Aug. 1, 1853, already well past eighty-four, he set out for Plymouth, in the heat of midsummer, in order to join in the celebration of the embarkation of the Pilgrims from Delft Haven for America. After arriving he discovered that his pocketbook, containing one hundred and fifty dollars and some valuable papers, was missing, and stooping to look for it, fainted. He died later in the day and was buried at East Bridgewater. In 1794 he had married Nabby, daughter of Silvanus Lazell, by whom he had five children, three girls and two boys.

[*Proc. Mass. Hist. Soc.,* Apr. 1854; *New-Eng. Hist. and Geneal. Reg.,* July 1847, July 1864; F. J. Metcalf, *Am. Writers and Compilers of Sacred Music* (copr. 1925); *Biog. Dir. Am. Cong.* (1928); *The Mass. Reg.,* 1802-26; *Fleet's Reg. and Pocket Almanac* (1799); *Daily Herald* (Newburyport, Mass.), Aug. 3, 1853.]
S. M—l.

MITCHELL, NATHANIEL (1753-Feb. 21 1814), governor of Delaware, Revolutionary soldier, was born near Laurel, Sussex County, Del., the son of James and Margaret (Dagworthy) Mitchell. His long and respectable record as an officer in the Revolutionary War commenced in 1775, when he was raised to the rank of captain and transferred to Col. Samuel Patterson's Delaware Battalion of the "Flying Camp." The next year he was again transferred (Jan. 20, 1777), this time to Col. William Grayson's Additional Continental Regiment, and on Dec. 23 of the same year was raised to the rank of major. Mitchell remained in the Continental Line to the end of active fighting. His regiment was consolidated, April 1779, with Col. Nathaniel Gist's Additional Continental Regiment, and later in the year he was made brigade-major and inspector to Gen. Peter Muhlenberg, serving only part time in this capacity, however. While campaigning under Lafayette in Virginia during the latter part of 1780, he was sent to Petersburg to obtain intelligence of the enemy and collect stores. During the campaign he was captured and made prisoner of war, being paroled on May 10, 1781. By resolution of Congress his detachment had been disbanded Jan. 1, but he did not know it, and his petition for pay from that date was unsuccessful (*Journals of the Continental Congress, 1774–1789*, XXI, 1039–40; *Papers of the Continental Congress, Letters, M 78*, vol. XVI, no. 243, MSS., Library of Congress).

Mitchell then probably retired to his home at Laurel. From 1786 until the date of his death, he held offices in Delaware almost continuously, but without special distinction. His political career began with his election as delegate to the Continental Congress. He presented his credentials on Jan. 18, 1787, and appeared on Feb. 1 of the following year with credentials of reelection (*Journals of the Continental Congress*, no. 1, vol. XXXVIII, MSS., Library of Congress). It was probably no descent from being delegate to the enfeebled Congress to the position of prothonotary of Sussex County, to which he was appointed in the fall of 1788; this office he held until 1805 (Conrad, *post*, II, 689). On Jan. 15 of that year he became governor of Delaware, having been elected over Joseph Haslet in 1804 by a very small majority, and served until 1808. From 1808 to 1810 he was a member of the Delaware House of Representatives, and from Jan. 2, 1810, to May 1812, of the state Senate (*Journal of the House of Representatives of the State of Delaware*, 1808–11; *Journal of the Senate of Delaware*, 1808–11, 1812–14). His wife was Hannah Morris Mitchell, daughter of Anthony C. Morris (*The Mitchell Family Magazine*, January 1917, p. 79); they had one son, Theodore. Mitchell died in Laurel and is buried at Christ Church.

[In addition to the above references, see H. C. Conrad, *Hist. of the State of Del.* (3 vols., 1908); H. H. Bellas, "A Hist. of the Delaware State Soc. of the Cincinnati," in the *Papers of the Hist. Soc. of Del.*, no. 13 (1895), which is inaccurate with respect to some of the dates.]   C. W. G.

MITCHELL, ROBERT BYINGTON (Apr. 4, 1823–Jan. 26, 1882), soldier, governor of New Mexico Territory, was born in Mansfield, Richland County, Ohio, of Scotch-Irish parents. Whether he graduated at Kenyon College, Ohio, or Washington College, Pa., is a controverted matter; neither school has a record of his attendance. He studied law in the office of John K. Miller at Mount Vernon, Ohio, was admitted to the bar, and began practice at Mansfield. In the Mexican War he served as first lieutenant in the 2nd Ohio Infantry. Later he resumed the practice of law, and in 1855 was elected Democratic mayor of Mount Gilead. In the same year he was married to Jennie, daughter of Henry St. John of Tiffin, Ohio.

A business trip to Kansas Territory in 1855 convinced Mitchell that it offered opportunities for advancement; accordingly in October 1856 he migrated thither and settled at Paris, Linn County. Throughout the Kansas struggle he was a conservative, law-and-order Free-State man. He was elected to the lower house of the territorial legislature in 1857 and was reëlected a year later. In 1858 he was a delegate to the Leavenworth constitutional convention. The following year he was appointed treasurer of the territory, serving until it became a state in 1861. When the Republican party supplanted the Free-State organization in 1859, he returned to the Democratic party, and was appointed delegate to the Charleston convention in 1860.

After brief service as adjutant on the staff of Gov. Charles Robinson [*q.v.*], Mitchell was commissioned colonel of the 2nd Kansas Volunteer Infantry. At the battle of Wilson's Creek he was severely wounded, but recovered and was transferred to a cavalry regiment. On Apr. 8, 1862, President Lincoln commissioned him brigadiergeneral, and at the battle of Perryville, Ky., he commanded the 9th Division. He was then stationed at Nashville for several months. As chief of cavalry in the Army of the Cumberland he made commendable contributions to Union successes in southeastern Tennessee in 1863. Severe wounds incapacitated him temporarily for field service, and Secretary Stanton ordered him to Washington for court-martial duty. Early in 1864 he was assigned to the district of Nebraska Territory in the department of Kansas. A year later he was transferred to the district of North Kansas, and when the two divisions of the state were combined, June 28, 1865, he was appointed to the command. Throughout the war he had the reputation of being a shrewd and energetic commander.

Late in 1865 President Johnson nominated Mitchell to be governor of New Mexico Territory. The nomination was confirmed Jan. 15, 1866, and he took office on the 16th of the following July. He soon quarreled with the legislature and his removal was requested. He was accused of making a vacancy appointment of delegate to Congress, of remaining in Washington during an entire session of the assembly, of removing officials appointed by the secretary during his absence, and of usurpation of power. In 1868 the organic act was amended to abrogate the governor's absolute veto. Mitchell relinquished the office in 1869 and returned to Kansas. In 1872 he was nominated for Congress by Liberal Republicans and Democrats, but was defeated. Subsequently, he removed to Washington, D. C., where he died.

[A sketch of his career, published in the La Cygne Weekly Jour., Apr. 26, May 3, 1895, was reprinted in Kan. Hist. Colls., XVI (1923–25); material relating to his Civil War career is in War of the Rebellion: Official Records (Army); for resolutions of the New Mexico legislature consult House Misc. Docs. 64 and 94, 40 Cong., 2 Sess. See also D. W. Wilder, The Annals of Kansas (1886); H. H. Bancroft, Hist. of Ariz. and New Mex. (1889); R. E. Twitchell, The Leading Facts of New Mex. Hist., vol. II (1912); Harper's Weekly, Apr. 4, 1863; Evening Star (Washington), Jan. 28, 1882.]
W. H. S—n.

MITCHELL, SAMUEL AUGUSTUS (Mar. 20, 1792–Dec. 18, 1868), geographer, publisher of geographical works, was the youngest son of William and Mary (Alton) Mitchell. His father came to America from Scotland when he was a lad of twelve, learned the clothier's trade, and settled in Bristol, Conn., about 1773. Samuel Mitchell was born at Bristol and died in Philadelphia. In August 1815 he married Rhoda Ann Fuller. Possessing literary as well as business talent, he devoted his early life to teaching, but, becoming dissatisfied with the treatment of geography in the textbooks then in use, transferred his attention to writing and publishing geographical works. Forty years of his life, in Philadelphia, were given over to preparing textbooks, maps, and geographical manuals, the demand for which became so great that, at one time, more than 400,000 copies were sold annually. More than 250 persons were employed in the manufacture of these books, and every effort was made to include in them the results of the latest geographical discoveries.

In 1831 he published A New American Atlas and the same year issued separate maps of several sections of the United States, following these by maps of the settled portions of the various territories. In 1832 appeared Mitchell's Traveller's Guide through the United States; it contained the latest information on stage, canal, and steamboat routes, and was reëdited annually for more than twenty years. In 1834 a series of

"Tourist's Pocket Maps" of the different states was begun, supplemented in 1836 by Reference and Distance Map of the United States. Keeping an eye on current events, Mitchell issued in 1846 a Map of Mexico and Mitchell's New Map of Texas, Oregon and California, and in 1847, Map of the Seat of War; while in 1849 there came from the press Description of Oregon and California . . . with a Map, and in 1861, at the outbreak of the Civil War, a Map of the United States and Territories, on which the various fortifications then existing were displayed. In the meantime, among other works, he had published Mitchell's Compendium of the Internal Improvements of the United States (1835); A General View of the World Comprising a Physical, Political, and Statistical Account of Its Grand Divisions (1842); An Accurate Synopsis of the Sixth Census of the United States (1843); A General View of the United States (1846), and in 1847, A New Universal Atlas, which went through many editions. He had early conceived the idea of a system of school geographies adapted to the progressively developing capacities of the student, and issued, among others: Mitchell's School Geography . . . Illustrated by an Atlas of Sixteen Maps (1839); Mitchell's Geographical Reader (1840); Mitchell's Primary Geography (1840); A Key to the Study of the Maps Comprising Mitchell's School Atlas (1841), later entitled Mitchell's Geographical Question Book; Mitchell's Ancient Atlas (1844); Mitchell's Ancient Geography (1845); Mitchell's Biblical and Sabbath School Geography (1849); Intermediate or Secondary Geography (1850). In this group may also be included Mitchell's Atlas of Outline Maps (1839), and Key for Exercise on Mitchell's Series of Outline Maps (1842). Most of these works went through many successive editions, some of them, in revised form, being reissued after the beginning of the twentieth century.

Many of Mitchell's earlier maps were engraved by J. H. Young, and compare favorably with the contemporary work of John Arrowsmith the younger, distinguished English mapmaker. Mitchell entered the field of cartography at an opportune moment, when national expansion, following the expeditions of Lewis and Clark, Pike, and others, stimulated an interest in the newer parts of the country and created a market for travel maps and guidebooks. He remains an outstanding figure in the development of American geography; he placed his subject accurately and popularly before the students of his day, and met the demand for maps with all the resources at his command.

[S. A. Allibone, *A Critical Dict. of English Lit. and Brit. and Am. Authors* (1870), II, 1328; *Bristol, Conn.* (1907); *Commemorative Biog. Record of Hartford County, Conn.* (1901); *Geneal. of Some Descendants of Edward Fuller* (1905); *Press* (Phila.), Dec. 19, 1868; Philadelphia directories; information from Hist. Soc. of Pa. and Conn. Hist. Soc.]   J.M.T.

MITCHELL, SILAS WEIR (Feb. 15, 1829–Jan. 4, 1914), physician, neurologist, poet, and novelist, was born in Philadelphia, Pa., the son of John Kearsley Mitchell [*q.v.*] and Sarah Matilda (Henry). He attended the "University Grammar School" at Fourth and Arch Streets, the descendant of the old Academy of Philadelphia from which the University of Pennsylvania sprang, and in 1844 entered the College Department of the University, remaining until illness compelled his withdrawal during his senior year. In 1906 he was granted the degree of bachelor of arts as of the class of 1848. In 1850 he graduated from the Jefferson Medical College, in which his father was a professor, and then spent a year abroad, studying chiefly with Claude Bernard, the physiologist, and Charles Phillippe Robin, the microscopist. Returning in the fall of 1851, he encountered heavy professional and family responsibility on account of the failing health of his father, whose assistant he became. He had very positive interest in research and was elected a member of the Academy of Natural Sciences of Philadelphia in 1853. His first paper, "Observations on the Generation of Uric Acid and Its Crystalline Forms," was published in the *American Journal of the Medical Sciences* in July 1852. In 1858 he read a paper before the biological section of the Academy of Natural Sciences, entitled "Observations on the Blood Crystals of the Sturgeon," which was published in the *Proceedings* of that year. This subject interested him through life and ended in the great work on the crystalography of hemoglobin published in 1909 by E. T. Reichert and A. P. Brown, in whose investigations Mitchell had a part. His next important contribution was "Researches upon the Venom of the Rattlesnake," which appeared in *Smithsonian Contributions to Knowledge* (vol. XII, 1860). He was the first to point out that snake venom is a double, not a single, poison. Hideyo Noguchi's great work, done many years later, had its origin in Mitchell's early researches.

Early in the Civil War he was appointed an acting assistant surgeon in the Union army, and improved the opportunity to study nerve wounds and diseases afforded by the Turner's Lane Hospital, Philadelphia. G. R. Moorehouse and W. W. Keen were associated with him in his army work. In collaboration with them he published two important studies: *Gunshot Wounds and Other Injuries of Nerves* (1864) and *Reflex Paralysis* (1864). The former was amplified and reissued in 1872 under the title *Injuries of Nerves and Their Consequences*. This work received immediate recognition and wide acclaim. It is an important contribution to knowledge of the peripheral nerves, both from the point of view of the symptomatology of peripheral nerve injuries and that of the treatment of such injuries.

The wide scope of Mitchell's investigations makes it difficult to classify, or, at least, to list, all his contributions. From the end of the Civil War to 1870 he wrote articles on toxicology, peripheral nerve paralyses, the physiology of the cerebellum, opium and its effects, and other subjects. From 1870 to 1878 he published thirty-four neurological articles, among them "Influence of Nerve Lesions on the Local Temperature" (*Archives of Scientific and Practical Medicine*, vol. I, 1873), "On the Spasmodic Diseases of Stumps" (*Philadelphia Medical Times*, Feb. 13, 1875), and "On a Rare Vaso-motor Neurosis of the Extremities and on the Maladies with Which It May Be Confounded" (*American Journal of the Medical Sciences*, July 1878). His description of this rare neurosis, erythromelalgia, is a masterpiece. He was the first to describe it adequately, and it has been named "Weir Mitchell's disease." In 1874 he called attention to a new clinical entity, post-paralytic chorea. His researches on the physiology of the cerebellum mark him as an experimental investigator of the first rank. They were carried on from 1863 to 1869, but he did not begin publishing his results until April of the latter year (*American Journal of the Medical Sciences*).

In 1871 appeared his *Wear and Tear*, a book calling attention to the inability or indisposition of Americans to play, and the increase in nervous disorders that was likely to follow. The book had a wide sale and made a deep impression. It was followed in 1873 and 1875 respectively by two articles on rest in the treatment of the neuralgia of locomotor ataxia (*American Journal of the Medical Sciences*, July 1873), and on rest in the treatment of disease (*A Series of American Clinical Lectures*, edited by E. C. Seguin, vol. I, no. 4, 1875). These were really preparations for his therapeutically important work *Fat and Blood*, which appeared in 1877. In this volume Mitchell advocated rest, overfeeding, massage, electrotherapy, and physiotherapy in the treatment of functional nervous disorders. These methods were viewed at first with skepticism, but, because of the success which followed Mitchell's use of them, they soon came to be regarded as important aids in treating nervous disorders. The demonstration of their value was one of his most significant contributions to medicine, and they have become known as the "Weir Mitchell Rest Cure." The book went through many editions, and was translated into French, German, Italian, and Russian. In 1881 he published a volume entitled *Lectures on the Diseases of the Nervous System, Especially in Women,* and in 1897, *Clinical Lessons on Nervous Diseases,* works which contain many original and valuable observations. Mitchell was a very keen clinician, and pointed out the seasonal relations of chorea, pre-hemiplegic and post-hemiplegic pains, the disorders of sleep, and the faulty reference of sensations of pain. His "Physiological Studies on the Knee-jerk" (*Medical News,* Feb. 13, 20, 1886), in collaboration with Morris Lewis, is still one of the best treatments of this subject.

Mitchell's contributions to medical literature covered many different fields. In all he wrote 119 neurological, and fifty-two pharmacological, physiological, and toxicological papers. Besides those already mentioned these included studies on the nerve supply to the skin, spinal arthropathies, neurotomy, the cremaster reflex, hysteria, tendon and muscle jerks, facial tics, sleep, and sciatica. To the knowledge of many of these subjects he made original contributions. Mitchell was a fine combination of the practitioner and investigator in medicine. Many of his original investigations were made in clinical subjects, but his studies of snake venom and of the functions of the cerebellum indicate that he was also a laboratory student of the first rank. He was never satisfied unless he was engaged in research of some sort. He was made a professor in the Philadelphia Polyclinic and College for Graduates in Medicine, but the hospital with which his name is most intimately associated is the Philadelphia Orthopædic Hospital and Infirmary for Nervous Diseases. To this institution he devoted over forty years of service, and under his influence it became a center for the treatment of nervous disorders. Here many came to study with him and here he gave most of his instruction. He was a member of numerous societies, American and foreign, and the recipient of many honors.

Mitchell did not, however, limit himself to medical interests; he became distinguished also in the field of literature. His first creative work was in verse. As early as 1856 he had made a collection of his poems which, upon the advice of Dr. Oliver Wendell Holmes, he did not publish, and his initial volume of verse, *The Hill of*

Stones, did not appear until 1882. His most important early poems are to be found in *A Psalm of Deaths, and Other Poems* (1890); *Francis Drake—A Tragedy of the Sea* (1893), in which he included his vivid dramatic narratives; and *The Mother and Other Poems* (1893), containing in the title poem one of his most appealing lyrics. In 1896, *Collected Poems* was published, and in 1901 *Selections from the Poems of S. Weir Mitchell* was issued in London. The last included his finest effort in verse, "Ode on a Lycian Tomb," inspired by the death of his only daughter, and written with a restraint and a distinction of phrase which make it one of the outstanding elegies in American literature. His ability was revealed also in his metrical adaptation of one of the most exquisite of Middle English poems, *Pearl* (1906), a father's symbolic vision of a little daughter in Paradise. Mitchell's last volume of verse, *The Comfort of the Hills,* appeared in 1909, and a definitive edition of his poetical works, *Complete Poems,* in 1914.

He began his career as a writer of fiction with "The Case of George Dedlow," published anonymously in the *Atlantic Monthly* as the leading article for July 1866. This satire on spiritualism, in which a soldier whose arms and legs have been amputated sees them revived at a seance, was so realistic that contributions were sent to the author under the impression that George Dedlow was a real person. The story is also of great interest because it portrays the real feelings of a soldier upon entering a battle, antedating the work of Stephen Crane [*q.v.*] by nearly thirty years. After three novelettes, published in one volume in 1880, the first two of which, "Hephzibah Guinness" and "Thee and You," dealt with life in Philadelphia in the early nineteenth century, Mitchell returned to the Civil War period in his first long novels, *In War Time* (1885), which appeared originally as a serial in the *Atlantic Monthly* (January to December 1884), and *Roland Blake* (1886). In the former, which has for its background the army hospital in Philadelphia, he portrays a number of characters, notable among whom is Dr. Ezra Wendell, the earliest of the writer's profound studies in human weakness. *Roland Blake,* so far as the hero, a Union soldier, is concerned, is a portrait of valor and mysticism; but the greatest character in the story, Octopia Darnell, who absorbs without mercy the emotional lives of those she dominates, is the first of the abnormal women in the depiction of whom Mitchell was unrivaled in his time.

Roland Blake represents in itself the two forms of fiction in which Mitchell was to excel—the novel of psychology and the historical romance. *Far in the Forest,* a dramatic story of the woodland region of Pennsylvania, appeared in 1889, and in *Characteristics* (1891), Mitchell created a different form of fiction, one in which the story consists largely of the conversations of a group of people whose center is Owen North, a physician. This conversation reproduces the flavor of the Saturday evening gatherings at the author's home. *When All the Woods Are Green* (1894) was based on Mitchell's summer experiences in Canada, and, while a favorite with those who love fishing as did he, has less framework than the most of his fiction. His great historical novel of the Revolution, *Hugh Wynne, Free Quaker,* first appeared in the *Century Magazine* (November 1896–October 1897) and was published separately in 1898. Mitchell spent seven years of study in preparation for the work, but the composition took but six weeks. While the hero is fictitious, Edward Wynne, an ancestor of the second Mrs. Mitchell, came over with Penn in 1682, and the story has the atmosphere of reality. Mitchell knew Philadelphia's history well, and his portrayal of life there in war time, and especially his portraiture of Washington, Hamilton, Rush, and others, give the book an unrivaled position among the romances of the Revolution.

His next work, *The Adventures of François* (1899), which had also appeared in the *Century Magazine* (January–September 1898), is a novel of the French Revolution, and its hero, a foundling and a thief "of whom Nature meant to make a gentleman," is one of Mitchell's most vivid portraits. His preparation as usual was thorough, and in his description of the seamy side of Paris life he showed the effect of his close study of the methods of the great realist Defoe, of whose works he possessed a complete collection, including a number of first editions. *The Autobiography of a Quack* (1900), an expansion of a story published in the *Atlantic Monthly* (October and November 1867), was followed by *Dr. North and His Friends* (1900), a sequel to *Characteristics,* in which the same group of characters appear, and, in addition, Sybil Maywood, probably the first example of dual personality in American literature. As early as 1888 Mitchell had published a scientific account of a woman living in a state of double consciousness (*Transactions of the College of Physicians of Philadelphia,* vol. X). *Circumstance* (1901), a story laid in Philadelphia immediately after the Civil War, contains another of his remarkable studies of women in Lucretia Hunter, the adventuress. In 1903 he published *Little Stories,* a collection

of tales notable for their compression and dramatic quality. "A Consultation" could have been written by no one else. The same may be said of *Constance Trescott* (1905), perhaps the most truly organized of all his novels. The account of Constance's revenge for the murder of her husband has seldom been equaled in modern fiction.

In 1907 Mitchell again revivified the past of Philadelphia in *The Red City,* giving a picture of the national capital when the struggle between Democrats and Federalists made Washington's administration a hotbed of intrigue. Washington the statesman is painted as accurately as Washington the soldier had been in *Hugh Wynne,* and the yellow-fever epidemic of 1793 is depicted with the skill which the knowledge of the physician made possible. *John Sherwood, Inn Master* (1911), while not on the same high level, contains an interesting study of insanity, while his last novel, *Westways* (1913), is one of his best. Here the Civil War is described from the point of view of a surgeon with Doubleday's Pennsylvania troops, the forces that held the center against Pickett's charge at Gettysburg.

Mitchell's own selection of his most significant work reveals his sound critical judgment. In a personal letter (to one of the writers of this article), he said: "Of course Hugh Wynne is regarded as the book which is likely to have any continuous life—let us say, the immortality of a decade. But François is the book of my affections and the only novel with which I can find no fault is Constance Trescott." To these must be added, however, as of special excellence, *Roland Blake, The Red City,* and *Westways,* pictures of life in great moments of the Republic, and *Characteristics* and *Dr. North* for their originality of form.

In 1858 Mitchell married Mary Middleton Elwyn, daughter of Alfred Langdon Elwyn of Philadelphia, who died in 1862 leaving two sons, John Kearsley, who became associated with his father in his profession, and Langdon Elwyn, playwright and poet. In 1875, Mitchell married Mary Cadwalader, daughter of Gen. Thomas Cadwalader of Philadelphia. It was in memory of their daughter that the "Ode on a Lycian Tomb" was written. While he never accepted public office, in a strict sense, he was constantly called upon for advice and help in progressive civic movements in Philadelphia. He preferred to limit his official duties to such semi-public offices as his trusteeship of the University of Pennsylvania, which began in 1875. Here he worked with Provost William Pepper in the development of the school of medicine and the foundation of the department of hygiene. Among his honorary degrees were the M.D. *honoris causa,* from the University of Bologna in 1888, and an LL.D. from Edinburgh in 1895. In 1902, upon the foundation of the Franklin Inn, the writers' club of Philadelphia, he became its first president, remaining in office till his death. It was in such associations, but more especially at his own residence at 1524 Walnut Street, where he was at home every Saturday evening to his friends, that he shone in repartee and presided over "the best talk in Philadelphia."

George Meredith, who read *Roland Blake* three times, said, "It has a kind of nobility about it," and this comment remains the best characterization of its author. He met financial loss after the failure of the Real Estate Trust Company, of which he was a director, with the same courage that had animated him in his early days of struggle. Liberal, tolerant, with a readiness to help younger men and accord them full credit for their achievement, a patrician to the finger tips, Weir Mitchell wore his many honors with the ease of those to whom great achievement brings no change of character.

[In 1894 *A Catalogue of the Scientific and Literary Work of S. Weir Mitchell,* containing an analytical bibliography of his publications from 1852, was printed under his direction. Additional items were added in MS., bringing the record up to 1907, and two copies were deposited in the library of the University of Pennsylvania. Neither this list nor that given in the only biography, *Weir Mitchell, His Life and Letters* (1929), by Anna Robeson Burr, is in all cases accurate. Appreciations of his character and achievements, read at the memorial meeting in Philadelphia, by Talcott Williams, Dr. William H. Welch, and Owen Wister, were published in 1914 under title of *S. Weir Mitchell, M.D., LL.D., F.R.S., 1829–1914—Memorial Addresses and Resolutions.* See also C. W. Burr, *S. Weir Mitchell, Physician, Man of Science, Man of Letters, Man of Affairs* (1920); *Proceedings of the Mitchell Memorial Meeting of the Phila. Psychiatric Soc.,* Dec. 13, 1929, containing "S. Weir Mitchell, Poet and Novelist," by F. E. Schelling, and "S. Weir Mitchell, Physician," by C. W. Burr; *Gen. Mag. and Hist. Chronicle of the Univ. of Pa.,* Apr. 1930; A. H. Quinn, "Weir Mitchell, Artist, Pioneer and Patrician," the *Century,* Jan. 1930; *Public Ledger* (Phila), Jan. 5, 1914.]   C. W. B.
          A. H. Q.

MITCHELL, STEPHEN MIX (Dec. 9, 1743–Sept. 30, 1835), jurist and statesman, was born at Wethersfield, Conn., the son of James Mitchell, a merchant and West-Indian trader who had emigrated about 1730 from Paisley, Scotland. Stephen was the only child of his father's second marriage. His mother, Rebecca, a first cousin of Jonathan Edwards, was a daughter of the Rev. Stephen Mix (Harvard, 1690), a native of New Haven and pastor of the First Church of Wethersfield. Prepared for college by the aid of a private tutor, Stephen entered Yale where he graduated with the class of 1763. He continued his studies there as a Berkeley scholar for the next three years. In the fall of 1766 he

began a three years' service as tutor at the college, and while carrying on his work as a teacher, he studied law under the direction of the elder Jared Ingersoll. On Aug. 2, 1769, he was married to Hannah Grant of Newtown, Conn., whose father had left her a large fortune. He was admitted to the bar in 1770 and practised first at Newtown, thereafter at Wethersfield, until in May 1779 he was made associate judge of the Hartford county court. He began here a judicial career which lasted with but one interruption (1793–95) until his retirement from the bench in 1814. In May 1790, after eleven years as associate judge, he was placed at the head of the county court. As an Assistant, 1784–85 and 1787–93, he was a member of the supreme court of errors. In October 1795 he was raised to the superior court of the state and when in 1807 the powers of a supreme court were transferred from the Council to his tribunal, he was made chief justice. This office he held until 1814 when he retired under the age limit. As a jurist he was less distinguished for deep learning and brilliance than for impartiality in the conduct of judicial proceedings; he was much more interested in justice than in the intricacies of the law. Not given to words, he wrote few of the opinions of his court, preferring to concur with, or dissent from, those of his associates.

During his service on the bench and in the interim from 1793 to 1795 Mitchell held numerous legislative positions. During the Revolution, from 1778 to 1783, he served in the lower house of the Connecticut legislature. In 1784 he was transferred to the Council where, except for 1786, he sat until 1793 when he was chosen to fill the unexpired term of Roger Sherman in the United States Senate. He retired from this post in 1795 to take his place in the superior court of his state. He had meanwhile been chosen to represent Connecticut in the Continental Congress from 1783 to 1788. Here he was partially responsible for securing Connecticut's title to the Western Reserve. In 1818 he served in the state constitutional convention. Throughout his life he was a stanch Federalist. In 1814 he retired to Wethersfield where he spent his last score of years. He was a benevolent patriarch with abundant white hair, clean-shaven face, and aquiline nose, a venerable figure dressed in knee breeches, woolen hose, and a long coat with capacious pockets, trudging about his farm with the aid of a great oaken staff or riding through the village in a low chariot specially constructed for him. He died in 1835 having outlived his wife and all but four of his eleven children. His six sons all graduated from Yale. The youngest was the father of Donald Grant Mitchell [*q.v.*], "Ik Marvel," whose descendants possess an admirable portrait of the Judge done by Samuel F. B. Morse in 1827. Another by the same painter is owned by the Connecticut Historical Society at Hartford.

[F. B. Dexter, *Biog. Sketches of the Grads. of Yale Coll.*, vol. III (1903); E. E. and E. M. Salisbury, *Family Hists. and Geneals.*, vol. I (1892); H. R. Stiles, *The Hist. of Ancient Wethersfield, Conn.*, vol. II (1904); 13 *Conn. Reports*, App.; *Biog. Dir. Am. Cong.* (1928); "The Supreme Court of Conn.," *Green Bag*, Oct. 1890; *Columbian Reg.* (New Haven, Conn.), Oct. 10, 1835.]   P.D.E.

MITCHELL, THOMAS DUCHÉ (1791–May 13, 1865), physician, was born in Philadelphia, of a family of proved "respectability and morality," established there for four generations. He received his English and classical education at Carson Academy, and the Friends' Academy. After spending almost a year in the drug store and chemical laboratory of Dr. Adam Seybert [*q.v.*], where he acquired his taste for chemistry, he took up the study of medicine under the preceptorship of a Dr. Parrish, with whom he continued for three years. In the meantime he attended lectures in the medical department of the University of Pennsylvania, receiving his degree there in 1812. He began the publication of papers on medical subjects while yet an undergraduate and the year of his graduation he was appointed professor of animal and vegetable physiology in St. John's College, Philadelphia. In 1813 he was appointed physician to the Philadelphia Lazaretto, which position he held for three years. From 1822 to 1831 he practised in Frankford, Pa.

In 1819 he published a small volume entitled, *Medical Chemistry; or a Compendious View of the Various Substances Employed in the Practice of Medicine.* The following year he was offered the professorship of chemistry in Ohio University at Athens, Ohio, but declined it. He was an early advocate of total abstinence from alcohol, and in 1826 he attempted to form a total-abstinence temperance society at Frankford, but was unsuccessful. Apparently, too few of his contemporaries shared his views. In 1831 he accepted the chair of chemistry at Miami University, but before the end of the year went to a similar position in the Medical College of Ohio. In 1832 he published his *Elements of Chemical Philosophy*, a volume of about 600 octavo pages, and his *Hints on the Connexion of Labor with Study, as a Preventive of Diseases Peculiar to Students*, a duodecimo. In 1832–33 he was co-editor of the *Western Medical Gazette*. He went to Louisville, Ky., in 1837 as professor of chem-

istry at the Medical Institute, but a month later, accepted a similar position in Transylvania University, Lexington. In 1839 he was transferred to the chair of materia medica and therapeutics, which he held until 1849, teaching obstetrics, also, in the session of 1845–46. In 1849 he became professor of theory and practice of medicine, obstetrics, and medical jurisprudence, at the Philadelphia College of Medicine. In 1850 he published his *Materia Medica and Therapeutics* (revised edition, 1857), an octavo of 750 pages, and also edited John Eberle's *A Treatise on the Diseases and Physical Education of Children*, to which he added notes and about 200 pages of new material. In 1857 he became professor of materia medica in Jefferson Medical College. At the time of his death he left unpublished a work of 600 pages on the "Fevers of the United States." He was the biographer of John Eberle [*q.v.*] in Samuel D. Gross's *Lives of Eminent American Physicians* (1861), and a frequent contributor to medical periodicals.

[Sketch by "Cato" in *Boston Medic. and Surgic. Jour.*, Dec. 10, 1851; August Schachner in H. A. Kelly and W. L. Burrage, *Am. Medic. Biogs.* (1920); Robert Peter, *The Hist. of the Medic. Dept. of Transylvania Univ.* (1905), being Filson Club Pub. No. 20; Otto Juettner, *Daniel Drake and His Followers* (1909); the *Press* (Phila.), May 17, 1865.]   P.M.A.

MITCHELL, WILLIAM (Dec. 20, 1791–Apr. 1, 1869), amateur astronomer, was born in Nantucket, Mass., the son of Peleg and Lydia (Cartwright) Mitchell, and a lineal descendant of several of the first settlers of the island, including Peter Folger [*q.v.*], the grandfather of Benjamin Franklin. Peleg Mitchell was the grandson of Richard who emigrated to Rhode Island in 1708. The Mitchells, like many other residents of Nantucket, belonged to the Society of Friends. They were in comfortable circumstances until the War of 1812, when their income, hitherto derived from whaling ventures, was greatly reduced. William was a natural student, with a scientific mind, and an innate fondness for astronomy. The strict discipline of the times, however, prevented his having any love for school or his teachers. He prepared for Harvard College but he did not enter, and at fifteen years of age he undertook to learn the cooper's trade. He was married, Dec. 10, 1812, to Lydia Coleman of Nantucket. They had ten children, two of whom, Maria and Henry [*qq.v.*], gained distinction in the scientific world. Giving up cooperage and work in an oil factory for the more congenial occupation of teaching school, Mitchell became, in 1827, master of the first free school of Nantucket. In 1830 he became secretary of the Phoenix Marine Insurance Company, and from 1837 until 1861 he was cashier of the Pacific Bank. His kind and sympathetic character, his love of peace, and his other sterling traits, won for him the affection of his pupils and of all with whom he came in contact. He was president of the Nantucket Atheneum for more than thirty years; a delegate to the Massachusetts constitutional convention of 1820; state senator in 1845; and a member of the council of Gov. George N. Briggs [*q.v.*] in 1848 and 1849. Astronomy was his favorite diversion. He had several telescopes and made observations of star positions for the United States Coast Survey and for his own use in rating chronometers for the Nantucket fleet of ninety-two whaleships. A scientific atmosphere pervaded his home and neighborhood, a fact somewhat remarkable when the isolated position of the island is considered. He was held in high esteem by scientific men of the day. Professors William Cranch Bond and George P. Bond [*qq.v.*], the first two directors of the Harvard Observatory, were his intimate friends. He was a member of the visiting committee of the Harvard College observatory from 1848 to 1865, its chairman after 1855, and an overseer of Harvard University from 1857 to 1865. The honorary degree of master of arts was conferred upon him by Brown University in 1848, and by Harvard in 1860. He was a fellow of the American Academy of Arts and Sciences and a member of the American Association for the Advancement of Science. After the death of his wife in 1861 he moved to Lynn, Mass. In 1865, when his daughter, Maria, became head of the Astronomical Department of Vassar College he went to Poughkeepsie to live. There he died.

[*Vital Records of Nantucket, Mass. to the Year 1850*, vols. II (1926), IV (1927); L. S. Hinchman, *Early Settlers of Nantucket* (2nd ed., 1901); *Proc. Am. Acad. Arts and Sciences*, vols. II (1852), VIII (1873); E. S. Holden, *Memorials of William Cranch Bond and of His Son George Phillips Bond* (1897); Phebe Mitchell Kendall, *Maria Mitchell: Life, Letters, and Journals* (1896); *The Am. Ann. Cyc. and Register of Important Events of the Year 1869*; original letters of William Mitchell filed in Memorial House of Nantucket Maria Mitchell Association.]   M. H.

MITCHELL, WILLIAM (1798–May 11, 1856), actor, dramatist, manager, was of British birth and peculiarly a product of the English theatres. He was born at Billquay in the County of Durham, England, and after fifteen years as actor and stage manager in the provincial and in London theatres, he came to America with his family in 1836, making his American début at the National Theatre, New York, on Aug. 29, as Grimes in *The Man with the Carpet Bag* and as Jem Baggs in *The Wandering Minstrel*, the latter a play in which he had been received with

great favor in London. Both of these plays were given as afterpieces to a performance of *The Merchant of Venice*, with Junius Brutus Booth as Shylock. He continued to act in New York with varying degrees of popularity until on Dec. 9, 1839, he took over the management of the hitherto unlucky Olympic Theatre on Broadway between Howard and Grand Streets, and then began what was to prove one of the most amazing series of seasons of managerial triumphs in the history of the New York, and indeed of the American, stage. His opening pieces were *His First Champagne, No!* and *High Life Below Stairs,* and thenceforth for almost ten years the words Mitchell's Olympic represented a diversified form of theatrical entertainment that has never been duplicated. His preliminary announcement read that his purpose was the production of "vaudevilles, burlettas, extravaganzas, farces, etc., the evening performances beginning at seven o'clock, and the prices being extremely low, 50 cents for the boxes, and 25 cents for pit seats."

As manager and actor Mitchell seemed to know exactly what the public of his day liked. Contemporary records testify to his great popularity, and permanent chronicles of the theatre emphasize and record it in phrases that would seem to be exaggerative were they not unanimous. Ireland says that "his various amusing burlesques and travesties, and his inimitable personation of Dickens's *Manager Crummles* raised him to the very summit of popular favor and insured for him an extraordinary patronage for several years" (*post*, p. 192). Odell records the fact that "he is one of the most interesting figures in our stage history; the world today laughs at his antics, in sheer envy of those who were fortunate enough to have laughed with him" (*post*, IV, p. 137). Among the most sensational of his productions was a burlesque of *Hamlet*, with Mitchell himself singing comic songs in the title character; and a burlesque of Fanny Elssler, who was then all the rage, was extremely popular. Mitchell's Olympic was a fashionable resort as well as a place of popular entertainment, but as inevitably happens its patronage eventually decreased, and its eleventh and last season came to a sudden close on Mar. 9, 1850, when Mitchell retired permanently from its management and from public life. He left a gap in the New York theatre, for the position and reputation of Mitchell's Olympic rightly deserved to be described as unique. Little is remembered, however, of Mitchell as an actor, so completely is his fame eclipsed by his theatre and his part in its direction. It was not simply the Olympic Theatre, it was Mitchell's Olympic. Joseph Jefferson (*Autobiography*, p. 107) describes him as "a manager of rare ability," but says nothing of his acting. Since his object was the laughter of the moment, and since he invariably portrayed grotesque characters, there was doubtless more rough comedy than artistic finesse in his impersonations. A long period of ill health intervened between his retirement from management and his death six years afterward.

[Sources include: *The Autobiography of Joseph Jefferson* (1889); J. N. Ireland, *Records of the N. Y. Stage* (1867), vol. II; T. Allston Brown, *A Hist. of the N. Y. Stage* (1903), vol. I; Arthur Hornblow, *A Hist. of the Theatre in America* (1919), vol. II; G. C. D. Odell, *Annals of the N. Y. Stage*, vol. IV (1928), vol. V (1931); the *New World*, July 11, 1840; *N. Y. Times*, *N. Y. Herald*, *N. Y. Daily Tribune*, May 13, 1856. Although several sources give May 12, 1856, as the date of Mitchell's death, the death notice in the *N. Y. Daily Tribune*, May 13, 1856, states that he died on Sunday, May 11.]   E. F. E.

MITCHELL, WILLIAM (Feb. 24, 1801–Oct. 6, 1886), jurist, the son of Edward and Cornelia (Anderson) Mitchell, was born in New York City. His grandfather, William Mitchell, was a stationer in Coleraine, Ireland, near Belfast. His father emigrated in 1791 and for many years was pastor of the Society of United Christians (Universalist) in New York City. His mother was a native of New York City, a descendant of Peter Andresson to whom a grant of land in the city of New Amsterdam was made in 1645 by the Dutch West India Company. William prepared for college at the school of Joseph Nelson, a blind teacher. He was at the head of his class and received from Nelson as a testimonial of esteem a rare copy of Quintilian. In 1820 he graduated with high honors from Columbia College, where he excelled in mathematics and classics. To the end of his life Greek and Latin authors continued to be his recreation from professional studies. His Commencement oration, delivered in Latin, was entitled, "*De Julii Caesaris vita et nece*." On June 2, 1841, he was married to Mary Penfold Berrien of New York City, a descendant of Cornelius Jansen Berrien who came to Long Island about 1670 from Rotterdam.

He studied law in the office of William Slosson and was admitted as attorney at law in 1823, solicitor in chancery in 1824, counselor at law in 1826, and counselor in chancery in 1827. In 1832 he published an edition of Blackstone's *Commentaries* with special references to American cases, which was one of the early efforts to correlate American decisions with English common law. He is said to have been too modest to acknowledge his editorship so he attributed the work to "A Member of the New York Bar." He

was made master in chancery in 1840 and was elected justice of the state supreme court for the 1st judicial district in 1849. In 1854 he became the presiding justice of the court and continued in that position until he retired in 1857, with the exception of the year 1856 when he was a member of the court of appeals. He was so learned and just in his decisions that, after his retirement from the bench in 1857, the court often chose him as referee in important cases, and individuals brought cases to him for trial and decision. He continued to hold his court regularly throughout the later years of his life. He served two terms as vice-president of the New York bar association. At the time of his death he had been a member of the New York bar sixty-three years and was said to be its oldest member. He died on a visit to his son at Morristown, N. J.

[Information from Cornelius von Erden Mitchell, a grandson, New York City; B. D. Silliman, "Memorial of Wm. Mitchell," *Asso. of the Bar of the City of N. Y. . . . Report . . . 1887* (n.d.); "In Memoriam," by J. A. Flack in the general minutes of the supreme court for Oct. general term, 1886; *N. Y. Times*, and *N. Y. Tribune*, Oct. 7, 1886.]   D. V. S.

MITCHELL, WILLIAM (Nov. 19, 1832–Aug. 21, 1900), judge, was the son of John and Mary (Henderson) Mitchell, both natives of Scotland. He was born in Welland County, Ontario. After a preparatory education in the local schools he matriculated at Jefferson College, Canonsburg, Pa., where he was graduated in 1853. At college he formed a friendship with Eugene M. Wilson, with whose father, Edgar C. Wilson of Morgantown, Va. (now W. Va.), he read law after a brief period of teaching. He was admitted to the bar in the circuit court of Virginia in 1857. On Sept. 3, 1857, he was married to Mrs. Jane (Hanway) Smith, the daughter of John Hanway of Morgantown. Almost immediately he went to the pioneer town of Winona, Minn., to practise with the younger Wilson until the latter removed to Minneapolis. A partnership with Daniel S. Norton, which was terminated by Norton's election to the United States Senate, was followed by one with William H. Yale. In 1859–60 Mitchell was a member of the second state legislature of Minnesota. He was interested in railroads, became president of the Winona & Saint Peter Railroad Co., and later was president of the Winona Savings Bank. His first wife died in 1867, leaving three daughters. On July 11, 1872, he was married to Mrs. Frances (Merritt) Smith of Chicago, the daughter of Jacob M. Merritt. They had one son, William DeWitt Mitchell.

Mitchell's real career began when he became

juage of the 3rd judicial district in 1874, to which position he was reëlected in 1880. His reputation as a sound lawyer and impartial judge made him one of the most respected members of the Minnesota bench and was the cause of his designation as temporary judge of the supreme court sitting on a case in which two of the regular justices had been previously connected as counsel. In 1881, shortly after his second election, he was appointed by Gov. John S. Pillsbury to one of the two newly created positions on the supreme bench. In 1882 he was elected for the regular term and twice thereafter reëlected, so that his service in this capacity extended from the spring of 1881 to December 1899, when he filed his last opinion. In 1898 he accepted nomination by the Democratic and Populist parties but was not indorsed by the Republicans, as he had been at the three previous elections. His Republican opponent was elected by a small majority, much to the regret of most of the bar. During the years he was an associate justice of the supreme court of Minnesota there were relatively few issues of great public significance that came before it for adjudication; it was, however, a period during which he had occasion to read many opinions that vitally affected the body of common law in Minnesota. The soundness of his reasoning, balanced between respect for past judicial dicta and a recognition that new times and new forces demanded modification of old formulae, drew the attention of lawyers and legal writers in all parts of the country. Sometime after Mitchell's death, Dean Woodruff of the College of Law in Cornell University wrote: "It has seemed to me, as I have read Judge Mitchell's opinions, that he belongs in the group with Chief Justice Shaw of Massachusetts, Chief Justice Gibson of Pennsylvania, and the few others who mark the highest achievement of our state courts. His mind was a quick solvent for the most refractory and opaque material of legal contention" (*Minnesota Law Review, post*, p. 386). He was an indefatigable worker and student. His opinions, and they averaged one every three days for the nineteen years on the bench, showed familiarity not only with contemporary decisions but a real knowledge of the history of the law. Coke, Littleton, or Blackstone were as often on his lips as the names of the foremost American jurists. "To him the common law was a living, growing organism" (*Minnesota Law Review, post*, p. 385) although he regarded precedent as a leader and not a master.

Without bitterness at his defeat he turned, for the remaining few months of his life, to private practice, for he had accumulated no fortune on which to retire. He declined to be considered for appointment as chief justice of Puerto Rico. In 1891 he had been nominated by President Harrison for the circuit court of appeals, but his name was withdrawn before action by the Senate. It was, however, probably no loss to legal development that he was left to carry on his invaluable work in a state court, whatever might have been his gratification at holding the more conspicuous position. He died at Lake Alexandria, Minn.

[*Great Amer. Lawyers*, ed. by W. D. Lewis, vol. VIII (1909); *Minn. Law Review*, May 1920; *Biog. and Hist. Cat. of Washington and Jefferson College* (1889); *Hist. of Winona County* (1883); *Progressive Men of Minn.*, ed. by M. D. Shutter and J. S. McLain (1897); *Portrait and Biog. Record of Winona County* (1895); *U. S. Biog. Dict. and Portrait Gallery* (Minn. vol., 1879); *Minnesotian* (Saint Paul), Mar. 2, 1860; *Daily Pioneer Press* (St. Paul), Nov. 2, 1898, Aug. 22, 1900; information in regard to date of birth and certain other matters from Hon. W. D. Mitchell.]

L. B. S.

MITCHILL, SAMUEL LATHAM (Aug. 20, 1764–Sept. 7, 1831), physician, United States senator and representative, promoter of science, was born of Quaker parents, Robert and Mary (Latham) Mitchill, at North Hempstead, L. I. He was the grandson of Robert Mitchill who came to America about 1694. His uncle, Dr. Samuel Latham, taught him the elementary principles of medicine while he was receiving his classical education; he studied for three years with Dr. Samuel Bard [*q.v.*] in New York City, and in 1783 went to Edinburgh, where in 1786 he graduated from the University with the degree of M.D. Returning to New York, he was licensed to practise medicine and commenced the study of law. In 1788 he was appointed one of the commissioners to negotiate with the Six Nations for the purchase of lands in western New York, and in 1791 he was a member of the state legislature.

His scientific career began in 1792, with his appointment to the chair of natural history, chemistry, and agriculture at Columbia College; from 1793 to 1795 he was professor of botany also. In Edinburgh he had studied chemistry under Joseph Black, and he now began to teach the new or antiphlogistic chemistry recently promulgated by Lavoisier, in defense of whose theories he carried on a controversy for some years with Joseph Priestley [*q.v.*] and others. In 1801 he published *Explanation of the Synopsis of Chemical Nomenclature and Arrangement*. He was among the early analysts of the Saratoga spring waters and his work on the salts in these waters attracted public attention to mineral springs in general. His theory of the septic action of a substance he called "septon," though fanciful and erroneous, was an incentive to the study of sanitary chemistry and hygiene and was one of the factors that led Davy to investigate problems in nitrous oxide. He made many contributions to problems in industrial chemistry, conspicuously those relating to gunpowder, soap, and disinfectants. In 1800 and soon afterwards he published papers on the "non-action" of nitric acid on silver, tin, and copper, on the history of muriate of soda, on the presence of soda, magnesia, and lime in the ocean, and on the use of ocean water for washing without the aid of soap. He collected minerals, displayed specimens in his lectures, and deposited them in a museum at the college for the use of future teachers. He also studied fertilizers and was greatly interested in the agricultural devolopment of his native state. In 1796, under the auspices of the Society for the Promotion of Agriculture, Arts, and Manufactures, which he had helped to found, he made a mineralogical exploration of the banks of the Hudson River, a pioneer piece of geological research. With Edward Miller [q.v.] and Elihu H. Smith he established, in 1797, the *Medical Repository*, which soon became a medium for scientific contributions of all kinds. Of this journal he was principal editor for twenty-three years. He was again a member of the New York legislature in 1798, and gave sturdy support to the act granting Livingston and Fulton a monopoly of steam navigation in the waters of New York. Through his marriage, June 23, 1799, to Catherine, daughter of Samuel Akerly and widow of William Cock, he came into the possession of comfortable means. There were no children.

He resigned his professorship at Columbia in 1801 to accept a seat in Congress, sitting in the House until 1804; in the Senate, 1804–09; and in the House again from 1810 to 1813. In 1810 he served a third term in the New York legislature. At Washington, he advocated the establishment of quarantine laws and made several reports on matters connected with the Library of Congress, and one urging the exploration of the Louisiana Purchase. During the War of 1812 he served on a commission to supervise the construction of a steam war-vessel, and with other citizens of New York labored for several days digging trenches for the defense of the city. In 1807, upon the organization of the College of Physicians and Surgeons in New York, he was chosen professor of chemistry, and the next year was transferred to the chair of natural history, which he held until 1820, when he became professor of botany and ma-

teria medica. Resigning with the rest of the faculty in 1826, he joined his colleagues J. W. Francis, David Hosack, W. J. MacNeven, and Valentine Mott [qq.v.] in forming the Rutgers Medical College, of which he was vice-president during the four years of its existence. For two decades he was a physician to the New York Hospital. He helped to found the New York Literary and Philosophical Society in 1814, and in 1817 was principal founder of the Lyceum of Natural History, forerunner of the New York Academy of Sciences. He was surgeon general of the state militia in 1818.

Throughout his life he wrote prolifically, contributing paper after paper to the transactions of the many societies to which he belonged, to literary journals, and especially to his own *Medical Repository*. His most notable contributions included papers on the fishes of New York (*Transactions of the Literary and Philosophical Society* and *Medical Repository*, 1815); "A Sketch of the Mineralogical History of New York" (*Medical Repository*, 1797, 1800, 1802); "A Discourse . . . Embracing a Concise and Comprehensive Account of the Writings which Illustrate the Botanical History of North and South America" (*Collections of the New York Historical Society*, vol. II, 1814); papers on the origin of the Indians, Indian poetry, and Indian antiquities (*Transactions and Collections of the American Antiquarian Society*, vol. I, 1820). To the New York edition of Thomas Bewick's *General History of Quadrupeds* (1804) he contributed notes on American animals. He was frequently called upon to deliver addresses, notably at celebrations in 1823 and 1825 of steps in the completion of the Erie Canal, of which he had been an enthusiastic supporter. Other discourses worthy of mention are *The Life, Precepts, and Exploits of Tammany*; the *Famous Indian Chief* (1795), chiefly an exposition of political mythology; and *A Discourse on the Character and Services of Thomas Jefferson, More Especially as a Promoter of Natural and Physical Science* (1826). It has been said with considerable truth that Mitchill "supported the Republican party because Jefferson was its leader and supported Jefferson because he was a philosopher" (Henry Adams, *History of the United States*, vol. I, 1889, p. 111), but his attachment to republican ideas is manifested in his endeavor to establish "Fredonia" as a name for the United States.

Characterized variously by contemporaries as "a living encyclopedia" and "a chaos of knowledge," Mitchill is perhaps "remembered more for the goodness of his heart than the strength of his head." His investigations resulted in no epoch-making discoveries, his theories were often erroneous, but through the sincerity of his interest, the extent of his learning, and the simple amiability of his character, he won renown both at home and abroad as a man of science and was able to exert a pronounced influence in the promotion of scientific inquiry and in the practical application of scientific principles to life.

[Mitchill himself published *Some of the Memorable Events and Occurences in the Life of Samuel L. Mitchill, of New York, from 1786 to 1821* (n.d.); see also: *Harper's Mag.*, Apr. 1879; James Herring and J. B. Longacre, *The Nat. Portrait Gallery of Distinguished Americans*, vol. I (1834); J. W. Francis, *Old New York* (1858); *Reminiscences of Samuel Latham Mitchill* (1859), repr. in S. D. Gross, *Lives of Eminent Am. Phys. and Surg.* (1861), and abridged in H. A. Kelly and W. L. Burrage, *Am. Medic. Biogs.* (1920); Félix Pascalis-Ouvière, *Eulogy on the Life and Character of the Hon. Samuel Latham Mitchill* (1831); E. A. and G. L. Duyckinck, *Cyc. of Am. Lit.* (1875), vol. I; C. R. Hall, in *Jour. Chem. Educ.*, Mar. 1928, in *N. Y. Hist.*, Apr. 1933, and "An American Scientist—Samuel Latham Mitchill" (1933), doctor's thesis at Columbia Univ.; E. F. Smith, *Chem. in America* (1914), and *Samuel Latham Mitchill* (1922), repr. from *Jour. Indus. & Engineering Chem.*, June 1922; W. J. Youmans, *Pioneers of Science in America* (1896); B. F. Thompson, *Hist. of L. I.* (1839); H. L. Fairchild, *A Hist. of the N. Y. Acad. of Sci.* (1887); G. B. Goode, *The Beginnings of Am. Sci.: the Third Century* (1888); F. L. Mott, *A Hist. of Am. Mags.* (1930); list (incomplete) of Mitchill's scientific papers in Royal Soc. of London, *Cat. of Sci. Papers* (1800–1863), vol. IV (1879).]   L. C. N.

MITTEN, THOMAS EUGENE (Mar. 31, 1864–Oct. 1, 1929), street-railway official, was born at Brighton, Sussex, England, the son of George and Jane (Lucke) Mitten. His parents emigrated to the United States in 1877 and settled on a farm near Goodland, Newton County, Ind. In the next seven years on the farm Thomas acquired a working knowledge of telegraphy from the Goodland station agent and at the end of that period became a telegraph operator and station agent at Wyndham (now Swanington), Ind., for the Chicago & Eastern Illinois Railroad. In 1887 he became local agent at Attica, Ind., for the same railroad and from 1890 to 1893 he held various minor positions with the Denver & Rio Grande Railroad and the Rio Grande Western Railroad. He then became general superintendent of the Denver, Lakewood & Golden Railroad, a suburban line, parts of which were electrified under his direction. His opportunity to enter the electric street-railway industry came in 1896 when he was made assistant superintendent and later general superintendent of the street-railway system of Milwaukee, Wis. He left this position in 1901 to become general superintendent of the International Railway Company, operating electric lines in and around Buffalo, N. Y., and for a year, 1904–05, was general manager of the system. In 1905 he went to Chicago to accept the presidency of the Chicago City Railway Company. He resigned this position in 1911 to become director and general supervisor of the physical properties of the lines of the Philadelphia Rapid Transit Company, then practically bankrupt. In June of this same year he was elected chairman of the executive committee and later president of the company, which post he held until February 1923 when he resigned, retaining, however, the chairmanship of the board of directors and of the executive committee. He had gained a reputation for interesting himself in the problems of labor and of turning labor into capital through the cooperation of men and management. One of his first projects in connection with the affairs of the Philadelphia Rapid Transit Company was the formation of the so-called "Mitten Co-Operative Plan," which gave employees a voice in matters affecting wages and working conditions, made employees stockholders of the company, and gave them representation on the board of directors. He also organized the Mitten Men and Management Bank and Trust Company.

The independent transit corporations in the city of Philadelphia Mitten brought under the control of Mitten Management, Incorporated, a company capitalized at $10,000 and incorporated under the laws of Delaware. In 1924 the company took over the operation of the Philadelphia Rapid Transit Company. Under Mitten management the Transit Company failed to submit annual reports to the city comptroller called for by the company's contract with the city and in July 1929 Mayor Mackey ordered an investigation of the accounts. As a result of the audit conducted by Milo R. Maltbie, revealing tremendous expenditures for the operation of the Transit Company, the city comptroller filed suit on Dec. 1, 1929, for an accounting of transit finances. Meanwhile, on Oct. 1, Mitten was drowned in Big Log Cabin Pond on his estate, "Sunnyland," about twelve miles from Milford in Pike County, Pa. In April 1931 the Transit Company was ordered into receivership. Judge Harry S. McDevitt of the Philadelphia court of common pleas, in making the order, condemned the Mitten Management as "'a colossal conspiracy against the taxpayers" (*New York Times*, Apr. 12, 1931). The bulk of Mitten's estate, which by the terms of a will drawn up a few days before his death, was to have been largely used in furthering friendly relations between capital and labor, was absorbed in the settlement of claims of the Philadelphia Rapid Transit Company against Mitten Management.

Mitten was married in 1887 to Kate M. Warner of Fowler, Ind. In 1904 he was married to Ruth Bissell of Lockport, N. Y., who divorced him in Paris in 1926.

[*Who's Who in America*, 1928–29; *Am. Mag.*, Mar. 1930, Nov. 1922; *World's Work*, July 1922, Mar. 1929; *Outlook*, Apr. 12, 1922, Mar. 30, 1927; *Collier's*, Feb. 7, 1920, Dec. 9, 1922; *Lit. Digest*, Apr. 1, 1922, Oct. 2, 1926; *Nat. Municipal Rev.*, Apr. 1932, pp. 252–53; and newspaper accounts of Mitten's affairs and the investigation of Mitten Management, especially the *N. Y. Times*, Mar. 16, 17, 1922, July 20, Aug. 29, Oct. 2, 3, 8, 9, 16, Dec. 1, 1929, Aug. 17, Sept. 17, 1930, Apr. 12, May 14, 15, July 17, Nov. 4, 1931, July 1, Aug. 3, 4, 1932.]   J. H. F.

MIXTER, SAMUEL JASON (May 10, 1855–Jan. 19, 1926), surgeon, was born in Hardwick, Mass., to William and Mary (Ruggles) Mixter. He was a descendant of Isaac Mixter (or Mixter), born in Suffolk County, England, who sailed from Ipswich for America on the *Elizabeth*, Apr. 10, 1634. Through Mary Ruggles his mother, he traced his ancestry to Gov. Thomas Prence of Plymouth Colony and to Elder William Brewster. Some of his ancestors were successful farmers and storekeepers; others were prominent in the business and political life of their communities. He received his early education in schools at Amherst and Boston, graduated as a bachelor of science from the Massachusetts Institute of Technology in 1875, and as a doctor of medicine from Harvard in 1879. In 1879 he became a surgical house officer at the Massachusetts General Hospital, and on Aug. 12 of this same year married Wilhelmina Galloupe, descended from John Gallop who came to America on the *Mary and John* in 1630, and was one of the earliest grantees of land in Boston. Soon after, they went to Vienna, where Mixter studied surgery, anatomy, and microscopic pathology. In 1882 he became assistant demonstrator of anatomy at the Harvard Medical School and in 1887 demonstrator. The Warren Museum of that institution possesses specimens prepared by him which testify to his skill and careful craftsmanship.

In 1886 he was appointed to the staff of the Massachusetts General Hospital, a connection which lasted to the end of his life. He was surgeon to out-patients, 1886 to 1894; visiting surgeon, 1894 to 1911; chief of West Surgical Service, 1911 to 1915; and on the board of consultation, 1915 to 1926. At one time or another he was upon the staff of other hospitals but his life work centered at the Massachusetts General. Here his surgical colleagues were C. B. Porter, H. H. A. Beach, J. Collins Warren [*q.v.*], Arthur T. Cabot [*q.v.*], John Homans, Maurice H. Richardson [*q.v.*], John W. Elliott,

and Francis B. Harrington. Even in such a group he was conspicuous. His knowledge of anatomy and pathology, his skilled surgical technique, his courage and sound judgment, and his resourceful mind made him a notably successful surgeon. His modification of the Abbe operation for the cure of trigeminal neuralgia was one of his outstanding contributions to neurological surgery and this operation was well known until superseded by section of the sensory root of the nerve. He was particularly interested and successful in surgery of the œsophagus. Some of the best known of the many instruments which he invented are those which he used in his œsophageal operations. He perfected the technique of skin grafting and devised special instruments for this purpose. The "Mixter colostomy" is one of the recognized procedures in intestinal obstruction. He made numerous contributions to medical literature, dealing particularly with unusual cases and original surgical methods, and delivered scholarly addresses on other subjects before some of the larger surgical societies of the country. To his interest in the practical problems of the hospital was due the reclaiming of surgical gauze at the Massachusetts General Hospital, by a process which has been of great economic value to hospitals all over the country. He was president of the American Surgical Association in 1917 and the first president of the New England Surgical Society.

Mixter was a friendly person; his greetings, invariably cheerful and happy. His physical appearance, even in his later years, was that of a man of robust health. He always dressed carefully and generally wore a flower in his buttonhole; his mobile face lighted and his eyes twinkled as he talked to his friends. He was a keen sportsman. No year was complete for him unless it contained its proper share of hunting and fishing. During the later part of his life the large Mixter farm at Hardwick came under his care. There he developed and perfected a herd of Guernsey cattle, which, at the time of its dispersal, was the largest and probably the best in the United States. He saw active service during the World War and returned a lieutenant-colonel in the Medical Reserve Corps. He died at Grand Junction, Tenn., where he happened to be when taken ill with pneumonia.

[Private family records; *Boston Medic. and Surgic. Jour.*, May 13, 1926; *Surgery, Gynecology and Obstetrics*, Nov. 1927; Records Mass. Soc. of Mayflower Descendants; H. A. Kelly and W. L. Burrage, *Dict. of Am. Medic. Biog.* (1928); *Mass. General Hospital, Memorial and Hist. Vol.* (1921); *Index Medicus*; *Who's Who in America*, 1926–27; J. C. Warren and A. P. Gould, *The International Text-book of Surgery by American and British Authors*, 2 vols. (1899–1900);

Boston Evening Transcript, Jan. 20, 1926; W. S. Bickham, Operative Surgery (1924), vol. V.]   F. A. W.

MODJESKA, HELENA (Oct. 12, 1840–Apr. 8, 1909), Polish-American actress, was born in Cracow, Poland. Her father, Michael Opid, was a music teacher, born in the Polish mountains. He died early, and his widow had to put all her children to work. Little Helena, who saw and was greatly moved by her first play at seven, from the first aspired to the stage. While still in her teens she was married to her guardian, a man much older than herself, named Gustav Modrzejewski, and by him she had one son. With his aid she secured a small place in the provincial theatre, and in 1863 she acted in Germany. Two years later she returned to Cracow where her talents were hailed and she became a favorite. In 1867 Dumas *fils* invited her to Paris, to play Marguerite Gauthier, but she refused the challenge, feeling she was not yet ready. Her first husband, meanwhile, had died, and in 1868 she married Charles Bozenta Chlapowski, a member of the Polish aristocracy, and joined the company at the Imperial Theatre in Warsaw. There she remained, the reigning actress of the nation, until 1876. That year the nationalistic views of her husband and herself made life in Warsaw difficult, under Russian régime, and with her husband, her son, and a group of Poles she journeyed to America.

The party visited the Philadelphia Exposition and then moved on to California, where it was proposed to found a Polish colony in what was supposed to be an earthly Paradise. A large ranch was purchased and the colonists lighted their Polish cigarettes, climbed into their hammocks, and proceeded to enjoy the climate. But, alas! oranges are not grown and marketed without labor, and the colonists knew little about labor. Their money was soon gone. Modjeska (as she abbreviated her name for America) learned to speak English in six months, at the suggestion of Edwin Booth, and went to San Francisco, where John McCullough, then managing the famous California Theatre, gave her a chance, in 1877, to appear in *Adrienne Lecouvreur*. In spite of her foreign accent (which she never wholly lost, though it soon became but a piquant sauce to her acting), the public welcomed her, and it was immediately apparent that she had a future career on the American stage. She was signed for a two-year tour in a repertoire of plays, making her New York début Dec. 22, 1877. In 1878 she revisited Poland, where she was warmly welcomed, but after a limited engagement there, she came back to America. In 1880 she went to London and acted

for the rest of the year in that city, in English. She then again returned to the United States, which thereafter became definitely the country of her adoption. Her husband became a citizen and purchased a ranch outside Santa Anna, Cal. Madame Modjeska for many years toured the country in a wide range of parts, though in 1882 and 1884 she again visited both Poland and London.

In 1882, in Warsaw, she produced Ibsen's *Doll's House*, under the title *Nora*, and with the "happy ending" then used on the Continent, in spite of the author's objections. This play she brought back to America and produced in Louisville, Ky., in 1883, probably the first production of Ibsen in English—certainly the first in America. It attracted no attention—as, indeed, it did not deserve to, with the whole point removed by the botched, sentimental ending. In 1889–90 she played a joint engagement with Edwin Booth, but by this time both actors were past their prime, and the union was less successful than it would have been ten years earlier. In 1892 she produced an American play, *Countess Roudine*, by Paul Kester and Minnie Maddern Fiske. At the World's Fair in 1893, Modjeska delivered a speech attacking the Russian government and was thereafter forbidden to enter Russian territory. Illness in 1895 caused her temporary retirement, but she reappeared in 1897. In 1900–01 she produced *King John,* and in 1902 made a "farewell tour" with Louis James. In 1905, at the Metropolitan Opera House, New York, a testimonial performance was given for her benefit. She attempted a brief tour in 1907, but was too frail to continue. She died Apr. 8, 1909, at Bay Island, East Newport, on the coast south of Los Angeles, and her body was taken by her husband, who had always acted as her manager, to Cracow for burial. Neither he nor she was practical in business matters, and though her earlier tours had made her much money, her last days were passed in comparative poverty, cheerfully endured (William Winter, *The Wallet of Time,* vol. I, p. 366).

Modjeska was of slim, aristocratic, and graceful figure, with a face interesting, expressive, and gracious, rather than conventionally beautiful. In Polish she had a repertoire of over a hundred rôles. In English she played nine heroines of Shakespeare, from Juliet and Rosalind to Cleopatra, and such well-known parts as Adrienne Lecouvreur, Camille, Julie de Martemar in *Richelieu* (which she created in America), Ibsen's Nora, Mary Stuart, Frou-Frou, and several more. Her personal preference, from girlhood, had been for Shakespeare, and she was essentially a poetic actress. She excelled not so much in sweep or profundity of emotion as in the depiction of womanly grace and charm, in piquant archness and especially in scenes where she impersonated a fine woman displaying affection, or suffering for it. Her technique was carefully studied, and she was conscious mistress of her effects. "Her movements," according to William Winter, "always graceful, were sometimes electrical in their rapidity and long and sinuous reach" (*The Wallet of Time*, I, p. 370). Although her technique was masterful, and her intellectual grasp of all her characters sure and steady, her hold on the public lay more, perhaps, in her personality, with its gleams of humor, its graceful dignity, its womanly sweetness, and always an indefinable atmosphere of poetic elevation. She even imparted those qualities to Camille and Magda, and possibly not wholly unintentionally. But in Viola, Rosalind, Queen Katherine, and similar rôles, the effect was exactly right, and her impersonations of such parts were long dwelt upon affectionately by those who saw them.

[William Winter, *The Wallet of Time*, vol. I (1913); L. C. Strang, *Famous Actresses of the Day in America* (1899); Brander Matthews and Laurence Hutton, *Actors and Actresses of Great Britain and the U. S.*, vol. V (1886); *Who's Who in America*, 1901–02; T. A. Brown, *A Hist. of the N. Y. Stage* (1903), vols. II and III; J. B. Clapp and E. F. Edgett, *Players of the Present*, pt. 2 (1900); *Los Angeles Daily Times*, Apr. 9, 1909.] W. P. E.

MOELLER, HENRY (Dec. 11, 1849–Jan. 5, 1925), Roman Catholic prelate, was the son of Bernard and Teresa (Witte) Moeller, who emigrated from Westphalia about 1845. Born in Cincinnati, Ohio, he was educated there in St. Joseph's German parochial school and St. Francis Xavier's College. His father, a bricklayer and building contractor, provided well for the education of his six children: the only daughter joined the Sisters of Charity at Mount St. Joseph on the Ohio; one son, Ferdinand, became a Jesuit; and another, Bernard, a distinguished secular priest of Cincinnati. Henry was sent by Archbishop Purcell to the American College at Rome in 1869, and there, according to the rector, F. S. Chatard, passed with honors an examination for the doctorate in divinity seven years later. Ordained by Archbishop Lenti at the church of St. John Lateran, Rome, June 10, 1876, he returned to Ohio and was assigned to St. Patrick's Church, Bellefontaine. During the next two years he taught in Mount St. Mary's Seminary, Cincinnati, then, after a few months as secretary to Bishop Chatard of Vincennes, became secretary to Archbishop William Henry Elder [q.v.], whom he assisted in the financial

reorganization of the Cincinnati archdiocese. In 1886 he was made chancellor in recognition of his unusual administrative skill. Fourteen years later, the Holy Father named him to the see of Columbus, for which he was consecrated by Archbishop Elder in St. Peter's Cathedral, Cincinnati, on Aug. 25, 1900. Here again his business ability was tested, for this diocese had been in such poor financial condition that its dissolution had been considered.

On the request of Elder for a coadjutor, the suffragan bishops failed to decide between Moeller and C. P. Maes [q.v.] of Covington for the nomination and sent both names to Rome. Moeller was selected, Apr. 27, 1903, as coadjutor *cum jure successionis* with the title of Archbishop of Aeropolis. Hence, upon the death of Elder in 1904, he automatically succeeded to the see, Oct. 31, 1904, and received the pallium in his cathedral at the hands of Cardinal Gibbons, Feb. 15, 1905.

Archbishop Moeller assumed direction of a well-organized, conservative diocese which had practically settled the old financial tangle bequeathed by Archbishop Purcell. During his tenure he accomplished a great deal: the number of priests and churches was increased; Mount St. Mary's Seminary was erected at Norwood; the new St. Francis Xavier College was established by the Jesuits with the archbishop's active support; the Fenwick Club was built; the Sisters of St. Ursula, the cloistered nuns of the Second Order of St. Dominic, and the Dominican Nuns of St. Catherine de Ricci were introduced into the diocese; St. Rita's School for the Deaf was established; diocesan charities were centrally organized under a Bureau of Catholic Charities; and parochial and secondary schools were raised to a standard which other dioceses sought to emulate. Moeller was deeply concerned with Catholic education and the National Catholic Educational Association. He was heartily interested in the National Catholic Welfare Council, and in 1922, with Bishop Schrembs of Cleveland, went to Rome in order to protect its threatened existence. His mission was evidently successful, for the reorganized National Catholic Welfare Conference was continued under the same management and given papal approbation. Two years later he was appointed an assistant to the pontifical throne. Chairman of the committee of the hierarchy on missions, president of the board of the Catholic Students' Mission Crusade, and an organizer of the languishing National Councils of Catholic Men and of Catholic Women, he was a recognized power in Catholic circles.

At his funeral mass, celebrated by Cardinal Hayes of New York, he was eulogized by Archbishop Glennon of St. Louis as an active priest of forceful character.

[J. H. Lamott, *Hist. of the Archdiocese of Cincinnati* (1921); *Am. Cath. Who's Who* (1911); *Who's Who in America*, 1924–25; annual Cath. directories; files of the *Catholic Telegraph* (the diocesan organ); Nat. Cath. Welfare Conference News Service, Jan. 6, 19, 1925; the *Sun* (Baltimore), Jan. 7, and *Cincinnati Enquirer*, Jan. 6, 1925; note on death of Moeller's sister, Sister Henrietta Maria, in *N. Y. Times*, Mar. 6, 1932.]

R. J. P.

MOFFAT, DAVID HALLIDAY (July 22, 1839–Mar. 18, 1911), capitalist, was born at Washingtonville, Orange County, N. Y. His parents were David Halliday and Katherine (Gregg) Moffat (*Who's Who in America*, 1910–11). After a common-school education he started work as a bank messenger in New York City (1851), and rose to the position of assistant teller. In 1855 he joined a brother at Des Moines, Iowa, and the following year became teller of the Bank of Nebraska at Omaha. When the bank closed in 1860, Moffat and a partner drove a wagonload of books and stationery to the new mining center at Denver. There they opened a store which soon handled also groceries, newspapers, and wall paper, contained the post office, and held the agency for the Western Union Telegraph Company. In 1861 Moffat returned East and on Dec. 11 married a boyhood sweetheart, Fannie A. Buckhout of Mechanicsville, N. Y., taking her to Colorado with him. In 1865 he became cashier of the First National Bank, Denver, and fifteen years later, president. This connection identified him thoroughly with the affairs of Denver and of Colorado and made him an influential citizen, so that a history of Moffat henceforward is almost a history of the city and state in which he lived. He invested widely in mining properties during and after the latter seventies. Among his best-known mines were the "Little Pittsburgh," "Robert E. Lee," and "Maid of Erin," and he was particularly interested in the regions of Leadville, Cripple Creek, and Creede. He was adjutant-general of the Colorado militia in 1865 and territorial treasurer, 1874–76. He helped organize the Denver Clearing House in 1885, was part owner of the *Denver Times* until 1902, was a director and sometime president of the Denver water company which built the Cheesman dam, was interested in the Denver Tramway Company during the nineties and later; and was an incorporator and director of the Central Colorado Power Company. He was also a large owner of Colorado farming lands and Denver real estate.

Moffat was one of the men who realized that Denver's future importance depended largely on the adequacy of its transportational facilities. He saw Denver as a railroad center, with roads radiating in every direction. When it became certain that the Union Pacific would not touch the town he became one of the backers of the Denver & Pacific, of which he was treasurer and John Evans president (*First Annual Report . . . of the Denver and Pacific . . .*, 1869, *passim*). He was a factor in the affairs of the Boulder Valley Railroad, built to Boulder; of the Denver, South Park & Pacific, opened between Denver and Leadville; and of the Denver & New Orleans, making connections to the Gulf. The last two of these roads are now parts of the Colorado & Southern. Moffat was also a director of the Denver & Rio Grande from 1883, and president from 1884 to 1891 (*Sixth Annual Report . . . of the Denver and Rio Grande*, p. 2). His most lucrative road was the Florence & Cripple Creek, built in the middle nineties to connect the Cripple Creek mines with the main line of the Denver & Rio Grande, but the best known was the Denver, Northwestern & Pacific, still called "the Moffat road." It was chartered in 1902 to create a direct route from Denver to Salt Lake City. The main difficulty encountered in building it was a tunnel at Long's Peak. Moffat planned a two and a half mile tunnel, but when it was completed it was six miles long. The chief promoter spent a considerable share of his personal fortune on the construction of the road, but by 1908 had been able to complete only 211 miles of a scenic line rising to 11,600 feet, as far as Steamboat Springs. His efforts to raise money in the East were blocked by E. H. Harriman [q.v.], who preferred not to have new competition. Moffat died in 1911, while on a trip to New York to finance the road. After his death the line became the Denver & Salt Lake, and the tunnel was completed in 1926 by means of public taxation.

[E. C. McMechen, *The Moffat Tunnel of Colo.* (2 vols., 1927); W. F. Stone, *Hist. of Colo.* (4 vols., 1918); J. C. Smiley, *Hist. of Denver* (1901); H. H. Bancroft, *Hist. of Nev., Colo., and Wyo.* (1890); *Hist. of the City of Denver, Arapahoe County, and Colo.* (1880); Frank Hall, *Hist. of the State of Colo.*, vol. III (1891); *Who's Who in America*, 1910–11; *Denver Republican* and *Rocky Mountain News*, Mar. 19, 1911; W. C. Williams, "Colorado's Great Tunnel," in *Rev. of Revs.* (N. Y.), Oct. 1922; G. F. Paul, "The Six-Mile Moffat Tunnel," in *Sci. American*, Apr. 1926; M. M. Rice, "Tunneling the Rockies," in *Rev. of Revs.* (N. Y.), Sept. 1926; Arthur Chapman, "Colorado Tears Down Her Mountains," in *World's Work*, Aug. 1927.]

R. E. R.

MOFFAT, JAMES CLEMENT (May 30, 1811–June 7, 1890), church historian, was born in Scotland, at Glencree. His father was David Douglas Moffat, his mother was Margaret Clement. Most of his early education he gave himself. From his tenth year to his sixteenth he was a shepherd-boy, and while at work read all the books he could lay hands on. For five years from 1828 he worked in a printing-shop, and out of hours studied Latin, Greek, French, German, and Hebrew. In 1833 he landed in New York, expecting to follow his trade, but a chance meeting with Professor (afterward President) John Maclean [q.v.] of Princeton led to his entering the junior class of that college. After his graduation in 1835 he was for two years a private tutor with two students at Yale, and himself studied there. The next two years he spent in Princeton College as tutor in Greek. In 1839 he went to Lafayette College as professor of Latin and Greek, and in 1841 began a service of eleven years as professor of Latin and esthetics at Miami University, Oxford, Ohio. The Presbytery of Oxford licensed him to preach on Jan. 5, 1851, and on Oct. 23 of the same year, ordained him, without his having taken a theological course. His long poem, *Alwyn: A Romance of Study* (1875), which is known to be autobiographical, doubtless interprets his life to this point. It recites the spiritual adventures of the hero, following him through many fields of reading and thought, wide travels in Europe for the sake of study, influences of many forms of art, and experiences with various philosophies. In the end he returns to the Christian faith in which he had been brought up. For a few months in 1852 Moffat taught Greek and Hebrew in a short-lived theological seminary in Cincinnati. Then followed eight years in Princeton College, as professor first of Latin and history and then of Greek. In 1861 he became professor of church history in Princeton Theological Seminary. This place he held for seventeen years. He taught for a year after his resignation, and a year later died in Princeton.

Moffat was not original in mind, and did not impress his students with force of personality, but his nature was refined and cultivated, and sensitive to beauty in nature and art. An industrious student and a copious writer, he was also a lover of the out-door world and a notable walker. While his main intellectual concern was with church history, his interests were varied and enthusiastic. He had poetic aspirations and wrote a good deal of verse, but recognized his own limitations in this faculty. His character was profoundly religious and marked by great simplicity and gentleness. Besides his poem *Alwyn* he published a *Life of Thomas Chalmers*

(1853), in the main an abridgment of William Hanna's biography; *An Introduction to the Study of Aesthetics* (1856); *A Comparative History of Religions* (2 vols., 1871–73); *Outlines of Church History* (1875); *The Church in Scotland* (copr. 1882), a history to the Reformation; *The Story of a Dedicated Life* (1887), a biography of Joseph Owen, missionary at Allahabad; *A Rhyme of the North Country* (1847), and *Song and Scenery: or a Summer Ramble in Scotland* (1874). He was married on Oct. 13, 1840, at Easton, Pa., to Ellen Stewart, who died in 1849, and on Dec. 26, 1850, at Oxford, Ohio, he was married to Mary B. Matthews. Five sons and three daughters survived him.

[*Necrological Report . . . Princeton Theol. Sem.* (1891); *Gen. Cat. Princeton Univ.* (1908); S. J. Coffin, *The Men of Lafayette* (1891); *New York Evangelist*, June 19, 1890; *Presbyt. Banner* (Pittsburgh), June 11, 1890; *Daily True American* (Trenton), June 9, 1890; Moffat's works.]   R. H. N.

MOFFETT, CLEVELAND LANGSTON (Apr. 27, 1863–Oct. 14, 1926), journalist, author, was born in Boonville, N. Y., the son of William H. and Mary (Cleveland) Moffett. After a common schooling in his home town, he entered Yale and was graduated A.B. in 1883. Four years of newspaper reporting followed, and then he was placed on the European staff of the *New York Herald,* where he served from 1887 to 1891. He was on the New York staff of the same newspaper during 1891–92, then joined the *New York Recorder* as foreign editor, 1893–94. At this point he abandoned the newspaper profession and thereafter devoted his time to the writing of books (fiction and non-fiction), plays, and magazine articles, save for one brief period in 1908–09 when he returned to the *New York Herald* as Sunday editor. One of his first literary tasks was the translation of Paul Bourget's *Cosmopolis* from the French in 1893. He was a rapid and versatile writer, usually with a journalistic touch, and in the next few years contributed many articles to magazines and newspapers on almost every imaginable subject, though current topics, often of a semi-scientific nature, were among his favorites. His first original book, *True Detective Stories from the Archives of the Pinkertons,* appeared in 1897; a series of articles, "Careers of Danger and Daring," first ran as a serial in *St. Nicholas* and appeared in book form in 1901; *A King in Rags* was published in 1907, and *Through the Wall,* a mystery story of Paris, where he was then living, in 1909. Other books of fiction from his pen were *The Mysterious Card* (1912), first published in the *Black Cat,* 1896; *The Bishop's Purse* (1913), written in collaboration with

Oliver Herford, and *The Land of Mystery* (1913), first published in *St. Nicholas.*

From the beginning of the World War in 1914 Moffett was much concerned as to America's attitude and was one of the earliest propagandists in favor of preparedness. After some correspondence from the war front, he returned to the United States and wrote in 1916 *The Conquest of America,* in which he pictured a possible invasion by the Germans five years later. When the United States entered the war, he assisted in the organization of the American Defense Society and was made one of its trustees. He made many patriotic addresses, wrote at length on the definition of treason, and was active in the operations of the Vigilantes, an organization formed to combat disloyalty. He was for some time its chairman. In his zealous pursuit of this work he took part in some exciting street incidents when he challenged "soapbox" orators whose utterances he considered seditious; and he appeared as complainant a number of times in court actions against such persons. He continued to write busily during the war, producing, *inter alia,* "How to Live Long —and Love Long" (*McClure's,* September–November 1916); "Glint of Wings," in collaboration with Virginia Hall, issued in book form in 1922; and several "prose poems." A novel, *Possessed,* appeared in 1920. He had written a number of successful plays earlier in his career, all on modern subjects. These included *Money Talks,* produced in 1906; *Playing the Game,* 1907; *The Battle,* a discussion of the antagonism between capital and labor, which had a long run in 1908–09 and caused much discussion; *For Better, For Worse,* produced in 1910; *Greater Than the Law,* 1912. During the last twenty years of his life he made his home for the most part in Paris and died there; though he also spent considerable time in California, adapting some of his books and plays for use in motion pictures and writing original stories for the screen. He was married on Feb. 11, 1899, to Mary E. Lusk who, together with a son and two daughters, survived him.

[*Who's Who in America, 1926–27; Yale, 1883: The Book of the Class Comp. after Its Quarter-Centenary Reunion* (1910); *Yale Univ. Obit. Record,* 1927; *Yale Alumni Weekly,* Oct. 29, 1926; *N. Y. Times, N. Y. Herald-Tribune,* and other papers, Oct. 16, 1926; numerous newspaper references during 1917–18; articles by Moffett in newspapers and magazines.]

A.F.H.

MOHR, CHARLES THEODORE (Dec. 28, 1824–July 17, 1901), botanist, was born in Esslingen, Württemberg, the son of Louis M. Mohr. Derived from a family noted for its representatives in chemistry and pharmacology, he entered the polytechnic high school in Stuttgart as a student of chemistry, pharmacy, and mineralogy, having as his instructor in chemistry Hermann von Fehling. Although he had become interested in natural history as a boy, his association at the Polytechnicum with Fehling (who had recently come from Liebig's laboratory at Giessen), with Wilhelm Hochstetter, and with the botanist Johann Hohenacker, decided him to devote himself entirely to natural history. After his graduation in 1845, he accompanied August Kappler to Dutch Guiana as botanical collector. In this work he engaged for a few months, until a protracted illness forced him to return to Germany at the end of 1846.

After the revolution of 1848 he decided, with his brother, to emigrate to the United States, and accordingly came to Cincinnati, then a German community of considerable magnitude, where he took employment as chemist with a chemical manufacturer. During this period he continued his botanical studies and built up a large herbarium, paying particular attention to plants of economic, especially medical, importance. He went to California with the gold rush in 1849, returning the following year with his health permanently impaired. From Cincinnati he removed to Louisville, where he engaged in business as a pharmacist and greatly extended his botanical studies. On Mar. 12, 1852, at Louisville, he married Sophia Roemer, a native of Zweibrücken, Bavaria, who became the mother of three sons and two daughters. In 1857 he moved because of his health to Mobile, Ala., which remained his home until nearly the end of his life.

Here he engaged in pharmacy, and began the extensive studies on the botany of Alabama which constitute his claim to fame. He published nearly a hundred papers on botanical subjects, the most important among them being a report on the forests of Alabama for the Tenth Census (vol. IX, 1884, pp. 525–30); an important memoir on the timber pines of the southern United States (*Bulletin No. 13,* Division of Forestry, United States Department of Agriculture, 1896); and an extensive memoir of over 900 pages on *Plant Life of Alabama* (Contributions from the National Herbarium, vol. VI, United States Department of Agriculture, 1901). The last was reissued, also in 1901, with a biographical sketch and portrait of the author, by the Geological Survey of Alabama. Mohr also made for various organizations important collections of plants and minerals of Alabama; and assembled exhibits for the expo-

Moïse

Moldehnke

sitions at Atlanta (1881) and New Orleans (1884).

Of his personality and character, a contemporary said: "Mohr is possessed of a true scientific spirit and great enthusiasm in his botanical work. . . . He has not only increased the sum of our knowledge, but has added to our powers of direct usefulness" (Lamson-Scribner, in Mohr's *Plant Life,* Alabama edition, p. xi). Dr. Eugene A. Smith, long his colleague on the Geological Survey of Alabama, writes: "Personally Dr. Mohr was the most lovable and unselfish of men, totally devoid of affectation and pretense . . . inspiring all who knew him with love and respect" (*Ibid.,* p. xii). A year before his death, he moved from Mobile to Asheville, N. C., there to work in the Biltmore Herbarium and finish seeing through the press his *magnum opus,* the *Plant Life of Alabama.* His death, at Asheville, cut short the completion of his projected "Economic Botany of Alabama," which he had planned as the crowning work of his career.

[*Pharmaceutische Rundschau,* Feb., Mar. 1887; *Pharmaceutical Rev.,* Sept. 1901; C. T. Mohr, *Plant Life of Alabama,* Alabama edition (Ala. Geol. Survey, 1901), pp. v–xii; *Who's Who in America,* 1901–02; *Asheville Daily Gazette,* July 18, 1901.]   S. W. G.

MOÏSE, PENINA (Apr. 23, 1797–Sept. 13, 1880), poet, was born in Charleston, S. C., the daughter of Abraham and Sarah Moïse. The death of her father, an Alsatian Jew who had first emigrated to Santo Domingo and had then fled to Charleston during the negro uprising in 1791, compelled her to leave school when she was twelve years old in order to help support the large family. Being very studious, she gave her spare time to study and attained a high degree of scholarship, at the same time cultivating her own literary talents. These early years were filled with self-sacrificing endeavor, for she devoted herself during the early part of her life to her home and community interests, being especially active in religious and welfare work, teaching, nursing, and writing hymns. In the latter years of her life, although handicapped by failing eyesight and finally total blindness, she conducted a small but exceptionally fine school for the young girls of her race. By 1830 she had begun writing poetry voluminously. In 1833 she published *Fancy's Sketch Book* and thereafter contributed many poems to the *Occident and American Jewish Advocate, Godey's Lady's Book,* the *Home Journal,* and the *Boston Daily Times,* the *Washington Union,* and *Heriot's Magazine,* besides many occasional pieces in New Orleans and Charleston papers. Her best-loved and most characteristic work is contained in the volume

of *Hymns Written for the Use of Hebrew Congregations* (1856), especially compiled for the use of the congregation of Beth Elohim, the synagogue of which she was a member. The quality of these poems and hymns is, in the main, not above the average, although some of them are beautiful and stately. The predominant note is reminiscent of eighteenth-century English classicism, but occasionally there is interspersed a hint of romanticism.

[*Secular and Religious Works of Penina Moïse, with a Brief Sketch of her Life* (1911), compiled and published by the Charleston section, Council of Jewish Women; B. A. Elzas, *The Jews of S. C.* (1905); L. C. Harby, "Penina Moise, Woman and Writer," *The Am. Jewish Year Book,* 1905–06; the *Critic,* Dec. 28, 1889; *News and Courier* (Charleston), Sept. 14, 1880.]
R. D. B.

MOLDEHNKE, EDWARD FREDERICK (Aug. 10, 1836–June 25, 1904), Lutheran clergyman, was born at Insterburg, East Prussia, the son of Franz August and Justine (Kessler) Moldencke. His father, an excise official and amateur inventor, was descended from an officer in the army of Gustavus Adolphus, his mother from one of the exiled Protestants of Salzburg. Her death when he was nine years old made his boyhood and youth dismal and cheerless. He attended the Gymnasium at Lyck, 1845–53, matriculated at the age of seventeen at the University of Königsberg as a student of philosophy and theology, and followed Prof. Justus L. Jacobi in 1855 to the University of Halle, where he remained till 1857. While in Halle he acted as secretary to Friedrich Tholuck, in whose household he lived. He was one of the founders of the anti-dueling students' society, Tuisconia. Having passed his examinations with distinction, he was made head, for a few months, of the parochial school at Eckersberg, East Prussia, and was called in 1859 to a professorship in the Lyck Gymnasium. In that same year he married Elise Harder, a descendant of the baronial house of Mannteufel.

Though eminently happy at Lyck, he was eager for the work of the ministry, and in 1861 agreed to come to the United States for five years of missionary work in the West. He was ordained at Königsberg July 23, 1861, and reached Wisconsin, with his wife and child, in August. For four years he led the hard and at times dangerous life of a traveling missionary among the remote settlements of Germans in Wisconsin and Minnesota. In 1865 he was elected president of the Lutheran Theological Seminary at Watertown, Wis., and became editor of the Wisconsin Synod's *Gemeindeblatt.* The University of Rostock made him an honorary doctor. He returned to Germany in August

78

1866 to become pastor at Johannisburg, East Prussia. This parish numbered 11,000 German and Polish members, and Moldehnke's post included the oversight of thirty-three schools and several prisons, poorhouses, and hospitals. During his incumbency the district was ravaged by epidemics of cholera and typhus; at one time Moldehnke himself was stricken and pronounced dead by his physician. Illness and overwork, aggravated by dissatisfaction with the Prussian State Church, led him to resign in 1869. Starting his career anew, he came to New York and organized a Lutheran congregation, Zion's, which worshiped temporarily in the Medical College at Twenty-third Street and Fourth Avenue. In 1871, this congregation was merged with St. Peter's, of which he served as pastor until his death thirty-three years later.

He was a man of commanding presence and great personal charm, conversed fluently in German, English, Latin, Polish, French, and Italian, and had few equals as an orator in German. He was a member of the committee that edited the General Council's *Kirchenbuch* (1877) and was president of the Council from 1895 to 1898. He was the author of: *Darstellung der Modernen Deutschen Theologie* (Watertown, Wis., 1865); a life of Luther in verse, *Lutherbüchlein* (Allentown, Pa., 1879); *Das Heilige Vaterunser* (Allentown, 1878); and *Durch Kampf zum Sieg* (New York, 1887), the last being a series of lectures delivered in Cooper Institute. His "Fünf Jahre in Amerika" was published in Hengstenberg's *Evangelische Kirchenzeitung* (Berlin, October 1868–February 1870). He wrote prolifically for various church periodicals in Germany and the United States, was the first editor of the *Lutherisches Kirchenblatt* of Reading, Pa. (1884), and edited *Siloah,* a paper founded in the interest of German home missions, 1882–88. He died at his summer home in Watchung, N. J., while preparing a sermon for the following Sunday. Of his four sons, Charles Edward became a well-known Egyptologist and Richard George Gottlob Moldenke [*q.v.*], a metallurgist.

[This article is based chiefly on material supplied by Moldehnke's son, Dr. Charles Edward Moldenke of Watchung, N. J. See also *Who's Who in America,* 1903–05; J. C. Jensson-Roseland, *Am. Luth. Biogs.* (Milwaukee, 1890); *North Plainfield Review,* July 9, 1904; *N. Y. Times,* June 26, 29, 1904; *New-Yorker Staats-Zeitung,* June 27, 29, 1904. The family name is variously spelled; the forms here adopted are those apparently preferred by the individuals mentioned.]

G. H. G.

MOLDENKE, RICHARD GEORGE GOTTLOB (Nov. 1, 1864–Nov. 17, 1930), metallurgist, was born in Watertown, Wis., the son of the Rev. Edward F. Moldehnke [*q.v.*], a Lutheran clergyman, and Elise (Harder) Moldehnke. Richard changed the spelling of the family name, and rarely used his second and third baptismal names. In 1870 he was taken to New York City, where he attended Columbia Grammar School and later the School of Mines, Columbia University, receiving the degree of E. M. in 1885 and that of Ph.D. in 1887. Late in life, in the course of a public address, he said, "I thank my father because he put me to school when I was three years old, and I have been to school ever since. . . . I shall stay there as long as I live" (*Transactions of the American Foundrymen's Association,* vol. XXXIII, p. xxvii). After two years with the Coast and Geodetic Survey, he organized the mechanical and electrical engineering-departments at the Michigan College of Mines and served as professor of mechanical engineering for one year (1889).

With the acceptance in 1890 of a position with McConway & Torley Company, Pittsburgh, Pa., he started on his active career of forty years as a metallurgist. His restless cravings for research led him to originate and follow through some of the most valuable investigations which have been undertaken in the field of foundry science. His cupola study served to revise charging methods and to effect great economies in plant operation. He worked out the action of carbon, silicon, and other basic elements in iron. His study of coke led to a new understanding of that fuel. He was a pioneer in improving practice in the gray-iron industry by substituting science for rule-of-thumb. Because of his great influence in stimulating the scientific study of foundry problems and particularly because of the improvements in the art of producing gray-iron castings which resulted from his investigations and studies, he was awarded in 1925 the Joseph S. Seaman gold medal of the American Foundrymen's Association.

He was an active and influential member of that organization almost from its inception, and was for fourteen years its secretary and treasurer. Through his membership in this and other technical societies in the United States and Europe, his attendance at meetings, and his generous and enthusiastic participation in their proceedings, he not only kept in touch with metallurgical developments but also earned for himself an international reputation as a metallurgist. During the last thirty years of his life he was retained as consultant by a large number of foundries and manufacturing firms both in the United States and abroad. As consultant for the federal government during the World War he supervised the casting of war materials and drafted the specifications for the castings used in the manufacture of Liberty motors.

Moldenke was a prolific writer on foundry and metallurgical subjects, contributing to the technical press, government publications, and the proceedings of technical societies. Two important works, *The Principles of Iron Founding* (1917; 2nd ed., 1930) and *The Production of Malleable Castings* (1910), are outstanding contributions to foundry literature. At Watchung, N. J., he built himself a replica of a German castle and behind it constructed a small foundry in which he performed his experimental work. He was married, Sept. 18, 1891, to Anne, daughter of John D. Heins of New York, who, together with a daughter and two sons, survived him. His death, following an operation, occurred at Plainfield, N. J., Nov. 17, 1930. On Nov. 20 the *Iron Age* remarked: "In his passing the castings industry has lost its great technician and its generous adviser."

[*The Foundry*, Dec. 1, 1930; *Trans. Am. Foundrymen's Asso.*, vol. XXXIII (1926); *Trans. and Bull., Am. Foundrymen's Asso.*, Dec. 1930; *Who's Who in America*, 1930–31; *N. Y. Times*, Nov. 18, 1930.]
B. A. R.

MOLLENHAUER, EMIL (Aug. 4, 1855– Dec. 10, 1927), violinist, conductor, was born in Brooklyn, N. Y., the son of Friedrich and Margaret (Pugh) Mollenhauer. The father was one of three brothers born in Erfurt, Germany, all of whom were excellent musicians. Friedrich and Eduard, who were violinists, came to America as members of the Jullien Orchestra which toured the United States in 1853. They remained as soloists, orchestral players, and teachers. Heinrich, the third brother, a 'cellist, emigrated in 1856 and established a school of music in Brooklyn. Friedrich Mollenhauer was the most brilliant of the three and in addition was an able teacher. Recognizing his son's musical talent, he gave him violin lessons and the boy progressed so rapidly that he made his début with the orchestra in Niblo's Garden before he was quite nine years old. When he was fourteen he became a member of the orchestra of Booth's Theatre and played throughout Joseph Jefferson's run of six months in *Rip Van Winkle*. At the age of seventeen he became one of the first violinists in the Theodore Thomas Orchestra, remaining for about eight years, when he joined the New York Symphony Society founded by Leopold Damrosch. He also became a member of both the New York and the Brooklyn Philharmonic societies.

Meantime he had developed into a well-equipped pianist and was frequently called upon to act as accompanist for soloists appearing on the orchestral programs. In 1884 he settled in Boston, having accepted a position as first violinist in the Boston Symphony Orchestra, but he resigned in 1888 to accept the more responsible position of conductor of the Germania Orchestra, later known as the Boston Festival Orchestra. He was also conductor of the Municipal Concerts until 1903. In 1899 he succeeded Reinhold L. Herman as conductor of the Handel and Haydn Society which was in need of reorganization. He remained head of this organization for twenty-eight years, resigning in May 1927, because of ill health. From 1901 until his death he conducted the Apollo Club of Boston and at various times the oratorio societies of neighboring towns, besides conducting the People's Symphony Orchestra (1920–25) and the Boston Band. For a number of years he toured the country with the Boston Festival Orchestra, visiting especially the cities in the East and Middle West which had excellent choral societies, and supplying the orchestral background for their festivals. In 1904 he conducted the Boston Symphony Orchestra at the St. Louis Exposition and in 1915 at the San Francisco Exposition.

According to Mollenhauer's own statement, Theodore Thomas exerted the greatest influence on his development as a musician, and as he entered the Thomas Orchestra in the most impressionable period of his life, he had ample opportunity to observe and learn from this conductor, whom he adored. He was a versatile musician—an able conductor and an excellent coach in the interpretation of opera, oratorio, and the *Lied*. He was conservative in his taste and extreme innovations did not appeal to him. He was a most serious musician and demanded the same quality of seriousness in those who played or sang under him. On Apr. 1, 1884, he married Mary E. Laverty, a singer of Boston, who survived him. He died suddenly at his home in Boston on the day before he was to have conducted a concert by the People's Symphony Orchestra, in Jordan Hall. At a presentation of the *Messiah* by the Handel and Haydn Society the following week he was to have been presented with a purse as an expression of appreciation of his service.

[*Who's Who in America*, 1926–27; W. F. Bradbury, *Hist. of the Handel and Haydn Soc.*, vol. II, no. 2 (1913); *Internat. Who's Who in Music* (1918); *Music*, Oct. 1892; *Musical America*, Dec. 17, 1927; *Boston Evening Transcript*, Dec. 10, 11, 1927; *N. Y. Times*, Dec. 11, 1927; information from Mollenhauer's friend, Reinhold Faelten.]
F. L. G. C.

MÖLLHAUSEN, HEINRICH BALDUIN (Jan. 27, 1825–May 28, 1905), traveler, author, was born on a small estate near Bonn on the Rhine. His father, Heinrich Möllhausen, began his career as a Prussian artillery officer, but later retired from the army to practise civil engineering. His mother was Elisabeth Baronesse von Falkenstein, who died early, leaving three children to be cared for by her family while the father roamed to the four corners of Europe. Balduin attended the Gymnasium at Bonn until his fourteenth year, when financial difficulties cut short his education. For a time he tried his hand at agriculture in Pomerania and weighed the possibility of becoming an Austrian officer, but after a bit of experience in the Revolution of 1848 his restless blood made its demands on him and in the fall of 1849 he sailed for America. He proceeded to the Middle West, where he "led the roving life of a hunter in the region of the Kaskaskia River in Illinois." On hearing that the Duke Paul William of Württemberg was on the point of setting out on a scientific expedition to the Rocky Mountains, he requested and was granted the privilege of joining the party. The expedition got as far as Fort Laramie, but soon collapsed in the face of repeated Indian attacks. Late in the autumn of 1851 the Duke and Möllhausen retreated alone to the Missouri and from there to Fort Kearny. At some distance from this place the Duke, fallen ill, was picked up by a United States mail coach, leaving Möllhausen alone to battle Indians, famine, snow, and cold for long months. He was ultimately rescued by friendly Indians, and after a considerable lapse of time joined the Duke in New Orleans.

In January 1853 Möllhausen was back in Berlin. Here he came into intimate contact with Alexander von Humboldt, who became his patron and friend. In this cultured home he met and later married (Feb. 6, 1855) Carolina Alexandra Seifert who had been reared as a foster child of the distinguished scientist. After less than four months in Berlin he sailed again for America, provided with letters of recommendation to influential persons in Washington. His arrival, in May 1853, could not have been more opportunely arranged. The United States government was on the point of sending out three different expeditions to chart the best course for a railroad to the Pacific. Möllhausen was assigned as topographer to that commanded by Lieut. A. W. Whipple, while the Smithsonian Institution commissioned him to make physical observations and to act as naturalist on this venture. His unusual ability to sketch played no little part in these appointments. With this expedition he made the trek from Fort Smith to

Pueblo de los Angelos. In August 1854 he was again in Berlin, the house guest of von Humboldt. His renowned patron prevailed upon King Frederick William IV to create for him the position of custodian of the libraries in the royal residences in and about Potsdam, a position which he held until his death. This fortunate turn of affairs gave him the comfort and the leisure necessary for his writing. Once more he heard and followed the call of the American West, accepting an appointment offered him by the United States government as assistant to an expedition to explore and survey the Colorado River (1857–58). The thrills of this adventure he later crystallized into a number of novels. During most of the remaining forty-seven years of his life he stayed at home and developed his art as a voluminous and facile writer of adventure stories. He died in Berlin, in 1905.

Forty-five large works in 157 volumes and eighty novelettes in twenty-one volumes bear emphatic witness to Möllhausen's industry and the fertility of his mind. This voluminous output may be roughly divided into two groups: first, the earlier novels whose action takes place wholly on American soil, such as *Der Halbindianer* (4 vols., 1861) and its sequels, and *Das Mormonenmädchen* (6 vols., 1864); secondly, the later stories, by far the more numerous, which have for their scenes of action both the old and the new country. He must be considered as one of the most prominent exponents of both Indian and emigration fiction. His biographer, P. A. Barba, has summed up his deserts excellently: "Balduin Möllhausen was the most prolific, and at the same time the last great exponent of transatlantic fiction in Germany. He did not write with the passionate pen of Sealsfield [Karl Postl]; he did not give the Indian so prominent a place in his novels as Strubberg did . . . he may lack Gerstäcker's facile style of narrative; but in point of form, and in the skillful motivation of a plot he is the master of all these. . . . In view of his splendid portrayals of Indian and pioneer life, and by virtue of the high character of his sea-novels, there is none who deserves so much the title of 'The German Cooper.'"

[P. A. Barba, *Balduin Möllhausen, The German Cooper* (Americana Germanica, vol. XVII, Pubs. of the Univ. of Pa., 1914), is dedicated to Carolina Alexandra Frau Balduin Möllhausen and opens with a German introduction by the lady; see also a short sketch by Franz Brümmer in *Biographisches Jahrbuch und Deutscher Nekrolog*, X (1907), 123–24; and the obituary article in *Berliner Tageblatt*, May 29, 1905.]

C.F.S.

MOLYNEUX, ROBERT (July 24, 1738–Dec. 9, 1808), Roman Catholic priest and educator, was born near Formby, Lancashire, a scion of a noteworthy North Briton cavalier family which contributed a number of members to the Society of Jesus. Educated by private tutors and reared in the seclusion enforced upon Catholics by the penal laws, he entered the Society of Jesus on Sept. 7, 1757, and studied theology in Belgium, teaching for a time in his community's college at Bruges. Soon after his ordination, he was assigned to the American missions, where a relative, Richard Molyneux, had previously labored as a Jesuit missionary and superior. Arriving in Maryland in 1771, he served two years on the missions and was then appointed to St. Mary's Church, Philadelphia, to succeed Robert Harding [q.v.], who had died in September 1772. Later he became joint pastor of St. Joseph's Church as well. Here after the suppression of his society he continued as a secular priest along with Ferdinand Farmer [q.v.]. During the Revolution he was a moderate patriot, taking the oath of allegiance to Pennsylvania, welcoming the attendance of members of Congress at two funeral masses for foreign envoys, tutoring the Chevalier de la Luzerne in English, burying himself in his library in order to avoid association with the invaders during the British occupation. He opened a parochial school, purchasing its site in 1781, and that same year improved the church. In 1783 he was one of the signers of a petition praying that Congress return to Philadelphia.

A zealous churchman, he urged his intimate friend, John Carroll [q.v.], to accept the appointment as prefect apostolic in order that the church in America might be freed from English jurisdiction. This step accomplished, he advocated the appointment of an American bishop, joining with Carroll and the Rev. John Ashton in a memorial to Rome on this subject. After papal approval had been secured (July 12, 1788), the convention of clergy met at Whitemarsh, Carroll's name was submitted to Rome, and he was forthwith named bishop. Meanwhile, Molyneux left Philadelphia for Bohemia Manor (1788) and later Newtown, Md. As Bishop Carroll's vicar general for the southern district, he took part in the diocesan synod of 1791. Soon afterwards he succeeded Father Robert Plunkett as president of Georgetown College, where he remained until transferred back to Newtown in 1796. Deeply concerned in the negotiations with the Rev. Gabriel Gruber, general of the Society of Jesus in Russia, Molyneux rejoiced in the preliminary restoration of the Society, of which he was named American superior, June 21, 1805. In 1806, upon the res-

ignation of Bishop Leonard Neale [q.v.], he again assumed the rectorship of Georgetown. Two years later, weary and realizing that his end was near, he named Charles Neale as acting superior of the Jesuit priests in America. He left no literary remains save a *Sermon on the Death of Father Farmer* (1786), which, incidentally, was one of the first Catholic publications in the United States.

[J. G. Shea, *Hist. of the Cath. Ch. in the U. S.*, vol. II (1888) ; Peter Guilday, *The Life and Times of John Carroll* (1922) ; Thos. Hughes, *Hist. of the Soc. of Jesus in North America* (1910) ; *Am. Cath. Hist. Researches* (1884–1912), see index volume, and esp. vol. XXIX (1912), pp. 267–78; J. L. J. Kirlin, *Catholicity in Phila.* (1909) ; *National Intelligencer and Washington Advertiser*, Dec. 26, 1808; *Am. Cath. Quart. Rev.*, Jan. 1886 ; J. S. Easby-Smith, *Georgetown Univ.* (2 vols., 1907.]

R. J. P.

MOMBERT, JACOB ISIDOR (Nov. 6, 1829–Oct. 7, 1913), Episcopal clergyman, author, was born in Cassel, Germany, the son of Dr. J. L. and Joanna M. Mombert. When twelve years old he went to England. In 1857 he was ordained a deacon of the Anglican church in the Chapel Royal, Whitehall, London, by Dr. Tait, later the Archbishop of Canterbury. Dean Stanley was one of the examiners. The following year he was priested by Bishop Mountain in Quebec, Canada, and served until 1859 as an assistant in Trinity Church, to which he had been called because of his ability to preach in English, French, and German. From 1859 to 1870 he was the rector of St. James Church, Lancaster, Pa., where, on July 5, 1860, he married Emma Elizabeth Muhlenberg, half-sister of Frederick Augustus Muhlenberg [q.v.]. His sermon, "The Open Door," preached before the Congress of Convocation held at Reading, Pa., Feb. 20, 1867 (Paterson *Morning Call*, Dec. 23, 1907), led to the erection of the Central Diocese of Pennsylvania, and his services at Bedford Springs brought about the establishment of a parish. During the Civil War he supported the Union, and jointly with Phillips Brooks ministered to the wounded and performed the last rites for the dead upon the field of Gettysburg. After leaving Lancaster he held the following rectorships: St. John's Dresden, Germany, 1870–76; Christ Church, Jersey City, N. J., 1877–78; St. John's, Passaic, N. J., 1879–82. The last years of his life were devoted to literary labors in Paterson, N. J., where he died, survived by two sons and four daughters.

His published works covered a considerable range. In the Biblical field his *Translation and Commentary on the Book of Psalms* (1858), from the German of Augustus Tholuck, was fraught with peculiar difficulties because Tholuck had taken as a basis Luther's version, for which the English Authorized had to be substituted with inevitable adjustments in the commentary. Mombert's translation of the Catholic Epistles in J. P. Lange's *A Commentary on the Holy Scriptures* (vol. IX, 1867) was enriched by a large number of signed notes. His edition of *William Tyndale's Five Books of Moses* appeared in 1884 (London and New York). His handbook called *English Versions of the Bible* (1883, 1890, 1906) is a learned and yet readable account of all the versions in the English tongue from the Anglo-Saxon to the Anglo-American Revision, with a description of the circumstances of the translation and of the sources employed.

In the field of general and ecclesiastical history, he published *A History of Charles the Great* (1888), intended for the general reader, but based on a thorough and critical use of the sources; *A Short History of the Crusades* (1894), a popular and colorful account; and *Great Lives* (First Series, all that appeared, 1886), a popular "course of history in biographies" from Hercules to Ulysses S. Grant, including Constantine, Charlemagne, and Luther. A volume published in 1882, *Faith Victorious,* is a vindication of Dr. Johann W. Ebel, a Lutheran clergyman of Königsberg, Prussia.

In a class by itself among his writings is *An Authentic History of Lancaster County in the State of Pennsylvania* (1869), a most diverse compilation, its topics ranging all the way from Mennonites to mineralogy and from archeology to agriculture, and presenting for the first time the colonial records, including the names of those from the county who served in the Revolution. His last publication was *Raphael's Sistine Madonna* (1895), an historical account and an artistic appreciation, for which he was fitted not only by his unusual linguistic and historical attainments, but also by an artistic taste which led him at the age of seventy to take up oil painting.

[*Who's Who in America,* 1912–13, slightly inaccurate; *Newark Churchman,* Jan. 1908, Nov. 1913; *N. Y. Times,* Oct. 8, 1913; *Paterson Press,* Dec. 21, 1907, on the occasion of the fiftieth anniversary of his ordination as a deacon; information as to certain facts from Miss Rietta A. Mombert of Paterson, N. J.]

R. H. B.

MONCKTON, ROBERT (June 24, 1726– May 21, 1782), British lieutenant-general, was the second son of John Monckton, created Viscount Galway in 1727, and of his wife Lady Elizabeth Manners, daughter of the second Duke of Rutland. He entered the 3rd Foot Guards in 1741, became captain in the 34th in 1744 and major in 1747. He served at Dettingen and at Fontenoy. In 1751 he became lieutenant-colonel of the 47th, and followed his father as member of Parliament for Pontefract. After joining his regiment in Nova Scotia in 1752, Monckton commanded at Fort Lawrence from August to June 1753, when he was appointed a provincial councilor. In December he quelled an insurrection of German immigrants at Lunenburg by "moderate management and most judicious measures" rather than by force. In June 1755, at the head of 270 regulars and nearly 2,000 New Englanders, he accomplished the only successful British action of the summer, taking Fort Beausejour in an admirably executed two weeks' campaign and destroying the French control of the isthmus. For his "zeal and ability" in this service he was made lieutenant-governor of Nova Scotia. Until November he remained in Chignecto and followed Gov. Charles Lawrence's orders in destroying French villages and in collecting 1,100 French inhabitants for removal southward. In 1756 he was disciplining the 600 new recruits of his regiment in his customary kindly, firm manner, and in December 1757 he was appointed colonel of the 2nd Battalion of the Royal American regiment. In 1758 he acted as governor in Lawrence's absence, commanded in Nova Scotia during Amherst's siege of Louisbourg, and from September to November led an expedition up the River St. John to reduce that section to British obedience. Though Amherst had designed him to succeed Forbes as commander in the south, he was selected by Wolfe in England, and approved by Pitt, as second in command of the Quebec expedition of 1759, with the temporary rank of brigadier-general. He was at the actions of Point Lévis and Montmorency, was wounded through the lungs at the battle of the Plains, and commanded in Canada until ill health forced him south. In October he became colonel of the 17th. In 1760 he received from Amherst the command of the southern district and was at various posts in Pennsylvania and western New York. The following year saw his merits gain full recognition, for he was named governor of New York, major-general and commander-in-chief of an expedition against Martinique. Sailing in November, he effected in conjunction with Admiral Rodney the surrender of the island by Feb. 5, in a sharp, soldierly campaign. In June he returned to assume his government of New York, where his "easy disposition" scarcely fitted him for rigorous administration, and a year later left for England. In 1764 a court-martial triumphantly acquitted him of a trumpery charge brought against him by a cashiered officer, Colin Campbell. In 1765 he became governor of Berwick-on-Tweed; in 1770 lieutenant-general. Three years later he petitioned both King and Parliament for the appointment in India as second in command under Warren Hastings; he was offered instead the chief command in North America, which he refused (Sir John Fortescue, *The Correspondence of King George the Third*, II, 1927, pp. 494–503). The next year he represented Pontefract in Parliament, and in 1778 Portsmouth, having been appointed governor of Portsmouth. There is no record of his marriage, but he left three sons and one daughter.

[D. H. Monckton, *A Geneal. Hist. of the Family of Monckton* (1887); *The Northcliffe Collection* (1926), containing 400 pages of Monckton's papers; *Selections from the Pub. Documents of the Province of Nova Scotia* (1869); E. B. O'Callaghan, *Documents Relative to the Colonial Hist. of the Province of N. Y.*, vols. VII–VIII (1856–57); A. G. Doughty and G. W. Parmelee, *The Siege of Quebec* (6 vols., 1901); Capt. John Knox, *An Hist. Jour. of the Campaigns in North America* (3 vols., 1914–16), ed. by A. G. Doughty; "The Letters and Papers of Cadwallader Colden," vol. VI, which is vol. LV of the *N. Y. Hist. Soc. Colls.* (1923); "Monckton's Report of his Expedition Against the French on the St. John in 1758," *New Brunswick Hist. Soc. Colls.*, No. 5 (1904); "Aspinwall Papers," *Mass. Hist. Soc. Colls.*, 4 ser. IX–X (1871); J. C. Webster, *The Forts of Chignecto* (1930); *Proc. of a General Court-martial . . . for the Trial of a Charge Preferred by C. Campbell* (1764); Public Record Office, W. O. 34, The Amherst Papers.]   S. M. P.

MONCURE, RICHARD CASSIUS LEE (Dec. 11, 1805–Aug. 24, 1882), jurist, was born at "Clermont," his family's ancestral Potomac River plantation, Stafford County, Va., the seventh of nine children of John and Alice Peachy (Gaskins) Moncure. He was descended from the Rev. John Moncure, born in Scotland, who emigrated to Virginia about 1734. Although of distinguished family he was not born to wealth and apparently received little formal schooling, but at the age of twenty he was admitted to the bar. The same year, Dec. 29, 1825, he married Mary Butler Washington Conway. In 1826 he became commonwealth's attorney for Stafford County, a post he long occupied. Although he served in the House of Delegates of 1827–28 he was not attracted by politics, but in the years 1847–49, when the statute law of Virginia was revised, he again represented his native county in the legislature and, as a member of the committee charged with the task of revision, played a prominent part in the promulgation of the code of 1849. The next year, as delegate to the state constitutional convention, he materially aided in framing the constitution of 1851. Already recognized by the bench and bar as a lawyer of the first rank, Moncure now enjoyed a state-wide reputation and in 1851 the legislature

appointed him to the supreme court of appeals. When the new constitution, providing for the popular election of judges, went into effect, he was chosen without opposition to continue on the bench, where he remained until the collapse of the Confederacy. After a brief retirement during the confusing days which followed Appomattox he returned to his judicial duties and became president of the court, but with the establishment of military rule during Reconstruction he was removed from office. In 1870, with the return of civil government under a new constitution, the legislature restored him to the bench and he again became president of Virginia's highest court.

The opinions handed down by Moncure during his long judicial career, contained in twenty-nine volumes of the *Virginia Reports* from 7 *Grattan* (47 *Va.*) to 1 *Matthews* (75 *Va.*) are those of an independent and incorruptible judge who was learned in the law and devoted to his task of administering justice. His best decisions, perhaps, are the ones in which he applied the great principles of equity. Plain and unadorned in style, without literary or oratorical pretensions, his opinions generally were clear expositions of the law, although in later years, through his desire to show that no point had been overlooked, they tended to become too detailed and tedious. Moncure labored diligently in his search for truth and justice. He read neither classical nor current literature and cared little for what is usually called pleasure; his happy domestic life, the law, and the "record" completely absorbed him. He seldom perceived a joke unaided, but was genial and could laugh heartily when it was explained to him. Sublime in his unconscious simplicity, free from display, and unoppressed by his heritage and attainments, he had an appropriate conception, however, of the dignity of his office. So thoroughly did he inspire public confidence and affection that when forced into retirement during Reconstruction he was frequently chosen as unofficial arbiter of disputes. He was a vestryman in the Episcopal Church for forty years, devout yet tolerant, basing his belief squarely on the Bible which he deemed the foundation-stone of the law. Strong and fearless in his faith, with a consciousness of life's task completed, he died at his home "Glencairne" in the county that gave him birth.

[H. E. Hayden, *Va. Geneals.* (1891), pp. 437, 443–44; Joseph Christian, "Judge R. C. L. Moncure" in 76 *Va.*, v–xiii; Resolutions by bench and bar on the death of Moncure in 76 *Va.*, xiii–xv; Robert Ould, "Hon. Richard C. L. Moncure," *Va. Law Jour.*, Jan. 1883; J. C. Lamb, "Some Anecdotes of Judge Moncure," *Ibid.*, Aug. 1885; R. W. Moore, address on Moncure in *Va. Law Reg.*, June 1924; S. S. B. Patteson, "The Supreme Court of Appeals of Va.," the *Green Bag*, Aug. 1893; *Daily Dispatch* (Richmond, Va.), Aug. 26, 1882.]   T. S. C.

MONETTE, JOHN WESLEY (Apr. 5, 1803–Mar. 1, 1851), physician, historian, was a native of Virginia, born in the Shenandoah Valley near Staunton, the son of Samuel and Mary (Wayland) Monett. Later he added an "e" to the family name. His father, an ordained Methodist minister and a practising physician, was a descendant of Isaac Monet, a French Huguenot who settled in Maryland sometime before 1707. When John was very young, the family moved to Chillicothe, Ohio, where the lad grew up, receiving at the academy there, under the tutelage of Rev. John McFarland, an excellent education. In 1821 Dr. Monett transferred his residence to the new state of Mississippi, settling at Washington, then the capital. The son, having decided to become a physician, was sent to Transylvania University, Lexington, Ky., where he made an excellent record in scientific studies and graduated with the degree of M.D. in 1825. He then joined his father at Washington, Miss., and thereafter made that place his home. On Dec. 10, 1828, he married Cornelia Jane Newman; four only of their ten children lived to maturity.

Monette gained considerable reputation as a physician from his study of yellow fever epidemics in Mississippi. The results of his observations he incorporated into numerous articles, among which are "An Account of the Epidemic of Yellow Fever that Occurred in Washington, Mississippi, in the Autumn of 1825" (*Western Medical and Physical Journal*, May 1827); *The Epidemic Yellow Fevers of Natchez* (1838); and *Observations on the Epidemic Yellow Fever of Natchez and of the Southwest* (1842). He is credited with being the earliest to suggest the quarantine as a means of preventing the spread of the disease, and the fact that Natchez escaped the epidemic of 1841 has been attributed to the employment of that means. He also recommended the use of oil of turpentine as an irritant, especially in the treatment of typhus fever, publishing "Oil of Turpentine as an External Irritant" (*Western Medical and Physical Journal*, June 1827).

Monette made a number of fortunate investments and accumulated a fortune sufficient to permit him to devote much time to literary and scientific studies. Although a Methodist and a trustee of the local church and college, his studies in physical geography and concerning the origin of man led him toward conclusions similar to those which his English contemporary, Darwin, later promulgated. His place in the history of science, however, is not a prominent one. He projected but never completed a "Physical History of the Human Race." When about thirty years of age he began collecting material for a work on the physical geography of the Mississippi Valley and in the course of his research he was led to study its history. This portion of his work was the first completed and resulted in his monumental volumes, *History of the Discovery and Settlement of the Valley of the Mississippi by the Three Great European Powers, Spain, France, and Great Britain, and the Subsequent Occupation, Settlement and Extension of Civil Government by the United States until the Year 1846* (2 vols., 1846). The prospectus circular stated that it would be followed by two more volumes on the physical geography of the Valley; but at his death the manuscript was left unfinished and was never published. Monette was one of the first to appreciate the share which the great central valley of the Mississippi River had in the history of the United States.

His work is one of great research and erudition. The style is easy and flowing and less ponderous than that of many histories of his time. He was not always able to refer to original documents and depended upon such authorities as F. X. Martin's *History of Louisiana* and Mann Butler's *History of the Commonwealth of Kentucky*, but the material is well organized and the treatment thorough. Monette was a frequent contributor to various periodicals, among his articles being "Geology of the Mississippi Valley" in *Commercial Review of the South and West* (February, March 1847), "Public Lands Acquired by Treaty," *Ibid*. (January, February 1848), and "Early Spirit of the West," *De Bow's Review* (April, May 1850). Not long before his death he established a home in Madison Parish, La. He is buried at Washington, Miss., however, and always regarded that place as his home. He was mayor and councilman of the town and one of its prominent citizens.

[O. E. Monnette, *Monnet Family Geneal.* (1911); *Miss. Hist. Soc. Pubs.*, vol. V (1902); F. L. Riley, "Life and Literary Services of Dr. John W. Monette," *Ibid.*, vol. IX (1906); H. A. Kelly and W. L. Burrage, *Am. Med. Biogs.* (1920); C. G. Forshey, "John W. Monette, Historian of the Mississippi Valley," in *De Bow's Rev.*, July 1851.]   L. P. K.

MONEY, HERNANDO DE SOTO (Aug. 26, 1839–Sept. 18, 1912), newspaper editor, lawyer, representative and senator from Mississippi, was born on a plantation in Holmes County, Miss., but in early childhood his family moved to Carrollton. His father, Peirson Money, came from Buncombe County, N. C.; his mother, Tryphena (Vardaman) Money, was a member of a pioneer Mississippi family. A private tutor directed part of his preliminary education. In 1860 he graduated from the law school of the University of Mississippi and began practice at Carrollton. With the beginning of the Civil War he entered the Confederate infantry and served until his defective eyesight caused him to be furloughed. He then joined the cavalry and served to the end of the war. On Nov. 5, 1863, he was married to Claudia Jane Boddie, of Hinds County; six children were born of this union.

After the war Money was for a time a planter in Leflore County. He then edited the *Conservative* at Carrollton and from 1873 to 1875 published the *Advance* at Winona. During the Reconstruction period, and particularly in the exciting times of 1875, he fought valiantly against the Carpet-bag régime, and his election to the lower house of the Forty-fourth Congress was an indication of the return of power to the native white people of the state. He continued to hold this office through five congresses (Mar. 4, 1875–Mar. 3, 1885). Though there was no opposition to his renomination, he retired to private life and practised law at Washington. At the end of eight years he was persuaded to represent his district once more and served through the Fifty-third and the Fifty-fourth congresses (Mar. 4, 1893–Mar. 3, 1897). In January 1896 he was elected by the legislature to fill the senatorial term beginning Mar. 4, 1899. Between these two dates Senator J. Z. George died and Money was first appointed by the governor (Oct. 8, 1897), and soon afterward elected by the legislature, to complete the term begun by George. He was reëlected for a second term and was thus in the Senate from 1897 until 1911, his total congressional career covering almost twenty-eight years. He was never defeated for nomination or election to any office, though he was singularly independent in his political activities, apparently spending little time or thought on his political fences.

His long career in Congress, as well as his ability, brought him a number of important committee appointments. In the House he was a member of the committees on foreign affairs, naval affairs, and for two congresses served as chairman of the committee on post-offices and post-roads, where he displayed strong leadership in the destruction of the "star route" system, in reducing letter postage from three to two cents, and in promulgating the idea that the postal system should not be considered a source of revenue, or even expected to pay its own way.

He was a member of the Democratic steering committee of the Senate, and was on the finance and foreign relations committees. During his last years he was interested in the cause of peace and believed that it could be best attained by preparedness. He personally favored the Swiss method of military training and was contemplating a book on this subject when his death occurred at his home on the Mississippi coast. He was buried in the family vault at Carrollton.

[Dunbar Rowland, *The Official and Statistical Reg. of the State of Miss.*, 1908, and *Mississippi* (1907), vol. II; F. M. Witty, "Reconstruction in Carroll and Montgomery Counties," *Pubs. Miss. Hist. Soc.*, vol. X (1909); *Cong. Record*, 62 Cong., 3 Sess., pp. 4818–19, and *Ibid.*, App., pp. 129–30, 133–34; *Who's Who in America*, 1912–13; *Daily Democrat* (Natchez), Sept. 19, 20, 1912.]
                                                    C. S. S.

MONIS, JUDAH (Feb. 4, 1683–Apr. 25, 1764), Hebrew scholar, theologian, educator, was born in Algiers or Italy and was educated in the Jewish schools of Leghorn and Amsterdam. After a residence in Jamaica he went to New York, where he was made a free citizen on Feb. 28, 1715/16, his occupation being given as that of merchant. In later years, however, he is described as "sometime Rabbi of the Synagogue in *Jamaica,* and afterwards in *New York.*" He appears next in Boston or Cambridge. On June 29, 1720, he submitted to the Corporation of Harvard College the draft of a Hebrew grammar, and, in consequence, at the Commencement of the same year he received the degree of M.A. About two years later (Mar. 27, 1722), he was baptized publicly and with great solemnity in the College Hall at Cambridge. Soon after that (Apr. 30, 1722), he was appointed instructor of Hebrew in Harvard College for one year. This appointment was renewed from year to year until 1760, when he resigned his instructorship and retired to Northborough, Mass. He died there four years later.

Of his life in Cambridge certain pertinent facts are known. In January 1723/24 he married a Christian woman by the name of Abigail Marrett; he owned property, kept a shop even while teaching at Harvard, acted on one occasion as Spanish interpreter to the government, was nominated to be a justice of the peace, and when pressed by straitened circumstances petitioned the legislature for a grant from the public treasury to supplement his meager income. The records of Harvard College contain references to his successive reappointments, to occasional increases in his salary, to regulations regarding attendance at his classes, to a quarrel with one of his colleagues over the use of a class room, to assistance granted to him in connection with the publication of his grammar, and to a promise of support in defense of his privilege of exemption from taxes. His name appears also on the pamphlet issued in 1744 by the Harvard officials against the Rev. George Whitefield. Though there was some misgiving as to the sincerity of his conversion, he was at once allowed by the First Church of Cambridge to partake with its members at the Lord's Supper. Later (Feb. 5, 1736–37), he joined that church as a member. He continued, however, throughout his lifetime to observe the seventh day as the Sabbath. Before his death he professed his firm belief in the Christian religion and left the bulk of his estate as a permanent fund for poor widows of Christian ministers.

Monis is chiefly noted for the circumstance that he was the first in several things—the first Jew to receive a degree from Harvard, the first teacher at Harvard to bear the title of instructor, and the author of the first Hebrew grammar published in America. He is the author of the following works: *Three Discourses . . . The Truth, The Whole Truth, and, Nothing But the Truth: One of Which was Deliver'd by him at his Baptism* (Boston, 1722, printed together with Benjamin Colman's *A Discourse Had in the College-Hall. At Cambridge, Mass., Mar. 27, 1722, Before the Baptism of R. Judah Monis*); *Dickdook Leshon Gnebreet: A Grammar of the Hebrew Tongue* (Cambridge, 1735); "Nomenclatura Hebraica: . . . Short Nomenclator or Vocabular in English and Hebrew," a manuscript in the Harvard College Library.

["Harvard Coll. Records, Part II," in *Colonial Soc. of Mass. Pubs.*, vol. XVI (1925); Hannah Adams, *The Hist. of the Jews* (1812), II, 210–13; Benjamin Peirce, *A Hist. of Harvard Univ.* (1833); Josiah Quincy, *The Hist. of Harvard Univ.* (1840), vol. I; G. A. Kohut, "Judah Monis, M.A., The First Instructor in Hebrew at Harvard Univ.," *Am. Jour. of Semitic Languages and Lits.*, July 1898; L. M. Friedman, "Judah Monis, First Instructor in Hebrew at Harvard Univ.," *Am. Jewish Hist. Soc. Pubs.*, no. 22 (1914); G. F. Moore, "Judah Monis," *Proc. Mass. Hist. Soc.*, vol. LII (1919); F. B. Dexter, *The Lit. Diary of Ezra Stiles* (1901), I, 423. Additional bibliographical data are to be found in Kohut, Friedman, and Moore.]   H. A. W.

MONROE, JAMES (Apr. 28, 1758–July 4, 1831), fifth president of the United States, was born in Westmoreland County, Va. His parents, Spence and Elizabeth (Jones) Monroe, were Virginians of good but not distinguished stock. The paternal line can be traced with considerable probability to Andrew Monroe, who settled in Maryland in 1647, opposed Lord Baltimore, and removed to Westmoreland County, Va. (*William and Mary College Quarterly*, Jan. 1907). James Monroe went to the private school of Parson Archibald Campbell, and at sixteen entered the College of William and Mary. But the advent of the Revolution soon interrupted his academic career, and at the age of eighteen, after some service as a cadet, he enlisted as a lieutenant in a Virginia regiment of the Continental line. He was present at the battles of Harlem, White Plains, and Trenton; in the last engagement he bore a rather conspicuous part and received a wound in the shoulder. In the campaigns of 1777 and 1778 he served as aide to the Earl of Stirling, with the rank of major, and saw further fighting at the Brandywine, Germantown, and Monmouth. By his promotion, however, he had lost his place in the Continental line, and, although he had aroused the friendly interest of Washington, he found it impossible to secure a suitable military position in the service of his state. Acting in part upon the advice of his uncle, Judge Joseph Jones [*q.v.*], in 1780 he formed a connection as a student of law with Thomas Jefferson, then governor of Virginia, that continued until 1783. The close friendship of the two men endured until the death of the elder in 1826.

In 1782 Monroe was elected to the Virginia legislature and in 1783 to the Congress of the Confederation, where he served until 1786. In the latter body he played a by no means inconspicuous rôle. He had begun to see the necessity of some political mechanism stronger than that set up by the Articles, but his caution, his strong localism, and his fear of centralization, made him espouse a very moderate course. He favored an amendment which would permit the Congress to regulate commerce, but which would leave the imposts to be collected under the authority of the individual states, and to be spent by the state authorities. Even this modest proposal, which he reported to the Congress on Mar. 28, 1785, he did not press vigorously. He made two trips into the western country, in 1784 and 1785, and in the Congress strongly opposed John Jay's negotiations with Gardoqui, which looked to a commercial treaty with Spain and involved the dropping of the claim to the free navigation of the Mississippi. The youthful delegate was not a dominating influence, however, in the great legislation of 1784 and 1785 for the organization of the West. It is difficult to determine his attitude with regard to slavery in these newly organized regions, but he was twice absent from a vote on the question, and in the last of these instances, had he been present, his action might have been decisive in barring slavery from all of Transappalachia. He at least showed no zeal for a policy of restriction.

Monroe was present at the famous Annapolis conference of 1786, but he was not a delegate to the great convention of 1787. His term in the Congress of the Confederation having expired, he returned to the Virginia legislature. He was, however, elected to the state convention called to ratify the Constitution in 1788. He maintained a cautious and neutral policy before his election, but in the convention aligned himself with the opponents of the Constitution. He based his opposition largely upon the tendency towards centralization which he believed to be involved. But the real explanation of his conservative stand seems to have lain in the sentiment of the district he represented, and in his strong sectional feeling. He had been jealous and alarmed all through Jay's negotiations with Gardoqui; and he did not hesitate to assail Jay's policy before the convention and to express his fears lest the federal government, if strengthened, would give up the American claim to the navigation of the Mississippi. That his attitude in this matter was not without influence may be inferred from the fact that of the members of the convention from the Kentucky districts ten out of fourteen voted against ratification (H. B. Grigsby, *The History of the Virginia Federal Convention of 1788*, 2 vols., 1890–91). The final vote was a close one, 79 to 89. Monroe accepted the result, and in the fall of the year he was a candidate against Madison for election to the First Congress. In this election he was badly beaten. In 1790, however, there occurred a vacancy in the Senate of the United States, and the choice fell upon Monroe. His friendship with Jefferson had now become closer than ever; in 1788, indeed, he had moved very near to "Monticello." From the beginning of his service he was severely critical of the Washington administration. He participated little in debate, but opposed the establishment of the Bank of the United States, the selection of Gouverneur Morris as minister to France, and, later, that of John Jay as minister to Great Britain. He was one of the senatorial committee which investigated in 1792 the charges against Alexander Hamilton's handling of the public funds, in the course of which the Secretary of the Treasury was compelled to lay bare his relations with Mrs. Reynolds. Monroe remained in possession of the papers and, before his departure for France, deposited them with a friend, "a respectable character in Virginia," in whose hands they still were in 1797. He disclaimed any agency in or knowledge of their publication that year by the unscrupulous James Thomson Callender [*q.v.*], leading to the publication by Hamilton himself of the famous Reynolds pamphlet (H. C. Lodge, *The Works of Alexander Hamilton*, VI, 1886, pp. 449–535). Monroe was

rather evasive in his comments on the bitterly partisan affair and the full circumstances are still shrouded in considerable mystery; but the fact that the papers saw the light of day, if it does not reflect upon his sense of honor, as Hamilton's defenders have claimed, reflects at least upon his discretion, or that of his unnamed friend.

Monroe's senatorial service was cut short by his appointment as minister to France in June 1794. The task which now confronted him involved great difficulties from the beginning. The French government was naturally suspicious and apprehensive with regard to the Jay mission to England; it was the task of the American minister to quiet these suspicions, if possible, to bring about cordial relationships, and to secure redress for French interference with American commerce and hardships suffered by American citizens. Under the circumstances, perhaps no one could have completely succeeded; but Monroe, in his efforts to command French esteem and secure French cooperation, and moved by his own decided sympathies, pursued a course by no means in accord with the desires of the State Department. On his arrival in France, he sought to be received by the National Convention, and made a speech before that body "the extreme glow" of which later brought him a reproof from Edmund Randolph, the secretary of state (*American State Papers, Foreign Relations*, I, 1832, p. 690). The negotiations with Great Britain seriously embarrassed him, and he was very much displeased with their result. Indeed, he neglected to defend the Jay treaty, finally signed in November 1794, though furnished by the State Department with arguments in partial justification of that document. Though at the outset relatively successful in securing redress for grievances, he soon suffered from what the French considered as the Anglophile policy of the American administration, and during his last year in France he satisfied neither the authorities in Paris nor those at home. He was recalled in 1796 by Randolph's successor, Pickering, and on his return published a vindication of his mission, entitled *A View of the Conduct of the Executive, in the Foreign Affairs of the United States* (1797). In this document wounded pride reveals itself side by side with political ambition and strong partisanship.

Monroe's defeats and discomfitures never shook the confidence of his Virginia supporters. In 1799 he became governor of the state, and held this post until December 1802. Early in 1803 President Jefferson sent him to France to cooperate with Robert R. Livingston [*q.v.*] in the negotiation of a treaty which should secure western interest in the free navigation of the Mississippi. Before the Virginian arrived in Paris, the astonished Livingston had been proffered the whole vast territory ceded to France by Spain and had virtually signified his willingness to negotiate on this basis. In the details of the discussion, however, the new envoy played a part, and from the beginning he was strongly in favor of taking advantage of the French offer. The treaty which resulted contained some ambiguities which were to lead to further negotiations with Spain. In particular, the title to West Florida was left ill-defined. In 1804 Monroe was instructed to proceed to Madrid to negotiate with Charles Pinckney with regard to this matter, and to secure the cession of the eastern portion of the Floridas, either by purchase, or as a setoff against American claims. His treatment by the Spanish government was anything but courteous, and, after months of arduous correspondence and patient waiting, he was compelled to leave Madrid. Once again he had been given an almost impossible task. His diplomatic notes of this period, however, make a favorable impression, revealing his grasp of the subject with which he was instructed to deal.

Monroe's next task, again an extremely difficult one, was to attempt to settle the vexing disputes which had arisen between the United States and Great Britain. In 1805 he proceeded to London. Apparently acting under political pressure, President Jefferson associated with him in this negotiation William Pinkney [q.v.] who commanded to a greater degree the confidence of the Anglophile elements in the United States. The two men carried on long negotiations, and concluded a treaty with the British ministry in December 1806. Monroe had been instructed to secure cessation of the practice of impressments, but he was obliged to content himself with a declaration by the British government that in exercising that "right" the utmost care would be used to avoid injury or molestation of American citizens. In the *Essex* case the British courts had declared that neutral trade between the French and Spanish colonies and their mother countries was prohibited, even when the goods were actually landed in the United States. Monroe secured a concession providing that if such goods paid a small duty in the United States, they might be re-exported. He also secured certain commercial concessions. At the last moment the British ministry made the acceptance of the treaty contingent upon the assurance of the American government that it would not submit to Napoleon's interference with neutral trade. The treaty was deemed so unsatisfactory by Jefferson and Madison that it was never submitted to the Senate. Indeed, it can hardly be said to have been in any sense superior to the Jay compact of which Monroe had been so severely critical eleven years before.

Whether or not presidential ambitions and the desire to gain Federalist votes motivated Monroe in signing a treaty so favorable to the British (Henry Adams, *History of the United States,* III, 413), he certainly came home in an aggrieved mood, and he permitted his friends to groom him for the presidential race. John Randolph, John Taylor of Caroline, and Littleton Waller Tazewell were among his supporters. In the summer of 1808 Monroe was writing directions for the campaign, and in October still hoped for success. As a matter of fact, he was decisively defeated, receiving in Virginia hardly a fifth of the vote of Madison, and not a single vote in the electoral college. He had not identified himself with the virulent opposition group headed by Randolph, nor had he himself criticized the administration. He continued to pursue this course after Madison's election, arguing that the Republican party must not be split into factions by any act of his. In November 1809, through the good offices of Jefferson, he was offered by Madison the governorship of Upper Louisiana. This post he refused, but he made it clear that he would not be averse to a reconciliation on what he considered proper terms. In the fall of 1810 he was reëlected to the Virginia legislature, and in January 1811 again became governor. In the meantime, factional politics had compelled Madison to remodel his administration. Monroe had political influence in Virginia which was badly needed. In March 1811, therefore, the President offered his former friend and associate the post of secretary of state, and Monroe accepted.

Monroe took office on the theory that he was to have a free hand, and that he would be able to solve the knotty problems raised by American neutrality in the European wars, and particularly to bring about a reconciliation with Great Britain. Just before he entered office, Congress had proclaimed non-intercourse with Great Britain, and the elections of 1810 had been highly unfavorable to any prospect of accord. None the less, he entered into negotiations with Foster, the newly arrived British minister, in July, apparently still hopeful of accommodation. He was doomed to disappointment. The British minister refused to consider the possibility of repealing the Orders in Council, contending, quite correctly, that the United States had not made its views respected by France, and that until it did so, there was little use in asking concessions from the government in London. By December Monroe seems to have been convinced that war must result. Subsequent negotiations, and the British Order in Council of Apr. 12, 1812, only deepened this impression. When, in June, war was actually declared, it apparently was Monroe who prepared the report of the House of Representatives, presented by Calhoun, on which the action was based (W. M. Meigs, *The Life of John Caldwell Calhoun,* 1917, I, 131; *American Historical Review,* Jan. 1908, pp. 303–10).

In this period of his incumbency of the State Department Monroe was in a measure involved in an episode not wholly to his credit. A strong sentiment existed in the South looking to the acquisition of East Florida. Congress indeed authorized taking possession of the province if its possession were threatened by another power. But there were those who were unwilling to wait for any such contingency. General George Mathews [*q.v.*], former governor of Georgia, visited Washington and talked with Madison in the summer of 1811. He also wrote twice to Monroe explaining the situation. The Secretary of State must have understood that what was in the wind was an attempt to revolutionize West Florida. He answered not a word, however, and Mathews went ahead with his plans, and in March 1812, carried out the projected coup. But his band of "patriots" met with considerable resistance, and Monroe was compelled to disavow his activities. The troops who had crossed over into East Florida, however, were withdrawn only after a congressional vote virtually compelled such action in May 1813.

Despite the withdrawal by the British of the obnoxious Orders in Council, Monroe continued to justify the war on other grounds, notably that of impressments. But he stood with Madison in accepting Russian mediation in March 1813, and he deserves part of the credit for the selection of the very able delegation which was sent to negotiate the peace. He had little influence upon the course of negotiations. He was compelled to forego his hope of securing from Great Britain recognition of American claims to Florida, and he was also obliged to abandon the ground which he took at the beginning with regard to impressments. But he accepted apparently without regret the treaty negotiated at Ghent. Throughout the war Monroe had strong presidential ambitions. He sought at various times to secure military command, and was intensely jealous of John Armstrong, who, in 1813, became secretary of war. After the defeat at Bladensburg in August 1814, Madison, at his insistence, dismissed Armstrong, and the Secretary of State became

also secretary of war, a post which he held until Mar. 1. In his discharge of these duties he exercised more energy and resolution than either of his predecessors. The military events of the fall of 1815, the victory at Plattsburg, and the still greater victory at New Orleans, doubtless did much to enhance Monroe's prestige. He was by now definitely in line for the presidency, yet in the congressional caucus of 1816, with the support of the administration behind him, he won by only eleven votes over his rival, William H. Crawford.

Monroe had been in his early years strongly sectional, narrowly partisan, and perhaps a little too ambitious. His diplomatic achievements, taken as a whole, had been anything but brilliant. Yet he had never ceased to command the loyalty of an influential following in Virginia, and after each defeat he had come back stronger than ever, and with his desire for high office unimpaired. He had now reached the summit of his ambition, and in the presidency he was to exhibit a capacity for administration and for the accurate interpretation of the mood of the country which compels respect. In the field of domestic politics few great issues confronted the administration in its eight years of office. On the important question of internal improvements, Monroe began by adopting the conservative course which had been followed by his predecessor. In his first annual message he declared his belief that the Constitution did not empower Congress to establish a system of internal improvements, and recommended an amendment to confer that power. In the course of time his views underwent some modification. In 1822 he vetoed a bill authorizing the erection of tollhouses, gates, and turnpikes on the Cumberland Road, but accompanied his veto message with one of the most formidable state papers on record, "Views on the Subject of Internal Improvements" (*Writings,* VI, 216–84). In this document, while denying to the federal government the right of jurisdiction and construction, he declared that Congress had unlimited power to raise money, "restricted only by the duty to appropriate it to purposes of common defense and of general, not local, national, not State, benefit" (*Ibid.,* VI, 265–66). This middle-of-the-road point of view, entirely characteristic of Monroe, opened the way for an act in 1823 appropriating money for the repair of the Cumberland Road, and for the passage of the first harbor act. In 1824 the President put his signature to the so-called Survey Act, which laid out an elaborate program of internal improvements for the future. He departed again from the strict constructionist point of view when he gave his approval to the tariff bill of the same year.

More important than the question of internal improvement was that of slavery, as it shaped itself in 1819 and 1820 in the struggle over the admission of Missouri. On this issue Monroe's sympathies were naturally with the South, while his conception of his presidential duties led him to abstain from all interference with the struggle over the Missouri bill until it came to him for signature. It is known, however, that he would have refused to sign any bill admitting Missouri "subject to restraint" (*Congressional Globe,* 30 Cong., 2 Sess., Appendix, p. 67). The measure which came to him provided for the admission of Missouri as a slave state, but prohibited slavery north of 36° 30' in the future. He was by no means sure that Congress had the constitutional power to exclude slavery from states formed in the future within this territory, and submitted the question to the cabinet, most of whose members shared his doubts. He finally decided, however, to permit this question to remain unsettled, and signed the measure, no doubt the most momentous of his administration.

At the very outset of his administration Monroe made a journey through the northeastern states. This kind of royal progress naturally came in for some criticism, but it seems to have accomplished useful results, and on the whole enhanced his popularity. A second tour through the South and Southwest followed. Despite the economic depression of 1819, Monroe received in 1820 the tribute of a virtually unanimous reëlection to the presidency. Only one vote was cast against him in the electoral college. He had interpreted with a good deal of accuracy the mood of the country; and he had given evidence that his point of view was no longer sectional, as in his early years. He had gathered about himself a group of excellent advisers. Calhoun was a vigorous and effective secretary of war. Wirt, the attorney-general, was one of the ablest lawyers of his day. Crawford, the secretary of the treasury, was highly regarded in his own time. And above all, the President recognized capacity and rose above sectional predilections in his appointment of John Quincy Adams as secretary of state. No choice for that great office has ever been a happier one, and the large discretion which Monroe left to Adams, while yet maintaining a supervision over foreign affairs, is highly creditable to him.

In the field of foreign politics a considerable number of important issues confronted the Monroe administration. Some of them were matters which had already been under discussion during his term as secretary of state. The great agree-

ment for the limitation of armaments on the Great Lakes had been discussed as early as the summer of 1818. The Newfoundland and Labrador fisheries dispute had also been a subject of consideration for some time when it was liquidated by the convention of 1818. The vexed question of the Northwest was temporarily settled by the principle of joint-occupation. More important was the question of the acquisition of Florida, which Monroe had attempted to broach both at Madrid and at Washington before he became president. Negotiations with Spain, vigorously pursued by Adams, were proceeding favorably when, in April 1818, General Andrew Jackson invaded Florida. Jackson claimed to have written to the President and received encouragement to go ahead. It seems more probable that Monroe, in this as in a former instance, maintained a silence that was somewhat equivocal. At any rate, the incident once having occurred, he was at first inclined to disavow the impetuous military leader, but was dissuaded by Adams. The conversations were resumed, and a treaty was signed on Feb. 22, 1819, and ratified after long delay two years later.

Meanwhile, the former Spanish colonies were clamoring for recognition of their independence, their cause being supported in the House of Representatives by Henry Clay. Monroe had received Mexican agents as early as 1811, and perhaps had even promised them a measure of aid (I. J. Cox, in *Annual Report of the American Historical Association for the Year 1911,* 1913, pp. 199–215); one of his first acts in the presidency was the sending of special agents to Latin-America. He was held in check by Adams, but recognition seemed imminent in the early winter of 1819. The Florida negotiations, however, provided a strong argument for delay and action was not taken until March 1822. Characteristically, even at this late date, Monroe sought to associate Congress with him in this step by the message of Mar. 8, 1822. Out of the recognition of the Spanish colonies grew the events leading up to the famous message of Dec. 2, 1823, enunciating what has come to be known as the Monroe Doctrine. In the fall of 1823, the administration received information from Richard Rush, minister to England, which led to the belief that the Continental powers contemplated the reconquest of Spain's former colonies, and their restitution to the mother country. The language of the Russian minister, Baron Tuyll, encouraged a similar hypothesis. Long cabinet discussions followed, in which the vigorous Adams played an undeniably influential and important part. But it was, almost beyond peradventure, Monroe who thought of dealing with the Spanish colonial question in his forthcoming message to Congress, and who drafted the famous paragraphs dealing with this problem. The clear-cut differentiation between Old World and New World politics may have been due in some measure to the Secretary of State, for the President wished to include a recommendation for the recognition of Greece, and a denunciation of the course of the Allied governments in sanctioning intervention in Spain. But both the initiative and the responsibility for the famous declaration belong to Monroe. On the other hand, the well-known principle that the American continents are no longer subject to European colonization, a principle enunciated in the negotiations with Russia over the northwest coast, was taken over verbatim by Monroe from Adams' report to him, and clearly owes its origin to the Secretary. Thus the Doctrine, considered as a whole, may be said to owe something to both men. It is worth noting that Monroe reiterated his views on Latin-America in the message of 1824. It is also to be observed that his administration carefully avoided making any more definite commitments when invited by the Colombian government to translate the language of the message into a treaty of alliance. Monroe's relations with Adams were cordial; one discerns a genuine respect on the part of the Secretary for his Chief, and an excellent combination of tact and definite-mindedness on the part of the President in dealing with the difficult, prickly New Englander. The caustic *Memoirs* of Adams reflect a remarkably favorable judgment of Monroe.

After the expiration of his presidential term, Monroe returned to Virginia and for a time to private life. His financial affairs were much involved, and in 1826 Congress voted him $30,000 in settlement of certain claims of his against the government. In 1828 he became a visitor of the young University of Virginia. In 1829 he was elected to the Virginia constitutional convention, and became its presiding officer. In this capacity, he was aligned with the conservatives, opposing a broadening of the suffrage, along with Madison, and taking very little interest in any action on the question of slavery. In February 1786 he had married Eliza Kortright, daughter of Lawrence Kortright, a merchant of New York and a descendant of a Dutch emigrant of 1663. In the spring of 1830, after the death of his wife, his private affairs being still involved, he moved to New York City, where he took up his residence with his daughter and her husband. There he died on July 4, 1831, and there he was buried, but in 1858 his remains were removed to Richmond.

Lacking the qualities of high imagination, unpretentious in appearance, far from brilliant in speech, without any genuine graces, Monroe yet attained distinction. "Untiring application and indomitable perseverance" were a part of his character (W. C. Rives, *History of the Life and Times of James Madison*, II, 1866, p. 20). He was undiscouraged by defeat or by failure. He seems never to have lost the loyal support of his friends. The longer grew his term of public service, the wider became the circle of his admirers. Jefferson and Madison, Calhoun, Adams, and Benton, all spoke in praise of him. All alike paid tribute, moreover, to the soundness of his judgment, and while such a tribute, applied to the rising Virginia politician, seems not wholly deserved, it is difficult not to accept it with regard to his years in the presidency. By the Doctrine which bears his name, he is now indissolubly connected with one of the major dogmas of American foreign policy. While in this he promulgated nothing very novel, he consolidated and fortified existing views and gave expression to a growing popular sentiment, in striking form. No colorless personality could have left behind him so favorable a judgment on the part of so many persons of such diverse views and temperaments as did Monroe. Less intellectual than either Jefferson or Madison, he surpassed them both as an administrator. If to this fifth president of the United States can never be assigned a place among the really great men who have held that high office, he must be numbered among the more useful and the more successful.

He was above the medium height, his mouth was rather large, his nose was well-shaped, his forehead was broad, and his eyes were blue-gray. His countenance was rather unexpressive in repose, and his manners were simple.

[Probably the best-known portrait of Monroe, by John Vanderlyn, is in the N. Y. City Hall; a portrait by Rembrandt Peale is owned by J. F. Lewis; one by Sully is at West Point. The most important collection of papers is in the Lib. of Cong., but the N. Y. Pub. Lib. has a considerable collection. Calendars are: Dept. of State, Bureau of Rolls and Library, *Calendar of the Correspondence of James Monroe* (1893); Lib. of Cong., Division of MSS., *Papers of James Monroe* (1904). S. M. Hamilton, *The Writings of James Monroe* (7 vols., 1898–1903), while by no means complete, is of very great value. Some of his letters are in the *Proc. of the Mass. Hist. Soc.*, vol. XLII (1909), and in the *Bulletin of the N. Y. Pub. Lib.*, Feb. 1900, Sept., Nov. 1901, June, July 1902. Much of his diplomatic correspondence, in the files of the Dept. of State, has been published in *Am. State Papers, Foreign Relations*, vol. III (1832).

There is no good general biography. D. C. Gilman, *James Monroe* (1883) is an interesting interpretation, but hardly complete or free from the note of eulogy. George Morgan, *The Life of James Monroe* (1921), is entertainingly written, but cannot be said to furnish a satisfactory picture, or to deal adequately with the more important problems. It is marred, too, by the tendency to justify Monroe's action at every turn. Among books dealing with particular aspects of his career, mention must be made of B. W. Bond, *The Monroe Mission to France* (Johns Hopkins Studies in Hist. and Pol. Science, ser. 25, nos. 2 and 3, 1907); the remarkable chapters in Henry Adams, *Hist. of the U. S.* (9 vols., 1890–91), invaluable for the Louisiana purchase, and the missions to Spain and Great Britain, though none too sympathetic with Monroe; and S. F. Bemis, ed., *The Am. Secretaries of State and their Diplomacy*, vol. III (1927), which contains a highly discriminating account of Monroe's career as secretary of state by Julius W. Pratt. For the period of the presidency, there is little of value on the side of domestic affairs, viewing the matter from Monroe's personal point of view, but on the side of foreign policy attention is paid to the rôle of the president in the account of John Quincy Adams' secretariat in *The Am. Secretaries of State and their Diplomacy*, vol. IV (1928), by Dexter Perkins; the rôle of the chief executive and of his principal adviser in the enunciation of the Monroe Doctrine has been treated by W. C. Ford in two articles, "John Quincy Adams and The Monroe Doctrine," in the *Am. Hist. Rev.*, July, Oct. 1902, and from a point of view more favorable to Monroe in Dexter Perkins, *The Monroe Doctrine, 1823–26* (1927). Further bibliographical data may be found in Gilman.]   D. P—s.

MONTAGUE, HENRY JAMES (Jan. 20, 1843–Aug. 11, 1878), actor, appears from records that are none too authentic to have been born in a Staffordshire village on the date here given, and to have been the son of an Anglican clergyman. His real name was Mann. His age at the time of his death, the date of which is undisputed, is given on the monument erected to his memory by Lester Wallack in Greenwood Cemetery, Brooklyn, as twenty-seven, but this is obviously inaccurate, since there are reliable records of his appearances in important characters in the London theatres as early as 1863. His first connection with the stage was probably in a secretarial capacity in London with Dion Boucicault, and for about ten years thereafter he was acting continuously at the St. James's, Princess, Vaudeville, Globe and other theatres, in such rôles as Lord Beaufoy in *School,* Charles Courtly in *London Assurance,* Claude Melnotte in *The Lady of Lyons,* and Careless in *The School for Scandal.* He came to the United States in 1874 and appeared here for the first time in Wallack's Theatre, New York, Oct. 6, as Tom Gilroy in *Partners for Life,* becoming an immediate favorite, especially with the feminine portion of theatre audiences, not so much for the quality of his acting, which· was of the conventional leading-man type, as for his striking face and figure, his graceful manner, his personal magnetism, and his ability to look the parts assigned to him without the addition or disguise of make-up. He was associated with Lester Wallack in that actor-manager's New York theatre, and on tour, throughout his entire American career, which continued less than four years. His appearance and technical skill confined him mainly to plays

of his own period, although on occasion he played such rôles as Gratiano in *The Merchant of Venice,* for which, says William Winter, he lacked animal spirits and dash, and also Harry Dornton in *The Road to Ruin* and Captain Dudley Smooth in *Money.* Winter sums him up definitely when he says that he "endeared himself by what he was rather than by what he did" (*Brief Chronicles,* p. 218). Among the impersonations by which he was best known in modern plays were Manuel in *The Romance of a Poor Young Man,* Julian Beauclerc in *Diplomacy,* Captain Molyneux in *The Shaughraun,* Captain D'Alroy in *Caste,* Arthur in *False Shame,* and Tom Dexter in *The Overland Route.* His health was failing during his last months on the stage, and going to San Francisco to play an engagement of four weeks at the California Theatre, he died suddenly of hemorrhage of the lungs. Funeral services were held both in San Francisco, and in New York at the Little Church Around the Corner, where a memorial window was later erected to his memory.

[Montague's career in England is well treated in the sketch of him in the *Dict. Nat. Biog.* See also: Wm. Winter, *Brief Chronicles* (1889), and *Vagrant Memories* (1915); Clement Scott and Cecil Howard, *The Life and Reminiscences of E. L. Blanchard* (2 vols., 1891); T. A. Brown, *A Hist. of the N. Y. Stage* (1903), vols. II and III; Lester Wallack, *Memories of Fifty Years* (1889); Marie and Squire Bancroft, *The Bancrofts: Recollections of Sixty Years* (1909); *Mail and Express: Illustrated Saturday Mag.,* Nov. 12, 1898; *Frank Leslie's Illustrated Family Almanac,* 1879; *N. Y. Times,* Aug. 13, 20, 1878. His name is given in some sources as Henry John Montague.]   E. F. E.

MONTEFIORE, JOSHUA (Aug. 7, 1762–June 26, 1843), lawyer, soldier, and author, was born in London, England, the sixth son in a family of seventeen. His father, Moses Haim (or Vita) Montefiore, had emigrated in 1758 from Leghorn, Italy, where his ancestors had been merchants of standing in the Jewish community. There Moses had been married to Ester Hannah Racah, daughter of a Moorish merchant. Most of the children of this union became identified with mercantile enterprises in various quarters of the globe. Joshua's roystering and free-hearted disposition unfitted him for a one-track life, and his career, though less prosperous, was much more colorful. At eighteen he began the study of law and in 1784 he was admitted as an attorney and a solicitor in chancery by Sir William Scott. Late in 1791 a group of naval officers and London merchants formed a society for the colonization of the island of Bulama, on the African coast near Sierra Leone. Moses Ximenes, a prominent Jew, was a director in the enterprise, and Montefiore became a subscriber. When in the spring of 1792 the 275 colonists set sail, Montefiore and his wife were members of the party. From the start the expedition was ill-starred. Disease and lack of discipline brought the colonists to their destination in bad humor. A hasty occupation of the island without negotiating with the natives for its purchase led to a raid in which lives were lost and many prisoners captured. Montefiore advocated a policy of negotiation and purchase and took an active part in the defense of the party. Having fallen ill, he was discharged at his own request in June 1792. Thereafter he traveled for a time among the tribes in Sierra Leone, and then returned home.

In 1794 Montefiore published a tract entitled *An Authentic Account of the late Expedition to Bulam, on the Coast of Africa; with a Description of the Present Settlement of Sierra Leone, and the Adjacent Country.* The bulk of his published writings, however, concerned his legal interests. These included a commercial dictionary, compendiums of mercantile and commercial law, and copyright law, and traders' manuals. They gave in convenient form extracts from tariffs and other commercial regulations, notes on judicial opinions, and short articles on commercial law. Since they were principally of contemporary importance, they were in time out-dated and superseded.

From Montefiore's family Bible, which besides being his spiritual guide was also his note book, it appears that "on the 3rd March, 1803, he was, by order of King George III, presented by Lord Boston to His Majesty," and that he was offered and declined the order of knighthood. He did seek a commission in the army, and is said to have been the first of his race to have this mark of favor. The *Army List* shows that he was paymaster of the York Light Infantry Volunteers from about 1807 to Jan. 30, 1812. During this service he was present at the taking of Martinique and Guadeloupe. On resigning from the army he emigrated to America where he practised law and published other volumes on commercial law. One characteristic of the author was his propensity for dedicating his works to various eminent judges. Eventually he settled at St. Albans, Vt. In his seventy-third year he was married a second time, and at his death eight years later left a family of seven children by this marriage. On his death bed he wrote from memory a translation of the Hebrew burial service. This was read as he had wished, and he was buried in his garden at St. Albans.

[*Jewish World*, Supp., Oct. 31, 1884; Philip Beaver, *African Memoranda* (London, 1805); W. H. Smyth, *The Life and Services of Capt. Philip Beaver* (London, 1829); Lucien Wolf, *Sir Moses Montefiore* (1884); Paul Goodman, *Moses Montefiore* (1925), p. 228; the *Vt. Chronicle* (Windsor), July 5, 1843.]
C. F.

MONTGOMERY, DAVID HENRY (Apr. 7, 1837–May 28, 1928), textbook writer, was born at Syracuse, N. Y., the only child of David and Sarah (Prescott) Montgomery. His father was a law partner of the first mayor of the city. Left an orphan at the age of seven, he lived with relatives until he went West and became a ranchman. He was at Brown for three years in the class of 1861, and gained some recognition there as a debater. After completing the course at the Harvard Divinity School (1863) he held Massachusetts pastorates at Leicester and West Bridgewater. He was not fitted by temperament to cope with church administration, and in 1880 he went to England. From unsuccessful business experiences there he returned in 1884 in poverty. John J. May of Boston gave him a desk in his office, and in gratitude Montgomery prepared an elementary history for May's grandchildren. This book, *Leading Facts of English History* (1886), was designed to illustrate, as he said, the great law of national growth in the light thrown upon it by the foremost English historians. On publication by Ginn & Company, it was immediately popular. A life of Franklin, the autobiography supplemented by the story carried on from 1757 to 1790, followed in 1888. *The Leading Facts of French History* (1889) was similar in treatment to the English history, and was likewise well supplemented with maps, chronological tables, and indexes. It has been said that several thousand copies were read by American soldiers in France during the World War. *The Leading Facts of American History* was published in 1890, followed in 1892 by *The Beginner's American History,* of which an edition in Spanish was published in 1901. *The Student's American History* (1897), enlarged from *The Leading Facts of American History* was one of the best textbooks of the period and was widely adopted. It contained maps, as well as illustrations of old letters and documents, and an appendix containing the Constitution and Declaration of Independence, useful tables, and a bibliography. His final work was *An Elementary American History* (1904), designed "to appeal to the eye as well as to the understanding."

Montgomery's works received constant revision. He would spend weeks in study, the only visible result of which would be a change in a shade of meaning. On one occasion, to insure the destruction of the electrotype plates of a superseded edition, he carried a hatchet to the press and demolished the old plates himself. Over nine million copies of his textbooks have been sold. He also published for school use editions of several literary classics. He was fond of travel and spent some fifteen years in England, often quoting Dr. Johnson's words: "He who gets tired of London gets tired of life." As he declined in health he rarely left his residence at 50 Frost Street, Cambridge, where he had surrounded himself with books, pictures, tapestries, statuary, and maps. He married Delia A. Bowman, daughter of Francis Bowman, of Cambridge, on Dec. 10, 1867, a woman of culture and some literary ability. She died in 1908, leaving a son. Harvard College, the Cambridge Hospital, and the Boston Athenæum were remembered generously in Montgomery's will. His copyrights went by gift to the College.

[Sources include: records of Harvard and Brown Universities; Montgomery's letters to C. N. Baxter and Linda F. Wildman at the Boston Athenæum; C. H. Thurber's memoir in *Intramural Stuff*, Ginn & Company leaflet for June 8, 1928; law files of James E. Kelley of Boston; recollections of Mrs. Fanny Knapp Palmer, of Oneida, N. Y., E. K. Robinson, Le Roy Phillips of Boston; librarian's report, Boston Athenæum, for 1930; *Boston Transcript*, May 31, 1928. Reviews of some of Montgomery's works may be found in the *Jour. of Educ.*, May 4, 1886, May 9, 1889; and in the *Am. Hist. Rev.*, Apr. 1898, July 1910.]

C. K. B.

MONTGOMERY, EDMUND DUNCAN (Mar. 19, 1835–Apr. 17, 1911), philosopher, was born in Edinburgh, Scotland, and died at "Liendo," his plantation near Hempstead, Tex. He was the natural son of Isabella Davidson Montgomery and Duncan MacNeill, later Baron Colonsay and Oronsay, an eminent Scottish jurist who rose to the position of lord justice-general in 1852. At the time of Montgomery's birth, his father was solicitor-general for Scotland in Peel's first administration. When but four years old the boy was taken to Paris, remaining there until 1844, when his mother took him to Frankfort. There he lived until 1852, in which year he matriculated as a student of medicine at Heidelberg. From his student notebooks of his Gymnasium days it is evident that he was unusually gifted in languages, science, and mathematics. According to contemporary testimony he was the most popular boy in his school, and it appeared that he would surpass his father, who had obtained the degree of M.D. at St. Andrews and a "first" in mathematics at Edinburgh. In his fourteenth year, however, an event occurred which was destined for many years to cast a shadow on his life. He refused to be confirmed, after having gone through the preliminary training, and was ostracized. Years after

the event Montgomery wrote that at this time he was driven by loneliness and religious perplexity almost to the point of suicide.

In 1848 Montgomery, still a boy, participated in the revolution at Frankfort to the extent of helping to build barricades. In 1850 he frequently saw Schopenhauer. During the years from 1852 to 1858 he studied at various German and Austrian universities (Heidelberg, 1852–54; Berlin, 1855; Bonn, 1856; Würzburg, 1857; and possibly Prague in 1858 and Vienna in 1859). He claimed for himself a degree in medicine, but the records of the universities that he attended yield no evidence to support his assertion. At Heidelberg he was a friend of Moleschott and Kuno Fischer, and at Bonn he was a pupil of Helmholz. He returned to England and became resident physician at the German Hospital (1860–61), Bermondsey Dispensary (1861–62), and demonstrator of morbid anatomy at St. Thomas' Hospital in London (1861–63). For some reason, possibly a tubercular infection, but more probably the discovery of his imposture, he left St. Thomas' and went to Madeira. It was here, Nov. 17, 1863, at the office of the British consul, that he married Elisabet Ney [*q.v.*], whom he had first met and loved while he was a student of medicine at Heidelberg. During the years 1863–69 he practised medicine at Madeira, Mentone, and Rome. In 1869 he retired from medical practice and in 1870 came to America.

The first two years of their residence in America Montgomery and his wife spent in a colony near Thomasville, Ga., devoted to the reclamation of the negro. The colony failed to advance its aims, and in 1872 they removed to Hempstead, Tex. "Liendo" was purchased in 1873. Here, isolated from the world, Montgomery for several years (1873–79) continued intensive researches on the nature of protoplasm which he had begun during his London days (*vide* his *On the Formation of So-Called Cells in Animal Bodies*, London, 1867). The fruits of his biological studies in Texas appeared in a number of papers published in the *Popular Science Monthly* (September, October 1878), *St. Thomas' Hospital Report* (1879), the *Index* (Dec. 25, 1884), *Jenaische Zeitschrift für Naturwissenschaft* (vol. XVIII, 1882), *Archiv für die gesammte Physiologie* (vol. XXV, 1881), and in a final monograph, *The Vitality and Organization of Protoplasm*, an octavo pamphlet of 83 pages, published independently in 1904. In these papers he maintained what may be called a neo-vitalistic point of view in contrast with the materialism current in his day. At the same time (1878–87), in *Mind, Index*, the *Journal of Spec-*

ulative Philosophy, New Ideal, the *International Journal of Ethics,* the *Monist, New Occasions,* and *Open Court,* he published an imposing series of philosophical articles preliminary to his *magnum opus, Philosophical Problems in the Light of Vital Organization* (1907).

Montgomery in his philosophical position is undoubtedly monistic, but his monism is of a double-aspect type, corresponding to that of Clifford and Hoffding. To him the fundamental philosophical problem was that of the mind-body relation. The principal effort of his thought was "to show, that the two disparate modes of existence, known to us under the name of body and mind, have a common origin in one and the same underlying reality" (*Open Court,* Aug. 21, 1890, p. 2462). He was firmly convinced that this and related problems must be solved by the scientific discovery and demonstration of a unitary substance in the very nature of which inhere the two contradictory attributes of permanence and change. His biological researches convinced him that living protoplasm was such a substance. On this same basis he concluded that nature is wholly teleological. Its highest achievement is human personality (*Index,* Oct. 9, 1884, p. 173), and his ethical theory, which is unique, is based upon this conception. His monism is likewise strikingly similar to that of Bergson, but to him the fundamental reality is not *élan vital,* but living substance. In his concept of the origin and nature of life he anticipated in detail that of the great biochemist, Benjamin Moore (*Problems of Philosophy in the Light of Vital Organization,* 1913, p. 300). He accounted for the appearance of novelties in the evolutionary series by a formulation strikingly anticipatory of the later theory of "emergent evolution."

In intellectual quality and personal appearance Montgomery resembled his father to an unusual degree. His photograph bears a most striking resemblance to Thomas Duncan's portrait of Duncan MacNeill in the National Portrait Gallery in Edinburgh. He was a gracious and outstandingly attractive person. The unfortunate circumstances of his birth, and complications rising out of his marriage with Elisabet Ney combined to make him an aloof figure. Yet he received from his contemporaries a degree of recognition of his ability. (See *Open Court,* Mar. 31, 1887, pp. 103–07, and the papers by Salter and Lane, cited below.) Following close upon the death, in June 1907, of Elisabet Ney, Montgomery sustained an apoplectic attack, and after a period of paralysis lasting over three years, died.

[*Proc. Forty-fourth Ann. Meeting, Free Religious Asso.* (1911); W. M. Salter, "A New Type of Naturalism—Montgomery," *Internat. Jour. Ethics,* Oct. 1908; C. A. Lane, "Edmund Montgomery," *Monist,* Oct. 1909; I. K. Stephens, "Edmund Montgomery, the Hermit Philosopher of Liendo Plantation," *Southwest Rev.,* Jan. 1931; Bride Neill Taylor, *Elisabet Ney, Sculptor* (1916), uncritical and one-sided; Eugen Müller-Münster, *Elisabeth Ney, die seltsamen Lebensschicksale der Elisabeth Ney und des Edmund Montgomery, 1833–1907* (1931); Montgomery's library, with a complete set of his numerous publications in the Library of Southern Methodist University.]
S. W. G.

MONTGOMERY, GEORGE WASHINGTON (1804–June 5, 1841), translator, diplomat, son of John Montgomery, was born in Alicante, Spain, where the father was a well-known American merchant. His mother was probably Spanish. He was educated at Exeter, in England, and returning to Spain, passed his entire life, in that country and in America, in the consular and diplomatic services of the United States. He will be remembered, however, chiefly for his definite and curious services to American literature in connection with Spain and Washington Irving.

He had been before 1826 private secretary in Madrid to the Marquis of Casa Yrujo, a friend of Irving's, but during the two years of Irving's first stay in Madrid, he was attached to the American legation, apparently as official translator. This intimacy with Irving led to his creating and publishing the first version of the writings of this author into Spanish, thus beginning a long list of translations, and laying the foundation for Irving's reputation in Spain. The first was a book, now exceedingly rare, called *Tareas de un Solitario* (1829). It included versions of "The Young Italian," "The Mutability of Literature," and "Rip Van Winkle." Called to account because the last story seemed to the Spanish censor to smack of "libel and treason against the King," Montgomery issued the book anonymously. It was remarkable for its pure and beautiful Spanish, and Longfellow introduced it into Bowdoin College for use in his classes. Its interest lies, however, in its sympathetic interpretation to the Spaniards of Irving's romantic themes. In 1831 Montgomery published his *Crónica de la Conquista de Granada,* an adaptation of Irving's book of similar title, and, in 1832, his *El Bastardo de Castilla,* an historical novel based upon the story of Bernardo del Carpio. "His Spanish works," says Obadiah Rich, the bibliographer, who also knew Montgomery in Madrid, "met with great applause in Spain, for the classical purity of their language, and have been adopted by many Spanish teachers as classbooks" (*post,* II, p. 329).

It is probable that Montgomery planned to

continue his translations of Irving and possibly of other American writers, but in December 1835 he was appointed United States consul at San Juan, Puerto Rico, and three years later he was sent from Washington to Guatemala. Afterward as consul at Tampico he incurred ill health which caused his death, at Washington, in 1841. During these last years he served intermittently in the Department of State as copier and indexer. Two years before his death appeared his *Narrative of a Journey to Guatemala*, a book reëmphasizing by its strong, clear English, Montgomery's odd but remarkable bilingual powers as an obscure man of letters.

[For a full account of Montgomery's writings see S. T. Williams, "The First Version of the Writings of Washington Irving in Spanish," in *Modern Philol.*, Nov. 1930. Briefer accounts of Montgomery occur in S. Austin Allibone, *A Critical Dict. of English Lit. and British and Am. Authors* (1870), and J. DeL. Ferguson, *Am. Lit. in Spain* (1916). Other details have been gleaned from the Ticknor Collection, in the Boston Pub. Lib.; the files of the Dept. of State, Washington; the files of the American embassy, Madrid; Obadiah Rich, *Bibliotheca Americana Nova* (London, 1846); *The Journals of Washington Irving* (1919), vol. III, ed. by W. P. Trent and G. S. Hellman; *Washington Irving Diary, 1828–29* (1926), ed. by C. L. Penny; *Daily Nat. Intelligencer* (Wash., D. C.), June 7, 10, 1841.]   S. T. W.

MONTGOMERY, JAMES (Dec. 22, 1814– Dec. 6, 1871), soldier and jayhawker, was born in Ashtabula County, Ohio, whither his parents had emigrated from New York. He was a great-grandson of James Montgomery, a Scotch Highland chieftain who came to America by way of Ireland. After receiving an academic education in Ohio, he moved to Kentucky in 1837 where he taught school and entered the ministry of the "Campbellite" church. In 1852 he emigrated with his second wife to Missouri, but soon after the passage of the Kansas-Nebraska bill he purchased a claim at Mound City, Linn County, Kan. Pro-slavery settlers were in the majority in the southeastern part of the Territory, and Montgomery soon became the recognized leader of the minority. He organized Free-State men into a "Self-Protective Company" in 1857, which drove pro-slavery advocates from the county and made predatory excursions into Missouri. He made several attempts to destroy Fort Scott, where a pro-slavery district judge pursued a policy of discrimination, and on one occasion he collided with Federal troops. Disturbances in the "infected district," some of which Montgomery created, were eventually quelled by the intervention of Governor Denver. In 1860 Montgomery and eastern associates planned to rescue two of John Brown's men imprisoned at Charles Town, Va. (now W. Va.), but the scheme did not materialize. He was

elected in 1857 to the "state" Senate under the Topeka constitution, but was defeated for the Territorial House of Representatives two years later. He represented Linn County in the Republican state convention of April 1860.

On July 24, 1861, Montgomery was commissioned colonel of the 3rd Kansas Volunteer Infantry which operated as a part of "Lane's brigade" in southeastern Kansas and western Missouri. His regiment soon gained a reputation for jayhawking or plundering. On Apr. 3, 1862, the 3rd was consolidated with other regiments to form the 10th Kansas with Montgomery colonel. Early in 1863 he was authorized to raise a colored regiment in South Carolina. From Hilton-head he made expeditions into Georgia and Florida, liberated slaves, and destroyed Confederate property. In 1864 he returned to Kansas and was chosen colonel of the 6th Militia Regiment when its commander refused to lead it against Gen. Sterling Price. As a fighter Montgomery excelled in bushwhacker tactics. With limited mental powers, he was daring and fearless, and usually fought without having formed a plan of campaign. At the close of the Civil War he retired to his farm in Linn County, abandoned the "Campbellite" faith, became a First-Day Adventist, and preached that doctrine at various places in Kansas. He died at Mound City.

[A few of Montgomery's letters are preserved in the Kan. State Hist. Lib. at Topeka. Reports of his military activities are scattered through the *Official Records*. Wm. P. Tomlinson, *Kan. in Eighteen Fifty-Eight* (1859), contains a chapter on his early Kansas career. Further sources include: A. T. Andreas, *Hist. of the State of Kan.* (1883); D. W. Wilder, *The Annals of Kan.* (1886); W. E. Connelley, *A Standard Hist. of Kan. and Kansans* (1918), vols. II and III; E. S. W. Drought, "James Montgomery," *Trans. Kan. State Hist. Soc.*, vol. VI (1900); "Col. Montgomery and His Letters," *Kan. State Hist. Soc. Colls.*, vol. XIII (1915); and scattered references in the *Transactions* and *Collections* of the State Hist. Soc.]

W. H. S—n.

MONTGOMERY, JOHN BERRIEN (Nov. 17, 1794–Mar. 25, 1873), naval officer, was born at Allentown, N. J., the son of Dr. Thomas and Mary (Berrien) Montgomery, and a descendant of William Morse Montgomery who was in East Jersey in 1702. He entered the navy as midshipman June 4, 1812, leaving home for war service along with his elder brother Alexander, a surgeon under Porter, and his younger brother Nathaniel Lawrence, who lost an arm in the *President-Belvidera* action and was made lieutenant at sixteen. John Montgomery served in the *Hamilton, Madison,* and *General Pike* on Lake Ontario, then joined Perry on Lake Erie in August 1813 and fought creditably in the *Niagara* at the Battle of Lake Erie, receiving with other officers a sword and thanks from Congress.

In the subsequent Perry-Elliott controversy, Montgomery, like most *Niagara* men, favored his ship-commander Elliott, and he served frequently under him later. In the *Niagara* he took part in the blockade and attack on Mackinac, Aug. 4, 1814. He was in the *Ontario* of Decatur's squadron against Algiers; on the African coast, 1818–20, after promotion to lieutenant; and in the *Erie* on a long Mediterranean cruise, 1821–26. In 1830 he was executive of the *Peacock,* and subsequently commanded the *Erie* on the coast of Mexico. After recruiting duty in Philadelphia and New York, 1833–35, he was executive under Elliott in the *Constitution* when she brought the American minister Livingston from France in 1835. He then returned to receiving-ship and recruiting service, with promotion to commander, 1839. In command of the *Portsmouth* of Sloat's squadron on the West Coast during the Mexican War, he raised the American flag at San Francisco and near-by settlements, July 9, 1846. The name Montgomery Street, San Francisco, commemorates the occupation. The *Portsmouth* also blockaded Mazatlan, March-April 1847, occupied several Lower California ports, and took part in the bombardment of Guaymas, October 1847.

In August 1820 Montgomery had married Mary, daughter of William Henry of New York. They had five sons and four daughters. Two sons were with him on this cruise, one an acting master and the other captain's clerk. Both mysteriously disappeared in November 1846 while in charge of a boat party taking money from the ships off San Francisco to forces ashore, circumstances indicating mutiny and the murder of the two youths. After service in the Washington Navy Yard, 1849–51, Montgomery was made captain, Jan. 6, 1853, and in the *Roanoke* brought back 250 of Walker's filibusters from Aspinwall in 1857. At the outbreak of the Civil War he was commanding the Pacific Squadron, which included four steam and two sailing ships, with the *Lancaster* as flagship. When news of war reached the *Lancaster* at Panama, Montgomery forestalled possible disturbances by requesting all officers to take the oath of allegiance, only one declining. In December 1861 he retired and went home, being promoted to commodore (retired) July 16, 1862. Thereafter he was still actively occupied as commandant of the Charlestown (Massachusetts) Navy Yard, May 1862—December 1863, and then of the Washington yard till October 1865, carrying out efficiently the important services of repair, supply, and training of men. In July 1866 he was made rear admiral (retired), and for two

years subsequently had charge at Sacketts Harbor. He was put on waiting orders, Sept. 1, 1869. His death occurred at Carlisle, Pa., and he was buried in Oak Hill Cemetery, Washington. A destroyer was named for him in 1918. He was of a modest nature, an eminently just man who made the Scriptures his daily study. No quarrels or serious mishaps marred his service career.

[T. H. Montgomery, *A Geneal. Hist. of the Family of Montgomery* (1863) ; *The Biog. Encyc. of N. J. in the Nineteenth Century* (1877) ; sketch in *Mag. of Am. Hist.,* July 1878 ; L. R. Hamersly, *The Records of Living Officers in the U. S. Navy and Marine Corps* (1870) ; *Army and Navy Jour.,* Apr. 26, 1873 ; *Evening Star* (Washington), Mar. 28, 1873.] A. W.

MONTGOMERY, RICHARD (Dec. 2, 1738–Dec. 31, 1775), soldier, was the third son of Thomas and Mary (Franklin or Franklyn) Montgomery, and a younger brother of the notorious and cruel Capt. Alexander Montgomery with whom some earlier historians confused him. He was born at Swords, County Dublin, Ireland, and educated at St. Andrews and Trinity College, Dublin. His father was a member of Parliament and he himself chose the army for a career. He was commissioned ensign in the 17th Foot, Sept. 21, 1756, and served with his regiment at the siege of Louisbourg, 1758, and in the Lake Champlain campaign in 1759. After the fall of Montreal he went with his regiment to the West Indies, where he was present at the captures of Martinique and Havana. By May 1762 he attained the rank of captain. When peace was signed in 1763 he was ordered to New York and two years later returned to England. There he became well known among prominent liberal members of Parliament who were friends of the colonies. Foreseeing no chance of military advancement in the peace, he sold out of the army, Apr. 6, 1772. For some reason, never fully determined, he appears to have felt that he had no future in England and that his friends either could not or would not help him. He wrote at this time that he had conceived a violent passion for farming, that he had no friends to advance him, that with little money he could cut no figure among "Peers, Nabobs, etc.," and that therefore he had cast his eye on America where his pride and poverty would be "much more at their ease" (*New York Genealogical and Biographical Record,* July 1871, p. 129). He was, however, by no means penniless and when he arrived in New York, in accordance with his decision to emigrate, he bought a sixty-seven-acre farm at King's Bridge. He became genuinely interested in agriculture and enjoyed rural life. On July 24, 1773, he was married to

Janet, daughter of Robert R. Livingston, 1718–1775 [*q.v.*], of New York City, and although at that time he bought other property, he spent the short remainder of his life at his wife's estate, "Grassmere," near Rhinebeck.

Montgomery's previous experiences in America, his friendship in England with such men as Burke and Fox, and his own views, all led him to adopt the colonial point of view as troubles thickened with the mother country, and although he had been in New York only three years by 1775 he was elected one of the members of the Provincial Congress. In June of that year he was appointed by the Continental Congress the second in rank of the eight brigadier-generals then designated, and with much honest regret and reluctance he accepted the appointment. It was from a sense of duty only that he left his new home and young wife and took up arms against England. He was made second in command of the expedition which was to proceed under Maj.-Gen. Philip Schuyler against Montreal. As a result of Schuyler's illness the command almost immediately devolved upon Montgomery. His troops, largely New Englanders, were poor military material. They were lacking in discipline, were constantly deserting, and at times practically mutinous. Montgomery deserves the highest praise for working them into shape for the expedition. He captured forts Chambly and St. Johns, and with the latter the first British colors, those of the 7th Fusiliers, taken in the war. Proceeding into Canada, he captured Montreal, and in December joined the forces under Benedict Arnold at Point aux Trembles. The combined forces then laid siege to Quebec. It was obvious that from lack of both morale and supplies, the American army was in no condition to maintain a winter siege. An assault was ordered and made on Dec. 31, and Montgomery was shot and killed. The English recognized his body and it was ordered "decently buried." In 1818 it was moved to St. Paul's Church, New York. Montgomery was a capable commander of high character, wholly unselfish in his adherence to the American cause. He left no children.

[There is a good biography of Montgomery in the *Dict. Nat. Biog.* A longer but less accurate account is John Armstrong's "Life of Richard Montgomery," in Jared Sparks's *Lib. of Am. Biog.*, vol. I (1834). Other sources include: T. H. Montgomery, "Ancestry of Gen. Richard Montgomery," *N. Y. Geneal. and Biog. Record*, July 1871; J. M. Le Moine, "Gen. R. Montgomery and His Detractors," *Ibid.*, Apr. 1891; N. H. E. Faucher de Saint-Maurice, *Notes pour Servir à L'Histoire du Gen. Richard Montgomery* (1893), reprinted from *Proc. and Trans. of the Royal Soc. of Canada*, vol. IX (1892); "Hist. Notes on the Defence of Quebec in 1775," *Trans. of the Lit. and Hist. Soc. of Quebec, ... 1876–77* (1877); J. H. Smith, *Our Struggle*

for the Fourteenth Colony (2 vols., 1907); John Codman, *Arnold's Expedition to Quebec* (1901); Louise L. Hunt, *Biog. Notes Concerning Gen. Richard Montgomery* (1876), reprinted in *Harper's*, Feb. 1885. The date of Montgomery's birth is given in some sources as 1736, in others as 1738. The statement that he was sixteen when he matriculated at Dublin on June 15, 1754, in G. D. Burchtaell and T. U. Sadleir, *Alumni Dublinenses* (1924), substantiates 1738.] J. T. A.

MONTGOMERY, THOMAS HARRISON (Mar. 5, 1873–Mar. 19, 1912), zoölogist and teacher, was born in New York City, a descendant of Robert Montgomery who emigrated to New Jersey in 1701. His father, Thomas Harrison Montgomery, was president of the Insurance Company of North America for twenty-three years. His mother, Anna, was the daughter of Samuel G. Morton [*q.v.*], the anthropologist. When Thomas Montgomery, Jr., was nine years of age, his family moved to the country near West Chester, Pa., and soon afterward he became interested in birds, gathered detailed notes on their habits, and made a collection of skins. He was a pupil at Dr. Worrall's School in West Chester and graduated from the Episcopal Academy in Philadelphia at the age of sixteen. He then attended the University of Pennsylvania (1889–91) and transferred from there to the University of Berlin (1891–94) where he attained his doctorate in philosophy with the dissertation: *Stichostemma eilhardi . . . Ein Beitrag zur Kenntnis der Nemertinen* (1894). On his return to Philadelphia in 1895 he continued his morphological research on nemerteans at the Wistar Institute of Anatomy (1895–98), brought out nine additional papers on their structure and phylogeny, and became interested in the hairworms, publishing *The Gordiacea of Certain American Collections, Parts I and II* (1898) and eight subsequent papers. His youthful interest in birds resulted in five papers, written between 1896 and 1906. In 1897 he was appointed lecturer in zoölogy at the University of Pennsylvania. He became instructor the next year and was made assistant professor in 1900. At the same time (1898–1903) he was also professor in biology and director of the museum at the Wagner Free Institute of Science. Most of his summers were spent at the Marine Biological Laboratory, Woods Hole, Mass. In 1901 he married Priscilla Braislin of Crosswicks, N. J.; three sons were born to them.

Montgomery developed two divergent specialties which finally received much of his attention. His brilliant cytological investigations resulted in a rapid succession of papers; in *A Study of the Chromosomes of the Germ Cells of Metazoa* (1901) he was apparently the first to suggest that synapsis might represent a juncture of maternal and paternal chromosomes. His investigations on the taxonomy and habits of spiders culminated with *The Significance of the Courtship and the Secondary Sexual Characters of Araneads* (1909), in which he presented arguments against Darwin's theory of sexual selection. In 1903 he went as professor in zoölogy to the University of Texas. During this period he published *The Analysis of Racial Descent in Animals* (1906). In 1908 he returned to the University of Pennsylvania as director of the department of zoölogy and there he devoted the last three or four years of his life primarily to the fulfilment of his plans for a new zoölogical laboratory. He was just thirty-nine years of age when pneumonia caused his untimely death. His last paper, "Human Spermatogenesis, Spermatocytes and Spermiogenesis: A Study of Inheritance," appeared after his decease as the leading article in the centennial volume of the Academy of Natural Sciences of Philadelphia (1912). Montgomery was a member of the American Philosophical Society, the American Society of Naturalists, and the American Society of Zoölogists, which he served one term as president.

[Edward G. Conklin, memoir and bibliography in *Science*, Aug. 15, 1913; *Old Penn*, Mar. 23, 1912; T. H. Montgomery, *A Geneal. Hist. of the Family of Montgomery* (1863); *Pub. Ledger* (Phila.), Mar. 20, 1912.]   H. B. B.

MONTGOMERY, WILLIAM BELL (Aug. 21, 1829–Sept. 25, 1904), agriculturist, editor, was born in Fairfield District, S. C. His father, Hugh Montgomery, and his mother, Isabelle (Bell), were of Scotch-Irish descent and members of families that were prominent in colonial days. They moved to Mississippi in 1835 when William was only six years old, and his boyhood was spent in the country. He was educated in the common-schools of Mississippi, in Erskine College, South Carolina, and the College of New Jersey (Princeton), where he was graduated B.A. in 1850. After some years spent in agriculture in Mississippi he became a cotton broker at Mobile, Ala. During the Civil War he was loyal to the South although he had opposed the war and himself took no active part in it. His health impaired by confinement in a broker's office, he returned to Mississippi in 1865, settling in Oktibbeha County, near Starkville, and resumed the practice of agriculture, which afforded him the outdoor life and physical exercise he needed. He introduced new grasses, began to raise fancy Jersey cattle, and soon became a leader in his section of the state, doing much, during a period of more than thirty years, to advance live stock and agricultural interests in Mississippi. In 1875 he founded the *Live Stock*

Journal of which he was editor, publisher, and owner. It was succeeded the next year by the *Southern Live Stock Journal,* published at Starkville and edited by his son. He continued to contribute articles to the new periodical, which for a time ranked as a leading agricultural magazine in the South. In 1870 he founded the Starkville Female Institute, which was operated successfully for a number of years, until the property was purchased by the City of Starkville and rebuilt as a public grammar-school. When the Agricultural and Mechanical College of the state was established in the seventies, he was appointed local trustee and served as such for a period of twenty-six years.

He was married first, in 1852, to Julia Gillespie, daughter of Dr. William and Marjorie Gillespie of Starkville, Miss., and second, in 1865, to Sarah A. Glenn, daughter of William and Elizabeth Glenn. Five children were born to each marriage, and surviving members of the family continue to live in the old homestead.

[*Southern Live Stock Journal*, vol. V (1880); D. B. Montgomery, *Geneal. Hist. of the Montgomerys and Their Descendants* (1903); Dunbar Rowland, *Mississippi* (1907), esp. vol. III; T. B. Carroll, *Hist. Sketch of Oktibbeha County, Miss.* (1931); *Southern Farm Gazette*, Oct. 1, 1904; private papers in the files of the family.]
                                              B. M. W.

MONTRÉSOR, JAMES GABRIEL (Nov. 19, 1702–Jan. 6, 1776), British military engineer, was born at Fort William, Scotland, the son of James Gabriel Le Tresor of Thurland Hall, Nottingham, who, though a native of Caen, Normandy, was a naturalized British subject, a major of the Royal Scots Fusileers, and lieutenant-governor of Fort William. His mother, Nanon de Hauteville, was also of Norman stock. Montrésor began his military career as a matross in the Royal Artillery at Minorca in 1727, and served a year at Gibraltar as bombardier. In 1731 he was commissioned as a practitioner engineer, and for the next twenty-three years, with a single intermission, he lived at Gibraltar, rising finally to be chief engineer there, a subdirector, but with no higher army rank than a lieutenancy in the 14th Foot. His knowledge of fortifications became as profound as his practical, if unimaginative, mind permitted. He improved the defenses of Gibraltar.

In 1754 Montrésor was selected as chief engineer in America, accompanied Braddock's expedition, and was wounded at the Monongahela. The order of 1757 giving army rank to engineers made him a major, and in 1758 he became director and lieutenant-colonel. His services throughout the war were confined to New York, for successive commanders distrusted both his ability to direct a siege and his physical endurance. They left to him the work for which his experience had fitted him, the administration of the corps of engineers and the designing and construction of forts, blockhouses, and such buildings as barracks, hospitals, and storehouses. He was more skilled than his colleagues in adapting European systems of fortification to frontier conditions, and more tactful in working with the provincial troops who performed most of the actual construction work. Montrésor planned and directed considerable building in northern New York, at Albany, along the Mohawk, up the Hudson, especially at Saratoga and Fort Edward, and at Fort William Henry. In 1757 he was with Webb at Fort Edward when Montcalm took Fort William Henry; in 1758 he remained at that post while an engineer of inferior rank directed Abercromby's disastrous attack on the lines before Ticonderoga; in 1759 Amherst left him in charge of the rebuilding of new Fort George at the lower end of Lake George. Following an accident in 1759, leave was given him. He returned to England in 1760 and for two years traveled abroad for his health. During the rest of his life he remained in England, in active service as an engineer, though he resigned his lieutenant's commission in the 14th. He designed and superintended the construction of powder magazines at Purfleet, served as chief engineer at Chatham, and in 1772 received his colonelcy. For his American services he was granted ten thousand acres to the east of Lake Champlain. He died at New Gardens, Teynham, Kent, where he was buried.

Montrésor was married, first, on June 11, 1735, to Mary, daughter of Robert Haswell, who was with him at Gibraltar and accompanied him to New York; second, on Aug. 25, 1766, to Henrietta, daughter of Henry Fielding, the novelist; and third, to Frances, daughter of H. Nicholls, and widow of William Kemp, who brought him New Gardens. John Montrésor [q.v.] was a son of his first marriage.

[Sir Bernard Burke, *A Geneal. and Heraldic Hist. of the Landed Gentry of Great Britain and Ireland* (1898); Whitworth Porter, *Hist. of the Corps of Royal Engineers* (2 vols., 1889); R. H. Vetch, in *Dict. Nat. Biog.*; G. D. Scull, "The Montrésor Jours.," in *N. Y. Hist. Soc. Colls.,* Pub. Fund Ser., vol. XIV (1882); correspondence with the Ordnance Board, including at least one formal journal, and with Amherst, in Public Record Office, London.]   S. M. P.

MONTRÉSOR, JOHN (Apr. 6, 1736–June 26, 1799), British military engineer, the son of James Gabriel Montrésor [q.v.] and his wife Mary (Haswell), was born at Gibraltar. There his father taught him as a youth something of engineering, and in 1754 he took him to America

to join Braddock's army. He became ensign and later lieutenant in 1755, and was appointed by Braddock as an additional engineer, though the ordnance board did not place him on the establishment as a practitioner engineer until 1758. During the Seven Years' War his work consisted principally in leading special scouting expeditions and carrying dispatches. He was wounded at the Monongahela, served along the Mohawk and at Fort Edward in 1756, went to Halifax with Loudoun in 1757, was present at Amherst's capture of Louisbourg and Wolfe's siege of Quebec, and served with Murray in the final campaign of 1760. His extra services included a winter expedition in 1758 to the interior of Cape Breton Island; an arduous overland journey in winter from Quebec to New England, in which his party suffered the extremes of hunger and cold; and the exploration, in 1761, of the Kennebec river route to Canada. For two years he was intermittently engaged upon a survey of the St. Lawrence River. He ended the war as a subengineer, with the rank of lieutenant.

In Pontiac's War, 1763, Montrésor carried dispatches from Amherst to the commander at Detroit, Maj. Henry Gladwin [q.v.]. His party was shipwrecked at the east end of Lake Erie, attacked by Indians soon after it came ashore, but succeeded finally in relieving the garrison. The next year he fortified the portage at Niagara, and went with Bradstreet to Detroit, where he improved the defenses. He was a hostile witness of the Stamp Act riots of 1765 in New York and Albany. In 1766 he solicited preferment in England, whence he returned as engineer extraordinary and captain-lieutenant, with a commission as barrackmaster for the ordnance in North America. During the next few years he improved the fortifications or repaired barracks at New York, Boston, Philadelphia, and the Bahamas, and surveyed the boundary line between New York and New Jersey. He purchased Montrésor's (Randall's) Island in New York harbor, where he lived with his wife and family, having married, Mar. 1, 1764, Frances, daughter of Thomas Tucker of Bermuda.

During the Revolution the British made little use of Montrésor's long American experience. He was commissioned as chief engineer in America in 1775, with the rank of engineer in ordinary and captain, was superseded, reappointed, and again superseded. He was present at Lexington, Bunker Hill, and the capture of Long Island; he drew the approaches before Mud Island (Philadelphia), which he himself had built; and acted as chief engineer at the Brandywine. As Howe's aide-de-camp, he brought to the American lines the news and a description of Nathan Hale's execution. In 1778, having incurred Clinton's displeasure, he returned to England, where for twenty years he struggled to pass his accounts at the Treasury. Testifying before a committee of the House of Commons in 1779, he was non-committal, and seemed to know "hardly anything" about the conduct of the war. After retiring from the army, he traveled for a year on the Continent, and spent the remainder of his life at Belmont, Kent, and Portland Place, London. He was a cousin of Susanna Haswell Rowson [q.v.], and is said (Elias Nason, *A Memoir of Mrs. Susanna Rowson*, 1870, p. 46) to have been the model from which the hero of *Charlotte Temple* was drawn.

[Sir Bernard Burke, *A Geneal. and Heraldic Hist. of the Landed Gentry of Great Britain and Ireland* (1898); G. D. Scull, "The Montrésor Jours.," *N. Y. Hist. Soc. Colls.*, Pub. Fund Ser., vol. XIV (1882); "Journal of a March Undertaken in Winter on Snowshoes from Quebec . . . to . . . New England," in *New-Eng. Hist. and Geneal. Reg.*, Jan. 1882; "Arnold's Letters on His Expedition to Canada in 1775," in *Me. Hist. Soc. Colls.*, 1 ser. I (1831); J. C. Webster, *Presidential Address: Life of John Montrésor* (1928), repr. from *Trans. Royal Soc. of Canada*, 3 ser. XXII, section II (1928); A. G. Doughty and G. W. Parmelee, *The Siege of Quebec* (6 vols., 1901); F. H. Severance, "The Achievements of Captain John Montrésor on the Niagara, and the First Construction of Fort Erie," *Buffalo Hist. Soc. Pubs.*, vol. V (1902); F. M. Montrésor, "Capt. John Montrésor in Canada," *Canadian Hist. Rev.*, Dec. 1924; H. P. Johnston, *Nathan Hale* (rev. ed., 1914); *The Detail and Conduct of the American War . . . with a Very Full and Correct State of the Whole of the Evidence as Given before a Committee of the House of Commons* (3rd ed., 1780).] S. M. P.

MOOD, FRANCIS ASBURY (June 23, 1830–Nov. 12, 1884), clergyman of the Methodist Episcopal Church, South, educator, was born at Charleston, S. C., the son of John Mood and Catherine McFarlane. His family name was originally Muth; his paternal ancestor came to Philadelphia from Württemberg about 1750. Mood pursued a classical course at the College of Charleston where he was graduated with honor in 1850. He received the master's degree two years later. During part of his college course he conducted a school in Charleston for the children of free negroes. His parents were warmly interested in the work of the Methodist Episcopal Church, South, and he gladly prepared himself to take up the duties of its ministry as his father had done, and as his two elder brothers were already doing, and, licensed to enter the itinerant ministry, began serving Cypress Circuit in the South Carolina Conference in 1850. He had other circuits in his charge later, and also held pastorates at Columbia, Greenville, and elsewhere. When the Civil War began he supported the Confederacy, and President Davis appointed him in 1863 chaplain to the army hospitals in Charleston.

In December 1865, with a few associates, he began to publish a weekly newspaper, the *Record*, but the unsettled condition of the South made it impossible to continue publication. In the same period he was instrumental in defending his branch of the church: a Northern Methodist clergyman had taken possession of parish property in Charleston and refused to relinquish it, whereupon Mood appealed to President Johnson, who issued an order directing that the property be returned to its rightful owner. While pastor of Trinity Church, Charleston, Mood was offered the presidency of Soule University at Chappell Hill, Tex., and in November 1868 he decided to accept. He had long been interested in educational work, and his address, *A Theory of Education* (Hendersonville, N. C., 1859), shows his firm grasp of principles. He extinguished the debt at Soule and attracted students. Next, drawing plans for the establishment of a college which might count upon the support of the entire body of Texan Methodism, he persuaded the church assemblies to accede to the project, thus fostering one college instead of starving several. Resigning from the presidency of Soule, he became head of Southwestern University, as it is called today, with the title of regent. The new institution opened its doors at Georgetown, Tex., in the autumn of 1873. The Regent worked hard to gain support for Southwestern, but also he found time to teach the courses in philosophy. Resources at his command were but few at first, and he struggled against any relaxation of standards. Surrounded by utilitarianism, he nevertheless continued to encourage students to cultivate the study of the classical languages as the best means of obtaining a liberal education. When he retired from the regency the college was on a firm footing.

Mood wrote one historical work, *Methodism in Charleston, S. C.* (1856), and a considerable number of pamphlets and contributions to the *Charleston Courier* and to the religious press. Some of these articles record impressions of his travels in Europe in 1857 and again in 1865. He went to London in 1881 as a delegate to the Ecumenical Methodist Conference. He was married to Sue Logan in 1858, and when he died, at Waco, Tex., was survived by his wife and nine children.

[C. C. Cody, *The Life and Labors of Francis Asbury Mood* (1886), based upon Mood's unpublished autobiography, now in the keeping of his son, Judge A. M. Mood, Amarillo, Tex.; *A Narrative of the Facts Relating to the Founding and Progress of Southwestern*

University, 1840–1882 (Galveston, n.d.) ; bibliography of Mood's uncollected writings, on deposit in the Harvard Univ. Lib.; catalogues of the College of Charleston; *Christian Advocate* (Nashville), Nov. 22, 29, 1884.]   F. M—d.

MOODY, DWIGHT LYMAN (Feb. 5, 1837–Dec. 22, 1899), evangelist, was born at Northfield, Mass., son of Edwin Moody, brick-mason, and his wife Betsey (Holton) Moody. He was of Puritan ancestry, a descendant in the sixth generation of John Moody, who emigrated from England in 1633 and was one of the original settlers of Hartford, Conn., in 1635, and of William Holton, who came from England in 1634 and also settled in Hartford. His father died when Dwight was four years old, leaving to his widowed mother the care of nine children, all under thirteen years of age. A healthy lad, full of energy and given to pranks, young Moody attended school until he was thirteen, then went to work in nearby farms or in adjacent towns. Restless and ambitious, he tired of this manner of life, and at seventeen left home to seek his fortune in Boston, finally securing employment in a shoe store conducted by two uncles, brothers of his mother.

With the rest of his family, he had been baptized by the minister of the Unitarian church in Northfield. In Boston he began to attend the Mount Vernon Congregational Church, and here, through the interest of his Sunday-school teacher, Edward Kimball, he experienced what he ever afterward recalled as his conversion. Applying for membership in this church, he was granted a probationary status only, because of his ignorance of its doctrines. Almost a year elapsed before, on May 3, 1856, he was received into full church-membership. Dissatisfied with his situation at Boston, in the fall of 1856 he removed to Chicago, where, first as a retail clerk, then as a traveling salesman for a wholesale firm dealing in shoes, he got started on the road to success in business. At twenty-three he had an income for the year, through salary and commissions, of more than five thousand dollars. Meantime, religion and human welfare began increasingly to claim his time and interest. At Plymouth Church, which he joined, he was soon renting four pews, filling them each Sunday with men whom he invited from hotels, boarding-houses, and street-corners. Volunteering to teach in a mission Sunday school, he gathered a class of youngsters from the slums. In 1858 he organized the North Market Sabbath School, which met in a hall over one of the city markets, and induced John V. Farwell [*q.v.*], prominent merchant, to become its superintendent. In connection with this school he developed a remarkable program of evangelistic services, prayer-meetings, home-visitation, social recreation, philanthropic relief, and welfare work. In 1860, after a struggle which he later described as the hardest of his life, he decided to give his entire time to this work, and resigned from business to become an independent city missionary, without salary or assured support.

For reasons of conscience, Moody did not enlist as a soldier in the Civil War; but, with John Farwell and B. F. Jacobs, he organized an army and navy committee of the Chicago Young Men's Christian Association, and later made this a branch of the United States Christian Commission. He threw himself actively into its work of promoting the "spiritual good, intellectual improvement, and social and physical comfort" of the soldiers. Nine times he served at the front as a delegate of the Commission. In the intervals between these periods of service with the army, he devoted himself to his missionary work in Chicago. In connection with his Sunday school he organized in 1863 an undenominational church, and erected for it a building. In 1866 he became president of the Chicago Young Men's Christian Association, which he had for some time been serving as a secretary, and erected for it Farwell Hall, the first Association building in the country. He gave considerable time to county, state, and national conventions of Sunday-school workers and of Association leaders, and aided in the national organization of these movements.

Moody visited Great Britain in 1867 and again in 1870, to get acquainted with Christian leaders there and to study their methods. In June 1873, at the invitation of British friends, he embarked for a third visit, this time to conduct evangelistic services. He took with him Ira D. Sankey [*q.v.*], organist and singer, who had been helping him as chorister in the Sunday school and church at Chicago. Beginning quietly at York, the evangelists labored for five months in the north of England, awakening such interest that they were invited to Edinburgh. Here they succeeded in enlisting the cooperation of ministers and university men of both the Church of Scotland and the Free Church in a series of meetings which continued for more than two months. Many professed conversion or a quickening of spiritual life; ecclesiastical party issues sank to a place of relative unimportance; reports of the meetings were given increasing place in the public and religious press; even the traditional Scotch antipathy to the use of instrumental music in the worship of God gave way before Sankey's organ After Edinburgh, a similar extensive and successful series of meetings was conducted in Glasgow; then four months were devoted to preaching, for shorter periods, in various places throughout Scotland. In September 1874 the evangelists landed in Ireland, where they labored for three months, receiving a warm welcome both at Belfast and at Dublin. The following winter months were devoted to meetings in Manchester, Sheffield, Birmingham, and Liverpool. The work of the evangelists culminated in a four months' mission in London, conducted in the largest buildings available in each of five sections of the city. In the course of this London mission, 285 meetings were held, attended by an estimated total of 2,530,000 people.

Moody and Sankey returned to America in August 1875. Their visit to Great Britain had been prolonged to more than two years, and they had been the instruments in a religious awakening comparable only to that under the preaching of Wesley and Whitefield. They had gone unheralded; they returned in a blaze of public curiosity and interest, which brought them many more invitations than they could accept. Moody went quietly to Northfield, where he henceforth made his home. Here, in this comparatively remote Massachusetts town, he conducted a two weeks' series of meetings; then, with excellent strategy, he selected Brooklyn, Philadelphia, and New York as the cities in which to undertake evangelistic campaigns in the fall and winter of 1875–76. Careful preliminary organization, the ensured cooperation of the churches, judicious advertising and generous publicity, admission by freely distributed tickets, and well-planned methods of handling the throngs that attended the meetings, helped to clear the way for the full persuasive effect of Moody's preaching and Sankey's music. Their success in these American cities was as notable as in Great Britain.

Moody had found his life work. He was experiencing, to use a phrase which was dear to him, "what God can do with a man wholly surrendered to His will." In 1876–77 he successfully met the test of extensive campaigns in Chicago, where he was best known, and in Boston, traditionally conservative and non-revivalistic. He devoted the year 1877–78 to the smaller cities of New England—Burlington and Montpelier, Vt.; Concord and Manchester, N. H.; Providence, R. I.; Springfield, Mass.; Hartford and New Haven, Conn. Changing his plan in the interest of yet closer cooperation with the churches, he spent the winter of 1878–79 at evangelistic work in Baltimore, 1879–80 in St. Louis, and 1880–81 in San Francisco. Meanwhile, his interests were broadening. He believed in the kind

of evangelism that issues in social service; he himself was a doer rather than a preacher merely. In 1879, aroused by the need of the young people in the hills around his home, and heartened by the counsel of Henry F. Durant [q.v.], who had recently founded Wellesley College, he established a school for girls, the Northfield Seminary, intended primarily for those of limited means. In 1881, along somewhat similar lines, he established a school for boys, Mount Hermon School, near Northfield. In the summer of 1880, in the buildings of the Northfield Seminary, he held a general conference of Christian workers, which has been followed by a like conference in each successive summer, except for three years when Moody was abroad.

His second extended evangelistic campaign in Great Britain was undertaken in the autumn of 1881 in response to invitations from Ireland, Scotland, England, and Wales, and culminated in an eight months' mission in London, which closed in June 1884. At one of the London meetings a young doctor, Wilfred T. Grenfell, was attracted by Moody's adroit closure of a clergyman's tedious prayer—"While our brother is finishing his prayer we will sing number 75"—and was inspired by Moody's sermon to give his life to work as a missionary physician in Labrador. In 1891–92 Moody engaged in a final year of work in Great Britain, and in the spring of 1892 visited Palestine.

The seven years between 1884 and 1891 he devoted to evangelistic work, for short periods, in many cities large and small of the United States and Canada. During the first four months of 1887 he conducted an evangelistic campaign in Chicago, which eventuated in his founding the Chicago Bible Institute, formally opened in 1889, primarily for the training of men and women who had not been privileged to receive a college education but felt impelled to enter home or foreign missionary service as lay workers. In connection with this school he organized, in 1894, the Bible Institute Colportage Association for the publication and sale of religious books at prices low enough to secure wide circulation.

In the eighties his mind turned toward college students. In 1876 he had visited Princeton, and in 1878, after conducting an evangelistic campaign in New Haven, he had accepted the invitation of Yale students to give a special series of addresses to them. In both of his extended visits to Great Britain he had interested university men, and many had assisted at his meetings. At his invitation J. E. K. Studd, a young graduate of Cambridge University, who was later to become Lord Mayor of London, visited America in 1885 and told to student audiences the story of the spiritual awakening in British universities. In July 1886 Moody conducted a conference of college students at Mount Hermon, which was attended by two hundred and fifty young men from eighty colleges in twenty-four states. Transferred to Northfield in the following year, the conference was made memorable by the participation of Henry Drummond, who gave an address on "The Greatest Thing in the World," which was later published and became one of the most widely read of his writings. Thereafter, the conference was held annually and a like conference for students in the women's colleges was begun in 1893. These conferences stimulated in the colleges the development of Young Men's Christian Associations and similar voluntary organizations of students devoted to Christian purposes. One of the immediate results of the first gathering was the initiation of the Student Volunteer Movement, an organization of college students pledged to seek appointment to foreign missionary service. With its enthusiastic slogan —"the evangelization of the world in this generation"—the Movement did much in the closing years of the nineteenth century and the opening decades of the twentieth to recruit the foreign missionary forces of the Protestant churches.

After his last visit to Great Britain Moody resumed work in various cities of the United States and Canada. Daring but successful was a six months' campaign of evangelistic services which he conducted in Chicago from May to November 1893, during the progress of the World's Fair. Among other cities in which he labored in this decade were New York, Boston, Philadelphia, Providence, Scranton, Washington, Richmond, Birmingham, St. Louis, Denver, Montreal, Toronto, and Winnipeg. He gave the early months of 1899 to meetings in the Southwest and on the Pacific Coast, and in November of that year he began a campaign in Kansas City. His work here was interrupted by illness and he traveled home to Northfield, where on Dec. 22, he died.

Moody was a layman. He never sought ordination. His work was characteristic of the growing assumption by laymen of responsibility for Christian enterprises, which began about the middle of the nineteenth century, and it powerfully stimulated that movement. A man of large administrative and executive ability, he commanded the confidence of business men, who received him as one of themselves and contributed to the support of his projects because they trusted his judgment as well as his sincerity. Not money-hungry, he refused to accept as personal profit the proceeds of his work, and he and Sankey turned over all royalties accruing from the sale of their hymnbooks to a board of trustees headed by William E. Dodge [q.v.], which devoted these funds chiefly to the endowment of the Northfield schools. Moody's preaching was direct, forceful, intimate. He talked to his audiences as man to man, simply, even colloquially. He used short sentences and the rugged Anglo-Saxon words of common life. His emphasis was upon the gospel of God's fatherly love, rather than the terrors of hell fire. His speech was vivid, moving, but not sensational. Understanding and using the methods of effective publicity, he disdained its cheaper and more personal forms. He believed in personal evangelism and never lost the individual in the mass. His gospel was one of friendship. The "inquiry room" for personal conferences was invariably included in the organization of his campaigns, and he was adept in enlisting and training helpers for this personal service. "Better set ten men to work than do the work of ten men," he often said. With singleness of purpose he combined largeness of spirit and an uncommon degree of common sense. He quite lacked the censoriousness which has marred the work of many itinerant evangelists, or the passion for statistics of the converted which has sometimes distracted them. Kindly and conciliatory, he let no personal quirks or sectarian differences stand in the way of the gospel he preached and lived. He worked effectively with men like Sir George Adam Smith and Henry Drummond, whose positions were in some respects far from his own. He withstood temptation to set up as a faith-healer, and refused to let that cult gain a foothold in his Chicago School. A man of prayer, he was tirelessly and far-sightedly a man of work. "There is no use asking God to do things you can do yourself," he said. A layman, Moody inspired ministers; an evangelist, he understood the importance of Christian education; unschooled, he commanded the admiration and cooperation of University students and teachers; a man of large business ability, he devoted himself unreservedly to what he conceived to be the greatest business in earth or heaven— the saving of souls.

On Aug. 28, 1862, he married Emma C. Revell, daughter of Fleming H. Revell, a Chicago ship builder, and sister of Fleming H. Revell [q.v.], who became a publisher of religious books. She entered into his work with sympathy and good judgment, and her influence on Moody's life was incalculable. She introduced him to certain social graces and increased greatly his charm and effectiveness. They had two sons and one daughter.

[W. R. Moody, *D. L. Moody* (1930), superseding *The Life of Dwight L. Moody* (1900) by the same author, contains an extensive bibliography. See also Lyman Abbott, *Silhouettes of My Contemporaries* (1921); J. V. Farwell, *Early Recollections of Dwight L. Moody* (1907); W. S. Carson and I. D. Sankey in *Boston Daily Globe*, Dec. 23, 1899; Gamaliel Bradford, *D. L. Moody, A Worker in Souls* (1927), with bibliography. Moody published eighteen volumes, chiefly sermons.]

L. A. W.

MOODY, JAMES (1744–Apr. 6, 1809), the most noted spy in British service during the American Revolution, was born in New Jersey. He was living quietly with his wife and three children on his large farm in its northernmost county, Sussex, during the first two years of the war. Like some of his neighbors he rejected the oaths of abjuration and allegiance prescribed by state law, which were tendered by the Council of Safety in 1777. Hence the Whigs molested and even shot at him. In April of that year he fled with seventy-four neighbors and friends to Bergen County and shortly enlisted in the brigade organized by Gen. Cortlandt Skinner, former attorney-general of New Jersey, and soon known as "Skinner's Greens." He served a year as a volunteer without pay, being soon sent back with a hundred men to annoy his former neighborhood. Later he penetrated the country and obtained intelligence about a Whig corps. Early in August 1777 the Council learned that Moody and two others were recruiting in New Jersey and ordered their apprehension. One was caught. In 1778 his property, like that of other Loyalists, was confiscated by the state and, after being cleared of obligations and claims, was sold.

In 1779 Moody was commissioned ensign in the first battalion of Skinner's brigade, and in June in the course of a raid to Tintonfalls, seized four Whig officers and several privates, and drove off three hundred head of live stock. Moody's party plundered a military magazine, and with the prisoners and booty reached their boats at Sandy Hook after repulsing thirty Whigs. He spied on the troops of Washington, Sullivan, and Gates, and in May 1780 undertook to execute the order of the Hessian officer, Lieut.-Gen. Wilhelm von Knyphausen, to bring to New York with their public papers Gov. William Livingston, other officials, and those persons in New Jersey concerned in the execution of three spies. A reward of 2,000 guineas had been offered by General Skinner for the achievement of this feat. The expedition failed, however, because one of Moody's men was apprehended and vaguely revealed its object. In a more successful exploit in July Moody with seven men captured eighteen committeemen and militia officers. For this he was hunted far and wide and taken near Eng-

lishtown by Captain Lawrence of the New York state levies. Falling into the hands of Gen. Anthony Wayne, he was transferred from one prison to another. He was finally lodged in a filthy dungeon at Westpoint and otherwise mistreated until Washington ordered the situation remedied. At length, fearing execution, Moody effected his escape on a stormy night. He received two rewards for waylaying "rebel" mails, and was promoted lieutenant, Aug. 14, 1781. Later in the same year he started for Philadelphia to get the books and papers of the Continental Congress, but learned by chance at the Delaware that the plot had been revealed.

His health was now impaired, and he was urged by Sir Henry Clinton to visit England. There he memorialized several government officials and at mid-June, 1782, was granted £100 a year by the Treasury. In 1783 he published in pamphlet form the *Narrative* of his exertions and sufferings, and in June of the following year testified before the commissioners on Loyalist claims who were so impressed by the nature of his service and the grave risks he had run that they broke their rules by allowing his claim in full for £1,330. They also promised to recommend him to Gov. John Parr of Nova Scotia on his departure for that province, where he expected to obtain a grant of six hundred acres. After a sojourn in Halifax Moody settled at Weymouth, Nova Scotia, in 1786. There he served as colonel of militia. He died in 1809. His younger brother John took part in some of his adventures and was executed in November 1781, at Philadelphia, for attempting to break into the state house there.

[*Lieut. Jas. Moody's Narrative of His Exertions and Sufferings in the Cause of Gov't.* (1782, revised and enlarged, 1783), was edited and republished with notes by C. I. Bushnell under the title: *Narrative of the Exertions and Sufferings of Lieut. Jas. Moody* (1865). See also: *The Royal Commission on the Losses and Services of Am. Loyalists* (1915), ed. by H. E. Egerton; W. S. Stryker, "The N. J. Volunteers" (1887); *Archives of the State of N. J.*, 2 ser. III (1906) and IV (1914); Lorenzo Sabine, *Biog. Sketches of Loyalists of the Am. Revolution* (2 vols., 1864); E. A. Jones, "The Loyalists of N. J.," *N. J. Hist. Soc. Colls.*, vol. X (1927).]

W. H. S—t.

MOODY, PAUL (May 21, 1779–July 8, 1831), inventor, was born in Byfield Parish, Newbury, Mass., the sixth son of Capt. Paul and Mary Moody. His father, a man of influence in Newbury, was a Byfield volunteer at Lexington, March 1776, and commanded a company of sixty-eight Newbury men in the Revolutionary War. At the age of twelve Paul evinced an interest in mechanics and entered a woolen factory at Waltham to learn the art of weaving; he next found employment in a nail-making plant in B field; in fact, for several years, he went from one establishment to another where mill machinery was in use, and by close study and handling of machines became a master mechanic. On July 13, 1800, he married Susannah Morrill of Amesbury, and then entered a co-partnership with Ezra Worthen in the operation of a cotton mill of that town. His contacts during the succeeding fourteen years' management of this plant were with those New Englanders who were ambitious to develop domestic manufacture so as to avoid foreign dependence. Accordingly when Francis C. Lowell [*q.v.*] formed the Boston Manufacturing Company about 1814, to manufacture cotton-mill and other machinery, Moody joined him in establishing the plant at Waltham, Mass. Here he remained for the succeeding eleven years, repairing and manufacturing machinery and inventing a number of improvements. On Mar. 9, 1816, he secured a patent for a new mechanism to wind yarn from bobbins or spools; on Jan. 17, 1818, he perfected soapstone rollers for Horrocks' dressing machine and doubled its efficacy; he improved the "double-speeder" for roping cotton and obtained a patent Apr. 3, 1819; and, finally, on Jan. 19 and February 19, 1821, respectively, he was granted patents for machines to make cotton roping and to rope and spin cotton. Moody's contributions did much to bring to its highest efficiency the Waltham system of cotton manufacture.

In 1823 he went to East Chelmsford, now Lowell, Mass., to superintend the building of new cotton-mills there. A large machine shop, called the Lowell Machine Works, was also established, and after its completion in 1825, Moody, together with a full force of experienced men, was transferred from Waltham to Lowell. Here under his direction the manufacture of cotton machinery was continued and new and improved designs of machinery perfected. In a comparatively short time the shop was manufacturing every item of equipment needed for the operation of a cotton-mill, and its reputation for good designs and workmanship was the highest in the country. Moody, however, enjoyed but little of the reward, for he died suddenly after a three-day illness, when only fifty-two years of age. His special interests outside of business were community welfare and education: he was also a stanch supporter of temperance. His widow and three sons survived him.

[J. L. Ewell, *The Story of Byfield, A New England Parish* (1904); *Vital Records of Newbury, Mass.* (1911); *Vital Records of Amesbury, Mass.* (1913); C. C. P. Moody, *Biog. Sketches of the Moody Family* (1847); J. D. Van Slyck, *Representatives of New Eng. Manufacturers* (1879); Alfred Gilman, "Francis Cabot Lowell," in *Contributions of the Old Residents' Hist.*

Asso. (Lowell, Mass.), vol. V, no. 2 (1876); L. B. Lawson, "Lowell and Newburyport," *Ibid.*, no. 3 (1877); Joseph Coffin, *A Sketch of the Hist. of Newbury, Newburyport, and West Newbury* (1845); H. A. Miles, *Lowell As It Was, and As It Is* (1845); F. W. Coburn, *Hist. of Lowell and Its People* (1920), vol. I; Nathan Appleton, *Introduction of the Power Loom, and Origin of Lowell* (1858); *Essex Reg.* (Salem, Mass.), July 11, 1831; *A List of the Patents Granted by the U. S. from Apr. 10, 1790, to Dec. 31, 1836* (1872).]   C. W. M.

MOODY, WILLIAM HENRY (Dec. 23, 1853–July 2, 1917), congressman, cabinet member, jurist, was born in Newbury, Mass. The first William Moody had come to America in 1634 and after a year at Ipswich removed to Newbury where his descendants continued their residence. William Henry Moody was born in the homestead which had been in the family for more than two centuries. His parents were Henry L. and Melissa A. (Emerson) Moody. When he was six years of age the family moved to Danvers where he received his early schooling—later attending Phillips Academy, Andover, from which he graduated in 1872. He then entered Harvard College and received the degree of A.B. *cum laude* with honors in history in 1876. In September of that year he entered the Harvard Law School but remained only until the following January. He continued his law studies in the office of Richard H. Dana, Jr., author of *Two Years Before the Mast,* and a prominent member of the Massachusetts bar. Although his period of study was only eighteen months rather than the usual three years he was permitted to present himself for the bar examinations—at that time a process of oral questioning—and was duly admitted to the bar at the April 1878 term of the supreme judicial court before Chief Justice Gray.

He began practice in Haverhill with Edwin N. Hill and later became associated with Joseph K. Jenness. Moody early laid down for himself the rule, "The power of clear statement is the greatest power at the bar" (*World's Work,* Nov. 1906, p. 8190). Because of his outstanding ability he soon came to be recognized as one of the leading lawyers in Essex County. He served on the Haverhill school board for three years and, 1888–90, was the city solicitor. In 1890 he was chosen district attorney for the Eastern District of Massachusetts. Moody's administration of this office brought him forward as one of the most successful trial lawyers in the Commonwealth; and, although the venue was not in his district, he was engaged specially to take part in the prosecution of the famous Lizzie Borden case in Fall River. The defendant was acquitted but Moody's activities in the case won him wide recognition. At a special election in November 1895, he was elected to succeed William Cogswell in the Fifty-fourth Congress. In this body (1895–1902), as already at the bar, he became a master of fact and detail, and during his second term he was appointed to the important appropriations committee.

His career as a member of the House of Representatives so commanded the notice of President Theodore Roosevelt that on May 1, 1902, he was appointed secretary of the navy. Moody had the obvious qualities of pugnacity and virility, and they appealed strongly to the Roosevelt temperament. A close friendship developed between the two and upon the resignation of Attorney-General Philander C. Knox in 1904 the President selected Moody as his successor. Although perhaps up to that time he had not become known throughout the country as the preeminent lawyer, his effective service as the nation's chief law officer soon established him as the leader of the American bar in title and achievement. Roosevelt's anti-trust activities reached their high point while Moody was attorney-general. He personally argued the so-called Beef Trust Case (*Swift & Co.* vs. *U. S.*; 196 *U. S.*, 375), wherein the government contended that a combination of corporations and individuals, after purchasing livestock and converting the same into fresh meat, sold the products in interstate commerce in such manner that competition, both in the purchase of cattle on the hoof and in the sale of meat, was suppressed. The government won the case. Moody also instituted prosecutions alleging restraint of trade against combinations engaged in the paper, fertilizer, salt, tobacco, oil, lumber, and other businesses. Roosevelt said of his work, "his record as Attorney-General can be compared without fear with the record of any other man who ever held that office" (*Outlook*, Nov. 5, 1910, p. 532).

When the retirement of Justice Henry B. Brown was followed by the announcement that the President was to appoint the vigorous Attorney-General to the Supreme Court, it was not met with universal approval. It was feared by some that his administrative attitude toward "big business" would be carried into his judicial functioning and that some of the "radical" ideas of the President with whom he was so friendly would be reflected from the bench. However, on Dec. 12, 1906, the Senate confirmed him and on Dec. 17 he was sworn in as an associate justice. Thus, within five years, Moody had the singular distinction of serving the legislative, executive, and judicial branches of the government.

During his service on the Court, Moody wrote sixty-seven opinions, of which five were dissents,

and he cast dissenting votes in ten cases. His principal dissenting opinion was in the group known as the Employers' Liability Cases (207 *U. S.*, 463), wherein the majority of the Court declared the first Federal Employers' Liability Act to be unconstitutional. Moody supported the proposition that since the Constitution gave Congress the power to regulate interstate commerce, coincidently that body had the right to regulate the relation of master and servant in the matters concerning interstate commerce. The majority opinion, however, declared that the act went beyond this realm and involved the regulation of intrastate commerce also. The burden of Moody's dissent was a contention that the statute could be so interpreted as not to have this effect. An important case having to do with so-called fundamental rights of the individual in which Moody wrote the majority opinion was *Twining* vs. *State of New Jersey* (211 *U. S.*, 78), wherein the state trial court had commented unfavorably upon the refusal of the defendants to testify. Unless such refusal was violative of a privilege guaranteed by the federal Constitution, the Supreme Court had no jurisdiction to inquire how it had been dealt with in the courts below. Moody's conclusion that the Constitution embodies no such guarantee either directly or by inference is set out in an opinion marked for its insight, clarity, and thoroughness of consideration.

His rather unusual practical experience in public life and his fundamental soundness as a lawyer promised to make Moody's service on the Court one of much usefulness. His work seemed to promise that he would become one of the great justices of that great body, but ill health beset him and in 1910 Congress by special act (because of his short term of service) granted him the retirement privileges ordinarily extended to federal judges who have served for at least ten years and attained the age of seventy. On Nov. 20, 1910, he resigned. He spent his remaining years in Haverhill, Mass., where on July 2, 1917, he died. He never married.

[*U. S. Supreme Court Reports*, vols. CCIII–CCXVIII; Official Records, Dept. of Justice, Washington, D. C.; 36 *Statutes at Large*, pt. II, 61 Cong., 2 Sess.; ch. ccclxxvii, Act of June 23, 1910; F. B. Wiener, Life and Judicial Career of William Henry Moody, Harvard Law School Thesis, 1930; I. F. Marcosson, in *World's Work*, Nov. 1906; George Whitelock, in *Green Bag*, June 1909; Theodore Roosevelt, in *Outlook*, Nov. 5, 1910; *Who's Who in Am.*, 1916–17; *Proc. at the Meeting of the Essex Bar in the Supreme Judicial Court in Memory of William Henry Moody, Apr. 26, 1919* (n.d.); obituaries in *N. Y. Times*, *Boston Evening Transcript*, July 2, 1917.]

C. P. S.

MOODY, WILLIAM VAUGHN (July 8, 1869–Oct. 17, 1910), poet, playwright, educator, was born in Spencer, Ind., the son of Francis Burdette Moody and Henriette Emily (Stoy) Moody. His father, originally from New York, was a steamboat captain, and the boy was brought up in New Albany, Ind. He early manifested a bent for scholarship and the character to achieve it in the face of obstacles. He taught school to earn money to fit himself for college, and he arrived at Harvard in September 1889 with just $25 in his pocket, but he completed what was then almost universally a four-year course in three years, meanwhile supporting himself and partially supporting a sister by typewriting, tutoring, and serving as a proctor. Furthermore, he found time to join in the active literary life of the college, writing both verse and prose, and becoming one of the editors of the *Harvard Monthly*. The group with whom he was associated in college included Daniel Gregory Mason, Robert Herrick, George Santayana, Philip Savage, Norman Hapgood, and other future writers. His senior year (1892–93) he spent in Europe, paying for his trip by accompanying a boy as tutor. Following his graduation he secured the degree of A.M. in 1894 and then served during 1894–95 as an assistant to Lewis E. Gates in the English department at Harvard and Radcliffe. In the autumn of 1895 he became an instructor in English at the University of Chicago. In 1899–1900 he withdrew for a year, living in Boston and East Gloucester, to complete his volume of poems. On his return to the University of Chicago in 1901 he was made an assistant professor, with considerable liberty of movement, and he continued to keep this title till 1907, when he finally resigned completely from teaching and devoted his entire attention to literary production.

Moody's first published book was a drama in verse, *The Masque of Judgment* (1900). This was followed by a volume of *Poems* (1901), and by a second poem in dramatic form, *The Fire-Bringer*, in 1904, originally intended for production by the Chicago Civic Theatre. Feeling the need of a year of leisure he wrote, with Robert Morss Lovett, a textbook, *A First View of English Literature* (1905), which enabled him to make a trip to the West, as well as to Europe, and to devote time to a prose drama which was shaping in his mind. This play, first called *The Sabine Woman,* he brought to Margaret Anglin early in 1906, and she produced it at the Garrick Theatre, Chicago, Apr. 12, 1906. With Henry Miller as Ghent and Miss Anglin as Ruth, and the title changed to *The Great Divide*, it was shown at the Princess Theatre, New York, Oct. 3, 1906, and was at once recognized

as an important contribution to American drama. It was acted in London, Sept. 15, 1909, has often been revived since, and in 1929 was made into a motion picture. Moody's next play, *The Faith Healer*, was acted by Henry Miller at Harvard College in 1909, in Saint Louis, Mar. 15, 1909, and in New York, Jan. 19, 1910. Unlike *The Great Divide,* it was not successful as a popular attraction, but its high merits were recognized, and Moody was looked upon as a leader among American dramatists. In 1908 Moody received the degree of Litt.D. from Yale and was elected to the American Academy of Arts and Letters. In the spring of that year he suffered a severe attack of typhoid fever, at his apartment in Waverley Place, New York, and was nursed by an old friend, Mrs. Harriet Tilden Brainard, of Chicago, whom he married on May 7, 1909. He recovered sufficiently to draft one act of *The Death of Eve,* a poetic drama, but never finished it, as a serious brain disease developed and caused his death at Colorado Springs, Oct. 17, 1910.

Moody was rather small in stature, wore a small, pointed beard, and was taciturn and shy. His college friends used to say, "It took Moody a pipeful to make a remark." At Chicago the students who had to write themes for him called him "The Man in the Iron Mask." But his native taciturn shyness and perhaps a certain academic aloofness developed at Harvard, concealed a man of fine critical as well as creative intellect, and profound feeling. Though outwardly his life was quiet and uneventful, his poetry and plays all came, as Dickinson puts it, "out of moral conviction and mental necessity" (*post*, p. 136). He was constantly striving to come "to grips with the spirit of the age, and expressing his message with force and pure beauty" (*Ibid.*, p. 135)—for beauty was with him a passion. The lyric quality of his verse, exhibited in such a poem as "Gloucester Moors," suggested the *Songs from Vagabondia* by his contemporaries, Carman and Hovey. But in his "Ode in Time of Hesitation" (1900) was visible his spiritual wrestling with problems of the day—here his revolt against "imperialism" in the Philippines. *The Masque of Judgment* is a dramatization of the dignity of the individual, even to rebellion against the Most High. *The Fire Bringer,* a Promethean drama, again stresses "the supreme duty of rebellion." Neither of these verse plays, though the latter was intended for the stage, has been produced (1933). Perhaps they were, in form, not sufficiently in revolt against the academic tradition of poetic drama. As late as 1904 Moody wrote to Percy Mac-

Kaye, "I am heart and soul dedicated to the conviction that modern life can be presented on the stage in the poetic mediums and adequately presented only in that way" (*Letters, post*, p. 148). But shortly thereafter he wrote *The Great Divide* in prose, and at last saw his work reach the stage. In this play of contemporary American life Moody transferred to Stephen Ghent, the rough Westerner, his ideal of personal independence, and to Ruth Jordan, daughter of a long line of Puritans, the inhibitions which choke the growth of the human spirit and may prevent the real conquest of evil, the real achievement of happiness, and the good life. In this play Moody kept his prose dignified and at times poetic, but it was human speech adapted to the ear trained on realistic drama, and therefore he was able to reach large audiences, who realized at once that in Moody the American theatre had found a dramatist who could, in contemporary terms, express philosophic ideas and bring to the theatre new spiritual values. *The Faith Healer* is in the same style and spirit, and shows the struggle between earthly love and consciousness of a "mission." Its failure on the stage was probably due to the extreme difficulty of dramatizing, in contemporary terms, occult religious phenomena. Few dramatists have ever succeeded. But Quinn declares this to be Moody's finest play. *The Death of Eve* was undertaken to complete the trilogy of poetic dramas Moody had planned. Had he lived, he would undoubtedly have contributed more dramas, in the current prose idiom, to the practical theatre, and would have achieved a most important place in the theatrical history of America. *The Great Divide*, alone, coming as it did in the first decade of the twentieth century, when the American theatre was struggling for deeper and more significant expression, marked an important step in the evolution of the drama. But Moody, the lyric poet, also continues to be read and admired, alike for form and content. He was a conscientious artist, and he was also a forward-looking intellect.

[*Some Letters of Wm. Vaughn Moody* (1913), with an Introduction by D. G. Mason; Bliss Perry, memoir in *Proc. Am. Acad. Arts and Letters*, vol. VI (1913), reprinted in the *Commemorative Tributes* (1922) of the Academy; *Selected Poems of Wm. Vaughn Moody* (1931), edited by R. M. Lovett, with biographical sketch; T. H. Dickinson, *Playwrights of the New Am. Theatre* (1925); A. H. Quinn, *A Hist. of the Am. Drama from the Civil War to the Present Day* (1927), vol. II; E. H. Lewis, *Wm. Vaughn Moody* (1914); *Harvard Grads'. Mag.*, Dec. 1910; *Chicago Tribune*, Oct. 19, 1910.]

                  W. P. E.

MOONEY, JAMES (Feb. 10, 1861–Dec. 22, 1921), ethnologist, son of James and Ellin (Devlin) Mooney, was born at Richmond, Ind. He began his education in the common-schools and later taught two terms. He was strongly interested in Indians, reading everything available on the subject, but his interest did not lead to any apparent avenue of support and he entered the office of the *Richmond Palladium*, where he worked both as a compositor and in an editorial capacity. After he had saved a little money he journeyed to Washington with a secret intent of going to Brazil to study the Indians of that country. In Washington he met Maj. J. W. Powell [*q.v.*] in 1885, and through him Mooney found an outlet for his enthusiasm in the Bureau of American Ethnology, where he remained for the rest of his life. His early Indian studies had taken the form of a list of tribes amounting to 3,000 entries, and this came into use as material for the *Handbook of American Indians* (2 vols., 1907–10, ed. by F. W. Hodge), in the preparation of which he took an active part. In North Carolina he studied the language, folk lore, mythology, and material culture of the Cherokees ("Myths of the Cherokees," *Nineteenth Annual Report of the Bureau of American Ethnology, . . . 1895–96*, 1900). At a fortunate juncture he discovered an ancient Cherokee ritual written in the Cherokee script ("The Sacred Formulas of the Cherokees," *Seventh Annual Report . . . 1885–86*, 1891). About 1890 the last ebullition of Indian race-consciousness took place with the outbreak of the Ghost Dance—an endeavor to rehabilitate the Indian to his former status—and this phase of Indian life Mooney studied exhaustively ("The Ghost-dance Religion and the Sioux Outbreak of 1890," *Fourteenth Annual Report . . . 1892–93*, 1896). Some of his best years were spent in the investigation of the Kiowa ("Calendar History of the Kiowa Indians," *Seventeenth Annual Report . . . 1895–96*, 1898), and at the time of his death he was engrossed with a large work on Kiowa heraldry. He also investigated the seemingly anomalous presence of Siouan language tribes on the borders of the Virginia Algonquians and his research went far to clear up the history of the migrations of this great stock ("The Siouan Tribes of the East," *Bulletin 22 of the Smithsonian Institution, Bureau of Ethnology*, 1894).

Mooney's parents had come from Meath, Ireland, and he was deeply ingrained with Irish lore. One of his first papers was "The Funeral Customs of Ireland" (*Proceedings of the American Philosophical Society, 1888*, vol. XXV, 1888, pp. 1–56). His scientific writing was mostly confined to large, thoroughly prepared monographs. A particularly lucid style characterized his writing. He was active in various scientific organizations and especially in the Anthropological Society of Washington, of which he was president, 1914–15. He threw his whole energy into all matters looking toward the advancement of his science. His own work was never subject to adverse criticism and his faculty of getting along with the Indians whom he studied was phenomenal. Of medium height, with gray eyes and dark hair, he was a true Irish type. In 1897 he married Ione Lee Gaut of Tennessee, who accompanied him on his journeys on the Western frontier.

[*Am. Anthropologist*, Apr.–June 1922; *Who's Who in America*, 1920–21; the *Evening Star* (Washington, D. C.), Dec. 23, 1921; personal recollections.]

W. H.

MOONEY, WILLIAM (1756–Nov. 27, 1831), one of the founders of the New York Society of Tammany, was probably born of humble parents in New York City. He is said to have been a soldier in the American army in the Revolution, but his term of service must have been in the early years of the war. In August 1780, three years before the British evacuation, he was engaged in business as an upholsterer and dealer in wall paper in William Street, New York City. He continued in this business at various locations until his retirement in 1821. In the great parade to celebrate the ratification of the Constitution, in 1788, he appeared on a float in the act of upholstering a presidential chair for General Washington.

Mooney and others in 1786 founded the New York Society of Tammany which, like the earlier Tammany societies, seems to have been a social and benevolent organization of the middle class, with strong prejudices against "aristocrats" on the one hand and "foreign adventurers" on the other. When the written constitution of the society was adopted in August 1789, he was chosen the first grand sachem. He was later prominent in all the activities of Tammany over a period of forty years, among others as a director of the museum established for the preservation of historic objects, and as a member of one of the committees for the interment of the remains of eleven thousand American soldiers and sailors who died on board British prison ships in New York harbor. Many charters granted to other Tammany societies bore his signature. When the society became involved in politics he promoted its activity and was eager to share in the spoils of office.

In February 1808, following a Republican victory in the municipal elections, the council made a place for Mooney as superintendent of the almshouse. The position allowed him an expense account and furnished accommodations for his family, besides a salary. Within a few months the commissioners of the almshouse complained of Mooney's incompetence and financial irregularities, and in September 1809 the council dismissed him. A committee appointed to investigate his accounts found that he had curtailed the expenditures for necessities for the inmates and had greatly increased the amounts spent for luxuries, especially for rum and other liquors. One heading for entries in his books—"Trifles for Mrs. Mooney"—long continued to be a byword among the opponents of Tammany Hall. Mooney's explanation of his accounts was that there had been an increase in the number of inmates, that the almshouse had been frequently visited by members of the Corporation, and that it had been made the resort of "certain other persons" (*Minutes of the Common Council, post,* V, p. 720). He had probably erred in being too liberal with his party associates. The Tammany Society was apparently satisfied with his explanation, for in 1811 it again chose him grand sachem, and reëlected him at the close of his term.

[E. P. Kilroe, *Saint Tammany and the Origin of the Soc. of Tammany* (1913); *N. Y. Gazette and Weekly Mercury*, Aug. 14, 1780; *An Account of the Interment of the Remains of Am. Patriots* (1865); I. N. P. Stokes, *The Iconography of Manhattan Island*, vol. V (1926); *Minutes of the Common Council of the City of N. Y., 1784–1831* (19 vols., 1917); *Commercial Advertiser* (N. Y.), Nov. 28, 1831.]

E. C. S.

MOORE, ADDISON WEBSTER (July 30, 1866–Aug. 25, 1930), philosopher, was born at Plainfield, Ind., the son of John Sheldon and Adaline (Hockett) Moore. His paternal ancestors came from Virginia by way of Kentucky. His father, an ardent Abolitionist, served throughout the Civil War. On his mother's side he came from a family of Quakers who emigrated from North Carolina to Indiana because of the slavery issue. The son, Addison, attended the Plainfield Academy near his home, then taught school, and at twenty years of age entered the neighboring De Pauw University, from which he received the degree of A.B. in 1890. On Sept. 1, 1891, he was married to Ella E. Adams whom he had known at the University. In 1893 he entered the graduate school of Cornell University as a candidate for the degree of Ph.D. At the end of the academic year 1893–94 he was attracted to the University of Chicago by the philosophy and personality of John Dewey. From that date until his retirement as professor emeritus in 1929, his connection with the Chicago School of Philosophy, as student or teacher, was unbroken and influential. He was granted the degree of Ph.D. in 1898 and in 1901–02 he studied in Berlin. In 1911 the Western Philosophical Association elected him to its presidency and in 1917 he was elected president of the American Philosophical Association. He died in London following a stroke of paralysis; he had just completed an automobile tour of six thousand miles on the continent of Europe.

At Cornell University Moore was methodically trained in the history of philosophical ideas and problems. His interest in historical scholarship was kept fresh during his entire teaching career. It proved to be one of the most valuable parts of his generous equipment for the guidance and instruction of a long line of graduate students. He had little sympathy with the doctrines of absolute idealism which the Cornell School had derived from Kant and the neo-Hegelians, particularly through the mediation of Bosanquet and Bradley. He was temperamentally and by bias of early education interested chiefly in the problems of will and of society, in a philosophy adjustable to the flux of action and purpose. A system of rigid and static reality was, in his opinion, useless for an empirical world of evolution. He rejected, therefore, absolute idealism in all of its forms and allied himself whole-heartedly with the Chicago school of instrumental pragmatism, of which Dewey was the creator and Moore the principal apologete. He believed that truth is identified with ideas that work, that solve our problems, that fit into the purposiveness of empirical processes. In his assumption that both fact and idea have their only being and meaning when they are applied to desiring and willing, to believing and working, that is, to human life, his philosophy was a form of Humanism. This accounts for his indifference to the ordinary problems of epistemology and metaphysics. His contribution to *Studies in Logical Theory,* edited by Dewey and published in 1903, was somewhat tentative and obscure, but in 1910 he published the most complete statement of his views in *Pragmatism and its Critics.* The volume is primarily a work of exposition and defense, although it contains instructive chapters on the historical backgrounds of absolute idealism and pragmatism. The first chapter of this work, "The Issue," rings out a challenge, and as challenger he stood for two decades, lance in hand, in the front rank of pragmatists. Although nearly all of his writings and addresses are controversial in character, few authors have illustrated more happily the amenities of polemical discourse.

His philosophical activity and influence are scarcely to be measured by the number or range of his publications, the chief of which are:

Pragmatism and its Critics (1910); "Bergson and Pragmatism" (*Philosophical Review,* July 1912); "Reformation of Logic," in the volume entitled *Creative Intelligence* (1917), edited by John Dewey; and "The Opportunity of Philosophy" (*Philosophical Review,* March 1918). Perhaps his greatest influence was exerted through the spoken word and the oral dialectic of his graduate seminary.

[*Who's Who in America,* 1930–31; J. M. and Jaques Cattell, *Am. Men of Sci.* (4th ed., 1927); *N. Y. Times, Chicago Daily Tribune,* Aug. 26, 1930; addresses by J. H. Tufts, Mathilde Castro Tufts, and George H. Mead at a memorial service held at the Univ. of Chicago, Nov. 8, 1930.]

W. A. H.

MOORE, ALFRED (May 21, 1755–Oct. 15, 1810), Revolutionary soldier and associate justice of the United States Supreme Court, was born in New Hanover County, N. C. In 1764 his parents, Judge Maurice [*q.v.*] and Anne (Grange) Moore, sent him to Boston for an education. He returned home before the Revolution, studied law under his father, and was licensed to practise in 1775. He married Susanna Elizabeth Eagles of Brunswick County. On Sept. 1, 1775, the Third Provincial Congress elected him a captain in the 1st North Carolina Continental Regiment, and he participated in the Moore's Creek campaign in February 1776 and in the gallant defense of Charlestown (later Charleston), S. C., in June. He resigned his commission, Mar. 8, 1777, and returned to his plantation "Buchoi" in Brunswick County, where until the end of the conflict he was active as a colonel of militia, particularly in harassing the British under Maj. James H. Craig, who occupied Wilmington in 1781. The war left his plantation plundered and his fortune greatly impaired, but by 1790 he was the owner of forty-eight slaves.

In 1782, as representative of Brunswick County in the Senate, Moore opposed the policy of extreme proscription of the Loyalists. On May 3 he was elected attorney-general of North Carolina, and for nearly nine years he executed the duties of the office with unusual distinction. On Jan. 9, 1791, displeased at an act of 1790 which expanded the court system and created the office of solicitor-general with the same powers and remuneration as that of attorney-general, he resigned, stating that no satisfactory division of the work could be arranged without injury to his health or private business. His legal career was brilliant. In his generation he shared the leadership of the North Carolina bar with only William R. Davie [*q.v.*]. His power as an advocate and his knowledge of the criminal law profoundly impressed his contemporaries. With small stature, frail physique, dark, piercing eyes, and clear voice, he was graceful in manner, chaste in style, quick in perception, animated in address, and powerful in analysis. He helped prepare the public mind for the establishment of the state university, contributed to its support, and served as a trustee, 1789–1807.

Moore was designated by the governor as a delegate to the Annapolis Convention in 1786, but no North Carolinian attended. He was a Federalist in politics and in 1788 favored the ratification of the Constitution as drafted. In 1792 he represented Brunswick County in the House of Commons; in 1795 he was defeated by Timothy Bloodworth, Republican, after a stubborn contest in the General Assembly for election to the United States Senate. On Jan. 8, 1798, President Adams nominated him as one of the three commissioners to conclude a treaty with the Cherokee nation of Indians, but he withdrew from the negotiations before the treaty was signed on Oct. 2. He was elected a judge of the superior court by the General Assembly, Dec. 7, 1798. In recognition of his legal eminence, President Adams appointed him an associate justice of the Supreme Court of the United States in December 1799 to succeed James Iredell, deceased. He delivered an opinion in only one case (*Bas* vs. *Tingy*, 4 *Dallas*, 37) followed *seriatim* by the opinions of the other judges. The court held in this case (1800) that a state of "limited, partial" war existed with France. The opinion was applauded by Federalists but condemned by Republicans. In 1804 Moore resigned on account of ill health, dying on Oct. 15, 1810, at the home of his son-in-law in Bladen County.

[*The Colonial Records of N. C.* (10 vols., 1886–90) ; *State Records of N. C.* (16 vols., 1895–1905) ; *Jours. of the Senate and House of Commons*, 1794–95, 1798 ; Governors' Papers, in N. C. Hist. Commission ; S. A. Ashe, "Alfred Moore," in S. A. Ashe, ed., *Biog. Hist. of N. C.*, vol. II (1905) ; W. H. Hoyt, ed., *The Papers of Archibald D. Murphey* (2 vols., 1914) ; address of Junius Davis, Apr. 29, 1899, in 124 *N. C. Reports*, 882–92 ; *Am. State Papers, Indian Affairs*, vol. I (1832) ; *Raleigh Reg.*, Nov. 1, 1810.]   A. R. N.

MOORE, ANDREW (1752–May 24, 1821), political leader, representative and senator from Virginia, was the son of Mary (Evans) and David Moore, who emigrated from the north of Ireland and settled in the Valley of Virginia. He was born at "Cannicello," about twenty miles south of Staunton, in that part of Augusta County which is now Rockbridge County. After attaining some education at the local log college, Augusta Academy (now Washington and Lee University) he went to Williamsburg, where he studied law under George Wythe. He qualified as an attorney about 1774. When the Revolution

began he asserted his leadership by persuading the neighborhood youths to enlist under him and, as head of a company of the 9th Virginia Regiment of the Continental Line, he had one or more important tours of service. He never advanced beyond a captaincy in the Revolution but, later, as a militia officer reached the rank of majorgeneral. Soon after the Revolution he married Sarah, the daughter of Andrew Reid of Rockbridge County. In his early thirties he had become a political leader of the very important Valley section of Virginia. This leadership was recognized in the state legislature, to which he was consistently elected during the decade before the organization of the federal government in 1789. He became one of Madison's chief lieutenants in the contests against such measures as the emission of paper money, an assessment for religion, and the confiscation of British debts. Likewise he joined with Madison and did service in the movements for religious liberty, the reform in the state court system, and the reorganization of the federal government. While he played a minor part on the floor of the Virginia ratification convention of 1788, he proved his worth to Madison and his colleagues by refusing to be influenced by a nearly successful attempt of the anti-federalists to change the sentiment of his constituents after he had been elected as a federalist. On June 28, 1788, he was elected a member of the privy council, for which he qualified on Nov. 4.

Though one of the younger Valley leaders he was chosen as the representative from his section to the First Congress in 1789 and was reelected for four successive terms. In the House he continued as a Madison lieutenant, opposing drastic amendments to the new Constitution, fighting against the Bank of the United States and, later, the Alien and Sedition Acts. He also joined heartily with Madison and White in the various maneuvers that finally succeeded in bringing the new capital to the banks of the Potomac. His independence, as well as his loyalty to his section, is indicated in his refusal to vote with Madison for the first tariff measures because they contained provisions unfavorable to his frontier section, such as the salt duties and the distillery excise. In 1799, after an absence of ten years, he returned with Madison to the Virginia legislature for the 1799–1800 session and helped to defeat the set of resolutions that proposed to repudiate those of 1798. In the next session, 1800–01, he served in the upper house of the legislature. In 1800 he was a presidential elector on the Republican ticket. The next year he was appointed as one of the commissioners to adjust the boundary line between Tennessee and Virginia, but he was prevented from serving because he accepted the federal appointment to be marshal of the western district of Va. (*Calendar, post,* vol. IX, pp. 205, 276). He was reëlected to Congress but, only after successfully contesting the election with Thomas Lewis, was he able to serve from Mar. 5 to Aug. 11, 1804, when he resigned in order to accept appointment to the United States Senate. He served in the Senate as an administration supporter until March 1809. In the following year he was appointed United States marshal for the state of Virginia and continued in that position until his resignation just before his death (*The Writings of James Monroe,* ed. by S. M. Hamilton, vol. VI, 1902, p. 176). His most important non-political service was in behalf of the academy he had himself attended. He was active in obtaining a charter from the legislature in 1782, served as a trustee from 1782 to 1821, and was largely instrumental in enlisting the sympathy and material aid of Washington for the permanent establishment of the institution which later became Washington and Lee University.

[Sketch by H. B. Grigsby, in *Washington and Lee Hist. Papers,* no. 2 (1890) ; *Biog. Dire tory Am. Cong.* (1928) ; *Calendar of Va. State Papers,* vols. I, p. 235, III, p. 75, IV, pp. 461, 508, 543, 586, V, pp. 241, 394, VIII, p. 477, IX, pp. 75, 205, 216, 276, 414, 425 ; *Va. Mag. of Hist.,* Oct. 1900, p. 123 ; J. A. Waddell, *Annals of Augusta County, Va.,* 2nd ed. (1902).]   F. H. H.

MOORE, ANNIE AUBERTINE WOODWARD (Sept. 27, 1841–Sept. 22, 1929), musician, author, translator, known also under the pseudonym Auber Forestier, was born in Montgomery County, Pa., the daughter of Joseph Janvier Woodward and Elizabeth Graham (Cox). Educated in private schools in Philadelphia, Pa., and later by private tutors, she specialized in music and the Scandinavian languages, thus preparing herself for the specific line of endeavor which she had in mind and in which she was to make her mark. One of the earliest students of Scandinavian music in America, she began in 1880 to give musical lecture-recitals, being a pioneer in that type of educational entertainment. She continued active on the lecture-stage for some years, giving talks in different cities on music and musicians with illustrative piano playing, and lectures on musical-literary subjects. In 1880 she published *The Spell-bound Fiddler,* a translation from the work of Kristofer N. Janson [*q.v.*]. Subsequently she collaborated with Rasmus Björn Anderson, professor of Scandinavian languages and literature at the University of Wisconsin, in the transla-

tion of Björnstjerne Bjørnson's *Synnöve Solbakken* (1881) ; *Arne* (1881) ; *A Happy Boy* (1881) ; *The Fisher Maiden* (1882) ; *Captain Mansana and Other Stories* (1882) ; *The Bridal March and Other Stories* (1882); *Magnhild* (1883) ; and under the pseudonym of Auber Forestier, in the compilation of *The Norway Music Album* (1881). In 1886 she assisted in translating into English Thuiskon Hauptner's *Voice Culture.* On Dec. 22, 1887, at Madison, Wis., she married Samuel H. Moore.

From 1900 to 1912 she conducted classes in the history and theory of music and musical appreciation and analysis at the Madison Musical College. She was also literary critic for the *Wisconsin State Journal,* from 1900 to 1911, and editor of the department of music in the *Simmons Magazine,* 1910–12. In these later years she published various musical works: *For My Musical Friend* (1900), *For Every Music Lover* (1902), *Faustina, A Venetian Queen of Song* (1918) ; and a collection, *Songs of the North* (1907), also a translation. She died in Madison, Wis.

[*Who's Who in America,* 1916–17; *N. Y. Times,* Sept. 24, 1929; *Capital Times* (Madison, Wis.), Sept. 23, 1929.]   F. H. M.

MOORE, BARTHOLOMEW FIGURES (Jan. 29, 1801–Nov. 27, 1878), lawyer, was born in Halifax County, N. C. He was the son of James Moore, a native of Virginia, and Sally Lowe Lewis of Edgecombe County, N. C. Entering the sophomore class of the University of North Carolina, he was graduated in 1820. He then studied law, was admitted to the bar in 1823, and began practice at Nashville, Nash County, where for twelve years he barely made a living. Employing these lean years in close study, he became, while still a young man, a very learned lawyer, well versed in statute law, and profound in his knowledge of the common law. In 1835 he returned to Halifax County and finally won professional success. Also in a modest way he entered politics. He had been a Crawford Republican, but he disliked intensely Jacksonian Democracy and cast his lot with Clay. In 1836, and again in 1840, 1842, and 1844, he was a member of the House of Commons where he was an active champion of internal improvements, public schools, and the establishment of asylums and hospitals for the unfortunate. From 1848 to 1851 he was attorney-general, resigning upon his selection as one of the commissioners to revise the statute law of the state. The *Revised Code of North Carolina . . . 1854* (1855) is a monument to his legal learning. He achieved his first wide reputation as a lawyer by his brief in *State* vs. *Will* (18 *N. C.*, 121), a case in which the court upheld him in affirming the right of a slave to protect himself by force from unlawful violence, even from his master. This marked a notable lessening of the rigor of the slave code. All of his cases were admirably prepared and forcibly presented, but without a trace of oratory or eloquence. In appearance and manner he was austere, and, utterly frank, he was frequently impetuous and irascible in speech.

As the Civil War approached, Moore found himself out of sympathy with the trend of Southern sentiment. While he believed that the South was justly aggrieved, he denied the right of secession and never changed his opinion. He refused to be a candidate for the secession convention, and his only concession to the Confederate cause was his acceptance of a place on the state board of claims. He refused to take the oath of allegiance to the Confederacy, although he was thereby debarred from practice in the Confederate courts, and, while he took no part in any peace movement, he made no secret of his love for the Union and his wish for its restoration. When the war closed, President Johnson summoned him to Washington for advice on North Carolina affairs, and on May 22, 1865, explained his plan of restoration in detail and showed him the amnesty and North Carolina proclamations which were ready to be issued. Moore vehemently opposed the whole plan, denying its constitutionality, and urged the President to employ the existing legislatures to summon conventions and thus preserve legal continuity. Johnson was friendly but firm, and when he invited Moore to participate in the selection of a provisional governor, the latter declined to have any part in it. He was, however, a member of the convention of 1865 and its outstanding leader. He drew the ordinance declaring the ordinance of secession null and void from the beginning, and favored vacating all offices, but he bitterly resented the President's insistence upon the repudiation of the war debt and voted against the ordinance. He served on the commission to suggest such changes in the laws as were made necessary by emancipation, and wrote the report, later adopted by the legislature, which recognized the citizenship of the freedmen and granted them substantial equality before the law.

In the second session of the convention in 1866 Moore drew up the new constitution, induced the convention to adopt it and submit it to the people, and, in a powerful argument, unsuccessfully urged its ratification. He had little sympathy with the conservatives who were in power in the state from 1866 to 1868, and even less

with the radicals. He opposed congressional reconstruction because he believed it unconstitutional and because he foresaw its evil results, but he saw no hope of immediate relief and took no active part in politics. In 1869, however, when certain justices of the supreme court and other judges took an active part in a political demonstration in behalf of the Republican party, he drew up a solemn protest which was signed by 107 other lawyers and published. The supreme court at its succeeding session ordered the signers disabled from appearing until they could show cause to the contrary, and served the rule upon Moore and two others. Upon their disavowal of intent to bring the court into contempt, the court, which found itself in an awkward position, discharged the rule. Moore continued in active practice, chiefly in the federal courts, until his death. His practice in the United States Supreme Court was large and successful. He was twice married: on Dec. 2, 1828, to Louisa, the daughter of George Boddie, of Nash County, N. C., who died in 1829, and on Apr. 19, 1835, to her sister Lucy.

[S. A. Ashe, ed., *Biog. Hist. of N. C.*, vol. V (1906); J. H. Wheeler, *Reminiscences and Memoirs of N. C.* (1884); J. G. deR. Hamilton, *Reconstruction in N. C.* (1914); E. G. Haywood, address in *Tribute to the Memory of Bartholomew Figures Moore* (1878); *Univ. Mag.* (N. C.), May 1878; the *Observer* (Raleigh, N. C.), Nov. 28, 1878.]   J. G. deR. H.

MOORE, BENJAMIN (Oct. 5, 1748–Feb. 27, 1816), second Protestant Episcopal bishop of New York and president of Columbia College, was a descendant of Rev. John Moore, one of the settlers of Newtown, Long Island. Benjamin was born in Newtown, the son of Samuel Moore, a farmer, and his wife Sarah, daughter of John Fish. He graduated at the head of his class at King's College in 1768, and after studying theology with Rev. Samuel Auchmuty [*q.v.*], went to England, where he received deacon's and priest's orders from the Bishop of London in June 1774 (Dix, *post*, II, 319–20). He became an assistant minister of Trinity Church, New York, in February 1775. After the flight of Myles Cooper [*q.v.*], the Loyalist president of King's College, in May of that year, Moore was made president *pro tempore* and retained the title until 1784. When the college building was taken over by the military officials in the spring of 1776, Moore moved his family and the remaining students to 13 Wall Street, where some instruction was carried on until the British took the city. He remained loyal to the King throughout the war, and acted as deputy chaplain for the hospital in the college building. In November

1783, before the British forces had evacuated New York City, the Loyalist rector of Trinity, Rev. Charles Inglis [q.v.], resigned, and Moore was elected in his place. The election was immediately challenged by the Whig members of the parish, because of Moore's "avowed sympathies with the British cause and his dislike of the new government," and he wisely withdrew (Dix, II, 3). Upon the reorganization of King's College as Columbia in 1784, he was appointed professor of rhetoric and logic, a position he held until 1786, and in December 1800, when the rectorship of Trinity was again offered him, he assumed office without opposition. After the resignation of Bishop Provoost [q.v.] in 1801, Moore was elected his successor, and was consecrated at Trenton, Sept. 11, 1801. In the same year, Rev. Charles Henry Wharton [q.v.] resigned the presidency of Columbia after a few months' service, and on Dec. 31, Moore was elected to that position. He held these three offices until February 1811, when an attack of paralysis incapacitated him for any further public service. An assistant bishop (John Henry Hobart) and an assistant rector (Abraham Beach) were elected to take over his church duties, and on May 6 he resigned the presidency of the college. After suffering repeated paralytic attacks, he died, early in 1816, "at his residence at Greenwich, near New York."

He filled with acceptance, if not distinction, the various offices to which he was called. Both Columbia and Trinity were in financial straits during his terms of office, and he left them unimproved, although it was under his rectorship that Trinity erected St. John's Chapel in Varick Street. As a preacher he commanded attention and respect by his dignity and unaffected solemnity of manner and the skilful management of a naturally feeble voice. In appearance he was slender and graceful, of medium stature, and long-faced. His only publications were sermons, of which a two-volume collection was published posthumously (1824) by his son.

On Apr. 20, 1778, he married Charity, daughter of Maj. Thomas Clarke, deceased, a British officer whose large estate, "Chelsea," in Greenwich Village, Manhattan, was ultimately inherited by the Moores (*New York Gazette*, May 2, 1778; *Collections of the New York Historical Society for the Year 1900*, 1901, p. 37). Their only child was Clement Clarke Moore [q.v.], theologian and lexicographer.

[W. B. Sprague, *Annals Am. Pulpit*, V (1859), 299–304; Morgan Dix, *A Hist. of the Parish of Trinity Ch. in the City of N.Y.* (4 vols., 1898–1906), John B. Pine, "Benjamin Moore," in *Columbia Univ. Quart.*, June 1900; N. Y. *Evening Post*, Feb. 28, 1816; J. W. Moore, *Rev. John Moore of Newtown, L. I. and Some of His Descendants* (1903).]   M. H. T—s.

MOORE, CHARLES HERBERT (Apr. 10, 1840–Feb. 15, 1930), artist, teacher, writer on the fine arts, was born in New York City, the son of Charles and Jane Maria (Benson) Moore. His early education was received in the New York public schools. He did not attend any college, but in 1890 he was given the honorary degree of A.M. by Harvard. In New York he received some training as a landscape painter, but while still a young man he moved to Catskill, where he lived for a number of years.

In 1871 he was called to Harvard as instructor in freehand drawing and water color in the Lawrence Scientific School. Three years later he was invited by Prof. Charles Eliot Norton [q.v.], who had just been appointed lecturer on the history of the fine arts, to offer to undergraduates in Harvard College a course on the principles of design, painting, sculpture, and architecture. This appointment marked the real beginning of his long career as a teacher, and also the beginning of the gradual establishment of fine arts on an equal footing with other subjects included under the general head of liberal education in American colleges and universities. Norton believed that an educated man should know something of the history and principles of the fine arts (the visual arts), and Moore insisted that some actual practice in drawing and painting was necessary as a means of thorough understanding and appreciation of works of art. In developing this rather revolutionary method of teaching fine arts, Moore had the vigorous backing of President Eliot. From this time on Moore was primarily a teacher. He was appointed assistant professor in 1891 and professor in 1896. When the Fogg Art Museum was built in 1895 he was made first curator, and the following year, director, a position which he held until he retired from active service in 1909.

Moore owed much to Ruskin as well as to Norton. The winter of 1876–77 he spent in Europe. He called on Ruskin at Brantwood with a letter of introduction from Norton, and later joined him in Venice. They worked together on Carpaccio's "Vision of St. Ursula," which was put into a separate room for Ruskin's benefit. A small study of the whole picture by Ruskin is in the drawing school at Oxford, and a full-sized copy of the head by Moore is in the Fogg Museum. In a letter to Norton from Venice in October 1876 Ruskin wrote: "I am very much delighted at having Mr. Moore for a companion —we have perfect sympathy in all art matters and are not in dissonance in any others. His voice continually reminds me of yours.—And he's not at all so wicked nor so republican as you, and minds all I say!" (E. T. Cook and Alexander Wedderburn, *The Works of John Ruskin*, 1909, vol. XXXVII, 211). Moore visited Ruskin in Verona and saw him also in Florence; and it must have been at this period that they returned together over the Simplon. The Fogg Museum owns a number of water colors or scenes in and about the Simplon village done by Moore in this and later years. As a painter Moore was perhaps the most accomplished of those who may be thought of as Ruskin's pupils. His handling of body-color and his general point of view place him with the English painter Brabazon, only that he was usually much more precise. A few of his copies—one especially of Botticelli's "Calumny"—have hardly been surpassed. His copies of paintings and most of his studies of natural form were made for use in connection with his teaching, and they are mainly in the collection of the Fogg Museum.

Moore's wide reputation came principally from his study of medieval architecture, to which he devoted much of his time from about 1885. The results of this study are embodied in a series of books, the best known of which is *Development and Character of Gothic Architecture* (1890, revised edition, 1899). He was inspired more especially by Viollet-le-Duc, and he stands close to the latter as a pioneer in the study of the structural side of medieval architecture. Since he found this exemplified notably in the French architecture of the Île de France, he proposed that the term Gothic be employed exclusively in this connection. Such limitation in the use of the term, as well as some of his conclusions in regard to the development and character of English architecture, was objected to, particularly by English writers, but many of them have expressed their great appreciation of the clearness and conviction with which his opinions were stated and the necessity he put upon them of defining their own views with more precision. Perhaps his most extreme statement of the case for expressiveness of function and structure is in *Character of Renaissance Architecture*, published in 1905.

It has been said that the keynote of Moore's character was his hatred of sham, and that in art, as in life, he demanded above all things honesty and simplicity. It was this quality which attracted him to the study of medieval architecture and endeared him to many of his students and to his friends. His former pupils remember him as a picturesque figure, dressed usually in warm-colored tweeds and an English cloth hat. Regular exercise, principally in the sawing of

wood for the fireplaces, kept him in good physical condition, and even when he retired from teaching his cheek showed a round and youthful outline through his full white beard.

On July 19, 1865, he married Mary Jane Tomlinson of Schenectady, N. Y., by whom he had a daughter, Elizabeth, who later assisted him in illustrating with pen-drawings his book on Gothic architecture. After the death of his first wife he married, Dec. 30, 1881, Elizabeth Fisk Hewins. Upon retiring, in 1909, he built a house at Hartfield, Hartley Wintney, Winchfield, Hants, in England, where he lived with his wife and daughter until his death. Here he continued his work on architecture, and in 1912 published *The Mediæval Church Architecture of England*. An interest in Swedenborg increased toward the end of his life and resulted in his publishing in 1918, *Swedenborg: Servant of God*.

[*Who's Who in America*, 1930–31; W. R. Lethaby, "The Late C. H. Moore, A.M.," in *Jour. of the Royal Institute of British Architects*, Mar. 22, 1930; *Times* (London), Feb. 18, 22, 1930; *Harvard Grads. Mag.*, June 1909; *Art News*, Feb. 22, 1930; *Boston Evening Transcript*, Feb. 17, 1930.]   A. P.

MOORE, CLARENCE LEMUEL ELISHA (May 12, 1876–Dec. 5, 1931), mathematician, the son of George Taylor and Lydia Ann (Bradshaw) Moore, was born in Bainbridge, Ohio. His father was a grain dealer and was descended from the early settlers. After some years of school teaching, Moore entered the Ohio State University, from which he was graduated in 1901. He then pursued graduate study in mathematics at Cornell University, from which he received the degree of M.A. in 1902, and that of Ph.D. in 1904. From this time until his death, he was associated with the Massachusetts Institute of Technology, where he was successively instructor, assistant professor (1909), associate professor (1916), and professor (1920). Shortly after going to the Institute, he spent a year in study abroad, principally at Turin under Segre, and the influence of the Italian geometers profoundly affected his later mathematical work. On June 11, 1913, he married Belle Pease Fuller of Springfield, Mass.

He was outstanding in all three of the fields of activity of an American educator: teaching, administration, and research. He conducted classes in mathematics as applied to aeronautics; for eleven years he was in charge of the course in general science and engineering. In creative mathematical work, he maintained a vigorous interest throughout his entire career, and his accomplishments were large, although he was all his life handicapped by deficient eyesight.

His numerous published papers deal principally with geometry. He began with problems concerning algebraic geometry in Euclidean space of three and higher dimensions, and later proceeded to the differential geometry of Riemannian manifolds. He also (partly with H. B. Phillips) did some work on the applications of vector analysis to geometry. Taken as a whole, his work possesses unusual unity, and gives evidence of a real feeling for vital problems and a keen geometric insight into them. His papers (partly with E. B. Wilson) applying the methods of Ricci to the geometry of hyperspace, a field since made popular by the interest in the theory of relativity, showed him to be one of the first American mathematicians to recognize the importance of these methods. His last few papers (partly with Philip Franklin) dealt with the geometry of Pfaffians. He was a member of various mathematical societies, and a fellow of the American Academy of Arts and Sciences. From 1921 to his death he edited the *Journal of Mathematics and Physics,* which was founded at the Institute of Technology largely through his efforts.

[D. J. Struik, in *Jour. of Math. and Phys.,* vol. XI (1932) gives a complete list of scientific publications; see also D. J. Struik, in *Bull. Am. Math. Soc.,* Mar. 1932; Philip Franklin, *Proc. Am. Acad. of Arts and Sciences,* vol. LXVII (1933); *Technology Rev.,* Jan. 1932; *Who's Who in America,* 1930–31; *Boston Transcript,* Dec. 5, 1931.]   P.F.

MOORE, CLEMENT CLARKE (July 15, 1779–July 10, 1863), Hebrew scholar, writer of verse, was born at "Chelsea" in New York, son of the Rev. Benjamin Moore [*q.v.*] and Charity, second daughter of Maj. Thomas Clarke, whose estate fell to Clement Clarke Moore's parents and was inherited by him, their only child. After tutoring the boy at home, his father sent him to Columbia College, where he was graduated in 1798. It was the father's hope that the son would take orders, but he preferred to serve the Church as a layman. If the ascription to him of the anonymous *Observations upon Certain Passages in Mr. Jefferson's Notes on Virginia Which Appear to Have a Tendency to Subvert Religion and Establish a False Philosophy* (1804) be correct, we have an indication of the temper and trend of the young man's thought. He regrets "that more of the well-disposed among his young countrymen do not devote their leisure hours to the attainment of useful learning, rather than to frivolous amusements or political wrangling" (p. 32). His own addiction to "the attainment of useful learning" is shown by his devotion to the study of Hebrew, and led to his publishing in 1809 *A Compendious Lexi-*

con of the Hebrew Language: In Two Volumes. It is a creditable piece of work and doubtless fulfilled his hope that "his young countrymen" would "find it of some service to them, as a sort of pioneer, in breaking down the impediments which present themselves at the entrance of the study of Hebrew" (p. xii). On Nov. 20, 1813, he was married to Catharine Elizabeth Taylor.

After his father's death he took an increasing interest in ecclesiastical affairs. In February 1819 he offered, through Bishop Hobart, sixty lots in New York City (including the present Chelsea Square) on condition that "the buildings of the theological school should be erected thereon." This gift, together with one from a New York layman two years later, made the General Theological Seminary possible. In 1821 he became professor of Biblical learning and interpretation of Scripture in the diocesan seminary at New York, and in 1823, a professor in the General Theological Seminary, into which the diocesan seminary was merged. In 1825 the first permanent seminary building was erected on the ground he had given. He continued to serve the Seminary as professor of Oriental and Greek literature until his resignation in 1850. This same year he published *George Castriot, Surnamed Scanderbeg, King of Albania.* It is based upon an English translation of Jacques Lavardin's work, and the author's task was to "concentrate Lavardin's history by rendering the language more concise" (Preface, p. 6). It is, as are all his serious works, written in a dignified prose based on Johnsonian standards.

Moore is chiefly remembered, however, for his ballad beginning "'Twas the night before Christmas, when all through the house . . ." According to tradition, he wrote the verses in 1822 as a Christmas gift for his own children; they were transcribed by a guest of the household, and by her given to the press in Troy, N. Y., the following year. First published anonymously in the *Troy Sentinel,* Dec. 23, 1823, the poem was reprinted in school readers and in a collection of the author's verse, *Poems* (1844). It has since been included in many different anthologies, and, losing none of its original freshness, has been loved by American children for more than a hundred years.

[J. W. Moore, *Rev. John Moore of Newtown, Long Island, and Some of His Descendants* (1903); E. A. Hoffman, "Hist. Sketch of the Gen. Theological Sem.," in W. S. Perry, *The Hist. of the Am. Episc. Ch. 1587–1883* (1885), vol. II; W. S. Pelletreau, *The Visit of Saint Nicholas . . . Facsimile of the Original MS. with Life of the Author* (1897); Clarence Cook, "The Author of 'A Visit from St. Nicholas,'" in *Century Mag.,* Dec. 1897; Journals of the N. Y. Diocesan Convention, and minutes of the trustees and faculty of the Gen. Theological Sem.; *N. Y. Times*, July 14, 1863.]

H. E. W. F.

MOORE, CLIFFORD HERSCHEL (Mar. 11, 1866–Aug. 31, 1931), classicist, was born in Sudbury, Mass., where his ancestors had lived since the earliest settlement of the town. His parents were John Herschel and Julia Ann (McCullough) Moore. He studied at the public school in Sudbury and the Framingham High School. Graduating from Harvard College in 1889, he immediately assumed duties as classical master in the Belmont School for Boys, Belmont, Cal. On July 23, 1890, he married Lorena Leadbetter of Charlestown, Mass. In 1892 he succeeded E. G. Coy as professor of Greek at Phillips Academy, Andover, Mass., and later (1902) became a member of its board of trustees. When (July 9, 1892) the National Education Association appointed the Committee of Ten, headed by President Eliot, to examine the state of secondary education in the United States, Moore's ability as a leader and counselor caused him to be chosen as one of the sub-committee which reported on the study of Greek. In 1894 he was appointed instructor in Latin at the University of Chicago, where he was soon promoted to an assistant professorship, which he held until 1898. Receiving leave of absence, he went to the University of Munich, and in 1897 received there the degree of Ph.D.

The following year he accepted President Eliot's invitation to return to Harvard as assistant professor of Greek and Latin. In 1900 he issued a revision of Frederic De Forest Allen's *Medea of Euripides*, in 1902, an edition of *The Odes, Epodes, and Carmen Saeculare of Horace*, and in 1906 *Elements of Latin* (with J. J. Schlicher). He contributed articles to various scientific periodicals and to the *New International Encyclopaedia*. Advanced to the professorship of Latin in 1905, he served that year at the American School of Classical Studies in Rome, Italy. In 1913 he was Harvard Exchange professor with Western colleges. In 1925 he was elected to the Pope Professorship of Latin at Harvard. In this year appeared the first volume of his *Histories of Tacitus* (Loeb Classical Library), followed in 1931 by the second. Combining interest in the more rigorous disciplines of Latin grammar and epigraphy with a wide knowledge of literature and philosophy, he made the religions of Greece and Rome the special field of his research at Harvard and the subject of his course before the Lowell Institute in Boston (1914). The substance of these lectures is embodied in *The Religious Thought of the Greeks, from Homer to the Triumph of Christianity* (1916, 1925), an admirable discussion of Hellenic ideas concerning the gods and the relations and obligations of men toward them. As president of the American Philological Association (1920), he delivered a notable address on "Prophecy in the Ancient Epic" (*Harvard Studies in Classical Philology*, vol. XXXII, 1921). In 1918 he gave at Harvard the Ingersoll Lecture on the immortality of man. His latest work, completed just before his death, was *Ancient Beliefs in the Immortality of the Soul* (1931).

As an administrative officer he worked with devoted industry, resourcefulness, and tact. During the last years of the World War he took an active part in the difficult task of organizing the Student's Army Training Corps. After the war his executive talents were promptly recognized by his promotion to the deanship of the Graduate School of Arts and Sciences, and later, to that of the Faculty of Arts and Sciences, in which capacity he displayed extraordinary ability as director of the budget and of the curriculum. His wide acquaintance in other colleges at home and abroad, with the hospitable welcome which he and his wife extended to all, made his house in Cambridge the congenial resort of old and young alike. Though he often suffered from ill health, he was fond of outdoor sports. His teaching was lucid and incisive, lighted with humor and apt illustration; his intellectual and moral standards were high. No man did more to improve the relations between secondary schools and the college, and none had greater influence in shaping the new policies of Harvard from 1918 until his death.

[*Class of 1889 Harvard College* (1914); *Report of the President of Harvard College for 1930–31* (1932); *Harvard University Gazette*, Dec. 5, 1931; *Boston Evening Transcript*, Aug. 31, 1931; the *Times* (London), Sept. 8, 1931; *Harvard Alumni Bull.*, Oct. 2, 1931); the *Nation*, Oct. 7, 1931; personal acquaintance.]

C. B. G.

MOORE, EDWARD MOTT (July 15, 1814–Mar. 3, 1902), surgeon, was born in Rahway, N. J., the son of Lindley Murray Moore and Abigail Lydia (Mott). His father was a native of Nova Scotia, the son of Samuel Moore, a New Jersey Quaker who joined the Loyalist emigration after the Revolution; his mother was descended from ancestors who settled about 1644 at Hempstead, L. I. After Edward's birth the family moved successively to New York City, to Westchester, where the father conducted a school, and in 1830 to Rochester, N. Y. Edward commenced his education under his father and began the study of Latin and Greek at the age of four. A robust boy, he was early interested in farming and became one of the prize broadcast sowers of grain in the vicinity. He prepared for college under his father's direction and entered the Rensselaer School at Troy (now Rensselaer Polytechnic Institute) in the class with James Hall [*q.v.*], who was for many years' state geologist of New York. He withdrew soon, however, and in 1833 began the study of medicine at Rochester with Dr. Anson Coleman and in 1835 entered the College of Physicians and Surgeons, New York. Later he became a medical student at the University of Pennsylvania, where he was graduated M.D. in 1838. Thereafter he spent one and a half years as interne at Blockley Hospital, where he was associated with Dr. C. W. Pennock. He is given credit for original work on the heart in Pennock's American edition of James Hope's *Treatise on the Diseases of the Heart and Great Vessels* (1842).

Unusually well equipped, he returned to Rochester in 1840 and entered upon the practice of his profession. His ability was immediately recognized and in 1842 he was called to the faculty of the Vermont Medical College, Woodstock, where he taught surgery for eleven years. For a part of that time he also taught surgery at the Berkshire Medical College, Pittsfield, Mass., and in 1852 he became professor of anatomy at Buffalo University. Resigning from these professorships in 1853 or early 1854, he taught surgery at the Starling Medical College, Columbus, Ohio, from 1853 to 1856. In the latter year he severed his Columbus connection and returned to the University of Buffalo, where as professor of surgery he was associated with Dalton, Flint, Hamilton, and others, and continued to teach for twenty-six years.

In 1882 he returned to Rochester. Here he was surgeon-in-chief of St. Mary's Hospital and organized the Infants' Hospital. He was president of the medical associations of Monroe County, Central New York, and New York State, of the American Medical Association, and of the American Surgical Association. In those years such was the lack of knowledge of fractures and dislocations and so great the deformities resulting therefrom that his interest was challenged, and he devoted much attention to the study of their cause and treatment. Before the microscope had come into common use, he examined ground bones microscopically, embodying his conclusions in many lectures and monographs. He contributed "Dislocations" to *A Reference Handbook of Medical Sciences*, ed-

ited by A. H. Buck (vol. II, 1886), and "Gangrene and Gangrenous Diseases" to the *International Encyclopaedia of Surgery,* edited by John Ashhurst (1st ed., vol. II, 1882; 2nd ed., vols. I, 1888, and VII, 1895). His studies of fracture of the collar bone, of the superior end of the humerus, of the elbow joint, and of Colles' Fracture are recognized as pieces of original work, the correctness of which has since been proved by the use of the X-ray. Interested in communicable diseases, he became a member of the Rochester board of health and was first president of the New York state board of health. As an educator, he became a member and president of the board of trustees of the University of Rochester. He early advocated parks and was first president of the Rochester Park Commission. He was a man of robust frame and cultivated manner, kind, helpful, generous, courageous, who freely gave to others all that was in him during a long and useful life. He was married in 1847 to Lucy Richard Prescott of Windsor, Vt. Eight children were born to them, two of whom became successful physicians.

[*Boston Medic. and Surgic. Jour.,* Mar. 13, 1902; *Buffalo Medic. Jour.,* Apr., July 1902; *Jour. Am. Medic. Asso.,* Mar. 15, 1902; *Trans. Medic. Soc. of the State of N. Y.,* 1903; H. A. Kelly and W. L. Burrage, *Am. Medic. Biogs.* (1920); T. C. Cornell, *Adam and Anne Mott: Their Ancestors and Descendants* (1890); *Rochester Democrat and Chronicle,* Mar. 4, 1902; personal acquaintance.]
                                                     G. W. G.

MOORE, EDWIN WARD (June 1810–Oct. 5, 1865), naval officer, was born in Alexandria, Va. After attending school at the Alexandria Academy he entered the navy as a midshipman, Jan. 1, 1825, in which rank he served first on board the *Hornet* of the West India Squadron and later on board the *Fairfield* of the Mediterranean Squadron. On reaching the rank of passed midshipman in 1831, he was again attached to the *Fairfield,* at this time stationed in the West Indies. Promoted lieutenant from Mar. 3, 1835, he on July 16, 1839, resigned from the service, as it offered little opportunity for advancement.

On Apr. 21, 1839, he had been offered by the Republic of Texas command of its navy, then consisting of the recently acquired armed steamer *Zavala* and a worthless brig. Between May and December 1839 the navy was increased by the addition of the flagship *Austin,* 20 guns, together with a brig and three schooners. Moore's commission, which was not issued until July 20, 1842, gave him the rank of "post captain commanding." His courtesy title was commodore. Before the last of the new fleet had left Schott & Whitney's Baltimore yard he visited New York, where, in attempting to enlist seamen, he came into conflict with the United States authorities and was compelled to leave the city. In 1840–41 he cruised off the Mexican coast with a fleet of five vessels to expedite the peace negotiations of the Texan diplomat James Treat. When these negotiations collapsed Moore not only swept Mexican commerce from the Gulf but also entered into a *de facto* alliance with Yucatecan rebels and captured the town of Tabasco, upon which he levied a contribution of $25,000. After refitting his ships he surveyed the Texan coast and made a chart of it, which was published in New York and also by the British Admiralty. In the winter of 1841–42 he again cruised with three vessels of his fleet off the coast of Yucatan, thereby saving the federalist Yucatecans from a hasty peace with centralist Santa Anna and continuing an advantageous alliance with the Texans. After capturing several small vessels, he returned to Galveston in May. Thence he proceeded to New Orleans to refit his fleet for the enforcement of a blockade of Mexico, proclaimed by President Sam Houston in retaliation for Mexico's invasion of March 1842. Finances delayed the refitting, by which time a favorable turn in Texan relations with the United States caused Houston to delay further the proposed naval offensive by withholding funds, but without taking Moore or the Yucatecan allies into his confidence. In February 1843 there arrived at New Orleans two commissioners appointed to carry out a secret act of the Texas Congress providing for the sale of the navy. Previous to their arrival Moore had agreed with the authorities of Yucatan, in consideration of the payment of a sum of money sufficient to finish refitting the fleet, to attack the Mexican squadron blockading the Yucatan coast. In accordance with this agreement he attacked the squadron on April 30 and again on May 16, 1843, and in both engagements defeated it. In the second engagement both sides suffered considerable loss and two Mexican ships, *Guadalupe* and *Montezuma*, were badly damaged. On June 1 Moore received a proclamation of Houston declaring that he was guilty of "disobedience, contumacy, and mutiny" and suspending him from his command. He proceeded at once to Galveston and asked for a trial. After a joint committee of the Texas House and Senate had completely vindicated him, he was tried by a court martial and found not guilty on eighteen counts and guilty in respect to matter and form on four counts. The decision, which was a victory for him, was disapproved by Houston. In 1843 he published *To the People of Texas,*

which, in addition to being a personal vindication, is today the best collection of source materials on the Texan navy.

No small part of Moore's later years was spent in prosecuting his claims, in the course of which he published a number of other pamphlets, against the governments of Texas and the United States. From Texas he received more than $20,000 in settlement of claims and payment for relief. A claim in behalf of himself and his fellow officers to incorporation into the federal navy was bitterly opposed by the federal naval officers. Finally, in 1857, Congress voted the Texan officers five years' pay. The last years of Moore's life were passed in New York City, where he was engaged in devising a machine which he believed would revolutionize marine engineering. He died suddenly of apoplexy, leaving, so far as known, no children. In 1849 he was married to Emma M. (Stockton) Cox of Philadelphia. He has been described by those who knew him as a man of science and undoubted gallantry, but having no head for details.

[Record of Officers, Bureau of Navigation, 1825–40; *Tex. State Hist. Asso. Quart.*, Jan. 1904, July, Oct. 1909; *N. Y. Herald*, Oct. 10, 1865; E. W. Moore, *To the People of Texas*, mentioned above; G. P. Garrison, "Diplomatic Correspondence of the Republic of Texas," *Ann. Report Am. Hist. Asso.*, 1907 (1908), vol. II and 1908 (1911), vol. II; Navy registers.]   C. O. P.

MOORE, ELY (July 4, 1798–Jan. 27, 1860), labor leader and congressman, was born near Belvidere, N. J., the son of Moses and Mary (Coryell) Moore and the descendant of John Moore who emigrated from England and settled in Lynn, Mass., before 1641. His education was received partly in the public schools of his birthplace and partly in New York City, where he studied medicine. After a few years of practice he abandoned the profession of medicine to become a printer at a time when great changes were taking place in the printing industry and when technical knowledge on the part of publishers was becoming of less importance than business ability. Men with ambitions and those wishing to promote some special interest, such as politics, agriculture, or labor were crowding into the trade. In 1833 he was elected the first president of the newly formed federation of craft unions of the city of New York, the General Trades' Union (*Address Delivered before the General Trades' Union of the City of New-York*, 1833), and he edited a paper, the *National Trades' Union,* which became its official organ. He was chosen a member of a special commission appointed to investigate the subject of the competition of convict labor from state prisons hired out to contractors. The commission's report approving the continuation of prison labor was not at all satisfactory to the workingmen, who held a public meeting, condemned the report, and demanded his resignation. The demand was not enforced, and the same year he was chosen for a more prominent position in labor politics. In 1834 there was convened in New York a national convention of trades unions with delegates from six eastern cities which took the name of National Trades' Union, electing him its chairman. This position of prominence became a stepping stone to political preferment. The early trade unions had taken a strong stand against political activities, and the politicians, on their side, distrusted the unionists because of their fondness for forming independent parties. However, in New York at this time a working agreement existed with Tammany Hall, and with Tammany support he was elected in 1834 as representative in Congress. Two years later, the workingmen claimed that Tammany had not kept its pledges, deserted, and joined the Equal Rights party. In spite of the fact that he was again a Tammany candidate he received the workingmen's votes and was reëlected to Congress. At the expiration of his second term in 1839 he was appointed surveyor of the port of New York, and in 1845 marshal for the southern district of New York. After a few years he retired to his birthplace in New Jersey where he became the publisher and editor of the *Warren Journal*. About 1850 he emigrated to Kansas and in 1853 became the agent for the Miami and other Indian tribes. Two years later he was appointed register of the United States land office at Lecompton, Kan. In this position he served until his death. He was married twice: first, to Emma Contant who bore him six children and, second, to Mrs. Clara Baker.

[*Biog. Directory Am. Cong.* (1928); J. R. Commons and others, *Hist. of Labor in the U. S.* (1918), vol. I; J. W. Moore, *Rev. John Moore of Newtown, Long Island, and some of his descendants* (1903); *U. S. Mag. and Democratic Rev.*, Oct. 1837, pp. 74–86; *Kan. Natl. Democrat* (Lecompton), Feb. 2, 1860.] P.W.B.

MOORE, FRANK (Dec. 17, 1828–Aug. 10, 1904), author, editor, was baptized Horatio Franklin Moore, but is known only as Frank Moore. He was born in Concord, N. H., the son of Jacob Bailey Moore [*q.v.*] and Mary Adams Hill, and was a brother of George Henry Moore [*q.v.*]. He went to New York City in 1839 with his parents, and attended public school there, moving to Washington, D. C., in 1841 when his father took a position in the post-office in that city. In 1849 he accompanied his father to California. As a secretary to Minister Wash-

burn, he was attached to the American legation at Paris, France, 1869–72, during the Franco-Prussian War, returning to New York in the latter year. He became a member of the New York Historical Society in 1856, and is known for the many books he wrote and edited. Beginning with *Songs and Ballads of the American Revolution* (1856), his works appeared very regularly and included: *American Eloquence: a Collection of Speeches and Addresses* (1857); *Diary of the American Revolution from Newspapers and Original Documents* (2 vols., 1859–60); *Materials for History* (1861); *Heroes and Martyrs: Notable Men of the Time* (1862); *The Rebellion Record* (11 vols. and 1 supp., 1861–68); the Red, White and Blue Series (3 vols., 1864), comprising *Songs of the Soldiers, Personal and Political Ballads of the War,* and *Lyrics of Loyalty; Rebel Rhymes and Rhapsodies* (1864); *Speeches of Andrew Johnson* (1865); *Women of the War* (1866); *Anecdotes, Poetry and Incidents of the War* (1866); *Record of the Year* (2 vols., 1876); *Songs and Ballads of the Southern People* (1886); and others. He contributed to the *New York Criterion,* 1855–56, and to other American literary periodicals. His books on the history of the Revolutionary War and the Civil War are considered valuable compilations. He married Laura M. Bailey, daughter of the Hon. John Bailey of Dorchester, Mass., who died in Boston, Nov. 11, 1904. They had no children. Moore died in Waverly, Mass.

[Sources include: manuscript notes made by J. B. Moore and Geo. H. Moore, gathered by Thomas E. V. Smith; manuscript records in the possession of the N. Y. Hist. Soc.; E. S. Stearns, *Geneal. and Family Hist. of the State of N. H.* (1908), II, pp. 491–92; *Boston Transcript,* Aug. 10, 1904. Moore's diary of 36 volumes, covering the years 1877–94, is in the library of the N. H. Hist. Soc.] A.J.W.

MOORE, GABRIEL (1785?–June 9, 1845?), representative and senator in the federal Congress, governor of Alabama, was the son of Matthew and Letitia (Dalton) Moore and the grandson of John and Frances (Jouett) Moore of Albemarle County, Va. He was born in Stokes County, N. C. He removed to Huntsville, Mississippi Territory, about 1810 and entered upon the practice of law. He was soon sent to represent Madison County in the legislature of the territory. After he had served in this capacity for several years the territory was divided in 1817, and Madison County became a part of the new Territory of Alabama. He continued as representative under the new jurisdiction and was at once elected to the speakership of the lower house of the Assembly. When Alabama became a state he sat in the convention of 1819 that framed her constitution. Immediately thereafter he was elected to the upper house of the new legislature, served in 1819 and 1820, and was chosen speaker in 1820. In 1821 he was sent to Congress and continued to hold this place until 1829, when he was elected without opposition to the governorship of Alabama. Alabama had been a supporter of the Jackson movement from its incipiency, and he was one of the local leaders in the cause. He had an ear for popular favor and was accused of the usual electioneering practices of his partisans. It was said that he made a habit of condemning his opponents as aristocrats and appealing to the reason of his adherents on the hustings through the agency of potent spirits (J. E. Saunders, *Early Settlers of Alabama*, 1899, p. 284). It was as a thoroughgoing Jacksonian that he was elected to the chief magistracy of his state, and his gubernatorial policy was in keeping with his pretensions. He advocated the graduation system for the sale of public lands, deprecated the nullification movement in South Carolina, and proposed that the congressional delegation from Alabama be instructed to vote against the recharter of the Bank of the United States. In local affairs he took an active interest in the beginning of the construction of the canal around Muscle Shoals and in the opening of the state university, both of which events occurred during his administration. He was also much interested in the establishment of a separately organized supreme court for the state, in the revision of the penal code, and in the establishment of a penitentiary (*Journal of the Senate of the State of Alabama*, 1830, pp. 43–47; *Ibid.*, 1831, pp. 7–15; Executive letter book, August 1830).

In 1831 he resigned the governorship in order to take a seat in the Senate of the United States. In this body he voted against the confirmation of Van Buren as minister to the Court of St. James's, and thus broke definitely with the Jackson party (T. H. Benton, *Thirty Years' View*, I, 1854, p. 215). The Alabama legislature requested his resignation, but, in spite of his support of the doctrine of instruction while he was governor, he now refused to comply and continued in his seat until the expiration of his term in 1837 (*Address of Gabriel Moore to the Freemen of Ala. . . . in Reply to Resolutions of the General Assembly Inviting him to Resign his Seat, 1835*). During this year he ran again for the House of Representatives, but the Jackson forces were arrayed against him, and he was defeated. Having thus brought an end to his

political life in Alabama, he removed to Texas in 1843. He is supposed to have died at Caddo in that state two years later, but there is a curious uncertainty in respect to this event (*Southern Advocate*, Huntsville, Ala., Sept. 6, 1844; Addie L. Booker to Marie B. Owen, Nov. 9, 1927. Both are in files of Alabama Department of Archives and History). He was married to a Miss Callier of Washington County, Ala., but an immediate divorce followed. This led to a duel with the bride's brother, who was slightly wounded in the affray. It appears that Moore never married again.

[Material in Ala. Dept. of Archives and Hist. at Montgomery; information from Miss Addie L. Booker, Malta Bend, Mo.; Willis Brewer, *Ala.* (1872); *Biog. Directory Am. Cong.* (1928); Wm. Garrett, *Reminiscences of Public Men in Ala.* (1872), pp. 757–69.]
T. P. A.

MOORE, GEORGE FLEMING (July 17, 1822–Aug. 30, 1883), judge, had the distinction of being twice elevated to the position of chief justice of the supreme court of Texas, with an interval of eleven years between the end of his first and the beginning of his second term of service. His parents, William H. and Mary Garland (Marks) Moore, were members of Virginia families, his mother being the younger half-sister of Meriwether Lewis [*q.v.*]. After their marriage they moved to Elbert County, Ga., where George Fleming Moore was born, the seventh son of a family of ten sons and two daughters. Later the family moved to Alabama. In 1839 he entered the University of Alabama and in 1840 was a law student at the University of Virginia, but, on account of his father's financial reverses, he did not graduate from either institution. He began the study of the law in 1842 and was admitted to the bar in 1844. After two years of practice in Alabama he removed to Texas, residing first in Crockett, then in Austin, and later in Nacogdoches, where he became the senior member of the well-known firm of Moore and Walker. In 1858, his firm was made reporter for the supreme court and brought out volumes 22–24 of the *Texas Reports* (1860–61). During the Civil War he served as colonel of the 17th Regiment of Texas Cavalry but resigned to accept a place on the supreme court of the state, to which he was elected in 1862 to fill the vacancy created by the retirement of Oran M. Roberts. When in 1866 the state, acting under President Johnson's plan of reconstruction, drafted a new constitution and elected a new state government, he was elected chief justice, but in 1867 upon the adoption of the congressional plan of Reconstruction he, with his associates of the supreme court, was removed by the federal military authorities. At the end of the Reconstruction period, when the people of Texas regained control of their government in 1874, he was appointed by Richard Coke as an associate justice of the state supreme court. After the adoption of the Constitution of 1876 he was elected as one of the two associate justices and was appointed chief justice in 1878, when Chief Justice Roberts resigned to become governor. In 1881, because of ill-health and impaired eyesight, he resigned from the court. He died in Washington, D. C. His body was sent to Austin for burial.

One of Moore's successors in the office of chief justice declared him to have been "possibly the greatest equity Judge in the history of the Court" (*Texas Jurisprudence, post*). One of the most important of his opinions may be found in *Ex parte F. H. Coupland* (26 *Texas Reports*, 387), in which he upheld the power of the Confederate Congress to raise an army by conscription. In 1864 he showed the quality of his courage by declaring in contempt of his court the military authorities in Texas who had seized for military punishment five citizens then held in custody by an officer of the supreme court, declaring in his opinion that "there is no officer or tribunal, civil or military, known to the law of the land, that could, without a violation of law and a contempt of this court, forcibly take from under its control, and without its consent, said prisoners, until the final adjudication by the court upon the matter before it" (*The State* vs. *Sparks, 27 Texas Reports,* 632). In the case of *Jacob Kuechler* vs. *Geo. W. Wright* (40 *Texas Reports,* 600) he wrote an exhaustive opinion, establishing the rule, ever since followed in Texas, that all executive officers except the governor are in proper cases subject to control by the writ of mandamus. He was married in Alabama, in 1846, to Susan Spyker, who with six of their seven children survived him.

[Information from Mrs. Mary L. Evans, Denton, Texas; *Texas Jurisprudence,* vol. I (1929), p. xli; J. D. Lynch, *The Bench and Bar of Texas* (1885); *Biog. Encyc. of Texas* (1880); *A Register of the Officers and Students of the Univ. of Ala.,* comp. by T. W. Palmer (1901); *Univ. of Va.* (1904), vol. II; W. T. Lewis, *Geneal. of the Lewis Family* (1893); L. H. A. Minor, *The Meriwethers and Their Connections* (1892), p. 62; *Galveston Daily News,* Aug. 31, Sept. 2, 9, 10, 12, 1883; *Austin Weekly Statesman,* Sept. 13, 1883.]

C. S. P.

MOORE, GEORGE FOOT (Oct. 15, 1851– May 16, 1931), theologian, Orientalist, and historian, was born at West Chester, Pa., the son of William Eves Moore, a Presbyterian minister, and Harriet Francina, daughter of Rev. George Foot, of Connecticut. The Moore stock was Scotch-Irish, the emigrant ancestor, William, having come from Londonderry, Ireland, early in the eighteenth century, to settle in New Castle, Del. George Foot Moore was prepared for college at the West Chester Academy and by his father. Entering Yale as a junior, he graduated in 1872, second in the class. After four years of teaching and private theological study he entered the senior class of Union Theological Seminary, New York, and graduated in 1877. On Feb. 8, 1878, he was ordained to the Presbyterian ministry at Columbus, Ohio, and on Apr. 25, he married Mary Soper Hanford of Chicago. After a pastorate at Zanesville, Ohio (1878–83), he went to Andover Theological Seminary to be professor of the Old Testament and from 1899 to 1901 served as president of the faculty. In 1902 he became professor of the history of religion at Harvard, where he remained until his retirement from active teaching in 1928.

In Moore's nearly twenty years at Andover his eminence as a critical scholar in the field of Hebrew and the Old Testament became recognized both in the United States and in Europe. He made frequent contributions to the *Andover Review,* of which he was assistant editor (1884– 93), and to other journals, and in 1895 published his important *Critical and Exegetical Commentary on Judges.* For the *Encyclopaedia Biblica* (1899–1903) he wrote nearly forty articles, that on "Historical Literature" and the influential article on "Sacrifice" being considerable treatises. At Harvard his personal attractiveness and distinction as a scholar made his position one of great dignity and importance in both the faculties (Arts and Sciences, and Divinity) of which he was a member. His universal knowledge became almost a myth, and he was consulted by all sorts of inquirers on every kind of subject. He was active in administrative matters, as syndic of the Harvard University Press (1913– 24), and as editor of the *Harvard Theological Review* (1908–14 and 1921–31); in the establishment and conduct of which he took the leading part. In 1909–10 as Harvard exchange professor he made the second of two visits to Germany, his only earlier stay having been for the greater part of 1885. His contacts with German scholars were always close, as were those with Jewish scholars in the United States and abroad. He was president of the American Academy of Arts and Sciences, the Massachusetts Historical Society, the American Oriental Society, and the Society of Biblical Literature and Exegesis. Yale conferred on him three honorary degrees.

Besides smaller but weighty books on *The*

Literature of the Old Testament (1913) and *The Birth and Growth of Religion* (1923), his chief later works were his *History of Religions* (2 vols., 1913–19) and *Judaism in the First Centuries of the Christian Era: the Age of the Tannaim* (3 vols., 1927–30). Important are also the articles in the *Harvard Theological Review* on "Christian Writers on Judaism" (July 1921), "Intermediaries in Jewish Theology" (January 1922), and "The Rise of Normative Judaism" (October 1924, January 1925). As befitted a life-long student of Greek philosophy, Moore's interest lay rather in the philosophical than the anthropological aspects of the history of religions, and he was concerned less with the beginnings of the several religions than with their whole history. It was "the religion of intelligent and religious men" which he chiefly studied and described. His *History of Religions* contains a masterly and very interesting account of the origins and whole history of Christian thought based on his own fresh study of the sources. His greatest work, *Judaism,* was the fruit of a critical knowledge of the rabbinical sources unique among Christian scholars in any age. He held that the Jewish religion of the second century of our era, which he portrayed, was but the culmination of a "normative" system of religious life and thought which had had a development continuous since the sixth century before Christ. From this latter date on, "the salient mark of the following centuries was not the elaboration of the Levitical law, however much of this there was, but the appropriation and assimilation of the religious and moral teachings of the prophets."

Moore was of large frame, disciplined in body as in mind, and tireless in work, but no ascetic. An admirable teacher, a lucid and interesting lecturer, he was also an impressive preacher. His promptness and keenness and power of statement made him formidable in controversy. Somewhat quick of temper, impatient of ignorant presumption, capable of severe judgment, not without his dislikes, he was full of kindness, and ready to do anything at any sacrifice for any one who wanted to learn. He was fond of society, and of music, art, and literature. His generosity, his courage, and his loyalty were the traits of a great soul as well as a great scholar.

[W. W. Fenn, in *Proc. Mass. Hist. Soc.,* vol. LXIV (1932); C. C. Torrey, in *Harvard Grads. Mag.,* June 1931; *Harvard Univ. Gazette,* Feb. 27, 1932; *Yale Univ. Obit. Record,* 1931; J. W. Moore, *Rev. John Moore of Newtown, L. I., and Some of His Descendants* (1903), App., p. 484; *Who's Who in America,* 1928–29; *Boston Transcript,* May 16, 1931.] J. H. R.

MOORE, GEORGE HENRY (Apr. 20, 1823–May 5, 1892), librarian, historian, bibli-ographer, brother of Frank Moore [*q.v.*], was born in Concord, N. H., the son of Jacob Bailey Moore [*q.v.*] and Mary Adams (Hill), and a descendant of Jonathan Moore who emigrated from Scotland to New Hampshire in 1650. His early education was received in Concord and at Holmes's Plymouth Academy. He attended Dartmouth College until the end of the first term of his sophomore year, after which he taught district school in Acworth, N. H., until his removal with his parents to New York City in 1839. There he entered the sophomore class of the University of the City of New York, from which he graduated in 1842.

In 1841, while still a sophomore in college, he entered the employ of the New York Historical Society as assistant librarian to George Folsom, the Society at that time having quarters in the University building. When his father, who was librarian of the Society from 1848 to 1849, resigned, the younger Moore was elected to that position. He had previously (Mar. 7, 1848) been elected secretary of the executive committee, on which he served until 1891. During these fifty years he was the central figure in all the activities of the Society, serving also as secretary to the trustees of the new building, which was completed in 1857. He was recognized as a patient investigator in the field of history, a lover of art and literature, with a wide knowledge of books. His research was confined chiefly to the colonial and revolutionary periods of American history, and among the pamphlets he published, perhaps the one which attracted the most attention, was *"Mr. Lee's Plan—March 29, 1777": The Treason of Charles Lee* (1860). He had addressed the New York Historical Society on this subject on June 22, 1858, and brought to light for the first time the character of that Revolutionary general. His writings also included: *Historical Notes on the Employment of Negroes in the American Army of the Revolution* (1862); *Notes on the History of Slavery in Massachusetts* (1866); *Notes on the History of Witchcraft in Massachusetts* (1883–85); *Washington as an Angler* (1887); *Libels on Washington* (1889); *Typographiae Neo-eboracensis Primitiae: Historical Notes on the Introduction of Printing into New York, 1693* (1888); *The First Folio of the Cambridge Press* (1889); *John Dickinson—The Author of the Declaration on Taking up Arms in 1775* (1890). He was also a frequent contributor to various New York newspapers under the signature of "E. Y. E." In addition to his other duties he acted as secretary of the Mexican Boundary Commission, having been appointed in 1850. He was an excellent public speaker and delivered addresses before various societies. In 1876 he was at his own request relieved of his duties at the New York Historical Society to take up the administration of the Lenox Library, of which he had been elected superintendent and trustee on Oct. 3, 1872. He served as secretary of the board from Jan. 6, 1876, until his death. He was a personal friend and adviser of James Lenox [q.v.], the founder of that library, who had rigid ideas as to the public use of it. The formality involved in gaining admittance to it resulted in much hostile public criticism, which was recalled by at least one editor at the time of the death of Moore, on whom he put the blame. The latter, however, was answerable to the board of trustees whose wishes he was obliged to carry out. He is remembered as a man of upright and kindly character. In politics he was originally a Whig and later an ardent Republican. On Oct. 21, 1850, he married, in New York, Mary Howe Givan, widow of Henry S. Richards. They had two children. The sale of his private collection of books and manuscripts in 1893 was one of the noted book auctions of the day.

[E. S. Stearns, *Geneal. and Family Hist., State of N. H.* (1908), vol. II; manuscript notes made by J. B. Moore and G. H. Moore, gathered by T. E. V. Smith; manuscript records in the N. Y. Hist. Soc.; Howard Crosby, in *Hist. Mag.,* Jan. 1870; H. M. Lydenberg, *Hist. of the N. Y. Pub. Lib.* (1923); *Gen. Alumni Cat. of N. Y. Univ.* (1906); *Lib. Jour.,* May 1892; *N. Y. Tribune,* May 6, 1892.]   A. J. W.

MOORE, Sir HENRY (Feb. 7, 1713–Sept. 11, 1769), colonial governor, was born in Vere, Jamaica, the son of Samuel and Elizabeth (Lowe) Moore, and grandson of John Moore, who settled in Barbados in the reign of Charles II and later removed to Jamaica. After receiving his education at Eton and the University of Leyden, he returned to Jamaica, where he married Catharine Maria Long, by whom he had one son. He became successively a member of the Legislative Assembly and of the Council, and secretary of the island. Later he became lieutenant-governor, and upon the departure of Admiral Sir Charles Knowles in June 1756, acting governor, serving in this capacity until 1762, with the exception of a short interval. During his administration he coped successfully with a serious negro insurrection which broke out on Easter Monday, 1760. While in personal command of the pursuing troops, he once narrowly escaped capture, and throughout the campaign displayed a "prudent intrepidity which compensated for the inexperience of his men" (Bridges, *post,* II, p. 97).

On his return to England, the government created him a baronet, Jan. 26, 1764, and in July of the following year appointed him governor of New York. He arrived at his post November 1765, in the midst of the disturbances due to the Stamp Act, to find the province in the utmost confusion and the acting governor, Cadwallader Colden, confining himself to Fort George and refusing to meet the people. Failing to receive the support of his Council, Moore adopted a policy of watchful waiting, trusting economic pressure to bring the inhabitants to terms. "As I had not the power to do, what my own inclination suggested on this occasion, I contented myself with shewing as much indifference as possible, being fully perswaded, that the distresses which must attend the suspension of the Act will facilitate the carrying it into execution, more than any attempts I could possibly make in its favour" (letter to Lord Dartmouth, Dec. 21, 1765, O'Callaghan, *post,* VII, p. 802). In pursuance of this policy he refused to permit the courts to function and denied vessels permission to sail. In general, he pursued a conciliatory policy, causing Colden to write in June 1766: "He openly caressed the Demagogues—Put on a Homespun Coat, the Badge of the Faction & suffered the Mob to insult the officers of Government without interposing" (Colden Letter Books, II, p. 112).

Moore devoted much effort to the settlement of boundary disputes with neighboring provinces, and in the case of Quebec was successful. Matters of Indian policy also occupied much of his attention, and in this connection he made two trips to the country of the Five Nations. On the second of these, in 1768, he suggested the possibility of improving the navigation of the Mohawk River at Little Falls by a "canal on the side of the Falls with Sluices on the same plan as those built on the great Canal in Languedoc" (O'Callaghan, *post,* vol. VIII, p. 93). His greatest difficulty, other than the Stamp Act disturbances, arose from his controversy with the Assembly over their failure to pass the quartering bill. This led to the prorogation of the Assembly in December 1766, and eventually to the signing by the King of the restraining act the following summer. Upon his death the *New York Gazette* could say with justice (Sept. 18, 1769) that he "conducted himself ... with such a Degree of Wisdom and Temper, as to gain the Approbation of his Sovereign and the Esteem of the People committed to his Care."

[Sources include: *Dict. Nat. Biog.;* G. E. Cokayne, *Complete Baronetage,* vol. V (1906); G. W. Bridges, *The Annals of Jamaica,* vol. II (1828); E. B. O'Callaghan, *Docs. Relative to the Colonial Hist. of the State of N. Y.,* vols. VII–VIII (1856–57); "The Colden Letter Books," *N. Y. Hist. Soc. Colls.*, Pub. Fund Ser., vols. IX–X (1877–78) and "The Letters and Papers of Cadwallader Colden," *Ibid.*, vols. LV–LVI (1923); "The Montrésor Jours.," *Ibid.*, vol. XIV (1882).]

D. C. H.

MOORE, JACOB BAILEY (Oct. 31, 1797–Sept. 1, 1853), journalist, printer, author, father of George Henry and Frank Moore [*qq.v.*], was born at Andover, N. H., the son of Jacob Bailey Moore (1772–1813) and Mary Eaton. His father was a physician whose ancestor, Jonathan Moore, of Scotch origin, had settled in Exeter, N. H., by 1650. Young Moore was of studious habits, and though without a college education, he acquired considerable knowledge of the classics and was noted for his love of historical reading, for his musical talents, and for his mechanical ingenuity. In 1813, at the age of sixteen, his father having died, he apprenticed himself to Isaac Hill [*q.v.*], owner and editor of the *New Hampshire Patriot*, at Concord, N. H. His articles in the newspaper attracted attention, and on Jan. 5, 1819, he became a partner of Hill, whose sister Mary Adams Hill he married Aug. 28, 1820. In 1823 his business partnership was dissolved owing to differences of political opinion, and he carried on printing, bookselling, and publishing, issuing the first three volumes of the *Collections of the New Hampshire Historical Society* (1824–32). Moore was one of the founders of that Society and was elected its first librarian on June 13, 1823, a position he held until 1830, and again from 1837 to 1839. On Sept. 11, 1826, he published at Concord the first issue of the *New Hampshire Journal*, supporting John Quincy Adams for a second term in the presidency, while his brother-in-law, Isaac Hill, supported Andrew Jackson in the *New Hampshire Patriot*. In 1827 Moore helped to prepare by-laws for the Second Congregational (Unitarian) Church in Concord, organized that year. In 1828 he was elected a member of the New Hampshire Assembly but resigned soon after his election. He served as sheriff of Merrimack County, N. H., 1828–33, and as justice of the peace, 1825–35.

Moore continued until December 1829 to edit the *New Hampshire Journal*, which attained a very large circulation throughout New England and was a strong political organ. The downfall of the Adams party in New Hampshire, and the bitter differences of political opinion with his brother-in-law, who in 1836 became governor of New Hampshire, caused him to withdraw from public life in his native state, and although he owned three mills, water rights, and considerable land, he was overwhelmed by financial difficulties and was forced into bankruptcy. He moved to New York City in 1839 and edited the *New York Daily Whig* from July 2 of that year to Mar. 18, 1840, in support of William Henry Harrison. In 1841 President Tyler appointed him a chief clerk in the Post-office Department in Washington, D. C., where he served until 1845, being removed by President Polk upon pressure from the New Hampshire Democrats. For a short time he was inspector of the post-office in New Hampshire. On Jan. 4, 1848, he was elected librarian of the New York Historical Society where his son George was acting as assistant librarian. He resigned on June 5, 1849, to accept an appointment of President Taylor to establish the post-office in California, and was made deputy postmaster at San Francisco by President Fillmore in September 1850.

During these many activities his interest in historical writing never ceased, and while in California he sent to his son at the New York Historical Society many of the daily newspapers of the West which form a good collection in the library of that Society. In February 1853 he returned to the East, and died at the home of his brother, John Weeks Moore [*q.v.*], in Bellows Falls, Vt., where he is buried. He had two daughters and four sons. Among his works may be mentioned: *A Topographical and Historical Sketch of the Town of Andover ... New Hampshire* (1822); *A Gazetteer of the State of New Hampshire* (1823), in collaboration with John Farmer [*q.v.*]; *Collections, Historical and Miscellaneous* (3 vols., 1822–24), also in collaboration with Farmer; *Annals of the Town of Concord ... New Hampshire* (1824); *The Principles and Acts of Mr. Adams' Administration Vindicated* (1828); *Laws of Trade in the United States* (1840); *Memoirs of American Governors* (vol. I, 1846).

[Sources include: manuscript notes made by J. B. Moore and Geo. H. Moore gathered by Thomas E. V. Smith; manuscript records in the possession of the N. Y. Hist. Soc.; J. O. Lyford, *Hist. of Concord, N. H.* (2 vols., 1903); E. S. Stearns, *Geneal. and Family Hist. of the State of N. H.* (1908), II, 490–91; *Memorial Biogs. of the New-Eng. Hist. Geneal. Soc.*, vol. II (1881); *N. H. Patriot and State Gazette* (Concord), Sept. 14, 1853.]

A. J. W.

MOORE, JAMES (d. 1706), colonial governor, is said to have been a descendant of Roger Moore, a leader of the Irish rebellion of 1641. He emigrated to America and located at Charlestown (now Charleston, S. C.) about 1675. There he married Margaret Berringer, the daughter of Lady Yeamans and the step-daughter of Sir John Yeamans [*q.v.*]. The blood of his rebellious ancestors seemed to evidence itself in Moore's own activities, for he soon identified himself with the discontented elements and was active in movements of protest. In 1684 he was prominent in the opposition to the prerogatives of the proprietors, took part in the overthrow of Governor Colleton in 1690, and was a leading spirit in 1693 and 1694 in the protest against quit rents. He had an important place in colonial politics and served as a member of the councils of Governors Morton, Archdale, and Blake. When Blake died in 1700 he was elected by the council to take his place as governor. He "is said at this time to have been in great debt, and determined if possible to improve his desperate circumstances during his lease of power" (McCrady, *post*, p. 374). In addition to his political activities he had engaged in cattle raising and was a prominent Indian trader. He had had to fight the accusation of enslaving the Indians and in 1692 had been forbidden to leave the colony to engage in trade except with the consent of the governor and council. He had even lost his councilorship when he attempted to reopen the peltry trade, closed by an Indian war. As governor he perhaps saw a way to strengthen his position in the trade, and he had a bill introduced into the Assembly that would have given him a monopoly of the Indian trade. When the bill was defeated he dissolved the Assembly. In the election of a new Assembly charges of illegal voting were raised, and when the Assembly, which was unfavorable to him, attempted to investigate the charges he prorogued it, a course he continued as often as the investigation was taken up. He showed himself a man of adventure, not only in his choice of the hazardous occupation of Indian trader but also in his leadership of expeditions and his aspirations as an explorer. As governor he led a force during Queen Anne's War against Saint Augustine and besieged the city for some weeks but on the appearance of two Spanish frigates burned his own ships and retreated by land. After Nathaniel Johnson arrived in the colony to assume the governorship in 1703 Moore advocated an offensive against the Apalachee Indians for the purpose of counteracting French influence and, possibly, advancing his own interests as a trader. The Assembly refused to support such a move, and he himself gathered an army of whites and Indians at Okmulgee and in 1704 made a successful raid, weakening French power and carrying off many Indians to be slaves. In his activities as a trader he found gold that was assayed in England and reported to be valuable, but he was unsuccessful in interesting the Lords of Trade in his investigations. In 1699 he also tried to obtain support from Edward Randolph in a project to explore the Mississippi, which he declared he could do with a force of fifty whites and a hundred Indians. Nothing

came of his dreams of exploration, however, and a few years later he died of yellow fever in Charlestown.

[Edward McCrady, *The Hist. of S. C. under the Proprietary Gov.* (1897); A. S. Salley, *Narratives of Early Carolina* (1911); Verner W. Crane, *The Southern Frontier* (1928); Mrs. St. Julien Ravenal, *Charleston* (1906); Yates Snowden, *Hist. of S. C.* (1920), vol. I; W. J. Rivers, *A Sketch of the Hist. of S. C.* (1856); Alexander Hewatt, *An Hist. Account of . . . S. C.* (1779), vol. I; B. R. Carroll, *Hist. Colls. of S. C.* (1836), vol. II.]   H. B-C.

MOORE, JAMES (1737–April 1777), Revolutionary soldier, was born in New Hanover County, N. C., the son of Maurice Moore, pioneer settler and a founder of Brunswick, and of his second wife, Mary (Porter) Moore. He was the brother of Maurice Moore [*q.v.*] and of Rebecca who married John Ashe (*c.* 1720–1781, *q.v.*). In the French and Indian War he was a captain and for a year was in command at Fort Johnston at the mouth of the Cape Fear River. He represented New Hanover County in the provincial House of Commons from 1764 to 1771 and in 1773. He was one of the leaders of the Cape Fear mob that marched to Brunswick in February 1766 to prevent the enforcement of the Stamp Act in North Carolina, and he was prominent in the subsequent activities of the Sons of Liberty. Supporting the established government, controlled by the eastern oligarchy of planters and merchants, in its contest with the Regulators, he participated as a colonel of artillery in Governor Tryon's armed expedition of 1768 and in the battle of Alamance on May 16, 1771.

Nevertheless, in the controversy with Great Britain he defied the royal governors. His name was the first signed to the circular letter of the committee that called the first Revolutionary provincial Congress, held at New Bern in August 1774 in defiance of Governor Martin, and he was conspicuous in the activity of the New Hanover Committee of Safety. On Aug. 8, 1775, he was chosen a delegate from New Hanover County to the Third Provincial Congress to be held at Hillsboro on Aug. 20; and on Sept. 1, on account of his military experience and ability, he was selected by this provincial Congress for the position of colonel of the 1st North Carolina Continental Regiment. Although he was absent from the final engagement, he directed the patriot maneuvers in the brief campaign ending on Feb. 27, 1776, in the victory at Moore's Creek Bridge over the Scotch Highlanders who were marching to join the British forces already on their way to Wilmington for the subjugation of the southern colonies. On Mar. 1, 1776, the Continental Congress appointed him brigadier-general in command of the forces in North Carolina. After Moore's Creek he did not accompany the North Carolina troops sent to assist in the defense of Charlestown, S. C., in June but remained relatively inactive at Wilmington, watching a small fleet left in the Cape Fear River when the British departed in May for South Carolina. The Provincial Congress ordered him on Nov. 29 to march at once to Charlestown, where he remained until February 1777. On Feb. 5 the Continental Congress ordered him and his troops to proceed north to join Washington; but, while engaged at Wilmington in preparations for the march that was delayed by lack of money for supplies, he died (Apr. 9, according to Heitman, *post*) from "a fit of Gout in his stomach" (*State Records, post,* XI, p. 454). Regarded as the ablest military leader in North Carolina at the beginning of the Revolution, he was thus denied the opportunity of showing his military ability in a major campaign. He was survived by his wife Ann (Ivie) Moore and their four children.

[Sources include *Biog. Hist. of N. C.,* ed. by S. A. Ashe, vol. II (1905); James Sprunt, *Chronicles of the Cape Fear River* (2nd ed., 1916); *The Colonial Records of N. C.,* esp. vols. I, VI–X (1886–90); *The State Records of N. C.,* esp. vol. XI (1895); *Jour. of the Continental Cong.,* ed. by W. C. Ford, vols. IV–IX (1906–07); *S. C. Gazette* (Charleston), July 5, Aug. 9, 1770. Although Jan. 15 is frequently given as date of death for both James and Maurice Moore, James apparently obeyed a Congressional order of Feb. 5. For his death F. B. Heitman, *Hist. Register of the Officers of the Continental Army* (1893), gives date of Apr. 9, and that he had died very recently is indicated by a letter of Samuel Johnston to Thomas Burke on Apr. 19, 1777 (*State Records, ante,* XI, p. 454).]   A. R. N.

MOORE, JAMES (1764–June 22, 1814), pioneer educator and clergyman of the Episcopal Church in Kentucky, came to that state from Virginia some time prior to April 1792. It is recorded that he was a man of engaging manners, superior natural endowments, and considerable learning, though what his ancestral and educational background had been seems to have been forgotten. His ecclesiastical connections were originally Presbyterian, and among his Virginia friends were Archibald Scott, long pastor of the churches in Hebron and Bethel, Augusta County, and John Brown, pastor of the Timber Ridge and New Providence congregations. Soon after his arrival in Kentucky, Moore was received as a candidate by the Transylvania Presbytery, Apr. 27, 1792. The following year he preached a trial sermon on the text, "Except ye repent, ye shall all likewise perish," which did not meet with the approbation of the Presbytery. He refused to be examined again and was dismissed. He then turned to the Episcopal Church and in 1794 was ordained by Bishop Madison of

Virginia (W. S. Perry, *The History of the American Episcopal Church,* 1885, II, 198).

Soon after his arrival in Kentucky Moore had been appointed principal or "director" of Transylvania Seminary, the first public educational institution of that region, which, conducted near Danville, had carried on a precarious existence for several years. He taught the school in his own house and in addition to his salary of twenty-five pounds, later increased to fifty, he was allowed four pounds, thirteen shillings, and fourpence for the portion of his dwelling used for educational purposes. On Apr. 8, 1793, the trustees voted to locate the seminary permanently at Lexington. Moore continued in charge until February 1794 when he was superseded by Harry Toulmin [*q.v.*]. The appointment of the latter, whose theology it was believed was tainted by Socinian errors, was offensive to the Presbyterians, who sought to control the school. Accordingly they established at Pisgah, some eight miles from Lexington, a rival institution, Kentucky Academy. Moore, though an Episcopalian, had the confidence of the Presbyterians, and in April 1796 he became the second principal of the new school. The following September, however, Transylvania Seminary called him back and made him president. In 1798, under a charter from the General Assembly granted Dec. 22, to take effect Jan. 1, 1799, the two schools were united under the name of Transylvania University. Moore was made acting president and professor of logic, metaphysics, moral philosophy, and belles-lettres, in which capacity he served until 1804, when he was succeeded by the Rev. James Blythe.

Throughout these years he had also been engaged in the work of the ministry. In 1796 he began conducting services for a little group of Episcopalians in Lexington, and in 1809 organized them into a church, becoming the first resident rector in Kentucky. He continued to serve them until shortly before his death, at which time he was fifty years old.

[Robert Davidson, *Hist. of the Presbyt. Ch. in the State of Ky.* (1847); G. W. Ranck, *Hist. of Lexington, Ky.* (1872); Lewis and R. H. Collins, *Hist. of Ky.* (1882); Robert and Joanna Peter, *Transylvania Univ.* (1896), being Filson Club. Pubs. No. 11; A. F. Lewis, *Hist. of Higher Educ. in Ky.* (1899).]   H. E. S.

MOORE, JAMES EDWARD (Mar. 2, 1852–Nov. 2, 1918), surgeon, was born in Clarksville, Pa., the son of George W. and Margaret (Ziegler) Moore. His father was a Methodist minister who supported himself by his trade and preached on the Sabbath. James attended the public schools of Western Pennsylvania and Poland Union Seminary at Poland, Ohio. His medical studies were begun at the University of Michigan and continued at Bellevue Hospital Medical College from which he received his degree of M.D. in 1873 after the customary two years' course of those days. He went to Ft. Wayne, Ind., to practise, and a year later returned to spend two years in the hospitals of New York City. In 1876 he settled in Emlenton, Pa., where for six years he followed the rather arduous duties of a country practitioner, making most of his calls on horseback and dispensing drugs carried in his saddle-bags. In the summer of 1880 he spent four months as an assistant to Paul F. Munde in the dispensary at Mt. Sinai Hospital, New York. By this time he became restless and felt the urge of ambition for a field in which he could develop a career, for he did not under-estimate his own powers even then. In 1882 he went to Minneapolis, Minn., where he was in general practice until 1885, when he sailed for Europe to study in Berlin, Paris, and London. On his return to Minneapolis in 1887 he confined himself to surgery and orthopedics, and after 1897, gave his entire time to surgery. He claimed for himself the distinction of being the first specialist in surgery west of New York. His book, *Orthopedic Surgery,* one of the first American works on the subject, was published in 1898.

Moore was one of the pioneers in medical education in the state, holding the rank of professor of orthopedics in the old Minneapolis College Hospital, and a connection with the St. Paul Medical School. With the absorption of these two schools into the newly formed medical school of the University of Minnesota in 1888, he continued to hold the chair of professor of orthopedics and in 1894 was appointed professor of orthopedics and adjunct professor of clinical surgery. In 1897 he resigned the chair of orthopedics but continued as clinical professor of surgery. In 1904 he was made professor of surgery and in 1908 professor and director of the department of surgery, a position which he held until his death in 1918. He took an active part in the reorganization of the medical school and was one of the original three about whom the new faculty was formed and with whom the selection of its members largely rested. He was intuitive, clear-minded, forceful, and a born teacher, excelling in clinical subjects. His courtesy, his earnestness, and his personal charm drew his students to him naturally and surely and made a lasting impression upon them. In his will he left the bulk of his estate, after the death of his widow, to the surgical department of the medical school.

In the medical societies Moore was an interested and active member and readily gained a wide circle of friends. He served as first vice-president of the American Surgical Association, 1905; president of the Western Surgical Association, 1902; member of the judicial council of the American Medical Association, and chairman of its surgical section, 1903; fellow of the American College of Surgeons and a member of the board of governors at its founding; president of the Minnesota Academy of Medicine; president of the Hennepin County Medical Society; and delegate from the University of Minnesota to the International Medical Congress at Rome. He was also a frequent visitor to the Southern Surgical and Gynecological Society. As chief of staff of the Northwestern Hospital and chief of the surgical division of the University Hospital, he aided materially in the development of both institutions. His numerous medical writings were mostly articles founded upon his clinical experiences. His original contributions treated mainly surgical technique and bone and joint surgery. In addition to his *Orthopedic Surgery* he wrote a chapter, "General Principles of Surgical Treatment," in *American Practice of Surgery* (J. D. Bryant and A. H. Buck, vol. I, 1906). He was married three times: in 1876 to Bessie Applegate, who died in 1882; in 1883 to Clara Collins, who died in 1884; and in 1887 to Louie (Heckler) Irving, who survived him. As a pioneer in the surgery of the Northwest he rendered a notable service and won a distinction which he well deserved.

[*Trans. Southern Surgic. Asso., 1918,* vol. XXXI (1919); *Minn. Medicine,* Dec. 1918; *Surgery, Gynecology and Obstetrics,* Dec. 1924; H. A. Kelly and W. L. Burrage, *Am. Medic. Biogs.* (1920); *Minneapolis Jour.,* Nov. 3, 1918; records at the Univ. of Minn.; information as to certain facts from Moore's relatives; personal recollections.]   A. T. M.

MOORE, JOHN (*c.* 1659–Dec. 2, 1732), colonial official of South Carolina and Pennsylvania, was born in England. He was of the Moore family of Fawley in Berkshire and was probably a son of Sir Francis Moore. About 1680 he emigrated to South Carolina, where he served as provincial secretary and receiver-general in 1682–83 and as deputy to Sir Peter Colleton, one of the lords proprietors, in 1684. In 1685 he married Rebecca Axtell, a daughter of Daniel Axtell, one of the landgraves of South Carolina. He was a friend and protégé of Robert Quarry, who was for a short time the governor of the province, and it was probably through Quarry's influence that he removed to Philadelphia in 1695 or 1696. The Bishop of London (Henry

Compton) and the English authorities were making an effort at that time to create an Anglican Tory party in Pennsylvania as a balance to the Quakers. As Moore was a devout Churchman and also interested in the spoils of office, he heartily sympathized with this movement. In 1698 he was appointed advocate of the court of vice-admiralty for Pennsylvania, the lower counties (Delaware), and West Jersey. During the next few years he and his friend Quarry, who was the judge of this court, were closely associated in the leadership of the Anglican party and in the efforts to enforce the acts of trade and navigation. They were both vestrymen of Christ Church, Philadelphia, which was the oldest Anglican Church in the province (founded in 1695) and the center of an aggressive movement against the Quakers. They played active parts in the long and complicated struggle with the Quakers over the right of affirmation and also in the effort to improve the administration of the imperial customs system.

In 1700 Moore was appointed the King's attorney-general for Pennsylvania. William Penn confirmed this appointment and also made him register-general of the province. He was disloyal to Penn, however, in the quarrel between Penn and Quarry and, after some legal difficulties, was removed from both of these positions in 1704. He held the post of advocate of the vice-admiralty most of the time until 1704 and then served as deputy judge until about 1713. On July 24, 1704, he wrote to the Bishop of London that John Bewley, the collector of the port of Philadelphia, had recently died and that Quarry had asked him (Moore) to fill the post until a permanent appointment was made by the commissioners of the customs (Board of Trade Manuscripts, Proprieties, vol. VII, 1702–04, M. 46). Owing probably to his Lordship's influence, the appointment was approved and Moore served as collector of the port until 1728 and then as deputy collector until 1732. He was also deputy register-general from 1724 to 1726. He died in Philadelphia and was buried in Christ Church. He was survived by his wife, two daughters, and five sons, one of whom was William Moore, 1699–1783 [q.v.]. In his zeal to enforce the imperial laws, to improve the system of imperial defense, and to advance the cause of the Church of England, Moore came into conflict with both the proprietor and the people of Pennsylvania, and knowledge of his character and his services is largely based upon their complaints. As a historical figure, he belongs in the same class with Edward Randolph, Joseph Dudley, and other early American Tories, who combined a lust for office with a sincere devotion to the cause of imperial unity.

[For genealogical data and material relating to Moore's life in South Carolina, see D. M. Hall, *Six Centuries of the Moores of Fawley, Berkshire, England, and their Descendants* (1904) and *S.-C. Hist. Soc. Colls.*, vol. I (1857). There is a copy of his will, made on Nov. 16, 1731, in the possession of the Hist. Soc. of Pa. For his public career in Pennsylvania, see the Board of Trade Manuscripts, Proprieties, vols. I–VII, the *Minutes of the Provincial Council of Pa.*, vols. I–II (1852), and *Correspondence between Wm. Penn and Jas. Logan* (2 vols., 1870–72), ed. by Edward Armstrong. The best secondary account is given by W. T. Root, *The Relations of Pa. with the British Govt., 1696–1765* (1912).]
W. R. S.

MOORE, JOHN (June 24, 1834–July 30, 1901), Roman Catholic bishop of St. Augustine, was born at Rosmead, County Westmeath, Ireland, of respectable parentage, his mother being an O'Farrell of Scurlockstown. On completion of his elementary schooling, he emigrated in 1848 to Charleston, S. C., where he attended the Collegiate Institute and the Seminary of St. John the Baptist. In 1851, he was sent by Bishop Ignatius Reynolds to the College of Courbrée in France, from which, four years later, he proceeded to the Urban College in Rome. Ordained there by Monsignor Luigi Busso, Apr. 9, 1860, he returned to Charleston where he served as a curate at St. Finbar's Cathedral during the Civil War. Like his ordinary, Bishop P. N. Lynch [q.v.], he was a stout Confederate, and his aggressive Southern sympathies were not abated by the destruction of church properties by Northern forces. He refused to take an oath of allegiance to the Union, and thereafter his mail was censored by the commander of the fleet in Charleston harbor. Despite various inconveniences, however, he managed his parish with the assistance of a single priest and attended the dying and wounded of both sides as confessor and nurse. At the end of the war he commenced a twelve-year rectorship of St. Patrick's Church, during the last few years of which he also served as vicar-general. On the death of Augustine Verot, he was appointed second bishop of St. Augustine and consecrated by Bishop Lynch in St. John's Pro-Cathedral, May 13, 1877.

Simple, studious, diffident, yet approachable, he proved a successful administrator. Without immigration, Catholic growth was slow, yet his tenure was marked by an increase of priests from twelve to thirty-one, of whom a larger proportion were English speaking, by the erection of a number of churches and parochial schools, the founding of a Colored Institute, the establishment of St. Leo's Benedictine College for boys and an orphanage at Jacksonville, and the introduction of the Jesuits into southern Florida. In 1887, the cathedral was burned and the Bishop brought to light old plans for a cathedral drawn by Renwick, the architect of St. Patrick's Cathedral in New York, in harmony with the Spanish tradition of St. Augustine. Seeking financial aid in the North, he obtained generous assistance in rebuilding from Henry M. Flagler [q.v.], who was engaged in the development of Florida. In Jacksonville he is especially remembered for his courageous work in the yellow-fever epidemic of 1888. He encouraged immigration to the state and fostered harmonious relations with other denominations. Somewhat liberal in his views, he befriended Fathers Burtsell and McGlynn of New York, actually interceding for McGlynn [q.v.] in Rome. He was a member of the Third Plenary Council of Baltimore, 1884, and was named along with Bishop Joseph Dwenger of Fort Wayne to carry its decrees to Rome. There, despite the doubts expressed by Bishops McQuaid of Rochester and Richard Gilmour of Cleveland (who was later also accredited by Cardinal Gibbons), he was largely successful in obtaining papal ratification. As a self-sacrificing bishop of an obscure diocese, however, he naturally had little part in the national affairs of the church.

[J. G. Shea, *The Hierarchy of the Cath. Ch. in the U. S.* (1886) ; F. J. Zwierlein, *The Life and Letters of Bishop McQuaid* (3 vols., 1925–27) ; annual Catholic directories ; *Florida Times-Union and Citizen* (Jacksonville), July 31, 1901 ; *Freeman's Jour.* (N. Y.), June 9, 1877 ; material furnished by an able associate of Moore.]   R. J. P.

MOORE, JOHN TROTWOOD (Aug. 26, 1858–May 10, 1929), Tennessee author and journalist, was born at Marion, Ala., the son of John and Emily Adelia (Billingslea) Moore. His father, a circuit judge in Alabama, came of a family distinguished in early South and North Carolina history, and served as captain in the Confederate army. His mother was of a pioneer Georgia family. After graduation in 1878 from Howard College at Birmingham, Ala., he edited the Marion *Commonwealth* for a year, publishing in it verses that were widely copied. For the next six years he taught school at Monterey and at Pineapple, Ala., establishing Moore's Academy at the latter place. Meanwhile he studied law and passed bar examinations, but never practised. In 1885 he married Florence W. Allen and moved to Maury County, Tenn., where on a farm near Columbia he began to raise blooded stock. Like the Southern gentlemen whose tradition he shared and understood, Moore knew and loved horses but was about equally inclined to literature. The spirit of the Middle Tennessee region into which he had

come stirred him to write, and he became its genial yet passionate interpreter, contributing first to the Columbia *Herald* and more prominently later to the Chicago *Horse Review.* "Trotwood," first chosen from *David Copperfield* as a pen-name, so clung to him that he adopted it as a middle name.

Moore's advocacy of the pacing horse, then coming into favor largely through performances of the Tennessee Hal strain, and his expert knowledge of the breed, got him a regular engagement with the *Review,* which he continued until 1904. In 1897 he published *Songs and Stories from Tennessee,* a collection of sketches and poems that had appeared in the *Review.* It contained his famous race-horse story, "Ole Mistis," and stories of Uncle Wash, a negro creation drawn from life and one of the most authentic representations of the Southern negro in American literature. In 1901 he published his first novel, *A Summer Hymnal,* a romantic story with a Tennessee setting, and began a series of works that won him a devoted following. Although he was a sincere romanticist and hero-worshipper, with a decided turn for the tradition of pathos and gallantry, he offset many of the faults of the sentimental school by his irresistible humor, good use of local detail, and variety of characters. He was himself the epitome of the Southern traits he interpreted—a personality genial and positive, leisurely yet fiery ; and his books were not only stories but garnerings of his philosophizing and observations. But with these qualities there appeared in *The Bishop of Cottontown* (1906) a social consciousness in advance of his time; it was perhaps the first important Southern novel to treat industrial forces that were changing Southern life. It was followed in 1910 by *Uncle Wash, His Stories,* and *The Old Cotton Gin,* a poem, and in 1911 by *The Gift of the Grass,* the autobiography of a race-horse, perhaps his best-written novel.

In 1905 Moore had established *Trotwood's Monthly,* into which he poured anecdote, history, story, and verse. In 1906 he moved to Nashville. Changing the title of the monthly to the *Taylor-Trotwood Magazine,* he edited it jointly with Senator Robert Love Taylor of Tennessee until 1911, when it was discontinued. After publishing *Jack Ballington, Forester,* in 1911, he turned his attention largely to Tennessee history. From 1919 until his death he was director of libraries, archives, and history for Tennessee and did extensive and valuable pioneer work in collecting original documents, erecting markers and memorials, and stimulating historical enterprises. In 1923, with Austin P. Foster, he published

Tennessee, the Volunteer State (4 vols.). His devotion to Andrew Jackson, whose career he had long studied, was the basis of his last novel, *Hearts of Hickory* (1926), a spirited historical romance in which he dramatized the episodes of Jackson's early battles. From 1926 until his death he wrote occasional articles on historical subjects, constantly made journeys and filled speaking engagements among the people to whom he had become a familiar and beloved figure, and was at work almost to his last moment on another, unfinished novel. He died of heart failure at his Nashville home, leaving three children. His first wife had died in 1896 and in 1900 he was married to Mary Brown Daniel, who survived him.

[T. M. Owen, *Hist. of Ala. and Dict. of Ala. Biog.* (1921), vol. IV; *Who's Who in America,* 1928–29; the *Horse Rev.,* May 15, 1929; *Nashville Banner,* May 10, 1929; *Nashville Tennessean,* May 11, 12, 19, 1929; family papers supplied by Mrs. John Trotwood Moore.]
D. D.

MOORE, JOHN WEEKS (Apr. 11, 1807– Mar. 23, 1889), editor of musical journals, and musical biographer, was the son of Dr. Jacob Bailey Moore, a physician, and Mary Eaton, and a brother of Jacob Bailey Moore [*q.v.*]. His father settled in Andover, N. H., in 1796; he was a fine singer and a writer of songs. His son was educated in the Concord (N. H.) High School and Plymouth Academy, and while still in his teens was apprenticed to learn the printer's trade in the office of the *New Hampshire Patriot.* In 1827 he began on his own account the publication of the *Androscoggin Free Press,* the first weekly newspaper in the state of Maine, which was printed in Brunswick. On Sept. 17, 1832, he was married to Emily Jane Eastman, of Concord, N. H. Six years later he removed to Bellows Falls, Vt., where for seventeen years he issued the *Bellows Falls Gazette.* In 1840 he began to devote himself more especially to the publication of musical works. He was a good musician and played the piano, violin, and flute. He edited for a time two musical journals, the *World of Music* and the *Musical Library.* His collections included *Sacred Minstrel* (1842?); the *American Collection of Instrumental Music* (1856) and the *Star Collection of Instrumental Music* (1858). At Portsmouth and Manchester he published in eighteen numbers *Puritanism of Music in America.* There followed the five volumes of his *Musical Record* (1867–70), and the *Songs and Song Writers of America* (1859–80), of which two hundred numbers were issued. In 1854 he published his *Complete Encyclopædia of Music, Elementary, Technical, Historical, Biographical,*

Vocal and Instrumental, supplemented in 1875 by an *Appendix,* and in 1876 he brought out *A Dictionary of Musical Information.* These served as source materials in the preparation of definitions of musical terms for general dictionaries. His last work was a product of his many years' experience as a printer: *Moore's Historical, Biographical and Miscellaneous Gatherings . . . Relative to Printers, Printing, Publishing, and Editing . . . from 1420 to 1886* (1886). His chief activity was laid in the period between 1825 and 1860 when musical activity was concentrated in a few metropolitan centers. His contributions to a more general spread of musical knowledge are deserving of respect, for while much of his work is crude, it represents valuable pioneer effort. Moore died in Manchester, N. H., at the age of eighty-two. His brother Henry Eaton Moore, 1803–1841, had a similar but briefer career as a printer and musician.

[E. S. Stearns, *Geneal. and Family Hist. of the State of N. H.* (1908), vol. II; S. P. Cheney, *The Am. Singing Book* (1879); *People and Patriot* (Concord, N. H.), Mar. 28, 1889; musical dictionaries.]
F. H. M.

MOORE, MAURICE (1735–1777), jurist and Revolutionary patriot, the son of Maurice and Mary (Porter) Moore, was born in New Hanover County, N. C., and educated in New England. He was the brother of James Moore and the father of Alfred Moore [*qq.v.*]. He married Anne Grange. He was an influential representative of the borough of Brunswick in the North Carolina House of Commons, serving 1757–60, 1762, 1764–71, and 1773–74. His early "disposition to support his Majesty's Interest" (*Colonial Records, post,* V, 948) elevated him to the governor's council from 1760 to 1761. Appointed to an associate judgeship of the province, he wrote a pamphlet, in 1765 after the passage of the Stamp Act, entitled *The Justice and Policy of Taxing the American Colonies in Great Britain, Considered* (printed in Boyd, *post,* pp. 163–74), maintaining that there could be no rightful taxation of the American colonies by a Parliament in which they had neither actual nor virtual representation, and he was suspended by Governor Tryon for his intemperate zeal and conduct in preventing the enforcement of the Stamp Act. Reinstated in 1768, he held the judgeship until the court ceased to function in 1773 because of a deadlock between the governor and Assembly over the new court law. He was appointed a commissioner to hold the courts established by royal prerogative in 1773, but the Assembly refused to defray their expenses.

He was prominent in the Regulator movement. At first he sympathized with the distressed Regulators and was accused of having encouraged the movement, though he denied the charge. He was a colonel in Governor Tryon's first armed expedition, a judge at the Hillsboro trial of 1768, an advocate of a drastic policy that culminated in the Johnston or Riot Act of 1771, and a judge at the special court in Hillsboro in June 1771 after the battle of Alamance that sentenced twelve Regulators to death on the charge of treason. Bitterly hated by the insurgents, he was attacked in 1770 in a public letter whose reputed author, Hermon Husbands [q.v.], was expelled from the House of Commons. Yet after the Hillsboro trial of 1771 he became lenient and sympathetic to the Regulators. The public letter of "Atticus" in 1771, severely criticising Tryon's policy toward the Regulators, was attributed to him (published *Colonial Records, post,* VIII, 718–27); and in 1772 he held in an opinion as judge that there could be no further prosecutions under the Riot Act, which he interpreted liberally, and he actively promoted a policy of leniency toward the leaders. The Third Provincial Congress on Aug. 21, 1775, appointed him on the committee to try to induce the Regulators to support the patriot cause. Representing the borough of Brunswick in this Third Provincial Congress, he served on important committees in the interest of the patriot cause; but he was too conservative to approve actual separation from Great Britain. On Jan. 9, 1776, in a letter to Governor Martin he expressed his belief that North Carolina, if there were opportunity, would renounce every desire of independence and accept reconciliation on the basis of the political conditions of 1763 (*Colonial Records, post,* X, 395–96), but the Moore's Creek campaign made negotiations impossible. Though elected a delegate from Brunswick County he did not attend the Fifth Provincial Congress of November 1776. He died some time before Apr. 20, 1777 (*State Records, post,* XI, 456). Governor Martin characterized him as a man of "considerable influence," but a "visionary in politicks" and "a zealous votary of the bubble popularity," whose political conduct had been fickle and undecided (*Colonial Records, post,* X, 400).

[Printed sources include sketch of life in *Some Eighteenth Century Tracts Concerning N. C.,* ed. by W. K. Boyd (1927); M. DeL. Haywood, *Gov. Wm. Tryon and his Administration in the Province of N. C.* (1903); W. E. Fitch, *Some Neglected Hist. of N. C.* (1905) for unfavorable interpretation with citations; G. J. McRee, *Life and Correspondence of James Iredell,* vol. I (1857), pp. 195, 201; *The Colonial Records of N. C.,* esp. vols. V, VI, VII, VIII, IX, X (1887–90); *The State Records of N. C.,* esp. vol. XI (1895); date of death as Jan. 15 has been rejected because the tradition includes the coincident death of James Moore, which seems impossible. See bibliography to sketch of James Moore.] A. R. N.

MOORE, NATHANIEL FISH (Dec. 25, 1782–Apr. 27, 1872), professor, librarian, and president of Columbia College, was the son of William Moore, M.D., Edinburgh 1780, a distinguished New York physician, and Jane, daughter of Nathaniel Fish. He was born in Newtown, L. I., and graduated from Columbia during the presidency of his uncle, Bishop Benjamin Moore [q.v.], in 1802. At Commencement he delivered the Latin salutatory, *De Astronomiae Laudibus.* Choosing the profession of law, he studied under Beverly Robinson and was admitted to the bar in 1805. His practice was never extensive, and in 1817 he accepted the more congenial occupation of adjunct professor of Greek and Latin at Columbia, succeeding Peter Wilson [q.v.], as professor in 1820. In 1835 he resigned his professorship and traveled for about two years in Europe. Upon his return he sold his library, a choice collection of about a thousand titles in the classics, philology, and theology of the sixteenth, seventeenth, and eighteenth centuries, to the college for $10,000. In January 1838 he was appointed librarian of the college. He was the first incumbent to devote his entire time to the office, and he classified and arranged the books and made with his own pen a huge catalogue in book form which continued to be used for thirty years. In 1839 he resigned and went abroad again, visiting Egypt, Greece, and Palestine, as well as Germany and England.

On Aug. 1, 1842, Moore was elected president of Columbia, succeeding William Alexander Duer [q.v.]. His duties included instruction in the classics to the seniors. During his presidency, the college was situated in one of the quiet, residential sections of the city; the enrolment was slightly over one hundred, the annual income and expenditures were about $23,000, and there was a debt of some $60,000. The duties of the presidency were not particularly congenial to Moore, whose previous life had been spent in scholarly seclusion and reflection among his books, and little more can be said than that the college held its own during his seven-year term. He relinquished his duties in October 1849, to be succeeded by the more worldly and active Charles King [q.v.]. While on a visit to London in 1851, Moore was greatly impressed with the specimens of the new art of photography on paper exhibited at Crystal Palace, and on his return he devoted himself assiduously to photography as a hobby. Some of his work is preserved at Columbia. The last sixteen years of his life were spent in retirement, and he died at his brother's home in the Highlands of the Hudson, Apr. 27, 1872 (*Evening Post, New-York Trib-*

une, *New York Times,* Apr. 29; elsewhere the date is erroneously given as Apr. 25). In *Through the Gates of Old Romance* (1903), W. Jay Mills records the love story of Moore and "the heavenly Ellen Conover, a belle of Chambers Street, New York," whom Moore was forbidden to marry because they were first cousins; perhaps this explains why Moore never married.

Moore's scholarship was in the English tradition rather than the German, and his profound interest in the beauties of the ancient writers inspired his pupils with a deep desire to know more of them and of their works. His publications include: *Remarks on the Pronunciation of the Greek Language, Occasioned by a late Essay . . . by John Pickering* (1819); *Ancient Mineralogy: or, An Inquiry Respecting Mineral Substances Mentioned by the Ancients* (1834), a work little noticed in America but highly appreciated in England; *Lectures on the Greek Language and Literature* (1835); *Addresses . . . at . . . Commencement* (1843); *A Short Introduction to Universal Grammar* (1844); *An Historical Sketch of Columbia College* (1846), an excellent little book, the second work published on this subject; and *An Address to the Alumni of Columbia College* (1848), on the library resources of the United States.

[Benj. I. Haight, *A Memorial Discourse of Nathaniel F. Moore, LL.D.* (N. Y., 1874); J. B. Pine, "Nathaniel F. Moore, LL.D.," *Columbia Univ. Quart.,* Mar. 1903.]   M. H. T—s.

MOORE, NICHOLAS [See MORE, NICHOLAS, d. 1689].

MOORE, PHILIP NORTH (July 8, 1849– Jan. 19, 1930), mining engineer, only child of Henry C. and Susan (North) Moore, was a descendant of John North who settled in Connecticut in 1635. Henry Moore was a canal and railroad builder, and Philip was born in Connersville, Ind., where a canal was being constructed. After graduating in 1870 from the classical course at Miami University, he went to the School of Mines, Columbia University, where he was a special student, 1870–72. The next six years he spent in geological work under such distinguished men as T. B. Brooks, Raphael Pumpelly, and N. S. Shaler [*qq.v.*], and then, after six months in Europe, went to Leadville, Colo., in 1878. Here he was superintendent of the first lead smelting works and built the second plant, the La Plata. After a couple of years he ventured into independent development. In 1879 he married Mary Eva Perry (July 24, 1852–Apr. 28,1931), daughter of Seely and Elizabeth (Benedict) Perry of Rockford, Ill., and a descendant of Massachusetts stock. She was a

graduate of Vassar College, with a background of European travel and a speaking knowledge of several languages. In 1882 they moved to Kentucky, where at Slate Creek Moore acquired a quarter interest in a smelting works of which he was also manager. In 1889 he moved to St. Louis to obtain better school facilities for his children, but retained charge of the Kentucky enterprise until it was worked out. Meanwhile he had acquired an iron property in Alabama, of which he was president for eighteen years, and during all this time he practised as a consulting mining engineer, sometimes traveling as much as 50,000 miles in twelve months. Among other enterprises he developed the Conrey Placer Mining Company, Montana, an important part of the estate which Gordon McKay left for the benefit of the mining school at Harvard University. During the period of the Great War he developed the Admiralty Zinc Company, Oklahoma. As president of the American Institute of Mining Engineers in 1917 he was an important factor in coördination work on strategic minerals through the War Minerals Committee. In that same year he organized the American Engineering Council, which cooperated with the Council of National Defense in stimulating the production of necessary minerals. In 1919 he was called to Washington to serve as chairman of the War Minerals Relief Commission, created by Congress to indemnify those who undertook mineral production at government solicitation but had not recouped their expenditures by the time of the Armistice. In this capacity he acted until 1921, when he returned to St. Louis. For many years one of the board of managers of the Missouri Geological Survey, he was active in bringing about cooperation between engineers and legislature to promote the best interests of the state and in awakening engineers to a sense of their civic responsibilities. His wife, too, was a leader in civic affairs, being an officer of the General Federation of Women's Clubs, 1894– 1912, except for the years 1901–05, when she was president of the Missouri Federation of Women's Clubs; president of the National Council of Women, 1916–25; and vice-president, 1920–30, of the International Council of Women. She was also a trustee of Vassar College and president, 1903–07, of the Association of Collegiate Alumnæ. From April 1917 till it disbanded in 1919 she served as a member of the Women's Committee of the Council of National Defense. She survived her husband only fifteen months, dying Apr. 28, 1931. They left a son and a daughter.

[T. A. Rickard, "Interviews with Mining Engineers," *Mining and Scientific Press* (San Francisco), 1922;

pp. 373–86; *Mining and Metallurgy*, Mar. 1930; *Am. Men. of Sci.* (1927); *Who's Who in America*, 1928–29; *St. Louis Post-Dispatch*, Jan. 20, 1930; Dexter North, *John North of Farmington, Conn., and His Descendants* (1921); information regarding Mary Eva Perry Moore contributed by Miss Katharine Twining Moody; sketch in *Am. Biog.*, vol. XLIX (Am. Hist. Soc. 1931), revised by Mrs. Moore, with additions by her daughter.]   T. T. R.

MOORE, RICHARD BISHOP (May 6, 1871–Jan. 20, 1931), chemist, was the son of William Thomas Moore [*q.v.*], a leading minister of the Disciples of Christ, and Mary A. (Bishop) Moore. He was born at Cincinnati, Ohio, but at the age of seven accompanied his parents to England where they resided till 1895. He attended Argyle College, St. Edmund's College, the Institut Keller in Paris, and University College, London. Here he studied from 1886 to 1890 under William Ramsay and became interested in rare gases and radium. Returning to the United States, he attended the University of Chicago for a year, receiving the degree of B.S. in 1896, and was retained as an assistant in chemistry one year. He then became instructor in chemistry at the University of Missouri, where in addition to his regular duties he did pioneer work in the investigation of radioactive substances. In 1905 he resigned, to accept the professorship of chemistry at Butler College, Indianapolis, Ind. He continued his investigations and during a leave of absence in 1907 worked in Sir William Ramsay's laboratory on the separation and purification of krypton and xenon and the determination of their properties. His work on rare gases became so well known that in 1911 he was called away from teaching by the United States government. Joining at first the staff of the Bureau of Soils, he was transferred the next year to the newly organized Bureau of Mines and as a physical chemist in charge of the chemistry and metallurgy of rare metals established headquarters in Colorado, where he made a survey of radium deposits, devised methods for concentrating the ore, and supervised the preparation of the first radium salts produced in the United States.

In the early years of the World War he and his co-workers devoted much attention to the use of the metals vanadium, tungsten, and molybdenum in making special steels. He was among the first to advocate the use of helium in balloons and airships, and largely through his arguments and insistence steps were taken, first by the Navy Department and later by Congress, to conserve this gas. In 1918 he was given charge of all helium experiments conducted by the Bureau of Mines. The following year he became chief chemist of the bureau, and in this capacity, during the next five years, organized the cryogenic laboratory in Washington, served on the helium board of the army and navy, and directed the work by which the cost of producing helium was reduced to a nominal sum and its use was correspondingly increased.

In 1923 he left the government service to enter commercial work with the Dorr Company, New York, of which he was general manager for two years. The position was not congenial, however, and in 1926 he resigned to become professor of chemistry and dean of the school of science at Purdue University, Lafayette, Ind., where he remained until his death. During his few years of active service at Purdue his work as a teacher, investigator, and executive resulted in permanent contributions to the progress of the University. While in the employ of the Bureau of Mines he published articles, individually or jointly, on helium, radium, and the rare metals uranium, vanadium, tungsten, cerium, thorium, titanium, and zirconium (see, especially, *United States Bureau of Mines Bulletin 70*, 1913, *104*, 1915, *212*, 1923, and *Serial 2363*, 1922). He was the author of several papers on metallurgical subjects published by the American Institute of Mining and Metallurgical Engineers; of a textbook, *A Laboratory Chemistry* (1904); and of a lecture, *The Rare Gases of the Atmosphere* (1927), delivered at Columbia University in 1926. For his work on radium, mesothorium, and helium he was awarded in 1926 the Perkin medal of the American Section of the Society of Chemical Industry. He had previously received the Longstreth and Potts medals of the Franklin Institute. As a public servant he was characterized by unusual ability to grasp the essential factors of large projects, by exceptional capacity to organize varied plans, and by personal power to enlist the cooperation of associates. He married, first, Callie Pemberton of Auxvasse, Mo., on June 11, 1902; and second, June 18, 1924, Georgie E. Dowell of Dallas, Tex.

[*Purdue Alumnus*, Feb. 1931; *Industrial and Engineering Chem.* (News Ed.), Feb. 10, 1931; *Mining and Metallurgy*, Feb. 1931; *Chem. and Met. Engineering*, Feb. 1931; *Who's Who in America*, 1930–31; *Indianapolis Star*, Jan. 21, 1931.]   L. C. N.

MOORE, RICHARD CHANNING (Aug. 21, 1762–Nov. 11, 1841), bishop of the Protestant Episcopal Church, was born in New York City, where his grandfather, John Moore, son of John Moore, c. 1659–1732 [*q.v.*], had attained wealth and eminence, being an alderman, a member of the colonial legislature, and of the King's council for the province. One of his eighteen children was Thomas, who married Elizabeth Channing and had twelve children, among whom was Richard. He received a good classical training under Alexander Leslie, professor of languages in King's College; but the Revolutionary War, which ruined his father's business and caused the removal of the family to West Point, interrupted his education. After a brief trial of sea-faring life, he settled down to the study of medicine under the direction of Dr. Richard Bayley, an eminent New York physician. He practised for a short period in that city, and later in the eastern part of Long Island. At the age of twenty-two he married Christian Jones of New York. About this time his mind became deeply exercised on the subject of religion, and he finally decided to enter the church. After preparation under Bishop Samuel Provoost, he was by him ordained deacon at St. George's Chapel, New York, in July 1787, and was admitted to priest's orders the following September. For about two years he was in charge of Grace Church, Rye, N. Y., and then became rector of St. Andrew's parish, Staten Island. Here for more than twenty years he had a fruitful ministry, eking out his slender salary at the start by continuing to practise medicine, and from 1793 to 1802 by conducting a school. On April 20, 1796, his wife died, leaving him with three children, and on Mar. 23, 1797, he married Sarah Mersereau. He was one of the deputies representing the diocese of New York at the General Convention, held in Baltimore in May 1808, where he was chairman of the committee which selected additional hymns for the use of the churches. In 1809, leaving his son David as his successor at Staten Island, he became rector of St. Stephen's, New York. After five years' service here, marked by notable success, in 1814 he was called to the rectorship of the Monumental Church, Richmond, Va., and to the episcopate of that state. On May 18, at St. James's Church, Philadelphia, he was consecrated bishop.

Owing to the effects of the Revolution, the outgoing of the Methodists, the secularization of the clergy, and a lack of effective leadership, the Episcopal Church in the South was in a prostrate condition. Parishes were impoverished and vacant, priests were few, and apathy and discouragement prevailed. Bishop Moore was ideally adapted to the needs of the situation. He was a man of distinguished ancestry, well-bred, and possessed of social qualities which made him everywhere acceptable. He was a speaker of magnetism and persuasiveness. He could exercise discipline with tact and kindliness. Although loyal to his own church, he was broad-minded, charitable, and disinclined to controversy. More important still, he was a man of deep and sincere piety, zealously devoted to the salvation of souls and the spiritual edification of his people. While warmly attached to the constituted ministry and government of the church and careful to keep enthusiasm within proper bounds, he was strongly evangelical, upholding prayer meetings, lecture-room services, and revivals. He did not escape opposition, but regard for him steadily grew, and under the sway of his wisdom and goodness the diocese began to revive. Discipline was restored, churches were reëstablished, the number of clergy increased, and the Virginia Theological Seminary, at Alexandria, was founded. After 1829 he was assisted by a coadjutor, Bishop William Meade [q.v.]. Together with Bishops John Henry Hobart and Alexander V. Griswold [qq.v.] he is credited with reconstructing the Episcopal Church in the United States, both in spirit and in character. After having directed the affairs of the diocese for twenty-seven years, he died while on a visitation to Lynchburg, and was buried in Richmond.

[J. P. K. Henshaw, *Memoir of the Life of the Rt. Rev. Richard Channing Moore, D.D.* (1842), containing seventeen sermons; W. B. Sprague, *Annals Am. Pulpit*, vol. V (1859); Wm. Meade, *Old Churches, Ministers, and Families of Va.* (1857); F. L. Hawks, *Contributions to the Ecclesiastical Hist. of the U. S.*, vol. I (1836); W. S. Perry, *The Hist. of the Am. Episc. Ch. 1587–1883* (1885); H. G. Batterson, *A Sketch-Book of the Am. Episcopate* (1878); C. C. Tiffany, *A Hist. of the Protestant Episc. Ch. in the U. S. A.* (1895); E. L. Goodwin, *The Colonial Ch. in Va. with Biog. Sketches of the First Six Bishops of the Diocese of Va.* (1927); D. M. Hall, *Six Centuries of the Moores of Fawley* (1904); *Richmond Enquirer*, Nov. 16, 1841.]
H. E. S.

MOORE, SAMUEL PRESTON (1813–May 31, 1889), surgeon general of the Confederate army, was born in Charleston, S. C., the son of Stephen West and Eleanor Screven (Gilbert) Moore. The founder of the Moore family in America was Dr. Mordecai Moore who came to America with Lord Baltimore, as his physician. Samuel graduated from the Medical College of South Carolina on Mar. 8, 1834. One year later he was commissioned assistant surgeon in the United States Army and entered upon a long service in the western posts of Iowa, Kansas, and Missouri. Afterward he went to Florida, where, in 1845, he married Mary Augusta Brown, the daughter of Maj. Jacob Brown. During the Mexican War his entire service was along the Rio Grande, mostly at Camargo, across the Rio Grande from what was later Fort Ringgold. On Apr. 30, 1849, he attained his surgeoncy, with the rank of major, which he held until his resignation in 1861.

The coming of the Civil War was to him, as

to many regular officers, the occasion for much distress of mind. He resigned from the service so as not to fight against his state, and entered the practice of medicine at Little Rock, Ark., apparently hoping that he need not fight against his country. Trained military surgeons were too few in the South, however, for one of so long service to remain unknown. In June 1861 he was made surgeon general of the Confederate army. His task was most difficult. There was a shortage of doctors, as well as of drugs, supplies, and hospitals. Owing to the general practice of organizations electing their own officers, including surgeons, many poorly qualified men were commissioned. Moore established examining boards to weed out the unfit, and introduced, so far as possible, the organization and methods obtaining in the medical department of the United States Army. Probably he succeeded as well as any one could under the circumstances, but when the Union army entered Richmond, the records of his office were almost entirely destroyed by fire, as were most of the books and private papers of his family, so that there is very little documentary evidence of his work. During the war he undertook two methods of keeping medical officers informed as to the progress of their profession. He organized in 1863 and was president of the Association of Army and Navy Surgeons of the Confederate States, and he encouraged the publication of the *Confederate States Medical and Surgical Journal* (January 1864–February 1865). The Association promoted meetings and discussions of medical subjects and, in general, the extension of knowledge, much as does the ordinary medical society. The *Journal* presented interesting articles in the way of case reports, original investigations, and reviews of foreign and Union books and journals. It was a useful publication and its relative value was greatly enhanced by the absence of any other such publication in the Confederacy.

After the war, Moore remained in Richmond, not practising medicine but devoting much time to the furtherance of education and agriculture, incidentally serving as a member of the Richmond school board (1877–89) and of the Virginia Agricultural Society. In the latter capacity he took an important part in the promotion and improvement of the state fairs. He lived quietly and in honor until his death. As surgeon general he was regarded as strict and exacting, and as a severe disciplinarian; yet personally he seems to have been kind, mild, philanthropic, and modest and reserved in manner.

[H. R. McIlwaine, in *Surgery, Gynecology and Obstetrics,* Nov. 1924; S. E. Lewis, in *Southern Practi-*

tioner, Aug. 1901; C. W. Chancellor, *Ibid.,* Nov. 1903; J. E. Pilcher, *The Surgeon Generals of the Army* (1905); *Southern Hist. Soc. Papers,* vol. XXIX (1901); *Va. Medic. Mo.,* June 1889; *Richmond Dispatch,* June 1, 1889.]   P. M. A.

MOORE, THOMAS OVERTON (Apr. 10, 1804–June 25, 1876), governor of Louisiana, was born in Sampson County, N. C., the son of John and Jean (Overton) Moore and the descendant of James Moore (d. 1706, *q.v.*), who emigrated from Ireland in the seventeenth century to what is now South Carolina and became the governor of the Carolinas in 1700. On his mother's side he was descended from William Overton who emigrated from England to Virginia about 1670. He received his education in his native county and remained there until 1829, when he moved to Rapides Parish, La., where his uncle, Walter H. Overton, lived. For some years he managed his uncle's sugar plantation. Later he acquired a plantation of his own in the same parish and soon became one of the important sugar planters of the state. In disposition fiery and inclined to be exacting and uncompromising, he was, nevertheless, a thorough politician and played the political game with great zest and effectiveness. He was active in local politics rather early and for a number of years served as a member of the police jury of his parish. In 1848 he was elected to the state House of Representatives and in 1856 to the Senate. He became the candidate of the regular faction of the Democratic party for governor in 1859. Although he was opposed by Thomas J. Wells of the same parish he was elected in the following November and inaugurated in January 1860.

After the deadlock in the National Democratic Convention at Charleston he supported the Breckinridge-Lane faction and did much towards the success of that ticket in Louisiana in November. With the election of Lincoln as president he issued a call, on Dec. 10, to determine what course Louisiana should pursue. In his message he said: "I do not think it comports with the honor and respect of Louisiana, as a slave holding state, to live under the government of a Black Republican President" (Greer, *post,* p. 622), and on his recommendation the legislature called a state convention to meet on Jan. 23, 1861, in order to decide the matter. Anticipating what the convention would do, he ordered the state troops to take Forts Jackson and St. Philip, which commanded the Mississippi River below New Orleans, and also Fort Pike on the Rigolets and the barracks and arsenal at Baton Rouge, the state capital. Following the adoption of an ordinance of secession by the state convention, he took the lead in making Louisiana a member of the Confederacy, organizing local companies for defense, establishing supply depots on the Red River, and building packing plants to feed the men under arms. He cooperated with the Confederate government in the prosecution of the war. In April 1861 he issued a call for 5,000 troops for the Confederate service in addition to the 3,000 already asked for by President Davis, and he continued to exert his authority to raise troops and supplies for the armies in the field. He had in the meantime requested the banks to suspend specie payments and had instructed them to accept and pay out Confederate treasury notes at par. His administration was disrupted in June 1862 when, after the capture of New Orleans by Benjamin F. Butler, the Federal government appointed George F. Shepley as military governor of Louisiana. Shepley's administration was effective, however, only in the southern part of the state, and Moore continued to act as governor over central and northern Louisiana, still within Confederate lines, until the end of his term early in 1864. He moved the capital from Baton Rouge to Opelousas and later to Shreveport. On reaching Opelousas he issued an address to the people of the state directing what to do under the circumstances. Among other things he forbade their trading with the enemy, entering the Federal lines, bearing Federal passports, or accepting Federal money, and he ordered that steamboats be burned rather than allowed to fall into the hands of the enemy (*Official Records, post,* 1 ser., vol. XV, pp. 504–10). He was greatly handicapped, however, by the loss of New Orleans and the lower river parishes and was therefore unable to carry on an effective administration or to render any great amount of assistance to the Confederate government. When Banks made a raid up the Red River in the spring of 1864, his plantation in Rapides Parish was confiscated and his home and sugar mill destroyed. After the surrender of E. Kirby-Smith in May 1865, Moore, whose arrest had been ordered by the Louisiana state Senate newly organized under the constitution of 1864, fled to Havana, Cuba. Through the intercession of friends he was finally allowed to return home with a full pardon, and he spent the remainder of his days trying to restore his plantation and recover the losses he had sustained in the war. He took no further part in party politics and died on his plantation near Alexandria. He was married on Nov. 30, 1830, to Bethiah Jane Leonard of Rapides Parish, the daughter of Edward Augustus and Sarah (Morris) Leonard. They had five children.

[A few papers in possession of his grand-daughter, Mrs. Shirley Bruce Staples, Alexandria, La., some of which are published in G. P. Whittington, "Thomas O. Moore," and "Concerning the Loyalty of Slaves" in *La. Hist. Quart.,* Jan. 1930, Oct. 1931; see also Alcée Fortier, *A Hist. of La.* (1909), vols. III, IV, and *La.,* vol. II (1909); M. L. McLure, "The Elections of 1860 in La.," *La. Hist. Quart.,* Oct. 1926; J. K. Greer, "La. Politics," *Ibid.,* July, Oct. 1930; *War of the Rebellion: Official Records (Army),* esp. 1 ser., vols. I, VI, XV, 4 ser., vols. I, II; *Jefferson Davis . . . Letters, Papers and Speeches,* ed. by Dunbar Rowland (1923), vols. V, VI.]

E. M. V.

MOORE, THOMAS PATRICK (1796?–July 21, 1853), Kentucky congressman and minister to Colombia, was born in Charlotte County, Va., but removed in early childhood to Mercer County, Ky. The first record of him in Kentucky history is that of his enlistment during the War of 1812. From August until October 1812 he was a private in the company of Capt. George Trotter of the 1st Regiment of Kentucky Light Dragoons (*Report of the Adjutant General of the State of Kentucky: Soldiers of the War of 1812,* 1891, p. 35). His service in this war is often confused with that of Major T. P. Moore of the Virginia troops. After the war he attended Transylvania University and studied law with Judge John Green. In 1819 and 1820 he served in the state House of Representatives from Mercer County. The *Journal of the House of Representatives . . . of Kentucky* shows that in his first term he was a member of the committee on grievances, and, in his second, of that on courts of justice (1819, p. 7, 1820, p. 7). From March 1823 until March 1829 he was a member of the federal House of Representatives, where his most important committee assignment was that on manufactures which he was holding at the close of his services. It does not appear that he was an active legislator, but as a pronounced partisan of Jackson he achieved considerable prominence. John Quincy Adams recorded his opinion that "his integrity is problematical, and his only public service, the servility of his prostitution to the cause of Jackson's election and the baseness of his slanders upon me," and again that he was "a man generally despised" (*Memoirs of John Quincy Adams,* ed. by C. F. Adams, VIII, 1876, 112, 189). He was named minister plenipotentiary to Colombia on Mar. 13, 1829, to succeed William Henry Harrison [*q.v.*]. He ingratiated himself with Bolivar and in the first few weeks of his ministry obtained important commercial concessions for the United States. After the withdrawal of Ecuador and Venezuela, he remained at Bogotá and exerted himself to bring about a reunion of the three states. When these efforts failed he asked to be recalled in 1832 but at Jackson's request stayed for another year.

In the Black Hawk War, as in the War of 1812, he has been credited with a military record belonging to some one else (F. B. Heitman, *Historical Register and Dictionary of the United States Army,* 1903, vol. I, p. 723). As a matter of fact he did not return from New Granada until June 1833 (*Niles' Weekly Register,* June 8, 1833) and then plunged at once into a campaign for election to Congress against Robert P. Letcher. He was given the certificate of election, but Letcher brought a contest before Congress on the grounds of fraud and that body ordered a new election, in which Moore was defeated (*Ibid.,* Sept. 7, 14, 1833). He remained in private life until the war with Mexico. In March 1847 he was appointed lieutenant-colonel of the 3rd Regiment, United States Infantry, and in April was given the same command in the 3rd Regiment, United States Dragoons. He was honorably mustered out July 31, 1848 (Heitman, *ante*). Returning to Kentucky he was elected a delegate to the constitutional convention of 1849 and served on the committee on miscellaneous provisions. This was his last public service. He died of paralysis at Harrodsburg. He was married three times and was survived by three children.

[H. Levin, *The Lawyers and Lawmakers of Ky.* (1897) ; Lewis and R. H. Collins, *Hist. of Ky.,* 2 vols. (1874) ; *Biog. Directory Am. Cong.* (1928) ; J. D. Richardson, *A Compilation of the Messages and Papers of the Presidents,* vol. II (1896), pp. 467, 595 ; *House Exec. Doc. 173,* 22 Cong., 1 Sess. (1832) ; *Louisville Daily Democrat,* July 26, 1853 ; *Report of the Debates and Proc. of the Convention for the Revision of the Constitution . . . of Ky.* (1849) ; date of birth from statement of age as 53, in 1849, *Ibid.,* p. 7.]   R. S. C.

MOORE, VERANUS ALVA (Apr. 13, 1859– Feb. 11, 1931), bacteriologist, pathologist, leader in veterinary science, was born at Hounsfield, Jefferson County, N. Y., the son of Alva and Antinette Elizabeth Moore. The physical and mental qualities of a hardy, industrious ancestry characterized his personality and work throughout his life. His early education was obtained in the public schools and at Mexico Academy, Oswego County, N. Y., where he graduated in 1883. He was unfortunate in meeting with an accident in his youth, which necessitated much medical attention and the use of crutches until he was twenty-five years of age. His physical suffering and his frequent contact with physicians aroused his interest in the medical profession, and with a view to entering it, he enrolled at Cornell University in the fall of 1883, graduating with the degree of A.B. in 1887. That same year he accepted a position in the division of animal pathology, United States bureau of animal industry, where he investigated livestock diseases. At night he studied at the Columbian (now George Washington University) Medical School, from which institution he received the degree of M.D. in 1890, and where he was immediately appointed demonstrator, and later, professor of normal histology. In 1895 he succeeded Dr. Theobald Smith as chief of the division of animal pathology, which position he held until 1896, when he resigned to become professor of comparative pathology, bacteriology, and meat inspection at the veterinary college, Cornell University. He served continuously at Cornell until his retirement on June 21, 1929, at the age of seventy. During the last twenty-one years he held the position of dean, and from 1898 to 1910 was also professor of pathology and bacteriology in the Ithaca division of the medical college. The veterinary college developed under his administration until it became an outstanding institution of its kind. It is said that during the thirty-three years he was connected with Cornell he never missed a class on account of personal disability. In the fall following his retirement as dean, he was appointed superintendent of the Ithaca Memorial Hospital, which position he retained until his death.

As a bacteriologist and pathologist Moore had an international reputation. President Theodore Roosevelt appointed him a member of the International Conference on Tuberculosis, and President Hoover made him a member of the Conference on Child Life. He was also one of a commission of scientists appointed by the secretary of agriculture in 1907 to pass judgment upon the federal meat inspection regulations. When the United States entered the World War, Moore was called to Washington to assist in organizing the veterinary corps of the United States Army.

As a research worker he was concerned with tubercle bacilli in milk, bovine tuberculosis, infectious leukemia (now called fowl typhoid), diphtheria in fowls, swine plague, rabies, rabbit septicemia, enterohepatitis, corn-stalk disease, actinomycosis, glanders, and infectious abortion. The incalculable services he rendered to the livestock industry were recognized everywhere and his researches contributed much toward extending the outposts of knowledge in the field of veterinary medicine. Among his principal publications are: *Laboratory Directions for Beginners in Bacteriology* (1898) ; *The Pathology and Differential Diagnosis of Infectious Diseases of Animals* (1902) ; *Principles of Mi-*

crobiology (1912); *Bovine Tuberculosis and its Control* (1913); *History of Veterinary Education and Service from 1896 to 1929* (1929). He also delivered many addresses and contributed numerous articles on infectious diseases to government and state publications, and to medical and veterinary journals. On July 12, 1892, he married Mary L. Slawson of Cicero, N. Y., by whom he had three children.

[*Who's Who in America*, 1930–31; J. M. Cattell and D. R. Brimhall, *Am. Men of Sci.* (3rd ed., 1921); *Veterinary Medicine*, Aug. 1929; *Report of the N. Y. State Veterinary Coll.*, *1928–29* and *1930–31* (1930, 1932); V. A. Moore, *N. Y. State Veterinary Coll., a Special Report to the President of Cornell Univ.* (1908); *N. Y. Times*, Feb. 12, 1931.]   J. R. M.

MOORE, WILLIAM (May 6, 1699–May 30, 1783), Pennsylvania jurist, was born in Philadelphia. He was the son of John Moore [*q.v.*], collector of the port of Philadelphia, and his wife, Rebecca Axtell of South Carolina. According to family tradition, he was educated in England and graduated at Oxford in 1719, but he does not appear in the list of matriculates of the institution. About 1722 he married Williamina Wemyss, a relative of the Earl of Wemyss in the peerage of Scotland. Shortly after his marriage, his father gave him a large tract of land in Chester County, a few miles from Valley Forge, and he lived there for more than fifty years. The stone house that he built on this estate is still called Moore Hall. During the French and Indian War, he was colonel of a Chester County militia regiment. He was a devout churchman and was a vestryman of St. James Church on the Perkiomen and later of the church at Radnor in Delaware County.

He was a member of the Provincial Assembly for Chester County from 1733 until 1740, when he refused to be a candidate for reëlection. He was a justice of the peace from 1741 to 1783 and was the presiding judge of the Chester County court during most of the period from 1750 to 1776. It is believed that he was associated with the Quaker or anti-proprietary party until 1755, when he became involved in a controversy with them over the question of military defense. The frontier settlements of Pennsylvania were ravaged by the Indians, after Braddock's defeat, and on Nov. 5, 1755, a petition was sent to the Assembly from Chester County demanding security and protection. Moore's name heads the list of signatures and he probably wrote the petition itself. This made him obnoxious to the Quaker majority in the Assembly and they organized an attack upon his integrity as a judge. They were helped by Isaac Wayne, the father of Anthony Wayne, who lived near Moore Hall and was one of Moore's personal enemies. Through Wayne's efforts, twenty-eight petitions were presented to the Assembly in 1757 urging Moore's removal as presiding judge on the ground that he had been tyrannical, unjust, and extortionate in the performance of his duties. Moore denied the jurisdiction of the Assembly, but an *ex parte* investigation was conducted and a formal address was sent to Gov. William Denny praying that he should be removed from office. As this document was printed and widely circulated, Moore decided that his answer, in which he referred to the conduct of the Assembly as "virulent and slanderous," should be given equal publicity. On Jan. 6, 1758, he was arrested for libel and for violating the privileges of the Assembly and was imprisoned in the common gaol in Philadelphia. The Rev. William Smith [*q.v.*], the principal of the Academy of Philadelphia, who had opposed the Assembly on the defense issue, was also imprisoned on the charge of assisting Moore in the preparation of his address. The Assembly forbade the courts to issue a writ of *habeas corpus* and both of the prisoners remained in gaol for almost three months, when the house adjourned and they were released by the governor. The governor and council also investigated the judicial charges that had been brought against Moore and he was completely exonerated.

After this episode, Moore returned to his home and his duties as a judge and led an uneventful life until the beginning of the American Revolution. He was too old to take an active part in that movement, but his sympathies were obviously with the Loyalists. When he was visited by a Whig committee in 1775 and asked to recant his views, he signed a curious and somewhat equivocal statement. It is doubtful whether his visitors fully appreciated the sarcasm of the following sentence: "I also further declare that I have of late encouraged and will continue to encourage learning the military art, apprehending that the time is not far distant when there may be occasion for it" (Futhey and Cope, *post*, p. 663). He was always noted for his hospitality, however, and he entertained Col. Clement Biddle and other American officers while Washington's army was encamped at Valley Forge. He died at Moore Hall on May 30, 1783, and was buried in the churchyard at Radnor. He was survived by his wife, who died in 1784; and by five of his twelve children.

[There is a volume of Moore's manuscripts in the possession of the Pa. Hist. Soc., but it contains very little biographical data. The Society also has a manu-

Moore

Moore

script volume entitled *Smith and Moore vs. the Assembly, 1758–59.* For the printed material see D. M. Hall, *Six Centuries of the Moores of Fawley, Berkshire, England, and their Descendants* (1904); H. W. Smith, *Life and Correspondence of the Rev. William Smith, D.D.* (2 vols., 1880); J. S. Futhey and G. Cope, *Hist. of Chester County, Pa.* (1881), containing sketch reprinted in S. W. Pennypacker, *Hist. and Biog. Sketches* (1883); W. R. Riddell, "Libel on the Assembly: A Prerevolutionary Episode," *Pa. Mag. of Hist. and Biog.*, Apr.–Oct. 1928; and the *Pa. Gazette*, June 18, 1783.]
W. R. S.

MOORE, WILLIAM (c. 1735–July 24, 1793), merchant, Revolutionary patriot, jurist, was born in Philadelphia, the son of Robert and Elizabeth Moore. His father, a native of the Isle of Man, was a shopkeeper of some means. Educated for a mercantile career, William became a successful merchant. His marriage to Sarah, daughter of Thomas and Susannah Lloyd, Dec. 13, 1757, allied him with one of the oldest and most influential families of provincial Pennsylvania. Although opposing the Stamp Act and subscribing to the non-importation agreements in 1765, he disapproved of more radical measures in the early revolutionary period, his son of sixteen bringing great distress to his parents by enlisting with the patriot army for the Canadian expedition, 1775–76. Before his return, however, both father and mother had "caught the delusion" of the patriots and from that time on Moore gave liberally of his time and money to the American cause. He supported the state constitution of 1776, not out of thorough agreement with it but from the conviction that the salvation of the state demanded such a course.

On Dec. 10, 1776, Moore was appointed by the assembly to the council of safety, and on Mar. 13, 1777, by the supreme executive council to the newly organized board of war. Elected to Congress, Feb. 5, 1777, he declined to serve owing to the pressure of business affairs. He was a member of the supreme executive council from October 1779 to October 1782, of which he was vice-president the first two years and president the third. Although a Constitutionalist, he was of a more sober temper than most of his party, and possessed the confidence and warm regard of many in the opposite party, as testified to by his almost unanimous election as president. During his tenure, a period of great financial distress for the state, the Anti-Constitutionalists made further inroads on their steadily weakening opponents. He disagreed with the paper-money views of his own party, accepting the more conservative position of Robert Morris, 1734–1806 [*q.v.*], for whom he entertained a warm friendship. A jealous guardian of executive privilege, he attacked the assembly for withdrawing money from the treasury without the council's consent. His letters while president reveal a man of character and energy, of broad education, remarkable for his practicality and cool deliberation. On Nov. 14, 1781, by virtue of being president, he was commissioned judge of the Pennsylvania high court of errors and appeals, the council reviewing his commission on Mar. 18, 1783. During and after his presidency he was active in promoting plans to solve Pennsylvania's financial difficulties, and in July 1784 presided at a public meeting in Philadelphia held for that purpose. He was elected to the assembly in 1784, was director of the Bank of Pennsylvania, trustee of the University of the State of Pennsylvania, 1784–89, and a conspicuous member of the St. Tammany Society. In later life he continued to play an important part in Philadelphia's civic affairs. Moore was a man of striking appearance, of dignified bearing, and possessed an agreeable manner. He left three children, his only daughter Elizabeth in 1784 having married François de Barbé Marbois, French chargé d'affaires, who later negotiated the treaty for the sale of Louisiana to the United States.

[J. P. Parke and Townsend Ward, *Geneal. Notes* (1898); W. C. Armor, *Lives of the Govs. of Pa.* (1872); C. P. Keith, *The Provincial Councillors of Pa.* (1883); *Pa. Archives*, 1 ser. VII–X (1853–54), 2 ser., I (1874), 4 ser. III (1900), 827–54; *Minutes of the Provincial Council of Pa.*, vols. XI–XIII (1852); *Pa. Mag. of Hist. and Biog.*, Oct. 1885, pp. 278–79, Oct. 1902, pp. 341–42; Oct. 1917, p. 435.]
J. H. P.

MOORE, WILLIAM HENRY (Oct. 25, 1848–Jan. 11, 1923), capitalist and promoter, was born in Utica, N. Y., the son of Nathaniel F. and Rachel (Beckwith) Moore, of colonial descent. His father was a banker and his mother was the daughter of a banker. After attending a seminary at Oneida and then the Cortland Academy at Homer, N. Y., he entered Amherst in 1867 but left in 1870 before graduation because of ill health. He studied law and was admitted to the bar at Eau Claire, Wis., in 1872, but in the same year went to Chicago, where he entered the offices of Edward A. Small, a leading corporation lawyer. After a year and a half as managing clerk he was made partner, under the firm name of Small, Burke, and Moore, and on Oct. 31, 1878, he married Ada W. Small, the daughter of his partner. They had three children. At Small's death in 1882 he took into partnership his younger brother, James Hobart Moore. They continued in active practice until 1887, and in later life Moore was commonly referred to as "Judge." He gained wide repute for his skill in the intricacies of corporation law, but gradually the brothers forsook legal practice for corporate promotion and management. They were among the first to recognize the possibilities of industrial mergers in America, and—next to Morgan—perhaps the most important in developing them.

Their first important venture was the reorganization of the Diamond Match Company with an increase of capitalization to $7,500,000 and later to $11,000,000. Six months later they reorganized a combination of strawboard manufacturers, with a capitalization of $7,000,000. In 1890 they brought several Eastern cracker factories together into the New York Biscuit Company, with a capitalization of $9,000,000. But Moore was playing for higher stakes than promotion returns. With other Chicago financiers to back him, he formed a pool to boost and sustain the price of Diamond Match in the Chicago Exchange. There was talk of technical improvements, and of negotiations with various foreign countries for contracts or the establishment of factories. It is not clear how much of this was genuine expectation on Moore's part, and how much unprincipled conjecture or less. Diamond Match rose from 120 in January 1896 to 248 in May; a similar sympathetic movement took place in New York Biscuit. The plan seems to have been to sustain the prices until some tangible favorable development would enable the holders to "unload" on outsiders at top prices. For six months there was a Diamond Match craze; for weeks almost the entire business of the exchange was in the Moore stocks. But the failure of the mysterious foreign negotiations to eventuate, and the Bryan Populist scare, took the strength out of the boom. Some of the insiders in the pool treacherously began unloading on the Moores. Finally after desperate efforts to bolster their margins—efforts which included the withdrawal of $800,-000 of the match company's funds for that purpose—the Moores gave up, and on the night of Aug. 3 the panicky leaders of the Exchange decided to close it the next morning. The panic was felt a bit on the New York Exchange, and there was even some liquidation in London, while the Chicago Exchange "did not find it convenient" to open for three months. While Moore's losses, which were originally estimated at about eight million, were scaled down to four, they meant a burden of debt and a blow to his prestige.

Moore went about imperturbably retrieving his career. His tall, thick-set, commanding figure, his sure and confident voice, his genial, self-sufficient smile were not those of a shattered man. He was forced out of Diamond Match, but

so successfully did he in his other venture, with the backing of Armour and Pullman, engineer a price war against the American Biscuit and Manufacturing Company that the only possible result was a merger—the National Biscuit Company, formed in February 1898 with a capital of $55,000,000 and a monopoly control of 90 per cent of the cracker-biscuit companies of the country. In its incorporation under the favorable New Jersey laws, in its capitalization not only of tangible assets but also of projected "good-will" and anticipated monopoly profits, and in the large "melon" reserved for promotion, the new company served as a model for subsequent consolidations. It was immediately and immensely successful. Moore's prestige was restored. He was besieged with requests to organize companies "from the marshes of Maine to the Pacific coast" (*Industrial Commission Report, post*, p. 963), of which he selected only a few and on his own terms.

Turning to the steel industry, he organized in rapid succession (December 1898–April 1899) the American Tin Plate Company, the National Steel Company, and the American Steel Hoop Company with a total capitalization of $142,-000,000, of which at least $20,000,000 went for promotion. Despite the fact that the stock of all three companies was plentifully watered and represented anticipated profits rather than actual properties, it was eagerly caught up and oversubscribed. The Moores seemed to have found the secret of successful promotion. Wall Street was probably not far wrong in guessing that it lay in the creation of monopolistic control, the contrivance of devices to avoid the operation of the anti-trust laws, the reorganization of production and marketing to effect economies, and the retention of control in the hands of a small group. This group consisted of the two Moores, Daniel G. Reid, and William B. Leeds, the latter two being accessions from the tin-plate industry. Together they formed the "Moore gang," the "Moore crowd," the "Moore interests," and "the Big Four from the Prairies," as they were variously known on Wall Street, and they continued to work together.

In May 1899 a syndicate headed by Moore agreed to pay $320,000,000 for the combined Carnegie-Frick properties. Carnegie insisted that the dealings should be with his partners Henry Clay Frick and Henry Phipps, Jr. [qq.v.], and gave them power of attorney. They joined the syndicate; Moore paid $1,000,000 for a ninety days' option and Frick and Phipps added $170,000. The negotiations seemed to have every chance of success, but the failure of expected financial support to materialize, and the presence on the market of too many "undigested securities" made it impossible for the syndicate to obtain the necessary cash. Carnegie relentlessly refused to extend the option, and kept the option money. The Moores now turned to other consolidations—that of the American Sheet Steel Company in February 1900, and that of the American Can Company in March 1901. Their companies formed one of the four main groups in the steel industry, the other three being the Carnegie, Morgan, and Rockefeller groups, and when Morgan succeeded in buying out Carnegie and launching the new $1,400,000 United States Steel Corporation in 1901, they were included. It was generally believed that the Moore companies, although the most heavily overcapitalized, received the best terms of all. Moore himself was placed on the board of directors of the new corporation, and Reid on the executive committee. But Morgan had no intention of admitting the Moore group to active control: their peculiar type of speculative and predatory activity was too unlike his own conception of business methods. Enormously wealthy now, they turned their money and attention elsewhere.

The West had been partitioned into four railroad empires—those of Hill, Harriman, Gould, and Morgan. But the Chicago, Rock Island, & Pacific Railway, as a comparatively minor road, had been left out of the calculations. Its management was conservative and responsible and paid good dividends, but lacked daring and imagination. These the Moores were ready to supply. After a stock-buying campaign of nine months, during which the stock rose from 80 to 160, Moore forced his way into the control. On June 4, 1901, he and Reid were elected to the board of directors of the Rock Island; on Dec. 12, Leeds was installed in the presidency and James Moore was added to the board of directors; finally on Jan. 30, 1902, the Moore interests placed four of their number on the executive committee of seven, pushing out the Cable interests, and took complete charge of the road. Despite suspicion and hostility on Wall Street, they set out on a brilliant campaign of expansion; technical matters were handled by Reid and matters of financial strategy by Moore himself. In rapid succession they bought up or leased a number of roads, acquiring mileage and terminal facilities that would make of the Rock Island an important transcontinental system. The stock continued to rise, reaching 200 in July 1902. The capitalization, which had remained at fifty million since 1880,

was increased to sixty in July 1901 and to seventy-five in June 1902. Applying to the new field the magnificence of operation that had characterized their steel finance, the Moores announced in August a proposed reorganization of the Rock Island, and a "rearrangement of securities." Wall Street, accustomed as it was to financial manipulation, was bewildered by the intricacies of the new scheme. Three companies were to be created, in a double-holding company arrangement, and each holder of $100 of stock in the original company was to receive $270 in bonds and stock (for details see *Poor's Manual of the Railroads of the United States*, 1903, pp. 1514–24). Albert W. Atwood, writing in *Harper's Weekly*, Mar. 28, 1914, called this reorganization "the most astounding piece of stock-watering the world has ever seen." To pay interest and dividends on an increase in capitalization of 270% placed an enormous burden upon properties and revenues, especially since the stock of the railway was replaced by the bonds of the operating company, with the consequent substitution of fixed charges for dividends. The financial world felt doubtful about the whole matter, and in Sunday newspapers, magazines, and financial weeklies the proposed reorganization was met with a burst of disfavor. But the plan was pushed through, and Moore went on with his career of conquest. In the winter of 1902 he added to the Rock Island system the St. Louis & San Francisco Railroad, with a mileage of over 5,000 miles, and B. F. Yoakum of the latter line was added to the inside group of the Rock Island. In 1904, to the great chagrin of Harriman, they captured a stock majority in the Chicago & Alton Railroad Company. Moore became known as the "Sphinx of the Rock Island." He went on his way with a complete indifference to public sentiment, and stood out in the first decade of the new century as the foremost and most daring promoter in American business, just as Morgan was the foremost financier. He had behind him the backing of a dozen banks and trust companies, and was the leader of a group that controlled fifteen thousand miles of railroad.

During the next few years Moore obtained control of the Lehigh Valley Railroad, and with the aid of an English syndicate (Pearson-Farquhar) he began to buy into the Denver & Rio Grande Railroad Company, the Missouri Pacific Railway Company, and the Wabash Railroad Company. But he met with reverses. The St. Louis & San Francisco had turned out to be a distinct loss, and in 1909 it was returned to the original owners with a loss of

$20,000,000. The Chicago & Alton had also been returned at a loss in 1907. The operations of Moore and the English syndicate were hampered by the tightening of the market, and were finally taken over by Kuhn, Loeb & Company. The holding company scheme of the Rock Island drained the road and placed an incubus on all future holdings. In the end the Rock Island went into receivership. The entire period of Moore control was described in periodicals as "the looting of the Rock Island." It was pointed out that the stock had declined from $200 in 1902 to $20 in 1914, although the road's earnings had steadily increased. A stockholders' protective committee was formed under N. L. Amster, with Samuel Untermeyer as counsel, the latter declaring that in comparison with the Moore maneuvers "the manipulators of the old Fisk-Gould days were artless children." In 1916 the Interstate Commerce Commission issued a drastic report, arraigning Moore, Reid, and the other members of the controlling group, and charging them with deliberate misrepresentation and with looting the railroad. The receivership was ended on June 24, 1917, and the Moore group was ousted from control.

Moore now retired from active business interests. He had built up a stable which was regarded as the equal of any in the turf world, and he had the best string of hackneys in the country. He entered his horses in international competitions and had an absorbing interest in the fashionable Madison Square Garden horse shows. His own skill as a four-in-hand driver was internationally known. He died of heart disease at his New York home.

[For Moore's early life and the first stages of his career, see Will Payne, "The Imperturbable Moores," *Everybody's Mag.*, June 1903; the obituaries in the *N. Y. Times* and other papers for Jan. 12, 1923; the accounts in the *N. Y. Times* of the Diamond Match episode on the Chicago Stock Exchange, especially for the week Aug. 3–10, 1896; the National Biscuit Co. house organ, *The N B C*, March 1923, pp. 5–8. For Moore's activities in the steel industry, see his testimony in *Industrial Commission. Preliminary Report on Trusts and Industrial Combinations* (1900), I, 959–67; *Report of the Commissioners of Corporations on the Steel Industry*, pt. I (1911), pp. 1–180, esp. 8–13, 85–91, 133–41, 176–79; the files of the *Commercial and Financial Chronicle*, 1898–1901, containing detailed announcements and comment on stock issues, directors' meetings and corporate reorganizations in the various Moore promotions; for differing versions of the Moore negotiations for buying out Carnegie, see George Harvey, *Henry Clay Frick the Man* (1928), pp. 204–15, and B. J. Hendrick, *The Life of Andrew Carnegie* (1932), II, 76–88, highly illuminating for their contrast; for the Morgan negotiations, see Lewis Corey, *The House of Morgan* (1930), ch. xxiii. For Moore's railroad career, see *Interstate Commerce Commission Reports*, vol. XXXVI (1916), pp. 43–61, the most valuable source; see also the following periodical accounts: C. M. Keys, "The Newest Railroad Power," and "The Overlords of the Railroad Traffic," *World's Work*, June 1905, Jan. 1907; R. W.

Vincent, "The Inside Story of Rock Island—'Frisco Financing,'" *Moody's Mag.*, Jan. 1909; A. Franklin, "Current Railroad Strategy," and "The Big R. R. Deal that Went Wrong," *Bankers Mag.*, July, Sept., 1910; A. W. Atwood, "Upsetting an Inverted Pyramid," *Harper's Weekly*, Mar. 28, 1914; T. Prince, "The Rock Island Situation," and "The Rock Island," *Moody's Mag.*, Mar. 1915, Aug. 1916; T. Gibson, "The Chicago, Rock Island & Pacific Ry. Co.," *Ibid.*, Sept. 1916.]

M. L.

MOORE, WILLIAM THOMAS (Aug. 27, 1832–Sept. 7, 1926), clergyman of the Disciples of Christ, was born in Henry County, Ky. His father, Richard Moore, was of Irish ancestry; his mother, Nancy M. (Jones), of Scotch extraction. They moved from Virginia to Kentucky and thence to Indiana, where Richard Moore died when William Thomas, the eldest son among six children, was nine years old. The family then returned to Kentucky, and William within a few years was its chief support. At eighteen he had received practically no schooling but had read the Bible and a few histories. In 1850 he entered an academy at New Castle, Ky. He then taught and preached, and in 1855 entered Bethany College, Va. (now W. Va.), graduating in 1858.

For six years thereafter he was pastor at Frankfort, Ky. In 1864 he married Mary A. Bishop, daughter of R. M. Bishop of Cincinnati, later governor of Ohio; Richard Bishop Moore [q.v.] was one of their children. From January 1865 to February 1866 he was pastor of the Jefferson Avenue Christian Church, Detroit, Mich. Thence he was called to a professorship in Kentucky University and later elected to a pastorate in Cincinnati, Ohio. He accepted the pastorate conditionally, served as professor at Kentucky University for one year, 1866–67, at the same time teaching sacred rhetoric and ecclesiastical history at the College of the Bible, Lexington, and for two years thereafter delivered a brief course of lectures annually at Kentucky University. During his Cincinnati pastorate he made his congregation the largest and most far-reaching in influence of any in his brotherhood.

He was a member of the executive committee of the American Christian Missionary Society and of the committee to revise the church hymnbook (1864). He was chairman of a committee of twenty which drafted a plan of work adopted in 1869 by the national convention of the Society at Louisville, Ky. In 1874, realizing that the "Louisville Plan" was unsatisfactory, he called a meeting and urged the organization of a foreign-missionary society. As a result, during the convention of 1875, the Foreign Christian Missionary Society was formed. Moore was vice-president, 1875–77, secretary, 1876–77, and member of the board of managers, 1883–84.

In July 1878 he entered the service of the Society. After preaching for three years in Southport and Liverpool, England, he was for ten years minister at the West London Tabernacle. While here, in 1881, he began to publish the *Christian Commonwealth,* which he edited actively for sixteen years, and by proxy through his eldest son, Paul, for five years more. His first wife died Apr. 14, 1888, and on Aug. 20, 1890, he married Emma S. Frederick of Carthage, N. Y. In 1896 he became dean of the Bible College of Missouri, a new school established in Columbia, Mo., by the Disciples of Christ, adjacent to the University of Missouri, to train young men for the ministry and to supply to university students such religious studies as a tax-supported institution cannot offer. He remained in Columbia until 1909, serving for part of the time as chaplain and professor in the Christian College there, an institution for women, of which his wife was president. From 1897 to 1900 he edited the *Christian Quarterly,* which he had founded and edited from 1869 to 1877. In 1909 he moved to Florida, where he spent his remaining years. He died at Orlando, at the age of ninety-four.

Moore was the author of a number of books on religious subjects and a contributor to periodicals. His best-known publications include *The Living Pulpit of the Christian Church* (cop. 1867), a series of sermons by representative ministers of the Disciples of Christ, with biographical sketches; a similar series, *The New Living Pulpit of the Christian Church* (1918); and *A Comprehensive History of the Disciples of Christ* (1909). He was more than six feet tall, weighed nearly two hundred pounds, and wore a patriarchal beard reaching to his waist. A man of tremendous vitality (he went swimming in Lake Michigan after he was ninety, and continued to preach until shortly before his death), he was a prominent figure in his denomination for more than half a century.

[F. M. Green, *Christian Missions and Hist. Sketches* (1884); J. T. Brown, *Churches of Christ* (1904); J. W. Monser, *The Literature of the Disciples* (1906); J. H. Garrison, *The Reformation of the Nineteenth Century* (1901) and *The Story of a Century* (1909); Archibald McLean, *The Hist. of the Foreign Christian Missionary Soc.* (1921); A. W. Fortune, *The Disciples in Ky.* (1932); *The Biog. Encyc. of Ky.* (1878); J. F. Brennan, *A Biog. Cyc. . . . of Ohio* (1879); *Who's Who in America,* 1910–11; *Pensacola Jour.,* Sept. 8, 1926; *N. Y. Times,* Sept. 9, 12, 1926; information as to certain facts from friends and relatives.]   G. D. E.

MOORE, ZEPHANIAH SWIFT (Nov. 20, 1770–June 30, 1823), Congregational clergyman, college president, was born in Palmer, Mass., the son of Judah and Mary (Swift) Moore. He was descended from John Moore who settled at Sudbury, Mass., in 1642. In 1778 the family moved to Wilmington, Vt., where Zephaniah worked for ten years on his father's farm. During this time he evinced a keen intelligence and so strong a desire for a college education that his parents at considerable sacrifice to themselves sent him to Bennington, Vt., for a brief preparatory course and afterwards to Dartmouth College, where he graduated with distinction in 1793. The next year he taught as principal of the academy in Londonderry, N. H. He then took up the study of theology with the Rev. Charles Backus of Somers, Conn., and was licensed to preach in 1796. Having received invitations to various places, he accepted a call in 1797 to the First Congregational Church at Leicester, Mass., where he remained for fourteen years. Throughout this period he served as trustee of Leicester Academy and from July 1806 to October 1807, was principal preceptor. Soon after settling at Leicester he was married, Feb. 21, 1799, to Phebe Drury of Ward (now Auburn), Mass. In 1811 he became professor of learned languages (Latin, Greek, and Hebrew) in Dartmouth College, his alma mater, where he taught with so much success that in 1815 he was elected to the presidency of Williams College. In recognition of this honor Dartmouth conferred on him the degree of doctor of divinity. As chief executive of Williams he proved to be highly efficient. He was, however, one of those who believed that the institution could not continue to prosper in its isolated location and that it should be removed to a more accessible place in the Connecticut Valley. Strong opposition to this plan developed and the controversy was continued until 1820 (Durfee, *post,* p. 157), when the legislature rejected the petition of the trustees for removal of the college to Northampton. Just at this time plans were being formed for the establishment of a college at Amherst, Mass., and Moore was invited to be its first president. He accepted the task in May 1821, and fifteen of the students at Williams accompanied him to Amherst. Under his able leadership, in spite of the meager resources then available in New England for such an enterprise, the institution was successfully launched. He lived, however, to complete barely two years of service in his new position. Weakened by excessive labors he succumbed after a brief illness to an attack of "bilious colic." He left no children, but his widow survived till 1857.

Moore was a large man of even temperament and kindly disposition. He wore the conservative knee-breeches when long trousers were becoming fashionable, and his manners while pleasant and unassuming were marked by a quiet dignity. He readily won the confidence and loyalty of those with whom he worked. He excelled especially as a college officer, governing the undergraduates with great firmness, but so wisely as to win their esteem and even their affection. As a preacher he employed little action or rhetorical embellishment, but by reason of a clear, concise, and logical exposition of the subject and great sincerity and earnestness of delivery he was uniformly impressive. His religious views were strictly orthodox, conforming to those prevalent in New England at that period. As an educationalist he held firmly to the importance of liberal studies as a preparation for professional work, insisting also that religious instruction was quite as essential as intellectual training.

[W. S. Tyler, *Hist. of Amherst Coll.* (1873); Calvin Durfee, *A Hist. of Williams Coll.* (1860); L. W. Spring, *A Hist. of Williams Coll.* (1917); W. B. Sprague, *Annals. Am. Pulpit*, vol. II (1857); L. B. Richardson, *Hist. of Dartmouth Coll.* (1932), vol. I; *Quarterly Register*, Feb. 1833; Emory Washburn, in *New-Eng. Hist. and Geneal. Reg.*, Oct. 1847; *Ibid.*, July 1903, Apr. 1904; *Christian Spectator*, Sept. 1, 1823; *Boston Daily Advertiser*, July 4, 1823. A number of Moore's addresses and sermons, some of them in manuscript, are preserved in the Amherst, Dartmouth, and Williams College libraries.]   H. P. G.

MOOREHEAD, WILLIAM GALLOGLY (Mar. 19, 1836–Mar. 1, 1914), United Presbyterian clergyman, Biblical scholar, was born on a farm near Rix Mills, Muskingum County, Ohio. His parents were David and Margaret (Henderson) Moorehead. He graduated at Muskingum College in 1858 and studied theology at the Allegheny and Xenia theological seminaries of the United Presbyterian Church, graduating from the latter in 1862. During his seminary course he was licensed to preach, April 1861, and acted as a stated supply at Urbana, Ohio, until some time in the early part of 1862. On July 1, 1862, he was ordained to the ministry in connection with his appointment by the General Assembly of the United Presbyterian Church as a missionary in Italy under the direction of the American and Foreign Christian Union. About seven years (1862–69) were spent in Italy, the first two being devoted to mastering the language, the last five to missionary work in Florence and Sienna. In 1869 he returned to America and the next year became pastor of the First United Presbyterian Church, Xenia, Ohio, continuing to serve until 1875. While in this pastorate he was elected in 1873 to the chair of New Testament literature and exegesis at Xenia Theological Seminary,

which position he retained until 1908, when he insisted on being relieved. In April 1875 he was called to the Fourth United Presbyterian Church of Allegheny, Pa., where he served until January 1876, without interrupting his classroom work. From 1878 to 1885 he was pastor of the Third Church of Xenia, this charge being an annex to his professorship. When the board of management of the seminary reluctantly consented to his withdrawal, in 1908, from the chair he had occupied since 1873, it induced him to take up the lighter duties of the Newburgh chair of English Bible and Biblical theology. To this work the last years of his life were given so that he completed four decenniums of continuous service as a professor in Xenia Theological Seminary before he died. In 1899 he had become president of the Seminary and he filled that office until his death.

Moorehead had a gracious personality and was an able preacher and teacher. In Bible Schools and at special conferences he was a notably successful lecturer. He was frequently heard at Winona, at Grove City, Pa., in various Chautauquas, at Niagara, and at the Moody Bible Institute, Chicago. He wrote a number of books dealing with the Bible: *Studies in the Mosaic Institutions* (1896), *Outline Studies in the Books of the Old Testament* (1893), *Studies in the Four Gospels* (1900), *Outline Studies in Acts ... Ephesians* (1902), *Outline Studies in the New Testament, Philippians to Hebrews* (1905), *Outline Studies in the New Testament, Catholic Epistles* (1910), and *Studies in the Book of Revelation* (1908). In addition to these publications he contributed to various periodicals articles dealing with subjects in the field of Biblical literature. For some time after 1908 he represented the United Presbyterian Church on the International Sunday School Lesson Committee. In 1892, 1896, and 1904 he was a delegate to the Council of Reformed Churches Throughout the World Holding the Presbyterian System.

He was married three times: first, on Aug. 9, 1864, to Helen King, who died Nov. 13, 1870; second, to Anna L. Beatty, who died Jan. 14, 1874; and third, to Elizabeth Ankeney, who survived him, dying Apr. 22, 1924. Two sons and two daughters survived him.

[*United Presbyterian*, Mar. 5, 12, 19, Apr. 9, 1914; *Christian Union Herald*, Nov. 15, 1928; *Testimonial and Memorial* (1913), issued in connection with the celebration of Dr. Moorehead's fortieth Seminary anniversary; *Who's Who in America*, 1914–15; *Cincinnati Enquirer*, Mar. 2, 1914.]   J. M.

MOOREHEAD, JAMES KENNEDY (Sept. 7, 1806–Mar. 6, 1884), Civil War congressman from Pennsylvania, canal builder, and pioneer in commercial telegraphy, was born in Halifax, Dauphin County, Pa. His father, William Moorhead, had emigrated from Ireland and settled in the United States in 1798. In 1814 he was appointed by President James Madison collector of internal revenue for the tenth district of Pennsylvania, but he died in 1817, leaving his wife, Elizabeth (Kennedy) Young Moorhead, a widow with several children to support and no other form of income than that which could be obtained from a farm. Under these circumstances, James's schooling ended when he was eleven years old after he had completed two years in the district school in Harrisburg. At fourteen he had the full responsibility of the farm and Moorhead's ferry. Two years later he served as an apprentice to a tanner, but he never followed the trade. Having gained a fair knowledge of building and a familiarity with water transportation, he offered a low bid and obtained the contract for the construction of the Susquehanna branch of the Pennsylvania Canal—a job which netted him almost four hundred dollars. He then remained as superintendent of the Juniata division and was the first to place a passenger packet on the system. During the ten years he spent in navigating the canal he gained a knowledge of the problems involved in managing canal transportation and in 1839 he began a connection with the Monongahela Navigation Company in Pittsburgh. In 1846 he became president of the company, retaining the position until his death thirty-eight years later. In this capacity he built many dams, locks, and reservoirs in Pennsylvania, Indiana, and Kentucky, and earned for himself the title "Old Slackwater" because of the slackwater dams. In 1840 he established the Union Cotton Factory in what is now the Northside district of Pittsburgh. Nine years later the factory burned along with his house. He rebuilt the latter but it was again destroyed in 1853 by fire. At this time he also owned a part interest in the Novelty Works in Pittsburgh.

Moorhead was one of the first to appreciate the possibilities of commercial telegraphy and it was largely through his efforts and direction, dating from 1853, that lines were established between Pittsburgh and Philadelphia. The operating company, of which he was president, was the Atlantic & Ohio Telegraph Company. He was also the president of the various companies owning lines to Cincinnati and Louisville. Afterward, when these lines were consolidated, they formed the basis of the Western Union System. In politics Moorhead was an active member of the Democratic party of that day and for

a short time held an appointment under President Van Buren as deputy postmaster of Pittsburgh (1840–41). But in the trying years from 1854 to 1858 he left the party and aided in the formation of the Republican party. In 1859 he was its successful candidate for Congress and served continuously in the lower house from 1859 to 1869. During the term of his membership he served on several important committees —commerce, national armories, manufactures, naval affairs, and ways and means—and was chairman of the two first named. In 1868 he served in his last political position, as delegate to the Republican National Convention at Chicago which nominated Ulysses S. Grant.

Moorhead always exhibited a great interest in the affairs of his church, the Presbyterian, in which he was the ruling elder, and in 1884 he went to Belfast, Ireland, as a delegate to the Pan-Presbyterian Council. Shortly afterward, upon his return to Pittsburgh, he died. He had lived to celebrate with his wife, Jane Logan, to whom he was married Dec. 17, 1829, their golden anniversary. Their family consisted of two sons and three daughters. Moorhead's native ability was the deciding factor in his success, overcoming almost total lack of material means. He brought to each task the experience gained from a previous undertaking and thus advanced step by step through his own efforts to a position of responsibility at the head of a large navigation company.

[*Memorial Vol.: Jas. Kennedy Moorhead* (privately printed, 1885); *Biog. Dir. Am. Cong.* (1928); Erasmus Wilson, ed., *Standard Hist. of Pittsburg, Pa.* (1898); the *Pittsburg Dispatch* and *Pittsburgh Post*, Mar. 7, 1884.]

A. I.

MOOSMÜLLER, OSWALD WILLIAM Feb. 26, 1832–Jan. 10, 1901), Roman Catholic priest of the Order of St. Benedict, was born into a wealthy family at Aidling in the Bavarian Alps. He was trained by tutors and in the old Benedictine College of Metten in the diocese of Ratisbon, where he learned of the pressing need for missionary priests among the German immigrants in the United States. He entered the Benedictine order, and at the end of his novitiate, in 1852, was sent to St. Vincent's Abbey at Latrobe, Pa., then under the distinguished Boniface Wimmer [*q.v.*]. Here he completed his theological studies and was ordained to the priesthood in 1856 by Bishop Michael O'Connor [*q.v.*]. After two years as an assistant in Father Gallitzin's old Carrolltown mission and in Holy Trinity Church, Brooklyn, N. Y., under the pioneer German priest, Vicar-General John Raffeiner, he was sent to St. Joseph's Church, Covington, Ky. In 1859, he went to Rio de Janeiro as a missionary to the newly arrived Germans and as a supervisor of the Benedictine program of agricultural and trade schools in Brazil. Although this task proved exceptionally difficult, because of the political anti-clericalism under Pedro II, permanent foundations were laid for subsequent work. After two years, he was transferred to Sandwich, Ont., as superior of a Benedictine monastery whose growth was thwarted by the economic consequences of the American Civil War. In 1863, he commenced a term of three years as prior of St. Mary's in Newark, N. J., a center of German missions for a large area in New York and New Jersey. He was then named procurator of the American congregation and director of St. Elizabeth's Seminary in Rome where, incidentally, he trained Hilary Pfraengle, later abbot of St. Mary's in Newark, and Innocent Wolf, later abbot of St. Benedict's monastery, Atchison, Kan. Upon the seizure of Rome by the Italian armies under King Victor Emmanuel, Dom Oswald returned to America, served as prior and treasurer of St. Vincent's Abbey, 1872–74; as superior of St. Benedict's Abbey in Atchison, 1874–77, where he also acted as an army chaplain and ministered among the Indians; and as superior of a colony of Benedictines who were working among the negroes in Alabama and Georgia. At Skidaway near Savannah he established an agricultural school in which his interest was so intense that he refused to leave it to accept election as first abbot of Belmont Abbey in North Carolina. In 1892, he was selected to organize the monastery of Cluny at Wetaug, Ill., where he labored in the fields and at the desk for the rest of his life. He died on a pallet of straw among the books in his library. Cluny was abandoned in 1903 and its monks were reëstablished at St. Peter's Abbey at Muenster in northern Saskatchewan, whither the remains of its founder were transferred in 1829.

Father Oswald was a gifted man of decided ability as a missionary and as a preacher in several tongues; but he was a visionary and a dreamer, and somewhat impractical. Despite his active, wandering life, he found opportunity to write a number of articles on the school question in *Katholische Volkszeitung* (Baltimore, 1867); sketches of America in the Cincinnati *Wahrheitsfreund,* republished as *Europäer in America vor Columbus* (1879) on the fourteenth centennial of the founding of the Order of St. Benedict; essays in his own historical magazine, *Der Geschichtsfreund* (1882–84); *A Manual of Good Manners* (1874), in English; and two authoritative little books on the Benedic-

tines in Pennsylvania, *St. Vincenz in Pennsylvanien* (1873) and *Bonifaz Wimmer, Erzabt von St. Vincent in Pennsylvanien* (1891). He was offered but did not accept a chair of history in the Catholic University of America at Washington. At Cluny, he published *Legende,* or lives of the saints, in monthly installments (1892–99), but so monumental and impractical was his plan that only the saints commemorated between Jan. 1 and Feb. 7 found place in the seven completed volumes.

[Felix Fellner, in *Records Am. Cath. Hist. Soc.,* Mar. 1923; Fidelis Busam, in *St. Vincent's Journal,* X, 217–30; *Central-Blat and Social Justice,* Feb.–Dec. 1927; annual Catholic directories; E. J. P. Schmitt, *Bibliographia Benedictina* (1893); material from confreres, especially Dr. Fellner.]   R.J.P.

MORAIS, SABATO (Apr. 13, 1823–Nov. 11, 1897), rabbi, was born at Leghorn, Italy, the son of Samuel and Buonina (Wolf) Morais and one of nine children. Descended from a Portuguese family which fled to Italy to escape the persecutions of the Inquisition, he inherited a love of liberty and an interest in republican government which manifested itself throughout his life and led to a friendship with Mazzini. He carried on his Hebrew studies under the rabbis Funaro, Curiat, and Piperno, the latter chief rabbi of Leghorn, acquiring a good knowledge of the Bible, the Talmud, and Jewish literature generally, and an ability to write and speak Hebrew fluently. Secular studies he pursued under Salvatore de Benedetti; in addition to his native Italian, he wrote and spoke French and Spanish with facility. During most of his student life he taught others in order to aid his father in the support of the family.

In 1845 he went to London as a candidate for the position of reader at the Spanish and Portuguese synagogue in Bevis Marks, but the fact that he knew no English prevented his election and he returned to Italy. The following year he was recalled to London to fill the post of Hebrew master of the orphan school of the same congregation. He came to America in March 1851 and the following month was elected minister of the Mikveh Israel Congregation of Philadelphia, which he served until his death. His duties were many; he read the services on Sabbaths and holidays, and preached in English, often using his pulpit for instruction, chiefly in Jewish history. In addition to this work, he visited widely those who were in distress, in his congregation and outside of it, and answered painstakingly all letters asking him for advice or comfort. In the early days he complained of his difficulty with English but as time went on he gained greater command of it, though his style retained a Latin warmth and richness. His most important articles were reprinted in 1926 under the title *Italian Hebrew Literature*, to commemorate the one-hundredth anniversary of his birth.

During the Civil War Morais, who was an ardent abolitionist and a passionate admirer of Abraham Lincoln, had several disagreements with his congregation over the partisan tone of his sermons. At one time a group to whom he refers as "copperheads" prevented his speaking in the pulpit for three months. His attitude won him recognition in another quarter, however, for the Union League Club of Philadelphia elected him an honorary member. Morais was much moved by the persecution of the Jews in Russia in 1881. Through an old schoolmate, Emanuel Felice Veneziani, the aide of Baron Maurice de Hirsch in his varied philanthropies, he was able to get a fund for the settlement of the immigrants from Russia in agricultural colonies in New Jersey. Nor did his interest end with securing the money. He often visited the colonies and burdened himself with countless details of their management.

He was a born teacher and was greatly interested in the local educational organizations. He gave private lessons gratuitously to any one who wanted to learn and collected about him a group of young men who carried on the various interests which he fostered or founded. He was professor of Bible and Biblical literature in the Maimonides College which was established in Philadelphia in 1867, and taught there until it closed in 1873. When the Hebrew Union College was founded in 1875 he hoped that it would serve as a seminary for all the Jews in America desirous of entering the rabbinate, but when he saw that the trend there was away from traditional Judaism, he immediately took steps to start another institution. As a result, the Jewish Theological Seminary was founded in New York in 1886, which from small beginnings has grown to be an important seat of learning. He was president of the faculty and professor of Bible in this institution until his death. He considered the Seminary the most important undertaking of his life and always referred to it as his Benjamin—the child of his old age. The chair of Biblical literature and exegesis there is now named after him.

Morais was a man of genuine humility, tall and spare, and ascetic in his habits. He married Clara Esther Weil in 1855, and they had seven children.

[The principal sources are personal recollections and unpublished letters and documents. Printed sources include biographical sketch by a son, Henry Samuel Morais, in *The Jews of Philadelphia* (1894); "Sabato Morais, a Memoir," also by H. S. Morais, in *Proc. of the Sixth Biennial Conv. of the Jewish Theol. Sem. Asso.* (1898); *Commemoration of the One Hundredth Anniversary of the Birth of the Rev. Dr. Sabato Morais by the Congregation Mikveh Israel, Apr. 18, 1923* (1924); William Rosenau, "Sabato Morais: An Appreciation on the Centenary of His Birth," in *Yearbook of the Central Conf. of Am. Rabbis*, XXXIII (1923), 356–70, and additional material by Marvin Nathan, pp. 370–74; *Jewish Exponent*, Nov. 20, 1897, Apr. 20, 1923; *N. Y. Times*, Apr. 15, 1923; *Pub. Ledger* (Phila.), Nov. 12, 1897.]   C. A.

MORAN, BENJAMIN (Aug. 1, 1820–June 20, 1886), diplomat and author, was born in West Marlboro township, Chester County, Pa. His parents, middle-class English immigrants, settled in the United States in the early nineteenth century, the father, William, first acting as manager of a textile mill in Trenton, N. J., and later setting up as a cloth manufacturer on Doe Run in Pennsylvania. Benjamin received a good public-school education, during which he developed a marked interest in literature. At its close, he entered the employment of a Philadelphia printer to learn his trade. He was there thrown into frequent contact with authors, cultivated their acquaintance and, at thirty-one, determining himself to become a writer, abandoned his craft and sailed for Great Britain. He toured England, Scotland, Wales, and Ireland on foot, and though very short of funds, managed to visit the important literary shrines and other points of interest, and sold to American periodicals a number of short sketches illustrated by drawings. His experiences were subsequently published in book form under the title *The Footpath and Highway: or, Wanderings of an American in Great Britain, in 1851 and '52* (1853), a work of no particular merit.

Moran was strongly attracted to England and, returning in 1853, spent most of the remainder of his life there. He first secured employment as temporary clerk at the American legation, perhaps because James Buchanan, then minister, had known his father through business connections. In 1854 he became Buchanan's private secretary and when his chief retired was appointed permanent clerk on his recommendation. He proved himself an indefatigable worker and gained an exceptional knowledge of the archives. In 1857 he was named assistant secretary of legation, and in 1864, secretary. The latter post he held until the close of 1874. On numerous occasions during this decade he served as chargé d'affaires in the absence of the minister.

His years of service in London coincided with the development of critical relations between the United States and Great Britain arising out of the Civil War, and his voluminous journal, kept with scrupulous care from 1857 to 1874, forms invaluable source material on the subject. As secretary and chargé d'affaires, affording continuity from one minister to another, Moran exercised considerable influence on the diplomatic relations between the two countries. He was stanchly loyal to the Union and, through his popularity in British political circles, played no small part in setting forth the Northern cause and preventing an open rupture. He was held in marked esteem in Great Britain, and the cautious *Times* on one occasion (Dec. 22, 1874) characterized him as a highly trained diplomat and the "ablest and most honest" representative the United States had ever had. In December 1874, in recognition of his services, he was named minister resident to Portugal, the first occasion on which an American secretary of legation had been thus promoted. When that office was discontinued in 1876, he became chargé d'affaires at Lisbon, filling the position until 1882, when he resigned, incapacitated by paralysis. He returned to England, a helpless invalid, and made his home with an intimate friend, Joshua Nunn, former American vice-consul, in Braintree, Essex County. Here he died four years later. The *Times* obituary stated that he had married "an English lady," but failed to give her name.

While closely associated with literary men during his entire official career, Moran made little attempt to carry out his early ambitions and, save for a history of American literature, embodied in *Trübner's Bibliographical Guide to American Literature* (2nd ed., London, 1859), he produced nothing of more than passing value. While at London, he suffered from a grossly exaggerated sense of his own importance which, while hidden from the world at large, becomes painfully apparent in the pages of his diary. He adopts a patronizing air toward legation callers and applies strongly derogatory adjectives to those failing to show him the desired deference; he is filled with scorn and contempt for minor personages in government service, and agonizes over what he considers slights at the hands of his superiors.

[Diary in 43 volumes (1851, 1857–75), "Notes and Queries" (1 vol.), and Moran clippings and drawings, MSS. Div., Lib. of Cong.; "Extracts from the Diary of Benjamin Moran, 1860–68," in *Proc. Mass. Hist. Soc.*, XLVIII (1915), 431 ff.; *Register of the Department of State*, 1874–82; State Dept. Appointments Bureau records; dispatches from London and Lisbon, State Dept.; *Appletons' Ann. Cyc., 1886* (1887); the *Times* (London), Dec. 22, 1874, June 22, 23, 1886; *N. Y. Times*, June 26, 1886; *Evening Telegraph* (Phila.), June 22, 1886.]
L. J. R.

MORAN, EDWARD (Aug. 19, 1829–June 9, 1901), marine painter, born at Bolton, Lancashire, England, was the eldest son of Thomas and Mary (Higson) Moran, and elder brother of Peter and Thomas Moran [*qq.v.*]. His father was a hand-loom weaver, and Edward was put to work at the loom while still a very small child. In 1844 the family emigrated to America and settled in Maryland, where the same occupation was carried on. But Edward, then in his teens, was dissatisfied with the slender wage he was receiving, and dreaming of some more congenial calling, started out on foot one day, without money in his pocket, and walked to Philadelphia in quest of new opportunities. For a while he worked in the shop of a cabinet-maker; then he was in a bronzing establishment, but eventually he was forced to go back to weaving at six dollars a week. While he was so engaged his employer one day found him making a drawing, and realizing that it showed unusual talent, was moved to introduce the youth to Paul Weber, a landscape painter of repute, who accepted him as a pupil. It was evident before long that he had found his vocation. Shortly, Weber passed him on to another painter, James Hamilton, who specialized in marine pictures and illustrations, and, after some hardships, the young man was at last enabled to take a little studio "over a cigar store, with an entrance up a back alley." From this modest start he gradually but steadily progressed in his profession, became an associate of the National Academy, and established himself as one of the earliest of a long line of American marine painters.

In 1862 he went to England and studied for a short time in the school of the Royal Academy, London. In 1871 he exhibited in Philadelphia a collection of seventy-five of his pictures, the entire profits being given in aid of the sufferers from the Franco-Prussian War. In 1872 he moved from Philadelphia to New York, where for some thirty years he was a conspicuous figure in the artistic life of the metropolis. One of his friends and pupils here was Joseph Jefferson, the actor. In 1879–80 he was domiciled in Paris where he sought to perfect himself in the painting of the human figure. He had married, in 1869, Annette Parmentier, a Southern woman of French descent, who was his second wife.

Unquestionably the influence of Turner and of Stanfield can be traced in Moran's sea pieces. His canvases reflect the dramatic element in Turner's work, and his important group of thirteen large paintings, illustrating salient episodes in the history of America, bear resemblance to Stanfield's spirited historical sea compositions.

The ground covered by his historical series extends from the landing of Leif Ericson to the close of the war with Spain in 1898. The subjects comprise such events as the landing of Columbus, the midnight mass for the repose of the soul of De Soto on the Mississippi River, Henry Hudson's little ship entering New York harbor, the embarkation of the Pilgrims, the first salute to the United States flag at sea, the burning of the frigate *Philadelphia,* the engagement between the brig *Armstrong* and the British fleet, the sinking of the *Cumberland* by the *Merrimac,* the farewell salute of the White Squadron to the body of Capt. John Ericsson, and the return of the victorious American squadrons of Dewey, Sampson, and Schley at the end of the Spanish-American War. The series was exhibited at the Metropolitan Museum of Art, New York, in 1904, and was subsequently seen in several other cities, including Washington, where it was installed as a loan in 1907 in the National Gallery of Art, Smithsonian Institution, remaining there for several years. In 1927 it was exhibited at the Ainslie Galleries, New York, and was acquired by Theodore Sutro, who presented it to the Pennsylvania Museum of Art, Philadelphia.

[Theodore Sutro, *Thirteen Chapters of Am. Hist.* (1905); *Am. Art Annual,* 1903–04; Richard Rathbun, *The Nat. Gallery of Art* (1909); Mich. State Lib., *Biog. Sketches of Am. Artists* (1924); G. W. Sheldon, *Am. Painters* (1881); magazine section of the *N. Y. Herald,* Nov. 6, 1904; *N. Y. Times,* June 10, 1901.]

W. H. D—s.

MORAN, PETER (Mar. 4, 1841–Nov. 9, 1914), landscape and animal painter, etcher, born at Bolton, Lancashire, England, was the son of Thomas and Mary (Higson) Moran, and younger brother of Thomas and Edward Moran [*qq.v.*]. He was brought to the United States by his parents in 1844. When he was sixteen his father apprenticed him to Herline & Hersel of Philadelphia to learn the art of lithographic printing. This specialty, however, failed to appeal to his taste, and after a few months it became so distasteful to him that he picked a quarrel with his employers as a result of which his indenture was canceled. He then made prompt use of his freedom by taking lessons in drawing, painting, and etching from his two elder brothers, who were already established as artists. At this period he was greatly impressed by some landscapes by Émile Lambinet which he had seen in the Philadelphia picture shops. A little later he was enamored of Rosa Bonheur's cattle-pieces and as he matured he came under the influence of Constant Troyon. Animal life chiefly engrossed him as a subject, and he cherished a natural desire to study Landseer's works in Lon-

don, a desire which he was able to gratify in 1863, when he returned to his native land for about a year's sojourn. He took with him a letter of introduction to Landseer, but he never presented it, possibly because of youthful shyness, but also because, when he came to see Landseer's originals in the galleries, he was somewhat disappointed in them.

He returned to Philadelphia in 1864, set up a studio, and passed the rest of his professional life there. On July 7, 1867, he was married to Emily Kelley, of Dublin, Ireland, who was also a painter and etcher. From the sixties on for a half-century he was incessantly at work painting and etching. In the field of animal painting he soon won a reputation not less well deserved than that of his elder brothers in their specialties of landscape and marine work. He made several long trips to the West and Southwest with his brother Thomas, and found in New Mexico a number of picturesque and novel motives in the old Indian pueblos. But it was more especially as a competent and prolific etcher that he made his mark. Few Americans of that period were producing such admirable and thoroughly artistic plates. For his group of etchings of animal subjects shown at the Centennial Exposition, 1876, he was honored by the award of a medal; no less than thirteen of his etchings and drypoints were in the noteworthy exhibition of prints held in the Boston Art Museum in 1881. He became president of the Philadelphia Society of Etchers, a member of several other artistic associations, including the Pennsylvania Academy of the Fine Arts, and received many honors. He died in Philadelphia in his seventy-third year. His second wife was Sarah D. C. Francis, of Philadelphia, whom he married in 1911.

[There is a two-volume grangerized edition of Geo. W. Sheldon's *Am. Painters* (1881) in the Boston Pub. Lib. which contains valuable material on Peter Moran. Other sources include: *Who's Who in America,* 1914–15; *Am. Art Rev.,* Feb. 1880, Aug. 1881; *Century Mag.,* Feb. 1883; *Art Jour.* (London), Feb. 1879; Frank Weitenkampf, *Am. Graphic Art* (1912); Mich. State Lib., *Biog. Sketches of Am. Artists* (1924); *Am. Art Annual,* 1915; *Pub. Ledger* (Phila.), Nov. 11, 1914.]

W. H. D—s.

MORAN, THOMAS (Jan. 12, 1837–Aug. 26, 1926), landscape painter and etcher, was born at Bolton, Lancashire, England, the son of Thomas and Mary (Higson) Moran. Edward and Peter Moran [*qq.v.*] were his brothers. The story of his early life runs closely parallel to that of his elder brother Edward. In 1844 he emigrated with the family to America; later he found his way to Philadelphia, and, after various vicissitudes, was apprenticed to a wood-engraver with whom he worked for two years. Aided by Edward, he began to paint, at first in water-colors, then, in 1860, in oils; his first picture was an illustration of Shelley's "Alastor." In 1862 he returned to England, and in the National Gallery, London, came at once under the spell of Turner, whose pictures he was copying. This influence remained with him throughout his life, coloring all his subsequent practice, and as it fell out, Turner's method and palette were well adapted to the grandiose motives that Moran most affected, especially in the Far West. In the sixties he made another European tour, this time traveling extensively in France and Italy, remaining abroad for several years and copying many of the works of the old masters. He secured at this time the material for the Venetian series which are among his best-known works.

After his return to America in 1871 he accompanied the United States geological expedition under F. V. Hayden to the Yellowstone region and painted the large panoramic picture entitled "The Grand Canyon of the Yellowstone." Two years later he made a second western exploration to the Grand Canyon of the Colorado, and painted the "Chasm of the Colorado." These two pictures were purchased by Congress for $10,000 each and were hung in the Capitol at Washington. Aside from their artistic aspects these works owed much of their importance and interest to the fact that they were the first adequate pictorial records of the stupendous scenery of still unfamiliar regions. For Louis Prang & Company of Boston, lithographers, he painted a series of water-colors of the Yellowstone country. In 1872 he had made his first visit to California, where he saw the Yosemite Valley. In 1874 he made in Colorado the studies for his celebrated painting of the "Mountain of the Holy Cross," for which he was awarded a medal at the Centennial Exposition of 1876. His name has been perpetuated in Mount Moran, of the Teton Range, in Wyoming, and in Moran Point, Ariz., the former in the Yellowstone and the latter in the Grand Canyon.

Moran was married, in April 1862, to one of his pupils, Mary Nimmo, daughter of Archibald Nimmo, of Strathaven, Scotland; she was also a painter and etcher. A son and daughter were born to them. The family made Philadelphia their home until 1872, when they moved to Newark, N. J., and a little later to New York City. In 1884 Moran was made a member of the National Academy. In the same year he built a summer studio at Easthampton, L. I., where he spent many summers. He traveled far and wide, going to Mexico in 1883, to Italy again in 1886, and to the Pacific Coast several times.

In 1916 he moved to Santa Barbara, Cal., where the last decade of his long life was spent. He worked to the end, and like Corot, lying in bed in his last hours, he saw his still-to-be-painted landscapes on the ceiling and talked of them. He died in his ninetieth year, the senior member of the National Academy of Design, and dean of his profession. If he was among the ablest painters of the great mountains, canyons, waterfalls, and other spectacles of nature in America, it was in large measure because he had assimilated the grand style of his exemplar, Turner, with its daring color, its visible atmosphere, and its spectacular splendor of effect, and knew how to adapt it to his own subject-matter.

In addition to his work in color he was an etcher and illustrator of more than common merit. He began as an engraver; produced many magazine and book illustrations; and was elected a fellow of the British Society of Painter-Etchers. One of his plates, exhibited in London, is said to have been pronounced by John Ruskin one of the best that had come out of America (*International Studio*, August 1924, p. 361). He also expressed in original lithographs his love of bold scenic effects. Two of his best-known lithographs are "Solitude," a wood interior, one of his set called "Studies and Pictures" (1868), and his "South Shore of Lake Superior" (1869).

[*Am. Mag. of Art*, Nov., Dec. 1926; *Am. Art Rev.*, Feb. 1880; *Internat. Studio*, Aug. 1924, Mar. 1927; *Brush and Pencil*, Oct. 1900; *Century Mag.*, Feb. 1883; *Mag. of Art*, Jan. 1882; Samuel Isham, *Hist. of Am. Painting* (1905); Frank Weitenkampf, *Am. Graphic Art* (1912); Chas. E. Fairman, *Art and Artists of the Capitol of the U. S.* (1927); *Cat. of the Thos. B. Clarke Collection of Am. Pictures* (1891); *N. Y. Tribune*, May 4, 1872; *Evening Star* (Wash., D. C.), Aug. 27, 1926.]

W. H. D—s.]

MORDECAI, ALFRED (Jan. 3, 1804–Oct. 23, 1887), soldier, engineer, was born at Warrenton, N. C., the son of Jacob Mordecai of Warrenton and Rebecca (Myers) of Newport, R. I. His adult life was sharply divided into two periods. Throughout the first he was an officer of the United States Army, with unusual opportunities and responsibilities, which came to him because of his exceptional abilities. Following his resignation from the army at the outbreak of the Civil War, he lived and died a civilian. Although circumstances dictated a complete change in his career, his ability brought him marked success in his later occupations.

He was appointed as a cadet at the United States Military Academy, June 24, 1819. Graduating first in his class, he was commissioned second lieutenant, Corps of Engineers, July 1,

1823. He was detailed as assistant professor at the Military Academy, but was relieved in 1825 to become assistant engineer in the construction of Fortress Monroe, Virginia, and in 1828 he became assistant to the chief of engineers. He was commissioned captain in the ordnance department on its creation in 1832, and from 1833 to 1838 commanded successively the Washington and the Frankford, Pa., arsenals. From 1838 to 1842 he was assistant to the chief of ordnance, becoming in 1839 a member of the ordnance board and retaining membership thereon for many years. During the war with Mexico he was in command of the Washington arsenal and was brevetted major in 1848 for meritorious services on this duty. He was commissioned major in the ordnance department, Dec. 31, 1854. As a member of the ordnance board he studied artillery in Europe, and published the results in *Artillery for the United States Land Service* (1849). In 1853 he visited Mexico in connection with war claims, and from 1855 to 1857 he served on the military commission to the Crimea. His observations made while on the latter duty were published by order of Congress in 1860 (*Senate Executive Document, No. 60, 36 Cong., 1 Sess.*). In addition to the two publications mentioned above, he was the author of numerous technical writings, among which are *A Digest of the Laws Relating to the Military Establishment of the United States* (1833), *The Ordnance Manual for the Use of the Officers of the United States Army* (1841, 1850), *Report of Experiments on Gunpowder* (1845), *Second Report . . .* (1849).

On the outbreak of the Civil War, Mordecai, in common with many other professional army officers of Southern birth, was confronted with the necessity for a momentous personal decision. He was a soldier of unusual ability, who had enjoyed many positions of trust in the service of his country; on the other hand he felt as keen obligations to his state. His decision was that he should fight against neither. His son, also Alfred Mordecai, who was just graduating from West Point, elected differently and fought throughout the war in the service of the Union, dying a brigadier-general of the United States Army. The father resigned from the army, May 5, 1861, and became a teacher of mathematics in Philadelphia. From 1863 to 1866 he was assistant engineer of the Mexico & Pacific Railroad, running from Vera Cruz through the City of Mexico to the Pacific Ocean. From 1867 to 1887 he was treasurer and secretary of canal and coal companies controlled by the Pennsylvania Railroad Company. His wife was Sara Hays of

Philadelphia, and they had six children. Mordecai died at Philadelphia.

[Personnel files, War Department, Washington, D. C.; files Army War College, Washington, D. C.; G. W. Cullum, *Biog. Reg. Officers and Grads. U. S. Mil. Acad.* (3rd ed., 1891), vol. I; *Nineteenth Ann. Reunion Asso. Grads. U. S. Mil. Acad. . . . June 11, 1888* (1888); *Army and Navy Jour.*, Oct. 29, 1887; *Public Ledger* (Phila.), Oct. 24, 1887.]   J. N. G.

MORDECAI, MOSES COHEN (Feb. 19, 1804–Dec. 30, 1888), ship-owner and merchant, son of David Cohen and Rinah (Cohen) Mordecai, was born in Charleston, S. C., where his grandfather had settled in 1772. This grandfather, Moses Cohen, was a member of the Grenadier Company of Charleston during the Revolution and fought at Fort Moultrie and Yorktown. Mordecai received but little formal education, leaving school when quite young, but he became one of Charleston's most prominent commercial figures and representative citizens in ante-bellum days. On Feb. 20, 1828, he married Isabel Rebecca Lyons of Columbia, S. C. He was the founder of the firm of Mordecai & Company, large ship-owners and extensive importers of Mediterranean fruits, Cuban sugar and tobacco, and Rio coffee. He established a line of steamers between Charleston and Havana and by making Charleston his port of entry, brought a vast amount of business to the city. He was interested in all public enterprises and movements for the improvement of Charleston, and the list of offices of trust he held between 1830 and 1861 is long. He was president of the ancient Synagogue Beth Elohim, then one of the most aristocratic synagogues in America, from 1857 to 1861. In the turbulent politics of his day he played a prominent part. He was a delegate to the Augusta convention in 1838, a representative in the legislature, 1845–46; and state senator, 1855–58. In July 1851, in conjunction with B. C. Pressley and Ker Boyce, he founded the *Southern Standard* (after 1853 the *Charleston Standard*) and in 1852 was joined in this enterprise by five other prominent citizens. The combined wealth of these eight stockholders was estimated at six million dollars, an indication of the wealth of ante-bellum Charleston. Pressley, the editor, was a Union man, and the *Standard* advocated an unpopular cause. It soon emphasized the policy of "no secession without co-operation," and in the fall of 1851, succeeded in bringing about a test vote of the people, the result of which was against separate secession. The paper continued to be published till 1858.

In 1860 Mordecai's steamer *Isabel,* named after his wife, was carrying the United States mail between Charleston and Key West. The rescinding of this contract on Jan. 2, 1861, led later to a lawsuit against the United States in the Court of Claims, which was decided against the plaintiff on Dec. 17, 1883 (*Mordecai* vs. *United States, 19 Court of Claims,* 11). The *Isabel* transferred Anderson and his men to the Federal fleet after the surrender of Fort Sumter and became a famous blockade runner during the Civil War (*Official Records of the Union and Confederate Navies in the War of the Rebellion,* 1 ser. IV, 250, 255, and *passim*). Mordecai was a heavy loser by the war. In 1865, he removed to Baltimore, carrying a goodly competence with him. With his son, he again established the firm of Mordecai & Company and undertook the agency for a line of steamers between Charleston and Baltimore. He never forgot his old home and continued to be a generous contributor to its charities. When the bodies of eighty-four South Carolina soldiers who had fallen at Gettysburg were removed to Charleston in 1870, Mordecai & Company furnished free transportation. For the last eighteen years of his life he was completely blind, but continued to carry on his various activities. A generation after his death he was remembered by old residents of Charleston as a philanthropist and cultured gentleman.

[For history of Mordecai's family, see *Lessee of Levy et al., vs. M'Cartee, 6 Peters,* 101. See also *Lineage Book, Nat. Soc. D. A. R.,* vol. II (1896); obituary notices in *Jewish Exponent* Jan. 4, 1889; *Am. Israelite,* Jan. 3, 1889; *Jewish Messenger,* Jan. 4, 1889; and *News and Courier* (Charleston, S. C.), Jan. 2, 1889; B. A. Elzas, *The Jews of S. C.* (1905); W. L. King, *The Newspaper Press of Charleston, S. C.* (1872); *A Brief Hist. of the Ladies' Memorial Asso. of Charleston, S. C.* (1880); *Sun* (Baltimore), Dec. 31, 1888.]

B. A. E.

MORE, NICHOLAS (d. 1689), first chief justice of Pennsylvania, was born in England. He was educated as a physician, but he did not practise his profession after he went to America. In 1682 he became the president of the Free Society of Traders, a body organized by a group of English merchants to purchase land, establish a manorial settlement, and engage in agriculture, trade, and manufacturing in the province of Pennsylvania. (He is referred to in the charter and other records of the Society as a medical doctor of London.) This Society was not particularly successful, but More's connection with it probably helped him in his political career and made it easier for him to buy land for himself on favorable terms.

He and his family migrated to Pennsylvania with William Penn in 1682 and settled in Philadelphia. There is a tradition that he was the chairman or speaker of the first provincial assembly, which met at Chester in December 1682, but the tradition is not corroborated by the records. He was, however, secretary of the provincial council in 1683, a member of the assembly in 1684–85, and speaker of the assembly in 1684. He was also presiding judge of the county courts of Philadelphia in 1683–84 and, on Aug. 4, 1684, was appointed prior judge or chief justice of the province and the lower counties (Delaware). On Aug. 7 of the same year, he purchased an estate of about 10,000 acres of land in Philadelphia County, which was called the manor of Moreland and is now a part of Moreland township. Shortly after his appointment as chief justice, More became involved in a dispute with the assembly which culminated in the first impeachment trial in American history. Ten charges were brought against him, May 15, 1685, based mainly on complaints from the lower counties. It was alleged that he had held circuit courts at inconvenient times and without consulting the provincial council; that he had summoned juries in an unlawful manner; that he had browbeaten a jury into finding an unjust verdict; and that he had committed various other high crimes and misdemeanors. He was expelled from the assembly and suspended from his judicial position (June 2, 1685) but the council refused to sanction the impeachment proceedings. In 1686 he was appointed a member of the board of five commissioners who were to act as the provincial executive, but his health was failing and he was unable to serve. He died at Moreland, in 1689, survived by his wife, Mary, whom he had married in England, and by four children.

More's troubles were largely due to the defects of his character. He had an ungovernable temper and a fluent vocabulary of abuse. In spite of his temperamental defects, he had some very devoted friends and it was probably owing to their influence that the impeachment proceedings were abandoned. It is also possible that the charges brought against him were exaggerated, because William Penn would hardly have selected as a member of his executive board a man who had been a complete failure as chief justice.

[For the charter and other material relating to the Free Society of Traders, see Samuel Hazard, *Annals of Pa., from the Discovery of the Delaware, 1609-1682* (1850); there are several references to More, including the articles of impeachment, in the *Minutes of the Provincial Council of Pa.,* vol. I (1838); see also the manuscript "Survey by Thomas Fairman, Showing the Division of the Manor of Moreland Between the Children of Nicholas More," in the library of the Hist. Soc. of Pa.; J. H. Martin, *Martin's Bench and Bar of Phila.* (1883); J. C. Martindale, *A Hist. of the Townships of Byberry and Moreland in Phila., Pa.* (1867); T. F. Gordon, *The Hist. of Pa.* (1829); and

Lawrence Lewis, Jr., "The Courts of Pa. in the Seventeenth Century," in *Pa. Mag. of Hist. and Biog.*, V (1881), 141–90: this *Magazine*, IV (1880), 445–53, also contains reprint of *A Letter from Dr. More . . . Relating to . . . the Province of Pa.*, which was first printed in London in 1687.]   W. R. S.

MOREAU DE SAINT-MÉRY, MÉDÉRIC-LOUIS-ÉLIE (Jan. 13, 1750–Jan. 28, 1819), historian, publisher, the son of Bertrand-Médéric and Marie-Rose (Beeson) Moreau de Saint-Méry, was born at Fort Royal, Martinique, where his ancestors, emigrants from Poitou, had settled in the seventeenth century. Members of his family, ever since that time, had occupied high judicial posts on the island. At nineteen he went to Paris, joined the king's guard, and later was admitted to the bar. He returned to Martinique, but soon left for Cap Français, Santo Domingo, to practise law. Here he made researches with a view to codifying colonial law, and also discovered the tomb of Columbus, which he restored at his own expense. He went back to Paris to arrange for the publication of his books, and the six volumes of his *Loix et Constitutions des Colonies françaises de l'Amérique sous le Vent* appeared there between 1784 and 1790. He helped to found the Museum of Paris and became its president in 1787. It was more of an incubator of revolutionary ideas than a museum, and in 1789 Saint-Méry's connection with it caused him to be appointed president of the Electors of Paris. When the Bastille fell, he received its keys from the hands of the leaders of the mob, and for the next three turbulent days he governed Paris with prudence and courage. It was he who persuaded the Electors to place Lafayette in command of the National Guard.

Having incurred the enmity of Robespierre, he narrowly escaped the guillotine by fleeing with his wife and two children to America, and landed at Norfolk, Va., on Mar. 8, 1794. After working there as a shipping clerk until May, he went to New York and obtained another similar job. In October, however, he moved to Philadelphia and by Dec. 10 had set himself up in business as a bookseller, printer, and stationer. His little shop became the rendezvous of the French *émigrés*. Noailles, Volney, Talon, Démeunier, La Colombe, La Rochefoucauld-Liancourt, de Beaumetz, and many others met there every night, and the Duc d'Orléans, who was later to become King of the French, came often. Saint-Méry's most intimate friend, however, was Talleyrand, and the two men spent hours together drinking Madeira and plotting how to seize Louisiana from the Spanish. In spite of the fact that Saint-Méry followed a humble calling, selling books, maps, music, and even woollen socks, gouty mittens, muffs, drawers, and "gallices," his erudition and intelligence gained for him many friends among the Anglo-Saxon intellectuals of the city. He had been a non-resident member of the American Philosophical Society since 1789, and in January 1795 was made a resident member.

The amount and quality of the printing that he turned out of his little press during the three and one half years it ran is quite amazing. There were numerous pamphlets written by him or by refugee friends, his own exhaustive two-volume *Description topographique et politique de la partie espagnole de l'Isle Saint-Domingue* (1796), and his equally bulky *Description topographique, physique, civile, politique et historique de la partie française de l'Isle Saint-Domingue* (1797–98), together with the translations of both of them by William Cobbett. In addition he printed and published in two volumes A. E. van Braam Houckgeest's handsomely illustrated *Voyage de l'Ambassade de la Compagnie des Indes Orientales Hollandaises, vers l'Empereur de la Chine, en 1794–1795* (1797), and he even did the composition and presswork for a daily newspaper, edited by Gaterau, called *Courrier de la France et des Colonies*. His publications were of such excellence, intellectually as well as typographically, that they entitle him to be classed among the best of the early American printers and publishers.

Since Frenchmen had come to be looked upon with grave suspicions, President Adams included Moreau de Saint-Méry's name in a list of persons to be deported under the Alien Bill. Saint-Méry thought it wise to anticipate any such action and so sailed for France on Aug. 23, 1798. In Paris he obtained a position as historiographer at the Ministry of Marine, became very popular among the intellectuals, and was elected to membership in various learned societies. In 1800 he was made councillor of state, and the following year sent as Resident to the Duke of Parma. Upon the Duke's death in 1802 he became administrator of Parma, Piacenza, and Guastalla, and ruled them until Napoleon recalled him in 1806 because he believed him to have been too lenient in suppressing a mutiny in the militia. The Emperor took him to task very harshly when he arrived in Paris, and it was then that Moreau de Saint-Méry made his famous answer: "Sire, I do not ask you to reward my probity; I only beg that it be tolerated. Do not be afraid, this disease is not catching." Napoleon never quite forgave his temerity, and stopped the payment of his pension and also of the 40,000 francs already owed him. Saint-Méry eked out the remainder of his life in penury, assisted by the Empress Josephine, his distant relative, and by scanty and intermittent pensions. He died in Paris in January 1819, at the age of sixty-nine.

[M. L. E. Moreau de Saint-Méry, *Voyage aux États-Unis de l'Amérique, 1793–1798* (1913), ed. by S. L. Mims, with a biographical sketch and numerous references to other material; H. W. Kent, "Chez Moreau de Saint-Méry, Philadelphie," in *Bibliographical Essays, A Tribute to Wilberforce Eames* (1924), with bibliography of Saint-Méry's American publications by G. P. Winship; A. F. Silvestre, *Notice Biographique de Moreau de Saint-Méry* (1819); François Fournier-Pescay, *Discours prononcé aux obsèques de Moreau de Saint-Méry le 30 janv. 1819* (1819) and article in *Biographie Universelle*, vol. XXX (1821); Claude Augé, *Nouveau Larousse Illustré*, vol. VI (1903); *Journal de Paris*, Jan. 30, 1819.] E. L. T.

MOREAU-LISLET, LOUIS CASIMIR ELISABETH (1767–Dec. 3, 1832), Louisiana jurist and politician, was born in Cap Français, Santo Domingo, a French dependency. He received in France a solid education both in languages and law, and came to New Orleans in his thirties, probably driven from his native land by the negro revolution under Dessalines. He married Anne Philipine de Peters who bore him one child, a daughter. He adopted the name Lislet to distinguish himself from an elder brother. In 1805, with Edward Livingston, Pierre A. C. B. Derbigny, and Étienne Mazureau [*qq.v.*], he won a judicial decision insuring the recognition of the Roman Civil Law in Louisiana. In the following year he published *Explication des Lois Criminelles du Territoire d'Orléans* (1806), and with James Brown was commissioned by the legislature to prepare a code, which under the title *Digeste des lois civiles maintenant en vigueur dans le Territoire d'Orléans* was published in both French and English editions in 1808. He served as a parish judge and worked on a translation of Spanish laws. In 1817 he became attorney-general but soon resigned to accept a state senatorship. Three years later, with the collaboration of Henry Carleton, he published *The Laws of Las Siete Partidas Which Are Still in Force in the State of Louisiana* (2 vols., 1820). He was immediately selected with Derbigny and Livingston to prepare a revised code, which, as *Civil Code of the State of Louisiana,* appeared in 1825. In the meantime Moreau continued as the representative of the second district of New Orleans in the state legislature. In 1828 he issued *A General Digest of the Acts of the Legislature of Louisiana, Passed from the Year 1804 to 1827, Inclusive.* His last public act was to sign a proclamation, June 26, 1832, calling a mass meeting to oppose

Nullification. He died less than six months later at the age of sixty-five.

Moreau-Lislet played a leading rôle in a troublous time. He fought for the interests of the French population, but ever in a spirit of compromise. Governor Claiborne praised his *Digeste* of 1808 for allaying jealousies, and assuring peace to a people living under three jurisprudences. In 1820, he was instrumental in the conciliatory gesture whereby Derbigny withdrew as candidate for governor in favor of Thomas B. Robertson. The deft hand of Moreau helped much in the work of pacification so necessary at his time. He possessed an excellent command of his mother tongue, a deep knowledge of Spanish legal history; and a trained mind thoroughly versed in the law.

[F. X. Martin, *The Hist. of La.*, vol. II (1829); Charles Gayarré, *Hist. of La.*, vol. IV (1866), and "The New Orleans Bench and Bar in 1823," in *Harper's Mag.*, Nov. 1888; Alcée Fortier, *A Hist. of La.* (1904), vol. III; Carleton Hunt, "Life and Services of Edward Livingston," in *Proc. La. Bar Asso.*, 1903; Henry Favrot, "The First Governor on the First Code," *Report La. Bar Asso.*, 1909; *Official Letter Books of W. C. C. Claiborne* (6 vols., 1917), ed. by Dunbar Rowland; *La. Hist. Quart.*, Jan. 1921; *Courier* (New Orleans), Dec. 6, 13, 1832.] L. C. D.

MOREHEAD, CHARLES SLAUGHTER (July 7, 1802–Dec. 21, 1868), Kentucky governor and congressman, was born in Nelson County, Ky., the son of Charles and Margaret (Slaughter) Morehead. He was the first cousin of James Turner Morehead and the second cousin of John Motley Morehead [*qq.v.*]. After graduating from Transylvania University in 1820, he became a tutor there, studied law, and received the LL.B. degree in 1822. He practised in Christian County and later in Franklin County. After serving in the legislature from 1828 to 1829 he was appointed attorney-general, a position that he filled for almost six years. In 1834 in collaboration with Mason Brown he published *A Digest of the Statute Laws of Kentucky,* a two-volume work authorized and supported by the legislature. Several times reëlected to the legislature, he served from 1838 to 1845 and again from 1853 to 1854. He was speaker from 1840 to 1842 and for the session of 1844–45. He was twice elected as a Whig to the federal House of Representatives and served from 1847 to 1851. In 1848, as a member of the committee on ways and means, he opposed the financial plans of the Polk administration (*Speech of Mr. C. S. Morehead of Kentucky on the Loan Bill,* 1848). In 1850, fearing that President Taylor's policy would disrupt both the party and the Union, he favored Clay's compromise measures and a new cabinet with

Webster as secretary of state. When the Whig party declined he joined the American party, primarily, he said, in the hope of saving the Union. In 1855 this party nominated him for governor. In a strenuous contest with the Democratic candidate, Beverly L. Clarke, involving the serious anti-foreign riot at Louisville known as "Bloody Monday," he was elected, and he was inaugurated in September. The only partisan reference in his messages was to the "foreign invasion" and the desirability of a longer naturalization period. He denounced Northern "nullification" of the Fugitive Slave Act, and declared that slaves could be taken into any territory. He also favored the increase of educational facilities, internal improvements by corporations, the limitation of state banks and of the currency, and the encouragement of agriculture. After 1859 he practised in Louisville with his nephew, Charles M. Briggs.

The secession movement brought him back into public life. In February 1861 he was a member of the peace conference, and, with others, had interviews with Lincoln and Seward. In May he was elected to the border states convention at Frankfort. He approved, with the other members, the plea for Kentucky to be neutral, but he refused to sign the address to the people of Kentucky because he did not indorse all the statements therein. Subsequently he accused Seward of inconsistency and publicly criticized cutting off trade with the South. It was doubtless such action that led to his arrest in September 1861 and his imprisonment, by order of the Secretary of War, without trial at Fort Lafayette in New York harbor and later at Fort Warren in Boston harbor. The Kentucky legislature and Louisville Unionists petitioned for his release on parole, which was obtained on Jan. 6, 1862, apparently largely through the influence of his friend, John J. Crittenden. On Mar. 19 he was discharged from the conditions of his parole, but, fearing arrest because of his refusal to take the oath of allegiance, he fled in June to Canada and then to Europe and Mexico. After the war, he resided on one of his plantations near Greenville, Miss., and died there.

[Lewis and R. H. Collins, *Hist. of Ky.* (2 vols., 1874); E. M. Coulter, *The Civil War and Readjustment in Ky.* (1926); H. Levin, *The Lawyers and Lawmakers of Ky.* (1897); W. E. Connelley and E. M. Coulter, *Hist. of Ky.* (1922), vol. II; *War of the Rebellion: Official Records (Army)*, 2 ser., vol. II; Mrs. Chapman Coleman, *The Life of John J. Crittenden* (2 vols., 1871); J. M. Morehead, *The Morehead Family* (1921); date of death from copy of inscription on tombstone and from statement of grand-daughter, Mrs. Malcolm Moncreiffe, Bighorn, Wyo., in files of the Congressional Joint Committee on Printing.]

W. C. M.

MOREHEAD, JAMES TURNER (May 24, 1797–Dec. 28, 1854), Kentucky governor and senator, first cousin of Charles Slaughter Morehead and second cousin of John Motley Morehead [*qq.v.*], was born near Shepherdsville, Bullitt County, Ky., his father, Armistead Morehead, having recently migrated from Virginia. The family soon moved to Russellville, where James began his education. After attending Transylvania University, 1813–15, he studied law under Judge H. P. Broadnax and John J. Crittenden. In 1818 he was admitted to the bar and began to practise in Bowling Green, where he became known as an able lawyer. On May 1, 1823, he married Susan A. Roberts of Logan County.

Morehead began his public career in 1816 by writing letters to the newspapers on public affairs. In the twenties he favored the proposed bankruptcy laws, but opposed the new court of appeals established by the Relief party. Elected to the lower house of the legislature, where he served from 1828 to 1831, he became chairman of the committee on internal improvements and in 1831 reported the bill for a state subscription to the Maysville-Lexington Turnpike Company. In that year he was a member of the National Republican Convention at Baltimore which nominated Henry Clay for the presidency, and was nominated by a state convention for the post of lieutenant-governor, to which he was elected, although a Democrat, Breathitt, was elected governor. On the latter's death, Morehead became governor, Feb. 21, 1834, and held the office until September 1836. He strongly urged the legislature to extend the river improvements already begun, and became *ex officio* the first president of the permanent Board of Internal Improvements, of which he was later appointed president by his successor in the governorship (1836–37). During this period, many Kentucky rivers were surveyed and many improvements projected, but the panic of 1837 prevented the execution of most of the plans. As governor, Morehead also favored judicial reform and popular education, and denounced the Abolitionists. He was again a member of the legislature, 1837–38; and in 1839–40 was, with J. S. Smith, a commissioner to arrange for the return of fugitive slaves from Ohio. In 1841, he was elected to the United States Senate over many competitors, and served from Feb. 20, 1841, to Mar. 3, 1847. He consistently supported the program of his colleague, Henry Clay, being especially prominent in defense of the Bank Bill and the nomination of Everett as minister to London. He opposed the annexation of

Texas, both by treaty and by joint resolution, and the acquisition of territory from Mexico, although, like most of the Whig senators, he felt compelled to vote for waging war on Mexico because it was felt that Mexico had begun the war.

Morehead was also interested in the American Colonization Society, being at one time president of the Kentucky branch. His large library contained many works on early Kentucky history, and in 1840 he published *An Address in Commemoration of the First Settlement of Kentucky,* largely based on earlier writers but containing some original material on the Boonesborough settlement. He was also the author of *Practice in Civil Actions and Proceedings at Law* (1846). During his latter years he practised at Covington, Ky., and there he died.

[Gov. J. T. Morehead's Letters and Papers, 1834–36 (MSS. in the Ky. State Hist. Soc., containing little of interest except on internal improvements); *Journals of the House of Representatives of Ky.,* 1828–38; *Journals of the Senate of Ky.,* 1834–36; W. R. Jillson, "Early Political Papers of Gov. James Turner Morehead," in *Register of the Ky. State Hist. Soc.,* Sept. 1924, Jan. 1925; Lewis and R. H. Collins, *Hist. of Ky.* (2 vols., 1874); J. M. Morehead, *The Morehead Family of N. C. and Va.* (1921), pp. 41–42; *Ky. Statesman* (Lexington), Jan. 2, 1855, reprinting article from *Louisville Courier,* Dec. 30, 1854.] W. C. M.

MOREHEAD, JOHN MOTLEY (July 4, 1796–Aug. 27, 1866), governor of North Carolina and leader in economic and social movements in that state, was born in Pittsylvania County, Va., the son of John Morehead and his wife, Obedience (Motley) Morehead, who were respectively of Scotch and Welsh descent. He was the second cousin of Charles Slaughter Morehead and James Turner Morehead [qq.v.]. The Morehead family had been identified with Virginia affairs since 1630, when Charles Morehead, probably an ancestor, settled in the Northern Neck. John Morehead removed to Rockingham County, N. C., in 1798. His son was sent to the "log college" of David Caldwell [q.v.], then entered at the University of North Carolina in 1815, and was graduated with the class of 1817. He read law with Archibald De Bow Murphey [q.v.] and began the practice of his profession in Wentworth, Rockingham County. On Sept. 6, 1821, he was married to Ann Eliza Lindsay, the daughter of Robert Lindsay of Guilford County, who bore him eight children. In that year he represented his county in the North Carolina House of Commons; removing to Greensboro, he represented Guilford County in the House of Commons in 1826 and 1827. In politics he was identified with the western group that advocated revision of the state constitution, the construction of rail-

ways by state aid, and public education, and he was a member of the constitutional convention of 1835. A Jacksonian Democrat before 1835, in that year he joined the rising Whig forces and in 1840 was elected governor of North Carolina, as he was again in 1842. As executive he advocated state aid to railways, the construction of highways, and the improvement of navigation, but he accomplished little because of a Democratic majority in the legislature. However, he did successfully urge the establishment of a state institution for the deaf, which was opened in Raleigh and to which the blind were admitted sometime later.

His greatest services were not in politics but in the realm of state business. A constant advocate of railroads he became the president of the North Carolina Railroad and was a promoter of the Atlantic & North Carolina Railroad and of the Western North Carolina Railroad, all being lines projected to give North Carolina a complete transportation system from the mountains to the sea. In 1858 he made his last appearance in the legislature for the purpose of obtaining the continuation of the policy of state aid for railway expansion. Distinctly a business man, he was identified with cotton-mills, commission and mercantile houses, and other enterprises. In national economy he believed in a protective tariff and a national banking system. As the crisis of 1860–61 approached he was a conservative, opposed to a dissolution of the Union, and was a delegate from North Carolina to the peace conference held at Washington in February 1861. After secession he represented North Carolina in the provisional Congress of the Confederacy, in which body he was influential in obtaining an extension of the Richmond & Danville Railroad from Richmond, Va., to Greensboro, N. C.

[B. A. Konkle, *John Motley Morehead and the Development of North Carolina* (1922); *Biog. Hist. of N. C.,* ed. by S. A. Ashe, vol. II (1905); R. D. W. Connor, *Antebellum Builders of N. C.* (1914); *In Memoriam Hon. John M. Morehead* (1868); J. M. Morehead, *The Morehead Family* (1921).] W. K. B.

MOREHOUSE, HENRY LYMAN (Oct. 2, 1834–May 5, 1917), Baptist clergyman, was born in Stanfordville, N. Y., the son of Seth S. and Emma (Bentley) Morehouse. On his father's side, he was descended from Thomas Muirhouse, a Scotch Covenanter, who because of the persecutions of King Charles and Archbishop Laud emigrated to Connecticut about 1640; on his mother's side, he was a descendant of William Bentley who came to Massachusetts from Kent, England, in 1635. His Baptist inheritance went back to 1751, when an ancestor participated in the founding of a Baptist church in Stratfield, Conn. Henry Morehouse prepared for college at the Genesee Wesleyan Seminary, Lima, N. Y., and his education was continued at the University of Rochester, from which he graduated in 1858, and at Rochester Theological Seminary. At the university he was under President Martin B. Anderson [q.v.], and at the seminary, under President Ezekiel Gilman Robinson [q.v.], both of whom exerted a strong influence upon him. In 1864 he was ordained at East Saginaw, Mich., and served as pastor there from October 1864 to January 1873. A second pastorate of more than six years followed at the East Avenue Baptist Church in Rochester, N. Y. During part of this period he was trustee of the New York Baptist Union for Ministerial Education as well as its corresponding secretary. For the next thirty-eight years, he was connected with the general work of the Northern Baptist denomination, acting as corresponding secretary of the American Baptist Home Mission Society from 1879 to 1893 and from 1902 to 1917, and as field secretary from 1893 to 1902, during which time he was also corresponding secretary of the American Baptist Education Society. From 1905 he was a member of the American Committee of the Baptist World Alliance. Of commanding stature, free from self-seeking, whole-heartedly devoted to his work, characterized by normal, mental, and spiritual balance, he was easily at the head of the statesmen of the Baptist denomination in the field of home missions during his generation. Except in 1891, when charges were made involving his integrity, but against which he vindicated himself, and his work in such a manner as to receive an enthusiastic reëlection as corresponding secretary, his supremacy as leader was unchallenged.

During the long period that he was connected with the American Baptist Home Mission Society, he succeeded in reorganizing it, expanding it, and making it more dynamic, the annual expenditures increasing from $115,083 to $987,-611, and the students in schools for negroes from 1,056 to over 7,000. Always interested in education, he was prominent in organizing the American Baptist Education Society. He was the trusted advisor of Frederick T. Gates and Thomas W. Goodspeed [qq.v.], prominent in the founding of the University of Chicago, and had some influence in persuading William Rainey Harper to become president of that institution. As early as 1892 he suggested extension courses and summer schools for theological students. A believer in Baptist solidarity, he endeavored to lessen the effects of the Baptist schism of 1845

over the question of negro slavery by suggesting the formation of the General Convention of Baptists of North America. Probably his efforts in behalf of the establishment of the Ministers and Missionaries Benefit Board of the Northern Baptist Convention will prove to be his most significant achievement. He was its president from 1911 until his death. His interests extended beyond the limits of his own denomination, and he was one of the promoters of the Federal Council of Churches of Christ in America. He was editor of missionary periodicals and author of numerous missionary pamphlets, of *Baptist Home Missions in America* (1883), and of *History of Seventy-five Years of the First Baptist Church, Brooklyn* (1898). He also wrote a number of poems, among which were the widely circulated "Led About," and "My Song at Seventy." His death occurred in Brooklyn, N. Y. He was unmarried.

[A. H. Newman, *A Century of Bapt. Achievement* (1901); L. A. Crandall, *Henry Lyman Morehouse, a Biog.* (1919); *Jour. and Messenger,* May 17, 1917; *Who's Who in America,* 1916–17; *N. Y. Times,* May 6, 1917.]   C. H. M.

MORELL, GEORGE WEBB (Jan 8, 1815–Feb. 11, 1883), soldier, engineer, lawyer, of French Huguenot descent, was born in Cooperstown, N. Y. His father, Judge George Morell, served through successive grades to that of major-general in the New York militia, and was chief justice of the supreme court of Michigan when he died in 1845. His mother, Maria Webb, was the daughter of Gen. Samuel B. Webb [q.v.] of the Revolutionary army. It was natural, therefore, that George Webb Morell should be inclined toward a career in the army. He entered West Point and graduated in 1835, first in a class of fifty-six cadets. After serving in the Corps of Engineers as assistant engineer in the improvement of the Lake Erie harbors, on the Ohio and Michigan boundary survey, and in the construction of Fort Adams, Newport, R. I., he resigned, June 30, 1837, to become assistant engineer of construction for the Charleston & Cincinnati Railroad. The following year he went to the Michigan Central Railroad, with which he remained until 1840, when he removed to New York City and studied law. In 1842 he was admitted to the bar and practised law until 1861. Upon the outbreak of the Mexican War he was commissioned major (July 23, 1846) of the 4th New York Volunteers, but the regiment was never mustered into the federal service. He became major and division engineer of the New York militia in 1849, and was promoted to colonel in 1852, which rank he held until 1861. He was commissioner of the United States circuit court for the southern district of New York from 1854 to 1861.

On Apr. 15, 1861, he was appointed colonel and served as quartermaster and chief of staff to Major-General Sanford, New York Volunteers, in organizing regiments in New York City and sending them to the seat of war. From May 20 to July 7, 1861, he was engaged in the defenses of Washington, D. C. While participating in the operations about Harper's Ferry, Va., July 7 to Aug. 21, 1861, he was promoted (Aug. 9) brigadier-general of United States Volunteers, and assigned to the Army of the Potomac. He was on duty guarding the approaches to Washington from Aug. 21, 1861, to Mar. 10, 1862, and from then until August, in the Virginia Peninsular campaign. During this period he commanded the 1st and later the 2nd Brigade of F. J. Porter's division and from May 1862, the 1st Division of Porter's V Corps. He participated in the following engagements: Howard's Bridge, Apr. 4, 1862; siege of Yorktown, Apr. 5 to May 4, 1862; capture of Hanover Court House, May 27, 1862; Mechanicsville, June 26, 1862; Gaines's Mill, June 27, 1862; and Malvern Hill, July 1, 1862. On July 4, 1862, he became major-general, United States Volunteers, but since his nomination was never made to the Senate, his recess appointment expired Mar. 4, 1863. He served in the campaign of Northern Virginia and the Maryland campaign, August to October 1862. He was engaged in the second battle of Bull Run (Manassas), Aug. 30, 1862, and Antietam, Sept. 17, 1862. From Oct. 30 to Dec. 16, 1862, he commanded the forces guarding the upper Potomac. He was in Washington awaiting orders until Dec. 15, 1863, when he was placed in command of the draft rendezvous in Indianapolis, Ind. He remained on this duty until Aug. 29, 1864, and was mustered out of the service Dec. 15, 1864.

In 1866 he married Catherine Schermerhorn Creighton, daughter of Rev. William Creighton of Tarrytown, N. Y., and settled in Scarborough, N. Y., where he engaged in farming until his death.

[G. W. Cullum, *Biog. Reg. Officers and Grads. U. S. Mil. Acad.* (1891), vol. I; War Department records; F. B. Heitman, *Hist. Reg. and Dict. U. S. Army* (1903), vol. I; *War of the Rebellion: Official Records (Army)*; *14th Ann. Reunion, Asso. Grads. U. S. Mil. Acad.* (1883); David McAdam and others, *Hist. of the Bench ad Bar of N. Y.*, vol. I (1897); *N. Y. Times*, Feb. 13, 1883.]   J. W. L.

MOREY, SAMUEL (Oct. 23, 1762–Apr. 17, 1843), inventor, was born in Hebron, Conn., which was also the birthplace of his parents, Israel and Martha (Palmer) Morey. Before he was four years old the family moved to New Hampshire and settled in Orford, where Israel Morey became proprietor of a tavern and an influential citizen. During the Revolutionary War he was made a colonel and commanded a body of New Hampshire militia on the frontier. Samuel was educated in the public school of Orford, and during his youth developed considerable mechanical ability and an intense interest in natural philosophy. He became a lumberman with a successful business in Orford but he took part also in the construction of the Connecticut River locks between Windsor, Conn., and Olcott Falls, being engineer in charge at Bellows Falls, Vt. As early as 1780 he began devoting his leisure hours to experimentation with heat and light, and in the course of ten years acquired considerable knowledge of general chemistry and of the properties of steam. His first patent, granted Jan. 29, 1793, was for a steam-operated spit. Two years later, Mar. 25, 1795, he patented a rotary steam-engine. Patents were also issued to him for a windmill, a water-wheel, and a steam pump.

Meanwhile, about 1790, he began his experiments with steamboats, and after three years of work devised a small craft equipped with a steam-engine mounted on the bow, which he operated on the Connecticut River at Orford. In 1794 he is said to have built a stern-wheel steamboat and to have run it from Hartford, Conn., to New York. Preble (*post*) says that this was the sixth steamboat built in the United States. In the hope of securing financial aid, Morey went to Bordentown, N. J., in 1797, and there constructed a side-wheel steamboat, which he demonstrated on the Delaware River; but this venture failed. When Fulton began his steamboat work in the United States, Morey went to New York with a model of his steamboat and tried to persuade Fulton to adopt it. He was not successful, however, and always claimed that his steamboat ideas were stolen by Fulton. He obtained two patents for steam-engine improvements in 1803 and 1815, respectively, and on Apr. 1, 1826, one of the first American patents for an internal combustion engine. Presumably Morey had been working on this invention for a number of years, for about 1820 he constructed a boat called *Aunt Sally,* and propelled it by a vapor engine on Fairlee Pond, now Lake Morey, at Fairlee, Vt. Morey contributed to Silliman's *American Journal of Science and Arts* a number of articles bearing on his work. He married Hannah Avery in Orford, and at his death in Fairlee, Vt., where he resided during the latter part of his life, he was survived by his widow and a daughter.

Morfit

Morford

[G. H. Preble, *A Chronological Hist. of the Origin and Development of Steam Navigation* (1883); W. A. Mowry, "Who Invented the American Steamboat?," *Colls. N. H. Antiquarian Soc.*, no. I (1874); Gabriel Farrell, Jr., *Capt. Samuel Morey* (1915); *Am. Jour. of Science and Arts*, vol. I (1819), II (1820), XI (1826); *Centennial Celebration of the Town of Orford, N. H., 1865* (n.d.); *A List of Patents Granted by the U. S. from Apr. 10, 1790, to Dec. 31, 1836* (1872).]

C. W. M.

MORFIT, CAMPBELL (Nov. 19, 1820–Dec. 8, 1897), chemist, son of Henry Mason Morfit, a native of Norfolk, Va., and Catherine (Campbell) Morfit, was born at Herculaneum, Mo. His father moved to Baltimore in 1861 and lived there until his death; he was a successful lawyer and held several public offices. Campbell Morfit was one of sixteen children. One brother, Charles, became a physician, and another, Clarence, a chemist. After an interrupted schooling Campbell Morfit enrolled as a student in Columbian College (now George Washington University), Washington, D. C., but before completing his course he went to Philadelphia to enter the private chemical laboratory which had recently been established there by James Curtis Booth [*q.v.*]. Becoming interested in industrial chemistry, he left the Booth laboratory, where the work was largely analytical, entered a laboratory in Philadelphia specializing in the manufacture of industrial chemicals, and in time became its owner. Meanwhile he associated himself with the University of Maryland. Realizing the need of instruction in industrial chemistry, in 1851 he offered to establish at his own expense a school of applied chemistry in connection with the medical department of the University. A plan of the proposed building, which was to be erected on the campus at a cost of $10,-000, accompanied the offer. His generous tender was declined, however, because the trustees decided that industrial chemistry did not fall within the field of a medical school, but in appreciation of Morfit's liberality and interest the University gave him the honorary degree of M.D. In 1854 he became professor of applied chemistry in the University and held the post until 1858, when he resigned and went to New York to resume analytical and industrial work.

His researches in industrial chemistry included studies in guano, salt, sugar, coal, gums, and glycerine. Accounts of this varied work were published in the *Journal of the Franklin Institute,* the *American Journal of Science and Arts,* and other scientific periodicals. He was joint author with Booth of three reports (1851–55) to the United States ordnance department on gun metal, published in *Reports of Experiments on the Strength and Other Properties of Metals for Cannon, by the Officers of the Ordnance Department, U. S. Army* (1856); most of the analytical work was done by Morfit in a laboratory established by himself at the Pikesville (Md.) Arsenal. He assisted Booth in preparing *The Encyclopedia of Chemistry* (1850), writing most of the longer and many of the smaller articles on subjects in industrial chemistry, *e.g.* fats, essential oils, dyes, starch, waxes, sugar, and varnish. He also cooperated with Booth in the monograph *On Recent Improvements in the Chemical Arts* (1852). He edited and revised an American edition of H. M. Noad's *Chemical Analysis* (1849). In addition he was the author of several books, the best known being *Chemistry Applied to the Manufacture of Soap and Candles* (1847); 2nd ed., *A Treatise on Chemistry Applied* (1856); *Chemical and Pharmaceutical Manipulations* (1849; 1857), in collaboration first with Alexander Mucklé and then with Clarence Morfit; *A Practical Treatise on the Manufacture of Soap* (1871), and *A Practical Treatise on Pure Fertilizers* (1872). In 1861 he settled permanently in England and thereafter devoted most of his time to the improvement of technical processes, such as the preparation of condensed food rations, the manufacture of paper, soap, and candles, and the refining of oils. His contributions to industrial chemistry were recognized by diplomas and awards from scientific societies and by his election as a Fellow of the Chemical Society of London. He was married, Apr. 13, 1854, to Maria Clapier Chancellor of Germantown, Pa. She died Apr. 26, 1855, leaving a daughter who became a chemist, worked with her father in London, and died there Feb. 21, 1916. Morfit never married again. He died at South Hampstead, a suburb of London, in his seventy-eighth year.

[Private communication from the Medical School of the Univ. of Md., Baltimore, Md.; *Am. Jour. Pharmacy*, Feb. 1898; Royal Soc. of London, *Cat. of Sci. Papers, 1800–1863*, vol. IV (1870); J. C. Poggendorff's *biographisch-literarisches Handwörterbuch . . . 1863–1904* (1926), vol. II; *Chemical News* (London), Dec. 17, 1897; *Times* (London), Dec. 9, 1897.]   L. C. N.

MORFORD, HENRY (Mar. 10, 1823–Aug. 4, 1881), journalist and author, was the son of William and Elizabeth (Willett) Morford, who were residents of what is now New Monmouth, N. J., where Henry was born (Ellis, *post*, pp. 568–69). Most of his youth and early manhood were spent in his native town, first as a merchant and later as postmaster of the village, but his leisure during these years was given to writing verses. At sixteen he was already contributing poems to the *New Yorker* and to the Philadelphia *Saturday Evening Post,* and in 1840 he published a thin pamphlet, *Music of the Spheres,* an immature poetical production showing the influence of Bryant. In 1852 he turned his talent for writing to a more lucrative end by establishing at Middletown Point (now Matawan) the *New Jersey Standard,* a weekly newspaper. Besides editing and managing this paper, he contributed to it frequent poems, and a series of supposedly autobiographical "Sketches of a Country Shopkeeper." In 1854 or 1855 he sold the *Standard,* and a year later went to New York, where for some time he served on the editorial staff of a newspaper or magazine. From 1862 to 1868 he acted as a clerk of the court of common pleas (*Manual of the Corporation of the City of New York,* 1862–68). He was for a time on the editorial staff of the New York *Atlas.* During this period he produced several novels having as a background the events of the Civil War, and a volume of humorous sketches, *Sprees and Splashes* (1863). In search of health and of fresh literary materials, he spent the summer of 1865 in England, France, and Scotland, later publishing his observations in *Over-Sea* (1867). Two years later he visited the Paris exposition, which he described in a volume called *Paris in '67* (1867). These short trips abroad suggested to him the possibility of publishing a guidebook to Europe which would benefit the person who had at his disposal but a few months for travel. This idea bore fruit in *Morford's Short-Trip Guide to Europe,* first published in 1868. A similar book, intended for Europeans visiting America, appeared in 1872 under the title *Morford's Short-Trip Guide to America.* In 1878 he again visited Europe, publishing a record of his experiences in *Paris and Half-Europe in '78* (1879). In January 1880 he established and edited the *Brooklyn New Monthly Magazine,* which continued until March 1881. From 1876 to the time of his death he kept a bookstore and travel office at 52 Broadway, where he made a specialty of guidebooks.

His work as an author was uneven. Perhaps the best of his poetical work is *The Rest of Don Juan* (1846), a continuation of Byron's poem, in which he sometimes handles the *ottava rima* as skilfully as the English poet, although the effort as a whole is unevenly sustained. Much weaker are the verses collected in *Rhymes of Twenty Years* (1859) and *Rhymes of an Editor* (1873). Morford undoubtedly possessed the journalist's instinct to turn to literary use the events of the passing moment. Three novels composed during the Civil War were addressed to a war audience—*Shoulder-Straps* (1863), *The Days of Shoddy* (1863), and *The Coward* (1864). With

the coming of the centennial of the Declaration of Independence in 1876, he published another novel, *The Spur of Monmouth,* whose subject was suggested no doubt by the battlefield near which he had lived as a boy. These tales are labored, discursive productions, weak for the most part in characterization, and abounding with trite and improbable incident. Of slightly greater literary value are his books of travel, which, although wholly informal in manner, lack the touch of a descriptive master. A drama, *The Bells of Shandon,* in which he collaborated with John Brougham, was produced at Wallack's Theatre, New York, in 1867, but has never been published (T. A. Brown, *A History of the New York Stage,* 1903, II, 164). Morford is particularly remembered, however, for his guidebooks, whose popularity in his day is evidenced by the many editions through which they passed.

[T. H. Leonard, *From Indian Trail to Electric Rail* (1923), pp. 110–11; Franklin Ellis, *Hist. of Monmouth County, N. J.* (1885); *Trow's New York City Directory,* 1858–82; H. S. Ashbee, "The Rest of *Don Juan,*" *Bibliographer,* July 1883; *N. Y. Times,* Aug. 7, 1881; bound file of the *New Jersey Standard,* Apr. 1, 1852– Apr. 1, 1854, in the N. Y. Hist. Soc.; four letters of Morford in the Hist. Soc. of Pa.]   N.F.A.

MORGAN, ABEL (1673–Dec. 16, 1722), Baptist clergyman and Biblical scholar, was born at Alltgoch in the parish of Llanwenog, Cardiganshire, South Wales. He was the son of Morgan ap Rhydderch ap Dafydd ap Gruffydd, an elder and later a minister of the Rhydwilym Baptist Church, and in accordance with the custom in Wales at a time when family names were almost unknown he took as a surname his father's Christian name. For a number of generations the family had been prominent for its devotion to literature, the best known member of it being Abel's uncle, Sion Rhydderch ("John Roderick"), who, besides being a printer, an antiquary, and something of a poet, compiled the first English-Welsh dictionary, wrote one of the first Welsh grammars, and translated into Welsh a number of religious works.

Abel began to preach before he was eighteen years old, and settled at Llanwenarth in Monmouthshire near Abergavenny. When, about 1696, the Blaenau Gwent branch was established as a separate church independent of Llanwenarth, he was called to preach there and four years later he was ordained its first minister. He soon rose to prominence in the affairs of the Welsh Baptists, but in 1711 he decided to emigrate to Pennsylvania, whither his brother Enoch and other members of the family with many Welsh Baptists had preceded him. He embarked at Bristol on Sept. 28, but the ship was detained by contrary winds and it was not until Feb. 14, 1712, that he arrived in Philadelphia after a stormy passage. On the voyage his wife, who was Priscilla Powell of Abergavenny, and his infant son died, leaving him with one daughter. Almost immediately upon his arrival he assumed charge of the Pennepek Baptist Church, with its branch in the city of Philadephia, which relationship he retained until his death. He quickly became one of the leaders among the Baptists of Pennsylvania, and also established churches in Delaware and New Jersey. He married in this country Martha Burrows, and, as his third wife, Judith (Griffiths) Gooding (daughter of the Rev. Thomas Griffiths), who, with four children, survived him.

He published nothing during his lifetime but is said to have translated into Welsh the Century Confession, adding to it certain articles embodying his own ideas on the subject of singing hymns and the laying on of hands, and a Catechism similarly modified. Eight years after his death his brother Enoch and his half-brother Benjamin Griffiths published his *Cyd-gordiad Egwyddorawl o'r Scrythurau: neu Daflen Lythyrennol o'r Prif Eiriau Yn y Bibl Sanctaidd. Yn Arwain, dan y Cyfryw eiriau, i fuan ganfod pob rhyw ddymunol ran o'r Scrythurau. A Gyfansoddwyd Drwy Lafurus Boen Abel Morgan, Gwenidog yr Efengyl er lle's y Cymru. Argraphwyd yn Philadelphia, gan Samuel Keimer, a Dafydd Harry. MDCCXXX.* This, the second Welsh book published in America, was the first real concordance to the Welsh Bible, and was long the only one. Of its author a recent writer (David Jones in the *Cambrian*) has said, "To this day his name is a household word in Wales and America among the Welsh People."

[Morgan Edwards, *Materials Towards a Hist. of the Baptists in Pa.* (1770); H. G. Jones, in *Pa. Mag. of Hist. and Biog.,* vol. VI, no. 3 (1882); J. Davis, *Hist. of the Welsh Baptists* (1835); Thomas Rees, *Hist. of Protestant Nonconformity in Wales* (1861); articles in the *Cambrian,* vol. XIII (1893); William Rowlands, *Cambrian Bibliog.* (1869); Charles Ashton, *Hanes Llenyddiaeth Gymreig* (n.d.; 1893?); *Enwogion y Ffydd* (1880).]   J. J. P.

MORGAN, CHARLES (Apr. 21, 1795–May 8, 1878), shipping and railroad owner, was descended from James Morgan, a Welshman who emigrated to Boston about 1636 and later settled in Connecticut. Here on a farm in Killingworth (now Clinton), Conn., Charles was born, the son of Col. George and Elizabeth (Redfield) Morgan. At fourteen he went to New York City, which became his permanent home. Starting as a grocery clerk, he was in business for himself at twenty-one, with a shop on Peck Slip, selling provisions to ships. He next began to import

fruit directly from the south. This venture led to a line of sailing vessels to the West Indies. Quick to realize the value of steam, he secured an interest in the *David Brown,* the first steamship on the New York-Charleston run.

In 1835, even before Texas secured its independence, Morgan invaded the Gulf waters which were to be the scene of his greatest activity and success, sending the steamer *Columbia* from New Orleans to Galveston. He soon had a regular line of mail steamers plying between those points. From Galveston, the Morgan service radiated to Indianola, Corpus Christi, and Vera Cruz, while from New Orleans a line ran to Mobile and there was another on Lake Pontchartrain. With Arnold Harris, Morgan established the Texas & New Orleans Mail Line, the Mexican Ocean Mail & Inland Company, and the Southern Mail Steamship Company. Though several of his steamers were lost without, it is said, a cent of insurance, he continued to expand his business. On the eve of the Civil War, Judah P. Benjamin stated to a congressional committee that Morgan's steamers did "all the business on the Gulf."

During the middle fifties came the "war of the three commodores" between Morgan, Cornelius Vanderbilt, and George Law [*qq.v.*]. When Vanderbilt opened the Nicaragua Transit and ran steamships on the Atlantic and Pacific in opposition to the Law-Aspinwall mail subsidy lines, he made Morgan and C. K. Garrison [*q.v.*] his agents in New York and San Francisco respectively, Morgan becoming president when Vanderbilt went to Europe in 1853. During his absence, Morgan and Garrison manipulated stock prices in such a way that they profited while Vanderbilt lost heavily. The latter, on his return, is said to have stormed at them, "I will not sue you, because the law takes too long. I will ruin you." While Morgan and Garrison made use of William Walker [*q.v.*], the filibuster, to get control of the Nicaraguan government and secure the transfer of the Transit concession to themselves, Vanderbilt sent Sylvanus H. Spencer to Nicaragua where, with Costa Rican troops, he definitely closed the Transit. Walker was ruined, but Morgan and Garrison survived.

The Civil War was naturally a crisis for a Northern man with much of his capital tied up in Southern waters. Three of Morgan's steamers were seized at New Orleans for the Confederate service on Apr. 28, 1861, but several others were chartered or sold for Union service, three of them bringing him approximately $650,-000, a sum far in excess of their value. In 1850 he had secured control of the T. F. Secor marine engine works in New York, changing the name to the Morgan Iron Works, but he turned over the actual control to his son-in-law, G. W. Quintard [q.v.], who built more machinery than anyone else for the Union navy. At the close of the war, Morgan picked up several steamers at auction for less than half of what they had cost the government. He started what is still known as the Morgan Line, from New York to New Orleans, and about 1870 was called "the largest shipowner in the United States."

About this time he began to interest himself in railroads. On May 25, 1869, he purchased for $2,050,000 the bankrupt New Orleans, Opelousas & Great Western Railroad, which ran eighty miles westward from New Orleans along the north side of the great swamp region to the foot of Grand Bay at Brashear City. This terminus was renamed Morgan City, while the road became "Morgan's Louisiana & Texas Railroad." With the Morgan Line and his Gulf steamers, it gave him an all-Morgan route from New York to Texas, with a virtual monopoly of transportation in the latter region. Extending his control still further, he acquired two short Texas lines. His master stroke, however, came a year before his death when, for some $4,400,000, he secured control of the 505-mile Houston & Texas Central Railroad. Then he organized "Morgan's Louisiana & Texas Railroad and Steamship Company" as a holding company for all these various lines. He was chairman of the board and his son-in-law Charles A. Whitney, president. In 1883 these lines were purchased from the Morgan heirs for $7,500,000 by the Southern Pacific Railroad, and became part of its system.

Morgan died at his home on Madison Square in New York City. In 1870 he had given $50,000 to establish a school in his native town of Clinton. Like almost everything else with which he was connected it bore the name of Morgan. He is said, however, to have been quiet and unostentatious, and a very kindly master to the thousands in his employ. Although he believed in one-man control, he had the happy faculty of choosing able lieutenants. Three of these, J. C. Harris, Quintard, and Whitney, were his sons-in-law. He was twice married: on Dec. 20, 1817, to Emily Reeves, who bore him five children, and after her death in 1850, to Mary Jane Sexton, June 24, 1852. There were no children by his second marriage.

[N. H. Morgan, Morgan Geneal. (1869); L. E. Stanton, An Account of the Dedication of the Morgan School Building, Clinton, Conn. (1873); James Parton and others, Sketches of Men of Progress (1870–71), pp. 419–23; W. O. Scroggs, Filibusters and Financiers (1916); W. V. Wells, Walker's Expedition to Nicaragua (1856); W. A. Croffut, The Vanderbilts and the Story of their Fortune (1886); Official Records of the Union and Confed. Navies, 1 ser. IV, 165; House Ex. Doc. 29, 30 Cong., 1 Sess.; House Ex. Doc. 337, 40 Cong., 2 Sess., p. 24; H. V. Poor, Manual of the Railroads of the U. S., 1870–71, p. 344, 1877, p. 849, 1878, p. 548; Commercial & Financial Chronicle (N. Y.), Feb. 24, 1883; and M. Y. Beach, The Wealth and Biog. of the Wealthy Citizens of N. Y. (13th ed., 1855); obituary in N. Y. Herald, May 9, 1878; advertisements of Morgan's various lines over a forty-year period.]   R. G. A.

MORGAN, CHARLES HILL (Jan. 8, 1831–Jan. 10, 1911), engineer, inventor, son of Hiram and Clarissa Lucina (Rich) Morgan, was born in Rochester, N. Y., where his father was employed as a mechanic. He was descended from Miles Morgan, one of the founders of Springfield, Mass., who emigrated from Bristol, England, in 1636. Charles Morgan enjoyed but a short schooling, for at the age of twelve he was put to work in a factory and at fifteen entered a machine shop in Clinton, Mass., as apprentice. Here he remained for six years, becoming an expert machinist and, through diligent work in night schools, a draftsman as well. In 1852 he entered the employ of the Clinton Cotton Mills and also served part time as draftsman for the Lawrence Machine Company. From 1855 to 1860 he was draftsman for the inventor and carpet manufacturer, Erastus B. Bigelow [q.v.], during which association he devised a system of designing and constructing cam curves for carpet-looms which proved of great value. In 1860 Morgan and his brother established a paper-bag manufacturing plant in Philadelphia, and designed an automatic machine for making bags, the great success of which placed paper-bag making for the first time on a commercial footing. The brothers sold this business to good advantage in 1864 and Morgan then became superintendent of I. Washburn and Moen, later Washburn & Moen Manufacturing Company, Worcester, Mass., makers of wire. Four years later he was made general superintendent and served in this capacity until 1887.

When Morgan joined this organization wire-rolling methods in the United States were far inferior to those in Europe. In 1865 he was sent abroad to study rolling-mill processes. In England, George Bedson had designed and constructed the first type of continuous rolling-mill, and on Morgan's recommendation the Washburn & Moen Company purchased one of Bedson's mills in 1869 and erected it in Worcester, Mass. While this was far superior to anything then existing in the United States, there was room for improvements and Morgan undertook the task of achieving them. After ten years of experimentation the power reel was perfected to handle the product of the mill, replacing the hand-operated reel. Morgan was greatly assisted in this work by Fred H. Daniels [*q.v.*], and they received patents no. 224,838, no. 224,-840, and no. 224,942, on Feb. 24, 1880. Morgan's second improvement was the perfecting of a continuous train of horizontal rolls, by providing intermediate twist guides which gave the metal the necessary quarter turn as it passed between successive sets of rolls. This was patented jointly with Daniels Oct. 23, 1883, patent no. 287,008 (correspondence with American Steel Wire Company, Worcester, Mass.), and is the only type of continuous mill in use today, being known as the Morgan Mill. His third contribution was that of automatic reels, both of the pouring and the laying type, such as are now in use in wire mills throughout the world. The successful trial of these was made on Mar. 10, 1886. In 1881 Morgan established the Morgan Spring Company in Worcester, and after 1887 he devoted much of his time to his duties as president of this successful enterprise. In 1891 he organized the Morgan Construction Company to manufacture rolling-mill machinery, particularly the pure continuous type of rod mill. This undertaking was likewise successful and today practically all of the continuous wire rod rolling-mills in the world are equipped with this company's products.

Beside attending to his own businesses, Morgan served as a consulting engineer for the American Steel & Wire Company from 1887 until his death. He was very closely identified with the Worcester Polytechnic Institute, being a member of its board of trustees from its founding until his death. He was president of the American Society of Mechanical Engineers in 1899; a member of the International Iron and Steel Institute of Great Britain; and an honorary member of the Société des Ingénieurs Civils de France. He was twice married: first, June 8, 1852, to Harriet C. Plympton of Shrewsbury, Mass., who died July 28, 1862; and second, Aug. 4, 1863, to Rebecca Ann Beagary of Philadelphia. At his death in Worcester he was survived by his widow and five children.

[C. G. Washburn, *Industrial Worcester* (1917); Charles Nutt, *Hist. of Worcester and Its People* (1919), vol. IV; *Trans. Am. Soc. Mech. Engrs.*, vol. XXXIII (1912); *Iron Age*, Jan. 12, 1911; Pat. Office records; *Who's Who in America*, 1910–11; *Boston Transcript*, Jan. 10, 1911.]   C. W. M.

MORGAN, DANIEL (1736–July 6, 1802), Revolutionary soldier, son of James and Eleanora Morgan, was of Welsh ancestry and born probably in Hunterdon County, N. J., though some authorities say just across the Delaware River in Bucks County, Pa., where his father was ironmaster at the Durham Iron Works. The meager records of his youth tell us that, after quarreling with his father, he made his way to the Shenandoah Valley in Virginia, where he worked as farm laborer and teamster until he had saved sufficient money to become an independent wagoner, in which capacity he accompanied Braddock's ill-fated expedition. Later, he transported supplies to the frontier posts of Virginia. For striking a British subaltern, the hot-tempered, impulsive youth received five hundred lashes on his bare back, yet freely forgave the officer upon the latter's expression of contrition. He served as lieutenant in Pontiac's War and in 1774 accompanied Lord Dunmore's expedition to western Pennsylvania. Meanwhile, his marriage to Abigail Bailey gradually transformed him from a boisterous, pugnacious youth into a high-spirited man, eager to improve his mind and to acquire a competence.

At the outbreak of the Revolution Congress commissioned him, June 22, 1775, captain of one of the two companies of riflemen to be raised in Virginia. Within ten days he enlisted his company and twenty-one days later reached Boston from Winchester, Va., his company intact. After a short period of comparative inactivity, he volunteered for Arnold's arduous expedition through the Maine wilderness to Quebec, and accompanied Arnold's column in the assault, Dec. 31. When Arnold was wounded, at the insistence of the other officers Morgan assumed command, captured the first barrier, being one of the first over, and penetrated a considerable distance into the lower city; but upon the failure of the other troops to join him he reluctantly surrendered to overwhelming odds. After his release the following autumn, Congress, Nov. 12, 1776, commissioned him colonel of a regiment to be raised in Virginia. Upon rejoining Washington, the following April, he organized, under the latter's order, a corps of five hundred sharpshooters, and participated in various movements in New Jersey until ordered north in August to assist Gates in opposing Burgoyne's advance. Here his troops rendered such signal service at the battles of Freeman's Farm and Bemis Heights that Gates, replying to Washington's request for their return, declared that he could not spare "the corps the army of General Burgoyne are most afraid of" (Sparks, *post*, II, 437). Morgan's indignant refusal to participate in the intrigues against Washington led to an estrangement between him and Gates, though the latter had warmly welcomed him upon his arrival. After Burgoyne's surrender, Washington recalled him to assist in the campaign around

Philadelphia in the fall and winter of 1777. Though not actually engaged at the battle of Monmouth, he effectively pursued the British after that engagement.

Impaired health and dissatisfaction with the course pursued by Congress regarding army promotions led him to resign in July 1779, and retire to Virginia, where he occupied himself in erecting his mansion, "Saratoga." Recalled to active service in 1780, he joined Gates, with whom he had become reconciled, shortly after the latter's disastrous defeat at Camden. When Greene succeeded Gates in command of the southern department, the former placed Morgan, recently created brigadier-general, in command of the troops in western North Carolina which were opposing the advance of the British northward from Charleston. Failing to obtain Greene's consent to his plan of creating a diversion by advancing into Georgia, Morgan gradually retired northward before the advancing British under Tarleton until he reached the Cowpens, a few miles south of the North Carolina boundary. Here, with the Broad River in his rear, he determined to make a stand with his small force of somewhat over eight hundred. On Jan. 17, 1781, largely by the effective work of his cavalry, he won the brilliant victory of Cowpens, one of the decisive victories of the war, for which he received the thanks of Congress and a gold medal. Fearing a union of Tarleton's shattered troops with the main army under Cornwallis and an effort to cut him off, he retreated rapidly northward, effecting a junction early in February with Greene's troops at Guilford Court House. Ill health shortly afterward again forced his retirement from active duty, though he joined Lafayette for a short time in July in the defense of Virginia.

At the conclusion of the war he advanced money, so far as his straitened circumstances permitted, to many of his needy soldiers, taking their scrip as security, subject to redemption. This act led for a time to the charge, which he bitterly resented, even to the point of personal encounter, that he was speculating in his soldiers' necessities. Retiring to "Saratoga," he devoted himself with such success to the restoration of his shattered fortune that by 1796 he owned more than 250,000 acres on the Monongahela and Ohio Rivers (Graham, *post*, p. 413). In 1794, in command of the Virginia militia, he assisted in suppressing the Whiskey Insurrection in western Pennsylvania and, after the withdrawal of the main army, remained in control of the district, where he successfully pursued a policy of conciliation. Defeated for Congress in

1795, he was successful in 1797, serving one term. Indicative of his intense partisanship is his comment in a letter of 1798 regarding the Democrats: "They at this time look like a parsell of Egg sucking Dogs that have been caut Breaking up Hens Nests" (letter to Presley Neville, in New York Public Library). Morgan was stout and active, six feet in height, "exactly fitted for the toils and pomp of war." Wild in his youth, in later years he became a devout member of the Presbyterian Church. His two daughters, Nancy and Betty, became the wives of Presley Neville and James Heard, respectively.

[James Graham, *Life of Daniel Morgan* (1856), and the *Cowpens Papers* (1881) reprint many documents from the Morgan papers in the New York Public Library; see also Henry Lee, *Memoirs of the War in the Southern Department* (2 vols., 1812), esp. I, 386 ff.; J. F. Folsom, in *Proc. N. J. Hist. Soc.*, July 1929; J. H. Brandow, in *Proc. N. Y. Hist. Asso.*, vol. XII (1913); J. H. Smith, *Arnold's March from Cambridge to Quebec* (1903) and *Our Struggle for the Fourteenth Colony* (2 vols., 1907); E. A. Duyckinck, *Nat. Portrait Gallery of Eminent Americans* (1862); Jared Sparks, *Correspondence of the Am. Rev.* (1853); *Virginia Argus* (Richmond), July 21, 1802.]   D. C. H.

MORGAN, EDWIN BARBER (May 2, 1806– Oct. 13, 1881), merchant and philanthropist, was born and lived throughout his life at Aurora, N. Y., on Cayuga Lake. James Morgan, from whom he was descended, emigrated from Wales to Massachusetts about 1636, removed to New London, Conn., about 1650, and later settled at Groton, Conn., where his descendants were substantial farmers. Thence young Christopher Morgan, whose wife was Nancy Barber, went to clerk of the company building the long bridge across the lower waters of Cayuga. In 1800 he became a merchant at Aurora. Edwin, the eldest of his sons, attended a school there, and when he was thirteen went to work in his father's store. At the age of twenty-one he took over his father's affairs, and soon created a large business in buying and shipping agricultural produce and in boat-building, his brothers becoming his partners. Some of the capital thus acquired he used in developing express companies. In this enterprise he was associated with Henry Wells [*q.v.*], also of Aurora, a pioneer in the express business and the first president of the American Express Company. At the organization, in 1852, of Wells, Fargo & Company's Express, Morgan became its president. He was one of the founders of the United States Express Company in 1854, and a lifelong director of the American. With his brothers he operated extensive gypsum beds at Grand Rapids, Mich., and had important interests in the starch-making industry at Oswego. Through these and other activities he gained a large fortune.

His energies found outlet in politics, also. He was elected representative in Congress in 1852, and twice reëlected, serving from Mar. 4, 1853, to Mar. 3, 1859. During his last term his cousin, Edwin Denison Morgan [q.v.], was chosen governor of the state. In the House Morgan actively expressed his anti-slavery convictions, and was one of the members who rescued Charles Sumner from Brooks's assault. From its formation he was attached to the Republican party. During the Civil War he devoted himself to raising and equipping troops, and the strong representation of central New York in the army was due considerably to his influence and gifts. Every colonel of a regiment from this region received from him a thousand dollars for his command, he also gave regular pay to all volunteers from Aurora and assisted soldiers' families. His work in the war brought him the title of colonel. He rendered an important public service through the *New York Times,* in which he was an original stockholder. In the thick of his fight against Tweed, George Jones [q.v.], the editor, feared that ownership of the paper would pass into unfriendly hands. Accordingly, in 1871, Morgan bought for $375,000 enough stock to assure the continuance of Jones's policy, thus materially contributing to Tweed's downfall.

Morgan's later years were chiefly devoted to education. He long maintained the Cayuga Lake Academy at Aurora, which he had attended, and was a trustee of Cornell University and other institutions in central New York. Soon after the founding of Wells College, at Aurora, by Henry Wells, Morgan became a trustee, and later was the president of the board of the college and its principal benefactor, giving to it much time and more than a quarter of a million dollars. Auburn Theological Seminary, situated near his home, also received from him strong support. Most of the cost of its dormitory was met by him, and he and William E. Dodge [q.v.] made possible its library building.

Morgan died at Aurora, survived by a son and a daughter. His wife, to whom he was married on Sept. 27, 1829, was Charlotte Fidelia Wood of Aurora. Physically and mentally he was quick-moving and incessantly active, even to old age. Extraordinary foresight and sagacity largely explain his commercial success, but in addition he had great self-reliance, determination, perseverance, and courage. Large interests elsewhere never lessened his devotion to his own village. His personal beneficences were innumerable. He helped many young people to get educations and many men to advance in business.

[*Biog. Dir. Am. Cong.* (1928) ; E. A. Storke, *Hist. of Cayuga County, N. Y.* (1879) ; E. S. Frisbie, in *Report of Regents of Univ. of State of N. Y.* (1888) ; W. I. Lowe, *Wells College and Its Founders* (1901) ; *Wells College Hist. Sketches* (1894) ; J. Q. Adams, *A Hist. of Auburn Theological Seminary, 1818–1918* (1918) ; Elmer Davis, *Hist. of the N. Y. Times, 1851–1921* (1921) ; *N. Y. Times,* Oct. 14, 1881.]   R. H. N.

MORGAN, EDWIN DENISON (Feb. 8, 1811–Feb. 14, 1883), governor of New York, United States senator, was a descendant of James Morgan, a Welshman, who came to Massachusetts about 1636 and about 1650 settled in New London, where he married Margery Hill. Edwin, the son of Jasper and Catherine (Copp) Avery Morgan and a first cousin of Edwin Barber Morgan [q.v.], was born in Washington, Berkshire County, Mass., but in 1822 removed with his parents to Windsor, Conn. During his boyhood he worked on his father's farm in summer and attended the village school in winter. In 1826 he entered Bacon Academy, Colchester, Conn., but two years later became a clerk in his uncle's grocery store at Hartford, Conn. At twenty, he became his uncle's partner. In 1832 he was elected a member of the Hartford city council. Desiring a wider sphere of activity, he removed to New York in 1836, and here, in partnership with Morris Earle and A. D. Pomeroy, established the wholesale grocery firm of Morgan & Earle. Upon its dissolution at the end of 1837, he began business on his own account. His enterprise and sagacity placed him in a few years among New York's leading merchants. On Jan. 1, 1842, he associated with himself his cousin, George D. Morgan, and the latter's partner, Frederick Avery, who retired one year later, his place being taken by one of Morgan's clerks, J. T. Terry. In 1854 Solon Humphreys joined the firm, and banking and brokerage were added to the wholesale grocery business. Largely through Humphreys, who had spent several years in Missouri, E. D. Morgan & Company in the two years 1858–60 handled over $30,000,-000 in securities issued by that state and by the city of St. Louis.

Meanwhile, in 1849 Morgan had been elected a member of the New York City Board of Assistant Aldermen, which acknowledged his ability by electing him its president. His valiant service during a cholera epidemic which swept over the city that year strengthened him in the public eye, and upon the expiration of his term as assistant alderman he was sent to the state Senate. Two years later he was reëlected after a severe contest with the Democratic Locofoco candidate. During both his terms he was president *pro tempore* of the Senate and chairman of its finance committee. He introduced and carried through the legislature the bill establishing Central Park in New York City. When in 1855 he declined to run for a third term he was appointed one of the state commissioners of emigration, a much coveted position which he held until 1858. Although up to 1855 he had been an assiduous Whig, and was an earnest opponent of slavery, he had not identified himself with the abolitionists because he did not believe in the wisdom of their methods. He was vice-president of the conference which made plans for the first Republican National Convention and was chairman of the Republican National Committee which conducted the Frémont campaign. This chairmanship he continued to hold until 1864.

In 1858 he was chosen by Thurlow Weed as Republican candidate for governor of New York. The odds were against him, but his fine personal character, his spotless record, and his reputation as a successful business man, coupled with the energy with which he conducted his campaign, carried him into office in a four-cornered contest by a plurality of over 17,000 votes. Far from being a mere satellite of Weed, he displayed independence and statesmanlike qualities, both in his messages to the legislature and in his use of the veto power. In 1860 he was reëlected by the largest majority which up to that time had ever been given to a gubernatorial candidate in the state. He succeeded during his first administration in improving the state's credit, strengthening its canal system, and making prisons, insurance companies, and charitable organizations more effective. His second administration was devoted to the success of the Union cause in the Civil War. Commissioned major-general of volunteers by Lincoln and placed in command of the military department of New York, he enrolled and equipped 223,000 soldiers. In 1862 he declined renomination for the governorship and upon the expiration of his term was commissioned under a legislative act to put New York harbor in a state of defense. He expended only $6,000 of the $1,000,000 appropriated for this purpose, returning the rest to the state treasury. In 1863 he was chosen United States senator to succeed Preston King. His career in the Senate was not characterized by oratorical display but by hard work both in the committee room and on the floor. In 1865 he declined appointment as secretary of the treasury. He voted with the minority on President Johnson's veto of the Freedman's Bureau Bill and for Johnson's conviction. In 1869 he was defeated for reelection after a bitter contest with Ex-Governor R. E. Fenton [q.v.]. From 1872 to 1876 he was again induced to head the Republican Commit-

tee, and in the latter year his name was mentioned in connection with the presidency. He stood for sound currency and civil service reform. In 1876 he was again nominated for governor, but the machine element of his party headed by Senator Conkling was dissatisfied with him, and he was defeated by Lucius Robinson. When Chester A. Arthur [q.v.], his old and ardent friend, succeeded to the presidency, he nominated Morgan for secretary of the treasury, but although the appointment was unanimously confirmed by the Senate, Morgan for a second time declined. During his last years he retired from all active participation in politics.

Morgan's fortune at the time of his death was estimated to be between eight and ten million dollars. His gifts during his lifetime totaled over a million dollars. Williams College, Union Theological Seminary, and the Women's, Presbyterian, and Eye and Ear hospitals in New York City especially benefited from his generosity. He was a patron of art well known both in America and on the continent of Europe, and a director of many business concerns. He was tall, well-proportioned, dignified, rather aristocratic in bearing. In 1833 he married his first cousin, Eliza Matilda Waterman, daughter of Capt. Henry and Lydia (Morgan) Waterman, of Hartford, Conn. Of their five children only one reached maturity, and he died in 1881, before his parents. The elder Morgan died at his home in New York City and was buried in Cedar Hill Cemetery, Hartford, Conn.

[*Jours. of the Senate and the Assembly of . . . N. Y.*, 1883; N. H. Morgan, *Morgan Geneal.* (1869); J. A. Morgan, *A Hist. of the Family of Morgan* (1902); George Wilson, *Portrait Gallery of the Chamber of Commerce of the State of N. Y.* (1890); C. Z. Lincoln, *State of New York, Messages from the Govs.* (1909), vol. V; Thurlow Weed Barnes, *Memoir of Thurlow Weed* (1884); D. S. Alexander, *A Pol. Hist. of the State of N. Y.*, vols. II, III (1906–09); S. D. Brummer, *Pol. Hist. of N. Y. State during . . . the Civil War* (1911); Frederick Phisterer, *N. Y. in the War of the Rebellion* (1912), vols. I, V; J. G. Wilson, *The Memorial Hist. of N. Y.* (1893), vols. III, IV; *N. Y. Daily Tribune*, Feb. 14, 1883; *N. Y. Times*, Feb. 15, 1883.]
H. J. C.

MORGAN, GEORGE (Feb. 14, 1743–Mar. 10, 1810), land-speculator and Indian agent, was born in Philadelphia, the brother of John Morgan [q.v.] and the son of Joanna (Biles) and Evan Morgan, a prosperous Philadelphia merchant who had emigrated from Wales probably about 1717. Both his parents were dead before he was six years old. He attended school in Philadelphia and at about thirteen years of age entered the service of Baynton and Wharton, merchants, as an apprentice. In 1763 he entered a new partnership with his employers, which became known as Baynton, Wharton, and

Morgan. On Oct. 21, the next year, he was married to Mary Baynton, the daughter of his partner, John Baynton. They had eleven children. At the end of Pontiac's War the firm, interested in the fur trade, undertook a venture to the Illinois country, recently acquired from the French by England, to profit at the same time from supplying Indian goods to the Crown and provisions to the military posts in the Illinois. He went to the Illinois as the representative of the firm and, though disappointed in his hopes for profits, became well known as a leader in the movement for the establishment of a civil government in the Illinois and as a judge in the civil court established there in 1768. When the trading venture failed the partnership went into a voluntary receivership, counting as the largest of its assets its share in the Indiana grant made by the Six Nations at Fort Stanwix in 1768 to the "suffering traders" whose goods had been destroyed by the Indians in 1763. The grant consisted of some 2,862 square miles of land in what is now West Virginia, just south of the Pennsylvania line. After a period of uncertainty the Indiana Company was reorganized in the spring of 1776 with Morgan as secretary-general and superintendent of the land office, with headquarters at Fort Pitt. The state of Virginia, claiming jurisdiction over this area, opposed the Indiana Company, and there ensued a long struggle in the legislature of Virginia, in the Continental Congress, and in the Supreme Court of the United States. Morgan was prevented from prosecuting his claim by the passage of the Eleventh Amendment to the Constitution in 1798.

During the Revolution he served in the double capacity of Indian agent for the United States in the middle department and deputy commissary-general of purchases for the western district, with the rank of colonel. Having served in these capacities, with headquarters at Fort Pitt, for about three years, he resigned in 1779. He retired to his farm, "Prospect," near Princeton, N. J., where he became a gentleman farmer. He dabbled in science in true eighteenth-century style and wrote several contributions to the proceedings of the two societies of which he was a member, the Philadelphia Society for the Promotion of Agriculture and the American Philosophical Society. His most notable study was an investigation of the life and habits of the Hessian fly, then attacking the eastern wheat fields. He published his results in various contemporary magazines, such as the *American Museum* (June, Sept. 1787).

In 1789, with the financial support of Don Diego de Gardoqui, Spanish minister to the United States, he founded the colony of New Madrid, in Spanish Louisiana, now Missouri; but Don Estéban Miró, governor of Louisiana, having other plans for the settlement of Americans in Spanish territory, threw obstacles in the way of the project, and Morgan retired again to "Prospect." The last years of his life were spent at "Morganza," his farm near Washington, Pa., whither he removed in 1796. There he continued his scientific farming, devoting special attention to grape culture. The quiet of his life there was broken only once, by the visit of Aaron Burr, who stopped at his house in an attempt to enlist him and his sons in the western scheme. He refused to be drawn into the project and later journeyed to Richmond to testify against Burr at his famous trial.

[Max Savelle, *George Morgan* (1932); C. R. Woodward, *The Development of Agriculture in N. J.* (1927); *Ill. State Hist. Lib. Coll.*, esp. vol. I ed. by H. W. Beckwith (1903); C. W. Alvord and C. E. Carter, "The New Régime" (1916) and "Trade and Politics" (1921); *Papers of Sir William Johnson*, vols. II, IV–VII (1922–31); *Calendar of Va. State Papers*, esp. vol. VI (1886), pp. 1–36; K. M. Rowland, *The Life of George Mason* (2 vols., 1892); Louis Houck, *The Spanish Régime in Mo.* (1909), vol. I.]   M. S.

MORGAN, GEORGE WASHINGTON (Sept. 20, 1820–July 26, 1893), soldier, lawyer, congressman, came of Welsh stock, being descended from George Morgan [*q.v.*], whose father, Evan, came to America from Wales early in the eighteenth century. The son of Thomas Morgan and his wife Katherine, daughter of William Duane [*q.v.*], he was born in Washington County, Pa. In his sixteenth year he left Washington College to enlist in a company raised by his brother, Thomas Jefferson Morgan, for service in the war for Texan independence. President Houston appointed him a lieutenant and he soon became a captain. Returning to his home in 1839, he entered the United States Military Academy in 1841 but resigned during his second year. He worked at various tasks, in different places, studying law as opportunity offered. Removing to Mount Vernon, Ohio, in 1843, he studied in the office of his future partner, J. K. Miller. Shortly after his admission to the bar, he became prosecuting attorney for Knox County, but resigned to raise a company for the war with Mexico, in 1846. He was shortly elected colonel of the 2nd Ohio Volunteers, though only twenty-six years old. He acquitted himself creditably under Taylor until Mar. 3, 1847, when he was commissioned colonel of the 15th United States Infantry, and assigned to Pierce's brigade of Scott's army. He was wounded at both Contreras and Churubusco, and in

Morgan

1848 was brevetted brigadier-general "for gallant and meritorious conduct." From 1848 until 1855 he combined law and farming at Mount Vernon. President Pierce appointed him consul at Marseilles in 1856. Two years later he became minister to Lisbon, which post he resigned at the outbreak of the Civil War.

He was appointed brigadier-general of volunteers in November 1861 and given command of the 7th Division of Buell's Army of the Ohio. With this division he drove the Confederates from Cumberland Gap. In 1863 he was transferred to Sherman's army and commanded a division in the Vicksburg campaign, and the XIII Corps at the capture of Fort Hindman, Ark. There was some disagreement between Morgan and Sherman (see Morgan's account of the fight at Chickasaw Bayou, *Battles and Leaders*, III, 462, and Sherman's comment in his *Memoirs*, I, 320), and within a few months illness and dissatisfaction with the policy of using negro troops caused Morgan's resignation, June 8, 1863. In the National Democratic Convention of the following year he defended General McClellan against the charge of "defeatism." In 1865 Morgan was defeated for governor of Ohio by Gen. J. D. Cox [*q.v.*], Republican. He was elected to Congress in 1866 and served from March 1867 to June 1868, when he was unseated in favor of his Republican fellow townsman, Columbus Delano [*q.v.*]. He was elected to the Forty-first and Forty-second congresses, however, and served 1869–73. He was a member of the committees on military affairs, on foreign affairs, and on reconstruction. In and out of Congress he vigorously opposed the harsh measures of reconstruction favored by the Radical Republicans. Blaine, who defeated him for the speakership, has testified to Morgan's ability. After leaving Congress Morgan resumed his law practice at Mount Vernon, Ohio. He was delegate-at-large to the National Democratic Convention of 1876. On Oct. 7, 1851, he had married Sarah H. Hall of Zanesville, Ohio, who with their two daughters survived him. His death occurred at Fortress Monroe, Va., and he was buried at Mount Vernon, Ohio.

["Extracts from the Reminiscences of Gen. George W. Morgan," with biog. note by J. M. Morgan, *Southwestern Hist. Quart.*, Jan. 1927; *Battles and Leaders of the Civil War*, vol. III (1888); *Appletons' Ann. Cyc.*, 1893 (1894); *Biog. Dir. Am. Cong.* (1928); Taylor's and Scott's reports in *House Exec. Doc. 60*, 30 Cong., 1 Sess.; *War of the Rebellion: Official Records (Army)*; J. G. Blaine, *Twenty Years of Congress* (2 vols., 1884–86); *The Biog. Encyc. of Ohio of the Nineteenth Century* (1876); *Personal Memoirs of Gen. W. T. Sherman* (3rd ed., 2 vols., 1890); J. H. Smith, *The War with Mexico* (2 vols., 1919); *Evening Star* (Washington, D. C.), July 27, 1893.] **M. L. B., Jr.**

MORGAN, JAMES DADA (Aug. 1, 1810–Sept. 12, 1896), Union soldier, merchant, and banker, of Welsh-English colonial ancestry, was born at Boston, the son of James Morgan, sea-captain and trader, and Martha (Patch) Morgan. He attended the common-schools in his native city until he was sixteen years of age, when the urge of the sea prompted him to start on a long voyage in a sailing-ship. When it was a month out of Boston, however, a mutiny arose, the vessel was burned, and, after drifting in a small boat for fourteen days, Morgan with certain companions finally reached the shores of South America. He made his way back to Boston, and in the year 1834 went to Quincy, Ill., where, for some twenty-seven years, he engaged in mercantile pursuits. Incidentally, he became interested in local military affairs, and helped organize the Quincy Grays and, later, the Quincy Riflemen. With the latter organization, he saw military service in Hancock County, Ill., during the Mormon difficulties of 1844–45, which ended with the death of the "Prophet," Joseph Smith, and a movement of the Mormon settlers to Utah.

Morgan entered the Mexican War as captain of the 1st Illinois Volunteer Infantry (June 18, 1846), was promoted major for conspicuous gallantry at the battle of Buena Vista, and was mustered out of the volunteer service on June 17, 1847. Returning to Quincy, he reëntered business, in which he continued to engage until the outbreak of the Civil War, when, Apr. 29, 1861, though suffering from a fractured leg, he assumed the duties of lieutenant-colonel of the 10th Illinois Infantry, becoming colonel on July 29 following. With his regiment he was mustered into federal service for three years. He participated in the engagement at Island Number Ten, where he commanded the 1st Brigade, 4th Division of Pope's army. For meritorious services at New Madrid, Mo., and in the capture of Corinth, Miss., where again he commanded a brigade, he was promoted brigadier-general of volunteers, July 17, 1862. He took an active part in the Atlanta campaign and accompanied General Sherman in his march to the sea and through the Carolinas, being brevetted, Mar. 19, 1865, major-general of volunteers for gallantry at Bentonville, N. C., where he contributed largely to saving the left wing of Sherman's army. He also distinguished himself at Buzzard's Roost Gap, Mar. 9, 1864.

He was mustered out of the military service, Aug. 24, 1865, and, returning to Quincy, became identified as a banker with many important corporations and institutions. He served as treasurer of the Illinois Soldiers and Sailors Home

171

from its incorporation in 1887, and as vice-president of the Society of the Army of the Cumberland. He died at his home in Quincy, and there his interment took place. Early in life he was married to Jane Strachan of Boston, by whom he had two sons who survived him. His wife died in 1855, and on June 14, 1869, he married Harriet Evans of Gloucester, Mass.

[*Soc. of the Army of the Cumberland, Twenty-sixth Reunion, Rockford, Ill., 1896* (1897); F. B. Heitman, *Hist. Reg. and Dict. U. S. Army* (1903); *Chicago Tribune,* Sept. 13, 1896; *Portrait and Biog. Record of Adams Co., Ill.,* (1892); *Battles and Leaders of the Civil War,* vol. IV (1888); H. M. Cist, *The Army of the Cumberland,* J. D. Cox, *Atlanta,* and *The March to the Sea,* M. F. Force, *From Fort Henry to Corinth,* all in Campaigns of the Civil War series (1881–82); information as to certain facts from a great-nephew, J. R. Wells, of Quincy, Ill.]　　　　　C. D. R.

MORGAN, JAMES MORRIS (Mar. 10, 1845–Apr. 21, 1928), Confederate naval officer, soldier, author, was descended from Evan Morgan, who migrated from Wales to Philadelphia early in the eighteenth century and married Joanna Biles. One of their children was Dr. John Morgan [*q.v.*], Washington's first surgeon-general. Another was Col. George Morgan [*q.v.*], who apprised Jefferson of Burr's suspicious activities. Thomas Gibbes Morgan, grandson of George, removed to Louisiana early in the nineteenth century. His first wife, Eliza McKennan, bore one child, Philip Hicky Morgan [*q.v.*]. James Morris, the eighth child of Sarah Fowler, the second wife, was born in New Orleans. He entered the United States Naval Academy in September 1860, where his class, the first to use "Old Ironsides" as a training-ship, became known as the "brood of the *Constitution.*" The secession of Louisiana ended his career at Annapolis, however, and he became a midshipman in the Confederate navy. Serving first in the sloop *McRae,* on the Mississippi, he was transferred to the James River, then to Charleston. Accompanying Commodore Matthew F. Maury [*q.v.*] to Europe in October 1862, he served on board the cruiser *Georgia* until May 1864, then ran the blockade into Wilmington. Assigned to the schoolship *Patrick Henry,* on the James River (a "realistic war college"), he was soon sent to the naval Battery Semmes, near Dutch Gap. Since he was connected by marriage with Mrs. Jefferson Davis (his brother had married her cousin), he was detailed by the secretary of the navy to accompany her on her flight from Richmond, shortly before its fall. Not yet twenty-one, Morgan married, in October 1865, Helen, daughter of G. A. Trenholm of Charleston, late Confederate secretary of the treasury. She died a year later, leaving an infant daughter. About

this time, through General Sherman, Khedive Ismail Pasha of Egypt engaged ten Union and ten Confederate veterans to drill his army, and Morgan, finding law and agriculture uncongenial, accepted an Egyptian commission. After three busy and exciting years, he returned to the United States in 1872.

He now tried farming and journalism in South Carolina, and participated in the campaign of 1876 which ousted the Carpet-bag rule. His second wife, whom he married in 1873, was Gabriella Burroughs, grand-daughter of Chancellor W. F. DeSaussure of South Carolina. She died in a few years, leaving him another daughter. After serving a while as messenger to a committee of the United States Senate, Morgan tried engineering and prospecting in Mexico. He also helped erect the Statue of Liberty. In 1885 his brother-in-law, F. W. Dawson [*q.v.*], editor of the Charleston *News and Courier,* procured from President Cleveland Morgan's appointment as consul-general to Australasia. He was accompanied to his post by his third wife, Frances, daughter of Judge Charles A. Fincke of New York. One child (another daughter) was born to this marriage. Returning to America in 1888, Morgan tried farming and horse breeding in Maryland until 1898, when he removed to Washington. Besides participating in various financial enterprises, he did some writing and speaking. In 1903, as the representative of a banking house, he was in Panama at the time of the birth of that republic. He contributed numerous articles to magazines, and in 1915, in collaboration with J. P. Marquand, published a small volume of stories, *Prince and Boatswain: Sea Tales from the Recollections of Rear-Admiral Charles E. Clark.* His masterpiece was his autobiography, *Recollections of a Rebel Reefer,* published in 1917. He was stricken with paralysis in January 1928, and died shortly after his eighty-third birthday.

[Besides *Recollections of a Rebel Reefer,* see Sarah Morgan Dawson, *A Confederate Girl's Diary* (1913); *Official Records of the Union and Confederate Navies in the War of the Rebellion,* 1 ser. II, 2 ser. I; M. L. Bonham, Jr., "The Rebel Reefer Furls His Last Sail," in *La. Hist. Quart.,* Oct. 1928; *Evening Star* (Washington, D. C.), Apr. 23, 1928.]　　　M. L. B., Jr.

MORGAN, JOHN (June 10, 1735–Oct. 15, 1789), physician, founder of the University of Pennsylvania medical school, medical director of the Continental Army, was born in Philadelphia, the son of Evan and Joanna (Biles) Morgan. His father, an emigrant from Wales and a successful merchant, was prominent in Philadelphia civic life. John attended Nottingham School, near Philadelphia, and the College of

Philadelphia (now the University of Pennsylvania), graduating with the first class from the latter institution in 1757. He served six years' apprenticeship under Dr. John Redman [*q.v.*], having begun his work with him about 1750, and for several years was lieutenant and surgeon with the provincial troops in the French war. In 1760, on the advice of Dr. Redman, he decided to continue his studies abroad. Carrying letters of introduction from Benjamin Franklin, he spent a year in London under William Hewson, John Fothergill, and John and William Hunter, and two years at the University of Edinburgh, where he was granted the degree of M.D. (1763), his thesis, on the formation of pus, winning recognition as a valuable contribution. The following winter he studied anatomy in Paris and subsequently spent several months with Giovanni Morgagni in Italy. A memoir (later published in the *Transactions of the American Philosophical Society,* vol. II, 1786) on the subject of making anatomical preparations by corrosion, an art in which he acquired skill in England, procured his admission to the Académie Royale de Chirurgie de Paris (July 5, 1764). He was also a member of the Royal Society of London and the Belles-Lettres Society of Rome, and a licentiate of the Royal Colleges of Physicians in London and Edinburgh.

While abroad Morgan conceived the idea of establishing a medical school in connection with the College of Philadelphia, and upon his return in 1765 he proposed such a project to the trustees. It was adopted, May 3, 1765, and he was appointed professor of the theory and practice of physic. At the annual Commencement that year he delivered *A Discourse upon the Institution of Medical Schools in America* (1765). This classic is an elaborate exposition of the nature and scope of medical science, its conditions in America, obstacles in the way of medical study, and reasons for the establishment of medical schools. Arguing the need for separating the functions of physician, apothecary, and surgeon, he declared it his intention to confine himself to the practice of internal medicine solely by prescription. His advanced ideas at first met with great opposition, his opponents asserting that they were not adaptable to conditions in America.

At the first sign of trouble with the mother country Morgan hoped for a peaceful settlement of all difficulties and won a gold medal from John Sargent for his paper, published with the work of others in *Four Dissertations on the Reciprocal Advantages of a Perpetual Union between Great. Britain and her American Colonies* (1766). At

the outbreak of war he cast his lot with the colonies, and on Oct. 17, 1775, Congress elected him director-general of hospitals and physician-in-chief of the American army. He joined the army at Cambridge and later followed it to New York. Drastic reorganization of the medical department followed his appointment, especially with respect to raising the standards of assistants and to the dispensing of medicines. His exacting methods provoked the jealousy and antagonism of his subordinates, who by false charges and political intrigue caused him to be "degraded," Oct. 9, 1776, to director of hospitals east of the Hudson only. Increasing abuses, over which he had no control, brought loud complaints against him from his enemies, and on Jan. 9, 1777, Congress removed him without explanation. The real reason seems to have been the feeling that while there were no particular charges against him, the numerous general complaints made his removal necessary for the good of the service (W. C. Ford, *Journals of the Continental Congress, 1774–1789,* vol. VIII, 1907, p. 626).

Morgan denounced the resolution dismissing him without reason as unfair, and published *A Vindication of His Public Character in the Station of Director-General of the Military Hospitals, and Physician in Chief of the American Army* (1777), in which he charged that *"a mean and invidious* set of men" had plotted his removal, and declared that the intermeddling of Congress had rendered efficiency and honesty impossible in his department. His dismissal was a severe blow to him, and though Washington exonerated him of neglect and wrong-doing and Congress decided that he "hath in the most satisfactory manner vindicated his conduct" and that as director-general he "did conduct himself ably and faithfully in the discharge of the duties of his office" (*Ibid.,* vol. XIV, 1909, p. 724), he considered himself disgraced and withdrew from public life. Thereafter, he confined his efforts to his private practice and to his duties as professor and as physician at the Pennsylvania Hospital.

Morgan was a handsome man, an indefatigable worker, and well versed in Latin and Greek. His writings, in addition to those already mentioned, include *A Recommendation of Inoculation, According to Baron Dimsdale's Method* (1776), and a journal, left in manuscript, which, edited by Julia Morgan Harding, was published in 1907 as *The Journal of Dr. John Morgan of Philadelphia, from the City of Rome to the City of London, 1764.* He possessed a choice medical library, containing many original manuscripts, which was destroyed during the Revolution. He was an active member of the American Philosophical Society, while the Philadelphia College of Physicians, organized in 1787, was the outgrowth of his suggestion. His wife, Mary, daughter of Thomas and Mary Hopkinson, whom he married Sept. 4, 1765, died in 1785. There were no children. Morgan's death occurred in Philadelphia.

[Morgan's writings; letters and other MSS. in the Hist. Soc. of Pa., Phila., and in the Papers of the Continental Cong., No. 63, and the Joseph Meredith Toner Papers, Lib. of Cong.; M. I. Wilbert, "John Morgan, the Founder of the First Medical School and the Originator of Pharmacy in America," in *Am. Jour. of Pharmacy*, Jan. 1904; Joseph Carson, *A Hist. of the Medic. Dept. of the Univ. of Pa.* (1869); G. W. Norris, *The Early Hist. of Medicine in Phila.* (1886); and G. B. Wood, *Hist. and Biog. Memoirs* (1872); H. A. Kelly and W. L. Burrage, *Am. Medic. Biogs.* (1920); *Pa. Mag. of Hist. and Biog.*, Apr. 1886, p. 43, Apr. 1894, p. 35, Oct. 1909, pp. 502, 503, July 1924, p. 22; *Phila. Jour. Medic. and Physic. Sci.*, vol. I, no. 2 (1820), pp. 439–42; J. A. Morgan, *A Hist. of the Family of Morgan* (1902).]   J. H. P.

MORGAN, JOHN HUNT (June 1, 1825–Sept. 4, 1864), Confederate raider, was born at Huntsville, Ala. His father, Calvin Cogswell Morgan, a merchant, was a Virginian; his mother, Henrietta, was the daughter of John W. Hunt, an influential business man of Lexington, Ky. About 1830 the Morgans moved to a farm in the neighborhood of that city and there John received a good common-school education. He enlisted for the Mexican War in 1846 and saw service at Buena Vista. Shortly after his return, he was married to Rebecca Bruce, who soon became a confirmed invalid and died in July 1861. Morgan prospered in business and, retaining his interest in military affairs, organized, in 1857, the Lexington Rifles.

In September 1861 he joined the Confederate army and immediately became a scout. Elected a captain, he was given a squadron to command, and early in 1862 began his famous raids, during which he harassed the Federals by penetrating their lines, capturing men and trains, and destroying supplies. He became a colonel on Apr. 4, 1862, took part in the Shiloh campaign, and then started a raid, beginning near Iuka, Miss., in which he fought near Columbia, Tenn., on May 1, taking 400 prisoners, but was badly defeated at Lebanon on May 5 by Federal cavalry under General Dumont. Nothing daunted, he rallied his men, and advanced into Kentucky, on May 11 reaching Cave City, where he wrecked the railroad and burned important stores. In June he was placed at the head of a brigade, with which, starting from near Knoxville, Tenn., July 4, 1862, he raided extensively in Kentucky, marching more than 1,000 miles, taking hundreds of prisoners and enormous stocks of sup-

plies, and returning safely to his base. Morgan acted rapidly, he fought hard to secure his objectives, then split his command, striking right and left to confuse his enemies. He withdrew quickly, avoiding fighting wherever possible. During the remainder of 1862, he raided the country between Nashville, Louisville, and Cincinnati. On Dec. 7 he captured a Federal force at Hartsville, Tenn., taking over 1,700 prisoners. For this victory he was appointed brigadier-general and given the command of a cavalry division. On Dec. 14, he was married to the daughter of the Hon. Charles Ready, of Murfreesboro, Tenn. He started a new series of raids in March 1863 and on May 1 the Confederate Congress gave him a vote of thanks for his "varied, heroic and invaluable services."

In June 1863 he secured authority from Gen. Joe Wheeler [*q.v.*] to raid Kentucky with 2,000 men. Nothing was said about going beyond Kentucky, but Morgan had that project in mind. Starting July 2, he crossed the Ohio into Indiana six days later. Pursued by superior forces, he commenced a wild ride through the suburbs of Cincinnati, and east. The ride was so fast, fifty to sixty miles a day, and his column was so harassed by swarms of home guards, that Morgan's men became exhausted, with the result that when their pursuers caught up with them on July 19, near Buffington Island, most of the command surrendered. Morgan himself rode on, but was surrounded near New Lisbon, Ohio, and on July 26 surrendered. This raid destroyed Morgan's division and inflicted only minor losses upon the Federals, but it drew large Federal forces from in front of Bragg's army, and saved East Tennessee to the Confederacy for several months.

Escaping from the Ohio State Penitentiary, Columbus, Ohio, on Nov. 26, Morgan was assigned in April 1864 to command the Department of Southwest Virginia. His forces were poorly equipped and badly disciplined, but he restored order and organized an efficient force, with which he raided Kentucky in June. This raid had some success, but losses were severe, and the troops committed excesses, which led to dissatisfaction on the part of the Confederate government over Morgan's failure to discover and punish the culprits. On Sept. 3, 1864, Morgan decided to attack Federal forces near Knoxville, Tenn., and encamped that evening at Greenville. In the night a Federal force passed unnoticed into his lines. Entering the town early the next morning, Morgan was surprised and killed while endeavoring to join his men. His body was buried at Abington, subsequently interred at Richmond,

Va., and finally buried in Lexington, Ky. Gentle and generous, Morgan was bold in thought and action. He was a thorn to his enemies, not because of military genius, but on account of untiring energy and continuous devotion to his cause.

[*War of the Rebellion: Official Records (Army)*; B. W. Duke, *Hist. of Morgan's Cavalry* (1867); A. C. Quisenberry, "Hist. of Morgan's Men," in *Reg. Ky. State Hist. Soc.*, Sept. 1917; S. K. Smith, *Life, Army Record, and Public Services of D. Howard Smith* (1890); *The Biog. Encyc. of Ky. of the Nineteenth Century* (1878); *Biog. Cyc. of the Commonwealth of Ky.* (1896); the *Sentinel* (Richmond), Sept. 10, 1864.]

C. H. L.

MORGAN, JOHN PIERPONT (Apr. 17, 1837–Mar. 31, 1913), banker and foremost leader of American finance, was the son of Junius Spencer Morgan [*q.v.*], a prominent international banker who did much to open the United States to European capital and left at his death in 1890 an impressively large fortune for his time. On the maternal side his inheritance was equally significant, if different. His mother, Juliet (Pierpont) Morgan, was a daughter of the Rev. John Pierpont [*q.v.*], poet, impetuous clergyman, and fiery reformer. The Morgan fortune did not begin with Junius Spencer; it was founded by the latter's father Joseph, who with his wife Sarah Spencer took up a farm near Hartford, Conn., in 1817. Joseph Morgan did not remain a farmer long, but amassed wealth, first in stage coaches, then in hotels, and finally in fire-insurance companies. He purchased a partnership for his son in a local drygoods firm, and shortly thereafter the eldest of Junius' five children, John Pierpont Morgan, known later as J. Pierpont Morgan or as J. P. Morgan, was born. The young Morgans soon moved from a small cottage on Asylum Street to a much larger and more comfortable house, surrounded by farm lands, which Joseph Morgan had built for them on Farmington Avenue. The eldest child entered a local school at the age of six, but when he was fourteen his parents moved to Boston, where his father became partner in one of the leading drygoods houses. There he entered English High, a noted school, from which he graduated in good standing at seventeen. The same year his father accepted a partnership with George Peabody, an American merchant who had become a great London banker. Although Pierpont was large and well built his health was poor for a time, and he was sent to the Azores to recuperate. From there he went to a school at Vevey on Lake Geneva in Switzerland, and then for two years to the University of Göttingen, in Germany, where mathematics was one of his chief studies.

Entering his father's house in London in 1856, he was sent to New York the following year to work in that of Duncan, Sherman & Company, American representatives of George Peabody & Company. From 1860 to 1864, as J. Pierpont Morgan & Company, he acted as agent in New York for his father's firm; in 1864–71 he was a member of the firm of Dabney, Morgan & Company, being associated with Charles H. Dabney, formerly a partner in Duncan, Sherman & Company; and in 1871 with the Drexels of Philadelphia he formed the New York firm of Drexel, Morgan & Company. Anthony J. Drexel, the head of the house, died in 1893, and in 1895 the New York firm became J. P. Morgan & Company. Closely associated with Drexel & Company of Philadelphia, Morgan, Harjes & Company of Paris, and J. S. Morgan & Company (after 1910 Morgan, Grenfell & Company), of London, it became one of the most powerful banking houses of the world, carrying through a long series of operations, of enormous variety and many of great scale. Certain very important ones were in the nature of reorganizations and consolidations, the success of which could generally be ascribed to the ability and leadership of Morgan.

During the trying days of the Civil War, young Morgan, concentrating on business, chiefly foreign exchange, made slow but sure progress. Two incidents of his relatively inconspicuous career during that era of profiteering and speculative orgy do not redound to his credit. To Simon Stevens, who sold to the Federal government obsolete Hall's carbines, he gave financial backing, though he withdrew from the case before Stevens finally brought successful suit for payment in full ("Government Contracts," *House Report No. 2, 37 Cong., 2 Sess.*, pp. lxiv–lxxvi, "Case No. 97—J. Pierpont Morgan, New York"; *2 Court of Claims Reports*, 95–103); and in 1863, with Edward Ketchum, he speculated in gold in a way that was hardly patriotic (*N. Y. Times*, Oct. 11, 16, 21, 1863; *American Gold, 1862–1876*, 1876). More characteristically, in 1869 he engineered a successful contest with Jay Gould and James Fisk [*qq.v.*], then at the zenith of their powers, over the control of the Albany & Susquehanna Railroad. Essentially an organizer and integrating force, he fought the financial buccaneers of his age with their own weapons, and, triumphing over them, became an influence, though not yet a conspicuous one, for stabilization (Corey, *post*, pp. 90–91). In a sense, his prominence dates from 1873, when by securing a division of a treasury loan between a Morgan syndicate and one organized by Jay Cooke [*q.v.*], he broke the monopoly of that financier in the vast refunding operations of the government. After the failure of Jay Cooke & Company in the panic of that year, the Morgan firm, increasing its already powerful international connections, became dominant in government financing.

Morgan, however, hardly became a large figure in the public eye until he was more than forty. In 1879 he sold a large block of New York Central stock direct to English investors, enabling William H. Vanderbilt to dispose of large holdings without unloading them on the American market and making a great impression on that magnate by his incisive action. The deal, unusual for those days, brought Morgan much prestige and may have influenced him to engage in the work of reorganizing American railroads, with a view to the restoration of faith abroad in American securities. Combatting tendencies toward reckless promotion and construction, unprofitable competition, and general demoralization, and extending centralized financial control, in 1885 he reorganized the New York, West Shore & Buffalo Railroad, causing it to be leased to the New York Central (*Commercial and Financial Chronicle*, Aug. 29, 1885), and forced the Pennsylvania to buy the South Pennsylvania Railroad, a competing line of the same type that was being built by Vanderbilt. In 1886 he reorganized the Philadelphia & Reading, and in 1888 the Chesapeake & Ohio. After the passage of the Interstate Commerce Act in 1887, Morgan, though unsympathetic with governmental regulation, by means of successive conferences (1889, 1890) of generally reluctant railroad presidents, sought to secure the enforcement of the act and agreements for the maintenance of "public, reasonable, uniform and stable rates" (*N. Y. Times*, Jan. 9, 1889). The conferences served at least to establish some community of interest among railroads hitherto engaged in ruthless and wasteful competition, and thus paved the way for the great consolidations of later years (Corey, ch. xvii).

Following the panic of 1893, Morgan was called upon to reorganize a large number of the leading railroad systems of the country, chiefly the Southern Railway, the Erie, the Philadelphia & Reading for a second time, and, with the Deutsche Bank, the Northern Pacific (Daggett, *post*). Moved by a desire to protect the good name of his country abroad, where investors had bought heavily of American securities, as well as the faith and reputation of his own firm, he assumed the greater part of the gigantic task of rehabilitation, after a period of frequently reck-

less and unscrupulous promotion. A characteristic feature of the reorganization effected by him was the creation in a particular road of a "voting trust," whereby the voting power of the stock was vested for a time at least in a small group of trustees selected by him. The device proved extremely useful in securing stability of control during a period of distress, but the immediate result was a vast concentration of power in his hands, much of which was retained by less direct means, such as directorships and fiscal agencies, after the crisis was relieved. By the end of the century, besides the lines under Morgan's unquestioned control which constituted one of the six major railroad "empires," and those controlled by him with James J. Hill, he had great influence in both the Vanderbilt and Pennsylvania systems. Only the Harriman and Gould systems were independent of him.

The power of this imperial financier was made clear to the general public in connection with the crisis of the national Treasury in 1895. Finding that its efforts to maintain by successive bond issues the dangerously depleted gold reserve were being frustrated by the withdrawal from the Treasury itself of gold with which to make the purchases, the Cleveland administration was forced to appeal to international bankers. Morgan formed a syndicate to furnish the government with some $65,000,000 in gold, half of which was obtained abroad, took bonds at 104½ in payment, and by vigorous methods prevented a further outflow of gold for a period of months. As events proved, this bold operation marked the turning point in the financial history of the decade, but both Cleveland and the Morgan-Belmont syndicate received severe criticism at the time because of the terms of the transaction. A disinterested historian has concluded that these were "extremely harsh," and that the financiers "measured with little mercy the emergency of the government" (Noyes, *post*, p. 234). The bonds were disposed of at 112¼ by the syndicate and rose to 119 on the open market. Despite the dangers and uncertainties under which Morgan labored, his profits, which he refused to reveal to a congressional committee, were probably excessive (Allan Nevins, *Grover Cleveland*, 1932, pp. 664–65; *Senate Document No. 187*, 54 Cong., 2 Sess., p. 297). Cleveland himself emphasized the public service that had been rendered, but to the leaders of the swelling popular revolt it appeared that the government itself was at the mercy of private financiers.

With the earlier stages of the consolidation of industry, Morgan, absorbed by his railroad activities, had had little to do. By financing the

Federal Steel Company, however, in 1898, and soon thereafter the National Tube Company and the American Bridge Company, he launched upon a course that led to his organization in 1901 of what was then the largest corporation in the world. With the reaction in the steel market in the middle of 1900, ruinous competition was threatened between the various over-capitalized consolidations that had been recently effected, and between them and Carnegie, the most powerful factor in the industry (Berglund, *post*). Many appeals were made to Morgan to form a combination, and especially to buy out Carnegie, who wanted to sell if he could get his price. The result was the United States Steel Corporation, representing a merger of the Morgan companies with the interests of Carnegie, William H. Moore, John W. Gates [*qq.v.*], and Rockefeller. With characteristic optimism and magnificence of operation, Morgan arranged to buy out the various companies at a very high figure. The new corporation, accordingly, was distinctly over-capitalized, but a Morgan syndicate carried through the colossal task of financing. There was a time when the stock slumped dangerously, but, because of the prosperous years that followed and the general efficacy of centralized financial control, the enterprise, under the direction of Elbert H. Gary [*q.v.*], proved highly successful. Community of interest was recognized in the directors, who in effect were selected by Morgan. About this time he financed the International Harvester Company (1902). He was less happy in organizing the grandiose International Mercantile Marine (1902). Including many but not a majority of the transatlantic lines, which were bought up at huge prices, this over-capitalized combination, after many vicissitudes, ultimately went into the hands of receivers. His prestige was also threatened by the fight with Edward H. Harriman [*q.v.*] over the control of the Northern Pacific Railroad, but, though Morgan was forced to recognize Harriman by giving him a place on the board of directors, his own ally James J. Hill remained in undisputed control after the dissolution of the Northern Securities Company in 1904.

Although Morgan was in his seventy-first year when the panic of 1907 burst upon the nation, the bankers turned instinctively to him for directions. His leadership, indeed, was recognized by the Secretary of the Treasury, who deposited with his house and affiliated banks large sums of government money to be used for purposes of financial relief, subject to the decision of conferences which he dominated (*Commercial and Financial Chronicle*, Oct. 26, 1907). He had able co-workers in George F. Baker and James Stillman [*q.v.*], but his personal influence was the decisive factor. At one time the only expedient of relief (advocated by Stillman) was the guaranteeing of deposits of certain weak trust companies in New York City by the stronger institutions, a few of which were stubbornly reluctant to join in such a commitment. Probably no one could have rescued the situation but Morgan, who here appeared at the height of his prestige. A final episode has perhaps been unduly emphasized. The brokerage firm of Moore & Schley, about to go bankrupt, were relieved of stock in the Tennessee Coal, Iron & Railroad Company, not readily salable, by the purchase of this by the United States Steel Corporation with its salable bonds (*Hearings before the Committee on Investigation of United States Steel Corporation. House of Representatives*, vol. I, 1911, p. 170). President Theodore Roosevelt approved the transaction, despite the antitrust laws, because of the emergency; and the Steel Corporation greatly extended its holdings. The action was hardly as important in ending the panic—which was already nearly over—as Roosevelt claimed, but the means employed were none the less effective, as well as profitable.

After the death of Harriman in 1909, Morgan stood without a challenging American rival in the field of finance, and, in the public mind, was the supreme symbol of financial power. Inevitably, during a period of rising economic and political discontent, he became an object of criticism and attack. The investigation of the alleged money trust by the Pujo committee of the House of Representatives in 1912 was aimed directly at him. His own testimony and battle of wits with the committee's counsel, Samuel Untermeyer, marked the high point of the hearings. The elderly banker was treated with deference and, in the prevailing opinion, emerged with unimpaired personal credit and prestige. His replies to questions were polite but generally non-committal; he denied the existence or the possibility of a money trust; he even denied that he himself possessed or desired great financial power. Nothing that was personally discreditable to him was revealed. His statement that the first requisite of credit is character and that he would not lend money to a man that he did not trust in spite "of all the bonds in Christendom," while not surprising to those who knew him, was widely commented upon at the time and afterward; it was strikingly characteristic of the man.

The findings, however, revealed unquestionably that there was vast centralization of financial control (*Money Trust Investigation*, III, pp. 55–106). The undisclosed resources of J. P. Morgan & Company, private bankers, and their deposits of $162,000,000, consisting often of the funds of great corporations for which the firm acted as fiscal agents and on whose boards of directors they were represented, constituted only the nucleus of their far-reaching power. The house controlled or had a powerful voice in banks and trust companies in New York City with resources of $723,000,000, besides the Equitable Life Assurance Society, with half a billion more (*Ibid.*, p. 60). They were closely allied with the powerful First National Bank, and, according to the committee, with the great National City Bank; on Wall Street, however, the general opinion was that their relationship with the latter was more often one of rivalry than of friendliness. In one way or another the company dominated or was intimately connected with a score of railroads, several street-railway systems, the International Mercantile Marine, and, among industrial corporations, United States Steel, International Harvester, General Electric, and American Telephone & Telegraph. Altogether, the eleven Morgan partners held seventy-two directorships in forty-seven of the larger corporations (*Ibid.*, p. 89). A brilliant critic of the "system," writing shortly afterward, said: "Investment bankers, like J. P. Morgan & Co., dealers in bonds, stocks and notes, . . . became the directing power in railroads, public service and industrial companies through which our great business operations are conducted—the makers of bonds and stocks. They became the directing power in the life insurance companies, and other corporate reservoirs of the people's savings—the buyers of bonds and stocks. They became the directing power also in banks and trust companies—the depositaries of the quick capital of the country—the life blood of business, with which they and others carried on their operations. Thus four distinct functions, each essential to business, and each exercised, originally, by a distinct set of men, became united in the investment banker. It is to this union of business functions that the existence of the Money Trust is mainly due" (L. D. Brandeis, *Other People's Money*, 1932, ed., pp. 5–6). In the prepared statement of the Morgan firm, financial concentration was defended on the ground that it was necessary in order that adequate banking facilities might be provided; and power was held to be dangerous only when in evil hands (*N. Y. Times*, Jan. 25, 1913). Nothing in Morgan's available record indicates that he had any doubts of the advantages of continued integration and combination; he said he did not mind a little

competition, but he seemed willing to extend his control or influence indefinitely. In his testimony, while denying the possibility of control, in effect he sought to justify it on the grounds of the wisdom, character, and good faith of those that exercised it.

The Pujo committee may have erred in attacking primarily the personal aspects of centralization rather than the system itself, but in seeking to explain the unparalleled position occupied by Morgan in American finance one cannot escape the conclusion that much of his power came from his personality. He had qualities of character that inspired absolute confidence. In his word, and his faith, implicit faith was reposed. His very physique was commanding. He had a large frame with massive shoulders, a big head with piercing eyes, shaggy brows, and a powerful nose. His eyes could be icy and his frown terrifying upon occasion. His manner at times was abrupt and dictatorial. He had a positive way of doing business; he dealt in ultimatums. All who came in contact with him felt the mental vigor, extraordinary ability to concentrate, reserve force, and power of decision of the man. The effect was heightened by long periods of silence and apparent aloofness from those about him. Even at important entertainments given by himself he was known to draw apart from guests, speaking to no one for long periods, or even playing cards alone at a small table. Under an exterior which frightened many there was much kindness, but his strong emotional nature harbored violent dislikes as well as likes. He refused to work with men he disliked, important though they might be. Despite his prejudices he was usually wise in his judgment of men; his knack of picking talented partners became one of the business traditions of America.

In business he was by no means infallible. He long seriously underestimated the abilities of Harriman, whose operations, while not precisely the same as his, had a very similar scope. His great shipping combine was anything but a success. In spite of his usual extraordinary instinct for soundness in finance, at times he lent his aid to the fashioning of instruments of capital inflation, as in the formation of the Northern Securities Company (Noyes, *post*, pp. 349–50). No other chapter of his career has been so criticized as his later connection as director and banker with the New York, New Haven & Hartford Railroad. He had been associated for many years with this company, but toward the end of his life its previous high credit and prosperity suffered a long and grave eclipse, partly because of the extremely costly expansion program of an over-ambitious management. It has been claimed that he bore opprobrium for the errors of others, but President Charles S. Mellen [*q.v.*], testifying before a congressional committee, left little doubt of Morgan's personal interest and dominance ("New York, New Haven and Hartford Railroad Company Evidence," *Senate Document No. 543*, 63 Cong., 2 Sess., 1914, vol. I, pp. 712–13). It would appear that here, as elsewhere, "the Morgan sins, if any, were the sins of magnificence" (Lerner, *post,* p. 313). With his British contacts, Morgan was perhaps the chief instrument by which foreign capital built up his native country. He believed in the phrase attributed to his father, "Never sell a bear on the United States." He was essentially, not the industrial pioneer, but the banker and conservator; while he was the foremost organizer of great corporations in his time, his interest was that of the protector of investors and depositors. In general, he personified legitimate investment throughout a period in which wreckers were typical of financial operations. He did not hesitate in various hearings and lawsuits to describe such men as "dangerous elements," and he emphasized his own moral responsibility to stockholders. As a witness in *Peter Power* vs. *Northern Securities Company,* he said: "I felt bound, since I had reorganized the property and assumed the responsibility for its policy, that I should protect it (*New York Tribune,* Mar. 27, 1902). If he was a somewhat ruthless force making for centralized control of industry and credit, he unquestionably contributed to corporate stability.

Morgan's breadth of view was not equal to changing social outlooks; he was not interested in social reform; Theodore Roosevelt and his anti-trust activities were to him anathema. He was essentially the aristocrat and his inbred attitude was not lessened by close and constant European associations. He cared next to nothing for public opinion, and had the instinctive shrinking from publicity of the man of breeding. Unlike many other great figures of his day he was master rather than slave of his business. His outside interests were varied and extensive. An enthusiastic yachtsman, he was four times prominently identified with defense of the *America's* Cup, and was president of the New York Yacht Club, holding the title of commodore. He traveled much, and was the leading art collector of his time.

His activities as a collector are not unworthy of comparison with his financial operations, for, as he was the organizer extraordinary, so was he the super-collector; they may also be regarded as an expression of his richly sensuous nature.

The year before his death he sent to the Metropolitan Museum of Art, of which for a number of years he was president, his collections that had been abroad, planning an exhibition of all his works of art. A preliminary exhibition was placed on view in January 1913, but Morgan died without ever having seen his collection as a unit. All his collections were left unconditionally to his son, J. Pierpont Morgan, Jr., who authorized the loan exhibition of 1914–16; this included enamels, ivories, bronzes, wood-carvings, glass, pottery, tapestries, furniture, miniatures, statuary, and paintings. Subsequently, the greater part of this loan was given outright to the Museum and was, with previous gifts of both Morgans, made permanently available to the public in the Pierpont Morgan Wing. Morgan's literary treasures, including manuscripts, illuminations, incunabula, and other early editions of books, were housed in a beautiful marble library adjoining his residence in New York City. In his lifetime the library was used for his personal pleasure and by a few research scholars. In 1924 it was conveyed by J. Pierpont Morgan, Jr., to six trustees, to be administered as a public reference library for the use of scholars as a memorial to his father. It contained some 25,000 books and manuscripts, besides collections of drawings, etchings, coins, and medals.

Morgan made great gifts during his life, to churches, cathedrals, art museums, and hospitals, but not along the studied, methodical lines followed by Rockefeller and Carnegie. He maintained no special bureaus or organizations for the purpose, but followed personal inclination and associations in his philanthropies. Besides his art collections, valued at *c.* $50,000,000, he left a net estate of more than $68,000,000, but a much larger total might have been expected in view of his influence and the greater accumulations of other men less active in finance than he. The largest single item was his interest in the New York and Philadelphia firms, appraised at $29,875,847. Strangely enough, his estate contained many worthless securities, tokens, no doubt, of friendships, rather than of business misjudgments.

He died at Rome, on Mar. 31, 1913, only a few months after his appearance before the Pujo committee, and was buried in Hartford, Conn. It was generally agreed that he would have no successor. The wording of his lengthy will, his gifts, his art and book collections, his friendships with so many rulers and others among the great of the earth, together with the magnificence of his business operations, have caused the adjective "princely" to be applied to him more often perhaps than to any other American. He was the most prominent and one of the most active lay members of the Protestant Episcopal Church, and in the first article of his will avowed his complete faith in the doctrine of the atonement.

In 1861, in Paris, he was married to Amelia Sturges, daughter of Jonathan Sturges of New York City. She died the next year, and in 1865 he married Frances Louise Tracy, daughter of Charles E. Tracy, a leader of the New York bar and vestryman in St. George's Church, with which Morgan became so closely identified. By his second wife, who survived him, he had four children, a son, John Pierpont Morgan, and three daughters.

[Morgan made practically no speeches, gave the rarest and briefest of interviews, wrote no articles or books. No collection of letters, if such exists, has been made available. Of biographical works, the best is Lewis Corey, *The House of Morgan* (1930); both Carl Hovey, *The Life Story of J. Pierpont Morgan* (1911), and J. K. Winkler, *Morgan the Magnificent*, lack documentation and suffer from the unavailability of source materials, though the latter work is entertaining and in certain respects fairly detailed. An interesting article is Max Lerner, "Jupiter in Wall Street," *American Mercury*, July 1930. The most valuable single source for Morgan's business activities is *Money Trust Investigation. Investigation of Financial and Monetary Conditions in the U. S. . . . before a Subcommittee of the Committee on Banking and Currency* (3 vols., 1913), containing Morgan's testimony, II, 1003–08, 1011–91, and the report, vol. III. For the business background, see works on his contemporaries and the following: B. H. Meyer, *A Hist. of the Northern Securities Case* (1906); Abraham Berglund, *The U. S. Steel Corporation* (1907); Stuart Daggett, *Railroad Reorganization* (1908); A. D. Noyes, *Forty Years of Am. Finance* (1909); John Moody, *The Masters of Capital* (1919). For his collections, see Gardner Teale, "An American Medici. J. Pierpont Morgan and his Various Collections," *Putnam's Mag.*, Nov. 1909; memoir in London *Times*, Apr. 1, 1913; F. J. Mather, Jr., "The Morgan Loan Exhibition," *Art and Progress*, Apr. 1914; "The Pierpont Morgan Library," *Lib. Jour.*, Mar. 1, 1924; Joseph Breck and M. R. Rogers, *The Metropolitan Museum of Art. The Pierpont Morgan Wing* (1929); *The Pierpont Morgan Library . . . 1924 . . . 1929* (1930). For ancestry, see N. H. Morgan, *Morgan Genealogy* (1869); J. A. Morgan, *A Hist. of the Family of Morgan . . .* (1902?). Obituaries appeared in almost all the important papers, Apr. 1, 1913. The above sketch is based in part upon personal information.]

A. W. A.

MORGAN, JOHN TYLER (June 20, 1824– June 11, 1907), senator from Alabama, was the son of George Morgan of New York, who married Frances, the daughter of John Tyler Irby of Virginia, and shortly afterward removed to Athens, Tenn., where their son, John Tyler Morgan, was born. In a pioneer school the boy received a thorough grounding in the Latin and Greek classics. His mother had him memorize long passages from the Bible and from the English classics. Moving in 1833 to Calhoun County, Ala., he was brought up to the pioneer life and, by making friends with the Indians in the neighborhood, obtained a valuable basis for his

important work as chairman of the Senate Indian affairs committee years later. He studied law with William P. Chilton [q.v.] of Tuskegee and in 1845 was admitted to the bar. On Feb. 11 of the following year he married Cornelia Willis of Talladega County. They had four children. In 1855 he moved to Selma, where he made his residence till his death. He was elector on the Breckinridge ticket in 1860 and a member of the state secession convention of 1861. At that time thirty-seven years old, he preferred military to political service. Enlisting as a private in the "Cahaba Rifles," he rose to be lieutenant-colonel of the 5th Alabama Regiment, resigned the next year to recruit the 51st Alabama Cavalry, and cooperated with Forrest in the Stone River campaign of 1862–63. For brilliant movements in the Chickamauga and Knoxville campaigns he was made brigadier-general on Nov. 17, 1863, but on Jan. 27 of the next year in eastern Tennessee he was routed and dispersed by the 2nd Indiana Cavalry. With a new command he harassed and scouted in the Atlanta campaign and, as a forlorn hope, he was raising negro troops in Mississippi at the close of the war (*Official Records, post,* 1 ser., XLIX, p. 1276).

After the war he resumed the practice of law, fighting for white supremacy, and in 1876 was elected to the Senate, where he served until his death. An unsuccessful attempt was made at the outset by his Republican colleague to bar his entrance, but despite this his first vote went to confirm the appointment of the negro, Frederick Douglass [q.v.], as marshal of the District of Columbia. The old order was changing. In 1879 he defeated the Force Resolutions of Senator Edmunds and fifteen days of filibuster (*Cong. Record,* 45 Cong., 3 Sess., pp. 839–48, 885–93, 960–61, 1003, 1008–27). Using the state-rights argument, he fought effectively from 1886 to 1888 against the Blair education bill for eradicating Southern illiteracy, which cut party lines. Yet with certain environmental limits he was fair and sincere in his approach to the race problem. Ever constructive in aim, his first legislative efforts succeeded in turning over large tracts of national coal and iron land to the University of Alabama and other lands to state normal schools, barring them from exploitation by syndicates. This conception of socializing public resources led him, beginning in 1879, to introduce a series of bills to reclaim from transcontinental railroads unearned land grants which, after a ten-year fight, resulted in a saving of millions of dollars. He planned extensively for improvement of navigation on the important Alabama tributaries of the Mississippi and the Gulf, and one of his earliest speeches was on the deepening of Mobile harbor. This plan was intimately connected with his long fight for an Isthmian Canal, which he envisaged as a means for raising the South from the ashes of the Civil War by opening a gateway for Southern trade to competing Pacific markets (Speech at Democratic Caucus, 1900, Scrap Book No. 1, p. 28, Morgan MSS.). Advocating a policy similar to Blaine's and Frelinghuysen's, he labored ceaselessly, as chairman of the inter-oceanic canals and foreign relations committees, for government control of the privately owned Maritime Canal Company of Nicaragua, reporting the third and fourth bills for this purpose, which passed the Senate but were lost in the House. The Nicaragua route was largely accepted as the American route before 1900 and his fight for it against the tremendous opposition of the railroads and other groups aroused general interest when it might have flagged. This brought him fame and distinction from all America. Rather than defeat the project, he voted for the Spooner amendment to the Hepburn Bill, changing the route to Panama if a treaty could be negotiated. Though shocked at the change, he secretly believed this would fail. He thought that Panama was used as a scheme by Hanna and the railroads to defeat the canal. In the meantime he advocated to Secretary Hay the annexation of Panama as the only solution, but said "Colombia . . . would be likely to be opposed" (W. R. Thayer, *The Life and Letters of John Hay,* 1915, II, 304). Roosevelt's coup d'état was a terrible disappointment, and he condemned it violently. He cooperated in the construction at Panama, but till his death remained a stanch believer in the superior merits of the Nicaragua route.

A strong expansionist, he urged Cuban intervention and then the annexation of Cuba and the Philippines. In order to readjust the balance of power in the Senate to the interest of the South he advocated statehood for Cuba, Puerto Rico, and Hawaii, believing them Southern in politics. In 1898 he was appointed one of three commissioners to draft legislation for Hawaii. Although decrying the show of force against smaller countries, he was very jealous of Great Britain and of other powers, opposing general treaties of arbitration (Letter to John Hay, Apr. 30, 1904, Morgan MSS.). When he served as arbitrator with Justice Harlan in the Bering Sea fisheries dispute to which he was appointed in 1892, he alone voted against Great Britain on every major question. His feelings for the justice of his cause permitted compromise only with great dif-

ficulty. An ardent silver senator during the nineties, he supported Bryan on the sixteen-to-one platform and generally fought for social and anti-trust legislation. Yet he did not mention bimetallism in his proposed Democratic platform in 1901 (Scrapbook, Morgan MSS.), and in 1904 dropped Bryan as leader for what he thought was the good of the party (letter to Alton B. Parker, Jan. 29, Morgan MSS.). His great characteristics were independence and courage. In 1906 his state-rights views made him vote against the Hepburn rate-regulation act contrary to the wishes of his constituents. He defied Cleveland or supported Republican policies with the same equanimity, and, with his extensive learning and subtle logic, he was always a power which it was not safe to disregard. Though an intense Southerner, his national vision made him a national figure to all sections.

[Morgan Coll. in Lib. of Cong.; some important printed speeches and *Letter from Morgan to the Selma Mirror, Mar. 4, 1909* (1900), filed with Morgan Coll.; *War of the Rebellion: Official Records (Army),* 1 ser., XVI, pt. 2, XX, pt. 1, XXX, pt. 2, XXXI, pts. 1, 3, XXXII, pt. 1, XXXVIII, pts. 3–5; T. M. Owen, *Hist. of Ala. and Dict. of Ala. Biog.* (1921), vol. IV; *Who's Who in America,* 1906–07; *John Tyler Morgan and Edmund Winston Pettus: Memorial Addresses* (1909); J. A. Morgan, *A Hist. of the Family of Morgan* (1902?); *Evening Star* (Washington), June 12, 1907.]
C. W. G.

MORGAN, JUNIUS SPENCER (Apr. 14, 1813–Apr. 8, 1890), international banker, and one of the chief links in the financial relationship between Great Britain and the United States in the middle portion of the nineteenth century, was in a sense the real founder of the great banking house which his son, John Pierpont Morgan [*q.v.*], later headed. A descendant of Miles Morgan, who settled in Springfield, Mass., in 1636, and the grandson of Joseph Morgan, a soldier in the Revolution, he was born in West Springfield, Mass., but spent most of his childhood, youth, and young manhood in Hartford, Conn. There his father, Joseph Morgan, had acquired a substantial fortune by the time Junius reached man's estate. His mother was Sarah (Spencer) Morgan. For several years the boy attended the academy that later became Norwich University (Vt.), but in his middle teens he became a clerk in a drygoods house. After some experience in New York with A. and M. Ketchum, brokers, he acquired a partnership, first in the Hartford mercantile house of Howe, Mather & Company, and then in one in Boston, J. M. Beebe, Morgan & Company. Levi P. Morton [*q.v.*] was a partner of the latter firm, one of the foremost of its kind in the country.

In 1854 Morgan became a partner in the important London firm of George Peabody & Company, engaged in international banking. Ten years later George Peabody [*q.v.*] retired and the firm name was changed to J. S. Morgan & Company. Morgan headed the firm until his own death in 1890, though his son had come to dominate its affairs by that time, and conducted it on as important a scale as Peabody had done. The firm favored the Union cause in the Civil War, though criticized by some because of its activities in reselling American securities abroad (*New York Times,* Oct. 26, 27, 31, 1866) ; and in 1877 the bankers of New York gave Morgan a dinner in recognition of his services. Gov. Samuel J. Tilden described him as "upholding unsullied the honor of America in the tabernacle of the Old World" (*New York Times,* Nov. 9, 1877). Morgan in his response said that his business aim was never to do anything to cause evil to be spoken of the American name. To him was attributed the injunction, "Never sell a bear on the United States," the term used at that time for selling short.

Possibly the most important event in Morgan's life was his placing of a $50,000,000 loan for France in the fall of 1870, during the war with Prussia. The French were in a distressing plight at the time, part of the government having been removed to Tours, and found it impossible to raise a loan in Paris or from British bankers. Morgan was approached and successfully carried through the loan. Bismarck publicly declared that a loan contracted by the Tours government would not be recognized by the French government with which Germany would make peace, and he even threatened to make non-recognition of the loan one of the conditions of peace. Despite this impressive opposition, the loan, which was at 6%, was successfully placed. For a short time it fell to a slight discount but later advanced and proved a great success. Its effect, besides assisting the French, was at once to place J. S. Morgan & Company in the front rank of issuing houses in London. During this period a large portion of all British investments made in America went through this banking firm, which naturally worked in close conjunction with Drexel, Morgan & Company in New York.

Morgan entertained extensively at "Dover House," Rochampton, where he had some seventy acres. He talked with lucid precision, had definite opinions, and acted upon them. He was a witty man and highly amusing in his conversation. Although he lived more than half his life abroad he always retained his interest in Hartford, Conn. Out of his large fortune he gave in his lifetime $100,000 to establish a free library

at Hartford, a gift which his son and family supplemented with a like amount. He subsequently made a substantial gift to the Hartford Orphan Asylum in memory of his mother. He gave to the Metropolitan Museum of Art in New York a picture by Sir Joshua Reynolds. Other gifts were made to Guy's Hospital in London, to the National Nurses' Pension Fund in England, to Yale University for the establishment of a professorship in the new law department, to Trinity College, and to the Wadsworth Atheneum in Hartford.

Morgan married Juliet, daughter of the Rev. John and Mary Pierpont, of Boston, on May 2, 1836. Of his five children, John Pierpont and three daughters grew to maturity; one son died in childhood. Morgan died at Monte Carlo from injuries received in leaping from his carriage, when the horses became unmanageable at a point near the village of Èze in the Riviera.

[Published material regarding Junius S. Morgan is of the slightest. The present sketch has been based in part upon personal information. Accounts of the banquet by N. Y. bankers appeared in *N. Y. Times* and *N. Y. Tribune,* Nov. 9, 1877; *N. Y. Times* gives an account of his accident and details of his career, Apr. 6, 1890, and an obituary, Apr. 9, 1890; *London Times,* Apr. 9, 1890, has an obituary. For further bibliographical details see sketch of John Pierpont Morgan.]

A. W. A.

MORGAN, JUSTIN (1747–Mar. 22, 1798), was an obscure New England teacher who owned and perhaps bred the most remarkable animal in the history of the American horse. Born at or near West Springfield, Mass., he acquired a common-school education there, and being always too frail and sickly for physical labor, supported himself and his family as best he could by giving lessons in singing and penmanship, at which he excelled. In 1774 he married Martha Day (*New-England Historical and Genealogical Register,* January 1875, p. 55). For a time he kept a wayside tavern, and for several years had charge of horses kept for stud service. In 1788 he removed to Randolph, Vt., where he was elected lister and later town clerk. His wife died there in 1791, leaving four small children. Within a short time the family was broken up, the children going to live with neighbors, while the tall, consumptive singing master seems thereafter to have had no home, but to have lived first in one neighborhood and then in another, wherever he could find employment.

According to the recollection of his son Justin, then nine years old, as written to the *Albany Cultivator* forty-seven years afterward, the father in 1795 made a trip to the old home in West Springfield to collect a debt, but instead of the money he received two young horses, one of which, a colt then two years old, he "always while he lived, called a Dutch horse." Though a mere pony in size—he was little more than fourteen hands (fifty-six inches) high—he was thick-set, docile, quick, and intensely energetic, and could outpull some of the largest horses to be found. When Morgan died at the home of William Rice, in Woodstock, Vt., three years later, this horse was apparently his only remaining possession. To compensate Rice for expenses incurred in connection with his last illness, Morgan made the horse over to him.

Long after "the Justin Morgan Horse," as he came to be known, had died of neglect at the age of twenty-nine, it became apparent that he was one of those rare animals having the power to project his own characteristics through succeeding generations to remote descendants. Before the middle of the nineteenth century Morgan horses had become a distinct type or breed, famed throughout the country for their attractive appearance and their endurance, docility, and utility as driving, riding, cavalry, stage, and general-purpose horses. The very popularity of the tribe almost compassed its ruin, through widespread and long-continued use of the best stallions for improving the common horse stock of the new West without perpetuating the original type from mares of their own kind. Representative specimens were fast disappearing when in 1906 the United States Department of Agriculture and the Vermont State Experiment Station began to assemble a small band of Morgan mares at Burlington. In the same year Joseph Battell, historian of the breed, who had collected a stud on his extensive farm near Middlebury, Vt., presented a farm to the United States government, to which the mares were removed in 1907. The establishment, to which Battell added another farm in 1908, became the United States Morgan Horse Farm, operated by the Department of Agriculture for the purpose of reviving and preserving the early Morgan type and distributing surplus stock to foreign and domestic breeders.

[D. C. Linsley, *Morgan Horses* (1857); Joseph Battell, *The Morgan Horse and Register* (2 vols., 1894–1905); "Breeding Morgan Horses," *U. S. Dept. of Agric. Circular 199* (1926); *Wallace's Monthly*, 1875–90; *passim*; W. H. Gocher, *Trotalong* (1928), vol. I; Justin Morgan, Jr., in the *Cultivator* (Albany), June 1842; John Morgan in the same, July 1842; F. J. Metcalf, *Am. Writers and Compilers of Sacred Music* (1925).]

G. C. G.

MORGAN, LEWIS HENRY (Nov. 21, 1818–Dec. 17, 1881), ethnologist, was born near Aurora, N. Y., ninth of thirteen children of Jedediah and Harriet (Steele) Morgan. On his father's side he was descended from James Morgan, who came to New England in 1636, settling first at Roxbury, Mass., and in 1650 moved to New London, Conn. Thence Lewis' grandfather, Thomas, migrated to Cayuga County, N. Y., becoming a farmer near Aurora, then surrounded by Iroquois Indians. On his mother's side Lewis was descended from John Steele, who settled in Newtown, now Cambridge, Mass., in 1641.

Morgan entered Union College, Schenectady, and was graduated in 1840. He then read law for four years, occasionally wrote articles for the *Knickerbocker* and other periodicals, was admitted to the bar, moved to Rochester, and there, Aug. 13, 1851, married his cousin, Mary Elizabeth Steele of Albany. In this same year he formed a partnership with George F. Danforth, afterward judge of the court of appeals. During his early residence in Rochester he was a member of "The Club," a select group of professional men, before which papers were read and current affairs discussed. In 1855 Morgan became legal adviser of a railroad in course of construction between Marquette, Mich., and the Lake Superior iron region, in which he also became financially interested and from which he acquired some wealth. Devoting much attention to political affairs, first as a Whig, afterward as a Republican, he served in the New York Assembly from 1861 to 1868 and in the state Senate in 1868–69, but was defeated for renomination in 1870.

It is as a man of science that he is best known, however. While he cannot be regarded as a "born" ethnologist, as some have characterized him, his researches, during a time when anthropology in America had scarcely reached the infant stage, gained for him in later years the title of "Father of American Anthropology." When he returned to Aurora from college, he joined a secret society called the "Gordian Knot," which through the influence and aid of young Ely S. Parker [q.v.], the later noted Seneca Indian, was patterned after the Iroquois Confederacy, with chiefs, sachems, and the like, its members wearing Indian garb during their "councils" by firelight in the woods. After making a study of the League of the Iroquois the society became known as "The Grand Order of the Iroquois," with Morgan as its leading spirit, and undertook, as its chief purposes, to study and to perpetuate Indian lore, to educate the Indians, and to reconcile them to the conditions imposed by civilization. Morgan's casual interest in Indian matters thus developed into a serious investigation of Iroquois institutions and customs which led him to further researches among other American tribes and then into the wider field of world anthropology. Sent by the "Grand Order" to Washington to defeat the ratification of a fraudulent treaty by which the Seneca would have parted with their lands in favor of the Ogden Land Company, he succeeded in his purpose and as a result became so popular among the Indians that he was adopted, Oct. 1, 1847, into the Hawk clan of the Seneca, as the son of Jimmy Johnson, nephew of the famous Red Jacket. He was given the name Tayadawahkugh, or "One Lying Across," signifying that he would serve as a bond of union between Indians and whites. This induction admitted him into the innermost councils of the tribe and gave him every facility for pursuing his studies.

The year before his adoption he had read before the New York Historical Society an essay on "The Constitutional Government of the Six Nations of Indians," which was not printed; but he presented before the "Grand Order of the Iroquois" several papers embodying results of his Seneca researches which in amplified form were published in the *American Review* (New York, February-December 1847) in the form of fourteen "Letters on the Iroquois, by Skenandoah." In 1849 the University of the State of New York made an appropriation for the enlargement of its Indian collection and entrusted the execution to Morgan, who added his own collections and submitted illustrated reports of high value to students of Iroquois material culture (*Second Annual Report of the Regents of the University on the Condition of the State Cabinet of Natural History*, 1849; *Third Annual Report*, 1850). Continuing his studies of the subject, he prepared a "Report on the Fabrics, Inventions, Implements and Utensils of the Iroquois," published in the *Fifth Annual Report of the Regents* (1852), while in the following year lists of other objects given by and purchased from him were published. His book, *League of the Ho-dé-no-sau-nee, or Iroquois* (1851), inscribed to his friend and collaborator, Ely S. Parker, and acknowledged as "the fruit of our joint researches," has been distinguished as the first scientific account of an Indian tribe given to the world. Stern (*post*) compares the work with *Notes on the Iroquois* (1847), by H. R. Schoolcraft [*q.v.*], to the disparagement of the latter, a comparison which compels realization of the advance Morgan's study marked in American ethnology; but, he adds, "it fails lamentably to measure up to Morgan's later standard . . . to describe Indian life in terms of itself and not in terms of the culture of the investigator" (*Social Forces*, March 1928, p. 349).

While still engaged in the practice of law,

Morgan read before the American Association for the Advancement of Science in 1857 a paper on "Laws of Descent of the Iroquois" (*Proceedings . . . 1857*, 1858), and in 1859 he published at Rochester a pamphlet under the title: *Laws of Consanguinity and Descent of the Iroquois,* which excited so much interest that he concluded to return actively to ethnological investigations. While in Michigan the previous year (1858) on business connected with his railroad interests, he had learned from some Ojibwa Indians that their kinship system corresponded closely to that of the Iroquois. This discovery led him to pursue similar inquiries among other tribes, for which purpose, in 1859–62, he visited Indians of Kansas and Nebraska and the upper Missouri, and penetrated as far as the Hudson Bay Territory, ultimately recording notes on the kinship systems of upward of seventy tribes and reaching the conclusion that the kinship system of the Iroquois was practically the same as that of the Indians throughout America. With a view to further enlarging his field of observation, he prepared a series of questions which, as *Circular in Reference to the Degrees of Relationship among Different Nations,* was widely distributed by the Smithsonian Institution in 1860. His inquiries were thereby extended to the primitive world in general. The materials thus gathered were classified, a preliminary paper thereon was published by the American Academy of Arts and Sciences under the title "A Conjectural Solution of the Origin of the Classificatory System of Relationship" (*Proceedings,* vol. VII, 1868), and in 1871 the work appeared in its final form in *Smithsonian Contributions to Knowledge* (vol. XVII), with the title: "Systems of Consanguinity and Affinity of the Human Family." It is a quarto of 600 pages which reveals a prodigious amount of labor and forms a valuable addition to the source materials of primitive society; but the fundamental basis of its arrangement has been justifiably questioned.

Morgan's *magnum opus,* his *Ancient Society or Researches in the Lines of Human Progress* (1877; reissued 1878), was the logical outgrowth of "Systems of Consanguinity and Affinity." In it he propounded the doctrine of the common origin and psychic unity of all races of men and asserted that they passed through successive stages of savagery, barbarism, and civilization. His conclusions had a far-reaching influence, but according to Dr. Stern, whose opinion is now that of anthropologists generally, Morgan's evolutionary scheme is extremely tenuous when applied to primitive society, and "the persistence of the application of his methods today is . . .

inexcusable" (*Social Forces*, March 1928, p. 354). Morgan's theory that the family evolved from a state of promiscuity and his interpretation of kinship terms brought forth much acrimonious criticism, particularly on the part of British anthropologists, among whom J. F. McLennan was especially bitter (see his *Studies in Ancient History*, 1886, pp. 249–76); yet the influence of Morgan's concept has been acknowledged by many even to the present day.

Believing that the social systems of the Indians exercised a pronounced influence on their customs and arts, and especially on their architecture, Morgan published a paper on "The 'Seven Cities of Cibola'" in the *North American Review*, April 1869, in which he argued that the remains of the great pueblo structures of the Southwest, as well as those of Mexico, rather than being the palaces of princes and potentates, were the communal dwellings of advanced tribes, and that their erection was due to the prevalence of a system of relationships identical with that observed among the tribes of the North. In criticism of H. H. Bancroft's statements of ancient Mexican culture based on accounts by early Spanish chroniclers, Morgan published in the *North American Review*, April 1876, an article entitled "Montezuma's Dinner." It was highly commended, and doubtless tended to disparage Bancroft's valuable work in the public mind. The subject of the migration of the tribes engaging Morgan's attention, he published two articles in the magazine last cited (October 1869, January 1870) in which he advanced the theory that the Columbia Valley had been a cradle of the tribes whence the overflow of population migrated to the north and east—a conjecture which, however, has not been substantiated.

Pursuing his studies of aboriginal American architecture, he wrote the article on that topic in *Johnson's New Universal Cyclopædia* (vol. I, 1875), and another on "Houses of the Mound Builders" in the *North American Review*, July 1876. His attention being directly attracted to the Southwest, in 1878 he studied various ruins and visited some of the existing pueblos, some of the results being embodied in a paper, "On the Ruins of a Stone Pueblo on the Animas River in New Mexico" (*Twelfth Annual Report . . . of the Peabody Museum of American Archæology and Ethnology, Harvard University*, 1880), and "A Study of the Houses of the American Aborigines; with Suggestions for the Exploration of the Ruins in New Mexico, Arizona, the Valley of the San Juan, and in Yucatan and Central America" (*Archæological Institute of America, First Annual Report*, 1880).

His keen interest and scholarly influence led to the appointment of A. F. Bandelier in 1880 to undertake, on the part of the Archæological Institute, a survey of the archaeology and early history of the Pueblo country which continued for several years. Morgan's interest in aboriginal habitations culminated in his last work, *Houses and House-life of the American Aborigines* (1881), published shortly before his death. During his visits to Michigan in the interest of his railroad, he not only pursued his ethnological studies but, following his earlier bent concerning the manifestation of mind by the lower animals, studied the beaver, and in 1868 published *The American Beaver and His Works*, long regarded as a classic on the subject.

Morgan is described as of medium stature and well proportioned; he was energetic and active, alert in manner and cheerful in disposition; an agreeable companion, easily approached, and helpful to those in need of advice. He was an ardent adherent of the Presbyterian faith; "religion was one of his prime interests: it dominated all his researches, and he never emancipated himself from his theological background" (Stern, *Morgan, post*, p. 22). Indeed, his correspondence shows that he entertained a fear lest his ethnological work was "detrimental to the true religion" (*Social Forces*, March 1928, p. 345). He was an enthusiastic advocate of temperance and renounced the use of tobacco late in life, but did not hesitate to engage in a round of poker. He was instrumental in organizing the Section of Anthropology of the American Association for the Advancement of Science in 1875, and was its first chairman. In recognition of his ethnologic researches he was elected a member of the National Academy of Sciences in 1875, and in 1879 became president of the American Association for the Advancement of Science. Although not possessed of great wealth, he bequeathed the better part of his fortune to the University of Rochester, for female education.

[J. W. Powell in *Pop. Sci. Mo.*, Nov. 1880; J. H. McIlvaine, *The Life and Works of Lewis H. Morgan* (1882), and W. H. Holmes, in *Nat. Acad. Sci. Biog. Memoirs*, vol. VI (1909), both repr. in *Rochester Hist. Soc. Pub. Fund Ser.*, vol. II (1923); *Proc. Am. Acad. Arts and Sci.*, vol. XVII (1882); B. J. Stern, in *Social Forces*, Mar. 1928, in *Am. Anthropologist*, Apr.–July 1930, Jan. 1933, and *Lewis Henry Morgan, Social Evolutionist* (1931); N. H. Morgan, *Morgan Geneal.* (1869); *The Morgan Centennial Celebration at Wells College, Aurora* (1919); *N. Y. Tribune*, Dec. 18, 1881.]
F. W. H.

MORGAN, MATTHEW SOMERVILLE (Apr. 27, 1839–June 2, 1890), cartoonist, painter, was born in Lambeth, London, England. His parents were Matthew Morgan, an actor and music teacher, and Mary Somerville, an actress and singer. They recognized his talent at an early age and permitted him to study art under Telbin, with whom he worked for some years, afterwards painting scenery at the Drury Lane and Princess theatres in London. A natural taste for caricature, however, earned him a connection with the *Illustrated London News* as artist and correspondent. He also found time to study in Paris, Italy, and Spain. In Spain he painted a number of large water colors. In 1858 he traveled to the interior of Africa by way of Algeria, but returned to Europe in 1859 in time to report the Austro-Italian War for the *News*. His next venture was an association with Frank C. Burnand and William S. Gilbert on the staff of a publication called *Fun,* in which Morgan's best-known work, his cartoons of the American Civil War, began to appear in 1862. Some of these were published in book form, with the work of others, as *The American War, Cartoons* (1874). In 1867 he became owner and illustrator of a paper called the *Tomahawk,* which, because of his cartoons ridiculing Queen Victoria and the Prince of Wales and attacking royalty in general, found little favor in England and soon expired. As a side line he occupied the post of scene-painter to the Royal Italian Opera, Covent Garden.

Frank Leslie [*q.v.*], apparently with the intention of pushing Morgan as a rival of Thomas Nast [*q.v.*], induced him to come to America in 1870 and work on *Frank Leslie's Illustrated Newspaper*. In New York also, Morgan did scene-painting on the side for several theatre managers. In 1880 he designed the decorative stone work for the *Ledger* Building in Philadelphia and shortly after the completion of that work went to Cincinnati as manager of the Strobridge Lithographing Company. While here he founded The Matt Morgan Art Pottery Company and the Cincinnati Art Student's League. In 1887 he returned to New York and in 1888 became art editor of the new magazine, *Collier's Once a Week*. Toward the close of his life he seems to have been affected by a desire to do things on a large scale. He painted a number of panoramas of battles of the Civil War, an oil painting thirty by fifteen feet of Christ entering Jerusalem, and a background for Buffalo Bill's Wild West Show in Madison Square Garden, this last work covering 15,000 square yards of canvas. He was married early in life and had nine children by his first wife; shortly before coming to America he was married a second time, and of this union seven children were born

(*New York Tribune,* June 3, 1890). He died in New York City.

[Ralph C. Smith, *Biog. Index of Am. Artists* (1930); C. E. Clement and Laurence Hutton, *Artists of the Nineteenth Century and Their Works* (1907); Frank Weitenkampf, *Am. Graphic Art* (1924); Ulrich Thieme and Felix Becker, *Allgemeines Lexikon der Bildenden Künstler,* vol. XXV (1931); *Art Journal* (N. Y.), Mar. 1875; *N. Y. Times,* June 3, 1890.]　　R. H.

MORGAN, MORRIS HICKY (Feb. 8, 1859–Mar. 16, 1910), classicist, was born in Providence, R. I., the son of Morris Barker Morgan and his wife, Isabelle Manton. Of his ancestors, Edward Manton came from England in 1634, Evan Morgan from Wales soon after 1700, Daniel Hicky from Ireland in 1740. Edward Manton was a friend of Roger Williams and followed him to Rhode Island. Evan Morgan's son, George [*q.v.*], ancestor of Morris Hicky Morgan, commanded Fort Pitt during the Revolution. Morgan was educated at St. Mark's School, Southboro, Mass., and at Harvard, where he received the degree of A.B. in 1881 and that of Ph.D. in 1887. From 1881 to 1884 he was a tutor at St. Mark's. He gave instruction in Latin and Greek at Harvard from 1887 to 1896; from 1896 to 1899 he was professor of Latin, and from 1899 to 1910, professor of classical philology. A man of boundless and infectious energy, he was at once an inspiring teacher, a productive scholar, and an effectual administrator in many fields of academic service. His spoken as his written word was charged with a freshness and buoyancy of spirit, a peculiar vivacity and playfulness, that gave adequate expression to his vigorous personality and intellectual ability. Endowed with a fine literary taste, he treated the ancient classics as literature, not as a field for the display of mere learning. Of permanent value is his conception of the study of literature, a study which "must be based upon the understanding of three things: first, the influence of time and surroundings which led the author to write what he has written; secondly, what was the author's message to his contemporaries; thirdly, what ought to be his message to us" (*Addresses and Essays,* 1910, which book has been said to incorporate the Harvard spirit in philology).

Among his publications may be mentioned: *An Illustrated Dictionary to Xenophon's Anabasis* (1892), in conjunction with Prof. J. W. White; two translations, *The Art of Horsemanship by Xenophon* (1893) and *The Phormio of Terence* (1894); an edition of *Eight Orations of Lysias* (1895); "Remarks on the Water Supply of Ancient Rome" (*Transactions and Proceedings of the American Philological Association,* vol. XXXIII, 1902); "The First Harvard Doctors of Medicine" (*Harvard Graduates' Magazine,* June 1909); "Some Aspects of an Ancient Roman City" (*Harvard Essays on Classical Subjects,* 1912, ed. by H. W. Smyth). He edited and completed George M. Lane's *Latin Grammar for Schools and Colleges* (1898, 1903), and prepared *A School Latin Grammar* (1899) based on the longer work. He published *A Bibliography of Persius* (1909), and presented to the Harvard College Library his private collection of 660 editions and treatises on that poet. His greatest scholarly achievement was a translation of Vitruvius' Architecture (*Vitruvius, the Ten Books on Architecture,* 1914), nearly finished before his death, and completed by Professor A. A. Howard. Morgan was married at Baltimore, June 3, 1896, to Eleanora Semmes Gibson, grand-daughter of Admiral Raphael Semmes [*q.v.*] of the Confederate navy.

[*Harvard Grads.' Mag.,* June 1910; B. L. Gildersleeve, in *Am. Jour. of Philol.,* Apr., May, June 1910; *Memorial Minute of the Class of 1881* (1910); *Harvard College Class of 1881 Fiftieth Anniversary* (1931); *Classical Philology,* July 1910; *Classical Jour.,* June 1910; J. A. Morgan, *A Hist. of the Family of Morgan* (1902?); *Boston Transcript,* Mar. 16, 1910.]
H. W. S—h.

MORGAN, PHILIP HICKY (Nov. 9, 1825–Aug. 12, 1900), jurist, diplomat, son of Judge Thomas Gibbes and Eliza (McKennan) Morgan, was born in Baton Rouge, La. On his father's side, he was a descendant in the fourth generation of Evan Morgan who emigrated from Wales to Pennsylvania; on his mother's side he was a nephew of Thomas M. T. McKennan [*q.v.*] and related to Thomas McKean [*q.v.*], signer of the Declaration of Independence, later chief justice and then governor of Pennsylvania. Thomas Morgan settled in Baton Rouge early in the nineteenth century, and practised law there. Philip was educated in the public schools of that city and at Paris, France, where he laid the foundation for his great knowledge of the civil law. As a very young man he spent some time in Havana, Cuba, and there learned to speak Spanish—one of several modern languages he later commanded with ease and fluency. He returned from his Parisian law studies just in time to enter the Mexican War as first lieutenant of a Louisiana volunteer company. Upon completing this service, he was admitted to the Louisiana bar, and is said to have spent the months immediately following in helping his father annotate the civil code of the state. On May 22, 1852, he married Beatrice Leslie Ford, daughter of Judge James Ford of Baton Rouge, by whom he had five children. Soon after his marriage, he went to practise law in New Orleans, and had not

lived there long before he was elected judge of the second district court of Louisiana, which office he held for four years.

Four of his half-brothers, one of whom was James Morris Morgan [*q.v.*], served the Confederacy, but Morgan was loyal to the Union and devoted his best efforts to its preservation. At a mass meeting on Canal Street, New Orleans, on the eve of the war, he told those assembled that if they would fight the abolitionists within the Union he would fight with them, but warned them that if they fired a shot at the Stars and Stripes their slaves would be their political masters within five years. Just then a large straw man bearing a placard with the words "P. H. Morgan—Traitor" was hoisted on a nearby telegraph pole and set on fire. He is supposed to have spent the Civil War period in England, but, if he did, he returned immediately after the conclusion of hostilities. President Johnson appointed him United States district attorney for Louisiana in December 1866, but the Senate rejected the appointment, Mar. 2, 1867. The following year he was again appointed and this time the appointment was confirmed (Jan. 7, 1869). From 1873 to 1876 he was one of the judges of the state supreme court—the so-called "carpet-bag court." In 1877 he became one of the judges of the recently organized international court in Egypt, for which he was admirably fitted by reason of his linguistic ability and knowledge of foreign codes, and served for one term. While still in Egypt he was appointed envoy extraordinary and minister plenipotentiary to Mexico by President Hayes, which post he occupied from January 1880 until his successor, appointed by President Cleveland, took office early in March 1885. After he returned from Mexico he practised law in New York City until his death there. He was buried in Allegheny Cemetery, Pittsburgh, Pa.

Morgan was a man of large and powerful physique. He had the moral courage to declare his convictions and remain true to them, for which he paid the price in unpopularity. In the end conditions became such that he left the South he loved, never to return, but he accepted his exile uncomplainingly as the fortune of war.

[Information from family records, supplied by Mrs. Miriam Morgan Shepherd of Pittsburgh, Pa., and other relatives. There are numerous references in the volume by his brother, J. M. Morgan, *Recollections of a Rebel Reefer* (1917); and in Ella Lonn's *Reconstruction in La. After 1868* (1918), there is an account of his activities during Reconstruction days. See also J. A. Morgan, *A Hist. of the Family of Morgan* (1902?); *N. Y. Tribune,* Aug. 14, 1900.]
M. J. W.

MORGAN, THOMAS JEFFERSON (Aug. 17, 1839–July 13, 1902), soldier, Baptist clergyman, educator, and denominational leader, was sixth in descent from Nathan Morgan, the first of his line to emigrate to the New World. The son of Rev. Lewis Morgan and his third wife, Mary C. Causey (or Cansey), he was born in Franklin, Ind. His grandfather had been a slave-holder, but his father was an anti-slavery advo-cate and a leader in religious, political, and edu-cational matters. Thomas was fitted for college in the preparatory school of Franklin College and received the degree of A.B. from that insti-tution in 1861, though he left in his senior year to enlist in the Union army. After three months' service, he took charge of public education at Atlanta, Ill., but on Aug. 1, 1862, was appointed first lieutenant in the 70th Indiana Volunteer Infantry. His period of military service con-tinued for over three years. Prominent in the enlistment of negro troops and eloquent in their defense, he became lieutenant-colonel of the 14th United States Colored Infantry on Nov. 1, 1863, and colonel on Jan. 1, 1864. He commanded a division at the battle of Nashville and was brevetted brigadier-general, Mar. 13, 1865. Throughout his life he maintained that war is sometimes justifiable, because the Old Testa-ment teaches that it has been a means of accom-plishing holy and gracious purposes of God toward mankind; because admittedly good con-sequences have issued from war; because his-torians reckon eras from great battles, such as Tours and Waterloo; because it is necessary to repel invasion, protect the innocent, punish na-tional wrong-doing; and because it is right to engage in a struggle for national independence. He defended nationalism even while pleading for internationalism and dedicating his life to the defense of freedom of conscience.

After leaving the army he entered Rochester Theological Seminary, graduating in 1868. He was ordained a Baptist minister, at Rochester, N. Y., in 1869, but held only one brief pastorate —at Brownville, Nebr., 1871–72. From 1872 to 1874 he was president of the Nebraska Normal School at Peru; from 1874 to 1881, he taught homiletics and ecclesiastical history in the Bap-tist Union Theological Seminary, Chicago, spending several months in Germany in 1879; from 1881 to 1883 he served as principal of the New York State Normal School at Potsdam, and from 1884 to 1889, as principal of the State Normal School at Providence, R. I. In the lat-ter year, he was appointed commissioner of In-dian Affairs by President Harrison. For four years he served with zeal, energy, and good judg-ment, insisting, in spite of much political and ecclesiastical opposition, that the principle of

separation of church and state must be recog-nized in the control of Indian schools, and that they must be placed upon the same basis as pub-lic schools.

In 1893 he renewed his denominational activ-ity, accepting the position of corresponding sec-retary of the American Baptist Home Mission Society, in which position he served until his death almost a decade later. The clarity of his thought and his unswerving loyalty to his con-victions, combined with rare ability wisely to choose and judge his coworkers, made him in-valuable as an associate of Dr. Henry L. More-house [q.v.], field secretary of the society. Un-der his skilful promotion, schools for thousands of negro men and women were established and equipped. He was editor of the *Baptist Home Mission Monthly,* 1893–1902, and author of *Reminiscences of Service with Colored Troops in the Army of the Cumberland, 1863–65* (1885); *Educational Mosaics* (1887); *Students' Hymnal* (1888); *Studies in Pedagogy* (1889); *Patriotic Citizenship* (1895); *The Praise Hymnary* (1898); *The Negro in America and the Ideal American Republic* (1898). In 1870 he married Caroline Starr. Their only son died before his father.

[*Who's Who in America,* 1901–02; F. B. Heitman, *Hist. Reg. and Dict. U. S. Army* (1903); Comfort Starr, *A Hist. of the Starr Family* (1879); J. A. Mor-gan, *A Hist. of the Family of Morgan* (1902?); *Ex-aminer,* July 24, 1902; *Bapt. Commonwealth,* July 24, 1902; *N. Y. Times,* July 14, 1902.]　　C. H. M.

MORGAN, WILLIAM (Aug. 7, 1774?–1826?), Freemason, was born probably in Culpeper County, Va., served an apprenticeship as a stone-mason in Madison County, removed to a west-ern state, possibly Kentucky, returned to Orange County, Va., and then went to Richmond. It has been claimed that he fought with Jackson in the War of 1812. For all these as well as for most of the other statements about his life there seems to be no proof and many of them have been denied in the course of the bitter, long-extended controversy over the circumstances of his death. It is agreed that about 1819 he was married to Lucinda Pendleton, that in 1823 he was in Rochester, N. Y., and that shortly afterward he went to live in the neighboring town of Batavia as a brick-and-stone mason. It has been asserted that at this time he was a respectable though not distinguished member of the community and, on the other hand, that he was a drunken knave. It has been denied that he was ever properly initi-ated into Freemasonry but there is no doubt that he gained admittance to the order and took an active part in its proceedings and that, on May 31, 1825, at Leroy, N. Y., he became a Royal

Arch Mason. The next year there were rumors that he was writing a book, to be published by David C. Miller of Batavia, in order to expose the secret ritual of the Masonic order. The records of the copyright office show that on Aug. 14, 1826, he made copyright registration of the title of the book, *Illustrations of Masonry.* That summer he was several times sued and imprisoned for small debts. On Sept. 11, arrested on a charge of petty theft, he was taken to Canandaigua to answer the charge. From that place he never returned, and of him there has never appeared any authentic trace. A body found a short time afterward near Oak Orchard, N. Y., was with equal show of probability declared to be that of William Morgan and to be that of one Timothy Munro. For a generation after his disappearance there sprang up various rumors of his existence in many parts of the world, as a merchant in Smyrna, an Indian chief in the Rocky Mountains, a pirate hanged in Havana, a hermit in northern Canada, and a professed Mohammedan on the shores of the Mediterranean.

His disappearance caused great excitement. It was freely charged that the Masons had murdered him in order to prevent the publication of the book he was believed to be writing on Masonic secrets. These charges were uniformly denied by Masons in good standing, and the claim was brought forward that he had disappeared of his own will. Gov. DeWitt Clinton, a high officer in the Masonic organization, offered a reward of $1,000 for his discovery, if alive, and $2,000 for the discovery and conviction of his murderers, if he were dead. Committees were organized by each faction to procure evidence in the matter. Later indictment and trial of several persons failed to reveal the facts. In the autumn of 1826, probably in October, was published the first edition of the *Illustrations of Masonry.* Of this book the Masons said, variously, that it was merely plagiarized from *Jachin and Boaz,* published in London in 1762, that it was actually the work of David C. Miller who corrected and rewrote Morgan's illiterate manuscript, and that it was unimportant since the true secret of Masonry was the development of the spirit rather than the outward form of a ritual. On the other hand, a group of men who had been Masons met to declare solemnly that it was true revelation of Masonic practice. The book was pirated, translated into several European languages, and sold widely. Almost at once the affair assumed a political aspect, furnishing the occasion for the organization of existing objections to all kinds of secret societies and for the rise of the Anti-

Masonic party in which various factors played a part and in which the fate of William Morgan soon lost its importance.

[Of the great number of books and pamphlets on the subject, a collection is in the State Hist. Lib. of Wis.; records of the copyright office are in the Lib. of Cong.; among the partisan accounts are Henry Brown, *A Narrative of the Anti-Masonick Excitement* (1829); Rob Morris, *Wm. Morgan* (1883); P. C. Huntington, *The True Hist. . . . of Wm. Morgan* (1886); S. U. Mock, *The Morgan Episode* (1930); David Bernard, *Light on Free Masonry* (copr. 1858); S. D. Greene, *The Broken Seal* (1870). For bibliography see Charles McCarthy, "The Antimasonic Party," *Am. Hist. Asso. Report . . . 1902,* vol. I (1903), which, however, does not discuss the Morgan episode.]   K. E. C.

MORIARITY, PATRICK EUGENE (July 4, 1804–July 10, 1875), Augustinian superior and preacher, was born, apparently, of well-to-do parents, who resided in Mount Joy Place, Dublin, Ireland. His early instruction was received at the Augustinian convent at Callan, and at Carlow College, where he came under the influence of the Rev. James Warren Doyle, the famous Irish patriot-bishop and publicist ("J. K. L."). At the age of sixteen he joined the order of the Hermits of St. Augustine, and later studied philosophy and theology in the Augustinian colleges at Lucca and Perugia, and finally in Rome, where he was ordained Jan. 28, 1828. For some years he served as a missionary preacher in Ireland, in France at the invitation of Cardinal Cheverus [*q.v.*], from whom he learned of America at first hand, and in Portugal. In 1834 he volunteered for the East Indian missions and was sent as a secretary and vicar-general of Bishop O'Connor of Madras, where he served as chaplain to the British forces and assisted in establishing the *Madras Expositor,* a journal of wide influence. Returning to Rome in 1839, he was awarded a doctorate in divinity by Pope Gregory XVI. Almost immediately he was commissioned by his general to go to America as superior or commissary of the Augustinian missions.

Moriarity had hardly landed in Philadelphia (July 4, 1839), when, as pastor of St. Augustine's Church, he became a temperance reformer and established St. Augustine's Catholic Total Abstinence Society (June 28, 1840), one of the first associations of its kind. Two months later, he instituted the Catholic Temperance Beneficial Society of Philadelphia. A suave gentleman of poise and sturdy physique, a linguist, a cosmopolitan, a raconteur, an eloquent preacher, and a fiery orator, Moriarity became the leading priest of the diocese. He preached everywhere throughout the East for charity-benefits, at ordinations, at temperance meetings, and at corner-stone ceremonies. In 1842 he founded Villa-nova College, just outside of Philadelphia. In 1850 and 1851 he aided in founding manual train-ing schools for orphans at Villanova and at Govanstown, Md. Popular with non-Catholic audiences, he was a frequent lecturer before the Athenian Institute and Mercantile Library Com-pany. Away on a speaking tour in South Caro-lina when his church and library were fired by a nativist mob (1844), Moriarity, on his return, did not hesitate to attack nativism and intoler-ance in a bitter sermon which worried the less bold Bishop F. P. Kenrick [q.v.], who feared that resentment on the part of the natives would prejudice the suit for damages. On behalf of St. Augustine's, he appealed for aid in Lyons, and in Ireland (*Catholic Directory*, Dublin, 1845), where he was stationed for a few years. In 1847 he was assistant-general of the order. Three years later, he was back in the United States as pastor of St. Augustine's, as commissary-gen-eral of the Augustinians (1851–57), and as pro-fessor of sacred eloquence in the seminary at Villanova, of which he became president in 1854. In 1855 he built Our Lady of Consolation Church at Chestnut Hill, where he was officially sta-tioned until his death. He inaugurated the Au-gustinian mission at Lansingburg, N. Y., aided the Sisters of St. Joseph in establishing their mother house in his parish (1858), attended the Councils of Baltimore, compiled a *Life of St. Augustine, Bishop, Confessor, and Doctor of the Church* (1873), and wrote a number of articles for the press, including a series in the *Catholic Record* on the "Marks of the Church" and "Let-ters to a Protestant Friend." As a church-build-er and organizer, he was not a success. In busi-ness, he remained unsophisticated, nor was he a collector of money save for charity. A fervid supporter of the Irish cause, he was not opposed to Fenianism, which Bishop J. E. Wood [q.v.] condemned. Advertised to deliver an address in the Academy of Music (May 23, 1864) on "What Right has England to rule Ireland?", Moriarity gave the lecture despite the inhibition of the bishop. Thousands heard him and many thousand copies of the address were sold for the relief of a parish in the West of Ireland. Wood disciplined Moriarity by withdrawing his facul-ties; these were restored a few months later, however, on his submission of a letter of self-humiliation and an apology from the altar steps to a congregation whose sympathy was with the pastor. His last public appearance was in a se-ries of public lectures in refutation of addresses delivered in Philadelphia by the English his-torian Froude.

[*Sadliers' Cath. Directory*, 1876, p. 57; items in *Am. Cath. Hist. Researches*, Jan. 1891, Apr. 1896, Oct. 1902; *Records of the Am. Cath. Hist. Soc.*, esp. vols. I (1887), 201 f., XII (1901), 139 f., 263 f., 387 f.; *Boston Pilot*, Oct. 24, 1857; F. E. Tourscher, *The Kenrick-Frenaye Correspondence* (1920); T. C. Middleton, *Hist. Sketch of the Augustinian Monastery, College, and Mission of St. Thomas of Villanova* (1893); *Phila. Inquirer*, July 12, 14, 1875; *Cath. Record*, Oct. 1875; *N. Y. Freeman's Jour.*, July 17, 1875.]   R.J.P.

MORINI, AUSTIN JOHN (Mar. 4, 1826–July 29, 1909), Catholic ecclesiastic, son of Paul and Anna (Bartolini) Morini, was born in Flor-ence, Italy. Trained in this cultural, religious center, the boy studied in its art galleries and worshiped at the Annuziata chapel. On June 2, 1844, he entered the Servite Order at its origi-nal novitiate of Monte Senario. Six years later he made his solemn profession and was ordained, May 1, 1850. After necessary training, he took charge of the students in humanities and rhetoric at the Annuziata, where his work won him a doctorate in divinity (1856). From 1864 to 1870, he served in England. Here he established his order, founded churches, and won the con-fidence of Cardinal Manning, who counseled with him on matters of discipline and theology. At the Vatican Council, the Servites were in-vited by Bishop Joseph Melchior of Green Bay, Wis., to establish a foundation in his diocese, and Morini was sent with a group of religious to the United States (July 1870).

He took charge of a congregation at Menasha, Wis., and four years later, on the invitation of Bishop Thomas Foley, established Our Lady of Sorrows Church in Chicago as a mother house. Subsequently, the Servites entered a half dozen dioceses. In the midst of parochial duties, Mo-rini gave missions and retreats and acted as vicar-general of the order. In 1884 he attended the Third Plenary Council of Baltimore, and four years later retired to Rome as one of the general consultors whose chief interest was in the work of the order in England and in the United States. Here he was honored with the privileges of an ex-general until his death at the convent of San-ta Maria in Via. A solid student who gave con-siderable time to researches in ecclesiastical history and doctrine, Morini wrote a number of articles for American and foreign Catholic peri-odicals and published *Poems in Honor of St. Philip Benizi* (1885), *Historical Essays on the Seven Holy Founders and Their Times* (1888), and *The Origin of Devotion to Our Lady of Sor-rows* (1893).

[A. T. Andreas, *Hist. of Chicago*, vol. III (1886); *Golden Jubilee, Our Lady of Sorrows Church, Chicago* (1924); annual Catholic directories; materials in the archives of the Ordo Servorum Beatae Mariae Vir-ginis, through the courtesy of the Am. provincial, Rev. J. Mulherin, O.S.M.]   R.J.P.

MORISON, GEORGE SHATTUCK (Dec. 19, 1842–July 1, 1903), bridge engineer, was born in New Bedford, Mass., the son of the Rev. John Hopkins and Emily (Rogers) Morison and a descendant of John Morison and his son Thomas who settled in Londonderry, N. H., in 1719. He was educated at Phillips Exeter Academy and at Harvard, where he received the degrees of A.B. in 1863 and LL.B. in 1866, was admitted to the New York bar, and became associated with the great law firm of Evarts, Southmayd & Choate. After a year of practice, however, he abandoned the legal career in which he was so well launched to enter the profession of civil engineering, for which he had no special training nor any advantageous connections to assist him. To offset these handicaps he brought to his new profession a mature and disciplined mind, exceptional mathematical talents and training, and a large degree of native constructive genius. His first work was on the construction of a large bridge over the Missouri River at Kansas City, under the direction of Octave Chanute [*q.v.*], a noted engineer (see Chanute and Morison, *The Kansas City Bridge,* 1870). In 1873, when Chanute became chief engineer of the Erie Railroad, Morison was chosen his principal assistant. In this position he soon acquired a wide experience in railway bridge construction, since the Erie was then replacing many of its old wooden bridges with metal structures.

Leaving the Erie in 1875, he became consulting expert on railway properties to the American agents of Baring Brothers, London. He also organized the firm of Morison, Field & Company, New York, bridge contractors, but in 1880 withdrew from the contracting firm and devoted his attention for the next fourteen years to consulting practice. He built in rapid succession more than a score of great railroad bridges: over the Missouri (at Bismarck, Sioux City, Blair, Omaha, Rulo, Nebraska City, Atchison, Leavenworth, and Bellefontaine Bluffs), over the Mississippi (at Winona, Burlington, Alton, St. Louis, and Memphis), one over the Ohio at Cairo, two over the Snake River and one over the Columbia River in Washington, one over the Willamette at Portland, Ore., one over the St. John's at Jacksonville, Fla., and many smaller bridges in all parts of the United States. Considering the magnitude and difficulty of most of the projects, this record stands unrivaled in the history of bridge construction. The Missouri River was regarded as the most treacherous stream in the country to bridge, and little precedent existed for such work. The perfection of methods for handling the pneumatic founda-

tion work involved in these projects was one of Morison's most notable achievements. This period also marked the transition from wrought iron to steel in bridge construction, and Morison was the great pioneer in the use of the latter metal. The Memphis bridge, the longest truss span in America when completed, practically set the standard for later steel bridge specifications.

During the last decade of his life Morison acted on commissions reporting on the Manhattan Bridge over the East River and the proposed bridge over the Hudson in New York City, as well as on a proposed bridge over the Detroit River—the last two colossal projects not realized until some forty years later. Though primarily a bridge engineer, he was also an expert on railway management and remained a valued consultant to Baring Brothers and other financial houses throughout his career. He was a member of the Isthmian Canal Commission, 1899–1901, and his powerful advocacy of the Panama route, backed as it was by an exhaustive study of the situation, proved an important factor in bringing about the final decision.

At the time of his death he stood at the very pinnacle of the engineering profession. He was regarded as the leading bridge engineer in America, perhaps in the world, and had an international reputation as an expert in railways and waterways. Gifted with a superb physical and intellectual endowment, a prodigious capacity for work, and an indomitable will, he supplemented his exceptional education by life-long habits of scholarship. He amassed a considerable fortune, never married, and was able to indulge to the full his love of travel. He observed keenly, read widely, and thought profoundly. Considering his scholarly bent, his professional publications are few. The most important include: "The River Piers of the Memphis Bridge," which won the Telford Medal of the British Institution of Civil Engineers (*Minutes of Proceedings,* vol. CXIV, 1893); "The Continuous Superstructure of the Memphis Bridge" (*Transactions of the American Society of Civil Engineers,* September 1893); "Suspension Bridges—A Study" (*Ibid.,* December 1896). In June 1895 he delivered the presidential address before the American Society of Civil Engineers. Toward the close of his life he prepared a small volume, published posthumously under the title: *The New Epoch as Developed by the Manufacture of Power* (1903), which presents the essentials of his social and economic philosophy. Though little known, it is a most original and carefully reasoned piece of work.

It was an unfortunate fact that with all his

rare talents, high character, and professional eminence, Morison was intensely unpopular with many of his colleagues. The very abundance of his powers made him somewhat arrogant and intolerant of the opinions of less gifted men; he usually arrived at any conclusion only after an exhaustive study of all the facts, and once his decision was made, he was inclined to enforce it with a tenacity and ruthlessness that bore down all opposition but, even when he was right, did not endear him to those holding different opinions.

[G. S., R. S., and Mary Morison, *John Hopkins Morison: A Memoir* (1897); L. A. Morison, *The Hist. of the Morison or Morrison Family* (1880); *Report of the Secretary of the Class of 1863 of Harvard College*, 1888, 1893, 1903; *Trans. Am. Soc. Civil Engineers*, vol. LIV (1905); *Who's Who in America*, 1901–02; *N. Y. Tribune*, July 3, 1903; recollections of personal acquaintances.]					J. I. P.

MORLEY, EDWARD WILLIAMS (Jan. 29, 1838–Feb. 24, 1923), chemist, physicist, was born in Newark, N. J., the son of Sardis Brewster and Anna Clarissa (Treat) Morley. Both parents were of good New England stock; the father was a Congregational minister and the mother had been a teacher under Catharine E. Beecher [*q.v.*]. The family lived at Hartford, Conn., and Attleboro, Mass., during most of Edward's childhood. Since Edward, though precocious, was very frail, his early education was acquired at home under the tutelage of his father. He could read at three years of age, began the study of Latin at six, and read Greek at eleven. His bent toward science soon became evident, for he found among his father's books a small volume entitled *Conversations in Chemistry* which he read with more interest than the *Arabian Nights*. When fourteen years of age he acquired a copy of Benjamin Silliman's newly published textbook on chemistry, and absorbed its contents so thoroughly that he found nothing new in his first course in chemistry in college. He entered Williams College as a sophomore in 1857 and graduated in 1860. In those days the science of astronomy was much better developed than that of chemistry and besides offered a field for exact measurement, in which young Morley already took an interest. He therefore stayed on at Williams for a year after graduation, working in astronomy under Prof. Albert Hopkins. During this year he mounted a transit instrument, constructed a chronograph, and made the first accurate determination of the latitude of the college observatory, which last achievement was the subject of his first scientific paper, read before the American Association for the Advancement of Science in January 1865 (*Proceedings*, vol. VI, 1866).

In accordance with a strong family tradition, he decided to become a minister and spent the years 1861–64 at Andover Theological Seminary. After graduation his health was so poor that he felt he ought not to enter the active ministry, but instead spent the year 1864–65 in the service of the United States Sanitary Commission in charge of the station at Fortress Monroe. During the next few years he taught in a private school at Marlboro, Mass. About this time, his health having improved, he was offered the pastorate of the church at Twinsburg, Ohio. Before really settling there, however, he accepted the professorship of natural history and chemistry at Western Reserve College, Hudson, Ohio (removed in 1882 to Cleveland as Adelbert College of Western Reserve University). He took up his duties in Hudson in January 1869, and just before moving thither married Isabella Ashley Birdsall of West Winsted, Conn. They had no children.

In 1878 he became interested in studying the variation of the oxygen content of the atmosphere, and in 1880 he determined the proportion of this element in the air on 110 consecutive days, for the purpose of accumulating data bearing on the so-called Loomis-Morley hypothesis. According to this hypothesis, there is a deficiency of oxygen at times of high atmospheric pressure, because downward currents bring air from high altitudes to the surface of the earth; and the results of Morley's measurements showed that this theory agreed fairly well with the facts. From 1883 to 1894 he was engaged on his *magnum opus,* a study of the densities of oxygen and hydrogen and the ratio in which they combine to form water. It was published in 1895 as No. 980 of the *Smithsonian Contributions to Knowledge,* and in shorter form in some of the chemical journals. During this same period Morley was collaborating with A. A. Michelson [*q.v.*] in developing the interferometer, an instrument for measuring lengths in terms of the wave length of light, which device they used in attempting to determine the motion of the earth with reference to the luminiferous ether. These experiments, of fundamental importance to modern physics, were later continued with the cooperation of Prof. Dayton C. Miller. With the latter, Morley also determined the velocity of light in a magnetic field and studied the thermal expansion of air, nitrogen, oxygen, and carbon dioxide. For these last experiments he devised a new form of manometer by which differences of gaseous pressure as small as 1/10,000 millimeter of mercury could be measured. He also was engaged in other researches on the expansion of metallic bars, the conduction of heat through water vapor, the relative efficiency of various drying agents, and the vapor tension of mercury. All of his research work was characterized by great ingenuity in devising and constructing apparatus and by his ability to make precise and accurate measurements. He received honorary degrees from many institutions and was awarded the Sir Humphry Davy Medal by the Royal Society of London in 1907, the Elliot Cresson Medal of the Franklin Institute, 1912, and the Willard Gibbs Medal from the Chicago Section of the American Chemical Society in 1917. He was president of the American Association for the Advancement of Science in 1895 and of the American Chemical Society in 1899. He published or read fifty-five scientific papers. In 1906 he retired from active work, and spent his declining years in West Hartford, Conn.

[Biographical notes and letters left by Morley and reports to the secretary of his class, Williams College; F. W. Clarke, in *Jour. Chem. Soc. of London, Trans.*, vol. CXXIII, pt. 2 (1923), and Memoirs Nat. Acad. Sci., vol. XXI (1926), with bibliog.; O. F. Tower in *Science*, Apr. 13, 1923, the *Jour. Am. Chem. Soc.*, June 1923, and *Bull. Western Reserve Univ.*, 1923, with bibliog.; *Hartford Times*, Feb. 24, 1923.] O. F. T.

MORLEY, MARGARET WARNER (Feb. 17, 1858–Dec. 12, 1923), educator, author, daughter of Isaac and Sarah Robinson (Warner) Morley, was born in Montrose, Iowa. The family removed to Brooklyn, N. Y., and there Margaret attended the public schools, the curricula of which were supplemented by private instruction. Her more advanced education was received at the Oswego, N. Y., Normal School and the New York City Normal College, from which she was graduated in 1878. Becoming interested in biology, she carried on special studies in that subject at Armour Institute, Chicago, and at the Woods Hole, Mass., marine laboratories. As a teacher she naturally found her way into normal schools and held positions in the Oswego and Milwaukee, Wis., State Normal Schools, as well as in the high school at Leavenworth, Kan. Later she was instructor in biology at Armour Institute and in the Free Kindergarten Association Training Class of Chicago. She also lectured on popular nature studies in Boston.

In connection with courses prepared for her classes, she began to gather material for books on the life of birds, insects, and small animals and it is as a writer she did her most important work. Coming at a time when nature study was being established as a definite part of gradeschool courses, her books had something of pioneer importance. In addition to their specific information, given in conversational form, they teach non-pedantic lessons of kindness to animals, tree and flower conservation, and the value of agriculture to industry and commerce, as well as in its primary support of all life. Those of her books written for the purpose of teaching children and young people the facts of sex and birth shocked many in the nineties but in comparison with the frankness of later writings on the subject they seem somewhat vague and sentimental. Her most important books of this type are: *A Song of Life* (1891); *Life and Love* (1895), a book for older children; *The Renewal of Life; How and When to Tell the Story to the Young* (1906); and *The Spark of Life; the Story of How Living Things Come into the World, as Told for Girls and Boys* (1913), which was designed for parents to read to young children. The last has an occasional religious note and teaches the importance of heredity and environment. Some of her most popular nature-study books are: *Seed Babies* (1896), botany for small children; *Flowers and their Friends* (1897); *The Honey Makers* (1899); *Little Wanderers* (1899), descriptions of plants for children; *Down North and Up Along* (1900), travels in Nova Scotia and Cape Breton, with good atmosphere and word pictures of the inhabitants and their customs; *Wasps and their Ways* (1900); *The Insect Folk* (1903); *Little Mitchell; the Story of a Mountain Squirrel* (1904); *Butterflies and Bees; the Insect Folk*, vol. II (1905); *Donkey John of the Toy Valley* (1909), the result of a visit to the Austrian Tyrol; *The Carolina Mountains* (1913), a rhapsody and a super-guide-book to her much loved North Carolina; *Will-o'-the-Wasps* (1913); and *The Apple-Tree Sprite* (1915). Margaret Morley loved out-door life and spent some months of each year in Tryon, N. C., where she observed for herself the growth of plants and the habits of animals. She often carried a pet squirrel in her pocket, which gave her the material for *Little Mitchell*. She died at Garfield Memorial Hospital, Washington, D. C., following an operation.

[*Who's Who in America*, 1922–23; *Woman's Who's Who of America*, 1914–15; *New Internat. Year Book*, 1923; Margaret W. Morley, "Nature Study and its Influence," *Outlook*, July 27, 1901; the *Evening Star* (Wash., D. C.), Dec. 13, 1923; *N. Y. Times*, Dec. 15, 1923.] S. G. B.

MORPHY, PAUL CHARLES (June 22, 1837–July 10, 1884), chess player, was born in New Orleans, the son of Alonzo Morphy, a distinguished member of the Louisiana bar, and his wife, Thelcide Louise Le Carpentier. The paternal grandfather was a native of Spain, possibly a descendant of an Irish *émigré* named Murphy. The mother's family was French, having come to New Orleans from Santo Domingo. At the age of ten Morphy was taught to play chess by his grandfathers. At the age of twelve he was recognized as the strongest player in New Orleans. In May 1850 he contested three games in New Orleans with the famous Hungarian expert, J. J. Löwenthal, winning two and drawing one. He prepared for college at the Jefferson Academy in New Orleans, entered Spring Hill College, Alabama, in December 1850, and graduated with honor in 1854. He continued there until October 1855, studying chiefly law and mathematics, then attended the law school of the University of Louisiana, graduating in April 1857 and being admitted to practice as soon as he should become of legal age. In early life he acquired a fluent command of French, Spanish, and German.

By urgent solicitation of the Committee of Management he was induced to participate in the first American Chess Congress, meeting at New York City in the fall of 1857. His overwhelming success here and his later games with American experts gave him immediate recognition as the foremost American player. A description of his playing at this time appeared in *Frank Leslie's Illustrated Newspaper* (Oct. 31, 1857): "Mr. Morphy is a most fascinating player for those looking on. . . . His attention is not by any means riveted on the game, and he makes his moves with a speed approaching rapidity. Knights are thrown away and bishops left carelessly *en prise*, but the young general has certain victory in his eye; and when his antagonist perchance thinks he can at last win one game . . . Morphy quietly suggests that mate may be given in five, six, or seven moves." An enthusiastic reception awaited him upon his return to New Orleans at the end of 1857. There he began seriously blindfold play, achieving six games.

In June 1858 he sailed for England, being desirous of testing his strength against Howard Staunton, the foremost English player and writer on chess, who had refused an earlier challenge, and other European experts. As Staunton again declined to play, a match was arranged with J. J. Löwenthal who had recently defeated Staunton in a tournament. Morphy won with nine to three and two drawn games. At a congress in Birmingham, England, he played eight games blindfold against first-rate players, winning six, losing one, and drawing one, a feat which he repeated with great success in Paris and again in England. In Paris, matches were arranged with Harrwitz, Mongredien, and Anderssen, the greatest European expert, all of which Morphy won decisively.

In April 1859 he sailed via England for New York, acclaimed as the recognized champion of the world and as an unparalleled chess genius. Receptions and gifts were showered upon him to his evident embarrassment. His public utterances at this time reveal the natural conflict between his passion for chess and the desire of a well-trained, gifted student for a normal career to satisfy personal and family ambitions. Possibly today Morphy's national prominence would have furthered his personal ambitions in law, but at that time in New Orleans there was no proper opening for him. This conflict, doubtless combined with some personal financial reverses and the general upheaval of the Civil War, proved disastrous to him. Considering chess primarily an amusement and wishing to please his devoted mother, who opposed his playing, Morphy never thought seriously of the game as offering a career, nor accepted compensation for his chess activities. During his stay in New York he formed an editorial connection with the *Chess Monthly*. D. W. Fiske [*q.v.*] has noted (manuscript letters to Seguin, John G. White Collection, Cleveland Public Library) that Morphy annotated hundreds of games and "made frequent suggestions as to the matter of the Chess Monthly which were generally adopted." In 1860, however, he withdrew his name as an editor of the *Chess Monthly* and terminated his connection with the *New York Ledger,* in which he had conducted a column since August 1859.

During 1861 his efforts to launch a legal career in New Orleans failed. During the years 1862 to 1864 he visited Havana and Paris, playing chess privately but, in view of the war, properly avoiding any matches or public performances. Upon his return to New Orleans he became involved in an unfortunate quarrel with the executor of his father's estate. Only occasional games, largely at odds with his friend Charles A. de Maurian, are recorded after 1864, the final recorded game being played in 1869. In 1867 he visited Paris, but apparently played no chess. He continued to live at his home in New Orleans with his mother. He undoubtedly suffered some mental disturbance accounted for by the conflict mentioned above and possibly by a disappointment in love. As late as 1875, however, he apparently gave serious consideration to the invitation to play in the Congress of the Centennial Exhibition at Philadelphia. In 1882, in connection with a projected biographical work on men of Louisiana, he wrote a long letter to the *New Orleans Bee* urging the superior achievements of his father and grandfather as compared with his own achievements in chess. He was short and slight of stature, with dark eyes and hair, careful in dress, and distinguished in appearance and bearing. His speech and his manner marked him as a cultured gentleman. He died, unmarried, at his home in New Orleans. He is universally recognized as the greatest chess genius of history.

[D. W. Fiske, *The Book of the First American Chess Congress* (1859); C. A. Buck, *Paul Morphy* (1902); Regina Morphy-Voitier, *Life of Paul Morphy* (1926); L. A. Morphy, *Poems and Prose Sketches, with a Biog. Memoir of Paul Charles Morphy* (1921); J. J. Löwenthal, *Morphy's Games of Chess* (1860), with a brief preface by Morphy; Max Lange, *Paul Morphy* (3rd ed., Leipzig, 1894); F. M. Edge, *The Exploits and Triumphs, in Europe, of Paul Morphy* (1859); P. W. Sergeant, *Morphy Gleanings* (1932); *Times-Democrat* (New Orleans), July 11, 1884; *Chess Monthly* (N. Y.), 1857-60.]   L. C. K.

MORRELL, BENJAMIN (July 5, 1795–1839), sealing captain and explorer, was born in Rye, N. Y., the son of Benjamin Morrell. His father, a ship-builder, removed his family to Stonington, Conn., when Benjamin was less than one year old. After a childhood of ill health and with only a village-school education, the boy ran away to sea at the age of sixteen (March 1812). Sailing from New York on the ship *Enterprise* under Capt. Alexander Cartwright, with a cargo of contraband provisions for Spain, he reached Cadiz in the midst of a heavy bombardment by the French. On the return voyage the ship was captured by a British sloop and Morrell and the rest of the crew were held in prison at St. John's, Newfoundland, for eight months. After reaching home, he joined the crew of the American privateer, *Joel Barlow*, in May 1813, but it was captured in the following July and Morrell was confined at Dartmoor prison until May 1815. He made a number of deep-sea voyages, always before the mast, since his education did not fit him to be an officer, until he shipped on the *Edward* of New York under Capt. Josiah Macy [*q.v.*], who conceived a deep interest in the young man, taught him navigation and promoted him as rapidly as was fitting, until he became master of his own ship.

Morrell thereupon commenced a series of sealing voyages into the South Seas, in the *Wasp* (1822–24), the *Tartar* (1824–26), and the *Antarctic* (1828–29, 1829–31), and it is upon his written narrative of these voyages that his reputation rests (*A Narrative of Four Voyages to the South Sea,* 1832). The South Seas at this period were little known. According to Morrell's account he was the first American sea-captain to penetrate the Antarctic circle. He reached 70° south which had been surpassed in that period only by Cook (71°) and Weddell (74° 15'). Both of these latter were for ex-

ploration, not commercial ventures. His voyages were made in typical sealers' small topsail schooners, the largest being the *Antarctic* of 175 tons. His voyages were combined with trading and the search for new sealing grounds and it is mainly the variety of his experience with the South Sea natives, many of whom saw white men for the first time with his arrival, that makes his book of interest. Presumably he was on the lookout for pearls. He also describes the building of drying sheds for *bêche-de-mer* and mentions other ventures which show that he was alert for any avenue of profit. His voyages averaged about 6,500 fur-seal skins.

Morrell married first in 1819. Upon his return from his first voyage as master, in June 1824, he found that his wife and two children had died. Before sailing on his second voyage he was married to a cousin barely fifteen years of age, named Abby Jane Wood. His wife accompanied him on his fourth voyage and in 1833 published a *Narrative* of the journey. It would appear that a number of the discoveries Morrell claimed were already known and possibly charted. Nevertheless, he gave a vivid first-hand description of certain parts of the South Seas that was the best obtainable information of his day. Nothing can be said for his literary style; there is much extraneous matter, and many of his conclusions are untenable. Morrell's later journeys included a voyage to the islands of the Pacific on the *Margaret Oakley,* which, according to rumor, he pirated, and which was wrecked at Madagascar. After further wanderings he died of a fever at Mozambique.

[In addition to Morrell's *Narrative of Four Voyages* and his wife's *Narrative of a Voyage . . . 1829, 1830, 1831,* see T. J. Jacobs, *Scenes, Incidents, and Adventures in the Pacific Ocean, . . . under Capt. Benj. Morrell* (1844); the *Am. Quart. Rev.,* June 1833; the *Monthly Rev.* (London), Oct. 1833; and the first census of the United States, 1790.]   C. W. A.

MORRIL, DAVID LAWRENCE (June 10, 1772–Jan. 28, 1849), clergyman, physician, United States senator, and governor of New Hampshire, was born at Epping, N. H., where his father, Samuel Morril, a Harvard graduate and a Congregational minister, had settled and married Anna, daughter of David Lawrence. He studied with his paternal grandfather, Isaac Morril, a Congregational minister at Wilmington, Mass., and went to Exeter Academy. He then studied medicine and began to practise at Epsom, N. H., when only twenty-one. Seven years later, as the result of a religious experience, he commenced to study for the ministry under the Rev. Jesse Remington, of Candia, and in 1802 he became pastor of a church at Goffstown, formed by a union of Presbyterians and Congregationalists. Owing partly to ill-health and partly to difficulties in the church, Morril ended his active ministry in November 1809, and his relations with the parish were formally severed in July 1811. During his years as a minister he had not entirely given up medicine. He had also served as town moderator (1808–14), justice of the peace (1808, and frequently thereafter), and as representative in the state legislature (1808–17). After resigning his pastorate he continued the practice of medicine but became more and more active in politics. In 1816 he was chosen speaker of the state House of Representatives and in the same year was elected for a six-year term in the United States Senate. Here he proved himself a ready speaker, advocating measures for preventing the illegal African slave-trade, opposing the requirement of state enforcement of the federal fugitive-slave laws (though declaring he had "no disposition to deprive slave-holders of that species of property"), and vigorously disapproving the Missouri Compromise. He spoke eloquently, if somewhat sentimentally, in favor of pensions for Revolutionary officers, opposed reimbursing Matthew Lyon for the fine exacted under the Sedition Act, and moved to dismiss from the army and navy, officers who had engaged in dueling.

During his term at Washington Morril and William Hale were both nominated (1820) for governor of New Hampshire against Samuel Bell, but Governor Bell swept the state. When his term as senator expired, however, Morril was immediately elected to the Senate of New Hampshire and was chosen president of that body in June 1823. The next year he was nominated again for governor by the "Adams men," or "old guard" of the Democratic-Republicans, in opposition to the incumbent, Levi Woodbury, who had been elected the preceding year by the "insurgents." Neither candidate received a majority of votes cast, but Morril, having a plurality of more than 3,000, was chosen by the legislature. His reëlection the following year was practically unanimous, 30,167 votes being cast for him out of a total of 30,770. In 1825 he had the honor of receiving Lafayette when the latter visited Concord. The following year he was elected governor for a third time, at the expiration of which tenure he retired to private life. He changed his residence in 1831 from Goffstown to Concord, where during his remaining years he was chiefly engaged in religious activities. He served as a vice-president of the American Bible Society, the Sunday-School

Union, and the Home Missionary Society, and for two years was editor of a religious paper, the *New Hampshire Observer*. Still active within ten days of his death, he died at Concord in his seventy-seventh year.

Morril was an unusual combination of the student and active man of affairs. Medicine, theology, and politics all interested him, and he continued his studies and activities in all three till almost the end of his life. He was strongly Calvinistic in religion, and a stanch, but not violent, anti-Federalist in politics. His intelligence, ability as a speaker, and knowledge of public affairs drew him naturally into political life and made him a popular candidate for office. He seems to have spent his last years in comparative leisure and retirement. He married first, Sept. 25, 1794, Jane Wallace of Epsom, who died Dec. 14, 1823, without children. On Aug. 3, 1824, he married Lydia Poore, of Goffstown, by whom he had four sons, three of whom survived him.

[See Nathaniel Bouton, *Hist. of Concord* (1856); E. S. Stackpole, *Hist. of N. H.* (1916), vol. III; G. P. Hadley, *Hist. of the Town of Goffstown, 1733–1920* (2 vols., 1922–24); and A. M. Smith, *Morrill Kindred in America* (2 vols., 1914–31). Hadley reproduces a portrait of Morril which is in the State House at Concord. The *New-Eng. Hist. and Geneal. Reg.*, Apr. 1849, gives a sketch of his life based on the best contemporary newspaper account, in the Concord *Democrat and Freeman*, Feb. 1, 1849. There is a brief account of him in the *Biog. Dir. Am. Cong.* (1928) and in N. F. Carter, *The Native Ministry of N. H.* (1906).]

E. V. M.

MORRILL, ANSON PEASLEE (June 10, 1803–July 4, 1887), governor of Maine and congressman, the son of Peaslee and Nancy (Macomber) Morrill and the descendant of John Morrill who was living at Kittery, Me., as early as 1668, was born in Belgrade, Kennebec County, Me. He had the advantages only of a common-school education, working during his spare time in a mill where corn was ground, wood sawed, and wool carded. At one time he taught school at Miramichi, New Brunswick, Canada. In early manhood he became the postmaster at Dearborn in Kennebec County, keeping at the same time a general store. Still a store-keeper, he was later postmaster at North Belgrade, and he lived for some time at Madison. In 1827 he was married to Rowena M. Richardson, who died in 1882. His great business opportunity came in 1844 when he was asked to take charge of a woolen-mill in Readfield, then on the verge of bankruptcy. Here his exceptional talents became evident. Putting the mill on a paying basis, he eventually became the owner of the factory and laid the foundations of a comfortable fortune. His political career began in 1834, when he served a term in the state legislature. He was sheriff of Somerset County in 1839 but lost this office in 1840, when Maine elected the Whig state and national ticket. In 1841 he refused reappointment from the newly elected Democratic governor. From 1850 to 1853 he was land agent of the state.

When the two questions, temperance and slavery, broke the unity of the Democrats in Maine, with considerable courage he led a bolting faction of the Democrats in 1853 on the temperance issue. His supporters were known as "Morrill Democrats," and as an independent candidate for the governorship he ran third. The following year, 1854, the Whigs and the Freesoilers joined the temperance forces to give him a vote of about 44,000 against 28,000 for his opponent, Albion K. Parris. Since, however, there were four candidates he did not have a majority of the votes cast and the legislature chose him when it met the next January. The fusion party that elected him governor took the name Republican for the first time in Maine on Aug. 7, 1854 (see W. F. P. Fogg, *The Republican Party . . . with the History of its Formation in Maine*, 1884). In the election of 1855 he again had a popular plurality, but the same Senate that elected his brother, Lot Myrick Morrill [*q.v.*], its president, appointed his Democratic opponent, Samuel Wells, governor. He was a delegate to the Republican National Convention of 1856. Elected to Congress in 1860, he served from 1861 to 1863 but declined reëlection, preferring to make way for the election of James G. Blaine. With the exception of one more term in the state legislature, 1881–82, this ended his political service. His independence and impetuosity frequently offended many friends. His own acts and words often impeded his political progress. Others, however, were attracted by his ruggedness, honesty, and integrity. His superior business ability was recognized when the railroad interests that had bought largely of the stock of the Maine Central elected him president of the road. During the year he occupied this position he took a special interest in improving the efficiency of operation. From Readfield he moved to Augusta in 1879, where he died after a short illness, leaving two children.

[L. C. Hatch, *Maine* (1919) vol. II; *Reminiscences of Neal Dow* (1898), pp. 482–95, 503–21; A. M. Smith, *Morrill Kindred in America*, vol. II (1931); *Harper's Weekly*, July 16, 1887; *Daily Eastern Argus* (Portland), July 6, 1887.]   R. E. M.

MORRILL, EDMUND NEEDHAM (Feb. 12, 1834–Mar. 14, 1909), congressman from Kansas and governor, the son of Rufus and Mary

(Webb) Morrill, was born at Westbrook, Cumberland County, Me., and received his education at Westbrook Seminary. He removed to Brown County, Kan., where he arrived on Mar. 12, 1857, and set up a sawmill, which he operated until 1860. On October 5, 1857, he was elected to the free-state territorial legislature. On Oct. 5, 1861, he enlisted in the 7th Kansas Cavalry and through the influence of Vice-President Hamlin of Maine was appointed, in August 1862, to be commissary of subsistence. He was mustered out with the rank of major, by brevet, in October 1865. On Nov. 27, 1862, he had married Elizabeth A. Brettun, the daughter of William H. Brettun of Leavenworth, Kan., who died in September 1868. On Dec. 25, of the next year, he married Caroline J. Nash of Roxbury, Mass., who bore him three children.

His life after the war was divided between business and politics. Although in political life almost continuously, he was not a professional politician in the usual sense. He was active in promoting the building of two railroads across the county in which he lived. He entered the banking business in 1871 at Hiawatha, later became interested in banks at Leavenworth and Kansas City, as well as in a loan company at Atchison, and acquired extensive land holdings. Toward the end of his life he was rated as one of the wealthiest men in the state. After his retirement from the governorship he developed one of the largest single apple orchards in the state, an orchard of 880 acres. He was active in promoting the educational and cultural interest of his community, established a public library in 1882, and assisted financially in establishing and maintaining the Hiawatha academy. He was a conservative in his general point of view on life and on public questions his attitude was further conditioned to a marked degree by his service as a Union soldier and by his interests as a banker.

From 1866 to 1872 he held county offices. In the latter year he was elected to the state Senate on the Republican ticket and was reëlected in 1876. In that body he became chairman of the committee on ways and means and president *pro tempore*. From 1883 to 1891 he was a member of the federal Congress, where he received an assignment on the committee on invalid pensions. The eight years spent in the House of Representatives was devoted almost exclusively to pension legislation. He declined to stand for reëlection in 1890. In 1894 he was brought forward against the Populists who then dominated Kansas, and was elected governor in spite of the charge that in his speculations in land with clouded titles he had defrauded large numbers of farmers of their homesteads and thereby built up a large part of his fortune (*Ottawa Journal*, Sept. 20, 27, Oct. 4, 1894, for excellent summary of charges; *Atchison Daily Champion*, Oct. 30, 1894, for defense). His administration was embarrassed in carrying out a program by a Populist Senate. Among the leading problems of his term as governor were those arising from drought and destitution in the western part of the state, from the mortgage laws and rates of interest, and from the prohibition law which he upheld in a conservative although sincere fashion. His conception of his office was that the governor should execute laws and not attempt to make them (Morrill to C. J. Hammonds, Jan. 30, 1895, correspondence of the governors of Kansas, Letter-press Books, vol. III, p. 294). His theory of government was expressed in his statement that "when the government has protected the individual in his life and property . . . he ought to hustle for himself to get bread" (Morrill to William A. Porter, Jan. 19, 1895, correspondence of the governors of Kansas, Letter-press Books, vol. III, p. 23). In 1896 he was renominated and in the bitterly fought campaign the opposing party, a Populist, Democratic, Free Silver combination brought up again the charge of 1894. He was defeated, although he ran ahead of the state ticket and the McKinley electors, and retired to Brown County to devote himself to his varied interests. He died in San Antonio, Texas.

[Private papers in the hands of his family; correspondence as governor of Kan. in State Hist. Soc. Lib., Topeka; F. W. Blackmar, *Kansas* (copr. 1912), vol. II; A. T. Andreas, *Hist. of the State of Kan.* (1883); *Kan. State Hist. Soc. Trans.*, vol. X (1908); *Kan. State Hist. Soc. Colls.*, vol. XII (1912); *Who's Who in America*, 1908–09; G. W. Harrington, *Annals of Brown County, Kan.* (1903); D. W. Wilder, *The Annals of Kan.*, new ed. (1886); *World* (Hiawatha, Kan.), esp. Mar. 15–20, 1909.]   J. C. M.

MORRILL, JUSTIN SMITH (Apr. 14, 1810–Dec. 28, 1898), representative and senator from Vermont, was the eldest of the ten children of Nathaniel and Mary (Hunt) Morrill. Of humble, sturdy, English stock, he was the descendant of Abraham Morrill who landed in Boston in 1632 and settled in Salisbury, Mass. The Morrills settled in Strafford, Vt., in 1795, where the boy was born and where his grandfather and father combined farming with the blacksmith's trade. He attended the village school and neighboring academies until the age of fifteen, when he became a clerk in the village store. He was in Portland, Me., from 1828 to 1831 learning merchandising and then returned to Strafford and became a partner of his friend, Jedediah H. Harris, in the village store, which as a center of news and a forum of discussion was an excellent training-school for politicians. As a merchant he prospered, and in 1848 he was able to retire to a quiet life of reading and farming. On Sept. 17, 1851, he was married to Ruth Barrell Swan of Easton, Mass. They had two sons. As an amateur politician he had served on county and state committees, and in 1852 he was chosen to represent the Whigs at their national convention. The dissension of the Whig party at this convention influenced him throughout his life to labor to preserve harmony in the Republican party, in the Vermont organization of which he had played a prominent part in 1855.

In 1854 he was elected as an Anti-Slavery Whig to the House of Representatives, commencing an unbroken service of twelve years in the House and almost thirty-two years in the Senate, to which he was elected in 1866 and was returned at each election with virtual unanimity. This service in the House and Senate constituted the longest period of continuous service in the United States Congress so far recorded. In the House he became an important member of the committee on ways and means, of which he was chairman from 1865 to 1867; and in the Senate he served effectively as a member of the committee on finance, of which he was chairman from 1877 to 1879, 1881 to 1893, and 1895 to 1898. After an experimental period in the House, in which though a stanch abolitionist he sounded a temperate and conciliatory note on the great question of slavery, he found his real work in problems of tariff and finance. As a member of the committee on ways and means he wrote a bill providing for the payment of outstanding treasury notes, authorizing a loan, and revising the tariff. This act, known as the Morrill Tariff Act, was intended to be a revenue as well as a protective measure, but amendments made it more strongly protectionist than he had desired. Although causing bitter resentment in the South, the bill was passed early in 1861. His tariff views were somewhat colored by a traditional distrust of Great Britain, and he never thoroughly mastered the principles of international trade, but as a conscientious and not uncompromising protectionist he remained throughout his career influential in tariff legislation, especially in the bill of 1883. In the field of finance lay his greatest talents. With an attack upon the legal tender bill, which, however, was passed in 1862, he began a long fight against inconvertible money and financial inflation. During the Civil War he prepared a series of internal revenue bills and became the champion of economy in the House. After the war he was a leader in the financial reconstruction and an inflexible advocate of a speedy return to specie payments. He was offered a position in the cabinet of President Hayes as secretary of the treasury but declined. In the Cleveland administration he attacked the free-silver heresy.

Perhaps his greatest accomplishment was his Land-Grant College Act, which led to the development of the important system of state educational institutions aided by the federal government. In 1857 he introduced a bill "donating public lands to the several States and Territories which may provide colleges for the benefit of agriculture and the mechanic arts" (*Cong. Globe,* 35 Cong., 1 Sess., p. 32). This was vetoed by Buchanan in 1859, but a similar bill was signed by Lincoln in 1862. In 1890 he introduced in the Senate the so-called Second Morrill Act, under which $25,000 is given annually by the federal government to each of the land-grant colleges. As chairman of the Senate committee on building and grounds he rendered valuable service. He was largely responsible for the plan and execution of the terraces, fountains, and gardens of the Capitol and the completion of the Washington Monument. To his original proposal and persevering legislation is also chiefly due the Library of Congress. His artistic and literary interests found further outlet in his numerous contributions to current periodicals, among them being his book, *Self-Consciousness of Noted Persons* (1882), his *Forum* series of "Notable Letters from my Political Friends" (Oct.–Dec. 1897), and other articles in the *Forum* from time to time (Aug. 1896, Jan., July 1889, Oct. 1898).

As a politician he was noted for sound reasoning, clear apprehension and statement, faithful labor, and temperate, courteous attitude. He was an exceptionally skilful legislator. In appearance he was imposing, being tall and angular and having stern Roman features and side whiskers. As a man he was characterized by urbanity and charm of manner, modesty, culture, and great love of country. He was a genial host at his home on Thomas Circle in Washington, and his birthday parties were among the important social events of the Capitol. In his later days in the Senate his prestige was great, and he was often referred to as "The Nestor of the Senate," "The grand old man of the Republican Party," and "The Gladstone of America." He died in Washington, survived by one of his two sons.

[Papers and letters are in Lib. of Cong.; published material includes W. B. Parker, *The Life and Public Services of Justin Smith Morrill* (1924); G. W. Atherton, *The Legislative Career of Justin Smith Morrill* (1900?); I. M. Tarbell, "The Tariff in Our Times," *Am. Mag.,* Dec. 1906, pp. 116–32; *Memorial Addresses on the Life and Character of Justin Smith Morrill* (1879); *Justin Smith Morrill: Centenary Exercises* (1910); A. M. Smith, *Morrill Kindred in America,* vol. II (1931); *Evening Star* (Washington), Dec. 27, 28, 1898. A discussion of the credit due to Jonathan Baldwin Turner [q.v.] for the Land-Grant College Act is in Parker, *ante,* pp. 278–84; the claim is set forth in some detail in E. J. James, "The Origin of the Land Grant Act of 1862," *Univ. of Ill. Studies,* vol. IV, no. 1 (1910); a brief consideration and decision against the Turner claim in I. L. Kandel, "Federal Aid for Vocational Education," *The Carnegie Foundation for the Advancement of Teaching Bulletin,* no. 10 (1917), p. 79.]

C. M. F.
A. R. B.

MORRILL, LOT MYRICK (May 3, 1812–Jan. 10, 1883), governor of Maine, United States senator, secretary of the treasury, one of the fourteen children of Peaslee and Nancy (Macomber) Morrill, was born in Belgrade, Me. After attending the common-school and the local academy he taught in order to obtain money to attend Waterville (now Colby) College, which he entered at the age of eighteen. He remained there but a short time, however. For a year he was principal of a private school in western New York. Returning to Maine, he began the study of law under Judge Fuller of Readfield. Admitted to the bar in 1839, he built up a considerable law practice chiefly among Democratic friends. Being much in demand as a speaker on temperance and political subjects, he won some local fame so that when he moved to the state capital, Augusta, in 1841, he was frequently employed before legislative committees. This was his school of politics. His law partners in Augusta were James W. Bradbury and Richard D. Rice. Becoming chairman of the state Democratic committee in 1849, he held that office until 1856, when he refused to attend the meetings of the state committee, writing, "The candidate [Buchanan] is a good one, but the platform is a flagrant outrage upon the country and an insult to the North" (Talbot, *post,* p. 232). The breach with his party, thus made complete, began in 1855 when he opposed pledging the Democratic party to further concessions to the slave states. The same step had already been taken by his brother, Anson Peaslee Morrill, and his friend, Hannibal Hamlin [qq.v.]. He was a member of the state House of Representatives in 1854 and of the Senate in 1856. His immediate election to the presidency of the Senate by the Democratic majority, from whom he had already shown divergence of principles, has been explained on the ground that his ability on the floor was more feared than his prestige as president. His Republicanism became definite in 1856 and, although his nomination to the governorship was opposed by some because of his late conversion, he was elected and twice reëlected governor, serving in 1858, 1859, and 1860. Both in the legislature and as governor he was a strong opponent of the repeal of Maine's prohibition law, against which there had been a reaction.

When Hannibal Hamlin resigned from the Senate to accept the vice-presidency under Lincoln, the state legislature, in January 1861, elected Morrill as his successor. Reëlected, he served to March 4, 1869, being succeeded by Hannibal Hamlin, who defeated him by one vote in the Maine Senate. In the so-called peace convention of February 1861 he opposed with conspicuous ability the arguments of Crittenden (L. E. Chittenden, *A Report of the Debates and Proceedings . . . of the Conference Convention, 1864*, pp. 144-50), and he maintained the same position when the Crittenden Resolutions were presented to Congress in March. In March 1862 he spoke in favor of a bill to confiscate the property and to emancipate the slaves of "rebels," seeing clearly that the question was not one of law but one of placing in the hands of the military authorities a weapon to help them win the war (*Speech . . . Delivered in the Senate . . . Mar. 5, 1862*, 1862, also in *Cong. Globe*, 37 Cong., 2 Sess., pp. 1074-78). In April 1862 he led the debate which resulted in the act emancipating slaves in the District of Columbia (*Ibid.*, p. 1516). Later, in June 1866, he was a prominent advocate of the act that conferred suffrage on the colored citizens of the District (*Ibid.*, 39 Cong., 1 Sess., pp. 3432-34). He was a strong adherent of congressional Reconstruction (*Reconstruction. Speech in the Senate . . . Feb. 5, 1868*, 1868; also in *Cong. Globe*, 40 Cong., 2 Sess., app. pp. 110-17), and voted for the impeachment of President Johnson, although his colleague from Maine, William P. Fessenden [*q.v.*], voted for acquittal. On the death of Fessenden in September 1869 he was appointed to fill out the unexpired term. He was reëlected by the state legislature in 1871.

Although he had previously refused to accept appointment as secretary of war, resigning from the Senate on July 7, 1876, he accepted Grant's appointment as secretary of the treasury to succeed Benjamin H. Bristow [*q.v.*]. His studies as chairman of the Senate committee on appropriations had fitted him for the duties of this office and he was a worthy successor to Bristow. When he left the treasury on Mar. 8, 1877, President Hayes offered him the ministry to Great Britain. Enfeebled health, following on a severe illness of 1870 and another attack of 1877, influenced him to accept the lucrative post of collector at Portland rather than a more important and responsible position. He held the collectorship at the time of his death in Portland. His wife, Charlotte Holland Vance, whom

he had married in 1845, and four daughters survived him.

[G. F. Talbot, "Lot M. Morrill," *Me. Hist. Soc. Colls.*, 2 ser., vol. V (1894); J. W. North, *The Hist. of Augusta* (1870); *Biog. Encyc. of Me.* (1885); C. E. Hamlin, *The Life and Times of Hannibal Hamlin* (1899); A. M. Smith, *Morrill Kindred in America*, vol. II (1931); *Advertiser* (Portland), Jan. 10, 1883; *Daily Eastern Argus*, Jan. 11, 1883; date of birth from his daughter, Anne Morrill Hamlin.]   R. E. M.

MORRIS, ANTHONY (Aug. 23, 1654–Oct. 23, 1721), Quaker leader of early Pennsylvania, son of Anthony and Elizabeth (Senior) Morris, was born in Old Gravel Lane, Stepney, London. In his youth he joined the Society of Friends "by convincement," and was married to Mary Jones, Mar. 30, 1676, in the Friends' Savoy Meeting House, in the Strand, London. Early in 1683 he removed to Burlington, West Jersey, and about three years later took up residence in Philadelphia, where he served on numerous committees, and held for some time the position of clerk (presiding officer) of the Monthly Meeting. In 1687 he was clerk of Philadelphia Yearly Meeting and as such signed an "Advice" to all Monthly Meetings against the sale of rum to the Indians. In 1688 he sat in the Quarterly Meeting of Philadelphia that considered the famous petition against slavery presented by the German Friends of Germantown, and signed on behalf of the meeting the Minute passing the matter on to the Yearly Meeting. When past middle life he began to speak in meetings for worship. Later he traveled in the ministry to New England and other parts of America, and to Great Britain.

He seems to have prospered financially, judging by the ample properties he owned in Burlington and Philadelphia. His business, in part at least, was brewing, in a day when no odium was attached thereto. He retired from active business, however, when he became engaged in the ministry. His interest in education is indicated by the fact that he signed, in 1697/98, the petition to the governor and council for the charter of a public school (the present William Penn Charter School) and was appointed by the charter as a member of the first board of overseers. As early as 1691 he was serving as a justice of the peace in Philadelphia, and he served in that capacity for some years. In 1693 he became presiding justice of the Court of Common Pleas for the city and county of Philadelphia and held that position for about five years. In August 1694 he was commissioned associate justice of the provincial supreme court, a position which he held, with his other judicial offices, until 1698. In the charter of 1691 incorporating the city of Philadelphia he was named one of six aldermen;

in the city charter of 1701 he was named again to the same office. For one year, 1703–04, he served as mayor of Philadelphia and in that capacity signed an interesting protest to the deputy governor in defense of the rights of the city (*Minutes of the Provincial Council of Pennsylvania*, II, 1852, p. 161). He was twice elected, in 1695 and 1696, a member of the provincial council and was a member of the Assembly from 1698 to 1704. Morris was married four times: in 1689 to his second wife, Agnes, widow of Cornelius Bom, in Philadelphia; in 1693/94 to Mary, widow of Thomas Coddington, at Newport, R. I.; and in 1700 to Elizabeth Watson, in Philadelphia. He had fifteen children.

[Sources include: R. C. Moon, *The Morris Family of Phila.* (5 vols., 1898–1909), esp. vol. I; J. W. Jordan, ed., *Encyc. of Pa. Biog.*, vol. X (1918); G. P. Donehoo, ed., *Pennsylvania: A Hist.* (1926), vol. IX; F. B. Lee, ed., *Geneal. and Memorial Hist. of the State of N. J.* (1910), vol. III; J. H. Martin, *Martin's Bench and Bar of Phila.* (1883); *Bull. of Friends' Hist. Soc. of Phila.*, May 1919; the *Friend*, July 21, 1855; John Smith, "The Lives of the Ministers of the Gospel among the People Called Quakers" (1770), a manuscript in the library of Haverford Coll.; and manuscript records of the Friends preserved at 304 Arch Street, Phila. A few manuscripts written or signed by Anthony Morris are in the library of the Pa. Hist. Soc.]   R. W. K.

MORRIS, ANTHONY (Feb. 10, 1766–Nov. 3, 1860), merchant, was born at Philadelphia, Pa., the son of Samuel and Rebecca (Wistar) Morris and a descendant of Anthony Morris, 1654–1721 [*q.v.*]. His father was a merchant and captain of the 1st Troop, Philadelphia City Cavalry, during the Revolution. He studied with private tutors, then attended the University of Pennsylvania, graduating in 1783. After studying law he was admitted to the Philadelphia bar on July 27, 1787, but he practised little for he was more interested in business and carried on an extensive trade with the East Indies. He was speaker of the Pennsylvania Senate, 1793–94, and from 1800 to 1806 was a director of the Bank of North America. From May 1810, after the American chargé at Madrid, George W. Erving, had been forced to leave the country because of the chaotic conditions of factional and civil war, Morris, together with Thomas L. Brent and Thomas Gough, was an unofficial representative of the United States in Spain. He was accused by his companions of seeking to obtain the appointment as minister to Spain and there is no doubt that he was a party to a rather discreditable intrigue, in which certain Spanish officials were involved, to make himself minister by discrediting Erving with the Spanish government. In 1814 when diplomatic relations were resumed Erving was renamed as minister to Spain and Morris returned to America. During his so-

journ at Madrid he suggested to the United States that East and West Florida could be purchased for a reasonable sum. Though this suggestion received no attention at the time, it was eventually realized in the Treaty of 1819 by which Spain ceded East and West Florida and the adjacent islands to the United States. He seems, however, to have taken no part in the negotiations. About 1830–31 he founded an agricultural school at Bolton Farms in Bristol Township, Bucks County, Pa., but this venture was not successful. He served as a trustee of the University of Pennsylvania from 1806 to 1817. His wife was Mary Pemberton whom he had married on May 13, 1790. They had four children. During the latter part of his life he resided with his daughter at "The Highlands," near Georgetown, D. C., where he died.

[J. L. Chamberlain, ed., *Universities and Their Sons: Univ. of Pa.*, vol. II (1902); R. C. Moon, *The Morris Family of Phila.*, vols. I and II (1898); H. B. Fuller, *The Purchase of Fla.* (1906); J. L. M. Curry, "Diplomatic Services of Geo. Wm. Erving," *Proc. Mass. Hist. Soc.*, 2 ser. V (1890).]   J. H. F.

MORRIS, CADWALADER (Apr. 19, 1741 o.s.–Jan. 25, 1795), merchant, was born in Philadelphia, Pa., the son of Samuel and Hannah (Cadwalader) Morris and a descendant of Anthony Morris, 1654–1721 [*q.v.*]. His father was a prominent lawyer. He attended a private school in Philadelphia and then joined his brother, Samuel C. Morris, in the importing business. He was the firm's representative in the West Indies for several years and lived for some time in Kingston, Jamaica, and elsewhere in the Islands. He was strongly sympathetic toward the cause of the colonists and took a prominent part in the Revolutionary War as a member of the 1st Troop, Philadelphia City Cavalry, commanded by his cousin, Capt. Samuel Morris. He was a signer of the paper bills of credit issued by order of the Pennsylvania Assembly on Mar. 21, 1772, and Apr. 7, 1781. When the Pennsylvania Bank was organized on June 8, 1780, for the purpose of supplying and transporting food to the army, he aided in its establishment by a subscription of £2,500 to its capital and for a time served as one of its inspectors. He was also one of the founders and a director (1781–87) of the Bank of North America. In 1783–84 he was a delegate from Pennsylvania to the Continental Congress and was elected for another term but declined to serve. In 1788 he moved to Birdsboro, Berks County, Pa., where, with some other Philadelphia capitalists, he had purchased two iron forges. In 1790, however, he sold his interests in this venture and returned to Philadelphia where he again engaged in the importing business. He was a member of the Democratic Society of Philadelphia which was organized as an act of good will toward the French Revolution. He died in Philadelphia. He had married, on Apr. 8, 1779, Ann Strettell, by whom he had five children.

[*Biog. Dir. Am. Cong.* (1928); *Hist. of the First Troop, Phila. City Cavalry, 1774–1874* (1874); R. C. Moon, *The Morris Family of Phila.*, vols. I and II (1898); M. L. Montgomery, "Early Furnaces and Forges of Berks County, Pa.," *Pa. Mag. of Hist. and Biog.*, Mar. 1884.]   J. H. F.

MORRIS, CASPAR (May 2, 1805–Mar. 17, 1884), physician, was born in Philadelphia, Pa., the third son of Israel Wistar and Mary (Hollingsworth) Morris, and a descendant of Anthony Morris, 1654–1721 [*q.v.*]. His father was a prosperous merchant. He attended private schools, the Pine Street Meeting House, David Dulles' school in Church Alley, and the William Penn Charter School. Later he studied medicine at the University of Pennsylvania and was graduated in 1826. While attending the school of medicine he studied also with Dr. Joseph Parrish. After his graduation he traveled to India as surgeon on the *Pacific,* returning to Philadelphia in 1828. He was appointed physician of the Philadelphia Dispensary soon after his return. The following year, on Nov. 11, 1829, he was married to his cousin, Anne Cheston of Baltimore. In spite of his social position, he chose to live near a poor district. He was one of the founders of the House of Refuge, which he served as physician from 1830 to 1834, and also helped to establish the Pennsylvania Institution for the Instruction of the Blind, serving as its manager and physician from 1833 until his death. In the early fifties he published a brief article emphasizing the need for increased hospital facilities in Philadelphia, the result of which was the movement to establish the Episcopal Hospital, which he served as manager for many years. A list of his writings includes *An Appeal on Behalf of the Sick* (1851); *Lectures on Scarlet Fever* (1851); *An Essay on the Pathology and Therapeutics of Scarlet Fever* (1858); an abridgment (1838) of Robert I. Wilberforce's life of William Wilberforce; and a small volume of poems, privately printed, entitled *Heart Voices and Home Songs.* In recognition of his experience in America and observation of foreign institutions he was appointed one of five men selected to submit suggestions for the building of the Johns Hopkins Hospital in Baltimore. His contribution, "Hospital Construction and Organization," was published in *Hospital Plans: Five Essays Relating to the Construction, Organization and Management of Hospitals* (1875).

Morris was a member of the National Academy of Sciences (1829–38) and of the American Philosophical Society (1851–60), and a fellow of the College of Physicians. He aided in founding in 1838 the Philadelphia Medical Institute and was a lecturer there until 1844. Suffering an impairment of his health in 1868, he never fully regained his strength thereafter and died in 1884, having survived his wife by three years.

[J. C. Morris, "Biog. Sketch of Caspar Morris, M.D.," *Trans. Coll. of Physicians of Phila., 1888,* 3 ser., vol. X (1888); H. A. Kelly and W. L. Burrage, *Am. Medic. Biogs.* (1920); R. C. Moon, *The Morris Family of Phila.* (3 vols., 1898); *Medic. and Surgic. Reporter,* Mar. 29, 1884; *Pub. Ledger* (Phila.), Mar. 18, 1884.]   R. L. B.

MORRIS, CHARLES (July 26, 1784–Jan. 27, 1856), naval officer, was born at Woodstock, Conn., of early New England ancestry, son of Charles and Miriam (Nichols) Morris. Though a reader and diligent student, he was occupied with farm work and had little regular schooling after his tenth year. Through his father, a naval purser during the American hostilities with France, he secured a midshipman's appointment, July 1, 1799, and made his first cruise in the *Congress.* By a fall from the mainmast in January 1800, he suffered a broken arm and concussion of the brain, but recovered, and after a winter on the West-Indies station was selected in June 1801 as one of the 159 out of 355 midshipmen retained in the peace establishment. Following nine months in Woodstock Academy he sailed in August 1803 in the *Constitution* of Preble's squadron against Tripoli. Already marked by professional ambition and enthusiasm, he achieved his first fame when he was selected by Decatur to share in the celebrated exploit of burning the frigate *Philadelphia,* held by the Tripolitans. Leaping with Decatur, he was first aboard the frigate and figured prominently in her capture and destruction. He took part in subsequent bombardments of Tripoli, and returning home in the *President,* received his lieutenant's commission (1807) during a second Mediterranean cruise in the *Hornet.*

After gunboat duty in Maine, and service in the *President,* 1809–10, Morris was first lieutenant under Hull in the *Constitution* at the outbreak of the War of 1812. He suggested warping the *Constitution* ahead with anchors in her extraordinary escape from Broke's squadron, July 17–19, 1812, and was highly praised by Hull for his part in the victory, Aug. 19, following, over the *Guerrière,* in which he was shot through the body while attempting to lash the ships together. This exploit won him promotion to captain, over the grade of master-commandant, though, owing to protests, his advancement was delayed to avoid his superseding Lawrence and Jacob Jones. Assigned next to command the *John Adams* (26 guns), he escaped from the Chesapeake Jan. 18, 1814, for a cruise on the African and Irish coasts. The *Adams* captured ten prizes, but after grounding on the Maine coast and retreating up the Penobscot, she was attacked, Sept. 3, 1814, by two British vessels with a landing force of over six hundred. Morris had mounted his guns ashore, but upon the flight of his supporting militia, was compelled to burn his ship and retreat. Cleared by a court of inquiry, he was ordered to the *Congress,* which, after the war, in August 1815, joined Decatur's squadron against Algiers. He remained in the *Congress* until 1817, commanding the forces in the Caribbean (1817) while on diplomatic missions to Haiti and Venezuela. His command of the Portsmouth (New Hampshire) station during the next five years was broken by a visit to Georgia (1819) to recover from pneumonia, and a short subsequent cruise to Buenos Aires (1819–20). In 1823 he was appointed to the Board of Navy Commissioners with John Rodgers and Isaac Chauncey. Earlier, in 1815, Rodgers had highly recommended Morris for this important administrative office as "of strong, discriminating mind, of considerable science, and uniting perhaps as much, if not more theoretical knowledge as any man of his age in the service" (C. O. Paullin, *Commodore John Rodgers,* 1910, p. 302). Morris' correspondence in this and later periods shows him constantly occupied with problems of naval construction, signals, regulations; in fact, every phase of naval activity.

Morris held the commissionership until 1827, except for a year, 1825–26, when he commanded the *Brandywine* in which Lafayette returned to France. He afterward visited Lafayette on his estate and made a tour of French and British naval establishments. Following command of the Boston yard, 1827–32, he was again navy commissioner until the board was abolished in 1841. Then, after commanding the Brazil and Mediterranean squadrons, 1841–44, he was head of the bureau of construction, and later the bureau of ordnance, until his death. Of his fifty-six years' service, twenty-two were at sea, and only two unemployed. A strict disciplinarian, Morris was noted for his influence over his men. Farragut called him "the ablest sea officer of his day" (*Autobiography,* note, p. 88). His appellation "Statesman of the American Navy" (*Providence Journal,* Jan. 29, 1856) was justified by the trust placed in his judgment and his

employment in important administrative work throughout his later years. His portrait by Scheffer, a gift from Lafayette, pictures a shrewd, kindly, self-controlled character, and, like his *Autobiography,* bears out contemporary testimony that "he combined in his manners, to a rare degree, unaffected simplicity and manly dignity" (*Ibid.*). He was married, Feb. 1, 1815, to Harriet, daughter of Dr. William Bowen of Providence, R. I., and had six daughters and four sons. The eldest son, Charles, a naval lieutenant, was killed in the Mexican War; another, George, commanded the *Cumberland* at the battle of Hampton Roads.

[The early sketch in Isaac Bailey, *Am. Naval Biog.* (1815), and the later one in Charles Morris, *Heroes of the Navy in America* (1907), are of slight value compared with *The Autobiog. of Commodore Charles Morris, U. S. Navy* (Boston, 1880, and also in *Naval Inst. Proc.,* vol. VI, 1880), covering his life to about 1840. Obituaries in the *Providence Jour.,* Jan. 29, 1856, and *Nat. Intelligencer,* Feb. 1, 1856, are reprinted in J. F. Morris, *A Geneal. and Hist. Reg. of the Descendants of Edward Morris* (1887). Many originals or facsimiles of Morris' letters and papers are in the Navy Dept. Lib.]

A. W.

MORRIS, CLARA (Mar. 17, 1848–Nov. 20, 1925), actress, was born in Toronto, Canada. Her mother, of Scotch-English ancestry, was Sarah Jane Proctor, a servant-maid, who, after being rescued from a mad dog by a French-Canadian cab-driver, Charles La Montagne, married him. The marriage was discovered to be bigamous after three children had been born, the eldest of whom was Clara. The mother assumed her grandmother's maiden name, Morrison, and fled to Cleveland, Ohio, with Clara. The other children were adopted: the daughter by a family in Buffalo; the son, who died at six, by a family in Cleveland. Mrs. Morrison, as she was known, had a struggle for existence, and the two suffered misery and hardship. Clara learned to read and write, however, and in 1862, at fourteen, was engaged by John Ellsler, manager of the Cleveland Academy of Music, as an extra at fifty cents for each public performance. She clipped her name to Clara Morris and began her stage appearances. Owing to a bad fall in childhood, which left her with spinal trouble, her health was permanently impaired and for the rest of her life she suffered ill health.

In 1869 she went to Cincinnati to play at Wood's Theatre and in the spring of 1870 she appeared at the National Theatre, Louisville, Ky., with Joseph Jefferson. By the fall of the year she had reached New York, where she was engaged by Augustin Daly to play in his Fifth Avenue Theatre. The opening play of the season was *Man and Wife*. By chance she was given the leading rôle, Anne Sylvester, which she played with sufficient effect to gain an ovation on the opening night, Sept. 13, 1870. She remained with Daly until 1873, when she went to A. M. Palmer of the Union Square Theatre. There, in November 1873, she appeared in *The Wicked World*. Her first season as a star took her to the West Coast, after which she returned to Daly's to appear on Nov. 22, 1875, in *The New Leah*. In November 1876 she appeared at the Union Square Theatre in *Miss Multon*, and a year later she appeared at Wallach's Theatre as Jane Eyre. Thereafter "season followed season until she was known throughout the United States as the most prominent if not the greatest emotional actress on the American stage" (Clapp and Edgett, *post*, p. 266). Her rôles included Camille, Lady Macbeth, Alixe, Blanche de Chelles in *The Sphinx*, Mercy Merrick in *The New Magdalen*, Cora in *L'Article 47*, and Fanny Ten Eyck in *Divorce*. In the nineties, at the height of her career, she was forced by the state of her health to give up regular performances and thereafter she returned to the stage only for occasional appearances and in variety shows.

The reason for Clara Morris' success was baffling even to her critics. It was said of her that she could draw bigger houses on short notice than any other actress, and in certain parts she excited and moved her audiences. Yet her abilities were distinctly limited. William Winter said of her (*Vagrant Memories*, pp. 239–40): "It would not be accurate to designate Clara Morris as either a tragedian or a comedian. She was, intrinsically, an expositor of human nature in self-conflict, of the revolt of humanity against affliction and suffering, of erring virtue tortured in the miserable bonds of fatal circumstance. . . . Her acting was pervaded by a bizarre quality and fraught with hysterical passion and intense tremulous nervous force, but it revealed neither definite intellectual method nor consistent artistic design. The structure of it was perplexed by aimless wanderings across the scene, motiveless posturings, facial contortions, wailing vocalization, extravagant gesture, and spasmodic conduct—as of a haphazard person taking the uncertain chance of somehow coming out right at last." To another critic she was a marvel of cunning. "Nym Crinkle," commenting in the New York *World* after seeing her in *Camille*, wrote: "The wet eyes, the sobs, . . . the hysterical tremor like a little wave of electricity that went through the house. . . . Nothing like it when Bernhardt or Modjeska plays *Camille*. Why? I give it up. Criticism has wrestled with that condition in and out of season—how she can play upon all sensibilities and sweep as with supernatural fingers the whole gamut of emotions, passes critical knowledge" (*World*, Sept. 25, 1885).

Clara Morris was married on Nov. 30, 1874, to Frederick C. Harriott of New York City. When she left the stage she retired to her home, "The Pines," in Riverdale, N. Y. She was an ardent horsewoman, kept birds and dogs in numbers, and painted and embroidered indefatigably. As her finances waned she took up writing for magazines and papers, and published some separate works. Included among these are: *A Silent Singer* (1899), a volume of short stories; *Life on the Stage* (1901); *A Pasteboard Crown* (1902); and *The Life of a Star* (1906). In 1909 her eyesight failed. After five years of blindness she partially regained her vision. Her husband died in 1914, her mother in 1917, and she herself passed away in 1925 in New Canaan, Conn., and was buried from "The Little Church Around the Corner." Her property, which would have escheated to the state, finally went to her sister, whom Clara Morris had been unable to trace during her own lifetime.

[Clara Morris' diaries, which she kept throughout her life, are in the possession of Mrs. George Mac-Adam, Scarsdale, N. Y. For printed sources consult: Wm. Winter, *The Wallet of Time* (1913), vol. I, and *Vagrant Memories* (1915); T. A. Brown, *A Hist. of the N. Y. Stage* (1903), vols. II and III; J. B. Clapp and E. F. Edgett, *Players of the Present* (1900); J. R. Towse, *Sixty Years of the Theatre* (1916); Brander Matthews and Lawrence Hutton, *Actors and Actresses of Great Britain and the U. S.* (1886); John Parker, *Who's Who in the Theatre*, 1922; *Theatre Arts Monthly*, Jan. 1926; *N. Y. Times*, Sept. 15, 1870, Nov. 21, 1925, Oct. 28, 1927.]
V. M.

MORRIS, EDMUND (Aug. 28, 1804–May 4, 1874), editor, writer on agriculture and other subjects, was born in Burlington, N. J., a descendant of Anthony Morris, 1654–1721 [*q.v.*]. His father was Richard Hill Morris and his mother was Mary, daughter of Richard S. Smith of Moorestown, N. J. He was married on Dec. 27, 1827, to Mary P. Jenks, daughter of William Jenks of Bridgetown, Bucks County, Pa. They had a son and three daughters. Morris spent his school days in Philadelphia and subsequently learned the printing trade in the office of the *Freeman's Journal*. In 1824, when he was nineteen years of age, he formed a partnership with S. R. Kramer of Philadelphia and bought the *Pennsylvania Correspondent*, published at Doylestown, the name of which was changed to *Bucks County Patriot and Farmers' Advertiser*. The partnership was dissolved in February 1827 and Morris conducted the paper alone until October of the same year, when he sold it. Subsequently he was associated with several Philadelphia publications including the *Ariel*, a literary weekly. He returned to his native town, and in 1846 became the editor of the *Burlington Gazette* with which he remained for two years. In 1854 he assumed the editorship of the *Daily State Gazette,* published at Trenton, N. J., resigning his post in 1856 when he returned to Burlington to remain until his death.

Throughout his life Morris was interested in rural pursuits and wrote on agriculture and other general subjects. He took up farm land in the neighborhood of Burlington and wrote several pamphlets embodying his experience. One of these, *Ten Acres Enough for Intensive Gardening* (1844), had a wide sale and was translated into several languages. This gave him a reputation and brought him into contact with those interested in agriculture and thus led him into the business of selling farms in the vicinity of Burlington. The town of Beverly on the Delaware River below Burlington owes its foundation to his efforts. He also became interested in silk culture and impoverished himself in experimenting with mulberry plants. He was an ardent opponent of slavery and was active with his pen in support of the Union cause. One of his friends was Horace Greeley, for whom he frequently wrote editorials. During and after the Civil War he was a regular contributor to the *New York Tribune,* the *Newark Daily Advertiser,* and the Philadelphia *Press.* He experimented with mechanical inventions, and it is claimed that he was one of the first persons in the United States to print in two colors. His published writings include *How to Get a Farm and Where to Find One* (1864) and *Farming for Boys* (1868). He edited *Derrick and Drill* (1865), a compilation of information regarding the oil fields of Pennsylvania.

[W. E. Schermerhorn, *The Hist. of Burlington, N. J.* (1927); W. W. H. Davis, *Hist. of Doylestown, Old and New* (1903); Mary Morris Ferguson, *The Family of Edmund Morris* (1899); *Report of the State Librarian of Pa., 1900* (1901); *Daily State Gazette* (Trenton), May 6, 1874.]   H. S.

MORRIS, EDWARD DAFYDD (Oct. 31, 1825–Nov. 21, 1915), Presbyterian clergyman, educator, was born at Utica, N. Y. His father, Dafydd Edward Morris, was a native of Wales who came to the United States in his youth; his mother, Anne (Lewis), was of Welsh descent. The father, a man of strong religious principles, was a shoemaker, later conducting a small grocery business. The son enjoyed speaking and preaching in the Welsh language during his public life. He attended private schools in Utica and prepared for college at Whitestown Seminary, N. Y. Entering the sophomore class at Yale in 1846, he ranked high in scholarship while earning his living. He made political speeches for the Free-Soil party and his writing attracted attention. He graduated at Yale in 1849, a classmate of Timothy Dwight [*q.v.*].

Graduating in 1852 at Auburn Theological Seminary, where he studied theology under Laurens P. Hickok [*q.v.*], Morris was ordained, by the Cayuga Presbytery, pastor of the Second Presbyterian Church of Auburn, N. Y. In 1855 he went to the Second Presbyterian Church of Columbus, Ohio. From this scholarly and productive ministry he was called in 1867 to the professorship of church history in Lane Theological Seminary, Cincinnati, and in 1874 was transferred to the chair of systematic theology, which he held until 1897 when he resigned and was made professor emeritus. Thereafter, he made his home at Columbus, for a time still lecturing at Lane besides speaking in various places and writing for publication. He was in responsible relation to Lane Seminary for thirty-four years, having become one of its trustees in 1863 and serving on the board until he became one of its faculty. He was again elected a trustee in 1870 in order to serve in an emergency as treasurer and superintendent of the Seminary, a task for which his business abilities specially fitted him. During the closing years of his professorship he won the gratitude of the trustees by his strenuous and successful efforts to assist the Seminary through a period of stress and peril.

Morris was moderator of the General Assembly of the Presbyterian Church in 1875. He was a member of the Church's committee on the revision of the creed, to which he gave active service. He was an earnest upholder of the theological standards of his Church, which he interpreted in a liberal spirit that accorded with his training and the temper of his mind. He was a vigorous exponent of the "New School" theology. His students were impressed with the lucidity, catholic range, and deeply evangelical spirit of his instruction, and appreciated his constant personal interest in them. His courtly bearing, brilliant dark eyes, and ruddy complexion gave him an appearance of vigor and distinction, enhanced in his later years by abundant white hair and beard. He was twice married: on July 29, 1852, to Frances Elizabeth, daughter of Dan and Fanny (Rowe) Parmelee of Fair Haven, Conn., who died in 1866; and on Mar. 26, 1867, to Mary Bryan Treat of Tallmadge, Ohio, who died in 1893. Four children were born of the first marriage; two, of the second. He died in Columbus three weeks after his ninetieth birthday, having maintained his mental activity to the end. His published works include: *Outlines of Theol-*

ogy (1880), *Ecclesiology* (1885), *Scripture Readings* (1887), *Is there Salvation after Death?* (1887), *Thirty Years in Lane* (1897), *Theology of the Westminster Symbols* (1900), *The Presbyterian Church, New School* (1905).

[*Ohio State Journal* (Columbus), May 6, 1895, and Nov. 22, 1915; *Herald-Dispatch* (Utica), Nov. 22, 1915; *The Continent* (N. Y.), Aug. 3, 1911, and Dec. 2, 1915; *Herald and Presbyter* (Cincinnati), Nov. 24 and Dec. 1, 1915; *Gen. Biog. Cat. Auburn Theol. Sem.* (1918); *Obit. Record Grads. Yale Univ.*, 1916; personal characteristics described in letters from Rev. Dr. Arthur Judson Brown, New York, and others.]

E. D. E.

MORRIS, EDWARD JOY (July 16, 1815–Dec. 31, 1881), legislator, diplomat, and author, was born in Philadelphia, Pa. He matriculated at the University of Pennsylvania in the class of 1835, left in his freshman year, and was graduated from Harvard College in 1836. He studied law in Philadelphia and was admitted to the bar in 1842, meanwhile being elected to the state Assembly in which he served during the years 1841–43. He was then elected as a Whig representative to the Twenty-eighth Congress for one term, 1843–45. He was an unsuccessful candidate for reëlection. On Jan. 10, 1850, he was appointed chargé d'affaires to the Two Sicilies and was stationed at Naples until Aug. 26, 1853. On his return from Naples he became a member of the board of directors of Girard College, Philadelphia, and was a member of the state House of Representatives in 1856. He took a leading part in the movement for the organization of the Republican party and was elected to the Thirty-fifth, Thirty-sixth and Thirty-seventh congresses and served from Mar. 4, 1857, to June 8, 1861, when he resigned. On the latter date President Lincoln appointed him minister to Turkey, where he served with zeal and fidelity until Oct. 25, 1870. While at Constantinople he negotiated a commercial treaty which was approved by the United States Senate in 1862.

Morris was a fine linguist, speaking French, Italian, and German fluently, was able to converse in Greek, and knew Turkish and Arabic. In manner he was said to be most agreeable and conciliating. He was a frequent contributor to American magazines and newspapers for many years and was also the author of several works. His *Notes of a Tour through Turkey, Greece, Egypt, Arabia Petræa to the Holy Land* (2 vols., 1842) is sometimes referred to as "Morris' Travels." He published in 1854 *The Turkish Empire: Its Historical, Statistical and Religious Condition*, translated from the German of Alfred de Bessé, giving an idea of the "past and present condition of the Ottoman people and empire." In it Morris incorporated ex-

cerpts from French writers and a "considerable amount of original matter suggested by his own travels." In 1854 he also published from the original of Theodor Mügge, *Afraja, a Norwegian and Lapland Tale, or Life and Love in Norway*, which Bayard Taylor called "one of the most remarkable romances of the generation." Another translation was his *Corsica, Picturesque, Historical and Social* (1855), from the German of Ferdinand Gregorovius, which contained a sketch of the early life of Napoleon.

Morris left Turkey in 1870 and returned to the United States. He had married, July 15, 1847, Elizabeth Gatliff Ella, daughter of John Ella, of Philadelphia. His wife having died sometime prior to 1870, he married Susan Leighton, in Philadelphia, in October 1876. By his first marriage he had two daughters, one of whom survived him. He died in Philadelphia and was buried in Laurel Hill Cemetery.

[*Biog. Dir. Am. Cong.* (1928); S. A. Allibone, *A Critical Dict. of English Lit. and British and Am. Authors*, vol. II (1870); *Pub. Ledger* (Phila.), Jan. 2, 1882; Probate Court records, Phila.; records of the U. S. Dept. of State.]

A. E. I.

MORRIS, ELIZABETH (*c.* 1753–Apr. 17, 1826), actress, known on the stage as Mrs. Owen Morris, was presumably born in England, but no information is available concerning her before she became the second wife of Owen Morris, comedian in the American Company, and even the date of her marriage remains undisclosed. Her first stage appearance of which there is a definite record was made at the Southwark Theatre, Philadelphia, in the fall of 1772 (G. O. Seilhamer, *History of the American Theatre*, I, 1888, p. 309). In 1773 she performed with the American Company at Charleston, S. C. (Eola Willis, *The Charleston Stage in the XVIII Century*, 1924, p. 67), and the same year made her New York début. During the Revolution the company withdrew to the West Indies, and there Mrs. Morris followed her profession until the troupe returned to the United States in 1785 (Seilhamer, *op. cit.*, II, 1889, pp. 136 ff., 175). In a few years dissension developed within the organization. Thomas Wignell, a prominent comedian, finding his ambitions thwarted by the managers, Lewis Hallam and John Henry, withdrew in 1791 to form a new company, taking with him Mr. and Mrs. Morris, the latter of whom was probably eager to escape the rivalry of Mrs. Henry (J. N. Ireland, *Records of the New York Stage*, I, 1866, p. 83).

While awaiting the completion of the Chestnut Street Theatre at Philadelphia, which was to be the headquarters of Wignell's players, the

Morrises had the distinction of participating, in 1792, in the first theatrical season ever known at Boston, a season conducted in defiance of the law and abruptly terminated after several weeks by the sheriff, who interrupted Mr. and Mrs. Morris as Sir Peter and Lady Teazle in *The School for Scandal* and placed them under arrest (William Dunlap, *A History of the American Theatre*, 1832, pp. 127–28). From the opening of the Chestnut Street Theatre in February 1794, Mrs. Morris was associated mainly with that house until 1810, the year after her husband's death. Two or three years later she apparently acted with an upstart company in Philadelphia, and there is reason to believe that she performed at New York as late as 1815 (G. C. D. Odell, *Annals of the New York Stage*, II, 1927, p. 448). The obituary notice (*Poulson's American Daily Advertiser*, Philadelphia, Apr. 19, 1826), which refers to her as "formerly an eminent actress," indicates that she retired some years before her death.

In her prime, shortly after the Revolution, Mrs. Morris was regarded as the greatest attraction on the American stage. Especially in high comedy rôles, to which her tall and elegant figure and her spirited acting in the grand manner admirably adapted her, she was considered unsurpassed. At least one contemporary, however, held that she was much overrated, that she was extremely defective in education, enunciation, and memory (W. B. Wood, *Personal Recollections of the Stage*, 1855, pp. 26–28). He attributed her appeal to her personal attraction and to a mysterious manner which she affected both on and off the stage. So successfully did she avoid exposure to the common gaze that on the few occasions when she did appear on the street in her extravagantly high heels and her costume of 1775, to which she clung to the end of her life, she never failed to create a sensation. It is doubtful, however, whether Wood's explanation alone can account for her reputation among early American playgoers as "the inimitable Mrs. Morris" (Odell, *op. cit.*, I, 1927, p. 254).

[The principal sources have been mentioned in the body of the article. See also: Thos. C. Pollock, *The Phila. Theatre in the Eighteenth Century* (1933). The date of her death is taken from the burial records of St. Peter's Church, Phila., and verified by the newspaper cited above. The probable year of her birth is arrived at from Wood's statement *op. cit.*, p. 139, that she died at seventy-three.]   O.S.C.

MORRIS, GEORGE POPE (Oct. 10, 1802–July 6, 1864), journalist and poet, was born in Philadelphia, Pa. Early in his youth he removed to New York, where for some years he was employed in a printing office and where he began to contribute verses to various New York newspapers. In 1823 he founded the *New-York Mirror and Ladies' Literary Gazette*, a periodical which he engaged Samuel Woodworth, then well known in literary circles, to edit. After a year's connection with the magazine, Woodworth withdrew, and Morris himself became the sole proprietor and editor of the paper. The importance of the *Mirror* in affording a medium of public expression for the early Knickerbocker school, cannot be overestimated. In a day when literary magazines in New York were few, the *Mirror* encouraged, through its patronage, a local talent then clamoring for expression. A glance over its pages reveals such contributors as William Cullen Bryant, James K. Paulding, Nathaniel P. Willis, and Fitz-Greene Halleck—the leading literary lights of the early New York school. In 1842 the *New-York Mirror* ceased publication, but in the following year the *New Mirror*, edited jointly by Morris and his friend Nathaniel P. Willis, took its place, carrying on the same journalistic tradition. A difficulty over "an interpretation of the postage laws," however, finally led to its discontinuance in 1844. In the same year Morris again associated himself with Willis in the editing of a daily paper called the *Evening Mirror*, which continued for several years. In the meantime (1845) he had started a weekly entitled the *National Press*. After about a year, Willis also became an associate in this enterprise, and the title of the periodical was changed to the *Home Journal*. This weekly, which proved very popular, Morris continued to edit until shortly before his death. In describing his qualifications as a journalist, Evert A. Duyckinck mentions "his editorial tact and judgment; his shrewd sense of the public requirements; and his provision for the more refined and permanently acceptable departments of literature" (*Cyclopædia of American Literature*, 1855, II, 348).

Morris occupies but a minor place in the early Knickerbocker school. His drama, *Brier Cliff*, founded upon incidents of the American Revolution, was produced in 1826 at the Chatham Theatre. It had a long run and is said to have yielded its author the sum of $3,500. The drama has never been published. In his collected works may be found the libretto of an opera in three acts, *The Maid of Saxony*, based "upon historical events in the life of Frederick the Second of Prussia." This opera, for which Charles E. Horn produced the music, had in 1842 a run of about two weeks. As a writer of poetry Morris in his day attained a genuine popularity, and his songs were frequently set to music by distinguished composers in the United States and abroad. Edgar Allan Poe considered "Wood-man, Spare that Tree" and "Near the Lake" "compositions of which any poet, living or dead, might justly be proud" (*Southern Literary Messenger,* April 1849, p. 219), and it was said in Morris' day that he could "at any time obtain fifty dollars for a song unread." But his verses were at times sharply censured by contemporary critics. One satirist called *Brier Cliff* a "paltry play," and another spoke of Morris himself as

A household poet, whose domestic muse
Is soft as milk, and sage as Mother Goose.

To a later audience his lyrics are uniformly insipid and sentimental. Occasionally, however, he leaves the purely banal for a strain of simple and quiet beauty to which is added a note of genuine pathos. In 1839 he published *The Little Frenchman and his Water Lots,* a volume of prose sketches mostly in a humorous vein.

Of a generous and hearty, though practical, nature, Morris represented well that spirit of *bonhomie* which distinguished New York life of the early nineteenth century. He has been described as "about five feet two or three inches high. . . . Short, crisp, dark curly hair, thinly streaked with silver threads, encircled a high, well-formed forehead, beneath which was a pair of bright, twinkling black eyes. . . . [His] complexion was fresh and florid" (G. W. Bungay, *Off-Hand Takings,* 1854, pp. 44–45). He was usually called "General" Morris—a title derived from his connection with the state militia. For many years he resided at his country estate situated in the Hudson River highlands, near Cold Spring. His personal letters which have survived reveal a domestic life of happiness and comfort, despite occasional financial reverses. His household consisted of his wife, Mary Worthington Hopkins, and several children. A son, William Hopkins Morris [*q.v.*], was a West-Point graduate who served in the Civil War.

[Sources include: "Am. Poetry," *People's and Howitt's Jour.,* vol. X (1850), p. 101; *U. S. Rev.,* June 1855; *North Am. Rev.,* July 1858; *Southern Lit. Messenger,* Oct. 1838; H. B. Wallace, *Lit. Criticisms and Other Papers* (1856); F. L. Mott, *A Hist. of Am. Magazines, 1741–1850* (1930); Timothy Hopkins, *John Hopkins, of Cambridge, Mass., 1634, and Some of His Descendants* (1932); J. G. Wilson, *Bryant and His Friends* (1886); *N. Y. Times,* July 8, 1864. The best collection of Morris' poems is the fourth edition published by Scribner (New York, 1860). The following institutions possess Morris papers and manuscripts: Lib. of Cong., Harvard Coll. Lib., Hist. Soc. of Pa., N. Y. State Lib., and the N. Y. Pub. Lib., which has several manuscript copies of *Brier Cliff.*] N.F.A.

MORRIS, GEORGE SYLVESTER (Nov. 15, 1840–Mar. 23, 1889), educator, philosopher, was born in Norwich, Vt., the son of Sylvester and Susanna (Weston) Morris. The family was of English stock traceable to Nazing, Essex, their original migration to America having occurred in 1636. Morris was educated first in the local district school and then in Kimball Union Academy, Meriden, N. H. In the autumn of 1857 he entered Dartmouth College. He seems to have shown marked ability and was regarded as the best scholar of his class. After graduation he taught for one year. He had planned to enter Auburn Theological Seminary, but the loyalties invoked by the Civil War led to his enlistment in the 16th Vermont Volunteers. Here he was given the detached service of mail carrier for the regiment. There is little doubt that his war experience had its broadening effect upon a boy hitherto too much of a recluse and too much dominated by a family atmosphere of a moralistic and pietistic type. At the end of his enlistment he became a tutor at Dartmouth. While teaching, he continued his studies and secured his master's degree. In September 1864, he entered Union Theological Seminary, New York, where he came in contact with liberal thought in the person of Prof. Henry Boynton Smith. The next important step in his education was a sojourn abroad for two years, spent chiefly in study at Berlin. Here he came under the influence of F. A. Trendelenburg, a noted Aristotelian scholar. This period in Europe brought Morris into touch with a different kind of social life and with art in its various forms. In 1868, at the age of twenty-eight, he returned to America, exceptionally equipped for an academic career.

While waiting for an opening in the college field, he was a tutor in the family of Jesse Seligman, a New York banker. After two years, in 1870, he was appointed to the chair of modern languages and literature in the University of Michigan, an institution with which his life was henceforth to be chiefly associated. His primary interest, however, was in philosophy. He undertook the translation of Friedrich Ueberweg's *History of Philosophy* and carried it through in an extremely creditable fashion, publishing the translation in two volumes, in 1871–73. In 1877 came an invitation to become lecturer on the history of philosophy and ethics in The Johns Hopkins University, a position which required his absence from Michigan for only a short time each year. It is worthy of note that he acted as one of the examiners of Josiah Royce, later the famous idealist philosopher of Harvard. This arrangement at Baltimore did not develop the possibilities which had been hoped from it, but it did lead to his transfer at Michigan to the department of philosophy in 1881. He now entered upon a period of scholarly production. In 1885, he was made head of the department of philosophy and henceforth devoted all his energies to his work at Ann Arbor and to his writing. He was in the full tide of his intellectual powers and much was hoped from him when death came to him suddenly, in March 1889, from the effects of a cold caught in an outing. He was only forty-nine years of age when he died. In June 1876 he had married Victoria Celle, who with a son and a daughter survived him.

Morris was a champion of the idealistic movement initiated by Kant and carried farther by Hegel. His was a point of view which was destined to dominate much of English and American thought during the latter part of the nineteenth century. Thus he can be regarded as a co-worker with W. T. Harris [q.v.] and the St. Louis movement on this side of the Atlantic and with men like T. H. Green and F. H. Bradley in England. This idealism was opposed to traditional empiricism and to Spencerian agnosticism. It was speculative and friendly to moral and religious pieties. It was also marked by a strongly developed historical sense. Aside from the translation already referred to, Morris published many articles dealing with art, education, and religion and wrote four books of some significance: *British Thought and Thinkers* (1880), *Kant's Critique of Pure Reason* (1882), *Philosophy and Christianity* (1883), and *Hegel's Philosophy of the State and of History* (1887). These works show careful scholarship. In appearance, Morris was of average height and rather spare of build. His face was sensitive and somewhat ascetic. A picture of him hangs in a room at the University called, in his honor, the Morris seminary.

[R. M. Wenley, *The Life and Work of George Sylvester Morris* (1917), a labor of love by a fellow idealist, which includes letters from Morris' niece and from various friends and colleagues; John Watson, *A Typical New England Philosopher*, repr. from *Queen's Quart.* (Queen's Univ., Kingston, Ont.), Jan. 1918; Morris' Commonplace book, MS., in Univ. of Mich. Library; *Detroit Free Press*, Mar. 24, 1889.]

R. W. S.

MORRIS, GOUVERNEUR (Jan. 31, 1752–Nov. 6, 1816), statesman, diplomat, was born in the manor house at Morrisania, N. Y., the son of Lewis Morris, second lord of the manor, by his second wife, Sarah Gouverneur. From his grandfather, Lewis Morris [q.v.], the first lord of the manor, and from his father, both of whom had served on the bench and in the assembly of New York, defending the rights of the colonists against the royal governors, he inherited traditions of public service and political autonomy. His mother was a descendant of a Huguenot family driven from France by the revocation of the Edict of Nantes in 1685; and it was doubtless the French strain in Morris' blood that lent to his conversation and his writings the charming combination of graceful manner, pervasive humor, and cynical philosophical detachment which contrasts so noticeably with the rather ponderous and prosaic rectitude of most of his revolutionary associates.

While he was at school in the Huguenot settlement of New Rochelle where he had frequent opportunity to hear his mother's language spoken, the French power was driven from America and the quarrel between the mother country and the English colonies drew rapidly to its crisis. In the year of the Stamp Act Morris entered King's College, New York, from which he graduated in 1768 at the age of sixteen, just as the British government was dispatching regiments of redcoats to Boston to enforce the provisions of the Townshend legislation. But if the atmosphere of that "provincial Oxford" under its Loyalist president affected the young man with either devotion or repugnance to King George and his friends in Parliament, there is nothing in Morris' record to show it. His bachelor's and master's essays were pretty conceits of rhetoric, the one on "Wit and Beauty" and the other on "Love." After a period of study in the office of William Smith, the historian and later the chief justice of the province, Morris was admitted to the bar at the age of nineteen and soon built up a practice which, had it not been constantly interrupted by his political and diplomatic activities, would have put him in the foremost rank of the lawyers of his day. But family influence, a brilliant intellect, unfailing self-assurance, and a remarkable social aptitude combined to make a political career inevitable for Gouverneur Morris. Before he had reached his majority he arrested the attention of the politicians by a vigorous attack upon a bill proposed by the provincial assembly providing for the emission of paper money to liquidate the debt incurred by the French and Indian War.

Until the clash of arms at Lexington made the breach with Great Britain inevitable, Morris was a conservative. As a member of the landed aristocracy he dreaded the social upheaval which he believed would follow in the train of a "democratic" revolution. "I see, and I see it with fear and trembling," he wrote in 1774, "that if the disputes with Britain continue, we shall be under the worst of all possible dominions . . . the domination of a riotous mob. . . . It is the interest of all men, therefore, to seek for reunion with the parent state" (Sparks, *Life,* I, 25). Yet when the breach came, Morris adhered unreservedly to the American cause, at no small cost to his family and social connections. Though his half-brothers Lewis and Richard [*qq.v.*], were active patriots, his half-brother Staats Long Morris became a major-general in the British army and married the Duchess of Gordon; and for writing even a filial letter to his Loyalist mother, Gouverneur Morris fell for a time under suspicion.

The last colonial legislature in New York under the royal governor adjourned in April 1775, and on May 22 a provincial congress of some eighty delegates met at New York City to assume the responsibility of governing the colony. Morris took his seat in this revolutionary body as a representative from Westchester County, and from the first took a leading part, holding the balance between the radical agitators who wished to inaugurate a reign of terror against the Loyalists and the strong Loyalist element who hoped that the British warships in the harbor would make short work of the revolutionary congress. Realizing that the colonists must present a united front if they were to win their rights from Great Britain either by remonstrance or by force, Morris was a strong defender of the dignity and power of the Continental Congress at Philadelphia. To that body, he insisted, should be entrusted the whole responsibility of the negotiations for reconciliation with England, as well as the control of the issue of paper money by the colonies. He was a nationalist before the birth of the nation.

When Washington arrived in New York with the Continental Army, after the British evacuation of Boston, the courage of the patriots in the congress and the colony was fortified; and when, three months later, Washington read the Declaration of Independence to his soldiers in Bowling Green, New York was ready to accept the responsibility of an independent state. Morris sat in the constitutional convention which met in July 1776, and with John Jay and Robert R. Livingston drafted the frame of government, adopted the following year, under which the state was to live for nearly half a century. His plea for religious toleration was successful, in spite of Jay's proposal to impose a special oath of loyalty on Roman Catholics, but the combined efforts of Morris and Jay failed to move the convention to abolish slavery in the state. Morris also labored hard for the creation of a strong executive, with powers of suspensive veto and of appointment, subject to the ratification of the legislature. He secured the provision for a single governor instead of an executive board,

but the fear of executive tyranny was still strong enough to hamper the governor by the cumbrous faction-ridden councils of revision and appointment which vexed the politics of the state for more than four decades. When the work of the convention was done Morris was appointed on committees, first to organize the new government, then to act as a council of safety until the new governor, George Clinton [*q.v.*], and the legislature were elected. As a member of the Council of Safety Morris visited the northern army which was resisting the advance of Burgoyne toward Albany. He was an ardent supporter of General Schuyler [*q.v.*], and with Jay went to Philadelphia on a belated mission to prevent Schuyler from being superseded by Horatio Gates.

Morris' versatility of talent and soundness of judgment were never more in evidence than during the two years 1778–79, when, as a young man in his middle twenties, he sat in the Continental Congress. Financial, military, and diplomatic matters engaged his chief attention. He was chairman of several leading committees and his facile pen was requisitioned for the draft of many an important document, such as the report on Lord North's conciliation offer of 1778 (reprinted in Morris' *Observations on the American Revolution,* 1779), a public paper on the significance of the treaty with France (*Address of the Congress to the Inhabitants of the United States,* 1778), the draft of instructions to Benjamin Franklin, first minister of the United States to the Court of Louis XVI, and a comprehensive letter of instructions for the envoy to be sent to Europe to negotiate a treaty of peace and commerce with Great Britain. These instructions, approved in August 1779, six weeks before John Adams was appointed to carry them out, formed the basis of important provisions in the final treaty of peace four years later. On an official visit of inspection to the army at Valley Forge, early in 1778, Morris came into close contact with Washington, to whom he remained devoted for life, and of whose military policies he became perhaps the most able and ardent defender in Congress. Because he refused to enlist the support of Congress for Governor Clinton and his New Yorkers in their claims to Vermont, Morris was defeated for reëlection to the Continental Congress in the autumn of 1779. He thereupon transferred his citizenship to Pennsylvania and resumed the practice of law and the cultivation of polite society in the gay city of Philadelphia. He could not remain long out of public life, however. A series of brilliant articles on the Continental finances which he contributed under the signature "An American" to the *Pennsylvania Packet,* February-April 1780, brought him a year later the invitation from Robert Morris [*q.v.*], newly created superintendent of finance, to serve as his assistant. This position the younger Morris (who was not a relative of the Superintendent) held from 1781 to 1785, his most notable service being a plan for a decimal system of coinage (Sparks, *Diplomatic Correspondence,* XII, 81) which was later simplified and perfected by Jefferson and Hamilton.

Morris was elected to the Pennsylvania delegation to the Constitutional Convention of 1787, and took part in the debates of that body more frequently than any other member on the floor, not even excepting James Madison. He favored a strong, centralized government in the hands of the rich and the well-born. He would have a president elected for life, with power to appoint a Senate of life members. The suffrage for presidential and congressional electors should be limited to freeholders: "Give the votes to the people who have no property," he argued, "and they will sell them to the rich" (Farrand, *post,* II, 203). The federal government should have "compleat and compulsive operation" (*Ibid.,* I, 34) throughout the country. Considering that "State attachments, and State importance" had been the "bane of this Country," Morris was willing to see "all the Charters & Constitutions of the States . . . thrown into the fire" (*Ibid.,* I, 531, 553). He strenuously opposed the equal representation of the states in the Senate, and the concessions to slavery in the three-fifths rule and the extension of the slave trade for twenty years. Yet when he was defeated in this extreme program he loyally accepted the bundle of compromises which compose the Constitution, and used his incomparable skill in putting the document into its final literary form.

None of the framers of the Constitution had better claims to high office under it than Gouverneur Morris. But his frankly cynical contempt for "democracy" was a poor asset for the solicitation of votes, and the large interests which he had acquired in various commercial ventures—some of them in association with Robert Morris—tempted him to forsake public life for business. He had purchased the family mansion at Morrisania from his elder brother and after the Convention he returned to his native state to live, but was hardly settled on the old manor when business took him to France as agent for Robert Morris to press a claim against the Farmers-General rising out of a tobacco contract (Sparks, *Life,* I, 265, 308). Business, diplomatic duties, and recreational travel kept him in Europe for

nearly a decade. He arrived in Paris in February 1789, in time to see the curtain rise on the great drama of the French Revolution. His fame as one of the founders of the American Republic had preceded him. Wealth, affability, family connections, a perfect command of the language, and that sprightly intellectual versatility which is so dear to the heart of the cultured French people opened all doors to him, even the doors of the Court.

After Jefferson's return to the United States at the close of 1789, Morris was the most influential American in Paris. He was engaged in plans for opening the tobacco trade on better terms for Americans, for supplying American wheat to the French market, getting the American debt to France transferred to private hands (his own and those of his associates), and selling American lands. These enterprises brought him often before French ministers and committees to urge the modification of the French customs system for the benefit of American trade. His wide range of friendships brought him into contact with leaders of all shades of political opinion, and his immunity from diplomatic responsibility during the first three years of the Revolution allowed him to dispense criticism and counsel freely. The voluminous diary which he kept during these years, supplemented by a diligent correspondence with Washington, Jay, Hamilton, Livingston, King, and other friends at home, furnishes a mine of information and shrewd comment on the men and measures of the Revolution. "You are constantly making remarkable prophecies which turn out to be true," said the French minister to Great Britain to him in July 1790 (*Diary and Letters,* I, 336). The historian Taine, who drew heavily on Morris in his volumes on the French Revolution, ranked him with Arthur Young, Mallet du Pan, and Mounier in value as a source (*Derniers Essais de Critique et d'Histoire,* 1894; 6th ed., 1923, p. 307). Morris believed in a constitutional monarchy for France; but he had little confidence in the capacity of a people without political training to make a workable constitution, and still less in the capacity of Louis XVI and his courtiers to provide the authority, order, and justice necessary for the maintenance of the monarchy. Nevertheless, if the monarchy were to be saved in France, Louis XVI must be saved: and Morris even went so far as to draft and urge the carrying out of a plan for the rescue of the king from his virtual imprisonment in the Tuileries.

Early in 1792 President Washington named Morris as minister to France. The nomination was bitterly fought in the Senate, partly because of Morris' aristocratic views and his unconciliatory manners, partly because of the disappointing results of his special mission to London in 1790–91, when he attempted to settle the controversies over debts, trading-posts, impressments, and commercial privileges left over from the peace treaty of 1783 (see S. F. Bemis, *Jay's Treaty*, 1923). Had the senators known that at the very moment of their deliberations Morris was deeply engaged in the plot to get the king out of Paris, they would certainly not have ratified his nomination—even by the narrow margin of 16 to 11 votes. Still, no one could have represented the United States at Paris better than Morris did in the stormy years 1792–94. Morris was the only foreign minister who refused to leave Paris when the reign of terror converted the city into a shambles. He stayed in the face of repeated insults and perils to vindicate with dignity and courage the full rights of his countrymen, and to offer the asylum of his house to many a refugee in danger of the guillotine. He was recalled at the request of the French government in the late summer of 1794, as a *quid pro quo* for the dismissal of "Citizen" Genet [*q.v.*] by President Washington. Morris did not return to America for another four years, however; he spent the intervening time traveling in various countries, from Scotland to Austria, attending to his manifold business interests, studying the confused European political scene, and writing letters to the British Foreign Office reporting his observations (S. F. Bemis, *The American Secretaries of State*, vol. II, 1927, p. 21; Sparks, *Life*, I, 424, III, 83–87, 89, 93).

Though he was but forty-two years old when he quitted his ministerial post at Paris, Morris was practically done with politics. To be sure, he had what he called in his diary "the misfortune" to be elected in April 1800 to fill an unexpired term in the United States Senate; but soon after he took his seat as a pronounced Federalist the Democratic-Republicans, under the leadership of Aaron Burr, got control of the New York legislature, and Morris was defeated for reëlection in the autumn of 1802, despite the fact that he had supported Jefferson's Louisiana policy. On the expiration of his term the following March, he retired to the new mansion which he had built at Morrisania and spent the remaining thirteen years of his life in cultivating his estate and his friends. On Christmas day, 1809, he married Anne Carey Randolph of Virginia, sister of Thomas Mann Randolph [*q.v.*]. One son was born of this union.

Morris was active in forwarding the plans for the Erie Canal, and for many years was chairman of the canal commission. His disgust with the rule of the Republicans at Washington drove him to unfortunate extremes in his opposition to the policies of the national government. He denounced the Embargo, condemned the War of 1812, approved the Hartford Convention, and even advocated repudiating the national debt incurred by the war. "In his hatred of the opposite party," says one of his biographers, "he lost all loyalty to the nation" (Roosevelt, *post*, p. 352). Perhaps this judgment is too harsh, yet it is distressing to see a man whose faith in the American Republic was so robust in the days of the Constitutional Convention and the mission to France writing to Timothy Pickering in 1814 that he would be "glad to meet with some one who could tell ... what has become of the union, in what it consists, and to what useful purpose it endures" (Sparks, III, 312). He rejoiced in the restoration of the Bourbons in 1814, but died two years làter with his faith in the future of his own country unrevived.

[Jared Sparks, *The Life of Gouverneur Morris, with Selections from his Correspondence* (3 vols., 1832); Anne Carey Morris (his grand-daughter), *The Diary and Letters of Gouverneur Morris* (2 vols., 1888); Theodore Roosevelt, *Gouverneur Morris* (1888), in the American Statesmen series; H. C. Lodge, "Gouverneur Morris," in the *Atlantic Monthly*, Apr. 1886, repr. in his *Hist. and Pol. Essays* (1892); Adhémar Esmein, *Gouverneur Morris, un Témoin américain de la Révolution française* (Paris, 1906); Daniel Walther, *Gouverneur Morris, Témoin de deux Révolutions* (1932), with extensive bibliography and list of manuscript sources; Jared Sparks, *The Diplomatic Correspondence of the Am. Rev.* (12 vols., 1829–30); *Am. State Papers, For. Rel.*, vol. I (1832); Max Farrand, *The Records of the Federal Convention* (3 vols., 1911); W. W. Spooner, *Hist. Families of America* (copr. 1907); MSS. in Washington Papers, Jefferson Papers, and William Short Papers, Lib. of Cong.]   D. S. M.

MORRIS, JOHN GOTTLIEB (Nov. 14, 1803–Oct. 10, 1895), Lutheran clergyman, was born at York, Pa., the youngest of the seven children of John and Barbara (Myers) Morris. His father, born in Germany at Rinteln on the Weser, emigrated to America in 1776, enlisted immediately in the Revolutionary army, and became a commissioned surgeon in the Marquis de la Rouerie's regiment. On the advice of friends who feared that the British might capture and execute him as a deserter, he changed his name from Moritz to Morris. After the Revolution he married and settled as a physician at York. John Gottlieb attended the York County Academy, entered the College of New Jersey in 1820, and transferred after two and a half years to Dickinson College, where he graduated in 1823. Having decided to enter the Lutheran ministry, he studied with the Rev. Samuel Simon Schmucker [*q.v.*] at New Market, Va., 1823–24, attended Princeton Theological Seminary, 1825–26, and then returned to Schmucker as a member of the first class in Gettysburg Theological Seminary, 1826–27. He was ordained at Frederick, Md., Oct. 15, 1827, and on Nov. 21 of the same year married Eliza Hay, who bore him several daughters and died in 1875. For the rest of his life he lived in Baltimore, where he was pastor of the First English Lutheran Church, 1827–60, librarian of the Peabody Institute, 1860–65, and pastor of the Third Church, 1864–73.

Even as a young man he was one of the leaders of his church. In 1831 he founded the *Lutheran Observer,* which in 1833 he turned over to Benjamin Kurtz [*q.v.*]. He served repeatedly as president of the Maryland Synod and in 1843 and 1883 of the General Synod. For over sixty years he was a director of Gettysburg Seminary and a trustee of Pennsylvania (now Gettysburg) College. He visited the two institutions annually from 1869 to 1894 to give special courses of lectures. In 1846, with Kurtz and S. S. Schmucker, he went to London to attend the first convention of the Evangelical Alliance. In 1851 he and Kurtz founded Lutherville, a suburb of Baltimore, which thereafter was his summer home. He published a number of books and contributed copiously to church papers, his last article appearing on the day of his death. From the theological dissensions that wracked the General Synod he stood, like his closest friend, Charles Philip Krauth [*q.v.*], apart, trusted and sometimes claimed by all factions, but at heart in sympathy with the moderate conservatives.

Morris was also a diligent student of history, bibliography, and natural science. He and his nephew, Charles Augustus Hay [*q.v.*], founded the Lutheran Historical Society and built up its great collection of books, documents, and other materials. He was a frequent lecturer before the Smithsonian Institution and presided for many years over the entomological section of the American Association for the Advancement of Science. His chief publications are: *Life of John Arndt* (1853); *Synopsis of the Described Lepidoptera of the United States* (1862); *Catalogue of the Described Lepidoptera of North America* (1860); *Bibliotheca Lutherana* (1876); *Fifty Years in the Lutheran Ministry* (1878); *The Stork Family in the Lutheran Church* (1886); and *Life Reminiscences of an Old Lutheran Minister* (1896). He retained into his ninety-second year much of the mental and physical vigor of his prime and enjoyed in the Lutheran Church the honors of a Nestor. His common sense, gruff kindliness, and independence of spirit became proverbial. His one extravagance was an indiscriminate passion for joining historical and scientific societies. Outside his denomination, he was the best-known Lutheran clergyman in the United States. He died at Lutherville and was buried at York, Pa.

[See Morris' *Life Reminiscences of an Old Lutheran Minister* (1896); P. C. Croll, "Rev. John G. Morris, D.D., LL.D.," *Pa.-German,* Feb. 1907; C. J. Hines, "The Beginnings of English Lutheranism in Baltimore," *Luth. Quarterly,* July 1926; the *Sun* (Baltimore), Oct. 11, 1895; A. R. Wentz, *Hist. Ev. Luth. Synod of Md.* (1920) and *Hist. Gettysburg Theol. Sem.* (1926). The first and last of these contain lists of his publications.]

G. H. G.

MORRIS, LEWIS (Oct. 15, 1671–May 21, 1746), chief justice of New York and governor of New Jersey, was the first lord of the manor of Morrisania in New York. His father, Richard Morris, after service in Cromwell's army had become a merchant in Barbados, where he married Sarah Pole, a lady of substantial fortune. In 1670 Richard and his brother Lewis, also a merchant of Barbados, purchased a tract of five hundred acres, known as Bronck's land, just north of the Harlem River in New York. There Richard and Sarah Morris died in 1672, leaving their infant son, Lewis, as the ward of the uncle for whom he had been named. The elder Lewis Morris, having assumed his responsibilities at Bronck's land in 1675, was greatly disturbed because young Lewis developed into a headstrong boy who resented the discipline of the Society of Friends upon which his uncle insisted and defied his guardian's authority. The youth mended his ways sufficiently to warrant forgiveness, however, and in 1691 inherited not only his uncle's equity in the Bronck's land estate, which had been increased to almost two thousand acres, but also 3,500 acres in Monmouth County, N. J.

The sense of being a man of property seems to have sobered Lewis Morris. On Nov. 3, 1691, he married Isabella, daughter of James Graham, attorney-general of the province of New York, and established a home at "Tintern" (later corrupted to "Tinton"), N. J., named in honor of the ancestral home of the Morrises in Monmouthshire. During the following year he was appointed a judge of the court of common right of East Jersey and was named a member of Gov. Andrew Hamilton's council. He vigorously supported Hamilton [*q.v.*], but in 1698 he opposed the appointment of Gov. Jeremiah Basse [*q.v.*] on the ground that the choice had been made by only ten of the required sixteen proprietors. His obstructive tactics resulted in his dismissal from the governor's council.

Although Governor Fletcher had issued royal letters patent in May 1697 erecting Morris' New York estate into the manor of Morrisania, the new lord was less interested in his manorial grant than in the politics of New Jersey. He went to England in 1702 to promote the transfer of political authority from the Jersey proprietors to the Crown. Ambitious to be the first royal governor of the province, he was keenly disappointed when the ministry named Lord Cornbury [*q.v.*] to be governor of both New York and New Jersey. As a member of Cornbury's council for New Jersey, Morris became an outspoken opponent of that unscrupulous official. Dismissed from the council, he was elected in 1707 to the assembly, where he collaborated with Samuel Jennings in formulating the protest to Queen Anne against Cornbury's reprehensible conduct, which was largely responsible for the governor's removal from office.

After 1710 Morris supported the admirable administration of his friend Robert Hunter [*q.v.*]. He spent more time in New York, especially after Hunter appointed him chief justice of the supreme court of that province (1715). He continued, however, to serve upon the governor's council for New Jersey under Burnet and Montgomerie. With the administration of Gov. William Cosby [*q.v.*] the lord of Morrisania found himself once more at odds with the representative of the Crown. When Cosby sought to establish a court of chancery to hear his suit against Rip Van Dam, chief-justice Morris pronounced the whole proceeding illegal, whereupon the governor removed him and appointed James De Lancey, 1703–1760 [*q.v.*], in his place (Aug. 21, 1733). Morris was elected to the assembly from the town of Eastchester, and joined James Alexander [*q.v.*] and William Smith in championing the popular cause against the "court party" led by Cosby and De Lancey. In 1734 he presented the assembly's grievances in London, where he failed to secure the removal of Governor Cosby but won a vindication of his own conduct as chief justice.

When the political connection between New York and New Jersey was severed, he became governor of the latter province (1738). Though he had challenged the royal prerogative as represented by Cornbury and Cosby, he permitted no questioning of his own authority. He frequently lectured the provincial assembly on its duties and complained to the lords of trade in 1740 that the legislators "fancy themselves to have as much power as a British House of commons, and more" ("Papers of Governor Lewis Morris," *post*, p. 123). His administration was marked by bitter and wordy quarrels with the assembly over taxation, support of the militia, issuance of bills of credit, and validity of land titles.

For many years Lewis Morris was an active churchman, serving from 1697 to 1700 as a vestryman of Trinity Church and encouraging the Society for the Propagation of the Gospel in its missionary enterprises. In 1702 he suggested to the Society that New York, as the center of English America, was a proper place for a college and that Queen Anne might be persuaded to grant her farm in New York toward the project. Morris' public career was never touched by the least suspicion of political jobbery. His enemies accused him of inordinate vanity, and no doubt he was fully conscious of his talents, which were great. The contentious spirit, manifest in his youth, grew stronger with the passing years and involved him in controversy until his death, which occurred at "Kingsbury" near Trenton. He was buried at Morrisania with simple rites in accordance with the terms of his will. The bulk of his estate was divided between his son Lewis, who became second lord of the manor, and his son Robert Hunter Morris [*q.v.*], who inherited the New Jersey property.

["The Papers of Lewis Morris, Governor of the Province of New Jersey," *N. J. Hist. Soc. Colls.*, vol. IV (1852); Robert Bolton, *A Hist. of the County of Westchester* (2 vols., 1848); William Smith, *The Hist. of the Late Province of N. Y.* (1829); *Archives of the State of N. J.*, 1 ser. IV–VII (1882–83); E. B. O'Callaghan, *Docs. Rel. to the Col. Hist. of the State of N. Y.*, vols. IV–VI (1854–55); E. M. W. Lefferts, *Descendants of Lewis Morris of Morrisania* (1907). A portrait of Morris, done by John Watson in 1715, may be a copy of an earlier portrait.]   J.A.K.

MORRIS, LEWIS (Apr. 8, 1726–Jan. 22, 1798), signer of the Declaration of Independence, the eldest son of Lewis Morris, second lord of the manor of Morrisania, and Tryntje (Staats) Morris, was born at Morrisania, Westchester County, N. Y. His father carefully supervised his early education and with some misgiving allowed him to enter Yale College. He completed the work for the degree of A.B. in 1746, the year that his grandfather, Lewis Morris [*q.v.*], first royal governor of New Jersey, died, and his father became lord of the manor. After being graduated he returned to Morrisania to assist his father in the management of the family estates. The task proved so congenial that for sixteen years he lived the pleasant life of an aristocratic landholder, satisfied with the quitrents and produce from his own and his father's extensive acres. Lacking the acquisitiveness which had characterized earlier generations of his family, he preferred to use wisely that which had already been accumulated rather than to strive to increase the estate. His marriage, Sept. 24, 1749, however, brought him additional wealth, for Mary Walton, his bride, daughter of Jacob and Maria (Beekman) Walton, was a member of a

New York family famed beyond the borders of the province for its possessions.

At the death of his father in 1762 Morris became the third (and last) lord of the manor of Morrisania. After coming into his inheritance he manifested a spirited interest in politics, probably stimulated by his brother Richard [q.v.] who was inclined to support the Livingstons and the Smiths in their quarrels with the De Lanceys. He served one term in the provincial assembly in 1769, but his growing criticism of British policy and the representatives of imperial authority in the province was not indorsed by all his neighbors in the borough town of Westchester, some of whom attributed his ultimate support of the Revolutionary movement to his resentment that he had not been treated more handsomely in the matter of public offices. Whatever his motives, he represented but a minority in his county when he persuaded certain local politicians from the southeastern towns to issue a call (Mar. 28, 1775) for a meeting at White Plains on Apr. 11 to choose Westchester's deputies to the provincial convention. The Philipses, De Lanceys, and Pells strove to defeat the purpose of the gathering, but Morris and his faction carried the day, securing the appointment of eight deputies to attend the convention scheduled for Apr. 20, 1775, in New York City. Morris was named chairman of the delegation, which was instructed to support a resolution to send representatives of the province to the Second Continental Congress. He was eager to be named on the delegation to represent New York at Philadelphia, an honor which came to him through the action of the provincial convention.

Lewis Morris took his seat in the Continental Congress on May 15, 1775. His service there was concerned with the administration of specific business transactions rather than with the determination of general public policies. He was early placed on the committee charged with the selection of the posts to be defended in the province of New York and somewhat later he was assigned to the committee formed to "supply these colonies with ammunition and military stores." Consequently his time was consumed with correspondence over the purchase of tent cloth, the manufacture of sulphur and saltpetre, and the acquisition of gunpowder. In September 1775 he made a trip to Pittsburgh, acting as commissioner for Indian affairs in the Middle Department, and discussed with representatives of the western tribes the possibility of establishing amicable trading relations. Later he became a member of the permanent committee on Indian affairs.

On June 7, 1776, the third provincial congress of New York made provision for an increase in the militia of Westchester County and appointed Morris brigadier-general in command, naming his son major of brigade. Securing a leave of absence from Congress, Morris assumed his military post promptly, apparently believing that it offered greater opportunity for military service than proved to be the case. He was absent from Philadelphia when the Declaration of Independence was finally adopted, but was present in the fourth provincial congress at White Plains on July 9, 1776, when the action of the Continental Congress was indorsed. Later in the year he returned to Congress and signed the Declaration. He participated in the New York campaign during the autumn of 1776, but thereafter his military duties were constantly interrupted by the responsibilities of civil office. He served as county judge in Westchester from May 8, 1777, until Feb. 17, 1778. From 1777 until 1790 he was intermittently a member of the upper house of the state legislature.

At the close of hostilities he retired with the rank of major-general of militia and set about the task of rehabilitating his estates, which had been burned and plundered by the British. Public duty called him frequently from his private affairs. In 1784 he became a member of the first Board of Regents of the University of the State of New York. Two years later he was named a member of the Council of Appointment. In 1788, at the Poughkeepsie convention, he labored valiantly as a member of the Hamiltonian forces in favor of ratification of the federal Constitution, in the drafting of which his much younger half-brother, Gouverneur Morris [q.v.], had had so prominent a part. His greatest joy, however, was to preside over his establishment at Morrisania, which he proudly insisted had been restored to its pre-war magnificence. Tall, handsome, erect despite his years, he remained a representative of the landed aristocracy until his death in 1798.

[Peter Force, *Am. Archives,* 4 ser. (6 vols., 1837–46), 5 ser. (3 vols., 1848–53); W. C. Ford, ed., *Journals of the Continental Congress, 1774–1789,* vols. II–VI (1905–06); "Letters to General Lewis Morris," in *N. Y. Hist. Soc. Colls.,* Pub. Fund Ser., vol. VIII (1876); Robert Bolton, *A Hist. of the County of Westchester* (2 vols., 1848); J. T. Scharf, *Hist. of Westchester County, N. Y.* (2 vols., 1886); W. W. Spooner, *Hist. Families of America* (copr. 1907).]   J.A.K.

MORRIS, LEWIS RICHARD (Nov. 2, 1760–Dec. 29, 1825), congressman, Vermont statesman, was born at Scarsdale, N. Y., the son of Richard [q.v.] and Sarah (Ludlow) Morris. His father was a landed proprietor of Westchester County and for a decade, chief justice of New York. Gen. Lewis Morris, signer of the

Declaration of Independence, and Gouverneur Morris [*qq.v.*] were his uncles. He received a common-school education, and during the Revolution saw military service in New York as aide to General Schuyler and General Clinton. From 1781 to 1783 he was first secretary under Robert R. Livingston, 1746–1813 [*q.v.*], secretary of the department of foreign affairs.

In 1786 he moved to Springfield, Windsor County, Vt. Here he built a stately residence, acquired extensive lands, engaged in business, furthered plans for bridging the Connecticut River and for locking it at Bellows Falls, and became active in politics. He served as selectman (1788), as town treasurer (1790–94), as clerk of the county court (1789–96), and sat in the Bennington convention of 1791 for ratifying the federal Constitution. He was one of the two commissioners to Congress to arrange for the admission of Vermont to the Union, was secretary of the constitutional convention at Windsor in 1793, and from 1791 to 1801 was the first United States marshal in the Vermont district. After serving as clerk (1790–91), the ubiquitous Morris represented Federalist Springfield in the state assembly in 1795, 1796, 1803, 1805, 1806, and 1808. During his first two years of membership he was speaker. In addition to his other offices, he was elected a brigadier-general of the militia in 1793 and promoted two years later to major-general, a position he held until 1817.

His career in Congress was less distinguished. Elected to the House of Representatives by a close margin in 1796, he sat in the Fifth, Sixth, and Seventh congresses. His six years' service was remarkable only for the part he played in making Jefferson president. When the House was choosing between Jefferson and Burr in the contested election of 1800, Jefferson, until the thirty-sixth ballot, received the votes of only eight of the sixteen states. Morris then absented himself, allowing his Republican colleague to cast the vote of Vermont for Jefferson. This act, combined with a similar procedure in the Maryland delegation and a blank ballot from Delaware, gave Jefferson more than the necessary majority. That Morris was a stanch Federalist was shown in his willingness to have Matthew Lyon [*q.v.*], his Republican colleague, expelled from the House in February 1798, for using objectionable language (*Annals of Congress*, 5 Cong., 2 Sess., p. 1008).

Some years before his death he retired from politics and business. He was married, first, in 1786, to Mary, daughter of Timothy and sister of President Timothy Dwight, 1752–1817 [*q.v.*], of Yale. He left her soon after their marriage.

His second wife was Theodotia, daughter of the Rev. Buckley Olcott of Charlestown, N. H., and his third, Ellen, daughter of Arad Hunt of Vernon, Vt. He died at Springfield, Vt., and was buried at Charlestown, N. H.

[W. H. Crockett, *Vt., the Green Mt. State* (5 vols., 1921), *passim*; *Biog. Dir. Am. Cong.* (1928); W. W. Spooner, *Hist. Families of America* (1907); E. M. W. Lefferts, *Descendants of Lewis Morris of Morrisania* (1907); Benj. Dwight, *The Hist. of the Descendants of John Dwight* (1874), I, 224; H. S. Olcott, *The Descendants of Thomas Olcott* (1874); E. P. Walton, ed., *Records of the Governor and Council of the State of Vt.*, vols. IV–VI (1876–78); W. H. Crockett, ed., *State Papers of Vt.*, vol. III (in 2 vols., 1928–29); A. P. Lee, "Pioneering with Forty Slaves," in *Daughters of the Am. Revolution Mag.*, July 1926; *Brattleboro' Messenger*, Jan. 7, 1826.]   E. W. S.

MORRIS, LUZON BURRITT (Apr. 16, 1827–Aug. 22, 1895), lawyer, governor of Connecticut, was born in Newtown, Conn., the second child of Eli Gould and Lydia (Bennett) Morris. On both sides of his family his ancestry stretched back through colonial days to England. When his father, a farmer with a small fortune, became an invalid, Morris left school at the age of seventeen and became a mechanic. Four years later he was manager of a tool factory at Seymour and had saved enough money to permit him to continue his education. After two years of college preparation at Suffield he entered Yale with the class of 1854. Here he made a reputation as a debater. By the beginning of his senior year he had decided to study law. To shorten the period of his education and to aid his former employer, who had fallen ill, he left Yale in the autumn of 1853 and resumed the management of the factory at Seymour, meanwhile reading law. He completed his legal training by a year at the Yale Law School, being admitted to the bar in March 1856. In 1858 Yale granted him the degree of A.B. as of the class of 1854.

Morris began practice at Seymour but moved in 1857 to New Haven, where he spent the rest of his life. As judge of probate from 1857 to 1863 he gained a reputation for honesty and fairness as well as learning. Upon retirement from the bench and in the interim between various political offices he devoted himself again to his legal practice, which consisted largely of the administration of estates and of service under the courts as appraiser, referee, and arbitrator. His sound judgment and high sense of honor fitted him admirably for this type of work, while a certain shyness made pleading at the bar distasteful to him.

His political career began soon after he left college. For two terms (1855–56), he represented Seymour in the lower house of the state legislature, of which body he was again a member in 1870, 1876, 1880, and 1881. In 1874 he served one term as state senator. Thanks to his wise counsel and genial personality, he soon took high rank among his fellow Democrats of the state. In 1888 they nominated him for governor. Morris stood for a revision of the constitution to permit a secret ballot and the election of officers by a plurality rather than a majority of votes. Population had increased rapidly in Connecticut's industrial centers in previous years but no redistribution of seats had followed. Hence the Democratic strongholds were under-represented. Morris failed to obtain a majority of popular votes, and lost the election when the choice was made by a Republican legislature. After a second campaign, in 1890, he seemed to have won the needed majority vote, but the two houses of the legislature disagreed over the accuracy of the ballot count. A tedious and acrimonious dispute followed. The courts failed to settle it and the legislature was deadlocked when the election of 1892 put an end to the matter by the choice of Morris with a clear majority. He carried out the duties of his office for one term with dignity and success, though he failed to effect the constitutional revision which his party desired. Upon retirement he resumed his professional activity, continuing practice until his death by apoplexy, Aug. 22, 1895.

In 1880 Morris was a member of the commission which settled the ancient dispute over the boundary between Connecticut and New York. In 1884 he presided over a commission which remedied various defects in the probate laws of his state. For many years he was an officer of the Connecticut Savings Bank and for a time director of the New York, New Haven & Hartford Railroad Company. His portrait by Thompson in the governor's room at Hartford shows a strong, kindly face. He married, June 15, 1856, Eugenia L. Tuttle of Seymour, by whom he had three sons and three daughters, one of whom, Helen, married Arthur Twining Hadley [*q.v.*], later president of Yale University.

[For biographical material see *Obit. Record Grads. Yale Univ.*, 1896; S. E. Baldwin, obituary sketch in 66 *Conn. Reports*, App.; J. E. Johnson, *Newtown's Hist. and Historian* (1917); F. C. Norton, *The Govs. of Conn.* (1905); *New Haven Evening Register*, Aug. 22, 1895. For the election contest see "Connecticut," in *Appletons' Ann. Cyc.*, 1888, 1890, 1891, 1892.]　P. D. E.

MORRIS, MARY PHILIPSE (1730–1825). [See MORRIS, ROGER, 1727–1794.]

MORRIS, NELSON (Jan. 21, 1838–Aug. 27, 1907), stock-breeder and meat-packer, was born in Hechingen, province of Hohenzollern, near the Black Forest in the southwest part of Germany. He came to America as a boy and reached Chicago in the fifties, looking for work, having walked most of the way from Buffalo, N. Y. He was first employed at the Myrick Stock Yards, one of a number of small stockyards which preceded the building of the Union Stock Yards. Later, by good fortune, he was given work by John B. Sherman, the founder of the Union Stock Yards. As Sherman's protégé he evolved into a head-hog renderer and after several years left Sherman's employ to become a cattle trader on a small scale. His trading tactics were somewhat unique. He was willing to bid on anything and buy anything at a price, usually named by himself. Frequently staying out of the market until late in the week he found his competitors with full coolers and the holders of stale cattle willing to accept any figure within reason to effect a clearance. These were his harvest periods, when with apparent reluctance, protesting that he could not handle more cattle than he had, he cleared the yards. Within a few years he acquired a leading position in the live-cattle trade, not only from Chicago to the Atlantic seaboard, but also in transatlantic shipments.

Morris was not an innovator, but he was a pioneer in transporting dressed beef from Chicago to the Atlantic seaboard. He early secured contracts to supply the French and other European governments with beef and he was also largely instrumental in supplying the commissariat department of the Union troops with livestock during the Civil War. By 1873 his company was earning more than eleven million dollars a year. In 1874 he entered into partnership with Isaac Waixel and for a while the firm was known as Morris & Waixel. Eventually it became Nelson Morris & Company and later simply Morris & Company. The Morris plant was one of the first packing houses to be opened in Chicago at the Union Stock Yards and finally occupied some thirty acres. Outside of Chicago Morris established packing plants at East St. Louis, Ill., St. Joseph, Mo., and Kansas City, Kan. In addition to these interests he owned large cattle ranches in the Dakotas and in Texas and was one of the first to import Polled-Angus and Galloway cattle. At one time he was the most extensive cattle feeder in the world, turning out approximately seventy-five thousand fat bullocks annually from his feedlots.

A man of many contacts, Morris became a director in various corporations. He was interested in a number of banks and other financial institutions, among which was the First National Bank of Chicago, in which he had always been a heavy stockholder and had taken a prominent part as a member of its board of directors. He also invested heavily in real-estate in Chicago. Throughout his life he kept his original simplicity of character. Although he did not care to have his name associated with many charities, he gave of his means for many worthy causes. He established the Nelson Morris Institute of Pathological Research, for the purpose of study and original research in connection with diseases of all kinds, and contributed generously to public institutions, notably to the Michael Reese Hospital. He was married, in 1863, to Sarah Vogel of Chicago. Of his five children, Edward succeeded him as president of Morris & Company, and Ira Nelson entered the diplomatic service of the United States. He died in Chicago.

[See: *Who's Who in America*, 1906–07; P. T. Gilbert and C. L. Bryson, *Chicago and Its Makers* (1929); R. A. Clemen, *The Am. Livestock and Meat Industry* (1923); the *Nat. Provisioner*, Aug. 31, 1907; *Chicago News*, Aug. 27, 1907; *Chicago Tribune*, Aug. 28, 1907. *Who's Who in America* gives Jan. 21, 1839, for date of birth, but the date given in this sketch is correct according to Morris' family.]   R. A. C.

MORRIS, MRS. OWEN [See MORRIS, ELIZABETH, *c.* 1753–1826].

MORRIS, RICHARD (Aug. 15, 1730–Apr. 11, 1810), jurist, was the third son of Lewis Morris, second lord of the manor of Morrisania, and Tryntje (Staats) Morris, and a brother of Gen. Lewis Morris [*q.v.*], signer of the Declaration of Independence. In temperament he was one of the most aristocratic of the Morrises, though, unlike his brother, Staats Long Morris, he finally supported the movement against British authority. Graduating from Yale in 1748, he followed the family tradition and read law in New York City. He was admitted to the bar in 1752, the year his half-brother, Gouverneur [*q.v.*], was born. He soon attained a reputation for legal learning which placed him among the prominent lawyers of the province. His father, who was judge of the court of vice-admiralty, named him deputy and authorized him to hold court in New Jersey. In 1762, under a royal commission issued in the high court of admiralty at London, he became judge of the vice-admiralty court having jurisdiction over New York, Connecticut, and New Jersey, a position which his father and grandfather had filled before him. He played no part in the rising revolt against British authority, but in the autumn of 1775 he tendered his resignation to Governor Tryon, who urged him to retain his post until the political disturbances of the period should be quieted. His hesitation in embracing the Patriot cause was responsible for his citation in June 1776 (Peter Force, *American Archives,* 4 ser. VI, 1368–69),

to the provincial committee to detect conspiracies, as a person of "equivocal neutrality." Nevertheless, when the provincial congress created a high court of admiralty on July 31, 1776 (*Ibid.,* 5 ser. I, 1461), it urged Richard Morris to become the first judge. He declined on the ground that his Westchester estate had been destroyed by the British and his family needed his assistance.

After the new state government had been established, Morris was named by the assembly in 1778 to serve the unexpired term of a senator from the southern district. He remained an inconspicuous member of the upper house until 1780. Meanwhile, he had been appointed in 1779 to succeed John Jay as chief justice of the supreme court of the state. As a member of the New York county delegation at the Poughkeepsie convention of 1788 he worked vigorously for the ratification of the proposed federal Constitution. On several occasions he ably seconded speeches of Hamilton and Jay, though he offered little that was original in his discussion of the ills which would befall the country if New York failed to indorse the work of the Philadelphia convention. The record indicates that he was absent when the final vote resulted in favor of ratification. The following year his friends urged his claims to the Federalist nomination for governor, but a few party leaders opposed him. Hamilton appreciated his ability and his loyalty to Federalist principles, but felt that the Chief Justice was not the best candidate to placate the more moderate anti-Federalists. Accordingly the nomination went to Robert Yates.

In 1790, Morris, having reached the age of sixty, retired from public life. His residence had originally been at Mount Fordham, not far from Morrisania, where he had established his home when he married Sarah Ludlow, June 13, 1759. Following the Revolutionary War he had purchased several farms in the town of Greenburgh and a delightful country-seat in Scarsdale. At the latter place he spent the last twenty years of his life, content to play the rôle of a gentleman farmer. A dignified though somewhat portly representative of the "tie-wig" aristocracy, he seems to have impressed his generation as a man of integrity and extensive knowledge of jurisprudence, attributes which probably explain his elevation to the post of chief justice. He died in Scarsdale in 1810 and was buried at New York in the family vault in Trinity churchyard. His daughter, Mary, wife of Major William Popham, inherited the Scarsdale seat, while the remainder of the estate was divided between his two sons, Lewis Richard [*q.v.*] and Robert.

[M. A. Hamm, *Famous Families of N. Y.* (1901), vol. II; Peter Force, *Am. Archives*, 4 ser. (6 vols., 1837–46), 5 ser. (3 vols., 1848–53); E. B. O'Callaghan, *Calendar of Hist. MSS., 1664–1776*, pt. II (1866); E. A. Werner, *Civil List of . . . N. Y.* (1889); Charles M. Hough, *Reports of Cases in the Vice-Admiralty of the Province of N. Y.* (1925); E. C. Benedict, *The Am. Admiralty* (1850); J. C. Hamilton, *The Works of Alexander Hamilton*, II (1850), 478–79; *N. Y. Evening Post*, Apr. 13, 1810.]   J. A. K.

MORRIS, RICHARD VALENTINE (Mar. 8, 1768–May 13, 1815), naval officer and diplomat, was born at Morrisania, Westchester County, N. Y. He was the youngest son of Lewis Morris, 1726–1798 [*q.v.*], signer of the Declaration of Independence, and Mary (Walton) Morris, member of a prominent shipbuilding family. After the Revolution, during which the family suffered severe hardships and losses, Richard became actively engaged in the maritime enterprises with which his relatives were identified; then, on Jan. 24, 1797, he married his cousin, Anne Walton. On June 8, 1798, he was commissioned captain in the United States Navy, and was placed in command of the U.S.S. *Adams*, then under construction at New York. So satisfactory did his services prove that in 1802 he was given command of a naval squadron which was being sent by the United States to operate against Tripoli. The scope of his authority was subsequently extended by instructions to superintend all negotiations of the United States with Tripoli, Tunis, Algiers, and Morocco.

His first attempt to reach Tripoli failed because of adverse winds, and, although he later blockaded the chief port of the enemy, he was unable to conclude peace on favorable terms (Goldsborough, *post*, pp. 203, 204). Moreover, the Emperor of Morocco demanded certain concessions which Morris quite properly refused to grant; whereupon the Emperor, in June 1803, declared war. The declaration was not followed by the seizure of any American vessels, but throughout the period of his Mediterranean command Morris' concentration upon his chief task was lessened by the hostility of Morocco. Additional difficulties arose when the Algerine government refused to commute, from naval and military stores to cash, certain annual payments which the United States had been accustomed to make to Algiers. The Bey of Tunis was also unfriendly, and constantly made threats against the United States. In order to placate him Morris, in February 1803, landed at Tunis. The Bey thereupon refused him permission to depart until Morris had granted certain concessions.

In June 1803 Morris was ordered to relinquish his command and to return to the United States. In consequence of the subsequent report of a court of inquiry that he had not displayed "the diligence or activity necessary to execute the important duties of his station," his commission was revoked. There were circumstances other than, or in addition to, lack of diligence on his part which contributed to the squadron's ineffectiveness in 1802–03: the armament was small, and some of the vessels were unseaworthy; means of communication were most unsatisfactory; and all the North African rulers were hostile. These factors Morris emphasized in an elaborate and, on the whole, convincing pamphlet, *A Defence of the Conduct of Commodore Morris During His Command in the Mediterranean* (1804). Since he incorporated in this work many official dispatches relative to the whole field of his Mediterranean activities, it is of considerable importance as a source for the study of relations between the United States and the Barbary Powers.

After thus seeking vindication in the public estimation, he retired with his family to Morrisania, where he busied himself with his estate and other private interests until his death. He was survived by his wife and three children, one son having died in 1798.

[E. M. W. Lefferts, *Descendants of Lewis Morris of Morrisania* (1907); W. W. Spooner, *Hist. Families of America* (copr. 1907); C. W. Goldsborough, *The U. S. Naval Chronicle* (1824); G. W. Allen, *Our Navy and the Barbary Corsairs* (1905); C. O. Paullin, *Diplomatic Negotiations of Am. Naval Officers* (1912); R. W. Irwin, *The Diplomatic Relations of the U. S. with the Barbary Powers* (1931); Dispatches: Algiers, Tunis, and Tripoli, in Archives of Dept. of State, Washington, D. C.; *N. Y. Evening Post*, May 15, 1815.]   R. W. I.

MORRIS, ROBERT (Jan. 31, 1734–May 8, 1806), financier of the American Revolution, was born in or near Liverpool, England. The name of his mother is unknown. At the age of thirteen he appeared in Maryland, where he joined his father, also Robert Morris, who was at the time engaged at Oxford on the Chesapeake in exporting tobacco. He was put to school in Philadelphia, but his time there was brief and his acquisitions were scanty. Soon he was in the service of the Willings, shipping merchants, who held a secure position in the commercial as well as in the social life of Philadelphia. By diligence and industry he won the respect and confidence of his employers to such a degree that in 1754 he was made a member of the firm. To Willing, Morris & Company, and its successors under other names, he gave his interest for thirty-nine years and, for a large part of that period, his active direction. The business of the house involved the importation of British manufactures and colonial produce, and the exportation of American goods for which there was a market abroad. It embraced the ownership of ships and a general exchange and banking business. Prudence, with courage and resolution, led to success and the accumulation of wealth, and Morris individually, as well as the firm, held a leading position in the trade of Philadelphia and of America in general when the first crisis was reached in the controversy with Great Britain on the question of taxation. His first appearance in public affairs occurred during the resistance to the Stamp Act, when he was one of those who signed the non-importation agreement of 1765. In October of that year he served on a committee of citizens appointed to force the collector of the stamp tax in Philadelphia to desist from performing the duties of his office. The following year he was warden of the Port of Philadelphia.

Although, when the first Continental Congress met in Philadelphia in 1774, Morris was not yet committed to the "Patriot" cause, he took his place a few months later among its leading representatives. It is related that the die was cast in his case on St. George's Day (Apr. 23), 1775, when, while he and others were attending a dinner of the Society of the Sons of St. George, a courier brought the news of the battle of Lexington. On June 30, 1775, he was made a member of the Council of Safety by the Assembly, and on Oct. 20 was reappointed on the new Council to serve during the ensuing year. His commercial experience was put to use at once; from the beginning he was a member of the committee charged with procuring munitions, and he frequently acted as its banker. In the absence of Franklin, he presided over the Council. In September, a secret committee of the Continental Congress contracted with Willing & Morris for the importation of arms and ammunition. Morris was elected in October to the last Pennsylvania Assembly held under the colonial charter; he was on the Committee of Correspondence, and in November 1775 was sent by the Assembly as a delegate to the Congress.

Within a fortnight after taking his seat he had been appointed to provide two swift vessels to carry dispatches. On Nov. 29 he succeeded his partner, Willing, on the Secret Committee for the procuring of munitions, and two weeks later, was placed on the committee for providing naval armament. He was appointed, Jan. 30, 1776, to the Committee of Secret Correspondence which during the following month drew up the instructions to Silas Deane [q.v.], envoy to France. In March, he was put on a committee to devise "ways and means" and on another to

consider the fortifying of one or more seaports. Meanwhile he continued, as a member of the firm of Willing & Morris, to import supplies for the army, and from time to time was charged with banking business for the Congress. An able business man, he lost no opportunity to make his profit in a deal, or, when acting as broker, to collect his commission. This fact was recognized by his colleagues, but it in no way lessened their confidence in him. In April John Adams wrote to Horatio Gates: "You ask me what you are to think of Robt. Morris? ... I think he has a masterly Understanding, an open Temper and an honest Heart. . . . He has vast designs in the mercantile way. And no doubt pursues mercantile ends, which are always gain; but he is an excellent Member of our Body" (Burnett, post, I, 433).

Morris voted against the Declaration of Independence in July 1776, thinking it premature (see his letter to Joseph Reed, July 21, 1776, Burnett, post, II, 19), but he signed it in August, and thereafter wished the whole attention of the country to be given to the prosecution of the war (Sumner, Financier, post, I, 197). He was returned to Congress in July by the Pennsylvania convention, and in August and September was directed by the Secret Committee to purchase tobacco for export in exchange for supplies. In November he was chosen to the first Pennsylvania Assembly under the new constitution, but was unable to give much time to its business, and in the following February another member was elected in his stead.

After the flight of Congress from Philadelphia in December 1776, Morris remained in the city to carry on the work of his committee. He bought supplies and borrowed money in the face of appalling difficulties, providing Washington and the leaders in the field moral support and material assistance without which the army must have been dispersed. In the spring of 1777 the Committee of Secret Correspondence became the Committee of Foreign Affairs, and in July was reconstituted as the Committee of Commerce. Through all these changes Morris remained a member, and frequently served as its banker. There is no doubt that he made large profits in his capacity as middleman, but he likewise took great risks, and he "employed for the public all the knowledge or opportunities which he possessed" (Sumner, I, 205). A contemporary observer, writing in October 1777 said that Congress was ruled by Richard Henry Lee, the Adamses, and Robert Morris; and in the following year, characterized Morris as "active, zealous, . . . Bold and enterprizing—of great mercantíle knowledge, fertile in expedients & an able financier. Very popular in & out of the Congress; grown extremely rich. . . . Is much Confided in by all the Cabals" (Paul Wentworth, in B. F. Stevens, *Facsimiles of Manuscripts in European Archives Relating to America, 1773–1780,* 1890, nos. 277, 487).

During the winter of 1777–78 the misbehavior of his younger half-brother, Thomas, for whom he had secured appointment as commercial agent of the United States at Nantes, France, caused a temporary misunderstanding between Morris and the commissioners Deane and Franklin, but the matter was cleared up after the death of the young man early in 1778. In March of that year Morris signed the Articles of Confederation on behalf of Pennsylvania, and in August he was made chairman of the congressional committee on finance, serving until the expiration of his term, Nov. 1, 1778.

Being ineligible to reëlection, under the democratic constitution of Pennsylvania, he retired from Congress, but continued his exertions in the Pennsylvania Assembly, to which he was immediately elected, taking his seat Nov. 6. In swearing allegiance to the new constitution he reserved the right to agitate for its amendment. During the following winter Congress was torn by arguments over the conduct of Silas Deane [*q.v.*]. Morris took no part in the controversy, although his sympathies were with Deane, with whom he had had commercial relations. In January 1779, however, Thomas Paine [*q.v.*], through the press, attacked Morris as well as Deane for conducting private commercial enterprises while holding public office, and in Congress, on Jan. 9, Henry Laurens [*q.v.*] made charges of fraudulent transactions against the firm of Willing & Morris. A congressional committee investigated the charges and at Morris' request examined his books, reporting as their opinion "that the said Robert Morris . . . has acted with fidelity and integrity and an honorable zeal for the happiness of his country" (State Dept. MSS., No. 137, App. 36, quoted by Sumner, I, 226). Nevertheless, this incident and the Deane controversy affected the opinion toward Morris of many of his political opponents who, being poor, resented his great wealth. A mass-meeting in May appointed a committee to investigate his conduct, and although he was vindicated by another mass-meeting in July, his popularity had declined sufficiently to permit his defeat at the polls in November. For a year he held no public office, but in November 1780 was again elected to the Assembly, where he served until June 1781.

In the winter of 1780–81 the outlook for the Continental cause was wholly dark, less for want of military strength and capacity of direction in the field than for the means of making these available. The paper currency was not worth the cost of printing it; on further loans in Europe hope might not confidently rest; the states had been called upon for their quotas, but the Union under the Articles of Confederation was a "rope of sand" and no importunities would avail without power of enforcement. The Treasury was empty, credit was gone. As early as February 1780 Pelatiah Webster had advocated the appointment of a single financier to supplant the committees, and the same proposition had been urged in September by Hamilton, who mentioned Morris for the post (H. C. Lodge, *The Works of Alexander Hamilton,* vol. I, 1885, p. 215). That a financial dictator was needed was recognized by Congress in February 1781, and on the 20th, without a dissenting vote, Morris was chosen superintendent of finance.

Before accepting this unique office, in which he would assume a burden such as had rarely been placed on the shoulders of one man, Morris insisted that Congress recognize his right to retain his private commercial connections, and that he be permitted to control the personnel of his department (Sparks, *post,* XI, 350). Congress at first hesitated to grant him the executive independence his task required, but in view of the desperate need of his services, it finally yielded most of what he asked. In his letter of acceptance, May 14, 1781, he expressed the view of the sound commercial banker, saying that the outstanding debt must be funded so that provision for its payment might be made: "The least breach of faith must ruin us forever. . . . Congress will know that the public credit cannot be restored without method, economy, and punctual performance of contracts. Time is necessary for each" (*Ibid.,* 363). The letter also contained the assertion: "The United States may command everything I have, except my integrity, and the loss of that would effectually disable me from serving them more" (*Ibid.,* p. 362). By "integrity" he meant the commercial honor of his signature (Sumner, I, 268, note), which time and again had made it possible for him to borrow money for the public cause. Although he began at once to organize his department, he did not formally assume his new duties for some weeks, but remained in the Pennsylvania Assembly in order to win the support of his own state in the policies he projected.

Morris took office with a definite program which included federal taxes laid in specie, to be used in paying interest on the debt; requisitions from the states, to be used to carry on the war; a possible loan from France; and vigilant economy. To save expense to the government he accepted himself the agency of marine, Sept. 8, and on Sept. 12, 1781, was authorized to fit out and employ the ships of the United States. He assumed the task of buying supplies for the armies, abolishing the wasteful system of regimental commissaries. He made himself unpopular with the medical department by investigating alleged extravagance in hospitals. He used notes which circulated only by reason of his own credit, pressed the states in impassioned phrase for their contributions, which he would have furnished him in cash and not in "specific supplies," called for accounting in reference to financial operations in Europe, and put vigor, as well as order, into civil administration. During all this period, however, he was being driven to greater risks and the use of daring financial sleight-of-hand by the desperate need of money. He has been harshly criticized for possessing the "art or abuse, of dazzling the public eye by the same piece of coin, multiplied by a thousand reflectors" (William Johnson, *Sketches of the Life . . . of Nathanael Greene,* 1822, II, 255), but only the possession of that art enabled him to finance the Yorktown campaign which resulted in the surrender of Cornwallis. A timely loan of $200,000 in specie, brought by the French fleet, made possible the formation of the Bank of North America, which opened its doors in January 1782. Morris was one of the heaviest subscribers, strengthening the bank by his personal credit. "I am . . . determined," he wrote to John Jay, "that the bank shall be well supported, until it can support itself, and then it will support us" (Sparks, VII, 440). From it he was able to borrow heavily on behalf of the Congress.

Despite all his efforts to arouse the states to a sense of their obligations, he failed to secure the revenue upon which he had counted, and in January 1783 there was as little prospect of paying the debts he had contracted since taking office as there had been two years before. In despair and disgust with the states and the impotent Congress, he tendered his resignation, Jan. 24: "To increase our debts, while the prospect of paying them diminishes does not consist with my ideas of integrity. I must therefore quit a situation which becomes utterly insupportable" (Sparks, XII, 326). When the fact became public, he was subjected to violent abuse in the press. In May, because there was no one else to undertake the task, he was prevailed upon to retain office until the army was paid and disbanded. A loan secured by John Adams in The Netherlands carried him through, and in September 1784 he extricated himself from the affairs of the states with his personal fortune unimpaired and the public credit as high as it could be placed under the circumstances.

The following year (October 1785) he was elected to the General Assembly of Pennsylvania for the special purpose of defending the Bank of North America. He and others hired Thomas Paine to write in favor of the Bank, and Morris is said to have paid Mathew Carey for publishing debates on the bank question. Reëlected the following year, he served on the committee appointed to consider the proposition of Virginia that a convention be held for the purpose of regulating commerce, and was a delegate to that convention (Annapolis, 1786). During this period he gave considerable attention to building up his own business. In 1785 he made a contract with the French Farmers-General which gave him the monopoly of the American tobacco trade with France. This circumstance aroused the antagonism of other American tobacco dealers, and had a marked effect on French politics (Nussbaum, *post*).

Convinced by experience that the Republic could not survive without a firm central government, he took his place naturally among the Federalists. Neither Hamilton, nor Washington, nor John Adams better understood the futility of direct democracy, without "checks and balances," or the danger that the new nation would face, if it were to remain a mere league of states. He sat in the convention at Philadelphia in 1787 which framed the Constitution of the United States, and though he took little part in debates or committee work, lent the weight of his opinion to the *Bundesstaat* rather than the *Staatenbund*. He probably agreed in almost every detail with his business associate and former assistant, Gouverneur Morris [*q.v.*], who was the most frequent speaker on the floor of the Convention. Robert Morris was offered and declined the position of secretary of the treasury in Washington's first cabinet, and was one of the two men whom Pennsylvania sent to the United States Senate immediately upon the organization of the new government, serving 1789–95.

Before his term had come to an end, he was deeply involved in land speculations which, at this period, brought so many to disaster. His belief in the potential value of the undeveloped lands west of the settled areas, together with his audacious confidence in himself by reason of the long-continued and unwavering success of his financial projects, especially his daring maneuvers during the Revolution, led to his downfall. He had not foreseen the Napoleonic wars, the paralysis of Europe, and the distress which at such a time must follow in the wake of a great extension of business founded upon borrowing and credit. He had bought great tracts of land in western New York and elsewhere. With a partner he held a large part of the site of the present city of Washington, a wilderness to which after ten years the capital of the Republic was to be removed. The foundations of a really vast fortune were shaken, and all went down together for want of the opportunity to sell what Morris had so hopefully acquired, and of means to pay the taxes upon it and to meet interest charges upon his loans. On the day of collapse, he had in course of construction a palatial marble house in Philadelphia, designed by L'Enfant [q.v.], architect of the Federal City. To a country estate, "The Hills," on the Schuylkill River, he retreated, and there, in February 1798, a small creditor caused him to be arrested. He was taken to "Prune Street," the debtors' prison in the city, in which, in a good deal of misery, not diminished in summer by devastating epidemics of yellow fever, he remained for three years, six months, and ten days. On Aug. 26, 1801, he was released under the federal bankruptcy law, and thereafter was supported by his wife's annuity, secured for her by Gouverneur Morris. He was by this time broken in body and in spirit and ended his days in a small dwelling house in Philadelphia, a nearly forgotten and much pitied man.

Morris' rise to eminence had been as spectacular as his fall. By sheer personal ability he won and merited the affectionate friendship of the most intelligent and discriminating of the public characters of his time. It has been said that few, if any, in the councils of the young nation so fully commanded the respect and confidence of Washington. Certainly there were none to whom the commander-in-chief owed more. The relationship between the two men was one of frank, open-hearted comradeship, though one was noted for a certain austerity of social manner, while the other was markedly accessible, free and radiant of spirit. Morris was the most generous and lavish of hosts, as many had reason to know who came to Philadelphia while that city was the meeting place of Congress and the capital of the country. At the age of thirty-five, Mar. 2, 1769, he married Mary White, of Maryland, daughter of Col. Thomas White and sister of William White [q.v.], who, as Bishop White, was a venerated figure in the American Episcopal Church for a period of fifty years. Mrs. Morris adorned her husband's house and increased the reputation of his hospitalities.

Morris' writing was terse and spirited, and few of the men who employed their talents in establishing the republic could put so much common sense, with good humor, into English phrase. Sentences from his letters and "Circulars" while he was superintendent of finance ring with eloquence no less than truth, as he pleaded with the states for money with which to prosecute the war. Though he was not a finished public orator, he could at need speak with directness and force, and draw to him attentive listeners. It was of him that William Pierce, a delegate in the Constitutional Convention from Georgia, wrote, while that body was still in session: "He has an understanding equal to any public object, and possesses an energy of mind that few Men can boast of. Although he is not learned, yet he is as great as those who are. I am told that when he speaks in the Assembly of Pennsylvania he bears down all before him" (Farrand, post, III, 91). Of his five sons and two daughters, two sons died before their father. His wife survived him until 1827. Morris died in his seventy-third year, and was buried in "the family vault of William White and Robert Morris," behind Christ Church, Philadelphia.

[Biographies include E. P. Oberholtzer, *Robert Morris, Patriot and Financier* (1903); W. G. Sumner, *The Financier and Finances of the American Revolution* (2 vols., 1891), condensed and abridged in *Robert Morris* (1892). Noteworthy biographical sketches are by Robert Waln, Jr., in John Sanderson, *Biog. of the Signers to the Declaration of Independence*, vol. V (copr. 1825); E. A. Duyckinck, *Nat. Portrait Gallery of Eminent Americans* (1862), vol. I; Joseph Delaplaine, *Delaplaine's Repository of the Lives and Portraits of Distinguished Americans*, vol. II, pt. 1 (1818); A. N. Hart, "Robert Morris," in *Pa. Mag. of Hist. and Biog.*, I (1877), 333; C. H. Hart, "Mary White—Mrs. Robert Morris," *Ibid.*, II (1878), 157. For the ramifications of Morris' tobacco enterprise, see F. L. Nussbaum, "American Tobacco and French Politics, 1783–89," *Pol. Sci. Quart.*, Dec. 1925. For his land speculations see Orsamus Turner, *Pioneer Hist. of the Holland Purchase* (1849) and *Hist. of the Pioneer Settlement of Phelps and Gorham's Purchase and Morris' Reserve* (1851); P. D. Evans, "The Holland Land Company," *Buffalo Hist. Soc. Pubs.*, vol. XXVIII (1924); A. C. Clark, *Greenleaf and Law in the Federal City* (1901). A thirty-four word obituary notice appeared in Duane's *Aurora* and Poulson's *Am. Daily Advertiser* (both Phila.), May 10, 1806. Published source materials include: "Letters to Robert Morris," in *N. Y. Hist. Soc. Colls., Pub. Fund Ser.*, vol. XI (1879); Jared Sparks, *The Diplomatic Correspondence of the Am. Rev.* (12 vols., 1829–30); E. C. Burnett, *Letters of Members of the Continental Congress* (1921 ff.); and the writings of contemporaries. The most important manuscript sources are the diaries and letter-books of Robert Morris and the Papers of the Continental Congress in the Lib. of Cong.]   E. P. O.

MORRIS, ROBERT (c. 1745–June 2, 1815), federal judge and chief justice of the supreme court of New Jersey, was the natural son of Chief Justice Robert Hunter Morris [q.v.] and the grandson of Lewis Morris, 1671-1746 [*q.v.*], first lord of the manor of Morrisania, who became royal governor of the province of New Jersey in 1738. He was born at New Brunswick, probably in 1745. His father died suddenly in 1764, but Robert was able to complete his legal studies, in which he manifested that aptitude which had characterized the Morrises for several generations. Admitted to the bar in September 1770, he was licensed as a counselor three years later. Though he had never presided over a court, he was chosen by the joint ballot of the legislature in 1777 as chief justice of the newly created supreme court of the state. The difficult task to which he was called had already been declined by Richard Stockton and John De-Hart. Upon Morris, versed only in the theory of judicial procedure, devolved the responsibility of formulating rules for the high court of the state and of organizing county courts and the court of oyer and terminer. Having entered upon his duties in February 1777, he was instructed by the council to hold a term of oyer and terminer in Sussex County in May. With his customary energy he carried out instructions, reporting in vigorous language to Gov. William Livingston the difficulty of holding court with inexperienced officers and with associate judges who were "but reputable farmers, doctors and shopkeepers" (Elmer, *post*, pp. 267–69). Zealous and fearless in meeting the demands from various parts of the state for the institution of courts, he was angered when the legislature inquired whether he was sufficiently diligent in the performance of his duties. He brusquely replied to his critics: "I accepted my present office to manifest my resolution to serve my country. . . . Whenever the legislature think they can fill it more advantageously the tenor of my commission shall not disappoint them" (*Ibid.*). The exacting nature of his work, aggravated by the legislators' interference, soon proved irksome to his independent spirit and he tendered his resignation in June 1779. Brief though his term had been, it had demonstrated his competence upon the bench and had marked the translation into reality of the plan for a system of state courts.

For a dozen years Morris practised law in New Brunswick, accumulating in the process a considerable estate in land. He was a member of the Protestant Episcopal Church and served the Christ Church parish almost twenty years as warden. His reputation as a jurist persisted and, being in the good graces of the Federalists of the state, he was recommended for a place on the federal bench. When the United States dis-

trict courts were organized under the Judiciary Act of 1789, President Washington named him judge in the New Jersey district, a position which he filled acceptably for twenty-five years. The docket in his court could not have been heavily burdened, for his prolonged absences, occasioned by serious illness, did not seem to interfere with the administration of justice. He died at New Brunswick on June 2, 1815.

[*Archives of the State of N. J.*, 2 ser. III (1906); L. Q. C. Elmer, "The Constitution and Government of . . . New Jersey," *N. J. Hist. Soc. Colls.*, vol. VII (1872); W. W. Clayton, *Hist. of Union and Middlesex Counties, N. J.* (1882); E. Q. Keasbey, *The Courts and Lawyers of N. J., 1661–1912* (1912), vol. II; W. H. Benedict, *New Brunswick in Hist.* (1925); *Proc. N. J. Hist. Soc.*, July 1920, Apr. 1921; N. Y. *Evening Post*, June 5, 1815.]   J. A. K.

MORRIS, ROBERT (Aug. 31, 1818–July 31, 1888), Masonic writer and lecturer, was born near Boston, Mass. His parents were schoolteachers, and he was educated for the same vocation and followed it for a number of years. Shortly after reaching his majority he left New England and settled in Oxford, Miss., where he became principal of Mount Sylvan Academy. On Aug. 26, 1841, he married Charlotte Mendenhall, who resided near Oxford. Three sons and three daughters were born to them. He moved to Lodgeton, Ky., in 1853, to La Grange in 1860, and later lived for some time in Louisville. In 1868 he visited the Holy Land and made extensive researches which are embodied in his work *Freemasonry in the Holy Land* (1872). For a brief period he was president of the Masonic College at La Grange. In addition to his interest in education, he was an ardent geologist and numismatist and at one time was secretary of the American Association of Numismatists. He was also an honorary member of several archeological societies. His contributions to the scientific and religious press were numerous, and he enriched Sunday-school literature with scores of odes, sketches, addresses, and songs. Many of his poems were composed in stage coaches, railway carriages, steamboats, and on horseback. The most famous of these is "The Level and the Square."

His personality is best expressed by one who referred to him as "lank as a rattlesnake and as swift at a witty stroke; nervous to the last degree; frightfully dyspeptic; extremely fond of nature and an indefatigable collector of shells, arrow-heads and eccentric stones; a glutton for books; fluent as the river and generous as the sea; speaking in all things from the heart, amiable and generous" (quoted by Kenaston, *post*, p. 73). The fact that a contemporary writer had the same name caused him to shorten his first name to Rob, his reason being that when the other Robert wrote anything which was not well received he got the blame for it.

He was made a Master Mason in Oxford Lodge, No. 33, Oxford, Miss., on July 3, 1846. Owing to changes of residence, his lodge membership was transferred, and in 1860 he is recorded as a Past Master of Fortitude Lodge, No. 47, La Grange, Ky. He was Grand Master of the Grand Lodge of Kentucky, 1858–59, held membership in other rites of Freemasonry, and has been called the founder of the Order of the Eastern Star. In his extensive travels he delivered thousands of lectures, and was crowned "Poet Laureate of Freemasonry" in the Masonic Hall, New York City, Dec. 17, 1884. To the Masonic fraternity he gave a new literature, the result of painstaking research, which has permanent value. Among his publications, besides innumerable articles in magazines, are *The Lights and Shadows of Freemasonry* (1852); *Life in the Triangle* (1854); *A Code of Masonic Law* (1856); *The History of Freemasonry in Kentucky* (1859); *Tales of Masonic Life* (1860); *The Masonic Martyr, the Biography of Eli Bruce* (1861); *Masonic Odes and Poems* (1864); *The Dictionary of Freemasonry* (1867); *Freemasonry in the Holy Land* (1872); *William Morgan; or, Political Anti-Masonry, Its Rise, Growth, and Decadence* (1883); *The Poetry of Freemasonry* (1884). He was the editor of a number of Masonic periodicals and publisher of the Universal Masonic Library in thirty volumes. His death occurred at La Grange, Ky., where he was buried with all honors of Masonry.

[T. R. Austin, *The Well Spent Life, the Masonic Career of Robert Morris* (1878); L. V. Rule, *Pioneering in Masonry, the Life and Times of Rob Morris* (1922); J. M. Kenaston, *Hist. of the Order of the Eastern Star* (1917); *Voice of Masonry and Family Mag.*, Sept. 1888; biographical notice in Morris' *Poetry of Freemasonry* (ed. in 1895); *Courier-Jour.* (Louisville, Ky.), Aug. 1, 1888.]   W. L. B.

MORRIS, ROBERT HUNTER (*c.* 1700–Jan. 27, 1764), chief justice of New Jersey and governor of Pennsylvania, was born at Morrisania, N. Y., the second son of Lewis Morris, 1671–1746 [*q.v.*], and Isabella (Graham). He received a "liberal education," as that term was understood in the eighteenth century, and was trained in political affairs by his father, whose argumentative ability he seems to have inherited. When Lewis Morris was appointed governor of New Jersey in 1738, the name of his son, Robert, appeared on the list of councilors. Within the year Governor Morris named Robert as chief justice of the province, his commission to run "during good behavior in same," though the war-

rant of the previous incumbent, Robert L. Hooper, had been phrased "during the royal pleasure." As chief justice, Morris "stuck to punctuality in the forms of the courts, reduced the pleadings to precision and method, and possessed the great qualities of his office, knowledge and integrity in more perfection than had often been known in the colonies" (Smith, *post,* p. 439).

While his father was governor, Morris belligerently defended the royal prerogative, using his influence on the council with telling effect. He became a member of the council of proprietors for East Jersey in 1742 and was soon one of the most active in protecting the interests of the landholders of the province. His great concern after 1745 was for the speedy suppression of the riots occasioned by disputes over land titles and by resentment on the part of tenants against the proprietors. Feeling that Gov. Jonathan Belcher [*q.v.*] was too lenient with the rioters, Morris secured a power of attorney from the East Jersey proprietors and sailed for England in 1749. Several projects besides the settlement of the land problem were in his mind. During the five years that he remained in England he worked against the plan to reunite the provinces of New York and New Jersey, tried to collect the arrears of salary which the assembly refused to pay his father's estate, and urged his friends to help him secure a suitable executive post in America. In 1754 John and Thomas Penn offered him the governorship of Pennsylvania, which he accepted.

The Pennsylvania interlude was far from happy for Governor Morris. At the outset he clashed with the assembly over his refusal to publish his instructions. The ill feeling thus engendered cropped out in a controversy concerning funds to be devoted to the protection of the frontier against the French and their Indian allies. As the assembly would not vote the money in accordance with the proprietors' instructions, Morris failed to secure adequate support for the militia and was bitterly denounced by the western counties. So ably did Benjamin Franklin present the cause of the legislators that the Governor finally gave up the struggle and resigned in 1756.

Returning to New Jersey, Morris resumed his post as chief justice, for his resignation, presented in 1754, had never been accepted. In 1757, however, he visited England, and during his absence William Aynsley was named chief justice and served until July 1758. When Morris announced his intention of resuming his judicial duties again, he learned that Nathaniel Jones, an unknown London barrister, had been appointed to succeed Aynsley. Jones presented himself in March 1760, but Judge Samuel Nevill of the supreme court ruled that his credentials were not satisfactory, since the commission of Robert Hunter Morris had never been surrendered. Since Jones did not contest the matter, Judge Morris remained on the bench until his death.

Despite his disputatious temperament, Morris was a great favorite socially. Of handsome countenance and imposing presence, he charmed his acquaintances by his facile conversation and compelled their admiration by the wide range of his interests. He was still active in public affairs when he dropped dead at a dance given near his home in Shrewsbury, N. J. Though he had never married, he had at least three natural children, one of whom, Robert Morris, c. 1745–1815 [q.v.], inherited most of his considerable estate.

[R. S. Field, "The Provincial Courts of New Jersey," *N. J. Hist. Soc. Colls.*, vol. III (1849) ; Samuel Smith, *The Hist. of the Colony of Nova-Cæsaria or N.J.* (1765) ; Benjamin Franklin's autobiography, in A. H. Smyth, *The Writings of Benjamin Franklin*, vol. I (1905) ; *Pa. Archives*, 4 ser. II (1900) ; *Archives of the State of N. J.*, 1 ser. V–IX (1882–85), and XXXII (1928), p. 298 ; E. B. O'Callaghan, *Docs. Rel. to the Colonial Hist. of the State of N. Y.*, vol. VI (1855) ; W. W. Spooner, *Hist. Families of America* (copr. 1907) ; *N. J. Hist. Soc. Colls.*, vol. IX (1916).]   J. A. K.

MORRIS, ROGER (Jan. 28, 1727–Sept. 13, 1794), British soldier and Loyalist, was the third son of Roger Morris of Netherby, Yorkshire, and of his wife Mary, daughter of Sir Peter Jackson. First commissioned in 1745, he accompanied Braddock to Virginia in 1755 as captain in the 48th Regiment and was wounded at the Monongahela. After serving as aide-de-camp to Generals Braddock, Shirley, and Webb successively, he became major of brigade in March 1757, attached to the staff of Webb, his intimate friend, at Fort Edward. Promoted to a belated majority in the 35th in February 1758, he served at Halifax during the summer, accompanied Monckton up the River St. John in September, and remained as commanding officer at Fort Frederic until the following spring. During the next two years in Canada he commanded detachments of grenadiers at the siege of Quebec and at Montreal, took part in the battle of Sillery, 1760, and became lieutenant-colonel of the 47th in May 1760.

In 1764 Morris resigned from the army to assume an entirely different station and mode of life as the husband of one of the wealthiest heiresses in New York, Mary Philipse (July 3, 1730–July 18, 1825), daughter of Frederic Philipse, second lord of Philipse Manor. Charming

"Captain Polly," adored by half the officers in New York, had given her hand to Morris, "a Ladys Man, always something to say," in January 1758, and with it 51,000 acres in Dutchess County, with 156 tenants, a rent-roll worth nearly £1,000 a year. For the next ten years Morris lived in New York, either at the town house on Stone Street, at the impressive Morris Mansion (later the Jumel Mansion) which he built in Harlem, or, for two months in the year only, in a comfortable "loghouse" on Lot Number Five. Though he paid little attention to his estates, he was regular in his attendance at the provincial council, of which he became a member in 1765. After the battle of Lexington he went to England, unwilling to commit himself to either side, and though he returned in December 1777, could not prevent the confiscation of all his property by an act of attainder of the state legislature, in which both he and his wife were named. Even then he took no commission in the British army, serving only as inspector of the claims of refugees with the temporary rank of colonel, and as councilor under Governor Robertson. In 1783 he left America forever with his wife, two sons, and two daughters, and settled in Yorkshire. He or his family subsequently received as compensation from the British government a fourth of the value of their American estates, and his heirs, who by Mary Philipse's marriage settlement had a right to those estates and had not been themselves attainted, sold their claims to John Jacob Astor in 1809 for £20,000. Both Roger Morris and his wife were buried in the churchyard of St. Savioursgate, York.

[See *The Northcliffe Collection* (Ottawa, 1926) ; W. O. Raymond, *The River St. John* (1910) ; John Knox, *An Hist. Jour. of the Campaigns in North America* (3 vols., 1914–16), ed. by A. G. Doughty for the Champlain Soc. ; E. H. Hall, *Philipse Manor Hall at Yonkers, N. Y.* (1912) ; W. H. Shelton, *The Jumel Mansion* (1916). In the Public Record Office, London, A. O. 12:21, ff. 185 sqq. is the examination of Morris' claim by the Commissioners . . . for enquiring into the Losses and Services of the American Loyalists.]   S. M. P.

MORRIS, THOMAS (Jan. 3, 1776–Dec. 7, 1844), senator from Ohio, was the fifth child in the family of twelve children of a Baptist preacher of Welsh descent, Isaac Morris, and of Ruth (Henton) Morris and his wife. He was the descendant of Thomas Morris who emigrated from England to Massachusetts in 1637. Soon after his birth in Berks County, Pa., his parents settled near Clarksburg, now in West Virginia. With the exception of three months in a common-school he was educated by himself and by his abolitionist mother and father who had a library composed of three Bibles, four New Testaments, a work on elocution, and a few other books. In 1795 he moved to Columbia, now part of Cincinnati, Ohio, where he studied and worked as clerk in a store for the Rev. John Smith, one of the first two United States senators from Ohio. He married Rachael Davis of Welsh descent on Nov. 19, 1797, and moved to Bethel, Ohio, in 1804, where he established his permanent home. He became the father of three daughters and eight sons, one of whom preached at his funeral in the Bethel cemetery and two of whom were elected later to Congress as Democrats. While leading the hard life of a frontier brick-maker he read Blackstone at night by the light of his log-cabin fireplace.

He entered politics after his admission to the bar in 1804 and was elected to the state legislature, where in 1806 he began fifteen terms of service as a state legislator, in the House of Representatives for the fifth, seventh, ninth, tenth, and nineteenth sessions from 1806 to 1821, and in the Senate for the twelfth, thirteenth, twentieth, twenty-first, twenty-fourth to twenty-seventh, thirtieth, and thirty-first sessions from 1813 to 1833. He was chosen judge of the state supreme court in 1809, but later legislation prevented his qualifying. In 1828, with Samuel Medary [q.v.], he established the *Ohio Sun* to support Andrew Jackson for president. After his defeat for Congress in 1832 the Ohio legislature elected him United States senator to serve a full term, 1833–39. He was an able speaker in spite of his diffidence. He wielded great power over juries with speeches filled with Biblical quotations. He was a stanch partisan but not of the pro-slavery wing of the Democracy. True Democracy meant to him the supremacy of the Bible in a society wherein men harmonized their lives with the laws of nature. His political doctrines were determined by his legalistic and moralistic temperament. He opposed lotteries, chartered monopolies, and imprisonment for debt, and he advocated temperance, the prohibition of alcohol, freedom of conscience in religion, education at state expense, and the recall of judges. As a Unionist he denounced nullification and secession as revolutionary and destructive of American liberty; as an expansionist and abolitionist he boldly opposed the extension of slavery. He believed slavery was a moral evil, a national calamity, the greatest national sin. At a time when it was political suicide in Ohio to be an aggressive radical he incurred the condemnation of the South and lost the support of tactful politicians in his own state by his introduction of petitions in the United States Senate to abolish slavery in the District of Colum-

bia. Probably his greatest speech was a defense of the abolitionists that he made in the Senate on Feb. 9, 1839, in answer to a severe condemnation of their principles and tactics by Henry Clay (*Congressional Globe*, 25 Cong., 3 Sess., 180–88, app., 167–75). In 1840 he went home ostracized, contemned, and martyred to his cause. The threats of mobs and riotous disturbances did not deter him in his anti-slavery crusade from 1841 to 1844. He was active in the campaign and election of 1844 as the nominee for the vice-presidency of the Liberty party and died of apoplexy soon afterward. His greatest contributions were made as chairman of judiciary committees on which he served for many years and as the abolitionist example and preceptor of the Ohio trio, Salmon P. Chase, Joshua R. Giddings, and Benjamin Wade.

[B. F. Morris, *The Life of Thomas Morris* (1856); C. B. Galbreath, *Hist. of Ohio* (1925), vol. II; *The Biog. Cyc. and Portrait Gallery . . . of the State of Ohio*, vol. I (1883); Henry Howe, *Hist. Colls. of Ohio*, centennial ed., vol. I (1889); J. B. Swing, "Thomas Morris," *Ohio Arch. and Hist. Soc. Quart.*, Jan. 1902; *Ibid.*, July 1922.]
W. E. S—h.

MORRIS, THOMAS ARMSTRONG (Dec. 26, 1811–Mar. 22, 1904), engineer, was born in Nicholas County, Ky. His father, Morris Morris, and his mother, Rachel (Morris) Morris, were cousins, grandchildren respectively of two brothers, James and John Morris, emigrants from Wales to Virginia. Thomas was the third son among their nine children. In 1821 the family moved to Indianapolis, where Morris Morris served on the commission which erected the state house, and as state auditor (1829–44). At the age of twelve, Thomas began work with a printer. Three years afterwards he entered a private school conducted by Ebenezer Sharpe, and finally, July 1, 1830, the United States Military Academy, West Point, N. Y. He graduated four years later, was made a brevet second lieutenant of artillery, and was commissioned second lieutenant, Feb. 25, 1835, but resigned the following year.

Settling in Indianapolis as a civil engineer, he was first given charge of the construction of the Indianapolis section of the Central Canal, which was completed from Broad Ripple into the city. He is also credited with the suggestion and execution of the "state ditch," which saved Indianapolis from recurrent floods and greatly lessened the prevalence of fever incidental to its early settlement. Meanwhile, the state began building the first of the railroads (the Madison & Indianapolis), which ultimately supplanted all the canals within its borders as means of transportation. Morris was chief engineer of this enterprise from 1841 to 1847, during which time it passed from the state into private hands. He finished its construction from North Vernon to Indianapolis, and conceived and carried through the plan of financing construction by taking subscriptions in land and issuing scrip on this security for payment of construction expenses. From 1847 to 1852 he was chief engineer of the Terre Haute & Richmond Railroad (now part of the Pennsylvania) and of the Indianapolis & Bellefontaine, Ohio (now part of the Big Four). Early in this period he prepared estimates and reports on the Peru & Indianapolis Railroad. He was chief engineer (1852–54) and president (1854–57) of the Indianapolis & Cincinnati (now part of the Big Four); president of the Indianapolis & Bellefontaine (1857–59); chief engineer of the Indianapolis & Cincinnati (1859–61). His services on these different roads suggested to Morris the idea of a union depot at Indianapolis, which he planned and built.

At the outbreak of the Civil War, Gov. Oliver P. Morton [q.v.] appointed him state quartermaster-general. On Apr. 27, 1861, the president commissioned him brigadier-general, and in the last week of May his brigade was ordered into the western part of Virginia by Maj.-Gen. George B. McClellan, who was then in command of the department of the Ohio. Morris insisted upon mustering in volunteer regiments of Western Virginia Unionists (*Official Records,* 1 ser. II, 673), in which move he was supported by McClellan, and the troops did good service. He drove the Confederate forces back from Philippi on June 3, and was well started in the task of driving them out of Western Virginia when McClellan took command in person of the campaign along the Great Kanawha. On July 3, McClellan harshly refused reinforcements which Morris had requested (*Ibid.,* 208–09), and on July 14, in his report, criticized him for not pursuing the Confederates more vigorously at Laurel Hill. A slight pursuit action at Carrick's Ford, July 13, virtually brought Morris' services to an end, since the term of enlistment of his regiments expired in July. He was honorably mustered out July 27. He expected another commission, but none came for more than a year. Believing his services were not really wanted, he declined a commission as brigadier-general in September 1862 and another as junior major-general in October of that year.

As chief engineer of the Indianapolis & Cincinnati Railroad (1862–66), he built the Lawrenceburg-Cincinnati section. From 1866 to 1869 he was president and chief engineer of the Indianapolis & St. Louis, and constructed the road between Terre Haute and Indianapolis. For the three following years he was receiver of the Indianapolis, Cincinnati, & Lafayette Railroad. On Nov. 19, 1840, he married Elizabeth Rachel Irwin, daughter of John Irwin of Madison: they had five children. He accumulated a considerable estate and the twenty-acre tract on which he built his home remained intact for many years after it was entirely surrounded by the growing city. He died at San Diego, Cal., at the age of ninety-three, and was buried at Crown Hill Cemetery, Indianapolis.

[B. R. Sulgrove, *Hist. of Indianapolis and Marion County, Ind.* (1884); *Indianapolis Journal,* Mar. 24, 1904; *Report of the Adjutant General of the State of Ind.,* vol. II (1865); Catherine Merrill, *The Soldier of Ind. in the War for the Union* (1866), vol. I; *War of the Rebellion: Official Records (Army),* 1 ser. II; F. B. Heitman, *Hist. Reg. and Dict. U. S. Army* (1903), vol. I; G. W. Cullum, *Biog. Reg. Officers and Grads. U. S. Mil. Acad.* (3rd ed., 1891), vol. I; *A Biog. Hist. of Eminent and Self-Made Men of the State of Ind.* (1880), vol. II; *Thirty-Fifth Ann. Reunion Asso. Grads. U. S. Mil. Acad.,* June 14, 1904.]
C. B. C.

MORRIS, WILLIAM HOPKINS (Apr. 22, 1827–Aug. 26, 1900), soldier, author, was born in New York City, the son of George Pope Morris [q.v.] and Mary Worthington Hopkins. After receiving a common-school education he attended West Point, graduating July 1, 1851, and being commissioned a second lieutenant of the 2nd Infantry. His permanent commission as second lieutenant was awarded Dec. 3, 1851. He served on garrison duty at Forts Columbus and Wood, New York, that year, and at Fort Yuma, Cal., in 1852 and 1853. Portions of the next two years he spent on recruiting service, after which he resigned from the service, Feb. 28, 1854, and aided his father in editing the *Home Journal.* In 1859 he invented a repeating carbine for which he and Charles Liston Brown received a patent in 1860. On Aug. 20, 1861, he was appointed staff captain, assistant adjutant-general, on the staff of Gen. J. J. Peck, in the defenses of Washington. He served until the following May, when he was present at the siege of Yorktown and the battle of Williamsburg. At the battle of Fair Oaks (May 31–June 1) he was commended and on Sept. 2, 1862, was elected colonel, 135th New York Infantry, which regiment soon became the 6th New York Heavy Artillery. He was appointed brigadier-general, United States Volunteers, Nov. 29, 1862, and his command was stationed at Maryland Heights, near Harpers Ferry, Va., until the summer. In July 1863, his command joined the Army of the Potomac and was in reserve at the battle of Gettysburg. Following this, he was in small operations in the vicinity, and was later given a brigade in the 3rd Division, III Corps. His brigade took part in the Bristoe, Va., campaign of October and in the advance of the Union forces to the Rappahannock in November.

On Apr. 30, 1864, Morris' brigade was transferred to the VI Corps. It engaged in the campaign from the Rapidan to the James and formed part of the forces operating against Richmond. His work at the battle of the Wilderness was, on the 13th of March, 1865, rewarded by appointment as major-general of volunteers, for "gallant and meritorious services." On May 9, 1864, he was wounded at Spotsylvania Court House and was sent to Washington on sick leave until July, when he served on courts-martial and military commissions until mustered out on Aug. 24, 1864. In the same year he published *Field Tactics for Infantry,* followed some time later by *Tactics for Infantry, Armed with Breech-loading or Magazine Rifles* (1882). While neither of these was revolutionary, both were sound attempts at bettering the clumsy infantry tactics of the period and provided one of the steps in the evolution of the squad formation. In 1866 Morris was appointed colonel, division engineer, New York National Guard, and the following year was appointed a brevet major-general of that organization. In 1867 and 1868 he was delegate to the New York state constitutional convention, from Putnam County, and was a member of the military committee. In 1869 he was appointed commissary general of ordnance, New York National Guard, with permanent rank of brigadier-general in addition to his brevet rank. He was married in 1870, to Catharine (Hoffman) Hyatt, daughter of Dr. Adrian Hoffman of Westchester County, N. Y., and widow of Charles C. Hyatt. After his marriage he retired to his estate, "Briarcliff," New York. He died at Long Branch, N. J.

[G. W. Cullum, *Biog. Reg. . . . U. S. Mil. Acad.* (3rd ed., 1891), vol. II; *Ann. Reunion Asso. Grads. U. S. Mil. Acad., June 8, 1901*; F. B. Heitman, *Hist. Reg. and Dict. of the U. S. Army* (1903), vol. I; *Ann. Report of the Adj.-Gen. of the State of N. Y.*, 1866–69, 1896; *War of the Rebellion: Official Records* (*Army*); *Documents of the Convention of the State of N. Y., 1867–68* (5 vols., 1868); correspondence with Commandery of the State of N. Y., Military Order of the Loyal Legion.]   D.Y.

MORRISON, JOHN IRWIN (July 25, 1806–July 17, 1882), educator, son of Robert and Ann (Irwin) Morrison, was born near Chambersburg, Franklin County, Pa. Of his boyhood little is known except that he received instruction from local clergymen. In 1824 he moved with his parents to Washington County, Ind., where he soon found employment as a teacher at Walnut Ridge. Early in April 1825 he was placed in charge of the Salem Grammar School which he conducted successfully until September 1827, when he resigned to enter Miami University at Oxford, Ohio. With two years' advanced credit, he fulfilled the requirements of the junior and senior years in one year and received the degree of A.B. in 1828. Immediately after graduation he returned to Salem, Ind., to take charge of the first Washington County Seminary, in the fall of 1828. Here, according to contemporary accounts, he achieved a distinguished reputation as a teacher, attracting students from many counties throughout the state. In 1832 he married one of his former pupils, who had just returned from the Friends' School at Westtown, Pa., Catherine Morris, daughter of Benoni and Rebecca (Trueblood) Morris. With her assistance he established in 1835 the Salem Female Institute, which he conducted as a private venture until 1839, when he was elected state representative.

At the end of his term in the House, in 1840, Morrison accepted an appointment as professor of ancient languages at Indiana University, resigning in 1843 to teach again in the Washington County Seminary. From 1847 to 1850 he served as state senator and was appointed senatorial delegate to the constitutional convention of 1850–51. His knowledge of educational matters was recognized at once in his election as chairman of the committee on education, in which position he drafted the article on education. He was also the author of Section 8 of the law which created the office of state superintendent of public instruction, June 14, 1852, and helped to secure the passage of the laws which provided for the establishment of teachers' institutes (1865), and which created the office of county superintendent of schools (1873). He served as trustee of Indiana University, 1846–49, 1850–55, and as president of the board in 1854–55 and from 1875 to 1878. From 1856 to 1860 he was treasurer of Washington County. During these busy years, he found time to engage in various newspaper ventures. In 1847 he purchased the *Washington Republican,* which he renamed the *Washington Democrat* (now the *Salem Democrat*). Three years later he founded, with J. F. Baird, the *Salem Locomotive,* which was short-lived. In May 1861 he became editor of the *Salem Times,* changing its name, in June of that year, to the *Union Advocate.* His editorial career came to an end with his appointment, by President Lincoln, as commissioner of enrolment, in 1863, with an office in Jeffersonville. He was state treasurer, 1865–67, changing his residence to Indianapolis at the beginning of his term. In 1872 he removed to Knightstown, Ind., where he continued his public services as president of the school board, 1874–77, and where he remained until his death.

[R. G. Boone, *A Hist. of Educ. in Ind.* (1892); Annie Morrison Coffin, "John Irwin Morrison and the Washington County Seminary," *Ind. Mag. of Hist.,* June 1926; Logan Esarey, *A Hist. of Ind.* (2 vols., 1915); J. H. Smart, ed., *The Ind. Schools and the Men who have Worked in Them* (1876); T. A. Wylie, ed., *Ind. Univ., its Hist. from 1820, when Founded, to 1890* (1890); *Indianapolis Jour.,* July 18, 1882.]

R. F. S.

MORRISON, NATHAN JACKSON (Nov. 25, 1828–Apr. 12, 1907), college president, Congregational clergyman, was born in Sanbornton, now Franklin, N. H., of Scotch-Irish lineage. He was the son of Nathan Smith and Susannah (Chase) Morrison, and a descendant of David Morrison who emigrated to Boston in 1718. Until he was twenty he had only the educational advantages of the district school during four months of the year. He prepared for college at academies in Sanbornton, Meriden, and New Hampton, and graduated from Dartmouth in 1853. He went West to study theology under President Finney of Oberlin, graduating at Oberlin Theological Seminary in 1857. During his seminary course he served as tutor in the classics in the preparatory department of the college. He was ordained, Feb. 11, 1858, pastor of the Congregational church in Rochester, Mich. In 1859 he became professor of Greek and Latin at Olivet College. He married, July 8, 1863, Miranda Capen Dimond, daughter of Isaac Marquand and Sarah Colton (Capen) Dimond of Brooklyn, N. Y.

The school which the founders of the village of Olivet, Mich., had established in the wilderness in 1844 was granted a college charter the year Morrison went there to teach, and a president was elected, who, however, continued in office for only a brief period. The Civil War reduced the struggling institution to a low ebb. It was under these adverse conditions that Morrison was in 1864 unanimously elected to the presidency, an office the duties of which he had already been performing for three and one-half years. He was also transferred to the chair of mental and moral philosophy. His tenacity of purpose and largeness of outlook enabled him to surmount the difficulties of the situation and the college made steady progress throughout his administration, which closed in 1872.

After resigning at Olivet, he became a leading spirit in the organization of Drury College, Springfield, Mo., and was elected its president. From 1873 to 1888 he built up the college, carrying it through the panic of 1873 and the subsequent financial depression, through local and regional misunderstandings of the function and methods of a college, and through the loss sustained by a fire that in December 1882 destroyed the college's finest building. After serving as professor of philosophy in Marietta College, Ohio, from 1888 to 1895, Morrison became interested in the project of raising Fairmount Institute, Wichita, Kan., to the rank of a college. In this enterprise again he was successful, becoming president at the age of sixty-seven and maintaining the struggle for twelve years with unabated enthusiasm through the reverses following the collapse of "boom" conditions in the community, until death closed his career.

Morrison united the ideals and the bearing of the New England educators of his youth with the energy, the ardor, and the optimism of western pioneers. He was nearly six feet in height, of rather slender build, and of dark complexion; in dress and manner he was distinctly the gentleman. His personal interest in his students was keen and of practical helpfulness. As an administrator he was autocratic; but he showed marked ability to secure able men for his faculty and to retain them in spite of meager salaries paid with painful irregularity. The confidence with which he pushed forward his enterprises sometimes appeared to the public and to his fellow workers visionary; but the outcome usually vindicated his judgment and rewarded his courage.

[W. B. Williams, *Hist. of Olivet Coll.* (1901); A. P. Hall, *Hist. Address at the Semi-Centennial of Drury Coll.* (1923); M. T. Runnels, *Memorial Sketches and Hist. of the Class of 1853 Dartmouth Coll.* (1895); *The Congreg. Year-Book,* 1907 (1908); *Congregationalist,* May 4, 1907; *Topeka State Jour.,* Apr. 12, 1907.]

E. D. E.

MORRISON, WILLIAM (Mar. 14, 1763–Apr. 19, 1837), pioneer merchant, was born at Doylestown, Bucks County, Pa., the son of John and Rebecca (Bryan) Morrison. His father, the son of Sir John Morrison, of County Cork, Ireland, came to America as a young man. William was probably only a boy when he entered the store of his uncle, Guy Bryan, a noted merchant of Philadelphia. Some time before August 1790, he went to Kaskaskia, Ill., as the western representative of the firm of Bryan & Morrison, and here in later years he was joined by his brothers Robert, James, Jesse, Samuel, and Guy. In this important trading center of pioneer days he rapidly built up a flourishing business, the range of his operations extending from Prairie du Chien, Wis., to New Orleans, and from the Rocky Mountains to Pittsburgh. About 1800 he established a store in Cahokia, Ill. In 1804 he sent Baptiste Lalande with a stock of goods to Santa Fé and was thus the first citizen of the United States to attempt the opening of trade with New Mexico. Though a business competitor and political antagonist of Pierre Menard [*q.v.*], he joined Menard in backing Manuel Lisa [*q.v.*] in his trapping venture to the mouth of the Big Horn in 1807, and, two years later, took part with him in organizing the St. Louis Missouri Fur Company. Most of his enterprises prospered, and he acquired great wealth.

In the bitter political contests that marked the early days of the Illinois country he and his brother Robert, with John Edgar, led the faction that opposed Gen. W. H. Harrison, then governor of Indiana Territory. He was also closely allied with the groups and individuals charged by Michael Jones, Harrison's register of the land office and one of the land commissioners at Kaskaskia, with gigantic frauds. He took a prominent part in the movement to oust Jones from office, and on the murder of Rice Jones, the principal attorney for the land speculators, Dec. 7, 1808, sought, with others, to fasten the crime on the register. For this defamation of character he was sued by the register, who had been formally acquitted of the charge, and was mulcted in $200 damages.

Morrison was married three times—to Catherine Thaumur, about 1794; to Euphrosine Huberdeau of Ste. Genevieve, Mo., Nov. 27, 1798; and to Elisa Bissell, of St. Louis, July 20, 1813— and had children by each marriage. About 1801 he built a large and handsome stone residence in Kaskaskia, which became in time perhaps as famous as the home of Menard. He is described by Governor Reynolds (*post*), who knew him well, as a man of ordinary size, in his later years inclined to corpulency, but of marked dignity and grace of manner. Though he had little schooling, his native intelligence enabled him to pick up a practical education. Reynolds, ignoring his connection with the land frauds, speaks of him as honest and upright, and adds that he was kind and benevolent. He died at his home.

[John Reynolds, *The Pioneer Hist. of Ill.* (1852), pp. 129–33; C. W. Alvord, *The Ill. Country, 1673–1818* (1920); Thomas James, *Three Years among the Indians and Mexicans* (1916), ed. by W. B. Douglas; F. L. Billon, *Annals of St. Louis and Its Territorial Days* (1888), pp. 219–21; Elliott Coues, ed., *The Expeditions of Zebulon Montgomery Pike* (1895), II, 500, 602–03; W. A. B. Jones, "Rice Jones," *Chicago Hist. Soc. Colls.*, IV (1890), 277.]   W. J. G.

MORRISON, WILLIAM McCUTCHAN (Nov. 10, 1867–Mar. 14, 1918), Southern Presbyterian clergyman, missionary to the Congo, was born on a farm near Lexington, Va., the eldest of the eight children of James Luther Morrison and his wife, Mary Agnes McCutchan. Descended on the paternal side from a line of Scotch-Irish Presbyterians and on his mother's side from a family which had produced many missionaries, he inherited a tradition of religious service which was heightened by the strictly pious atmosphere of his home life. Indeed, almost at his birth his parents had "consecrated William to God." Young Morrison kicked against the pricks, however, and throughout most of his college course at Washington and Lee University he was resolved to become a lawyer. It was only at the death of his father in 1886, the year before his graduation, that he surrendered this ambition for the career to which his parents had destined him. Financial considerations compelled the postponement of his ministerial training. Only after six years of teaching in the South did he enter the Presbyterian Theological seminary in Louisville, Ky., where he graduated in 1896. Soon afterward, having been ordained to the ministry, he set out for Africa as a missionary of the Southern Presbyterian Church (Presbyterian Church in the United States). Six months out of Philadelphia he reached his station at Luebo in the heart of the Congo Free State. Here and in the surrounding country he passed the rest of his life, save for the furloughs which took him back occasionally to America.

Morrison was successful from the beginning. Brought up on a farm, he knew how to use his hands to perform the innumerable practical tasks incident to life in the jungle. Strongly built and of sturdy constitution, he kept his health in spite of incessant labor in the trying climate of the Congo. Knowing from infancy the negro character, he had little difficulty in dealing with the natives; almost instinctively he knew how to win their confidence and affection. Trained as a teacher, he entered immediately into the educational work which is the first step in the civilizing activity of the missionary and a capital one in the training of native evangelists. He early began the study of the native language with the aim of reducing it to writing and of translating the Scriptures. He had a quick ear, a retentive memory, and considerable linguistic training. By dint of great patience and persistent labor, aided by some of the more intelligent natives, he completed in 1906 his *Grammar and Dictionary of the Buluba-Lulua Language as Spoken in the Upper Kasai and Congo Basin,* which was printed in the United States. This work, intended for the use of the missionaries, was followed by translations of Bible paraphrases, of the catechism, of various tracts, and finally of the New Testament. The translation of the last named had proceeded only through Acts when Morrison died. His work was the more useful because the Buluba tongue was a sort of a *lingua franca* over large sections of the Congo. He also edited the *Kasai Herald,* established in 1901 and discontinued sixteen years later.

Morrison's most notable work was his defense of the interests of the natives against the Free State government and its concessionary companies. A man of his humane but aggressive and courageous temper could not remain silent in the face of such outrages as he witnessed in the rubber districts of the Congo. His protests began soon after his arrival at Luebo; they continued until the needed reforms were introduced. At London, in 1903, where the reform movement was already under way, he cooperated with the Congo Reform Association, addressed Parliament on the subject, and wrote several stirring articles for the press. In America he continued the campaign through the press and on the platform. A vigorous and forceful speaker, capable of real eloquence on occasion, he moved his auditors deeply. Calls for American interference in the Congo situation resulted; the government at Washington, not being a signatory to the treaty of Berlin, felt unable to act. Morrison continued his agitation and won the support of numerous American editors and of Mark Twain, whose book, *King Leopold's Soliloquy* (1905), was based in part upon data supplied by Morrison. Undoubtedly his work was effective. He helped to form that public sentiment which, translated into pressure from the British government, caused the appointment by King Leopold of an investigating commission. The resulting revelations, plus the continued campaign in which Morrison had his part, set in train the movement toward reform, effected only after Belgian assumption of sovereignty in the Congo. In 1909 Morrison, with his colleague, W. H. Sheppard, was sued for damages by the Kasai Company on account of an allegedly libelous article written by Sheppard and published by Morrison in the *Kasai Herald.* The missionaries were defended at the trial by Émile Vandervelde, Socialist leader from Brussels, who had long been known as a champion of Congo reform. Thanks to his efforts the missionaries were acquitted. Morrison continued his work at Luebo until March 1918, when he died of tropical dysentery. His wife, Bertha Marion Stebbins, whom he had married in 1906, died in Africa in 1910. They had no children.

[*Who's Who in America,* 1914–15; T. C. Vinson, *William McCutchan Morrison* (1921); S. H. Chester.

Behind the Scenes (1928) ; *Missionary Review of the World,* June 1918; files of the *Missionary* and the *Missionary Survey,* Nashville, Tenn.]   P. D. E.

MORRISON, WILLIAM RALLS (Sept. 14, 1824?–Sept. 29, 1909), congressman from Illinois and chairman of the Interstate Commerce Commission, was an influential Democratic leader for four decades at the end of the nineteenth century. His parents, John and Ann (Ralls) Morrison, of Anglo-Saxon ancestry, were natives of southern Illinois, where he was born near the present town of Waterloo. His mother died early in the boy's life, and his father left the farm at Prairie du Long, remarried, and took over the management of the inn at Waterloo, Ill. There the boy absorbed politics as he grew, for the tavern was the community center and his father was active in local politics, serving as justice of the peace, sheriff, state assemblyman, and county judge. At twenty-two the son became deputy sheriff but soon left that office to serve as a private in the Mexican War and then went to California in the gold rush. When he returned to Illinois he spent two years in the preparatory department of McKendree College and in 1852 settled down in Waterloo as circuit court clerk. In that year he was married to Mary Jane Drury, who bore him two sons both of whom died young. After her death he was married, in 1857, to her half-sister, Eleanora Horine, who proved an able and industrious assistant in all his political undertakings. They had one child who also died in infancy. From 1854 to 1860 he was a member of the state legislature as a Douglas Democrat and was chosen speaker in his third term. During this period he was admitted to the bar and began the practice of law. At the outbreak of the Civil War he organized a Union regiment, the 49th Illinois Volunteer Infantry, from his border-line region and was elected colonel. He was wounded while leading an attack at Fort Donelson but recuperated sufficiently to take part in the move on Corinth.

Meanwhile his friends at home elected him to the federal House of Representatives as a Democrat. He did not distinguish himself at Washington, 1863–65, and failed of reëlection by seventy-five votes. Except for a season in the state legislature in 1871, he did not appear in politics again until 1872, when, in spite of his tariff-reform campaign, a Republican district sent him to Congress and kept him there from 1873 to 1887. He was chairman of the committee on ways and means, 1875–77 and 1883–87, but throughout his congressional service his influence was greater than committee assignments and speeches indicate. Tariff reduction was his chief concern. In 1876 he stated his principles: "Protection . . . other than that incidental to revenue, is spoliation, because it takes the earnings of the labor of one person or class of persons and gives these earnings to other persons" (*Congressional Record,* 44 Cong., 1 Sess., p. 3313). He achieved a few minor reductions, but his general bills were unsuccessful except as they popularized the idea of reform. His most noted proposal was that of 1884 providing for a general horizontal tariff reduction of 20 per cent., which attached to him the nickname of "Horizontal Bill." Opponents assailed the measure as unscientific, an accusation he himself admitted, but the attacks were impelled by hatred of reduction rather than by abhorrence of unscientific procedure. Although a real reform seems to have been impossible, this attempt failed by only five votes. A strict and active party man, he attended almost all the state and national Democratic conventions and did much committee work. He was a candidate for senator in 1885, when he and John A. Logan fought one of the most spectacular elections in Illinois history. For almost five months the legislature balloted evenly on the two candidates before a well-planned ruse gave Logan the necessary extra vote. Morrison was several times a prominent possibility for the presidential nomination, notably in 1892 and in 1896. Perhaps the decisive obstacle preventing his obtaining this honor was his refusal to barter his bi-metallism principles. Tenacity of ideals was both his strength and his weakness politically.

Defeated in the 1886 election by secret machinations of Pennsylvania manufacturers and the Knights of Labor, he was appointed, in 1887, by Cleveland to the new Interstate Commerce Commission, of which Thomas McIntyre Cooley [*q.v.*] was chairman. As a member of this body and as chairman after Mar. 19, 1892, he labored diligently to guide it through the difficulties of its first period of authority. He conducted a vigorous campaign against railroad privilege, established new rates to displace those declared unjust, and attacked discriminations and rebates that had aroused public feeling. When a series of court decisions, based on defects in the act of 1887, temporarily robbed the commission of real power, he could not have felt disappointed that McKinley refused to reappoint him in 1897. He retired to his home in Waterloo, Ill., and lived quietly until his death.

[Collection of newspaper clippings and some correspondence in the possession of relatives at Waterloo, Ill.; F. D. Scott, "The Political Career of Wm. R. Morrison," *Ill. State Hist. Soc. Trans.,* no. 33 (1926);

J. M. Palmer, *Bench and Bar in Ill.* (1899), vol. II; *Who's Who in America,* 1908–09 ; *Report of Adjutant-General of . . . Ill.* (1867), vol. II; *Ill. State Register* (Springfield) and *Chicago Daily Tribune,* Sept. 30, 1909 ; date of birth from McKendree College records.]
F. D. S.

MORRISSEY, JOHN (Feb. 12, 1831–May 1, 1878), gambler, prizefighter, congressman, and state senator, son of Timothy Morrissey, was born at Templemore, Tipperary, Ireland. There were eight children in the family, seven girls and John. The Morrisseys emigrated to Canada when the boy was a few years old. After three months there the family was destitute and moved to Troy, N. Y., where the father managed to find enough work to keep the children from starving.

It was in Troy that John Morrissey started the career that, like the chapters of a romance, led from rags to riches and from poverty to power. A big boy for his age, he was wild in school and soon began to roam the streets, picking up bad habits and a very definite skill in rough-and-tumble fighting. He worked first in a wall-paper factory and later in the Burden Iron Works, giving up both jobs in disgust. He became something of a local gang leader and a hero for his exploits in street fights. At the age of seventeen he took a job as deckhand on a Hudson River steamer, under Capt. Eli Smith, whose daughter Sarah he later married. By her he had one son, who died at an early age.

Morrissey's first exploit upon arriving in New York City was to invade the Empire Club, a sporting saloon owned by one "Dutch Charley," and challenge all hands to combat. He was worsted in the free-for-all fight that followed but decided that he liked New York City and would remain there. He became a "runner" for a boarding house, his task being to entice to it as many immigrants as possible. The competition in that business led to more fighting and the job just suited the belligerent Irish boy. Soon he began to take up prizefighting in earnest and to hurl challenges at the leading fighters of the day, Tom Hyer, Yankee Sullivan, and others. Lured to California by the gold rush reports and the hope of fighting Hyer, he "bummed" his way across the Continent. He did fight Hyer's trainer, George Thompson, at Mare Island in 1852. While in that area he undertook what practically amounted to a pirate cruise to Queen Charlotte's Island when the rumor arose that the Sitka Indians had discovered gold. The gold was not found and Morrissey returned to the East and prizefighting. He beat Yankee Sullivan at Boston Four Corners (now Boston Corners), N. Y., Oct. 12, 1853, in thirty-seven rounds for $2,000 prize money. This victory gave him something of a claim on the heavy-weight championship. Later he fought a man named Poole on a dock in New York City. Not long after the bout Poole was assassinated, al-legedly by Morrissey's friends, and Morrissey was arrested but was soon released. In the next few years he rose rapidly to power as a gambler, saloon-keeper, labor leader, and politician. Chal-lenged by John C. Heenan [*q.v.*] for the cham-pionship, he accepted and announced that the fight would be his last, win or lose. On Oct. 20, 1858, at Long Point, Canada, he defeated Hee-nan in eleven rounds for $2,500 a side.

He became a huge, flamboyant, and belligerent figure in New York sporting, political, and even financial life. He made Commodore Vanderbilt his friend by presenting him with a fine race horse and is supposed to have profited greatly by financial tips from Vanderbilt in later years. He lost $124,000 in one night to Benjamin Wood at his gambling house. In 1866 he ran for Con-gress from the fifth district, mainly to annoy the great number of people who said that it was a disgrace to consider him for such an office. He was elected and served for two terms, Mar. 4, 1867, to Mar. 3, 1871. As early as 1862 he had a gambling house in Saratoga, N. Y., his resi-dence in his late years, and in 1870 he opened a "new clubhouse" there. In 1875 he was elected state senator from the fourth district. In 1877 he was elected again, this time from the seventh district. When he died, the following year, he owned three-eighths of the gambling casino at Saratoga, one-third of the racetrack and build-ings, and real estate here and there in the town.

He had made and lost several fortunes in Wall Street. Though he was a turbulent character in turbulent times, his fighting exploits, his kind-heartedness, his loyalty to his friends, and other redeeming qualities covered a multitude of his sins. He was buried at Troy, N. Y., with state senators as pall-bearers and 15,000 people fol-lowing his body to the cemetery in the rain.

[W. E. Harding, *John Morrissey, His Life, Battles, and Wrangles* (1881); *Biog. Dir. Am. Cong.* (1928); A. J. Weise, *Hist. of the City of Troy* (1876); *N. Y. Times, N. Y. Tribune,* May 2, 1878.]   J.K.

MORROW, DWIGHT WHITNEY (Jan. 11, 1873–Oct. 5, 1931), lawyer, banker, diplomat, was born at Huntington, W. Va. His parents James Elmore and Clara (Johnson) Morrow were both of pre-Revolutionary Scotch-Irish stock and both were scholarly. Five surviving children, including Dwight, all taught school. Reared in western Pennsylvania, he won a com-petitive examination to West Point but was de-nied the appointment because his elder brother Jay Johnson Morrow, later a brigadier-general, was already at the Military Academy. He there-fore decided to go to Amherst College, entering with the Class of 1895, which included Calvin Coolidge. His devotion to Amherst lasted all his life. After graduation with honors, he worked as a clerk for a year. Entering the Columbia Law School in 1896, he paid his expenses by tutoring and graduated in 1899, once more with distinction.

Morrow was first employed by the firm of Reed, Simpson, Thacher and Barnum, of which former Speaker Thomas B. Reed was the newly installed head. His advancement in the law was rapid and by 1905 he had won a partnership in the firm. He continued active in the profession for nine years. His practice was concerned with the larger business affairs of the period, the complicated details of which he could quickly master. Thomas D. Thacher afterward said that he had "an uncanny knack of quickly finding the common ground upon which the conflicting claims of divergent interests could be resolved" (*Bar Association Year Book,* p. 386). This gift was repeatedly shown later in banking and diplomacy. He made his home in New Jersey, at Englewood, and rendered valuable service to the state by drafting, with Col. R. C. Bolling, the workmen's compensation law of 1911. Sub-sequently he served as chairman of the New Jersey Prison Inquiry Commission (*Report,* 2 vols., 1917), and, as the first president of the State Board of Control (1918–20), carried into effect significant reforms in the administration of penal and corrective institutions. On the eve of the World War (1914) Morrow entered the banking house of J. P. Morgan & Company, and continued there until 1927. In the new oc-cupation he speedily gained the same distinction that he had earned in law. The firm was called upon to finance the purchases of American goods and munitions required by the Allied Powers. In all the financial transactions of the house aris-ing from the war and from the reconstructive efforts following the peace, Morrow participated. When the United States entered the war Mor row's first work was with the National War Savings Committee, as director of New Jersey. His subsequent service as adviser to the Allied Maritime Transport Council was probably his most important in the war itself. He advised General Pershing on his transportation prob-lems and was awarded the Distinguished Serv-ice Medal by that officer "for the first intelligent epitomization of the complete Allied tonnage situation and his able presentation of the situation to the Allied countries" (quoted in Howland, *post,* p. 30; McBride, *post,* p. 114). His experiences widened Morrow's acquaintance with the leading men of Europe which in the post-war period developed into friendship and confidence. In 1920 there was an economic and financial collapse in Cuba and Morrow was asked to study the situation and to prepare a plan by which the credit of the government could be restored. After his death there was a recession but his immediate success won the confidence of the government of Cuba.

In 1925 Morrow was chairman of a board appointed by President Coolidge to examine the national interest in aeronautics and its application to national defense. The *Report of the President's Aircraft Board* (1926) led to the separation of control of aircraft for national defense from that of aircraft for commercial purposes, and the adoption of means of encouragement for commercial aviation. Morrow was appointed ambassador to Mexico by President Coolidge in 1927 when relations with that republic were strained. Once more he was changing professions and again success was to attend him. Rare understanding and sympathy marked his mission. Under his intelligent and tactful guidance good relations were reëstablished and a variety of disputes, including those over oil and the agrarian question, were adjusted or put in the way of adjustment. An example of his diplomatic skill was the termination by non-official intervention of the differences between the Mexican government and the Roman Catholic Church, and the return to the country of the expelled clergy of the church. President Hoover named him as one of the delegates to the London Naval Conference in 1930 and so capably did he perform his part that before he died he had been requested by the President to lead the American delegation to the World Disarmament Conference, which was held at Geneva after his death.

Morrow was elected as a Republican to the United States Senate from New Jersey in 1930 with a plurality in the primary of 300,000 and in the election of 200,000. In his campaign he attracted wide attention by his frank advocacy of the repeal of the Eighteenth Amendment and the restoration of the control of the liquor traffic to the states. He served in the Senate only through the short session, from December 1930 to March 1931, and during this time did not make a single speech or offer a single resolution. He revealed to friends that it was his definite plan first to master the rules and procedure of the body, and thoroughly to acquaint himself with its members. In his votes he was entirely regular. His un-

timely death at Englewood, in the midst of an international economic depression, was widely deplored. Sir Arthur Salter, in the London *Times* (Oct. 7, 1931), characterized it as a "world disaster"; and Walter Lippmann in the *New York Herald Tribune* (Oct. 7, 1931) said: "No man of our time has had the complete trust of so many different kinds of people."

Morrow was a trustee of Amherst College, Union Theological Seminary, the Smithsonian Institution, and the Association for the Improvement of the Condition of the Poor in New York, and he held honorary degrees from many institutions of learning. On June 16, 1903, he married Elizabeth Reeve Cutter of Cleveland; with their three daughters and son she survived him.

[M. M. McBride, *The Story of Dwight W. Morrow* (1930), a laudatory account; H. H. Howland, *Dwight Whitney Morrow. A Sketch in Admiration* (1930), of the same type; "Memorial of Dwight Whitney Morrow," in the *Asso. of the Bar of the City of New York Year Book 1932*, pp. 381–405; Carleton Beals, "The Diplomat who won the Mexicans," *N. Y. Times*, Sept. 21, 1930; Edmund Wilson, "Dwight Morrow in New Jersey," in *The American Jitters* (1932), a critical but fair article on the Senate campaign in New Jersey; comments on his career in the Senate, in *N. Y. Times*, editorial, Mar. 5, 1931, and *New Republic*, Mar. 25, 1931; *Who's Who in America*, 1930–31; obituary articles in *N. Y. Times*, Oct. 6, 7, 1931.] M. E—n.

MORROW, JEREMIAH (Oct. 6, 1771–Mar. 22, 1852), first representative from the state of Ohio, senator, and governor, was the grandson of the Scotch-Irish Covenanter, Jeremiah Murray who left Londonderry for the New World about the middle of the eighteenth century and settled near Gettysburg, Pa., in a neighborhood as Scotch and Presbyterian as any parish in Scotland. Jeremiah Murray's son, John, a Federalist farmer (who spelled his name Morrow), had married in 1768 Mary Lockart. Their son Jeremiah was born on the farm near Gettysburg, where he spent his first twenty-three years but managed to obtain a rather good education, particularly in mathematics. This latter attainment he turned to account in 1794, when he went to the Ohio country as a surveyor. He arrived in the Miami Valley in the spring of 1795, surveyed land, grew corn, taught school, and invested in land in Warren County. Four years later, on Feb. 19, 1799, in Pennsylvania, he was married to his cousin, Mary Parkhill, and took her west to share his home on the frontier. He won the esteem of his neighbors, who chose him in October 1800 to represent them in the second territorial legislature. In the legislature he, with the "Chillicothe Junto," opposed the efforts of St. Clair to postpone Ohio's statehood. Two years later he was a delegate to the convention that drew up a constitution for the new state and was a member of the first state Senate in 1803. He was then chosen by the Jeffersonians to represent the state in Congress and took his seat on Oct. 17, 1803. He was regularly reëlected and served in the House of Representatives from 1803 to 1813, when he entered the Senate and served six years. His career in Congress, while not spectacular, was notable for constructive lawmaking. He became expert in matters pertaining to the public lands. He consistently advocated three changes in existing legislation: the sale of land in smaller units, cash payment, and lower price. The act of 1820 that established a minimum cash price of $1.25 an acre for units as small as 80 acres was the result of his advocacy (P. J. Treat, *The National Land System*, 1910, pp. 132, 139). In 1818 he declined reëlection to the Senate.

In 1822 he was elected governor and was reelected in 1824. As governor he inaugurated the canal-building program and was influential in establishing the public-school system. He retired in December 1826, but his interest in politics remained active. He served in the state Senate for the session of 1827–28 in the House of Representatives for the session 1829–30 and 1835–36. He represented Ohio's tariff interests in the Harrisburg convention in 1827; he supported Adams in the election of 1828; he was later a leader of the Whig party in the state; he was a Clay elector in 1832; and he was chairman of the Ohio Whig convention which indorsed Harrison in 1836. In 1840 he was elected to Congress and served from Oct. 13, 1840, to Mar. 3, 1843, but he felt that he belonged to an older generation and declined renomination. He was president of the Little Miami Railroad Company, chartered in 1836, which built the first railroad out of Cincinnati. He seems to have regarded his association with this project more as a piece of constructive statesmanship than as a means of enriching himself. He served without pay and resigned when the road was an assured success. His greatest pleasure was in the management of his flour mill and his large farm. His nature was most unassuming; he lived in "republican simplicity." He died near Lebanon, Ohio. Of a family of six children only his eldest son survived him.

[Manuscripts of Jeremiah Morrow in the Ohio State Lib. and in the Ohio State Arch. and Hist. Soc. Lib., Columbus; W. A. Taylor, *Ohio Statesmen and Hundred Year Book* (1892); biography by Josiah Morrow, his grandson, in The *"Old Northwest" Geneal. Quart.*, Jan., Apr., July 1906; W. H. Smith, "Gov. Jeremiah Morrow; or a Familiar Talk about Monarchists and Jacobins," *Mag. of Western Hist.*, Oct. 1889, and *Ohio Arch. and Hist. Quart.*, June 1888.]   W. T. U.

MORROW, PRINCE ALBERT (Dec. 19, 1846–Mar. 17, 1913), physician, sociologist, was born at Mount Vernon, Christian County, Ky., his parents being Col. William C. Morrow, who at one time represented Christian County in the lower branch of the Kentucky legislature, and Mary (Cox) Morrow. In 1864, he received the degree of A.B. from Princeton College, Kentucky. Soon afterward he began the study of medicine. Through the influence of his uncle, Dr. Thomas V. Morrow [q.v.], who was one of the founders of the Eclectic Medical College of Cincinnati, Morrow received his early medical education in an eclectic school. He then studied at the École de Médecine in Paris and later spent about fifteen months in the hospitals of London, Paris, Berlin, and Vienna. In 1874 he graduated in medicine from the University Medical College, New York, and the following year began practising medicine in New York City. The honorary degree of A.M. was conferred upon him by the University of the City of New York in 1883.

Soon after beginning his medical career, Morrow specialized in diseases of the skin, becoming a lecturer in this subject at his medical alma mater in 1882. In the same institution (now New York University and Bellevue Hospital Medical College) he became successively clinical professor of venereal diseases in 1884, professor of genito-urinary diseases in 1886, and emeritus professor in 1890. In the last-mentioned year he was appointed attending physician of the skin and venereal department of the New York Hospital, continuing in this capacity until 1904. From 1884 to 1904, he was attending physician to the City Hospital, and he was also consulting dermatologist to St. Vincent's and to the City Hospital.

Morrow early recognized the importance of the problem of venereal diseases from the social, moral, and economic standpoints. Foreseeing that treatment of these diseases was the least important factor in their control, he purposed to attain their prevention through dissemination of knowledge to the laity. His task was indeed a difficult one. He lived during a period in which there was deep-seated feeling, chiefly the result of tradition, that such a subject should be kept *sub rosa*. His earliest endeavors were met with apathy and indifference. He worked indefatigably, however, and by degrees interested physicians, lawyers, educators, and leaders in all walks of life. Public interest increased and he became a leader in a great social movement. His proposed reforms included the wholesome teaching of sex hygiene to the young, thus appeasing a natural curiosity and encouraging a proper outlook on life. The true nature of venereal diseases was brought to the attention of the public through the medium of press and platform, and Morrow, personally, wrote many pamphlets on the subject. He openly discussed measures for the control of prostitution and advocated the registration of those suffering from venereal diseases as communicable. He was a facile and convincing writer. Among his more important contributions were *Syphilis and Marriage* (1881), translated from the French of Alfred Fournier; *Venereal Memoranda* (1885); *Drug Eruptions* (1887); *An Atlas of Skin and Venereal Diseases* (1888–89); *A System of Genito-Urinary Diseases, Syphilology and Dermatology, by Various Authors* (3 vols., 1893–94), which he edited; *Personal Observations of Leprosy* (1889), written after visits to the Hawaiian Islands, Mexico, and Louisiana; *Social Diseases and Marriage* (1904). He was one of the founders and for sixteen years the editor of the *Journal of Cutaneous Diseases* (now *Archives of Dermatology and Syphilology*). A member of numerous professional societies both American and European, he was president of the American Dermatological Association in 1890–91 and of the American Society of Sanitary and Moral Prophylaxis from its inception in 1905.

He married Lucy B. Slaughter, daughter of Thomas Jefferson and Mary (Henry) Slaughter of New York City, on Apr. 23, 1874. Two sons and a daughter survived him, one of the sons becoming a practising surgeon in New York City. Morrow was a man of strong convictions and a tireless worker. He rarely took a long vacation, but for many years was accustomed to spend weekends at Madison, N. J., where he had a summer home, and here he did much of his early writing. He enjoyed all forms of out-door exercise but especially walking and golf. Though giving little time to it, he was fond of social life and was a prominent figure at the meetings of the Southern Society and the Kentuckians. The last few years of his life were devoted almost solely to social reform and he will probably be remembered more as a pioneer and leader in this field than for his important work in former years in the field of dermatology.

[*Who's Who in America*, 1912–13; *N. Y. Times*, Mar. 18, 1913; E. B. Bronson, in *Jour. of Cutaneous Diseases*, Oct. 1913, p. 775; *Bull. de la Société française de dermatologie et syphilologie*, vol. XXIV (1913); *Jour. Am. Medic. Asso.*, Mar. 29, 1913; *Lancet* (London), Apr. 19, 1913; *Social Diseases*, July 1913; H. A. Kelly and W. L. Burrage, *Am. Medic. Biogs.* (1920); personal interview with Morrow's son, Dr. Albert S. Morrow.]
G. M. L.

MORROW, THOMAS VAUGHAN (Apr. 14, 1804–July 16, 1850), pioneer in eclectic medicine, was born at Fairview, Ky. His father, Thomas Morrow, was of Scotch descent, though the occasional appearance of the name as Moreau indicates a French origin. His mother, Elizabeth Vaughan, was of English stock. He attended Transylvania University and then went to New York, where he attended a regular medical school and was later graduated from the Reformed Medical College conducted by Dr. Wooster Beach [*q.v.*], the "founder of eclecticism." After a short period as professor of obstetrics at the latter institution he settled at Hopkinsville, Ky., for practice. In 1830 the Reformed Medical Society of the United States determined to establish a medical school in the Ohio River Valley and accepted the offer of Worthington College to form its medical department. The new school was called the Reformed Medical College of Ohio. Morrow was chosen to head the college as president, dean, and professor of materia medica, obstetrics, and theory and practice of medicine. The *Western Medical Reformer* was established in 1836 in connection with the school. After a stormy career culminating in a mob attack upon the institution it was closed in 1839. Morrow continued practice and private instruction at Worthington until 1842, when he removed to Cincinnati and began at once the organization of a school to succeed the Worthington venture. First named the Reformed Medical School of Cincinnati, Ohio, it was incorporated as the Cincinnati Eclectic Medical Institute in 1845 and as the Eclectic Medical College graduated classes until 1929, when it became extinct. In the Cincinnati school Morrow was appointed dean, treasurer, and professor of physiology, pathology, and theory and practice of medicine, which positions he held until his death. He died from dysentery at the early age of forty-six, and was buried in Wesleyan Cemetery, Cincinnati.

Morrow's claims to remembrance rest upon his championship of the eclectic system of medicine and his part in the foundation of the first schools of that cult in the West. When the National Eclectic Medical Association was inaugurated in Cincinnati in 1848 he was elected its first president. He was a forceful speaker, an able teacher, and a highly successful practitioner both in Worthington and in Cincinnati. His writings include introductory addresses to the classes of the Cincinnati school and many clinical articles and editorials for the pages of the *Western Medical Reformer* and its successor, the *Eclectic Medical Journal*. He was engaged upon the preparation of a "Theory and Practice of

Medicine" at the time of his death. This work was incorporated in *The American Eclectic Practice of Medicine* (2 vols., 1853–54), by I. G. Jones, Morrow's former associate in the Worthington school. Physically Morrow was well over six feet in height, weighing two hundred and fifty pounds. During his stay in Worthington he married Isabel Greer of that place. Prince Albert Morrow [*q.v.*], noted dermatologist and sociologist, was his nephew.

[*Hist. of the Eclectic Medic. Inst., Cincinnati* (1902); *Eclectic Medic. Jour.* (Cincinnati), Aug. 1850; Alexander Wilder, *Hist. of Medicine* (1901); C. T. Greve, *Centennial Hist. of Cincinnati* (1904), vol. II.]

J. M. P.

MORROW, WILLIAM W. (July 15, 1843–July 24, 1929), jurist, congressman from California, was born near Milton, Wayne County, Ind., of Scotch-Irish parentage, the son of William and Margaret (Hood) Morrow. When he was about three years of age, his parents moved to Adams County, Ill., where he attended the common-schools and heard Lincoln, Douglas, and Trumbull trying cases and speaking upon political issues. In 1859 he moved to Santa Rosa, Cal., where he worked as a harness-maker and taught school. Early in 1862 he rode from Santa Rosa to Oregon and, while lost on the way, discovered rich placers which soon led to the development of Cañon City, Ore. Later in the same year he went east and enlisted in the Union army. He was detailed to California in June 1865 as a special agent of the Treasury Department in charge of $5,000,000 in money, and during the next four years he was employed in a confidential position under the secretary of the treasury. In 1869 he was admitted to the bar and entered upon the practice of law in San Francisco, serving from 1870 to 1874 as assistant United States district attorney. He won some distinction in prosecuting officers of merchant ships for cruelty to sailors and assisted in obtaining important reforms by legislation and shipping regulations in the interest of merchant seamen. In 1872 he assisted in the organization of the San Francisco Bar Association and twice served as its president. Between 1880 and 1885 he was attorney for the state board of harbor commissioners, and special attorney for the United States in connection with the *Alabama* claims and before the French and American claims commission. Interested in politics, he was chairman of the California Republican state central committee from 1879 to 1882 and in 1884 attended the Republican National Convention at Chicago as chairman of the California delegation. That fall he was elected to Congress as

representative from the San Francisco district and served during the Forty-ninth, Fiftieth, and Fifty-first congresses (1885–91). He was active in introducing private or local bills and resolutions but made few extended speeches, although he advocated a more stringent Chinese exclusion law, the free coinage of silver, and a survey of the possibilities of irrigating arid lands in the Far West. He was a member of the committees on commerce, foreign affairs, appropriations, and importation of contract laborers.

In 1891 Morrow entered upon a long judicial career, first as judge of the federal district court for the northern district of California. Three cases which he decided as district judge were especially important: *In re Ezeta* (62 *Fed.*, 964), involving questions of extradition; *United States* vs. *Cassidy et al.* (67 *Fed.*, 698), resulting from the Pullman strike in 1894; and *In re Wong Kim Ark* (71 *Fed.*, 382), in which his dictum that a person born in the United States of Chinese parents is a citizen of the United States, under the Fourteenth Amendment, was afterward sustained by the Supreme Court. His charge to the jury in the second case was said at the time to have been the longest ever delivered in a criminal case in the United States. In 1897 President McKinley advanced Morrow to the federal circuit court. One of the best-known cases coming before him as circuit judge was *In re Noyes* (121 *Fed.*, 209), or the "Nome Case," growing out of the gold discovery in Alaska. The facts in this case formed the basis of Rex Beach's novel, *The Spoilers*. (See Morrow's explanatory article, "The Spoilers," *California Law Review*, January 1916.) He wrote the opinion of the circuit court of appeals in the Salton Sea cases (172 *Fed.*, 792), in the Bisbee deportation cases (1918) involving members of the I. W. W. in Arizona (*United States* vs. *Wheeler et al.*, 254 *Fed.*, 611), in *Fireman's Fund Insurance Company* vs. *Globe Navigation Company et al.* (236 *Fed.*, 618), and in the *Marconi Wireless Telegraph Company of America* vs. *Kilbourne and Clark Manufacturing Company* (265 *Fed.*, 644). Upon his completion of thirty years upon the federal bench in 1921, the bar of San Francisco tendered him a public reception. Two years later he retired from active service. During his judicial career, he is said to have handed down more than 650 decisions.

Morrow was selected by Andrew Carnegie in 1900 to be a trustee of the Carnegie Institution in Washington. In 1905 he became an incorporator of the American National Red Cross, upon its reincorporation by Congress, and received a medal for his relief work in connection with the San Francisco fire in 1906. For his services as a member of the American Association for International Conciliation, he was awarded the d'Estournelles de Constant medal by that society in 1925. His wife, Margaret Hulbert, whom he had married at Santa Rosa on June 18, 1865, died in 1926. On Dec. 31, 1927, he was married to Julia E. Neill. She and two children by his first marriage survived him. He died at San Francisco and was buried with Masonic honors in Cypress Lawn Cemetery.

[See: J. G. Jury, "Wm. W. Morrow," *Cal. Law Rev.*, Nov. 1921; *Who's Who in America*, 1928–29; *Biog. Dir. Am. Cong.* (1928); O. T. Shuck, *Sketches of Leading and Representative Men of San Francisco* (1875), pp. 1071–73; *San Francisco Chronicle, San Francisco Examiner*, July 25, 1929. A letter from Morrow in the Lib. of Cong. states that his middle initial does not represent a name.]   P. O. R.

MORSE, ANSON DANIEL (Aug. 13, 1846–Mar. 13, 1916), educator and historian, brother of Harmon Northrop Morse [*q.v.*], was born at Cambridge in one of the most rugged parts of Vermont, the son of Harmon and Elizabeth Murray (Buck) Morse of ancestry reaching back to the earliest years of the settlement of New England. His early training was obtained in the schools of the neighborhood and he was graduated from Amherst College with high honors in the class of 1871. From 1872 to 1875 he taught at Williston Seminary, Easthampton, Mass., then, after a year of study at Heidelberg, he was brought back to teach at his alma mater, to which he was to give more than forty years of most devoted and useful service. In 1876 he was a lecturer on political economy in Amherst College; in the following year he became professor of political economy and instructor in history, in 1879 he was appointed Otis Professor of History and Political Science and in 1885 he was transferred to the Winkley chair. After 1892 this professorship was divided and he became professor of history, which title he held till his retirement in 1907. He had studied again at Heidelberg in 1883. After almost fifty years of residence in Amherst, he died in 1916, a greatly beloved figure.

Morse was a leader in a small group of scholars who in the last quarter of the nineteenth century began to teach that the political party is the most effective organ for expressing and enforcing the popular will. They further pointed out that the United States, through its freedom from deeply rooted antagonistic customs and institutions, offers the most favorable field for the study of the sweep toward democracy, which has characterized the development of civilized government since the eighteenth century. In three

notable articles: "The Place of Party in the Political System" (*Annals of the American Academy of Political and Social Science*, vol. II, no. 3, 1892); "What is a Party" (*Political Science Quarterly*, March 1896); and "The Natural History of Party" (*Yale Review*, May 1893), Morse presented a philosophical study of the conditions which bring parties into existence, of their nature and organization, their behavior in and out of power, and, finally, the causes and circumstances of their dissolution. These ventures into the realm of political theory were supplemented by a number of purely historical studies of great value, dealing with American parties and political figures. The most important of these studies were collected and published in 1923 in a volume entitled *Parties and Party Leaders*. Thus a relatively few articles and a small book entitled *Civilization and the World War* (1919), published after its author's death, constitute the whole of his published work. Throughout his life he was a most thorough and diligent student of history but he was often reluctant to commit his thought to print. Furthermore his early leaning toward economics and political science led him, in teaching history, to emphasize its bearing upon the present, and his recognition of the rapidly changing character of economic and political experiences may have contributed also to his reluctance. However this may be, his best work was done as a teacher. His method was profoundly suggestive and provocative of discussion; he was never didactic. His presentations were always dignified and quietly persuasive, so much so that he was singularly successful with generations of students, many of whom in public and professional life remained true to his teachings. Morse was married, on Sept. 3, 1878, to Margaret Duncan Ely. She, with six of their seven children, survived him.

[The Introduction to *Parties and Party Leaders* by Dwight W. Morrow and to *Civilization and the World War* by John B. Clark contain biographical information. See also: *Amherst Grads.' Quart.*, May 1916; *Amherst Coll., Biog. Record of the Grads. and Nongrads.* (1927); *Who's Who in America*, 1914–15.]
F. L. T.

MORSE, CHARLES WYMAN (Oct. 21, 1856–Jan. 12, 1933), promoter and speculator, was born in Bath, Maine. His parents, Benjamin Wyman and Anna E. J. (Rodbird) Morse were fairly well-to-do, his father having a large part of the control of towing on the Kennebec River. While at Bowdoin College he was already deep in the shipping business and when he graduated in 1877 he had accumulated a considerable capital. He joined forces with his father and a cousin, and as C. W. Morse & Company the firm entered on an extensive ice-shipping and lumber-transporting business. Within a few years Morse outgrew Bath; soon he outgrew even State Street, in Boston; to Wall Street he came in 1897.

Morse first made his fame and fortune in New York in ice. After forming his own Consolidated Ice Company he succeeded, through persuasion or the devious methods of business coercion, in merging it with other companies into the American Ice Company. Formed in 1899 with a capitalization of sixty million, this was one of the earlier and more flagrant instances of corrupt and overcapitalized promotion in the annals of the American trust movement. It gave Morse almost overnight a dubious public prominence as the "Ice King." On May 1, 1900, the trust announced an advance in the price of ice for New York City from twenty-five and thirty to sixty cents per hundred pounds. There was a public outcry, and the *New York Journal and Advertiser* found that disconcertingly large blocks of American Ice stock were held by Mayor Van Wyck, Boss Croker, and other Tammany leaders. Suit was instituted and in the course of the testimony it emerged that Morse had let Van Wyck have the stock at half of par, and had in addition lent him the money with which to buy it; also that the docking commissioners had given Morse's company privileges so favorable as practically to exclude serious competition from independents (32 *Misc. N. Y. Reports*, 1; 55 *Appellate Division Reports*, 245; *Outlook*, June 16, 1900). The Van Wyck administration was turned out at the next election and the price of American Ice stock fell drastically; but not before Morse had formed a holding company, the Ice Securities Corporation, had maneuvered its stock weirdly, and withdrawn with an estimated fortune of twelve million dollars.

He now turned intensively to banking and to shipping. His method in both fields was that of rapid consolidation of individual firms either through peaceful or military penetration; pyramiding of their assets with a bewildering swiftness and complexity; criss-crossing of his two groups of ventures so that the shipping companies bolstered the banks and the banks financed the shipping companies; and the formation of syndicates to take up the flotation of the overcapitalized stock of the consolidated companies. Through a series of brilliant operations he managed to obtain before 1907 something close to a monopoly of the coastwise shipping from Bangor to Galveston and came to be termed "Admiral of the Atlantic Coast." His Consolidated Steam-

ship Company, formed in 1905, combined most of the important lines outside of the New Haven Railroad interests. So close had he come to his monopolistic objective that he frightened not only Wall Street but also President Theodore Roosevelt himself. When the New Haven road was considering in 1907 Morse's offer of twenty million dollars for its Long Island Sound lines, Roosevelt promised President Mellen of the railroad immunity from government interference in his shipping holdings if he would promise not to sell to Morse (*Senate Document No. 543, 63* Cong., 2 Sess., vol. I, p. 875). In banking Morse joined forces with F. Augustus Heinze [*q.v.*], a prominent copper speculator, and E. R. Thomas, a young man of considerable inherited fortune. Together they gained a foothold in a dozen New York banks, the principal ones being the Bank of North America and the Mercantile National Bank; but the United Copper pool, which collapsed according to Heinze because of secret unloading of stock by Morse, reacted fatally on their banking ventures. The Heinze-Morse banks became the storm center of the panic of 1907, and on Oct. 20 a "vigilance committee" of fifteen delivered to them an ultimatum to sell out and retire permanently from banking (C. A. Conant, *A History of Modern Banks of Issue*, 1909, p. 713).

An investigation of the Bank of North America by the United States district attorney, Henry L. Stimson, resulted in the indictment and conviction of Morse for false entries in the books of the bank and for criminally misapplying its funds. He was sentenced in November 1908 to a fifteen-year term in the Atlanta penitentiary, and, despite appeals, he had finally to depart for Atlanta on Jan. 2, 1910. "There is no one in Wall Street who is not daily doing as I have done," he said in an interview. "The late administration wanted a victim; the System wanted a scapegoat" (quoted in *Current Literature*, Feb. 1910, p. 153). The kernel of truth in this statement was the continued hostility which the dominant and conservative group of Wall Street bankers felt toward him. This "fat, squatty little man" with the "masterful, inquiring eyes," as he was described by contemporary journalists, had either not played the game or else had played it all too well. Since the ice scandals the white light of publicity had never receded from him. The attempt of his relatives, in 1903, to annul his second marriage, to the divorced wife of a Pullman car conductor, had resulted in unsavory publicity, and one of the lawyers in the case, Abraham H. Hummel [*q.v.*], was sentenced to a year's imprisonment. This episode had embittered Morse and estranged him even further from the reigning Wall Street group.

In little over two years Morse was out of jail. The main outlines of the processes by which his release was accomplished were clarified and documented by Senator Caraway ten years later on the floor of the United States Senate (*New York Times*, May 21, 23, 1922). Every exertion by Morse's friends and relatives to secure a pardon or a commutation of sentence from President Taft had been unavailing. Finally Harry M. Daugherty, later in the Harding cabinet as attorney-general, contracted with Morse, for a retainer of five thousand dollars and the promise of an additional twenty-five thousand in case of success, to secure his release. A commission of doctors was eventually appointed to investigate the report that Morse was a dying man. It reported negatively, but a second commission of army doctors assured the President that Morse had only a few more weeks if he were kept in prison, that he was suffering from a complication of ailments including Bright's disease, and that even if released he could not survive for more than a year. Taft signed his pardon and Morse departed for medical treatment in Wiesbaden. But Daugherty's fee remained unpaid; and the attorney-general's office received information that before his examinations Morse had drunk a combination of soapsuds and chemicals calculated to produce temporarily the effects the army commission noted. President Taft later charged that he had been deluded in the whole matter, and said that the case "shakes one's faith in expert examination" (*New York Times*, Nov. 16, 1913).

On his return from Europe Morse reëntered business with renewed energy, throwing down his gauntlet to the Wall Street group. He reconquered something of his old dominion in the shipping field, until in July 1915 his Hudson Navigation Company was already being sued for unfair competition. On Jan. 11, 1916, he came back to the front pages of the metropolitan newspapers with a grandiose scheme for organizing an American transoceanic shipping combination. This assumed reality in the incorporation of the United States Shipping Company, a holding company for whose stock was exchanged the stock of sixteen separate subsidiary companies, each organized around a steamship. The entrance of the United States into the World War gave Morse an even greater opportunity. He was now given contracts by the Shipping Board for building thirty-six vessels, and he borrowed from the Emergency Fleet Corporation the money with which to do so. Twenty-two of the ships

were eventually completed. But in the investigation of "war frauds" by the Harding administration the findings of a special legal staff attached to the Department of Justice resulted in the charges that Morse had misrepresented his facilities for ship construction, that he had applied much of the money he borrowed to the building of shipyards rather than ships, that he had failed to turn over to the government the profits of the ships it had leased to him, and that he had appropriated some of the equipment for his own purposes (*New York Times*, Apr. 28, 1922). Before an indictment could be found, Morse sailed for Havre. Attorney-General Daugherty sent him a cable to return. Morse, professedly surprised at the whole pother, and insisting that his trip was an innocent attempt to consult with his Italian physician, nevertheless returned to New York. He was arrested and later indicted for conspiracy to defraud the government. Before the case could be brought to trial he was again indicted with twenty-three others of his group, on a charge of using the mails to defraud prospective investors in United States Steamship stock. The long and costly trial on the Shipping Board charges resulted in an acquittal, but a subsequent civil suit in 1925 against Morse's company, the Virginia Shipbuilding Company, on charges growing out of the same transactions, resulted in a judgment for the government of over eleven and a half million dollars. The mail fraud case had a chequered career, but Morse was finally adjudged too ill to stand trial, and after a jury had disagreed the charges against his sons were dismissed. On Sept. 7, 1926, he was placed under guardianship by the probate court of Bath as incompetent to handle his affairs. He suffered several strokes and died in Bath, of pneumonia, on Jan. 12, 1933. He had married Hattie Bishop Hussey of Brooklyn on Apr. 14, 1884. She bore him four children and died probably in 1897. He had no children by his second wife, Clemence (Cowles) Dodge, whom he married in 1901 and who died in 1926.

[For the main outlines of Morse's career until the 1907 panic, see Owen Wilson, "The Admiral of the Atlantic Coast," *World's Work*, April 1907; and C. F. Speare, "Career of a Great Promoter," *Moody's Mag.*, July 1907. For the ice-trust episode, see *N. Y. Times*, Apr. 15, 16, 1899, May 6, 1900; comments in the *Outlook*, May 9, June 9, 16, July 7, 1900, and in the *Independent*, May 31, 1900; and "Water Still Freezes," in *Fortune*, May 1933. For his shipping activities before his imprisonment, see in addition to the above the testimony of Mellen in the investigation of the New Haven Railroad by the Interstate Commerce Commission, reported in *N. Y. Times*, May 22, 1914. For his banking activities, see C. M. Keys, "Regulating Banks by Vigilance Committee," *World's Work*, Dec. 1907, and "The Story of Morse," *Current Literature*, Feb. 1910. For the details of Morse's pardon, see *N. Y. Times*, May

21, 23, 1922; for Daugherty's official statement, *Ibid.*, May 28, 1922. For Morse's later shipping career see especially a feature article, *Ibid.*, July 25, 1926. See also *N. Y. Times*, Jan. 13, 1933; P. M. Reed, *Hist. of Bath and Environs, Sagadahoc County, Me., 1607–1894* (1894).]					M. L.

MORSE, EDWARD SYLVESTER (June 18, 1838–Dec. 20, 1925), zoölogist and museum director, was born at Portland, Me., a son of Jonathan Kimball and Jane Seymour (Beckett) Morse. He began in boyhood to collect and classify shells and minerals. He attended the Bethel (Maine) Academy, then served for a time as mechanical draftsman at the Portland locomotive works. Most important for his development, he registered as a special student of Louis Agassiz at the Lawrence Scientific School, Harvard University, specializing for three years in conchology. His study of the brachiopods led to his undertaking a systematic exploration of the Atlantic Coast from Maine southward, and his publication of this research attracted the attention of Darwin and other European naturalists. After 1866 he made his home at Salem, Mass. He had married, on June 18, 1863, Ellen Elizabeth Owen. He helped to found the *American Naturalist* and in 1869 became a fellow of the American Academy of Arts and Sciences. He was professor of zoölogy and comparative anatomy at Bowdoin College, 1871–74. In 1876 he was elected a vice-president of the American Association for the Advancement of Science, and served in 1886 as president.

The Pacific Ocean brachiopods lured Morse to Japan in 1877. The expedition started the young conchologist in studies which brought him eminence and led to his writing extensively upon archeology, anthropology, architecture, ceramics, ballistics, folk-lore, and astronomy. This versatility was natural, for Morse's mentality was encyclopedic. He was, however, intensely emotional and often prejudiced, as when he allowed his anti-religious bias to cause him to ignore much of the mythological lore and ceremonial life of ancient Japan. Admitted this disqualification, his journals of the Japanese years, carefully kept and illustrated with his expressive and descriptive drawings, are very important documents.

Morse opened a laboratory at Eno-Shima and was invited to teach zoölogy at the Imperial University, Tokyo. His tenure of this professorship (1877–80) witnessed the introduction among the Japanese of modern methods of collecting and classifying objects of natural history. From the train between Eno-Shima and the capital Morse's alert eye detected some shell heaps, ignored by the native savants. His excavation of these kitchen-middens with their pre-historic artifacts was an epoch in the annals of anthropology. While visiting Yezo and the Hokkaido Morse first saw the Aino and perceived their probable kinship with the brunette white races. Having found at Omori the earliest of Japanese potteries he set out to form a complete collection of the national ceramics, including the works of living potters. In association with the Boston collectors, William Sturgis Bigelow and Ernest F. Fenollosa [*qq.v.*], he took part in the preservation of almost countless objects of art at a time when the Japanese were inclined to dispose of them. A friendship formed with Percival Lowell [*q.v.*], astronomer and author of *The Soul of the Far East* (1888), preceded the astronomical observations and researches to be embodied later in a book on Mars.

Morse's first residence in Japan ended in 1880 when he returned to Salem to take up his lifework as director of the Peabody Museum. He revisited Japan in 1882, extending his journey to China. In 1898 the Japanese Emperor decorated him with the Order of the Rising Sun. He was the first American to be so honored. Beginning with his Lowell Institute lectures on Japanese folkways in 1881, Morse gave to many persons their initial appreciation of the beauty and dignity of the arts and life of *daimyo* and *samurai*. He was an ideal popular lecturer, spontaneous, dramatic, witty, and always well informed. He drew brilliantly, on occasion, with both hands. The Peabody Museum, meantime, became primarily Morse's museum, with his multifarious collections, attractively arranged. His foremost achievement, however, the Morse collection of Japanese potteries, was deposited in 1890 in the Boston Museum of Fine Arts as a loan. It was bought by the museum in 1892 and Morse was made its curator. His great catalogue of the collection, scholarly, discriminating, and readable, was published in 1901. In 1925 the aged author received a copy of the Japanese translation of this work, sponsored by the imperial government. His publications, which concerned, besides the subjects already mentioned, music, archery, numismatics, and other topics, were numerous and yet, apparently, never superficial or casual. He was painstaking if not always patient. A vivid emotionality and an accompanying irritability gave to his writing and conversation a piquant charm, and an obvious limitation. The books, besides the ceramic catalogue mentioned, by which he is best represented are: *First Book of Zoölogy* (1875); *Japanese Homes and their Surroundings* (1886); *Glimpses of China and Chinese Homes* (1902);

Mars and its Mystery (1906); *Japan Day by Day* (2 vols., 1917).

[Copious manuscript materials for a life of Morse await a biographer. *Japan Day by Day* is autobiographical. The Boston Museum of Fine Arts possesses the notes o₁ which the *Cat. of the Morse Collection of Japanese Pottery* (1901) was based. See especially the obituary article by F. S. Kershaw in the *Museum of Fine Arts Bull.*, Feb. 1926, and the obituary, *Boston Herald*, Dec. 21, 1925.] F. W. C.

MORSE, FREEMAN HARLOW (Feb. 18, 1807–Feb. 6, 1891), carver of figure-heads, congressman from Maine, United States consul at London, the son of William and Eliza (Harlow) Morse, was born in Bath, Me. Until the age of fourteen he attended the public schools. Without serving the usual apprenticeship, he immediately commenced ship-carving in which he attained great skill. Nearly all of his spare time he spent in reading, first on art and poetry, then as his interests changed, on history and politics. A young men's debating society of which he was a member gave him his first training in the preparation and delivery of speeches. His ability attracted the attention of local politicians and as a Whig he represented his district in the state legislature in 1840, 1841, and 1843. Twice he was the Whig candidate for the speaker's office. He was elected to the Twenty-eighth Congress on the Whig ticket in a Democratic district. His first speech before the House was a defense of the Maine commissioners on the Northeastern boundary and of Webster as negotiator of the Treaty of Washington. His last speech before his retirement, Mar. 3, 1845, was in opposition to the annexation of Texas. The Liberty party in Maine so divided the vote in Morse's district that, in spite of the general opposition there to annexation, an annexationist was elected. Morse returned to Bath and resumed ship-carving, entering politics briefly in 1845 only to suffer defeat as the Whig candidate for governor. He was mayor of Bath in 1849, 1850, and 1855, and again served in the state legislature in 1853 and 1856. Becoming a zealous advocate of the principles of the Republican party, he was returned to Congress, serving two terms, Mar. 4, 1857, to Mar. 3, 1861. As a congressman from Maine he attended the so-called Peace Convention of 1861.

On Mar. 22, 1861, Morse accepted appointment from President Lincoln as United States consul at London. As the war proceeded, this office became of increasing importance. Morse was closely associated with Charles Francis Adams in the task of gathering evidence regarding British-built privateers. President Johnson continued Morse in the consulship, while President Grant, in spite of the almost unanimous op-

position of the Maine delegation in Congress, advanced him to consul-general on Apr. 16, 1869. But he was not to hold this post long; Gen. Adam Badeau [*q.v.*] replaced him in July 1870. Unhappy over his retirement, which he ascribed to narrowly partisan politics, Morse refused to return to America. He became a British citizen, continuing, however, to perform many friendly services for Americans in England. He contributed two articles on foreign trade to the *International Review* (January, May 1879) and two articles on civil service to *Harper's New Monthly Magazine* (July 1877, May 1878). His wife, Nancy Leavitt of Bath, whom he had married on Apr. 21, 1834, returned to America with their two daughters and lived for a time in Wellesley Hills, Mass. Morse died of old age in Surbiton, Surrey, England, and is buried in the churchyard of the parish of St. Mary's, Long Ditton.

[Abner Morse, *Memorial of the Morses* (1850), App., p. xc; H. D. Lord, *Memorial of the Family of Morse* (1896); *Souvenir of the 300th Anniversary of Am. Shipbuilding, Bath, Maine*, Aug. 5–9, 1907; obituary in Bath (Me.) *Daily Times*.] R. E. M.

MORSE, HARMON NORTHROP (Oct. 15, 1848–Sept. 8, 1920), professor of chemistry, was born at Cambridge, Vt., where his early years were spent on his father's farm. He was the son of Harmon and Elizabeth Murray (Buck) Morse and a brother of Anson Daniel Morse [*q.v.*]. His first paternal ancestor, John Morse, came to America in 1639 from England and settled at New Haven, Conn. Morse graduated from Amherst in 1873 and after two years in Germany he received the degree of Ph.D. from Göttingen in 1875. After returning to America he taught for one year at Amherst. When The Johns Hopkins University was opened he was made one of the first fellows of that institution but before entering upon the fellowship he was promoted to a position on the staff of the chemistry department of that university and remained connected therewith until his retirement, becoming successively associate professor (1883), professor of analytical chemistry and adjunct director of the laboratory (1892), professor of inorganic and analytical chemistry and director of the chemistry laboratory from 1908 until his retirement in 1916. In 1916 he was awarded the Avogadro Medal offered by the Turin Academy of Sciences. He was also fellow of the American Academy of Arts and Sciences, foreign member of the Utrecht Society of Arts and Sciences, of the American Philosophical Society, and of the National Academy of Sciences. For many years preceding his retirement he was research associate of the Carnegie Institution of Washington, D. C.

Morse's first contributions were in the field of organic chemistry. He made but three contributions in this field, however, when it was necessary for him to give his attention to inorganic and analytical chemistry. His investigations in these fields included many new methods of quantitative analysis both gravimetric and volumetric and a well-known method for the calibration of volumetric apparatus. Besides researches on methods of analysis his work on *The Atomic Weight of Zinc as Determined by the Composition of Its Oxide* (1889), written in collaboration with W. M. Burton, and "A Redetermination of the Atomic Weight of Cadmium" (*American Chemical Journal*, April 1892), in collaboration with H. C. Jones, deserve special mention. Up to this point Morse's work consisted of isolated researches on a variety of analytical problems in which there was frequently exhibited a high order of skill and ingenuity. In 1896 he began his first extended investigation. This was on permanganic acid and its salts and was continued for several years. This work led by accident to what later proved to be his most conspicuous investigation. It was noticed occasionally that the porous clay cell used in the preparation of permanganic acid solutions became filled with finely divided manganese dioxide. From this observation an electrolytic method was developed for depositing semipermeable membranes. The utilization of these membranes in accumulating accurate experimental data on the osmotic pressure of aqueous solutions occupied Morse's whole outstanding accomplishment. In all, Morse published about sixty articles on original researches. All of these except the first three were published in the *American Chemical Journal*. In addition he was the author of *Exercises in Quantitative Chemistry* (1905) and *The Osmotic Pressure of Aqueous Solutions* (1914), monograph No. 198 of the Carnegie Institution of Washington, which is a complete report of the investigations of himself and associates on the subject of osmotic pressure carried out at The Johns Hopkins University under grants from the Carnegie Institution. His death occurred suddenly at his summer home at Chebeague, Cumberland County, Sept. 8, 1920. He had married, Dec. 13, 1876, Caroline Augusta, daughter of John Brooks, a merchant of Montpelier, Vt. In 1887 his wife died leaving four children, and on Dec. 24, 1890, he was married to Elizabeth Dennis Clarke of Portland, Me. There were no children by the second marriage.

[Biographical memoirs in *Memoirs Nat. Acad. Sci.*, vol. XXI (1926), with bibliography; *Who's Who in America*, 1920–21; *Daily Eastern Argus* (Portland, Me.), Sept. 9, 1920.]   J. C. W. F.

MORSE, HENRY DUTTON (Apr. 20, 1826–Jan. 2, 1888), diamond cutter, was born in Boston, Mass., the seventh of the eleven children of Hazen and Lucy (Cary) Morse. Of English descent, he belonged on his father's side to the seventh, and on his mother's to the sixth, generation of native-born New Englanders. His father was a well-known bank-note engraver, in whose office Henry mastered the craft while still a boy in school. From the beginning he had sharp eyes, a cunning hand, and the instinct of workmanship. When eighteen years old he set up for himself as an engraver and designer in gold and silver and a few years later learned jewelry-making in the workshops of Clark & Currier, whom he paid $300 for six months' instruction. For some years he manufactured jewelry; then he became a partner in the retail firm of Crosby, Hunnewell & Morse (later Crosby, Morse & Foss) on Washington Street; on the dissolution of the partnership in 1875 he opened a shop of his own on Tremont, confining himself to a trade in precious stones, and two years later organized the Morse Diamond Cutting Company. He was the first American to learn the technique of diamond-cutting. Although his Dutch workmen took their usual precautions to guard the secrets of their trade, Morse spied them out, experimented until he became expert, imparted his skill to American apprentices, and finally made improvements that revolutionized the whole art of diamond cutting. He invented labor-saving machinery for sawing and polishing the stones and, after studying the application of the laws of optics to the work, boldly sacrificed weight to proportion and so cut the first modern full-fashioned brilliants with their fifty-six facets and dazzling powers of refraction. Absolute precision in cutting was his basic principle. No radical changes have been made in the art since his time. The most famous of Morse's early feats was the cutting in 1859 of the so-called Dewey diamond, an ill-shaped, discolored, badly flawed, but well-advertized "rock," which a laborer turned up in a Manchester, Va., street in 1854. After other cutters had given it over as a bad job, he succeeded in obtaining from it an octahedron, with slightly rounded faces, weighing almost twelve carats. Years later, when his hand, eye, and brain were at their best, he cut the largest diamond ever handled in the United States, the Tiffany No. 2 of 125 carats, which was reduced to 77 carats in the cutting. Morse was married May 22, 1849, to Ann Eliza Hayden, daughter of Ezekiel and Elizabeth (West) Hayden, who with two of their four daughters survived him. Artistic taste, keen eyesight, and manual skill were as evident in his recreations as in his professional work. He was an amateur painter, frequently exhibiting his landscapes and animal pictures at Boston shows, an expert rifle shot, and an ornithologist and bird-stuffer. He died at his home at Jamaica Plain, Mass., of a stroke, after an illness of two days.

[H. D. Lord, *Memorial of the Family of Morse* (1896), pp. 340–42; S. C. Cary, *John Cary, the Plymouth Pilgrim* (1911); *Jeweler's Weekly*, Jan. 5, 12, 1888; G. F. Kunz, *Gems and Precious Stones of North America* (1890), pp. 16–17, 316–17; W. R. Cattelle, *Precious Stones* (1903), pp. 60–61; *Boston Daily Advertiser*, Jan. 3, 1888; *Boston Transcript*, Jan. 3, 5, 1888.]
G. H. G.

MORSE, JEDIDIAH (Aug. 23, 1761–June 9, 1826), Congregational clergyman, "father of American Geography," was born in Woodstock, Conn., the eighth child of Jedidiah and Sarah (Child) Morse. After a rather frail boyhood he entered Yale College with the class of 1783, in which "he had a very fair reputation as a scholar . . . though he scarcely gave promise of the eminence which he finally attained" (Sprague, *Annals, post,* p. 251). As a student, he was a member of the Linonian Society and of Phi Beta Kappa. On the eve of graduation he decided to enter the Christian ministry, and with this end in view remained in New Haven for two more years studying theology and supporting himself by teaching and by writing a school textbook in geography. He was licensed to preach in 1785, and for a time taught school and preached in Norwich, Conn., returning to Yale as tutor in June 1786. Overwork, a desire to further his geographical studies by travel, and the attractions of an evangelical ministry led him, a few months later, to seek ordination (Nov. 9, 1786) and take the vacant pulpit in Midway, Ga., where he remained for five months. The following year he preached as candidate for settlement in the Collegiate Presbyterian Churches of New York and in the First Congregational Church of Charlestown, Mass., finally accepting a call from Charlestown. Following his installation, Apr. 30, 1789, he married, May 14, Elizabeth Ann Breese of Shrewsbury, N. J., the daughter of Judge Samuel Breese and the grand-daughter of Samuel Finley [*q.v.*], president of the College of New Jersey. Over the church in Charlestown Morse remained settled for thirty years. As a preacher he was unusually acceptable and popular. Of his sermons and occasional addresses, some twenty-four were published.

In his theological views Morse was a Calvinist and a stanch supporter of orthodoxy. With growing concern, therefore, he observed the inroads of "Arminianism, blended with Unitarianism" in the Congregational churches of eastern Massachusetts. To combat the progress of these "liberal views" became one of the dominant purposes of his ministry, and it was early his hope to separate the Unitarians from the Orthodox and then draw the Orthodox of different shades into more cordial relations. As the champion of Orthodoxy, Morse stepped to the front following the election of Henry Ware [*q.v.*] as Hollis Professor of Divinity at Harvard in 1805. One of the board of overseers, he vigorously opposed this choice on the ground that Ware's theological views were not the orthodox views of the donor, and that his election was a violation of the terms and spirit of the Hollis bequest. Furthermore, he made public the orthodox position in his *True Reasons on which the Election of a Hollis Professor of Divinity in Harvard College was opposed at the Board of Overseers, 14 February, 1805* (1805), the appearance of which proved decisive in joining the issue between the liberal and the orthodox within the Congregational order in Massachusetts. Determined that the liberal clergy should not wholly carry the day, he launched the *Panoplist* in 1805 to uphold and unify the orthodox cause, and this periodical he edited for five years. Equally important in behalf of orthodoxy were his labors in the organization of the General Association of Massachusetts, and in the establishment of Andover Theological Seminary (1808), of which he was one of the most active founders. In Boston itself, he assisted in founding a bulwark of orthodoxy in the Park Street Church (1809), and finally, in publishing the pamphlet, *American Unitarianism; or a Brief History of "The Progress and Present State of the Unitarian Churches in America"* (1815), extracted from Thomas Belsham's *Memoirs of the Life of the Reverend Theophilus Lindsey* (1812), he did more, perhaps, than any one man to force the Unitarian churches out from the Congregational fold. Morse's own church did not escape division, for a Unitarian defection took place in 1816, and continued friction led to his own request for dismissal in 1819.

Not all Morse's energies went into the Unitarian controversy, however. Quite as important, perhaps, were his efforts to further the progress of evangelical truth. He was among the first in America to see the value of tract distribution, and he helped found the New England Tract Society (1814). Equally active were his efforts in the distribution of the Bible, and in 1816 he aided in establishing the American Bible Society. In 1811 he was elected to the American Board of

Commissioners for Foreign Missions, and served on the prudential committee of that board until 1819. As secretary of the Society for Propagating the Gospel among the Indians and others in North America, he took an active interest in the Indians, as well as in the poor whites on the Isles of Shoals. This interest lasted throughout his ministry, and upon leaving Charlestown in 1819 he was commissioned by the government to study the condition of the Indian nations and to render a report, which he published in 1822 (*A Report to the Secretary of War . . . on Indian Affairs, Comprising a Narrative of a Tour Performed in the Summer of 1820*).

In politics Morse was as conservative as in religion, and quite as outspoken. A strong Federalist, he was startled and dismayed in the 1790's by the rising tide of republicanism and by the prevalence of the "French influence," which seemed to him to threaten "orderly" government and religion in the United States. In 1798 he firmly believed that he had discovered the secret cause of these evils in the spread of Illuminism to this side of the Atlantic, and, giving wide publicity to this rather dubious discovery in three sensational published sermons, he contributed not a little to the wave of popular hysteria which followed the outbreak of the quasi-war with France. So vigorous was his defense of the existing political order that to some of his contemporaries he appeared as a "Pillar of Adamant in the Temple of Federalism." His political convictions led him in 1801 to assist in founding *The Mercury and New England Palladium,* a vigorous Federalist periodical.

Jedidiah Morse is best remembered, however, as the "father of American Geography." It was while teaching school in New Haven that his interest in geography developed. Dissatisfied with the treatment of America in the existing English texts, he prepared a series of geographical lectures, which were published in 1784 as *Geography Made Easy,* the first geography to be published in the United States. During the lifetime of its author this famous little text passed through twenty-five editions. So successful was this first effort that he at once projected a larger work which he published in 1789 as *The American Geography,* and in its later editions as *The American Universal Geography.* This work passed through seven American and almost as many European editions, and firmly established its author's reputation as "the American Geographer." Largely in recognition of his geographical services the University of Edinburgh honored him with its degree of S.T.D. in 1794. In 1795 he published *Elements of Geography,*

for children, followed in 1797 by *The American Gazetteer* and in 1802 by *A New Gazetteer of the Eastern Continent,* prepared in collaboration with Elijah Parish, all of which passed through several editions, as did abridgments of these more basic works. During their author's lifetime the Morse geographies virtually monopolized their field in the United States. He was essentially a compiler, drawing his information from the best American and European sources available, as well as from letters and documents sent him from all parts of the country in response to widely published requests for geographical information. At the request of the publisher Morse wrote the article on America for the American edition of the *Encyclopedia Britannica* (1790), which was also published separately. In collaboration with Elijah Parish he wrote *A Compendious History of New England* (1804), the appearance of which gave rise to a famous literary controversy with Hannah Adams [*q.v.*]. Almost his final literary effort was his *Annals of the American Revolution* (1824).

Following his removal from Charlestown Morse went to New Haven, where he devoted the closing years of his life to Indian affairs, writing, and occasional preaching. In personal appearance he was very prepossessing. "The tall, slender form, the well shaped head, a little bald, but covered thinly with fine silken powdered hair, falling gracefully into curls, gave him, when only middle-aged, a venerable aspect, while the benignant expression of his whole countenance and especially of his bright, speaking eye won for him at first sight respect and love" (S. E. Morse, quoted in Sprague, *Life, post,* p. 281). In dress and manners he was "a gentleman of the old school." Temperamentally he was inclined to be sanguine, impulsive, and rather sensitive, which tendencies made him, perhaps, over controversial at times; but his most marked characteristics were his tremendous industry and intellectual activity. To his friend Timothy Dwight, 1752–1817 [*q.v.*], he was "as full of resources as an egg is of meat" (Prime, *post,* p. 4). Of the eleven children born to him and his wife, three survived infancy: Samuel Finley Breese Morse, Sidney Edwards Morse [*qq.v.*], and Richard Cary Morse.

[The chief source for the life of Morse is a manuscript life by his son, Richard Cary Morse, the property of the late Richard Cary Morse of New York. Published sources include W. B. Sprague, *The Life of Jedidiah Morse* (1874), and *Annals Am. Pulpit,* vol. II (1857); F. B. Dexter, *Biog. Sketches Grads. Yale Coll.,* vol. IV (1907); S. I. Prime, *The Life of Samuel F. B. Morse* (1875); E. L. Morse, *Samuel F. B. Morse; His Letters and Jours.* (2 vols., 1914); *Columbian Register* (New Haven), June 10, 1826. For his part in the

Illuminati episode see V. Stauffer, *New England and the Bavarian Illuminati* (1918).]   W. R. W.

MORSE, SAMUEL FINLEY BREESE

(Apr. 27, 1791–Apr. 2, 1872), artist, inventor, was born in Charlestown, Mass., in the Edes House on Main Street, the eldest child of the Rev. Jedidiah Morse [*q.v.*] and his wife, Elizabeth Ann Breese. He was sixth in descent from Anthony Morse of Marlborough, Wilts, who emigrated to Massachusetts in 1635 and settled in Newbury. Anthony's grandson, Peter, removed before 1698 from Newbury to New Roxbury, which, by a relocation of the colonial boundary, became Woodstock, Conn., in 1749 but remained the seat of the family down to Jedidiah's birth in 1761. Morse's mother was the only child of Samuel Breese by his first wife, Rebecca, daughter of Samuel Finley [*q.v.*]. Breese, whose father had been a purser in the British navy and later a thriving merchant in New York, lived on his estate at Shrewsbury, N. J., was a district judge, and a colonel in the Continental Army. Mrs. Morse managed her household with shrewd practical sense, held her husband's Calvinist and Federalist convictions without mitigation or dilution, and bore with heroic resignation the death at birth or in infancy of eight of her eleven children. To his surviving brothers, Sidney Edwards Morse [*q.v.*] and Richard Cary Morse (1795–1868), as to his parents, he was affectionately attached throughout life. The characteristics of the parents descended with little modification to the children; in Finley, as his family called him, the energy and enterprise of the father were fused with the strong will and sense of the mother.

At the age of eight Morse was taken to Phillips Academy, Andover, of which his father was a trustee. He was unhappy under Mark Newman's discipline and twice was so homesick that he fled back to Charlestown. He entered Yale College in 1805, was summoned home, however, during his first year, and did not graduate until 1810. While in residence at Yale he acquired a local reputation for his miniatures on ivory, but his father was reluctant to let him adopt art as a profession.

While he was working as a clerk in a Charlestown bookstore, his pictures of "Marius on the Ruins of Carthage" and "The Landing of the Pilgrims at Plymouth" gained him the approval of Washington Allston and Gilbert Stuart; his parents consented; and on July 13, 1811, he sailed with Allston and his wife for England. Except for two portrait-painting expeditions to Bristol, he spent the next four years in London studying under his master Allston, whom he never ceased to admire, and at the Royal Academy, where he received courteous attention from Benjamin West. He lived frugally; made a warm friend of his room-mate, Charles Robert Leslie [*q.v.*]; met a few notables; read Chaucer, Spenser, Dante, and Tasso as part of his education in art; and painted assiduously. He produced three works of distinction: in 1812 a terra-cotta statuette of "Hercules," that won the gold medal of the Society of Arts; in 1813 a large canvas, "The Dying Hercules," which was hung in the spring exhibition that year of the Royal Academy and received much flattering comment; and in 1815 a second painting, "The Judgment of Jupiter," which would probably have won the cash premium of the Royal Academy if Morse had stayed to receive it. That summer, however, he returned to Boston and opened a studio, full of ambition "to be among those who shall revive the splendor of the fifteenth century."

His hopes were soon dashed. He was socially successful, and people visited his studio to admire "The Dying Hercules" and "The Judgment of Jupiter," but no one offered to buy them or gave him commissions for similar work. As a young artist in London he had disdained portrait-painting, but he soon found that portraits were the only works of art that Americans would buy. Since there were not enough commissions to keep him in Boston, he was compelled to lead a rather vagrant existence. The chief centers of his activity, besides Boston, were Concord, N. H., the home of his father-in-law, which he visited for the first time in the summer of 1816; New Haven, the home of his parents in their latter years; Charleston, S. C., where he spent the winters of 1818–21 and achieved his initial successes; and New York, where he made his headquarters after 1823. In four or five years his art reached its maturity. To the vigor and honesty fundamental to his own nature, he added a profound insight into character and a free, delicate technique. He was thus an admirable portrait painter, and though he had to paint many a dull face for the sake of the fee, he seldom failed to respond to a sitter worthy of him. The level excellence of his portraits is high. Perhaps the best known were the two of Lafayette painted in Washington in 1825, the full-length owned by the City of New York and the half-length owned by the New York Public Library. His landscapes and subject-pictures are much fewer in number and are, for the most part, cold and unimaginative. An exception, however, is "The Old House of Representatives" (Corcoran Gallery, Washington), which he painted in 1821–22. With its eighty-six portraits and masterly rendering of the effect of candle-light, it has its own magnificence and has elicited warm admiration. A similar but lesser feat of virtuosity was "The Exhibition Gallery of the Louvre" (College of Fine Arts, Syracuse University), done in 1831–32. Morse painted these pictures in the hope of making money by exhibiting them around the country, but the public was indifferent to them, and both pictures disappeared for some years. He was the leading spirit among the founders of the National Academy of Design and as its first president, 1826–42, made it an active and even aggressive institution. He organized efficient classes for instruction and waged a pamphlet war against the rival American Academy of Fine Arts, which he denounced as exclusive and moribund. His inventive fancy led him to devise ingenious theories about the combination of colors and to make various experiments. For one of his most beautifully executed pictures, a portrait of his wife and their two children, he ground his pigments in milk; for another picture, with results unrecorded, he ground them in beer.

In the intellectual and artistic circles of New York his urbanity, conversational powers, and commanding presence found their appropriate sphere. His income, however, was uncomfortably small and irregular; and the successive deaths of his wife in 1825, his father in 1826, and his mother in 1828 were hard to bear. In 1829 he went to Europe and spent three years in study, travel, and painting. He divided his time chiefly between Italy and Paris, and cultivated close friendships with James Fenimore Cooper and Horatio Greenough. He was too old, unfortunately, to benefit much by the change of environment.

In October 1832 he returned to New York from Havre on the packet *Sully*. The voyage marked the turning point of his career, but the transition from artist to inventor occupied another five years. In 1832 he was appointed professor of painting and sculpture (later professor of the literature of the arts of design) in the University of the City of New York (now New York University). He retained the title for life, but the position was only nominal; he received no salary, and the fees from his pupils did not pay the rent of his rooms in the University Building on Washington Square. To this period 1832–35 belongs his lapse into anti-Catholic and Native-American agitation. He had come home from Italy with a strong aversion to Catholicism; he fell an easy victim to Maria Monk's imposture, and was inveigled into writing and sponsoring several widely circulated anti-Catholic and Na-

tive-American tracts. In 1836 he ran for mayor of New York on the Native-American ticket, polling about 1500 votes. His example conferred on the movement such respectability as it possessed. In his riper years, he disentangled his facts and his prejudices and grew more tolerant. Several causes contributed to his final withdrawal, about 1837, from painting. The contumelious rejection by a committee of Congress of his application to fill one of the four large vacant panels in the rotunda of the Capitol was probably the deciding factor; but he was weary of the struggle for recognition and even for subsistence; he had reached the limit of his powers as an artist, and a new career was opening before him. But he took the step unwillingly and grieved over it for years (E. L. Morse, *post*, II, 31).

Morse's preoccupation with the telegraph dates from the voyage on the *Sully* in October 1832. A fellow passenger, Charles Thomas Jackson [*q.v.*], led the dinner conversation one day to electricity and exhibited apparatus that he had acquired in Europe. Morse remarked, "If the presence of electricity can be made visible in any part of the circuit, I see no reason why intelligence may not be transmitted instantaneously by electricity." There is evidence that his mind had already toyed with the idea, but the conception of an electro-magnetic recording telegraph came to him now with the power of a revelation, and during the rest of the crossing he lived in a state of intense intellectual excitement, sketching in his note-book a rude but sufficient plan of his invention. His qualifications for the work ahead of him were curiously variegated. Though he had developed little mechanical skill, he had the inventive type of mind. With his brother Sidney he had patented in 1817 a workable, though unremunerative, flexible piston-pump for fire-engines, and five years later he constructed a marble-cutting machine that infringed unluckily on a previous patent. His interest in electrical phenomena had been awakened by the college lectures and demonstrations of Benjamin Silliman and Jeremiah Day. Early in 1827 he attended a course of lectures on electricity delivered before the New York Athenæum by James Freeman Dana [*q.v.*], who included in his topics a detailed, extremely able exposition of the electro-magnet discovered in 1824 by the Englishman, William Sturgeon. Among Dana's auditors, unknown to each other, were Joseph Henry, Leonard Dunnell Gale (1800–1883), and Morse. Henry went from the lecture room to Albany to embark on his great career; Gale was employed on a geological survey; and Morse continued with his painting. He and Dana became friends, but Dana died Apr. 14, 1827, and the possibilities latent in their association came to an end. What Morse knew about electricity in October 1832 he had learned from Dana; he was ignorant of the progress of the last five years, of Henry's discoveries in electro-magnetism and the several European experiments with an electro-magnetic needle telegraph.

The essential features of his invention, as set down in the 1832 note-book, were: (1) a sending-apparatus to transmit signals by the closing and opening of an electric circuit; (2) a receiving-apparatus, operated by an electro-magnet, to record the signals as dots and spaces on a strip of paper moved by clock-work; (3) a code translating the dots·and spaces into numbers and letters. From this original conception Morse wrought his invention through elaboration to eventual simplicity. The sending-apparatus became a "port-rule," through which notched lead types were run to break the circuit automatically in the required sequences of dots and spaces, but this arrangement gave way at last to the simple finger-key. The recording-apparatus went through a similar development before the embossing stylus took the place of clumsier methods of recording. Rather early in the process Morse noticed that the signals could also be read by ear and worked out an efficient sounder. The code went through another series of changes before it became the "Morse code" of American telegraphy. At the outset Morse did not dream of the telegraph as one of the conveniences of daily life; it was to be government-controlled and used only for communications of momentous importance. With this idea in mind, he wasted much time on devising a semi-secret code that required the use of a huge dictionary. He saw from the beginning, however, that another system would be needed for sending proper names. The dash was added to the signals, and dots, dashes, and spaces were translated directly into the letters of the alphabet.

In January 1836 Morse took Gale, now his colleague at the University of the City of New York, into his confidence and showed him his working model. The magnet, however, would not function at a greater distance than forty feet from the battery. Gale's service to the inventor was to bring his knowledge of electro-magnetism up to date. For the one-cup battery and simple Sturgeon magnet he substituted Henry's many-cup battery and intensity magnet, after which they were able to send messages through ten miles of wire wound on reels around Gale's lecture room. Gale also brought Morse into personal contact with Henry, who from time to time gave essential advice and encouragement. At this time, too, Morse worked out a system of electro-magnetic renewers or relays to be placed in the telegraph line at those points where the electric current became too feeble either to print or to project a signal. This was his most brilliant contribution, for it made both possible and practicable the transmission of intelligence from one point on a line through indefinitely great distances, to any number of branch lines, and to an indefinite number of stations, with registration at them all by the manipulation of a single operator at a single station. The general idea was anticipated by Henry and was incorporated in the patents of Morse's contemporaries in England, Wheatstone and Edward Davy, but its practical application, fully described by Morse in his caveat filed in the Patent Office in 1837, would indicate that this was an original discovery. In September 1837 Alfred Vail [q.v.] was also taken into partnership. He provided money for carrying on the work, gave Morse needed moral support, and lent his mechanical skill to the simplifying of the apparatus.

Morse filed his caveat at the Patent Office in September 1837 and went to Europe to secure patents. In England his application was rejected without ceremony; in France he was fêted by scientists and scholars, but the French government was not interested, and he returned empty handed, having been unable to comply with the French patent law. Seven lean years followed, during which Morse preferred poverty and actual hunger to going into debt. Even the Vail family refused him further advances, and Morse's courage almost faltered, but in the confused last minutes of the closing session of 1843, Congress voted $30,000 for an experimental line from Washington to Baltimore. Meanwhile he had been advertising his invention by exhibitions in New York and in 1838 before President Van Buren at Washington, and had been making drastic changes in the apparatus. The Washington-Baltimore line was built by Ezra Cornell [q.v.], and on May 24, 1844, Morse sent the famous salutation, "What hath God wrought!" from the Supreme Court room in the Capitol to Vail in Baltimore. Vail returned the message correctly; and a brief conversation ensued over the wire. The Morse telegraph was in operation.

The telegraph having proved its worth, Morse entered upon the last phase of his career. He and his associates were willing to sell their rights to the government for $100,000, and Morse, satisfied with a competence, would have resumed his painting; but Cave Johnson, the postmaster-general, opined that the invention would not pay its way, Congress adjourned without acting, and the development of the telegraph was left in private hands. The inventor himself had little knowledge of business methods and was sometimes scandalized by what he chanced to discover; though want had taught him to value money, he was too versatile to become engrossed in its acquisition; and he had an artist's repugnance to the necessary routine. It was therefore one of his greatest strokes of luck that he engaged Amos Kendall [q.v.], to manage his business and legal affairs, leaving himself comparatively free. He could not escape, however, from the harassments of almost continuous litigation and detraction. Of all his enemies Francis Ormond Jonathan Smith, a former Congressman from Maine, who had championed Morse in Congress and had become one of his partners, proved the most unscrupulous and implacable, pursuing the inventor even to his death-bed. Morse's rights were upheld in the courts, and in the last analysis the most deplorable feature of his many controversies was the rupture with Joseph Henry. The breach began with an oversight in Vail's book on the telegraph and was rapidly widened by a series of misunderstandings, by the sensitive nature of both men, and by the intrigues of rival entrepreneurs. Morse, usually grateful to his friends and at times magnanimous, was finally goaded into making a headlong, hysterical assault on Henry's integrity. The charges were baseless and have left an unfortunate stain on Morse's reputation. He lived to realize the enormity of his folly and tried awkwardly to make amends, but pride kept him from offering the full confession of guilt that the case demanded.

Otherwise he enjoyed the acclaim, honors, and emoluments of a great inventor and public personage. Yale conferred her LL.D. on him, and European governments, while consistently denying him patents, showered him with medals and decorations until his coat-front, on state occasions, glittered like a lieutenant-general's. In 1858 France, Austria, Belgium, the Netherlands, Piedmont, Russia, the Holy See, Sweden, Tuscany, and Turkey united to give him an honorary gratuity of 400,000 francs, part of which he was compelled to hand over to F. O. J. Smith. His first dividends from the telegraph he gave for church uses. For years his income was slender and uncertain. Kendall's benign efforts to make him rich were constantly thwarted by Morse's open-handed benefactions and the ease with which he could be duped by swindlers, but ultimately both men attained to wealth. In 1854 he ran for Congress on the Democratic ticket and was defeated. In 1857–58 he was electrician for Cyrus W. Field's Company, engaged in laying the transatlantic cable, but resigned when he found himself maneuvered off the board of directors. He distrusted the insulation used on the second cable and, during the few weeks of its operation, predicted its failure. He was one of the founders of Vassar College in 1861 and served again that year as president of the National Academy of Design. In 1864 he made a last effort to paint but found that his skill had departed. His home during these years was a two-hundred-acre estate, "Locust Grove," on the Hudson two miles below Poughkeepsie, which he had bought in 1847. In 1859 he acquired a brownstone house at 5 West 22nd Street, New York City, as a winter residence.

His family life matched his two-fold career as artist and inventor. On Sept. 29, 1818, he married Lucretia Pickering Walker, daughter of Charles and Hannah (Pickering) Walker of Concord, N. H. She died in 1825, and for twenty-three years Morse was a widower. On Aug. 9, 1848, he married Sarah Elizabeth, daughter of Samuel and Catharine (Breese) Griswold of Utica, N. Y., Mrs. Griswold being his first cousin. His second wife was his junior by thirty-one years, but he lived to within a year of their silver wedding. He had four children by each marriage. His youngest son, Edward Lind Morse, graduated from Yale College sixty-eight years after his father.

On June 10, 1871, the telegraph operators of America unveiled a bronze statue of Morse in Central Park, N. Y. It was the work of Byron M. Pickett and was presented to the city by William Cullen Bryant. Morse's last public appearance was on Jan. 17, 1872, when he and Horace Greeley unveiled a statue of Franklin in Printing House Square. His health was now failing. One of his last acts was to take his youngest son downtown to buy him his first gold watch. He died at his city home Apr. 2 and was buried in Greenwood Cemetery.

It was Morse the inventor whose death was commemorated by Congress and at memorial meetings held throughout the nation, the artist having been forgotten. Though his specific inventions have long since been obsolete, even the Morse code giving way to automatic dispatching and printing machines, he remains the greatest figure in the history of the telegraph. Recognition of him as an artist has come slowly, but the exhibition of his paintings at the Metropolitan Museum of Art in 1932 enhanced a reputation that had already begun to grow. The most recent students of American art have been warmest in their appraisal of his successes as a painter and of his influence on the national culture, but his full significance as one of the representative men of his time is revealed only by a study of his whole career and his stalwart, many-sided personality.

[*Samuel F. B. Morse: His Letters and Journals, Edited and Supplemented by his Son, Edward Lind Morse* (2 vols., 1914) is the most authoritative biography but does not wholly supersede the earlier official biography, S. I. Prime, *The Life of Samuel F. B. Morse, LL.D.* (1875). Both were founded on Morse's papers (63 vols., including letter books), now in the Division of Manuscripts, Lib. of Cong. There is other manuscript material in the Yale Univ. Lib. and among the F. O. J. Smith papers in the Me. Hist. Soc. Lib. The U. S. Nat. Museum has the certified copy of the 1832 note-book and various relics of the first Morse telegraph; Cornell Univ. has a few others. Additional biographical material may be found in: *Memorial of Samuel Finley Breese Morse . . . Pub. by Order of Cong.* (1875); Justin Winsor, ed., *The Memorial Hist. of Boston*, III (1881), 552–53; *Personal Reminiscences of the late Mrs. Sarah Breese Walker* (privately printed, 1884); E. G. Porter, "The Morse Tablet at Rome," *Proc. Mass. Hist. Soc.*, 2 ser. XI (1897); J. H. Morse and E. W. Leavitt, *Morse Geneal.* (1903), esp. pp. 216–17; F. B. Dexter, *Biog. Sketches of the Grads. of Yale Coll.*, vol. VI (1912)—the only bibliography of Morse's own writings; *Correspondence of Jas. Fenimore Cooper* (2 vols., 1922); *Diary of Wm. Dunlap, 1776–1839* (3 vols., 1930); T. F. Jones, ed., *N. Y. Univ., 1832–1932* (1933); L. L. Morse, "Samuel F. B. Morse," and H. W. Reynolds, "The Story of Locust Grove," *Year-Book, Dutchess County Hist. Soc.*, vol. XVII (1932). On his work as artist see: *Hist. of the Rise and Progress of the Arts of Design in the U. S.* (1834; rev. ed., 3 vols., 1918, ed. by F. W. Bayley and C. E. Goodspeed); T. S. Cummings, *Hist. Annals of the Nat. Acad. of Design* (1865); E. L. Morse, "Samuel F. B. Morse, the Painter," *Scribner's Mag.*, Mar. 1912; F. J. Mather, Jr., *Estimates in Art, Ser. II* (1931); H. B. Wehle, *Samuel F. B. Morse, Am. Painter* (Met. Museum of Art, 1932)—with finding list of Morse's known paintings and numerous photographic reproductions. On his invention of the telegraph see: *Ann. Report . . . Smithsonian Institution . . . 1857* (1858); E. N. Horsford, *Address at the Morse Memorial Meeting in Faneuil Hall, Apr. 16, 1872* (1872); E. L. Morse, "The Dot-and-Dash Alphabet," *Century Mag.*, Mar. 1912; "The Invention of the Electro-Magnetic Telegraph," *Electrical World*, July 20, 1895–Mar. 28, 1896 —a series of articles by F. W. Jones, F. L. Pope, J. J. Fahie, Rudolf Petsch, A. M. Tanner, E. L. Morse, Jas. D. Reid, Stephen Vail, and Mary A. Henry, together with letters, editorial comment, and other items. For his Native-American activities see: L. D. Scisco, *Pol. Nativism in N. Y. State* (1901) and F. J. Connors, "Samuel Finley Breese Morse and the Anti-Cath. Pol. Movements in the U. S.," *Ill. Cath. Hist. Rev.*, Oct. 1927. The writer is indebted to Carl W. Mitman of the Smithsonian Institution for the passage on the relay.]

G. H. G.

MORSE, SIDNEY EDWARDS (Feb. 7, 1794–Dec. 23, 1871), inventor and author, was born in Charlestown, Mass., the second son of Jedidiah [*q.v.*] and Elizabeth Ann (Breese) Morse. He was graduated A.B. at Yale in 1811, and studied law at Tapping Reeve's law school in Litchfield, Conn. Fresh from college, he set forth his views on the growing preponderance of the South in national affairs in a series of twelve articles signed "Massachusetts," published in the *Columbian Centinel* of Boston, beginning

Dec. 30, 1812. These were reprinted as *The New States, or a Comparison of the . . . Northern and Southern States; with a View to Expose the Injustice of Erecting New States at the South* (1813). The charge of plagiarism brought against his father by Hannah Adams [*q.v.*] caused him to publish *Remarks on the Controversy between Dr. Morse and Miss Adams, together with Some Notice of the Review of Dr. Morse's Appeal*, of which two editions appeared at Boston in 1814.

He definitely cast his lot with the newspaper world when his father and Jeremiah Evarts [*q.v.*], editor of the Boston religious monthly, the *Panoplist*, suggested the establishment of a religious newspaper. On Jan. 3, 1816, the first number of the *Recorder* appeared at Boston, with a prospectus written by Morse setting forth its hopes and ideals. The paper long remained a Boston institution, maintaining its identity until 1867 when it merged with the *Congregationalist*. Morse left it after about a year to enter Andover Theological Seminary, where he studied from 1817 to 1820. In 1823, with his younger brother, Richard Cary Morse, he moved to New York to establish the *New York Observer*, a religious paper of the same type as the Boston *Recorder*, the first number appearing May 17. With Samuel Irenæus Prime [*q.v.*] he made it an influential instrument in Protestant evangelical circles for many years. His obituary notice in the *Observer* (Dec. 28, 1871) records him as "senior editor and proprietor until the year 1858, when he sold his interest to its present senior editor, and retired to private life."

In 1820 he had worked with his father in revising the latter's *Geography*, and father and son joined in editing *A New System of Modern Geography . . . Accompanied by an Atlas*, published at New Haven in 1822. About 1835 (Prefatory note to *The Cerographic Atlas of the United States*, 1842) he began experimenting, with Henry A. Munson, on a new method of printing maps with the letterpress of a book instead of issuing them as plates engraved on metal, wood, or stone. With the *Observer* of June 29, 1839, appeared a map of Connecticut, the first example of what he called "the new art of cerography." He kept the process a secret, but it obviously consisted of engraving on wax and from the wax engraving making a plate to be inserted into the form with the type; the process probably utilized the principles of electrotyping, which had been introduced in 1840. On Oct. 3, 1817, Sidney Morse, with his brother Samuel F. B. Morse [*q.v.*], had been granted a patent for a device for "raising and forcing water and other fluids," usually referred to as "a flexible piston pump." After his cerographic process was established and after he was freed from the daily grind of newspaper work he turned his attention to a "bathometer," for rapid exploration of the depths of the sea, a patent for this "sounding apparatus" being granted him and his son as No. 56,436, July 17, 1866.

A large man of sedentary habits, Morse retained his native strength until he was well along in years. He had a mathematical and statistical mind which found pleasure in the most abstruse, perplexing, and extended calculations. On Apr. 1, 1841, he married Catharine Livingston, daughter of Rev. Gilbert R. Livingston of Philadelphia, and to them were born one son and one daughter. After his death a controversy arose as to whether he or Nathaniel Willis deserved the credit for establishing the *Recorder* as the first religious newspaper (see Frederic Hudson, *Journalism in the United States from 1690 to 1872*, pp. 289–95; also letters in the New York *Evening Post*, Jan. 16, 22, 29, Feb. 15, 22, 1872). Besides the works mentioned above Sidney Edwards Morse was the author of *An Atlas of the United States* (1823); *A Geographical View of Greece, and an Historical Sketch of the Recent Revolution in that Country* (1824); *North American Atlas* (1842); *The Cerographic Atlas of the United States* (1842–45), *The Cerographic Bible Atlas* (1844), and *The Cerographic Missionary Atlas* (1848), the last three being issued as supplements to the *Observer*; *A System of Geography for the Use of Schools* (1844); *A Geographical, Statistical and Ethical View of the American Slaveholders' Rebellion* (1863); *Memorabilia in the Life of Jedidiah Morse* (1867).

[H. D. Lord, *Memorial of the Family of Morse* (1896); obituary notice in the *N. Y. Observer*, Dec. 28, 1871; F. B. Dexter, *Biog. Sketches Grads. Yale Coll.*, vol. VI (1912), with bibliog. of Morse's publications; *Obit. Record Grads. Yale Coll.*, 1872; *N. Y. Times, N. Y. Herald,* and *World* (N. Y.), Dec. 24, 1871; *N. Y. Tribune*, Dec. 25, 1871; biographies of Jedidiah, S. F. B., and Richard Cary Morse.]

H. M. L.

MORTIMER, MARY (Dec. 2, 1816–July 14, 1877), teacher and first principal of Milwaukee College, was a pioneer in the higher education of women in the decades before and after the Civil War. In collaboration with Catharine Esther Beecher [*q.v.*], she inaugurated in Milwaukee, Wis., in 1851, a college system of instruction for young women. She was a native of Trowbridge, Wiltshire, England, the sixth child of William Mortimer, a blacksmith, and of Mary Pierce Mortimer. When she was five years old her family moved to America, and, after a brief stay of two years in New York City, settled on a farm in western New York in the town of Phelps, and here the transplanted English child grew up. Both of her parents died when she was twelve. At the age of twenty-one (1838), she rounded out her education by two years' study at Geneva Seminary, New York, after which she taught there and in other seminaries near-by; in 1849, she started a school of her own in Ottawa, Ill., only to have it fail on account of an outbreak of cholera. At this juncture she met Catharine Beecher and, as a result, entered upon the task of carrying into practice Miss Beecher's theories for the reform of feminine education, particularly the formation in the West of endowed, nonsectarian schools for young women, organized on the college plan. It was a singularly congenial partnership. In Mary Mortimer, Catharine Beecher found one of the "original, planning minds" for which she and her sister, Harriet Beecher Stowe, had been looking. A private seminary in Milwaukee was selected as the basis for the experiment, with the cooperation of its founder, Mrs. Lucy A. Parsons. Mary Mortimer was made a member of its staff and immediately set in motion such changes embodying the reform ideas that by 1851 there evolved a new institution with a college charter, a board of trustees, and herself as principal; and in the two years following a new building was acquired and also a new name: Milwaukee Female College. In 1852 Catharine Beecher and Mary Mortimer spent June and July at Harriet Beecher Stowe's home in Brunswick, Me., working out a course of study; they also formed the American Woman's Educational Association largely to secure an endowment for the infant college and for similar institutions which it was hoped would spread over the nation in imitation of Milwaukee's example. For two periods: 1850–57, and 1866–74, fifteen years in all, Miss Mortimer served the college, harassed by unceasing financial difficulties. In the interval between she was for a time principal of a seminary in Baraboo, Wis. The last three years of her life she spent at her home, "Willow Glen," Milwaukee, giving lectures, building up a post-graduate course, initiating and organizing the Woman's Club of Wisconsin. Frances E. Willard, a student at the college in 1856, describes Miss Mortimer as a small, plump woman with an astonishingly impressive head. In 1895 Milwaukee Female College merged with Downer College of Fox Lake, and the new institution took the name of Milwaukee-Downer College.

[W. W. Wight, *Annals of Milwaukee Coll., 1848–91* (1891), based on Mary Mortimer's autobiographical sketch and records of the college; Minerva Brace Norton, *A True Teacher: Mary Mortimer* (1894), which contains many private letters; information from a few former students of Milwaukee College.]   A. C. F.

MORTON, CHARLES (*c.* 1627–Apr. 11, 1698), Puritan clergyman and schoolmaster, was born at Pendavy in Cornwall, the home of his mother, Frances (Kestell) Morton, and was baptized Feb. 15, 1626/27. His father was the Rev. Nicholas Morton, chaplain of St. Saviour's, Southwark. Charles was admitted pensioner at Queen's College, Cambridge, in 1646, but transferred to Oxford, became a scholar and fellow of Wadham College, B.A. 1649, M.A. 1652, and was admitted *ad eundem* at Cambridge the next year. In 1655 he was installed rector of Blisland, Cornwall. When the Restoration forced him out of that post, he preached privately at St. Ives, until, in 1666, he set up at Newington Green, near London, what became the most famous of the Dissenters' academies. Here, although chiefly interested in the training of ministers, Morton provided a sound university education for the sons of Nonconformists, then denied admittance to the universities. Among his pupils were Samuel Wesley and Daniel Defoe, both of whom praised his ability. Calamy, historian of the Nonconformists, says of Morton: "He had indeed a Peculiar Talent, of winning Youth to the Love of Virtue and Learning, both by his Pleasant Conversation, and by a Familiar Way he had of making difficult Subjects easily Intelligible" (*Account, post,* II, 145). Nevertheless, constant harassment from the court of the bishop of London, who looked upon such schools as centers of sedition and heresy, finally determined Morton to emigrate to New England, where he expected to become president of Harvard ("The Hutchinson Papers," *Prince Society Publications,* vol. II, 1865, pp. 287, 293). Accompanied by Samuel Penhallow [*q.v.*], he landed in Boston in July 1686.

Unsettled conditions in Massachusetts preventing his being chosen president, he became minister at Charlestown instead. His fame as a teacher attracted pupils to him there, including some rebellious Harvard students; but early in 1687, pressure from the Harvard authorities forced him to give up his teaching, and what might have become a rival college was throttled in infancy (*Collections of the Massachusetts Historical Society,* 4 ser., vol. VIII, 1868, pp. 111 f.). Harvard made use of his ability, however, by electing him fellow in 1692, and vice-president in 1697, Morton being the first to occupy that newly created office. He was an active member of the corporation and an occasional lecturer on scientific subjects. His "Compendium Phys-

icae," a popular work on science, and his "System of Logic" were used in many manuscript copies as textbooks at Harvard far down into the eighteenth century. Treatises by him appeared in the *Philosophical Transactions* of the Royal Society for April 1675, and in *The Harleian Miscellany* (vol. II, 1744). He was the author of about a dozen separate volumes, generally short, on Biblical and religious subjects, including "Two little things in English meeter." His best known work was *The Spirit of Man* . . . (1693).

A leading minister from the time of his arrival, Morton associated himself in matters of polity with the Mathers. Judge Sewall [*q.v.*], a connoisseur of sermons, used often to go over to Charlestown to hear him preach. His popularity was enhanced by an unsuccessful prosecution in 1689 for seditious speaking against the Andros régime. In 1690 he founded an association of twenty-two leading ministers from the vicinity of Boston, who met at Harvard College every six weeks for mutual counsel (Manuscript record book in Harvard University Library; sections reprinted in *Proceedings of the Massachusetts Historical Society,* vol. XVII, 1880, pp. 262–80). He is said to have been the first minister in New England to perform marriages, a right previously reserved to the civil authorities (Budington, *post,* p. 184). He also began what is known among Congregationalists as the ceremony of "installation," when he refused to be reordained by the laying on of hands at his induction into the Charlestown church. His wife, Joan, of whom little is known, died in 1693 and there were no children (T. B. Wyman, *The Genealogies and Estates of Charlestown,* p. 687).

[Sources for Morton's life in England include Edmund Calamy, *An Account of the Ministers . . . Who Were Ejected or Silenced after the Restoration in 1660, by or before the Act of Uniformity,* vol. II (1713), and *A Continuation of the Account of the Ministers, etc.,* vol. I (1727); Joshua Toulmin, *An Hist. View of the State of the Protestant Dissenters in Eng.* (1814); Walter Wilson, *Memoirs of the Life and Times of Daniel De Foe* (1830), vol. I; Luke Tyerman, *The Life and Times of the Rev. Samuel Wesley* (1866); John MacLean, *The Parochial and Family Hist. of the Deanery of Trigg Minor in the County of Cornwall,* vol. I (1873); *Dict. of Nat. Biog.*; Joseph Foster, *Alumni Oxonienses* (1891), vol. III; John and J. A. Venn, *Alumni Cantabrigienses,* pt. I, vol. III (1924). For his life in Mass., besides miscellaneous material printed in the publications of the Mass. Hist. Soc., see: "Harvard College Records," *Pubs. Colonial Soc. of Mass.,* vol. XVI (1925); Josiah Quincy, *The Hist. of Harvard Univ.,* vol. I (1840); "Diary of Samuel Sewall," *Colls. Mass. Hist. Soc.,* 5 ser., vol. V (1878); W. I. Budington, *The Hist. of the First Church, Charlestown* (1845); J. F. Hunnewell, *Records of the First Church in Charlestown, Mass., 1632–1789* (1880); Richard Frothingham, Jr., *The Hist. of Charlestown, Mass.* (1845); W. B. Sprague, *Annals Am. Pulpit,* vol. I (1857); T. B. Wyman, *The Geneals. and Estates of Charlestown* (1879), vol. II. Works of Morton in MS. are to be found in the libraries of Harvard Univ. and Bowdoin Coll.]

W. J. B.

MORTON, GEORGE (1585–June 1624), Pilgrim father, was probably the son and heir of Anthony Morton, a wealthy Catholic gentleman living near Bawtry or Harworth, not far from the little village of Scrooby, in Nottinghamshire, England. When still very young, he was converted by William Brewster [q.v.] to Puritanism. He was a member of the Scrooby congregation before their emigration and either went to Holland with them or followed them after a residence at York. He is one of the three emigrants to America who can be traced to the Scrooby district, the others being Brewster and William Bradford [q.v.]. On July 23, 1612, he was married at Leyden to Juliana Carpenter. Morton was possessed of considerable means, was entered in his marriage record (facsimile in *Mayflower Descendant*, October 1909, p. 193) as a merchant from York, was apparently one of the financial mainstays of the Pilgrims at Leyden, and was certainly closely associated with the leaders. He was one of those who went to London in 1619 to negotiate with the merchants, living probably at Aldgate, where his brother-in-law, Edward Southworth, was already established. Here he changed his name to Mourt, perhaps to escape the displeasure of his Catholic relatives.

While Robert Cushman [q.v.] was absent in America, Morton was probably chief Pilgrim agent in London. He received the writings sent in the *Fortune* from Plymouth in 1622, and published them under the title: *A Relation or Iournall of the beginning and proceedings of the English Plantation setled at Plimoth in New England . . . London, Printed for Iohn Bellamie* (1622), which is still the only contemporary account of the voyage of the *Mayflower* and the first months of the colony. Tradition has assigned to him the authorship, and it has always been known as "Mourt's Relation." It has been conjectured that Bradford and Winslow were the authors and Morton merely the publisher (Alexander Young, *Chronicles of the Pilgrim Fathers*, 1841; Edward Channing, *A History of the United States*, vol. I, 1905, p. 318; W. T. Davis, *Bradford's History of Plymouth Plantation*, 1908, pp. 11–14), but since the narrative Bradford wrote and sent back on the *Fortune* was retained by the captain of the French privateer which captured the *Fortune* on its return voyage (*Calendar of State Papers, Colonial Series, 1574–1660*, 1860, p. 124), it is possible that Morton wrote a narrative from information brought back by those

returning on the *Mayflower* and the *Fortune* and published it together with material by Winslow and others not retained by the French captain. The authorship of the book cannot now be definitively established.

Morton was one of the organizers of the voyage of the *Anne* and the *Little James* in 1623 and came himself with his wife and four children, and his wife's sister, Alice Southworth, a widow, who married Governor Bradford the following year. He was assigned an excellent piece of land in 1624, but died in June of that year. His property having by this time been spent in the Pilgrim service, Bradford assumed care of his wife and children. Morton's descendants have been numerous and influential. His eldest son, Nathaniel [q.v.], was secretary of the colony for many years.

[Accounts of Morton's life appear in J. K. Allen, *George Morton of Plymouth Colony and Some of His Descendants* (1908); J. A. Goodwin, *The Pilgrim Republic* (1888); Joseph Hunter, *Colls. Concerning the Church or Congregation of Protestant Separatists Formed at Scrooby . . . The Founders of New Plymouth* (1854); H. M. and M. Dexter, *The England and Holland of the Pilgrims* (1905). The best edition of the *Relation* is *Mourt's Relation or Iournal of the Plantation at Plymouth* (1865), with intro. and notes by H. M. Dexter.]

R. G. U.

MORTON, HENRY (Dec. 11, 1836–May 9, 1902), scientist, first president of Stevens Institute of Technology, was born in New York City, the son of Rev. Henry J. and Helen (MacFarlan) Morton. His father was rector of St. James's Episcopal Church in Philadelphia for more than fifty years. Henry's early education was received at the Episcopal Academy, Philadelphia, and at the age of seventeen he entered the University of Pennsylvania, graduating with the class of 1857. Toward the close of his college course he suggested to some of his classmates that they undertake the translation of the famous Rosetta Stone that had been discovered in Egypt during the occupation of Napoleon, a plaster cast of which had been presented to the Philomathean, a philosophical undergraduate society, of which Morton was a member. Although this stone had been studied by others no complete translations had been made. The inscriptions were in Greek, demotic, and hieroglyphic; Morton undertook the translation of the hieroglyphic inscription while two of his associates worked on the Greek and demotic inscriptions. All of the translations were completed and Morton drew a rich color design for most of the pages of a 160-page book; then, to minimize costs, he drew all the designs on stone for lithographing. Within each page-design was a portion of the translation in Morton's bold, clear, characteristic penmanship. The work was published in 1858 (2nd edition, 1859) under the title: *Report of the Committee of the Philomathean Society of the University of Pennsylvania to Translate the Inscription on the Rosetta Stone.*

In 1859 Morton studied law for a short time, but as a result of his success in teaching chemistry and physics at the Episcopal Academy, he soon gave up law to devote himself to science. His lectures were so "novel, . . . entertaining and instructive" that his lecture room had to be enlarged and finally a new wing added to the academy building. The fame of them spread, and in 1863 he became professor of chemistry at the newly organized Philadelphia Dental College and the next year was appointed resident secretary of the Franklin Institute. To upbuild and augment the financial resources of the Institute, he undertook a series of public lectures on light, sound, and cognate topics. His reputation had become such that the Philadelphia Academy of Music, then one of the largest auditoriums in the country, seating 3,500 people, was engaged. Before the first lecture every seat in the house was sold, as was also the case at a repetition of the lecture a few days later. He was made editor of the *Journal of the Franklin Institute* in 1867, serving in this capacity until July 1871. In 1868 he occupied the chair of chemistry and physics at the University of Pennsylvania during the year's leave-of-absence of the regular professor. The following year a separate department of chemistry was created for him. He was employed by the United States Nautical Almanac Office in 1869 to organize and conduct an expedition to Iowa to make photographs of the total eclipse of the sun on Aug. 7. In this connection, he was the first to prove that the bright line on the sun's disk adjacent to the edge of the moon was a photographic phenomenon and not an optical one.

In 1870 he accepted the presidency of Stevens Institute of Technology, then in process of organization, and, together with a strong faculty that he gathered about him, he developed the first curriculum in mechanical engineering in America. He continued his researches and his writings, one of his early laboratory accomplishments at Stevens being the scientific development of plastic materials for filling teeth, work which resulted in widespread changes in dental treatment. He was soon called into consultation in New York by lawyers engaged in patent litigation. From this labor he received sufficient remuneration to leave him a comfortable fortune, even after he had given back to Stevens

Institute a larger total sum for the development of the college than he had received in salary. It is said that his printed testimony given in patent litigation, if collected, would equal in volume a set of Scott's novels (Sellers and Leeds, *post*). He wrote extensively on the subjects of fluorescence, galvanic batteries, pneumatic pyrometer, conservation of energy, gaseous compounds, Roentgen rays, photometry, liquid air, artificial illumination, electric storage, engineering fallacies, and dynamo-electric machines, his articles appearing in various American and European papers, notably in *Engineering* (London). A student of Biblical criticism, he wrote in 1897, at the request of the editor of *Bibliotheca Sacra,* two articles on "The Cosmogony of Genesis and its Reconcilers," published in the April and July issues of that year. He was also a contributor to the *New York Tribune,* the *Churchman,* the *Outlook,* and the *Church Eclectic.* He was interested in archeology and was a member of the committee in charge of the expedition for excavating Ur of the Chaldees and other Babylonian sites, to which enterprises he contributed generously. He had strong artistic instincts and was an art connoisseur throughout his life. "With him," it was said, "poetry was a natural form of expression," but very little of his verse was published. On Aug. 20, 1862, he married Clara Whiting Dodge, and they had two children.

[Coleman Sellers and A. R. Leeds, *Biog. Notice of Prest. Henry Morton* (1892); F. DeR. Furman, *Morton Memorial, A Hist. of the Stevens Inst. of Technology* (1905); *Who's Who in America,* 1901–02; *Science,* May 30, 1902; *Engineering* (London), July 18, 1902; E. L. Nichols, "Biog. Memoir of Henry Morton" (1915), in *Nat. Acad. Sci. Biog. Memoirs,* vol. VIII; name of mother and date of marriage from a grandson.]

F. DeR. F.

MORTON, JAMES ST. CLAIR (Sept. 24, 1829–June 17, 1864), soldier, engineer, and author of works on engineering and fortification, was born in Philadelphia, Pa. He was the son of Dr. Samuel George Morton [*q.v.*] and Rebecca Grellet (Pearsall) Morton. After attending the University of Pennsylvania four years, he entered West Point in 1847 and graduated on July 1, 1851, second in a class of forty-two. He was assigned to the Corps of Engineers as brevet second lieutenant and served as assistant engineer in the construction of the defenses of Charleston harbor, S. C., from 1851 to 1852, and in the building of Fort Delaware, Del., from 1852 to 1855. Promoted second lieutenant, Apr. 1, 1854, he was detailed as assistant professor of engineering at West Point. On July 1, 1856, he was promoted first lieutenant and on June 17 of the following year became assistant engineer in operations preliminary to the construction of

Sandy Hook Fort (Fort Hancock), N. J. Following this assignment, from 1858 to 1859, he was lighthouse engineer of the third district (from Gooseberry Point, Mass., to Squam Inlet, N. J.). Next he was in charge of the Potomac Water Works (1859–60), then engineer in charge of the Chiriqui Expedition to Central America, and from 1860 to 1861 of the Washington Aqueduct.

He was promoted captain of engineers Aug. 6, 1861. Later that year he became superintending engineer of the construction of Fort Jefferson, Dry Tortugas, Fla., and in 1862 was in charge of repairs at Fort Mifflin, Pa. From June 9 to Oct. 27, 1862, he was chief engineer of the Army of the Ohio. He was appointed brigadier-general, United States Volunteers, Nov. 29, 1862. From Oct. 27, 1862, to Aug. 22, 1863, and from Sept. 17 to Nov. 14, 1863, he was chief engineer of the Army of the Cumberland and from Nov. 3 to Nov. 7, 1863, commanded the pioneer brigade attached to the XIV Corps of that army. He participated in the Tennessee campaign and for gallant and meritorious services in the battle of Stone River, Dec. 31, 1862–Jan. 2, 1863, was brevetted lieutenant-colonel of engineers of the Regular Army. Until June 1863 he was engaged in fortifying Nashville and Murfreesboro, Tenn. He was promoted major, corps of engineers, July 3, 1863, and participated in the advance on Tullahoma, June 24 to July 4, and in the crossing of the Cumberland Mountains and the Tennessee River, Aug. 15 to Sept. 4 of that year. He was wounded in the battle of Chickamauga and on Sept. 20, 1863, was brevetted colonel for gallant and meritorious services at that battle. From September to November of the same year he was engaged in fortifying Chattanooga, and on Nov. 7 was mustered out of the volunteer service.

He was superintending engineer of the defenses of Nashville, Murfreesboro, Clarksville, and Fort Donelson, Nov. 14, 1863, to Jan. 30, 1864, when he became assistant to the chief engineer at Washington, D. C. On May 18, 1864, he was appointed chief engineer of the IX Army Corps and participated during the Richmond campaign in the battles of North Anna, May 24, 1864; Totopotomoy, May 28–29, 1864; Bethesda Church, May 30, 1864; and the assault of Petersburg, Va., June 17, 1864, where he was killed while leading the attack. On the same day he was brevetted brigadier-general, United States Army, for gallant and meritorious service. He lies buried in Laurel Hill Cemetery, Philadelphia.

He was the author of a *Memoir on Fortification* (1858); *Memoir on the Dangers and Defences of New York City* (1858); *Memoir on American Fortification* (1859). These are analytical studies of European fortifications, and of American fortification as it should have been. Written in the days when cannon had a maximum range of less than 5,000 yards, their value today is entirely in their historical interest. His *Memoir of the Life and Services of Captain and Brevet Major John Sanders, of the Corps of Engineers, U. S. Army* (1861) is an appreciation of the work of a great military engineer.

[G. W. Cullum, *Biog. Reg. Officers and Grads. U. S. Mil. Acad.* (1891), vol. II; War Dept. records; F. B. Heitman, *Biog. Reg. and Dict. U. S. Army* (1903), vol. I; Clarence Pearsall, *Hist. and Geneal. of the Pearsall Family in England and America* (1928), vol. II.]

J. W. L.

MORTON, JOHN (*c.* 1724–April 1777), signer of the Declaration of Independence, was born after his father's death in Ridley, Chester (now Delaware) County, Pa., the son of John Morton and Mary Archer. His great-grandfather, Morten Mortenson, had sailed from Gothenburg, Sweden, in 1654, a member of the Tenth Swedish Expedition under Johan Classon Rising, the last governor of New Sweden. Young Morton received only three months of public schooling, but he was efficiently educated at home in all common branches of learning by his foster father, John Sketchley, an Englishman of excellent training and a surveyor by profession, who had married the widowed Mrs. Morton and had taken an affectionate interest in her son. Possessed of an alert, mature mind, great industry, and a fondness for precision, the stepson was soon able to share the work of his teacher, so that his early employment consisted in surveying lands and cultivating his "patrimonial farm." Many tracts on Tinicum Island were surveyed by Morton. In 1754 he married Ann Justice (or Justis), a descendant of the Delaware Swedes, and had by her three sons and five daughters, who survived him. Their descendants are numerous and many have attained distinction.

Morton was early called into public life and served his state and country with unusual faithfulness. Elected a member of the Provincial Assembly from Chester County in 1756, he was reëlected to the same office for ten consecutive years. In February 1767 his position was filled by another—apparently because of political disagreements with the views of Morton—but he was returned to the Assembly in 1769 and served seven more terms, acting after Mar. 15, 1775, as speaker of that body. Beginning in October 1766, he held for three years the position of high sheriff of Chester County. In 1757 he had been chosen justice of the peace for Chester County and in 1770 a judge for the trial of negroes. He also served for a time as president judge of the court of general sessions and common pleas of his county, and became in April 1774 an associate judge of the supreme court of the province. In 1765 he was one of the four Pennsylvania delegates to the Stamp Act Congress and was a delegate to the Continental congresses from 1774 until early in 1777. In the session of July 1776, his vote together with those of Benjamin Franklin and James Wilson placed Pennsylvania on the side of independence by a majority of one. While in Congress Morton served on many important committees and was chairman of the committee of the whole on the adoption of the Articles of Confederation finally ratified after his own death. After the battle of Lexington he had been offered the colonelcy of a volunteer corps in Pennsylvania, but he declined the honor because of his other duties.

Morton was essentially a self-made man, of pleasant social and domestic qualities, sound in judgment, and modest in manner. His character is revealed in his unrelenting stand in favor of colonial freedom, in a state where opinion on the matter was seriously divided. A museum of Swedish-American interests erected in Philadelphia has been named the John Morton Memorial Building.

[Sources include: *Minutes of the Provincial Council of Pa.*, vols. IX and X (1852); *Pa. Archives*, 2 ser. IX (1880); M. A. Leach, "John Morton," *Am. Scandinavian Rev.*, July–Aug. 1915; J. H. Martin, *Chester (and Its Vicinity), Delaware County, in Pa.* (1877); Geo. Smith, *Hist. of Delaware County, Pa.* (1862); H. D. Paxson, *Sketch and Map of a Trip from Phila. to Tinicum Island, Delaware County, Pa.* (1926). There are brief biographies of Morton in the various works on the Signers, though they are for the most part mere eulogies of character. Since there were several contemporaries by the same name, no portrait of Morton, the Signer, is considered authentic. His tombstone in St. Paul's churchyard at Chester, Pa. and the tablet to his memory in the Independence Chamber of the State House in Philadelphia give 1724 as the year of birth, but it may have taken place early in 1725, N.S.]

A. B. B.

MORTON, JULIUS STERLING (Apr. 22, 1832–Apr. 27, 1902), agriculturist, was born at Adams, Jefferson County, N. Y., of New England lineage, the son of Julius Dewey and Emeline (Sterling) Morton. In 1834 Julius Morton followed the tide of emigration into the west, locating first at Monroe, Mich., and later at Detroit, where he became a well-known and prosperous citizen. Young Julius Sterling Morton, who showed signs of mental alertness at an early age, was given excellent educational opportunities. He spent two years at the University of Michigan, but, owing to his independence of the constituted authorities, he was expelled in his senior year. Although he was apparently never in residence at Union College, Schenectady, N. Y., he received the A.B. degree there in 1856. In 1858 the Regents of the University of Michigan voted to confer the A.B. degree as of the class of 1854. On Oct. 30, 1854, he was married to Caroline Joy French, the daughter of Hiram Joy and the adopted daughter of David and Cynthia French of Detroit. The wedding trip was the journey to a new home in Nebraska, then much advertised by reason of the discussion Douglas' Kansas-Nebraska Act had aroused. After a short stay at Bellevue, Neb., he located at Nebraska City, where for a number of years he edited a pioneer newspaper, the *Nebraska City News,* writing, as he was also accustomed to talk, vigorously and with small regard for the consequences.

He early interested himself in territorial politics. As a member of the territorial legislature, the second assembly, 1855–56, and the fourth, 1857–58, he opposed the efforts of Omaha and the North Platte country to dominate the affairs of the territory, and he fought valiantly against the numerous wild-cat banking projects then so generally approved by local speculators. In 1858 his leadership in territorial affairs was recognized when he was appointed by President Buchanan to be secretary of the territory, an office he held until 1861. For several months of that time he also served as acting-governor. He was a Democrat, and as such he was repeatedly a candidate for office. Twice he ran for territorial delegate to Congress, and four times he was his party's nominee for governor. Many times, also, he received the Democratic vote of the legislature for United States senator. In the days when the railroads figured largely in Nebraska politics, he was regarded as the especial friend of the Chicago, Burlington & Quincy Railroad. His highest political honor came in 1893, when he was appointed secretary of agriculture by President Cleveland, a post in which he distinguished himself by his emphasis upon economy. Among other things he eliminated temporarily the free distribution of seeds by congressmen, in his opinion a sheer waste of money.

Cleveland's appointment came to Morton not merely because of his political record and his low-tariff, hard-money views but also because of his standing as an agriculturist. He was a student of agriculture; he owned and lived upon a quarter-section of land adjacent to Nebraska City, and he esteemed it his duty to instruct the people of the state in the subject of farming by precept, perhaps, even more than by example.

Tree-planting was his hobby, and he set out literally hundreds of trees with his own hands. To encourage the same practice on the part of others, he urged that one day each year, to be known as Arbor Day, should be especially dedicated to that purpose, and from 1872 to 1885 some day in April was generally so observed throughout the state (see sketch of Robert W. Furnas). In the latter year the legislature designated his birthday, Apr. 22, as Arbor Day and declared it a legal holiday. From Nebraska the idea spread to many other states and even outside the United States. The success of Arbor Day was to him the crowning achievement of his life. His political and agricultural activities made him a well known figure in Nebraska, as did his editorial and literary activities. Throughout his life he made numerous speeches in Nebraska and elsewhere (*A Speech Delivered at the Nebraska State Fair*, 1873; *A Commemorative Pamphlet, ... 1876, at Nebraska City, ... Containing ... an Oration*, 1876; *Addresses ... at Chicago ... 1893*, 1893). In 1897 he undertook the editorship of *The Illustrated History of Nebraska*, planned the volumes, and arranged for some of the contributions before he persuaded another editor to complete the work (edited by J. S. Morton, succeeded by Albert Watkins, 3 vols., 1905-13). The next year, 1898, he began to publish the *Conservative*, a periodical devoted to political and economic discussions, which was suspended soon after his death. His aggressive personality, so well reflected in his sturdy figure, his keen blue-gray eyes, and his prominent features, won admiration even from his enemies. His emergence into national prominence gratified the pride of his fellow citizens, who, before the advent of William Jennings Bryan, were unaccustomed to such honors. While his own fortune was very modest, the extraordinary financial success of his four sons, the second of whom was Paul Morton [*q.v.*], also attracted attention to him. Up to the time of his death, at his son's home in Lake Forest, Ill., he was generally regarded, by friend and foe alike, as one of Nebraska's foremost citizens. Many years after his death his Nebraska City home, "Arbor Lodge," together with the surrounding groves, **was given to the** state by his heirs as a memorial and a park.

[*Illustrated Hist. of Neb.*, ed. by J. S. Morton succeeded by Albert Watkins, vol. I (1905); A. E. Sheldon, *Nebraska* (1931), vol. I; J. M. Woolworth, *In Memory of Caroline Joy French Morton* (1882); *Univ. of Mich. Regents' Proceedings, 1837-64* (1915); letters from D. Richard Weeks of the Graduate Council of Union College and from Lunette Hadley of the Alumni Catalogue Office of Univ. of Mich.: *Arbor Day*, ed. by R. W. Furnas (1888); *Neb. State Journal* (Lincoln), Apr. 28, 1902.]   J. D. H.

MORTON, LEVI PARSONS (May 16, 1824-May 16, 1920), minister to France, vice-president of the United States, and governor of New York, was primarily a banker whose prominence in New York business extended from the Civil War until after the panic of 1907. He came of old New-England stock, a descendant of George Morton [*q.v.*], and with perhaps no ancestor who arrived in America after 1650. His father, the Rev. Daniel Oliver Morton, was pastor at Shoreham, Vt., when Levi was born. The name, Levi Parsons, was contributed by a missionary brother of his mother, Lucretia (Parsons) Morton. The young man gained much of his early business experience as store-keeper and forwarder at Hanover, N. H., where he lived in the household of a professor at Dartmouth College, but he had neither time nor means for a collegiate career. He met in Hanover his first wife, Lucy Young Kimball, of Long Island, whom he married on Oct. 15, 1856. The channel of wholesale and importing business carried him through Boston, where he was for a time in the same firm with Junius Spencer Morgan, to New York, where on Jan. 1, 1855, he became head of the wholesale house of Morton, Grinnell & Company. He failed, when Southern debts became worthless in 1861, but he reorganized his business and paid his creditors in full, and in 1863 he launched a banking firm in Wall Street. His mastery of the uncertain trends of finance after the Civil War was so complete that, in the operations under the refunding law of 1870 his firm, since 1869 Morton, Bliss & Company, with its London agent, Morton, Rose & Company, found itself, with Drexel, Morgan & Company, on the upward curve, supplanting in some measure the firm of Jay Cooke, that had for ten years been dominant in American finance.

Morton's English partner, Sir John Rose, was go-between in the conversations that preceded the Joint High Commission of 1871, and both Rose and Morton were in frequent communication with President Grant and Secretary Fish during the critical moments of the Geneva arbitration. This concluded, the firm handled the transfer of the Geneva award, and Morton began to see vistas of political preferment. He was nominated for Congress by the Republican party of the eleventh New York district (a residential district on upper Fifth Avenue), in 1876, and was defeated after cutting down the normal Democratic majority. He was successful, however, in the two ensuing elections of 1878 and 1880. He did not sit during the second term to which he was elected, having accepted the post of minister to France, after declining the vice-presidential nomination and the post of secretary of the navy. He would have preferred a seat in the Senate, which went to Platt, or the Treasury, but President Garfield would not bestow that office upon a Wall-Street banker. Paris was to his liking, although he preferred not to have the legation offices over a grocer's shop. His first wife having died in 1871, he was married on Feb. 12, 1873, to Anna Livingston Read Street. With abundant wealth, they entertained lavishly and acquired a fondness for European residence. Morton's diplomatic responsibilities were not heavy, involving nothing more than matters of nationality and citizenship, the ceremonies surrounding the gift of the Bartholdi statue of liberty, and interminable correspondence regarding the status of the American hog in France. He came home vainly aspiring to the Senate, in 1885 and again in 1887, but willing to accept the vice-presidency, which he gained in 1889.

Morton had by this time set up a great country estate, "Ellerslie," near Rhinecliff on Hudson, and now as vice-president he bought a house on Scott Circle and established his family in Washington society. As presiding officer over the Senate he was his own master, unyielding to party pressure; yet he was a faithful servant of the Senate rules, showing none of the ambition to command that Reed exhibited in the House and none of the zeal to reform that his next banker-successor, Dawes, displayed in 1925. He was chagrined, but dignified, when accident deprived him of the barren honor of a renomination in 1892. In 1895 he became governor of New York, after twelve years of Democratic rule, succeeding his neighbor Roswell P. Flower who had in 1881 taken his place as congressman. He became governor with the support of Senator Thomas C. Platt, now boss of the state, but he was in no sense a cog in Platt's machine; and in the many moments in which he showed a determination to be a real governor, Platt tried in vain to discipline him by threats of withholding support for the presidential nomination of 1896. He was a firm and moderate advocate of civil-service reform and lent deliberate and constructive aid to the movement for the consolidation of Greater New York. As a banker, he strongly supported the gold standard. He finally received the support of Senator Platt and became a favorite son in 1896, but the support was only for bargaining purposes since before the Republican convention met Hanna and McKinley were already in control of its des-

tiny. Morton supported the party ticket with increasing zeal as the maintenance of the gold standard became the campaign issue, and returned placidly to his banking house after leaving office as governor on Jan. 1, 1897. In 1899 he rearranged his affairs, launching at the age of seventy-five the Morton Trust Company, which increased in wealth and influence until it was amalgamated with the Guaranty Trust Company in 1909. After this amalgamation, he retired from active business to spend much of his time in travel and in contemplation of his various benefactions, among which were generous contributions to the cathedral of St. John the Divine. After the death of his wife in 1918 he lived in almost complete retirement until he followed her on his ninety-sixth birthday, in 1920. Three of his daughters survived him.

[Morton outlived his prominence and received less obituary notice than might have been expected, although there is a good article in the *N. Y. Times*, May 17, 1920. The campaign biography of 1888, by George Alfred Townsend [Gath], was printed in Lew Wallace, *Life of Gen. Ben Harrison* (1888), but is unimportant. There is a somewhat unusual collection of eulogistic speeches by the senators of the Fifty-second Congress in *Testimonial to Vice-President Levi P. Morton* (1893). But all of these are supplanted by the excellent official biography, Robert McElroy, *Levi Parsons Morton: Banker, Diplomat and Statesman* (1930), in which extensive use is made of the Morton papers now deposited in the N. Y. Pub. Lib. For genealogical details, see J. G. Leach, *Memoranda Relating to the Ancestry and Family of Hon. Levi Parsons Morton, Vice-President of the U. S., 1889–93* (1894).]

F. L. P.

MORTON, MARCUS (Feb. 19, 1784–Feb. 6, 1864), jurist, governor of Massachusetts, was born in Freetown, Mass., the son of Nathaniel and Mary (Cary) Morton, and a descendant of George Morton [*q.v.*] who emigrated to America in 1623. His early education was received at home, and when he was fourteen years of age he was placed under the Rev. Calvin Chaddock, at Rochester, Mass., for further instruction. In 1801 he entered Brown University with the sophomore class. Here he began to show much interest in the doctrines of Jefferson with their appeal to reason against custom and precedent and their emphasis on the rights of man. His Commencement oration argued for one of the principles he maintained throughout his life—economy in public affairs, since extravagance leads to privilege and inequality. After graduation in 1804, he studied law for a year in the office of Judge Seth Padelford, at Taunton, and then entered Tapping Reeve's law school at Litchfield, Conn., where he was a schoolmate of John C. Calhoun.

Admitted to the Norfolk bar in 1807, he began to practise in Taunton, and on Dec. 23 of the same year married Charlotte Hodges, daughter of James and Joanna (Tillinghast) Hodges, by whom he had twelve children, among them Marcus Morton [q.v.]. Almost at once he became active in politics, and after holding a number of minor offices was from 1817 to 1821 representative in the Fifteenth and Sixteenth congresses. He was lieutenant-governor of Massachusetts, 1824–25, and in the latter year became acting governor on the death of Gov. William Eustis [q.v.]. In 1825 Gov. Levi Lincoln [q.v.] appointed Morton to the Massachusetts supreme court, a position he held until his resignation in January 1840. His accomplishments as a judge were marked by his ready knowledge of legal principles, his sound judgment in applying them, his patience, courtesy, and strength of character.

Morton's perennial candidacy for governor on the Democratic ticket was one of the most significant features of his life. From 1824 to 1848 the political forces in Massachusetts were fairly definitely aligned. The two major parties were the conservative element, consisting of the wealthy aristocrats, the shipowners, bankers, and manufacturers, largely concentrated in Boston; and the more liberal and progressive element comprising the farmers, workingmen, and recent immigrants. It was at the head of the latter group that Morton placed himself, and for sixteen successive years (1828–43) was its candidate for governor. Only twice during that period was he successful. In 1839 he defeated Edward Everett [q.v.] by the majority of a single vote, and in 1842 he was chosen over John Davis by the Senate, neither candidate having received a majority. As governor he advocated and secured retrenchment in public expenditures, reduced the number of supreme court justices from five to three, and abolished the right of appeal from the court of common pleas to the supreme court except on questions of law, this privilege having made the administration of justice slow, expensive, and uncertain.

In 1845 Morton was appointed collector of the port of Boston, which position he held for four years. In 1848 he refused to run for vice-president with Van Buren, for he could not bring himself to bolt his party. Later, however, his life-long opposition to slavery led him to join the Free-Soil party, of which he was delegate to the state constitutional convention in 1853, and by which he was elected to the state legislature in 1858. He was a man of unquestioned probity, whose poise, serenity, and character made him generally admired. In his championship of the lower classes, his distrust of over-large corporations, and his advocacy of shorter hours for the working man he was ahead of his

time, and perhaps partly for this reason a large measure of political success was denied him. He was for thirty-two years an overseer of Harvard. He died at Taunton.

[J. K. Allen, *George Morton of Plymouth Colony and Some of His Descendants* (1908); *A Hist. of Freetown, Mass.* (1902); *Biog. Dir. Am. Cong.* (1928); *U. S. Mag. and Democratic Rev.*, Oct. 1841; *Colls. of the Old Colony Hist. Soc.*, no. 7 (1909); *Law Reporter*, Feb. 1840; A. B. Darling, *Political Changes in Mass., 1824–1848* (1925); "Necrology of Brown Univ., for the Year 1863–4," *Providence Daily Jour.*, Sept. 6, 1864; *Boston Daily Courier*, Feb. 8, 1864; Morton's letter books in possession of the Mass. Hist. Soc; date of birth from *Brown Hist. Cat.*: some sources give Dec. 19.]

S.H.P.

MORTON, MARCUS (Apr. 8, 1819–Feb. 10, 1891), chief justice of the supreme court of Massachusetts, was born in Taunton, Mass., the son of Marcus [q.v.] and Charlotte (Hodges) Morton. He attended Bristol County Academy, was graduated from Brown University in 1838, and from the Harvard Law School in 1840. After one year in the Boston office of Judge Peleg Sprague [q.v.], he was admitted to the Suffolk bar in 1841 and practised in Boston for seventeen years. His first appearance in a public position was as a member of the constitutional convention of 1853, in which he sat for Andover, Mass., his home from 1850. In 1858 he served in the state House of Representatives, where he was chairman of the committee on elections and rendered reports on important questions regarding election law, which the House has since followed.

His judicial service began with his appointment in 1858 to the superior court of Suffolk County and continued unbroken for over thirty-two years. During these years he was one of the original ten members of the state superior court, organized in 1859; justice of the supreme judicial court of Massachusetts from Apr. 15, 1869; and chief justice from Jan. 16, 1882, to Aug. 27, 1890, at which time he resigned because of ill health. He died of heart failure in Andover, leaving his widow, whom, as Abby B. Hoppin of Providence, R. I., he had married on Oct. 19, 1843, a son, and five daughters.

Morton was by temperament an excellent judge, thorough, strong, and reliable rather than brilliant, rapid in assimilating materials and in dispatching business, forbearing and patient in court, always accessible, of sufficient learning, courageous in deciding according to his convictions, and of unusual practical sagacity and native shrewdness. Possessed of a direct and vigorous sense of justice, he viewed cases comprehensively, aiming at substantial justice rather than "the sharp quillets of the law." His summaries to juries were characterized by their simplicity, intelligibility, accurate sense of proportion, and impartiality. His judgments, of which over twelve hundred are recorded in the *Massachusetts Reports,* are compact, clear, and forcible, and, in the opinion of his associates, contain few dicta which will require overruling or qualifications. As a *nisi prius* judge he is said to have had few equals in the history of the Commonwealth of Massachusetts. In private life he was plain and unassuming and, though of great personal charm and popularity, averse to public display.

[J. K. Allen, *George Morton of Plymouth Colony and Some of His Descendants* (1908); "Brown University Necrology for 1890–91," *Providence Daily Jour.,* June 17, 1891; 153 *Mass. Reports,* 601–08; *Boston Herald, Boston Transcript,* Feb. 11, 1891.]

C. M. F.

MORTON, NATHANIEL (1613–June 29, 1685 o.s.), Pilgrim father, author, was born at Leyden in the Netherlands, the eldest son of George Morton [*q.v.*] and Juliana (Carpenter) of Bath. His mother's sister Agnes married Samuel Fuller, later the Pilgrim doctor, and her sister Alice married at Leyden Edward Southworth and later at Plymouth, Gov. William Bradford [*q.v.*]. Nathaniel came to Plymouth with his father and family on the *Anne* in 1623 and when his father died in 1624 was taken into the family of Governor Bradford, who had just become his uncle by marriage with Alice Southworth. He was educated at Plymouth by Bradford, Brewster, Standish, and Fuller, and well educated, for about 1634 he became his uncle's clerk and amanuensis and apparently his agent in many transactions. His association with Bradford was extremely close until the Governor's death in 1657. From December 1647 to 1685, Nathaniel Morton was secretary of the colony and keeper of the records, and as such was entrusted with most of the routine work of government, which he executed with great fidelity and accuracy. He probably drafted most of the colony's laws, and thus the statute book was largely his work. A part of his duty consisted in making copies of the statutes in longhand for the use of the officers and judges in the other towns, but he seems to have been more than a copyist. He probably resided at Plymouth throughout his life, though he sold land at Duxbury in 1652 and may have lived there for a time (*Mayflower Descendant,* October 1899, p. 214). In the town of Plymouth, he was extremely active as tax collector and assessor, and was constantly member of committees to survey land, determine boundaries, lay out roads, and settle disputes. He was town clerk of Plymouth in

1674 and 1679, and probably in later years. Doubtless as a recompense for his extended and varied services, the colony and the town of Plymouth made him many grants of land at various times, several of sufficient value to be readily sold; and it seems certain that he was one of the wealthier men of the colony during the later half of his life. In 1671 he became member and secretary of the council of war to conduct the campaigns against King Philip, and he remained one of its most active members throughout the war (E. W. Peirce, *Peirce's Colonial Lists,* 1881, p. 93). In the Pilgrim church, he also served for many years as secretary and compiler of the records and was prominent in its management and affairs. Certainly he was one of the most important men at Plymouth from about 1640 until his death in 1685.

On Bradford's death, Morton became custodian of his writings and soon became reputed the best informed man at Plymouth on Pilgrim history. At the request of many, soon reinforced by the requests of the commissioners of the four New England colonies, he prepared *New Englands Memoriall,* printed at Cambridge in 1669. He declared in his preface that it had been prepared from Bradford's papers and from those of Winslow. Until the recovery of Bradford's *History of Plimoth Plantation* in 1855, it was the chief authority for the early history of the colony, but now has little value as far as the earliest period is concerned, although it remains the only authority for the list of the signers of the Compact in 1620, for the name of the *Speedwell,* for many minor biographical details, and for the period after 1646. Criticized at the time for the brevity of his account of the earlier years, Morton prepared a longer account which was completed in 1676; the manuscript was burned in that year, however, and he undertook to rewrite it, finishing the task in 1680. This account, largely from Bradford's papers, was printed in the Congregational Board's edition of the *Memoriall* (*post*), together with a "Dialogue" of Bradford's edited by Morton. He wrote also and included in the *Memoriall* many commemorative verses which deserve notice as some of the earliest verse written in America.

Morton was married twice: in 1635 to Lydia Cooper, who died in 1673, and on Apr. 29, 1674, to Ann (Pritchard), widow of Richard Templar. Most of the later Mortons, however, were descended from Nathaniel's brother, Ephraim.

[J. K. Allen, *George Morton of Plymouth Colony and Some of His Descendants* (1908); J. A. Goodwin, *The Pilgrim Republic* (1888); *Records of the Colony of New Plymouth* (12 vols., 1855–61), ed. by N. B. Shurtleff; *Records of the Town of Plymouth,* vol. I

(1889); "Plymouth Church Records," vol. I, being *Col. Soc. Mass. Pubs.*, vol. XXII (1920); the best edition of *New Englands Memoriall* is the facsimile edition (1903), with introduction by Arthur Lord; the sixth edition, *New England's Memorial, by Nathaniel Morton* (Congreg. Board of Pub., 1855), contains numerous notes, now somewhat out of date. On the various editions and copies see *Mayflower Descendant*, Apr. 1922, Apr. 1924, and for the alleged London edition of 1669, see Albert Matthews, "A Ghost Book," *Col. Soc. Mass. Pubs.*, vol. XIV (1912).]   R. G. U.

MORTON, OLIVER PERRY (Aug. 4, 1823–Nov. 1, 1877), governor of Indiana and senator, was born in the decaying frontier village of Salisbury, Wayne County, Ind. His full name was Oliver Hazard Perry Throck Morton. Both his parents, James Throck and Sarah (Miller) Morton, were of New Jersey birth, and on the paternal side the ancestral line began with John Throckmorton who emigrated from England with Roger Williams in 1631 and later settled in Providence Plantations. Oliver's father was the first to write his surname as Morton. When the boy was less than three years old his mother died, and he was taken to the farm of his maternal grandparents near Springfield (now Springdale), Ohio, where two of his aunts gave him their solicitous care. Scotch Presbyterianism pervaded their home, and he seems to have received an overdose of it, for he never became a church member, and later he was credited, quite properly, with exceedingly unorthodox views on religion. One of his aunts taught a neighboring school, which he attended, but much of his early education came from a rather indiscriminate reading of all the books he could get. For one year he attended the Wayne County Seminary at Centerville, Ind., to which his father had removed when the village of Salisbury sank into hopeless decline. On his grandfather's death in 1838 he went to work as became a frontier youth of fifteen years, at first as a drug clerk, and later, when he quarreled with his employer and lost his job, as an apprentice to his brother William, who was a hatter. He thoroughly disliked the hatter's trade and obtained his release from service six months before the four years for which he was bound had ended. Financed by a little money from his grandfather's estate, he entered Miami University, where he spent two years in study, excelling in mathematics, learning to write good English, and enjoying himself thoroughly in debate.

In 1845 he left college to read law in a Centerville office, and in spite of his dwindling financial resources he was married on May 15, 1845, to Lucinda M. Burbank, also of Centerville. Five children were born to them, of whom the three sons survived him. Faced with the necessity of maintaining a home of his own, he speedily began the practice of law, gained some advertising through an unsuccessful race for prosecuting attorney in 1848 on the Democratic ticket, and when he was only twenty-nine years old served out the unfinished term of a circuit judge who had died in office. Doubtless his brief judicial career, less than eight months, convinced him that he needed further legal training, for, before resuming his practice at Centerville, he attended one term at the Law School of the Cincinnati College. After this his progress in his profession was rapid, and in a few years he became the leader of the Wayne County bar. Since he was an unusually effective pleader, his services were in great demand, especially by railway corporations, whose fees helped out his income materially. His formal entrance into politics coincided with the beginnings of the Republican party. Earlier he had no particular sentiment on the slavery question and had even opposed the Wilmot proviso as prejudicial to harmony within the Democratic ranks. By 1854, however, his views had changed. He revolted openly against the Kansas-Nebraska Bill, and when the Democratic state convention of that year indorsed the Douglas measure he went over to the People's party, the forerunner of the Republican party in Indiana. He helped with the formation of the new party along national lines, and in 1856 he was its unsuccessful candidate for governor of Indiana. For the next four years he divided his time between politics and his profitable law practice, doubtless expecting to be the Republican candidate again in 1860. But this was not to be. For reasons of expediency the party leaders gave the nomination to Henry S. Lane, who had been a Whig, consoling Morton, who had been a Democrat, with second place on the ticket and the promise that in case the Republicans won the legislature Lane should be speedily transferred to the United States Senate, and Morton should succeed to the governorship.

All fell out as planned, and thus it happened that he became Indiana's war-time governor, according to James Ford Rhodes, "the ablest and most energetic of the war governors of the Western States" (*History of the United States*, vol. IV, p. 182). Believing that war was necessary and inevitable, he visited Washington soon after Lincoln's inauguration to use his influence in favor of a vigorous policy towards the South, and he did what he could to prepare his state for the impending struggle. When at last the president's call for troops came, Indiana responded loyally, offering more than twice the number of men asked. Morton expected the war to be a hard-fought contest, and he was determined that none of those who volunteered should be refused the opportunity to serve. He therefore called the legislature into special session to provide ways and means for accepting into state service such men as the national government could not use at the moment. To this and to other requests of the governor, who believed that the war should be made "instant and terrible" (Foulke, *post,* I, 118), the legislature responded with alacrity. Throughout the struggle he put the full power of his office and of his personality behind every request of the administration for men. Thanks in no small part to his efforts, there were over 150,000 enlistments from Indiana during the four years with only a negligible number of men drafted.

He was at his best in his repeated and notable triumphs over the discouraged and disloyal agitators who tried to weaken the state's effective support of the war. Indiana, like the rest of the Old Northwest, had a large Southern element in its population in which sympathy with the Southern cause and opposition to the war soon became rife. Orders like the Knights of the Golden Circle, the Order of American Knights, or the Sons of Liberty did their best to retard enlistments, encourage desertions, free Confederate prisoners, and even form a new and independent northwestern confederacy. When the election of 1862 was held, Union military reverses and the absence of thousands of voters at the front strengthened the forces of discontent so that the Democratic legislature and state officers elected in Indiana that year were of pacifist views. According to a provision of the Indiana constitution that gave the governor a four-year term, he remained in office, providentially commissioned, he felt, to thwart all "Copperhead" plots. In order to accomplish this end heroic measures were required; for example, a scheme of the majority in the legislature to take his military power from him and to vest it in a board of its own choosing was frustrated only by the withdrawal of the Republican legislators and, ultimately, by the adjournment of the session for want of a quorum. Since the usual appropriation bills had not been passed, he faced the alternative of calling the obnoxious legislature together again or himself raising the money to keep the state government in operation. To the surprise and chagrin of the Democrats, he chose the latter course. He used some profits from the manufacture of munitions in an arsenal he had established, obtained advances from private citizens and from loyal county officials, and borrowed heavily from the government at Washington. The legislature was not recalled, the state government functioned normally except that the governor reigned as a sort of dictator, and the business of helping win the war went on without relaxation. In 1864 he was reëlected governor, and a Republican legislature was chosen with him, which in the main supported him in what he had done.

The arduous labor of war time told on him physically, and during the summer of 1865 he was visited by a stroke of paralysis that left him a hopeless cripple but did not cloud his brain. A trip to France in search of medical aid was of no avail for that purpose, but he delivered a personal message from President Johnson to Napoleon III, which pointed out the wisdom of the removal of the French troops from Mexico without formal demand from the United States and which was doubtless of some consequence. Returning to the United States he refused, in spite of his infirmity, to retire from politics, and he attacked the Democrats in the campaign of 1866 with a ruthlessness and a ferocity that set the pace for Republican orators for many a year. In an age of extreme partisanship his partisanship was rank. He saw no good in the Democratic party, the war-time record of which he never forgave, and he viewed individual Democrats with grave suspicions. Any Democratic victory seemed to him a dire calamity.

In 1867 he was elected to the United States Senate, where he served until his death. Reconstruction was then the all-absorbing problem, and to it he devoted much thought. Immediately at the close of the war he had favored some such generous terms as were proposed by Lincoln and Johnson, but party necessities drew him irresistibly in the direction of the harsher policies advocated by the congressional leaders, and in the end he became one of the ablest and one of the least compromising of the supporters of "thorough" Reconstruction. Probably he did more than any other man to obtain the ratification of the negro suffrage amendment to the Constitution (Foulke, *post,* II, 117–18). His record on financial matters was as inconsistent as his record on reconstruction. In his earlier senatorial career he was quite free from soft-money heresies. Indeed, he formulated and introduced in 1868 a bill for the resumption of specie payments on Jan. 1, 1872, that differed little from the bill under which later on resumption was actually accomplished, but hard times following the panic of 1873 seem to have changed his opinions on the money question. Familiar with the problems of the western debtors, he saw clearly their point of view, and he came to ridicule as fanaticism the same kind of insistence upon a return to specie payments of which, as he freely confessed, he had once been guilty himself. The hard times emergency, he thought, justified further, strictly limited, issues of paper (Foulke, *post*, II, 319–20).

He was a formidable contender for the Republican nomination of 1876, but his physical condition, his soft-money tendencies, and his strict partisanship with its attendant lack of enthusiasm about civil reform, all told against him, while Hayes had no such liabilities. He took an active part in the dispute over the election of that year and was convinced that the Republicans had won. He opposed the plan embodied in the electoral bill for settling the contest because of the chance it gave the Democrats to secure the presidency, but as a member of the electoral commission established when the bill became a law, he had a chance to do his full duty by his party. After the contest was over he went to Oregon to help investigate charges of bribery made against a newly elected senator from that state. He was unsparing of himself on the trip and perhaps on this account suffered, in August 1877, another stroke of paralysis. Returning at once to Indiana, he went first to the residence of his wife's mother in Richmond and later to his own home in Indianapolis, where he died.

He was to a remarkable degree the typical politician of his period. He had, to be sure, a much higher sense of honor than some, and in money matters he was incorruptible. Yet his fanatical devotion to party, his glory in combat, his intolerance of opposition, his heated rhetoric were distinctly of his time. Powerful physically, of commanding voice and presence, he feared no man, nor did the affliction of his later years abate his courage. He was an able lawyer, but he preferred politics, and probably he was not greatly tempted by Grant's offer of the chief-justiceship on the death of Chase. To the end of his life he was a power to be reckoned with in American politics, loved and honored by his friends, cordially hated by his enemies, and almost never ignored. Like many another he coveted the presidency, but his failure to obtain it did not in the least embitter him.

[Wm. D. Foulke, *Life of Oliver P. Morton* (2 vols., 1899); W. M. French, *Life, Speeches, State Papers and Public Services of Gov. Oliver P. Morton* (1864); *Memorial Addresses on . . . Oliver P. Morton . . . in the Senate and House of Representatives* (1878); *Oliver P. Morton . . . by direction of the Ind. Republican State Central Committee* (1876); J. A. Woodburn, "Party Politics in Ind. during the Civil War," *Am. Hist. Asso. Report, 1902*, vol. I (1903); Logan Esary, *A History of Indiana* (1918), vol. II; *Indianapolis Journal*, Nov. 2, 1877.]   J. D. H.

MORTON, PAUL (May 22, 1857–Jan. 19, 1911), business executive, secretary of the navy for one year after July 1, 1904, was the son of Julius Sterling [*q.v.*] and Caroline (Joy) Morton. His parents, of native stock, were early Nebraska pioneers who resided at Nebraska City, although Paul was born at Detroit, Mich., his mother's home. Impatient of formal education, Paul joined the Burlington Railroad at fifteen and by 1890 had become its general freight agent. He served the Colorado Fuel & Iron Company for the next six years, and the Atchison, Topeka & Santa Fé Railroad for eight years after 1896. A "gold Democrat," like his father, he became a Roosevelt Republican. As second vice-president of the Santa Fé, he handled freight rates on a competitive basis, not caring to deny the illegalities involved when in 1901 the Interstate Commerce Commission questioned him. His "unusual mental poise, energy, and executive ability" (New York *Evening Post*, Jan. 20, 1911) made him a marked figure on the witness stand, developing a tradition that he could "look any man in the eye and tell him to go to hell" (G. B. Clarkson, *Industrial America in the World War*, 1923, p. 44). These traits, perhaps, rather than his record as a rebater, attracted the interest of President Roosevelt, who called him to Washington at the close of the Republican National Convention of 1904; and the next day it was announced that Morton was to become secretary of the navy, vice Moody who was transferred to be attorney-general.

Morton took over the new post July 1, 1904, and shortly declared in Chicago that the United States navy "should be the most formidable in existence" (New York *Evening Post*, July 15, 1904). In his only annual report, in November, he recited the General Board arguments for strengthening the navy, taking pride in the unusual number of fleet additions of the year. But in December 1904, the traffic manager of the Santa Fé admitted the granting of illegal rebates to the Colorado Fuel & Iron Company while Morton was his superior officer, in spite of an injunction against such practices of Mar. 25, 1902, and the Anti-Rebate Law of Feb. 19, 1903, and Morton became "grotesquely out of place in the cabinet of a president who is engaged in declared and open war" against rebates (*Milwaukee Sentinel*, June 3, 1905). The Interstate Commerce Commission handed down the Santa Fé opinion, Feb. 1, 1905 (10 *Interstate Commerce Reports*, 472), forwarding the testimony to the attorney-general who employed Judson Harmon and Frederick N. Judson to inquire into its sufficiency as a basis for prosecution. But the attorney-general, backed by Roosevelt, declined to prosecute Morton, and the special counsel resigned their commission on June 5. Before the resignation was made public, Morton had announced that he would on July 1 leave the cabinet, and early in June he was made chairman of the board of directors of the Equitable Life Assurance Association, the stock of which Thomas Fortune Ryan had bought after the insurance scandals of the spring. On June 21 Roosevelt gave out long letters to Moody and Morton explaining why no personal guilt adhered to the latter in spite of the behavior of his subordinates in the Santa Fé (*New York Tribune,* June 22, 1905). Morton spent the rest of his life in the rehabilitation of the affairs of the Equitable. He was rejected by his own company for a life policy in December 1910, and the rejection was justified when his heart failed him suddenly in January 1911. He was survived by his wife, Charlotte Goodridge of Chicago, whom he married on Oct. 13, 1880, and by two daughters.

[There is a good obituary of Paul Morton in the N. Y. *Evening Post,* Jan. 20, 1911. See also: *Who's Who in America,* 1910–11; Edwin Lefèvre, "Paul Morton—Human Dynamo," *Cosmopolitan Mag.,* Oct. 1905; the *Nation,* June 30, 1904, June 22, 29, 1905.]

F. L. P.

MORTON, SAMUEL GEORGE (Jan. 26, 1799–May 15, 1851), physician and naturalist, son of George and Jane (Cummings) Morton, was born in Philadelphia, Pa., the youngest of nine children. His father, who had emigrated from Ireland in his youth, died when the boy was but six months of age, and his mother then took her family to Westchester, N. Y. His early education was obtained at various boarding schools conducted by the Society of Friends. In 1812, his mother having married Thomas Rogers, the family returned to Philadelphia, and Morton attended the Quaker school in Westtown. His mother died when he was but seventeen. It seems that during her illness the attending physicians became interested in the boy and helped him toward the study of medicine. In 1817 he began his medical education in the office of Dr. Joseph Parrish, and among his associates in this period was the brilliant naturalist, Richard Harlan [*q.v.*], who exerted a marked influence upon him in turning his thoughts toward science. During his period of study under Parrish, Morton attended lectures at the medical department of the University of Pennsylvania and in 1820 was awarded the degree of M.D. It was at this time that he became a member of the Academy of Natural Sciences of Philadelphia, an institution which he served for the period of his life, holding the office of president at the time of his death.

His education was broadened by study in Europe where he attended the medical college of Edinburgh University (M.D., 1823). In 1827 he was married to Rebecca Grellet Pearsall. James St. Clair Morton [*q.v.*] was their son.

Morton's first paper, "An Analysis of Tabular Spar from Bucks County, Pennsylvania" (*Journal of the Academy of Natural Sciences of Philadelphia,* vol. VI, 1829) gives a fair idea of his varied interests, for his researches extended through the fields of medicine, geology, vertebrate paleontology, and zoölogy. In 1834 he published a "Synopsis of the Organic Remains of the Cretaceous Group of the United States," in which were described the fossils brought back by the Lewis and Clark Expedition. This work gave its author a deserved scientific reputation, and according to Marcou, it is the starting point of all paleontological and systematic work on American fossils. In 1830 he published a "Synopsis of the Organic Remains of the Ferruginous Sand Formation of the United States" in the *American Journal of Science and Arts* (vols. XVII and XVIII, 1830). This contribution dealt with many interesting fossil forms including plesiosaurus, crocodiles, horses, elephants, and mastodons found near the Raritan River in New Jersey. His zoölogical papers included his description of a new species of hippopotamus, determined from a skull received from Dr. Goheen of Liberia. In the field of medicine he published an essay, "Observations on Cornine," in 1825 (*Philadelphia Journal of the Medical and Physical Sciences,* vol. XI, 1825). In 1834 appeared his "Illustrations of Pulmonary Consumption" in which he followed Parrish in recommending the open-air treatment of the disease. In 1836 he published in two volumes *Principles of Pathology and Practice of Physics,* an American edition of the work of John Mackintosh. He at first lectured under Parrish and then in 1839 he was elected to the professorship of anatomy in Pennsylvania College, holding this position until his resignation in 1843. In 1849 he published a substantial work, *Human Anatomy,* considered a volume of permanent value and one upon which much of his lasting reputation rests.

Morton's major interests in research consisted of collecting for comparative studies a large series of human skulls. This material is estimated to have cost Morton somewhere between ten and fifteen thousand dollars to assemble, in spite of the fact that most of the specimens were contributed by about one hundred of his friends. Louis Agassiz declared that this collection alone was worth a journey to America. After a careful study of his collection, Morton prepared two technical works, *Crania Americana* (1839) and *Crania Ægyptiaca*. His studies in the field of anthropology led him to conclude that the races of man were of diverse origin. For this conclusion he was bitterly assailed by many persons, including several ministers, who claimed that he was denying the authority of the Scriptures. In 1847 he published an essay on hybridity in the *American Journal of Science and Arts* (January, March 1847). Agassiz accepted in the main Morton's views on this subject. According to Marcou, Morton was second only to Cuvier in his influence upon Agassiz's mind and scientific opinion. Morton died in Philadelphia at the age of fifty-two.

[G. B. Wood, memoir of Morton in *Quart. Summary of the Trans. of the Coll. of Physicians of Phila.*, n.s. vol. I, no. 9 (1853); C. D. Meigs, *A Memoir of Samuel Geo. Morton* (1851); H. S. Patterson, *Memoir of the Life and Scientific Labors of Samuel Geo. Morton, M.D.* (1854); Jules Marcou, *Life, Letters and Works of Louis Agassiz* (1895), II, 28–29; H. A. Kelly and W. L. Burrage, *Am. Medic. Biogs.* (1920); *Pa. Inquirer*, May 16, 1851.]
D. M. F.

MORTON, SARAH WENTWORTH APTHORP (1759–May 14, 1846), considered by her contemporaries the chief American poetess, was baptized at King's Chapel, Boston, Aug. 29, 1759. Her parents, James and Sarah (Wentworth) Apthorp, soon after removed to Braintree, where she was brought up. She was given an unusual education for her day and was reared in the traditions of cultured ancestors, her grandfathers having been wealthy and distinguished merchants of Boston. Her unusual beauty and charm and her poetic talent won the affections of a brilliant young Boston lawyer, Perez Morton, who had gained local fame by his funeral oration over the body of General Warren. After their marriage, Feb. 24, 1781, they occupied the Apthorp family mansion on State Street, where their five children were probably born and where they lived on intimate terms with the families of Governor Bowdoin and Vice-President Adams. In 1789 the newly established *Massachusetts Magazine* enlisted Mrs. Morton's support, and a number of her moralizing or eulogistic lyrics appeared in the issues of the next four years, mostly over her pseudonym "Philenia." Her first published volume, *Ouâbi, or the Virtues of Nature, an Indian Tale* (Boston, 1790), an idealized narrative on the "noble savage" theme, in stilted Popean couplets, was well received in America and in England (*Monthly Review*, September 1793, pp. 72–77), where James Bacon used its plot for his play, *The American Indian* (1795). Her poems continued to appear in the Boston *Columbian Centinel*, the *New York Magazine*, Joseph Dennie's *Tablet*, and other papers; and

"Philenia" became the object of extravagant praise by such contemporary critics as Dennie and Thomas Paine (later Robert Treat Paine, Jr.), who eulogized her as the "American Sappho" and the "American Mrs. Montague."

Many of her verses, like Whittier's favorite, "The African Chief" (*Columbian Centinel*, June 9, 1792), were widely copied. A portion of her most ambitious undertaking, a versified account of the Revolution, was published in 1797 as *Beacon Hill, a Local Poem, Historical and Descriptive*. A second part appeared as *The Virtues of Society* (1799), but the work, if completed, was never published in entirety. In 1797 the family moved to a house of Mrs. Morton's designing in Dorchester, and thence about 1808 to another residence called "the Pavilion," where in later years she and her husband, now attorney-general of Massachusetts, enjoyed the society of many distinguished guests. In 1802 Mrs. Morton visited Washington and Philadelphia, where Stuart painted for her three of his finest portraits, though the third was never finished. These show her to have been a woman of rare personal beauty, which, with her social charm, doubtless enhanced her reputation as a poet. Her verses, called forth by various national and local events and causes, still appeared, some as broadsides, some in the *Port Folio* and the *Monthly Anthology*, and others in the newspapers. Her fame had considerably declined by 1823, however, when she published her miscellany of short didactic prose pieces and fugitive lyrics, with autobiographical notes, under the title *My Mind and Its Thoughts*. Soon after her husband's death, Oct. 14, 1837, she moved to her old Braintree home, by that time in the town of Quincy, where she died, aged eighty-six, having outlived her children and all of her near relatives.

Over thirty years after her death, Mrs. Morton's name was first linked in print with the earliest American novel, *The Power of Sympathy* (by F. S. Drake in *The Town of Roxbury*, 1878, p. 134), which has since usually been attributed to her in bibliographies of American fiction. The sole reason for this attribution appears to be that an episode in the novel was based upon a scandal involving Mrs. Morton's husband and her sister. The real author was probably the Mortons' neighbor, William Hill Brown (1765–1793), a minor novelist, playwright, poet, and essayist.

[See Emily Pendleton and Milton Ellis, *Philenia, the Life and Works of Sarah Wentworth Morton* (1931), University of Maine Studies, 2nd ser., no. 20. The evidence indicating Brown's authorship of *The Power of Sympathy* is summed up in Milton Ellis, "The Authorship of the First American Novel," *Am. Lit.*, Jan. 1933, pp. 359–68. The novel has been twice reprinted: by Walter Littlefield in 1894, with an introduction attributing it to Mrs. Morton; and serially in the *Bostonian*, Oct. 1894–June 1895, accompanied by an article, Dec. 1894, "The Real Author of *The Power of Sympathy*," by A. W. Brayley, in which Brown's authorship was first asserted.]   M. E—s.

MORTON, THOMAS (fl. 1622–1647), adventurer, was probably a lawyer and "of Clifford's Inn, Gent" as he designated himself. He seems to have come first with Andrew Weston's party in 1622, remaining at Wessagusset during the summer, and returning to England in the autumn. He was fond of hunting and outdoor life, and later came back to Massachusetts with the Wollaston company, settling within the limits of the present Quincy. His manner of life, which was distinctly licentious and convivial, made him anathema to the Pilgrims of Plymouth, and it was hinted darkly that he had had a horrible past. Wollaston had enough of New England in one winter and went to Virginia, but Morton remained and built his house at Merry Mount, where, in 1627, the Pilgrims came and cut down the Maypole he had erected. He was a fur-trader and enormously increased his business to the danger of the pockets and polls of everyone on the coast by selling guns to the Indians. He forestalled the trading activities of the Plymouth colonists on the Kennebec and, in 1628, was captured by a band under Capt. Standish and was sent to England, with charges. In a year and a half he had returned, brought by Isaac Allerton. By this time the Puritans had arrived at Boston and times had changed. John Endecott [*q.v.*] had visited Merry Mount and the Maypole had again been cut down, and most of Morton's old companions had been scattered. Trouble soon began and in 1630 Morton was once more taken into custody, sentenced to have all his goods confiscated, his house burned, and himself shipped back again to England. After some delay the sentence was carried out. On reaching England, he was confined in Exeter jail but was soon set at liberty, probably through the influence of Gorges. In London he was a useful witness against the Massachusetts colony. He seems to have spent some years in England, ready to the hand of Gorges, who, however, claimed to have set him adrift in 1637. It was in that year that he published his *New English Canaan* in which he somewhat incoherently proclaimed his opinions of New England and gave a description of the country. In 1643 he turned up again in Plymouth. He was ordered to leave and the next spring went to Maine. He was next heard of in Rhode Island but ventured into Massachusetts and was promptly taken and placed in prison. The only charge was that he had com-plained against the colony to the Privy Council, which as an English citizen he had a legal right to do. He was kept in prison for a year when it was decided he was too expensive for the country to support and was fined and released. By this time he was old and infirm and a winter in Boston jail had not improved his health. He died within two years after. He was himself a worthless rake, in spite of efforts which have been made to rehabilitate his character as a persecuted churchman.

[C. F. Adams, Jr., edited *The New English Canaan of Thos. Morton* with a long biographical introduction, for the Prince Society (1883). Contemporary references in Bradford, Winthrop, and others may be found noted there. A more popular account is given by Adams in his *Three Episodes of Mass. Hist.* (1892), vol. I. Charges against Morton in letters to the Council for New England appear in the *Mass. Hist. Soc. Colls.*, 1 ser. III (1794), 62–64.]   J. T. A.

MORTON, WILLIAM JAMES (July 3, 1845–Mar. 26, 1920), neurologist, was born in Boston, Mass., the year before his father, William Thomas Green Morton [*q.v.*], then a young and struggling dentist, began his experiments with ether as an anaesthetic. His mother was Elizabeth (Whitman) Morton. The boy, the only child, attended the Boston Latin School and then Harvard College, graduating in 1867, the year before his father died. After some months of teaching, he entered the Harvard Medical School in 1868, and graduated in 1872. He began practice in Boston that same year, but being restless and venturesome, closed his office in 1873 and went to Vienna. A few months later he became physician to a mining company in Cape Town, South Africa, and a prospector and big game hunter as well (1874–76). Returning to Boston, he contributed to the *Bulletin* of the American Geographical Society an account of his experiences which was reprinted in pamphlet form under the title *South African Diamond Fields, and the Journey to the Mines* (1877). In 1877 he was called to Europe to care for or to decide upon the medico-legal status of a psychotic patient there. This is possibly the event that turned his attention to psychiatry and neurology.

In 1878 he resumed practise in New York City. He became a member of the American Neurological Association the following year, at which time he presented a paper on the toxic effects of tea as seen in tea-tasters (*Journal of Nervous and Mental Disease*, October 1879). In 1880 he was in Paris at the Salpêtrière, that Mecca of all neurologists of the day, attending Charcot's memorable clinics; and in the same year he was appointed professor of mental diseases in the medical department of the University of Vermont, where he gave a series of summer courses, 1880–84. In 1881 he was back in New York, deep in the study of electrical energy. Physics and chemistry had always attracted him and at this time he made some notable experiments in high-frequency currents, inventing what he then called his "static induced current." He read a paper, "On Statical Electro-Therapeutics," before the New York Academy of Medicine, Mar. 3, 1881, which was published in the *Medical Record* of Apr. 2 and 9. His practice as a neurologist grew rapidly, for his personality was attractive and his originality and verve quite sweeping. In 1882, with C. L. Dana, he published a description of the brain of Guiteau, assassin of President Garfield (*Medical Record,* July 5, 1882), and in the same year became editor and publisher of the *Journal of Nervous and Mental Disease,* then the leading neuropsychiatric publication in the United States. He continued as editor until 1885 when he was joined by Dr. B. Sachs, to whom in 1886 he turned over the entire work. He was president of the New York Neurological Society in 1883. Before the American Neurological Association he read a number of papers: *A Contribution to the Subject of Nerve Stretching* (1882), *Neuritis following Dislocation* (1883), *An Apparatus for Scrivener's Palsy* (1883), and *Treatment of Migraine* (1883). These early papers were full of promise, but his attention became more and more engrossed in his electrotherapeutic work and an ingenious and original mind was in large measure lost to neurology. From 1890 to 1909, however, he was professor of diseases of the mind and nervous system and of electrotherapeutics at the New York Post Graduate Medical School and Hospital, and for some time was neurologist to the Metropolitan Throat Hospital and the New York Infant Asylum.

Working incessantly at his electrotherapeutics, Morton hoped great things from his many experiments. In 1890, before the New York Neurological Society, he read a paper on "The Franklinic Interrupted Current; or My New System of Therapeutic Administration of Static Electricity" (*Medical Record,* Jan. 24, 1891). He was very enthusiastic in his experiments on cataphoresis, hoping to perfect a means of driving metallic and other remedies into the body by other than the hypodermic method now so much in vogue (*"Cataphoresis," or Electric Medicamental Diffusion as Applied in Medicine, Surgery and Dentistry,* 1898) ; and his various publications on this subject contributed definitely to the development of the therapeutic method later known as ionization. He was also one of the first physicians in America to use the X-ray in the treatment of skin disorders and cancerous growths, publishing in the years 1902–07 several papers based on his experiments.

Morton's manner was courteous and pleasing, although to some of his colleagues he seemed shut in and reserved, as if the bitterness of his father's disappointment had left its effect upon him. His later years, like those of his father, were not happy. His adventurous and daring spirit led him to speculate in certain Canadian mining properties, which despite his lack of experience he endeavored to develop, in association with some friends and one Albert Freeman, a promoter. In November 1912, with his associates, he was indicted, and in March 1913 convicted of using the mails to defraud, in promoting the sale of stock. Morton and one of his friends were sentenced to a year and a day in the Atlanta penitentiary, while Freeman received a sentence of five years (*New York Times,* Mar. 15, 1913). In October, however, Morton and his friend were released on parole (*Ibid.,* Oct. 16, 1913), and in December were pardoned by President Wilson (*Ibid.,* Dec. 17, 1913). In the following June Morton was restored to his status as a medical practitioner by the State Board of Regents at the request of prominent physicians and other citizens (*Ibid.,* June 26, 1914). Six years later he died of heart disease at Miami, Fla. He had married Elizabeth Campbell Lee, May 20, 1880. There were no children.

[I. A. Watson, *Physicians and Surgeons of America* (1896) ; classbooks, Class of 1867, Harvard College; C. L. Dana, in *Jour. Nervous and Mental Disease,* Mar. 1921 ; *N. Y. Medic. Jour.,* May 1, 1920; *Boston Medic. and Surgic. Jour.,* Apr. 15, 1920 ; *Semicentennial Vol. of the Am. Neurological Asso., 1875–1924* (1924) ; C. H. Farnam, *Hist. of the Descendants of John Whitman* (1889) ; *N. Y. Times,* Apr. 4, 1920.]
S. E. J.

MORTON, WILLIAM THOMAS GREEN (Aug. 9, 1819–July 15, 1868), dentist, anaesthetist, was born at Charlton, a village in Worcester County, Mass. He was the son of James Morton, a farmer of that town, by his wife, Rebecca, daughter of William Needham of Charlton. Morton's ancestor, Robert Morton, had emigrated from Scotland early in the seventeenth century and settled in Salem, Mass. After receiving a New England common-school education at Northfield and Leicester Academies, William, at the age of seventeen, went to Boston, where he became clerk and salesman in various business houses, but finding these occupations distasteful he betook himself to Baltimore in 1840 and there began the study of dentistry at the College of Dental Surgery. Two years later he settled at Farmington, Conn., and acquired a moderate dental practice. In 1842 he met Horace Wells [*q.v.*] of Hartford, Conn., who later (1844) employed nitrous oxide for the extraction of teeth. During the winter of 1842–43 these two dentists practised together at 19 Tremont St., Boston, but since the partnership proved unremunerative it was amicably dissolved in the autumn of 1843, Wells returning to Hartford and Morton remaining in Boston. In March 1844 Morton, conscious of his inadequate medical training, matriculated at Harvard Medical School, but, having married in that same year, he was compelled by financial difficulties to practise dentistry; consequently he never received a medical degree from Harvard.

During 1844 he lived with Prof. Charles T. Jackson [*q.v.*] and in July, at Jackson's recommendation, he used ether in drops as a local anaesthetic during the filling of a tooth (Hodges, *post*, p. 11). Morton at this time had become especially interested in the manufacture of artificial teeth and in order to render his work effective found it necessary to remove the roots of all old teeth remaining in the jaw. Few patients would submit to this painful procedure, and he had tried intoxicants, opium, mesmerism, and other questionable methods to deaden pain, but none were effective. Jackson had demonstrated before his chemical classes that inhalation of sulphuric ether causes loss of consciousness. Morton accordingly tried ether upon himself, but before using it on patients he tested it further, during July and August 1846, by anaesthetizing a goldfish, a hen, and his pet spaniel; as they all recovered without obvious impairment of faculties he decided to use ether upon human beings. On Sept. 30, 1846, he had a conference with Jackson during which, for some unaccountable reason, he professed complete ignorance of the effects of ether inhalation (Hodges). That afternoon, however, a patient named Frost came to Morton in agony with a toothache. Morton let him breathe the fumes of the ether which he had borrowed that morning from Jackson, and within less than five minutes the tooth was painlessly extracted. Public notice of this incident, which appeared in the *Boston Daily Journal* of Oct. 1, 1846, read as follows: "Last evening, as we were informed by a gentleman who witnessed the operation, an ulcerated tooth was extracted from the mouth of an individual without giving him the slightest pain. He was put into a kind of sleep, by inhaling a preparation, the effects of which lasted for about three-quarters of a minute, just long enough to extract the tooth." Other successful extractions followed. This announcement attracted the attention of Henry Jacob Bigelow [*q.v.*], a young surgeon of Boston, who called upon Morton to obtain further details. Through Bigelow the news reached the ears of John Collins Warren [*q.v.*], who made arrangements with Morton to try his new discovery at the Massachusetts General Hospital. The day set was Oct. 16, 1846, and Warren was to remove a vascular tumor from the left side of the neck of a young man named Gilbert Abbott. The growth was excised in five minutes and the patient showed no evidence of pain, though toward the end of the operation he moved slightly, owing to incomplete etherization. Again under Morton's supervision a second operation was carried out on the following day by Dr. George Hayward [*q.v.*] with equal success. During the next two weeks a disagreement arose as to the advisability of continuing the procedure, since Morton was not a medical man and refused to tell the composition of the anaesthetic agent. The difficulties were finally overcome and the discovery was first announced by H. J. Bigelow on Nov. 18, 1846, in the *Boston Medical and Surgical Journal.*

Morton at once sought to secure profit from his discovery and applied for a patent to protect his rights. He did not reveal that the anaesthetic agent was sulphuric ether, but designated it by the mysterious name of "letheon." On Oct. 27, 1846, he applied (with Jackson, whom he had been forced to include by legal advisers) for letters patent, which were issued Nov. 12, 1846 (patent no. 4848) for a period of fourteen years. On Nov. 26, 1846, Morton stated publicly that he was prepared to grant licenses for use of his apparatus and discovery, but on Bigelow's advice agreed to repay the fee should the United States government adopt his invention (*Circular—Morton's Letheon*). On Nov. 28 he stated that certain charitable hospitals might use "letheon" free of charge (Warren Papers, *post*, vol. xxiii). A few months later the Monthyon prize of 5,000 francs was awarded by the French Academy of Medicine to Jackson and Morton jointly, but Morton refused to take his share, saying that the discovery was entirely his. In 1847 a memorial was sent to Congress by the surgeons and physicians of the Massachusetts General Hospital, praying that adequate compensation be given to the discoverer of the anaesthetic uses of ether. In 1849, however, when his patent and the memorial to Congress had brought him nothing, Morton solicited Congress himself for financial reward. As a result of this and other pressure which was

brought to bear, two bills appropriating $100,-
000 for the discovery of practical anaesthesia
were introduced into Congress at three separate
sessions of that body, but, owing to the activities of the supporters of Jackson, Wells, and
Crawford W. Long [*q.v.*], the appropriations
were never carried. The deliberations of committees and sub-committees were drawn out for
nearly two decades. Valuable reports and hearings were published (*Statements Supported by
Evidence of Wm. T. G. Morton, Submitted to
the . . . Committee Appointed by the Senate of
the United States, Jan. 21, 1853*, 1853), but
when the Civil War came the cause was lost in
a maze of unfinished business. Several plans
were instituted to give Morton financial support, but these brought him honor without
riches. The last twenty years of his life were
spent in the perpetual torment of bitter controversy and litigation, as a result of which he was
reduced to dire poverty. He died from apoplexy
which came on while driving in Central Park,
New York. The seizure was thought to have
been induced by reading a publication just then
issued in behalf of Jackson in order to prejudice
another testimonial subscription which was being raised for Morton.

Personally Morton was tall, dark-haired, quick
of thought and movement, methodical in his
habits, neat in personal appearance, and of
agreeable manners. In the heat of controversy
he often exerted remarkable forbearance and he
is said never to have attempted to retaliate upon
his enemies. His education was faulty, however,
and the fact that he sought personal benefit from
his discovery will, perhaps rightly, always be
held against him. He married Elizabeth Whitman of Connecticut in May 1844, and they had
one son, William James Morton [*q.v.*], a pioneer in the use of the X-ray in the United
States.

In the discovery of surgical anaesthesia Crawford W. Long, Horace Wells, and Charles T.
Jackson all shared, yet Morton acted independently and conducted experiments with ether on
his own initiative. Moreover, he took entire responsibility for the outcome of his first public
demonstrations upon human beings, and in so
doing he, before any one else, convinced the
surgical world of the value of the discovery; for
this contribution alone one may allow him credit as the discoverer, and this, indeed, was the
opinion of those of his contemporaries most
competent to judge (Welch, *post*, p. 11). The
fact that the demonstration was a triumph of
the experimental method makes Morton's position even more secure. The regrettable features

of his conduct may lessen but cannot rob him
of the honor which is his due.

His published works relating to ether are rare
and little known. Beginning on Nov. 26, 1846,
he issued, usually weekly and at his own expense, a little publication entitled *Circular—
Morton's Letheon*, in which he communicated
the results of his experiments on anaesthetiza-
tion and cautioned others concerning the use of
the new agent (see back page, *Boston Medical
and Surgical Journal*, Dec. 9, 1846). These
sheets soon became a receptacle of newspaper
articles and correspondence from all parts of the
world reporting the success of surgical anaesthesia, and were then issued in pamphlet form
(Rice, *post*, p. 115), under the same title. Of
this brochure five editions appeared under Morton's direction. (The Surgeon General's Library has a 14-page edition of the pamphlet,
evidently issued in 1846, which is probably the
first edition.) In 1847 he published his most important work, *Remarks on the Proper Mode of
Administering Sulphuric Ether by Inhalation*,
a small duodecimo of forty-four pages, dedicated
"To the surgeons of the Mass. Gen. [*sic*] Hospital . . . as an evidence that their early and continued interest in the administration of sulphuric ether is gratefully appreciated." It contains detailed direction concerning the use of
ether in dentistry, general surgery, and obstetrics, and gives a list of "the symptoms indicating danger" during its administration. A 60-
page pamphlet, *Mémoire sur la découverte du
nouvel emploi de l'éther sulfurique, suivi des
pièces justificatives*, containing a carefully documented statement of Morton's claims to priority in the introduction of anaesthesia, was issued
in Paris in 1847. A brochure, *On the Physiological Effects of Sulphuric Ether, and Its Superiority to Chloroform*, was published in Boston in 1850, called forth largely by the claims
of Simpson in Edinburgh as to the virtues of
chloroform. In addition to controversial matter and a history of the discovery of ether, it
contains a clear description of the two stages of
etherization (p. 10), and a discussion of the sequence of action of ether upon various parts of
the central nervous system. There is also an appendix containing six pages of testimonials. The
foregoing works are all that Morton published
on ether, except for a small 48-page booklet bearing the title, *Remarks on the Comparative Value
of Ether and Chloroform, with Hints upon Natural and Artificial Teeth* (1850), on the back
cover of which appeared a print of a building
labeled "Morton's tooth factory." A paper written in 1864, "On the First Use of Ether as an

Anesthetic [*sic*] at the Battle of the Wilderness in the Civil War," was published by his son in the *Journal of the American Medical Association,* Apr. 23, 1904. Morton wrote also several pamphlets on dentistry, such as *On the Loss of the Teeth and the Modern Way of Restoring Them* (1848).

[Of the many accounts of Morton's career the most reliable are the following: N. P. Rice, *Trials of a Public Benefactor, as Illustrated in the Discovery of Etherization* (1859); B. P. Poore, *Hist. Materials for the Biog. of W. T. G. Morton, M.D.* (1856); H. J. Bigelow, "A History of the Discovery of Modern Anaesthesia," in *A Century of Am. Medicine* (1876); R. M. Hodges, *A Narrative of Events Connected with the Introduction of Sulphuric Ether into Surgical Use* (1891); W. H. Welch, *A Consideration of the Introduction of Surgical Anaesthesia* (n.d.), Ether Day address, Mass. Gen. Hosp., Oct. 1908; William Osler, "The First Printed Documents Relating to Modern Surgical Anaesthesia," *Proc. Roy. Soc. Med.,* Sect. Hist. Med. (London, 1918), XI, 65–69, and in *Annals Medic. Hist.* (N. Y.), Dec. 1917. See also G. B. Roth, "'Original Morton Inhaler' for Ether," *Annals Medic. Hist.,* July 1932; and a useful account by W. J. Morton, "Memoranda Relating to the Discovery of Surgical Anaesthesia and Dr. William T. G. Morton's Relation to This Event," *Post-Graduate,* Apr. 1905. The *Bibliotheca Osleriana* (1928) contains a *catalogue raisonné* of the most extensive collection of documents relating to the history of anaesthesia which has yet been assembled, and is invaluable on all points of reference. A volume of Morton's letters and MSS. relating to the introduction of ether, deposited by Mrs. Morton, Nov. 13, 1869, is available at the Mass. Hist. Soc., Boston, where the Warren Papers are also to be found. Notices of Morton's death appeared in *Evening Post* (N. Y.), July 16, and *Boston Transcript,* July 17, 1868.]

           J.F.F.

MORWITZ, EDWARD (June 11, 1815–Dec. 13, 1893), physician and publisher, the son of a wealthy merchant, was born in Danzig, Prussia. After receiving his Jewish education in his native city, he was sent to Halle, where he studied Semitic languages, Oriental literature, and theology. Deciding upon a career as a physician he began the study of medicine in the college at Danzig and continued at Leipzig University and finally at the University of Berlin, receiving the degree of M.D. from the latter institution in 1841. After his graduation he was appointed first assistant of the Hufeland clinic in Berlin, remaining for two years. In 1843 he settled in Konitz, where he began to practise his profession, specializing in the treatment of nervous and mental disorders. His success was gratifying, and he opened a hospital for the sick poor, supporting it himself. While thus engaged in this small town he began to write his *Geschichte der Medicin* (2 vols., 1848–49) which was published in Leipzig. As the work was coming from the press, the Revolutionary movement in Central Europe and France began to assume an ominous phase, and Morwitz, who was strongly inclined to democratic principles,

threw in his lot with the Revolutionists. His views became well known and he found himself an object of political hatred. On one occasion, the carriage in which he was riding was overturned by the royalists, and he was severely injured. Upon his recovery he was obliged to emigrate.

He had invented a breech-loading mechanism for field guns, and as he could not offer it to Germany he went to England to seek a purchaser. Failing there in his efforts he decided in 1850 to go to the United States, where at first he fared no better, but his love for democracy influenced him in determining to remain. He made a visit to Europe to settle his affairs and then returned in 1852, taking up his residence in Philadelphia, Pa. In that city he once more engaged in the practice of his profession and in time established a German dispensary for the poor. He took an active interest in the affairs of the city and began to contribute articles to the *Philadelphia Demokrat,* a daily printed there in the German language. About 1853 he bought a controlling interest in the paper from John S. Hoffmann. Morwitz formulated many plans for the improvement of Philadelphia and through the *Demokrat* strongly supported the consolidation of the city. In 1855 he began the publication of a political weekly, *Die Vereinigte Staaten Zeitung,* and was active in securing the election of Richard Vaux as mayor of the city in 1856. In the same year he started a Sunday literary paper, *Die Neue Welt,* which was virtually the Sunday edition of his daily. As a Democrat, he advocated the election of James Buchanan for president, and for campaign purposes purchased a newspaper called the *Pennsylvanian,* but sold it in 1860 when Stephen A. Douglas and John C. Breckinridge were separately nominated for the presidency. Confining his efforts to the *Demokrat,* he tried to use his influence in preventing the Civil War, but when the die was cast he remained loyal to the Union and assisted in raising regiments to send into the field of operations. In 1866 he issued the *Abendpost,* which he continued to publish for some years.

He took a prominent part in the organization of the German Press Association of Pennsylvania and in 1870 called a meeting to raise funds to assist German soldiers in the Franco-Prussian War, which resulted in the collection of $600,000 for the purpose. In 1874 he purchased the *Age,* a Philadelphia daily, but the following year sold it. He published German newspapers in several sections of Pennsylvania. It is said that at one time three hundred newspapers in both the German and English languages were printed by the Newspaper Union, which he organized. This was "the most extensive German establishment of its kind in the United States" (Scharf and Westcott, *post,* III, p. 2012). It was in his establishment that the so-called "patent-inside" was adopted. By this method miscellaneous matter and advertisements were printed on the second and third pages, then the papers were shipped to the country newspaper offices where the local news, editorials, and local advertisements were printed on the other pages. In 1873 Morwitz began the publication of *Uncle Sam's Almanac,* a cheap annual which had a large sale, and in 1875 he started the *Jewish Record,* which he carried on for eleven years. With others he compiled the *New American Pocket Dictionary of the English and German Languages* (in 2 parts, 1883), the forty-seventh edition of which was published in Milwaukee in 1911. Morwitz died in Philadelphia, leaving one son, Joseph, who carried on his publishing business.

[J. T. Scharf and Thompson Westcott, *Hist. of Phila.* (1884), vol. III; H. S. Morais, *The Jews of Phila.* (1894); the *Jewish Encyc.*; the *North American* (Phila.), *Phila. Inquirer,* and *Pub. Ledger,* Dec. 14, 1893.]   **J.J.**

MOSBY, JOHN SINGLETON (Dec. 6, 1833–May 30, 1916), Confederate ranger, was born at Edgemont, Powhatan County, Va., the eldest child of Alfred D. Mosby of Amherst County, and of Virginia, daughter of the Rev. Dr. McLaurine, of Edgemont. In 1838 the family moved from Nelson County to a farm near Charlottesville. In 1849 Mosby entered the University of Virginia, where he showed special aptitude in his studies. While an undergraduate, he was sentenced to six months in jail and fined $1,000 for shooting and wounding a fellow student in an altercation. The sentence was annulled by the legislature. In 1855 he was admitted to the bar at Bristol, Va., and in 1857 married Pauline, daughter of Judge Beverly L. Clarke, of Kentucky. With the outbreak of the Civil War in 1861, he enlisted in the cavalry, participating in the Bull Run campaign. In February 1862 he became adjutant of his regiment, and commenced to work as a scout. Failing of reëlection to the adjutancy in April, he was attached to Gen. J. E. B. Stuart's staff, and served with him during the campaigns in the Peninsula, at Manassas, and at Antietam, except for about a month's absence while he was a prisoner of war.

On Jan. 2, 1863, Mosby commenced independent operations as a ranger, in Loudoun County, Va., with only nine men. He acted under the partisan ranger law, which permitted the division of captured property among the captors. Mosby attacked isolated pickets and men with success from the first, and was commissioned a lieutenant in February. His rangers never had camps. Within limits, they boarded where they chose. Each man furnished his own food, horse, arms, and uniforms. After an engagement the command scattered, to meet at a future date and place as agreed upon. Besides dividing captured public property, the men freely took personal belongings, and were soon regarded as robbers by the Federals. Mosby, personally, however, never received anything. There were no drills; revolvers were the principal weapons, carbines were few; sabers were not used. The life with its booty and adventures, free from camp drudgery, fascinated many, and the rangers were constantly increasing in numbers through the recruiting of bold riders and fearless fighters. Mosby's first great success was on Mar. 9, 1863, when silently and unseen he crept within the Federal lines in the small hours of the morning, and entering Fairfax Court House, seized General Stoughton, about 100 others, and mounts for all. For this achievement he was appointed a captain, and for a raid on Chantilly in April, a major. Directed to organize a regular company, he declined, stating that he wanted rangers, not regulars. His request was granted, and on June 10, his men became Company A, 43rd Battalion Partisan Rangers. Additional companies were organized later.

In June, operations were extended across the Potomac into Maryland. Mosby performed valuable scouting at the commencement of the Gettysburg campaign, but he was unable to accompany Lee's army North. In the autumn, the rangers were the only disciplined force in northern Virginia. By common consent, Mosby acted as judge and administrator and maintained order. He was well liked, and in turn the people helped him in his military expeditions, the country becoming popularly known as "Mosby's Confederacy." In February 1864, he was promoted lieutenant-colonel. He was mercilessly hunted by the Federals, but since his forces dispersed when danger threatened, he was never caught. Two famous raids occurred this year: one, July 4, on Point of Rocks, Md., obtained much plunder; the other, Oct. 14, the "greenback raid," seized some $168,000, which was divided among the men and used to buy new uniforms and equipments. In this year, Mosby operated extensively in the Shenandoah Valley.

In November he hung seven prisoners, selected by lot, as a reprisal for the execution by the Federals of seven of his men, charged with being outlaws. (*Official Records*, 1 ser. XLIII, pt. 2, p. 920). Mosby informed General Sheridan of what he had done, and why, adding that he hoped it would not be necessary so to act again. It never was. In December he was promoted colonel and in the same month was severely wounded. His last engagement was on Apr. 10, 1865. The rangers had now grown to eight companies, and were never more efficient, better equipped, or better mounted. When Lee surrendered, Mosby realized that the war was over, and on Apr. 21, he reviewed his men at Salem, Va., and disbanded them. He himself surrendered at the end of June.

Settling at Warrenton, Va., he practised law, and later joined the Republican party. Because of this affiliation he was subjected to severe criticism, and his popularity with Southerners suffered. He was a great admirer of General Grant, however, and was willing to make personal sacrifices on this account. In 1878 he was appointed consul at Hong Kong, serving until 1885. Soon after, he became a land agent in Colorado, and from 1904 to 1910 was an assistant attorney for the Department of Justice. In 1887 he published *Mosby's War Reminiscences, and Stuart's Cavalry Campaigns*; and in 1908, *Stuart's Cavalry in the Gettysburg Campaign*. He was also the author of some minor publications. He died at Washington, D. C., survived by three daughters and a son, and was buried at Warrenton, Va. Mosby was of medium height, slender, with deep eyes and large features; he was smoothshaven except during the war, when he wore a full beard. Genial and energetic, he was more of a thinker than a talker.

[*War of the Rebellion; Official Records (Army)*; J. J. Williamson, *Mosby's Rangers: A Record of the Operations of the Forty-third Battalion Va. Cavalry* (1896); *The Memoirs of Col. John S. Mosby* (1917), ed. by C. W. Russell; *Richmond Times-Dispatch*, May 31, 1916.]   C. H. L.

MOSCOSO DE ALVARADO, LUIS de

(fl. 1530–1543), *maestre de campo* or second in command under Hernando de Soto [*q.v.*] during the "conquest" of Florida by the latter, was born in Zafra, Spain, a son of the Comendador Alonso Hernández de Diosdado and Isabel de Alvarado, two brothers being Juan de Alvarado and Christóbal de Mosquero. After serving under Pedro de Alvarado in Guatemala and Quito, 1530–35, Moscoso sailed from San Lucar with Soto in April 1538, in command of the galleon *La Concepción*. His two brothers accompanied the army. That Moscoso enjoyed the confidence and trust of his superior is shown by the fact that he lodged with him, for instance at the house of the chief of Ucita in Florida, that he was trusted with separate commands, as at Cale, and was sent in advance from Tallise to Tascaluça to announce to the chief the coming of his commander. His cautious spirit made him advise against entry of Mauvila, fearing a trap; had his advice been heeded, the defeat there might have been avoided. But when it appeared that Moscoso was partially to blame for the disaster at the Chicaça winter camp in 1541, he was replaced by Baltazar Gallegos. There is no record of complaint at this discipline, and Soto dying made him his successor.

The new governor then, "longing to be again where he could get his full measure of sleep" rather than search mythical kingdoms, undertook to reach New Spain. From Guachoya (near Arkansas City) on June 5 the army struggled to do so overland. Probably Moscoso moved west through broken timber country to Naguatex, held by a northern branch of the Natchitoches Indians, in the bend of the Red River; thence he turned southeast through villages of Caddoans to Guasco, then southwest some two hundred miles to the Daycao (probably the Brazos) River, not crossing nor entering the buffalo plains. There, despairing, he returned to the Mississippi to essay the journey by the Gulf. Seven brigantines were built by June 1543. The voyage, begun on July 2, was marked by hard Indian fighting for several of the seventeen days to the Gulf; fifty-two more days by hazards ensued before Pánuco was reached. There an army of 311 survivors out of six to nine hundred enlistments was royally received by the surprised settlers, for they had been counted lost. Food and clothing were lavished upon them; they sold their armor for horses, or walked, traversing sixty leagues to Mexico city. They were welcomed by the viceroy, Antonio de Mendoza, and replenished at royal expense. Moscoso delivered to him a copy of the narrative of the expedition written by Luis Hernández de Biedma, and it was sent to Charles V.

[Moscoso's route from Guachoya was studied by T. H. Lewis in *Spanish Explorers in the Southern United States* (1907). The direction is turned southwestward from that of Lewis by H. E. Bolton, in an unpublished study. This correlates the Soto sources with the topography and ethnography of the La Salle episode and the La Salle literature and that of the Spanish expeditions sent to expel the French after 1685. See: J. E. Kelly, *Pedro de Alvarado, Conquistador* (1932); Antonio del Solar y Taboada and José de Rújula y de Ochotorena, *El Adelantado Hernando de Soto* (1929); and the bibliography following the sketch of Hernando de Soto.]   H. I. P.

MOSELEY, EDWARD AUGUSTUS (Mar. 23, 1846–Apr. 18, 1911), lawyer, public official, was born in Newburyport, Mass., the eldest child of Edward Strong and Charlotte Augusta (Chapman) Moseley. He was a descendant in the seventh generation from John Maudesley or Moseley, an English Puritan, who emigrated to America in the seventeenth century. His maternal grandfather was George T. Chapman, an Episcopal clergyman, who was born in Devonshire, England. His father early in life was a prominent and successful shipowner but as the trade between New England and the East declined, he turned to banking and for the forty years preceding his death was president of two banks of Newburyport. The son first attended private schools, and later the public high school, though he did not graduate. At the age of sixteen he shipped to Africa and India as a sailor before the mast on one of his father's vessels. The voyage was a miserable experience and he returned at the end of a year, wasted and racked by Asiatic dysentery. After his recovery, he turned to business and eventually at the age of twenty-six formed the lumber firm of Moseley & Wheelwright. Business interests took him to the Gulf states, Central and South America, the West Indies, and Europe. He served two successive terms as city alderman and in 1885 and 1886 was elected to the state legislature. On Apr. 13, 1869, he married Kate Montague Prescott, the daughter of Joseph Newmarch and Sarah (Bridges) Prescott.

After the enactment of the Interstate Commerce Act, Moseley applied for an appointment as one of the commissioners. Cleveland had determined to appoint the commissioners in accordance with a geographical plan which did not admit of the appointment of a Democrat from the New England States, but he suggested Moseley's appointment to the secretaryship. The commissioners elected him at their first meeting on Apr. 19, 1887. The chairman of the Commission, Thomas M. Cooley, was not at first cordial to Moseley, but as the routine of the office settled the two men became fast friends, and it was at Cooley's suggestion and with his aid that Moseley studied law and became a member of the bar in 1889. Moseley's work as secretary, aside from the routine of the office, was devoted to one great cause—the protection of railroad employees and travelers from the dangers of trains operated without proper safety appliances. His work took him into the courts, before congressional committees, into conferences with politicians, railroad executives, labor unions, and lawyers. He also wrote numerous articles and pamphlets setting forth detailed arguments in support of his position. After some twenty years the railroads were required by law to equip their trains with the automatic coupler, the air brake, the block signal, and similar devices to insure safety to trainmen.

In 1902, at the request of Gen. Leonard Wood, then military governor of Cuba, Moseley went to Havana to assist in the revision of the island's railway laws. In the actual drafting of the laws, he performed services of great value and many measures were introduced to safeguard the public and employees. In the same year, President Roosevelt appointed him an assistant recorder of the Anthracite Coal Strike Commission; upon his assuming office, he was made disbursing officer. The only unpleasant incident that marred Moseley's long tenure of office occurred in 1904 when charges of misconduct in office were made against him. At once he laid aside his duties and absented himself for six months, giving the investigators free access to all private and official records. He was completely exonerated. He died in 1911, while working in Washington, and was buried in Newburyport. One of his three children survived him.

[Sources include: Jas. Morgan, *The Life Work of Edward A. Moseley in the Service of Humanity* (1913); manuscript autobiography of Moseley deposited in the library of the Interstate Commerce Commission, Wash., D. C.; *Ann. Reports of the Interstate Commerce Commission,* 1887–1911; the *Evening Star* (Wash., D. C.), Apr. 18, 1911; information as to certain facts from F. S. Moseley.]   H. Ca—s.

MOSES, BERNARD (Aug. 27, 1846–Mar. 4, 1930), political scientist and historian, was born in Burlington, Conn., the son of Richard and Rachel (Norton) Moses and a descendant of John Moses who was in Windsor, Conn., in 1647. He was educated at the University of Michigan, where he took his bachelor's degree in 1870, and at Heidelberg, Germany, where he received the degree of Ph.D. in 1873. After a year as professor of history at Albion College in Michigan, he accepted an appointment to the faculty of the University of California in 1876, continuing in service at that university, either actively or as professor emeritus, until his death in 1930. During the first quarter-century of his work there, he built up a reputation as a scholar in the fields of his activities. Gradually, however, he became drawn more and more to a hitherto neglected phase of history, at least by Anglo-American students, the colonial era of Spanish America. Most of his research efforts were henceforth directed to that subject, and with such enthusiasm that even when past eighty years of age he was still engaged in productive work. His best-known books were the following: *The Establishment of Spanish Rule in America* (1898); *South America on the Eve of Emancipation* (1908); *The Spanish Dependencies in South America* (2 vols., 1914); *Spain's Declining Power in South America, 1730–1806* (1919); *Spanish Colonial Literature in South America* (1922); *The Intellectual Background of the Revolution in South America, 1810–1814* (1926); and *Spain Overseas* (1929). A pioneer in this work, he had to write his own monographs. In consequence his books had a somewhat novel style. The story he told was not necessarily a continuous and united whole, but more often a series of essays which bore a relation to the general title. Often some rare or little-known work in a foreign tongue would be digested to serve as the basis for a single chapter, with other volumes being used in like manner as the foundation of other chapters. Always his investigations were painstaking and scholarly.

Moses is to be remembered especially for the impulse that he gave to the study of Hispanic-American history in the United States. He established a course in 1894–95 and at the beginning of the twentieth century he was perhaps the only professor in the United States devoting his full time to Hispanic-American subject matter. As a teacher he inspired others to follow in his footsteps until universities generally in the United States offered such courses. He became widely known as a specialist in his field and was often invited to be a member of various commissions upon which his knowledge of Hispanic institutions would be valuable. Most noteworthy in this connection was his service as a member of the United States Philippine Commission in the important years from 1900 to 1902, when American policies in the recently acquired Philippine group were in the early stages of formulation. He was also a member of various Pan-American congresses in the United States and Hispanic America and in 1910 was one of the United States ministers plenipotentiary to Chile on the occasion of the one-hundredth anniversary of the beginning of the Chilean war of independence. On June 15, 1880, he was married to Mary Edith Briggs, by whom he had one daughter. During the last twenty years of his life he was rarely in active service at the University of California. Much of his time he spent abroad, especially in Paris, pursuing his researches. When in California he resided at his Walnut Creek ranch, a few miles from the University.

Moses was tall and distinguished in appearance. His extreme dignity gave him an outward austerity of manner, but he was most genial and kindly to those who were in the inner circle of his acquaintance. Although his studies in his special field were his most important contributions to scholarship, his other works deserve mention. They include: *Politics* (1884), with W. W. Crane; *The Federal Government in Switzerland* (1889); *Democracy and Social Growth in America* (1898); *The Railway Revolution in Mexico* (1895); *The Establishment of Municipal Government in San Francisco* (1889); and *The Government of the United States* (1906).

[This article is based largely on records on file at the University of California, on personal acquaintance, and on information from others who were personal friends of Moses. For printed sources see: *Who's Who in America*, 1928–29; Zebina Moses, *Hist. Sketches of John Moses, of Plymouth.... John Moses, of Windsor and Simsbury.... Also a Geneal. Record of Some of Their Descendants* (2 vols., 1890–1907); *San Francisco Chronicle, San Francisco Examiner*, Mar. 6, 1930.]   C. E. C.

MOSES, FRANKLIN J. (1838–Dec. 11, 1906), governor of South Carolina, had a career that fulfilled in most details the conventional Southern conception of a scalawag. He was born in 1838 in Sumter District, S. C., the son of Franklin J. and Jane (McLelland) Moses. His original name was Franklin Israel Moses, but for reasons unknown he and his father, for whom he was named, both dropped Israel entirely and substituted the initial J. His father belonged to a Jewish family that had served the state with distinction, and was, himself, an able and successful lawyer, a member of the state Senate from 1842 to 1862, commissioner of South Carolina before the North Carolina secession convention, a circuit judge in 1865, and, after the accession of the Republicans to power in 1868, chief justice of the state, in which position he served with great distinction until his death in 1877. The younger Moses was a freshman in South Carolina College in 1855 but withdrew without finishing the course. On Dec. 20, 1859, he married Emma Buford Richardson, the daughter of James S. G. Richardson, a distinguished lawyer. He began his public career in December 1860, as private secretary to Gov. Francis W. Pickens, and he became an influence in politics. He raised the Confederate flag over Fort Sumter when the Federals surrendered that stronghold. He was made an enrolling officer with the rank of colonel under the Confederate conscription act. On Nov. 28, 1866, he was admitted to the bar, and the following April he was elected a vestryman of the Sumter Episcopal Church. During 1866 and 1867, as editor of the *Sumter News,* he favored President Johnson's Reconstruction plans and in 1866 was a delegate to a state convention called to indorse the president.

In 1867 he suddenly became a renegade to all his previous code of conduct. His writings became so radical that he was dismissed from his editorship, and it was discovered that he was closely affiliated with the Union League. Blessed with great gifts of personality and eloquence and cursed with underlying moral weakness, he yielded to the temptation to seize the opportunity of leading the black majority that was gaining the political mastery of the state. Elected a delegate from Sumter District to the constitutional convention of 1868, he became chairman of an important committee and in his speeches advocated those measures calculated to please the negroes. In the new government he served, simultaneously, as speaker of the House of Representatives, as adjutant and inspector-general of the armed forces of the state, and as trustee of the state university. In 1872 he was elected governor by an overwhelming majority over the candidate of the reform faction of the Republican party, and he served for two years. In his public service he was thoroughly unscrupulous; while he was speaker he issued fraudulent pay certificates and accepted bribes for influencing legislation; as adjutant-general he misappropriated funds for the purchase of arms for the militia; as governor he accepted bribes for his approval of legislation, for pardons, and for official appointments. In his private life his extravagance and immorality caused public scandal.

When he finished his term as governor he was a ruined man. His ill-gotten gain passed from him as easily as it had come; in May 1874 it became known that he was a hopeless bankrupt. His associates deserted him; there was no thought of nominating him for reëlection in 1874. When Gov. Daniel Chamberlain [*q.v.*] refused to commission him as a circuit judge in 1875 after the legislature had elected him to that position, the action of the governor won universal applause. To save himself from prison Moses testified against his former associates. In 1878 his wife divorced him, and the knowledge of his career was hidden from his children. Some of the members of his family, feeling the disgrace of his career, changed their name to Harby. From 1878 until his death he was a hopeless wanderer, a victim of poverty and of the drug habit. His sole asset was his ingratiating manner. For a time he was moderator of the town meeting of Winthrop, Mass.,

and editor of a local newspaper. Several times he was convicted of petty frauds and thefts and served short terms in various prisons. He died at Winthrop, a victim of accidental asphyxiation.

[F. B. Simkins and R. H. Woody, *S. C. during Reconstruction* (1932); R. H. Woody, "Franklin J. Moses, jr.," *N. C. Hist. Rev.,* Apr. 1933; J. S. Reynolds, *Reconstruction in S. C.* (1905); B. A. Elzas, *The Jews of S. C.* (1903); *Report of the Joint Investigating Committee on Public Frauds and Election of Hon. J. J. Patterson to the United States Senate Made to the General Assembly of S. C.* (1878); *Sumter News,* Dec. 6, 1866, Apr. 25, 1867; (Columbia) *State* and (Charleston) *News and Courier,* Dec. 12, 1906; *Charleston Mercury,* Jan. 15, 1868; register of the Church of the Holy Comforter at Sumter; a few details of personal history from members of the Moses family of Sumter.]   F. B. S.
                    R. H. W.

MOSESSOHN, DAVID NEHEMIAH (Jan. 1, 1883–Dec. 16, 1930), lawyer, editor, business executive and arbiter, was born at Ekaterinoslav, Russia, the son of Dr. Nehemiah and Theresa (Nissenson) Mosessohn. The home of his father, at one time chief rabbi of Odessa, was characterized by religion, scholarship, and ideals of public service. In 1888, when David was five years old, the family emigrated to the United States, and after brief sojourns in Philadelphia and Dallas, finally settled in Portland, Ore. After graduating from the Portland high school in 1900, he studied law at the University of Oregon and received the degree of LL.B. in 1902. That same year he was admitted to the bar and began practising law in Portland in partnership with his brother Moses Dayyan. From 1908 to 1910 he was deputy district attorney for Multnomah County. He served as president of the district grand lodge of the Independent Order B'nai B'rith in 1917, and took an active part in civic and Jewish communal affairs in the Northwest. On July 9, 1905, at Alameda, Cal., he married Manya Lerner, who with one son survived him.

In 1918 he moved to New York and devoted himself to war activities, in the course of which he met J. J. Goldman, a leader in the garment trade. At that time, although New York was the center of America's dress industry, and the annual business done, the capital invested, and the human, social, and economic factors involved were all on a colossal scale, the industry was in a chaotic condition. Uncontrolled individualism and cutthroat competition were weakening its whole structure. Goldman invited Mosessohn to examine the situation and report how it could be improved. Within thirty days, he presented a plan which resulted in the organization, in 1918, of the Associated Dress Industries of America. He was appointed its executive director, and from 1923 was its executive chairman and supreme arbiter, with wellnigh dictatorial powers. Through his high gifts of organization, he made the Associated Dress Industries a clearing house for ideas and methods pertaining to manufacture and distribution, the expansion of markets, the prevention of overproduction, and the handling of credit problems. Perhaps his greatest personal achievement was that of educating the industry in the advantage of arbitration over litigation. His eminent fairness gained for him implicit confidence, and he achieved widespread distinction as an impartial arbitrator. In recognition of his position in the dress trade, President Hoover, in December 1929, named him a member of the National Business Survey Conference.

Mosessohn was also an able publicist. While still in his teens he gained newspaper experience with the *Oregon State Journal*. In 1903 he and his brother began publishing in Portland a weekly magazine, the *Jewish Tribune*, with his father as editor, a publication which they transferred to New York on coming East. After his father's death in 1926, David Mosessohn assumed the editorship. Manifesting in this capacity the impartiality which characterized his business activities, he conducted the periodical as a non-partisan organ of Jewish enlightenment, defense, and good will, dedicated to the promotion of unity and harmony in Israel. In his communal activities in New York, he showed special interest in educational work among the Jewish youth. He was a leader in the Jewish Education Association, and in the Avukah Organization of the Zionist student youth, and was a founder of the council on American Jewish student affairs. To the United Synagogue of America, of which he was a director, to Zionism, and to charitable and philanthropic campaigns, he gave both active personal service and generous space in the *Jewish Tribune*. He was a thirty-second degree Mason, a past grand master of the Odd Fellows, and past chancellor of the Knights of Pythias. In addition he found time for participation in numerous business, social, and civic organizations. His intellectual interests were wide, and he was a member of several legal, historical, and other learned societies. His outstanding characteristics were executive ability, a keen mind, an energetic personality, a tender heart, and a touching loyalty to the inspiration of his father's life.

[Annual reports of the Associated Dress Industries of America; *Who's Who in America*, 1930–31; *Who's Who in American Jewry* (1928); *Popular Finance*, Sept. 1923; *Jewish Tribune*, Dec. 19, 26, 1930; *N. Y. Times*, Dec. 17, editorial Dec. 18, 1930.] D. deS. P.

MOSHER, ELIZA MARIA (Oct. 2, 1846–Oct. 16, 1928), physician, educator, civic worker, daughter of Augustus and Maria (Sutton) Mosher, was born in Cayuga County, N. Y., of conservative Quaker ancestry. She overcame the objections interposed by family and friends and at the age of twenty entered the New England Hospital for Women and Children as the first step in the medical career to which she was determined to devote herself. On Oct. 3, 1871, she matriculated in the medical course of the University of Michigan which had only the year before opened its doors to women. She received her degree of M.D. in 1875, and with a classmate, Dr. Elizabeth Hait Gerow, opened her office for private practice in Poughkeepsie, N. Y. In 1877 she was made resident physician at the Massachusetts State Reformatory Prison for Women at Sherborn, Mass. Resigning in 1879 in order to study in Europe, she returned in 1881 as superintendent of the institution. An injury to her knee forced her to abandon this position, but while she was still on crutches her friend and former associate at the University of Michigan, Alice E. Freeman, then president of Wellesley College, induced her to lecture for two semesters in that young institution. With Dr. Lucy Hall, with whom she had been associated at Sherborn, she opened an office in 1883 for private practice in Brooklyn, N. Y., but was almost immediately called to Vassar College as resident physician and professor of physiology and hygiene. Here she instituted the systematic physical examination of students. In 1886 she resumed her practice in Brooklyn. Ten years later President James B. Angell asked her to the University of Michigan to become the first dean of women, and first professor of hygiene, sanitation, and household economics, positions which she held until 1902, when she again returned to her Brooklyn practice. Here she continued to work until in March 1928 she suffered an accident which caused her death a few months later.

Eliza Mosher made important studies in posture, designed the seats in several types of rapid-transit streetcars, and invented a kindergarten-chair. She was the author of a book, *Health and Happiness, a Message to Girls* (1912), and for more than twenty years was senior editor of the *Medical Woman's Journal*. At a dinner given in her honor on Mar. 25, 1925, at the Hotel Roosevelt in New York City, five hundred persons from all parts of the country gathered to do her honor, and to celebrate the fiftieth anniversary of her medical service. Testimony was forthcoming as to her services to the colleges she had served; to the Union Missionary Training Institute where she had established a medical training department and herself taught the course in anatomy; to the Chautauqua Summer School which she had served twenty years as a member of the board of directors; to the American Posture League, of which she was a founder; to the American Women's Hospitals, of which she was a founder and a member of the board of governors for eleven years; to the Medical Women's National Association, of which she was honorary president; to Plymouth Congregational Church; to the medical societies; and to the city of Brooklyn. At the University of Michigan she shaped with dignity, understanding, and great humanity, the position of dean of women. She was the first woman physician in the university and organized the women's department of physical education. She also instituted physical examinations for women and was chiefly instrumental in securing the Barbour Gymnasium for women at the university. In June 1927, nearly fifty-four years after her matriculation, she turned the first sod for the construction of the Women's League Building of the University of Michigan in which "The Eliza M. Mosher Hostess Room" is dedicated to her.

[See *Mich. Alumnus*, Oct. 27, 1928, May 16, 1925; *Woman's Who's Who of America*, 1914–15; B. A. Hinsdale, *A Hist. of the Univ. of Mich.* (1906); the *Medic. Woman's Jour.*, July 1924, May 1925—the latter devoted to Dr. Mosher; *Jour. Am. Medic. Asso.*, Oct. 27, 1928; *N. Y. Times*, Oct. 17, 1928; information from friends and associates of the subject of the sketch.]   L. K. M. R.

MOSHER, THOMAS BIRD (Sept. 11, 1852– Aug. 31, 1923), publisher, was born in Biddeford, Me., the son of Benjamin and Mary Elizabeth (Merrill) Mosher. His forebears were mainly seafaring people but his parents were familiar with good literature. He attended the grammar-school and was to go to a private school in Boston, but his father, then in Hamburg, sent for his young son to accompany him on a sea voyage in the winter of 1866–67. "Thus," said Mosher, "I escaped college." On a trip to the Rhine the indulgent parent bought his son, for reading on shipboard, a set of Bell's *British Theatre* (1792) in thirty-four volumes. This set young Mosher devoured from Milton's *Comus* to Wycherley's plays, declaring that "with it I unlocked the gate and entered the enchanted garden of literature." The voyage did not end until the winter of 1870. In 1871 he began his career in the book world as a clerk in a publishing house on Exchange Street, Portland, Me., above which his office was afterward situated, and in 1882 he became one of the firm of McLellan, Mosher & Company. He had in mind the production of beautiful books at low cost, which should introduce to the American public little-known masterpieces of literature. Uninfluenced by the revival of printing in heavy types and sumptuous forms led by William Morris in England in 1890, Mosher followed classical models and made his books not only beautiful in type and paper, but in small and inexpensive format. He selected for their contents, with rare discrimination, the best literature of all times and all countries. In 1891 he produced the first of the "Mosher Books"—George Meredith's *Modern Love and Other Poems*—then all but unknown. Some of the works of English authors who had failed to secure American copyright, Mosher appropriated for his books. His reprint of Andrew Lang's *Aucassin and Nicolette* (1896) so aroused Lang's ire as an act of piracy that he never forgave him. On the other hand, many authors, like William Sharp, were glad to have their works reprinted in the United States, and in many cases Mosher paid substantial honorariums to authors unprotected by American copyright.

Though not a practical printer, Mosher followed very definite ideas and ideals in the more than five hundred works which he designed and published. In January 1895 he brought out the first number of *The Bibelot*, "a reprint of poetry and prose from scarce editions and sources not generally known." Produced in monthly parts of some twenty-four pages each, he continued it for twenty years, the series ending in 1915 with an index volume. Everything that he published bore the mark of his good taste. Two volumes of *Amphora* (1912–26) contain selections made by him from opuscula printed in his catalogues. The second, issued after his death by Flora Macdonald Lamb, holds tributes to his memory by noted authors. He was better known as a publisher in London literary circles than in Portland, and he was internationally known as a collector. He formed a large library of his favorite authors, though he was not primarily a collector of first editions. He was a genial person. Of medium height, rather thick-set and somewhat portly in later life, with his twinkling blue eyes and quizzical smile, he was in appearance far from the ascetic scholar. He was a member of the Bibliographical Society of London, the Grolier Club of New York, and the Authors', Omar Khayyam, and City clubs of Boston. He died in Portland. He had married, on July 2, 1892, Anna M. Littlefield of Saco, Me.

[A. E. Newton, "The Decay of the Bookshop," *Atlantic Monthly*, Jan. 1920, and *This Book-Collecting Game* (1928); "Thos. Bird Mosher — Publisher," *Pub-*

lisher's Weekly, Sept. 15, 1923; F. A. Pottle, "Aldi Discipulus Americanus," Lit. Rev. of the N. Y. Evening Post, Dec. 29, 1923; H. L. Koopman, "Modern Am. Painting," Am. Mercury, May 1924; Richard Le Gallienne, "In Praise of a Literary 'Pirate,'" Lit. Digest Internat. Book Rev., Oct. 1924; Christopher Morley, "A Golden String," Saturday Rev. of Lit., July 11, 1925; Maine Lib. Bull. (Augusta), Jan. 1921; Sun-Up (Portland), June 1927; Will Ransom, Private Presses and Their Books (1929), containing a bibliography of Mosher's publications; Alice F. Lord, article in the magazine section of the Lewiston Jour., July 7, 1928; Portland Press Herald, Sept. 1, 1923; original papers and letters.]   G. H. S.

MOSLER, HENRY (June 6, 1841–Apr. 21, 1920), genre painter, was the son of Gustav and Sophie (Wiener) Mosler, Germans living in New York City. His father was a lithographer. The family moved to Cincinnati, Ohio, in 1851; thence to Nashville, Tenn., in 1854, but after a year there returned to Cincinnati in 1855. Young Mosler was precocious; he acquired some knowledge of wood-engraving and painting without much assistance, and while still a youth made drawings for the Omnibus, a humorous weekly published in Cincinnati. His first serious instruction came from James H. Beard, who was his teacher from 1859 to 1861. In 1862–63 he was attached to the staff of Gen. R. W. Johnson as special war artist for Harper's Weekly with the Army of the West. Then, at the instance of Buchanan Read, the poet, he went to Düsseldorf, in the spring of 1863, entered the Royal Academy, and studied drawing and painting under H. K. A. Mücke and A. Kindler for some two years and a half. From Düsseldorf he proceeded to Paris in 1865, and for a half-year worked in the atelier of A. A. E. Hébert. In 1866 he returned to Cincinnati, and three years later he was married to Sarah Cahn. He remained in Cincinnati until 1874, when, with his wife and son, he went to Munich and passed three years there, studying under Ferdinand Wagner and Karl von Piloty. In 1877 he moved to Paris, where he lived for seventeen years, with two or three trips to America and many summer vacations in Brittany. He began to send his works to the Salon in 1878 and continued to exhibit there fairly regularly until he left Paris in 1894.

Mosler's first painting to gain notable recognition was "Le Retour," 1879, which was bought by the French government for the Luxembourg Museum, being the first picture by an American thus honored. On his return to America in 1894 he established his studio in New York. His "Wedding Feast in Brittany," 1892, a large composition with nearly a score of figures, quite typical, was bought by the Metropolitan Museum of Art, New York. Standing behind a long table set with the marriage feast, surrounded by his family and friends, the bridegroom is proposing a toast, while brimming glasses are raised in response. In 1896 an important exhibition of his paintings was held at Avery's Galleries in New York. Among his works in public collections, besides those in Paris and New York, may be mentioned his "Saying Grace" in the Corcoran Gallery, Washington; "The Rainy Day" in the Pennsylvania Academy, Philadelphia; "Return of the Shrimp Fishers" and "Head of a Monk" in the Cincinnati Museum; "The Biskarin Minstrel" in the Toledo Museum; "The Village Tinker" in the Springfield (Mass.) Museum; and other examples in the museums of Sydney, N. S. W., Grenoble, France, and Louisville, Ky. The artist's death occurred in New York in his seventy-ninth year. Muther sums up in a few words the verdict on Mosler's pictures when he says they "are good genre pictures"; they tell their stories well, with obvious pathos or humor.

[Catalogue of the Mosler exhibition, Avery Gallery, N. Y. (1896), with appreciation by J. S. Covington; W. A. Cooper, article in Godey's Mag., June 1895; Am. Art Ann. 1915; L. M. Bryant, Am. Pictures and their Painters (1917); Illustrated Cat.: Paintings in the Metropolitan Museum of Art (1905); Richard Muther, The Hist. of Modern Painting (1896), vol. III; Mich. State Lib., Biog. Sketches of Am. Artists (1924); Am. Art News, Apr. 24, 1920; N. Y. Times, Apr. 22, 1920.]   W. H. D—s.

MOSS, FRANK (Mar. 16, 1860–June 5, 1920), reformer, was born in Coldspring, Putnam County, N. Y. His father, John R. Moss, had emigrated from England in 1850. Eliza (Wood) Moss, his mother, was of English and Dutch parentage. He was educated in the public schools and studied for some time at the College of the City of New York. He also took courses in science and literature in the Chautauqua University. Meanwhile he was reading law and at the age of twenty-one was admitted to the New York bar. New York City in 1881 offered many opportunities to a young lawyer with ability and a crusading spirit. Tammany Hall, defeated after the exposure of the "Tweed ring" ten years before, had come back into power. A small group of unscrupulous politicians, manipulating masses of ignorant, foreign-born voters, controlled the city government. Gamblers and prostitutes plied their trades openly under police protection. Moss first came into public notice when, in 1887 as counsel for the Society for the Prevention of Crime, he successfully prosecuted the keepers of disorderly houses in the "Tenderloin" and the police captain who had protected them. The president of the society, Howard Crosby [q.v.], wrote that he had "established a reputation for wisdom, boldness, and energy, which any lawyer might covet . . ." (Parkhurst, *post*, p. 144). He continued to act as counsel for the society and in 1892 became a member of its executive board. In 1891 Charles H. Parkhurst [*q.v.*] was chosen president of the society and, inaugurating a radical change in policy, he made the society the instrument of a vigorous attack on the police administration and on Tammany. In the two-year battle that ensued the famous preacher aroused public opinion by his dramatic denunciations of the mayor and his subordinates, but it was Moss and his associate, Thaddeus D. Kenneson, who accumulated evidence, examined witnesses, and prepared cases. This service, to which a large part of their time and energy was devoted, was performed entirely without compensation. At a critical point in the struggle, the New York Senate appointed the Lexow investigating committee, which selected Moss as one of its counsel (see sketch of Clarence Lexow). In this position he added to his reputation as a persistent prosecutor and investigator. The elections of November 1894 resulted in the defeat of Tammany, and the reformers' candidate, Mayor William L. Strong, came into office. When after two years of strenuous service Theodore Roosevelt, the president of the board of police commissioners, resigned, Moss was chosen to succeed him. Two years later, in 1899, when the municipal administration was again under legislative scrutiny he was chosen as leading counsel for the Mazet investigating committee. For a number of years thereafter he devoted himself to private law practice. Although nominally a Republican in politics he was too independent to be a favorite with the machine. He reëntered political life, however, in 1909 as first assistant to District Attorney Whitman. In this capacity he served until 1914, conducting the successful prosecution of the four gunmen who murdered the gambler Rosenthal, and participating actively in the trial of Police Lieutenant Becker.

It was not merely a zealot's hatred of wrongdoing which inspired his work; he was moved also by genuine love and pride for his city. These sentiments inspired him to write *The American Metropolis* (3 vols., 1897), which does not conform to the standard type of local history but is "a reminiscent, observant, reflective journey on historical lines" (Author's Preface, p. xiii). The reader is conducted on a tour of lower Manhattan, and as the successive landmarks are reached he is taught their history. The description of life on the East Side incorporates many incidents that the author must

have witnessed. Crime and criminals occupy a large part of the third volume. In 1919 he published *America's Mission to Serve Humanity,* which he wrote to show that President Wilson's foreign policy was consistent with that of American statesmen since the days of Washington. He was married on Jan. 24, 1883, to Eva Estelle Bruce, who with their two children survived him.

[C. H. Parkhurst, *Our Fight with Tammany* (1895), esp. pp. 142–44, 204–07, 251 ; *Who's Who in America*, 1920–21 ; *N. Y. Times,* June 6, 1920 ; *Sun and the N. Y. Herald,* June 6, 1920.]   P.W.B.

MOSS, JOHN CALVIN (Jan. 5, 1838–Apr. 8, 1892), pioneer photoengraver, was born near Bentleyville, Washington County, Pa., the son of Alexander J. and Mary (Calvin) Moss. His mother intended him for the ministry, but the youth learned the printer's trade instead. The daguerreotype was then a sensation, and Moss learned something about making portraits in that manner. On learning of William Robert Grove's attempts to turn a daguerreotype into a printing plate, Moss made a Grove battery and began to experiment in that direction. This probably started him toward what later became his life work. In 1856 he married Mary A. Bryant, who became as ardent as himself in the search for a method of engraving through the aid of photography. In 1859 he became publisher of the *Colleague,* at Washington, Pa., but in 1860 he was again working at his trade as a printer in Philadelphia. Here he haunted the libraries, studying optics, chemistry, photography, acquiring knowledge that would help him toward a realization of his ambition to engrave by the aid of the camera. After the Civil War he got work at his trade in New York, and turned his home in Jersey City, N. J., into a laboratory. His wife carried out experiments in the daylight while he was setting type to earn a living for them both. He became so confident that he had solved the problem that he induced a friend to invest some money and they founded in January 1871 the Actinic Engraving Company, 113 Liberty Street, New York. Printers would not accept his engravings so the enterprise failed. Obtaining more capital (Moss established the Photoengraving Company, May 2, 1872, which he moved later to 67 Park Place, New York. Here he was successful. He depended upon secrecy to protect himself from competition, but his workmen would leave him and begin business for themselves in a small way. Finally he decided to go into business on a large scale, employ hundreds of men, and retain his leadership.

In 1881 he accordingly sold out his business

and established the Moss Engraving Company at 535 Pearl Street, New York. Here the dreams of nearly a quarter century came true; he became the best-known photoengraver in the world. In attempting to supplant the wood-cut he found that he must train pen-and-ink draftsmen to imitate the line of the wood engraver in the treatment of portraits, figures, architecture, and landscapes, in order to sell his photoengravings. So successful was he in counterfeiting the work of the wood-engraver that the public could not distinguish the new from the old methods of engraving. He trained a new school of draftsmen from which many famous illustrators graduated. Moss's printing blocks were stereotypes, so shallow that it required a large staff of trained wood-engravers to deepen them between the lines. When printers complained that they could not get results from his engravings Moss established his own printery to prove that the fault was with the printer. In the meantime other experimenters had devised methods of photoengraving that were improvements upon his and more artistic in quality. Moss was obliged to adopt these newer methods and died in 1892 a disappointed man. From his plant went forth photoengravers who carried the knowledge gained under his tutorage into other places and cities and in many instances became more successful financially than their master. To him, however, remains the credit of being the first to establish photoengraving in the United States as a commercial business.

["John Calvin Moss," *Photo-Engravers' Bull.* (Chicago), Feb. 1926; *Appletons' Ann. Cyc.*, 1892; *N. Y. Times*, Apr. 9, 1892; *Ann. Reports of the Commissioner of Patents*, 1877–78; personal acquaintance.]
S. H. H.

MOSS, LEMUEL (Dec. 27, 1829–July 12, 1904), Baptist clergyman, editor, educator, was born in Boone County, Ky., the son of Rev. Demas and Esther (Lewis) Moss, pioneer Baptists of southern Indiana. On Dec. 24, 1851, he married Harriet Bingham of Cincinnati. After following the printer's trade for nine years, he entered the University of Rochester in 1853 as a special student. President Martin B. Anderson [*q.v.*] soon persuaded him to pursue the full course, and he graduated from the University with high honors in 1858 and from the Rochester Theological Seminary in 1860.

Ordained at Worcester, Mass., he served as pastor of the First Baptist Church there from 1860 to 1864, when he accepted the secretaryship of the United States Christian Commission. He was the author of the only published account of the work of that body—*Annals of the United States Christian Commission* (1868). His educational work began at Bucknell University, where from 1865 to 1868 he held the professorship of systematic theology. For the next four years the editorship of the *National Baptist* interrupted his teaching career, but in 1872 he was installed as professor of New Testament interpretation at Crozer Theological Seminary. Two years later, he assumed the presidency of the old, moribund Chicago University, and from 1875 to 1884 he was president of Indiana State University. After a few years without charge, he became in 1889 editor of the *Ensign* of Minneapolis, Minn., which position he occupied until 1893. Returning to the pastorate for a brief period, he was minister of the First Baptist Church, Woodbury, N. J., 1894–96. In 1897 he was editor of the *Baptist Commonwealth*, Philadelphia. During the last eight years of his life, he promoted the work of the American Baptist Historical Society, acting as president from 1895 to 1900 and as vice-president, 1900 to 1904; from 1898 to 1904 he also lectured on social science at Bucknell University.

In 1902 he averted a serious crisis at the National Baptist Anniversaries at St. Paul. For many years the Baptists of the North had conducted their national and international work through three societies, the Missionary Union, the Home Mission Society, and the Publication Society. Criticisms of inefficiency, overlapping, and waste had been repeatedly made. Considerable feeling was developing, and at the St. Paul meeting Moss offered resolutions, enthusiastically adopted, providing for the appointment of a committee of fifteen charged with the function of promoting harmony and consolidation. By serving upon this commission, he paved the way for larger endeavor and more harmonious cooperation among these societies. Truly democratic in his attitude toward their consolidation, he insisted that the Baptist constituency decide upon the type of national Baptist organization. The ultimate result was the provisional organization in 1907 of the Northern Baptist Convention. Liberal in his intellectual attitude, he occasionally appeared upon the platform of the Baptist Congress and by apt suggestion and comparison stimulated the movement toward a broader interpretation of Christianity. Among his publications were *The Baptists and the National Centenary: A Record of Christian Work* (1876) and *A Day with Paul* (1894). Loyal to Baptist principles but not sectarian in his religious attitude, by nature fearless and courteous, given to ceaseless mental toil although long a sufferer from bodily ills, he used his pen to promote the best interests of his denomination. He died in New York City, survived by his wife and three children.

[*Rochester Theological Sem., Gen. Cat.* (1910); *Am. Baptist Year Book*, 1868–1904; *Who's Who in America*, 1901–02; *Watchman*, July 21, 1904; *Examiner*, July 21, 1904; *N. Y. Times*, July 13, 1904.]
C. H. M.

MOST, JOHANN JOSEPH (Feb. 5, 1846– Mar. 17, 1906), anarchist, was born in Augsburg, Germany, the son of Josef Most, a lawyer's copyist who was unable because of poverty to secure a marriage license until two years after the son was born. His mother was educated and a liberal but died when he was ten. His childhood embittered by a five years' illness (following exposure when intoxicated at seven years), an operation which left his face disfigured for life, a cruel stepmother, and a brutal employer, he started forth at seventeen equipped with the trade of bookbinder, a meager general education, a love of reading, extreme sensitiveness because of his deformity, and a thwarted ambition to become an actor. After wandering for five years through Germany, Austria, Italy, and Switzerland, encountering difficulty in getting work and making friends, he joined the International Workingmen's Association in Zurich and threw his feverish energy into the Socialist movement. Between 1868 and 1878 he edited Socialist papers in Vienna, Chemnitz, and Berlin, spent two years in prison in Austria and three in Germany, was elected twice to the Reichstag, lectured frequently, wrote many pamphlets and labor songs, and was expelled first from Austria and finally from Germany. In 1878 he established in London a weekly organ, *Die Freiheit*. Gradually his ideas became more extreme, he became an anarchist, and in 1880 was expelled from the German Socialist party. An article glorifying the assassination of Alexander II, in March 1881, led to the suppression of his paper and to a sentence of sixteen months' imprisonment. Upon his release he transferred himself and *Freiheit* to New York, where he landed on Dec. 12, 1882, and was welcomed as a martyr by a mass meeting of social revolutionists—a man slightly above medium height, with a large head, bushy hair and beard, and mild blue eyes. Later he made a series of tours advocating violence against rulers and capitalists and inspiring terror among the timid.

A magnetic speaker with a sinister power of hatred and invective, and a brilliant writer full of biting wit and sarcasm, Most became leader of the extreme faction of American anarchists, most of them German-speaking, and dictated the declaration of principles adopted by the Pittsburgh convention of 1883 which became the Bible of communist anarchism in America. Just before the Chicago Haymarket tragedy of May 1886, he was sent to Blackwell's Island for a year for inciting to violence, and after his release was almost immediately returned there because of his pamphlet on "the scientific art of revolutionary warfare" which described how to use bombs and other methods of destruction. By the end of this second year's sentence Most had begun to doubt the efficacy of direct individual action and when, in 1892, he repudiated the act of Alexander Berkman in attempting the life of Frick he lost his influence among the younger anarchists. Nevertheless, after the assassination of McKinley in 1901 he served a third term on Blackwell's Island. In his later years, with only a small following and slight power to attract attention, he took to drink but continued *Freiheit* and was on a lecture tour when he died at Cincinnati. Early in life he married in Germany but this connection is lost in as much obscurity as his frequent later emotional experiences. Though not one of the constructive theorists of anarchism he is widely known as the apostle of "propaganda by deed." Yet his many imprisonments were all for what he said and not for what he did. Except for his influence over others he might be considered primarily as an example of twisted psychological development.

[The most recent and extensive biography is Rudolf Rocker, *Johann Most, Das Leben eines Rebellen* (1924). Most wrote an autobiography, entitled *Memorien, Erlebtes, Erforschtes und Erdachtes,* which was published in four parts, beginning in 1903. In addition, his numerous pamphlets and files of the papers he edited, practically all in German, furnish biographical material. A list of his writings and speeches, as well as a brief biography, is contained in Ernst Drahn, *Johann Most: Eine Bio-Bibliographie* (1925), in the *Bio-Bibliographishe Beiträge zur Geschichte der Rechts- und Staatswissenschaften.* This study also contains a list of the principal German works relating to his place in the socialist and anarchist movements. With reference to his career in the United States, consult John R. Commons and associates, *Hist. of Labour in the U. S.* (1918), vol. II; Morris Hillquit, *Hist. of Socialism in the U. S.* (1903); Richard T. Ely, *The Labor Movement in America* (1886) and *French and German Socialism* (1883); Robert Hunter, *Violence and the Labor Movement* (1914). A biographical sketch by Emma Goldman is contained in the *Am. Mercury* for June 1926, and an article by Karl Kautsky reviewing Rocker's biography is contained in *Die Gesellschaft* (Berlin), vol. I, 1924, pp. 545–64.]
H. S. W.

MOTLEY, JOHN LOTHROP (Apr. 15, 1814–May 29, 1877), historian, diplomat, was born in Dorchester, a suburb of Boston, Mass. He was descended from a long New England ancestry, mostly merchants on his father's side, clergymen on his mother's. His father, Thomas

Motley, and his father's brother, Edward Motley, were well-to-do Boston merchants; his mother, Anna Lothrop, was a daughter of the minister of the Old North Church. From his parents John Lothrop Motley inherited the handsome face and fine presence which were marked characteristics and he was surrounded from his birth by ease and typical Boston culture. Through life he was a member of an enviable group of friends: in America, Holmes, Prescott, Longfellow, Emerson, Hawthorne, Lowell, Agassiz, Dana, Sumner, Amory, and others; in England, the Russells, Bright, Dickens, Hughes, and other cultured and prominent members of the nobility, gentry, and learned and literary groups; on the Continent, the royal, court, and diplomatic personages with whom his position as United States minister and his repute as an historian brought him in contact. He was naturally intelligent, a ready speaker and writer. His early years were spent at private schools; at Round Hill, Northampton, one of his teachers was George Bancroft, the future historian. Much attention was paid at these schools to languages and Motley learned languages easily; at eleven he wrote a letter to his brother in French as an exercise, and in the same year he was studying Greek, Latin, and Spanish. He was a great reader, reading Hume's *History of England* before he was twelve and Scott's and Cooper's novels as they appeared. He entered Harvard in 1827 and graduated in 1831, at the age of seventeen. College life made little impression upon him, apparently, except as it gave him opportunity for reading, a little writing, and social enjoyments. He was elected to Phi Beta Kappa, although at the bottom of the list. Two years' study in Germany, first in Göttingen, then in Berlin, followed. Such studying as he did, apart from steady drill in the German language, as part of which he translated Goethe's *Faust* into English, was in Roman and international law; but he made interesting observations and acquaintances, among the latter, Bismarck, whose affectionate remembrances of their young men's life together were renewed at several intervals when the great statesman had reached his later eminence.

After a trip through Austria, Italy, France, and Great Britain in 1834 and 1835, Motley returned to Boston, living with his parents, nominally studying law, actually trying his hand at literature. On Mar. 2, 1837, he married Mary Benjamin, sister of Park Benjamin [*q.v.*], the writer, who lived for a time with his sisters in Boston. They were a refined and attractive family and Motley's marriage was a particularly

happy one. His long and vivacious letters to his mother, his wife, and his three daughters (his one son had died young), whenever they were separated, and those to his friends, vie in bulk and interest with the written remains of his historical and diplomatic life. After his marriage he lived in a house built for him by his father on his estate at Riverdale near Boston.

Motley's principal adventures in literature were two novels, *Morton's Hope,* published in 1839, and *Merrymount,* written near the same time but not published till 1849. Neither of them was of great significance or reached appreciable recognition. Nor did a term in the Massachusetts House of Representatives in 1849 give promise of success in local political life. On the other hand it was during this decade, between 1840 and 1850, that the two lines of his future life work were indicated, diplomatic service abroad and the writing of history. He wrote to his wife that he would prefer the profession of diplomacy to any other and considered himself especially well fitted for it. It was to be his fortune to find each of his three experiences in it unsatisfactory. The first was brief and uneventful. In the fall of 1841 he was appointed secretary of legation at St. Petersburg, but he found the climate there unpleasant, his duties uninteresting, and living expensive. As he had left his wife and children in the United States he soon resigned and returned to Boston. His first piece of historical writing may have been suggested by his Russian experience. It was an essay on Peter the Great, published in the *North American Review* (October 1845) in the form of a review of two recent works on Peter, one French, the other English. It has little importance from the historical point of view, indicating no knowledge of the subject beyond what was drawn from the works reviewed and no special powers of criticism or interpretation. On the other hand it showed, as did his other two essays of the same period, "The Novels of Balzac" (*Ibid.,* July 1847) and "Polity of the Puritans" (*Ibid.,* October 1849), a clear and picturesque style, the flow of humor and the eloquence which characterized his later historical writings.

It was apparently in the year 1847 that he settled on the field of history that was to be his interest for the rest of his life, the attainment of independence by the Netherlands and the struggles of their early years. Just why he chose that subject does not appear, though he told a Dutch scholar long afterward that he was struck with the analogies between the United Provinces and the United States and between William of Orange and Washington. He said at one time, "I had not first made up my mind to write a history and then cast about to take up a subject. My subject had taken me up, drawn me on, and absorbed me into itself" (Holmes, *post*, p. 63). Hearing that Prescott, already famous, was planning to follow the *Conquest of Mexico* with a life of Philip II, Motley called on him to offer to give up his own newly formed plan, but the older scholar encouraged him to proceed, offered him any help he could give, and called attention to Motley's forthcoming work in the preface of his next volume.

Motley wrote his first large work practically three times, once in the United States, a second time in Germany, a third time in Holland. Without training as an historian and with little conception of the requirements of original historical work, he labored for some time with such materials as he could find in Boston. Then realizing the necessity for better access to at least the printed sources, in 1851 he took his family with him to Europe and settled for two years in Dresden, working steadily in the excellent collections of the Saxon royal library, which possessed almost half a million volumes. He wrote that he was "working as hard as a wood sawyer," and was digging "raw material out of subterranean depths of black-letter folios in half a dozen different languages" (*Correspondence*, I, 145–46). He was occupied "ten hours a day, with folks who lived three centuries ago" (*Ibid.*, I, 142). By the early part of 1853 he had worked through that portentous list of sixteenth-century chronicles and other contemporary materials that he gives in the preface of his first volume and refers to in his footnotes, writing as he collected his material, and had brought to seeming completion the three volumes he had planned as the first part of his work, covering the period down to the death of William of Orange. Going next to The Hague and then to Brussels for the purpose of subjecting his work to some revision, in the archives there he found so much new and unexpected matter, mostly in manuscript, that he confesses to have been almost in despair, but set to work emending, reorganizing, and rewriting. He wrote to Holmes, "Whatever may be the result of my labors, nobody can say that I have not worked hard like a brute beast; but I do not care for the result. The labor is in itself its own reward and all I want" (*Ibid.*, I, 163), almost the same words that another great American historian, Henry C. Lea, used privately, though neither of them was by any means uninterested in the subsequent reception by the public of his writing. As a

matter of fact, Motley was supremely happy in his work, and after some eight months in the Netherlands, by the middle of 1854 had his book in satisfactory shape and set out with the manuscript for London to find a publisher. Murray, to whom he had letters of introduction, kept the manuscript for some weeks but finally declined it on account of its considerable length and unfamiliar subject. After some further negotiations Chapman agreed to publish it in England simultaneously with Harper & Brothers in America, at the author's expense. Motley's father and uncle joined him in defraying the cost. *The Rise of the Dutch Republic* appeared in London and New York early in 1856. Both by scholars and the public it was received with praise from which there were but few dissenting voices. Instead of the sales of less than a hundred which Motley had feared and the unremunerative response the publishers had apprehended, some 17,000 copies were sold in little more than a year in England alone, and almost as many more in the United States. A second edition was immediately required.

The reasons for this acclaim and the lasting repute of the work are obvious. It is a picturesque, dramatic narrative of a striking series of events, gathering around a group of clearly marked personalities, and is suffused with a warm glow of love of political and religious liberty. "If ten people in the world hate despotism a little more and love civil and religious liberty a little better in consequence of what I have written, I shall be satisfied," he wrote to a friend (Mildmay, *post*, p. 42). The faithful investigation Motley had made of the sources gave him sureness of touch, his eager spirit provided the illumination, and his literary gifts gave him the ability to draw a series of pictures almost unrivaled in their brilliancy in historical literature. His view of history is of a series of episodes, interesting in themselves, and illustrative of his general conception of the time and its lessons. On the other hand his warm partisan admiration for William and hatred of Philip II, his personal addiction to liberty, as he considered it to exist in America and England and among the patriot party in the Netherlands, and his dislike of Catholicism undoubtedly lessened the value of the work as true history. It shows more learning than insight and more enthusiasm than sobriety. It is almost purely political and religious, paying scarcely any attention to economic or social matters. It can never be considered a definitive history of its period. It will always remain a brilliant personal interpretation of it. Later editions and translations into

Dutch, French, German, and Russian appeared within the next few years and there were several abbreviated and unauthorized publications founded upon it.

In the intervals of a short visit to America, European travel with his family, and his next diplomatic appointment, Motley continued his work. It was now more largely drawn from manuscript sources. He worked with the assistance of copyists in the British Museum and state paper office in London, in the archives at The Hague and Brussels, and among the copies from the Simancas Archives in Paris. He wrote from The Hague, "I work every morning at home two hours before breakfast, then to the Archives till three, after which, in the course of the day and evening I get a few hours more" (*Correspondence*, I, 307). The *History of the United Netherlands* was published almost simultaneously in England and America, the first two volumes in 1860 in London (New York, 1861), the second two in 1867 (New York, 1868). This work covers the period from the death of William to the truce of 1609 only, though he had originally intended to extend it to the entrance of the Netherlands into the Thirty Years' War. His remaining work, *The Life and Death of John of Barneveld, Advocate of Holland; with a View of the Primary Causes and Movements of the Thirty Years War* (2 vols., 1874), filled in this interval. The *United Netherlands* is occupied more with the general affairs of Europe, especially with Dutch relations with England and France, than his earlier work; it has not its dramatic interest, though it has still its devotion to personal and picturesque occurrences and to what he called "fruitful examples of the dangers which come from superstition and despotism, and the blessings which flow from the maintenance of religious and political freedom." In *John of Barneveld*, Motley's analysis of the tortuous and troubled interplay of religious and political dissension and his inevitable sympathy with the Arminian side subjected him to more criticism in the Netherlands than did his earlier works (see Groen van Prinsterer, *Guillaume Maurice et Barneveldt. Étude Historique*, Utrecht, 1875). On the other hand he was already deeply entrenched in the national admiration and affections of the Dutch; for some time he lived in a house set apart for him at The Hague by the queen, with whom he and his family were on friendly terms, and later in the old de Witt mansion. The history of the Thirty Years' War, bringing the work down to 1648, which he had planned from the first, and which led him to visit Bohemia in

search of local color in 1871, was never written. With ill health, beginning with a slight stroke of paralysis in 1873, with the death of his wife on the last day of 1874, and with the disappointments of his later diplomatic career, he lost energy and spirit for further study or writing.

The long interval between the appearance of the first and the second two volumes of the *United Netherlands*, 1860 and 1867, was due partly to Motley's absorption in the occurrences of the Civil War, partly to his duties as minister to Austria. He was appointed to that post by President Lincoln while he was on a visit to America, on the strong urgency of Senator Sumner, Aug. 12, 1861. There was some opposition on the ground of too many appointments having been made from Massachusetts. He went to Vienna by way of England and France, conversing informally while in England with Lord John Russell, whom he visited at his summer home in Scotland and by whom he was taken to visit the Queen and Prince Consort at Balmoral. These and other interviews in 1860 and 1861, two long letters he wrote to the London *Times* (May 23, 24, 1861) which were immediately republished in England and America, and his reports on what he knew of English opinion given to Lincoln, Seward, and others while in Washington before his appointment, although not a part of his formal diplomatic service, were of the greatest value in the increase of good understanding between Great Britain and the United States. He remained in Vienna from November 1861 to July 1867. Early in 1862 Secretary Seward, at the suggestion of Gustavus Körner, who had been appointed minister to Spain, offered Motley the opportunity to exchange Vienna for Madrid, on the ground that he might be able better to prosecute there his studies of the Dutch revolt from Spain. Motley declined, partly from his belief that Körner, being by birth a German, would not be welcome at Vienna, partly because he had already secured all the material needed for his present work, whereas for the history of the Thirty Years' War which he hoped to write next, Vienna was the fountain head of knowledge. Of the two hundred and thirty-six official dispatches sent home during the six years of his ministry a large part consisted of reports of European reactions to the Civil War, of his negotiations concerning the election of Maximilian to the throne of Mexico, and of his observations on Austrian and general European society. The Austrian government responded in a friendly spirit to American protests against their attitude on Mexican affairs, although in 1866 Motley informed the foreign minister that he had received orders to withdraw from Vienna if the rumored plan for sending Austrian troops to Mexico were carried out, and later American efforts to prevent the execution of Maximilian were acknowledged gratefully. Motley's dispatches at this period are almost as full, intimate, and interesting as are his family letters, and Seward repeatedly expressed his appreciation and gratitude for them.

These pleasant relations were suddenly broken by a dispatch from the Department of State, dated Nov. 21, 1866, in which Seward informed him that a "citizen of the United States," whose name Motley afterward learned was George W. McCrackin, but whom he did not know, had written from Paris to President Johnson, saying that he had observed during his recent travels in Europe that the ministers and consuls of the United States were for the most part bitterly hostile to the President and his administration and expressed their hostility openly. More especially he charged Motley with expressing his "disgust" for the President's conduct, with saying that Seward was "hopelessly degraded," and with showing general contempt for American democracy. Seward asked Motley, as he did the other American ministers named in the letter, to deny or confirm the charges. Immediately on the receipt of this dispatch, Dec. 11, 1866, Motley wrote with his own hand a long statement of his views on Reconstruction, which certainly differed somewhat from those of President Johnson, but explained that he had carefully avoided any public expression of his views and characterized as a "vile calumny" the assertion that he had spoken disrespectfully of the President or Secretary or of American democracy. Resenting being questioned on such charges he closed his letter by resigning his position as minister. In acknowledging this dispatch, Jan. 5, 1867, Seward said that the President did not find Motley's answer to be unsatisfactory, and since there seemed no consideration of public policy requiring his resignation it lay within his own choice whether this should be considered absolute or not. Johnson, however, insisted on the recall of Seward's dispatch, and Motley had no reply to his letter of Dec. 11 until he received a brusque dispatch dated at Washington, Apr. 18, 1867, accepting his resignation and instructing him to present his recall to the Emperor and to hand over the embassy to the chargé d'affaires, which he did early in June 1867. This controversy, which was evidently part of the political struggle in which President Johnson was engaged, became a matter of wide discussion, and much sympathy was expressed for Motley. (*Senate Executive Document No. 8*, 39 Cong., 2 Sess.; *No. 9, Ibid.*; *No. 1*, 40 Cong., 2 Sess.; John Bigelow, "Mr. Seward and Mr. Motley," *International Review*, July–August, 1878.)

During 1868, while Motley was again in America, he delivered two addresses which were printed, and in London he published a pamphlet in 1869, *Democracy the Climax of Political Progress*. In March 1869, again on the urgency of Sumner, President Grant appointed Motley minister to Great Britain. It was a time of strained relations between the two countries. A number of subjects were in dispute, the most serious being the *Alabama* claims. Before Motley left America he went through the official correspondence, drew up a general account of these disputes, and submitted a memorial on them to Hamilton Fish, secretary of state. This was however laid aside, and instructions were handed him the day he sailed. With the most sincere intention of following out his instructions, either because of their indefiniteness or because of his long-settled opinions, he did not succeed in representing in his early conversations with the British foreign secretary the President's exact intentions, and although other negotiations were left in his hands he was instructed to ask that the *Alabama* claims should in future be discussed in Washington, not in London. This was apparently an indication of dissatisfaction of Grant and Fish with his mission, but Motley was quite unaware of this and believed he still had their entire confidence. In June 1869 Fish told him he had stated American claims well and forcibly, and as late as May 27, 1870, congratulated him warmly on his success in negotiating the naturalization treaty. Even when in June 1870 it was stated in the English newspapers that he was to be recalled, he could not believe he was to be so discourteously treated and supposed the report mere gossip. On June 30, 1870, however, he received a dispatch from Washington stating that the President wanted to make a change in the mission to Great Britain and offering him the opportunity to resign. Secretary Fish, on July 13, wired him for a reply and Motley telegraphed back his refusal, explaining at length in a letter written the same day his unwillingness to admit by such resignation that he had failed in any way in his duty to his country. For the next four months official relations were kept up, though on somewhat strained terms, until a dispatch, dated Nov. 10, 1870, reached Motley, enclosing a letter to the queen announcing his recall, and ordering him to commit the property of the embassy to the secretary of legation. On Dec. 7 Motley sent a long letter of protest, which was answered by a still longer and certainly a much exaggerated letter of complaint from Secretary Fish, addressed not to him but to the secretary of the embassy. It is hard to believe that Motley's dismissal was not influenced by the anger of Grant against Sumner, Motley's friend, who had opposed Grant in his Santo Dominican policy. The matter was discussed in the Senate and the whole correspondence called for and published (*Senate Executive Document No. 11*, 41 Cong., 3 Sess.; *New York Herald*, Jan. 4, 1878). Motley should have made an ideal ambassador. He was traveled, polished, rich, attractive, conciliatory, intensely patriotic, yet not unwilling to follow official instructions; his ill-success was part of the political misfortunes of that time.

He died at the house of one of his married daughters in England, from a stroke of apoplexy, May 29, 1877, and was buried with his wife in Kensal Green Cemetery, just outside of London, Dean Stanley reading the service to a notable gathering, including John Bright, the Duke of Argyll, Froude, Thomas Hughes, Lord Houghton, Lecky, the ministers of the Netherlands and Belgium, and others. His daughters all married and remained in England.

[*John Lothrop Motley. A Memoir* (1879), by his friend O. W. Holmes, an excellent memoir based on personal knowledge and his correspondence; *The Correspondence of John Lothrop Motley* (2 vols., 1889), ed. by G. W. Curtis; *John Lothrop Motley and His Family. Further Letters and Records* (1910), ed. by his daughter Susan St John Mildmay and Herbert St John; Ruth Putnam, "Prescott and Motley," *Cambridge Hist. of Am. Literature*, II (1918), pp. 131–47; bibliography of his works, *Ibid.*, pp. 501–03; a study of his last diplomatic mission in Beckles Wilson, *America's Ambassadors to England, 1785–1929* (1929); letters to the secretary of state in Dept. of State, Washington; obituary in *Boston Evening Transcript*, May 30, 31, 1877; memorials in *Proc. Mass. Hist. Soc.*, XV (1878); *The Writings of John Lothrop Motley* (17 vols., 1900).]   E. P. C.

MOTT, GERSHOM (Apr. 7, 1822–Nov. 29, 1884), Union soldier, was born at Lamberton, now part of Trenton, N. J., the youngest of five children of Gershom and Phoebe Rose (Scudder) Mott. He received schooling at Trenton Academy until he was fourteen years old, when he became a clerk in a drygoods store in New York. On Apr. 23, 1847, he received appointment as second lieutenant, 10th United States Infantry, and was presented a sword by citizens of Trenton. He served throughout the Mexican War without distinguishing incident. On Aug. 8, 1849, he married Elizabeth, daughter of John E. Smith of Trenton, by whom he had one child.

Following his discharge from the army, he served as collector of the port, Lamberton, N. J., until his appointment in 1850 to a position with the Bordentown, Delaware & Raritan Canal Company. In 1855 he became teller of the Bordentown Banking Company, continuing in that position until the outbreak of the Civil War.

His military career was one of promotions earned by distinguished service. In August 1861 he was appointed lieutenant-colonel of the 5th New Jersey Volunteers, and remained with that regiment until his promotion to colonel of the 6th New Jersey Volunteers, May 7, 1862, for achievement at the battle of Williamsburg. His active service was with the Army of the Potomac. His regiment was in support during the Seven Days' battles, but saw action at the second battle of Bull Run, where Mott was wounded. He was promoted brigadier-general of volunteers Sept. 7, 1862, and assigned to command a brigade of Hooker's Center Grand Division, which operated against Lee. He was wounded again at the battle of Chancellorsville in May 1863. His brigade took part in the operations of the summer and fall of 1863 against Lee, being present during the Mine Run Campaign in Meade's attempt to surprise Lee on the Rapidan, and operated from the Rapidan to the James in the winter and spring of 1864. During the battles of the Wilderness and at Spotsylvania Court House in May and June 1864, he earned special recognition. At the latter, he was particularly selected to command the 4th Division and restore its fighting efficiency after casualties and hardships had so lowered its morale that its officers could not control the men. In this task he succeeded admirably. As a division commander on July 30, 1864, he personally led his 3rd Division in making important gains at the crater of Petersburg. Appointed brevet major-general of volunteers on Aug. 1, for distinguished services, he continued with his division through the Richmond campaign until its completion. In May 1865, he was appointed major-general of volunteers and ordered to Washington for duty, serving there until discharged on Feb. 20, 1866.

Although appointed colonel of the 33rd United States Infantry in 1868, he declined the appointment, wishing to reënter civil life. His civilian pursuits included appointments as paymaster of the Camden & Amboy Railroad in 1866; treasurer of the state of New Jersey, 1875; keeper of the state prison, 1876–81; member of the Riparian Commission of New Jersey from 1882 until his death. He was a member of the iron-foundry firm of Thompson & Mott,

1873–76, and was a director of the Bordentown Banking Company. From 1873 until his death he was major-general, commanding the New Jersey National Guard. His memory was publicly honored at Trenton, N. J., in 1896, when the Mott School was named after him.

[*Colls. N. J. Hist. Soc.*, vol. IX (1916); E. M. Woodward and J. F. Hageman, *Hist. of Burlington and Mercer Counties, N. J.* (1883); *Record of Officers and Men of N. J. in the Civil War* (2 vols., 1876); F. B. Heitman, *Hist. Reg. and Dict. U. S. Army* (1903); *The Soc. of the Cincinnati in the State of N. J.* (1898); *Report of the Adj. Gen. of the State of N. J., 1906* (1907); *Boyd's N. J. State Directory*, 1874; *War of the Rebellion: Official Records* (Army); *N. Y. Geneal. and Biog. Record*, Apr. 1894; *N. Y. Times,* Nov. 30, 1884.]
D. Y.

MOTT, JAMES (June 20, 1788–Jan. 26, 1868), reformer, abolitionist, was born in North Hempstead, Long Island, N. Y., the son of Adam and Anne (Mott) Mott, through both of whom he inherited the blood of a seventeenth-century English emigrant, Adam Mott, and of a long line of Quaker ancestors. His father was a farmer and miller. Both parents were worthy people, moderately strict in following the principles of their religion, but they appear to have influenced the intellectual and moral development of their son less than did his mother's father, also named James Mott, a man of unusual intelligence and culture, interested in the advancement of education and in the movements for temperance and abolition. The boy received his education chiefly in the Friends' boarding school at Nine Partners, about fifteen miles from Poughkeepsie, N. Y., where he was a student for ten years and assistant and teacher for two years. There he met Lucretia Coffin and on Apr. 10, 1811, the two were married. In the spring of 1810 he had gone to Philadelphia, where he became a partner of Lucretia's father in the manufacture and sale of cut nails. When the hard times following the War of 1812 brought reverses he tried various business positions in an effort to make an adequate living for his family but met with little success. About 1822 he went into the commission business in Philadelphia, dealing especially in cotton.

He prospered in this enterprise but eight years later gave it up, for he had reached the decision that it was wrong to have even such an indirect part in slavery, since cotton was produced by slave labor. Though the step meant a serious financial loss at first, he was able to turn to the wool commission business, from which he retired in 1852 with a fair competence. In deciding that indirect participation in slavery was wrong he was influenced by the teachings of Elias Hicks, the leader of the liberal movement

in the Society of Friends, with whose theological views he also sympathized. After the separation in the Society in 1827 the Motts aligned themselves with the Hicksite group of Friends. During these years of spiritual and moral upheaval they became very active against slavery, at the time defended by many Quakers, and for these activities as well as for their religious heterodoxy were the objects of bitter attack. In 1833 both were present at the Philadelphia convention that founded the American Anti-Slavery Society, and James Mott was a member. Both he and his wife were delegates to the world anti-slavery convention held in London in 1840, and on his return he published his experiences in a little book called *Three Months in Great Britain* (1841). After the passage of the fugitive-slave law of 1850, the Mott home in Philadelphia became a refuge for runaway negro bondmen.

He took an advanced attitude, rare for the period, toward the position of women and early spoke in favor of giving them additional recognition in the Society of Friends. Fully appreciating his wife's superior abilities as a public speaker, he accompanied her on extensive preaching and lecturing tours, thus saving her from the criticism to which, as a woman, she would have been liable at that time. When, under the lead of Lucretia Mott, Elizabeth Cady Stanton, and a few other women, the first woman's rights convention was held at Seneca Falls, N. Y., in 1848, he presided over some of the sessions. His ability to express ideas in writing, his sympathy, and his judgment were potent factors in the development of his wife's reputation and usefulness. In 1857 the Motts gave up their large house in Philadelphia and moved to a little farm, called "Roadside," eight miles out of town on the old York road, but he continued his activity in the anti-slavery cause until emancipation was achieved. During the last few years of his life he worked insistently in the interest of better educational facilities for young people of the Society of Friends, and partly as a result of his efforts Swarthmore College was founded in 1864. Four years later, while visiting a daughter in Brooklyn, N. Y., he died from an attack of pneumonia.

[*James and Lucretia Mott: Life and Letters*, ed. by A. D. Hallowell (1884); *Three Months in Great Britain*, ante; T. C. Cornell, *Adam and Anne Mott* (1890); *N. Y. Tribune*, Jan. 27, 1868.]
M. W. W.

MOTT, LUCRETIA COFFIN (Jan. 3, 1793–Nov. 11, 1880), reformer and preacher of the Society of Friends, was born on the island of Nantucket, the descendant of Tristram Coffin who emigrated from Devonshire, England, and became one of the original purchasers of the island. She was the second cousin of Isaac and John Coffin [*qq.v.*]. Her parents were Quakers, as were most of her forebears for some generations. Her mother, Anna Folger, a descendant of Peter Folger [*q.v.*], was an energetic, capable, conservative woman whose family had stood firmly on the British side during the Revolution. Thomas Coffin, her father, appears to have been of a milder, more democratic bent. During her early childhood he was a ship's captain who voyaged to China, but about 1803 he gave up the sea and took his wife and six children to Boston, where he engaged in business. This journey, when Lucretia was eleven years old, was her first trip to the "continent," as the islanders called the mainland. In Boston she was sent to the public school for a time because her father thought his children ought to acquire democratic sympathies, but at the age of thirteen she entered the Friends' boarding school at Nine Partners near Poughkeepsie, N. Y. There she spent almost two years in study and two more as assistant and teacher in the girls' section before she returned to her father's home, now removed to Philadelphia. Shortly afterward a fellow pupil and teacher at Nine Partners, James Mott [*q.v.*], joined her father in business and on Apr. 10, 1811, she was married to him. They had six children, of whom five lived to adult life.

The death of an infant son in 1817 gave her thoughts a decidedly religious turn. The next year she began to speak in meeting and soon showed such marked gifts that she was made an "acknowledged minister" of the Society. But her views were so liberal as, before long, to excite some criticism. She sympathized with Elias Hicks, whose teachings brought about a controversy in the Society of Friends early in the 1820's, and after the separation and reorganization in the Society she, like her husband, aligned herself with the liberal or Hicksite group and remained thereafter a member of it. She became known as one of the most eloquent preachers in Philadelphia and traveled extensively to speak at Quaker meetings in different parts of the country. With William Penn she felt that "men are to be judged by their likeness to Christ, rather than by their notions of Christ" (Hallowell, *post,* p. 92) and consequently in her religious discourses she emphasized righteousness and ignored technical theology. Many of her sermons and addresses were concerned directly with reform subjects, especially temperance, peace, woman's rights, and antislavery.

Her most notable work was connected with the question of woman's rights and antislavery. Her interest in woman's wrongs and woman's rights began at Nine Partners school, where, merely because of her sex, she was paid but half as much salary as were the men doing the same work. In the years that followed she occasionally spoke in public on the unjust status of women. Her interest in the subject was further roused by the refusal of the world anti-slavery convention held in London in 1840 officially to recognize herself and a number of other women who were delegates from the United States. One result of this rebuff was the first woman's rights convention, held on July 19 and 20, 1848, in the Wesleyan Methodist Church at Seneca Falls, N. Y., at which was formally launched the woman's rights movement in the United States. The chief promoters of the gathering were herself and Elizabeth Cady Stanton [*q.v.*]. Her greatest interest, however, was the abolition of slavery, to the importance of which Elias Hicks first roused her. When she first began to speak against it, slavery was defended by many Friends, and, consequently, her activities led to persistent but futile efforts to depose her from the ministry and to drop her from the Society. She attended the convention that met in Philadelphia in 1833 and organized the American Anti-Slavery Society. Immediately afterward she helped form the Philadelphia female anti-slavery society, of which she was president during most of its existence. At the anti-slavery gathering of 1840 in London she made her influence felt, in spite of her failure to be recognized as a delegate, and she was referred to as the lioness of the convention. Following the passage of the new fugitive-slave law, she and her husband gave much attention to the protection of runaway bondmen, to whom the Mott home was an asylum.

In 1857 the family moved from Philadelphia to a quiet farm place called "Roadside" near the city, but she kept up her interest in preaching and in various reform movements, especially in activities for improving the condition of the negro. Her last public address was made in May 1880 at the Philadelphia yearly meeting of the Society of Friends. She was sprightly, impulsive, cheerful, and energetic, and, though very fond of approbation, showed firmness and courage in what she believed to be right. In her busy life she found time to be a good cook, was a careful housekeeper equal to the many emergencies incident to a growing family, and was able to manage a large and hospitable household with a grace to be envied by many women of lesser attainment in the world of affairs.

[*James and Lucretia Mott: Life and Letters,* ed. by A. D. Hallowell (1884); *Hist. of Woman Suffrage,* ed. by E. C. Stanton (6 vols., 1881–1922), esp. sketch in vol. I; T. C. Cornell, *Adam and Anne Mott* (1890); *N. Y. Tribune,* Nov. 12, 1880.]   M. W. W.

MOTT, VALENTINE (Aug. 20, 1785–Apr. 26, 1865), surgeon, was born in Glen Cove, Long Island, the son of Henry and Jane (Way) Mott and a descendant of Adam Mott, an English Quaker who emigrated to America about the middle of the seventeenth century. Henry Mott was a physician, and at the age of nineteen his son entered the office of a kinsman, Dr. Valentine Seaman, a surgeon to the New York Hospital, to study medicine. Here he remained until 1807, meanwhile obtaining his medical degree in 1806 from the Medical Department of Columbia College. During these undergraduate years he became a devoted pupil of Dr. Wright Post, the professor of surgery and New York's ranking surgeon. In 1807 he went to London for post-graduate instruction. He was a pupil of Astley Cooper in surgery and surgical anatomy and assisted him in numerous operations, but studied also under other London surgeons and later in Edinburgh.

Returning to New York in 1809, he opened an office and within a few months began to give a private course of lectures and demonstrations on surgery in the anatomical rooms of Columbia College. He was appointed professor of surgery here in 1811 and retained his chair when, in 1813, the Columbia medical school merged with the College of Physicians and Surgeons. Here he continued until 1826, when with other members of the faculty he resigned to found the short-lived Rutgers Medical College, under the leadership of David Hosack and S. L. Mitchill [*qq.v.*]. This institution closed in 1830, and Mott resumed his old chair in the College of Physicians and Surgeons, but resigned it again in 1835 because of ill health. He spent the next six years abroad, visiting not only Europe but Asia and Africa as well, and on his return assisted in founding the medical department of the University of the City of New York, where he became professor of surgery and surgical anatomy. Resigning this post in 1850 he again visited Europe, and upon his return rejoined the faculty of the College of Physicians and Surgeons. Although his nominal status was that of professor emeritus, he was active in teaching up to the time of his death.

Very early in his career Mott became known as a bold and original surgeon, and a few daring operations gave him a world-wide reputation. In 1818 he was the first to tie the innominate artery with the object of preventing death from a subclavian aneurism. This operation was a technical success, the patient living for three weeks, but his death at the end of the period was charged up to an error in placing the ligature. Mott at once reported the case in a series of medical and surgical reports which appeared during the years 1818–20. In 1827 he successfully tied the common iliac artery for an aneurism of the external iliac, and the patient survived (*American Journal of the Medical Sciences,* vol. XIV, 1827). He was one of the first to perform a successful amputation at the hip joint, and to excise the jaw for necrosis, and was a pioneer in surgery of the veins, which he resected and sutured, chiefly in the course of major operations. During his career he performed nearly a thousand amputations, operated 150 times for stone in the bladder, and ligated forty large arteries. According to his former teacher, Sir Astley Cooper, he performed more major operations than any surgeon in history, up to his time. So great was his reputation that when living in Europe he was summoned to operate on the Sultan of Turkey. After the introduction of surgical anaesthesia (1846), he soon became an authority on the subject, and during the Civil War prepared by request of the Sanitary Commission a report entitled *Pain and Anaesthetics* (1862). Like many of the pre-anesthetic surgeons he was an extremely rapid and skilful operator and was ambidextrous.

He wrote no major work, and it is stated that he had a repugnance to authorship, although he published some twenty-five medical papers, including eulogies on his friends Wright Post, John Revere, and John W. Francis, and supervised the publication of *New Elements of Operative Surgery* (3 vols., 1847), translated by P. S. Townsend from the French of A. A. L. M. Velpeau, which he augmented with notes and observations. On his return from his six-year sojourn in the Old World, he published *Travels in Europe and the East* (1842). He was co-editor of the *Medical Magazine,* 1814–15, and of the *Medical and Surgical Reporter,* 1818–20, but after that period showed little interest in medical journalism. He assembled a library which he bequeathed to the medical profession, and also a surgical and a pathological museum which were ultimately merged with larger units. During his entire active life and for many years after his death his reputation was of the highest as a surgeon, a progressive member of the medical profession, a citizen, and a man. He was brilliant, free from any erratic quality, and without any of the reactionary element so often encountered in men who have become famous. In 1819 he married Louisa Dunmore Mums, by whom he had nine children. After his death, she erected a building to house the Mott Memorial Library. He died in New York City after a very brief illness, having retained his surgical deftness and much of his physical vigor until within a few days of the end.

[S. D. Gross, *Memoir of Valentine Mott* (1868); A. C. Post, *Eulogy on the Late Valentine Mott* (1866); S. W. Francis, *Memoir of Valentine Mott* (1865); G. S. Bedford, in *Trans. Medic. Soc. of the State of N. Y.*, 1866; *Boston Medic. and Surgic. Jour.*, Dec. 11, 1850; *Medic. and Surgic. Reporter*, May 21, 28, 1864; *Lancet* (London), May 20, 1865; *Pacific Medic. and Surgic. Jour.*, Oct. 1865; *Annali universali di medicina* (Milano), Feb. 1868; *Bull. N. Y. Acad. of Medicine*, Aug. 1925.]   E. P.

MOULTON, ELLEN LOUISE CHANDLER (Apr. 10, 1835–Aug. 10, 1908), writer of verse and juvenile stories, daughter of Lucius Lemuel and Louisa Rebecca (Clark) Chandler, was born in Pomfret, Conn. She attended the school of the Rev. Roswell Park there and then went for a year to Emma Willard's Female Seminary at Troy, N. Y. Her parents were rigid Calvinists and her upbringing, from which all frivolity was excluded, may have been responsible for the strain of melancholy in her mature personality. One of her Pomfret schoolmates was James McNeill Whistler, who gave her one of his juvenile paintings, which she always preserved. She later knew him well in London. When she was only fifteen, her writing began to find a magazine market and her first volume, *This, That, and the Other*, a miscellaneous collection, was published in 1854. On Aug. 27, 1855, a few weeks after leaving school, she was married to William U. Moulton, a Boston journalist and publisher, who died Feb. 19, 1898. After her marriage she resided in Boston, where her Friday salon was frequented by artists, musicians, and writers, among them Lowell, Whittier, Longfellow, and Holmes. From 1876 on, she spent summers and autumns in Europe and came to be quite at home in London, where she numbered among her friends Monckton Milnes (Lord Houghton), Browning, Carlyle, Holman Hunt, Madox Brown, Burne-Jones, the Rossettis, William Morris, Swinburne, Watts-Dunton, Pater, the Meynells, Hardy, and Meredith.

Though devoted to her only child, a daughter, she was not domestic in her tastes and found her happiness in her writing and in friends whose pursuits were similar to her own. She wrote for many newspapers and magazines. From 1870 to 1876 she was Boston literary correspondent for the *New York Tribune*, and from 1886 to 1892 contributed a weekly letter on books to the *Boston Sunday Herald*. Her published volumes include several books of bed-time stories for children and some travel reminiscences, of which the best known, perhaps, is *Lazy Tours in Spain and Elsewhere* (1896). In *The Poems and Sonnets of Louise Chandler Moulton* (1909), published in the year after her death, are collected many of her verses which had appeared in earlier publications. She edited, with biographies, *A Last Harvest* (1891) and *The Collected Poems of Philip Bourke Marston* (1893), by the blind poet Marston, and *Arthur O'Shaughnessy, His Life and His Work, with Selections from His Poems* (1894). For *Recent English Dramatists* (1901) she wrote the life of Stephen Phillips.

Her place in American literature she achieved through her poetry, which is intensely personal. Lady Wilde, mother of Oscar Wilde, once said to her: "I have read your poems, but they deal with the sorrows and emotions of one individual; they have naught in them of the passion of the world" (Rittenhouse, *post*, p. 606). Though there is truth in the statement, some of her poetry escapes this judgment. It is subjective, often melancholy, and burdened with a sense of the fleeting quality of all happiness. It reveals an unfulfilled longing for the ideal in life and love, and a reaching out for religious belief in the midst of doubts. It is essentially the expression of a woman's feeling, and in form, it has beauty, fancy, and melody. Her sonnets are her best work and have been highly praised. She died in Boston, after a long illness from Bright's disease. During the last year of her life she carried on a correspondence with Clara Louise Burnham, through whose instrumentality she endeavored to find help in the teachings of Christian Science.

[See: Harriet Prescott Spofford, biographical introduction to *The Poems and Sonnets of Louise Chandler Moulton* (1909); Lilian Whiting, *Louise Chandler Moulton, Poet and Friend* (1910); *Who's Who in America*, 1908–09; Frances E. Willard and Mary A. Livermore, *Am. Women* (1897), vol. II; A. F. Johnson, "The Poetry of Louise Chandler Moulton," *Poet-Lore*, winter 1908; Jessie B. Rittenhouse, "Louise Chandler Moulton and her London Friendships," *Bookman*, Feb. 1909; obituaries in the *Boston Herald*, Aug. 11, 1908, and *Boston Evening Transcript*, Aug. 10, 1908, and an appreciation by T. W. Higginson in the *Transcript* for Aug. 12, 1908. Mrs. Moulton's library was presented to the Boston Pub. Lib.; the bulk of her correspondence, classified by Arlo Bates, went to the Lib. of Cong., and a considerable collection of letters and original manuscripts of her poetry and fiction was given to the American Antiquarian Soc., Worcester, Mass.]   S. G. B.

MOULTON, RICHARD GREEN (May 5, 1849–Aug. 15, 1924), college professor, lecturer, and author, was born in Preston, England, the sixth child of Rev. James Egan Moulton, a Wesleyan Methodist minister, and Catherine

(Fiddian) Moulton. When he was six years old his mother died, and he was brought up by a step-mother, a woman of Huguenot descent who had been reared in France, and to whom, he felt later, he owed much. He attended schools at Northampton and Bath, and in 1869 received the degree of A.B. from London University, and in 1874, from Christ College, Cambridge. Just at this time the university extension movement was developing, and Cambridge was a center of its influence. Soon after his graduation young Moulton became one of its most enthusiastic representatives, giving hundreds of lectures. In 1890 he visited America, where he also had immediate success as a lecturer and shared in the organization of the American Society for the Extension of University Teaching. In 1892 he became the professor of literature (in English) at the newly organized University of Chicago, at first dividing his time between university lectures and university extension work. In 1901 his title was changed to professor of literary theory and interpretation, and he became the head of the department of general literature. On Aug. 13, 1896, he married Alice Maud Cole. Retired from his professorship in July 1919 because of having reached the age limit, he returned to England, where he lived until his death, five years later, at Hallauleigh, Tunbridge Wells.

Moulton was an evangelist in the field of literature. By lecture and by published volume he sought to interest all classes of persons in understanding literature as an interpretation of life and as a source of spiritual culture. He felt that an understanding of the forms of different literatures would disclose a universal philosophy of life. His own interest lay chiefly in Shakespeare, ancient classical drama, and the Bible. The unity which he found in these various fields, each the object of technical study on the part of others, was a group of principles which governed a "world literature."

His personality was forcible and unique. He was gifted as a musician; had a memory which enabled him to recite all of the masterpieces which he expounded; and was capable of a dramatic delivery which few if any lecturers of his time could equal. To him form was an important element in the interpretation of literature, but literature to him was much more than form. His early writings dealt with Shakespeare and the classical drama, but throughout his life he emphasized the literary study of the Bible. Probably his most significant work was *The Modern Reader's Bible* (21 vols., 1896–98; one-volume edition, 1907). With a stimulating ingenuity, he so analyzed and printed the text as to enable the

reader, even though unacquainted with the original languages, to appreciate the dramatic quality of the Biblical material. Technical Biblical scholarship has not altogether accepted his ideas or methods, but the wide circulation of this work shows that, as in his lectures and university work, he popularized literature as an aid to culture, and stimulated interest in an intelligent reading of the Bible as an instrument of culture rather than as a quarry for systems of theology. Among his other publications were *Shakespeare as a Dramatic Artist* (1885); *Shakespeare as a Dramatic Thinker* (1907); *The Ancient Classical Drama* (1890); *The Literary Study of the Bible* (1895); *World Literature and Its Place in General Culture* (1911); *The Modern Study of Literature* (copr. 1915).

[W. F. Moulton, *Richard Green Moulton* (1926); *Biog. Reg. of Christ's Coll.*, vol. II (1913); *Who's Who in America*, 1918–19; *Univ. Record* (Univ. of Chicago), Oct. 1924; *Times* (London), Aug. 16, 1924.]

S. M—s.

MOULTRIE, JOHN (Jan. 18, 1729–Mar. 19, 1798), physician, lieutenant-governor of East Florida, Loyalist, was the eldest of six sons of Dr. John Moultrie, an eminent physician of Charlestown (Charleston), S. C., and descendant of an ancient Scotch family whose seat was Seafield Tower on the Firth of Forth, County Fife. The father was educated at Edinburgh and emigrated to Charlestown about 1728, where on Apr. 22 of that year he married Lucretia Cooper. The son also went to Edinburgh and was graduated M.D. in 1749, his thesis being *De Febre Maligna Biliosa Americæ.* He returned to Charlestown and on Apr. 30, 1753, was married to Dorothy Dry, widow of John Morton, by whom he had a daughter. After her death he was married on Jan. 5, 1762, to Eleanor Austin, daughter of George Austin, by whom he had four sons and two daughters. Meantime, he acquired several plantations and many slaves and became a major in the militia. In 1761 he accompanied Lieut.-Col. James Grant's expedition against the Cherokees. When Grant formed the government of East Florida in the autumn of 1764 he appointed Moultrie and his brother James, then acting attorney-general of South Carolina, members of his council. The latter was also made chief justice, but died on Aug. 6, 1765. For James's children John Moultrie took up grants of land totaling some three thousand acres and for himself others amounting to more than fourteen thousand. Among the latter was his residential plantation, "Bella Vista," four miles south of St. Augustine, where his artificers erected a large stone mansion and numerous other buildings, laid out a park and garden, and planted a great number of fruit trees of various kinds.

Grant was in poor health and sailed for England on leave early in May 1771, having recommended Moultrie, the president of the council, for lieutenant-governor. A few days later thirty inhabitants presented an address congratulating Moultrie, complaining of the decline of population in the province, and calling for a legislative assembly. Inaugurated in August, he sold his plantations near Charlestown, and brought eighty more slaves to Florida. Soon differences arose between Moultrie and two members of his council, Chief Justice William Drayton and Dr. Andrew Turnbull [qq.v.]. The two members resigned their seats but Drayton was soon restored by the King, only to be suspended by Moultrie for "obstructing public business." Both antagonists sent their complaints to Lord Dartmouth, who in a few weeks communicated notice of the appointment of Col. Patrick Tonyn as governor. Otherwise Moultrie was occupied with locating new roads, building a state house, completing St. Peter's church, and remodeling the Spanish bishop's house for public offices. Retaining his post after Tonyn's arrival, Mar. 1, 1774, he prejudiced his successor against the Drayton-Turnbull faction and obtained from him many grants of land. With the outbreak of the Revolution, which cut off supplies from the neighboring colonies, Moultrie induced his fellow-planters to raise more provisions. At the end of the war he shipped his slaves to the Bahamas, sold his live stock and effects, and in July 1784, sailed with his family for England, where they became dependent upon his wife's life annuity of £500. In 1787 he was awarded £4,479 11s. of his claim of £9,432 for losses. He seems to have passed his closing years obscurely in Oxfordshire and in Shropshire, where, in St. Andrews Parish, in Shifnal, he was buried. Three of his brothers, Alexander, Thomas, and William [q.v.], fought in the Continental Army.

[W. H. Siebert, *Loyalists in East Fla., 1774 to 1785* (1929), vol. II; *S. C. Hist. and Geneal. Mag.*, Oct. 1904, Apr. 1924; Colonial Office Papers, 5/540, 5/545, 5/552, 5/553, 5/562, 5/563; *S. C. Gazette*, June 5, 1755, April 1, 1761, Aug. 25–Oct. 1, 1764, Aug. 3–10, 1765, Apr. 7, May 9, 23, 30, Oct. 24, 31, 1771; manuscript Minutes of the Council of East Fla., Aug. 7, 1771, to July 6, 1772, July 20, Aug. 2, 20, 1773; Carita Doggett, *Dr. Andrew Turnbull and the New Smyrna Colony of Fla.* (1919); *Gentleman's Mag.*, Mar. 1798.]
W. H. S—t.

MOULTRIE, WILLIAM (Nov. 23/Dec. 4, 1730–Sept. 27, 1805), Revolutionary general, governor of South Carolina, was born in Charlestown (Charleston), S. C., the son of Dr. John and Lucretia (Cooper) Moultrie, and the brother of John Moultrie [q.v.]. He was married on Dec. 10, 1749, to Elizabeth Damaris de St. Julien. On Oct. 10, 1779, he was married to Hannah (Motte) Lynch, the daughter of Jacob Motte and widow of Thomas Lynch. By his first marriage and by purchase he acquired a large estate in St. John's Berkeley, and he made his home there. It was perhaps the weight of his property that sent him, a month after he became of age, to the House of Commons where for eight years he played an inconspicuous part. But as a captain in the provincial regiment during the Cherokee War he found his rôle, and during ten more years of almost continuous service in the Assembly, he became a recognized leader in the military affairs of the province. From 1775 to 1780 he was member, successively, of the two provincial congresses, and of the legislative council and Senate, but these duties were incidental, for the first Congress had elected him colonel of the 2nd Regiment. The fort on Sullivan's Island, which guarded one of the entrances to the harbor, was a sixteen-foot wall of sand held in place by palmetto logs. Here on June 28, 1776, with four hundred men and thirty-one guns, Moultrie received the attack of the British fleet. His courage and judgment were vindicated, though his preparations for the battle offered some ground for the criticism that he was too easy-going and neglected his opportunities, a criticism that followed later incidents in his career. The next September his regiment was taken over by Congress, and Moultrie shortly afterward was promoted to brigadier-general in the Continental service. On the fall of Savannah, in December 1778, he was sent to the southwest part of the state, and though subject to Lincoln's orders, was on detached command. In February he defeated a force of the enemy at Beaufort. In May, when the British commander took advantage of Lincoln's invasion of Georgia to march on Charlestown, Moultrie saved the city by a rapid and skilful retreat, and by a determined stand against surrender. In May 1780 he was captured with the garrison of Charlestown and was quartered for nearly two years with other Continental officers who were held as prisoners on parole at Haddrell's Point, opposite the town. His own moderation and his Loyalist connections were responsible for an attempt of the British to win him over to their cause. His reply was courteous but resolute. In February 1782 he was exchanged and served to the end of the war, being made major-general in October 1782.

In 1783 Moultrie sat in the state House of Representatives, the next year was elected lieutenant-governor, and in February 1785 was made governor. The violent political divisions in the state made the military hero an ideal choice, and his good sense and experience enabled him to serve successfully. He urged the reëstablishment of the state's credit, the better organization of the militia, and the improvement of internal navigation. At the end of his term in 1787 he was elected from his parish to the Senate, and also represented the same district in the convention which ratified the Federal Constitution. In 1791 he resigned from the Senate but a year later was again elected for a two-year term as governor. After this he retired to private life. He suffered heavy losses during the Revolution, and his fortune further declined afterward. He continued, however, high in public esteem, and was president of the state Society of the Cincinnati from its organization to his death.

[Moultrie's *Memoirs of the Am. Revolution* (2 vols., 1802), composed largely of his own correspondence, is the chief source for his campaigns and is of great value for the history of the Revolution in South Carolina and Georgia. His political career must be traced from the manuscript journals of the legislative bodies of the state. Other sources include: *S. C. Hist. and Geneal. Mag.*, Oct. 1904, Apr. 1928; *Reg. of St. Philip's Parish, . . . 1754–1810* (1927), ed. by D. E. Huger Smith and A. S. Salley, Jr.; Edward McCrady, *The Hist. of S. C. in the Revolution* (2 vols., 1901–02); Wm. Hollinshed, *A Discourse Commemorative of the Late Maj.-Gen. Wm. Moultrie* (1805); S. C. Soc. of the Cincinnati, *Remarks of Wilmot G. De Saussure, . . . 4th July, 1884* (n.d.).]   R. L. M.

MOUNT, WILLIAM SIDNEY (Nov. 26, 1807–Nov. 19, 1868), painter, was born at Setauket, Long Island, N. Y., one of the five children of Thomas Shepard and Julia (Hawkins) Mount. His father, a farmer, died when William was seven years old, and the family removed to the Hawkins homestead at Stony Brook, near Setauket. "To the age of 17," Mount later told William Dunlap, "I was a hard working farmer's boy" (*post*, vol. III, p. 263). An elder brother, Henry S. Mount, had established himself as a sign-painter in New York, and in 1824 William became his apprentice. At about the same time another brother, Shepard A. Mount, also became an apprentice and all three brothers were ambitious to qualify as artist painters, and all eventually attained membership in the National Academy of Design. William, while still painting signs, "eagerly sought and examined pictures" (Dunlap, III, 263). He greatly admired Benjamin West, whose "Madness of Lear" and "Ophelia" he studied attentively. In 1826 he entered the Academy as a student and a year later, his health affected by overwork, he returned to Setauket. Here he painted three canvases that were exhibited: a self-portrait and two large compositions—"Christ Raising the Daughter of Jairus" and "Saul and the Witch of Endor."

In 1829 he was again in New York, eager to paint portraits. An amusing legend of the studios had it that Luman Reed, a wealthy art collector whose paintings afterward went to the New York Historical Society, bought Mount's first exhibited work for $1,000, and that the young painter, who hardly knew that so much money existed, planned to live on it for the rest of his life at Stony Brook. T. S. Cummings, however, the Academy's annalist, discredits this story by insisting that Mount was "by no means so ridiculous a person as these statements would make him appear to be" (*post*, p. 141). His first Academy picture was bought, Cummings contends, by a Mr. Kemble and not by Luman Reed. Mount acquired associate membership in the Academy in 1832; full membership a year later. His full-length portrait of Bishop Onderdonk in the 1833 exhibition "elicited a universal burst of applause" (Dunlap, III, 263). Throughout his career he was popular, "endeared," as said a minute of the Academy's council, passed Nov. 30, 1868, "by his frank, cheerful and manly character, by the wit and humor that brightened his social hours."

Love of the country led Mount to spend much of his time at Setauket where he made the studies for his popular genre pictures, such as "Raffling for the Goose," now in the Metropolitan Museum of Art, New York; "The Long Story," at the Corcoran Gallery of Art, Washington; "Coming to the Point," New York Public Library; and "The Truant Gamblers," "The Fortune Teller," and "Bargaining for a Horse," New York Historical Society. Among his many portraits were those of Gen. Jeremiah Johnson, mayor, at the Brooklyn City Hall; Daniel Webster; the Rev. Zachariah Green; Selah B. Strong; Robert Schenck; and Benjamin F. Thompson, historian of Long Island. His likeness of the last named, a former neighbor at Setauket, is reproduced as a frontispiece in Thompson's *History of Long Island*. About 1859 Mount constructed a portable studio, on wheels, which greatly interested his fellow artists. In his last ten years he painted but little as his health steadily declined. He never married. He can hardly be said to have attained great distinction but his portraits and figure pieces have a sturdy honesty and constructive solidity that entitle them to respect. He was represented in 1925 at the National Academy's centennial exhibition by his "Power of Music," lent by the Century Association.

[Wm. Dunlap, *A Hist. of the Rise and Progress of the Arts of Design in the U. S.* (1918), vol. III; T. S. Cummings, *Hist. Annals of the Nat. Acad. of Design* (1865); B. F. Thompson, *Hist. of Long Island* (1918), vol. I, p. xxviii, vol. IV, pp. 290, 293; *N. Y. Times*, Nov. 21, 1868; manuscript memorandum prepared for the author of this article by Clara Brewster Mount, Setauket, N. Y., great-niece of the artist.] **F. W. C.**

MOURT, GEORGE [See MORTON, GEORGE, 1585–1624].

MOUTON, ALEXANDER (Nov. 19, 1804–Feb. 12, 1885), governor of Louisiana and senator, was born on the Bayou Carencro, in Attakapas County, now Lafayette Parish, La., the son of Jean and Marie Marthe (Bordat) Mouton and the descendant of Acadian exiles on both sides of his family. He received his elementary education in the district schools of his county and later attended Georgetown College in the District of Columbia. He spoke French as his native tongue and received his instruction in the district schools altogether in that language, but during his youth he acquired a good knowledge of English, which he spoke fluently and effectively. He studied law in the offices first of Charles Antoine and later of Edward Simon of St. Martinville, La., in 1825 was admitted to the bar, and began to practise in Lafayette Parish. He soon gave up practice, however, to manage a plantation given him by his father near Vermilionville, the present town of Lafayette, La., where he became one of the more prosperous sugar planters of the state. In 1826 he was married to Zelia Rousseau, a grand-daughter of Jacques Dupre, one of the wealthiest cattle raisers in the Opelousas country and later acting-governor of Louisiana. They had four children. In the same year he was elected from Lafayette Parish to the lower house of the state legislature and served from 1829 to 1832. He was speaker in 1831 and 1832. He was named presidential elector on the Democratic ticket in the elections of 1828, 1832, and 1836. In 1836 he was again elected to the state legislature, which, in 1837, chose him to the United States Senate to fill out the unexpired term of Alexander Porter, who had resigned. At the end of that term he was re-elected and served from Jan. 12, 1837, to Mar. 1, 1842, when he resigned to campaign for the governorship of Louisiana on the Democratic ticket. While he was senator he was married in 1842, to his second wife, Emma K. Gardner, the daughter of Charles K. Gardner [q.v.]. They had six children.

He was inaugurated governor in January 1843 for a term of four years but, under the new constitution of 1845 which made some rearrangements in the terms of the state officers, he retired in February 1846. At the beginning of his administration the state was deeply in debt, but by its close most of the indebtedness had been liquidated and provision had been made for the payment of the rest by 1872. He was very active in the presidential campaign of 1844 in behalf of Polk and Dallas and contributed effectively toward carrying the state in their behalf. He was interested in the development of railroads in Louisiana and was president of the southwestern railroad convention held at New Orleans in January 1852. He was also made president in 1858 of the vigilance committee of the Attakapas country, which was organized for the purpose of ridding that part of the state of bandits and marauders. In 1856 and in 1860 he was a delegate from Louisiana to the Democratic conventions in Cincinnati and Charleston respectively. In 1861 he was a delegate to the Louisiana secession convention, served as president of that body, and voted for secession. He was subsequently a candidate for the senate of the Southern Confederacy but was defeated. During the Civil War he sustained heavy losses both in his family and in his fortune. To the end of his life he remained a picturesque type. He is said to have been the original for George W. Cable's brief description, in "Carancro" (*Century Magazine*, Jan. 1887, p. 355), of "the Acadian of the Acadians," the grandson of the Acadian widow who took refuge in Louisiana, whom the people of Louisiana made "Senator, Governor and President of the Convention."

[Alcée Fortier, *Louisiana* (1909), vol. II and *A Hist. of La.* (4 vols., 1904); W. H. Perrin, *Southwest La.*, 1891; *Biog. and Hist. Memoirs of La.*, 1892, vol. II; *Biog. Dir. Am. Cong.* (1928); *Times-Democrat* (New Orleans), Feb. 14, 1885; the spelling of the Christian name follows that printed on the form of the official certificate of appointment in the Lib. of Cong.]

E. M. V.

MOWATT, ANNA CORA OGDEN (Mar. 5, 1819–July 21, 1870), writer, actress, was the daughter of Samuel Gouverneur and Eliza (Lewis) Ogden. Her father, a New York merchant, was the son of the Rev. Uzal Ogden [q.v.]; her mother was the grand-daughter of Francis Lewis [q.v.], a signer of the Declaration of Independence. Anna Cora Ogden was born at Bordeaux, France, near which place she lived until her seventh year, when her family returned to New York. She attended private schools, but got her education mainly by extensive reading at home in French and English authors, especially Shakespeare. As a child she wrote verse, and frequently wrote, acted, and directed dramatic pieces with her brothers and sisters, taking part also in school plays. On Oct. 6, 1834, at the age of fifteen, she married James Mowatt, a well-to-do New York lawyer, and lived happily with him at Flatbush, Long Island, continuing her studies and literary efforts. Her first published work, signed "Isabel," was *Pelayo; or, The*

Cavern of Covadonga (1836)—an imitative historical verse romance in six cantos, which was followed by a sharp verse satire in its defense, *Reviewers Reviewed* (1837). Advised to take a sea voyage, because of a serious breakdown from tuberculosis, she spent fifteen months abroad, visiting London (where she saw and admired Madame Vestris at her theatre), Hamburg, Bremen, and other cities. In Paris she was greatly impressed by the impassioned acting of Rachel in her famous rôles. Here she began a short blank-verse play in five acts, finishing it after she returned to America in restored health; this was *Gulzara; or, The Persian Slave,* acted at her home, and published in the *New World,* Apr. 24, 1841.

Since her husband had lost his fortune, she determined to earn money by giving public readings of poetry and made her first appearance Oct. 28, 1841, before an enthusiastic audience at the Masonic Temple in Boston. Later she appeared in New York, but in 1842 was obliged to give up this work because of a recurrence of illness. During her convalescence, which she attributed to mesmerism, she wrote under the name of "Helen Berkley" for *Godey's Lady's Book, Graham's,* and other magazines; compiled books on etiquette, cooking, and miscellaneous subjects, and in 1842 was awarded a prize of $100 by the *New World* for a novel, "The Fortune Hunter; or, The Adventures of a Man about Town," with realistic hits at contemporary New York Society. She also published, in 1844, a life of Goethe under the pseudonym Henry C. Browning, and an abridged edition of the *Memoirs of Madame d'Arblay,* and wrote, under Frederika Bremer's influence, a two-volume domestic tale, *Evelyn,* which appeared in 1845.

Her most important imaginative work was a play entitled *Fashion; or, Life in New York,* first published in February 1850. Undertaken at the suggestion of Epes Sargent and rapidly written, it was produced at the Park Theatre in New York on Mar. 24, 1845, running for three weeks. Immediately afterward it was produced in Philadelphia, and later in other leading American cities, everywhere with notable success, and in January 1850, ran for two weeks at the Olympic Theatre, London. In 1924 it was revived at the Provincetown Playhouse, New York, in a burlesqued version arranged by Brian Hooker and Deems Taylor, with songs of the Victorian period inserted. A five-act farcical comedy, *Fashion* deals with members of a new-rich New York family and their circle who ape French manners and are unfavorably contrasted with a true-hearted prosperous farmer and his

grand-daughter. Though it has touches of lively humor and characterization and is well adapted to the stage, its effects are generally exaggerated, and its plot is conventional. The author's enthusiasm for democratic institutions appears also in *Armand, The Child of the People,* a five-act romantic pseudo-historical play of the reign of Louis XV, in prose and blank verse, first produced Sept. 27, 1847, at the Park Theatre, New York. It met with favor here, in other American cities, and also in London when Mrs. Mowatt acted in it there in January 1849. It was first published as *Armand; or, The Peer and the Peasant* (1849).

Following the production of *Fashion,* Mrs. Mowatt received flattering invitations from managers to go on the stage. She made a highly successful début as Pauline in *The Lady of Lyons* at the Park Theatre, June 13, 1845, and during the next eight years acted in most of the important American cities, with E. L. Davenport [*q.v.*], after her first season, as her leading man. Among her rôles were Juliet, Beatrice, Rosalind, Desdemona, Ariadne, Blanche in *Armand,* and Gertrude in *Fashion.* Poe, who was a severe critic of *Fashion,* joined in the general commendation of her qualities as an actress, praising her "brilliant and expressive" eyes, her "radiantly beautiful smile," her charming grace and naturalness of manner, and her singularly rich voice. She was slight in figure, with light auburn hair and prominent, distinguished features. From December 1847 to July 1851 she played with E. L. Davenport in England and was warmly received in London and other large English cities, as well as in Dublin. During this period she worked under grave difficulties owing to her husband's ill health, a serious attack of brain fever which disabled her for some months in 1850, and fresh financial reverses. In 1851 James Mowatt died in London.

Returning to America in August of that year, she appeared at Niblo's Garden, New York, and then undertook a new American tour. Again disabled by ill health, she devoted some months in 1853 to writing her *Autobiography of an Actress; or, Eight Years on the Stage* (1854), which had a large sale. It is facile and vivacious in style, idealistic in tone, and gives vivid glimpses into the life and theatre of the day. On June 3, 1854, in New York, she made her final appearance on the stage, and on June 6, married William Foushee Ritchie, editor of the *Richmond Enquirer.*

After her retirement, she published *Mimic Life; or, Before and Behind the Curtain* (1856), three romantic narratives of stage life with some realistic pages based on her own experiences; and in the same vein, *Twin Roses* (1857). Soon afterward she became active in the movement for the purchase and preservation of Mount Vernon, was secretary of the state committee organized in Richmond, and from 1858 to 1866 was vice-regent (representing Virginia) of the Mount Vernon Ladies' Association of the Union. After 1861 she lived abroad (apart from her husband, with whom, it is said, she differed over Civil War issues), mainly in Florence, writing romantic novels: *Fairy Fingers* (1865), *The Mute Singer* (1866), and *The Clergyman's Wife and Other Sketches* (1867); and occasional articles on events in Florence which appeared after her death in a volume with historical sketches entitled *Italian Life and Legends* (1870). She died in Twickenham, England.

[Autobiography and other writings mentioned above; *New World* (ed. by Park Benjamin), Jan. 22, 1842; E. A. Poe, notices in *Broadway Journal*, of Mar. 29, Apr. 5, July 19, 29, 1845, and article in *Godey's Lady's Book*, June 1846, repr. in *The Complete Works of Edgar Allan Poe*, Virginia Edition (1902), ed. by J. A. Harrison, vols. XII, XV; *Howitt's Journal*, Mar. 4, 11, 18, 1848; W. J. Clapp, Jr., *A Record of the Boston Stage* (1853); Laurence Hutton, *Curiosities of the American Stage* (1891); Laurence Hutton and Brander Matthews, *Actors and Actresses of Great Britain and the United States* (1886), vol. IV; A. H. Quinn, *A Hist. of the Am. Drama from the Beginning to the Civil War* (1923); M. J. Moses, *Representative Plays by Am. Dramatists*, 2 ser., 1815–58 (1925); R. S. Hammer, *A Daughter of Firenze* (1924); Grace King, *Mount Vernon on the Potomac* (1929); T. A. Brown, *A Hist. of the N. Y. Stage* (3 vols., 1903); W. O. Wheeler, *The Ogden Family in America* (1907); J. N. Ireland, *Records of the N. Y. Stage*, vol. II (1867); *N. Y. Times*, June 7, 1854, July 30, 1870; *N. Y. Tribune*, July 30, 1870; G. C. D. Odell, *Annals of the N. Y. Stage*, vols. V, VI (1931); information as to certain facts from Archives Municipales, Bordeaux, France; Register of Deaths, District of Brentford, England, and relatives and acquaintances; memoirs of actors of the period.]

H. M.

MOWBRAY, GEORGE MORDEY (May 5, 1814–June 21, 1891), pioneer oil refiner, inventor of explosives, was born in Brighton, England. As a youth he studied chemistry in England, France, and Germany, becoming a manufacturer of drugs in his native land. Later he joined a firm of wholesale druggists. In 1854 his health became impaired and he took a long sea voyage around South America. Landing in California, he there filled an important need as doctor, surgeon, and chemist in the gold fields. In 1858 he moved to New York and became associated with Schieffelin Brothers & Company, wholesale druggists. In the following year, however, when at Titusville, Pa., Edwin L. Drake [*q.v.*] drilled the first successful oil well and thus initiated a new industry, Mowbray was among the first to remove to the oil field. He produced the first refined oil there, and was the first to use nitroglycerin (or tri-nitro-glycerin as he preferred to call it) in the shooting of dormant wells. He obtained several patents for devices and methods relating to the production of oil.

Depression following the speculation of the period 1859–65 forced him to close his refinery in 1866, but he remained in Titusville and turned his attention to the manufacture of nitroglycerin. His advertisements in the *Scientific American*, which show him to be the only manufacturer in America offering nitroglycerin in quantity, won the interest of the Massachusetts commissioners who were building the Hoosac Tunnel and they invited him to North Adams to furnish the explosives for the work. He arrived on Oct. 29, 1868, and the next day began to build his plant on a site provided by the state. By the end of the year the plant was completed. Up to this time most of the nitric acid used in the United States was imported from abroad, but Mowbray began to make his own. He also manufactured the insulation (guttapercha) and fuses needed for the work. His manufacturing method, which was very simple, is described in full in his *Tri-nitro-glycerin* (1872), which went through three editions and was the first treatise on this subject in America. The Hoosac Tunnel, considered one of the great engineering feats of the time, was the first to show the possibilities of high explosives in tunneling.

Mowbray manufactured over a million pounds of nitroglycerin, with such care and success that he dominated the explosives market in the northeastern and central parts of the United States long after the modern type of dynamite was introduced. He supplied, without accident, the one hundred thousand pounds required for the building of the Canadian Pacific Railway in lots of twenty thousand pounds, fifty pounds to a can. For shipment by rail, cars divided into compartments were used, each can being placed in a separate compartment, padded with thick hair felt and provided with ice to keep the product in frozen condition. When the train reached Fargo, N. Dak., the cans were carried to a Red River steamboat by Indians, the only help available. Unloaded from the steamer, they were placed on two-wheeled ox-carts and hauled 110 miles to the Lake of the Woods, thence across the lake by boat, and finally carried on men's backs to the construction camps. Finding that an explosive of less shattering power would be better for some work, Mowbray developed a method of diluting nitroglycerin with finely divided scales of mica. Although all his improvements were the results of his own research, some of them were declared to infringe the Nobel patents held in the United States by the Atlantic Giant Powder Company, and, following an injunction, Mowbray gave up the manufacture of nitroglycerin.

His interest continued along related lines, however, and he did valuable work in the developing of zylonite (celluloid), serving as technical manager for the American Zylonite Company from 1881 until his death. In 1886 he turned his attention to research in ammunition and contracted with Sir Hiram Stevens Maxim [q.v.] of the Maxim-Nordenfeldt Guns and Ammunition Company of England to turn over to that concern all patents for smokeless powder that might result from his experiments. He received patents for a long series of improvements in explosives, the earliest being No. 76,499 (Apr. 7, 1868) and the last, No. 443,105 (Dec. 23, 1890). During the last year of his life he directed his experiments from his bed, one of his assistants being Hudson Maxim [q.v.]. He died in North Adams at the age of seventy-seven.

Mowbray and his wife, Annie Fade, had no children of their own, but adopted Mrs. Mowbray's five-year old orphaned nephew, who as Henry Siddons Mowbray [q.v.] became a distinguished painter. He is quoted as saying (Mowbray, post, p. 11): "There was never, to my mind, a man quite like my foster father. Strong and masterful to the world, to me he showed a surprising tenderness and affection, and never ... do I recollect an unkind word or action on his part. We became close comrades. He had a wonderful way of smoothing out youthful trouble, clearing away the unessentials, and setting forth the thing so simply that all the clouds disappeared."

[A. P. Van Gelder and Hugo Schlatter, *Hist. of the Explosives Industry in America* (1927), with portrait; Florence Millard Mowbray, *H. Siddons Mowbray* (privately printed, 1928); *Atlantic Giant Powder Co., Complainant, v. George M. Mowbray et al., Defendant; Pleading and Evidence* (1876); *Boston Transcript,* June 23, 1891.]   A. I.

MOWBRAY, HENRY SIDDONS (Aug. 5, 1858–Jan. 13, 1928), figure and mural painter, was born at Alexandria, Egypt, of English parents, John Henry and Eliza (Fade) Siddons. His father had gone from England to Egypt as the representative of an English banking house and died in 1859. The widow returned to England with her infant son and shortly determined to come to the United States. Not long after their arrival she was burned to death in Brooklyn, and the boy was adopted by his uncle and aunt, George [q.v.] and Annie (Fade) Mowbray who were then living at Titusville, Pa.

They moved from Titusville to North Adams, Mass., when the boy was about eleven years old. He was sent to the Drury Academy at North Adams from 1869 to 1878, with a brief interregnum. An appointment had been obtained for him to the United States Military Academy at West Point, but he stayed there only a short time. He returned to North Adams and then at the age of twenty went to Paris and entered the atelier of Léon Bonnat. A year after his arrival in Paris his "Young Bacchus" was hung in the Salon. In the spring of this year (1879), in company with Henry Walker, he went to Spain, spent a month in Madrid, copying the Velasquez pictures, and, after visiting Toledo, Seville, and Granada, returned to Paris, where he sold his first picture. In 1883 he exhibited at the Salon "The Etchers" and "Le Récit," both of which were sold. He remained in France eight years, spending several summers at Rablay, in Anjou. "In those impressionable years," he wrote, "I acquired an affection for France and its people that has always remained" (*H. Siddons Mowbray, post,* p. 24). Returning to the United States in 1886, he settled in New York, became an academician, a member of the Society of American Artists, and took charge of the men's life classes at the Art Students' League. One of his first patrons was Thomas B. Clarke, who bought four of his pictures, "Scheherazade," "Aladdin," "The Evening Breeze," and "The Last Favorite." On June 7, 1888, he married Helen Amelia Millard, daughter of Henry S. Millard, of North Adams, Mass. A son was born to them. His wife died on Aug. 5, 1912, and three years later he married her sister, Florence Gertrude Millard, by whom he had a son and a daughter. In 1890 he had bought a house in West Eleventh Street and converted the upper floor into a studio. There he lived until 1907 when he moved to Washington, Conn., where he passed the rest of his life.

In an undated note Mowbray wrote: "A fondness for the Italian art of the Renaissance came over me. I wanted above all things to do mural work" (*H. Siddons Mowbray,* p. 56). His first small commission came from Thomas B. Clarke in 1889. It was for an over-mantel panel for the reception room of an athletic club. In 1892 a more important opportunity was offered him: this was a series of twenty-one lunettes in the main hall of Collis P. Huntington's New York mansion, a commission which kept him busy for two years. From this time until the end of his life his desire to do mural work was fully gratified. In 1896 he painted "The Transmission of the Law," a frieze in the Appellate Court

House, New York. In 1897 he decorated the ceiling of the drawing-room in the F. W. Vanderbilt mansion at Hyde Park, N. Y. The oval central panel, ten by eighteen feet in dimensions, represents a scene from the legend of Ceres and Proserpine—Mercury bringing back the daughter for whom her mother has mourned. The color scheme is opalescent, with a play of rose pinks, blue-greens, violets, mauves, and reds. From 1900 to 1927 he was kept busy with mural painting. He collaborated with E. H. Blashfield in the work in the board-room of the Prudential Life Insurance Company at Newark, N. J. He decorated the J. P. Morgan library; Larz Anderson's house in Washington; the United States court room in the Federal Building at Cleveland, Ohio; the ceiling of the Gunn Memorial Library, Washington, Conn.; a gallery in the home of Breckenridge Long, St. Louis, Mo.; the chancel of St. John's Church, Washington, Conn.; the chancel of St. Michael's Church, Litchfield, Conn.; a triptych in a private chapel; and the pediment of the Madison Square Presbyterian Church, New York. But his most important and most brilliant work was the decoration of the library of the University Club, New York. For the purpose of studying Pinturicchio's wall paintings of the Borgia apartments in the Vatican, upon the general style of which he had decided to base this work, he went to Rome in 1902, and while there he was appointed director of the American Academy in Rome, an office which he filled acceptably through 1903–04. In 1921 President Wilson appointed him a member of the National Commission of Fine Arts. He held this office for seven years, or until his death, which occurred at his home in Washington, Conn., in 1928. After his death a very complete and impressive memorial exhibition, held by the Century Association, New York, May 6 to 29, 1928, served to confirm the most favorable estimate of his work.

[A full account of the life and work of Mowbray is given in *H. Siddons Mowbray, Mural Painter, 1858–1928* (1928), the privately printed volume issued by his wife and edited by H. F. Sherwood. Other sources are: Royal Cortissoz, article in *Scribner's Mag.*, May 1928; Pauline King, *Am. Mural Painting* (1902); Mich. State Lib., *Biog. Sketches of Am. Artists* (1924); *Am. Art Annual*, 1923–24; *N. Y. Times*, Jan. 14, 1928; *Hartford Daily Times*, Jan. 16, 1928; Mobray's first name often appears as Henry.]

W. H. D—s.

MOWER, JOSEPH ANTHONY (Aug. 22, 1827–Jan. 6, 1870), soldier, was born at Woodstock, Vt., the youngest of the five children of Nathaniel and Sophia (Holmes) Mower. When he was six years old the family moved to Lowell, Mass., where Joseph received a common-school education. A distinguishing trait of his early years was a love of reading military and naval history. In 1843 he matriculated at Norwich (Vt.) University and was a student there two years. Upon leaving he became a carpenter. When the Mexican War broke out he enlisted as a private of engineers, serving throughout the war, and being discharged July 25, 1848. On June 18, 1855, he was commissioned second lieutenant in the regular army, advancing to the grade of first lieutenant, Mar. 13, 1857, and to that of captain, Sept. 9, 1861.

Mower's combat record during the Civil War was one rarely equaled in the American army, and it is a fair deduction that had the war not ended in 1865 he would probably have attained command of an army. Within a period of two years commencing in March 1862 he was commended by his superiors in orders or official letters no less than twelve times, most of these stressing his conspicuous personal bravery, though, with the exception of Vicksburg and the final campaigns of the war under Sherman, he was not in particularly conspicuous theatres of action. His brevet commissions in the regular army were additional to more rapid promotions in the volunteer forces. These brevet commissions were: major, May 9, 1862, for gallant and meritorious service at Farmington, Miss.; lieutenant-colonel, Sept. 19, 1862, battle of Iuka, Miss., where, though forced back, his regiment camped on the field and found no enemy in the morning; colonel, May 14, 1863, for gallant and meritorious service at the capture of Jackson, Miss.; brigadier-general, Mar. 13, 1865, for gallant and meritorious conduct at the capture of Fort de Russy, La., a year previously, when he rode in on horseback ahead of his troops; major-general, Mar. 13, 1865, for gallant and meritorious conduct at the passage of the Salkehatchie, Georgia.

The above-mentioned events appear as high spots in a military career which properly commenced its period of command at his election as colonel of the 11th Missouri Volunteers, May 3, 1862, after his successful capture of New Madrid, Mo., in March. At the capture of Corinth, Mo., he discovered the dispositions of the Confederate General Lovell, and was wounded, captured, and recaptured in the course of the battle. During May 1863, his regiment planted itself on the ramparts of Vicksburg and stayed until relieved by Sherman in person. Following Vicksburg, Mower was a man marked for distinction, and was given many minor independent commands in Mississippi and northern Louisiana in preparation for his projected employment by

Sherman against Forrest. In spite of repeated efforts of Sherman, however, he was not made a major-general until Aug. 12, 1864, by which time Forrest's raids had ceased to be a danger. Ordered to join Sherman in the Nashville campaign, Mower first obeyed prior orders to accompany the expedition into Missouri against Price, where the rapid marches and maneuvering of his division were noteworthy. Upon joining Sherman in the Atlanta campaign, November 1864, he was given a division, commanding it through the march to the sea, and subsequently serving in the Carolinas, where he was given command of the XX Corps.

Mustered out as a brevet major-general in February 1866, he was reappointed in the regular army as colonel, 39th Infantry, July 28, serving as such until his transfer, as colonel, to the 25th Infantry in March 1869. At the time of his death in New Orleans he was in command of the department of Louisiana. On June 6, 1851, he married Betsey A. Bailey.

[Data on Mower's early life are in the Norman Williams Public Library, Woodstock, Vt. See also, W. L. Mower, *Mower Family Hist., A Geneal. Record of the Me. Branch* (1923); G. M. Dodge and W. A. Ellis, *Norwich Univ. 1819–1911* (1911), vol. II; F. B. Heitman, *Hist. Reg. and Dict. U. S. Army* (1903); *War of the Rebellion: Official Records (Army)*; *Am. Ann. Cyc. and Reg. of Important Events of the Year 1870* (1871); *Army and Navy Jour.*, Jan. 15, 22, Mar. 26, 1870; tribute by Gen. Sherman in *Vermont Standard* (Woodstock), Jan. 20, 1870.]   D. Y.

MOWRY, WILLIAM AUGUSTUS (Aug. 13, 1829–May 22, 1917), educator and author, was born in Uxbridge, Mass., the only son of Jonathan and Hannah (Brayton) Mowry and the descendant of Nathaniel Mowry who in 1672 was made a freeman of Providence. His parents were both members of the Society of Friends, but he became a member of the Congregational Church. Left fatherless at the age of three, he shared the life of his grandfather's farm and from the age of four attended the district school. After his thirteenth year he was self-supporting, working on farms and in mills, selling books, and teaching school. His early youth was a constant, although apparently joyous, struggle with grim necessity. Among his chief characteristics were tireless industry, cheerful common sense, originality, keen insight, and a never waning buoyancy of spirit. Terms of district school taught in Rhode Island and in Massachusetts alternated with attendance at Uxbridge Academy and at the Phillips Academy at Andover, which he entered in 1851. At the age of twenty-five he entered Brown University in the class with John Hay and worked his way through the junior year, when he broke down in health and withdrew from college, but in 1866 he received an honorary degree of A.M., and was elected to the Phi Beta Kappa society. He received an honorary Ph.D. degree from Bates College in 1882.

His comprehension of the needs of school children and teachers was gained from ample experience. After teaching boys for four years in the Providence High School and serving a period as captain in the 11th Rhode Island Volunteers during the Civil War, he opened in Providence the English and Classical School for boys, popularly known as Mowry and Goff's, and served as its principal for over twenty years. This notable school was a demonstration of the most enlightened ideas of school hygiene, equipment, methods of teaching, and discipline. There he had that contact with school problems which made him a national authority on many phases of practical pedagogy. In the teachers' institutes, which were the main source of assistance for the entire mass of public school teachers, he was a leader for over half a century, during which time he gave more than 1800 lectures to teachers in twenty-six states. For nineteen years he was executive head of the pioneer summer school for teachers, the famous Martha's Vineyard Summer Institute, which was established in 1878 and was a forerunner of the now almost universal summer schools of pedagogy. During his long career he served on Providence and Boston school boards, was superintendent of schools in Cranston, R. I., and in Salem, Mass., edited educational journals in Rhode Island and in Massachusetts, and was the author of many books. His various elementary books of history and civil government, widely used as texts, have influenced the ideas concerning citizenship of school children for several generations. He compiled several books of genealogy such as *The Descendants of Nathaniel Mowry* (1878) concerning his own ancestral line and *The Descendants of John Mowry* (1909), of a collateral line. He also published *The Uxbridge Academy* (1897), partly devoted to his own schooldays, and *Talks with my Boys* (1885), which went through several editions. His *Recollections of a New England Educator* (1908) was a review of school conditions in New England from 1838 to 1908. On Nov. 15, 1849, he married Rufina M. E. Weaver, of Slatersville, R. I., who died four months later. On Apr. 29, 1858, he married Caroline E. Aldrich of Woonsocket, R. I., who died in January 1897. They had three children.

[Biog. material in own books, *ante*; *Memories and Appreciations of Wm. Augustus Mowry*, ed. by R. M.

Brown (1918); *Hist. Cat. of Brown Univ.* (1914);
Whitman College *Pioneer,* May 1902; *Providence
Daily Journal,* May 23, 1917.]   J. L. A.

MOXHAM, ARTHUR JAMES (Sept. 19,
1854–May 16, 1931), steel manufacturer, was
born at Neath, Glamorganshire, South Wales,
the son of Egbert and Katherine (Morgan)
Moxham. His father was an architect of some
prominence who died when the boy was quite
young, and he was educated in the Clapton Orphan Asylum near London, from which he graduated in 1869 and came to America. He settled
first in Louisville, Ky., and was employed in
an iron foundry, where he learned the business
and at the same time educated himself along
general and engineering lines.

In 1878 he went to Birmingham, Ala., and
organized the Birmingham Rolling-Mill Company, planning and building the Birmingham
Rolling Mills, which he operated for several
years. About 1883 he moved to Johnstown, Pa.,
where, in partnership with Tom L. Johnson
[*q.v.*], inventor of an iron girder rail, he formed
the Johnson Company. At the start the rails
were made by the Cambria Steel Company, but
the business grew rapidly and in a few years the
Johnson Company had its own plant at Wood-
vale, just above Johnstown. This plant was
wiped out by the Johnstown Flood in 1889, but
was rebuilt in another suburb named Moxham.
The business expanded to such an extent that the
company at length controlled over ninety per
cent. of the girder-rail business of the United
States, which at that time was of very considerable volume due to the development of street
railways throughout the country. This increase
in business was largely due to Moxham's ingenuity in organization and production. The Johnson Company subsequently moved to Lorain,
Ohio, and became the Lorain Steel Company.
In 1899 Moxham was instrumental in the formation of the Illinois Steel Company through the
merging of the Lorain Steel Company and the
Minnesota Iron Company. It was later absorbed
by the United States Steel Company. Soon afterward Moxham retired from active business
for a year and took a trip around the world in
his yacht. Later, he formed a partnership with
H. M. Whitney of Boston, Mass., and went to
Sydney, Nova Scotia, where he built the Dominion Iron & Steel Company. He left there
in 1902 and became associated with T. C. du
Pont in forming the E. I. du Pont de Nemours
Powder Company, of which he was a vice-president, director, and member of the executive
committee until 1914, when he resigned to become president of the Ætna Explosives Com-

pany, which he organized and which, under his
direction, operated on a large scale to meet the
demands occasioned by the World War.

Resigning from this position in 1917, he spent
much of the later part of his life in the study of
special processes for the enhancement of ore
values. He was regarded as one of the foremost
steel experts both in the United States and
abroad. At the time of the Johnstown Flood,
he was named, by common acclaim of the citizens, chairman of the relief committee, and as
such acted as virtual dictator over the stricken
community until the authorities appointed by
the governor of Pennsylvania took charge. On
July 3, 1876, he married Helen Jilson Coleman
of Louisville, Ky., and they had three children.
He died at Great Neck, Long Island, N. Y.

[A. P. Van Gelder and Hugo Schlatter, *Hist. of the
Explosives Industry in America* (1927); D. J. Beale,
Through the Johnstown Flood (1890); *N. Y. Times*
and *N. Y. Herald Tribune,* May 17, 1931; information
as to certain facts furnished by a son, Egbert Moxham
of New York City.]   J. H. F.

MOXOM, PHILIP STAFFORD (Aug. 10,
1848–Aug. 13, 1923), clergyman, was born in
Markham, Ontario, Canada. His father, Job
Hibbard Moxom, a grenadier in the British
army, came to Canada as a member of a regiment sent out to suppress the famous Papineau
rebellion among the French-Canadians. After
peace had been restored, the elder Moxom left
the army to study for the ministry, and became
pastor first of a Methodist, and later of a Baptist church. With his wife, Anne Turner, who
had been brought to Canada from England by
her parents when three years' of age, he emigrated in 1857 to the United States, settling first
at Dement, and then at DeKalb, Ill. At the outbreak of the Civil War, the father offered his
services to the government and was promptly
commissioned a second lieutenant. Philip, only
thirteen years old, but man-grown, was also
eager to enlist. Though rejected on account
of his youth, he was permitted to go to the
front as a "captain's boy," and saw active service at Fort Donelson. Two years later, after a
period of illness at home, he was accepted as a
member of Company C, 17th Illinois Cavalry,
and served with this regiment until the end of
the conflict.

The young man now decided to become a lawyer. Supporting himself by teaching school, he
spent two years at Kalamazoo College (1866–
68), and two years more at Shurtleff College,
Alton, Ill., where he was graduated in 1870. He
then began reading law in a Kalamazoo office,
but the next year received a most unusual "call"
to the ministry. His father, pastor of a Baptist

church in Bellevue, Mich., had announced his resignation and the date of a farewell sermon. Prevented from being present on this date, he directed his son to take his place. The young man so pleased his surprised audience that they asked him to come again, and then to be their regular pastor. This experience marked the turning-point of his career. He was ordained at Bellevue on Sept. 19, 1871, and the following year he went to a Baptist church at Albion, Mich., where he remained three years. In 1875, feeling the need of a proper education, he entered the Rochester Theological Seminary, at the same time preaching each Sunday at a Baptist church in Mount Morris, N. Y. After receiving his theological degree in 1878, he entered Rochester University, and a year later was granted a bachelor's degree.

It was in his thirty-first year (1879) that Moxom began his brilliant career in the Christian ministry. A superb specimen of manhood, six feet four inches tall, graceful, forceful, eloquent, devoted, he was called to the First Baptist Church in Cleveland, Ohio. Six years later (1885), he went to the First Baptist Church in Boston, where he remained for eight years. It was during this period that he became generally known and admired as one of the most progressive and fearless preachers in the orthodox pulpit. It was at this time, also, that he found certain restrictions of the Baptist church irksome —its rigorous practice of immersion, and its exclusion of the unbaptized from the communion table. Unable to conform or be silent, he suddenly in December 1893 resigned his Boston pulpit, "not knowing where he would go." In quick succession, however, he received invitations from five different churches—a Baptist, a Presbyterian, a Congregational, a Universalist, and a Unitarian. Accepting a call to the South Congregational Church, Springfield, Mass., in March 1894, he was installed on Apr. 3, and entered upon a distinguished pastorate of twenty-one years.

He was of an ardent, enthusiastic, often impulsive temperament. In his opinions he was "strong-bitted," as he put it, and free, sometimes blunt, in their expression. In personal relations he was warm-hearted, expansive, companionable, yet frank and independent. In public, whether alone in the pulpit or mingled with others in a hall or on the street, he was a notable figure. He held his own with such contemporaries as Phillips Brooks, Minot J. Savage, George A. Gordon, Edward Everett Hale, as one of the most popular and influential preachers of his day. He was always welcome at the

colleges, and for three years (1894–97) served as university preacher at Harvard. His greatest hour, perhaps, came in 1893, at the World Parliament of Religions in Chicago, where he was selected to present to that remarkable assembly the Christian argument for immortality. His theological attitude was liberal; from the orthodox point of view, radical. He sought always the essentials of belief, and was impatient of petty refinements of doctrine or practice. An ardent patriot and active civic leader, he insisted upon identifying the church with public affairs, and was a pioneer in the idea of social centers and institutional features of church life. He attacked unflinchingly the social evils of his time, identified himself with progressive political causes, and was conspicuous for years as a worker for world peace. He visited Europe seventeen times, frequently to attend international peace conferences and church councils. His scholarship was wide and deep. No parish minister of his time was more familiar with the literature of theology. In addition, he mastered philosophy, history, and literature in various languages. Among his manuscripts were found after his death an unfinished translation of Rousseau's "Confessions" and a study of the Hebrew vocabulary of the Psalms. He published the following books: *The Aim of Life* (1894), *From Jerusalem to Nicaea: the Church in the First Three Centuries* (Lowell Institute Lectures, 1895), *The Religion of Hope* (1896), *Two Masters: Browning and Turgenief* (1912).

He was twice married: first, on Sept. 6, 1871, to Isabel Elliott (died in May 1919), by whom he had three sons and one daughter, and second, in June 1920, to Mrs. Jessie Braman Daggett, of Indiana. He resigned his Springfield pulpit June 30, 1917, owing to age and serious impairment of health, but maintained his connection with the South Church as pastor emeritus.

[*Rochester Theolog. Sem. Gen. Cat.* (1910); *The Congregational Year-Book*, 1923; *Congregationalist*, Aug. 23, 1923; *Springfield Republican*, Aug. 14, 1923; *Who's Who in America*, 1922–23; collection of clippings from *Springfield Republican* for entire time of Moxom's stay in Springfield and now preserved in the public library of that city.]   J. H. H.

MOYLAN, STEPHEN (1737–Apr. 13, 1811), Revolutionary soldier, was born in Cork, Ireland, son of John Moylan, a merchant of substance. The family was Catholic and as a result of the severe penal laws Stephen was educated in Paris. He engaged in the shipping business in Lisbon for three years before coming to Philadelphia in 1768, where he gained wealth and social prestige. In 1771 he became the first president of the Friendly Sons of St.

Patrick. At the outbreak of the Revolution his friend John Dickinson [*q.v.*] commended him to Washington as a zealous patriot; Moylan joined the army at Cambridge and became muster-master general, Aug. 11, 1775. In this position he fitted out several privateers which in the early months of the war considerably damaged British shipping. From January 1776 he actively agitated for the complete independence of the colonies; at the same time he entertained the vain hope of being appointed American ambassador to Spain. He became secretary to Washington in March; in June Congress elected him quartermaster-general of the army to succeed Thomas Mifflin [*q.v.*]. Moylan attempted, with little success, to block the progress of Lord Howe up the Hudson River; he also attempted to reorganize the army. Under the circumstances this latter task was impossible and a congressional committee of investigation could only recommend a change of quartermaster-general. Moylan promptly resigned and wrote a lengthy letter of vindication to Washington. Refusing several minor appointments, he remained with the army as a volunteer; a bitter snowstorm kept him out of the victory over the British at Trenton, but at the battle of Princeton he served with distinction: "I know I never felt so much like one of Homer's Deities before. We trod on air—it was a glorious day!" (Griffin, *post*, p. 48).

In December 1776 Washington requested him to organize and command a regiment of cavalry or light dragoons. The regiment was prepared for active service the following April and became a part of the American cavalry commanded by Casimir Pulaski [*q.v.*]. Moylan quarreled with Pulaski and Zielinski, another Polish officer, so that in October 1777 he was tried by a court martial for his unseemly conduct. He was acquitted, but in December Zielinski had the satisfaction of "unhorsing" Moylan in a tilt. When in March 1778 Pulaski resigned his command of the cavalry to form an independent corps of dragoons, Moylan was appointed, in spite of Pulaski's protests, to the command. The cavalry, though poor in numbers and equipment, became more efficient and useful. In May 1781 Moylan and his cavalry were sent to join Lafayette in Virginia; after the surrender of Cornwallis at Yorktown ill health forced Moylan to return to Philadelphia. At the end of the war the military establishment was reduced and his services were no longer needed. Congress, on Nov. 3, 1783, made him a brevet brigadier-general.

In the midst of the distresses of war he had become engaged to Mary Ricketts Van Horn of Phil's Hill, N. J. She was the daughter of a retired merchant, whose five daughters all found husbands during the war. She was captivated by Moylan's jovial nature and by his very remarkable uniform, consisting of a red waistcoat, buckskin breeches, bright green coat and bearskin hat. On Sept. 12, 1778, Moylan married her, "a lady possessed of every accomplishment to render the married state happy." An interesting glimpse of the Moylans and Van Horns is given by the Marquis de Chastellux (*post*, I, 141–73), who dined with them and who "conceived a great friendship" for Moylan. Washington appointed him commissioner of loans in Philadelphia in 1793; and in 1796 he was again elected the president of the Friendly Sons of St. Patrick.

[Marquis de Chastellux, *Travels in North America* (2 vols., London, 1787); M. J. Griffin, *Stephen Moylan* (1909); Frank Monaghan, "Stephen Moylan in the American Revolution," in *Studies: an Irish Quart. Rev.* (Dublin), Sept. 1930; *Poulson's Am. Daily Advertiser*, Apr. 16, 1811.]
                F. M—n.

MOZIER, JOSEPH (Aug. 22, 1812–Oct. 3, 1870), sculptor, was born in Burlington, Vt. Although he entered business in New York City, he is said to have spent much of his early manhood in Mount Vernon, Ohio, and to have married there. In the forties he was reported as a successful Broad Street merchant in New York, pursuing art only as a recreation. Like the sculptors Gould and MacDonald, he gave up business to devote himself wholly to sculpture. He went to Italy and made some preliminary studies in Florence. In 1845 he established himself in Rome, where he spent the rest of his life, aside from at least one visit made to his native land to show his works in the Tenth Street Studio, New York. In his day, the theme in a work of art was regarded as particularly important. Most of Mozier's themes had a strong literary or historic or anecdotic appeal, and both critics and clients appraised his output first of all from the point of view of the subject. One of his best works is in New Haven, Conn. It is the "Wept of Wish-ton-Wish," a life-size marble figure representing in nondescript Indian costume the heroine of Cooper's novel of that name. His "White Lady of Avenel" issues from the pages of Scott, and his "Indian Girl" illustrates a stanza from Bryant. Of his "Il Penseroso," Miltonic in derivation, a life-size draped female figure in marble, one copy is in the National Gallery of Art, Washington, D. C., and one is in Horticultural Hall, Fairmount Park, Philadelphia. His "Peri," representing another poetic theme, is in Mt. Olivet Cemetery, Nashville, Tenn.

Mozier's Old Testament figures include "Queen Esther," of which at least two copies were sold in the sixties, "Jephthah's Daughter," "Rebecca at the Well," "Rizpah," now in seclusion at the Metropolitan Museum, New York, and the marble group of the "Prodigal Son," owned by the Pennsylvania Academy of the Fine Arts. Of all his works, this group is the most ambitious and impressive. The emotion of the moment of meeting is well rendered in the action of both figures; the laborious carving of the details of the father's costume does not materially impair the effect of the whole. Samuel Osgood, writing in 1870, commented: "Mozier deals chiefly with subjects of feeling.... He designs somewhat in the tone of Thompson's 'Seasons.' ... He studies faithfully, and is content with completing one statue each year" (*post*, p. 422). In 1878, Clark enthusiastically included the "Prodigal Son" in *Great American Sculptures*. Few of Mozier's critics were as severe as Nathaniel Hawthorne, who, friendly enough toward Powers and Harriet Hosmer, was not attracted by the art of "Mr. ——," as he cautiously designated Mozier; admitting meanwhile that "Mr. —— is sensible, shrewd, keen, clever ... nor did I hear a single idea from him that struck me as otherwise than sensible." Probably present-day criticism would in general find Hawthorne correct in most of his estimates of the various works he saw in Mozier's studio, although even he approved of two genre pieces, "Boy Whittling," and "Girl with Cat and Dog." Two well-known works were the companion pieces, "Truth" and "Silence," formerly seen in the Lenox Library, New York City, and the oft-repeated "Pocahontas." Unlike most of his confrères, Mozier dealt little with the portrait bust, choosing as his province the draped ideal or genre figure. After twenty-five years of honorable activity in Rome, he died at Faido, Switzerland. His "Undine," which won the grand prize in Rome in 1867, was acquired by the University of Dayton in 1930 (*Dayton News*, Mar. 16, 1930).

[Rodman J. Sheirr has an article on Mozier, with eight illustrations, in *Potter's Am. Monthly*, Jan. 1876. Nathaniel Hawthorne, in his *Italian Note-Books* (1858), vol. I, pp. 154–56, gives a penetrating contemporary description of Mozier's productions and personal characteristics. From another point of view, Samuel H. Osgood, in "Am. Artists in Italy," *Harper's Magazine*, Aug. 1870, writes a friendly notice of this sculptor's studio work and social position in Rome. H. T. Tuckerman, in his *Book of the Artists* (1867), and Wm. J. Clark, Jr., in *Great Am. Sculptures* (1878), give additional data. C. E. Fairman's *Art and Artists of the Capitol of the U. S.* (1927) has a note, p. 317, on "Il Penseroso." Lorado Taft, *The Hist. of*

Am. Sculpture (1930), has the best general summary, with special descriptions and one full-page illustration. The *Art Jour.* (London), Apr. 1, 1859, has a comment on the "Prodigal Son" and on Jan. 1, 1871, an obituary. For other obituaries see the *Cincinnati Commercial*, Oct. 24, 1870, and the *N. Y. Times*, Oct. 30, 1870.]

A. A.

MUDD, SAMUEL A. [See Booth, John Wilkes, 1838–1865].

MUDGE, ENOCH (June 28, 1776–Apr. 2, 1850), Methodist Episcopal clergyman, the son of Enoch and Lydia (Ingalls) Mudge, was born in Lynn, Mass. Both his parents were of old New England ancestry, his father being a descendant of Thomas Mudge, born in 1624, and in 1657 a resident of Malden, Mass. In 1791 Jesse Lee [*q.v.*] of Virginia, the pioneer Methodist evangelist of New England, preached his first sermon in Lynn. He made a deep impression on several persons who had been members of the local Congregational church, which was then rent with internal strife. Among these were Enoch and Lydia Mudge, who joined the Methodist class which Lee organized, the first in Massachusetts, of which Mudge became the leader. The younger Enoch, a lad of fifteen, was stirred by what went on in the meetings and by the religious conversation he heard in his home, and with the help of John Lee, another Methodist itinerant, he, too, reached the satisfying experience of conversion. From the first he was an evangelist, winning his companions, and as a youthful exhorter making addresses in the neighboring towns. In 1793, at the age of seventeen, he was received into the New England Conference on trial as a Methodist preacher and appointed to the Greenwich circuit, which covered the state of Rhode Island and parts of Massachusetts. Thus he was the first native of New England to enter the ministry of this aggressive sect that was getting a hearing for the first time in territory long monopolized by the Puritan churches. The next year he was junior preacher on the New London, Conn., circuit, and in 1795 he was appointed to Readfield in the District of Maine. In 1796, though still a minor, he was ordained elder, and appointed to Bath, from which he pushed on farther east to Penobscot, pioneering new territory. Here, with his young companion, Timothy Merritt, one of his own Connecticut recruits who became a leader of New England Methodism, he formed numerous societies in rural hamlets and fishing villages.

On Nov. 29, 1797 (Alfred Mudge, *post*), he married Mrs. Jerusha Hinckley, daughter of John Holbrook, and settled on a farm at Orrington, Me., ceasing to travel as a member of the

Conference, though he continued to exercise the functions of a minister. On this account he was prosecuted for solemnizing a marriage, though the court dismissed the case as "malicious persecution." On another occasion, when he publicly denounced some young people for a "frolic," he was prosecuted for defamation. In 1811–12 and in 1815–16 he represented Orrington in the Massachusetts legislature, where he aided in the passage of the "religious freedom bill," which relieved the younger churches from the disabilities imposed upon them by the old laws giving special privileges to original Puritan churches. In 1817 Mudge reëntered the traveling ministry, serving as pastor in Boston (1817–18), Lynn (1819–21), Portsmouth (1821–22), Providence (1823–24), Newport (1825–26), and other city churches. While stationed at Lynn he was a delegate to the constitutional convention of Massachusetts (1819). From 1831 to 1844, when his health failed, he was port chaplain at New Bedford, where his kindliness, sympathy, and good cheer greatly commended him to the seamen of that flourishing whaling port. The last seven years of his life were spent in his native town of Lynn. He was a short, thickset man, of ruddy countenance, ready of speech and quick of wit. Common sense, a simple practical mind and a marked ability to command the confidence and support of other men were among his distinguishing traits. He made no pretensions to scholarship, but had a plain, direct style of discourse. He was an incorporator of Wilbraham Academy (1824), and served on the committee in the same year to establish a Methodist weekly in Boston. His publications include sermons, lectures to young people, a system of Biblical instruction, *Camp-Meeting Hymn Book* (1818), *The Parables* (1832), and "History of the Missions of the Methodist Episcopal Church," in *History of American Missions to the Heathen from Their Commencement to the Present Time* (1840).

[W. B. Sprague, *Annals Am. Pulpit*, vol. VII (1873); *Vital Records of Lynn, Mass.* (1905), vol. I, births; Alfred Mudge, *Memorials: Being a Geneal., Biog., and Hist. Account of the Name of Mudge in America* (1868); Stephen Allen and W. H. Pillsbury, *Hist. of Methodism in Me.* (1887); *Minutes of the Ann. Conferences of the M. E. Ch.;* 1850; Abel Stevens, *Memorials of the Early Progress of Methodism in the Eastern States* (1852); James Mudge, *Hist. of the New Eng. Conference of the M. E. Ch.* (1910); *Zion's Herald*, May 8, 1850; *Boston Journal*, Apr. 5, 1850.]
J. R. J.

MUDGE, JAMES (Apr. 5, 1844–May 7, 1918), Methodist clergyman and missionary, was born at West Springfield, Mass., the son of the Rev. James and Harriet Wilde (Goodridge) Mudge,

and a descendant of Thomas Mudge, who was a resident of Malden, Mass., as early as 1657. James attended the public schools of South Harwich and Lynn, and at the age of seventeen entered Wesleyan University, Middletown, Conn., from which he received in 1865 the degree of A.B. He spent the two succeeding years as a teacher of Greek and Latin in the seminary at Pennington, N. J., and then entered the newly opened Boston University School of Theology, from which he received the degree of S.T.B. in 1870. He was ordained on Mar. 30, 1868, at a session of the New England Conference of the Methodist Episcopal Church, and was assigned shortly afterwards to the North Avenue Church, Cambridge, Mass. Upon the completion of his theological course, he took charge for three years of a church at Wilbraham, Mass., to which he had been appointed in Apr. 29, 1870, by the Springfield Conference. He married, on Apr. 29, 1873, Martha Maria Wiswell of New Haven, Conn., whom he had met while she was a teacher in Wilbraham Academy.

Shortly before his marriage, Mudge's mind was turned toward missionary service in India by a specific request from J. M. Thoburn [*q.v.*], of Lucknow, for a "first class, scholarly young man of literary turn" to act as editor of books and periodicals. He received appointment by the mission board of his Church and on July 1, 1873, sailed with his bride for India by way of Europe. Upon their arrival in Lucknow, Oct. 25, 1873, he assumed charge at once of the *Lucknow Witness,* a religious periodical published in English. During his ten years in India he carried on editorial work, issued various pamphlets, contributed numerous articles to American papers, compiled, mostly from materials which had appeared in the *Witness,* three volumes of *Good Stories and Best Poems,* prepared a Methodist catechism (in Hindustani), and published a history of Methodism. He had charge for a time of a vernacular Sunday school in Lucknow, and from 1878 to 1882 was pastor of the English-speaking Methodist congregation of that city. During 1882–83 he was stationed at Shahjahanpore as a general missionary in charge of vernacular work, a change of mission policy having ordained that missionary service should be devoted to native rather than to English constituencies. In 1883, with his wife and three children (a fourth, the eldest, having died in Lucknow), he returned to America, deeming himself ill-fitted for a general missionary career.

He resumed pastoral service under the auspices of the New England Conference, and for the next twenty-five years served churches in eastern Massachusetts. From 1888 to 1913 he was secretary and treasurer of the missionary society of the New England Conference; from 1888 until 1904, lecturer on missions at the Boston University School of Theology; and from 1889 until 1918, secretary of the New England Conference. He was also book editor of *Zion's Herald* (1908–12). He compiled *Poems with Power to Strengthen the Soul* (1907, 1909) and *The Best of Browning* (1898), edited *Sunday School Missionary Speaker* (1905), thirty volumes of Conference minutes, and *Hymns of Trust* (1912), and was the author of the following books: *Faber* (1885), *In Memoriam, or a Portraiture of the Rev. Zachariah Atwell Mudge* (1890), *Pastors' Missionary Manual* (1891), *Growth in Holiness* (1895), *Honey from Many Hives* (1899), *China* (1900), *The Life of Love* (1902), *The Land of Faith* (1903), *The Saintly Calling* (1905), *The Life Ecstatic* (1906), *Fenelon the Mystic* (1906), *The Riches of His Grace* (1909), *History of the New England Conference of the Methodist Episcopal Church* (1910), *The Perfect Life* (1911), *Religious Experience* (1913), and *Heart Religion as Described by John Wesley* (1913). He died in Malden, Mass., and was buried in the lot with his father in Pine Grove Cemetery, Lynn. Enoch Mudge [*q.v.*] was his great-uncle.

[Alfred Mudge, *Memorials: Being a Geneal., Biog., and Hist. Account of the Name Mudge in America 1638 to 1868* (1868); *Minutes of the New Eng. Conference of the M. E. Ch.*, 1919; *Who's Who in America*, 1918–19; *Zion's Herald*, May 15, 1918; *Boston Transcript*, May 7, 1918.]   J. C. A—h—r.

MUHLENBERG, FREDERICK AUGUSTUS (Aug. 25, 1818–Mar. 21, 1901), Lutheran clergyman, teacher, college president, grandson of Gotthilf Henry Ernest Mühlenberg and great-grandson of Henry Melchior Mühlenberg [*qq.v.*], was born at Lancaster, Pa., the second of the five children of Frederick Augustus Hall Muhlenberg (1795–1867) by his first wife, Elizabeth Schaum. His father, a physician, banker, and prominent citizen of Lancaster, had been a pupil of Benjamin Rush and was a graduate in arts and medicine of the University of Pennsylvania; his mother was a granddaughter of John Helfrich Schaum, who was sent from Halle to Philadelphia in 1745 to work as a catechist under H. M. Mühlenberg. Frederick Augustus entered Pennsylvania (now Gettysburg) College in 1833, only a few months after its opening, but transferred later to Jefferson (now Washington and Jefferson) College at Canonsburg, where he graduated in 1836. While at Jefferson he was much influenced by its

president, Matthew Brown, a Calvinist of deepest dye, whose character was more genial than his doctrine. After a year's breathing spell at home, studying anatomy and physiology with his father, he spent the year 1837–38 at Princeton Theological Seminary and entered on his long career as an educator. In generous measure he possessed the vigor of mind and body, the executive capacity, and the strong sense of duty that were recurrent traits in his family. Though he wrote little, he was a notable scholar, especially in Greek, and an excellent teacher, inculcating, at least in his apter pupils, an accurate, appreciative knowledge of the Greek classics and efficient habits of study and thought. As professor or president he contributed richly to the life of five colleges of his native state. He was a member, 1840–50, of the faculty of Franklin College at Lancaster, of which his grandfather had been the first president, and in 1849 proposed the union of Franklin, Marshall, and Pennsylvania colleges. This motion led to the transfer to Pennsylvania College in 1850 of the Lutheran interest in Franklin College and to the organization in 1852–53 of Franklin and Marshall College as an institution of the German Reformed Church.

Muhlenberg was the first incumbent, 1850–67, of the Franklin professorship of ancient languages in Pennsylvania College, his tenure corresponding almost exactly with the presidency of Henry Louis Baugher [*q.v.*]. He was licensed in 1854 and ordained in 1855 by the Ministerium of Pennsylvania, preached regularly in Christ Church, and was librarian of the college. During the Gettysburg campaign his house was pierced by a shell and pillaged by marauding soldiers. In 1867 he removed to Allentown to become the first president of Muhlenberg College. For nine years, besides teaching Greek, the mental and moral sciences, and the evidences of Christianity, he bore the burdensome responsibility of organizing and administering a college that was crippled from the start by financial difficulties. With the able cooperation of two of the professors, Matthias Henry Richards and Theodore Lorenzo Seip [*q.v.*], he kept the college alive, and when he resigned in 1876 its continuance and usefulness seemed assured. For the next twelve years he was professor of the Greek language and literature in the University of Pennsylvania. For the first time since his graduation from college he recrossed the Alleghanies in 1891 to assume the presidency of Thiel College at Greenville, which was in dire need of his firm, orderly control. Having reorganized the institution, he retired in 1893 at the age of seventy-five. Muhlenberg was married on Aug. 8, 1848, to Catharine Anna (1827–94), daughter of Maj. Peter Muhlenberg, U. S. A., and grand-daughter of John Peter Gabriel Muhlenberg [q.v.]. Four of their six sons outlived him. He spent his last years in Reading, where he died and was buried in the Charles Evans Cemetery.

[H. M. M. Richards, "Descendants of H. M. Mühlenberg," *Proc. and Addresses Pa.-Ger. Soc.*, vol. X (1900); biog. sketch by H. E. Jacobs in S. E. Ochsenford, *Muhlenberg Coll.* (1892); *Biog. and Hist. Cat. Washington and Jefferson Coll.* (1902); J. H. Dubbs, *Hist. of Franklin and Marshall Coll.* (1903); *Necrological Report, Princeton Theol. Sem.*, 1901; sketch of F. A. H. Muhlenberg in J. L. Chamberlain, *Univ. of Pa.*, vol. II (1902); *Press* (Phila.), Mar. 22, 1901.]
G. H. G.

MUHLENBERG, FREDERICK AUGUSTUS CONRAD (Jan. 1, 1750–June 4, 1801), Lutheran clergyman, politician, first speaker of the federal House of Representatives, was born at Trappe, Montgomery County, Pa., the third child and second son of Henry Melchior Mühlenberg [q.v.] by his wife, Anna Maria Weiser, daughter of the younger John Conrad Weiser [q.v.]. He was sent to Halle in 1763 with his brothers, John Peter Gabriel and Gotthilf Henry Ernest [qq.v.], attended the schools of the Francke Stiftungen and the University, returned to Philadelphia in 1770 with Gotthilf and their future brother-in-law, John Christopher Kunze [q.v.], and was ordained at Reading, Oct. 25, 1770, by the Ministerium of Pennsylvania. On Oct. 15, 1771, he married Catharine (1750–1835), daughter of Frederick Schaefer, a Philadelphia sugar refiner, by whom he had three sons and four daughters. His ministerial career extended until the summer of 1779. After his ordination he acted as assistant to his brother-in-law, Christian Emanuel Schulze, preaching and performing other ministerial duties at Tulpehocken, Schaeferstown, Lebanon, and other points in that region. In 1771 he made two arduous trips to Sunbury. In November 1773 he went to New York as pastor of Christ Church ("The Old Swamp Church") at Frankford and William Streets. In 1775 he wrote to his brother Peter rebuking him for mixing revolutionary and martial activities with the ministry of the Word, but he himself was known to be in sympathy with the Revolution. As a measure of precaution he sent his wife and two children to Philadelphia in February 1776 and late in June, when Howe's fleet appeared in the offing, he followed them. A month later he removed to Trappe with his family and relieved his father of the charge at New Hanover. He also preached regularly at Oley Hills and New Goshenhoppen and occasionally at Reading.

The turning-point of his life was his election Mar. 2, 1779, to fill the unexpired term of Edward Biddle in the Continental Congress. He had been an honest, faithful, laborious clergyman, but his choice of that profession had been dictated by circumstance rather than by his own volition, and to the political career now opening ahead of him he turned with renewed hope and energies. He was reëlected to the Continental Congress Nov. 12, 1779, his term expiring Oct. 28, 1780, when he became ineligible for three years. Meanwhile he had been elected to the General Assembly, of which he was speaker 1780–83. He was president of the Council of Censors 1783–84, and one of the party striving for a revision of the state constitution. He was commissioned justice of the peace Mar. 9, 1784; and on the organization of Montgomery County that autumn he was made registrar of wills and recorder of deeds. He wrote occasionally for the press, both in German and English, and his private letters are enlivened with racy comments on the politics and politicians of the day. In 1787 he presided over the convention called to ratify the Federal Constitution, and the next year he was elected to the First Congress as a Federalist from the Philadelphia district. Financial necessity compelled him, meanwhile, to engage in business: he was a partner in the firm of Muhlenberg & Wegmann, importers, and in that of Muhlenberg & Lawersweiler, sugar refiners, in Philadelphia, and owned a house and fifty acres of land at Trappe, with which a store of some kind was connected. When Congress assembled at New York, Muhlenberg came to it with the reputation of an experienced, urbane, impartial presiding officer and was elected speaker, the choice being undoubtedly influenced by the consideration that, since the President came from the South and the Vice-President from New England, it was desirable to select the speaker from the most powerful of the middle states. He was reëlected to the Second, Third, and Fourth congresses as a Federalist, but was displaced as speaker in the Second Congress by Jonathan Trumbull, the change being motivated probably by the fact that Muhlenberg's Federalism had been growing lukewarm. When the Third Congress was organized he was elected speaker again, this time by the help of Republican votes. During the ensuing years he steered a political course that must have been as puzzling sometimes to himself as it has since been to historians. As the Federalist candidate for governor of Pennsylvania, he was badly beaten by Thomas McKean [*q.v.*] in 1793 and overwhelmingly in 1796, while in Congress he worked harmoniously with Jefferson's supporters. In 1796, as chairman of the House acting as a committee of the whole, he cast the deciding vote to refer again to the House the bill appropriating money for the ratification of Jay's Treaty. It was a courageous, statesmanlike act, and cost him his popularity in Pennsylvania. About two years before his death he abandoned the Federalist party and threw his support to the Republicans. John Adams attributed the Federalist loss of Pennsylvania in the national elections to the influence of Frederick Muhlenberg and his brother Peter. On Jan. 8, 1800, Gov. Thomas Mifflin [*q.v.*] appointed him receiver-general of the Pennsylvania Land Office, and he moved to Lancaster, then the seat of the government. He was extremely corpulent, and his death in 1801 resulted from an apoplectic stroke. He was buried in the Lutheran churchyard at Lancaster.

[H. M. M. Richards, "Descendants of H. M. Mühlenberg," *Proc. and Addresses Pa.-Ger. Soc.*, vol. X (1900); D. M. Gregg, "Three Pennsylvania Statesmen of the Olden Time" (unpublished, written 1932); letter to Gen. Peter Muhlenberg, and MSS. in the Gregg Collection (vol. I), Lib. of Cong.; B. M. Schmucker, "The Luth. Ch. in the City of N. Y., II," *Luth. Ch. Rev.*, Apr. 1885; Oswald Seidensticker, "Friedrich August Conrad Mühlenberg," *Deutsch-Amerikanische Geschichtsblätter*, Jan. 1909; W. J. Mann, *Life and Times of H. M. Mühlenberg* (1887); *Doc. Hist. Ev. Luth. Min. of Pa. 1748–1821* (1898); M. P. Follett, *The Speaker of the House of Representatives* (1896); *The Journal of William Maclay* (1927); *Aurora and Gen. Advertiser* (Phila.), June 22, 1801.]   G. H. G.

MÜHLENBERG, GOTTHILF HENRY ERNEST (Nov. 17, 1753–May 23, 1815), Lutheran clergyman, botanist, was born at Trappe, Montgomery County, Pa., the fifth child and third son of Henry Melchior [*q.v.*] and Anna Maria (Weiser) Mühlenberg. Accompanied by his brothers, John Peter Gabriel and Frederick Augustus Conrad Muhlenberg [*qq.v.*], he was sent to Germany in April 1763 to be educated at Halle. There he spent six years in the Waisenhaus, mastering Greek, Latin, Hebrew, and French, and exhibiting at times a spirit as fiery as that of his brother Peter. In September 1769 he matriculated at the University, and a year later, with Frederick and their future brother-in-law, John Christopher Kunze [*q.v.*], he returned to Philadelphia. Though he was still a stripling, the members of the Lutheran Ministerium of Pennsylvania were so impressed by his scholarship and had such faith in the Mühlenberg name that they ordained him at Reading, Oct. 25, 1770, with but slight misgiving. For the next few years he was his father's assistant at Philadelphia and in the Raritan Valley in

New Jersey, and in April 1774 he was elected third pastor at Philadelphia. On July 26 of that year he married Mary Catharine Hall (Dec. 26, 1756–May 1, 1841) of Philadelphia, who bore him four sons and four daughters. As the British forces approached Philadelphia, he sent his family to his father's house at New Providence (Trappe), and on Sept. 22, 1777, four days before the occupation, he himself retired thither. After the British withdrawal in June 1778 he returned. In April 1779, as the upshot of a misunderstanding with Kunze, he resigned abruptly. The next year he succeeded J. H. C. Helmuth [*q.v.*] as pastor of Holy Trinity, Lancaster, where he remained till his death thirty-five years later. He was secretary of the Ministerium of Pennsylvania for six terms and president for eleven. He was the first president (1787) of Franklin College.

He began the study of botany in the spring of 1778 during his enforced rustication and was an accomplished botanist when Johann David Schöpf [*q.v.*] visited him in 1783. Schöpf gave him confidence in the soundness and value of his work and brought him into correspondence with various European botanists. Thereafter Mühlenberg exchanged letters and specimens with scientists in England, France, Switzerland, Germany, and Sweden, and was elected to honorary membership in several learned societies. In his own country he was even better known. He did as much field work as his arduous professional duties would permit, kept a calendar of the flowering plants of his neighborhood, and by 1791 had listed more than 1,100 plants growing within three miles of Lancaster. In the precision and accuracy of his descriptions, his scrupulous regard for correct nomenclature, his aversion to splitting species into numerous varieties on the basis of minute variations, and his recognition of the necessity for collaborative effort in compiling a complete flora of North America, he was a true forerunner of Torrey and Gray. He also gave much attention to the economic and medicinal uses of plants. His total contribution to descriptive botany—some hundred species and varieties—is the more remarkable because of the restricted area that he explored personally.

His publications include: *Eine Rede, gehalten den 6ten Juny 1787, bey der Einweihung von der Deutschen Hohen Schule oder Franklin Collegium in Lancäster* (Lancaster, 1788); "Index Florae Lancastriensis" and "Supplementum Indicis," *Transactions of the American Philosophical Society*, vols. III (1793) and IV (1799); *Observations on the Genera Juglans, Fraxinus,*

Muhlenberg

and Quercus, in the Neighbourhood of Lancaster, in North America (copr. 1801); *English-German and German-English Dictionary* (2 vols., Lancaster, 1812), in collaboration with Benedict J. Schipper; *Catalogus Plantarum Americae Septentrionalis Huc Usque Cognitarum Indigenarum et Cicurum: Or, A Catalogue of the Hitherto Known Native and Naturalized Plants of North America, Arranged According to the Sexual System of Linnæus* (Lancaster, 1813); and *Descriptio Uberior Graminum et Plantarum Calamariarum Americae Septentrionalis Indigenarum et Cicurum* (Philadelphia, 1817). He also left much work unpublished.

A representative both of the later phase of German Pietism and of the Enlightenment, Mühlenberg was a man of exemplary character and great personal charm. In his prime he had a strong body and enjoyed traveling on foot between Lancaster and Philadelphia, a distance of more than sixty miles. In later life he suffered repeated apoplectic attacks, to which he finally succumbed. He was buried in his churchyard at Lancaster.

[Muhlenberg papers are in the archives of the Am. Phil. Soc., the Ev. Luth. Min. of Pa., and the Hist. Soc. of Pa. Printed materials include: "Kurze Nachricht von dem Leben und Tode des Hochwürdigen Hrn. Doctor Mühlenbergs," *Evangelisches Magazin,* 1816, pp. 13–16 (probably by J. H. C. Helmuth); G. F. Krotel, *Memorial Vol. of the Ev. Luth. Ch. of the Holy Trinity* (Lancaster, 1861); *Doc. Hist. Ev. Luth. Min. of Pa. 1748–1821* (1898); J. H. Dubbs, *Hist. Franklin and Marshall Coll.* (1903); *Reliquiae Baldwinianae: Selections from the Correspondence of the Late William Baldwin, M.D.* (1843); Wm. Darlington, *Memorials of John Bartram and Humphry Marshall* (1849); "The Muhlenberg Herbarium," *Bull. Torrey Botanical Club,* July 1881, pp. 80–81; J. M. Maisch, "G. H. E. Mühlenberg als Botaniker," *Pharmaceutische Rundschau* (New York), June 1886; *Life, Journals and Correspondence of Rev. Manasseh Cutler, LL.D.* (1888); W. J. Youmans, *Pioneers of Science in America* (1896); *Poulson's Am. Daily Advertiser* (Phila.), May 26, 1815.] G. H. G.

MUHLENBERG, HENRY AUGUSTUS PHILIP (May 13, 1782–Aug. 11, 1844), Lutheran clergyman, politician, diplomat, was born at Lancaster, Pa., the third of the eight children of Gotthilf Henry Ernest Mühlenberg [*q.v.*] and Mary Catharine Hall. He received a thorough classical training from his father, studied theology with his uncle, John Christopher Kunze [*q.v.*], and, having been licensed by the Ministerium of Pennsylvania, became pastor in April 1803 of Trinity Church, Reading, Pa. He was ordained at Easton in 1804. The next year he married Mary Elizabeth, daughter of Joseph Hiester [*q.v.*]. She died in childbed in 1806, and in 1808 Muhlenberg married her sister Rebecca. His official call to Reading stip-

ulated that he should receive, in addition to his salary and perquisites, "all love and friendship which a faithful and conscientious pastor should have, so that he may fulfill his office among us with joy and not with grief" (Fry, *post,* p. 134), and this proved to be more than a pious wish, for under him the congregation enjoyed a quarter-century of peace, good will, and prosperity. During these years he maintained an extensive correspondence with other Lutheran clergymen and served as secretary and as president of the Ministerium. His only known published sermon is *Busstags-Predigt Gehalten Donnerstags den 20sten August 1812* (Reading, 1812). In 1828, because of indifferent health, he resigned his charge and removed to a farm on the outskirts of the town, but he continued to preach to his congregation until his successor, Jacob Miller, was installed in March 1829.

Meanwhile, taking advantage of his prestige among the Pennsylvania Germans, the Democrats of Berks County nominated him for Congress. He was readily elected, took his seat Mar. 4, 1829, in the Twenty-first Congress, and served continuously until his resignation, Feb. 9, 1838. Muhlenberg took to politics as a duck to water. In Berks County he had a large personal following that gave its vote to the entire Democratic ticket, and the county became known —in the words of campaign orators—as "the tenth legion of the Democracy." In Congress he served continuously as chairman of the House committee on Revolutionary claims, gave loyal, intelligent support to President Jackson's measures, and made a good friend of Martin Van Buren. Meanwhile in state politics he was less fortunate. As a result of internal dissensions, the Democrats put two candidates for governor into the field in 1835, George Wolf, who was running to succeed himself for the second time, and Muhlenberg. The ensuing defeat engendered bitterness that lasted for years, and finally it became obvious that in the interests of party harmony Muhlenberg would have to be removed, at least temporarily, from Pennsylvania politics. Van Buren offered him the secretaryship of the navy and the ministry to Russia, but Muhlenberg felt that he could not afford to accept them. Then it was decided to send a legation to Austria, and on Feb. 8, 1838, he was made the first American minister to Austria. John Randolph Clay, later minister to Peru, was his secretary of legation. Muhlenberg did something to promote the use of American cotton in Austria, enjoyed the society of Prince Metternich, and traveled in Germany, Switzerland, and Italy; but the legation was a severe drain on his resources, and on Sept. 18, 1840, he was recalled at his own request. In 1844 he was again nominated for governor of Pennsylvania, and with the united support of his party his election was assured, but he died, in the midst of the campaign, of a stroke of apoplexy. He was buried in the Charles Evans Cemetery.

[H. M. M. Richards, "Descendants of H. M. Mühlenberg," *Proc. and Addresses Pa.-Ger. Soc.*, vol. X (1900); Jacob Fry, *The Hist. of Trinity Luth. Ch., Reading, Pa.* (1894); *Doc. Hist. Ev. Luth. Min. of Pa. 1748–1821* (1898); "Biog. Memoir of the Late Henry A. Muhlenberg," *U. S. Mag. and Dem. Rev.*, Jan. 1845; the *Pennsyvanian* (Phila.), Aug. 13, 15, 1844; W. U. Hensel, "Sidelights on an Early Political Campaign," *Lancaster County Hist. Soc. Papers*, Apr. 1914; Van Buren Papers, MSS. Div., Lib. of Cong.]

G. H. G.

MÜHLENBERG, HENRY MELCHIOR (Sept. 6, 1711–Oct. 7, 1787), Lutheran clergyman, was born at Einbeck, Hanover, the seventh of the nine children of Nicolaus Melchior and Anna Maria (Kleinschmid) Mühlenberg. His father was an hereditary member of the Brewers' Company, a master-shoemaker by trade, and an officer of St. Mary's Church. His mother was the daughter of a retired army officer. The father's death in 1723 left the family in narrow circumstances, so that for three years Mühlenberg had to forgo his studies and work for an elder brother. He learned meanwhile to play the organ and completed his preliminary education later in classical schools at Einbeck and Zellersfeld. The close connection between the University of Göttingen and American cultural life begins with Mühlenberg, who was one of its first matriculants in March 1735. While a student at the University he lived in the household of a Dr. Oporin, a member of the theological faculty, opened a school, which still exists, for the elementary instruction of poor children, and gained the friendship of several men of influence, among them Count Reuss of Koestritz and Count Henkel of Poeltzig. Having completed the theological course in 1738, he made a short visit to the University of Jena and then was appointed teacher in the famous Waisenhaus at Halle. The year under G. A. Francke at Halle was decisive. He thought of going to the East Indies as a missionary, but since no opening occurred, he became in 1739 co-pastor and inspector of an orphanage at Grosshennersdorf in Upper Lusatia, where the Baroness von Gersdorf, an aunt of Count von Zinzendorf, was his patroness. His ordination took place at Leipzig Aug. 24, 1739. While Mühlenberg was visiting in Halle on his birthday, Sept. 6, 1741, Francke, acting for himself and for F. M. Ziegenhagen, German court-preacher in London,

laid before him a call to the United Congregations (Philadelphia, New Providence, New Hanover), in Pennsylvania. This call had been unfinished business with him and Ziegenhagen for eight years, but rumors of Zinzendorf's efforts at church union among the Germans of the colony had at last galvanized them into action. Mühlenberg took six weeks to consider the proposal and on Oct. 18 accepted by letter. After a pleasant farewell journey through Saxony and Hanover he reached London Apr. 17, 1742, and spent nine weeks with Ziegenhagen, familiarizing himself with conditions in America and practising his English, the rudiments of which he had acquired in his student days at Göttingen. A harrowing voyage of twelve weeks brought him to Charleston, S. C., whence he proceeded to Ebenezer, Ga., for a week's conference with Johann Martin Boltzius [*q.v.*]. On Nov. 25, 1742, after a two weeks' sail from Charleston, he landed at Philadelphia.

Since no one expected him, no one welcomed him. The Philadelphia congregation was split between Zinzendorf and a clerical vagabond, Valentine Kraft. His rural congregations were known in the vernacular by the sinister names of "Die Trappe" and "Der Schwamm." When he found out where they were and reached them, over miles of wretched road and through unbridged streams, he was received with skepticism. He soon made a friend, however, in the Swedish pastor, Peter Tranberg, the more intelligent members of the congregations came to his support, and he was duly installed. The conflict with Zinzendorf, deplorable but inevitable, was fortunately brief; a month later the Count abandoned his great dream and departed for Europe. Dismal as was Mühlenberg's reception in Pennsylvania, it began an epoch in the history of his denomination. He saw his task, almost from the beginning, not as the serving of three isolated congregations but as the planting of a Church, and to that great enterprise he brought talents of the highest order. Though of but medium stature and hardly an athlete, he grew strong and active of body, capable of enduring long days in the saddle, exposure to every inclemency, and an unending round of duties. His intellect was clear, vigorous, alert, not original, but able to assimilate whatever nutriment it required. He had been a good scholar in Germany, and in Pennsylvania he did not forget what he had learned. His Biblical and theological scholarship was sound, and his personal religious life was warmed and mellowed by a mild type of Pietism. He was a good linguist: his German was pure and idiomatic, uncorrupted by the fashionable barbarities and complexities of the time; he spoke Latin with ease and learned, with amazing rapidity, to preach in English and Dutch. Among his minor assets were a well-trained tenor voice, some familiarity with legal principles, and a rather greater knowledge of medicine and hygiene. He was dignified in manner, urbane and affable, and wholly devoid of any desire for self-aggrandizement. To his fundamental pastoral and missionary zeal he added a genius for organization.

Nominally, he remained pastor of the United Congregations till almost the close of his life, but he soon made them the nucleus of an organization that spread rapidly wherever German Lutherans had settled in the middle colonies. In January 1745 his first helpers—Peter Brunnholtz, John Nicolas Kurtz, John Helfrich Schaum—arrived from Halle. On Apr. 22, of that year, he married Anna Maria, daughter of the younger John Conrad Weiser [q.v.], who bore him six sons and five daughters and outlived him by many years. Her mother was long believed to have been an Indian woman; she was, however, Anna Eve, daughter of Peter Feg (Feck), an immigrant from the Palatinate. As new congregations were formed or old ones allied themselves with Mühlenberg, the need of closer organization became apparent, and on Aug. 26, 1748, the first convention of the Evangelical Lutheran Ministerium of Pennsylvania was held at Philadelphia. By that date he had already made trips to the Raritan Valley in New Jersey, to Frederick, Md., and to various points in eastern Pennsylvania. Until the outbreak of the Revolution he continued to visit Lutheran congregations scattered all the way from the Hudson River to the Potomac. During parts of 1751 and 1752 he resided in New York, ministering temporarily to the churches there and at Hackensack; in 1758 and 1759 he made similar stays in the Raritan Valley. In 1774-75 he made a notable journey to the Salzburgers at Ebenezer, Ga. Until 1761 his home was at New Providence; from 1761 to 1776 he lived in Philadelphia; but with the oncoming of the Revolution he found it safest to return to his rural retreat at New Providence. With the addition to his forces of such men as J. H. C. Helmuth, John Christopher Kunze [qq.v.], and Christian Emanuel Schulze—the two latter became his sons-in-law—he was the leader of a highly intelligent, constantly expanding society. He remained its revered leader even after the infirmities of age compelled him to restrict his activities.

In 1779 he formally resigned as rector of St. Michael's and Zion's in Philadelphia; two years

later he made his last appearance at a meeting of the Ministerium. In 1784 the University of Pennsylvania made him a doctor of divinity. He did most of the editorial work on the *Gesangbuch* published by the Ministerium in 1786. Though his mind was still clear and active, he was confined more and more to New Providence and finally to his own house, where he died Oct. 7, 1787, of a complication of diseases. He is buried beside the Augustus Church at New Providence (Trappe). At the time of his death his significance as the virtual founder of the Lutheran church in America was recognized on all sides, and his fame has grown with the church. Thanks to the remarkably full records of his life, he is still one of the molding forces of his denomination.

[The chief repositories of Mühlenberg's papers are the Ostindische Bibliothek of the Franckesche Stiftungen at Halle and the Archives of the Ministerium of Pa. in the Theological Seminary at Mount Airy, Phila. The Francke Nachlass in the Preussiche Staatsbibliothek in Berlin and the Lutheran Hist. Soc. Library at Gettysburg contain some additional matter. The Library of Congress has photostats of the material at Halle and Berlin, and the Ministerium Archives eventually will have copies of all papers not in its possession; see C. H. Kraeling, "In Quest of Muhlenbergiana," *Luth. Ch. Quarterly*, Apr. 1929. Printed materials comprise *Nachrichten von den vereinigten Deutschen Evangelisch-Lutherischen Gemeinen in Nord America, absonderlich in Pensylvanien* (2 vols., Halle, 1787; new ed., by W. J. Mann and B. M. Schmucker, the first volume richly annotated, Allentown, Pa., 1886-95); *Heinrich Melchior Mühlenberg—Selbstbiographie, 1711-43*, ed. by Wm. Germann (Allentown, 1881); "The Autobiog. of H. M. Muhlenberg," tr. by J. W. Early, *Luth. Ch. Rev.*, Oct. 1914; "Jour. of a Voyage from Phila. to Ebenezer, Ga., in the Years 1774-75," tr. by J. W. Richards, *Evangelical Rev.*, Jan. 1850-Oct. 1852; "Account of the march of the Paxton Boys against Phila. in the Year 1764" and "Extracts from the Rev. Dr. Muhlenberg's Jours. of 1776 and 1777 relating to Military events about that period," tr. by H. H. Muhlenberg, *Colls. Hist. Soc. of Pa.*, Nov. 1851, May 1852; "Abstract of a letter . . . on the Constitutional Convention of Pa., 1776," *Pa. Mag. of Hist. and Biog.*, Notes and Queries, Apr. 1898, pp. 129-31. The first biog. accounts were two memorial sermons: J. H. C. Helmuth, *Denkmal der Liebe und Achtung, Welches seiner Hochwürden dem Herrn D. Heinrich Melchior Mühlenberg . . . ist Gesetzet Worden* (1788) and J. C. Kunze, *Elisas Betränter Nachruf bei der Hinwegnahme seines Gottesmannes Elias* (1788). M. L. Stoever, *Memoir of the Life and Times of Henry Melchior Muhlenberg* (1856) was several times reprinted. W. J. Mann, *Life and Times of Henry Melchior Mühlenberg* (1887; German ed., 1891), reviewed by H. E. Jacobs, *Luth. Ch. Rev.*, July 1887, is the standard biog. and a masterpiece of scholarship and understanding. See also his "Conservatism of Henry Melchior Mühlenberg," *Luth. Ch. Rev.*, Jan. 1888, and "Lutherans in America before Mühlenberg," *Ibid.*, Apr. 1887. For family data consult: H. M. M. Richards, "Descendants of H. M. Mühlenberg," *Proc. and Addresses Pa.-Ger. Soc.*, vol. X (1900) and "The Weiser Family," *Ibid.*, vol. XXXII (1924); H. M. Oakley and J. C. Schwab, *Muhlenberg Album* (privately printed, 1910); J. C. Schwab, *The Descendants of H. M. Muhlenberg* (privately printed, 1912), a chart.]

G. H. G.

MUHLENBERG, JOHN PETER GABRIEL (Oct. 1, 1746–Oct. 1, 1807), Lutheran clergyman, Revolutionary soldier, politician, was born at Trappe, Montgomery County, Pa., the eldest of the eleven children of Henry Melchior Mühlenberg [*q.v.*] and his wife, Anna Maria Weiser. As a boy he displayed frontiersman-like traits, natural enough in a grandson of John Conrad Weiser [*q.v.*] but perturbing to his father. After learning a little Latin at the Philadelphia Academy, he was sent to Halle in 1763, with his brothers Frederick and Gotthilf [*qq.v.*], to be educated at the Waisenhaus or, at the discretion of its director, Gotthilf August Francke, to be apprenticed to a merchant. Francke ill-advisedly bound the high-spirited, quick-witted youth for a term of six years to a petty Lübeck grocer. When Peter could endure his situation no longer, he absconded, joined the 60th (Royal American) Regiment of Foot, and as secretary to one of the officers, a friend of his father, returned to Philadelphia and was discharged early in 1767. He then prepared for the ministry with Carl Magnus von Wrangel, provost of the Swedish churches on the Delaware, preached in various pulpits with more than ordinary approval, and in February 1769 took charge, as his father's assistant, of the Lutheran churches at Bedminster and New Germantown, N. J. On Nov. 6, 1770, he married Anna Barbara Meyer of Philadelphia, who bore him four sons and two daughters and died a year before him. In 1771 he accepted a call to the German Lutheran congregation at Woodstock, Va., and, in order to secure the privileges of a clergyman of the Established Church, went to England and was ordained priest, Apr. 23, 1772, by the bishop of London. William White [*q.v.*] was ordained at the same time. Apparently Muhlenberg never received Lutheran ordination, and his status as a Luthero-Episcopalian is of considerable interest. His grandnephew, William Augustus Muhlenberg [*q.v.*], may well have had this precedent in mind when he proposed in 1853 that Episcopal ordination, under certain circumstances, be conferred on ministers of other denominations. Muhlenberg began work at Woodstock in the late summer or early autumn of 1772, and was soon the leader of the community. He was elected to the House of Burgesses in 1774, associated with the leaders of the Revolutionary party, and was made chairman of the committee on public safety for Dunmore County. In January 1776 he preached his farewell sermon, with Ecclesiastes, iii, 1, for his text, and at the close of the service cast off his clerical gown, revealing beneath it the uniform of a militia officer.

He raised and commanded the 8th Virginia Regiment, composed largely of Germans from the Shenandoah Valley, and gave a good account of himself at the battle of Sullivan's Island in June 1776. On Feb. 21, 1777, he was commissioned brigadier-general in the Continental Army and ordered north to Morristown, N. J. On Sept. 11 his brigade and Weedon's bore the brunt of the fighting at Brandywine, and on Oct. 8 he distinguished himself again at Germantown. He was stationed at Valley Forge that winter; was in charge of the second line of the right wing under Greene at Monmouth Court House, July 28, 1778; was with Putnam's division on the North River later in the year; and during the winter, while Putnam was detailed for other duties, commanded the division. He was in winter quarters at Middlebrook, N. J., 1778–79, and the next summer supported Anthony Wayne in the assault on Stony Point. In December 1779 Washington sent him to Virginia to take chief command in that state, but heavy snowfalls and impassable roads prevented him from reaching Richmond until March. In December Major-General Von Steuben succeeded to his position, and Muhlenberg became Steuben's second-in-command. He was engaged in most of the numerous but indecisive actions at this stage of the war, was in charge of the troops on the south bank of the James when Cornwallis was bottled up at Yorktown, and on Oct. 14, 1781, he commanded the American brigade that stormed one of the two British redoubts. In this action Alexander Hamilton, as senior colonel of the brigade, led the advance force. At the close of the war, on Sept. 30, 1783, Muhlenberg was brevetted major-general. He had proved himself a courageous, level-headed officer, strict in discipline, but vigilant for the welfare and comfort of his men, and possessed of marked executive ability.

After settling his affairs at Woodstock, he removed in 1783 to Philadelphia and made two journeys to Ohio and Kentucky to attend to the military bounty lands assigned to him and several of his friends, among them Von Steuben. His health had been permanently impaired by the war, and he was uneasy about his finances. A political career, however, was opening to him, for among the Germans of his native state he was a hero second only to Washington. He was elected to the Supreme Executive Council of the state in 1784, was vice-president of Pennsylvania, Franklin being president, 1785–88, and was influential in securing the early adoption of the Federal Constitution. Up to this time his inclinations had been toward the Federalists, but in 1788 the Republicans nominated him and his brother Frederick for congressmen-at-large, and they were triumphantly elected. Peter was thus a representative at large in the First Congress, 1789–91, and a representative for Montgomery County in the Third and Sixth congresses, 1793–95 and 1799–1801. In 1790 he was a member of the state constitutional convention. As a presidential elector he voted for Jefferson in 1796 and again as a member of the House of Representatives in 1801. He was president of the German Society of Pennsylvania in 1788 and 1801–07. On Feb. 18, 1801, he was elected to the United States Senate but resigned a month later in order to accept the appointment as supervisor of revenue for Philadelphia. From 1802 until his death he was collector of customs for Philadelphia.

In his political views he was a thorough Jeffersonian, but Jeffersonianism in him, as in its author, was not incompatible with a fundamentally aristocratic temper. In person he was tall, active of body, strikingly handsome, and courtly in manners. He died at his suburban home at Gray's Ferry on the Schuylkill (now part of Philadelphia) and was buried beside his father at the Augustus Church at Trappe. Patriotic historians and poets have commemorated his virtues and his deeds, and statues of him stand in City Hall Plaza, Philadelphia, and in Statuary Hall in the national Capitol.

[H. A. Muhlenberg, *The Life of Major-Gen. Peter Muhlenberg* (1849); H. M. M. Richards, "Descendants of H. M. Mühlenberg," *Proc. and Addresses Pa.-German Soc.*, vol. X (1900); William (Wilhelm) Germann, "The Crisis in the Early Life of General Peter Mühlenberg," *Pa. Mag. of Hist. and Biog.*, July, Oct., 1913, translated, without acknowledgment, from H. A. Rattermann's *Deutsch-Amerikanisches Magazin*, Oct. 1886, Jan., Apr., 1887; J. C. Honeyman, "Zion, St. Paul, and Other Early Luth. Churches in Central N. J.," *Proc. N. J. Hist. Soc.*, Apr., July 1928; C. W. Cassell, W. J. Finck, E. O. Henkel, *Hist. of the Luth. Church in Va. and East Tenn.* (Strasburg, Va., 1930); "Orderly Book of Gen. John Peter Gabriel Muhlenberg, Mar. 26–Dec. 20, 1777," *Pa. Mag. of Hist. and Biog.*, July, Oct. 1909, Jan.–July 1910, Jan.–July 1911; Gaillard Hunt, *Calendar of Applications and Recommendations for Office during the Presidency of George Washington* (1901); "Letter to Col. Richard C. Anderson," *Mag. of Am. Hist.*, Nov. 1887, p. 440; *The Works of John Adams*, X (1856), p. 121; *The Journal of William Maclay* (1927); Washington and Jefferson Papers, Lib. of Cong.; Allan Nevins, *The Am. States During and After the Revolution, 1775–89* (1924); *Doc. Hist. Ev. Luth. Min. of Pa., 1748–1821* (1898); "Journal of Rev. Peter Muhlenberg in London, 1772," *Luth. Ch. Rev.*, Oct. 1885; *Aurora and General Advertiser* (Phila.), Oct. 2, 1807.]   G. H. G.

MUHLENBERG, WILLIAM AUGUSTUS Sept. 16, 1796–Apr. 8, 1877), Episcopal clergyman, was born in Philadelphia, the eldest of the three children of Henry William and Mary (Sheaff) Muhlenberg, and a grandson of Frederick Augustus Conrad Muhlenberg [*q.v.*]. He

was baptized in the Lutheran Church by J. H. C. Helmuth and attended the Lutheran services for a few years of childhood, although he understood no German; but when his widowed mother sold a lot to St. James' Episcopal Church, the vestry gave her a pew, which she was too thrifty to leave unoccupied, and Muhlenberg accordingly grew up an Episcopalian. Even as a boy he displayed the delicate sensibilities and profound religious feeling that characterized him as a man. After graduating in 1815 from the University of Pennsylvania, he studied with Bishop White and Jackson Kemper, his assistant, was ordained deacon in 1817 and priest in 1820, and, having assisted White for three years, went to Lancaster in December 1820 as co-rector with Joseph Clarkson of St. James' and two filials. He remained at Lancaster until July 1826 and for the next two years was rector of St. George's, Flushing, L. I. These early years of his ministry were a period of preparation, busy but not altogether happy, for the half century of achievement still before him. His life was to be a series of experiments in broadening and enriching the work of the church.

For seventeen years his primary interest was in education. He was the founder, chief stockholder, and headmaster of Flushing Institute, a boys' school, which opened to receive pupils in the spring of 1828. Having purchased the tract of land on Long Island Sound known as College Point, he established St. Paul's College in 1838. Muhlenberg is traditionally regarded as one of the great schoolmasters of recent times: although the two institutions had but a short life, they proved what could be done in the way of education under Christian auspices, and they provided a model for many subsequent enterprises. The death of his beloved brother, Frederick Augustus, who had been closely associated with him in the work, the panic of 1837, the refusal of the New York legislature to grant degree-conferring privileges to a denominational school, and perhaps, too, his own restless imagination, made Muhlenberg lose interest in St. Paul's, and in 1843, after a visit to England and the Continent, he turned to a new enterprise.

This was the Church of the Holy Communion, which was erected at the corner of Sixth Avenue and 20th Street, New York, by his sister, Mrs. Mary A. Rogers, and of which he became rector in 1846. It was the first important free church of his denomination in the United States and became the seat of a highly developed and, at that time, unique parish life. One episode in the development of the parish was the founding in 1852 of the Sisterhood of the Holy Communion, with Anne Ayres [*q.v.*] as the first member of the order. In this, as in several other innovations, Muhlenberg seems to have been inspired by Lutheran example. The best known of his many philanthropies, St. Luke's Hospital, originally built at Fifth Avenue and 34th Street, was also an outgrowth of the Church of the Holy Communion. Meanwhile, Muhlenberg became the leader of what was later known as the Memorial Movement and drafted the Memorial presented in 1853 to the House of Bishops. Among other things, the signers of the Memorial asked for certain reforms of the liturgy and for the episcopal ordination, under definite safeguards, of clergymen of other denominations. The Memorial, a noble, carefully reasoned statement of Muhlenberg's conception of the church, had little effect at the time, but it has been a subterranean influence on the thought of the Episcopal Church ever since. St. Luke's Hospital was incorporated in 1850, and after its opening in 1858 Muhlenberg resigned from the Church of the Holy Communion in order to give all his time to the Hospital, in which he made his home till his death. Like his other enterprises it was highly successful and has been frequently imitated. The last of his foundations was St. Johnsland, incorporated in 1870, an experiment in Christian communal life. It consisted of a small industrial community on the north side of Long Island, with schools, a church, an orphanage, and a home for old people. Less successful than his earlier experiments, it was in some ways the most characteristic, and was the darling of his old age.

He also influenced strongly the development of hymnody in the Episcopal Church. Of his own compositions, the sentimental "I would not live alway" (written 1824) was the best known. In later years its author became ashamed of it and tried to rewrite it in conformity with his maturer thought, but without effect. Much more representative of his religious verse is the fine baptismal hymn, "Saviour, Who Thy flock art feeding" (1826). He made visits to Europe in 1855 and again in 1872. In 1874 an attack of malarial fever left him permanently weak, and thereafter body and mind declined slowly together. Reverenced as one of the prophets of his church, he died in his hospital on Apr. 8, 1877, and was buried at St. Johnsland.

[Anne Ayres, *The Life and Work of William Augustus Muhlenberg* (1880; 4th ed., 1889) ; W. W. Newton, *Dr. Muhlenberg* (1890) ; H. E. Jacobs, " 'A Common-Place Lutheran,' " *Luth. Ch. Rev.*, Apr. 1890 ; Alonzo Potter, *The Memorial* (1857) ; Hall Harrison, *Life of the Right Rev. John Barrett Kerfoot* (2 vols., 1886) ; N. O. Halsted, "Dr. Muhlenberg and Saint Johnland," *Pa.-Ger.*, Apr. 1905 ; Robert Abbe, "A New

View of the Boyhood of the Rev. Dr. Muhlenberg," *Medic. Jour. and Record*, Nov. 17, 1926 ; *N. Y. Tribune*, Apr. 9, 1877 ; *Eve. Post* (N. Y.), Apr. 6, 9, 1877 ; John Julian, *A Dict. of Hymnology* (rev. ed., London, 1907). C. C. Tiffany, *A Hist. of the Protestant Episcopal Church in the U. S. A.* (1895) ; E. Harwood and G. D. Wildes, *In Memory of William Augustus Muhlenberg, D.D., LL.D.* (1877) ; E. A. Washburn, *Sermons in Memorial of William Augustus Muhlenberg, D.D.* (1877) ; *Churchman* (Hartford, Conn.), Apr. 14, 21, 1877 ; E. A. Washburn, "Dr. Muhlenberg," *Ibid.*, May 5, 1877.]
           G. H. G.

MUIR, JOHN (Apr. 21, 1838–Dec. 24, 1914), naturalist and explorer, was born at Dunbar, Scotland. His ancestry was Scotch both on his father's and on his mother's side. Daniel Muir married Anne Gilrye of Dunbar in 1833. John Muir was the eldest son and the third in a succession of five daughters and three sons. His early education, to the age of eleven, was secured in the schools of Dunbar. The ordinary subjects of instruction included also Latin and French, and in addition to the school tasks his father imposed the daily memorizing of a certain number of verses in the King James version of the Bible. This extra task was exacted by his father with military precision and enforced with much corporal punishment. Though grievous at the time, this memory work undoubtedly contributed much to the formation of his engaging English style. In 1849 Daniel Muir emigrated to America, taking along with him three of the older children, Sarah, David, and John. The remainder of the family followed after a homestead had been established in the wilds of Wisconsin, not far from Portage. Muir's autobiographical volume, *The Story of My Boyhood and Youth* (1913), furnishes a vivid account of his experiences on the Wisconsin farm. With relentless severity his father exacted from him all kinds of adult labor when he was a mere boy. Such farm labor included rail-splitting, fencing, plowing, hoeing maize, mowing with the scythe, and cutting grain with the cradle. He was no doubt right in thinking that the long hours and severe labor of the farm so far exceeded his strength that it checked his growth. John had a consuming desire for knowledge and read every book he could buy, exchange, or borrow for miles around. His father would not let him read in the evening, but said he might rise as early as he liked. Fearing to lose precious morning hours, and being "an ingenious whittler," he made a wooden clock, pivoted his bed on a crossbar, and hitched the clock to it by a special contrivance which he called "an early-rising machine" and which could be depended upon to set him on his feet at any desired time in the morning. By this heroic means he managed to acquire a sufficient general education to enable him to enter the University of Wisconsin when he came of age. A variety of astonishingly ingenious mechanical inventions, exhibited in 1860 at the Wisconsin State Fair in Madison, brought him to the favorable notice of the university authorities.

Muir took no degree when he left his university in 1863, because he preferred to choose his studies rather than conform to a prescribed curriculum. Chemistry and geology were his major interests. At the close of his college career botany became an absorbing passion which sent him on extensive foot-tours through Wisconsin, Iowa, Illinois, Indiana, and into Canada. In 1867, while employed in a wagon factory in Indianapolis, he suffered an accidental injury to one of his eyes. This occurrence decided him to "bid adieu to mechanical inventions" and devote the rest of his life "to the study of the inventions of God." Under the urge of this determination he started off at once on foot from Indiana to the Gulf of Mexico. He kept a journal in which he entered day by day his observations on the flora, the forests, physiography of the country, and experiences with the inhabitants. He also confided to it his personal reflections on man's attitude toward nature, the animal world, and the processes of life and death. The journal is important for an understanding of Muir at this stage of his career. It was edited by the writer after Muir's death under the title of *A Thousand-Mile Walk to the Gulf* (1916). He arrived in California in 1868 and immediately went to Yosemite Valley which remained the center of his studies and explorations for about six years. Then Nevada, Utah, the Northwest, and Alaska attracted him. On all his excursions he kept a journal in which he noted his observations, interspersed with abundant pencil sketches. These notebooks, of which seventy or more survive, formed the raw materials of his books and articles.

On Apr. 14, 1880, Muir married Louie Wanda Strentzel, the only surviving child of Dr. John Strentzel, an expatriate Pole who sought refuge in America after the unsuccessful Polish revolution of 1830. After some years of pioneering in Texas, where he had married Louisiana Erwin, a native of Tennessee, Strentzel had joined the Clarksville train of emigrants to California in 1849. Settling in the Alhambra Valley near Martinez, he soon became one of the most noted of the early horticulturists of the state. After his marriage Muir first rented and later bought from his father-in-law a part of the Strentzel fruit ranch, and then proceeded with great thoroughness to master the art of horticulture, for which

he possessed natural aptitude. During the decade from 1881 to 1891 he wrote and traveled little, devoting his attention wholly to the winning of a competence. This he did so successfully that at the end of this period he had, by his own testimony, enough money to provide permanently for his wife, his two daughters, and his own needs. He then sold a part of the ranch and leased the rest, in order to be able to devote the remainder of his life to travel and study.

As a naturalist Muir was interested in all the life and phenomena of the natural world. But he gave the most enthusiastic and continuous study to glaciers and forests. He was the first to demonstrate the origin of Yosemite Valley by glacial erosion (Badè, *Life and Letters of John Muir,* vol. I, ch. ix), opposing the views of Whitney and other scientists of the time. The generic use of the word "yosemite" was originated by him, for he saw clearly that it was only a type of valley similarly formed. After his discovery of residual glaciers in the Sierra Nevada, he extended his explorations into Alaska, discovering and describing many great glaciers, among them the one which now bears his name. The study of trees, particularly the sequoias and the pines, was another great passion of his life, and he made special journeys to Australia, Africa, and South America, in order to see the most impressive forest trees of these countries. On some of his expeditions to study trees in Alaska and in the Alleghanies he was accompanied by Charles S. Sargent [*q.v.*], director of the Arnold Arboretum, who dedicated to him the eleventh volume of his *Silva,* devoted to the *Coniferæ.*

In 1889 John Muir took Robert Underwood Johnson, then one of the editors of the *Century Magazine,* on a camping tour in the region of Yosemite Valley and the adjacent Tuolumne watershed, and showed him the devastation wrought by uncountable hordes of sheep. At Johnson's suggestion, they jointly determined to initiate a campaign for the establishment of what is now the Yosemite National Park. During the preceding decade Muir had written for *Scribner's Monthly* and the *Century* a series of brilliant articles on Western forests and scenery, which had a profound educative effect upon the public mind. One result was that public-spirited men all over the country rallied to the support of the Muir-Johnson movement; and one of the great conservation eras of our country began with the passage of the Yosemite National Park bill by Congress in October 1890. In the following year Congress passed an act empowering the president to create forest reserves. As early as 1876 Muir had proposed the appointment of a national commission to inquire into the fearful wastage of forests, to make a survey of existing forest lands in public ownership, and to recommend measures for their conservation. When at last such a commission was appointed in 1896, Charles S. Sargent, its chairman, invited John Muir to accompany the party on its tour of investigation. The Forestry Commission reported in 1897 and on the basis of its recommendations President Cleveland created thirteen forest reservations comprising more than twenty-one million acres. Predatory interests immediately sought to nullify the reserves by congressional action, and through their tools in Congress, succeeded in restoring to the public domain until Mar. 1, 1898, all forest reservations created by Cleveland, except those of California.

In the battle which now was joined, in Muir's phrase, "between landscape righteousness and the devil," he found his greatest opportunity for public service. Two brilliant articles, one in *Harper's Weekly* (June 5, 1897), entitled "Forest Reservations and National Parks," the other written at the request of Walter Hines Page for the *Atlantic Monthly* (August 1897) on "The American Forests," turned the tide of public sentiment. In both these articles Muir's style rose to the impassioned oratory of a Hebrew prophet arraigning wickedness in high places and preaching the sacred duty of so using the country we live in that we may not leave it ravished by greed and ignorance, but may pass it on to future generations undiminished in richness and beauty. Muir's invective caught the public ear and became effective in Congress, for when in 1898 enemies of the reservation policy again started a move to annul the reservations it failed. John F. Lacey, then chairman of the public lands committee of the House, insisted that Muir's judgment was probably better than that of any of his opponents. Muir had now become the acknowledged leader of the forest conservation movement in the United States. In the spring of 1903 he went on a brief camping trip in and about Yosemite with Theodore Roosevelt, then in his first term as president. Muir used the opportunity to expound to a willing and sympathetic listener his views on the urgent need of more forest reserves and national parks. The following six years of Roosevelt's presidency were distinguished by the setting aside of 148,000,000 acres of additional forest reserves, the establishment of sixteen national monuments, and the doubling of the number of national parks. In the accomplishment of this result Muir's informed enthusiasm played an imponderable but

influential part. The last six years of Muir's life were saddened by the unsuccessful struggle to preserve the beautiful Hetch-Hetchy Valley in the Yosemite National Park from conversion into a reservoir. Although a Board of Army Engineers had reported that "several sources of water supply could be obtained and used by the city of San Francisco," political intrigue, misrepresentation, and commercial considerations prevailed, to quote Muir, "over the best aroused sentiment of the entire country." One result of his leadership of the opposition was the consolidation of public sentiment against any possible repetition of such a raid.

Muir was a man of medium height, lithe, spare of frame, and during his prime was possessed of extraordinary powers of physical endurance. He was auburn-haired, had inquiring blue eyes, and an engaging personality. "The impression of his personality," wrote David Starr Jordan, "was so strong on those who knew him, that all words seem cheap beside it." His conversation was easy, vivid, and interspersed with flashes of delicious humor. In a conversational argument Muir was a formidable opponent, for he was quick at repartee and had an instinctive gift for seizing the essence of an issue and condensing it into a pungent phrase, like his description of sheep in forests as "hoofed locusts." According to the unanimous testimony of friends who knew him during the seventies and eighties he was an absorbingly fascinating talker, and it was the effect produced upon them by his conversation and letters that led them persistently to urge him to write for publication (*Life and Letters,* vol. II, pp. 6–7), a task which he always found more or less irksome. In his nature philosophy he was a theist with strong leanings toward Emerson and Thoreau, yet quite unlike either of them. With the mechanistic tendencies of his friend and contemporary John Burroughs he found himself at variance. He was a fellow of the American Association for the Advancement of Science, a member of the American Academy of Arts and Sciences, and he was the recipient of honorary degrees from the universities of Harvard, Wisconsin, Yale, and California, in the order mentioned. He died in Los Angeles and his remains were laid to rest beside those of his wife on his ranch near Martinez. Muir's books published during his lifetime, in addition to *The Story of My Boyhood and Youth,* include: *The Mountains of California* (1894); *Our National Parks* (1901); *Stickeen* (1909); *My First Summer in the Sierra* (1911); and *The Yosemite* (1912). Published posthumously were: *Travels in Alaska* (1915); *A Thousand-Mile Walk to the*

Gulf (1916) ; *The Cruise of the Corwin* (1917) ; and *Steep Trails* (1918).

[See: W. F. Badè, ed., *The Life and Letters of John Muir* (2 vols., 1923–24) ; S. Hall Young, *Alaska Days with John Muir* (1915) ; H. F. Osborn, *Impressions of Great Naturalists* (1924) ; R. U. Johnson, *Remembered Yesterdays* (1923) and "John Muir," in *Proc. Am. Acad. Arts and Letters*, vol. IX (1916) ; *Who's Who in America*, 1912–13 ; *Los Angeles Daily Times*, Dec. 25, 1914.]   W. F. B.

MULFORD, ELISHA (Nov. 19, 1833–Dec. 9, 1885), Protestant Episcopal clergyman, teacher, and author, was born in Montrose, Pa., the son of Silvanus Sandford Mulford. He prepared for college in the academy at Homer, N. Y., and entered the sophomore class at Yale, from which institution he graduated in 1855. Deciding to enter the ministry, he studied at Union Seminary, New York City, and at Andover Seminary, Andover, Mass. Later, he traveled abroad, studying at Berlin, Heidelberg, and Halle. He then became a clergyman in the Episcopal Church, being ordained deacon by Bishop Williams at Middletown, Conn., Apr. 20, 1861, and priest, by Bishop Odenheimer, at South Orange, N. J., Mar. 19, 1862. On Sept. 17 of the latter year he was married to Rachel Price Carmalt of Lakeside, Pa. After serving as rector in South Orange, he retired from the active ministry in 1864 (because of deafness) and moved to Lakeside, Pa., where he devoted himself to study and writing. In 1870 he published *The Nation,* and ten years later, *The Republic of God* (1880). Removing to Cambridge, Mass., in 1880, he became a lecturer in theology and apologetics in the Episcopal Theological School (1881 to 1885). He died at Cambridge and was buried in Sleepy Hollow Cemetery, Concord, Mass.

Mulford was preëminently a student, scholar, and writer. He was especially influenced in his philosophical and religious thinking by Hegel, Stahl, Trendelenburg, and Bluntschli, and, among English theologians, by Frederick Denison Maurice, whom he personally knew. He read largely in science, economics, social philosophy, art, and literature. His book *The Nation* is a well ordered and serious effort to define the substance and purpose of the state, reviewing the theories of its origin and development from Plato's ideas to those of Rousseau and modern philosophical writers. In it he attempts to show that the doctrines which regard the nation as an historical accident, or as a jural society or an economic society, are vague and partly untrue. The nation is an organism, a personality responding in its total life to ethical ideals, and cannot perform its proper function of progress and helpfulness without an everliving ethical conscious-

ness, fulfilling a divine purpose. The nation and its history is God in history working to a purposeful end. The later work, *The Republic of God,* was more distinctly a theological book, written with a background of historical religious scholarship and a new and modern spiritual outlook. The central theme of theism and Christianity is illustrated by skilful arguments drawn from literature, science, and art, as well as from philosophy. The antithesis between the kingdom of God and the republic of God brings out the dignity and responsibility of the individual who in human society becomes a kingly citizen to benefit the whole. As a teacher in the theological school, Mulford was inspiring and reverent, always connecting religion with life as well as with thought.

[*Obit. Records of Grads. of Yale Coll.,* 1886; C. D. Warner, *Lib. of the World's Best Literature,* vol. XVIII (1897) ; T. T. Munger, in *Independent,* Jan. 7, 1886, and *Century,* Apr. 1888 ; *Boston Transcript,* Dec. 10, 1885; appreciation by A. V. G. Allen (MS.) in Wright Memorial Lib., Cambridge, Mass.; information as to certain facts from members of the family.]

D. D. A.

MULFORD, PRENTICE (Apr. 5, 1834–*c.* May 27, 1891), journalist, philosopher, was born to Ezekiel and Julia (Prentice) Mulford at Sag Harbor, Long Island. Named for his maternal grandfather, Amos Prentice, he seems never to have used the first name. He grew up in Sag Harbor, at sixteen was working in his father's hotel, spent a few months at the state normal school but soon abandoned the idea of becoming a teacher, held a job as clerk in New York City for a year, then one in Illinois, and, having returned to Sag Harbor, at twenty-one shipped on board the clipper *Wizard,* bound for San Francisco. Upon reaching that port late in 1856, he was told by the captain that he was "not cut out for a sailor," and discharged from the crew. After a few months in San Francisco, he shipped with the schooner *Henry* down the California coast. Lured by the gold fields, he went in 1858 to Hawkins' Bar on the Tuolumne River, but prospecting proved unprofitable and accordingly, he taught school for two years in a mining camp in Tuolumne County. During the copper fever of 1862–63, he became, he says, "a copper expert," sinking unsuccessful shafts on his gold claim near Swett's Bar. Next came the silver excitement, but by this time he was finding more remuneration in other fields. In March 1865 he tramped to Sonora, Cal., to begin his career as a comic lecturer, and about the same time began to contribute poems and essays to the Sonora *Union Democrat* under the pen name, "Dogberry." In the political campaign of 1866–67 he was a candidate for the state assembly, but failed of election.

Through his "Dogberry" articles in the *Union Democrat,* he had, he says, "gained a small county but cashless reputation" (*Prentice Mulford's Story,* ed. of 1913, p. 260) and in 1866 Joseph Lawrence of the *Golden Era,* then the leading literary weekly west of the Mississippi, numbering among its contributors Bret Harte and Mark Twain, called him to San Francisco. During the next five years he wrote for several papers, including the *Dramatic Chronicle,* forerunner of the *San Francisco Chronicle,* and for a few months in 1868 edited the Stockton *Gazette,* a Democratic campaign paper. In 1872 he sailed for Europe, "to advance by writing and talking the good and glory of California" (*Ibid.,* p. 296), the mission being financed by San Francisco business men. He remained for a time in London, recording his impressions in letters to the San Francisco *Bulletin,* for which he also reported the Vienna world's fair. When he returned to New York in 1873 with but nine dollars in cash, he brought a young English girl as his bride. According to all accounts she was charming and exceedingly attractive, but the marriage was not successful and after a few years there was an amicable separation. In New York Mulford lectured for a time, but in the middle seventies joined the *Daily Graphic,* then under David G. Croly [*q.v.*], creating the column of condensed local news called "The History of a Day." Sick, after six years, of the sordid routine of this work, he gave up his job and retired alone to a small cabin which he built himself in the New Jersey woods near Passaic. In *The Swamp Angel,* published in 1888, he humorously described some of his experiences. The following year he published *Prentice Mulford's Story,* an account of his life up to the time of his leaving California.

While in the New Jersey wilderness, Mulford began to write the philosophical essays known as the White Cross Library. He published the first of these in Boston in May 1886, and for several years thereafter issued one a month, in pamphlet form. They were later collected in six volumes under the title, *Your Forces and How to Use Them.* In these essays and in the lectures he gave during the same period he expounded many of the ideas comprehended in the system of popular philosophy which came to be known as "New Thought." He maintained that the individual, by controlling his thought, directing it toward worthy objects, and cultivating a serene and confident attitude of mind, can achieve health and success. He believed in the evolu-

tion of man through a series of reincarnations leading toward the final perfection of the spirit and the loss of the "material parts that decay." Though his literary style lacked grace and was often actually crude, it was characterized by a directness and force which gained him an increasing number of readers, who found encouragement in his teachings. The quality of his thought brought a tribute from Whittier, who in the little poem, "Mulford," speaks of him as "a sage and seer." On May 24, 1891, having been troubled and depressed for some time (*National Magazine,* September 1906, p. 568), he set out in a dory for a solitary cruise along the south shore of Long Island, seeking quiet and a chance to order his thoughts. On May 30 he was found dead in his boat, which had been anchored in Sheepshead Bay since the morning of the 27th. His body, identified the next day by an intimate friend, was placed on June 2 in the family vault at Sag Harbor.

[*About Prentice Mulford* (1891), White Cross Library, no. 64; C. W. Stoddard, in *Nat. Mag.,* Apr. 1905; Sept. 1906; *Prentice Mulford's Story* (London, 1913); E. M. Martin, *Prentice Mulford, "New Thought" Pioneer* (1921); *Occult Review,* Mar. 1910, Jan. 1916; *A Hist. of Tuolumne County, Cal.* (1882); E. S. C. Mighels, *The Story of the Files* (1893); C. J. F. Binney, *The Hist. and Geneal. of the Prentice or Prentiss Family* (1883); *N. Y. Times,* June 1, 1891; information as to first name from H. D. Sleight, Sag Harbor, L. I.]   I. V.–F.

MULHOLLAND, ST. CLAIR AUGUSTIN (Apr. 1, 1839–Feb. 17, 1910), Union soldier, was a native of Ireland, being born in Lisburn, County Antrim, the son of Henry and Georgina (St. Clair) Mulholland. When he was but a boy, his parents emigrated to the United States and settled in Philadelphia, where young Mulholland received his early education. He became active in local militia organizations, and as a first lieutenant, assisted in organizing the 116th Pennsylvania Volunteers for Civil War service. He was appointed lieutenant-colonel of the regiment, June 26, 1862, and received his first wound in the charge of the Irish Brigade up Marye's Heights, Fredericksburg, Va., Dec. 13, 1862. His regiment being subsequently consolidated into a battalion, Mulholland was mustered out Feb. 24, 1863, and three days later, recommissioned major. At the battle of Chancellorsville, May 3–4, 1863, he distinguished himself by recapturing the guns of the 5th Maine Battery, and brilliantly commanded the picket-line covering the withdrawal of the Army of the Potomac across the Rappahannock River. The latter hazardous duty won for him the official commendation of Maj.-Gen. John Hancock, and the award, years later (Mar. 26, 1895), of the Congressional Medal of Honor. At Gettysburg, July

1–3, 1863, his own regiment having been seriously disorganized in the first day's battle, Mulholland led the 140th Pennsylvania Volunteers into action; and upon the reorganization of the 116th Pennsylvania Volunteers, was commissioned its colonel, May 3, 1864. In the Wilderness, May 5, 1864, he received his second wound, and for gallantry in action was subsequently brevetted (Mar. 13, 1865) brigadier-general of volunteers. At Po River (May 10, 1864), he was again wounded, but after a short convalescence returned to his command and on May 31 was dangerously wounded at Tolopotomy Creek. On Oct. 15, 1864, he assumed command of the 4th Brigade, 1st Division, II Army Corps, and participated in all the operations around Petersburg, Va. For gallantry at Boydton Plank Road, Oct. 27, 1864, in charging and capturing Confederate fortifications, he received, Mar. 13, 1865, the brevet of major-general of volunteers. He was honorably mustered out of the military service, June 3, 1865, and returned to his home in Philadelphia, where he served efficiently (1868–71) as the city's chief of police. President Cleveland appointed him United States pension agent at Philadelphia, which office he held for twelve years, through the administrations of Presidents McKinley and Roosevelt. In his spare hours, Mulholland devoted much time to art studies, and to the preparation of articles and lectures on the Civil War. He was also regarded as an authority on the subject of penology. In the year 1864 he was married to Mary Dooner, by whom he had three daughters and a son; and subsequently, to Mary Josephine Leeman, by whom he had two daughters.

[See Mulholland's *The Story of the 116th Regiment, Pa. Infantry* (1899) and *Mil. Order: Cong. Medal of Honor Legion of the U. S.* (1905); F. B. Heitman, *Hist. Reg. and Dict. of the U. S. Army* (1903), vol. I; D. P. Conyngham, *The Irish Brigade and Its Campaigns* (1867); *Who's Who in Pa.* (2nd ed., 1908); *The Cath. Encyc.; Cath. Standard and Times* (Phila.), Feb. 26, 1910; the *Press* (Phila.), Feb. 18, 1910. The spelling of Mulholland's middle name follows *Who's Who in Pa.* Heitman gives Agustin; the *Cath. Encyc.,* Augustine.]   C.D.R.

MULLAN, JOHN (July 31, 1830–Dec. 28, 1909), explorer, pioneer road-builder, was the son of John Mullan, a native of Ireland, and of Mary (Bright) Mullan, an American. He was born at Norfolk, Va., the first of ten children, but when he was three years old the family moved to Annapolis, Md. His parents, though poor, determined to give him an education. At nine he entered the grammar school of St. John's College, where he was graduated A.B. in 1847. In 1848, finding himself without a job or a profession, he sought admission to the United States Military Academy, interviewing President Polk, who soon afterward gave him an appointment. In 1852 he graduated, fifteenth in his class, and was assigned first to the topographical engineers and then to the artillery.

In 1853 he joined Gen. I. I. Stevens [*q.v.*] in exploring a route for a railroad from St. Paul to the Pacific. Stevens sent him on a mission of friendship to the Flatheads who were reported in camp on the Mussel-shell River, and Mullan followed the Indians, who were moving about, and brought them to a conference. He was then sent, during the winter, to the Bitterroot to examine the mountain passes. He explored the Rocky Mountains southward to Fort Hall on the Snake River and north to Canada, discovering Mullan Pass. According to General Stevens, he "made remarkable contributions to existing knowledge, both of the snows and the geography of the country, at a season of the year and under circumstances when most men would have done nothing" ("Narrative," *post*, p. 182).

Promoted first lieutenant in 1855, Mullan was recalled to active military duty and spent two years in the South fighting the Seminoles. Meanwhile Congress authorized the construction of a military road from Fort Benton to Walla Walla to connect navigation on the Missouri with that on the Columbia. Mullan's fine record of exploration won for him the position of chief of construction. While he was on his way to begin work the Indians became hostile and he found that his first task was to fight them. He distinguished himself in the battle of the Four Lakes, Sept. 1, 1858, and in other encounters. When the Indian war was over he found his resources exhausted and went to Washington to secure a new appropriation. He was aided by Stevens, then delegate to Congress, and in March 1859 that body appropriated $100,000 to begin construction. Mullan's surveys of 1853 and 1854 made selection of a route easy; work was begun in the summer of 1859, and continued till the spring of 1863 (John Mullan, *Report on the Construction of a Military Road from Fort Walla Walla to Fort Benton,* 1863). In 1860, while the road was under construction, Maj. Blake with 400 troops conducted the first wagon train over it and for the next twenty years it was a highway for immigrants to the Northwest. In 1862 Mullan urged the building of a new road from Deer Lodge Valley to the Yellowstone, then south to the Platte, anticipating the Bozeman road, but the government was too busy with war to pay attention to this recommendation.

On Apr. 28, 1863, Mullan and Rebecca Williamson were married. To them five children were born, three of whom survived their father. Soon after his marriage he resigned from the army and started a huge ranch near Walla Walla which failed the next year. He then obtained a four-year contract to carry the mail from Chico, California to Ruby City, Idaho, a distance of 600 miles, at the rate of $75,000 a year, and attempted to establish an express business, but within a year was forced out of business by a competitor and gave up his contract. Settling in San Francisco, he began the practice of law and was quite successful. In 1865 he published *Miners' and Travelers' Guide to Oregon, Washington, Idaho, Montana, Wyoming, and Colorado via the Missouri and Columbia Rivers*. He moved to Washington, D. C., in 1878, and there continued his legal work until failing health forced his retirement. He died in Washington.

[I. I. Stevens, "Narrative and Final Report of Explorations for a Route for a Pacific Railroad . . . from St. Paul to Puget Sound," in *Explorations and Surveys . . . for a Railroad Route from the Mississippi River to the Pacific Ocean*, vol. XII (1855) ; Lawrence Kip, *Army Life on the Pacific* (1859) ; G. W. Cullum, *Biog. Reg. Officers and Grads. U. S. Mil. Acad.* (3rd ed., 1891) ; *Army and Navy Jour.*, Jan. 1, 1910 ; *Evening Star* (Washington), Dec. 29, 1909 ; Mullan's journal from Fort Dalles to Fort Walla Walla, July 1858, ed. by Pal Clark, in *The Frontier* (Missoula, Mont.), May 1932 ; *Contribs. to the Hist. Soc. of Mont.*, VIII (1917), 162–69 ; D. A. Willey, "Building the M. R.," in *Sunset*, June 1910 ; clippings and memoir by Rebecca W. Mullan in the possession of a daughter, Mrs. Henry H. Flather, Tulip Hill, Md., and Washington, D. C.]
P. C. P.

MULLANY, JAMES ROBERT MADISON (Oct. 26, 1818–Sept. 17, 1887), naval officer, was born in New York, the son of Col. James R. Mullany, quartermaster-general of the army, and Maria (Burger) Mullany. Appointed midshipman from New Jersey on Jan. 7, 1832, he served for three years on the *Constellation*, and, after an intermission, for two years on the *United States*, both of the Mediterranean Squadron. His first assignments to sea duty, after being warranted passed midshipman in 1838, were to the *Dolphin* of the Brazil Squadron in 1839 and to the *Missouri* of the home squadron in 1841. After serving as acting master of the *Somers*, he was in July 1844, a few months after obtaining his lieutenancy, ordered to the Coast Survey where he remained for four years. In the years 1848–50 he served on the *St. Louis* and the *Brandywine* of the Brazil Squadron; and from 1852 to 1855 on board the *Columbia* of the home squadron. After a term of four years at the New York navy yard on ordnance duty, he in 1859 again joined the home squadron and was serving therein on the *Sabine* at the outbreak of the Civil War.

During April and May, 1861, Mullany commanded. successively, the *Wyandotte* and *Supply*

at Pensacola and aided in the defense of Fort Pickens. Promoted commander from Oct. 18, 1861, he was in the spring of the following year placed in command of the *Bienville*, a position that he held for more than three years, with the exception of a few days in August 1864, at the time of the battle of Mobile Bay. As the *Bienville* was not fit to engage the Confederate forts defending Mobile, he volunteered for service on some other vessel and was assigned the *Oneida* by Admiral Farragut. This ship held a position at the rear end of the line of battle and suffered considerable damage while passing the forts. In her engagement with the ram *Tennessee* Mullany received several wounds, one of which necessitated the amputation of his left arm. For his brave conduct he was commended by Admiral Farragut. During the war he was elsewhere several times under fire. In 1862 he captured off the South Carolina coast several blockade runners and in 1863 he commanded a division of the West Gulf blockading squadron operating off the coast of Texas.

Mullany was promoted captain in 1866, commodore in 1870, and rear admiral in 1874. In the years 1868–70 he commanded the *Richmond* of the European fleet; in 1870–71, the Mediterranean Squadron; and from 1874 to 1876, the North Atlantic station. At the time of his retirement on Oct. 26, 1879, he was governor of the naval asylum at Philadelphia, in which city he made his home. Mullany was twice married. He was a communicant of the Roman Catholic Church. The torpedo boat destroyer *Mullany* was named for him.

[*Record of Officers, Bureau of Navigation, 1832–93* ; *War of the Rebellion : Official Records (Navy)*, 1 ser. IV, XII, XIII, XX–XXII ; *Army and Navy Jour.*, Sept. 24, 1887 ; *N. Y. Tribune*, Sept. 18, 1887.]
C. O. P.

MULLANY, PATRICK FRANCIS [See AZARIAS, BROTHER, 1847–1893].

MÜLLER, WILHELM MAX (May 15, 1862–July 12, 1919), Orientalist, was born at Gliessenberg, Bavaria, the son of Frederic and Pauline (Barthel) Müller. He was reared in a devoutly religious home and, when prepared for university studies, went to Erlangen, then a center of Lutheran theological learning. Later he attended the universities of Berlin, Munich, and Leipzig, receiving from the last-mentioned the degree of Ph.D. He was an able linguist. It is said that he could speak both Greek and Hebrew, but his fame as a scholar rests upon his contributions to the science of Egyptology. He was well grounded in Egyptian, having been at Berlin a pupil of Adolf Erman, and, while working in the Museum at Munich, made his first important contribution to the subject. In 1888 he came to the United States, and on Apr. 13, 1889, he was married to Bettie Caspar of New York. In 1890 he was made professor of ancient languages and Old and New Testament exegesis in the Theological Seminary of the Reformed Episcopal Church in Philadelphia, a position which he held until his death. He was an excellent teacher and his accurate scholarship and simple piety made a deep impression upon his students. Here for almost thirty years he taught Hebrew and Greek, although nearly all of his publications were in the field of Egyptology. His Egyptological researches were carried on in his spare hours.

His earliest book, *Asien und Europa nach altägyptischen Denkmälern* (1893), at once took its place as the chief authority on the subject. His next book, *Die Liebpoesie der alten Ägypter* (1899), which contained Egyptian poems in hieroglyphic and demotic, together with translations into German, placed within the reach of students of the Bible Egyptian expressions of the tender passion, comparable in many ways to the Song of Songs. Like his earlier book, it gave evidence of competent scholarship. Through the good offices of Dr. S. Weir Mitchell [*q.v.*], Müller was sent to Egypt by the Carnegie Institution in the summer of 1904 to prosecute researches there. Although summer is the worst time to visit Egypt, it was the only time that his duties as a teacher would permit him to go. His work was so successful that he was sent back in 1906 and again in 1910. This last visit proved so great a strain upon his health that he did not go again. The fruit of these expeditions he published in *Egyptological Researches,* Volumes I and II (1906–10). A third volume, nearly ready for publication at the time of his death, was edited by H. F. Lutz and published in 1920. His other principal work was "Egyptian Mythology" in Volume XII of Louis H. Gray's *Mythology of all Races* (1918). In addition to these books, he was a contributor to the *Encyclopædia Biblica,* the *Jewish Encyclopedia,* to various revisions of Gesenius' Hebrew dictionary, and to Oriental journals.

During the last few years of his life he became assistant professor of Egyptology in the University of Pennsylvania in connection with his professorship in the Theological Seminary. He was never fully understood by some persons and possessed in his adopted country a narrower circle of friends than many scholars. Foreign scholars, however, appreciated his work, and, when passing through Philadelphia, many of

them sought him out. During the trying years of the World War he was thoroughly loyal to the United States. He borrowed money with which to buy a "liberty bond" and paid it back in instalments at considerable sacrifice. He was drowned at Wildwood, N. J., while swimming alone.

[*Jour. Am. Oriental Soc.,* Oct. 1919; *Who's Who in America,* 1918–19; *Pub. Ledger* (Phila.), July 13, 1919; *N. Y. Times,* July 13, 1919; personal information.]

G. A. B.

MULLIGAN, CHARLES J. (Sept. 28, 1866– Mar. 25, 1916), sculptor, was born in Riverdale, County Tyrone, Ireland, in humble circumstances, and came to this country at the age of seventeen. A vigorous boy, with a passion for work, he found employment as a stone-cutter in Pullman, near Chicago, Ill. Here he was discovered by the sculptor Lorado Taft, who was trying to forward artistic craftsmanship by means of a small vocational school in Pullman. Soon Taft received him as pupil-assistant in his own studio in Chicago and first called upon the apprentice to help in the carving of a marble bust. The master noted that this young Irishman of twenty had not only a skilful hand and an active imagination, but also a radiant personality which kindled the enthusiasm of the students in the evening classes of the Art Institute of Chicago, where "Charley," not content with hard work all day long, spent three evenings a week in modeling. Perhaps his greatest service to art was the inspiration he gave to others. In addition to his Art Institute training, he had a brief period of study in Paris, under Alexandre Falguière. In 1891 he was chosen by Taft to be the foreman of his Exposition workshop. Though cleverer artists than the new director were busy there, the manliness and tact of Mulligan minimized friction and brought about an atmosphere of harmony. His earliest attempts in creative work revealed his aspiration to become "the prophet of hopeful, cheerful labor." At the Buffalo Exposition, 1901, his statue "The Digger" attracted attention by its lively sincerity, while his four architectural figures of workingmen for the Illinois building stood forth as unusually good examples in this field. Later, his "Miner and Child," or "Home," an interesting pyramidal group in marble, showed his advance in technical competence, and in the expression of profound feeling. It is now in Humboldt Park, Chicago. Garfield Park, of the same city, has his statues of "Lincoln as Railsplitter," and of John F. Finerty; his "President McKinley" is in McKinley Park.

Mulligan never turned over his plaster models to be carved and finished in stone or marble by a practitioner, as is often the case. His ideal was to do his carving himself, and as he did not despise valuable mechanical aids, he had a pneumatic tool outfit in his studio. He was popular among his artist companions in Chicago and was instrumental in forming the nucleus of the artist colony, "Eagle's Nest," later established in Oregon, Ill. He was one of the founders of the Palette and Chisel Club; a member of the Society of Western Artists, Society of Chicago Artists, Beaux Arts Club, the Cliff Dwellers, and the Irish Fellowship Club. After Taft's resignation as head of the department of sculpture at the Art Institute, Mulligan was chosen to this position, in which he remained until his death. Among his many works in the West and South are "Justice and Power," with "Law and Knowledge," a pair of entrance groups for the State House, Springfield, Ill.; an impressive statue of Gen. George Rogers Clark, Quincy, Ill.; the soldiers' monument at Decatur, Ind.; and the Illinois monument, depicting Lincoln, the president, Grant, the warrior, and Yates, the governor, at Vicksburg, Miss. There was a tragic side to his career. "Much work he did," wrote Taft, "but never sufficiently recompensed to permit of adequate study" (*History of American Sculpture*, 1924, p. 540). In 1889, Mulligan married Margaret Ely, of Chicago. He died in St. Luke's Hospital, Chicago, from the effects of an operation, leaving a widow and three sons.

[The *Monumental News*, May 1916, published a sketch of Mulligan's life, with complete list of works, and Taft's tribute. Taft's *Hist. of Am. Sculpture* (1924, 1930) has brief references and one illustration. Other illustrations are found in *Harper's Weekly*, Nov. 27, 1909, p. 11, and in the *Art Interchange*, June 1904, p. 150. See also: *Bull. of the Art Inst. of Chicago*, Apr. 1916; *Art and Archæology*, Sept.–Oct. 1921; *Am. Art News*, Apr. 1, 1916; *Chicago Tribune*, Mar. 26, 27, 1916.]

A. A.

MULLINS, EDGAR YOUNG (Jan. 5, 1860–Nov. 23, 1928), Baptist clergyman, educator, and author, was born in Franklin County, Miss., the son of Seth Granberry and Cornelia Blair (Tillman) Mullins. His father and paternal grandfather were Baptist ministers and successful planters; while his maternal grandfather, Stephen Tillman, was a planter and politician, being for some years a member of the Mississippi legislature. When Edgar was eight years old the family moved to Corsicana, Tex., where the father became pastor and also established a school. Here Edgar grew to manhood and prepared for college. Because the family was large and the income very moderate, it was necessary for him to go to work early. He was at intervals printer's devil, newsboy, typesetter, printer, messenger boy, and telegrapher. Proving dependable

and efficient, he was put in charge of a telegraph office on full pay at fifteen years of age. This business experience was excellent preparation for the management of the greater interests which were later entrusted to his care. His father was a graduate of Mississippi College, a Baptist institution, but Edgar chose to enter Texas Agricultural and Mechanical College, where he graduated in 1879.

He then began the study of law, but was converted in 1880 and decided to follow his father's profession. Entering the Southern Baptist Theological Seminary, Louisville, Ky., in 1881, he spent four years in theological preparation. Upon graduation in 1885, he was ordained and became pastor of a town-country church at Harrodsburg, Ky., where he remained until 1888. His other pastorates were those of Lee Street Baptist Church, in downtown Baltimore from 1888 to 1895, and the wealthy, cultured suburban church at Newton Centre, Mass., from 1896 to 1899. For a few months in 1895–96 he was assistant secretary of the Foreign Mission Board. While in Baltimore he continued his studies in The Johns Hopkins University and also served as correspondent for the *Examiner*. During his three pastorates, which gave him experience in three different types of churches, he developed into an exceedingly effective preacher. His sermons were distinguished by universal appeal, freshness and vigor of thought, lucidity of language, and aptness in illustration.

When, in 1899, the presidency of the Southern Baptist Theological Seminary became vacant, he was elected to the position, which he held until his death. Here, as president and professor of theology, he did his greatest work. He was an able administrator, a clear and vigorous theological thinker, a stimulating teacher, and a prolific author. His more important works included: *Why Is Christianity True?* (1905); *The Axioms of Religion* (1908); *Baptist Beliefs* (1912); *Freedom and Authority in Religion* (1913); *Studies in Ephesians and Colossians* (1913); *The Life in Christ* (1917); *The Christian Religion in Its Doctrinal Expression* (1917); *Spiritualism a Delusion* (1920); *Christianity at the Cross Roads* (1924). In addition to the above, he wrote many tracts and pamphlets on religious subjects and was a frequent contributor to the religious press. As a theologian, he was a moderate Calvinist. His theological position was based on a careful interpretation of the scriptures and was little affected by current scientific thought. He was conservative as to position and progressive as to method. He was thoroughly evangelical, holding the generally recognized views of the great body of Protestant scholars, but reaching them in an independent way. His later writing was devoted largely to the problems arising from the impact of the natural sciences upon Christianity, and had a considerable influence upon the thought of Southern Baptists with regard to these questions. He was president of the Southern Baptist Convention from 1921 to 1924, and of the Baptist World Alliance from 1923 to 1928. In these positions he exercised a powerful influence in the promotion of unity, harmony, and progress among the Baptists of the world, seeking to avoid extremes and to hold the discordant elements of his people together in harmonious fraternal cooperation.

On June 2, 1886, he was married to Isla May Hawley of Alabama, a charming and cultured woman who made a worthy companion to her husband. To this union were born two children, neither of whom lived beyond childhood. He died in Louisville, Ky., at the age of sixty-eight; his wife survived him.

[Isla May Mullins, *Edgar Young Mullins* (1929); B. J. W. Graham, *Bapt. Biog.*, vol. I (copr. 1917); Isla May Mullins, *Captain Pluck* (1923); *Who's Who in Louisville*, 1926; *Who's Who in America*, 1928–29; *Hist. of Ky.* (1928), vol. IV; *Review and Expositor*, Apr., July, Oct. 1929; *Baptist*, Dec. 8, 1928; *Watchman-Examiner*, Nov. 29, 1928; *Courier-Journal* (Louisville), Nov. 24, 1928.] W. J. M.

MULRY, THOMAS MAURICE (Feb. 13, 1855–Mar. 10, 1916), Vincentian, son of Thomas and Parthenia (Crolius) Mulry, was born in Greenwich Village, New York, the second child in a family of fourteen, of whom one became a Sister of Charity and four, members of the Society of Jesus. The father, one of five brothers who came from Roscommon, Ireland, about 1837, had developed into a successful building contractor. Thomas' schooling at St. Joseph's parochial school and the De La Salle Academy was broken by two temporary removals of the family to a farm at Pleasant Prairie, Wis., but after returning to New York, while working with his father, to whose business he succeeded, he attended night classes at the Cooper Institute. On Oct. 6, 1880, he married Mary E. Gallagher, a school-teacher, and set up housekeeping in Greenwich Village, where he reared a large family. Three of his sons became Jesuits and a daughter, a Sister of Charity. Deeply religious in a practical way, Mulry so sympathized with the poor inhabitants of the cellars and tenements of the congested Village and with the impoverished immigrants landing at Castle Garden that he gave all his spare time to charity and poor relief. This work, he believed, could be best accomplished through the Society of St. Vincent de Paul, with which he became affiliated in 1872. He was scrupulously honest and dependable, and his business prospered until he became recognized as one of the solid men of the city: a trustee of the Emigrant Industrial Savings Bank (1901), of which he was elected president in 1906, and a director in a number of real-estate corporations and trust companies. After the insurance scandal, he served on a committee under former President Cleveland which sought to rehabilitate the Mutual Life Insurance Company. No politician, he held no official positions, although he refused offers of Democratic nominations for controller and mayor (1905) when such nominations would have virtually insured election. Apparently he knew the temptations of office too well. A delegate to the state constitutional convention in 1915, he defended private charitable institutions against the onslaught of professional philanthropists.

It is as a Vincentian that Mulry was nationally known. A member of the Superior Council of New York in 1885, he became its secretary in 1887 and was its president from 1905 to 1915. For some time he had an editorial interest in the *St. Vincent de Paul Quarterly.* In 1915, he aided in the reorganization of the society on provincial, diocesan, and parochial lines, with a Superior Council in the United States responsible to the Council-General at Paris. He was elected national president in recognition of his character as an "American Ozanam." A founder of the National Conference of Catholic Charities (1910), he won the support of the Vincentians for its program of cooperative effort and scientific means of relief and reformation. A frequent speaker and reader of papers at the conventions of the National Conference of Charities and Corrections, at meetings of the New York State Charity Conference (of which he was president in 1903), and at the meetings of the City Conference of Charities and Corrections (over which he presided in 1912), he was so direct, earnest, and informative that he won recognition in the field as a sane counselor with solid business acumen. Hence he was named to positions on a number of boards: member of the State Board of Charities; president of the board of managers of Manhattan Hospital for the Insane; chairman of the committee on children of the National Conference of Charities, of which he was president at the Minneapolis meeting in 1907; and vice-president of the White House Conference on the Standards of Child Welfare (1909), which President Roosevelt declared was successful largely because of Mulry's cooperation. In the field of Catholic charities, he was a patron of the Marquette League for Indian Welfare, a trustee of the Catholic Summer School, founder and president of the Catholic Home Bureau for Dependent Children, and founder of St. Elizabeth's Home for Children, the St. Vincent de Paul Summer Home for Children, St. Elizabeth's Home for Convalescent Women and Girls. He was also a patron of the Ozanam Association for promotion of boys' clubs, a manager of the New York Foundling Asylum, and vice-president of the Friendly Sons of St. Patrick. For his services, he was not without honors: the knighthood of the Pontifical Order of St. Gregory was conferred upon him by Pope Pius X; the honorary degree of LL.D. by the Catholic University of America (1915); and the Laetare Medal, annually awarded to an outstanding Catholic layman, by Notre Dame University (1912). His last public appearance was in defense of the State Board of Charities before the Strong Commission of Investigation (1915). He died the following year, and with services in St. Patrick's Cathedral presided over by Cardinal Farley and Bishops Hayes and Shahan, was buried in Calvary Cemetery.

[T. F. Meehan, *Thomas Maurice Mulry* (1917); Patrick Mulry, *A Memoir of George Mulry, S. I.* (1891); *St. Vincent de Paul Quart.*, May 1916, memorial number, containing tributes by leaders in Church and State; an appreciation by W. J. Kerby, in *Cath. World*, July 1916; *America*, Mar. 18, 1916; *N. Y. Herald*, Mar. 11, 1916; *Truth*, Oct. 1933.]   R. J. P.

MUMFORD, JAMES GREGORY (Dec. 2, 1863–Oct. 18, 1914), surgeon and author, was born in Rochester, N. Y., the son of George Elihu and Julia Emma (Hills) Mumford and a descendant of Thomas Mumford who settled in Rhode Island in 1655. He prepared for college at St. Paul's School, an institution of which he was eventually a trustee, and was graduated by Harvard College in 1885 and the Harvard Medical School in 1890. After an internship at the Massachusetts General Hospital he settled in practice in Boston as a surgeon. He became a fairly successful surgeon, although he could not be considered an unusual one. For many years he was on the staff of the Massachusetts General Hospital, where he did excellent work. He never held more than a minor teaching position at the Harvard Medical School. He wrote eight books, as well as fifty or sixty papers, the great majority of them on surgical subjects. In 1903 appeared his *Clinical Talks on Minor Surgery*, in 1905 *Surgical Aspects of Digestive Disorders*, written in collaboration with A. K. Stone, in 1908 *Some End Results of Surgery*, and, in 1910, a textbook on *The Practice of Surgery*, a second edition of which appeared in 1914. In 1911 came a minor book entitled *One Hundred Surgical*

Problems; the Experiences of Daily Practice Dissected and Explained. All these books were sound contributions to American surgery. Early in his career he also showed a marked interest in the history of medicine and one of his first books, in 1903, was *A Narrative of Medicine in America*. Two years later he edited *The Harvard Medical School* (3 vols.), written by Thomas Francis Harrington [*q.v.*]. In 1908 he published *Surgical Memoirs and Other Essays* and in 1912 one of the most delightful of his short works, *A Doctor's Table Talk*. These latter publications were written in a charming, winsome style.

He was somewhat of a medical reformer, although not of the aggressive, disagreeable type. He became interested in the relations between religion and medicine and identified himself with the Emmanuel Movement, led by the Rev. Elwood Worcester of Boston. He foresaw the establishment of great medical centers, including hospitals and medical schools, and with full-time teachers upon the staff. He was also interested in providing good medical care for persons of moderate means and in 1910 he planned such a hospital; but the scheme got no farther than its prospectus. The idea was partly realized, however, at the Clifton Springs Sanitarium, New York, where he spent the last two years of his life. He was a member of many medical societies and social clubs and he took an active interest in bodies for civic uplift, such as the Economic Club and the Reform Club. His health was never good in the last dozen years of his life, for he suffered from a severe cardiac disease, of which he finally died. Greatly beloved by many of his contemporaries, he characterized himself, in a letter written in 1910, at the time of the twenty-fifth anniversary of his graduation by Harvard College, as follows: "I like teaching; students pass me out the usual compliments due to credulous senility. I like practising surgery; patients toss me roses mingled with thorns. I like writing about people and things, for the reviewers deal me comments which chasten the soul. Altogether, life continues a pleasant experience." His writings were characteristic of the man, for they exhibit sound judgment, keen perception, and a clarity of statement which is seldom found in scientific or lay literature. Mumford married, in 1892, Helen Sherwood Ford of Troy, N. Y.; there were no children.

[*Trans. Am. Surgic. Asso.*, vol. XXXIV (1916); *Boston Medic. and Surgic. Jour.*, Apr. 1, 1915, Feb. 6, 1919; *Class of 1885, Harvard Coll., Secretary's Report No. 7* (1910); *Johns Hopkins Hospital Bull.*, vol. XXVI (1915); J. G. Mumford, *Mumford Memories, Being the Story of the New Eng. Mumfords from the*

Year 1655 to the Present Time (1900); *Boston Transcript*, Oct. 19, 1914.]   H. R. V.

MUNDÉ, PAUL FORTUNATUS (Sept. 7, 1846–Feb. 7, 1902), physician, was born in Dresden, Germany. His mother, Bertha, was the daughter of Baron von Hornemann, a councilor of the King of Saxony. His father, Dr. Charles Mundé, a man of intense democratic ideals, participated actively in the Revolution of 1848, was proscribed, and as a political exile fled with wife and child to America. The family settled in Florence, Mass., where Dr. Charles Mundé conducted a sanatorium until his return to Germany. The son inherited intrepidity and a sturdy physical constitution from his father. His studious nature was early exhibited; he entered the Boston Latin School, and at the age of seventeen years was prepared to start the study of medicine at Yale. The Civil War interrupted his studies, but the spirit of adventure which seems to have been one of his essential characteristics was not satisfied by service in the garrison at Boston, and after six months he returned to the study of medicine at Harvard. He graduated with high honors in 1866 and spent the next seven years in Germany.

He arrived just in time to take part in the War of 1866 as an assistant surgeon in the Bavarian army. Upon his release from service in 1867 he went to Würzburg, where the famous gynecologist and obstetrician, Scanzoni, was in charge of the Maternity Hospital. Mundé was resident physician for three years and here obtained the training which determined his future work and gave him the ideals of German scientific medicine. Again a war interrupted his studies. He joined the Bavarian army at the outbreak of the Franco-Prussian conflict, and at the siege of Paris had charge of a hospital which was destroyed by the enemy's fire. During the conflagration he rescued the wounded personally and received the Iron Cross for this deed. It is characteristic of Mundé that the honors which he won in both these foreign wars were unknown to most of his friends until after he had died. At the close of the war he traveled throughout Europe and visited the centers where medical thought was particularly active—Heidelberg, Berlin, Vienna, London, Edinburgh, and Paris.

After this extraordinary preparation he returned to America in 1873 and entered practice in New York City. In November of that year he married Eleanor Claire Hughes of New Haven, Conn. His subsequent life was one of devotion to scientific medicine. The time was propitious for the development of the specialties. New York City was the scene of labors of J. M.

Sims, T. A. Emmett, and Abraham Jacobi [*qq.v.*], but there was great need for such well-trained men as Mundé. His assiduity marked him as fitted for positions which require painstaking energy and these he filled with such skill that only the physical incapacities of later years relieved him of his labors. In 1874 he became chief editor of the *American Journal of Obstetrics* and he retained that position until 1892. In this time the *Journal* rose to a position of preeminence in its field. He was secretary and (1886–88) president of the New York Obstetrical Society and treasurer (1876–83), vice-president (1884), and president (1898) of the American Gynecological Society. He became gynecologist to Mount Sinai Hospital in 1881, and its Gynecological Outpatient Department was his creation. As professor of gynecology he taught in the New York Polyclinic and at Dartmouth College.

His publications include over one hundred scientific articles and three textbooks: *Minor Surgical Gynecology* (1880), *Diagnosis and Treatment of Obstetrical Cases by External Examination and Manipulation* (1880), and *A Practical Treatise on the Diseases of Women* (1891), rewritten and reëdited from the original of Theodore Gaillard Thomas. Mundé exerted a powerful influence on the course of the gynecological specialty in America, not because of any important scientific discovery but because he brought excellent training, a passion for scientific truth, and weighed judgment to a country which still lacked workers of quality. In this activity of transferring European ideals to American soil he was aided by a charming personality which was energetic and resourceful but not combative or zealous. He died in New York City in his fifty-sixth year.

[*Mount Sinai Hosp. Reports, 1901–02*, vol. III (1903); H. A. Kelly and W. L. Burrage, *Am. Medic. Biogs.* (1920); *Trans. Am. Gynecol. Soc.*, vol. XXVII (1902); *Am. Jour. Obstet.*, Apr. 1902; *Boston Medic. and Surgic. Jour.*, Feb. 13, 1902; *Medic. News* (N. Y.), Feb. 15, 1902; *N. Y. Times*, Feb. 8, 1902.]   H. S. R.

MUNFORD, ROBERT (d. 1784), Revolutionary soldier and dramatist, was born at "Whitehall," Prince George County, Va., of aristocratic stock, son of Robert Munford (2nd) and his wife Anna Bland. He was educated at Wakefield, Yorkshire, England, along with other sons of the Virginia gentry, and while quite a young man was a soldier in the French-Indian wars, serving as captain in the 2nd Virginia Regiment, under William Byrd III, in the campaign of 1758. There are extant several letters written by him from Fort Cumberland to his uncle Theodorick Bland, Sr., which give interesting details of his military experience as well as his estimate of Colonel Washington. When Mecklenburg County was formed in 1765 he was made county-lieutenant and continued in that office until his death, the while representing the district in the House of Burgesses, 1765–75, and in the General Assembly, 1779 and 1780–81. In the pre-Revolutionary period he followed a temperate but courageous part in resisting British aggressions, and he was among those who signed the Williamsburg Association, a non-importation agreement, on June 22, 1770. During the war he saw much service of different kinds, his efforts in recruiting soldiers for the American army being especially beneficial, and rose to the rank of major. He married his first cousin, Anne, daughter of William Beverley of "Blandfield," Essex County.

A fine type of the cultured colonial gentleman and planter, Munford found diversion in literature from his professional activities. His reputation as a writer depends, save for occasional letters, upon his single posthumous volume, *A Collection of Plays and Poems* (1798), published, with a preface, by his son William [*q.v.*]; but this miscellany suffices to demonstrate, besides an aim to combine instruction with entertainment, his grace and vigor of expression, shrewd observation of men and events, broad humor, and turn for trenchant satire. Save for a spirited "Patriotic Song" and an amusing narrative, "The Ram," ridiculing feminine vanity, the half-score original poems lack distinction. More should be said, however, for the two prose plays and for the rhymed translation of Book I of Ovid's *Metamorphoses*—his death prevented the completion of this task—which is both scholarly and pleasing. *The Candidates,* written apparently several years before the Revolution, is a three-act satire upon country election practices which spares neither the heedless voter nor the unscrupulous aspirant; in spite of certain limitations, it mixes sound sense and passable farce with its gibes, and "it introduces in Ralpho probably the first negro character in the American drama" (A. H. Quinn, *A History of the American Drama from the Beginning to the Civil War,* 1923, p. 55). *The Patriots* (first published in Philadelphia, 1776, although seemingly never acted) is a much more significant piece, not only in structure, characters, dialogue, and particularly in plot, but also in its general temper. Avowedly a contrast between real and pretended patriotism, this early purpose drama from the pen of a man whose devotion and services to his country were above question is of added interest for its undertone of al-

most pacifistic hatred of war and its impatience with extremes of conduct and precept, whether Whig or Tory.

[See: Philip Slaughter, *A Hist. of Bristol Parish, Va.* (2nd ed., 1879); *Tyler's Quart. Hist. and Geneal. Mag.,* Jan. 1922; *Va. Mag. of Hist. and Biog.,* Jan.–Apr. 1928; *Va. Hist. Reg.,* Jan. 1850, pp. 17–24; B. B. Munford, *Random Recollections* (1905); and Chas. Campbell, ed., *The Bland Papers* (2 vols., 1840–43). Detailed data concerning Munford are relatively scarce, partly no doubt owing to the destruction by fire of "Richlands," his Mecklenburg plantation, in the early nineteenth century.]   A. C. G., Jr.

MUNFORD, WILLIAM (Aug. 15, 1775–June 21, 1825), legislator, court reporter, poet, and classicist, was born in Mecklenburg County, Va., the eldest child and only son of Col. Robert [*q.v.*] and Anne (Beverley) Munford. He was educated in the grammar school connected with the College of William and Mary and later at the college itself. His early training might have terminated with his father's death and the resulting straitened circumstances had not Chancellor Wythe, then professor of law at Williamsburg, enabled him to continue. From Wythe, Munford gained a deep insight into the law and learned to love the classics. Completing his legal education at the age of twenty-one he almost immediately entered politics. During the session of 1797–98 he represented his native county in the House of Delegates, to which he was returned from 1800 to 1802 when he was elected to the state Senate. In that year, 1802, he was married to Sally Radford, daughter of William Radford of Richmond. After four years in the upper house he was placed on the privy council or council of state and thereafter made his home in Richmond. In 1811 he was appointed clerk of the House of Delegates, holding this office until his death. From 1808 to 1811, in conjunction with William W. Hening, he reported the decisions of the Virginia supreme court of appeals for the years 1806–10, the four volumes (11–14 *Va.*) bearing both names. After Hening's death Munford continued as reporter until 1821, publishing the decisions for the years 1810–21 in *Munford's Reports* (15–20 *Va.*). Under the direction of Benjamin Watkins Leigh he materially assisted in preparing the Code of 1819. He was an Episcopalian and from 1815 to 1824 served as secretary and treasurer of the Convention of the Diocese of Virginia.

The son of one of Virginia's early poets and dramatists, Munford was to achieve his greatest distinction, perhaps, in the field of letters rather than in public service or the law. In 1798 he published *Poems and Compositions in Prose on Several Occasions,* comprising poems on various themes, translations from Horace and Ossian, and a five-act tragedy, *Almoran and Hamet,* a dramatized story of the East. Designed to benefit his readers, enhance his reputation, and afford economic return, it was, however, a rather juvenile adventure into the realms of literature. But Munford's love for the classics was to produce one noteworthy contribution to literature, his translation into blank verse of the *Iliad.* Not content with existing translations, he undertook one of his own. For many years he labored painstakingly at his cherished work and completed it just before his death. Published in 1846, twenty-one years later, it received warm contemporary praise and was hailed as one of the greatest accomplishments in the history of classical scholarship in Virginia. Although it lacked, perhaps, Homer's poetic fire, it succeeded to a considerable degree in reproducing the beauty and magnificence of the original. It still stands as a significant milestone in the progress of American letters—an honorable and fitting close to a busy professional life.

[G. D. Fisher, *Hist. and Reminiscences of the Monumental Church* (1880); G. W. Munford, *The Two Parsons* (1884); F. V. N. Painter, *Poets of Va.* (1907); Preface to *The Revised Code of the Laws of Va.* (2 vols., 1819); *The Hist. of the Coll. of Wm. and Mary* (1874); *Wm. and Mary Coll. Quart.,* Jan. 1900, Oct. 1909; *Tyler's Quart. Hist. and Geneal. Mag.,* Jan. 1922; E. G. Swem and J. W. Williams, *A Reg. of the Gen. Assembly of Va., 1776–1918* (1918); *North Am. Rev.,* July 1846; the *Am. Rev.: A Whig Jour.,* Oct. 1846; *Christian Examiner,* Sept. 1846; family data supplied by Mrs. W. S. Robertson, Richmond, Va., Munford's grand-daughter.]   T. S. C.

MUNGER, ROBERT SYLVESTER (July 24, 1854–Apr. 20, 1923), inventor, manufacturer, was born in Rutersville, Fayette County, Texas, the son of Henry Martin and Jane C. (McNutt) Munger and a descendant of Nicholas Munger who emigrated from England to Connecticut in the seventeenth century. His father was a successful merchant and farmer and, in addition, was engaged in a small way in the manufacture of cotton-gins. When Robert was sixteen years old the family moved to Mexia, Tex. He had attended the public schools at Rutersville and he now entered the preparatory department of Trinity University, soon after its establishment at the old town of Tehuacana. After three years there, but before graduating, he returned to his home and took charge of his father's ginning plant, where he quickly developed a keen interest in the machinery, and soon manifested a considerable inventive talent. He conceived the idea of a pneumatic system for handling seed cotton and conveying it from the wagon to the gin, but a number of years elapsed before he devised a practical system. Meanwhile he patented several machines essential to cotton

ginning, including three saw cleaners, patented Apr. 23, 1878, May 20, 1879, and July 22, 1879, respectively, and a saw-sharpening tool, patented Oct. 10, 1882. In 1885 he attempted to get manufacturing companies interested in exploiting his patents but was unsuccesful, and accordingly established a manufacturing plant of his own at Dallas, which he operated for three years. Then, in 1888, he organized the Munger Improved Cotton Machine Company of Dallas and assumed the office of president. He resigned this position the following year and shortly thereafter moved to Birmingham, Ala., where he organized the Northington-Munger-Pratt Company in 1892 for the manufacture of cotton-gin machinery. During this time he had made progress in the perfection of his idea for pneumatic handling, and on July 12, 1892, obtained patent No. 478,883 for a machine "for handling, cleaning and distributing seed cotton." The Munger system, as it came to be known, was a revolutionary improvement over the old system used at cottongins and was quickly adopted throughout the cotton-states and the world generally. Although serving as vice-president and director of both Dallas and Birmingham companies, Munger found time to continue with his inventive work and patented a duplex cotton-press (Oct. 4, 1892); an improvement in his pneumatic system (Nov. 28, 1893); a baling machine and a cotton elevator, cleaner and feeder (both Aug. 6, 1901); and an additional improvement on his cotton cleaner (Aug. 5, 1919). He is recognized as the pioneer of most of the improved ginning machinery used in the United States today. He retired from active management of his companies in 1902, following their purchase by the Continental Gin Company of Dallas, and thereafter devoted his attention mainly to real-estate interests. He was an active philanthropist and much interested in educational enterprises throughout the South. He married Mary Collett of Austin, Tex., May 2, 1878, and at the time of his death in Birmingham was survived by eight children.

[T. M. Owen, *Hist. of Ala. and Dict. of Ala. Biog.* (1921), vol. IV; L. B. Hill, *A Hist. of Greater Dallas and Vicinity* (1909), vol. II; J. B. Munger, *The Munger Book* (1915); Patent Office records; *Birmingham Age-Herald,* Apr. 20, 21, 1923; *Dallas Morning News,* Apr. 21, 1923.]   C. W. M.

MUNGER, THEODORE THORNTON (Mar. 5, 1830–Jan. 11, 1910), Congregational clergyman, was born in Bainbridge, N. Y., the fifth child of Dr. Ebenezer and Cynthia (Selden) Munger, and a descendant of Nicholas Munger who emigrated from England to New Haven probably about 1639. On his father's side he was of the sixth generation from John Eliot [*q.v.*], apostle to the Indians, and by his mother he was in direct descent from Thomas Selden who came to Hartford, Conn., with Thomas Hooker in 1636. When he was six years of age the family removed to Homer, N. Y. Entering Yale in 1847, he gave himself more to general reading than to the prescribed course of studies. He graduated in 1851, and from the Yale Divinity School in 1855. After spending a term in Andover Theological Seminary, he accepted a call to the village church (Congregational) of Dorchester, Mass., in which he was ordained Feb. 6, 1856. He served successively churches in Haverhill, Mass., Providence, R. I., Lawrence, Mass., San José, Cal., East Hartford, Conn., and North Adams, Mass. In 1885 he became minister of the United Church, New Haven, Conn., continuing until, having reached the age of seventy, he resigned and was made pastor emeritus. He was married to Elizabeth Kinsman Duncan of Haverhill, Mass., Oct. 12, 1864, and to Harriet King Osgood of Salem, Mass., Mar. 5, 1889.

An unassertive man, his rise to general recognition was slow. He studied seriously and made himself a master of prose style; from time to time he wrote articles for the religious press. He was fifty, however, before his first book was published—a series of sermons to young people entitled *On the Threshold* (1880), of which more than 25,000 had been sold when the publishers reissued it as one of the Cambridge Classics. *Lamps and Paths,* a companion volume for younger readers, appeared in 1883, and the next year, a second edition, enlarged by four chapters. His most characteristic thought found expression in *The Freedom of Faith* (1883), which Whittier welcomed as being "refreshing and tonic as the north wind." It attracted wide attention, for, coming at a time of great religious unsettlement, it shed light on fundamental spiritual problems, and also revealed the essential vitality of the newer ways of thinking. With his eager, intuitional mind and his ardent faith in an ever-increasing revelation of truth, Munger was constitutionally sympathetic with the New Theology. Instinctively he had been drawn to Horace Bushnell; he was also greatly inspired by F. D. Maurice; but it was Frederick Robertson who molded his manner of thinking. Robertson's six principles of thought, he affirmed in his last years, told him "how to know under what principles of thought to express myself." The first three, especially, go far to explain his ideals and methods—"the establishment of positive truth, instead of the negative destruction of error;

truth is made up of two opposite propositions, spiritual truth is discerned by the spirit, instead of intellectually in propositions, and therefore should be taught suggestively, not dogmatically." These principles, early adopted, guided him through life. In the heated debate between the champions of the old and the new ways of religious thinking, Munger was a recognized leader. Under his touch theology became literature. In a volume of sermons and essays called *The Appeal to Life* (1887) he characteristically interpreted truth through human experience. In 1897 appeared a book of sermons bearing the title *Character Through Inspiration*. Next to *The Freedom of Faith* his most important book was *Horace Bushnell, Preacher and Theologian* (1899), a masterly interpretation of a spiritual predecessor to whom he was much indebted. If Munger's talent was slow in maturing, it continued fruitful in old age, for after his retirement he wrote frequently for current periodicals and published an important book, *Essays for the Day* (1904), in his seventy-fourth year.

A devoted pastor, his chief distinction was as a preacher and writer. Though lacking the peculiar gifts which make one popular with the masses, he was effective in reaching select minds of every class and condition. In his sermons there was an intensity of conviction, a swiftness of movement, a penetration and rich suggestiveness of thought, a stimulating terseness of expression, which brought light and power to his hearers. Thoughtful students in the university sought his counsel because of a certain mental flexibility which enabled him to think out their problems with them. Memorial tablets in his honor have been placed in Woolsey Hall, Yale University, and in the United Church, New Haven.

[J. B. Munger, *The Munger Book* (1915); *Obit. Record Grads. Yale Univ.,* 1910; *The Congregational Year-Book,* 1911; *Who's Who in America,* 1908–09; B. W. Bacon, *Theodore Thornton Munger* (1913); J. W. Buckham, *Progressive Religious Thought in America* (1919); *Congregational and Christian World,* Jan. 22, 1910; *New Haven Evening Register,* Jan. 12, 1910.]   C. A. D.

MUNN, ORSON DESAIX (June 11, 1824– Feb. 28, 1907), editor, publisher, was the youngest son of Rice and Lavinia (Shaw) Munn and was born in Monson, Mass., where his father was engaged in business. His first direct American ancestor was Benjamin Munn who in 1649 removed from Hartford, Conn., and settled in Springfield, Mass. Orson was educated at Monson Academy, and, having decided upon a commercial career, began work at the age of nineteen as a clerk in a bookstore in Springfield.

Mass. After two years he became a clerk in a general store in Monson and was so engaged when, in 1846, he was asked by his friend and schoolmate, Alfred E. Beach [q.v.], to join him in the purchase of a publication called the *Scientific American,* which had been founded Aug. 28, 1845, by Rufus Porter [q.v.]. Munn accepted, the firm of Munn & Company, consisting of Beach, Munn, and Salem H. Wales, was established, and office space was secured in New York in the building occupied by the New York *Sun,* a paper then owned by Beach's father.

The first issue of the *Scientific American* under the new firm appeared July 23, 1846, and from that time until his death, sixty-one years later, Munn gave his whole attention to its interests. Inasmuch as it was the first American periodical devoted purely to science and mechanics, the partners were constantly brought into contact with inventors seeking information and advice regarding patents. Consequently, they established a patent department, which, coming at a time when patent attorneys were practically unknown, met with immediate response. Under the directorship of Judge Charles Mason [q.v.], a former commissioner of patents, the business grew at a rapid rate, necessitating the opening of an office in Washington, D. C., and at the time of Munn's death over 100,000 patents had been secured by the department for clients. Properly to describe and illustrate the interesting exhibits at the Centennial Exhibition of 1876, the partners began in that year the publication of the *Scientific American Supplement.* Its success led them to continue it as a weekly review of current scientific literature and to add also articles too long or too technical for the ordinary reader. About 1890 they began still another publication, *La América científica e industrial,* designed for the Spanish-speaking peoples of South America. One of the features of the *Scientific American* was its information bureau; and in view of the many requests for data on home building and furnishing, Munn began in 1885 the publication of a monthly magazine devoted to this subject. It appeared for a time as the Building Edition of the *Scientific American,* but in 1905 it was remodeled and issued under the name *American Homes and Gardens.* Aside from his business, Munn's chief interest centered in his farm near Orange, N. J., and in his prize stock of Dutch belted cattle. He married Julia Augusta Allen of Monson, Mass., in 1849, and at the time of his death was survived by a son.

[*Sci. Am.,* Mar. 9, 1907; *Who's Who in America,* 1906–07; *N. Y. Times,* Mar. 2, 1907.]   C. W. M.

MUÑOZ-RIVERA, LUIS (July 17, 1859– Nov. 15, 1916), resident commissioner of Puerto Rico at Washington, poet, editor, political leader, was born in Barranquitas, a small town in Puerto Rico, eldest son of Luis Ramón Muñoz-Barrios and Monserrate Rivera-Vásquez. He largely educated himself, aside from instruction received in the elementary schools of his native town, by diligent reading in Spanish and French literature. As a young man he began writing poetry, designed particularly to inspire his people with a spirit of nationalism and with patriotic ideals, which was published in various papers from 1882; later he became more interested in editorial writing directed to the same ends. In 1887 he was a member of the assembly of protest at Ponce which demanded from Spain for Puerto Rico autonomy, decentralization of administration, and the right to vote upon the island's budget. Moving to Ponce he launched *La Democracia* (July 1, 1890) as an organ for expounding its program. His editorials aroused opposition from the Spanish administration and led to many lawsuits, but they evoked the enthusiastic support of many liberals, and soon he became a leader of the Autonomist party. A small extreme group, which desired independence obtained by insurrection, organized a Puerto Rican branch of the Cuban Revolutionary party, but he persuaded his party to send a commission to Spain (1896), of which he was a member, where an agreement was made with Sagasta and the Liberals that, when that party should again return to power, they would grant autonomy to Puerto Rico. Those who accepted this pact became the Insular Liberal party (1897), with *El Liberal* which he founded in San Juan as its organ; those who rejected it were known as "*Puros.*"

The assassination of the Conservative leader, Cánovas, led to the return to power of the Liberals and a royal decree of Nov. 25, 1897, granted autonomy to Cuba and Puerto Rico. In the first Autonomist cabinet (Feb. 12, 1898), consisting of three Liberals and three *Puros,* Muñoz-Rivera was secretary of grace, justice, and government, but later he became president. War between Spain and the United States interrupted these plans and resulted in the transfer of sovereignty to the latter (Oct. 18, 1898). The resignation of the Autonomist cabinet was not accepted by General Brooks, the first military governor, and its members continued to serve until he was succeeded by Gen. Guy V. Henry, who sought to abridge the powers they were exercising, accepted their resignation, and reorganized the cabinet in another form (1899). Muñoz-Rivera then went to Washington to secure free trade with the United States on behalf of the agriculturists of the island. Opposing the Foraker Act, which initiated civil government, as inadequate and unsatisfactory, he organized the Federal party and launched *El Diario de Puerto Rico* as its organ (1900). His party being in the minority—and he claimed harshly treated—he went to New York in 1901 and launched the *Puerto Rico Herald*. In 1902 a fusion of the Federals with dissatisfied Republicans became the Unionist party. He returned to the island, campaigned for it, and was elected to the Puerto Rican House of Delegates (1906–10). The Unionists then elected him resident commissioner for Puerto Rico to the United States. While in Washington he continued his articles for *La Democracia* as a means of informing the people of Puerto Rico of conditions in the United States and gained a speaking knowledge of English after he was fifty so that he could present his country's needs to Congress.

His last and most important speech in Congress (*Congressional Record,* 64 Cong., 1 Sess., pp. 7470–73) was in favor of the Jones Bill, which became Puerto Rico's organic act, although he did not live to see its passage. After securing the postponement of the general elections until this should be in force, he returned to San Juan to receive a great welcome from his people (Sept. 20). But the following day he fell ill and died at Santurce, a suburb of San Juan, on Nov. 15, 1916. Accompanied by thousands his body was carried to his birthplace and buried at Barranquitas. He had married, on Jan. 3, 1893, Amalia Marín. Among his own people he is famed as a poet, as an editor, as an orator, and as a statesman; his birthday is celebrated each year, and his character held up for imitation to the young people of the island. It has been said, "in politics, he harmonized the promptings of idealism with the needs of reality, as he cooperated more than any one else to form governing parties of the Island's liberal elements, thus facilitating the fulfilment of Porto Rico's desires and the solution of its problems" (*El Libro de Puerto Rico, post,* p. 1037).

[Muñoz-Rivera's writings, *Obras Completas de Luis Muñoz Rivera* (Madrid, 4 vols., 1925), edited by his son, Luis Muñoz-Marín, include his important editorials and contributions to newspapers and the poems published in 1902 under the title *Tropicales.* See also: José Gonzáles Ginorio, *Luis Muñoz Rivera, a la Luz de sus Obras y de su Vida* (1919); Eugenio Fernández García, *El Libro de Puerto Rico* (1923); *Boletín Histórico de Puerto Rico,* 1914–27; *Puerto Rico Illustrado,* Nov. 18, 25, Dec. 7, 1916.]   C. R. W—s.

MUNRO, DANA CARLETON (June 7, 1866–Jan. 13, 1933), historian, was born in Bristol, R. I., where his ancestors had lived for five generations. His father was John B., his mother Abby Howland (Batt) Munro. He graduated from Brown University in 1887, and was given the degree of A.M. by the same university in 1890. He studied at Strassburg in the autumn and winter of 1889 and at Freiburg in Breisgau in the spring of 1890. Here he came under the influence of Professor Paul Scheffer-Boichorst and began the interest in the Crusades which remained his throughout life. In 1890 he returned to America and taught for two years in a grammar school in Haverford, Pa. During this time he continued his post-graduate study at the University of Pennsylvania where in 1893 he became instructor and later assistant professor of medieval history. It was at this time that along with Professor J. H. Robinson and E. P. Cheyney he established and prepared eight numbers of the series of *Translations and Reprints from the Original Sources of European History,* published 1895–99, the pioneer effort in America to take students back to the sources. It was during this period also that he became intimate with the historian Henry C. Lea [*q.v.*], in whose library he read, and whose methods of work he has interpreted in various articles.

From the beginning Munro insisted on the most rigorous scientific method. He laid down a rigorous rule that no statement must be made in historical writing for which a satisfactory reference to a contemporary source cannot be given. His influence has thus been marked on a long series of younger scholars. This practice also was probably responsible, at least in part, for the slow progress of what was to be his *magnum opus,* a detailed and scholarly history of the Crusades, based on an exhaustive and critical use of the contemporary sources and vivified by a careful study on the ground of the regions traversed and occupied by the Crusaders. For the latter purpose he made two visits to the Near East. The work was still incomplete at his death. The Crusades were in the meantime the subject of many special studies, seminar and lecture courses, and detached papers and of a series of Lowell lectures delivered in Boston in 1924. Several of these studies were published.

In 1902 Munro was called as professor of European history to the University of Wisconsin, where he remained thirteen years. While there he acted as director of the Summer School and fulfiled other administrative duties. Although these interfered with the progress of his larger work, as a member of the active teaching group in that university he published textbooks and other material for teaching and started several younger scholars on their career. He was an active member of the Wisconsin State Historical Society, and president of the Wisconsin Academy from 1912 to 1915. In 1915 he went to Princeton University as professor of medieval history and remained there during the succeeding eighteen years of his life. American entrance into the World War in 1917 brought him into government service, first, as one of the principal research assistants to the Committee on Public Information, then as chairman of the National Board of Historical Service. In this capacity he prepared two pamphlets, *German War Practices* (1917) and *German Treatment of Conquered Territory* (1918). He was responsible for preserving in many government publications a tone of moderation in criticism of German actions and policy, though he was convinced of the rightfulness of the allied cause and confident of future restriction of war's barbarities. He contributed also to the collection of material for the "Inquiry," to be used by the American representatives at the Paris peace conference. He was chairman of the New Jersey State War History Commission from 1919 onward. He was president of the American Historical Association in the years 1925–26, and served as managing editor of the *American Historical Review* for 1928–29. He became chairman of the advisory board of the American Council of Learned Societies in 1928, when it was formed, and served in that capacity till his death. He was active in the affairs of the American Philosophical Society. In 1930 he became president of the Medieval Academy.

The published historical work of Munro is a slight though not unworthy measure of his accomplishments. *The Middle Ages*, first published in 1902, and subsequently revised and enlarged, is more than a textbook; it is an original contribution to knowledge drawn directly from medieval documents. His edition of L. J. Paetow's *A Guide to the Study of Medieval History* (1931), the preparation of which occupied much of his time in his later years, required a breadth of scholarship and an industry which might well have produced independent work. The volume, edited by L. J. Paetow, *The Crusades and Other Historical Essays* (1928), presented to him in manuscript by his former students when he retired from the presidency of the American Historical Association in 1926, gives testimony to much work on his part vicariously performed. There are some historians, like Lord Acton in England, whose contribution to the writing of history is to be sought in the incentive to production they have given to others, the standards they have set by their own work, scanty as it may be

in bulk, and their preparation of materials for later work. The writing of history in modern times is largely a cooperative task, and in this general activity of workers probably no other American historian of his time was better known, more valued, or more useful than Munro. He was married on July 16, 1891, to Alice Gardner Beecher and left two sons and three daughters. He died in New York from a sudden attack of pneumonia, Jan. 13, 1933.

[*Who's Who in America*, 1932–33; *N. Y. Times*, Jan. 14, 1933; E. P. Cheyney, in *Am. Hist. Review*, April 1933, pp. 618–20; personal acquaintance and private information.]   E. P. C.

MUNRO, GEORGE (Nov. 12, 1825–Apr. 23, 1896), publisher, was born at West River, Pictou County, Nova Scotia. He was a member of a large family and was dependent upon his own efforts for anything more than an elementary education. He learned printing in the office of the Pictou *Observer*, attended Pictou Academy three years, and, after teaching three years at New Glasgow, became instructor of mathematics and headmaster of the Free Church Academy in Halifax. He was winning a reputation as a teacher, when, in 1856 with several hundred dollars saved up, he suddenly departed for New York City. There he worked at various jobs; he was for a time in the employ of the American News Company, and, about 1863, he became a clerk in the firm of Beadle & Adams, dime-novel publishers. Beadle, in speaking one day to Edward S. Ellis, according to a story told by the latter, nodded toward an outer room where Munro, then forty years old, was tying up bundles and remarked, "That man has worked for us nearly two years. I pay him sixteen dollars a week; he is perfectly content with that; he will never wish to change his situation or try to improve it" (Pearson, *post*, p. 84). Scarcely a year later Munro began his own publishing house, and a decade later he was Beadle's most formidable rival. "Munro's Ten Cent Novels" were patterned after Beadle's original dime novels, and the series soon numbered several hundred titles. He began the publication, in 1867, of the *Fireside Companion*, a cheap family paper of entertainment and amusement that reached a phenomenal circulation figure. In 1872 he published *Old Sleuth the Dectective* by Harlan P. Halsey, the first of the famous Old Sleuth Series by that author, which eventually totaled over one hundred titles. This was followed by the scarcely less popular Old Cap Collier Series. However, his most successful venture was the "Seaside Library," a series of reprints of English works in paper-covered, octavo pamphlets, which could be forwarded in the mails at news-paper rates. The works of Scott, Dickens, Charlotte Brontë, George Eliot, Charles Reade, and other standard British writers were printed in this manner with no thought of compensation to the authors. Through the medium of the American News Company the nearly 2,000 titles that eventually were included in the series were scattered broadcast through the country and sold for ten cents each. Though the margin of profit was small, he rapidly became rich. On Vandewater and Rose streets he erected in 1883 a nine-story building with the most up-to-date equipment then known to care for his tremendous output. Though his reprints undoubtedly brought to the masses cheap and, at the same time, good reading material, they also hastened the passage of the international copyright law, when the more dignified publishers at last arrayed themselves in favor of the copyright side.

His interest in education led him to give liberally for education purposes. He was of great assistance to Dalhousie University at Halifax, when for a time its very existence was at stake, and endowed it with professorships of English literature, history, physics, metaphysics, and constitutional and international law. He also established tutorships in the classics and mathematics and an endowment for competitive scholarships. His total benefactions to this school amounted to about half a million dollars. He was also a benefactor and long a member of the council of the University of the City of New York. In build he was sturdy of frame and slightly below the average height. He was simple and frank in character, eminently practical, and possessed a high capacity for application to his business. He was married to Catherine, the daughter of Alexander Forrest of Halifax, who, together with their two sons and two daughters, survived him. His sons assumed control of the publishing business shortly before their father's death and continued to carry it on into the present century.

[E. L. Pearson, *Dime Novels* (1929) ; *Encyc. of Contemporary Biog. of N. Y.*, vol. IV (1885) ; J. P. MacPhie, *Pictonians at Home and Abroad* (1914) ; *New York University*, ed. by T. F. Jones (1933) ; *One Hundred Years of Dalhousie* (1919), pp. 24–30 ; *Publishers' Weekly*, May 2, 1896 ; *N. Y. Times*, Apr. 25, 1896.]　　　　　　　　　　　　　　O. W. H.

MUNRO, HENRY (1730–May 30, 1801), clergyman, army chaplain, Loyalist, or Harry Munro, as he signed his name, was born in Scotland, the son of Robert Munro of Dingwall, near Inverness, and Anne (Munro) Munro, both connected with the landed gentry. He attended the University of St. Andrews, where he took the degrees of bachelor and master of arts, after which he studied divinity at the University of Edinburgh. In 1757 he took orders in the Church of Scotland and purchased the chaplaincy of the 77th Regiment of Highlanders, which proceeded in the same year to America. He served in this capacity for a period of six years, seeing much active service. He accompanied the regiment on the expedition against Fort Duquesne in 1758, was present at the taking of Ticonderoga and Crown Point in 1759, and at the capture of Montreal in 1760. He later served in the West Indies with the forces which took Dominica and Martinique. His health being undermined by yellow fever, he obtained leave to return to New York, where he arrived about the close of the year 1762.

With the coming of peace and the reduction of his regiment, he left the military service and for a while made his residence at Princeton, N. J. During this period his religious views appear to have undergone a change and he decided to become a member of the Church of England. He proceeded to England toward the end of 1764 and was ordained on Feb. 10, 1765. Returning to America in the same year, he became missionary at Philipsburgh (now Yonkers), to which position he had been appointed by the Society for the Propagation of the Gospel in Foreign Parts. Early in 1768 he removed to Albany, where he became rector of St. Peter's Church and also missionary of the Society for the Propagation of the Gospel. He was appointed chaplain to the military garrison at Albany in July 1770. From 1768 until the Revolution, he was active in that portion of the New York frontier extending from Albany to Fort Stanwix. He preached in the frontier settlements and exercised considerable influence among the Indians, particularly the Mohawks. He seems to have worked in close understanding with Sir William Johnson, with whom he occasionally corresponded. As a veteran of the French war, he was granted a considerable tract of land between the Hudson and Lake Champlain, which he was endeavoring to settle on the eve of the Revolution. Being a Loyalist in his sympathies, Munro was seized and imprisoned at Albany late in 1776 or early in 1777. He succeeded in escaping in October 1777 and joined the British forces in Canada, with which he again served for a time as chaplain. He returned to England in 1778 and in 1783 went to Scotland, where he resided until his death, which occurred in Edinburgh in 1801. He received a grant from the British government by way of compensation for the loss of his property in America.

Munro enjoyed a considerable reputation as a

scholar. In 1773 he had been awarded the honorary degree of master of arts at King's College, New York, and in 1782 the University of St. Andrews conferred upon him the degree of doctor of divinity. He was married three times. The name of his first wife is unknown; his second was a Miss Stockton of Princeton; while his third, whom he married Mar. 31, 1766, was Eve Jay of New York, sister of Chief Justice John Jay [q.v.]. By her he had a son, Peter Jay Munro, who attained some distinction later in the state of New York.

[The best sketch available is E. F. DeLancey's "Memoir of the Rev. Dr. Harry Munro, the Last Rector of St. Peter's Church, Albany, under the English Crown," in *N.Y. Geneal. and Biog Record*, July 1873; this treatment is based in large part upon Munro's personal papers, the present repository of which is unknown. See also "American Loyalists: Transcript of the Manuscript Books and Papers of the Commission of Enquiry into the Losses and Services of the American Loyalists . . .," vol. XLV, bk. 5, in N. Y. Pub. Lib., and E. A. Jones, "The Loyalists of N. J.," in *Colls. N. J. Hist. Soc.*, vol. X (1927), pp. 150–51. A few letters are contained in E. B. O'Callaghan, *Documentary Hist. of the State of N. Y.*, vol. IV (1851); biog. note on p. 410 should be used with caution.]   W. E. S—s.

MUNSELL, JOEL (Apr. 14, 1808–Jan. 15, 1880), printer and antiquarian, was born at Northfield, Mass., the son of Joel and Cynthia (Paine) Munsell. In the public schools of Northfield he received his early education, which was continued by private study throughout the succeeding years. Beginning with the trade of wheelwright, young Munsell soon turned his attention to the printer's trade, obtaining his first lessons at the case in Greenfield, Mass. Going to Albany, N. Y., in 1827, he was not long in finding employment in a printing shop. Albany even at that day was a center of political contention and newspaper activity. Thurlow Weed was soon to exhibit his powers of editorial leadership, and the "Albany regency" was in the ascendant, with Edwin Croswell giving expression to its policies in the *Albany Argus*. Munsell never wholly surrendered to the emotions which were absorbing much of the journalistic ability of the country. After a brief period of adjustment to the new environment, he entered upon a career as a printer that is singular for the variety of its interests and a certain degree of detachment from the main currents of public activity. This is illustrated by a list of newspapers and periodicals that issued from his presses. The *Albany Minerva*, a semi-monthly of which only eight numbers saw the light, heads a series comprising the following publications, some of which he edited: The *New York State Mechanic*, the *Mechanics' Journal*, the *Lady's Magazine*, the *American Literary Magazine*, the *Northern Star and Freeman's Advocate*, the *Albany Religious Spectator*, the *Gavel*, an Odd Fellows' journal, the *Daily Unionist*, the *State Register*, a daily, the *New York Teacher*, a monthly, the *Albany Morning Express*, the *Albany Daily Statesman, Webster's Calendar, or the Albany Almanac*, and for three years, 1862–64, the *New-England Historical and Genealogical Register*.

In addition to these, Munsell produced various compilations. They include: *Outline of the History of Printing* (1839); *Annals of Albany* (10 vols., 1850–59); *The Every Day Book of History and Chronology* (1843); *A Chronology of Paper and Paper Making* (1856); *Collections on the History of Albany* (4 vols., 1865–71); and *The Typographical Miscellany* (1850), a limited edition. He also published books of reference relating to the early wars and settlements of America, a service which has given him a secure place among the pioneer workers who, by their labors in source material, have opened to others more inviting fields of historic production. A catalogue of the works which had issued from his press appeared in 1872 under the title *Bibliotheca Munselliana*. His general library was rich in *Americana* and comprised many writings connected with the early life of Albany. On Apr. 18, 1876, he read before the Albany Institute a paper thus introduced: "I now propose to take you on a tour about the streets within the purlieus of these quaint old walls for the purpose of pointing out . . . some interesting localities as they existed two-hundred years ago, and to revive a memory of men and things long since departed" (*Men and Things in Albany Two Centuries Ago*, 1876, p. 5). The purpose of that talk was an animating principle of Munsell's activities in the transmission of local annals, knowledge that is as perishable as it is important. Interested in the history and practical adaptations of the printing art, he gathered a large collection of works on printing which was purchased in part by the New York State Library. His collection of newspapers, comprising 10,000 specimens, is a notable instance of his interest in the progress of journalism. He was one of the founders of the Albany Institute, which is now a corporate part of the Institute of History and Art. Munsell was married on June 17, 1834, to Jane C. Bigelow; and after her death was married, on Sept. 11, 1856, to Mary Anne Reid.

[Sources include: Publications in the N. Y. State Lib., including newspaper files; in the same library Munsell's scrapbooks, one of which contains a personal narrative essentially autobiographical; G. R. Howell and Jonathan Tenney, *Hist. of the County of Albany* (1886); J. H. Temple and Geo. Sheldon, *Hist. of the Town of Northfield, Mass.* (1875); G. R. Howell, "Biog. Sketch of Joel Munsell," *New-Eng. Hist. and*

Geneal. Reg., July 1880; J. J. Latting, sketch in the N. Y. Geneal. and Biog. Record, Apr. 1880; Albany Evening Jour., Jan. 18, 1880.]　　　　　R. E. D.

MUNSEY, FRANK ANDREW (Aug. 21, 1854–Dec. 22, 1925), publisher, the son of Andrew Chauncey Munsey, a Maine farmer and builder, and Mary Jane Merritt Hopkins, his wife, was born at Mercer, Me. His father, who served his country for three years during the Civil War, was known in the various places in which he lived as a hard worker of severely rigid opinions. His mother, according to a genealogist employed by her son, was the lawful descendant of four passengers on the *Mayflower*; hers was therefore "the better family." Despite his father's industry, there was but a small income to maintain his large family, as a member of which Frank Munsey enjoyed little schooling and suffered much from illness. At fifteen his ambition made him hire himself out to the local postmaster for $100 a year. From this he graduated into the service of the Western Union Telegraph Company in Portland, first as night and Sunday operator, in due course becoming manager of the Augusta, Me., office. It was here, in a boarding house, that he met a successful mail-order publisher and became inspired by him to enter the publishing field himself. With only forty dollars of his own and two hundred and sixty dollars of borrowed money, but without training, experience, tradition, or backing, he arrived in New York on Sept. 23, 1882, to begin a career which was carried to success by extraordinary pluck and determination and by his ability to devote himself entirely to his work. He was at first his own office-boy, bookkeeper, clerk, advertising solicitor, manager, editor, and serial-story writer —as he himself set forth in his latter years in a booklet covering the first twenty-five years of his publishing career.

His first venture was the *Golden Argosy*, established in 1882, a magazine for boys and girls. It is said that he had twenty salesmen on the road east of the Mississippi before he engaged a stenographer or bookkeeper (Duffus, *post*, p. 299). The first ten years were financially fruitless; but from 1894 to 1907 inclusive his magazines earned him $8,780,905.70 in net profits. Throughout his career he never took a partner, nor created else than a dummy board of directors, nor yielded any of his authority to a powerful legal advisor. Nor did he marry. He never held staff conferences, seldom took suggestions, and supervised all details himself. The Munsey Publishing House was Frank A. Munsey, and his life was so ordered that he could live for his business and for success alone. He was not a reformer, nor an idealist, nor was he deeply interested in any causes. His passion was to found or purchase magazines and, later, newspapers. If one of his magazines failed to earn well he killed it and began another; if public taste passed from one of his productions he dropped it to develop another. As he progressed from cheap, inconsequential magazines to more important ones and then to daily newspapers, so he turned later to the stock market, became owner of the chain of Mohican grocery stores and at least one hotel (The Mohican) in New London, Conn., in search of wider fields to conquer.

So quick was he to destroy not only the creations of his own imagination but various newspapers which he bought to suppress in order to increase the power and influence of others he possessed that the phrase "Let Munsey kill it" became current newspaper slang whenever a daily was reported in distress. Thus he destroyed, merged, or renamed among magazines the *Scrap Book*, the *Quaker*, the *Puritan*, the historic *Godey's Magazine* (eagerly sought by collectors), *Peterson's Magazine*, the *Live Wire*, *Junior Munsey*, *Woman*, the *Cavalier*, the *Railroad Man's Magazine*, and the *All-Story Magazine*. He failed in his effort to create a successful tabloid daily only to see the New York *Daily News* succeed. In the newspaper field he similarly merged or destroyed the New York morning *Sun*, the *New York Press*, the *Daily Continent*, the *Globe*, the *Mail and Express*, the *Herald* (by sale to the *Tribune*), the Baltimore *Star*, and the Philadelphia *Times*. After owning them for a time he also sold the *Boston Morning Journal*, the Washington *Times*, the *Baltimore American* and the *Baltimore News*, thus meriting the description of him as "a dealer in dailies." At his death there survived him as his possessions the New York evening *Sun*, one of the three most successful New York dailies, and the *Evening Telegram*. Of the magazines there were left only the *Argosy All-Story Weekly*, *Munsey's Magazine*, and *Flynn's Weekly Detective Fiction*; yet Munsey was able to boast in 1907 that *Munsey's* was then the leading magazine in the world in circulation and earning power. Although in the daily field he more often failed than succeeded, he was able to carry on by the millions made in the Mohican stores, through the Munsey Trust Company of Washington, D. C., and by successful speculation in Wall Street; he indignantly and specifically denied on Aug. 28, 1922, published charges that he was a war-profiteer in munitions-making, declaring, "I made no money whatever, directly or indirectly, out of the war or anything associated with the war" (*New York*

Herald, Aug. 28, 1922). After his death his estate was appraised at $19,747,687, the bulk of which went to the Metropolitan Museum of Art in New York.

A lifelong adherent of the Republican party, Munsey bolted with Theodore Roosevelt in 1912 and with his dailies espoused the Progressive cause because of his admiration for the former president rather than for any belief in his platform. This was the only time that his journals took a liberal position; for the rest they were usually conventional and conservative under his management, though opposed to what he called (in the *New York Herald*) "damn fool protectionism," ship subsidies, and the soldier bonus. There was in them no editorial illumination, or passion, or power. He stood with the great capitalists, of whom he was one, and his dailies safeguarded their interests. But they were also clean and respectable (as well as dull) both in their news and advertising columns. No salacious stories crept into them. It is to his credit that he never stooped to the gutter to succeed; he preferred to kill or sell a daily rather than to degrade it. In other words, his newspapers reflected the viewpoint of the average prosperous American concerned with his own affairs and his own success. None the less he once declared that America "has cut loose from the conservatism of our fathers and penetrated deep into the wilderness of radicalism" (*An Address by Frank A. Munsey before the American Bankers' Association,* 1922, p. 14). While there was much feeling against him in journalistic circles, because of his killing of historic dailies and turning their employees into the street, it came to be recognized that he was merely illustrating dramatically a trend toward consolidation and combination and decreasing competition, which became the most striking phase of the newspaper business. While in his early days Munsey wrote fiction and sport news, and in later years numerous editorials for his dailies, he was without distinction as a writer. He died in New York City following an operation for appendicitis.

[Of Munsey's writings, see especially *The Founding of the Munsey Publishing House* (1907); *The Daily Newspaper; Its Relation to the Public* (1910); *Getting on in Journalism* (1898); and *Militant Am. Journalism* (1922), a pamphlet consisting of editorials reprinted from the *N. Y. Herald.* Other sources include: O. G. Villard, *Some Newspapers and Newspaper-Men* (2nd ed., 1926); E. J. Ridgway, *Frank A. Munsey: An Appreciation* (1926); R. L. Duffus, "Mr. Munsey," *Am. Mercury,* July 1924; Allan Nevins, *McNaught's Monthly,* Mar. 1926; R. H. Titherington, "In Memoriam: Frank A. Munsey," *Munsey's Mag.,* Mar. 1926; D. O. S. Lowell, *A Munsey-Hopkins Geneal., Being the Ancestry of Andrew Chauncey Munsey and Mary Jane Merritt Hopkins* (1920); the *N. Y. Times,* Dec. 23, 1925; Jan. 10, 1926; the *Sun* (N. Y.), Dec. 22, 1925.]   O. G. V.

MUNSON, THOMAS VOLNEY (Sept. 26, 1843–Jan. 21, 1913), viticulturist, horticulturist, son of William and Maria (Linley) Munson, was born near Astoria, Fulton County, Ill., and died at Denison, Tex. His father was of New Hampshire stock, and his mother was from Kentucky. After an elementary education in the country schools, he taught in Illinois (1861–64) to earn money for his course at the University of Kentucky, which he attended with his brother, William B. Munson, receiving the degree of B.S. in 1870. On June 27, 1870, he married Ellen Scott Bell, daughter of Charles Stuart Bell, a horticulturist and nurseryman of Lexington, Ky. They had two sons and five daughters. During the years 1870–71 he was professor of science in the University of Kentucky, and from 1871 to 1873 he was engaged in the nursery business with his wife's father in Lexington. He established himself in Lincoln, Nebr., in 1873, and three years later, at the solicitation of his brother William, removed his business to Denison, Tex., his home until his death.

It was here that all of his scientific and horticultural work was done. He developed a vineyard and experimental grounds, while at the same time he became one of the most prominent general horticulturists of the South. In 1883 he published his "Forests and Forest Trees of Texas" (*American Journal of Forestry,* July 1883) for which the Agricultural and Mechanical College of Kentucky conferred on him the degree of M.Sc. In the eighties, at the instance of the French government, he sought for and experimented with American species of wild grape resistant to the phylloxera pest of the French grape, and received, in recognition of his work, membership in the Legion of Honor, election as foreign corresponding member of the Société Nationale d'Agriculture de France (1898), and honorary membership in the Société des Viticulteurs de France. His admirable work on the grape appears in his "Classification and Generic Synopsis of the Wild Grapes of North America" (*United States Department of Agriculture, Division of Pomology, Bulletin No. 3,* 1890); in *Texas Agricultural Experiment Station, Bulletin No. 56,* 1900; in articles in L. H. Bailey, *Cyclopedia of American Horticulture,* vol. II (1900); and in his own *Foundations of American Grape Culture* (1909). He was a prominent member of numerous scientific and horticultural societies in America, lecturer for years in the farmers' institutes of Texas, a member of the Texas World's Fair Commission (1903–04), and one of the international jury of awards at the St. Louis Exposition (1904). His death, which occurred in his seventieth year, was due to influenza, followed by pneumonia.

Munson was gifted with a singular ability to see the possibilities of horticultural stocks. By his hybridization and selection experiments, he was able to give hundreds of new horticultural varieties to the world. His work on the grape is almost without a parallel. What is said to be the most complete botanical display of the whole grape genus ever made was prepared by him for the Chicago World's Fair (1893) and is now in the United States Department of Agriculture. His work on the culture of the American grape is a monumental achievement. With all his abilities and accomplishments, he was a man of singularly modest disposition, and was widely loved. "Probably no man ever lived in Texas whose character attracted greater admiration, or whose removal caused more general regret . . . he loved his kind and was lavish in his benefactions to those, who, helpless, appealed to his sympathy" (Johnson and Barker, *post*, IV, 1722).

[F. W. Johnson and E. C. Barker, *A Hist. of Texas and Texans* (1914), vol. IV; *Dallas Morning News,* Jan. 23, 1913; family papers.]   S. W. G.

MUNSON, WALTER DAVID (Feb. 18, 1843–Apr. 24, 1908), ship-owner, developer of the Munson Line, was descended from Thomas Munson, an Englishman who had settled at Hartford by 1637. He was born on a farm in Cheshire, Conn., fifth of the six children of Barnabas Daniel and Delia (Canfield) Munson. He was only three when his father died. His mother later married David W. Wood, a widower whose daughter Emily M. Wood became Munson's wife on Dec. 31, 1863. He was brought up on the farm, with a fair schooling. At eighteen he enlisted as a private in Company E of the 8th Connecticut Volunteers and fought through the Civil War. He became second lieutenant, first lieutenant, and finally captain in the 2nd United States Cavalry and served as assistant adjutant-general of the 3rd Division of the XVIII Army Corps. Remaining in the army for a year after the war, he was with Sheridan's force which was sent to the Rio Grande in protest against the French occupation of Mexico. Finally mustered out early in 1866 in Texas, he settled in Brownsville for two years. In 1868 he moved to Havana and from that time until his death he was intimately connected with Cuba. He became interested in the refining of petroleum there and eventually that led to shipping, which became his most important field of activity.

The nucleus of the future Munson Line was a schooner with which he began regular freight service between New York and Havana in 1873. By 1882, when he moved to New York, he had five sailing vessels regularly engaged in trade between the two ports. Three of his five children were born by that time and Munson took a very keen interest in their upbringing. It is said that the principal reason for his leaving Cuba was the desire to give them better surroundings and educational opportunities. For the remainder of his life he made his home in Brooklyn and conducted his business from New York. He continued to develop the line of ships between New York and Cuba, adding steamships to the sailing vessels. The line specialized in freight, but he later put some excellent passenger ships on the New York-Havana run. The Munson freighters connected New York not only with Havana but also with Matanzas, Santiago, and many other ports on the island. He extended his service to Mexico and developed a regular service between Havana and Mobile and other Gulf ports. In 1894 he was also serving as agent for the Prince Steamship Company which connected Haiti, Jamaica, Central America, and Colombia. This shipping business was at first Munson's private venture, but in 1899 it was incorporated as the Munson Steamship Line, remaining a fairly close corporation. Munson himself was president and a director.

Munson also extended his shipping line northward to Nova Scotia and the Maritime Provinces where pulpwood and other bulky commodities offered good freight. He was president of the Cameron Steamship Company, vice-president of the Atlantic & Mexican Gulf Steamship Company, and secretary-treasurer of the International Coal Company. He was a director of the Compania Maritima Cubana and of the Cuban & Pan-American Express Company. The Munson Line itself, however, was his chief interest. By the time of his death, it had expanded in thirty-five years from a single schooner to sixty steamships. In size and volume of trade, it was the largest freighting organization in the American coastal trade and was a powerful influence in Caribbean commerce. His sons Carlos W. and Frank C. Munson became respectively president and vice-president-treasurer of the line after his death. Munson himself was a large and kindly man, bald and with a drooping moustache. He was liberal in his views, being non-sectarian in religion and non-partisan in politics. Devoted to business and his family, he took almost no part in public life.

[The principal source is M. A. Munson, *The Munson Record* (1895), vol. I. See also the *Munson Line Bull.* (later the *Cuba Bull.*, *Cuba Rev. and Bull.*, and finally the *Cuba Rev.*); *Directory of Directors in the City of N. Y.*, and the *N. Y. Herald*, Apr. 25, 1908.]

R. G. A.

MÜNSTERBERG, HUGO (June 1, 1863–Dec. 16, 1916), psychologist, was born in Danzig, Germany. His father, Moritz Münsterberg, was a lumber merchant who bought lumber in Russia and sold it in England. The business took his father frequently abroad and he always returned with glowing accounts of foreign countries, which undoubtedly stimulated the young son's imagination. His mother, Anna Münsterberg, was an artist and although she took devoted care of her four sons, and supervised her household in true German thoroughness, she had sufficient time to continue her painting and pen-and-ink drawings. The boys were encouraged in their love of good books, and Hugo and his brother Otto also devoted much time to music, the former playing the 'cello and the latter the violin. It was in this atmosphere of broad and intelligent thinking and reverence for the arts that Münsterberg spent a happy, care-free childhood. The influence of his early environment was a strong factor in his future development. It is true that he became primarily a scholar, rather than an artist, but the love of beauty remained always with him. He wrote his first poem at the age of seven. At fourteen he wrote a ballad, and some years later published a volume of poems under the *nom de plume* of Hugo Terberg. He also retained his passion for music throughout his life. It is necessary to realize the two sides of his nature in order to understand the man and his works, for the artistic had a profound influence upon the structure and the expression of his thought.

Münsterberg's education began with kindergarten. After a few years at a private school, he entered the Gymnasium of Danzig at the age of nine. His mother died when he was twelve, and this first and great sorrow changed him from a child into a thoughtful and serious youth. During his school years he engaged in many intellectual pursuits outside of the regular curriculum. When he was only fifteen he diverted himself by compiling a dictionary of foreign words used in German. He also amused himself with the study of Arabic and Sanskrit, and dipped into archeology. He was by no means a grind, however, for he had ample time to engage in outdoor sports, and he was also fond of dancing with his numerous girl companions. In 1882 he passed the final examination of the Gymnasium with credit, and as he desired to see more of the world, he spent a semester at the University of Geneva, where he improved his knowledge of the French language and literature. In September of the same year he began his serious studies at the University of Leipzig. He started with social psychology but soon changed to medicine. In 1883 he attended lectures by Wilhelm Wundt and was so deeply impressed by the great teacher of psychology that he determined to devote himself to that subject, and entered the psychological laboratory at Leipzig, which has been the training ground of many American psychologists. He continued his study of medicine, however, along with psychology and passed the preliminary examination in the former subject in 1884. In July 1885, he received his Ph.D. degree in psychology, his dissertation being upon the doctrine of natural adaptation. He then went to Heidelberg to continue his medical studies, and in the summer of 1887 he received his medical degree and also passed an examination which permitted him to lecture as "privatdocent" at Freiburg. On Aug. 7, 1887, he was married to Selma Oppler of Strassburg.

During this period he lectured principally in philosophy. There was no psychological laboratory in the university, so he equipped rooms in his own house with apparatus, and attracted many students from Germany and foreign countries. In 1891 he was promoted to an assistant professorship. In 1889 he had attended the First International Congress of Psychology at Paris, and here it was that he first met William James. They corresponded frequently for the next few years, and James was so impressed by the young man's genius that in 1892 he invited him to come to Harvard for three years to take charge of the psychological laboratory, which was then in old Dane Hall. Münsterberg accepted, after obtaining leave of absence from Freiburg. He was highly successful as a teacher and an administrator and was offered a permanent professorship at the end of his three years' appointment, but he preferred to postpone the decision to settle in America and returned to Freiburg for two years. Harvard, however, sent him urgent invitations to return, and in 1897 he yielded to the persuasive letters of President Eliot and William James. The decision was, as it turned out, a crucial one in his career, for he remained at Harvard until his death, and devoted himself without reserve to the furtherance of American psychology and to the education of the American youth. His ability was early recognized beyond the Harvard Yard. In 1898 he was elected president of the American Psychological Association. He also soon began to give public lectures in various cities throughout the country, an activity that occupied much of his time in later years.

The department of philosophy was sorely in need of a building of its own, and Münsterberg was one of the most active members in arousing interest in this project, and in raising funds for the purpose. On Monday, May 25, 1903, the hundredth anniversary of the birth of Ralph Waldo Emerson, the cornerstone of Emerson Hall was laid, and soon thereafter Münsterberg saw his dream come true of a laboratory especially equipped for experimental psychology. In the same year he took a prominent part in insuring the success of the Congress of Arts and Science at the St. Louis Exposition. Besides his scientific and literary work, he gave numerous lectures throughout the country on both psychological and cultural subjects. He carried on an extensive correspondence with the leading men of Europe and America and also found time to test his belief in the application of psychological methods to practical affairs, one of his first ventures being in the detection of crime. He also paved the way for the more extensive use of psychology in industry, medicine, arts, and education, and may justly be called one of the pioneers in the field of applied psychology. In the laboratory he directed the research of a large group of students, and occasionally he gave psychotherapeutic treatment to patients whose cases seemed likely to yield data of scientific value. He was interested in psychic research, and although firmly convinced from his experience and his theory of mind that there was no such thing as mental telepathy or spiritism, he took part in a few scientific investigations of such alleged phenomena. In 1910 he was appointed exchange professor from Harvard to the University of Berlin. Inspired by the belief that harmony among nations could be brought about only by fostering the cultural ties between them, he devoted much of his time while in Berlin to the creation of the America Institute.

On his return to Harvard, he became more engrossed than ever in applied psychology and devised many ingenious tests which he and his students tried out on the personnel of a number of large industrial plants. With characteristic impulsiveness, he made a hurried trip to Berlin in April 1912, to attend the meeting of German experimental psychologists. His last visit to his fatherland was in the summer of the same year, and although he was needing a vacation, the inner drive for creative work kept him busy on a book on applied psychology for part of the time. The last years of his life were full of stress and sorrow. He was devoted to America,

but he always remained loyal to his own country, and so from the first days of war until his death, he continued to write books and numerous newspaper and magazine articles in defense of Germany's action and in explanation of her motives and ideals. He was violently criticized and attacked from many quarters, and lost numerous friendships of long standing. He faced the storm courageously, but he felt the situation keenly, and the strain undoubtedly undermined his strength. On Dec. 16, 1916, he had to walk to his lecture at Radcliffe against a stiff, cold wind. He was exhausted on his arrival and died on the lecture platform before he had finished his opening sentence.

He was a large man of dignified appearance. He always maintained a certain reserve, so characteristic of the German professor, especially towards his students. He was never familiar, yet always gracious and genial. He had a keen sense of humor, generosity of spirit, and warmth of heart, and delighted in the companionship of his friends. He was firm in his own opinion, and aggressive in debate, yet tolerant of the views of others. He took little physical exercise, but he had great energy and his mind was never idle. He was an unusually logical and clear thinker. He had a great love of beauty in every form, and his esthetic nature showed itself in the balance and smoothness of his literary style, and the well-developed pattern of his lecture. He had the constructive imagination of the genius, and also that other characteristic so often possessed by men accustomed to think in the abstract, a certain childlike simplicity and naïveté. As a lecturer he was fluent and convincing, and never failed to hold his audience. He seldom, if ever, used notes, and his extemporaneous speeches seemed as finished as his well-prepared lectures. In philosophy, he was an idealist of the type of Fichte. In psychology he had two principles. He believed that the causal law held for mental phenomena in so far as they were correlated with physiological processes. Here he was a determinist. When, however, he considered the mental from the viewpoint of values, he believed in freedom. His chief contribution to theoretical psychology was probably his "action theory" which defined attention in terms of the openness of the nerve paths to the muscles of adjustment. His insistence upon the motor response as an essential factor of consciousness makes him a forerunner of modern behaviorism.

He composed rapidly and usually by dictation. Some of his books were produced in less than a month. His first comprehensive publication was

Die Willenshandlung (1888) in which he placed emphasis upon the motor process. His *Beiträge zur experimentellen Psychologie* (1889–92), in two volumes, contains an account of the experiments he performed before coming to Harvard, and it was followed by the *Grundzüge der Psychologie* (1900), which was one of his most profound treatises. In it he set forth his views upon the philosophical presuppositions of psychology, views which formed the structure for much of his future thinking. While at Harvard he edited four volumes of *Harvard Psychological Studies* (1903–15), which presented the work of the students of the laboratory. In *The Principles of Art Education* (1905) he described his views, both philosophical and psychological, upon esthetics, and elaborated them in *The Eternal Values* (1909). This latter book was based upon his idealistic principles in the fields of philosophy, morals, and beauty. In *American Traits from the Point of View of a German* (1901) he endeavored to interpret and explain the life of the American people and their political institutions. He wrote a number of semi-popular books on applied psychology: *On the Witness Stand* (1908); *Psychology and the Teacher* (1909); *Psychotherapy* (1909); *Psychology and Industrial Efficiency* (1913); and *Psychology and Social Sanity* (1914). His *Grundzüge der Psychotechnik* (1914) was an ambitious attempt to explain the use of psychological methods in industry and was influential in furthering the cause of industrial psychology both in America and Germany. His only textbook was *Psychology, General and Applied* (1914). During the stress of war, he wrote his last book, *Tomorrow* (1916), which looked toward peace and the restoration of international relations.

[The sketch is based mainly upon *Hugo Münsterberg: His Life and Work* (1922), by Margaret Münsterberg, and upon the writer's impressions during a long acquaintance with Münsterberg. Other sources include: Wm. Stern, "Hugo Münsterberg: In Memoriam," *Jour. of Applied Psychol.*, June 1917; H. E. Burtt, "Prof. Münsterberg's Vocational Tests," *Ibid.*, Sept. 1917; J. W. Baird, "Hugo Münsterberg: 1863–1916," *Jour. of Philos., Psychol. and Sci. Methods*, Feb. 15, 1917; R. M. Yerkes, "Hugo Münsterberg," *Philos. Rev.*, July 1917; *Science*, Jan. 26, 1917; *Boston Transcript*, Dec. 16, 1916.]   H.S.L.

MURAT, ACHILLE (Jan. 21, 1801–Apr. 15, 1847), author, christened Charles Louis Napoléon Achille, was born in Paris, France, the elder son of Joachim Murat and Caroline (Maria Annunciata Carolina Buonaparte) Murat. When Joachim was created Grand Duke of Berg and Cleves (1806), Achille became heir apparent to the duchies; and when in 1808 his father was made King of Naples, Achille became the crown prince. His education was suitable to his rank.

After Joachim's defeat by the Austrians at Tolentino, May 3, 1815, Caroline and her children took refuge at Trieste, where the mother lived as the Countess Lipona (Napoli). After the father's death, the widow and her children removed to Schloss Hamburg, thence in 1817 to Frohsdorf near Vienna. The Neapolitan Revolution (1820) naturally threw suspicion upon them, and to avoid persecution Achille determined to emigrate to the United States. After three months in Hamburg, where he spent almost half his fortune, he arrived in New York on May 19, 1823. According to the story he later related to Hortense Bonaparte, after visiting Joseph Bonaparte in New Jersey, he sailed for Spain to join the Constitutionalist party, but after spending 40,000 francs fruitlessly, returned to the United States. At Washington in 1824 he met Richard Keith Call, territorial representative of Florida in Congress, who advised him to settle in that region. Murat went to Tallahassee, near which he bought and developed the plantation known as "Lipona." Here he married, July 12, 1826, Catherine Daingerfield (Willis) Gray, daughter of Byrd C. Willis of Virginia and a great-grandniece of Washington. The next year Murat and his wife made a northern tour; on the vessel from St. Augustine to Charleston he met Emerson, with whom he conversed on philosophical and political subjects, and with whom he later corresponded. At Point Breeze they visited Joseph Bonaparte whom Murat later served as agent in Europe.

In Florida Murat took an active part in the life of the rising community about Tallahassee. He was admitted to the bar in 1828; he was active in promoting the Florida Institute of Agriculture, and in developing the resources of the country; and he held various minor offices, including a postmastership. At this period he regarded himself as an American; his *Lettres sur les États-Unis . . . à un de ses amis d'Europe* (1830) addressed to Count Thibeaudeau and originally printed in the *Revue Trimestrielle* (1828), are a republican manifesto to Europe. From these later developed his important *Esquisse morale et politique des États-Unis de l'Amérique du Nord* (1832), a philosophic account of American institutions.

The Revolution of July took Murat to Europe, and though, on leaving Florida, he informed his fellow citizens that it was his duty as a Frenchman to support the present government of France, he did not expect the July monarchy to endure and hoped to advance the fortunes of the Bonapartes, with whose Parisian agents he was in correspondence. His arrival in London in 1830 alarmed Metternich, and he was unable to penetrate the Continent farther than Belgium, where he was compelled to give up the command of a regiment which had been given him. The Murats spent some time in London (1831), where they were socially popular, and then returned to Florida to resume their life there. His *Exposition des principes du gouvernement républicain, tel qu'il a été perfectionné en Amérique* (Paris, 1833), widely distributed on the Continent, was regarded by the reactionaries as a dangerous work. He served in the Seminole War as aide-de-camp to General Call and was later commissioned colonel and appointed to the command of the frontier. He died in 1847 and was buried with Masonic ceremony in the Episcopal cemetery at Tallahassee. An editorial in the *Floridian* (Apr. 17, 1847) justly speaks of him as "a man of great eccentricity of character," but "gifted with a high order of mind, which was enriched by solid literary acquirements, . . . withal a most interesting and agreeable companion." In person he is said to have resembled Napoleon. His three books on the United States are those of a candid observer; if they are not as philosophic as de Tocqueville, they are often more graphic. In the year after his death his wife was made a princess of the Second Empire by Louis Napoleon and provided with an annuity.

[On the earlier life of Murat see especially *Lettres et documents pour servir à l'histoire de Joachim Murat, 1767–1815, publiés par S. A. le Prince Murat* (8 vols., 1908–14), ed. by Paul le Brethon, and the *Diario Napoletano, 1798–1825* (1906), of Carlo de Nicola. For his American career see Emerson's *Journals*, vol. II (1909); Georges Bertin, *Jos. Bonaparte en Amérique* (1893); "Personal Reminiscences of Madame Murat. By a Friend and Relative," *Potter's Am. Monthly*, Feb. 1882. In his relation to Bonapartist politics see Valérie Masuyer, "La Reine Hortense et le Prince Louis en Angleterre (Mai–Juin 1831)," *Revue des Deux Mondes*, Mar. 1, 1915; and Richard de Metternich, ed., *Mémoires, documents, et écrits divers laissés par le Prince de Metternich*, vol. V (1882). For general accounts see "The Murats of Fla.," the *Galaxy*, June 1875; J. F. Bouchelle, "An Am. Prince and Princess," *Gulf States Hist. Mag.*, Sept. 1903; M. L. McConnell, "The Prince and Princess Achille Murat in Fla.," *Century Mag.*, Aug. 1893; Caroline M. Brevard, *A Hist. of Fla. from the Treaty of 1763 to Our Own Times*, vol. I (1924); and B. C. and R. H. Willis, *A Sketch of the Willis Family of Va.* (1898). Murat's *Esquisse morale et politique* was translated twice: as *A Moral and Political Sketch of the U. S. of North America*, etc. (London, 1833), and as *America and the Americans* (New York, 1849). The translations differ in important respects.]   H. M. J.

MURDOCH, FRANK HITCHCOCK (Mar. 11, 1843–Nov. 13, 1872), actor, playwright, was born at Chelsea, Mass., the eldest of the six children of George Frank and Mary (Murdoch) Hitchcock, and the eighth in descent from Luke Hitchcock, a shoemaker, who took the freeman's oath at New Haven in 1644 and died in Wethers-field, Conn., in 1659. In 1861, through the interest of his uncle, James Edward Murdoch [*q.v.*], whose name he adopted, he secured employment at the Arch Street Theatre, Philadelphia, of which Louisa Lane Drew [*q.v.*] had just become manager. He remained with her company, playing juvenile and light comedy parts, until his death. A half-century later her son still remembered him as "a fine actor" (John Drew, *My Years on the Stage*, 1922, p. 32). He was a modest, agreeable young man with a good sense of his vocation and ambition for honors as a dramatist. Four plays are ascribed to him. Of *The Keepers of Lighthouse Cliff* the time and place of production are unknown; David Belasco, however, told William Winter that James A. Herne [*q.v.*] had acted in it and had lifted from it the climax of *Shore Acres* (*The Life of David Belasco*, 1918, vol. I, p. 200). *Only a Jew* was produced by John T. Raymond, Feb. 24, 1873, at the Globe Theatre, Boston, three months after Murdoch's death. A flimsy, impossible little comedy of parted lovers and a stolen will, it was rendered entertaining and even charming by the novel scenes in a pawnshop and by the sweet amiableness of Nathan Rosenthal, the *deus ex machina* of the piece (*Boston Evening Transcript*, Feb. 25, 1873; *Boston Daily Advertiser*, Feb. 26, 1873). As Murdoch was acting in Philadelphia at the time, he did not see the production of his *Davy Crockett*, which he wrote for Frank Mayo [*q.v.*], at the Opera House, Rochester, N. Y., Sept. 23, 1872 (*Rochester Democrat and Chronicle*, Sept. 23, 1872). It was received somewhat tepidly, but Mayo believed in the piece, wrote encouragingly to its author, continued to tinker the script, and from time to time tried it out on audiences. After a few years it gained favor and for two decades it was immensely popular. To the actual Davy Crockett the play owed only its name, but to Scott's ballad of young Lochinvar and to the youthful Natty Bumpo of the *Deerslayer* it owed almost everything. An idyl of the backwoods, its famous scenes showed Davy barring the door with his arm while wolves gnawed their way almost through the floor and wall of the log-cabin, and later confessing bashfully to his cultured sweetheart that he could not read or write. Hamlin Garland has testified to the relief felt by the spectators when the girl offered to teach Davy his letters (Introduction to *The Autobiography of David Crockett*, 1923, p. 3). Critics pining for an autochthonous drama beheld great virtues in what was essentially a piece of claptrap (Brander Matthews, "The American on the Stage," *Scribner's Monthly*, July 1879, pp. 327–28; Laurence Hutton, *Curi-*

osities of the American Stage, 1891, pp. 30–35). Murdoch himself took the part of Bob Tangent, a "sensation writer," in his fourth play, *Bohemia, or The Lottery of Art,* which was put on for the usual week's run at the Arch Street Theatre Oct. 28, 1872, and which was ascribed on the program to a "young gentleman of Philadelphia." Intended for a satire on the venality and unscrupulousness of dramatic critics, and motivated perhaps by newspaper treatment of his wife, Jennie Workman, a member of the Arch Street company, Murdoch mixed too much indignation with his humor, and the result was a flat failure. The critics, impenitent and unabashed, made the most of the situation. Although they attributed the play to Barton Hill, Mrs. Drew's leading man, and praised Murdoch's own acting warmly, the young author was deeply grieved. He was still brooding over his fiasco when he was stricken twelve days later with meningitis and died after a brief illness.

[Mrs. Edward Hitchcock, Sr. (M. L. J. Hitchcock), *The Geneal. of the Hitchcock Family* (1894); *Phila. Inquirer* and *Public Ledger,* Nov. 14, 1872; *Press* (Phila.), Oct. 29, Nov. 15, 1872; A. H. Quinn, *A Hist. of the Am. Drama from the Civil War to the Present Day* (1927), vol. I.]
G. H. G.

MURDOCH, JAMES EDWARD (Jan. 25, 1811–May 19, 1893), actor, lecturer, teacher of elocution, was the eldest of four sons of Thomas and Elizabeth Murdoch of Philadelphia, Pa. His father, although a book-binder and paper ruler by trade, was also interested in local politics and acted as a volunteer fireman. James Murdoch, after a few years of common-school education, became an apprentice in his father's shop. His interest in the stage first manifested itself when he joined a local group of amateur Thespians and in his spare time devoted himself under the instruction of two teachers to studies of elocution. His father, although disappointed at the boy's unwillingness to pursue further the family trade, started him on his career as an actor by engaging for him the Philadelphia Arch Street Theatre and its company for the night of Oct. 13, 1829. Murdoch chose for his début the rôle of Frederick in Kotzebue's *Lovers' Vows,* and during the remainder of the season he was assigned a few other rôles, although without pay. With the hope of securing a more lucrative opening Murdoch went in the following year to Halifax, Nova Scotia, but when the troupe of actors shortly afterward found itself without funds, he was forced again to seek financial aid from his father. A barnstorming tour in South Carolina and Georgia under the management of Vincent De Camp was equally unsuccessful. While playing minor rôles at the Arch Street Theatre in 1832 he seriously impaired his health by taking a dose of arsenic which he had mistaken for medicine. Throughout his career as an actor he was forced at all times to husband carefully his strength.

Leaving the Arch Street shortly after this accident he played as leading juvenile at the Chestnut Street Theatre opposite Frances Ann (Fanny) Kemble [*q.v.*], but was soon forced by reason of his health to go to New Orleans to recuperate. During the next ten years he appeared intermittently in many theatres: at the St. Charles in New Orleans; at the Emmanuel Street in Mobile; in Pittsburgh and Philadelphia under the management of Francis Courtney Wemyss; at the Park Theatre, New York, supporting Ellen Tree; and at the Tremont and National Theatres in Boston. In 1842 he retired temporarily from the stage and gave a series of lectures on "The Uses and Abuses of the Stage" and on Shakespearian characters. He also gave lessons in elocution to students of law and theology and collaborated on a book called *Orthophony, or Vocal Culture in Elocution* (1845). His most important period as an actor was from 1845 to 1860, during which time he established a national reputation both as tragedian and comedian. Noah Miller Ludlow praised his Hamlet as "the best representation of the Danish prince that I have ever seen." Sol Smith declared that Murdoch had very few if any equals as a light comedian—a tribute corroborated by the sound judgment of Wemyss. In 1853, after many successful engagements throughout the East and the Middle West, Murdoch went for a short season to California where he achieved great popularity. Three years later he visited England, playing one hundred and ten nights at the London Haymarket, and later appearing for a short engagement in Liverpool. On his return to the United States he engaged in intermittent starring tours, after which he would retire for long periods of rest to a farm which he had bought near Cincinnati. During the Civil War he visited the Federal camps and aroused the fervor of the soldiers by eloquent recitals of patriotic poems. After the war he returned to his Ohio farm. His wife, Eliza Middlecott, whom he married in 1831, was English by birth.

[Consult: Biographical sketch by J. Bunting prefacing J. E. Murdoch, *The Stage, or Recollections of Actors and Acting* (1880); J. N. Ireland, *Records of the N. Y. Stage,* vol. II (1867); G. C. D. Odell, *Annals of the N. Y. Stage,* vols. V and VII (1931); N. M. Ludlow, *Dramatic Life as I Found It* (1880); Sol Smith, *Theatrical Management in the West and South for Thirty Years* (1868); O. S. Coad and Edwin Mims, Jr., *The Am. Stage* (1929); C. T. Greve, *Centennial Hist. of Cin-*

cinnati and Representative Citizens (1904), vol. II; Cincinnati Commercial Gazette, May 20, 1893.]

E. M., Jr.

MURDOCK, JAMES (Feb. 16, 1776–Aug. 10, 1856), Congregational clergyman, author, was born at Westbrook, Conn., of Protestant Scotch-Irish ancestry, being a descendant of Peter Murdock who emigrated to Long Island in 1700. His father, Abraham, a farmer, died in his twenty-sixth year (1777), leaving James, then fourteen months old, another child, and a widow, Hannah (Lay) Murdock, who married again. The son picked up his early education in the midst of severe manual labor, yet was able to enter Yale at seventeen and to graduate in 1797, second in a class of distinguished men, among whom was Lyman Beecher. The next few years were spent in theological study, pastoral supply, and teaching. During this period, Oct. 8, 1799, he married Rebecca Lydia, daughter of Jeremiah Atwater of New Haven; they had ten children. In January 1801 he was licensed to preach by the Oneida Association of Congregational Ministers and on June 23, 1802, he was ordained as pastor of the church in Princeton, Worcester County, Mass., at a salary of $366. His ministry produced a revival in 1810. In 1815 he became professor of the learned languages in the University of Vermont, and also of mathematics and natural philosophy. In 1818 he was elected to, but declined, the professorship of languages in Dartmouth College. He was appointed Brown Professor of Sacred Rhetoric and Ecclesiastical History in the Theological Seminary at Andover in 1819, but in 1828 was dismissed because of his unwillingness to see ecclesiastical history crowded out of the curriculum in favor of sacred rhetoric. Settling in New Haven in 1829, he devoted the remainder of his life to Christian scholarship. He was a member of a committee of the Connecticut Academy of Arts and Sciences which in 1842 reported that the customary suppers following the meetings were "a bad example to be exhibited in the vicinity of the college." The suppers ended and the Academy declined. In 1844 Murdock gathered the like-minded into the Philological Society of Connecticut. In 1848 he became a member of the American Oriental Society. He died at the home of his son in Columbus, Miss., and was buried in New Haven.

Among his original works may be noted a sermon, *Nature of the Atonement* (1823), in which he developed the governmental theory of Grotius, and thereby gave occasion for "some imputations against his orthodoxy" (Richardson, *post*, p. 10). The rôle was reversed when he tilted against Hegel's "pantheism," "this species of

Atheism" (*Church Review*, July 1851, p. 257). Murdock's chief original work was called *Sketches of Modern Philosophy, Especially Among the Germans* (1842, 1844). One chapter was devoted to France and two to the influence of German philosophy through Coleridge on America. Almost an original production was *Institutes of Ecclesiastical History* (3 vols., 1832), a translation of the work of J. L. von Mosheim, with notes so copious as to constitute nearly an independent treatment. In 1852 he edited the translation of the first and translated the eleventh volume of Mosheim's *Historical Commentaries on the State of Christianity*. When seventy years old he resumed the study of Syriac and brought out a translation of the Peshito version of the New Testament (1851), being led on by "the pleasing thought that the words were, probably, in great part, the very terms which the Saviour and his Apostles actually uttered in their discourses and conversations."

[F. B. Dexter, *Biog. Sketches Grads. Yale Coll.*, vol. V (1911); N. S. Richardson, *Biog. Sketch of Rev. James Murdock* (1856), reprinted in *Church Rev.*, Jan. 1857; *Trans. Conn. Acad. Arts and Sciences*, vol. II, pt. II (1901–02); J. B. Murdock, *Murdock Geneal.* (1925); Francis Atwater, *Atwater Hist. and Geneal.* (1901); *Am. Congreg. Year-Book*, 1857; C. T. Russell, *The Hist. of Princeton, Worcester County, Mass.* (1838); *A Memorial of the Semi-Centennial Celebration of the Founding of the Theol. Sem. at Andover* (1859); *The Independent*, Aug. 28, 1856; *Columbian Weekly Reg.* (New Haven), Aug. 23, 1856.]

R. H. B.

MURDOCK, JOSEPH BALLARD (Feb. 13, 1851–Mar. 20, 1931), naval officer, was born at Hartford, Conn., son of Rev. John Nelson and Martha (Ballard) Murdock, and descendant of Robert Murdock, a Scotchman who came to Massachusetts sometime before 1692. Appointed to the Naval Academy in 1866, he spent five years after graduation in the Atlantic and Caribbean, four years in the coast survey, and three as instructor in physics at the Naval Academy, 1880–83. Here began the specialization in science, particularly in electricity, which gave added distinction to his professional career. Subsequently, during a year's leave, he was assistant in physics at the University of Pennsylvania, and thereafter engaged in tests of incandescent lights and dynamos under the Franklin Institute, in recognition of which work he was made honorary member of the Institute.

Following a year in the *Dolphin*, the first ship of the new steel navy, he spent two years developing electrical equipment at the Newport Torpedo Station; then served on Admiral Belknap's staff in the Orient, 1888–91; and, after returning through Europe to inspect electrical equipment in foreign navies, carried on electrical work at the New York Navy Yard, 1891–94. In 1886 he was elected to membership in the American Philosophical Society. From December 1894 to March 1897 he was in the Mediterranean as navigator of the *Minneapolis,* which rendered effective service in checking Turkish massacres in the Near East. The Spanish-American War called him from the War College, Newport, where he was an instructor then and twice thereafter, to be executive of the transport *Panther,* which landed a marine battalion at Guantanamo, June 10–14, 1898, and assisted in its occupation and defense. Made lieutenant commander (1899), and commander (1901), he was executive of Sampson's flagship *New York,* 1899–1901, commander of the *Alliance* and later the *Denver,* and commander of the battleship *Rhode Island,* 1907–09, during the world cruise of the American fleet. Upon promotion to rear admiral (November 1909), he commanded a division of the Atlantic Fleet, May 1910–April 1911, and subsequently the Asiatic Fleet, May 1911–July 1912, during the revolution which set up a Chinese republic. In this troubled period he stood firmly for protection of American interests, on one occasion insisting effectively—alone among foreign officers —on the right of foreign shipping to occupy the international anchorage near Shanghai (*Army and Navy Journal,* Feb. 15, 1913).

Retired for age Feb. 13, 1913, after brief duty on the General Board, he was again in active service during the World War, May 1918–May 1919, as president of general courts martial, Portsmouth Navy Yard. He was married June 26, 1879, to Anne, daughter of Dr. Simeon Dillingham of Philadelphia, but had no children. After retirement he spent the summers in Hill, N. H., and the winters usually in travel. He took active interest in public affairs, was twice elected to the New Hampshire House of Representatives (in 1921 and 1923), served on the state forestry commission and as trustee of the state historical society, and made a special study of genealogy and American history. He was author of *Notes on Electricity and Magnetism* (1884), *Murdock Genealogy* (1925), and articles on electricity and professional subjects, notably "The Naval Use of the Dynamo Machine and Electric Light," *Proceedings of the United States Naval Institute,* April 1882, and "Torpedo Tubes on Battleships," *Ibid.,* September 1903.

[*Who's Who in America,* 1930–31; J. B. Murdock, *Murdock Geneal.* (1925); L. R. Hamersly, *Records of Living Officers of the U. S. Navy and Marine Corps* (6th ed., 1898); *Manchester Union* (Manchester, N. H.), Mar. 21, 1931; *N. Y. Times,* Mar. 21, 1931; brief autobiographical service record and other data supplied by Harold Murdock, Chestnut Hill, Mass.] A. W.

MUREL, JOHN A. [See Murrell, John A., fl. 1804–1844].

MURFEE, JAMES THOMAS (Sept. 13, 1833–Apr. 23, 1912), educator, was born in Southampton County, Va. His parents, James Wilson and Anne (Parker) Murfee, were of the Tidewater gentry of Virginia. His preparatory education was done under his father and private tutors and in Stone's popular academy at Stony Mount. At the age of twenty he was graduated from the Virginia Military Institute with highest honors in civil engineering, and immediately after graduation he began the profession of teaching which he pursued for fifty years. In 1854 he became professor of natural sciences in Madison College, Pa., and the following year he served as professor of mathematics and commandant of cadets at Lynchburg College, Va. The next two years he gave to preparing his younger brothers for college. In 1860 the University of Alabama adopted the Virginia Military Institute system of discipline and appointed Maj. Caleb Huse commandant. Murfee, who was familiar with the system, was made professor of mathematics. In 1862 he was appointed commandant of cadets at the university. He was commissioned lieutenant-colonel by the Confederate government and was in charge of the university cadets when Gen. Croxton invaded Tuscaloosa and burned the university. At the end of the war Murfee was employed to design and erect new buildings for the University.

In 1871 he was elected president of Howard College, a Baptist institution then situated at Marion, Ala., and remained in this position for sixteen years. He nurtured the college through the troublous days of Reconstruction, expunged its debt, and established it upon a firm basis. When it was moved to Birmingham he declined to go with it. In the old college buildings he set up, in 1887, the Marion Military Institute of which he was superintendent until 1906. Here his academy, founded upon the old Virginia Military Institute plan, was a boon to the young men of Alabama when educational opportunities were pitifully meager. It became well known, and from various states and sections candidates for admission to West Point and Annapolis came to Marion to make their preparations. Murfee's work led President Harrison to appoint him a member of the Board of Visitors to the West Point Military Academy. He retired from active service upon an award of annuity given by the Carnegie Foundation because of "long and distinguished service" to the cause of education in Alabama. Murfee was married in July 1861

Murfree   Murfree

to Laura Owen of Tuscaloosa, Ala. A historian
of Alabama has written of him: "There are hundreds of men adorning the different vocations in
this state and in others,—who gratefully trace
the inception of their success to this great teacher of youth" (Riley, *post*, p. 318).

[T. M. Owen, *Hist. of Ala. and Dict. of Ala. Biog.*
(1921), vol. IV; B. F. Riley, *Makers and Romance of
Ala. Hist.* (n.d.); M. B. Garrett, "Sixty Years of
Howard College," *Howard Coll. Bull.*, Oct. 1927; the
Montgomery Advertiser, Apr. 25, 1912; information
as to certain facts from members of Murfee's family.]
A. B. M—e.

MURFREE, MARY NOAILLES (Jan. 24,
1850–July 31, 1922), novelist and short-story
writer, better known under her pen-name, Charles
Egbert Craddock, was born near Murfreesboro,
Tenn., at "Grantlands." Her mother, Priscilla
Dickinson, inherited this estate from her father,
David Dickinson, owner of extensive plantations
in both Tennessee and Mississippi. Her father,
William Law Murfree, a prominent lawyer, was
the grandson of Lieut.-Col. Hardy Murfree, an
officer of distinguished North Carolina ancestry
in the Continental Army who, settling in Tennessee in 1807, became a large landholder and gave
his name to Murfreesboro. Both families were
of English descent, though there was also a strain
of Huguenot blood in Mary Murfree, which came
through the Maney and Noailles families. Her
early childhood was passed happily at "Grantlands" until a fever left her partially paralyzed
and somewhat lame for the remainder of her life.
When she was six, her family moved to Nashville where she made rapid progress in school,
always leading her classes. A governess taught
her to speak French, and after the war she attended a boarding school in Philadelphia. As a
pianist she acquired a technique unusual for an
amateur. Early becoming an omnivorous reader,
she read extensively in history, in English,
French, Italian, and Latin literature, and in law
under the direction of her father. For many
years her summers were spent in the Cumberland Mountains where she became thoroughly
familiar with both scenery and mountaineers,
and was inspired to portray them in fiction.

Her literary career began with the publication
of some short stories in *Lippincott's Magazine*
(May 1874, July 1875) under the name R. Emmet Dembry. In May 1878 her "Dancin' Party
at Harrison's Cove" appeared in the *Atlantic* under the pen-name Charles Egbert Craddock.
This story with seven others from the *Atlantic*
appeared in 1884 in a collection of her stories
entitled *In the Tennessee Mountains*, which
created a literary sensation and contributed to
that year's being called "the climactic year in the

history of the short story" (F. L. Pattee, in *Cambridge History of American Literature*, II, 388).
Her masculine pseudonym, taken from the name
of the hero in one of her earliest stories, suited
her virile, robust, forthright style as well as her
bold, heavily shaded handwriting, which caused
Aldrich to write, "I wonder if Craddock has laid
in his winter's ink yet, so that I can get a serial
out of him" (Baskervill, *post*, p. 372). The editor
of the *Atlantic*, completely deceived, was astonished, on meeting "Mr. Craddock" the following year, to find the person to be a little lady,
slightly a cripple, who quietly remarked that she
was Charles Egbert Craddock. Other stories of
the mountains followed: namely, *Down the
Ravine* (1885); *The Prophet of the Great Smoky
Mountains* (1885); *In the Clouds* (1887); *The
Story of Keedon Bluffs* (1888); *The Despot of
Broomsedge Cove* (1889); *In the "Stranger Peoples'" Country* (1891); *His Vanished Star*
(1894); *The Phantoms of the Footbridge and
Other Stories* (1895); *The Mystery of Witch-
Face Mountain and Other Stories* (1895); *The
Juggler* (1897), and *The Young Mountaineers*
(1897).

With simplicity and originality she revealed
in these stories in a singularly rhythmical prose
the pathos of the lonely, frustrated lives of the
mountaineers and the solemn poetic beauty of
their surroundings. The dialect is faithfully reproduced, with its dry caustic wit and drawling
intonations. Her style is marred by too many
landscape pictures, and grandiloquent phrases
and unusual and pedantic words. Her dénoue-
ments are sometimes weak, and the characters
of her heroes are not always sustained with the
promise of her opening chapters. Yet her talent
for graphic description and her charm as a story-
teller carry the reader forward with interest.
The best work of the latter half of her literary
career belongs to historical fiction, after the manner of her first novel, *Where the Battle Was
Fought* (completed in 1876 but not published until 1884), a picture of the devastation wrought
by the Civil War. *The Story of Old Fort Loudon*
(1899), *A Spectre of Power* (1903), *The Frontiersmen* (1904), and *The Amulet* (1906) are
based upon the colonial history of the Old Southwest. *The Storm Centre* (1905) has the Civil
War for its background; while *The Bushwhack-
ers and Other Stories* (1899) and *The Raid of
the Guerilla and Other Stories* (1912) interweave
mountain characters in the incidents of the Civil
War. Of her remaining stories, *The Champion*
(1902) is a juvenile, *The Windfall* (1907) and
The Ordeal (1912) have their setting partially
in the mountains, while *The Fair Mississippian*

(1908) and *The Story of Duciehurst* (1914) portray the region with which Mary Murfree had become familiar in her youth. Her later works are free from some of the stylistic imperfections of her earlier stories, but they do not have the unstudied naïveté and charming spontaneity of her romances of the Tennessee mountains. As an author, she had a passion for accuracy and exactness, often quoting Scott's saying, "I love to be particular." She had a well-poised "judicial mind," was devoted to nature, and was sincerely religious. A vivacious and interesting conversationalist, she drew friends to her through her generosity and hearty responsiveness. In appearance, she had a "blond complexion and lightbrown, almost golden hair, bright, rather sharp face, with all the features quite prominent—forehead square and projecting, eyes gray, deep-set, and keen, nose Grecian, chin projecting, and mouth large" (Baskervill, *post*, p. 373). Failing eyesight prevented her from doing much literary work during her last years. Her death occurred at Murfreesboro in 1922. She was never married. Another novel of Mississippi River life, entitled "The Erskine Honeymoon," was left nearly completed at the time of her death and appeared as a serial in 1930 in the *Nashville Banner.*

[Sources include: W. M. Baskervil, *Southern Writers* (1897), vol. I; F. L. Pattee, *A Hist. of Am. Lit. Since 1870* (1915); *The Cambridge Hist. of Am. Lit.* (1918), vol. II; H. A. Toulmin, Jr., *Social Historians* (1911); Mildred L. Rutherford, *The South in Hist. and Lit.* (1907); *Lib. of Southern Lit.*, vol. VIII (1907); H. S. Fiske, *Provincial Types in Am. Fiction* (1903); *Nashville Banner*, Aug. 1, 1922; memoranda and manuscript material supplied by Miss Murfree's sister, Fanny N. D. Murfree, Murfreesboro, Tenn.]
C.L.L.

MURIETTA (MURIETA), JOAQUIN
[See MURRIETA, JOAQUIN, *c.* 1832–1853].

MURPHEY, ARCHIBALD DE BOW
(1777?–Feb. 1, 1832), jurist, pioneer in social and economic reforms in North Carolina, was born in Caswell County, N. C., the son of Archibald and Jane (De Bow) Murphey. After preparatory training at the log college of David Caldwell [*q.v.*] near Greensboro, he entered the University of North Carolina and graduated in 1799. There he was retained as tutor and professor of ancient languages for two years. On Nov. 5, 1801, he was married to Jane Armistead Scott. They had four sons and one daughter. In 1802 he qualified for the bar and began the practice of law in Hillsboro. He soon won distinction as an equity pleader and in the handling of testimony. From 1818 to 1820 he was superior-court judge and frequently acted as special justice of the supreme court when cases were heard in which one of the three regular justices had been of counsel or on the lower bench during the litigation leading to appeal. He also edited three volumes of reports consisting of the cases heard from 1804 to 1819 by the supreme court and its antecedent, the court of conference (*Reports of Cases in the Supreme Court . . . 1804 to 1819*, 3 vols., 1821–26).

His prime interests were not in the law but in the improvement of economic and social conditions in North Carolina. From 1812 to 1818, inclusive, he was a member of the state Senate from Orange County and assumed a distinct leadership in many public causes. Believing that the chief factor that retarded prosperity in North Carolina was its lack of adequate transportation facilities, he advocated a system of internal improvements with aid from the state, proposing a comprehensive program that included the improvement of harbors, the dredging of rivers, the construction of canals and turnpikes, and the drainage of swamp lands. A number of navigation companies had been chartered before 1815, and the policy of state aid had been recommended without results, but after proposals in that year by a committee on internal navigation, of which he was chairman, appropriations were made by the state to various enterprises. In 1819 he set forth a comprehensive survey of the transportation problem in his *Memoir on the Internal Improvements*. In the same year the state established a fund for internal improvements, its income to be used to finance transportation enterprises. Unfortunately most of the enterprises were too expensive for the financial resources available, and not until the advent of railroads was transportation adequately improved in North Carolina. Along with internal improvements he urged public education. Of this he was by no means the first advocate, but a *Report on Education . . . to the General Assembly of North Carolina* (1817), written by him, offered the first definite plan for public education submitted in North Carolina. That plan was not unlike one proposed by Thomas Jefferson for Virginia; primary schools and academies should be established and larger support given the university, but free education was to be confined to poor children. Nothing was accomplished in his lifetime, except the establishment of a literary fund in 1826; not until 1838 was a public-school law enacted. In other reforms, also, he was interested, notably the revision of the state constitution, the colonization of the free negroes, humanizing the criminal law, and the abolition of imprisonment for debt. He was instrumental in obtaining the passage of a statute in 1820 abolishing the imprisonment of debtors, but the law was repealed the following year; and in 1829 he was compelled to spend some time in jail as part of the procedure by which his property was turned over to his creditors. Another of his projects was the writing of a history of North Carolina. To this end he collected materials and memorialized the legislature for appropriations with which to copy documents in the British archives. He was granted permission to float a lottery which, however, was not successful. Only the introductory chapter of his history was ever completed. He was preëminently a scholar and idealist in politics with social concepts too advanced for his day and time; but in later years he came to be regarded as the prophet of a new era.

[*The Papers of Archibald D. Murphey*, ed. by W. H. Hoyt (2 vols., 1914); W. A. Graham, "Memoir of Hon. Archibald D. Murphey," *N. C. Univ. Mag.*, Aug. 1860; *Index to the . . . Records of N. C.*, vol. IV (1914), pp. 15–29; W. H. Hoyt, "Archibald D. Murphey," *Biog. Hist. of N. C.*, ed. by S. A. Ashe, vol. IV (1906); K. P. Battle, *Hist. of the Univ. of N. C.* (2 vols., 1907–12); C. L. Coon, *The Beginnings of Public Education in N. C.* (2 vols., 1908).]   W. K. B.

MURPHY, CHARLES FRANCIS (June 20, 1858–Apr. 25, 1924), political boss, was the son of John and Mary (Prendergrass) Murphy, Irish immigrants. Born in New York City, he and seven brothers and sisters were reared in an East Side neighborhood. His formal education, like the family means, was limited; he worked at one time or another in a wire factory, as caulker in a shipyard, and as a horse-car driver. He had become a leader of the youths of the neighborhood and organized a highly successful baseball team before he opened in 1878 a small saloon, which prospered and became the headquarters of his gang. Murphy soon established himself as the friend and counselor of dockyard men, gas-house workers, clerks, and politicians who lived in the neighborhood. He later opened a couple of other saloons and a hotel. He identified himself with Tammany and was so successful in politics that in 1892 he was elected leader of the eighteenth assembly district. Six years later he was rewarded for his services by Mayor Van Wyck, who appointed him dock commissioner. This was the only salaried political office he ever held. It subsequently appeared that his board leased piers and granted contracts to members of the organization without public bidding (Report of the Mazet committee, *New York Tribune*, June 17, 1903).

Murphy's great opportunity came with the forced retirement of Richard Croker [*q.v.*] from the leadership of Tammany Hall in 1901. After the unsuccessful attempt of Lewis Nixon, Croker's political heir, to assume his power, a tri-

umvirate consisting of Murphy, McMahon, and Haffen was appointed in May 1902. In September, by vote of the executive committee, the leadership was vested in Murphy alone, though the general expectation was that he would not long retain it. His rule, which continued until his death nearly twenty-two years later, was longer than that of any other of Tammany's absolute bosses. During that period, he may be said to have elected three mayors, George B. McClellan in 1903 and again in 1905, William J. Gaynor [*q.v.*] in 1909, and John F. Hylan in 1917 and 1921. In his second term, however, McClellan turned against Murphy and tried unsuccessfully to overthrow him, while Gaynor proved far from pliable. Like Tweed, Murphy conjoined with the control of Tammany the Democratic leadership of New York state. He procured the election of John A. Dix as governor in 1910, and of William Sulzer in 1912, but the latter proved a disappointment to him in matters of patronage, was impeached at his instance, and removed from office. In the next municipal election, the Tammany candidate was defeated by John Purroy Mitchel [*q.v.*], and in 1914 the state was carried by the Republicans. There was considerable agitation at this time for the removal of Murphy, who was distinctly out of favor with the Wilson administration and seemed at the lowest point of his leadership. In 1917, however, he recovered the city and in 1918, under Alfred E. Smith, a Tammany man, the Democrats swept the state. At the time of Murphy's death, Tammany was at the highest point of its prestige and power.

Much of his success may be attributed to his mastery of a taciturn diplomacy. He substituted for Croker's assertiveness the quiet purpose of an umpire. Silent, unspectacular, and extraordinarily tactful, he held together the warring elements in his organization, even at the lowest point of his political fortunes. He was gifted with great political intuition. In his first municipal campaign, when Tammany was being denounced by the reform element as nothing but a graft ring, he took the wind out of the opposition's sails by nominating on the Democratic ticket two of the most important Fusion candidates. In 1909, in effect, he repeated this coup by nominating Gaynor, a man above reproach, to oppose William Randolph Hearst, who advocated civic reform. Many unusual persons who later held high office were discovered and nurtured by Murphy. The so-called "New Tammany" took its name because of these protégés of his. There was something hopeful and stimulating about the relationship of Murphy with his young men during the later years of his life. He sat with them and challenged their arguments, and when they convinced him backed them up. He found, it was said, a demonstration of independence a sure mark of the fundamental courage necessary for the welfare of his own organization. Murphy's insistence that the police must be kept out of politics was as much the expression of profound political wisdom as of stern opposition to the exploitation of commercialized vice. He knew that though the public might philosophically accept "honest" graft, the discovery of police corruption would have an inflammatory effect. The Becker-Rosenthal débâcle, in the middle of his leadership, brought him bitter confirmation of this axiom. Tammany figured in no scandals of this sort during the latter half of his period of rule. The schools and the judiciary were also kept rigorously out of politics.

There is no doubt that Murphy was a clever business man and that his wide acquaintance inevitably opened the way to profits. His real-estate investments enabled him to live comfortably. But it is greatly to his credit that his fortune was no larger when he died than when he became leader of Tammany Hall. He married Mrs. Margaret Graham, a widow, when he was over forty. The year he became leader of Tammany, newspapers described him as resembling an Irish clergyman. As he grew older he became stouter and ruddier, but he by no means created the impression of joviality. His cold gray eyes and austere silence preserved his air of detachment and dignity. Although he received any one who came to Tammany Hall, he remained a shadowy figure in the public mind, for he never made speeches, never gave interviews, and, with the one exception noted above, never held or sought public office. If he had any theory or philosophy of government, if he had political views on any subject, he never expressed them publicly. His life was a masterpiece of reticence.

[J. J. Hoey, in *Jour. of the Am. Irish Hist. Soc.*, XXIII (1924), pp. 231–40, also reprinted in *The Soc. of the Friendly Sons of St. Patrick . . . One Hundred and Forty-Second Anniversary Dinner, Mar. 17, 1926*; Isabel Paterson, "Murphy," *Am. Mercury*, July 1928; M. R. Werner, *Tammany Hall* (1928); Harold Zink, *City Bosses in the U. S.* (1930); *N. Y. Times*, and *N. Y. World*, Apr. 26–28, 1924; *Outlook*, May 7, 1924; *Literary Digest*, May 17, 1924; *Nation*, May 21, 1924. The press comments after his death were rather favorable to the man, but wholly condemnatory of the system he represented. The above sketch is based in part on information supplied by Judge James Foley and others in personal interviews.]   R. M.

MURPHY, DOMINIC IGNATIUS (May 31, 1847–Apr. 13, 1930), pension commissioner, consular officer, was born in Philadelphia, Pa., the son of Dominic J. Murphy, a cotton manufacturer. He was educated in the private and public schools of that city, graduating from the Central High School with the degree of A.B. in 1865. He entered the Pension Office in Washington as a clerk on Mar. 22, 1871, and made an especially good record there, rising grade by grade to be chief of division, supervising special examiner, and chief clerk of the office. In 1893 he became deputy commissioner, and in 1896 President Cleveland appointed him commissioner of pensions, in which office he served with unusual efficiency for a year. From 1902 to 1904 he engaged in private practice as a patent attorney in Washington, and also, from 1903 to 1905, he edited and published a weekly journal entitled the *New Century*, devoted to the interests of the Catholic Church. He was prominent in Catholic societies and was a trustee of the St. Vincent Orphan Asylum.

On Apr. 30, 1904, he was appointed secretary of the Isthmian Canal Commission and served until May 23, 1905, when President Roosevelt appointed him consul at Bordeaux, France. While at that post he acted also, in 1907, as honorary commissioner to the International Maritime Exposition at Bordeaux. His next post was at St. Gall, Switzerland, where he served from 1909 to Feb. 7, 1914, when he was transferred to Amsterdam. On Feb. 22, 1915, he was promoted to consul general and assigned to Sofia, Bulgaria. He was temporarily detailed to the American consulate-general at London, England, from May 20 to Oct. 15, 1915, for special duty in the war claims department in charge of claims against the British government. He then returned to Sofia, where during the World War his services were particularly important and valuable, both to his own country and to Bulgaria; they were subsequently recognized by the naming of a hospital and a street in Sofia after him, and in various other ways. He is credited with having induced the Bulgarian government to ask the Allies for an armistice. After the war General Ludendorff wrote with feeling of Murphy's influence (*Ludendorff's Own Story*, 1920, II, 162, 367). While at Sofia he was also in charge of British interests in Bulgaria, and was presented by the British government with a silver bowl for "very special services" there to British prisoners of war and interned subjects. On July 8, 1919, he was transferred to Stockholm, where he remained until July 1, 1924, when he retired. During his term at Stockholm, he contributed efficiently to the development of the commercial and cultural relations between Sweden and the United States. After his retirement he continued to reside there until his death. He married, Oct. 24, 1904, Mrs. Bessie (Throckmorton) Atkinson, of

Washington, D. C., who with two sons survived him.

[Information from U. S. Pension Office; records of the Dept. of State; *Who's Who in America,* 1924–25; *N. Y. Times,* Apr. 14, 1930.]　　　A. E. I.

MURPHY, EDGAR GARDNER (Aug. 31, 1869–June 23, 1913), Episcopal clergyman, publicist, the son of Samuel W. and Janie (Gardner) Murphy, was born at Fort Smith, Ark. He was educated in the schools of San Antonio, Tex., at the University of the South, Sewanee, Tenn., and the General Theological Seminary, New York City, but took no degree. On Aug. 31, 1891, he married Maud King of Concord, Mass. Two sons were born to them. Ordained deacon (1890) and priest (1893) in the Protestant Episcopal Church, for more than a decade he served with distinction as rector of churches in San Antonio and Laredo, Tex., Chillicothe, Ohio, Kingston, N. Y., and Montgomery, Ala. The intensity of his devotion to the Kingdom of God as represented by his church is revealed in his books, *Words for the Church* (1897) and *The Larger Life* (1897). In Montgomery, he was instrumental in the founding of an Episcopal church for negroes. The erection and equipment of the Young Men's and Young Women's Christian Association buildings, in the city were largely due to his initiative, and Andrew Carnegie's gift to Montgomery of the first public-library building in Alabama was made in response to Murphy's efforts.

While in Montgomery he became vitally interested in the social problems of the new industrial era then rapidly opening in the South, and from this period the subjects of child-labor and popular education, and the race problem, largely dominated his life. With the assistance of a strong local committee he organized a conference for the free discussion of the race problem and conditions in the South. This was held in Montgomery in 1900, with Hilary A. Herbert [*q.v.*] as the presiding officer and Murphy as secretary. While the conference was under the direction of Southern men, the speakers were representative of both races and of all sections of the country. Its spirit was one of notable fairness and candor, and the published proceedings aroused wide interest in both America and Europe. Keenly sensitive to conditions in the textile industry, Murphy was responsible for the organization of the Alabama child-labor committee. Investigation disclosed that a number of Alabama cotton-mills were owned and controlled by Northern capitalists, whose influence had been effective in securing the repeal of laws enacted for the protection of women and chil-

dren working in factories (Murphy, *Problems of the Present South,* 1904, pp. 309–29). Murphy thus realized that child-labor was not a local problem, and became the leading spirit in the organization of the National Child Labor Committee. Convinced, however, of the need for an aroused and sustained public opinion, expressing itself in local rather than national legislation, he opposed the efforts of the committee to secure congressional action regulating child-labor. His open letter on national child-labor legislation to Senator Albert J. Beveridge (New York *Evening Post,* Mar. 9, 1907) was a brilliant defense of constitutional principles, later sustained by the Supreme Court of the United States. On account of differences on this issue between him and the majority of the National Child Labor Committee Murphy later resigned from it, but his interest in its work never abated. After his death, the statement was made that it was he "who pricked the conscience of the country alive to the existence of child labor as a shame and a curse to America" (*Child Labor Bulletin,* November 1913, p. 9).

A more intimate acquaintance with industrial, social, and racial problems showed him the necessity for a broader support, and more effective policies of public education. Realizing that his best work could be done outside the official ministry of the church he withdrew from that ministry (1903), and became executive secretary of the Southern Education Board (1903–08). The sincerity of his purposes, the clarity of his vision, and the statesmanlike quality of his thinking drew to him the leaders of the educational revival in his section and won for him an honored place among them. Besides editing the reports of several conferences on race problems and education in the South, and contributing to the *Outlook,* the *North American Review,* the *Century Magazine,* and other periodicals, he presented the results of his constructive thinking in two influential books, *Problems of the Present South* (1904) and *The Basis of Ascendancy* (1909). In the *Outlook* (July 5, 1913), he was described as "a leader not merely of Southern liberalism, but of national progress in social welfare," and the statement was made that "no man in this generation has succeeded so well in interpreting the South to the rest of the country."

He was compelled to give up active public work in 1908, but his physical sufferings in no way diminished the vigor of his intellect. Lying on his cot on the roof of his New York apartment he gave himself to the study of the heavens, and in 1912, under the pseudonym Kelvin Mc-

Kready, published *A Beginner's Star Book* (quarto), which won favorable notices in scientific journals. He was engaged in preparing an unfinished volume on the subjects to which he had devoted his life, at the time of his death, June 23, 1913.

[T. M. Owen, *Hist. of Ala. and Dict. of Ala. Biography* (1921), vol. IV; *Annals of the Am. Academy of Pol. and Social Science*, May 1905, Mar. 1906; *Who's Who in America*, 1912–13; obituaries in *Montgomery Advertiser*, June 24, 1913, and *Living Church*, June 28, 1913; letter of O. R. Lovejoy in N. Y. *Evening Post*, July 2, 1913.]   N. L. A.

MURPHY, FRANCIS (Apr. 24, 1836–June 30, 1907), temperance reformer, was born at Tagoat, County Wexford, Ireland. He was the younger of two sons of a poor tenant farmer, who died three months before Francis' birth. His schooling, not over four years in all, was received in a parish school conducted by a priest who apparently treated him unkindly, so that the boy was glad to be put to service at an early age in the household of his mother's landlord. For some years he contributed to the support of his widowed mother, who was a devout Catholic.

At the age of sixteen he emigrated to the United States. Landing in New York, he fell in with a group of convivial companions and lost all his money in a week of dissipation. Without a trade, he drifted from job to job and eventually into the country, where he worked on an upstate farm. He fell in love with his employer's daughter, Elizabeth Jane Ginn, and, overcoming strong parental objections, on Apr. 10, 1856, he married her. They had seven children, six of whom lived to maturity. His first wife died in 1870, and in 1890 he married Mrs. Rebecca Johnstone Fisher, of Council Bluffs, Iowa, who had been prominent in the work of the Woman's Christian Temperance Union and who became his faithful co-worker in temperance activities.

At the outbreak of the Civil War, Murphy enlisted as a private in the 92nd Regiment, New York Infantry, and served a three-year term in the army. In 1865, with the financial assistance of his brother James, who had also come to America, he became proprietor of the Bradley Hotel, Portland, Me. The habit of drinking formed in his youth fastened itself upon him here, and he sank rapidly in the social scale. In 1870 he was sentenced to jail for a drunken assault in his tavern. While in prison he was visited by Cyrus Sturdevant, a pious sea captain, whose appeals led, Apr. 3, 1870, to his conversion and the signing of a total-abstinence pledge.

After his release he was induced by friends to testify in meetings and found, to his surprise, that his endeavors provoked an enthusiastic response. He became president of a state reform club, and his evangelistic work soon extended to adjoining states and the Middle West. He adopted the blue ribbon as the badge of his crusade for "gospel temperance," and framed the Murphy pledge. In 1876 he was invited to conduct meetings in Pittsburgh and for a decade he made his headquarters there. During his first campaign of ten weeks he induced 40,000 men to sign his pledge, some $15,000 was raised by business men to support his work for sobriety among their employees, and 500 saloons in Allegheny and adjoining counties are said to have closed for lack of trade. During the Centennial Exhibition in Philadelphia he held meetings promoted by John Wanamaker. Assisted by his sons, he made a memorable tour through England, Scotland, and Ireland, during which he was received by Queen Victoria. He later conducted campaigns in Canada, Hawaii, and Australia. During his entire career he is said to have secured over 12,000,000 signatures to his pledge, and to have addressed more than 25,000 meetings.

He served in the Spanish-American War as chaplain of the 5th Pennsylvania Volunteers. In 1901 he moved from Pittsburgh to Los Angeles to spend his declining years, though he continued active until his last illness.

Murphy's power lay almost entirely in the charm of his personality. He was a man of fine physique and bearing, with heavy mustache, bushy eyebrows, and a shock of white hair. His manner was simple, earnest, and transparently honest, his smile constant, and his handclasp magnetic. His oratory was unstudied and extemporaneous, making large use of his personal experience, practical argument, and emotional appeal. From the standpoint of organization, however, his work was weak and the results not of real permanence. Religiously he was orthodox and evangelical, having become a Protestant after his conversion, but he never accepted ordination, though it was offered him in the Methodist Church. He had the broadest tolerance for the views of others and was eagerly supported by religious leaders of every faith. He never joined in the drive for legislative prohibition through the Prohibition Party or the Anti-Saloon League, believing that the public could not be permanently influenced by institutional or coercive methods.

[*Memories of Francis Murphy* (n.d.), by his wife; *Talks by Francis Murphy* (1907); E. H. Cherrington, *Standard Encyc. of the Alcohol Problem*, vol. IV (1928); A. F. Fehlandt, *A Century of Drink Reform in the U. S.* (1904); H. M. Chalfant, *Father Penn and John Barleycorn* (1920); J. S. Vandersloot, *The True*

Path; or, Gospel Temperance, Being the Life, Work, and Speeches of Francis Murphy, Dr. Henry A. Reynolds, and Their Co-laborers (1878); Pittsburgh Gazette, Nov. 29, 1876, and ff.; Los Angeles Times, July 1, 1907.]   K. M. G.

MURPHY, FRANKLIN (Jan. 3, 1846–Feb. 24, 1920), manufacturer, governor of New Jersey, was born in Jersey City, N. J., the son of William Hayes and Abby Elizabeth (Hagar) Murphy. He came of colonial stock, being a descendant of Robert Murphy, who settled in Connecticut in 1756, and whose son moved to New Jersey in 1766, and later fought in the Revolutionary War. Through his grandmother, Sarah (Lyon) Murphy, he was descended from another soldier in the Revolution—Benjamin Lyon, who was a private in the Essex New Jersey Light Horse. When Franklin was ten years old, his parents moved from Jersey City to Newark. The boy attended the Newark Academy until he was sixteen. Leaving school in July 1862, he enlisted as a private in the 13th Regiment, New Jersey Volunteers. During nearly three years of active service, he took part in nineteen battles, including Antietam, Chancellorsville, Gettysburg, Missionary Ridge, and Lookout Mountain. He was mustered out as a first lieutenant in June 1865. Immediately upon returning to civil life, though only nineteen years of age, he organized in Newark the firm of Murphy & Company, varnish manufacturers. This concern grew steadily until in 1891 it was incorporated as the Murphy Varnish Company, with its founder as president. Under his direction a system of profit-sharing for all employees was introduced, and also a pension system. In 1915 he resigned as president, to be succeeded by his son, Franklin Murphy, Jr., but he remained chairman of the board of directors until his death.

After securely establishing himself in business, Murphy entered politics as a Republican. He became a member of the Newark common council in 1883, and served until 1886, in the last year as president. In 1885 he was elected to the state Assembly. The range of his public interests is shown by his work as a trustee of the state reform school at Jamesburg, 1886–89; as the commissioner who planned Essex County's system of parks, 1895–1902; as one of the American commissioners to the Paris Universal Exposition in 1900; as a member of the board of managers of the National Home for Disabled Volunteer Soldiers, 1905–12; and as president-general of the national society of the Sons of the American Revolution, 1898–1900. In 1897 he declined the ambassadorship to Russia. He was for many years chairman of the Republican

state committee, and from 1900 to 1918 was a member of the Republican National Committee. In 1908 he was a candidate for the Republican nomination for vice-president, receiving seventy-seven votes at the national convention in Chicago, and in 1916 was defeated by Joseph S. Frelinghuysen as a candidate for the nomination for United States senator. He was a delegate to five national conventions (1900–16). The most valuable public service which he rendered, however, was during his three years as governor of New Jersey. Elected in 1901, he entered office at the beginning of 1902, and immediately applied the methods of the successful business man to the affairs of state. The result was that during his administration New Jersey enacted its first primary-election law, child-labor law, workshop-ventilation law, and tenement-house-commission law. Moreover, he introduced a complete audit system of state expenditures, and compelled banks to pay interest on state deposits. He abolished the fee systems in state and county offices. Largely through his efforts the state sanitarium for tuberculous patients was established at Glen Gardner, and an appropriation was made for the industrial school for colored children at Bordentown. Even after he retired from the governorship, he exerted considerable influence on the politics of the state.

In private life he was well liked for his courtesy and good humor. He was a man of culture, interested in American history and particularly in patriotic societies. He was married, June 24, 1868, to Janet Colwell of Newark. She died in 1904, leaving two children who survived him. His death occurred at Palm Beach, Fla.

[Lyon Memorial, vol. II (1907); Manual of the Legislature of N. J., 1904; Who's Who in America, 1918–19; N. Y. Times, N. Y. Tribune, Feb. 25, 1920; Newark Evening News, Feb. 24, 1920.]   J. E. F.

MURPHY, HENRY CRUSE (July 5, 1810–Dec. 1, 1882), lawyer, political leader, scholar, was born in Brooklyn, N. Y. His paternal grandfather, Timothy Murphy, an Irish physician, emigrated to New Jersey before the Revolution. John G. Murphy, his father, a skilled mechanic and millwright, married Clarissa Runyon of an old Dutch family of Princeton, N. J., and about 1808 established himself in Brooklyn. Henry, the eldest son, graduated with honors from Columbia in 1830, studied law with the Hon. Peter W. Radcliffe, and, after admission to the bar, began to practise in Brooklyn. In 1834 he became city attorney, and the following year he joined John A. Lott, then the ablest lawyer in Brooklyn, in partnership. Shortly afterwards John Vanderbilt was admitted, and the firm entered upon a long and prosperous career.

All of its members were able politicians, and so completely did they control the local affairs of the Democratic party that in the words of Stiles, the Brooklyn historian, to write a history of the firm "would be to write the political history of Brooklyn from 1835 to 1857" (*post*, p. 10). Murphy, at the age of thirty-one (1842) was elected mayor of Brooklyn. Before his term was completed he was sent to Congress, where he served from 1843 to 1845, and again from 1847 to 1849. At the state constitutional convention of 1846 he contended vainly for a notably advanced program of city charters, taxation, and government, and repeated his efforts, without effect, at the constitutional convention of 1867–68. In 1852, when the Virginia delegation introduced the name of Franklin Pierce into the deadlocked National Democratic Convention, with the result that he was nominated and subsequently elected, it was only after Pierce had won the delegation's preference over Murphy by one vote. In 1857 he was appointed minister to the Netherlands by Buchanan, and served until recalled by Lincoln. The period was a quiet one in the relations of the two countries until the secession crisis, when Murphy communicated to the Dutch government a notably able statement of the Federal viewpoint (*Papers Relating to Foreign Affairs*, 1861, I, 327 ff.). Upon his return he was elected without much effort on his part for six successive terms in the state Senate, 1861–73. He urged support of the war by the Democratic party in speeches at the state convention, and before the Tammany Society. At the National Democratic Convention of 1868, as chairman of the committee on resolutions, he battled vainly against the Greenbackers and their Ohio program. The same year he lost a bitterly fought battle at the Democratic state convention for nomination for governor, being supported by the opponents of John T. Hoffman [*q.v.*], the Tammany candidate. He was the party's unsuccessful nominee for the United States Senate in 1867 and 1869, and his hopes for the same office in 1875 were dashed when Governor Seymour supported his henchman, Francis Kernan [*q.v.*]. During the entire period after his return from The Hague Murphy's political career was handicapped by the fact that he belonged to a minority faction of a minority party.

In the meantime he had been turning more and more to business and scholarly pursuits. He aided in securing many local improvements for the city. His interest in the development of Coney Island led him to accept the presidency of the Flatbush & Coney Island Railroad and to build Brighton Beach Hotel at its terminus. He drafted and secured the passage of the legislation necessary for the building of Brooklyn Bridge, and was president of the private company which, in the beginning, conducted the enterprise, and also of the corporation which succeeded it. He relentlessly fought all opposition, and worked against both natural and legal obstacles, remaining at his post "when almost any other man would have retired in disgust" (editorial, New York *Sun*, Dec. 2, 1882).

While studying law he had served as the chief editorial writer of the *Brooklyn Advocate* and as a rising party leader he contributed political articles to the *United States Magazine and Democratic Review* and to the *North American Review*. Having persuaded a few friends of the desirability of establishing a Democratic newspaper in Brooklyn, he issued in October 1841, the first number of the *Brooklyn Eagle*, of which he remained proprietor and associate editor for almost a year, placing the paper upon a firm foundation. His increasing interest in early American history led him to collect, with rare discrimination, a library of Americana, which at his death was rivaled by only two or three collections in the country. His chief contributions to American history were his translations of works relating to New Netherland, especially *The Representation of New Netherland* (1849), from the Dutch of Adriaen van der Donck, *Voyages from Holland to America* (1853), from the Dutch of D. P. deVries, and the valuable journal of Jasper Dankers and Peter Sluyter, which he discovered in manuscript in an Amsterdam bookstore, purchased, and translated for the first volume (1867) of the *Memoirs* of the Long Island Historical Society. A unique piece of work was his *Anthology of New Netherland; or Translations from the Early Dutch Poets of New York* (Bradford Club Series, no. 4, 1865). His *Henry Hudson in Holland* (1859) is still valuable, having been reprinted with notes, documents, and bibliography by Wouter Nijhoff in 1909. In his *Voyage of Verrazzano* (1875), however, he unfortunately took the view that Verrazzano's claims of discovery were unfounded.

Murphy married, July 29, 1833, his cousin, Amelia, daughter of Richard Greenwood of Haverstraw, N. Y., who survived him; to them were born two sons.

[H. R. Stiles, in *N. Y. Geneal. and Biog. Record*, Jan. 1883; Frederick Greenwood, *Greenwood Geneals.* (1914); D. S. Alexander, *A Political Hist. of the State of N. Y.*, vol. III (1909); *Proc. at the Dinner ... to the Hon. Henry C. Murphy* (1857); *Cat. of the Magnificent Lib. of the Late Henry C. Murphy* (1884);

U. S. Mag. and Democratic Rev., July 1847; *Brooklyn Eagle, N. Y. Times, N. Y. Tribune*, Dec. 2, 1882.]
O. W. H.

MURPHY, ISAAC (Oct. 16, 1802–Sept. 8, 1882), governor of Arkansas, was born near Pittsburgh, Pa., the son of Hugh and Jane Murphy. In 1830 he settled in Tennessee, where he taught school. In 1834 he moved to Arkansas and taught in Fayetteville and the surrounding country. The next year he was admitted to the bar and for several years taught, practised law, and surveyed public lands. He was elected to the legislature in 1848 but went to California in 1849 and remained until 1854. On returning to Arkansas he moved to Huntsville, where he and two of his daughters conducted the Huntsville Female Seminary. His impress upon the educational system of northwest Arkansas was good. In 1856 he was elected to the state Senate to fill a vacancy, and thereafter he devoted himself to the law and politics. In 1861 he was elected a delegate from Madison County to the state convention which had been called to consider secession. A majority of the delegates, including Murphy, opposed secession, but they allowed the secessionists to put through a resolution submitting "secession" or "cooperation" to the people to be voted upon in August. After the bombardment of Fort Sumter the convention was called together again and voted secession with only five negative votes (May 6). Four of the five members were won over by the secessionists but Murphy remained impervious to all appeals for unanimity (*Journal, post*, pp. 123–24). He remained in the convention, however, until it adjourned in June. He then returned to his home, but the situation became unbearable and after the battle of Pea Ridge he fled (April 1862) to the Union army commanded by Gen. Samuel R. Curtis, leaving his family at Huntsville. There his wife and daughters suffered many hardships at the hands of Confederate sympathizers.

Murphy was made a member of General Curtis' staff and remained with the Union army until the capture of Little Rock, Sept. 10, 1863. He then became active in forming a loyal state government. President Lincoln issued an order on Jan. 20, 1864, for an election to be held on Mar. 28, but the loyalists had already anticipated him and a convention, assembled at Little Rock on Jan. 8, elected Murphy provisional governor. Lincoln then directed the military authorities to cooperate in the establishment of a government. In March the revised constitution was adopted by popular vote, mainly in the counties north of the Arkansas River, and Murphy was elected governor. His program included cooperation with the Federal authorities to crush the Confederates, the abolition of slavery, the education of the masses, and the rebuilding of the state by encouraging the immigration of people with capital. Confederate sympathizers gave him much trouble and he appealed to Lincoln several times. He reported that loyalists were dying of starvation, but he could not help them. There was no money in the treasury when he was elected, but he conducted the government economically, paid expenses, and had $167,221.27 in greenbacks and bonds in the treasury when the Carpet-bag convention met in 1868. In 1866 former Confederates captured the legislature and passed numerous laws and resolutions distasteful to him, but he was never swept into the camp of the Radical Republicans and thereby regained to a large extent the confidence and respect of his opponents. When displaced by the new government he returned to his home in Madison County and remained there until his death, passing his last days in obscurity. He had married, on July 31, 1830, Angelina A. Lockhart in Tennessee. Six daughters were born of this marriage. He was not a forceful leader, but he was honest and straightforward and held tenaciously to his opinions.

[Fay Hempstead, *A Pictorial Hist. of Ark.* (1890); T. S. Staples, *Reconstruction in Ark., 1862–74* (1923); C. H. McCarthy, *Lincoln's Plan of Reconstruction* (1901); M. W. Downes, *The Murphy Family* (1900); journals of the House and Senate of Arkansas, 1864–65; *Jour. of Both Sessions of the Convention of the State of Ark., Little Rock* (1861); *Daily Ark. Gazette*, Sept. 12, 1882.]
D. Y. T.

MURPHY, JOHN (Mar. 12, 1812–May 27, 1880), book-publisher, son of Bernard and Mary (McCullough) Murphy, was born in Omagh, Tyrone, Ireland, and was brought by his parents to New Castle, Del., in 1822. Here he attended the New Castle Academy and worked in a store until he was sixteen years of age, when he went to Philadelphia to learn the printing trade. Becoming a skilled craftsman, with an artistic touch, and possessing business acumen, he was soon superintendent of a thriving concern. About 1835 he established a printing and stationery house in Baltimore, where the trade was less crowded, and two years later he added the publication of books. In 1852, he married Margaret E. O'Donnoghue of Georgetown, D. C., who died in 1869, leaving two sons and four daughters.

As a publishing house of high standards and laudable ideals, Murphy & Company did a substantial general business, although its specialty was Catholic books. Catholic writers, some of whom became prelates, owed Murphy a debt of gratitude, for he courageously undertook ponderous theological works for which there was a restricted market, and assumed losses which were met by the profits from commercial printing and the sale of textbooks. Furthermore, he was available when secular publishing houses practically refused manuscripts by Catholic writers. He also brought out Bibles, hymnals, prayerbooks in various languages, and devotional guides, putting them on the market at a commendably low price; through translations issued by him foreign Catholic writings were made known to the American public. He printed *The Religious Cabinet,* the first number of which appeared in January 1842. A year later he became proprietor of the periodical, and the name of it was changed to the *United States Catholic Magazine,* under which title he published it until December 1848. He also published *The Metropolitan; A Monthly Magazine* (1853–59), a monthly devoted to religion, education, literature, and general information; the *Metropolitan Catholic Almanac and Laity's Directory;* the *Catholic Youth's Magazine* (1857–61); *The Works of the Right Reverend John England* (5 vols., 1849); theological writings of the Kenricks and the Spaldings; Peter Fredet's popular histories, Gibbons' *Faith of Our Fathers,* which proved a best seller; and numerous works of lesser clergymen. The foreign books brought out by him included Butler's *Lives of the Saints,* Faber's writings, Thomas Moore's *Travels of an Irish Gentleman in Search of a Religion, Rituale Romanum Pauli V,* John Lingard's *Abridgment of the History of England,* J. M. V. Audin's *Life of Luther,* Cardinal Wiseman's works, Hendrik Conscience's Belgian novels, Châteaubriand's *Genius of Christianity,* and Balmes's *Protestantism and Catholicity Compared.* For the publication of the *Definition of the Dogma of the Immaculate Conception,* Murphy was awarded a papal medal of merit (1855); for his *Acts and Decrees of the Second Plenary Council of Baltimore,* he was honored with the title of "typographer to the Apostolic See" (1866). Among his secular publications were James McSherry's *History of Maryland* (1850), the new constitution of Maryland of 1851 and also those of 1864 and 1867, and *The Maryland Code, Public General Laws* (2 vols., 1860), with later supplements, which won the encomium of his friend, Chief Justice Taney. It was said justly that Murphy elevated the standard of law publications and uplifted the publishing business to a higher ethical basis. A man of integrity, he lived quietly through the trying Civil War years and paid off all liabilities when many businessmen took refuge in bankruptcy. On his sudden death from paralysis, he was buried from the cathedral in Baltimore, attended by an unusual concourse of friends of various ranks, who bore witness to his character and numerous charities.

[*Gazette* (Baltimore), May 28, 1880; *Sun* (Baltimore), May 28, 31, 1880; *Stationer* (N. Y.), June 3, 1880; *N. Y. Freeman's Journal,* June 5, 1880; *Catholic Review* (Baltimore), June 5, 1880; information from Murphy's son and successor, Frank K. Murphy.]

R. J. P.

MURPHY, JOHN BENJAMIN (Dec. 21, 1857–Aug. 11, 1916), surgeon, was born of Irish parents, Michael and Ann (Grimes) Murphy, on a farm near Appleton, Wis. After a preliminary education in the public schools and some medical studies under Dr. John R. Reilly of Appleton, he entered Rush Medical College, Chicago, where he was graduated in 1879. Following an internship in the Cook County Hospital, he spent two years in graduate study in Vienna. Returning to Chicago, he associated himself in practice with Dr. Edward W. Lee. In 1884 he became lecturer in surgery at Rush Medical College. His later teaching positions were as follows: professor of clinical surgery in the College of Physicians and Surgeons, Chicago, 1892–1901; professor of surgery, Northwestern University Medical School, 1901–05; professor of surgery, Rush Medical College, 1905–08; and again professor of surgery, Northwestern University Medical School, 1908–16. He became chief of the surgical staff of Mercy Hospital in 1895, which position he held until his death. For much of his career he was an attending surgeon at Cook County Hospital.

Murphy began his professional career at a time when bacteriological investigation and antiseptic methods were greatly increasing the possibilities of abdominal surgery. It was to this field that he turned his early efforts. He was one of the first to investigate the cause and treatment of peritonitis following appendicitis. Being of an inventive turn of mind, he produced in 1892 the Murphy button, a mechanical device for making rapid and accurate intestinal and gastro-intestinal anastomosis. This device revolutionized the gastro-intestinal surgery of the time and made possible life-saving operations that never would have been attempted without its help. Though the Murphy button will be remembered as his outstanding contribution to surgery, he advanced the surgical knowledge of every region of the abdomen. Later, he devoted himself to the principles underlying the surgery of the lungs and of the nervous system, and his later years were largely devoted to the surgery of bones and joints, particularly to deformities due to infections. He was a rapid operator with mechanical skill of the highest order. He was also the first of the master-surgeons of Chicago to whom surgical asepsis was a matter of intuition. It was as a teacher of surgery, however, that he was preëminent. Despite a high shrill voice, he had an eloquence and a force of personality that made him one of the greatest interpreters of surgery that America has produced. His presentation was dramatic. Dr. William J. Mayo has said that as a teacher of clinical surgery he was "without a peer," characterizing him as "the surgical genius of our generation" (Kelly and Burrage, *post*, p. 839).

Murphy was the recipient of many honorary degrees, from both American and foreign universities. He was awarded the Laetare medal by Notre Dame University in 1902 and in 1916 the Pope made him Knight-Commander of the order of Saint Gregory the Great. He held membership in the principal surgical societies of America and Europe and was president of the American Medical Association, 1910–11, and of the Clinical Congress of Surgeons, 1914–15. His writings were largely confined to contributions upon clinical surgery to journals. He wrote the article entitled "Surgery of the Appendix Vermiformis" in W. W. Keen's *Surgery, Its Principles and Practice* (1908), and published *General Surgery* in 1911. His other most noteworthy work is *The Surgical Clinics of John B. Murphy, M.D., at Mercy Hospital, Chicago* (5 vols., 1912–16).

Physically he was tall and powerfully built, with a florid complexion, thin hair, a red beard, carefully parted, and a red moustache. He had extraordinary energy, which showed in his quick movements and terse decisive speech. He was invariably kind and courteous, deeply religious, and scrupulous in his religious obligations. The stress of his work brought on attacks of angina pectoris, from which he was invalided for several months before his death, which took place at Mackinac Island, Mich. He was married on Nov. 25, 1885, to Jeannette C. Plamondon of Chicago, who survived him; they had five children, one son and four daughters. In 1926 the American College of Surgeons inaugurated in Chicago the John B. Murphy Memorial, a monumental building to house the headquarters of the college. His name is also borne by the Murphy Hospital opened in 1921 on Belmont Avenue.

[*Surgery, Gynecology and Obstetrics*, Aug. 1916; *Ibid.*, Dec. 1920; *Bull. Am. Coll. of Surgeons*, July 1926; *Trans. Am. Surgic. Asso.*, vol. XXXVI (1918); H. A. Kelly and W. L. Burrage, *Am. Medic. Biogs.* (1920); *Chicago Daily Tribune*, Aug. 12, 1916.]
J. M. P.

MURPHY, JOHN FRANCIS (Dec. 11, 1853–Jan. 30, 1921), landscape painter, was born at Oswego, N. Y. He attended the public schools of Oswego but took slight interest in any line of study save that of painting. In his art he was wholly self-taught. At the age of seventeen he went to Chicago and found employment as a painter of advertising signboards, but he soon lost this job because of laziness. Returning to the East, he spent several years in New Jersey, not far from Orange, where he sketched and during the summer months taught a group of girl students, one of whom, Adah Clifford, later became his wife. In 1875 he opened a studio in New York, and a year later he exhibited his first picture at the National Academy. His early years in New York were a period of severe struggle for a living. He was elected a member of the Salmagundi Club in 1878 and thereafter for nearly a half-century was closely identified with that organization. He struck his gait in the early eighties and began to experience the satisfactions of relative prosperity. He was awarded the second Hallgarten prize at the National Academy in 1885 and became an academician in 1887. At the same time he built a summer home and studio at Arkville, N. Y., a hamlet at the western edge of the Catskill region. There, from that time to the end of his life, he spent many happy summers and autumns in leisurely contemplation; he never painted out-of-doors, and his pictures were never literal portraits of places, but he made pencil notes and was constantly observing.

In time numerous honors as well as higher prices for his pictures told the story of his popularity. The list of prizes lengthened; the museums were eager to acquire his works; and at the time of his death in the winter of 1921, he was at the acme of his renown. He was given a funeral at the Fine Arts building, and he was buried at Arkville. Five exhibitions of his work were opened soon after his death. The Lotos Club opened a memorial exhibition of seventy-five of his landscapes; the Salmagundi Club exhibited a somewhat smaller collection of his works; there was an exhibition at the Macbeth Gallery; the Kansas City Art Institute displayed a group of nineteen pictures; and in Boston the Vose Gallery placed on view a collection of landscapes. Examples of his art are to be seen in the leading museums of the United States. The chief merit of his landscapes, to which, perhaps, there is a certain sameness, is their poetic sentiment. The designs are simple and good; the quiet phases of nature are pictured with harmony of tone. Of all his work, some of his small early canvases are among his best productions.

[Eliot Clark, *J. Francis Murphy* (1926), containing bibliography; F. F. Sherman, *Am. Painters of Yesterday and Today* (1919); Elliott Daingerfield, article in *Scribner's Mag.*, Jan. 1917; Royal Cortissoz, in *N. Y. Herald-Tribune*, Feb. 6, 1921; C. L. Buchanan, in *Internat. Studio*, July 1914 and Mar. 1921; *Am. Art News*, Feb. 5, Dec. 3, 10, 1921; Handbook of loan exhibition, Macbeth Gallery, 1921; H. T. Lawrence, article in *Brush and Pencil*, July 1902; Mich. State Lib., *Biog. Sketches of Am. Artists* (1924); S. G. W. Benjamin, article in *Am. Art Review*, Mar. 1881; catalogues of the memorial exhibitions at the Lotos Club, Salmagundi Club, and Vose Gallery; Sadakichi Hartmann, *A Hist. of Am. Art* (1932), vol. I; the *Arts*, Feb.-Mar. 1921; *N. Y. Times*, Jan. 31, 1921.]
W. H. D—s.

MURPHY, JOHN W. (Jan. 20, 1828–Sept. 27, 1874), bridge engineer, was born at New Scotland, N. Y. When he entered Rensselaer Polytechnic Institute, he was already a practical surveyor, seasoned by a sound apprenticeship; and after he was graduated, in 1847, he obtained a position of some responsibility on the Erie Canal. During the next twenty-five years he explored many fields of engineering: in 1851–52 he erected the levees on the Alabama River; in 1860-61 he served as chief engineer of Montgomery, Ala.; in 1864 he constructed the Union Hall, in Philadelphia, which was taken over by the Pennsylvania Railroad; in 1869 he built the aqueduct over the valley of the Wissahickon; but he is remembered primarily as a pioneer in the design, construction, and manufacture of bridges.

On the Erie Canal he became assistant to Squire Whipple [q.v.], who, in 1840, had built an iron bridge with wrought-iron tension and cast-iron compression members. Under Whipple's influence he advanced rapidly in his profession. While engaged on the construction of a wooden bridge at Easton, Pa., he substituted a temporary bridge for the falsework usually employed; and this method he developed more fully in the erection of the aqueduct at Germantown. Another of his more notable innovations was a testing machine for determining the elasticity of construction materials. His chief contribution to the art of bridge-building sprang, however, from his association with Whipple, who, in 1848, introduced the type of truss bridge which bears his name. As modified by Murphy, it soon came to be known as the Murphy-Whipple bridge. In its final form, which was in wide use throughout the United States until 1885, the struts were vertical and the ties intersected twice. As early as 1859, in a bridge on the Lehigh Valley Railroad, Murphy initiated the use of pin connections, long a characteristic feature of American metal bridge construction. In this instance the pins were turned and the eyes formed by bending the bars around the pins and welding the ends. In 1863, he designed for the Lehigh Valley Railroad a pin-connected bridge in which all the members were of wrought iron. This was the first bridge of its kind in the United States. His chief monument is the Broad Street Bridge, in Philadelphia, in the erection of which he had to overcome unprecedented difficulties. In 1855 he entered into partnership, at Trenton, N. J., with his classmate, George Washington Plympton, who was associated with him in the development of his testing machine. In 1859, with several of his fellow alumni of Rensselaer, including George Brooke Roberts [q.v.] and Percival Roberts, he organized a company which constructed many important bridges of the Murphy-Whipple type during the era of railroad expansion.

Murphy, who was twice married, was popular in social and musical circles. He was a pleasant companion, an entertaining anecdotist, an effective speaker, and a composer of some ability. By his first marriage he had a son and a daughter. He died in Philadelphia.

[Zerah Colburn, "American Iron Bridges," *Minutes of Proc. of the Inst. of Civil Engineers* (London), XXII (1863), 540–75; W. C. Unwin, *Wrought Iron Bridges and Roofs* (1869); J. A. L. Waddell, *Bridge Engineering* (2 vols., 1916); R. P. Baker, *A Chapter in Am. Educ.* (1924); H. B. Nason, *Biog. Record Officers and Grads. Rensselaer Polytechnic Inst.* (1887); the *Press* (Phila.), Sept. 29, 1874.]
R. P. B.

MURPHY, MICHAEL CHARLES (Feb. 28, 1861–June 4, 1913), coach, pioneer of athletic training in the United States, was born at Westboro, Mass. As a boy, he was frail and slim. Early in life he took up physical exercise in the form of athletic competition, hoping to improve his physique. Ambitious to become an athlete, he soon excelled in running and in baseball. He even tried long-distance running and walking, but it was as a sprinter that his talent was best displayed. Possessing an unusually keen and active mind, he studied closely the methods of every professional athlete with whom he came in contact and adapted the hints thus obtained to his own use with marked success. In the middle eighties he established a training camp for athletes near his home in Westboro, and put his ideas into practice. His success in improving the performance of his pupils brought him in 1887 to the attention of A. B. Coxe, who induced him to become athletic trainer at Yale. After two years there, he went to the Detroit Athletic Club, where he stayed three years. He returned to Yale in the summer of 1892 as coach of the track team and trainer of the football team, remaining until the summer of 1896, when the University of Pennsylvania secured his services. After a four-year period of tremendous success at Pennsylvania, he returned to Yale in the fall of 1900, remaining in New Haven until 1905, when he again returned to the University of Pennsylvania. In this connection he continued until his death. During most of his summer vacations he coached the track team of the New York Athletic Club. He was elected without question to coach the American Olympic teams of 1908 at London and of 1912 at Stockholm, both of his teams winning overwhelming victories. He was again chosen coach for the American team of 1916, an appointment canceled by his death in 1913. The Olympic Games themselves were canceled by the World War.

Murphy had an alert mind and an inquiring spirit, and was quick to catch the meaning of any innovation or suggestion that his athletes had to offer. The nervousness of Charles H. Sherrill on the starting line of the sprint was turned by Murphy from a handicap to an advantage when he introduced the crouching start, the greatest contribution to the art of sprinting in modern times. He continually studied and remembered the little tricks and devices that went to improve the technique of jumping, pole vaulting, hurdling, and weight throwing, until he had a knowledge of these feats which was unique. He was a keen judge of character and had an astonishing ability to get the best out of his athletes by persuasion, flattery, or the lash of sarcasm, each used to suit the case. He had supreme confidence in himself and was fearless in upholding his views; above all, he had the evangelist's ability to work himself up to a state of fervor that communicated itself to his athletes and inspired them to superhuman efforts. A list of the victories of his teams at Yale and Pennsylvania would be a history of the intercollegiate championships of his time. In his later years, Pennsylvania became the place to which coaches from all over America and abroad came for advice and counsel, which was always freely given. His trainer's lore and his theories were written down by E. R. Bushnell and published after his death in a book entitled *Athletic Training, by Michael C. Murphy* (1914). Apart from this work, he was author of little except some small handbooks in the Spalding Athletic Library and ephemeral newspaper articles. He died in Philadelphia. His wife was Nora B. Long.

[*Old Penn* (Univ. of Pa.), June 14, 1913; *Phila. Record*, June 5, 1913; *North American* (Phila.), June 5, 1913; intro. by E. R. Bushnell to *Athletic Training, by Michael C. Murphy* (1914); F. A. M. Webster, *Athletics of Today* (1929); C. H. Mapes, *The Man Who One Day a Year Would go "Eelin'"* (1915); certain facts and dates from E. R. Bushnell.]   R. T. M.

MURPHY, WILLIAM SUMTER (1796?– July 13, 1844), chargé d'affaires in Texas, was born in South Carolina and removed to Chillicothe, Ohio, in 1818. He married Lucinda Sterret in 1821. He was a practising lawyer with a taste for politics and military affairs, a taste so strong that his place in the history of the Ohio bar is not an important one. His oratorical powers, however, were considerable, and it is said that he was in demand as counsel for the defense in criminal cases and that his friends liked to refer to him as "the Patrick Henry of the West." His only public service in Ohio was as one of the commissioners who in 1835, after the "Toledo War," remarked the disputed portion of the Ohio-Michigan boundary (*Special Message of Governor Lucas . . . in regard to the Northern Boundary Line . . . Dec. 8, 1835*, 1835, p. 8). A brigadier-general in the militia, he was always known as General Murphy. The story is told that, at first a Democrat, he became soured by his failure to obtain a nomination for Congress in 1832. At any rate, he was a supporter of Harrison in 1836 and 1840 and after that a supporter of Tyler.

In 1843 Tyler, by a recess appointment, made him minister extraordinary to Central America and chargé d'affaires to Texas. The Central-American mission amounted to little, but for a year he was the representative of the United States in Texas. He was not, however, entrusted with much responsibility, though serving as a useful instrument in the promotion of the annexation plans of Tyler and his secretaries of state. Neither the Washington nor the Texan government kept him informed as to what was going on, so that he, an ardent annexationist, believed that Great Britain's power over President Houston was complete. In fact the burden of his dispatches was the dark machinations of the British, and in this way they were equally acceptable at Washington and at the capital of Texas. In January 1844 negotiations for annexation were promising after Secretary Upshur had assured Houston, through Murphy, that a clear two-thirds of the Senate was in favor of a treaty. Houston at once obtained from the eager Murphy a promise of military protection by the United States pending the conclusion of the affair, and Murphy went so far as to order an American vessel to Vera Cruz to warn other naval units that they would soon be needed to repel a Mexican invasion of Texas. This was a little too much, and Washington informed the charge that he had pledged the president to action unwarranted by the Constitution. However, by the time this dispatch reached Texas, on Apr. 11, 1844, the treaty of annexation was signed. Soon the treaty came before the Senate and was rejected, while the confirmation of Murphy's appointment was refused at the same time. "The tail went with the hide," he pleasantly remarked in reporting the rejection and his recall to the Texan government (Reeves, *post*, p. 160). Within a few weeks he died of yellow fever at Galveston.

[*Hist. of Ross and Highland Counties, Ohio* (1880), p. 77; L. S. Evans, *A Standard Hist. of Ross County, Ohio* (1917), vol. I; J. S. Reeves, *Am. Diplomacy under Tyler and Polk* (1907); J. H. Smith, *The Annexation of Texas* (1911); G. P. Garrison, "Diplomatic Correspondence of the Republic of Texas," *Am. Hist. Assoc. Report . . . 1908*, vol. II, pts. 1, 2 (1911); "Calhoun Correspondence," *Ibid. . . . 1899*, vol. II (1900); L. G. Tyler, *The Letters and Times of the Tylers*, vol. II (1885); *Sen. Doc., 341, 349, 28* Cong., 1 Sess. (1844); *Southwestern Hist. Quart.*, Jan. 1913, July 1915; *Niles' National Register*, June 15, 1844, Aug. 17, 1844.]   H. D. J.

MURPHY, WILLIAM WALTON (Apr. 3, 1816–June 8, 1886), United States consul-general, was born at Ernestown, Canada, but was brought to Ovid, Seneca County, N. Y., at an early age. As a youth of nineteen he joined the pioneer emigration from New York State to Michigan and entered the United States land office at Monroe as a clerk in 1835, when the speculation in land was at its height. He remained in the land office for two years and studied law in his leisure hours. In 1837 he removed to the pioneer community of Jonesville and with William T. Howell opened the first law office in Hillsdale County, continuing in practice until 1861, the firm from 1848 being that of Murphy & Baxter. In addition to practising law, he conducted a land agency, founded a newspaper, the *Jonesville Telegraph,* and was a partner in the banking firm of E. O. Grosvenor & Company. He served one term as prosecutor of Hillsdale County and in 1844 was elected representative in the Michigan legislature. For many years he was an ardent Democrat, but his strong anti-slavery views impelled him to join the Free-Soil party in 1848. After the passage of the Kansas-Nebraska bill in May 1854, he supported Isaac P. Christiancy in his efforts to have the Free-Soil party withdraw its state nominations during the coming campaign and call a mass convention of all anti-slavery elements, which resulted in the convention at Jackson, July 6, 1854, the first Republican state convention ever held, at which Murphy was one of the vice-presidents. He was a member of the Michigan delegation which supported Seward at the Repub-

lican National Convention held at Chicago in May 1860. In July 1861 he was appointed by President Lincoln consul-general for the free city of Frankfort-on-the-Main, Germany.

On his arrival at Frankfort in November 1861, Murphy found that his predecessor, Samuel Ricker, was aiding the Confederate cause, and was remaining in Frankfort with the hope of establishing a consulateship there for the Confederate states. Murphy frustrated this hope by persuading Frankfort's Senate to permit him to place the flag of the United States on the consular premises, thus recognizing him as consul-general for the entire Union rather than for the Northern states alone. When Ricker negotiated with a banking firm to take up a Confederate cotton-loan, Murphy obtained a statement from the head of the banking house of M. A. von Rothschild, which influenced the more conservative houses against participating in the loan. Murphy also had published in the *Neue Frankfurter Zeitung* and other journals the latest annual reports of the Confederate secretary of the treasury, and Jefferson Davis' defense of repudiation of the bonds of the South. Gaining the friendship of the editor of *L'Europe,* he was permitted to use its columns for articles written by himself and his friends in aid of the Union cause. Thus, when the English and French exchanges were closed to the sale of United States bonds issued to prosecute the War they found a ready market in Germany, and large sales were made in Frankfort. Murphy remained consul-general at Frankfort until 1869, after which he settled in Heidelberg as the financial agent of several American railway companies. He died on June 8, 1886. He had married, in 1849, Ellen Beaumont.

[*Hist. of Hillsdale County, Mich.* (1879); S. D. Bingham, *Mich. Biogs.* (2 vols., 1924); *Hist. Colls. . . . Mich. Pioneer and Hist. Soc.*, vol. XI (1888); H. M. Utley and B. M. Cutcheon, *Mich. as a Province, Territory, and State* (1906), vol. III; *100 Years of the Am. Consulate Gen. at Frankfort on the Main, 1829–1929* (1929); *Autobiog. of Andrew Dickson White* (1905), I, 97–99.]   J. L. R.

MURRAY, ALEXANDER (July 12, 1754 or 1755–Oct. 6, 1821), naval officer, was born at Chestertown, Md., one of eight children of Dr. William Murray and Ann (Smith) Murray. Of Highland-Scotch descent, the Murrays emigrated to America after a residence in Barbados. Alexander was regularly bred to the sea and at the age of nineteen commanded a vessel trading with Europe. On the outbreak of the Revolution he obtained a lieutenancy in the 1st Maryland Regiment and rose to the rank of captain, taking part in Washington's campaign of 1776–77 in New York and New Jersey. As he was a mariner by profession, he applied for a lieutenancy in the navy and was promised one by John Hancock and other members of Congress. While awaiting his appointment he entered the privateer service and commanded successively the *General Mercer, Saratoga, Columbus,* and *Revenge.* He captured several British merchantmen and privateers and was himself twice captured, losing the *Saratoga* and the *Revenge.* On July 20, 1781, he finally obtained a naval lieutenancy and a few days later went to sea on board the frigate *Trumbull.* He was wounded when that ship was captured by the frigate *Iris,* after a severe engagement. On being exchanged he went to Richmond, Va., took command of the privateer *Prosperity,* and sailed for the West Indies with a cargo of tobacco. On this voyage he displayed skill and courage in a fight with a privateer of superior force. In 1782 he took part in a joint Spanish-American expedition that effected the capture of New Providence. Returning to the Continental Navy as a lieutenant in the *Alliance,* he remained in the service until 1785, one of the last officers to leave it.

After the Revolution Murray established himself in Philadelphia as a merchant, a calling that he followed with much success. In 1794 when the navy under the Constitution was organized he offered his services to President Washington and early in the war with France was appointed captain, taking rank from July 1, 1798. Ordered to the *Montezuma,* he cruised for nine months in the West Indies, capturing one small prize and convoying many merchantmen. He contracted yellow fever and was compelled to give up his ship. He next went to sea as the commander of the *Insurgente,* with a roving commission, and made an extended cruise, visiting, among other places, the Azores, Lisbon, Cayenne, Jamaica, and Havana. In the last year of the war he cruised in the West Indies as commander of the *Constellation,* and for a time served as commander of the Santo Domingo station.

Retained under the peace establishment of 1801 and ranking sixth in the list of captains, Murray in 1802-03 commanded the *Constellation* of the Mediterranean Squadron, and for some two months blockaded Tripoli. On one occasion he attacked the Tripolitan gunboats, doing them considerable damage. In the latter part of 1805 he commanded the *Adams* and cruised off the Carolina coast for the protection of American commerce. This was his last sea duty. After serving as president of the *Chesapeake* and *Leopard* court of inquiry, he in 1808 was made commanding naval officer at Philadelphia, an office that he held until his death, which occurred

at his country residence near that city. He had been the ranking officer of the navy since 1811. On June 18, 1782, he was married to Mary Miller of Philadelphia. A son, Alexander M. Murray, died when a midshipman in the navy; and a grandson, Alexander Murray, entered the navy and rose to the rank of rear admiral.

[The earliest sketch of Murray's life, not entirely to be relied on, is found in the *Port Folio,* May 1814. See also S. P. Waldo, *Biog. Sketches of Distinguished Am. Naval Heroes in the War of the Revolution* (1823); G. A. Hanson, *Old Kent: The Eastern Shore of Md.* (1876); G. W. Allen, *Our Naval War with France* (1909) and *Our Navy and the Barbary Corsairs* (1905); *Poulson's Am. Daily Advertiser* (Phila.), Oct. 8, 10, 1821. The *Port Folio* and Waldo give year of birth as 1755, while Hanson gives 1754.]   C. O. P.

MURRAY, DAVID (Oct. 15, 1830–Mar. 6, 1905), educator, author, the son of William and Jean (Black) Murray, both of Scotch extraction, was born at Bovina, Delaware County, N. Y. After obtaining his early education at Delaware Academy, Delhi, and Fergusonville Academy, he entered the sophomore class of Union College. He was a graduate of Union College (1852), and from 1852 to 1863 was connected with Albany Academy (New York) as teacher and principal. He then went to Rutgers College as professor of mathematics and astronomy for a decade (1863-73). During that period, according to the testimony of a pupil, he was able to make his courses seem so valuable that several students elected to study calculus "because we wished to study under our favorite professor." In 1873 he was invited by the Japanese government to become superintendent of educational affairs and adviser to the minister of education. For six years (1873-79), he rendered good services in the establishment of a universal educational system, largely along American lines. Particularly valuable was his work in laying the foundations for women's education. During this engagement, Murray was appointed a commissioner to the Centennial Exhibition at Philadelphia; he also assisted in the collection of materials for a Tokio educational museum. His *Outline History of Japanese Education* (1876) was the first official presentation abroad of that subject. He devoted himself also to arousing public sentiment in favor of returning to Japan America's share ($750,000) of the Shimonoseki Indemnity Fund, and he lived to see the fruition of his efforts (1883).

Soon after his return to America Murray became secretary of the board of regents of the University of the State of New York and served from 1880 to 1889 in this capacity, displaying marked administrative ability. He was also author of a history of the board of regents. In

1889, on account of ill health, he retired to private life in New Brunswick, N. J., and engaged chiefly in literary labors, of which a *History of Education in New Jersey* (United States Bureau of Education, 1899), and the volume on *Japan* in the Story of the Nations Series (1894; revised edition, 1906), were notable results. When the centenary of the establishment of Delaware County was celebrated in 1897, he was the editor and one of the authors of *Delaware County, New York: History of the Century, 1797–1897* (1898), and he prepared a paper, "The Antirent Episode in the State of New York," which was published in the American Historical Association *Annual Report for 1896* (vol. I, 1897). In his later years he was a trustee of Rutgers College and secretary of the board, and was officially connected with New Brunswick Theological Seminary and Wells Memorial Hospital. In 1867 he had married Martha Neilson who survived him. He died in New Brunswick.

[The best sketch of Murray is W. I. Chamberlin, *In Memoriam, David Murray* (1915), containing a list of unpublished manuscripts by Murray in the Lib. of Cong. See also: the *New Brunswick Weekly Fredonian*, July 26, 1866; the *New Brunswick Times*, May 3, 1873; the *Christian Intelligencer* (N. Y.), June 3, 1908; and the *Sunday Times* (New Brunswick), Jan. 16, 1927, and Feb. 5, 1928.]   E. W. C.

MURRAY, JAMES ORMSBEE (Nov. 27, 1827–Mar. 27, 1899), clergyman, first dean of Princeton University, was born at Camden, S. C. His grandfather, John Murray, whose parents came from Scotland, was a merchant in Philadelphia. John Murray's wife, Elizabeth, was a daughter of Philip Syng [*q.v.*], an original member of the American Philosophical Society and friend of Benjamin Franklin. Their son, James Syng Murray, removed to Camden, S. C., where he was engaged in business. He married Aurelia Pearce, of English descent, grand-daughter of William Blanding and Lydia Ormsbee, New Englanders. James Ormsbee Murray, son of James and Aurelia, was eight years old when his father, being opposed to slavery, emancipated some of his slaves, provided for the emancipation of the others, and removed with his family to Springfield, Ohio. Here the boy was prepared for college. He entered Brown University with the class of 1848, but was obliged by ill health to drop back two years, graduating as valedictorian in 1850. He spent the next year as instructor in Greek at Brown, then entered Andover Theological Seminary, where he graduated in 1854. From 1854 to 1861 he was pastor of the Congregational church at South Danvers, now Peabody, Mass.; from 1861 to 1865 pastor of the Prospect Street church in Cambridgeport, Mass.; and then became associate pastor with Dr. Gardiner Spring [*q.v.*] of the Brick Church (Presbyterian) in New York City. From 1873 to 1875 he was sole pastor of this church. During these years in the ministry he wrote many articles on literary subjects and gained a reputation for his wide acquaintance with English letters. In 1875 he was elected to the Holmes Professorship of Belles Lettres and English Language and Literature in the College of New Jersey (Princeton). His lectures at Princeton dealt principally with writers of the sixteenth and eighteenth centuries and were of a broad and human, rather than a narrowly scholastic kind. In the latter years of the administration of President James McCosh [*q.v.*] matters of internal administration fell more and more into Professor Murray's hands, and in 1883 he was appointed dean of the faculty. The office was at first a difficult one, for it included discipline and the enforcement of standards of scholarship; but Dean Murray soon obtained general good will without sacrificing just severity. He had an enthusiastic, impulsive, and affectionate disposition. In his teaching and his administrative methods he formed a link between the men of an older generation whose equipment consisted chiefly of general culture and the later generation of trained specialists. He was retained in the deanship by President Patton and died in office at the dean's house, Mar. 27, 1899. On Oct. 22, 1856, at Brookline, Mass., he had married Julia Richards Haughton, who with four sons and a daughter survived him.

In collaboration with other editors, Murray compiled a hymnbook, *The Sacrifice of Praise* (1869). He edited *Orations and Essays with Selected Parish Sermons by J. L. Diman* (1882) and *Selections from the Poetical Works of William Cowper* (1898); and was the author of *George Ide Chace: A Memorial* (1886), *William Gammell: A Biographical Sketch* (1890), *Francis Wayland* (1891).

[John DeWitt, *James Ormsbee Murray: a Memorial Sermon* (1899); *Princeton Bull.*, May 1899; *Hist. Cat. Brown Univ.* (1905); *Daily True American* (Trenton), Mar. 28, 1899; communications from Murray's daughter, Mrs. A. C. Armstrong, Middletown, Conn.; personal acquaintance.]   G. M. H.

MURRAY, JOHN (1737–Oct. 11, 1808), Quaker merchant, was born on Swatara Creek, near Lancaster, Pa., the son of John Murray who emigrated from Scotland in 1732, and a younger brother of Robert Murray [*q.v.*]. In 1753 the two brothers removed to New York City, and entered into a mercantile partnership, importing on a large scale and becoming the chief ship-owners in the colonies. They also obtained valuable landholdings on Manhattan Island, in a locality which was to become one of the fashionable centers of the city. In the political contests which agitated the city before the outbreak of the Revolution they took no part. John, however, was involved with Robert in the difficulties with the Committee of Sixty occasioned by landing a part of the cargo of the ship *Beulah*, February 1775, in violation of the non-importation agreement. During the War of Independence they remained in their homes, preserving the attitude enjoined by the Quakers' conscientious repugnance to the appeal to arms. Both were distinguished by acts of kindness to American prisoners. As members of the Chamber of Commerce, which, from July 1779 to the end of the struggle, directed largely the internal affairs of the city, they shared responsibilities for which the military command had little fitness, thus easing the rigor of the military control.

After the war, the Chamber of Commerce received a new charter from the legislature, and on Feb. 13, 1787, John Murray, with thirteen others belonging to the old colonial body, was admitted to membership. From 1798 to 1806 Murray was its president. He was also elected in 1789 a director of the Bank of New York established in 1784, and was director of an insurance association. He took a leading part in the philanthropic activities of the city. With Thomas Eddy [*q.v.*] and others he was appointed on a commission to build one of the state prisons in New York City (1796). In 1805, with Eddy, he issued a call for a meeting, at his house in Pearl Street, to provide means for the education of neglected children. From this invitation came the "Act to incorporate the Society instituted in the City of New York, for the Establishment of a Free School for the Education of Poor Children who do not belong to, or are not provided for by, any religious society." DeWitt Clinton was the first president, and Murray the first vice-president. Murray was also associated with Eddy in efforts for improvement of the Oneida and other central New York Indians. He was a director of the Humane Society, organized for the relief of distressed prisoners at a time when insolvent debtors were subject to peculiar hardships. It is related (Scoville, *post*, I, 294) that Murray was once perilously near bankruptcy, but at the last moment was rescued by a turn of fortune through a ticket purchased in an English lottery. Although the importation of English goods, in which the transactions of the Murrays largely consisted, was seriously affected before the Revolution by the cessation of American demands and during the war by the activity of privateers, John, at death, owned valuable property on Murray Hill, and his entire estate was estimated to be worth half a million dollars. In December 1766 he was married to Hannah Lindley, daughter of James and Susanna (Lownes) Lindley and a niece of his brother Robert's wife.

[J. M. Lindly, *The Hist. of the Lindley, Lindsley-Linsley Families in America, 1639–1924*, vol. II (1924); I. N. P. Stokes, *The Iconography of Manhattan Island, 1498–1909* (6 vols., 1915–28); J. G. Wilson, *The Memorial Hist. of the City of N. Y.* (4 vols., 1892–93); J. A. Scoville, *The Old Merchants of New York City*, 1 and 2 series (1863); A. M. Schlesinger, *The Colonial Merchants and the Am. Revolution, 1763–1776* (1917); J. A. Stevens, *Colonial Records of the N. Y. Chamber of Commerce, 1768–1784, with Hist. and Biog. Sketches* (1867); *American Citizen* (N. Y.), Oct. 12, 1808.]

R. E. D.

MURRAY, JOHN (Dec. 10, 1741–Sept. 3, 1815), founder of Universalism in America, was born in Alton, Hampshire, England, into a family comfortably circumstanced but subject to stern religious discipline. The paternal grandmother, a Frenchwoman converted to the Church of England, sacrificed an inheritance for her new faith, and in her son this firmness became an extreme rigor of Calvinist conviction. The boy John, merry by nature but schooled to the belief that he was predestined to eternal misery, became excessively emotional. When in 1751 the family removed to Cork, Ireland, the father intensified the family discipline to a morbid absorption in worship and chastisements, refused an offer of school and university education for his son, and being himself now incapacitated by pulmonary disease placed the boy in an occupation.

Happier days began for the son, however, when—though still an unrelenting Calvinist—the father joined the Wesleyan group and won the friendship of John Wesley. Appointed by Wesley as leader of a boys' class, John soon became facile in singing, in public prayer, in examining the soul experiences of his mates. Now admired and praised, he had emotional ecstasies that assured him of eternal joy. A welcome visitor in the home of a Mr. Little, a man of means who had been converted to Methodism, he had access, without his father's knowledge, to the novels, plays, and poems current in that age of luxurious sentiment, and fell in love with a lady ten years his senior. The spell was broken when his letter offering eternal devotion was returned by her to his irate father. Then the death of one of his friends, Mr. Little's son, his own illness, and the death of his father brought him back to intensities of religious concern. His widowed mother consenting, he joined the Little family to replace the lost son, but the lure of London soon made him part with home and friends.

Before leaving Ireland he had a transport of enthusiasm for the Calvinist Methodism of Whitefield, whom he heard in Cork. In London his susceptible temperament yielded to the fascination of music, dancing, theatre going, and convivial parties until embarrassing debts and Whitefield's preaching at the Tabernacle brought him again to sober seriousness. Employment in a broadcloth factory paid his debts and a romantic courtship of Eliza Neale, a devotee of the Tabernacle, led to a marriage blest with "as much of happiness as ever fell to the lot of humanity" (*The Life of the Rev. John Murray,* ed. of 1869, p. 144). But after some years of this felicity, a crisis developed. Evangelical circles in London were now disturbed by James Relly's preaching of universal redemption finally effective for each and every man, and the hatred which Murray felt for such a "destroyer of souls" was embittered by defeat in argument with one of Relly's adherents. With fear and trembling he read Relly's *Union* (1759), then with his wife visited Relly's meeting and agreed with his wife that the sermon had unadulterated truth. The result was attendance on Relly's preaching, searching study of Scripture in the light of the new doctrine, excommunication from the Tabernacle, the loss of all friends, and serious financial distress. Then came the death of his child, soon followed by the death of his wife and his own arrest for debt. Though rescued by his wife's brother, he was now in emotional collapse. Conceiving America as a vast wilderness where he might bury a ruined life, he embarked in July 1770, at Gravesend, on the brig *Hand-in-hand.*

What happened on his arrival in America was ever after viewed by him as a supernatural calling to an independent apostolate. The brig grounded on a shoal in Cranberry Inlet, New Jersey, and much of the cargo was transferred to a sloop of which Murray was put in charge. Going ashore for provisions, he found a farmstead and a meeting-house which the farmer, Thomas Potter, had built in hope that heaven would send a preacher in whose belief all men were equally dear to God. An inward voice assured the farmer that the approaching stranger was the divinely sent preacher. Before sailing Murray reluctantly discoursed to the neighbors, and he soon returned to Potter's farm at "Good Luck," proposing to help in the farm labor and to preach without monetary reward. Unordained, untrained in theology, shrinking from conflicts that his doctrine would excite, he was nevertheless led on by popular response to his warm emotional speech into two years of itinerant evan-

gelism with "Good Luck" as a center. Though he was later accused of concealing his faith in universal redemption, the purport of his preaching was seen from the outset. When, for this departure from orthodoxy and his presumption in preaching without church authorization, pulpits were closed to him, the hearing given him in homes, court houses, or in the open fields assured him that like St. Paul he had an apostolate conferred not by ecclesiastical officers but by the Spirit active in his heart.

In 1772 invitations led him to New England, where he won admiration from laymen of high repute and hostility from clergy of the Standing Order. Reaching Newport he was engaged by prominent parishioners of the Rev. Ezra Stiles [*q.v.*], who was absent, to preach on Sunday, Sept. 27, and on several weekdays thereafter. When Stiles returned, Oct. 10, he forbade further preaching from a wanderer without credentials. Abundant entries in Stiles's diary record that clergyman's credulous acceptance of slanderous rumors concerning Murray in contrast to the marked respect shown him by the laymen. A year later, October 1773, Murray, again in Newport, was invited by the Governor to preach in the State House and was offered a new church if he would remain. The itinerant went on. Arriving in Boston, Oct. 26, he became the guest of the noted Thomas Handasyde Peck, preached in Manufacturing House, in a private home, and on return from pulpits in Newburyport and Portsmouth, in Andrew Croswell's church and Faneuil Hall. In the autumn of 1774, in spite of Croswell's bitter opposition, he was again invited to preach by action of the proprietors. On one occasion stones were hurled at him through the church window and he needed the escort of a body of friends to reach his dwelling.

In the midst of these disturbances, Winthrop Sargent, a prosperous ship-master, representing a group in Gloucester who had studied Relly's *Union,* secured his service in the place of the Gloucester pastor, Rev. Samuel Chandler, who was ill. When Murray explained his heretical view, Chandler refused him further permission to preach and in the *Salem Gazette,* Feb. 14, 1775, printed a warning against the dangerous doctrine. Murray, however, remained in Gloucester, preaching in Sargent's mansion and in neighboring towns, refusing all compensation beyond his simple necessities. In the following May his friendly admirers, Varnum, Greene, and Hitchcock, commanding the Rhode Island regiments camped near Boston, made him their chaplain, and when other chaplains protested against him, Washington in General Orders, Sept. 17,

1775, announced that "The Rev. Mr. John Murray is appointed Chaplain to the Rhode Island Regiments, and is to be respected as such" (Eddy, *post*, p. 14, quoting Order Book). Illness cut short his chaplaincy but did not prevent arduous winter journeys to raise money for Gloucester families made destitute by the war. In May 1776 a pamphlet by the Rev. John Cleaveland of Ipswich, one of the protesting chaplains, attacked the heresy of "a certain stranger who calls himself John Murray" (*An Attempt to Nip in the Bud the Unscriptural Doctrine of Universal Salvation . . .*). The gift of a bit of land to make Murray a freeholder foiled an attempt to expel him as a vagrant, but letters like that of Ezra Stiles (Dec. 24, 1777; see Eddy, pp. 162–65) which called him a Romanist in disguise and an enemy to the American cause led the town authorities to order him to leave. These accusations against his character and patriotism were brought to an end by a letter from Major-General Greene, May 27, 1777.

In January 1779, sixty-one persons, including some fifteen suspended members of Gloucester First Church, united to form the Independent Church of Christ, with Murray as its minister. When on their refusal to pay taxes for the First Church their goods were sold at auction, the members brought suit under the bill of rights of the new constitution of Massachusetts. Repeated trials ended with a decision in their favor, June 1786. Fined for performing a marriage ceremony without an ordination recognized as sufficiently public, Murray with the support of his congregation, petitioned the legislature for relief, which was granted in 1788. While the petition was pending Murray visited old scenes in England (January–July 1788). In October 1788 he married Judith (Sargent) Stevens, widowed daughter of Winthrop Sargent [see Judith Sargent Stevens Murray], and on Christmas Day was re-ordained in more formal and public manner. On Oct. 23, 1793, he was installed as pastor of a Universalist society in Boston, and, being now responsible for a family, at last accepted a modest salary. His pastoral activity and preaching tours were ended by a stroke of paralysis, Oct. 19, 1809, though he lived nearly six years longer. He was buried first in the Granary Burying Ground, but in 1837 his remains were moved to Mount Auburn Cemetery, where a monument was erected over his grave by the many churches which owe their existence chiefly to him.

Murray's departure from the Old Calvinists lay in the belief "that *every individual* shall in due time be separated from sin, and rendered fit to associate with the denizens of heaven" (*Letters and Sketches of Sermons*, I, 144). This faith was based on texts that show Christ as dying for the redemption of all men. Murray prided himself on his ability to make all texts consistent with this belief, but the consistency required some arbitrary efforts at allegorical interpretation.

[The main sources are *Records of the Life of the Rev. John Murray, Preacher of Universal Redemption, Written by Himself, with a Continuation by Mrs. Judith Sargent Murray* (1816, and many later editions); John Murray, *Letters and Sketches of Sermons* (3 vols., 1812–13); documentary materials in Richard Eddy, *Universalism in Gloucester, Mass.* (1892). See also F. B. Dexter, *The Lit. Diary of Ezra Stiles* (3 vols., 1901); *The Diary of William Bentley* (4 vols., 1905–14); F. A. Bisbee, *1770–1920, From Good Luck to Gloucester* (1920); *Columbian Centinel*, Sept. 6, 1815.]

F. A. C.

MURRAY, JOHN GARDNER (Aug. 31, 1857–Oct. 3, 1929), first elected presiding bishop of the Protestant Episcopal Church, was born at Lonaconing, Md., the only son among the four children of James and Anne (Kirkwood) Murray. He grew up at Lonaconing and passed through its public schools, and in 1876 entered the Wyoming Seminary, near Wilkes-Barre, Pa. The following year the family moved to Osage City, Kan., where his father became a coal dealer. Having decided to enter the ministry of the Methodist Episcopal Church, in which he had been brought up, Murray became a student at Drew Theological Seminary, Madison, N. J., in the fall of 1879, expecting to spend four years there. Before he had finished the course, however, his father died, and to help support the family Murray abandoned his preparation for the ministry and entered upon a business career. He became the trusted agent and confidential clerk of Col. T. J. Peter, principal owner of the Carbon Coal Company of Osage City, whose business interests were later extended to central Alabama. In 1882 Murray was transferred to Brierfield, Ala., and made secretary and treasurer of the Brierfield Iron Company. Seven years later, Dec. 4, 1889, he married Clara Alice Hunsicker of Osage City, and established a home at Selma, Ala., where he became a wholesale grocer and a dealer in real estate, in both of which ventures he was successful.

While at Brierfield he had transferred his church connection from the Methodist Episcopal Church to the Protestant Episcopal Church, being confirmed July 4, 1886. Throughout his business career his desire to become a minister persisted and he held religious services as he had opportunity. In 1891 he was licensed to act as lay reader in the Episcopal Church; in 1893 he was made deacon by Coadjutor Bishop Henry

M. Jackson, and in 1894 was ordained priest by Bishop Richard Hooker Wilmer. He was now thirty-six years old. For two years he served as diocesan missionary and had charge of the Alabama River Mission, consisting of eight small stations which he reached on horseback. So signal was his success that in 1896 he was elected rector of the Church of the Advent, Birmingham, the largest parish in the Diocese of Alabama, and here soon took a leading place in the city as well as the Church. He remained there nearly seven years. When Bishop Wilmer died in 1900, Murray came within a few votes of being elected his successor.

In January 1903 he was chosen rector of the largest parish in the Diocese of Maryland, the Church of St. Michael and All Angels, Baltimore, and at once gained prominence because of his great popularity, especially among men. He continued as rector of this church for six years. The Diocese of Kentucky and the Diocese of Mississippi each elected him to be its bishop; but he declined both offices. In May 1909 he was elected almost unanimously to be bishop coadjutor of Maryland, and was consecrated in his own church on Sept. 29 by Bishops Paret, Adams, Randolph, Nelson, and DuMoulin of Canada. Upon the death of Bishop Paret, Jan. 18, 1911, Murray succeeded at once to the office of bishop of Maryland. Owing to his exceptional business ability and his personal popularity the diocese made great progress during his episcopate of twenty years.

At the General Convention of the Protestant Episcopal Church held at New Orleans, La., in October 1925, Bishop Murray was elected presiding bishop of the Church. Previously the senior bishop had automatically succeeded to that office; Murray was the first to hold it through the choice of his brother bishops. To share his labors as bishop of Maryland he was granted a coadjutor the following year. His most distinctive services to the Church as a whole were executive and administrative; he succeeded in eliminating the deficit and raising funds to balance a generous budget. In addition, however, as a leader possessing spiritual depth and power as well as the gift of inspiring oratory, he was responsible for an awakening felt throughout the Church. He gave himself so unreservedly to the discharge of his duties that he overtaxed his strength. Death came to him suddenly while he was presiding over a special session of the House of Bishops held in the Church of Our Saviour at Atlantic City, N. J. Being greatly beloved, he was greatly mourned. His funeral took place in the Church of St. Michael and All Angels, Baltimore, and he was interred in the Druid Ridge Cemetery. His wife and five children survived him.

[M. P. Andrews, *Tercentenary Hist. of Md.* (1925), vol. II; *Who's Who in America,* 1928–29; *The Living Church Annual,* 1931; *Living Church,* Oct. 12, 1929; *Sun* (Baltimore), Oct. 4, 1929; information as to certain facts from Mrs. Murray; personal acquaintance.]
A. C. P.

MURRAY, JOSEPH (*c.* 1694–Apr. 28, 1757), lawyer, was born in Queen's County, Ireland, the son of Thomas Murray, and emigrated to New York early in life, appearing at the New York bar in 1718 (Mayor's Court Minutes, 1718–20, fol. 28). He interrupted his legal practice in New York to attend the Middle Temple, where he was admitted in 1725. Returning to New York, where he was voted the freedom of the city in 1728, he quickly gained recognition as an erudite lawyer. He appeared in the Mayor's Court in most of the principal cases in his generation, and his arguments reveal a thorough grounding in the civil as well as the common law. His form books are models of eighteenth-century pleading. He was associated as counsel or arbiter in some of the most important real-estate litigation in New York and New Jersey. He appeared for the proprietors of the Oblong or Equivalent Lands (Colden Papers, *post,* II, pp. 203, 232); again, with James Alexander, for the plaintiffs in 1752 in the suit of the Earl of Stair and other proprietors of East New Jersey against Bond and others; and for the city of New York in its boundary dispute with the town of Harlem (*Minutes of the Common Council, post,* V, p. 345), and in its protracted litigation with Brooklyn over ferry rights (*Ibid.,* pp. 110–11). He was a New York commissioner in the boundary dispute with Massachusetts in 1754 and in the same year rendered an extensive report to the counsel with regard to the boundary dispute with New Jersey.

Murray appears to have had a principal share in amending and completing a draft of the Montgomerie Charter, in which task, according to the official resolution of thanks, he was said to have given "a lasting Instance of his great Learning Ability and Integrity in his Profession as well as for his Regard to this Corporation" (*Minutes of the Common Council, post,* IV, p. 43). Through his marriage in 1738 with Grace (Cosby) Freeman, widow of Thomas Freeman and a daughter of Governor Cosby, Murray was brought into close alliance with the governor and undertook a defense of the prerogative against the attacks of William Smith [*q.v.*], arguing before the Assembly in 1734 the legality of the court of exchequer. Murray's

"Opinion Relating to the Courts of Justice in the Colony of New York" (appended to Smith's *Opinion*, 1734), his only published work, is one of the few really important contributions to legal history penned in the American colonies. The author enlisted the full weight of common-law precedent against the assertion that courts of law could be established only by statute, and set forth convincingly the view that "Fundamental Courts" are a part of the constitution of England. He appears on less solid ground, however, in claiming that the authority of the colonial legislatures and courts is derived, not from the King's commission, but from the common law to which the colonies are entitled. He concluded his argument by citing colonial precedents of 1702 and 1729, when the New York Supreme Court of Judicature sat as a court of exchequer. The substance of his arguments was embodied by Governor Cosby in an aggressive opinion in defense of the Court of Chancery the following year (*Rex* vs. *Birdsall et al.*, Chancery Minutes, 1720-48, pp. 67-68). Once again Murray and Smith clashed. In the election dispute between Garret Van Horne and Adolph Philipse in 1737, when the question was raised whether Jews were qualified to vote, Murray argued in the affirmative, because the law mentioned all freeholders of competent estate.

A member of the executive council under George Clinton [*q.v.*], Murray was soon prominently identified with the opposition faction headed by Chief Justice James De Lancey, ultimately breaking with Clinton and Colden and effectually tying up the governor's military program. The joy of De Lancey and Murray when Sir Danvers Osborne succeeded Clinton in the governorship was soon tempered when that official, while a guest of Murray, committed suicide as a result of private grief. With De Lancey in the saddle, Murray was made one of the New York delegates at the Albany Congress of 1754. In addition, he was a member of the first board of trustees of the New York Society Library and a governor of that institution. A strict Episcopalian, he was active in the affairs of Trinity Church and was named one of the governors of King's College in the charter of 1754. Murray devised to King's College his residuary estate, including a fine library, the origin of the Columbia collection. Unfortunately the greater part of this collection was destroyed or scattered during the occupation of the British or the fire of 1776.

[Obituary notices are found in the *N.-Y. Mercury*, and the *N.-Y. Gazette, or the Weekly Post-Boy* for May 2, 1757. See also: *N. Y. Hist. Soc., Colls., Pub. Fund Series*, vol. XXVIII (1896), p. 454, and vol.

XXIX (1897), pp. 165-66; "The Letters and Papers of Cadwallader Colden," *Ibid.*, vols. LI-LII (1910-20); *Minutes of the Common Council of the City of N. Y., 1675-1776* (8 vols., 1905); E. B. O'Callaghan, *Docs. Relative to the Colonial Hist. . . . of N. Y.*, vol. VI (1855); Thos. Jones, *Hist. of N. Y. during the Revolutionary War* (1879), I, 136-37; E. A. Jones, *Am. Members of the Inns of Court* (1924). Murray's pleadings and other legal papers are available in part in the Office of the Commissioner of Records, New York City; a Form Book is in the Columbia Law Lib., and miscellaneous correspondence may be found in Alexander MSS. V, N. Y. Hist. Soc.]   R. B. M.

MURRAY, JUDITH SARGENT STEVENS (May 1, 1751–July 6, 1820), author, was the daughter of Capt. Winthrop Sargent, a prominent citizen and merchant of Gloucester, Mass., and his wife, Judith Saunders, descendant of an active seafaring family. She was given an unusual education, sharing the studies of her brother Winthrop [*q.v.*], in his preparation for Harvard. She early began writing verses and essays, some of which were printed in the *Gentleman's and Lady's Town and Country Magazine* at Boston in 1784, over her pen-name, "Constantia." She married first, Oct. 3, 1769, Capt. John Stevens of Gloucester, who, after financial difficulties, sailed in 1786 for the West Indies, where he died on the island of St. Eustatius shortly afterward. In the meantime the Gloucester Sargents had been converted to Universalism by the Rev. John Murray, 1741-1815 [*q.v.*], who had begun his ministration in the town in 1774. A warm friendship and mutual admiration between Murray and Mrs. Stevens culminated in their marriage, Oct. 6, 1788. She was devoted to him and his religious interests and shared his preaching tours, notably a visit to Philadelphia in 1790, of which she wrote an interesting account in her letters (*Universalist Quarterly*, April 1881, April 1882).

In 1789 she began actively contributing poetry to the *Massachusetts Magazine*, the first contribution appearing in the issue for January 1790. Her most important work, however, was a series of essays called "The Gleaner," begun in that magazine in February 1792 and continued with few interruptions to August 1794. When the managers of the newly established theatre in Boston called for original dramas by American writers, she was apparently the first to respond (see G. O. Seilhamer, *History of the American Theatre*, vol. III, 1891, p. 248, which wrongly attributes her play to Royall Tyler) with a comedy, *The Medium, or A Happy Tea-Party* (called for publication, *The Medium, or Virtue Triumphant*), produced at the Federal Street Theatre, Mar. 2, 1795. Neither this play nor its successor, *The Traveller Returned*, was a success, though the latter survived two performances, the first on Mar. 9, 1796. It was caustically criticized by Robert Treat Paine, Jr. (quoted in J. T. Buckingham, *Specimens of Newspaper Literature*, 1850, II, 243), who supposed John Murray to be the author. These two plays, with her essays and other short prose pieces and her poems, were collected in three volumes and published by subscription at Boston in February 1798 under the general title, *The Gleaner*. Mrs. Murray's later work, except for seven poems in the *Boston Weekly Magazine* (Oct. 30, 1802–Mar. 19, 1803), and one in the *Boston Magazine* (Dec. 14, 1805), was of an editorial nature. During her husband's decline she prepared for publication his *Letters, and Sketches of Sermons* (3 vols., 1812–13); and after his death in 1815, she added the three concluding chapters to his autobiography. The value of both works she lessened by conscientiously suppressing material of a personal application, deleting dates and names of persons and places. She died at the home of her daughter, Julia Maria (Murray) Bingaman, near Natchez, Miss. Her work as a poet and dramatist is negligible; but her essays rival in firmness of texture and in interest those of Joseph Dennie, Freneau, and Noah Webster, her best contemporaries.

[The authoritative biography is Vena B. Field, *Constantia, A Study of the Life and Works of Judith Sargent Murray* (1931), in Univ. of Maine Studies, 2 ser. See also E. W. and C. S. Sargent, *Epes Sargent of Gloucester and His Descendants* (1925); *Boston Commercial Gazette*, Aug. 7, 1820. The extensive family MSS. stored on the Bingaman plantation near Natchez, have become illegible. Two fine portraits of Mrs. Murray, by Copley and Stuart, are displayed in the Sargent-Murray-Gilman House at Gloucester, which was her residence as wife to John Stevens and John Murray.]
                                        M. E—s.

MURRAY, LINDLEY (June 7, 1745–Jan. 16, 1826), grammarian, was born on Swatara Creek in what is now Dauphin County, Pa., the eldest, and the last to survive, of the twelve children of Robert [*q.v.*] and Mary (Lindley) Murray. His father, who had emigrated from Scotland in 1732, was at the time of his son's birth a miller. Later he embarked in the West Indies trade, tried his luck for a few years in North Carolina, and in 1753 settled as a merchant in New York, where he rose to affluence. Brought up in the Westminster Confession, he joined the Quakers but lived with a sumptuousness that scandalized poorer members of the sect. He sternly denied his son's desire for a literary education until finally the boy ran away from home and enrolled in a school at Burlington, N. J. A compromise was then effected and Lindley studied law in the office of Benjamin Kissam, with John Jay for a fellow pupil. He was called to the bar and acquired a lucrative practice among the Quakers. On June 22, 1767, he married Hannah Dobson, who died Sept. 25, 1834. They had no children.

With the outbreak of the Revolution he retired to Islip, Long Island, on Great South Bay, hunted and fished, and experimented with the making of salt, but in 1779 he returned to New York and, with capital supplied by his father, set up as a merchant. Having amassed a comfortable fortune, he retired in 1783 to his estate, "Bellevue," the site of which is now occupied by Bellevue Hospital. In the hope of restoring his failing health he made a leisurely tour through New Jersey and eastern Pennsylvania and in 1784 went to England, which he had already visited in 1770–71. He bought a small estate at Holgate, just outside York, and made his home there until his death forty-two years later. In these years of retirement he cultivated a garden which was said to rival those at Kew, and gave considerable time to writing. He moved about as little as possible, seldom ventured further than the Friends' Meeting House in York, and for many years before his death never left the house.

He produced a number of schoolbooks, including an *English Grammar* (1795); *English Exercises* (1797); *A Key to the Exercises* (1797); *The English Reader* (1799); *Sequel to the English Reader* (1800); *Introduction to the English Reader* (1801); *Lecteur François* (1802); *Introduction au Lecteur François* (1807); *An English Spelling-Book* (1804); and *An English Grammar* (1818), this last a complete revision and elaboration of his first publication. These books were widely circulated in England and the United States; for a time the grammars virtually monopolized the field. According to R. L. Lyman (*post*, p. 80), "A very conservative estimate of the total number of Murray's grammars, including his own and his followers' before 1850, is 200 editions, totaling between 1,500,000 and 2,000,000 copies." They were eclectic in principle and well arranged for pedagogical purposes; but rival grammarians, often with much heat, pointed to numerous shortcomings, and Murray was frequently charged with forgetting his own rules; for half a century, nevertheless, he was to grammar what Hoyle was to whist. Goold Brown [*q.v.*] and Samuel Kirkham ultimately displaced him.

Of Murray's religious tracts the most popular was *The Power of Religion on the Mind in Retirement, Sickness, and Death* (1787), the first edition of which was printed privately for presentation to his friends. His other publications include: *The Sentiments of Pious and Emi-*

nent Men, on the Pernicious Tendency of Dramatic Entertainments and Other Vain Amusements (c. 1789); *Some Account of the Life and Religious Labours of Sarah Grubb* (1792); *A Selection from Bishop Horne's Commentary on the Psalms* (1812); *A Biographical Sketch of Henry Tuke* (1815); *A Compendium of Religious Faith and Practice* (1815); and *The Duty and Benefit of a Daily Perusal of the Holy Scripture in Families* (1817). "A purified edition of the British Poets" was another project dear to his heart, but was never completed. In sentiment and deportment Murray was an almost perfect Sir Charles Grandison; decorum, virtue, propriety were his watchwords. By his own generation he was admired unreservedly; visitors thronged to Holgate to see the famous garden, to meet its proprietor, and to be edified by his conversation. For eleven years he was a recorded minister of the Society of Friends. His many years of confining illness he bore cheerfully. He died at York and was buried there.

[The major source is *Memoirs of the Life and Writings of Lindley Murray: In a Series of Letters, Written by Himself, with a Preface, and a Continuation of the Memoirs by Elizabeth Frank* (1826). See also Joseph Smith, *A Descriptive Catalogue of Friends' Books* (2 vols., 1867) and *Supplement* (1893); C. F. Smith, article in *Dict. Nat. Biog.*, vol. XXXIX (1894); W. H. Egle, *Pa. Geneals.* (1886); J. M. Lindly, *The Hist. of the Lindley Lindsley-Linsley Families in America*, vol. II (1924); *Biog. Cat. . . . of the . . . London Friends' Inst.* (1888); W. C. Abbott, *N. Y. in the Am. Rev.* (1929), p. 198; R. L. Lyman, *English Grammar in Am. Schools before 1850* (1922); S. A. Leonard, *The Doctrine of Correctness in English Usage 1700–1800* (Madison, Wis., 1929); *Gentleman's Mag.* (London), Feb. 1826; letters (MS.) Oct. 6, 1799, and Mar. 26, 1804, MSS. Div., Lib. of Cong. Some authorities give Apr. 22 as day of birth, but June 7, 1745, is given by Lindly (*ante*, p. 330) as from the family Bible, and appears also in the *Memoirs*, p. 189).   G. H. G.

MURRAY, LOUISE SHIPMAN WELLES (Jan. 2, 1854–Apr. 22, 1931), archaeologist and local historian, daughter of Charles Fisher and Elizabeth (Laporte) Welles, was born at Athens, Pa. Descended on the paternal side from Thomas Welles, a colonial governor of Connecticut, and on the maternal side from Bartholomew Laporte, one of the French *emigrés* who founded Asylum, Pa., she had by inheritance a particular interest in the history of the two principal elements of population that settled the region about Athens. She attended the Athens Academy, the Moravian Seminary at Bethlehem, Pa., and Brown's School at Auburn, N. Y. In 1870 she entered Wells College, Aurora, N. Y., where she was graduated in 1872. She married Millard P. Murray, June 27, 1876, and to them were born three daughters.

Excavations for their home in Athens in 1882 revealed an unusual Indian burial plot containing portrait pottery and skeletal remains of great size. For nearly fifty years thereafter Mrs. Murray followed up the theory that the Andastes or Susquehannocks of Captain John Smith's account were the Indians who left these remains; her last publication, on which she was at work at the time of her death and which was published posthumously, was concerned with this theory. Stimulated by these archaeological discoveries, she founded the Tioga Point Historical Society, which opened and maintained the Tioga Point Museum. In 1898 this institution was installed in the Spalding Memorial Building, a model museum structure secured through her efforts. As director and archaeologist of this museum, she spent more than three decades of indefatigable labor endeavoring to correlate museum activity with school and community aims. With this end in view, she made a study of museums in Buffalo, Cleveland, Ann Arbor, Chicago, and Milwaukee. Her bulletins and pamphlets, her scheduled lectures for school children, and her methods of exhibition reveal a body of progressive museum criteria not often found in small-town institutions.

Meanwhile, in addition to her educational work with the museum, she carried on independent researches in local history and for this purpose accumulated at the museum valuable manuscript and other primary sources. In 1903 she published her first study, *The Story of Some French Refugees and their "Azilum," 1793–1800*; in 1908 appeared her most important work, *A History of Old Tioga Point and Early Athens, Pennsylvania*. Both of these studies reveal an aptitude for research in original sources, are well documented, and remain the standard authority for the subjects they treat. In 1921 she contributed articles to the *American Anthropologist* on the aboriginal sites in and near "Teaoga" (Athens). In 1929 she published *Notes . . . on the Sullivan Expedition of 1799*, a series of documents drawn from the Tioga Point Museum and other archives. In 1931 the Society for Pennsylvania Archæology, of which she was a charter member and second vice-president, issued as its first publication her *Selected Manuscripts of General John S. Clark Relating to the Aboriginal History of the Susquehanna*. She was a founder of the Athens Library Club and was active in patriotic and historical societies. Possessed of the instincts of a genuine scholar, she was also adept and persevering in the recruiting of finances with which to execute her archaeological and historical projects. Her personality and her achievements are best appreciated when it is recognized that, over a period of several decades, neither lack of finances, domestic cares, lack of formal training in research, nor the apathy of a small town were sufficient to thwart her.

[*Elmira Star-Gazette*, Apr. 24, 1931; *Sayre Times*, Apr. 23, 1931; bulletins of the Tioga Point Museum.]

J. P. B.

MURRAY, ROBERT (1721–July 22, 1786), Quaker merchant, was born in Scotland, and emigrated to America with his father, John, in 1732. At Swatara Creek, now in Dauphin County, Pa., a region noted for its thriving agriculture, the younger Murray in early life operated a small flour mill, in which he shared an interest with other members of his family. Later he undertook trading voyages to the West Indies, and from 1750 to 1753 he lived in North Carolina. In 1753 he engaged in general trade in New York with a younger brother, John [*q.v.*], as a partner. The import and export trade of the brothers with England and her colonies, carried on in their own ships, gradually advanced the Murrays to the foremost rank of American merchants. From 1767 to 1775 Robert was on business in England.

When the interests of commerce were required to yield to a patriotic consideration, and New York merchants agreed, in opposition to the tea duty, to exclude British goods from the domestic market, Murray acquiesced in the policy of non-importation. In February 1775, however, the ship *Beulah* arrived from London and, failing to get past the boat of the Committee of Sixty, went to Sandy Hook, where a part of its cargo was taken off by a boat from Elizabethtown. Robert and John Murray confessed to the Committee that they were principals in the affair and promised to reship the goods in seven days' time. In May 1775 they petitioned Congress for restoration of former commercial privileges (Schlesinger, *post*, pp. 491, 565). That Murray's sympathies were with the British may be inferred from the fact that in 1779 Gen. Alexander McDougall, describing in a letter to Governor Clinton a plot to get supplies to the King's troops, said this of the Quaker merchant: "Robert Murray is on Long Island, with a store of goods, which makes one link of the chain" (*Public Papers of George Clinton*, vol. IV, 1900, p. 511). There is little doubt that Murray's ocean trade was brisk, and profits approached the normal magnitude, when British warships were able to keep the lanes of commerce open. It is significant that Murray's house "on the Heights of Inklenberg" (Murray Hill) was exempted from seizure by the British during their occupation (Stokes, *post*, I, 325).

Murray was an original member of the New York Chamber of Commerce, formed Apr. 5, 1768, and served on a committee of the chamber to consider the condition of the coinage and the embarrassments springing from variations in colonial standards. In 1768 he invested money in the whale fishery. His country house on Murray Hill was famous for its elegance and its hospitality. Murray's wife, whom he married in 1744, was Mary Lindley; their son, Lindley [*q.v.*], the grammarian, was the eldest of twelve children. Mary Lindley Murray is remembered because on Sept. 15, 1776, when the British, with a view to capturing Manhattan, landed at Kip's Bay, she invited the officers to avail themselves of the hospitality of her home on what is now Murray Hill. They accepted and thereby, intentionally or unintentionally, she delayed the British force, while General Putnam and his men were quietly leaving Manhattan to join the main army on Harlem Heights.

[W. H. Egle, *Pa. Geneals.* (1886); J. M. Lindly, *The Hist. of the Lindley Lindsley-Linsley Families in America 1639–1924*, vol. II (1924); I. N. P. Stokes, *The Iconography of Manhattan Island, 1498–1909* (6 vols., 1915–28); J. G. Wilson, *The Memorial Hist. of the City of N. Y.* (4 vols., 1892–93); *Memoirs of the Life and Writings of Lindley Murray* (1826); J. A. Scoville, *The Old Merchants of N. Y. City*, 1 and 2 ser. (1863); C. H. Haswell, *Reminiscences of an Octogenarian* (1896); A. M. Schlesinger, *The Colonial Merchants and the Am. Revolution, 1763–1776* (1917).]

R. E. D.

MURRAY, THOMAS EDWARD (Oct. 21, 1860–July 21, 1929), consulting engineer, inventor, was the son of John and Anastatia (McGrath) Murray and was born in Albany, N. Y., where his parents also were born and where his father was employed as a carpenter. He attended the public schools until he was nine years old, when, owing to the death of his father, he was compelled to go to work. Thereafter, he attended night school and for two years worked in the drafting rooms of local architects and engineers. He then served his machinist apprenticeship for four years in various shops in Albany, and in 1881 became an operating engineer at the pumping plant of the Albany Waterworks.

In 1887 Anthony N. Brady [*q.v.*] employed Murray to take charge of the power station of the Municipal Gas Company at Albany, and in that company his rise was rapid. He was soon in complete charge of the company's activities and was called into consultation in connection with other Brady properties, including the Troy City Railway Company, the Troy Electric Light Company, the Kings County Electric Light and Power Company, and the Albany Railway Company. He also had a part in consolidating Brady electric companies in Brooklyn and the formation of the Edison Electric Illuminating Company, later known as the Brooklyn Edison Company. During this period, too, his inventive genius, which was to secure for him over eleven hundred patents, began to assert itself. In 1895, having been intrusted by Brady with the task of consolidating the electric properties in Manhattan, Murray moved with his family to New York, and when, five years later, this consolidation was effected through the organization of the New York Edison Company, he was made second vice-president and general manager. In 1913, he became vice-president, in 1924 senior vice-president, and finally, after the merging of the New York Edison Company and the Brooklyn Edison Company in 1928, vice-chairman of the board of directors. Under Murray's general direction many of the great electric power stations which supply the various boroughs of New York City were built. Among these are Waterside No. 1 and No. 2, Sherman Creek, Hell Gate, Gold Street, Hudson Avenue, and East River stations, and the Williamsburg power house. He was also the designer of steam-power plants in Albany, Utica, and Rochester, N. Y., as well as in Dayton, Ohio; and of hydro-electric-power plants, in Chattanooga, Tenn., and in Trenton Falls and Cohoes, N. Y. It is believed that the total capacity of these plants is greater than that of those designed by any other man in the electrical industry.

Murray also organized and maintained supervision over several corporations of his own— Thomas E. Murray, Inc., the Metropolitan Device Corporation, the Metropolitan Engineering Company, and the Murray Radiator Company. Although most of his earlier engineering and inventive work was in the electrical and gas-appliance fields, the influence of his activities has been felt in almost every phase of industry. His inventions were exceeded in number only by those of Thomas A. Edison and included water wall furnaces for steam boilers, electrical protection devices, copper radiators, cinder catchers, pulverized fuel equipment, and automatic welding. His method of welding shells was found to be the only one that could be used for the production of the 240 mm. mortar shell, and because of it he received high commendation from the War Department. For the numerous safety appliances he invented he received in 1913 the gold medal of the American Museum of Safety, New York. He served as president of the Association of Edison Illuminating Companies; he was an active member of the American Society of Mechanical Engineers for thirty-five years; and he was a fellow of the American Institute of

Electrical Engineers. Among his publications were several technical works which include *Electric Power Plants* (1910), *Power Stations* (1922), and *Applied Engineering* (1928). He was active in charitable and religious work, taking a prominent part in the affairs of the Roman Catholic Church, for which service membership in the orders of the Knights of St. Gregory and in the Knights of Malta was conferred on him. In 1887 he married Catherine Bradley of Brooklyn, N. Y., and at the time of his death, at his summer home, "Wickapogue," Southampton, L. I., he was survived by eight children.

[*Jour. Am. Inst. Electrical Engineers*, Aug. 1929; *Electrical World*, July 27, 1929; *N. Y. Herald Tribune, N. Y. Times, World* (N. Y.), July 22, 1929; *Jour. of Commerce* (N. Y.), July 23, 1929; information from Edison Pioneers, Asso. of Edison Illuminating Companies, and Thomas E. Murray, Inc.; Patent Office records.]   C. W. M.

MURRAY, WILLIAM VANS (Feb. 9, 1760– Dec. 11, 1803), diplomatist, was born in Cambridge, Md., the son of Dr. Henry Murray, a prominent physician and influential citizen of Dorchester County. His mother was Rebeckah Orrick, the daughter of John Orrick of Anne Arundel County and Baltimore. William Vans Murray received his early education in Maryland and later went to London, where he entered upon the study of law at the Middle Temple, Apr. 28, 1784. While in England he married Charlotte Hughins. Here also he became interested in politics and diplomacy and wrote *Political Sketches* (1787), inscribed to John Adams, minister plenipotentiary from the United States to Great Britain. He returned to Cambridge at the close of the summer in 1787, was admitted to the bar, and began the practice of law. He was chosen to represent Dorchester County in the Maryland legislature but resigned to serve in Congress, where he continued from Mar. 4, 1791, to Mar. 3, 1797. A loyal Federalist, he was frequently consulted by Washington upon matters of patronage, and the appointments of James McHenry as secretary of war and Samuel Chase to the federal bench were made after his advice was taken. His longest and most important speech in the House of Representatives was delivered Mar. 23, 1796, against the resolution calling upon the President to produce the correspondence and documents relating to Jay's treaty with Great Britain.

In the campaign of 1796, Murray warmly advocated the election of Adams to the presidency and wrote numerous "pieces for the press" in his behalf. When his friends suggested early in 1797 that he be given a diplomatic post, Washington had already determined to appoint him minister to the Netherlands. The nomination was sent to the Senate on Feb. 27 and was confirmed Mar. 2. Murray was eager to enter upon the mission and, accompanied by his wife and secretary, sailed on the ship *Friend* and landed at the Helder June 7, 1797. He arrived at The Hague during a very critical period. The misunderstandings and disputes between the United States and France were already beyond mending. Within a year the envoys sent by President Adams had returned to report their shameful reception at the hands of Talleyrand's agents, X, Y and Z. Diplomatic relations were severed, and Adams, supported by the people of the United States, insisted that a renewal of friendly intercourse awaited advances on the part of the French government. The first overtures came through conversations between M. Pichon, secretary of the French legation at The Hague, and Murray. Although Pichon displayed a letter from Talleyrand, the suggestions therein contained were so indefinite that Murray thought them of little value. But Talleyrand continued to pursue negotiations for a reconciliation through the channel opened up at The Hague, and in September 1798 assured Murray that "whatever plenipotentiary the government of the United States might send to France, in order to terminate the existing differences between the two countries, would undoubtedly be received with the respect due to the representative of a free, independent, and powerful nation" (*American State Papers, Foreign Relations,* vol. II, 1832, p. 239). When this declaration was communicated to President Adams, he nominated Murray as minister plenipotentiary. A few days later he decided to send a commission and added the names of Oliver Ellsworth [*q.v.*] and Patrick Henry. Henry was unable to serve and Gov. W. R. Davie [*q.v.*] of North Carolina was chosen in his stead.

When Murray met the other commissioners in France in February 1800, they found that the Directory had been overthrown and the Consulate set up, with Napoleon Bonaparte at its head. It was to Napoleon that they presented their credentials on Mar. 8, in the hall of the ambassadors in the Tuileries. The French commissioners were Joseph Bonaparte, M. Fleurieu, formerly minister of marine, and M. Roederer, counselor of state. The negotiation continued throughout the summer until, "at ½ past 3 in the morning" of Oct. 1, the convention between France and the United States, though not entirely satisfactory, was signed. Murray returned to his post at The Hague to remain until Sept. 2, 1801, when he resigned. The remaining days of his life he spent on his farm near Cambridge.

"He had," said John Quincy Adams (*post,* p. 5), "a strong and genuine relish for the fine arts, a refined and delicate taste for literature, and a persevering and patient fondness for the pursuits of science." Because Murray was pleasing in his manners and also amusing and instructive in his conversation, he was able to carry through to a successful conclusion negotiations which, in the hands of a duller man, would likely have failed.

[The materials for the life of William Vans Murray are nearly all in manuscript. The Murray MSS. in the Lib. of Cong. contain his diary written at The Hague and "Some Remarks on the Stages of Our Negotiations at Paris, 1800." His commonplace book, begun at London and Chelsea, 1786, and renewed at Cambridge, 1795, is in the Princeton Univ. Lib. Numerous letters from Murray to John Quincy Adams are printed in the *Ann. Report Am. Hist. Asso., 1912* (1914). See also extracts from his diary, in *Proc. Am. Antiq. Soc.,* n.s. XII (1899), 245–55; J. Q. Adams, in *Port Folio,* Jan. 7, 1804; B. C. Steiner, *The Life and Corresp. of James McHenry* (1907); C. F. Adams, *The Works of John Adams* (10 vols., 1850–56); E. A. Jones, *Am. Members of the Inns of Court* (1924); *Biog. Dir. Am. Cong.* (1928); G. N. Mackenzie, *Colonial Families of the U. S. A.,* vol. II (1911); *Poulson's Am. Daily Advertiser* (Phila.), Dec. 17, 1803.]

W. S. C.

MURRELL, JOHN A. (fl. 1804–1844), outlaw, was the leader of a clan purporting to number more than a thousand members, whose activities touched eight states of the Old Southwest. Apart from a few court records and dates from documentary sources there is little contemporary information about Murrell himself (whose name is also spelled Murrel and Murel), except the narrative written by his captor, Virgil A. Stewart, who wormed his way into the desperado's confidence, took the oath of allegiance to the clan, and thus secured the leader's story. According to Murrell's statement, as retailed by Stewart (*post*), he was born in Middle Tennessee in 1804. His parents (unnamed and unknown) were poor, his father, "an honest man, I expect," but his mother a woman who "learnt me and all her children to steal so soon as we could walk." His name first appears in the court records of Williamson County in 1823 when he was fined for "riot." In 1825 he was before the court for gaming, and in 1826 he was twice tried for horse stealing, being sentenced the second time to twelve months in prison. As he told Stewart, he "began to see the value of having friends in this business," and with an older hand, Daniel Crenshaw (whom tradition sometimes makes the real leader of the clan), he set off on a round of highway robberies which took him from Georgia to New Orleans and back to Tennessee. Valuable connections were made with local groups of bandits and the framework of his organization was created. Channels of exchange were organized whereby the spoils—money, horses, or negroes—were traded from one part of the country to another to be disposed of. Negro-stealing became Murrell's specialty. By promises of freedom he would entice a negro from his owner, sell him several counties distant, steal him again, and repeat the process until the negro became so well known by the posting of repeated rewards that he could no longer be sold. He was then murdered and his body disposed of so that no tales were told.

Captured by Stewart in 1834 after a reign of some eight years, Murrell was brought to trial before the circuit court in Jackson, Tenn., in July of that year. He was convicted of negro-stealing and sentenced to a ten-year term in the state penitentiary. The most sensational part of Stewart's testimony against him, however, was the assertion that for some time Murrell and his agents had been planning a great negro rebellion in the Southwest. So strongly did this allegation affect the imaginations of the people that when in the summer of 1835 several outbreaks did occur and some of the instigators confessed to belonging to Murrell's gang, more than a score were hanged before the excitement was allayed. Murrell was discharged from the Nashville penitentiary Apr. 3, 1844 (*Journal of the House of Representatives of the State of Tennessee, October 1845*, 1846, App., p. 317), and lived but a few years longer, dying of consumption at Pikesville, Tenn.

[A. Q. Walton (pseud.), *Hist. of the Detection, Conviction, Life, and Designs of John A. Murel* (Athens, Tenn., 1835) is the first edition of the Stewart narrative, while *The Hist. of Virgil A. Stewart* (New York, 1836), compiled by H. R. Howard, is an expanded version. The stilted dialogue, the melodramatic style, and the dime-novel fashion in which events occur in the Stewart narratives lessen one's confidence in them. See also "Uses and Abuses of Lynch Law," *Am. Whig Rev.*, Nov. 1850, Mar. 1851; Park Marshall, "John A. Murrell and Daniel Crenshaw," *Tenn. Hist. Mag.*, Apr. 1920; James Phelan, *Hist. of Tenn.* (1888), ch. xxxii; Douglas Anderson, "A Famous Outlaw of the Early Southwest," *Nashville Banner*, Mar. 20, 1921; S. C. Williams, *Beginnings of West Tenn.* (1930); R. M. Coates, *The Outlaw Years* (1930). The Murrell gang receives fictional treatment in W. G. Simms, *Richard Hurdis* (1838) and *Border Beagles* (1840), and in Vaughan Kester, *The Prodigal Judge* (1911).]   O.W.H.

MURRIETA, JOAQUIN (*c.* 1832–July 25, 1853), brigand, was the most noted of the California bandits of the gold-discovery days. Herrera (*post*) says that he was born in Santiago, Chile, in 1830; but the weight of evidence makes him a native of Sonora, Mexico, and gives him a later birthyear. His surname may have been Carrillo. He arrived in California probably in 1849, when prejudice against Latin-Americans in the mines was beginning to express itself in numerous outrages. He is said to have been driven from a claim on Stanislaus River, in the early spring of 1850, by men who abused his wife or mistress, and later to have been driven from the placers on Calaveras River. At Murphy's Diggings, Calaveras County, where he worked for a time as a monte dealer, he is said to have been flogged and his half-brother hanged for the alleged theft of a horse.

Accounts of his life are contradictory, and few of the details given can be fully authenticated. By Latin-American writers and by Bancroft he has been invested with a considerable degree of romantic glamor, but the probability is that he was a ruffian, brutal, avaricious, and lawless. The account by Hittell (*post*), drawn largely from a rare book by F. L. Ridge, is perhaps the safest guide to his character and career. Because of some grievance, real or imagined, Murrieta vowed vengeance against the Americans, and for more than two years, at the head of a band of desperadoes, he ranged over a large part of the state and committed an appalling number of robberies and murders. In 1852, in Mariposa County, he narrowly escaped capture at the hands of Capt. Harry S. Love, deputy sheriff of Los Angeles County, who on his own initiative had tracked the bandit to one of his hiding places. A fresh series of robberies and murders in the spring of 1853 caused the legislature to pass an act authorizing Love to organize a company of mounted rangers to pursue him. Love, with his company, soon took the field, and on a morning in July surprised a part of Murrieta's band at a point west of Tulare Lake. In a running fight the bandit chief and three others were killed and two captured, while two or three escaped. For purposes of identification Murrieta's head was cut off and preserved in alcohol, and was later exhibited in various parts of the state.

[T. H. Hittell, *Hist. of Cal.*, III (1897), 712–25; H. H. Bancroft, *Hist. of Cal.*, VII (1890), 203, and *Cal. Pastoral* (1888), p. 645; Ireneo Paz, *Life and Adventures of the Celebrated Bandit, Joaquin Murrieta* (1925), translated by Frances P. Belle; Ignacio Herrera, *Joaquin Murrieta, El Bandido Chileno en Cal.* (1926), a pamphlet; Jos. Gollomb, *Master Highwaymen* (1927); Horace Bell, *Reminiscences of a Ranger* (1881), reprinted in 1927 with an introduction by A. M. Ellis; J. L. Cossley-Batt, *The Last of the Cal. Rangers* (1928); W. N. Burns, *The Robin Hood of El Dorado* (1932); *Joaquin Murrieta, the Brigand Chief of Cal.* (1859), reprinted in 1932 with notes by F. P. Farquhar; J. R. Ridge, *The Life and Adventures of Joaquin Murieta* (1854, and later editions).] W.J.G.

MURROW, JOSEPH SAMUEL (June 7, 1835–Sept. 8, 1929), missionary to the Indians, son of John and Mary Amelia (Badger) Murrow, was born in Jefferson County, Ga. His paternal grandfather had been a member of Marion's band of revolutionary heroes in South Carolina, and his maternal great-grandfather is said to have held a patent to Sullivan's Island. Young Murrow was early converted and united with the Green Fork Baptist Church, Burke County, Ga., in 1854, was licensed to preach in 1855, and entered Mercer University, Macon, Ga., as a sophomore in January 1856. He did not complete his studies there, but was ordained in September 1857 to go as a missionary to the Indians in the West. He was appointed by the Domestic and Indian Mission Board of the Southern Baptist Convention but was supported by the Rehoboth Association of Georgia.

Setting out for his future field of labor at once, he married on the way Mannie Elizabeth Tatom, and arrived at old North Fork Town, Indian Territory, now Eufaula, Okla., Nov. 13, 1857. Rev. H. F. Buckner, then the only white missionary in the Creek nation, who had been on the field since 1845, welcomed his new colleague and assisted him in many ways. They worked a good deal together among the Creeks, Seminoles, and Choctaws, Murrow riding a pony over wide areas and preaching through interpreters. He lost his young wife within ten months, and in 1859 married Clara, daughter of Rev. Willis Burns, who had come to the territory as a missionary the year before. Soon after his second marriage, he moved into the Seminole nation and established a mission there, organizing in 1861 the first church in that tribe. When the Civil War broke out the United States government withdrew its soldiers from the various forts in the territory, leaving the Indians to the care and control of the Confederate government. Murrow was selected by the Seminole council as agent in dealings with this government, a position which he held throughout the war, acting after 1863 as subsistence commissary in providing food for the Seminole, Comanche, Osage, and Wichita refugees along the Red River. While attending to these temporal matters, he was carrying on as far as possible his missionary work. Near the end of the war he was forced to remove to Texas for the safety of his family, where, at Linden, he engaged in teaching.

On his return from Texas in 1867 he settled at Atoka in the Choctaw nation, which became the center of his operations thereafter. For some years he spent considerable time in reëstablishing and reviving among the Choctaws, Creeks, and Seminoles the mission work which had been disrupted by the war. At his call representatives of sixteen churches met at Atoka in July 1872 and organized the Choctaw and Chickasaw Baptist Association, a body which has done much for the spread of Christianity among the Indians.

He was also largely instrumental in beginning mission work among the wild or blanket Indians through the native Indian preacher, John McIntosh. In 1876 he began a movement for the organization of all the Indian associations into a general body which could promote a larger fellowship and more vigorous work. As a result the Baptist Missionary and Educational Convention was organized in 1881, of which he was president for seventeen years. The founding at Bacone of Indian University, or Bacone College, was also due to his activities. In 1885 the American Baptist Home Mission Society appointed him superintendent of its Indian mission work and he severed his connection with the Southern Baptist Convention. Two years later, the Atoka Baptist Academy was founded; it was operated for some eighteen years and then merged into the Murrow Indian Orphans' Home, which was Murrow's last important contribution to the welfare of the Indians. For seventy years he lived among them, building many churches, a college, and an orphanage, preaching the gospel and serving their interests in all possible ways. He was greatly loved by the Indians of the entire territory, being known everywhere as "Father Murrow."

[Narrative (MS.) by A. J. Holt in archives of Home Mission Board, Atlanta, Ga.; "Fifty Beautiful Years" (MS.), narrative by Murrow's daughter, Clara A. McBride; minutes of Southern Baptist Convention; minutes of Baptist Home Mission Soc.; *Hist. of the Bapt. Denomination in Ga.* (1881); the *Baptist*, Sept. 28, 1929; *Muskogee Daily Phoenix*, Sept. 10, 1929.]

W. J. M.

MUSIN, OVIDE (Sept. 22, 1854–Nov. 24, 1929), violinist and composer, was the son of Jaques Musin, a civil engineer, and Louise de Milles, of Nandrin near Liège, Belgium, where he was born. He was admitted to the Liège Conservatory at the age of nine, and in 1867 he shared with Eugène Ysaye the second prize of the Conservatory. When Henri Léonard was appointed professor of violin at the Conservatory in 1870, Musin became his pupil and followed the Belgian master to the Paris Conservatory, where he won the gold medal for solo and quartet-playing. He began his professional career at fifteen as solo violinist of the Théâtre Royale in Spa. His first concert tours (1873–74) were made, on the recommendations of Léonard and Vieuxtemps, to fill concert engagements they could not undertake, and until 1882 Musin toured Europe triumphantly as a virtuoso violinist, appearing with leading orchestras in London, Vienna, and Paris, under various conductors: Hans Richter, Edvard Grieg, Edouard Colonne, Charles Lamoureux. In 1875 he organized in Paris a stringed quartet to popularize newer ensemble works and was the first to acquaint Parisians with Brahms's chamber music. In 1876 the King of Holland appointed him court violinist, but the following year he went to London. He remained in Great Britain for five years, touring England, Scotland, and Ireland, playing at Sir Julius Benedict's *soirées*, and in the homes of the nobility. He made his first appearance in America in the eighties with the New York Symphony Society, under Leopold Damrosch, and with the New York Philharmonic Society under Theodore Thomas, playing the Godard violin concerto for the first time in the United States.

He made various tours in the United States and Canada with a concert troupe of his own. In 1892 he visited Australia, New Zealand, and Mexico, and in the late nineties he appeared in Japan, China, the Philippines, and Hawaii. From 1898 to 1908 he was head of the advanced class for violin at the Liège Conservatory, but he spent half of his time in New York. In 1908 he resigned his position and established a violin school of his own in New York. Here he was prominent as a teacher for some twenty-one years, until he died in his home in Brooklyn. On Oct. 7, 1891, he had married Annie Louise Hodges-Tanner of New York.

Musin wrote a number of works for the violin and orchestra and for violin and piano. They include the "Valse de Concert," "Mazurka de Concert," "Extase," "Valse Lente," "Berceuse et Prière," and "Mazurka Élégante." His compositions for the most part were brilliant virtuoso pieces after the manner of Vieuxtemps and Wieniawski; he also arranged a number of transcriptions. His chief contributions to the teaching literature of the violin were his *System of Daily Practise* (1899) and *The Belgian School of the Violin* (1916), four volumes of studies which represent a combination of Léonard's methods and his own. *My Memories* (1920) is his record of a half-century as a globe-trotting violin virtuoso. He was the recipient of many orders and decorations, including the Order of Leopold (Belgium) and the Order of Bolivar (Venezuela).

[In addition to *My Memories* see: *Who's Who in America*, 1924–25; *Le Monde Musical*, Jan. 31, 1930; *Musical America*, Dec. 10, 1929; *Musical Observer*, Nov. 1907; *N. Y. Times*, *N. Y. Herald-Tribune*, Nov. 25, 1929.]   F. H. M.

MUSSEY, REUBEN DIMOND (June 23, 1780–June 21, 1866), surgeon, was born in Pelham, Rockingham County, N. H., the son of a country doctor, John Mussey, and his wife, Beulah Butler. He obtained his early education in Pelham, and later attended the district school

of Amherst, N. H., and Dartmouth College, where he was graduated A.B. in 1803. He began the study of medicine under Nathan Smith and Luke Howe, and devoted a portion of each winter, during the period 1803–05, to teaching school in Peterborough, N. H., in order to secure money to finish his medical education. The degree of bachelor of medicine was conferred upon him by the Medical Department of Dartmouth College in 1805, and that of doctor of medicine by the University of Pennsylvania in 1809.

Following his graduation from the University of Pennsylvania, he opened an office in Salem, Mass., and for five years enjoyed a large practice in association with Dr. Daniel Oliver. Besides practising general medicine, he gave courses of lectures on chemistry. He left Salem in 1814 to teach the theory and practice of medicine, materia medica, and obstetrics at Dartmouth, becoming professor of anatomy and surgery there in 1822. He spent ten months in Paris and London during the year 1830. In addition to his work at Dartmouth, he lectured on anatomy and surgery at Bowdoin College, 1831–35, and on surgery at the College of Physicians and Surgeons, Fairfield, Herkimer County, N. Y., 1836–38. In 1838 he resigned his professorship at Dartmouth to become professor of surgery in the Medical College of Ohio. This post he held until 1852, when the Miami Medical College was organized in Cincinnati, and he accepted the chair of surgery in the new institution. He continued in this capacity until 1857, then went to live with his daughter and son-in-law, Mary and Lyman Mason, in Boston, where he died.

Aside from six pamphlets which are in the library of the Cincinnati General Hospital, Mussey published a book: *Health, Its Friends and Foes* (1862), largely devoted to matters of hygiene and sanitation, and *Essay on Ardent Spirits and Its Substitutes as a Means of Invigorating Health* (1835), reissued the same year together with an essay by Dr. Harvey Lindsly, in a volume entitled: *Temperance Prize Essays*. His earliest research was undertaken to prove that the skin possesses powers of absorption, the idea being in direct conflict with the teaching of the eminent physician Benjamin Rush. Mussey proved his contention by making experiments upon himself (*Philadelphia Medical and Physical Journal*, 3rd supplement, May 1809). The cataphoric action of galvanism was demonstrated by him in 1821, while still a student at the University of Pennsylvania. In 1830, while in London, he discussed with Sir Astley Cooper the possibility of bony union after fracture of the neck of the femur, having taken with him specimens to prove his contention that such union is possible. These specimens are now in the Museum of the Cincinnati General Hospital. Mussey began very early to use chloroform and ether as anesthetics, reporting his experiences in a letter to Dr. Isaac Parrish, published in the *Transactions of the American Medical Association*, vol. I (1848). He was president of the American Medical Association in 1850, being the fourth to hold that office. He was a total abstainer from the use of both tobacco and alcohol, and seems to have written more upon this subject than any other. He was a vegetarian, very religious, and quite musical. He was married twice; his first wife, Mary Sewall, died May 31, 1807, and in 1813 he married his second wife, Mehitable Osgood, daughter of Dr. Joseph Osgood, an army surgeon. They had two daughters and seven sons, two of whom, William H. Mussey and Francis B. Mussey, became physicians.

[Otto Juettner, *Daniel Drake and His Followers* (1909); H. A. Kelly and W. L. Burrage, *Am. Medic. Biogs.* (1920); Minutes of Faculty Meetings of the Medical College of Ohio, 1838–52 (MSS.); J. B. Hamilton, "Life and Times of Dr. Reuben D. Mussey," *Jour. Am. Medic. Asso.*, Apr. 4, 1896; A. B. Crosby, *An Address Commemorative of Reuben Dimond Mussey* (1869), repr. from *Trans. N. H. Medic. Soc.*; H. S. Webster, *Thomas Sewall; Some of His Ancestors and All of His Descendants* (1904); *New-Eng. Hist. and Geneal. Reg.*, Jan. 1849, p. 73; *Autobiog. of Samuel D. Gross, M.D.* (1887), vol. II; *Boston Transcript*, June 25, 1866; pamphlets, reprints, and books by Mussey in the Library of the Cincinnati General Hospital; correspondence with a grand-daughter, Miss Theodora Mussey of Denver, Colo.]   J.C.O.

MUYBRIDGE, EADWEARD (Apr. 9, 1830–May 8, 1904), a pioneer in motion photography, was born at Kingston-on-Thames, England, the son of John Muggeridge, a grain dealer, and his wife Susannah. His name was originally Edward James Muggeridge, but at an early age he changed it to Eadweard Muybridge. After receiving a common-school education in England, he emigrated to the United States. Engaged at first in mercantile pursuits, he shortly became interested in photography, and in the course of time his skill in the art led to his employment as a photographer in the United States Coast and Geodetic Survey, for photographic survey work on the Pacific Coast. While so engaged, in May 1872 his services were secured by Leland Stanford [q.v.] of Palo Alto, Cal., to prove by photography whether a running horse at any period of his stride has all his feet entirely off the ground. Using one camera and a string stretched across the path of the horse to operate the shutter, Muybridge secured a series of photographs in silhouette which proved that at certain times all four feet of a running horse are off the ground.

This investigation projected him into a most interesting field of experiment, namely, animal locomotion, which occupied his attent.on for the remainder of his life. With the financial aid of Stanford, he made a series of elaborate experiments, covering a period of six years, at the former's stud farm in Palo Alto. A course similar to a running path was built, one side being bounded by a white background, and opposite it, twelve to twenty-four cameras were set up in a line and arranged to obtain photographs from three different points of view. The best of the results of these experiments were published in book form by Muybridge in 1878, under the title *The Horse in Motion*. The book excited worldwide interest, and particularly that of Dr. E. J. Marey of Paris, the renowned physiologist. Between 1878 and 1881 Muybridge continued his experiments in California, photographing athletes, oxen, dogs, and birds. He also developed in 1879 an apparatus which he called the zoopraxiscope, by the aid of which he successfully reproduced the moving figures in large size on a screen. In this machine, photographs of the successive phases of the analyzed motion were reproduced around the rim of a large glass disk. This was placed on a shaft connected to a projection lantern, and when the disk was rapidly revolved the enlarged images were projected upon the screen, giving the impression of the original motion. In 1881 and 1882 Muybridge spent most of his time in Europe working with Dr. Marey and lecturing on the subject of animal motion both in Paris and in London.

After returning to the United States in 1883 he continued his lectures for a time and in 1884 began a series of new experiments in Philadelphia under the auspices of the University of Pennsylvania. For these he developed a timing mechanism and an electro-magnetic latch to release the camera shutters. The work continued for two years, and the results were published in eleven volumes containing 100,000 photographic plates, under the title, *Animal Locomotion; An Electro-photographic Investigation of Consecutive Phases of Animal Movements, 1872–1885* (1887). Upon the completion of this work Muybridge returned to England and, except for a few brief visits to the United States, resided henceforth at his birthplace. During the World's Columbian Exposition in Chicago in 1893, he gave illustrated lectures to pay audiences in a specially erected building called "Zoopraxographical Hall." He also published *Descriptive Zoopraxography* (1893) and *The Human Figure in Motion* (1901). He never married. He died in England and his remains were cremated at Woking. His pioneer work in motion photography was commemorated by an inscribed tablet bearing his portrait which was placed in the Public Library at Kingston-on-Thames, England, July 17, 1931. In this institution is preserved his original zoopraxiscope.

[Waldemer Kaempffert, *A Pop. Hist. of Am. Invention* (2 vols., 1924); L. F. Rondinella, "Muybridge's Motion Pictures," *Jour. Franklin Inst.*, Sept. 1929; Merritt Crawford, "Men in the Movie Vanguard," *Cinema*, June 1930; *Gen. Mag. and Hist. Chron.* (Univ. of Pa., Alumni Soc.), Apr. 1928; *Notices of the Proc. at the Meetings of the Members of the Royal Inst. of Great Britain*, vol. X (1884); *Dict. Nat. Biog.*, second supplement; *Times* (London), May 10, 1904; *Illustrated London News*, July 18, 1931.]   C.W.M.

MYER, ALBERT JAMES (Sept. 20, 1829–Aug. 24, 1880), soldier, signal officer, founder of the Weather Bureau, was born in Newburgh, N. Y., the son of Henry Beekman Myer and Eleanor Pope (McLannan) Myer. While he was still a child his mother died, and he was brought up by an aunt, with whom, about 1836, he moved to Buffalo. He graduated from Hobart College (A.B.) in 1847 and from Buffalo Medical College (M.D) in 1851. On Sept. 18, 1854, he entered the army as an assistant surgeon. From the close of his college days he had known how to operate a telegraph instrument, and while serving on the Texas plains where the clearness of the air made it possible to see objects at a great distance, he became enthusiastic over the possibilities of visual signaling. In 1856 he drafted a memorandum on his signal devices, and in 1858 succeeded in having a military board authorized to consider them. Two more years of effort on his part resulted in an act of Congress adding to the staff of the army one signal officer with the rank and pay of major, and on June 27, 1860, Myer was appointed to the post. He had as yet, however, no organization to carry on his work, and almost immediately was ordered to the West, where until March 1861 he took part in General Canby's expedition against the Navajos in New Mexico. He carried his enthusiasm with him, and his visual signaling, with a code of three elements, was successfully used in that campaign. On the outbreak of the Civil War he called attention to the need for a signal service, and in June 1861 was ordered to Washington to organize and command the Signal Corps of the army. He also furnished plans for naval signaling at the request of the secretary of the navy. Although still handicapped by lack of personnel, he succeeded in having signal schools organized, and himself conducted signal communications in the Army of the Potomac. He was on the staffs of Generals Butler, McDowell, and McClellan, serving from the first battle of

Bull Run through much of the fighting in Northern Virginia. He was brevetted lieutenant-colonel, May 27, 1862, for gallant services in the battle of Hanover Court House, and colonel, July 2, 1862, for similar services at Malvern Hill.

In the meantime he was busy in Washington extending the scope of his activities. He succeeded finally in securing the establishment of the Signal Corps through the enactment of the Sundry Civil Act, Mar. 3, 1863. This gave him the position of colonel and chief signal officer. He held the appointment as colonel until it expired and was revoked July 21, 1864. The expansion of his activities—he supervised the building of some five thousand miles of telegraph lines to frontier posts—kept him in conflict with the United States Military Telegraph, which was under the direct supervision of an assistant secretary of war, and at length, owing to the friction between the two services, he was relieved as chief signal officer (November 1863) and ordered to a reconnaissance of the Mississippi River. From May 1864 to the end of the war he was signal officer of the Division of West Mississippi, and participated in operations along the river. He published *A Manual of Signals: For the Use of Signal Officers in the Field* (1864). On May 13, 1865, he was brevetted brigadier-general for his services as chief signal officer and for special service Oct. 5, 1864, when the post of Allatoona was saved by relief secured through signal communication.

On July 28, 1866, an act of Congress reorganized the Signal Corps and gave Myer the permanent rank of colonel as chief signal officer. He assumed charge Aug. 21, 1867. For some years prior to the Civil War the Smithsonian Institution had issued weather predictions and storm warnings based on telegraphic weather reports; but this work was interrupted by the war, and its resumption afterward delayed by a fire at the Smithsonian. In his report of 1869 Myer proposed that the peacetime activities of the Signal Corps be extended to include the sending out of storm warnings. His arguments, in conjunction with those of certain others interested in the matter, led Congress, in February 1870, to authorize the establishment of the United States Weather Bureau under the direction of the Signal Corps. During the first ten years of its existence Myer supervised the new bureau, which was soon rendering an extremely valuable service to commerce. He represented the United States at meteorological congresses in Vienna (1873) and Rome (1879), and by his perseverance and tact succeeded in bringing about the establishment of a uniform international system of simultaneous meteorological observations. On June 16, 1880, he was promoted brigadier-general in conformity with legislation giving the chief signal officer that rank. He died at Buffalo, N. Y., two months later, while still in active service.

Myer was married early in his military career to Catherine, daughter of Judge Ebenezer Walden, who with two sons and four daughters survived him. Fort Myer, Virginia, is named for him.

[Personnel files, War Dept., Washington, D. C.; files of Army War College, Washington, D. C.; *The Army of the United States* (1896); *War of the Rebellion: Official Records (Army)*, 1 and 2 ser.; F. B. Heitman, *Hist. Reg. and Dict. U. S. Army* (1903); Cleveland Abbe [*q.v.*], in *Am. Jour. Sci.*, Aug. 1871; G. M. Kober, "General Albert J. Myer and the United States Weather Bureau," *Mil. Surgeon*, July 1929; *Frank Leslie's Pop. Mo.*, Sept. 1878; *Pop. Sci. Mo.*, Jan. 1880; *Harper's Mag.*, May 1866, Aug. 1871, Dec. 1873; obituaries in *Army and Navy Jour.*, Aug. 28, 1880; *Buffalo Commercial Advertiser*, Aug. 24, 1880; *Buffalo Express*, Aug. 25, 1880; year of birth and spellings of family names from a daughter, Miss Gertrude W. Myer, Washington, D. C.]   J. N. G.

MYERS, ABRAHAM CHARLES (May? 1811–June 20, 1889), first quartermaster-general of the Confederate Army, the son of Abraham Myers, a lawyer, and the descendant of Moses Cohen, the first rabbi of Charleston, was born in Georgetown, S. C. He entered the United States Military Academy from South Carolina on July 1, 1828, but because of deficiency in his studies was turned back to the next class at the end of his first year. He was graduated on July 1, 1833, was appointed brevet second lieutenant, and was stationed at Baton Rouge. He served in the Indian wars in Florida in 1836–38 and again in 1841–42. In November 1839 he became a captain in the quartermaster department. He served under Gen. Zachary Taylor in Texas and northern Mexico and was brevetted major for gallant and meritorious conduct in the battles of Palo Alto and Resaca de la Palma. Transferred to Scott's army, he was brevetted colonel for gallant conduct at Churubusco and was chief quartermaster of the Army of Mexico from April to June 1848. During the next thirteen years, still in the quartermaster service, he was stationed at various posts in the southern states. In the meantime he married Marion Twiggs, the daughter of Gen. David E. Twiggs, the commander of the Department of Texas.

At the beginning of 1861 he was stationed at New Orleans, where on Jan. 28, on demand of the state officials, he surrendered the quartermaster and commissary stores in his possession. On the same date he resigned his position in the United States Army. On Mar. 16, 1861, he was appointed lieutenant-colonel in the quartermaster-general's department of the Confederate States Army. On Mar. 25 he was announced as acting quartermaster-general. He became quartermaster-general in December and was raised to the rank of colonel on Feb. 15, 1862. During the first months of the war he procured supplies by purchase in the open market; but when this source approached exhaustion in the fall of 1861 he made contracts throughout the country with local manufacturers for cotton and woolen cloth and with tanners for leather, and he established government shops for making clothing, shoes, tents, wagons, and other equipage. He purchased horses and mules at market prices as long as possible; but by the spring of 1862, much against his inclination, he was forced to resort to impressment. He was constantly hampered by the inability of the treasury to furnish him sufficient funds, by the rapid deterioration of the currency, and by poor railway transportation. By the middle of 1863 he had built up an extensive organization of purchasing agents, post quartermasters, shops, and supply depots; but he was never able to provide adequately for the armies, especially in the essentials of clothing and shoes. His bureau therefore became the target of severe criticism. A careful survey of the records and correspondence of Myers's office indicates that he was very efficient as an accountant, but that he was unable to rise above the routine he had learned in the old army or to overcome the laxity, carelessness, and inefficiency of remote subordinates.

On Aug. 7, 1863, by order of Jefferson Davis, he was superseded as quartermaster-general by Brig.-Gen. Alexander R. Lawton. The only reason ever given for the change was that it was in the interest of efficiency (*Journal, post*, III, 627). Myers and his friends resented his removal, and the senate on Jan. 26, 1864, resolved that, since Lawton had not been nominated to that body, Myers and not Lawton was legally quartermaster-general. Davis then submitted Lawton's nomination, and on Feb. 17 it was confirmed. Myers refused to serve under Lawton and presently found himself, on a technicality, "out of the army" (*Official Records, post*, ser. 4, vol. 3, pp. 318–20; letters from Myers to General Bragg, June 13, Aug. 9, 1864, in Bragg Papers, Western Reserve Historical Society, Cleveland, Ohio). He lived during the rest of the war in Georgia, "almost in want, on the charity of friends" (*Ibid.*). He was never reconciled with Davis. Of his life after the war, little is known. He is said to have traveled in Europe from 1866 to 1877. He seems to have made his home at

Lake Roland, Md., and then in Washington, D. C., where he died.

[G. W. Cullum, *Biog. Register of the Officers and Grads. of the U. S. Military Acad. at West Point*, vols. I, III supplement (1868–79); *War of the Rebellion: Official Records (Army)*, for dates esp. 4 ser., vols. I–III, 2 ser., vols. III–V, 3 ser., vol. I; *Jour. of the Cong. of the Confederate States of America*, vols. I–V (1904–05); *Jefferson Davis*, ed. by Dunbar Rowland (1923), vol. VII; *Times-Democrat* (New Orleans), June 21, 1889; information supplied by Mabel L. Webber, Librarian of the S. C. Hist. Soc.]   C. W. R.

MYLES, JOHN (*c.* 1621–Feb. 3, 1683), pioneer Baptist minister, whose name also appears as Miles, was probably the John Myles, son of Walter Myles of Newton, Herefordshire, who matriculated at the University of Oxford from Brasenose College on Mar. 18, 1635/36, at the age of fifteen (Joseph Foster, *Alumni Oxonienses*, 1891, III, 1012). But the first certain glimpse of John Myles comes on Oct. 1, 1649, when he and Thomas Proud, after a visit to the Baptist society at the Glasshouse in Broadstreet, London, formed one of the earliest Baptist churches in Wales, at Ilston, near Swansea. Myles became pastor of the church and an active leader among the Welsh Baptists. The act of Parliament of Feb. 22, 1650, "for the better Propagation and Preaching of the Gospel in Wales" names him as one of the twenty-five Welsh ministers who should recommend "godly and painful men" as worthy to preach and teach in Wales (C. S. Firth and R. S. Rait, *Acts and Ordinances of the Interregnum, 1642–1660*, 1911, II, 345). He helped to form an association of Welsh Baptist churches, which in 1651 sent him as delegate to a meeting of Baptist ministers in London. At the Restoration he was ejected from his parish, and, after the passage of the Act of Uniformity (Aug. 24, 1662), decided to leave the country (Edmund Calamy, *A Continuation of the Account of the Ministers . . . Eject . . . after the Restoration*, 1727, II, 747). Taking the records of the church at Ilston, he and several friends emigrated to New England.

At Rehoboth in Plymouth Colony in 1663 he helped to organize one of the earliest Baptist churches in America, and became its pastor. It is evident that he no longer advocated strict communion as he had in Wales, for his church at Rehoboth was unusually liberal in admitting paedobaptists to the Lord's Supper (Bicknell, *post*, p. 226). On July 2, 1667, Myles and another member were fined £5 each by the General Court of Plymouth Colony "for theire breach of order in seting up of a publicke meeting without the knowlidge and approbation of the Court," and were ordered to leave Rehoboth within the month (*Records of the Colony of New Plymouth*,

vol. IV, 1855, p. 162). Accordingly, the Baptists migrated a short distance into Wannamoisett and erected a meeting house there. On Oct. 30 of the same year the Court meeting at Plymouth granted the land at Wannamoisett to "Capt Willett and Mr Myles, and others theire naighbours" (*Ibid.*, IV, 169). On this land they built the town of Swansea. Myles became the minister of the settlement and master of the first school. When the members of his congregation were scattered by King Philip's War, he went to Boston and became acting pastor of the First Baptist Church there. Although he was invited to remain, he later resumed his pastorate at Swansea, and held it until his death. Cotton Mather, in his *Magnalia Christi Americana* (1702), characterized Myles as one "of those Persons, whose Names deserve to live in our *Book* for their *Piety*," and added that he had "a respectful Character in the Churches of this Wilderness" (Bk. III, p. 7). Thomas Hutchinson, in his *History of the Colony of Massachusets-Bay* (1764), testified to Myles's catholic spirit (I, 228). Myles married Ann, daughter of John Humphreys and widow of William Palmes, or Palmer. Their son Samuel Myles (*c.* 1664–1728) graduated from Harvard, was incorporated M.A. at the University of Oxford on July 15, 1693 (Foster, *op. cit.*, III, 1012), and became the second rector of King's Chapel, Boston.

[The old record book of the church at Ilston which Myles brought with him in 1663 is still in the possession of the First Baptist Church, Swansea, Mass. It was used by Isaac Backus in writing *A Hist. of New-England, with Particular Reference to the Denomination of Christians Called Baptists* (2 vols., 1777), and was the source of his information about Myles. See also Joshua Thomas, *A Hist. of the Bapt. Asso. in Wales* (1795); A. H. Mason, *Book A. Records of the Town of Swansea* (1900); Francis Baylies, *An Hist. Memoir of the Colony of New Plymouth* (1830); Leonard Bliss, *The Hist. of Rehoboth* (1836); T. W. Bicknell, "John Myles: Religious Toleration in Massachusetts," *Mag. of New England Hist.*, Oct. 1892; David Benedict, *A Gen. Hist. of the Bapt. Denomination* (1848); H. M. King, *Rev. John Myles and the Founding of the First Bapt. Ch. in Mass.* (1905); for Samuel Myles, H. W. Foote, *Annals of King's Chapel* (2 vols., 1882–96).]   D. M. D.

MYRICK, HERBERT (Aug. 20, 1860–July 6, 1927), agricultural editor, publisher, publicist, was born at Arlington, Mass., the son of Henry L. and Lucy Caroline (Whittemore) Myrick. He was educated at Massachusetts Agricultural College and Boston University, being graduated B.S. in 1882. He earned much of his own way, and while setting type in a printing shop, saw a copy of the *New England Homestead*, of Springfield, Mass., which decided him to become an agricultural editor. He found work with this journal during vacation, at two dollars a month and commissions on what subscriptions he could get. After leaving college he bought for $1449.57 a one-twelfth interest in the Phelps Publishing Company, which issued the paper, raising $49.57 in cash and giving his note for the rest. He lived on $4.50 a week until the note was paid.

Myrick's tremendous energy and peppery editorship increased circulation rapidly; the company prospered and began taking over other publications. It issued *Farm and Home* at Springfield and Chicago for more than forty years. The *Orange Judd Farmer* of Chicago was taken over in 1889 together with the *American Agriculturist* of New York, and *Southern Farming* of Atlanta in 1913. Although these periodicals were theoretically edited in various cities, Myrick, who for many years was president of the company, was editor in chief of them all. He likewise headed the company publishing the *Dakota Farmer;* and from 1905 until his death, the American Educational Press, which for some years issued the little paper, *Current Events.* In 1900 his Phelps Company purchased a small magazine called *Good Housekeeping,* which in a short time he developed into one of the most popular of women's publications. In connection with it he founded the Good Housekeeping Institute, where articles offered for advertisement in the magazine were tested before acceptance. This magazine was sold to the Hearst interests in 1911.

Myrick was always a crusader, and usually a fiery one. In 1883 he organized the United States Postal Improvement Association, which helped to enlist public opinion in behalf of rural free delivery and later induced Congress to grant lower mail rates on bulbs, seeds, and plants. In the same year he was instrumental in organizing the New England Tobacco Growers' Association and later, the Nurserymen's Protective Association. He was one of the first advocates of cooperative dairying and cooperative buying and selling by farmers, and was from the first in favor of the farmer's taking a more active part in politics. In 1901 he organized the Farmers' Political League, which did much to influence legislation in New England, New York, and Pennsylvania, and was the germ of the so-called Farm Bloc which in later years wielded much power in Congress. He aided in the passage of the Massachusetts credit union law, which was copied by several other states, also the Massachusetts farmland bank act. He spent much time and money in promoting the Hatch Act of 1887 which established a federal system of agricultural experiment stations. In behalf of the beet-sugar industry he campaigned for more than a quarter of a century. In 1900 he helped organize the League of Domestic Producers (of sugar, tobacco, cotton, wool, fruit, and nuts) which exerted an influence on tariff legislation. In 1916 he toured the United States, lecturing on the new Federal Farm Loan System, published a book upon the subject (*The Federal Farm Loan System,* 1916), aided in locating twelve banks and their districts, and became a director of the Springfield bank. He advocated an international institute of agriculture until such an organization was established at Rome by the King of Italy.

In addition to his other activities, he developed a device for drawing the fiber of cotton, and to manufacture it organized the Metallic Drawing Roll Company in 1891, of which he was president until 1923. He was long prominent in civic affairs in Springfield, and donated to the city an extensive right of way for a new street, Broadway. He wrote a number of books, including *Cooperative Finance* (1912) and *Rural Credits System for the United States* (1922). In 1926 he published *Ode to the Organ and Other Poems by Mother and Son,* a collection of verses by his mother and himself. He died in Bad Nauheim, Germany, whither he had gone for medical treatment, and was survived by his wife, Elvira Lawrence (Kenson) Myrick, together with a son and two daughters.

[*Who's Who in America,* 1926–27; obituary notices in *Springfield Republican, N. Y. Times,* July 7, 1927, and in the *New England Homestead,* July 16, 1927; J. E. Tower, *Springfield, Present and Prospective* (1905); information from Myrick's associates in the Phelps Publishing Company.]   A. F. H.

NACK, JAMES M. (Jan. 4, 1809–Sept. 23, 1879), "deaf and dumb poet," was born and reared in New York City. Cut off from educational advantages through financial reverses which came to his father, he was taught by a sister in her spare time, and was able to read at four and to write verses before he was nine. As a small boy he imitated preachers he heard at church and made up couplets in the style of hymns. In his eighth year, while carrying a playmate, he fell on a stairway and dragged a heavy fire screen down upon his head. When he recovered consciousness, after some weeks, his hearing was gone. Through his inability to hear his own voice, gradually his power of speech decayed also, though he could make himself understood to those who were closest to him. From August 1818 to December 1823 he was an inmate of the New York Deaf and Dumb Asylum, where he showed ability in grammar and arithmetic. His passion for poetic composition never waned, however, and it became the means by which he rose above the poverty and misery of his lonely life. He wrote a tragedy at twelve and another at fifteen, "on his knees," in a cold garret, without a table, with the stump of a pen; both of which productions, like many other early ones, he destroyed. But a poem of his, "The Blue-Eyed Maid," attracted the notice of Abraham Asten, clerk of the city and county of New York. Asten first secured the boy employment with a lawyer, a man of taste possessing a fine library, but eventually took him into his own office as an assistant, and introduced him to the *literati* of the city.

With the publication of his first volume, *The Legend of the Rocks and Other Poems* (1827), Nack became the literary sensation of the day. The New York *Critic* praised the music of a mind cut off from all sounds; another periodical hailed him as an intellectual wonder and a second Byron; Samuel Knapp pronounced him the most promising young writer he had ever met, and became his friend. In 1833, he published his *Ode on the Proclamation of President Jackson*; in 1839, *Earl Rupert and Other Tales and Poems,* including some prose selections and dedicated to Washington Irving; in 1850, *The Immortal, a Dramatic Romance,* with dedicatory verses to Dickens, reprinted under the title, *Poems,* in 1852; and *The Romance of the Ring and Other Poems,* with a portrait and facsimile signature, in 1859. Many of the early poems reappeared in subsequent volumes. He married Martha W. Simon, whom he had known from childhood, in 1838, and his married life was one of great felicity. Throughout his career he saw his poems quoted and reprinted; but he died regretting he had not done more as a poet.

The best that can be said of Nack is that his achievement in becoming a poet in spite of physical handicaps was a greater one than his poetry itself. Haunted by the material of Scott and the landscape of Byron, and stirred by a passion for adventure that he must satisfy second-hand, he never rose to the level of the poets he imitated. He wrote for a period, and his poems have been buried with the obvious sentimentality of that day.

[S. L. Knapp, *Sketches of Public Characters* (1830); memoir by J. Hancock, in *An Ode on the Proclamation of President Jackson* (1833); memoir by Prosper M. Wetmore, in *Earl Rupert and Other Tales and Poems* (1839); memoir by G. P. Morris, in *The Immortal* (1850); E. A. and G. L. Duyckinck, *Cyc. of Am. Lit.* (1875), vol. II; records of the N. Y. Institution . . . for the Deaf and Dumb; *N. Y. Tribune,* Sept. 25, 1879.]
R. P. T. C.

NADAL, EHRMAN SYME (Feb. 13, 1843–July 26, 1922), author, was born in Greenbrier County, Virginia (now West Virginia), the son of Bernard Harrison and Jane (Mays) Nadal. His father, then minister of the Methodist church in Lewisburg, Va., later served parishes in Maryland and Pennsylvania, became professor of English in Indiana Asbury, now De Pauw, University in 1854, and at the time of his death was acting president at Drew Theological Seminary. Because his father's place of employment was so frequently changed, Nadal attended a variety of elementary and secondary schools. In 1860 he entered Columbia College, transferring in 1862 to Yale, from which he was graduated in 1864. The next year he was an instructor in Dickinson Seminary, Williamsport, Pa., and from 1865 to 1867 he taught in schools in Dansville, N. Y., and Leavenworth, Kan. From 1867 to 1870 he was employed by the federal government, first in the Philadelphia mint and afterwards in the dead-letter office, Washington. He was a secretary of legation in London, from Jan. 28, 1870, to May 12, 1871, and was in England for eighteen months. During the next five years he wrote for various periodicals, including the *Nation,* and for some time was employed by the New York *Evening Post.* On June 8, 1877, he was commissioned second secretary to the London legation, and held that office until Nov. 26, 1883. After his return to the United States, he served for some time as secretary to the three civil-service boards of examiners in New York City, contributed to magazines, wrote for the *Evening Post,* and, in 1892–93, was lecturer on English composition at Columbia. From 1900 until his death, at Princeton, N. J., though he continued to engage in literary work, his principal occupation was dealing in horses, chiefly saddle horses. He never married.

Nadal's interest in writing was stimulated by his father, who contributed to various denominational periodicals. His own first literary venture was an editorial on civil-service reform, written while he was a government employee. It was printed by the New York *Evening Post,* and Nadal's connection with that journal was thus established. During his first residence in London, he began to write essays on various aspects of English life that interested him, and these were collected in 1875 under the title *Impressions of London Social Life.* A rather shrewd observer, he made some illuminating comments on British customs, and the essays still have value as reflections of the life of that time. A second collection, containing some critical articles, followed in 1882—*Essays at Home and Elsewhere.* In 1895 appeared *Notes of a Professional Exile,* a slight volume made up of impressionistic comments on English and Americans at a German resort. He contributed an essay on Milton to *The Warner Classics: Poets* (1899). In 1917 he published *A Virginian Village,* which reprinted a number of essays that he had written for periodicals during the preceding two decades. One of Nadal's last essays was a rather valuable account of Henry James ("Personal Recollections of Henry James," *Scribner's Magazine,* July 1920). He belongs to the group of informal essayists that enjoyed some popularity in the later decades of the nineteenth century. He wrote with no great distinction, and literature was with him only an avocation, but he was able to impart to his work enough charm to win at least a small circle of readers. Though he wrote more or less on literary subjects, and though his judgment was independent and at times keen, he was too little disciplined to become a first-rate critic, and his best essays are descriptions of social customs. In tone his work is invariably personal.

["Autobiog. Notes," in *A Virginian Village* (1917); *Decennial Record of the Class of 1864, Yale Coll.* (1875); *Hist. of the Class of 1864, Yale Coll.* (1895); *Yale Univ. Obit. Record,* 1923; *Who's Who in America,* 1922–23; *N. Y. Times,* July 28, 1922.]   G. H.

NAIRNE, THOMAS (d. April 1715), South Carolina assemblyman and Indian agent, was probably born in Scotland, though it is possible that he was born of Scottish descent in one of the plantations. He was first mentioned in the Carolina records in 1698 as a landowner on St. Helena Island. Sometime before this he had married Elizabeth Quintine, by whom he had one son. As a large planter on the extreme southern border of the English settlements he acquired an influence over the Indians that made him the most remarkable frontier figure of the South in the period of Queen Anne's War. He was captain of a company in Gov. James Moore's unsuccessful attack upon St. Augustine in 1702, and a partizan leader in the later destructive raids into Florida. In 1702 he was employed by the Assembly to regulate the traders among his neighbors, the Yamasee. He was also active in efforts to procure missionaries to the Indians through the agency of the Society for the Propagation of the Gospel. As a representative of the Colleton County dissenters he first clashed with the governor, Sir Nathaniel Johnson, over the conformity and church acts; and in the assembly of 1707 he became the aggressive leader of the country party in the successful struggle to wrest administrative powers from the governor. The issues were the appointment of the public receiver and the regulation of Indian affairs under control of the Commons. His Indian act of 1707 laid the basis of the southern regulative system. Under it he served as the first provincial Indian agent with a jurisdiction as "itinerary justice" and diplomatic agent as far westward as the Mississippi. In this office he launched an ambitious scheme for extending British influence among the western tribes and driving the French from Louisiana. He himself at great risk made peace with the Choctaw, the bulwark of the French colony. His memorial of July 10, 1708, to the secretary of state, elaborating his project, was a remarkable statement of the expansionist aims of the Carolinians. Yet his activities in regulating the traders had brought him again into conflict with the governor, and in June 1708 he had been thrown into prison on an obviously manufactured charge of high treason. He was later denied his seat in the Assembly and discharged as agent. Apparently he was never tried; and by a journey to England in 1710 he won the favor of the Lords Proprietors, on whose nomination to the Admiralty he was appointed judge advocate of South Carolina. In England he was energetic in stimulating the settlement of the Port Royal region, and was probably the author of the promotion tract, *A Letter from South Carolina* (1710).

Restored to his Indian agency in 1712, he was engaged in parleys with the discontented Yamasee at Pocotaligo Town, when, on Apr. 15, 1715, the great southern Indian war broke out, a revolt against the abuses of a trade to whose reform he had directed his efforts. He died at the stake after tortures prolonged, a contemporary reported, for several days.

[This sketch is based upon materials cited in V. W. Crane, *The Southern Frontier, 1670–1732* (1928), which contains a fuller account of Nairne's activities. A manuscript note, apparently contemporary, in the British Museum copy of *A Letter from South Carolina* (1710), says by "Capt. Tho. Nairn a North Britain"; this ascription is supported by internal evidence.]
V. W. C.

NANCRÈDE, CHARLES BEYLARD GUÉRARD de (Dec. 30, 1847–Apr. 12, 1921), surgeon, was born in Philadelphia, Pa., the son of Thomas Dixey and Mary Elizabeth (Bull) Nancrède. His father, a wholesale importer, was the son of Paul Joseph Guérard de Nancrède [*q.v.*] who came to America with the French army of Count Rochambeau and served at the battle of Yorktown. Nancrède's premedical education was obtained in private schools of Philadelphia and at the University of Pennsylvania, from which institution he obtained his degree of M.D. in 1869. In 1883 he obtained a similar degree from Jefferson Medical College. Following an internship in the Protestant Episcopal Hospital he began practice in Philadelphia, where, during the following twenty years, he developed into one of the foremost surgeons of the city. From the beginning of his medical career he kept in the forefront of professional progress, particularly in the art of surgery. He early joined the following of Lord Lister in the advocacy, first of antiseptic, later of aseptic, surgery. Together with Doctors W. W. Keen and J. E. Mears, he was instrumental in establishing these procedures in Philadelphia surgical practice. He is credited with being the first surgeon in Philadelphia to operate for bullet wounds of the stomach and intestines and to have participated in the first operation for appendicitis in that city. He made a specialty of the diagnosis and surgical treatment of brain abscess and tumors and of cortical epilepsy. He was at various times on the surgical staffs of the Protestant Episcopal, Jefferson, and St. Christopher's hospitals.

Nancrède began his teaching career as an instructor in physiology while still a medical student at the University of Pennsylvania. Later he became successively demonstrator in anatomy and lecturer on regional anatomy. In 1882 he was appointed professor of general and orthopedic surgery at the Philadelphia Polyclinic. After this active and varied experience he was called to the chair of surgery and clinical surgery at the University of Michigan at Ann Arbor in 1889, which position he held for the remainder of his life. This appointment also made him chief of the surgical service of the university hospital and clinic. He had been appointed lecturer on surgery at Dartmouth Medical College in 1887, and in 1900 he was promoted to professor, which post he held until his retirement in 1913. His courses at Dartmouth were held during the summer months. His teaching was marked by enthusiasm, with a genial sympathy and understanding of his students. He was keen and critical in analysis and positive from a broad knowledge of his subject. His two text-books, *Essentials of Anatomy* (1888) and *Lectures upon the Principles of Surgery* (1899), went through several editions. He contributed articles on injuries to the bursae and injuries to the head to Ashhurst's *International Encyclopædia of Surgery;* a section on "Symptoms, Diagnosis, and Treatment of Inflammation, Abscess, Ulcer, and Gangrene" to *System of Surgery* (vol. I, 1895), edited by F. S. Dennis and J. S. Billings; and "The Surgical Treatment of Croup and Diphtheria" to C. H. Burnett's *System of Diseases of the Ear, Nose, and Throat* (1893, vol. II). He discussed "Hæmorrhoids" and "Hæmorrhage" in Wood's *Reference Handbook of the Medical Sciences* and contributed articles for Park's *Treatise on Surgery,* Bryant and Buck's *American Practice of Surgery,* and *An American Text-Book of Surgery,* edited by W. W. Keen and J. W. White. In his early years he took an active

part in the meetings of the Philadelphia Pathological Society, presenting papers and specimens and acting as editor of the society's proceedings.

An inherited martial spirit led Nancrède into the Spanish-American War at its outbreak in 1898. He was commissioned a major in the volunteer army and went to Cuba as chief surgeon of the 3rd Division, II Army Corps, in which capacity he participated in the battle of Santiago. He continued his military connection as a reserve medical officer and member of the Association of Military Surgeons, but his age precluded active service in the World War. Though known primarily as a surgeon, he kept up his knowledge and interest in internal medicine and described himself as a medical man who operated. He had marked artistic ability, was fond of sketching and drawing, and was a member of the Philadelphia Sketching Club. He was also a member of the Philadelphia Choral Society. In addition to the organization already mentioned he was a member of the International Society of Surgery, the Philadelphia Academy of Natural Sciences, and the American Surgical Association of which he was elected president in 1908. He was also a corresponding member of the Royal Academy of Medicine of Rome. He was married on June 3, 1872, to Alice, daughter of Francis P. Dunnington of Baltimore, Md. He died at his home in Ann Arbor.

[*Jour. Mich. State Medic. Soc.,* Jan. 1922; *Trans. Am. Surgic. Asso.,* vol. XXXIX (1921); *Jour. Am. Medic. Asso.,* Apr. 30, 1921; *Who's Who in America,* 1918–19; *Detroit Free Press,* Apr. 14, 1921.]

J. M. P.

NANCRÈDE, PAUL JOSEPH GUÉRARD de (Mar. 16, 1761–Dec. 15, 1841), soldier, instructor, bookseller, editor, and printer, was born at Héricy, near Fontainebleau, France, the son of Jean Joseph and Louise Françoise (Gautier) Guérard. On Aug. 19, 1779, he enlisted in the French army under the name of Joseph Guérard. As a private in the regiment of the Soissonnais, company of Jean-Baptiste Marin, which embarked at Brest, Apr. 6, 1780, he participated in all the important operations of the army of Rochambeau including Yorktown, returning to France, upon the close of the war, some time in March 1783. Two years later he came back to America, going to Boston, where he married Hannah Dixey, Nov. 11, 1788. From 1787 to 1797–98, he was instructor of the French language and literature at Harvard College. In a letter to the gentlemen of the Corporation of Harvard, signing his name as Joseph de Nancrède, he complains of the difficulties that confront him in his teaching on account of the lack of suitable French texts: "With a view to supply this deficiency, I have been engaged, for upwards of twelve months, in collecting pieces, in several different styles, from our best authors" (Nancrède correspondence, Harvard Library).

This collection, which was published in 1792 under the title of *L'Abeille Françoise,* is undoubtedly the first French school text composed especially for use in American colleges. It is filled with the philosophical sentiments of Rousseau and Helvétius. He had previously attempted to supply suitable class-room material in the publication of a French newspaper which was to serve also as an organ of intelligence to the French inhabitants of Boston. Through the personal influence of Brissot de Warville he was inspired to publish this French paper, the *Courier de Boston,* a political and literary journal, appearing weekly from Apr. 23 to Oct. 15, 1789, which was intended to disseminate the theories of Brissot in America. It was through this journalistic enterprise that he became associated with Samuel Hall, the printer of his newspaper. This relationship opened up a new field of endeavor to him, that of printing, which he successfully pursued in addition to his duties at the University until 1804. For a time, Hall and Nancrède were partners in the printing and book-selling business. In 1796, however, Nancrède went into business for himself, opening up a shop at 49 Marlborough Street, Boston. From the nature of the French and English works that issued from his press one sees further exemplified the ideas which pervaded *L'Abeille Françoise:* "l'humanitarianisme sentimental." And from the number, which is considerable, of the editions of French authors published by him one cannot help realizing how zealously he worked to introduce in America the Rousseauistic *genre* of French literature. In 1804, with eight of his nine children he went to France, where he remained until 1812, when he returned to the United States, this time to transfer his business from Boston to Philadelphia. Practically nothing is known about this period of his life. Some time later he made his last trip to Paris, where he died, Dec. 15, 1841. One of his sons was Joseph Guerard Nancrede, who became a well-known Philadelphia physician.

Two strikingly different estimates of Nancrède have been made by his contemporaries. In the diary of the Rev. W. A. Bentley there is the following entry: "This week Nancrede has a very valuable sale of Books. . . . His domestic affairs & his general manners have not contributed to the public confidence" (*post,* III, p. 73). De Sales La Terrière, on the other hand, says of him: "I came to have a close friendship

with him, as he was a most estimable person. He rendered me great services and wherever I or any of my sons may be let us be mindful of them. He was married to a very pretty woman" (translated by David Heald in the *Boston Medical and Surgical Journal,* Apr. 21, 1910).

[Important dates were obtained from copies of original documents in the possession of Mrs. De Nancrède Pond, great-grand-daughter of Nancrède. Printed sources include: Alexandre Belisle, *Histoire de la Presse Franco-Americaine* (1911); G. P. Winship, "Two or Three Boston Papers," *The Papers of the Bibliog. Soc. of America,* vol. XIV, pt. 2 (1920); Albert Schinz, "Un 'Rousseauiste' en Amérique," *Modern Language Notes,* Jan. 1920; Fernand Baldensperger, "Le Premier 'instructeur' de Français à Harvard Coll.: Jos. Nancrède," *Harvard Advocate,* Dec. 5, 1913; *The Diary of Wm. Bentley, D.D.,* vols. II and III (1907–11).]
A. J. B—d.

NANUNTENOO [See CANONCHET, d. 1676].

NAPTON, WILLIAM BARCLAY (Mar. 23, 1808–Jan. 8, 1883), jurist, the son of John and Susan (Hight) Napton, was born near Princeton, N. J. He attended the grammar school at Lawrenceville, and in 1826 was graduated from the College of New Jersey. For three years thereafter he served as tutor in the family of William Fitzhugh Gordon [*q.v.*] near Charlottesville, Va. His spare time he devoted to the study of law under John Tayloe Lomax at the University of Virginia and in 1830 he was graduated from the department of law of the university with high honors. During his five or six years of residence in a "strict-construction" atmosphere he naturally imbibed much that tended to make him a lifelong advocate of state rights. In 1832 he moved to Fayette, Mo., where he took up the practice of law, and at the same time for a few years edited the *Boone's Lick Democrat.* Governor Boggs appointed him attorney-general in 1836, an office which he held for three years. In 1838 he married Malinda Williams, the daughter of Judge Thomas L. Williams, who was for several years chancellor of eastern Tennessee and also a judge of the supreme court of Tennessee. Nine of their ten children lived to maturity.

In 1839 Napton was appointed a judge of the supreme court of Missouri and held the office until his defeat in the election of 1851. He was the chief if not the sole author of the famous Jackson Resolutions (instructions to Senator Thomas H. Benton to uphold the extreme pro-slavery program in Congress) passed by the state legislature in 1847. He first admitted and then, to save the face of their legislative sponsor, Claiborne F. Jackson, denied that he formulated the resolutions. When the trouble over slavery arose in Kansas, Napton, whose home was in Saline County—a strong pro-slavery section of western Missouri—aligned himself against the abolitionists. While this struggle was growing more acute a pro-slavery convention of considerable proportions was held (July 1855) at Lexington, then the largest town in western Missouri. Napton was the chairman of the resolutions committee, prime mover and general mouthpiece of this convention. It took, practically unanimously, a belligerent stand against the abolition movement and condemned the "diabolical" activities of the Emigrant Aid Society in Kansas.

Napton was elected to the state supreme bench in 1857 but was automatically retired from the position when he refused to take the specially devised oath of office in 1861. Apparently he took no active part in the Civil War. For a decade after 1863 he was a successful lawyer in St. Louis, and then (1873) was again chosen to the supreme court. He was generally considered the leading member of the bench until his voluntary retirement on Dec. 31, 1880. He takes unusually high rank among Missouri jurists. His judicial decisions bear the earmarks of painstaking research and were always clothed in beautiful and clear diction. In the jurisprudence of commercial law, land titles, and equity, the principles and conclusions which he set forth are counted as valuable and lasting contributions. Except perhaps where his favored doctrine of state rights was involved he was forward-looking in the adjustment of legal principles to new social and economic conditions. In this respect he helped to create precedents and through them to shape the course of legal development.

[*The Bench and Bar of Mo.* (1899); W. B. Napton, *Past and Present of Saline County, Mo.* (ed. 1910); *76 Mo. Reports,* i–xiii; *The Bench and Bar of St. Louis . . . and other Mo. Cities* (1884); L. C. Krauthoff, *The Supreme Court of Mo.* (1891); *Address to the People of the U. S., Together with the Proc. and Resolutions of the Pro-Slavery Convention of Mo., Held at Lexington, July 1855* (1855); J. F. Philips, *Reminiscences of Some Deceased Lawyers of Central Mo.* (1914); Wm. Hyde and H. L. Conard, *Encyc. of the Hist. of St. Louis* (1899), vol. III; W. B. Davis and D. S. Durrie, *An Illustrated Hist. of Mo.* (1876); A. J. D. Stewart, *The Hist. of the Bench and Bar of Mo.* (1898); *Jefferson Inquirer,* Aug. 18, 1849, June 4, 1853; *Mo. Republican,* Jan. 10, 1883.]

H. E. N.

NARVÁEZ, PÁNFILO de (c. 1478–1528), Spanish conquistador, was born in Valladolid, about 1478. Entering upon the profession of arms at an early age, he had already acquired considerable reputation as a soldier when he went to the Indies during the early years of the sixteenth century. He served at first in Jamaica, but when Diego Velázquez was sent to Cuba (then called Fernandina), Narváez, by special request, as he and Velázquez were old friends, was transferred thither, together with his thirty

specially trained archers. As chief captain of Velázquez, he took an active and ruthless part in pacifying and settling Cuba. In recompense, he was granted several Indian towns and amassed considerable wealth. In Cuba he married a widow, María de Valenzuela, who possessed other Indian towns. He acted in a civil capacity as accountant and special agent (*procurador*), and in the latter capacity, together with Antonio Velázquez, presented many petitions for the betterment of Cuba (1515–18), one being for better roads. In 1520, Velázquez commissioned Narváez to seize or kill Cortés who was charged with disobedience and disloyalty in the conquest he had undertaken. Accordingly, on Mar. 11, with title as captain-general of the Mexican conquest, thus superseding Cortés, he left Cuba with eighteen or nineteen vessels and a force numbering at least nine hundred Spaniards and some Indians—all well equipped. On May 23, however, he was defeated by Cortés, losing an eye in the encounter, besides being captured with all his men, most of whom were added to those of his rival. He was held prisoner until 1521, when he was freed by direct order of the council of the Indies.

In 1526, he obtained concessions granting titles of grand constable, governor, captain general, and *adelantado* to himself and his heirs and successors forever, with the right to make an expedition of conquest and settlement to Florida, the usual obligations, privileges, and exemptions being annexed. He left San Lúcar, Spain, on June 17, 1527, with five vessels and six hundred soldiers, colonists, and friars, with Alvar Núñez Cabeza de Vaca as treasurer. One hundred and forty men deserted during the forty-five days he spent at Santo Domingo. Two vessels, sixty men, and twenty horses were lost in a hurricane along the Cuban coast. After wintering in Cuba, the expedition (now four hundred men and eighty horses) set sail on Feb. 20, 1528, for Havana, but could not make that port, being held for a fortnight on a reef and then driven northward to Florida, reaching land on Apr. 14, near Clement's Point on the small peninsula west of Tampa Bay and about five leagues from the mouth of the bay which they had missed. On Apr. 16, possession of Florida was taken for the King, Narváez causing to be read aloud the long, absurd proclamation usual in such cases. A few explorations and forays among the sullen and hostile Indians netted little, except the crossing of the small peninsula and the discovery of the inner waters of Tampa Bay.

Understanding that great riches abounded in the town of Apalache, Narváez, after dispatching his ships along the coast toward Mexico (against the advice of Cabeza de Vaca), on May 1, 1528, led a shore party of three hundred men northward. They never saw their ships again. Crossing the Withlacoochie and Suwanee rivers, they turned west and after great suffering reached Apalache (in the neighborhood of the present Tallahassee), only to find it a wretched village of forty huts, whose Indians were hostile. Twenty-five days later they turned south and in a nine days' march through swamps, lakes, and dense forests, ever pursued by the Indians, they reached the town of Auté, at about the present St. Marks. This marked the end of the expedition. Narváez and others fell sick. Their only hope now was to reach Mexico. With but one carpenter and without tools or materials, they contrived to build five crazy boats on one of the many bays of South Florida. The horses were killed and eaten and from their hides were fashioned bellows, water bottles, and other necessities. From their weapons, stirrups, and other appliances, they made tools and nails. On Sept. 22, the two hundred and forty men left were divided among the boats and they set out along the coast, no person among them having a knowledge of navigation. The water bottles rotted and the men were assailed by thirst, hunger, storms, and sickness and death. For over a month they wandered about the gulf, finding but little comfort among the few Indians they saw. Three of the boats were wrecked or foundered at sea. Finally at a place probably near Matagorda Bay, toward the end of October or during the first few days in November 1528, Narváez was swept out to sea by a sudden storm that came up during the night. He had remained alone on his boat with the coxswain and a boy, all the others having gone ashore. He was never heard of again.

[Colección de Documentos Inéditos . . . de las antiguas Posesiones Españolas, 1 ser. (42 vols., 1864-84), esp. vols. X, XI, XII, XIV, XVI, XXII, XXIV, XXV, XXXV, 2 ser. (21 vols., 1885-1928), esp. vols. I and IV; Bartolomé de las Casas, Historia de las Indias, vol. IV (1876); Gonzalo Fernández de Oviedo y Valdéz, Historia General y Natural de las Indias (4 vols., 1851-55), vol. III; Alvar Núñez Cabeza de Vaca, La Relación (1542, 1555), pub. in English translation by Buckingham Smith under the title, The Narrative of Alvar Núñez Cabeça de Vaca (1871); translation of Narváez's proclamation in B. F. French, Hist. Colls. of La. and Fla., 2 ser. (1875), pp. 153-58; Morris Bishop, The Odyssey of Cabeza de Vaca (1933); A. P. Maudslay, The True Hist. of the Conquest of New Spain (5 vols., 1908-16), translated from the Spanish of Bernal Díaz del Castillo; Francisco López de Gómara, La Historia General de las Indias (1553); Antonio de Herrera y Tordesillas, Historia General (4 vols., 1601-15), pub. in English translation by John Stevens under the title, The Gen. Hist. of the Vast Continent and Islands of America (6 vols., 1725-26); Juan de Torquemada, Segunda Parte de . . . Monarchia Indiana (1723).]
                                  J. A. R.

NASBY, PETROLEUM V. [See LOCKE, DAVID ROSS, 1833–1888].

NASH, ABNER (c. 1740–Dec. 2, 1786), governor of North Carolina and delegate to the Continental Congress, was born at "Templeton Manor," his father's plantation in Amelia County, later Prince Edward County, Va. He was the third son of Ann (Owen) Nash, the daughter of Hugh Owen of Tenby, Pembrokeshire, Wales, and John Nash who had emigrated from Wales to Virginia about 1730, and was the brother of Francis Nash and the father of Frederick Nash [qq.v.]. In 1761 and 1762 he represented Prince Edward County in the Virginia House of Burgesses. Removing to North Carolina in 1762, he settled at Halifax, where he rose quickly to prominence in local politics and in the practice of law, as he did also at New Bern to which he removed in the early 1770's. Twice he was married advantageously: first, to Justina (Davis) Dobbs, the widow of Gov. Arthur Dobbs [q.v.], through whom he was involved in the famous Dobbs land suit, and, second, in 1774 to Mary Whiting Jones. His representation of Halifax town in 1764 and 1765 and Halifax County from 1770 to 1771 in the House of Commons, his connection with the Dobbs land suit, and his rôle in the Regulator and Revolutionary movements brought him considerable reputation. In the Regulator disturbance he supported the conservative eastern interests and the established government under Gov. William Tryon, who appointed him a major of brigade in 1768. From the beginning of the contest with the mother country he was a zealous and active patriot. He was a leader in the local events that induced Gov. Josiah Martin to flee from New Bern in May 1775, was the choice of the borough of New Bern as delegate to each of the five Revolutionary provincial congresses from 1774 to 1776, was a member of several prominent committees in the congresses, notably those that drafted the Halifax resolution of Apr. 12, 1776, and the constitution of 1776, was a member of the Provincial Council in 1775 and 1776, and was an agent of the Council in 1776 to confer with the South Carolina authorities at Charleston in regard to defense. His conspicuous revolutionary activity led Governor Martin, who admitted he was "an eminent lawyer," to brand him as "a most unprincipled character," one of four persons in the province "foremost among the patrons of revolt and anarchy" whose "unremitted labours to promote sedition and rebellion" had marked them as proper objects of proscription (Colonial Records, post, IX, 1155, X, 98).

Under the new government he was speaker of the first House of Commons and was the second governor. He represented New Bern for 1777 and Craven County for 1778 in the House of Commons, and Jones County in the Senate for 1779, when he was also chosen speaker. His greatest responsibility, however, was as governor during the military crisis of 1780 and 1781. Elected in the spring of 1780, he displayed energy in preparing for British invasion from the south; but, embarrassed by the constitutional weakness of his office, he requested the General Assembly to create a board of war to share responsibility while the Assembly was not in session. The board of war, as created by the radical Assembly in the fall of 1780, was given and exercised the constitutional powers of the governor and was independent in its attitude toward him. Already piqued in the spring by the Assembly's unconstitutional action of selecting Richard Caswell to command the militia, he resented the usurpation of the board of war, refused to fill a vacancy, and wrote that the executive power was so divided that "men not knowing who to obey, obey nobody" (*State Records, post*, XVII, 882). He expressed to the Assembly in January 1781 his determination to resign the "useless and contemptible" office unless it was restored to a condition of respectability (*State Records, post*, XV, 228–29). The board of war was merely replaced by the council extraordinary which likewise was given unconstitutional powers. On June 24, 1781, learning that he had been nominated for reëlection, he requested the withdrawal of his name on account of "excessive Fatigues of late and want of Health" (*State Records, post*, XVII, 802).

However, he soon reëntered public life as representative from Jones County in 1782, 1784, and 1785, and was an unsuccessful candidate for governor in 1784. In the House he was a leader in opposition to the restoration to the Loyalists of such of their confiscated property as had not been sold and to the repeal of all laws inconsistent with the treaty of 1783. He declined election to the Continental Congress in 1778, but accepted election in 1782, 1783, and 1785. In Congress he soon recognized the necessity of a stronger federal government. He was appointed delegate to the Annapolis Convention in 1786 but did not attend. In his personal life he was genial, suave, luxurious in habit and taste, improvident, convivial, and gracious in hospitality. He died while in New York to attend Congress and was buried with elaborate ceremony in St. Paul's Churchyard. Later his remains were removed to "Pembroke," his home near New Bern.

[Governors' papers and letter books in the Lib. of the N. C. Hist. Commission, Raleigh; *The Colonial Records of N. C.*, vols. II, VI–X (1888–90); *The State Records of N. C.*, vols. XI–XXIV (1895–1905); *Jours. of the House of Burgesses of Va., 1761–65*, ed. by J. P. Kennedy (1907); *Jours. of the Continental Cong.*, vols. XXII–XXV (1914–22); G. J. McRee, *Life and Correspondence of James Iredell*, vol. I, pp. 396–97, vol. II, pp. 35–36 (1857–58); *Presentation of Portrait of Governor Abner Nash, Address of J. G. deR. Hamilton* (1909); *Biog. Hist. of N. C.*, ed. by S. A. Ashe, vol. I (1905); A. R. House, *The Reads and their Relatives* (1930).]

A. R. N.

NASH, ARTHUR (June 26, 1870–Oct. 30, 1927), originator of the "Golden Rule Nash" plan of copartnership with workers, was born in a log-cabin in Tipton County, Ind., the eldest of nine children of Evermont Nash and Rachel Mitchel. Both his parents were zealous Seventh Day Adventists, and after attending high school at Greentown, Ind., he went to the Adventist Theological Seminary at Battle Creek, Mich. Ordained in 1894 he became instructor in a school for Adventist missionaries at Detroit, but within a few months he was dismissed because he refused to affirm that a humanitarian woman who had not been an Adventist, had gone to hell. There ensued a period of painful religious readjustment during which he fed his mind on atheistic literature while wandering about the Middle West as a box-car hobo, carrying a hod, plastering, making brooms, and working on bridge construction. In 1898 he returned to Detroit and organized a laundry and other measures for the relief of the unemployed. He met there a Y.W.C.A. worker, Maud Lena Southwell, whom he married at Cleveland, Ohio, on Apr. 9, 1899, and who turned him back to religion. In 1900 he entered the ministry of the Disciples of Christ and took a pastorate at Bluffton, Ohio, only to be asked to resign some two years later because in a memorial sermon he had eulogized the virtues of a kind-hearted but professedly unreligious man. He then began selling clothing for a Chicago house and was so successful that in 1909 he established himself as a manufacturer of men's clothing in Columbus, Ohio. In 1913 he moved to Cincinnati and there organized in June 1916 the A. Nash Company which produced clothing by cutting the garments in its own establishment and "farming out" their making to a contractor. Early in 1917 he accepted an invitation to preach a sermon on the theme, "What is the matter with Christianity?" After two months of reading and hard thinking he became convinced that the way to establish on earth the Kingdom of Heaven was to apply literally the Golden Rule.

Late in 1918, on taking over the business of the contractor who had been making his clothing, he discovered that the wage scale paid by a sweatshop did not square with the Golden Rule and, though his balance sheet for 1918 showed a loss, at once raised wages throughout the shop. At the same time he prepared to liquidate his business. But two months later he found that his employees were voluntarily working far more rapidly and efficiently than before and that his business was growing by leaps and bounds. From that time until his death Nash spent a large part of his time preaching with fiery oratory and sincere fervor the Golden Rule to business men's and social-welfare organizations throughout the country. By 1925 the Nash Company had grown to the largest establishment producing direct maker-to-consumer clothing in the United States. Meanwhile Nash lowered prices, stabilized employment, inaugurated a five-day week with eight hours a day, increased wages repeatedly, and paid his workers cash dividends based on time worked. In 1920 he began issuing stock dividends to employees and in May 1924 distributed among them his own share of a stock dividend, giving them, at the expiration of the five years, control over the business. In December 1925 he called together his employees, the majority of whom were anti-union, and, after a dramatic struggle which attracted nation-wide attention, persuaded them to consent to the unionization of the entire plant by the Amalgamated Clothing Workers of America. This struggle he called the supreme hour of his life. A shrewd business man, with a *flair* for leadership and a full understanding of the value of the publicity secured by his speeches, Nash was by nature and training a sincere and aggressive evangelist. To him the "Golden Rule in Business" was a religion and not merely a successful advertising slogan. Shortly after having placed a representative of the union on his board of management Nash died of heart disease in Cincinnati. In addition to several magazine articles he told the story of his life and his experiment in *The Golden Rule in Business* (1923, rev. ed., 1930). Nash also founded and endowed a movement called the "Brotherhood of Man," an organization intended to aid young Turks in Turkey and promote amity between them and their Christian neighbors.

[In addition to *The Golden Rule in Business*, see Nash's articles: "A Bible Text that Worked a Business Miracle," *Am. Mag.,* Oct. 1921, and "Bigger Dividends —No More Labor Troubles," *Collier's,* Aug. 22, 1925; and *Who's Who in America,* 1926–27. For several years there was much newspaper and magazine discussion of his ideas, including articles in the *N. Y. Times,* June 1, 1924; *Collier's Weekly,* July 28, 1923; *Lit. Digest,* July 12, 1924; *Nation,* Jan. 6, 1926; *New Republic,* Mar. 10, 1926; *Century Mag.,* Oct. 1926, and *Survey,* Jan. 1, 1926, May 1, 1927. Obituaries were published in the *N. Y. Times* and the *Cincinnati En-*

quirer, Oct. 31, 1927, *Survey,* Dec. 15, 1927, and other periodicals. Additional information was secured from Nash's daughter Mrs. Erwin Strachley, Jr., of Cincinnati.]
H. S. W.

NASH, CHARLES SUMNER (Feb. 18, 1856–Nov. 22, 1926), Congregational clergyman, educator, was born in Granby, Hampshire County, Mass., the son of Lorenzo Smith and Nancie Swinington (Knight) Nash. He graduated from Amherst College in the class of 1877, and was at once appointed instructor in Robert College, Constantinople, Turkey, where he taught for three years. Returning to America in 1880, he entered Hartford Theological Seminary, Hartford, Conn., and after receiving the degree of B.D. in 1883, pursued graduate study for another year. He was ordained to the Congregational ministry on Oct. 22, 1884, and served the First Congregational Church of East Hartford as pastor from 1884 until 1890. On May 15, 1889, he married Marie Louise Henry of Hartford. Their only children were a boy who did not survive infancy, and a girl who died at the age of ten.

In 1890 he was appointed instructor in Biblical theology and elocution in Hartford Seminary. The following year he resigned to become professor of homiletics and pastoral theology in Pacific Theological Seminary, then located in Oakland, Cal., but in 1901 removed to Berkeley. To this school, still in its pioneer stage when he came to it, he thenceforth devoted all his energies, serving as professor from 1891, as dean from 1906 to 1911, and as president from 1911 until his resignation in 1920. Thereafter as president emeritus and professor of church polity he continued in active association with the school until his death.

Nash was a man of earnest religious convictions and constantly enlarging vision, as is well illustrated in his little book entitled *Our Widening Thought of God* (1914). His outreaching personality and influence filled a large place in the religious life of the Pacific Coast. As teacher and administrator his career was noteworthy. Under his leadership Pacific Theological Seminary—up to that time a Congregational school—became in 1912 an undenominational institution, and at its fiftieth anniversary in 1916 changed its name to Pacific School of Religion. During his administration new departments were added and the funds of the school greatly enlarged.

He was a member of the Commission of Nineteen which formulated the plan adopted in 1913 for the reorganization of the National Congregational Council and a member of the Commission on Polity of the Council of 1921. In 1908-09 he delivered the Carew Lectures at Hartford

Seminary, published under the title *Congregational Administration* (1909). He was an earnest advocate of church unity and was one of the framers of an overture adopted by the National Congregational Council inviting the union of the Universalist with the Congregational churches. Although thoroughly attached to his profession and convinced of its large responsibilities and opportunities, he was not narrowly professional. He was one of the founders of the Outlook Club of Oakland, a well-known social and discussion group, and kept in close touch with world affairs. Fond of outdoor life he found the Berkeley Hills an unfailing source of health and recreation. He was a member of the Sierra Club, and an ardent lover of the High Sierra.

[*Pacific School of Religion Bull.*, Dec. 1926; C. S. Nash and J. W. Buckham, *Religious Progress on the Pacific Slope* (copr. 1917); *Congregationalist*, Dec. 9, 1926; *Who's Who in America*, 1924–25; *San Francisco Chronicle*, Nov. 23, 1926.] J.W.B.

NASH, DANIEL (May 28, 1763–June 4, 1836), Protestant Episcopal clergyman, frontier missionary in New York State, was born not far from the western border of Massachusetts in what is now Great Barrington, a descendant of Thomas Nash, who signed the Fundamental Agreement of New Haven in 1639. Daniel's father, Jonathan, son of Daniel and Experience (Clark) Nash, had married Anna Maria Spoor of Taghkanick, Columbia County, N. Y., and Daniel was the youngest of their nine children. He prepared for college and entered Yale, graduating in the class of 1785. President Ezra Stiles records in his diary under date of July 6, 1783, that after the forenoon sermon Daniel Nash, sophomore, among others, was admitted to the College Church (F. B. Dexter, *The Literary Diary of Ezra Stiles*, 1901, III, 78). For some years after his graduation he engaged in teaching, first at Pittsgrove, N. J., and later at Swedesboro. During this period changes in his ecclesiastical views led him to leave the Congregational for the Episcopal Church, and at Swedesboro he studied theology under Rev. John Croes, principal of the academy where Nash was teaching, and rector of the local church. In 1794 he became head of an academy in New Lebanon Springs, N. Y., and served as a lay reader for the Episcopalians of that town. In January 1796 he married Olive Lusk of Richmond, Mass.

Under the influence of Rev. Daniel Burhans who had been instrumental in establishing the church at New Lebanon Springs, Nash became imbued with intense missionary zeal. He was ordained deacon by Bishop Samuel Provoost on Feb. 8, 1797, and at once began work on the west-

ern frontier, making his first home at Exeter, Otsego County. For nearly forty years thereafter, indifferent to discomfort and hardship, abounding in labors and fervent in spirit, he devoted himself to extending the teachings and worship of what he had come ardently to believe was the Apostolically established church. Because he felt that Bishop Provoost did not display a proper missionary ardor, he did not wish to be ordained priest by him, and waited until Oct. 11, 1801, when the recently consecrated Bishop Benjamin Moore ordained him. His field was a difficult one, not only because it was frontier territory, but also because the settlers had Presbyterian traditions behind them; but Nash had great success. He lived in log-cabins, was content with few possessions, traveled on horseback, often with his wife holding a child behind him. Her help in the music and responses, he testified, was invaluable. He was not a great preacher, nor especially keen mentally, but he was diligent in season and out of season, entering the homes of the people, baptizing and catechizing the children, and conducting private and public worship. He came to be affectionately known everywhere as "Father Nash." In the annual Conventions he was styled "Rector of the Episcopal Churches in Otsego County." Others built on his foundations, but he established practically all the Episcopal churches of that county and extended his labors to some eight other counties, going as far north as Ogdensburg. Whatever his peculiarities and limitations, he was admirably fitted physically for his work, being "of rugged health, six feet in height, full in figure, over two hundred pounds in weight" (Ralph Birdsall, *The Story of Cooperstown*, 1917, p. 155). On Jan. 1, 1811, due to his activities, Christ Church, Cooperstown, was formally organized, and he was chosen rector. This position he informally held until his death, still continuing his missionary labors. He is supposed to have been the original of Rev. Mr. Grant in J. Fenimore Cooper's *The Pioneers*. He died in the home of a daughter in Burlington, N. Y., and was buried in the churchyard of Christ Church, Cooperstown, under a pine tree, a spot which he had chosen.

[F. B. Dexter, *Biog. Sketches Grads. Yale Coll.*, vol. IV (1907); W. B. Sprague, *Annals Am. Pulpit*, vol. V (1859); F. W. Halsey, *The Old N. Y. Frontier* (1901); G. P. Reese, *Hist. Records of Christ Ch., Cooperstown, N. Y.* (n.d.); J. N. Norton, *Pioneer Missionaries; or the Lives of Phelps and Nash* (1859); Philander Chase, *Reminiscences* (1844); Sylvester Nash, *The Nash Family* (1853).] H.E.S.

NASH, FRANCIS (*c.* 1742–Oct. 7, 1777), Revolutionary soldier, the fourth son of John and Ann (Owen) Nash and the brother of Abner Nash [*q.v.*], was born at "Templeton Manor" in Amelia, later Prince Edward County, Va. In early manhood he settled at Childsburg, later Hillsboro, in the frontier North Carolina county of Orange. Of superior training, handsome in person, affable, and industrious, he rose quickly to local prominence as merchant and attorney and, in 1763, to position as justice of the peace and clerk of the court of pleas and quarter sessions. He was representative to the House of Commons for Orange County in 1764, 1765, and 1771, and for the borough of Hillsboro from 1773 to 1775. He married Sarah, the daughter of Maurice Moore and the niece of James Moore [*qq.v.*]. Two of their children survived him. Holding the most lucrative county office, he was obnoxious to the Regulators and was charged by them with taking excessive fees. Station, temperament, and position fixed his sympathies with the established government, and he served as captain in Governor Tryon's army that crushed the Regulators in the battle of Alamance on May 16, 1771. In 1774 and 1775 he was judge of the court of oyer and terminer in Hillsboro district.

In the contest with Great Britain he supported the patriot cause, representing Orange County in the second revolutionary Provincial Congress of April 1775 and the town of Halifax in the third Congress of August 1775. However, it was in the field of military affairs that he excelled. Brave and high-spirited, he had risen to the rank of colonel of militia; and at Alamance he acquired experience and a reputation for courage and ability. On Sept. 1, 1775, the Provincial Congress elected him lieutenant-colonel of the 1st North Carolina Regiment of Continental troops and promoted him to colonel seven months later, on Apr. 10. He was with the expedition commanded by James Moore to aid Charleston in the winter of 1776–77. The Continental Congress elected him brigadier-general on Feb. 5, 1777, and ordered him to recruit soldiers in western North Carolina and to proceed northward in March with Moore and his Continental regiments. At Moore's death he succeeded to command and after some delay led the North Carolina brigade northward to join Washington's army. Placed in the reserves commanded by Lord Stirling at Germantown on Oct. 4, the brigade became involved in the confusion and disorder of that fog-obscured battlefield; and he, while leading his men bravely but ineffectually, was mortally wounded. Three days later he died and was buried at Kulpsville, Pa. He was regarded by Washington as a brave man and a valuable officer and by Gov. Richard Caswell as the ablest North Carolina officer in the field at the time of his death. Nash County, N. C., and Nashville, Tenn., were named in his honor, and, at the Guilford Battleground, a monument was erected to his memory by congressional appropriation.

[*The Colonial Records of N. C.*, vols. VI–X (1888–90); *The State Records of N. C.*, vols. XI–XV, XVII, XXII, XXIV (1895–1905); *Journals of the Continental Cong.*, vols. IV, VII–IX (1906–07); *Biog. Hist. of N. C.*, ed. by S. A. Ashe, vol. III (1905); A. M. Waddell, "Gen. Francis Nash," *The N. C. Booklet*, Oct. 1914; A. R. Rouse, *The Reads and their Relatives* (1930).]

A. R. N.

NASH, FREDERICK (Feb. 19, 1781–Dec. 4, 1858), jurist, was born in Tryon's Palace at New Bern, N. C., during the governorship of his father, Abner Nash [*q.v.*], whose death in 1786 left the cares of the family to the mother, Mary (Jones) Nash. Prominent family connections, a devout mother, religious training, the experience of exhortation from President Washington in 1791, and responsibility as the eldest of the children operated to make him from youth manly, serious, sensitive to duty, and lacking in humor. He was educated by the Rev. Henry Patillo at Williamsboro, at the academy of the Rev. Thomas P. Irving in New Bern, and at the College of New Jersey (Princeton), from which he was graduated with high rank in 1799. After studying law in the office of Edward Harris, he commenced practice in New Bern in 1801. On Sept. 1, 1803, he was married to Mary G. Kollock of Elizabethtown, N. J. His public career began as a representative from New Bern in the House of Commons, in 1804 and 1805; but his later career was associated chiefly with Hillsboro, to which he moved in 1807. In an extensive law practice and in the House of Commons, as representative of Orange County in 1814, 1815, 1816, 1817, and of Hillsboro in 1828 and 1829, he achieved reputation as an able advocate, a man of sturdy character and sound judgment, and an orator of pleasing voice, fine diction, lucid reasoning, and persuasive power. Intensely religious and devoted to the Presbyterian Church, he was, to a degree marked even in his generation, motivated by a sense of personal accountability to an ever-present God. He was particularly interested in judicial reforms, banking, and humanitarian legislation. He introduced bills in 1815 to prevent dueling and in 1817 to erect a state penitentiary, and he vigorously opposed the popular anti-bank movement in the session of 1828–29. He was speaker in 1814.

However, he attained chief distinction as a jurist. A notable career as superior court judge from 1818 to 1826 and again from 1836 to 1844 brought about his appointment in 1844, upon the death of William Gaston, to the supreme court, of which he remained a judge until his death, and in 1852 he was chosen by his associates as chief justice, succeeding Thomas Ruffin. Though not so brilliant as Gaston, or so powerful in logic as Ruffin, he was a worthy successor and a sound and able judge, whose learning, industry, evenness of temper, character, courtesy, and respect for truth and justice brought distinction to him and greater popular respect to the court. His opinions are characterized by clearness of legal conception, terseness of style, and cogency of reasoning (54–56 *N. C. Reports*).

In his political career he was a nominal Republican, though he voted against legislative resolutions praising the national administration in 1804 and 1815. He indorsed Jackson's nullification proclamation in 1832, but his opposition to the anti-bank policy of the administration and to what he considered a pronounced trend from republicanism toward pure democracy, led him into the Whig party. However, during his judicial career, he scrupulously refrained from public interest or activity in politics.

[Francis Nash Collection in possession of the N. C. Hist. Commission; Willie P. Mangum Papers in Lib. of Cong.; *The Papers of Thomas Ruffin*, ed. by J. G. deR. Hamilton, vols. I–III (1918–20); *The Papers of Archibald D. Murphey*, ed. by W. H. Hoyt (2 vols., 1914); *Biog. Hist. of N. C.*, ed. by S. A. Ashe, vol. I (1905); K. P. Battle, "An Address on the Hist. of the Supreme Court," 103 *N. C. Reports*, pp. 500–01; John H. Bryan "Memoir," *N. C. Univ. Mag.*, Dec. 1859.]
A. R. N.

NASH, HENRY SYLVESTER (Dec. 23, 1854–Nov. 6, 1912), Episcopal clergyman, teacher, and author, was born in Newark, Ohio, the son of Francis and Elizabeth (Burdett) Nash. He graduated at Harvard in the class of 1878, and at the Episcopal Theological School, Cambridge, Mass., in the class of 1881. He was ordained to the priesthood by Bishop Benjamin H. Paddock of Massachusetts, June 1, 1882, and at once became instructor in Biblical study and church polity in the Episcopal Theological School, being appointed later professor of literature and interpretation of the New Testament. Believing that a student should have practical experience in parochial work, he served for a time as assistant at Christ Church, Waltham, and on June 26, 1883, married Bessie Kiefler Curtis of that town. From 1889 to 1902, he was in charge of the Church of the Redeemer, Chestnut Hill, Newton, Mass. He was a preacher of rare power and originality and all his life was in frequent demand as a special preacher and lecturer, particularly in Massachusetts, Rhode Island, and New York.

On a generation of students for the ministry, he left the impression of a brave, versatile, original, and spiritual scholar, lifting them above the details of the lesson, opening up to them a wide vision, and forming within them a will to serve. In addition to his teaching and preaching, he found time for much writing. The first of his published works was *Genesis of the Social Conscience* (1897), originally prepared and delivered as the Lowell Lectures, Boston. This was followed by *Ethics and Revelation* (1899), *The History of the Higher Criticism of the New Testament* (1900), *The Belief in Democracy and Justification by Faith* (1903–04), and *The Atoning Life* (1908). His articles include "The Exegesis of the School of Antioch" (*Journal of Biblical Literature*, vol. XI, 1892), "The Nature and Definition of Religion" (*Harvard Theological Review*, January 1913). His *Genesis of the Social Conscience* was a book of much significance in its generalization and originality of statement, and discloses an intense interest in humanity. The supreme need, as he saw it, was "to get the world personalized." He was "a glad participant in the struggle for a truer democracy. . . . His own superb faith was a bridge for many who could not find their way alone" (New York *Evening Post*, Nov. 23, 1912). He was a brilliant conversationalist, and was fond of making extreme statements to emphasize his point. His spiritual nature expressed itself in beautiful devotional utterances which are preserved in *Prayers and Meditations* (1915).

[E. S. Drown, *Henry Sylvester Nash* (1913); *Official Bull. of the Episc. Theol. School*, Nov. 1912; *Who's Who in America*, 1912–13; *Harvard Coll., Class of 1878, Fiftieth Anniversary Report* (1928); *Harvard Grads. Mag.*, Mar. 1913; *Am. Ch. Almanac*, 1913; *Boston Transcript*, Nov. 6, 1912.]
D. D. A.

NASH, SIMEON (Sept. 21, 1804–Jan. 17, 1879), judge and author, the son of Simeon and Amy (White) Nash, was born at South Hadley, Mass. Both his mother and father were of English origin and of early colonial ancestry, his paternal ancestor, Thomas Nash, having been one of the signers of the Fundamental Agreement of New Haven in 1639. Prepared for college in the schools of South Hadley and in Hopkins Academy at Hadley, in spite of paternal opposition he entered Amherst College in 1825, where he was graduated in 1829. He began the study of law with Edward Hooker of South Hadley, while teaching Greek and mathematics in Woodbridge High School for boys there. On Dec. 16, 1831, he married Cynthia Smith of Granby, Mass. They had seven children. He left South Hadley to go to Gallipolis, Ohio, where he continued the study of law in the office of Samuel F. Vinton who represented his district for some time in Congress. In 1833 he was admitted to the bar of Ohio and settled in Gallipolis, which continued to be his home for the remainder of his life. He soon acquired an extensive legal practice. Elected to the Senate of Ohio, he sat in that body from 1839 to 1843. Refusing a third term he returned to the practice of law. In 1845 he was a member of a commission created by the legislature to inquire into the manner of spending the $14,000,000 which had been used in public works. The committee spent two years in its investigation and it is said that he traveled over 10,000 miles along the lines of public work and about the state gathering evidence. At the end of two years the committee made a report revealing much corruption and fraud. In 1850 he was elected a member of the convention called to draft a new constitution of that state. He was one of the most active and distinguished members of the body and as much as any one was responsible for the results accomplished. In 1851 he was elected a judge of the court of common pleas of Ohio, in which position he served with distinction for the following ten years. After leaving the bench he returned again to the practice of law in the city of Gallipolis, Ohio, for the remainder of his life.

Distinguished as he was as a lawyer and as a judge and in public office, it is probably as an author that he was best known. He was the author of *A Digest of Decisions of the Supreme Court of Ohio* (1853), devoted to the cases in the *Ohio Reports* from 1821 to 1851. By far the most important of his books was that on the civil code. Although raised under the common law pleadings and bitterly opposed to the adoption in 1851 of the civil code, after it was adopted he felt the need of a book upon the subject for the use of the lawyers of the state who were unfamiliar with anything but the common law pleadings. He, therefore, set himself to the task of writing such a work and his *Pleadings and Practice under the Civil Code* (1856) was of invaluable service to the bar. In fact, so useful was this book that it ran into five editions, the latest edition being published in two volumes in 1906-07, under the editorship of Hiram L. Sibley. He also wrote two books of less purely professional interest, *Morality and the State* (1859), a philosophical attempt to analyze man's moral and spiritual nature, and *Crime and the Family* (1876) which expressed some early ideas that later were embodied in the juvenile-court movement.

[*The Biog. Encyc. of Ohio* (1876); *Amherst College Biog. Record of the Grads.* (1927); Henry Howe, *Hist. Colls. of Ohio* centennial ed., vol. I (1889); *The*

Nash Family; or Records of the Descendants of Thomas Nash (1853), collected by Sylvester Nash.]
                                                A. H. T.

NASON, ELIAS (Apr. 21, 1811–June 17, 1887), schoolmaster, writer, lecturer, and Congregational clergyman, was born at Wrentham, Mass., the son of Levi and Sarah (Newton) Nason, and a descendant of Willoughby Nason who came to Massachusetts before 1691. His father was a farmer at Wrentham, Hopkinton, Medway, and Ashland successively, and Elias attended schools in all these towns. In 1826 he entered the paper-mill of David Bigelow & Company at Framingham, and for five years divided his time between making paper and attending school. In 1831, after a year's study under Chauncey Colton and Justin Perkins at Amherst, he entered Brown University, where he supported himself by teaching school during the winters. He graduated in 1835, and for five months was principal of the Cambridge Latin Grammar School. He then sailed for Charleston with John E. Holbrook [*q.v.*], the naturalist, and lived for four years in Georgia, where he edited a newspaper, was principal of an academy at Waynesboro, and lectured on botanical subjects. His active sympathy for the negroes more than once endangered his life. On Nov. 28, 1836, he married Myra Anne Bigelow, of Framingham, Mass., by whom he had six children.

Moving to Newburyport, Mass., in 1840, he opened a school for young ladies, and in 1844 became principal of the high school, and later of the Latin School. He also kept a book store in partnership with his brother, contributed to magazines, gave popular lectures on a variety of subjects, and is said to have edited a periodical called the *Watch Tower*. In the year 1849 he was licensed to preach, and became principal of the high school at Milford. After missing by two votes election as master of the Boston Latin School, he was in May 1852 ordained minister of the Congregational church in Natick. In 1858 he took charge of the Mystic Church, Medford, and from 1861 to 1865 was pastor of a church at Exeter, N. H. During the Civil War he served on the Christian Commission, visited the seat of war, and was an ardent advocate of the Union. In 1865 he bought a farm at North Billerica, which remained his home until his death. In 1866 and 1867 he edited the *New-England Historical and Genealogical Register*. From 1876 to 1884 he served as pastor of a church in Lowell (variously known as the Pawtucket Church and as the Centre Church of Dracut). He traveled widely as a popular lecturer, and contributed often to Congregationalist periodicals.

Nason knew something of every branch of

science, could read twelve languages, and was a skilled musician. As a lecturer he was distinguished by his pleasing address, his fervor of manner, and the apt and homely illustrations which he derived from conversations with mechanics and laborers. He published some thirty-nine books and pamphlets, of which the most important were *Congregational Hymn Book* (1857); *Sir Charles Henry Frankland, Baronet: or Boston in the Colonial Times* (1865); *A Memoir of Mrs. Susannah Rowson* (1870); *The Life and Public Services of Hon. Henry Wilson* (1872), in collaboration with Thomas Russell; *The Life and Times of Charles Sumner* (1874); *The American Evangelists, Dwight L. Moody and Ira D. Sankey* (copr. 1877); *A Gazetteer of the State of Massachusetts* (1874); *A History of Dunstable, Mass.* (1877), and *A Literary History of the Bible* (1881).

[W. B. Trask, in *New-Eng. Hist. and Geneal. Reg.*, Jan. 1889; *Hist. Cat. Brown Univ.* (1914); *Congregationalist*, June 23, 1887; A. C. Varnum, *Hist. of Pawtucket Church and Society* (1888); J. J. Currier, *Hist. of Newburyport, 1864–1905*, vol. I (1906); *Boston Post*, June 18, 1887.]   H. B. P.

NASON, HENRY BRADFORD (June 22, 1831–Jan. 18, 1895), educator, was born at Foxboro, Mass., the son of Elias and Susanna (Keith) Nason. His father and Levi, the father of Elias Nason [*q.v.*], were half-brothers. Henry was graduated from Williston Seminary, Easthampton, Mass., in 1851, and from Amherst College in 1855, then studied at Göttingen (1855–57), where he obtained his doctor's degree, at Heidelberg, and at Freiberg. Returning to the United States, he taught for a year at the Raymond Collegiate Institute, Carmel, N. Y., and in 1858 became professor of natural history in Rensselaer Polytechnic Institute. Until 1866, when he was appointed professor of chemistry and natural science at Rensselaer, he also taught natural history at Beloit College, Beloit, Wis., dividing his time between the two institutions. He retained his professorship at Rensselaer until his death. In Troy he married, Sept. 7, 1864, Frances Kellogg Townsend, by whom he had a son and a daughter.

As adviser to the Standard Oil Company, 1880–90, he introduced a number of improvements in the process of treating crude oil. In 1881 he was appointed inspector under the New York State Board of Health to eliminate nuisances due to the use of petroleum. He was later delegated by the United States, which he had represented at the Paris Exposition of 1878, to attend the International Congress called to consider the same subject. In connection with his studies in geology and mineralogy, to which, be-

cause of traditions at Rensselaer Polytechnic Institute, he was increasingly attracted, he also visited most countries in Europe and all the principal mining areas of the United States. Except, however, for advancements in technique, particularly in the analytical procedures applicable to the problems of geology and mineralogy, he appears to have done little original work in chemistry. Even his *Table of Reactions for Qualitative Analysis* (1865) and his *Table for Qualitative Analysis in Colors* (1870) are largely compilations based to a considerable extent upon results obtained in the laboratories of the Institute. His most useful service was that of translator, editor, and organizer of scientific activities. At Rensselaer he not only continued the scholarly traditions established by his predecessors, William Elderhorst and Charles Anthony Goessman [*q.v.*], both of whom were educated in Germany, but he also published *Handbook of Mineral Analysis* (1871), translated, with some revision, from the German of Friedrich Wöhler, and with Charles F. Chandler [*q.v.*] edited *Elderhorst's Manual of Qualitative Blowpipe Analysis, and Determinative Mineralogy* (6th ed., 1873, and subsequent editions).

Gifted with an easy address and an affable manner, he was prominent in the organization of the Geological Society of America and the American Chemical Society, of which he was president in 1889–90, and participated actively in the affairs of the General Alumni Association of Rensselaer Polytechnic Institute, which he served as secretary, 1872–86. In this capacity he prepared the *Proceedings of the Semi-Centennial Celebration of the Rensselaer Polytechnic Institute, Troy, N. Y., with a Catalogue of Officers and Students, 1824–74* (1875) and the more important *Biographical Record of the Officers and Graduates of the Rensselaer Polytechnic Institute, 1824–86* (1887), which throws considerable light upon the development of science and engineering in the United States.

[*Proc. of the Semi-Centennial Celebration of the Rensselaer Poly. Inst.* (1875); H. B. Nason, *Biog. Record Officers and Grads. Rensselaer Poly. Inst.* (1887); P. C. Ricketts, *Hist. of Rensselaer Poly. Inst.* (1914); W. P. Mason, in *Jour. Am. Chem. Soc.*, May 1895; *New-Eng. Hist. and Geneal. Reg.*, Jan. 1889; files of the *Polytechnic*, esp. issue for Jan. 26, 1895; *N. Y. Tribune*, Jan. 19, 1895.]   R. P. B.

NASSAU, ROBERT HAMILL (Oct. 11, 1835–May 6, 1921), missionary in Africa, the son of Charles William and Hannah McClintock (Hamill) Nassau, was born at Montgomery Square, near Norristown, Pa. He pursued the studies of the freshman year at Lafayette College, where his father was for some time a professor. The next year he spent in the high school at Lawrenceville, N. J., conducted by his mother's brothers. He then entered the College of New Jersey, from which he graduated in 1854. After teaching in Lawrenceville, he studied three years in Princeton Theological Seminary (1856–59). In 1859 he asked the Presbyterian Board of Foreign Missions to send him to its most difficult and dangerous post. He was appointed to the Corisco or West Africa mission, on the west coast, a degree north of the equator. To prepare himself further, he studied medicine at the University of Pennsylvania, receiving his degree in 1861. On July 2 of that year he was ordained to the Presbyterian ministry; September saw him at Corisco.

In this region, a French protectorate inhabited by Bantu tribes, there had been American missionaries since 1842. On Corisco Island, the headquarters of the Presbyterian mission, Nassau taught and preached for four years, working also over a wide stretch of mainland coast. He was married on Sept. 17, 1862, to Mary Cloyd Latta, a missionary in his station, who died in 1870. After he had mastered the Benga language, his pioneering instinct moved him to take charge of the mission's first station on the mainland, at Benito, fifty miles north of Corisco. Here he worked for six years, going out to preach along a hundred miles of coast, and penetrating as far up the Benito River. During a furlough in the United States in 1872–73, he was instructed to found a missionary station in the interior, a project which native opposition had thus far prevented. In 1874 he ascended the Ogowai (Ogowe) River, which enters the Atlantic seventy miles south of the equator, and there served for seventeen years. He learned well the Mpongwe and Fang dialects and the characters of the peoples. He established two stations—the furthest two hundred miles up the Ogowai—which proved permanent missionary centers, and organized four churches. On a furlough in 1881 he was married at Lakewood, N. J., Oct. 10, to Mary Brunette Foster, who died in 1884. Relieved in 1891, he spent two years in the United States, and then had three more terms in Africa, in 1893–98, 1900–03, and 1904–06. In these years he worked at Libreville and at Batanga, on the coast a hundred and twenty-five miles north of Corisco. There his duties were so arranged as to allow him to write his *Fetichism in West Africa* (1904). In 1906 he retired, after forty-five years of service. During 1907–08 he had charge of churches in Florida. His last eleven years, in which he wrote several books, were passed in Ambler, Pa.

To make Nassau an effective missionary there combined rare linguistic ability, intimate knowledge of African thought and customs, shrewd judgment of the character of the natives and skill in managing them, a resourceful, original mind, and never-flagging zeal. Somewhat conventional in his piety, he was anything but this in his methods. He was ahead of his time in using industrial training for missionary purposes. His cherished Winchester rifle figures largely in his journals of missionary labors. He was selfless in surrender to his task, yet amusingly egotistical. Along with consuming missionary devotion he carried other interests. He did valuable work in recording African folkstories, published in *Where Animals Talk* (1912), *In an Elephant Corral* (1912), and *Batanga Tales* (1915). His *Fetichism in West Africa* is a treasury of knowledge of African religion, and contains also a sketch of Bantu sociology. He sent home zoölogical and entomological specimens. With associates he translated the Old Testament and part of the New into Benga. These versions were published in original and revised forms between 1863 and 1881. His missionary activity was described, often minutely and vividly, in books of which the most important are *Tales Out of School* (1911), *Corisco Days: the First Thirty Years of the West African Mission* (1910), and *My Ogowe* (1914). During his furloughs he made many missionary speeches and became a well-known and striking figure in ecclesiastical meetings. By his first wife he had three sons, and by his second, a daughter.

[Annual reports of the Board of Foreign Missions of the Presbyterian Church in the U. S. A.; personal information and autobiog. sketch (MS.) in library of this board; *Biog. Cat. Princeton Theol. Sem.* (1933); *Princeton Theol. Sem. Bull., Necrological Report*, Aug. 1921; *Presbyterian* (Phila.), May 26, 1921; *Who's Who in America*, 1920–21; *Public Ledger* (Phila.), May 8, 1921.]
                                        R. H. N.

NAST, THOMAS (Sept. 27, 1840–Dec. 7, 1902), cartoonist, was born in Landau, Germany, where his father was a musician in the 9th Bavarian Regiment. In 1846 his mother took him to New York, where four years later his father, who had left Germany for political reasons and had enlisted in the French navy, joined them. The elder Nast, whose name is given in the city directory as Thomas, became a member of the Philharmonic Society and of various theatrical orchestras, while the boy attended the public schools. A gift of crayons by a neighbor led young Nast to develop a passion for drawing. After attending a class taught by the artist Theodore Kaufmann, he entered the

Academy of Design, receiving also much personal instruction from Alfred Fredericks. At fifteen he showed some of his sketches to the publisher Frank Leslie, received a trial commission to draw the Sunday-morning crowd at Christopher Street Ferry, and was promptly engaged by *Frank Leslie's Illustrated Newspaper* at four dollars a week. The office, frequented by some of the best illustrators of the period, was an excellent practical school. Sol Eytinge of the staff gave him invaluable technical training, while Nast carefully studied the methods of the English illustrators, Leech, Gilbert, and Tenniel. When in 1857 *Harper's Weekly* began its career he resolved to contribute, and his first important drawing, a page savagely satirizing a current police scandal in New York, appeared in it on Mar. 19, 1859. When later that same year the *New York Illustrated News* was established he left *Leslie's*, and covered important assignments for the new periodical, including the funeral of John Brown. The great Heenan-Sayers fight in 1860 drew him to England, and Garibaldi's revolt of that year led him to extend his tour to Italy, whence he sent pictures of the fighting to both London and New York periodicals. He returned to America on Feb. 1, 1861, with a dollar and a half in his pocket, and on Sept. 26, 1861, the day before his twenty-first birthday, he was married to Sarah Edwards. It was characteristic both of his self-confidence and love of music that his first purchase was a $350 piano on credit.

Following the outbreak of the Civil War, Nast quickly found his true rôle. He hurried to Baltimore and Washington, publishing his drawings at first in the tottering *New York Illustrated News*, then briefly renewing his connection with *Leslie's*, and finally contributing sketches to *Harper's Weekly*. In the summer of 1862 he became a staff artist for the last-named journal. Fletcher Harper, who was in charge of the *Weekly*, perceived his talent, and encouraged him to follow his own bent, making pictures with ideas rather than illustrations of events. By 1863 he was recognized as one of the pillars of the journal. His spirited drawing, "After the Battle," on Oct. 25, 1862, aimed at those who opposed vigorous prosecution of the war, his touching double-page Christmas picture of that year, his pictorial arraignments of guerrilla warfare in the border states, and his "Emancipation" of Jan. 24, 1863, depicting negro life of the past and the future, all produced a powerful impression. Several pictures of 1864, notably his spirited "On to Richmond" on June 18, and his sardonic sketch, "Compromise with the South"

on Sept. 3, just after the Democratic Convention (showing a triumphant Southerner clasping hands with a crippled Northern soldier over the grave of Union heroes), were circulated in tremendous numbers. Lincoln declared near the close of the war: "Thomas Nast has been our best recruiting sergeant" (Harper, *post,* p. 188). The Reconstruction cartoons expressed a bitterness which often became intemperate, notably in the portrayal of Andrew Johnson as a bully and dictator, and of Southerners as engaged in outrages upon the defenseless negroes; but they marked an advance in the art of political caricature. In 1866 he began his very effective use of Shakespearian situations as vehicles for his ideas. Ablest of all were the fierce attacks he maintained in the years 1869-72 upon the "Tweed ring," to the overthrow of which he contributed as much as any single man. Caricature has seldom if ever been more eloquent and impressive than in his drawings, "The Tammany Tiger Let Loose" (Nov. 11, 1871), "Who Stole the People's Money?" (Aug. 19, 1871), and "A Group of Vultures Waiting for the Storm to 'Blow Over'" (Sept. 23, 1871). His final triumph was the apprehension of Tweed in Spain through a cartoon which made him recognizable even in that country.

Throughout the 'seventies and until 1886 Nast remained one of the greatest influences in American journalism. While the policies of *Harper's Weekly* were dictated by G. W. Curtis and Fletcher Harper, Nast's pen was the most distinctive element in the journal. He made Greeley ludicrous in the campaign of 1872, mercilessly ridiculed the political hobgoblin of Grant's "Caesarism," defended Hayes against Tilden, and forsook the Republican party only when Blaine was nominated. The Tammany tiger, which he had popularized, was borrowed from the Americus Club emblem, but the Democratic donkey and Republican elephant were his own inventions, both becoming fixed in his pictures in 1874. Following his own inclination as well as that of the editors of *Harper's Weekly,* he stanchly upheld sound money and currency reform and was a devoted adherent of Grover Cleveland. In 1885 and 1886 his contributions to the *Weekly* grew fewer, he chafed under restrictions which he felt robbed his pen of its old slashing vigor, and his Christmas picture of 1886 was his last. For a time he contributed to other journals and in 1892-93 briefly managed a sheet called *Nast's Weekly,* but his great days were over. He had lost most of his savings, amassed in lecturing as well as journalism, by the Grant & Ward failure. In May 1902, Theodore Roosevelt appointed him consul at Guayaquil, Ecuador, where he succumbed to the climate.

[A. B. Paine, *Th. Nast: His Period and His Pictures* (1904), is an exceptionally interesting biography, fully illustrated, but sometimes lacking in definite facts. A few details are supplied by J. Henry Harper in *The House of Harper* (1912). A son, Cyril Nast, published "Thomas Nast as I Knew Him," in the *Am. Art Student*, Feb. 1927. A three-volume scrapbook collection of Nast's pictures is available in the N. Y. Pub. Lib. He illustrated a number of books, but the indispensable repository of his work is the files of *Harper's Weekly*. Obituaries appeared in *N. Y. Times*, Dec. 8, 1902; *Harper's Weekly*, Dec. 29, 1902.]   A. N.

NAST, WILLIAM (June 15, 1807–May 16, 1899), Methodist Episcopal clergyman and editor, founder of the first German Methodist church in the United States, was born in Stuttgart, Württemberg. His father, Johann Wilhelm, was a government official; his mother, Elisabetha Magdalena Ludovika (Böhm), the daughter of an Austrian officer. Both parents died in Nast's early childhood and his rearing was left in the hands of an elder sister, Frau Dr. Süsskind. He attended school at Stuttgart and at Vaihingen-an-der-Enz, and after his confirmation (1821) he entered the theological seminary at Blaubeuren. Earlier, he had attended meetings of the Pietists, and had read Arndt, Spener, Francke, and Thomas à Kempis. At the seminary Nast had as his roommate David Friedrich Strauss, later the well-known disciple of Ferdinand Christian Baur, and though for a time young Nast fought against the current rationalistic intellectual tendencies, he finally gave way to the *Zeitgeist,* and at the age of eighteen entered the University of Tübingen. After two years of study he left the university in a whirl of doubt, and after wandering about, visiting Vienna, Munich, and Dresden, he finally took the advice of his brother-in-law, Dr. Süsskind, and came to America.

Arriving in 1828, he secured a position as tutor in a Methodist family on Duncan's Island, near Harrisburg, Pa., where he had a pleasant home, gained his first impressions of Methodism, and became acquainted with several Methodist ministers. In 1832 he went to West Point as librarian and instructor in German, and here amidst the "godless atmosphere of the military academy" he felt again the call to the ministry. Another period of confusion of mind now followed. Wandering more or less aimlessly about, he finally came to the communistic community of Württembergers at Economy, Pa., where he remained for a time, working in the fields. Through Bishop McIlvaine of the Protestant Episcopal Church he secured a position as teacher of Greek and Hebrew at Kenyon College, Gambier, Ohio. Here he became acquainted with

a pious Methodist shoemaker, who took him to a nearby Methodist quarterly meeting. Finally, he made the definite decision to enter the Methodist ministry, and was admitted on trial to the Ohio Conference.

Just at this time T. A. Morris, editor of the *Western Christian Advocate,* the Methodist journal at Cincinnati, was urging that work be begun among the rapidly increasing German population, and in 1835 Nast was appointed German missionary to Cincinnati. Among his early converts was John Swahlen, who became the co-founder with Nast of German Methodism. Nast was soon traveling over Ohio and adjoining states, averaging some three hundred miles per month, visiting German communities. In 1838 he was able to organize the first German Methodist church in the city of Cincinnati. In September of the same year a German church-paper, *Der Christliche Apologete,* was founded (first issue January 1839), with Nast as the editor, a position which he held for some fifty-three years. Besides editing this paper, he busied himself with extensive writing and translating and was the founder of German Methodist Christian literature in America. Among his most important publications were *Das Leben und Wirken des Johannes Wesley und Seiner Haupt-mitarbeiter* (1852); *Die Aufgabe der Christlichen Kirche im neunzehnten Jahrhundert* (1857); a commentary in German on the gospels of Matthew and Mark (*c.* 1862), with an English edition in 1864; *Das Christentum und seine Gegensätze* (1883).

Nast made several journeys to Europe in the interest of his work; in 1844 he was permitted by the General Conference to visit Germany; in 1857 he attended the meeting of the Evangelical Alliance at Berlin, where he delivered an address on Methodism; and in 1877 he again visited Germany and Switzerland. He was one of the founders of German Wallace College at Berea, Ohio, originally a department of Baldwin University, and a separate institution from 1863 to 1913, when it was merged with Baldwin to form Baldwin-Wallace College. For many years he was nominally its president. On Aug. 1, 1836, he married Margaret Eliza McDowell, of a Scotch Presbyterian family of Cincinnati. Of the five children born to them, three were living at the time of Nast's death.

[The best source is C. Golder, J. H. Horst, and J. B. Schall, *Geschichte der Zentral Deutschen Konferenz, Einschliesslich der Anfangsgeschichte des deutschen Methodismus* (Cincinnati, n.d.) ; see also Adam Miller, *Experience of German Methodist Preachers* (1859) ; files of *Der Christliche Apologete* ; Rudolf Krauss, in *Biographisches Jahrbuch und Deutscher Nekrolog.*, vol. IV (1900) ; *Western Christian Advocate*, Feb. 10, 1837; *Cincinnati Enquirer*, May 17, 1899.]   W. W. S.

NATION, CARRY AMELIA MOORE (Nov. 25, 1846–June 9, 1911), temperance agitator, was born in Garrard County, Ky., the daughter of George Moore, a prosperous stock-dealer and planter who was the descendant of a pioneer Irish settler in the region, and of Mary Campbell who was descended by way of Virginia from the Scotch clan of Campbell and related to Alexander Campbell, the religious leader. The name "Carry" is correctly so spelled because her unlettered father wrote it thus in the family Bible at her birth. Her mother developed a psychosis, probably of a manic-depressive type with grandiose delusions that she was Queen Victoria, and her appetite for extravagant dress and equipage was humored by her family. Mrs. Moore spent the last three years of her life in the Missouri State Hospital for the Insane, and her mother, brother, and sister were also insane. The Moores and Campbells were slave-holders, and Carry's childhood was strongly influenced by the superstitious lore and religious excitements of the negroes. At ten she underwent a spectacular conversion in a "protracted meeting." Moore had a *Wanderlust,* and before Carry was sixteen the family had lived in a dozen counties of Kentucky, Missouri, and Texas. Her schooling was brief and sporadic. She attended for a time boarding schools in Missouri and the State Normal School at Warrensburg, where she received a teaching certificate. Throughout this period she was a semi-invalid from digestive troubles.

Moore's fortunes were broken by the Civil War. Stripped of his property and slaves after a disastrous venture in Texas, he returned in 1865 to Belton, Mo. There Carry met and married (Nov. 21, 1867) her first and only love, Dr. Charles Gloyd, a young physician and Union veteran from Ohio. Gloyd was addicted to liquor, and all his bride's reform efforts were wasted. He was a Mason and spent much time roistering at the lodge, which incited in her a permanent hatred of fraternal orders. After a few wretchedly unhappy months she was persuaded by her parents to abandon Gloyd, who died of alcoholism six months later, leaving her with an infant daughter, Charlien, her only child, who lived to a weak and insane maturity. For the next four years she taught in a primary school at Holden, Mo., supporting her child and her mother-in-law. In 1877 she married David Nation, a lawyer, minister, and editor nineteen years older than herself. They had little in common and were constantly bickering. Nation assisted her in some of her public activities but he disapproved of her extremism in religion and reform. The

Nations spent ten futile years in small towns of Texas, where Carry, with the most arduous labor, supported the family by running hotels. At this period she had many mystic experiences. In 1889 Nation removed to Medicine Lodge, Kan., near the Oklahoma border, to become pastor of the Christian Church, but shortly resigned to practise law. He divorced her for desertion in 1901.

Kansas was one of the original prohibition states, a constitutional amendment having been voted in 1880. Despite stringent enforcement laws, there were numerous "joints" where liquor was sold more or less openly. In 1890 the United States Supreme Court held that liquor shipped into Kansas and sold from the "original package" was subject only to the interstate commerce laws. The "wets," financed by distilleries which flooded the state with liquor, almost secured the resubmission of the amendment. Carry Nation was soon deeply involved in this struggle. She organized a branch of the Woman's Christian Temperance Union and with a few militant women began a campaign to expel the "jointists" from Medicine Lodge. So far as she had a definite theory of action, it was that since the saloon was illegal in Kansas, it was permissible for any citizen to force his way in and destroy not only liquor but furniture and fixtures. Saloon property, she avowed, "has no rights that anybody is bound to respect."

In the spring of 1900, always supported by "visions" of her divinely infallible mission, her activities spread rapidly and with increasing violence to neighboring towns and counties. In Wichita she wrecked the Hotel Carey and other expensive saloons, smashing mirrors, windows, bars, panelling, pornographic paintings, and liquor stocks valued at thousands of dollars. It was here that she first used the hatchet which became her distinctive weapon, and was confined in the Sedgwick County jail for seven weeks, when she was released on a writ of *habeas corpus.* In her subsequent career through Enterprise, Danville, Winfield, and Leavenworth, to Topeka, the capital, where she invaded the governor's chambers, and later in New York, Washington, Pittsburgh, Rochester, San Francisco, and other large cities, she was arrested some thirty times, usually on such charges as "disturbing the peace." Her numerous fines she paid from her earnings by the sale of souvenir hatchets, lecture tours, and stage appearances. She never became wealthy, but for half a dozen years she sometimes earned as much as $300 a week. At one time she was under the managership of the Furlong Lyceum Bureau, and later employed her own manager, Harry C. Turner. She had little business sense and was excessively generous, giving large sums to the poor and to temperance projects, and was easy prey for swindlers. She built a home for drunkards' wives at Kansas City, Kan. Among other propaganda methods she carried on several short-lived publishing ventures, such as *The Smasher's Mail, The Hatchet, The Home Defender,* and published her autobiography. She was often in physical danger of reprisal from her enemies and was frequently clubbed, cut, shot at, or otherwise attacked.

Her later years were marked by numerous melodramatic experiences, for her notoriety was now international. She visited several American universities, including Harvard and Yale, which she denounced as "hellholes"; the students greeted her with wild burlesque. In 1908 she toured the British Isles but was antagonistically received. Increasing feebleness compelled her retirement to a farm in the Ozark Mountains of Arkansas. Her last five months were spent in a Leavenworth hospital with a clouded and apathetic mind. She was buried in the family plot at Belton, Mo., where friends later erected a monument inscribed, "She hath done what she could."

Carry Nation was a woman of commanding presence, nearly six feet tall, weighing 175 pounds, with extremely muscular arms. She dressed in a sort of black-and-white deaconess uniform. Her fierceness and garrulity when aroused were proverbial. Her invective was amazingly vigorous, couched in a King James version of billingsgate. An ignorant, unbalanced, and contentious woman of vast energies, afflicted with an hereditary paranoia, she was subjected to early hardships and mystic seizures which fused all her powers into a flaming enmity to intoxicating liquor and its corrupt purveyors. During her crusading years the temperance advocates were sharply divided on the righteousness of her tactics, and although many indorsed her work, she never received the whole-hearted support of any national body. The tangible results of her activities in her own lifetime were slight beyond the closure and intimidation of many saloons and the probable prevention of a "backward step" by the Kansas legislature. In a very real sense, however, she was the spearhead as well as the goad of an aroused public opinion against the saloon. When in 1920 the long drive for constitutional prohibition reached its goal, Carry Nation had been largely forgotten, but a just appraisal of the social and psychological forces contributing to that end must certainly give her a large, if unpremeditated, place in the furthering of the program for forcible prohibition.

[Her autobiography, *The Use and Need of the Life of Carry A. Nation* (1904), of which 56,000 copies were sold in five years; Herbert Asbury, *Carry Nation* (1929), a definitive life, on the whole sympathetic and impartial, by a sophisticated modern; J. L. Dwyer, "The Lady with the Hatchet," *American Mercury,* March 1926; *American Monthly Review of Reviews,* March 1901; *Current Literature,* March, 1901; *Outlook,* Feb. 9, 1901; *Literary Digest,* Feb. 15, 1919; obituaries in *N. Y. Times, Leavenworth* (Kan.) *Times,* June 10, 1911.]
K. M. G.

NAVARRE, PIERRE (Mar. 28, 1790?–Mar. 20, 1874), fur-trader and scout in the War of 1812, was born in Detroit. His grandfather was a well-known settler, Robert Navarre; his father, François *dit* Hutro (or Utreau) Navarre. His mother, through her mother, was a member of the Campau family, probably Marie Louise Godet, though Pierre at one time gave her name as Marie Louise Panat Campau. He was also inconsistent in giving his age and was generally considered to be eighty-nine at the time of his death, although he was probably five years younger. The family moved to the River Raisin country when Pierre was still young, but it was not until about 1807 that he and his elder brother, Robert, built the cabin near the mouth of the Maumee which was to be Pierre's permanent home. The boy, inured to the woods and skilled in Indian ways, became a fur-trader, and is said to have traded with the Miamis at Fort Wayne, where he made the friendship of Chief Little Turtle [*q.v.*].

When the War of 1812 disrupted the border trade, Navarre and three of his brothers joined the army of Gen. William Hull. They were included in the surrender of Detroit, but, released on parole, went to the River Raisin, where they served as scouts to Gen. James Winchester. They managed to escape from the massacre in January 1813, and a little later, Navarre became a scout in William Henry Harrison's army. Many tales were told in later years of his daring adventures: of his great speed in carrying messages over the wilderness trails; of his courageous escape after capture by the British; of his racing the British to carry the news of their approach to Fort Stephenson. He was present at the battle of the Thames, where his services were valuable because of the respect that the Indians in the British service had for his abilities. Navarre himself said that he witnessed the death of Tecumseh and that he was one of the soldiers detailed to bury that chief.

After the war, he devoted himself again to the fur trade, and was probably the Pierre Navarre who was employed as a trader in the St. Joseph's and Kankakee Outfit of the American Fur Company in 1820. After a disagreement with his superior, Navarre was discharged, only to be hired by William H. Wallace, another Company trader, to trade near Terre Haute, Ind. He was again discharged. Later Navarre left the fur trade and spent the rest of his life on his farm near Toledo. In 1864 a special bill was introduced into Congress to grant him a pension of eight dollars a month. The bill was reported adversely by the Senate committee, but the pension was later granted and helped to swell his scanty income in the last years of his life. As an old settler and a veteran of the War of 1812, he was held in some respect at Toledo. He served for a time as president of the Maumee Valley Pioneer Association. He was twice married: in 1825 to Geneveva Robert, who died in 1827, and some time later, to Catherine Bourdeau. He was survived by several children, two of his sons having served in the Civil War.

[Clark Waggoner, *Hist. of the City of Toledo and Lucas County, Ohio* (1888); H. L. Hosmer, *Early Hist. of the Maumee Valley* (1858); *Pioneer Colls., Report of the Pioneer Soc. . . . of Mich.*, esp. vol. V (1884); *Cong. Globe*, 38 Cong., 1 Sess., pp. 1531, 2272, 2274, 2279; Christian Denissen, *Navarre, or Researches after the Descendants of Robert Navarre* (1879); *Toledo Times*, Feb. 2, 1931; Am. Fur Company Letterbooks (photostats), in Burton Hist. Coll., Detroit.]
W. B—*t*.

NEAGLE, JOHN (Nov. 4, 1796–Sept. 17, 1865), portrait painter, was born in Boston, his parents, Philadelphians, being in that city on a visit at the time of his birth. His father was a native of Doneraile, County Cork, Ireland; his mother, *née* Taylor, was the daughter of a New Jersey farmer. His father died when John was four years old and his mother married again. Her second husband, a grocer, was "no friend to John or to the arts." From Edward F. Petticolas, afterwards a well-known portrait painter and miniaturist in Richmond, Va., the boy received his first elementary instruction in drawing. After leaving the grammar school he was sent to a drawing school conducted by Pietro Ancora. For a short time he worked in his stepfather's grocery store; then, at his own suggestion, he was apprenticed to one Thomas Wilson, "coach and ornamental painter." This man had artistic aspirations, and was taking painting lessons of Bass Otis [*q.v.*], the portrait painter. Like master, like man: young Neagle, brought into casual contact with Otis, began to form plans to make an artist of himself. Out of his regular working hours he gave much time and energy to independent drawing and painting.

During his apprenticeship, which lasted more than five years, his employer allowed him to take painting lessons from Otis for about two months,

and Otis took him to call on Thomas Sully [*q.v.*] in his studio. He had already made his first essays in portraiture and his work had won the praise of Otis, Sully, and C. W. Peale. From the first he had a remarkable faculty for getting a good likeness. When his apprenticeship came to its end in 1818, he undertook what was then an arduous journey, traveling over the mountains all the way to Lexington, Ky., with the intention of settling there as a portrait painter; but to his surprise he found Matthew Harris Jouett [*q.v.*], an accomplished painter, was already well established in that part of the country, and it seemed useless to attempt to compete with him. Accordingly, Neagle determined to try New Orleans, but there he was wholly unknown and had no success in getting sitters. He returned, therefore, by sea to Philadelphia, deeply discouraged. William Dunlap [*q.v.*] gives a picturesque account of this episode (*post*, III, 167–68), which must have been given him by Neagle himself, with full details as to the precarious methods of financing his travels. After his return to Philadelphia the artist had little difficulty in securing all the sitters he could conveniently attend to. Beginning by charging only fifteen dollars for a head, he gradually increased his stipend as he became better known, until he could ask and get $100, which was then a handsome figure.

In May 1826 he married Mary Chester Sully, niece and step-daughter of Thomas Sully. In that year his picture, "Pat Lyon the Blacksmith," a full-length portrait commission, had a most enthusiastic reception and added greatly to his reputation. It was exhibited in Philadelphia and New York, and, owing partly to its intrinsic merit as a picture, but probably still more to certain interesting stories about Pat Lyon, had an amazing success. Lyon was a picturesque local figure. A master locksmith, he had been unjustly convicted of complicity in a bank robbery in Philadelphia and sentenced to a term in prison. When the real culprits were discovered, he was set free and awarded damages. The background of Neagle's picture is a glimpse of the city prison, seen through an open door or window. One can in imagination hear the brawny smith telling with relish of his adventures as he poses in his shirtsleeves and grimy leather apron to Neagle.

Neagle was fond of a good story. He went to Boston to see Gilbert Stuart, and there painted the best existing likeness of Stuart, now in the Boston Museum of Fine Arts. His notes of his studio intercourse with Stuart, which he placed at Dunlap's disposal, are of great value; he could not resist the temptation to record also the preposterous yarn told him by Stuart apropos of the pernicious habit of taking snuff. Neagle had his full share of eminent sitters, most of them Philadelphians. His portrait of Washington hangs in Independence Hall; that of Henry Clay is in the possession of the Union League Club. A replica of "Pat Lyon the Blacksmith" is in the Boston Athenæum. The Corcoran Gallery, Washington, owns his portrait of Col. Richard M. Johnson [q.v.], vice-president of the United States, 1837–41. In the Thomas B. Clarke collection of early American portraits there are eight by Neagle, including those of John Davis, governor of Massachusetts and United States senator, William Rush, the Philadelphia sculptor, and several other men of mark. For some years before his death Neagle was paralyzed. He died in Philadelphia in 1865.

[Wm. Dunlap, *A Hist. of the Rise and Progress of the Arts of Design in the U. S.* (2 vols., 1834; rev. ed., 3 vols., 1918); H. T. Tuckerman, *Book of the Artists* (1867); Samuel Isham, *The Hist. of Am. Painting* (1905); F. F. Sherman, *Early Am. Painting* (1932); Cat. of Gallery of Nat. Portraiture, Penn. Acad., 1905; Cat. of Thos. B. Clarke Coll. of portraits by early Am. artists, 1928; H. W. Henderson, *The Pa. Acad. of the Fine Arts* (1911); Virgil Barker, "John Neagle," *The Arts*, July 1925; *Art in America*, Aug. 1916, Aug. 1918; dates of birth and marriage from C. H. Hart, *A Reg. of Portraits Printed by Thos. Sully* (1909), which contains information from the Sully family Bible, *Press* (Phila.), Sept. 20, 1865.]　W. H. D—s.

NEAL, ALICE BRADLEY [See Haven, Emily Bradley, 1827–1863].

NEAL, DAVID DALHOFF (Oct. 20, 1838–May 2, 1915), historical and portrait painter, born at Lowell, Mass., the son of Stephen B. and Mary (Dalhoff) Neal, was of Dutch descent. His early education was received in the Lowell grammar schools, the Lawrence high school, and a private academy at Andover, N. H. Before coming of age he went to New Orleans, and thence via the Isthmus of Panama to San Francisco, where he found employment in making drawings on wood and painting an occasional portrait, though his artistic training had been of a very elementary character. In 1861 a rich Californian, S. P. Dewey, convinced that Neal had unusual talent and needed only the right sort of training to achieve fame as an artist, offered to supply him with sufficient money to take him to Europe and support him there for several years. He forthwith went to Munich and entered the Bavarian Royal Academy, where he worked in the antique classes for two years, and then became a pupil of Max Emanuel Ainmiller, best known as a painter on glass, whose daughter Marie he had married on Dec. 9, 1862. She died Sept. 29, 1897.

In 1869 Neal entered the atelier of Karl von Piloty, the historical painter, with whom he remained until 1876. He now began to devote himself wholly to figure painting. His first historical painting of importance was completed in 1876, and for it he was awarded the great medal of the Bavarian Royal Academy. The subject was "The First Meeting of Mary Stuart and Rizzio." Bought by D. O. Mills of San Francisco, it was exhibited in all the chief cities of the United States and was also extensively reproduced. The leading critics of the time were enthusiastic. Dr. Foerster wrote in the *Wartburg* of Munich that the scene was excellently conceived and represented in a most masterly manner; the critic of the *Zeitschrift für bildende Kunst* (1878) was equally emphatic in his praise.

Neal lived many years in Munich. Before coming under the influence of Piloty he had painted several interiors, including the "Chapel of the Kings, Westminster Abbey," and a "St. Mark's, Venice," both of which were exhibited at the Munich international exposition of 1869 and later at the National Academy in New York. Following the success of the "Mary Stuart and Rizzio" he produced his important picture of "Oliver Cromwell of Ely Visiting Mr. John Milton," which was shown in Munich, Vienna, Boston, and many other cities. It shows Cromwell when he was but a simple farmer and Milton in the full vigor of his youth, and has undeniable human interest. In execution it is typical of the Munich school of the nineteenth century, with bravura in the brushwork, and a heavy color scheme. Another large historical canvas, "James Watt," which was exhibited at the Royal Academy, London, became the property of Sir Benjamin S. Phillips, a former lord mayor of the City of London. In 1884 an exhibition of Neal's pictures was held at the galleries of Noyes & Blakeslee in Boston. The later years of the artist's life were for the most part devoted to portrait painting. Among his subjects were Whitelaw Reid, Mark Hopkins, D. O. Mills, William Henry Green, Adolph Sutro, and Judge Ogden Hoffman of California. He now divided his time between Europe and America, but Munich continued to be his home and he died there in 1915. Neal is one of the Americans trained in Munich of whom Isham remarks that they mastered the Munich technique and assimilated the Munich ideals so thoroughly that they reveal no trace of anything distinctly American.

[*Boston Transcript*, Mar. 19, 1884; Catalogue of Boston exhibit, Mar. 7–15, 1884; *Wartburg* (Munich), no. 9, 1876; *Chicago Tribune*, Mar. 24, 1878; E. Ransoni in *Neue Feie Presse* (Vienna), 1882; Samuel Isham, *The Hist. of Am. Painting* (1905); J. R. Tait, "David Neal." in *Mag. of Art*, Jan. 1886; Ulrich

Thieme and Felix Becker, *Allgemeines Lexikon der Bildenden Künstler*, vol. XXV (1931); *Who's Who in America*, 1914–15; *Am. Art News*, June 12, 1915; *Münchner Neeste Nachrichten*, May 4, 1915.]

W. H. D—s.

NEAL, JOHN (Aug. 25, 1793–June 20, 1876), author, editor, man of affairs, was the son of a Quaker schoolmaster of the same name, who died in September 1793, at Falmouth, now Portland, Me., leaving to his wife, Rachel (Hall) Neal, the rearing of their month-old twins, John and Rachel. The boy proved strong, active, and self-reliant, and after brief schooling was soon supporting himself as clerk in a succession of shops and then as itinerant teacher of penmanship and drawing in the Kennebec River towns. At twenty-two he found himself stranded in Baltimore, after the failure of a business venture there in partnership with John Pierpont [*q.v.*]. He then turned to the study of law, meanwhile writing for a living. During the next eight years he worked prodigiously, studying history, languages, and literature, besides the law, editing for brief periods the *Baltimore Telegraph* and the *Portico,* a magazine projected by the Delphians, a club of which he and Pierpont were members; compiling a considerable portion of *A History of the American Revolution* (2 vols., 1819) credited to Paul Allen [*q.v.*]; and writing actively for the *Portico* and other publications. His own works during this period include two spirited narrative poems published together as *Battle of Niagara, a Poem, without Notes; and Goldau, or, the Maniac Harper* (1818), under the pseudonym "Jehu O'Cataract"; a tragedy in verse, *Otho* (1819); and five novels: *Keep Cool* (1817); *Logan, a Family History* (1822), a highly romantic fictionizing of the celebrated Indian chieftain; *Errata, or the Works of Will Adams* (2 vols., 1823); *Seventy-Six* (1823), a historical romance, probably his best work; and *Randolph* (1823). Neal boasted (*Blackwood's*, February 1825, p. 197) that the novels were written in odd hours at breakneck speed—*Logan* in six or eight weeks, *Randolph* in thirty-six days, and *Seventy-Six* in twenty-nine—but this is doubtful. Aspersions in *Randolph* on the deceased William Pinkney brought a challenge from the latter's high-spirited son, Edward Coote Pinkney [*q.v.*], which Neal, who in *Keep Cool* had ridiculed the practice of dueling, rather ostentatiously ignored. At this time, according to his own account, he was dismissed from the Society of Friends "for knocking a man who insulted him head over heels; for paying a militia fine; for making a tragedy; and for desiring to be turned out, whether or no" (*Ibid.*, p. 190). His novels had a considerable sale, *Logan* and *Seventy-Six*

achieving English reprints, and he was the closest American rival of Cooper in fiction.

In December 1823, desirous of extending his literary reputation, he sailed for England. There he won access to the pages of *Blackwood's Magazine* in May 1824, with an astute survey of the candidates and issues in the current American presidential campaign. Then followed, in the chief British periodicals, some two dozen or more other long articles, written partly from the assumed viewpoint of an Englishman familiar with the United States, and with the design of creating better understanding and respect for America in England. Most notable was "American Writers" (*Blackwood's*, September 1824–February 1825), critical estimates of 135 different American authors, based solely upon memory and ranging in length from a single curt sentence to ten pages for Irving, eight for himself, four for Charles Brockden Brown, and a half page for his rival, Cooper. His own poems he characterized as "abounding throughout in absurdity, intemperance, affectation, extravagance—with continual, but involuntary imitation: yet, nevertheless, containing, altogether, more sincere poetry, more exalted, *original,* pure, bold poetry, than *all* the works, of *all* the other authors that have ever appeared in America" (issue of February 1825, p. 194). Blackwood published in July 1825 Neal's novel, *Brother Jonathan,* containing some good scenes from New England life. The later months of his stay abroad were spent in the household of the aged utilitarian, Jeremy Bentham, for whom Neal later became an enthusiastic spokesman in America, publishing in 1830 a translation of Bentham's *Principles of Legislation* from Dumont's French rendition, with a memoir of the author.

In the summer of 1827, Neal landed in New York, intending to practise law there. On a visit to his home, however, hearing of threats against him, based upon supposed reflections on local characters in his novels, he changed his plans and settled in Portland for life. Within ten years he had overcome prejudice against him; received the honorary degree of M.A. from Bowdoin (1836); published three more novels: *Rachel Dyer* (1828), *Authorship* (1830), and *The Down-Easters* (1833); done valuable pioneer work in organizing gymnasium classes; won some note as a public speaker, and established a fortune by prudent investments in Maine granite quarries. On Oct. 12, 1828, he married Eleanor Hall, his cousin, by whom he had five children. From January 1828 to the end of 1829 he edited a literary periodical, the *Yankee,* published first at Portland, later at Portland and

Boston in fusion with the *Boston Literary Gazette*. As writer of most of the articles he voiced his opinions on temperance, phrenology, utilitarianism, and other hobbies, and encouraged young contributors, among them Whittier and Poe. The latter remarked that Neal gave him "the very first words of encouragement I ever remember to have heard" (the *Yankee*, December 1829). Later Neal edited for short periods the *New England Galaxy*, at Boston, and a Portland newspaper. Stories and poems of his were published in the annuals, the *Atlantic Souvenir* and the *Token;* in Lowell's magazine, the *Pioneer;* and later in *Godey's, Graham's,* and several other periodicals.

After 1840 Neal devoted less attention to the law (*Wandering Recollections*, p. 182) and more to real-estate promotion and civic interests. His activities in the latter field brought him occasionally into bitter conflict with his cousin, "mischief-making, meddlesome Neal Dow" [q.v.]. In January and February 1843, at the New York Tabernacle, he delivered a series of addresses in behalf of woman's rights, culminating in a debate with Park Benjamin and Col. William L. Stone (Daggett, *post*, pp. 30–51). Later in that year, from May to December, he succeeded N. P. Willis [q.v.] as editor of the weekly *Brother Jonathan*, at New York, in which his novel "Ruth Elder" appeared as a serial. After 1850 he continued writing actively for periodicals, with contributions to the *North American Review, Harper's Magazine*, the *Northern Monthly* (Portland), the *Atlantic Monthly*, and numerous others. His later books included *One Word More* (1854), a religious treatise; another novel, *True Womanhood* (1859); three dime novels for Beadle, *The White Faced Pacer* (1863), *The Moose Hunter* (1864), and *Little Moccasin, or, Along the Madawaska* (1866); and *Great Mysteries and Little Plagues* (1870), a book "for and about children." The great fire of 1866 in Portland destroyed much of his property, but he threw himself whole-heartedly into the task of rebuilding the city. His pride in it is shown in *Portland Illustrated* (1874) and in frequent passages in his autobiography. This work, published as *Wandering Recollections of a Somewhat Busy Life*, was suggested to him by his lifelong friend, Longfellow, in 1859, but though thrice rewritten, it did not appear until 1869. Garrulous, ill-proportioned, and not wholly reliable, it is invaluable as self-portraiture. Neal died at Portland after a brief illness, in his eighty-third year.

His appearance was striking: his frame was not large but he was finely built and his physical strength and agility were remarkable. At seventy-nine, he threw into the street a hoodlum who persisted in smoking in a horsecar. He was fearless, energetic, easily angered by injustice or insult, but was ordinarily kindly and courteous, sympathetic to children, and chivalrous toward women. He was always enthusiastic about something—a characteristic which proved both a strength and a weakness in his writing. He wrote too hastily and voluminously. Poe in the *Southern Literary Messenger* (February 1836) and Lowell in *A Fable for Critics* (1848) attest his strength and genius but lament his wastefulness and lack of restraint.

[The major sources are Neal's *Wandering Recollections*, his sketch of himself in *Blackwood's*, Feb. 1825, and several hundred letters to his friends Pierpont, Longfellow, and others. An admirably full and authoritative biography, with an inclusive bibliography of other sources and of Neal's works, has recently been compiled by Irving T. Richards, but is as yet (1933) unpublished. An extensive collection of Neal's letters is also being edited by Professor Richards. Certain phases of his life are discussed in Windsor P. Daggett's preliminary sketch, *A Down East Yankee from the District of Maine* (1920). See also Hervey Allen, *Israfel* (2 vols., 1926); F. L. Mott, *A Hist. of Am. Mags., 1741–1850* (1930); W. B. Cairns, *A Hist. of Am. Lit.* (1912), pp. 208–09; *Daily Eastern Argus* (Portland), June 21, 1876.]

M. E—s.

NEAL, JOSEPH CLAY (Feb. 3, 1807–July 17, 1847), journalist and humorist, was born in Greenland, N. H., the only son of the Rev. James A. Neal and Christina (Palmer) Neal. The father had been principal of a school for girls in Philadelphia, but was compelled by failing health to live in the country, where he served as a Congregational minister. Upon his death in 1809 his widow returned to Philadelphia, and there her son grew to manhood. After the discovery of the anthracite coal fields near Pottsville, he spent some time in that vicinity, but returned to Philadelphia in 1831 to engage in newspaper work. The *Pennsylvanian*, a Democratic daily newspaper established in 1832, attracted him, and he soon became its editor. In 1836, with Morton McMichael and Louis A. Godey [qq.v.], he established the *Saturday News and Literary Gazette*, later *Neal's Saturday Gazette and Lady's Literary Museum*, of which he was editor until his death. In 1841–42 he visited Europe and Africa in the interest of his health. Six months before his sudden death, he married, in December 1846, Emily Bradley of Hudson, N. Y., who under the pen name of Alice G. Lee had sent many contributions to the *Saturday Gazette* [see Haven, Emily Bradley Neal].

As a political writer at a time when violent partisanship gave rise to vituperation and abuse, Neal was distinguished for his mild, urbane, and courteous attitude towards his political opponents. He met them with argument, or turned aside their shafts with pleasant irony and grotesque humor. But it was not as a political writer that he was best known. He is memorable chiefly as one of the most popular humorists of his day. His first humorous sketches, published under the title of "City Worthies," appeared in the *Pennsylvanian*. The "worthies" that he depicted were the idlers, the spendthrifts, the pretenders to fashion, and generally those who were the victims of the minor follies and difficulties of city life. These sketches at once became extremely popular and were reprinted and praised in many newspapers. In 1838 Neal published eighteen of them in *Charcoal Sketches: or Scenes in a Metropolis*, with illustrations by David Claypoole Johnston [*q.v.*]. They passed through six editions in four years and were reprinted in the second volume of *The Pic Nic Papers* (3 vols., London, 1841), edited by Charles Dickens. Another collection, *In Town and About*, followed in 1843, and *Peter Ploddy, and Other Oddities* came in 1844. After Neal's death his widow published *Charcoal Sketches: Second Series* (1848). Another posthumous volume, *The Misfortunes of Peter Faber, and Other Sketches*, appeared in 1856, and as late as 1865 forty-six of his sketches were reprinted in *Charcoal Sketches: Three Books Complete in One*.

An abundant geniality is the pervading quality in his mildly satirical portraits. Their similarity to the early work of Dickens is obvious, but unlike Dickens, Neal coined no memorable phrases and created no memorable characters. His humor lacked substance and originality. His popularity, considerable in his day, waned as the Civil War approached, and in the generation that followed him—the generation of Artemus Ward, Josh Billings, Petroleum V. Nasby, and Mark Twain—his fame was eclipsed by a more vigorous and original humor, American in background and spirit.

[Registers of the Second Presbyterian Church of Phila.; *Pennsylvanian* (Phila.) and *Public Ledger* (Phila.), July 19, 1847; *North American* (Phila.), July 20, 1847; R. W. Griswold, *The Prose Writers of America* (1847); Henry Simpson, *The Lives of Eminent Philadelphians Now Deceased* (1859); A. H. Smyth, *The Phila. Mags. and Their Contributors* (1892); F. L. Mott, *A Hist. of Am. Mags., 1741-1850* (1930).]

N. E. M.

NEALE, LEONARD (Oct. 15, 1746–June 18, 1817), Roman Catholic prelate, a direct descendant of Capt. James Neale, a favorite of Charles I who settled in Lord Baltimore's colony before 1642, was born on the family manor near Port Tobacco, Md. His father, William, died early in life, leaving seven sons and three daughters to the care of his widow, Anne (Brooke) Neale, who also came of substantial old Maryland stock.

Leonard obtained his first schooling from the Jesuits at Bohemia Manor, but the penal laws made it necessary to send him to an English Catholic refugee college on the Continent for his further education. In 1758, accordingly, he entered the Jesuit College of St. Omer in Flanders and later went to Bruges. Following the family tradition, he entered the Society of Jesus at Ghent, on Sept. 7, 1767, as did four of his brothers, including Charles, who founded the Carmelite Order in the United States, and Francis, who was at one time president of Georgetown College. Later he completed the course in theology at Liège and was ordained. On the suppression of the Society he went to England where he labored as a missionary until 1779, when he volunteered for service in Demerara, British Guiana. Here he labored among the pagans and vicious settlers until 1783, then petitioned for removal to the United States. He was captured en route by a British cruiser but apparently freed, for in April 1783 he arrived in Maryland and was welcomed by his family and the group of former Jesuit priests.

While stationed at St. Thomas Manor, he took part in the Whitemarsh meeting which led to a reorganization of the church and to the appointment of John Carroll [*q.v.*] as prefect apostolic. Although Neale was not in favor of the foundation of a college or the establishment of an American bishopric lest it be prejudicial to Jesuit property interests if the Society were revived, he thoroughly approved of Carroll's promotion and was an active participant in the first diocesan synod (1791). Two years later he was sent to Philadelphia during the yellow-fever plague, as pastor of St. Mary's Church and Carroll's vicar-general. As priest and nurse, he was exposed to the fever, but without harm, though in the later epidemic of 1797–98 he fell ill and narrowly escaped death. In 1799, he was selected president of Georgetown College by Carroll. During his régime, ending in 1806, he transformed the school from an academy into a *bona fide* college which soon won a reputation for classical scholarship. When Father Graessl [*q.v.*] died, Carroll with the consent of his clergy urged that Neale be named bishop coadjutor with the right of succession. The bulls of appointment were issued by Pius VI on Apr. 17, 1795, but did not reach Baltimore until 1800. On Dec. 7 of that year Neale was consecrated by Carroll as coadjutor, with the title of bishop of Gortyna.

While nursing the victims of yellow fever in Philadelphia, Neale had been aided by three devoted women, led by Alice Lalor, later Mother Theresa [*q.v.*], who wished to become nuns.

Upon his removal to Georgetown in 1799 he invited them to establish an academy there. Following him, they lived for a time in a small convent of Poor Clares, of which community Neale's sister, Anne, was a member at Aire in Artois. When the Poor Clares returned to France, Neale purchased their house for his society (1805), which, on the restoration of Pius VII to his freedom and prerogatives in 1816, was finally affiliated with the Visitation Order. The establishment of this community was one of Neale's principal achievements, for the Visitation nuns have since developed into a large body with a number of academies and schools throughout the United States.

As a coadjutor, Neale was not especially active, but apparently Carroll was satisfied with the assurance that the Church's organization would continue under a bishop who would automatically succeed him. Among contemporaries, at least John Thayer, a convert priest, thought Neale a man of no great ability; and James Barry wrote that "there is no danger of Neale setting the Potomac on fire" (Guilday, *post*, II, 577). When upon the death of Carroll he did succeed to the archbishopric of Baltimore, Dec. 3, 1815, he was too feeble to enjoy his opportunities for distinguished service. He soon petitioned for a coadjutor, and Ambrose Maréchal [*q.v.*] was appointed, but before the papal briefs arrived, Neale died from a stroke of apoplexy. His remains were interred in the crypt of the Visitation chapel at Georgetown.

[J. G. Shea, *Hist. of the Cath. Ch. in the U. S.* (1888–90), vols. II, III; Peter Guilday, *The Life and Times of John Carroll* (2 vols., 1922); *Cath. Encyc.*, X, (1911), 728; R. H. Clarke, *Lives of the Deceased Bishops of the Cath. Ch. in the U. S.*, vol. I (1888); Mary Paulina Finn (M.S. Pine), *A Glory of Maryland* (1917); Thomas Hughes, *Hist. of the Society of Jesus in North America*, vol. I, pt. I (1908), pt. II (1910); *Messenger* (Georgetown, D. C.), June 23, 1817; manuscript life in the files of the Visitation Academy of Georgetown.]   R. J. P.

NEEDHAM, JAMES (d. September 1673), explorer, a young Englishman, arrived in the southern Carolina settlement from Barbados in September 1670. Possibly he was the son of George Needham, Esq., of Little Wymondley, Hertfordshire, and his wife Barbara Fitch; it is evident that he belonged to a family of some social rank and was a man of education. He soon had a seat on the Ashley River. When Dr. Henry Woodward was sent by Sir John Yeamans in July 1671 to make discoveries in Virginia, Needham may have been one of the company. And when in August of 1672 Woodward was sent by the colonial council to arrest and overtake a traitor who was attempting to escape through the wilderness from Carolina to St. Augustine in the Spanish Dominions, Needham was named to accompany him. Again when Col. Abraham Wood residing on his plantation at Fort Henry, the present site of Petersburg on the James River, fitted out an expedition to trade with the Indians and discover a passage by water to the southwest, James Needham was selected to head the party. His companion was Gabriel Arthur, an uneducated but very intelligent lad, who was probably an indentured servant of Wood. The party also included eight Indians. The journey was begun from Wood's post on Apr. 10, 1673. Proceeding westward they were turned back by hostile Occaneeches who were encamped on the Roanoke River near the present site of Clarksville. The party reformed and again left Fort Henry in May 1673. They met some friendly Cherokees and safely passed the Occaneechi stronghold and pushed on to the west, crossing nine eastward-flowing streams. Beyond the Yadkin the party struck due west over the North Carolina Blue Ridge Mountains. About two weeks later, after traversing the northwest-flowing headwaters of the New River, they came down into the valley where the water flowed to the southwest and were soon at the main Cherokee village which stood on a high bluff on the headwaters tributary of the Tennessee River, in what is now the state of Tennessee. While Needham was viewing the Valley of the Tennessee as he crossed the Alleghanies, Marquette and Joliet first saw the Tennessee country on their trip down the Mississippi.

While returning from his travels Needham readily effected a treaty with the Cherokees, and leaving Arthur to learn the language of the Indians, returned to Fort Henry accompanied by a band of Cherokees. Wood welcomed him and refitted him for a return trip, which was begun in September 1673. Everything went well until the party passed the Occaneechi village, when on the Yadkin "Indian John," who had been hired as a guide by Wood, fell upon Needham and murdered him in cold blood. So far as is known Needham was the first Englishman to penetrate the domain of the over-hill Cherokees. Of him Wood wrote: "Soe died this heroyick English man whose fame shall never die if my penn were able to eternize it, which had adventured where never any English man had dared to atempt before" (Alvord and Bidgood, *post*, p. 217).

[There is no available primary source material for information on James Needham. It was through the researches of C. W. Alvord and Lee Bidgood and the subsequent publishing of their findings in a volume entitled *The First Explorations of the Trans-Allegheny Region, . . . 1650–1674* (1912) that Needham's work became known. The account of Needham's travels was found in a letter by Abraham Wood to his friend John Richards, treasurer of the Lords Proprietors of Carolina in London, dated Aug. 22, 1674. The letter was found with the Shaftsbury Papers, section ix, bundle 48, no. 94, and first appeared in the above-mentioned publication. There is also evidence that Needham left a journal of his expedition but it has been lost for a century. Further printed sources include: S. C. Williams, *Early Travels in the Tenn. Country, 1540–1800* (1928); W. R. Jillson, "The Discovery of Ky.," in *Ky. State Hist. Reg.*, May 1922; *Va. Mag. of Hist. and Biog.*, July 1903; Oct. 1912; Sir Henry Chauncy, *The Hist. Antiquities of Hertfordshire* (1826), II, 111.]   F. W. S.

NEEF, FRANCIS JOSEPH NICHOLAS (Dec. 6, 1770–Apr. 6, 1854), educator, was born at Soultz, Alsace, the son of Francis Joseph and Anastasia (Ackerman) Neef. His father, a miller who had built up a substantial, thriving business, had hopes of seeing his son in holy orders, but at twenty-one Joseph, as he preferred to style himself, decided that nature had not intended him for the life of the priesthood, and enlisted in the French army under Napoleon. Within a few years, various promotions came to him in recognition of his courage and efficiency. He distinguished himself especially during the Italian campaign. Severely wounded in the battle of Arcole, Nov. 15–19, 1796, he resigned his commission and left the army. After a brief period of wandering, he was engaged by Pestalozzi, in 1799, as a teacher of languages and gymnastics in the famous institution at Burgdorf, in the canton of Berne, Switzerland. Here, July 5, 1803, he married one of his students, Eloisa Buss, sister of the drawing and music master at the school. Later in the same year, when Pestalozzi was asked by a group of French philanthropists to send a teacher to Paris to conduct a school there according to his own ideas, he honored Neef by selecting him for the task. Neef's success at Paris justified his choice. Two years later a similar honor was conferred upon him: during a sojourn in Switzerland in the summer of 1805, William Maclure [q.v.], a wealthy Philadelphian, visited Pestalozzi's school at Yverdun and became so enthusiastic over the methods employed in the classroom that he at once asked Pestalozzi to suggest some one qualified to establish and conduct a similar school in Philadelphia. Following Pestalozzi's recommendation, Maclure called on Neef in Paris, and persuaded him to come to the United States, allowing him two years in which to learn the English language.

Neef came to Philadelphia in 1806, and was so successful in his efforts to master the language that he was able to publish, in 1808, a book entitled *Sketch of a Plan and Method of Education, Founded on an Analysis of the Human Faculties and Natural Reason, Suitable for the Offspring of a Free People and for All Rational Beings,* frequently called "the first strictly pedagogical work published in the English language in this country" (Carman, *post*). The essence of his master's teaching is clearly and briefly stated: "All possible knowledge, which we shall in any way be able to derive from our senses and immediate sensations, shall be exclusively derived from them. . . . Books, therefore, shall be the last fountain from which we shall endeavor to draw our knowledge." This treatise was followed by *The Logic of Condillac. Tr. by Joseph Neef, as an Illustration of the Plan of Education Established at His School near Philadelphia* (1809). About 1808 or 1809, he established at the Falls of the Schuylkill, some five miles from Philadelphia, the first Pestalozzian school in the United States. During this period, he acquired a small reputation as a naturalist: on June 4, 1812, he was elected a corresponding member of the Academy of Natural Sciences of Philadelphia. In 1813 he removed his school to Village Green, Delaware County, Pa., where he completed his *Method of Instructing Children Rationally in the Arts of Writing and Reading,* published in that year. Among his pupils there was David Glasgow Farragut [q.v.], later admiral in the United States Navy. Financially unsuccessful in Village Green, Neef moved in 1814 to Louisville, Ky., where he maintained a school until 1826. Then, at the invitation of Robert Owen, of New Lanark, Scotland, Neef and his wife took charge of the educational program in the recently founded experimental community at New Harmony, Ind. They taught here until the failure of the venture, two years later. From New Harmony, Neef went to Cincinnati, and then to his last school at Steubenville, Ohio. After a brief period of retirement on a farm in Jeffersonville, Ind., he returned, in 1834, to New Harmony to spend the remainder of his life.

[R. G. Boone, *A Hist. of Educ. in Ind.* (1892); N. A. Calkins, "The History of Object Teaching," *Am. Jour. Educ.*, Dec. 1862; Paul Monroe, *A Cyc. of Educ.* (1912), IV, 404; C. D. Gardette, "Pestalozzi in America," *Galaxy*, Aug. 1867; C. H. Wood, "The First Disciple of Pestalozzi in America," *Indiana School Jour.*, Nov. 1892; W. S. Monroe, *Hist. of the Pestalozzian Movement in the U. S.* (1907), and "Joseph Neef and Pestalozzianism in America," *Education*, Apr. 1894; Ada Carman, "Joseph Neef: A Pestalozzian Pioneer," *Pop. Sci. Mo.*, July 1894; Caroline Dale Snedeker, *The Town of the Fearless* (1931), reminiscences and family traditions recorded by Neef's great-grand-daughter; copy of baptismal certificate, and date of death, from another great-grand-daughter, Mrs. Aline Owen Neal, New Harmony, Ind.; G. B. Lockwood, *The New Harmony Movement* (1905); Robert Dale Owen, *Threading My Way* (1874).]   R. F. S.

NEELY, THOMAS BENJAMIN (June 12, 1841–Sept. 4, 1925), Methodist Episcopal bishop and writer, was born in Philadelphia, Pa., the son of Thomas and Frances (Armstrong) Neely. He studied at Dickinson Seminary and at Dickinson College, receiving from the latter institution the honorary degree of A.M. in 1875. He was admitted to the Philadelphia Conference of the Methodist Episcopal Church in 1865, and rose rapidly to a position of leadership in that body. He held thirteen pastorates, chiefly in Philadelphia and vicinity, and from 1889 to 1894 was presiding elder. In March 1882 he married Elizabeth Cheney Hickman of Philadelphia.

His talents were most conspicuous in the deliberative assemblies of the Church. In 1884, at the age of forty-two, he was elected to the General Conference, where he seized upon the first opportunity that offered to break lances with the veteran champions of that tilting-ground. A member of the five succeeding quadrennial sessions, also, he came to be recognized as one of the most influential members of that body. Years of indefatigable study of the history, laws, and constitution of the denomination, and of the broad principles which underlie all law, were the foundations of his power. Intense application to the study of special questions equipped him with a reserve fund of information which few of his opponents could match. His mind worked with order and precision in the presentation of his argument. Moreover, his self-control seldom relaxed in the heat of forensic strife, and he was ever ready to thrust the thin blade of fact and logic between the joints of his adversary's armor. The attitude of his mind was conservative. An expression in his maiden speech in the General Conference, "Radical changes should be approached with great caution," was the keynote of his public life, and his habitual caution heightened with the years.

As early as 1888 he began to receive votes for the episcopacy. In 1900, when he failed of election, he was chosen secretary of the Sunday School Union and the Tract Society. In this capacity he traveled widely among the churches, and showed himself to be an intelligent, industrious, and vigorous executive. Numerous improvements were introduced into the educational material of which he was editor. In 1904 he was elected bishop and assigned to Buenos Aires, Argentina. He had been the champion of the party which resisted the High Church theory that the Methodist episcopacy was a distinct order in the ministry. He held that it was but an office to which an ordained elder was commissioned for a special service. His own period of service was a troubled one. He was no longer young, and his field, the South American continent, subjected him to hardships of travel, altitude, and climate. His assertion of authority was not always acceptable among a people unaccustomed to the close supervision of one who conscientiously tried to be "every inch a bishop." In 1908 he was transferred to New Orleans, La., a residence which did not please him and the climate of which perhaps hastened the death of his wife in 1912. His uncompromising assertion of episcopal prerogative in the use of the appointing power in certain annual conferences in the North, where he held temporary assignments, added to the growing feeling of dissatisfaction with him as bishop. At the General Conference of 1912 he was retired by a vote of 496 to 297, no reasons being formally stated. He believed himself to be the victim of injustice, and protested bitterly, though he acquiesced in the decision.

Returning to Philadelphia, he devoted himself to studies which resulted in several learned treatises on Methodist polity and doctrine. He spoke and wrote against Methodist unification, against the idea of granting a degree of autonomy to the churches in mission lands, against uniting with other denominations in the joint support of missionary institutions, and against the ambitious and, as he believed, disastrous, plans of missionary expansion known as the Centenary Movement (1919) and the Interchurch World Movement. He fired his heaviest guns against the League of Nations. He lacked traits which make for the widest popularity, but his place is assured among American churchmen, as a productive legislator, an acute parliamentarian, an erudite historian, and a worthy expounder and defender of Methodist doctrine and polity. In his long list of published works, the most important are: *Parliamentary Practice* (1883); *The Evolution of Episcopacy and Organic Methodism* (1888); *A History of the Origin and Development of the Governing Conference in Methodism* (1892); *The Bishops and the Supervisional System of the Methodist Episcopal Church* (1912); *The Minister in the Itinerant System* (1914); *American Methodism, Its Divisions and Unification* (1915); *Doctrinal Standards of Methodism* (1918); *The League—the Nation's Danger* (1919); *Present Perils of Methodism* (1920); *The Only Condition* (1920); *The Methodist Episcopal Church and Its Foreign Missions* (1923).

[R. C. Wells, in *Jour. of the General Conference of the M. E. Ch.*, 1928; *Christian Advocate* (N. Y.), Sept. 17, 1925; *Who's Who in America*, 1924–25; *Public Ledger* (Phila.), Sept. 6, 1925.]   J. R. J.

NEF, JOHN ULRIC (June 14, 1862–Aug. 13, 1915), chemist, the eldest son of Johann Ulric Nef and Katherine (Mock) Nef, was born in

Herisau, Switzerland. In 1864, his father came to the United States and was employed as superintendent of a textile factory in Housatonic, Mass. Four years later the family joined him and they settled on a farm near Housatonic. John attended school at Great Barrington, four miles from his home, walking each way daily. He had one year in a high school in New York City. Funds were meager, and during the summers he worked diligently on the farm. In 1880 he entered Harvard with the intention of studying medicine but soon became fascinated with chemistry and proved to be so brilliant a student that in 1884 he was awarded the Kirkland Traveling Fellowship. After his graduation he went to Munich and began studying at once under Adolph von Baeyer, receiving the degree of doctor of philosophy in 1886. His thesis, entitled *Ueber Benzochinoncarbonsäuren,* treated of the compounds related to succinosuccinic-ethyl-ester.

In 1887 he returned to the United States as professor of chemistry at Purdue University. Two years later he went to Clark University as assistant professor of chemistry and was made acting head of the department shortly afterward, following the resignation of Professor Michael. Here he remained until 1892, when he responded to the invitation of President Harper to organize and head the department of chemistry at the University of Chicago. This position he held until his death. It was at Chicago that he met Louise Bates Comstock who became one of his students, and his wife on May 17, 1898. She died Mar. 20, 1909. To them one son was born.

Nef was small of stature, with a massive brow and bright, penetrating eyes. He had an all-consuming and contagious love for his science. The rapidity of his thought so outdistanced the speed of his words that his students could take only sketchy notes which they would later piece out and amplify in order to get the full value of his lectures. His restless enthusiasm for the problems in which he was engrossed developed in him an appearance of brusqueness which amounted almost to impatience when the research did not progress smoothly. Back of this intellectual eagerness, however, dwelt kindly human qualities. He was by temperament intense and found his relaxation in long walks which he pursued at an uncompanionable speed. He loved music and was a weekly attendant during the season of the concerts of the Chicago Symphony Orchestra. He died of heart disease at Carmel, Cal., while traveling with his son.

Nef's pioneer work on bivalent carbon, on the fulminates, on the sugars, on the mechanism of organic reactions, and on many other subjects contributed greatly to the advance of chemical knowledge. It was his signal research at Purdue University on the structure of quinone which led to his call to Clark University. This work forms a very important part of the chemistry of dyes and is universally accepted. As a result of his research in organic chemistry, he published thirty-seven independent articles, most of which were written in German. Thirty-six others represent work carried on under him, twenty-eight of which were the theses of those taking the doctorate of philosophy with him. He may be said to have stood for an individual school of thought in organic chemistry, a fact recognized by its separate treatment in advanced texts in this field, but he never assembled his theories of organic chemistry in a single volume, nor wrote a textbook. His scientific papers may be found scattered through *Justus Liebig's Annalen der Chemie* from vol. CCLXX (Apr. 27, 1892) to vol. CCCCIII (Sept. 28, 1913) and *Berichte der Deutschen Chemischen Gesellschaft.* His students Hedenburg and Glattfeld assembled after his death the remaining unpublished results of his researches, and published them in the *Journal of the American Chemical Society,* August 1917. Articles prepared in collaboration with his students appeared in the *American Chemical Journal* and the *Journal of the American Chemical Society* during the period of his active work.

[The chief sources for the above sketch are a memorial by Prof. L. W. Jones in the *Proc. Am. Chem. Soc.,* 1917 (incorporated in *Jour. Am. Chem. Soc.,* Feb. 1917), and personal acquaintance. See also Julius Stieglitz, "John Ulric Nef," in *Univ. of Chi. Mag.,* Nov. 1915; *San Francisco Chronicle,* Aug. 14, 1915. A biography by Prof. Stieglitz for the *Memoirs of the National Academy of Sciences* is in course of preparation.]
W.L.L.

NEGLEY, JAMES SCOTT (Dec. 22, 1826– Aug. 7, 1901), Union soldier, congressman, and railway executive, was born in East Liberty, Allegheny County, Pa., the son of Jacob and Mary Ann (Scott) Negley. On his paternal side he was descended from Swiss-German ancestors who spelled the name Nägeli. From the public schools he went to the Western University of Pennsylvania, the institution later known as the University of Pittsburgh. On the outbreak of war with Mexico, as a member of the Duquesne Grays, he entered the 1st Pennsylvania Regiment. Mustered into service, Dec. 16, 1846, he served throughout the remainder of the war, rose to the rank of sergeant, and was honorably discharged, July 25, 1848. On his return to civilian life, he engaged for a time in business, but soon took up the pursuit of horticulture in which he became well known. Meanwhile, maintaining his connection with the local militia, he was elected brigadier-general of the 18th Division, Pennsylvania Militia. At the beginning of the hostilities of the Civil War in April 1861 he was placed in command of military affairs in Pittsburgh, where the vigor with which he organized and equipped forces gave great satisfaction.

In the summer of 1861 he served under Maj.-Gen. Robert Patterson in Pennsylvania, Maryland, and Virginia, and on the disbandment of his three months' volunteer troops, returned to Pittsburgh where he raised a new brigade which in October was sent to Kentucky. Under General Buell he played an important part in the movements in central Tennessee and northern Alabama in the summer of 1862, at one time threatening the capture of Chattanooga. But on the dramatic Confederate advance across Tennessee into Kentucky late in the summer, he was drawn back by Buell and left in command of Nashville, where he ably held his position until the return of the Union forces. In the midwinter battle of Stone River, he commanded the Union center and by conspicuous skill and gallantry won promotion to the rank of major-general. He again figured prominently in the advance of General Rosecrans against Chattanooga in the autumn of 1863, but in the battle of Chickamauga, along with other commanders on the right wing of the Union line, he was swept back from the battlefield. Criticized by Generals John M. Brannan and Thomas J. Wood, he was relieved from command by General Rosecrans. Appeals to the latter's successors were in vain and, though a court of inquiry cleared him of the charges of cowardice and desertion (*Official Records,* 1 ser. XXX, pt. 1, pp. 1004–53), he failed to secure reassignment to command. He resigned from the army Jan. 19, 1865. He always bore resentment for the way he had been treated and said it was due to jealousy between West Pointers and "civilian soldiers." (See *Congressional Globe,* 41 Cong., 2 Sess., p. 1850.)

Returning to Pittsburgh, Negley again entered business. He was elected to Congress in 1868 on the Republican ticket and was reëlected in 1870, 1872, and 1884. In Congress he was an ardent Republican and a faithful representative of his constituency. He presented many petitions in favor of tariff protection and supported this policy in votes and speeches. His chief interest, however, was inland waterways, and he several times introduced bills for the improvement of navigation of the Ohio, Monongahela, and Allegheny rivers. He also introduced a bill "to complete a water highway from tidewater on the James river to the Ohio river at the mouth of the Kanawha" (*Congressional Globe,* 42 Cong., 3 Sess., p. 83).

In the interval between the Forty-third and Forty-ninth congresses, Negley resided in Pittsburgh. In local administration he was made gas inspector, while in business he was vice-president of the Pittsburg, New Castle, & Lake Erie Railroad in 1879, and president of the New York, Pittsburgh & Chicago Railway in 1884–85. During his final term in Congress, while maintaining his earlier activities, he displayed particular interest in the National Home for Disabled Volunteer Soldiers (*Congressional Record,* 49 Cong., 2 Sess., p. 611), of which he later became one of the managers. Defeated for the Republican nomination in 1886, by John Dalzell, he removed to New York, where he organized the Railroad Supply Company with which he was still connected at the time of his death at his home in Plainfield, N. J., Aug. 7, 1901. He was twice married. By his first wife, Kate de Losey, whom he married in 1848, he had three sons who predeceased him. By his second wife, Grace Ashton, he left three daughters. He was a man of large physique and fine appearance, affable and urbane, but of an independent spirit.

[J. W. Jordan, *Encyc. of Pa. Biog.,* vol. V (1915); *Biog. Dir. Am. Cong.* (1928); *Who's Who in America,* 1901–02; A. P. James, "Gen. Jas. Scott Negley," *Western Pa. Hist. Mag.,* Apr. 1931; memoriam obituary in the *Year Book of the Pa. Soc. of N. Y.,* 1902; *War of the Rebellion: Official Records (Army);* Pittsburgh directories, 1856–87; the Pittsburgh *Post,* the title of which varies, for Dec. 18, 1846, July 18, 26, 1848, Apr. 15–25, 1861, Aug. 8, 1901; inscription on tombstone, Allegheny Cemetery, Pittsburgh.]

A. P. J.

NEHRLING, HENRY (May 9, 1853–Nov. 22, 1929), ornithologist, horticulturist, was born in the town of Herman, near Howard's Grove, Sheboygan County, Wis., the son of Carl and Elizabeth (Ruge) Nehrling. His family on both sides was of German descent. His early education was received from his mother and grandfather and he was later sent to a Lutheran parochial school situated several miles from his home. His daily walks to and from school through what was then primeval forest familiarized him with every aspect of nature and helped to develop the passionate love for the outdoors—especially for birds and flowers—that was to characterize his entire life. From 1869 to 1873 he attended the State Normal School at Addison, Ill., and upon graduation taught in various towns in Illinois, Missouri, and Texas. In 1887 he accepted an appointment as deputy collector and inspector of customs at the port of Milwaukee, a position which he held until 1890 when he became secretary and custodian of the Public Museum of Milwaukee, a post much more to his liking. During his connection with the museum he made many important additions to the collections and laid the foundations for the future usefulness of the institution. Owing to politics, a factor with which he was unable to cope, he lost his position in 1903 after several years of service.

As early as 1884 Nehrling had bought a tract of land at Gotha, Fla., not far from Orlando. Thither he now repaired after a short association with the Philadelphia Commercial Museum. Always a lover of flowers, he had become somewhat of a horticulturist and during his residence in Milwaukee had built a greenhouse and had interested himself in growing various tropical plants, an interest greatly stimulated by the horticultural exhibits at the Columbian Exposition at Chicago. He now set about more seriously and developed a notable botanic garden, devoting himself particularly to the breeding of the amaryllis and caladium of which he developed many new forms while he maintained a correspondence with horticulturists in all parts of the world. In view of his outstanding knowledge of the subject he was appointed a collaborator of the Bureau of Plant Industry of the United States Department of Agriculture in 1906 and at the convention of garden clubs in Miami in 1929 was awarded the Meyer Medal for distinguished service in his field. Unfortunately, like many another gifted scientist, he lacked business sense, and was constantly in financial difficulties, losing, in the end, his gardens and practically all of his other worldly possessions. Worry over his losses brought on the breakdown that resulted in his death.

Nehrling was married on July 20, 1874, to Sophia Schoff of Oak Park, Ill., and had a family of seven children. After the death of his wife (1911), he married, June 7, 1916, Mrs. Betty B. Mitchell. His outstanding publication was his *Die Nordamerikanische Vogelwelt*, published in Germany. An English edition appeared simultaneously in America under the title: *North American Birds* (1889–93), later changed to *Our Native Birds of Song and Beauty* (2 vols., 1893–97), illustrated with colored plates by German and American artists. This work was designed to fill the gap between the very expensive and the merely technical ornithological books. He also published many popular articles on North American birds in various journals and newspapers in Germany and America and an account of the birds of various parts of Texas, in the *Bulletin of the Nuttall Ornithological Club* (January,

July, October 1882), an important volume entitled *Die Amaryllis* (1908). He was not primarily a scientist but rather a man of high literary attainments with a broad knowledge of birds and plants, an intense lover of the beautiful in nature with an ambition to impart that interest to others regardless of the cost to himself. In personality he was of a lovable and kindly disposition but with a child-like lack of business acumen.

[J. M. and Jaques Cattell, *Am. Men of Science* (1927); *Who's Who in America*, 1928–29; the *Auk*, Jan. 1930; letters from Nehrling's friends, and a brief personal acquaintance.]   W. S.

NEIDHARD, CHARLES (Apr. 19, 1809–Apr. 17, 1895), pioneer homeopathist and physician, was born at Bremen, Germany, the son of Friedrich Neidhard and his wife, the daughter of Prof. David Christoph Seybold. He came of an old and distinguished patrician family of Ulm, in the Cathedral of which town is the Neidhard Chapel more than five hundred years old. His grandfather was a Lutheran bishop of eminence; in the Austrian branch of the family was Cardinal Nithard, who later became prime minister of Spain. His father died when Charles was six years old. His mother then married Professor Georg Friedrich List [*q.v.*] of Württemberg, a distinguished political economist. The boy's early education was obtained at the Buxweiler College, in Alsace, and at the Gymnasium at Stuttgart. His career at the latter institution was interrupted summarily at the end of the first year, that is in 1825, because List had incurred the displeasure of the government and was banished, whereupon he soon removed to America. Neidhard accompanied his step-father and shortly after his arrival in America began the study of medicine in the office of a physician at Reading, Pa. He took two courses in the Philadelphia Medical Institute, two years of clinical lectures at the Pennsylvania Hospital, Philadelphia, and three and one-half courses at the University of Pennsylvania. Through his arduous studies he became broken in health. Regular treatment proving unavailing he consulted Dr. William Wesselhoeft, of Bath, Pa. The result was good and Neidhard became a convert to homeopathy. In 1834 he accompanied his step-father to Leipzig, Saxony, to which city the latter had been appointed United States consul. While there he continued his studies and joined the Leipzig Medical Society in 1835 and later graduated at Jena. He returned to America in 1836 and took up the practice of homeopathy, which he continued up to the time of his death.

In 1837 Neidhard was graduated from the Allentown Homœopathic Medical College. In 1839, associated with Dr. Constantine Hering and Dr. Walter Williamson, he organized and incorporated the Hahnemann Medical College of Pennsylvania. For the first three years of the institution's existence he held the chair of clinical medicine. He then resigned from the faculty because facilities for clinical instruction had been afforded in the hospital. In 1862 he received the honorary degree of M.D. from the Hahnemann Medical College of Chicago. He was one of the charter members of the American Institute of Homeopathy and for many years was very active in the work of various scientific committees. He was by nature a studious man and possessed strong literary tastes. He was an associate editor of the *American Journal of Homeopathy* in 1838 and a co-editor of the *North American Journal of Homeopathy* from 1862 to 1868. He was a voluminous contributor to various homeopathic medical journals. He published provings of realgar, calcarea phosphorica, cinnabaris, oxalic acid, oleum jecoris asseli, antimonium sulphuratum auratum, cannabis indica, formic acid, mephitis putorius, rhus tox., sanguinaria, phytolacca decandra, tarentula, balsam of Peru, and calcarea arsenica. His most notable contributions to literature were *Neidhard on Diptheria, as it Prevailed in the United States from 1860 to 1866* (1867), and *On the Efficacy of Crotalus Horridus in Yellow Fever* (1860, 1868), both of which were leading authorities of their day.

Neidhard was ordinary and corresponding member of the medical societies of Leipzig, Paris, Munich, Brazil, and of the state societies of Massachusetts and Rhode Island. He built up a large practice in Philadelphia. As a physician he exhibited a kind personality, was ever observant of phenomena of illness. He died of heart disease, suddenly, on Apr. 17, 1895. He had married Isabella Taylor, the daughter of Richard Taylor, an English geologist. They had five daughters. His sole interests in life were his patients and the promotion of the organization of homeopathy as a healing art. Though an intense believer in his school of medicine, he was always tolerant of the views of others.

[T. L. Bradford, *Homœopathic Bibliog. of the U. S.* (1892), *Hist. of the Homœopathic Medic. Coll. of Phila.* (1898), and "Biogs. of Homœopathic Physicians," vol. XXIII, in the library of the Hahnemann Medic. Coll. of Phila.; *Trans. Fifty-first Session Am. Inst. of Homœopathy,* 1895; T. L. Montgomery, *Encyc. of Pa. Biog.,* vol. XIV (1923); *Pub. Ledger* (Phila.), Apr. 18, 1895; personal acquaintance.]
C. B—t.

NEIGHBORS, ROBERT SIMPSON (Nov. 3, 1815–Sept. 14, 1859), Texas pioneer, Indian agent, was a native of Virginia. He went from Louisiana to Texas, either in 1833 or in 1837; but as there is evidence that he was in the Texas army at San Jacinto the earlier date seems more probably correct. He was a man of imposing personality, tall, and notable for his courage, energy, and strength of character. In January 1840 he was commissioned a lieutenant in the Texas army and in December 1841 was made a captain. He was one of the prisoners taken by the Mexican General Woll in the raid upon San Antonio in 1842 and was confined in Castle Perote, Mexico, for two years. In February 1845 he was appointed sub-agent of the Republic of Texas for the Lipan and Tonkawa Indians. In May 1846 he was a state commissioner to a great council on the upper Brazos at which the United States commissioners, P. M. Butler and M. G. Lewis, made a treaty with the Comanche and other wild tribes. After this he conducted a delegation of Indian chiefs to Washington to visit President Polk. In 1847 he was commissioned special agent of the United States for the Texas Indians with instructions to go out among the tribes, keep them friendly but away from the settlements, prevent the sale of intoxicating liquors to them, and keep the whites from intruding into the Indian country. This extremely difficult task he performed well, but entire success was impossible since the United States did not extend its Indian intercourse laws over Texas, the state owned the public lands and granted them to settlers who constantly encroached upon the Indian country, and the loose authority of the chiefs could not restrain the warriors from depredations. He made long visits to the Indians, studied them carefully, and sent in reports that constitute the most reliable information extant of the tribes in Texas, especially of the Comanche, for that period.

He was removed from office by the Whig administration in 1849, and in the spring of that year he led an expedition to locate a route from Austin to El Paso. Early in 1850 Governor Bell sent him to organize new counties in the El Paso-Santa Fé region; but because of the attitude of the federal authorities, who disputed the jurisdiction of Texas, he could accomplish nothing. His report to the governor caused great excitement in Texas and almost brought about a conflict of arms. In 1851 he was a member of the Texas legislature from San Antonio, and the next year he was a Democratic presidential elector. In 1853 he returned to his former post as general United States agent for the Texas Indians. His advocacy of reservations for the Indians resulted in an agreement between the state and federal governments for two reservations on the upper Brazos; and, with the aid of Capt. Randolph Barnes Marcy, he selected the sites and induced the smaller tribes to settle on one and a portion of the Comanche on the other. However, the experiment proved an unhappy one, for the white settlements soon spread to the neighborhood and the wild prairie tribes continued their depredations. The incensed settlers came to believe the reservation Indians guilty of the raids and, under a group of reckless leaders, threatened to attack them. After trying in vain to settle the difficulty, he recommended that the Indians be removed from Texas into the Indian Territory, and in the summer of 1859 he led the more peaceful tribes to their new homes. The Comanche on the upper reserve returned to the prairies and to the war-path. On his return to Fort Belknap in Texas to wind up the affairs of his agency, he was assassinated by an outlaw. He left a wife and two small children.

[Photostats from files of the Office of Indian Affairs, Neighbors Papers, Maverick Papers, and manuscript Memoirs of John S. Ford in Univ. of Texas Lib.; Texas Indian Papers in Texas State Lib., Austin; *Texas Almanac,* 1859, p. 136; R. B. Marcy, *Thirty Years of Army Life* (1866), pp. 170–223; W. B. Parker, *Notes Taken ... through Unexplored Texas* (1856), esp. pp. 116, 130–31, 139, 152, 168, 237–38; R. N. Richardson, *The Comanche Barrier* (1933); W. C. Binkley, *The Expansionist Movement in Texas* (1925); *Southwestern Hist. Quart.,* Apr., Oct. 1925, Oct. 1927; *State Gazette* (Austin, Tex.), esp. Sept. 24, 1859; information from Mrs. Alice Atkinson Neighbors, grand-daughter-in-law.]   C.W.R.

NEILL, EDWARD DUFFIELD (Aug. 9, 1823–Sept. 26, 1893), clergyman, educator, historian, a brother of John and Thomas Hewson Neill [qq.v.], was born in Philadelphia, Pa., the son of Dr. Henry and Martha R. (Duffield) Neill. After two years at the University of Pennsylvania, he went to Amherst College in 1839 and was graduated in 1842. He then spent a year in Andover Theological Seminary and completed his theological studies in Philadelphia. In 1847 he was licensed by the presbytery of Galena, Ill., to preach among the lead-miners of the vicinity. In the same year, on Oct. 4, he was married to Nancy, daughter of Richard Hall. On Apr. 26, 1848, he was ordained, and a year later he went to St. Paul, Minnesota Territory, where he established the First Presbyterian Church, of which he was pastor, 1849–54. From 1851 to 1863 he was secretary of the Minnesota Historical Society and contributed numerous articles to its *Collections.* From 1855 to 1860 he was pastor of the House of Hope Presbyterian Church, which he had organized. He promoted education as well as religion: he helped establish public schools in St. Paul, was the first

superintendent of instruction for Minnesota Territory, 1851–53, founded and became president of the Baldwin School and the College of St. Paul, both abortive institutions, was chancellor of the state university, 1858–61—at this time a university without students—and state superintendent of public instruction, 1860–61. In 1858 he published the first edition of his *History of Minnesota.*

In the next decade Neill's activities lay outside of Minnesota. He was chaplain of the First Minnesota Infantry, 1861–62, and United States Army hospital chaplain in Philadelphia, 1862–64. From February 1864 to 1869 he served as assistant secretary to Presidents Lincoln and Johnson, after which he was consul in Dublin for two years. These various services gave him opportunity for historical research which resulted in his most important works, *Terra Mariæ; or, Threads of Maryland Colonial History* (1867), *History of the Virginia Company of London* (1869), and *The English Colonization of America during the 17th Century* (1871). Returning home, Neill flung himself again into educational projects. In 1872 he opened in Minneapolis "Jesus College," a religious but nonsectarian institution, with himself as provost. This being unsuccessful, he persuaded Charles Macalester of Philadelphia to give a building, contingent upon the raising of an endowment fund, for a Christian but nonsectarian college. The fund was raised, and in 1874 Macalester College was started with Neill as president. In the same year he deserted the Presbyterians to become "presbyter in charge" of Calvary Reformed Episcopal Church. In 1880 Macalester College was transferred to the control of the Presbyterian synod, in 1883 it was removed to St. Paul, and in 1884 Neill resigned as president. From 1885 until his death he occupied the chair of history, English literature, and political economy, and for some years he was also librarian. He published two volumes of *Macalester College Contributions* (series 1 and 2, 1890–92), containing papers on historical subjects.

Neill's works are lacking in organization and interpretation and have been largely superseded, but he made valuable contributions to historical knowledge by bringing to light important documentary material. In education he was rather the promoter than the successful administrator, with more versatility than tenacity of purpose. In an era of beginnings in Minnesota this versatility was not to his disadvantage. It enabled him to turn from one venture to the next with undiminished enthusiasm and faith in his own abilities. He is noteworthy as a prophet of the mind and spirit at a time when most of his associates were preoccupied with material things.

[W. W. Folwell, *A Hist. of Minn.*, vol. IV (1930); Warren Upham, memoir in *Minn. Hist. Colls.*, vol. VIII (1898); H. D. Funk, *A Hist. of Macalester Coll.* (1910); E. D. Neill, *John Neill of Lewes, Del., 1739, and His Descendants* (1875); *Obit. Record of Grads. of Amherst Coll., for the Academical Year Ending June 27, 1894* (1894). The Neill papers of the Minn. Hist. Soc. are described in *Minn. Hist. Bull.*, Aug. 1916.]   S. J. B.

NEILL, JOHN (July 9, 1819–Feb. 11, 1880), surgeon, brother of Edward Duffield and Thomas Hewson Neill [*qq.v.*], was born in Philadelphia, Pa., the son of Dr. Henry and Martha R. (Duffield) Neill, and a grandson of Dr. Benjamin Duffield, one of the founders of the College of Physicians of Philadelphia. He was descended from John Neill who probably emigrated from Tyrone, County Ulster, Ireland, to America about 1739. He was graduated from the University of Pennsylvania in 1837, with the degree of A.B., and in 1840 received the degree of M.D. He then made a voyage to the West Indies, in charge of a patient, and in 1842 returned to his native city to begin practice. In the autumn of the same year he was made an assistant demonstrator, and in 1845 he became demonstrator of anatomy, in the medical department of the University of Pennsylvania. In 1849, during the epidemic of cholera in Philadelphia, he contracted the disease, probably while making post-mortem examinations of patients in the Southeast Cholera Hospital. In 1852 he was elected surgeon to the Pennsylvania Hospital, but he resigned this position in 1859. From 1854 to 1859 he was professor of surgery in the medical department of Pennsylvania College; he was also for some years surgeon to the Philadelphia Hospital at Blockley.

During the Civil War Neill's enterprise and activity were much in evidence. On the day of the announcement of the fall of Fort Sumter, he drove about the city in search of public buildings adaptable to hospital purposes. He found such a place on Christian Street above Ninth and obtained permission from the mayor of the city to take possession of it. Later, with authority obtained from the surgeon-general of the army, he established there the first United States Military Hospital in Philadelphia. About the same time, upon the organization of the home guard, Neill was appointed medical director of that body. In 1863, upon the invasion of Pennsylvania by Lee's army, he was appointed medical director of the forces from the state, and, under Gen. William F. Smith, he established military hospitals at Carlisle and Pine Grove, Pa., and at Hagerstown, Md. In 1862

he had been given rank as surgeon of volunteers, and in 1863, for meritorious services in the Gettysburg campaign, he was brevetted lieutenant-colonel.

In 1874 Neill was elected to the chair of clinical surgery in the University of Pennsylvania, but it appears that he was not entirely in sympathy with the removal of the University to West Philadelphia, and he resigned his chair the next year. About this time he lost his eyesight and remained totally blind until his death. Early in life he acquired a certain popularity with medical students, not only by his "quiz" classes, but by the publication of three little books with colored figures, on the arteries, the veins, and the nerves, and by the compilation, in conjunction with Dr. Francis Gurney Smith, of *An Analytical Compendium of the Various Branches of Medical Science* (1848). It is said that in later life he frequently expressed regret that "he had ever been connected with a publication, however successful, which contributed so largely to make medical education superficial" (Shippen, *post*, p. cliv). He published in 1852 *The Principles and Practice of Surgery*, an American edition of the work of William Pirrie, and just before his last illness is said to have projected an original work on the principles of surgery. He is remembered more for his work during the war than for his activities in civil life. He left a reputation of not getting along well with his colleagues, and of being always dissatisfied with the positions he held. He invented an apparatus for the treatment of fractures of the leg and modified Desault's splint for fractures of the femur. He died in Philadelphia in his sixty-first year. He had married, Sept. 24, 1844, Anna Maria Wharton Hollingsworth, daughter of Samuel Hollingsworth.

[Edward Shippen, "Memoir of John Neill, M.D.," *Trans. Coll. of Physicians of Phila.*, 3 ser. V (1881); T. G. Morton and Frank Woodbury, *The Hist. of the Pa. Hospital* (1895); H. A. Kelly and W. L. Burrage, *Am. Medic. Biogs.* (1920); E. D. Neill, *John Neill of Lewes, Del., 1739, and His Descendants* (1875); *Proc. Am. Phil. Soc.*, vol. XIX (1882); *Phila. Medic. Times*, Feb. 28, 1880; the *Press* (Phila.), Feb. 12, 1880.]   A. P. C. A.

NEILL, THOMAS HEWSON (Apr. 9, 1826–Mar. 12, 1885), soldier, was born in Philadelphia, Pa., a brother of John and Edward Duffield Neill [*qq.v.*] and the son of Dr. Henry and Martha R. (Duffield) Neill. After an elementary education in the public schools of his native city, he entered the University of Pennsylvania, but left that institution at the close of his sophomore year. On July 1, 1843, he was appointed a cadet at the United States Military Academy. Commissioned brevet second lieutenant of infantry,

July 1, 1847, he was regularly promoted through the intermediate grades and made captain on Apr. 1, 1857. During the Mexican War he served in garrison, and on the frontier until 1853 when he became assistant professor of drawing at the Military Academy, continuing in this capacity till 1857. He was with the Utah expedition in 1858 and remained in the West until 1861, when he was made mustering officer at Philadelphia.

Throughout the Civil War he rendered notable service, which received appropriate recognition. During Patterson's campaign on the upper Potomac in the summer of 1861 he was on General Cadwalader's staff. Commissioned colonel of volunteers on Feb. 17, 1862, he assumed command of the 23rd Pennsylvania Infantry and served with his regiment in McClellan's Peninsular campaign (March to August 1862). For gallantry in the battle of Malvern Hill he was brevetted, July 1, major, regular army. He took part in the Antietam campaign, but his regiment did not participate in the battle of Antietam. Made a brigadier-general of volunteers on Nov. 29, 1862, he assumed command at Fredericksburg, after its previous commander had been wounded, of the 3rd Brigade, 2nd Division, VI Army Corps. At Chancellorsville he took part in the operations of Sedgwick's VI Corps. With his brigade he participated in the assault on Marye's Heights, May 3, 1863, and on the following day defended the rear of Sedgwick's position at Salem Church, for which service he was brevetted lieutenant-colonel in the regular army. After a forced march of over thirty miles, his brigade reached Gettysburg on the afternoon of July 2, 1863, and supported elements of the I and XII corps on Cemetery Hill. The following day he held the extreme right of the Union line. During the pursuit of Lee, he commanded a division made up of his own brigade and McIntosh's cavalry brigade. On May 7, 1864, at the battle of the Wilderness, after General Getty was wounded, he took command of the 2nd Division, VI Corps. He was brevetted colonel, regular army, for gallantry at Spotsylvania and participated in the Cold Harbor and Petersburg campaigns. On June 21, 1864, he was transferred to the staff of the XVIII Army Corps, where he served until Sept. 12; then joining Sheridan's army in the Shenandoah Valley, he commanded the base at Martinsburg and served as an inspector. Later he was on duty in Washington, D. C., and in command of Fort Independence. On Mar. 13, 1865, he was brevetted brigadier-general, regular army, and major-general of volunteers for gallant and meritorious service during the Civil War. He reverted, Aug. 24, 1865, to the rank of major, 11th Infantry, to which he had been promoted Aug. 26, 1863.

After the war he served in various capacities until Feb. 22, 1869, when he was promoted to lieutenant-colonel. The following year, Dec. 15, he was transferred to the 6th Cavalry and went to the frontier to take part in the Indian campaigns. From 1875 to 1879 he was commandant at West Point, and on Apr. 2 of the latter year was made colonel of the 6th Cavalry. He retired from active service, Apr. 2, 1883, for disability contracted in line of duty, and died in Philadelphia almost two years later. His wife, whom he married, Nov. 20, 1873, was Eva D. Looney, and he was survived by one of their three children.

[War Department records; *War of the Rebellion: Official Records (Army)*; F. B. Heitman, *Hist. Reg. and Dict. U. S. Army* (1903); G. W. Cullum, *Biog. Reg. Officers and Grads. U. S. Mil. Acad.* (3rd ed., 1891), vol. II; *Sixteenth Ann. Reunion Asso. Grads. U. S. Mil. Acad.* (1885); S. P. Bates, *Martial Deeds of Pa.* (1875); G. J. Fiebeger, *Campaigns of the Am. Civil War* (1914); *Press* (Phila.), Mar. 13, 14, 1885; E. D. Neill, *Hist. Notes on the Ancestry and Descendants of Henry Neill, M.D.* (1886).]   H. O. S.

NEILL, WILLIAM (d. Aug. 8, 1860), Presbyterian clergyman and educator, was born near McKeesport, Pa., in 1778 or 1779, his family later fixing Apr. 25 as the probable day. His father, also William Neill, who was of Irish descent and had removed with his family from Lancaster County about 1775, was killed by Indians on his farm during William's infancy. The mother, Jane (Snodgrass) Neill, of Scottish ancestry, rapidly failed in health, and died when the boy was not more than four years old. After a boyhood in the homes of relatives, and several years' attendance at country schools, he became clerk of a country store in Canonsburg. Without early religious training, as an adolescent he was influenced by the pioneer minister, Rev. John McMillan, was deeply affected by a two months' illness, and later was led to attend prayer meetings at Canonsburg Academy by some of the students. In 1797 he entered the academy, determined to become a minister, and in 1800 enrolled in the College of New Jersey, from which he graduated in 1803. Thereafter for two years he was tutor in the college and studied theology under Dr. Henry Kollock, pastor of the church at Princeton.

Licensed by the Presbytery of New Brunswick in 1805, he immediately took charge of the Presbyterian church at Cooperstown, N. Y. There he was tutor of Samuel and James Fenimore, sons of Judge William Cooper. From Cooperstown, in 1809, Neill went to Albany to succeed Dr. John B. Romeyn as pastor of the church attended by the governor and several state judges. Both at Albany and at Philadelphia, where he took charge of the Sixth Church in 1816, he was notably successful in Bible-class work. The Albany class was one of the first formed in the United States. He believed that he influenced more people to join the church by his teaching in these classes than by his preaching. He succeeded John M. Mason [*q.v.*] as president of Dickinson College in 1824, serving for about five years. Like his predecessor he encountered serious difficulties, due largely to the partial control over the institution exercised by the state legislature. During his administration, however, the attendance and faculty were doubled. From 1829 to 1831 he performed laborious pioneer work as secretary of the board of education of the Presbyterian Church, and from 1831 to 1842 was stated supply of the church at Germantown.

Returning to Philadelphia, he was a volunteer city missionary, supplying vacant pulpits and ministering to the Widows' Asylum, a Magdalen Asylum, and other charitable institutions. During this period he published his *Lectures on Biblical History* (1846) and his *Practical Exposition of the Epistle to the Ephesians* (1850). He issued also some occasional discourses and other small publications. He married, Oct. 5, 1805, Elizabeth Van Dyke of Princeton, who died in 1809; on Feb. 25, 1811, Frances, daughter of Gen. Joshua King of Connecticut, who died in 1832; and on Apr. 15, 1835, Sarah, daughter of Dr. Ebenezer Elmer of Bridgeton, N. J. There were two children by the first marriage, three by the second, and two by the third. He was moderator of the Presbyterian General Assembly in 1815, helped organize the American Bible Society, and was a director of Princeton Theological Seminary from its founding. Ranking among the more distinguished clergymen of his time, he was known as a man of unselfish and beneficent disposition, unusually attractive manner, and direct, methodical, and persuasive preaching.

[J. H. Jones, *Autobiog. of William Neill, D.D., with a Selection from His Sermons* (1861), including a sermon on Neill's life and character; Neill's *Discourse Reviewing a Ministry of Fifty Years* (1857); W. B. Sprague, *Presbyterian Reunion: A Memorial Vol.* (1870); E. H. Gillett, *Hist. of the Presbyterian Church in the U. S. A.* (2 vols., 1864); Alfred Nevin, *Encyc. of the Presbyterian Church in the U. S. A.* (1884); J. M. Wilson, *The Presbyterian Hist. Almanac,* 1861; *The Centennial Memorial of the Presbytery of Carlisle* (2 vols., 1889); *Phila. Daily News,* Aug. 11, 1860.]   P. P. F.

NEILSON, JOHN (Mar. 11, 1745–Mar. 3, 1833), officer in the Revolution and member of the Continental Congress, was born at Raritan Landing, near New Brunswick, N. J., the only son of Dr. John Neilson, who came to America from Belfast, Ireland, and Joanna Coejeman, of the Albany family of that name. Losing his father when he was but eight days old, he was adopted by his uncle, James Neilson, a shipping merchant in New Brunswick. He was brought up in the business and later succeeded to it. On Dec. 31, 1768, he married Catherine, daughter of John and Catherine (Schuyler) Voorhees, of the same city. On the outbreak of the Revolutionary War, "bitterly resenting the attempt of a venal Parliament, bought by an oppressive ministry, to tax his country," he raised a company of militia, was appointed its captain, and was called into service at the east end of Long Island under General Heard, to disarm the Loyalists. On Aug. 31, 1775, he was appointed by the Provincial Congress colonel of a battalion of Minute Men of Middlesex County. Early the next year he was urged to take a seat in the Continental Congress but declined, believing he could be more useful in the military service of the state. He read in public the Declaration of Independence when it first appeared and then began recruiting for the army. In August 1776 he was appointed colonel of the 2nd Regiment, Middlesex militia, and served with it in Essex and Bergen counties, where the Loyalists were prominent. In December he retired with the army under Washington to the west bank of the Delaware, but in a few days (Dec. 31), Washington directed him to return to New Jersey to call out more of the state militia. On Feb. 18, 1777, with a detachment of his regiment, he surprised and captured an outpost of Loyalist refugees on the Island Farm, near New Brunswick. In acknowledgment of this service he was appointed, on Feb. 21, brigadier-general of militia, but he acted so little in that capacity that the name "Colonel Neilson" always followed him. While the British were at New Brunswick that winter Lord Howe made Neilson's house his headquarters.

Neilson served the rest of 1777 with the militia of Middlesex and Somerset counties, and in 1778 in Monmouth County, part of the time under General Dickerson, but otherwise holding a separate command. During this year he was again chosen to be a delegate to the Continental Congress but again declined. In 1779 he commanded the militia at Elizabethtown and Newark, aiding in the attempts to ward off the British raids from New York. The same year he intercepted the Simcoe raid, which was doing so much damage in Somerset County. On Sept. 20, 1780, he was appointed deputy quartermaster-general for New Jersey, in which position he continued until January 1783. In the meantime, on June 18, 1782, he was appointed a commissioner to settle, in terms of a depreciated currency, the pay of the New Jersey Line. He enjoyed the confidence of Washington, as published letters from the latter show, and their friendship continued after the war. Lafayette, on his visit to America in 1824, presented Neilson with his sword. The war over, Neilson returned to his business and carried on an extensive trade with Lisbon, Madeira, London, Dublin, and the West Indies. He also held various public offices. He was a member of the state convention which adopted the Constitution of the United States; from 1795 to 1798 he was judge of the court of common pleas; in 1800 and 1801 he was a member of the state Assembly, and from April 1796 to February 1821 he was successively register and recorder of New Brunswick, N. J. He was an elder and trustee in the First Presbyterian Church of New Brunswick, and a trustee of Rutgers College from 1782 until his death. His wife died Aug. 2, 1816. They had eleven children, the best known being James, who served with the rank of captain in the War of 1812 and was later a colonel of militia, and who succeeded his father as trustee of Rutgers College.

[W. W. Clayton, ed., *Hist. of Union and Middlesex Counties, N. J.* (1882); W. H. Benedict, *New Brunswick in Hist.* (1925); F. B. Lee, *Geneal. and Memorial Hist. of the State of N. J.* (1910), vol. IV; E. W. Van Voorhis, *A Geneal. of the Van Voorhees Family in America* (1888); *Newark Daily Advertiser*, Mar. 6, 1833.]

A. V–D. H.

NEILSON, WILLIAM GEORGE (Aug. 12, 1842–Dec. 29, 1906), mining engineer, the son of William Smith Neilson of Philadelphia and Esther (LaCoste) of Trinidad, who was of French descent, was born in Philadelphia and died in that city. He graduated from the Polytechnic College of the State of Pennsylvania in 1862, and shortly after became an instructor in mathematics there. Later he was connected with Booth & Garrett, a prominent firm of analytical chemists in Philadelphia.

In 1867 he was associated with the interests of Jay Cooke [q.v.] in the Adirondacks, spending three years in those mountains operating forges at Elizabethtown, Essex County, N. Y. He was next, for a short time, with the Pennsylvania Steel Company. During 1871, when the Logan Iron & Steel Company of Burnham, Pa., failed, Neilson was appointed its receiver

and upon subsequent reorganization of the company was made its general manager. In the meantime he became interested in the Freedom Forge of the same place, and with William Burnham of Philadelphia laid the foundations for what later became the Standard Steel Works, an affiliated interest of what was then called Burnham, Parry, Williams & Company, and is now known as the Baldwin Locomotive Works. He was manager of the Standard Steel Works for thirteen years (1877–90), and in 1878 was given charge of the first consignment of American-made locomotives to Russia. He was accompanied by a picked crew of men from Baldwin's for the purpose of placing these engines in service at Eydtkuhnen, an important railroad point on the border of East Prussia (now Lithuania). In 1890 he resigned from the Standard Steel Works to accept a position with the Chester Rolling Mills, later becoming vice-president of the Wellman Iron & Steel Company (1890–92). From 1893 to 1895 he was general manager of the Taylor Iron & Steel Company of Highbridge, N. J., and subsequently, for a period of eight years, treasurer of the Keystone Drop Forge Works at Chester, Pa.

With William Burnham and Edward Nichols, who subsequently became the president of the Brooks Locomotive Works, Tarrytown, N. Y., now a part of the American Locomotive Works system, Neilson, in 1882, purchased the Ridge Valley Iron Company, makers of charcoal pig-iron, in Floyd County, Ga.; and in that year formed the Republic Mining & Manufacturing Company for purchasing and operating mineral properties in the South. Bauxite, the ore from which aluminum metal is derived, was first discovered in the United States the following year at Hermitage, about one mile from the Ridge Valley Furnace. Neilson became a pioneer in the bauxite industry and was closely associated with its remarkable development. He was president of the Republic Mining & Manufacturing Company from 1892 until his death.

In 1888, with a few friends, he purchased land which was about to be sold for its timber and established the Adirondack Mountain Reserve, one of the largest and most attractive forest reserves in New York State. Its area, which includes Mount Marcy and the Ausable lakes, still retains its original wildness and beauty and has served as a game refuge to the present time. Neilson served as president of the controlling organization from its formation until 1903. He was also for many years a member of the Pennsylvania Forestry Association.

His religious interests covered a broad field,

his activities centering chiefly in the Protestant Episcopal Church of the Epiphany, Philadelphia, of which he was long a vestryman, and in the Philadelphia Branch of the Young Men's Christian Association, which he served as director and for three years as president. He was secretary of the centennial committee of the American Institute of Mining Engineers and his tact and the charm of his personality are attested by the successful manner in which he carried out the work of this office at the Centennial Exhibi-·tion at Philadelphia in 1876. For his services he received distinguished recognition from foreign governments. In 1872 he married Mary Louise Cunningham, of Philadelphia. He was survived by two sons and four daughters.

[*Trans. Am. Institute of Mining Engineers,* vol. XXXVIII (1908); *Who's Who in America,* 1906–07; *North American* (Phila.), *Public Ledger* (Phila.), Dec. 30, 1906; information from a son, Winthrop C. Neilson.]
F. L. G.

NELL, WILLIAM COOPER (Dec. 20, 1816–May 25, 1874), negro writer, was born in Boston. He was the son of William G. and Louisa M. Nell, the latter a native of Brookline, Mass., and the former of Charleston, S. C. The father, a tailor by trade, was steward on the ship *General Gadsden* when she escaped from the British brig *Recruit* in July 1812, and became a member of the General Colored Association of Massachusetts in 1826. Young Nell attended one of the separate primary schools, which had been established for negro children in Boston in 1820, and subsequently graduated with honors from the Smith School, of grammar grade, opened in 1835. He looked on while the white children were given prizes which he, although of equal scholarship, was debarred from receiving on account of his color.

This incident made a deep impression on him and henceforth he worked unceasingly for equal school rights to all children irrespective of the color of their skins. He read law for a time in the office of William I. Bowditch but, on the advice of Wendell Phillips, refrained from applying for admission to the bar, an act that would have entailed the taking of an oath to support the Constitution of the United States, which, in Phillips' opinion, compromised with the slave power. Nell then became affiliated with the anti-slavery movement as an organizer of meetings, at some of which he spoke acceptably. He also made himself useful by carefully preserving data and documents that would be helpful to the cause. In 1840 his name headed the list of signers of the first petition presented to the Massachusetts legislature asking for the opening of the public schools to negro children. For many years

thereafter he was to agitate this reform, since it was not until Apr. 28, 1855, that a law was passed abolishing the separate schools for colored children.

In the meantime he had developed into a journalist and author. During 1851 he assisted Frederick Douglass [*q.v.*] in the publication at Rochester, N. Y., of the *North Star*. In May of the same year he issued a pamphlet entitled *Services of Colored Americans in the Wars of 1776 and 1812*. This was followed in 1855 by a larger volume, *The Colored Patriots of the American Revolution,* to which Harriet Beecher Stowe wrote an introduction. In this book Nell paid a tribute to Crispus Attucks [*q.v.*], the first martyr of the Revolution, for whom, on Mar. 5, 1851, he had unsuccessfully petitioned the Massachusetts legislature to erect a monument. In it he also dwelt on the injustice of making only free white persons eligible for positions in the federal service. When, however, John G. Palfrey was named postmaster of Boston in 1861 he ignored this restriction and appointed Nell one of his clerks; thus he became the first colored man to hold a post under the federal government. This position he filled until the time of his death. A wife survived him.

[*William Lloyd Garrison, 1805–1879: the Story of His Life, Told by His Children* (4 vols., 1885–89); S. J. May, *Some Recollections of Our Anti-Slavery Conflict* (1869); W. W. Brown, *The Rising Sun* (1874); John Daniels, *In Freedom's Birthplace* (1914); Vernon Loggins, *The Negro Author: His Development in America* (1931); *Liberator,* Dec. 18, 1846, Feb. 11, 1848; C. G. Woodson, *The Mind of the Negro as Reflected in Letters Written During the Crisis 1800–1860* (1926); *Boston Daily Globe,* May 26, 1874; *Boston Transcript,* May 26, 29, 1874.]
H. G. V.

NELSON, CHARLES ALEXANDER (Apr. 14, 1839–Jan. 13, 1933), librarian, bibliographer, and expert indexer, was born in Calais, Me., the son of Israel Potter and Jane (Capen) Nelson, both members of old New England families. His early education was obtained at private schools in Fredericton and St. John, New Brunswick, and in Eastport, Me. In the fall of 1854 he entered the Male Academy at Gorham, Me., but a year later, December 1855, his family having moved to Cambridge, Mass., he joined the college class of the Cambridge High School. Entering Harvard College in 1857, he graduated in 1860. For one year he was tutor in Latin and Greek in the Albany Male Academy, then spent a year in the Lawrence Scientific School, and for more than a year was in business in Boston. In the fall of 1863 he became sub-master and professor of mathematics in the Collegiate School of Boston and resumed his studies at Harvard College, receiving the degree of master of arts in 1863.

From April 1864 to March 1865, he served as civil engineer and draftsman in the quartermaster's department of the United States Army at New Bern, N. C. After the war he remained in New Bern until 1873, serving as superintendent of schools and justice of the peace, and holding various other civil positions. In the spring of 1865 he was acting superintendent of white refugees, and in 1867 had charge of registration work in Craven County, under the reconstruction acts. From 1865 to 1871 he was also interested in the furniture business in New Bern, and from 1866 to 1873 was cashier of the Freedman's Savings & Trust Company. He returned to Boston in 1874 and was engaged in the book business and literary work until 1879, when he became professor of Greek and librarian at Drury College, Springfield, Mo., but returned to Boston one year later. For two years he was manager of the Old South Bookstore and editor of the firm's publications.

For the remainder of his life Nelson was engaged in library and bibliographical work at various institutions, holding numerous offices in professional organizations, contributing constantly to professional library journals, and publishing many bibliographical works of significance. His interest in library work began when as a boy of sixteen he served as librarian of the Male Academy, Gorham, Me. While a student in Harvard he worked as assistant in the college library under the tutelage of John Langdon Sibley and Ezra Abbot [qq.v.], whose work aroused his interest in cataloguing. In 1881 Nelson went to the Astor Library, New York, as catalogue librarian, to prepare a continuation of the catalogue made by Joseph G. Cogswell [q.v.]. This supplement was published in four volumes (1886–88), and gained for Nelson the diploma of honorable mention at the Pan-American Exposition in Buffalo in 1901, and at the exposition held in Charleston, S. C., in the same year. He left the Astor Library in 1888 to become the first librarian of the Howard Memorial Library at New Orleans, which was intended by its donors to excel in size and value all other libraries of the South. Having established a reputation as an expert cataloguer through his work on the catalogue of the Astor Library, he was called to the Newberry Library, Chicago, in 1891, to prepare a dictionary catalogue, but in 1893, before the work was completed, he accepted an appointment as deputy librarian of Columbia University, where he remained until he was retired on a pension from the Carnegie Foundation in 1909. In November 1913 he joined the staff of the Merchants' Association of New York, where

he organized and maintained an index-digest of the activities of the Association until his final retirement in July 1926.

The most important of Nelson's published works, in addition to the catalogue of the Astor Library, were: *Waltham, Past and Present* (1879); *Catalogue of the Avery Architectural Library* (1895); *Books on Education in the Libraries of Columbia University* (1901); *Catalogue raisonnée; Works on Bookbinding, Practical and Historical . . . from the Collection of Samuel Putnam Avery . . .* (1903); *Analytical Index to Volumes 1–25 of the Educational Review* (1903); Index to *Minutes of the Common Council of the City of New York, 1675–1776* (8 vols., 1905–06). In 1872, at New Bern, N. C., Nelson married Emma Norris of Slaterville Springs, N. Y., who died Apr. 6, 1926. Two daughters survived him.

[*Who's Who in America,* 1932–33; H. M. Lydenberg, *Hist. of the N. Y. Pub. Lib.* (1923); *Lib. Jour.,* Feb. 1, 1933; *Bull. of the Am. Lib. Asso.,* Feb. 27, 1933; *N. Y. Times,* Jan. 14, 1933; autobiographical material supplied by a daughter, Mrs. R. A. Wetzel, Mount Vernon, N. Y.]

C. C. W.

NELSON, DAVID (Sept. 24, 1793–Oct. 17, 1844), Presbyterian clergyman, educator, abolitionist, was born near Jonesboro, Tenn., one of a family of Presbyterian ministers. His parents, Henry and Anna (Kelsey) Nelson, of English and Scotch extraction respectively, had migrated to East Tennessee from Rockbridge County, Va. David studied under the Rev. Samuel Doak [q.v.] at Washington College, two miles from his home. Upon his graduation at the age of sixteen he determined to become a physician, and after an apprenticeship to Dr. Ephraim McDowell [q.v.] at Danville, Ky., he went to Philadelphia for further study. He began his active practice as surgeon in the War of 1812 with an expeditionary force that invaded Canada, and later served with Andrew Jackson's army in Alabama and Florida. After peace was declared he returned to Jonesboro, and during the ensuing decade built up a lucrative practice in his profession.

While studying medicine, Nelson had been captured by the naturalistic doctrines then rife among members of his profession, and had become "an honest, unreflecting deist." He was big, fun-loving, and attractive; he drank and played cards to an extent distressing to his family, and after settling in Jonesboro, he eloped at the age of twenty-two with the charming young daughter of David Deaderick, a prominent merchant. She appears to have been sincerely religious, however, and her influence, together with several years of reflection upon his deistical principles, brought him back to the Presbyterian Church. His return from deism to Calvinism he later recorded in a powerful tract, *The Cause and Cure of Infidelity*, written in 1836, of which more than a hundred thousand copies were distributed by the American Tract Society, and many thousands more by tract societies in England. With time his convictions deepened; in April 1825 he was licensed to preach by the Abingdon Presbytery, and six months later he gave up his medical practice and was ordained as an evangelist. From 1827 to 1829 he was one of the editors of the *Calvinistic Magazine* and in 1828 he succeeded his brother, Samuel Kelsey Nelson, as pastor of the Presbyterian church at Danville, Ky. Though careless in dress and eccentric in manner, he was a pulpit orator of great ability (R. J. Breckinridge, in Sprague, *post*, p. 687) and became one of the notable preachers of his day in his denomination.

In 1831 he founded and became president of Marion College, near Palmyra, Mo., "for the training of pious young men," converts of the Great Revival of 1830. The next year the "modern abolition" movement invaded the Presbyterian Church in the West. At Western Reserve College, Theodore D. Weld, abolition revivalist extraordinary, started among the faculty an anti-slavery discussion whose repercussions were heard throughout the Western Reserve. The next year among the students at Lane Theological Seminary in Cincinnati he inspired a debate on slavery that converted the student body and disrupted the school. At St. Louis, Mo., Elijah P. Lovejoy [*q.v.*] echoed the perilous agitation in the columns of the *St. Louis Observer*, the Presbyterian paper for the Far West. Nelson's convictions had led him, before he went to Missouri, to free his own slaves, and now, surrounded as he was by the agitation, he could not remain unmoved: at the Presbyterian General Assembly of 1835, in Pittsburgh, Theodore Weld found him ready for the abolition gospel. Together with more than one-fourth of his fellow delegates, he "pledged himself openly to the Cause" (*Emancipator*, Boston, June 16, 1835).

Nelson was no faint-hearted reformer. A month after his return to Marion College he accepted a regular agency from the American Anti-Slavery Society, and in 1836, from the pulpit of his Presbyterian church in Palmyra, he called upon the slave-holders of his congregation to repent their sins and free their slaves. He was straightway expelled from Marion College and from Missouri, not escaping mob violence on the way, and the faculty of Marion College published a manifesto, nervously asseverating

their loyalty to the institutions of the community. At Quincy, Ill., he now founded a new college, a "manual labour institution," where students were to support themselves by building their own dwellings and raising food for their sustenance on the college farm. The school did not survive its first year, and Nelson again took up agency work for the American Anti-Slavery Society. As anti-slavery lecturer in western Illinois, he was only moderately successful, partly on account of increasing disability from epilepsy. Intermittently he labored for the slave until 1840, when his health gave way completely. He died at Oakland, Ill., four years later.

[A short biography of Nelson is in the second American edition (n.d.) of his *Cause and Cure of Infidelity*; and a biographical sketch, with reminiscences of several colleagues, appears in W. B. Sprague, *Annals Am. Pulpit*, vol. IV (1858). Contemporary events are recorded in the *Calvinistic Mag.*, 1827–28; *St. Louis Observer*, 1835–36; *Alton Observer*, 1837; *Philanthropist*, 1836–40; and Minutes of the Agency Committee, Am. Anti-Slavery Soc., 1835–40. An obituary appears in *Presbyterian of the West* (Springfield, Ohio), Nov. 21, 1844. D. L. Leonard, *The Story of Oberlin* (1898).]

G. H. B.

NELSON, HENRY LOOMIS (Jan. 5, 1846–Feb. 29, 1908), author, editor, and teacher, was born in New York City, the son of Theophilus and Catherine (Lyons) Nelson. He was graduated from Williams College in the class of 1867, and among its members he was known as an original thinker, a picturesque speaker, and a friendly and delightful companion. From Williams College he went to the law school of Columbia University, received the degree of LL.B. in 1869, was admitted to the New York bar, and began the practice of law. On Oct. 14, 1874, he married Ida Frances Wyman of Brooklyn. Business called him to Kalamazoo, Mich., in the year of his marriage; during his two years of residence in that city his interest in public questions prompted him to send frequent letters to the newspapers, and ultimately resulted in shifting his attention from law to journalism. In 1876 he moved to Greenfield, Mass., where he became owner and editor of the *Franklin County Times*. From the concerns of a small New England city he was soon attracted to the national capital. He was Washington correspondent of the *Boston Post* from 1878 to 1885. His shrewd common sense, political sagacity, and lively style not only commended him to his Boston readers but also brought him to the notice of men prominent in public life. Eventually, while continuing to act as correspondent for the *Post*, he became private secretary to John G. Carlisle, then speaker of the House of Representatives. In 1885 he was called from Washington to become editor of the newspaper that he had been representing. A year later a change in the ownership of the *Post* set him adrift. He returned to New York and for eight years he engaged in editorial work, first for the *Star,* then for the *Mail and Express,* then for the *World.* From 1894 to 1898, during the turbulent final years of the Cleveland administration, the free-silver campaign of 1896, and the tumult of the Spanish-American War, he was editor of *Harper's Weekly.* A supporter of Cleveland, an opponent of Bryan, and a sceptical and suspicious observer of the rising star of Theodore Roosevelt, he made his periodical a powerful factor in the thought of the time.

The succeeding years he gave to free-lance writing, until in 1902 Williams College called him to the newly created David A. Wells Professorship of Political Science. He was markedly successful as a teacher, bringing to his new work a vigorous mind and a sense of realities. During his professorial life he continued to write on political problems and personalities for the leading magazines and kept in touch with men and affairs. He died suddenly in 1908 from an attack of angina pectoris while on a visit to New York. Aside from the editorials in *Harper's Weekly,* numerous essays in periodicals, and unidentifiable contributions to newspapers, his chief works are *John Rantoul,* a novel, published in 1885, and two small books, *Our Unjust Tariff Laws* (1884), and *The Money We Need* (1895). A man of strong convictions, a good hater and a loyal friend, he was typical of the best of that group of Americans who were proud to call themselves Cleveland Democrats. He was a fighter for civil-service reform, a free-trader, a believer in the gold standard, an anti-imperialist. Politically he typified a party and an era. As an educator he was eloquent in support of the humanities, upheld the intellectual life against the excesses of organized athletics, employed the project method years before the term was known to college men, and in the classroom stirred his students by his piquant speech and his faculty of revealing the simple principles underlying complicated governmental problems. His positive, dynamic personality made itself felt in all of his undertakings.

[*Who's Who in America,* 1907–08; sketch by H. W. Mabie, in *Obit. Record of the Soc. of Alumni, Williams Coll.,* May 1908; *Thirty-fifth Anniversary Papers of the Class of 'Sixty-Seven, Williams Coll.;* sketch by E. S. Martin, in *Harper's Weekly,* Mar. 14, 1908; L. W. Spring, *A Hist. of Williams Coll.* (1917); *N. Y. Daily Tribune,* Dec. 20, 1894; *N. Y. Times,* Mar. 1, 1908; *Springfield* (Mass.) *Republican,* Mar. 1, 1908; personal recollections.]   G. B. D.

NELSON, HUGH (Sept. 30, 1768–Mar. 18, 1836), politician, jurist, diplomat, was of the third generation of the Nelson family born on the soil of York County, Virginia, in the then thriving Yorktown, to play a conspicuous rôle in the public affairs of the Old Dominion. He was the fifth child of Thomas Nelson [*q.v.*], Revolutionary governor of Virginia, and his wife Lucy, daughter of Philip and Mary Randolph Grymes of Middlesex. He was of the vintage of Revolutionary Virginia sons who were not sent like their fathers to old England but were given their education at the College of William and Mary at Williamsburg, where he was graduated in 1790. Soon after reaching manhood he moved to Albemarle County. On Apr. 28, 1799, he was married to Eliza, only child of Francis Kinloch and Mildred Walker, granddaughter of Jefferson's guardian, Dr. Thomas Walker. Through his wife the estate of "Belvoir" came into his possession and he lived there among the Albemarle hills for many years with an ever increasing family to add liveliness to rural seclusion. There were nine children of this union who reached maturity.

Nelson practised law in Albemarle and began his official career as delegate from the county in the Virginia Assembly from 1805 to 1809. In the interval between his service in the Virginia legislature and his congressional services he was judge of the General Court of Virginia. In 1811 he was sent to Congress from his district and was returned continuously to that body until he resigned in 1823 to accept appointment by his former neighbor, President Monroe, as minister plenipotentiary to the Court of Spain. During the years of his congressional office he kept in close touch with Jefferson, reporting to him from the inside such critical issues as the Missouri question. Monroe constantly esteemed him as a loyal, dependable friend. On his request he was relieved of his Spanish post in 1825, just before Monroe left the presidency, and returned to Albemarle. There he spent the declining years of his life with a brief interruption when he again represented that county in the Virginia House of Delegates of 1828–29. Through his father he had had intimate knowledge of the Revolutionary leaders in Virginia and was frequently consulted in his later years for information on figures even then becoming legendary. It is on his authority that Patrick Henry has enjoyed the reputation for having read Livy every year. Church affairs had his keen interest and hearty support. He served as a vestryman in the Episcopal Church in his Albemarle parish, was often a member of the annual diocesan convention, and on several occasions represented the church in Virginia in the General Convention of the Protestant Episcopal Church in the United States.

[Material on the career of Hugh Nelson is fragmentary and scattered. The best brief sketch is to be found in R. C. M. Page, *Geneal. of the Page Family in Va.* (2nd ed., 1893). See also: C. F. Adams, ed., *Memoirs of John Quincy Adams*, vols. IV–VI (1874–75); S. M. Hamilton, *The Writings of Jas. Monroe* (7 vols., 1898–1903); E. C. Mead, *Hist. Homes of the South-west Mountains, Va.* (1899), pp. 163–64; and *Southern Churchman*, Apr. 1, 1836. There are some forty of Nelson's letters, written for the most part between 1808 and 1818, in the Division of Manuscripts of the Lib. of Cong.]
M. H. W.

NELSON, JOHN (1654–Nov. 15, 1734), New England trader, statesman, was the son of Robert Nelson, a member of Gray's Inn, and of Mary (Temple) Nelson, the daughter of Sir John Temple of Stanton Bury, Buckinghamshire, and the sister of Sir Thomas Temple, proprietor and governor of Nova Scotia, 1656–70. Probably shortly after 1670 when Sir Thomas settled in Boston Nelson came from his home in England to join him. When Sir Thomas died in 1674 the nephew inherited his uncle's pretensions to land and trade in Nova Scotia. As early as 1677 Nelson was engaged in the fur trade in the Kennebec country. In the interest of this trade he went to Canada in 1682 where he became acquainted with prominent French officials. In Boston he married Elizabeth, the daughter of William Tailer and the niece of William Stoughton. To them were born two sons and four daughters. He was an outspoken opponent of Randolph and Andros, and when news of the overthrow of James II reached Boston in 1689 he joined in demanding the surrender of Andros and led the militia that captured him. Nelson was ignored in the reorganization of the colony. Hutchinson explained that it was because he was an Anglican and "of a gay free temper" (*post*, I, p. 378). Probably a bitter personal and political rivalry existing between himself and William Phips also prevented his receiving recognition. In 1691, however, the colony sent him on an expedition to Nova Scotia. He was captured by the French and held prisoner in Quebec for a year. The French treated him kindly but feared him, and when his captors learned that he had sent military information to Boston they sent him to France where he was confined in a dungeon of the castle of Angoulême for two years. In 1694 his importance was sufficiently recognized to secure his transfer to the Bastille. There French officials entered into discussions with him regarding a project for gaining the neutrality of America during the war and Nelson wrote to Blathwayt regarding the proposition. The French king finally offered him a parole to go to London to discuss the matter.

In London Nelson was reprimanded by the Privy Council for entering into negotiations with the French, but the Board of Trade listened to his views. He informed the latter of French designs to establish a colony on the Mississippi and to develop there the fur trade, upon which their power in America depended. He urged that the English encourage the "bush-lopers" to extend their trade, and that plans be formed to unite the colonies under one head to resist the French. Then the conquest of Canada could be accomplished. Blathwayt and apparently the whole Board of Trade were impressed with his arguments and his memorial was discussed by the Board years afterward. England was not then in position to demand the cession of Canada but Nelson's arguments apparently were conclusive in establishing the southern boundary of Acadia at the St. George River instead of at the Kennebec as claimed by the French. After the Peace of Ryswick Nelson was released from parole and returned to Boston. During the War of the Spanish Succession he continued to address arguments to Blathwayt for the expulsion of the French from America, and especially from the country south of the St. Lawrence. It was due in no small measure to his propaganda that Nova Scotia and Newfoundland were ceded to England at the Peace of Utrecht. After the peace Nelson continued his efforts to have the boundaries of New France restricted by the boundary commission. After his return to Boston he was appointed a commissioner to treat with the Indians. Although still an Anglican he supported Benjamin Colman in his efforts to liberalize the New England church. He opposed the intrigues to supplant Governor Dudley by Sir Charles Hobby. He resumed his fur trade with the Indians of the northeast and he succeeded in regaining some of the lands his uncle had held in Nova Scotia. He was a capable business man and died wealthy.

[Temple Prime, *Descent of John Nelson and of his Children* (1886, 4th ed., *Some Account of the Temple Family*, 1899); Timothy Cutler, *The Final Peace. . . . A Sermon Deliver'd at Christ-Church in Boston Nov. 28, 1734, on the Occasion of the Death of John Nelson, Esq.* (1735); Thos. Hutchinson, *The Hist. of the Colony of Mass. Bay*, vol. I (1764); A. H. Buffington, "John Nelson's Voyage to Quebec in 1682," *Col. Soc. Mass. Pubs.*, vol. XXVI (1927); "Papers of the Lloyd Family of . . . Lloyd's Neck," *N. Y. Hist. Soc. Colls.*, Pub. Fund Series, vols. LIX–LX (1927); *Mass. Hist. Soc. Colls.*, 3 ser. I (1825), 4 ser. VIII (1868), 5 ser. VIII (1882); *Proc. Mass. Hist. Soc.*, 1 ser. VII (1864); *Me. Hist. Soc. Colls.*, 2 ser., "Doc. Hist.," X (1907); E. B. O'Callaghan, *Docs. Rel. to the Col. Hist. . . . of N. Y.*, vol. IV (1854), vol. IX (1855); W. T. Morgan, "A Crisis in the Hist. of the Hudson's Bay Company," *N. Dak. Hist. Quart.*, July 1931; *Calendar of State Papers, Colonial Ser., America and West Indies . . . 1696 . . . 1697* (1904); *Jour. of the Commissioners for Trade and Plantations . . . 1704 . . . 1709*

(1925) and *1718 ... 1722* (1925); J. B. Brebner, *New England's Outpost, Acadia, Before the Conquest of Canada* (1927); *Collection de Manuscrits ... Relatifs à la Nouvelle-France* (4 vols., 1883–85).]   P. C. P.

NELSON, JULIUS (Mar. 6, 1858–Feb. 15, 1916), biologist and specialist in oyster culture, was born in Copenhagen, Denmark, the son of Christian and Julia (Jörgensen) Nelson. In 1863 his family came to America and settled near Waupaca, Wis. The young man prepared for college in the Waupaca High School and entered the University of Wisconsin, graduating with the degree of B.S. in 1881. For a time he served as principal of the high school at Rio, Wis., but he continued his studies and received the degree of M.S. from the University of Wisconsin in 1884. He enrolled for further graduate study at Johns Hopkins University where subsequently he was appointed to a fellowship. Shortly after finishing his studies there with the doctor's degree in 1888, he was appointed biologist of the New Jersey Agricultural Experiment Station and professor of biology at Rutgers College, positions he held until the time of his death.

During his first ten years at the New Jersey Station he conducted extensive investigations of cattle diseases and their relation to public health. To the knowledge of bovine tuberculosis, then in a primitive stage, his studies yielded valuable results. His investigations also embraced contagious abortion and garget in cattle, poultry diseases, egg production by virgin fowls, dairy bacteriology, sewage disposal, and home sanitation. His greatest contributions, however, were made subsequent to 1900 in the field of oyster culture. Aided by special state appropriations and with the cooperation of progressive oystermen, he established laboratories on the New Jersey coast where through successive summers he studied the life history and habits of the oyster. His findings were put into practical application by the oyster industry of New Jersey. As a result of his studies, Nelson came to be recognized as the outstanding American authority on oyster culture and was frequently called upon for expert testimony before such bodies as the National Board of Food and Drug Inspectors and the United States Fish Commission. In 1915 he was engaged by the Biological Board of Canada to make a survey of oyster-producing resources in Canadian waters. His sudden death in 1916, resulting from an attack of pneumonia, cut short a scientific career that had just begun to enjoy the full fruition of pioneering and painstaking labor. Nelson had married, on Aug. 9, 1888, Nellie Cynthia Chase of Madison, Wis. They reared a family of three sons and three daughters.

Nelson's writings include a long list of studies, most of which were published in the annual reports and bulletins of the New Jersey Agricultural Experiment Station. In addition he was the author of "Heredity and Sex" (*American Journal of Psychology*, January 1890), and a *Descriptive Catalogue of the Vertebrates of New Jersey* (New Jersey Geological Survey, 1890). He was also a contributor to Bailey's *Cyclopedia of American Agriculture*. He was a member of the Nature Study Society of America, of the National Association of Shell Fish Commissioners, of the New Jersey Tuberculosis Commission, and of the New Jersey State Science Teachers' Association, and served as president of the New Jersey State Microscopical Society, 1896–97. He was also vice-president and consulting advisor of the Lederle Laboratories, New York.

[See the annual reports and bulletins of the N. J. Agric. Experiment Station, 1888–1916; the *Targum*, Rutgers College, Feb. 23, Mar. 8, 1916; *Rutgers Alumni Quart.*, Apr. 1916; and the *Daily State Gazette* (Trenton), Feb. 17, 1916. Nelson's oyster investigations are summarized in the *Thirty-Seventh Ann. Report of the N. J. State Agric. Experiment Station* (1917); they are treated in further detail in Carl R. Woodward and Ingrid N. Waller, *New Jersey's Agric. Experiment Station, 1880–1930* (1932).]
C. R. W—d.

NELSON, KNUTE (Feb. 2, 1843–Apr. 28, 1923), governor of Minnesota, United States senator, was born at Evanger in the district of Voss, Norway. His mother, Ingeborg Kvilekval, brought him to the United States when he was six years old, and, after a brief period of much hardship in Chicago, the two went to La Grange, Wis. There the mother was married to Nels Nelson, an immigrant from Norway, and the boy assumed his name. In 1853 the family settled on a farm in the town of Deerfield, about twenty miles east of Madison. After attending local schools the youth at fifteen entered Albion Academy, a school conducted by Seventh-Day Adventists and chosen by Nelson because it was only fourteen miles from his home. He worked for the principal of the academy to pay for his tuition and a room, and he fetched supplies of fuel and food from his home. In the winter of 1860–61 he taught a district school; and in May 1861 he enlisted in the 4th Wisconsin Infantry, a regiment which, after 1863, was mounted and designated as the 4th Wisconsin Cavalry. He participated in Butler's expedition against New Orleans and Sherman's first expedition against Vicksburg. He was wounded during the siege of Port Hudson and was held prisoner within the city for a month until its capitulation. After recovering from his wound he served with his regiment until the expiration of his enlistment, July 1864. In 1863 he had become a corporal. Returning to Wisconsin, he reëntered Albion Academy in the fall of 1864, completed his course, and was graduated with the degree of Ph.B.

Having already determined upon a career in politics, Nelson read law with William F. Vilas of Madison and was admitted to the bar in 1867. In that year also he married Nicholina Jacobson, and was elected to the Wisconsin Assembly, in which he served two terms. After living a short time at Cambridge, Wis., he removed to Alexandria, Minn., at that time (1871) a frontier county seat. He took up government land and combined homesteading with law practice, managing, as he said, "to get on one side or the other of about every case of importance in the six or seven counties in my part of the country" (*Minnesota History Bulletin*, February 1924, p. 350). His first public office in Minnesota was that of county attorney for Douglas County (1872–74); he was thereafter state senator, 1874–78. In 1882 he was elected to Congress as a Republican, after a bitter fight for the nomination had resulted in a split in the party in his district. He served three terms in Congress and then refused a fourth nomination and returned to his law practice. In 1892 the Republicans in Minnesota, alarmed by the tendency of the Scandinavian settlers to join the Populists, selected Nelson as their candidate for governor. He was elected, and was reëlected in 1894 but resigned the office in 1895 upon being chosen by the legislature as United States senator.

The office of senator Nelson held by successive reëlections until his death. During these years he was member of the committees on Indian affairs and public lands, and member and chairman of the judiciary committee. He was interested in legislation relating to Chippewa Indian lands in Minnesota and to the development of Alaska. Among the more notable measures ascribed to him are the Nelson bankruptcy act (1898) and the act creating the Department of Commerce and Labor (1902). His Republican conservatism was modified by low tariff leanings. He advocated a federal income tax and the constitutional amendment necessary to secure it, supported the prohibition amendment and the Volstead Act, was active in establishing the Interstate Commerce Commission, fought amendments designed to weaken the Sherman Anti-trust law, was violently opposed to the Adamson law, and arrayed himself against his party in advocating the entrance of the United States into the League of Nations. In appearance he was short and broad of stature, blue-eyed, with black hair and chin whiskers which turned gray soon enough to win him the sobriquet of "the grand old man of Minnesota." His habits were simple and frugal; he died possessed of a modest competence. He was politically astute, especially in his earlier years when astuteness was necessary to his political survival. The first Norwegian-born American citizen to serve as congressman, as a state senator, or as United States senator, he had the vote of his countrymen behind him in his early career, though later agrarian unrest and the increasing liberalism of his compatriots alienated many. A statue of Nelson, erected by popular subscription, stands before the state capitol of Minnesota.

[See M. W. Odland, *The Life of Knute Nelson* (1926); J. A. O. Preus, "Knute Nelson," in *Minn. Hist. Bull.*, Feb. 1924, followed by two autobiographical letters; E. E. Adams, "Nelson-Kindred Campaign of 1882," in *Ibid.*, May 1923; *St. Paul Sunday Pioneer Press*, Apr. 29, 30, 1923. Nelson's papers are in the possession of the Minn. Hist. Soc.]   S. J. B.

NELSON, NELSON OLSEN (Sept. 11, 1844–Oct. 5, 1922), manufacturer and promoter of profit-sharing, was born in Lillesand, Norway, the son of Anders and Gertrude Nelson. His father emigrated to the United States in 1847 and settled in Buchanan County, Mo. Nelson's boyhood years were divided between work on a farm in summer and attendance at rural school in winter. At the outbreak of the Civil War he enlisted in the Union army and served throughout its duration. Upon reëntering civil life he settled in St. Louis and took employment with a wholesale grocery firm. A year later he started a business of his own in St. Joseph, Mo. In April 1868 he was married to Almeria Posegate. From 1870 to 1872 he was established in Hiawatha, Kan., but in the latter year he again went to St. Louis and in 1877 he founded the N. O. Nelson Manufacturing Company, makers of building and plumbing supplies, which became one of the largest concerns of its kind in the world.

The problems of labor had for a long time attracted Nelson's interest, and in 1886, because of the reputation for wisdom and justice he had established among business and labor elements, he served as conciliator and arbitrator of a strike on parts of the Gould system of railroads. He then began to study the basic causes of industrial disharmony and acquainted himself with several plans of profit-sharing, especially with those of the Maison Leclaire in Paris, and Godin in Guise, France. He became convinced that the essentials of such a system possessed all the attributes necessary to the maintenance of a just and practicable relationship between capital and labor. Capitalism, notwithstanding its shortcomings, was preferable, so he held, to any alternative order, and he believed that a major reason for the practicability of profit-sharing was that it rested "automatically upon conditions already in effect." The plan of profit-sharing in his plant Nelson put into operation in 1886. After allowance had been made for "customary salaries, wages, expenses, and interest," the remainder of the firm's income for the year was to be divided pro rata upon the total amount of wages paid and capital employed. The dividends were payable in cash or in stock in the firm. In 1890 a tract of land near Edwardsville, Ill., was purchased, and upon it Nelson founded the village of Leclaire, in which were built factories and employees' dwellings and which was laid out as a model community. For many years it was the worthy boast of its residents that it had no policemen, no pauperism, and an extraordinarily low rate for death and infant mortality. In 1905 Nelson extended the provisions of the profit-sharing plan to the customers of the firm.

In his effort to minimize economic waste and to increase in all feasible ways the incomes of his employees, Nelson started in 1902 a cooperative store in Leclaire based upon the Rochdale plan. By 1916 it had about 150 members. The success of this project heightened Nelson's belief in the practicability of cooperation in merchandizing. In 1911, during a visit to New Orleans, he was affected by the evidence of want on the part of the inhabitants of the poorer districts, and he established at his own expense a grocery-store in which commodities were sold at the lowest possible margin of profit. He developed the enterprise into a chain and in 1915 organized a cooperative association. The business grew to consist of sixty-three stores, a bakery, a creamery, a condiment factory, and the stock and equipment on a farm. Notwithstanding early prospects of success, the enterprise as expanded, experienced a succession of losses culminating in 1918 in its failure, and Nelson filed a personal petition for bankruptcy on the New Orleans undertaking.

For many years Nelson had been strongly interested in numerous matters of civic, social, and philanthropic import. In 1887 and 1890 he was a member of the St. Louis City Council. In 1895 he was a delegate to the meeting in London of the Profit-Sharing and Co-operative Associations of the World. He organized the Fresh Air Mission for children in the downtown districts of St. Louis, free-steamboat excursions for poor children and mothers, and built free swimming-pools. He aided in founding work-

ingmen's self-culture clubs and lecture courses; he started traveling libraries for country-school districts. In politics he was for many years a Republican but with the passage of the McKinley tariff, which he strongly opposed, he allied himself with the Democratic party. He favored free trade, and believed in "free silver" and the single tax. In religion he was until middle life a Lutheran, but in later years he became a Unitarian. His character, personality, and intellect, combined with his energy and superior business sense, were the basis for his accomplishments. But it seems fair to say that he at no time appreciated the deeper implications of a system of profit-sharing or recognized the limitations operating against its widespread and permanent adoption. He failed to understand that the success accomplished in his own plant was more personal than institutional. The collapse of his venture in New Orleans hastened his loss of interest, already considerably diminished, in the major business in St. Louis. For three years preceding his death he lived in California.

[Nelson wrote occasional articles treating of his business experiments. For the best of these see the *Independent*, Feb. 21, 1901, May 25, 1905, Feb. 13, 1913, Jan. 19, 1914; the *North Am. Rev.*, Apr. 1887; and *System*, Oct. 1915. For biographical details see *Who's Who in America*, 1914–15; H. L. Conard, *Encyc. of the Hist. of Mo.* (1901), vol. IV; Wm. Hyde and H. L. Conard, *Encyc. of the Hist. of St. Louis* (1899); *St. Louis Globe Democrat*, Oct. 7, 1922. Nelson's correspondence was made available to the writer of this sketch by his private secretary.]   G. W. S.

NELSON, RENSSELAER RUSSELL (May 12, 1826–Oct. 15, 1904), Minnesota jurist, was born at Cooperstown, N. Y., the son of Catherine Ann (Russell) and Samuel Nelson [*q.v.*]. He was of mixed New England and Irish ancestry, with a dash of Dutch and Scotch. The boy was prepared for college at a military academy at Cooperstown and at Haerwick Seminary. He was graduated from Yale in 1846, read law in the offices of James R. Whiting of New York and George A. Starkweather of Cooperstown, and was admitted to the bar in 1849. After practising a short time in Buffalo, he went to Minnesota Territory in 1850 and opened a law office in St. Paul, although informed by the landlord of his hotel that the population of the town (about a thousand) included "fifty lawyers, mostly starving." Soon thereafter he joined with five other St. Paul men in a land speculation, which in August 1853 took them as settlers to Superior, Wis. Having helped to organize Douglas County, with Superior as the county seat, Nelson was appointed county attorney by the governor, and at the first election, in November 1854, he was elected to the same office. But the vision of Superior as a great inland port was not to be realized at so early a day, and he returned to St. Paul in 1855.

In 1857 Nelson was appointed by President Buchanan associate justice of the supreme court of Minnesota Territory. In the same year he rendered an important decision, refusing a writ of mandamus to compel the territorial officers to remove the capital from St. Paul to St. Peter. A bill for this removal had passed both houses of the legislature but had been sequestered by the chairman of the committee on engrossed bills until the legislature had adjourned. Nelson ruled that, the power to fix the location of the territorial capital having been granted to and exercised by the first territorial legislature, no subsequent legislature had the power to change that location; he further ruled that the bill substituted for the missing bill and signed by the governor was not the bill passed by the legislature and that hence no act had been passed.

In May 1858, when Minnesota became a state, Nelson was appointed a United States district judge for Minnesota. A Democrat in a normally Republican state, he had no temptation to forsake the bench for politics and did not retire until 1896. He was married on Nov. 3, 1858, to Emma F. Wright (*née* Beebe) of New York. From 1862 to 1864 he was vice-president of the St. Paul & Pacific Railroad Company. He was reputed to be an unprejudiced and liberal-minded judge whose decisions were seldom reversed; he had "a serene composure which seemed natural to the man, becoming to a judge," and "the courteous gentility of the old school of which he was one of the best examples."

[W. H. C. Folsom, *Fifty Years in the Northwest* (1888); H. F. Stevens, *Hist. of the Bench and Bar of Minn.* (2 vols., 1904); J. F. Williams, *A Hist. of the City of St. Paul* (1876); "Proceedings in Memory of the Honorable Rensselaer R. Nelson," in 93 *Minnesota,* xxi–xxxvi; *Bull. of Yale Univ., First Ser., No. 5, July 1905: Obit. Record of Grads.*; obituaries in St. Paul and Minneapolis newspapers, Oct. 15, 16, 1904.]
S.J.B.

NELSON, REUBEN (Dec. 16, 1818–Feb. 20, 1879), Methodist Episcopal clergyman, educator, and administrator, was born in New York City, one of the twelve children of Abraham and Huldah Nelson. In his early youth he lost his right arm below the elbow while working in a woolen mill. When a lad of fifteen he joined the church, and within a year he was licensed as an exhorter; at the end of another year, in spite of his youth, he was licensed to preach. He early saw his need of education and was keen to avail himself of every opportunity for intellectual and cultural development. For a period he studied at Hartwick Seminary, Otsego County, N. Y. On Aug.

19, 1840, he was admitted on trial to the Oneida Conference of the Methodist Episcopal Church and was appointed as third preacher on the Otsego circuit; the next year he held a similar appointment on the Westford circuit. He was ordained deacon Aug. 10, 1842, and in that year married Jane Scott Eddy, daughter of Col. Asa Eddy of Milford, N. Y. In addition to his work as a preacher, he performed the duties of principal of Otsego Academy at Cooperstown, N. Y. When, in 1844, the Oneida Conference founded Wyoming Seminary at Kingston, Pa., he was chosen its first principal. His ordination as elder occurred July 22, 1846. For twenty-seven years he served as principal at Wyoming Seminary, and placed it in the forefront of institutions of its class.

Having risen to a place of leadership of his church, he was elected, in 1872, a publishing agent of the Methodist Book Concern at New York. Although this great publishing house at that time was passing through the most critical period of its long existence, Nelson proved remarkably well fitted for his new position with its many complicated and difficult problems. He was held in high regard by his associates in the ministry, and represented his Conference five times as a delegate to the General Conference, holding at each of these sessions committee positions of commanding importance and responsibility. In addition to his service as publishing agent, he was, from 1872 to the time of his death, treasurer of the Missionary Society of the Methodist Episcopal Church, an office involving the most careful scrutiny of contributions, investments, and expenditures of world-wide range. He died in New York City, and was buried in the Cemetery at Forty Fort, Pa.

[*Hist. of Wyoming Conference* (1904); *Jour. of the General Conference of the M. E. Ch.* (1880); *Methodist Quart. Rev.*, Oct. 1879; the *Christian Advocate*, Feb. 27, 1879; H. C. Jennings, *The Methodist Book Concern* (1924); J. W. Jordan, *Encyc. of Pa. Biog.*, vol. VII (1916); *N. Y. Times,* Feb. 20, 21, 1879.]
S.J.H.

NELSON, ROGER (1759–June 7, 1815), Revolutionary soldier, congressman, jurist, youngest son of Dr. Arthur and Lucy (Waters) Nelson, was born at their homestead near Point of Rocks, Frederick County, Md. After completing his preparatory work, he studied at the College of William and Mary. Commissioned a lieutenant in the 5th Regiment of the Maryland Line July 15, 1780, he was sent south immediately to the army commanded by General Gates. At the battle of Camden the following month he fought with courage but fell wounded in the retreat. Surrounded by a band of British, and further wounded, he was left on the field for dead but was later discovered, only to be carried off a prisoner to Charleston. After several months of hardship on British prison-ships he was exchanged, whereupon he was transferred to the regiment of cavalry commanded by Col. William Washington. At the battle of Guilford Court House, Mar. 15, 1781, he took part in the charge against the British guards led by Colonel Washington. He engaged in the battle of Eutaw Springs, September 1781, and was present at the surrender at Yorktown. In 1793 he engaged in the suppression of the Whiskey Rebellion by organizing and leading a troop of cavalry. He closed his military career as brigadier-general of militia.

Meanwhile he had embarked upon his career of civilian service. After his return from the Revolutionary War he studied law and was admitted to the bar about 1785. After a brief residence at Taneytown, Md., he moved to Frederick where he soon gained a large practice. After serving in the Maryland House of Delegates, he was elected without opposition to fill a vacancy in the federal House of Representatives caused by the death of Daniel Heister [q.v.]. Reëlected for three successive terms, he served from November 1804 until his resignation in May 1810. He was named by the House one of the managers for the impeachment proceedings against Associate Justice Chase but refused to serve because of the latter's Revolutionary record. Although he supported Jefferson in an embargo policy which bore heavily upon the rural districts in depressed agricultural prices, he weathered the political storm in the election of 1808 which swept out many fellow Democrats—an evidence of his great personal popularity. He thus maintained a record of never having been defeated in an election. His final public service was as associate judge of the sixth judicial circuit of Maryland, which post he filled from 1810 to his death in 1815. He married Mary Brooke Sim in 1787. Though not regarded as a learned or profound lawyer, it was said of him that his persuasiveness was irresistible with a Frederick County jury. As a political speaker he was eloquent and dramatic and was a force in Congress. For many years he was the recognized Democratic leader in his county. He died at Frederick.

[There is an account of Nelson in T. J. C. Williams, *Hist. of Frederick County, Md.* (1910), vol. I. See also: *Ancestral Records and Portraits* (1910), vol. II; J. T. Scharf, *Hist. of Western Md.* (1882), vol. I; *Archives of Md.*, vols. XVIII (1900) and XLVIII (1931); *Biog. Dir. Am. Cong.* (1928); *Army and Navy Chronicle*, Mar. 14, 1839; *Md. Republican*, June 17, 24, 1815, *Baltimore Patriot and Evening Advertiser*, June 9, 1815.]   E. L.

NELSON, SAMUEL (Nov. 10, 1792–Dec. 13, 1873), jurist, was born in Hebron, Washington County, N. Y. His parents, John Rogers and Jean McArthur (Jane McCarter according to some accounts) Nelson were Scotch-Irish who came to America about 1760. He spent his boyhood on a farm and attended the district school where his aptness as a pupil led to plans for his entrance into the ministry. At fifteen he went for two years to the Washington Academy at Salem, N. Y., and for one year to Granville Academy. He entered Middlebury College as a sophomore and graduated in 1813. To the disappointment of his parents he entered the law office of Savage & Woods in Salem as a clerk. After two years he moved with Judge Woods to Madison County and remained with him for two more years. Upon admission to the bar in 1817 he opened an office in Cortland, N. Y., where he developed a remunerative practice.

Nelson's entrance into public life occurred in 1820 when he served as a presidential elector for James Monroe and was also appointed to the postmastership of Cortland, which he held for three years. In 1821 he was a delegate to the New York constitutional convention where he strongly advocated the abolition of property qualifications upon the suffrage. In 1823 he was appointed as judge of the sixth circuit under the new arrangements set up by the constitution of 1821. He held this post until 1831 when he was appointed associate justice of the supreme court of New York. In 1837 he became chief justice and held that position for eight years. In 1845 he received the support of a substantial group of Democrats in the New York legislature for the United States Senate but failed of election. He was a member of the state constitutional convention of 1846 but took no active part in its proceedings.

In February 1845 President Tyler nominated Nelson, unexpectedly to him and to his friends, to the associate justiceship on the Supreme Court of the United States left vacant by the death of Smith Thompson. In spite of the Senate's bitter hostility to Tyler the nomination was confirmed without delay and Nelson took his seat on the Court on Mar. 5, 1845. He became one of the most useful and hard-working members of the Court and a recognized authority in the fields of admiralty and maritime law, international law, patent law, and conflict of laws. As a result of his attention to these more technical problems his interest in questions of constitutional law was correspondingly less, or perhaps it may be said that his training as a common-law lawyer and judge made him somewhat less willing than some of his colleagues to blaze new trails in the politico-judicial realm of judicial review and constitutional interpretation. Ten years elapsed after he entered the Court before he delivered a majority opinion upon a constitutional question (*Pennsylvania* vs. *Wheeling & Belmont Bridge Company,* 18 *Howard,* 421). During his twenty-eight years on the Court he wrote but twenty-two majority opinions in constitutional cases as against three hundred and seven in other cases. He ·wrote four concurring and seventeen dissenting opinions. His opinions delivered on the circuit bench for the second circuit were of importance in the fields in which he was expert and his decisions were seldom appealed from. There was little about him or his work as a judge which was spectacular or scintillating, but his opinions could be relied upon for logic, lucidity, brevity, and freedom from *obiter dicta* and academic digressions.

Nelson's unwillingness to play politics under the guise of constitutional interpretation is well illustrated by his attitude in the case of Dred Scott [*q.v.*]. The issue presented in this case (19 *Howard,* 393) was the citizenship in Missouri of Scott, such citizenship being requisite to the jurisdiction of any federal court. By its own earlier decision in the case of *Strader* vs. *Graham* (10 *Howard,* 82) the Court had supposedly settled this matter by holding that the status of a negro slave taken by his master into free territory and then back into a slave state was determined by the law of the latter state. The Court's original intention was to dispose of the Dred Scott case in this manner, dismissing it for want of jurisdiction, and to Nelson was assigned the writing of the opinion. On the grounds just outlined he held Scott to be not a citizen of Missouri, the Missouri courts having so held, and consequently incapable of bringing suit as a citizen in a federal court; and he omitted as irrelevant all consideration of the validity of the Missouri Compromise Act of 1820. Stirred by the information that Justices Curtis and McLean were preparing elaborate opinions upholding the citizenship of Scott and the power of Congress to exclude slavery from the territories, the majority of the Court decided to deal with these larger problems and withdrew its support from the narrower and sounder position which Nelson had assumed. Taney's famous opinion and those of his concurring colleagues were the result. But Nelson stood his ground and his opinion remains today as the only one in the case free alike from *obiter dictum* and evidences of political bias.

Nelson's attitude during the Civil War was that of the conservative but loyal Northern Democrat. He doubted the constitutionality of coercing the Southern states and acted with Justice John A. Campbell as an intermediary early in 1861 between the Southern commissioners and Secretary Seward. He strongly urged a policy of conciliation and when Lincoln refused to support Seward to this end he withdrew from the negotiations and left Washington. He looked askance upon what seemed to him to be unwarranted accretions of power to the executive and military branches of the government. He dissented from the majority decision in the Prize Cases and joined with the majority in the Milligan decision. He was one of the original majority in the Legal Tender Cases denying the validity of the Legal Tender Acts and dissented both against the Court's decision to rehear the case and its final judgment of reversal. The Legal Tender Cases were the last in which he participated.

In 1871 Nelson was named by President Grant as a member of the Joint High Commission to negotiate the settlement of the *Alabama* claims, a task for which his knowledge of international law, his tact, and his firmness made him eminently fit. This arduous work extending over several months withdrew him from the bench temporarily. It also hastened his death. A protracted conference in an unheated room induced an illness from which he never fully recovered. He resigned from the Court on Nov. 28, 1872, retiring upon full pay under the Act of 1869. Had he delayed his resignation for a few months, he would have rounded out a full fifty years of service on the state and federal bench. In 1819 Nelson had married Pamela Woods, the daughter of his partner. She died in 1822, leaving one son. In 1825 he moved to Cooperstown, N. Y., where he married Catherine Ann Russell, by whom he had two daughters and a son, Rensselaer Russell Nelson [*q.v.*]. He always maintained a home in Cooperstown and became an intimate friend of James Fenimore Cooper. He died there of apoplexy on Dec. 13, 1873.

[See Alden Chester, *Courts and Lawyers of N. Y.* (1925), vol. III; Edwin Countryman, "Samuel Nelson," *Green Bag,* June 1907; Charles Warren, *The Supreme Court in U. S. Hist.* (1922), vols. II and III; H. L. Carson, *The Supreme Court of the U. S.* (1891); E. J. Wiley, *Cat. of the Officers and Students of Middlebury Coll.* (1917); E. S. Corwin, "The Dred Scott Decision, in the Light of Contemporary Legal Doctrines," *Am. Hist. Rev.,* Oct. 1911; tributes at the time of retirement from the bench in 14 *Wallace,* vii–x; *N.-Y. Tribune,* Dec. 15, 1873. Nelson's Supreme Court decisions are to be found in 4 *Howard* to 12 *Wallace,* inclusive. His circuit court reports are in 1–10 *Blatchford's Circuit Court Reports* (2nd circuit).]

R. E. C.

NELSON, THOMAS (Dec. 26, 1738–Jan. 4, 1789), merchant, signer of the Declaration of Independence, soldier, governor, was the eldest son of William Nelson [q.v.] of Yorktown, Va., and his wife Elizabeth Burwell. He was sent to England to be educated and after attending a private school at Hackney, he entered Christ's College, Cambridge, in May 1758, to stay until Ladyday in 1761. In the year after his return from England, on July 29, 1762, he was married to Lucy, daughter of Philip and Mary (Randolph) Grymes, who bore him eleven children, among them Hugh Nelson [q.v.]. While yet on board the vessel returning from England he had been chosen by the voters of York County to represent them in the House of Burgesses, but he soon took his place among his fellow planters in His Majesty's Council of Virginia in 1764. As the first stages of the Revolution passed in Virginia he was an articulate member of the conventions and supported ardently the preparation for war, especially Patrick Henry's motion to arm Virginia in March 1775. He went to the Continental Congress in 1775, resigning as colonel of the 2nd Virginia Regiment. The none too kindly pen of John Adams described Nelson, when they met in Philadelphia, as "a fat man, like the late Colonel Lee of Marblehead. He is a speaker, and alert and lively for his weight" (C. F. Adams, *The Works of John Adams*, II, 1850, p. 422). In the Virginia convention of 1776 he introduced the resolutions drafted by Edmund Pendleton and advocated by Patrick Henry calling upon Congress to declare the colonies free and independent. These resolutions passed the Virginia convention on May 15 and were taken by Nelson to the Congress in Philadelphia. Thus Thomas Nelson, the embodiment of wealth and established position in Virginia, stood shoulder to shoulder with the then impecunious frontiersman Henry as they swung their followings into the path of independence.

When the Declaration of Independence was adopted Nelson was one of the Virginia signers. Ill health, however, forced him to give up service in the Congress and he returned to Virginia in the spring of 1777. Although he was an ardent revolutionist, he was in no sense a radical and he keenly opposed the Virginia Act of Sequestration of British property in 1777 and is said to have declared that he would pay his debts like an honest man. Appointed by the governor and council of Virginia brigadier-general and commander-in-chief of the forces in the commonwealth, he raised a company with large personal expenditure and marched to Philadelphia in 1778, but these troops were disbanded when Congress felt unable to support them. In 1779 Nelson returned to Congress but was ill again after several months of service and returned to Virginia to serve for the remainder of the conflict in the rôle of financier, governor, and commander of the militia of his state. In 1781 he was elected in succession to Jefferson governor of Virginia, the first conservative to hold that office. His powers were strengthened by the legislature to meet the military crisis, but he even exceeded these grants of authority in his virtual position as military dictator. In September with over three thousand Virginia militia he joined Washington in the siege of Yorktown. His aid brought expressions of gratitude from Washington and his selfless patriotism in offering his own mansion in the town as a target for the bullets of his fellow countrymen has become one of the lasting tales of the Revolution in Virginia. Again the burden of office proved too great a strain for his constitution and he was forced to resign from the governorship before the end of 1781.

With the victory of the American cause Nelson reaped the ruin of his personal fortune. He sacrificed his private means to pay his public debts, accumulated in security for Virginia's loan of 1780 and in fitting out and provisioning troops. This course with the other hazards of the Revolution left him a poor man with a wife and eleven children. He moved to a small estate, "Offley," in Hanover County, and there spent in simple surroundings the last years of his life. Asthma, the foe he had fought so long, brought his death early in 1789. He was buried in the old churchyard at Yorktown.

[Family Bible of Thos. Nelson in the possession of the Va. Hist. Soc.; "Letters of Thos. Nelson, Jr.," *Va. Hist. Soc. Pubs.*, n.s., no. 1 (1874); *Official Letters of the Govs. . . . of Va.*, vol. III (1929); R. C. M. Page, *Geneal. of the Page Family in Va.* (2nd ed., 1893); Wm. Meade, *Old Churches, Ministers and Families of Va.* (1857); M. V. Smith, *Virginia, 1492–1892, . . . A Hist. of the Executives of the Colony and of the Commonwealth* (1893).]   M. H. W.

NELSON, THOMAS HENRY (c. 1823–Mar. 14, 1896), lawyer, diplomat, was born near Maysville, Ky., an elder brother of William Nelson [q.v.], and the son of Dr. Thomas W. Nelson and Frances (Doniphan) Nelson of Mason County, Ky., in whose home the Clays, the Crittendens, and other members of the old Kentucky aristocracy were familiar guests. After completing his studies in the Maysville schools, he went in 1844 to Rockville, Ind., where he studied and practised law for six years, and then moved to Terre Haute, which became his permanent home. In 1855 he formed a law partnership with Abram Adams Hammond, who afterward became governor of Indiana, and in 1856 a partnership with Isaac N. Pierce. In his active law practice in western Indiana and eastern Illinois he met as a legal opponent, and presently as a friend, Abraham Lincoln. He became a leader of the Whig party, and was one of the founders of the Republican party in the Middle West. Several times he was a delegate to state and national conventions. Only once, however, was he a candidate for a public office: in 1860 he made a joint canvass with Daniel W. Voorhees in a campaign for Congress, and his rival won the election. On June 1, 1861, Nelson was appointed minister to Chile by his old friend Lincoln.

Tall and soldierly in bearing, distinguished in appearance, vigorous in action, a brilliant and compelling orator, skilful in public affairs, gifted with a contagious friendliness, he exerted his best efforts to win the friendship of Chile for the United States, and was notably successful, even while he was bringing American claims outstanding against Chile to a speedy and satisfactory settlement. Perhaps the high point of Chilean enthusiasm for Nelson was reached after the terrible fire in the Church of Campañia in Santiago on Dec. 8, 1863, in which about 2,000 persons perished. On this occasion Nelson, with other Americans, showed great heroism in rescuing several individuals. The people of Santiago devoted the following Fourth of July to a celebration to do him honor. In 1865, when hostilities broke out between Chile and Spain, Chile believed that the United States would become her ally. Nelson labored tirelessly to bring about a peaceful settlement between the two warring countries, but was not authorized to involve the United States as a belligerent. The people of Chile were much disappointed, even resentful, but the Minister's policy of neutrality was subsequently indorsed by the State Department.

Returning to the United States in 1866, he campaigned vigorously in favor of the Fourteenth Amendment to the Constitution. In 1869 he was appointed minister to Mexico, and served there ably and faithfully until 1873, although no outstanding incident marked this period of service. The death of his wife, Elizabeth (Key) Nelson, in Mexico city in 1872 was a severe blow to him. The daughter of Col. Marshall Key, a Kentucky political leader, she was possessed of great charm, intelligence, and many accomplishments, and since her marriage in 1844 had taken an important part in her husband's career. (See the article on Mrs. Nelson written by William Cullen Bryant, in the *Annual Cyclopedia* for 1872.) After his resignation from the diplomatic service, Nelson returned to Terre Haute, where he

again practised law and took a prominent part in politics. He died there in 1896, survived by two of his six children.

[*A Biog. Hist. of Eminent and Self-Made Men of the State of Ind.* (1880), vol. II; H. C. Bradsby, *Hist. of Vigo County, Ind., with Biog. Selections* (1891); Osgood Hardy, "When the Monroe Doctrine Was Forgotten," in *Chile* (N. Y.), Mar. 1930; C. C. Oakey, *Greater Terre Haute and Vigo County* (1908), vol. I; U. S. Dept. of State, Diplomatic Correspondence, Chile, vols. XVIII–XXIII, Mexico, vols. XXXVI–XLVIII; *Papers Relating to the Foreign Relations of the U. S.*, 1863 (pt. 2), 1864 (pt. 4), 1866 (pt. 2), 1870, 1871, 1872 (pt. 1), 1873 (pt. 1); Thomas H. Nelson, Official Letter Books, 1861–65 (MSS.), MSS. Div., Lib. of Cong.; "Report and Accompanying Documents . . . on the Relations of the United States with Mexico," *House Report No. 701*, 45 Cong., 2 Sess.; F. F. Hamilton, *Ancestral Lines of the Doniphan, Frazee, and Hamilton Families* (1928); *Sunday Journal* (Indianapolis), Mar. 15, 1896. Date of birth, given in secondary accounts as Aug. 12, 1824, is incompatible with date of Sept. 27, 1824, given for birth of his brother William.]
I.L.T.

NELSON, WILLIAM (1711–Nov. 19, 1772), merchant, planter, councilor, was born in the region of Yorktown, a notable member of the first generation of the Nelson family who bore so vital a part in eighteenth-century Virginia. He was the son of Margaret Reade and Thomas Nelson, "Scotch Tom," as he was called, who emigrated to Virginia at the close of the seventeenth century from Penrith, on the English side of the Scotch border, where the Nelsons were numerous and were occupied in various trades and callings. Scotch Tom settled about 1700 at Yorktown, where he became a successful merchant and landholder. As early as 1738 William Nelson was made sheriff of York and represented that county in the House of Burgesses from 1742 to 1744. He became a member of the Virginia council in 1744 and retained membership until his death in 1772. He served as president of the council and hence was generally known as President Nelson. On the death of Governor Botetourt he was *ex officio* acting governor from October 1770 to August 1771. He was a member of the Committee of Correspondence of the Virginia Assembly, established in 1759, and took a leading part in opposing the taxation policy of England in the decades before the Revolution. In 1770 he declared that the colonists were learning to make many things for themselves and boasted that he wore a "good suit of cloth of my son's wool, manufactured as well as my shirts, in Albemarle, my shoes, hose, Buckles, Wigg & hat, etc., of our own country, and in these we improve every year in Quantity as well as Quality" (*William and Mary College Quarterly*, July 1898, p. 26).

Interested in sports as well as politics, he was keenly concerned in the horse racing of his generation and is credited with having promoted distance racing at the earliest subscription meets. He was a zealous communicant of the Anglican church and stanchly sought to train his children in that faith and with something of austerity he censored their social habits. He patented lands widely scattered over Virginia, thus adding to the considerable patrimony inherited from his father. He cooperated in the forming of the Dismal Swamp Company of 1763 to take up and drain the vast domain of the Dismal Swamp. As a merchant in the thriving town of York, building on the trade inherited from his father, he became the leading merchant of that region and one of the best known in the colonies. For many years he served on the board of visitors of the College of William and Mary. In his marriage he allied himself to two of the most prominent families of the Virginia aristocracy. In 1738 he married Elizabeth, only daughter of Nathaniel Burwell, of Gloucester County, and Elizabeth Carter, second daughter of "King Carter" and his wife Judith Armistead. There were of this union six children who reached maturity, among them Thomas Nelson [q.v.], signer of the Declaration of Independence and Revolutionary governor of Virginia. On his death in 1772 Nelson was buried in the churchyard at Yorktown. In his will he left bequests for the relief of patients, in the Public Hospital and to the poor of the parish of York-Hampton.

[Nelson's letter book is preserved at the Episcopal Seminary in Alexandria, Va. Extracts from his letter book appear in the *Wm. and Mary Coll. Quart.*, July 1898, and his will is reprinted in R. C. M. Page, *Geneal. of the Page Family in Va.* (2nd ed., 1893). See also: Wm. Meade, *Old Churches, Ministers, and Families of Va.* (1857), vol. I; and the *Va. Mag. of Hist. and Biog.*, Apr. 1902, Apr. 1903, Apr. 1909, Apr. 1925 (reprint of will), Oct. 1927 (article by Fairfax Harrison), Jan. 1929.]
M. H. W.

NELSON, WILLIAM (Sept. 27, 1824–Sept. 29, 1862), naval officer, Union soldier, was born near Maysville, Ky., youngest son of Dr. Thomas W. Nelson and Frances (Doniphan) Nelson. His elder brothers were Anderson Doniphan Nelson, who became an army officer, and Thomas Henry Nelson [q.v.]. William was appointed midshipman in the United States Navy, Jan. 28, 1840, and became passed midshipman July 11, 1846. He served with the fleet which supported Scott's invasion of Mexico and commanded a battery during the siege of Vera Cruz, Mar. 9–29, 1847. Later he served with the Mediterranean Squadron and on board the *Niagara* when that ship was used to return to Africa the slaves taken from the slaver *Echo*. He was promoted master in September 1854 and lieutenant, Apr. 18, 1855.

During the spring of 1861, Nelson, who was devoted to the Union, made several visits to his native state to study conditions there, reporting his observations to the President, who in April sent him into Kentucky to arm the loyalists and to organize regiments for the Union Army. Some five thousand stand of arms were distributed to the Kentucky Home Guard, the Unionist military organization of the state. Early in August, Nelson established Camp Dick Robinson in Garrard County and began to organize troops for an expedition into East Tennessee. He was commissioned brigadier-general of volunteers, Sept. 16, 1861, and later in the fall was sent into Eastern Kentucky to supervise recruiting camps. During November he expelled a small Confederate column which had invaded the state. Later he joined Buell's Army of the Ohio before Louisville and was given command of the 4th Division. He marched with Buell's command to Pittsburg Landing. Nelson's division was the first element of the Army of the Ohio to arrive on the field of Shiloh. He reached the battlefield with his leading brigades about 5:00 P.M., Apr. 6, 1862, and checked the victorious Confederate advance near the river bank. He bore an important part in the Union counterattack on Apr. 7 and participated in the occupation of Corinth, Miss. After Corinth, he participated in the advance against Chattanooga. On July 17, 1862, he was commissioned major-general of volunteers.

In that month he was ordered, with his division, to Nashville to protect Buell's communications against raid by Forrest's Confederate cavalry. When the Confederate armies of Bragg and E. Kirby-Smith [qq.v.] invaded Kentucky, Nelson was sent thither to organize troops. On Aug. 30, he was wounded at Richmond, Ky., while attempting to rally two of his brigades which had been severely defeated. Later he was placed in command at Louisville to organize its defense. While thus engaged, he had occasion to reprimand Brig.-Gen. Jefferson C. Davis [q.v.] for alleged negligence. A few days later, Sept. 29, 1862, Davis, in company with Gov. O. P. Morton of Indiana, encountered Nelson in the lobby of the Galt House in Louisville. During the altercation which ensued, Davis shot Nelson, who died in about half an hour. Nelson was a strong and dominating character, of great energy, a strict disciplinarian, and intolerant of neglect of duty. His untimely death lost a valuable officer to the Union cause.

[*War of the Rebellion: Official Records (Army)*; F. B. Heitman, *Hist. Reg. and Dict. U. S. Army* (1903); *Battles and Leaders of the Civil War* (4 vols., 1887–88); Thomas Speed, *The Union Cause in Ky.* (1907); W. C. Goodloe, *Kentucky Unionists of 1861* (1884); C. A. Evans, *Confed. Mil. Hist.* (1899), vol. IX; E. M.

Coulter, *The Civil War and Readjustment in Ky.*
(1926); G. J. Fiebeger, *Campaigns of the Am. Civil
War* (1914); A. M. Ellis, "Major General William
Nelson," *Reg. Ky. State Hist. Soc.*, May 1906; J. B.
Fry, *Military Miscellanies* (1889); *Cincinnati Daily
Commercial*, Sept. 30, Oct. 1, 1862; date of birth from
Ellis and Fry.]   H. O. S.

NELSON, WILLIAM (Feb. 10, 1847–Aug.
10, 1914), lawyer, historian, was born in Newark,
N. J., the son of William and Susan (Cherry)
Nelson. He attended the Newark public schools,
graduating from the high school in 1862. The
next year, when only sixteen, he became reporter
for the *Newark Daily Advertiser*, and the following two years he taught English in German
schools in Newark and South Orange, and general subjects in a district school at Connecticut
Farms (now Union), N. J. Deciding to devote
more time to journalism he took up his residence
in Paterson in June 1865, and for ten years was
a reporter for the *Paterson Daily Press*. In
April 1868 he was elected a member of the Paterson board of education. In May 1871 he was
appointed clerk of the Passaic County Board of
Chosen Freeholders, serving as such until May
1894, a period of twenty-three years. In the
meantime, for ten years (1877–87), he was clerk
of the Paterson district court. As a young man
he had begun to study law in a desultory way.
In his late twenties he entered the office of Hon.
John Hopper in Paterson and at the June Term,
1878, was admitted as attorney at the New Jersey
bar. In February 1900 he became counselor-at-
law and also a master and special examiner in
Chancery and from 1902 until his death he served
as United States commissioner. From the time
of his admission to the bar he practised in Paterson. He amassed the most valuable private law
library in the state, consisting of about 10,000
volumes.

In 1872 Nelson read a paper upon the discovery and early history of New Jersey before the
Passaic County Historical Society. From that
period onward, during the forty-two years of his
remaining life, while in a measure active in law
practice, he gave most of his time to historical,
ethnological, and antiquarian subjects. In 1880
he became recording secretary of the New Jersey
Historical Society, in 1890 its corresponding
secretary, and this position he retained until his
death. While so serving he edited the *Proceedings* of the Society, some dozen volumes, and
was brought into wide correspondence with other
historians and societies. In 1897, by appointment of the legislature, he was made chairman
of the Public Records Commission of New Jersey.
While in politics a Republican, he did not care
to hold party offices, although he was frequently
a delegate to local and national conventions. He

was active in religious and social groups, serving as elder and clerk of the session in the First
Presbyterian Church of Paterson, on the advisory
board of the Paterson General Hospital, and as
trustee of the Pennington Seminary. He held
membership in many of the leading scientific, historical, and genealogical societies throughout the
country. A bibliography of his books and pamphlets, including a few magazine articles reproduced in pamphlet form, comprises about one
hundred and thirty titles. His chief contributions to New Jersey history are in the *Archives
of the State of New Jersey*, six volumes of which
he edited jointly, and fourteen of which he alone
edited, with copious notes, and in a few cases
with lengthy historical preliminary monographs.
Some other important works were: *The Indians
of New Jersey* (1894); *Genealogy of the Doremus Family in America* (1897); *Personal Names
of Indians of New Jersey* (1904); *The Law and
Practice of New Jersey . . . Concerning the
Probate of Wills* (1909); and *Nelson's Biographical Cyclopedia of New Jersey* (2 vols.,
1913). He also wrote a three-volume *History
of Paterson and Its Environs* (1920), published
after his death, and he left various other uncompleted manuscripts, all on historical topics. A
nearly complete list of his publications may be
found in the *Proceedings of the New Jersey Historical Society* (April 1918). He died at Mata-
moras, Pa., where he had gone to regain his
health in the early summer, but was buried in
Cedar Lawn Cemetery, Paterson. He was twice
married, in 1872 to Martha Buckley, daughter of
Mayor Benjamin Buckley of Paterson, who died
in 1885, and, on July 25, 1889, to Salome Williams Doremus, daughter of Henry C. and Ann
Eliza (Banta) Doremus, who survived him. He
left no children.

[E. Q. Keasbey, *The Courts and Lawyers of N. J.*
(1912), vol. III; J. F. Folsom, "Wm. Nelson," *Proc.
N. J. Hist. Soc.*, July, Oct. 1914; M. D. Ogden, *Memorial Cyc. of N. J.*, vol. II (1915); *N. J. Law Jour.*,
Sept. 1914; *N. Y. Times*, Aug. 11, 1914.] A. V–D. H.

NELSON, WILLIAM ROCKHILL (Mar.
7, 1841–Apr. 13, 1915), journalist, son of Isaac
DeGroff Nelson, who emigrated in 1836 from
New York state to Indiana, and Elizabeth Rockhill Nelson, whose father had removed in 1819
from New Jersey, was born in Fort Wayne,
where he spent a rough-and-tumble boyhood.
He was put down as "unruly" and his father,
though a vestryman in the Episcopal church,
sent him "for discipline" to Notre Dame College,
a Catholic institution, from which, at the end of
his second year, he carried home a note saying
he should not return. Studying law, he was admitted to the bar and entered practice, but not

for long. Immediately after the Civil War—his absence from the front is ascribed to parental opposition—he forsook the law and with a companion sought a fortune growing cotton in the southland. This venture ended disastrously. Reestablished in his native town, he became a contractor, built roads and bridges, and introduced wooden-block pavement into numerous midwestern cities. His incessant energy had accumulated for him, at thirty-three, the then amazing sum of $200,000 which was swept away in the collapse of his former partner whose notes he had indorsed too freely.

Meanwhile, Nelson had become an enthusiastic Democrat and figured as manager of the Tilden campaign in Indiana. This experience led him, in 1878, to acquire part ownership in the *Fort Wayne Sentinel,* the local Democratic organ, and to take on its active conduct. Two years convinced him his true calling lay in journalism. Desiring a larger field, he chose Kansas City, and with Samuel E. Morss, previously associated with him on the *Sentinel* but soon retired by ill health, he launched the *Kansas City Evening Star,* Sept. 18, 1880. From that time until his death, Nelson had sole control of the publication and every copy irradiated his personal characteristics and aims. At the very outset the editor announced his newspaper ideals. He wanted a paper made particularly for the reader, presenting all the day's happenings concisely without distortion, attractively printed and easily legible, combined with useful information and entertaining reading matter—a family journal in the best sense. He rated the reporter as most important in producing a newspaper.

The paper avowed its independence politically: it was to be "independent but never neutral." The corollary that it had "no fixed policy" was reflected later in strangely contradictory turns and alliances. Disgusted when Tilden was not renominated, Nelson had renounced all party ties but found a successor to worship as his political idol in Cleveland, whom he supported steadfastly, and again in Roosevelt, whose name the *Star* listed as a contributing editor for a time. The chronic inconsistency of the paper convinced its readers of Nelson's complete freedom from "the bosses" and stimulated confidence in his integrity of purpose. The *Star* attacked election frauds, crusaded against vice and gambling and corrupt protection of lawlessness, and forced the construction of cable and electric street-railways. It urged unceasingly, well-paved streets, winding boulevards, and beautiful parks. Its constant tugging "pulled Kansas City out of the mud" and set it on the way to primacy among Missouri Valley cities. Nelson's warranted boast that his papers were read in every home in Kansas City rested upon his policy of recouping the entire cost of production from the advertisers. Originally the *Star* was a six-day, four-page, two-cent sheet, sold to subscribers for ten cents a week. It was successively enlarged, a Sunday issue was added in 1894, and then, on the purchase of the *Kansas City Times* in 1901, a morning paper, giving thirteen copies of a metropolitan daily for ten cents, barely the press-room and delivery expense. The *Star* was to be cheap in price but not in quality. Willing or unwilling, the advertisers had to pay the bill and handsome profits as well. Recalcitrants begged his forgiveness after boycotts or alternative measures taught them that they could not get along in Kansas City without using its columns. Similarly a weekly issue of the paper circulated widely in rural districts of the Southwest at twenty-five cents a year.

Nelson did almost no writing but vigilantly directed the preparation or selection of all that he published. He withstood the lure of office, stressing the superior opportunities for public service of the faithful journalist. Easily accessible to both coworkers and public, he kept aloof from outside enterprises except the Associated Press, of which he was a director, and a papermill, erected in Kansas City as a stroke of independence, which, like his cotton-growing, proved a failure. He is to be credited, however, for his fruitful efforts to promote home-building and to develop the city's residential suburbs. A big man physically, the picture of tenacity and pugnacity, his face conveyed at the same time an impression of "massive dignity." By familiars he was called "Colonel," though at no time in military ranks. On Nov. 29, 1881, he was married to Ida Houston of Champaign, Ill. To her, jointly with their daughter, Laura, wife of Irwin R. Kirkwood, he bequeathed his newspapers in trust, to be sold on the death of the survivor to provide an art foundation and museum for Kansas City.

[See *Wm. Rockhill Nelson* (1915), a memorial volume published by members of the staff of the *Kansas City Star; Who's Who in America,* 1914–15; W. G. Bleyer, *Main Currents in the Hist. of Am. Journalism* (1927); O. G. Villard, *Some Newspapers and Newspaper-men* (1923); W. B. Stevens, *Centennial Hist. of Mo.* (1921), vol. III, and "The New Journalism in Mo.," *Mo. Hist. Rev.,* Jan. 1925; W. A. White, "The Man Who Made the 'Star'," *Collier's,* June 26, 1915; *Kan. City Star,* Apr. 13, 14, 15, 1915.]   V. R.

NERINCKX, CHARLES (Oct. 2, 1761–Aug. 12, 1824), Roman Catholic missionary, was born in Herffelingen, Belgium, the eldest son of Dr. Sebastian and Petronilla (Langendries) Nerinckx, one of fourteen children. Educated at the preparatory schools of Enghien and Gheel and at Louvain University, Charles followed the traditions of a religious family, when, at the seminary of Mechlin, he began preparation for the priesthood. His uncle was a priest and two aunts were nuns; three of his sisters became nuns; his brother, Peter, was a Brother of Charity; and another brother, John, became a priest on the English missions; three of his cousins also became nuns, while a nephew, F. X. Decoen, S. J., labored in America. After his ordination (1785), Father Nerinckx was a curate at St. Rumoldus, Mechlin, where he interested himself in the welfare of the laboring class. In 1794, he became pastor of Everberg-Meerbeke. His uncompromising manner so aroused the hatred of Revolutionists that the French Directory ordered his arrest. He eluded the police by living in studious seclusion in Dendermonde, where he acted secretly as substitute for the chaplain of the Hospital of St. Blase, who had been sentenced to penal servitude on the Isle of Rhé. Of his writings there remain a treatise on missionaries and an exposition of the reign of Satan, both in Latin (edited by A. F. Vandewyer, Mechlin, 1844). By stealth he visited his abandoned parish, but refused a reappointment in 1801, because he could not accept the Concordat. He was considering service at the Cape of Good Hope or in England, when he learned of opportunities in America. Since his archbishop was in prison, he sought aid from Princess Gallitzin, mother of Demetrius Gallitzin [q.v.], who wrote to Bishop John Carroll [q.v.]. In sore need of priests, the bishop welcomed Nerinckx, who arrived in Baltimore, Nov. 14, 1804. After a few months at Georgetown College, he set out for Kentucky and joined Father Stephen T. Badin [q.v.] in July 1805.

Nerinckx and Badin became warm friends, but neither relished the coming of the Dominicans (1806), who took over their parish on Cartwright's Creek. Indeed, the relations between the rival missionaries were long strained and far from edifying. In Nerinckx's view, the Dominicans were too lax in parish rule; while the religious regarded him as tainted with Jansenist rigorism and as too fearful of republicanism. Carroll refused to take sides, and time healed their petty differences. Nerinckx won the people, even frontiersmen of no faith, who appreciated his self-discipline and courageous acceptance of danger, whether from Indians or the swollen rivers which he was accustomed to swim on his missionary tours. Of powerful physique, he lifted logs heavy enough to tax the strength of two or three men as he built his log chapels at Rolling Fork, Lexington, Hardin's Creek (1806), on Long Lick (1812), and Casey's Creek (1812), and at stations in the wilderness. Nor did he hesitate to carry the hod when erecting a brick church at Danville (1807). He refused a titular bishopric with administrative control over Louisiana (1809), probably realizing that his conscience would render him unfitted for episcopal responsibilities. During a number of journeys to Europe, he obtained financial aid, secured art treasures and paintings, which are now cherished by the Louisville diocese, and brought over novices for his convent, as well as a number of missionaries and Jesuit recruits. He is said to have brought the first organ and the first stoves into Kentucky. In 1812 he founded the Sisters of Loretto at the Foot of the Cross, with Mothers Ann and Mary Rhodes as first superiors. He not only served as spiritual director and author of their strict rule, but aided materially in building their mother house at Loretto, where he lived in a log cabin. Bishop Flaget [q.v.] described this community as "the most valuable legacy which good Mr. Nerinckx had left to his diocese"; it has come to comprise more than 900 nuns, who have the care of two colleges, thirty-one high schools, seventy-one parochial schools, a negro school, two Indian schools, and a branch in Han Yang, China.

In trouble with Rev. Guy I. Chabrat who regarded him as too rigorous and who wished to modify the rules of the Lorettines, Nerinckx left Loretto for The Barrens, Mo., in 1824, although Bishop Flaget made no decision regarding Chabrat's complaints. Accepting his cross, he asked Bishop Rosati for an assignment to his most needy mission, but death came to him while he was visiting at Ste. Geneviève. His remains were interred at The Barrens, and later removed to the sisters' cemetery at Loretto.

[C. P. Maes, *The Life of Rev. Charles Nerinckx* (1880); W. J. Howlett, *Life of Charles Nerinckx* (1915); *Cath. Encyc.*, X (1911), 752; *Cath. Miscellany and Monthly Repository* (London), Apr. 1825; *Cath. Hist. Rev.*, Apr. 1920; M. J. Spalding, *Sketches of the Early Cath. Missions of Ky.* (1844); *Metropolitan Cath. Almanac* (1854); *Am. Cath. Quart. Rev.*, July 1880; B. J. Webb, *The Centenary of Catholicity in Ky.* (1884); *Loretto Centennial Discourses* (1912); A. C. Minogue, *Loretto, Annals of the Century* (1912); V. F. O'Daniel, *The Rt. Rev. Edward Dominic Fenwick* (1920); W. J. Howlett, *A Review of Father O'Daniel's Estimate of the Early Secular Missionaries of Ky.* (n.d.); John Rothensteiner, *Hist. of the Archdiocese of St. Louis* (1928).]   R. J. P.

NESBITT, JOHN MAXWELL (*c.* 1730– Jan. 22, 1802), merchant, was born in Loughbrickland, County Down, Ireland, the son of Jonathan Nesbitt and his wife, whose maiden name was Lang. He emigrated to Philadelphia in 1747 and was apprenticed by his uncle, Alexander Lang, to Redmond Conyngham, a distant relative, to learn the shipping trade. In 1756 he was admitted to partnership by his employer and the firm became Conyngham & Nesbitt. The company was one of the most prosperous and highly regarded mercantile organizations in the city of Philadelphia. Nesbitt took a prominent part among the citizens of Philadelphia during the Revolution. He was appointed a member of the Committee of Correspondence, May 20, 1774, paymaster of the state navy, Sept. 14, 1775; treasurer of the Council of Safety, July 27, 1776, by virtue of which he was treasurer of the state navy board, and treasurer of the state board of war for land service. When the Pennsylvania Bank was organized in 1780 to supply the Continental Army with provisions his firm subscribed five thousand pounds sterling to its funds and he acted as one of the first five inspectors for the bank. He was one of those who cooperated most generously with Robert Morris in the latter's efforts to sustain the public credit and provide for the continuance of the Revolution.

In March 1776 Nesbitt was elected a member of the First Troop, Philadelphia City Cavalry, and remained an active member of this organization during the Revolution, serving principally in its New Jersey campaign. On his resignation he was made an honorary member of the troop, Sept. 10, 1787. When the Bank of North America was organized in November 1781 he was made one of the directors and continued in that capacity until Jan. 9, 1792. He served on the organization committee of the Insurance Company of North America, and upon completion of its organization, Dec. 10, 1792, was chosen as its first president, a position he held until Jan. 13, 1796. He served as one of the wardens for the Port of Philadelphia in 1788 and as an alderman in 1790. In 1793 he was a member of the committee of merchants which collected information regarding the capture or detention of vessels belonging to citizens of the United States by cruisers of European nations then at war. He wrote the report of this committee and was one of those who laid it before the president of the United States. He was one of the original members of the Friendly Sons of St. Patrick, serving first as vice-president of the society (1771–73) and later as president (1773–74, 1782–96). He was never married and died in Philadelphia.

[J. T. Scharf and Thompson Westcott, *Hist. of Phila.* (1884), vol. I; J. H. Campbell, *Hist. of the Friendly Sons of St. Patrick and of the Hibernian Soc.* (1892); B. T. Hartman, *A Geneal. of the Nesbit, Ross, Porter, Taggart Families of Pa.* (1929); T. H. Montgomery, *A Hist. of the Insurance Company of North America* (1885); H. E. Hayden, ed., *The Reminiscences of David Hayfield Conyngham* (1904); *Reg. of Pa.,* July 10, 1830; *Hist. of the First Troop, Phila. City Cavalry* (1874); *Poulson's Am. Daily Advertiser,* Jan. 27, 1802.]   J. H. F.

NESMITH, JAMES WILLIS (July 23, 1820–June 17, 1885), pioneer, lawyer, soldier, legislator, was born in New Brunswick, Canada, while his parents were visiting there. Descended from James Nesmith, a Scotch-Irish founder of Londonderry, N. H., he was the son of William Morrison Nesmith, of Washington County, Me., and Harriet Willis, who died before he was a year old. His father's extensive holdings in New Brunswick were destroyed in 1825 by a forest fire from which the family barely escaped, the step-mother dying from resulting exposure. James then lived with various relatives in New England, learning at a tender age to earn his own living. Winters he attended common-schools desultorily, and as a strapping boy worked near Cincinnati for some years where he had his last chance at schooling. But he loved books, mastered their contents almost without effort, and retained what he had learned, an aspiring spirit in a superb body. At seventeen or eighteen he drifted to Missouri, then to western Iowa, and spent the season of 1842 working as a carpenter at Fort Scott, Kan. From there he joined the Great Emigration of 1843 which established the Oregon colony. He was a natural leader of men, for he was handsome, rugged, democratic, and fun-loving. He was elected orderly sergeant of the Emigrating Company. In Oregon he read some law, was elected supreme judge under the provisional constitution in 1845, was a member of the legislature later, was commissioned captain of volunteers in the Cayuse War in 1848 and in the Rogue River War of 1853, and colonel in the Yakima War of 1855–56. In the years 1857–59 he was superintendent of Indian affairs.

In 1860, as a Douglas Democrat, he gained one of two United States senatorships owing to a combination of Republicans and Douglas men in the legislature against the Lane followers, Edward Dickinson Baker, Republican, winning the other. Powerful in debate, whole-hearted in defense of the Union, Nesmith was a tower of strength to the Lincoln cause. He took an independent stand as a Democrat to vote for the Thirteenth Amendment and he came to the administration's rescue in several critical situations. But fallible judgment betrayed him into supporting McClellan for the presidency in 1864, and this mistake, together with his ardent friendship for Andrew Johnson, virtually terminated his political course. In 1873, as a purely personal triumph, he was elected to Congress, and in 1876 he had the votes to be chosen senator but lost the prize. He had married in 1846 Pauline Goff and settled on a farm at Rickreall, Ore., which was thereafter his home, and there he was buried. Though most men loved him, others hated or feared him. Few were indifferent. He nourished bitter animosities, and George H. Williams, for preventing Nesmith's confirmation as minister to Austria, later found himself checkmated by Nesmith when Grant wished to make him chief justice of the Supreme Court. But he was essentially genial, humorous, and kindly.

[There are important Nesmith letters in the Deady Collection, Ore. Hist. Soc. An intimate sketch by Harriet K. McArthur, his daughter, is in the *Trans. . . . Ore. Pioneer Asso.*, 1886. See also: Nesmith's address, *Ibid.*, 1875, "A Reminiscence of the Indian War, 1853," *Quart. Ore. Hist. Soc.*, June 1906, and his reports as superintendent of Indian affairs. Other sources include: G. H. Williams and W. D. Fenton, "Pol. Hist. of Ore. from 1853 to 1865," *Quart. Ore. Hist. Soc.*, Mar., Dec. 1901; W. C. Woodward, "Rise and Early Hist. of Pol. Parties in Ore.," *Quart. Ore. Hist. Soc.*, Mar. 1912; R. C. Clark, *Hist. of the Willamette Valley, Ore.* (1927), vol. I; C. H. Carey, *Hist. of Ore.* (1922).]   J. S.

NESMITH, JOHN (Aug. 3, 1793–Oct. 15, 1869), merchant, manufacturer, inventor, was born in the part of Londonderry, N. H., that is now Windham, son of John and Lucy (Martin) Nesmith. The father, a successful farmer, was a grandson of Deacon James Nesmith, one of the Irish Presbyterians who settled Londonderry. John, after scanty schooling, was apprenticed at fourteen to John Dow, a merchant of Haverhill, Mass. Having learned the business, he returned to Windham where with his brother Thomas (1788–1870) he opened a general store. The two also worked up a profitable trade in buying and selling linen thread, then manufactured in the neighborhood by the Irish descendants. In 1822 they opened a second store, in Derry. They might have continued to be country merchants but in the thirties, attracted by the opportunities developing at Lowell, Mass., they sold their New Hampshire interests and bought the estate on which Judge Edward St. Loe Livermore had lived in the confluence of the Merrimack and Concord rivers, and to which he had given the name "Belvidere." There the Nesmiths laid out streets and house lots on which were built many of the most pretentious residences of a fast-growing community. Their own houses were large, solidly constructed, and in good taste. Of the brothers, John Nesmith, positive, aggressive, and yet public-spirited, became the more prominent in business and politics. Educating himself broadly, he studied the sciences and made himself an expert mechanic. He operated woolen-mills at Lowell, Dracut, and Chelmsford, Mass., and at Hookset, N. H.; he invented machines for shawl fringing and for weaving wire fence; and he inaugurated a system of using several New Hampshire lakes as storage basins to regulate the flow of the Merrimack River. As a member of the Essex Company he was one of the founders of the city of Lawrence.

As a young man he served a term in the New Hampshire legislature. His interest in the antislavery and temperance movements made him later in life an active member of the newly formed Republican party, and as a presidential elector he voted twice for Abraham Lincoln. In 1862 he was elected lieutenant-governor of Massachusetts. Declining a renomination in 1863 he was appointed collector of internal revenue for his district, an office which he held until just before his death. His enthusiasm for the temperance cause was intense and practical. He gave liberally to the local charities. He was interested in the arts of design, a generous patron of the portrait painter Thomas B. Lawson, for several years resident at Lowell. His death was said to be due to his suddenly wearing out after a life of unusual physical and mental activity. Resolutions of the Massachusetts State Temperance Society, of which he was a vice-president, stated: "We tenderly remember his benignant countenance and gentle manly bearing, his form somewhat bowed with the weight of age but his heart aglow with the sensibilities of youth." He had married three times: in June 1825, Mary Ann, daughter of Samuel Bell [*q.v.*], of Chester, N. H.; in 1831, Eliza Thom, daughter of John Bell, of Chester; in October 1840, Harriet Rebecca, daughter of Aaron Mansur, of Lowell. He had nine children.

[See: L. A. Morrison, *The Hist. of Windham* (1883); C. C. Chase's "Lowell," in D. H. Hurd, *Hist. of Middlesex County, Mass.* (1890), vol. II; *Illustrated Hist. of Lowell and Vicinity* (1897), published by the Courier-Citizen Company; F. W. Coburn, *Hist. of Lowell and Its People* (1920), vol. II; J. C. Chase, *Hist. of Chester, N. H.* (1926); obituaries and editorials in the *Lowell Daily Citizen* and *Lowell Courier*, Oct. 15, 1869. The author of this sketch was given access to letters and other manuscript material in the possession of the family.]   F. W. C.

NETTLETON, ALVRED BAYARD (Nov. 14, 1838–Aug. 10, 1911), soldier, journalist, financier and associate of Jay Cooke in his Northern Pacific operations, was born in Berlin township, Delaware County, Ohio, the son of Hiram and Lavina (Janes) Nettleton. After the customary earlier schooling of his day he entered Oberlin College with the class of 1863, but his college days were cut short when he enlisted as a private in the 2nd Regiment of the Ohio Volunteer Cavalry, September 1861. His rise from the ranks was rapid and spectacular, for when he was mustered out in June 1865, he was brevet brigadier-general. He had seen service in nearly every part of the country to which the military operations of the Civil War extended, from Kentucky and Missouri, where his regiment was first sent, to the campaigns in North Carolina and about Richmond when he was in Sheridan's cavalry corps. In all he participated in more than seventy battles and minor engagements.

While Nettleton left Oberlin at the close of his sophomore year and did not reënter college after the war, his degree, as of the class of 1863, was subsequently bestowed upon him. He read law and was admitted to the bar, but for many years his real interest lay in the field of journalism and finance. During his stay at Oberlin he had worked on the *Oberlin News*. In 1866 he became editor of the *Sandusky Register* and two years later was financial editor of the Chicago *Advance*. It was while at Sandusky that he became acquainted with Jay Cooke who was accustomed to spend much time in the summer at "Gibraltar," his island home in Lake Erie, and, through Nettleton, Cooke got into print his views on the national banking system and on the resumption of specie payments. It was apparent that the financial magnate was impressed by the abilities of the young journalist, for when he took over the moribund Northern Pacific one of the first things he did was to engage him to take charge of the publicity work which was involved in marketing the securities of the railroad. In preparation for this task Nettleton traversed the whole of the proposed route of the road in Minnesota and Dakota Territory. He then made his home at Chelten Hills, Philadelphia, near Cooke's "Ogontz," while his office was at Cooke's bank in town. When the Northern Pacific proved too heavy a burden even for the famous banking concern of Jay Cooke & Company, Nettleton was out of his publicity job, but he was retained for some time to work out a plan of reorganization satisfactory to the bondholders of the railroad.

The brief connection with this type of high finance ended, Nettleton turned again to journalism. After a connection with the *Philadelphia Inquirer*, in 1885 he bought a half interest in the *Daily Minnesota Tribune*, published in Minneapolis, which he made over into a morning daily. Five years later he sold his interest and for the next five years was the Minneapolis representative of various eastern banks and capitalists, placing mortgage loans and dealing in investments generally. In July 1890 he was appointed by President Harrison assistant secretary of the treasury, a position which made him director of the United States Immigration Bureau, and in that capacity he supervised the enlarging and

rebuilding of the facilities at Ellis Island. For a brief interim after the death of Secretary Windom and before the appointment of Charles Foster, he served as acting secretary of the treasury. A subsequent appointment to the World's Columbian Exposition Commission and diverse other interests kept him in Washington for a few more years.

In 1899 Nettleton removed to Chicago where he resided until his death. Those twelve years found him occupied with various business enterprises and with occasional journalistic and magazine work. His interest in Oberlin was always strong and for twenty-two years (1870–92) he was a trustee of that institution. On Jan. 8, 1863, he had married Melissa R. Tenney; she, with three children, survived him when he died in 1911.

[*Annual Reports of the President and the Treasurer of Oberlin Coll.*, 1910–11; E. P. Oberholtzer, *Jay Cooke, Financier of the Civil War* (1907), vol. II; G. E. Warner and C. M. Foote, *Hist. of Hennepin County and the City of Minneapolis* (1881); Military Order of the Loyal Legion of the U. S., Minn. Commandery, *In Memoriam, Companion Bvt. Brig. Gen. A. B. Nettleton* (Circular No. 12, 1912, whole no. 444); Frederick Janes, *The Janes Family* (1868); *Who's Who in America*, 1910–11; *Minneapolis Morning Tribune*, Aug. 12, 1911.]   L.B.S.

NETTLETON, ASAHEL (Apr. 21, 1783–May 16, 1844), Congregational evangelist, was born in what is now the town of Killingworth, Conn., second child of Samuel and Anne (Kelsey) Nettleton. He grew up on his father's farm with only the ordinary advantages of a country boy. His parents were Half-Way Covenant members of the Congregational Church, and he received a good grounding in religious and moral principles. After a period of painful conflict and uncertainty, when he was eighteen years old he became conscious of a change of heart. As the eldest son, the death of his father, shortly afterwards, brought added responsibilities to him. While he went about his duties on the farm, however, the desire to be a means of saving souls possessed him with increasing force, and the reading of missionary literature made him resolve to go to non-Christian lands. With some assistance from the local pastor, Rev. Josiah B. Andrews, he prepared himself for college, and entered Yale in 1805. Here his thoughts were much occupied with religion, and he took but ordinary rank as a student. Graduating in 1809, he served as college butler for a year, studying theology in the meantime, and later, under Rev. Bezaleel Pinneo of Milford, Conn. The Western Association of New Haven County licensed him to preach on May 28, 1811.

Since opportunity to enter the foreign missionary field did not then open, he engaged in evangelistic work in eastern Connecticut, where the excesses and strife engendered by the revival of 1740 were most conspicuous, and many of the churches were without pastors. A study of the causes which had produced these disorders did much to determine the sane and effective spirit and methods which he himself came to employ. The success that accompanied his early labors, together with the solicitation of his brethren, led him to postpone his entrance upon a missionary career, and he was ordained as an evangelist by the Consociation of Litchfield County, Conn., on Apr. 9, 1817. Ill health, following an attack of typhus fever in 1822, finally forced him reluctantly to abandon the missionary project.

Nettleton is said to have been instrumental in the conversion of thousands. He never had a settled pastorate, never married, never asked remuneration for his services, but with single-minded zeal devoted himself to the awakening of souls. He was strictly Calvinistic in his theological views; of no exceptional intellectual power or oratorical ability; simple, searching, practical, and energetic in his preaching. There was nothing fanatical about him or sensational in his methods. To effective address from the pulpit, he added house-to-house visitation, personal conference, and inquiry meetings for instruction. Converts were always thoroughly schooled in the fundamentals of the Christian faith. During the first ten or eleven years of his ministry his labors were chiefly in Connecticut with excursions into neighboring states. After his health broke in 1820 his activities were curtailed. While recuperating he prepared *Village Hymns for Social Worship, Selected and Original* (1824). This same year there also appeared *Zion's Harp; or, a New Collection of Music, Intended as a Companion to "Village Hymns for Social Worship."* Gradually, so far as his strength permitted, he resumed his former manner of life. He spent three winters (1827–29) in Virginia, and a little more than a year (1831–32) in England. The revival methods of Charles Grandison Finney [q.v.] he strongly opposed (see *Letters of the Rev. Dr. Beecher and Rev. Mr. Nettleton on the "New Measures" in Conducting Revivals of Religion*, pamphlet, 1828). Sympathizing with those who were averse to the "New Haven Theology," he joined with them in forming the Connecticut Pastoral Union, which in 1834 founded the Theological Institute of Connecticut at East Windsor Hill, Conn., later transferred to Hartford and named Hartford Theological Seminary. He declined a professorship, but made his home in East Windsor until his death, occasionally lecturing at the Institute,

and preaching in various places as he was able. After his death appeared *Remains of the Late Rev. Asahel Nettleton, D.D., Consisting of Sermons, Outlines and Plans of Sermons, Brief Observations on Texts of Scripture, and Miscellaneous Remarks* (1845), compiled by Bennet Tyler.

[Bennet Tyler, *Nettleton and His Labours, Being the Memoir of Dr. Nettleton . . . Remodelled in Some Parts* (1854); F. B. Dexter, *Biog. Sketches Grads. Yale Coll.*, vol. VI (1912); W. B. Sprague, *Annals Am. Pulpit*, vol. II (1857); *Christian Review*, June 1845; *The New Englander*, Jan. 1845; F. G. Beardsley, *A Hist. of Am. Revivals* (1904); F. J. Metcalf, *Am. Writers and Compilers of Sacred Music* (1925).]
H. E. S.

NETTLETON, EDWIN S. (Oct. 22, 1831–Apr. 22, 1901), civil and irrigation engineer, was born on a farm near Medina, Ohio, the son of Lewis Baldwin and Julia (Baldwin) Nettleton, both of whom were natives of Washington, Conn. He had no middle name but adopted the initial "S" when he started business for himself. Although his formal education was cut short after a period at Oberlin College (1853–54), by reason of lack of funds, he never ceased to be a student of engineering subjects.

Upon leaving college, he went into the lumber business with his cousin, Frank Broadwell, at Kalamazoo, Mich. Removing to Pleasantville, Pa., early in 1865, he took an interest in some oil wells and served as county surveyor. In the spring of 1870, he started West. At Council Bluffs he met and joined the Union or Greeley Colony, organized by Nathan C. Meeker [q.v.], agricultural editor of the *New York Tribune*, then on its way to Colorado. As engineer of the colony, he surveyed the town site of Greeley and laid out its irrigation ditches, which aggregated forty-six miles in length. This system was built out of a common fund and the rights transferred to the water-using farmers, probably the first instance where the use of water for irrigation was put on a truly practical and cooperative basis. Later, Nettleton built the Larimer and Weld Canal for the Colorado Mortgage & Investment Company, commonly known as the English Company. This irrigation system was the largest in Colorado up to that time, covering, in 1881, 60,000 acres of land between Greeley and Fort Collins. He also built the High Line Canal, known as the English Ditch because it was under the financial control of the English Company. A weir invented by Nettleton was first built for the English Company. He surveyed the town sites of Colorado Springs in 1871, Manitou in 1872, and South Pueblo, now a part of Pueblo, in 1873. For a few years he was president of a flour-milling company in Pueblo. From 1883 to 1887 he served as state engineer of Colorado, during which time he inaugurated the work of gauging the streams and ditches. To him more than to anyone else is due the excellent system of stream control and water distribution in irrigation which Colorado now possesses. Following this period, he engaged in consulting work, laying out for construction a number of irrigation works in Wyoming and Idaho. He was chief engineer in diverting the Yaqui River in Mexico for irrigation purposes.

When the first investigation of irrigation was made by the United States government, Nettleton was appointed consulting engineer, acting in that capacity from 1889 to 1893. He was sent to Spain in 1889 and to Spain and Italy in 1892, to investigate irrigation systems, the manner of reforesting denuded tracts, and methods of preventing destruction of forests. The results of his investigation are included in *A Report on Irrigation and the Cultivation of the Soil Thereby* (1893), Part II, published by the United States Department of Agriculture. His last two years were spent as irrigation expert, under Dr. Elwood Mead of the United States Department of Agriculture. In this capacity he made a number of studies in Idaho, Wyoming, and Colorado, and was concerned in devising instruments for the better measurement of water. Shortly before his death, the Department of Agriculture published a bulletin by him, entitled *The Reservoir System of the Cache La Poudre Valley* (1901).

He was one of the founders and one of the first trustees of Colorado College, at Colorado Springs. He established the weather bureau on Pike's Peak, taking the levels up twice, the second time simply to verify the first. An owner of real estate in the suburbs of Denver when the boom began in 1898, he became wealthy, but lost much of his fortune in the failure of one of the Denver banks. On Oct. 17, 1861, he married Lucy F. Grosvenor, of Medina, Ohio; they had four children. Nettleton died in Denver and was buried in Forest Hill Cemetery, Kansas City, Mo.

[*Science*, May 3, 1901; *Denver Republican*, Apr. 23, 24, 1901; David Boyd, *A Hist.: Greeley and the Union Colony of Col.* (1890); J. F. Willard, *The Union Colony at Greeley, Colo., 1869–71* (1918); A. T. Steinel, *Hist. of Agriculture in Colo.* (1926); C. C. Baldwin *The Baldwin Geneal.* (1881); letter from a daughter, Mrs. Willis N. Pickhard, and information from Dr. Elwood Mead, a former associate.] B.A.R.

NEUENDORFF, ADOLPH HEINRICH ANTON MAGNUS (June 13, 1843–Dec. 4, 1897), musician, conductor, impresario, was born in Hamburg, Germany. In 1854 he accompanied his parents to New York, where he studied violin with George Matzka and Joseph Wein-

lich, and piano with Gustav Schilling. He made his début as a concert-pianist at Dodworth Hall in 1859. The record of his subsequent years is one of practically uninterrupted activity as a solo player, conductor, operatic manager, and composer. After serving for a year as concert-master of the orchestra at the old Stadt Theatre in New York in 1860, he toured South America from 1861 to 1863 as a violinist. Upon his return he took over the musical directorship of the German Theatre in Milwaukee (1864–65). He then went to New York as chorus master for Karl Anchütz at the new Stadt Theatre, succeeding the latter as director in 1867. At his theatre *Lohengrin* was performed for the first time in America on Apr. 3, 1871. In the same year he brought to America the famous German tenor, Theodor Wachtel, to sing in concert and opera. In 1872 he conducted at the Academy of Music in New York, and from 1872 to 1874 was manager of the Germania Theatre. In 1875 he gave a season of German opera in New York with Wachtel and Eugenie Pappenheim, and two years later he acted as director and conductor of the Wagner Festival in New York at which *Die Walküre* was given for the first time in this country, Apr. 2, 1877. Gustav Kobbé, in *The Complete Opera Book* (1919), calls this première, at the Academy of Music, "an incomplete and inadequate performance with Pappenheim as Brünnhilde" (p. 163).

In 1876 Neuendorff had attended the first performance of the *Nibelungen Ring* at Beyreuth as the correspondent of the *New Yorker Staats-Zeitung*. During 1878–79 he conducted the New York Philharmonic Society, succeeding Theodore Thomas. In the year 1881 he transferred the Germania Theatre to the building vacated by Lester Wallack and there lost a fortune in two years' time. He was subsequently active as conductor of the Promenade Concerts in Boston (1884–89); as conductor of the Emma Juch Opera Company (1889–91); and of English grand opera in New York (1892). From 1893 to 1895 he conducted at the Vienna *Hofoper*, where his wife, Georgine von Januschowsky, was one of the *prime donne*. He returned to New York in 1896 and became director of music in the Temple Emanu-El, the following year succeeding Anton Seidl as conductor of the permanent orchestra of the Metropolitan Opera House. His last appearance in public was as conductor of this organization at the Madison Square Roof Garden concerts during the summer of 1897. He died in New York City later in the same year. He had conducted opera and choral societies in practically all of the larger cities of the United States and produced

434

some forty operas while at the Stadt Theatre in New York. In spite of his uninterrupted activity as a practical musician he was a prolific composer. His comic operas include *The Rat-Charmer of Hamelin* (1880), *Don Quixote* (1882), *Prince Waldmeister* (1887), and *The Minstrel* (1892); he also composed two symphonies and several overtures, cantatas, and a number of songs. He probably did more to bring German drama to a high state of development in New York than any other one man.

[See: the *Musical Courier*, Dec. 8, 1897; *Musical Record*, Jan. 1, 1898; *Grove's Dict. of Music and Musicians, Am. Supp.* (1920); *Appletons' Ann. Cyc.*, 1897; *N. Y. Times*, Apr. 4, 1871; *N. Y. Tribune*, Dec. 5, 1897.]   F. H. M.

NEUMANN, JOHN NEPOMUCENE (Mar. 28, 1811–Jan. 5, 1860), Roman Catholic prelate, son of Philip and Agnes (Lebisch) Neumann, was born in Prachatitz, Bohemia, where his father operated a stocking factory and his uncle ruled as mayor. Reared by devout parents, two of whose six children became Sisters of St. Charles, John evidenced remarkable religious fervor in the elementary school which he attended and in the Cistercian college at Budweis. Despite paternal urging to study medicine, he managed to enter the seminary at Budweis although only a fourth of the candidates could be admitted. A laborious student, he gained a deep knowledge of canon law, scriptures, and Hebrew, and also found opportunity to study English at the University of Prague, with the intention of going on the American missions, in which a crusading interest had been aroused by the publications of the Leopoldine Society. In vain he sought adoption by the dioceses of Vincennes and Philadelphia. Undaunted, he set forth for New York, where he was received by Bishop Dubois, who ordained him in old St. Patrick's (June 25, 1836). Assigned to Williamsville, N. Y., Father Neumann attended a number of missions, journeying on foot as often as by wagon as he ministered to scattered and impoverished immigrant congregations. His self-sacrifice and zealous acceptance of privations attracted the attention of the Redemptorist Fathers who were establishing a monastery at Pittsburgh. He in turn, appreciating the value of their rigorous rule, joined the congregation on Oct. 13, 1840. After a period of probation he took the full vows in St. James's Church, Baltimore, Jan. 16, 1842.

As a Redemptorist, Neumann's life and work were changed but little. He continued to preach on missions in the German centers of New York, Pennsylvania, Virginia, Maryland, and Ohio, until he was appointed superior of the community at Pittsburgh (1844). Here he carrried a heavy burden, building the elaborate St. Philomena's Church and winning the gratitude of Bishop O'Connor [q.v.] for his effective work among the Germans. In 1847 he was chosen vice-provincial with headquarters at Baltimore. During his tenure, he established a number of parishes and schools and stimulated vocations. Interested in their work among the negroes, he saved the Colored Oblate Sisters from dissolution. As a confessional priest who courted seclusion and shunned worldly applause and influence, he rejoiced when, in 1851, he was permitted to become pastor of the unfinished church of St. Alphonsus, Baltimore. This interim of comparative ease was brief, however, for Neumann was named successor to Francis P. Kenrick [q.v.] as bishop of Philadelphia, to the intense satisfaction of the German element who were under-represented in the hierarchy. Neumann sought relief from episcopal honors, but under the rule of obedience accepted and was consecrated in his parish church by Archbishop Kenrick on Mar. 28, 1852. He was a determined promoter of parochial education. His diocese built about a hundred elementary schools, which were assigned to the various teaching sisterhoods, among which were the Sisters of Notre Dame of Munich, whom he aided in coming to America; the Sisters of the Holy Cross, whom he introduced from France; and the sisters of St. Francis, whose Philadelphia branch he founded. To the Christian Brothers, he assigned boys' schools. Meanwhile, he compiled such doctrinal aids for children as the *Kleiner Katechismus* (1853), and *Katholischer Katechismus* (1855), which appeared in later German and English editions. In an effort to encourage priestly vocations, he established a model preparatory seminary and improved the standards at the major seminary of St. Charles Borromeo. Yet it was not as a builder primarily that Neumann was notable, but as a writer of spiritual pastorals, a retreat master, an exact ritualist, a promoter of devotional practices, a lover of children, and a friend of the poor and the unfortunate. Even the bitterest Know-Nothings found little to condemn in a man who could accept affronts with forgiving humility. Together with his brother he assigned his patrimony for the endowment of a hospital in his native village, where he received every possible honor when he visited the town in connection with his journey to Rome for the promulgation of the doctrine of the Immaculate Conception (1854).

The tradition of Neumann's sanctity strengthened when miracles were said to have occurred at his tomb in St. Peter's Church. A commission was instituted to inquire into his life and furnish testimony to Rome with the view of his ultimate beatification (1886). Ten years later (Dec. 15), he was declared venerable and his cause is still under advisement before the Sacred Congregation of Rites.

[There are several lives: one by J. A. Berger (a nephew), translated from the German by Eugene Grimm (1884); one by J. Magnier (1897); and, in Dutch, another by J. L. Jansen (Amsterdam, 1899); see also *Funeral Obsequies of Rt. Rev. John Nepomucene Neumann* (1860); U. S. Cath. Hist. Soc., *Records and Studies*, Oct. 1900; R. H. Clarke, *Lives of the Deceased Bishops of the Cath. Church in the U. S.*, II (1888), 431–67; G. F. Houck, *The Church in Northern Ohio* (1887); Neumann's notebook in *Records Am. Cath. Hist. Soc.* (1930); *Cath. Encyc.*, X, 773; J. G. Shea, *Hist. of the Cath. Church in the U. S.*, IV (1892); *Ave Maria*, Feb. 1890; *Cath. World*, Dec. 1892; *Morning Pennsylvanian*, Jan. 6, 10, 1860; *Philadelphia Daily News*, Jan. 10, 1860; *Cath. Herald* (Phila.), Jan. 14, 1860; *Ecclesiastical Rev.*, June 1930.]
R. J. P.

NEUMARK, DAVID (Aug. 3, 1866–Dec. 15, 1924), Jewish philosopher, was born in Szczerzec, Galicia, the son of Solomon and Schifrah Schuetz Neumark. His father was a private scholar who devoted himself altogether to study, while the maintenance of the family devolved upon the mother, a woman of energy and resourcefulness. Her great ambition was to have her only son, David, the youngest of three children, study for the rabbinate. He was a child of exceptional gifts. His schooling began in the *cheder*, the communal Jewish school, when he was but two and one half years old; at the age of six he began the study of the Talmud under his father's tutelage. Upon the death of the father a year later, the mother at great personal sacrifice decided that the child must continue his studies. He attended the Beth ha-Midrash (Hebrew Academy) and also studied privately. After a time he frustrated his mother's hope that he would prepare for an active rabbinical position by deciding to enter a university. Leaving home in 1887 without her consent, he proceeded to the Galician metropolis, Lemberg, where, after studying for three and one half years, he took the entrance examinations for the Obergymnasium. Here he specialized in philosophy, devoting particular attention to Kant, and graduated in 1892.

In November of that year he proceeded to Berlin where he matriculated at the University and entered also the liberal rabbinical seminary known as the Hochschule für die Wissenschaft des Judenthums. Here he again specialized in philosophy and also studied intensively Semitic languages and literature. At this time he wrote the essay which was awarded the Mendelssohn

prize in 1894—"Die Verschollenheit des Ehegatten im rabbinischen Rechte." This was soon followed by a study of Nietzsche's philosophy which was published in the Hebrew periodical *Mimizrach umimaarab,* Vienna. He received the degree of doctor of philosophy from the University of Berlin on Mar. 26, 1896. Professor Hans Vaihinger of the University of Halle, president of the Kant Society, thought so highly of Neumark's thesis that he recommended it to a well-known publishing firm, and it appeared under the title *Die Freiheitslehre bei Kant und Schopenhauer* (1896). A year later Neumark was graduated from the rabbinical seminary. His thesis here was an outline of the history of dogmas in Judaism, which sketch he elaborated and published in Hebrew in two volumes some years later (Odessa, vol. I, 1913; vol. II, 1919).

He obtained his first and only rabbinical post in Rakonitz, Bohemia, where he served from March 1897 to February 1904. While here he married, June 7, 1898, Dora Turnheim of Przemysl. In 1903 he was considered for the position of chief rabbi of Rome, but about that time he accepted the position of editor in chief for the sections of Jewish Philosophy and Talmud in the new Hebrew encyclopedia, launched by the Achiasaf, a Hebrew publishing society of Warsaw. It established a branch bureau for him in Berlin, to which city he removed in February 1904. While in the German metropolis he taught for a while in the Lehrerinnen-Seminar of the central Jewish congregation (Haupt Gemeinde). In 1907 he was elected to succeed the noted scholar Dr. Moritz Steinschneider as professor of Jewish philosophy in the Veitel-Heine-Ephraimische Anstalt. He had scarcely been named for this position when the invitation came from Cincinnati, Ohio, to occupy the chair of Jewish philosophy at the Hebrew Union College. He finally determined to go to the United States, where he arrived with his family on Nov. 28, 1907. A week later he reached Cincinnati and entered at once upon his work, continuing therein for the remainder of his life.

At the time of his death Neumark was generally conceded to be the leading student of Jewish philosophy. He made the entire field of Hebrew learning his own and was a daring and original thinker. His philosophical studies comprised "Jehudah Hallevi's Philosophy in its Principles," his first publication in English, which appeared in the *Catalogue* of Hebrew Union College in May 1908; "Crescas and Spinoza," which was published in the *Year Book of the Central Conference of American Rabbis* (vol. XVIII, 1909); and "Steinthal and Lazarus" and "Historical and Systematic Relations of Judaism to Kant," the latter in commemoration of the two-hundredth anniversary of the birth of Kant, both of which appeared in the *Year Book* (vol. XXXIV, copr. 1925). He published also a work entitled *The Philosophy of the Bible* (1918). His *magnum opus,* however, was to be a history of medieval Jewish philosophy, which he planned on a comprehensive scale, but did not live to complete. Two volumes only, the second in two parts, were published under the title *Geschichte der Jüdischen Philosophie des Mittelalters* (1907-28). A Hebrew edition was also issued (1921-29). At the time of his death he had done the preliminary work for the remaining volumes, but had asked that his notes should not be given to anyone else to use, though he hoped that someone would be inspired by his work to continue a history of Jewish philosophy. Neumark contributed extensively in the form of essays and reviews to Hebrew, German, and English periodicals. A glance at the titles of these articles makes clear how broad was his outlook and how encyclopedic his learning. In order to make the most important of these studies more accessible to scholars the Central Conference of American Rabbis published a volume in 1929 entitled *Essays in Jewish Philosophy by David Neumark.* To this volume is appended a full bibliography of his writings.

In 1919 he founded a quarterly review under the title *Journal of Jewish Lore and Philosophy.* After four numbers had appeared, he suggested that the authorities of the Hebrew Union College take it over and publish it as an official organ of the institution. This suggestion was adopted in 1921, but in place of a quarterly it was issued as an annual publication under the title *Hebrew Union College Annual.* Neumark was a member of the board of editors until his death.

[*Hebrew Union Coll. Mo.,* Jan., Feb. 1924; *Hebrew Union Coll. Ann.,* vol. II (1925); *Year Book Central Conf. of Am. Rabbis,* vol. XXXV (1925); *Jewish Exponent,* Dec. 19, 1924; *Cincinnati Enquirer,* Dec. 16, 1924; *Jewish Tribune,* Dec. 26, 1924; *Who's Who in America,* 1924-25.]   D. P—n.

NEVILLE, JOHN (July 26, 1731–July 29, 1803), Revolutionary soldier, was the son of George and Ann (Burroughs) Neville. George Neville apparently came to the colonies in his early youth (family tradition recorded in *Potter's American Monthly,* February 1876), settled on the headwaters of the Occoquan River in Virginia, and acquired a large estate, which appears on Pownall's, Fry's, and Jefferson's maps and on the map accompanying the 1787 edition of Jefferson's *Notes on the State of Virginia.* There John Neville was born and reared. On Aug. 24,

1754, he married Winifred Oldham. He served under Washington in Braddock's expedition (1755) and then settled near Winchester, Va., where he was elected sheriff. He later made large purchases of land on Chartier's Creek, near Pittsburgh, and for his services in the Dunmore War (1774) received, with Valentine Crawford, a joint patent for 1,000 acres. This region was in dispute between Pennsylvania and Virginia and the inhabitants elected Neville a delegate to the Virginia convention of 1774, but he was too ill to attend. In August 1775 the Virginia Committee of Safety ordered him to proceed to Pennsylvania with the militia company which he commanded and occupy Fort Pitt. This accomplished, he was appointed justice of "Yohogania County," the new county organized by Virginia for the government of the disputed area. Neville declined to take any further part in the boundary dispute and remained commandant at Fort Pitt during the first two years of the Revolution. With George Morgan, Indian agent, he tried to keep the tribes friendly, but only the Delawares responded. On Nov. 12, 1776, Neville was promoted lieutenant-colonel and later was ordered to join Washington's army, to which he was attached for the remainder of the war. He was promoted colonel in 1777 and brevetted brigadier-general in 1783. After the Revolution he was elected to the Supreme Executive Council of Pennsylvania, to the Pennsylvania convention which ratified the federal Constitution, and to the Pennsylvania constitutional convention of 1789-90. As "inspector of survey" for the collection of the whiskey tax in western Pennsylvania (1792-95) he was a central figure in the Whiskey Rebellion of 1794. His house was repeatedly threatened and finally destroyed by the volatile citizenry (*Olden Time,* Pittsburgh, October 1846, December 1847). Neville escaped and with other "exiles" returned with the army sent to put down the rebellion. In 1796 he served as federal agent for the sale of public lands northwest of the Ohio. During his later years he lived at his estate on Montour's Island, near Pittsburgh, where he entertained visitors of note, including Louis Philippe, the duc d'Orléans (King of the French, 1830-48), and his two brothers, the duc de Montpensier and the comte de Beaujolais (1797). Neville died on the island in 1803. His descendants, bearing the surnames Neville and Craig, were of considerable importance in Pittsburgh and Cincinnati for the next fifty years. His son, Col. Presley Neville, married Nancy, daughter of Gen. Daniel Morgan [*q.v.*].

[R. G. Thwaites and L. P. Kellogg, *The Revolution on the Upper Ohio, 1775-77* (1908); Morgan Neville,

"Reminiscence of Pittsburgh," *Cincinnati Chronicle and Lit. Gazette,* Jan. 8, 1831, reprinted in *Western Pa. Hist. Mag.,* Oct. 1922; Samuel Wilkeson, "Early Recollections of the West," *Am. Pioneer* (Cincinnati), May 1843; W. H. Egle, *Pa. Geneals.* (2nd ed., 1896); Neville B. Craig, *The Hist. of Pittsburgh* (1851, new ed. with index, 1917); Boyd Crumrine, *Hist. of Washington County, Pa.* (1882); H. M. Brackenridge, *Recollections of Persons and Places in the West* (1834) and *Hist. of the Western Insurrection in Western Pa.* (1859).]   F.E.R.

NEVILLE, WENDELL CUSHING (May 12, 1870–July 8, 1930), commandant of the United States Marine Corps, was born at Portsmouth, Va., the son of Willis H. and Mary Elizabeth (Cushing) Neville. He was educated at Galt's Academy, Norfolk, Va., and entered the United States Naval Academy Sept. 13, 1886. Completing the four years' academic course in June 1890, he served two years at sea as a naval cadet on board the *Kearsarge* and the *Newark.* He was commissioned a second lieutenant in the United States Marine Corps July 1, 1892, his first station being the marine barracks, Washington, D. C., where he spent two years. This was followed by service on various vessels. On Jan. 4, 1898, he was married to Frances Adelphia Howell of Washington, D. C. While on duty with the marine battalion of the North Atlantic Squadron in 1898 he participated in the battle of Guantanamo Bay, Cuba, and was appointed captain by brevet for conspicuous service in this battle. Upon the outbreak of the Philippine Insurrection, he became a member of the 4th Battalion organized for duty in the Philippines. This battalion, however, was diverted to China, thus giving Neville the opportunity to participate in the Boxer Campaign from Aug. 5 to Oct. 9, 1900. This service was followed by a tour of duty in the Philippine Islands where he commanded the barracks of Isabela de Basilan in the Moro country of the southern islands. His return in March 1903 was followed by various assignments and duties in the United States; by this time he had reached the grade of major.

When the United States intervened in Cuba, he served as a battalion commander in the initial phase of the occupation of the island during the month of October 1906. This was followed during the next few years largely by sea duty, but it also included service in Nicaragua. Early in 1914 he embarked at Pensacola in command of the 2nd Regiment and in April participated in the engagement which resulted in the occupation of Vera Cruz, Mexico. For this service he received the Naval Medal of Honor with commendation for conspicuous courage, coolness, and skill in the conduct of the fighting. From December 1915 to October 1917 he commanded the marine detachment of the American legation

at Peking, China. Upon his return to the United States late in 1917, he was immediately ordered to France. He arrived there Dec. 28, 1917, assumed command of the 5th Regiment of Marines, and at the end of the month received his commission as colonel. His long and varied service had qualified him for the training of a regiment for the great conflict and the command of it on the battlefields of France. His regiment, together with the 6th Marines, constituted the 4th Brigade of the 2nd Division. While in command of the 5th Regiment he participated in the Aisne-Marne defensive, at Château-Thierry and in the battle of Belleau Woods. As commander of the 4th Brigade he participated in the battle of Soissons, the St. Mihiel offensive, the offensive in the Champagne (Blanc Mont), and in the Meuse-Argonne offensive. He was promoted brigadier-general on Aug. 28, 1918. The award of the Distinguished Service Medal cites these actions in which he participated and states most simply: "In all of these he proved himself to be a leader of great skill and ability." An American military officer could hardly ask greater distinction than to have exercised command in the 2nd Division in these actions.

After the signing of the armistice Neville served with the Army of Occupation in Germany and returned to the United States in the summer of 1919. He was promoted to the grade of major-general with rank from Dec. 10, 1923. He occupied important positions including that of assistant to the major-general; commandant; commander of the Department of the Pacific; commanding general of the Marine Corps Expeditionary Force, United States fleet; commanding general of Quantico; and finally commandant of the United States Marine Corps, to which position he was appointed Feb. 7, 1929, by President Coolidge, succeeding Gen. John A. Lejeune. He died on July 8, 1930, survived by a daughter, and was buried in the Arlington National Cemetery. He was the recipient of numerous decorations.

[*Who's Who in America,* 1930–31; *Army and Navy Reg.,* July 12, 1930; *Outlook,* Mar. 20, 1929; *Washington Post,* July 9, 1930; *N. Y. Times,* July 9, 10, 1930; official records of the U. S. Navy Dept.]
                                                            M.E.S.

NEVIN, ALFRED (Mar. 14, 1816–Sept. 2, 1890), Presbyterian clergyman, editor, and author, was a native of Shippensburg, Pa., the second son of Maj. David and Mary (Peirce) Nevin, a younger brother of Edwin H. Nevin [*q.v.*], and first cousin of John Williamson Nevin [*q.v.*]. He was educated at Jefferson College and at Judge Reed's law school, which was the law department of Dickinson College, receiving his degree in 1837. That same year he was admitted to the bar, but appears not to have practised the profession, for he at once entered Western Theological Seminary at Allegheny, graduating and being licensed to preach by the Presbytery of Carlisle in 1840. For twenty years he served in the pastorate, acquiring an experience of life and a wide acquaintance with other ministers which was invaluable in his later career as a writer, editor, and publisher in the religious field. His pastorates were at Cedar Grove, Pa., 1840–45; Chambersburg, where he served the German Lutheran Church, 1845–52; Second Presbyterian Church, Lancaster, 1852–57; and in Philadelphia, where, in 1857, he organized the Alexander Presbyterian Church, named in honor of Dr. Archibald Alexander [q.v.], first professor of Princeton Theological Seminary, and was its pastor four years.

He resigned from the Alexander Church in order to edit and publish a weekly religious periodical, the *Standard,* at a period when such denominational papers were issued in large numbers throughout the country, and when many of them were financially profitable. In 1866 ill health compelled him to relinquish control of the *Standard* and it was merged with the *Northwestern Presbyterian.* After a time he published the *Presbyterian Weekly,* which in a few years became the *Baltimore Presbyterian,* and for a number of years, until 1880, he was editor-in-chief of the *Presbyterian Journal,* Philadelphia. Each of these papers has since passed through one or more changes in name and ownership, the *Standard* and the *Journal* now being represented by the *Presbyterian Advance,* published at Nashville, Tenn. From the early years of his ministry Nevin was the author of books, *Churches of the Valley* (1852), being his first volume of note. Among the others, which totaled more than twenty, were *The Age Question* (1868); *Notes on Exodus* (1874); *Centennial Biography: Men of Mark of the Cumberland Valley, Pa., 1776–1876* (1876); *Parables of Jesus* (1881); *Letters Addressed to Col. Robert G. Ingersoll; or Infidelity Rebuked and Truth Victorious* (1882); and *Encyclopædia of the Presbyterian Church in the United States of America* (1884). In editing the last work he was assisted by his youngest brother, David Robert Bruce Nevin.

During Nevin's editorship of the *Standard* he was also an army chaplain, serving at Satterlee General Hospital, Philadelphia, from November 1863 to July 1865. He was a member of the first board of trustees of the Presbyterian Historical Society, of the state historical societies of Pennsylvania and Wisconsin, and of the Presbyterian Board of Education. While he was located at Lancaster he was elected moderator of the Synod of Pennsylvania, and he attended several of the annual sessions of the General Assembly as an elected commissioner. In 1841 he married Sara, daughter of Robert Jenkins, of Lancaster.

[See Nevin's *Encyc.* and his *Hist. of the Presbytery of Phila.* (1888); also, F. B. Heitman, *Hist. Reg. and Dict. U. S. Army* (1903); *Biog. and Hist. Cat. of Washington and Jefferson Coll.* (1902); *The Western Theol. Sem. Gen. Biog. Cat.* (1927); *Presbyterian Banner,* Sept. 10, 1890; *Presbyterian,* Sept. 10, 1890; *Phila. Inquirer,* Sept. 3, 1890.]   P. P. F.

NEVIN, EDWIN HENRY (May 9, 1814–June 2, 1889), clergyman, educator, and author, was born at Shippensburg, Cumberland County, Pa., son of Maj. David and Mary (Peirce) Nevin, a brother of Alfred Nevin [q.v.], and a cousin of John Williamson Nevin [q.v.]. His father served in the defense of Baltimore during the War of 1812, and was a member of the convention which revised Pennsylvania's state constitution (1837–38). He was a successful merchant, and was known for his enterprise and philanthropies. Edwin Nevin was graduated from Jefferson College in 1833, and from Princeton Theological Seminary in 1836, after having taken his first year of theology in Western Seminary at Allegheny, Pa. Following his licensure by the First Presbytery of Philadelphia in 1836, he served the church at Portsmouth, Ohio, and from 1839 to 1841 was pastor at Poland in the same state.

When only twenty-six years old he was elected president of Franklin College, New Athens, Ohio, where he was received as "a young man of ardent temperament, with a well cultured mind, and . . . an attractive pulpit orator" (*Franklin College,* 1908). Under his administration the college gained wide repute, considerable funds were raised, and a new building was erected. He was instrumental in having a bell for this building cast in exact facsimile of the bell on Independence Hall, Philadelphia, even to the inscription: "Proclaim liberty throughout the land, and to all the inhabitants thereof." He resigned in 1844 to accept a pastorate in Cleveland. Though ill health hampered his activities during much of his later life, he served the Presbyterian church at Mount Vernon, Ohio, several Congregational churches in New England, St. Paul's Reformed Church at Lancaster, Pa., and the First Reformed Church of Philadelphia. In 1875 he retired from the active ministry.

In addition to his pastoral work he wrote many articles for the religious press, numerous hymns and poems, and books on religious subjects. Among the last-named were *Mode of Baptism*

(1847); *Warning Against Popery* (1851); *Faith in God, the Foundation of Individual and National Greatness* (1852); *The Man of Faith* (1856); *The City of God* (1868). He had a wide reputation in his day as an impressive preacher, a ready debater—particularly in opposition to slavery—a man of comprehensive literary knowledge, and a warm advocate of conservative religious belief. Late in life he was elected a member of the Victoria Philosophical Society of Great Britain. His wife was Ruth C. Little, whom he married in 1837.

[Alfred Nevin, *Encyc. of the Presbyterian Ch. in the U. S. A.* (1884), and *Centennial Biog.: Men of Mark of the Cumberland Valley, 1776–1876* (1876); *Princeton Theol. Sem. Biog. Cat.* (1909); *The Western Theol. Sem. Gen. Biog. Cat.* (1927); *Presbyterian Banner*, June 12, 1889; *Presbyterian*, June 8, 1889; *Public Ledger* (Phila.), June 3, 1889.]   P. P. F.

NEVIN, ETHELBERT WOODBRIDGE (Nov. 25, 1862–Feb. 17, 1901), composer, was among the first native-born American composers to display strongly individual qualities of style. He was born at Edgeworth, near Pittsburgh, Pa., the fifth in a family of eight children. His ancestors, of Scottish origin on both sides, had been in America since the early eighteenth century. His father was Robert Peebles Nevin [*q.v.*]. His mother, Elizabeth Duncan (Oliphant) Nevin, of Uniontown, Pa., was descended from Duncan Oliphant, who had come to America from Gash, Scotland, in 1721. She was a trained musician of wide culture, and the first grand piano to be carted over the Alleghany Mountains into Western Pennsylvania was for her girlhood home. Her love of music made a powerful impression upon Ethelbert. At the age of three he learned to sing the stirring songs of the times and at five he played his own accompaniments at the piano while he sang. At ten he took his first formal piano lessons from Von der Heide and a little later from William Guenther, both of Pittsburgh, and at eleven he played in a public concert in Pittsburgh. In 1877–78 his parents took him abroad for a year's travel and study and placed him for a time for piano instruction under Franz Böhme in Dresden. On his return to Edgeworth he entered the Western University of Pennsylvania but remained only till the end of his freshman year in 1879, when he decided to enter the path of the professional musician.

He overcame his father's opposition to such a career, and in the early fall of 1881 he went to Boston and for two years studied piano with Benjamin Johnson Lang and harmony and composition with Stephen A. Emery. Ambitious to perfect himself as a concert pianist, he went to

Berlin in August 1884 and spent two years with Karl Klindworth (piano) and Carl Bial (theory), also a short period with Hans Von Bülow (piano) and Otto Tiersch (composition). A few weeks after his return to America he made a successful début as a pianist in Pittsburgh, Dec. 10, 1886, then settled in Boston, where he remained for nearly five years, teaching, concertizing, and composing. The rapidly growing popularity of his earlier compositions (notably the *Sketch Book*) made him turn more and more to composition as his life-work. Feeling the need for further study, he sailed for Europe in May 1891, spending a year in Paris composing and teaching and eight months in Berlin given wholly to study and composition. In December 1892 he was in America again, but he was overworked and ill, and to recuperate he made a brief trip to Algiers in the early months of 1894. Midsummer found him at "Vineacre," the old home at Edgeworth, preparing for the most successful concert tour of his career—and the last. Abandoning concert-life, he again went abroad early in 1895 to find there a more serene and inspiring atmosphere for composition. The stay in Europe included sojourns in Florence, Montepulsiano in the Tuscan Apennines, Venice, and then Paris. He returned to America in October 1897 and established himself in New York. In the late autumn of 1900 he moved to New Haven, Conn., where he lived quietly and in increasing ill health till his death. The funeral service was held in the Presbyterian Church at Sewickley, Pa., and he was buried in the little cemetery close by. He was married on Jan. 5, 1888, to Anne Paul of Pittsburgh, who with two children survived him.

Nevin was slender and rather frail in figure, never robust nor fond of any sport. Though struggling much with ill health, he possessed a happy, buoyant, lovable nature and rare social gifts. As a pianist of ample technical equipment he was happiest in the interpretation of his own compositions, which always evoked enthusiasm. His total published compositions number about one hundred and thirty (seventy songs, forty-two for piano, three for violin, sixteen for chorus). His genius was essentially lyrical. Aside from the fine early song "Herbstgefühl" (1889), there are but few dramatic passages in all his music. Recognizing this, he had the wisdom to confine himself to the smaller instrumental and vocal forms, of which he was a complete master. The exceptional popularity of many of his compositions is due to their unaffected simplicity, spontaneity, grace, and melodic charm. His music reflects his instinctive love for light rather than shadow, for joy rather than sorrow. His love for nature finds full expression in such groups as *Water Scenes* (*opus* 13, 1891), *In Arcady* (*opus* 16, 1892), *May in Tuscany* (*opus* 21, 1896), and *A Day in Venice* (*opus* 25, 1898). He was fortunate in gaining early recognition for his talent. The *Sketch Book* (*opus* 2, 1888), a versatile collection of thirteen songs and piano pieces, had a remarkable sale and contained several of his finest compositions—"Im wunderschönen Monat Mai," "Lehn' deine Wang," and "Oh! that We Two Were Maying." "One Spring Morning" (from *opus* 3, 1888) and "'Twas April" (from *opus* 4, 1889) also made wide appeal. He attained international fame when he published *Water Scenes,* owing largely to one of the group, "Narcissus," which soon became a world favorite. The same measure of popularity has also been accorded to "The Rosary" (1898), which was the most famous song written by an American after the melodies of Foster, who was an intimate friend of Nevin's father. This song was first publicly sung by Francis Rogers accompanied by the composer, Feb. 15, 1898, in Madison Square Garden Concert Hall, New York. His most pretentious work is *The Quest* (1902), a cantata on which he was working when he died. The orchestration was completed by Horatio Parker.

[Vance Thompson, *The Life of Ethelbert Nevin* (1913), based upon Nevin's letters and his wife's memories; Francis Rogers, "Some Memories of Ethelbert Nevin," *Musical Quart.*, July 1917; J. T. Howard, *Our Am. Music* (1931); Rupert Hughes, *Contempory Am. Composers* (1900); L. C. Elson, *The Hist. of Am. Music* (1904); Louis Tipton-Campbell, *Music*, Apr. 1901; Willa Cather, "The Man Who Wrote 'Narcissus,'" *Ladies' Home Jour.*, Nov. 1900; the *Musician*, Mar. 1901; *Pittsburg Dispatch*, Dec. 11, 1886; *N. Y. Times*, Feb. 18, 1901.]   R. G. C—e.

NEVIN, GEORGE BALCH (Mar. 15, 1859– Apr. 17, 1933), composer, was born in Shippensburg, Pa., a descendant of Daniel Nevin who settled in the Cumberland Valley in the eighteenth century. His father, Samuel Williamson Nevin, was a prosperous farmer who married Harriet Macomb Balch. George Nevin passed his boyhood on his father's farm. He rode the saddle horses, learned to fish and hunt, and had for his hobby a completely equipped carpenter shop, from which one of his proudest products was a banjo made with his own hands. He was educated at the Cumberland Valley State Normal School, and for one year at Lafayette College as a member of the class of 1883. In later years Lafayette awarded him two honorary degrees. At the normal school Nevin specialized in chemistry and in drawing, but at the same time he spent part of his time for three years studying singing with Julia E. Crane, who helped him develop a baritone voice that enabled him to sing regularly in church choirs for twenty-five years. On leaving Lafayette College he went to Philadelphia, where he had a position for a few years with the firm of John Wanamaker. In Philadelphia he was a member of the choir of Holy Trinity, where David Bispham was soloist. During these years he was also a member of the Philadelphia Cecilian Society. About 1884 he returned to the town in which he had attended college—Easton, Pa.—where he opened a wholesale paper business at 320 Ferry Street. He conducted this enterprise until 1919.

Simultaneously with the conduct of his business Nevin continued his activities as a singer, becoming a member of various church choirs and of the Orpheus Glee Club. He also became interested in composing music, particularly for the church, and in this field he achieved a distinction that won him a national reputation. Sitting at his desk in his paper store, he would work on the anthem or song, "while overhead a battery of six or more printing presses was pounding out that many conflicting rhythms" (*Diapason*, Dec. 1, 1929, p. 10). In 1918, during the World War, Nevin organized the Victory Drummers, with a membership of forty men who averaged sixty years in age. This group was much in demand for patriotic rallies. During his later years he spent much of his time lecturing for women's clubs, with programs of his own compositions. He was physically and mentally active until two weeks before his death, when he was stricken with paralysis at his home in Easton. He had married, Apr. 25, 1888, Lillias Clara Dean of San Francisco, who became the mother of his three children, two of whom survived him. His wife wrote the texts of many of his anthems, songs, and cantatas.

As a composer Nevin was termed "a well-schooled musician, abundantly supplied with a pleasing melodic flow." He published a quantity of music, principally for the church. Among his larger works were the cantatas: *The Adoration, The Crown of Life, The Crucified, The Incarnation, The Gift of God,* and *The Angel of the Dawn.* It is said that *The Adoration* achieved a sale of sixty thousand copies. He also wrote many shorter anthems, among them "At the Sepulchre"; "The Walk to Emmaus"; a setting of "Crossing the Bar"; "Let this Mind Be in You"; "Hail, Gladdening Light"; "The Gift of God"; "Beloved, Let Us Love One Another"; "There Were Shepherds," and more than fifty others. Among his songs, sacred and secular, was a setting of Sidney Lanier's "Into the Woods my Master Went," and his part-songs numbered, among many others, "My Bonnie Lass, She Smileth"; "It Was a Lover and his Lass"; "O Mistress Mine"; "Smile Again, my Bonnie Lassie"; and "O, Little Mother of Mine." During the World War he published "When the Flag Goes By," a song which had wide use.

[See *Who's Who in America*, 1932–33; Gordon B. Nevin, "George Balch Nevin as Biographically Viewed by his Son," the *Diapason*, Dec. 1, 1929; "George B. Nevin," *Etude*, Sept. 1910; *Easton Express*, Apr. 17, 1933; *N. Y. Times, New York Herald Tribune*, Apr. 18, 1933.]   J.T.H.

NEVIN, JOHN WILLIAMSON (Feb. 20, 1803–June 6, 1886), theologian, educator, came of Scotch-Irish ancestry. His grandfather, Daniel Nevin, settled as a young man in the Cumberland Valley of Pennsylvania, where he took up land and married Margaret Williamson. John, the elder of his two sons, married Martha Mc-Cracken, became a prosperous farmer, and reared a family of nine children of whom John Williamson was the eldest. The family were devout Presbyterians; the father had graduated from Dickinson College (1795) when that institution was under Presbyterian control, and the son was sent, at fourteen years of age, to Union College, Schenectady, N. Y., where he graduated in 1821, the youngest member of his class. Poor health caused him to remain two years on his father's farm after graduation, and in 1823, when he entered Princeton Theological Seminary, he had not yet definitely chosen his life work.

Upon completing his course at Princeton in 1826, he was appointed to fill temporarily the place of Dr. Charles Hodge [*q.v.*], while the latter spent two years in foreign study. During this period Nevin prepared *A Summary of Biblical Antiquities* (2 vols., 1828), which for many years had wide use. On the completion of his instructorship at Princeton he was offered the professorship of Biblical literature in a new Presbyterian institution, Western Theological Seminary, then being organized at Allegheny, Pa. He began his work here in 1830 and remained for ten years, gaining a reputation as a scholar and a thoughtful preacher. He became a mild abolitionist and although he took no part in the doctrinal controversy which in 1837–38 divided the Presbyterian Church, he came gradually to a position out of harmony with Old-School Calvinistic orthodoxy. Commencing the study of German, he began to read the works of contemporary German theologians and church historians. He was especially influenced by Neander, and began to emphasize, more and more, the churchly and sacramental side of Christianity. In 1840, entirely without his knowledge, he

was unanimously elected by the General Synod of the Reformed Church to a professorship in their seminary at Mercersburg, Pa., and was finally persuaded to accept the call. Transferring his ecclesiastical relationship from the Presbyterian to the Reformed Church, he was soon exercising a large influence within that body, especially through his writings. His teachings came to be the cause of controversy within the denomination. In 1843 he published a pamphlet called *The Anxious Bench—A Tract for the Times,* in which he opposed the revivalistic methods which were gaining considerable acceptance among all the Protestant churches. At once the pamphlet caused a flood of replies from writers in several denominations.

The coming of Dr. Philip Schaff [*q.v.*] to Mercersburg Seminary from Berlin in 1844 greatly influenced Nevin's career. He and Schaff were in full sympathy in their points of view. Schaff's inaugural address, "The Principle of Protestantism as Related to the Present State of the Church," delivered in German, was translated into English by Nevin and published, together with a sermon of Nevin's on "Catholic Unity" (*The Principle, etc.,* 1845). At once bitter attacks were made upon the publication, and especially upon Nevin for the position he had taken in regard to the Catholic Church. Nevin now set forth in numerous articles, pamphlets, and books his position in regard to tradition, the sacraments, mystical union, and the church question, which came to be known as the "Mercersburg theology." His most important work was *The Mystical Presence: A Vindication of the Reformed or Calvinistic Doctrine of the Holy Eucharist* (1846) and *History and Genius of the Heidelberg Catechism* (1847). At this period Schaff was beginning the publication of the first volumes of his monumental *History of the Christian Church,* though he took little part in the controversy. The year 1849 was marked by the establishment of the quarterly *Mercersburg Review,* of which Nevin was editor and chief contributor until 1853. Altogether about a hundred of his articles appeared in the *Review,* filling nearly three thousand pages.

During the years 1841 to 1853 he was not only a professor in the Seminary but was acting president of Marshall College, also located at Mercersburg. In the latter year an agreement was reached with Franklin College at Lancaster to unite the two institutions, and when this had been accomplished, Nevin, whose health had failed, retired to private life. Some years later, after his removal to a small farm near Lancaster, he again became connected with the college as lecturer, holding this position from 1861 to 1866, when the institution was reorganized and at the request of the trustees he assumed the presidency. He was at the head of Franklin and Marshall College thenceforward until advancing age caused his final resignation in 1876. For the next ten years he lived in retirement at his country home near Lancaster, where he died in 1886 of old age.

Nevin was a quiet man, of grave countenance, with a strong, deep voice, which, added to his great earnestness and logical presentation, gave to his pulpit ministration and public address singular impressiveness. He was married in 1835 to Martha Jenkins, second daughter of Robert Jenkins, a wealthy iron-master of Lancaster County. They had seven children, but three of the five sons died in infancy. Nevin's brother, Robert Peebles Nevin [q.v.], father of the composer Ethelbert Nevin [q.v.], was a well-known journalist and man of affairs, while two first cousins, Alfred and Edwin H. Nevin [qq.v.], were Presbyterian ministers of some note.

[Theodore Appel, *The Life and Work of John Williamson Nevin* (1889); A. R. Kremer, *A Biog. Sketch of John Williamson Nevin* (1890); *Centennial Biog.: Men of Mark of the Cumberland Valley, Pa., 1776–1876* (1876); *Princeton Theol. Sem. Biog. Cat.* (1909); *Phila. Inquirer*, June 7, 1886.]   W. W. S.

NEVIN, ROBERT PEEBLES (July 31, 1820–June 28, 1908), journalist, pioneer oil-refiner, was born in Shippensburg, Pa., the son of John and Martha (McCracken) Nevin and a brother of John Williamson Nevin [q.v.]. While an infant he was taken by his parents to a farm in Cumberland County where the father died in Robert's ninth year. At the age of twelve the boy went to Chillicothe, Ohio, and subsequently lived at various times in Niles, Mich., and Pittsburgh. He received his elementary schooling partly at Chillicothe Academy, later attended Sewickley Academy, of which his brother, William M. Nevin, was in charge, and at length entered Jefferson College, Canonsburg, Pa. (now Washington and Jefferson, Washington, Pa.), from which he was graduated in 1842.

He then entered into partnership with a brother as a dealer in drugs and white lead, at Pittsburgh, and was engaged in this business until 1870. He had begun to write verse at the age of twelve, and he now devoted his leisure to writing poems and sketches for newspapers and magazines. He also became a correspondent of the *Washington Reporter* and during the presidential campaign of 1844 was one of the most popular writers of campaign songs, his "Our Nominee" being widely reprinted. Later he contributed several noteworthy articles to magazines, among them being "Stephen C. Foster and Negro Minstrelsy" (*Atlantic Monthly*, November 1867), and "Tom, the Tinker" (*Lippincott's Magazine*, October 1868), dealing with a romantic character of the Whiskey Rebellion. He also wrote *Black-Robes, or Sketches of Missions and Ministers in the Wilderness and on the Border* (1872), taking up in order the Jesuit, Moravian, Methodist, and Presbyterian missionaries and ministers. In 1888 he published *Les Trois Rois*, in which he likened William Thaw (transportation), Andrew Carnegie (steel), and George Westinghouse, Jr. (natural gas), to the three magi of the early legend. During 1887–88 he published "Tracks of a Traveller" as a serial in the Pittsburgh *Leader*. In 1899 he made a collection of his poems, including verses written at the age of twelve, his campaign song, "Our Nominee," and "Tracks of a Traveller," which he published in a volume entitled *The "Beautiful River" and Other Poems* (1899). These verses are not remarkable in any sense; for the most part they were written for specific, local occasions and they have no universal appeal.

Retiring from the drug business in 1870, Nevin purchased an interest in the *Weekly Leader*, a Sunday paper, and as part owner and editor made it over into a daily newspaper. In 1880 he founded the *Pittsburg Times*, which he sold four years later. In the field of oil refining, far removed from literary interests, he took a leading part, being among the first, if not the first Pittsburgher to become interested in petroleum. In 1855, more than three years before Edwin L. Drake [q.v.] sank the first oil well at Titusville, Pa., Nevin bought the crude oil which came to the surface of the salt wells at Tarentum, Pa., and refined it for illuminating purposes, producing three barrels a week. After Drake's discovery, Nevin with associates drilled a well near Titusville, but lost most of their product by a fire, and sold out the same year.

Nevin died at his home, "Vineacre," near Pittsburgh, just before reaching the age of eighty-eight, after two years' illness. His wife, Elizabeth Duncan Oliphant, whom he married Jan. 9, 1851, had died in 1898. The daughter of Gen. F. H. Oliphant, prominent in the iron trade, she was an accomplished musician, and one of her eight children (of whom four survived their father) was Ethelbert Woodbridge Nevin [q.v.] the composer.

[*Who's Who in America*, 1906–07; Vance Thompson, *The Life of Ethelbert Nevin* (1913); *Biog. and Hist. Cat. of Washington and Jefferson Coll.* (1902); Erasmus Wilson, *Standard Hist. of Pittsburg, Pa.* (1898); *Pittsburg Dispatch, Pittsburgh Post*, June 29, 1908.]   A. I.

NEVIUS, JOHN LIVINGSTON (Mar. 4, 1829–Oct. 19, 1893), missionary in China, was of the seventh generation after the Joannes Nevius who became *schepen* of New Amsterdam in 1654. About 1818 John P. Nevius, then the head of the family, had moved from New Jersey to a farm in the township of Ovid, Seneca County, among the "Finger Lakes" of western New York. His son, Benjamin Hageman Nevius, in 1826 married Mary Denton, of English descent; and on the day when Andrew Jackson was first entering office as president, their son, John Livingston Nevius, was born. During his early years on the farm the boy developed a sturdy physique and some acquaintance with the mysteries of farming. With his brother Reuben he attended Ovid Academy and then entered Union College. Upon graduating in 1848, he yielded to the lure of new country and went south to Georgia. There he taught school for a year with a considerable measure of success. The year's greatest significance to him, however, was that it dated his conversion. From his intimate letters to his brother Reuben it is evident that the conversion was the result not of sudden influences from without but of months of inner questioning. Returning north, he entered Princeton Theological Seminary; and by the time of his graduation in 1853 he had received appointment from the Presbyterian Board as missionary to China. He was ordained by the Presbytery of New Brunswick on May 23; in June he married Helen Sanford Coan, a school friend of Ovid Academy days; and in September they sailed, by way of the Cape of Good Hope, for China.

Their first years in China were full of uncertainties. The climate of Ningpo, to which they had been assigned, is notoriously difficult. Mrs. Nevius' health failed, and in 1857 she had to return to the United States for a period. Nevius became pastor of a church at Ningpo and started evangelistic work in San-Poh, an inland district "north of the hills." He and his wife were pioneers in a mission station in Hangchow in 1859, but had to withdraw because of political unrest. They then spent several months in Japan, and on their return to China proceeded north to aid in the establishment of a mission in Shantung province.

There Nevius toiled with characteristic energy for more than thirty years. His evangelistic zeal prepared the way for many local churches, the work in each locality being delegated as far as possible to native residents. He kept up a steady output of written material both in Chinese and in English. This included at least sixteen tracts or books or translations in Chinese, and several works in English: *San-Poh* (1869); *China and the Chinese* (1869); *Methods of Mission Work* (1886); and *Demon Possession and Allied Themes* (1894), which was published after his death. A lasting benefit to China's material well-being resulted from his experiments in acclimatizing Western fruits and vegetables. The statesmanship of his contribution to the missionary program was recognized in China by his appointment as American chairman of the Second Missionary Conference in Shanghai, 1890; and in America by the prominence accorded to his counsels and addresses. Study of the "Nevius method" became a part of the preparation of missionary candidates. The commanding presence and the powers of concentration which this record suggests were characteristic of Nevius, but equally characteristic were qualities of geniality and sympathy and good comradeship. His life continued active and full to the last day; and it ended peacefully at his desk after daily prayers in "San-lou," the house which he had himself erected on a hill overlooking the Chinese city of Chefoo.

[The chief source of information is *The Life of John Livingston Nevius* (1895), by his wife, Helen S. C. Nevius. See also A. Van Doren Honeyman, *Joannes Nevius . . . and His Descendants . . . 1627–1900* (1900); H. P. Beach, *Princely Men in the Heavenly Kingdom* (1903); F. F. Ellinwood, "Rev. John L. Nevius, D.D.," in *Church at Home and Abroad*, Feb. 1894; Gilbert Reid, "The Rev. John L. Nevius, D.D.," in *Missionary Review of the World*, May 1894; C. A. Clark, *The Korean Church and the Nevius Methods* (1930); *Necrological Report . . . Princeton Theol. Sem.*, 1894; records of the Board of Foreign Missions, Presbyt. Ch. in the U. S. A.]
H. Cl—s.

NEWBERRY, JOHN STOUGHTON (Nov. 18, 1826–Jan. 2, 1887), lawyer, manufacturer, congressman, was born at Sangerfield, Oneida County, N. Y., the son of Elihu and Rhoda (Phelps) Newberry. He was a descendant of Thomas Newberry who emigrated from Devonshire, England, to Dorchester, Mass., in 1634. Oliver and Walter Loomis Newberry [*qq.v.*] were John's uncles. Elihu moved from Oneida County westward, finally settling at Romeo, Mich., where John prepared for college. Later he entered the University of Michigan, took high rank as a student, and graduated in 1847.

Having acquired a practical knowledge of civil engineering, he spent two years with the Michigan Central Railroad. Then, after a year of travel, he entered a law office in Detroit, and was admitted to the bar in 1853. He was soon recognized as an expert in admiralty cases and in 1857 published *Reports of Admiralty Cases in the Several District Courts of the United States*. In 1855 he married Harriet Newell Robinson, who died in 1856 leaving one son; on Oct. 6, 1859, he married Helen Parmelee Handy and to this union were born two sons. From his majority he had supported and voted the Whig ticket, but upon the formation of the Republican party he joined forces with it and thereafter remained a stanch supporter. President Lincoln appointed him provost-marshal of Michigan in 1862, with the rank of captain of cavalry, an office which he held until 1864, during which time he organized two drafts. Familiar with the needs of the army, he was one of a company of Detroit capitalists who established in 1862 or 1863 the Michigan Car Company to build freight cars for the Union forces; of this company he became president, continuing as such until 1880. Although this venture led him to abandon the practice of law, it developed into a highly profitable enterprise and formed the basis of his large personal fortune, estimated at his death to be from three to four million dollars. The firm soon had branches in London, Ontario, and St. Louis, and employed some five thousand men. In 1878, with James McMillan [q.v.], who was associated with the Michigan Car Company, he formed the firm of Newberry & McMillan, capitalists. As the car-building enterprise prospered, so did his other ever-widening business ventures. He helped organize a corporation to build the Detroit, Mackinac & Marquette Railroad. He also established the Vulcan Furnace Company at Newberry, Mich. As investor he held large interests in banks, factories, and centrally located Detroit real estate. So wide and varied were these holdings that at his death he was a director in almost every local industry.

With the exception of his term as provost-marshal, he held public office but twice. In 1862 he was elected to the Detroit board of education, and in 1878 he won the Republican nomination for representative to Congress from the First District, and was elected. He served on several important committees and was chairman of the committee on commerce. After one term he retired, feeling that his business interests demanded his full attention. A Congregationalist in his youth, he later joined the Jefferson Avenue Presbyterian Church, where he was noted for regular attendance and his stanch support of church activities. He was interested in philanthropic projects and one of his last undertakings was the establishment, together with James McMillan, of the Grace Homeopathic Hospital, to which Newberry gave $100,000. His will contained bequests of $650,000 to institutions and charities.

[J. G. Bartlett, *Newberry Geneal.* (1914); *Cyc. of Mich.* (1890); Charles Moore, *Hist. of Michigan*

(1915); Henry Hall, *America's Successful Men of Affairs*, vol. II (1896); *Biog. Dir. Am. Cong.* (1928); *Detroit Free Press*, Jan. 3, 1887; *Evening News* (Detroit), Jan. 3, 1887.]
J. J. S.

NEWBERRY, JOHN STRONG (Dec. 22, 1822–Dec. 7, 1892), geologist and paleontologist, son of Henry and Elizabeth (Strong) Newberry and a descendant of Thomas Newberry who came from Devonshire, England, to Dorchester, Mass., about 1634, was born in the town of Windsor, Conn. When he was but two years of age his father moved the family to Ohio, where he founded the town of Cuyahoga Falls in the Western Reserve. Engaging in various enterprises including coal mining, then an entirely new industry, he prospered and was able to bring up his family of nine children in reasonable comfort and amid agreeable surroundings. John received his early education in the local schools and a special school in the adjoining town of Hudson, then entered Western Reserve College, where he graduated in 1846 at the age of twenty-four. During his last two years in college he also studied medicine, and in 1848 graduated from the Cleveland Medical School. In the autumn of 1849 he went abroad to study in the medical schools of Paris, where he also attended geological lectures by distinguished scientists.

Returning to America in 1851, he settled down to the practice of medicine in Cleveland, Ohio, and is said to have been very successful. While thus engaged, he received an appointment as assistant surgeon on an expedition under command of Lieut. R. S. Wilkinson, organized for the purpose of exploring the country along the line of the projected Pacific Railroad from San Francisco Bay to the Columbia River. In January 1856, the work completed, he accompanied the rest of the party to Washington, where they spent the remainder of the year in the preparation of the report. While here Newberry became associated with the Smithsonian Institution and also received appointment as professor of geology in Columbian (now George Washington) University. In 1857 he was appointed physician and naturalist to the expedition under Lieut. J. C. Ives [q.v.], sent out to make a military exploration of the Colorado River. After ascending that stream from its mouth to a point called Fortification Rock, north of the 40th Parallel, the explorers returned to Washington in the early summer of 1858. The following year Newberry was again in the field, this time as member of a topographic surveying party under Capt. J. N. Macomb, exploring the region northwest of Santa Fé as far as the Colorado and Green rivers. With the outbreak of the Civil War, he entered upon duty with the United States Sanitary Commission (June 1861), remaining in this service until the close of the war.

In 1866, after a short association with the Smithsonian Institution, he was chosen professor of geology and paleontology in the School of Mines of Columbia University, New York, a position which he held for the rest of his life. As a teacher he was eminently successful. His relations with his students were always kindly; he was never too busy to receive a caller; never trivial, flippant, or superficial. He is to be credited with an influential part in the organization of the School of Mines. In addition to his academic responsibilities, he was state geologist of Ohio, 1869–74. In this capacity he met with the usual obstacles of an unappreciative legislature, aggravated perhaps by the fact that he postponed publication of the economic results of the survey until the last, thereby giving cause for the complaint that too much attention was being devoted to the academic subject of paleontology.

As a scientist Newberry was of the old school, a general naturalist rather than a specialist. He had been attracted in boyhood by the abundant plant remains in the coal mines near Cuyahoga Falls and had made large collections. Fossil plants and fishes remained always his favorites; he rarely touched upon the broader tectonic problems. His first scientific paper, "Description of the Quarries Yielding Fossil Fishes, Monte Bolca, Italy," was published in the *Family Visitor* in 1851, while he was abroad. His best-known works and those upon which his reputation largely rests were his two volumes on the paleontology of the Ohio Survey (*Report of the Geological Survey of Ohio,* vol. I, pt. 2, 1873, and vol. II, pt. 2, 1875); *Fossil Fishes and Fossil Plants of the Triassic Rocks of New Jersey and the Connecticut Valley* (1888); and *The Paleozoic Fishes of North America* (1889), the last two published as Monographs XIV and XVI of the United States Geological Survey. He received many scientific honors, including membership in the National Academy of Sciences, the presidency of the American Association for the Advancement of Science in 1867, the vice-presidency of the Geological Society of America in 1889, and the presidency of the International Geological Congress in 1891. In 1888, he was awarded the Murchison Medal of the Geological Society of London.

Personally, Newberry is represented by those who knew him best as of a cheerful and buoyant temperament, fond of companionship, but with a sensitive and delicate spirit that sometimes sub-

jected him to periods of depression. He was fond of music and played the violin. In 1848 he married Sarah Brownell Gaylord of Cleveland, Ohio. They had five sons and one daughter. Though his domestic ties were strong, he was separated from his family in his early days by his western explorations and army service; and later, with his family in Cleveland or in New Haven, where they settled at the close of his Ohio work, he lived a lonely life in his rooms at Columbia. He died at his home in New Haven in 1892 from a stroke of apoplexy sustained some two years earlier.

[C. A. White, in *Nat. Acad. Sci. Biog. Memoirs,* vol. VI (1909); J. F. Kemp, in *School of Mines Quart.,* Jan. 1893; memoir by H. L. Fairchild and bibliography by J. F. Kemp, in *Trans. N. Y. Acad. Sci.,* vol. XII (1893); *Proc. Second Joint Meeting of the Scientific Alliance of N. Y. Mar. 27, 1893, in Memory of Prof. John Strong Newberry* (1893); bibliography of Newberry's writings, purporting to be complete, in each of the foregoing publications; J. G. Bartlett, *Newberry Geneal.* (1914); *New Haven Reg.,* Dec. 8, 1892.]

G. P. M.

NEWBERRY, OLIVER (Nov. 17, 1789– July 30, 1860), merchant, ship-builder, known as the "Admiral of the Lakes," was born in East (now South) Windsor, Conn., the son of Amasa and Ruth (Warner) Newberry. His father, a soldier of the Revolution, moved to Oneida County, N. Y., in 1805. In 1808 Oliver left for the Ohio country, where he worked until the opening of the War of 1812. Enlisting in the army, he marched to Sacketts Harbor. At the close of the war he opened a store in Buffalo and was later joined by his brother Walter [*q.v.*]. A visit to Detroit so impressed him with the prospects there that he sold the Buffalo store and in 1826 moved to Detroit. Here he opened a store that carried everything from oxbows to hairpins. He soon became agent for the American Fur Company and entered the commission and forwarding business, took government contracts, and began to build sailing vessels at Newport, Mich. (now Marine City). He was one of the first to foresee the future of Chicago and opened a branch office there. This office dealt in salt meats, which were shipped to Detroit, and helped to build up the large business of Newberry's ever-growing fleet of ships. By 1832 he was the owner of eight vessels. In 1833 he built the steamship *Michigan,* then the largest on the Great Lakes, and two years later he established regular steamship service between Detroit and Chicago. This service aided him in taking care of his ever increasing shipping business. It is said his boats carried the first bituminous coal sent to Chicago by water. During this period he was sutler for Fort Dearborn and made money on the contract. About this time, however, he refused to "profiteer" in flour, thus winning popular support. He built the first lightship at the Strait of Mackinac and was instrumental in opening the Chicago River to large ships by dredging.

In Detroit his interests were many and varied. He was a large holder of real estate; he bought and sold everything; his warehouse was the largest on the lakes. He was the "ready money man" of the city, one of the stockholders in the Detroit & St. Joseph Railroad, and a director in the company. He is often credited with coining the term "wild cat" money, and his adventures in stopping cutthroat competition between the Milwaukee banks and the Bank of Michigan show his ability to meet situations quickly.

In 1859 Newberry made his last complete inspection of his branch offices and shipping interests. The panics of 1837 and 1857 had reduced his wealth, but at the time of his death he was a man of comparatively large means. He left few records of his activities, for he handled his papers carelessly, depositing those needed for each day's business in his hat. He was never married. John Stoughton Newberry [q.v.] was his nephew.

[J. G. Bartlett, *Newberry Geneal.* (1914); G. B. Catlin, *The Story of Detroit* (1926); A. T. Andreas, *Hist. of Chicago*, vols. I, II (1884–85); *Detroit Free Press*, July 31, 1860; Woodbridge Papers, Burton Collection, Detroit Pub. Lib.]   J. J. S.

NEWBERRY, WALTER LOOMIS (Sept. 18, 1804–Nov. 6, 1868), merchant, banker, philanthropist, son of Amasa and Ruth (Warner) Newberry, and a descendant of Thomas Newberry who emigrated from Devonshire in 1634, was born in East (now South) Windsor, Conn. Save through heritage, however, New England influenced him but little, for when he was only a year old the family moved to Sangerfield, Oneida County, N. Y. His father saw active service in the Revolution, and later was a captain in the Connecticut militia. Walter Newberry's limited schooling was obtained at an academy in the neighboring town of Clinton, and in 1820 he received an appointment to West Point, but failed to pass the physical examination. Leaving school, he went to Buffalo and entered the employ of his brother Oliver [q.v.]. In 1826 his brother moved to Detroit and Walter accompanied him, established a drygoods business, and prospered. He took an active interest in public affairs, serving as adjutant-general of the Territory of Michigan from 1829 to 1831, and as alderman of the little frontier city of Detroit in 1832.

Newberry's first extensive land investments, from which he afterwards gained a fortune, were made in 1833, when, in company with his brother Oliver, W. B. Astor, and Lewis Cass [qq.v.], he bought large tracts of land in Wisconsin, northern Michigan, and in the newly established town of Chicago. The raw little colony at the southern end of Lake Michigan attracted him from his first visit; he had the imagination to see its future importance, and determined to grasp the business opportunities it presented. Closing up his affairs in Detroit, he removed to Chicago in 1833 and made that city his home for the rest of his life, seeing it grow, during his thirty-five years' residence, from a straggling board-shack settlement of less than four thousand to a city of nearly three hundred thousand inhabitants. Engaging in the commission business and later in banking, and prospering in both, he invested his profits for years in Chicago real estate. What he bought by the acre he sold later by the front foot, and the increase in value provided him a fortune ample for that period. As the city developed he was active in large business enterprises. He was head of the banking house of Newberry & Burch; founder (1857) and director for years of the Merchants Loan & Trust Company; and a director (from 1857) and president (1859) of the Galena & Chicago Union Railroad Company, which in 1864 became a part of the Chicago & North Western system. He held many positions of trust and honor, a fact indicative both of the esteem of his contemporaries and of his interest in civic affairs. He was a member (1843) of the Chicago board of health, city comptroller (1851), and for a time acting mayor. He was a founder and the first president (1841) of the Young Men's Library Association, the modest institution which more than any other was the forerunner of the Chicago public library. His interest in its affairs very probably influenced him in providing in his will for the Newberry Library. From 1859 to 1863 he was a member of the board of education and in the latter year its president. In 1857 he became a member of the newly organized Chicago Historical Society, was its vice-president from 1858 to 1860, and its president from 1860 until his death eight years later. He gave land to several religious congregations, on which churches were built, and his gifts of money to various enterprises were doubtless greater than is now known. He married, Nov. 22, 1842, Julia Butler Clapp, daughter of James and Julia (Butler) Clapp, of Oxford, N. Y., by whom he had four children, two sons who died in infancy, and two daughters who died unmarried. Newberry's death occurred at sea while he was on his way to join his family in Paris. His body was brought back to Chicago and buried in Graceland Cemetery.

As a result of a contingent provision in Newberry's will, one half of his estate, or about $2,-100,000, went in 1887 to the founding of the independent free public reference library in Chicago that bears his name. Much of the property bequeathed was in undeveloped real estate, which in later years greatly increased in value. Under a cooperative agreement with other reference libraries of the city, the Newberry Library has specialized almost exclusively in the fields of literature, history, philology, and music. Within these limits, its collection of about 500,-000 books and manuscripts has given the institution an international reputation.

[Will of Walter Loomis Newberry, probated 1868; J. G. Bartlett, *Newberry Geneal.* (1914); H. R. Stiles, *The Hist. and Geneals. of Ancient Windsor, Conn.*, vol. II (1892); Silas Farmer, *The Hist. of Detroit and Mich.* (1884); A. T. Andreas, *Hist. of Chicago*, vols. I, II (1884–85); Joseph and Caroline Kirkland, *The Story of Chicago* (2 vols., 1892–94); H. J. Galpin, *Annals of Oxford, N. Y.* (1906); E. O. Gale, *Reminiscences of Early Chicago* (1902); *Chicago Tribune*, Nov. 20, 1868.]   G. B. U.

NEWBOLD, WILLIAM ROMAINE (Nov. 20, 1865–Sept. 26, 1926), philosopher, psychologist, Orientalist, was of English lineage, in the eighth generation from Michael Newbould who settled in Burlington County, N. J., before 1681. He was born at Wilmington, Del., the eldest child of William Allibone Newbold by his second marriage, to Martha Smith Baily, and one of seven children. Marked by special devotion to books and to languages, as a boy he taught himself Hebrew and on entering the University of Pennsylvania as a sophomore in 1884 he organized a group of fellow students to whom he taught that language. He induced M. W. Easton, professor of English, to offer Sanskrit, and pursued the subject for two years. In college he won all the prizes for which he competed, against classmates of later distinction who freely admitted his preëminent qualities.

Receiving the bachelor's degree in 1887, he taught Latin two years in the Cheltenham Military Academy, and then became instructor in Latin and lecturer in philosophy at the University of Pennsylvania. His graduate studies, begun in 1887, brought him the doctorate of philosophy in 1891, and he then studied abroad for one year, chiefly in Berlin. On returning, he resumed teaching at his alma mater, with which he was connected for the rest of his life: as lecturer in philosophy, 1892–94; assistant professor, 1894–1903; professor, 1903–07; and Adam Seybert Professor of Intellectual and Moral Philosophy from 1907 until his death. As dean of the Graduate School, 1896–1904, he rendered

important service in raising the standards of graduate work.

His interests were many, his knowledge encyclopedic. At first particularly interested in psychology and in the work of the Society for Psychical Research, he next turned to philosophy, and became a master in expounding Plato and Aristotle. By these studies he was led from a state of religious unrest to a firm Christian orthodoxy; he gave a course at the University on the development of early Christian thought and twice (1923–25) gave a similar course at the General Theological Seminary of the Protestant Episcopal Church in New York. He was even invited, though a layman, to assume the chair of ecclesiastical history in this seminary, but declined it.

Between 1892 and 1902 he published a number of brief papers and reviews on psychological and philosophical subjects. His more important published writings include: "Bardaisan and the Odes of Solomon" (*Journal of Biblical Literature*, vol. XXX, pt. 2, 1911); "The Descent of Christ in the Odes of Solomon" (*Ibid.*, vol. XXXI, pt. 4, 1912); "A Syriac Valentinian Hymn" (*Journal of the American Oriental Society*, February 1918); "The Syriac Dialogue 'Socrates'" (*Proceedings of the American Philosophical Society*, vol. LVII, 1918); "The Great Chalice of Antioch" (*Ladies' Home Journal*, November 1924); "The Eagle and the Basket on the Chalice of Antioch" (*American Journal of Archaeology*, October–December 1925); "Five Transliterated Aramaic Inscriptions" (*Ibid.*, July–September 1926). His lectures on the Valentinian Gnosis, delivered in 1920 at Philadelphia on the Bohlen Foundation, were left in manuscript. Perhaps his best-known achievement was the partial decipherment of the Roger Bacon Manuscript owned by the late W. M. Voynich of New York, which had previously defied all efforts of cipher experts. His studies of the manuscript were begun in 1919, but were left incomplete by his sudden death; the material found among his papers was edited by a colleague and published under the title, *The Cipher of Roger Bacon*, in 1928.

Newbold was a short, slight man, with a pointed beard trimmed close on the cheeks; he habitually read and studied until well after midnight, despite his lack of robust health, but was fond of outdoor life during his vacations, and was expert with a sailboat. His black hair never became thin nor touched with gray; his keen brown eyes revealed his unusual intellectual and spiritual gifts. Of his inclusive human sympathy he gave freely to all who came to him; in colleagues and in students alike, he inspired a love that approached worship. His course on Greek philosophy was regularly elected by about a hundred students, who gave a tribute of applause at the hour's end (a rarity at his University); in his last year the course was taken by over a hundred and fifty. He was married on Apr. 9, 1896, to Ethel Kent Sprague Packard of Boston, who survived him; they had no children. He died in Philadelphia in his sixty-first year.

[*Newbold Memorial Meeting* (Univ. of Pa., 1927), ed. by R. G. Kent, containing portrait and bibliography; *Gen. Mag. and Hist. Chronicle* (Univ. of Pa.), Jan. 1927; *Public Ledger* (Phila.), Sept. 27, 1926; *Am. Jour. Archaeology*, Jan.–Mar. 1927; *Jour. Am. Oriental Soc.*, Dec. 1927; *Who's Who in America*, 1926–27; F. A. Virkus, *The Abridged Compendium of Am. Geneal.*, I (1925), 946; H. V. Cubberly, *Bloomsdale: Sketches of the Old-time Home of the John Newbold Family and Geneal. Notes* (1930); Foreword to *The Cipher of Roger Bacon* (1928), ed. by R. G. Kent.]
R. G. K.

NEWBROUGH, JOHN BALLOU (June 5, 1828–Apr. 22, 1891), founder of Shalam religious community, was born near Springfield, Ohio, the son of Jacob and Mary Newbrough. He left home at the age of sixteen and worked for a dentist, Dr. Slauson, in Cleveland. In 1849 he graduated from a Cincinnati dental college. Within a few months, however, he joined the gold rush for California and in 1851 went to the goldfields of Australia. After six years of travel he returned to Cincinnati, where he practised medicine and dentistry. In 1860 he was married in Scotland to Rachel Turnbull, and returned with his bride to Philadelphia, where he practised dentistry until 1862, when he moved to New York. In 1865 he published *A Catechism on Human Teeth*, in which he speaks of his experience abroad. He continued to practise his profession until 1884 and is credited with the invention of a rubber plate.

During these years he became increasingly interested in spiritualism and finally discovered that he had an unusual gift for automatic writing. In order to facilitate his communication with angels, he undertook a systematic discipline of "purification," avoiding meat and stimulants. In 1881, according to his own account, "one morning the light struck both my hands on the back and they went for the typewriter, for some fifteen minutes, very vigorously. I was told not to read what was printed. . . . For fifty weeks this continued . . . and then it ceased, and I was told to read and publish Oahspe" (preface to 1932 edition of *Oahspe*.)

Oahspe: A New Bible (first edition, 1882) was written in Biblical idiom for "faithists." It outlines in elaborate detail the history and structure of the universe and announces the dawn of the "Kosmon Age," beginning in 1848, during which "Jehovih's [*sic*] Kingdom on Earth" is to be established. The revelations of *Oahspe* induced Newbrough to collect a large number of orphans and foundlings at Pearl River, N. Y., and, with the help of a faithful band of followers, to organize the communistic society of Shalam, N. Mex. This community controlled about 1,000 acres of irrigated land near Doña Ana in Mesilla Valley. It was planned to build another community for adults, named Levitica, nearby, but the limited resources of the group made this venture impossible. The children were legally adopted by Shalam Community and were given a systematic, practical education, which was intended to make them competent to do the work of the community and to despise the "filth and luxury" of "the land of UZ" (the cities of the world). A "Faithist's Infants' Home" was established in New Orleans for castaways, foundlings, and orphans: "said babes are to be taken to a place in the country, distant from vice, such as drunkenness, using tobacco, flesh-eating and so on" (*The Castaway, post*, p. 101). Newbrough labored in and with this community until his death, and the work was continued for about ten years longer under the direction of A. M. Howland of Boston, who had provided most of the funds for the venture. Divorced from his wife because she refused to follow him to New Mexico, he married Frances Van de Water. He had a son by his first marriage, and a daughter by his second. He was a 33rd degree Mason and his grave is in the Masonic Burial Grounds at Las Cruces, N. Mex.

[W. A. Hinds, *Am. Communities* (1902); L. H. Gray, "Oahspe," in James Hastings, *Encyc. of Religion and Ethics*, vol. IX (1917); *Vohu Esfoma* (London, 1927); *The Castaway* (New Orleans, 1889); preface to 1932 ed. of *Oahspe* and other publications of the Kosmon Press, London, and the Oahspe Publishing Asso., Los Angeles; obituary in *Santa Fé Daily New Mexican*, Apr. 25, 1891.]
H. W. S—d—r.

NEWCOMB, CHARLES LEONARD (Aug. 7, 1854–Mar. 13, 1930), mechanical engineer, inventor, was born at West Willington, Conn., the son of Charles Leonard and Martha Jane (Hudson) Newcomb, and a descendant of Andrew Newcomb who was in New England as early as 1666. After obtaining a common-school education and while still in his teens, Charles, having a natural interest in the metal trades, went to work in an iron foundry. After several years of experience in this field, he began a machinist apprenticeship, upon the completion of which he spent upwards of ten years practising his trade in various places in Connecticut. He was millwright and stationary engineer for the Florence Mills; millwright and machinist of the

Rock Manufacturing Company at Rockville; master mechanic for the Pratt & Whitney Company at Hartford; and a machinist for the American Clutch Company at Middletown. Feeling the need of a technical education, he entered the Worcester Free Institute (later the Worcester Polytechnic Institute), Worcester, Mass., from which he was graduated with the degrees B.S. and M.E. in 1880.

Following his graduation, he was made superintendent of the American Electric Lighting Company, New Britain, Conn., and established there the first municipal electric lighting plant in the United States. In 1881 he moved to Holyoke, Mass., to accept the position of superintendent of the Deane Steam Pump Company, makers of pumping machinery. Until his retirement in 1927 he was directly connected with this establishment, and through his engineering and executive ability developed it into one of the most important manufacturing enterprises of New England. When in 1899 the International Steam Pump Company obtained control of the Deane Works, Newcomb was elected president and general manager of the reorganized concern. Later he was influential in bringing the Worthington Pump & Machinery Corporation to Holyoke, and when that corporation gained control of the Deane Works in 1914, Newcomb became general manager, continuing in that capacity until his retirement. From 1907 to 1911 he also served as general manager of the Blake-Knowles Works of the International Steam Pump Company at East Cambridge, Mass. Newcomb not only managed the affairs of these organizations but also employed his mechanical training and ingenuity in effecting the remarkable improvements in pumping machinery that took place between 1880 and 1930. Nationally recognized as an authority on mechanics and hydraulics, he acted in a consulting capacity as an expert in various lines of engineering.

In addition to his business and engineering work, Newcomb was active in the human relations side of industry. As an executive of the Silver Bay Industrial Conference Board he took part in its annual conferences and became well known throughout the world for the ideas he projected looking toward improved working conditions in manufacturing plants. He was vitally interested in national affairs affecting the metal trades. He helped to found the National Foundry Association in 1898 and was its first vice-president; he was instrumental in forming in 1899 the National Metal Trades Association; and he was an active member of the American Society of Mechanical Engineers from 1883 until his

death, a manager from 1919 to 1921, and vice-president in 1926–28 under the leadership of Charles M. Schwab. He was also the organizer in 1919, and the first president of the Engineering Society of Western Massachusetts; a member of the American Society of Naval Architects and Marine Engineers; and a member of the executive committee of the Associated Industries of Massachusetts. From the very beginning of his residence in Holyoke, he took an active part in municipal affairs. He served two terms as councilman (1886–87) and one as alderman (1888). When, in 1893, the newly created fire commission was established he was named chairman, a position which he occupied for seventeen years. While on this commission he devised the rotary deluge nozzle, for which he received patent No. 616,200 on Dec. 20, 1898. By the use of this nozzle in connection with the aerial fire ladder, the latter was converted into a water tower. He did much research work looking toward the improvement of fire hydrants, and the standards developed by him were adopted by the National Board of Fire Underwriters and by the American Water Works Association. During the whole of his extremely busy life he wrote prolifically for the technical press. At the time of his death he was president of the Holyoke Cooperative Bank; a director of the Holyoke Valve and Hydrant Company; and a member of the board of trustees of the Worcester Polytechnic Institute. On Jan. 20, 1874, he married Inez Louise Kendall of Rockville, Conn.; he was survived by his widow and six children.

[B. M. Newcomb, *Andrew Newcomb 1618–1686 and His Descendants* (1923); *Who's Who in America,* 1928–29; *Mechanical Engineering,* June 1930; *Power,* Apr. 1, 1930; *Springfield Republican,* Mar. 15, 16, 1930; *Holyoke Daily Transcript,* Mar. 13, 14, 1930; *N. Y. Times,* Mar. 14, 1930; Pat. Off. records.]

C. W. M.

NEWCOMB, HARVEY (Sept. 2, 1803–Aug. 30, 1863), Congregational clergyman, editor, and author, a descendant of Capt. Andrew Newcomb who was in America as early as 1666, was born in Thetford, Vt., the son of Simon and Hannah (Curtis) Newcomb. In 1818 the family moved to Alfred, N. Y., where Harvey taught school for eight years. Turning his attention to journalism, he became the owner and editor of the *Western Star* of Westfield, N. Y. (1826–28), editor of the Buffalo *Patriot,* an anti-Masonic paper (1828–30), and of the Pittsburgh *Christian Herald,* a paper for children (1830–31). The following ten years were devoted to writing books for children and young people.

Without a college or seminary training, but with the preparation afforded by his years of teaching and writing, Newcomb turned toward the ministry. He was licensed in 1840 and supplied the Congregational church in West Roxbury, Mass., during the two following years. On Oct. 6, 1842, he was ordained pastor of the church in West Needham, now Wellesley, Mass., where he remained till July 1, 1846, when with twenty-six of his parishoners he withdrew and founded the church at Grantville, now Wellesley Hills. Returning to journalism in 1849 he was assistant editor of the *Boston Traveller* for a year and of the *New York Observer* for two years. He then settled in Brooklyn, where he conducted a private school for young ladies and engaged in authorship and in Sunday-school and mission work. In 1859 he became pastor of a church in Hancock, Pa., and remained as such till ill health forced his retirement to Brooklyn, in which city he died.

Newcomb had a genius for assimilating and imparting information and his literary output is estimated at as high as 178 volumes, some of which were published anonymously. He had an intelligent conception of Bible study and in some respects anticipated the historical criticism of a later generation. He probably, also, came as near as any author of his day to adapting his writings to the mental capacity of children and young people. His series of nineteen Sunday-school question books had a circulation of 300,000 copies, and his fourteen volumes of church history had wide popularity. His *How to be a Man* (1847) and *How to be a Lady* (1846; 8th ed., 1850) had a circulation of 34,000 copies each. A series on the Indians of North America and missionary work among them was abandoned at the end of the second volume for lack of popular interest in the subject. His most important work was his *Cyclopaedia of Missions* (1854), in which the enterprises of all denominations and the fields occupied were fully described, together with the histories of individual missions and missionaries. His writings are characterized by taste, judgment, wide and accurate information, and an intense desire to benefit humanity. He was an ardent and zealous worker, but in his contact with people his zeal sometimes outran his tact, a factor which tended to make his pastorates of short duration. He was deeply interested in city mission work and has been called the father of the mission Sunday school. He wrote constantly for the press and was a frequent contributor to such papers as the *Boston Recorder,* the *Puritan Recorder,* and the *New York Evangelist.* His contributions to the *Youth's Companion* cover a period of many years. He left in manuscript an interesting autobiography.

On May 19, 1830, he was married to Alithea A. Wells by whom he had two sons and two daughters.

[J. B. Newcomb, *Geneal. Memoir of the Newcomb Family* (1874); B. M. Newcomb, *Andrew Newcomb and His Descendants* (1923); *Congregational Quart.,* Oct. 1863; E. H. Chandler, *Hist. of the Wellesley Congregational Ch.* (1898); G. K. Clarke, *Hist. of Needham, Mass., 1711–1911* (1912); *N. Y. Observer,* Sept. 3, 1863.]

F. T. P.

NEWCOMB, JOSEPHINE LOUISE LE MONNIER (Oct. 31, 1816–Apr. 7, 1901), philanthropist, was born in Baltimore, Md., the youngest daughter of Alexander Louis and Mary Sophia (Waters) LeMonnier. Her mother was of English extraction and her father had emigrated to America from France. She lost her mother when very young and, being almost penniless, went to New Orleans to live with a married sister. There she received a large part if not all of her education, and there she met her future husband, Warren Newcomb, a man of New England ancestry then on a visit to New Orleans from Louisville, Ky., where he was a member of the firm of H. D. Newcomb & Brother, merchants. After their marriage they lived for a time in New York City, where they had a son, who died in infancy, and a daughter, Harriott Sophie, who was born on July 29, 1855. In 1866 Newcomb died, leaving his fortune to his widow and to their daughter, with whom she continued to live in New York until the child died on Dec. 16, 1870. Already saddened by the death of her husband and her son and harassed by the efforts of her husband's relatives to set aside his will, this death of the last member of her immediate family was an unusually severe blow. She lived in retirement for a number of years, and then vainly sought relief in travel.

Finally she decided to give her money to found a woman's college in memory of her beloved daughter, and she returned to New Orleans to make the necessary arrangements. The H. Sophie Newcomb Memorial College, in the Tulane University of Louisiana, for the higher education of white girls and young women, came into existence with her initial gift of $100,000 to the Tulane educational fund on Oct. 11, 1886. From that time until her death the welfare of the institution was her greatest personal interest. She made other gifts to it during her lifetime, and by her will, dated May 12, 1898, she made the university her residuary legatee, a bequest amounting to about $2,700,000. She was small in stature, modest, and retiring, and would not allow her philanthropies to be extolled in her presence. She had a clear idea of the value and administration of wealth and under her care the fortune of about half a million dollars left by her husband grew to important proportions and provided abundant means for the charities of her long life. Her gifts were by no means confined to Newcomb College; wherever she saw that money was needed she gave freely. During her lifetime she built a memorial chapel to Robert E. Lee at Lexington, Ky.; she made gifts to the Confederate orphans' home at Charleston, S. C., and to a deaf mutes' school in New York City; and in the Eye, Ear, Nose, and Throat Hospital of New Orleans she established a bed and named it after her daughter. She died on Easter Sunday 1901 in New York City and was buried in Greenwood Cemetery, N. Y.

[Records of the Tulane University; *Bulletin of the Tulane University of La.*, 31 ser., no. 4 (1930); *Newcomb College, Pictures and Practical Information,* May 1930; B. V. B. Dixon, *A Brief Hist. of H. Sophie Newcomb Coll.* (1928); B. M. Newcomb, *Andrew Newcomb ... and His Descendants* (1923); *Daily Picayune* (New Orleans), Apr. 9-11, 14, 1901; date of birth from certificate of registra of St. Paul's parish, Baltimore, Md.; spelling of daughter's name from *In Memoriam* (n.d.), a booklet placed in archives of Newcomb Coll. by Mrs. Newcomb, through courtesy of Alice M. Labouisse, Newcomb Coll.]   M. J. W.

NEWCOMB, SIMON (Mar. 12, 1835-July 11, 1909), astronomer, was born in humble circumstances at Wallace, Nova Scotia. His father, John Burton Newcomb, was an itinerant school teacher of New England and Pennsylvania Scotch-Irish ancestry, his mother, Emily (Prince) Newcomb, a village girl of good mind, descended from a family of New England country preachers. Although showing precocity in school, at sixteen years of age Simon was apprenticed to a herbalist doctor, whom he soon discovered to be no more than a quack. At the age of eighteen, he ran away empty-handed, to make his career. After walking nearly a hundred miles, he reached St. John, New Brunswick. Finding no means of support there, he pressed on in great distress till he reached Calais, Me. Thence a kindly ship-captain allowed him to work his passage to Salem, Mass., for he hoped that opportunities for intellectual occupation might be found in the United States.

Drifting to Maryland, he taught country school for several years. Sometimes he traveled in high leather boots over the muddy or dusty road the long way to Washington. On one occasion he introduced himself to Joseph Henry [*q.v.*], first secretary of the Smithsonian Institution, and then the most influential man of science in America. Seeing promise in the boy, Henry recommended him to J. E. Hilgard [*q.v.*], then in charge of the Coast Survey. By the loan and recommendation of books, and in other ways, they both encouraged the hard-working, en-

thusiastic youth. Newcomb even undertook to read Newton's *Principia* and Bowditch's translation of Laplace's *Mécanique céleste,* but with the meager mathematical knowledge he then possessed found it impossible to master these abstruse works. Through the recommendations of Henry and Hilgard, Newcomb was appointed a computer in the Nautical Almanac Office, then located at Harvard University. He says in his *Reminiscences of an Astronomer* (p. 1), "I date my birth into the world of sweetness and light on one frosty morning in January, 1857, when I took my seat between two well-known mathematicians, before a blazing fire in the office of the 'Nautical Almanac.'" At Cambridge, he availed himself of the opportunity to attend the Lawrence Scientific School of Harvard University, from which he was graduated (B.Sc.) July 2, 1858. In 1860 he published his first important research, done while still a computer at the Nautical Almanac Office. The astronomer Olbers had suggested that the minor planets of the solar system had originated in the disruption of a larger planet. Newcomb was able to show that the orbits of these bodies had never intersected, so that this origin is impossible (*Proceedings of the American Association for the Advancement of Science,* vol. XIII, 1860; *Memoirs of the American Academy of Arts and Sciences,* n.s. VIII, pt. 1, 1861). In 1860 he and William Ferrel [*q.v.*] were sent to the wilderness of Saskatchewan north of Lake Winnipeg to observe a total eclipse of the sun. Upon reaching their station after many adventures, they found it inundated. They set up their instruments in puddles of water and slept in their canoe, but the eclipse was entirely hidden by thick clouds. On Sept. 21, 1861, Newcomb was commissioned professor of mathematics in the United States Navy. In this service he continued at the Naval Observatory and the Nautical Almanac Office until his retirement for age with the naval rank of captain in 1897. He was promoted to be rear-admiral (retired) in 1906.

Although he was assigned to the new 8-inch transit circle in 1862, and made many observations during his connection with the Naval Observatory, he was primarily a mathematical rather than an observational astronomer. In 1866 and in 1873 he published in the *Smithsonian Contributions to Knowledge* (vols. XV, XIX) fundamental investigations and tables of the orbits of Neptune and of Uranus. In recognition of these investigations he was awarded the gold medal of the Royal Astronomical Society of London in 1874. Having arranged his observing with a view to determining errors in the catalogue positions of the stars, he published a memoir on the right ascensions of the equatorial fundamental stars, and on the corrections required to reduce existing observations of star positions in right ascension to a homogeneous system (*Astronomical and Meteorological Observations Made during the Year 1870, at the United States Naval Observatory,* generally cited as *Washington Observations,* App. 3, 1873).

About 1868 he began his celebrated studies of the motion of the moon, to which he gave much of his attention up to the very end of his life. They first led him to search the early European records for occultations of stars. He carried on this search at the Paris Observatory during the reign of the Commune in 1871, while the city was besieged by the National forces. He had such success as to push back a fairly exact knowledge of lunar positions from the year 1750 to about 1645, and in this way disclosed an unsuspected inadequacy of Hansen's tables of the moon's motion, which till then had been regarded as definitive. About this time, he became deeply concerned with the question of the sun's parallax. All approaches to it interested him. He took part in observing the total solar eclipses of 1869 and 1870, as well as in the preparations and observations relating to the transits of Venus in 1874 and 1882. While in Vienna in 1883, he was able to rescue from discredit the records made by Father Maximilian Hell, S.J., of the transit of Venus as observed at Wardhus in Norway in 1769, which were regarded as of great importance if trustworthy (*Monthly Notices of the Royal Astronomical Society,* May 1883; *Reminiscences of an Astronomer,* pp. 154–60). With the assistance of A. A. Michelson [*q.v.*] he redetermined the velocity of light by the revolving-mirror method. Gravitational approaches through the lunar and planetary inequalities of motion were also investigated by him. His revision of the value of the solar parallax published in *Washington Observations, 1865* (1867) remained standard for many years, but was itself superseded by his own new revision of 1895 (published in *The Elements of the Four Inner Planets, and the Fundamental Constants of Astronomy,* 1895, which was issued as a supplement to the *American Ephemeris . . . for 1897*). This second revision since then has been slightly improved in its turn by later results depending on the discovery of the minor planet Eros.

With his achievements so widely recognized that already he had been elected to the principal academies and societies of the world, and had received their most honorable decorations and medals, he was appointed, Sept. 15, 1877, to be superintendent of the American Ephemeris and Nautical Almanac. When he assumed charge, the Nautical Almanac Office was cramped into a dilapidated old dwelling-house in Cambridge, and much of the computing was done as piecework at high prices by distant college professors. Newcomb found this piecework method well suited to economical administration after he had, little by little, brought in the work to less expensive computers in Washington. He removed the offices to more commodious quarters, where they remained until the completion of the present Naval Observatory. Inefficient personnel, which had received appointment by influence in those days antedating civil-service reform, he succeeded in removing. Thus the office was reorganized to do its great work.

Immediately after assuming his new responsibilities, Newcomb conceived the astonishing program of critically reforming the entire basis of fundamental data involved in the computation of the Ephemeris. The fundamental star places, the mass and distance of the sun, the motion of the moon, and the masses and orbits of the planets and their satellites, all were to be redetermined and new tables computed to suit the revised theory. Surprising to relate, he was able to accomplish all of this during his own lifetime excepting new tables of the moon's motion, which have since his death been computed by Prof. Ernest W. Brown of Yale University. Newcomb's program involved the discussion of all the worthwhile observations of the positions of the sun, moon, and planets, as well as those of many of the fixed stars, which had been made at the principal observatories of the world since 1750. These observations numbered several hundred thousands. The work also involved investigating the mathematical theory of the perturbations caused by the several planets upon the motions of each other. In this highest type of practical mathematical research, he was fortunate in enlisting the services of George William Hill [*q.v.*], to whom was assigned the theory and tables of motion of Jupiter and Saturn. Newcomb himself discussed the orbits of Neptune, Uranus, and the four inner planets, Mercury, Venus, Earth, and Mars, and computed tables of their motions. He also expended enormous labor on lunar theory. As Hill remarked: "He seems to be determined that no inequality of sensible magnitude should escape him" (Hill, *post,* p. 356). In 1896 he took a leading part at the Paris Conference on a common international catalogue of fundamental stars. Different portions of the required research being assigned to different astronomers, Newcomb worked up for international use the best value of the constant of precession (*Astronomical Papers*, vol. VIII, pt. 1, 1897), and following this he published a catalogue of about fifteen hundred fundamental star positions (*Ibid.*, pt. 2, 1898).

To the *Astronomical Papers Prepared for the Use of the American Ephemeris and Nautical Almanac*, of which he was the founder, he contributed a great number of classic memoirs. In the opinion of his colleague Hill, some ten of these, in addition to the two just mentioned, were of outstanding importance. His "Discussion and Results of Observations on Transits of Mercury, from 1677 to 1881" (*Astronomical Papers*, vol. I, pt. 6, 1882) corroborated Leverrier's assertion that a secular motion of the perihelion of the planet amounting to 40" is unaccounted for by gravitational theory. This is the peculiarity of Mercury's orbit that in recent years has become celebrated as evidence of the soundness of Einstein's theory of relativity (see "Einstein's Appreciation of Simon Newcomb," *Science*, Mar. 1, 1929). A memoir on the velocity of light (*Astronomical Papers*, vol. II, pt. 3, 1885), the work in which he collaborated with Michelson, gave an account of the investigation by Foucault's method made at Washington in the years 1880–82. An exhaustive discussion of the observations of the transit of Venus in 1761 and 1769 and their bearing on the solar parallax and the position of the node of Venus appeared in 1890 (vol. II, pt. 5) and a memoir on the constant of nutation as determined by observations with the transit circles of Greenwich and Washington, in 1891 (vol. II, pt. 6).

Deeming "that improvements could be made in the mode of deriving the periodic expressions needed in the subject of planetary perturbations" (Hill, p. 355), he elaborated his method of treatment in "A Method of Developing the Perturbative Function of Planetary Motion" (*American Journal of Mathematics*, September 1880), and, more extensively, in "Development of the Perturbative Function and Its Derivatives in Sines and Cosines of Multiples of the Eccentric Anomaly and in Powers of the Eccentricities and Inclinations" (*Astronomical Papers*, vol. III, pt. 1, 1884). Finally, he applied this method to the four interior planets in "Periodic Perturbation of the Longitudes and Radii Vectors of the Four Inner Planets of the First Order as to the Masses" (*Ibid.*, vol. III, pt. 5, 1891). "For certain long-period inequalities in these planets," says Hill (*loc. cit.*), "it was found convenient to employ expressions involving time-arguments; this led to the composition of two memoirs in Volume V of the same collection" (*Astronomical Papers*,

pts. 1, 2, 1894). "The secular variations of the elements of these planets are derived and the mass of Jupiter determined from observations of Polyhymnia in parts 4 and 5 of the same volume" (1894–95). In 1884 (vol. III, pt. 3) appeared a memoir on the retrograde motion of the line of Jupiter's satellite Hyperion, which he ascribed to the disturbing influence of Titan; while a highly important memoir on the elements of the four inner planets and certain fundamental constants of astronomy was published (1895) as a supplement to the *American Ephemeris* for the year 1897. Following this were issued the actual tables of motion of these planets (*Astronomical Papers*, vol. VI, pts. 1–4, 1895–98). In 1899, Newcomb's revision of the motions of six planets was completed by publication of the tables of motion of Uranus and Neptune (*Ibid.*, vol. VII, 1899). Other work laid out by him but finished by his colleagues appeared in later volumes.

After his retirement in 1897, some slight provision was made by Congress for several years to employ his great powers for the benefit of the Nautical Almanac Office. The Carnegie Institution, however, almost immediately after its establishment, made grants which enabled him to go on with his work till the end of his life. Among his later investigations, besides those of a purely astronomical type, were some relating to meteorology and the influence of sunspots on terrestrial climate. He took a prominent part in procuring the 26-inch telescope of the United States Naval Observatory, in the foundation of the Lick Observatory, and in other important steps in astronomical progress both in America and abroad. As a presiding officer, he was a most extraordinary and impressive figure. Not unconscious of the high worth implied by the numerous honors, doctorates, and decorations heaped upon him from all parts of the world (see *Who's Who in America*, 1908–09), he conducted himself with great dignity, heightened by the massive leonine head with its crown of iron-gray hair and the strong mouth framed by beard and mustache. To see him presiding at a meeting of astronomers was indeed a serious sight, well calculated to inspire awe of the profession in a youthful mind. Besides the classic memoirs of the *American Ephemeris* which issued under his direction, and a long memoir on the lunar theory, *Investigation of Inequalities in the Motion of the Moon, Produced by the Action of the Planets* (Carnegie Institution of Washington, 1907), Newcomb published numerous articles in astronomical journals both in America and abroad. These treated in masterly fashion almost every conceivable subject in astronomy. In addition, he published a number of mathematical textbooks and several outstanding astronomical books for the general reader, including *Popular Astronomy* (1878), *The Stars* (1901), *Astronomy for Everybody* (1902), and *Reminiscences of an Astronomer* (1903). The author's good sense of humor is often betrayed in these writings. He did not at all confine his thoughts to astronomy, but wrote a romance, *His Wisdom, the Defender* (1900); *The A B C of Finance* (1877), consisting in large part of articles that had first appeared in *Harper's Weekly*, 1875–76; *Principles of Political Economy* (1886); and *A Plain Man's Talk on the Labor Question* (1886). He used to say that while astronomy was his vocation, political economy was his avocation. He was also the first president of the American Society for Psychical Research.

Throughout most of his career he was closely associated with collegiate work. In 1879–80, he delivered four lectures in a course on political economy at Harvard University. For two years, 1884–86, he was nominally professor of astronomy at Columbian College (now George Washington University). In October 1884, he was appointed professor of mathematics and astronomy at The Johns Hopkins University, and lectured there twice a week till 1894, and again 1898–1900. In 1885, he was invited to assume the presidency of the University of California, but declined.

He married, Aug. 4, 1863, Mary Caroline Hassler, daughter of Dr. C. A. Hassler, United States Navy, and grand-daughter of Ferdinand Rudolph Hassler [*q.v.*], first superintendent of the United States Coast Survey. Three daughters were born of this marriage. His death occurred at Washington in his seventy-fifth year.

[Newcomb's notebooks, MSS., and letters are in the MSS. Div., Lib. of Cong. For biography, in addition to his *Reminiscences of an Astronomer* (1903), see W. W. Campbell, "Simon Newcomb," with bibliography by R. C. Archibald of Newcomb's writings and articles about him, in *Memoirs Nat. Acad. Sci.*, vol. XVII (1924); Orville Stone, in *Ann. Report ... Smithsonian Inst., 1909* (1910); *Proc. Am. Phil. Soc.*, vol. XLIX (1910); R. C. Archibald, "Simon Newcomb," a collection of facts and dates, in *Science*, Dec. 22, 1916; G. W. Hill, "Professor Simon Newcomb as an Astronomer," *Science*, Sept. 17, 1909; Irving Fisher, in *Economic Jour.* (London), Dec. 1909. For genealogy, see B. M. Newcomb, *Andrew Newcomb, 1618–1686, and His Descendants* (1923).]   C. G. A.

NEWCOMER, CHRISTIAN (Jan. 21, 1749–o.s.–Mar. 12, 1830), one of the founders of the Church of the United Brethren in Christ, was born in Lancaster County, Pa. His father, Wolfgang Newcomer, emigrated with his parents from Switzerland to America some time between 1719 and 1729. He married a Miss Baer—who died about a year later—and as his second wife,

Elizabeth Weller. Christian was one of their eight children. The family was identified with the Mennonite faith.

At the age of seventeen Christian experienced a religious conversion. At this time there was a small but growing body in the ministry and laity of different churches, which gave special emphasis to the inner experiential elements of religion. The movement which it furthered contributed, among English-speaking people, to the development of American Methodism, and among the Germans to the organization, in 1800, of the Church of the United Brethren in Christ, under the leadership of Philip William Otterbein [*q.v.*], a minister of the German Reformed Church. Newcomer, some time subsequent to his conversion and partly as a result of a critical illness which led to a more serious consideration of spiritual matters, became inwardly convinced that he was divinely called to preach the Gospel, but through natural timidity he remained in a state of indecision for a number of years. He had been married, Mar. 31, 1770, to Elizabeth Baer, and in 1775, during this period of vacillation, he moved to Frederick County, Md., his residence later being included, by change of boundary, in Washington County. Finding no peace of mind as a fugitive from duty, as he regarded himself, he finally yielded to his convictions, entering upon the work of the ministry in 1777. Withdrawing from the Mennonite communion, he became identified with the movement headed by Otterbein, which, though lacking in compact organization, was assuming considerable proportions and wielding a growing influence. He took a leading part in the founding of the Church of the United Brethren in Christ and became a most ardent promoter of its activities. In his zeal for extending the work he made excursions into western Pennsylvania, Kentucky, Ohio and Indiana, and did much to establish his Church west of the Alleghany mountains. He early perceived the necessity of effective organization, and wherever conditions permitted he formed local congregations, at the same time urging and developing a more complete plan for missionary enterprise. He was among the first to attempt to formulate a discipline for the government of the general body, and to promote organic unity of the congregations east and west of the Alleghanies. In his itineraries, he made at least nineteen trips through the mountains, invariably on horseback. Later historians are much indebted for information regarding the early history of the Church to the diary, known as "Newcomer's Journal," which records, though incompletely, his labors from 1795 to 1830. This journal, translated and edited by John Hildt, was published in 1834, under the title, *The Life and Journal of the Rev'd. Christian Newcomer, Late Bishop of the Church of the United Brethren in Christ.* He was elected bishop in 1813, being the third to occupy that office, and was successively reëlected to that position in 1814, 1817, 1821, 1825, and 1829. His strength as a preacher was more in his intense earnestness and spiritual zeal than in any marked oratorical ability, though he was recognized as possessing a high degree of persuasive power and ability to expound the Scripture.

[In addition to *The Life and Journal*, see Daniel Berger, *Hist. of the Ch. of the United Brethren in Christ* (1897); H. A. Thompson, *Our Bishops* (1889); A. W. Drury, *Hist. of the Ch. of the United Brethren in Christ* (1924).]   W. E. S—r.

NEWEL, STANFORD (June 7, 1839–Apr. 6, 1907), lawyer, diplomat, was the son of Stanford and Abby Lee (Penniman) Newel. He was born in Providence, R. I., but at the age of fifteen went with his parents to St. Anthony Falls (now Minneapolis), Minn. He graduated from Yale College in 1861 and in 1864 he completed the course in Harvard Law School. Returning to Minnesota he was admitted to the bar and began the practice of law in St. Paul. On June 24, 1880, he was married to Helen F. Fiedler, daughter of Ernest and Helen F. Fiedler of New York. With a private income which made it unnecessary to depend upon his profession for support, he took less and less interest as time went on in litigation, and made it his aim to keep his clients out of lawsuits whenever possible. Nevertheless he was known as one of the outstanding lawyers of the Northwest. A large part of his practice was devoted to giving counsel to those who could not afford to pay regular fees. For many years he was a member of the St. Paul park board and was active in other civic affairs. He was the principal founder and many times president of the Minnesota Club of St. Paul. He took great interest in state and local politics, and while he never ran for public office, his advice on Republican policies and candidates had great influence; he was said to have been the confidential friend and adviser of nearly every prominent man in Minnesota politics between 1880 and 1896. He was chairman of the state Republican central committee for six years and was twice delegate to national Republican conventions. Several times he drafted the party platforms of the Minnesota Republicans.

It was not merely as a reward for his political services, however, that Newel received the appointment of United States minister to the Netherlands from President McKinley in 1897.

His background of culture, learning, and experience, his record of quiet and unpretentious but effective public service, his capacity for making and keeping friends, combined with a keen mind, quick perceptions, and a gift for turning a happy and meaningful phrase, made him most valuable as a diplomatic representative abroad. He soon became popular with the diplomatic corps at The Hague and with the people of the Netherlands, and won respect as an able representative of American national interests. He arrived at The Hague in July 1897. A year later, on Sept. 6, 1898, he attended the coronation of the youthful Queen Wilhelmina as the specially accredited representative of the United States, and on Feb. 7, 1901, attended her marriage to Duke Hendrik of Mecklenburg-Schwerin. His most important work at The Hague was as a member of the American delegation to the first Hague Peace Conference in 1899. He was a member of the Second Committee, which had reference to the extension of the Red Cross rules of 1864 and 1868 to maritime warfare, and the revision of the declaration of 1874 concerning the laws and customs of war. With the other members of the delegation he signed the Hague Agreements at the end of the Conference for the United States. He subsequently shared in the organization of the Hague Permanent Court of Arbitration. Newel was the first accredited diplomatic representative of the United States to Luxemburg, to which he was appointed minister on June 5, 1903, in combination with his duties as minister to the Netherlands. In 1905 he resigned from the diplomatic service and returned to St. Paul, where he died a little less than two years later.

[Newel's diplomatic dispatches are preserved in the archives of the State Department; a portion are published in *Papers Relating to the Foreign Relations of the U. S.*, 1898–1905. Biographical articles are found in *Minn. Hist. Soc. Colls.*, vol. XII (1908); Warren Upham and Rose B. Dunlap, "Minn. Biogs.," *Ibid.*, vol. XIV (1912); *Obit. Record of Grads. of Yale Univ.*, 1907; *Sunday Pioneer Press* (St. Paul), Apr. 7, 1907; *Am. Rev. of Revs.*, May 1899; *Who's Who in America*, 1906–07.]   I. L. T.

NEWELL, FREDERICK HAYNES (Mar. 5, 1862–July 5, 1932), civil engineer, was born in Bradford, Pa., the son of Augustus William and Annie Maria (Haynes) Newell. He lost his mother when he was a child and was reared in Newton, Mass., by his maiden aunts, graduating from the high school of that city in 1881. In 1885 he received the degree of B.Sc. in mining engineering from the Massachusetts Institute of Technology. He was then engaged for three years in various surveys in Pennsylvania, Colorado, and other states, and was appointed, Oct. 2, 1888, as assistant hydraulic engineer in the United States Geological Survey under **Maj.** John Wesley Powell [*q.v.*]. For nearly fourteen years he was engaged in irrigation surveys as hydrographer in charge of stream measurements, selection and survey of reservoir sites, and irrigation projects in the arid West.

On the passage of the Reclamation Act in 1902, in the preparation of which he had been prominently concerned, he was made chief engineer of the Reclamation Service under Charles D. Walcott, director of the Geological Survey. In 1907, he was made director of the Reclamation Service, which then became an independent bureau of the Department of the Interior. In this position he continued until 1914, when he was succeeded by Arthur P. Davis, and became consulting engineer for the same service. During his incumbency of these positions the Reclamation Service surveyed and began construction of twenty-five irrigation projects in eighteen different states, involving an investment of nearly $100,000,000 in dams, reservoirs, tunnels, canals, and power and pumping plants. These and auxiliary minor works served about 1,500,000 acres of arid land.

A good speaker, of pleasing personality, he delivered many lectures on irrigation before schools and scientific and civic organizations in various parts of the country. In 1915, he became head of the department of civil engineering of the University of Illinois, but resigned from this position in 1920 and returned to his former home in Washington, D. C. He was associated with others in the organization of the American Association of Engineers, of which he became president in 1919. In 1924, with A. B. McDaniel, he founded the Research Service, in Washington, D. C., an organization of engineering consultants, of which he became president. He was at various times a member of the United States Land Commission, Inland Waterways Commission, Advisory Board on Fuels and Structural Materials, and Illinois State Board of Examiners of Structural Materials. During his career he wrote *Hydrography of the Arid Regions* (1891); *Report on Agriculture by Irrigation in the Western Part of the United States* (1894), published by the 11th Census; *The Public Lands of the United States and Their Water Supply* (1895); *Irrigation in the United States* (1902); *Hawaii, Its Natural Resources and Opportunities for Home-Making* (1909); *Principles of Irrigation Engineering* (1913), with D. W. Murphy; *Irrigation Management* (1916); *Water Resources, Present and Future Uses* (1920). He was joint editor of *Engineering as a Career* (1916), a series of papers by distinguished members of the profes-

sion; and editor of *Planning and Building the City of Washington* (1932). In 1918, he was awarded the Cullum Gold Medal by the American Geographical Society for his achievements in irrigation. He died suddenly in Washington, D. C., of heart failure. On Apr. 3, 1890, he married Effie Josephine Mackintosh of Milton, Mass., who with one son and two daughters survived him.

[*Who's Who in America*, 1932–33; memoir prepared by Allen B. McDaniel for *Trans. Am. Soc. Civil Engineers*; *The Semi-Centennial Alumni Record of the Univ. of Ill.* (1918); F. H. Newell, "Descendants of Walter Haynes and Peter Noyes of Sudbury, Mass.," *New-Eng. Hist. and Geneal. Reg.*, Jan. 1893; *Evening Star* (Washington, D. C.), July 6, 1932; reminiscences of A. B. McDaniel and Mrs. F. H. Newell; personal acquaintance.]					A. P. D.

NEWELL, PETER SHEAF HERSEY (Mar. 5, 1862–Jan. 15, 1924), cartoonist and illustrator, son of George Frederick and Louisa N. Newell, was born near Bushnell, MacDonough County, Ill. In spite of an early predilection for sketching and caricaturing, at the age of sixteen he attempted to work in a cigar factory. This experiment lasted three months and was followed by an apprenticeship to a maker of crayon portraits in Jacksonville, Ill. He made enlargements, thereby gaining his first knowledge of drawing, and though he later studied in an art school he may be said to have been largely self-taught, for his work was free from the prevailing influences in illustration and he evolved a definitely original technique. At about this time he sent a humorous drawing to *Harper's Bazar* with a note asking the editor whether it showed talent. The reply came back: "No talent indicated," but a check was enclosed. Successful contributions to the New York *Graphic* and various periodicals took him to New York in 1882, where he studied at the Art Students' League. He tolerated academic training only three months, believing that the value of his work —its originality—would be sacrificed by adapting it to accepted methods. In 1893, using negro subjects in his new flat-tone technique, he achieved success with *Harper's Magazine* (August 1893) and sudden popularity by an amusing bit of naïveté: "Wild Flowers."

He contributed full-page illustrations to holiday numbers of *Harper's Weekly* and *Harper's Bazar*, continued to do comics with captions of his own invention, and then turned this knack to making children's books, starting with *Topsys and Turvys* (1893). This reversible little volume resulted from the distressing occasion upon which he discovered one of his children scrutinizing a picture-book upside down. He determined to produce a book which could be looked at from any angle. Thereafter he illustrated contemporary fiction, notably: John Kendrick Bangs's *A House-Boat on the Styx* (1896) and *The Pursuit of the House-Boat* (1897), and in 1901 tried his hand at *Alice in Wonderland*. The appearance of substitutes for Sir John Tenniel's inimitable illustrations was attended by considerable controversy. Newell defended the new edition in an article in *Harper's Monthly Magazine* (October 1901), in which he asserted that any distinctly personal reaction to character justifies a new version of interpretation.

Considered by his contemporaries to be an illustrator of ability and conspicuous originality, Newell has survived by reason of his good humor rather than on grounds of artistic merit. Whenever his work lacks the animation of wit its execution appears unimpressive. The flat decorative use of wash does not conceal an inadequacy of drawing and composition. His strength lay in whimsical interpretation of nonsense set forth in simple and direct terms. He was inventive rather than imaginative, giving a certain zest to his own cartoons which is not felt in his illustrations of the ideas of others. Newell was married, Feb. 5, 1884, to Leona Dow Ashcraft. They had two daughters. He died in his sixty-second year at Little Neck, L. I.

[*Peter Newell's Pictures and Rhymes* (1899) contains a biographical sketch by John Kendrick Bangs. See also: C. B. Loomis, "Interesting People—Peter Newell," *Am. Mag.*, May 1911; Albert Lee, "Book Illustrators—Peter Newell," *Book Buyer*, July 1896; Louise M. Sill, "Mr. Newell's Latest Drawings," *Harper's Bazar*, Sept. 1902; Mich. State Lib., *Biog. Sketches of Am. Artists* (1924); Regina Armstrong, "The New Leaders in Am. Illustration," *Bookman*, June 1900; P. L. Allen, "Illustrations of Alice in Wonderland," *Ibid.*, Feb. 1908; Peter Newell, "Alice's Adventures in Wonderland from an Artist's Standpoint," *Harper's Monthly*, Oct. 1901; *N. Y. Times*, Jan. 16, 1924.]   F. B.

NEWELL, ROBERT (Mar. 30, 1807–November 1869), trapper, Oregon pioneer, was born in Muskingum County, Ohio. The names of his parents are not known. After meager schooling he became a saddler's apprentice in Cincinnati. On Mar. 17, 1829, he left St. Louis with a trapping party for the mountains, forming on the way a lasting friendship with a youth of nineteen, afterward well known, Joseph L. Meek [*q.v.*]. He remained a trapper for eleven years. In 1833 he married a Nez Percé woman, and at some time he acquired the nickname of "Doc" (or "Doctor"), which ever afterward he bore. In 1840 he and Meek, with their Indian families, accompanied by two white men, started from Fort Hall for Oregon, taking with them three wagons, and thus brought the first wheels to the Columbia. Newell and Meek settled near the present Hillsboro, in the Willamette Valley. Newell from the first actively interested himself in the affairs of the settlements and soon became a leader. In the meeting of May 2, 1843, which took the first effective steps toward the formation of a government, he was chosen a member of the legislative committee which drew up the constitution ratified on July 5. Throughout the life of the Provisional Government he was a member of the House of Representatives, and for two sessions the speaker.

In 1844 he removed to a place near Champoeg. About this time he built two keelboats, probably the first on the upper Willamette, and engaged in transportation. His Indian wife died in December 1845 and in 1846 he married Rebecca Newman. In the winter of 1848–49 he joined the gold rush to California but returned in the fall of 1850, when he engaged in merchandizing. He commanded a company of scouts in the Indian troubles of 1855–56, and in 1860 he was elected to the state legislature. The floods of December 1861 destroyed most of his property except his residence. He moved to Lapwai, Idaho, where for six years he served as an interpreter and a special commissioner at the army post and the Indian agency. His second wife died in May 1867. He became agent on Oct. 1, 1868. In June 1869 he married a Mrs. Ward, and in July he was replaced as agent. He then moved to Lewiston, where, four months later, he died of heart disease. His wife and several children of his second marriage survived him.

Newell was an Episcopalian and a Mason. He holds a place of unique importance in the early history of Oregon. With the death of Ewing Young he assumed a leadership in the affairs of the colony which was maintained for some years. Like Meek he was a jester; but unlike Meek he was sober, studious, prudent, and dependable. The early chroniclers, with but one outstanding exception, pay tribute to his high character and recount his notable services to the community.

[T. C. Elliott, "'Doctor' Robt. Newell: Pioneer," *Quart. Ore. Hist. Soc.*, June 1908; H. W. Scott, *Hist. of the Ore. Country* (6 vols., 1924); C. H. Carey, *Hist. of Ore.* (1922); Mrs. F. F. Victor, *The River of the West* (1870).]   W. J. G.

NEWELL, ROBERT HENRY (Dec. 13, 1836–July 1901), American journalist, poet, and humorist, who wrote under the pen-name Orpheus C. Kerr, was born in New York, the son of Robert and Ann Lawrence Newell. His father was a manufacturer and inventor, the designer of a patent lock and a sewing machine, whose work received the award of a gold medal at the "Great Exhibition" in London, 1851. Robert Henry Newell attended a private academy but the death of his father left the family in straitened circumstances and he was denied a college education. He began to write fugitive pieces for the New York press in which work he achieved immediate recognition and employment. He became an assistant editor of the New York *Sunday Mercury* in 1858, for which during the next two years he contributed a variety of verse and current comment all of which has proved as ephemeral as it was successful. The outbreak of the Civil War gave him the opportunity and the occasion to write the Orpheus C. Kerr papers, originally initiated in the form of Washington correspondence to the *Mercury*, continued for other journals, and published later in three volumes (1862–65). The name was a supposedly laughable transposition of "office seeker." The flood of applicants for office, when President Buchanan went out and Lincoln came in, was an outstanding political feature of the moment and the "office seeker" became a stock character of political lampoonery.

The Orpheus C. Kerr papers possess now only a historical interest as a sort of comic commentary on the history of the Civil War. They contain a mixture of what is meant to be funny dialogue, imaginary episodes and war incidents, interspersed with various verses and poems intended to be pathetic but rarely more than sentimental. One chapter of the papers (Letter no. VIII of the First Series) deserves perhaps a permanent place in the history of American burlesque writing, containing parodies of the best-known authors of the day in their supposed attempts to compose a new national anthem. The style of the papers represents a mixture of the mock heroic style adopted and popularized by Dickens, written in correct orthography and grammatical language, but with a false elevation of tone, and the loose, comic humor of gargantuan exaggeration, gross misspelling, and wilful irreverence for solemnity which had been already initiated in the West (Artemus Ward, Mark Twain). On Sept. 24, 1862, Newell married Adah Isaacs Menken [*q.v.*], an actress, who divorced him in 1865. His connection with the *Mercury* (1858–62) was followed by his occupancy of various literary editorships in New York. He was a war correspondent for the *New York Herald*, an editor of the New York *World* (1869–74), editor of the *Daily Graphic*, and later of a weekly journal called *Hearth and Home*, his last position as a journalist.

A painful nervous affliction which rendered writing physically difficult and impaired his sight removed Newell in 1876 from active employment and the last quarter-century of his life was spent in the shadow. Apart from *The Orpheus C. Kerr Papers* by which his name is chiefly remembered, Newell collected and published two volumes of his verse, *The Palace Beautiful and Other Poems* (1865) and *Versatilities* (1871). While still active as a journalist he had written *Avery Glibun, or Between Two Fires* (1867). After his retirement he wrote a romance, *There was once a Man* (1884), a story intended to satirize the still novel and still wicked Darwinian theory of the descent of man. He also wrote a book called *The Cloven Foot*, one of the many attempts to interpret and complete (1870) Charles Dickens' unfinished *Mystery of Edwin Drood*. Newell introduced a novel feature in transferring the setting of the story to American conditions, but his work appears to have passed without recognition in the voluminous Edwin Drood controversies. He also published a novel of New York life in 1872 under the title of *The Walking Doll, or the Asters and Disasters of Society*. He died in Brooklyn early in July 1901. His writings are marked with the conventional merits and defects of his time and show nothing to elevate him above the crowd. His pathos is based upon genuine feeling but runs easily to sentiment, his tears flow kindly but easily run to drivel, his humor demands an uproarious reader. His work is interesting nowadays only as illustrating, for those who care to know it, the current way of writing, joking, and weeping, which has been replaced by our own.

[Jennette Tandy, *Crackerbox Philosophers in Am. Humor and Satire* (1925) ; W. P. Trent, "A Retrospect of Am. Humor," *Century Mag.*, Nov. 1901 ; Robt. Ford, *Am. Humorists* (1897) ; *Who's Who in America*, 1901–02 ; *Appletons' Ann. Cyc.*, 1901 ; *N. Y. Daily Tribune*, July 13, 14, 1901 ; *Brooklyn Daily Eagle*, July 12, 13, 28, 1901.]

S. L.

NEWELL, WILLIAM AUGUSTUS (Sept. 5, 1817–Aug. 8, 1901), congressman and governor of New Jersey, was born in Franklin, Ohio, the son of James Hugh and Eliza D. (Hankinson) Newell of Freehold, N. J. His parents had temporarily moved to Ohio but returned to New Jersey when he was three years of age. He attended school at New Brunswick, N. J., and was graduated from Rutgers College in 1836. He received the M.D. degree from the medical department of the University of Pennsylvania in 1839 and began the practice of medicine with his uncle at Manahawkin, Ocean County, N. J. He went to Imlaystown and about 1844 settled at Allentown, N. J., where he built up a large and lucrative practice. The same year he began practice his attention was called to a shipwreck off the coast near his home, and, appalled at the loss of life when thirteen bodies were brought ashore, he began to experiment with lines and with a mortar to reach a wrecked vessel in the hope of preventing future accidents. He was so far successful that, eight years later when serving in Congress, he had plans for a life-saving service, which gave impetus to the establishment of a federal life-saving service that was adapted for the entire sea and lake coasts (*Remarks of William A. Newell . . . Aug. 3, 1848,* 1848; *Letter from William A. Newell . . . to Hon. William J. Sewell,* 1898, with useful citations). He served two terms in Congress as a Whig, from 1847 to 1851, and then resumed practice in Allentown.

In 1856 he had identified himself with the American party and was elected governor of New Jersey; he served two terms from 1857 to 1861. In these critical years he led in the unification of the interests of the American and Republican parties in the state. By 1860 he had become a Republican and was a delegate to the Republican convention at Chicago. Under Lincoln's administration he was appointed superintendent of the life-saving service in New Jersey. He was for a period examining surgeon of drafted soldiers in his state. In 1865 he returned to Congress for one term. He was defeated for reëlection as he was in several later efforts to be elected to the House and to the Senate as well as to the governorship. Nevertheless he continued to keep a firm hold on party patronage in the state. In 1875 he became president of the New Jersey state board of agriculture, and his efforts were important in the establishment of the federal agricultural bureau. In 1880 President Hayes appointed him governor of Washington Territory, in which office he served four years. Then he was appointed Indian inspector for the same territory. He practised a year in Olympia and was resident surgeon in the soldiers' and sailors' home there. He returned to Allentown, N. J., in 1889, where he continued to practise until the time of his death. He was married in early life to Joanna Van Deursen of New Brunswick, N. J., who died while he was governor of Washington Territory. They had three children.

[Information from Mrs. Wm. S. Meek, Elizabeth, N. J.; *The Biog. Encyc. of N. J.* (1877); *The New Jersey Coast* (2 vols., 1902); *Biog. Dir. Am. Cong.* (1928); *Who's Who in America,* 1901–02; C. M. Knapp, *N. J. Politics during the Period of the Civil War* (1924); C. A. Snowden, *Hist. of Wash.* (1909), vol. IV; *Newark Evening News,* Aug. 8, 11, 1901.]
A. V–D. H.

NEWELL, WILLIAM WELLS (Jan. 24, 1839–Jan. 21, 1907), scholar, folklorist, and editor, was born in Cambridge, Mass., the son of the Rev. William Newell, minister of the First Parish Church, Cambridge, and Frances Boott (Wells) Newell. He came by his studious tastes naturally, as both his father and William Wells, his mother's father, were well-known classical scholars. His early education was in the Cambridge schools, from which he entered Harvard College, graduating with the class of 1859. He then studied for the ministry, taking his degree from the Harvard Divinity School in 1863. At first he served as assistant to the Rev. Edward Everett Hale at the South Congregational Church, Boston, but after a short time left to join the Sanitary Service of the War Department in Washington. Returning to ministerial work again at the close of the war, he was settled for a time at the Unitarian Church in Germantown, Pa., but later, feeling that he had mistaken his vocation, he gave up the ministry and turned to teaching. From 1868 to 1870 he was tutor in philosophy at Harvard College, leaving to open a school in New York City. In this he was very successful, but wishing to have more leisure for scholarly pursuits, he gave up teaching in the early eighties and after a year or two of travel and study in Europe, settled down in Cambridge to the pleasant life of the private scholar. His major interests had long lain in the fields of literature and the fine arts, and already his attention had been turned in the direction of folklore, of which he had acquired a wide and accurate knowledge.

His more purely literary work comprised *King Œdipus: The Œdipus Tyrannus of Sophocles Rendered into English Verse* (1881), and *Sonnets and Madrigals of Michelangelo Buonarroti* (1900). In 1895 he published a small volume of original poems, entitled *Words for Music,* later (1904) reprinted at a small private press which he had set up at Wayland. His interest in the fine arts had always been keen, and during his residence in New York he was closely in touch with artistic circles there. An able and discerning student of painting, he discovered and acquired during his stay abroad a number of canvases of real distinction, which later found their way into the Metropolitan Museum in New York and other public and private collections.

Newell is best known, however, for his work in folklore and related subjects. It was largely through his efforts and enthusiasm that the American Folk-Lore Society was founded in 1888, and he served as the permanent secretary of the organization and editor of the *Journal of American Folk-Lore* and the *Memoirs* of the American Folk-Lore Society until his death in

1907. Although his best-known studies lay largely in the European field, his interests were wide, and one of his earliest publications was *Games and Songs of American Children* (1883). Current superstitions, negro practices and beliefs, and those of the American Indians all strongly attracted his attention, and his enthusiasm enlisted the services of many students and collectors in gathering data. He contributed many papers on diverse topics to the *Journal of American Folk-Lore* and to the *Publications* of the Modern Language Association, but his major interest for many years was concerned with the Arthurian romances and kindred literary materials of the medieval period. In 1897 he published *King Arthur and the Table Round* and in 1902 issued *The Legend of the Holy Grail and the Perceval of Crestien of Troyes,* a collection of papers originally appearing in the *Journal.* A third study on which he was engaged at the time of his death, *Isolt's Return* (1907) was printed posthumously at his Wayland press.

Newell was a fine example of the private scholar. He made no parade of his learning, gave freely of his time and energy to aid and advise other students both young and old, and inspired with his enthusiasm all with whom he came into contact. His influence in the development of folklore studies in America was great, and in the related field of anthropology he did much to inculcate the value of the historical method of approach. He had much charm of personality, and his wit and vivacity made him a delightful companion.

[*Jour. of Am. Folk-Lore,* Jan.-Mar. 1907; *Harvard Grads.' Mag.,* Mar. 1907; *Who's Who in America,* 1906–07; *Boston Evening Transcript,* Jan. 23, 1907.]
R. B. D.

NEWHOUSE, SAMUEL (Oct. 14, 1853–Sept. 22, 1930), mine owner and operator, financier, the son of Isaac and Babetta Newhouse, was born in New York City. His father was a pioneer merchant in the anthracite coal region of Pennsylvania. After graduating from the Central High School, Philadelphia, Pa., Samuel read law in Scranton until 1873, when he was appointed clerk of the court in Luzerne County. He served in this capacity until 1879, and then went West, arriving in Leadville, Colo., at the height of the mining boom. He soon engaged in freighting, which proved so profitable, especially before the railroad reached Leadville, that he accumulated sufficient capital to invest in mining prospects. The Leadville and San Juan districts, the Prussian tunnel in Boulder County, and the region around Idaho Springs, all in Colorado, were fields for his mining ventures. In 1891 he originated and in 1894 became president of the Denver, Lakewood & Golden Railroad. During this period he projected the Argo (more commonly called the Newhouse) tunnel, with portal at Idaho Springs, perhaps the most celebrated mining tunnel in the world. Begun in January 1894 and completed in November 1910, it is over five miles long, with nearly twenty miles of workings. The mines under which it passes are estimated to have produced gold, silver, lead, and copper to the value of about $75,000,000. The tunnel provided cheaper drainage, ventilation, and transportation facilities than would otherwise have been possible, permitted mining at greater depths and the profitable extraction of comparatively low-grade ore. In the driving of this tunnel and in other enterprises Newhouse secured the interest of English capitalists.

From 1888 to 1896 he made his headquarters in Denver, but in the latter year removed to Salt Lake City, since his Utah holdings were becoming more important than those in Colorado. In Utah, he opened the Highland Boy mine at Bingham and through its sale made his first large fortune. He then became head of the Boston Consolidated Mining Company at Bingham Canyon, which in 1910 was merged into the Utah Copper Company. In working the property of this concern he used the first steam-shovel ever operated on a copper mine. Upon his pioneer work with this style of mining was subsequently based the success of the great Utah copper mine. He also organized and operated the Newhouse Mines & Smelters, at Newhouse, Beaver County, Utah. In 1907 he introduced modern steel skyscraper construction into Salt Lake City: the Newhouse and Boston buildings and the Newhouse Hotel still stand (1933) as monuments to his memory. He did much to improve and beautify his other property holdings in this city, and was one of the organizers of the National Copper Bank. At one time his interests were so widespread that in addition to his headquarters at Salt Lake City he had offices in New York and London. He was married, Jan. 1, 1883, to Ida H. Stingley, daughter of Hiram Stingley of Virginia. He retired from business about 1925 because of failing health, and spent the last years of his life in Europe, dying at his château at Marnes La Coquette, Seine et Oise, seven miles from Paris.

[*Who's Who in America,* 1899–1929; *Engineering & Mining Journal,* Oct. 9, 1930; *Deseret News* (Salt Lake City), Sept. 24, 1930; Arthur Lakes, "The Newhouse Tunnel," *Engineering Mag.,* Oct. 1895; *Mines Handbook* (1926), p. 570; letter from Lafayette Hanchett of Salt Lake City, long-time friend of Samuel Newhouse and manager of his mining operations.]
B. A. R.

461

NEWLANDS, FRANCIS GRIFFITH (Aug. 28, 1848–Dec. 24, 1917), representative and senator from Nevada, was born in Natchez, Miss., the son of Scottish parents, James Birney and Jessie (Barland) Newlands. His father, a physician, went to Troy, N. Y., but soon removed to the South. He might have been content to remain there in the congenial society of the cotton-planters, but his wife, an accomplished musician, desired better opportunities for the education of her children, and so they went to Quincy, Ill. When Francis was but three years old, the father died leaving his wife with four sons and a daughter. They were in reduced circumstances, for the income that professional skill had won easily had been liberally spent in living. The marriage of the mother, however, to Eben Moore, a banker and mayor of Quincy, so lightened the family burden that Francis could go from the schools of Quincy and Payson to high school in Chicago and have private tutoring in Washington, D. C., to prepare for Yale College. He entered at the age of sixteen with the class of 1867, in which he quickly gained distinction, but, even though friends wished to provide funds in order that he might stay, he decided to withdraw from college in the middle of his junior year. He knew that his step-father had lost heavily in the panic of 1857; his mother's small fortune, too, was gone; moreover, he had long thought of becoming a lawyer and seeking a public career. He returned to Washington, obtained a position in the service of the government, attended the evening sessions of the law school of Columbian College (George Washington University), and gained admission to the bar in 1869.

As the death of his step-father threw more of the family responsibility upon him, he decided to begin his practice of law in a newer community. He, therefore, accepted a loan from a classmate, James Allen, and went to San Francisco in 1870. At first he was dependent upon the court for his cases; but his ability quickly attracted the attention of persons prominent in business; and he turned from criminal to corporation law. By 1873 he had become well established. On Nov. 19, 1874, he was married to the daughter of William Sharon, Clara Adelaide Sharon, who bore him three daughters and died in February 1882, on the day following the birth and death of their son. Newlands gave himself over intensively to business and politics for the next six years. He became trustee of the Sharon estate in 1885 and continued in that capacity through difficult litigation. While in England, he was married, on Sept. 4, 1888, to Edith McAllister, the daughter of Hall McAllister [q.v.]. Both their sons died in infancy. The Civil War and the reconstruction of the South had deeply affected him, and he had gone to California with inclinations toward the Democratic party. Before an infuriated audience in the Democratic state convention of June 1884, he indorsed for president Stephen J. Field [q.v.] of the United States Supreme Court, who had aroused bitter feeling by his decisions concerning the rights of those who had supported the Confederacy, of the railroads, and, particularly, of the Chinese in California. Newlands himself was actually in danger of violence; but his self-possession and his determination won a hearing, and he gained recognition as a man of political promise.

The fulfilment of his political ambitions came soon after his removal to Nevada, in the winter of 1888. Beyond his hope for the future of that state and personal concerns there in connection with the Sharon properties, he saw the possibility of a national program. To him the silver issue involved not only the interest of Nevada's mines but the advancement of all those productive areas where men needed to be able to borrow money easily. He thought it a matter of justice that the quantity of money should be increased to aid those who, under previous conditions of artificially inflated prices, had incurred financial obligations in endeavoring to develop the country. Definitely turned from the law to politics, therefore, he proceeded from his work for the National Silver Committee in Washington to seek a place in Congress as the representative of Nevada. In 1892 as the candidate of the Silver party, with the indorsement of the Republican organization in the state, he won election to the House of Representatives and was reëlected, but, when the national Democratic party took over the cause of silver in 1896, he returned to the party of his youth. He became a member of the Senate in 1903.

He had a significant rôle in the councils of his party; there was hardly an economic plank in any of its platforms that was not shaped by his thinking. In the House of Representatives he was an active member of the committee on foreign relations, but he was far more interested in his work on the committee on ways and means and in domestic problems. The reclamation act in 1902, the act in 1913 for mediation and conciliation of labor disputes, the law of 1914 establishing the federal trade commission, his successive proposals for a waterways commission finally enacted in the river and harbor legislation of 1917, his support of the movement for a federal bureau of fine arts, and his persistent demand that the problem of the tariff should be placed in charge of a board of experts, all bore witness to his conception of democratic government by scientific services and administrative boards with delegated authority from Congress. He was among the ablest critics of Republican financial policy and of the program of Nelson W. Aldrich [q.v.] for reorganizing the banking system. His plan for national incorporation of the railroads, long opposed, came finally to impressive indorsement in its practical acceptance by railroad executives. His years of activity in the important committee of the Senate on interstate commerce culminated during the Wilson administration in the chairmanship of the commission of inquiry which sat in 1916–17 to make an entire reappraisal of the problems of transportation. In the midst of this undertaking, as President Wilson was about to take control of the railroads in the war with Germany, Newlands died. In framing the transportation act of 1920, however, fellow members of the commission drew heavily upon the fund of knowledge that had been gathered under his guidance. Kindliness in debate, a serene persistence in introducing defeated measures again and again, skill in applying theory to detail, and astuteness in business undertakings marked his public life; intimate friends remembered his appreciation of the beautiful, his considerateness for men of all kinds and classes, and his joyous love of children.

[The Newlands Collection, deposited in Yale Univ. Lib.; other papers in the possession of the family; *The Public Papers of Francis G. Newlands*, ed. by A. B. Darling (2 vols., 1932); H. H. Bancroft, *Chronicles of the Builders of the Commonwealth*, vol. IV (1892); *Senator Francis G. Newlands; his Work*, comp. by M. F. Hudson (1914); *Francis Griffith Newlands . . . Memorial Addresses . . . in the Senate* (1920); *Supplementary Record of the Class of 1867 in Yale College* (1914); *Evening Star* (Washington, D. C.), Dec. 25, 1917.]   A. B. D.

NEWMAN, HENRY (Nov. 20, 1670–June 26, 1743), philanthropist, the son of the Rev. Noah and Joanna (Flynt) Newman, was born in Rehoboth, Mass., the town founded by his grandfather, the Rev. Samuel Newman. Brought up by his maternal grandmother after the death of both parents in his early youth, he prepared for college in the grammar schools at Dorchester, Roxbury, and Braintree. He graduated from Harvard with the degree of A.B. in 1687, and was awarded the degree of A.M. in 1690. His preference for other things, notably mathematics, and his Anglican leanings, which soon carried him over to the Church of England, led him to abandon his original intention of entering the

Congregational ministry. Instead, after graduating he engaged for the time being in a variety of occupations, ranging from librarian at Harvard to merchant at St. John's, Newfoundland.

About 1703 he moved to London, where he was to spend the rest of his life. Early contact with the Rev. Thomas Bray [q.v.] and members of his philanthropic circle shaped the main outlines of Newman's career. For some years he was the secretary of Bray's Trustees for Erecting Parochial Librarys: and Promoting Other Charitable Designs. He was also one of the Commissioners for the Relief of Poor Proselytes, a body formed to administer relief to needy converts from the Roman Church among the French Protestant population in England. Most important, however, was his connection with the Society for Promoting Christian Knowledge, the earlier of Bray's two great religious-philanthropic organizations. Elected a corresponding member in 1703, he was chosen its secretary in 1708, remaining in that position until his death. No branch of the society's multifarious activities escaped his careful and efficient attention, but among them the charity schools, the missions in India, and the transporting of persecuted Protestant Salzburgers to the newly founded colony of Georgia clearly appealed most strongly to him.

A New Englander with his qualifications and connections, resident in London, was a likely man for a colonial agent. Hence it was that, sponsored at the outset by Governor Dudley, he was occasionally employed in that capacity by New Hampshire from 1709 to 1720 and permanently from the latter date until the Belcher administration. He always considered himself a loyal New Englander, though he was an ardent prerogative man, and his interest in affairs at home was further fostered by his work as agent for Harvard College, the more formal side of which he supplemented by zealous endeavors to procure money and books for his alma mater. His early liking for mathematics and astronomy had led him to prepare and publish two almanacs, *Harvard's Ephemeris* (1690) and *News from the Stars* (1691). Throughout his life this field remained something of an avocation for him. Because of this fact his services were frequently sought by friends at home, whether to get communications from New Englanders like Cotton Mather before the Royal Society, with many of the members of which he had an acquaintance, or to select astronomical apparatus for Yale College.

It is in his work for the Society for Promoting Christian Knowledge, however, that the man himself is most clearly revealed, his deep but unobtrusive piety, his broad tolerance, and his joy in giving himself for the welfare of others. All of these qualities made him deeply sympathetic with that movement of reform which, slowly gaining momentum in the later seventeenth century, branched out into a wide variety of humanitarian endeavor during the years of his London life. He was never married.

[A sketch of Newman is in J. L. Sibley's *Biog. Sketches of Grads. of Harvard Univ.*, III (1885), 389-94, but the bulk of the source material is in the archives of the Society for Promoting Christian Knowledge, London, including, besides the official Minutes, etc., many volumes of Newman's letter-books, which contain both personal and official correspondence.]

A. B. F.

NEWMAN, HENRY RODERICK (*c.* 1843-1918), painter of architectural subjects and flower pieces, was born at Easton, N. Y. His father, Roderick Newman, a physician and surgeon, worked so incessantly that he undermined his health. He thereupon sold his home and his practice in Easton and moved to New York City. His son, at that time eleven years old, was a delicate boy, and his studies were often interrupted by sickness, but in spite of this handicap he always kept his place at the head of his class. Dr. Newman hoped that Henry would become a physician, but his artistic bent was strong and his mother encouraged his ambition in this direction. When Henry was eighteen years of age his father died. Soon afterward the youth left his New York home and went to Stockbridge, Mass., where he spent six months making studies and sketches from nature. His work was received with so much favor on his return to New York that his purpose of becoming a painter was confirmed. He then went to the Green Mountain region of Vermont and passed another year in field work. Again returning to New York, he taught an art class in the Cooper Institute until he fell ill from overwork, but shortly he was able to go to Stockbridge for a second time, taking his mother with him. In 1868 she died. He spent the winter of 1868-69 in Florida and then determined to go to France for the purpose of continuing his studies.

After a few weeks in Fontainebleau, he found himself in Paris at the moment of the outbreak of the Franco-Prussian War. He pursued his studies in Gérôme's class for about three weeks, but the German armies were then advancing toward Paris, and he betook himself to Chartres, where he spent two months making careful and elaborate studies of the cathedral. After this he went to Switzerland and to Italy, arriving in Florence late in the summer of 1870. His work soon came to the attention of John Ruskin, who

was extremely enthusiastic about his draftsmanship, and expressed himself so strongly on the subject that Newman's drawings began to find many eager buyers in Italy, England, and America. His personal relations with Ruskin became more and more intimate, during the decade from 1870 to 1880, and more than once he was a guest at Coniston. Ruskin bought his watercolors and persuaded his friends to do likewise; the two men rambled about the old Italian cities together, making sketches; and they jointly assembled the materials for the illustrations for the *Stones of Venice*. Newman's motives included such historic architectural monuments as the Duomo, the Bigallo, Or San Michele, the Palazzo Vecchio, the Mercato Vecchio, and Santa Maria Novella. His flower pieces were also in high favor among amateurs. After his marriage to a cultured English woman in 1884, his home and studio in the Piazza dei Rossi, Florence, became an interesting and attractive social center, more especially for the British and American colony. Such personages as the Brownings, the De Morgans, Henry James, and Nathaniel Hawthorne were among the friends who foregathered there. The Newmans traveled widely. They spent several winters in Egypt, where the artist made a series of pictures of the temples and royal tombs along the valley of the Nile. He died at Florence in 1918 and was survived by his widow. His view of the Church of St. Martin of Lucca is in the Birmingham (England) Museum.

[H. B. Forman, "An Am. Studio in Florence," *Manhattan*, June 1884; *Continental Times* (Geneva), Dec. 31, 1881; E. T. Cook and A. Wedderburn, eds., *The Works of John Ruskin* (1907), vol. XXX; *Cat. of Paintings, Museum of Fine Arts, Boston* (1921); *Am. Art News*, Feb. 9, 1918; *N. Y. Times*, Jan. 31, 1918.]

W. H. D—s.

NEWMAN, JOHN PHILIP (Sept. 1, 1826-July 5, 1899), Methodist Episcopal bishop, was born in New York City. His father, Philip Newman, was a thoughtful, studious man of German descent, who died when John was eight years old, leaving seven children and his wife, Mary D'Orfey Allen, a vivacious and richly intelligent woman of Huguenot ancestry. At sixteen the lad underwent a spiritual experience which gave him an ambition and directed him to the Methodist ministry. After a few terms in Cazenovia (N. Y.) Seminary, he began to preach with crude eloquence in country churches, and in 1847 was admitted to the Oneida Conference. At Fort Plain, N. Y., a blunt schoolmaster punctured his self-esteem by telling him that his pronunciation and grammar were abominable. Immediately Newman began to toil with passionate diligence to remedy these and other defects. His wife, Angeline Ensign, whom he married in 1855, was an inspiring companion. He wrote out and memorized his sermons, sparing no pains to have every word correct. Imagination, a noble presence, and a rich and musical voice were his natural gifts. Soon he was stationed in Albany with the governor listening in admiration to his preaching; then, in New York City, where he crowded the largest churches (Bedford Street, 1859; Washington Square, 1862–64). Meantime, a year abroad expanded his horizons and enabled him to write a respectable volume on Palestine. From 1864 to 1869 he was at New Orleans, charged with reëstablishing the Methodist Episcopal Church in the Southwest, which was then in control of Union troops. Here he "blew both the Federal and Gospel trumpets," founded schools, a paper, and several Conferences.

In 1869 he was appointed to the new Metropolitan Church in Washington, D. C. President Grant, Vice-President Colfax, Chief Justice Chase, Major-General Logan, and other notables, were members of his great congregation. His rôle was almost that of "court preacher." From 1869 to 1874 he was also chaplain of the Senate. When his three years' term as pastor expired, his friend at the White House created him "Inspector of United States Consulates," and with his accomplished wife as secretary he made a leisurely trip around the world. Although the appointment evoked criticism, Newman took his commission seriously and his report yielded valuable suggestions. Returning to the Metropolitan Church for a second term (1876–79), he found the presidential pew vacant, but all others filled. His next pastorate (1879–82) was in Central Church, New York City, of which his faithful friend, Grant, became a trustee. When the operation of the three-year limit again moved him, he yielded to the invitation of a Congregational society (Church of the Disciples), taking the status of "acting pastor" and Methodist local preacher, to the scandal of the stricter Methodists, and of some Congregationalists. He soon sought readmission to the Methodist Conference and was reappointed to his former church in Washington.

In 1868, 1872, and 1880 he was a delegate to the General Conference. As early as 1872 his influential lay friends had been proposing his name for office, and in that year he received 100 votes for bishop. In 1880 he had 121 votes for missionary secretary. In 1888, with the active help of the Grant family and Grand Army friends, he was elected bishop on the fourteenth ballot, over determined opposition. His official resi-

dences were Omaha (1888–96) and San Francisco (1896–99); he also made visitations to Japan, South America, and Mexico. As an administrator he was not distinguished. He was accused of pomposity and self-esteem, but his fine spirit, which mellowed with the years, and his broad sympathy, redeemed some of these faults. His rather grandiose style, with rehearsed gesture and pose, and a wealth of allusion and illustration from literature and foreign travel, delighted the prevailing taste. His sermons and lectures were laboriously prepared to the last detail. Doubtless his commanding and ingratiating countenance, his stalwart figure, his distinguished bearing, and his musical and sonorous voice, made his audience uncritical of his thought, which was not analytical or profound. In the public mind he was "Grant's pastor." That famous friendship never waned. Newman watched by his hero's bedside at Mount McGregor, administered the rite of baptism, and pronounced the official eulogy. Childless himself, he had a deep interest in ambitious youth, and joined with Mrs. Newman in educating scores of young men who met his specifications of "piety, poverty, pluck and brains." He died at Saratoga, N. Y., where he had long maintained a summer residence. His estate was divided between Drew Theological Seminary and a school in Jerusalem. He has been described as "one of the most superbly ornamental figures that ever took its stately walk through Methodism" (Kelley, *post*, p. 616). Among his published writings are *From Dan to Beersheba* (1864); *The Bible and Polygamy* (1874), a debate with Orson Pratt, Salt Lake City; *Sermons* (1876); *Thrones and Palaces of Babylon and Nineveh* (1876); *Christianity Triumphant* (copr. 1883); *Supremacy of Law* (1890); *Conversations with Christ* (1900).

[J. M. Buckley, in *Christian Advocate* (N. Y.), July 13, 1899; J. E. King, in *Christian Advocate* (N. Y.), May 4, 1911; L. C. Matlack, *The Antislavery Struggle and Triumph in the M. E. Ch.* (1881); W. W. Sweet, *The M. E. Ch. in the Civil War* (1912); W. V. Kelley, in the *Meth. Rev.*, July 1900; *Official Journal . . . N. Y. Conf. M. E. Ch.*, 1900; *N. Y. Tribune*, July 6, 1899; manuscript records and journals in possession of Mrs. Emma Manson, Saratoga Springs, N. Y.]   J. R. J.

NEWMAN, ROBERT LOFTIN (Nov. 10, 1827–Mar. 31, 1912), figure painter, was born at Richmond, Va. The family moved to Louisa Court House, Va., then when Robert was eleven years old, to Clarksville, Tenn. As a boy he read much about art and artists, and at the age of seventeen he had already begun to experiment for himself with paints and brushes. Six years later he was enabled to go to France to take up the serious study of painting. He entered the atelier of Thomas Couture in Paris but remained there only a few months and never received any subsequent academic instruction. After a year's absence from home he returned to Tennessee in 1851. During a second journey to France in 1854 he formed the acquaintance of William Morris Hunt [q.v.], another pupil of Couture, who took him to Barbizon and introduced him to Jean François Millet. Newman at once bought "Le Vanneur" and other paintings by Millet, but in later years he was obliged to part with them. He returned to the United States in 1855. Upon the outbreak of the Civil War in 1861 he was employed by the Confederate government at Richmond as a draftsman, and in 1864 he was conscripted and served in the 16th Virginia Regiment. After the war was over he pursued his art in obscurity, for a time in Baltimore, where he worked in a sign-painter's loft, and afterward in New York, where he had a studio in West Tenth Street.

In 1882 and twice thereafter he found his way back to Barbizon. Altogether he spent a year and a half there. He was deeply in sympathy with the tendencies of the Barbizon painters, and had much in common with them in his ideals and sentiment. After making New York his home he exhibited rarely, and those artists and collectors who knew him and appreciated his work were obliged to seek him out in his studio. Nevertheless, in the course of a few years, such men as Wyatt Eaton, William M. Chase, Richard Watson Gilder, Thomas B. Clarke, Stanford White, Francis Lathrop, John Gellatly, R. U. Johnson, and Sir William Van Horne not only bought his pictures but tried to bring him into popular favor. It was not until 1894 that an adequate loan exhibition of his work was opened at Knoedler's Gallery, New York, when a collection of oil paintings was shown. After the close of this New York exhibition the same collection was shown at the Museum of Fine Arts in Boston. The foreword in the catalogue alluded very justly to his delicate and beautiful sense of color, his poetic feeling, and the suggestiveness of his work. An article in the *Critic* (Mar. 10, 1894) gave him credit for "that rare and delightful characteristic which we call quality"; and other New York and Boston critics were greatly impressed. "That Newman was a great colorist in the best sense," wrote F. F. Sherman, "is evident in all of his finished work. . . . In all his pictures it is the poetry of color and of life rather than the prose that one finds" (*post*, pp. 16–17). Nevertheless, Newman's name was all but unknown, and he was never financially successful. At the sale of the studio effects of Francis Lathrop after that artist's death a number of Newman's pictures were sold for insignificant prices. He died in his eighty-fifth year. His death, which may have been accidental, was caused by asphyxiation.

[F. F. Sherman, *Landscape and Figure Painters of America* (1917); Nelson Sanborn, "Robt. Loftin Newman," *Brooklyn Museum Quart.*, Oct. 1921; Sadakichi Hartmann, *A Hist. of Am. Art* (1932), vol. I; catalogue of the loan exhibition, Boston Art Museum, 1894; *Metropolitan Museum of Art Cat. of Paintings* (1921); *Critic*, Mar. 24, 1894; *Am. Art News*, Apr. 6, 1912; *N. Y. Tribune*, Apr. 1, 1912.]   W. H. D—s.

NEWMAN, SAMUEL PHILLIPS (June 6, 1797–Feb. 10, 1842), preacher, author, teacher, was born in Andover, Mass., the son of Rev. Mark Newman, third principal of Phillips Academy (1795–1810) and Sarah Phillips Newman, daughter of William Phillips, a merchant of Boston. As a boy he attended Phillips Academy and in 1816 he was graduated with honors from Harvard College. For a year after his graduation he was a private instructor in a family in Lexington, Ky.; he then studied for one year at Andover Theological Seminary. In 1818 he went to Bowdoin College as a tutor, with the privilege of continuing his theological studies under President Appleton. The next year he was elected professor of Greek and Latin, and upon the establishment of the professorship of rhetoric and oratory in 1824, he was transferred to that chair. Although his time was chiefly devoted to the teaching of English, he was also, from 1824 to 1839, lecturer on civil polity and political economy. His versatility is also shown by the fact that in 1820 he was licensed to preach as a Congregationalist (although in those searching times he was somewhat suspected of Unitarian leanings) and for nearly three years, 1830–33, during the absence of President Allen, was the acting-president of the college. He had a decided bent not only for the art of teaching but also for the conduct of business, the administration of affairs, and the leadership of men. A Bowdoin historian writes of him: "During the whole period of his professorship at Brunswick he was probably the most influential member of the college government" (Cleaveland and Packard, *post*, p. 131). On May 31, 1821, he married Caroline, daughter of Col. William A. and Charlotte (Mellen) Kent of Concord, N. H., and before he left Brunswick in 1839 he had a family of five daughters.

In 1827 Newman published a textbook, *A Practical System of Rhetoric or the Principles and Rules of Style*, which for a score of years was widely used in the schools and colleges of the country. It went through more than sixty editions in the United States and was republished in England. Although the terms used are a bit different from those in modern rhetorics, and the philosophical principles and abstract qualities of style more heavily stressed, it is clearly and pleasantly written. Both in this book and also in an important address, "A Practical Method of Teaching Rhetoric," delivered before the American Institute of Instruction in Boston in 1830, he advocated principles and suggested methods, such as teaching by illustrative examples, by translation of other languages, by "talking lectures," and by individual conferences, for many years regarded as good devices. In 1835 he published *Elements of Political Economy*. Largely based upon the writings of Adam Smith, the book could not lay much claim to originality, but it did expound in clear language the principles of the then rapidly rising subject and in the opinion of Professor Amasa Walker of Harvard was "the best work of its kind in the United States" (Hatch, *post*, p. 49). In 1839, after twenty-one years of efficient service at Bowdoin, he "yielded to an application of the Massachusetts Board of Education" and became head of the newly established State Normal School at Barre. But after two years his health broke and he returned to his birthplace, dying there at the age of forty-four. Those closest to him at Bowdoin regarded him not only as an understanding and sagacious teacher and an able administrator, but as a lovable and loyal friend.

[Nehemiah Cleaveland and A. S. Packard, *Hist. of Bowdoin Coll. with Biog. Sketches of its Grads.* (1882); L. C. Hatch, *The Hist. of Bowdoin Coll.* (1927); W. W. Lockwood, "An Early Bowdoin Economist," *Bowdoin Alumnus*, June 1931; *Zion's Herald and Wesleyan Jour.*, Sept. 21, 1864; *Portland Evening Advertiser*, Mar. 7, 1842.]   W. B. M.

NEWMAN, WILLIAM TRUSLOW (June 23, 1843–Feb. 14, 1920), federal judge, was born near Knoxville, Tenn., the son of Henry Baker and Martha (Truslow) Newman. At the outbreak of the Civil War he volunteered as a private soldier in the 2nd Tennessee Cavalry. After some months of service he was promoted to the rank of lieutenant. In 1863 he was wounded and captured by Federal skirmishers in Kentucky. Exchanged, he was again wounded the next year near Jonesboro, Ga., and lost his right arm. At the close of the war he went to live in Atlanta, Ga., read law with Judge John L. Hopkins, was admitted to the bar in 1866, and began practice. From 1871 to 1883 he was city attorney. During these years he built up a substantial private practice and became prominent in the life of the community. On Sept. 20, 1871, he was married to Frances Percy Alexander of Knoxville, Tenn.

In August 1888 he was appointed by President Cleveland to be federal judge of the northern district of Georgia, in which position he continued to serve until his death. He discouraged litigation and brought to bear all the weight of his influence to obtain settlements out of court. His rulings in bankruptcy cases and in cases involving public regulation of utilities became important in determining practice in his district. Yet it was for more unusual qualities that his judicial career made a profound impression on the people among whom he administered federal justice for nearly two generations. Without any claim to erudition his decisions never lacked the essential quality that was recognized as justice by both parties, and his rendering of justice was always tempered with mercy. He made it his custom to parole rural prisoners until they had gathered their crops and, in spite of rumors of some official disapproval, continued to exercise his prerogative of paroling prisoners whenever he thought the situation warranted and to enjoy the kind of respect that brought the paroled men back to prison without violation of trust.

Of his six children one daughter, Frances Newman (Sept. 13, 1883–Oct. 22, 1928, from records of West View Cemetery Assoc., Atlanta) attained distinction as a magazine writer and novelist of the radical sentiment of a changing South. Perhaps *The Hard Boiled Virgin* (1926) is the best-known of her writings, but her book reviews and *Frances Newman's Letters*, ed. by Hansell Baugh (1929) show a curious combination of her father's independence of mind and the spirit of revolt typical of another generation.

[Information from his son, Henry A. Newman and Judge Blanton Fortson; *Report of the Thirty-seventh Ann. Session of the Ga. Bar. Asso. . . . 1920* (1920); *Who's Who in America*, 1918–19; *Atlantic Journal*, Feb. 14, 15, 1920; *Ibid.*, Nov. 18, 1928, and Emily Clark, *Innocence Abroad* (1931) for material on daughter.]   J. H. T. M.

NEWPORT, CHRISTOPHER (d. August 1617), mariner, began his sea-faring career during the reign of Queen Elizabeth. He served with Drake's Cadiz expedition of 1587 (Corbett, *post*, pp. 160, 163) and in 1592 commanded a successful privateering expedition of the West Indies, taking nineteen Spanish vessels and plundering three small towns in Hispaniola and one on the mainland of Honduras. Upon his return, he assisted Sir John Burgh off the Azores in the capture of the "great carrack," the *Madre de Dios* (Aug. 3, 1592), and brought the prize into Dartmouth. He doubtless made other voyages to America in subsequent years (early in

1603 an unfounded rumor spread that he had taken an entire plate fleet), and in September 1605 he presented King James I with "two young Crocodiles and a wild Bore" brought alive from the West Indies (Howes, *post*, p. 871). The next year he entered the service of the newly chartered Virginia Company and was given charge of its early voyages. The first expedition, consisting of three vessels (the *Susan Constant*, the *Godspeed*, and the *Discovery*) and about 120 settlers, left London Dec. 20, 1606, went by way of the southern route and the West Indies, and entered Chesapeake Bay Apr. 26, 1607. The site of Jamestown was selected May 13. Between May 21 and 27, Newport, in accordance with his instructions, ascended the James as far as the falls, near the present Richmond. On June 22, after a fruitless endeavor to persuade the members of the council to maintain harmony during his absence, he sailed for England, leaving provisions expected to last thirteen and a half weeks, and promising to return in twenty.

Arriving at Plymouth on July 29, he raised high the hopes of the Council for Virginia by his announcement of gold, remained sanguine even after the goldsmiths had reported, and continued the vain quest on subsequent voyages. On Oct. 8 he was off with the "first supply" of two ships and 120 emigrants, of whom about a hundred survived the voyage. He arrived at Jamestown six weeks behind his schedule, on Jan. 2, 1608, to find only some forty alive of the 104 he had left, the president of the council, E. M. Wingfield [*q.v.*], imprisoned, and Capt. John Smith [*q.v.*] about to be hanged. Newport effected the liberation of Smith and Wingfield and restored a measure of harmony, but renewed exertions were paralyzed by the fire which destroyed the settlement on Jan. 7. Toward the close of February Newport and Smith visited Powhatan at Werowocomoco on the York River and returned well supplied with corn. On Apr. 9 Newport returned to England, carrying back Wingfield and the troublesome Archer.

On his third voyage (August 1608–January 1609) he brought out one ship and some seventy settlers, including the first skilled craftsmen the Company had attempted to send the colony. He brought gifts and a crown for Powhatan, and performed the somewhat ridiculous ceremony of his coronation at Werowocomoco. Later he conducted an expedition several days' march beyond the falls of the James, and may have reached the mouth of the Rivanna. Before his fourth voyage the Company was reorganized. In 1609 Newport, with the title of vice-admiral, brought out Sir Thomas Gates [*q.v.*] and Sir George Somers.

Attempting the northern route, he was wrecked with them on the Bermudas (Sept. 28), and reached Virginia in May 1610, using pinnaces built on the island. On July 15, he embarked on the return voyage with Gates. The next year, in March, he brought out Sir Thomas Dale [*q.v.*] with three vessels and about three hundred colonists. On their arrival in Virginia in May Sir Thomas pulled Newport's beard and threatened to hang him, apparently for having indorsed Sir Thomas Smyth's too optimistic account of the state of the colony ("A Briefe Declaration of the Plantation of Virginia," *Colonial Records of Virginia*, 1874, p. 79).

Newport returned to England in mid-December 1611, taking home Gates's daughters, and shortly afterward left the service of the Virginia Company for that of the East India Company. Howes's statement is credible, that he took this step "seeing the necessary yeerely supplies for this plantation not to proceed as was requisite for so honourable an action" (Howes, p. 1018). He made three voyages to the East Indies. On the first (Jan. 7, 1613–July 10, 1614), he carried back Sir Robert Sherley, the Persianized Englishman and Shah's ambassador, and established a new record for speed. On the second (Jan. 24, 1615–*c.* September 1616), Newport, second in command to Keeling, carried out Sir Thomas Roe on his famous embassy to the Mogul emperor of Hindustan. The third (November 1616) was his last. He died at Bantam in the last days of August 1617.

Newport was thrice married: Oct. 19, 1584, to Katharine Procter; Jan. 29, 1590, to Ellen Ade; and Oct. 1, 1595, to Elizabeth Glanfield, who survived him (G. W. Hill and W. H. Frere, *Memorials of Stepney Parish*, 1890–91, pp. 25–26, note 6). He left two daughters and two sons, one of whom, John, lived to acquire land in Virginia in return for his father's investment of £400. Newport is generally well spoken of by his contemporaries, with the exception of Smith, who speaks well of no one but himself. He seems to have taken a very genuine concern in the Virginia enterprise, and to have served it to the best of his considerable abilities. His position as intermediary between colonists and Company in the early days was not an easy one.

[A narrative of the voyage of 1592 appears in Richard Hakluyt's *The Principal Navigations, Voyages, Traffiques & Discoveries of the English Nation* (see MacLehose ed., 1904, vols. VII, XII), and narratives of the voyages of 1607, 1609, and 1613 in Samuel Purchas, *Hakluytus Posthumus, or Purchas His Pilgrimes*, vols. III, IV, XVI, XVIII, XIX (ed. of 1905–06). See also J. S. Corbett, *Papers Relating to the Navy during the Spanish War, 1585–87* (1898), being Pubs. Navy Records Soc., vol. XI; Alexander Brown, *The Genesis of the U. S.* (2 vols., 1890) and *The First*

Republic in America (1898); *Travels and Works of Captain John Smith* (2 vols., 1910), ed. by Edward Arber and A. G. Bradley; *Calendar of State Papers, Domestic* and *Colonial Ser.*; Edmund Howes, *Annales, or, A Generall Chronicle of England, Begun by John Stow: Continued and Augmented* (1616; ed. used, that of 1631); William Strachey, *The Historie of Travaile into Virginia Britannia* (Hakluyt Society, 1849); Newport's and his son's wills, summarized in *New-Eng. Hist. and Geneal. Reg.*, Apr. 1894.]   D. H. M.

NEWSAM, ALBERT (May 20, 1809–Nov. 20, 1864), lithographer, was born in Steubenville, Ohio. He was a deaf mute from birth. His father, William, an Ohio River boatman, was accidentally drowned while the boy was a small child, and nothing is known of his mother. The afflicted boy was brought up by Thomas Hamilton, an Irishman, who kept a small hotel in the village. Without any advantages, and with only the inspiration born of the sight of a few prints in the very few books within his reach, he early displayed a considerable talent for drawing. When he was about ten years of age, a deaf-mute impostor, who called himself William P. Davis, came to Steubenville and lodged at Hamilton's hotel. Detecting the talent of the boy, he proposed to the inn-keeper that he take Albert and provide for him, which was assented to. The pair were not long on the road from Steubenville before it became evident that the boy was being used to display his talents for the purpose of exciting the interest of the charitable. He revolted, but the man appeased him with the argument that he was taking him to Philadelphia for the purpose of having him educated. To all who questioned him Davis told the same story, and always referred to Albert as his brother.

When they arrived in Philadelphia in May 1820, they took lodgings in a small hotel and then ventured to the marketplace to see the town. At the corner of Fifth and Market streets there was a watchman's box on the side of which Newsam began to sketch the busy scene before him. A group assembled around the young artist, and later it was joined by the aged Bishop William White, who was then president of the recently organized Asylum for the Deaf and Dumb. The Bishop heard with interest the tale told him by Davis, and the upshot of the meeting was that the managers of the asylum gave an outfit of clothing to both of the strangers; gave Davis a sum of money to take him South, ostensibly to seek relatives; and admitted Newsam to the institution as a state pupil, first protégé of the legislature of Pennsylvania. The boy learned rapidly, spending six years (1820–26) in the institution, and after his graduation remaining as monitor for a year. His talents brought him into contact with Sully, Inman, Rembrandt Peale, Neagle,

and J. R. Lambdin. The last-named sought to teach him to paint portraits, but found he was not likely to succeed because he could not animate his model by conversation. In 1827 he attracted the attention of Col. Cephas G. Childs [*q.v.*], whose engraving establishment in Philadelphia was widely known. He was apprenticed to Childs, and remained with him for four years. During this period lithography in the United States was slowly advancing as a commercial enterprise. Newsam was taught the new process by Duval, whom Colonel Childs had brought from Paris, and thus became a lithographer instead of an engraver. During his apprenticeship he attended the classes in the Pennsylvania Academy of the Fine Arts, and improved himself in his art by remarkable industry. His beautiful and accurate drawings of portraits soon became noted and he remained at the head of American lithographic artists until illness forced his retirement. In 1853 he designed the monument to Thomas H. Gallaudet [*q.v.*] in Hartford, Conn. In 1857 he became partly blind, and in 1859, partly paralyzed. After a year spent in the Pennsylvania Hospital, his funds were exhausted, and he was removed to the city almshouse, where he remained for two years. Then some of his old friends collected a fund and had him placed in the Living Home, near Wilmington, Del., where he died in November 1864. His remains were interred in Laurel Hill Cemetery, Phila. Newsam was married Mar. 26, 1834, to Rosanna Edgar, a Philadelphia woman who was not a mute, but the pair separated a week after the ceremony.

[The Hist. Soc. of Pa. has a large collection of lithographs by Newsam, principally proofs once owned by the artist himself. J. O. Pyatt, *Memoir of Albert Newsam* (1868) is the chief authority for his career; see also sketch by D. M. Stauffer, in *Pa. Mag. of Hist. and Biog.*, Oct. 1900, and lists of Newsam's lithographs, *Ibid.*, Jan., Apr. 1901, Oct. 1902; D. M. Stauffer, *Am. Engravers Upon Copper and Steel* (1907), vol. I; J. T. Scharf and T. Westcott, *Hist. of Phila.* (1884), vol. II; *Pennsylvanian* (Phila.), Mar. 31, 1834 (note of marriage); *Phila. Inquirer*, Nov. 22, 1864.]   J. J.

NEWTON, HENRY JOTHAM (Feb. 9, 1823–Dec. 23, 1895), manufacturer and inventor, was born at Hartleton, Pa., the younger son of Dr. Jotham and Harriet (Wood) Newton, both originally of Connecticut. When the father, a young physician of promise, died within a year of his son's birth, the mother returned to her father's home in Somers, Conn. Henry was sent to school there and afterwards finished at the Literary Institute of Suffield. He was then apprenticed for four years to Whittlesey Brothers, piano-makers of Salem, Conn. His progress was so rapid that in three years he became a member of the firm. Five years later (1849) he went to New York City, where he associated himself with Ferdinand Lighte in the piano business. In 1853 William B. Bradbury [q.v.] and his brother Edward G. Bradbury also became partners, and the firm Lighte, Newton & Bradbury soon won a leading place in the trade. In 1858 Newton retired with a competency, which he invested so judiciously in New York City real estate that he died a millionaire. Except for the attention which his real-estate holdings required and for his presidency after 1884 of the Henry-Bonnard Bronze Company, a successful business run chiefly by his son and son-in-law, he was free for the rest of his life to devote himself to his various hobbies.

The chief of these was photography. His early steps in the art were taken under the guidance of Charles A. Seely, publisher of the *American Journal of Photography*. The top floor of Newton's home at 128 West 43rd St. soon became an amateur's photographic laboratory as he experimented with different kinds of emulsions, developing solutions, washes, and sensitized papers, in different processes and under varying conditions. The history of photography in this period is confused, and there were so many workers in the field that his exact contributions are difficult to determine. He made a number of improvements in the dry-plate process, however, and so popularized it that he came to be known as "the father of the dry-plate process in America." He experimented with the use of various alkalis in developing dry plates. He was also a pioneer in the preparation of ready-sensitized paper, and is credited with working out the paraffin paper process. His findings were usually presented orally at the meetings of the American Photographical Society, and are merely referred to, or summarized, in the reports in the *American Journal of Photography* of that society's meetings. He was long treasurer of the organization, which in 1867 became the Photographical Section of the American Institute of the City of New York, and after 1873 served as its chairman.

A scientific interest in spirit photography led Newton to study the subject of Spiritualism, and he spent much time and money in the investigation of various mediums. He exposed a number of them, including the famous Etta Roberts, by apparatus and tests which he originated. Despite such fakes, he became a convert to Spiritualism, and his faith was unshaken to the last. He was trustee and, for the last twenty years of his life, president of the First Society of Spiritualists in New York, the society benefiting greatly from his scientific support and from his generous donations. He was also a founder of the Theosophical Society (1875), and its treasurer during the first few years. He always claimed that the society was organized for the scientific study of occultism, and after the publication by Madame Blavatsky [q.v.] of her *Isis Unveiled* (1877), which became the Bible of a new religion with teachings hostile to Spiritualism, he resigned in much bitterness. He was instrumental in effecting the first scientific cremation of a human body in America, Dec. 6, 1876, at the crematory in Washington, Pa., erected by F. J. Le Moyne [q.v.], when, as an executor of the Baron de Palm's will, he carried out the Baron's last wishes in regard to the disposition of his body. The event was viewed by a number of scientists and received nation-wide newspaper publicity.

It is significant that at Newton's death newspaper obituaries emphasized his Spiritualist and Theosophic connections, his more tangible contributions having been almost forgotten. In later years his gray hair and long gray beard gave him somewhat the appearance of a self-appointed prophet. His wife, Mary A. Gates of Wethersfield, Conn., whom he married in 1850, was an accomplished musician, a woman of culture and social charm, who encouraged her husband's unorthodox interests. They entertained frequently, and were members of many organizations. Newton was run down by a street car during an evening rush hour as he was crossing Broadway between 22nd and 23rd Streets, then "the most dangerous spot in New York." Besides his wife, a son and two daughters survived him.

[*Sun* (N. Y.) and *N. Y. Herald*, Dec. 24, 1895; *Photographic Times*, Feb. 1896; files of the photographical magazines for the 60's and 70's; proceedings of Photographical Section, in *Ann. Reports* of the Am. Inst. of the City of N. Y.; H. S. Olcott, *Old Diary Leaves* (1895); for father's family, E. N. Leonard, *Newton Geneal.* (1915), p. 189.]   O. W. H.

NEWTON, HUBERT ANSON (Mar. 19, 1830–Aug. 12, 1896), mathematician, was the fifth son of a family of seven sons and four daughters, children of William and Lois (Butler) Newton, of Sherburne, N. Y. He was of good New England stock, his ancestors on both sides being among the first settlers in Massachusetts and Connecticut. Prepared for college in the local schools of Sherburne, he entered Yale at the age of sixteen, graduating with the class of 1850. For the next three years he pursued mathematical studies at his home and in New

Haven. He was only twenty-three when, on the death of Prof. Anthony Dumond Stanley (1810–53), he was called upon to take control of the department of mathematics in his alma mater. Upon receiving the rank of professor two years later, he was given a leave of absence for a year, and spent his time studying at Paris under the eminent French geometer, Michel Chasles (1793–1880). Upon his return to Yale, he cultivated an interest in astronomy, paying considerable attention to the subject of meteors. The results of his investigations were published in the *American Journal of Science,* 1860–62, and in an elaborate paper, "On Shooting Stars," which was read before the National Academy of Sciences in 1864 and appeared in the first volume (1866) of its *Memoirs.*

According to a colleague (Gibbs, *post,* p. 118), the most important side of his life was that identified with the organic life of the University. His scientific studies, which he loved, were almost "the recreations . . . of one whose serious occupation has been that of an instructor." Despite his preference for a quiet, scholarly existence, he was for one term an alderman of New Haven. His influence upon mathematics and astronomy was rather due to his expository articles and his connection with learned societies than to original investigations. He was a member of many scientific organizations, including the National Academy of Sciences and the American Philosophical Society, and was president of the American Association for the Advancement of Science in 1885, and for several years president of the Connecticut Academy of Arts and Sciences. He was an ardent advocate of the metric system of weights and measures, and one of the founders of the American Metrological Society. He realized, however, that the practice of generations could be successfully altered only after a period of education, and therefore labored to interest the makers of scales and rulers and to secure the inclusion of metric tables in school arithmetics. Perhaps his most important single contribution to the cause was a set of tables, *The Metric System of Weights and Measures* (1868), reprinted with corrections from the *Report* for 1865 of the Smithsonian Institution. Among his most notable publications in addition to those already mentioned were "Explanation of the Motion of the Gyroscope" (*American Journal of Science,* September 1857); "On the Origin of Comets" (*Ibid.,* September 1878); "The Story of Biela's Comet" and "The Biela Meteors of Nov. 27th, 1885" (*Ibid.,* February and June 1886); "On the Transcendental Curves $\sin y \sin my = a \sin x \sin nx + b$," in collabora-

tion with A. W. Phillips (*Transactions of the Connecticut Academy of Arts and Sciences,* vol. III, 1874–78, p. 97). He also contributed articles on meteors to *Johnson's Universal Cyclopedia* (1877) and the *Encyclopædia Britannica* (1883), and mathematical and astronomical definitions to *Webster's International Dictionary* (1890). On Apr. 14, 1859, he married Anna C. Stiles. He died in New Haven.

[J. W. Gibbs, in *Nat. Acad. Sci. Biog. Memoirs,* vol. IV. (1902); M. Faye, in *Comptes rendus . . . de l'Académie des Sciences,* vol. LXIV (1867); *Obit. Record Grads. Yale Univ.,* 1897; *New Haven Evening Register,* Aug. 13, 1896.]   D. E. S.

NEWTON, ISAAC (Jan. 10, 1794–Nov. 23, 1858), steamboat designer and proprietor, was born in Schodack, Rensselaer County, N. Y., the son of Abner and Alice (Baker) Newton. Little is known of his youth; but that his attention was early drawn to steamboats is shown by his vivid recollections in later years of witnessing at the age of thirteen the *Clermont's* first trip up the Hudson. In 1826 he was associated with several others in establishing the first line of tow boats on the Hudson. In 1839 he brought out the *Balloon,* a small passenger steamer which attracted attention because of its speed. He then associated himself with Daniel Drew [*q.v.*] in the promotion of the People's Line and became president and manager, while Drew became treasurer. For this line he designed the *North America* and *South America,* built in 1840 and 1841, which set the style for river boats of the day. On these two vessels he introduced the burning of anthracite coal, the first instance of practical success with a fuel that was both cheaper and more economical of stowage space than wood, and which was to permit rapid advances in the size and speed of boats. He designed and added to the line the *Hendrick Hudson* (1845), the *Isaac Newton* (1846), and the *New World* (1847), each in its turn the largest steamer on the Hudson. They were also fast boats, participating in many races which made exciting river history. The People's Line Association was incorporated in 1854 as the New Jersey Steamboat Company. In 1855 the *Isaac Newton* and the *New World* were renovated and lengthened and put on night service. They were the first inland river steamers to have a double tier of staterooms above the main deck, and in them Newton introduced the grand saloon extending through both decks and surrounded by galleries leading to the staterooms, a feature of river steamers which has become standard in America. The ornate saloon decorations, the gas-lighting fixtures, the rich cabin furnishings, made the boats the most popular on the river and established the success and fame of the line. Newton was also interested in a railroad connection to the Great Lakes, and was for a time president of the Mohawk & Hudson, resigning in 1846. He extended his steamboat interests to the Great Lakes, and in 1854 the *Western World* and *Plymouth Rock* were built after his design by John Englis & Son of New York who sent their crew to a Buffalo yard to do the work. These were for a time the finest steamers on the lakes. Altogether Newton is said to have designed and supervised the construction of more than ninety barges, river boats, and ocean steamers. He lived most of his adult life in New York City and was a member and long a Sunday-school teacher in the old Oliver Street Baptist Church. He married Hannah Humphreys Cauldwell who survived him many years, and had ten children. Of these Henry Newton won some fame as a geologist and Isaac Newton became an engineer of note.

[D. L. Buckman, *Old Steamboat Days on the Hudson River* (1907) ; F. E. Dayton, *Steamboat Days* (1925); Joel Munsell, *The Annals of Albany*, vols. VIII (1857), X (1859) ; S. W. Stanton, *Am. Steam Vessels* (1895) ; J. H. Morrison, *Hist. of Am. Steam Navigation* (1903) ; *Hist. Mag.* (N. Y.), Jan. 1859 ; *Evening Post* (N. Y.), Nov. 23, 1858 ; *N. Y. Daily Tribune*, Nov. 24, 1858; will in the Hall of Records, New York City.]

O. W. H.

NEWTON, ISAAC (Mar. 31, 1800–June 19, 1867), first United States commissioner of agriculture, was born in Burlington County, N. J., the son of Isaac and Mary (Newton) Newton, of English ancestry and orthodox Quaker stock. His father, a farmer, died young, and his mother, left a widow at eighteen when Isaac was only a few months old, continued to live in the home of her father-in-law, a prosperous farmer of Burlington County. Isaac's education was gained mostly in the county and state schools of New Jersey and Pennsylvania, and he was thoroughly taught the principles of farming on his grandfather's farm. He was married Oct. 18, 1821, to Dorothy Burdsall of Philadelphia. A few years later he was asked to take charge of two adjoining farms in Springfield, Delaware County, Pa., which under his care became celebrated for their neatness, order, and productiveness. To make use of the surplus of milk and cream from his farm he opened an ice-cream and confectionery shop in Philadelphia. He was one of the early and active members of the Pennsylvania State Agricultural Society and the United States Agricultural Society and for years was prominent in urging upon Congress the policy of establishing a department of agriculture. About 1854, acting on the advice of a friend, he purchased a thousand-acre tract of farm land in Prince William County, Va., but this venture later proved unsuccessful, partly because of the outbreak of the Civil War.

Early in 1861 Newton, who was personally acquainted with Lincoln, was appointed by him superintendent of the agricultural division of the Patent Office, the small bureau which at that time had charge of national agricultural interests. This was enlarged the following year by the Act of May 15, 1862, establishing a department of agriculture with a commissioner at its head. To this post Newton was appointed by President Lincoln and was thus the first incumbent of the office. Within the first few months, a skilled horticulturist, William Saunders [*q.v.*] of Pennsylvania, was appointed botanist and superintendent of the propagating garden, and C. M. Wetherill [*q.v.*], department chemist. Other early appointments were those of Lewis Bollman to be statistician, and Townend Glover [*q.v.*] to be entomologist. These appointments were the beginnings of the present large bureaus of plant industry, chemistry, agricultural economics, and entomology. In his first and second annual reports Newton dwelt upon the vital importance in agriculture of the weather and climate. In his third report, that for 1864, he advocated (p. 10) that daily weather reports be communicated by telegraph over the whole country under the supervision of the government. His recommendations were among the factors that contributed to the organization of the government meteorological service, or Weather Bureau, first established in the office of the chief signal officer of the army [see Myer, Albert James], and in July 1891 transferred to the Department of Agriculture. Newton obtained land in Washington on the Mall, between 12th and 14th Streets, for an experimental farm, and he secured from Congress the appropriation for a new building to house the Department.

In July 1866, while on the Department experimental field, he suffered a sunstroke, and though he partially recovered, he died from its effects within a year. Despite his limited education, the evidence indicates that he was a man of good sense and vision and earnestly devoted to the interests of agriculture. The foundations of the Department which he laid were solid and not unworthy of the superstructure of later years. The important records of his efforts are contained in the annual *Report of the Commissioner of Agriculture* for the years 1862–66. His *Circular on the Present Agricultural, Mineral, and Manufacturing Condition and Resources of the United States,* issued in 1862, was his initial plea to the "farmers and friends of agriculture" for co-operation with the new Department in carrying into effect "the beneficent and important ends contemplated by its organization."

[J. W. Stokes, "Death of Hon. Isaac Newton," in *Monthly Report of the Agric. Dept.*, May–June 1867; C. H. Greathouse, *Hist. Sketch of the U. S. Dept. of Agric.* (1898); J. M. Swank, *The Dept. of Agric. Its Hist. and Objects* (1872); "Isaac Newton, first United States Commissioner of Agriculture," by Amanda A. Newton, a grand-daughter (typewritten; copy in the U. S. Dept. of Agric. Lib.); *Evening Star* (Washington, D. C.), June 20, 1867.]   C. R. B.

NEWTON, JOHN (Aug. 24, 1823–May 1, 1895), soldier, engineer, was born in Norfolk, Va., the son of Thomas Newton, 1768–1847 [*q.v.*], and his second wife, Margaret (Jordan) Pool. His father was a representative in Congress for twenty-nine years. John Newton was graduated second in his class at the United States Military Academy, July 1, 1842, and was commissioned second lieutenant of engineers. Prior to the Civil War, he served as assistant to the Board of Engineers, as instructor at West Point, and on fortification, lighthouse, and river and harbor work. His name is identified with the construction of Fort Warren, Mass., Fort Trumbull, Conn., Forts Porter, Niagara, and Ontario, New York, Fort Wayne, Mich., and Forts Pulaski and Jackson, Ga. He became first lieutenant, Oct. 16, 1852, and captain, July 1, 1856. He was chief engineer of the Utah Expedition of 1858. In 1848 he was married to Anna M. Starr, daughter of Jonathan Starr, a leading banker of New London, Conn. They had five sons and one daughter.

The outbreak of the Civil War found him engaged in fortification work on Delaware Bay. He was successively chief engineer of the Departments of Pennsylvania and of the Shenandoah, was in action at Falling Waters, Va., June 30, 1861, and did much field reconnaissance. Promoted to major Aug. 6, 1861, and made brigadier-general of volunteers Sept. 23, he was on duty as engineer in constructing the defenses of Washington from Aug. 28 of that year to March 1862. He constructed Fort Lyon, one of the larger works of the Washington defenses. Subsequently he commanded a brigade at West Point, Va., May 7, 1862, and at Gaines's Mill, Glendale, South Mountain, and Antietam. He selected the Union position at West Point, and showed good judgment and skill in handling troops. At South Mountain he ordered his men to advance with the bayonet, without firing, until the enemy should begin to retreat. He accompanied them and carried the enemy's position with a rush. His corps commander recommended him for promotion to major-general for conspicuous gallantry and important services at Antietam. He commanded a division at Fredericksburg, Chancellorsville, and Gettysburg. In the Chancellorsville campaign, he was ordered to attack Marye's Heights, which had defied attack in the memorable battle of Fredericksburg. He carried the position with the bayonet in three minutes, with the loss of 1,000 out of 3,500. On the first day at Gettysburg, General Meade selected him to command the I Corps, upon the death of Gen. John F. Reynolds.

When the I Corps was broken up in March 1864, he was ordered to report to General Sherman and was assigned to the 2nd Division, IV Corps, Sheridan's old division. At the beginning of the Atlanta campaign, he carried Rocky-face Ridge. He was in the operations around Dalton and Adairsville, and the battles of Dallas, Kenesaw Mountain, Peach Tree Creek, Jonesborough, and Lovejoy's Station. Never did his soldiership show to better advantage than at Peach Tree Creek. His division prevented the penetration of Sherman's forces. "The blow was sudden and somewhat unexpected," said Sherman in his report, "but General Newton had hastily covered his front by a line of rail piles, which enabled him to meet and repulse the attack on him" (*Official Records*, 1 ser. XXXVIII, pt. 1, p. 71). After the fall of Atlanta, he commanded the District of West Florida, where he showed great activity. He was brevetted lieutenant-colonel, colonel, brigadier-general, major-general of volunteers, and major-general, United States Army, and held the rank of major-general of volunteers from Mar. 30, 1863, to Apr. 18, 1864.

After the close of the war, he became lieutenant-colonel of engineers, Dec. 28, 1865, was mustered out of the volunteer service, Jan. 15, 1866, and returned to fortification and river and harbor work. His most notable achievements were the removal of obstructions in the East River, New York. He blasted away Pot Rock, a large, submerged stone that had caused many wrecks and had baffled previous efforts to remove it. He mined a reef, three acres in area, projecting at Hallet's Point into Hell Gate, and placed in it 50,000 pounds of high explosives. To allay public excitement, he let it be known that he and his family would be at the electric batteries, near the shaft, and that his daughter Mary, two years old, would touch the electric button. The mines were exploded Sept. 24, 1876, with complete success. He blew up, with 200,000 pounds of dynamite, Flood Rock, or Middle Reef, nine acres in area, in Hell Gate, Oct. 10, 1885. Earth tremors were recorded 183 miles away. He had been promoted to the rank of colonel,

June 30, 1879, and on Mar. 6, 1884, he became brigadier-general and chief of engineers, but he retained personal charge of the Hell Gate operations until Dec. 31, 1885. He was retired at his own request, Aug. 27, 1886, and on the following day accepted the office of commissioner of public works of New York City. He declined a reappointment two years later and accepted the presidency of the Panama Railroad Company, a position which he held until his death in New York City, May 1, 1895. He was buried in Post Cemetery, New York. Newton was a handsome man of commanding presence and pleasing personality. From early manhood he was a devout member of the Roman Catholic Church. He was awarded the degree of LL.D. by St. Francis Xavier College in 1886, and was a member of the National Academy of Sciences and an honorary member of the American Society of Civil Engineers.

[G. W. Cullum, *Biog. Reg. Officers and Grads. U. S. Mil. Acad.* (3rd ed., 1891), vol. II; *Professional Memoirs, Corps of Engineers, U. S. Army*, Mar.–Apr. 1912; *Twenty-sixth Ann. Reunion Asso. Grads. U. S. Mil. Acad.* (1895); *Ann. Report of the Chief of Engineers, U. S. Army*, 1843-62, 1867-87; *War of the Rebellion: Official Records (Army)*, 1, 2, 3 ser. (see Index vol.); *Nat. Acad. Sci. Biog. Memoirs*, vol. IV (1902); *N. Y. Times*, May 2, 1895.]   S. C. V.

NEWTON, RICHARD (July 26, 1812–May 25, 1887), Protestant Episcopal clergyman, was born in Liverpool, England. His parents, Richard and Elizabeth (Cluett) Newton, with their family of six children, settled in Philadelphia in August 1824. After a little schooling in that city, Richard left home rather than work in his father's store on Sunday, and earned his board and tuition at a manual-training school in Wilmington, Del. He entered the University of Pennsylvania, was graduated in 1836, and spent three years in study at the General Theological Seminary, New York. On July 4, 1839, he was made deacon by the Rt. Rev. H. U. Onderdonk, and on July 26, 1840, was ordained priest by the same bishop. On July 31, 1839, he married Lydia, daughter of Lawrence Greatorex of Wilmington. He became rector of Holy Trinity Church, West Chester, Pa., immediately upon his ordination, but shortly afterward accepted a call to St. Paul's Church, Philadelphia, of which he was rector until 1862. This was the most fruitful period of his ministry. He became a stanch evangelical, and one of the leaders of that party in his church. Notable features of his parish work were his sermons to children and his missionary services. A very large per cent of young men confirmed under him became clergymen. In many ways he anticipated modern methods in church administration. During the

Civil War he was a firm supporter of the Union. In 1862 he accepted a call to the Church of the Epiphany, Philadelphia. During the disputes of the early seventies over ritualism, which led to the secession of the Reformed Episcopal Church, it was expected that Newton, as a pronounced "Low Churchman," would follow Bishop George David Cummins [*q.v.*], but he refused to leave his Church and retained his rectorship until 1881 when his health broke down and he resigned. After a year's rest, however, he felt fit for duty again, and accepted the rectorship of the less burdensome Church of the Covenant, where he remained until his death.

Newton was a man of deep evangelical piety and the most evident sincerity. Although extremely dignified in manner, he was famous for his success with children. His sermons for them fill no less than eighteen volumes, of which more than a hundred thousand copies have been sold. Translations of these discourses appeared in eighteen different languages, including Siamese, Japanese, Arabic, and even Zulu, and they were very largely used in missionary work. He was also the author of a number of books, including *The King's Highway* (1861); *The Jewish Tabernacle and Its Furnishings* (1864); *Bible Jewels* (1867); *Illustrated Rambles in Bible Lands* (1875); *The Life of Jesus Christ for the Young* (1876). Like most works of the sort their usefulness declined with changes of taste and religious outlook.

Though small of stature, Newton was strongly built. He was always plainly but carefully dressed. He died in Philadelphia in his seventy-fifth year, leaving two sons, Richard Heber Newton and William Wilberforce Newton [*qq.v.*], both clergymen. His wife predeceased him by a few weeks.

[Bibliography of Newton's writings in *The New Schaff-Herzog Encyc. of Religious Knowledge*, vol. VIII (1910); memoir by W. W. Newton prefixed to *The Heath in the Wilderness, or Sermons to the People, by the Late Rev. Richard Newton, D.D.* (1888); N. S. Barratt, *Outline of the Hist. of Old St. Paul's Ch., Phila.* (1917); *Churchman*, June 4, 1887; *Public Ledger* (Phila.), May 26, 1887; personal acquaintance.]
                    J. C. Ay—r.

NEWTON, RICHARD HEBER (Oct. 31, 1840–Dec. 19, 1914), Protestant Episcopal clergyman, generally known as Heber Newton, was born in Philadelphia. He was the son of the Rev. Richard [*q.v.*] and Lydia (Greatorex) Newton and the elder brother of William Wilberforce Newton [*q.v.*]. He was educated in Philadelphia, spending the years 1857–59 at the University of Pennsylvania. Forced to leave college on account of his health, he was later awarded the degree of A.B. as of the class of 1861. In

1863 he graduated from the Divinity School of the Protestant Episcopal Church in Philadelphia. Ordered deacon, Jan. 19, 1862, by the Rt. Rev. Alonzo Potter, he was ordained priest by the same prelate in 1866. He was successively assistant minister at St. Paul's Church, Philadelphia, 1862–63, minister-in-charge of Trinity Church, Sharon Springs, N. Y., 1864–66; and rector of St. Paul's Church, Philadelphia, 1864–69. On Apr. 14, 1864, he married Mary Elizabeth Lewis, daughter of Charles S. Lewis, by whom he had four children. In 1869 he accepted a call to All Souls' Church (Anthon Memorial) in New York City. Here he found his real career and remained for more than thirty years, establishing a reputation as the foremost liberal preacher in his denomination. Resigning this charge in 1902, he removed to California and became resident preacher at the Leland Stanford, Jr., University, where he enjoyed great popularity with the students because of his clear and fearless handling of current theological and moral questions. His last years were spent in retirement at East Hampton, L. I., where he died.

Heber Newton had a keen and powerful mind and a wide range of interests. As a theologian he was especially interested in the modern critical and historical study of the Bible, a matter which was just beginning to attract attention in the early years of his ministry. Although not an original student or investigator, he endeavored to make the results of the "Higher Criticism" common property. In this field his best and most popular work was *The Right and Wrong Uses of the Bible* (1883), of which in the first edition 25,000 copies were sold in a year. Two attempts were made to bring him to trial, the failure of which strengthened the position of the liberals who held that there was a place in the Church for such critical views.

Since he belonged to a transition age when the new type of theology was establishing itself, Newton's work was almost wholly for his own generation. As yet there were few who were interested in the subjects in which he was absorbed and fewer still who had the fearlessness or the opportunity to discuss them in public. He added nothing to the substance of theological learning, but accomplished much in its dissemination; his more spiritual message, however, did not find embodiment in works of permanent value. Personally he was interested in the teaching of F. D. Maurice and F. W. Robertson, but himself lacked the mystic appeal of the former or the religious fervor of the latter. His appeal was preëminently intellectual and ethical. He gave

much attention to evolutionary science, was one of the first serious American students of psychic research and the phenomena of spiritualism, and was deeply interested in civic and labor questions. The scope of his interests is suggested by the list of his publications, among which were, in addition to that already mentioned, *The Children's Church* (1872), a Sunday-school service book; *The Morals of Trade* (1876); *Studies of Jesus* (1880); *Womanhood* (1881); *Book of the Beginnings* (1884); *Philistinism* (1885); *Social Studies* (1887); *Church and Creed* (1891); *Christian Science* (1898); *Parsifal* (1904); and *The Mysticism of Music* (1915), published posthumously. His appearance was intellectual and forceful, his voice was rich and carefully modulated. No rhetorician, he had a sense of humor, was at times epigrammatic, and was always incisive.

[*Churchman*, Jan. 23, 1915; *A Service to Honor the Memory of the Rev. R. Heber Newton, D.D.* (1915); N. S. Barratt, *Outline of the Hist. of Old St. Paul's Ch., Phila.* (1917); *N. Y. Times*, Dec. 20, 1914; personal acquaintance.   J. C. Ay—r.

NEWTON, ROBERT SAFFORD (Dec. 12, 1818–Oct. 9, 1881), eclectic physician and editor, was born on a farm near Gallipolis, Ohio. His father, John Newton, and his mother, a daughter of Robert Safford, were early Ohio pioneers of Massachusetts Puritan stock. After the log schoolhouse of his home district, he attended academies at Lewisburg, Va., and Gallipolis. While engaged in farming and school-teaching he studied medicine with a pharmacist-physician in Gallipolis, and later attended the Medical College of Ohio at Cincinnati and the Louisville Medical College, where he was graduated in 1841. He settled in Gallipolis for practice, and on Sept. 14, 1843, married Mary M. Hoy of that town. His choice of cancer for a specialty brought him the questionable title of "cancer doctor" and some disrepute with his fellow practitioners. This name and fame followed him to Cincinnati, whither he moved in 1845, and soon led him to become an eclectic practitioner. In 1849 he went in Memphis, Tenn., to accept the chair of surgery in the Memphis Institute. Following the death of Dr. T. V. Morrow [*q.v.*], founder of the Eclectic Medical Institute of Cincinnati, he was invited in 1851 to the chair of surgery in that institution, thus made vacant. In 1853 he transferred to the chair of medical practice and pathology, continuing an active member of the faculty until 1862. During this period he also conducted Newton's Clinical Institute, a hospital and school, assisted by Dr. Zoheth Freeman.

These were years of storm and strife in the

Eclectic Medical Institute, and Newton was in the midst of every controversy. His early professional troubles caused him to take up writing on medical reform, and in 1852 he founded the *Eclectic Medical Journal*, which he edited for the next ten years. During this period and later he wrote *The Eclectic Treatise on the Practice of Medicine, Embracing the Pathology of Inflammation and Fevers* (1861); aided Dr. John King [*q.v.*] in preparing the *American Dispensatory (Eclectic)*, first published in 1852; and collaborated with Dr. W. B. Powell in writing *The Eclectic Practice of Medicine* (1854), and *The Eclectic Practice of Medicine (Diseases of Children)* (1858). He edited an American edition of James Syme's *Principles and Practice of Surgery* (1865) and several other works. At various times he was editor or co-editor of the *Western Medical News* of Cincinnati (1851–59); the *American Eclectic Medical Review*, New York (1866–72); the *American Eclectic Register*, New York (1868); the *Medical Eclectic*, after 1878 the *New York Medical Eclectic* (1873–81); and the *New York Quarterly Journal* (1875).

As a surgeon his chief interest was the pathology and treatment of cancer. He is credited with having originated the circular incision for removal of the breast. With the outbreak of the Civil War he interested himself in the recruitment of men for the Union Army. Later he was a severe and constant critic of the treatment of patients in the military hospitals and of the sanitation of army camps. He instituted a movement for the recognition of eclectic practitioners in the army, in which he was successful. He was appointed surgeon to a brigade of Cincinnati home guards. In 1863 he moved to New York City, where he secured a charter for and organized the Eclectic Medical Society of the State of New York, of which he was president for the three following years. In 1865 he participated in the founding of the Eclectic Medical College of the City of New York. He held the chair of surgery in this institution and continued one of the most conspicuous figures in American Eclectic medicine for the rest of his life. He died at this home in New York, from apoplexy. A son, Robert Safford, Jr., became a prominent member of the faculty of the New York school.

[*Medical Truth* (N. Y.), Apr. 1883; H. W. Felter, *Hist. of the Eclectic Medical Inst., Cincinnati, Ohio* (1902); H. A. Kelly and W. L. Burrage, *Am. Medic. Biogs.* (1920); *N. Y. Tribune*, Oct. 11, 1881.]

J. M. P.

NEWTON, THOMAS (June 10, 1660–May 28, 1721), New England colonial official, was born and educated in England. His profession was the law and he doubtless received his training in England, although his name does not appear in the list of those called to the bar during his early years in any of the Inns of Court. He arrived in Boston during the régime of Edmund Andros [*q.v.*], was sworn as an attorney June 7, 1688, and found early and important employment of an official character. In 1691 he was in New York as attorney for the Crown in the trial of Jacob Leisler [*q.v.*], Milborne, and others for high treason. In 1692 he was secretary of New Hampshire; and he was still a member of the council of that province in 1698. In 1702 he was appointed deputy judge of the court of Admiralty for Massachusetts Bay, Rhode Island, and New Hampshire. In 1707 he became comptroller of the customs in Massachusetts, and in 1720, attorney-general.

Meanwhile his private practice of the law flourished. Conditions of life in Boston were becoming less simple and judges and attorneys began to have more frequent recourse to the principles and precedents of the English common law than theretofore. Newton quickly became a leading member of the bar in Massachusetts, and is given credit for having "a greater influence in molding the early jurisprudence" of the province, "than any of his contemporaries" (Goodell, *post*, p. 371). In particular, he appears to have been the first to use the title "barrister" in the courts of Massachusetts (Alger, *post*, p. 206), a title that did not receive an official sanction and rating until 1761. In 1701–02 he appeared as counsel for a slave seeking to establish his freedom under an act of manumission granted by his master. His law library, advertised for sale after his death, was estimated by his contemporaries to be the largest and best collection of law books to be found in America.

When in May 1692 a special commission of oyer and terminer was appointed for the trial of the supposed witches at Salem, of the ten commissioners only Newton was a trained lawyer. Accordingly he was appointed attorney for the Crown and served in that capacity from May 27 to July 26, 1692, when he was superseded by Anthony Checkley, the attorney general. It is clear, from a letter written by Newton from Salem a few days after taking up his work there, that he was as completely obsessed by the prevailing delusion as his fellows who were not trained in the law (C. W. Upham, *Salem Witchcraft*, 1867, II, 255). Spectre evidence was admitted, confessions were extorted, and menaces used against those who denied their guilt while he was attorney for the Crown as well as later. In fact, it was only after Newton had been superseded that the Salem juries began to acquit. His connection with the "judicial murder" of Leisler, Milborne, and others in New York has been noted. In 1705, when some twenty men were placed on trial in Boston for alleged piracy, he was the principal attorney for the Crown. The evidence admitted and the procedure used in this trial were indefensible even according to the common-law precedents then prevalent. His conduct of these trials seems to have been "not only greatly to his discredit but morally criminal" (Goodell, p. 397).

As a citizen of Boston, he bore his fair share of the duties of government and frequently placed his legal talents at the disposal of the town. He became a member of the Ancient and Honorable Artillery Company in 1702. He was a communicant of King's Chapel, the first Episcopal church in Massachusetts, and a leading member in its early and difficult days, serving as vestryman and churchwarden on numerous occasions. He married an English woman, Christian Phillips (?), and by her had four children, Hibbert, Elizabeth, Christian, and Hannah. His son Hibbert was appointed collector of customs in Nova Scotia in 1711, and had a worthy if not distinguished career in that province and in Boston.

[Boston records; A. C. Goodell, *The Acts and Resolves of the Province of Mass. Bay,* vol. VIII (1895); Nathaniel Bouton, *Provincial Papers: Docs. and Records Relating to the Province of N. H.,* vol. II (1868); E. B. O'Callaghan, *Docs. Rel. to the Col. Hist. of the State of N. Y.,* vols. III, IV (1853–54); *Pubs. Col. Soc. of Mass.,* I (1895), 93–99; *Mass. Hist. Soc. Colls.,* 5 ser. V–VI (1868–72); *Proc. Mass. Hist. Soc.,* vols. XX, XXI (1884–85); *Proc. Am. Antiq. Soc.,* n.s. II (1883), 170–71; O. A. Roberts, *Hist. of the Military Company of the Massachusetts,* I (1895), 344–45; E. N. Leonard, *Newton Geneal.* (1915), p. 799; H. W. Foote, *Annals of King's Chapel* (2 vols., 1882–96); A. M. Alger, in *New-Eng. Hist. and Geneal. Reg.,* Apr. 1877; obituary from *Boston News-Letter,* May 29–June 5, 1725, repr. in *New-Eng. Hist. and Geneal. Reg.,* Apr. 1893; see also *Ibid.,* Jan. 1914, p. 102.]   W. O. A.

NEWTON, THOMAS (Nov. 21, 1768–1847), congressman from Virginia, was the son of Thomas and Martha (Tucker) Newton and the descendant of George Newton who was living in lower Norfolk County as early as 1670. His great-grandfather was educated in England and was the first mayor of Norfolk chosen by the council under the charter, and his father was a colonel of militia and a member of the House of Burgesses and of the committee of safety. The boy was educated at the College of William and Mary and studied law privately in Norfolk. From 1796 to 1799 he served in the Virginia House of Delegates. He was elected to Congress as a Republican. Taking his seat on Dec. 7, 1801,

he was placed on the committee of commerce and manufactures. During the impeachment trial of John Pickering, federal judge for the district of New Hampshire, in 1804 he was one of the managers chosen by the House of Representatives. In Congress he acted in the interests of the seacoast commercial classes. The commercial dispute with Great Britain, brought to a head by the Chesapeake affair, caused him to take a bellicose stand. He advocated arming the militia, building a navy, and going to war with Great Britain. In speeches and resolutions in Congress and in letters to the governor he urged adequate defenses for Norfolk. The best defense, he said, would be a large navy rather than coastal forts. Such measures as the Embargo would have lasting effect, since it would force Europe to recognize the value of American commerce and would place a premium on American friendship. In 1818 he was made chairman of the committee on commerce and manufactures and his activity on the floor of Congress ceased. The few speeches he made were on technical subjects. He presented his credentials to the Twenty-first Congress, but the election was contested, and after serving one year of the term he relinquished the seat to George Loyall on Mar. 9, 1830. In the next election he was clearly the victor. At the expiration of this term he retired.

He returned to Norfolk, resumed his law practice, and acted as recorder of the hustings court. He was twice married. His first wife was Mrs. Myers, a widow of Barbados, who bore him one daughter. His second wife was Margaret (Jordan) Pool, the widow of Howard Pool. They had nine children, among them John Newton [*q.v.*]. A quiet, kind, and unostentatious person, he was regarded as Norfolk's leading citizen. His speeches were short and were adorned with statistics and Latin quotations. Always ready to protect and advance the economic interests of his city, he clothed his utterances with a fine patriotic sentiment. He attributed to Great Britain the cause of the commercial distress of the East and characterized her as an "insidious foe, who never gave notice when ... about to strike a blow" (*Annals of Congress,* 10 Cong., 1 Sess., 1852, col. 1029). In state politics he was active as member of the committee to frame a Republican ticket and to choose electors. Both he and his father were in constant correspondence with the various governors of Virginia on such needs of the Tidewater district as new docks for Norfolk harbor and the draining of the Dismal Swamp. The date of his death is given variously. The probate of his will, on Oct. 27, 1847, is recorded in Norfolk.

[W. S. Forrest, *Hist. and Descriptive Sketches of Norfolk and Vicinity* (1853); T. J. Wertenbaker, *Norfolk* (1931); *Memoirs of J. Q. Adams*, ed. by C. F. Adams, vols. IV–VII (1875); *William and Mary College Quart.*, Jan. 1912; *Va. Mag. of Hist.*, Oct. 1921, Jan., July 1922; *Cal. of Va. State Papers*, vols. IX, X (1890–92).]   F. T. W.

NEWTON, WILLIAM WILBERFORCE (Nov. 4, 1843–June 25, 1914), Protestant Episcopal clergyman, was born in Philadelphia, the son of the Rev. Richard Newton [*q.v.*] and his wife, Lydia Greatorex, and younger brother of Richard Heber Newton [*q.v.*]. He was educated in Philadelphia, graduating at the University of Pennsylvania in 1865 and at the Divinity School of the Protestant Episcopal Church in Philadelphia in 1868. Ordered deacon, June 19, 1868, by the Rt. Rev. W. B. Stevens, he was ordained priest Feb. 19, 1869, by the same bishop. On Nov. 16, 1870, he married Emily Stevenson Cooke of Philadelphia, by whom he had one son. After serving one year at the Church of the Epiphany as assistant to his father, he became successively rector of St. Paul's Church, Brookline, Mass., 1870–75; Trinity Church, Newark, N. J., 1875–77; St. Paul's, Boston, 1877–78; and St. Stephen's, Pittsfield, Mass., 1881–1900. On account of a severe affection of the throat, which rendered public speaking almost impossible, he gave up the pastoral ministry in 1900.

Like his father, he was markedly successful in preaching to children. He published the Pilgrim Series of sermons for children in six volumes (1877–90), *The Gate of the Temple, or Prayers for Children* (1876), and edited the *American Church Sunday School Magazine* from 1885 to 1906. His best works for adults were his *Essays of To-day: Religious and Theological* (1879), and an excellent life of the Rev. W. A. Muhlenberg, *Dr. Muhlenberg* (1890), in the series of American Religious Leaders. He wrote several novels including *The Priest and the Man; or, Abelard and Heloisa* (1883) and *Philip MacGregor* (1895). Other works were *The Voice of St. John* (1881, and later editions), poems; *The Vine out of Egypt* (1887), sermons; *A Run through Russia* (1894), travels, including an account of a visit to Tolstoy; *The Child and the Bishop* (1894); *The Abiding Value of First Principles* (n.d.). In the years of his retirement he contributed many articles and stories to periodicals. His writings were of merit but not such as to secure any permanent place in literature. In theology he was a Broad Churchman and sympathized with the liberalizing tendencies in his Church. He organized the American Congress of Churches, a shortlived attempt at bringing about greater comity among churches, which met at Hartford, Conn., in 1885, and at Cleveland, Ohio, in 1886. He was tall and spare in build; his complexion was florid, his manner hearty and affable. He had a delicate sense of humor, and before his throat affection developed, a ringing voice, which, with his pleasing personality and appearance, made him an effective speaker.

[Biographical sketch revised by Newton himself in *The New Schaff-Herzog Encyc. of Religious Knowledge*, vol. VIII (1910); journals of the diocese of Pa.; *Boston Transcript*, June 26, 1914; personal acquaintance.]
                                                  J. C. Ay—r.

NEY, ELISABET (Jan. 26, 1833–June 29, 1907), sculptor, daughter of Johann Adam and Elisabeth (Wernze) Ney, was born in Münster, Westphalia, and was christened Franzisca Bernardina Wilhelmina Elisabeth. At an early age she was seized with a desire to become a sculptor and worked in the atelier of her father, a well-known sculptor of ecclesiastical works. After attending the schools of her native town, she determined, as a seventeen-year-old girl, to go to Berlin to study sculpture under the great master, Christian Daniel Rauch. For two years her parents steadfastly opposed her purpose but finally compromised in permitting her to attend the Academy of Fine Arts at Munich. While there she met, as a medical student, her future husband, Edmund Duncan Montgomery [*q.v.*], who was destined to exert a very great influence upon her development. After two years in the academy at Munich, during which time her brilliant work made her a marked student, she transferred in 1855 to Berlin, where Rauch accepted her as a student. With him she continued until his death two years later. Her extraordinary gifts, her unusual beauty, and her indomitable will carried her to heights of popularity. In 1856 she exhibited her work at the Berlin Exposition and gained warm praise. After the death of Rauch she took over some of his uncompleted commissions. She became a warm friend of the philosopher, Arthur Schopenhauer, and the naturalist, Alexander von Humboldt, and made busts of them. During the years 1859–60 she spent several months in Hanover, engaged in making a colossal bust of King George V of Hanover. At this time, Friedrich Kaulbach made a famous portrait of her, and this, with her bust of the King, is now one of the most striking objects in the Museum of the province of Hanover.

In 1860 Elisabet Ney returned to her native town and remained there for three years, engaged in numerous works, largely busts and statues of historical personages of the province. As a result, Münster possesses the best array of her early work in public and private collections. During the summer of 1863 she made two visits to England. On Nov. 17, 1863, she was married to Montgomery in Madeira and then spent the following year in art travels in Egypt, Greece, and Italy. She returned to Munich early in 1865. After a few weeks, she left with her husband for Mentone and Rome and made a bust of Garibaldi during a year's sojourn in Italy. She returned with Montgomery to Munich in the spring of 1867 and rode the crest of a wave of unprecedented popularity. Among the many commissions that she received during the year were one from King Wilhelm I of Prussia for a bust of Bismarck, and busts of the chemists Justus von Liebig and Friedrich Wöhler for the Polytechnicum of Munich. In 1869 King Ludwig II of Bavaria had her make a statue of himself. She also received commissions for two classical figures to be cast in bronze for the Polytechnicum in Munich.

Although Elisabet Ney had been legally married to Montgomery in the office of the British consul at Madeira, she always, by an incomprehensible whim of hers, denied her marriage, even to her parents and closest friends, in the face of subsequent social ostracism in America and Europe. At Munich, in 1870, this insistence, coupled with her very close association with Montgomery, brought down upon her head the marked disapprobation of society, and finally ostracism. The result was that she determined to leave Europe and go to America, where her ideas might be "free," and so, at the end of December 1870, accompanied by Montgomery and a faithful servant, "Cencie," she left Munich. She made one of a company of free spirits who formed a colony at Thomasville, Ga. The colony later disintegrated and at the end of 1872 Ney and Montgomery traveled to Texas. Elisabet's indomitable and stiff-necked pride would not allow her to admit failure to her European friends, and hence she accepted banishment from cultured Europe and its artistic associations. In March 1873 Montgomery purchased a plantation, "Liendo," near Hempstead, Tex. For twenty years the sculptress was here isolated from all contact with the artistic world. In the meantime she bore two children, one of whom died. In 1892, after many years of deprivation, in furtherance of her lifelong, insatiable hunger for recognition as a sculptor, she moved to Austin, the capital of Texas. There, with the aid of Montgomery, she built a studio (now the "Elisabet Ney Museum"). About this time she received a commission to make statues of Stephen F. Austin and Samuel Houston for the Texas Building at the World's Columbian Exposition at Chicago. When state-wide recognition of her gifts as a sculptor followed upon the completion of these statues, she executed a number of works, chiefly busts of Texans prominent in the history of the state. Three visits to Germany followed during the next ten years. Her first (1895) was in the nature of a triumphal return. Subsequent visits (1902, 1903) saw the completion of her most ambitious works, "Prometheus Bound" (now in the Bavarian royal castle at Linderhof) and the Albert Sidney Johnston Memorial, now in the state cemetery at Austin, Tex. Lorado Taft (*The History of American Sculpture*, 1924, pp. 214-15) said of her: "She is one of the best equipped of women sculptors. . . . Her sketches and compositions are admirable, as are her virile, simply handled heads of the forceful sons of Texas. . . . The details of the features are epitomized with great discrimination and with an easy mastery of form which is unknown to the majority of our sculptors."

Elisabet Ney was marked by an independence of spirit that broke everything to her will; this was especially true of her treatment of her husband and her surviving son. She possessed a haughtiness and uncalculating ambition that surmounted all personal and material obstacles, and this, together with a pride that could not bend, conspired to rob her of opportunities by means of which she might have risen to world-wide acclaim as a sculptor. The isolation of her twenty years at "Liendo," and her semi-isolation for another fifteen years at Austin, prevented the growth to be expected in one of her genius. Without constant friendly criticism her work was destined to show qualities of unevenness.

[Bride Neill Taylor, *Elisabet Ney, Sculptor* (1916); Eugen Müller-Münster, *Elisabeth Ney, die seltsamen Lebensschicksale der Elisabeth Ney und des Edmund Montgomery* (1931); Alfred von Mensi-Klarbach, *Vor und hinter den Kulissen der Welt- und Kulturgeschichte* (1925); I. K. Stephens, "Edmund Montgomery, The Hermit Philosopher of Liendo Plantation," *Southwest Rev.*, Jan. 1931; *Biographisches Jahrbuch und Deutscher Nekrolog*, 1907; *Der Grosse Brockhaus*, vol. XIII (1932); *Galveston Daily News*, July 1, 1907.]

S. W. G.

NG POON CHEW (Apr. 28, 1866–Mar. 13, 1931), Chinese editor, lecturer, was born in South China, 150 miles southwest of Shuang Hu, on the fourteenth day of the third moon, in the Chinese lunar calendar. He was the son of Ng Yip and Wong (Shee) Hok. Among Americans he was always addressed as if his family name were Chew instead of Ng (or Wu, as it is pronounced in the Mandarin dialect). In early years he was placed under the tutelage of a Taoist priest in the hope of entering the priesthood of that faith, but in 1879 an uncle, after spending eight years in California, returned to China with $800 Mexican. This seemingly fabulous sum, spread out on the table in eight sacks containing $100 each, so impressed the boy's imagination that he resolved in 1881 to go to San Francisco under the care of a relative. From there he proceeded to San José, where for several years he worked in the daytime and attended public school at night. Converted to Christianity in 1882, he resolved to utilize the pulpit to elevate the lot of his people. After some years of preparation in Occidental College, he entered San Francisco Theological Seminary in 1889, graduating in 1892. He was ordained the same year by the Presbytery of San Francisco and was appointed assistant pastor of the Chinese church of that city. In 1894 the Presbyterian Board of Foreign Missions appointed him to Los Angeles to look after the Chinese missions of southern California. In 1899 he resigned from the ministry in the hope of influencing his countrymen in secular as well as religious matters. Believing that his purpose could be accomplished through a newspaper, he persuaded friends to cooperate with him in establishing at San Francisco in 1899 the *Hua Mei Hsin Pao* (Chinese American Weekly). Although many prophesied that Chinese readers would be too few and that the venture would fail, the success was great enough to warrant the paper's becoming a daily in 1900, at which time its name was changed to *Chung Sai Yat Po* (Chinese Western Daily)—the first Chinese daily newspaper to be published in the United States. With the exception of one week during the San Francisco earthquake, this paper has appeared regularly ever since. Ng furthered the cause of Sun Yat-sen in China, not only by the policy of his paper, but by securing the release of that leader from the immigration office in San Francisco, and providing him with financial aid to proceed to London. During the last sixteen years of his life he lectured extensively on Chautauqua and Lyceum platforms, visiting every state in the Union, and crossing the continent for this purpose no less than eighty-six times. His keen sense of humor, his expansive good will, and his boundless optimism made him a very acceptable speaker. He did much to promote among Americans an appreciation of the best in Chinese culture, and among the Chinese a recognition of the superiority of western civilization on the material side. The University of

Pittsburgh in 1913 conferred upon him the honorary degree of Litt.D. He was a thirty-second-degree Mason, and the first Chinese in California to become a Shriner. An authority on all phases of the Chinese exclusion question, he did much to promote mutual understanding in this matter. For some years (1906–13) he was adviser to the Chinese consulate general of San Francisco, and from 1913 till his death, vice-consul in that city. He married, May 4, 1892, Tso Chun Fah, of San Francisco. At the time of his death he left, beside his widow, a son and four daughters, all engaged in professional or humanitarian work.

[*Who's Who in America*, 1930–31; *Gen. Assem. Presbyt. Ch., U. S. A., Reports of the Boards*, 1895; E. A. Wicher, *The Presbyt. Ch. in Cal., 1849–1927* (1927); *Chung Sai Yat Po*, Mar. 14, and 17, 1931; *San Francisco Examiner*, Mar. 14, 1931.] A.W.H.

NIBLACK, ALBERT PARKER (July 25, 1859–Aug. 20, 1929), naval officer, was born in Vincennes, Ind. He was the fifth generation in descent from John Niblack of Scotland, who came to America in 1760 and settled in Salisbury, N. C. His father was William Ellis Niblack [*q.v.*]; his mother, Eliza Ann Sherman. Niblack had his early education in the public schools, and entering the United States Naval Academy at seventeen, was graduated four years later (1880). After two years on the South Pacific Station, he was sent to the Smithsonian Institution for instruction and then spent four years in survey and exploration in Alaska. Written during this period was his treatise, "The Coast Indians of Southern Alaska and Northern British Columbia," published in the *Annual Report of the Board of Regents of the Smithsonian Institution . . . 1888* (1890). In May 1887 he was instrumental in saving the crew of the *Ocean King,* which foundered off the northwest coast, and for this he received a letter of commendation. Varied duty afloat followed. In the years 1896–98 he was naval attaché in Berlin, Rome, and Vienna. His interest in writing continued, and in 1890 and again in 1896 he was the prize essayist of the United States Naval Institute. In the Spanish-American War he took part in the blockade of the Cuban coast and in the battle of Nipe Bay. On being ordered to the East, he assisted in the suppression of the Philippine insurrection. In 1900, at the time of the Boxer trouble, he served in the North China Expeditionary Force. Later he was in the Philippine Islands, where, under the United States navy hydrographic office, he acted as secretary to the naval commission and was personally charged with the surveys made for several of the naval stations. On Nov. 24, 1903, he was married to Mary A. Harrington of San Francisco.

After commanding several ships in the Pacific and the Atlantic, he served again as naval attaché, first for a year and a half in South America at Buenos Aires, Rio de Janeiro, and Santiago, and then for somewhat less than two years in Europe at Berlin and The Hague. He had been promoted captain in 1911, and in 1914 when he was in command of the battleship *Michigan* he took part in the occupation of Vera Cruz. Later he was ordered to Newport for the long course at the Naval War College, with which for some time he had had a close relation both as student and lecturer, and was graduated in December 1916. At the outbreak of the World War he was given command of the First Division and later of the First Squadron of Battleships of the Atlantic Fleet. In November 1917 he was given command of the Second Squadron, Patrol Force, of the Atlantic Fleet based on Gibraltar, and had this most important duty until after the signing of the armistice. It was estimated that more than one-fourth of the convoys which reached the Allies either rendezvoused at this point or passed through the straits. His force here consisted of forty-one ships and a personnel which averaged 314 officers and 4,660 men (Sims, *post,* p. 161). The American ships attending the convoys provided approximately seventy per cent. of the escorts between Gibraltar and the United Kingdom as well as twenty-five per cent. of those required for the Allied forces in the Mediterranean. Secretary Josephus Daniels said of his service: "Admiral A. P. Niblack . . . directed our forces at Gibraltar to the end of the war, with fine judgment and ability. He and his force became a tower of strength in that region, to the Allies as well as our own Navy" (*Our Navy at War,* 1922, pp. 117–18). Herbert Hoover, director-general of relief, wrote with like enthusiasm of his subsequent work when in 1919 he was commander of the United States forces operating in the Eastern Mediterranean, saying: "It would not have been possible to have secured any relief to these people but for your co-operation" (letter from Hoover to Niblack).

In the final years of his naval career Niblack was successively director of naval intelligence, Washington; naval attaché, London; commander of the United States naval forces in Europe, with the rank of vice-admiral; and commandant of the sixth naval district and navy yard, Charleston, S. C. He had been promoted to the grade of rear-admiral in 1918 and was retired in that grade in 1923 at the statutory age of sixty-four. In 1924 he became representative of the United States in the International Hydrographic Bureau, Monaco, and in 1927 was elected president for a term of five years. He died in Nice, France. His published work, in addition to the treatise mentioned and many articles that appeared in magazines, consisted of *Why Wars Come* (1922) and *Summary of Data on Coastal Signals, with Proposals for Their Unification* (Monaco, 1926). In recognition of his services in the World War and later he received many decorations.

[W. S. Sims, *The Victory at Sea* (1920); *Who's Who in America,* 1928–29; *Proc. U. S. Naval Inst.,* Nov. 1929; annual reports of the secretary of the navy; *Army and Navy Jour.,* Aug. 24, 1929; *N. Y. Times,* Aug. 21, 1929; data from the Navy Dept. and from private sources.]   C. S. A.

NIBLACK, WILLIAM ELLIS (May 19, 1822–May 7, 1893), congressman, judge, was the eldest of the seven children of Martha (Hargrave) Niblack and John Niblack, who was of Scotch-Irish descent and who, about 1817, removed from Kentucky to Dubois County, Ind., where he was married and where his son was born. After a boyhood on his father's farm William entered Indiana University but soon withdrew, and for the next few years he worked on the farm, taught school, assisted in managing a trading boat, and was assistant surveyor of Dubois County. During these years he studied law and on Apr. 25, 1845, he was admitted to the bar and began practice in Martin County, Ind. He married Belvina Reily in January 1848. She died the following April, and on Oct. 4, 1849, he married Eliza Ann Sherman of Cazenovia, N. Y. They had five children, one of whom was Albert Parker Niblack [*q.v.*]. This same year, 1849, he became a Democratic member of the Indiana House of Representatives, and in 1850 the party elected him to the state Senate. In January 1854 Gov. Joseph A. Wright appointed him as circuit judge to fill out the unexpired term of Alvin P. Hovey. He succeeded himself in the October election that year. In December 1855 he removed to Vincennes and in 1857 went to Congress from the Vincennes district to fill the seat of James Lockhart, who had died in September. He was a successful candidate for re-election in 1858 but declined to run in 1860. Knox County sent him to the state legislature in 1862.

In 1864 he became a member of the Democratic national committee on which he served until 1872. In the National Democratic Convention of 1864 he supported the nomination of McClellan on the platform of peace. On this platform he was reëlected to Congress in 1864, but the war was over before he took his seat. He served until 1875. In 1876 he was elected to the supreme court of Indiana. He suffered his first defeat in the election of 1888, and after the expiration of his term in 1889 he removed to Indianapolis, where he engaged in private practice until his death. He represented the thought of southern Indiana. He voted for the Lecompton constitution, because he believed the best remedy for slavery troubles was the organization of Kansas into a state and that the views of Buchanan on the validity of the Lecompton constitution were correct (see speech of Mar. 31, 1858, *Cong. Globe,* 35 Cong., 1 Sess., App., 1858, pp. 297–98). He was typical of that class of Northern Democrats who during the Civil War represented that paradoxical combination of union and peace but not Copperhead principles. During the Reconstruction period he supported Johnson and opposed the radical Reconstruction measures as too harsh and militaristic. Ever a strong Democrat and imbued with a highly legalistic mind, he continually opposed the encroachments on what he believed were state's rights.

[Papers in the possession of the family in Indianapolis; *Memorial on the Death of Judge William Ellis Niblack by the Ind. State Bar Asso. Mag. of 1893* (1893); G. I. Reed, *Encyc. of Biog. of Ind.,* vol. I (1895); J. G. Blaine, *Twenty Years in Cong.,* vol. II (1886); *Indianapolis Sentinel,* May 8, 1893.]

            J. L. N.

NIBLO, WILLIAM (1789–Aug. 21, 1878), hotel and theatre manager, was born in Ireland and came to America in his youth. With his first apprenticeship to a coffee-house proprietor of 43 Pine Street he entered upon the career which made his name familiar through half a century of New York history. Hotel and theatre were often associated in those days, especially in the form of outdoor gardens with platform stages connected with hotels where guests and neighbors and their friends gathered in the evenings to listen to some simple and often topical entertainment, while they partook of light refreshments and discussed the news of the day. After he had conducted the Bank Coffee House for several years, Niblo decided to invest in the concert garden business as an outlet for both his ambitions and his products. In 1823 he leased the Columbian Gardens at Broadway and Prince Street on the site of the old circus and started summer night entertainments there, later developing this into the Sans Souci Theatre. In 1829 he reopened the place as Niblo's Garden. Leaving the old circus arena as it was, he built a small theatre which at once became so great a success that he soon built another, finer and larger than the first. By 1837 this was the fashionable entertainment center in New York life with such attractions as the Ravels (the famous

family of acrobats and rope dancers) and a vaudeville company headed by the elder Jefferson, with a dramatic season under the lead of John Sefton, a concert series, and a season of opera in which the outstanding production was *The Barber of Seville* with Fornasari.

Later Niblo's Garden passed through many changes and vicissitudes. The theatre burned in 1846 and was not rebuilt until 1849. The actual direction of the theatre passed through diverse hands, including such competent theatre managers as Henry Palmer and James J. Wallack. Niblo himself does not seem to have been in any more direct relation to the performances than that of lessee of the property. But his personality was strong and his popularity was great, and to him are generally credited the success and distinction of the entire venture, including the long procession of famous theatre folk who were attracted by the quality of the audience at Niblo's Garden and played there during Niblo's management. In 1850 William Florence made his first New York appearance there. Among the other performances there were Mathilda Heron in *Camille,* Charles Kean in *Hamlet* and *Macbeth,* Edwin Forrest in a series of his tragic impersonations, Henry Wallack, Henry and Thomas Placide, Anna Cora Mowatt, the author of *Fashion,* E. L. Davenport who made his first New York appearance there, J. H. Hackett in his first New York appearance as Falstaff in *The Merry Wives of Windsor,* Charlotte Cushman, Dan Rice, Dion Boucicault, Agnes Robertson, George Holland, and Adelina Patti; and in 1866, after Niblo had retired, *The Black Crook* which carried the fame of Niblo's Garden around the world. Although Niblo was not highly educated, he picked up a knowledge of literature and art and as he grew more affluent, became somewhat of a collector. After the death of Francis Lister Hawks [*q.v.*] he purchased the latter's American history library and presented it to the New York Historical Society. Niblo retired in 1861 and died in 1878. His wife, Martha (King) Niblo had died in 1851.

[See: T. A. Brown, *The Hist. of the N. Y. Stage* (1903), vol. I; G. C. D. Odell, *Annals of the N. Y. Stage,* vols. III–VII (1928–31); J. N. Ireland, *Records of the N. Y. Stage from 1750 to 1860,* vol. II (1867); *Appletons' Ann. Cyc.,* 1878; *Wm. Niblo: Seven Plates Illustrative of New York's Early Dramatic Hist.* (n.d.); *N. Y. Daily Tribune,* Aug. 22, 1878. The catalogue of the books in the Hawks library presented to the N. Y. Hist. Soc. occupies pages 47–166 of *A Memorial of Francis Lister Hawks, D.D., LL.D.* (1871), by E. A. Duyckinck.]   E. J. R. I.

NICHOLAS, GEORGE (1754?–June 1799), Virginia politician and Kentucky pioneer, brother of John, Wilson Cary, and Philip Norborne

Nicholas [*qq.v.*], was the eldest son of Robert Carter [*q.v.*] and Anne (Cary) Nicholas. Born at Williamsburg, he attended the College of William and Mary and entered the army on the outbreak of the Revolution, rising from the rank of captain to that of colonel. In 1778, at an officers' ball in Baltimore he met Mary Smith, daughter of John and sister to Robert and Samuel Smith of that city, a family notably conspicuous for its part in the political and commercial life of Maryland. Retiring from the army, he married her, studied law, and entered politics. In 1781 he removed from Hanover to Albemarle County with his mother and brothers, his father having died the year before. During 1781 he made his political début in the House of Delegates by moving an investigation into the conduct of Governor Jefferson during Arnold's invasion. The charges were later dropped and no ill feeling arose between the two men because of the incident (H. S. Randall, *The Life of Thomas Jefferson*, 1858, I, p. 351), Nicholas presently becoming one of Jefferson's leading supporters. In the Assembly he cooperated with Madison in the struggle for religious freedom in 1784. In 1787 he at first supported and then deserted him when he advocated the payment of British debts (*The Writings of James Monroe*, ed. by S. M. Hamilton, I, 1898, p. 178). During the same period he opposed the issuance of paper money by Virginia. He was a member of the Virginia convention of 1788 and was an ardent advocate of the adoption of the Federal constitution. During the debates on this subject, Nicholas and Patrick Henry hurled at each other certain implications regarding land speculations, which indicated that each had information concerning the investments of the other (Wm. W. Henry, *Patrick Henry*, 1891, II, pp. 355–56). Harry Innes [*q.v.*], whose friendship with Nicholas dated from their college days, had gone to Kentucky in an official capacity after the Revolution, and had become closely associated with James Wilkinson and others in land speculations and in trade with the Spanish at New Orleans. In 1790 Nicholas removed to Kentucky and became interested in the operations of these men. He was a member of the convention which, in 1792, drafted the first Kentucky constitution. One of the remarkable features of that instrument, for which Nicholas was said to be largely responsible, was a clause requiring all cases involving land titles to be tried before the supreme court of the state. Nicholas became the first attorney-general when Kentucky was admitted to statehood. In 1797 he was involved in the last phase of the Spanish Conspiracy (R. M. McElroy, *Kentucky*

in the Nation's History, 1909, pp. 200–08) and in 1798 took a leading part in the framing and advocating of Jefferson's famous anti-Federalist resolutions of that year, thus becoming one of the leaders of the rising Republican party in Kentucky (*The Writings of Thomas Jefferson*, Memorial Edition, X, 1904, p. 104). He died, however, during the next year.

In personal appearance George Nicholas was stocky, blond, and bald. Taciturn in public, he is said to have been genial and humorous in private conversation. He must have been a man of great energy and restless enterprise. In Virginia his associations with Madison and Jefferson were entirely creditable to him, and his policy was enlightened as was theirs. In Kentucky his associations with Wilkinson and Innes were certainly devious. Though he probably had no treasonable intent in connection with the Spanish Conspiracy, it is certain that he worked in harmony with a group of land speculators and that he used his public position in order to promote his private interests. In most of his political activities he had the cooperation of his brother, Wilson Cary, who later became governor of Virginia.

[There is a good brief account of Geo. Nicholas in H. B. Grisby, *The Hist. of the Va. Fed. Convention of 1788*, II (1891), 281–98. The biographies and published correspondence of Thos. Jefferson throw some light on his political career in Virginia. Humphrey Marshall's *Hist. of Ky.* (2 vols., 1824), and the papers of Harry Innes in the Lib. of Cong. furnish the best clues to his Kentucky connections. See also: Temple Bodley, ed., *Reprints of Littell's Pol. Trans. . . . and Letter of Geo. Nicholas* (1926); and Robt. Peter, *Transylvania Univ.* (1896), Filson Club Pubs., no. 11. In the Durrett Collection, Univ. of Chicago, there is a volume of letters, papers, and speeches in the handwriting of Geo. Nicholas.]   T. P. A.

NICHOLAS, JOHN (1756?–Dec. 31, 1819), member of Congress from Virginia, brother to George, Wilson Cary, and Philip Norborne Nicholas [*qq.v.*], and son of Robert Carter [*q.v.*] and Anne (Cary) Nicholas, was born in Williamsburg, Va. Almost nothing is known of his early life, but being the second son of the Treasurer of the Colony, he doubtless received every advantage that the little provincial capital afforded. It appears that he attended the College of William and Mary, studied law, and practised for a time in Williamsburg, but his career was interrupted by the outbreak of the Revolution, which occasioned the removal of his family to the comparative safety of an estate in Hanover County. Though at some time during his career John lost the use of one of his eyes, he appears to have continued his studies or his practice during the war, and to have taken no part in military operations. In 1781, on the death of his father, his family removed from Hanover to Albemarle County. It is not clear that John followed them to their new home, for we presently find him located in Stafford County, where he married Anne Lawson, daughter of Gavin Lawson, by whom he had eleven children. In 1793 he was elected to the Federal House of Representatives and, being thrice reelected, served until 1801. He came to be recognized as one of the leading supporters of the Republican cause on the floor of the House. He was effective in debate, and his speech advocating repeal of the Sedition Act was published in 1799 as a Republican pamphlet and later included by Alexander Johnson in his collection of *Representative American Orations* (1884, I, 83–95). Nicholas appears to have suffered financially as a consequence of his public service, and in 1799 desired to give up his seat in Congress but consented to serve another term in the interest of the Republican cause. It was presumably due to this economic situation that he finally retired from public life in 1801 and two years later removed to Geneva, Ontario County, New York (Manning J. Dauer, "The Two John Nicholases," *American Historical Review*, January, 1940, 338–53). In his new home he engaged in agricultural pursuits and in 1806 was elected to the state senate, which place he held until 1809. From 1806 until 1819 he acted as judge of the court of common pleas of Ontario County. He died at his home in Geneva on Dec. 31, 1819, and was interred in Glenwood Cemetery. Little is known of his private life except that he was a devout member of the Episcopal Church.

[There is a meager account of John Nicholas in the *Biog. Dir. Am. Cong.* (1928); and another in Alexander Brown, *The Cabells and their Kin* (1895), pp. 200–01. See also: Louise P. du Bellet, *Some Prominent Va. Families* (n.d.), vol. II; *Va. Mag. of Hist. and Biog.*, July 1901; Ori: Clark, *A Funeral Address, Delivered at the Interment of the Hon. John Nicholas ... 1820* (n.d.); *Richmond Enquirer*, Jan. 15, 1820.]

T. P. A.

NICHOLAS, PHILIP NORBORNE (1775?–Aug. 18, 1849), Virginia jurist and politician, brother of George, John, and Wilson Cary Nicholas [*qq.v.*], was the youngest son of Robert Carter [*q.v.*] and Anne (Cary) Nicholas. He was born in Williamsburg, Va., and was named for Norborne Berkeley, Lord Botetourt, the governor of the Province. He attended the College of William and Mary, studied law, and in 1800 became attorney-general of Virginia (*The Writ-*

ings *of James Monroe,* ed. by S. M. Hamilton, III, 1900, p. 170). In 1804 he was made a director of the first bank to be established in Richmond, and for years was president of the Farmer's Bank of that city. In 1817 he was made a director of the Richmond branch of the Bank of the United States, of which institution his brother Wilson Cary was for a short while president. In 1823 he was made judge of the General Court of Virginia and retained this position until his death in 1849.

These activities stamp him as a substantial citizen rather than as a man of action and ideas. He spent his entire active life in Richmond, establishing his home on Shockoe Hill where John Marshall and other notable citizens had their residences (C. H. Ambler, *Thomas Ritchie, 1913*, p. 16). He was appointed on civic committees and presided over civic rites on important occasions when internal improvements were to be considered or when the death of a Jefferson or a Monroe was to be mourned. Though never a great political figure, he yet took a very active part in politics and was one of the guiding forces in the establishment of the Jacksonian party in Virginia. As early as 1800 he consulted with Jefferson on tactical political moves (*The Writings of Thomas Jefferson,* Memorial Edition, X, 1904, p. 163), and doubtless worked in concert with his brothers, George and Wilson Cary, for the promotion of the Jeffersonian cause in Virginia. He apparently devoted his time to his banking interests during the long rule of the Virginia Dynasty, but when this period came to an end, his noted brothers were dead, and he carried on the tradition of the family by taking a powerful, though quiet, part in the political transition that followed. Like most of the state-rights men of the Jeffersonian school in Virginia, he supported William H. Crawford for the presidency in 1824 (H. H. Simms, *The Rise of the Whigs in Virginia,* 1929, p. 16), but on Crawford's failure, he and Thomas Ritchie [*q.v.*], of the *Richmond Enquirer,* along with certain others who came to be known as the "Richmond Junta," decided to throw their support to Andrew Jackson. They carried their state for him and continued to control it in his interest. Now a thoroughgoing Jackson man, Nicholas wrote articles condemning nullification, and he appeared against Lieut. R. B. Randolph in the case of the personal attack upon Jackson by that young hot-spur. Though opposed to the sub-treasury, as a banker should have been, Nicholas remained faithful to Van Buren, as did his associates of the Junta. It was, in fact, in collaboration with Van Buren that the Virginia group had made the transition from the Crawford to the Jackson camp (C. H. Ambler, *op. cit.*, p. 106). On one of the very few occasions when Nicholas became a candidate for office, he was elected a member of the convention which framed Virginia's second constitution in 1829. He was married twice: his first wife was Mary Spear of Baltimore, Md., and his second, Maria Carter Byrd, of Clark County, Va.

[The works which deal with the Jackson movement in Virginia contain scattered references to Philip Norborne Nicholas. A little personal information is to be found in R. A. Brock, *Va. and the Virginians* (1888), I, 121–29; W. A. Christian, *Richmond, her Past and Present* (1912); Louise P. du Bellet, *Some Prominent Va. Families* (n.d.), II, 320–21; *Richmond Enquirer*, Aug. 21, 1849.]   T. P. A.

NICHOLAS, ROBERT CARTER (Jan. 28, 1728–Sept. 8, 1780), colonial official and Revolutionary patriot, was the eldest son of Dr. George and Elizabeth (Carter) Burwell Nicholas. His mother was daughter to Robert, the famous "King" Carter, of Virginia, and widow of Nathaniel Burwell. His father, after having served as a surgeon in the British Navy, emigrated about 1700 from Lancashire to Williamsburg, Va. (Louise P. du Bellet, *Some Prominent Virginia Families*, n.d., II, pp. 310 ff.). Robert was educated at the College of William and Mary and presently took up the practice of law, becoming in time the recognized head of the provincial bar. Probably in 1751 he was married to Anne, daughter to Wilson and Sarah Cary of Virginia. In 1756 he was elected to represent York County in the House of Burgesses, and for years he took an active part in the proceedings of that body (*Journals of the House of Burgesses of Virginia*, 1752–55, 1756–58, ed. by H. R. McIlwaine, 1909, p. x). In 1765 he opposed Patrick Henry's Stamp Act resolves. At the same time he took a leading part in exposing the irregularities in the treasury, and on the death of Speaker John Robinson [*q.v.*] in 1766, Nicholas' friends were instrumental in inducing Governor Fauquier to consent to the separation of the speakership and the office of treasurer and the appointment of Nicholas to the latter post ("The Preston and Virginia Papers," *post*, I, p. 59; *Journals of the House of Burgesses of Virginia*, 1766–69, ed. by John P. Kennedy, 1906, pp. xv–xviii). Though opposing revolutionary measures, Nicholas did not favor unconditional submission to the British Parliament. In 1769 he helped to frame resolutions condemning the attitude of that body on the questions of taxation and the transportation of criminals for trial in England. By 1771 his other interests had become so pressing that he offered his unfinished legal business to Thomas Jefferson, but Jefferson was unable to accept it and it was turned over to Patrick Henry in 1773.

When news of the closing of the port of Boston reached Williamsburg, Jefferson, Henry, and their radical friends persuaded the conservative and religious Nicholas to offer a resolution which they had drafted setting aside a day of prayer and fasting (Lyon G. Tyler, *History of Virginia*, 1924, II, p. 121). A pamphlet criticizing this action and upholding the British policy was published anonymously, but it is believed to have been written by the attorney-general, John Randolph. Nicholas answered with another publication in which he defended the American cause and his own actions (*Considerations on the Present State of Virginia, Attributed to John Randolph—and Considerations on the Present State of Virginia Examined, by Robert Carter Nicholas*, ed. by Earl G. Swem, 1919). When Dunmore seized the supply of powder at Williamsburg in 1775, Nicholas helped to prevent a clash between the Governor and the outraged colonists led by Henry. It was during this anxious time that he opposed Henry's resolutions proposing to arm the colony for defense, but the measure having passed despite his efforts, he was placed upon the committee charged with its execution.

Alone of all the important men in the Virginia Assembly, Nicholas opposed the adoption of the Declaration of Independence, but he was a member of the committee appointed to draft a declaration of rights and a new form of government. In this capacity he opposed the assertion that "all men are by nature equally free and independent" as being the forerunner of civil convulsion (Kate Mason Rowland, *The Life of George Mason*, 1892, I, p. 240). This reluctant acceptance of the changing situation classified him as a stanch conservative Patriot, and he further entrenched himself with the conservatives when he became one of the leading defenders of the established Church against the liberals who worked for religious freedom. On the organization of the new state government, Nicholas, largely through the influence of Jefferson, was defeated by George Wythe in the contest for the speakership of the House of Delegates (J. H. Eckenrode, *The Revolution in Virginia*, 1916, p. 172). His duties as treasurer now came to an end, and in 1779 he was placed on the bench of the High Court of Chancery. In 1780 he was appointed on the committee charged with the construction of public buildings which were to be erected in Richmond, but he died within the year.

At the outbreak of hostilities in 1775, Nicholas removed his family from Williamsburg to "The Retreat," his estate in Hanover County. It was here that he died in 1780. After the invasion of

Cornwallis in 1781, his widow removed her family to a tract of land which her father-in-law had purchased in the piedmont county of Albemarle. Here her promising children grew up under the influence of Thomas Jefferson. Four of her sons, George, John, Wilson Cary, and Philip Norborne [qq.v.] took active parts in political life. Her daughter Elizabeth became the wife of Edmund Jennings Randolph [q.v.]. The conservative father of this family of Democrats was an unusual man in his time. A close friend to Governor Botetourt, an important member of the colonial régime, and a stanch defender of the established Church, there was yet much of puritanical austerity in his character. He exposed fraud in high places and administered the treasury with scrupulous honesty. He opposed most of the plans of the Revolutionists, but was trusted by them to aid in carrying out the very designs against which he had argued.

[Material is scattered through the works dealing with the Revolutionary history of Virginia, such as C. R. Lingley, *The Transition in Va. from Colony to Commonwealth* (1910); and J. H. Eckenrode, *The Revolution in Va.* (1916). The only good characterization is in Henry S. Randall, *The Life of Thomas Jefferson* (1858), I, 198–99. See also: Wm. Meade, *Old Churches, Ministers, and Families of Va.* (1857), vol. I; *Va. Mag. of Hist. and Biog.*, July 1901; R. A. Brock, *Va. and the Virginians* (1888), vol. I; H. B. Grigsby, *The Va. Convention of 1776* (1855); "The Preston and Va. Papers of the Draper Collection of MSS.," *Wis. Hist. Soc. Pubs., Calendar Series*, vol. I (1915); *Sons of the Revolution in Va. Quart. Mag.*, Apr. 1923.]   T. P. A.

NICHOLAS, WILSON CARY (Jan. 31, 1761–Oct. 10, 1820), congressman, United States senator, and governor of Virginia, brother of George, John, and Philip Norborne Nicholas [qq.v.] was the third son of Robert Carter [q.v.] and Anne (Cary) Nicholas. He was born at Williamsburg, Va., but removed with his parents to Hanover County in 1775. At an early age he became a student at the College of William and Mary but withdrew in 1779 to join the Revolutionary army. He became commanding officer of Washington's Life Guard, which post he held until the dissolution of the corps in 1783. During the period of his service in the army, his father had died and his mother had removed to Albemarle County. He now joined the family in the new abode, and shortly thereafter married Margaret Smith, daughter of John Smith, a prominent citizen of Baltimore. Another daughter of the house, Mary, had married his brother George. After his marriage, Wilson Cary Nicholas made his home at "Warren" in Albemarle. In 1784 he was elected to the House of Delegates and in that body disregarded his father's example and his mother's advice by supporting Madison in his stand for religious liberty. He also sup-

ported him in his effort to remove legal obstructions to the payment of British debts in accord with the treaty of 1783. He remained in the House of Delegates until 1789, serving meanwhile in the convention of 1788 and acting again in accord with Madison in championing the adoption of the Federal constitution. Like Jeffersonians in general, he was in thorough sympathy with the ideals of the French Revolution (*The Writings of James Madison*, ed. by Gaillard Hunt, vol. VI, 1906, p. 132). In most of his early political activities he cooperated with his elder brother George, who went with him to the convention of 1788.

From 1794 until 1799 Nicholas again served in the Assembly. In 1798 he and his brother George consulted with Jefferson in the framing of the famous anti-Federalist resolutions of that year. He then passed them on to his friend John Breckinridge for enactment by the Kentucky Assembly, while he himself championed those presented to the Virginia Assembly by Madison (D. R. Anderson, *William Branch Giles*, 1914, pp. 62–64). In 1799 he was elected to the United States Senate, where he quickly became a leader of the Jefferson forces. In 1804 he resigned in order to become collector of the port of Norfolk, but Jefferson still needed his help in Congress and in 1807 he was elected to the House of Representatives. He favored war as a result of the *Chesapeake* and *Leopard* affair but restively supported Jefferson's Embargo. In 1808 he was one of the organizers of Madison's candidacy for the presidency (*Ibid.*, pp. 123–24). Though elected for a second term in Congress, Nicholas resigned in 1809 because of ill health and retired for some years from active public life. In 1814, however, he was elected governor of Virginia and served during the final period of the War of 1812. As soon as this struggle was ended, he turned his attention to the problems of internal improvement and education, and, in his official capacity, collaborated with Jefferson in the foundation of the institution which presently became the University of Virginia (P. A. Bruce, *History of the University of Virginia*, I, 1920, p. 87). On his retirement from office he served for a short time as president of the Richmond branch of the Bank of the United States, but again his health failed and he was forced into his final retirement.

With his brother George he had been a heavy speculator in western lands, and for this or other reasons, his financial affairs became heavily involved in the panic year of 1819. His default on a twenty-thousand-dollar note which Jefferson had indorsed was the crowning blow which brought economic calamity upon his old friend and patron (H. S. Randall, *The Life of Thomas Jefferson,* 1858, III, p. 533). In 1820 Nicholas was stricken and died at the home of his son-in-law, Thomas Jefferson Randolph in Albemarle County, and he was buried in Jefferson's plot at "Monticello." He was a man of solid ability rather than one of brilliant parts; he was worker rather than creator. Throughout his life he was a devoted follower of his great political mentor. Nicholas' son, Robert Carter Nicholas, was United States senator from Louisiana; his daughter Jane married Thomas Jefferson Randolph, grandson of Jefferson.

[There are sketches of the life of Wilson Cary Nicholas in H. B. Grigsby, *Hist. of the Va. Fed. Convention of 1788,* II (1891), 299–310; in L. G. Tyler, *Hist. of Va.* (1924), II, 449; and in R. A. Brock, *Va. and Virginians* (1888), I, 121–29. There is considerable material concerning him in H. S. Randall, *The Life of Thos. Jefferson* (1858), and in Jefferson's published correspondence.]   T. P. A.

NICHOLLS, FRANCIS REDDING TILLOU (Aug. 20, 1834–Jan. 4, 1912), Confederate general, governor and chief justice of Louisiana, was born at Donaldsonville, La., the fifth and youngest son of Louisa Hannah (Drake) Nicholls, the sister of Joseph Rodman Drake [*q.v.*], and Thomas Clark Nicholls, a member of the legislature and judge of the court of appeals. He was the descendant of Edward Church Nicholls who, when disinherited for refusing to become a Roman Catholic priest, emigrated from Cornwall, England, to Maryland and later removed to Louisiana. The boy received his preparatory training at Jefferson Academy in New Orleans, and then, more by accident than because of military taste, entered the United States Military Academy at West Point. He was graduated in 1855, assigned to a second-lieutenant in the artillery, served in Florida in the Seminole campaign, and then was sent to the lonely outpost of Fort Yuma, Cal. The resignation of his commission in 1856 may have been due to overhearing the regimental physician predict his death unless he left that climate. He studied in the law school of the University of Louisiana, now of Tulane University, but, tempted by the offer of an exceedingly large fee, he left the law school before graduation, passed his examination, and won the case. He was married to Caroline Zilpha Guion, the daughter of George Seth Guion, on Apr. 26, 1860.

The outbreak of the Civil War found him a counselor-at-law in Napoleonville, practising with his brother Lawrence, and already attracting attention. Although he did not favor secession, when confronted with the necessity of a choice he chose to go with his state. He entered the Confederate army as captain of a company of infantry, the Phoenix Guards, that he and a brother raised in Ascension and Assumption parishes, but was promptly chosen as lieutenant-colonel of the 8th Louisiana Regiment. Ordered to Virginia he participated in the first battle of Manassas and saw service subsequently with Taylor's brigade in northern Virginia. In the spring of 1862, taking part in Stonewall Jackson's Valley campaign, he fought at Front Royal and Winchester, in which latter battle he was taken prisoner and sustained a wound that cost his left arm. By the following September, when he was exchanged, he had been commissioned colonel of the newly organized 15th Louisiana, but before he could join it he was promoted to the rank of brigadier-general. Although he had lost one arm, he was given command of the 2nd Louisiana brigade. This command he led gallantly in the battle of Chancellorsville, where his horse was shot from under him and his left foot torn off by a shell. He was recognized in Lee's report (*War of the Rebellion, post,* 1 ser. XXV, pt. 1, p. 803) and rewarded by Davis with the offer of a major-generalship, which he was too conscientious to accept since his days of active service at the front were ended. After his convalescence he was placed in command of the post at Lynchburg and on July 28, 1864, was made superintendent of the conscript bureau of the Trans-Mississippi Department, where he served until the close of the war.

He resumed his practice in Napoleonville, until his state again demanded his fighting services, this time in the political arena, for his friends nominated for governor at the Democratic convention in 1876 "all that is left of General Nicholls." His task was to rid the state of negro and Carpet-bag rule. One-armed and one-legged he stumped the state, inspiring courage and awakening enthusiasm. When the returning-board declared his Republican opponent, Packard, elected, the grim warrior ignored the decision, established a *de facto* government, and was ultimately recognized by the federal authorities after a period of dual governments. When a group of city politicians obtained control of his party and succeeded in calling a constitutional convention in 1879 that reduced his term to three years, he declined to be a candidate again and took up his profession in New Orleans. It was during this period of eight years of semi-retirement from public life that he was appointed by President Cleveland to the board of visitors for West Point. In the moral and economic crisis of 1888, while the Louisiana lottery company was bargaining for an extension of its charter by specious offers of revenue without taxation to a debt-ridden state, the people seeking a man with the requisite moral courage and political daring to lead the fight turned once more to him for their gubernatorial candidate. He was elected in the most bitter campaign of Louisiana's history and during his term of office, 1888 to 1892, succeeded in destroying the lottery.

His third period of service, which covered almost the entire remainder of his life, lay in the field of jurisprudence. In 1892 he accepted appointment as chief justice of the supreme court of Louisiana for a term of twelve years. In accordance with the provision of the constitution of 1898 that the judge senior in date of appointment should hold the chief post, a change he recognized as an effort to improve the system, he became associate justice upon his reappointment in 1904 and served until 1911 when ill-health compelled his retirement. He enjoyed the unusual honor of continuing on the pay-roll. In his nineteen years on the bench, he wrote voluminous reports, lucid and painstakingly elaborate, through which he molded Louisiana constitutional law. He spent the year after his retirement on his plantation near Thibodeaux. In the public service that was thrust upon him he served his state well and gained from his fellow citizens a degree of respect rarely accorded. It is significant of the modesty of the man that he died thinking that his sacrifice had hardly been worth the price he had paid, not because of his physical loss but because his services had been of so little worth to the Confederate cause.

[*Asso. of the Grads. of the U. S. Military Acad. Ann. Reunion . . . 1912* (1912); *Biog. Reg. of the Officers and Grads. of the U. S. Mil. Acad.*, Supp., vol. VIA, ed. by Wirt Robinson (1920); *Confed. Mil. Hist.*, ed. by C. A. Evans (1899), vol. X; *War of the Rebellion: Official Records (Army)*, esp. 1 ser. XXVII, pt. 2, XXIX, pt. 2, XXXVII, pt. 1, XL, pt. 3, 2 ser. IV; "The Nicholls Family in La.," *La. Hist. Quart.*, Jan. 1923; *Daily Picayune*, Jan. 5–7, 1912, and *Times-Democrat*, Jan. 5, 1912, of New Orleans; *L'Abeille de La Nouvelle Orleans*, Jan. 6, 1912.]   E. L.

NICHOLLS, RHODA HOLMES (Mar. 28, 1854–Sept. 7, 1930), artist and educator, was born in Coventry, England. The daughter of the Rev. William Grome Holmes, a graduate of Oxford University and vicar of Little Hampton, and Marion (Cooke) Holmes, she was named Rhoda Carleton Marion Holmes. Governesses were her first teachers but as she developed a marked talent for art she was sent to London, to the Bloomsbury School of Art, where she won the Queen's Scholarship, a prize of sixty pounds for three years. She also studied in one of the schools of the Kensington Museum. Lured by the brilliant color of the South, she sacrificed two years of the Queen's prize to go to Italy, where she studied with Vertunni and Cammerano in Rome and became a member of the Circello Artistico Club, in which were gathered artists of many nationalities who criticized each other's work. Her own work immediately attracted attention and she exhibited in Rome, Turin, the Royal Academy in London, and elsewhere. She spent three years in South Africa on her brother's large ostrich farm, returning to England with many beautiful canvases of rich and brilliant colors in oil and water-color. While in Italy she met in Venice Burr H. Nicholls, an American painter. They were married in Lyminster, Sussex, England, in 1884 and they sailed for America almost immediately, where she at once won enthusiastic recognition. She was active as a teacher, her pupils coming from all parts of the country, especially for out-of-door study. For many years she was in charge of the water-color department at the William Chase School at Shinnecock, L. I. She also taught at the Art Students' League, in New York, and for many years conducted summer classes at Gloucester and Provincetown, Mass., or at Kennebunkport, Me. She was on the staff of the *Art Interchange* and the *Art Amateur* and was co-editor of *Palette and Brush*. Aside from her professional activities she was an early champion of the political emancipation of women.

Mrs. Nicholls was also known as an illustrator. Her work ranged all along the line of painting, water-color, wash drawings, crayons, and pastels. She had few rivals and her acute knowledge of drawing and genius for composition are apparent in all her work. She devised a method for water-color painting which came to be widely employed. By having a saturated blotting paper under her water-color paper she could work with more freedom and less speed because the paper could be kept wet indefinitely. A critic writing of the exhibition of the American Water-color Society, says: "In her two works 'Cherries' and 'A Rose,' Mrs. Rhoda Holmes Nicholls shows us a true water-color, executed by a master hand. The subject of each is slight, each stroke of her brush is made once and for all, with a precision and dash that are inspiriting, and you have in each painting the sparkle, the deft lightness of touch, the instantaneous impression of form and coloring that a water-color should have" (*International Studio*, March 1901, p. 80). Her water-colors are well known through their repeated reproduction. It is said that her picture "Those Evening Bells" for which she won the gold medal at the New York Prize Fund Exhibition in 1886, she sold for $100 to a publisher, who eventually realized $30,000 from the reproductions. She was a member of many art groups and won numerous awards, among them medals at the World's Columbian Exposition, 1893; Atlanta, 1895; Nashville, 1897; Buffalo, 1901; and St. Louis, 1904. She is represented in the principal museums and galleries. A special exhibition of her water-colors was given at the Corcoran Gallery of Art in Washington in 1924. She died at Stamford, Conn., having been a sufferer from arthritis for several years. A daughter, a son, and two grand-children survived her.

[*Who's Who in America*, 1926–27; *Am. Art Annual*, 1930; Mich. State Lib., *Biog. Sketches of Am. Artists* (1924); *Art Digest*, Sept. 1930; *Special Exhibition of Water Colors by Rhoda Holmes Nicholls, Corcoran Gallery of Art, Washington, D. C.* (1924); *Hartford Daily Courant*, Sept. 9, 1930; *Evening Star* (Washington), Feb. 17, 1924; *N. Y. Times*, Sept. 8, 1930.] H. W.

NICHOLS, CHARLES HENRY (Oct. 19, 1820–Dec. 16, 1889), physician, psychiatrist, was born at Vassalboro, Kennebec County, Me., the son of Caleb Nichols. He received his academic training in the schools of his native state and at the Friends' School of Providence, R. I. He studied medicine at the University of the City of New York and the University of Pennsylvania, receiving his degree from the latter institution in 1843, after which he practised for a short time at Lynn, Mass. From 1847 to 1849 he served Dr. Amariah Brigham [*q.v.*], one of the pioneers in mental medicine, at the New York State Lunatic Asylum, Utica, N. Y., and from 1849 to 1852 he was resident physician at the Bloomingdale Asylum, New York City.

Nichols is best known as the first superintendent of the Government Hospital for the Insane (now St. Elizabeth's Hospital) at Washington, D. C. In 1852 he was selected by President Fillmore to superintend and take charge of the establishment of that institution. An appropriation of $200,000 was made for the purchase of a site, consisting of 200 acres, and for the construction work required. Nichols prepared the plans for the original building and personally supervised the entire work, meeting the deficiency of this small appropriation by manufacturing the bricks out of the earth dug for the foundation. Architecturally the building was a modified type of the old Kirkbride style, and consisted of a central administrative portion, with wings on each side. Nichols' construction, differing from the older type in that the wings were in echelon, is said to have been twenty-five years in advance of its time, and was reproduced by many of the state hospitals and those of Australia and New-

foundland. A well-appointed lodge for the colored insane, probably the first distinct provision of the kind ever made for the people of that race, was attached to the institution. For a quarter of a century Nichols remained at St. Elizabeth's, erecting additional buildings, acquiring considerable additional land, and at the same time keeping the institution abreast of the most modern curative methods in the treatment of the insane. During the Civil War he acted as volunteer surgeon of the St. Elizabeth's General Army Hospital, and was present as one of General McDowell's staff at the battle of Bull Run.

In 1877 he resigned to accept the position of medical superintendent of the Bloomingdale Asylum in New York City, and when it was decided to build the new hospital at White Plains, he was sent to Europe to study the newest methods of hospital construction. He visited many foreign institutions and the ideas which he obtained were utilized to great advantage in his new construction program. He died shortly after his return to Bloomingdale, and is buried in Congressional Cemetery at Washington, D. C. For a number of years he was president of the Association of American Superintendents of Institutions for the Insane, and was an honorary member of the Medico-Psychological Association of Great Britain. He was one of the most eminent forensic psychiatrists of his time and appeared in many *causae celebrae*. Chiefly remembered perhaps is his testimony for the defense in the trial of the United States *vs.* Charles J. Guiteau, who assassinated President Garfield.

In appearance, Nichols was imposing. Well over six feet tall and broad in proportion, with a commanding presence, he was well fitted by nature to be a leader. The betterment of the conditions of the mentally ill occupied the greater portion of his life. No doubt his interest in this particular class of unfortunates was due to his upbringing among the Quakers, a sect which has supplied so many pioneers in the field of psychiatry. In 1860 he married Ellen G. Maury, daughter of John Maury, at one time mayor of Washington; they had one daughter, who died at an early age, and a son. His first wife having died June 12, 1865, he married in 1872 Sallie (Lathrop) Garlic of Pittsfield, Mass.

[*Joint Select Committee to Investigate the Charities and Reformatory Institutions in the District of Columbia*, pt. III (1898); H. M. Hurd and others, *Institutional Care of the Insane in the U. S. and Canada*, vol. IV (1917); *Am. Jour. of Insanity*, Jan. 1889, Jan. 1890; *Report of the Government Hospital for the Insane*, 1890; *Report of the Proc. in the Case of the U. S. vs. Charles J. Guiteau* (3 vols., 1882), pt. I; *Jour. of Mental Sci.*, Apr. 1890; *N. Y. Tribune*, Dec. 18, 1889; *Evening Star* (Washington, D. C.), Dec. 17, 1889.] W. A. W.

NICHOLS, CHARLES LEMUEL (May 29, 1851–Feb. 19, 1929), physician, bibliophile, author, was the son of Dr. Lemuel Bliss and Lydia Carter (Anthony) Nichols, and grandson of Dr. Ezra and Waity Grey Nichols of Bradford, N. H. Born in Worcester, Mass., he was a "blue baby," whom only infinite care preserved through a precarious infancy for a long life of useful activities, distinguished attainments, and many beneficences. Graduating from Brown University in 1872 with first rank in chemistry, he stayed on at Brown for a year as assistant in that subject. The Cambria Iron Works offered him $10,000 a year as resident chemist; but, holding to his purpose to follow his father's footsteps, he graduated at Harvard Medical School in 1875, served a year as interne in Ward's Island Hospital in New York harbor, and returned to Worcester in 1876 to practise medicine, according to the homeopathic school, to which his father had belonged. A college classmate termed him "a very prince among physicians . . . his patients' physician, friend, and counsellor." His entire life was one of unselfish devotion to parents, family, church, college, and community (Kellen, *post*, pp. 9, 11). He was a founder and long president of the Worcester Associated Charities, president of county and state medical societies, founder of the Worcester Welfare Association, trustee of Brown University, director of the Worcester Free Library, trustee of Westboro Hospital, and an active member of many clubs in Worcester, Boston, Providence, and London. From 1887 to 1907 he lectured on medical history at the Boston University Medical School.

Once firmly established in his profession, he took up bibliography as a hobby, being afflicted with "the incurable disease, Biblio-mania," as he termed it. Elected in 1897 to membership in the American Antiquarian Society, he long served it as recording secretary, councillor, and finally, as president (1927–29). From 1917 he was a member of the Massachusetts Historical Society. These two organizations he enriched with generous gifts of books, historical manuscripts, money, and literary contributions, including printed memoirs of G. Stanley Hall, Albert J. Beveridge, Henry Vignaud, L. P. Kinnicutt, Nathaniel Paine, Franklin Pierce Rice, and Henry E. Huntington. His other publications include: *Bibliography of Worcester* (1899); *The Library of Rameses the Great* (1909), for the Club of Odd Volumes; *Some Notes on Isaiah Thomas and His Worcester Imprints* (1900); *Isaiah Thomas, Printer, Writer and Collector* (1912); *Notes on the Almanacs of*

Massachusetts (1912); *Justus Fox, a German Printer of the Eighteenth Century* (1915); *The Portraits of Isaiah Thomas* (1921); *The Various Forms of the Columbus Codex* (1926); *Samuel Salisbury, a Boston Merchant in the Revolution* (1926); *The Boston Edition of the Baskett Bible* (1927); *Checklist of Maine, New Hampshire and Vermont Almanacs* (1929).

He was twice married: first, in 1877 to Caroline Clinton Dewey, who had one daughter, and died in 1878; second, in 1884, to Mary Jarette Brayton, who died in 1910 leaving two sons and a daughter. In All Saints Church his children placed cloister windows, picturing subjects of his special interest: Gutenberg printing the Bible, Tyndale translating it, and the resulting Reformation.

[W. V. Kellen, *Charles Lemuel Nichols; a Tribute* (1929); L. C. Wroth, "Dr. Nichols of Worcester," *Brown Alumni Monthly*, May 1929; unpublished records of the Class of 1872, Brown University; *Proc. Am. Antiquarian Soc.*, 1929; *The Parish* (pub. by All Saints Church, Worcester), Feb. 24, Nov. 3, 1929; *Worcester Evening Gazette* and *Worcester Evening Post*, Feb. 19, 1929; *The Pastoral Staff* (Springfield, Mass.), Apr. 1929; *Boston Transcript*, Feb. 20, 1929.]   F. W. A.

NICHOLS, CLARINA IRENE HOWARD (Jan. 25, 1810–Jan. 11, 1885), reformer, editor, publicist, was born in Townshend, Windham County, Vt., of English and Welsh ancestry. She was the daughter of Chapin and Birsha (Smith) Howard and the grand-daughter of Levi Howard or Hayward who removed to Townshend from Milford, Mass., about 1775. She became a teacher in public and private schools and is said to have founded a young ladies' seminary in Herkimer, N. Y., about 1835. On Apr. 21, 1830, at Townshend she was married to her first husband, Justin Carpenter. On Mar. 6, 1843, she was married, also at Townshend, to George W. Nichols who was the publisher of the *Windham County Democrat* at Brattleboro. His illness forced her, soon after their marriage, to take the financial and editorial control of his paper. It was in these columns that she began the work for woman's rights that marked the whole of her long career. She wrote editorials from 1843 to 1853, when the paper was discontinued. A series of articles, published in 1847 and addressed to the voters of Vermont, dealt with the property disabilities of women and were important in influencing the passage, in 1848, of the Vermont law to secure to a wife the real estate owned at marriage or thereafter acquired by gift, devise, or inheritance even against the debts of the husband, with the corollary right of disposing of her property by will as if "sole." In 1850 she began speaking for woman's suffrage in her native state, in New Hampshire, and in Massachusetts.

In September and October 1853 she traveled 900 miles in the state of Wisconsin as agent of the woman's state temperance society. As a result of her work and that of others, a law was passed by the Wisconsin legislature to secure to the wives of drunkards their own earnings along with the custody and earnings of their minor children.

In October 1854, with her two eldest sons, she joined a company of 225 emigrants to Kansas. She went directly to Lawrence and at once began lecturing and speaking on woman's rights. Her husband followed with another party but died a few months after his arrival. She returned to Vermont to settle his estate and, while in the East, lectured on Kansas and its problems. In the winter and spring of 1856 she also wrote for the *Herald of Freedom,* published at Lawrence, Kan., a series of articles dealing with women's legal disabilities. Upon her return to Kansas in 1857 with her daughter and her youngest son she went to Wyandotte County, where for some years she made her home. When in 1859 the constitutional convention for Kansas met at Wyandotte, she, knitting in hand, the only woman present, sat through its sessions, "watching every step of the proceedings, and laboring with members to so frame the Constitution as to make all citizens equal before the law" (*History of Woman Suffrage, post,* III, 704). After the Kansas woman's rights association was formed in 1859, as its representative she attended the session of the first state legislature at Topeka in 1860 and by invitation addressed both houses. For the two years preceding this legislative session she had spoken in the towns and hamlets of Missouri that lay along the Kansas border. In 1860 and 1861 she lectured in Wisconsin and Ohio. From December 1863 to March 1866 she was in Washington, D. C., writing in the military and revenue departments, and acting as matron in the home for colored orphans. She returned to Kansas in 1869 and two years later removed to Mendocino County, Cal. She died in Potter Valley. "A good writer, an effective speaker, and a preëminently brave women," she was "gifted with that rarest of virtues, common sense." She "may be said to have sown the seeds of liberty in three states in which she resided," Vermont, Kansas, and California (*History of Woman Suffrage, post,* III, pp. 764–65).

[*Hist of Woman Suffrage,* ed. by E. C. Stanton, S. B. Anthony, and M. J. Gage, esp. vols. I, III (1881–87); *Annals of Brattleboro,* ed. by M. R. Cabot, vol. I (1921); *Gazetteer . . . of Windham County, Vt.,* comp. by Hamilton Child (1884), p. 304; P. W. Morgan, *Hist. of Wyandotte County, Kan.* (1911), vol. I; records in office of secretary of state, Montpelier, Vt.; clipping from *Ukiah* (Cal.) *City Press,* Jan. 16, 1885, in library of the Kan. State Hist. Soc.]   L. K. M. R.

NICHOLS, ERNEST FOX (June 1, 1869–Apr. 29, 1924), physicist, teacher, college president, was born in Leavenworth, Kan., in the Reconstruction period following the Civil War. His father, Alonzo Curtis Nichols, a photographer especially interested in daguerreotypes, and his mother, Sophronia (Fox) Nichols, succumbed to the struggle against poverty and ill health while Nichols was yet a boy, and left him to the care of his maternal uncle, Gen. S. M. Fox, of Manhattan, Kan. His ancestry on both sides was American for many generations back, the family coming from English-Scotch stock which had settled in New England during the early part of the seventeenth century. A frail child, Nichols obtained his elementary education at home. His first institutional schooling was received at the Kansas State Agricultural College at Manhattan, from which he obtained the degree of B.Sc. in 1888. While there he attended an illustrated talk on experimental physics given in the college chapel by Professor Edward L. Nichols of Cornell University. This lecture so stimulated his interest in physics that he decided to devote himself to the study of that subject, and after a year of graduate study in Kansas he went to Cornell to undertake advanced work. The next four years he spent at Ithaca in study and in acquiring experimental technique in his chosen field of radiation. He was appointed associate professor of physics at Colgate University in the fall of 1892 and received the degree of M.Sc. from Cornell the following spring. At Hamilton he made the acquaintance of Katharine Williams West, whom he married on June 16, 1894. She and a daughter survived him.

His first published paper appeared on page 1, Volume I (July-August 1893) of the *Physical Review.* Although this contribution came from Colgate, the work which it described was done at Cornell during the summer of 1892. It consisted of an experimental study of the transmission spectra of a number of substances in the infra-red region extending as far as the wave length 3μ. For this investigation Nichols devised a weak-field galvanometer of such high sensitivity that he was able to measure currents of 10^{-10} amp. The difficulty of working with an instrument so susceptible to external disturbances led him to consider other methods of studying radiation and resulted in the later development of the Nichols radiometer, an instrument which he used in all his more important researches.

In 1894 Nichols obtained leave of absence from Colgate to go to Emil Warburg's laboratory in Berlin. The first task undertaken there was the adaptation of Sir William Crookes's radiometer to the measurement of energy in the infra-red spectrum. Aided by suggestions from Ernst Pringsheim, who had already studied this instrument, Nichols constructed a radiometer with blackened mica vanes hung by a quartz fiber the suspended parts of which weighed only 7 mg. (*Physical Review,* January-February 1897, p. 297). This instrument was so sensitive that a candle 6 meters away produced a deflection of 60 scale divisions. With it he investigated the reflecting powers of silver and of quartz up to 9μ, finding that silver became an almost perfect reflector for wave lengths between 4μ and 9μ and that quartz possessed such strong absorption bands between 8μ and 9μ that it exhibited the properties of metallic reflection.

In this investigation Nichols took his first step in bridging the unexplored region between the visible spectrum and the electro-magnetic waves of Heinrich Hertz, a task which he made one of the principal objectives of his life, and which he successfully completed only on the day of his death. The work under consideration extended the known spectrum from 3μ, to which point it had been brought by Heinrich Rubens, up to 9μ. Nichols' investigation of the absorption bands of quartz led him to develop with Rubens (*Physical Review,* January-February 1897) a new method of isolating a limited portion of the long-wave spectrum without the difficulties attendant upon the use of prisms or gratings. This method of "residual rays" consists in the successive reflection of radiation from surfaces of a substance like quartz which has a narrow absorption band at the wave length to be studied surrounded by regions of transparency. Radiation of the critical wave length is almost completely reflected, while that on either side passes through the surface. Using fluorite the investigators were able to study residual rays of a wave length of 30μ. To measure the wave length accurately, recourse was had to a diffraction grating of fine gold wires and a bolometer, use of the radiometer being precluded by the fact that no substance transparent to these long waves could be found of which to construct the window.

In later papers (*Physical Review,* August, September 1897), Rubens and Nichols studied the residual rays from rock salt and mica as well as those from quartz and fluorite. In these investigations a radiometer with a silver chloride window was used in place of a bolometer, as it had been found that silver chloride was sufficiently transparent to the long waves involved to make the radiometer a much more sensitive detector than the bolometer. The longest radiation investigated was that obtained by reflection from rock salt, which was estimated to be not far from 50μ. Thus the known spectrum of heat rays was extended from the red end of the visible region to a wave length of a twentieth of a millimeter, approximately the thickness of a sheet of paper.

In addition to this extension of the spectrum, the September 1897 paper contained an experimental confirmation of the electromagnetic character of infra-red radiation. As a verification of James Clark Maxwell's electromagnetic theory of light, this work was second in importance only to the famous experiments of Hertz. The method consisted in measuring the radiation reflected from a glass plate covered by minute rectangular silver resonators. In accord with theory and with the results which Augusto Righi had obtained for short electrical waves, the reflection was found to be much greater when the lengths of the resonators approximated a whole number of half-wave lengths than when near an odd number of quarter-wave lengths.

On his return from Germany Nichols completed the requirements for the D.Sc. which was conferred upon him by Cornell in 1897. The following year he left Colgate to accept a professorship of physics at Dartmouth. Here he spent five of the most productive years of his life applying his radiometer to the investigation of important physical problems. His first research, carried out at the Yerkes Observatory during the summers of 1898 and 1900, consisted in the measurement of the relative heat received by the earth from the stars Vega and Arcturus and the planets Jupiter and Saturn. Several years before, Charles Vernon Boys had made a similar attempt with his radiomicrometer, but without success. The sensitivity of the radiometer used by Nichols in this work was sufficient to detect one fifty-millionth of the heat coming from a candle one meter distant, a sensitivity twenty-six times as great as that of Boys's instrument.

Nichols' next investigation, undertaken at Dartmouth with the collaboration of Gordon F. Hull (*Physical Review,* November 1901, *et seq.*), was the crowning achievement of his life. Maxwell had shown as early as 1873 that light, if electromagnetic in nature, should exert a pressure on an obstacle placed in its path, which is twice as great for a perfect reflector as for an ideal absorber. The minuteness of the predicted effect, however, had discouraged experimenters from attempting to detect it. Nichols, nevertheless, had planned as early as his Berlin days to make an effort to measure light pressure with the sensitive radiometer which he had designed. For this purpose the blackened vanes of the instrument were replaced by silvered vanes of high reflecting power and a series of preliminary experiments were made to find the pressure (16 mm. of Hg) at which the effect of the bombardment of gas molecules was a minimum. For gas action, although an advantage in the measurement of heat energy, would only mask the effect of light pressure in the present work. Since gas action increases with the time of exposure, this effect was further reduced by allowing the light to fall on the radiometer vane for a very short time, and measuring the pressure by the ballistic throw. The intensity of the incident light was determined at first by a bolometer, but later more accurately by means of the rise in temperature occasioned by its absorption. Not only was light pressure detected, but the theoretical formula connecting the pressure with the energy per unit volume was verified within a probable error of less than one per cent. Unknown to Nichols and Hull, Peter Lebedew in Moscow was working on the same problem at the same time, and through a strange coincidence the first complete reports of the two independent investigations appeared simultaneously in November 1901 in the *Physical Review* and in Drude's *Annalen der Physic*. Lebedew's results were in complete accord with those of Nichols and Hull, although his method differed in a number of important details.

In 1903 Nichols left Dartmouth to become professor of physics at Columbia University. Here he remained until 1909, with the exception of the winter of 1904–05, spent on leave of absence at Cambridge University, England. During this period he carried out further work on residual rays (*Physical Review*, October 1908), consisting particularly of exact measurements of wave length. Incidentally he showed the complete absence in sunlight, even at the altitude of Mt. Wilson Observatory, of long-wave radiation of the order of 50µ (*Astrophysical Journal*, July 1907).

In addition to being a brilliant investigator, Nichols combined the power of the artist with that of the scientist in devising demonstration experiments to illustrate his lectures and had the rare gift of inspiring his students with a love of productive scholarship. Moreover he exhibited the wise judgment, the eloquence of speech, and the sympathetic appreciation of the viewpoints of others characteristic of a successful administrator. Hence it was natural that the board of regents of Dartmouth College should turn to him in 1909 to fill the vacancy in the presidency caused by the retirement of W. J. Tucker. Although he realized that acceptance would halt his scientific activities, he served in this position for seven years. At the end of that time he had established the college on a secure financial and scholastic basis and felt free to resign in order to accept a professorship of physics at Yale. But before he could resume research the United States entered the World War, and he spent the next two years in investigating schemes proposed by others to combat the submarine menace and in making contributions of his own. In 1920 he left Yale to become director of the Nela Research Laboratory in Cleveland, and a few months later he succeeded Richard Cockburn MacLaurin [*q.v.*] as president of Massachusetts Institute of Technology. Unfortunately he was stricken by a serious illness which made it necessary for him to resign from this position even before he had stepped into active service.

The remaining years of his life were spent at the Nela Laboratory in completing the exploration of the region between the longest known heat rays and the shortest known electrical waves which he had begun twenty-five years earlier. In the intervening time the gap had been shortened to the region from 0.4 mm. to 7.0 mm. This time he approached the unexplored territory from the long-wave length side, developing, in collaboration with James DeGraff Tear, a Hertzian oscillator consisting of a spark gap in kerosene between tungsten cylinders only 0.01 mm. apart. The receiver was a radiometer whose vanes carried minute platinum resonators which absorbed the waves to which they were tuned. With this apparatus fundamental wave lengths were obtained as short as 0.9 mm. and harmonics down to 0.22 mm. The work was completed in time for Nichols to report the complete closing of the gap between heat rays and electrical waves at the spring meeting of the National Academy of Sciences in 1924. In the middle of his paper, the speaker's heart stopped, and before medical aid could arrive he had passed away. Among other honors Nichols received the Rumford medal of the American Academy of Arts and Sciences in 1907, and was given honorary degrees by Dartmouth, Colgate, Clark, Wesleyan, Vermont, Pittsburgh, and Denison. He was chairman of the physics and engineering section of the National Academy of Sciences from 1917 to 1920, a member of the American Philosophical and many other societies, and a fellow of the American Physical Society.

[E. L. Nichols, "Ernest Fox Nichols," *Nat. Acad. Sci. . . . Biog. Memoirs*, vol. XII (1929); Philip Fox, "Ernest Fox Nichols," *Astrophysical Jour.*, Jan. 1925; Augustus Trowbridge, "Ernest Fox Nichols," *Science*,

May 9, 1924; *Electrical World*. May 10, 1924; *Light*, June 1924; *N. Y. Times*, Apr. 30, 1924.]   L. P.

NICHOLS, GEORGE WARD (June 21, 1831–Sept. 15, 1885), promoter of art education and music in Cincinnati, was born in the village of Tremont, Mount Desert, Me., the son of John and Esther Todd (Ward) Nichols. His father and grandfather were sea-captains. In 1835 the family moved to Boston, Mass., where George received a public-school education. He appears to have entered journalism promptly upon leaving school. Later he went to Kansas and was active in the political and military struggle which attended the organization of that state. In 1859 he spent some time in Europe, principally in Paris, where he studied painting under the direction of Thomas Couture, and upon his return was art editor on the New York *Evening Post*, writing also for magazines. On Apr. 25, 1862, he entered the Union army as a captain, and served at first on the staff of Frémont. Subsequently (1863), he was detailed to assist the provost-marshal general's department in Wisconsin, after which duty he was a recruiting officer until 1864, when he was made aide-de-camp on the personal staff of General Sherman. He accompanied Sherman on his march to the sea and was with him until the conclusion of the war. Upon his resignation he was brevetted lieutenant-colonel of volunteers.

From a full diary which he kept while in the service, Nichols immediately compiled a volume entitled *The Story of the Great March* (1865), which had a sale of 60,000 copies within a year, besides being reprinted in English newspapers and being translated (it is said) into Spanish, French, and German. Perhaps hoping to repeat this success—which, however, resulted from the fame of Sherman's exploits rather than from Nichols' literary skill—he utilized the same matter in the composition of a war-novel, *The Sanctuary* (1866). This artless story, conventional in motivation and stilted in language, attracted no widespread attention and was soon completely forgotten.

Shortly after the close of the war, Nichols went to Cincinnati with Sherman, and there met Maria Longworth, aunt of Nicholas Longworth, 1869–1931 [*q.v.*], whom on May 6, 1868, he married. From this time Cincinnati was his home, and he quickly made himself felt there as an energetic, commanding force, promoting the cultural development of the city. He had much to do with the founding of the School of Design, which was at first a part of the University of Cincinnati and was later transferred to the Art Museum. Convinced that a large and profitable field awaited the employment of trained artists and craftsmen in industry, he busied himself in advancing the cause of art education. In 1877 he published *Art Education Applied to Industry*, and in 1878 *Pottery: How it is Made, its Shape, and Decoration*. These are straightforwardly written and well-arranged manuals, on the whole skilfully adapted to their purpose. His most conspicuous and important service to the arts, however, lay in another direction. The Harmonic Society of Cincinnati under his presidency and management gave a series of concerts which were so successful as to suggest a more elaborate undertaking, and in 1872 the May Festival Association was organized with Nichols at its head. The first musical festival took place in 1873, and he continued to direct the affairs of the Association until 1880, during which time three festivals were held. Meanwhile, in 1879, with the aid chiefly of Reuben R. Springer [*q.v.*], he established the College of Music of Cincinnati and became its first president, a position which he held until his death from pulmonary tuberculosis. He was a born "promoter," with remarkable executive capacity, determination, and self-confidence, with the result "that his career often seemed to those about him too full of his own individuality for the most comfortable enjoyment of easy social friendship" (Cox, *post*, p. 25). Yet it may be said, in general, that Cincinnati owes its importance as a musical center very largely to his audacity and diligence.

[*Cincinnati Enquirer* and *Cincinnati Commercial Gazette*, Sept. 16, 1885; *Cincinnati Times-Star*, Sept. 15, 1885; *Circulars, Papers and Annual Meeting of the Ohio Commandery of the Military Order of the Loyal Legion During the Year 1885* (1887); J. D. Cox, in *Memorial Services in Honor of George Ward Nichols . . . Mar. 4, 1887* (1887); C. T. Greve, *Centennial Hist. of Cincinnati* (1904), vol. I; *The Biog. Cyc. and Portrait Gallery with an Hist. Sketch of the State of Ohio*, vol. IV (n.d.); *Harper's Weekly*, Sept. 26, 1885; local records, Town of Mount Desert, Me.]
R. S.

NICHOLS, JAMES ROBINSON (July 18, 1819–Jan. 2, 1888), chemist, son of Stephen and Ruth (Sargent) Nichols, was born at West Amesbury (now Merrimac), Mass., and died at Haverhill, Mass. His early life was spent on his father's farm, where he acquired an interest in agriculture and utilized his spare hours in study. At the age of eighteen he became associated with his uncle, Moses Nichols, who was a druggist in Haverhill. His desire for a formal education was not gratified; in fact the only academic connection he had was attendance on a course of lectures at the medical school of Dartmouth College in 1841–42. This connection was broken by illness and he did not graduate.

His work there, however, supplemented by numerous specific contributions to chemistry, pharmacy, and science in general, was recognized by the institution a quarter of a century later, and he was granted the degree of M.D. in 1867 and the honorary degree of M.A. He returned to the drug business in Haverhill in 1843, but left most of the work to assistants so that he could pursue his investigations in the laboratory. He gave considerable time also to studying chemistry, lecturing, and writing. After an extended tour through Europe, he gave up his drug business in Haverhill in 1857 and established in Boston the firm of J. R. Nichols & Company, for the manufacture of fine chemicals and medical preparations. Its property was destroyed by the great fire of 1872 and Nichols retired from the firm, but the business was resumed by his partners under the name of Billings, Clapp & Company. During his connection with the concern he made several trips to Europe in an effort to learn the process of manufacturing the finer chemicals, *e.g.*, those used in medicine, photography, dyeing, and painting, his aim being to supply these products which had previously been imported at considerable expense. He was responsible for the introduction of new chemical and pharmaceutical compounds, and of more economical methods for manufacturing them. Soda-water apparatus, the carbonic-acid fire extinguishers and the leather-board industry, were the results of inventions which he made. An improved form of hot-air furnace of his devising had extensive use (*Popular Science News*, Feb. 1, 1888).

In July 1866 he founded the *Boston Journal of Chemistry and Pharmacy,* which was the first publication in the United States devoted to the exposition of chemistry in a popular but accurate way. The following year the name was changed to *Boston Journal of Chemistry* and remained as such until January 1881, when it was merged with a scientific periodical having a wider field, and was known first as the *Boston Journal of Chemistry and Popular Science Review,* and later, as *The Popular Science News and Boston Journal of Chemistry*. This journal, of which, under its various names, he was the editor-in-chief until his death, had a large circulation and exercised a marked influence on the growth of interest in the simpler aspects of chemistry. Besides numberless editorials and articles he wrote *Chemistry of the Farm and the Sea* (1867), *Fireside Science* (1872), *From Whence, What, Where?* (1882), the sixth edition (1883) being entitled *Whence, What, Where?* and *Science at Home* (1883). Always

interested in books, he founded the Merrimac Public Library in 1877, presented it with a large number of volumes, and continued his interest and help from year to year until his death.

His unbroken interest in agriculture led him in 1863 to buy a large tract of land in Haverhill. Here he built a summer home called "Winnekeni Castle" and tried out many experiments with chemical fertilizers. His investigations led to practical results of value which were freely given to farmers. In 1878 he was made a member of the state Board of Agriculture. From 1873 to 1878 he was president of the Vermont & Canada Railroad, and from 1873 until his death, a director of the Boston & Maine Railroad. In 1844 he married Harriet Porter and in 1851 Margaret Gale. His only son was associated with him in many enterprises.

[Information from a descendant; H. A. Kelly and W. L. Burrage, *Am. Medic. Biogs.* (1920); *Biog. Encyc. of Mass. of the Nineteenth Century,* vol. II (1883); *Haverhill Gazette,* and *Daily Evening Bulletin* (Haverhill), Jan. 3, 1888; *Popular Sci. News,* Feb. 1, 1888; *Boston Jour.,* and *Boston Herald,* Sept. 21, 1870.]

L. C. N.

NICHOLS, MARY SARGEANT NEAL GOVE (Aug. 10, 1810–May 30, 1884), author, reformer, and water-cure physician, was born in Goffstown, N. H., the daughter of William and Rebecca Neal. Her girlhood was spent in Craftsbury, Vt., her parents having moved to this village when she was a small child. She had little formal schooling but educated herself as completely as possible by wide reading. Books on anatomy and physiology held a special fascination for her, and in spite of ridicule she persisted in studying them. As a young woman she taught in a district school, contributed tales and verse to local papers, and believed that she was destined for some peculiar mission in the world. In 1831 she married Hiram Gove, of Weare, N. H. This marriage proved most unhappy. After the birth of a daughter in 1832, Mrs. Gove began to devote herself to a study of books on health, receiving help and encouragement from kindly physicians. About 1837 her husband removed to Lynn, Mass., and there she found opportunity to use her knowledge in teaching anatomy and physiology to young women. Her work aroused interest and she was invited to lecture in other New England towns. Opposed by her husband in her beliefs and way of life, she separated from him in 1840, and the same year assumed for a brief period the editorship of the *Health Journal and Advocate of Physiological Reform,* a periodical published in Worcester, Mass., setting forth the principles of vegetarianism.

Ill health and difficulty in obtaining the custody of her child darkened the next few years of her life, but she persevered in her chosen field and by 1844 had established herself in New York as a water-cure physician. From 1845 to 1853 she contributed extensively to the New York *Water-Cure Journal,* published *Lectures to Women on Anatomy and Physiology* (1846), *Experience in Water-Cure* (1849), and several novelettes. She was included by Poe in his account of *The Literati,* and became well known in reform circles for her advocacy of mesmerism, spiritualism, Fourierism, temperance, and dress reform. On July 29, 1848, divorced from her first husband, she married Thomas Low Nichols [*q.v.*]. One child was born of this marriage. From 1851 to 1853 they carried on a school in New York for the training of water-cure practitioners, both of them speaking and writing, meantime, for almost all the radical causes of the day. In 1853 they joined in editing *Nichols' Journal,* a monthly magazine, published in Cincinnati, Ohio, setting forth the theory of "individual sovereignty," especially the theory of freedom in love. In 1854 they published a volume called *Marriage: Its History, Character, and Results,* expounding the same ideas. Later Mrs. Nichols published *Mary Lyndon; or Revelations of a Life* (1855), a frank account of her own career.

When the Civil War broke out, Mrs. Nichols and her husband left America for England, where they spent the remainder of their lives. They established a hydropathic institution at Great Malvern and continued their efforts to spread knowledge of sanitary science. Mrs. Nichols contributed frequently after 1875 to the London *Herald of Health,* and was well known in English vegetarian and spiritualistic societies. During her later years she was a great sufferer, but the energy and will power that had carried her through many vicissitudes enabled her to continue her work almost to the last day of her life. She died in London in her seventy-fourth year, a dauntless crusader for many unpopular causes.

[In addition to *Revelations of a Life* see: Sarah J. Hale, *Biog. of Distinguished Women* (1876); files of the *Water-Cure Jour.,* 1845–54; E. A. Poe, *The Literati* (1850); *Nichols' Health Manual* (1887); *Dietetic Reformer and Vegetarian Messenger,* July 1884.]

B. M. S.

NICHOLS, THOMAS LOW (1815–1901), pioneer dietician, hydrotherapist, author, and editor, was a descendant of early English settlers in Massachusetts. He spent an uneventful boyhood in his native village, Orford, N. H., and some quiet years at the end of his life in France. Between these two periods he was engaged in ceaseless activity to bring about some radical social or sanitary reform. He began the study of medicine at Dartmouth College, abandoned it for journalism, served an apprenticeship on newspapers in Lowell and New York, and in 1837 became the editor and part proprietor of a political paper called the *Buffalonian.* This he edited with such vehemence that he was sentenced to four months' imprisonment for libel. His first book, *Journal in Jail* (Buffalo, 1840), is a lively egotistical account of this experience. The next fifteen years of his life he spent in New York City, advocating with voice and pen the ideas of Sylvester Graham on vegetarianism and the social theories of Fourier, Josiah Warren, and J. H. Noyes. On July 29, 1848, he married Mary S. Gove [see Nichols, Mary Sargeant Neal Gove], a water-cure physician, and after completing his medical course at the University of the City of New York (1850), joined her in founding a school for the training of water-cure practitioners. He published *Esoteric Anthropology* in 1853, *Marriage: Its History, Character, and Results,* written jointly with his wife, in 1854, and wrote voluminously for the *American Vegetarian and Health Journal* and for the *Water-Cure Journal.* When his views on social questions became too radical for these papers, he and his wife established, in 1853, *Nichols' Journal of Health, Water-Cure, and Human Progress.* In 1855 they removed to Cincinnati, where they continued their paper as *Nichols' Monthly* (1855–57), setting forth in it the doctrines of free love, spiritualism, health reform, and individual liberty. For a short time (1856–57) they conducted a water-cure and "School of Life" at Yellow Springs, Ohio. Soon after this they became converts to Catholicism, were received into the church, and for two years gave lectures on hygiene in Catholic institutions in the Mississippi Valley.

With the outbreak of the Civil War they left the United States. Nichols did not believe in the war and felt that he owed no duty to a "military despotism." Thereafter he made his home in England. In 1864 he published *Forty Years of American Life,* two volumes of vivid, well-written social history. From 1867 to 1875 he and his wife conducted a hydropathic institute at Great Malvern. There he wrote a widely popular little volume entitled *How to Live on Sixpence a Day* (1871). In 1875 he began the publication of the London *Herald of Health,* and continued as its editor until 1886, trying through its columns to raise the standard of health and to teach temperate living. He established a Sanitary Depot in London as a distributing center for his publications and for the health foods and sanitary appliances which he invented. He said little during his later years on the subject of his radical social theories but lectured frequently on food reform, which he had come to regard as the root of all questions. Of his later works *Eating to Live* (1881), *Dyspepsia* (1884), and *Nichols' Health Manual* (1887) are most important. The last years of his life were spent in complete retirement. He died at Chaumont-en-Vezin, France, at the age of eighty-five, widely known as a great pioneer of food reform.

[In addition to the *Jour. in Jail* and *Forty Years of Am. Life* see: *Nichols' Health Manual* (1887); files of the New York *Water-Cure Jour., Nichols' Monthly,* the London *Herald of Health* and *Dietetic Reformer.*]

B. M. S.

NICHOLS, WILLIAM FORD (June 9, 1849–June 5, 1924), second Protestant Episcopal bishop of the diocese of California, was born in Lloyd, N. Y. His father, Charles Hubert, a business man, was of old colonial stock, his first American ancestor being Francis Nichols, one of the proprietors of Stratford, Conn. His mother, Margaret Emilia (Grant) of Hobart, Delaware County, N. Y., was of Scotch descent and vigorous Scotch character. At Dutchess County Academy and at the Poughkeepsie Collegiate School, from which he graduated in 1866 first in his class, William prepared for Trinity College, Hartford, Conn. His decision to enter the ministry, although reached only after long deliberation, was the normal outcome of his training and character. He entered the Berkeley Divinity School, Middletown, Conn., in the autumn of 1870. Through the latter part of his course and for three years after his graduation, he served as secretary to the bishop of Connecticut, Dr. John Williams [*q.v.*], who became a determinative influence in his life.

He was made deacon on June 4, 1873, and ordained priest exactly a year later. His first parish was St. James', West Hartford, with the care of Grace Church, Newington. On May 18, 1876, he married Clara Quintard, daughter of Edward Augustus Quintard of New York. To them two sons and three daughters were born. In 1877 he became rector of Christ Church, Hartford, and there his gifts as pastor and administrator were quickly revealed. From 1885 to 1887 he added the duties of professor of church history at Berkeley Divinity School. In 1887 he accepted the rectorship of St. James' Church, Philadelphia. The following year he declined an election as assistant bishop of Ohio; but when California elected him in February 1890 to a like position he accepted and was consecrated on June 24. Bishop William I. Kip [*q.v.*], then over eighty, placed the entire administration in Nichols' hands, and after the death of the former in April 1893, Nichols succeeded him. The area, still administered from San Francisco, was very large; churches were widely scattered; unity of action was difficult. Los Angeles and the southern part of the state were beginning to grow with unexampled rapidity. Nichols saw that for effective church work there must be a division of territory. Such a division was made in 1895 by the erection of the diocese of Los Angeles; and fifteen years later, the vast central valley of San Joaquin with the mountains to the east was in its turn separated from the parent diocese.

Bishop Nichols' episcopate was notable for many reasons other than the general growth of the Church. He founded in 1893 at San Mateo the Church Divinity School of the Pacific (moved in 1930 to Berkeley), acted as its dean for thirty years, and also served as professor of church history. From its foundation in 1907 in Berkeley he guided the work of the Deaconess Training School of the Pacific. He organized the Cathedral chapter of the diocese, and after the earthquake and fire of 1906 secured the gift of a strategic site and began the building of Grace Cathedral. He reorganized completely the administration of the diocese, established sound financial policies, and vastly increased its resources. Through his initiative there was established in 1904 the House of Churchwomen, an official body acting in collaboration with the Convention. After the earthquake and fire he rendered distinguished service not only through his leadership in rehabilitating parishes and rebuilding churches, but also as a member of the citizens' committee in general relief work. He was early associated with General Convention as assistant secretary of the House of Bishops, was deputy from Pennsylvania in 1889, and after he became bishop was a member of many important commissions and committees. In 1902 he went to the Hawaiian Islands to carry out the transfer of the property and jurisdiction of the Church of England there to the Protestant Episcopal Church. When provinces were organized by General Convention in 1915 he was elected first president of the Province of the Pacific (comprising the coast and adjacent mountain states), holding the office until failing health led to his resignation in 1921. He continued the administration of his diocese alone until 1919, when a coadjutor was elected, to whom the Bishop surrendered the heavier work.

He traveled extensively, twice going to Europe officially; first in 1884, as delegate to the Seabury Centenary at Aberdeen, and in 1897, as a member of the Lambeth Conference. In 1911 he went around the world, commemorating the journey in a considerable book of reminiscences—*Some World-Circuit Saunterings* (1913). Among his other publications were *On the Trial of your Faith* (pamphlet, 1895); *A Father's Story of the Earthquake and Fire in San Francisco April 18, 19, 20, 1906* (pamphlet, 1906); *Apt and Meet; Counsels to Candidates for Holy Orders at the Church Divinity School of the Pacific* (1909); *Days of My Age* (1923), an autobiography; *Memories Here and There of the Fourth Bishop of Connecticut* (pamphlet, 1924).

In churchmanship Nichols was commonly accounted conservative; but his mind was unusually alert to world movements of thought, he welcomed the advances of science, and his sympathies were broad; he belonged to no school. In character he was well poised, wise, judicious, slow in forming judgments, inflexible in carrying them out when formed.

[In addition to autobiography mentioned above, see D. O. Kelley, *Hist. of the Diocese of Cal. from 1849 to 1914* (1915); C. C. Tiffany, *A Hist. of the Protestant Episcopal Ch. in the U. S. A.* (rev. ed., 1898); W. S. Perry, *The Bishops of the Am. Ch. Past and Present* (1897); *Who's Who in America, 1924–25; San Francisco Chronicle*, June 6, 1924.]   E. L. P.

NICHOLSON, ALFRED OSBORNE POPE (Aug. 31, 1808–Mar. 23, 1876), United States senator and jurist, the son of O. P. Nicholson and Saachy Hunter, was born in Williamson County, Tenn. After graduation from the University of North Carolina in 1827, he attended lectures in Jefferson Medical College in Philadelphia. He never practised medicine, however; instead, he became editor of the Columbia, Tennessee, *Mercury*, and a member of the local bar. In 1829 he married Caroline O'Reilly. He was an able lawyer; in cooperation with R. L. Caruthers he prepared *A Compilation of the Statutes of Tennessee* (Nashville, 1836); and in 1851, on the appointment of Gov. William Trousdale, he served for a few months as chancellor for the Middle Division of Tennessee. He was prominently identified with the development of railroads in Tennessee, as a director of the Nashville & Chattanooga and other railroads, and as an able advocate of the granting by the state of financial aid in railroad construction. In 1847 he was president of the Bank of Tennessee. Like many young lawyers, Nicholson entered actively into political life. In 1833 he began a series of three consecu-

tive terms in the Tennessee House of Representatives, and subsequently (1843–45), he was a member of the state Senate. In 1835 he gave temporary support to the presidential candidacy of Hugh Lawson White, but he soon returned to the Jacksonian camp, supported Van Buren's candidacy, and thereafter was a faithful and prominent worker in the Democratic party. Upon the death of Felix Grundy he was appointed by Gov. James K. Polk to serve a portion (1840–42) of Grundy's unexpired term in the United States Senate. He was an ardent supporter of Polk's presidential candidacy in 1844, and on the solicitation of the President-elect he became editor of Polk's organ and the leading Democratic newspaper in Tennessee, the *Nashville Union*. As a reward for his effective services in this capacity during the state campaign of 1845, it was expected that he would be sent again to the United States Senate. Polk desired this and the Democratic legislative caucus nominated Nicholson, but a combination of the Whig minority with anti-administration Democrats prevented his election. Nevertheless, he was recognized soon as the leader of his party in Tennessee. He supported the presidential candidacy of Lewis Cass in 1848 and was the recipient of the famous "Nicholson Letter" in which Cass sought to explain his views on the Wilmot Proviso (W. L. G. Smith, *Fifty Years of Public Life: The Life and Times of Lewis Cass*, 1856, pp. 607–16). He was a member of the Tennessee delegation in both sessions of the Southern Convention that met in Nashville in 1850, but his influence in that body was conservatively against secession and in advocacy of the acceptance of the compromise measures of 1850. He became a close friend of President Pierce but refused a place in the cabinet. Instead, as a result of the President's influence, he assumed the editorship of the administration organ, the Washington *Daily Union* (though not very effectively), and was chosen public printer to the House of Representatives. In 1857 he was elected to succeed John Bell upon the expiration of the latter's senatorial term in 1859. By no means a "fire eating" secessionist, he gave his support to the Confederacy after Tennessee's withdrawal from the Union, and for this he was expelled from the Senate on July 11, 1861. After the Civil War he was one of the leaders of the majority in Tennessee that were disfranchised by the Radicals. He was an influential member of the constitutional convention of Tennessee in 1870 that completed the overthrow of the Radical régime. For the remaining years of his life, 1870–76, he was chief justice of the supreme court of his state. He died at Columbia, Tenn.

[W. S. Speer, *Sketches of Prominent Tennesseans* (1888), pp. 332–33; J. W. Caldwell, *Sketches of the Bench and Bar of Tenn.* (1898), pp. 227–30; Roy F. Nichols, *Franklin Pierce* (1931); J. T. Moore, *Tenn.: The Volunteer State* (1923), vol. II; *Biog. Dir. Am. Cong.* (1928); Philip M. Hamer, *Tenn.; A Hist.* (1933).]   P. M. H.

NICHOLSON, ELIZA JANE POITE-VENT HOLBROOK (Mar. 11, 1849–Feb. 15, 1896), newspaper proprietor and poet, was born near Pearlington, in Hancock County, Miss., the daughter of William J. Poitevent and Mary A. (Russ) Poitevent. Her mother being an invalid, Eliza grew up under the care of an aunt near what is now Picayune, Miss. In July 1867 she was graduated from the Amite (Louisiana) Female Seminary. She began to write verses "while still almost a mere girl," contributing to New Orleans papers, and to the *Home Journal* and the *Ledger* of New York. Her first productions were published in a little sheet called the *South,* whose editor, J. W. Overall, gave her encouragement. Her verses appeared over the signature Pearl Rivers, a *nom de plume* most happily chosen, since the Pearl River ran close to her girlhood home, and in its valley she spent her most impressible years. Her poems attracted the attention of Col. A. M. Holbrook, editor of the New Orleans *Picayune,* and in the summer of 1870 poems by Pearl Rivers began to be a feature of the Sunday issue. Her career and that of the paper from that time were closely connected. It has been frequently stated that she became literary editor of the *Picayune* in 1874 at a weekly salary of $25, and that she and Holbrook were married a few months later. Actually, her poems began to appear after July 1870, and according to the legal records the marriage took place on May 18, 1872. Her position as "literary editor" seems to have meant that her verses were regularly printed on the front page of the *Picayune,* for she signed no books reviews or dramatic criticisms, although she did contribute some short prose narratives.

Holbrook sold the paper to a company of New Orleans merchants in January 1872. A selection from her newspaper verses was printed in 1873 entitled *Lyrics by Pearl Rivers.* The volume was warmly reviewed in the *Picayune* on Apr. 6, 1873, and was praised by many, including Paul Hamilton Hayne. In December 1874 Holbrook regained control of the *Picayune,* but his illness and death (January 1876) prevented him from putting the paper on its feet, so that his wife was left with a debt of $80,000 and a dubious title to the paper. About six months after Holbrook's death George Nicholson acquired an interest in the paper. A native of Leeds, England, he had gone to New Orleans in 1842 and had worked up to the position of business manager of the *Picayune.* On June 27, 1878, Mrs. Holbrook and Nicholson were married. From that time on the affairs of the paper gradually improved, until it became a prosperous enterprise. Mrs. Nicholson took an intimate interest in her paper. She introduced a society column into the Sunday issue, an innovation which conservative New Orleans society regarded at first with mild dismay. She supported many public movements, particularly the efforts of Sophie B. Wright to improve public education. Her decisions were rapid and intuitive rather than cautious, but were usually lucky. She was the first woman in the South to become proprietor of an important newspaper.

The *Lyrics* of 1873 and three small pamphlets contain all her accessible poems, numbering about fifty in all. Her best poems deal with some phase of country life and are filled with memories of swamp maples in bud, wild briers, and partridge-calls. The ambitious dramatic monologues *Hagar* and *Leah,* in spite of some good lines, are rhetorical rather than passionate. The sincerity of her emotions is usually evident, though sometimes obscured by inadequate technique and expression. It was the feeling in her poems which appealed to her many readers. Although she was slight in build and unassuming in manner, she succeeded in leaving vivid impressions of her personality. She was particularly fond of travel. She died ter. days after her husband, in an influenza epidemic, leaving two sons.

[Information from files of the *Picayune* and the New Orleans *Times;* J. H. Harrison, *Pearl Rivers, Publisher of the Picayune* (1932), pub. by the Dept. of Education, Tulane Univ.; *Biog. and Hist. Memoirs of La.* (1892), vol. II; *Lib. of Southern Lit.,* vol. IX (1909); *La. Hist. Quart.,* Oct. 1923; *Times-Democrat* (New Orleans), and *Daily Picayune,* Feb. 16, 1896.]
                                      R. P. M.

NICHOLSON, FRANCIS (Nov. 12, 1655–Mar. 5, 1728), colonial governor, was born at Downholme Parke, near Richmond, in Yorkshire, England, on a part of the vast Bolton estate, but his parentage is not known. It has been suggested (Dalton, *post*) that he was a natural son of Lord St. John, later Duke of Bolton, who came into possession of the property shortly before Nicholson's birth. But more probably, he was the son or grandson of a certain Francis Nicholson, who had assisted the Earl of Sunderland, former owner of the estate, in arranging his children's inheritance in 1629 ("Yorkshire

Royalist Composition Papers," vol. I, *Yorkshire Archæological Society. Record Series,* vol. XV, 1893, pp. 56–57). In either case, the Duke of Bolton took an active interest in Nicholson's career. In his youth Nicholson served as page to his patron's wife. He entered the army in 1679 and spent a few years in Tangier, acting as courier and aide-de-camp to the governor. After returning to England with his regiment, he is said to have knelt during mass in the tent of James II on Hounslow Heath, though his later career shows him to have been a stanch Anglican. His long connection with the colonies began in 1686 with his appointment as captain of a company of foot sent to New England under Sir Edmund Andros [*q.v.*]. Soon afterward, Nicholson was sworn a member of the Council for the Dominion of New England, and in 1688 he was commissioned lieutenant-governor. Andros was at Pemaquid and Nicholson at New York when news came of the Revolution in England. The latter handled the local situation badly. His indiscreet remarks angered the followers of Jacob Leisler [*q.v.*], while the concessions which he made to popular feeling only resulted in his losing control of the fort. Eventually he decided to sail for England, ostensibly to report on the uprising but probably in reality to avoid imprisonment.

He was disappointed in his hope of returning to New York as governor, but the home officials showed their confidence in him by appointing him lieutenant-governor of Virginia, the absentee governor of which was the Roman Catholic, Lord Howard of Effingham. Nicholson now began what was probably his most successful administration. Always taking a broad, and even continental, view of colonial affairs, he made several trips to the interior to study frontier conditions. He also sent a personal agent through the northern colonies to report on the situation there. He encouraged the establishment of postal services within Virginia and between that province and New York. His most enduring service to Virginia was the support and financial assistance he gave to the commissary, the Rev. James Blair [*q.v.*], in the founding of the College of William and Mary. In 1692 Nicholson was replaced as chief executive by Sir Edmund Andros, who had succeeded Lord Howard as governor. But two years later Nicholson was back in America, this time as governor of Maryland. Here, as in every colony in which he served, he labored to advance the causes of the Anglican church and of education, the two matters closest to his heart. His activities in these directions were so exten-

sive as to lead to the report in England a few years later that he had established "two universities and 28 churches" in America (Narcissus Luttrell, *A Brief Historical Relation of State Affairs,* 1857, vol. V, 292). As far as education was concerned, the report was exaggerated, for Blair deserves most of the credit for the College of William and Mary, while the little King William's School at Annapolis (later St. John's College), which Nicholson helped to found, did not attain collegiate rank during the colonial period. Yet, everywhere he went, Nicholson encouraged the building of schools and churches, both by appeals to the assemblies for necessary legislation and by generous gifts from his own funds. He was largely responsible for the removal of the Maryland capital from St. Mary's to the more centrally located Annapolis. He was less successful in persuading the assemblies of Maryland and Virginia to aid in the defense of New York. The Maryland legislature did agree in 1694 to send £133 if he would advance the sum, but when he offered to repeat the loan a year later, the assembly refused to accept it. The last years of this administration were marred by a series of bitter personal quarrels, during which Nicholson's ungovernable temper destroyed much of his earlier popularity. But, on the whole, he showed more than average ability in office and his services were rewarded in 1698 by his promotion to the full governorship of Virginia.

His second term in this colony was far less successful than the first. His temper became more violent than before and led to his estrangement from Commissary Blair after the latter had read him a lecture on conduct. Nicholson's dictatorial behavior aroused the opposition of several leading councilors, who accused him of trying to dominate the Council. The charge was doubtless true, although his opponents, who represented the colonial aristocracy, were equally as guilty as the governor of attempting to dominate provincial affairs. Yet he managed to do much for the good of the colony. He was the leading spirit in the removal of the capital from Jamestown to Williamsburg and in the establishment there of adequate facilities for governmental offices. He greatly improved the provincial finances and succeeded, at least partially, in making the local administration more efficient. He continued his interest in intercolonial affairs and once went personally to New York to confer with Governor Cornbury on problems of mutual concern. His downfall came, not because of a hostile Assembly, for the House of Burgesses continued friendly to the end, but because of the little group of aristocratic councilors whom he had antagonized. He was recalled in 1705.

Of his life in England during the next four years we know little except that he was elected a fellow of the Royal Society in 1706. When a joint attack upon Canada and Port Royal was proposed in 1709, he volunteered to accompany its commander, Samuel Vetch [q.v.]. Although Nicholson had attained the rank of colonel several years before, his actual military experience was slight. But he was so active in organizing the northern colonies for the enterprise that their governors persuaded him to command the contingent which was to march northward from New York. However, the whole scheme fell through when the promised troops failed to arrive from England. Nicholson returned to that country with a request from Massachusetts to renew the attack upon Port Royal the following year. The British government agreed and Nicholson, now a brigadier-general, was made commander in chief of the expedition. With 400 marines and 1,500 colonial troops, he effected a bloodless conquest of Port Royal in October 1710, thus establishing British military supremacy on the Acadian peninsula. In 1711 another joint military and naval attack upon Quebec was proposed. Nicholson was given a commission as lieutenant-general in America and made commander of the troops which were to go by land from New York. But the shipwreck of part of Admiral Walker's fleet in the St. Lawrence led to the abandonment of the entire expedition. Late in 1713 Nicholson was named governor of Nova Scotia, but he spent only a few weeks there, for he also had a series of commissions to inquire into provincial finances, clandestine trade, prize money, and ecclesiastical affairs, throughout the northern colonies. As a sort of "Governour of Governours," he proved a failure, for his temperament irritated the other colonial executives. Governor Robert Hunter [q.v.] of New York, who did not sympathize with his high-church views and who directed his farce Androborus against him, called him "that eternall teazer," and declared that "for the present folks have no manner of occasion for madmen" (New York Colonial Documents, V, 400, 453). On the other hand, the Anglicans of Newbury, Mass., praised Nicholson as "that worthy patron of vertue and religion" (Calendar State Papers, Colonial . . . 1712–1714, 1926, p. 258). His various commissions were not renewed after the accession of George I and he retired to England. During the next few years the Board of Trade often called upon him for advice on colonial matters, but he was never rewarded for his American services with knighthood as has commonly been supposed.

In 1720 he undertook his last colonial governorship, that of South Carolina, whose inhabitants had declared in favor of royal rather than proprietary control. Nicholson won the confidence of the colonists and his administration was relatively quiet. But he gained the hostility of the Charlestown merchants, chiefly by failing to oppose the issue of large quantities of paper money. Eventually they petitioned for his recall. He himself was failing in health and asked for a leave of absence which was granted. He sailed for England in 1725 and died there three years later without returning to the province. He never married though he is said to have courted a daughter of Major Burwell in Virginia, and to have threatened if she were married to another, to cut the throats of the bridegroom, the clergyman, and the justice of the peace giving the license (Perry, post, p. 90). At his death he left most of his estate to the Society for the Propagation of the Gospel in Foreign Parts, of which he had long been an ardent member.

Nicholson's long and varied career in America was very nearly unique. As governor or lieutenant-governor in five colonies and as supervising official or military organizer in several others on the continent, he was almost the only Englishman of his times who might be called a professional colonial governor. His usefulness was seriously impaired by his unrestrained temper which made it difficult for other officials to work with him. An Indian, who once saw him in a fit of rage, is said to have remarked that he was "born drunk." But despite this lack of self-control, his constructive energy, zeal for education and religion, and breadth of vision, entitle him to a high rank among colonial governors.

His Journal of an Expedition . . . For the Reduction of Port Royal (1711), first appeared in the Boston News Letter, Oct. 30–Nov. 6, 1710; it was reprinted, under a slightly different title, in Reports and Collections of the Nova Scotia Historical Society, vol. I (1879). He also published An Apology or Vindication of F. Nicholson, His Majesty's Governor of South-Carolina, from the Unjust Aspersions Cast on Him by Some of the Members of the Bahama-Company (1724).

[Official documents connected with Nicholson's career are given, in full or in abstract, in Calendar of State Papers, Colonial Series, America and West Indies, 1685–1721 (1899–1933); Jour. of the Commissioners for Trade and Plantations, 1704–28 (1920–28); Colls. of the N. Y. Hist. Soc., Publication Fund Ser., vol. I (1868); Colls. of the S.-C. Hist. Soc., I (1857),

228–93; E. B. O'Callaghan, *Docs. Relative to the Colonial Hist. of the State of N. Y.*, III–V (1853–55); A. M. Macmechan, ed., *Nova Scotia Archives*, II (1900). A sketch of Nicholson by Charles Dalton, in *George the First's Army, 1714–1727* (1912), II, 54–62 (1912), corrects some errors in the article in the *Dict. of Nat. Biography*. The best accounts of Nicholson's administrations are in H. L. Osgood, *The American Colonies in the Seventeenth Century*, III (1907), and *The Am. Colonies in the Eighteenth Century* (4 vols., 1924). See also W. S. Perry, *Papers Relating to the Hist. of the Church in Va.* (1870); H. R. McIlwaine, *Executive Journals of the Council of Colonial Va.*, vols. I–III (1925–28).]

L. W. L.

NICHOLSON, JAMES (*c.* 1736–Sept. 2, 1804), naval officer, was a member of a notable Maryland family, many of whose members have been officers of high rank in the navy. The immigrant, William Nicholson, who was born at Berwick-upon-Tweed in Scotland, settled at Annapolis early in the eighteenth century. His grandson, James Nicholson, was born in Chestertown, Md., the son of Joseph and Hannah (Smith) Scott Nicholson. Educated in England, he went to sea at an early age and was with the British fleet at the capture of Havana in 1762. In the following year, on Apr. 30, he married Frances Witter and became for a time a resident of New York City. Early in the Revolution, having moved to the Eastern Shore of Maryland, he offered his services to his native state and was appointed captain of the *Defence*, the chief vessel of the Maryland navy. In March 1776 he checked the advance up Chesapeake Bay of the sloop-of-war *Otter* and recaptured several prizes. On June 6 Congress appointed him captain in the Continental navy and later when it fixed the rank of the captains placed him at the head of the list. From Jan. 2, 1778, when Esek Hopkins [*q.v.*] was dismissed from the service, until the Continental navy was disbanded at the end of the Revolution, Nicholson was its senior officer. He successfully maintained his right to this rank against the claim of John Paul Jones [*q.v.*]. His first Continental command, the frigate *Virginia*, built at Baltimore, was not ready for sea until early in 1777.

In the meantime Nicholson and his crew had temporarily joined the army and participated in the battle of Trenton. Because of the close blockade of the Chesapeake maintained by the British, the *Virginia* was forced to remain idle until Mar. 30, 1778, when she sailed from Annapolis for the West Indies. Running on to a shoal the next day, within sight of two British men-of-war, the ship was captured, but Nicholson escaped in a boat, with the ship's papers. An inquiry into the loss of the *Virginia* instituted by Congress acquitted him of blame, and he was never brought before a court-martial. Somewhat earlier he had been suspended by Congress for a brief period for writing a "contemptuous" letter to the governor of Maryland. As the number of captains was greatly in excess of the number of ships, Nicholson did not obtain another vessel until September 1779, when he was made commander of the frigate *Trumbull*, fitting for sea at New London, Conn. Late in May of the following year he sailed on a cruise and to the northwest of Bermuda fought with the Liverpool letter of marque *Watt*, 32 guns, one of the most hotly-contested actions of the Revolution. After an engagement of two hours and a half both vessels withdrew seriously disabled and with difficulty reached friendly ports. The Continental Board of Admiralty congratulated Nicholson on his gallantry.

In the spring of 1781, while he was temporarily in command of a fleet consisting of the privateer *Nesbit* and two other small vessels, Nicholson convoyed Lafayette's army from the head of Elk to Annapolis. In August he again went to sea on board the *Trumbull*, this time bound for Havana, having shipped an ill-assorted crew composed of British deserters. Dismasted in a storm, his vessel was overtaken by the British frigate *Iris*, 32 guns. When called to quarters, three-fourths of her crew, by reason of disaffection or cowardice, refused to fight. With the remaining fourth, Nicholson, aided by Lieuts. Richard Dale and Alexander Murray [*qq.v.*] fought his ship for an hour and a half until forced to surrender. His next command was the frigate *Bourbon*, but the war came to an end before she was ready for sea.

In 1785 Nicholson still regarded himself as liable for naval service, for in that year he asked Congress for permission to go to sea in command of a merchantman. A few years later he was living in New York as a retired naval captain in good circumstances and active in Republican politics and in the social life of the city. His house on William Street, one of the most valuable in the metropolis, was the headquarters for the followers of Burr and Jefferson. The "commodore," as he was now called, could always be counted upon to grace and dignify the ceremonies of state occasions. In April 1789 he commanded the decorated barge that transported Washington from New Jersey across New York harbor. He once had a tiff with Alexander Hamilton and the duel that threatened possessed considerable charm for him, now a choleric old man. He had eight children. One of his daughters married Albert Gallatin [*q.v.*]. His two brothers, Samuel [*q.v.*] and John, like himself, were captains in the Continental navy. In 1801 he sought and obtained from Jefferson the commissionership of loans for New York, a post that he was filling when he died.

[*Ancestry of Albert Gallatin . . . and Hannah Nicholson* (1916), revised by W. P. Bacon; G. W. Allen, *Naval Hist. of the Am. Revolution* (1913); Henry Adams, *The Life of Albert Gallatin* (1879); C. O. Paullin, *Out-Letters of the Continental Marine Committee and Board of Admiralty* (2 vols., 1914); *Jours. of the Continental Cong.*, 1776–82.]　C. O. P.

NICHOLSON, JAMES BARTRAM (Jan. 28, 1820–Mar. 4, 1901), bookbinder, fraternal official, was a son of John and Eliza (Lowry) Nicholson, both natives of Philadelphia, and a grandson of John Nicholson, a gunsmith who came from Scotland in 1755 and settled in that city, where, during the Revolutionary War, he manufactured firearms for the Continental Army. He is said to have designed the firelock, or musket, which was adopted by the Committee of Safety. James was born in St. Louis, Mo., while his parents were temporarily residing there.

In 1822 John and Eliza Nicholson returned to Philadelphia, which was henceforth James's home. At the age of twelve he was placed in a lawyer's office as errand boy; later he was similarly employed for a drygoods house and for a grocery. At sixteen he was apprenticed to a house carpenter, but because of poor health and ill treatment he left his master. The latter attempted to force his return, but it was decided that the terms of his indenture did not demand it, and he went into the shop of Weaver & Warnick, where he learned the trade of bookbinding. After completing his apprenticeship, in 1848 he joined in a partnership with James Pawson, an English binder, and under the style of Pawson & Nicholson began a business which was continued by descendants of the original partners until about 1911. Nicholson retired from active business in 1890, his house having become one of the leading binderies in this country. He was a thorough student of his craft, which he followed as a fine art, and in 1856 published *A Manual of the Art of Bookbinding,* the first practical manual of the subject by an American. Although it was founded upon John Hannett's *Bibliopegia* (1835), it went farther than that popular work and came to be regarded as the most nearly complete treatise yet published in America.

Nicholson was as prominently identified with the life of the Independent Order of Odd Fellows in the United States as he was with the bookbinding trade. He joined the Order in 1845, was elected Grand Sire of the Sovereign Grand Lodge in 1862, Grand Secretary of the Grand Lodge of Pennsylvania in 1866, and Grand

Scribe of the Grand Encampment of Pennsylvania in 1869. He held this last office at the time of his death. His efforts as Grand Sire of the national lodge were largely responsible for the fact that "the Order issued intact from the chaos of the Civil War, the only Order of the kind in the whole country, it is said, which was not disrupted by that four year struggle between North and South" (*Public Ledger*, Philadelphia, Mar. 5, 1901). His own account of the experience was privately printed in 1896 as *I.O.O.F.: The Story of '65*. He gained a national reputation for oratory, and as Grand Scribe introduced reforms into the business of the Order regarding questions of dues and benefits by which he is said to have "conferred untold blessings" upon its members (*In Memoriam*, p. 15).

While addressing a meeting at Berwyn, Pa., in December 1892, he was stricken with paralysis, which rendered useless the right side of his body and caused his death in Philadelphia nine years later. He was married, Oct. 5, 1841, to Adelaide Broadnix, and they had three sons, two of whom carried on the business their father founded. Although Nicholson was buried in Odd Fellows Cemetery, Philadelphia, the Pennsylvania Grand Lodge, I.O.O.F., in 1917 erected a large bronze statue of him in Mount Peace Cemetery.

[Nicholson family MSS., and information from a son, the late C. G. Nicholson, Philadelphia; *In Memoriam: James B. Nicholson, Past Grand Sire of the Sovereign Grand Lodge . . . I.O.O.F. of Pennsylvania* (1901); *Public Ledger* (Phila.), Mar. 5, 1901.]　J. J.

NICHOLSON, JAMES WILLIAM AUGUSTUS (Mar. 10, 1821–Oct. 28, 1887), naval officer, born in Dedham, Mass., was the son of Nathaniel Dowse and Hannah (Gray) Nicholson. His father served as an officer of the navy in the War of 1812, and his grandfather, Capt. Samuel Nicholson [*q.v.*], in the Revolution. Appointed midshipman on Feb. 10, 1838, James saw his first active service on board the *Levant* of the West India Squadron. Later, after a cruise in the Mediterranean, he was for a time attached to the New York navy yard and then to the Philadelphia naval school. In 1844, when he was promoted to the grade of passed midshipman, he was ordered to the steamer *Princeton* on special service. After a tour of duty in the Pacific, he served as acting master in the home squadron. In 1852 he was advanced to a lieutenancy and in the following year was ordered to the *Vandalia,* one of the ships of Commodore M. C. Perry [*q.v.*] destined for service in Japanese waters. For several months he was stationed with a guard on shore at Shanghai, China, to protect the foreign settlement from contending

Nicholson

Chinese. From 1857 to 1860 he was on board the *Vincennes* of the African Squadron, assisting in the suppression of the slave trade.

In April 1861 Nicholson volunteered to assist in the relief of Fort Sumter and took part in the expedition thereto as an officer of the *Pocahontas*. He was serving as her executive officer a few months later when she engaged the Confederate batteries at Aquia Creek below Washington. In October he received his first command, the *Isaac Smith,* one of the ships of Flag Officer S. F. Du Pont [*q.v.*], and participated in the battle of Port Royal. In the following year he assisted in the capture of Jacksonville, Fernandina, and St. Augustine, Fla., and for a time commanded the last-named city, as well as the waters of St. John's River where he defeated a party of Confederate riflemen. After a period of service on ordnance duty at the New York navy yard, during which he was promoted commander from July 16, 1862, he joined the West Gulf Blockading Squadron and participated with his ship, the *Manhattan,* in the battle of Mobile Bay, engaging the forts and the Confederate ram *Tennessee.*

In 1865–66 Nicholson commanded the *Mohongo* of the Pacific station and was present at Valparaiso when that city was bombarded by a large Spanish fleet. He was promoted captain from July 15, 1866. After commanding the *Wampanoag* on her trial voyage and the *Lancaster* of the South Atlantic station, he attained the grade of commodore, taking rank from Nov. 8, 1873. From 1876 to 1880 he was commandant of the New York navy yard. In 1881 he was chosen to command the European station, with the rank of acting rear admiral. In June 1882, under orders from the Navy Department, he visited Alexandria, Egypt, and when that city was bombarded by a British fleet he rescued the archives of the American consulate and received the American and other refugees on board his ships. After the bombardment he reëstablished the consulate, and, landing a detachment of marines, rendered timely aid in extinguishing fires, burying the dead, and restoring order. For his services he was commended by the Navy Department, thanked by Great Britain and several other foreign governments, and presented with a gold medal by the king of Sweden. On Mar. 10, 1883, he was retired as rear admiral. He died at his residence in New York City, leaving a widow, Mary (Heap) Nicholson, and at least one son.

[*New-Eng. Hist. and Geneal. Reg.,* Oct. 1858, for name of mother; Record of Officers, Bureau of Navigation, 1832–88; *War of the Rebellion: Official Records (Navy),* 1 ser., vols. XII, XIII, XXI; *House Misc. Doc. No. 46, 47 Cong., 1 Sess., Army and Navy Jour.,* Nov. 5, 1887; *Memorials of the Mass. Soc. of the Cincinnati* (1890).]
C. O. P.

NICHOLSON, JOHN (d. Dec. 5, 1800), comptroller general of Pennsylvania, land-company promoter, was born in Wales and with his brother Samuel emigrated to Philadelphia prior to the American Revolution.

In 1781 he was chosen one of the three commissioners of accounts of Pennsylvania. The following year (Apr. 13, 1782) the legislature abolished the commission and appointed John Nicholson comptroller general of the state, as "a person of known integrity, diligence and capacity." He was given Draconic powers to settle all accounts to which the state was a party and collect all debts, except taxes, due the state. His decisions could not be appealed from and became liens on the lands of all debtors. He could issue subpoenas and commit for contempt. By giving such far-reaching powers to one man, Pennsylvania was the first state to bring order into its financial affairs during the turmoil of the Revolution. When peace was finally proclaimed, the comptroller was also given, by an act of Apr. 1, 1784, the duties of issuing certificates for pay and for depreciation on pay to the disbanded militia. He handled over six million dollars in various forms of certificates. In 1785, in addition to being comptroller, he was appointed receiver general of taxes, and in 1787, escheator general to liquidate the estates of those attainted of treason. An attempt was made to remove him from office in 1790 but his services in settling the Revolutionary accounts of Pennsylvania with the new federal treasury could not be dispensed with. On this occasion he published *Address to the People of Pennsylvania Containing a Narrative of the Proceedings against John Nicholson* (1790). Three years later he was impeached by the Pennsylvania House for redeeming certain of his own state certificates instead of funding them in federal certificates. He was acquitted by the Senate in 1794 but resigned all his offices (Edmund Hogan, *The Pennsylvania State Trials,* vol. I, 1794).

After his resignation, Nicholson became the partner of Robert Morris [*q.v.*], the financier of the American Revolution, with whom, as early as 1780, he had been interested in a glass works. He was by now regarded as one of the wealthiest men of the day. The firm of Morris & Nicholson acquired seven thousand lots in the new Federal City (Washington) and built one-third of the structures which were standing there when it became the nation's capital. They also promoted the Asylum Company with a million acres on

the Susquehanna as a haven for French and
Santo Dominican refugees. The North American
Land Company, formed in 1795 by Morris,
Nicholson, and James Greenleaf, had four million acres in various states, one-half in Georgia.
The Pennsylvania Land Company, formed in
1797, was their final venture. Nicholson alone
promoted the Pennsylvania Population Company
in 1794, with a million acres, and the Territorial
Company with lands in the South Western Territory in 1795. He did much to encourage settlers to move onto the new lands, promoted industries such as Hayden's Forge, the first of the
Allegheny iron works, and had agents all over
Europe to induce immigration.

The financial stringency which began in 1795
and the defeat of the Federalists in Pennsylvania
in 1796 brought confusion into the affairs of the
land speculators. Morris was arrested for debt
in 1798, but Nicholson struggled on till 1800
when he joined his partner in the debtor's prison.
Here he edited *The Supporter or Daily Repast.*
When he died in December of that year, he left
a wife, eight children, and debts amounting to
more than four million dollars. The career of
John Nicholson was very similar to that of Robert Morris. Both rendered invaluable financial
assistance during the Revolution, both did much
to develop and settle the new territories, and
both were finally broken by being too sanguine
of the rapid growth of the country.

[Henry Simpson, *The Lives of Eminent Philadelphians now Deceased* (1859); E. P. Oberholtzer, *Robert Morris* (1903); W. G. Sumner, *The Financier and
Finances of the American Revolution* (2 vols., 1891);
J. B. Anthony, *Report on Liens of the Commonwealth
upon the Lands of John Nicholson and Peter Baynton*
(1839); *First Report of the Commissioners . . . to
Settle the Estates of John Nicholson and Peter Baynton*
(1841); *Extracts from the Diary of Jacob Hiltzheimer*
(1893), ed. by J. C. Parsons; A. C. Clark, *Greenleaf
and Law in the Federal City* (1901); Franklin Ellis,
Hist. of Fayette County, Pa. (1882); *Poulson's Am.
Daily Advertiser,* Dec. 8, 1800.]   G. E. H.

NICHOLSON, JOSEPH HOPPER (May
15, 1770–Mar. 4, 1817), jurist, congressman, was
born probably in Chestertown, Kent County, Md.,
the second child of Joseph Nicholson, Jr., and
Elizabeth (Hopper) Nicholson, and a nephew of
James and Samuel Nicholson [qq.v.]. Colonel
Joseph Nicholson, his grandfather, was high
sheriff of Kent County, and for many years colonel of the county militia. Joseph Nicholson, Jr.,
was a member of the council of safety, or committee of observation, which shared in the government of Maryland in 1776–77. Joseph Nicholson, Jr., provided his son with a good education.
When the latter was twenty-three years old he
married (Oct. 10, 1793) Rebecca Lloyd, the attractive second daughter of Col. Edward Lloyd,

1744–1796 [q.v.], of "Wye House," near Easton,
Md., and of the Chase House, in Annapolis.
Nicholson studied law, moved to Centerville,
now in Queen Annes County, Md., and rapidly
became one of the prominent men in his community.

From 1796 to 1798 he was a member of the
Maryland House of Delegates. He served in
Congress from 1799 to 1806, and during the session of 1801–02 gained renown by insisting, although he was dangerously ill, upon being carried into the House for seventeen successive days,
to cast his ballot in favor of Jefferson in the contest between Burr and Jefferson for the presidency. Nicholson displayed great ability in the
House and soon, with Nathaniel Macon [q.v.]
of North Carolina and John Randolph [q.v.] of
Roanoke, became one of its three leaders. Between Randolph and Nicholson a strong friendship developed. Nicholson, who acted as the
right-hand man for his friend in the affairs of
the House, shared many of his burdens, such as
the conduct of the impeachment proceedings
against Judge John Pickering, 1737–1805 [q.v.].
On May 13, 1803, Jefferson wrote to Nicholson
and suggested that he take the necessary steps
to arrange for the impeachment of Justice Samuel Chase [q.v.]; but Nicholson was a candidate
for Chase's office, which, it appears to have been
well understood, he was to receive if Chase was
impeached. Accordingly at a hint from Macon
that no candidate for the judge's office should be
the leader in the proceedings, he passed the President's charge to Randolph. Nicholson sponsored many important measures in the House
and his position was such that even Jefferson,
according to Henry Adams, "was glad to conciliate Joseph Nicholson, next to Randolph, the
most formidable 'old Republican' in public life"
(*History, post,* III, 166–67). In 1805 the governor and council of Maryland unanimously chose
him as fiscal agent to sell English funds held by
the state and to reinvest the proceeds in American securities. He was a poor man with a wife
and six children to support; his pay as a representative was only six dollars a day and not
sufficient to meet his needs. When the governor
and council first offered him a position as associate judge of the second judicial district of
Maryland, which carried with it a salary of $1400
a year, he declined the offer, but when in March
1806 he was offered the chief judgeship of the
sixth judicial district at $2200 a year, he ac-
cepted. His letter of resignation was read to
the House on Apr. 9, 1806, by the speaker. At
once Randolph wrote him: "I was not in the
House when your letter to the speaker was read

but I got it from Beckly and paid it the willing tribute of my tears. God bless you, Nicholson" (quoted from Nicholson Manuscripts by Bond, *post,* p. 106).

Nicholson served as a judge of the Maryland court of appeals from 1806 until his death in 1817. In one of the earliest cases over which he presided he stated that "he had uniformly been of opinion, that it was improper for the court in the last resort, to assign their reasons for the final judgment. In the inferior court it was proper that they should give the reasons of their decision, because it afforded counsel an opportunity, when they came before the court of appeals, to show the fallacy of the reasoning of the court below, if it was fallacious. He had therefore, on this account, always given the reasons of the court in which he presided. But here there was no necessity of that kind, because the decision of the court of appeals became the law of the land, whether that or their reasoning was or was not correct; and where the reasoning was bad, it was too often blended with the decision of the court, and considered likewise as the law" (*Beatty* vs. *Chapline,* 2 *Harris & Johnson,* 7, 26). He deviated from this rule in only two or three instances and his longest opinion does not exceed a page and a half. As a circuit judge, however, he wrote full-length opinions, which reveal the ability for which he was so highly regarded by the bar and the public. In 1810 he became the first president of the important Commercial and Farmers' Bank of Baltimore, and during the War of 1812 raised at his own expense and commanded a company of artillery. He was present at the battles of Bladensburg and Fort McHenry. Francis Scott Key [*q.v.*] married Mary Tayloe Lloyd, a sister of Nicholson's wife; Nicholson, becoming acquainted with Key's poem, "The Star Spangled Banner," caused it to be published. His death was sudden; the mayor and city council of Baltimore attended his funeral in a body and the bar and judges of the court of appeals resolved to wear crepe in his honor until the end of the court's session. He was buried at "Wye House."

[Nicholson MSS., Lib. of Cong.; C. T. Bond, *The Court of Appeals of Md., A Hist.* (1928); Henry Adams, *John Randolph* (1883); *Hist. of the U. S. A.,* vols. I–IV (1889–90); W. C. Bruce, *John Randolph of Roanoke, 1773–1833* (1922); *Niles' Weekly Reg.,* Mar. 8, 1817; H. D. Richardson, *Sidelights on Md. Hist.* (1913); *Biog. Dir. Am. Cong., 1774–1927* (1928); *Sun* (Baltimore), Sept. 25, 1904; *American and Commercial Daily Advertiser* (Baltimore), Mar. 6, 1817; Nicholson Papers, Md. Hist. Soc.]   H. Ca—s.

NICHOLSON, SAMUEL (1743–Dec. 29, 1811), naval officer, was born in Maryland, the son of Joseph and Hannah (Smith) Scott Nichol-

son and the brother of James Nicholson [*q.v.*]. Regularly bred to the sea, he was active in the patriot cause during the first months of the Revolution. Obliged to go to London on private business, he remained there for a time without official duties. On visiting Paris he was employed by the American commissioners in the line of his profession and on Dec. 10, 1776, was commissioned captain in the Continental navy. When ordered to procure a vessel at French or English ports, he went to England and returned with the cutter *Dolphin,* which he purchased at Dover. In May, having armed and fitted out this vessel, he sailed as the junior commodore in a small fleet, of which Capt. Lambert Wickes [*q.v.*] was the senior officer. In June the fleet cruised to the northward of Ireland and in the Irish Sea and Nicholson shared in the success of the venture, which included the capture of eighteen prizes. One of them was a Scottish armed brig, which surrendered to the *Dolphin* after a half-hour's engagement.

On the completion of the frigate *Deane,* 34 guns, which was built for the American commissioners at Nantes, Nicholson was placed in command of her and ordered to America, where he arrived in May 1778. Early in the following year he cruised for upwards of four months, chiefly in the West Indies, and captured several prizes, one of which, the *Viper,* mounted 16 guns. In the summer of 1779 he made a successful cruise in company with the frigate *Boston,* during which eight prizes were taken, including the ships *Sandwich* and *Thorn,* each of 16 guns. The two frigates returned to Boston with 250 prisoners, among whom were several army and navy officers. Nicholson was congratulated on his success by the marine committee. He cruised rather fruitlessly off the coast of South Carolina in 1780 and in the West Indies in 1781. In the spring of 1782 he was again in the West Indies, and captured several prizes, one of which, the *Jackal,* 20 guns, was the last naval prize taken by a Continental vessel. On his return to the United States he was relieved of his command, for a reason now unknown, and in September 1783 he was tried by a court martial and honorably acquitted.

On June 4, 1794, Nicholson was commissioned captain in the new navy organized that year, taking rank next to its senior officer. His first duty was to superintend the construction of the frigate *Constitution* at Hartt's navy yard, Boston. On her completion in the summer of 1798 he went to sea and cruised off the Atlantic coast in search of French ships. He captured the British privateer *Niger,* mistaking her for a

French vessel, and was forced to release her. In the winter and spring of 1799 he cruised in the West Indies, but with little success, since the *Constitution* was too large to chase the smaller privateers. He captured the *Spencer,* but gave her up, under a misapprehension respecting his authority, because she was unarmed. On his return to Boston in May he was detached from his ship and henceforth until the end of the war was employed on shore. Retained by Jefferson under the peace establishment of 1801, he became the first superintendent of the navy yard at Charlestown, Mass., where he died, having been the senior officer of the navy since 1803. On Feb. 9, 1780, he was married in Trinity Church, Boston, to Mary Dowse, a niece of Sir John Temple. Four of his sons were naval officers; James W. A. Nicholson [*q.v.*] was a grandson. In 1901 the torpedo boat *Nicholson* was named for him.

[G. W. Allen, *A Naval Hist. of the Revolution* (1913); *Our Naval War with France* (1909); C. O. Paullin, *Out-Letters of the Continental Marine Committee and Board of Admiralty* (1914); E. E. Hale, and E. E. Hale, Jr., *Franklin in France,* vol. I (1887); *Ancestry of Albert Gallatin . . . and of Hannah Nicholson* (1916), revised by W. P. Bacon; *Repertory and Gen. Advertiser* (Boston), Dec. 31, 1811.]   C. O. P.

NICHOLSON, SAMUEL DANFORD (Feb. 22, 1859–Mar. 24, 1923), mining operator, United States senator, was a native of Springfield, Prince Edward Island, Canada, the eldest of the thirteen children born to Donald M. and Catherine (McKenzie) Nicholson, sturdy Scotch settlers. His boyhood was spent on the island, where he attended village school and the Presbyterian kirk, and worked on his father's farm. At the age of nineteen he went to Bay City, Mich., and continued his schooling there while living with an uncle and earning his board and room. After working for a short time on a farm in Nebraska, in 1881 he moved to Colorado, reaching the booming mining camp of Leadville with twenty-five cents in his pocket. A tall, reddish-haired youth, he had a good physique, courage, and perseverance. He worked for several years as a mine laborer; then advanced to positions of foreman, superintendent, and manager of various mines, his most important position being that of president and manager of the Western Mining Company. Hard-earned savings he invested in mining prospects, the first of which proved failures. Further efforts met with better results, his leases of the Colonel Sellers, the Maid of Erin, and other mines bringing him good returns. Part of the mining profits he invested in banking and public-utility enterprises in Leadville and Denver. On Nov. 28, 1887, he married Anna Neary of Clifton Springs, N. Y.

Being so closely identified with silver mining,

he naturally became a leader among the Populists when that party championed free silver. He was elected mayor of Leadville on the Populist ticket in 1893, and reëlected in 1895. A miners' strike and other difficult local problems he handled with considerable executive ability. He was sent as delegate to the Populist National Convention of 1896. A zinc-bearing aragonite ore found in a mine under Nicholson's management was named for him, "nicholsonite." Its discovery was a boon to Leadville. After the decline of the Populists, Nicholson resumed his connection with the Republican party. He had close business relations with the American Smelting and Refining Company, controlled by the Guggenheims, and worked for the election of Simon Guggenheim to the United States Senate in 1906. Nicholson was an unsuccessful candidate for governor of Colorado at the Republican primaries in 1914 and 1916. During the World War he served as state chairman of the Liberty and Victory Loan campaigns, and of the Salvation Army drive, and was a member of the fuel administration for Colorado. In 1920 he was elected to the United States Senate on the Republican ticket. In that body he concerned himself more with local than national affairs, being especially active on the committee for mines and mining. He introduced a measure providing for a secretary of mining in the president's cabinet, but it failed of enactment. His senatorial career was cut short by death in 1923. He was survived by a son and a daughter.

[W. F. Stone, *Hist. of Colo.,* vol. III (1918); J. H. Baker and L. R. Hafen, *Hist. of Colo.* (1927), vol. V; *Samuel D. Nicholson. Memorial Addresses Delivered in the U. S. Senate . . . Mar. 9, 1924* (1925); *Biog. Dir. Am. Cong., 1774–1927* (1928); *Who's Who in America, 1922–23; Denver Post* and *Rocky Mountain News* (Denver), Mar. 25, 1923; data from associates and relatives.]   L. R. H.

NICHOLSON, TIMOTHY (Nov. 2, 1828–Sept. 15, 1924), Quaker humanitarian, was born near Belvidere, N. C., the son of Josiah and Ann (White) Robinson Nicholson, and a descendant of Edmund Nicholson, who about 1660 settled in New England. Timothy's early boyhood was spent in a typical pioneer Quaker home on a farm which offered ample outlet for his boundless energy. After attending the local Friends academy, he entered Friends (now Moses Brown) School at Providence, R. I. On his return to North Carolina he was made principal of Belvidere Academy, which flourished under his six years' direction. On Nov. 8, 1853, he married Sarah N. White. He was appointed teacher in the preparatory department of Haverford College, Pa., in 1855 and in 1859 was made general superintendent of that institution. At the age of thirty-three he removed with his family to Richmond, Ind., where he soon established himself in the book business with a brother. At the time of his death he was widely known in the book trade as the Nestor of American booksellers.

It was in the field of human betterment, however, that he won state and national recognition. In him was embodied the Quaker ruling passion for social amelioration. With this social impulse he combined the scientific spirit which gave directness and effectiveness to his work in the field of reform. During the Civil War period he was a leader among American Friends in administering relief to the colored freedmen in the South. The work for which he was best known began in 1867 when he was appointed as a member of the Indiana Yearly Meeting's committee on prison reform. It was chiefly through the persistent efforts initiated by this committee that the state schools for delinquent boys and girls, the Woman's Prison, and later the Board of State Charities were established by state legislation. For forty years Timothy Nicholson was a leader in this work, both on and off the committee. From 1889 to 1908 he was a prominent member of the state board. In 1901 he was elected president of the National Conference on Charities and Corrections. He was an early advocate of temperance and prohibition legislation. His association with the educational development of his state was long and intimate. In 1862 he was appointed a trustee of Earlham College at Richmond, in which capacity he gave forty-nine years of distinguished service. In 1868 he was appointed by the governor as a trustee of the state normal school and served during the formative years of that institution. He was indefatigable in laboring for the furtherance of peaceful methods of settling disputes among nations.

In the Society of Friends he was a distinguished leader. He filled various offices of trust in Indiana Yearly Meeting, of which he was for some years presiding clerk. He was instrumental in promoting the General Conferences of Friends, the first of which was held at Richmond in 1887, which eventuated in 1902 in a national organization, the Five Years Meeting of Friends in America. Uniformly benign and courteous, he was fearless and outspoken on occasion, especially when the cause of the unfortunate was involved. Once when criticism and reprimand of a state official were required, the State Board of Charities laid the unpleasant duty upon Timothy Nicholson. Accepting it, he said: "Sometimes we Friends have to use very plain language. But when a duty like this is to be performed, I have long ago learned first to dip my sword in oil in order that it may heal as well as cut" (Wood-

ward, *post*, p. III). His first wife died in 1865, and on Apr. 30, 1868, he married her sister, Mary White.

[Primary source material consists chiefly of 200-page autobiographical sketch in MSS., private correspondence, and proceedings of social welfare organizations with which Nicholson was connected; see esp. *Proceedings* of the Ind. State Conf. of Charities and Corrections, 1892–1924. For secondary accounts see W. C. Woodward, *Timothy Nicholson, Master Quaker* (1927); Alexander Johnson, *Adventures in Social Welfare* (1923); *Am. Friend*, Sept. 25, 1924; *The Friend*, Sept. 25, 1924; *Indianapolis Star*, Sept. 16, 1924; *The Survey*, Oct. 15, 1924.]
W. C. W.

NICHOLSON, WILLIAM JONES (Jan. 16, 1856–Dec. 20, 1931), soldier, came of a family represented in many wars of the United States. He was born in the city of Washington, his father being Commodore Somerville Nicholson, United States Navy, and his grandfather, Maj. Augustus Nicholson, first quartermaster of the United States Marine Corps. His mother, Hannah, was the daughter of Dr. William Jones, a surgeon who took part in the battle of Bladensburg in the War of 1812. A brother, Reginald Fairfax Nicholson, reached the grade of admiral, United States Navy.

Young Nicholson attended the schools of the Jesuit Fathers in Washington and later (1867–68), the preparatory school of Georgetown College. In 1876, the 7th United States Cavalry having become depleted of officers by reason of the so-called "Custer Massacre," Nicholson was appointed by President Grant a second lieutenant in that regiment, in which he subsequently served for some thirty-seven years. He shared hardships with his regiment in campaigns against the Apaches, Nez Percés, and Sioux, culminating in the sanguinary battle of Wounded Knee (1890). During the war with Spain, he served on the staff of General Sanger as major and chief ordnance officer, United States Volunteers. Promoted through all the intermediate grades, he reached the rank of colonel, Aug. 24, 1912. Later, as a participant in General Pershing's punitive expedition into northern Mexico, he commanded the 11th Cavalry. With the outbreak of the World War, he was commissioned brigadier-general, National Army, and commanded first the training camp at Camp Meade and later a similar one at Camp Upton. In 1918 the War Department sent him overseas in command of the 157th Brigade, 79th Division, composed in large part of soldiers from Pennsylvania and Maryland. He participated with marked distinction in the military operations of the Avocourt sector, the Meuse-Argonne offensive, and the Bois Belleu-Côte sector, until hostilities were terminated by the Armistice. The most notable achievement of his brigade was perhaps its leading part in the capture of Montfaucon.

In recognition of his record overseas, he was awarded the Distinguished Service Medal for "exceptionally meritorious and distinguished services," and the Distinguished Service Cross for "distinguished and exceptional gallantry at Bois de Beuge on September 29, 1918." The French Republic made him an officer of the Legion of Honor. Tall, wiry, active in his movements, affable and just in his relations with subordinates, but forceful in the administration of his brigade, he possessed to a marked degree the qualities of a successful leader of soldiers.

He was retired from active service as a colonel of cavalry Jan. 16, 1920, by operation of law, and seven years later was advanced to the grade of brigadier-general by special act of Congress. On Feb. 6, 1883, while a student officer at the Infantry and Cavalry School, from which he graduated, he was married to Harriette Fenlon of Leavenworth, Kan. His death occurred at Washington, D. C., from a stroke of paralysis, following a hunting trip some months before in the high altitudes of Colorado, and he was buried with military honors in Arlington National Cemetery. His widow, a son, and a daughter survived him.

[Information from Nicholson's family; sketches of his career in the *Evening Star* (Washington) and *Washington Post*, Dec. 21, 1931, and in the *Army and Navy Reg.* and *Army and Navy Jour.*, Dec. 26, 1931; *Who's Who in America*, 1930–31; military facts from War Department records, *U. S. Army Reg.*, 1931, and F. B. Heitman, *Hist. Reg. and Dict. U. S. Army* (1903).]

C. D. R.

NICHOLSON, WILLIAM THOMAS (Mar. 22, 1834–Oct. 17, 1893), inventor, manufacturer, son of William and Eliza (Forrestell) Nicholson, was born in Pawtucket, R. I., but shortly after his birth his father, a machinist, moved with his family to Whitinsville, Mass. Here the boy attended the common-schools, afterwards spending a year at the academy at Uxbridge, Mass. At the age of fourteen he began his machinist apprenticeship in Whitinsville, and upon completing it three years later, went to Providence, R. I., to obtain a more varied experience. After two or three years in various machine shops in that city, he entered in 1852 the shop of Joseph R. Brown [q.v.], where he remained six years—the last two as manager—meanwhile studying mechanics and mechanical drawing. In the spring of 1858 he established a general machine business of his own in partnership with Isaac Brownell. A year later he bought Brownell's interest and then enlarged his shop so as to manufacture a spirit level and an egg-beater, both of

which he patented in 1860. His plans were thwarted by the outbreak of the Civil War, but in due time the demand for war materials gave him the opportunity to manufacture special machinery for the production of small arms. For this work he took Henry A. Monroe into partnership, but in 1864 sold his interest in the ordnance work to his partner and turned his attention to the development of a machine for cutting files, an invention which he had long desired to perfect.

Two patents were granted to him for a file-cutting machine on Apr. 5, 1864, and shortly thereafter he organized the Nicholson File Company in Providence and began to devise the necessary machinery not only for cutting but also for forging and grinding files. Years were required to accomplish the purpose he had in mind, and meantime he completed forty inventions and produced four hundred different kinds of files. One of the most serious problems confronting him was the task of establishing a market for his product. Trade unions combined to prevent the use of, and consumers were disposed not to buy, files made by machinery, one of the many objections being that the machine-made file required more labor in use than the hand-made file. Nicholson, however, overcame all difficulties and lived to see his business grow to be the greatest of its kind in the world. He was president and general manager of his company from the time of its inception until his death. He served as an alderman of the City of Providence for three years and was a trustee of the Providence Public Library from the time of its organization. He was director in several Rhode Island public utilities and banks and was a member of the American Society of Mechanical Engineers. He married Elizabeth Dexter Gardiner at Smithfield, R. I., in 1857, and at the time of his death in Providence was survived by his widow and five children.

[*Machinist*, Oct. 26, 1893; *Trans. Am. Soc. Mech. Engrs.*, vol. XIV (1893); *Providence Daily Journal*, Oct. 18, 1893; *The Biog. Cyc. of Representative Men of R. I.* (1881); Caroline E. Robinson, *The Gardiners of Narragansett* (1919); information from Nicholson File Company, Providence; Patent Office records.]

C. W. M.

NICOLA, LEWIS (1717–Aug. 9, 1807), Revolutionary soldier, public official, editor, merchant, appears to have been born in France, of Huguenot stock, and to have been educated in Ireland (*Pennsylvania Magazine of History and Biography*, July 1922, p. 269). He had twenty-six years' experience as a military officer before migrating from Dublin to Philadelphia in or after 1766 (*A Treatise of Military Exercise*, p. 88).

A Ludwick Nichola, who lived in Berks County and was naturalized in Philadelphia Nov. 18, 1769, seems to be an earlier arrival. He may have practised surveying in his new homeland; it is certain that he set up as a wholesale and retail merchant in Philadelphia, maintained a circulating library, and edited *The American Magazine, or General Repository*, all before 1770. His magazine (nine numbers published, January–September 1769), "the least unsuccessful" of several similar attempts in the Colonies, 1760–74, sought to promote public progress as well as to entertain and instruct its readers. Elected to membership in one of Philadelphia's two scientific organizations (1768), Nicola was a negotiator of the merger (1769) by which the American Philosophical Society was formed, repeatedly served as one of the Society's curators, published the *Transactions* as a supplement to his magazine, and gave special emphasis to scientific news and articles (Richardson, *post*). In 1774 he was appointed a justice in Northampton County, Pa., where he had established a home for his wife and daughters.

During the Revolutionary War Nicola frequently displayed his aptitude for framing ingenious projects for public service. He published three military manuals for American use, *A Treatise of Military Exercise* (1776), and two translations from the French, *L'Ingénieur de Campagne: or Field Engineer* (1776), and *A Treatise, on the Military Service, of Light Horse and Light Infantry* (1777). Early in 1776 he was appointed barrack master of Philadelphia, and from December of that year to February 1782 was town major, commanding the "home guards." He also was active as a recruiting officer, and made an historically valuable map showing the effects of the British occupation of Philadelphia in 1777–78. Doubtless irked by Benedict Arnold's misrule in Philadelphia following the British evacuation, Nicola (May 1780) proposed the appointment of a military governor for the city, recommending himself for the post. The plan was not adopted but meanwhile Nicola had been appointed (June 1777) colonel of the invalid regiment recently established by Congress. With his utilization of invalid veterans, incapacitated for field service, Nicola combined the systematic instruction of fresh recruits. From the summer of 1781 to the spring or summer of 1783 Nicola was at the main cantonment of the Continental Army, on the Hudson, and here, in May 1782, wrote the most famous of his proposals, suggesting to Washington that a change of government to monarchical institutions was in order and recommending

that Washington become king, perhaps with a title modified to allay popular prejudice against monarchy. Due to the breaking down of government under the Congress of the Confederation similar sentiments were held by numerous persons, but Nicola was not their spokesman. Washington's reply, a stern rebuke, called forth agitated yet dignified apologies from Nicola (W. C. Ford, *The Writings of George Washington*, vol. X, 1891, pp. 23–25; Dunbar, *post*, appendix).

Nicola has been severely criticized for his monarchical propositions; however, they were kept secret at the time and subsequently (November 1783) he was brevetted brigadier-general, and from time to time was entrusted with positions of responsibility in Philadelphia. He was a member of the Pennsylvania Society of the Cincinnati, and was elected to its standing committee in 1784 but did not complete his term, it being announced (March 1785) that he had "removed to a distant part of the state," probably to Northumberland County where he held property. By 1788 he was again in Philadelphia, was made commandant of the Invalid Corps, and till 1793 served as keeper of Philadelphia's "model" workhouse. Subsequently he was brigade inspector of the Philadelphia militia (his name now appearing officially as Nicolas) and maintained, it is said, a broker's shop. In 1798 he removed to Alexandria, Va., where he died Aug. 9, 1807, aged ninety. Nicola frankly regarded public appointments as a means of livelihood where "private advantage" should "coincide with the public utility." He discharged his public trusts with much diligence.

[*Pa. Mag. of Hist. and Biography*, July 1922; Nicola's letters to Washington, May 1782, in MSS. Division, Lib. of Cong.; *The American Magazine*, Jan.–Sept. 1769, one of the best files of which is in the William L. Clements Lib., Univ. of Mich.; *Proc. Am. Phil. Soc.*, vols. XXVII (1889), LXVI (1927), p. 24; J. C. Fitzpatrick, *Calendar of the Correspondence of George Washington . . . with the Officers* (4 vols., 1915); *Proc. of the Pa. Soc. of the Cincinnati* (1785); *A Synopsis of the Records of the State Soc. of the Cincinnati of Pa.* (1909); Bureau of the Census, *Heads of Families at the First Census of the U. S.* (1908); J. C. Fitzpatrick, "The Invalid Regiment and Its Colonel," in *The Spirit of the Revolution* (1924); J. T. Scharf and Thompson Westcott, *Hist. of Philadelphia* (3 vols., 1884); *Mag. of Am. Hist.*, Nov. 1883, pp. 358–60; Justin Winsor, *Narrative and Critical Hist. of America*, vol. VI (1887); L. B. Dunbar, "A Study of 'Monarchical' Tendencies in the U. S., from 1776 to 1801," *Univ. of Ill. Studies in the Social Sciences*, March 1922, vol. X, no. 1; C. S. R. Hildeburn, *Issues of the Pa. Press, 1685–1784*, vol. II (1886); F. L. Mott, *A Hist. of Am. Magazines, 1741–1850* (1930); L. N. Richardson, *A Hist. of Early Am. Magazines, 1741–1789* (1931), pp. 153–56; obituary in *Poulson's Daily Am. Advertiser*, Aug. 13, 1807.] L. B. D.

NICOLAY, JOHN GEORGE (Feb. 26, 1832–Sept. 26, 1901), private secretary and biographer of Lincoln, was an immigrant German-American in whose career one may read the triumph of American opportunity, aided by self-education, over the limitations of poverty, hardship, and physical frailty. He was born in the village of Essingen, near Landau, in the Rhenish Palatinate, Bavaria, the son of John Jacob and Helena Nicolay. The family, with its five children, sailed from Havre to New Orleans in 1838, lived for a time at Cincinnati, moved to Indiana, shifted to Missouri, and later settled in Pike County, Ill., where the father and brothers operated a flour mill for which John George acted as scribe and business interpreter. Thrown upon his own resources by the death of his parents, young Nicolay clerked for a year in a store at White Hall, Ill.; he then entered the establishment of the *Free Press,* published in the picturesque town of Pittsfield, county seat of Pike County, a New England town settled from Pittsfield, Mass., and surrounded by the primitive environment whose tang and flavor are preserved in John Hay's *Pike County Ballads.* From printer's devil and typesetter he became editor-proprietor of the paper in 1854. In 1851 the brilliant John Hay [see Hay, John Milton] of Warsaw, Ill., came to Pittsfield to prepare for college; Nicolay and Hay at once became chums, and they remained fast friends for life. Denied the college training for which he yearned, Nicolay found his education in the *Free Press* office, in type-setting, in editorial tasks, in reading the Bible "for recreation," and in the study of books. In 1856 he sold the *Free Press* and became a clerk for the secretary of state in Springfield. Now an ardent Republican, he became acquainted with Lincoln, whose private secretary he became upon Lincoln's nomination for the presidency. Nicolay obtained Hay's appointment as assistant secretary; and the two chums thus stepped together upon the escalator of fame.

Sharing a room in the White House, the secretaries enjoyed the intimate friendship of the President, whom in their own chitchat they lovingly termed the "Tycoon," or the "Ancient." Few men, indeed, were as close to Lincoln as Nicolay or so fully enjoyed his confidence. Sometimes his duties were more than secretarial, as when he attended the Republican convention at Baltimore in June 1864 to "watch proceedings," that is, to promote Lincoln's interests. Nicolay served as consul at Paris, 1865–69; in 1872 he became marshal of the Supreme Court of the United States, serving until 1887. For fifteen arduous years, 1875–90, he collaborated with Hay on the ten-volume biography entitled *Abraham Lincoln: A History* (1890). The plan

was conceived in 1861; and before they began to write Nicolay had spent six years in collecting and arranging the elaborate mass of Lincoln papers loaned by Robert Lincoln, and had blocked out the chapters. There was constant consultation; each chose the chapters he preferred; and the manuscript of each was passed to the other for criticism. Such is the literary blending of the final product that it is practically impossible by reading the text to distinguish the style of one author from that of the other. Prepared under the scrutiny of Robert Lincoln, and written by Republicans who were "Lincoln men all through" (Thayer, *post,* II, 33), the work is caustic in treating Lincoln's opponents; yet it stands as an impressive monument, not only because of the vastness of the undertaking, but also because of its enduring historical significance.

On June 15, 1865, Nicolay was married to Therena Bates of Pittsfield, Ill., who died in November 1885. His later years were spent in Washington where he died in 1901, survived by his daughter. A son had died in infancy. He was of slight build and frail health, and labored under the handicap of severe eye trouble. Beneath a grave exterior he revealed a charming vein of humor to his intimate friends. He was interested in music and drawing, and was an inventor of various mechanical devices. Literary labors and historical interests occupied his later years. With the collaboration of Hay he edited the works of Lincoln in two volumes (1894), subsequently enlarged and published in twelve (1905). His other writings include *The Outbreak of Rebellion* (1881), which was the initial volume of a series published by Scribner's entitled *Campaigns of the Civil War;* the article on Lincoln in the ninth edition of the *Encyclopaedia Britannica* (vol. XIV, 1882); *A Short Life of Abraham Lincoln* (1902); the Civil War chapters (XIV–XVI, XVIII) in the *Cambridge Modern History* (vol. VII, 1903); and numerous magazine articles.

[The above sketch is based largely upon manuscripts furnished by Nicolay's daughter, Miss Helen Nicolay. Fragmentary data are to be found in W. R. Thayer, *The Life and Letters of John Hay* (2 vols., 1915); *Letters of John Hay and Extracts from Diary* (3 vols., 1908); Helen Nicolay, *Personal Traits of Abraham Lincoln* (1912); Tyler Dennett, *John Hay: From Poetry to Politics* (1933). See also *Who's Who in America,* 1901–02; obituaries in *Washington Post* and *Evening Star* (Washington, D. C.), Sept. 27, 1901.]
J. G. R.

NICOLET, JEAN (1598–Nov. 1, 1642), French explorer, was the discoverer of Lake Michigan, Green Bay, and Wisconsin. He was a native of Cherbourg, France, whence his father, Thomas Nicolet, was carrier of the mail to Paris. His mother, Marguerite de la Mer, was from a neighboring town, both parents being of Norman ancestry. Jean was familiar with the sea and ships and was quick to respond when Samuel de Champlain, founder of New France, asked the lad to accompany him to the New World. It was Champlain's policy to bring over promising French youths and to place them among the Indians to learn their languages in order to become interpreters. They were also to learn the lore of the wilderness and to be able to explore the unknown hinterland. In Nicolet Champlain found the qualities he sought—persistence, steadfastness, love of the wilderness, and a talent for adventuring.

Nicolet was twenty years old when he landed in New France; the same year he went with some of the French-allied Indians to live on Allumette Island, high up on Ottawa River. There he dwelt for two years, learning the native language and Indian woodcraft, but, unfortunately, he never learned to swim. During his residence on Allumette Island he went on a peace mission to the Iroquois. On his return, Champlain sent him further from the colony to live among the Nipissing. In 1624 he was appointed their official interpreter, dwelling somewhat apart, much revered by the tribesmen. In 1633, after the English occupation, he returned to Canada and became official interpreter for the colony with headquarters at Three Rivers.

Jean Nicolet's name was practically unknown until the middle of the nineteenth century, when John G. Shea, studying the sources of early Canadian history, found in the *Jesuit Relations* an account of Nicolet's western journey and discovered that he was the first known visitor to Lake Michigan and Wisconsin. Shea dated his voyage west in 1639 (*History of the Discovery of the Mississippi River*, 1852, p. xx). Immediately, Western historians took up the subject, and published all that could be found about the man and his discoveries. Benjamin Sulte proved conclusively that the voyage took place in 1634, the year before Champlain's death. Nicolet's biographers give a short but vivid description of his voyage. He accompanied a mission flotilla to Huronia, where he secured a large canoe with seven Hurons to paddle it. Mounting Lake Huron, he passed the Straits of Mackinac, entered a deep bay on the west side of Lake Michigan, and there, near the bottom of Green Bay, found the tribe he was seeking, called the Winnebago or "Men of the Sea." He had hoped to find Orientals and discovered only a new tribe of Indians. With them he made a

treaty of alliance; hundreds came to see the "Manitou-iriniou"—that is, the "wonderful man." They feasted him and admired him and thought him descended from the gods.

How far Nicolet explored in this region is a matter of controversy. Probably he did not go far inland, for he returned to Huronia by the autumn. The next year he was again at his post at Three Rivers, which he never again left for western traveling. He was drowned during a storm on the St. Lawrence, calling to his companion as his boat overturned: "Sir, save yourself; you can swim, I cannot; as for me, I depart to God." Nicolet's biographers were the Jesuit missionaries who highly esteemed him and declared he was "equally and singularly loved" by both French and Indians. He was married at Quebec, Oct. 7, 1637, to Marguerite Couillard.

[R. G. Thwaites, *The Jesuit Relations and Allied Documents*, vols. XVIII (1898), XXIII (1898); *Early Narratives of the Northwest* (1917), ed. by L. P. Kellogg; Benjamin Sulte, in *Wis. Hist. Soc. Colls.*, vol. VIII (1879) and Henri Jouan, in vol. XI (1879); L. P. Kellogg, *The French Régime in Wis. and the Northwest* (1925).]

L. P. K.

NICOLL [See also Nicolls].

NICOLL, DE LANCEY (June 24, 1854–Mar. 31, 1931), lawyer, born at Shelter Island, L. I., belonged to a family prominent in New York for nearly three centuries. He was a son of Solomon Townsend Nicoll, a successful East India merchant, and of Charlotte Ann (Nicoll) Nicoll; and through both his parents was descended from Matthias Nicolls [*q.v.*], a London barrister who came to New York in 1664 as secretary of the Duke of York's commission. After attending various private schools, De Lancey Nicoll completed his college preparatory work at St. Paul's School, Concord, N. H. He was graduated from the College of New Jersey (Princeton) in 1874 and from the Columbia Law School two years later. After his admission to the bar in 1876 and a short apprenticeship in the offices of Clarkson N. Potter and of Julien T. Davies, he began practising in partnership with Walter D. Edmonds. In 1885, while still comparatively unknown at the bar, he was appointed assistant district attorney of New York County. A series of brilliant prosecutions brought him immediate recognition as an outstanding trial lawyer. Among others he convicted Frederick Ward, the partner of General Grant, of brokerage frauds; and four of the notorious "boodle" aldermen, or "combine of thirteen" (the rest having fled to Canada), of having accepted bribes to grant a street railway franchise on Broadway. In 1887 he was the unsuccessful candidate of independent Democrats and Republicans for district attorney; but three years later he was elected on the Tammany ticket. The duties of the office were administrative, and Nicoll was chiefly engaged in directing and advising a group of able assistants whom he had appointed.

At the close of his term he refused a renomination and resumed his practice. Among his clients were labor organizations, the New York *World*, the Interborough Rapid Transit Company, and the American Tobacco Company. Three cases which he argued before the Supreme Court of the United States were of unusual interest. In the Panama Libel case (*U. S.* vs. *Press Publishing Co.*, 219 *U. S.*, 1) which concerned the publication by the *World* of sensational exposures of scandals in the acquisition of the Canal Zone, Nicoll was pitted against the whole executive department of the government from the President down. Basing his defense chiefly on narrow legal grounds, but with some attention to the constitutional aspects of the case, he won a significant victory for a free press. In the case of *Hale* vs. *Henkel* (201 *U. S.*, 43), a contempt proceeding against an officer of a corporation for refusing to testify or to produce books and papers, Nicoll, though not sustained on several important points, established the principle that papers of corporations are not subject to indiscriminate subpoena by the courts. In defending the American Tobacco Company in anti-trust proceedings (*U. S.* vs. *American Tobacco Co.*, 221 *U. S.*, 106), he argued for a reasonable interpretation of the Sherman Act and perhaps suggested the "rule of reason" which the Supreme Court announced in another case and considerably extended in this case. After the decision, which went against his client, he successfully applied the "rule of reason" in the dismemberment of the company.

Besides utilizing the resources of precedent and legal principles, Nicoll showed great originality in the preparation and presentation of cases. He liked difficult cases and was at his best before judges who were unsympathetic toward his clients. In politics he was always a Democrat except in 1896, when he voted for McKinley. As a member of the state constitutional conventions of 1894 and 1915 he supported the short ballot and other genuine reforms but fought against specious proposals. He hated demagogues and professional altruists. In private life he was a brilliant wit and a rare friend. He married Maud Churchill of Savannah, Ga., on Dec. 11, 1890, and had a son and a daughter. Only the son survived him.

[J. S. Auerbach, *De Lancey Nicoll, An Appreciation* (1931), is an excellent presentation of Nicoll as a lawyer and as a man. Obituary sketches in the *N. Y. Herald Tribune* and the *N. Y. Times*, Apr. 1, 1931, give additional details, but need to be checked carefully. The published arguments in the Panama and American Tobacco cases show Nicoll's methods of presenting cases; and the *Revised Record* of the conventions of 1894 (5 vols., 1900) and of 1915 (4 vols., 1916), his opinions on public questions. See also for certain biographical details, *Who's Who in America, 1930–31; N. Y. County Lawyers' Asso. Year Book, 1931.*]

E. C. S.

NICOLL, JAMES CRAIG (Nov. 22, 1847– July 25, 1918), marine painter and etcher, the son of John Williams and Elizabeth Phillips (Craig) Nicoll, was a descendant of John Nicoll, a Scotchman who emigrated to America in 1711. Born in New York City, he attended the Quackenbos School there, then worked for two years in the studio of M. F. H. de Haas, the marine painter, who was his adviser and critic rather than his master, for Nicoll always insisted that he was not the pupil of any man or any school. He went out into the country frequently on sketching trips, with De Haas and with Kruseman van Elten. Very soon he began to specialize in marine and coast subjects, and from 1868, when he began to exhibit at the National Academy of Design, he was incessantly busy painting his favorite subjects all the way along the Atlantic coast from the Gulf of St. Lawrence to the tip of Florida. His ability to suggest the appearance of water in motion, the *sine qua non* of a marine painter, was beyond all question; his waves are surely rolling; but in respect of color his pictures are not especially noteworthy. There is, at times, a certain brilliance, but depth is lacking. Textures are skilfully indicated, as in pictures of the sea, rocks, sand, and sky; this is especially true of his water colors, which were perhaps better known and more popular than his oil paintings. His "On the Gulf of St. Lawrence" and "Foggy Morning, Grand Manan" were shown at the Centennial Exhibition, Philadelphia, in 1876, and he sent two water colors to the Paris Exposition of 1878. His "Squally Weather" belongs to the Metropolitan Museum, New York. He was among the earliest etchers in New York, and his etching, "In the Harbor," was praised for its understanding of the sea. The list of his honors comprises medals from Paris, New York, Boston, and New Orleans.

Nicoll was a man of executive ability. For nine years (1870–79) he served as secretary of the American Water Color Society, of which he was the founder; and later (1904–10) he was its president. For some years he was secretary of the National Academy of Design, of which he was elected a member in 1885. He was active in the affairs of at least a half-dozen other artistic organizations in New York. He acted as secretary of the Etching Club for several years, and was president of the Artists' Fund Society in 1887. He was also secretary of the international jury of awards for paintings at the World's Columbian Exposition of 1893 in Chicago. He married Cora Anna Noble, in New York, June 4, 1873, and they had four children, two sons and two daughters. He died at his summer home at Norwalk, Conn., in the seventy-first year of his age.

[*Am. Art News*, Aug. 17, 1918; *Am. Art Annual*, 1918; *Boston Transcript*, July 27, 1918; Frank Weitenkampf, *Am. Graphic Art* (1912); *Art Jour.* (N. Y.), Mar. 1875; *Metropolitan Museum of Art, Catalogue of Paintings* (1924); *Who's Who in America*, 1916–17, which is authority for date of birth; Ulrich Thieme and Felix Becker, *Allgemeines Lexikon der Bildenden Künstler*, vol. XXV (1931); W. L. Nicoll, *The Nicoll Family of Orange County, N. Y.* (copr. 1886).]

W. H. D—s.

NICOLLET, JOSEPH NICOLAS (July 24, 1786–Sept. 11, 1843), explorer and mathematician, erroneously called Jean, came in 1832 to the United States from France. He was born in Cluses, Savoy, of poor parents and passed his early years as a herdsman on the slopes of the Alps. A priest of the locality, having discovered that the boy was very intelligent, taught him to read and secured for him a scholarship in the college at Cluses. There he proved to be a mathematical prodigy and at the age of nineteen was teaching at Chambéry. Some years later he went to Paris, where he was naturalized and in 1817 became secretary and librarian at the Observatory, working with Pierre Simon Laplace. In 1821 he discovered a comet in the constellation of Pegasus. The next year he was made astronomical assistant at the bureau of longitude and was sent to measure an arc of latitude in southern France. He became professor of mathematics at the Collège Louis-le-Grand, for which he wrote *Cours de Mathématique à l'Usage de la Marine* (Paris, 1830). Having become involved in speculations in the Bourse during the Revolution of 1830, he determined to emigrate to the United States, where he had been invited to visit. Arriving in 1832 at New Orleans, he sought first the regions of the former French occupation. At St. Louis he became intimate with the Chouteau family, members of which encouraged his plans for exploration.

His first expedition occurred in 1836, when he ascended the Mississippi in the attempt to find its source. On July 26 he arrived at Fort Snelling, where he was cordially welcomed by the officers and encouraged in his purpose to continue to the headwaters of the Mississippi. Two months later he returned to Fort Snelling having had many adventures among the Chippewa, especially those of Leech Lake, whose chief he persuaded to accompany him to the fort. On Sept. 29, 1836, the Indian agent at the fort wrote Governor Dodge of Wisconsin: "Mr. Nicollet who has just returned (Sept. 27) from the sources of the Mississippi found the Chippewa of Leech Lake in great excitement; his situation was critical and unpleasant" (Indian Office files, Washington). The explorer spent the winter with the officers at the fort and the next year was invited by Secretary Poinsett to visit Washington. In 1838 he headed an official expedition for a survey of the upper Missouri. On this occasion he was accompanied by Lieut. John C. Frémont [*q.v.*], who joined him at St. Louis. Notwithstanding a slight physical frame, unsuited to the hardships of exploration, Nicollet's eager spirit urged him to continue his adventures. In 1839 he made a second survey up the Missouri in the steamboat *Antelope*, reaching Fort Pierre in seventy days. From this point he rode northward across the plains towards the sources of the Red River of the North, exploring as far as Devil's Lake in North Dakota. Upon his return to Washington he devoted his time to the preparation of a map of the region northwest of the Mississippi, dwelling with Ferdinand R. Hassler [*q.v.*], chief of the Coast Survey. He prepared also *Report Intended to Illustrate a Map of the Hydrographical Basin of the Upper Mississippi* (1843), published by the government after its author's death, which occurred at Washington.

Nicollet was an urbane, polished gentleman, with a superior mind. He was a musician as well as a mathematician and was a great favorite in social circles, particularly in New Orleans and St. Louis, where he felt at home among the residents of French descent. The Western states are indebted to him for his early surveys and his enthusiastic descriptions of primitive conditions. Minnesota has several place names in his honor.

[J. C. Frémont, *Memoirs of My Life* (1887); *Minn. Hist. Soc. Colls.*, vols. I (1872), VI (1894), VII (1893); *La Grande Encyc.*, vol. XXIV; *Globe* (Washington, D. C.), Sept. 11, 1843; Journals and Reports (MSS.) in Lib. of Cong.]

L. P. K.

NICOLLS, MATTHIAS (Mar. 29, 1626–Dec. 22, 1687?), provincial secretary of New York, jurist, was born at Plymouth, England, the son of the Rev. Matthias Nicolls and his wife, Martha Oakes. The family, whose name was variously spelled Nicolls, Nicoll, or Nicholls, had been established at Islip, Northamptonshire, since the fifteenth century. Following his education at Plympton grammar school and Lincoln's Inn, where he was admitted Nov. 27, 1649, Matthias took up the practice of law in London. In 1663 Samuel Maverick, who had been appointed one of the royal commissioners to investigate conditions in New England, secured for him the position of secretary to the commission (*Collections of the New York Historical Society,* Publication Fund Series, vol. II, 1870, p. 57). Together with his wife, the former Abigail Johns, and their two children, Nicolls accompanied the expedition to America in the following year. The principal member of the commission, Richard Nicolls [*q.v.*], to whom Matthias was not related, was also appointed governor of New York by the Duke of York and charged with the task of wresting that province from the Dutch. After the conquest, the new English governor named Matthias Nicolls secretary of the province, a position he held continuously until 1680 except for the short period of Dutch reoccupation in 1673–74. In his capacity as secretary he was a member of the council and served as presiding judge in the court of assizes. He also held a number of other offices. He was captain of a military company and was twice appointed mayor of New York City, 1671–72 and 1674–75. After the abolition of the court of assizes and the reorganization of the provincial judicial system in 1683 he became judge of the court of oyer and terminer and continued to act in that capacity during the remainder of his life. In 1683 he was also chosen speaker of the first assembly called in the province. Matthias Nicolls is best known, however, as the reputed principal author of the legal code known as the "Duke's Laws" promulgated by Governor Nicolls in 1665. Unquestionably the provincial secretary, with his legal training, had a large part in the drafting of the document, though his exact contribution cannot be determined. Many sections were drawn from codes of New England, since the inhabitants first affected by its provisions were those of Long Island and Westchester, a large proportion of whom had originally come from the Puritan colonies. Other sections of the code were simply adaptations of familiar English practices to the immediate circumstances of the province. The system of government established by this code served on the whole as a highly satisfactory and adequate arrangement during the transition period of the colony's history. (See A. E. McKinley, "The Transition from Dutch to English Rule in New York," *American Historical Review,* July 1901.)

Nicolls acquired a considerable tract of land at Cow Neck (now Manhasset), Long Island, where he established an estate. He is said to have had several children, but according to family tradition all except one daughter and one son, William [*q.v.*], were drowned in an accident in the East River near Hell Gate, the latter saving himself by swimming to the shore. According to family tradition, Nicolls died Dec. 22, 1687, but his name appears in a list of those appointed Apr. 16, 1688, to a special court of oyer and terminer in New York (*Calendar of Council Minutes, post,* p. 58), and letters of administration on his estate were not granted until 1693.

[*The Records of the Honorable Society of Lincoln's Inn,* vol. I, "Admissions" (1896), p. 261; *Docs. Rel. to the Col. Hist. of the State of N. Y.,* vols. III (1853), XIV (1883); I. N. P. Stokes, *The Iconography of Manhattan Island,* vols. IV, VI (1922, 1926); New York State Library, *Calendar of Council Minutes, 1668–1783* (1902); N. Y. Hist. Soc. Colls., Pub. Fund Ser., XXV (1893), 219–20; B. F. Thompson, *Hist. of Long Island* (3rd ed., 4 vols., 1918); De Lancey Nicoll, *Matthias Nicolls 1626–1687* (address delivered before the Society of Colonial Dames of the State of New York, Jan. 21, 1915, privately printed); E. H. Nicoll, *The Descendants of John Nicoll of Islip, England* (n.d., Pref. 1894); and information supplied from family records by De Lancey Nicoll, Jr.]   L. W. L.

NICOLLS, RICHARD (1624–May 28, 1672), the first English governor of New York, was the fourth son of Francis Nicolls, a barrister of Ampthill, Bedfordshire, and his wife Margaret, daughter of Sir George Bruce. The family was stanchly royalist, and in 1643 Richard took command of a troop of horse against the parliamentary forces. The words used in this connection on his epitaph, *"relictis musarum castris,"* have led writers to assert that he abandoned a university career to enter the army, but no record of his matriculation at either Oxford or Cambridge has been found. In 1663, however, Oxford conferred a doctorate of laws upon him (Anthony à Wood, *Fasti Oxonienses, The Second Part,* 1820, ed. by Philip Bliss, p. 275). Nicolls, together with two brothers, followed the Stuarts into exile, where he attached himself to the Duke of York, serving under the latter's command in the French army (*Documents Relative to the Colonial History of the State of New York,* III, 133). It was probably during this service that he gained the title of colonel by which he was always subsequently known. He was never knighted as sometimes has been said. Upon the Restoration, he became a groom of the bedchamber to the Duke of York.

In 1664, when Charles II determined to seize the Dutch colony of New Netherland and conferred the lands between the Connecticut and

Delaware rivers upon the Duke of York, the latter appointed Nicolls governor of the province about to be acquired. The king also made him the principal member of a commission of four men empowered to investigate the condition of affairs in New England, to hear complaints and appeals in the colonies of that region, and to bring them under closer control of the Crown. Nicolls and his associates, accompanied by three companies of troops and a squadron of four vessels, sailed from England in May. After spending a few weeks on the New England coast the squadron blockaded New Amsterdam on Aug. 18 (Aug. 28, new style) and shortly afterwards Nicolls sent a summons to Peter Stuyvesant [q.v.], the director general, to surrender. Stuyvesant favored resistance, but was opposed by the leading inhabitants when they learned that Nicolls offered liberal terms for submission to English authority. The capitulation took place without bloodshed on Aug. 29 (Sept. 8, new style), and subordinates of Nicolls soon effected the occupation of all other Dutch posts.

The new governor began at once the difficult task of organizing the administration in conformity with his instructions from the Duke of York. He wisely made the transition to English institutions of local government as gradual as possible and appointed many of the Dutch inhabitants to minor offices. Since many towns on Long Island had been settled by New Englanders, Nicolls promised them equal, if not greater, freedoms and immunities than any of his Majesty's colonies in New England (*Documents . . .*, XIV, 561). Nevertheless, the authority given to the Duke of York by his charter was extensive and he never intended that his governor should establish an elective legislature. In March 1664/65, Nicolls issued a legal code, known as the "Duke's Laws," which he had prepared with the assistance of the secretary, Matthias Nicolls [q.v.], and the court of assizes. The new code, which was largely drawn from the codes of Massachusetts and New Haven, was put in force at once in the English parts of the colony and was gradually extended to the Dutch communities as well. Some outspoken criticism arose among the Long Islanders at the absence of any provision for an assembly such as they had expected from Nicolls' earlier promises, but in spite of his arbitrary powers, he ruled so fairly and well that he gained almost universal respect and esteem.

He was so much occupied with the affairs of New York that he was able to devote little time to his duties as head of the royal commission to New England. After the other commissioners had met with some success in Plymouth, Rhode Island, and Connecticut, Nicolls joined them in Boston in May 1665. But the theocratic leaders of Massachusetts were so determined to preserve their system of control without interference that the royal appointees were able to accomplish nothing. The Massachusetts General Court defended its actions in an address to the king in which it charged all the commissioners except Nicolls with acting in a spirit of partisanship (*Records of the Governor and Company of the Massachusetts Bay*, vol. IV, pt. 2, 1854, p. 274).

Nicolls remained in office in New York until his resignation as governor, which took effect in August 1668. His departure was accompanied with every evidence of the high regard in which the colonists held him. Once more in England, he resumed his place as groom of the bedchamber to the Duke of York. On the outbreak of the Third Dutch War in 1672 he volunteered to serve in the fleet and was killed at the battle of Solebay. He was buried in Ampthill Church, where a monument was erected enclosing in its upper portion the cannon ball which had killed him, and bearing the words *"Instrumentum mortis et immortalitatis."*

[E. B. O'Callaghan, *Docs. Rel. to the Col. Hist. of the State of N. Y.*, vols. II, III (1858, 1853); and Berthold Fernouw, *Ibid.*, vol. XIV (1883); *Notes & Queries*, Mar. 14, 1857; Charles Wolley, *A Two Years Journal in New York* (1860), ed. by E. B. O'Callaghan which quotes Nicolls' epitaph; J. R. Brodhead, *Hist. of the State of N. Y.* (2 vols., 1853, 1871); sketch by E. H. Nicoll in *N. Y. Geneal. and Biog. Reg.*, July 1884; A. E. McKinley, "The Transition from Dutch to English Rule in New York," *Am. Hist. Rev.*, July 1901; manuscript correspondence of Nicolls, especially with Governor Berkeley of Va., in the Huntington Lib., San Marino, Cal.]   L. W. L.

NICOLLS, WILLIAM (1657–May 1723), colonial lawyer and politician, was born in England, the son of Matthias Nicolls [q.v.], the first secretary of the province of New York, and of Abigail (Johns) Nicolls. He probably accompanied his father to America in 1664, but went back to England in 1677 and spent two years in the army, seeing service in Flanders. Following his return to New York, he began the practice of law. He was appointed clerk of Queen's County in 1683 and became attorney general of the province in 1687. When the Leislerian revolt took place in 1689, he ranged himself at once on the side of the conservatives. In a private letter he forcefully though indiscreetly described the *de facto* lieutenant-governor as "that incorrigeable brutish coxcomb Leisler," and with reference to the party in control declared that "out of hell certainly never was such a pack of ignorant, scandalous, false (malitious), impudent, impertinent rascalls herded together" (*Documents . . ., post,* III, 662–63). The interception of this letter in January 1690 gave Leisler [*q.v.*] an excuse for the arrest and imprisonment of Nicolls. The latter remained in custody until the collapse of Leisler's administration in March 1691, with the arrival of Governor Sloughter, in whose instructions Nicolls was named a councillor. For the next seven years his star was in the ascendent. He was one of the prosecutors who brought about the conviction of Leisler and his associate Milborne. Governor Sloughter's successor, Fletcher, added to Nicolls' already large holdings in Suffolk County until his estate at Islip contained more than one hundred square miles. At various periods he also acquired large tracts of land on Shelter Island. In 1695 he was one of two agents sent to England to discuss measures for the colony's defense. On the voyage he and his colleagues were captured by the French, but ultimately were exchanged and reached London, where they made a strong plea for the total reduction of the French in Canada.

In 1698 Fletcher was replaced as governor by Richard Coote [*q.v.*], Earl of Bellomont, who was soon identified with the Leislerian party in colonial politics. Nicolls was one of the first to suffer, being suspended from the council on charges of having participated in Fletcher's profitable negotiations with pirates. The Board of Trade thought the evidence sufficiently conclusive to justify Nicolls' definite removal as councilor. Bellomont also accused him of bribery in the passage of an act injurious to the interests of New York City. Nicolls' political ambitions had now to be satisfied through the assembly rather than through the council. At first he contented himself merely with electioneering. Bellomont, who later admitted that he was "the most sensible man of the [anti-Leislerian] party, and the hottest," declared that in the election of 1698 Nicholls "rode night and day about the country with indefatigable pains" (*Documents,* IV, 783, 507). In 1701 he was chosen to represent Suffolk County in the assembly and came within one vote of election as speaker, but the Leislerian majority brought about his disqualification as a deputy on the ground that he was not a resident of Suffolk County although he was one of its most important freeholders. Thereupon he built a house upon his Islip estate and made it his permanent residence. In 1702 he was again chosen deputy and this time was the successful candidate for speaker. He held this office continu-

ously until 1718 when he resigned because of ill health, though he retained his seat as deputy during the remaining five years of his life. In his capacity as speaker he took an active part in the assembly's successful efforts to gain control of finance at the expense of the governor.

Nicolls was recognized as one of the ablest lawyers in the colony and participated in many important cases. Among these, besides the prosecution of Leisler and Milborne, were the trials of Nicholas Bayard [*q.v.*] for treason in 1702 and of the Rev. Francis Makemie [*q.v.*] in 1706 for preaching without the governor's license. In both cases Nicolls represented the defense and in both cases the accused were ultimately freed. In 1693 Nicolls married Anne, daughter of Jeremiah Van Rensselaer and widow of her cousin Kiliaen Van Rensselaer. His will, drawn up in 1719, mentions six sons and three daughters.

[E. B. O'Callaghan, *Docs. Rel. to the Colonial Hist. of the State of N. Y.,* vols. III, IV (1853–54), and *Doc. Hist. of the State of N. Y.,* vol. II (1849); *Jour. of the Votes and Proc. of the Gen. Assembly of the Colony of N. Y.,* vol. I (1764); B. F. Thompson, *Hist. of Long Island* (4 vols., 1918); J. R. Brodhead, *Hist. of the State of N. Y.,* vol. II (1871); Nicolls' will in *N. Y. Hist. Soc. Colls.,* Pub. Fund Ser., vol. XXVI (1894).]

L. W. L.

NIEDRINGHAUS, FREDERICK GOTTLIEB (Oct. 21, 1837–Nov. 25, 1922), manufacturer, congressman, was born in Lübbecke, Westphalia, the son of Frederick William and Mary (Siebe) Niedringhaus. His entire academic training was received before he left Germany. In 1855, with the other members of his family, he came to the United States, settling immediately in St. Louis. He first worked at a tinner's bench, making such common household articles as he could market in his immediate neighborhood. In 1862 his brother, William, became his partner. Until this time tinware vessels of all kinds had been made by soldering pieces together; the stamping of entire articles from single sheets of tin, then a new French process, had not as yet been introduced into the United States. Niedringhaus was instrumental in bringing to America a Frenchman who was familiar with this stamping process, and the new method was introduced by the Niedringhaus Brothers into their factory, which they incorporated in 1866 under the name of the St. Louis Stamping Company, with Frederick G. Niedringhaus as president. In addition to the new stamping process, which was a complete success from the beginning, Niedringhaus himself conducted a long series of experiments by which he tried baking many different kinds of chemicals on steel plates, and at length developed and introduced a method of enameling steel plates which added greatly to the cleanliness of cooking utensils and made them rust proof. The business grew so rapidly that new quarters had to be found. Accordingly, after a survey, a tract of farm land in Illinois, just across the river from St. Louis, was acquired, and a large group of influential investors were interested who assured adequate capital. When the plant was moved to its new location, the name of the concern was changed to the National Enameling & Stamping Company, but Niedringhaus continued as president until his retirement in 1908, after which he served as chairman of the board of directors. The new enameling process gave the name to Granite City, Ill., where the factory was established.

In 1888 Niedringhaus was elected to the Fifty-first Congress of the United States, from the eighth congressional district of Missouri. He served one term, Mar. 4, 1889–Mar. 4, 1891, and became a stanch supporter of protection, especially of the tin-plate industry. With his business well founded, with adequate protection by means of the tariff from outside competition, he turned his attention to the labor question within his own plant. At considerable expense to himself, he brought to the United States a colony of Welshmen and established them near his factory in Granite City, Ill. His other business connections were numerous. He was president of the Granite Realty & Investment Company, a director of the Blanke-Wenneker Candy Company, president of the St. Louis Press Brick Company, vice-president of the Granite City Gas Company, and a director of the Louisiana Purchase Exposition Company. He was a member of Grace Methodist Church, St. Louis, and was affiliated with several St. Louis clubs. His chief recreations were reading and walking. In 1860 he married Dena Key of St. Louis. Ten children were born to them. He died at his home in St. Louis, in his eighty-sixth year.

[*St. Louis Star, St. Louis Globe-Democrat,* and *St. Louis Post-Dispatch,* Nov. 26, 1922; Wm. Hyde and H. L. Conard, *Encyc. of the Hist. of St. Louis* (1899), III, 1643; *The Book of St. Louisans* (1912); *Who's Who in America,* 1922–23.]   O. B.

NIEMEYER, JOHN HENRY (June 25, 1839–Dec. 7, 1932), artist, teacher of drawing, was born in Bremen, Germany, a son of Charles Henry and Margareta Dorettea (Otto) Niemeyer. In his childhood his parents removed to the United States, settling in Cincinnati, where the boy grew up and was educated in the city schools. About 1858 he was living in Indianapolis and working in a sign painter's shop. In November 1860 he moved to New York City,

and later taught in a school in New Jersey until he had enough money to go to Europe. In 1866 he was in Paris, where he pursued his studies for about four years. At the École des Beaux Arts he worked under Jean Léon Gérôme and Adolphe Yvon. He also studied with Sébastien Cornu. His main work as a student, however, was done under Jacquesson de la Chevreuse, who was then carrying on the atelier of Ingres and the classical traditions of that master. Of all his teachers, de la Chevreuse influenced him most. During this time, Augustus Saint-Gaudens [*q.v.*], who had come to Europe to study, was supporting himself by cutting cameos in Paris. His evenings he spent with Niemeyer, who taught him what he himself had learned during the same day in the studio of de la Chevreuse. Saint-Gaudens in his greatness never forgot his youthful teacher. Later pupils who won renown were Frederic Remington and Bela Lyon Pratt [*qq.v.*].

After receiving three medals in the government schools, Niemeyer returned home in 1870, and in 1871 became professor of drawing in the Yale Art School. Here he remained until his retirement with the title emeritus in 1908, having in the interval been made Street Professor of Drawing. He came to be a great teacher of drawing, by some considered unsurpassed in the entire country. On the walls of the room in which he gave instruction he placed a quotation from Ingres, "Drawing is the probity of art." For some years he gave lectures on the fine arts at Smith College, and assisted in laying the foundations of the art school and collection there. He exhibited his canvases in the annual exhibitions of the National Academy of Design, of which he was made an associate member in 1905. He was also a member of the Society of American Artists and of the American Art Association of Paris. Competent critics, among them George De Forest Brush, considered his work unexcelled by any artist of his day in beauty and precision of line and perfection of modeling.

In the Graduates Club (New Haven), Niemeyer is represented by fine portraits of President Woolsey (a full-length, painted in 1876), Prof. Bernadotte Perrin, Prof. William Dwight Whitney, and Prof. Thomas R. Lounsbury. The Yale School of the Fine Arts owns his "Gutenburg Discovering Movable Types" (1872), a "Portrait of a Lady," and a number of his masterly drawings from the antique, dating from his student days in Paris. In his private collection were examples of the work of Julian Alden Weir and John H. Twachtman, both lifelong friends, and of John La Farge. One of Niemeyer's most admired canvases is his portrait of the late Theodore S. Gold, of Cream Hill, Cornwall. He was also notably successful in his portraits of Prof. Hubert Newton—a fine piece of characterization and composition and beautiful in color—and of Dr. John Slade Ely, sometime dean of the Yale School of Medicine. Niemeyer also executed some bas-reliefs, among them a large medallion of William M. Hunt (1883) and "Lilith Tempting Eve" (1883). Among his etchings is a notable portrait of President Woolsey of Yale. His self-portrait hangs in the dean's office of the Yale School of the Fine Arts.

He was married, July 10, 1888, to Anna Beekman Talmage, a daughter of the Rev. Goyn Talmage of Port Jervis, N. Y., and a niece of Rev. T. DeWitt Talmage [q.v.]. She was a woman of strong mentality and had a keen appreciation of the fine arts. After Niemeyer's retirement they spent much time abroad, especially in Paris, Normandy, and Brittany. He died in New Haven.

[G. D. Seymour, in *Yale Alumni Weekly*, Dec. 16, 1932; M. Q. Burnet, *Art and Artists of Ind.* (1921); *Am. Art Annual*, 1923; *Who's Who in America*, 1930–31; *New Haven Jour.-Courier*, Dec. 8, 1932.] G. D. S.

NIES, JAMES BUCHANAN (Nov. 22, 1856–June 18, 1922), Protestant Episcopal clergyman and archaeologist, was born at Newark, N. J., the son of Simon and Antoinette Fredrika (Landano) Nies. While he was still a boy, his family removed to New York City, where he began his education in the public schools. After attending Trinity College, Hartford, Conn., for a term, he studied successively at Columbia College, from which he received the degree of A.B. in 1882, and at the General Theological Seminary, from which he graduated in 1885. Ordered deacon that same year and priested in 1886, he was meanwhile in charge of a mission of Holy Trinity, Harlem. From 1886 to 1887 he was rector of St. John's, Tuckahoe, N. Y., with charge of St. John's, Upper New Rochelle, and then for five years (1887–92) vicar of Christ Chapel, Brooklyn. In the meantime he had done graduate work at Columbia and was awarded the degree of Ph.D. in 1888. From 1892 to 1898 he was rector of the Church of the Epiphany, Brooklyn. He then retired, on account of rheumatism, from the active ministry, except for two years (1905–07) when he served as rector of Christ Church, Sharon, Conn. Possessed of private means, he devoted himself to travel and archaeology. His chief interest lay in southern Italy, Greece, Egypt, and especially Palestine; but he also visited other regions, such as Lake Titicaca, Peru. On Sept. 3, 1891, he married Jeanie Dows, daughter of Alexander E. Orr of Brooklyn, and after her death, having no children, he made his home in that city with his brother, Frederick Nies.

Deeply interested in the archaeology of the Holy Land, Nies sought successfully to organize systematic excavation there by his compatriots through endowment of the American School for Oriental Study and Research at Jerusalem, of which he was field-director in 1901. It was there that he died, having returned to erect for the School a building named in honor of his wife. He also bequeathed to it gifts valued at some $25,000, while to Yale University he left his rich collection of Babylonian clay tablets, together with $50,000 for their augmentation. He was a member of many learned societies, among them the American Association for the Advancement of Science, of which he was a fellow, and the American Oriental Society.

Nies wrote comparatively little, his published volumes being *Ur Dynasty Tablets* (Leipzig, 1920) and *Historical, Religious and Economic Texts and Antiquities* (volume II of *Babylonian Inscriptions in the Collection of James B. Nies*, New Haven, 1920). He also contributed a few articles to technical journals, among which may be mentioned "Kufic Glass Weights and Bottle Stamps" (*Proceedings of the American Numismatic and Archaeological Society*, 1902), and "A Pre-Sargonic Inscription on Limestone from Warka" (*Journal of the American Oriental Society*, June 1918). Although his published works were few, he rendered service of much importance by collecting material, by making research possible for others, and, above all, by his labors for the American School at Jerusalem. He possessed a remarkable, almost intuitive, talent for reading cuneiform, and his personality won the hearty cooperation of all associated with him. Theologically he belonged to the evangelical (Low Church) wing of his communion, but with liberal (Broad Church) tendencies.

[A. T. Clay, in *Bull. Am. Schools of Oriental Research*, Oct. 1922; *Who's Who in America*, 1922–23; *N. Y. Times*, June 20, 1922; information from a sister-in-law.] L. H. G.

NIES, KONRAD (Oct. 17, 1861–Aug. 10, 1921), poet, was born in Germany at Alzey in Rhenish Hesse, the third of the four sons of Franz and Katharina Margarethe (Breyer) Nies. His father was a prosperous baker. Nies attended the public school of his native town, was apprenticed for two years to a dry-goods merchant at Worms, and at the age of seventeen entered an actors' training school at Leipzig. He played for brief engagements in a stock company at Aachen and in guest performances at Chemnitz and Kaiserslautern, but even the roving life of a young actor could not satisfy his inveterate *Wanderlust,* and in August 1883 he emigrated to the United States, making his headquarters at first with his brother Philip at Newark, Ohio. For a short time he attended Doane Academy at Granville. Through his boyhood friend, Fannie Bloomfield (later Fannie Bloomfield-Zeisler), he secured introductions to various people in Chicago and Milwaukee and became a traveling representative of the Freidenker Publication Company. In Milwaukee he met Elisabeth Waldvogel, whom he married in 1887. She remained loyal to him throughout all the vicissitudes of his career and supported him by her labor when he himself was too ill to work. They had two children, a son and a daughter.

For a short time after his marriage Nies lived at Omaha, Nebr., where he began to edit a monthly publication of his own. In 1888 he became a teacher of German in the Newark, Ohio, high school, but his literary ambition soon took him to New York, where, during the years 1888–90, he continued his monthly, *Deutsch-Amerikanische Dichtung,* devoted to the cultivation of German literature in America. His first volume of verse, *Funken,* was published at Leipzig in 1891. He visited his home in Germany in the summer of 1892. Meanwhile he had developed tuberculosis of the larynx from which he sought relief in brief residences at Palenville, N. Y., and Orlando, Fla. In 1894–95 he visited the literary centers of Germany and Austria, became acquainted with many persons of note, but avoided the men and methods of the naturalistic movement. He lectured on "German Literature in America" in Berlin, Breslau, and Wiesbaden. Discontented, he returned to America and took over the direction of the Victoria Institute, a private school for girls in St. Louis. But he was not the man to stick to one task for any length of time. He began traveling again far and wide over the United States and Canada, lecturing and reading poetry wherever Germans resided in large numbers. He thus visited at least seventy-three cities on the North American continent, returning to some of them more than ten times. In this way he became known and liked everywhere. By his example and by inspiring others he hoped to keep alive the appreciation of German poetry among the Germans of America. Between 1900 and 1905 he published at St. Louis four short verse-dramas: *Deutsche Gaben* (1900), *Rosen im Schnee* (1900), *Im Zeichen der Freiheit* (1902), and *Die herrlichen Drei* (1905). While he was desperately ill again in 1900–02, his friends collected funds which en-

abled him to rest and travel abroad during 1905–07. He now published a second volume of poetry, *Aus Westlichen Weiten* (Leipzig, 1905). To this period belongs his ardent and, in the end, disillusioning, friendship with a young Russian noblewoman, Olga Khripounoff.

Partly because of his own shiftlessness his family life was wrecked, many friends estranged, and valuable connections severed. A modest inheritance from his mother, however, enabled him once more to unite with wife and children under one roof. He took up residence in San Francisco in 1909. For the peace of his soul he turned to spiritualism, theosophy, and later to the anthroposophy of Rudolf Steiner. The economic problem of his life he hoped to solve by founding a quasi-communistic colony in California, but the plan did not materialize. With the help of generous friends in Denver, Colo., he acquired a cottage on the southeastern slope of Mount Tamalpais, Marin County, Cal. There, in his "Waldnest," overlooking San Francisco Bay, he spent the last seven years of his life in solitude, poverty, and greatest simplicity. During these years he wrote some of his most mature poetry, *Welt und Wildnis* (Leipzig, 1921). This period of retirement was interrupted when Nies was called to become editor-in-chief of the *Colorado Herold* during the critical year 1916–17. It was his dearest hope that the country of his adoption would not take up arms against the country of his birth. Disappointment made him age rapidly and visibly. He died after a belated appendectomy in the German Hospital at San Francisco on Aug. 10, 1921.

Nies had a lovable, winning, even inspiring personality; yet he was irresponsible and unreliable in his dealings with many, including those nearest to him. He had a remarkable command of written and spoken German. He wrote English well, but spoke it with a noticeable accent. He was conservative in the selection of subject matter and form of his poetry. He achieved unusual mastery of the sonnet; he introduced the "quintine" as a stanza and rhyme-sequence into German literature. Nies's poetry is determined by his reactions to nature, love, friendship, and fatherland, by his struggle for self-mastery and his metaphysical longing. Some of his finest poems have been inspired by various aspects of American life and nature, notably the ballad, "Die Rache der Wälder," calling attention to the destruction of American forests. He was the most talented and accomplished of German poets who had made America their permanent home.

[G. A. Zimmermann, *Deutsch in Amerika* (2nd ed., 1894); G. A. Neeff, *Vom Lande des Sternenbanners*

(Heidelberg, 1905); *Daily Leader* (Davenport, Iowa), May 11, 1899; Amalie von Ende, "Konrad Nies, eine Dichterindividualität Deutschamerikas," *New Yorker Staatszeitung*, Mar. 9, 1902; *Denver Post*, Oct. 5, 1903; *Baltimore News* and *Evening Star* (Washington, D. C.), May 14, 1904; *Lit. Digest*, Feb. 24, 1906; *Springfield Union* (Springfield, Mass.), Jan. 26, 1914; *San Francisco Chronicle*, Aug. 12, 1921; editorial and letter by Ferdinand Freytag, *Nation* (N. Y.), Aug. 31, Oct. 5, 1921; Werner von Elpons, "Über Konrad Nies," *Die Neue Zeit* (ed. Oscar Illing, New Ulm, Minn., 1928); Ernst Jockers, "Deutschamerikanische Dichtung," *Auslanddeutsche: Mitteilungen des Deutschen Ausland-Instituts* (Stuttgart, 1928; vol. XII, no. 10); C. R. Walther Thomas, "Konrad Nies, ein deutscher Dichter in Amerika," in manuscript; Nies's papers, diaries, and letters.]
C. R. W. T.

NILES, HEZEKIAH (Oct. 10, 1777–Apr. 2, 1839), editor, was born at Jefferis' Ford, Chester County, Pa., whither his parents had gone for safety just before the battle of the Brandywine. His father, Hezekiah Niles, a plane-maker of Philadelphia, had married Mary Way of Wilmington, Del., and moved to the latter place. Both were of the Quaker faith, though the father was "disowned" a few years after going to Wilmington. Though definite record is lacking, it is probable that the younger Hezekiah attended the Friends' School in Wilmington. At seventeen he was apprenticed to Benjamin Johnson, a printer of Philadelphia, with whom he worked for three years, until 1797, when he was released because of his master's lack of funds. Niles's first writing was done in Philadelphia; in 1794 he published in newspapers several essays favoring protection, and in 1796 arguments against Jay's Treaty. He married Ann, daughter of William Ogden, of Wilmington, May 17, 1798, and they had twelve children. She died in 1824, and two years later Niles married Sally Ann Warner, by whom he had eight children. At the time of his second marriage he was described by an acquaintance as "a short stout-built man, stooping as he walked, speaking in a high key, addicted to snuff, and with a keen gray eye, that lighted up a plain face with shrewd expression" (J. E. Semmes, *John H. B. Latrobe and His Times*, 1917, p. 184).

Upon returning to Wilmington in 1797 Niles assisted in publishing an almanac and did job printing. After two years he formed a partnership with Vincent Bonsal, but the partnership was dissolved because of losses incurred in the publication of *The Political Writings of John Dickinson* (2 vols., 1801). In 1805, following the failure of a short-lived literary magazine, the *Apollo*, Niles moved to Baltimore and became editor of the *Baltimore Evening Post*. This paper supported the Jeffersonian party in all of its policies; it was sold in June 1811, and Niles immediately issued the prospectus for his *Weekly Register* (later *Niles' Weekly Register*) which after seven years of publication had over 10,000 subscribers. This paper he edited and published until 1836, with the assistance of his son, William Ogden Niles, from 1827 to 1830, and on it his reputation is based. In these twenty-five years he made it the strongest and most consistent advocate of union, internal improvements, and protection to industry, in the country. Niles was probably as influential as any in the nationalist economic school which sponsored the American System after the War of 1812. He was the intimate associate of Mathew Carey and Henry Clay. He was a principal mover in the protectionist conventions at Harrisburg in 1827 and at New York in 1831; for the former he wrote the address to the people of the United States; of the latter he was the chief secretary (*Niles' Weekly Register*, Aug. 11, Oct. 13, 1827; Nov. 5, 1831). In each instance he gave spirit and form to the work of the convention, and utilized, besides, his remarkable talents and opportunities as a propagandist in its behalf. His opinions and advocacies developed as he advanced. He opposed the recharter of the first Bank of the United States in 1811, believing it to be unconstitutional and a harmful monopoly. But he espoused the recharter of the second Bank of the United States in Jackson's administration, declaring that it had become a necessity to prosperity. In politics, Niles was a Jeffersonian until 1816 or 1817, when he described himself as a no-party man. On Jan. 10, 1824, he wrote: "I cannot believe that either [Jackson or Calhoun] will be elected, and should regret votes thrown away. I esteem both, personally and politically; and though my private wish is rather for Mr. Adams, I shall be content to accept any other than Mr. Crawford" (Darlington Collection, *post*). When Jackson came into office in 1829, Niles differed sharply with his policies, and became a Whig.

Niles devoted many editorials to the institution of slavery, which he declared should be abolished, though gradually. While in Delaware he was an officer of the state abolition society. In his arguments for the protective tariff, he exerted himself with much ingenuity to win the agricultural interest to his side. His writing was characterized by vigor and decision. He was a tireless worker, and supplied statistical evidence where many in his group were content with eloquence. Besides a number of pamphlets, he published the *Principles and Acts of the Revolution in America* (1822). He never held national office, but in Wilmington was twice town clerk and twice assistant burgess; in Baltimore he served two terms in the first branch of the city council. He was elected and reëlected (1818–19) grand high priest by the Masonic Order in Maryland. He was a leading figure in the Baltimore Typographical Society. He died in Wilmington.

[R. G. Stone, *Hezekiah Niles as an Economist* (1933) ; biographical notices in *Niles' National Register* (as it was then called), Apr. 6, 13, 1839 ; Philadelphia *North American*, Apr. 4, 1839 ; *Baltimore Patriot and Commercial Gazette*, Apr. 3, 1839 ; "Village Record, West Chester, Pa., Notae Cestrienses, No. 34," in *Genealogical Soc. of Pa. Colls.* The *Register* is the best source for his opinions and activities. See also Clay and Darlington collections in MSS. Div., Lib. of Cong.; E. T. Schultz, *Hist. of Freemasonry in Md.*, II (1855) ; J. S. Futhey and Gilbert Cope, *Hist. of Chester County, Pa.* (1881) ; Edward Stanwood, *Am. Tariff Controversies in the Nineteenth Century* (1903), vol. I.]

B. M.

NILES, JOHN MILTON (Aug. 20, 1787–May 31, 1856), editor, United States senator, postmaster general, was born into a family of moderate means residing in that part of Windsor, Conn., known as Poquonock. His parents, Moses and Naomi (Marshall) Niles, found it no easy task to rear their five children, and John, consequently, received no better education than could be gained from the common-schools of the period. As a young man of some ambition, he applied himself to a course of self-improvement, reading largely in the fields of history and politics. To his public career, he brought also a strong sense of moral uprightness, derived from his Puritan ancestors.

In 1817 he was admitted to the Hartford bar, and in the same year he founded the *Hartford Weekly Times,* a liberal paper, designed to further the cause of political reform in Connecticut. He was an ardent Republican, or Tolerationist, and when his party had secured a new state constitution in 1818, he hoped for still further democratic reforms, which were not soon realized. From 1821 to 1829 he was a judge of the Hartford County court; in 1826 he served one term in the state legislature; and a year later he was a candidate for the United States Senate, being defeated, however, because of his liberal views. He had, by 1827, become a leader of the Jacksonian party, which did not secure a strong hold on conservative Connecticut until 1833. He was made postmaster of Hartford in 1829. Six years later he was chosen by Gov. Henry W. Edwards [*q.v.*] to fill a vacancy in the Senate, caused by the death of Nathan Smith, and being subsequently elected he served until March 1839.

At the outset of his senatorial career, he displayed independence of judgment, refusing to vote immediately for the recognition of Texas, which annoyed his fellow Democrats very much (*Congressional Globe,* 24 Cong., 1 Sess., pp. 438–

39). Some of his other actions during the term were more pleasing to his constituents, especially his plea for a memorial to Nathan Hale, and several speeches in support of the sub-treasury (*Ibid.,* 24 Cong., 1 Sess., p. 145; 25 Cong., 1 Sess., pp. 44–45, 2 Sess., p. 179). Niles believed the latter institution would protect the interests of the laboring classes, whose cause strongly appealed to him. His speeches were not brilliant, but evidenced an accurate and discriminating mind. Because of his uncompromising democracy he was an object of loathing to Connecticut Whigs, who could hardly mention his name without adding vile and insulting epithets. After his first senatorial term he ran unsuccessfully for the governorship of Connecticut in the elections of 1839 and 1840, and was for a short time, May 25, 1840, to Mar. 3, 1841, postmaster general in Van Buren's cabinet. During his second term as senator, 1843–49, he was even less strictly partisan thàn before, although he held firmly to the doctrine of strict construction, and the belief that the activities of the federal government should be restricted to the smallest possible sphere. In 1844 he was stricken with a severe illness, which temporarily affected his mind, giving hope to his enemies that he might be removed from office on the ground of insanity, but to their discomfiture he recovered (*Ibid.,* 28 Cong., 1 Sess., pp. 564–65, 602). Shortly afterward his friends began to fear that his illness had actually altered his democratic principles, for he turned protectionist, and later showed himself very lukewarm in support of the Mexican War (*Ibid.,* 30 Cong., 1 Sess., pp. 328–29).

Leaving the Senate in 1849, he retired to a quiet horticultural life; he made a trip to Europe in 1851–52; and just before his death from cancer, in 1856, was about to found a new Hartford paper, the *Press,* as an organ of the newly formed Republican party. Throughout his life this quiet-demeanored man was kind-hearted and benevolent, although continual political strife threw over his behavior a cloak of diffidence, and often bitterness, which made him appear unsociable. He married, June 17, 1824, Sarah Robinson, widow of Lewis Howe, and after her death in 1842, he took for his second wife, Nov. 26, 1845, Jane Pratt, of Columbia County, N. Y. There were no children.

Niles combined considerable literary ability with his taste for politics; he edited the first American edition (1816) of *The Independent Whig,* and was either joint or sole author of other works, including *A Gazetteer of the States of Connecticut and Rhode-Island* (1819), *The Life of Oliver Hazard Perry* (1820), *The Con-*

necticut Civil Officer (1823), *A View of South America and Mexico* (1825), enlarged and republished under the title *History of South America and Mexico* (1838). He was interested in the Wadsworth Athenæum and the Connecticut Historical Society, leaving his personal library to the latter; he also bequeathed to the city of Hartford a large sum of money to be used as a charity fund. Niles could hardly be called a nationally prominent figure, but in Connecticut he was outstanding, not only because he was for over thirty years the power behind the local Democratic party, but because he refrained from the mean personalities of politics and dealt only with broad and worthy principles. He died in Hartford.

[H. R. Stiles, *The Hist. and Geneals. of Ancient Windsor, Conn.*, vol. II (1892); Green's *Connecticut Register;* files of the *Hartford Times* and the *Connecticut Courant; Biog. Dir. Am. Cong.* (1928); scattered letters in the Daggett Papers, Yale Univ. Lib.; Boardman collection of Conn. MSS., Conn. State Lib.; miscellaneous papers of the legislature in the office of the secretary of state.]   J. M. M.

NILES, NATHANIEL (Apr. 3, 1741–Oct. 31, 1828), inventor, theologian, preacher, politician, and man of business with a somewhat less happy dash of the poet, was born at South Kingston, R. I., the son of Samuel and Sarah (Niles) Niles and the grandson of Samuel Niles [*q.v.*]. His parents were cousins german. Like his father and grandfather, Nathaniel was sent to Harvard College but because of illness he left that institution after his first year. Later (1765), with his brother Samuel, he entered the College of New Jersey where he graduated in 1766. His many interests proved at first somewhat of a handicap; he could not decide upon his life work. For a time he studied medicine, then law, and finally turned to theology under the direction of Joseph Bellamy. Though he preached in several New England towns, he was never ordained. Shortly before the Revolution he settled in Norwich, Conn., where he married Nancy, the daughter of Elijah Lathrop, a prosperous trader and manufacturer. He entered Lathrop's factory and is said to have invented an improved type of wool card and to have discovered a new method of applying water power to the drawing of wire from bar iron. These inventions, however, seem to have left no mark upon American industry. Meanwhile he was preaching frequently at Norwich and elsewhere. Several of his sermons he published. He also found time for politics, serving in the Connecticut legislature for three sessions (1779–81). Toward the end of the Revolution he bought a large tract of land in Orange County, Vt., and in 1782 or 1783, he abandoned his business career to move with several friends

into the northern forest. They were the first settlers in what became the township of West Fairlee.

The rest of his strenuous life Niles spent in Vermont, preaching frequently, attending the sick when physicians were not available, writing on theology, but devoting himself primarily to the management of his land and to politics. His position as the largest proprietor in the neighborhood, his undoubted intelligence, his positive and democratic ideas, his forceful and aggressive character, all contributed to his success in politics. From 1784 to 1814, when at the age of seventy-three he retired to his farm, he was almost always in office, on occasion filling two positions simultaneously. For eight terms he sat in the lower house of the Vermont legislature. From 1784 to 1787 he was a member of the supreme court of the state; hence his title of judge by which he was called thereafter. For many years he was a member of the Council, a popularly elected executive and legislative body. From 1791 to 1795 he sat in the federal House of Representatives. He took a leading part in the state convention of 1791 which ratified the federal Constitution, and in another of 1814 which revised the fundamental laws of the state. Unlike most New England clergymen he was a Jeffersonian Democrat. Leading his party in Vermont, he fought against slavery and against banks; he gave vigorous support to the second war with England and as vigorous condemnation of the Hartford Convention. His influence, however, was not widespread for the Federalist triumph in Vermont in 1794 kept the state Democrats out of national office for many years.

In 1793 he was made trustee of Dartmouth College, a position he held until 1820. Characteristically he took his duties with the utmost seriousness. In temperament and in religious and political ideas he was in sharp contrast to President John Wheelock. He early became convinced that the college was suffering under the latter's direction and he soon headed the opposition in the board of trustees. When matters came to a crisis in 1815, he joined with his Federalist fellow members to oust the president and to defend the institution against the state authority. Besides his sermons he published numerous theological articles. His one attempt at poetry, an ode called *The American Hero,* was written in celebration of the battle of Bunker Hill. Set to music it gained wide popularity during the Revolutionary War. Posterity will not regret that thereafter Niles turned his talents to other fields. Despite weak health in his youth his physical and mental vigor was remarkable; even in extreme age he spent long hours renewing his knowledge of Latin. He left nine children, five of them by his second wife, Elizabeth Watson of Plymouth, Mass., whom he married on Nov. 22, 1787.

[J. A. Vinton, *The Vinton Memorial* (1858); F. M. Caulkins, *Hist. of Norwich, Conn.* (2nd ed., 1866); A. M. Hemenway, *The Vt. Hist. Gazetteer*, vol. II (1871); W. B. Sprague, *Annals of the Am. Pulpit*, vol. I (1857); J. M. Comstock, *A List of the Principal Civil Officers of Vt.* (1918); J. G. Ullery, *Men of Vt.* (1894); J. K. Lord, *A Hist. of Dartmouth Coll.* (1913); E. B. Huntington, *A Geneal. Memoir of the Lo-Lathrop Family* (1884); *Vt. Watchman and State Gazette* (Montpelier), Nov. 18, 1828.]   P. D. E.

NILES, NATHANIEL (Dec. 27, 1791–Nov. 16, 1869), diplomatist, was the son of Nathaniel Niles, 1741–1828 [*q.v.*], pioneer settler of Fairlee, Vt., dubbed by his contemporaries "the Athenian of the East Side of the Green Mountain." His mother, Elizabeth (Watson) Niles, daughter of Judge William Watson of Plymouth, Mass., if less famous than her husband was hardly less talented and devout. Judge Samuel Niles of Braintree, Mass., was Nathaniel's grandfather, and Dr. Samuel Niles, famous New England clergyman, his great-grandfather. The founder of the Niles family came from England soon after the Massachusetts colony was established. Graduating from the Harvard Medical School in 1816, Nathaniel practised medicine for several years in Boston and then went to Paris for further study. There he married an accomplished French woman, Mme. Rosella Sue, widow of Dr. Sue, physician to King Louis XVIII. When William C. Rives, American minister at Paris, resigned in 1830 to return to the United States, he left Niles in charge of the legation. Niles was officially appointed secretary of legation on Nov. 9, 1830, and remained until 1833, when a new chargé d'affaires replaced him. Losing interest in a medical career, he returned to America and sought another opening in the diplomatic service. On June 7, 1837, he was appointed special diplomatic agent to Austria-Hungary, to find a market for American tobacco and to induce the Austrians to lower the high barriers against American commerce. For more than a year he worked hard collecting information and negotiating with high officials, and when Henry A. P. Muhlenburg [*q.v.*], the new American minister, arrived at Vienna to take over his work in 1838, Niles was able to report substantial progress.

At Vienna the Count de Sambuy, Sardinian minister to Austria, suggested to Niles the desirability of forming diplomatic relations with Sardinia and the United States, which at this time had no relations with any of the Italian states. Niles reported the conversation to the State Department and was immediately given power to negotiate such a treaty, if it could be done within three months. He reached Turin in September 1838, and on November 26 a most-favored-nation treaty of commerce and navigation was signed. It was transmitted to the Senate, which voted for its ratification notwithstanding the fact that it had not been consulted as to the negotiations. This treaty stood until superseded in 1871 by the treaty with Italy following the union of the Italian states. In 1839 Niles left the foreign service, but went again to Sardinia as chargé d'affaires from Jan. 4, 1848, to Aug. 20, 1850. During this period he submitted two interesting projects to the State Department, one involving the building of a Panama canal, to be under international control, the cost of construction and maintenance to be borne by the chief maritime nations; the other, a scheme for the exchange, free of duty, between the United States and Italy, Switzerland, and other European countries, of cheap editions of the national literature of each country in the original language, the main object of which was to promote international good feeling through mutual understanding of national cultures. From 1850 until his death Niles's home was in New York City.

[Manuscript sources include: Nathaniel Niles Papers, 2 vols. (letters to Niles), U. S. Lib. of Cong., Division of MSS.; U. S. Dept. of State, "Diplomatic Correspondence," France, vols. XXV and XXVI, Austria, vol. I, Sardinia, vols. IV and V, Special Agents, vol. XII. Published sources include: *House Executive Document 40*, 23 Cong., 2 Sess.; *House Executive Document 229*, 26 Cong., 1 Sess.; *Senate Document 246*, 27 Cong., 2 Sess.; *Senate Document 118*, 29 Cong., 1 Sess.; *Senate Executive Document 1, House Executive Document 5*, 31 Cong., 1 Sess.; *Senate Executive Document 7*, 32 Cong., 1 Sess.; H. M. Wriston, *Executive Agents in Am. Foreign Relations* (1929); T. F. Harrington, *The Harvard Medic. School: A Hist., Narrative and Documentary* (1905), vol. III.]   I. L. T.

NILES, SAMUEL (May 1, 1674–May 1, 1762), clergyman, religious controversalist, and historian, was born on Block Island, between Narragansett Bay and Long Island, the son of Nathaniel and Sarah (Sands) Niles, and a grandson of John Niles who was in Dorchester, Mass., as early as 1634 and later moved to Braintree. Samuel attended school at Braintree, but in 1689 his education was interrupted. As he afterwards wrote: "the great spoil made on the island by the French, in their repeated visits, and particularly on my father's interest, occasioned my staying from school six years. . . . In this time I turned my hand to husbandry, and sometimes to handicraft. . . . After the space of six years thus employed I returned to school, so that by reason of this delay, I was near two-and-twenty years old when I entered into the college at Cambridge" (*Collections of the Massachusetts Historical Society,* 3 ser. VI, 274). There he received the degree of A.B. in 1699, the first Harvard degree granted to a Rhode Islander.

He then studied for the ministry, probably with the Rev. Peter Thacher [*q.v.*] of Milton, whose daughter Elizabeth he married on May 29, 1701. From 1702 until 1710 he engaged in difficult missionary work at Kingstown, R. I. In the latter year he removed to Braintree, where on May 23, 1711, he was ordained minister of the Second Church. His long pastorate there, which continued until his death, was a prosperous one. It is recorded that he administered baptism to 1,200 persons, and received 312 into the full communion of the church. His first wife died on Feb. 10, 1715/16, and in accordance with her death-bed request he married, Nov. 22, 1716, Ann Coddington of Newport, R. I., granddaughter of Gov. William Coddington [*q.v.*]. His third and last wife was Elizabeth (Adams), widow of the Rev. Samuel Whiting, to whom he was married on Dec. 22, 1737.

Niles took a prominent part in the religious controversies of the period. He was moderator of an Association of Ministers convened at Weymouth in January 1744, which attacked George Whitefield in a pamphlet entitled *The Sentiments and Resolutions of an Association of Ministers* . . . (1745). Niles himself published *Tristitiæ Ecclesiarum or, a Brief and Sorrowful Account of the Present State of the Churches in New England* (1745), deploring the effects of Whitefield's preaching; *A Vindication of Divers Important Gospel-Doctrines* (1752); and *The True Scripture Doctrine of Original Sin* (1757). Two years later Harvard awarded him an A.M. degree. The most important of his writings is "A Summary Historic Narrative of the Wars in New England with the French and Indians" (*Collections of the Massachusetts Historical Society,* 3 ser. VI, and 4 ser. V). A work in rhyme entitled *A Brief and Plain Essay on God's Wonder Working Providence for New England in the Reduction of Louisburg* (1747) and his "Summary Historic Narrative" have gained him a small place in the history of American literature. Niles was included by a contemporary, the Rev. John Barnard [*q.v.*], among prominent preachers who were all "men of learning, pious, humble, prudent, faithful and useful men in their day" (*Ibid.,* 1 ser. X, 170). That he was humble may be questioned, however. He had a talent for obstinacy. He refused to permit the new way of singing from notes to be introduced in his church at Braintree, held services in the parsonage rather than yield, and surrendered only when some of his flock went over to the Episcopalians. The town of Braintree had to accept a most inconvenient boundary line because he refused to let the line cross his farm. He ordinarily rode a horse that no one else could and to him "were brought for breaking all the rebellious colts and young religious innovators of Braintree" (Shipton, *post,* IV, 490).

[*Colls. Mass. Hist. Soc.,* 1 ser. X (1809), 3 ser. VI (1837), 4 ser. V (1861); J. A. Vinton, *The Vinton Memorial* (1858); Wilkins Updike, *A Hist. of the Episcopal Ch. in Narragansett, R. I.* (2nd ed., 1907), vol. I; preface of Niles's *A Vindication* . . . (1752); C. K. Shipton, *Sibley's Harvard Grads.,* vol. IV (1933); diary of Niles containing his mother's lineage, a record of baptisms, and a history of Braintree during the time that he lived there, in the possession of Asa P. French of Randolph, Mass.]   H. M. N.

NIPHER, FRANCIS EUGENE (Dec. 10, 1847–Oct. 6, 1926), physicist, was born at Port Byron, N. Y., the son of Peter Nipher and Roxalana Powell Tilden. His paternal great-grandfather, Michael Niver, born in Württemberg, Germany, came to America in 1756 at the age of ten years, and later served in the Revolutionary War. On his mother's side, Nipher was of English descent through Nathaniel Tilden, who settled in Massachusetts in 1634, and who was a brother of one of the London merchants who fitted out the *Mayflower.* Peter Nipher, with his wife and three children, moved in 1863 to Iowa City, where the Nipher family owned a government grant of land. The principal purpose of the move was to enable the son Francis to take advantage of the educational opportunities offered at the State University of Iowa. Here he specialized in the natural sciences and mathematics, and in 1870 received the degree of Ph.B. For several years thereafter he served the same institution as instructor in the physics laboratory, at the same time continuing his studies as a candidate for the master's degree which was conferred in 1873. In the same year he married Matilda Aikens, of Atalissa, Iowa, who had been one of his students, and who, with their five children, survived him.

Called to the chair of physics at Washington University in 1874, Nipher began a career which continued without interruption until his retirement in 1914. Probably the greatest influence he exerted as a teacher was due to his insistence upon the inductive method of arriving at physical laws from actual observations and measurement, utilizing to an unusual extent the algebraic interpretation of graphs. It was as an original investigator, however, rather than as class-room or laboratory teacher, that he will be remembered. The variety of his interests is attested by the long list of his published papers, of which the most important are to be found in the *Transactions* of the Academy of Science of St. Louis. Among his important contributions are a series of reports on magnetic observations in Missouri, beginning with the summer of 1878 and continuing for four summers thereafter. This work led to the publication, in 1886, of a book entitled *Theory of Magnetic Measurements*. When electrical engineering began to develop as a major division of technology, Nipher was one of the first to offer courses of study in that branch of science. The course of lectures he developed culminated in 1895 in the publication of *Electricity and Magnetism: A Mathematical Treatise for Advanced Undergraduate Students*.

The measurement of wind pressure on stationary and moving structures engaged his attention for over ten years beginning in 1896, at the time of the disastrous St. Louis tornado. Nipher developed apparatus which made it possible to separate the static from the dynamic pressure head at any point of a structure, and when Washington University took possession of its new campus in 1905 the physics building was completely equipped with an elaborate apparatus exhibited at the Louisiana Purchase Exposition of 1904 and which was there awarded a gold medal for excellence of design. The apparatus, in modified form, was used to measure the frictional effect of railway trains upon the air, a paper on that subject appearing as Volume X, Number 10, of the *Transactions* of the Academy of Science of St. Louis. Other researches included a long series of original experiments on the properties of photographic plates. At the same time that this work was in progress, he contributed to the Academy of Science a series of interesting papers on the thermodynamics of gaseous nebulae. Later, in St. Louis and at his summer home in northern Michigan, he undertook a study of the causes of local variations of the earth's magnetic field. His last, and probably his most important, work was an experimental study of the nature of the electric discharge, the results of which appear in a series of five papers in the *Transactions* of the Academy of Science of St. Louis, summarized in a book, *Experimental Studies in Electricity and Magnetism* (1914). The last years of his life were spent in quiet retirement at his home in Kirkwood, Mo., where he died.

[*Who's Who in America*, 1926–27; *St. Louis Globe-Democrat*, Oct. 7, 1926; information from Nipher's daughter, Mrs. James C. Dawson; personal recollections.]
A. S. L.

NISBET, CHARLES (Jan. 21, 1736–Jan. 18, 1804), Presbyterian clergyman and first president of Dickinson College, son of William and Alison Nisbet, was born at Haddington, Scotland. Graduating from the University of Edinburgh at the age of eighteen, he studied theology for six years at Divinity Hall, and in 1760 was licensed by the Presbytery of Edinburgh. After preaching for two years in Glasgow, on May 17, 1764, he was ordained by the Presbytery of Brechin and installed as pastor at Montrose. In 1766 he was married to Anne, daughter of Thomas Tweedie of Quarter, by whom he had four children. He possessed natural abilities of a high order, enhanced by an extraordinary memory. He soon rose to an influential position in the General Assembly of the Church of Scotland, participating freely in discussion as a champion of strict Calvinistic theology. In 1783 the College of New Jersey conferred upon him the degree of D.D.

Nisbet ardently defended the cause of the American Colonies in the Revolutionary struggle. This fact together with his renown as a scholar led Benjamin Rush and John Dickinson [*qq.v.*], in 1784, to offer him the presidency of Dickinson College at Carlisle, chartered in 1783. After considerable urging, he accepted the invitation and arrived in Philadelphia, June 9, 1785. The bright prospects with which he entered upon his duties were soon obscured. A lingering fever fastened upon his body, while the poverty, demoralization, and gloom of the postwar period depressed his spirit. Within a few months he resigned, intending to return to Scotland, but a strong prejudice of his own forbade his sailing in a vessel commanded by an Irish captain. In the ensuing delay his health so improved that he consented to an unanimous re-election, and served at his post with unabating vigor until his death eighteen years later. Simultaneously with his inauguration as president of Dickinson, he was chosen co-pastor of the Presbyterian church at Carlisle with Dr. Robert Davidson [*q.v.*].

As college president Nisbet lectured on logic, mental and moral philosophy, and belles-lettres, and in addition, for the accommodation of students for the ministry, he prepared and delivered a course of 418 lectures on systematic theology and twenty-two lectures on pastoral theology. In the solidity and variety of his erudition he excelled most of the learned men of his age; he was master of nine languages, ancient and modern, was versed in their literatures, and was equally distinguished for his acquirements in sacred and secular knowledge. His manner of speaking was calm and dignified, his style clear and direct; he appealed to intelligent and serious minds. He was a man of fixed habits and prejudices, outspoken in his opinions and inclined to caustic expression. According to Chief Justice Taney of the United States Supreme Court, who was a student under the Scotch divine, Nisbet's classes were warmly and affectionately attached to him. He was cheerful and animated, full of anecdote and classical allusion, seasoned with playful and lively wit. His sarcasm and wit were at times severe and cut deep. His lectures were written out and read slowly that the students might copy them. In his examinations he always preferred an answer in the student's own language, though it might not be as accurate; his object was to teach the student to study, to think, to reason, to form an opinion. He was anti-republican, had no faith in American institutions, did not believe in their stability. The class was good-natured about such utterances, but would not write them down; against such views from any other professor they would have rebelled (Samuel Tyler, *Memoir of Roger Brooke Taney*, 1872, p. 2).

Many of Nisbet's classroom lectures are preserved in manuscript in the Museum of Dickinson College. His publications, which were few, include a review of Wesley's system of doctrine, written in 1771, according to Nisbet's biographer, Miller (*post*), and published some years later in a periodical; his inaugural sermon at Dickinson, *The Relation Between Learning and Piety* (1785); *Address to the Students of Dickinson College* (1786) on the occasion of his reëlection to the presidency; a sermon, *The Usefulness and Importance of Human Learning* (1786). After his death, *Miscellaneous Writings* (1806) appeared.

Nisbet was of portly habit and florid complexion. In his youth he was remarkable for physical agility and endurance, frequently jogging twenty miles before breakfast as a morning exercise. Pneumonia terminated his earnest and active career and his body was interred in the Old Graveyard at Carlisle.

[W. B. Sprague, *Annals Am. Pulpit*, vol. III (1858); Samuel Miller, *Memoir of the Rev. Charles Nisbet, D.D., Late President of Dickinson Coll.* (1840); C. P. Wing, *A Hist. of the First Presbyt. Ch. of Carlisle, Pa.* (1877); Alfred Nevin, *Centennial Biog.: Men of Mark of Cumberland Valley* (1876); *Centennial Memorial of the Presbytery of Carlisle* (2 vols., 1889); G. R. Crooks, *Dickinson Coll.: The Hist. of a Hundred Years* (1883); J. H. Morgan, *Dickinson Coll.: The Hist. of One Hundred and Fifty Years* (1933); C. F. Himes, *Sketch of Dickinson Coll.* (1879); S. W. Parkinson, *Charles Nisbet, First President of Dickinson Coll.* (1908); H. C. King, *Hist. of Dickinson Coll.*, reprinted from the *Am. Univ. Mag.*, Feb., Mar., Apr., May 1897.]
L. C. P.

NISBET, EUGENIUS ARISTIDES (Dec. 7, 1803–Mar. 18, 1871), Georgia legislator and supreme court judge, congressman, was born in Greene County, Ga., the son of Penelope (Cooper) and James Nisbet, a physician who removed from North Carolina to Georgia in 1791, was a member of the convention that framed the constitution of 1798, and for twelve years served on the board of trustees of the University of Georgia. He was the descendant of John Nesbitt, whose father had emigrated to America from the North of Ireland and who, himself, changed the spelling of his name to Nisbet and removed from Lancaster County, Pa., to Rowan County, N. C., about 1741. The boy received an excellent education at Powelton Academy, at South Carolina College (now the University of South Carolina), and at the University of Georgia, where he was graduated in 1821 with highest honors. He began to read law in the office of Judge Augustin S. Clayton but soon went to the law school established by Tapping Reeve and James Gould [*qq.v.*] at Litchfield, Conn. Returning to practise his profession, he obtained a special act of the legislature to admit him to the bar, since he was still under the legal age, an unusual procedure that provoked a spasm of opposition and brought him valuable publicity. He located at Madison in the Ocmulgee circuit, where, gifted in tongue, pen, and bearing, he met immediate success. On Apr. 12, 1825, he married Amanda Battle, his boyhood sweetheart. Of their twelve children, five boys and seven girls, nine reached maturity. He was a member of the General Assembly for eight terms, two in the House, 1827–29, and six in the Senate, 1829–32, 1834, 1835. He was a follower of Troup, and later, like many of the Troup adherents, he became successively a member of the State-Rights, Whig, and Know-Nothing parties. He was known at this time for his support of education and of all liberal movements and for his literary ability. He was offered the chair of belles-lettres in the University of Georgia, and, later, in Oglethorpe College, a Presbyterian institution at Midway, of which he was one of the founders.

In 1837 his growing practice led to his removal to the larger center of Macon. The following year he was elected to Congress on the Whig ticket and in 1840 was reëlected. He resigned before the expiration of his second term to assume the burden of a heavy debt for which, during his absence, his firm had become liable as surety. When the supreme court of Georgia was inaugurated in 1845, he, Joseph Henry Lumpkin, and Hiram Warner received the honor of selection as judges by the General Assembly. During the first difficult years of the existence of the court he contributed all the force of his vigorous mind. Of the opinions he wrote several are notable. In *William Culbreath* vs. *James M. Culbreath and Daniel C. Culbreath* (*7 Ga. Reports,* 64) he maintained, along a delicate line of reasoning, that there existed a well-defined distinction between ignorance of the law and a mistake in understanding the law and that the courts were bound to recognize such a difference; in *Wiley Mitchum* vs. *The State of Ga.* (*11 Ga. Reports,* 615) he held that a new trial should be granted because, in argument to the jury, counsel overstepped the rules of justice in commenting on facts not proven, and this opinion had the distinction of being used as the decision of another court without acknowledgment of the quotation (see *Green Bag, post,* p. 23). Resuming his law practice in Macon in 1853, he soon became, in cooperation with Benjamin Harvey Hill, a leader of the Know-Nothing party in Georgia. To the secession convention that assembled in Milledgeville on Jan. 16, 1861, he had been chosen as a delegate, though known as a Union man and an opponent of the Democratic majority in the state, and he proved an unexpected accession to the leadership of secession. On Jan. 18, he proposed a resolution that it was the right and duty of Georgia to secede from the Union and to cooperate with such of the other states as had done or would do the same for the purpose of forming a Southern Confederacy, and that a committee be appointed to report an ordinance to assert the right and fulfil the obligation of the state. Notwithstanding the opposition of Herschel V. Johnson, Benjamin H. Hill, and Alexander H. Stephens, the committee was appointed. Nisbet, as chairman, drafted the ordinance of secession that was prepared by the committee and presented to the convention. In 1861 he was his party's candidate against Joseph E. Brown but was unsuccessful. He declined election to the provisional Congress of the Confederacy and continued to practise in Macon until his death.

[Sketch by J. R. Lamar, in *Great Amer. Lawyers,* ed. by W. D. Lewis, vol. IV (1908); George White, *Hist. Colls. of Ga.* (1854); I. W. Avery, *The Hist. of the State of Ga.* (1881); L. L. Knight, *Georgia's Landmarks* (2 vols., 1913–14); W. J. Northen, *Men of Mark in Ga.,* vol. III (1911); B. T. Hartman, *A Geneal. of the Nesbit, Ross . . . Families of Pa.* (1929); *Green Bag,* Jan. 1892.]   J. H. T. M.

NITCHIE, EDWARD BARTLETT (Nov. 18, 1876–Oct. 5, 1917), teacher of the deaf and author of textbooks on lip-reading, was born in Brooklyn, N. Y., the son of Henry Evertson Nitchie and Elizabeth Woods Dunklee. At the age of fourteen he became almost totally deaf but he persisted in his efforts to obtain an education and attended successively the Adelphi Academy, Brooklyn, the Brooklyn Latin School, and Betts

Academy, Stamford, Conn. By occupying a front seat, using an ear-trumpet, and interviewing his instructors after class he managed not only to attain but to keep up high grades. He entered Amherst in 1895, made Phi Beta Kappa in his junior year, became editor-in-chief of the *Amherst Literary Magazine,* was "ivy poet" at Commencement, and was graduated in 1899 *magna cum laude.* In spite of his brilliant record he had difficulty in finding employment. After several unsuccessful attempts he studied lip-reading and essayed to teach it and to devise simpler and easier methods of acquiring it. His own personal experience taught him to lay "less stress on technicalities and phonetic analysis and the mechanical phases of speech and speech-reading, and more on the mental processes involved" (Wright, *post,* p. 787). He believed that lip-reading must be largely self-taught. With the advice and sympathy of Alexander Graham Bell he put the results of his studies into his first book, *Self-Instructor in Lip-Reading,* published in 1902. In 1903 he started the New York School for the Hard-of-Hearing, which after his death became the Nitchie School. He was a rarely sympathetic and understanding teacher. In the fourteen years before his death he taught 1,100 pupils, and owing to the simplicity of his methods 117 of them became teachers much sought after by lip-reading schools everywhere. His second book, *Lessons in Lip-Reading for Self Instruction,* was published in 1905, and the revised edition in 1909. In 1912 appeared *Lip-Reading Principles and Practice,* which became the standard textbook in most schools. He also published a pamphlet, *Lip-Reading Simplified* (n.d.).

In 1910 the Nitchie Alumni Association was formed to facilitate social intercourse and to award scholarships to deserving pupils without means, and this association expanded two years later into the Nitchie Service League. The program included recreation, instruction, and employment. Nitchie was largely responsible for breaking down the prejudice against deaf employees and for securing opportunities for them to earn their own living in occupations for which deafness was no serious bar. Two years later the organization became, at Nitchie's own suggestion, the New York League for the Hard-of-Hearing that there might be no misapprehension as to its purpose. This League was the parent of similar groups organized in many cities of the United States and Canada, united in a national federation, the membership composed mainly of the hard-of-hearing, but including many eminent otologists. Nitchie created a life-work out of his deafness. It gave him understanding and suggested courses of action. His fertility in devising social amusements for the deaf, such as lip-reading contests, was amazing. For three out of the last six years of his life his work was interrupted by ill-health, but as often as the doctor permitted he went back to his work. He made wonderful use of the small pittance of life allowed him. His pupils placed a memorial tablet in the Volta Bureau at Washington, and six of his teachers erected one in the Nitchie School. He had married, June 18, 1908, Elizabeth Logan Helm in New York. They had one son.

[Juliet D. Clark, "Edward Bartlett Nitchie: An Appreciation," *Volta Rev.*, Nov. 1917; tributes by Alice N. Trask and Elizabeth Brand in *Ibid.*, Dec. 1917; J. D. Wright, "In Memory of Edward Bartlett Nitchie," *Ibid.*, Dec. 1918; Elizabeth Helm Nitchie, "Edward Bartlett Nitchie," *Ibid.*, Jan. 1919; *N. Y. Times*, Oct. 6, 1917; information as to certain facts from Nitchie's widow and from the N. Y. League for the Hard-of-Hearing.]   E. E. Ca--s.

NITSCHMANN, DAVID (Dec. 27, 1696–Oct. 8, 1772), bishop of the Renewed Unitas Fratrum or Moravian Church, was born at Zauchtenthal, Moravia, the son of George Nitschmann, a pious and well-to-do citizen, in the line of a family that had given leaders to the Ancient Unitas Fratrum for over a century. The son possessed a strain of evangelical enthusiasm that, at an early age, brought him into conflict with his environment and with the pious but conforming habits of his father. In 1722 he and four like-minded young men made the acquaintance of Christian David who had persuaded Count Nicholas von Zinzendorf to found a refuge for the persecuted remnant of the Ancient Brethren's Church on his estate at Berthelsdorf, Saxony. In May 1724 these five young men, outcasts from their homes, escaped by devious mountain passes to the Saxon haven and were present when the cornerstone of the first building of Herrnhut was laid. For a year Nitschmann remained in this growing asylum and learned the carpenter's trade. Then he visited his home as an evangelist and persuaded, among others, his invalid father and his uncle, also a David Nitschmann, to abandon their homes and enter the new community, and they were all present in 1727 when the Renewed Unitas Fratrum or Moravian Church was formed. On this trip, Nov. 12, 1726, he married Rosina Schindler.

Count Zinzendorf, recognizing the inherent power of the young man, promptly made use of him for the furtherance of evangelistic work. He was sent to various courts and centers in Europe, going as far as Denmark, Russia, and England. It was at David Nitschmann's instigation that the official center for Moravian work was placed at London, just at the moment when English supremacy in the trade world was becoming an assured fact. And it was this quiet, practical-minded carpenter who realized that the hopes of Herrnhut could be brought to fruition by attaching them to the power of England. In August 1732 he was sent with Leonard Dober to establish a mission among the black slaves of St. Thomas, W. I. This work having been accomplished he returned to Europe in 1733. In 1735 he was consecrated bishop.

Zinzendorf's plans for the evangelization of the North American Indians and for the unification of the migrant Germans of Pennsylvania opened with the attempt at Savannah, Ga., in 1735. Nitschmann arrived early in 1736 and ordained Anton Seifert (or Seiffert) as the first pastor of the Savannah group. This was the first ordination, by a Protestant bishop, in America. In March 1736 he went to Pennsylvania and then sailed for Europe to meet Zinzendorf in England. For the next two years he was constantly in motion from country to country seeking support for the Pennsylvania plan. In 1740, accompanied by his uncle, David Nitschmann the elder, he started for America to establish centers for the evangelization of the Indians. The Savannah settlement was abandoned and the entire company proceeded to Pennsylvania. Nitschmann bought five hundred acres at the confluence of the Lehigh River and the Monocacy Creek in Pennsylvania, and on this tract David Nitschmann the elder began, with the rest of the party, the erection of the town of Bethlehem. From this period on, the headquarters of the sect at Bethlehem was entirely in the hands of Nitschmann. He was unquestionably the founder of all the Moravian work in America, though his uncle, because he held title and directed most of the physical operation, has often mistakenly been called the founder of Bethlehem. In 1744 the administration of the American work was given to Bishop Augustus Gottlieb Spangenberg and Nitschmann started for Europe. His vessel was captured by a Spanish frigate and he was carried to St. Sebastian as a prisoner, not reaching Herrnhut until 1745. He renewed his organization work but before 1750 he had returned to America, and between this time and 1756 he was constantly in motion, making over forty journeys across the Atlantic. His last voyage took him to Pennsylvania in 1755. At the age of sixty-five he returned to Bethlehem where he lived in retirement until his death in 1772. His first wife having died in 1753, he later married Mary Barbara (Leinbach) Martin, widow of Frederick Martin.

[Manuscript materials include the "Autobiog. of David Nitschmann" (1765), the "Bethlehem Diary, 1740–72," and the certificate of consecration from Daniel Jablonsky, June 14, 1737, in the archives of the Bethlehem Church, as well as correspondence and diaries of itinerant workers, 1735–72. Published material includes: J. M. Levering, *Hist. of Bethlehem* (1896); Edmund deSchweinitz, "David Nitschmann, First Bishop of the Renewed Brethrens Church," in *Trans. Moravian Hist. Soc.*, vol. II (1886), section I, and *The Hist. of the Church Known as the Unitas Fratrum* (1885); Adelaide L. Fries, *The Moravians in Ga., 1735–40* (1905); L. T. Reichel, *The Early Hist. of the Church of the United Brethren Commonly Called Moravians in North America* (1888), and *Memorials of the Moravian Church* (1870); J. T. Hamilton, *A Hist. of the Church Known as the Moravian Church or the Unitas Fratrum* (1900) and *Moravian Missions* (2 vols., 1904).]   A. G. R.

NIXON, JOHN (Mar. 1, 1727–Mar. 24, 1815), Revolutionary soldier, was born in Framingham, Mass., the son of Christopher Nixon or Nickson and his wife, Mary Seaver. At the age of eighteen he enlisted in Capt. Ephraim Baker's company of Sir William Pepperell's regiment and served in the expedition of 1745 against Louisbourg. At the outbreak of the French and Indian War, he enlisted (Mar. 27, 1755) in Capt. Ebenezer Newell's Roxbury company and was commissioned lieutenant. Subsequently transferred to Capt. Jonathan Hoar's Concord company and promoted (Sept. 8) to be captain, he took part in the expedition against Crown Point. In the following year he served in the provincial force organized to capture Ticonderoga. In 1758 he was captain of a company in Colonel Ruggles' regiment at Half Moon, N. Y. He also saw considerable service in the closing years of the struggle. In the meantime he had acquired a farm in Sudbury and a wife, Thankful Berry, whom he married on Feb. 7, 1754. In the course of time ten children, five sons and five daughters, were born.

Family and fireside could not hold him back when the Revolution began. He commanded a company of minute-men in the fighting at Lexington and Concord of Apr. 19, 1775. His keen sense of discipline is illustrated by the fact that when he was ordered to hold his detachment in check and one of his men impatiently accused him of cowardice, he replied: "I should rather be called a coward by you, than called to account by my superior officer, for disobedience of orders" (Temple, *post*, p. 276). A week later, under authority of the Massachusetts Committee of Safety, he proceeded to raise a regiment. He was wounded in the battle of Bunker Hill and participated in the siege of Boston. On Jan. 1, 1776, he became colonel of the 4th Continental Infantry, and later moved with the army to New York. On Washington's recommendation, Congress elected him brigadier-general (Aug. 9).

He was placed in command of two regiments of infantry and a detachment of artillery on Governor's Island, and took part in the operations on the mainland subsequent to the capture of New York. In 1777 his brigade, as part of the northern army, participated in the movements resulting in the defeat of Burgoyne. On one occasion a cannon-ball passed so near to his head as to impair his sight and hearing on one side. He was detailed to escort the captive British from Saratoga to Cambridge, Mass. Granted a furlough of several months because of ill health, he took occasion to marry, on Feb. 5, 1778, his second wife, Hannah (Drury) Gleason, widow of a comrade-in-arms. Upon his return to the colors, he served on the court martial appointed to try General Schuyler. His health continuing poor, he resigned Sept. 12, 1780, receiving an honorable discharge. About 1806 he removed from Sudbury to Middlebury, Vt., where he died. Notwithstanding his soldierly bearing and firmness of character, he was a man of engaging manners, who in later years especially enjoyed recounting stories of his military career for the pleasure of his grandchildren.

[J. H. Temple, *Hist. of Framingham, Mass.* (1887); Peter Force, *Am. Archives* (9 vols., 1837–53); Wm. Barry, *A Hist. of Framingham, Mass.* (1847); S. A. Drake, *Hist. of Middlesex County, Mass.* (2 vols., 1880); A. S. Hudson, *The Hist. of Sudbury, Mass.* (1889); D. H. Hurd, *Hist. of Middlesex County, Mass.* (1890), II, 402; *Mass. Soldiers and Sailors of the Revolutionary War*, vol. XI (1903); F. B. Heitman, *Hist. Reg. of Officers of the Continental Army* (1914); J. M. Merriam, *Five Framingham Heroes of the Am. Rev.* (1925); *Hist. Mag.*, Dec. 1860, Jan. 1861; *Repertory* (Boston), Apr. 11, 1815.]   E. E. Cu–s.

NIXON, JOHN (1733–Dec. 31, 1808), Revolutionary patriot, merchant, financier, was born in Philadelphia, Pa., the son of Richard and Sarah (Bowles) Nixon, and on Apr. 17, 1735, at the age of two, was baptized in Christ Church. His father was a prominent shipping merchant and the proprietor of Nixon's Wharf on the Delaware River in Philadelphia. John received but little education except in his father's business, which he inherited in 1749. He early took a leading part in public affairs and in March 1756 was chosen lieutenant of the Dock Ward Company, a home-guard organization. In 1765 he was one of the signers of the non-importation agreement and from that time ranked as one of the leaders of the patriot cause in Philadelphia. The following year he was appointed a warden of the port, and in 1767 was one of the signers of the paper money issued by Pennsylvania.

He became a member of the first Committee of Correspondence in June 1774 and a deputy to the General Conference of the Province of Pennsylvania, July 15; he was a delegate to the Convention for the Province in January 1775; and in April of that year helped organize and was chosen lieutenant-colonel of the 3rd Battalion of Associators, known as the "Silk Stockings." On Oct. 20, 1775, he was made a member of the provincial Committee of Safety, serving and acting as president *pro tempore* whenever the president and vice-president, Benjamin Franklin and Robert Morris, were absent. He was also chairman of the committee on accounts of this organization. In May 1776 he commanded the defenses of the Delaware at Fort Island and in July was placed in command of the Philadelphia city guard. During this year he was also a member of the Continental navy board. On July 8, 1776, appointed by the sheriff of Philadelphia for the task, he had the distinction of publicly reading and proclaiming the Declaration of Independence to an assemblage of citizens, for the first time after its adoption. Immediately after this his Battalion of Associators was called upon to aid in the defense of Amboy, N. J. Six weeks later they returned to Philadelphia, where they remained until December when, Nixon having succeeded to the command of the organization, they joined General Washington in the campaign against Trenton and took part in the battle of Princeton, Jan. 3, 1777. He was a member of the committee to settle and adjust the accounts of the Committee and Council of Safety in 1778; and in 1779 was one of the auditors of public accounts, whose chief business was to settle and adjust the depreciation of the Continental currency. In the spring of 1780 he was one of the organizers of the Bank of Pennsylvania for the purpose of supplying the army of the United States with provisions and supplies. He contributed the sum of five thousand pounds sterling and was appointed as one of the two directors. In 1784 he became a director of the Bank of North America and in 1792 was elected its president, which post he held until his death. From 1789 to 1796 he was an alderman of the city.

Throughout his life Nixon maintained his interest in the business which his father had founded and at the time of his death was senior member of the firm of Nixon & Walker, shipping merchants. He was a member of and officer in numerous social and business organizations, was one of the managers of the Pennsylvania Hospital, 1768–72, and a trustee of the College of Philadelphia, 1789–91. In October 1765 he married Elizabeth Davis, who bore him four daughters and a son. He died in Philadelphia and was buried in St. Peter's Church Yard. Dignified and reserved in manner but noted for his kindness, he was recognized as a man of honor, integrity, and decision.

[C. H. Hart, *Memoir of the Life and Services of Col. John Nixon* (1877), reproducing portrait by Gilbert Stuart, repr. from *Pa. Mag. of Hist. and Biog.*, vol. I (1877); Henry Simpson, *The Lives of Eminent Philadelphians Now Deceased* (1859); J. L. Chamberlain, *Universities and Their Sons: Univ. of Pa.*, vol. I (1901); J. T. Scharf and Thompson Westcott, *Hist. of Phila.* (1884), vol. I; E. P. Oberholtzer, *Phila., A Hist. of the City and Its People* (n.d.), vol. I; J. H. Campbell, *Hist. of the Friendly Sons of St. Patrick and of the Hibernian Soc.* (1892); Michael Hennessy, "Col. John Nixon," in *Hist. Mag. and Notes and Queries*, Dec. 1860, Jan. 1861; Lawrence Lewis, Jr., *A Hist. of the Bank of North America* (1882); W. W. Bronson, *The Inscriptions in St. Peter's Church Yard, Phila.* (1879), p. 14.]

J. H. F.

NIXON, JOHN THOMPSON (Aug. 31, 1820–Sept. 28, 1889), jurist, was born in Fairton, a small village about four miles from the county seat of Cumberland County, N. J. He was the son of Jeremiah S. Nixon and his wife Mary Shaw (Thompson). The Nixon family was one of the leading families of the county. After the usual preliminary education, John entered the College of New Jersey (now Princeton University) in 1837, graduating in 1841, and for a time was employed in teaching languages there. About 1843 he went to Staunton, Va., as a tutor in the family of Judge Isaac S. Pennybacker of the United States court for the western district of that state, and while so engaged he studied law and was admitted to the Virginia bar in 1844. The retirement from practice of a prominent lawyer of Bridgeton, N. J., brought him back to his native county as a partner of Charles E. Elmer. He was admitted to the New Jersey bar at the October term 1845 as an attorney and at the July term 1849 as a counselor.

On September 24, 1851, he married Mary H. Elmer, the daughter of Lucius Q. C. Elmer [q.v.], who in 1838 had rendered a great service to the bar and people of the state by compiling and publishing *A Digest of the Laws of New Jersey*, a compendium of the general statutory law then in force which came to be known as "Elmer's Digest." In 1852 Elmer was appointed to the state supreme court, and since the new constitution of 1844 had intervened and the arrangement of the revised statutes of 1847 was unsatisfactory, Nixon undertook the preparation of a second edition of Elmer's *Digest*. It appeared in 1855 with Elmer's name above Nixon's on the title-page, but was generally known as "Nixon's Digest." A third edition appeared in 1861, and a fourth in 1868, all compiled by Nixon but continuing to bear Elmer's name.

Meanwhile Nixon had diligently pursued the practice of his profession and had also entered the field of politics. He served in the New Jersey Assembly in 1849 and 1850, and in the latter year was speaker. In 1858 he was elected a representative in Congress from his district, and served for two terms, until Mar. 3, 1863. In 1864 he was elected a trustee of Princeton College and served as such until his death. He was also a trustee of Princeton Theological Seminary from 1883 until his death, and for many years was an active and valued participant in the councils of the Presbyterian Church. His judicial career began in April 1870 when President Grant appointed him judge of the district court of the United States for the district of New Jersey; and for nearly twenty years he handled the difficult specialties of admiralty, bankruptcy, and patents in a manner which caused his court to be sought out as a forum for important litigation, particularly in the field of patent law. His outstanding characteristics were indefatigable industry, thorough and profound knowledge of the law, sturdy honesty, a keen and delicate sense of honor, and a geniality without undue familiarity which endeared him to the bar and drew to his court a volume of business which ultimately wore him out. He carried an increasing load of work until failing eyesight in 1887 forced him to permit others to aid him. In the summer of 1889 he went to Maine for his vacation, but on the way home died at Stockbridge, Mass., Sept. 28. Three children survived him.

[*Gen. Cat. of Princeton Univ.* (1908); T. F. Fitzgerald, *State of N. J., Manual of the Legislature,* 1889; *N. J. Law Jour.,* Oct. 1889; *Rules of the Supreme Court of the State of N. J. . . . 1885* (1885); Wm. Nelson, *Nelson's Biog. Cyc. of N. J.* (1913), vol. I; *Daily True American* (Trenton), Sept. 30, 1889; personal information from Nixon's grandson, J. N. Brooks of Trenton, N. J.]   C. W. P.

NIXON, WILLIAM PENN (Mar. 19, 1833–Feb. 20, 1912), journalist, derived from his ancestors two highly dissimilar strains. His father, Samuel Nixon, was the son of a famous Quaker preacher, a Virginian of English ancestry and an early protestant against human slavery; while from his mother, Rhoda Hubbard (Butler) Nixon, who was descended from Cherokee Indians, he may have acquired the quality of patient persistence which, coupled with a Quaker's devotion to the right as he saw it, made him a power in his profession. Born in Fountain City, Wayne County, Ind., he sought his education mainly in the schools adjacent to his home, going at fourteen years of age to Turtle Creek Academy, Warren County, Ohio, then entering Earlham College, Richmond, Ind. In 1854 (according to *Who's Who in America*) he was graduated at Farmers' (now Belmont) College

near Cincinnati, having interrupted his scholastic endeavors from time to time by months of teaching. A four-year course in law and graduation (LL.B.) at the University of Pennsylvania in 1857 completed his academic training.

Like many others destined to win later success in journalism, he embarked first upon the practice of law. In Cincinnati between 1860 and 1868 he attained a measure of success as an attorney, though his taste for politics, already apparent, interfered with a single-minded devotion to his profession. He was elected to the state legislature in 1864 and through reëlection served until 1868. In that year he joined his brother, Dr. O. W. Nixon, in the establishment of the *Cincinnati Daily Chronicle,* an evening newspaper. The position of financial editor, which he held at first, he soon abandoned for the post of publisher and general manager, and as such continued until 1872 when the paper was merged with the *Times.* He had, in the meantime, been married twice; in September 1861 to Mary Stites of Cincinnati, who died a year later, and on June 15, 1869, to Elizabeth Duffield of Chicago.

In 1872 Nixon went to Chicago, which was just beginning to be rebuilt upon the charred ruins of its great fire. Here he found that the chief Republican paper of the city and state, the *Chicago Daily Tribune,* was at odds with its party on the fundamental issue of the tariff, while an almost moribund paper, the *Inter Ocean,* was feebly attempting to make its way. In May 1872 he became business manager of the latter journal. After serving for a time in this capacity, he secured with his brother a controlling interest, and in 1875 became general manager and editor. Thenceforth until 1897 he gave his personal attention to every department of the paper.

Under his editorship the *Inter Ocean* was always what the politicians call a "reliably" Republican newspaper. The party platform was its sufficient guide in matters economic and political. Believing thoroughly, as he did, in the worth of the policy of protection to American industries, Nixon made the paper the most unfaltering advocate of that policy in the Middle West. It was generally believed that some beneficiaries of protection were among its owners, for the period was one in which newspaper management had not reached its present business stage, and the profits of many papers were based as much on their political associations as upon legitimate advertising receipts. The journals of that time were more scholarly, however, than the press of a later day—less sensational, more world-wide in their viewpoint—and Nixon's own editorial endeavors impressed these characteristics especially upon the *Inter Ocean*. In 1896 he was chosen delegate-at-large to the Republican National Convention. It was the year of the struggle over free silver, and those who recalled that he had printed "Coin's Financial School" in the *Inter Ocean* (greatly to the advantage of the paper's circulation) apprehended that he might not follow his party on that issue. But the life-long habit of regularity was not easily interrupted, and during the heated campaign he earnestly advocated the election of William McKinley. In December 1897 he was appointed collector of the port of Chicago, and reappointed in 1902. His paper passed into other hands, and his later years were spent in retirement.

In what was perhaps the stormiest period of Chicago's social and political development, Nixon displayed a quiet and kindly demeanor, an aversion to anything which savored of self-assertion or a desire for political domination. He went with his party with little endeavor to lead it, yet his influence was extended and in the main for good. He did not succeed in making his paper financially successful, but at least he made it eminently respectable and, within its own party, exceedingly influential. In all the progressive and esthetic public activities of the day he took a leading part, not merely as a journalist but as a public servant. He was a member of the Lincoln Park Board in 1896 and its president in 1897–98. For some time he was president of the Associated Press.

[Paul Gilbert and C. L. Bryson, *Chicago and Its Makers* (1929); *Who's Who in America*, 1908–09; *The Book of Chicagoans* (1911); A. T. Andreas, *Hist. of Chicago*, vol. III (1886); *Rev. of Revs.* (N. Y.), June 1895; clippings, etc., in files of Chicago Hist. Soc.; *Inter Ocean* (Chicago), Feb. 19, 21, 1912.] W. J. A.

NIZA, MARCOS de (d. Mar. 25, 1558), Franciscan missionary, author, and explorer, was born in Nice, in the duchy of Savoy. He went to Santo Domingo as a missionary in 1531 and from there to Peru. He is said to have been present at the capture and execution of the Inca, Atahualpa, and is credited with having founded the Franciscan province of Lima, with having written several works which deal with the conquest and native races of Ecuador and Peru (see Juan Velasco, *Historia del Reino de Quito*, 3 vols., 1841–44), and with having supplied Las Casas with information concerning the treatment of the Indians of Peru by the Spaniards. From Peru, Fray Marcos went to New Spain by way of Central America and soon was sent to the province of Nueva Galicia, of which Francisco Vazquez Coronado [*q.v.*] became governor in 1538. Fray Marcos was highly esteemed, and in 1539 became vice-commissary-general of the Franciscan Order in New Spain. The following year he was elected provincial of the province of Santo Evangelio and held that office for three years.

By Viceroy Mendoza, he was sent in 1539 to investigate reports brought to New Spain in 1536 by Núñez Cabeza de Vaca [*q.v.*] concerning a high civilization in the present states of New Mexico and Arizona, and it is for this expedition that he is best known. A former negro slave who accompanied Núñez was selected as guide and went on in advance. Upon reaching one of the Zuñi pueblos in western New Mexico he was murdered by the inhabitants. Accordingly, Fray Marcos contented himself with viewing the pueblo from a safe distance, and returned to New Spain to report that he had seen a city that was "greater than the city of Mexico." Bandelier (*post*, p. 172) believes that he did not deliberately lie, reasoning that in the desert atmosphere the pueblo appeared larger from a distance than was the case; he argues, furthermore, that the comparison was with the newly founded Spanish town of Mexico, not with the old city which had been destroyed in 1521. Whatever his intentions, Fray Marcos' report was exaggerated and quickly spread over New Spain, with the result that Coronado was commissioned to conquer the region. When his spectacular expedition set out in 1540 the Franciscan went along as a guide. Zuñi proved to be disappointing and the prestige of Fray Marcos waned correspondingly; in fact, "such were the curses that were hurled upon him" by the disappointed treasure-seekers that he soon returned to New Spain. The chief result of the Coronado expedition which the earlier report of Fray Marcos had inspired was the military occupation by the Spaniards of the upper Rio Grande Valley for two winters.

On his northern expeditions the friar lost his health. The date of his death is disputed but according to Vetancurt (*post*) he died in the city of Mexico on Mar. 25, 1558.

[Niza's report appears in *Colección de Documentos Inéditos Relativos al Descubrimiento, Conquista y Colonización de las Posesiones Españolas en América y Oceanía*, III (1865), 325–69; with translation and notes by P. M. Baldwin, in *Hist. Soc. of N. Mex., Pubs. in Hist.*, vol. I (1926), and in translation, in *N. Mex. Hist. Rev.*, Apr. 1926. See also H. H. Bancroft, *Hist. of Ariz. and N. Mex.* (1889), pp. 27–68; A. F. Bandelier, in *Papers of the Archæological Institute of America*, V (1890), 106–78; H. E. Bolton, *The Spanish Borderlands* (1921), pp. 80–105; Fray Antonio de la Rosa Figueroa, "Promptuario General y Específico" (MS., Mexico, 1770; original MS. in García Collection, Univ. of Tex.); Woodbury Lowery, *The Spanish Settlements within the Present Limits of the United States, 1513–1561* (1901), pp. 260–336; G. P. Winship, "The Coronado Expedition, 1540–1542," in *Fourteenth Ann. Report, Bureau of Ethnology*, pt. I (1896), pp. 329–613; Agustín de Vetancurt, "Menologio Franciscano," *Teatro Mexicano*, IV (Mexico, 1871), 117–19.] C. W. H.

NIZZA, MARCOS de [See NIZA, MARCOS DE, d. 1558].

NOAH, MORDECAI MANUEL (July 19, 1785–Mar. 22, 1851), lawyer, playwright, journalist, was born in Philadelphia, Pa., of Portuguese-Jewish ancestry. His father, Manuel M. Noah, a Jewish patriot of Charleston, S. C., is said to have served with General Marion and to have contributed a considerable sum to the Revolutionary cause. His mother, Zipporah Phillips Noah, was the daughter of Robert Phillips, a Jewish merchant of Philadelphia. Noah's early youth was spent in Charleston, S. C. At the age of ten, after the death of his mother, he was sent to live with his maternal grandfather in Philadelphia. Here, after a short period at school and after a brief apprenticeship to a carver and gilder, he was appointd a clerk in the auditor's office of the United States Treasury. Upon the removal of the national capital to Washington in 1800, Noah became a reporter at the sessions of the Pennsylvania legislature at Harrisburg, where he acquired his first experience in journalism, a profession which he was to follow, with few interruptions, for the rest of his life.

In early manhood Noah returned to Charleston, where he engaged in politics and possibly studied law. An ardent patriot, he advocated war with Great Britain and the maintenance of American rights on the high seas; many of his vigorous communications to the Charleston press bore the signature "Muley Malack." He had become interested in the theatre in Philadelphia, had published a play, and in 1812 wrote a melodrama, *Paul and Alexis,* adapted from *Le Pélerin blanc* (1802) of *Pixerécourt.* This, his first acted play, was afterward produced under the title *The Wandering Boys.*

In April 1813 Noah was appointed consul to Tunis, with a special mission to Algiers. He was instructed to negotiate for the release of some Americans held as prisoners by the Algerine pirates. On May 23, 1813, he sailed from Charleston, but his vessel being captured by the British, he was taken to England and detained two months. In October he arrived in Cadiz, where he contracted with Richard R. Keene, an American who had become a Spanish subject, to effect the release of the twelve Americans held for ransom by the Algerines. After being delayed in France and Spain for more than a year, Noah finally arrived in Tunis. On July 30, 1815, he received a letter from James Monroe, secretary of state, revoking his commission and hinting at irregularities in his accounts. Monroe's treatment of Noah was never satisfactorily ex-

plained, though his association with Keene, who had been accused of treason, was doubtless detrimental to his prestige. In January 1817, however, Noah received a letter from the Department of State which vindicated his conduct and returned several thousand dollars due him in the enterprise which resulted in the release of the American captives. He wrote a defense of his actions, published as *Correspondence and Documents Relative to the Attempt to Negotiate for the Release of the American Captives at Algiers* (1816), the substance of which was embodied in his *Travels in England, France, Spain, and the Barbary States* (1819). Returning to America in 1816, Noah entered the field of journalism in New York City. In 1817 he became editor of the *National Advocate,* a daily journal founded by the Tammany faction of the Democratic party. During this period of editorship which continued for almost ten years, Noah engaged in a project which he had cherished for many years. Always strongly attached to his own people, he desired to establish in America a colony for the oppressed Jews of all nations. Accordingly, in 1825, with imposing ceremonies, he laid the corner-stone of "Ararat, a City of Refuge" which he hoped to establish on Grand Island in the Niagara River. Though the project came to naught, it affords an interesting commentary upon an otherwise practical mind. Shortly upon his return to America Noah's patriotic impulses sought dramatic expression. His play, *She Would be a Soldier* (1819), based upon the battle of Chippewa, held the stage for many years. *The Siege of Tripoli,* first produced in 1820, later played in Philadelphia under the title *Yuseff Caramalli,* has not been preserved. *Marion, or the Hero of Lake George,* performed in 1821, a drama of the Revolution, uses the battle of Saratoga for background. His last play, *The Grecian Captive* (1822), though an adaptation from a French melodrama, is charged with patriotic sentiments.

In 1822 Noah was appointed sheriff of New York, an office which he held for less than a year, and, in 1823, he was admitted to the New York bar. In 1826 he married Rebecca Esther Jackson, by whom he had six sons and one daughter. In this same year he left the *National Advocate* and established the *New York Enquirer,* which, in 1829, was merged with the *Morning Courier* under the title *Morning Courier and New York Enquirer,* a paper which supported Jackson's first administration. In 1829 President Jackson appointed Noah surveyor of the Port of New York, but in 1833 Noah resigned this office, and the following year **he**

founded the *Evening Star* to support the new
Whig party. In 1841 Governor Seward appointed him associate judge of the New York court
of sessions, an office which he resigned the following year. He then became successively editor
of the *Union,* and *Noah's Times and Weekly
Messenger.* The last-named paper he edited to
the end of his life. *Gleanings from a Gathered
Harvest* (1845) is a collection of his newspaper
essays. He died of a stroke of apoplexy in his
sixty-sixth year.

[See Simon Wolf, *Mordecai Manuel Noah, a Biog.
Sketch* (1897); C. P. Daly, *The Settlement of the Jews
in North America* (1893); L. F. Allen, "Founding of
the City of Ararat on Grand Island by Mordecai M.
Noah," *Buffalo Hist. Soc. Pubs.,* vol. I (1879); M. J.
Kohler, "Some Early Am. Zionist Projects," *Am.
Jewish Hist. Soc. Pubs.,* no. 8 (1900); G. H. Cone,
"New Matter Relating to Mordecai M. Noah," *Ibid.,*
no. 11 (1903); Noah's speech on the laying of the
corner-stone of "Ararat" in *Ibid.,* no. 21 (1913); letters from the Van Buren papers relating to Noah, *Ibid.,*
no. 22 (1914); Wm. Dunlap, *A Hist. of the Am. Theatre* (1832), pp. 380-84; A. H. Quinn, *A Hist. of the
Am. Drama from the Beginning to the Civil War*
(1923); Samuel Lockwood, "Major M. M. Noah," *Lippincott's Mag.,* June 1868; Anita L. Lebeson, *Jewish
Pioneers in America, 1492–1848* (1931), useful for references; *N. Y. Tribune,* Mar. 24, 1851.]
                                        H.W.S—g—r.

NOAILLES, LOUIS MARIE, Vicomte de
(Apr. 17, 1756–Jan. 5, 1804), French soldier,
man of affairs, was born in Paris, France, the
second son of Philippe, duc de Mouchy, and his
man of affairs, was born in Paris, France, the
Duc d'Arpajon. On Sept. 19, 1773, at the age of
seventeen, he married his cousin, Louise de
Noailles, a daughter of the Duc d'Ayen, whose
sister later married Lafayette. It was rather as
a "modern" and fashionable young man than as
a crusader that Noailles welcomed the revolt of
the American colonies. Lack of an independent income prevented his departure with Lafayette; but as an officer in the French army he
later took part in d'Estaing's campaign in the
West Indies, commanded a trench with credit
in the siege of Savannah, and arrived at Newport with Rochambeau in 1780 as colonel *en
second* of the regiment of Royal-Soissonais. As
the real commander of this regiment he took a
distinguished part in the Yorktown campaign
and was chosen to represent the French army
in negotiating the terms of surrender with Cornwallis. He returned to France and served both
in the Assembly of Notables of 1787 and in the
Estates-General of 1789. He is forever associated with one of the most radical steps taken
by the National Assembly. On the night of Aug.
4, 1789, Noailles in a brief and very effective
speech proposed that the privileged orders take
the first step toward the abolition of social and

economic privilege by giving up freely their antiquated feudal status. This speech started an
orgy of verbal altruism, and before the night
was over the *ancien régime* was abolished, at
least on paper. Noailles attempted to serve as
an officer in the new army but could not completely repudiate his blood and his upbringing.
He left France in 1792, and his name was placed
on the list of *émigrés*—a step which meant the
confiscation of his property. After a brief stay
in England he went to Philadelphia in 1793,
probably for economic reasons. His second stay
in America is perhaps more interesting, save to
military and diplomatic history, than his first,
for he built up a moderate fortune for himself
in the Philadelphia business world. He became
a partner in the banking house of Bingham &
Company and seems to have speculated successfully on the stock exchange. With Robert Morris and John Nicholson [*qq.v.*] he promoted the
Asylum Company, organized to buy and sell
lands, especially in an attempt to provide a
refuge for French *émigrés*. The colony was established in what is now Bradford County, Pa.
In 1800, Noailles's French possessions were restored to him, and his name was erased from the
list of *émigrés*. He did not, however, return to
France. But having gone to Santo Domingo on
business, he accepted a commission under Rochambeau, son of his former commander. He
held Môle St. Nicolas against a large force of
blacks and a blockading British squadron for
five months, and then ran the blockade, escaping
with his men to a Cuban port. Proceeding with
a few men toward Havana on the schooner *Courrier,* he met an English corvette of seven guns,
the *Hazard,* fooled her commander by his knowledge of English, and got close enough to board
and capture her in one of the most romantic
struggles in French naval history. He died of
wounds received in this action, after having
brought the *Hazard* to Havana as a prize.

Noailles was clearly a man of great personal
charm and social flexibility. He was a brave
and capable officer, and a good man of business.
Living as he did in eighteenth-century France,
he had the radical sympathies of the most active
of his order. But there are no signs that he
really thought out for himself the consequences
of his devotion to liberty, novelty, and progress.
He left his wife in France to be guillotined and
never returned to see his sons. He was apparently somewhat vain, and shared with Lafayette a thirst for glory. Yet his speeches, his letters to the Robinsons, and his activities in Philadelphia reveal a man of common sense, to whom
the ideas of 1776 and of 1789 were neither a faith

nor a goal, but something to be accepted, and used, like a fashion.

[A. M. R. A. Noailles, *Souvenirs d'Amérique et d'Orient* (Paris, n.d.); Marquis de Castellane, "Gentilshommes démocrates: le Vicomte de Noailles," *Nouvelle Revue*, Sept. 1, 15, 1890; A. H. Wood, "The Robinson Family and their Correspondence with the Vicomte and Vicomtesse de Noailles," *Newport Hist. Soc. Bull.*, no. 42, Oct. 1922; C. A. Pontgibaud, *Mémoires du Comte de Moré* (Paris, 1898), of which an English edition, translated by R. B. Douglas, was published in Paris in 1897; Louise W. Murray, *The Story of Some French Refugees and Their "Asilum," 1793–1800* (2nd ed., 1917); J. B. P. J. Courcelles, *Histoire Généal. et Heraldique des Pairs de France*, vol. VIII (1827).]   C. B—n.

NOBILI, JOHN (Apr. 8, 1812–Mar. 1, 1856), Catholic missionary and educator, was born at Rome, where his father was a lawyer of repute. Trained in a Roman college, he entered the Society of Jesus in 1826, and after following the regular Jesuit course of study he taught in the Society's colleges at Rome, Loretto, Placentia, and Fermo. Ordained in 1843, he volunteered for the American missions and accompanied Father Pierre-Jean De Smet [*q.v.*] to the Rocky Mountains. Here in the wild regions of Oregon and of New Caledonia as far as Fort Stuart, this Roman, accustomed to the mild Italian climate, spent six years of terrible suffering from hunger and cold. Often reduced to a diet of herbs and of the flesh of dogs and wolves, he labored with desperate intensity as a missioner and as superior of the Oregon–Rocky Mountain missions among the Okanagans, Flatheads, and Kalispels, of whom he is said to have baptized about 1,500.

In 1849, because of failing health, he was ordered to California and assigned to duties in San Francisco, where he is said to have been the first priest to preach. He won the merited approval of its rough inhabitants in the severe cholera epidemic of 1850, during which he nursed the sick and comforted the dying. A year later, Bishop José S. Alemany [*q.v.*] assigned him to a mission at Santa Clara, where he opened a school for boys with the assistance of two lay teachers and a matron. The institution attracted attention because of its technical instruction in mining and grew rapidly as the population of the state increased. In 1855 the college was incorporated as a university with Nobili as president. A scholarly, urbane man of excessive zeal, with the aid of brother Jesuits expelled from Sardinia, he made this pioneer school unequaled on the Pacific Coast. His death, at a comparatively early age, was from lockjaw, occasioned by his stepping upon a nail.

[*The Metropolitan Cath. Almanac for the Year 1857*, p. 298; *N. Y. Freeman's Jour.*, Apr. 5, June 14, 1856; *Records of the Am. Cath. Hist. Soc.*, June 1906; H. M. Chittenden and A. T. Richardson, *Life, Letters, and Travels of Father Pierre-Jean De Smet, S. J.* (1905); J. W. Riordan, *The First Half Century of St. Ignatius Church and College* (1905); *San Francisco Daily Herald*, Mar. 3, 1856.]   R. J. P.

NOBLE, ALFRED (Aug. 7, 1844–Apr. 19, 1914), civil engineer, was born in Livonia, Wayne County, Mich. His father, Charles, and his mother, Lovina (Douw) Noble, were the descendants of several ancestors who saw military service in the American Revolution, and his grandfather, Norton Noble, was a soldier in the War of 1812. Alfred's early education in the public schools of his native town was interrupted when he was eighteen years of age by service in the Civil War. Enlisting in the 24th Michigan Volunteers, he participated between October 1862 and February 1865 in most of the important campaigns and battles of the Army of the Potomac. For two years, 1865–67, he was a clerk in the War Department at Washington, then entered the sophomore class at the University of Michigan, where he was graduated C.E. in 1870, despite an absence of a year and a half as recorder of the federal Lake survey. His first work after graduation was in connection with surveys of harbors on Lake Michigan, but from September 1870 until 1882 he was engaged in the improvement of navigation in the St. Mary's River between Lakes Superior and Huron and in the enlargement of the St. Mary's Falls Canal at Sault Ste. Marie, Mich. As assistant engineer, 1873–82, under Maj. Godfrey Weitzel [*q.v.*] he had an important part in the construction of the Weitzel Lock at the "Soo." In 1882 he became resident engineer of the Shreveport Bridge across the Red River, and then, 1883–86, was assistant engineer in charge of bridge construction on the Northern Pacific Railroad. Subsequently, he became resident engineer of the Washington Bridge, New York City (1886–87), under William R. Hutton; of the Cairo Bridge over the Ohio River (1887–89), under G. S. Morison and E. L. Corthell [*qq.v.*]; and of the Memphis Bridge over the Mississippi (1888–92), under Morison. Upon the completion of the last-named work he formed a limited partnership with Morison during which he was assistant chief engineer of bridges at Alton, Ill., Bellefontaine, Mo., and Leavenworth, Kan.

Upon the expiration of this partnership in 1894, he opened an office as consulting engineer in Chicago. In April 1895 he was appointed by President Cleveland a member of the Nicaragua Canal Commission, with Gen. William Ludlow and Commander Mordecai Thomas Endicott [*qq.v.*] as his colleagues. The commission visited many points in Central America with a view to the construction of an inter-oceanic canal, and in October 1895 submitted its final report. Thereafter, Noble was engaged in private practice, mostly as a consulting engineer, until appointed by the secretary of war to membership in the Deep Waterways Commission, to study ship-canal routes from the Great Lakes to the sea (1897–1900). By appointment of President McKinley, 1899–1903, he was member of the Isthmian Canal Commission, which was charged with determining the route of the Panama Canal. Subsequently President Theodore Roosevelt appointed him (1905) to the board of consulting engineers on the Panama Canal. Although a majority of this board favored the construction of a sea-level canal, Noble was one of those who held out strongly for a lock-canal, the type finally adopted. (See his statement before a Senate sub-committee, *The Isthmian Canal*, 1902; and his statement before the Senate Committee on Interoceanic Canals, *Investigation of Panama Canal Matters*, 1906, pp. 441–94.) In 1900 he served on a board of engineers to advise the state engineer of New York with regard to plans for the projected State Barge Canal. From 1901 to 1905 he and Ralph Modjeski were associated in the building of a bridge across the Mississippi at Thebes, Ill., Noble having special charge of the substructure. From 1902 to 1909 he was chief engineer of the East River division of the Pennsylvania Railroad, supervising important tunnel construction under the river and terminal improvements which included the foundations of the Pennsylvania Station, New York City. As consulting engineer, he was connected with the construction of the Galveston seawall, the New York rapid-transit subways, the Pearl Harbor (Hawaii) Dry Dock, the new Welland Canal and the new Quebec Bridge, the Catskill Aqueduct, and a number of important water-power developments.

Throughout his life, he contributed papers and studies to the Western and the American societies of civil engineers, and to the Chicago Academy of Sciences. He became president of the Western Society of Civil Engineers in 1897, of the American Society of Civil Engineers in 1903, and of the American Institute of Consulting Engineers in 1913. In 1910, he was awarded the John Fritz Medal of the American Institute of Mining Engineers "for notable achievements as a civil engineer," and in 1912, the Elliott Cresson Medal of the Franklin Institute "for distinguished achievement in the field of civil engineering." At the time of his death, follow-

ing a serious operation, he held a position in the front rank of his profession. He was survived by his wife, Georgia Speechly of Ann Arbor, Mich., whom he married May 31, 1871, and by one son, also a civil engineer.

[*Trans. Am. Soc. Civil Engineers*, vol. LXXIX (1915), containing memoir, bibliography, tributes, and reprints of numerous obituaries; W. F. Johnson, *Four Centuries of the Panama Canal* (1907); *Who's Who in America*, 1914–15; R. W. Raymond, in *Engineering Record* (N. Y.), Apr. 25, 1914; *Railway World*, May 1914; *N. Y. Times* and *N. Y. Herald*, Apr. 20, 1914.]
C. D. R.

NOBLE, FREDERICK ALPHONSO (Mar. 17, 1832–Dec. 31, 1917), Presbyterian and Congregational clergyman, was born in Baldwin, Me., the son of James and Jane (Cram) Noble. The characteristics of his parents—the father of Scotch descent, unremittingly industrious as farmer and cooper, a captain of militia, scornful of unrighteous living, gifted with effective speech in town-meetings; the mother tall, dignified, alert, hospitable—appear distinctly in their son, the first-born of twelve children.

Early determined to obtain an education, he worked his way through Kimball Union Academy, Meriden, N. H., and borrowed money for his college course at Yale, graduating in 1858. After two years at Andover Theological Seminary he entered Lane Seminary, Cincinnati, Ohio, from which he graduated in 1861. On Sept. 15, 1861, he married Lucy A. Perry of Dummerston, Vt. He was invited to supply the pulpit of the House of Hope Presbyterian Church, St. Paul, Minn., and there, July 16, 1862, he was ordained and installed pastor. The church had but sixty members and an indebtedness exceeding the value of its entire property. Under the leadership of the young pastor it grew steadily in membership and influence, and his eloquent patriotism made helpful contribution to the Union cause throughout the war. In 1867 he was called to the Third Presbyterian Church of Pittsburgh, Pa. He was already recognized as a vigorous writer and administrator: a progressive conservative, he became an advocate of woman's suffrage. From Pittsburgh he was called in 1875 to the First Church of Christ (Congregational), New Haven, Conn.

In 1879 he was recalled to the interior by a challenging invitation to Union Park Congregational Church, Chicago. The great fire of 1871 had left this church struggling with a crushing indebtedness and its future was problematical. Here Noble entered upon his largest work, achieving the apparently impossible in effecting the extinction of the debt, and organizing the church upon widely serviceable lines. In the meantime he advanced steadily to prominence among the recognized leaders in the Congregational body. Of impressive physique, a wide reader, a consecutive and practical thinker and convincing speaker, a sympathetic pastor, a sagacious counselor, a public-spirited citizen, a coworker in world-wide religious undertakings, he became during his twenty-two years at Union Park an outstanding example of statesmanship in the ministry. His dominating will and forthright utterance were tempered by his friendliness and just appreciation of others. He was a founder of the New West Education Commission and its president, 1879–98; a founder of the Chicago City Missionary Society; moderator of the National Congregational Council, 1898; president of the American Missionary Association, 1898–1900; and editor of *The Advance,* Chicago, 1886–88. He was also the author of *The Divine Life in Man* (1896), *Discourses on Philippians* (1897), *Our Redemption* (1898), *Typical New Testament Conversions* (1901), *The Pilgrims* (1907), *Spiritual Culture* (1914), besides pamphlets on civic, educational, and religious subjects.

In 1901 he closed his pastorate, continuing active in a general ministry. Mrs. Noble had died, June 7, 1895; and on July 1, 1897, he married Leila M. Crandon of Evanston, Ill. For several years he was much in New England. It had long been his custom to visit the Rangeley Lakes (Maine) in summer, and his had been the leading influence in the erection of a church-building and later a public library at Rangeley. After 1910 he made his home in Evanston.

[*Obit. Record Grads. Yale Univ.,* 1918; editorial and obituary in *The Congregationalist and Advance,* Jan. 17, 1918; *Who's Who in America,* 1916–17; a study of Noble's life and character by his son Frederic Perry Noble of Spokane, Wash. (1918, unpublished); *The Treasury* (New York), Jan. 1891.]

E. D. E.

NOBLE, JAMES (Dec. 16, 1783–Feb. 26, 1831), senator, was born in Clarke County, Va., the second of the fifteen children of Elizabeth Claire (Sedgwick) and Thomas Noble, a physician of Scotch descent. Toward the end of the century the family moved to Campbell County, Ky., where Thomas Noble had a grant of 210 acres on the Bank Lick. There James received the self-directed and informal education typical of the frontier. About the time of his marriage, on Apr. 7, 1803, to Mary Lindsay of Newport, Ky., he began to read law in the office of Richard Southgate of Newport. Some six or eight years later he removed to Indiana, where his two younger brothers, Noah and Lazarus, soon followed him and where his family continued to be important in Indiana politics for many years.

He was admitted to the bar and became one of the first lawyers in Lawrenceburg. There were, perhaps, other men who knew more law than he, but, as an orator who could appeal to the emotions of the crowd, he was unsurpassed. He was popular, ambitious, and a political opportunist.

When Franklin County was formed in 1810, he was appointed prosecuting attorney and thereafter made Brookville his home. In 1811 he became lieutenant-colonel of militia and the next year, when his regiment was called out to protect the frontiers of the county, he became colonel. In 1815 he operated a ferry across the Ohio from his lands in Switzerland County. On Apr. 25, 1815, Gov. Thomas Posey appointed him to fill an unexpired term as judge of the third circuit. The following year he was sent by the voters of Franklin County to represent them in the Indiana state constitutional convention. Legislative work was not new to him for he had served as clerk of the territorial House of Representatives as early as 1810. In the convention he was chairman of the committees on the legislative department, elections, and banks and banking companies, and was a member of the committees on the militia, judicial department, and school lands. Characteristically, he was one of the chief leaders of the convention and when forced to a vote usually carried his point. On Nov. 8, 1816, four days after the meeting of the first state legislature, to which he was a representative, he and Waller Taylor were elected as Indiana's first two senators. To this same office he was reëlected in 1821 and again in 1827. He fought for internal improvements and the development of the west, and he pushed along the bill in Congress to authorize the selling of the public lands in quarter sections. His work in Congress did not bar him from other activities. In 1820 he became a director of the Brookville branch of the Vincennes Bank, and, when that institution became involved in difficulties with the United States, he was assigned by the government to settle the affair, which he did to the satisfaction of all. He died in Washington, D. C.

["Executive Journ. of Ind. Territory," ed. by W. W. Woollen, D. W. Howe, and J. P. Dunn, *Ind. Hist. Soc. Pubs.,* vol. III (1900); *Journ. of the Convention of the Ind. Territory* (1816); *Ind. Hist. Colls.,* "Governors Messages and Letters. Messages . . . of Wm. Henry Harrison," ed. by Logan Esarey (1922), vol. II; *Ibid.,* "Messages of Jonathan Jennings, Ratliff Boon, and Wm. Hendricks" (1924); W. W. Woollen, *Biog. and Hist. Sketches* (1883); A. J. Reifel, *Hist. of Franklin County* (1915); Archibald Shaw, *Hist. of Dearborn County* (1915); L. M. Boltwood, *Hist. and Geneal. of the Family of Thomas Noble* (1878); state treasurer's account book for 1810 and manuscript, "Family Hist. of Noah Noble," by E. N. Carter, in Ind. State Lib. at Indianapolis; date of birth from letter of Mrs. Esther Noble Carter of Indianapolis, giving data copied from family Bible of Philip Sweetser.]

J. L. N.

NOBLE, JOHN WILLOCK (Oct. 26, 1831– Mar. 22, 1912), soldier, lawyer, secretary of the interior, was born at Lancaster, Ohio, the son of John and Catherine (McDill) Noble, Pennsylvania Presbyterians who had migrated early to Ohio. After attending the public schools of Cincinnati, he spent three years at Miami College, before his graduation with honors from Yale in 1851. The year following he received his law degree from the Cincinnati Law School but continued to study in the office of Henry Stanbery before his admission to the bar. In 1855 he moved to St. Louis, but, shortly becoming convinced that, as a Free-Soiler and a Republican, he could not succeed in the pro-slavery atmosphere there, he moved to Keokuk, Iowa, where from 1856 to 1861 he acquired an extensive practice and shared with Samuel Freeman Miller the leadership of the state bar. In August 1861 he enlisted in the 3rd Iowa Cavalry and during the Civil War served with distinction in every grade from lieutenant to colonel, seeing service in various western campaigns and in raids into the lower South. He also acted as judge-advocate-general of the Army of the Southwest. "For gallant and meritorious services" he was brevetted brigadier-general in 1865. On Feb. 8, 1864, he married Lisabeth Halsted, of Northampton, Mass., a woman of marked intellectual power and a leader in early social-welfare movements.

In 1865 Noble returned to St. Louis. His subsequent career was divided between professional and public interests. At the instance of his former teacher, Stanbery, he was appointed in 1867 United States district attorney for the eastern district of Missouri. During three years of hard work and of harder fighting Noble prosecuted with intelligence and thoroughness numerous violaters of the internal-revenue laws. The chief offenders were certain of the whiskey and tobacco interests and their corrupt and entrenched governmental allies, a notorious combination which defrauded the government of huge sums. Against this group, the forerunner of the Whiskey Ring, Noble fought with some success and set in operation forces which eventually exposed the ramifications of the system. In 1870 he resumed practice and won immediate success. His clients included large corporate and railroad interests of the Southwest. He was very effective both in trial and in appellate practice, despite a too frequent reliance upon oratory. He declined in 1872 the position of solicitor-general.

He was considered well qualified for the secretaryship of the interior to which Harrison named him in 1889 (*St. Louis Globe-Democrat,* Mar. 4, 1889). As an esteemed Grand Army man and as an exponent of the orthodox Republican view that the surplus collected largely under the tariff laws should properly be distributed in pensions, Noble favored a policy of great liberality and repeated in his reports many of the platitudes concerning the old soldier. He absolutely refused, however, to sanction the highly irregular and illegal administrative activities and rulings of "Corporal" James Tanner, the commissioner of pensions. A sharp difference arose over the policy of reratings, and the two men clashed frequently. Harrison supported Noble in the controversy, and Tanner, "insubordinate in the last degree," finally resigned (W. H. Glasson, *Federal Military Pensions in the United States,* 1918).

The pension act of 1890 received Noble's cordial approval, although its administration was beset with fraudulent claimants, political sentimentalists, and astute claim attorneys whom he found impossible to control. With reference to the timber lands, his practice was to dispose of the thousands of cases in the Land Office by a more liberal interpretation of the land laws in favor of the settler (*Report of the Secretary of Interior,* 1889, 1891). In this manner the cases were rapidly settled but probably many fraudulent claims received approval. In 1890 Noble strongly supported the views of the American Forestry Association and the Division of Forestry and was responsible for the introduction of the forest reserve sections in the revision of the land laws in 1891 (John Ise, *The United States Forest Policy,* 1920). Harrison acted immediately and withdrew for national forests millions of acres of valuable lands. The act of 1891 remains Noble's most significant achievement. At his retirement from office in 1893, the general administrative functions of the department were efficiently conducted. Politically, he was generally regarded as a follower of the president rather than of Blaine. He was austere and formal in his official relations but friendly and democratic in his personal contacts. Upon his return to St. Louis he reëntered his profession but found it difficult to regain his practice. Concerning his public life he ruefully declared, "I spent my whole fortune living up to the office. My house cost me more than my salary. . . . I thought I was doing well but when I came home I had no practice and came near starving" (I. H. Lionberger, "Glimpses of People and Manners in St. Louis," 1920). A mining interest provided him with necessary resources. He was not again active in political affairs but remained an interested and benevolent figure at veterans' gatherings and college reunions. He died in St. Louis after a month's illness.

[L. D. Ingersoll, *Iowa and the Rebellion* (1866); B. E. Fernow, *A Brief Hist. of Forestry* (1907); I. H. Lionberger, "Glimpses of People and Manners in St. Louis" (1920); J. T. Scharf, *History of St. Louis City and County* (2 vols., 1883); D. L. McMurry, "The Bureau of Pensions during the Administration of President Harrison," *Miss. Valley Hist. Rev.*, Dec. 1926; annual reports of the secretary of the interior, 1889–92; *Who's Who in America*, 1912–13; *Obit. Record of Yale Grads.*, 1911–12.]   T. S. B.

NOBLE, SAMUEL (Nov. 22, 1834–Aug. 14, 1888), ironmaster, founder of the city of Anniston, Ala., was born in Cornwall, England, the son of James Noble and Jenifer Ward Noble. The family emigrated to Pennsylvania in 1837 and at Reading Samuel received an elementary education. More important, however, was the early training in ironmaking from his father; he was brought up in the atmosphere of the furnace and forge. When the family moved to Georgia in 1855, Samuel became the leading spirit of the firm of James Noble & Sons, whose plant consisted of a rolling-mill, foundry, and nailery in Rome, and a furnace in Cherokee County, Ala. Their business prospered and they expanded it to meet the needs of the Confederacy by building Cornwall Furnace in the same county to provide more iron for war materials. Both the furnace and the factory at Rome were destroyed by the Federal forces in 1864.

Noble typified in many ways the industrial pioneer of the post-war period who undertook the task of building a new South. Successful in enlisting capital from the North, he soon rebuilt the works at Rome. Meanwhile he was in search of larger ore deposits in the hill country of northeastern Alabama. After prospecting near Oxford he secured financial aid in New York with which to buy in Calhoun County extensive brown-ore properties and a large acreage of yellow pine for charcoal. On a visit to Charleston, S. C., he chanced to meet Gen. Daniel Tyler, a northern capitalist, who was so impressed by the young man's enthusiasm that he explored the ore fields in company with Noble. The result was the formation of the Woodstock Iron Company in 1872 with Gen. Tyler's son Alfred as president and Samuel Noble as secretary-treasurer and general manager. In April 1873 their charcoal blast furnace No. 1, of forty-ton capacity, was blown in and ran almost continuously for twenty years. It produced a high quality of car-wheel iron which found a ready market in the North. The steady demand for this iron en-

abled the company to survive the panic and depression of the mid-seventies, to construct furnace No. 2 in 1879, and to enlarge No. 1 the following year.

Meanwhile the town of Woodstock had been organized in July 1873 as Anniston, named for the wife of Gen. Tyler. Samuel Noble, dynamic spirit of the enterprise, with visions of the "model city of the South" (as it was later advertised), directed the policy of the company in laying out streets and parks, erecting schools, and providing lots for churches of every denomination. When the first boom of the eighties appeared, Anniston grew by leaps and bounds. During the period 1880–85 Noble and his associates organized the Clifton Iron Company at Ironaton where they built two forty-ton charcoal furnaces and enlarged an older one, the Jenifer. In Anniston a cotton-mill with 12,000 spindles was erected and the car-wheel works of Noble Brothers was moved thither from Rome. In 1883 the Woodstock Company, which had retained possession of all property, formally opened the city to the public and encouraged new industries. Noble, always a progressive ironmaster, acquired valuable coal properties and constructed two two-hundred-ton coke furnaces to make pig iron for the manufacture of cast-iron pipe, a pioneer enterprise embodied in the Anniston Pipe Works Company, organized in 1887.

That the progress of Anniston, social as well as economic, was always Noble's primary consideration, was evidenced in the schools, the Anniston Inn, and the first newspaper—the *Weekly Hot Blast*—which he founded. People of every sect and worthy cause were recipients of his gifts, and his employees, both white and colored, were devoted to him. He built the Episcopal church, of which he was the leading member. At the height of his achievements, when Anniston's industrial capital represented an investment of more than eleven million dollars, he died suddenly. Convinced that the southern iron industry needed a protective tariff, he consistently supported the Republican party. In 1861 he married Christine Stoeckel of Philadelphia, Pa., by whom he had one son and three daughters.

[A contemporary sketch of Samuel Noble and the early years of Anniston is found in *Northern Ala. Hist. and Biog.* (1888), pp. 112, 470–77, and in *Anniston, "The Model City of the South." A Description of Anniston* (1887). The *Memorial Record of Ala.* (1893), vol. I, contains a biographical sketch. An article in the *Anniston Star*, Mar. 6, 1924, is the report of an interview with Noble's sister, Miss Mary Noble, who provided most of the material on Noble in Ethel Armes, *The Story of Coal and Iron in Ala.* (1910). See also T. M. Owen, *Hist. of Ala. and Dict. of Ala. Biog.* (1921), vol. I, and the *Daily Reg.* (Mobile), Aug. 16, 1888.]   L. J. C.

NOEGGERATH, EMIL OSCAR JACOB BRUNO (Oct. 5, 1827–May 3, 1895), physician, was born in Germany, at Bonn on the Rhine. His father, Jacob John Noeggerath, professor of mineralogy at the University of Bonn, was an authority on subjects concerning mining and ore-refining, but his interests extended beyond his special field to literature and politics. He was apparently personally acquainted with Goethe and his home was a center for the dormant liberalism of the post-Napoleonic period. The maiden name of Emil's mother was Primavesi; her family was originally Italian. Emil Noeggerath began his medical education at the University of Bonn in 1848 and received the degree of M.D. in 1852. From Bonn he went to Berlin, started special work in gynecology, and in 1853 passed the official state examinations. He then visited Vienna, Prague, and Paris. Upon his return to Bonn he served as first assistant in the obstetrical clinic and in 1856 entered upon private practice in Neuwied on the Rhine.

The following year he came to America to accept a position on the faculty of a prospective medical school in St. Louis, Mo., but the plan was frustrated by the financial failure of the institution and he was forced to enter general practice in New York City. He soon gained a reputation for special abilities in gynecology and obstetrics and all his subsequent practice was in these specialties. He was associated with the German Hospital, Mount Sinai, and other prominent medical institutions, was one of the founders of the American Gynecological Society and of the New York Obstetrical Society, and professor of obstetrics and gynecology at the old New York Medical College. In 1885 his life-long ailment, tuberculosis, forced him to return to Germany, where he died in 1895. He had married a kinswoman, Rolanda Noeggerath, and had a daughter and three sons.

Noeggerath was probably one of the most talented American physicians of his time. He combined an acute sense of biological mechanism with an appreciation for the totality of the organism. In this characteristic he fused the old and new systems of medicine in a blend whose virtue was not appreciated until recent times. He was among the first to use pathology at the sick-bed itself in that he advised the microscopic examination of the uterine tissues removed by curettage. At a time of operative enthusiasm, he taught that conservative treatment must always be the method of choice. This attitude he assumed despite the fact that he was himself a brilliant surgeon and developed new operative methods. He deplored the development of virtuosity in surgical technique at the cost of surgical diagnosis. For many years he stood alone in his belief that the cervical tear was an innoxious deformity and that the operations devised for its repair were needless and dangerous. He was interested in bacteriology at a time when this subject was still only an interesting biological curiosity. He developed a surgical aseptic technique for gynecological examinations which transcended the bounds of Lister's antisepsis. Again, it was many years before gynecologists appreciated the potential sources of infection which the examining finger or instrument represented and instituted the measures which Noeggerath had proposed.

His greatest work is his publication: *Die Latente Gonorrhoe im Weiblichen Geschlecht* (Bonn, 1872). In this brochure, which was written in the hours of relaxation from a busy practice, he stated and supported the following theses: 1) that gonorrhea is a chronic disease which retains its infective power long after the acute stage has passed; 2) that every male in such a latent stage will perforce infect the female with whom he cohabits; 3) that the disease can also produce a latent stage in the female from which it can be awakened by sexual activity, by parturition, or by simple mechanical interference, such as medical instrumentation; 4) that most of the inflammations of the genital tract in females are due to gonorrheal infection; 5) that sterility is often due to the same agent and that the male in many sterile unions is the deficient member. This book was published three years before Robert Koch made bacteriology an exact science and seven years before Neisser discovered the gonococcus. So fundamental are these theses that they have become commonplaces of medical knowledge today.

It is remarkable that a man of such talent and achievement should have made so little impression on his age that he was all but forgotten by medical historians. His critical mind aroused animosity among his American colleagues and the extramural scientific activities of a self-made specialist received a cold welcome at European universities. He thus never succeeded in founding a school of thought. Close upon the heels of his publications came the dramatic discoveries of the classical bacteriologists who were the fortunate possessors of Koch's golden key to discovery, and in the flush of the new era all previous work was forgotten.

[Paul Diepgen, "Emil Noeggerath," *Klinische Wochenschrift*, Oct. 1, 1927; F. H. Garrison, *An Intro. to the Hist. of Medicine* (4th ed., 1929); H. S. Reichle, "Emil Noeggerath (1827–1895)," in *Annals of Medic. Hist.*, Mar. 1928; Zinsser, "Emil Noeggerath,"

Münchener Medizinische Wochenschrift, Sept. 30,
1927; Archiv für Pathologische Anatomie und Physiologie und für Klinische Medicin, Mar. 9, 1896; J.
Pagel, Biographisches Lexikon hervorragender Ärzte
des Neunzehnten Jahrhunderts (1901); information
concerning wife and children from a son, Prof. Carl
Noeggerath, Univ. of Freiburg, Germany.]   H.S.R.

NOGUCHI, HIDEYO (Nov. 24, 1876–May
21, 1928), bacteriologist, parasitologist, and im-
munologist, was born at Inawashiro in northern
Japan, the son of a peasant, Sayosuke Kobiyama,
and his wife, Shika Noguchi, who adopted her
husband in order to give her son her family
name. Owing to the poverty of his family and
to a deformation of his left hand following a
severe burn in infancy, he was, in childhood, so
heavily handicapped that his opportunities for
securing an education were threatened. Fortunately, his native ability was discovered by the
principal of an academy, a certain Kobayashi,
who made suitable arrangements for his schooling. A successful operation upon his hand by
Dr. K. Watanabe, led the boy to decide upon
medicine as a career. Serving at first as errand
boy and apprentice to Watanabe and attending
to the household affairs and medical practice of
the latter during his absence because of the war
between Japan and China, Noguchi (whose
childhood name was "Seisaku," changed to
"Hideyo" on the attainment of manhood) in
1894 entered the Tokyo Medical College where
he graduated in 1897. He then became assistant
to Surgeon-General Satow at the General Hospital, edited the hospital journal, and lectured
on general pathology and oral surgery at the
Tokyo Dental College. In September 1898 he
joined Kitasato's staff at the Government Institute of Infectious Diseases and when bubonic
plague broke out in China he was sent by the International Sanitary Board to New Chwang, and
became physician-in-chief to the Central Bureau
in charge of the hospital and the bacteriological
laboratory. The plague dying out there, he was
sent to Manchuria under a Russian medical commission but, on the development of the Boxer
movement, he was recalled to Kitasato's Institute in Tokyo, where he wrote textbooks on
pathology, bacteriology, and dentistry, and translated part of Hueppe's manual of hygiene into
Japanese.

Early in 1899 Noguchi became acquainted with
Simon Flexner, who, on his way to the Philippine Islands as a member of a Johns Hopkins
Medical Commission, visited Kitasato's Institute. The young Japanese expressed the desire
to go to America to study pathology and bacteriology, and though this was not strongly encouraged by Flexner, Noguchi, after earning the

money for the journey and receiving a promise
from Kobayashi that his family would be looked
after, went to Philadelphia at the end of 1899
and started work in the laboratory of pathology
of which Flexner had just been made head at the
University of Pennsylvania. After consultation
with Dr. Silas Weir Mitchell, Noguchi was assigned to the study of immunity against snake-
venoms, receiving support from the National
Academy of Sciences and the Carnegie Institution of Washington. In this study, he investigated most carefully the problems relating to the
hemolysins and agglutinins of snake venom and
the protective sera. With his clarity of interest,
his technical skill, and his prodigious industry
he was able quickly to obtain brilliant results,
which were published in a series of important
articles, and, finally, in an illustrated volume on
the subject, The Action of Snake Venom upon
Cold-blooded Animals, brought out by the Carnegie Institution in 1904, a work that, in itself,
established Noguchi's reputation as a keen observer and an experimenter of the first order.

In 1903, pending the transfer of his activities
to the Rockefeller Institute of Medical Research,
Noguchi, attracted by the immunochemical researches of Madsen and Arrhenius, worked in
Copenhagen. On taking up work at the Rockefeller Institute after it opened in 1904, he applied
Madsen's ideas to the study of the Wassermann
reaction and devised a new and important method
for the diagnosis of syphilis. As a result of this
study, he was led into his most important researches upon methods for obtaining pure cultures of spiral organisms, modifying the method
of Theobald Smith (in which a fragment of
sterile rabbit's kidney was added to culture
media). In these investigations, Noguchi displayed his extraordinary ability to adapt technical methods by means of subtle alterations to
make them successful for varying purposes. Not
only was he able to grow in pure culture the
spiral organism that causes syphilis (previously demonstrated in the lesions of syphilis by
Schaudinn) but he also obtained in pure culture
a large variety of pathogenic spiral organisms
as well as many saprophytic spiral forms. The
isolation of the Treponema pallidum in pure culture made possible, too, the preparation of luetin,
a soluble extract analogous to tuberculin, useful
for the diagnosis of latent and of congenital lues.
In 1913, with J. W. Moore, Noguchi demonstrated the presence of Treponema pallidum in
the cerebral cortex of patients dead of general
paralysis; the post-mortem recovery of this
parasite in the central nervous system in both
general paresis and tabes dorsalis settled once

and for all the nature of the etiological agent in these two serious maladies.

His discovery of the great value of media containing rabbits' testis for the growth of the etiological agent of syphilis in large numbers and for freeing it from associated contaminating bacteria was further applied by him to the cultivation of the globoid bodies in poliomyelitis, to the study of Rocky Mountain spotted fever, and to the enrichment and purification of the virus of vaccinia (so as to free it from the miscellaneous bacteria of the bovine product). During the last ten years of his life Noguchi directed his investigations to the clearing up of the etiology of yellow fever, of Oroya fever, and of trachoma. As a result of his four expeditions to South America he concluded that the yellow fever there was due to infection with *Leptospira icteroides,* for he was able to isolate this organism from the blood of more than twenty per cent. of the patients called yellow fever by clinical experts. Later, the studies of Stokes and others indicated that the yellow fever of Africa is due to a filter-passing virus, and there is now doubt whether the South American yellow fever studied was another infectious disease (confused with yellow fever and due to *Leptospira*) or is the same as African yellow fever but complicated by an associated secondary or concomitant infection with *Leptospira.*

In his studies of the Oroya fever of Peru, Noguchi was able to grow Barton's rod-shaped bodies in special media and by animal experiments to prove that the general febrile process, Oroya fever, and the clinically widely different warty or verrugous local process, Verruga peruviana, are due to the same micro-organism, *Bartonella bacilliformis,* an infectious agent that entomologists have since shown is carried by nocturnal blood-sucking insects of the Phlebotomus class. The much-studied problem of the etiology of trachoma among American Indians was finally solved by Noguchi through a series of painstaking researches in which he eliminated successively many types of bacteria that live in or upon the conjunctiva of trachomatous patients until he was able to isolate one, *Bacterium granulosis,* that will produce the characteristic lesions in certain monkeys.

In 1927 Noguchi went to Africa to study the yellow fever there. He confirmed the findings of Stokes of the presence of a filterable virus and of the absence of *Leptospira,* but, just as he was ready to return, contracted yellow fever himself and died at Accra on May 21, 1928, thus succumbing to a disease of which Stokes had already become a victim and from which Young, who

was to have continued the experiments, also died eight days later. Physically, Noguchi was frail but he exhibited extraordinary powers of endurance. By disposition he was kindly, cheerful, and affectionate, and he was inspired by an intense desire to serve humanity in a practical way through discovery of the causes of disease. His originality, his capacity to formulate problems clearly, his power of inventiveness of new technical methods, his prodigious industry, his indomitable will, and his good fortune in establishing intimate and sympathetic associations in an environment that supplied him with adequate facilities for his work account for the achievements that made him, at the age of fifty-two, the outstanding figure in microbiology since Pasteur and Koch. He was the recipient of many honors from governments and learned societies and after his death the Order of the Rising Sun was conferred by his native country. He was survived by his wife, Mary Dardis, whom he had married on Apr. 10, 1912. His birthplace has been bought to be made into a shrine in which the records of his life and work will be permanently preserved.

[See: Gustav Eckstein, *Noguchi* (1931); *Japan Medic. World,* July 15, 1928; *Schweizerische medizinische Wochenschrift,* July 14, 1928; *Current Hist.,* July 1928; *Science,* June 28, 1929; *Sci. Monthly,* July 1928; *Bull. N. Y. Acad. of Medicine,* Sept. 1929; *N. Y. Times,* May 22, 1928.]   L. F. B.

NOLAN, PHILIP (*c.* 1771–Mar. 21, 1801), contraband trader, is said to have been born at Frankfort, Ky. (Hale, "The Real Philip Nolan," *post,* p. 282), though according to his own questionable declaration in 1794 (census report, Nacogdoches, Texas), he was a native of Belfast, Ireland, twenty-three years old. A reference to him by Gen. James Wilkinson [*q.v.*] as "a child of my own raising" (King, *post,* p. 92) and the fact that Nolan once referred to Wilkinson as "the friend and protector of my youth" (Wilkinson, *post,* II, App. 2) give some ground for the belief held by Spanish officials in Louisiana that he was reared in the General's family. As early as 1790 he was Wilkinson's agent in tobacco dealings at New Orleans. The following year he made the first of four trading ventures into Texas. Suspected as a spy in Mexico and cheated of his goods (according to his own account, *Ibid.*) he lived for a time among the Indians, but subsequently went back to the Spaniards, and having sold skins and caught a number of wild horses, returned in 1794 to Louisiana. From his second expedition (1794–96), to San Antonio, he took back 250 horses, selling some in Natchez and Kentucky, though he was legally entitled only to supply mounts for the Spanish cavalry in Louisiana. Sharing in the profits of his enterprises, Spanish officials both there and in Texas winked at his illicit trading, and he was even permitted to pasture his wild horses with the cavalry horses at San Antonio until they were gentle. He had corrals also and a "pasture" on the Trinity River, in East Texas.

At the beginning of his third expedition he fell in with Andrew Ellicott [q.v.], then on his way to survey the Southwestern boundary. Seizing the opportunity to obtain instruction in Ellicott's profession, he accompanied him as far as Natchez, and in the summer of 1797 set out with instruments and a passport from Governor Gayoso [q.v.] of Louisiana to explore and map for him the north Texas region. After his death it was said that he had intended to gather information for General Wilkinson to use in a projected conquest of Mexico (Deposition of Samuel P. Moore, 1810, Wilkinson, II, App. 3). After penetrating apparently as far south as the Rio Grande in the state of Tamaulipas, he returned with some 1,300 horses. Before his return the suspicions of Gayoso had been aroused and the Texan authorities warned to look out for Nolan, and after this expedition his license to do horse-trading was revoked. Accordingly, when he set forth the next year, it was with the avowed purpose of bringing into the United States horses from his "pasture" on the Trinity River, but it is evident that he planned to do other trading also. Gayoso's warnings against him now became effective, however, and a hundred men under Lieut. M. Musquiz were sent out from Nacogdoches to arrest him. In a skirmish between this force and Nolan's party near the present Waco, Nolan was killed. He had married on Dec. 19, 1799, Frances Lintot, daughter of Bernard Lintot, a merchant of Natchez. An only son, born after his father's death, died at the age of twenty-one.

The testimony of those who knew him shows Nolan to have been a man of magnetic personality; reputed to possess an exceptional knowledge of the Spanish frontier. Daniel Clark, 1766–1813 [q.v.], in a letter to Thomas Jefferson written in 1799, characterized him as "that extraordinary and enterprising Man . . . whom Nature seems to have formed for Enterprises of which the rest of Mankind are incapable" (Quarterly of the Texas State Historical Association, April 1904, pp. 309–10). William Dunbar [q.v.] attributed to him "energy of mind not sufficiently cultivated by education, but which under the guidance of a little more prudence might have conducted him to enterprises of the first magnitude" (Ibid., p. 315). According to Professor

E. C. Barker, "Nolan's connection with Wilkinson, Jefferson's desire to get information from him concerning the habits of wild horses, and Clark's vague references to 'a man who will at all times have it in his Power to render important Services to the U. S.' (Ibid., p. 310) have enveloped his smuggling adventures in an atmosphere of mystery and international intrigue which candid scrutiny of available sources tends to dispel."

[Information concerning Nolan, including manuscripts in the Nacogdoches and Bexar Archives and transcripts and photostats from Mexican archives, is collated in an unfinished master's thesis by Maurine T. Wilson, at the Univ. of Tex. The original *testimonios* taken in the examination of Nolan's companions in 1801 are in the Yale Univ. Lib. Much of the information in the foregoing sketch has been furnished by Professor E. C. Barker. Published sources include J. A. Quintero, "Philip Nolan and his Companions," in *The Texas Almanac*, 1868, pp. 60–64; E. E. Hale, "The Real Philip Nolan," in *Miss. Hist. Soc. Pubs.*, IV (1901), 281–329, in which he explains that the historical Nolan is not the prototype of "The Man Without a Country"; Grace King, "The Real Philip Nolan," in *La. Hist. Soc. Pubs.*, vol. X (1918); James Wilkinson, *Memoirs of My Own Times* (1816), vol. II, pp. 232–42 and Apps. 2, 3, 28; *Quart. Tex. State Hist. Asso.*, Apr. 1904; Dunbar Rowland, *Mississippi* (1907), II, 342–45; Henderson Yoakum, *Hist. of Tex.* (1855), I, 403–07. E. E. Hale, *Philip Nolan's Friends* (1876) is a novel based on the real Nolan's career.]
H. C. B.
E. R. D.

NOONAN, JAMES PATRICK (Dec. 15, 1878–Dec. 4, 1929), labor leader, was born in St. Louis, Mo., the son of Thomas P. Noonan and Bridget Kemmey. His father was a farmer in St. Louis County whose family came from Ireland and settled in Missouri in 1850. Young Noonan attended school until he was about thirteen but, left an orphan at an early age, he spent his boyhood mainly in manual labor of various kinds. On the outbreak of the Spanish-American War in 1898 he enlisted as a private and after his discharge the next year became an electric lineman in St. Louis. He married, at Clayton, Mo., Inez M. Mitchell on June 26, 1901. In the same year he joined the International Brotherhood of Electrical Workers and for the next twenty-eight years was identified with the history of that organization. At twenty-four he was president of his local union, the next year president of the Missouri and Illinois District Council, and in 1904 vice-president of the international organization with headquarters at Springfield, Ill. In this capacity Noonan served throughout the internal struggle of 1908 to 1913 which threatened to disrupt the union, and in 1917, when President Frank Joseph McNulty [q.v.] went on leave of absence, became acting president and two years later president, with headquarters after 1920 in Washington. He had an enormous capacity for work and was thorough and conscientious, a good fighter when the need arose but more often a skilled diplomat who won the respect of the employers who sat opposite him at the council table. Under his pacific and progressive leadership from 1919 to 1929 his organization made rapid progress toward solidarity and business efficiency. Meanwhile he was elected in 1922 fifth vice-president of the Building Trades Department of the American Federation of Labor, later a member of the National Board of Jurisdictional Awards for the Building Trades, and in 1924 a member of the executive council of the Federation. He was fifth vice-president of the American Federation of Labor and third vice-president of the Building Trades Department at the time of his death. As an authority on the effect of electric power on labor and labor organizations Noonan was made the only American labor delegate to the World Power Conference at London in 1924 and submitted a paper on "Labour's Part in Power Production" (*Transactions of the First World Power Conference,* London, 1925, vol. IV, pp. 1414–20). He was also appointed by Governor Pinchot a member of Pennsylvania's Giant Power Board and by Secretary of Commerce Hoover a member of the St. Lawrence Waterway Commission. He served on numerous committees, including the committee on seasonal operation in the construction industry of the President's Conference on Unemployment from 1921 to 1924. He was a member of the Elks and of the Congressional Country Club. His death resulted from burns received when he fell asleep while smoking in his Washington apartment, and his funeral in St. Louis where, because of the large amount of traveling required by his official duties, he kept his family home, was attended by several hundred members, many of them from distant points, of the International Brotherhood of Electrical Workers. A heavy-set man, broad-shouldered and almost completely bald but erect, alert, and energetic in his movements, Noonan owed his popularity to his friendliness, his personal charm, and his frank and candid manner of approaching all questions. But the qualities which kept him for many years an outstanding figure in the labor movement were his practical common sense, his honesty, his broad interests, and his ability to adapt himself to circumstances and opportunities.

[Obituaries were published in the *N. Y. Times,* and *St. Louis Globe-Democrat,* Dec. 5, 1929, in the *Jour. of Electrical Workers and Operators,* Dec. 1929 and Jan. 1930, and in other journals. Biographical material is also contained in M. A. Mulcaire, *The Internat. Brotherhood of Electrical Workers* (1923); the *Jour. of Electrical Workers and Operators;* the *Proc.* and the *Reports of Officers of the Internat. Brotherhood of Electrical Workers* from 1904 to 1929; and in the *Re-*

ports of Proc. of the . . . Ann. Conventions of the Building Trades Dept., Am. Federation of Labor from 1922 to 1930. Additional information has been secured from Noonan's son, Robert E. Noonan of St. Louis.]
H. S. W.

NORCROSS, ORLANDO WHITNEY (Oct. 25, 1839–Feb. 27, 1920), master-builder, second son of Jesse Springer and Margaret Ann (Whitney) Norcross and eighth in descent from Jeremiah Norcross, a proprietor in Watertown, Mass., as early as 1642, was born in Clinton, Me. Removing with his family to Salem, Mass., at the age of four, he attended the grammar schools there, but started to work at about thirteen because his father had joined the gold rush of 1849 and never returned. After following for several years his father's trade of carpenter, he enlisted as artificer July 5, 1861, in the company which became Company D, 1st Heavy Artillery, Massachusetts Volunteers. As road and bridge-builder during his three years with the Army of the Potomac, he was often under Confederate fire.

Honorably discharged in the summer of 1864, he formed a partnership, as building-contractor, with his elder brother James, who managed the clerical and financial affairs of the firm while Orlando directed the constructional work, to which he was always, heart and soul, devoted. After completing successfully their first large contract, the Leicester Congregational Church, the firm established permanent headquarters at Worcester, Mass., in 1868. The financial panic of 1873 yielded them an unexpected dividend, for building prices dropped substantially shortly after they had signed a contract for the erection of Trinity Church, Boston. This contract had other important results. Executed between 1872 and 1877, it brought young Norcross into personal contact with H. H. Richardson [*q.v.*], the eminent architect, who during fifteen years regarded him as his right-hand man on all matters of practical construction.

Norcross was quick to adopt new methods and materials. To him is to be credited the flat-slab construction of reinforced concrete, which he invented. His practical inventiveness and resourcefulness often put the technical judgments of engineers to rout, notably in the case of a stone arch at the Springfield, Mass., railway station. At West Point, the erection of the Battle Monument, a granite monolith 41.6 feet high, weighing eighty-one tons, at that time (1893) the largest polished shaft in the world, presented almost insuperable difficulties, over which, however, Norcross as usual triumphed. He came to be widely recognized as a leader in his field. In 1875 he was appointed by the Secretary of the Treasury as one of three commissioners to inspect the Chicago Federal Building. The first edition of Frank E. Kidder's *Architect's and Builder's Pocket-Book* (1885), known as the "contractor's Bible" for nearly half a century, was dedicated to him. His firm's important contracts included Custom House Tower and Harvard Medical School, Boston; Harvard Union, Cambridge; Rhode Island State Capitol; New York Public Library; Bank of Montreal; D.A.R. Building, Pan-American Building, Corcoran Art Gallery, and Masonic Temple in Washington, D. C.; Howard Memorial Library, New Orleans; and the Ames Memorial Monument of the Union Pacific Railroad at Sherman, Wyo.

To the financial side of his work Norcross was always indifferent, and in later years he suffered as a consequence. From early life he was devoted to books, seeking to atone by wide and constant reading for his lack of formal education. His absorption in work was proverbial. His Civil War experiences and abundant contacts with labor having impressed him keenly with the waste and suffering entailed by strong drink, he was always a firm temperance advocate. He was a disciple of nature and fond of tramping; he loved his home and shunned club life. He was a vestryman of two Episcopal churches and a trustee of Clark University, an office he, a self-educated man, particularly prized. He married in May 1870, Ellen Sibley of Salem, who bore him five children, of whom two sons died in infancy. At the age of eighty he was seized with apoplexy while on his way to business and died within a few hours. On his eighty-first birthday a bronze tablet bearing a bas-relief portrait of him was unveiled in the Worcester City Hall.

[T. H. Gage, *Memorial Address, Oct. 25, 1920* (n.d.); Charles Nutt, *Hist. of Worcester and Its People* (1919), vol. IV; *Who's Who in America,* 1918–19; *Record of the Mass. Volunteers 1861–65,* vol. I (1868); *Trans. Am. Soc. Mech. Engineers,* Feb. 1921; *Trans. Am. Soc. Civil Engineers,* vol. LXXXIV (1921); *Worcester Evening Gazette* and *Boston Transcript,* Feb. 27, 1920; *Sunday Telegram* (Worcester), Mar. 7, 1920.]
R. K. S.

NORDBERG, BRUNO VICTOR (Apr. 11, 1857–Oct. 30, 1924), mechanical engineer, the son of Capt. Carl Victor and Dores (Hinze) Nordberg, was born at Björneborg, Finland. His father, a prominent and successful shipbuilder, died while Bruno was still at the preparatory school, where he studied theology, history, and languages. When he entered the University of Helsingfors and discovered that his inclination was toward technical subjects, he found that his early schooling had given him little of value for his later career. Close association with Prof. Rudolf Kolster, a physicist at the University,

confirmed his desire to become an engineer, but it required his greatest efforts to build up the foundation in science and mathematics which had previously been neglected and at the same time to progress in his studies.

In 1879, about two years after his graduation, he came to the United States and obtained work in Buffalo. Four months later he pushed westward to Milwaukee, and there came upon the works of the E. P. Allis Company, where he found employment detailing Corliss engine parts. Soon thereafter he seized upon an opportunity to design a blowing engine, an achievement which revealed his unusual skill as a designer and engineer and resulted in his further advancement. In an endeavor to improve the economy of slide-valve engines, he designed a poppet valve cut-off governor, and in 1886, with the financial aid of friends, organized the Bruno Nordberg Company for the manufacture of such governors. The first shop was in small rented quarters.

Increased demand for Corliss engines led Nordberg to design such units, the first of which was built at the Wilkins Manufacturing Company of Milwaukee. In 1890 the need for enlarged quarters was felt and the Nordberg Manufacturing Company was organized, of which, during the years which followed, Nordberg served as president and chief engineer. An existing building was equipped with machinery, where governors, Corliss-valve, and poppet-valve engines were built. There followed the building of compressors, pumps, blowing engines, hoists, condensers, and heaters. The reputation of the Company grew rapidly and to it were referred all manner of difficult engineering problems. The economy of Nordberg's steam engines was soon recognized, and what became known as the Nordberg generative cycle was developed. This cycle is used at the present time (1934) in modern turbine plants.

Among the works of the company were the Champion Copper Company's compressor at Painesdale, Mich., and the pumps built for the Wildwood Water Works, Wildwood, Pa., both still known as record-holding plants. Nordberg's compound steam stamps were epoch-making in the milling operation of Northern Michigan Copper Mines. Hoists were improved with such rapid strides that the demand for them came from all metal mines. He designed the hoist for the Tamarack Mining Company, which remarkable piece of work was followed some years later by the famous hoist built for the No. 2 Shaft at the Quincy Mining Company, Hancock, Mich., the largest one so far built. The chemical industry profited by a great variety of special vacuum pumps and gas compressors which he devised. The company built the largest uniflow engine in the country for rolling-mill work, as well as some of the largest compressors for mining work. Nordberg's greatest work, however, was the building of the pneumatic hoisting system for the Anaconda Copper Company, Butte, Mont.

He had taken out some seventy United States patents before his death. In his private laboratory he was active in electrical and chemical experiments, and developed many new ideas. As early as 1890, he was awarded a gold medal by the French Academy for noteworthy inventions. His genius attracted to the Nordberg Manufacturing Company a class of men notable for their ability, and as his enormous capacity for work diminished, these men gradually took responsibilities from his shoulders. His hobby was sailing his yacht. He designed yachts and spent much of his spare time in making yacht models. His mechanical genius was reflected even in the fittings of his boats. On Sept. 24, 1882, he married Helena Hinze, and his married life was an inspiration to all with whom he came in contact. He had two sons, one of whom died at the age of thirty-four. Nordberg's death occurred in his sixty-eighth year, at Milwaukee.

[*Trans. Am. Soc. Mech. Engineers*, vol. XLVI (1925), repr. from *Mechanical Engineering*, Dec. 1924, portr.; *Engineering* (London), Nov. 21, 1924; Paul Langer, in *Zeitschrift des Vereines Deutscher Ingenieure*, Dec. 20, 1924; C. E. Holmbery, in *Finlands Svenska Tekniker* (Helsingfors, Finland), ed. by Jonatan Reuter, pt. 1, 1923; *History of Milwaukee County* (1895), II, 7; *Men of Progress of Wis.* (1897); *Who's Who in America*, 1924–25; *Milwaukee Sentinel*, Oct. 31, 1924.]   D. K.

NORDHEIMER, ISAAC (1809–Nov. 3, 1842), Orientalist, was born in Memelsdorf, Bavaria, to Meyer and Esther Natal (Strauss) Nordheimer. Six years spent in the Yeshiba (Rabbinical Academy) at Presburg under the renowned Talmudist Moses Sofer gave him a thorough grounding in Hebrew and Aramaic literature. Thereafter, at the Gymnasium in Würzburg and at the Universities of Würzburg and Munich he gained his classical education and his knowledge of cognate Semitic languages, receiving the degree of Ph.D. at Munich in 1834. In response to the urging of some American friends there, he left Germany for the Western world, landing in New York in 1835. His mastery of Hebrew obtained for him in 1838, Jew though he was and remained, the position of instructor in sacred literature at Union Theological Seminary, where all the other members of the faculty had to profess the Westminster Confession. Attempts were made to draw him into

religious controversy, but when his interpretations were challenged, he studiously limited himself to grammatical issues and was able to avoid all theological questions. From 1839 to 1840 he was also acting professor of Hebrew in the faculty of science and letters of the University of the City of New York, and from 1840 till his death, professor of German and of Oriental languages. Never marrying, he lived with his sister Jeanette in the University building and gave himself unremittingly to his exacting toil, winning the esteem of students and colleagues both for his simple-hearted, childlike, affectionate nature, and for his devotion, enthusiasm, and skill as a teacher. The eminent Semitic scholar Edward Robinson [*q.v.*], in his report to the board of directors of Union Theological Seminary on June 28, 1842, testified to the great ability and fidelity with which Nordheimer instructed his classes, and to the very important aid which his labors gave to the reputation and best interests of the Seminary. By that time, however, Nordheimer, whose frame had always been frail, was exhausted by overwork, and four months later, at the early age of thirty-three, he died of tuberculosis. He was buried in the little Jewish cemetery on Twenty-first Street near Sixth Avenue, New York. His death destroyed the promise of the most brilliant Semitic grammarian of nineteenth-century America.

On his voyage to America he had conceived the idea of writing a textbook of Hebrew grammar according to the laws governing philology and the development of speech. He offered the completed manuscript of his first volume to the printer B. L. Hamlen in New Haven. Hamlen, pointing to shelves filled with copies of Hebrew grammars by Gesenius, Stuart, and Bush, for which there was virtually no demand, would not even look at it. To Nordheimer's plea that the original discoveries on every page of his volume would make it live, Hamlen replied coldly, "Your book also will die." Whereupon Nordheimer, pale with emotion, threw his manuscript on the counter, and said, "Den I will die wid my book." Touched by the depth of feeling of the gentle, curly-headed scholar, Hamlen relented, accepted the manuscript for examination, and on a favorable report, printed the book. This was *A Critical Grammar of the Hebrew Language* in two volumes (1838–41) on which Nordheimer's reputation is based. It is an original and penetrating piece of clear and profound scholarship, which attempts to show lexical and grammatical relations with Indo-European as well as with Semitic forms. Nordheimer's other writings were *A Grammatical Analysis of Selections from* the Hebrew Scriptures (1838); an elaborate review of Fürst's Hebrew concordance to the Bible, in the *Biblical Repertory and Princeton Review*, July 1839; "Hebrew Lexicography" (*American Biblical Repository*, April 1838); "The Philosophy of Ecclesiastes" (*Ibid.*, July 1838); "The Talmud and the Rabbies" (*Ibid.*, October 1839); and "The Rabbies and Their Literature" (*Ibid.*, July 1841). He issued a prospectus of a *Complete Hebrew and Chaldee Concordance to the Old Testament* in the year of his death.

[A. Rhine, in *The Jewish Encyc.* (1925), vol. IX; Henry Neill, in the *New Englander*, July 1874 (repr. for private circulation by William Nordheimer, London, 1906); G. L. Prentiss, *The Union Theol. Sem. in the City of N. Y.* (1889); C. R. Gillett, *Alumni Cat. of the Union Theol. Sem.* (1926); *Gen. Alumni Cat., N. Y. Univ.* (1906); "The Tomb of Nordheimer" (poem), in *Morning Courier and N. Y. Enquirer*, Nov. 17, 1842; Edward Robinson, *Bibliotheca Sacra: or Tracts and Essays* (1843).]   D. deS. P.

NORDHOFF, CHARLES (Aug. 31, 1830–July 14, 1901), journalist and author, was born in Erwitte, Westphalia, in the Kingdom of Prussia. When he was five years old his parents, Charles and Adelheid (Platé) Nordhoff, emigrated with him to the United States. After attending school in Cincinnati he was apprenticed at the age of thirteen to a printer. He served a year and then went to Philadelphia, where he worked as compositor on a newspaper. Enlisting in 1844 in the United States Navy he served three years and made, in that time, a voyage around the world. After the expiration of the term of his enlistment he spent several years on merchant vessels and in the New England fisheries. At the age of twenty-three he gave up seafaring and took up journalism as a profession. While employed as newspaper reporter he wrote a series of books inspired largely by his own experiences as a sailor. They were the three volumes, *Man-of-War Life* (1855), *The Merchant Vessel* (1855), and *Whaling and Fishing* (1856) that were later collected as *Nine Years a Sailor* (1857), and a fourth book, *Stories of the Island World* (1857). His life at sea not only provided the material for his first literary production, but, by hard physical training and by broadening his field of experience and quickening his powers of observation, it gave him an invaluable training for his later career as a newspaper correspondent. In 1857 Harper & Brothers engaged him as an editor and four years later he became managing editor of the New York *Evening Post*. During the Civil War he strongly advocated the Union cause both in the columns of his paper and in a number of books and pamphlets. He published *Secession*

is Rebellion (1860), *The Freedmen of South-Carolina* (1863), and *America for Free Working Men* (1865). He resigned from the *Post* in 1871 and spent the following two years in travel visiting California and Hawaii. In 1874 the *New York Herald* engaged him for its Washington correspondent, a position which he filled with great success until his retirement in 1890. In Washington "he won the friendship of the leading men of the day, and a high place among the political writers of the country. His letters were recognized as the authoritative presentation of the news, and the final word on the moral merits of a controversy. He . . . was not only one of the few correspondents in whom public men confided, but one of still fewer whom they consulted" (*Harper's Weekly, post*, p. 761). Some of his newspaper assignments led to rather important publications. His *Communistic Societies in the United States* (1875) was a valuable contribution to the social history of the United States. It was based on visits to a number of communities and on personal observation of their method of life. In *The Cotton States in the Spring and Summer of 1875* (1876), he set a high standard of impartiality for investigators of controversial political and economic questions. Holding no brief for party or section, his book records his own painstaking and systematic inquiries (see J. F. Rhodes, *History of the United States*, VII, 1906, p. 126). The strongly moral and religious trend of his thinking is displayed in two books written particularly for the instruction of his children and those of his friends. They are *Politics for Young Americans* (1875), which had considerable vogue as a school textbook, and *God and the Future Life* (1883). All of his writing was characterized by a direct and forceful style and by a preference for simple words and short sentences. His personality was like his writing, straightforward and downright. He spent the last years of his life in Coronado, Cal., partly because of his fondness for the region and partly because of the delicate health of his wife, Lida (Letford) Nordhoff. He died in San Francisco.

[*Harper's Weekly*, July 27, 1901; *Who's Who in America*, 1899–1900; *San Francisco Call*, July 15, 1901.]   P. W. B.

NORDICA, LILLIAN (May 12, 1859–May 10, 1914), prima donna, was born in Farmington, Me., the daughter of Edwin and Amanda (Allen) Norton, and the grand-daughter of a well-known revivalist preacher, familiarly known as "Camp-meeting John Allen." Her parents were talented and she was reared in a musical atmosphere. After studying with John O'Neill at the New England Conservatory of Music, she made her concert début at Madison Square Garden in New York City as the soprano soloist with Patrick Gilmore's band. In 1878, after two years of successful concert work, she accompanied Gilmore's band on a European tour in the same capacity and sang in London and in Liverpool, and at the Trocadéro in Paris. But in Germany her objection to open-air singing led her to sever her connection with Gilmore and study operatic rôles with the famous singing-master Antonio San Giovanni of Milan, who gave her the stage name by which she is known. On Apr. 30, 1879, she made her début as an operatic soprano as Brescia, in *La Traviata*, with immediate success. After singing in Genoa, Danzig, Königsberg, and Berlin, she first appeared as prima donna at the Grand Opera in Paris as Marguerite in Gounod's *Faust*, on July 21, 1882, scoring an instant success in a part in which her coloratura work was considered inimitable. That same year she married Frederick A. Gower, scientist and inventor, who accompanied her to the United States where, at the New York Academy of Music, she appeared for the first time in opera in America, Nov. 26, 1883, in the same rôle that had won her success in Paris. For a time she withdrew from the stage. Her marriage had not been happy and in 1886 when legal steps were being taken to secure a separation, Gower vanished into oblivion in a balloon.

She resumed her activity as a prima donna in 1887, appearing at the Covent Garden Theatre, London, where, until 1893, she continued as one of the stars of the London operatic season. In the latter year she first sang at the Metropolitan Opera House in New York as a member of an Italian company managed by Henry Eugene Abbey and Maurice Grau, and which included Melba, Calvé, Eames, Plançon, and the de Reszkés. But she was not content to remain an exponent of French and Italian operatic rôles. Her ambition was fixed upon Wagnerian opera, and after studying the rôle of Elsa with Julius Kniese and Cosima Wagner, she sang it at the Bayreuth *Festspielhaus* in 1894 with outstanding success. After further intensive study with Kniese at Bayreuth, she scored a triumph at the Metropolitan Opera House in New York, Nov. 27, 1895, when she sang Isolde to Jean de Reszké's Tristan. Thenceforward her successes in Germany, France, and England were achieved in Wagnerian rôles. In 1896 she married in Indianapolis, Ind., the Hungarian tenor, Zoltan Döme, from whom she was divorced in 1904. From that time on, with occasional intermissions, she sang at the Metropolitan Opera House until

1907. During the season of 1907–08 she was a member of Oscar Hammerstein's Manhattan Opera Company, but thereafter her operatic appearances were only occasional, and she devoted herself chiefly to extended concert tours. On July 29, 1909, she was married to the American banker George W. Young, in London, and only now and again made use of her repertory of forty operas, as when she sang Isolde and Brünnhilde in Paris (1910), and Isolde (1912) with the Boston Opera Company. Her last concert tour, which began in 1913, was to have taken her around the world. But as a result of exposure after the grounding of the *Tasman* on Bramble Cay in the Gulf of Papua in December 1913, she contracted pneumonia and died in Batavia, Java, on May 10 of the following year. Nordica was a singer rather than an actress. She had a voice rich in tone, notable coloratura range, and consummate artistic ability. She may be regarded as one of the very great Wagnerian sopranos. *Lillian Nordica's Hints to Singers*, containing also many letters written by Nordica and her mother, was published in 1923 by William Armstrong.

[In addition to *Lillian Nordica's Hints to Singers* see: *Who's Who in America*, 1912–13; Mabel Wagnalls, *Stars of the Opera* (1899); H. E. Krehbiel, *More Chapters of Opera* (1919); Anton Seidl, *The Music of the Modern World* (1895), vol. I; Wm. Armstrong, "Nordica: A Study," *Music*, Nov. 1900; *Musical Courier*, May 13, 1914; *Musical Observer*, June 1914; *New Eng. Conservatory Mag. and Alumni Rev.*, June 1914; *Foyer*, June 1914; *N. Y. Times*, May 11, 1914; and the Robinson Locke Collection, N. Y. Pub. Lib.]

F. H. M.

NORELIUS, ERIC (Oct. 26, 1833–Mar. 15, 1916), Swedish Lutheran clergyman, was born at Hassela, Helsingland, Sweden. At the age of nine he underwent an intense religious awakening, and after his confirmation he secured his parents' grudging consent to study. In January 1849 he entered school at Hudiksvall, where he heard of the Rev. L. P. Esbjörn [q.v.] and his work in America. Norelius decided to emigrate, and arrived in New York on Oct. 31, 1850. He went to Princeton, Ill., and thence to Andover, Ill., to see Esbjörn, who sent him to Capital (Lutheran) University, Columbus, Ohio, where he studied from 1851 to 1856. He served a congregation at West Point, Ind., which sent him in the fall of 1855 to find a better location for a settlement, when he chose Red Wing and Vasa, Goodhue County, Minn. After another year in school, he was ordained in the fall of 1856 at Dixon, Ill., and entered upon a ministry at Vasa and Red Wing, which, with interruptions, covered a period of sixty years. In spite of recurrent hemorrhages of the lungs, he was a zealous pastor, an active missionary, and an indefatigable literary worker throughout his long life. At his death his congregations had expanded into fifteen parishes served by nine pastors.

In 1857 Norelius and Jonas Engberg began the publication at Red Wing of *Minnesota Posten,* a Swedish paper. At the end of 1858 this was merged with *Hemlandet,* the paper of Dr. T. N. Hasselquist [*q.v.*], of Galesburg, Ill., and issued from Chicago by the Publication Society. In 1877–78 he issued *Ev. Luthersk Tidsskrift* at Vasa. He contributed regularly to the secular and religious press, and in recognition of his work he was made editor of the Augustana Synod's official organ, the *Augustana,* but resigned after a year on account of ill health. In a reminiscent mood he wrote "Memories of Sixty Years at Vasa" (*My Church,* vol. I, 1915), and "A Pioneer Boy's First Christmas in America" (*My Church,* vol. XIII). He issued an historical handbook, *The Ev. Lutherska Augustana-synoden i Nord Amerika och dess Mission* (Lund, 1870), and *The Life and Work of Rev. J. Ausland* (Red Wing, 1878). His more pretentious publications are the large biographical work, *Dr. T. N. Hasselquist* (Rock Island, n.d.), and *De Svenska Lutherska Församlingarnas och Svenskarnes Historia i Amerika* (Rock Island, vol. I, 1890; vol. II, 1916).

Norelius founded an orphanage at Vasa in 1865 which he conducted for eleven years. More enduring was a private school, which he started in 1862 at Red Wing, Minn., and which later expanded into the present Gustavus Adolphus College, St. Peter, Minn. He witnessed the growth of his synod from the Ev. Lutheran Synod of Northern Illinois to the Scandinavian Augustana Synod (1860). Of this synod he was president twice, from 1874 to 1881, and from 1899 to 1911. At the end of his second term of office he declined reëlection on account of ill health. He was then made president emeritus. He also served as president of the Minnesota Conference of the synod for four years. In recognition of his services, the King of Sweden made him a Knight and later a Knight Commander of the Order of the North Star, first class.

[*Who's Who in America,* 1903–05; *My Church,* vol. II (1916); J. C. Jensson, *Am. Lutheran Biogs.* (Milwaukee, 1890); *Minneapolis Jour.,* Mar. 16, 1916.]
J. M. R.

NORMAN, JOHN (*c.* 1748–June 8, 1817), engraver and publisher, seems to have been born in England. The published London parish registers do not give his name among christenings, nor has any authoritative statement been found concerning his parentage and early training. In May 1774 he advertised himself in the *Pennsyl-* *vania Journal,* Philadelphia, as "John Norman, Architect and Landscape Engraver, from London," offering assistance to "booksellers in any part of America" in preparing "frontispieces of any kind." A considerable record of his subsequent crude but prolific work has been amassed, though little has been discovered that concerns his personality. It is probable that he had a continuous struggle, echoes of which are noted in the distribution of his insolvent estate (25,285 in the probate records of Suffolk County, Mass.). Norman and Ward, "Engravers and Drawing Masters," advertised in the *Pennsylvania Journal,* Aug. 17, 1774, adding that "they have likewise opened an Evening Drawing School." The next year, Norman, styling himself "Architect-Engraver," made the copper-plate illustrations for Robert Bell's edition of *Swan's British Architect, or the Builders' Treasury of Staircases.* In 1776, from his shop in Second Street, near Spruce, he published *A Map of the Present Seat of War.* Apparently still in Philadelphia, about 1789 he engraved a portrait of General Washington, which appeared in *The Philadelphia Almanack for the Year of Our Lord 1780.*

In 1781 he was in Boston, and there engraved the title-piece and music of *The Psalm-singers' Amusement* (1781), by William Billings. Beginning two years later, in November 1783, the *Boston Magazine,* projected by gentlemen of historical tastes, several of whom subsequently formed the Massachusetts Historical Society, was issued by Norman & White "at their office in Marshall's Lane." With the magazine was printed at intervals a *Geographical Gazetteer of Massachusetts,* now prized by collectors. The publishing firm's name was changed to Norman, White & Freeman and then, in July 1784, presumably after a disagreement, Norman dropped out. He published in 1789 the first *Boston Directory,* in which his own address is given as 75 Newbury St. Others took over the directory, but Norman printed and sold *Weatherwise's Federal Almanack for the Year of our Lord 1790,* and in 1791 began his publication of *The American Pilot.* He continued for many years to engrave portraits which neither in his own time nor among later connoisseurs were universally esteemed. His plates made for *An Impartial History of the War in America between Great Britain and the United States* (2 vols., 1781–82) had a scathing criticism from the *Freeman's Journal* (Philadelphia), Jan. 26, 1795, the portraits of Samuel Adams, Henry Knox, and Nathanael Greene being pronounced especially bad. These and other Norman portraits are justly described by Weitenkampf (*post,* p.

64) as "a mixture of graver-work and stipple" foreshadowing the "'mixed manner' which in the middle of the 19th century degenerated into the production of a characterless, machine-made sauce."

Norman died of a slow fever and was buried on Copp's Hill. The records of the administration of his estate reveal that his wife's name was Alice and that his affairs were in bad shape. The inventory discloses a great mass of unsold publications and materials, together with household furniture on which a total valuation of $620.47 was placed.

[S. A. Green, "Remarks on the Boston Magazine, The Geographical Gazetteer of Mass., and John Norman, Engraver," published in *Proc. Mass. Hist. Soc.,* May 1904, corrected by C. H. Hart in "Some Notes Concerning John Norman," *Ibid.,* Oct. 1904. See also Frank Weitenkampf, *Am. Graphic Art* (1924) ; W. C. Ford, *Broadsides, Ballads, etc. Printed in Massachusetts 1639–1800* (1922) ; D. M. Stauffer, *Am. Engravers upon Copper and Steel* (1907) ; *A Descriptive Cat. of an Exhibition of Early Am. Engraving, at the Boston Museum of Fine Arts* (1904) ; *One Hundred Notable Am. Engravers* (N. Y. Pub. Lib., 1928) ; *Boston Daily Advertiser,* June 10, 1817.]　　F. W. C.

NORRIS, BENJAMIN FRANKLIN (Mar. 5, 1870–Oct. 25, 1902), journalist and novelist, known both in private life and in the literary world as Frank Norris, was born in Chicago, Ill., the son of Benjamin Franklin Norris and Gertrude (Doggett) Norris. His father, lame because of hip disease and consequently unfitted for the severe toil of a Michigan farm, became at the age of fourteen unpaid assistant to a village watchmaker, learned the trade, saw something of the world as itinerant clock-mender and pedler, prospered, and ultimately founded his own jewelry firm in Chicago. Frank's mother, born of mixed New England and Virginia ancestry on a Massachusetts farm, was before her marriage a teacher in the public schools of Chicago and an actress who had enjoyed considerable success on the professional stage. Of their five children, but two, Frank and a brother Charles, eleven years his junior, also destined to win distinction as a writer, survived the perils of infancy and childhood.

In 1884, largely on account of the health of the elder Norris, the family moved to California, residing first at Oakland and a year later in San Francisco. Frank was sent to a school for boys at Belmont, some twenty miles south of the city. In 1886 he was kept out of school for a time by a fracture of the left arm, and to relieve the tedium of its convalescence he went to a local artist for lessons in drawing. He showed such aptitude that his father resolved to give him the best opportunities for its development. In 1887 the parents took their two sons

first to London and then to Paris where Frank enrolled in the Atelier Julien. The family remained in Paris for more than a year and then returned to California, leaving the young artist to pursue his studies. But these studies came to an abrupt end in 1889 when the elder Norris, convinced, it is said, by the discovery of a serial romance with which Frank was entertaining his younger brother by mail, that his time in Paris was not being profitably employed, cabled him instructions to return home. The next year he definitely committed himself to literature rather than art by entering the University of California. In college he exercised his talents on student plays and class books, with an occasional story or poem. Having come under the influence of Zola, whom he read with the devotion of a disciple, he adopted realism as a creed and began the first chapters of a story of San Francisco to be later completed and published as *McTeague.* Prevented by unfulfilled requirements in mathematics from graduating with his class in 1894, he spent the next year at Harvard, as a special student in English, electing among others a course in English composition with Lewis E. Gates, who recognized and encouraged his literary ambition. Parts of *Vandover and the Brute* were written under this stimulus.

In the autumn of 1895 Norris went to South Africa with credentials from the *San Francisco Chronicle,* arriving just in time to become involved in Dr. Leander Starr Jameson's disastrous raid on Johannesburg. He was captured by the Boers and ordered to leave the country. A severe attack of African fever prevented him from doing so at once, and he was not able to return to San Francisco until the spring of 1896. There he was taken on the staff of a literary weekly known as the *Wave* and wrote diligently for its columns. "Moran of the Lady Letty," a tale of love and adventure at sea, based, it is said, upon material secured from a sailor in the coast guard, was written at this time. Within two years he was in New York City, where he was associated with *McClure's Magazine.* As correspondent for the same periodical he was in Cuba during the Santiago campaign and suffered there a severe recurrence of the African fever. Upon his recovery he returned to New York and in 1899 entered the service of Doubleday, Page & Company. He resumed his literary work, the quality of which speedily won him recognition as a novelist of unusual vigor and originality. *Moran of the Lady Letty* appeared in book form in 1898 and *McTeague* and *Blix* in 1899. *McTeague,* which some regard as his strongest work, is a tale of passion and violence, beginning in the office of a charlatan dentist in the older section of San Francisco and ending in the scorched distances of Death Valley. It is the stuff of romance realistically set forth in scenes new to most readers.

A less successful novel, *A Man's Woman*, a story of love and arctic exploration, followed in 1900, and then began a more ambitious undertaking, his "Epic of the Wheat." This was to consist of "The Octopus," a story of California and the growing of the wheat, "The Pit," a Chicago tale of wheat in the commerce of the world, and "The Wolf," which should show the wheat consumed as bread in some famine-stricken village of the old world. *The Octopus* appeared in 1901. It was a novel with a purpose, an ardent defense of the wheat-growers in their struggle against the dominating greed of the railroad trust, and through it ran the epic story of the life-giving wheat, impersonal and irresistible, in the end engulfing the odious figure of the railway agent. *The Pit* was posthumously issued in 1903, and as a novel and as a play enjoyed a great success. A collection of essays, *The Responsibilities of the Novelist*, was published in the same year and *Vandover and the Brute* in 1914.

Norris was married Jan. 12, 1900, to Jeannette Black of California, and one child, a daughter, was born to them. *Blix* is said to be in some degree the story of his own wooing and of his struggle for literary recognition. He died in a hospital in San Francisco of peritonitis following an operation for appendicitis. He had returned to California in 1902 and had purchased a ranch near Gilroy, intending to make it his home. A projected trip to India for material for "The Wolf" and a second trilogy, to deal with the battle of Gettysburg, were frustrated by his death, which brought to a close a life of real literary promise. His works were published in collected editions in 1903 and 1928.

[See Franklin Walker, *Frank Norris, A Biog.* (1932); Introduction by Kathleen Norris in 1925 edition of *Blix* and by Henry S. Pancoast in 1918 edition of *McTeague*; W. D. Howells, "Frank Norris," *North Am. Rev.*, Dec. 1902; editorial, "Memories of Frank Norris," in the *Bookman*, May 1914; C. C. Dobie, "Frank Norris, or Up from Culture," *Am. Mercury*, Apr. 1928; F. T. Cooper, *Some Am. Story Tellers* (1911); *San Francisco Chronicle* and *San Francisco Examiner*, Oct. 26, 1902.]   J.C.F.

NORRIS, EDWARD (d. Dec. 23, 1659), Congregational clergyman, is said to have been a native of Gloucestershire, England, and to have been either seventy or eighty years of age at his death. His name is often spelled Norice, and at least one of his extant letters is so signed. He may be identical with an Edward Norris who was probably the son of Edward Norris, vicar of Tetbury in Gloucestershire, was born in

1584, matriculated at Balliol College, Oxford, in 1599, was awarded the degree of B.A. by Magdalen Hall in 1606/7 and that of M.A. in 1609, and was rector of Anmer in Norfolk in 1624 (Joseph Foster, *Alumni Oxonienses*, 1891, vol. III, early series, p. 1076). It was said by a contemporary, John Traske, that he lived at Tetbury and Horsley, Gloucestershire, as a teacher of youth, as well as minister (Felt, *post*, I, 387). In 1635 he published *A Treatise Maintaining that Temporall Blessings Are to Bee Sought and Asked with Submission to the Will of God. Wherein Is . . . Also a Discovery of the Late Dangerous Errours of Mr. John Traske . . .* ; in 1637 he issued *Reply to John Traske's True Gospel Vindicated*; and in 1638, a second reply entitled *The New Gospel Not The True Gospel*. John Traske was an antinomian in London, and Norris mingles theological argument with coarse personal abuse. From these pamphlets it appears that his congregation had sailed for America about 1636, and that he had hoped to accompany them. Incidentally Norris shows no love for the "Jacobites or semi-separatists," believing evidently in remaining inside the establishment.

In July 1639 Norris and his wife, Eleanor, were in New England, where they became members of the Boston church. In September, in response to invitations, he obtained permission to move to Salem as assistant to Hugh Peter [*q.v.*]; and on Mar. 18, 1639/40, he was installed as teacher over the Salem church, almost all the ministers of the colony being present. He received one hundred acres of land and sixteen of meadow, and a salary of sixty pounds. In 1642 Norris wrote a defense of the standing council in answer to a pamphlet by Richard Saltonstall [*q.v.*]; in 1646 he preached the election sermon; in 1647 he was named first of the seven ministers commissioned to draw up a confession of faith; in 1651 he was joined with John Cotton and John Norton [*qq.v.*] to convince William Pynchon that his book, *The Meritorious Price of our Redemption* (1650), was heretical; in 1653 he urged the Commissioners of the United Colonies, by speech and letter, to prosecute vigorous war against the Dutch of New Amsterdam (the letter is quoted by Ebenezer Hazard in *Historical Collections*, vol. II, 1794, p. 255); in 1656 he received John Whiting as assistant in his ministry; in 1658 he was stricken speechless in the pulpit; and in May 1659 his death was so imminent that the town voted to pay the funeral expenses.

Norris is said to have been unusually tolerant, taking no part against the Gortonists or the

Baptists, and never adopting into his own church the Cambridge Platform. According to William Bentley (*post*), he was successful in opposing accusations of witchcraft in Salem in 1655, and his influence was against violent means toward the Quakers, though he died before the Quaker troubles were at their height. He diverted the fury of fanaticism by encouraging spinning in families, "he quieted alarms by inspiring a military courage, and in . . . a well directed charity, with a timely consent to the incorporation of towns around him, he finished in peace the longest life in the ministry which had been enjoyed in Salem" (Bentley, p. 259). Winthrop called him "a grave and judicious elder"; he was certainly an able and learned theologian; but he does not appear to have been so commanding a personality or so formative an influence on the institutions of New England as were some of his fellow clergymen.

[*Winthrop's Journal* (2 vols., 1908), ed. by J. K. Hosmer; John Eliot, *A Biog. Dict.* (1809); J. B. Felt, *The Ecclesiastical Hist. of New England* (2 vols., 1855–62); Sidney Perley, *The Hist. of Salem*, vol. II ((1926); William Bentley, "A Description and History of Salem," in *Colls. Mass. Hist. Soc.*, 1 ser. VI (1800); L. A. Morrison, *Lineage and Biogs. of the Norris Family in America* (1892); "Town Records of Salem, 1634–1659," in *Essex Inst. Hist. Colls.*, 2 ser. I (1868).]   H. B. P.

NORRIS, FRANK [see NORRIS, BENJAMIN FRANKLIN, 1870–1902].

NORRIS, GEORGE WASHINGTON (Nov. 6, 1808–Mar. 4, 1875), surgeon, was born in Philadelphia, Pa., the sixth son of Joseph Parker and Elizabeth Hill (Fox) Norris and a descendant of Isaac Norris, 1671–1735 [*q.v.*]. He was graduated from the University of Pennsylvania in 1827, with the degree of A.B., and in 1830 from the same institution as M.D. After serving from 1830 to 1833 as resident physician in the Pennsylvania Hospital, he went to Paris where he attended the lectures of Dupuytren, Velpeau, Roux, and Magendie. Returning to Philadelphia in 1835, he was in 1836 elected surgeon to the Pennsylvania Hospital and served that institution faithfully and with distinction until his resignation in 1863. In 1848 he was elected to succeed Dr. Jacob Randolph as professor of clinical surgery in the University of Pennsylvania and this post he resigned in 1857 upon his election as a member of the board of trustees of the university. He was married, in 1838, to Mary Pleasants Fisher, daughter of William W. Fisher. William Fisher Norris [*q.v.*] was their son. Of Norris's marriage his grandson has written: "Born a Quaker, he was thrown out of meeting for marrying a 'worldly'

woman, to wit, an Episcopalian, and thereafter always and regularly attended the Episcopal Church."

Norris is remembered as a sound and "conservative" surgeon. He was excellent in practical surgery and he trained many young men who became distinguished surgeons. He left a reputation for care and neatness in the dressing of wounds, and for insisting strenuously upon personal cleanliness in his assistants. He was gentle both in spirit and in touch, and was revered by many of his patients for his sympathy and kindness. He wrote comparatively little, but his few professional papers show careful preparation and thorough familiarity with the subjects. He took a lifelong interest in historical matters, and in 1886, some years after his death, his son published a volume from his pen entitled *The Early History of Medicine in Philadelphia*. He published *Practical Surgery* (1838), an edition of the work of Robert Liston; *A System of Practical Surgery* (1843), an edition of the work of Sir William Fergusson; and *A System of Surgery* (3 vols., 1847) an edition of G. F. South's translation of the work of M. J. von Chelius. In 1873, under the title *Contributions to Practical Surgery*, he published a collection of his more important "fugitive papers." Among these was the treatise, "On the Occurrence of Non-union after Fractures," which was very highly regarded at the time. His interest in the institutional life of Philadelphia may be inferred from his connection with the American Philosophical Society, the Historical Society of Pennsylvania (president, 1858–60), the Philadelphia Medical Society (vice-president, 1859), Academy of Natural Sciences of Philadelphia, the College of Physicians of Philadelphia (censor, 1848–1875, vice-president, 1864), and the Philadelphia Library Company. For a year, 1850–51, he was vice-president of the American Medical Association. He was consulting surgeon to the Children's Hospital of Philadelphia, and president of its board of managers, and for several years (1868–75) consulting surgeon to the Philadelphia Orthopædic Hospital.

[Wm. Hunt, "Memoir of George W. Norris, M.D.," *Trans. Coll. of Physicians of Phila.*, 3 ser. II (1876); T. G. Morton and Frank Woodbury, *The Hist. of the Pa. Hospital* (1895); H. A. Kelly and W. L. Burrage, *Am. Medic. Biogs.* (1920); the *Press* (Phila.), Mar. 6, 1875.]   A. P. C. A.

NORRIS, ISAAC (July 26, 1671–June 4, 1735), wealthy merchant and mayor of Philadelphia, official of the province of Pennsylvania, was born in London, England, the son of Thomas Norris or Norrice, a Quaker merchant, and Mary

(Moore) Norris. The family emigrated to Port Royal, Jamaica, about 1678 and Isaac served an apprenticeship in his father's business. In 1692 he was sent to Philadelphia to consider the prospects of removing to that city. On his return he found that his father had perished in the great earthquake of June 7, 1692, and that most of his other relatives had died. He went back to Philadelphia in 1693 and soon became a successful merchant. On Mar. 7, 1694, he was married to Mary Lloyd (1674–1748), a daughter of Thomas Lloyd [q.v.].

Norris was a member of the Assembly from 1699 to 1703 and again in 1705. In the years 1706–08 he visited England where he helped to rescue William Penn from a debtors' prison and played a leading part in settling the dispute between Penn and Philip Ford, Sr., and his son, over the proprietary rights to Pennsylvania. In return for these services he was appointed one of the five commissioners who acted as agents for the mortgage trustees and he was later named in Penn's will as a trustee of the province. He was an alderman of Philadelphia from 1708 to 1724 and was elected mayor in 1724. From 1709 to 1735 he served in the governor's council and, contrary to the usual custom, was also a member of the Assembly, 1710–13, 1715–16, 1718–20, 1734, and speaker in 1712 and 1720. He was likewise a justice of the Philadelphia county courts from 1715 to 1735 and a master in chancery for several years before his death. In 1731 he was chosen to succeed David Lloyd [q.v.] as chief justice of the supreme court but refused to serve. He attended the Indian conference at Albany in 1722 and was appointed a commissioner in the settlement of the boundary dispute with Maryland in 1734. He died in Germantown, Pa., June 4, 1735, survived by his wife and seven of his fourteen children.

Next to James Logan [q.v.], Norris was the chief representative of proprietary interests in Pennsylvania from 1708 until his death. John Penn wrote to him, May 1, 1732, acknowledging "the many and great obligations I am under to you for your constant good advice and friendly assistance for many years, both to my late Father and since his decease to us his children" (Norris Letter Books, II, 142). Norris's fortune was largely invested in real estate. In 1704 he and William Trent purchased from William Penn, Jr., a large tract of land on the Schuylkill River, including the site of Norristown, and, in 1712, he bought Trent's share of the property. He also owned the "Slate-roof House" in Philadelphia, celebrated as the residence of Penn on his second visit to Philadelphia, and a mansion,

"Fair Hill," in the Northern Liberties, where he lived from 1717 until his death. He was fond of books and his library was the nucleus of a collection that was later given to Dickinson College. A letter that he wrote to his son Isaac [q.v.] on the latter's visit to England in 1722 is interesting in this connection and also as an illustration of the workings of the Quaker conscience: "Thou may omit of my orders by thee, *The Arabian Nights Tales* and bring me Milton's *Paradise Lost*—octavo, large print" (Letter Books, II, 55).

[The Norris Papers in the Hist. Soc. of Pa. contain a copy of the journal kept by Norris on his visit to Philadelphia in 1692 and several letter books. There are also Norris letters in the Penn, Logan, and Pemberton collections. Some of his letters have been published in "Correspondence Between Wm. Penn and Jas. Logan," ed. by Edward Armstrong, in *Memoirs of the Hist. Soc. of Pa.*, vols. IX and X (1870–72). Other printed sources include: *Minutes of the Provincial Council of Pa.*, vols. II and III (1852); C. P. Keith, *The Provincial Councillors of Pa.* (1883); and J. W. Jordan, *Colonial Families of Philadelphia* (1911), vol. I.]
W. R. S.

NORRIS, ISAAC (Oct. 23, 1701–July 13, 1766), Philadelphia merchant, leader of the Quaker party and speaker of the Pennsylvania Assembly, was the son of Isaac Norris [q.v.] and Mary (Lloyd) Norris. He was born in Philadelphia and was educated at the Friends' school. In 1722 he spent a few months in England and in the years 1733–34 he made a longer visit to England and the Continent. He was a common councillor of Philadelphia, 1727–30, an alderman, 1730–42, a member of the Assembly of Pennsylvania, 1734–66, speaker of the Assembly, 1750–64, and a representative of Pennsylvania at the Indian Conferences held at Albany in 1745 and 1754. During his first term as speaker (1751), the old state house or Liberty bell was ordered from England and it was at his suggestion that the famous inscription was placed upon it: "Proclaim liberty throughout the land, unto all the inhabitants thereof."

Norris's militant pacifism is the pride of Quaker historians. In 1739, when Deputy-Governor George Thomas asked the Assembly to provide for the defense of the colony against the Spaniards, they replied that they had conscientious scruples and would put their trust in God and the mother country. In accordance with this decision, they refused to enact a militia law or to appropriate funds for military purposes. The quarrel, which was later complicated by a dispute over the right of the Assembly to tax the proprietary estates, lasted until the close of the Seven Years' War. Norris played so prominent a part in this conflict that the Quaker majority in the Assembly was frequently called the Norris party. He was selected to go to England with Benjamin Franklin in 1757 to represent the anti-proprietary faction, but, owing to ill health, was compelled to refuse. Although he continued to oppose the proprietors, he was not in sympathy with the petition sent to the King in 1764 asking for a change from proprietary to royal government. There is a difference of opinion as to whether he resigned the speakership at this time (May 1764) because of his health, which was undoubtedly poor, or because he disapproved the policy of the Assembly. It is possible that he was influenced to some extent by his son-in-law, John Dickinson [q.v.], who was associated with the proprietary party. He was again elected speaker by the new Assembly in the following October and again resigned after a few days' service. He retained his seat in the house, however, and was reëlected in 1765, but his health continued to fail and he died at his home, "Fair Hill," near Philadelphia, July 13, 1766.

The mercantile establishment of Norris & Company was one of the largest firms in Philadelphia. Norris managed it during the latter part of his father's life and became the senior partner after his father's death. He lived in the famous "Slate-roof House" in Philadelphia for several years, but in 1742 he removed to "Fair Hill" in the Northern Liberties, where he spent the remainder of his life (Logan Papers, XIII, 63–64). He was married to Sarah Logan, the eldest daughter of James Logan [q.v.], June 6, 1739. She died Oct. 13, 1744. He was survived by two daughters—Mary, who married John Dickinson, and Sarah, who died in 1769. With his father's books as a nucleus, he built up a large and well-selected library which in 1784 was given by his son-in-law to Dickinson College. He was interested in education and was a trustee of the Academy and College of Philadelphia from 1751 to 1755.

[Sources include the Norris and Logan Papers in the Hist. Soc. of Pa.; *Votes and Proc. of the House of Representatives of Pa.*, 1752–76; *The Jour. of Isaac Norris . . . During a Trip to Albany in 1745* (Philadelphia, 1867); J. W. Jordan, *Colonial Families of Philadelphia* (1911), vol. I; G. W. Norris, "Isaac Norris," *Pa. Mag. of Hist. and Biog.*, vol. I, no. 4 (1877); C. P. Keith, *The Provincial Councillors of Pa.* (1883).]

W. R. S.

NORRIS, MARY HARRIOTT (Mar. 16, 1848–Sept. 14, 1919), author and educator, the daughter of Charles Bryan and Mary Lyon (Kerr) Norris, was born at Boonton, N. J. Before the opening of Vassar College in 1865 her parents decided to send their daughter there. She was prepared in a private school, where she was the only girl studying Latin and, in spite of the disapproval of her mother's friends, made

her entrance, taking with her the water-proof cloak and other modest equipment required in the pamphlet issued by the college. Her own account of the early days at Vassar, *The Golden Age of Vassar* (1915), reveals a life of frugality and hard work. Hannah Lyman, the first lady principal, said of her that she was "as greedy for learning as many people are for food" (*Golden Age, ante*, p. 30). In 1870 she was graduated with the A.B. degree. In 1872 she delivered the annual address at the Vassar Commencement. In 1873 she published her first fiction, *Fräulein Mina; or, Life in a North American German Family*, which was so successful that she continued to write and published more than a dozen books of transient popularity. Among them were *School Life of Ben and Bentie* (1874) of the Ben and Bentie Series, *Dorothy Delafield* (1886), and *The Gray House of the Quarries* (1898). In the writing of such stories she showed some descriptive and story-telling ability, much sentiment, and an orthodox religious outlook. She also contributed to periodicals and edited for use in schools *George Eliot's Silas Marner* (1890); *Sir Walter Scott's Marmion* (1891); *Henry Wadsworth Longfellow's Evangeline* (1896); *Kenilworth by Sir Walter Scott* (1899); *Quentin Durward* (1900).

In 1880 she founded a private school in New York City and was its principal until 1896. In 1898 she became the first regularly elected dean of women of Northwestern University. She held this position as well as that of assistant professor of English literature for only a year, as she had stipulated that only for so long could she withdraw herself from her literary and other activities. During that time she organized a students' self-governing association and started a library for the woman's hall. Another change in which she took pride was that during her year the young women almost entirely abandoned the custom "of appearing at breakfast in wrapper and dressing sacks," she wrote, "a custom I found almost universal in the Hall on my arrival there" (Wilde, *post*, p. 100). Her Tuesday morning chapel talks on religious themes and her Thursday evening talks on etiquette and personal hygiene were considered very helpful to the students. She was made an honorary member of the class of 1899 of the university. During her later years she resided at Morristown, N. J.

[Biog. material in *The Golden Age of Vassar, ante*; *Who's Who in America*, 1918–19, 1920–21; *Men and Women of America* (1910); A. H. Wilde, *Northwestern Univ.* (1905), vol. II.]

S. G. B.

NORRIS, WILLIAM (July 2, 1802–Jan. 5, 1867), locomotive builder, was the son of William and Mary (Schaefer) Norris and was born in Baltimore, Md., where his father had a dry-goods store. He was a descendant of Henry Norris who emigrated from England to Virginia in 1680. After graduating from St. Mary's College, Baltimore, Norris was associated in business with his father for a few years and in 1828, with his father's help, opened a whole-sale dry-goods store in Philadelphia. His father failed in business the following year and Norris was forced to close his store and look about for other work.

He had always been keenly interested in steam engines and he now designed and built a steam carriage with an upright boiler and wooden wheels, which he demonstrated on the streets of Philadelphia. This achievement brought about his meeting with Col. Stephen H. Long [q.v.], Corps of Engineers, United States Army, who was also interested in locomotive building, and in 1832 the two organized the American Steam Carriage Company, with Long as president and Norris as secretary. They began the construction of a locomotive, designed by Colonel Long, which was to use anthracite coal as fuel, but it proved a failure. A second engine, the "Black Hawk," was completed in 1833 and used first on the Philadelphia & Columbia Railroad and later on the Philadelphia & Germantown Railroad. This locomotive, however, was not entirely successful and all members of the company withdrew their interest, leaving Long and Norris alone. The two then built three anthracite-coal-burning locomotives for a New England railroad, which were completed in 1834, but while these were entirely successful they were soon relegated to sand and gravel trains, because "the coal fires required more attention from the enginemen than did fires of wood." About this time Norris bought Colonel Long's interest in the locomotive works and soon after completed the successful locomotive "Star" for the Philadelphia & Germantown Railroad. In 1835 he moved his shop from Kensington, Pa., to Bush Hill, Philadelphia, and there with six employees began the construction of another locomotive of his own design. The "George Washington," as it was called, was completed in 1836 for the Philadelphia & Columbia Railroad, and by its initial performance of hauling a train weighing 19,200 pounds to the top of an inclined plane in Philadelphia at a speed of fifteen miles per hour, with a boiler pressure of only sixty pounds, it brought world-wide fame to Norris as a locomotive designer and builder. The year after the successful demonstration of the "George Washington," Norris received an order for seventeen

similar engines from the Birmingham & Gloucester Railroad in England, and by 1855 his locomotive works had shipped one hundred engines to France, Austria, Prussia, Italy, Belgium, South America, and Cuba, besides constructing many engines for the railroads of the United States.

In 1841 Norris had formed a partnership with his brother Richard, but three years later he resigned from the company to take charge of the government locomotive shops near Vienna. He remained abroad five years and on his return to the United States he accepted the appointment of chief engineer of the eastern division of the Panama Railroad. When he again returned to the United States in 1855, he organized a company in New York City for the purpose of constructing a fast steamship of his own design, capable of making the voyage to England in six days. The company failed, however, and Norris was obliged to abandon his project before its completion. For his services abroad he received many valuable presents from the Emperor of Austria, Louis Philippe of France, and the Czar of Russia. His great interest outside of locomotive design was music, and when but fifteen years of age he was organist and choir leader of a church in Baltimore. He composed sacred music and on Feb. 8, 1841, produced in Musical Fund Hall, Philadelphia, at his own expense, Mozart's opera, *The Magic Flute*. Norris was married in Baltimore in 1825 to May Ann Heide. A son survived him.

[Henry Hall, *America's Successful Men of Affairs*, vol. II (1896); Zerah Colburn, *Locomotive Engineering and the Mechanism of Railways* (2 vols., 1871); *The Railway and Locomotive Hist. Soc., Bull. No. 10* (1925); *U. S. Mag. of Science, Art, Manufactures, Agriculture, Commerce, and Trade*, Oct. 1855; data from Am. Antiquarian Society.] C. W. M.

NORRIS, WILLIAM FISHER (Jan. 6, 1839–Nov. 18, 1901), ophthalmologist, was born in Philadelphia, Pa., the son of George Washington Norris [q.v.], a prominent surgeon, and Mary Pleasants Fisher. He received his preparatory education at Ferris' private school in Philadelphia and then entered the University of Pennsylvania, receiving the degree of A.B. in 1857. In 1861 he received the degree of M.D. from the same institution and was appointed resident physician to the Pennsylvania Hospital, which institution he served for a period of eighteen months. He then (1863) entered the United States army as assistant surgeon and served until October 1865 when he resigned with the brevet rank of captain. The greater part of his army experience was in connection with the Douglas Hospital in Washington, D. C., where in conjunction with Dr. William Thomson he experimented considerably with photography and microphotography and demonstrated the feasibility of the photographic record for important medical and surgical cases which was subsequently utilized in the preparation of the elaborate *Medical and Surgical History of the War of the Rebellion.* This work probably led to his subsequent intensive study of ophthalmology.

In 1865, when he was twenty-six years of age, he went to Europe for this purpose and visited the clinics of Arlt, Jaeger, and Mauthner. It was this early contact with Vienna that shaped his subsequent career, and while he was there he carried on extensive studies in the histology and pathology of the cornea in collaboration with Stricker at the Pathologic Institute which were quite creditable. Upon his return to Philadelphia in 1870 he began the practice of ophthalmology. He was appointed lecturer in ophthalmology at the University of Pennsylvania and soon after this appointment, with Doctors Strawbridge and Ezra Dyer, was elected an attending surgeon to Wills Eye Hospital, Philadelphia. In 1871 in association with Dr. Horatio C. Wood and Dr. William Pepper he conceived the idea of the hospital of the University of Pennsylvania and in three years these men brought this idea to a successful issue by the construction of the hospital and the opening of its doors for the reception of patients. He was appointed clinical professor of ophthalmology at the University in 1873 and full professor of the same subject in 1876. In the interval between these appointments he was given the chair of honorary professor of ophthalmology, an unusual distinction. The yeoman work and accomplishment necessary for the creation of this hospital in the face of almost insuperable obstacles doubtless accounted for the great influence Norris wielded in connection with it since not only was he the ophthalmologist to the hospital during his lifetime but also president of the board of trustees over a long period. He was made a fellow of the College of Physicians in 1866, a member of the Academy of Natural Sciences in 1868, and a member of the American Ophthalmological Society in 1870. In 1877 he acted as vice-president of the Pathological Society and from 1894 to 1897 he was chairman of the section on ophthalmology of the College of Physicians of Philadelphia.

Norris' accomplishments in the literature of American ophthalmology began with his paper read before the American Ophthalmological Society in 1871 entitled "Paralysis of the Trige-

minus followed by Sloughing of the Cornea." It was followed by more than thirty papers, including the investigation of double staining in microscopic work, in collaboration with Dr. Edward O. Shakespeare, and that of the microscopic anatomy of the human retina with special consideration of the terminal loops of the rods and cones, in collaboration with Dr. James Wallace. The studies made early in his career covering hereditary optic atrophy, orbital growths, brain tumors, and tabes stamp him as a scientific investigator of merit. His major works include his contribution to James Tyson's *Treatise on Bright's Disease and Diabetes* (ed. 1881) and to John Ashhurst's *Principles and Practice of Surgery* (1871), and the section on medical ophthalmology in William Pepper's *System of Practical Medicine* (vol. IV, 1886). In collaboration with Charles A. Oliver he wrote *A Text-Book of Ophthalmology* (1893) and with the same associate he published *System of Diseases of the Eye* (4 vols., 1897–1900), a monumental work utilizing contributions from nearly all of the contemporary authorities in the world. Norris was married twice. His first wife was Rosa Clara Buchmann of Vienna, daughter of Hieronymous Buchmann, whom he met while a student in Vienna and married on July 4, 1873. She died in 1897. Three sons were born of this union. His second wife was Annetta Culph Earnshaw of Gettysburg, Pa., whom he married June 12, 1899, and who with two sons by his first marriage survived him. In 1901 Norris became the subject of recurring attacks of double pneumonia, complicated by a diabetes of long standing, and he died in November of that year.

[C. A. Oliver, *Memoir of Wm. Fisher Norris* (1901); *Trans. Am. Ophthalmol. Soc.*, vol. X (1905); *Trans. Coll. of Physicians of Phila.*, vol. XXIV (1902); J. L. Chamberlain, *Universities and Their Sons: Univ. of Pa.* (1901); *Alumni Reg., Univ. of Pa.*, Dec. 1901; *Phila. Medic. Jour.*, Nov. 23, 1901; *Univ. of Pa. Medic. Bull.*, Aug.–Sept. 1902; *Annals of Ophthalmol.*, Jan. 1902; *N. Y. Medic. Jour.*, Nov. 23, 1901; *Pub. Ledger* (Phila.), Nov. 19, 1901; communications from contemporaries.]   L. W. F.

NORSWORTHY, NAOMI (Sept. 29, 1877–Dec. 25, 1916), psychologist, educator, was born in New York of Devonshire stock. Her father, Samuel Bowden Norsworthy, a mechanical engineer with experience in the navy, brought his bride, Eva Ann Modridge, to the United States from England. To the mother's stern, Puritanic training was due Naomi Norsworthy's characteristic refusal to compromise with the second best, and her unswerving devotion to ideals. A delicate shyness was intensified by the social restrictions and seclusions involved in the family's adherence to the beliefs of the religious sect known as the Plymouth Brethren. A natural generosity was trained into unquestioning sharing of goods, home, time, personal interest with any who made worthy demand. The fun-loving, vivacious child developed into a radiant, sensitive, winsome woman whose charm was magnetic. Slender, dark, slightly over medium height, she appeared fragile; but an inner vitality was manifested by her restless, expressive hands and chiefly by her big, dancing brown eyes.

Educated in the public schools of Rutherford, N. J., she entered the state normal school at Trenton in 1893, where she was recognized as possessing a rare intellect with an unusual memory and a passion for clear thinking. Graduating in 1896, she taught a third grade in Morristown, N. J., till 1899, when she matriculated at Teachers College, Columbia University. The next year she was selected as student assistant in psychology. She received the degree of B.S. and higher diploma in 1901, and the degree of Ph.D. in 1904. Appointed on the staff of Teachers College as assistant in 1901, she rose through the ranks of tutor, instructor, assistant professor, to associate professor in 1912. Her doctor's dissertation, *The Psychology of Mentally Deficient Children* (1906), established the idea of feeblemindedness as a matter of degree of intelligence rather than of special type, in a period before the concept of mental age had become familiar. It was her fortune similarly to do pioneer work in other lines, though in none did she go very far. Thus in an article entitled "The Validity of Judgments of Character," contributed to *Essays, Philosophical and Psychological, in Honor of William James* (1908), she exemplified the use of the method of group ratings of personality traits. Later, she collaborated in planning the experimental teaching which preceded the formulation of the phrase "project method." Though she was joint author of the two books *How to Teach* (1917) and *The Psychology of Childhood* (1918), her reputation lay rather in her skill as a teacher than as a writer. Immediate disciple of Thorndike, McMurray, and Dewey, she combined, transmuted, and demonstrated their teachings, while evidencing rare gifts in guiding discussion and stimulating thought, whether on the public platform or in the classroom. Conscientious to an extreme degree, scorning superficiality, she inspired students with something of her own fearless truthfulness. Ever responsive, but with no sentimentality, her unofficial function at the college was adviser, counsellor, friend at large.

[Records on file at Teachers College; F. C. Higgins, *The Life of Naomi Norsworthy* (1918); *Teachers Coll. Record*, Jan. 1917; *Who's Who in America*, 1914–15; *Woman's Who's Who of America*, 1914–15; personal recollections.]   M. T. W.

NORTH, EDWARD (Mar. 9, 1820–Sept. 13, 1903), educator, classicist, was a native of Berlin, Conn. His father, Reuben North, was a son of Col. Simeon North, 1765–1852 [*q.v.*]; his mother, Hulda (Wilcox), was the daughter of Daniel Wilcox, owner of a large landed property in East Berlin. Edward spent his early years in Berlin, but at the age of fifteen he went to Clinton, N. Y., to live in the family of his uncle, Simeon North, 1802–1884 [*q.v.*], president of Hamilton College. He was graduated at Hamilton in the class of 1841 with the rank of valedictorian. After a year as a private tutor in a family in Paterson, N. J., and a few months spent in a law office, he was appointed principal of the Clinton Grammar School, and soon thereafter, on Dec. 27, 1843, professor of ancient languages in Hamilton College. In 1862 he was made Edward Robinson Professor of Greek, and held this position until his resignation, Nov. 16, 1901, after fifty-seven years of service. The greater part of the college year 1871–72 he spent in Athens, holding a position as secretary under John M. Francis [*q.v.*], United States minister to Greece. After the death of President Henry Darling [*q.v.*], he was appointed acting president of Hamilton College, serving from Apr. 21, 1891, until November 1892.

During his active connection with the faculty he was preëminently a teacher, with a singular skill in interpreting the masterpieces of Greek poetry. In addition to his classroom duties he did a great amount of editorial work, preparing the copy for the annual catalogue under at least three presidents. For thirty-four years he contributed news items concerning graduates to the college literary magazine. It was he who first undertook to prepare accurate obituary records of deceased alumni. He had a wide acquaintance with the public and private schools of the state and many teaching appointments were made upon his recommendation. In 1864 he declined the principalship of the State Normal School at Albany. In 1865 he was president of the New York State Teachers' Association. From 1881 until his death he occupied a unique position as trustee of the college in which he was a professor. In his earlier years he appeared frequently as a lyceum lecturer. His classroom lectures were remembered by his students for their singular charm. A part of one of these was published in the *North American Review*, July 1857 (pp. 168–77). He took a deep interest in local history and tradition and contributed frequently to current publications. He was an elder in the

Presbyterian Church from 1865 until his death, and sat twice, 1870 and 1876, in the General Assembly. He married Mary Frances Dexter, daughter of Hon. S. Newton Dexter, of Whitesboro, N. Y., July 31, 1844. Her death occurred May 27, 1869. Simon Newton Dexter North [q.v.] was their son.

One of Edward North's marked traits was a love of nature and a sympathy with country life. His feeling of companionship with trees inspired some of the most characteristic utterances quoted in the memoir, *Old Greek,* compiled by his son. Other published works of his are: *Dedicatory Address for the Sunset Hill Cemetery, Clinton* (1857); *Uses of Music* (1858); *Memorial of Henry Hastings Curran* (1867).

[S. N. D. North, *Old Greek: An Old-Time Professor in an Old-Fashioned College; a Memoir of Edward North, with Selections from His Lectures* (1905); Dexter North, *John North of Farmington, Conn., and His Descendants* (1921); Catharine M. North, *Hist. of Berlin, Conn.* (1916); *Who's Who in America,* 1901–02; *N. Y. Times,* Sept. 14, 1903.]   E. F.

NORTH, ELISHA (Jan. 8, 1771–Dec. 29, 1843), physician, was born in Goshen, Conn. He was a lineal descendant of John North who emigrated from England in 1635 and settled in Farmington, Conn. His father was Joseph North of Goshen, who married Lucy Cowles of Farmington. Although Joseph North had no regular medical education, he became a local practitioner, and it was under his guidance that his son first began the study of medicine. Later, Elisha studied under Dr. Lemuel Hopkins [q.v.] of Hartford, one of the celebrated "Hartford Wits" and one of the most prominent physicians of his day. In the fall of 1793 he entered the University of Pennsylvania, where he spent the greater part of two years but did not graduate. He then returned to his native town and prepared to settle down to his life work. In 1797 he married Hannah, the daughter of Frederick Beach of Goshen. Three years later, shortly after vaccination had been introduced in America, he made a trip to New Haven to obtain as he says "some Vaccine Fluid," and during 1800 and 1801 the "business of vaccination" was extensively carried on by himself and Jesse Carrington in Goshen. In May 1801 North recognized the first example of kine-pox in the country and it was through his efforts that the first kine-pox used for vaccination purposes was introduced into the city of New York. In 1807 a new disease known as "Spotted Fever" came to North's attention. His experience with the condition was very extensive and his treatment unusually successful. In one year he treated sixty-five patients afflicted with this dread disease and lost only

one. Four years after the appearance of the disease he published his notable work on the subject, *A Treatise on a Malignant Epidemic Commonly Called Spotted Fever* (1811), and became thereby the author of the first volume on cerebro-spinal meningitis to be found in medical literature.

In 1812 he was invited to remove to New London, Conn., an important seaport, where he established the first eye dispensary in the United States, at the same time carrying on a general medical practice. He was actively interested in medical society activities and in 1813 the Connecticut Medical Society conferred upon him the degree of M.D. Although possessed of a large clientele, he had pecuniary difficulties which led him to observe, "Judging from the lowness of medical fees in Connecticut, one would suppose that property regarded as a means of health, was held by the community in higher estimation than health itself." In 1829 he published in Connecticut papers several essays under the title "The Rights of Anatomists Vindicated" and signed Vesalius. In the same year he published a volume of 200 pages entitled *Outlines of the Science of Life; Which Treats Physiologically of Both Body and Mind,* a work showing wide acquaintance with current English literature on physiology; and in 1836, *The Pilgrim's Progress in Phrenology,* by "Uncle Toby." He was also the author of a number of essays in addition to those already mentioned. He lived to be seventy-three years of age and except for deafness in his latter years enjoyed splendid health. His life even to its close was devoted to study and to reading and writing. To him and his wife were born eight children.

[Dexter North, *John North of Farmington, Conn., and His Descendants* (1921); H. C. Bolton, "Memoir of Elisha North," in *Proc. Conn. Medic. Soc.,* vol. III, no. 4 (1887); W. R. Steiner, "Dr. Elisha North," in *Johns Hopkins Hosp. Bull.,* Oct. 1908; H. A. Kelly and W. L. Burrage, *Am. Medic. Biogs.* (1920).]   H. T.

NORTH, FRANK JOSHUA (Mar. 10, 1840–Mar. 14, 1885), scout and plainsman, second son of Thomas Jefferson and Jane Almira (Townley) North, was born in Ludlowville, Tompkins County, N. Y. Though named Frank Joshua, he rarely used his middle name. His early boyhood was spent in Richland County, Ohio. In the spring of 1856, the family moved on to the new settlement of Omaha, Nebraska Territory, and in 1858 to a still newer location, Columbus, on the Loup Fork of Platte River, Nebr. Through intimate association with the Pawnees, North learned their language and also the Indian sign language. In 1860, he drove a freight outfit to the Colorado gold fields. Returning to Nebraska, in 1861 he became clerk-interpreter at the Pawnee reservation on the Loup. In 1864, Gen. S. R. Curtis [q.v.], while organizing a campaign against the hostile Indians who had practically stopped overland stage travel and wagon traffic across the plains, took into service seventy-six Pawnee volunteers, with Joseph McFadden, a reservation employee who had formerly served under Gen. W. S. Harney, as captain of the company, and Frank North as lieutenant. North and two Pawnees were soon detached as scouts and guides for General Curtis and his escort to Fort Riley,. Kan., the remainder of the Pawnees and Captain McFadden accompanying Gen. R. B. Mitchell farther west.

Curtis authorized North to enlist a regular Pawnee scout company as Civil War volunteers, and on Oct. 24, 1864, he was commissioned captain by Alvin Saunders, governor of Nebraska Territory. Early in 1865, the company was ordered on the Powder River Indian Expedition, under Gen. Patrick E. Connor [q.v.]. It participated in several skirmishes and the battle of Aug. 28, 1865, on Tongue River, Dakota Territory (now northwestern Wyoming). Later, North and some Pawnees were sent out to locate Col. Nelson Cole, whose force had missed Connor's main column and nearly perished in Montana from short rations and severe weather. This object was accomplished, and the entire expedition united at Fort Connor (later Fort Reno). Discharged in the spring of 1866, North returned to the Nebraska Pawnee reservation; but early in 1867 was authorized by Gen. C. C. Augur [q.v.], commanding the Department of the Platte, to organize and command, as major of cavalry, a battalion of four Pawnee companies, mainly for the protection of surveys and construction work on the Union Pacific Railroad against hostile Indians. On Aug. 17, part of his command won a running fight with the Cheyennes at Plum Creek, Nebr. The same general duties continued, with varying members of companies, until after the completion and opening of the railroad. Among later engagements was the battle of Summit Springs, Colorado Territory, July 11, 1869, where North and the Pawnee scouts led the charge into the hostile village of Tall Bull, renegade Cheyenne chief, whose defeat saved the frontier settlements in adjacent Colorado and Nebraska from attacks by that band.

North was afterwards guide-interpreter at Fort D. A. Russell, Wyo., and Sidney Barracks, Nebr., participating frequently in scouts and occasionally in scientific explorations. In August 1876 he was sent by Gen. P. H. Sheridan to the Indian Territory to enroll and bring up 100 Paw-

nee Indians (including many veterans of previous expeditions) for service with Gen. George Crook [q.v.] in the fall and winter campaign. This last Pawnee company assisted Col. R. S. Mackenzie [q.v.] in his round-up of Red Cloud and Red Leaf on Chadron Creek, Nebr., Oct. 23, and formed a part of the Powder River Expedition. On Nov. 25, 1876, North and his Pawnees led the attack on the village of Dull Knife's Northern Cheyennes in the Big Horn region of Wyoming. They also accompanied the command to and from the Belle Fourche River in search of Crazy Horse [q.v.] and his band. Returning to the line of the Union Pacific, they were mustered out of service at Sidney Barracks, Nebr., late in April 1877. For about five years Frank and Luther H. North were partners of William F. Cody [q.v.] in a ranch on the Dismal River, Nebr. In the fall of 1882, Frank North was elected to the Nebraska legislature from the Platte County district. Later he joined Cody's "Wild West" show, and led the Pawnees in exhibitions of Indian warfare. In the summer of 1884 he was severely injured at Hartford, Conn.; and although later he rejoined the troupe, he never fully recovered, and died at Columbus, Nebr., after returning from New Orleans in the spring of 1885. On Dec. 25, 1865, he married Mary L. Smith, and they had one daughter.

Frank North had no superior as frontiersman and guide in his day, which was somewhat later than that of James Bridger and Christopher Carson [qq.v.]; he was probably the best revolver shot then on the plains, having beaten "Wild Bill" (James Butler) Hickok [q.v.] and others in competition in 1873. He was the only leader of Indian scouts thoroughly acquainted with the language and customs of his men, who called him Pani La Shar ("Pawnee Chief"), by which name he is still remembered among the tribe. Though often exposed to dangers, he was never wounded in the service. He kept the Pawnees in discipline, ready for emergencies; during six campaigns under his leadership, only one Pawnee was killed in battle and a few wounded, though greatly superior numbers were encountered and defeated. North was never a regular army officer; he was employed by the Quartermaster's Department only for stated periods overlapping the several enlistments of Pawnee scouts, but his rank and title corresponded to those involving similar duties in the regular establishment.

[G. B. Grinnell, *Two Great Scouts and Their Pawnee Battalion* (1928) and *Pawnee Hero Stories and Folk-Tales* (1889; 1909); Robert Bruce, *The Fighting Norths and Pawnee Scouts* (1932); Dexter North, *The Caleb North Genealogy* (1930); *Trans. and Reports Nebr.*

State Hist. Soc., vol. II (1887); Omaha Daily Herald, Mar. 15, 1885; various histories of the Indian wars, 1864-77.]   R. B.

NORTH, SIMEON (July 13, 1765–Aug. 25, 1852), manufacturer of pistols and rifles for the United States government for more than fifty years, was born in Berlin, Conn., the fourth son of Jedediah and Sarah (Wilcox) North, and of the sixth generation in descent from John North, who came from England in 1635 and settled in Farmington, Conn. Like his father and grandfather, he began life as a farmer. On his sixteenth birthday, in 1781, he shouldered his gun and walked to Saybrook, where he attempted to enlist in the Continental Army, but he was rejected by the recruiting officer. In 1786 he married Lucy, daughter of Jonathan and Elizabeth Ranney Savage of Berlin, Conn. She died in 1811, after bearing him five sons and three daughters. His second wife, Lydia, whom he married Mar. 2, 1812, was the daughter of Rev. Enoch Huntington of Middletown, Conn. She bore him one daughter. In 1795 he began a business of making scythes in an old mill adjoining his farm, and on Mar. 9, 1799, he secured his first contract with the War Department for 500 horse-pistols to be delivered within one year. It is probable that previously he had made some pistols for private sales. Other government contracts followed, some of which were for pistols for the Navy Department. It is not definitely known whether it was North or the more famous Eli Whitney [q.v.] who first devised tools and machines for making separate parts and was, therefore, the first American manufacturer to make arms whose parts should be interchangeable one with the other, but it is quite certain that the system of interchangeable parts had its birth in the work of these two men, both engaged in manufacturing arms for the federal government. In North's contract for 20,000 pistols, dated Apr. 16, 1813, there was this provision which he himself had recommended: "The component parts of pistols are to correspond so exactly that any limb or part of one Pistol may be fitted to any other Pistol of the twenty thousand." The contract price per pistol was $7.00.

His work for the government was invariably well done. His last pistol contract was made Aug. 18, 1828; all subsequent contracts were for rifles and carbines. His first rifle contract was dated Dec. 10, 1823, and called for 6,000 rifles to be delivered at the rate of 1,200 a year for five years. He delivered them all in four years. The last order received by him from the government was dated Feb. 5, 1850, for 3,000 guns. In 1825 he made a multicharge repeating rifle capable of

firing ten charges without reloading. One of these weapons is now owned by the Winchester Repeating Arms Company of New Haven, Conn.

In 1811 North was elected lieutenant-colonel of the 6th Connecticut Regiment, but resigned the office in 1813, although the title "Colonel" clung to him. While he had not the advantages of college training, he had a well-disciplined mind, was well-informed, and kept abreast of the world's affairs by reading the New York papers. He indicated his appreciation of education by participating in the establishment of the first Berlin Academy which was incorporated in 1802. He was a man of stalwart and erect figure, tireless energy, genial temperament, quiet and modest manner. Although a generous supporter and regular attendant of the village Congregational church, he was not a member of any religious body. He brought up his children strictly in accordance with his own principles of personal honor, the dignity of conscientious labor, the need of square dealing with every one, and the necessity of self-reliance. His four older sons were associated with him in business, but the youngest, Simeon [q.v.], was sent to Yale, where he graduated as valedictorian of his class, was ordained to the ministry, and became president of Hamilton College.

[North's papers were destroyed after his death. S. N. D. North and Ralph North, Simeon North, First Official Pistol Maker of the United States (1913), is based on official records of the War and Navy Depts., which are copiously used. See also J. W. Roe, English and American Tool Builders (1916); Dexter North, John North of Farmington, Conn., and His Descendants (1921); Catharine M. North, Hist. of Berlin, Conn. (1916); death notice in N. Y. Daily Tribune, Sept. 6, 1852.]   J. W. L.

NORTH, SIMEON (Sept. 7, 1802–Feb. 9, 1884), educator, clergyman, was born in Berlin, Conn., the son of Col. Simeon North [q.v.] and Lucy (Savage) North. While his elder brothers, Reuben, James, Alvin, and Selah, were engaged with their father in manufacturing firearms, Simeon, the youngest, entered Yale College and was graduated in 1825 with the rank of valedictorian. After spending two years in the Yale Divinity School he was appointed tutor in Yale College in 1827. In 1829, having before him a choice between one of the best parishes in Connecticut and a professorship of ancient languages in Hamilton College, Clinton, N. Y., he chose the latter.

On arriving at the scene of his labors he found the fortunes of the college at their lowest ebb. Owing to internal dissensions ten of the trustees had resigned and the faculty consisted of the president, Henry Davis [q.v.], and the professor of chemistry, Josiah Noyes. Only nine students remained, and these were members of the lower classes. Nothing daunted, the young professor entered upon his duties and had the satisfaction of seeing the regular succession of graduating classes resumed, after an intermission of two years, and never again interrupted. After serving ten years as a teacher he was elected fifth president of the college, and held that office until 1857. In 1840 he was elected a trustee of Auburn Theological Seminary and served nine years. In May 1842 he was ordained to the ministry by the Oneida Association of Congregational Churches. Five years later he delivered the oration before the Yale chapter of Phi Beta Kappa: *Anglo-Saxon Literature* (1847). Other published addresses and discourses are *The College System of Education* (1839), his inaugural address; sermons at the funeral of his colleague and intimate friend, Professor Marcus Catlin (1849), and of his predecessor in the presidency, Dr. Henry Davis (1852). In 1879 he made his last contribution to the literature of the College in the form of a Half-Century Letter of reminiscence, marking the fiftieth anniversary of his election to the chair of ancient languages. The years following his resignation, 1857 to 1884, were spent at his home near the campus, where, as a trusted counselor of three succeeding presidents, he lived quietly, finding satisfaction in cultivating old friendships and in reading the classics, ancient and modern. His administration was marked by substantial additions to the equipment of the college, including the building of the Litchfield Astronomical Observatory, and the founding of the Maynard professorship of law and history, first held by Theodore W. Dwight [*q.v.*].

He married on Apr. 21, 1835, Frances Harriet Hubbard, daughter of Dr. Thomas Hubbard, professor of surgery in Yale Medical College. Her death occurred Jan. 21, 1881; their only son died in boyhood. Edward North [*q.v.*] was North's nephew.

[*Memorial of Rev. Simeon North, D.D., LL.D.* (1884), comp. by Edward North; S. N. D. North and R. H. North, *Simeon North, First Official Pistol Maker of the U. S.* (1913), ch. ii; C. M. North, *Hist. of Berlin, Conn.* (1916); *Doc. Hist. of Hamilton Coll.* (1922); *Obit. Record Grads. Yale Coll.*, 1884; Dexter North, *John North of Farmington, Conn., and His Descendants* (1921); *The Congreg. Year Book* (1885); *N. Y. Times*, Feb. 11, 1884.]   E. F.

NORTH, SIMON NEWTON DEXTER (Nov. 29, 1848–Aug. 3, 1924), editor and statistician, was born in Clinton, N. Y., the son of Edward [*q.v.*] and Mary Frances (Dexter) North. He was educated at Hamilton College, and as an undergraduate displayed ability in journalism which led to his employment, im-

mediately after graduation in 1869, as managing editor of the *Utica Morning Herald*. A few years later he acquired a financial interest in the paper, of which he remained editor until 1886. On July 8, 1875, he married Lillian Sill Comstock of Rome, N. Y., by whom he had two daughters and two sons. He was one of the first newspapermen to make use of the typewriter. In 1885 he was elected president of the New York State Associated Press, and in 1886 became editor and part owner of the *Albany Express*. When after two years the paper was sold, he was employed for a short time as an editorial writer on the *New York Press*. In 1889 he went to Boston to become secretary of the National Association of Wool Manufacturers. As editor of the association's quarterly *Bulletin,* he began the collection of wool prices and other statistics important to the industry. Much of his time was spent in Washington, however, where during the tariff revisions of 1894 and 1897 he presented before congressional committees the case for the domestic manufacturers. He also acted as clerk for a sub-committee of the Senate Finance Committee during the tariff discussions of 1894 and 1897 (letter, *Congressional Record*, 63 Cong., 1 Sess., pp. 1659ff.).

In 1903 he was appointed director of the United States Census, a position for which he was well qualified by previous experience. For the Tenth Census (1880) he had prepared an exhaustive study, *History and Present Condition of the Newspaper and Periodical Press of the United States* (1884); he was the author of a special report, "Wool Manufacture," in *Report of Manufacturing Industries . . . at the Eleventh Census, 1890* (1895, pt. 3; also published as "A Century of American Wool Manufacture," in *Bulletin of the National Association of Wool Manufacturers,* September 1894–March 1895); and had been chief statistician for manufactures for the Twelfth Census. His appointment as director came at a critical period in the history of the census bureau. In response to the urging of economists and statisticians, Congress, by the act providing for the Census of 1900, had made the Bureau of the Census, placed in the Department of the Interior, substantially independent of the secretary. In 1903, however, the census bureau was transferred by executive order to the newly created Department of Commerce and Labor, and immediately differences of opinion arose between Director North and Secretary George Bruce Cortelyou. North opposed the Secretary's attempts to control the bureau on the ground that the director's authority as defined by statute could not be limited by executive orders. Legally, North's position appears to have been impregnable, but strategically he was at a great disadvantage in dealing with a cabinet member. He proceeded to reorganize and expand the work of the Bureau, but the administrative conflict, continually renewed, threatened to interfere with the plans for the Thirteenth Census, and finally President Taft, acting on a report from Secretary Charles Nagel, forced North to resign (*Evening Star*, Washington, May 26, June 1, 1909).

He was then sixty years old. Turning again toward editorial work, he spent a few months in Concord, N. H., associated with Messrs. Chandler, Rossiter, and others in building up the Rumford Press. In 1911 he returned to Washington to become assistant secretary of the Carnegie Endowment for International Peace, in which position he remained until 1921, when failing health caused his retirement. He died at the home of a daughter in Wilton, Conn., three years later.

North was a member of the United States Industrial Commission by appointment of President McKinley in 1898, and one of three commissioners sent to Germany by President Roosevelt in 1906 to investigate complaints regarding the administration of American customs laws. He was a prolific writer. His publications, in addition to those already mentioned, include "An American Textile Glossary" (*Bulletin of the National Association of Wool Manufacturers*, March 1893–September 1896); *Old Greek* (1905), a memoir of his father; *Simeon North, First Official Pistol Maker of the United States* (1913), in collaboration with Ralph H. North, a biography of his great-grandfather; and a large number of magazine articles of an historical or statistical nature. He edited *The American Year Book, 1910* (1911).

[W. F. Willcox, "The Development of the American Census Office Since 1890," *Pol. Sci. Quart.*, Sept. 1914; *Bull. Nat. Asso. of Wool Mfrs.*, Oct. 1924, with bibliog. of North's articles published in that journal; *Who's Who in America*, 1922–23; *Independent*, Apr. 15, 1909; Dexter North, *John North of Farmington, Conn., and His Descendants* (1921), which is authority for date of birth; W. L. Downing, *Thirty Years Post Graduate Record of the Class of 1869, Hamilton Coll.* (1899); *Hamilton Coll. Bull.*, *Necrology*, Apr. 1925; *Evening Star* (Washington) and *N. Y. Times*, Aug. 4, 1924.]
P. W. B.

NORTH, WILLIAM (1755–Jan. 3, 1836), Revolutionary soldier, was born at Fort Frederic, Pemaquid, Me., the son of Capt. John North and his second wife, Elizabeth Pitson. After his father's death in 1763, William removed with his mother to Boston where he was educated and began training for a mercantile career. At the outbreak of the Revolution, he desired to accompany Arnold's expedition to Quebec but illness prevented. On May 9, 1776, he was "engaged" as second lieutenant in Col. Thomas Crafts's train of artillery. Subsequently he served as an officer in various regiments of Massachusetts infantry, including Col. Henry Jackson's, the 4th, and the 16th. In May 1779 he was appointed aide-de-camp to the Baron von Steuben [q.v.]. This was the beginning of a romantic friendship terminating only with Steuben's death. North accompanied the baron on his campaigns, assisted him in reorganizing the army, was adopted by him as a son, became one of his heirs and executors, erected a monument over his grave, and wrote a biographical sketch of him which was used by Steuben's biographer Friedrich Kapp.

After the war North served for a time as inspector of the army with the rank of major. On Oct. 14, 1787, he married Mary, daughter of James Duane [q.v.], mayor of New York City. He acquired an estate in Duanesburg, N. Y., and was the father of three sons and three daughters. In 1794, when war with England seemed imminent, he served on a commission to devise measures for strengthening the defenses of the state. He was several times elected to the assembly as a Federalist. In 1795, 1796, and 1810 he was honored with the speakership. Upon the resignation of John Sloss Hobart [q.v.] as United States senator, he was appointed by Governor Jay, during the recess of the legislature, to fill the vacancy. After taking his seat on May 21, 1798, he voted for the Alien and Sedition laws (though not for the Naturalization Act), for increases in the military and naval establishments, and for suspension of commercial relations with France. His experience as a soldier led to his appointment (sometimes as chairman) upon various committees charged with the consideration of military affairs, such as the arming of the militia and the expense of raising a regiment of artillerists and engineers.

On July 19, the last day of the executive session, he was nominated by President Adams to be adjutant-general of the provisional army, and the nomination was at once confirmed. He served in this capacity until June 1800, when he was honorably discharged. By concurrent resolution of Mar. 13–15, 1810, the New York legislature appointed him member of a commission to report upon the feasibility of a canal between Lakes Erie and Ontario and the Hudson River. He entered upon his duties in July, and after study of the project joined the other commissioners in framing a report which helped to pave the way for the building of the Erie Canal. He died in

New York City and was buried in Duanesburg. He was a man of strong prejudices who combined in rare fashion joviality of temper with zeal in the performance of duty.

[Letters of North among the Steuben Papers in N. Y. Hist. Soc.; Friedrich Kapp, *The Life of Frederick William von Steuben* (1859); J. W. North, *The Hist. of Augusta* (1870); J. B. Doyle, *Frederick William von Steuben and the Am. Rev.* (1913); J. D. Hammond, *The Hist. of Pol. Parties in the State of N. Y.* (4th ed., 2 vols., 1846); *Buffalo Hist. Soc. Pubs.*, vol. II (1880); *Mass. Soldiers and Sailors of the Rev. War* (16 vols., 1896–1907); F. B. Heitman, *Hist. Reg. of Officers of the Continental Army* (rev. ed., 1914); *National Intelligencer* (Washington, D. C.), Jan. 12, 1836.]   E. E. Cu—s.

NORTHEN, WILLIAM JONATHAN (July 9, 1835–Mar. 25, 1913), governor of Georgia, was, in the course of his varied life, teacher, farmer, legislator, editor, writer, and soldier. He was born in Jones County, Ga., the son of Peter and Louise Maria Louisa (Davis) Northen and a descendant of Edmund Northen of English descent who emigrated to Virginia probably in the middle of the seventeenth century. His father moved to Penfield, where Mercer University had been established, and became a steward of the college and treasurer of the Baptist Convention. There the boy was graduated in 1853. He taught a private school in Mt. Zion until 1856, when he became assistant principal of Mt. Zion High School near Sparta in Hancock County. In 1857, upon the retirement of Carlisle P. Beman, he was made principal. He married on Dec. 19, 1860, Martha Moss Neel, the daughter of Thomas Neel of Mt. Zion. They had two children. During the Civil War he was a Confederate private in a company commanded by his father. In 1871 he moved his school to Kirkwood near Atlanta and at the end of 1874 resigned his school and returned to Hancock County, where he became a farmer. Until 1890 he farmed with success, being especially interested in cattle breeding and in producing large proportions of butter fat. He mixed with his farming no small measure of politics; he became permanent president of the Hancock County Farmers' Club, president of the Georgia State Agricultural Society, 1886–90, and he was representative of the county in the General Assembly, 1877–78 and 1880–81, and state senator, 1884–85. He was active in efforts to educate farmers to improved methods and to crop diversification, was a leader in the boycott to prevent an advance in the price of the jute bagging used to cover cotton bales, and supported the attack on the monetary system. In 1890 he was elected governor as the candidate of the Democratic party with the support of the farmers of the Georgia State Agricultural Society and the Farmers' Alliance. In 1892 he was reëlected for a second term against the Populist candidate. During his administration he advocated the interests of agriculture and urged the importance of such state undertakings as the geological survey, prison reform, and the improvement of the common-schools.

As ex-governor he continued to reside in Atlanta. He became manager of the Georgia Immigration and Investment Bureau, a position in which he was instrumental in bringing many desirable settlers into the state and, particularly, a group of Union veterans from Indiana who founded the town of Fitzgerald. He became editor of an extensive collection of biographical sketches published in six volumes from 1907 to 1912 under the title of *Men of Mark in Georgia* and himself wrote a number of the contributions. He published a seventh volume with uniform binding and title page in 1912 which, however, is not registered in the records of the copyright office and is not usually included in a description of the set. He took a prominent part in the councils of the Baptist Church, serving fourteen years as president of the Georgia Convention and three years as president of the Southern Baptist Convention. He was a trustee of Mercer University from 1869 to his death and held other positions of trust. On the death of Allen D. Candler he was appointed his successor as compiler of state records and edited in part *The Colonial Records of Georgia*, vol. XXII, pts. 1, 2 (1913). He maintained a constant and active interest in agriculture and education and was a strong advocate of prohibition. He was a frequent contributor to agricultural, educational, and religious journals. He was buried in Oakland Cemetery at Atlanta.

[Papers in the possession of his daughter, Annie B. Northen, Atlanta, Ga.; A. B. Caldwell, "William Jonathan Northen," *Men of Mark in Ga.*, IV (1908); L. L. Knight, *Reminiscences of Famous Georgians* (2 vols., 1907–08); and *Georgia's Landmarks* (2 vols., 1913–14); *Who's Who in America*, 1912–13; A. M. Arnett, *The Populist Movement in Ga.* (1922); *Atlanta Constitution*, Mar. 26, 1913.]   J. H. T. M.

NORTHEND, CHARLES (Apr. 2, 1814–Aug. 7, 1895), educator, was born at Newbury (now Newburyport), Mass., the descendant of Ezekiel Northend, who emigrated from Yorkshire, England, and settled in Newbury before 1691, and the son of John and Anna (Titcomb) Northend. His father, a studious, well-read man played an active part in the affairs of the town, serving as selectman and representative to the Massachusetts General Court. As a student in the public schools at Newbury and, later, at Dummer Academy at South Byfield during the period of his preparation for college, Charles

Northend achieved a reputation for scholastic accomplishment. He entered Amherst College in 1831 but was obliged, for financial reasons, to withdraw at the close of his sophomore year. Upon leaving college he was engaged as an instructor in Dummer Academy and remained there several terms. On Aug. 18, 1834, he was married to his cousin Lucy Ann Moody, the daughter of William and Abigail (Titcomb) Moody, of Newbury. They had three sons. In 1836 he accepted an appointment as principal of the First Grammar School in Danvers, Mass. Five years later he removed to Salem to take charge of the Epes Grammar School, in which position he served until 1852, when he returned to Danvers as superintendent of public schools. During this period he worked untiringly to improve conditions in the common schools. He organized teachers' associations and conducted institutes for the discussion of teaching problems. To his efforts were due many reforms in various phases of educational practice. The Essex County Teachers' Association recognized his contributions by electing him president for three successive terms, 1846, 1847, 1848. His success at Danvers attracted considerable attention throughout New England.

When the town was divided, in 1855, and his opportunities there were consequently curtailed, he was invited to New Britain, Conn., as school visitor, a position corresponding to that of assistant superintendent of public schools. He accepted this election in 1856 and devoted the remainder of his professional life to the New Britain school system. As in Massachusetts, he gave unsparingly of his time and energy to the cause of the common-school. From 1856 to 1866 he was an editor of the *Connecticut Common School Journal*. In 1878 he became an associate editor of the *New England Journal of Education* (later the *Journal of Education*). Among other activities, he delivered many addresses on educational topics before county, state, and national associations; and he became known as one of the most progressive superintendents of his time. The American Institute of Instruction elected him president for the year 1863–64. He became a member of the New Britain school board in 1872 and secretary in the following year. In 1879 he was elected superintendent of schools, a position which he held until his retirement in 1880. The last years of his life were spent in New Britain. Although he had withdrawn from public office, he continued his interest in educational affairs, brought out later editions of his books, and contributed articles to professional journals. He was a prolific writer of school-

books, some of which went through many editions. Among those best known are: *The Common School Book-Keeping* (1845), *The American Speaker* (1848), *Dictation Exercises* (1851), *The Teacher and the Parent* (1853), *The Teacher's Assistant* (1859), *Selections for Analysis and Parsing* (1864), *Gems for the Young* (1864), and *Entertaining Dialogues* (1876).

[*Amer. Jour. of Education*, June, Sept. 1865; Alfred Andrews, *Geneal. and Eccles. Hist. of New Britain* (1867); "The Northend Family," *Essex Institute Hist. Colls.*; vol. XII (1874); *Vital Records of Danvers, Mass.*, vol. II (1910); *Vital Records of Newbury, Mass.* (2 vols., 1911); *Hartford Courant*, Aug. 8, 1895.]

R. F. S.

NORTHROP, BIRDSEY GRANT (July 18, 1817–Apr. 27, 1898), educator, was born in Kent, Conn., the son of Thomas Grant and Aurelia (Curtiss) Northrop, and a descendant of Joseph Northrop who emigrated from England to Boston, Mass., in 1637, settling, two years later, at Milford, Conn. Since his grandfather, Amos Northrop, had attended Yale College, the boy wrote to the president of Yale, Jeremiah Day [*q.v.*], asking him "what school or schools are the best and most celebrated." "I wish," he added, "to attend a good school in a preparatory course for college" (*New England Magazine*, May 1900, p. 269). Presumably upon the advice of Dr. Day, but against the wishes of his father, the young man went to school in Ellington, Conn., and from there to Yale, from which he was graduated in 1841. He then entered the Yale Theological School and was graduated in 1845. During his college course he was troubled by ill health but, although he gave up study for a time, he was able to teach in Elizabethtown, N. J. In 1846 he married Harriette Eliza Chichester of Troy, N. Y. Five children were born to them.

In 1846 Northrop was called to the pastorate of the Congregational church at Saxonville, Mass., where he remained for ten years. In 1857 he resigned and was appointed agent of the Massachusetts State Board of Education, a position which he held until 1867, when he was appointed secretary of the Connecticut State Board of Education. He helped to inaugurate a free-school system in the state and to establish compulsory school attendance. After his resignation in 1883, he began to devote his energies to the establishment of Arbor Day, a project in which he had been actively interested since 1876, and to the improvement and beautifying of towns. To this latter activity is due much of the beauty of such towns as Barre, Great Barrington, and Lenox, Mass., Litchfield, New Milford, and Norfolk, Conn., and Geneseo, N. Y. In 1872 the government of Japan invited him to initiate a system of public education, but his duties kept him at home. Aside from his interest in the establishment of Arbor Day and village improvement societies, Northrop's great desire was to induce the United States government to return the Japanese indemnity exacted because of the Shimonoseki episode in 1863. In a bulletin issued from the "State House, New Haven, Conn.," dated Jan. 1, 1873, he gave a statement of the situation and sent out a petition for signatures, which was later presented to the Senate by Senator Joseph Hawley of Connecticut. The matter of the indemnity was before Congress at intervals for a number of years, but finally, in 1883, the whole amount paid by Japan was returned to be used for educational purposes. Northrop acted as the guardian of some of the first Japanese students who came to the United States. His advice in educational matters was frequently sought. It was after consultation with him that Daniel Hand [q.v.] gave over a million dollars to help the Southern freedmen. Charles Pratt [q.v.], who founded Pratt Institute, Brooklyn, N. Y., also consulted him. He was one of the original trustees of Smith College and was for some years a trustee of Hampton Institute. When he was nearly eighty years old he went to Japan and the Hawaiian Islands, giving many lectures, and in 1897 he went through the Southern states, lecturing and visiting numerous negro schools.

His publications, the titles of which suggest their character, include the following: *Education Abroad* (1873); *Lessons from European Schools* (1877); *The Legal Prevention of Illiteracy* (1878); *Village Improvement* (1878); *Schools of Forestry and Industrial Schools of Europe* (1878); *Tree Planting and Schools of Forestry in Europe* (1879); *Schools and Communism, National Schools and Other Papers* (1879); *Menticulture and Agriculture* (1881); *Rural Improvement* (1882); *Forests and Floods* (1885); *Arbor Day in Schools* (1892).

[A. J. Northrup, *The Northrup-Northrop Geneal.* (1908); *Obit. Record Grads. Yale Univ.*, 1898; *Semi-Centennial Hist. and Biog. Record of the Class of 1841 in Yale Univ.* (1892); E. B. Peck, "The Founder of Arbor Day," in *New England Mag.*, May 1900; *New Haven Evening Register*, Apr. 28, 1898.] A. B. M—h.

NORTHROP, CYRUS (Sept. 30, 1834–Apr. 3, 1922), second president of the University of Minnesota, was born on a farm near Ridgefield, Conn. His mainly peaceful and prosperous life divides itself roughly into three ample blocks: the period of nonage (1834–1857), the Yale professorship (1863–1884), and the presidential tenure, active and retired, lasting from 1884 to 1922.

Six years of fluctuation and uncertainty divide the first of these periods from the second.

He was a descendant of Joseph Northrop who emigrated from England in 1637 and two years later settled in Milford, Conn. His father's family, poor, industrious, thrifty, long-lived, God-fearing men, farmed the soil of Connecticut, without recorded interruption, from 1639 to the later nineteenth century. The elder Cyrus Northrop, father of the educator, married in 1822 Polly Bouton Fancher, whose ancestry, French on both sides, reached America in 1635 with John Bouton, Huguenot and refugee. It was only in Cyrus junior, the sixth and youngest child, that this devout and hardworking breed emerged from rusticity, a rusticity not incompatible with terms in the Connecticut legislature for two of the older brothers. Cyrus was sent to Williston Seminary in Easthampton, Mass., then at the zenith of its merited fame under Josiah Clark—first, for all time, among his teachers for the young Cyrus. To Yale College, in 1852, by a family decision which family poverty made touching and even heroic, the lad of eighteen betook himself. He graduated, third in his class, in 1857, and from the Yale Law School in 1859. Even at this early age his personality in conversation and his eloquence on the rostrum made impressions on practically everybody that were both instantaneous and ineffaceable.

In 1860 he was admitted to the bar. Two rasping years of small-town law practice in Norwalk and South Norwalk, Conn., in which fees were even rarer than clients, were alleviated by clerkships in the two houses of the state legislature, and ended by his acceptance of the editorship of the New Haven *Palladium*, a newspaper which opposed slavery and upheld Lincoln. His conduct of this paper was vigorous and inspiring, but fifteen months in its office showed him that the hopes of income on the strength of which he had married Anna Elizabeth Warren of Stamford, Conn., Sept. 30, 1862, were chimerical, and in 1863 he was led by "poverty" to accept the chair of rhetoric and English literature in Yale College. The fact marks a curious angle in his career. The young man predestined, as it seemed, to reach politics via law, actually drifted into instructorship by way of journalism. The new post was at once a step upward and a step aside.

Cyrus Northrop filled this post for twenty-one years with efficiency and with distinction. He mended his income by adding to his college work the collectorship of duties for the port of New Haven (1869–81), and he enlivened its routine by an unsuccessful canvass for a seat in Congress on the Republican ticket in 1867. In this snug academic harbor the man—not the teacher—was, in a sense, becalmed. Half the man was more than enough to perform his work efficiently; the other and richer half was unemployed. From this beguiling monotony he was released by an offer of the presidency of the University of Minnesota (1884) tactfully pressed upon his first unhesitating refusal and his slowly diminishing reluctance. Admirable teacher as he was, the classroom was both too large and too small to give scope for a personality which reached its perfection in the cabinet or on the rostrum. His gift was both public and intimate. He persuaded; he convinced; he impressed; he diverted; he controlled. It is impossible to trace here the steps (not to say the leaps and bounds) by which a small and shrinking institution of less than 300 students, subsisting on meager doles from an inconstant legislature, became in twenty-seven years a great and various body numbering its faculty by the hundred; its students by the thousand, and its income by the million. To this advance Cyrus Northrop contributed by judgment, address, resolution, fearlessness, and liberality. He helped even more perhaps by personifying the university in a form which dignified and magnified it in its own eyes and in the eyes of its constituents. He was not a thinker in education, not by instinct an innovator. Left to himself, he might have been content with an education predominantly classical and predominantly masculine; but he was never for a moment ungracious or uncordial to the movements which brought sciences and women to the front. He owed much of his success, both with communities and with individuals, to a humor which made a trifle or a nothing delectable by putting behind it the whole ironic weight of his majestic personality.

He retired from the presidency in 1911, at the age of seventy-seven. Pecuniary and domestic afflictions clouded his last years. He survived his three deeply loved children, of whom the eldest died in early childhood; the second, after an attack of scarlet fever, suffered from life-long mental infirmity; a third, Elizabeth, wife of Joseph Warren Beach, after years of tottering health, died in 1918, leaving two young sons, the president's only surviving descendants. He died of a ruptured heart, Apr. 3, 1922, and, three days later, was buried in the family lot in Lakewood Cemetery, Minneapolis. Throughout his life he was faithful to the Congregationalist Church, in which he had been born and to which, at nineteen, he had pledged his loyalty.

A volume of *Addresses, Educational and Patriotic* from his hand was published in 1910. An imposing auditorium on the campus of the University of Minnesota bears his name and protects his memory.

[A. J. Northrup, *The Northrup-Northrop Geneal.* (1908); *Yale Univ. Obit. Record*, 1922; O. W. Firkins, *Cyrus Northrop* (1925); *Minneapolis Jour.*, Apr. 4, 1922.]   O. W. F.

NORTHROP, LUCIUS BELLINGER (Sept. 8, 1811–Feb. 9, 1894), Confederate commissary-general, was born in Charleston, S. C., the son of Amos Bird Northrop and Claudia Margaret Bellinger. The Northrop family was well known in Charleston and was descended from Joseph Northrop, who emigrated from England and settled in Milford, Conn., in 1639. Lucius was graduated from West Point in 1831. He was made brevet second lieutenant of the 7th Infantry but in 1833 was transferred to the 1st Dragoons. He was stationed with this regiment in the West on Indian service and was for a time associated with Jefferson Davis. In 1834 he was promoted first lieutenant. During the Seminole War of 1839 in Florida he received a severe wound and was retired from the army on a permanent sick furlough. He then studied medicine at Jefferson Medical College, Philadelphia. Returning to Charleston, he was in 1848 dropped from the army for practising medicine on charity patients there. Later in the year, however, he was reinstated by Jefferson Davis, secretary of war, and was promoted captain. From 1853 to 1861 he practised medicine in Charleston. About 1841 he had married Maria Euphenia Joanna de Bernabeu, daughter of Juan Baptisto de Bernabeu, United States consul from Spain.

Shortly after the secession of South Carolina, Northrop resigned his commission and upon the urgent request of President Davis accepted the position of colonel and commissary-general in the Confederate army. He was entrusted with the enormous task of providing food for the Southern armies and also, after 1862, for all the Northern prisoners. Though at first his position was considered rather insignificant, as the food supply began to decrease it became quite important. Next to Bragg, and perhaps Benjamin, Northrop was deemed the special favorite of Davis, and soon he was bitterly criticized. Early in 1864, Senator Foote of Tennessee introduced a measure into the Confederate Senate for Northrop's removal, but it was defeated. Meantime, against the wishes of several officers, he had introduced a system by which he appointed state commissary agents and held them responsible directly to himself. He was accused of inadequately feeding Federal prisoners but in January 1865 the Confederate Senate acquitted him of the charge. On Jan. 18, 1865, J. B. Jones wrote that Northrop was "still held by the President, contrary to the wishes of the whole Confederacy" (*post,* II, p. 390). A month later, after the Confederate House of Representatives had passed a bill seeking his removal, Davis finally consented to take this step. After Lee's surrender, Northrop was arrested by Federal troops and imprisoned, but no charges were preferred against him and he was released in a few months.

After Bragg, Northrop was probably the most unpopular of Davis' appointees. The Confederate army officers thought him inefficient; Lee had little patience with him, and finally asked for his removal. Northrop was peevish, obstinate, condescending, and fault-finding. He was secretive, indirect, and inclined to regard every suggestion as interference. On the other hand, his work could hardly have been conducted without receiving criticism. He had to contend with the lack of sufficient funds and the necessity of buying with a depreciated currency, with the capture of supplies and the possession of productive country by the invading armies, and with the necessity of resorting to the hated methods of price-fixing and impressment. But during the last two years of the war, his worst trouble was with the transportation system. This was under control of the separate Quartermaster's Bureau. Even in January 1865 there were sufficient supplies in the lower South for Lee's army. Yet Northrop's urgent requests for the improvement of the railroad service were not sufficiently heeded. All in all, Northrop seems to have been a rather good, if "crusty, routine" executive, who was forced to resort to harsh methods. Upon his release from imprisonment after the war, he retired to a farm near Charlottesville, Va. He and Jefferson Davis now renewed their friendship. Northrop's letters to Davis reveal his bitterness toward Beauregard, J. E. Johnston, and others. In 1889 his wife died, and the next year he suffered a stroke of paralysis. He then entered the soldiers' home at Pikeville, Md., where he spent his few remaining years.

[There are a considerable number of Northrop papers in the N. Y. Pub. Lib. Printed sources include: *Confed. Mil. Hist.,* vol. I (1899); *War of the Rebellion, Official Records (Army)*; Dunbar Rowland, *Jefferson Davis, Constitutionalist* (10 vols., 1923), containing correspondence between Davis and Northrop; Northrop's article, "The Confederate Commissariat at Manassas," in *Battles and Leaders of the Civil War,* vol. I (1887); J. B. Jones, *A Rebel War Clerk's Diary* (2 vols., 1866); F. A. Pollard, *Southern Hist. of the*

War (1866), vol. II, pp. 477–83; G. C. Eggleston, *A Rebel's Recollections* (1875), pp. 203–09; A. J. Northrup, *The Northrup-Northrop Geneal.* (1908); the *Sun* (Baltimore), Feb. 10, 1894.]   R. D. M.

NORTON, ALICE PELOUBET [See Norton, Mary Alice Peloubet, 1860–1928].

NORTON, ANDREWS (Dec. 31, 1786–Sept. 18, 1853), a man of letters and a Biblical scholar of distinction, was born in Hingham, Mass., the youngest child of Samuel and Jane (Andrews) Norton, and a descendant of William, a brother of Rev. John Norton [*q.v.*]. He was graduated from Harvard College in 1804, pursued graduate studies for four years, preached for a brief period in Augusta, Me., taught for a year at Bowdoin College, in 1811 was appointed tutor at Cambridge, and in 1813 librarian of Harvard College and lecturer on the Bible. In 1819 he became Dexter Professor of Sacred Literature in the Harvard Divinity School. He resigned his professorship in 1830, but continued his literary and theological work at Cambridge until his death, which occurred twenty-three years later at his summer residence at Newport, R. I.

His most important work was his treatise on *The Evidences of the Genuineness of the Gospels,* of which the first volume was published in 1837, and the second and third volumes in 1844. This work, dealing with the history of the New Testament canon on the basis of a careful investigation of the evidence outside the Bible itself, was one of the earliest studies of Biblical literature from the critical point of view to be published in America. It antedates most of the New Testament criticism by nineteenth-century German scholars, who dealt primarily with questions of text and of internal evidence and to whom Norton owed less than he did to English writers. It ran through several editions in this country and in England (the latest being an abridged edition, Boston, 1867), brought him wide recognition as a scholar, and was an influential contribution to theological literature. In 1852 he published a volume entitled *Tracts on Christianity,* a collection of essays and discourses previously printed in various forms. After his death *Internal Evidences of the Genuineness of the Gospels* (1855), which among other things contained a critique of Strauss' *Life of Jesus,* and *Translation of the Gospels with Notes* (2 vols., 1856), appeared. He was actively concerned in the theological controversies of the time, in which, with a certain fastidiousness of thought and statement, he occupied the position of conservative Unitarianism. But, while he accepted the point of view of liberal

Christianity, he was disinclined to enter any associations formed on denominational lines. He established and wrote for the short-lived *General Repository and Review* (January 1812–October 1813), and contributed many reviews to the *Christian Examiner* and several to the *North American Review*. In 1833 he printed *A Statement of Reasons for not Believing the Doctrines of Trinitarians*. His address in 1839, *On the Latest Form of Infidelity*, was commonly interpreted as a reply to Emerson's famous *Divinity School Address* of the preceding year. By many persons who know nothing of Norton's substantial achievements its unfortunate title has been remembered to the disparagement of his just reputation.

In the field of general literature he played an influential part through the editing, with Charles Folsom, of *The Select Journal of Foreign Periodical Literature* (4 vols., 1833–34). He also edited *Poems by Mrs. Hemans* (1826–28). A volume of his own poems, *Verses,* was published in the year of his death. His poetry was of a reserved and formal type, reminiscent of the eighteenth century, but two of his hymns, "My God, I thank thee! may no thought E'er deem thy chastisements severe" (1809), and "Where ancient forests round us spread" (1833) are to be found in modern hymnbooks.

He was an independent and solitary thinker, but his learning enabled him to speak with an authority possessed by few American scholars of his generation, and his influence upon the literary and religious life of his time was constructive and beneficent, thanks to the clarity of his thought and the integrity of his character.

On May 21, 1821, he married Catharine, daughter of Samuel Eliot of Boston. They had six children, of whom four survived infancy. One of these, Charles Eliot Norton [*q.v.*], became a distinguished scholar, and another, Grace Norton, was well-known for her work on Montaigne. Andrews Norton lived in Cambridge at "Shady Hill," a mansion which he erected about the time of his marriage, and which, during the life of his son, became widely known as a center of influence in art and letters.

[William Newell, in *Christian Examiner*, Nov. 1853; W. B. Sprague, *Annals of the American Pulpit*, vol. VIII (1865); A. P. Peabody, *Harvard Reminiscences* (1888), pp. 73–78; S. A. Eliot, ed., *Heralds of a Liberal Faith* (1910), vol. II; *New-Eng. Hist. and Geneal. Reg.*, July 1859; Sara Norton and M. A. DeW. Howe, *Letters of Charles Eliot Norton* (2 vols., 1913.).]

H. W. F.

NORTON, CHARLES ELIOT (Nov. 16, 1827–Oct. 21, 1908), editor, author, teacher, was born in Cambridge, Mass., the fifth child and only surviving son of Andrews Norton [*q.v.*], then Dexter Professor of Sacred Literature in the Harvard Divinity School, and his wife, Catharine Eliot, daughter of Samuel Eliot of Boston. His parents made their home at "Shady Hill," an estate of some fifty acres in Cambridge, where their six children were born, and where Charles died. This home, with its simple but spacious and scholarly elegance, was the hospitable center of the life of the Nortons. Andrews had also a summer place in fashionable Newport. Charles made a retreat at the little town of Ashfield, in northwestern Massachusetts. Wherever domiciled he entered into the life of the place and was a factor in its civic betterment. By inheritance he was endowed with financial competence, scholarly tastes, and a pervasive moral sense. The thoroughness of his scholarship, and his ethical poise were accompanied by personal charm, qualities which combined to make a personality of rare and enduring influence.

Graduating from Harvard in 1846, at the age of nineteen, Norton spent three years with a Boston importing firm. To business he gave conscientious days: his evenings were spent in the congenial tasks of establishing night schools for men and boys in Cambridge and helping the almost blind Francis Parkman prepare for the press his *Oregon Trail*. In 1849, Norton went to India as supercargo. The business instinct of the Eliots, the ways and means of making money, he had not inherited; he was interested in commerce simply as an exchange of commodities. He spent a leisurely two years in Egypt, Italy, France, and England, indulging his bent in studying social conditions and making friendships. In Paris he met "the longhaired and sweet-visaged" George William Curtis [*q.v.*], fresh from his Nile experiences, and the two quickly began a lifelong association. In Florence he became on familiar terms with the Brownings. In England he enjoyed the Ascot races, and the literary society of the day.

Returning to Boston in 1851, Norton began on his own account a modest business in the East India trade. This faded out in 1855, leaving him free to indulge fully his propensity for a literary life. He began by editing the translations of the Gospels, discourses, and poems of his father, who had died in 1853. The doctors ordered Norton abroad in 1855, and with no reluctance he, accompanied by his mother and two sisters, went to Rome. His studies, observations, and opinions, embodied in *Notes of Travel and Study in Italy* (1860), came to be modified but never were essentially changed. He translated *The New Life of Dante Alighieri*

(1867, privately printed 1859) as a prelude to his prose rendering of *The Divine Comedy* (3 vols., 1891–92). In Switzerland he began the intimate friendship with Ruskin, recorded in the *Letters of John Ruskin to Charles Eliot Norton* (2 vols., 1904). James Russell Lowell joined the Nortons in Italy for mule rides, continuing a companionship which widened and deepened with their lives, as may be read in their published letters, those of Lowell in the two volumes Norton edited (1894); Norton's in the two volumes of his own letters. In England he met Thackeray, and was taken into companionship with the Pre-Raphaelites (*Letters*, I, 175). He visited his close friends, the Gaskells and the A. H. Cloughs.

Returning in 1857, Norton wrote articles and reviews for the *Atlantic Monthly*, just established with Lowell as its editor. He enjoyed companionship with its contributors—Lowell, Holmes, and Emerson especially. The impending Civil War engrossed him. Intimacy with the Middleton family of Charleston, S. C., whose summer home was at Bristol, R. I., gave him occasion to study slavery under its most favorable conditions, and to convince him that bad as that institution was for the blacks, it was even worse for the whites. John Brown's rash invasion of Virginia, his conviction, and his heroic death on the gallows, seemed to Norton to place Brown among the Covenanters and the Puritans, and, despite the wrongness of the means adopted, to "set up a standard by which to measure the principles of public men" (*Letters*, I, 201). He was undismayed by the prospect of war and had no fear for the result; but he looked forward "with the deepest sorrow and compassion to the retribution" the South was preparing for itself (*Ibid.*, I, 216). If his early confidence in Lincoln wavered at times, he was quick to readjust his judgment. As editor of the Loyal Publication Society broadsides, for three years he furnished local newspapers with copies of the most effective editorial writings of the day. In 1864, Lowell and Norton as editors made the *North American Review* convincingly loyal. On May 21, 1862, Norton married Susan Ridley Sedgwick, daughter of Theodore Sedgwick, 3rd, of Stockbridge and New York. After an ideal domestic life at "Shady Hill" and Ashfield, she died in February 1872, at Dresden, Germany, while the family (which included three sons and three daughters) were spending five years in Europe.

In March 1869, Norton met Thomas Carlyle, then seventy-four years old, at the latter's London home. Norton said Carlyle was "the

Court-jester of the century," and that like all great talkers, he said much for immediate effect and forgot it as soon as said (*Letters*, I, 332–33). Again, Norton wrote of Carlyle: "Like Dante, his face was black with the smoke of Hell" (*Ibid.*, II, 147). Emerson and Norton directed to Harvard, Carlyle's gift of a large portion of his library, as a sort of reparation for his attacks on the United States. In 1882, Froude, as Carlyle's literary executor, published a garbled version of the intimate journals of Jane Welsh Carlyle, thereby creating a literary sensation. "I could not have believed, even of Froude, bad as I thought him," wrote Norton, "a capacity for such falseness, for such betrayal of a most sacred trust, for such cynical treachery to the memory of one who had put faith in him" (*Ibid.*, II, 135). The family appealed to Norton, and he edited Carlyle's letters, reminiscences, and two notebooks, together with the Carlyle-Emerson and the Goethe-Carlyle correspondence—in all eleven volumes (1883–91).

Norton's work as a teacher covered the years from 1873 to 1897, from his forty-sixth to his seventieth year. Called to service by his cousin, the youthful, innovating President Charles W. Eliot [*q.v.*], Norton began at Harvard the first continuous university instruction in the history of the fine arts as related to social progress, general culture, and literature (manuscript letter, Harvard Library). Eliot Norton wittily and aptly called his father's courses "Lectures on Modern Morals as Illustrated by the Art of the Ancients" (*Letters*, II, 8). All his gathered learning, his discriminating judgment, the results of close companionship with world-worthies, he lavished on the students who flocked to him. The quiet, pervasive charm that had endeared him to the Brownings, to Carlyle, Ruskin, Emerson, Curtis, Lowell, and Longfellow was exercised in his crowded classroom and was expanded in the rare companionship of his home, where he exemplified the attributes of a gentleman. The purchase and gift to the Harvard Library of his rare books, by his students; the creation of The Norton Fellowship in Greek Studies by one of his pupils, and by another the foundation of the Charles Eliot Norton Lectureship of Poetry are manifestations of a sway which came to be accounted by many as the determining influence in their lives. His book, *Historical Studies of Church-Building in the Middle Ages* (1880), is a treasure to practitioners of architecture as a fine art. Another book, *History of Ancient Art* (1891), was prepared by H. F. Brown and W. H. Wiggin from his lectures.

The range of Norton's activities in literature and life was great. He edited *The Poems of John Donne* (2 vols., 1895), *The Love Poems of John Donne* (1905), and *The Poems of Mrs. Anne Bradstreet* (1897), as well as the *Orations and Addresses of George William Curtis* (3 vols., 1894). The Archaeological Institute of America, the American School of Classical Studies at Athens and in Rome, and the movement to preserve Niagara Falls owe to him inspiration and effective support. His sympathies were fresh and catholic. One of the first (*Putnam's Monthly*, Sept. 1855) to recognize Walt Whitman, as combining "the characteristics of a Concord philosopher with those of a New York fireman" (*Letters*, I, 135), he was equally quick to see the merits of Kipling and to enjoy Mr. Dooley. (See *Rudyard Kipling; A Biographical Sketch*, 1899, and *Atlantic Monthly*, Jan. 1897.) The Chicago Fair of 1893 was to him a foretaste of "the ideal Chicago, which exists not only in the brain, but in the heart of some of her citizens. I have never seen Americans from whom one could draw happier auguries for the future of America, than some of the men whom I saw at Chicago" (*Letters*, II, 218).

In 1865, E. L. Godkin, F. L. Olmsted, J. M. McKim, Norton, and others founded the *Nation* as a critical journal to maintain standards in politics, literature and art, familiarly known as "the weekly day of judgment." During forty years of intimacy with Godkin, Norton gave to him active support morally, financially, and by reviews and criticisms in art and letters. During summers at Ashfield, Norton and Curtis, in 1879, started for the benefit of local charity, a series of annual dinners at which Choate, Howells, Moorfield Storey, Booker Washington, and others advocated reform of the tariff and the civil service, the promotion of negro education, and especially anti-imperialism. Stigmatized as mugwumps and party renegades, the speakers through the press found a nation-wide audience. With Curtis' death and Norton's failing health the dinners ceased in 1903.

The breadth of Norton's intelligence, the unflinching clearness of his reasoning, the intensity of his moral convictions aroused antagonisms which he neither sought nor avoided. Companionship with Chauncey Wright, Cambridge mathematician and philosopher, developed a philosophy of life which led him out of the creeds of his ancestors and into a position "almost solitary in my open profession of freethinking" (*Ibid.*, II, 249), . . . "perplexed indeed by the mighty mystery of existence, and of the universe and happy in the conviction that the chief lesson of life is that of love" (*Ibid.*, II, 364). To him God and immortality were inconceivable, but "the motives which impel an intelligent man . . . to virtuous conduct, are the strongest which can be addressed to a human being, because they appeal directly to the highest qualities of his human nature" (*Ibid.*). Thus to him came "a new sense of the value of life to the individual, and of his infinite unimportance to the universe; . . . he can be a help or a harm to his fellows, and that is enough" (*Ibid.*, II, 347). His religious opinions caused momentary hesitation as to his confirmation as professor, and always colored estimates of him.

Norton's advice to his students that they ponder the question as to their duty to enlist for the Spanish-American War aroused widespread criticism, and the vituperations of his classmate, Senator G. F. Hoar, which were afterwards regretted by the latter, also an anti-imperialist. His insistence on *ethos* as the fundamental element in beauty in art brought about conflict with the architect, Charles F. McKim, who in reality practised Norton's precepts, and whose lifework in the American Academy in Rome, was later united with Norton's in the School of Classical Studies in the Eternal City. At times he failed to perceive that the principles he advocated were the very ones which actuated artists to create works he criticized. So, too, in politics the critic in his censures often was unmindful of exigencies which statesmen might guide but could not control.

Recognition of Norton's influence and service came in honorary degrees from Cambridge and Oxford, as well as from Harvard, Yale, and Columbia; also in original membership in the American Academy of Arts and Letters, and in appointment as grand officer of the Order of the Crown of Italy for his Italian studies. In 1907 his eightieth birthday was marked by a group of letters from friends, expressing the esteem he had won for himself. Edith Wharton sent a sonnet, appropriately entitled "High Pasture" (*Harvard Graduates' Magazine*, Dec. 1907); and in 1913, G. E. Woodberry paid his tribute in a Phi Beta Kappa poem (*Ibid.*, Sept. 1913). President Eliot put the climax to Norton's career in sober, prophetic words (*Ibid.*, Dec. 1907, p. 222): "Thousands of Harvard students attribute to his influence lasting improvements in their modes of thought, their intellectual and moral interests, and their ideas of success and true happiness. His work and his training for it were both unique, and are not likely to be parallelled in the future."

[Sara Norton and M. A. DeW. Howe, *Letters of Charles Eliot Norton with Biographical Comment*, containing a list of his writings (2 vols., 1913), a permanent piece of literature; Jane Whitehill, ed., *Letters of Mrs. Gaskell and Charles Eliot Norton, 1855–1865* (1932); W. R. Thayer, in *Harvard Grads. Mag.*, Dec. 1908; E. T. Cook and Alexander Wedderburn, *Works of John Ruskin*, vol. XXXV (1908), Præterita, II, chs. 2–3; *Development of Harvard University, 1869–1929* (1930), ed. by S. E. Morison, ch. v; *Proc. Am. Academy of Arts and Letters*, no. IV, 1910–11 (1911); E. W. Emerson and W. F. Harris, *Charles Eliot Norton* (1912); Barrett Wendell, in *Atlantic Monthly*, Jan. 1909; W. D. Howells, in *No. Am. Rev.*, Dec. 1913; *Boston Evening Transcript*, Oct. 20, 21, 22, 1908.]

C. M.

NORTON, ELIJAH HISE (Nov. 21, 1821–Aug. 5, 1914), congressman, jurist, was born near Russellville, Logan County, Ky. His father, William F. Norton, was the son of Quakers, but he became a Baptist when he married Mary Hise. She was of sturdy Pennsylvania German stock, was a pronounced Baptist, "loved to talk, talked much and talked well." About 1817 they moved from Pennsylvania to Kentucky, where William F. Norton engaged in farming and salt merchandizing. Elijah Hise Norton, their son, obtained most of his preliminary education at Centre College, Danville, Ky. He then entered the law department of Transylvania University, graduated in 1842, was admitted to the bar, and practised law at Russellville for about two years. But the strong pioneer spirit of the times soon took control of him, and in 1845 he moved west, to settle in the promising Platte Purchase country of northwest Missouri. Here, at the town of Platte City, he hung his shingle over the door of a two-room log cabin and soon won recognition as a leading lawyer among a dozen competitors. Upon being elected county attorney, with a salary of $100, he felt sufficiently prosperous to marry on May 28, 1850, Malinda C. Wilson, the daughter of an older and prominent lawyer of Platte City. She died in 1873, leaving a family of seven children, and on Sept. 17, 1877, he married Missouri A. (Green) Marshall.

During the fifties Norton was looked upon as the leading anti-Benton Democrat of northwest Missouri. In 1852 he was elected circuit judge of the Platte Purchase district and ably fulfilled the duties of this office until 1860. He was then nominated and elected to the stormy Thirty-seventh Congress (1861–63), where he took a decided stand in opposition to secession, although he stated that he did not favor war to prevent it. He was defeated when he stood for reëlection to Congress in 1862. As a leading delegate to the state convention of 1861 to consider the relations of Missouri to the federal government, he labored stubbornly and effectively against the

movement to take Missouri out of the Union. He was an outstanding member of the Missouri constitutional convention of 1875. The constitution then formulated and adopted was so permeated with his sound and statesmanlike proposals that it was subsequently not infrequently denominated the "Norton Constitution." It is still (1934) the fundamental law of the state.

When a vacancy occurred on the state supreme bench in 1876, Gov. C. H. Hardin [*q.v.*] appointed Norton to fill the place. Two years later he was elected to the office for the ensuing term and served until Dec. 31, 1888, when he declined renomination. He was chief justice in 1887–88. Among the scores of supreme-court decisions which he rendered, students of jurisprudence may read with profit his citations and conclusions in such cases as *State* vs. *Shock* (68 *Missouri*, 552), dissenting opinion; *Kitchen* vs. *St. Louis, Kansas City & Northern Railway Co.* (69 *Missouri*, 224); *St. Louis* vs. *St. Louis Gaslight Co.* (70 *Missouri*, 69); and *The Julia Building Association* vs. *The Bell Telephone Co.* (88 *Missouri*, 258). He was an able judge, though he did little to construct new bases of legal reasoning or re-direct the course of legal evolution. From 1890 until his death he lived on his large farm near Platte City. He was a successful farmer and business man.

[L. C. Krauthoff, *The Supreme Court of Mo.* (1891); R. P. C. Wilson, "Memorial Address upon Judge Elijah Hise Norton," *Proc. . . . Mo. Bar Asso.*, 1914; A. J. D. Stewart, *The Hist. of the Bench and Bar of Mo.* (1898); *Jour. and Proc. Mo. State Convention . . . 1861* (1861); *Jour. Mo. Constitutional Convention of 1875* (2 vols., 1920), ed. by Isidor Loeb and F. C. Shoemaker; W. M. Paxton, *Annals of Platte County, Mo.* (1897); *A Hist. of Northwest Mo.* (1915), ed. by Walter Williams, vol. II; J. C. Maple and R. P. Rider, *Mo. Bapt. Biog.*, vol. III (1918); H. C. McDougal, *Recollections* (1910); *Mo. Hist. Rev.*, Oct. 1914; *Boonville Daily Advertiser*, Jan. 20, 22, 1877; *Jefferson Inquirer*, Sept. 25, 1852; *St. Joseph Gazette*, Aug. 6, 1914.]

H. E. N.

NORTON, JOHN (May 6, 1606–Apr. 5, 1663), Puritan clergyman, was born at Bishop's Stortford, Hertfordshire, England, the eldest son of William and Alice (Browest) Norton, and grandson of William Norton of Sharpehow, Bedfordshire (*New-England Historical and Genealogical Register*, July 1859, pp. 225–30). The boy studied under Alexander Strange of Buntingford, and at fourteen proceeded to Peterhouse, Cambridge, where he received the degree of B.A. in 1623/4 and that of M.A. in 1627 (John and J. A. Venn, *Alumni Cantabrigienses*, vol. III, 1924; T. A. Walker, *Admissions to Peterhouse or S. Peter's College . . . Cambridge*, 1912, p. 16). For a short time he was an usher at Stortford Grammar School and curate there. He then became private chaplain to Sir William

Masham of High Lever, Essex, and a determined foe of Antinomianism. It is said that his uncle offered him a good benefice and also that he was offered a fellowship at Cambridge but that he declined them both because of his growing Puritanism. Having married "a gentlewoman both of good estate and of good esteem" (Mather, *post,* I, 289), he took ship for New England in the fall of 1634, in company with Thomas Shepard [*q.v.*], but was turned back by a severe storm and did not make another attempt to embark for nearly a year. He reached Plymouth in New England in October 1635. Here he preached and was invited to remain, but he preferred to settle in Massachusetts Bay, and became "teacher" in the church at Ipswich. He was admitted as a freeman May 17, 1637, but was not ordained until Feb. 20, 1638.

At once upon his arrival, he took his place among the leaders of the colony. He had come just in time for the Antinomian controversy and in 1637 was an influential member of the Synod convened to adjust the differences arising from it. Incidentally, he is partly responsible for the loss of valuable papers connected with it. John Cotton's son, charged by his father with destroying all his papers, hesitated to do so and put the question as a point of conscience to Norton, who decided for their destruction (Hutchinson, *post,* I, 179, note). In 1646 Norton was chosen to go with Winthrop as a special agent to England, but the plan was abandoned. The same year he took a leading part in the Synod and in 1648 he was active in drawing up the famous Cambridge Platform. When John Cotton [*q.v.*] was dying, he suggested Norton as his successor in the pastorate of the First Church of Boston, and after his death (Dec. 23, 1652), Norton took his place. He had some thought of returning to England, however; the church at Ipswich was reluctant to dismiss him, and it was only after three years and a sharp dispute between the Ipswich and Boston churches as to which should have the benefit of his ministry that he was installed at Boston, July 23, 1656. Meantime, on Oct. 18, 1654, he had been appointed an Overseer of Harvard and a week later, with Richard Mather, had been chosen to offer the presidency of the College to Charles Chauncy [*q.v.*].

Norton took a prominent part in the persecution of the Quakers at the end of that decade, showing himself bigoted, narrow-minded, and tyrannical. In spite of the succeeding popular reaction, he was one of the few who held out firmly for the passage of laws inflicting the death penalty (Bishop, *post,* p. 101). In 1662 he ac-

companied Simon Bradstreet [*q.v.*] as agent to present the colony's petition to Charles II, an embassy which signally failed, owing in no small part to the Quaker persecution. On the return of Norton and Bradstreet the disgruntled elements in Massachusetts did not hesitate to say that their liberties had been sold out by the agents, and Norton lost much of his popularity with the reactionary party. It is said, though without much foundation, that the criticism hastened his death. He died suddenly of apoplexy just after preaching his Sunday morning sermon.

Norton was a learned man but with a narrow and technical mind, not at all comparable in humane outlook and breadth of vision to his predecessor, Cotton. He was a fairly prolific writer whose pen was at the service of the authorities. In 1645 he wrote a treatise in Latin on the government of the New England churches, in reply to inquiries from the Dutch clergy (*Responsio ad Guliel. Apollonii Syllogen, ad Componendas Controversias in Anglia*) which was published at London in 1648. With Cotton and Edward Norris [*q.v.*] he was appointed in 1651 to convince William Pynchon [*q.v.*] that his book, *The Meritorious Price of Our Redemption* (1650) was heretical. Norton's answer, *A Discussion of That Great Point in Divinity, The Sufferings of Christ* (1653), was published by order of the General Court, and for his labor in preparing it he received £20. The following year he published *The Orthodox Evangelist* (1654), an extremely technical exposition of the Puritan system of theology. Other works were *Abel Being Dead Yet Speaketh; or the Life and Death of . . . John Cotton* (1658); and *The Heart of N– England Rent at the Blasphemies of the Present Generation,* a bitter attack on the Quakers written by order of the General Court and published at Cambridge in 1659. His will disposed of an estate valued at the large sum of £2,095, of which his library of 729 volumes amounted to over £300 (*New-England Historical and Genealogical Register,* October 1857). The day of his installation in Boston he married a second wife. Her Christian name was Mary and she has sometimes been confused with the Mary Mason who married Norton's nephew, John Norton, in 1678 (*Ibid.,* July 1859, p. 229). Norton left numerous collateral relatives, but no children.

[Cotton Mather, *Magnalia Christi Americana* (ed. of 1853), I, 286ff.; A. W. M'Clure, *The Lives of John Wilson, John Norton, and John Davenport* (1846); W. B. Sprague, *Annals Am. Pulpit,* vol. I (1856); W. H. Whitmore, *A Geneal. of the Norton Family* (1859), repr. from *New-Eng. Hist. and Geneal. Reg.,* July 1859; N. B. Shurtleff, *Records of the Gov. and Company of the Mass. Bay,* vols. I–IV (1853–54); T. F. Waters, *Ipswich in the Mass. Bay Colony,* vol. I (1905); *Colonial Soc. of Mass. Pubs.,* vol. XXI (1920); Thomas Hutchinson, *The Hist. of the Colony of Mass. Bay.*, vol. I (1764); George Bishop, *New England Judged by the Spirit of the Lord* (1703).]   J. T. A.

NORTON, JOHN NICHOLAS (1820–Jan. 18, 1881), Protestant Episcopal clergyman, was born in Waterloo, N. Y., the son of George Hatley Norton and his wife, Maria Gault. The father, a Virginian and one of the founders of the Episcopal Church in Western New York, soon settled at Allen's Hill, in the township of Richmond, Ontario County, but his sons apparently were educated in Geneva. John Norton's *Allerton Parish* (1863) is the story of Allen's Hill; and his first book, *The Boy Who Was Trained Up To Be a Clergyman* (1853), is autobiographical. The hero's college is evidently Hobart (then Geneva) College, which Norton entered in 1838. His picture of college life a century ago has real value; it is sadly trustworthy. Much chapel and little religion seems to have been his impression, and yet his class produced two other able clergymen. Graduated in 1842, Norton went to the General Theological Seminary in New York and in 1845 was duly ordained and became assistant at St. Paul's, Rochester. In 1847 he became rector of the Church of the Ascension, Frankfort, Ky., where he was to spend nearly twenty-four years.

He found little to work upon, but he worked very hard; from a dozen families developed a large and prosperous congregation; a small building gave way to a fine church and that also had to be enlarged. He was as generous as he was indefatigable. When poor he gave away all he could, and later on with money at command he still gave all he could. He preached a peculiar type of sermon, but people of all sorts and ages heard him gladly. Objection was made to his use of very homely illustrations, stories that to some seemed undignified; but the people came. He had the instinct of the good teacher—to begin where his hearers had left off, on their plane, not his. He could fill a church with children. In the midst of his zealous service at Frankfort he married, in 1855, Mary Louisa Sutton, daughter of George Washington Sutton of Lexington. She was in deepest sympathy with her husband's work and she commanded considerable means. In 1870 Norton became associate rector of Christ Church, Louisville. Again he worked incessantly, gave money to almost any one who asked for it, went anywhere, saw anybody, wherever there was work for him to do. He found the negroes without a church, and built them one and maintained it.

As soon as his work at Frankfort was well under way, he had begun to publish. His *Sketches, Literary and Theological* (1872) show an extraordinary range of interest. He subscribed, it appears, to innumerable magazines and newspapers, out of which he culled the stories that attracted so much attention in his sermons. He left to Hobart College a collection of several thousand pamphlets, which he had apparently had bound as he gathered them. His published sermons were very widely circulated, running sometimes into a dozen editions, and his lives of Episcopal bishops—some twenty biographies—were well known. His biographical work is very simple and unostentatious. The complexities of modern biography would doubtless have appalled him.

Norton had no doubts. Shy and retiring, he had entire courage; small and rather frail, he showed a most persistent and devoted diligence. He was a follower of the great Bishop Hobart in his high claims for his Church, but as he once remarked: "The member of an old and well-established family does not feel called upon to be forever proclaiming his pedigree." Having marked off boldly the inferior position of dissent, he proceeded with all diligence to serve the dissenter.

Among his published works not already mentioned are: *Full Proof of the Ministry* (1855); *Rockford Parish* (1856); *Short Sermons* (1858); *Life of Dr. Franklin* (1859); *Pioneer Missionaries; or, the Lives of Phelps and Nash* (1859); *Life of General Washington* (1860); *Lectures on the Life of David* (1860); *Life of Cranmer* (1863); *Life of Archbishop Laud* (1864); *The Lay Reader* (1870); *Milk and Honey* (1870); *Every Sunday* (1873); *Golden Truths* (1875); *The King's Ferry Boat* (1876); *Warning and Teaching* (1878); *Old Paths* (1880).

[*In Memoriam: John Nicholas Norton* (1881); *Churchman*, Feb. 5, 1881; *Louisville Commercial*, Jan. 19, 1881; information as to certain facts from a daughter, Mrs. Paul E. Johnson, Washington, D. C.]
M. H. T—k.

NORTON, JOHN PITKIN (July 19, 1822–Sept. 5, 1852), educator, agricultural chemist, was born in Albany, N. Y. His father, John Treadwell Norton, was a successful farmer and his mother, Mary Hubbard (Pitkin), was the daughter of Timothy Pitkin [*q.v.*], lawyer, statesman, and historian. John Treadwell, governor of Connecticut in 1809–11, was his great-grandfather. Of his own choice young Norton decided to become a farmer, to which plan his father agreed, but on the unusual condition that he should be broadly and thoroughly educated for that pursuit. Accordingly the boy spent his summers at work upon his father's farm, and his winters in a strenuous program of study in Albany, New York City, New Haven, and Boston, with some of the best masters of that day. He had little liking for the ordinary courses of study, particularly Latin and Greek, but manifested an absorbing interest in natural science which appears to have been first aroused by his study of mineralogy. He studied chemistry with the elder Silliman at Yale and in 1844 he went abroad, spending two years with Professor James F. W. Johnston at Edinburgh, and nine months with Professor Gerardus J. Mulder at Utrecht. While yet a student his ability as an analyst and his resourcefulness as an investigator attracted the favorable attention of his teachers.

In 1846 he was appointed professor of agricultural chemistry at Yale and, in association with the younger Benjamin Silliman [q.v.] who had at the same time been appointed professor of practical chemistry, he initiated that department of scientific education at Yale which was later to become the Sheffield Scientific School. The labors of the first years of this new school were severely taxing, particularly to Norton, who shortly assumed entire responsibility for the new enterprise because of the withdrawal of his colleague to accept a post of duty in another institution.

He was an indefatigable worker, compelled not only by an intense devotion to his chosen subject but also by a sense of duty to the public welfare. He always maintained an intelligent and sympathetic interest in the practical problems of the farmer, and his influence as an educator extended far beyond the walls of his classroom and laboratory. In addition to numerous articles of a popular character upon agricultural topics contributed to the agricultural press, he was the author of a number of scientific papers, among which may be cited his comprehensive prize study, "On the Analysis of the Oat," made in 1845 while he was a student at Edinburgh and published in the *Transactions of the Highland Agricultural Society of Scotland,* July 1846, and later in the *American Journal of Science and Arts,* May 1847; "The Potato Disease" (*American Journal of Science and Arts,* November 1846, July 1847) ; "Account of Some Researches on the Protein Bodies of Peas and Almonds, and a Body of Somewhat Similar Nature Existing in Oats" (*Ibid.,* May 1848) ; and another prize essay written in 1850, submitted to the New York State Agricultural Society and afterwards published under the title *Elements of Scientific Agriculture* (1850) as a textbook for schools.

On Dec. 15, 1847, he married Elizabeth P. Marvin of Albany, N. Y. They had two sons, one of whom died in infancy. Their home was a center of hospitality and it does not appear that in Norton's devotion to work he failed to enjoy the social activities of his community. He was possessed of an engaging personality into which entered the charm of cheerfulness, modesty, and quiet humor, blended with the dignity of culture. He was deeply religious and Christian motives controlled his life. With a future brilliant with promise of a highly useful career, he was stricken by illness which his overtaxed strength could not resist and died in Farmington, Conn., on Sept. 5, 1852. In his brief span of life he had come to be regarded as "the most practical agricultural writer and thinker of his time" (editor of the Albany *Cultivator,* quoted in *New Englander,* November 1852, p. 627), and had established a place for himself among the distinguished men of the age.

[*Am. Jour. Sci. and Arts,* Nov. 1852; Wm. A. Larned, in *New Englander,* Nov. 1852, and *Biog. Sketch of John Pitkin Norton* (1852) ; *Memorials of John Pitkin Norton* (1852), printed for private distribution ; A. P. Pitkin, *Pitkin Family of America: A Geneal. of the Descendants of William Pitkin* (1887); Elizabeth A. Osborne, *From the Letter-Files of S. W. Johnson* (1913) ; R. H. Chittenden, *Hist. of the Sheffield Scientific School of Yale Univ.* (1928), vol. I ; private correspondence with Norton's son, the late John T. Norton.]

E. M. B.

NORTON, MARY ALICE PELOUBET (Feb. 25, 1860–Feb. 23, 1928), teacher of home economics, daughter of Rev. Francis Nathan Peloubet [q.v.] and Mary Abby (Thaxter) Peloubet, was born at Gloucester, Mass., in a parsonage home of simple living. Named Mary Alice, she rarely made use of her first name. She was descended from Joseph Alexander de Chabrier de Peloubet, who came from Perigord, France, to the United States in 1803. In 1882 she received the degree of A.B. from Smith College; and on June 6 of the following year she was married, at Natick, Mass., to Lewis Mills Norton, of the chemistry department of the Massachusetts Institute of Technology. He died in 1893, and she faced a struggle to support her five children. Ellen H. Richards [q.v.], home-economics pioneer, became her counselor and directed her into a life of further study, teaching, and lecturing until she herself was recognized as one of the leaders in the home-economics movement. She held positions as teacher or lecturer in home economics at Lasell Seminary, 1893–99; the Hartford School of Sociology, 1894; the Boston Young Women's Christian Association School of Domestic Science, 1895–1900; the Boston Cooking School, 1898–1900; the High School at Brookline, Mass., where she was also supervisor of grammar-school work, 1896–1900; the Chicago Institute, 1900–01; the

University of Chicago, where she was assistant professor in home economics in the School of Education, 1901–04, and assistant professor in household administration, 1904–13. She was dietitian, 1913–14, of the Cook County, Ill., public institutions. During the summers of 1900 to 1905 and 1915 to 1917, she served as director of the Chautauqua, N. Y., School of Domestic Science.

She was one of the founders of the American Home Economics Association (1908), which developed from annual conferences held at Lake Placid, N. Y., beginning in 1899. At these conferences she was a constructive contributor on the subjects of teacher training and home economics in colleges. She was secretary of the Association, 1915–18, and editor of the *Journal of Home Economics*, 1915–21. During the World War she served as an editor for the United States Food Administration (1917–18) and was with the war-savings division of the treasury department (1919), where she helped to issue *Thrift Leaflets*. In 1921 the American Home Economics Association raised a sum of money to pay the salary of a professor of home economics at the Constantinople Women's College, and Mrs. Norton consented to occupy this position in a country where housework was considered a menial occupation suitable only for servants or peasants. She remained for over two years, making a survey of the elementary schools of the city, acquiring equipment, building up a permanent department, and giving lectures to the nurses' training class in the American Hospital at Stambul.

After her return from Constantinople, she substituted as head of the home-economics department of Indiana University (1924–25). Thereafter she made her home in Northampton, Mass., and carried on a study for the Institute for the Coördination of Women's Interests at Smith College. Shortly before her death her Institute bulletin, *Cooked Food Supply Experiments in America* (1927), was published. Her life was so full of changing activities that her writing was confined to articles and bulletins on home-economics subjects. Considering the many professional demands on her time and her personal economic problems (she provided college education for all her five children), the number of her civic and educational interests is remarkable. In addition to membership in many professional societies, she was a more or less active member of the American Association of University Women, the Religious Education Association, the College Political Equality League, the Drama League, the Chicago Women's Club,

the League of Women Voters, the Foreign Policy Association, and the Women's International League of Peace and Freedom.

[*Cat. of Officers, Grads., and Non-Grads. of Smith Coll.* (1925); *Who's Who in America, 1928–29; Woman's Who's Who of America,* 1914–15; Joseph Peloubet, *Family Records of Joseph Alexander de Chabrier de Peloubet* (1892); "In Memory of Alice Peloubet Norton," *Jour. of Home Economics,* Sept. 1928; *Boston Transcript,* Feb. 25, 1928.]   S. G. B.

NORTON, WILLIAM EDWARD (June 28, 1843–Feb. 28, 1916), marine painter, was born in Boston, Mass., the son of Daniel and Mary (Carr) Norton and a descendant of a family of shipbuilders. His father was a sailmaker and his mother was descended from George Carr, ship's carpenter of the *Mayflower*. Norton was educated in the public schools of Charlestown. From the time he could hold a pencil he began to draw, and when he was about ten he made a drawing of the statue of Gen. Joseph Warren on Bunker Hill which so impressed one of the members of the school board that he advised the boy to go to the Lowell Institute, but his parents would not allow him to do so. On leaving school he went to work in an office on Rowe's Wharf, Boston, where at odd moments he made sketches of the stevedores, the horses, the shipping and docks; then he went to sea on a merchant ship for a long voyage before the mast. Two episodes gave him standing with the tough company in the forecastle: he whipped "Dutch Louis" for attempting to bully him, and while off watch he drew lifelike sketches of his shipmates, their rude quarters, and various scenes on the deck. On his return to Boston he found employment as a house and sign painter. He now entered the night classes of the Lowell Institute, where he came under the excellent instruction of George Hollingsworth, studying perspective, light and shade, and color. He also studied anatomy both in the Lowell Institute and at the Harvard Medical School, where he made over five hundred drawings in the dissecting room. His daylight hours were devoted to house and sign painting, and, later, to fresco work and decorating; the early hours of the evening he gave to study; and from nine o'clock to midnight, in the paint shop of his employer, he often painted sea pictures with house paints, which he sold for trifling sums to his fellow workmen.

At the age of twenty-one he ventured to open a studio in Boston, and George Inness [*q.v.*] gave him counsel and encouragement. After two more voyages before the mast, in 1877 he found himself in London, where he remained for about a year, then went to Paris for further training under Antoine Vollon and Jacquesson de la

Chevreuse and in the École des Beaux-Arts. During the ensuing three years he visited Italy and other European countries, then opened a studio in London, where he continued to live until 1902. He exhibited three pictures at the Royal Academy in 1878, and was for about twenty years a constant and regular exhibitor there as well as at the Paris Salon and many other places. A number of his sea pieces were sent to the American exhibitions, and four cash prizes with three or four gold medals were among his honors. His picture of "The English Channel" is owned by the Boston Chamber of Commerce; his "Fight of the Alabama and the Kearsarge" belongs to the Historical Society of Portland, Me.; his "Fish Market, Dieppe, France" is in the Public Library of Malden, Mass., and his "Crossing the Grand Banks" is in the Abbot Hall collection at Marblehead, Mass. Other good examples of his work are owned by the Boston Art Club, the Boston Athletic Association, Essex Hall at Salem, Mass., and the Black Heath Art Club of London. His paintings of sailing vessels are spirited and full of movement. Nothing could be more thoroughly suggestive of the atmosphere and color of the ocean and the old-time clipper-ships than his mid-Atlantic compositions. His work has sailor-like qualities and could never have been done by a landsman.

On Sept. 23, 1868, he married Sarah D. Ryan of Grand Manan, N. B., who died in 1904. They had two daughters. Norton's death occurred in New York in 1916.

[F. T. Robinson, in *Art Interchange*, Feb. 1894; *N. Y. Herald*, June 20, 1909; *N. Y. Times*, Feb. 29, 1916; *Boston Transcript*, Mar. 1, 1916, Jan. 30, 1920; *Am. Art News*, Mar. 4, 1916; Cat. of exhibition at Vose Gallery, Boston, Jan.–Feb. 1920; *Am. Art Annual*, vol. XIII (1916); *Who's Who in America*, 1914–15; Ulrich Thieme and Felix Becker, *Allgemeines Lexikon der Bildenden Künstler*, vol. XXV (1931).] W. H. D—s.

NORWOOD, ROBERT WINKWORTH (Mar. 27, 1874–Sept. 28, 1932), Episcopal clergyman, was born at New Ross, Nova Scotia, the son of Rev. Joseph William Norwood and Edith Matilda (Harding). After coming to the United States he dropped his middle name. Joseph William Norwood had come to New Ross as rector of Christ Church (of the Church of England in Canada) after having been a sea captain, a soldier in the Union Army in the Civil War, and a missionary to the coast of Africa. Robert had a particular devotion to his father, and an admiration for his father's life and ministry; therefore, after going to school at Coaticock Academy in Quebec and studying at Bishops College, Lennoxville, Que., and at Kings College, Wind-

sor, N. S., he determined to enter the same calling, and was ordained deacon and priest of the Church of England in Canada in 1897 and 1898 respectively. On Sept. 12, 1899, while he was missionary in charge of St. Andrew's Church, Neil's Harbour, Cape Breton, he married Ethel McKeen. A few months later, his father, who was then rector of St. Luke's Church, Hubbards, N. S., was taken ill, and Robert went there as curate to carry on the work. In this early ministry in Hubbards he revealed the characteristics which always afterwards marked him—an unusual sensitiveness to all beauty, and a warm and friendly approach toward people which, beginning in his contacts with the fisher-folk of his Nova Scotia coast, broadened afterward to include persons of every kind. Subsequently, he became successively rector of Trinity Church, Bridgewater, N. S. (1901–07); All Saints' Church, Springhill (1908–10); assistant rector, Trinity Church, Montreal (1910–12); and rector of Memorial Church, London, Ont. (1912–17). In 1917 his life entered a new chapter with his removal from Canada to the United States to become rector of St. Paul's Memorial Church at Overbrook, Pa.

In 1925 when Dr. Leighton Parks resigned the rectorship of St. Bartholomew's Church in New York City, Norwood was called to succeed him. In Overbrook his preaching had drawn overflowing congregations, not only from his own community but from other suburbs of Philadelphia and the city itself. In New York his magnetism proved equally great. He had a musical voice, unusual dramatic vividness in utterance and gesture, and the gift of putting his thought into flashing pictorial form. Moreover, he was one of those rare persons who possess a mystical experience. In his look and in his message he conveyed to his congregation the sense of a man who was in touch with an invisible world. Both in his theology and in his impatience of ecclesiastical restraints he belonged to the liberal group in the Protestant Episcopal Church. He insisted upon interpreting truth not in terms of old formulas but of new experience, and he was a leader in efforts for close cooperation with other Christian churches, and for a better understanding, also, of the non-Christian religions. As tangible evidence of his ministry he left behind him at St. Bartholomew's a great community house and many enrichments of the church's structure, including the completion of its dome.

His religious thinking, as expressed in his published Lenten sermons—*The Steep Ascent* (1928), *His Glorious Body* (1930), and *Increasing Christhood* (1932), and in his life of Paul, entitled *The Heresy of Antioch* (1928), and in his life of Christ, entitled *The Man Who Dared to Be God* (1929)—was not systematic nor profound. Like his teaching, it was intuitive, impulsive, and poetic. He always liked to be regarded as primarily a poet—a poet of the goodness of life. His published poems include *His Lady of the Sonnets* (1915); *The Witch of Endor* (1916); *The Piper and the Reed* (1917); *The Modernists* (1918); *The Man of Kerioth* (1919); *Bill Boram* (1921), which is a description of the Nova Scotian country and people among whom he had grown up; *Mother and Son* (1925); and *Issa* (1931), a final volume, introspective and intimate in self-revelation. All these books are marked by a strong religious note. Measured by purely poetic standards, they are notable for their lyrical spontaneity and their colorful imagination.

[C. D. G. Roberts, "The Poetry of Robert Norwood," introduction to *Issa*; W. R. Bowie, "The Ministry of the Poet," introduction to *Increasing Christhood*; *The Churchman*, Oct. 8, Nov. 12, 1932; *The Canadian Theosophist* (Hamilton, Ont.), Oct. 15, 1932; A. D. Watson, *Robert Norwood* (Toronto, 1923); J. D. Logan and D. G. French, *Highways of Canadian Literature* (Toronto, 1924); *Canadian Poets*, ed. by J. W. Garvin (Toronto, 1926); *Who's Who in America*, 1932–33; *Publisher's Weekly*, Oct. 8, 1932; *N. Y. Times*, Sept. 30, 1932.]   W. R. B.

NOSS, THEODORE BLAND (May 10, 1852–Feb. 28, 1909), educator, was born on a farm at Waterloo, Juniata County, Pa., the son of George and Isabella (Coulter) Noss. His maternal grandfather, the Rev. John Coulter, was a prominent Presbyterian minister. Young Theodore attended the rural schools and helped in the work of his father's farm, store, and tannery. In 1868 the family moved to Strasburg, Va. At the age of nineteen he began teaching in a district school near Hagerstown, Md. He entered the Cumberland Valley State Normal School at Shippensburg, Pa., and was graduated in 1874. For some years thereafter he taught in the Shippensburg public schools; in Dickinson Seminary, Williamsport, where he was principal of the preparatory department; and in the Pittsburgh Female College. He was graduated from Syracuse University in 1880 and received there the degrees of A.M. (1882) and Ph.D. (1884). He made four trips to Europe for study, spending a total of approximately three years in residence at the universities of Vienna, Berlin, Jena, and Paris. On May 17, 1883, he was married to Mary B. Graham, of Monongahela, Pa. They had two children.

In 1883 Noss became principal of the Southwestern State Normal School, at California, Pa., of which he had previously been vice-principal,

and remained there until his death twenty-six years later. This long period of identity with one institution, which he built up to high standing, brought him a national reputation as a progressive educator. He was an active member of the National Education Association and in 1898–99 served as president of its normal department. He was a frequent contributor to educational journals and was in demand for the platforms of teachers' institutes. His special field of scholarship was educational psychology. On his European tours he became impregnated with the doctrines of Froebel, Herbart, and Pestalozzi, which he endeavored to adapt to American normal-school practice. Much of his time abroad was spent observing the technique of the Continental schools, especially those for training teachers. In his own school he insisted upon the admission of only the best-qualified students and also upon a maximum of personal attention to the needs of the individual. Intense moral earnestness was the outstanding trait of his character. During his administration more than 1,500 young persons were graduated from the institution, all of whom felt deeply the impress of his personality.

Noss's published works include *Outlines of Psychology and Pedagogy* (1890) and *Child Study Record* (1900). He was general editor of *The School Year Books* (Chicago, 1898–1907), a series of manuals of methods for elementary grades, and he compiled *The Chapel Hymnal* (1900), a collection of standard hymns and reading for use in schools which reached twelve editions. He was throughout his life a devoted layman of the Methodist Episcopal Church, serving as lay delegate to its General Conference in 1896. He was also an active leader in local community movements. He died of pneumonia at the Auditorium Hotel, Chicago, while on his way to a session of the National Education Association. At the largely attended memorial services held in the chapel of the Normal School at California, Pa., William Jennings Bryan, a friend of long standing, led the eloquent tributes. In May 1930 the new Theodore B. Noss Demonstration School, built by alumni of the Normal School, was dedicated to his memory.

[*Who's Who in Pa.* (2nd ed., 1908); *California* (Pa.) *Sentinel*, Mar. 10, 1909; the *Normal Rev.* (California, Pa.), Mar. 1909; *The Syracusan* (Syracuse, N. Y.), Apr. 1909; *Christian Advocate* (Pittsburgh), May 13, 1909; *Alumni Record and Gen. Cat. of Syracuse Univ., 1872–1910*, vol. III (1911), pt. I; Pittsburgh newspapers at the time of Noss's death; personal notes supplied by Mrs. Theodore B. Noss, Athens, Ohio.]   K. M. G.

NOTT, ABRAHAM (Feb. 5, 1768–June 19, 1830), jurist and member of Congress from

South Carolina, was born at Saybrook, Middlesex County, Conn. He was the second son of Deacon Josiah Nott and Zerviah Clark and the grandson of Abraham Nott, a prominent Congregational clergyman. He received his early education from the Rev. John Devotion of Westbrook Parish in Saybrook and, with the intention of becoming a minister, entered Yale College. He graduated from that institution in 1787, but finding in himself no distinctly religious convictions he felt that it would be sacrilegious for him to enter the pulpit. As he was not in good health, in 1788 he went to a plantation on Sapelo River, McIntosh County, Ga., where he found employment as a tutor in the family of the father of George M. Troup, the future governor being one of his pupils. The next year he removed to South Carolina where he studied law in the office of Daniel Brown, another Yale graduate, at Camden, and was admitted to the bar in Charleston in 1791. After his admission to the bar he settled at Union Court House where he practised law for three years. In August 1794 he was married to Angelica Mitchell and moved to a plantation on the Pacolet River where he continued the practice of his profession.

Nott was a Federalist member of the Sixth Congress (1799–1801). In the momentous struggle for the presidency in 1800 he at first voted for Aaron Burr but finally abstained from voting and thus assisted in the election of Jefferson. In the fall of 1804 he moved to Columbia, S. C., where he practised his profession with distinct success until 1810 when he was elected as a Law Judge to succeed Samuel Wilds. In 1816 the South Carolina legislature initiated a constitutional amendment giving to itself the power to fix the time and meetings of the Constitutional Court of the state and, in anticipation of the ratification of the amendment by the people, proceeded to enact a law ordering the judges to clear the dockets at Charleston and Columbia. Nott, together with his associates, declared this law unconstitutional on the ground that it was passed before the authority to enact it had been completely established. This decision, especially one of its statements, "that which was conceived in sin must be brought forth in iniquity," aroused a storm of protest and almost resulted in his removal from the court. In 1817 the salaries of the judges of the state were increased and when he resigned in order to obtain the benefit of the increase by reëlection he was returned to his position by a very narrow majority. He recovered his popularity, however, and in 1824 when the court of appeals was organized he was placed at its head by an overwhelming vote. In

this position he remained for the rest of his life and doubtless hastened his death by his industry in the discharge of his duties. He contracted tuberculosis in January 1830 and died on June 19 of the same year at the home of his friend, Dr. Davis H. Means, in Fairfield District, while on the way to his plantation in Union District. He is buried in the First Presbyterian Churchyard in Columbia. Nott's opinions both in law and equity bear comparison with those of any judge in the state. In the courtroom he enjoyed anecdotes and frequently "broke the tedium of an argument by some playful, witty, question." He was small and somewhat unimposing in person, but his face was well-featured and highly intellectual. His two sons, Henry Junius and Josiah Clark Nott [qq.v.], also had distinguished careers.

[Biog. Dir. Am. Cong. (1928); J. B. O'Neall, Biog. Sketches of the Bench and Bar of S. C. (1859), vol. I; F. B. Dexter, Biog. Sketches of the Grads. of Yale Coll., vol. VI (1907); Charleston Courier, June 25, 30, 1830.]   J. W. P.

NOTT, CHARLES COOPER (Sept. 16, 1827–Mar. 6, 1916), jurist, was born at Schenectady, N. Y., the son of Joel B. and Margaret Cooper Nott. His paternal ancestors were of early Connecticut stock but for two generations the family life had been interwoven with that of Union College of which Nott's grandfather, Eliphalet Nott [q.v.], had been president, and in which his father was professor of chemistry. It was but natural that the boy's education, uneventful in its earlier phases, should culminate in his graduation from the college in 1848. For two years thereafter he studied law in Albany and was admitted to the bar in 1850. He then moved to New York City where he practised successfully until the outbreak of the Civil War. He was a fairly active Republican and in 1860 was one of the committee responsible for bringing Lincoln to New York to deliver his Cooper Institute speech. A friendship between the two men began at this time. Shortly thereafter Nott secured from Lincoln the manuscript of his address which, with Cephas Brainerd, he published with notes in September 1860. After the outbreak of the war he entered the Union army under an appointment by General Frémont as captain in the Frémont Hussars. He later served in the 5th Iowa Cavalry and in the New York volunteers. He finally became colonel of the 176th New York Regiment. In June 1863 he was captured at Brashear City, La., and remained a Confederate prisoner for thirteen months. He did not see further active service and emerged from prison seriously impaired in health. He returned to the practice of law in New York.

The entire course of Nott's later life was determined by his appointment by President Lincoln as judge of the United States Court of Claims on Feb. 22, 1865. He remained a member of that tribunal for forty years, retiring Dec. 31, 1905, and from the time of his promotion by President Cleveland in 1896 he served as chief justice. When Nott took office the Court of Claims was still in its formative period and his life was spent in aiding in the establishment of a system of jurisprudence under which the claims of a contractual or business nature of the citizen against the federal government might be recognized and enforced. The record of his labors is found in opinions spread through forty-eight volumes of the *Cases Decided in the Court of Claims.* No small part of Nott's service to the Court lay in his reporting of its decisions. From 1867, when the publication of regular reports began, until 1914, Nott served as reporter. Until 1872 he was aided in this labor by Judge Samuel H. Huntington and from that date on by his brother-in-law, Archibald Hopkins. This long series of his reports is broken only in 1882–83 when his illness necessitated a year's absence from all official duties.

During his adult years Nott was a fairly voluminous contributor to the press and to more substantial publications. Much of his writing was done anonymously in the form of editorials and reviews. His longer works include: *A Treatise on the Mechanics' Lien Laws of the State of New York* (1856); *Sketches of the War* (1863); *Sketches in Prison Camps* (1865); *The Seven Great Hymns of the Mediæval Church* (1865); and *The Mystery of the Pinckney Draught* (1908). Nott was married on Oct. 22, 1867, to Alice Effingham Hopkins, the daughter of Mark Hopkins [*q.v.*], president of Williams College. Of this marriage there were born a son and a daughter. He died at the home of his son in New York City on Mar. 6, 1916.

[See *Who's Who in America*, 1914–15; *N. Y. Times*, *N. Y. Herald*, Mar. 7, 1916.]   R. E. C.

NOTT, ELIPHALET (June 25, 1773–Jan. 29, 1866), college president, Presbyterian clergyman, inventor, was born in Ashford, Conn., the son of Stephen and Deborah (Selden) Nott. His father proved himself a failure in each of his undertakings, but his mother was a woman of superior culture. She instructed the boy in the rudiments, and he prepared for college under the supervision of his brother Samuel [*q.v.*], pastor of the Congregational church at Franklin, Conn. At sixteen, he taught in the district school at Franklin. A year later, he became principal of the Plainfield Academy, and studied

Latin, Greek, theology, and mathematics with the Rev. Dr. Joel Benedict, pastor of the local Congregational church. In 1795 he entered Rhode Island College (Brown University), and without completing a full year there, was admitted to the degree of master of arts upon passing a special examination. On June 26, 1796, he was licensed to preach by the New London Congregational Association. In the following month, July 4, 1796, he married Sarah Maria, eldest daughter of Joel Benedict.

Commissioned by the Domestic Missionary Society of Connecticut, he set out for the wilderness of upper New York State, and in the fall became pastor of the Presbyterian church at Cherry Valley. Here he founded an academy which he conducted successfully while discharging the obligations of his pastoral office. His reputation as a preacher grew, and in 1798 he removed to Albany, where, on Oct. 13, he was ordained and installed as pastor of the First Presbyterian Church. At Albany, he established himself as a peculiarly gifted preacher, learned, eloquent, and convincing, and was soon considered one of America's greatest pulpit orators. Among the most celebrated of his published sermons was *A Discourse . . . Occasioned by the Ever to be Lamented Death of General Alexander Hamilton* (1804), delivered at the invitation of the Common Council of Albany. His interest in education expressed itself in his persistent efforts to reform the antiquated public-school system of Albany. As a result of his recommendations, first outlined in March 1803, the Albany Academy was finally incorporated, in 1813. On Mar. 11, 1804, his wife died, and on Aug. 3, 1807, he married Gertrude (Peebles) Tibbitts, widow of Benjamin Tibbitts of Troy. After her death, early in 1840, he married Urania E. Sheldon of Utica, Aug. 8, 1842.

Meanwhile, in 1804, he had succeeded Jonathan Maxcy [*q.v.*] as president of Union College, Schenectady, of which he had been a trustee since 1800. He found the college laboring under a heavy debt, while its income was far less than its necessary expenditures. His executive abilities were manifest at once in his admirable, far-sighted program. The state legislature responded to his appeal, Mar. 30, 1805, by authorizing four lotteries for the purpose of raising the sum of $80,000 for the college, and the following year Nott secured a loan of $15,000 from the state to defray pressing current expenses. Eight years later, when the drawing finally took place, the college realized but $76,000. By this time, there was an urgent need for a larger sum, and again Nott appealed to the legislature, which on Apr. 13, 1814, made an additional grant of $200,000, to be raised in the same manner. After waiting eight years without results, Nott took upon himself the management of the lotteries, and with such success that he was able to extricate the college from its embarrassments. By heroic personal efforts, he placed the endowment fund upon a secure basis. The building program went forward satisfactorily, the college developed rapidly from within, and achieved a high reputation for the excellence of its instruction. His form of control enabled the students to enjoy a larger measure of self-government than was customary in American colleges at that time. Among his innovations was the introduction of the scientific course as an alternative to the traditional classical curriculum.

His interest was not confined to the affairs of the college; as early as 1811, in baccalaureate addresses, he advocated the abolition of slavery; he often served as moderator in church trials; the religious revival of 1838 inspired some of his most memorable sermons, which added further to his reputation as a preacher. He was president of the American Association for the Advancement of Education at its second meeting, held in 1850 at Philadelphia. As an instructor of youth, he saw the dangers of intemperance, and became one of the most active and influential advocates of temperance in his time. His addresses on the subject, *Ten Lectures on the Use of Intoxicating Liquors* (1846), *Lectures on Temperance* (1847), *Lectures on Biblical Temperance* (1863), were published and circulated widely. Another of his publications which went through numerous editions was *Counsels to Young Men on the Formation of Character* (1840). His *Miscellaneous Works* had appeared in 1810. In addition to his prodigious labors as an educator, he experimented with the properties of heat. The results of his research are recorded in some thirty patents, granted for applications of heat to steam boilers and generators. Among his inventions was the first base-burning stove for the use of anthracite coal.

Nott's extraordinary influence over men—exemplified in his influence over the New York legislature—led him sometimes to accomplish his purposes by indirect means that laid him open to the accusation of double-dealing (Francis Wayland, quoted in Francis and H. L. Wayland, *A Memoir of the Life and Labors of Francis Wayland*, 1867, I, 90–92). In 1851, after a legislative inquiry concerning the financial condition of Union College, he was accused, in many newspapers, of misappropriating college funds. Upon examining the books of the institution, an Assem-

bly commission reporting in February 1852 completely vindicated him of all charges of dereliction. As a fitting sequel to this unpleasant affair, he donated in 1854 to the endowment fund $600,000 of his own fortune. His active career was terminated by a paralytic stroke, which forced him, in 1859, to relinquish some of the duties of his office. He presided at commencements, however, until 1862. At his death, in 1866, he had been president of Union for sixty-two years, an unprecedented period in the annals of higher education in America.

[Cornelius Van Santvoord and Tayler Lewis, *Memoirs of Eliphalet Nott* (1876); *Am. Jour. of Educ.*, Mar. 1863; H. L. Ellsworth, *A Digest of Patents Issued by the U. S. from 1790 to Jan. 1839* (1840); G. P. Schmidt, *The Old Time College President* (1930); J. T. Backus, *Address at the Funeral of the Rev. Dr. Nott* (1866); *Albany Evening Journal*, Jan. 29, 1866.]
R. F. S.

NOTT, HENRY JUNIUS (Nov. 4, 1797–Oct. 9, 1837), educator, author, was the son of Judge Abraham Nott [*q.v.*], and Angelica (Mitchell) Nott, and a brother of Josiah Clark Nott [*q.v.*]. He was born in Union District, S. C. His schooling was obtained at the Columbia Academy, from which he entered the sophomore class of the South Carolina College in 1810. Graduating in December 1814, he studied law in the office of William Harper, was admitted to the bar in 1818, and formed a partnership with David J. McCord [*q.v.*]. The firm did not enjoy a very large practice. The partners published two volumes of law reports, which have been considered valuable, although the reports of cases were very brief. Nott's health failing, he sailed for Europe in 1821, where he spent the next three years in study, for the most part in France and Holland. In the former country he met and married a French woman. On Dec. 7, 1824, he was elected professor of the elements of criticism, logic, and the philosophy of language in his alma mater, and for thirteen years he held the chair with marked success. Maximilian LaBorde [*q.v.*], who knew him, says of him in his *History of the South Carolina College:* "Perhaps no one ever filled the department with more ability" (p. 211). He adds that he was remembered as occupying a place among the most brilliant professors: "He had great enthusiasm in the cause of letters, was well fitted for presenting it in its most inviting and entertaining aspects, and very apt, therefore, to awaken a love for it in the bosom of others" (p. 213). When the South Carolina College was reorganized in 1835, he alone of the professors was retained; he served during that year as chairman of the faculty.

Nott was a frequent contributor to the *South-*

ern Review. His Novellettes of a Traveller; or, Odds and Ends from the Knapsack of Thomas Singularity, Journeyman Printer (2 vols., 1834) is the only other work that came from his pen. It was received with enthusiasm at the time and was regarded as "full of fun"; but the modern reader finds in it little merit. The sketch of Singularity is a dull narrative of his by no means interesting adventures. Of the other tales the "Dwarf's Duel" may still engage the attention of the reader. On Oct. 7, 1837, Nott left New York for Charleston on the unfortunate steamer Home. The vessel was wrecked two days later off the coast of North Carolina. He could have saved his life, according to all accounts, but he perished with his wife rather than survive her. He left one daughter.

[J. B. O'Neall, Biog. Sketches of the Bench and Bar of S. C. (1859), vol. II; E. J. Scott, Random Recollections of a Long Life (1884); G. A. Wauchope, The Writers of S. C. (1910); the Charleston Courier, Oct. 13, 14, 17, 19, 20, 1837; Morning Herald (N. Y.), Oct. 18, 19, 1837.]   E. L. G.

NOTT, JOSIAH CLARK (Mar. 31, 1804–Mar. 31, 1873), physician, ethnologist, was born at Columbia, S. C., the son of Abraham Nott [q.v.] and Angelica Mitchell, and the brother of Henry Junius Nott [q.v.]. He graduated from South Carolina College in 1824 and began his medical education in Columbia under the preceptorship of Dr. James Davis. In 1825 he entered the College of Physicians and Surgeons in New York City but a year later moved to Philadelphia and graduated in medicine from the University of Pennsylvania in 1827. He remained at the University for two years as demonstrator in anatomy and then began private practice in Columbia. In 1835 he went abroad and for a period of several months studied in Paris. Upon his return he settled in Mobile, Ala., and during the course of his long active practice in that city became one of the leading surgeons of the South and Southwest. He took an active part in the formation of the Mobile Medical Society in 1841 and in framing an act to revise the Alabama state law regulating the practice of medicine. During 1857 and part of 1858 he served as professor of anatomy at the University of Louisiana. Returning to Mobile in 1858, he helped to found the Medical College of Alabama, to which he was appointed professor of surgery. During the Civil War he served in the Confederate army. He moved to Baltimore in 1867 and to New York City the following year, where he became a charter member of the New York Obstetrical Society. Forced to retire because of ill health, he went to Aiken, S. C., in 1872, and soon afterward to Mobile. He died at Mobile on his birth-

day, Mar. 31, 1873, his death being registered as due to "laryngeal phthisis." He had married, in 1832, Sarah Deas, daughter of James Deas of Columbia, S. C. There were eight children from this union, four of whom died from yellow fever during the Mobile epidemic of 1853. One son died from exposure and fatigue after the battle of Shiloh and another was killed in action at Chickamauga.

Besides participating actively in civic affairs and caring for a large general and consultation practice, Nott wrote extensively on a variety of medical and scientific subjects including yellow fever, surgery, hypnotism, and ethnology. In a paper published in 1844 (New Orleans Medical Journal, May–July 1844), he stressed the importance of a knowledge of the anatomy and physiology of the nervous system as a background for treating certain types of cases. He reported in this paper the case of the removal of the coccyx of a patient who was suffering from severe lumbar pains, stating that he knew of no similar operation on record. In 1866 he published Contributions to Bone and Nerve Surgery, which was intended for young practitioners. Written in a confident, authoritative style, the book describes the pathology of bone and joint injuries sustained in the war and outlines proper methods of surgical treatment. He had expressed his belief in "animal magnetism" or "magnetic influences" in 1846 ("A Lecture on Animal Magnetism," Southern Journal of Medicine and Pharmacy, May 1846), citing as examples of this phenomenon several persons hypnotized by himself, and recommending mesmerism as a form of treatment for ill-defined nervous disorders. He was also interested in ethnology and in 1854, with George R. Gliddon, he published Types of Mankind, a volume of more than seven hundred pages, which ran through ten editions. The authors attempted to prove that each of the different races of man sprang from a fixed type, "permanent through all recorded time"—a doctrine later contradicted by the Darwinian theory. Indigenous Races of the Earth, by the same authors, followed in 1857.

Nott is perhaps best known for his views regarding yellow fever which have been discussed by Walter Reed and several other investigators. (See the New Orleans Medical and Surgical Journal, March 1848, March 1854.) Making use of his own observations in Mobile and those made elsewhere, among the conclusions he reached were the following: that the spread of yellow fever cannot be explained by any of the laws governing gases, vapors, and emanations, but that the disease has an inherent power of propagation independent of atmospheric conditions; that yellow fever is a clinical entity, distinct from malaria and intermittent fevers; and that yellow fever must be caused by an insect or some lower form of animal life. He mentioned mosquitoes only casually along with other flying insects. There is no reason to believe that he had any conception that the virus is carried by the mosquito as an intermediate host. He apparently recognized, however, that the cause of yellow fever is a living organism—a doctrine well in advance of the theories accepted by the majority of physicians in the middle of the nineteenth century.

[W. H. Anderson, memoir in *Trans. Am. Medic. Asso.*, vol. XXIX (1878); C. B. Partlow, Address delivered at the unveiling of the portrait of Josiah Clark Nott at the medical school of the Univ. of Ala., Univ., Ala., Oct. 3, 1930; *Am. Jour. of Obstetrics*, May 1913; H. R. Carson, *Yellow Fever* (1931); "Yellow Fever," *Senate Document 822*, 61 Cong., 3 Sess.]   G. H. R.

NOTT, SAMUEL (Jan. 23, 1754–May 26, 1852), clergyman, for seventy years pastor of the Congregational church in what is now Franklin, Conn., was the son of Stephen and Deborah (Selden) Nott, the grandson of Rev. Abraham Nott, minister of the Second Ecclesiastical Society of Saybrook, and a descendant of John Nott who came to America from Nottingham, England, about 1640 and settled in Wethersfield, Conn. At the time of Samuel's birth his father was keeping a small store in that portion of Saybrook which is now the town of Essex, Conn. Later he was a tanner in East Haddam, and after 1772, a farmer in Ashford, Conn. He never prospered and Samuel's youth was one of poverty. At the age of eight he was apprenticed to a blacksmith. He worked at this trade for four years and at a half dozen others in the years that followed. His schooling was meager, but he was a bright, ambitious, resourceful boy. Having taught a district school with some success, he determined to get a college education, and in 1774 began his preparation under Rev. Daniel Welch of Mansfield, Conn. Two years later he entered Yale College. During his course there he did considerable teaching, for which he seemed to have special aptitude, and at the end of his junior year took over the school in New Haven formerly taught by Joel Barlow [q.v.]. During his senior year and for some months after his graduation in 1780 he studied theology under the younger Jonathan Edwards [q.v.]. He was licensed to preach by the New Haven Association of Ministers on May 29, 1781, and for a short time supplied the Presbyterian church in Bridgehampton, L. I. Called to the Second Parish in Norwich, Conn., Norwich West Farms,

now Franklin, he was ordained there on Mar. 18, 1782. A month before, Feb. 14, he had married Lucretia, daughter of Josiah and Abigail Taylor of Mansfield, Conn., by whom he had eleven children.

His abilities, character, and especially the extraordinary length of his pastorate gave him in time an almost unique ecclesiastical position in eastern Connecticut. On Mar. 13, 1832, he preached a half-century sermon, *Reasons for Ministerial Fidelity*; ten years later he preached and published, *The Sixtieth Anniversary Sermon*. During 1844, when he was ninety years of age, he received fifty-four members into his church. It was not until he was ninety-five that a colleague pastor was called. His home was an educational institution. Between two and three hundred young men came there for instruction: some were fitted for college, and a few were given a theological training. He took his younger brother, Eliphalet [q.v.], into his family and instructed him for some years. When they were grown, two of his daughters conducted a school for young ladies in the parsonage. He also secured the nucleus of a public library and for years school visitor. Outside his parish he was esteemed as one well versed in practical affairs, an excellent administrator, and an exceptional presiding officer. For eighteen years he was a director of the Missionary Society of Connecticut, and he also served as president of the Connecticut Bible Society and of the Norwich Foreign Missionary Society. His death in his ninety-ninth year was caused by burns received when his dressing gown caught fire from a stove in his room. Seventeen of his sermons were published.

[W. B. Sprague, *Annals Am. Pulpit*, vol. II (1857); F. B. Dexter, *Biog. Sketches Grads. Yale Coll.*, vol. IV (1907); Cornelius Van Santvoord and Tayler Lewis, *Memoirs of Eliphalet Nott* (1876); *Conn. Quart.*, Apr.–June and July–Sept. 1897; *Hartford Courant*, May 31, 1852.]   H. E. S.

NOTZ, FREDERICK WILLIAM AUGUSTUS (Feb. 2, 1841–Dec. 16, 1921), educator, was born at Lehrensteinsfeld in the Weinsberg district of Württemberg, the eldest child of the Lutheran pastor, Gottlieb Notz, and his wife, Wilhelmina Louisa Burger. He received his early schooling in the Lateinschule at Leonberg and the Königliche Gymnasium at Stuttgart and was admitted in 1855 to the Klosterschule at Maulbronn, where he came under the decisive influence of Wilhelm Bäumlein, equally noted as classical scholar and pedagogue. He matriculated in the Evangelische Stift of the University of Tübingen in 1859, studied philosophy, theology, and classical philology under Ferdinand

Christian Baur, Johann Tobias Beck, Gustav Öhler, Wilhelm Sigismund Teuffel, and Karl Ludwig Roth, won the Freiherr von Palm prize with an essay on Roman history in the regal period, and took his doctor's degree in 1863 with a dissertation on the same subject. Having passed the theological examinations, he remained at the University for another year, was appointed vicar to his father, became a tutor in a noble family, and in 1866 came to the United States as tutor in a family living at Darien, Ga.

He decided to remain in America and, having established relations with Lutheran officials in the East, became professor of German in Pennsylvania (Gettysburg) College in 1868. The next year he accepted a professorship in Muhlenberg College, where the theological atmosphere was better suited to his own rigorous orthodoxy, and took part in the founding of the American Philological Association. He was secretary of the German-American Press Association in 1870 and president of the German School Association of Pennsylvania in 1871, began his career as an industrious writer for Lutheran periodicals in America and Germany, and in the summer of 1871 was pulpit supply in Philadelphia for his Tübingen friend, Adolph Spaeth. Meanwhile he had become interested in the work of C. F. W. Walther [q.v.] in the West. At first Walther wanted him for a professorship at St. Louis but, with his usual eye for strategy, decided instead to send him to Wisconsin to build up the educational work of the Wisconsin Synod. Accordingly, Notz became professor of Greek and Hebrew in Northwestern University (now College) at Watertown, Wis., and remained there for forty years, retiring because of impaired health in 1912. For many years he was "inspector" of the school, which in its organization, curriculum, and methods of instruction was modeled on the plan of a German Gymnasium.

His influence extended far beyond the sphere of the school itself. He was a member of the board of official visitors and later of the board of regents of the University of Wisconsin and gave valuable aid to various Lutheran educational institutions. In person he was the very embodiment of the German schoolmaster, genuinely learned, and with an inordinate respect for every detail, but mitigating the rigors of instruction and discipline with a wholesome South German humor. He was one of the chief opponents in 1889–90 of the notorious Bennett Law. His one separate publication was a German translation of Johann Conrad Dietrich's *Institutiones Catecheticae* (1876; 2nd ed., 1896). He was

married June 20, 1875, to Juliana Friederike Schulz of Watertown, by whom he had two sons and three daughters. He spent his last years in Milwaukee, where he died in his eighty-first year.

[This article is based chiefly on material supplied by Notz's son, William Frederick Notz. See also: J. C. Jensson, *Am. Luth. Biogs.* (1890); *Milwaukee Sentinel*, Dec. 17, 1921; *Lehre und Wehre*, Jan. 1922.]

G. H. G.

NOYAN, GILLES-AUGUSTIN PAYEN de (1697–Feb. 26, 1751), French officer in Louisiana, was born in France, the second son of Pierre Payen de Noyan, a naval officer, and Catherine Jeanne Le Moyne, sister of Bienville and Iberville [qq.v.]. It is probable that he received some sort of military training under his father and uncles. He came to Louisiana in 1717 or 1718, with the rank of lieutenant, and saw his first important service in 1719, when Bienville sent him, with a troop of Indians, to relieve Chateaugué in the recently captured Pensacola. Noyan arrived just after the Spanish had retaken the fort; presumably he took part in the second seizure by the French a month later. He next served for a year in command at New Orleans, and was given charge of a company of infantry. When Bienville was removed from office and recalled to France, Noyan appeared before the Superior Council to defend him, and in 1726 with his younger brother was dismissed from service and possibly recalled to France. If so, he soon returned, and through the years of Bienville's absence acted as his uncle's agent, showing much activity in disposing of his lands. Upon Bienville's reappointment to his old post in 1732, he showed his appreciation of his nephew's service by obtaining for him the position of adjutant at Mobile, and a year later transferred him to a similar post at New Orleans.

Bienville's great task for the next years was to stiffen the Choctaws' resistance to their old enemies, the Chickasaws, and the English behind them. Noyan was entrusted with diplomatic missions to the Choctaw chiefs, and on occasion took command in war raids. He was severely wounded in the campaign of 1736, but recovered to carry on his activities. Three years later he was sent up the Mississippi to find suitable headquarters and explore the country preparatory to an attack upon the Chickasaws by the combined French and Indian forces from Louisiana and Illinois. After months of inactivity at Fort Assomption on the Chickasaw Bluffs, ascribed to heavy rains and lack of pack animals, the expedition returned with nothing achieved, and Noyan, who had spent much for the campaign to his own impoverishment, was blamed for the selection of an impossible route.

He was made *lieutenant du roi* in 1741, and sat frequently as a member of the Superior Council of Louisiana; in 1748 he was for a time acting governor. He married, May 1, 1735, Jeanne Faucon Dumanoir, daughter of the agent for the Company of the Indies, and widow of Jean Baptiste Massy. His eldest son, Jean Baptiste Noyan, was executed in 1769, with his father-in-law, Nicholas Lafrénière, for protests against the Spanish régime.

Noyan is often confused with his brothers, Pierre-Jacques [*q.v.*], who rendered notable service at Detroit, and Pierre-Bénoit, who also served in Canada and Louisiana and died in France in 1766.

[Archives des Colonies, esp. C 13, A 5:303; F 3, 24:112; D 2 C, 4; D 2 C, 50; D 2 C, 51:105 (transcripts in Lib. of Cong.) give important unpublished material. Printed sources are: N. M. Surrey, *Calendar of MSS. in Paris Archives . . . Relating to . . . the Mississippi Valley* (2 vols., 1926–28), for date of death see II, 1173; *La. Hist. Quart.*, Oct. 1919, July, Oct. 1920, Apr. 1921, Apr. 1923, Jan. 1925, Jan. 1927–July 1928, Jan. 1929–Oct. 1932; F. A. A. de LaChesnaye-Desbois, *Dictionnaire de la Noblesse*, XV (1869), 535; Bénard La Harpe, *Journal Historique de . . . la Louisiane* (1831); Dunbar Rowland and A. G. Sanders, *Mississippi Provincial Archives, 1729–1740*; *French Dominion*, vol. I (1927); Grace King, *Jean Baptiste Le Moyne, Sieur de Bienville* (1892); Charles Gayarré, *Hist. of La.* (4th ed., 1903), vols. I, II; B. F. French, *Hist. Colls. of La.*, vol. V (1853).]   H. C. B.

NOYAN, PIERRE–JACQUES PAYEN de (Nov. 3, 1695–*c.* 1763), French-Canadian officer, was born at Montreal, the eldest son of Pierre Payen de Noyan and Catherine Jeanne Le Moyne. Allied through his mother to Bienville and Iberville [*qq.v.*] in Louisiana, and to the Longueuils in Canada, he and his younger brothers were fairly predestined to the colonial service. Whatever his early training may have been, he appeared in 1721 as commandant at Fort Frontenac (now Kingston, Ont.), and from that time on, in spite of persistent ill health, was constantly active along the Great Lakes. A few years later he visited Niagara, reporting on English relations to the Iroquois, and he took part in Lignery's expedition to the Sioux country in 1728, gaining a first-hand knowledge of the region. This he embodied in two memoirs, dated 1730 (*post*), which were favorably recommended to the attention of the French ministry by the intendant Hocquart. He urged, as a means of keeping the English from the Lakes, the better regulation of trade with the Indians, strict control of the traders, and the establishment of permanent settlements. Not only the fur trade, but the growing of wheat to supply the needs of the posts, the building of boats on the Lakes, and the development of copper and lead mines in the region deserved attention. He advocated in addition to these projects, an attack upon the Fox Indians to put the fear of the French into that tribe and their allies, the Iroquois. In full confidence of his own ability and disinterestedness, he asked for the command at Detroit, a request which was not granted until 1738. In the meantime he was appointed to Michilimackinac, but on the ground of his ill health was sent to Point à Chevalure (the later Crown Point), instead. When finally he went to Detroit, he had some success in establishing "Police, Order, and Love for Agriculture" among its inhabitants, but his greatest service was in keeping the Indians firmly attached to the French.

He complained of lack of support from the governor and made himself disliked by a prolonged dispute with other officers over the methods of paying the troops. He was succeeded by Céloron de Blainville [*q.v.*] in 1742, and with the reputation of "a man of talent, who has governed well," returned to Lower Canada. His influence among the Iroquois, by whom he had been adopted, was of great service as the last struggle with England drew near. He commanded again at Crown Point (Fort St. Frédéric), at Three Rivers, and in 1758 was sent to Fort Frontenac. Here, with a garrison of fifty men, he was wholly unable to withstand an attack by a force of 3,000 under Col. John Bradstreet [*q.v.*], to whom he surrendered on Aug. 27. Permitted to go to Montreal on parole, he was soon exchanged for Col. Peter Schuyler. It was said that Governor Vaudreuil had sacrificed Noyan to cover his own neglect to raise adequate forces.

Noyan's active career was now over. He went to France, and in 1761 was put on trial, with the intendant Bigot and others, for maladministration in Canada, but after a year's imprisonment, he was set free with a judicial admonition and a light fine (*Jugement rendu dans l'affaire du Canada*, 1763). Beyond this point nothing has been found concerning his life or death.

Noyan married Louise Catherine d'Aillebout, widow of Jean Baptiste Charly, on Nov. 17, 1731. He is said to have been a poet, something of a physician, possessed of a sharp wit which made enemies, and a high sense of his own merit. He has frequently been confused with his brother Gilles-Augustin [*q.v.*].

[Aegidius Fauteux, *La Famille d'Aillebout* (1917); Cyprien Tanguay, *Dictionnaire Généalogique des Familles Canadiennes*, vol. VI (1889); F. A. A. de LaChesnaye-Desbois, *Dictionnaire de la Noblesse*, XV (1869), 535; E. B. O'Callaghan, *Docs. Rel. to the Colonial Hist. of . . . N. Y.*, vols. V, IX, X (1855–58); Noyan's memoirs of 1730 and other material in *Hist. Colls. . . . Mich. Pioneer and Hist. Soc.*, vol. XXXIV (1905) and *Wis. Hist. Soc. Colls.*, vol. XVII (1906); *Mémoires sur le Canada, depuis 1749 jusqu'à 1760* (1838); F. H. Severance, "An Old Frontier of France," *Buffalo Hist. Soc. Pubs.*, vols. XX–XXI (1917); *Collection des Manuscrits du Maréchal de Lévis*, vol. VII (1895); Alex. Jodoin and J. L. Vincent, *Histoire de Longueuil et de la Famille de Longueuil* (1889).]   H.C.B.

NOYES, CROSBY STUART (Feb. 16, 1825–Feb. 21, 1908), journalist, was born on a farm in Minot, Me. He was a grandson of Nicholas and Rachel (Hill) Noyes and descended from Nicholas Noyes who came from England in 1633 and later settled at Newbury, Mass. Though frail of body, after a day's work in the fields Crosby Noyes would make a ten-mile trip on foot to borrow books from a neighbor. He spent much of his boyhood in Lewiston, Me., where he made and mended harness and worked in a cotton-mill to earn money with which to gain an education. Later he taught school. From early boyhood he wrote and published. At fifteen he issued a diminutive four-page weekly, the *Minot Notion*, written by hand and devoted to the "promotion of science, literature and the fine arts." Not much later he wrote a dialect sketch relating the unhappy experiences of "A Yankee in a Cotton Factory," first printed in the *Yankee Blade* of Boston. Some of his juvenile productions were reprinted in *The Harp of a Thousand Strings* (1858), pieces by American humorists. In December 1847, in quest of a milder climate and a more promising opening in the field of journalism, he went to Washington, D. C., arriving with less than two dollars in his pocket. His first employment was in a bookstore and as route agent for a newspaper; he also ushered in a theater. Soon he found employment on the weekly *Washington News* and began to send news and descriptive letters and character sketches to the *Lewiston Evening Journal*, the *Yankee Blade*, the *Spirit of the Times* (New York), and the *Saturday Evening Post* (Philadelphia), receiving an average of one dollar per column. In 1855 he traveled in Europe, following Bayard Taylor's example in *Views Afoot* and describing his experiences in a series of letters which were published in the *Portland* (Me.) *Transcript*. On his return late in 1855 he became a reporter on the Washington *Evening Star*, a four-page paper established in 1852. He covered sporting events, political meetings, debates in Congress, church affairs. During the Civil War he enjoyed acquaintance with Lincoln and Stanton and official announcements were frequently made through the *Star*, as a trustworthy newspaper.

After the war Washington's population decreased so greatly that the owner of the *Star* decided to sell it. Noyes had become assistant editor and was practically manager, also. Offered, in 1867, a forty-eight-hour option to buy the paper at the seemingly extravagant price of $100,000, he promptly organized a company, of which Alexander R. Shepherd [*q.v.*] was a member, bought the *Star*, and became its editor-in-chief. He decided to devote the paper to local welfare and succeeded also, according to a fellow editor, in making it "the most influential newspaper in Washington . . . which shapes more legislation than any other paper in the United States" (quoted in the *New York Tribune*, Feb. 22, 1908, p. 7). He advocated equitable municipal finances, enlargement of park areas, reclamation of the Potomac flats, and other projects that paved the way for the development of the capital city. He kept the *Star* independent in politics, praising or rebuking policies and acts, not parties. He was a conservative, not from cowardice, but from reserve, and so was the more effective when he went into action. He loathed coarseness, obscenity, and "yellow journalism," and his policy succeeded in winning devoted local esteem for the *Star* and in making it one of the most conspicuously prosperous of American newspapers. In 1904 he read a paper on "The Journalistic Outlook" before the World's Press Parliament at St. Louis and in June 1907, a particularly able and vigorous paper, "Journalism Since Jamestown," before the National Editorial Association at the Jamestown Tercentennial Exposition. He traveled widely, visiting practically all civilized and some semi-civilized countries, and sent a stream of letters to the *Star*. He gathered an extensive collection of Japanese prints, original drawings, and illustrated books which he presented in 1906 to the Library of Congress. He endowed a chair in Bowdoin College. He served as an alderman of Washington for two terms, from 1863, but after that foreswore public office, except on boards of charitable institutions. He was tall and slender in build, and modest almost to the point of shyness. The respect and affectionate regard accorded him alike by humble citizens and by statesmen were attested by the outpouring at the memorial meeting held in the National Theater, Washington, Apr. 5, 1908. In 1856 he married Elizabeth S. Williams of Maine. Of their sons, Theodore W. Noyes succeeded his father as editor of the *Star*, and Frank B. Noyes became president of the Evening Star Newspaper Company and in 1900 of the Associated Press.

[*Crosby Stuart Noyes, 1825–1908* (n.d.), a memorial pamphlet containing speeches and a biographical sketch; *Evening Star*, Washington, D. C., Feb. 22, 1908; *Washington Post*, Feb. 22, 1908; *N. Y. Tribune*, Feb. 22,

1908; G. T. Little, *Geneal. and Family Hist. of the State of Me.,* vol. IV (1909); H. E. and H. E. Noyes, *Geneal. Record of Some of the Noyes Descendants of James, Nicholas and Peter Noyes* (1904), vol. I.]
G. F. B.

NOYES, EDWARD FOLLANSBEE (Oct. 3, 1832–Sept. 4, 1890), governor of Ohio and minister to France, was born at Haverhill, Mass., the son of Theodore and Hannah (Stevens) Greely Noyes; he was a descendant of James Noyes who emigrated about 1633 with his brother Nicholas, the ancestor of John Humphrey Noyes [*q.v.*], and settled in Newbury, now Newburyport, Mass., where he was an influential clergyman for a quarter of a century. Left an orphan at three, Edward Follansbee Noyes spent his boyhood with his grandfather and his guardian in New Hampshire. A four years' apprenticeship to a printer was followed by study at the academy in Kingston and at Dartmouth College, where he was graduated in 1857. Visiting a classmate the following winter in Cincinnati he remained to study law and graduated from the law school of Cincinnati College in 1858. A law practice in that city was interrupted by his entering the Union Army in July 1861 as a major in the 39th Ohio Infantry. He served under Frémont and on the staff of Pope in Missouri. Becoming a colonel and participating in operations in Mississippi and Tennessee, he was designated by his superior commander as being "as efficient and faithful as he is brave and determined" (*War of the Rebellion: Official Records, Army,* 1 ser., XVII, pt. I, p. 186). Near Nickajack Creek, Ga., on July 4, 1864, a musketball entering his left ankle necessitated amputation. Later he was assigned to command at Camp Dennison, Ohio, and was brevetted brigadier-general. Resigning in April 1865 he became city solicitor and then probate judge of Hamilton County.

In 1871 his war record and the favor of prominent politicians and of Liberal Republicans won him the Republican nomination for governor by acclamation. Although he was elected by a decisive majority, his administration was undistinguished. He was renominated in 1873, but charges of personal corruption, jealousy among state leaders, general financial distress, and the aggressive opposition of William Allen [*q.v.*] combined with the scandals of the Grant régime to elect by a narrow plurality the first Democratic governor in almost twenty years. At the Republican National Convention of 1876, as chairman of the Ohio delegation, he made the speech placing Hayes in nomination, but its effect was largely lost because of Ingersoll's brilliant presentation of Blaine's candidacy (J.

B. Foraker, *Notes of a Busy Life,* 1916, I, 97). An over-night adjournment, however, made possible shrewd maneuvering by Noyes and others that resulted in Hayes's nomination. The candidate preferred Noyes for national committee chairman, but Zachariah Chandler was selected. After the fall elections he became a visiting statesman, going to Louisiana and then to Florida, where he presented the Republican case before the canvassing board. He was appointed minister to France by Hayes but visited the United States in 1878 to testify before the House committee as to his conduct in Florida. The evidence indicated that he made no promises to members of the canvassing board until after their work had been completed (*House Miscell. Docs. No. 31,* 45 Cong., 3 Sess., vols. IV, V, 1879). As minister he assisted in negotiations for the international monetary conference of 1878, received French assurances that no protectorate over Liberia was intended, and visited Africa in the interests of American commerce. He was an American representative at the Paris conference on industrial property in 1880.

Returning to Cincinnati in 1881 he encountered difficulty in reëstablishing his law practice. He was elected to the superior court at Cincinnati in 1889. A year later he died suddenly on the street. He was survived by his wife, Margaret Wilson (Proctor) Noyes, to whom he had been married on Feb. 15, 1863, and by their one son.

[*The Biog. Encyc. of Ohio* (1876); Whitelaw Reid, *Ohio in the War* (1868), vol. I; C. R. Williams, *The Life of Rutherford Birchard Hayes* (2 vols., 1914); R. C. McGrane, *William Allen* (copr. 1925); H. E. and H. E. Noyes, *Geneal. Record of Some of the Noyes Descendants* (1904), vol. II; *Papers Relating to the Foreign Relations of the U. S.,* 1877–81; *Cincinnati Commercial Gazette,* Sept. 5, 1890; the spelling of the middle name follows that in *Geneal. Record, ante* and in *Gen. Cat. of Dartmouth Coll.,* ed. by C. F. Emerson (1910–11).]
F. P. W.

NOYES, GEORGE RAPALL (Mar. 6, 1798–June 3, 1868), Unitarian clergyman, professor of Oriental languages at Harvard, was a native of Newburyport, Mass., a son of Nathaniel and Mary (Rapall) Noyes and a descendant of Nicholas Noyes who settled in Newbury in 1635. George's parents intended him for the ministry but were able to do little toward his education. Nevertheless he entered Harvard at sixteen, supporting himself largely by teaching for three winters at Bradford, Bolton, and Lexington, having as his pupil in the last-named place Theodore Parker [*q.v.*]. After his graduation in 1818 he taught for a year at Framingham Academy and entered the Harvard Divinity School the year following. He had been reared in the strictly orthodox Old South Presbyterian

Church of Newburyport, whose pastor, Dr. Daniel Dana, had given him much help and encouragement during his school and college course, but in the liberal atmosphere of Harvard he outgrew the theology of his earlier environment and prepared to enter the Unitarian ministry. After graduating from the Divinity School in 1822, he remained at Harvard for five years longer engaged in Biblical studies, serving at the same time as teacher and college tutor. In 1827 he was ordained and became pastor of the Unitarian church at Brookfield, Mass., where he remained till 1834, when he assumed the pastorate of the more important church at Petersham. During his ministry, which was faithfully and successfully performed, he continued his Biblical studies and published *An Amended Version of the Book of Job* (1827) and *A New Translation of the Book of Psalms* (1831). These, together with a number of scholarly articles on Biblical and theological subjects which appeared chiefly in the *Christian Examiner*, revealed him as one of the ablest Biblical scholars of his day and led to his dual appointment in 1840 as Hancock Professor of Hebrew and Oriental Languages and Dexter Lecturer on Biblical Literature and Theology in the Harvard Divinity School. These positions he held for the remainder of his life.

Noyes published translations of the entire Old Testament except the historical books, but the work which probably constitutes his most secure title to remembrance is his translation of the New Testament (1869), based on the text of Tischendorf. Completed during the last months of his life, it was not published till after his death. It is characterized by faithfulness to the original, clearness, simplicity, and dignity, and is often rated as one of the best ever made. Like his other scriptural translations, however, it is somewhat lacking in the poetic and imaginative qualities.

For nearly thirty years Noyes was a leading spirit in the teaching and administration of the Harvard Divinity School and a formative influence in the lives of generations of students in a time of theological ferment and transition. He was thoroughly familiar with German scholarship and a pioneer in the United States in the critical study of the Bible, early reaching conclusions which have long since become widely accepted, but were then branded as heretical. He was entirely reverent and conservative in temper but his intellectual honesty was so great that he often went counter to his own predilections in his logical following of the critical method. That he had the courage of his convictions

is shown by his publication, at a time when it made him liable to prosecution for blasphemy under an old statute, of a statement that he found no prediction in the Prophets of Jesus as the Messiah ("Christology of the Old Testament," *Christian Examiner*, July 1834).

On May 8, 1828, Noyes was married to Eliza Wheeler Buttrick of Framingham, Mass. Of their five children to grow to maturity, four sons were graduates of Harvard.

[S. A. Eliot, *Heralds of a Liberal Faith* (1910), vol. III, contains a good account of the life of Noyes, with a full bibliography of his works. Other sources are: H. E. and H. E. Noyes, *Geneal. Record of Some of the Noyes Descendants of James, Nicholas and Peter Noyes* (1904), vol. I; *Vital Records of Framingham, Mass.* (1911); A. P. Peabody, *Harvard Reminiscences* (1888); Sarah A. Emery, *Reminiscences of a Nonagenarian* (1879), pp. 116–18; *Christian Examiner*, July 1868; *Monthly Jour. of the Am. Unitarian Asso.*, Sept. 1868; *Christian Register*, June 6, 13, and 20, 1868; *Boston Transcript*, June 5, 1868.]   F. T. P.

NOYES, HENRY DRURY (Mar. 24, 1832–Nov. 12, 1900), ophthalmologist, was born in New York City, the son of Isaac Reed Noyes, a merchant, and his wife, Sarah Flint (Drury), both natives of Massachusetts. He was descended from James Noyes who emigrated from England in 1633. After taking the degree of A.B. from the University of the City of New York in 1851 and that of A.M. in 1854, he graduated from the College of Physicians and Surgeons of New York City in 1855. An interneship in the New York Hospital followed from 1855 to 1858, after which he studied in England, France, and Germany under the masters who founded ophthalmology. He returned to New York in 1859 and began to practise, being at once appointed to the position of assistant surgeon to the New York Eye and Ear Infirmary. He evidently filled this position faithfully and well for in November 1864 he was elevated to the office of full surgeon, and to executive surgeon in 1873. These responsibilities gave full scope to his unusual executive powers. He was particularly active in developing the Infirmary to one of the world's best special hospitals. He was elected first secretary of the American Ophthalmological Society in 1864, was first president of the American Otological Society (1868–73), and later (1879–84) served as president of the American Ophthalmological Society. His genius for organization soon became recognized and respected, and he was appointed to the chair of ophthalmology and otology at Bellevue Hospital Medical College, serving from 1868 until 1892, when the department was divided and he become professor of ophthalmology. His incumbency of this post lasted until his death.

Noyes was one of the first in the United States

to employ cocaine as a local anesthetic for eye operations. He kept abreast of the literature of his specialty and made many valuable contributions to a wide variety of subjects. In 1881 he published *A Treatise: Diseases of the Eye,* in Woods' Library of Standard Medical Authors, and in 1890 revised and expanded it into *A Text-Book on the Diseases of the Eye.* The list of his published papers numbers nearly one hundred. As his writings indicate, he was particularly interested in the surgical aspects of ophthalmology and was unusually skillful in operative procedures, but like so many men of attainments, he had interests so broad as to embrace many fields beyond the medical horizon.

He married Isabella Beveridge of Newburgh, N. Y., in 1859, soon after his return from his European studies. She died some ten years later, and in 1870 he married Anna M. Grant, likewise of Newburgh. He died at his summer home in Mount Washington, Mass., survived by his wife, two daughters, and a son. Two children had died in childhood.

[C. A. Wood, *The Am. Encyc. and Dict. of Ophthalmology,* vol. XI (1917); H. E. and H. E. Noyes, *Geneal. Record . . . of James, Nicholas and Peter Noyes* (2 vols., 1904); *Archives of Ophthalmology* Jan. 1901; *Jour. Am. Medic. Asso.,* Nov. 24, 1900; *Medic. News,* Nov. 17, 1900; *Medic. Record,* Nov. 17, 1900; *Ophthalmic Record,* Dec. 1900; *Trans. Am. Ophthalmological Soc.,* vol. IX (1902); *Trans. Am. Otological Soc.,* vol. VII (1901); *N. Y. Times,* Nov. 14, 1900; information as to certain details from friends and relatives.]

J. N. E.

NOYES, JOHN HUMPHREY (Sept. 3, 1811–Apr. 13, 1886), social reformer, founder of the Oneida Community, was born in Brattleboro, Vt., the descendant of Nicholas Noyes who with a brother, James, the ancestor of Edward Follansbee Noyes [*q.v.*], emigrated from England about 1633 and settled in Newbury, now Newburyport, Mass. His father, John Noyes, graduated from Dartmouth College, developed agnostic views that caused him to abandon his study of theology, attained unusual success in business, and was a member of Congress. His mother Polly (Hayes) Noyes, an aunt of Rutherford B. Hayes [*q.v.*], was a woman of strong character who devoted much attention to the religious education of her nine children, the eldest of whom became the mother of Larkin Mead, William R. Mead [*qq.v.*], and Elinor, the wife of William Dean Howells [*q.v.*]. As a boy, John Humphrey Noyes was thoughtful and was said to be passionate and violent when provoked. Strongly built and fond of outdoor life, he was the leader of his playmates. When he was ten, the family removed to Putney but he was sent back to Brattleboro to prepare for Dartmouth

College, which he entered at the age of fifteen. He was diligent in his studies and graduated in 1830 with high honors. For a year he devoted himself to the study of law at Chesterfield, N. H., in the office of Larkin G. Mead. At this time New England was experiencing a great "religious awakening." Having been "converted" at last, he abandoned his legal studies and began to prepare himself for the ministry. In the autumn of 1831 he entered the Theological Seminary at Andover. His burning zeal found the attitude of the students there too worldly, and after a year he transferred to the Theological Department at Yale College. There he became associated with a group of revivalists and with them organized a free church. Sharing the current reaction against the Calvinistic doctrine of human depravity, he became convinced that it was possible in this life to attain perfect holiness. He also developed a unique view of the second coming of Christ, fixing it not in the future but in the past, in 70 A.D.

Perfectionist and adventist beliefs received wide-spread acceptance during the intense religious excitement of the early 1830's, but he, with remarkable exegetical ingenuity, combined both views and from them derived religious sanction for an audacious social experiment. After his announcement, in February 1834, that he had attained a state of perfection or sinlessness, he was deprived of his license to preach, was requested to withdraw from the college, and was dismissed from the free church. For a few years he led a wandering life, during which he visited groups of perfectionists in New York and Massachusetts and also endeavored to interest reformers such as William Lloyd Garrison and Lyman Beecher in his new theology. Discouraged finally with the difficulty of welding together the scattered and somewhat disreputable perfectionist groups, in 1836 he returned to his home in Putney. There he gathered his family and their friends and expounded to them his views, which he later gathered together in *The Berean* (1847). From this "Bible School" developed a society known as the Bible Communists whose aim was to spread by means of its publications the gospel of perfectionism. Communism was adopted as for expediency rather than on principle, for his converts were well-to-do people, and he was more interested in changing their ideas than in improving their economic condition. As early as 1834 he became convinced that monogamic marriage was not compatible with perfectionism and in his famous "Battleaxe Letter" of 1837 he asserted his belief in promiscuity or free love (*Bibliotheca Sacra, post,* p.

186). Later, in the letter in which he proposed marriage to Harriet A. Holton, he stated his radical views, which, however, did not prevent their marriage in 1838. Complex marriage, or promiscuity within the bounds of the community, was first practised in the Putney community in 1846. A storm of indignation arose in the neighborhood, which was not abated by the claims of miraculous healing powers put forth by the community. He was arrested on a charge of adultery, but he broke bail and fled to central New York. Thither the Bible Communists followed him and established in 1848 the Oneida Community.

For a period of thirty years he was undisturbed in his social and economic experiments. In these years he set forth his religious and sociological views in various publications. Of these several are notable, *Bible Communism* (1848), *Male Continence* (1848), *Scientific Propagation* (c. 1873), and *Home Talks* (1875). In 1870 he published a study of communistic experiments, *History of American Socialisms*. His genius for organization and his dominating personality made Oneida Community the most successful of all American Utopias. When in 1881 the Community was reorganized as a business corporation, its property was found to be worth $600,000. By a rather harsh discipline Noyes enforced on his followers birth control and stirpiculture. The number of children to be born each year was predetermined and their parents were selected so as to produce the best possible offspring. In his character the extreme views of the reformer were strangely combined with the astuteness of the opportunist. In 1879, recognizing imminent decline of his personal leadership and sensing the growing strength of outside opposition, he proposed to the Community the formula under which it abandoned its peculiar sex relations. The members then married legally among themselves. By emigration to Canada he put himself beyond the reach of legal action. He died at Niagara Falls, Ontario.

[*Religious Experience of John Humphrey Noyes* (1923) and *John Humphrey Noyes: The Putney Community* (1931) both ed. by G. W. Noyes; autobiog. material in writings, esp. *American Socialisms, ante,* and *Dixon and His Copyists* (1874); Charles Nordhoff, *Communistic Societies of America* (1870); W. A. Hinds, *American Communities,* rev. ed. (1902); Gilbert Seldes, *The Stammering Century* (1928); B. B. Warfield, "John Humphrey Noyes and his 'Bible Communists,'" *Bibliotheca Sacra,* Jan.–Oct. 1921.]

P. W. B.

NOYES, LA VERNE (Jan. 7, 1849–July 24, 1919), inventor, manufacturer, the son of Leonard R. and Jane (Jessup) Noyes. was born on his father's farm in Genoa, Cayuga County,

N. Y. He was descended from James Noyes who emigrated from England and in 1633 became pastor of the Congregational church in Newbury, Mass. When La Verne Noyes was five years old his parents journeyed west to Springville, Linn County, Iowa, and there undertook the conversion of wild prairie land into a farm and home. In this arduous labor the boy did his part, but prepared for college as well, and entered Ames Agricultural College, now Iowa State College, Ames, Iowa, in 1868. The year before his graduation in 1872 he was assistant in the department of physics. His duties involved particularly the design and construction of much of the equipment used in the classroom and this experience, coupled with his earlier mechanical training on the farm in repairing machinery and tools, stimulated his genius for invention. After graduation he returned to his home where he again assisted his father and for a time had charge of the sale of farm implements in the village store at Marion, near by. He thus had opportunity to perceive the shortcomings of the existing farm machinery and to note the direction in which it needed improvement. In 1874, when twenty-five years old, he established a business in Batavia, Ill., for the manufacture of haying tools and carried it on successfully for about five years. Among the improvements he perfected during this time was a horse hay fork, patented June 22, 1878.

He was married, May 24, 1877, to Ida Elizabeth Smith of Charles City, Iowa. In 1879 he moved to Chicago and established a plant for the manufacture of a wire dictionary holder which he had first devised at the request of his wife. This undertaking was extremely profitable almost from the start, and gave him the opportunity to continue his inventive work in farm machinery. Thus in the succeeding decade he sold manufacturing rights to twelve patented inventions, including tractor wheels (Aug. 4, 1885), a harvester reel (Aug. 4, 1885), a sheaf carrier for self-binding harvesters (Nov. 13, 1888), and a cord-knotter for grain binders (Feb. 19, 1889). About 1886 he began giving serious attention to the possibilities of improving the windmill. After three years of experimentation resulting in the invention of numerous improvements, he organized the Aërmotor Company in Chicago and began the manufacture of steel windmills, which reduced the cost of wind power to one-sixth of what it had been previously. The business grew so rapidly that it required the enlargement of the manufacturing plant until it covered some ten acres. Besides his "air motors," he manufactured specially designed steel towers for his windmills and for electric power lines and wireless stations, gasoline engines, and water-supply goods. He was particularly interested in the utilization of his air motor for the generation of electric power.

While his business absorbed much of his attention, he was engaged in many enterprises for the public good. He worked for the organization of the Department of Commerce and Labor; and was one of the first advocates of the creation of the Interstate Commerce Commission. He was president of the Illinois Manufacturers' Association for two years and also of the board of trustees of the Chicago Academy of Sciences and of many other educational and charitable institutions. He made generous gifts to his alma mater, Iowa State College, and to a number of charities in Chicago, but his two outstanding philanthropies were gifts to the University of Chicago: first, the Ida Noyes Hall, a social center for women, erected as a memorial to his wife, who died in 1912, and second, the La Verne Noyes Foundation for the education of honorably discharged soldiers of the World War and their descendants. He died in Chicago in his seventy-first year.

[Although Noyes' name frequently appears as La Verne W., the middle initial is not perpetuated in the title of his estate or in that of the La Verne Noyes Foundation. Sources include: T. W. Goodspeed, "La Verne Noyes," in *Univ. Record* (Univ. of Chicago), Oct. 1918, and *Univ. of Chicago Biog. Sketches*, vol. I (1922); Alumni Records, Iowa State College; *The Alumnus of Iowa State College*, vols. VIII (1912–13), X (1914–15), XIII (1917–18); *Descendants of Rev. William Noyes* (1900); H. E. and H. E. Noyes, *Geneal. Record of Some of the Noyes Descendants of James, Nicholas, and Peter Noyes* (1904), vol. II; *The Book of Chicagoans* (1917); *Who's Who in America*, 1918–19; *Chicago Daily News*, July 24, 1919; Patent Office records. Preferred form of name and date of marriage have been confirmed by Estate of La Verne Noyes, Chicago.]　　　　　　　　　　C. W. M.

NOYES, WALTER CHADWICK (Aug. 8, 1865–June 12, 1926), jurist, was born in Lyme, Conn., to Richard and Catherine (Chadwick) Noyes. He was the sixth lineal descendant of the Rev. Moses Noyes to own and occupy the lands set apart to the Reverend Noyes as the minister in charge of the church established by the first settlers of the town of Old Lyme. He was a grand-nephew of Chief Justice Morrison R. Waite [*q.v.*]. After attending private schools Noyes went to Cornell University for a year (1884–85) and then entered upon the study of law in the office of Samuel Parks in New London, Conn. He studied also in the office of Judge Augustus Brandegee, one of the leading lawyers and political leaders of the state. After his admission to the bar he practised in New

London for many years in association with Judge Brandegee and his son, Frank B. Brandegee [*q.v.*], in the firm of Brandegee, Noyes & Brandegee. In 1895 Noyes became judge of the court of common pleas of New London County, a post which he held for twelve years. In 1904 he became president of the New London Northern Railroad Company. In 1907 he was appointed by President Roosevelt as United States circuit judge of the second judicial circuit. This made him a member *ex officio* of the United States circuit court of appeals in New York. During his tenure of the federal bench he participated in many important cases. These included a number of cases in patent law in which he became expert. He also participated in the famous Patten cotton corner case as well as in the proceedings against the American Tobacco Company.

In 1913 Noyes drew nation-wide attention to himself by resigning from the bench with the statement that his judicial salary of $7,000 was too low for the comfortable maintenence of his family and the education of his children (*New York Times*, June 6, 7, 1913). Much editorial comment on low judicial salaries ensued. Noyes resumed private practice in New York City where he at once assumed a position of importance at the bar. His practice was largely corporate in character and was highly lucrative. It included much business which brought him before the United States Supreme Court. He became general counsel for the Delaware & Hudson Company and he was peculiarly successful in the administration of important receiverships assigned to him. Perhaps the most conspicuous of these was that of the Rock Island Company in the management of which he was able to recover a substantial amount accruing to the benefit of bonds previously thought worthless. He served as chairman of the Connecticut corporation which operated the street and interurban railways of the state from 1914 until they were returned to the New York, New Haven & Hartford Railroad in 1925. Among his more notable cases in the United States Supreme Court was that of *The Kronprinzessin Cecilie* (224 *U. S.*, 12), in which he successfully argued that the abandonment of a voyage in reasonable anticipation of war did not entitle shippers to damage for breach of contract. In 1909–10 he served as a representative of the United States at the third international conference on maritime law at Brussels at which two treaties were negotiated. He published two legal works: *A Treatise on the Law of Intercorporate Relations* (1902, 1909) and *American Railroad Rates* (1905).

On Oct. 22, 1895, Noyes was married to Luella Shapley Armstrong; they had three daughters and one son. He always maintained the ancestral home in Lyme, Conn., as a country residence, although after his appointment to the federal bench it ceased to be the main family residence. It was known as "Indian Rock Farms." His death occurred in New York on June 12, 1926, after an illness of three months.

[See *Who's Who in America*, 1926–27; *Case and Comment*, Dec. 1911; Henry E. and Harriette E. Noyes, *Geneal. Record of Some of the Noyes Descendants of James, Nicholas, and Peter Noyes* (1904), vol. II; *N. Y. Times*, June 14, 1926.]   R. E. C.

NOYES, WILLIAM CURTIS (Aug. 19, 1805–Dec. 25, 1864), New York lawyer, was born in Schodack, N. Y., the son of George and Martha (Curtis) Noyes and a descendant of James Noyes who came to New England in 1633. He received a common-school and academy education, and at the age of fourteen years entered as a student the law office of Welcome Esleeck of Albany. He completed his studies in the office of Storrs & White of Whitesboro, was admitted to the bar as attorney in 1827 and as counselor in 1830. He practised law successively in Rome and Utica and became district attorney of Oneida County before his thirtieth year. In 1838 he removed to New York and rapidly advanced to the front ranks as an advocate.

Lacking a college education, he possessed the capacity to educate himself. He gradually built up a remarkable library, valued at $60,000, consisting of about five thousand law books and two thousand general works, all of which he bequeathed to Hamilton College on his death. He possessed a taste for miscellaneous reading and was a profound student of the law. His success as an advocate was enhanced by his exhaustive researches into the law and facts of his cases. He reduced his briefs to writing, memorized his speeches, and delivered them as though unpremeditated. In the "Huntington case" his masterly analysis of moral insanity secured the conviction of Huntington, a Wall Street broker on trial for forgery, who had set up a plea of insanity. Another notable suit was the Rose Will case (4 *Abbott's Court of Appeals Decisions*, 108), in which Noyes ably presented the history and doctrine of charitable uses. His greatest triumph occurred in the suit of the *Mechanics' Bank* vs. *New York & New Haven R.R. Co.* (13 *N. Y. Reports*, 599). In this trial in the New York court of appeals Noyes defended the stockholders of the railroad against the claim that they should be deprived of their holdings without compensation, because the transfer agent of the railroad had issued fraudulent stock to a third party.

Although he was sincerely interested in public affairs and politics, he was never a politician in the ordinary sense. Originally a Whig, he became a Republican upon the dissolution of the former party (1856). He was defeated for the office of state's attorney general in 1857, though running ahead of the party ticket. As a stanch Republican, he publicly attacked the Kansas-Nebraska Bill and Fugitive Slave Law. He was a delegate to the Peace Conference in Washington (1861), where he labored to harmonize conflicting views between the sections. His unionist convictions are summed up in the title of an address, which he delivered in 1862 to support the Emancipation Proclamation: *One Country! One Constitution! One Destiny!* In 1857, with Alexander W. Bradford and David Dudley Field he was appointed to codify the state laws, and in this work engaged chiefly in the revision of the penal code, which he completed just before his death. Though the code was rejected in New York, it was adopted at a later date by several western states. Noyes was a consistent Christian and philanthropist. For years he supported a home missionary without hinting of it to others. He was on the executive committee of the American Temperance Union, and was chosen president of the New England Society three days before he died. He was twice married, first to Anne Tracy, who bore him three children, and second to Julia A. Tallmadge, to whom two children were born. He was survived by one daughter of each marriage.

[H. E. Noyes and H. E. Noyes, *Geneal. Record of . . . James, Nicholas and Peter Noyes* (1904), vol. II; 43 *Barbour's Supreme Court Reports* (N. Y.), 649–73; S. W. Fisher, *William Curtis Noyes, a Baccalaureate Discourse* (1866); *Am. Ann. Cyc. . . . 1864* (1865); David McAdam and others, *Hist. of the Bench and Bar of N. Y.*, vol. I (1897); C. A. Alvord, printer, *Library of William Curtis Noyes* (1860); Charles Warren, *A Hist. of the Am. Bar* (1911); *N. Y. Herald*, Dec. 27, 1864; letters from Noyes to G. C. Verplanck, Apr. 18, 1840 and 1842, Mar. 31, 1846, Nov. 21, 1859 (MSS.), N. Y. Hist. Soc.]   A. L. M.

NUGENT, JOHN FROST (June 28, 1868–Sept. 18, 1931), United States senator, was born at LaGrande, Ore., the son of Edward and Agnes P. (Frost) Nugent. He grew up at Silver City, Idaho, where, after attending the public schools until the age of fifteen, he entered the mines and soon became a superintendent, having charge of several different workings in Idaho and, for a time, a mine in Australia. Returning to Idaho, he became court reporter for the third judicial district, of which his father was judge. At the same time he studied law, was admitted to the bar in 1898, and began practice at Silver City.

He was elected prosecuting attorney for Owyhee County for four terms, and was chairman of the county Democratic central committee for two terms. He then moved to Boise, where on May 15, 1895, he married Adelma Ainslie, by whom he had one son. He was associated with Clarence S. Darrow in 1907 in the defense of William D. Haywood [q.v.], George A. Pettibone, and Charles H. Moyer, officials of the Western Federation of Miners, against the charge of complicity in the assassination of former Gov. Frank Steunenberg. These defendants were accused in a confession of Harry Orchard (Alfred E. Horsley), the slayer, but were acquitted.

Idaho political control, at the time Nugent began his public career, was in the hands of Fred Thomas Dubois, who had been territorial representative in Congress, and later became the first senator from Idaho. Dubois was first a Republican, and opposed the Mormons and espoused free coinage of silver. He bolted the party in 1896 on the latter issue, and became a Democrat after election to the Senate for the term 1901–07. This shift in allegiance lost him strength in Idaho, and Nugent, as chairman of the state Democratic central committee, fought to oust him from leadership, completing the work by opposing Dubois' proposed anti-Mormon plank in the Democratic National Convention in 1908. Gov. Moses Alexander, in whose election Nugent had been most instrumental, appointed him United States senator in January 1918, to fill the unexpired term of James H. Brady. In the election of November 1918, the Non-Partisan League routed the Democrats in Idaho, but Nugent defeated former Gov. Frank R. Gooding for the Senate for the remainder of the term, receiving much League support. He defended the reconstruction policies of President Wilson and espoused American adherence to the League of Nations. Nugent resigned from the Senate, effective Jan. 14, 1921, President Wilson having appointed him, Dec. 20, 1920, a member of the Federal Trade Commission. In 1926 he ran unsuccessfully for the Senate. Retiring from the Federal Trade Commission in 1927, he practised law in Washington, D. C., until his death, which occurred in that city.

Nugent was a handsome man, with regular features and forceful presence. He was an excellent public speaker, took an active interest in fraternal organizations, and used his aptitudes to acquire an enthusiastic political following. He not only shone in campaign meetings, but proved himself an adroit political manager, and remained Democratic leader of his state from 1908 to 1920.

[*Biog. Dir. Am. Cong.* (1928); *Who's Who in America*, 1930–31; C. S. Darrow, *The Story of My Life* (1932); *Boise Capital News*, Sept. 18, 1931; *Idaho Daily Statesman* (Boise), Sept. 19, 1931.]
B. M.

NÚÑEZ CABEZA DE VACA, ALVAR (*c.* 1490–*c.* 1557), Spanish colonial official and explorer, was born in Jerez de la Frontera, Spain, toward the close of the fifteenth century and died (evidently at Seville) probably in 1556 or between that year and 1559. His father, Francisco de Vera, was a member of the municipal council of Jerez, and his paternal grandfather, Pedro de Vera Mendoza, one of the conquerors of the Canaries and their governor. His mother, Teresa Cabeza de Vaca, was descended from that shepherd, Martín Alhaja, who was ennobled and given the name Cabeza de Vaca by Sancho, King of Navarre, for showing the Christians a pass through the mountains by placing a cow's head at its entrance and thus enabling them to win the battle of Las Navas de Tolosa (June 11, 1212) from the Moors. Instead of bearing his father's name, Alvar was named for a maternal ancestor who was captain of the fleet of Jerez. In 1511 and 1512 he fought in Italy, in 1520 against the *comuneros* in Spain, and still later in Navarre against the French.

On Feb. 15, 1527, he was appointed treasurer and alguacil mayor of the expedition of Pánfilo de Narváez [q.v.] which set out to conquer and settle Florida. While wintering in Cuba, he and another officer were sent with two ships to get provisions at Trinidad, but both ships were lost in a sudden hurricane. Shortly afterward he was made commander of Narváez's fleet at Jagua, Cienfuegos Bay. When the expedition reached the coast of Florida in April 1528, he vainly advised Narváez not to abandon the fleet. After the costly overland march to Apalache, when the remnant of the expedition embarked on Sept. 22, 1528, in five rude boats made near the site of the present St. Marks, he was given command of one of them. Two only of the boats finally came through stress of weather to a small desolate island off the coast of Texas, dubbed Mal Hado (Bad Luck) by the men. The eighty survivors, succored for the moment by the wretched Indians of the island, were soon reduced by hunger, cold, and disease to fifteen, who were enslaved by the Indians and separated one from another.

In February 1530, Cabeza de Vaca escaped to a friendly tribe and became a trader, bartering articles from the coast for others from the interior. Once a year he returned to Mal Hado to try to persuade a Spaniard, Lope de Oviedo, to escape with him, and in 1532 succeeded, but shortly after, Oviedo, fainthearted, turned back. In 1534, Cabeza de Vaca and three others—Andrés Dorantes, Alonso del Castillo, and the latter's black slave Estavanico—took refuge among the Avavares or Coahuiltecas, among whom they plied the art of the medicine man with success. At last, in the spring of 1535, they set out in earnest on their long trek westward, traveling triumphantly from tribe to tribe, healing as they went. Their route led them across the continent, through what is now southern Texas and northern Mexico. In March 1536 they came to the Sinaloa River, and on July 23, to Mexico City, where they were met by Cortes and Mendoza. In 1537, despite the wishes of Mendoza, who desired to employ him in other expeditions, Cabeza de Vaca returned to Spain. Finding that the Florida expedition which he wished to obtain for himself had been given to Hernando de Soto [q.v.], he remained inactive for about two years.

On Mar. 18, 1540, he was commissioned to lead an expedition to the Rio de la Plata region in South America. Its most noteworthy incident was the thousand-mile march from the Brazilian mainland opposite Santa Catalina Island to Asunción, Paraguay, during which for the first time Europeans gazed upon the falls of the Iguazú. On Apr. 25, 1544, festering dissatisfaction among some of his men came to a head; he was arrested and held in close confinement for some months, and then sent back to Spain to be tried on certain definite charges, some of which seem to have been trumped up. Reaching Seville in August 1545, he was kept in prison until Mar. 18, 1551, when he was sentenced to deprivation of all offices and titles, permanent banishment from the Indies, and exile to Oran for five years. Later in that year his exile to Oran was repealed, and on Sept. 15, 1556, being ill, he was given a royal grant of 12,000 maravedis.

In *La Relacion que Dio Alvar Nuñez, Cabeça de Vaca de lo Acaescido enlas Indias* (Zamora, 1542), Cabeza de Vaca, first of all Europeans, described the opossum and the American bison and gave information of the Texas Indians. He also brought the first reports of the Pueblo Indians, although he did not see their towns. His reports led directly to the Coronado expedition and to the martyrdom of Fray Marcos de Niza [q.v.]. Cabeza de Vaca was sane, capable, adaptable, honest, and sincere. His narrative may contain some exaggerations and some inaccuracies, but he was no lover of the marvelous. He was thoroughly imbued with the religious faith of his day and his success in healing he attributed to divine intervention. Working alone, or almost alone, with the Indians, he was resourceful and successful, but with men of his own race, he ran almost immediately into difficulties, although he inspired devotion in not a few.

[Sources for the Florida expedition are the *Relacion* of 1542, of which notable English translations are Buckingham Smith, *Relation of Alvar Nuñez Cabeça de Vaca* (1871) and Fanny R. Bandelier, *The Journey of Alvar Nuñez Cabeza de Vaca* (1905); the account sent to the Audiencia of Santo Domingo, probably written jointly by Cabeza de Vaca and Dorantes in 1536 or 1537 and utilized by Oviedo in his *Historia General y Natural delas Indias* (Madrid), III (1853), 579–618; a short summary relation, perhaps given to the king by Cabeza de Vaca in 1537 (MS. in Archivo de Indias), reproduced in *Coleccion de Documentos Inéditos Relativos al Descubrimiento . . . de América*, XIV (1870), 265 ff.; and a letter of Feb. 11, 1537, written to the king by Viceroy Mendoza (MS. in Archivo de Indias, 2-2-2/5). Sources for the South American expedition are the *Comentarios*, perhaps dictated in part by Cabeza de Vaca, in *La Relacion y Comentarios del Gouernador Aluar Nuñez Cabeça de Vaca* (1555) and translated into English in Luis L. Domínguez, *The Conquest of the River Plate, 1535–1555* (Hakluyt Soc., 1891); Ulrich Schmidel's narrative of 1567, translated in Domínguez, *ante*; and Francisco López de Gómara, *La Historia General de las Indias* (1554). The best life of Cabeza de Vaca is Morris Bishop, *The Odyssey of Cabeza de Vaca* (1933), containing numerous references to other works. Andrés Bellogin García, *Vida y Hazanas de Alvar Núñez Cabeza de Vaca* (Madrid, 1928) has much to commend it but must be used with discretion. See also A. F. Bandelier, in *Hemenway Southwestern Archæological Expedition* (1890), pp. 24–67; Woodbury Lowery, *The Spanish Settlements* (1911); R. B. Cunningham Graham, *The Conquest of the River Plate* (1924); Enrique de Gandía, *Historia de la Conquista del Rio de la Plata y del Paraguay* (1932).]   J.A.R.

NUNÓ, JAIME (Sept. 8, 1824–July 17, 1908), conductor, composer, impresario, was born in San Juan de las Abadesas, Spain. He studied music in Barcelona under Mateo Ferrer, director of the cathedral choir, and at ten was admitted to the choir. After singing and studying there for six years he undertook the direction of an orchestra at Sabadell and conducted other small orchestras. He also composed religious music. In 1851 he became a Spanish army bandmaster and was sent to Cuba to establish military bands in the regiments there on duty. In 1853 the Mexican dictator, Antonio Lopez de Santa Anna, then in exile in Havana, met Nunó and was so impressed by his ability that on his recall to Mexico as president that same year, he took Nunó with him as general band inspector of the Mexican army. Soon afterward Nunó was appointed one of the two directors of the new National Conservatory of Music in Mexico city. In 1855, when Santa Anna was again overthrown, Nunó, like most of his protégés and partisans, fled the country, and in 1856 was active in the United States, managing

tours for Italian opera singers, acting as orchestra conductor for Sigismund Thalberg,
then concertizing in America, and afterward
conducting both French and Italian opera in
Havana. From 1863 to 1869 he directed opera
troupes in Cuba, the United States, Mexico,
and Central America, and on June 12, 1864,
when the Emperor Maximilian made his state
entry into Mexico city, Nunó assisted as bandmaster in the welcome given him. In 1869 he
settled in Buffalo, N. Y., as a teacher of singing. For four years, 1878–82, he was in Rochester as organist and choirmaster at the cathedral, then he returned to Buffalo and for a time
conducted the Buffalo Symphony Orchestra.
During these years he wrote many sacred compositions. He died in Bayside, L. I., where he
was spending the summer, at the age of eighty-
four. He was survived by a wife and two children.

Nunó's outstanding achievement was the
writing of the Mexican national hymn, to a
poem by Francisco Gonzalez Bocanegra. Henri
Herz, the pianist, touring Mexico in 1849, was
surprised to find that the country lacked a national hymn. He offered to set to music a com-
petitively selected poem, and did so. Neither his
setting nor the one by Bottesini, composed to
Bocanegra's verses (which won a prize offered by Santa Anna in 1853) won popular recognition, however, and in 1854 the Mexican
government officially adopted Nunó's "Himno
Nacional Mejicano"—already unofficially a favorite. On Sept. 15, 1854, it was given an inaugural performance in the Teatro de Santa
Anna in Mexico city with a display of the national flag, speeches, and a salute of cannon.
In 1901, Mexican visitors to the Pan-American Exposition in Buffalo discovered Nunó in
that city. As a result he was invited to Mexico
to conduct the singing of his hymn at the ninety-
first anniversary of Mexican independence
(Sept. 16, 1901). It was performed by a large
chorus of school children in Mexico city, and
Nunó, after depositing a wreath of flowers on
the poet Bocanegra's tomb, was crowned with a
golden chaplet and accorded a great ovation.

[See: Enrique de Olavarría y Ferrari, *Historia del
Himno Nacional y Biografía de Don Jaime Nunó*
(1901); "El Himno Nacional Mexicano," in *Anales
del Museo Nacional de Arqueologia, Historia y Etno-
grafia*, vol. XXII, no. 1; *Musical America*, July 25,
1908; *La Gaceta Comercial*, Sept. 5, 12, 13, 14, 1901;
Buffalo Express, *N. Y. Times*, July 19, 1908.]
F. H. M.

NURSE, REBECCA (1621–July 19, 1692),
victim of the Salem witchcraft delusion, was
born in Yarmouth, England, the daughter of
William Towne and Joanna (Blessing), and

was baptized Feb. 21, 1621. It is not known
when she came to America, but she married
Francis Nurse, a tray-maker, who lived in
Salem, Mass., for forty years after 1638. He
then purchased a farm in Salem Village (the
present Danvers) and removed thither with his
wife and eight children. The Nurse family
were involved in various local squabbles and
had acquired some enemies who took advantage
of the witchcraft frenzy which started in this
community in 1691. By absenting themselves
from meeting out of disgust at the commotions
raised by "possessed" wenches of Danvers, they
attracted unfavorable attention and Rebecca
was denounced. Although she was feeble, ill,
and seventy years old, and although thirty-eight
respectable citizens testified that "her life and
conversation were according to her profession"
and had given no cause to be suspected, she was
arrested and examined, Mar. 24, 1692, in the
presence of her four accusers. She repeatedly
denied her guilt: "I can say before my Eternal
Father, I am innocent, and God will clear my
innocency"; but the wenches counteracted this
by throwing fits timed to her every movement.
She was indicted on June 2; a jury of women
examined her and found what the majority believed to be a mark of the devil. Two of the
women, however, dissented, and Goody Nurse
petitioned for another examination, a plea which
the court evidently disregarded. At her trial,
June 29, the jury at first returned a verdict of
"not guilty," but the judges demanded if they
had well considered one expression of the prisoner's, how when she was confronted with one
Goody Hobbes, a confessing witch, Mrs. Nurse
had muttered, "She is one of us." The jury retired for further debate, returned to ask the accused what her remark had meant, and, upon
receiving no answer from her, reversed their
verdict. She later explained that she had only
meant that she and Goody Hobbes had been held
in prison together, and that "being something
hard of hearing and full of grief" she had not
been aware of the jury's question. Governor
Phips granted her a reprieve, whereupon her
accusers renewed their outcry and certain gentlemen of Salem prevailed upon him to recall
his order. On July 3 Rebecca Nurse was solemnly excommunicated by her church and on
July 19 was executed at Gallows Hill. With
the rapid reaction of the colony from the excesses of the delusion, her innocence speedily
became apparent; in 1712 the very pastor who
had cast her out of the church had the congregation by a formal and public act cancel the excommunication.

[The documents concerning Rebecca Nurse are found in W. E. Woodward, *Records of Salem Witchcraft, Copied from the Original Documents* (2 vols., 1864), and in *The Hist. Colls. of the Topsfield Hist. Soc.*, vol. XIII (1908), pp. 39–58; see also C. W. Upham, *Salem Witchcraft; With an Account of Salem Village* (2 vols., 1867); and C. S. Tapley, *Rebecca Nurse, Saint but Witch Victim* (1930).]   P. M.

NUTHEAD, WILLIAM (c. 1654–1695), printer of Virginia and Maryland, was probably of English birth and professional training. His name occurs for the first time in colonial records in a minute of the Governor and Council of Virginia, dated Feb. 21, 1683, in which it appears that, sponsored by John Buckner, Gentleman, of Gloucester County, he had set up a press at Jamestown and printed, without license, several papers and two sheets of the acts of assembly of November 1682. From Buckner's testimony before the Council, it became clear that in this instance the printer had acted prematurely. Because of the official dislike of "the liberty of a presse," Nuthead and his sponsor were thereupon required to give bond jointly that nothing else should be printed until the royal pleasure were known. In response to the Council's immediate representations, the king's orders of Dec. 14, 1683, forbade that any person in Virginia "be permitted to use any press for printing upon any occasion whatsoever," and it was not until the coming to Williamsburg of William Parks [*q.v.*] in 1730 that the press was reëstablished in Virginia. None of the papers or trial sheets of the acts printed by Nuthead at Jamestown is known to have survived, and his record as an American printer would consist of what has been said above if the government of the neighboring province of Maryland had not been more liberal in its policy than the Virginia Council at the time of this critical situation in his affairs. In the appropriation act of the Maryland Assembly of October 1686, three years after the inhibition of the Jamestown press, occurred the item: "To Wm. Nutthead Printer five Thousand five Hundred & fifty pounds of Tobaccoe." It is uncertain whether Nuthead had come to Maryland immediately after the stopping of his Virginia press, or whether this entry represents his first association with the government of that province. If the payment had been made for services rendered, however, it would mean that he had been at work in St. Mary's City for a year at least at the time of passage of the money act of October 1686. It is certain that he remained there from that time until his death in 1695. His name, with the designation "printer," appears in land records in 1686 and 1687; he was reproved by the Council in 1693 for actions that seemed to show par-

tiality to the party of the dispossessed Proprietary; and in the same year he was engaged by that body for a service of some delicacy. In October 1694 he signed an address protesting the removal of the capital from St. Mary's City to Annapolis. Nuthead died sometime before Feb. 7, 1694/5, on which day his widow Dinah, who later received the Governor's license to print in his place, asked to be appointed administratrix of his estate. Only a single imprint from the Maryland press of Nuthead remains—*The Address of the Representatives of Their Majestyes Protestant Subjects, in the Provinnce of Maryland Assembled*, Aug. 26, 1689—but he is known to have printed a week or two earlier the more extensive *Declaration* of the same body. Among his accounts, moreover, was found a list of sums owed him by various persons and officials, which suggests a moderate activity of his press during the years of his Maryland residence. Nuthead set up in Jamestown the earliest press in this country south of Massachusetts. Because of this fact and because of his persistence in the operation of his later Maryland press in spite of poverty and governmental interference, he has place in typographical history with Stephen Day [*q.v.*] of Massachusetts and William Bradford [*q.v.*] of Pennsylvania.

[W. W. Hening, *Statutes at Large . . . of Va.* (2nd ed., 1823), II, 517–18; *Calendar of State Papers, Col. Ser., America and West Indies, 1681–1685* (1898); records in Land Office, Annapolis, Md.; *Archives of Md.*, vols. VIII (1890), XIII (1894), XIX (1899), XX (1900); L. C. Wroth, *A Hist. of Printing in Colonial Md., 1686–1776* (1922).]   L. C. W.

NUTTALL, THOMAS (Jan. 5, 1786–Sept. 10, 1859), botanist and ornithologist, the son of Jonas Nuttall, was born in humble circumstances at Settle in Yorkshire. He was apprenticed to a printer and later entered the printing shop of an uncle in Liverpool. He seems to have been of a studious nature and lost no spare moment that was available for reading and study. In 1808 he emigrated to Philadelphia. He had apparently given some attention to the study of mineralogy before leaving England and must have had a general interest in nature, but it remained for the Philadelphia botanist Benjamin Smith Barton [*q.v.*] to introduce him to the pleasure found in the study of plants. He at once began collecting and investigating the native flora, extending his explorations southward from the valley of the Delaware and the pine barrens of New Jersey, through the Delaware-Maryland peninsula, to Virginia and the lowlands of North Carolina, and later to Mississippi and Florida. Embracing every opportunity for distant exploration, he went in 1809–11 with

John Bradbury, a Scotch naturalist, up the Missouri River beyond the Mandan Indian villages; in 1818–20, explored along the Arkansas and Red rivers in Arkansas, Louisiana, and Indian Territory; and in 1834–35, accompanied the Wyeth Expedition to the mouth of the Columbia River, in company with John K. Townsend [q.v.], the ornithologist, returning by himself through California and thence to the Hawaiian Islands and around Cape Horn.

After the first of these expeditions he was elected a fellow of the Linnæan Society of London (1813), a member of the American Philosophical Society (1817), and a correspondent of the Academy of Natural Sciences of Philadelphia (1817), in whose rooms he studied his botanical collections. His outstanding contributions to botany are: *The Genera of North American Plants, and a Catalogue of the Species, to the Year 1817* (1818), the greater part of the type of which he set with his own hands; his continuation (vols. IV–VI, 1842–49) of *The North American Sylva* of F. A. Michaux [q.v.]; numerous descriptions of new species and reports on collections, published in the *Journal of the Academy of Natural Sciences*, the *Transactions of the American Philosophical Society*, and Silliman's *American Journal of Science*; and a little treatise entitled *An Introduction to Systematic and Physiological Botany* (1827). In 1821 he published *A Journal of Travels into the Arkansa Territory, during the Year 1819*, with appendices dealing with the history of the Indian tribes and meteorological observations.

In 1822 he accepted a call to be curator of the Botanical Garden of Harvard University, where he remained for ten years, giving a few lectures on botany but devoting most of his time to the culture of rare plants. He resigned to accompany the Wyeth expedition to the Pacific Coast. While in Cambridge, his attention seems to have been turned more actively to ornithology, which had always attracted him to a certain degree, and in 1832 he published *A Manual of the Ornithology of the United States and Canada*. Upon this book and one paper, "Remarks and Inquiries Concerning the Birds of Massachusetts" (*Memoirs of the American Academy of Arts and Sciences*, n.s. I, 1833), rests his entire ornithological reputation. So great, however, was the need of such a work as his *Manual*, with only the expensive folios of Wilson and Audubon available, that it brought him a great and deserved reputation, and the first ornithological club in America was named in his honor. The *Manual* is well written, as were all of his works, and the preface and numerous notes show a remarkable famili-

arity with the literature of ornithology, while the pages are replete with original observations. One of the unique features is the painstaking effort to record the songs of birds by the syllabic method.

Several papers on mineralogy and a period devoted to the study of shells further illustrate the breadth of Nuttall's learning and his ability to turn from one field to another, maintaining in all the high quality of his writings. A paper which he read in December 1820 before the Philadelphia Academy of Natural Sciences, "Observations on the Geological Structure of the Valley of the Mississippi" (*Journal*, January 1821), in which he found the Secondary formations of Iowa to resemble the mountain limestone of Derbyshire, was the first attempt in America to correlate, by means of the fossils contained therein, geological formations widely separated geographically. It antedated by nearly fifteen years the similar work of Samuel George Morton [q.v.], who is generally considered the pioneer of American paleontology. (See Keyes, *post.*)

How Nuttall subsisted during his residence in Philadelphia his friends never knew; yet he is reported to have saved a certain sum of money. He was disorderly in his dress and excessively economical, living the life of a recluse, with few friends besides the botanists with whom he associated at the Academy. In 1842 an uncle bequeathed to him his estate, "Nutgrove," near Liverpool, on condition that he live there during nine months of the year for the remainder of his life, and he returned to England. While the estate did not yield a great income, it enabled him to devote his time to the cultivation of exotic plants, especially rhododendrons. He made one visit to Philadelphia in 1847–48, and plunged at once into his favorite work at the Academy, describing the collections brought from the Far West by Dr. William Gambel. He was never married and died on his estate in 1859.

[Elias Durand, "Biog. Notice of the Late Thomas Nuttall," *Proc. Am. Phil. Soc.*, vol. VII (1861); autobiographical sketch in Preface to vol. IV (1842) of *The North American Sylva*; F. L. Burns, "Miss Lawson's Recollections of Ornithologists," *The Auk*, July 1917; J. W. Harshberger, *The Botanists of Phila.* (1899); *Proc. Linnæan Soc. of London*, 1859; *Pop. Sci. Mo.*, Mar. 1895, with complete bibliography; *Ibid.*, Jan. 1909; C. R. Keyes, *Ibid.*, Feb. 1914; G. E. Osterhout, in *Plant World*, Apr. 1907.]   W. S.

NUTTING, CHARLES CLEVELAND (May 25, 1858–Jan. 23, 1927), ornithologist and marine zoologist, son of the Rev. Rufus and Margaretta Leib (Hunt) Nutting, was born at Jacksonville, Ill. Later, the family moved to Indianapolis, where Nutting received his high-school education. One of his teachers was David Starr Jordan [q.v.], who encouraged him in his natural taste for scientific studies and undoubtedly influenced the direction of his future career. Appointment of the father to the chair of Greek at Blackburn University brought the Nuttings to Carlinville, Ill., where Charles graduated in 1880 with the degree of A.B. and was awarded that of A.M. in 1882. The Presbyterian collegiate environment was a strong factor in his life and manifested itself in his open disapproval of Sunday scientific work by members of the parties he headed, and in his narratives.

Having developed a desire for travel, he opened correspondence with Spencer F. Baird [q.v.], which resulted in a commission from the Smithsonian Institution to investigate Nicaragua and Costa Rica where, in 1881 and 1882, he collected birds and antiquities. On Aug. 10, 1886, he married Lizzie B. Hersman, of Hersman, Ill., and a month later went to Iowa City as professor of zoology and curator of the museum in the State University of Iowa. His classes were small at first, and his teaching duties light, thus allowing him to devote his major effort to museum development, which was always his favorite enterprise. He was a natural collector, a good taxidermist for his day, and he had the ability to interest others in his projects. A trip to the Bahamas with his wife in 1888 gave him his first intimate acquaintance with marine life. Up to this time he had been particularly interested in ornithology, but now his tastes seemed to turn in the direction of the coelenterates. In 1889 his first serious paper, "Contribution to the Anatomy of Gorgonidae," appeared as an *Iowa University Bulletin.*

The death of his wife, after the birth of a daughter, early in 1891, was a heavy bereavement. In seeking distraction, he made a trip with two of his students to the muskeg country of the Saskatchewan district, where the party secured a considerable collection of birds. His "Report on Zoological Explorations on the Lower Saskatchewan River" (*Iowa University Bulletin*) appeared in 1893. In that year he organized and headed a party of twenty-three, mostly students, which chartered a ninety-ton schooner and made a three months' cruise for the purpose of studying the natural history of the Bahamas and adjacent seas. After his return he published "Narrative and Preliminary Report of Bahama Expedition," which also appeared as a *Bulletin* in 1895. It attracted wide and favorable attention, and brought him into communication with many influential zoologists. In 1895 he studied at the marine laboratories of Plymouth and

Naples, further enlarging his professional acquaintance. On June 16, 1897, he married M. Eloise Willis of Iowa City, by whom he had two sons. He went on the Hawaiian cruise of the U.S.S. *Albatross* in 1902 as a civilian member of the scientific staff, and was so impressed by the bird rookeries on Laysan Island that he became fired with the idea of reproducing the scene in a cyclorama for the museum—a plan carried out years later.

At the request of many students, he organized and directed another trip to the West Indies in 1918, but this time the steamer route was used and the work confined principally to shore and littoral stations on Barbados and Antigua. The scientific results, however, were of considerable interest (*Barbados-Antigua Expedition: Narrative and Preliminary Report,* 1919). His last enterprise of this nature was to lead a small party from the University of Iowa faculty to Fiji and New Zealand in 1922, an account of which trip he published under the title *Fiji-New Zealand Expedition* (1924). Meanwhile, he had been busy studying marine invertebrates and had brought out an important series of reports, *American Hydroids* (1900-15), and a mass of shorter articles, many of the later ones of a controversial nature in support of his views on evolution. At the end of this academic year he retired from his administrative duties as curator and departmental head but continued teaching until a few days before his death, which came suddenly in an attack of angina pectoris.

Nutting was a man of forceful character and manners, energetic in organizing and executing projects in which he was interested. His passion for collecting was a great aid to him in his museum development, while his industry, attention to detail, and aptitude in drawing fitted in well with his taxonomic studies. He was a good teacher, a man of strong religious convictions, and although his health had been failing visibly for many years he maintained his interests and his activity to the end.

[J. M. Cattell and D. R. Brimhall, *Am. Men of Science* (1921); *Science,* Feb. 11, 1927; *Who's Who in America,* 1926-27; personal association for forty-two years, and information as to certain facts from Mrs. Chas. C. Nutting.]   H.F.W.

NYE, EDGAR WILSON (Aug. 25, 1850-Feb. 22, 1896), "Bill" Nye, journalist, humorous writer and lecturer, was born at Shirley, a hamlet of Piscataquis County, Me. His parents, Franklin and Elizabeth Mitchell (Loring) Nye, were farming people of good New England stock, the father descended from Benjamin Nye who settled at Lynn, Mass., in 1635. Poverty prompted their removal to the new West in the migration which poured into Wisconsin after its admission as a state. On the St. Croix River in 1852 they took up, as Bill Nye has recorded, "one hundred and sixty acres of beautiful ferns and bright young rattlesnakes" (*Century*, November 1891, p. 60). Edgar's boyhood was spent in the typically American surroundings of a bush farm. The Nyes built themselves a cabin of basswood logs, and a year later, were able to add to it the luxury of a glass window. Bill Nye himself tells us that he went to school between Indian massacres. Later on his parents were able to send him for a time to an academy at River Falls. His studies, though much broken into by "vacations" during which he worked out by the month, were turned towards the law. For a time he worked in the law office of Bingham & Jenkins in Chippewa Falls, sleeping on the premises at night and keeping his blankets in the office safe. After an interlude of teaching school, in a final effort to achieve admission to the bar he removed to the county seat of Burnett County, which "consisted at that time only of a boarding-house for lumber men, surrounded by the dark-blue billows of a boundless huckleberry patch" (*Ibid.*, November 1892, p. 156). Here Bill Nye had his first taste of journalism, conducting for two weeks a newspaper housed in a log hovel. He left Wisconsin in 1876, drifted westward to Wyoming Territory, and brought up at the new settlement of Laramie City, ever after associated with his name. An informal examination by a "committee of kindly but inquisitive lawyers" admitted him to the bar. But he never practised. His legal status merely served to obtain him the position of justice of the peace. "The office was not a salaried one," he wrote, "but solely dependent upon fees. . . . So while I was called Judge Nye and frequently mentioned in the papers with great consideration, I was out of coal half the time, and once could not mail my letters for three weeks because I did not have the necessary postage" (*Ibid.*, November 1891).

Neither the bench nor the bar was destined to be his vocation in life. Soon after his arrival at Laramie and even before he had been elected a justice of the peace, he had done some casual work on a local paper, the *Laramie Daily Sentinel*. He seems to have acted as reporter and writer of anything and everything at a salary of fifty dollars a month. His connection with the *Sentinel* brought to him an offer from the *San Francisco Chronicle* to accompany, as a reporter, General Custer's ill-fated expedition against Sitting Bull (1876). Nye explains with

characteristic drollery that a difficulty about getting his trunk checked in time to catch the right train deprived him of the opportunity offered. He varied his work as reporter and justice of the peace by random contributions to other western journals, such as the *Cheyenne Daily Sun* and the *Denver Tribune*. During this period he married (Mar. 7, 1877) Clara Frances Smith of Chicago, by whom in due course of time he had two sons and two daughters.

In 1881, with the aid of Judge Jacob Blair, his associate and friend from his first arrival, he started the famous *Laramie Boomerang* with which his memory has ever since been connected. Nye edited this paper for about three years. His droll comments and *obiter dicta*—before the days of the "columnist"—and his humorous yarns of frontier life brought the *Boomerang* a continental reputation, though its editor assures us that he made no money out of it. Many of Nye's "pieces" which were collected to form his books appeared first in the *Boomerang*. The first collection, *Bill Nye and Boomerang* (1881), was followed in short order by *Forty Liars and Other Lies* (1882) and *Baled Hay* (1884). Meanwhile he had served as postmaster of Laramie from August 1882 until October 1883, when he resigned. His health had broken, and from time to time for the rest of his life he suffered from meningitis, the disease which eventually caused his death. Advised to seek a lower altitude, he went first to Greeley, Colo., then back to Wisconsin, buying a farm in Hudson, near the home of his parents. In 1886 he moved East and early in the following year accepted a position on the staff of the New York *World*, from which time on his name and his writings obtained a national circulation.

In 1885 he had appeared in a new and entirely successful rôle as a public lecturer. To vary his entertainment, at first too monotonously funny to be sustained, he united in 1886 with James Whitcomb Riley, thus forming a combination of gravity and gayety whose merit justified its success. For the rest of his life his services were in constant demand on the platform. He appeared with Riley until January 1890, and subsequently with Alfred P. Burbank and with William Hawley Smith. For some time he lectured under the management of James Burton Pond [*q.v.*], the famous lyceum organizer. In 1891 he moved his home to Arden, N. C., where after repeated periods of ill health he died five years later.

Edgar Wilson Nye's place in American literature belongs among that brilliant and distinctive group of the middle and later nineteenth century, represented chiefly by Mark Twain and Artemus

Ward, who first made American humor a distinct and truly national branch of literature. His work, like that of all the school, is often disfigured by the haste of its casual production and by its frequent reliance upon the cheap devices of verbal form. But the real merit of it lies in its essential point of view—broad, kindly, and human, and reflecting the new American analysis of traditional and conventional ideas. In addition to the volumes already mentioned, many others appeared both before and after his death. With Riley he wrote *Nye and Riley's Railway Guide* (1888). His most ambitious books were *Bill Nye's History of the United States* (1894) and *Bill Nye's History of England* (1896). He was also the author of two plays: *The Cadi*, based on his experience as postmaster of Laramie, which had moderate success, and *The Stag Party*, completed under pressure shortly before his last illness, which was a failure.

[Nye left two fragmentary chapters of autobiography in the *Century*, Nov. 1891 and Nov. 1892, while *Bill Nye, His Own Life Story* (1926), comp. by his son, F. W. Nye, is largely autobiographical. J. B. Pond, *Eccentricities of Genius* (1900), contains two delightful chapters upon Nye as a lecturer. See also G. H. Nye and F. E. Best, *A Geneal. of the Nye Family* (1907); Stephen Leacock, "American Humour," *Nineteenth Century*, Aug. 1914; "Letters of Riley and Bill Nye," *Harper's Mag.*, Mar. 1919; J. L. Ford, "A Century of American Humor," *Munsey's Mag.*, July 1901; Robert Ford, *Am. Humorists* (1897); F. B. Beard, *Wyoming* (1933), vol. I; *World* (N. Y.), Feb. 23, 1896; *N. Y. Times*, Feb. 23, 1896.]   S. L.

NYE, JAMES WARREN (June 10, 1814–Dec. 25, 1876), governor of Nevada Territory, United States senator, was the son of James and Thankful (Crocker) Nye and a descendant of Benjamin Nye who emigrated from England to settle in 1635 at Lynn, Mass. Born at De Ruyter, Madison County, N. Y., James grew up amidst the severe limitations of poverty. He secured secondary schooling at Homer Academy, however, and then studied law in Hamilton, N. Y., where he practised for some years. He was surrogate of Madison County, 1844–47, and judge of the county court, 1847–51. In 1848, running for Congress as a Free-Soil or "Barnburner" Democrat, he was defeated by the Whig candidate, William Duer. In 1851 he removed to Syracuse, continuing to enjoy a successful practice. Six years later, in 1857, he became one of the police commissioners of the metropolis under an act of that year amending the city charter.

When Fort Sumter was fired upon, Nye became an enthusiastic supporter of Lincoln, using his remarkable gift as a stump orator in behalf of the administration, and he was soon appointed governor of the newly created territory of Nevada. Upon arrival in Carson City, Nev., July 8, 1861, he was confronted with the difficult task of organizing the territory. The bulk of the population was included in what had been Carson County, Utah Territory. Without friction, Nye absorbed the government of the old county into that of the new territory, and guided the latter swiftly into the position of an effective governmental organization, a task the more difficult because the $30,700 a year in greenbacks, voted by Congress for support of the territory, was worth hardly more than half its face value.

When in 1864 Nevada was advanced to statehood, and Nye County, newly created, was named for him, Nye logically became a candidate to represent the new state in the United States Senate and was elected in company with William M. Stewart [q.v.]. The two cast lots in the state Senate for the long term, Nye drawing the short term. Reëlected to the Senate in 1867 after a hot contest with Charles E. DeLong, he served with honor on important committees, always stanchly loyal to the Republican party which had sent him to Washington. He concluded his term on Mar. 3, 1873, having been defeated for reelection by John Percival Jones [q.v.]. This was his last political office. About two years later he sailed from San Francisco for New York, apparently in good health, but during the voyage he lost his mind, and after living many months under this cloud he died on Dec. 25, 1876, at White Plains, N. Y.

Nye was of medium height, weighed nearly two hundred pounds, but was well built, with small hands and feet. His dancing black eyes, expressive features, and shoulder-length snow-white hair gave him in his later years a striking appearance, while his genial humor, quick repartee, and natural gift for oratory gave him power in social as well as in political life. The name "Gray Eagle" was bestowed upon him in recognition of his abundant life and vitality. The friend of Captain Jim of the Washoe Indian tribe as well as of President Lincoln, he swapped stories with both. He was a prolific user of Bible quotations, though not always in anecdote of the choicest character. In Fabius, N. Y., he had married Elsie Benson, and they had two children.

[G. H. Nye and F. E. Best, *A Geneal. of the Nye Family* (1907); *Frank Leslie's Illus. Newspaper*, Mar. 20, 1858, Sept. 14, 1872; *Hist. of Nev.* (1881), ed. by Myron Angel; H. H. Bancroft, *Hist. of Nev., Colo., and Wyo.* (1890); *Biog. Dir. Am. Cong.* (1928); *Daily Territorial Enterprise* (Virginia City, Nev.), Dec. 29, 1876; *N. Y. Times*, Dec. 28, 1876; *Daily Alta California*, May 24, 27, 1875, Dec. 29, 1876, Jan. 19, 1877.]
                    J. E. W.

OAKES, GEORGE WASHINGTON OCHS (Oct. 27, 1861–Oct. 26, 1931), editor, was born in Cincinnati, Ohio, the son of Julius Ochs [*q.v.*] and Bertha (Levy) Ochs. In 1865 the family moved to Knoxville, Tenn., where George attended public and private schools and earned a little money by delivering newspapers. In the fall of 1876, he entered East Tennessee University (later the University of Tennessee). On the completion of his junior year in 1879 he joined his family in Chattanooga. He won the highest distinction in his class in mathematics and Greek in his sophomore and junior years, and when his class graduated in 1880, on account of his high record during his three years, he was awarded the B.A. degree along with the other graduates. Some two years before, his elder brother, Adolph S. Ochs, had become owner of the *Chattanooga Daily Times,* and after leaving college George began his journalistic career as a reporter on this paper. In two years' time he was made city editor; a year later, news editor; and in 1884, managing editor. This position he occupied until late in the eighties, when he assumed charge of the *Tradesman,* a semi-monthly industrial magazine controlled by the *Times,* returning to the latter as general manager in 1896 when Adolph Ochs purchased the *New York Times.*

During these years he took a lively interest in public affairs and served locally in various official capacities. In 1891 he was appointed police commissioner. A delegate to the National Democratic Convention the following year, he delivered a speech in support of Cleveland and was active in his interests during the campaign that followed. On Oct. 10, 1893, he was elected mayor of Chattanooga and assumed office Oct. 16; he was reëlected in 1895, and served until October 1897. His administration was characterized by such economy and business efficiency that the city debt was practically wiped out and a low tax rate maintained, although new school buildings were erected and a park system and city hospital established. In 1895 he served as vice-president of the National Municipal League. During the Bryan campaign of 1896 the *Chattanooga Times* supported John M. Palmer, the candidate of the Gold Democrats, much to the annoyance of local politicians, some of whom demanded that Ochs resign as mayor. After the completion of his second term as mayor, he served as president of the board of education. He was active in the establishment of the earliest public library in the city and became its president. In 1891 he made the first of numerous trips to Europe, during which he recorded his experiences in a series of letters which were published in the *Chattanooga Times.*

In 1900 his brother Adolph placed him in charge of the publication of a daily edition of the *New York Times* at the Paris Exposition Universelle. He carried through the project with great success and for his services was made a Chevalier of the Legion of Honor. Upon his return to the United States he became general manager of the Philadelphia *Times,* which his brother had purchased on May 5, 1901. The following year the *Public Ledger* was acquired and merged with the *Times* and Ochs was made publisher and general manager. This publication became the reform newspaper of Philadelphia and was in part responsible for the election of Rudolph Blankenburg [*q.v.*] as mayor. On Jan. 30, 1907, he married Bertie Gans of Philadelphia, by whom he had two sons. In 1912, Cyrus H. K. Curtis bought the *Ledger* from Adolph Ochs, and George remained as publisher. Finding himself out of sympathy with Curtis's policies and methods he resigned at the end of 1914.

In the summer of 1915 he went to New York at the invitation of his brother to become editor of the *New York Times Current History* (after February 1916, *Current History*) and of the *Mid-Week Pictorial,* also an auxiliary of the *Times.* With the former he was associated for the remainder of his life. It was founded to record impartially the economic, political, and military developments growing out of the World War, and at the close of the war it was continued as a journal of significant happenings throughout the world.

Greatly embittered against the Germans by the events of the war, he determined that he would not hand down to his descendants a name of German origin, and early in 1917 he was given permission by the Philadelphia court of common pleas to change his name to George Washington Ochs Oakes. He was too old to be accepted for service in the war and was unwilling to accept a "swivel-chair position with a commission"; but he enlisted as a private in the New York militia. Few did more to develop public opinion on the issues of the struggle than did he. In New York he abstained from political activities, but was a member of numerous civic and social organizations.

He was a sagacious editor, a man of delightful personality, and had an unquenchable interest in things of the mind. He had nearly completed the requirements for the degree of Ph.D. at Columbia at the time of his death. Perhaps his most marked characteristic was his tolerance. Himself conservative, orthodox in economic beliefs, and austere in morals, he welcomed and sought for *Current History* all shades of thought. After his death selections from his voluminous writings, arranged and edited by William M. Schuyler, were published under the title, *The Life and Letters of George Washington Ochs-Oakes.*

[In addition to the above, see *Current Hist.*, Dec. 1931; *N. Y. Times*, Oct. 27, 28, 1931; *Chattanooga Times*, Oct. 27, 1931; *Am. Hebrew*, Oct. 30, 1931.]

A. B. H.

OAKES, THOMAS FLETCHER (July 15, 1843–Mar. 14, 1919), railroad executive, was born in Boston, Mass., the son of Francis Garaux and Caroline Comfort (Paige) Oakes, and a descendant of Nathaniel Oak who emigrated to Massachusetts, probably from Wales, about 1660. He was educated in the public schools and under private tutors. When he was twenty years of age he began work with a firm of contractors engaged in the construction of the Kansas Pacific Railroad, the eastern division of the Union Pacific. From this company he entered the service of the railroad itself in 1865 as purchasing agent and assistant treasurer. For the following six years he was general freight agent. He was then elected vice-president and after serving in this capacity for seven years he was appointed general superintendent. During this period James F. Joy of Detroit, with the aid of Boston capitalists, was endeavoring to build up a transcontinental system out of the Michigan Central, the Chicago, Burlington & Quincy, the Kansas City, Fort Scott & Gulf, and other shorter lines, but after the panic of 1873 the system disintegrated and the western lines were shifted from one group to another. Oakes had attracted the attention of the Boston owners by his ability, and in 1879 he was asked to become general superintendent of the Kansas City, Fort Scott & Gulf and the Kansas City, Lawrence & Southern Railroad companies, which with their branches made up about six hundred miles. He had occupied this position only a year when in May 1880 he was asked by Henry Villard to take the managership of the Oregon Railway & Navigation Company, which had been organized shortly before. Villard was at this time obtaining control of the Northern Pacific Railroad Company, and with the company just mentioned he practically monopolized both the north and south shores of the Columbia River as well as the navigation of the stream itself. When Villard became president of the Northern Pacific in June 1881, Oakes was elected director and vice-president, in which position he remained until his election as president in 1888.

As vice-president Oakes was in charge of the operating and construction departments, and also of the traffic and land departments, acting as executive officer to the president. When he assumed these duties the eastern division of the Northern Pacific had pushed west as far as Dickinson, Dakota Territory, while the western division stopped at Sprague, Washington Territory. The gap remaining to be built to connect these termini was about a thousand miles and embraced the most difficult portions of the work on the main line, including the crossing of the mountains and the building of two long tunnels. Yet in a little over two years he not only completed this work but built an additional thousand miles. He also reorganized the system of operation and increased its effectiveness. The panic of 1893 affected the Northern Pacific very severely, and in that year Oakes resigned the presidency and was appointed general receiver, in which capacity he acted from 1893 to 1895. After his retirement from this work he resided in Concord, Mass., but for several years maintained a connection with the banking firm of Taylor, Cutting & Company at 7 Wall Street, New York. He died at Seattle, Wash., where he had spent the last years of his life. His wife was before her marriage Abby Rogers Haskell of Gloucester, Massachusetts. They had five children, four of whom survived him.

[Biographical data concerning Oakes are meager. See *Who's Who in America*, 1910–11; *The Biog. Directory of Railway Officials of America*, 1913; *Railway Age*, Mar. 21, 1919; E. V. Smalley, *Hist. of the Northern Pacific Railroad* (1883); R. E. Riegel, *The Story of the Western Railroads* (1926); H. L. Oak, *Oak-Oaks-Oakes: Family Reg.* (1906); the *Post-Intelligencer* (Seattle, Wash.), Mar. 14, 1919. Information as to certain facts was supplied by Oakes's son, Prescott Oakes.]

E. L. B.

OAKES, URIAN (c. 1631–July 25, 1681), colonial poet, clergyman, and college president, was born in England, probably in London, in 1631 or 1632, and was brought to Cambridge, Mass., by his parents, Edward and Jane Oakes, about the year 1640. He received the degree of B.A. at Harvard with the class of 1649 and was named fellow of the college in the charter of 1650. The annual Cambridge almanac for 1650 was prepared by Oakes, who filled the blank spaces with an outline history of the world. On the title-page appears the epigram "Parvum parva decent; sed inest sua gratia parvis," the first three words (Horace, *Ep.* I, vii, 44) being a playful allusion to the author's diminutive stature. Returning to England after three years' tutoring of Harvard students, he became minister of Tichfield, Hants. Silenced by the Act of Uniformity in 1662, he became for a time headmaster of the Southwark Grammar School (John Oldmixon,

The British Empire in America, 1741 ed., I, 219); and then, when the persecution of dissenters had abated, organized a Congregational church at Tichfield. Eventually the Church of Cambridge, Mass., gave him a call, which he accepted in 1671.

Oakes had a high reputation in his day for social qualities, classical wit, and elegant Latinity (see example in *Magnalia,* Bk. IV, chap. vi). He is best remembered for his one published poem, the *Elegie* on Thomas Shepard, which, in the opinion of Moses C. Tyler "reaches the highest point touched by American poetry" in the colonial era (*post,* II, p. 16). His prose style was flexible, energetic, and dignified. As official orator on notable occasions, he lent the vigor of his English and grace of his delivery to the service of the orthodox cause; for unlike many New-England divines who had sojourned in the old country, Oakes stanchly supported early New-England principles, and frankly regarded "an unbounded Toleration as the first born of all Abominations" (*New-England Pleaded With,* 1673, p. 54). With Increase Mather and two other divines, he was appointed a censor of the Massachusetts press (*Proceedings of the Massachusetts Historical Society,* 2 ser. IX, 1895, p. 444); but his respect for authorities did not extend to those of Harvard College. Out of disappointment, perhaps, at not being offered the presidency after the death of Charles Chauncy, Oakes became ringleader of those who wrecked the promising administration of Leonard Hoar [*q.v.*]. After Hoar had been driven out, Oakes twice declined to be his successor; but while continuing his duties to the Cambridge church, he consented to be "acting President." Jasper Danckaerts' depressing picture of the unshepherded Harvard student body (*Journal,* 1913, ed. by B. B. James and J. F. Jameson, pp. 266–68) was during Oakes's "acting," or rather inactive, presidency of five years. Only twenty-two students—fewer than at any similar period in the college history—were graduated; but these included Cotton Mather, John Leverett, and the two Brattles; and Oakes did get a much-needed new building, the first Harvard Hall, completed. Upon being again elected president, Feb. 9, 1679/80 (correct date in *Colonial Society of Massachusetts, Publications,* XV, p. clii) and being voted a salary of £50 and a new President's Lodge, Oakes consented to be formally installed; but before having much opportunity to mend matters, he died.

[Contemporary estimates may be found in John Sherman's preface to Oakes's *Soveraign Efficacy of Divine Providence* (1682); in *A Poem Dedicated to the Memory of . . . Mr. Vrian Oakes* (Boston, 1682), Cotton Mather's first published work, reprinted in *Proc. Mass. Hist. Soc.,* 2 ser. XII (1899), and in the same author's *Magnalia Christi Americana,* Bk. IV, chap. v. J. L. Sibley, *Biog. Sketches of Grads. of Harvard Univ.,* I (1873), 173–85, is uncritical, but has a bibliography of Oakes's published writings; M. C. Tyler, in *A Hist. of Am. Lit. During the Colonial Time* (rev. ed., 1897), II, 15–18, 163–67, is even more eulogistic than contemporaries. Josiah Quincy, *The Hist. of Harvard Univ.* (1840), I, 34–38, is somewhat severe. Oakes's elegy on Shepard (Cambridge, 1677) has been reprinted in *Elegies and Epitaphs* (1896), ed. by J. F. Hunnewell, and there are selections in Tyler, *op. cit.* The unique copy of his *Almanack for the Year of our Lord 1650* is in the H. E. Huntington Library; but it will be found in Charles L. Nichols, *A Coll. of Photographic Reproductions of Mass. Almanacs, 1646–1700.* The records of his college administration are in *Colonial Soc. of Mass. Pubs.,* vols. XV and XVI (1925). A feeble elegy on Oakes by Daniel Gookin, Jr., is printed *Ibid.,* XX (1920), 248–52.]
                                        S. E. M.

OAKLEY, ANNIE (Aug. 13, 1860–Nov. 3, 1926), markswoman, was born in a log-cabin in Patterson Township, Darke County, Ohio, the sixth of the eight children of Jake Mozee and his wife Susanne, and was named Phoebe Anne Oakley Mozee. Her parents had emigrated to Ohio from Pennsylvania. When she was four years old her father died as the result of exposure in a blizzard, and until her mother's remarriage made a home for her Annie suffered to the full the hardships of the unfriended orphan. When nine years old she began to shoot rabbits and quail and was, almost from the start, a dead shot. In the course of five years she paid off the mortgage on the farm with game that she shipped by stagecoach to the Cincinnati market and gained a local reputation as a markswoman. A year or so later she was taken to Cincinnati to shoot a match with Frank E. Butler, a vaudeville performer, and defeated him by one point. Butler fell in love with the girl, kept up a correspondence with her for several years, married her, and, when his partner fell sick, used her as an assistant in his act. On the stage her girlish charm and inerrant shooting won her instantaneous success; she became the feature of the act, and Butler, with a self-effacement almost unbelievable in an actor, became her assistant and personal manager. While trouping with Sells Brothers Circus they played New Orleans when Buffalo Bill was there with his Wild West Show, and, liking the friendly spirit of his outfit, they joined it the next spring (1885) at Louisville. Nate Salsbury, Cody's perspicacious manager, lost no time in making Annie Oakley a star, and for seventeen years, with but one interruption, she was one of the chief features of the show. Rifle or shotgun in hand, she seemed to become a shooting machine. At thirty paces she would slice a playing-card held with the thin edge toward her, hit dimes tossed in the air, or shatter a cigarette held in her husband's lips. A play-ing-card flung in the air she would perforate a half-dozen times before it fluttered to the ground; to this day theatrical passes, meal tick-ets, and complimentary tickets of all kinds are known as "Annie Oakleys," because of the punch-marks in them. In the course of her ca-reer she smashed more glass balls than any one else that ever lived. In one contest, with a .22 rifle, she broke 943 out of 1000. In a single day she made a record of 4772 out of 5000. In Eng-land and on the continent of Europe she was almost as great a favorite as in the United States. Queen Victoria was especially charmed by her, and the Crown Prince of Germany (later Wil-liam II) insisted, to the consternation of every-one but himself and the markswoman, that she shoot a cigarette from his lips. In 1901 she was severely injured in a railroad wreck, and for a time her career seemed at an end. She recov-ered, however, and, though partially paralyzed for a while, made some of her most sensational records during the next two decades. For a number of years her home was at Nutley, N. J. Later she lived at Pinehurst, N. C., and in Flor-ida, and frequently returned to her native coun-ty. Herself childless, she supported and edu-cated some eighteen orphan girls. To the last her favorite reading was in the New Testament. In 1903 she brought suit against more than fifty newspapers for printing a libelous article on her and won all but a few of them. She died at Greenville, Ohio, in her sixty-seventh year and was buried at Brock, near her birthplace. Her husband died three weeks later.

[C. R. Cooper, *Annie Oakley—Woman at Arms* (1927) is based on the autobiographical notes and scrap-books that Mrs. Butler gave to Fred Stone, the comedian, but the material has been carelessly used. See also F. E. Wilson, *Hist. of Darke County, Ohio* (1914), I, 348–52, and the *N. Y. Times*, Nov. 5, 6, 14, 24, Dec. 28, 1926. Many American newspapers print-ed editorials and extended biographical notices of her at the time of her death.]   G. H. G.

OAKLEY, THOMAS JACKSON (Nov. 10, 1783–May 11, 1857), jurist, was born in Beek-man, Dutchess County, N. Y., the son of a Revo-lutionary officer and farmer, Lieut. Jesse Oak-ley, and Jerushah (Peters) Oakley. He was graduated from Yale in 1801, studied law in Poughkeepsie, and practised there after his ad-mission to the bar in 1804. In 1808 he was mar-ried to Lydia S. Williams, the daughter of Rob-ert Williams, a Federalist lawyer of Pough-keepsie. Through his father-in-law's influence he was appointed surrogate of Dutchess County (1810) but lost this position a year later by a party reversal. As a Federalist member of the Thirteenth Congress (1813–15) he was a critic

of the administration and of the War of 1812. From 1816 to 1820 he was a member and Fed-eralist leader of the state Assembly. He sup-ported the Erie Canal project, the bill for found-ing the state library, and was counsel for the de-fendant in the impeachment trial of Judge W. W. Van Ness, in which the latter was acquitted. In 1819 he succeeded Martin Van Buren to the office of attorney-general of the state but was removed in 1821 for political reasons. Asso-ciated with Thomas A. Emmet and opposed by Daniel Webster and William Wirt, he repre-sented New York state in *Gibbons* vs. *Ogden* (9 *Wheaton*, 1). Because of his able arguments in this case and in others before the Supreme Court, he rose to the front ranks as an advocate. He represented the claimants, Astor and Fowl-er, in a case which involved a large tract of land in Putnam County, confiscated during the Revolution because of Tory ownership, and he was conspicuous in litigation in New York state between landlords and their tenants which even-tually degenerated into the anti-rent disturb-ances. In 1826 he was elected as a Clinton Dem-ocrat to the Twentieth Congress but resigned in 1828 to become a judge of the superior court of New York City. He remained on the bench until his death, becoming chief justice in 1847. As a judge he was noted for his impartiality, his quick grasp of the controlling factors of a case, and his clear and direct charges to the jury. He was a member of the Kent Club, an organi-zation composed of leading lawyers and judges who met on Saturday nights for legal and scien-tific discussions after which "reports of cham-pagne bottles were preferred to law reports" (Allan Nevins, ed., *The Diary of Philip Hone*, 1927, I, p. 396). He was a member of the Cal-vary Church and for many years an active mem-ber of the diocesan conventions of the Protes-tant Episcopal Church. After the death of his first wife in 1827 he was married, on Mar. 29, 1831, to Matilda Caroline Cruger. Four chil-dren by the second marriage survived him. In private life he was simple in habits, approach-able and unostentatious. On the bench he was punctual, rigorous, and formal. He had a ma-jestic bearing and spoke easily with "but little rhetoric or gesticulation."

[F. B. Dexter, *Biog. Sketches of the Grads. of Yale Coll.*, vol. V (1911); "In Memoriam," 24 *Superior Court* (City of N. Y.) *Reports*, pp. xv–xxii; Charles Warren, *A Hist. of the Am. Bar* (1911); David Mc-Adam and others, *Hist. of the Bench and Bar of N. Y.*, vol. I (1897); M. B. Flint, *A Peters Lineage* (n.d.); H. W. Reynolds, ed., *The Records of Christ Church, Poughkeepsie, N. Y.*, vol. II (1919); D. R. Fox, *The Decline of Aristocracy in the Politics of N. Y.* (1918); the *Green Bag*, Sept. 1892; *N. Y. Herald*, May 13, 1857.]   A. L. M.

OATES, WILLIAM CALVIN (Nov. 30, 1835–Sept. 9, 1910), Confederate soldier, congressman, governor of Alabama, was born in Pike (now Bullock) County, Ala. His father's ancestors, of Welsh descent, had settled in South Carolina before the Revolutionary War, and his father, William Oates, had moved into Alabama some years before the birth of his son. His mother, Sarah (Sellers) Oates, had an Irish and French heritage. The family lived in extreme poverty, and Oates for only a few months at rare intervals was able to attend a country school. When he was sixteen years old he went to the Southwest, where he made a precarious living as a painter and a carpenter. Returning to Alabama, he taught a few months, attended school for a few months, and taught again. In this way he graduated from the Lawrenceville academy and financed himself while he studied law at Eufaula. He was admitted to the bar in 1858 and began practice in Abbeville in 1859, supplementing his small income by editing a Democratic newspaper. He raised a company of infantry for the Confederate army in 1861. It became a part of the 15th Alabama Infantry, and he served as its captain until 1863 when, having commanded the regiment at Sharpsburg (Antietam), he received the rank of colonel upon the recommendation of General Hood. He held the extreme right of the Confederate line during the assault on Little Round Top at the battle of Gettysburg, and, when his regiment had been transferred to the west, he took part in the battles of Chickamauga and Lookout Mountain. In 1864, he was assigned to command the 48th Alabama Infantry and returned to Virginia. He was wounded at Brown's Ferry and lost his right arm at Fussell's Mill near Petersburg in August 1864. At that time he had been recommended for promotion to the rank of brigadier-general.

In 1865 he resumed his law practice and entered politics. He was a delegate to the National Democratic Convention in 1868, served in the Alabama House of Representatives from 1870 to 1872, and in 1875 was chairman of the judicial committee in the state constitutional convention. He was elected to Congress from the 3rd district in 1880, reëlected six times, and resigned in 1894, when he was elected governor of his state. In Congress he was the only member of the Alabama delegation to support Cleveland in his demand for the repeal of the Sherman Silver Purchase Act. In 1890, when the Farmers' Alliance was strong, he bitterly opposed the sub-treasury scheme and led the hard-money forces of the state. His gubernatorial

campaign of 1894 against Reuben F. Kolb [*q.v.*] was one of the most exciting in the history of the state after the Reconstruction period. As "the one-armed hero" of Henry County he stumped the state for sound money and succeeded in carrying the election by a good majority. His two years in office were not years of achievement. It was not an easy time to be the governor of an agricultural state, when prices were low, money scarce, and taxes hard to collect. The state could not borrow money, and part of the time salaries were unpaid. In 1897 he was a candidate for the nomination of his party to the United States Senate, an honor that he had refused seven years earlier, but the Silver men were in the saddle and gave the nomination to Gen. Edmund W. Pettus. Made brigadier-general of volunteers by President McKinley, he served through the Spanish-American War at Camp Meade, Pa., where he commanded three different brigades. He served as a delegate-at-large to the state constitutional convention in 1901, where he acted as chairman of the committee on the legislative department and of the committee on suffrage and elections. He was one of the few men who opposed the soldier and grandfather clauses and demanded an equal standard of fitness for members of both races who should be granted suffrage (*Speeches . . . in the Constitutional Convention . . . 1901*, n.d.). The last years of his life were spent in the practice of law at Montgomery and in writing. He published "Gettysburg—the Battle on the Right" in *Southern Historical Society Papers* (Oct. 1878) and "Industrial Development of the South," *North American Review* (Nov. 1895). He also published *Speeches of Hon. W. C. Oates in the House of Representatives, 1880 to 1894* (n.d.), and wrote his recollections of the Civil War, *The War between the Union and the Confederacy* (1905). He was survived by his wife, Sallie (Toney) Oates, to whom he had been married on Mar. 28, 1882.

[T. M. Owen, *Hist. of Ala. and Dict. of Ala. Biog.* (1921), vol. IV; J. B. Clark, *Populism in Ala.* (1927); J. Sparkman, "The Kolb-Oates Campaign of 1894" (Univ. of Ala. thesis, 1924); *War of the Rebellion: Official Records (Army)*, 1 ser., XIX, XXVII, XXX–XXXII; *Montgomery Advertiser*, Sept. 10, 1910.]
H. F—r.

OATMAN, JOHNSON (Apr. 21, 1856–Sept. 25, 1922), gospel hymn writer, was born near Medford, N. J., and died at the home of his daughter in Norman, Okla. His parents were Johnson Oatman and Rachel Ann Cline. He learned to sing with his father, was educated at Herbert's Academy, Vincentown, and at the New Jersey Collegiate Institute, Bordentown, now the Bordentown Military School. He joined the Methodist church, was licensed as a local preacher, and was ordained deacon by Bishop Stephen M. Merrill at Burlington on Mar. 24, 1895, but he did not enter the itinerant ministry. For a while he was in business with his father at Lumberton, N. Y., later conducting the business of a life-insurance company at Mount Holly. On July 21, 1878, he was married to Wilhelmina Ried of Lumberton, with whom he lived until her death in 1909. A son and two daughters were born to them. Failing health in 1893 compelled Oatman to retire from his business and he then settled at Ocean Grove. The summer meetings at this resort were congenial to his religious nature and with returning health and strength, and encouraged by his surroundings, he found what proved to be the outlet for his spiritual nature. It was not his desire to take charge of a church, but to do his preaching through songs. His first gospel song, "I am walking with my Master," was written in 1892 and was set to music by John R. Sweney, who published it the following year. Encouraged by the latter he began to feel that his real work in life was to spread the gospel through his songs and he began to express in verse the emotions and sentiments of his own life. "When our Ships come sailing home," inspired by his stay near the ocean, was also set to music by Sweney, and was one of the favorites of its author, but it did not become so popular as some of his other hymns. "No, not one," has appeared in more recent hymn books than any other of his songs. Written in 1895, it was copied into thirty-five different collections within a single year, and it has been translated into many languages. "Count your Blessings" was likewise incorporated into many hymnals, and "Higher Ground" and "Sweeter than all" were widely sung. He wrote the words of at least seven thousand hymns which have been set to music by such composers as J. Howard Entwisle, Adam Geibel, A. J. Showalter, Charles H. Gabriel, George C. Hugg, and William J. Kirkpatrick.

[J. H. Hall, *Biog. of Gospel Song and Hymn Writers* (1914); C. H. Gabriel, "The Singers and Their Songs," *Epworth Herald,* Apr. 10, 1915; *Minutes, N. J. Conf., Meth. Episc. Ch.,* 1886; *Minutes of Ann. Conferences of the Meth. Episc. Ch.,* 1895; the *Music Teacher and Home Mag.,* June 1924; information as to certain facts from Oatman's daughter, Mrs. Frederick F. Blachly, Washington, D. C.]   F. J. M.

OBER, FREDERICK ALBION (Feb. 13, 1849–May 31, 1913), ornithologist, was born in Beverly, Mass., the eldest child of Andrew Kimball and Sarah Abby (Hadlock) Ober. On his father's side he was descended from Richard Ober who emigrated from Abbotsbury, England, to the Salem colony and settled in Mackerel Cove, later Beverly, on a grant of land from the King. From early childhood he was interested in natural history, but the lack of funds prevented him from getting far in his schooling. Before he reached manhood he had stuffed and mounted a collection of local birds which interested Alexander Agassiz of the museum at Harvard University. Later his collection was bought by the university and that gave young Ober the means to begin his life work. In 1872–74, having a connection with *Forest and Stream* and the Smithsonian Institution, he collected birds in Florida and explored the Lake Okechobee region. He wrote several articles on his experiences for *Forest and Stream* under the pen name of Fred Beverly. Later (1876–78, and 1880) he collected extensively in the Lesser Antilles, discovering twenty-two species of birds new to science, two of which were named after him—a flycatcher, *Myiarchus oberi,* and an oriole, *Icterus oberi.* The results of the first Antilles expedition were published under the title "Ornithological Exploration of the Caribee Islands" in the *Annual Report of the Board of Regents of the Smithsonian Institution . . . for the year 1878* (1879). He subsequently made several trips to Mexico, and still later to Spain, northern Africa, South America, and again to the West Indian islands. He served as United States commissioner for the Columbian Exposition at Chicago, having supervision of the ornithological exhibits. The government awarded him a diploma and bronze medal for his services.

Ober was a prolific writer and made use of his knowledge of Mexico and the West Indies in books of travel and adventure and historical tales. In his Heroes of American History Series he published the biographies of ten early explorers. Perhaps best known is his *Guide to the West Indies* (1908) of which a third edition was published in 1920. In 1908 Ober entered the real-estate business in Hackensack, N. J., and remained there until his death. He was married three times. When he was twenty-one years old he was married to Lucy Curtis of Wenham, Mass., but she died within a few months. In the early nineties he married Jean MacCloud of New Hampshire, and she died within a couple of years. His travels in out-of-the-way places were partly attempts to assuage his grief. In 1895 he married Nellie MacCartny of Cambridge, Mass., who survived him about a year. She left two children. Ober's lasting work, with which his name will always be connected, was his zoölogical exploration of the Lesser Antilles.

[*Who's Who in America*, 1912–13; *Forest and Stream*, June 7, 1913; the *World* (N. Y.), June 2, 1913; information as to certain facts from Ober's relatives.]   H. F—n.

OBERHOLTZER, SARA LOUISA VICKERS (May 20, 1841–Feb. 2, 1930), author, leader in movement for school savings, was born in Uwchlan, Chester County, Pa., the daughter of Paxson and Ann (Lewis) Vickers. Her father's ancestors were Quakers who came from England to Eastern Pennsylvania about the time of William Penn's second visit to Philadelphia. Her great-grandfather and grandfather, Thomas and John Vickers, were owners of earthenware potteries in Chester County. She was educated by private tutors, at the Friends' Boarding School, and at the Millersville State Normal School. On Jan. 1, 1862, she married John Oberholtzer of Chester County, who became a merchant in Philadelphia. Having from an early age shown considerable literary talent, she contributed articles to magazines and other periodicals and published hymns, letters of travel, pamphlets, and several volumes of verse, including *Violet Lee* (1873); *Come for Arbutus* (1882); *Daisies of Verse* (1886); and *Souvenirs of Occasions* (1892). She was also the author of *Hope's Heart Bells* (1884), a novel of Quaker life in Pennsylvania. She wrote the "Burial Ode" for the funeral services of Bayard Taylor at Longwood, verses for the dedication of the monument at Antietam Bridge, and many other commemorative poems. While John Greenleaf Whittier was engaged in anti-slavery work in Philadelphia he formed a close friendship with her that lasted until his death.

Mrs. Oberholtzer devoted much time to social and philanthropic as well as literary activities. Organizing the Anti-Tobacco Society in 1881 and the Longport Agassiz Microscopical Society in 1884, she served as president of both organizations for several years. She was president of the Pennsylvania Woman's Press Association, 1903–05, and took a prominent part in the World's and in the National W.C.T.U. Becoming interested in 1888 in methods of thrift teaching used in the public schools of Europe, especially in France and Belgium, she became an ardent advocate of school savings banks. She wrote letters, articles, and pamphlets, spoke in nearly every state in the union urging women's organizations to promote the idea and teachers to undertake the work, and labored with banks and trust companies to persuade them to receive the small deposits. For many years she edited *School Savings,* published from 1907 until 1923 under the name of *Thrift Tidings,* a periodical devoted to the promotion of the project. She saw the movement develop until in 1929 there were 15,598 schools using the system in forty-six out of the forty-eight states, with 4,222,935 depositors, while it had the support of legislators, teachers, and bankers. Mrs. Oberholtzer died at her home in Philadelphia and was survived by two sons.

[*Who's Who in America*, 1920–21; J. S. Futhey and Gilbert Cope, *Hist. of Chester County, Pa.* (1881); *Woman's Who's Who of America*, 1914–15; W. E. Albig, *A Hist. of School Savings Banking* (1930), a pamphlet published by the Am. Bankers Asso.; *N. Y. Times,* Feb. 4, 1930; information as to certain facts from Mrs. Oberholtzer's son, E. P. Oberholtzer of Philadelphia.]   A.L.L.

O'BRIEN, EDWARD CHARLES (Apr. 20, 1860–June 21, 1927), merchant, diplomat, was born in Fort Edward, N. Y., the son of James O'Brien, a well-to-do Irish farmer, and Mary (Walsh) O'Brien. Following his education in the public schools and in the Granville (N. Y.) Military Academy, he engaged for several years in the flour-commission business in Plattsburg, N. Y. The transportation phase of this business turned his attention toward deep waterways, foreign commerce, and maritime shipping, and these were to remain his major interests through life. He served as disbursing clerk in the United States House of Representatives during the Fifty-first Congress (1889–91). In 1892 and 1893 he was United States commissioner of navigation, and, as chief of the Bureau of Navigation of the Treasury Department, he won recognition for his satisfactory handling of the Norwegian and Swedish tonnage rate case. In 1895 he was appointed by Gov. Levi P. Morton commissary-general of the state of New York with the rank of brigadier-general. He resigned three months later to become commissioner of docks of New York City under Mayor Strong. During his four years in office he accomplished extensive dock improvements, acquired for the city over four million square feet of additional wharfage space by securing permission from the War Department to extend the pier head line farther into the North River, and constructed the city's first six recreation piers. Appreciation of his activities in behalf of inland deep waterways, particularly with regard to a proposed ship canal connecting the Great Lakes with the Hudson River, was shown in his appointment as chairman of the opening session of the first annual convention of the International Deep Waterways Association at Cleveland in September 1895. Following his retirement to private life in 1898 he organized and became president of the International Express Company, and of the Cuban and Pan-American Express Company.

In March 1905 O'Brien was appointed envoy extraordinary and minister plenipotentiary of the United States to Uruguay and Paraguay by President Roosevelt. During his four years' residence in Montevideo and Asunción he negotiated and signed a naturalization convention between the United States and Uruguay (Aug. 10, 1908), and an arbitration convention between the United States and Paraguay (Mar. 13, 1909). He was dean of the diplomatic corps at Asunción when the Paraguay revolution of July 2, 1908, occurred. With great coolness and diplomacy, and with the cooperation of his colleagues, he succeeded through his friendly offices in bringing about a cessation of hostilities, risking his life several times during the two days of heavy street fighting. He was afterward thanked by both the successful revolutionists and the defeated government leaders for his service in preventing a much greater loss of life and property than that which actually occurred. He resigned from the diplomatic service in 1909 and subsequently engaged in many enterprises connected with the development of South American ports and internal communications, and Latin-American trade with the United States, at the same time neglecting no opportunity to promote understanding and good will between the South American countries and the United States. At the time of his death he was visiting Montevideo on business connected with the construction of a motor highway joining the capitals of Uruguay and Argentina. He was buried in Troy, N. Y. He had never married.

[*Proc. First Ann. Convention, Internat. Deep Waterways Asso.,* 1895; *Municipal Affairs* (N. Y.), Sept. 1897; U. S. Bureau of Navigation, *Reports of the Commissioner of Navigation,* 1892, 1893; *Papers Relating to the Foreign Relations of the U. S.,* 1908; *Who's Who in America,* 1920–21; *Who's Who in N. Y. City and State* (3rd ed., 1907); *N. Y. Times,* June 22, 1927.]   I. L. T.

O'BRIEN, FITZ-JAMES (*c.* 1828–Apr. 6, 1862), journalist and author, son of James and Eliza O'Driscoll O'Brien, was born in County Limerick, Ireland, where his father was an attorney-at-law. His characteristic exaggerations and the destruction of records in Ireland have deprived us of accurate knowledge of his early years. He received an excellent education, but not, as is often asserted, at Trinity College, Dublin. At an early age he evinced a certain facility in writing verse and he seems to have determined upon a literary career. When he was about twenty-one he settled in London and during the course of two years, there and in Paris, he is said to have spent his inheritance of £8,000. Francis Wolle has recently established that before he came to America O'Brien had contributed at least twenty-seven poems, one story, and twelve articles to English and Irish periodicals. He came to America, probably early in 1852, with letters of introduction to George Pope Morris and others. Through them he was quickly welcomed into New York's literary and Bohemian circles where he became a conspicuous figure. He contributed poems, short stories, and articles to a number of periodicals, the *American Whig Review, Putnam's Magazine, Harper's Weekly, Vanity Fair,* and the *Atlantic Monthly,* but his most important literary association was that of regular contributor to *Harper's Magazine.* From time to time he contributed to the *Evening Post* and the *New York Times,* and for the latter he was once an editorial writer. For James W. Wallack he wrote several plays which gained some popular favor; one of these, *A Gentleman from Ireland,* was presented successfully as late as 1895. He adapted a play for Joseph Jefferson, who was the manager and principal actor at Laura Keene's Theatre, and he once traveled for a short time as literary assistant to H. L. Bateman who was directing a professional tour of Matilda Heron, the actress.

There have been several efforts to arouse public interest in O'Brien as "a neglected genius" and "an enchanted Titan," but they have met with indifferent success. The best of his voluminous poetry is hardly more than clever, spirited verse, and the most effective of his short stories, said to have "electrified" the reading public of the late fifties, have lost the greater part of their appeal. He possessed a facile talent but was hasty and careless in his work. Like many another gifted Irish writer, he was too impatient and undisciplined to cultivate his promising talent. Like several other flickering lights of American literature, he was more significant as a personality than as an author. He was one of the most colorful figures of that Bohemian society that flourished at Windust's, the old Hone House, and Pfaff's in the New York of his day. But the Bohemian "orgies" which afforded him pleasure were confined to late hours, the foaming flagon, and boisterous hilarity. His florid complexion, dark-blue eyes, tiny chin, his heavy, brown cavalry mustache, and his checkered tweed suit were a familiar and welcome sight in those gay and restless circles. He tried to lead the life of a poet and gentleman, retiring with the rising sun and breakfasting at two in the afternoon. During his first six years in New York he lived surrounded by all the trappings of a man of means—an elegant apartment, a large library, and a costly wardrobe. But, beginning in 1858, as a result of that convivial improvidence which marked his career, his waking hours were haunted by waiting landladies, who gradually acquired, in the course of his peregrinations, all his worldly goods. While at times he partially solved his domestic problem by moving into the rooms of such friends as Thomas Bailey Aldrich and William Winter, he was often reduced to the point where he had neither pen, ink, nor paper. The chief distresses of this proud and combative spirit were occasioned by the painful discrepancy between a gentleman's tastes and a hackwriter's income.

Upon the outbreak of the Civil War, O'Brien quickly joined the 7th Regiment of the New York National Guard. When the regiment returned to New York he became active for a time in gathering recruits for a volunteer regiment to be called the McClellan Rifles, but this failed. In January 1862 he was taken on the staff of Gen. Frederick W. Lander. The next month for his gallantry at the battle of Bloomery Gap, he received special and honorable mention, but on Feb. 16 he received a shoulder wound in a skirmish with the enemy which was improperly treated and he died of tetanus on Apr. 6 at Cumberland, Md.

[*Poems and Stories of Fitz-James O'Brien*, collected and edited, *with a sketch of the author by Wm. Winter* (Boston, 1881) contains reminiscences by O'Brien's friends and reprints contemporary comment on his death. It is the best source of information; later articles have added virtually nothing to this publication. Prof. Francis Wolle of the University of Colorado has supplied information about his early career abroad. See also: R. H. Stoddard, "The Best of the Bohemians," *Critic*, Feb. 26, 1881; Paul Fatout, "An Enchanted Titan," *South Atlantic Quart.*, Jan. 1931; Albert Parry, *Garrets and Pretenders: A Hist. of Bohemianism in America* (1933); *War of the Rebellion: Official Records (Army)*, 1 ser. V, p. 406; *N. Y. Times*, Apr. 7, 9, 10, 1862.]　　　　　　　　F. M—n.

O'BRIEN, FREDERICK (June 16, 1869–Jan. 9, 1932), journalist, author, was born in Baltimore, the son of William James and Catherine (McCarthy) O'Brien, and a grandson of an Irish immigrant, John O'Brien, who settled in Baltimore in 1820. His father was a lawyer, a Democrat in the national House of Representatives from 1873 to 1877, and in his later years a judge of the city orphans' court. He died in 1905 a highly regarded citizen and magistrate. Of his four sons two had respectable, commonplace careers in business and law, and a third became a Jesuit and a monsignor, but in Frederick the conventional middle-class pattern was crossed with a thread of waywardness. After a few years (1882–85) at Loyola College, where

he read Herman Melville to more effect than the prescribed books, he shipped out of Baltimore as a common sailor and returned with memories of adventures in Brazil, Venezuela, and Trinidad. When the study of law grew unbearably irksome, he went to sea again—this time to Liverpool on a cattle-boat—trudged the sidewalks of the London East End between the boards of a "sandwich," got back to the United States on a freighter, and until 1894 was a hobo and casual laborer. Then he happened into reporting for the Marion, Ohio, *Mirror*, at $8.00 a week, but soon went over to its rival, Warren Gamaliel Harding's *Star*, at $9.00 a week.

For the next twenty-five years, with respites devoted to globe-trotting, he was a newspaperman, likeable, competent, but hardly distinguished. After serving various papers in New York and San Francisco, he was news editor of the Honolulu *Advertiser*, 1900–01; editor and publisher of the Manila *Cablenews*, 1902–09; and manager of the Riverside, Cal., *Enterprise* and the Oxnard *Courier*, 1910–13. He had been married, May 26, 1897, to Gertrude, daughter of Wakefield Gale Frye of Belfast, Me. They had no children and ultimately separated, O'Brien disappearing among the islands of the South Seas to loaf and invite his soul indefinitely. He returned, however, in wartime, was connected with the California railroad commission and the United States food administration, edited the *Manilla Times* for a few months after the Armistice, and then set out on his second trip around the globe.

His first book, *White Shadows in the South Seas* (1919), was an account of his sojourn in the valley of Atuona, on Hivaoa, in the Marquesas. It was published just in time to strike what was virtually a new reading public, weary of war and of the discipline of military life, baffled by the complexities of contemporary society, and eager to escape, in imagination, to the only half-ruined paradise of O'Brien's romantic narrative. The astounding success of *White Shadows* called forth a number of imitators, helped to revive interest in the work of Herman Melville, Charles Warren Stoddard, and Robert Louis Stevenson, and ensured a ready market for O'Brien's subsequent books, magazine articles, and lectures. *Mystic Isles of the South Seas* (1921) dealt with his travels and experiences on Tahiti and Moorea, and *Atolls of the Sun* (1922) with Paumotu or the Low Archipelago. Like the earlier work, they were written in fluent journalese, showed marked sympathy not only for the native races but for individual natives, and were well laden with anecdote and adventure and a tolerant attitude toward the world in general. O'Brien himself lived the last years of his life at Sausalito on San Francisco Bay. Genial, unpretentious, and reticent about himself, he had friends throughout the world, but perhaps no intimates. He died of a heart ailment, after an illness of six months. His body was cremated, with none of his relatives present, and the ashes strewn on the ocean.

[*Who's Who in America*, 1930–31; J. J. Ryan, *Hist. Sketch of Loyola Coll., Baltimore, 1852–1902* (copr. 1903); E. F. Barker, *Frye Geneal.* (1920); Frederick O'Brien, "The Author of 'White Shadows,'" *Bookman*, Dec. 1920; *The Literary Spotlight* (1924), ed. by John Farrar; *Sun* (Baltimore), Nov. 14, 1905, Jan. 10, 1932; *San Francisco Chronicle*, Jan. 10, 11, 1932; *N. Y. Times*, Jan. 10, 12, 1932.]   G. H. G.

O'BRIEN, JEREMIAH (1744–Sept. 5, 1818), naval officer, was born in Kittery, Me., the eldest son of Morris and Mary (Hutchins) Cain O'Brien. Early in life Morris O'Brien followed the tailoring trade, first in his native city of Dublin, Ireland, and later in the towns of Kittery and Scarborough, Me. In 1765 he moved to Machias, Me., then a frontier town recently settled, and, aided by his sons, engaged with much success in lumbering, the main industry of the settlement. At the outbreak of the Revolution he and his family eagerly espoused the cause of the patriots. On June 2, 1775, there arrived at Machias the Boston sloops *Unity* and *Polly*, convoyed by the schooner *Margaretta*, under the command of Midshipman James Moore of the Royal Navy, for the purpose of obtaining a cargo of lumber for the use of the British army. Determined to prevent the shipping of the lumber, Jeremiah O'Brien with about forty volunteers, including his five brothers, armed with guns, swords, axes, and pitchforks, seized the *Unity*, and after a considerable chase, on June 12 engaged and captured the *Margaretta*, 4 guns, with a loss of seven men on each side. Midshipman Moore was mortally wounded. O'Brien exhibited much enterprise and daring in this "Lexington of the seas," the first naval engagement of the war. By a resolution, dated June 26, 1775, the Massachusetts General Court thanked him and his compatriots for their courage and good conduct.

Under the orders of the Machias Committee of Safety, O'Brien took command of the *Unity*, renamed the *Machias Liberty* and armed with the guns of the *Margaretta*. When, a few weeks after his first fight, the British naval schooner *Diligent* with her tender *Tapnaquish* appeared off Machias, he, with the aid of another vessel, captured the two British ships without firing a

gun. In August 1775 the General Court, recognizing his ability, placed him in command of the *Machias Liberty* and the *Diligent*, thus taking these vessels into the service of the state, the first ships of the Massachusetts navy. O'Brien cruised intermittently with his small fleet, taking a few prizes, until it was put out of commission in the fall of 1776. He next became a privateersman and in 1777 went to sea in command of the ship *Resolution* and captured the British ship *Scarborough* off Cape Negro. Continuing in this service he was captured in 1780 with his vessel, the *Hannibal*, and was confined first in the Jersey prison ship at New York and later in Mill Prison, England, where he suffered considerable hardship. Escaping, he returned to America and in 1781 commanded successively the *Hibernia* and the *Tiger*.

After the Revolution O'Brien lived a retired life at Machias until 1811 when President Madison appointed him collector of customs for the Machias district, a position he held at the time of his death. He was married, to Elizabeth Fitzpatrick, but appears to have left no descendants. In 1900, in recognition of his valuable services in the Revolution, Secretary of the Navy John D. Long named one of the torpedo boats, then under construction, after this gallant officer.

[A. M. Sherman, *Life of Capt. Jeremiah O'Brien* (1902), and *The O'Briens of Machias, Me.* (1904); *Memorial of the Centennial Anniversary of the Settlement of Machias* (1863); G. W. Allen, *Naval Hist. of the Am. Revolution* (1913); G. W. Drisko, *Narrative of the Town of Machias* (1904); *Boston Daily Advertiser*, Sept. 26, 1818.]   C. O. P.

O'BRIEN, MATTHEW ANTHONY (May 1804–Jan. 15, 1871), Roman Catholic preacher and missionary, son of John and Grace (Meagher) O'Brien, was born in the village of Bawn, County Tipperary, Ireland, where his father managed to rear a family of thirteen children from the profits of a distillery. Trained in a local hedge school and at Nenagh, the boy was poorly educated when in April 1826 he sailed on an immigrant ship for Quebec. From Canada, he managed to work his way to Savannah, Ga., and thence to New Orleans, where he had maternal uncles. Apparently, he had a desire to enter the priesthood, because he tramped and labored on boats for his passage until he reached Bardstown, Ky., where he presented himself to Bishop Flaget [*q.v.*], who urged that he become a lay brother in view of his age, irregular education, and aptitude for a trade. This he did in 1827, but the institute at Bardstown failed and was dissolved, whereupon he was enrolled at St. Rose's, Springfield, Ky. This time ill health thwarted his hopes, but he found a friend in an Irish priest, William Byrne, who had established St. Mary's College, Marion County, Ky. Here, from 1829 to 1835, he taught elementary subjects and was tutored in the classics by the rector and by the Jesuit Fathers who took over the institution. At length he was prepared to enter the Dominican seminary of St. Rose's, where he subscribed to the final vows of the Dominicans on Sept. 8, 1837, and was ordained by Bishop R. P. Miles [*q.v.*] in 1839. As submaster and master of novices, he continued his studies and reading. There was little expectation that he would develop into a preacher because of his awkward bearing, diffidence, piercing voice, and wretched memory, but he made an ideal novice-master because of his sound common sense, sincere piety, and marked tact. Hence, in 1842, he was assigned to a similar position at St. Joseph's House of Studies in Perry County, Ohio. Not until 1844 was he given a parish—that of St. Patrick's on Rush Creek near by, a German and Irish settlement, where he built a new church, and as procurator for his order superintended its general construction work. His controversy with a Protestant divine, Thomas Harper, and his missionary tours made him a familiar character in Kentucky, Tennessee, and Ohio.

Soon after returning from a short vacation in Ireland, O'Brien was elected American provincial of the Dominicans, Oct. 30, 1850. While St. Rose's remained his center, he was engaged in establishing St. Joseph's College, which died with the Civil War, in building a number of churches, schools, and convents, including St. Dominic's in Washington, D. C., and in promoting vocations for his own order as well as for the Dominican sisterhoods. He brought the Dominicans to the seaboard and won popularity for the order as he preached missions from the Gulf states to New England. Moreover, he became a magnetic if not a brilliant or erudite preacher, whose heartfelt sermons, interspersed with homely illustrations and unvarnished truths, appealed not only to the lowly but challenged critical scholars like J. A. McMaster and Orestes Brownson [*qq.v.*]. At the end of his term he became prior and pastor at St. Rose's, where he remained from 1854 until ordered to organize a Dominican parish in London, Ontario, in 1861. Two years later, he was recalled to work among the soldiers in Kentucky and to compromise warborn hostilities among the people. He himself was no violent Northern partisan.

As a visiting preacher, O'Brien continued to win attention and incidentally made his share of converts. There were few bishops who were not friends and admirers of the friar and few centers from New York to the Mississippi where he was unknown, stationed as he was at St. Vincent Ferrer's in New York and St. Louis Bertrand's in Louisville. A temperance advocate and a reformer, he had the courage to invade the gambling dens of New Orleans and attack that protected vice. At sixty-six, aged far beyond his years, he fell a victim to pneumonia in Louisville and was buried in the community cemetery at St. Rose's in Kentucky.

[V. F. O'Daniel, *An American Apostle: Matthew A. O'Brien, O. P.* (1923), a detailed, accurate, panegyric; B. J. Webb, *The Centenary of Catholicity in Ky.* (1884); *Freeman's Journal* (N. Y.), Feb. 4, 1871; *Louisville Commercial*, Jan. 17, 1871.]   R. J. P.

O'BRIEN, RICHARD (*c.* 1758–Feb. 14, 1824), mariner, United States consul-general to Algiers, was born in Maine and died in Washington, D. C. In his later years he spelled his name as given above, but during much of his life used the spelling, O Bryen. He was a son of William O Bryen and Rebecca Crane, who were married in 1757 and a few years later went with their four children to Ireland. The father died soon thereafter, leaving his family destitute. Richard, in order to visit his relatives in America, became apprenticed to a sea-captain, and until 1785 led a seafaring life. His formal schooling in consequence of these circumstances was slight; and, according to his own testimony, his reading in youth was limited to a primer, a collection of Aesop's Fables, an arithmetic, the Bible, and a few newspapers (O'Brien to J. L. Cathcart, Nov. 12, 1794, Despatches: Tripoli, II, State Department). The effects of this deficiency O'Brien deplored in later life, although native ability and devotion to the task of becoming a skilful navigator offset them to some extent. During the American Revolution he engaged in privateering and for a time served as a lieutenant on board the brig *Jefferson*. At the end of the war he became master of the ship *Dauphin*, owned by two Philadelphia merchants, but while sailing near Lisbon on July 30, 1785, was captured by Algerine pirates. During the period of his captivity he carried on an extensive correspondence with prominent Americans regarding Algerine affairs; then, when peace was made between the United States and Algiers in September 1795 and he was released, he conveyed a copy of the treaty to Lisbon to be countersigned by the United States' peace commissioner, David Humphreys [*q.v.*]. From Lisbon O'Brien went to London for funds to put the treaty into operation; then returned to Algiers in March 1796; and in June sailed to the United States to transact further business relative to the treaty. The following October he was commissioned to conclude a treaty of peace with Tripoli, and within less than a month had successfully performed the task. In July 1797 he was appointed consul-general to Algiers, in which capacity he served creditably until November 1803. On Mar. 25, 1799, he married Elizabeth Robeson, an Englishwoman, who prior to her marriage had been a maidservant in the household of J. L. Cathcart [q.v.], in America and for a time in Algiers (Cathcart, *Tripoli, post*, pp. 51, 52).

While the United States was at war with Tripoli, O'Brien found living in Barbary more and more irksome, and frequently expressed a desire to return to America. In November 1803 he was relieved by Col. Tobias Lear [q.v.]. For a time thereafter O'Brien aided Commodore Preble in negotiating with the Pasha of Tripoli; then, in December 1804, he returned to the United States. He settled in Philadelphia temporarily, and in 1808 became a member of the Pennsylvania legislature, serving one term in the lower house. In 1810 he established residence on a farm near Carlisle, Pa., and there spent the greater portion of his remaining years.

[*Am. State Papers: Foreign Relations*, vols. I–II (1832–33); Correspondence of J. L. Cathcart (MSS.), in the *N. Y. Pub. Lib.*; Despatches: Algiers, Tripoli, Tunis, etc. (1793–1805), in Archives of Dept. of State, Washington; autobiographical letter in *New-Eng. Hist. and Geneal. Reg.*, Jan. 1896; J. L. Cathcart, *Tripoli, First War with the U. S.* (1901); *Daily National Intelligencer* (Washington, D. C.), Feb. 16, 1824.]

          R. W. I.

O'BRIEN, WILLIAM SHONEY (c. 1826– May 2, 1878), capitalist, operator of Nevada silver mines, was born in Queen's County, Ireland, of humble parentage. He came to America before reaching his majority and took out citizenship papers in the New York marine court on Nov. 3, 1845. For a time he considered going to Texas to seek his fortune, but chose to remain in New York, where he found a job in a store. When gold was discovered in California, however, he was one of the first of the "argonauts" to go. He sailed in the ship *Tarolinta* around the Horn and arrived in San Francisco on July 6, 1849, an event which was yearly celebrated by the passengers of the ship as long as O'Brien lived. In San Francisco he was glad to earn a few dollars by helping to discharge the cargo of the vessel and also to accept a pair of boots, whose donor he unsuccessfully sought in later years. In 1850 he went to Poor Man's

Gulch on Feather River to mine, and there met James C. Flood, his later partner. In the fall of 1851 he returned to San Francisco, where until May 1854 he was a partner successively of Col. W. C. Hoff and Capt. W. J. Rosener in operating mercantile lines.

He then joined James C. Flood in the proprietorship of the Auction Lunch Saloon on Washington Street near Sansome, which during the next twelve years was increasingly patronized by mining men and stock-dealers. From these customers the partners obtained advantageous mining information and thus were able to become successful stock-brokers. They also became interested in several mines in the Grass Valley region and in 1866 felt justified in selling their saloon and concentrating upon the mines. The previous year, with J. M. Walker and John William Mackay [q.v.] they had obtained control of the Hale and Norcross mine on the Comstock lode in Nevada, and here they got their first real start on the road to wealth. In combination with Mackay and with James G. Fair [q.v.], who joined them in 1868, they purchased the Consolidated Virginia and the California mines. Soon thereafter the "Big Bonanza" was struck, from which by January 1875 each of the four had derived a princely fortune. In that year they opened the Nevada Bank of San Francisco, with a capital of $5,000,000 which was subsequently increased to $10,000,000.

O'Brien did not live long to enjoy his good luck. Bright's disease, induced by too generous living, killed him within three years. He died at San Rafael, whither he had been taken in hopes of relief, and was buried in a previously prepared mausoleum in Calvary Cemetery, San Francisco, after a pontifical requiem mass at St. Mary's Cathedral. He was never ostentatious of his fortune and although he bought an elegant private residence he remained more or less foreign to his new surroundings. He was noted for his geniality, being called "the jolly millionaire." He was a life member of the Society of California Pioneers and also of the Exempt Firemen California Engine Company Number 4, whom he had served as foreman in 1855–56, when he was given a silver trumpet. Except for the ownership of his mining stock, his partnership with Flood had been dissolved before his death. His vast fortune, with the exception of $100,000 for charities, went to his two sisters and their children.

[*Daily Alta California* (San Francisco), Sept. 3, 1856, Jan. 13, 1877, May 8, 1878, Oct. 20, 1878; Alonzo Phelps, *Contemporary Biog. of California's Representative Men* (1881); Hugh Quigley, *The Irish Race in Cal. and on the Pacific Coast* (1878); *The Exempt Firemen of San Francisco, Their Unique and Gallant*

Record (1900); Rollin Daggett Scrapbook, I, 118, in Cal. State Library.]   J. E. W.

O'CALLAGHAN, EDMUND BAILEY (Feb. 28, 1797–May 29, 1880), physician, historian, was born in Mallow, near Cork, Ireland, the youngest of a large family. His education included courses at Dublin, Paris, and Quebec, and he was admitted to the practice of medicine in Canada in 1823. His tastes were literary, however, and he became editor of the *Vindicator* at Montreal in 1834. After a year in the Canadian parliament (1836) he participated in Papineau's revolution of 1837, and found it necessary to flee the country. It would have been easy for him to return later, but he chose to remain in Albany, N. Y., where he resumed the practice of medicine and was for a time treasurer of the Albany County Medical Society. At the same time his literary proclivities were manifested. Interest in the anti-rent agitation led him to a study of the Dutch land grants and thence into early New York history. During the years 1842–44 he contributed poetry and historical articles to *The Northern Light*, a monthly published at Albany in the interest of the working class. In these articles was revealed a casual acquaintance with the mass of Dutch records, at that time undamaged by fire, in the office of the secretary of state. O'Callaghan's interest deepened. His early linguistic studies helped him to master Dutch and to produce the *History of New Netherland* (2 vols., 1846–48). This was a much needed antidote for Irving's burlesque *Knickerbocker* and won immediate commendation. Happily the state of New York realized its opportunity and induced the medical practitioner to give all his time to editing the old records, and for twenty-two years (1848–70) this native of Ireland and fugitive from Canada revealed to New Yorkers their Dutch beginnings. The man's energy was prodigious, as is evidenced by the scores of volumes published during those years, and scholars of three generations later marvel at the breadth of knowledge and the accuracy of workmanship shown by the sharp-eyed collator. The volumes most prized by all research students are *The Documentary History of the State of New York* (4 vols., octavo, 1849–51; 4 vols., quarto, 1850–51), and *Documents Relative to the Colonial History of the State of New York* (vols. I–XI, 1853–61). The second series was continued by Berthold Fernow [q.v.], who edited *Documents Relating to the Colonial History of the State of New York* (vols. XII–XV, 1877–87).

Amiability and a fund of Irish wit stood O'Callaghan in good stead with legislators. During his state service he became familiar with the colonial records of the metropolis down the river, had indeed translated some of the minutes of the New Amsterdam burgomasters. His translation was used later by Fernow in *The Records of New Amsterdam, 1653–74* (7 vols., 1897). Finally in 1870 Mayor A. Oakey Hall induced him to change his residence and undertake the editing of the common-council minutes of New York City. In two years' time the editorial work was completed and under the direction of C. A. Alvord [q.v.] the press work had begun (see fifteen volumes, two completely bound and the rest ready for binding, in the custody of the New York Historical Society), but Comptroller Andrew H. Green [q.v.], in the course of his financial reforms after the corrupt reign of the "Tweed ring," halted the publication, leaving the work to be done all over again a generation later (see *Minutes of the Common Council of the City of New York*, 8 vols., 1905). Other noteworthy publications by O'Callaghan include: *A List of Editions of the Holy Scriptures, and Parts Thereof, Printed in America Previous to 1860* (1861); *Journal of the Legislative Council of the Colony of New York . . . 1691 . . . 1775* (2 vols., 1861); *The Register of New Netherland, 1626 to 1674* (1865); *Calendar of Historical Manuscripts in the Office of the Secretary of State, Albany* (2 vols., 1865–66); *Laws and Ordinances of New Netherland, 1638–1674* (1868).

O'Callaghan was twice married: first, to Charlotte Augustina Crampe, who died in 1835, a native of Ireland who was brought to Canada in childhood; and second, May 9, 1841, to Ellen Hawe of Albany. There was one child by each marriage, but both died in infancy.

[J. J. Walsh, "Edmund Bailey O'Callaghan, of New York," with portrait, *Records Am. Cath. Hist. Soc.*, Mar. 1905; J. G. Shea, "Edmund Bailey O'Callaghan," *Mag. of Am. Hist.*, July 1880; *N. Y. Hist. Soc. Quart. Bull.*, Oct. 1923; *Hist. Mag.* (N. Y.), Apr., May 1873; letters (MSS.) in N. Y. Hist. Soc., N. Y. Pub. Lib., and Lib. of Cong.; information regarding marriages from Francis Shaw Guy, "Edmund Bailey O'Callaghan: His Position in American Historiography" (thesis in preparation at Catholic University); Wm. Schroeder, in H. A. Kelly and W. L. Burrage, *Am. Medic. Biogs.* (1920).]   A. E. P.

O'CALLAGHAN, JEREMIAH (1780–Feb. 23, 1861), Roman Catholic priest and writer, was born in County Cork, Ireland, one of fifteen surviving children of Jeremiah and Mary (Twohig) O'Callaghan, pious farmers. Educated for the priesthood, he was ordained in 1805 by Dr. William Coppinger, Bishop of Cloyne and Ross, and appointed to curacies on the Island of Cape Clear and at Aghnakishey. At the latter place, a controversy raged concerning the righteousness of taking interest, especially usurious interest, and O'Callaghan became a fanatic on the subject. Holding cobbeen-men and brokers responsible for the economic ills of the land, such as rack-rents and tithes, he denounced the tacit acceptance of usury by the Church in Ireland and made war upon the interest-takers in the vicinity. When his preaching involved him in difficulty, he applied for a decision to his bishop, who in 1818 transferred him to Ross Carberry, and when he got into trouble again, censured him for not remaining silent on the question of usury.

For more than a decade thereafter, although he carried an *exeat* guaranteeing that he was "of good fame and conversation, under no excommunication," he was something of a wanderer. He went to the College of Picpus in Paris and served at Soissons; returning to Cork in 1820, he opened a classical school at Ross Carberry. Three years later he emigrated with high hopes to New York, but despite the intercession of his friend, John Power [q.v.], Bishop Connolly, who did not relish his anti-capitalistic views, refused to place him. Neither was he accepted by Archbishop Maréchal [q.v.] of Baltimore, nor by Bishop Plessis of Quebec. In Montreal, he wrote *Usury, or Interest, Proved to be Repugnant to the Divine and Ecclesiastical Laws, and Destructive to Civil Society,* for which an irregular publisher was procured in New York. The volume appeared in 1824 and sold readily. The author maintained that the attack on trusteeism which it contained saved the church in New York $3,000 per annum. William Cobbett [q.v.] republished the work (1825, 1828) without the author's knowledge and forwarded him the profits. Cobbett also included a eulogy of O'Callaghan's work in his *History of the Protestant "Reformation" in England and Ireland* (2 vols., 1824–27), which was republished in Rome under the censor. O'Callaghan's book caused no sensation in the Sacred Congregation. Rome ordered him to make peace with his bishop, but the latter would not relent. Neither was O'Callaghan accepted in London, despite the shortage of priests; for a time he gained a livelihood by tutoring in Cobbett's household. In 1830, he returned to New York where Power, now vicar general, recommended him to Bishop Fenwick [q.v.], who accepted him for the diocese of Boston.

Assigned to Vermont, O'Callaghan did such noble service that he is referred to by local historians as the "apostle of Vermont," where "his influence and pastoral zeal radiated far and wide for nearly a quarter of a century" (Byrne, *post,*

II, 467). He traveled enthusiastically through the frontier settlements of French Canadians and Irish emigrants and gathered scattered congregations; he built the first Catholic church in Vermont at Burlington, and rebuilt an enlarged structure after an incendiary fire in 1838; he organized schools and Sunday Schools. Continuing to be a vigorous controversialist, he published *A Critical Review of Mr. J. K. Converse's Calvinistic Sermon* (1834); *The Creation and Offspring of the Protestant Church; also the Vagaries and Heresies of J. H. Hopkins, Protestant Bishop, and Other False Teachers* (1837); *The Hedge around the Vineyard* (1844); *Atheism of Brownson's Review, Unity and Trinity of God, Divinity and Humanity of Christ Jesus; Banks and Paper Money* (1852); and *Exposure of the Vermont Banking Companies* (1854). He renounced none of his views, but republished his *Usury* in 1834 and again in 1856, when he included an account of Jackson's war against the second United States Bank and a reprint of his "Exposure" of banking in Vermont. Removing to Holyoke, Mass., in 1854, he organized a congregation and built St. Jerome's Church. Here, worn out by missionary labors and intellectual harassments, he died seven years later and was buried in his church, where a monument was erected to his memory by loyal parishioners.

[Memoir in *Usury,* etc. (ed. of 1828 and subsequent eds.); William Byrne, *Hist. of the Cath. Church in the New Eng. States* (2 vols., 1899); *Cath. Encyc.,* vol. XV (1912); James Fitton, *Sketches of the Establishment of the Church in New England* (1872); W. S. Rann, *Hist. of Chittenden County, Vt.* (1886); J. R. Jackson, *Hist. of Littleton, N. H.* (1905), vol. II; Zadock Thompson, *Hist. of Vermont* (1842), pt. II, pp. 201–02; E. P. Walton, *The Hist. of the Town of Montpelier, Vt.* (1882), ed. by A. M. Hemenway.]

R.J.P.

OCCIDENTE, MARIA DEL [See BROOKS, MARIA GOWEN, c. 1794–1845].

OCCOM, SAMSON (1723–July 14, 1792), Indian clergyman and missionary, was born at Mohegan, near New London, Conn., and reared, according to his own account, "in heathenism" until he was between sixteen and seventeen years of age, when he was influenced by the exhortations of the Rev. James Davenport [q.v.], an evangelist of the "Great Awakening," to adopt the religion of his white neighbors. From 1743 to 1747 he was a docile and reasonably intelligent pupil of the Rev. Eleazar Wheelock [q.v.], of Lebanon, being the first of the Indians to be trained by that clergyman. Prevented by weakness of the eyes from taking a college course, in 1749 Occom became schoolmaster and minister to the Montauk tribe, on the eastern tip of Long Island, receiving £20 a year from the London

Society for the Propagation of the Gospel, but supporting himself mainly by labors as a farmer, fisherman, cooper, and bookbinder. In the autumn of 1751 he married Mary Fowler, a Montauk Indian, by whom he had ten children. His success among the Indians attracted much attention and in 1759, despite his lack of theological training, he was ordained by the Long Island Presbytery. In 1761 he was sent by Dr. Wheelock on a mission to the Oneida tribe in New York and repeated the journey in the two years following. He left Montauk in 1764 for a home in his native Mohegan and at the end of the following year he accompanied Rev. Nathaniel Whitaker [q.v.], of Norwich, on a journey to England to secure money for Wheelock's Indian Charity School.

Under the patronage of George Whitefield and his followers, including the second Earl of Dartmouth, the mission was an immediate success. An Indian preacher with the garb, mannerisms, and habits of thought of the Puritan divine was a novelty in England, and Occom attracted much attention. He conducted himself with great propriety, modesty, and dignity, winning for himself many friends. In the two years of their stay the envoys collected in England and Scotland over £12,000. Upon his return in 1768 Occom was disinclined to enter upon the missionary work among the Iroquois which Wheelock wished him to undertake, and was strongly opposed to his patron's plan to use the fund collected for the establishment of Dartmouth College; as a result the relations between the two men came to an end. Subsequently he acted as an itinerant preacher to the New England tribes and fell into extreme poverty and occasional intemperance. In 1773 he formed the plan of securing a grant of land from the Oneida tribe, upon which a selected group of New England Indians might settle and there live, undisturbed by encroachments of the whites. The movement was interrupted by the Revolution, but it was resumed in 1784, and Brothertown was established in the next year. Occom finally removed from Connecticut to that region in 1789 and spent the remainder of his life as pastor and adviser of his people.

His appearance was dignified, his voice pleasant, his fluency in English sufficient to enable him to preach without notes, while in the Indian language his brethren esteemed him a great orator. He paid little attention to the dogmas of theology, but centered his efforts upon the emphasis of rules of personal conduct with the citation of simple and pertinent illustrations. His *Sermon Preached at the Execution of Moses*

Paul, an Indian, a moving plea for temperance delivered in New Haven in 1772, was published and went through nineteen editions. He composed a number of hymns, the best known of which is "Awaked by Sinai's Awful Sound," and published an Indian hymnal, *A Choice Selection of Hymns* (1774), which attained three editions. He was a sturdy and uncompromising leader of his people in resisting white encroachment upon Indian lands, an activity which brought upon him great unpopularity in Connecticut, and which was successful in preserving to his followers their possessions in New York.

[Samuel Buell, *A Sermon Preached at Easthampton, Aug. 29, 1759, at the Ordination of Mr. Samson Occum* (1761), contains a biographical sketch. See also W. D. Love, *Samson Occom and the Christian Indians of New England* (1899); M. G. Humphreys, *Missionary Explorers Among the Am. Indians* (1913); L. B. Richardson, ed., *An Indian Preacher in England* (1933), letters of Occom and Whitaker; J. K. Lord, *A Hist. of Dartmouth Coll.* (1913); L. B. Richardson, *Hist. of Dartmouth Coll.* (2 vols., 1932). The greater part of Occom's manuscript diary is in the library of Dartmouth Coll., with a smaller portion in the collections of the Conn. Hist. Soc.]   L. B. R.

OCCONOSTOTA [See OCONOSTOTA, d. 1785].

OCHS, JULIUS (June 29, 1826–Oct. 26, 1888), merchant, promoter of civic welfare, was born at Fürth, in the Kingdom of Bavaria, Germany, where for generations his ancestors had lived. He was the son of Lazarus and Nannie (Wetzler) Ochs. Lazarus Ochs was a man of education and ability; he spoke several languages fluently, and was an authority on rabbinical law. Julius had his father's linguistic gifts and, having received his preliminary schooling at the Hyman-Schwabacher Institute, Fürth, was proficient at an early age in the classics and able to converse in German, English, French, and Italian. When he was thirteen years of age he went to Cologne, where he pursued further studies and, permitted access to the military post there, acquired knowledge which later stood him in good stead. By scholastic ability and taste he seemed destined for a professional career, but at the death of his father he was apprenticed by an elder brother to a bookbinder at Frankfurt-am-Main. Dissatisfied with his lot, he walked 600 miles to Bremen, embarked for New York, at which port he arrived in the summer of 1845, and then made his way to Louisville, Ky., where a brother and two sisters, who had emigrated earlier, were living.

His knowledge of languages attracting attention, he was soon engaged to teach in the Female Academy at Mount Sterling, Ky. Circumstances again conspired to thrust him into business, however, for in a short time the institution met with financial difficulties and was unable to pay salaries. While he was in Mount Sterling the Mexican War began and young Ochs enlisted in a company formed there, of which he was made sergeant and drill master. Its services were not required, however, and he returned to Louisville. During the next dozen years he was associated with various business enterprises, spending much of his time in the South, where his contacts with slavery made him an ardent abolitionist. In Nashville, Tenn., on Feb. 28, 1855, he was married to Bertha, daughter of Joseph Levy. A resident of Cincinnati during the Civil War, he took an active part in local military affairs, organizing in 1861 a company, known as "Julius Ochs Company," which became a part of Lieut.-Col. A. E. Jones's Independent Battalion of Ohio Volunteers and did guard duty in the state. Ochs served both as captain and as adjutant to Colonel Jones. In 1864, having removed to Knoxville, Tenn., he again enlisted, and was an officer in a regiment organized to protect the city from anticipated attack. He continued to reside in Knoxville until 1878 when he went to Chattanooga to become treasurer of the *Chattanooga Times,* which his twenty-year-old son, Adolph, had recently acquired.

Julius Ochs was a man of incorruptible integrity, firm but kind, devoted to the faith of his fathers, yet tolerant, active in public affairs and philanthropically inclined. While living in Knoxville, he was a delegate to the state convention which nominated William G. Brownlow [*q.v.*] for governor and campaigned in his behalf. From 1868 to 1872 he was justice of the peace and member of the Knox County court. As a delegate to the national convention of Liberal Republicans in 1872 he supported Horace Greeley for the presidency. He was one of the commissioners who built the first bridge across the Tennessee at Knoxville. For the little group of Jews in Knoxville he acted as rabbi. At Chattanooga he organized the first humane society there, helped to establish Erlanger Hospital, and was chaplain of the G. A. R. post. Here, too, he was influential in building up a prosperous Jewish congregation, of which he acted as rabbi, and a synagogue erected in 1927 bears the name, Julius and Bertha Ochs Memorial Temple. He was a lover of music and composed some light operas, among them, *The Megilah; or The Story of Esther,* for performance by Sabbath-school children. He died at Chattanooga, where he was buried with distinguished honors. He was survived by three daughters and three sons, the latter all prominent in the journalistic world,

Adolph Simon, publisher of the *New York Times,* George Washington [see Oakes, George Washington Ochs], and Milton Barlow.

[*Official Roster of the Soldiers of Ohio in the War of the Rebellion,* vol. I (1893) ; William Rule, *Standard Hist. of Knoxville, Tenn.* (1900) ; *Chattanooga Times,* June 13, 1927 ; G. W. O. Oakes, *Julius Ochs* (1927).]

H. E. S.

OCHSNER, ALBERT JOHN (Apr. 3, 1858–July 25, 1925), surgeon, was the son of Henry and Judith (Hottinger) Ochsner, Swiss pioneers who settled at Sauk City, Wis. The family claimed direct descent from the great physician Vesalius. Albert was born in Baraboo, the county seat where his father was serving as county treasurer. He was educated in the common schools of Sauk City and Baraboo, and took the degree of B.Sc. at the University of Wisconsin in 1884. After graduation from Rush Medical College, Chicago, in 1886, and an interneship in the Presbyterian Hospital, 1886–87, he took post-graduate work in Vienna and Berlin. He returned to Chicago in 1889 and in 1891 he became chief surgeon of Augustana Hospital, a position he occupied for the rest of his life. Throughout his subsequent career he was connected with medical instruction, first as instructor in histology at Rush Medical College, later as associate professor in surgery. In 1900 he was appointed to the professorship of clinical surgery at the University of Illinois College of Medicine, which he filled for twenty-five years. Though he spoke in a halting manner, without fluency, his words commanded a hearing given to few surgeons of his time. For a quarter of a century his Augustana clinic was one of the outstanding surgical clinics of the country. He was one of the first to remove tonsils as a part of the operation for removal of tubercular glands of the neck, to remove carious teeth as prevention of rheumatism, and to emphasize care of diet in peritonitis and appendicitis and the value of complete rest in septic infections. More than any other Chicago surgeon, he created a school of surgery to carry on his traditions. In addition to his work at Augustana he was chief surgeon at St. Mary's Hospital from 1896 to 1925.

Besides being a frequent contributor to periodical literature, Ochsner was the author of a number of books. Most noteworthy of these are *A Handbook on Appendicitis* (1902), *Clinical Surgery* (1902), *Organization, Management and Construction of Hospitals* (1907), and *The Surgery and Pathology of the Thyroid and Parathyroid Glands* (1910), written in collaboration with R. L. Thompson. He edited *Surgical Diagnosis and Treatment,* which was published in four volumes (1920–22). He was a fellow and one-time president of the American College of Surgeons, a fellow of the Royal Society of Surgeons of Ireland, and of the Royal Microscopical Society of London. He was given the honorary degree of LL.D. from the University of Wisconsin in 1909. During the World War he served in the army in the grade of major. A man of amiable disposition, he yet had strong convictions and was a fearless crusader without thought of compromise in any cause he espoused. He was married on Apr. 3, 1888, to Marion H. Mitchell of Chicago. He died of coronary thrombosis, after a few days' illness, and was buried alongside his parents in the churchyard cemetery at Honey Creek, Wis.

[*Proc. Inst. of Medicine of Chicago*, vol. VI (1926); *Trans. Southern Surgic. Asso.*, vol. XXXVIII (1926); *Medic. Jour. and Record*, Aug. 19, 1925; *Chicago Tribune*, July 26, 1925.]   J. M. P.

OCKERSON, JOHN AUGUSTUS (Mar. 4, 1848–Mar. 22, 1924), engineer, was born in the province of Skane, Sweden, the son of Jans and Rose (Datler) Akerson. When he was two years old, the family, together with a group of relatives and friends, emigrated to America with Chicago as their destination. On the trip overland from New York, both parents and the eldest son died of cholera. John was brought up by relatives who settled near Elmwood, Ill., and received his early training in the Elmwood public schools. After coming to America, the family Anglicized the spelling of their name to Ockerson, conforming to the Swedish pronunciation. In the spring of 1864, when only sixteen, the boy enlisted in the 132nd Illinois Infantry, but was mustered out after less than six months' service. In January 1865, he again enlisted, this time in the 1st Minnesota Heavy Artillery, with which he served until the end of the Civil War.

In 1869 he entered the civil-engineering course at the University of Illinois, graduating in 1873. Upon leaving the University he became principal assistant engineer in the federal Great Lakes Survey, for which he had been recorder during a college vacation, and for five years was engaged in hydrographic, topographic, and triangulation surveys, including the survey for the famous jetties at the mouth of the Mississippi constructed by James Buchanan Eads [*q.v.*]. When the Mississippi River Commission was established in 1879 by act of Congress, Ockerson was appointed its principal assistant engineer in charge of surveys and physical examinations from the source of the river to the Gulf. Nine years later, when the work of the Commission temporarily slackened because appropriations were reduced, he left the service for a short period to engage in a mining venture in Colorado. He returned to his old position in 1890, however, and occupied it until 1898, when he was appointed to a membership on the Commission, which he held until his death. His expert technical knowledge of all the problems connected with river improvement made him at once a leading member of that body and toward the end of his period of service he was the dominant figure on the Commission, usually heading its most important committees.

In his later years, Ockerson was internationally recognized as a leading authority on river and harbor improvement, navigation, and related problems, and developed a large consulting practice at home and abroad. One of his greatest individual achievements, undertaken in 1910, was the construction of levees to control the flood waters of the Colorado River, which threatened to overflow into the Salton Sea. This was not only an engineering achievement of the first magnitude, but since some of the construction and much of the hauling of materials had to be done in Mexican territory, was a task involving many delicate problems in international diplomacy and required administrative skill of a very high order. For the successful completion of this work, Ockerson received personal commendation from President Taft. He was the delegate from the United States to four International Congresses on Navigation (1900, 1905, 1908, 1912) and received many honors and decorations from foreign governments. In 1912 he was elected to the presidency of the American Society of Civil Engineers. His numerous contributions to technical literature were mostly in the form of official reports issued in connection with his work for the Mississippi River Commission. An especially elaborate report, on the opening and maintaining of navigation channels in rivers by hydraulic dredging, based as it was on original observation and experiment, will stand as one of the greatest contributions to this important field: "Dredges and Dredging of the Mississippi River" (*Transactions of the American Society of Civil Engineers*, vol. XL, 1898).

Ockerson was twice married: on Nov. 3, 1875, to Helen M. Chapin, who died in March 1886, and on June 4, 1890, to Clara W. Shackelford, who survived him. His was an outstanding personality; he possessed a powerful and commanding physique and unusual dignity and charm of manner. He was a gifted and persuasive talker on the platform or in private, and one of the most beloved as well as most highly respected members of his profession. He died at his home in St. Louis after an apoplectic stroke.

[Trans. Am. Soc. Civil Engineers, vol. LXXXVIII (1925); Who's Who in America, 1924–25; Illinois Alumni News, May 1924; St. Louis Globe-Democrat, Mar. 23. 1924; personal reminiscences.]   J.I.P.

O'CONNOR, JAMES (Sept. 10, 1823–May 27, 1890), Roman Catholic bishop of Omaha, was born at Cobh, Ireland, where he received his early schooling. At about sixteen years of age, he accompanied his brother, Michael [q.v.], who had just accepted the rectorship of the Seminary of St. Charles Borromeo, Philadelphia, to that city, and began his studies for the priesthood in the seminary. Sent to Rome, he completed his work in theology at the Propaganda and was ordained, Mar. 25, 1848, by Cardinal Franzoni. Returning to America, he served as a missionary priest under his brother, then bishop of Pittsburgh, until 1857, when he was named to the rectorship of St. Michael's Seminary. In addition to the duties of this office, he acted as vicar-general during the bishop's absence in Europe (1859–60). In 1862 he was relieved of his assignment at the seminary by Bishop Michael Domenec, and accepted the rectorship of the Seminary of St. Charles Borromeo, which he retained until June 1872, when he was transferred to the pastorate of St. Dominic's Church, Holmesburg, Pa. Four years later he was appointed second vicar-apostolic of Nebraska and consecrated as titular bishop of Dibona at the Philadelphia seminary by Patrick J. Ryan [q.v.], coadjutor-bishop of St. Louis, on Aug. 20, 1876.

Bishop O'Connor's jurisdiction, which included Nebraska, Wyoming, Montana, and the Dakotas, grew rapidly with the development of the Union Pacific and Burlington railroads, and in 1885, Omaha was made a see, with O'Connor as first bishop, his diocese covering Nebraska and Wyoming. A man of simple habits and marked ability, he won the frontiersmen and retained their good will. Approachable, he ruled his priests with tact, never disturbing any "man who does an honest day's work." Foreseeing the importance of Omaha and cleverly distinguishing permanent from boom towns, he judiciously invested in church properties. Through the generosity of Edward Creighton [q.v.] and his wife Mary, he established a college in Omaha (1879), which, under Jesuit control, became Creighton University. He introduced into the diocese the Franciscan Fathers, Poor Clares, Sisters of Mercy, Religious of the Sacred Heart, Sisters of Providence, and Benedictines, thus ensuring a parochial school system. Along with Katherine Drexel of Philadelphia and Archbishop Ryan, he established the Sisters of Divine Providence (1889), for missionary work among negroes

and Indians. About the same time, he aided in organizing the Catholic Mutual Relief Society of America. A director of the Irish Catholic Colonization Association, he was deeply concerned with the Irish colony of General O'Neil and John McCreary in Greeley County, Nebr., which centered around the town of O'Connor. During his episcopate the original diocesan area, which had twenty-seven priests and 23,000 Catholics, developed into five bishoprics with 210 priests and about 300,000 people; the city of Omaha, which in 1876 had two churches and 2,000 Catholics, had in 1890 nine churches, including the cathedral, and 20,000 parishioners. Of literary remains O'Connor left little, save several articles in the Catholic Quarterly Review. At the time of his death the Daily World-Herald (May 28, 1890) depicted him, editorially, as follows: "A scholar, liberal, though churchly, ambitious yet not arrogant, broadly charitable, actively beneficent, daring yet not aggressive, he stood for the best that can be represented by the churchman in this country."

[Cath. Encyc., XI (1911), 249; A. A. Lambing, Hist. of the Cath. Ch. in the Dioceses of Pittsburg and Allegheny (1880); R. H. Clarke, Hist. of the Cath. Ch. in the U. S. with Biog. Sketches of the Living Bishops, vol. II (1890); Hist. of the State of Nebraska (1882); Appletons' Ann. Cyc. for the Year 1890 (1891); L. B. Palladino, Indian and White in the Northwest (1894); Sadliers' Catholic Directory, 1891; Records Am. Cath. Hist. Soc., vol. III (1891); Omaha Daily Bee, May 28, 1890; Daily World-Herald (Omaha), June 5, 1890.]   R.J.P.

O'CONNOR, MICHAEL (Sept. 27, 1810–Oct. 18, 1872), Roman Catholic prelate, was born near Cork, Ireland, and received his preliminary schooling in Cobh. At the age of fourteen years, he was sent to college in France and then to the Propaganda, Rome, where he was a fellow student of the later Cardinal Cullen of Dublin, F. P. Kenrick [q.v.], and M. J. Spalding [q.v.], and gained distinction in theology, languages, and mathematics. Ordained June 1, 1833, he was awarded a doctorate in divinity the following year and then taught in the Propaganda and in the Irish College. Employed as a linguist, he became intimately acquainted with Gregory XVI. Returning to Ireland, he was a curate in Fermoy and chaplain of the Presentation Convent at Doneraile. About 1839 he accepted Bishop Kenrick's offer of the rectorship of the Seminary of St. Charles Borromeo, Philadelphia. In addition to teaching, he found time to serve stations at Norristown and Westchester and to build St. Francis Xavier's Church in Fairmont.

Transferred to Pittsburgh as vicar-general and rector of St. Paul's Church, which had 4,000 communicants (1841), he built a school and founded a Catholic literary institute (1843). While he was in Rome petitioning that he be allowed to join the Society of Jesus, he was named first bishop of Pittsburgh at the request of the American bishops, and was consecrated in the Irish College by Cardinal Franzoni on Aug. 15, 1843. Obtaining financial aid from the Leopold Verein, seminarians from Maynooth, and a colony of sisters of Our Lady of Mercy from Carlow, Bishop O'Connor returned to Pittsburgh in 1844 and inaugurated a period of diocesan development in keeping with the rapid growth of Western Pennsylvania. Within a decade, when the diocese of Erie was carved from that of Pittsburgh, churches and chapels had increased from thirty-three to eighty-two, priests from sixteen to sixty-four, and communicants from 25,000 to 50,000, of whom one-third were Germans; Boniface Wimmer [q.v.] had established the foundation of his Abbey of St. Vincent's at Beatty; a chapel had been erected for colored people (1844); and *The Catholic* had been established (1844) as a diocesan organ. In addition many educational and philanthropic activities had been put into operation. A cathedral was completed in 1855, for which the bishop procured Pietro Gagliardi's "Crucifixion" when in Rome the previous year. He brought the Passionist Order to the United States, with its establishment in Pittsburgh. During the Know-Nothing excitement, Bishop O'Connor courageously went his way, though he advised his priests to lay aside their clerical garb in order to avoid annoyances.

On the division of the diocese, O'Connor, with characteristic self-effacement, accepted the poorer see of Erie (1853), and Rev. Joshua A. Young was named to Pittsburgh. As a result of popular demand, however, Bishop O'Connor returned to Pittsburgh and Young took Erie. Worn out by his labors, O'Connor sought rest in a tour of Europe and Palestine (1856), and returned more determined than ever to change the mitre for the garb of the religious. Leaving his brother, Father James O'Connor [q.v.], as administrator, he went to Rome with his petition in 1859, and the following year his resignation was accepted (see valedictory, *The Catholic*, June 18, 1860). He thereupon entered the Jesuit novitiate at Gorheim, Sigmaringen, in Germany, and two years later, Dec. 23, 1862, made his solemn profession in Boston. After teaching for a year in Boston College, he was named socius to the provincial of Maryland, with residence at Loyola College, Baltimore. Always interested in the negroes, he founded St. Francis Xavier Church in Baltimore, and even

asked to be sent as a missionary among the slaves of Cuba. This request was denied. In 1871 he returned from a visit to England, with a group of Josephites who were dedicating themselves to the colored missions. Finally, after ten years as a Jesuit missionary during which he traveled from Maine to Louisiana, and into Cuba and Canada, he retired to Woodstock, Md., where on his death he was buried in the Community cemetery.

[R. H. Clarke, *Lives of the Deceased Bishops of the Cath. Ch. in the U. S.* (1888), III, 560–82; A. A. Lambing, *A Hist. of the Cath. Ch. in the Dioceses of Pittsburg and Allegheny* (1880); J. J. O'Shea, *The Two Kenricks* (1904); *Cath. Encyc.*, XII (1911), 122 f.; M. E. Herron, *Sisters of Mercy in the U. S.* (1929); J. G. Shea, *Hist. of the Cath. Ch. in the U. S.* (1890–92), vols. III, IV; Felix Ward, *The Passionists* (1923); *N. Y. Freeman's Jour.*, Jan. 25, Feb. 5, Mar. 26, 1859; *Biog. Sketch of Fr. Michael O'Connor, S. J.* (Woodstock College Press, 1873); *Pittsburgh Commercial* and *Sun* (Baltimore), Oct. 19, 1872; material contributed from the Society's archives at Woodstock, Md.]
R. J. P.

O'CONNOR, WILLIAM DOUGLAS (Jan. 2, 1832–May 9, 1889), journalist, author, civil servant, friend and champion of Walt Whitman, was born in Boston and was of Irish stock with an admixture of Scotch. In his youth he read widely in several literatures and studied art, intending to make it his career, but on coming of age he turned journalist and was employed on the Boston *Commonwealth* in 1853 and on the Philadelphia *Saturday Evening Post*, 1854–59. In 1856 he married Ellen M. Tarr of Boston, whose sympathy and helpfulness were his lifelong good fortune. Their happiness was marred only by the death of their two children. O'Connor was gaining a reputation as a journalist and literary man when he was summarily dismissed from the *Post* for writing too favorably about John Brown of Osawatomie. His rejoinder, concocted in his enforced leisure, was a vivid, vehement Abolitionist novel, *Harrington* (1860), which is still readable. The rest of his life he spent in the government service in Washington as corresponding clerk of the Light House Board, 1861–73; chief clerk, 1873–74; librarian of the Treasury Department, 1874–75; clerk in the Revenue Marine Division (with which the Life Saving Service was connected), 1875–78; and assistant general superintendent of the Life Saving Service, 1878–79. He wrote the annual reports of the Service, giving to them, and especially to the narrative portions, a literary quality seldom encountered in such documents. Years later Sumner Increase Kimball [q.v.] published a volume of extracts from them, *Heroes of the*

Storm (1904), as a tribute to his old friend and adjutant.

The most significant episode in O'Connor's life was his friendship with Walt Whitman, which began with a casual meeting in the office of Thayer & Eldridge, publishers, in Boston, in June 1860. When the poet came to Washington, penniless and friendless, in December 1862, it was O'Connor who came to his assistance, gave him shelter, and found him employment. Of all his services to Whitman, the most famous was the publication of *The Good Gray Poet* (1866), an eloquent philippic against James Harlan [*q.v.*], who, as secretary of the interior, had dismissed the poet from his clerkship. In "The Carpenter" (*Putnam's Magazine*, January 1868) O'Connor made his friend the hero of a tale in which he appears, unnamed, as a mystic savior of mankind. After O'Connor's death three of his stories were republished, with a preface by Whitman, as *Three Tales: The Ghost, The Brazen Android, The Carpenter* (1892). Of his poems the most ambitious was "To Fanny" (*Atlantic Monthly,* February 1871), remarkable for its metrical finesse.

O'Connor was strikingly handsome, graceful, and magnetic, and had the highly combustible temperament of a romantic Irishman of genius: eloquent, high-minded, impetuous, and chivalrous. As the result of a dispute over the merits of negro suffrage, Whitman and he quarreled and were partially estranged from 1872 to 1882; but when Whitman was again in need of a defender O'Connor was at his side, and their friendship remained close until the end. O'Connor was also an ardent Baconian and the author of two pamphlets on the subject: *Hamlet's Notebook* (1886) and *Mr. Donnelly's Reviewers* (1889). In Washington his home was the meeting place of a group of intellectuals that included John Burroughs, Spencer Fullerton Baird, and other men of note. He died in Washington, of paralysis, after a long illness.

[*Appletons' Ann. Cyc.*, 1889; Ellen M. Calder (Mrs. W. D. O'Connor), "Personal Recollections of Walt Whitman," *Atlantic Monthly*, June 1907; S. I. Kimball's introduction to *Heroes of the Storm* (1904); Horace Traubel, *With Walt Whitman in Camden* (3 vols., 1906–14); W. S. Kennedy, *The Fight of a Book for the World* (1926); Clara Barrus, *Whitman and Burroughs, Comrades* (1931); *Evening Star* (Washington), May 10, 1889.]
G. H. G.

O'CONOR, CHARLES (Jan. 22, 1804–May 12, 1884), lawyer, born in New York City, was the son of Thomas and Margaret (O'Connor) O'Connor and the great-grandson of Charles O'Conor who wrote a history of Ireland. In 1839–40, upon visiting Ireland and discovering that his ancestors spelled the name with one "n," he adopted that form. Thomas O'Connor incurred the disapproval of the British authorities by engaging in the Irish rebellion of 1798 and found it wise to emigrate to New York in 1801. He earned a precarious living by writing editorials for the local press, and after his marriage to the daughter of Hugh O'Connor, and the birth of Charles, was able to give his son scarcely any educational advantages. The mother died in 1816, after which Charles was apprenticed to a tar and lampblack manufacturer. At the end of a year he began his legal education as errand boy in Henry Stannard's office, from which he graduated to the office of Stephen P. Lemoine and finally into the office of Joseph D. Fay, where he served as clerk and law student. He was admitted to the bar in 1824, and at the age of twenty, with a capital of only $25, opened his own law office. This was the inauspicious beginning of a career in which he became nationally famous.

Politically O'Conor was a Democrat, with an aspiration for public office, to which, however, he never attained. He attributed his failure to win political recognition to the fact that he was a Roman Catholic and the son of an Irish emigrant. He was nominated for the office of lieutenant-governor of New York in 1848 but was not elected; and in 1872, at the Louisville Convention, he was nominated for president of the United States by the "Straight-out" Democrats. His popularity among Southern Democrats was due to his belief in slavery as a "just, benign and beneficent" institution, and to his firm conviction, often expressed, that there was no constitutional warrant for coercing seceding states. After the Civil War he served as senior counsel for Jefferson Davis when he was under indictment for treason, and along with Horace Greeley went surety for his bail bond. He held only two semi-political offices. In 1846 he was elected a member of the New York state constitutional convention, and in 1853 he was appointed United States district attorney for the southern district of New York, an office in which he served with distinction for fifteen months. He was for ten years treasurer of the New York Law Institute, and in 1869, its president; and he served also as vice-president of the New York Historical Society. Five institutions of learning conferred upon him the doctorate of law. Late in life he retired from practice, built a house on the Island of Nantucket, and there, surrounded by his library of 18,000 volumes, spent his last years.

O'Conor's fame is due almost entirely to his phenomenal success as a lawyer. It was literally true that his life was in his cases, so that they constitute his true biography. He was not a law reformer, did not believe in codification, and opposed it, says David Dudley Field, "with might and main." The papers in his principal cases, bound and bequeathed by him to the New York Law Institute, fill 100 volumes. They cover a period of fifty years. One of the earliest is the case of *Bowen* vs. *Idley* (1 *Edwards Chancery Reports,* 148), in which succession to property depended upon establishing the parentage of an illegitimate child. His most famous cases were probably the following: two cases involving the status of slaves temporarily brought into free states—*Jack* vs. *Martin* (12 *Wendell,* 311; 14 *Wendell,* 507) and *Lemmon* vs. *People* (20 *N. Y.,* 562, see article on William M. Evarts); four testamentary cases, the Parish and Jumel will cases, the Roosevelt Hospital case (43 *N. Y.,* 254), and *Manice* vs. *Manice* (43 *N. Y.,* 303); the Tilden-Hayes election contest; the Tweed cases; and the Forrest divorce case. He was a master of the law of uses and trusts, and of the law of wills, and seemed equally at home in commercial and corporation law, a fact evidenced by his conduct of the North American Trust & Banking Company cases (15 *N. Y.,* 9); and of the case of *Ogden* vs. *Astor* (4 *Sandford,* 311). This latter case involved intricate commercial dealings between Ogden and the two Astors, John Jacob and William B., running over a period from 1816 to 1850.

The two cases which brought him most fame were the Tweed litigation and the Forrest divorce suit. In the former of these he represented the state of New York, as special deputy attorney-general. The chief counsel opposed to him was David Dudley Field [*q.v.*]. Although these suits resulted in the dissolution of the "Tweed ring," they did not, in the judgment of O'Conor, give to the law an interpretation necessary to protect the public from corruption in office. His view of the result is expressed in the title given by him to a collection of documents which he published in 1875: *Peculation Triumphant: Being the Record of a Four Years' Campaign against official Malversation in the City of New York. A. D. 1871 to 1875.*

Twenty years before the Tweed cases, O'Conor, by his brilliant conduct of the Forrest divorce case, had established himself as the ablest member of the New York bar. In 1837, Edwin Forrest, the tragedian, married Catherine N. Sinclair in England. In 1849, after having made their home in New York for several years, they agreed upon a permanent separation. Subsequently Forrest unsuccessfully sought a leg-islative divorce in Pennsylvania, and then cross-suits for divorce were brought by both in New York. O'Conor appeared for Mrs. Forrest in a trial which lasted from Dec. 16, 1851, to Jan. 26, 1852, and resulted in a decree of absolute divorce with alimony. Justice Benjamin R. Curtis said at the time that O'Conor's management of the case was "the most remarkable exhibition of professional skill ever witnessed in this country" (Curtis, *post,* p. 167). The validity of the divorce and the award of alimony were bitterly contested by Edwin Forrest through legal proceedings which were finally decided against him on last appeal in 1862. Twenty-five years after the original suit, it was charged in the New York papers that, far from acting for Mrs. Forrest without compensation, O'Conor had in fact kept most of the awarded arrears of alimony for himself, contrary to an actual understanding with his client, and contrary to a public belief which he had allowed to go uncorrected. The venerable counselor, then seventy-two years old, himself presented these charges to the Association of the Bar of the City of New York and demanded an investigation. A committee was appointed which, after examination of evidence, reported that the charges were without foundation.

O'Conor was married in 1854 to Cornelia (Livingston) McCracken, the daughter of Francis A. Livingston and the widow of L. H. McCracken. Their married life was unhappy and they agreed to live apart. Physically O'Conor was tall and spare, and possessed of a physique which for strength, said Joseph H. Choate, seemed to be made of gutta-percha and steel springs. He was renowned as a pedestrian and in his long walks from Wall Street to Washington Heights, wearing an ill-fitting suit of black broadcloth and a rusty high hat, was the counterpart of the early stage lawyer. He had piercing gray eyes, a finely chiseled Irish face, and a square chin fringed with a white beard.

[H. E. Gregory, "Chas. O'Conor," in *Great Am. Lawyers,* vol. V (1908), ed. by W. D. Lewis; John Bigelow, "Some Recollections of Chas. O'Conor," *Century Mag.,* Mar. 1885; Irving Browne, "Chas. O'Conor," the *Green Bag,* Jan., Feb., 1895; J. C. Walsh, "Chas. O'Conor," *Jour. Am. Irish Hist. Soc.,* vol. XXVII (1928); Theron G. Strong, *Landmarks of a Lawyer's Lifetime* (1914); *Address of Chas. O'Conor to the Bar Asso. of the City of N. Y.* (1876); *Superior Court of the City of N. Y.: Catharine N. Forrest, Respondent, against Edwin Forrest, Appellant* (1855); B. R. Curtis, *A Memoir of Benjamin Robbins Curtis* (1879), vol. I; *N. Y. Times,* May 14, 1884.]
F. C. H.

OCONOSTOTA (d. 1785), Cherokee chief, lived at Great Echota, the Overhill town of sanctuary on the south side of the Little Tennessee River in what is now Monroe County, Tenn. His name was spelled in various ways, such as Ouconnastote or Occonostota, and he was often called Great Warrior. In 1756, while DeBrahm was building the ill-fated Fort Loudoun five miles away from his home, Oconostota, with Attakullaculla, organized an expedition to divert possible French interference. Three years later he led thirty-two Cherokee to Charleston in order to offer satisfaction for the ravages of the young warriors who, outraged at the treatment they received in Virginia on their way home from helping the Americans in the expedition against Fort Duquesne, had attacked the straggling frontier settlements. When his delegation was repulsed by Gov. William Henry Lyttelton [q.v.] against the advice of Lieut.-Gov. William Bull [q.v.], seized, and, in violation of its safe-conduct, was imprisoned at Fort Prince George, he himself was released through the efforts of Attakullaculla. Under such circumstances he signed an agreement to reëstablish peace and to consider his imprisoned companions as hostages, but neither he nor any other Cherokee ever showed any evidence of considering himself bound by that agreement. Instead he devoted all his energies to repaying treachery with equal treachery. During the attack on Fort Prince George early in 1760, he gave the signal to shoot down Lieutenant Cotymore as he emerged from the stockade in answer to an invitation to parley. When his forces proved unable to take the fort and to rescue his companions, whom he did not yet know to have been massacred immediately after the murder of Cotymore, he led the Cherokee against the frontier settlements. A little later he appeared in command of the Indians before Fort Loudoun and was responsible for the massacre of its defenders upon their surrender.

As it became evident that he could not overcome the white forces he seems to have reconciled himself to the situation, at least for the moment. It is probable that he went to England in 1762 with Timberlake's party in which Outacity [q.v.] cut so picturesque a figure (*Journals of the House of Burgesses, 1761–65*, p. xvii). He was the leader of the Cherokee and made the principal speech for the treaty of peace with the Iroquois at Johnson Hall in 1768. In the negotiations with Richard Henderson [q.v.] at Sycamore Shoals in 1775 he opposed the sale of Cherokee lands with great eloquence (for his speech see James Phelan, *History of Tennessee*, 1888, pp. 18–19), but in the end he seems to have signed the deed, although after his death his signature was denied by the Cherokee (Ramsey,

post, p. 120; *American State Papers: post*, p. 42). During the Revolution he fought on the side of Great Britain. Defeated, driven to a retreat in the mountains, helpless at seeing his lands ravaged by war and overrun by settlers, he made his peace with the state governments. In 1782, old and broken, he resigned his leadership to his son, Tuksi, the Terrapin, from whose uncertain grasp, however, it at once passed to the Tassel, a chief friendly to the newly organized states.

[*A Short Description of the Province of S. C. . . . Written in . . . 1763* (1770), repr. in B. R. Carroll, *Hist. Colls. of S. C.* (1836), vol. II; Alexander Hewat, *An Hist. Account of . . . S. C.* (1779), II, 201–54; J. H. Wynne, *A General Hist. of the British Empire* (1770), II, 273–82; "DeBrahm's Account," *Early Travels in the Tenn. Country* (1928), ed. by S. C. Williams, p. 193; E. B. O'Callaghan, *Docs. Rel. to the Col. Hist. of . . . N. Y.*, vol. VIII (1857); John Haywood, *The Civil and Pol. Hist. of Tenn.* (1823), App., pp. 488–500; *Journals of the House of Burgesses of Va., 1758–61* (1908), *1761–65* (1907), p. xx, *1770–72* (1906); *Cal. of Va. State Papers* (1875–93), I, 380, 602, III, 171, 234, 398, 527, IV, 54; J. G. M. Ramsey, *The Annals of Tenn.* (1853), pp. 50–61, 117–215; date of death from *Am. State Papers: Indian Affairs*, vol. I (1832), p. 42, and *Cal. of Va. State Papers*, IV, 54.]   K. E. C.

ODELL, BENJAMIN BARKER (Jan. 14, 1854–May 9, 1926), governor of New York, was born at Newburgh, N. Y., the eldest son of Benjamin Barker and Ophelia (Bookstaver) Odell and a descendant of William Odell who emigrated from England and settled in Fairfield, Conn., about 1644. His father was in business at Newburgh and, attaining prominence in politics, served for several terms as mayor. At eighteen, after attending the public schools and the Newburgh academy, the son joined the freshman class of Bethany College in West Virginia but transferred to Columbia College (Columbia University), where he excelled in athletics. He left before graduation, however, to enter business. Beginning on an ice-delivery route in Newburgh owned by his father, he engaged in the work with zest, quickly developed initiative, and succeeded in winning new customers. In a few years he had greatly widened his acquaintance, so that when he began to take an interest in politics he already had a large circle of personal friends in and about Newburgh. He was able, without great difficulty, to replace local Democratic majorities with Republican.

When thirty years of age he was made a member of the Republican state committee, and for twenty-five years thereafter he was a power to be reckoned with in the party councils. In 1894, without seeming to have personal ambition in the matter, he was persuaded to take the nomination for Congress in the Newburgh district and was reëlected, but his service at Washington was without distinction. His interest in state politics, however, was stronger than ever. Before the end of his second term in Congress he was made chairman of the Republican state executive committee. When the war with Spain gave prominence to Theodore Roosevelt, Odell was quick to suggest him as the Republican candidate for governor. The victory of the Republican nominee in a doubtful year, 1898, enhanced the state chairman's prestige among the party chieftains. In 1900 Odell himself was named for the governorship and in the McKinley-Roosevelt sweep of that year had no difficulty in carrying the state by a large majority. On entering office he promised a business man's administration. His first efforts were directed toward economies in the state government and in this he made marked headway. He understood and decried the wasteful organization and working of state bureaus. Most of the hostile criticism in his first term had to do with his retention of the party chairmanship while serving as governor. In 1902 he was nominated for a second term and was elected by a greatly reduced plurality. In his administration the state policy of indirect taxation was carried to the point where direct taxation practically ceased. Even his political opponents conceded his efficiency in office. He was called the most successful governor since Tilden (J. L. Heaton, *The Story of a Page*, 1913, pp. 178, 188).

He was the first of the so-called "machine" Republicans to defy the boss rule of Thomas C. Platt. He made appointments without consulting Platt and after the expiration of his second term as governor he continued his independent attitude as chairman of the Republican state committee. He was a thorough-going realist in politics; his whole success was based on his capacity to analyze and predicate actualities. In that, too, he was like Tilden. After his return to unofficial life his career as a party leader was uneven. Having declared himself in favor of Frank S. Black to succeed Chauncey M. Depew in the United States Senate, he felt compelled to withdraw his support from that movement and to acquiesce in Depew's reëlection in January 1905. The insurance investigation of 1905 and 1906 upset his plans and gave Hughes the Republican nomination. Thereafter Odell never scored an important success; in 1910 he announced his retirement from politics. He was married first, in 1877, to Estelle Crist, who was drowned in the Hudson River in 1888; and second, in 1891, to Linda (Crist) Traphagen, the widowed sister of his first wife. She, with two sons and a daughter, survived him.

[*Public Papers of Benjamin B. Odell* (4 vols., 1907); C. W. Thompson, *Party Leaders of the Time* (1906), pp. 104–08, 399–411; *Official New York from Cleveland to Hughes*, ed. by C. E. Fitch (1911), vol. I; *Who's Who in America*, 1924–25; H. F. Gosnell, *Boss Platt and his N. Y. Machine* (1924); *The Autobiog. of Thomas Collier Platt*, ed. by L. J. Lang (1910), p. 460; *Portrait and Biog. Record of Orange County, N. Y.* (1895); *Pedigree of Odell of U. S. and Canada* (1894), comp. by Rufus King; Robert Bolton, *The Hist. of ... Westchester* (1881), vol. II; *N. Y. Herald*, Dec. 28, 1902; *N. Y. Tribune*, Jan. 3, 14, 22, May 6, 1906; *N. Y. Times*, May 10, 1926; Odell's testimony in *Barnes* vs. *Roosevelt* on May 2, 1915, 3 *N. Y. Supreme Court Reports, Appellate Division, 4th Department*, 1826–36.]
W. B. S.

ODELL, JONATHAN (Sept. 25, 1737–Nov. 25, 1818), Loyalist, was born in Newark, N. J. His father, John, was descended from William Odell who came from England to Concord, Mass., in 1639 or earlier and some five years later settled at Fairfield, Conn.; his mother, Temperance, was a daughter of the Rev. Jonathan Dickinson [*q.v.*], first president of the College of New Jersey, now Princeton University. Young Odell was graduated from the College of New Jersey in 1759, was educated as a physician, and served as a surgeon in the British army. While stationed in the West Indies he left the army to go to England, where he studied for the ministry, being made deacon Dec. 21, 1766, in the Chapel Royal, St. James's Palace, and ordained priest in January 1767. During his stay in England he exhibited a talent for poetry. In July 1767 he was inducted by Gov. William Franklin [*q.v.*] into the office of missionary to St. Ann's Church (afterward St. Mary's) in Burlington, N. J., under the Society for the Propagation of the Gospel. In the same capacity he also served a church at Mount Holly. On July 25, 1771, as a side issue to help sustain his family, he began to practise medicine at Burlington. He married Anne, daughter of Isaac De Cou of Burlington, May 6, 1772. On Nov. 8, 1774, he was elected a member of the New Jersey medical society.

With the outbreak of the Revolution, Odell was found a strong partisan on the side of the Crown. On June 4, 1776, verses of his assailing the American position were sung by British prisoners then confined in the Burlington jail. This circumstance brought upon him much condemnation by the public and his case came up before the Provincial Congress. On July 20 he was ordered to be placed on parole whereby he should keep within a circle of eight miles from the Burlington County courthouse and on the east side of the Delaware River. He kept this parole till December, when he took refuge in Governor Franklin's house, and on Dec. 18 escaped to New York City. Later, Oct. 3, 1778, the grand jury of Burlington County brought in an inquisition against him for treason. He remained within British lines until the close of the war and was held in such esteem as to be intrusted with an important rôle in the negotiations between Benedict Arnold and British headquarters. From the beginning of the secret correspondence, in 1779, Odell acted as André's go-between, meeting the messengers, deciphering the letters received, and, under various pseudonyms, corresponding with Arnold's agent. At the same time he had the approval of Headquarters in writing and publishing sharp essays and satirical verses in Rivington's *Royal Gazette* and other newspapers. These stinging verses engaged much attention on both sides, and were among the most influential published during the period. Many of them were collected by Joel Munsell [*q.v.*] in *The Loyal Verses of Joseph Stansbury and Doctor Jonathan Odell* (Albany, 1860). Less poetic than Stansbury [*q.v.*], seldom showing playfulness or humor, Odell has been described as possessing "invincible tenacity, a deathless love, a deathless hate," while the same critic says that no one on the Loyal side "approaches Odell either in passionate energy of thought or in pungency and polish of style" (Tyler, *post*, II, 129, 80). Few public men in New Jersey escaped the lampoons of his verse or his prose. He became chaplain of a regiment of Pennsylvania Loyalists, translated French and Spanish papers, and was assistant secretary to the Board of Directors of Associated Loyalists. On July 1, 1783, he became assistant secretary to Sir Guy Carleton, then commander-in-chief of the British forces. He accompanied Carleton to England soon after the evacuation of New York, taking with him his wife and three children. In 1784, however, he returned to the Loyalist province of New Brunswick, Canada.

The Doctor had been greatly beloved by his Burlington congregation despite his attitude toward the war, and upon settling in New Brunswick he became registrar and clerk of the province, with a seat in the executive council, at a salary of £1,000. He continued in the former office until 1812, when he was succeeded by his only son, William Franklin Odell, godson of Gov. William Franklin. The younger Odell held the office for thirty-two years, dying in 1844. Jonathan Odell died at Fredericton, N. B., in 1818. His wife survived him, remaining in Fredericton until her death in 1825.

[E. M. Woodward and J. F. Hageman, *Hist. of Burlington and Mercer Counties, N. J.* (1883), pp. 76–77; E. A. Jones, "The Loyalists of New Jersey," *N. J. Hist. Soc. Colls.*, X (1927), 155; Lorenzo Sabine, *Biog. Sketches of Loyalists of the Am. Rev.* (1864), II, 122–23; G. M. Hills, *Hist. of the Church in Burlington* (1876); *Archives of the State of N. J.*, 2 ser. II (1903), 543; F. B. Lee, *N. J. as a Colony and as a State* (1902), II, 299–305; *Winslow Papers, A.D. 1776–1826* (1901), ed. by W. O. Raymond; J. W. Lawrence, *The Judges of N. B. and Their Times* (n.d.), ed. by A. A. Stockton; *New-Eng. Hist. and Geneal. Reg.*, Jan. 1892, pp. 20–21; M. C. Tyler, *The Lit. Hist. of the Am. Rev.* (1897), II, 97–129; information from the Sir Henry Clinton Papers in the Wm. L. Clements Lib., through the courtesy of Miss Jane Clark.]
A. V–D. H.

ODENHEIMER, WILLIAM HENRY (Aug. 11, 1817–Aug. 14, 1879), Episcopal bishop, was born in Philadelphia, the son of John W. and Henrietta (Burns) Odenheimer. He received his early education at St. Paul's College, Flushing, L. I., under Dr. W. A. Muhlenberg [*q.v.*], graduated at the University of Pennsylvania in 1835, and at the General Theological Seminary in 1838. He was made deacon Sept. 2, 1838, and ordained priest Oct. 3, 1841, by Bishop Henry U. Onderdonk. Upon admission to the diaconate he became assistant rector of St. Peter's Church, Philadelphia, where in 1841 he succeeded William Heathcote De Lancey [*q.v.*] as rector, remaining in this position until his elevation to the episcopate. St. Peter's Church became during his rectorship one of the most flourishing parishes in the community. He was among the first of Episcopal clergymen in America to establish in his parish a daily service and a weekly celebration of the Holy Communion, practices which have long since become common. So effective was his administrative work, as well as his ministry to his people, that he became known as the "model parish priest." During his rectorship he made two journeys to Europe, one of which, in 1852, was extended to include a visit to the Holy Land. On his return he delivered a series of lectures in St. Peter's on his travels, which formed the basis of a volume, *Jerusalem and Its Vicinity*, published in 1855.

Elected bishop of New Jersey, May 27, 1859, he was consecrated in St. Paul's Church, Richmond, Va., Oct. 13, 1859, during the session of the General Convention in that city. He carried on the work of his diocese with marked ability, combining distinguished scholarship with unusual administrative capacity. He was twice elected assistant secretary to the House of Bishops. During his episcopate the diocese, which included the entire state of New Jersey, grew so rapidly that it became necessary to divide the territory into the Diocese of New Jersey and the Diocese of Northern New Jersey (later the Diocese of Newark). Bishop Oden-heimer was elected to the latter, thus becoming its first bishop. Soon after his removal to the northern diocese in November 1874, his convention granted him a leave of absence for six months because of failing health. This period he spent in England. Though he returned improved in health, he suffered for the remainder of his life through physical infirmity, but carried on his work with energy and courage.

While he was of gentle disposition, both his sermons and his charges to his convention were marked by forthrightness. His published works include: *The True Catholic No Romanist* (1843); *Thoughts on Immersion* (1843); *The Origin and Compilation of the Prayer Book* (1844); *Bishop White's Opinions* (1846); *The Young Churchman Catechized* (2 parts, 1846, 1859); *The Private Prayer Book* (1851); *The Devout Churchman's Companion* (1853); *The Clergyman's Assistant in Reading the Liturgy* (1847); *The Sacred Scriptures, the Inspired Record of the Glory of the Holy Trinity* (1862); *The Church's Power in Her Controversy with Anti-Christ* (1865); *Canon Law* (1868). In 1881 his widow published a volume of his sermons, with a memoir. The essay on Canon Law, written for the alumni of the General Theological Seminary, was the first contribution on the subject of church law published for the Protestant Episcopal Church in the United States. Odenheimer edited *The Celebrated Treatise of Joach. Fortius Ringelbergius, De Ratione Studii* (1847), translated from the Latin, and, in collaboration with Frederic M. Bird, published *Songs of the Spirit* (1871). He died at Burlington, N. J., survived by his wife, Anne D. R. (Shaw), and by two daughters.

[*Sermons by the Rt. Rev. Wm. H. Odenheimer, with an Introductory Memoir* (1881); W. S. Perry, *The Bishops of the Am. Church* (1897); H. G. Batterson, *The Am. Episcopate* (3rd ed., 1891); *The Churchman*, Aug. 23, 30, 1879; *Newark Daily Advertiser*, Aug. 16, 1879. Names of mother and wife obtained from newspaper files at Hist. Soc. of Pa., through the courtesy of Rev. E. M. Jefferys.]

G. E. S.

ODIN, JOHN MARY (Feb. 25, 1801–May 25, 1870), Roman Catholic prelate, was born at Ambierle, France. Although he was the seventh child of a family of ten, his parents, Jean and Claudine Marie (Seyrol) Odin, were able to send him to classical schools at Roanne and Verrière and, later, to colleges at L'Argentière and Alix. Deeply religious, he entered the Sulpician seminary at Lyons, where he became interested in the American missions. He answered the appeal of Bishop Louis G. V. Dubourg [*q.v.*] for volunteers and accompanied

him in 1822 to New Orleans. Immediately he was sent to the Lazarist seminary at the Barrens, Mo., where he studied theology under Dr. Joseph Rosati [*q.v.*]. Joining the priests of the Mission, he was ordained May 4, 1823. As a missionary to Arkansas, as an instructor in theology, and as director of the seminary at the Barrens, Father Odin gained renown for both zeal and scholarship. In 1833, he was selected by Bishop Rosati as his theologian at the Second Provincial Council of Baltimore, which commissioned him to take its decrees to Rome. For two years he carried on a crusade in behalf of the western missions, seeking money and recruits in the Continental seminaries. On his return to the United States, he was assigned to Cape Girardeau, where he opened a school and attended outlying stations.

In 1839 Odin, as the Vice-Prefect Apostolic of Bishop John Timon [*q.v.*], departed for Texas, where he was destined to serve for a score of years as a simple missionary, journeying on horseback among the Comanche and Tonakanie tribesmen, visting Catholic communities, tracing isolated co-religionists, repairing Spanish missions, building churches and chapels in far-flung settlements, fostering colonization, and training disciples. In 1841 he refused the coadjutorship of Detroit, since Timon insisted that a bishop could easily be found for Detroit while Texas might wait long for another apostle. Tactful in handling politicians and empresarios who solicitously gave him attention because of his colonizing activities, he obtained the restoration of the old Spanish church properties, including the Alamo. In 1842 Texas was erected into a vicariate-apostolic with Odin as administrator under the title of Bishop of Claudiopolis; he was consecrated on Mar. 6, by Archbishop Antoine Blanc [*q.v.*]. Three years later, while in Europe, he secured the services of a number of French, German, and Irish priests, as well as material assistance from Belgium, the Society of the Propagation of the Faith at Lyons, and the Leopoldine Society of Vienna. He returned in time to attend the Sixth Provincial Council, which, in view of the political situation, urged that Texas be made a bishopric. Such action was taken and Rome appointed Odin to the see of Galveston in 1847. Convinced of the need of schools, he appealed to the religious communities for aid. The Ursulines from New Orleans established a convent and academy at Galveston (1847); the Ladies of the Incarnate Word came to Brownsville (1852); the Oblates of Mary Immaculate appeared in 1849 and soon founded the College of the Immaculate Conception; the

Brothers of Mary established St. Mary's College, long known as the French school, at San Antonio (1852), with other academies at Brownsville, Brazoria, and Laredo; the Conventual Franciscans busied themselves with the care of German and Polish settlers (1852); and the Benedictines revived the mission of San José (1860). Tender in the treatment of priests and people, devoted to the exiled Mexicans, appreciative of Protestant good will, and ready to minimize the Know-Nothing persecutions, Odin was esteemed as a saintly man and a loyal Texan. It was with regret that he accepted promotion to the archbishopric of New Orleans (Feb. 15, 1861) and withdrew from his well-ordered diocese.

No longer young but still indomitable, Odin continued to work energetically in the New Orleans of Civil War days. A Southern adherent of moderate views, he managed to survive the militarism of General Butler and General Banks and to meet the problems of physical and spiritual reconstruction. That he did so with boldness his printed pastorals indicate. In 1867 he journeyed to Rome in the interest of his diocese; two years later, despite feeble health, he attended the Vatican Council, where he obtained the appointment of Napoleon J. Perché [*q.v.*] as his coadjutor with the right of succession. Worn out, he sought relief from the sessions of the Council in his native village, where he died, his body being buried in the shrine at which he had worshipped as a child.

[R. H. Clarke, *Lives of the Deceased Bishops of the Cath. Church in the U. S.,* vol. II (1888) ; *Cath. Encyc.,* XI (1911), 208 ; J. G. Shea, *A Hist. of the Cath. Church in the U. S.,* vol. IV (1892) ; *Vie de Mgr. Jean-Marie Odin* (Paris, 1896), translated in part in *Annals Cong. of the Miss.,* vols. II, III (1895–96) ; M. A. Fitzmorris, *Four Decades of Catholicism in Texas, 1820–1860* (1926) ; C. G. Deuther, *The Life and Times of Rt. Rev. John Timon* (1870) ; *Records of the Am. Cath. Hist. Soc.,* June 1903, Sept. 1904 ; *N. Y. Freeman's Jour.,* June 8, 1861, Sept. 26, 1863, Feb. 27, 1864, July 9, 16, 1870 ; *Morning Star and Cath. Messenger* (New Orleans), June 26, 1870.]   R. J. P.

O'DONNELL, THOMAS JEFFERSON (June 2, 1856–June 11, 1925), lawyer, lived and died in the fighting spirit of his Irish forebears. His father, Michael, and his mother, Amy Winifred O'Connell, the latter a relative of the great Irish liberator, Daniel O'Connell, came to America from Ireland in search of political liberty and economic opportunity. Their son Thomas Jefferson, one of ten children, was born in Mendham Township, Morris County, N. J. The boy, who was educated in the local public school and in William Rankin's academy in Mendham, attracted attention in the community by his mental ability and oratorical powers. Soon after he

was graduated from the academy in 1873 he was made sub-editor of the *Morris Republican* of Morristown; four years later he founded the *Morris County Chronicle.* During his journalistic days he acted as correspondent for the *Sun* and the *New York Herald* and published a handbook history of Morristown. From 1876 to 1878 he read law in the offices of Frederick A. De Mott and of George T. Werts of Morristown. In 1879 he moved to Denver, Colo., and there spent the remainder of his life in the practice of law. Alert, tenacious, independent, and fearless, he became one of the most noted trial lawyers of the Rocky Mountain region. He was at his best when representing some unfortunate person against whom was arrayed, unjustly in his opinion, the power of the State, or of wealth, or of a hostile press. He was one of the organizers of the Denver Bar Association and its president in 1894, president of the Colorado Bar Association in 1916–17, and for many years one of the most active members of the American Bar Association.

Active in politics, O'Donnell was a power in the Democratic party in his adopted state and a delegate to the national conventions of the party of 1892, 1896, and 1904. At the first of these conventions he violently objected to President Cleveland's currency and financial policies, opposed his renomination, and on the adjournment of the convention returned to Colorado to join with other disaffected Democrats in a bolt of the party ticket. He was chairman of the convention of Colorado Democrats in 1892 which indorsed the candidacy of the Populist leaders, James B. Weaver and James G. Field. In the Democratic National Convention of 1896 he represented Colorado on the steering committee of the silver forces which dominated the session. He was several times a candidate for public office but never won an election. In 1883 he received the Democratic nomination for county judge in Denver; in 1890 he was defeated as a candidate for a seat in the House of Representatives; in 1911 he was one of the unsuccessful contestants for the United States senatorship before a deadlocked state legislature in which ninety-two ballots were taken in a vain attempt to fill a vacancy; and in 1912 he was defeated in the state primary election by John F. Shafroth for the Democratic nomination for United States senator.

An uncompromising fighter by nature, and a master of denunciation and invective, he naturally made enemies who struck back at him whenever opportunity presented itself in a political campaign. Through the midst of acrimonious personal and party contests, he continued to serve the public in various non-partisan capacities; he was a member of Denver's charter convention in 1903; was vice-president and active head of the Colorado commission to the St. Louis Exposition in 1904; a member of the National Conference of Commissioners on Uniform State Laws; and an ardent champion of the Allied and American cause in the World War, in which he took a leading part in relief and patriotic organizations. He was married, on Oct. 24, 1881, to Kathrine Dwyer of St. Louis who with three of their five children survived him.

[See *Who's Who in America*, 1924–25; T. H. Hood, "Thomas J. O'Donnell," *Report of the Colo. Bar Asso.*, vol. XXVIII (1925); W. F. Stone, *Hist. of Colo.*, vol. III (1918); J. C. Smiley, *Semi-Centennial Hist. of the State of Colo.* (1913), vol. II; *Rocky Mountain News* (Denver), June 12, 1925; *Denver Bar Asso. Record*, July 1926.]

C. B. G—z.

O'DONOVAN, WILLIAM RUDOLF (Mar. 28, 1844–Apr. 20, 1920), sculptor and painter, son of James Hayes and Mary Bright O'Donovan, was born in Preston County, Va. (now W. Va.). In his eighteenth year he entered the Confederate army, in which he served until the close of the Civil War as a member of the Staunton Artillery. Though little is known about his education, apparently in art he was self-taught. In the early seventies he settled in New York City, where he was to pass a half-century of active professional life. He established a studio and soon became favorably known for his portrait busts and bas-reliefs of eminent citizens. At the National Academy of Design he exhibited in 1874 his bust of Peter Gilsey; in 1876, that of J. A. Kennedy, ordered by the Odd Fellows as a cemetery memorial; in 1877, that of the painter Thomas Le Clear. In 1878 he showed portrait busts of his artist friends William H. Beard, Winslow Homer, and William Page. On the strength of the "Page" he was made an associate member of the Academy; a group of New Yorkers presented the work to that body, which still possesses it. O'Donovan was an artist who as a painter felt the coloring of his subject, while as a sculptor he sought to express absolute truth of characterization, yet with details so subordinated as to preserve unity. Evidently his ideals in sculptural portraiture were fully abreast of the times, perhaps even in advance of them. Among his sitters were Walt Whitman, Theodore Tilton, E. C. Stedman, Alexander S. Drake, the painters Arthur Quartley and Thomas Eakins, Gen. Daniel E. Sickles, Gen. James Grant Wilson, and Judge Charles P. Daly. A well-known bronze portrait bust is that of Gen. Joseph Wheeler, an old friend of the sculptor. Made in 1899, it was some years

later given by Henry Clews and others to the National Gallery of Art, Washington, D. C. His Dr. Talcott Williams was shown at the San Francisco Exhibition in 1915.

O'Donovan's early monumental works include a colossal statue of Father Matthew, the bronze statue of John Paulding, chief captor of André, for the André Capture Monument, Tarrytown, N. Y. (1881), and a soldier's monument for Lawrence, Mass. In collaboration with his friend Thomas Eakins, primarily a painter, but also a sculptor and an expert in the anatomy of the horse, he modeled the two life-size equestrian high reliefs of Lincoln and of Grant, cast in bronze, and placed in 1894 on the piers of the Soldiers' and Sailors' Memorial Arch, Prospect Park Plaza, Brooklyn, N. Y. No pains were spared to make these reliefs historically accurate; weeks were spent in trying to find as a model a horse similar to Grant's favorite mount (Cleveland Moffett, *Munsey's*, vol. V, pp. 419–32). A statue of Washington by O'Donovan is in Caracas, Venezuela; another crowns the shaft of the Battle Monument, Trenton, N. J. (1893); yet another, said to be a copy from Houdon's original, is a feature of the Peace Monument, Newburgh, N. Y. (1882). His statue of Archbishop Hughes is in St. John's College, Fordham, N. Y. For the Oriskany Battle Monument, Oriskany, N. Y., he made two anecdotic bas-reliefs (see description and illustrations in the *Magazine of American History*, August 1884). Cornell University at Ithaca, N. Y., has his memorial tablet to Bayard Taylor.

O'Donovan had a broad interest in art. He was among the half-dozen founders of the famous Tile Club (1877); in 1909 he served on the decorations' committee of the Hudson-Fulton Commission. He often expressed himself by painting landscapes. In 1919 an exhibition of his landscape studies, in tempera, praised for their poetic quality, was held at Cottier's, New York City. He was married to Mary Corcoran of New York in 1893. He died of "old age" at Flower Hospital, New York City.

[*Who's Who in America*, 1918–19; "A Sculptor's Method of Work," *Art Jour.* (N. Y.), Feb. 1878; Clara E. Clement Waters and Lawrence Hutton, *Artists of the Nineteenth Century* (1907); *Cat. of the Works of Art Belonging to the City of N. Y.* (1909), pp. 207, 208; Sadakichi Hartmann, *A Hist. of Am. Art* (1932), vol. II; *Am. Art News*, Apr. 24, 1920; *N. Y. Times*, Apr. 21, 1920.]

A. A.

O'DWYER, JOSEPH (Oct. 12, 1841–Jan. 7, 1898), physician, the first successfully to employ intubation for asphyxia in diphtheria, was born in Cleveland, Ohio. His parents moved to the vicinity of London, Ontario, where he received a common-school education and commenced the study of medicine in the office of a Dr. Anderson. Having served two years of apprenticeship, he matriculated at the College of Physicians and Surgeons, New York, where after two terms (four months each) he was graduated in 1866. His graduation thesis dealt with pyemia. On competitive examination he was appointed resident physician to the Charity (now City) Hospital on Blackwell's Island. During an epidemic of cholera there, he contracted the disease. When another cholera epidemic developed in New York City, he was among the volunteers who went to Hart's Island to care for the patients. He again contracted the disease and a little later, typhus.

Following two years' service on Blackwell's Island, he took up private practice and married Catherine Begg. They had eight sons, four of whom died of "summer complaint," victims of the infected milk of the period. In 1872 he was appointed to the staff of the New York Foundling Asylum. Diphtheria was the scourge of institutions for children at that time and in many cases death occurred from asphyxia: the false membrane, from which diphtheria in its Greek etymology is named, choking up the tiny larynx. O'Dwyer experimented with many ways of keeping the larynx open. Intubation proved successful, after he had worked long to devise a satisfactory tube. He saved the lives of many children and reported his results to the New York Academy of Medicine. Specialists in children's diseases who heard his paper declared that his idea was not new, that it had been tried unsuccessfully by the ancient Greeks and by the French in the modern time, and that it had been condemned by the Academy of Medicine in Paris. All agreed that intubation was infeasible, since the larynx would not tolerate a foreign body. Extremely sensitive, O'Dwyer was much hurt by this reception of the report of his years of labor, and for several days would not leave his house. He continued his work, however, and physicians who visited the Foundling Asylum were soon convinced of the life-saving value of intubation. Dr. Abraham Jacobi [q.v.], the distinguished children's specialist, shared in the first objection to O'Dwyer's report, but later, as president of the Academy of Medicine, he recanted and highly praised O'Dwyer's work because of his successful solution of all the problems connected with it. Others were soon won over. O'Dwyer showed that his tube could also be used with great benefit for adults suffering from constriction of the larynx. By special invitation he discussed the subject at the annual meeting of the British Medical Association in

Bristol, England, July 1894, in a paper published in the *British Medical Journal,* Dec. 29, 1894, under the title, "Intubation in the Treatment of Chronic Stenosis of the Larynx." Dr. W. P. Northrup, well-known children's specialist, praised O'Dwyer's "genius as an inventor, his achievement in adding a great operation to the equipment of the profession, thus making the most conspicuous real contribution to medical progress within the last fifty years" (*Medical Record,* New York, Mar. 12, 1898).

He was also among the first to recognize the value of diphtheria serum as a remedy, though there were many skeptics in the medical profession in the early years of its use, and the success of this remedy would mean inevitably lessened need for intubation. In his later years he was occupied with special research on the treatment of pneumonia. His results were bringing encouragement when a brain abscess put an end to his career. His first publication on intubation, "Intubation of the Larynx," appeared in the *New York Medical Journal,* Aug. 8, 1885; other articles include "Intubation in Laryngeal Stenosis Caused by Diphtheria," *American Lancet,* December 1893; "The Present Status of Intubation in the Treatment of Croup," *New York Medical Journal,* Mar. 10, 1894; and "The Evolution of Intubation," *Transactions of the American Pediatric Society,* vol. VIII (1896).

[W. P. Northrup, in *Archives of Pediatrics,* Jan. 1898; J. J. Walsh, *Makers of Modern Medicine* (1907); Roswell Park, in *Janus* (Amsterdam), May–June 1898; Abraham Jacobi, in *Pediatrics,* Feb. 1, 1898; G. McNaughton, in *Brooklyn Medic. Jour.,* June 1898; H. von Ranke, in *Münchener Medizinische Wochenschrift,* Mar. 15, 1898; G. Variot, in *Journal de clinique et de thérapeutique infantiles* (Paris), Feb. 24, 1898; H. A. Kelly and W. L. Burrage, *Am. Medic. Biogs.* (1920); *N. Y. Tribune,* Jan. 8, 1898.]   J.J.W.

OEHMLER, LEO CARL MARTIN (Aug. 15, 1867–Nov. 3, 1930), musician, composer, was born in Pittsburgh, Pa., the son of German-American parents—Rudolph Christian Oehmler and his wife, Elizabeth (Foerster). Oehmler was musically inclined from boyhood. At six he began his first lessons in music and continued them under local instructors until 1885, when he finished a course in the Western University of Pennsylvania (now University of Pittsburgh). He then went to Germany, and for a while studied at the conservatory at Schwartzburg-Sondershausen under Paul E. M. Gruenberg (violin), Ritter (piano), and Adolph Schutze (composition). Later he went to the Stern Conservatory at Berlin and worked with Émile Sauret, Keyser, and Heinrich Ehrlich, and, in composition, with Robert Radecke. While in Germany he became interested in Heinrich Ger-mer's piano methods, which fact influenced both the teaching and editorial work of his later career. About 1891 he returned to the United States and spent the next sixteen years teaching and concertizing in Pittsburgh and nearby cities. Among his pupils during these years was the young Charles Wakefield Cadman, destined to become one of the leading American composers of his time. In 1907 Oehmler moved to Pasadena, Cal., where he lived until his death. On Dec. 25, 1911, he married Lillian Katharine Heche of Pomona, Cal., one of his pupils in piano, violin, and harmony.

As a composer, Oehmler's contribution was valuable chiefly for the large quantity of teaching pieces he produced. Altogether his printed works numbered over three hundred. His most ambitious published composition was a sonata for violin and piano, issued in Germany. For the same instrumental combination he wrote "Elegy," "Saltarella," "Romanezco," "Gypsy's Serenade," and "Sandman's Lullaby." For piano alone he composed a "Cleopatra Suite," "California Romance," "Indian Tomahawk Dance," "Moonlight in the Forest," "Autumn Nocturne," "Reverie Romantique," "Purple Sunset." His songs included "When You I Beheld," "Ae Fond Kiss," "A Sailor's Life for Me," "Sleep Little Birdie," "God, My Father, Lend Thine Aid," and "Jesus, Lead Me to Thy Side."

Oehmler was of a romantic nature, a lover of sentiment, generous, cordial, with a gift for telling humorous anecdotes. He enjoyed the pursuit of several hobbies—nature study, painting, versification, and retouching photographs. He was both a pianist and violinist, playing the violin with warmth and vigor. He enjoyed robust health until the year before his death, when he suffered his first stroke of apoplexy. A second stroke followed a year later, and his death occurred within a few months.

[Material for this sketch has been furnished chiefly by Mrs. Leo Oehmler; for printed sources see *Who's Who in America*, 1930–31; *The International Blue Book*, 1926; *The Étude*, June 1919; *Musical America*, Nov. 25, 1930; *N. Y. Times*, Nov. 5, 1930.]
J. T. H.

OEMLER, ARMINIUS (Sept. 12, 1827–Aug. 8, 1897), physician, agriculturist, and promoter of the oyster industry in Georgia, was born at Savannah, Ga., son of Augustus Gottlieb and Mary Ann (Shad) Oemler, daughter of Maj. Solomon Sigismond Shad of Revolutionary fame. Augustus was born in Hettstedt, Germany, son of a Lutheran pastor, a direct descendant of Nicholas Oemler, who married Martin Luther's sister, and to whom Luther dedicated his translation of the Bible. He came to Amer-

ica when he was about eighteen and settled in Savannah, Ga. He was a pharmacist, botanist, and entomologist, and from him Arminius inherited his scientific tastes. His mother died when he was eight years old. He first attended school at the Chatham Academy in Savannah, but when he was about twelve his father took him to Germany. During 1846 to 1848 he was a student at the Dresden Technische Bildungsanstalt. After graduating with honors he returned to Savannah and began the study of medicine in the office of Dr. Stephen N. Harris, continuing it at the University of the City of New York, from which he received the degree of M.D. in 1856. He then began to practise in Savannah. On Apr. 10, 1856, he married Elizabeth P. Heyward, daughter of John and Constantia Pritchard Heyward of Charleston and Grahamsville, S. C. To them were born six children, three boys and three girls. Oemler practised medicine for only a short time, since the strain on his sympathies affected his health. He was advised to lead an outdoor life and decided to take up farming. When the Civil War broke out he joined the Confederate army and was made captain of the Second Company of DeKalb Riflemen. He was soon afterwards placed in the engineering corps under Major McCreary and assigned to the duty of making topographical maps, being stationed at the fortifications of Savannah. He made the first map of Chatham County.

After the close of the war he went to live on his plantation ("The Shad"), Wilmington Island, near Savannah, where he engaged in truck farming. He was among the first to introduce scientific diversified farming into the South and was president of the Chatham County, Georgia, Fruit and Vegetable Growers Association. His book entitled *Truck Farming at the South,* published first in 1883, was for many years the chief authority on the subject, later editions being published in 1888, 1900, and 1903. An article by him on "Truck Farming" appeared in *Report of the Commissioner of Agriculture,* 1885. He also wrote for the *American Agriculturist* and *Meehan's Monthly.* For several years he was inspector of fertilizers in Savannah. In his scientific investigations he anticipated by two years the discovery, made in 1888 by Hellriegel and Wilfarth in Germany, of the presence of nitrogen-fixing bacteria in the nodules of leguminous plants. In a letter to the United States Department of Agriculture, May 30, 1886, he expressed the conviction that such bacteria exist. In reply, the chemist of the Department wrote him as follows: "Your idea . . . that clover or cow-peas or any kind of plant might possibly be a source of utilizing the free nitrogen of the air must be regarded at the present time as untenable" (Letter in possession of family). This reply discouraged Oemler from further experiments along this line and thus he lost the credit which otherwise might have been his for this important discovery. His broad scientific knowledge is further attested by the fact that he was well known among American entomologists of his day as a keen entomological observer.

With his son Augustus he launched on Wilmington Island the first commercial oyster packing plant in the South. After six years' investigation of the oyster industry he presented his findings in an essay entitled "The Life History, Propagation, and Protection of the American Oyster," which he read before the Georgia Historical Society, Mar. 4 and Apr. 1, 1889, in the interest of a proposed bill for the protection and development of the oyster industry of Georgia. This presentation of facts was largely instrumental in influencing the legislature to enact the "Georgia Oyster Law" (1889). At the World's Fisheries Congress in 1893 he read a paper on the "Past, Present, and Future of the Oyster Industry of Georgia" (*Bulletin of the United States Fish Commission for 1893*, 1894). Through his various public-spirited activities he contributed much both to this industry and to the agricultural development of the South. He died at the Savannah Hospital after a brief illness caused by an apoplectic stroke, and was buried at Wilmington Island.

[Most of the information in the foregoing sketch is taken from Oemler family records; see also obituary in *Savannah Morning News*, Aug. 9, 1897, which is incorrect in some particulars.]   C. R. B.

OERTEL, JOHANNES ADAM SIMON (Nov. 3, 1823–Dec. 9, 1909), artist, Episcopal clergyman, was born in Fürth, Bavaria, the son of Thomas Friedrich Oertel, a metal-worker, and Maria Magdalena (Mennensdörfer) Oertel. Dedicated from childhood to the church, he began in his thirteenth year to study with a Lutheran clergyman, expecting to become a foreign missionary. He revealed such talent for drawing, however, that his preceptor urged him to study art. Accordingly, he became the pupil of J. M. Enzing-Müller, an engraver, with whom he spent some time in Munich, where he was much influenced by the painting of Wilhelm von Kaulbach. In 1848 he came to the United States and settled at Newark, N. J., where he was soon joined by his parents and two brothers. Here he gave lessons in drawing and in 1851 married Julia Adelaide Torrey. She became the mother

of four children, and until her death in 1907 was the "balance wheel" of her husband's life.

In the winter following his marriage Oertel made sketches for a series of four great paintings which should illustrate the redemption of mankind. Thereafter he looked upon the completion of these pictures as the major purpose of his life, and most of his work, during more than fifty years of moving from place to place, was undertaken in an effort to secure means for accomplishing it. From 1852 to 1857 he made steel-engravings for banknotes, painted portraits, and even colored photographs. In 1857–58 he designed the decorations for the ceiling of the House of Representatives in the Capitol at Washington; a few months of 1862 he spent with the Army of the Potomac, gathering material for several war paintings. In the sixties, at Westerly, R. I., he painted a picture first called "Saved, or an Emblematic Representation of Christian Faith," which came to be widely known in chromo reproductions under the title "Rock of Ages." An amazing number of photographs and lithographs after the original were sold, bringing to the publisher a handsome income in royalties, but through a flaw in the copyright, the artist was deprived of all profits after the first few years.

He had been confirmed in the Protestant Episcopal Church in 1852 and at Westerly occasionally acted as lay reader. In 1867, upon the urging of his rector, he was admitted to deacon's orders by Bishop T. M. Clark. Two years later he moved to Lenoir, N. C., where he assumed charge of a rural church and two mission stations—being ordained priest in 1871—and founded a school for girls. Here he remained until 1876. Later he was rector of another church at Morganton, N. C., for eighteen months; and after a year in Florida he lived for various periods at Washington, D. C., Sewanee and Nashville, Tenn., and St. Louis, Mo., where in 1889–91 he was instructor in fine arts at Washington University. He always looked upon religious art as his chief vocation, however, and his paintings and ecclesiastical wood carving were his principal means of support. The former are to be seen in churches in New York, Glen Cove, L. I., Lenoir, N. C., St. Louis, Mo., Jackson, Tenn., Emmorton and Belair, Md., and Washington, D. C., in many instances accompanied by elaborate wood carvings from his hand. An especially notable work was his altar and reredos for the Church of the Incarnation, Washington.

The last eighteen years of his life were spent near Washington, D. C. For a while he took charge of the church at Emmorton, Md., during the illness of its rector, his friend. In 1895, his sons having relieved him of the necessity for gaining a livelihood, he began at last to paint the first picture in his "Redemption" series: "The Dispensations of Promise and the Law." This was followed by "The Redeemer," "The Dispensation of the Holy Spirit," and "The Consummation of Redemption." The last of the four was completed in 1902. In 1897 he had declined an offer of $10,000 for the first painting, because he was unwilling to break the series, which he ultimately gave to the University of the South. There, in 1902, he received at the hands of Bishop Gailor the degree of D.D. Thenceforth he lived with a son at Vienna, Va., where he painted prolifically in his characteristic vein until the end. In 1906–07 he produced the paintings and designed the woodwork for the reredos of the Cathedral at Quincy, Ill. He died at Vienna at the age of eighty-six.

Oertel's draftsmanship was excellent from the beginning. At the outset of his painting career his delineation of form was far superior to his use of color; frequently his canvases were done in monochrome. In his later years, however, notably in the "Redemption" series and in the work for the Cathedral at Quincy, he used color with striking results. Always having a didactic purpose, his pictures sometimes include symbolic detail at the cost of artistic effect. Nevertheless, his composition is forceful and his rendering of the human figure and of animals thoroughly able. The University of the South has a number of his works besides the "Redemption" series; "The Walk to Gethsemane" is in the National Gallery at Washington; "It is Finished," "The Church Militant," and "The Burial of Moses" are at Washington Cathedral.

[J. F. Oertel, *A Vision Realized: A Life Story of Rev. J. A. Oertel* (1917); C. E. Fairman, *Art and Artists of the Capitol* (1927); D. M. Stauffer, *Am. Engravers Upon Copper and Steel* (1907); W. H. Holmes, *Smithsonian Inst., The Nat. Gallery of Art; Cat. of Colls.,* vol. I (1922); *Boston Transcript,* July 30, 1907; *Churchman,* Dec. 25, 1909; *Evening Star* (Washington), Dec. 10, 1909.]   W. H. D—s.

O'FALLON, BENJAMIN (Sept. 20, 1793–Dec. 17, 1842), Indian agent and trader, born in Kentucky, probably at Lexington (Parish, *post,* p. 260, note), was the son of Dr. James O'Fallon [*q.v.*] and Frances Eleanor (Clark), the youngest sister of William and George Rogers Clark [*qq.v.*]. Dr. O'Fallon died soon after Benjamin was born and the infant came under the guardianship of his uncle William Clark, who resided at St. Louis. Here the boy was reared and attended a school conducted by a Mr. Fay.

In 1816 Benjamin wrote from St. Louis to his brother John [*q.v.*] that he had sold his mill establishment and was about to set out to trade with the Sioux because his pride would not permit him to do business on so small a scale as he had done in St. Louis (O'Fallon papers, Missouri Historical Society). He became Indian agent at Prairie du Chien and in 1817 made treaties between the United States and the Otos and Poncas. In 1819 he was appointed Indian agent for the Upper Missouri, acquiring the title of major. Under his jurisdiction were the Pawnees, Otos, Missouris, and Omahas. With his deputy and interpreter, John Dougherty, he joined the Yellowstone Expedition led by Maj. Stephen H. Long [*q.v.*] at St. Charles and accompanied it to Council Bluffs, where he made his headquarters. The expedition was designed for the several purposes of protecting the growing fur trade, controlling the Indian tribes, and lessening the influence which the British trading companies were believed to exert upon them, but it failed to get sufficient appropriation from Congress to complete its work. The copies of Major O'Fallon's speeches at the councils with the Indians at Engineers Cantonment quoted by Major Long (R. G. Thwaites, *post,* vols. XIV–XVII) show that he was an orator of no mean ability and that he possessed a remarkable knowledge of Indian customs, habits, and characteristics. During the winter of 1821 O'Fallon acted as a guide for a group of Pawnees who visited the chief cities of the Eastern states, performing for the curious. On his return to Council Bluffs he resumed his duties as "Father" to the tribes. While at St. Charles, in November 1823, he married Sophia Lee, who bore him six children. In 1825 he signed fifteen treaties between the United States and Indian tribes in the Upper Missouri country. He resigned his position as agent in 1827 and returned to St. Louis. The following year he was named presidential elector for General Jackson from Missouri. He retired to Jefferson County, where he died fourteen years later. O'Fallon had become one of the principals of the Missouri Fur Company and to him is due the comparative friendliness of the Western tribes with that company. Honest and courageous, his bravery reaching the point of foolhardiness, he was efficient in the discharge of his duties, though he occasionally lost control of his temper. His memory is perpetuated in the West by O'Fallon's Creek in Montana, which was named in his honor by Gov. William Clark on the Lewis and Clark Expedition, while Benjamin was yet a boy. It is believed that O'Fallon's Bluff, seventeen miles west of North Platte on the Overland Trail, was named for him also, although the statement has been made that it was named for a hunter who was killed there.

[O'Fallon MSS. in the Mo. Hist. Soc.; records in the office of Indian affairs, Department of Interior, Washington; J. S. Morton, Albert Watkins and G. L. Miller, *Illustrated Hist. of Nebr.*, II (1906), 140; M. A. Leeson, *Hist. of Mont.* (1885); R. G. Thwaites, ed., *Early Western Travels*, vol. XI–XII, XIV–XVII (1905); Thomas James, *Three Years Among the Indians and Mexicans* (1916), ed. by W. B. Douglas; *Am. State Papers: Indian Affairs*, vol. II (1834); J. C. Parish, "The Intrigues of Dr. James O'Fallon," *Miss. Valley Hist. Rev.*, Sept. 1930.]   F. W. S.

O'FALLON, JAMES (Mar. 11, 1749–1794?), physician, Revolutionary soldier, political adventurer, and dabbler in foreign intrigue in the troublous days of James Wilkinson, George Rogers Clark, and Citizen Genêt [*qq.v.*], was born in Ireland, the son of William and Anne (Eagan) Fallon, or O'Fallon. As a youth he traveled extensively on the Continent, and studied medicine at the University of Edinburgh. In 1774 he came to North Carolina and became interested in public affairs as well as in the practice of his profession. The committee of safety of Wilmington caused him to be jailed in January 1776, for inflammatory writings. He served in the Revolution, at first with troops, but later as senior surgeon.

At the close of the war he removed to Charleston, S. C., where he was involved in politics as secretary of an extreme anti-Loyalist organization, first known as the Smoking Society, later converted into the Marine Anti-Britannic Society. Up to this time he had been known as James Fallon. He now added the prefix and was henceforth James O'Fallon. In 1788 he unsuccessfully approached Spanish officials with a project for the promotion of a Spanish colony in northern Florida. Having been appointed general agent of the South Carolina Yazoo Company in 1790, he left Charleston for Kentucky to arrange for colonizing a tract of land near the mouth of the Yazoo River, which had been granted to the company by the state of Georgia. He associated himself with James Wilkinson and opened a remarkable correspondence with Esteban Rodriguez Miró [*q.v.*], Spanish governor at New Orleans, in which he insisted that the intention of the company was to separate from the United States and form an independent government allied to Spain. In Kentucky he began to gather colonists and organize a battalion for military defense. Wilkinson supported him at first but soon discredited him with Miró, and undermined him in Kentucky and Charleston. Miró pretended acquiescence in O'Fallon's plans but secured a promise from the Choctaw and Chickasaw to attack any colonial venture in the Yazoo country. Meantime, in September 1790, O'Fallon had written to President Washington giving him a more patriotic version of the company's plans and asking for the cooperation of the United States. He took the occasion to divulge the activities of Wilkinson and his associates, and suggested that he (O'Fallon) could be of much use to the United States as a spy. During the winter he joined forces with George Rogers Clark, to whom he gave the command of his battalion, and in February 1791, he married the General's younger sister, Frances Eleanor Clark. His letters to Miró took on a more threatening cast, and his military plans assumed the aspect of offensive rather than defensive preparations.

A proclamation by Washington in March 1791, warning the West against O'Fallon, proved disastrous to his immediate plans. He dropped into the background and practised medicine in and about Louisville, but continued his intrigues and was instrumental in securing the appointment of George Rogers Clark by the French government as commander of troops in Genêt's projected attack upon Louisiana in 1793. About this time, however, he broke with Clark, and his wife separated from him, taking with her the two children, John and Benjamin [*qq.v.*]. His death apparently occurred during the first three months of 1794. Although his failures were constant, his audacity gave him prominence in the international contest for the Mississippi Valley. Wilkinson himself rightly characterized O'Fallon as possessed of talent but lacking in the judgment necessary for great enterprises.

[Manuscript material is available in the Spanish archives (see *Descriptive Catalogue of the Documents Relating to . . . the U. S. in the Papeles Procedentes de Cuba . . . at Seville*, 1916), and in various collections in the United States, notably that of the State Historical Society of Wisconsin. Contemporaneous printed matter is found in *The Colonial Records of N. C.*, vol. X (1890), *The State Records of N. C.*, vol. XIV (1896), the newspapers of S. C. and Ky., and *An Extract from the Minutes of the S. C. Yazoo Company* (1791). A sketch of O'Fallon is given in an introduction by L. P. Kellogg to a letter from Thomas Paine to James O'Fallon, in the *Am. Hist. Rev.*, Apr. 1924. Incidental accounts are contained in C. H. Haskins, "The Yazoo Land Companies," in *Papers of the Am. Hist. Asso.*, vol. V (1891), pt. 4; in Charles Gayarré, *Hist. of La.* (4th ed., 1903), vol. III; and in A. P. Whitaker, *The Spanish-American Frontier* (1927). For family history see W. H. English, *Conquest of the Country Northwest of the River Ohio . . . and Life of George Rogers Clark* (1896), II, 1151. The most extended treatment is J. C. Parish, *The Intrigues of Doctor James O'Fallon* (n.d.), reprinted from the *Mississippi Valley Hist. Rev.*, Sept. 1930.]   J. C. P.

O'FALLON, JOHN (Nov. 17, 1791–Dec. 17, 1865), soldier, merchant, and philanthropist, was born near Louisville, Ky. His father, Dr. James

O'Fallon [*q.v.*], a native of Ireland, had married in 1791 Frances Eleanor Clark, a sister of the two celebrated brothers, George Rogers Clark and William Clark [*qq.v.*], and of the union were born two children, John and Benjamin [*q.v.*]. The education of the two boys was looked after by their uncle, William Clark, whose correspondence with John, then in school, contains the following advice: "I must recommend you to court the company of men of learning, sober, sedate and respectable characters. You will not only gain information from them but respectability and influence" (O'Fallon papers, Missouri Historical Society).

Having been a student in Kentucky, first at an academy in Danville and later at an incipient college near Lexington, young O'Fallon entered in 1811 upon a military career. He served as a private (as did also his cousin, George Croghan [*q.v.*], the future hero of Fort Stephenson) in Gen. William Henry Harrison's campaign of that year against the Indians. Wounded severely in the battle of Tippecanoe, he went for convalescence to St. Louis, where he entered the service of his uncle William, at that time superintendent of Indian affairs in the West. During the War of 1812 he was in turn ensign, second lieutenant, first lieutenant, and captain; he also became private secretary to General Harrison, his acting deputy adjutant-general at Fort Meigs, and his regular aide-de-camp. "I live," the young soldier wrote to his mother in January 1813, "with Gen. Harrison, who manifests a strong attachment to me and expresses every confidence" (*Ibid.*). Later, when, in the heat of political controversy, attempts were made to belittle Harrison's military record, the General appealed to O'Fallon, asking him to write from his intimate personal knowledge for publication a letter in which the actual facts regarding Harrison's participation in the battles of Tippecanoe, Fort Meigs, and the Thames should be truthfully set forth. This request O'Fallon complied with in a remarkable letter, dated St. Louis, Feb. 26, 1840, in the course of which he observes: "I doubt whether there is another living who has possessed equal opportunities with myself of forming a correct opinion of Gen. Harrison's military character. I served under him during the greater part of the period he was in active service, near his person, commencing with the Tippecanoe expedition and continuing to its termination; . . . I can safely say that I never in my life saw a braver man in battle, one more collected, prompt, and full of resources than Gen. William Henry Harrison" (Scharf, *post*, I, 348).

Having been in command at Malden, which Canadian post he delivered to the British at the end of the War of 1812, O'Fallon in 1818 resigned at Mackinaw his commission in the army, prospects of promotion being slender, and went to St. Louis with the ambition, which he frankly avowed, of making a fortune in business. In this endeavor he eminently succeeded, becoming in turn Indian trader, army contractor, and merchant on a large scale. Within a year of his arrival in the West, he wrote to his mother that he was making money "at the rate of $1000 a month." Shrewd real-estate investments added largely to his means and in the end he became one of Missouri's wealthiest citizens. His reputation for personal integrity was widespread, and this, together with his well-known business acumen and great private fortune, gave him a position of unique influence in the community. He was president of the St. Louis branch of the United States Bank during the entire period of its existence, and president also of the Mississippi & Ohio Railroad and of the North Missouri Railroad. His benefactions were constant and included liberal gifts to O'Fallon Polytechnic Institute, St. Louis and Washington universities, and to churches of various denominations, especially his own, the Methodist Episcopal Church South. "The fact is," wrote Abel Rathbone Corbin to him in 1851, "you have done so much for religion, scientific and public purposes that it is difficult to make out a list of beneficiaries; not a fire-company, not a library association, not a church, not anything but appeals to Col. O'Fallon in their hour of need" (Scharf, *post*, I, 353). John O'Fallon was twice married: in 1821 to Harriett Stokes, an Englishwoman; and, on Mar. 15, 1827, to Ruth Caroline Sheets of Maryland. He died in St. Louis, survived by four sons and one daughter.

[O'Fallon papers in Mo. Hist. Soc. (St. Louis) and in the Draper Collection, State Hist. Lib. (Madison, Wis.); J. T. Scharf, *Hist. of St. Louis City and County* (1883), I, 344–54; Richard Edwards and M. Hopewell, *Edwards's Great West and Her Commercial Metropolis* (1860); W. H. English, *Conquest of the Country Northwest of the River Ohio 1778–1783 and Life of George Rogers Clark* (1896), vol. II; J. F. Darby, *Personal Recollections* (1880); Alfred Pirtle, *The Battle of Tippecanoe* (1900), being Filson Club Pubs., no. 15; Logan Esarey, "Messages and Letters of William Henry Harrison" (1922), being *Ind. Hist. Colls.*, vols. VII, IX; *Daily Mo. Democrat* (St. Louis), Dec. 18, 22, 1865.]   G. J. G.

O'FERRALL, CHARLES TRIPLETT (Oct. 21, 1840–Sept. 22, 1905), congressman, governor of Virginia, the son of John and Jane Green (Lawrence) O'Ferrall, was born in Frederick County, Va. At the age of fifteen he was appointed clerk *pro tempore* of the circuit court of Morgan County, Va. (now W. Va.). At seventeen he was elected clerk of the county court and held this position until the outbreak of the Civil War. When Virginia seceded, he followed her, in spite of the strong union sentiment in his county. Joining the 12th Virginia Cavalry, he rose rapidly to the rank of captain. With this organization he participated in the Valley campaign of 1862, in the second battle of Manassas, and in the cavalry engagements of June 1863 at Brandy Station, Aldie, and Upperville. He was severely wounded in the last engagement. Upon his recovery, he reëntered the service in December 1863 as a major in a battalion that became part of the 23rd Virginia Cavalry, and he fought with this regiment in the Valley of Virginia until the end of the struggle, attaining finally the rank of acting colonel of cavalry. On Feb. 8, 1865, he was married to Annie E. (McLain) Hand, and at the close of the war, engaged in business at Staunton, Va. In the autumn of 1868 he entered the law class of Washington College, under the presidency of Robert E. Lee.

Graduating in 1869, he located at Harrisonburg, Va., and represented Rockingham County in the House of Delegates for two terms, 1871–72, and 1872–73. He was elected to the legislature as an opponent of the funding bill that provided for the funding of all the former state debt except the third to be assumed by West Virginia. Nevertheless, he remained a Democrat in the party struggles with the Readjusters over the adjustment and the settlement of the ante-bellum state debt. From 1874 to 1880, he was judge of the county court of Rockingham County. On Jan. 12, 1881, he was married to his second wife, Jennie (Knight) Danforth. In 1882 he was nominated for Congress by the Democrats, carried the contested election to Congress, where a Readjuster, John Paul, had obtained the seat, and, after a delayed contest in Congress, was allowed the seat. He served from May 5, 1884, to Dec. 28, 1893, when he resigned. As a member of the committee of commerce in 1886 he advocated the proposed interstate commerce act, yet condemned those "always ready to engage in idle clamor against railroad monopolies" (*Congressional Record,* 49 Cong., 1 Sess., p. 7293); a strict constructionist, he favored federal aid for public education on the ground that the federal government, having freed the negroes, should assist in their education (*Ibid.*, 49 Cong., 2 Sess., pp. 1165–70). In regard to the tariff and the silver issue, he supported the policies of President Cleveland and voted to repeal the Sherman Silver Act of 1890. As governor of Virginia from 1894 to 1898, he made a determined effort to wipe out lynching, and, during the first two years of his term, largely because of his vigilance and free use of the militia, he was successful. In his last two years, however, his administration was marred in this respect by three lynchings. He proposed in one of his messages that the locality where mob violence occurred should be forced to pay into the school fund two hundred dollars per thousand population, and that the local officials should be removed from office and also be liable for damages to the relatives of the victim (*Rockbridge County News,* Dec. 12, 1895). This proposed legislation, however, was not enacted. Refusing to support Bryan in 1896 upon the silver platform and thereby losing favor with the dominant element in the Democratic party, at the expiration of his gubernatorial term he retired from public life, wrote his reminiscences, *Forty Years of Active Service* (1904), and practised law in Richmond until his death.

[C. T. O'Ferrall, *Forty Years of Active Service* (1904); L. G. Tyler, *Men of Mark in Va.*, vol. V (1909); *Who's Who in America*, 1903–05; *Times-Dispatch* (Richmond), Sept. 23, 1905.]   W. G. B.

OFFLEY, DAVID (d. Oct. 4, 1838), merchant, diplomat, and consul, member of a Philadelphia Quaker family, first appears as lieutenant and quartermaster in a regiment of volunteers enrolled when war with France was impending in 1799. In 1811 he went with a cargo of merchandise to Smyrna in Asia Minor, founding there the first American commercial house in the Levant. Feeling against England was bitter in the United States when he left, and he imported this antagonism into Turkey, where the lack of a treaty made American trade dependent upon British protection. Formerly American goods had paid the same duties as British, but recently the Turkish government had doubled the rate because New England captains had indiscreetly passed the Dardanelles without proper papers. Influenced by ardent nationalism, Offley erroneously attributed this to English intrigues and suspected that it lacked the Sultan's approval. When he refused to pay the increased duties, his property was seized, and he carried the case to Constantinople. Four months of negotiation and the judicious expenditure of several thousand dollars in bribes produced little result until he threatened to present a petition directly to the Sultan. A spirit of accommodation was then suddenly discovered and an agreement made which was practically a private treaty. The duty on American goods was fifteen per cent. more than that of nations having treaties, but the added expense was no greater than the cost of foreign protection. Returning to Smyrna, he was mortified to find other Americans unwilling to risk their goods under this arrangement. Trade was suspended during the war with England, but in 1815 he induced his countrymen to abandon British protection by agreeing to be responsible personally for any losses. In 1816 he gained the favor of Husrev Pasha, Turkish minister of marine, under whose powerful protection American trade prospered for fifteen years.

Settled in Smyrna with an Armenian wife and handling most of the growing American trade, Offley became wealthy enough to play successfully the part of unofficial ambassador, greatly respected by natives and foreigners. In 1823 his services were rewarded by appointment as consular commercial agent. Meanwhile Secretary John Quincy Adams, convinced of the need for a formal treaty, sent out several secret agents, and in 1826 sponsored a meeting between Husrev Pasha and Commodore John Rodgers of the American Navy. Greatly impressed by Offley's knowledge of the people and manners of Turkey, Rodgers took him along as adviser, but nothing definite came of the interview. Husrev kept suggesting a direct negotiation at Constantinople to Offley, who urged it upon the American government, feeling certain that success would be easy while Turkey was embarrassed by the Greek Revolution and war with Russia. In 1828 he and Commodore William M. Crane were commissioned to negotiate, but several months of labor in the capital were rendered fruitless by insufficient funds and foreign influence. A year later he was appointed on another commission with Commodore James Biddle and Charles Rhind. Since Offley was widely known, Rhind went alone to Constantinople and secretly concluded a most-favored-nation treaty on May 7, 1830. When the other commissioners arrived to add their signatures, Rhind disclosed a secret article against which they protested violently. Refusal to sign would have wrecked the whole negotiation. After an acrimonious quarrel they unwillingly signed and distributed the customary presents to the Ottoman negotiators. In 1832 Offley was raised to the rank of consul, a position he held at Smyrna until his death. A man of great vigor, keen judgment, wide knowledge of Turkey and the Turks, he was the founder of American commerce in the Levant, for he bestowed freely upon his countrymen the advantages won by his own liberal expenditure, energy, and bold diplomacy.

[Many of Offley's official letters are printed in *House Document 250, 22* Cong., 1 Sess., and in *Senate Document 200, 25* Cong., 3 Sess. These may be supplemented by MSS. in the volume "Negotiations with Turkey" in the State Dept. Archives and letters among the Rodgers Papers in the Lib. of Cong. A report by Charles Folsom in the Navy Dept. Archives, Captains Letters, 1820, vol. III, no. 27, gives his own account of Smyrna trade to 1820. See also C. O. Paullin, *Diplomatic Negotiations of Am. Naval Officers* (1912), chap. v, and H. M. Wriston, *Executive Agents in Am. Foreign Relations* (1929), *passim*.]   W. L. W., Jr.

OFTEDAL, SVEN (Mar. 22, 1844–Mar. 30, 1911), Lutheran clergyman, theologian, was born in Stavanger, Norway, the son of Svend L. and Gunhild (Stokke) Oftedal. After training in the Stavanger Latin school, he entered Christiania University in 1862 and graduated in theology in 1871, his stay there having been interrupted by two years of travel in southern Europe. He continued his studies for a year in Paris, where he formed a life-long friendship with Georg Sverdrup [q.v.], later his colleague for thirty years. Married in 1873 to Marie L. Gjertsen, he emigrated with her to the United States, where he became professor of theology at Augsburg Seminary, Minneapolis, Minn. In June 1874 he was elected president of the board of trustees, which position he held, except for one year, until his death.

Educationally, his conviction was that ministers should be trained in a religious, not a secular college, but that they should be educated so that they would not become a caste estranged from the men of every-day life and the priesthood of general believers. Ecclesiastically, he favored the congregationed church polity, viewing the local church as the body of Christ, and the group-church, or synod, as a human organization. He formulated these beliefs in a spirited, personal declaration of independence, *Aaben Erkläring* (1874). This document, enthusiastically received by many as a manifesto against a Romanizing tendency at work among the Norwegian Lutherans in America, was hotly contested for years, especially in the "Declaration of the Thirty," presented in 1882 by fourteen ministers and sixteen laymen, members of the Norwegian Lutheran Conference, of which also Oftedal was a member. He weathered the storm; but in 1893 it blew up again, this time in the United Norwegian Lutheran Church, into which the Conference and two other church bodies had merged three years before. On this occasion the educational issue was added to the ecclesiastical. The new body would give no guarantees that the college department of Augsburg Seminary would be continued as an integral department of the school, though the agreement had been that the institution was to be the training school for ministers in the new body. A conflict between the Church board and that of Augsburg arose, and the latter with Oftedal as president, was sued, losing in a lower court, but winning before the supreme court in 1898. The clash of issues and the resulting litigation and newspaper comments created ill feeling and even the questioning of Oftedal's honesty, though he had labored more than anybody else for the economic support of the school.

In teaching theology, Oftedal aimed more at the practical than at the theoretical. He defended lay preaching, and attached little value to doctrinal and ecclesiastical formularies. Among German theologians he found much to admire in Michael Baumgarten; among the French, Godet attracted him. He wrote and lectured equally well in English and Norwegian; he was also thoroughly familiar with the classics and at home in the languages of southern Europe, including modern Greek, which he spoke with ease. He was an able preacher and some of his published sermons may be found in *Aand og Liv* (Minneapolis, 1898). From 1877 to 1883 he edited, with Sverdrup, a newspaper, *Folkebladet*; and continued to be a leading contributor to its columns till his death. From 1875 to 1881 he was joint editor of *Kvartalskrift for den norsk lutherske Kirke i Amerika,* a theological periodical; from 1885 to 1890, joint editor of *Lutheraneren,* and from 1890 to 1893 of *Kirkebladet.* For ten years, from 1878, he was a member of the Minneapolis board of public education, being for four years its president; he was also member of the public-library commission from 1886 to 1896, and is known as the father of the Minneapolis branch library and branch high school. As he had been a leader in the Conference, so he was the leader among the "Friends of Augsburg," a group which was an informal successor to the merged Conference, and in 1897 was organized into the "Lutheran Free Church," which rallied to the support of Augsburg Seminary. He retired as professor at the age of sixty, and went to Greece, but in 1907, at the death of Georg Sverdrup, was again drafted into service by the Seminary, his work now being of a supervisory nature solely. In 1908 King Haakon VII of Norway made him Knight of the first class in the Order of St. Olaf. A lifelong enemy of dogmatism and clericalism, he did not permit the formidable opposition that beat upon him to bend his physical frame or sour his outlook on life. At his death, shortly after his sixty-seventh birthday, he was survived by his wife and four children.

[H. B. Hudson, *A Half Century of Minneapolis* (1908) ; J. C. Roseland, *Am. Lutheran Biogs.* (1890) ; *Who's Who Among Pastors in All the Norwegian Lutheran Synods of America, 1843–1927* (1928) ; Lars Lillehei, *Augsburg Seminary and the Lutheran Free Church* (1928) ; *Minneapolis Jour.,* Mar. 31, 1911 ; *In the District Court of the State of Minn. . . . Fourth Judicial District . . . : In the Matter of the Application of Nils C. Brun . . . Affidavits of Sven Oftedal . . . and Others* (1907) ; *Minn. ex rel. Nils C. Brun and Others vs. Sven Oftedal and Others* (72 *Minn. Reports,* 498).]
J. O. E.

OGDEN, AARON (Dec. 3, 1756–Apr. 19, 1839), soldier, lawyer, United States senator, governor of New Jersey, steamboat operator, was born at Elizabethtown (now Elizabeth), N. J., where his ancestor, John Ogden, had been a pioneer settler in 1664 after emigrating from Hampshire, England, to Long Island in 1640. Aaron was the son of Robert, at one time speaker of the colonial House of Assembly, and Phebe (Hatfield) Ogden. At sixteen he was graduated from the College of New Jersey (later Princeton) in the class of 1773 with "Light-Horse Harry" Lee and a year behind Aaron Burr, a boyhood companion. For three years he taught school, first at the Nassau Hall Grammar School and then at Barber's Grammar School in his native town. He had an active military career in the Revolution. His first exploit, with some Elizabethtown volunteers, was the capture of a British supply ship off Sandy Hook. From Nov. 26, 1776, until 1783, he was a "regular" officer in the 1st New Jersey, a line regiment of which his brother Matthias was finally colonel. Aaron rose from first lieutenant to brigade major, serving all the way from Brandywine to Yorktown, where he led the van of Hamilton's regiment in storming a redoubt. He bore to Clinton Washington's proposal to exchange André for Arnold. At the close of the war he studied law with his brother Robert, becoming successively attorney, counselor, and sergeant-at-law.

In the years between the two wars with England, he was reckoned as one of the leaders of the New Jersey bar. He had "strong analytical and logical powers of mind," unusual industry and thoroughness, and considerable effectiveness as an orator, revealing intimate acquaintance with the classics. The title of "colonel" which was generally attached to him came from the French war scare between 1797 and 1800 when he commanded the provisional 15th Infantry and was lieutenant-colonel of the 11th Infantry, as well as deputy quartermaster-general of the army. For a number of years he was clerk of Essex County. A prominent Federalist, he was chosen United States senator in 1801 to fill the remaining two years of an unexpired term. He served as one of the commission which, in 1807, discussed the boundary between New York and New Jersey. His principal activity, however, was legal. He resided in Elizabethtown, where on Oct. 27, 1787, he had married Elizabeth, daughter of Judge John Chetwood. She bore him two daughters and five sons. In the fall of 1812, Ogden was elected governor of New Jersey on a peace ticket, but a year later the war party rallied and elected William S. Pennington. Madison nominated Ogden major-general in 1813, intending probably to give him a command in Canada. He declined the appointment, however, saying that he preferred to remain in command of the state militia for defense purposes.

The war period marked a turning point in Ogden's career. He turned from the law to a steamboat venture which wrecked his fortune. In 1811 he built the steamer *Sea Horse*, with engines designed by Daniel Dod, to run between Elizabethtown Point and New York City. In 1813, however, the New York legislature, upholding the Fulton-Livingston monopoly, barred his boat from New York waters. The New Jersey legislature's attempts at reprisal were unsuccessful, so in 1815 Ogden submitted to the monopoly and paid heavily for a ten-year monopoly of steamboat navigation between his native town and New York. That soon brought him into conflict with the rival line of the irascible Georgian, Thomas Gibbons [*q.v.*]. Both men were stubborn fighters and the monopoly case was fought from the New York courts, where Ogden was successful, to the United States Supreme Court, which in 1824 reversed the decision, giving the occasion for Marshall's celebrated opinion. The expensive litigation wrecked the fortune which Ogden had accumulated in law. His only satisfaction came when Gibbons came to his home with a challenge for a duel, whereupon Ogden won five thousand dollars in a trespass suit. In 1829 Congress created specially for him the post of collector of customs at Jersey City, which was thereafter his home. He was soon imprisoned for debt in New York, but, thanks apparently to Burr, the New York legislature rushed through a bill prohibiting the debt imprisonment of Revolutionary veterans. Ogden continued as collector until his death. He was a man of powerful physique and massive features, with an expression fully as truculent as that of his antagonist Gibbons.

[Ogden's *Autobiography* (1893) is a brief sketch, chiefly military, written for his children. See also: W. O. Wheeler, *The Ogden Family in America* (1907), and accompanying genealogical chart; L. Q. C. Elmer,

The Constitution and Government . . . of N. J., with . . . Reminiscences of the Bench and Bar (1872); E. F. Hatfield, *Hist. of Elizabeth, N. J.* (1868); S. D. Alexander, *Princeton Coll. during the Eighteenth Century* (1872), p. 168; *Gen. Cat. of Princeton Univ., 1746-1906* (1908), pp. 9, 19, 97; F. B. Heitman, *Hist. Reg. of Officers of the Continental Army* (1914); L. H. Stockton, *A History of the Steam-Boat Case* (1815); and the *Newark Daily Advertiser*, Apr. 20, 1839. For his litigation see: 17 *Johnson*, 488; 6 *Wheaton*, 448; 9 *Wheaton*, 1; and 2 *Southard*, 598, 987.]   R. G. A.

OGDEN, DAVID (1707–1798), lawyer, judge, Loyalist, was born in Newark, N. J., the son of Josiah Ogden, chief founder of Trinity Episcopal Church at Newark, and his first wife, Catharine Hardenbroeck. He was descended from John Ogden who emigrated to Long Island from Hampshire, England, in 1640, and in 1664 settled in Elizabethtown, N. J. In 1728, ranking second in his class, he was graduated from Yale College. He read law in New York City but practised in Newark, where he soon exhibited distinguished ability and independence. From 1744 until 1750 he was prominent with James Alexander and Robert Hunter Morris, in matters of proprietary titles, which had caused various riots in three counties of the state. The rioters claimed title from the Indians and ejectment suits and various indictments followed. By 1751, when he was appointed one of His Majesty's Council for the Province of New Jersey, he was considered "at the head of the Bar in his native State." For a period of twenty-four years he served with great acceptability as a member of the Council, most of the time at the head of it. In the dispute in 1760 between Robert Hunter Morris and Nathaniel Jones, as to which one was entitled to be chief justice, he was the main counsel for Morris, whose cause succeeded. In 1761 he was one of several commissioners to try the cases of pirates. By 1764, in which year he was made sergeant-at-law, the threats of an American Stamp Act made him suggest a meeting of the colonies to see if the act could be averted. To the Congress which met in New York City Nov. 28, 1765, he went as a delegate from New Jersey. He disagreed wholly with the measures there taken and withdrew from the deliberations. In 1770, owing to the feeling against him because of his leanings toward the English Crown, his stables and out-buildings were burned.

Until 1772 he had practised law both in New Jersey and in New York City and was counsel for the East Jersey Proprietors, besides acting as a member of Council. But in that year, on May 18, he was appointed associate justice of the New Jersey supreme court and went upon the bench as the second justice in that court. He acted in this capacity until deprived of the office in 1776. On Jan. 5, 1777, although no warrant had been issued against him, he feared arrest and made his escape with two sons to New York City. The next day a regiment of Continental troops went to his house in Newark and plundered it of most of his valuable effects. In June 1778 the remainder of his personal property and most of his real estate, consisting of twenty-three pieces of property in Newark and other parts of the state, were confiscated and sold for the benefit of the state. He valued these possessions at £15,231 sterling; his aggregate losses totaled £18,528 sterling. While in New York City he became a member of the Board of Refugees and devised a plan of government for such time as the American colonies should submit to Great Britain; a time, he said, "certain and soon to happen." In November 1783, the war being over, he sailed with his son Peter for England, where he asked for compensation for his loss of property and salary, printing a pamphlet stating his claims. He also acted as agent for other Loyalists seeking remuneration for losses. The British government awarded him £9,415 for property and salary losses, and because of his previous distinguished position, gave him a pension of £200 per year. On returning from England in 1790 he settled at Whitestone, Long Island. His wife, who had been Gertrude Gouverneur, daughter of Isaac Gouverneur and Sarah Staats, had died in 1775, during his residence in Newark. He died at Whitestone between May 19, 1798, the date of his will, and Aug. 6 of that year, when it was probated. He had eleven children. His son, Isaac, lawyer and Loyalist, after serving as clerk of the New Jersey supreme court, went to Canada and gained distinction there as a judge of the Court of Queen's Bench. Nicholas, also Loyalist, obtained a lucrative office in Nova Scotia. Abraham adhered to the American cause and became the first appointed United States attorney for New Jersey. Samuel [q.v.], also a patriot, removed to Pennsylvania, where he became active in the politics of the state. His daughter Sarah married Nicholas Hoffman of New York City and was the mother of Josiah Ogden Hoffman [q.v.].

[E. A. Jones, *The Loyalists of N. J. in the Revolution* (1927); R. S. Field, *The Provincial Courts of N. J., with Sketches of the Bench and Bar* (1849); W. H. Shaw, *Hist. of Essex and Hudson Counties, N. J.* (1884), vol. I; W. O. Wheeler, *The Ogden Family in America* (1907); F. B. Dexter, *Biog. Sketches of the Grads. of Yale Coll.*, vol. I (1885); Lorenzo Sabine, *Biog. Sketches Loyalists of the Am. Revolution* (2 vols., 1864); the *Green Bag*, Aug. 1891; *N.-Y. Hist. Soc. Colls.*, vol. VIII (1876).]   A. V–D. H.

OGDEN, DAVID BAYARD (Oct. 31, 1775–July 16, 1849), lawyer, was born at Morrisania,

N. Y., the eldest of the twelve children of Samuel [q.v.] and Euphemia (Morris) Ogden. He received the degree of A.B. from the University of Pennsylvania in 1792; read law with his uncle Abraham Ogden; and was admitted to the New Jersey bar as attorney in 1796, becoming a counselor three years later. Desiring a wider scope for his legal career, he moved in 1803 from Newark to New York City, where he thereafter made his home. He married Margaretta Ogden, the daughter of his legal preceptor, and had eight children. Facilitated by family prestige and legal ability, he quickly gained social prominence and a flourishing practice. His chief fame arose from his practice before the Supreme Court. With a great fund of legal learning, he was able to present his cases with remarkable directness and simplicity of statement. Marshall said of him that "when he stated his case, it was already argued" (Warren, *post*, p. 304). His first appearance before the Supreme Court was apparently on Feb. 4, 1812, in *Fitzsimmons et al.* vs. *Ogden et al.* (7 *Cranch*, 2). He was one of the counsel for the defense, in which his uncle, Gouverneur Morris, was concerned. He appeared again in 1815 (9 *Cranch*, 244); four times in 1817; and eight times in 1818. From that time on until his final case in 1845, he was in constant demand and received some of the heaviest fees of any lawyer in the country.

The most celebrated case in which Ogden participated was *Cohens* vs. *Virginia* in 1821 (6 *Wheaton*, 264). Ogden, Pinkney, and Wirt supported Cohens while Webster represented Virginia. The case involved the jurisdiction of the Court. Ogden declared: "It is no objection to the exercise of the judicial powers of this court, that the defendant in error is one of the states of the Union. . . . We deny, that since the establishment of the national constitution, there is any such thing as a sovereign state, independent of the Union" (p. 346). Such federalist views naturally appealed to Marshall and were reflected in his decision. In *Sturges* vs. *Crowninshield* in 1819 (4 *Wheaton*, 122) and *Ogden* vs. *Saunders* in 1824 and 1827 (12 *Wheaton*, 212), both involving bankruptcy laws, Ogden was on the losing side, but his logic was impressive. One of the most difficult cases was that of *John Inglis, Demandant,* vs. *The Trustees of the Sailor's Snug Harbour* in 1830 (3 *Peters*, 99). In 1837 he successfully supported the constitutionality of a municipal regulation of passengers on vessels coming to New York from foreign ports or ports of other states in *City of New York* vs. *Miln* (11 *Peters*,

102). Two years later, in *Bank of Augusta* vs. *Earle* (13 *Peters,* 519), his arguments for the plaintiff did much to secure a decision which facilitated the interstate influence of corporations. His final appearance was in December 1845, when with Webster he supported the plaintiff in *Smith* vs. *Turner,* concerning the right of New York to tax passengers on ships arriving from foreign ports (7 *Howard,* 283).

Unlike most of his prominent colleagues at the bar, Ogden held no important public office, though he ran unsuccessfully for Congress in 1828. He was a Federalist and then a Whig. He sat in the New York Assembly in 1814 and again in 1838. Supported by Thurlow Weed, he was surrogate of New York County from 1840 to 1844, though Weed described him shortly before as "confiding even to credulity and as guileless as a child, but when roused . . . intellectually strong" (*The Life of Thurlow Weed,* vol. I, p. 408). William Kent called him a "good, pompous kind of man" (*Ibid.,* vol. II, p. 73), while his obituary stressed his kindness and urbanity, amenity of manners, kind and conciliating conduct at the bar, and his benevolence of heart. He was for years a trustee of Columbia and was a devoted Episcopalian. He died on Staten Island.

[In addition to the Supreme Court reports see: W. O. Wheeler, *The Ogden Family in America* (1907); Jas. Parker, *Hist. Sketches . . . of the Protestant Episc. Ch. in N. J.* (1889); Charles Warren, *A Hist. of the Am. Bar* (1911); *The Life of Thurlow Weed* (2 vols., 1884), ed. by H. Weed and T. W. Barnes; A. J. Beveridge, *The Life of John Marshall,* vol. IV (1919); C. M. Fuess, *Daniel Webster* (1930), vol. II; *Niles' Weekly Reg.,* Oct. 18, Nov. 15, 1828; E. A. Werner, *Civil List . . . of the Colony and State of N. Y.* (1889); *N. Y. Commercial Advertiser, N. Y. Herald,* July 18, 1849. Although the *Gen. Alumni Cat.* of the Univ. of Pa. gives Ogden's middle name as Boonton, it appears in the *Columbia Univ. Alumni Reg.* (1932) as Bayard, and his son is mentioned in Wheeler, *op. cit.,* as David Bayard Ogden, Jr.]   R. G. A.

OGDEN, FRANCIS BARBER (Mar. 3, 1783–July 4, 1857), engineer, consul, was born at Boonton, N. J., son of Gen. Matthias and Hannah (Dayton) Ogden, and a descendant of John Ogden who emigrated from Hampshire, England, to Long Island about 1640 and in 1664 settled in Elizabethtown, N. J. Matthias was a man of marked intelligence and natural ability and had gained his title of General through his distinguished services in the Revolution. Following the war, he had resumed his occupation of tanner and currier in Boonton, and there young Ogden obtained his primary education and grew to manhood. He had shown from early youth a keen interest in mechanics and as he matured this interest was confined more and more to studies and experiments with the steam engine

as a propelling power for boats. That such should have been the case was natural enough, since the most important experimental work on the steamboat was being done almost at his door by John Stevens, Nicholas Roosevelt, Daniel Dod, and Robert Fulton [*qq.v.*]—men whom Ogden probably knew well. His uncle, too, Aaron Ogden [*q.v.*], governor of New Jersey, had established a stagecoach line from Bristol, N. J., to Elizabeth, N. J., and in 1811 had constructed the steamboat *Sea Horse* to carry his stage passengers from Elizabeth to New York. There seems little doubt, in view of his interest, that Francis had much to do with this steamboat, both in its construction and operation. In 1812 Ogden entered the army and remained in the service until after the battle of New Orleans (1815), in which he saw action as aide-de-camp under Gen. Andrew Jackson.

Following the war, he returned to Boonton to resume his studies, and in 1817 went to England, presumably to be near the great master James Watt. In Leeds he designed and built for steamboat service a low-pressure condensing engine with two cylinders in which the steam worked expansively and the cranks were adjusted at right angles. In 1830 he was appointed United States consul at Liverpool, by President Jackson, and continued in the consular service until his death twenty-eight years later. During this time he remained keenly interested in steam navigation and sometime in the 1830's he formed the acquaintance of John Ericsson [*q.v.*], who had just devised his screw propeller. Ogden at once saw the probable value of this invention and confident of its success, placed money at the disposal of Ericsson for the building of an experimental boat, which, on its completion, the latter named the *Francis B. Ogden.* In addition, Ogden succeeded in bringing Ericsson's invention to the attention of the British Admiralty and in staging a demonstration of its capabilities, with the aid of the new craft. Little interest was manifested, but later Ogden brought about the meeting of Ericsson and Capt. Robert F. Stockton [*q.v.*], as a result of which Ericsson built the screw-propelled tug-boat *Robert F. Stockton,* demonstrated it to officials of the United States Navy, and a few years later, designed and superintended the construction of the U. S. S. *Princeton,* the first screw-propelled steam war vessel ever built. Meanwhile, in 1840, Ogden was made consul at Bristol, England, by President Van Buren. He remained at this post to the day of his death and was buried there. In 1837 he married Louisa Pownall of Liverpool, who survived him.

[W. O. Wheeler, *The Ogden Family in America* (1907); G. H. Preble, *A Chronological Hist. of the Origin and Development of Steam Navigation* (1883); J. H. Morrison, *Hist. of Am. Steam Navigation* (1903); R. H. Thurston, *A Hist. of the Growth of the Steam Engine* (3rd ed., 1893).] C. W. M.

OGDEN, HERBERT GOUVERNEUR (Apr. 4, 1846–Feb. 25, 1906), cartographer and topographer, the son of Morgan Lewis and Eliza Glendy (McLaughlin) Ogden and great-grand-son of Rev. Uzal Ogden [*q.v.*], was born in New York City. A descendant of John Ogden who came to America in 1640 and finally settled in New Jersey, he numbered also among his ancestors Francis Lewis [*q.v.*], signer of the Declaration of Independence. Ogden was educated in the grammar schools of New York City, at Rugby Institute, Washington, D. C., and under private tutors. He became a clerk in the office of the register of wills in Washington, serving in this capacity until Apr. 22, 1863, when he was appointed aid in the United States Coast and Geodetic Survey, with which he remained connected up to the time of his death. During the Civil War he was assigned to detached service and was engaged in the construction of the defenses of Washington (1863), under Gen. John G. Barnard [*q.v.*] of the corps of engineers. From November 1863 to May 1864 he saw duty on the North Atlantic blockade at Beaufort, Hatteras Inlet, N. C., and was on the gunboat *Commodore Hull* as volunteer watch officer when the Confederates besieged New Bern, N. C. In 1865 he went with the Nicaraguan expedition, and five years later served as topographer with the first naval exploring expedition to the Isthmus of Darien. He was promoted to sub-assistant in the Coast and Geodetic Survey, Jan. 1, 1869, and on Jan. 1, 1872, was made assistant.

In the regular course of his duties he eventually directed nearly every branch of the work. He was given charge of the engraving division in 1880, which position required an extensive and varied knowledge of chart construction and publishing. On Nov. 1, 1898, he was made inspector of hydrography and topography. Under his direction three editions of the *United States Coast Pilot* (1899, 1903, 1904), covering the coast of the United States and Alaska, were published. "Of the thousands who traverse our coasts in ships few are aware of the extent their safety depends on the integrity and completeness of his charts" (D. B. Wainright, *post*, p. 227). His best-remembered service was his work in connection with the boundary of Alaska and British Columbia. In 1893 he carried on original explorations and made maps, on the basis of which the present international boundary in southeastern Alaska was determined. His memory is perpetuated there by the names Mount Ogden, and Ogden Passage—an important Alaskan waterway on the southwestern coast of Chichagof Island.

From Sept. 4, 1890, till his death he served on the United States Board of Geographic Names. His interest led him to catalogue 2,400 names of places in southeastern Alaska, and these comprise 72 per cent. of those listed by Marcus Baker [*q.v.*] in his Geographic Dictionary of Alaska (1906), a work with which Ogden was for some time connected. Among his publications are an article under the title "Map" in *Johnson's Universal Cyclopaedia* (vol. V, 1897) and "Geography of the Land," in the *National Geographic Magazine* (vol. I, no. 2, 1889). He was a fellow of the American Association for the Advancement of Science and a member of several other learned societies. On May 28, 1872, he married Mary A. Greene of Brooklyn, N. Y., by whom he had five children. He died at Fortress Monroe, Va.

[W. O. Wheeler, *The Ogden Family in America* (1907); *Who's Who in America*, 1906–07; D. B. Wainright, "Herbert Gouverneur Odgen," *Proc. Washington Acad. of Sci.*, Dec. 24, 1908; *Fifth Report of the U. S. Geographic Board 1890 to 1920* (1921); records of U. S. Board of Geographic Names; records in Office of U. S. Coast and Geodetic Survey; *Evening Star* (Washington), Feb. 27, 1906.] F. W. S.

OGDEN, PETER SKENE (1794–September 1854), fur trader and explorer, youngest son of Isaac and Sarah (Hanson) Ogden, was born at Quebec, Canada, and died at Oregon City, Oregon. His parents, following events of the Revolution, removed from Newark, N. J., by way of England to Canada. Isaac Ogden, the son of David Ogden [*q.v.*], served many years as judge in the admiralty and other courts in Canada and his son in turn was schooled for the legal profession. Breaking away from social and cultural environment at home, Peter Skene, when near the age of majority, decided to enter active service in the fur trade, which was then the most lucrative business in Canada. He began as clerk in the North West Company and was stationed at Isle à la Crosse, but about 1818 he was transferred to the Columbia district beyond the Rocky Mountains and there spent the remainder of his life. With the merger in 1821 of the North West Company with the older and larger Hudson's Bay Company he remained with the latter company and at his death was at the head of the business in the district.

In Canada and in the Oregon Country the fur trader was by force of circumstances an explorer. For many years Ogden was in charge of the annual hunting and trading expedition sent to the so-called Snake Country to make contact with the Indian tribes and compete with American traders from St. Louis. It was a life of hardship, danger, and exposure which took him into almost every valley in southern Idaho and eastern Oregon and also to the head of Jefferson River in Montana. In this connection he was one of the first white men to visit the region of Great Salt Lake (where the city of Ogden was named in his honor) and actually the first to traverse the valley of the Humboldt River, first charted as Ogden's River, in northern Nevada; and his journals contain the first known mention of the name Shasta in northern California. From that service he was transferred to the trade in ships along the northwest coast of British Columbia and Alaska in competition with the Russians from Sitka. About 1836 he was sent to take charge of the difficult district known as New Caledonia on the Fraser River and remained there nearly six years. Beginning with 1844 his station was Fort Vancouver, the headquarters of the entire trade on the Columbia.

Ogden was a man of unusual force of mind and personal charm. His associates at Fort Vancouver were Dr. John McLoughlin and James Douglas, afterward Sir James Douglas, prominent in Oregon and British Columbia history, and he was especially trusted by Gov. George Simpson of the Hudson's Bay Company. In 1844, returning from a year's leave in Canada and England, he was assigned to escort to the Columbia two British army officers, Warre and Vavasour, who were sent incognito to examine the Columbia with reference to defense by British troops in the event of war with the United States for the possession of Oregon. Later Ogden was in command at Vancouver upon the arrival of the American officers and men after the treaty of 1846 and his urbane conduct and tact prevented possible friction then. His acquaintance with early travelers and settlers in Oregon was very wide, and the Indians knew him as a man of fair dealing but of authority. This made it possible for him singly to rescue the fifty or more women and children held as captives by the Cayuse tribe following the massacre of Marcus Whitman in November 1847 near Walla Walla, Wash. He was twice married, each time to a native woman, as was the custom with many of the officers in the fur trade.

Ogden was familiar with many Indian dialects and the Chinook jargon and spoke French as readily as English. By his voyageurs he was known as "M'sieur Pete." He enjoyed literature and wrote a small book entitled *Traits of American Indian Life and Character,* published anonymously in London in 1853. He left considerable property and Sir George Simpson was his executor.

[For biographical details see T. C. Elliott, "Peter Skene Ogden, Fur Trader," in *Quart. Ore. Hist. Soc.,* Sept. 1910, and W. O. Wheeler, *The Ogden Family in America* (1907). Ogden's journals of his expedition into the Snake Country were published in the *Quart. Ore. Hist. Soc.,* Dec. 1909, June, Dec. 1910.]

T. C. E.

OGDEN, ROBERT CURTIS (June 20, 1836–Aug. 6, 1913), merchant, and promoter of education, was born at Philadelphia, Pa., a son of Jonathan and Abigail (Murphey) Ogden. His father was a descendant of Richard Ogden, who in the seventeenth century settled at Stamford, Conn., and at Fairfield, N. J. His mother came of Scotch Presbyterian stock from County Antrim, Ireland. All of Robert's formal schooling was obtained before his fourteenth year, chiefly at a city academy that prepared students for the University of Pennsylvania. At fourteen he was working in a dry-goods store and in 1852, when Jonathan Ogden removed to New York as a partner in the clothing house of Devlin & Company, the son went with him and continued his apprenticeship to trade. Within a few years he had been admitted as a junior partner in the Devlin firm, had married on Mar. 1, 1860, Ellen Lewis, a young woman of Welsh descent, and had established a home in Brooklyn. His part in the Civil War was mainly confined to a month of soldiering with the 23rd Regiment of the New York National Guard in the defense of Pennsylvania towns threatened by Lee's invasion in 1863.

Ogden's earliest contacts with the South were formed on a journey during the opening months of 1861 as an agent of his clothing house. After peace came, the work of his friend Samuel C. Armstrong [q.v.] in founding and conducting Hampton Institute in Virginia had a profound influence upon his life and ideals. He saw that Armstrong was giving his life to the problem of negro education and the example inspired him to devote his own abilities to some like form of public service. His business and his growing family, however, made financial demands that could not be ignored or postponed, and a series of bad years in the seventies made his position precarious. In 1879, when his situation in New York had grown almost impossible, John Wanamaker invited him to become an associate in his Philadelphia retailing enterprises. Ten years later, upon Wanamaker's joining President Harrison's cabinet, Ogden took over the management of the entire business, which remained in his hands, much to Wanamaker's satisfaction, until the close of the Harrison administration in 1893. At the age of sixty he returned to New York to open the Wanamaker store in that city. Then followed more than ten strenuous years in which activities and exertions such as usually fall to the lot of younger men were required of him in the rapid expansion of the business.

Meanwhile, as a trustee of Hampton, Ogden had never lost interest in Southern education, but the schooling of the white population was taking a more central place in his thought. He was fortunate in his contacts with progressive Southern school men and with several Southern-born men of influence who lived and worked in the North. Cooperating heartily with both groups, he was able, through annual conferences held in Southern cities, to enlist the effective support of public opinion for ambitious educational programs. In the opening years of the twentieth century this "Ogden movement," as it was called, was an effective factor in the educational revival that swept over the Southern states. Ogden headed the Southern Education Board which vigorously promoted campaigns for increased school taxes and higher standards of supervision for both white and negro schools, and lengthening of terms, and later sponsored farm demonstration work in many communities. He was also a member of the General Education Board and was instrumental in dispensing large funds for Southern education. His kindliness and humor made him an irresistible campaigner. Encountering much opposition in the early years, he continually gained support until the time came when few Northerners were so favorably known in the South.

As old age approached, Ogden developed heart trouble and in 1907 felt compelled to retire from business. Within three years his wife died. He was still president of the Hampton board of trustees, a trustee of Tuskegee Institute, and a director of Union Theological Seminary. He had long been an elder in the Presbyterian Church, especially active in Sunday-school work, and was a leader of the liberal element in that denomination. He died at his summer home in Kennebunkport, Me., survived by two daughters.

[The authorized biography of Ogden, entitled *An Unofficial Statesman*, was written by Philip W. Wilson (1924). See also: *A Life Well Lived* (1914), a collection of memorial addresses on the life of Ogden by Francis G. Peabody, S. C. Mitchell, and William H. Taft; H. A. Gibbons, *John Wanamaker* (2 vols., 1926); Albert Shaw, "An Ogden Memorial," *Am. Rev. of Revs.*, Nov. 1915; the *Southern Workman*, Sept. 1913; F. G. Peabody, *Education for Life: The Story of Hampton Institute* (1918); *The Gen. Educ. Board: An Account of its Activities, 1902–14* (1915); *Southern Educ. Board: Activities and Results, 1904–10* (1911); *Report of the Commissioner of Education for the Year 1903* (1905), vol. I; *N. Y. Times*, Aug. 7, 1913.]

W. B. S.

OGDEN, SAMUEL (Dec. 9, 1746–Dec. 1, 1810), iron founder and land promoter, was the son of David [*q.v.*] and Gertrude (Gouverneur) Ogden and was born in Newark, N. J. While two brothers of Samuel adopted the profession of law and gained position, he engaged in business, chiefly the manufacture of iron, which had some years before enlisted the attention of the Ogdens of Newark. In the War of Independence his iron works at Boonton, Morris County, figured with other prominent concerns as affording supplies of ammunition for the American troops and material for the fortifications on the Hudson River. In 1781 he advertised nail manufacture "in all its branches"; and later, it is said, he built the forge at Hopewell, N. J. In spite of his contributions to the American cause and his rank as colonel in the patriot militia, general knowledge that his father and three of his brothers were stout Loyalists sometimes bred doubts of his steadfastness. A memorandum sent to Gov. George Clinton of New York in 1781, purporting to give names of persons in the secret service of the King, conveys the charge that Samuel Ogden of "Boon Town" furnished a rendezvous for a very active Loyalist, "when on his Rout to Sussex and Other ways in Jersey" (*Public Papers of George Clinton*, VII, 1904, p. 492). The weight of the accusation is relieved by the circumstance that the accuser had rendered aid to the enemy and was recommending himself for pardon by alleged disclosures. No conclusion need be drawn from the recorded fact that Ogden quarreled with the mettlesome William Livingston, New Jersey's war governor.

In the period following the war Samuel Ogden had important land transactions in Northern New York. Most of the area of the state was forest, held by the Six Nations. By a series of treaties from 1789 to 1795 aboriginal titles were extinguished and lands thrown open in northern New York. Ogden made his first investment on the St. Lawrence River in 1792, obtaining a tract in "mile squares," which was to become the town of Oswegatchie, St. Lawrence County. Immediate settlement was impossible because the frontier posts from Niagara to Oswegatchie were retained by the British. Persons in Canada procured leases within Ogden's tract from Oswegatchie Indians and under the guns of the fort stripped the trees from the soil. Ogden was soon in York (now Toronto) and in Quebec, protesting to Lord Dorchester, the governor-general, and to Simcoe, the lieutenant-governor of Upper Canada, in behalf of his property rights. He appointed as a resident agent Nathan Ford, a man who counts largely in the pioneer history of the region. The strife did not cease however until British troops were withdrawn from the posts by the Jay treaty, and one more treaty was framed to settle Indian claims.

The activity in sales and improvements which ensued is impressive. The foundation of the city of Ogdensburg at the mouth of the Oswegatchie River was laid by Samuel Ogden. Samuel's brother, Abraham, had purchased with others of the family a tract that later became the town of Madrid; and along the river enterprising communities sprang up during the first three decades of the nineteenth century. Samuel Ogden married Euphemia Morris, sister of Gouverneur and Lewis Morris [qq.v.], on Feb. 5, 1775. They had twelve children, one of whom was David Bayard Ogden [q.v.]. The latter years of his life were spent in New York City.

[F. B. Hough, *A Hist. of St. Lawrence and Franklin Counties, N. Y.* (1853); Gates Curtis, ed., *Our County and Its People: Memorial Record of St. Lawrence County, N. Y.* (1894); *A Hist. of Morris County, N. J.* (2 vols., 1914); W. O. Wheeler, *The Ogden Family in America* (1907); *Public Papers of Geo. Clinton* (10 vols., 1899–1914), ed. by Hugh Hastings; N. Y. *Evening Post,* Dec. 4, 1810.]   R. E. D.

OGDEN, THOMAS LUDLOW (Dec. 12, 1773–Dec. 17, 1844), lawyer, was descended from John Ogden, who emigrated from England to Southampton, Long Island, in 1640, later settling in Elizabethtown, N. J. Thomas' grandfather, Judge David Ogden [q.v.], was an influential Loyalist, and after the Revolution prosecuted Loyalist claims in English courts. His son, Abraham, Thomas' father, was a distinguished lawyer, surrogate of Morris County, N. J., and after his removal to Newark, was appointed United States attorney for that district (1791–98) by George Washington. Ogden was born probably in Morristown, N. J. Here, in the winter of 1776–77, Washington spent much time with the Ogden family, and according to family tradition, young Thomas often rode mounted on the saddle in front of Washington, on the General's tours of inspection of the army. It is recorded also that during the progress of a playful duel between the two, the button flew off the boy's foil, and Washington received a small flesh wound in the hand. Owing to the Loyalist sentiments of David Ogden, a rumor of attempted assassination got abroad, but was soon dissipated. In 1788 Thomas entered Columbia College, and four years later delivered his graduation oration, "On the Rising Glory of America."

He studied law with his father and Richard Harison and was admitted to the New York bar in 1796. In the same year he was married, on Jan. 23, to Martha Hammond, and formed a law partnership with his elder brother, David. Later, he was associated in practice with Alexander Hamilton. He became one of the most active corporation lawyers in New York City, specialized in trusts and will and equity jurisprudence, and served as counsel for prominent families in the city. He was eminently successful when, as temporary counsel for the Holland Land Company, which owned a three-million-acre tract of land in the western part of the state, he secured through political influence at Albany the passage of a law which the corporation had desired for twenty years. This law enabled it "to re-enter lands sold under the foreclosure of mortgages" and allowed the transfer of lands to aliens on equal terms with natives.

Outside his professional life, his interests and activities centered around religious and philanthropic enterprises. He was vestryman or warden of Trinity Church, New York, from 1807 to 1844, and for many years was "an able and and judicious delegate" to special councils of the Episcopal Church. He was one of the founders and vice-presidents of an Episcopal society for promoting religion and learning in New York, and a trustee of the General Theological Seminary; was trustee of Columbia College, 1817–44, and served in the same capacity for Sailors' Snug Harbor. The vigorous support which he gave a treaty which in his opinion offered the Indians a chance to "be saved from extinction and become a civilized people," further illustrates his breadth of interest (Ogden to Verplanck, manuscript collection, New York Historical Society). Socially prominent, he was vice-president of the banquet at the city hall in honor of Washington Irving's return to America (1832) and committeeman of the public dinner for Chancellor Kent (1843). He is described as a modest, courteous, public-spirited gentleman of the old school. He had seven sons and four daughters.

[W. O. Wheeler, *The Ogden Family in America* (1907); David McAdam and others, *Hist. of the Bench and Bar of N. Y.,* vol. I (1897); J. A. Scoville, *The Old Merchants of N. Y.,* 3rd ser. (1865); *The Diary of Philip Hone* (2 vols., 1889, ed. by Bayard Tuckerman); P. D. Evans, "The Holland Land Company," *Buffalo Hist. Soc. Pubs.,* vol. XXVIII (1924); C. H. Haswell, *Reminiscences of an Octogenarian* (1896); Wm. Berrian, *An Hist. Sketch of Trinity Church New-York* (1847); *Proc. Relating to the Organization of the Gen. Theol. Sem. of the Protestant Episcopal Church* (1854); MSS. in N. Y. Hist. Soc.; N. Y. *Jour. and State Gazette,* May 7, 1791; N. Y. *Commercial Advertiser,* Dec. 19, 1844; N. Y. *Spectator,* Dec. 21, 1844; N. Y. *Daily Tribune,* Dec. 20, 1844.]   A. L. M.

OGDEN, UZAL (1744–Nov. 4, 1822), clergyman, controversialist, was born in Newark, N.

J., the son of Uzal Ogden and Elizabeth Charlotte (Thébaut), daughter of Gabriel Lewis Thébaut of Antigua. On his father's side he was descended from John Ogden of Hampshire, England, who having emigrated to America about 1640, settled in Elizabethtown, N. J., in 1664. The elder Uzal was a merchant of Newark and one of the founders of Trinity Church in that city. As early as 1770 the younger Ogden seems to have interested himself in missionary work in Sussex County and was instrumental in forming the parish of Newtown (now Newton). He pursued theological studies under the Rev. Dr. Thomas B. Chandler [q.v.], rector of St. John's Church, Elizabethtown, and in the summer of 1773 went to England, where, on Sept. 21, he was ordained by the Bishop of London. Upon his return, he continued his missionary work in Sussex County. In April 1779 he was invited to minister occasionally to the needs of Trinity Church, Newark, of which his father was warden, and in November 1785 he was asked to become its rector, but did not accept until 1788, having in the meantime served as assistant rector of Trinity Church, New York. By his intellectual gifts and forceful personality he soon rose to leadership.

On Aug. 16, 1798, he was elected, by a substantial vote, the first bishop of New Jersey. The usual certificate was signed for presentation to the General Convention, which met at Philadelphia in June 1799; that body, however, refused to consent to his consecration, ostensibly because of doubts as to the regularity of his election, and referred the matter back to a future convention of the diocese. A special convention, meeting in October 1799, affirmed that the previous election had been regular in every respect. The matter was again considered by the General Convention held at Trenton, Sept. 8–12, 1801, which held to its previous action, and New Jersey did not have a bishop till some fourteen years later. Behind the refusal to consent to Ogden's consecration lay, probably, a wide-spread objection to his churchmanship, based upon his reputation for laxity in doctrine and disregard for the order of the Episcopal Church. Nothing was urged against his personal character (Hills, *post*, pp. 714, 286–93).

In 1803 he had trouble with his Newark congregation. The matter was brought before a special diocesan Convention in 1804, which requested that he resign on a pension from Trinity Church. Ogden refused and on May 9, 1805, the standing committee, with the aid and consent of Bishop Moore of New York, suspended him from the exercise of any ministerial duties in New Jersey. On Oct. 15, 1805, the Presbytery of New York received him as a member of that body and he remained such until his death. He never had a stated charge but preached as he found opportunity. In 1776 he married Mary, daughter of Samuel Gouverneur, who died in 1814, having had six children. Ogden's death occurred in Newark, in 1822, and four years later the city received by bequest from his estate four thousand dollars for poor orphaned children. He published numerous pamphlets and sermons and a two-volume treatise, *Antidote to Deism: The Deist Unmasked* (1795), refuting Thomas Paine's *Age of Reason*.

[W. O. Wheeler, *The Ogden Family in America* (1907); W. B. Sprague, *Annals Am. Pulpit*, vol. IV (1859); *Jours. of the Conventions of the Protestant Episcopal Ch. in N. J.*, 1785–1815 (1890); G. M. Hills, *Hist. of the Ch. in Burlington, N. J.* (2nd ed. 1885); *N. Y. Evening Post*, Nov. 5, 1822.]   H. S.

OGDEN, WILLIAM BUTLER (June 15, 1805–Aug. 3, 1877), railroad executive, was born in Walton, Delaware County, N. Y., the son of Abraham and Abigail (Weed) Ogden and a descendant of John Ogden who settled in Elizabethtown, N. J., in 1664. He was educated in the public schools and planned to study law, but when he was only fifteen his father suffered a paralytic stroke and the boy was compelled to devote himself to the management of his father's interests, which consisted of property in what was then an undeveloped country. William devoted himself to the improvement and sale of this land, and in this work showed the executive and financial ability which marked his later career. In 1834 he was elected to the New York legislature on a platform advocating the construction of the New York & Erie Railroad by state aid, which was obtained in 1835. In that year, Charles Butler, a New York capitalist, who had married Ogden's sister, urged his brother-in-law to move to Chicago to take charge of his real-estate interests there. Accordingly, Ogden went to Chicago and laid out a tract for subdivision. With characteristic energy he held an auction at which he sold one-third of the property for more than one hundred thousand dollars or enough to cover the original cost. He then established a land and trust agency and made purchases of land on his own account; in 1843 he formed a partnership with William E. Jones. His success in business and the rise in the value of his real estate later created for him a large fortune.

When Chicago was incorporated as a city in 1837 Ogden was elected its first mayor on the Democratic ticket. The population of the town was only 4,179, and the first problem was the improvement of the streets, which were in a bad condition, and the building of bridges to connect the three parts of the city. After his term as mayor Ogden served many years on the city council and was instrumental in having bridges and many miles of improved streets built. Ogden avenue was named after him. He next devoted himself to the construction of railways east and west from Chicago. One of the first roads projected was the Galena & Chicago Union Railroad which was to run to the then important lead mines. A charter was obtained in 1836 but the panic of the following year prevented the continuation of work, though the charter was kept alive. In 1846 Ogden was elected president of the company. By 1849 the road was built with strap rails to the Des Plaines River, a distance of ten miles, and in April of that year the first locomotive started west from Chicago on the line. Thereafter Ogden devoted himself entirely to railroad development. In 1853 he was chosen one of the directors of the Pittsburg, Ft. Wayne & Chicago Railroad Company, and when the road was made insolvent by the panic of 1857 he was appointed general receiver in 1859 and restored it. He presided over the National Pacific Railway Convention of 1850, held to advocate the building of a transcontinental railroad. In 1857 he became president of the Chicago, St. Paul & Fond-du-Lac Railroad, which later became part of the Chicago & Northwestern. He logically became president of the latter road in 1859 and continued in that office until 1868. When the Union Pacific was organized Ogden was elected its first president in 1862 in order to give prestige to the project. But subscriptions to the needed $2,000,000 capital were not forthcoming until Congress doubled the land grant, when the military character of the road was emphasized by the election in 1863 of Gen. J. A. Dix to the presidency. Ogden also served as president of the Illinois & Wisconsin Railroad, of the Buffalo & Mississippi, and of the Wisconsin & Superior Land Grant Railroad.

Ogden's executive ability was called into service in many lines of civic enterprise. He was the first president of Rush Medical College, a charter member of the Chicago Historical Society, and president of the Board of Trustees of the University of Chicago. When the Merchants Loan & Trust Company was organized in 1857 he was one of its first directors. When the slavery question arose he allied himself with the Free-Soil party and in 1860 was elected by the Republicans to the Illinois Senate, but he split with the party over the Emancipation Proclamation and retired from politics. In 1866 he

purchased an estate at Fordham Heights, just outside of New York City, where he made his home until his death. Late in life, on Feb. 9, 1875, he married Maryanne Arnot, daughter of John and Mary (Tuttle) Arnot, of Elmira, N. Y. He was a man of commanding presence, whose most striking characteristic was his self-reliance. He contributed liberally to educational and charitable institutions, and his name was given to the Ogden Graduate School of Science at the University of Chicago which a bequest from his estate helped to found.

[References to Ogden's life and services are found in a great many scattered references, of which the following are the best: A. T. Andreas, *Hist. of Chicago* (3 vols., 1884–86); I. N. Arnold, *Wm. B. Ogden and Early Days in Chicago* (Fergus Hist. Ser., no. 17, 1882); *The Biog. Encyc. of Ill. of the Nineteenth Century* (1875); D. W. Wood, ed., *Chicago and its Distinguished Citizens* (1881); *Yesterday and Today: A Hist. of the Chicago and North Western Railway System* (3rd ed., 1910); T. W. Goodspeed, *The Univ. of Chicago Biog. Sketches*, vol. I (1922).]   E. L. B.

OGILVIE, JAMES (d. Sept. 18, 1820), teacher and lecturer, was born in Aberdeen, Scotland, and emigrated to Virginia at the age of nineteen. He opened an academy at Milton, in Albemarle County, where he taught the entire curriculum, from grammar and geography to literature, ethics, natural philosophy, and political economy. Later, he moved to Richmond and there, as at Milton, had for pupils the sons of the most prominent families. With the maturer students he employed the lecture, or "expostulatory and explanatory" method, admirably suited to his emotional temperament, his high enthusiasm, and his *flair* for oratory. Another innovation of his was the "semi-annual academical examinations and exhibitions; at which, his pupils exhibited specimens of their proficiency and skill in composition and elocution" (see his *Philosophical Essays*, Supplementary Narrative, pp. ii, iii). On these public occasions he delivered sample orations of his own. Their enthusiastic reception encouraged him to plan a weekly course of orations for the people of the vicinity. President Thomas Jefferson attended one of these and was so favorably impressed that he sent Ogilvie an elegant edition of the works of Cicero and later gave other evidences of interest and regard. Popular applause proving far more stimulating and gratifying to his eccentric, if not psychopathic, mind, than the drudgery of teaching, which even a liberal use of opium did not relieve, he conceived the plan of abandoning teaching altogether and devoting himself exclusively to public lecturing.

Accordingly, in 1809 he closed his school and

put his plan into execution. Marked success in his new undertaking was outrun by a still greater ambition, and forthwith he conceived the idea of establishing in all the American colleges professorships of rhetoric, and of having erected in each of the large cities a spacious and magnificent hall for the exhibition of oratory. In pursuance of this idea, after delivering orations in many cities, he arrived in Columbia, S. C., and was invited by President Jonathan Maxcy [*q.v.*] of the South Carolina College to deliver three orations in the chapel of that institution. Their success was phenomenal. In March 1815 he returned to the college and gave oratorical lectures for the remainder of the session. During this time he delivered an oration before the legislature, making an impassioned plea for the establishment of a professorship of oratory at the college. "In vain! The feelings of his respectable auditors, after venting themselves in a loud and protracted plaudit, evaporated 'into thin air' " (*Ibid.*, p. lxvi). This and other bitter disappointments suffered during seven years of struggle to win support for his project convinced him that further efforts would be futile, unless he could manage to acquire a "permanent and extended celebrity, as a philosophical writer." The need of a greater prestige than would be accorded even the best elocutionist and the urgings of an ever-mounting ambition called for the display of "other and higher qualifications and accomplishments, than those of a popular declaimer."

Despite misgivings as to his philosophical competency and the handicap of his reputation as an elocutionist, he set to work, therefore, to win fame as a philosopher. In a few months the three essays, which were to bring the much hoped-for renown, were completed, and these together with "Copious Notes . . . A Supplementary Narrative [autobiographical], with an Appendix," he published in one volume, *Philosophical Essays*, at Philadelphia, in 1816. The second essay, "On The Nature, Extent, and Limits of Human Knowledge, so far as it is Founded in the Relation of Cause and Effect, and Concerns Mind and Matter"—the only one that could possibly lay claim to the term philosophical—was a restatement of Hume's skepticism. The few reviews the book received condemned both its substance and its style. In 1820 he embarked for London on his way to Scotland, to prosecute his claim to the earldom of Findlater. During his stay in London he was invited to lecture before a distinguished audience, but the effort (owing perhaps to the effect of opium) was a dismal failure. His claim to the earldom was not en-

tertained, and in September 1820 he committed suicide at Aberdeen.

[*"Recollections of James Ogilvie, Earl of Finlater, By One of his Pupils," Sou. Literary Messenger, Sept. 1848; William Crafts, "The Late Mr. Ogilvie, the Orator," A Selection in Prose and Poetry from the Miscellaneous Writings of W. Crafts* (1828), pp. 277–81; *Sou. Literary Messenger,* Jan. 1852, p. 8; *Analectic Mag.,* Dec. 1816; *North Am. Rev.,* Mar. 1817; *Blackwood's Edinburgh Mag.,* Feb. 1825; J. P. Little, *Hist. of Richmond* (1933); Joseph Irving, *The Book of Scotsmen* (1881); *Dict. of Nat. Biog.*] J. M—e.

OGILVIE, JOHN (1724–Nov. 26, 1774), a clergyman of the Church of England, prominent for twenty-five years in the Province of New York, was of Scotch descent, born, it is commonly assumed, in New York City, his first known residence. He graduated from Yale College in 1748, and having officiated as a lay reader in Norwalk and Ridgefield, Conn., went abroad for Episcopal ordination. With him he carried a letter to the Bishop of London from Rev. Henry Barclay, then rector of Trinity Church, New York, but formerly in charge of the Albany mission, which states: "I have engaged the bearer hereof, Mr. John Ogilvie, to undertake the mission to Albany and the Mohawk Indians, if your Lordship shall find him duly qualified for Holy Orders. . . . I look upon him as the best qualified for the Indian Mission of any person I could have found on account of his speaking the low Dutch language, which I found very useful to me, both on account of its conformity to the Indian in pronunciation as well as the service I was thereby enabled to do a considerable number of the Dutch inhabitants who are entirely destitute of religious instruction" (Joseph Hooper, *A History of St. Peter's Church in the City of Albany,* 1900, p. 86). Ogilvie was duly ordained by the Bishop of London and on June 30, 1749, licensed by him to officiate in the Plantations, his appointment to the mission at Albany having been approved by the Society for the Propagation of the Gospel in Foreign Parts.

Returning to America, he commenced his labors in the spring of 1750, taking charge of St. Peter's Church and beginning his ministry to the Mohawks. He found the work both among the Indians and at Albany much demoralized because of the border warfare that until recently had been going on, and reorganized it with great success. His ability, sound judgment, social qualities, and unselfish devotion to his calling gave him a high place in the esteem of the people; St. Peter's flourished, and in 1751 the church edifice was rebuilt with a "handsome Steeple, and a very good Bell," and all the "proper ornaments." He acquired a knowledge of the Mohawk language and his activities among the

Indians were as successful as those among the English. About 1755 he married Susanna Catharine, daughter of Lancaster Symes, Jr., of New York. They had a daughter and a son, George, who became an Episcopal clergyman. The Earl of Loudoun, impressed by Ogilvie's "great pains in the performance of his duties," appointed him, probably in 1756, chaplain to the 62nd or Royal American Regiment of Foot, and in 1759 he accompanied Sir William Johnson on the expedition against Fort Niagara. At the end of the year he was hard at work again in Albany. In 1760 his missionary zeal carried him as far west as Oswego. His work as chaplain had been of such an order that General Amherst commanded him to accompany the army of occupation to Canada. From Montreal he sent to the Society for the Propagation of the Gospel a detailed account of the state of religion there, thus helping to prepare the way for the establishment of the Church of England in Canada.

After the treaty of peace in February 1763, Ogilvie did not resume his work at the Albany mission, and in the autumn of 1764 was appointed an assistant minister of Trinity Church, New York. Here he labored with characteristic fidelity and achieved considerable popularity as a preacher. In 1769 there was published *The Order for Morning and Evening Prayer . . . Collected and Translated into the Mohawk Language Under the Direction of the late Rev. Mr. William Andrews, the Late Rev. Dr. Henry Barclay and the Rev. Mr. John Oglivie* [sic]. That same year, Apr. 17, his first wife having died, Ogilvie married Margaret (Marston) Philipse, daughter of Nathaniel Marston, Jr., and widow of Philip Philipse of New York. On Friday, Nov. 18, 1774, while he was officiating in St. George's Chapel, he suffered a cerebral hemorrhage and died Nov. 26, in his fifty-first year. Mrs. Anne Grant wrote of him, "His appearance was singularly prepossessing; his address and manners entirely those of a gentleman. His abilities were respectable, his doctrine was pure and scriptural, and his life exemplary . . . add to all this a talent for conversation, extensive reading, and a thorough knowledge of life" (*Memoirs of an American Lady*, 1808, II, 93–94). An elegy on his death appeared in *Rivington's New York Gazetteer* for Jan. 5, 1775.

[F. B. Dexter, *Biog. Sketches Grads. Yale Coll.*, vol. II (1896) contains a comprehensive bibliography. See also Hooper, *ante*, who gives an excellent account of Ogilvie's Albany career; Chas. Inglis, *A Sermon . . . Occasioned by the Death of John Ogilvie, D.D.* (1774); Morgan Dix, *A Hist. of the Parish of Trinity Ch. in the City of N. Y.*, pt. I (1898); *Colls. N. Y. Hist. Soc. . . . 1870*, Pub. Fund Ser., III (1871), 250–52, 262–63.]   H. E. S.

OGLE, SAMUEL (*c.* 1702–May 3, 1752), colonial governor of Maryland, was born in Northumberland County, England, where the Ogle family had become prominent as early as the eleventh century. The son of Samuel Ogle of Bousden, who represented Berwick-on-Tweed in the House of Commons, and of his second wife, Ursula, the daughter of Sir Robert Markham and the widow of Lord Altham, he was a captain of cavalry in the British army, when in 1731 he sailed for Annapolis, Md. He arrived on Dec. 2, and five days later was sworn in as proprietary governor of the province, in which his predecessor, Benedict Leonard Calvert, the brother of the lord proprietor, had failed to procure the cooperation of the popular branch of the General Assembly. Tobacco, the staple crop, was yielding small returns for labor, and the boundary dispute with the Penns was so serious that the lord proprietor visited the province and from Dec. 18, 1732, to July 11, 1733, administered the government in person. From the latter date until Aug. 23, 1742, Ogle was again governor, and he served a third term from Mar. 16, 1747, until his death.

As governor, he made it his first care not to show a disregard for any faction, and he was somewhat successful in his efforts to win the support of the leaders of the opposition by promises of lucrative offices. He issued effective proclamations for the apprehension and punishment of persons guilty of inciting mob violence for the destruction of tobacco plants. By accepting a compromise he brought to a close the dispute over the question of the extension of the English statutes to Maryland, a question that since 1722 had been a chief source of discord between the governor and the Assembly. He ably defended the interests of Maryland in a petty border warfare arising from the boundary dispute with Pennsylvania. He met his first and only serious defeat as governor, when in 1739 he attempted to force the passage of a bill for continuing the levy of a tobacco duty for the purchase of arms and ammunition. Disputes over other money bills contributed to a deadlock, and to break this the lord proprietor appointed his own brother-in-law, Thomas Bladen, to succeed Ogle. When Bladen proved to be incompetent, Ogle was restored and from his restoration until his death he was popular. Acting on his recommendations the Assembly, at its first session of his third term, not only passed an acceptable bill for the purchase of arms and ammunition but also passed a bill for the inspection of tobacco and the limitation of officers' fees. The limitation of fees removed a large source of discord between the executive and legislative branches. The inspection of tobacco was the salvation of the tobacco industry and contributed to the successful floating of a paper currency.

In 1741 he married Anne, the daughter of Benjamin Tasker, through whom he came into possession of "Belair," an estate of 3600 acres in Prince George's County twenty miles west of Annapolis. The house was a fine specimen of architecture, and the estate was laid out with a deer park of perhaps six hundred acres, a race track, kennels, and a bowling green. Here and on the highways in a four-in-hand coach with outriders, he maintained the traditions of the English gentleman. He was a lover of sport and took a prominent part in the organization of the Maryland Jockey Club. At his death in Annapolis he was characterized as a man of ability and understanding, whose conversation was affable and instructive but never assuming. He had five children; among them Benjamin, who was governor of Maryland from 1798 to 1801.

[*Archives of Md.,* esp. vols. XXV, XXVIII, XL, XLII (1905–23); "The Calvert Papers," no. 2, *Md. Hist. Soc. Fund Pub.* no. 34 (1894); N. D. Mereness, *Md. as a Proprietary Province* (1901); J. M. Hammond, *Colonial Mansions of Md. and Del.* (1914); *Md. Gazette,* May 7, 1752; H. A. Ogle, *Ogle and Bothal* (1902), pp. 211–13.]   N. D. M.

OGLESBY, RICHARD JAMES (July 25, 1824–Apr. 24, 1899), governor of Illinois and senator, was born in Oldham County, Ky., the son of Jacob and Isabella (Watson) Oglesby. His father was a farmer, owned a few slaves, and was a member of the Kentucky legislature. In 1833 his parents, two brothers, and a sister died of the cholera and the family property was sold, including the slaves. He maintained that it was the sale of these slaves, especially of Uncle Tim, whom he later bought and freed, that made him an abolitionist. An uncle took the orphaned boy to Decatur, Ill., where he attended the district school a few months before be began his struggle for a livelihood as farmer, rope-maker, and carpenter. He studied law in the office of Silas W. Robbins of Springfield, was admitted to the bar in 1845, and practised his profession at Sullivan, Ill., until the outbreak of the Mexican War. During the war he served as first lieutenant in the 4th Illinois Volunteers, participating in the battles of Vera Cruz and Cerro Gordo. After the war he resumed his law practice and attended a course of lectures at the law school in Louisville. In 1849 he went to California to dig for gold and returned to his profession at Decatur in 1851. Five years later he went abroad for twenty months' travel in Europe, Egypt, and the Holy Land.

On his return to Decatur he entered politics. He had been a Whig and had served as a Scott elector in 1852 but joined the Republican party upon its formation. In 1858 he ran for Congress on the Republican ticket and was defeated by only a small majority in a strong Democratic district. In 1860 he was elected to the state Senate, but he served only one term, resigning at the outbreak of the Civil War to become colonel of the 8th Illinois Volunteers. He served as brigade commander under Grant at Fort Henry and Fort Donelson and was severely wounded at the battle of Corinth. In April 1863 he returned to the army and was promoted to the rank of major-general. He resigned in May 1864. In November 1864 he was elected governor of Illinois on the Republican ticket. He was an ardent advocate of Lincoln's war policies; however, later he denounced Johnson bitterly and sent a formal demand to Washington for action against him. During his administration, Illinois ratified the Thirteenth and the Fourteenth Amendments and repealed her "Black Laws." Further enactments provided for a home for the children of deceased soldiers, a school for the feeble-minded, the location of the Illinois industrial college at Urbana, and the construction of a southern Illinois penitentiary. At the end of his term he returned to his law practice, but in 1872 he was again the Republican nominee for governor, the party realizing that he was the only Republican who could carry the state. There was an understanding, however, that the lieutenant-governor should succeed to the governorship immediately after inauguration and that Oglesby in turn should receive election to the United States Senate. A few days after his inauguration, therefore, he was elected to succeed Lyman Trumbull. As senator, he served as chairman of the committee on public lands and on the committees of Indian affairs, pensions, and civil service. As a member of the pensions committee, he was an earnest champion of the soldiers' interests. He retired at the end of his term in the Senate. In 1884 the Republican party nominated him governor by acclamation, and he was elected, the first man in Illinois to receive that honor three times. During this administration his general policies were carried out in laws providing for a soldiers' and sailors' home, a home for juvenile delinquents, and the creation of various pension funds. In 1889 he retired to his home at "Oglehurst," Elkhart, Ill. In 1891 he was nominated for the Senate, but he failed of election.

The last years of his life were spent in comparative quiet. He was married twice: to Anna

White in 1859 and, after her death in 1868, to Emma (Gillet) Keyes in 1873. He was a fine-looking man with a bluff, friendly manner that appealed to the people. This, added to his wit and good humor, his sincerity and enthusiasm, and his ability to speak to the people in the vernacular, made him an excellent stump speaker, and as such he acquired considerable fame. He believed in the people and in their ability to govern themselves; in return, he was dearly beloved by them, to whom he was known as "Uncle Dick."

[Correspondence in possession of Ill. State Hist. Lib., Urbana, and of his son, John G. Oglesby, Elkhart; J. M. Johns, *Personal Recollections of Early Decatur* (1912); *The Bench and Bar of Ill.*, ed. by J. M. Palmer (1899), vol. II; *The Biog. Encyc. of Ill.*, ed. by Charles Robsen (1875); G. B. Raum, *Hist. of Ill. Republicanism* (1900); John Moses, *Ill., Hist. and Statistical*, vol. II (1892); A. C. Cole, *The Era of the Civil War* (1919); E. L. Bogart, *The Industrial State* (1920); *Ill. State Register* (Springfield), Apr. 25, 1899.]   E. B. E.

VOLUME VII, PART 2
OGLETHORPE - PLATNER

(VOLUME XIV OF THE ORIGINAL EDITION)

CROSS REFERENCES FROM THIS VOL-
UME ARE MADE TO THE VOLUME
NUMBERS OF THE ORIGINAL EDITION.

CONTRIBUTORS
VOLUME VII, PART 2

CHARLES DAVID ABBOTT . . . . C. D. A.
THOMAS P. ABERNETHY . . . . T. P. A.
ADELINE ADAMS . . . . A. A.
JAMES TRUSLOW ADAMS . . . . J. T. A.
RAYMOND WILLIAM ADAMS . . R. W. A.
DANIEL DULANY ADDISON . . D. D. A.
NELSON F. ADKINS . . . . . . N. F. A.
ROBERT GREENHALGH ALBION . R. G. A.
WILLIAM F. ALBRIGHT . . . . . W. F. A.
CARROLL S. ALDEN . . . . . . C. S. A.
EDMUND KIMBALL ALDEN . . . E. K. A.
RICHARD ALDRICH . . . . R. A.
WILLIAM H. ALLISON . . . . . W. H. A.
KATHARINE H. AMEND . . . . K. H. A.
MARGUERITE APPLETON . . . . M. A.
RAYMOND CLARE ARCHIBALD . . R. C. A.
CHARLES F. ARROWOOD . . . . C. F. A.
PERCY M. ASHBURN . . . . . P. M. A.
ASTLEY P. C. ASHHURST . . . . A. P. C. A.
JOSEPH CULLEN AYER . . . . J. C. A.
SAMUEL GARDINER AYRES. . . . S. G. A.
ELIZABETH M. BACON . . . . . E. M. B—n.
CHRISTINA H. BAKER . . . . . C. H. B.
HORACE B. BAKER . . . . . . H. B. B.
THOMAS S. BARCLAY . . . . . T. S. B.
LEWELLYS F. BARKER . . . . . L. F. B.
VIOLA F. BARNES . . . . V. F. B.
CLARIBEL R. BARNETT . . . . C. R. B.
DAVID P. BARROWS . . . . . . D. P. B.
CLARENCE BARTLETT . . . . . C. B—t.
HOWARD R. BARTLETT . . . . H. R. B.
GEORGE A. BARTON . . . . . G. A. B—n.
EDSON S. BASTIN . . . . E. S. B—n.
ALAN M. BATEMAN . . . . . A. M. B.
ERNEST SUTHERLAND BATES . E. S. B—s.
GEORGE GORDON BATTLE . . G. G. B.
WILLIAM G. BEAN . . . . . W. G. B—n.
ROBERT P. BELLOWS . . . . . R. P. B.
ORVAL BENNETT . . . . O. B.
C. C. BENSON . . . . C. C. B.
PERCY W. BIDWELL . . . . . . P. W. B.
THEODORE C. BLEGEN . . . . . T. C. B.
WILLARD GROSVENOR BLEYER . . W. G. B—r.
LOUISE PEARSON BLODGET . . . L. P. B—t.
LANSING B. BLOOM . . . . . L. B. B.
G. ALDER BLUMER . . . . . . G. A. B—r.
ERNEST LUDLOW BOGART . . . . E. L. B.
HERBERT E. BOLTON . . . . . H. E. B.
ROBERT W. BOLWELL . . . . . R. W. B.

EDWIN M. BORCHARD . . . . . E. M. B—d.
SARAH G. BOWERMAN . . . . . S. G. B.
JULIAN P. BOYD . . . . J. P. B.
WILLIAM K. BOYD . . . . . . W. K. B.
ELIZABETH BRECKENRIDGE . . . E. B.
CRANE BRINTON . . . . C. B—n.
JEAN LAMBERT BROCKWAY . . . J. L. B.
ROBERT C. BROOKS . . . . . . R. C. B.
L. PARMLY BROWN . . . . L. P. B—n.
PAUL E. BRYAN . . . . P. E. B.
G. MacLAREN BRYDON . . . . . G. M. B.
F. LAURISTON BULLARD . . . . F. L. B.
EDMUND C. BURNETT . . . . . E. C. B.
WILLIAM MILL BUTLER . . . . W. M. B.
HENRY J. CADBURY . . . . . . H. J. C.
HUNTINGTON CAIRNS . . . . . H. C.
ISABEL M. CALDER . . . . . . I. M. C.
WILLIAM S. CARPENTER . . . . W. S. C.
ZECHARIAH CHAFEE, JR. . . . . Z. C., Jr.
WAYLAND J. CHASE . . . . . W. J. C.
FRANCIS A. CHRISTIE . . . . F. A. C.
JANE CLARK . . . . J. C.
ROBERT C. CLARK . . . . . . R. C. C—k.
HUGH McD. CLOKIE . . . . . H. M. C.
FREDERICK W. COBURN . . . . F. W. C.
ROBERT P. TRISTRAM COFFIN . . R. P. T. C.
FANNIE L. GWINNER COLE . . . F. L. G. C.
FLORENCE CONVERSE . . . . . F. C.
ROBERT SPENCER COTTERILL . . R. S. C.
GEORGE S. COTTMAN . . . . . G. S. C.
ROBERT C. COTTON . . . . . . R. C. C—n
E. MERTON COULTER . . . . . E. M. C.
THEODORE S. COX . . . . . . T. S. C.
KATHARINE ELIZABETH CRANE . K. E. C.
ROBERT IRVIN CRATTY . . . . . R. I. C.
EDWARD E. CURTIS . . . . . E. E. C.
EDWARD E. DALE . . . . . . E. E. D.
CHARLES B. DAVIS . . . . . . C. B. D.
RALPH DAVOL . . . . R. D.
RICHARD E. DAY . . . . R. E. D.
BABETTE DEUTSCH . . . . . . B. D.
IRVING DILLIARD . . . . I. D.
JOHN J. DOLAN . . . . J. J. D.
HAROLD I. DONNELLY . . . . . H. I. D.
WILLIAM HOWE DOWNES . . . W. H. D.
STELLA M. DRUMM . . . . . S. M. D.
EDWARD A. DUDDY . . . . . . E. A. D.
RAYMOND S. DUGAN . . . . . R. S. D.
ANDREW G. DU MEZ . . . . . A. G. D—M.

Contributors

Walter A. Dyer	W. A. D.
Rosamonde Hopkins Earle	R. H. E.
J. Harold Easterby	J. H. E.
Edward Dwight Eaton	E. D. E.
Walter Prichard Eaton	W. P. E.
Edwin Francis Edgett	E. F. E.
Everett E. Edwards	E. E. E.
Barnett A. Elzas	B. A. E.
Amos A. Ettinger	A. A. E.
Daniel Evans	D. E.
Paul D. Evans	P. D. E.
Herman L. Fairchild	H. L. F.
Charles Fairman	C. F.
Paul Patton Faris	P. P. F.
Hallie Farmer	H. F.
Ethel Webb Faulkner	E. W. F.
Harold U. Faulkner	H. U. F.
James Kip Finch	J. K. F.
Mary Elizabeth Fittro	M. E. F.
Paul J. Foik	P. J. F.
Henry Wilder Foote	H. W. F.
Harold N. Fowler	H. N. F.
Dixon Ryan Fox	D. R. F.
L. Webster Fox	L. W. F.
John H. Frederick	J. H. F.
John C. French	J. C. F.
Claude M. Fuess	C. M. F.
Joseph V. Fuller	J. V. F.
John F. Fulton	J. F. F.
Paul N. Garber	P. N. G.
Lee Garby	L. G.
F. Lynwood Garrison	F. L. G.
George Harvey Genzmer	G. H. G.
John H. Gerould	J. H. G.
W. J. Ghent	W. J. G.
William Frederic Giese	W. F. G.
Lawrence H. Gipson	L. H. G.
Harry Gehman Good	H. G. G.
Colin B. Goodykoontz	C. B. G.
Armistead Churchill Gordon, Jr.	A. C. G., Jr.
Kenneth M. Gould	K. M. G.
E. Allison Grant	E. A. G.
Charles Graves	C. G.
Anne King Gregorie	A. K. G.
Ernest S. Griffith	E. S. G.
Richard M. Gummere	R. M. G.
Sidney Gunn	S. G.
James Samuel Guy	J. S. G.
Charles W. Hackett	C. W. H.
LeRoy R. Hafen	L. R. H.
Percival Hall	P. H.
Marguerite Bartlett Hamer	M. B. H.
Philip M. Hamer	P. M. H.
J. G. deR. Hamilton	J. G. deR. H.
Talbot Faulkner Hamlin	T. F. H.
George McLean Harper	G. M. H.
Fred E. Haynes	F. E. H—s.
Earl L. W. Heck	E. L. W. H.
Samuel J. Heidner	S. J. H.
H. H. Henline	H. H. H.
Amos L. Herold	A. L. H.
Granville Hicks	G. H.
John Donald Hicks	J. D. H.
William Ernest Hocking	W. E. H.
John Haynes Holmes	J. H. H.
Oliver W. Holmes	O. W. H.
Ivan Lee Holt	I. L. H.
B. Smith Hopkins	B. S. H.
Walter Hough	W. H.
John Tasker Howard	J. T. H.
Leland Ossian Howard	L. O. H.
Theodora Kimball Hubbard	T. K. H.
Harry M. Hubbell	H. M. H.
Francis Edwin Hyde	F. E. H—e
Albert Hyma	A. H.
Asher Isaacs	A. I.
Edith J. R. Isaacs	E. J. R. I.
Joseph Jackson	J. J.
Alfred P. James	A. P. J.
Willis L. Jepson	W. L. J.
Rufus M. Jones	R. M. J.
Charles H. Judd	C. H. J.
Louis C. Karpinski	L. C. K.
Louise Phelps Kellogg	L. P. K.
Rayner W. Kelsey	R. W. K.
Ruth Anna Ketring	R. A. K.
Edward L. Keyes	E. L. K.
Alma Dexta King	A. D. K.
Edward S. King	E. S. K.
Louis A. Klein	L. A. K.
John R. Kline	J. R. K.
Grant C. Knight	G. C. K.
G. Adolf Koch	G. A. K.
Max J. Kohler	M. J. K.
Alois F. Kovarik	A. F. K.
E. B. Krumbhaar	E. B. K.
Charles B. Kuhlmann	C. B. K.
Elbert C. Lane	E. C. L.
William Chauncy Langdon	W. C. L.
Kenneth S. Latourette	K. S. L.
George M. Lewis	G. M. L.
Orin G. Libby	O. G. L.
Anna Lane Lingelbach	A. L. L.
Charles Sumner Lobingier	C. S. L.
Mildred E. Lombard	M. E. L.
Ella Lonn	E. L.
Charles E. T. Lull	C. E. T. L.
Thatcher T. P. Luquer	T. T. P. L.
Harry Miller Lydenberg	H. M. L.
Thomas Ollive Mabbott	T. O. M.
Thomas McCrae	T. M.
Roger P. McCutcheon	R. P. M.
Joseph McFarland	J. McF.
Reginald C. McGrane	R. C. McG
Kenneth McKenzie	K. McK.

Contributors

Donald L. McMurry	D. L. M.
Katherine McNamara	K. McN.
James C. Malin	J. C. M.
W. C. Mallalieu	W. C. M.
H. A. Marmer	H. A. M.
Frederick H. Martens	F. H. M.
William R. Maxon	W. R. M.
Robert Douthat Meade	R. D. M.
Leila Mechlin	L. M.
Lafayette B. Mendel	L. B. M.
Clarence W. Mendell	C. W. M—l.
A. Howard Meneely	A. H. M.
George P. Merrill	G. P. M.
Frank J. Metcalf	F. J. M.
Adolf Meyer	A. M.
Raymond C. Miller	R. C. M—r.
Florence Milligan	F. M.
Harvey C. Minnich	H. C. M.
Broadus Mitchell	B. M.
Wilmot B. Mitchell	W. B. M.
Carl W. Mitman	C. W. M—n.
Conrad Henry Moehlman	C. H. M.
Robert E. Moody	R. E. M.
Warren King Moorehead	W. K. M.
Samuel Eliot Morison	S. E. M.
Frank Luther Mott	F. L. M.
Edmund C. Mower	E. C. M.
John Herbert Nelson	J. H. N.
Thomas K. Nelson	T. K. N.
H. Edward Nettles	H. E. N.
Allan Nevins	A. N.
Lyman C. Newell	L. C. N.
Roy F. Nichols	R. F. N.
J. Bennett Nolan	J. B. N.
Joe L. Norris	J. L. N.
Walter B. Norris	W. B. N.
Grace Lee Nute	G. L. N.
Frank M. O'Brien	F. M. O.
Francis R. Packard	F. R. P.
Laurence B. Packard	L. B. P.
Victor H. Paltsits	V. H. P.
Scott H. Paradise	S. H. P.
Charles W. Parker	C. W. P.
Henry Bamford Parkes	H. B. P.
James W. Patton	J. W. P—n.
Charles O. Paullin	C. O. P.
Theodore C. Pease	T. C. P.
James H. Peeling	J. H. P—g.
Josiah H. Penniman	J. H. P—n.
Hobart S. Perry	H. S. P.
Charles E. Persons	C. E. P.
Frederick T. Persons	F. T. P.
A. Everett Peterson	A. E. P.
James M. Phalen	J. M. P—n.
Francis S. Philbrick	F. S. P.
Frank L. Pleadwell	F. L. P.
John M. Poor	J. M. P—r.
Charles Shirley Potts	C. S. P.
Julius W. Pratt	J. W. P—t.
Richard J. Purcell	R. J. P.
Belle Rankin	B. R.
Albert G. Rau	A. G. R.
P. O. Ray	P. O. R.
Thomas T. Read	T. T. R.
Herbert S. Reichle	H. S. R.
Alfred E. Richards	A. E. R.
Thomas A. Rickard	T. A. R.
Robert E. Riegel	R. E. R.
Donald A. Roberts	D. A. R.
George Roberts	G. R.
Burr Arthur Robinson	B. A. R.
Edwin Arlington Robinson	E. A. R.
William A. Robinson	W. A. R.
J. Magnus Rohne	J. M. R.
Lois K. M. Rosenberry	L. K. M. R.
Marvin B. Rosenberry	M. B. R.
Victor Rosewater	V. R.
Joseph Schafer	J. S—r.
Israel Schapiro	I. S.
Leslie M. Scott	L. M. S.
Horace Wells Sellers	H. W. S.
James Lee Sellers	J. L. S.
Thorsten Sellin	T. S—n.
Robert Francis Seybolt	R. F. S.
Robert Shafer	R. S.
Benjamin F. Shambaugh	B. F. S.
William Bristol Shaw	W. B. S.
Guy Emery Shipler	G. E. S.
Lester B. Shippee	L. B. S.
Kenneth C. M. Sills	K. C. M. S.
Alexander Silverman	A. S.
Francis Butler Simkins	F. B. S.
Theodore Sizer	T. S—r.
David Stanley Smith	D. S. S.
Edward Conrad Smith	E. C. S.
Herbert Solow	H. S.
E. Wilder Spaulding	E. W. S.
Oliver L. Spaulding, Jr.	O. L. S., Jr.
Thomas M. Spaulding	T. M. S.
C. P. Stacey	C. P. S.
Harris Elwood Starr	H. E. S.
Henry P. Stearns	H. P. S.
Raymond P. Stearns	R. P. S.
Leo F. Stock	L. F. S.
Witmer Stone	W. S.
R. H. Sudds	R. H. S.
James Sullivan	J. S—n.
Charles S. Sydnor	C. S. S.
David Y. Thomas	D. Y. T.
Charles M. Thompson	C. M. T.
Ernest Trice Thompson	E. T. T.
Herbert Thoms	H. T.
Irving L. Thomson	I. L. T.
Edward S. Thorpe	E. S. T.
Edward Larocque Tinker	E. L. T.
Elizabeth Todd	E. T.

Contributors

Charles C. Torrey . . . . . C. C. T.
Harry A. Toulmin, Jr. . . . . H. A. T., Jr.
Aaron L. Treadwell . . . . . A. L. T.
Alonzo H. Tuttle . . . . . . A. H. T.
George B. Utley . . . . . . G. B. U.
William T. Utter . . . . . . W. T. U.
John T. Vance . . . . J. T. V.
Thomas C. Van Cleve . . . . T. C. V—C.
Henry R. Viets . . . . H. R. V.
Harold G. Villard . . . . . . H. G. V.
Eugene M. Violette . . . . . E. M. V.
James J. Walsh . . . . . . J. J. W.
Harry R. Warfel . . . . . . H. R. W.
Aldred S. Warthin . . . . . . A. S. W.
W. Randall Waterman . . . . W. R. W.
Francis P. Weisenburger . . . F. P. W.
Paul Weiss . . . . P. W.
Charles L. Wells . . . . . . C. L. W.

F. Estelle Wells . . . . . . F. E. W.
Elizabeth Howard West . . . E. H. W.
Allan Westcott . . . . A. W.
Arthur P. Whitaker . . . . . A. P. W.
Jerome K. Wilcox . . . . . . J. K. W.
Estelle Parthenia Wild . . . E. P. W.
Herbert U. Williams . . . . . H. U. W.
Mary Wilhelmine Williams . M. W. W.
Stanley T. Williams . . . . . S. T. W.
Helen Sumner Woodbury . . H. S. W.
Robert M. Woodbury . . . R. M. W.
Maude H. Woodfin . . . . . M. H. W.
Thomas Woody . . . . T. W.
Walter L. Wright, Jr. . . . . W. L. W., Jr.
Lawrence C. Wroth . . . . . L. C. W.
Donovan Yeuell . . . . D. Y.
Edwin H. Zeydel . . . . . . E. H. Z.

DICTIONARY OF

AMERICAN BIOGRAPHY

Oglethorpe — Platner

OGLETHORPE, JAMES EDWARD (Dec. 22, 1696–June 30, 1785), soldier, philanthropist, founder of the colony of Georgia, was born in London, the son of two stanch Jacobites, Sir Theophilus and Lady Eleanor (Wall) Oglethorpe, who endowed him with an abiding loyalty to the Crown, the military and parliamentary family tradition, strong moral courage, and a high purpose. Educated at Eton and Corpus Christi College, Oxford, he held a succession of army commissions until 1715, when he migrated to Paris, whence in 1717 he took service under Prince Eugene of Savoy against the Turks. Having gained a deservedly high military reputation, he later joined his family as a satellite at the quasi-court of James III at Saint Germain, France, and Urbino, Italy. For two years he was wholly engulfed in the Jacobite maelstrom, serving the cause in England, France, and Italy; but his return to England in 1719 marked the definite cessation of his Jacobite interest, and he soon succeeded his elder brother as incumbent of the family estate of Westbrook in Godalming, Surrey. Here he seems to have remained quietly until in 1722 he emerged from his rural retreat as a candidate for Parliament.

Succeeding his father and two elder brothers, Oglethorpe represented Haslemere for thirty-two years, despite virulent Whig opposition in the elections of 1722, 1734, and 1741. He placed himself on record as a mild High Tory, an advocate of restrictions on the use of distilled spirits, an opponent of both royal extravagance and Walpole's autocratic mismanagement in domestic affairs, a protagonist of national defense and anti-continental isolation, an ardent advocate of the spiritually oppressed, and a strong supporter of the budding Industrial Revolution. Persistently advocating naval preparedness and the expansion of imperial commerce and voicing his colonial and commercial policy in phrases which, presaging the principles of Burke, Franklin and Jefferson, proclaimed at once the unity of the empire and the equality of all its citizens, whereever situate, Oglethorpe favored imperial preference, not isolated protection. His humanitarian bent was manifested in his reports of 1729–30 concerning penal conditions, especially in the debtors' prisons, in his exposé of the evils of impressment in a pamphlet, *The Sailor's Advocate* (1728), which went through eight editions, and in his avowed antipathy to negro slavery.

His interest in penal reform led him to conceive the idea of sending newly freed and unemployed debtors to America. While his plans matured and two sums of money came to aid him, the position of Carolina on the southern frontier of the English colonies, exposed to predatory raids of Indians, Spaniards, and the French, led the British government to seek a sound program of simultaneous colonial expansion and defense. Hence, after a long period of many trials, Oglethorpe and nineteen associates received a charter on June 9/20, 1732, creating them "Trustees for establishing the colony of Georgia in America," for a period of twenty-one years. The motives for the grant were threefold: to relieve domestic unemployment, to strengthen the colonies and increase imperial trade and navigation, and to provide a buffer state for Carolina. Oglethorpe played a major rôle in securing proper publicity and adequate revenues for the venture. In the former endeavor he utilized the newspapers and produced a prospectus, *A New and Accurate Account of the Provinces of South-Carolina and Georgia* (1732). With the help of royal approbation he secured, among other contributions, the grant originally intended for Bishop Berkeley's Bermudan and Rhode Island projects. The death of his mother in June 1732 left him unencumbered by domestic ties, and he determined to accompany the first band of emigrants.

From his landing at Charleston on Jan. 13, 1733, until his return to England late in 1734, he gave his attention chiefly to problems of administration. The neighboring Indians were conciliated at a convention where Oglethorpe secured a grant of the site of Savannah and the promise of the Indians to cease communication with the French and Spaniards. Fortifications were built and a rigorous system of military training established. Efforts were made to attract further immigration—a policy distinctively Oglethorpe's, for the British government opposed it—and resulted in the arrival in 1734 of the Salzburger Lutherans, the first religious body to seek asylum in Georgia. Lack of interest on the part of some trustees, together with constant need of money and certain neglect in his correspondence, led Oglethorpe to return to England in 1734. The press welcomed him and his Indian companions, and his presence revived the interest of his fellow trustees. Largely at his instigation, they now enacted important measures prohibiting the sale of rum, prohibiting negro slavery, and providing for the regulation of peaceful dealings with the Indians by means of a licensing system.

Rumors of insurrection led Oglethorpe to return to Georgia in December 1735, taking with him Charles and John Wesley to minister to the spiritual needs of his settlers. The policy of religious toleration brought results. To the flourishing congregation of Salzburger Lutherans were now added a colony of Scotch Highlander Presbyterians, equally valuable for military purposes. Three bands of Moravians under A. G. Spangenburg, David Nitzchmann, and Peter Boehler [qq.v.] came in 1735, 1736, and 1738, respectively. The Georgian careers of the Wesleys, despite Oglethorpe's best endeavors, were both brought to abortive conclusions through lack of sympathy with pioneer conditions and unfortunate encounters with the daughters of Eve. Charles sailed for England in 1736; John in 1737.

Almost immediately upon his return in 1736 Oglethorpe had founded Frederica on the Altamaha as a southern outpost against the Spaniards. To promote the military establishment he now incurred huge debts which the trustees, in sheer desperation, referred to the British government. Simultaneously Carolina rose in its wrath over the licensing of the Indian trade which deprived that colony of a lucrative traffic.

The storm now broke over Oglethorpe's head. Spain's complaints of his encroachments at Frederica, the trustees' ire at his failure to make regular reports, tales spread in London by returned malcontents, and the embattled Carolinians' prompt appeal to Whitehall drew him once more to England (1736–37). There, with honeyed words and a more equable balance sheet, he pacified the trustees; the Carolina question was compromised; the malcontents were silenced; but the Spanish issue remained. Early in 1737 Oglethorpe sought a parliamentary grant for the defense of his colony, and when it appeared that Walpole had intended to use Georgia as a pawn in his temporizing with Spain, the former bluntly criticized the Prime Minister and, ultimately gaining his desires, returned to Georgia in September 1738, with a regiment of seven hundred men.

Henceforth the vital concern in the life of Georgia and its governor was the war with Spain. By virtue of its proximity to Florida and its status in Spanish eyes as *terra irredenta*, Georgia was the logical point of first attack. Opening with a mutiny which, quelled by Oglethorpe, made him but the more determined to save his colony, the war developed into a futile attack on St. Augustine in 1740 by the Georgians, loyally aided by the Carolinians, and an equally unsuccessful Spanish riposte against Frederica in 1742. Despite the inertia of the trustees and the British government, Oglethorpe, by borrowing on all his English property, provided an adequate defense and saved Georgia to the empire. This period was also notable for the passing of the Moravians, who, reluctant to bear arms, removed to Pennsylvania; for the growth of the Anglican, Lutheran, and Calvinist elements in the colony; and for the missionary labors of George Whitefield [q.v.], whose orphanage Oglethorpe particularly befriended. The calm of domestic affairs was disturbed by the unwarranted expenditures of the storekeeper, the problems of primogeniture and tail male, and the protests of malcontents against the prohibitory laws. Oglethorpe gradually lost most of his great administrative powers. An attack on St. Augustine in 1743 failed, and an ever-deepening discontent and dissatisfaction with his policy, together with charges against him by a subordinate, drew him home in September 1743. He was brought before a court martial; the charges against him were dismissed as "frivolous . . . and without foundation"; but his colonizing days were ended.

The rest of his life was perhaps an anticlimax. Marriage on Sept. 15, 1744, to Elizabeth Wright, heiress of Crantham Hall, Essex; imperfect leadership in the campaign against the Young Pretender in 1745, resulting in a court martial in which he was acquitted; and the sop of promotion to lieutenant-general in 1746 and general in 1765, led him to a ripe old age, passed in the literary circle of Samuel Johnson, Boswell, Goldsmith, Horace Walpole, Edmund Burke, and the Georgian Ladies' Clubs, with Hannah More, Mrs. Vesey, Mrs. Carter, and Mrs. Montagu. His death on June 30, 1785, closed a career full of promise and replete with achievement in the expansion of the British empire beyond the seas: the career of an imperial philanthropist.

[The chief sources for Oglethorpe's early life are the various volumes of Reports of the Historical MSS. Commission, and the King's Collection of Stuart Papers at Windsor Castle (see *Calendar of the Stuart Papers ... Preserved at Windsor Castle*, 7 vols., 1902–23). For his parliamentary career, see Wm. Cobbett, *Cobbett's Parliamentary Hist. of England* (1811), vols. VIII–XV, and *Journals of the House of Commons*, vols. XX–XXVI; and for the colonization of Georgia see the *Gentleman's Magazine*, 1730–85; *MSS. of the Earl of Egmont: Diary of Viscount Percival Afterwards First Earl of Egmont* (3 vols., 1920–23); *The Colonial Records of the State of Ga.* (26 vols., 1904–16), ed. by A. D. Candler, esp. vols. XXI–XXV; and *Ga. Hist. Soc. Colls.*, vols. I–III (1840–73), vol. VII (3 pts., 1909–13). For the Johnsonian era see Geoffrey Scott and F. A. Pottle, *Private Papers of James Boswell . . . in the Coll. of Lt.-Col. Ralph Heyward Isham* (19 vols., 1928–34). Among secondary works, see V. W. Crane, "The Philanthropists and the Genesis of Georgia," *Am. Hist. Rev.*, Oct. 1921; R. A. Roberts, "The Birth of an American State: Georgia: An Effort of Philanthropy and Protestant Propaganda," *Trans. Royal Hist. Soc.*, 4 ser. VI (London, 1923); J. R. McCain, *Georgia as a Proprietary Province: The Execution of a Trust* (1917); A. E. Clark-Kennedy, *Stephen Hales, D.D., F.R.S.* (1929); James Boswell, *The Life of Samuel Johnson* (1791); Nehemiah Curnock, *The Jour. of John Wesley*, vol. I (1909); John Telford, *The Letters of the Rev. John Wesley* (1931), vol. I. For biographies of Oglethorpe, see Robert Wright, *A Memoir of General James Oglethorpe* (1867); Austin Dobson, *A Paladin of Philanthropy* (1899); Henry Bruce, *Life of General Oglethorpe* (1890); L. F. Church, *Oglethorpe* (1932). A forthcoming study, with a full bibliography, will be A. A. Ettinger, "James Edward Oglethorpe, Imperial Idealist."]   A. A. E.

O'GORMAN, THOMAS (May 1, 1843–Sept. 18, 1921), Catholic educator and prelate, son of John and Margaret (O'Keefe) O'Gorman, was born in Boston. In 1848 his parents moved to Chicago, and later, to St. Paul, Minn., in which cities Thomas received his early schooling. Bishop Joseph Crétin [*q.v.*] sent O'Gorman and John Ireland [*q.v.*] to study for the priesthood at the French seminaries of Meximieux and Monthel. Ordained, Nov. 5, 1865, in the St. Paul Cathedral by Bishop Thomas L. Grace, O'Gorman was stationed as pastor of St. John's Church, Rochester, Minn., until he joined the Congregation of St. Paul the Apostle (1878). As a Paulist, he served at the Church of St. Paul the Apostle, New York, and traveled throughout the United States on the mission band. Returning to

St. Paul diocese, he was given the parish of the Immaculate Conception in Faribault (1882). Three years later, Bishop Ireland appointed him first rector of St. Thomas College, St. Paul, where he also taught dogmatic theology. In 1890 he was called to the chair of ecclesiastical history in the recently established Catholic University of America in Washington. While there he wrote *A History of the Roman Catholic Church in the United States* (1895), for the American Church History Series, which was well received, although hardly more than a good summary of J. G. Shea's monumental work. Besides this book, a printed lecture, *How Catholics Come To Be Misunderstood* (n.d.), and an occasional fugitive article, he did little writing. Of imposing appearance and a winning personality, he is said to have been an inspiring teacher and a good lecturer.

In 1896, through the nomination of Archbishop Ireland, he was appointed second bishop of Sioux Falls, S. D., and consecrated, Apr. 19, in St. Patrick's Church, Washington, D. C., by Cardinal Satolli, the papal delegate. In 1902 he was selected by President Roosevelt to accompany Judge Taft on his mission to Rome for the settlement of the friar-land claims in the Philippines. As bishop, he saw his diocese thrive for a quarter of a century, the Catholic population grow from 30,000 to 70,000, the number of priests more than double; churches and missions increase, and large hospitals erected at Sioux Falls, Aberdeen, Milbank, Mitchell, Pierre, and Yankton. Especially interested in education, he built eighteen parochial schools; gave ample patronage to a number of academies; and founded in 1909 Columbus College at Chamberlain, S. D., under the Clerics of St. Viator, which in 1921 was superseded by a new institution at Sioux Falls, under specially trained diocesan priests. Death came from a paralytic stroke, and the bishop was buried from his recently dedicated St. Joseph's Cathedral.

[G. W. Kingsbury and G. M. Smith, *Hist. of Dakota Territory*, etc. (5 vols., 1915), vol. IV; Doane Robinson, *South Dakota* (1930), vol. I; *Who's Who in America*, 1920–21; *The Am. Cath. Who's Who* (1911); *Cath. Univ. Bull.*, Apr. 1896, II, 215; annual Cath. directories; *Daily Argus-Leader* (Sioux Falls), Sept. 19, 22, 1921; *Sioux Falls Press*, Sept. 20, 1921.]   R. J. P.

O'HARA, JAMES (1752–Dec. 16, 1819), Revolutionary soldier, manufacturer, was born in Ireland, the son of John O'Hara. It is said that he was educated at the seminary of St. Sulpice in Paris, gave up the ensign's commission given him by his relative, Lord Tyrawley, and entered a ship-broker's office in Liverpool to learn business methods before sailing for America. Upon receiving a legacy from a cousin he left England and settled in Philadelphia in 1772. The following year he entered the employ of Devereaux Smith and Ephraim Douglas of Pittsburgh in carrying on trade with the Indians. This work took him to the wilderness of western Virginia. Later he became a government agent among the Indians. At the outbreak of the Revolution he volunteered as a private, later equipped a company of volunteers, and was elected captain. His company saw much service on the frontier at Kanawha and then, as part of the forces of George Rogers Clark, during the expedition to Vincennes. In 1779 all but twenty-nine of his company had been killed in action, and those survivors were thereupon placed under Daniel Brodhead's command. He was selected by the general to carry an important message to Washington asking for supplies. Later he became commissary at the general hospital and was stationed at Carlisle, Pa. The years 1781–83 found him serving as the assistant-quartermaster for General Greene.

After the Revolution he married Mary Carson of Philadelphia. In their home at Pittsburgh he placed some of the first carpets brought across the Alleghany Mountains, and it is said that the neighbors called them coverlets and were amazed to see them laid on the floor. The O'Haras had six children. He entered business and filled many large contracts for the government. In 1792 President Washington appointed him quartermaster of the United States army, and he served during the Whisky Rebellion and General Wayne's expedition against the Indians. He is credited with "saving the army" by his efficient business methods and remarkable understanding of the Indian character and varied dialects. Resigning in 1796, he again became a government contractor and continued in that capacity until 1802. Sometime earlier he had formed a partnership with Maj. Isaac Craig, with whom he erected the first glassworks in Pittsburgh. To superintend the work he hired a German chemist, William Peter Eichbaum, with whom he journeyed from Philadelphia on foot. Their first successful product, the result of costly experimentation, was glass bottles, and their plant became famous. This plant was one of the first of its kind to use coal as fuel. He next turned his attention to the salt industry. He found that salt was carried overland on pack horses from New York state and was therefore very expensive. He built boats for the purpose of transporting this important product more cheaply. On the outward trip he loaded the boats with flour, provisions, and other merchandise in salt barrels, which were

reserved in his contracts and, when empty, were filled with salt for the return trip. He also built vessels to carry cotton to Liverpool and was one of the pioneers in this trade. His *General Butler* was captured by a Spanish vessel in 1807. He became a director and then president of the Pittsburgh branch of the Bank of Pennsylvania. He was interested in iron works at Ligonier in partnership with John Henry Hopkins [*q.v.*]. Having invested heavily in real estate in the rapidly growing town of Pittsburgh, he found himself "land poor" during the crisis of 1817 and was saved from bankruptcy by his friend, James Ross. Nevertheless, by the time of his death, two years later, he had cleared his estate of all debt. He was buried in the churchyard of the First Presbyterian Church, but his remains were subsequently moved to the Allegheny Cemetery.

["Letter-Book of Major Isaac Craig," *Hist. Reg.: Notes and Queries*, Sept. 1884; *Fort Pitt and Letters from the Frontier*, comp. by M. C. Darlington (1892); *Western Pa. Hist. Mag.*, Oct. 1926; *Hist. of Allegheny County, Pa.* (1889); R. M. Knittle, *Early American Glass* (copr. 1927).]　　　　　　　　　　A.I.

O'HARA, THEODORE (Feb. 11, 1820–June 6, 1867), journalist, soldier, was born at Danville, Ky. His father, Kean O'Hara, was one of three brothers who were implicated in Lord Edward Fitzgerald's Irish conspiracy in 1798 and fled with their father to the United States. He became famous in Kentucky as a schoolmaster, married a woman of Maryland Irish lineage, and bestowed affectionate care on the training of his son. After graduating in 1839 from St. Joseph's College, Bardstown, O'Hara read law in the office of William Owsley [*q.v.*] at Frankfort, made a lifelong friend of his fellow clerk, John Cabell Breckinridge [*q.v.*], and was admitted to practice in 1842. Soon thereafter he secured an appointment in the Treasury at Washington, but finding a clerk's life unbearably tame he returned to Frankfort and joined the staff of the *Yeoman*. During the Mexican War he served from June 26, 1846, to Oct. 15, 1848, as captain and assistant quartermaster of Kentucky volunteers, was brevetted major Aug. 20, 1847, for gallant and meritorious conduct at Contreras and Churubusco, and participated in the battle of Chapultepec as a member of Franklin Pierce's staff. After another sojourn in Washington he went back to the *Yeoman*. In the winter of 1849–50 he joined Narciso Lopez's expedition to "liberate" Cuba and was made colonel of the Kentucky regiment, which numbered about 240 men. They landed at Cardenas early in the morning of May 19, 1850, but O'Hara's filibustering on Cuban soil lasted only a few hours. He was shot in the legs while leading an attack on the Spanish barracks, was taken aboard ship, and conveyed safely to the United States. In 1852 he became one of the six editors, every man of them a colonel, of the Louisville *Times,* a militant anti-Know-Nothing sheet that was extinguished by its opponents' victory in the elections of 1855. He was a captain in the 2nd United States Cavalry from Mar. 3, 1855 to Dec. 1, 1856, and an editor of the Mobile *Register* from then until the oncoming of the Civil War. With his usual enthusiasm he raised the Mobile Light Dragoons and in January 1861, with the assistance of kindred spirits, seized Fort Barrancas in Pensacola harbor. Later he was colonel of the 12th Alabama Infantry and a staff officer to Albert Sidney Johnston and, after Johnston's death at Shiloh, to his old friend Breckinridge. After the war he became a cotton merchant at Columbus, Ga., but a fire destroyed his warehouse and other property. He never married. The story of his connection with William Walker, the Nicaraguan filibuster (Collins, *post,* I, 411), is apocryphal, and his movements during several periods of his career have not been traced.

O'Hara was of medium height, with black hair, hazel eyes, and regular features, was fastidious in his dress, and comported himself like the Irish gentleman that he was. Besides the social charm and derring-do that were natural to him, he possessed a magniloquence that his friends amiably mistook for evidence of literary genius. He is remembered for a single poem, "The Bivouac of the Dead," a sonorous dirge commemorating the re-interment at Frankfort, July 20, 1847, of the Kentuckians slain in the battle of Buena Vista. The poem exists in two versions, of which the earlier and longer is also the better. Certain lines from it have been carved in marble or cast in bronze on soldiers' monuments or over the gates of military cemeteries throughout the country. His scanty literary remains also include a short dirge for Daniel Boone and a eulogy of William Taylor Barry. The latter was long regarded as a masterpiece of Southern oratory. O'Hara spent his last days on a friend's plantation near Guerryton, Ala., where he died of malaria. His body was re-interred in 1874 in the state military cemetery at Frankfort, Ky.

[*Commonwealth* (Frankfort), June 14, 1867; *Louisville Daily Democrat,* June 14, 1867; Lewis and R. H. Collins, *Hist. of Ky.,* vol. I (1874); G. W. Ranck, *O'Hara and His Elegies* (Baltimore, 1875; reviewed in the N. Y. *Nation,* June 29, 1876, by C. E. Norton) and *The Bivouac of the Dead and Its Author* (Cincinnati, 1898); T. H. S. Hamersly, *Complete Regular Army Reg. . . . 1779–1879* (1880); *War of the Rebellion: Official Records* (*Army*), 1 ser. II, X, XX (pt. 1), XXXVIII (pt. 4), LII (pt. 3), 2 ser. III, 4 ser. I; D.

E. O'Sullivan, "Theodore O'Hara," *Southern Bivouac,* Jan. 1887; S. B. Dixon, "The Bivouac of the Dead," *Ibid.,* Mar. 1887; R. B. Wilson, "Theodore O'Hara," *Century Mag.,* May 1890; A. C. Quisenberry, *Lopez's Expeditions to Cuba, 1850–51* (Filson Club Pubs., no. 21, 1906); J. S. Johnston, "Sketch of Theodore O'Hara," *Reg. Ky. State Hist. Soc.,* Sept. 1913; J. W. Townsend, *Ky. in Am. Letters* (1913).]   G. H. G.

O'HIGGINS, HARVEY JERROLD (Nov. 14, 1876–Feb. 28, 1929), novelist, journalist, who has been called the prose laureate of the commonplace man, was born in London, Ontario, Canada, the son of Joseph P. and Isabella Stephenson O'Higgins. He received his education in the common schools and was a member of the class of 1897 at the University of Toronto. He left the University without a degree to begin his long career as a journalist. In July 1901 he married Anna G. Williams of Toronto. He soon began writing for American periodicals, chiefly *Scribner's,* the *Century, McClure's, Collier's,* and *Everybody's,* short detective stories and, later, articles on political and social questions. The sentiment and the love of common types apparent in the short stories appeared in his first full-length works such as *The Smoke-Eaters* (1905), *Don-a-Dreams* (1906), *A Grand Army Man* (1908), and *Old Clinkers* (1909). His success as a practical journalist led naturally to a series of volumes on matters of contemporary political or sociological interest. These he did in collaboration with others possessed of special knowledge in the fields presented. The first, *The Beast* (1910), written with Judge Ben B. Lindsey, deals with the social environment of city-bred youth and presents the reform measures advocated by Judge Lindsey. This volume was followed by *Under the Prophet in Utah* (1911), with Frank J. Cannon, dealing with the organization and functioning of the Mormon Church; *On the Hiring Line* (1909), with Harriet Ford; *The Doughboy's Religion* (1920), with Ben B. Lindsey; and *The American Mind in Action* (1924), with Dr. Edward H. Reade, an attempt to psychoanalyze several eminent Americans (Morris Fishbein, "The Typical American Mind," *Bookman,* June 1924; "The American Mind," *Current Opinion,* May 1924).

The last-mentioned volume indicates a turning point in O'Higgins' career. Serious illness caused him to seek various methods of cure, but the one that seemed to him most effective was that offered by psychoanalysis. He presented a general though spirited view of the subject in *The Secret Springs* (1920) but first applied it in a truly literary manner in *Some Distinguished Americans* (1922) in which he depicted with characteristic clarity and economy a series of characters motivated by the unconscious. His literary use of the psychoanalytic method was more effective than his application of it to actual persons in *The American Mind in Action*. And although he was deeply interested in his newly found literary mode he was not carried to any extreme by his enthusiasm. A good journalist, and the author of many volumes designed to popularize special information, he never became a press agent. His true literary instinct saved him and enabled him finally to produce his best work in *Julie Crane* (1924) and *Clara Barron* (1926), mature and sympathetic studies of modern American women. In these novels he was master not alone of his sure technique but also of his special concepts of character (*Saturday Review of Literature*, Nov. 15, 1924). In collaboration with Harriet Ford, he wrote several successful plays: *The Argyle Case* (1912), a detective drama in which W. J. Burns assisted, *The Dummy* (copyrighted in 1913 under the title *Kidnapped*), a detective comedy, *Polygamy* (1914), a tense drama of marriage under Mormonism, and *Main Street* (1921), which, though not important as drama, enjoyed much popular favor. The last was an endeavor to dramatize the novel by Sinclair Lewis (*Bookman*, December 1921, p. 373).

Throughout his life O'Higgins gave himself constantly and generously to every cause that affected the well-being and dignity of his craft. He devoted himself most assiduously to the work of the Authors' League with which he was actively associated from its establishment until his death. Officially through the League and unofficially through innumerable personal contacts with young authors he worked for the advancement and protection of American writers with a devotion and selflessness gratefully remembered by his co-workers (*Authors' League Bulletin*, March 1929). During the World War (1917–18) he entered the government service under George Creel as associate chairman of the Committee of Public Information. His special task was to answer the propaganda designed to arouse racial animosities within the United States. His patience and humanity admirably fitted him for the task while his inherent liberalism enabled him to see more clearly and to speak more temperately—though with no diminution of effect—on highly controverted matters (*Century*, December 1917, p. 302, January 1918, p. 405). O'Higgins was a man of great personal charm, and perhaps in this fact lies his truest claim to fame. For though he wrote many pleasing short stories and novels and was master of an authentic style he produced no one volume that will place him among the outstanding writers of America.

[*Who's Who in America*, 1928–29; Heywood Broun, "Literary Portraits: Harvey O'Higgins," *Bookman*, Oct. 1921; Burns Mantle, *Am. Playwrights of Today* (1929); Burns Mantle and G. P. Sherwood, *The Best Plays of 1909–19* (1933); "The Man Who Writes Irish Stories," *Current Opinion*, Oct. 1914; *Harper's*, Apr. 1929; *N. Y. Times*, Mar. 1, 1929.]   D. A. R.

OHLMACHER, ALBERT PHILIP (Aug. 19, 1865–Nov. 9, 1916), physician, pathologist, was born in Sandusky, Ohio, the son of Christian John and Anna (Scherer) Ohlmacher. He attended high school at Sycamore, Ill., and took his medical training at Northwestern University, graduating M.D. in 1890. On June 14, 1890, he was married to Grace M. Peck of Sycamore, Ill. He then launched upon a varied medical career. From 1891 to 1894 he was professor of comparative anatomy and embryology at the College of Physicians and Surgeons, Chicago, serving also for two years, 1892–94, at the Chicago Polyclinic. In the latter year, 1894, he went to the medical department of Ohio Wesleyan University as professor of pathology and bacteriology until 1897. For the next four years he was director of the pathological laboratory of the Ohio Hospital for Epileptics at Gallipolis. He then went to the medical department of Northwestern University as professor of pathology, but after a year, 1901–02, returned to the Ohio Hospital for Epileptics as superintendent. In 1905 he became director of the biologic laboratory of Frederick Stearns & Company in Detroit. After serving in this capacity for two years he entered private practice in Detroit and continued in it until his death. In practice he specialized in bacterial and vaccine therapy, and in the treatment of epilepsy. He was the author of various articles in the *American Text-book of Pathology* (1902) and the *Reference Handbook of the Medical Sciences* (vol. VII, 1904). He wrote numerous papers based on original investigations, on blood-platelets, thymus gland, lymphatic constitution, cancer parasite, microtechnique, diphtheria antitoxin, typhoid meningitis, vaccine therapy, epilepsy, and other subjects. He was a fellow of the American Medical Association, and a member of the American Association of Pathologists and Bacteriologists, the National Association for the Study of Epilepsy, the Society of American Bacteriologists, and the National Association for the Study and Prevention of Tuberculosis.

Ohlmacher's chief contributions to science were his studies on the pathology of epilepsy. In cases of idiopathic (primary) epilepsy, he noted the almost constant association of the thymic-lymphatic constitution, as shown by persistence of the thymus, general lymphadenoid hyperplasia, and arterial hypoplasia. From both morphological and physiological grounds he suggested that a relationship exists between genuine epilepsy and rachitis, eclampsia infantilis, thymic asthma and thymic sudden death, tetany, and possibly exophthalmic goiter. He called attention to the frequent occurrence of brain tumors and cerebral developmental disturbances in cases of secondary epilepsy, advancing the opinion that the presence of the neoplasm accounted for the epileptic seizures from which the patients suffered. While his general conclusions have not been confirmed in all respects by later work, Ohlmacher's studies are of importance in that they anticipated by some years the modern conceptions of the epileptic and hyperthyroid constitutions.

[*Who's Who in America*, 1914–15; H. A. Kelly and W. L. Burrage, *Am. Medic. Biogs.* (1920); *Bull. Ohio Hospital for Epileptics*, vol. I (1898) and vol. II (1904); *Jour. Am. Medic. Asso.*, Nov. 18, 1916; the *Detroit Free Press*, Nov. 11, 1916.]   A. S. W.

O'KELLY, JAMES (c. 1735–Oct. 16, 1826), was a pioneer Methodist preacher, who seceded from the Methodist Episcopal Church in 1792 and founded a sect the members of which first called themselves Republican Methodists and later simply "Christians." Whether he was born in Ireland or in America is uncertain. As a young man he seems to have lived in Surry County, Va., and there, about 1760, to have married Elizabeth Meeks; later they moved to Chatham County, N. C. By the time of the Revolution, during which he suffered hardships because of his zealous devotion to the American cause, and saw some army service, he had become a Methodist and was preaching as opportunity offered with much effect.

The first official mention of him appears in the minutes of the Conference held at Leesburg, Va., in May 1778. That year, and the year following, he traveled on the New Hope Circuit, N. C., and in 1780 on the Tan River Circuit. From 1782 his appointments were in Virginia, where for a number of years he served as presiding elder of districts. During this period he became one of the most influential of the Methodist leaders. At the "Christmas Conference" in Baltimore, 1784, at which the Methodist Episcopal Church in the United States was organized, he was one of those elected and ordained elder. A contemporary is quoted as saying of him that he was " 'laborious in the ministry, a man of zeal and usefulness, an advocate for holiness, given to prayer and fasting, an able defender of the Methodist doctrine

and faith, and hard against negro slavery, in private and from the press and pulpit' " (W. W. Bennett, *Memorials of Methodism in Virginia*, 1871, p. 315). He was independent, wilful, and fiery, however, resentful toward any display of authority on the part of individuals in the Church, and, increasingly antagonistic to Asbury, as time went on he became more and more obstreperous. He was a member of the first Council, a body made up of the bishops and presiding elders according to a plan originated by Asbury, who was then averse to General Conferences, for the purpose of directing the affairs of the Church. Immediately after its session, however, he returned to Virginia and began violently to oppose the institution, and to attack Asbury. In January 1790 he wrote the Bishop a letter charging him with exercise of power, and bidding him "stop for one year," or he would use his influence against him. He also wrote to Bishop Coke in England, complaining of Asbury's unwillingness to accede to the demand for a General Conference. Asbury at length yielded, and at the Conference held in Baltimore, Nov. 1, 1792, O'Kelly offered an amendment to the law investing bishops with the power of fixing the appointments of the preachers. After a long debate it was defeated. Subsequently, its author and some of its supporters left the Conference. At Asbury's suggestion the Conference voted him forty pounds per annum on condition that he forbear to excite division. He accepted it for only a short time. The charge that in addition to being opposed to the government of the Church, he had also become heretical in doctrine (see Jesse Lee, *A Short History of the Methodists in the United States of America*, 1810, p. 180) lacks substantiation. About 1798 he published, under the signature "Christicola," *The Author's Apology for Protesting Against the Methodist Episcopal Government*. Based upon material secured by Asbury, Rev. Nicholas Snethen issued in 1800, *A Reply to an Apology. . . .* These were followed by *A Vindication of an Apology* (1801) and, on Snethen's part, by *An Answer to James O'Kelly's Vindication of His Apology*. As a result of his secession, the Methodist Episcopal Church suffered a considerable loss in membership, and O'Kelly devoted the remainder of his life to the new organization which he and his followers established in 1793, then called the Republican Methodist Church, congregational in polity and with the Scriptures as its only creed and rule of faith and practice. A year later its adherents began to call themselves simply "Christians." He published pamphlets, tracts, and books, among them, *Essay on Negro Slavery*

(1784) ; *Divine Oracles Consulted* (1800) ; *The Christian Church* (1801) ; *Letters from Heaven Consulted* (1822) ; and *Hymns and Spiritual Songs Designed for the Use of Christians* (1816).

[In addition to works cited above see, W. E. Mac-Clenny, *The Life of Rev. James O'Kelly* (1910), a partisan defense of O'Kelly; John McClintock and James Strong, *Cyc. of Biblical, Theological, and Ecclesiastical Literature*, vol. VII (1877) ; *Jour. of Rev. Francis Asbury* (3 vols., 1852) ; L. M. Lee, *The Life and Times of the Rev. Jesse Lee* (1848) ; Robert Paine, *Life and Times of Wm. M'Kendree* (2 vols., 1869) ; E. J. Drinkhouse, *Hist. of Meth. Reform* (2 vols., 1899) ; M. T. Morrill, *A Hist. of the Christian Denomination in America* (1912). Authority for the date of death is *Raleigh Register and N. C. Gazette*, Nov. 3, 1826, which says that O'Kelly was then in his eighty-eighth year; MacClenny, *ante*, p. 229, quotes a statement that he died in his ninety-second year.]

H. E. S.

OKEY, JOHN WATERMAN (Jan. 3, 1827–July 25, 1885), judge and author, the son of Cornelius and Hannah (Weir) Okey, was born near Woodsfield, Monroe County, Ohio. His father was of English and his mother of Scotch-Irish descent. He received his education in the common-schools, under private instruction, and at the Monroe academy. He read law in an office at Woodsfield and was admitted to the bar in October 1849. In March of the same year he married May Jane Bloor of St. Clairsville, Ohio. In 1853 he was appointed and the next year elected probate judge of Monroe County. From 1856 until his resignation in 1865 he was common-pleas judge. Removing to Cincinnati, he practised law until 1875. With William Yates Gholson [*q.v.*] he published in 1867 the *Digest of the Ohio Reports,* which, though long since superseded, was considered an excellent work at the time. A committee of the bar in his day said of it that "it could not have been better done and the merits of no legal publication have ever been more universally acknowledged by the legal profession throughout the state" (43 *Ohio Reports*, vi). In 1869 he joined S. A. Miller in the publication of *The Municipal Code of Ohio,* and in 1875 he was appointed by Gov. William Allen a member of the commission to revise and consolidate the laws of Ohio. In 1877 he was elected a judge of the supreme court of Ohio on the Democratic ticket and in 1882 was reëlected to the same position. While serving this second term he died at Columbus, survived by four children.

Though in active practice in Cincinnati for ten years, it is not believed that he achieved great distinction at the bar. It is as a writer and more particularly as a judge that he is best known. His fame as a common-pleas judge extended far beyond his own district, and while on the supreme court bench he seems to have been looked upon by his colleagues and by the bar as a judge of ability. The reason for the unusual place assigned to him is not to be found in his reported opinions. These are with a few exceptions short and, although clear, logical, and well-written, are in no sense great opinions. His reputation as a judge is to be found in the fact that "he brought to this position a more ample and more accurate knowledge of our statutory law and the decisions of our court than was ever possessed by any one of whom we have any knowledge or tradition" (*Ibid.*). His paternal grandfather settled in Ohio before it became a state and upon the organization of Monroe County was elected an associate judge; his father was a member of the state legislature; he, himself, was steeped in the early history of Ohio. This, coupled with his long experience as a common-pleas judge and the knowledge he gained in editing the digest and in serving on the commission to revise the laws of Ohio, gave him a knowledge and understanding of the laws and decisions of Ohio possessed by no man of his generation. He was an omnivorous reader and was familiar with the decisions of other courts and the works of legal authors, but his peculiar distinction as a judge lies in his grasp of the polity of Ohio. "This polity Judge Okey knew, and he knew wherein it differed from all others; and he regarded it as better than any other" (*Ibid.,* viii).

[Information from his son, George B. Okey; "In Memoriam," 43 *Ohio Reports*, v–x; G. I. Reed, *Bench and Bar of Ohio* (1897), I, 31 ; *Cincinnati Commercial Gazette*, July 26, 1885.]

A. H. T.

O'LAUGHLIN, MICHAEL (*c.* 1838–Sept. 23, 1867). [See BOOTH, JOHN WILKES.]

OLCOTT, CHANCELLOR JOHN [See OLCOTT, CHAUNCEY, 1860–1932].

OLCOTT, CHAUNCEY (July 21, 1860–Mar. 18, 1932), actor, singer, whose given name was Chancellor John, was born of Irish ancestry in Buffalo, N. Y. His father was Mellon W. Olcott. He was educated in the public schools and made his first public appearance at the Academy of Music in Buffalo. In the late seventies he was appearing with traveling companies of entertainers and in 1880 he found employment with R. M. Hooley, well-known manager of minstrel shows. In 1882 he joined the Haverly Minstrels, and was also with the Thatcher, Primrose, and West Minstrels, and the Carncross Minstrels in Philadelphia. His voice had developed into a light tenor. While a "black face," he frequently sang "When the Robins Nest Again," to the great delight of audiences. His musical ability led him into other fields. For a time he sang in *The Old Homestead,* and also with the Duff Opera company. In 1891 he went to England and in London secured an Irish romantic rôle in a light opera, *Miss Decima,* at the Criterion Theatre. His success in this rôle suggested to him his future career, and on his return to the United States he joined forces with August Pitou, who both managed his tours and sometimes wrote his plays, and succeeded to the mantle of W. J. Scanlan as a star in Irish musical dramas. One of his first acts on his return to the United States was to introduce the song "Mother Machree." In 1894 he appeared in *The Irish Artist,* for which he wrote both the words and music, and in 1896 in *Edmund Burke,* and so on in a long list of now quite forgotten sentimental and romantic Irish comedies, with plentiful songs. Some of the songs he made famous were "I Love the Name of Mary," and "My Wild Irish Rose"; the latter he himself wrote. His success continued for two decades. He did not as a rule play in the so-called "first-class" theatres, at top prices, but in the more popular houses, at popular prices, and his audiences were to a great extent composed of men and women— especially women—of his own race. But they were immensely loyal, and responded to him year after year.

In spite of the fact that he was both a tenor and an Irishman, Olcott had a good business sense, so that he not only made but saved a tidy fortune. He built a summer house at Saratoga Springs, which was a tasteful adaptation of colonial architecture to modern summer living, with a charming garden, and it was widely copied by other home builders. There was, of course, a limit to the romantic appeal of even an Irish tenor, and after the World War Olcott's popularity waned. He reappeared in 1924, in a revival of *The Rivals,* however, in which Mrs. Fiske played Mrs. Malaprop, and he played Sir Lucius, and in the course of the play he sang a song, always followed by tumultuous and laughing applause by the audiences. In 1925 he was taken sick and never recovered. He went to Monte Carlo to live, where he died in March 1932 of anemia. He was married at least three times. His last wife was Margaret O'Donovan of San Francisco, to whom he was married on Sept. 28, 1897, and who survived him. He was never a great actor, nor a great singer. But he was pleasantly competent in both capacities, and he had a charming Celtic personality, well suited to the light sentimental or romantic rôles which he assumed. His audiences were not ex-

acting, but quickly responsive to sentiment, to a tear and a smile. These he gave them with sincerity. His plays had little relation to the realistic Irish drama developed by the Abbey Theatre in the twentieth century, and both plays and playing belong to an era of Irish-Americanism which is fast vanishing.

[*Who's Who in America,* 1930–31; *Who's Who on the Stage,* 1906; A. D. Storms, *The Players Blue Book* (1901); E. L. Rice, *Monarchs of Minstrelsy* (1911); August Pitou, *Masters of the Show* (1914); *Variety* (N. Y.), Mar. 22, 1932; *Boston Transcript,* Mar. 18, 1932; *N. Y. Times, N. Y. Herald Tribune,* Mar. 19, 1932; Robinson Locke Collection, N. Y. Pub. Lib.]
W. P. E.

OLCOTT, EBEN ERSKINE (Mar. 11, 1854– June 5, 1929), mining engineer and transportation executive, was born in New York City, the second son among four sons and four daughters of John Nathaniel Olcott and Euphemia Helen (Knox). His father was descended from Thomas Olcott, who settled in Connecticut in the seventeenth century. After attending the College of the City of New York, Eben entered the School of Mines of Columbia University and graduated there in 1874. His first position was that of chemist for a Hunt & Douglas process plant in North Carolina of which he later became superintendent; next he was assistant superintendent of the Pennsylvania Lead Company works, at Mansfield Valley, Pa. From 1876 to 1879 he was superintendent of a gold mine in Venezuela; later he held a similar position in Colorado. After superintending the St. Helena Mines, Sonora, Mexico, 1881–85, he opened an office as consulting engineer in New York. Partly on the basis of his professional studies of the copper deposits at Cerro de Pasco, Peru, mining was initiated in that region, which has since developed into one of the most important copper districts of the world. Two exploring expeditions in Guiana and Colombia were less productive of permanent enterprise. In 1890– 91 Olcott similarly explored the gold and copper district of eastern Peru, an undertaking of great hardship because of the high elevation, remoteness of the region, and difficulties of transportation.

By his marriage in 1884 to Kate Van Santvoord, he became the son-in-law of "Commodore" Alfred Van Santvoord, founder of the Hudson River Day Line of steamers running between New York and Albany. On the death of Van Santvoord's only son, he accepted in 1895 the management of this important line, to which he gave the greater part of his time for the rest of his life. He built the company's fleet up from two large steamships to seven and gave every detail of their operation his close supervision. His agreeable personal qualities gained him the loyalty of his employees and the friendship of his business associates. Shortly after assuming the management of the Day Line, he became senior member of the firm of Olcott, Fearn & Peele, consulting engineers. In connection with this firm and its successors, Olcott, Corning & Peele and Olcott & Corning, he continued to practise in an advisory capacity for a number of years. He was also a trustee, officer, or director, of several banking corporations, and a director of the Catskill Evening Line. He belonged to numerous professional societies, and in 1901–02 was president of the American Institute of Mining Engineers. He was on the council of the American Geographical Society, the Board of Foreign Missions of the Reformed Church in America, and the Board of Managers of the American Bible Society; was a trustee of the American Seaman's Friend Society, and treasurer and trustee of the American Indian Institute. He took an important part in the organization of the Hudson-Fulton celebration of 1909. At the time of his death, in New York City, he was survived by his widow, three sons, and a daughter.

[*Mining and Metallurgy*, July 1929; *Trans. Am. Soc. Civil Engineers*, vol. XCIV (1930); Nathaniel Goodwin and H. S. Olcott, *The Descendants of Thomas Olcott* (1874); *Who's Who in Mining and Metallurgy* (1908); *Who's Who in America*, 1928–29; *N. Y. Times*, June 6, 1929.]   T. T. R.

OLCOTT, HENRY STEEL (Aug. 2, 1832–Feb. 17, 1907), president-founder of the Theosophical Society, has been variously considered a fool, a knave, and a seer, and was perhaps a little of all three. He was born in Orange, N. J., the son of Henry Wyckoff and Emily (Steel) Olcott; was educated in the schools of New York City, and for one year attended the University of the City of New York; and from 1848 to 1853 was engaged in farming in northern Ohio. While there he became interested in spiritualism which, however, did not yet displace agriculture in his affections. In 1853 he returned to New York and, after taking a course in agricultural chemistry, started the Westchester Farm School at Mount Vernon, N. Y., where he attempted the culture of sorghum, on which he published a treatise, *Sorgho and Imphee* (1857). He visited Europe in 1858 to study its agricultural conditions and for the next two years was associate agricultural editor of the *New York Tribune*. On Apr. 26, 1860, he was married to Mary E. Morgan of New Rochelle, N. Y., from whom he was later divorced. At the outbreak of the Civil War he enlisted and served as signal officer in Burnside's North Carolina campaign until he caught fever and was invalided home. Appointed by Secretary Stanton a special commissioner, with the title of colonel, to investigate military arsenals and navy yards, he is said to have uncovered a great deal of corruption. After the war he studied law, was admitted to the bar, and practised for some years in New York City.

In the summer of 1874 he published in the New York *Daily Graphic* a series of articles on the alleged spiritualistic phenomena of the Eddy brothers at Chittenden, Vt. These were later published, with supplementary material, in book form as *People from the Other World* (1875). They sufficiently convict their author of credulity or chicanery or both (see D. D. Home, *Lights and Shadows of Spiritualism*, 1877, pp. 301–28). At Chittenden Olcott made the acquaintance of Helena Petrovna Hahn Blavatsky [*q.v.*], and during the ensuing winter they became very intimate. Under her tutelage he plunged into a study of occultism. When the Theosophical Society was formed in September 1875, he became its first president. He edited Madame Blavatsky's imperfect English in her *Isis Unveiled* (1877), and for years was her devoted press agent. But with all his efforts, the Society did not prosper; so on Dec. 18, 1878, "the Theosophic Twins," as Madame Blavatsky called them, sailed for India to carry Hindu philosophy to the Hindus. They settled first at Bombay, later at Adyar, a suburb of Madras. While Madame Blavatsky spread the faith of occultism by means of her "physic phenomena," Olcott attempted mesmeric healing but had so many failures that his colleague begged him to desist. As a lecturer he was more successful, particularly among the Buddhists, whose religion he formally adopted. In 1881 on a trip to Ceylon he urged the Buddhists to establish their own schools, and for use as a textbook compiled *A Buddhist Catechism* (1881), which was translated into twenty-three languages.

When, in 1885, Madame Blavatsky was exposed by the London Society for Psychical Research, opinions differed as to whether Olcott had been her dupe or her accomplice. It now seems probable that he began as the first and ended as the second. He was a man of plausible manners and dignified appearance, with a long sage-like beard, but one eye did not focus properly; it is said that occasionally that eye "got loose and began to stray suspiciously and knavishly, and confidence [in him] vanished in a moment" (V. S. Solovyoff, *A Modern Priestess of Isis*, 1895, pp. 36–37, 84). But although he can hardly be vindicated from some complicity in Madame Blavatsky's frauds, he was temperamentally an organizer rather than an occultist, and after her departure had left him in peace he settled down to the sober work of developing the Theosophical Society on a legitimate basis. For its enormous growth during the next twenty years the credit should be largely his. Tireless in lecturing and writing on its behalf, he paid several trips to Europe for the sake of harmonizing discordant factions. He edited until his death its official organ, the *Theosophist*, and wrote *Theosophy, Religion and Occult Languages* (1885), and *Old Diary Leaves*, an intimate history of the movement, in three volumes (1895, 1900, 1904). At the time of his death the Society had over six hundred branches in forty-two different countries.

Olcott also opened in India four free schools for pariahs which came to have 1,700 members. In 1889, on a lecture tour to Japan in response to an invitation from the eight Japanese Buddhist sects, he formulated fourteen points of agreement among all Buddhists, and persuaded the Japanese to enter into cordial relations with the Ceylonese Buddhists for the first time in history. He was on equally good terms with the Brahmins and received from one of their pundits, Taranath Tarka Vachaspati, the sacred thread of the Brahmin caste and adoption into his gotra—a unique favor to a foreigner. While traces of the charlatan remained with him till the end—seen in the occasional trick, learned from Madame Blavatsky, of invoking the authority of the Mahatmas for his own plans—nevertheless his genial kindliness of heart and genuine love of spiritual things made him, in the long run, a friend of humanity.

[Olcott's *Old Diary Leaves*, covering his life from the time of his first meeting with Mme. Blavatsky, must be read with due caution but is nevertheless invaluable; the form in which it first appeared, in the *Theosophist*, Mar. 1892–Dec. 1906, is more complete and candid than the revision for book publication. *The Theosophical Movement, 1875–1925* (1925) gives a very unfavorable view of Olcott from the pro-Blavatsky standpoint. Other references are: Nathaniel Goodwin and Henry Steel Olcott, *The Descendants of Thomas Olcott* (1874); the Hodgson report in the *Proc. of the Soc. for Psychical Research* (London), May and June 1885; Emma Coulomb, *Some Account of My Intercourse with Mme. Blavatsky from 1872 to 1884* (London, 1885); *Letters of H. P. Blavatsky to A. P. Sinnett* (1925); *The Mahatma Letters to A. P. Sinnett* (1923); obituary by Annie Besant, *Theosophist*, Mar. 1907; *Who's Who in America*, 1906–07; *N. Y. Daily Tribune*, Feb. 18, 1907.]   E. S. B—s.

OLDEN, CHARLES SMITH (Feb. 19, 1799–Apr. 7, 1876), governor of New Jersey, was a quiet, unpretentious Quaker who, after a successful career in business, was drawn into politics by those who respected his sagacity and honesty. He was the son of Hart and Temperance (Smith) Olden and was born on the family farm at Stony Brook near Princeton, N. J., originally purchased in 1696 by his ancestor, William Olden, who had come from England some time earlier. This farm had been the scene of the major action of the Revolutionary battle of Princeton. Charles began his education in Princeton and was continuing it at the Lawrenceville school nearby when, at fifteen, he gave up school to assist his father in running the little general store in Princeton. He was soon given an opening in the larger business of Matthew Newkirk in Philadelphia. Then, from 1826 to 1832, he engaged in business at New Orleans so successfully that he was able to return to Princeton, purchase part of the family farm, erect a fine house, and settle down to the life of a gentleman farmer. That was his chief occupation for the remainder of his life, though he became a director of the Trenton Banking Company in 1842. Upon his return to Princeton from the South, he married Phoebe Ann Smith. They had no children of their own but adopted a daughter.

Modest and retiring, he did not seek political office, but in 1844 he was persuaded to run for a seat in the state Senate from Mercer County. He won the election and held the position for six years. In 1859 an opposition group, composed of Republicans, Whigs, and National Americans, unanimously nominated him for the governorship, to run against the Democratic candidate, E. R. V. Wright. He was no orator, but he was popular with the farmers of the state and won the election by a close margin. His inaugural address indicated a desire to accomplish several reforms, particularly in connection with the state prison and the treatment of the insane. These were overshadowed, however, by the Civil War. Working quietly but incessantly, he tried to inject life into the obsolete state military system and obtain funds for the almost empty state treasury. A strong Union man, he cooperated in every possible way with the federal government. Though he had no formal legal training, he was a judge of the New Jersey court of errors and appeals and a member of the court of pardons from 1868 until his resignation in 1873. He was also a riparian commissioner from 1869 to 1875 and served as head of the New Jersey electors in the presidential election of 1872. He was treasurer of the College of New Jersey (Princeton) from 1845 until 1869 and was a trustee of Princeton from 1863 to 1875. He rendered the college a great service when, in 1866, he wrote a letter outlining Princeton's needs to his old school friend, John C. Green [*q.v.*]. He died at Princeton and was buried in the old Friend's burying ground not far from his home.

[Manuscript "Personal Reminiscences" of C. P. Smith in N. J. State Lib., Trenton; J. F. Hageman, *Hist. of Princeton and Its Institutions* (1879), I; *Geneal. and Personal Memorial of Mercer County, N. J.* (1907), ed. by F. B. Lee, vol. II; John MacLean, *Hist. of the Coll. of N. J.* (1877), vol. I; *Gen. Cat. of Princeton* (1908); C. M. Knapp, *N. J. Politics* (1924); *Beecher's Mgg.*, Apr. 1871.]   R. G. A.

OLDHAM, JOHN (*c.* 1600–July 1636), colonist and trader, was born in England, probably in Lancashire, about 1600 and emigrated to America in 1623, arriving at Plymouth in July by the ship *Anne*. He was one of the few passengers who did not intend to become members of the general body of the Plymouth colonists or join in their communal economic life but came on "their perticuler," as Bradford described it. Agreements were made with these new-comers, establishing their peculiar status and forbidding them to trade with the Indians until the period of "joint trading" as practised by the colonists should have ended. Oldham had considerable practical ability but was heady and self-willed and had an ungovernable temper. In the spring of 1624 the Rev. John Lyford arrived from England, and he and Oldham soon united with various malcontents in the colony to make trouble. They dispatched complaining letters to the party of the Adventurers at home opposed to the interests of the Pilgrims. Bradford secretly opened these letters and read them before the ship sailed which carried them. Oldham and Lyford next set up a church of their own. They were brought to trial and sentenced to banishment. Oldham left the colony but his wife and family were allowed to remain until he could remove them comfortably. He returned in March and exploded his wrath upon the colony's magistrates. They "committed him until he was tamer" and then beat him out of town with their muskets (Bradford, *post*, I, p. 411). He settled at Nantasket and soon after at Cape Ann where there was a small fishing settlement. He was an enterprising merchant and engaged in trade between Massachusetts and Virginia, and also carried on an extensive trade with the Indians. In time he made his peace with the authorities at Plymouth.

In 1628 he returned to England, taking charge of Thomas Morton [*q.v.*] of Merry Mount. While in England he suggested a commercial scheme to the Massachusetts Bay Company, then planning to settle the colony of that name. He not only failed in his negotiations but the Company forbade him to trade with the Indians.

The next year John Gorges, who claimed to be heir to the Gorges grant, conveyed to Oldham a large tract but the Massachusetts Bay Company refused to recognize his title. On Feb. 12, 1629/30 the Council for New England granted to Oldham and Richard Vines a tract of land lying on the south side of the Saco River in Maine. Oldham, however, took no interest in this patent. He returned to New England and settled at Watertown, where he became a substantial citizen. He took the oath as freeman, May 18, 1631, and was elected a representative to the General Court in 1632 and was reëlected in 1634. In 1633 he made an expedition to the Connecticut River and the following year was granted 500 acres by the Court lying near "Mt. ffeakes" on the Charles River (*Records of the Court of Assistants,* II, 1904, p. 43). The same year he was made one of the overseers of powder and shot for the colony, and in 1635 he was appointed by the Court one of the committee to consider the problem presented by Endecott's having cut the cross out of the flag (*Records of the Governor and Company of the Massachusetts Bay* I, 1853, pp. 125, 145). In the following July while on a trading expedition to Block Island Oldham was murdered in his shallop by Pequot Indians with the connivance of certain Narragansett sachems. The murder was one of the chief episodes leading to the Pequot War.

[Wm. Bradford, *Hist. of Plymouth Plantation* (2 vols., 1912), ed. by W. C. Ford; Alexander Young, *Chronicles of the First Planters of the Colony of Mass. Bay* (1846); *Winthrop's Journal* (2 vols., 1908), ed. by J. K. Hosmer; *Proc. Mass. Hist. Soc.*, 1 ser., XIV (1876) and XX (1884); *The New English Canaan of Thos. Morton* (1883), ed. by C. F. Adams; S. F. Haven, *Hist. of Grants under the Great Council for New England* (1869), p. 31.]   J. T. A.

OLDHAM, WILLIAMSON SIMPSON (June 19, 1813–May 8, 1868), jurist, Confederate senator from Texas, the son of Elias and Mary (Bratton) Oldham, was born in Franklin County, Tenn. Elias was a poor farmer and could not give his son an education, but the boy studied at night by the light of a brushwood fire, read law in Judge Nathan Green's office, and was admitted to the bar when twenty-three years old.

In 1836 he moved to Fayetteville, Ark., where he became a successful lawyer. His marriage, Dec. 12, 1837, to Mary Vance McKissick, the daughter of the wealthy and influential Col. James McKissick, and his own personality and untiring energy soon brought him recognition. In 1838 he was sent to the General Assembly from Washington County; he was elected speaker of the House of Representatives four years later; he was one of the presidential electors in

1844; and a few months thereafter was elected associate justice of the supreme court of Arkansas, a position he filled with distinction. Preferring a political to a judicial career, he ran for Congress in 1846, but was defeated. In 1848 he was a candidate for the United States Senate but was again defeated in a bitter campaign. He resigned his judgeship June 30, 1848.

In the spring of 1849 he moved to Austin, Tex. His wife died on the way, leaving him with five children. On Dec. 26, 1850, he married Mrs. Anne S. Kirk of Lockhart, Tex., and after her death, on Nov. 19, 1857, married Agnes Harper of Austin. He engaged in his profession and took part in all the social, economic, and political discussions of the time. From 1854 to 1857 he was one of the editors of the *Texas State Gazette* (after June 1855, the *State Gazette*), the Democratic organ in Texas. He played an important part in the controversy of 1855–57 between the Democratic party and the Know-Nothings. In 1859 he was defeated for nomination for Congress, because at this time he was not a radical "Southern rights man" and was opposed to the reopening of the slave trade. In that year he published, with the aid of George W. White, his law partner, *A Digest of the General Statute Laws of the State of Texas* (1859). As a member of the secession convention in 1861, he voted for secession, and was then sent as a delegate to the convention of the Southern states at Montgomery, Ala. He was a member of the Confederate Provisional Congress and was appointed by President Davis a commissioner to Arkansas in an unsuccessful attempt to get the state to secede at that time. Under the permanent government, he was sent to the Confederate States Senate from Texas, where he became the champion of state rights on every occasion. He opposed conscription bitterly, because he believed that the leaders wanted to destroy the state governments (Oldham, "The Last Days of the Confederate States," p. 187). He also opposed granting President Davis power to suspend the writ of *habeas corpus*. He was a member of a committee which reported on Jan. 25, 1865, that the government had enough men and military supplies to carry on the war indefinitely. After the downfall of the Confederacy, he went back to Texas, but soon fled to Mexico and later to Canada. He was allowed to return to Texas but he refused to apply for a pardon and remained an unreconstructed believer in state rights until his death from typhoid fever in Houston.

[Oldham's "History of a Journey from Richmond to the Rio Grande from March 30 until June 26, 1865, or, The Last Days of the Confederate States with a Re-view of the Causes That Led to Their Overthrow" (MS. at Univ. of Tex.), gives his opinions about measures in Congress. *Jour. of the Cong. of the Confederate States of America, 1861–1865* (7 vols., 1904–05) contains valuable information. The material for his life in Ark. is based on public documents and the files of the *Arkansas Banner* (Little Rock), 1843–48, and *Arkansas State Gazette* (Little Rock), 1837–42. The file of the *Texas State Gazette* (Austin), 1849–65, is valuable for the later period. See also *Ark. Banner*, Dec. 25, 1844; J. D. Lynch, *The Bench and Bar of Tex.* (1885); E. Fontaine, "Hon. Williamson S. Oldham," in *De Bow's Mo. Rev.*, Oct. 1869; *Houston Daily Telegraph*, May 9, 1868; A. D. King, "The Political Career of Williamson Simpson Oldham" (thesis, Univ. of Tex., 1929); Oldham family records.]   A. D. K.

OLDSCHOOL, OLIVER [See SARGENT, NATHAN, 1794–1875].

OLIN, STEPHEN (Mar. 2, 1797–Aug. 16, 1851), Methodist Episcopal clergyman, educator, son of Henry and Lois (Richardson) Olin, was born in Leicester, Vt. His father was a lawyer and a prominent political figure in that state. As a student in Middlebury College, Olin won high scholastic honors and was valedictorian of the class of 1820. He secured these honors, however, at the expense of his health. Close application to his studies and lack of physical exercise so undermined his constitution that the rest of his life was a continual struggle with disease. He had intended to enter the legal profession but in 1820, hoping to benefit by the climate, he went to South Carolina, where he became an instructor in Tabernacle Academy. While there he joined the Methodist Episcopal Church and in 1824 was admitted on trial to the South Carolina Conference. From January to July 1824 he served as junior preacher in Charleston, S. C., but the rigorous life of the early Methodist itinerancy proved too strenuous for him, and he was soon forced to retire from the active ministry. In 1826, while recuperating at Madison Springs, Ga., he was elected professor of ethics and belles-lettres in Franklin College, Athens, Ga., which position he held from 1827 to 1833. On Nov. 20, 1828, he was ordained elder by Bishop William McKendree [*q.v.*].

In March 1834 he became president of Randolph-Macon College, then located in Mecklenburg County, Va., but by 1837 his health was again depleted, and he spent the next three years recuperating in Europe and the Holy Land. Returning to America in 1840, his health partially restored, he accepted in 1842 the presidency of Wesleyan University, Middletown, Conn. This office he held until his death in 1851. As president of two pioneer Methodist colleges, he did much to arouse his denomination to its educational task. By his official visits to the annual Conferences and by his articles in the *Christian*

Advocate and Journal he did much to enlist the support of both clergy and laity to the early educational program of Methodism. He was one of the few Methodists prior to 1850 who championed the cause of theological education.

As a delegate to the General Conference of 1844 from the New York Conference, which opposed slavery, Olin found himself in a peculiar position, for during his stay in the South he had owned slaves. He endeavored to prevent the schism in the Church and was a member of the committee appointed to find a basis of agreement for the pro-slavery and anti-slavery groups. Buckley states that "the only speech delivered in the General Conference of 1844 which exhibited a full comprehension and just estimate of all sides of the subject was that of Stephen Olin who was as familiar with the North as with the South" (J. M. Buckley, *post*, II, 119). Although Olin voted for the Finley resolution which requested Bishop Andrew to desist from episcopal duties until he had freed himself from all connection with slavery, yet, immediately after the adjournment of the Conference, he became the leader in the movement for securing fraternal relations between the two branches of Episcopal Methodism. He was vitally interested, also, in fostering a closer friendship among the various Protestant denominations, and was instrumental in organizing the Evangelical Alliance. In 1846 he represented the New York and New England conferences of the Methodist Episcopal Church at the meeting of the Alliance in London.

In addition to his many contributions to Methodist periodicals, he published in 1843, *Travels in Egypt, Arabia Petraea, and the Holy Land* (2 vols.). After his death two volumes of his manuscript sermons and addresses were published under the title, *The Works of Stephen Olin* (1852). In 1853 *The Life and Letters of Stephen Olin* appeared. Other posthumous publications of his include: *Youthful Piety* (1853); *Greece and the Golden Horn* (1854); *College Life; Its Theory and Practice* (1867). Olin was married twice: first, Apr. 10, 1827, to Mary Ann Eliza Bostick of Milledgeville, Ga., who died in Naples, Italy, May 7, 1839; second, at Rhinebeck, N. Y., Oct. 18, 1843, to Julia M. Lynch. A son born to them in 1847 died in youth.

[Matthew Simpson, *Cyc. of Methodism* (1881); J. M. Buckley, *A Hist. of Methodism in the U. S.* (2 vols., 1897); J. M'Clintock, "Stephen Olin," in *Meth. Quart. Rev.*, Jan. 1854; R. Irby, *Hist. of Randolph-Macon Coll., Va.* (copr. 1898); *Meth. Quart. Rev.*, Oct. 1851; *Hartford Daily Courant*, Aug. 18, 1851.]
P.N.G.

OLIVER, ANDREW (Mar. 28, 1706–Mar. 3, 1774), lieutenant-governor of Massachusetts, was born in Boston of a wealthy and distinguished colonial family. He was the son of Daniel Oliver, a member of the Provincial Council, and Elizabeth Belcher, and the brother of Chief-Justice Peter Oliver [*q.v.*]. His great-grandfather, Thomas Oliver, emigrated from England in 1632. In Andrew's boyhood the political and social connections of the family were of the best, and the boy passed through Harvard, graduating at eighteen in 1724. Four years later, on June 20, 1728, he was married to Mary, daughter of the Hon. Thomas Fitch, by whom he had three children before her death on Nov. 26, 1732. Andrew Oliver [*q.v.*] was a son by this marriage. On Dec. 19, 1734, he was married to Mary, daughter of William Sanford, by whom he had fourteen children. His second wife was the sister of the wife of Gov. Thomas Hutchinson, and thus during most of his active life Oliver was in close family relations, as well as political sympathy, with Hutchinson and his party.

For some years Oliver represented Boston in the General Court and in 1748 served as a commissioner, with Hutchinson, at the meeting in Albany for the purpose of negotiating with the Six Nations. Meanwhile he had been elected to the Provincial Council in 1746 and continued to be elected annually to and including 1765. In December 1756 Josiah Willard, who had served as secretary of the province for more than a generation, died, and on the 13th Acting-Governor Phips appointed Oliver to the vacant post until the King's pleasure might be known. Oliver continued in the office until Mar. 11, 1771, being twice commissioned by the King, Mar. 2, 1758, and Apr. 10, 1761 (Colonial Society of Massachusetts, *Publications*, vol. II, 1913, vol. XVII, 1915).

After the passage of the Stamp Act, Oliver accepted an appointment as stamp-officer. This proved to be an extremely unpopular and even dangerous step. In 1765 he was reëlected to the Council, for the last time, by a majority of only three or four votes (Hutchinson, *post*, III, p. 117). On Aug. 14 he was hanged in effigy on the Liberty Tree. In the evening the mob razed a building said to have been intended for the stamp office and then attacked Oliver's house. The marauders broke windows, smashed down the doors, destroyed much of the fine furnishing, and greatly terrified the family. On the next day Oliver resigned his post but the mob was not satisfied and attacked the houses of Oliver's brother, the chief-justice, and of Hutchinson. After some months an unfounded rumor was spread abroad that Oliver intended after all to act as stamp officer. He received two threatening anonymous letters, and having already suffered enough from the mob, he agreed to appear again on Dec. 17 at the Liberty Tree and make oath before a justice of the peace that he would never act in that capacity. On Oct. 19, 1770, he was commissioned by the King as lieutenant-governor and sworn into office Mar. 14, 1771, serving until his death. He had always retained his interest in Harvard and in 1772 he fostered medical instruction there by gifts of anatomical preparations imported from London (Colonial Society of Massachusetts, *Publications,* vol. XIX, 1918, p. 284).

In 1773 he was again a storm center of popular rage. In the late sixties he, as well as Bernard, Hutchinson, and others, had written to England certain letters describing the unsettled conditions in the colonies and advising remedies. Benjamin Franklin, while in England, obtained these private letters and forwarded copies to the popular party in Boston. They were made public in 1773 and, although the incident reflects little credit upon Franklin and his Boston correspondents, the popular rage broke over Oliver. In addition, Arthur Lee, in England, concealing his identity under a pseudonym, accused Oliver of perjury in the public press. "Scarce any man," as Hutchinson wrote, "ever had a more scrupulous and sacred regard to truth" (Hutchinson, *post,* p. 456), and after an examination of evidence Oliver was completely exonerated, but his unpopularity and the threatenings of the mob had accented certain physical disorders and his health gave way. He sank slowly and died on Mar. 3, 1774. The petty vindictiveness of the popular party followed him to his grave. As lieutenant-governor, according to the custom of the day, he was accorded a public funeral but as a result of a childish dispute over a trifling matter of precedence between members of the two houses of the legislature, the lower house refused to attend. In addition, John Hancock, as commander of the "Cadets," insisted that they should form part of the procession as an honor due the office of lieutenant-governor if not the man. Samuel Adams made furious opposition. The feeling was so violent that Chief-Justice Oliver was afraid to attend his brother's burial. Indecent attacks were made upon the cortège, and in the presence of the family the Sons of Liberty cheered as the coffin was lowered into the grave.

[Thos. Hutchinson, *The Hist. of the Province of Mass. Bay,* vol. III (1828) ; J. H. Stark, *The Loyalists of Mass.* (1910) ; *Copy of Letters Sent to Great Britain, by His Excellency Thos. Hutchinson, the Hon. Andrew Oliver, and Several Other Persons* (1773); J. K. Hosmer, *The Life of Thos. Hutchinson* (1896); *New-Eng. Hist. and Geneal. Reg.,* Apr. 1865; *Coloni.. Soc. Mass. Pubs.,* vol. XXVI (1927).]   J.T.A.

OLIVER, ANDREW (Nov. 13, 1731–Dec. 6, 1799), jurist, scientist, was born in Boston. He was the son of Andrew Oliver [*q.v.*], secretary and lieutenant-governor of Massachusetts, and his wife Mary, daughter of the Hon. Thomas Fitch. He graduated from Harvard in 1749. On May 28, 1752, he married Mary, daughter of Chief Justice Benjamin Lynde [*q.v.*]. A few months prior to this he had moved to Salem, where his wife's family lived. Salem became his permanent home and with its interests he was closely identified. On Nov. 19, 1761, he was appointed judge of the inferior court of common pleas for Essex County, a position which he continued to occupy until the outbreak of the Revolution. In 1762, when one of the Salem representatives in the General Court was elected to the governor's council, Oliver was chosen at a special election, held June 9, to take his place. He continued to represent Salem in the provincial legislature until 1767, refusing to accept any compensation for his services. At a town meeting, Oct. 21, 1765, it was voted to request him to use his efforts to effect a repeal of the Stamp Act and at the same time to prevent "lawless violence and outrage." On Aug. 9, 1774, he was appointed one of the mandamus councilors but refused to serve. During the troublous years that followed, when all the other members of his family because of Loyalist sympathies went into exile, he stayed quietly at Salem.

Law and politics were by no means the whole of life to him. While proficient in mathematics and fond of music and history, his deepest interest, especially in later years, lay in scientific studies. He was a founder of the American Academy of Arts and Sciences and a member of the American Philosophical Society, to which he was elected on Jan. 15, 1773. Several papers composed by him were read at meetings of the society, and two were published in the second volume of the *Transactions* (1786). One of these, entitled "A Theory of Lightening and Thunder Storms," attempted to show that the electric charges in thunderclouds "reside, not in the cloud or vapors of which it consists, but in the air which sustains them." The other, entitled "Theory of Water Spouts," sought to explain these phenomena by analogy to the suction of liquid through a quill. His most significant contribution to colonial science was *An Essay on Comets, in Two Parts,* published in 1772 and reprinted in 1811, wherein he strove to account for the tails of comets "upon philosophical Principles" and to show that "in Consequence of these curious Appendages, Comets may be inhabited Worlds." This venture into the field of astronomy was dedicated to John Winthrop [*q.v.*], Hollis professor of mathematics and natural philosophy at Harvard, to whose inspiring instruction Oliver confessed that his interest in science was due. The work was translated into French and drew favorable comment from scholars at home and abroad. From science he is said to have turned occasionally to poetry. He appears to have been the author of an "Elegy on the late Professor Winthrop," first published in the *Independent Chronicle* of June 9, 1779.

A man of considerable means, he was not harried by the necessity of earning a livelihood. To those less fortunate than himself, he gave generously. Studious tastes and defective health induced him to lead a life of some seclusion. Afflicted for thirty years with a distressing chronic disease, he bore it with exemplary cheerfulness. He died at Salem, with an enviable reputation for learning and benevolence.

[John Winthrop and Andrew Oliver, *Two Lectures on Comets* . . . (1811), contains an excellent appreciation, and the elegy on Winthrop. See also *Jour. and Letters of the Late Samuel Curwen* (1842), ed. by G. A. Ward; J. B. Felt, *Annals of Salem* (2nd ed., 2 vols., 1845–49); *The Diaries of Benj. Lynde and of Benj. Lynde, Jr.* (1880); *Proc. Mass. Hist. Soc.*, 2 ser. III (1888) and vol. LXI (1928); W. T. Davis, *Bench and Bar of the Commonwealth of Mass.* (1895), II, 394.]

E. E. C.

OLIVER, CHARLES AUGUSTUS (Dec. 14, 1853–Apr. 8, 1911), ophthalmologist, was born in Cincinnati, Ohio, the son of George Powell Oliver, M.D., and Maria Louisa Oliver. His great-grandfather, Nicholas B. Oliver, was born in Kent, England, in 1740, educated at Oxford University, and emigrated to Philadelphia before the Revolutionary War in which he served as infantryman. His father served in the Union Army during the Civil War and settled in Philadelphia during the boyhood of Charles Augustus. He attained prominence as a surgeon in that city and became the founder and first president of the Medico-Chirurgical College of Philadelphia, later merged with the graduate school of medicine of the University of Pennsylvania. The son received his preliminary education in the public schools of Philadelphia and at the Central High School and was graduated M.D. from the medical department of the University of Pennsylvania in 1876. His thesis was entitled "Opium *vs.* Belladonna." He was married on June 6, 1888, to Mary Schermerhorn Henry of New York. A son and a daughter were born of this union.

Upon graduating from the University of Penn-

sylvania, Oliver served as interne in the Philadelphia Hospital (Blockley) from January 1877 to May 1878 and in 1894 he became ophthalmic surgeon to the institution. In 1878 he became affiliated with the Wills Hospital in Philadelphia through his appointment as clinical clerk in the service of William Fisher Norris [*q.v.*]. His association with Norris was instrumental in shaping his subsequent career which was devoted entirely to ophthalmology. His association with Wills Hospital was continuous from the time of his first appointment until his death. In 1890 he was elected attending surgeon to this institution and served as secretary of the staff during the whole period of his association with the hospital as surgeon. The eye clinics at St. Mary's, St. Agnes', and the Presbyterian hospitals owe their establishment to his enterprise, and upon his retirement from active service in them he was made consulting ophthalmic surgeon to each. He was made associate clinical professor of ophthalmology in the Woman's Medical College of Pennsylvania in 1897 and became full clinical professor of the same subject in 1906. He was also consulting ophthalmologist to the Friends' Asylum for the Insane in Philadelphia, and to the State Hospital for the Chronic Insane of Pennsylvania at Norristown, Pa.

In the literature of ophthalmology Oliver found the greatest field for his endeavors. *A Textbook of Ophthalmology*, written in 1893 in collaboration with his teacher and colleague Norris was one of his outstanding accomplishments. This was translated into Chinese and was adopted as a textbook in the medical schools of China. With the same associate he published *System of Diseases of the Eye* (1897–1900) which appeared in four volumes and represented the work of more than sixty contributors of eminence. He also published *Ocular Therapeutics for Physicians and Students* (1899), translated from the German of F. W. M. Ohlemann; *Injuries to the Eye in their Medico-Legal Aspect* (1900), a revised edition of A. J. Osterheimer's translation of the work of S. Baudry; *An Essay on the Nature and the Consequences of Anomalies of Refractions* (1899), a revised edition of the work of F. C. Donders, and contributed to Wood's *System of Ophthalmic Operations* (2 vols., 1911). Among his numerous monographs, that entitled *A Description of Some of the Important Methods Employed in the Recognition of Peripheral and Central Nerve Diseases* (1897) was translated into French and German. In addition to over one hundred and twenty-five monographs of record he found time to edit the ophthalmic section of Charles Sajous's *Annual of the Medi-*

cal Sciences over a period of several years in collaboration with Dr. Thompson Wescott, later with Dr. William Zentmayer, and still later with Dr. William Campbell Posey, and also to function in an editorial capacity in connection with the *Annals of Ophthalmology, Annales de Oftalmologia, Ophthalmoscope,* and *Annales d'Oculistique.* He was a member of many scientific societies in America and abroad.

[*Trans. Coll. of Physicians of Phila.,* 3 ser. XXXV (1913) ; *Who's Who in America,* 1910–11 ; *Who's Who in Pa.,* 1908; *Gen. Alumni Cat. of the Univ. of Pa.* (1917) ; *Annals of Ophthalmol.,* July 1911 ; H. A. Kelly and W. L. Burrage, *Am. Medic. Biogs.* (1920) ; J. W. Croskey, *Hist. of Blockley* (1929) ; *Pub. Ledger* (Phila.), Apr. 10, 1911 ; personal communications with Oliver's contemporaries.]   L. W. F.

OLIVER, FITCH EDWARD (Nov. 25, 1819–Dec. 8, 1892), physician and historian, was born in Cambridge, Mass., the son of Daniel and Mary Robinson (Pulling) Oliver. He was descended from Thomas Oliver, a physician, who emigrated to America in 1632, and was the great-grandson of Andrew Oliver, 1731–1799 [*q.v.*]. Daniel Oliver (1787–1842), his father, was professor of intellectual philosophy at Dartmouth College (1823–37) and also taught chemistry and materia medica in the medical school (1820–38). Oliver entered Dartmouth College when fifteen years of age, taught in rural schools during the long winter vacations, and was graduated in 1839. After a few months devoted to the study of law, he entered the Harvard Medical School and received the degree of M.D. in 1843, part of his medical education having been obtained at Dartmouth College, the Medical College of Ohio in Cincinnati, where his father had gone as a teacher, and by private instruction under Oliver Wendell Holmes [*q.v.*], a distant relative. After receiving his degree, he spent a year in Europe, particularly in Paris and Italy, returning to Boston to practise in 1844.

At first Oliver took an interest in general medicine. He became one of the district physicians of the Boston Dispensary, served on the staff of the Boston City Hospital, and was an instructor in materia medica in the Harvard Medical School (1860–70). From 1860 to 1864 he edited, with Calvin Ellis [*q.v.*], the *Boston Medical and Surgical Journal.* He was a member of the important local medical societies and his chief medical publications were a translation, with W. W. Morland, of A. F. Chomel's *Elements of General Pathology* (1848), an important paper, "The Use and Abuse of Opium" (*Third Annual Report of the State Board of Health of Massachusetts,* 1872), a much discussed subject at the time, and "The Health of Boston, 1875" (*Seventh Annual Report . . . Board of Health of Massachusetts,* 1876). His real interest, however, was in the history of Massachusetts, in which his direct as well as collateral family lines had borne an important and conspicuous part. His first historical publication was *The Diaries of Benjamin Lynde and of Benjamin Lynde, Jr.* (1880). A few years later he gave assistance to P. O. Hutchinson, who edited *The Diary and Letters of His Excellency Thomas Hutchinson, Esq.* (London, 2 vols., 1883–86; Boston, 2 vols., 1884–86) and, in 1878, he issued a completed edition of William Hubbard's *History of New England,* which had been published, in part, by the Massachusetts Historical Society in 1815. There followed, in 1890, *The Diary of William Pynchon of Salem,* whose daughter had married his grandfather. Besides these volumes Oliver wrote a number of papers which appeared in the *Proceedings* of the Massachusetts Historical Society. He joined the Society in 1876 and was appointed cabinet keeper in 1880, a position which he held, with distinction, until his death. He left to the Society a large and valuable collection of *Oliverana,* comprising all the publications he could find of those bearing his name.

For many years he was an active member of the Church of the Advent, Boston, and he wrote, for use in his church and elsewhere, *A Selection of Ancient Psalm Melodies, Adapted to the Canticles of the Church in the United States of America* (1852, 2nd ed., enlarged, 1858), in which is found an excellent arrangement of *"De Profundis." A Sketch of the History of the Parish of the Advent in the City of Boston, 1844–94* (1894) was largely written by him. As a physician, Oliver is said to have "brought to his duties fresh and abundant learning, conscientiousness, unsparing devotion, and the most scrupulous care" (Slafter, *post,* p. 478). As a historian he had "the instincts and habits of a scholar. . . . When he entered upon a theme of study he was not content till he had patiently surveyed the whole field, and gathered in all that was necessary to know" (*Ibid.,* 485). His writings and annotations are models of their kind, clear, concise, and in pure, faultless English. In social life he is said to have been somewhat reticent but modest, courteous, and dignified. On July 17, 1866, he married Susan Lawrence Mason, a descendant of a distinguished family of Boston. His wife and six children survived him.

[E. F. Slafter's memoir in the *Proc. Mass. Hist. Soc.,* 2 ser. VIII (1894), is the best account of Oliver. See also: *Boston Evening Transcript,* Dec. 9, 1892; and the *Boston Medic. and Surgic. Jour.,* Dec. 15, 22, 1892.]   H. R. V.

OLIVER, GEORGE TENER (Jan. 26, 1848–Jan. 22, 1919), steel manufacturer, lawyer, newspaper publisher, and United States senator from Pennsylvania, was born at Donaghmore, near Dungannon, County Tyrone, Ireland, while his parents, Henry William and Margaret (Brown) Oliver, were on a visit to the latter's old home. The father had been a merchant in Ireland and active in the Liberal party of that day; his emigration to America in 1842 followed the defeat of his party. George was educated in the public schools of Allegheny (now the Northside of Pittsburgh) and in Pleasant Hill Academy at West Middletown, Pa. He then attended Bethany College in West Virginia, graduating in 1868. For a short time thereafter he taught school in Peebles Township (now Hazelwood) but soon began the study of law in Pittsburgh in the office of Hill Burgwin. In 1871 he was admitted to the bar and on Dec. 19 of that year married Mary D. Kountze of Omaha, Nebr. During the ten years which followed Oliver built up a successful law practice in association with William B. Rogers. Against the advice of the latter he gave up this practice to become vice-president and later president of the Oliver Wire Company, organized by his brother Henry William Oliver [q.v.]. During his presidency he exhibited a regard for his employees rarely shown in those days. It was his practice to keep the plants running even though operating without profit in order to give employment to his men. In 1899 the company sold its plants. Between 1889 and 1897 Oliver was also president of the Hainsworth Steel Company. In the last-named year when this company merged with Oliver & Snyder Steel Company, he remained as president of the new company and served until 1901.

At the age of fifty-two Oliver disposed of his manufacturing interests and embarked upon a career, covering the remaining nineteen years of his life, as a newspaper publisher. In June 1900 he purchased the oldest newspaper west of the Allegheny Mountains, the *Pittsburgh Gazette*, a morning paper. Next he became owner of the *Pittsburgh Chronicle-Telegraph*, an evening paper. In 1906 he bought the *Pittsburg Times* which he consolidated with the *Gazette* and called the *Gazette Times*. He directed the papers and their policies throughout his ownership, often writing the editorials. He had long been interested in politics. In 1884 he was a presidential elector on the Blaine-Logan ticket; in 1890, the supervisor of the federal census for his district. In 1904 and again in 1916 he served as a delegate to the Republican National con-

ventions at which Roosevelt and Hughes were nominated. But his larger field of activity was in the United States Senate. Although he refused to fill the unexpired term of Senator Quay in 1904, he consented to step into the place made vacant in 1909 when President Taft appointed Philander C. Knox to the cabinet. After completing two years he was elected for the full term, 1911–17, thus serving during the trying days of American neutrality. His chief activity in the Senate was the support of the protective tariff in general and the iron and steel tariff in particular. He declined a second term and retired to private life on the death of his wife who was his constant companion. He survived her by less than two years. He was buried in Allegheny Cemetery in Pittsburgh.

[The sketch of Oliver in J. W. Jordan, *Encyc. of Pa. Biog.*, vol. XI (1919), is reprinted in G. T. Fleming, ed., *Hist. of Pittsburgh and Environs* (1922), vol. III. See also the *Biog. Dir. Am. Cong.* (1928); and the *Pittsburgh Dispatch* and *Pittsburgh Post*, Jan. 23, 1919.]

A. I.

OLIVER, HENRY KEMBLE (Nov. 24, 1800–Aug. 12, 1885), teacher, treasurer and commissioner of labor of Massachusetts, superintendent of cotton-mills in Lawrence, musician, was born in Beverly and died in Salem, Mass. He traced his ancestry from Thomas Oliver, who emigrated to America in 1632 and settled in Boston not far from the present Old South Church on Washington Street. The Rev. Daniel Oliver, a graduate of Dartmouth in 1785, was his father, and Elizabeth Kemble of Boston his mother. His name, Thomas Henry Oliver, he changed to Henry Kemble Oliver in 1820 to preserve that of his mother. From the Boston Latin School he went to Phillips Academy at Andover, divided his college course between Harvard and Dartmouth, and graduated in 1818 from the latter. Harvard granted him the degrees of A.B. and A.M. in 1862, placing his name with the class of 1818. He began his teaching career in Salem as usher of the Latin Grammar School and in 1827 he became the first master of its English High School. Owing to his interest in mathematics, he had his senior classes compute the times of all the total eclipses visible in the United States for the last seventy years of the century. In 1830 he erected on Federal Street in Salem a building for an academy and for five years conducted a school for boys, converting it then into a school for girls. He devoted twenty-five years to school work in that city. In 1830 he was one of the committee of seven who prepared the plan which resulted in the founding of the American Institute of Instruction, a forerunner of the National Education Association, and in 1858–59 he was agent for the state board of education.

From 1844 to 1848 Oliver was adjutant-general of the Massachusetts militia. His preparation for this office began in 1821 when he entered the Salem Light Infantry. Twelve years later he was lieutenant-colonel of the 6th Massachusetts Infantry and was soon promoted to its colonelcy. In the Ancient and Honorable Artillery of Boston he gained a captaincy by 1846. It was during the period of his state service that the Mexican War occurred, and it fell to him to raise the only volunteer regiment to go to Mexico from New England, known as the 1st Massachusetts Volunteers. During this time he was also a member of the board of visitors for West Point. For ten years, 1848–58, he served as superintendent of the Atlantic Cotton Mills in Lawrence. To provide for the better education of his employees he proposed a library for their use. He offered one hundred volumes and a loan of fifty dollars for new purchases and in a short time the number of volumes reached 3,500. He added bathing rooms to the mills and provided free lectures and concerts for its employees. From 1860 to 1865, during the years of the Civil War, he was treasurer of the state. During that time he handled almost eighty thousand dollars of the state's money at an annual salary of $2,300.

While still a young boy Oliver sang in a Boston church, and at the age of twenty-three he began his long career as an organist, serving two years at St. Peter's Church in Salem, two in the Barton Square Church, twenty in the North Church, and twelve in the Unitarian Church in Lawrence. He organized the Salem Mozart Association, serving as its president, organist, and director; was a member of the Boston Handel and Haydn Society, the Salem Oratorio Society, and the Salem Glee Club; and an honorary member of the Portland Haydn Society. He wrote church music and in 1848, with two others, joined in publishing *The National Lyre,* which contained many of his own compositions. In 1860 he published *Oliver's Collection of Hymn and Psalm Tunes,* followed in 1875 by *Original Hymn Tunes,* dedicated to the Salem Oratorio Society. "Federal Street" is his best-known tune. The climax of his musical career may be said to have occurred at the Peace Jubilee in Boston on June 25, 1872, when he was called from his place among the basses of the Salem Choral Society group to conduct the singing of his "Federal Street," set to his own words, "Hail gentle peace," and rendered by 20,000 voices. During the centennial year he was given a place at the exposition in Philadelphia as a judge of instruments of precision and of music.

The crowning work of Oliver's life was the organization and development of the Massachusetts Bureau of Statistics of Labor, a pioneer institution of its kind. It was authorized by a resolve of the legislature, approved June 23, 1869, and on the July 31 following he was appointed its first chief. His first report, covering the seven months to March 1870, dealt largely with wages and hours of labor. Subsequent reports showed cost of living, habits and education of families, and factory conditions. Oliver made four reports as chief of this bureau and in 1873 retired to spend the later years of his life at his home in Salem. He was mayor of that city from 1877 to 1880. He had married, on Aug. 30, 1825, Sarah Cook, daughter of Samuel Cook and Sarah Chever of Salem. They had seven children. He was a member of the North Street Unitarian Church in Salem and from its altar his public funeral was conducted. His writings consist chiefly of addresses on educational subjects and reports of the Bureau of Labor. He also published in 1830 a work on the construction and use of mathematical instruments, and in 1868 *Genealogy of Descendants of Thomas Oliver of Bristol, England, and of Boston, New England.*

[The best sketch of Oliver is that by J. H. Jones in *Seventeenth Ann. Report of the* (Mass.) *Bureau of Statistics of Labor* (1886). See also: the *Musical Herald,* Jan., Mar., Apr. 1882; F. J. Metcalf, *Am. Writers and Compilers of Sacred Music* (1925); C. S. Osgood and H. M. Batchelder, *Hist. Sketch of Salem* (1879); *Essex Inst. Hist. Colls.,* vol. XLIX (1913); *Fifty-Seventh Ann. Meeting of the Am. Inst. of Instruction,* 1886; *Salem Gazette,* Aug. 14, 1885.] F. J. M.

OLIVER, HENRY WILLIAM (Feb. 25, 1840–Feb. 8, 1904), ironmaster, was born at Dungannon, County Tyrone, Ireland, one of six children of Henry William Oliver, a Scotch-Irish harness-maker, and Margaret (Brown) Oliver. George T. Oliver [*q.v.*] was his younger brother. The family emigrated to Pittsburgh in 1842, where Henry attended the public schools and Newell's Academy until the age of thirteen. He then became a messenger boy for the National Telegraph Company, along with Andrew Carnegie. For eight years he was employed by Clark and Thaw, forwarding agents, and by Graff, Bennett & Company, iron manufacturers. At Lincoln's first call for troops in 1861 he enlisted in the 12th Pennsylvania Volunteers and served a three months' term. When Lee invaded Pennsylvania in 1863 he again enlisted and fought in the battle of Gettysburg.

In 1863 he organized the firm of Lewis, Oliver & Phillips for the manufacture of nuts and bolts on a small scale and in 1866 his brothers David and James were admitted to the firm. Upon the retirement of W. J. Lewis in 1880 the company adopted the name Oliver Brothers & Phillips. Still later (1888) it was incorporated as the Oliver Iron & Steel Company, with Henry W. Oliver as chairman of the board. In the twenty years following the Civil War the business grew to gigantic proportions. Oliver was identified with a great variety of ferrous industries, such as sheet and tin plate, steel wire, and pressed steel cars. He was also a builder of railroads, which he saw were essential to the industrial future of Pittsburgh. He was one of the original owners of the Pittsburgh & Lake Erie Railroad, was president of the Pittsburgh & Western Railway Company from 1890 to 1893, and promoted the Akron & Chicago Junction Railroad (now part of the Baltimore & Ohio) to secure better freight facilities with the West. As a railroad man he introduced important improvements, including the use of steel cars for safety.

With his practical knowledge of iron and steel, Oliver foresaw the necessity of large mineral reserves, and his chief distinction is as a pioneer in opening the vast iron-ore region of Minnesota. Hearing in 1892 of the discovery by the Merritt brothers of the great Mesabi range north of Duluth, he hastened to inspect the diggings. When Leonidas Merritt showed Oliver specimens of high-grade ore lying practically on the surface, which could be loaded with one scoop of a steam-shovel at a labor cost of five cents a ton, Oliver needed little argument. He leased an enormous annual tonnage, organized the Oliver Iron Mining Company, built a railroad to Lake Superior, and began the great ore traffic from the lake ports to the Pittsburgh mills. Andrew Carnegie was sceptical of the value of "ore prospecting" and considered Oliver a harebrained enthusiast, but Oliver's logic impressed Henry Clay Frick, then the active head of the Carnegie Steel Company, who, against Carnegie's orders, joined forces with Oliver to exploit the Minnesota treasures. Eight years later the Oliver iron-ore interests, originally organized on a cash investment of some $600,000, were bought by the newly formed United States Steel Corporation for $17,000,000. The "Oliver luck" became a Pittsburgh legend, but it was based more upon sound knowledge and driving energy than upon chance. Oliver invested heavily in Pittsburgh real estate and business structures, and also became an organizer and the largest stockholder of the Pittsburgh Coal Company. In the far West he held extensive interests in Arizona copper mines.

Oliver was a lifelong adherent of the Republican party. He served three years (1879–82) as president of the Common Council of Pittsburgh, was a delegate to four Republican National conventions (1872, 1876, 1888, 1892) and a presidential elector-at-large in 1880. In 1881 he was nominated by caucus for United States senator but was defeated on account of factional divisions in the party. He was highly influential in both state and federal policies, however, and in 1882 was appointed by President Arthur as representative of the iron and steel interests on a commission to draw up the metal schedules of the new tariff. He died in 1904. He had married in 1862 Edith A. Cassidy of Pittsburgh by whom he had one daughter. His estate built as a memorial the Henry W. Oliver Building, long the largest office building in Pittsburgh. Oliver himself was instrumental in the widening of a downtown street later renamed Oliver Avenue.

[J. N. Boucher, *A Century and a Half of Pittsburg and Her People* (1908), vol. III; J. W. Jordan, *Encyc. of Pa. Biog.*, vol. IX (1918); G. I. Reed, ed., *Century Cyc. of Hist. and Biog. of Pa.* (1904), vol. II; G. T. Fleming, ed., *Hist. of Pittsburgh and Environs* (1922), vol. IV; Paul DeKruif, *Seven Iron Men* (1929); *Pittsburgh Dispatch, Pittsburgh Gazette*, Feb. 8, 1904, personal information from members of the family.]

K. M. G.

OLIVER, JAMES (Aug. 28, 1823–Mar. 2, 1908), inventor, manufacturer, was born in the parish of Liddesdale, Roxburghshire, Scotland, the son of George and Elizabeth (Irving) Oliver. His father was a shepherd, and in the hope of bettering his circumstances he emigrated with his family to America in 1835, where several of his older children had preceded him, and settled on a farm near Geneva, N. Y. James had had a little schooling in Scotland, but when he arrived in the United States, although only twelve years old, he immediately went to work as a farm hand in the neighborhood of his home. In the spring of 1836 the Olivers moved to a leased farm near Alloway, N. Y., and in the following fall they migrated to Indiana and obtained a farm site at Mishawaka, four miles from South Bend. During the succeeding nineteen years Oliver engaged in a variety of occupations. In 1838 he was apprenticed to a builder of the Fox threshing machine; later, he obtained employment in a foundry owned by the South Bend Iron Works in Mishawaka; when this company discontinued business in 1840, he became a cooper's apprentice and after completing his apprenticeship followed his trade successfully in Mishawaka for a number of years. He was more interested in foundry work, however, and late in 1845 obtained employment with the St. Joseph Iron Company in the same town.

In 1855, while on a visit to South Bend, he met a young foundryman and purchased a one-fourth interest in his business there. He entered upon his new work most energetically and in 1857 purchased the entire establishment. Two years later the plant was destroyed by fire but he immediately rebuilt it, and to help defray the expense he took in two business friends as part owners. He continued in general foundry work with fair success until 1864, when his plant was again burned. Following its immediate reconstruction, he determined to go into the manufacture of plows in addition to regular foundry stock. Soon he was experimenting with chilled iron in an effort to make hard-faced plows, as many foundrymen and others had done before him. After four years of labor, he had proceeded with the problem sufficiently to obtain patents for a "mould board for plows" (No. 76,652) and "casting mould boards" (No. 76,939) on Apr. 14 and 21, 1868, respectively. Some time later he made his first important discovery in the matter of successful chilling; namely, that by circulating hot water through the "chills" he could prevent the castings from cooling too rapidly or unevenly. For this discovery he received patent No. 86,579 on Feb. 2, 1869, the patent being entitled "chill for casting mould boards." Confident that he was proceeding in the proper direction, he next worked on the improvement of moulding patterns. This undertaking resulted in a second important discovery—a method of ventilating the chills by curves along the face of the mould which allowed the escape of the gases that form within the flasks when molten iron is poured in. The use of this method permitted the liquid metal to come into direct contact with the face of the chill, removing all of the soft spots in the mould boards and leaving the surface smooth and perfect. For this improvement he received a number of patents between 1871 and 1876. His last great discovery was a process of annealing the plow castings so that the soft portions became pliable enough to work out their strains from shrinkage in cooling without affecting the hardness of the chilled faces. Even before the incorporation into his plow of this last discovery, Oliver's product was much in demand, for it was low in price, adaptable to any kind of soil, cut a very smooth furrow, and procured a lighter draft than any other metal plow then in use. In 1878, in order to increase his output, he bought thirty-two acres of land in the southwestern part of South Bend, and the following year began the erection of a new plant. Building followed building as the business increased, and at his death, the Oliver Chilled Plow Works covered sixty-two acres, employed 2,000 men, and produced annually upwards of 200,000 plows. Oliver, as president, conducted the affairs of this great business up to the time of his death, continuing also his inventive work.

He was very much interested in the civic betterment of South Bend. He built the Oliver Hotel, and erected a large opera house and the city hall. On May 30, 1840, he married Susan Doty of Mishawaka and at the time of his death in South Bend was survived by two children.

[Who's Who in America, 1908–09; Waldemar Kaempffert, A Popular Hist. of Am. Invention (1924), vol. II; R. L. Ardrey, Am. Agricultural Implements (copr. 1894); Anderson and Cooley, South Bend and the Men Who have Made It (1901); Farm Implement News, Mar. 5, 1908; Indianapolis News, Mar. 2, 1908; Patent Office records.]   C. W. M—n.

OLIVER, PAUL AMBROSE (July 18, 1830– May 17, 1912), soldier, inventor, manufacturer, the youngest of five children of Capt. Paul Ambrose Oliver and Mary Van Dusen, was born in the English Channel on board the *Louisiana*, a vessel built by his grandfather, Matthew Van Dusen, shipbuilder of Kensington, Pa., and owned and commanded by his father. Shortly after the birth of his youngest child, Captain Oliver settled with his family at Altona, Germany, and remained there ten years. During this time Paul Ambrose imbibed a knowledge of German military science at the local gymnasium which he later made of practical use. In 1849 he came to the United States, settled in New Orleans, and engaged in the cotton export trade. Later he settled at Fort Hamilton, N. Y., where he was also engaged in the shipping business. In 1856 he organized and was made president of the Fort Hamilton Relief Society, an association instrumental in preventing an epidemic of yellow fever in New York City.

He joined the army and on Oct. 29, 1861, was commissioned second lieutenant in the famous 12th New York Volunteers. His promotion was rapid, owing largely to the fact that he perfected in his own company a German bayonet drill which was widely approved by his superiors. He rose to the captaincy, was successively offered commissions as major, lieutenant-colonel, and colonel of the 5th New York Volunteers, all of which he declined, and served as aide on the staffs of Generals Butterfield, Meade, Hooker, and Warren. He was a principal witness at an investigation of the conduct of Gen. Carl Schurz, during which Schurz criticized Oliver for presuming to give as his own orders which really came from Hooker (*War of the Rebellion: Official Records, Army*, 1 ser. XXXI, pt. 1, p. 187).

By order of General Grant, Oliver was assigned to duty with General Patrick, Headquarters Armies of the United States, January 1865. As provost-marshal, he assisted in paroling the Confederate army at Appomattox, a service which General Sharpe called "invaluable and highly meritorious" (*Ibid.*, XLVI, pt. 3, p. 853). Oliver left the service on May 6, 1865; two days later he was brevetted brigadier-general of volunteers. He had taken part in twenty-five battles and was favorably mentioned in the official reports of Hooker, Butterfield, and others for the coolness, bravery, and intelligence he displayed in action (*Official Records*, 1 ser. XI, XII, XXXI and XLVI). At Resaca, Ga., on May 15, 1864, Oliver "assisted in preventing a disaster caused by Union troops firing into each other" (General Butterfield to the Secretary of War, May 26, 1892). The brigade being fired into was led by Col. Benjamin Harrison. Appropriately enough, when Harrison became president, Oliver was decorated with the Congressional Medal of Honor.

After the war Oliver engaged in the anthracite coal trade but soon gave that up to experiment in the manufacture of explosives. Between 1868 and 1889 he secured several patents for formulas for explosives and for machines for their manufacture. His machines were designed to mix the ingredients in small quantities with an excess of moisture so as to prevent violent explosions; his powders were especially adapted for blasting in coal mining. He is generally credited with the invention of dynamite and black powder; but his discoveries in this field were contemporaneous with, and probably independent of, the similar inventions of Nobel in France, Schultze in Germany, and Von Lenck in Austria (J. B. Bernadou, *Smokeless Powder*, 1901; J. P. Cundill, *A Dictionary of Explosives*).

Oliver settled in Wilkes-Barré, Pa., in 1868, and set up a small powder mill. As he was in close touch with the coal operators in the anthracite region, his business "grew to a large importance" (*Coal Trade Journal*, May 22, 1912, p. 478). His mill experienced several disastrous fires and explosions, but by 1873 he was regularly employing 100 men and producing 900 kegs of powder per day. His mills were purchased in 1903 by E. I. du Pont de Nemours & Company, and are still in operation; the principles of manufacture evolved by him have continued in use with some modifications. The enormous expansion of the anthracite coal trade following the Civil War and the increasing industrial uses of explosives meant a corresponding expansion in his business, and Oliver was enabled to retire after amassing a considerable fortune. Among

other things, he was interested in the forestry movement in his state, being stimulated, no doubt, by the denuding of thousands of acres of virgin timber in the adjacent mountains.

Oliver was a communicant of the Episcopal Church. He never married. Genial in manner, of distinguished presence, he made his home at Fern Lodge, overlooking the historic Wyoming Valley, typical of the resplendent hospitality and luxury of the new industrial order which he had done much to advance.

[Sources include: H. E. Hayden, "Oliver Family," *N. Y. Geneal. and Biog. Record*, July, Oct. 1888, Jan. 1889; H. C. Bradsby, *Hist. of Luzerne County, Pa.* (1893); *Circular No. 8*, ser. 1913, Pa. Commandery, Mil. Order of the Loyal Legion; *Ann. Reports of the Commissioner of Patents*, 1878–1889; A. P. Van Gelder and Hugo Schlatter, *Hist. of the Explosives Industry in America* (1927); *War of the Rebellion: Official Records (Army)*, 1 ser. XI, XII, XXV, XXVII, XXXI, XXXII, XXXVIII, XLII, XLVI; *Wilkes-Barré Record*, May 18, 1912; and records of E. I. du Pont de Nemours & Company, Wilkes-Barré office. A volume of newspaper clippings in the possession of Miss Adelaide Bonnell, Elizabeth, N. J., includes a copy of the letter from Gen. Butterfield of May 26, 1892, referred to above.]
J. P. B.

OLIVER, PETER (Mar. 26, 1713–October 1791), Loyalist, was born in Boston, Mass., the son of Daniel and Elizabeth (Belcher) Oliver and the brother of Lieutenant-Governor Andrew Oliver [*q.v.*]. The family was descended from Thomas Oliver who came to Massachusetts from England in 1632 and at the time of the Revolution its members occupied distinguished social and political positions. Peter graduated in 1730 from Harvard where he had ranked high in scholarship but had been disciplined for stealing a turkey and a goose. On July 5, 1733, he was married to Mary, daughter of William and Hannah (Appleton) Clarke, by whom he had six children. They lived in Boston until 1774 when Oliver bought land and settled at Middleboro', Plymouth County, about thirty miles from the capital. He established iron works there and built one of the finest residences in New England, called "Oliver Hall," celebrated for its size and elegance and the beauty of its grounds. He lived there until his exile; later, about 1782, the place was burned by the Americans.

On Dec. 12, 1747, Oliver was appointed judge of the inferior court of common pleas of Plymouth County and served for nine years. He was then made judge of the superior court, Sept. 14, 1756, and in 1771 became chief justice. The most famous case in which he sat, as an associate justice, was the trial of the British soldiers in 1770. "A Loyalist by birth, education and instinct, a man of courage, firmness, learning and character," he became a marked man as the troubles with England came to a crisis. The judges of the superior court received niggardly pay from the General Court, £120 a year for the associate justices and £150 for the chief justice. The British government determined to augment the salaries by annual grants, which immediately inflamed patriotic sentiment in the colony. In view of the threatening attitude of the people, four of the judges, after having decided to accept the grants, recanted, but Chief Justice Oliver held firm. He claimed that he had expended about £2,000 as justice since his appointment and offered to settle the question by resigning if the General Court would reimburse him to the extent of one-half his expenditures. The only answer was a categorical inquiry as to whether or not he would accept the Crown grant and he replied affirmatively. The legislature then proceeded to draw up articles of impeachment but Governor Hutchinson, whose daughter had married Oliver's son, refused to countenance the impeachment proceedings. Matters came to a head at Worcester, Apr. 19, 1774, when the grand jury in writing refused to serve under him. The grand jurors of Suffolk County similarly refused to serve under him in August.

Oliver had already been a member of the Council and in 1774 was appointed one of the "Mandamus Councillors." On Oct. 14, 1775, he was one of the signers of the Address to General Gage, and, with his niece, was among those who left for Halifax with the British forces when they evacuated Boston in March 1776. He continued to England where he was hospitably received by the King and was given the degree of D.C.L. by Oxford University. He resided at Birmingham until his death, the government having granted him a pension. At his death he left a manuscript entitled "The Origin and Progress of the American War to 1776" the interest of which is mainly personal as the bias is so strong as to invalidate the value of the account as history. He was greatly interested in history and wrote both in verse and prose, among the items printed being *A Speech . . . After the Death of Isaac Lothrop* (Boston, 1750); *A Poem Sacred to the Memory of the Honorable Josiah Willard* (1757), and *The Scripture Lexicon* (1787), which was used as a text at Oxford and several times reprinted.

[Sources include: Thos. Weston, "Peter Oliver," *New-Eng. Hist. and Geneal. Reg.*, July–Oct. 1886, and genealogy, *Ibid.*, Apr. 1865; J. H. Stark, *The Loyalists of Mass.* (1910); *Colonial Soc. of Mass. Pubs.*, vol. V (1902) and vol. XXV (1924); *Proc. Mass. Hist. Soc.*, vol. XIV (1876); P. O. Hutchinson, *The Diary and Letters of His Excellency Thos. Hutchinson* (2 vols., 1883–86); and Thos. Hutchinson, *The Hist. of the Province of Mass. Bay*, vol. III (1828). *The Alumni Oxonienses* and the *Gentleman's Mag.*, Oct. 1791, give Oct. 12, 1791, for date of death; the *New-Eng. Hist.* and *Geneal. Reg.*, Apr. 1865, gives Oct. 13. Oliver's "Origin and Progress of the American War to 1776" is with the Egerton MSS. in the British Museum; there is a transcript of the document in the Lib. of Cong., Manuscript Division.]
J. T. A.

OLMSTEAD, GIDEON [See OLMSTED, GIDEON, 1749–1845].

OLMSTED, DENISON (June 18, 1791–May 13, 1859), scientist and teacher, was the youngest and fourth child of Nathaniel Olmsted, a farmer living near East Hartford, Conn. His mother (his father's second wife) was Eunice Kingsbury of Hebron, Conn. He was the grandson of Nathaniel and Sarah (Pitkin) Olmsted of Hartford, and a direct descendant of James Olmsted who emigrated from Fairsted, Essex, England, to Connecticut in 1632. After his father's death, his mother married again and moved to Farmington, Conn., where Denison received his early education in the district school and privately from Gov. John Treadwell, who instructed him in arithmetic (not taught then in public schools) and in whose home Olmsted did "such offices as a boy could do for his board" (Woolsey, *post*, p. 577). Later, he was a clerk in the store of Governor Treadwell's son. At sixteen he decided to study further in order to enter Yale College, and after teaching a district school for one season he entered the school of James Morris at Litchfield South Farms. Rev. Noah Porter [*q.v.*], the parish minister at Farmington, was also his instructor. In 1809 he entered Yale and there received the degree of A.B. in 1813. Having nearly exhausted his patrimony, he taught at the Union School, New London (1813–15), before continuing further study. In 1815 he was appointed a tutor at Yale, where he also studied theology under President Timothy Dwight [*q.v.*]. His M.A. oration in 1816 was on "The State of Education in Connecticut," and contained ideas relating to a seminary for school-masters (normal school), plans for the establishment of which he hoped to carry out at the end of his tutorship.

Somewhat reluctantly, therefore, in 1817, he accepted a call to the professorship of chemistry at the University of North Carolina. He was granted a year for preparatory study under Benjamin Silliman [*q.v.*] at Yale, and in 1818 married Eliza Allyn of New London. At the University of North Carolina he successfully advocated in 1821 a state geological survey, legally established in 1822. He was appointed state geologist and mineralogist and made the first survey of and reports on the state's natural resources. In 1825 he was called to Yale to fill the chair of mathematics and natural philosophy.

Eleven years later he prevailed on the college authorities to establish a separate chair of mathematics, and after that time he filled the chair of natural philosophy and astronomy until his death. His wife died in 1829 and in 1831 he married Julia Mason of Rensselaer County, N. Y. He had five sons and two daughters. A teacher by nature, he assisted the friends of common-schools by writing, lecturing, and appearing before legislative bodies. While he was unable to carry out the normal-school idea himself, he nevertheless wrote much on the necessity of such a project.

As an instructor of scientific subjects, he introduced experiments into his lectures and inaugurated laboratory work for the students. He advocated an astronomical observatory for the use of students, and another for scientific research. A lamentable lack of textbooks led him to prepare such aids, not only for the colleges, but for academies and the general reader. His *Introduction to Natural Philosophy* (2 vols., 1831–32) was used for many years after his death in the edition revised by E. S. Snell of Amherst. It was followed by *Compendium of Natural Philosophy* (1833), which went through more than a hundred editions; *Introduction to Astronomy* (1839); *A Compendium of Astronomy* (1839), for schools; *Letters on Astronomy, Addressed to a Lady* (1840), prepared for school libraries by request of the Massachusetts Board of Education; and *Rudiments of Natural Philosophy and Astronomy* (1844), which also appeared in raised letters for the use of the blind. All his books show excellent arrangement of material, and thoroughness and clearness of presentation.

His contributions in physics and astronomy were mainly on meteors, hailstorms, aurora, and zodiacal light. The papers dealing with the famous meteoric showers of Nov. 13, 1833 (*American Journal of Science and Arts,* January–April 1834, January 1836), brought him scientific fame. In these he collected and arranged in logical and orderly manner all the available data on the subject. The cause of such showers, he concluded, is due to particles of cosmic origin (suggesting comets) passing through the earth's atmosphere and proceeding from a definite radiant (γ-Leonis), and, recalling similar observations of other times, he assumed a probable periodicity of occurrence of the phenomenon. Although he refers to the November showers of 1799, it was left for later generations to connect meteoric showers with a definite comet. His study of hailstorms led him to show the electrical theory then held (especially in France) to be incorrect and to give substantially the ex-

planation, accepted today, based on dynamics and thermodynamics of the atmosphere (*Ibid.,* April 1830). His work on geological subjects was mainly concerned with the mineral resources and their utilization. He invented a process for "gas light from cotton seed," patented July 21, 1827, a useful stove, patented Nov. 5, 1834, and a lubricant of lard and rosin for machinery. He wrote many articles on religious subjects and also a number of biographical sketches.

[F. B. Dexter, *Biog. Sketches Grads. Yale Coll.,* vol. VI (1912) contains full bibliog. See also T. D. Woolsey, in the *New Englander,* Aug. 1859; C. S. Lyman, in *Am. Jour. of Science and Arts,* July 1859; H. K. Olmsted and G. K. Ward, *Geneal. of the Olmsted Family in America* (1912); K. P. Battle, *Hist. of the Univ. of N. C.* (2 vols., 1907–12); Alexander von Humboldt, *Cosmos* (London, 1850, trans. by Edward Sabin); *Columbian Weekly Reg.* (New Haven, Conn.), May 21, 1859.]

A. F. K.

OLMSTED, FREDERICK LAW (Apr. 26, 1822–Aug. 28, 1903), landscape architect, was born in Hartford, Conn. His paternal forbears had been numbered among the intelligent townsmen and farmers of the region since its settlement in 1636, when James Olmsted, an emigrant of 1632 from Essex County, England, came thither from Boston. His father, John Olmsted, a prosperous merchant, took a lively interest in nature, people, and places, which was inherited by both Frederick Law and his younger brother, John Hull. His mother, Charlotte Law (Hull) Olmsted, died when he was scarcely four years old, to be succeeded in 1827 by a congenial step-mother, Mary Ann Bull, who shared her husband's strong love of nature and had perhaps a more cultivated taste.

Frederick was sent to be educated, first to dame schools and then to a succession of rural parsons, but his lessons were broken by solitary country rambles from the home of one friend or relation to another. Moreover, holidays took the form of long tours mostly by carriage, in which his father and step-mother, accompanied by the two boys, took great pleasure. When Frederick was sixteen he had thus made four journeys, each over a thousand miles, in New England, New York State, and Canada, during which he observed populous towns as well as various types of rural scenery, and was encouraged to discuss what he saw. When he was almost ready to enter Yale in 1837, sumach poisoning weakened his eyes and, giving up college plans, he spent two and a half years studying engineering with Frederick A. Barton, first at Andover, Mass., and later at Collinsville, Conn. In August 1840, he went to work for Benkard & Hutton, French dry-goods importers in New York, remaining until March 1842, but finding mercantile employment uncongenial after the out-door life he loved. For the next year, he at-tended lectures in a desultory way at Yale, leav-ing in April 1843, before the mast in the bark *Ronaldson* for China in search of adventure; during a year-long voyage his eyes were open for strange people and scenes.

On his return, he determined to take up farm-ing as a career, and spent some months at his Uncle Brooks's farm in Cheshire, Conn., fol-lowed by a summer (1845) on Joseph Welton's farm at Waterbury, Conn., and a winter attend-ing scientific lectures at New Haven, more en-joyable socially because of his brother John's presence at Yale. Frederick's Yale affiliations later caused him to be made an honorary member of his brother's class, that of 1847, and the circle of his brother's friends, there and in New York, numbering among them Charles Loring Brace [*q.v.*], brought him in touch with the great so-ciological problems of the period. From April to October 1846, he pursued his agricultural ap-prenticeship on the prize farm of George Geddes, "Fairmount," near Owego, N. Y., and in 1847 he felt himself ready to begin independent farm-ing, first on a small place at Guilford, Conn., and from January 1848, on the more adequate Ackerly farm, "South Side," Staten Island, N. Y., purchased for him by his father, and op-erated with enthusiasm for several years until literary activities came to overshadow agricul-tural interests. He himself in later life con-sidered this practical experience in agriculture, combined with his attempts at home landscaping and his modest nursery business, and also his active participation in local county affairs, an important part of his preparation for his career.

In 1850 he began the series of travels which were to draw forth his literary ability, and sailed with his brother and Charles Brace for Europe—following four weeks on the Continent by a walking tour of rural Britain, recorded in *Walks and Talks of an American Farmer in England* (1852). While farming and writing, he had made the acquaintance of Andrew Jack-son Downing [*q.v.*], who, in consequence of Olmsted's earlier contributions to the *Horticul-turist*, sent him letters of introduction. He vis-ited Downing at Newburgh, and they must have compared impressions of foreign parks and gar-dens. Late in 1852, impelled by a stirring dis-cussion with William Lloyd Garrison, who was visiting the farm with Charles Brace, Olmsted started on his first Southern journey, commis-sioned by Henry J. Raymond, editor of the *New York Times*, to write his unbiased impressions of slavery and of actual economic and social con-ditions in the South. The success of his letters, later published as *A Journey in the Seaboard Slave States* (1856), suggested a second tour, also largely on horseback, which took Frederick with his brother John into Texas, followed by a solitary return journey from New Orleans to Richmond, described respectively in *A Journey Through Texas* (1857) and *A Journey in the Back Country* (1860). Acclaimed as the most accurate picture of conditions in the South prior to the Civil War, the three books were con-densed and published in America as *The Cotton Kingdom* (2 vols., 1861), and in England as *Journeys and Explorations in the Cotton King-dom* (2 vols., 1861). His service in his South-ern books, however, was not limited merely to a fair record of what he saw. "Olmsted did what he could to save the pot from boiling over. . . . For passion he sought to substitute thoughtful-ness, for raving rationality, and for invective a calm examination of facts and their histor-ical antecedents that should induce tolerance" (Mitchell, *post*, p. xi).

Meanwhile, brief sojourns on the somewhat neglected Staten Island farm, shortly to be sold, editorial work for *Putnam's Monthly Maga-zine,* and, in company with George William Cur-tis [*q.v.*], a financially disastrous dabbling in the publishing business of Dix & Edwards, led up to further travels in Europe (1856), partly on pub-lishing matters. A pleasure visit to Italy with his sister yielded much in landscape inspiration. In 1857, somewhat at loose ends, he was still try-ing to wind up the publishing business, when chance gave him the opportunity for which his variety of experience had given him extraordi-nary preparation. The City of New York, in-spired by the appeals of William Cullen Bryant and Andrew Jackson Downing, had embarked on the novel undertaking of providing a great public pleasure ground comparable with those of Europe.

Indorsed by such notables as Asa Gray, Washington Irving, and Peter Cooper, on Sept. 11, 1857, he was appointed superintendent of the new Central Park in New York, then under construction from the design of Captain Egbert L. Viele; and there Olmsted, at thirty-five, learned to engage in the bitterly fought but gen-erally victorious battles between art and poli-tics which were to tax his energies throughout the rest of his professional career. Associating himself with Calvert Vaux [*q.v.*], a young English architect whom he had previously met as Downing's pupil, he entered the competition for a new design for the park, which the two young men won under the name of "Greensward." On May 17, 1858, Olmsted was appointed architect in chief of the Central Park, and, with Vaux, strove in the face of almost insuperable political difficulties, to make the first American park not only a work of art but also a successful municipal enterprise. (The full story of this great undertaking, told partly in Olmsted's own reports, may be found in Olmsted and Kimball, *post,* vol. II.)

On June 13, 1859, Olmsted married the widow of his brother John (who had died in 1857), Mary Cleveland (Perkins) Olmsted, thus becoming step-father to her three children, among them John Charles Olmsted [*q.v.*]; and to this family, first living in the Central Park, and then mainly in New York, were added two children that survived infancy, a daughter and a son, Frederick Law, Jr. In the fall of 1859, Olmsted paid an official visit to the parks and gardens of Europe to procure information of advantage for the development of Central Park, which, by 1860, to a large degree took the form intended by its designers and acquired a gratifying measure of public use and popularity. In that year, Olmsted and Vaux were appointed "landscape architects and designers to the Commissioners North of 155th Street," and thus began certain significant phases of city planning.

Shortly after the outbreak of the Civil War, Olmsted secured leave of absence from the Park to go to Washington, at the invitation of Henry W. Bellows [*q.v.*], to become general secretary of the United States Sanitary Commission, the parent of the American Red Cross; in some respects this was his most important single public service (F. L. Olmsted, Jr., *post*). Worn out by his arduous labors behind the battle-lines, the more difficult because of lameness caused by an accident during the Park's construction, Olmsted in 1863 was obliged to resign from the Sanitary Commission, but not before its work was thoroughly established and its ideals perpetuated in the newly formed Union League Club, of which he was a founder. To regain his health, Olmsted, having with Vaux resigned from the Park work largely for political reasons, accepted (August 1863) the superintendency of the Frémont Mariposa mining estates in California, where he was joined by his family in the early spring of 1864. The primitive life in Bear Valley, exploratory camping trips in the Yosemite and the High Sierras, and landscape designing in the region of San Francisco Bay, redirected Olmsted's thoughts to his career in landscape architecture. Two notable achievements resulted from his two-year sojourn: the erection of the Yosemite as a state reservation, Olmsted

serving as first president of the commission, and the design of the grounds and residential village for the new University of California at Berkeley.

In the summer of 1865, Olmsted and Vaux having been reappointed landscape architects to the commissioners of Central Park, and also designers of the new park for Brooklyn, Olmsted decided to return to New York, bringing his landscape work for the San Francisco park, the Oakland Cemetery, and the University of California to be completed by the firm of Olmsted, Vaux & Company. From 1865 dates the steady development of his national practice of the new art of landscape architecture, for seven years in close combination with Vaux, who supplied the architectural background which Olmsted himself lacked, and ultimately, after looser arrangements with Vaux and Jacob Weidenmann, with John Charles Olmsted and his own son Frederick Law, Jr., and other pupils. During this New York period to 1878 when, after ups and downs, political machinations finally removed him from Central Park, the most important other enterprises of Olmsted and Vaux were the laying out of upper New York, including Riverside Park, Prospect Park in Brooklyn, the suburban village at Riverside near Chicago, a park for Buffalo, the Chicago South Park, Staten Island improvement, and land subdivisions at Tarrytown and Irvington, N. Y. In 1874, Olmsted was commissioned to design the grounds of the United States Capitol at Washington, and in 1875 began his connection with what was to become the Boston park system. Early in 1878, accompanied by his stepson John, Olmsted sought relief from political persecution by a four months' holiday in Europe during which the two men studied parks and scenery with keen enjoyment. After Olmsted's return, he made the vicinity of Boston his principal headquarters, devoting himself to the plans of the Arnold Arboretum with Professors Asa Gray and Charles Sprague Sargent [*qq.v.*], the Boston parks, and the campaign for the protection of Niagara Falls in association with his friend Charles Eliot Norton [*q.v.*], which resulted in the general approval of Olmsted's scheme in 1879. Mount Royal Park in Montreal (1874–76), too, belongs to this period.

Although the permanent Olmsted home combined with office on Warren Street, Brookline, was not purchased until 1883, from 1881 Olmsted himself resided mainly in Brookline, leaving John in New York. The chief work of the next few years concerned the Albany State Capitol (with Leopold Eidlitz and H. H. Richardson), Belle Isle Park in Detroit, the Boston parks in which John became especially interested, the improvement of station grounds along the Boston & Albany Railroad near Boston, and numerous land subdivisions, grounds of educational and other institutions, and private estates, small and large, all over the country. (An extensive list of public and private clients of the Olmsted firm, which was constantly developing as a working organization, may be found in Olmsted and Kimball, *post*, vol. I.) In the later 1880's, the selection of site and development plans for Governor Leland Stanford's new university in Palo Alto, Cal., the publication of the improvement plan for the whole Niagara Reservation by Olmsted and Vaux, and Olmsted's participation with Charles Sprague Sargent in the founding of the journal *Garden and Forest,* were combined with work on the parks of Rochester, N. Y., and a large number of land subdivisions East and West, and advice to the City of New York, with Vaux, on Morningside Park and other matters.

The outstanding works which particularly filled Olmsted's mind during the last six years of active professional life were the "Biltmore" estate for George W. Vanderbilt at Asheville, N. C., other Vanderbilt and Rockefeller estates, the Boston and Hartford parks, parks for several Southern cities, especially Louisville, Ky., and above all the World's Fair at Chicago, to which, with "Biltmore," he personally gave the greater part of his time, although still traveling about the country to visit other works of the firm then in progress. When Henry Sargent Codman, who had been a member of the Olmsted firm since 1889, died suddenly, early in 1893 before the completion of the World's Fair grounds, Olmsted, refreshed by a rest and study tour abroad in 1892, was able to take charge and bring the landscape development to a successful outcome. At the famous dinner of Mar. 25, 1893, in New York, marking the collaboration of artists in creating the White City, Olmsted's life was summed up by Charles Eliot Norton: "Of all American artists, Frederick Law Olmsted, who gave the design for the laying-out of the grounds of the World's Fair, stands first in the production of great works which answer the needs and give expression to the life of our immense and miscellaneous democracy" (Charles Moore, *Daniel H. Burnham,* 1921, vol. I. 79). To this appreciation, Burnham added his own, "Each of you knows the name and genius of him who stands first in the heart and confidence of American artists. . . . he paints with lakes and wooded slopes; with lawns and banks

and forest-covered hills; with mountainsides and ocean views. He should stand where I do to-night, not for his deeds of later years alone, but for what his brain has wrought and his pen has taught for half a century" (*Ibid.,* I, 74).

Two more years of professional work were vouchsafed Olmsted, who leaned more and more on John and on young Charles Eliot [*q.v.*], a partner since 1893. The last year was spent, with his son as apprentice, largely at "Biltmore," and there in the spring his portrait was painted outdoors by John Singer Sargent. On his last tour abroad in 1895–96 he had "Biltmore" much at heart, although he had definitely retired from practice in the fall of 1895. Subsequently his mind failed after nearly forty years of professional activity in landscape architecture. He died at Waverly, Mass. In 1898 his firm had become Olmsted Brothers, having successively been called F. L. & J. C. Olmsted (1884–89); F. L. Olmsted & Company (to include Henry S. Codman); Olmsted, Olmsted & Eliot (1893–1897), and F. L. & J. C. Olmsted (for the remainder of 1897), until F. L. Olmsted, Jr., became a full participant.

It is difficult to choose the most significant of the many great works through which Olmsted, with his various partners, shaped the art of landscape architecture in America. Aside from the World's Fair, which gave the first impulse to the cooperation of designers and which profoundly influenced the art and science of city planning, and Central Park, which set a new ideal of municipal amenity and constructive development, perhaps the Prospect Park at Brooklyn, and Franklin Park in Boston together with its related parks and parkways, are the living examples in which the beholder may catch the spirit of repose and relief from urban distractions which Olmsted sought.

He was the more able to advocate his ideals because of his literary ability, applied not only to his earlier books, but freely to the reports and documents which explained his professional landscape problems. Among such very numerous writings, perhaps the most interest attaches to reports on Central Park written in 1873 (Olmsted and Kimball, II, p. 569) when a favorable turn of political events enabled him to control its policies for a short period, and to the retrospective pamphlet, *The Spoils of the Park* (1882), written in a lighter vein after the bitterness of his overthrow had subsided, but laying bare the political filth which had constantly retarded his efforts to do justice to the public interest. His article "Park" in Appleton's *New American Cyclopaedia* (vol. XII, 1863) was the first on the subject in any American encyclopaedia; and his two addresses, before the American Social Science Association, published as *Public Parks and the Enlargement of Towns* (1871) and *A Consideration of the Justifying Value of a Public Park* (1881), were milestones in the development of American civic consciousness. His interest in *Garden and Forest*, largely editorial, promoted increased public appreciation of the landscape art, and a late report on Central Park (1889) prepared with J. B. Harrison, "Observations on the Treatment of Public Plantations," represented his long experience in park planting as it reached approximate maturity. Among the reports for specific designs, in addition to the original "Greensward" document, that for Franklin Park, Boston, is perhaps the most illuminating of all in expressing his considered ideals for park scenery. By his writings he gave definition to the terminology of landscape art, establishing, with Vaux, the term landscape architect as applied to the professional designer and the term park as connoting scenery to be preserved and defended from urban encroachment.

Olmsted found landscape art in America at a low ebb. Even Downing reflected the horticultural taste which pervaded public as well as private landscape work, and, except for H. W. S. Cleveland [*q.v.*] and a very few others, "landscape gardeners" were usually ill-trained and interested rather in specimen plants than in picturesque compositions. Downing, however, had the ideal of public parks, which, deprived of his advocacy by his sudden death in 1852, descended to Olmsted who transmuted it into a living force. In him was the rare combination of philosopher and fighter; his conceptions, ardently expressed, could be comprehended by many who were originally hostile to them and thus be transformed on the ground into great instruments of public service. He was slightly built and never physically strong, yet his inborn vision, his qualities of leadership, and his penetrating sincerity, enabled him incomparably to direct urban life towards outdoor recreation and to leave in dozens of American cities continuing memorials to his foresight and genius.

[The most extensive source, consisting chiefly of his professional papers, is F. L. Olmsted, Jr., and Theodora Kimball, eds., *Frederick Law Olmsted, Landscape Architect, 1822–1903* (2 vols., 1922, 1928); vol. I, "Early Years and Experiences," contains a chronology and some autobiographical passages; vol. II bears the subtitle, "Central Park as a Work of Art and as a Great Municipal Enterprise, 1853–1895." To this should be added Broadus Mitchell, *Frederick Law Olmsted, A Critic of the Old South* (1924), prepared after a thorough analysis of unpublished manuscripts in possession of the family, as well as of the three books on the South. A brief sketch by F. L. Olmsted, Jr., is in *A Journey in the Seaboard Slave States* (1904 ed.), I, xi–xxvi. M. G. Van Rensselaer, a friend, published, on the basis of a long interview, "Frederick Law Olmsted" in the *Century Illustrated Monthly Mag.*, Oct. 1893. See also a serial article by John Nolen, "Frederick Law Olmsted and His Work," *House and Garden*, Feb.–July 1906, with the accepted photographic portrait of his later years; H. K. Olmsted and G. K. Ward, *Genealogy of the Olmsted Family in America* (1912); *N. Y. Times*, Aug. 29, 1903.]   T. K. H.

OLMSTED, GIDEON (Feb. 12, 1749–Feb. 8, 1845), sea captain and privateersman, was born at East Hartford, Conn., the son of Jonathan and Hannah (Meakins) Olmsted and a descendant of James Olmsted or Olmstead, who came to Boston in 1632. In youth he shipped on vessels engaged in the West Indies trade, and in 1775–76 served with Connecticut militia around Boston. Back at sea later in 1776, he became master of the sloop *Seaflower*, but returning from Guadeloupe was captured Apr. 6, 1778, by the British privateer *Weir*. Upon his release at Cape François he took command of the French privateer *Polly* (16 guns). Off Jamaica on July 8 the *Polly* engaged H. M. S. *Ostrich* (16 guns) and had fairly beaten her when the British *Lowestoffe's Prize* (10 guns) entered the action and after three hours' hard fighting forced the *Polly* to surrender, with a loss of fifty-five of her 102 men. While still a prisoner Olmsted was sent from Jamaica to New York as second mate in the British sloop *Active*, with three other Americans in his watch. About midnight on Sept. 6, off Long Island, he and his watch confined the remaining nine officers and men below, overcame resistance (in which struggle Olmsted suffered a pistol wound) by firing a four-pounder into the cabin, and steered for the Delaware. They were escorted in by the Pennsylvania state brig *Convention*, which subsequently laid unjustified claim to the *Active* as prize. In the litigation over ship and cargo, the latter alone worth $98,800, the Pennsylvania Admiralty court granted Olmsted only a fourth part, but with the support of Gen. Benedict Arnold he secured in December 1778 a wholly favorable decision in the court of appeals established by Congress. Because of the dangerous conflict between state and union, no immediate action was taken, and the state's share was retained by the Pennsylvania treasurer, David Rittenhouse, as stakeholder. Olmsted's prosecution of his claim in state and federal courts during the next thirty years made his case celebrated but not until 1809 did he gain substantial restitution; then a peremptory *mandamus* from the United States Supreme Court was served on the Rittenhouse heirs, despite a guard of Pennsylvania militia.

Olmsted returned to Connecticut in June 1779 and commanded successively the privateers *Gamecock* (August 1779), *Hawk* (spring of 1780), *Raven* (September 1780–June 1781), and *General Green* (spring of 1782), cruising chiefly off Long Island and taking numerous prizes. The *General Green* was captured in May 1782 by the much larger enemy privateer *Virginia*, and Olmsted probably remained prisoner in New York till the peace. Thereafter he commanded vessels in the Caribbean and European trade. His last privateering adventure began at Charleston in June 1793, when he converted his schooner *Hector* into a French privateer, taking out French citizenship papers and narrowly escaping prosecution when he entered Wilmington, N. C., in July with a British prize. Evidence suggests that he continued in this activity until 1795. He was married in 1777 to Mabel, daughter of Capt. Eliphalet Roberts of Hartford, but had no children. Until about 1809 he resided in Philadelphia, and later at East Hartford, where he was buried.

[For Olmsted's career see L. F. Middlebrook, *Capt. Gideon Olmsted, Conn. Privateersman* (1933), with detailed references to MSS. and printed sources; L. F. Middlebrook, *Hist. of Maritime Conn. during the Am. Revolution* (2 vols., 1925); H. K. Olmsted, *Geneal. of the Olmsted Family in America* (1912). Among many sources on the Olmsted claim see *U. S.* vs. *Judge Peters, 5 Cranch,* 115; *The Whole Proceedings in the Case of Olmsted and Others vs. Rittenhouse's Executrices* (1809); *Sundry Docs. Rel. to the Claim of Gideon Olmsted Against the Commonwealth of Pa.* (1808); *Jours. of the Continental Cong.,* 1779.] A. W.

OLMSTED, JOHN CHARLES (Sept. 14, 1852–Feb. 24, 1920), landscape architect, was born in Geneva, Switzerland. He was the eldest of the three children of John Hull Olmsted, who, after studying at Yale, in 1851 married Mary Cleveland (Perkins), received the M.D. degree from the College of Physicians and Surgeons in 1852, and then went abroad. After interludes in America, in 1857 John Hull died at Nice, leaving his wife and young family in charge of his brother Frederick Law Olmsted [*q.v.*], who married the widow in 1859. There was a strong bond of common interest between Frederick Law and the young John Charles, who, even at the age of twelve, demonstrated his enjoyment of the outdoor world during the family's residence in California, and especially during an exploring trip made in 1864 eastward through the High Sierras. Late in 1865 the family returned to New York, which remained its actual headquarters until 1881. Largely on account of the travels of his parents, John Charles

received his early education from private teaching. He graduated from the Sheffield Scientific School at Yale in 1875 with the degree of Ph.B.

From 1859 when, before their western trip, the Olmsted family resided for a time in the Central Park in New York, then developing under his step-father's charge, John Charles lived in the midst of the designing and construction of works of landscape architecture, and came to apprehend the social and political phases through which esthetic success in public works had to be achieved. After graduation from Yale, he entered the landscape office of his step-father (then at 209 West 46th St., New York), and in 1878 was given a financial interest in the practice. Although he always emphasized the professional character of landscape architecture, he early showed marked business ability and the power to keep a large number of projects—for public and private clients—moving steadily along. In this, he was an invaluable aid to his step-father, whose genius could be in some measure released for expression of the philosophical and esthetic phases of the art as these appeared in the ever-widening and diversified practice of the office. The calm, stable, practical abilities of John Charles Olmsted established the professional practice of the firm on such a sound basis that it not only advanced the profession in the eyes of the world but also influenced the organization of the offices of many later firms of landscape architects in the United States.

In 1884, following removal of the office to Brookline, Mass., John Charles became a full partner in F. L. and J. C. Olmsted. After his step-father's retirement in 1895 he became senior partner in the firm, which after 1898 was called Olmsted Brothers, and shared responsibilities with his half-brother Frederick Law, Jr., and other later partners until his death in Brookline in 1920. Although he traveled extensively in the course of his more than forty years of professional practice, he kept in the closest touch with the office organization. During the period when he was senior partner, approximately 3,500 jobs came to the firm; and the proportion of these with which he made himself familiar was very large. He was concerned alone or with his partners in the design of hundreds of private estates, large and small, in all parts of the country, and the grounds of many institutions, including Smith College, Mt. Holyoke College, and Ohio State University, of industrial plants (notably the National Cash Register Company of Dayton, Ohio), public buildings, state capitols, and exposition grounds, including the Chicago World's Fair in 1893, the Lewis and Clark Exposition at Portland, Ore., 1906, the Seattle Exposition of 1909, the San Diego Exposition of 1915, and the Canadian Industrial Exposition at Winnipeg. Of the many parks in the design of which he participated, the Hartford (Conn.) parks, the Boston municipal parks and parkways, the Essex County (N. J.) park system, and the Chicago Southside Playgrounds which set a new standard in community playgrounds, engaged his special interest; and the parks of Bridgeport, Conn., Trenton, N. J., Buffalo and Rochester, N. Y., Dayton, Ohio, Detroit, Mich., Milwaukee, Wis., Seattle and Spokane, Wash., Portland, Ore., Louisville, Ky., Atlanta, Ga., and New Orleans, La., are evidences of his far-reaching influence for the public benefit, exercised in conjunction with Frederick Law Olmsted, Sr., or other partners. He kept in close touch with the operation of parks through his active membership in the American Association of Park Superintendents. He made an early contribution, also, to the still inchoate science of city planning in his solutions of difficulties in connection with park system design and in his interpretations to civic leaders. He served as the first president of the American Society of Landscape Architects (founded 1899) and for many years on the executive board. He was also active in the formation of the Boston Society of Landscape Architects.

Unlike his partners, F. L. Olmsted, Sr., and Jr., J. C. Olmsted has only a very brief list of writings to his credit. Many of his letters containing valuable statements of the principles of park system design were incorporated into reports by the firm without differentiation as to authorship. As an example of his writing on parks, an extract from the *Report of Olmsted Brothers on a Proposed Parkway System for Essex County, N. J.* (1915) was published as "Classes of Parkways," in *Landscape Architecture* (Oct. 1915). A report which he wrote during the first year of his partnership on Beardsley Park, Bridgeport, Conn., was privately printed in Boston (1884), and a description by him of the Hartford parks appeared in the *Hartford Courant,* July 10, 1901. Of his travels abroad he made many notes, especially on English gardens, but these remained unpublished, although in style and manner of treatment they have been compared to the intelligent discussion of landscape problems by the French writer, the Duc d'Harcourt.

Olmsted was short of stature but possessed of quiet dignity, retiring but abounding in vigor, gentle and kindly but firm and always possessed of the courage of his convictions. With his in-

dustrious methods of mastering a problem, and his wide knowledge of practical community affairs, he inspired confidence in citizens charged with responsibility for large undertakings within the field of landscape architecture, and was thus able to see realized to a very considerable extent the projects to which his "independence of thought, great fertility of resource, a pains-taking care for the details of his schemes," and his thorough knowledge of materials gave potency (Pray, *post,* p. 105).

On Jan. 18, 1899, in Brookline, he married Sophia Buckland White; they had two daughters.

[J. S. Pray, "John Charles Olmsted. A Minute on His Life and Service," with portrait, in *Trans. Am. Soc. of Landscape Architects, 1909–1921* (1922), which has been interpreted by the writer of this sketch in the light of her editorial work on the Olmsted papers and her personal acquaintance with J. C. Olmsted; E. T. Mische, "In Memoriam, John Charles Olmsted," with another portrait, in *Parks and Recreation,* April 1920; *Yale University, Obit. Record of Grads. Deceased during the Year Ending July 1, 1920* (1921); *Boston Evening Transcript,* Feb. 25, 1920; H. K. Olmsted and G. K. Ward, *Genealogy of the Olmsted Family in America* (1912).]

T. K. H.

OLMSTED, MARLIN EDGAR (May 21, 1847–July 19, 1913), lawyer, congressman, son of Henry Jason and Evalena Theresa (Cushing) Olmsted, was seventh in descent from Richard Olmsted who came to America with his uncle, James, in 1632 and eventually settled at Norwalk, Conn. Born in Ulysses Township, Potter County, Pa., Marlin Edgar was educated in public schools and at Coudersport Academy, entered politics, and was elected auditor of the borough of Coudersport at the age of twenty-two. He had already been appointed assistant corporation clerk of the state in charge of corporation-tax collection. Continued in this position by Auditor-General Harrison Allen, he gave deep study to corporation taxation, and made valuable suggestions which were adopted in Pennsylvania law and practice. When a Democratic victory at the polls resulted in his removal from office in 1875, he turned at once to the study of law, reading in the office of a local judge. Admitted to the local bar on Nov. 25, 1878, to the bar of the supreme court of Pennsylvania, May 16, 1881, and to the bar of the Supreme Court of the United States, Nov. 12, 1884, he quickly found himself engaged in important practice. He was attorney for many corporations and his pleas resulted in some of the most important American decisions in corporation-tax law (see especially *Commonwealth* vs. *Texas & Pacific Railroad Co.,* 98 Pa. Reports, 90; *Commonwealth* vs. *Standard Oil Company,* 101 Pa., 119; *Common-*

wealth vs. *Westinghouse Electric & Manufacturing Co.*, 151 *Pa.*, 265; *Western Union Telegraph Co.* vs. *Pennsylvania*, 128 *U. S.*, 39).

While thus engaged in extensive legal practice, he again entered politics, serving in the select council of Harrisburg. Elected to Congress in 1896 by a heavy majority, he was continuously returned until his voluntary retirement from public life in the elections of 1912. In Congress he rapidly rose to distinction. He was earnest in defense of the Republican party and its policies. Tariff protection and the gold standard, the dominant Republican measures, received his immediate and lasting support. Appointed at once on Committee on Elections No. 2, he rendered able service and is credited with having done much during the next decade to establish the committee as a judicial rather than a political tribunal. Placed, in his second term, on the Committee for the Revision of Laws, he was influential in framing and securing the adoption in 1900 of the governmental code of Alaska. By reason of his mastery of parliamentary procedure, he was often chairman of the Committee of the Whole and at times speaker *pro tempore*. After his death, it was stated in a eulogy in Congress that he was slated as the Republican successor of Speaker Cannon, a plan which was ruined by the Democratic control of the House after the congressional elections of 1910.

Late in his congressional career, Olmsted served on the important Committee on Appropriations, but his name is best known in connection with his work on the Committee on Insular Affairs, of which he became chairman in the Sixty-first Congress. Here he was actively connected with legislation for Puerto Rico, the Philippines, and other insular possessions of the United States. When in 1909 the Puerto Rican legislature adjourned without having made new governmental appropriations, Olmsted, in the face of strong opposition, secured, by an amendment of the Foraker Act of 1900, the passage of a bill extending to Puerto Rico legislation already adopted in regard to the Philippines and Hawaii, by which old appropriations should run until new appropriations should be made. Probably more significant was the civil government program for Puerto Rico which he presented in 1910, but which was held up in the Senate and put into operation in modified form only after his death.

When he retired to private life in 1913, his health was badly shattered. A brief vacation did him little good and on July 19, 1913, he died suddenly in New York City, following an operation. He was survived by his wife, Gertrude (How-

ard) Olmsted, daughter of Maj. Conway R. Howard, of Richmond, Va., whom he had married at Lynchburg on Oct. 26, 1899, and by five children. Olmsted was a man of distinguished appearance and by arduous study, clear analysis, and acute logic, established a high reputation as a lawyer and legislator.

[*A Biog. Album of Prominent Pennsylvanians*, 2 ser. (1889); *Year Book of the Pa. Soc.*, 1914; L. R. Kelker, *Hist. of Dauphin County, Pa.* (1907), vol. III; *Biog. Dir. Am. Cong.* (1928); *Who's Who in America*, 1912–13; H. K. Olmsted and G. K. Ward, *Geneal. of the Olmsted Family in America* (1912); *Patriot* (Harrisburg, Pa.), July 21, 1913; *N. Y. Times*, July 20, 1913.]   A. P. J.

OLNEY, JESSE (Oct. 12, 1798–July 30, 1872), author of textbooks, was born at Union, Conn., the eighth of the ten children of Ezekiel Olney and his second wife, Lydia Brown. His ancestor, Thomas Olney, emigrated to Salem, Massachusetts, in 1635 and later aided Roger Williams in the founding of Providence. His grandfather, Jeremiah, and his father, as well as many other relatives, were officers in the Revolutionary army. His mother's family was of English stock long resident in America. The boy obtained most of his education at Whitesboro, N. Y. He was a precocious student with a special bent for the classics and geography. For a few years he taught in New York state; then moved to Hartford, Conn., where for twelve years, beginning in 1821, he was principal of the Stone School. He was a born teacher; effective pedagogical methods were instinctive with him. Dissatisfied with the classroom manuals in use, he sought to replace them with better ones and shortly proved himself a most successful textbook maker. His first venture was *A Practical System of Modern Geography* (1828), followed the next year by *A New and Improved School Atlas* (1829). It was immediately successful. The study of geography had but recently been introduced into American elementary education and was still a tail to the cosmographical kite. Its texts were dull and uninteresting, quite beyond the comprehension of elementary students. Olney's book was suited to his pupils. Beginning with the simple and known facts of their immediate surroundings, it carried them forward to a knowledge of distant lands and complex phenomena. Rudimental as the method seems now, it was new at the time. The book passed through nearly a hundred editions and millions of copies were sold. There were few American school children of that generation whose ideas of the outer world, both true and false, were not formed by it. If our grandfathers believed that "Italians are affable and polite . . . but they are effeminate, superstitious, slavish, and revengeful," Olney no doubt must be held accountable.

Three years after the book's appearance he abandoned teaching to devote the rest of his life to textbook writing and to politics. Among his publications of the next twenty years were various readers, the most popular of which was *The National Preceptor; or Selections in Prose and Poetry* (2nd ed., 1829) ; a common-school arithmetic; a history of the United States; and several new books of geography. Being a firm believer in visual education, he prepared outline maps with accompanying exercises. The success of his textbooks gave him both financial independence and a reputation. When he stood for a seat in the Connecticut legislature in 1835, he was easily elected. For eight terms he represented Southington, where he lived from 1833 to 1854. For two years (1867–68) he was state comptroller of public accounts. Throughout his political career his interest lay primarily in education. He was a strong supporter of the movement which culminated in the organization of a state board of commissioners of public schools (1838) and a vigorous advocate of generous appropriations for the support of elementary education. In religion, as in other things, he was a liberal, and in middle life he joined a Unitarian church. He married Elizabeth Barnes of Hartford in 1829; of their six children one, Ellen Warner (Olney) Kirk, gained some reputation as a writer of fiction. In 1854 Olney moved to Stratford, Conn., where he died in 1872.

[J. H. Olney, *A Geneal. of the Descendants of Thomas Olney* (1889) ; *The Am. Ann. Cyc. for 1872* (1873) ; Charles Hammond and H. M. Lawson, *The Hist. of Union, Conn.* (1893) ; H. R. Timlow, *Ecclesiastical and Other Sketches of Southington, Conn.* (1875) ; *Am. Hist. Record*, Sept. 1872; *Hartford Daily Courant*, Aug. 1, 1872.]   P. D. E.

OLNEY, RICHARD (Sept. 15, 1835–Apr. 8, 1917), lawyer, attorney-general, secretary of state, was born at Oxford, Mass. His father, Wilson Olney, was a descendant of Thomas Olney, a follower of Roger Williams ; his mother, Eliza L. (Butler), was connected with the Sigourney family, Huguenot settlers of Oxford. At Leicester Academy, Brown University (A.M., 1856), and the Harvard Law School (LL.B., 1858), he successively won distinction. He was admitted to the bar in 1859 and entered the Boston office of Benjamin F. Thomas, whose daughter, Agnes, he married, Mar. 6, 1861, and to whose practice he succeeded. Confining himself to testamentary and corporation cases, which he conducted personally, he attained a respected position in professional and business circles but did not appear in the courts or in public. Square-

hewn and forbidding of figure and face, with drooping mustache and stern dark eyes, he attracted and sought no social intimacies. His adherence to the Democratic party afforded him little chance for a political carer. He was elected to the state legislature in 1873, but, after successive defeats for reëlection and for two other offices, he gave up politics. He was, therefore, hardly known to the people even of his own state in 1893, when he was selected by Cleveland as attorney-general to represent New England in the cabinet.

Besides the concern of his department with the test case of the Sherman Anti-Trust Law brought by his predecessor against the sugar refiners, which was dismissed by the Supreme Court in January 1895 (*U. S.* vs. *E. C. Knight Co.*, 156 *U. S. Reports*, 1), he gave much attention in his first year to outside affairs. His insistence that any action toward undoing the effects of the recent *coup d'état* in Hawaii should be predicated on an amnesty to the leaders prevented a restoration of Queen Liliuokalani, although the treaty of annexation negotiated by the provisional government was dropped. By making a preliminary draft he materially assisted President Cleveland in preparing his message to Congress asking repeal of the silver purchase clauses of the Act of 1890.

The economic unrest which found overt expression in the spring of 1894 in the march of Coxey's Army on Washington was prevented from assuming more serious proportions by the prompt action taken under Olney's orders to protect the trains on the Western railroads from seizure by additional contingents of unemployed demonstrants. When, later that summer, the American Railway Union, in support of the striking employees of the Pullman Company, paralyzed several roads by strikes growing out of the refusal to handle Pullman cars, the Administration made a straight case against the Union on the ground of obstruction of the mails. Olney directed the protection of mail trains by deputy marshals and obtained from Federal judges in Chicago an injunction restraining the activities of Eugene V. Debs, president of the Union, and other leaders. Federal troops were moved into Chicago, Debs [*q.v.*] and his lieutenants were arrested, and the strike collapsed. Olney directed the argument in the Supreme Court, in March 1895, against their unsuccessful appeal from a sentence for contempt of court (*In re Debs, Petitioner*, 158 *U. S. Reports*, 564). While he had shown throughout no concern with the underlying issues of the case, handling it opened his eyes to their gravity. He afterwards upheld the rights of organized labor and supported the movement which brought about the arbitration act of 1898. His last important task as attorney-general was the defense before the Supreme Court of the income tax provisions of the Wilson-Gorman tariff act. Despite his forceful arguments, the Court ruled against the Government, May 20, 1895, by a vote of five to four (*Pollock* vs. *Farmers' Loan and Trust Co.,* 158 *U. S. Reports,* 601).

Upon the death of Walter Q. Gresham [*q.v.*] Olney, who had become a pillar of the administration and whose harsh personality had been mellowed by the social life of the capital, was chosen by Cleveland to fill his place as secretary of state. He was commissioned in his new office, June 8, 1895. Undertaking to push to a conclusion the repeatedly frustrated efforts of his predecessors toward inducing the British government to arbitrate the boundary dispute between Venezuela and British Guiana, he dispatched to Thomas F. Bayard, the ambassador at London, on July 20, 1895, with Cleveland's enthusiastic approval, the spirited declaration that, by withholding from arbitration a part of the disputed territory, the British were constructively extending their colonization in America in opposition to the "established policy" of the United States defined by President Monroe. His statement that, owing to its isolation and resources, "the United States is practically sovereign on this continent, and its fiat is law upon the subjects to which it confines its interposition," was not put to the test of an immediate comparison between the forces of the United States and those of Great Britain, because Great Britain, concerned with new and threatening international problems in Europe and South Africa, could not meet the challenge with a free hand. President Cleveland's seriousness of purpose in backing Olney was demonstrated by his appointment, under authority asked of Congress, of a commission to fix a line beyond which any extension of British authority would be resisted by the United States. After complicated negotiations, Olney secured Lord Salisbury's agreement to an arbitration safeguarding British settlements of fifty years' standing, under which the award of 1899 gave Venezuela the smaller portion of the territory that Great Britain had demanded.

The Venezuelan controversy was the occasion for the renewal of discussion of the project of an Anglo-American general treaty of arbitration, already under consideration for some years. When suggested by Salisbury in January 1896, Olney took up the subject earnestly. He endeavored in the correspondence which followed to secure the greatest possible extension of arbitrable subjects and assurance of the binding force of awards. A treaty largely satisfying his desires through a combination of ingenious formulae was signed in January 1897, but was not acted on by the Senate until after his retirement, when consent to ratification was denied.

Throughout his secretaryship Olney was vexed by problems connected with a new revolt in Cuba, which demanded constant activity: on the one hand, in preventing filibustering and, on the other, in pressing claims for the redress of injuries to nationals of the United States. Like Secretary Hamilton Fish under similar circumstances, he resisted the pressure for recognition of the belligerency of rebel forces which had no responsible organization capable of constituting a government. He likewise strove to persuade Spain to adopt a constructive program of reforms; but a note to this effect sent to the Spanish minister on Apr. 4, 1896, met with a dilatory response. The subsequent political weakness of the Cleveland administration prevented it from going forward with any strong policy.

In the disorders prevailing in China and Turkey, Olney insisted as vigorously and firmly as in the case of Cuba on the protection of American lives and property and on reparation for injuries. When the situation was reversed and Italians were lynched in Colorado and Louisiana, he readily admitted, subject to determination of the facts and to the reserved rights of the states, the obligation of the federal government to indemnify the families of the victims.

After his retirement, on Mar. 5, 1897, he returned to his law practice and did not again enter political life; but he served on the boards of many foundations, wrote and spoke on public questions, and remained a prominent figure in the Democratic party. He declined offers from President Wilson of the posts of ambassador to Great Britain and governor of the Federal Reserve Board, but supported all the policies of the Wilson administration in its foreign relations, including those with Germany. He died from a cancer two days after the declaration of war in 1917. His wife and two daughters survived him.

[Henry James, *Richard Olney and His Public Service* (1923), based on Olney's papers, with list of his published articles and addresses; Grover Cleveland, *Presidential Problems* (1904); A. L. P. Dennis, *Adventures in American Diplomacy* (1928); *Papers Relating to the Foreign Relations of the U. S.,* 1895–97; sketch by Montgomery Schuyler in S. F. Bemis, ed., *The Am. Secretaries of State and Their Diplomacy,* vol. VIII (1928); *Boston Daily Globe,* Apr. 10, 1917.]

J.V.F.

OLYPHANT, DAVID WASHINGTON CINCINNATUS (Mar. 7, 1789–June 10, 1851), merchant and philanthropist, was born at Newport, R. I., the son of David (1720–1805) and Ann (Vernon) Olyphant. His father, a nephew of Lord Olyphant, was educated as a physician, in his youth supported the Stuarts, and after the eclipse of the Jacobite cause in the battle of Culloden emigrated to South Carolina. In the Revolution he served the colonies in several capacities, among them as director of Southern hospitals. After the Revolution, he was a member of the General Assembly of South Carolina. He was also a member of the Society of the Cincinnati. In 1785 he moved to Rhode Island, apparently because of failing health, and there married.

In 1806, shortly after the death of his aged father, young David went to New York to seek his fortune. Here he entered the counting-room of his cousin, Samuel King, senior partner of King & Talbot, a firm engaged in the then flourishing trade with China. In 1812 he removed to Baltimore, forming a business connection with a Mr. Bucklin of that city. The stormy years during and after the War of 1812 worked the ruin of that venture, and in 1817 Olyphant, in debt, returned to New York. Here he was associated with George W. Talbot, formerly of King & Talbot, and succeeded in paying his obligations. In 1818 he entered the employ of Thomas H. Smith, a picturesque figure with a somewhat meteoric career, who for a time was one of the most notable merchants in the China trade. From 1820 to about 1823 Olyphant was in Canton as Smith's agent, then returned to America for a few years, after which period he again held the Canton agency of the Smith firm —from 1826 until the spectacular failure of his employer (1827 or 1828). Thereupon, he formed in Canton, with C. N. Talbot, the son of his early friend, the firm of Olyphant & Company, and, returning to the United States, organized in New York a house under the name of Talbot, Olyphant & Company. In these business connections he continued until his death. Twice again he was in China—from 1834 to 1837 and from 1850 to 1851. It was while returning from the last trip that he died in Cairo.

Olyphant is remembered even more for his religious and philanthropic activities than for his business career. While in Baltimore, in 1814, he formally announced himself a Christian, and, as was natural for one with his Scotch heritage, he became active in the Presbyterian Church. It was in part as a result of his interest that the first American Protestant missionary to China,

Elijah C. Bridgman [q.v.], went to Canton. Bridgman and David Abeel [q.v.]—the latter an agent of the American Seaman's Friend Society, in which Olyphant was also interested— arrived in Canton in 1830, having been given free passage by Olyphant's company on one of its ships. Olyphant and his partners provided quarters for the mission free of rent for thirteen years. Olyphant also underwrote the famous publication of this early American mission, the *Chinese Repository.* He and his partners provided free passage to China for many missionaries, including the distinguished S. Wells Williams [q.v.] and the first Protestant medical missionary in China, Peter Parker [q.v.]. In 1836 his firm purchased a vessel, the *Himaleh,* for the purpose of aiding in the distribution of Christian literature along the coast of China, and it was the *Morrison,* another of the company's ships, which in 1837 made a voyage to Japan in a memorable attempt to open that country to intercourse with Americans while restoring seven shipwrecked Japanese sailors to their homes. Olyphant was a member of the American Board of Commissioners for Foreign Missions and of the executive committee of the Presbyterian Board of Foreign Missions, and it was largely in the interest of missions that he made the trip to China which cost him his life. It was, moreover, from deep moral conviction that he and his firm refused to participate in the profitable opium traffic which bulked so large in the foreign imports to China in his day. He was married to Mrs. Ann Archer in May 1815, and his sons, one of whom was Robert Morrison Olyphant [q.v.], continued his business.

[J. N. Arnold, *Vital Record of R. I., 1636–1850,* vols. IV (1893), pt. 2, pp. 52, 107, XIV (1905), p. 148, XX (1911), p. 216; Harrison Ellery, "The Vernon Family," *New-Eng. Hist. and Geneal. Reg.,* July 1879; Thatcher Thayer, *A Sketch of the Life of D. W. C. Olyphant, Who Died at Cairo, June 10, 1851, with a Tribute to His Memory* (1852); *Chinese Repository,* July 1851; W. C. Hunter, *The 'Fan Kwae' at Canton before Treaty Days, 1825–1844* (Shanghai, 1882); K. S. Latourette, "The Hist. of Early Relations Between the U. S. and China, 1784–1844," *Trans. of the Conn. Acad. of Arts and Sciences,* vol. XXII (1917); F. W. Williams, *The Life and Letters of Samuel Wells Williams, LL.D.* (1889).]   K.S.L.

OLYPHANT, ROBERT MORRISON (Sept. 9, 1824–May 3, 1918), merchant, railroad president, was born in New York City. He was the youngest son of David W. C. Olyphant [q.v.] and his wife, Ann. His father was a member of Talbot, Olyphant & Company, merchants in the China trade, whose record of cooperation with missionaries and refusal to engage in the opium trade gained for their office in China the nickname of "Zion's Corners." As a child, Robert attended private schools in Troy, N. Y., Middletown, Conn., and New York City. He entered Columbia College with the class of 1843, at the age of fifteen, and graduated in three years (1842). On Oct. 13, 1846, he married Sophia, daughter of William Vernon of Middletown, R. I., and after her death, 1855, he married her sister Anna, Aug. 13, 1857.

After his graduation from Columbia, he entered the employ of his father's firm and in 1844 visited China, returning a year later. He was rapidly advanced and soon became a partner. Shortly before 1858 he reorganized his father's old firm, Olyphant & Company, Canton, China, and engaged in a general importing, shipping, commission, and mercantile business with the Orient, being careful to maintain the high standards which had characterized the concern under his father's direction. He resided in China four years and upon his return directed the business from New York until he retired from foreign trade in 1873.

During the later years of this period he turned his attention to the Delaware & Hudson Canal Company (later Delaware & Hudson Company), in which members of his family had been interested since 1852. This company was principally engaged in operating railroads and anthracite coal mines, though it also operated a canal, a gravity road, and steamboat lines on Lake Champlain and Lake George. He served as a member of its board of managers, 1867–68, 1873–74, and 1883–1918; was elected assistant president, 1876; vice-president, 1882; acting president, 1884; and president, Oct. 24, 1884. In this last capacity he served until his seventy-ninth year, retiring from active management, May 13, 1903. He was then made chairman of the executive committee, an honorary position. Olyphant's presidency was a quiet period in which the company reaped the advantages of previous construction and consolidation of its railroad properties. His policy was improvement rather than enlargement. He maintained the property at a high degree of efficiency and substantially increased the assets of the company in spite of sacrifices involved in the abandonment of the canal and gravity road during his administration. He dealt firmly with employees during strikes at the company's mines, and he regarded the award of the anthracite strike commission which followed the strike of 1902 as a concession to humanity and not to the strikers.

He liked to consider himself an old-fashioned business man. In his investments he preferred safety to large returns. He rarely took a vacation, and when he left the city he kept up a con-

stant supervision over his business concerns. He had, also, numerous interests in art, science, and philanthropy, and he formed a noteworthy collection of American works of art. As a fellow of the National Academy of Design he assisted in raising funds for the erection of its first building. He gave liberally toward missionary work in China and was a patron of the Canton Christian Church. His death occurred in New York City in his ninety-fourth year; he had ten children.

[*Reg. of Saint Andrew's Soc. of the State of N. Y.*, 2 ser., pt. II (1922?); MS. notes and clippings in the library of the N. Y. Hist. Soc.; *A Century of Progress: Hist. of the Del. and Hudson Co., 1823–1923* (1925); printed and MS. material from the records of the company; *World* (N. Y.), May 17, 1903; "The Oldest Living Graduate," *Columbia Alumni News*, Apr. 5, 1912; *N. Y. Times*, May 4, 1918.] E. C. S.

O'MAHONY, JOHN (1816–Feb. 6, 1877), Fenian leader, was born near Mitchelstown, County Cork, Ireland, not far from Kilbeheny in Limerick, where his father, Daniel O'Mahony, held some lands. The family was popular on account of its nationalist feeling and its opposition in the past to the Earls of Kingston, whose estates were near by. Both O'Mahony's father and an uncle are said to have been concerned in the rebellion of 1798. Like his elder brother, Thomas Daniel, John attended Hamblin's School at Middleton in Cork and went thence to Trinity College, Dublin, where he was admitted as a "pensioner" on July 1, 1833, but never took a degree. Apparently the death of his father and brother left him in possession of their property, and he settled down to the life of a gentleman farmer. When the enthusiasts of the "Young Ireland" party broke away from O'Connell in disgust with his caution, O'Mahony adhered to them. He was then living on "a small paternal property" near Carrick-on-Suir, and he organized in the district one of the clubs which the "confederates" hoped to utilize in a revolt. In 1848, he shared the fortunes of Smith O'Brien and others in their brief and abortive insurrection, but escaped arrest, and remained in hiding until September, when he and John Savage for some days carried on a guerrilla campaign in the valley of the Suir, and had several conflicts with the police. On Sept. 26 Dublin Castle offered a reward of £100 for O'Mahony's apprehension; nevertheless, after a whole series of hairbreadth escapes, he got safely away to France. There he lived in poverty until, apparently, late in 1853, when he went to New York. The next year he helped organize a military body called the Emmet Monument Association, designed to turn Britain's difficulties in the Crimean War to Irish advantage. This organization disbanded when the war ended, but was the foundation of the later Fenian movement. About this time O'Mahony had a fit of insanity and was temporarily confined in an asylum; but his friend John O'Leary (*post*) affirms his belief that he was quite sane during the rest of his life.

In 1857 O'Mahony published a translation of Geoffrey Keating's seventeenth-century Gaelic History of Ireland (*Foras feasa ar Eirinn . . . The History of Ireland*) which, though hastily executed and taken from bad texts, seems to have commanded respect from scholars. This work gave much attention (*e.g.*, pp. 343 ff.) to the Fenians (*Fiann*), the legendary defenders of Ireland in the time of Finn, and here probably O'Mahony got the idea of a name for a new militant organization. Towards the end of 1857 he and other Irishmen in New York suggested to James Stephens (see *Dictionary of National Biography*, 2nd Supp.), an 1848 rebel still in Ireland, that he should organize a revolutionary society there. On being promised financial support, Stephens inaugurated his secret movement in Dublin on Mar. 17, 1858. In Ireland the society, known later as the Irish Republican or Irish Revolutionary Brotherhood, was headed by Stephens; the American branch, called the Fenian Brotherhood, was directed by O'Mahony as "Head Centre." The movement spread in America—slowly at first—and modest sums were transmitted to Stephens. In 1860–61 O'Mahony visited Ireland and had a violent interview with Stephens, who accused him of affording him too little support; complete confidence was never restored between the two men afterwards. During the Civil War, O'Mahony worked to obtain Irish recruits for the Union army. Early in 1864 he raised the 99th Regiment, New York National Guard; became its colonel; and did duty with it at the Elmira prison camp.

At the end of the war the Brotherhood was prosperous, and O'Mahony sent drillmasters and large financial aid to Stephens. Disputes now arose between O'Mahony and hostile elements in his organization, growing worse after the British government nipped Stephens's conspiracy in the bud in September 1865. In October' a Fenian congress in Philadelphia adopted a new constitution styling O'Mahony president and providing a senate to check his powers. In December an open quarrel occurred over the sale of Fenian bonds, O'Mahony desiring to proceed with it at once to aid those still conspiring in Ireland, while the senate enjoined delay. The organization split in two, each faction claiming to be the Fenian Brotherhood. The senate party elected W. R. Roberts [*q.v.*] as president and

made plans to invade Canada. In January 1866, a congress of O'Mahony's adherents voted confidence in him and restored the old constitution. In April, however, he gave a reluctant consent to a hostile demonstration against Campobello Island (part of the province of New Brunswick), which proved a fiasco and was fatal to his popular reputation. Soon afterwards, Stephens, who had escaped from prison, arrived in New York, and on May 11 accepted O'Mahony's resignation. In 1872 O'Mahony was called out of retirement to resume the leadership of the Brotherhood, then only a shadow of the formidable organization of 1865; he now bore the title of executive secretary, but in 1875 again took that of "Head Centre," and held it until immediately before his death. His body was sent from New York to Ireland, and on both sides of the Atlantic there were impressive memorial demonstrations. He was buried in Glasnevin Cemetery, Dublin, on Mar. 4, 1877.

O'Mahony never married. O'Leary spoke of him as physically "perhaps the manliest and handsomest man" he ever saw, and believed him to be "the soul of truth and honour." Whatever may be said of his methods, the sincerity of his Irish patriotism is undoubted. With Stephens he shares, for better or worse, the credit of founding the formidable Fenian society. He was indifferent to money, and although he handled large sums of Fenian funds he died in poverty. His judgment was faulty and his behavior autocratic; but he remains one of the most attractive figures in the history of Irish nationalism.

[John O'Leary, *Recollections of Fenians and Fenianism* (2 vols., 1896), and article in *Dict. Nat. Biog.* (less valuable); John Savage, *Fenian Heroes and Martyrs* (1868); Joseph Denieffe, *A Personal Narrative of the Irish Revolutionary Brotherhood* (1906); C. G. Duffy, *Four Years of Irish History* (1883); Michael Doheny, *The Felon's Track* (1849); John Rutherford, *The Secret Hist. of the Fenian Conspiracy* (2 vols., 1877); Frederick Phisterer, *N. Y. in the War of the Rebellion* (1912), vol. I; *Alumni Dublinenses* (1924), ed. by G. D. Burtchaell and T. U. Sadleir; files of the *Times* (London), *Irish American* (N. Y.), *N. Y. Herald*, *N. Y. Tribune;* well-informed obituary notices, *N. Y. Herald*, Feb. 7, 1877, and *Irish World* (N. Y.), Feb. 17, 1877, and succeeding issues.]

C. P. S.

O'MALLEY, FRANK WARD (Nov. 30, 1875–Oct. 19, 1932), writer, was born in Pittston, Pa., the son of William and Catherine (Ward) O'Malley. His academic education was limited to the Wilkes-Barre, Pa., high school, but his ambition to be either an architect or an artist led him to spend ten years in pursuing special courses at the Art Students League, Washington, D. C. (1894–95), the University of Notre Dame (1896–98), and the Pennsylvania Academy of the Fine Arts in Philadelphia (1899–

1902). The time devoted to art was not justified by the results. O'Malley, in a facetious auto-biographical sketch, once said that while in Washington he spent too much time in the Senate gallery; in Notre Dame, too much time with the football team; and in Philadelphia, too much time in a burlesque theatre.

When he arrived in New York in 1902 he found no place for artistic expression except as a commercial illustrator. Seeing that his casual light verse and humorous articles found a fair market in newspapers, he became a special writer on the *Morning Telegraph,* a daily devoted to racing, the theatre, and the night life of Broadway. His articles attracted the attention of the *Sun,* which engaged him as a reporter in 1906. His success was instant, not only on account of his humorous treatment of trivial happenings, but also because of his accurate and dramatic relation of serious events. Read today, most of these articles lack the flavor of their time and the color of their setting. A few—notably O'Malley's interview with the mother of a young police-man who was killed on duty (*Sun,* Oct. 23, 1907) —have been used as models by teachers of journalism. The account of the Triangle shirt-waist factory fire, in which 150 persons lost their lives (*Ibid.,* Mar. 26, 1911), is a good example of his ability to write "straight news." Much of O'Malley's product concerned the people and events of the "white light district" of New York in pre-prohibition days. Himself of fine moral character, he regarded the Tenderloin as a sort of fairyland. He wrote of himself that he was "a reporter on the *Sun* for fourteen years, thirteen of which were spent in Jack's restaurant" (*New York Times,* Oct. 20, 1932, p. 21). The Bohemian life which centered about Jack's saw little of him after his marriage in 1917. He resigned from the *Sun* in 1920 with the intention of writing something less ephemeral than newspaper articles. From 1920 to 1932 he wrote for the *Saturday Evening Post* twenty-eight articles, humorous or satirical, touching on life both in the United States and in Europe. Two of his articles, published in the *American Mercury* (May, September 1929), dealt with the virtues and weaknesses of the Irish in the United States. He wrote two books, *The War-Whirl in Washington* (1918) and *The Swiss Family O'Malley* (1928), and in collaboration with E. W. Townsend, two plays, *The Head of the House* (1909) and *A Certain Party* (1910); the plays had little success. His greatest days were those in which he was regarded as one of the best reporters of his generation.

O'Malley's lack of valuable productivity in his later years may be laid to the fact that he was more interested in life itself than in the portrayal of it. He was a delightful companion, ever eager to discuss any subject, and much sought for his candor, graciousness, and wit. His only bitterness was directed at prohibition, which he denounced publicly and privately with vehemence and to which he attributed his long stays in Europe. This hatred was not lessened when diabetes prevented him from using spirits. He died in Tours, France. On Sept. 1, 1917, he was married to Grace Edsall Dalrymple who, with a son and a daughter, survived him.

[*Sun* (N. Y.), Oct. 19, 1932; *N. Y. Times,* Oct. 20, 1932; F. M. O'Brien, *The Story of the Sun* (1918); *Who's Who in America,* 1930–31; personal acquaintance.]
F. M. O.

OÑATE, JUAN de (*c.* 1549–*c.* 1624), frontiersman of New Spain (Mexico) and colonizer of New Mexico, was born of illustrious parentage in New Spain, but when and where it is uncertain. His father, Cristóbal de Oñate, became governor of Nueva Galicia in 1538, and during the next ten years, through the discovery of mines in Zacatecas, became one of the richest men in America. Juan's mother, Doña Cathalina de Salazar, was the daughter of the royal *factor,* Gonzalo de Salazar, who was the bitter enemy of Cortés. Little is known of Juan's youth. On the northern frontier, where he early became active for his king, his general services covered "bloody encounters with the Chichimecs, and the discovery of the rich mines of Zichú, Charcas, and San Luis Potosí, which he peopled with Spaniards" (quoted by Cornish, *post,* p. 459). He married Isabel Tolosa, a descendant of both Cortés and Montezuma. Of this union two children were born.

His chief claim to fame rests upon his services as founder of New Mexico. A revival of interest in that region after 1583 resulted in a spirited competition for the right to conquer it. Royal authorization for the appointment of a suitable person for this purpose was received by the viceroy of New Spain in 1583. Delays ensued, but on Sept. 21, 1595, the coveted contract, calling for the "exploration, pacification, and conquest of New Mexico," was awarded to Oñate. Disappointments awaited him. A new viceroy modified his contract, but, despite attendant delays, by September 1596 Oñate's large and well-equipped expedition was at the Nazas River, in the present Durango, prepared to enter the more than six hundred miles of unoccupied territory between there and the upper Rio Grande Valley. Meanwhile, in Spain, the Council of the Indies had shown interest in the New Mexico venture being entrusted to Pedro Ponce de León of Spain, and in July 1596, Viceroy Monterey had received instructions to cancel Oñate's contract. To this, Oñate offered vigorous protest—at the same time endeavoring to keep his expedition intact, pending an appeal—for he "had spent 100,-000 ducats in equipping the expedition, while the captains and soldiers who were to accompany him had spent an additional 200,000 ducats" (Hackett, *post*, I, 203). Confidence in De León being shaken, Oñate finally was authorized to proceed, and in August 1597 the expedition, somewhat depleted in men and supplies, advanced northward. On Apr. 30, 1598, a few miles south of the present El Paso, Tex., Oñate took formal possession "of all the kingdoms and provinces of New Mexico." By early autumn the upper Rio Grande pueblos had been reached, a capital had been founded at San Juan, missionary work had been begun, and the submission of the Indians received. This submission, save for the rebellion of Ácoma, which was suppressed with great cruelty early in 1599, was definitive for nearly a hundred years.

Oñate's contract—partly because of the king's interest in anticipating other European nations in the discovery of the supposed northwest passage—called for exploration, and in September 1598 the first of a series of expensive exploring expeditions was dispatched from San Juan. Others followed in rapid succession, notably one to Kansas in 1601, and one to the Gulf of California in 1605. In protest against these expeditions, which sapped the energy and resources of the colony, some of the settlers fled to Santa Bárbara but they were arrested and returned.

Meanwhile Oñate had been obliged to ask for reinforcements. Royal interest in New Mexico was still high and in 1605 twenty-four additional soldiers and two missionaries were sent. This aid proved insufficient, and for the next three years New Mexico's fate hung in the balance. Apparently for the purpose of bluffing the viceroy into sending reinforcements, Oñate resigned in August 1607, and notified the viceroy that if reinforcements were not forthcoming by June 1608 the province would be abandoned. The viceroy called Oñate's bluff and accepted his resignation, but instructed him to remain in the province. Soon thereafter the *cabildo* at the new capital, San Gabriel, elected him governor *ad interim*, and upon his refusal to serve, chose his son, Cristóbal. Since Cristóbal was an unsatisfactory choice, the viceroy in Mexico sent Don Pedro Peralta [*q.v.*] as governor, with sixteen soldiers, and orders were given for Oñate to return within three months.

Oñate went back to Mexico, and was tried on charges of misrepresenting the value of New Mexico, mistreatment of his soldiers and the Indians, and disobedience to vice-regal orders. He was found guilty on some of the charges in 1614 and sentenced to perpetual banishment from New Mexico, and from Mexico city for four years, and fined 6,000 ducats. In 1622 he appealed against the judgment, but though he had the support of the Council of the Indies, he failed to obtain the pardon of the king. He may have been successful later, for in 1624 he was in Spain trying to obtain a position in Mexico, Guadalajara, or the Philippines. His endeavor was not successful, but he was entrusted with the visitation of mines in Spain. His death, therefore, must have occurred in or after that year.

[Printed sources for the work of Oñate are *Colección de Documentos Inéditos, Relativos al Descubrimiento . . . de América*, vol. XVI (1871), and in C. W. Hackett, *Hist. Documents Relating to New Mexico . . .*, vol. I (1923). English translations of original sources are in Hackett, *op. cit.*, and in H. E. Bolton, *Spanish Exploration . . .* (1916). A contemporary account, written by a member of the expedition, is Gaspar Pérez de Villagrá, *Historia de la Nueva Mexico del Capitan Gaspar de Villagra* (1610), reprint with notes (2 vols., 1900). See also Beatrice Q. Cornish, "The Ancestry and Family of Juan de Oñate," in H. M. Stephens and H. E. Bolton, *The Pacific Ocean in Hist.* (1917) ; H. E. Bolton, *The Spanish Borderlands* (1921) ; G. P. Hammond, "Don Juan de Oñate and the Founding of New Mexico," in *Hist. Soc. of N. Mex. Pubs. in Hist.*, vol. II (Oct. 1927), also in *N. Mex. Hist. Rev.*, Jan. 1926–Apr. 1927 ; G. P. Hammond, "The Conviction of Don Juan de Oñate, New Mexico's First Governor," in *New Spain and the Anglo-American West. Hist. Contributions Presented to Herbert Eugene Bolton* (1932), I, 67–79.]   C. W. H.

ONDERDONK, BENJAMIN TRED-WELL (July 15, 1791–Apr. 30, 1861), bishop of the Protestant Episcopal Church, was born and died in New York City. He was the son of Dr. John and Deborah (Ustick) Onderdonk, and a descendant of Andries Onderdonk, a native of New Castle, Del., who died in 1687 ; Bishop Henry Ustick Onderdonk [*q.v.*] was Benjamin's brother. He was graduated at Columbia College in 1809, studied theology, and was ordained deacon at St. Paul's Chapel, New York, Aug. 2, 1812, and priest, in Trinity Church, Newark, N. J., July 26, 1815, by Bishop John Henry Hobart. In 1813 he married Eliza Moscrop. That same year he was appointed assistant minister of Trinity Church, New York, which position he held until his elevation to the episcopate, gaining a reputation as an excellent preacher and an energetic worker. From about 1821 he served as professor of ecclesiastical history at the General Theological Seminary, New York, and also as professor of the nature, ministry, and polity of the Church; from 1816 to 1830 he was secretary of the New York diocesan convention. On Nov. 26, 1830, he was consecrated bishop of New York, in St. John's Chapel, by Bishops William White, Thomas Church Brownell, and Henry Ustick Onderdonk.

In November 1844 he was presented for trial upon the charges of "immorality and impurity" by Bishops William Meade of Virginia, James Hervey Otey of Tennessee, and Stephen Elliott, Jr., of Georgia. On Jan. 3, 1845, after a trial by the court of bishops provided for by the canons of his Church, he was suspended "from the office of a Bishop in the Church of God, and from all the functions of the sacred ministry." It was the first trial of a bishop ever held under the canons of the Episcopal Church (since the suspension of his brother the previous year had been effected without a trial) and was the most sensational episode in the history of the Church up to that time. The canon which gave the right of presentment to any three bishops, as well as to the bishop's own diocese, had been passed only three months previous to the trial. The *Churchman*, at that time representing the High Church party, charged that the presentment and condemnation of Bishop Onderdonk were the result of a Low Church conspiracy. The trustees of the General Theological Seminary refused to remove him from his professorship in that institution. It is recorded that "the proceedings of the court were almost universally reprobated." In 1859 a resolution was offered in the New York diocesan convention requesting "the House of Bishops to remit and terminate the Judicial Sentence of Suspension, under which the Bishop of the Diocese of New York is now suffering disability." In presenting the resolution, Dr. Francis Vinton argued that the canon under which Onderdonk was tried was responsible for the indefinite character of the sentence, since it provided only for "admonition, suspension or degradation"; that its injustice had been officially recognized, since the next General Convention (1847) had revised the canon to provide remission or modification, and had adopted another specifying that under no circumstances should any similar indefinite sentence be passed on any one in the future. He pleaded that the convention should ask to have done in Onderdonk's case what the later canon provided—a time limit set for such suspension. In 1850, furthermore, a canon had been passed establishing procedure for the resignation of a suspended bishop, thereby demonstrating that Onderdonk still retained his jurisdiction. In the same year another canon provided for a provisional incumbent to serve during the suspension of a bishop, thus indicating that the Church intended to make possible a suspended

bishop's restoration. A memorial to the General Convention from Bishop Onderdonk was read, in which he begged "the mercy of the removal of my sentence," and stated that he could not acknowledge all the crimes imputed to him, adding, "I cannot but believe parts of my conduct to have betrayed indiscretion." The resolution was passed in the diocesan convention by vote of 147 to 19 (clerical) and 75 to 46 (lay). The General Convention of 1859 did not act on the petition, and before the next General Convention, Onderdonk had died. His conduct during his years of suspension was a matter for high commendation on all sides. He was a stanch and vigorous High Churchman, an aggressive, able administrator and opponent. His only written works were episcopal addresses, charges, and pastorals.

[Elmer Onderdonk, *Geneal. of the Onderdonk Family in America* (1910); W. S. Perry, *The Bishops of the Am. Church* (1897); H. G. Batterson, *A Sketch-Book of the Am. Episcopate* (1878); *Proc. of the Court . . . for the Trial of the Rt. Rev. Benjamin T. Onderdonk, D.D.* (1845); *Bishop Onderdonk's Statement: A Statement of Facts and Circumstances Connected with the Recent Trial of the Bishop of N. Y.* (1845); *Appeal from the Sentence of the Bishop of N. Y. in Behalf of His Diocese* (1845), and other pamphlets on the controversy; *Jour. of . . . the Seventy-sixth Convention of the Prot. Episc. Ch. in the Diocese of N. Y.* (1859); *Churchman*, 1844–45, 1861; *Church Jour.*, 1844–45, 1861.]
G. E. S.

ONDERDONK, HENRY (June 11, 1804– June 22, 1886), teacher, local historian, was born at Manhasset, in North Hempstead, N. Y., the son of Joseph Onderdonck (*sic*) and Dorothy Monfoort, his wife, and the seventh child in a family of ten. He was descended from two old Long Island families, being fourth in descent from Andries Onderdonk, who purchased land in Flatbush, L. I., in 1672. In 1827 Henry was graduated at Columbia. On Nov. 28, 1828, he was married to his cousin, Maria Hegeman Onderdonk. At an early period he devoted himself to teaching, becoming principal of Union Hall Academy, at Jamaica, an institution opened in 1792. To the duties of principal he added instruction in the classics, then the leading course in preparatory schools; but equally congenial was that which he made his recreation, the study of Long Island antiquities. He also as occasion arose delivered lectures on temperance. After following the teaching profession for thirty-three years, he retired and engaged wholly in the work for which he had been preparing by his investigations in history and genealogy.

In the preface to *Revolutionary Incidents of Suffolk and Kings Counties,* Onderdonk declares: "The present volume completes a plan the compiler had some years since conceived, of collecting and arranging in chronological order, the scattered and fragmentary notices of the events that occurred on Long Island, during our Revolutionary struggle" (p. 5). In respect for original documents as the source of knowledge and the basis of opinion, Onderdonk may rightly be pronounced a forerunner of a later school, whose claims are pronounced with much more emphasis than he ever employed. Official and military papers, diaries, old newspapers, and the conversations of aged people contributed material, and sometimes by their simplicity and bare reality they create an impression beyond the power of any literary presentation. Onderdonk understood the historic value of church records, which embody constant and unobtrusive influences in the life of communities, as important as the forces which give dramatic interest to political and military history. His work represents the painstaking collection and compilation of such materials as yield no great reputations but bring honor in the end to those who lay these foundations for prouder structures. Included in his published writings are: *Antiquities of the Parish Church, Jamaica (including Newtown and Flushing)* (1880); *The Annals of Hempstead, N. Y., 1643 to 1832, also the Rise and Growth of the Society of Friends on Long Island and in New York 1657 to 1826* (1878); *Antiquities of the Parish Church, Hempstead, including Oysterbay and the Churches of Suffolk County* (1880); *The Bibliography of Long Island* (1866); *Documents and Letters Intended to Illustrate the Revolutionary Incidents of Queens County* (1846); *History of the First Reformed Dutch Church of Jamaica, L. I.* (1884); *Queens County in Olden Times* (1865); *Revolutionary Incidents of Suffolk and Kings Counties* (1849).

[See the *Hist. of Queens County, N. Y.* (1882); Onderdonk's *Revolutionary Incidents of Suffolk and Kings Counties* (1849); Elmer Onderdonk, *Geneal. of the Onderdonk Family in America* (1910); *N. Y. Daily Tribune*, June 24, 1886.]   R. E. D.

ONDERDONK, HENRY USTICK (Mar. 16, 1789–Dec. 6, 1858), bishop of the Protestant Episcopal Church, was born in New York City, the son of Dr. John and Deborah (Ustick) Onderdonk; Benjamin T. Onderdonk [*q.v.*] was a younger brother. His ancestry is traced back to one Andries Onderdonk of New Castle, Del., who married Maria Van der Vliet, and died in 1687. Henry was graduated from Columbia College in 1805 and then studied medicine in London and Edinburgh, receiving the degree of M.D. from the University of Edinburgh. Returning to New York City, he became a prac-

tising physician, and from 1814 to 1815 was associate editor of the *New York Medical Magazine*. On Apr. 15, 1811, he married Eliza Carter. Dissatisfied with his profession, he studied for orders under the oversight of Bishop John Henry Hobart [*q.v.*], who ordained him deacon in St. Paul's Chapel, New York, Dec. 8, 1815, and priest, in Trinity Church, New York, Apr. 11, 1816. After four years in Canandaigua, then a missionary frontier post of the Episcopal Church in Western New York, he was elected, in 1820, to the rectorship of St. Ann's Church, Brooklyn, N. Y.

Having been elected assistant bishop of Pennsylvania, after a bitter partisan controversy between the High Churchmen and Low Churchmen of the day, he was consecrated at Christ Church, Philadelphia, Oct. 25, 1827, thereby becoming associated with Bishop William White [*q.v.*]. At that time Onderdonk was one of the most noted churchmen in the ministry of the Episcopal Church. On the death of Bishop White in 1836 he became the second bishop of Pennsylvania. In 1844 he wrote to the House of Bishops confessing his habitual abuse of intoxicating liquor, tendering his resignation of his jurisdiction, and asking for discipline. His resignation was accepted (*Journal of . . . General Convention*, 1844, p. 104), and he was suspended by the House of Bishops from "all public exercise of the offices and functions of the sacred Ministry, and in particular from all exercise whatsoever of the office and work of a Bishop in the Church of God" (*Ibid.*, pp. 171–72). He accepted his sentence in a spirit of humility, spending part of his period of suspension in writing. So exemplary was his conduct that he was restored to the active ministry by the House of Bishops in 1856, two years before his death.

Onderdonk was known as one of the outstanding theological scholars of his day and an expert controversialist. In the early part of 1844 he had been the cause of an extensive controversy, carried on chiefly in the church press. Learning that Bishop John H. Hopkins [*q.v.*] of Vermont intended to give a series of fifteen lectures on Romanism in Philadelphia, occupying in rotation the pulpits of five parishes, he wrote Hopkins that he had received the information with "regret and astonishment"—regret, because he felt the subject calculated to cause undue agitation and excitement, and astonishment, because he had not been consulted as head of the diocese. Bishop Hopkins canceled the proposed lectures, with a threat that he would take the matter to the General Convention. Among Onderdonk's published works are: *An Appeal to the Religious*

Public of Canandaigua (1813); *Episcopacy Tested by Scriptures* (1830); *Episcopacy Examined and Reexamined* (1835); *Essay on Regeneration* (1835); *Family Devotions from the Liturgy* (1835); *Thoughts on Some of the Objections to Christianity* (1835); *Sermons and Episcopal Charges* (2 vols., 1851). He wrote several hymns and versions of the Psalms, which appeared in the collection of Psalms and hymns appended to the prayer book of that day.

[Elmer Onderdonk, *Geneal. of the Onderdonk Family in America* (1910); W. S. Perry, *The Bishops of the Am. Ch.* (1897); H. G. Batterson, *A Sketch-Book of the Am. Episcopate* (1878); *Jour. of the Proc. of the Bishops, Clergy and Laity of the Protestant Episcopal Ch. in the U. S. A., Assembled in a Gen. Convention,* 1844, 1856; the *Churchman,* 1844–58; *Episcopal Recorder,* 1844–58; *Pennsylvanian* (Phila.), Dec. 7, 1858.]   G. E. S.

O'NEAL, EDWARD ASBURY (Sept. 20, 1818–Nov. 7, 1890), Confederate soldier, governor of Alabama, was born in Madison County, Ala., while Alabama was still a territory. His father, Edward O'Neal, a native of Ireland, and his mother, Rebecca (Wheat) O'Neal, of Huguenot extraction, had removed from South Carolina shortly before his birth. When Edward was very young, his father died, and his mother, who appears to have been a woman of great force of character, managed the business affairs of the family and taught her two sons until they were ready to enter the academy. He not only graduated from the academy but also graduated from LaGrange College in 1836. On Apr. 12, 1838, he was married to Olivia Moore at Huntsville. He studied law, was admitted to the bar in 1840, and began practice at Florence, Ala. Within a year he was chosen by the state legislature to serve as solicitor of the 4th circuit and held this office for four years. He was always interested in politics. He was a candidate for Congress in 1848 but was defeated. He became one of the leaders of the movement for secession in northern Alabama. In 1861 he enlisted in the Confederate army and was chosen major of the 9th Alabama Infantry. His promotion was rapid. In October of that year he became lieutenant-colonel, and the next spring he was raised to the rank of colonel and assigned to the 26th Alabama Infantry. He led his regiment in the battles of the Peninsular campaign, was wounded at the battle of Seven Pines and again at Boonsboro, led Rodes's Division in the battle of Chancellorsville, where he was again wounded, and he was in command of the same division at Gettysburg. Early in 1864 the 26th Alabama was returned to the state to recruit its ranks. From there it was sent to Dalton, Ga., to aid in the defense against Sherman. He

led Canty's Brigade at Marietta and at Peachtree Creek. He was relieved of his command after this campaign and placed on detached duty. When the war closed he was in Alabama arresting deserters from the Army of the Tennessee. For the last eighteen months of the war he acted as brigadier-general, but he never received a commission.

At the close of the war he returned to Florence to resume the practice of his profession and his activity in politics. He was the leader of the Democratic party in northern Alabama during the Reconstruction period and a member of the constitutional convention of 1875. In 1882 he was elected governor of the state and was reelected in 1884. His administration was a turning point in the history of Alabama. The development of the state, which had been arrested by the war and Reconstruction, was taken up again; the state was prosperous, and for the first time money was available for something more than necessities. His major interests during his administrations were education and prison reform. Normal schools were established, and greatly increased appropriations were made for other state schools through his influence. The first steps toward prison reform were taken with the establishment of the board of convict inspectors. At the close of his administration he returned to Florence and lived there until his death.

[Manuscript material in the State Department of Archives and History, Montgomery; Willis Brewer, *Alabama* (1872); J. E. Saunders, *Early Settlers of Ala.* (1899); *Confederate Mil. Hist.,* ed. by C. A. Evans (1899), vol. VII; T. M. Owen, *Hist. of Ala. and Dict. of Ala. Biog.* (1921), vol. IV; *Gov. Edward A. O'Neal . . . Proceedings of the Joint Session of the Senate and House of Representatives of Ala.* (1927); *Daily Reg.* (Mobile), Nov. 8, 1890.] H. F.

O'NEALE, MARGARET (1796–Nov. 8, 1879), was the wife of John H. Eaton [*q.v.*], secretary of war under Andrew Jackson. Few careers have been as varied, colorful, and dramatic as that of "Peggy" O'Neale. Her father, William O'Neale, was a tavern-keeper of Washington, D. C., from the founding of the city. Peggy was a pretty child and was spoiled by guests at her father's inn. Her mother, Rhoda Howell, was apparently a woman of refinement and, according to her daughter (*Autobiography, post,* p. 1), a sister of Richard Howell [*q.v.*], governor of New Jersey. Peggy attended Mrs. Hayward's Seminary in Washington and for a little while Madame Day's school in New York. At an early age she was married to John B. Timberlake, a purser in the navy, and by him had a son and two daughters. When John H. Eaton first came to Washington in 1818 as senator from Tennessee, he took lodgings at the O'Neale tavern and became acquainted with the vivacious daughter of his host. When Andrew Jackson also came to Washington in 1823 as senator, he took up his quarters with his friend Eaton and wrote home to Mrs. Jackson of the "amiable" O'Neale family, and particularly of Mrs. Timberlake, who "plays on the Piano Delightfully, & every Sunday evening entertains her pious mother with Sacred music to which we are invited" (Jackson Papers, Dec. 21, 1823, Library of Congress). Presently rumors began to circulate to the effect that Eaton had become too familiar with Mrs. Timberlake. Then in 1828 her husband died while on duty in the Mediterranean. It was rumored that he had committed suicide. Within the year Eaton proposed to marry the fetching widow and consulted his friend Jackson, who had just been elected President, as to the propriety of his intentions. Jackson, who had always been fond of Peggy, advised the match as a means of discrediting the rumors, and the wedding accordingly took place on Jan. 1, 1829.

It was now time for the new President to select his cabinet and Eaton was docketed for the secretaryship of war. Other prominent Tennesseeans had reason to expect the place, but Eaton was one of those personal followers in whom Jackson gloried. A great clamor was raised by the élite of Washington because of Eaton's wife; but Jackson, whose beloved wife had just died under the sting of unjust imputations, would not heed it. He was enough of a gentleman to be chivalrous and enough of a frontiersman to be simple, direct, and stubborn. He would stand by his friend and his own prerogatives. His family broke up and his cabinet dissolved in the heat of the social war, but the President did not desert Peggy. Eaton resigned from the cabinet in 1831 and in 1834 he was appointed governor of Florida. In 1836 he was sent to Madrid as minister to the court of His Catholic Majesty. Here his wife basked for four years in the brilliance of a society which had no prejudice against her. In 1840 the Eatons returned to the United States and settled down again in Washington. There Eaton died in 1856. Peggy, a wealthy widow, devoted herself to the rearing of her grandchildren but soon succumbed to the charms of an Italian dancing master, Antonio Buchignani, and married him. After a few years of married life her husband defrauded her of her property and eloped with her grand-daughter. It was a desolate old woman who dragged out her existence until 1879 in the city which had seen her fortunes rise and sink so strikingly.

[*The Autobiog. of Peggy Eaton* (1932), dictated in 1873, is revealing if not reliable. The manuscript was left in the hands of Mrs. Eaton's pastor in New York City, the Rev. Chas. F. Deems, and its publication was undertaken by his son, the Rev. Edward M. Deems. The popular biography by Queena Pollack, *Peggy Eaton, Democracy's Mistress* (1931), is apparently based upon authentic source materials, but is not documented. There are accounts of Margaret O'Neale in Jas. Parton, *Life of Andrew Jackson* (1860), vol. III, and Meade Minnigerode, *Some Am. Ladies* (1926), and there are references to her in the works dealing with the administration of Andrew Jackson. Her maiden name is variously spelled, but two deeds in the office of the Recorder of Deeds of the District of Columbia are signed by her father "William O'Neale."] T. P. A.

O'NEALL, JOHN BELTON (Apr. 10, 1793–Dec. 27, 1863), author and jurist, was born on Bush River, Newberry District, S. C. The son of Anne (Kelly) and Hugh O'Neall, he was of Irish ancestry on both sides. He was a descendant of Hugh O'Neill or O'Neale who, about 1730, deserted from a British ship at anchor in the Delaware River and settled on the Susquehanna River, where he is said to have changed his name to O'Neall in order to escape detection. As a child John Belton O'Neall possessed a precocious mind with a remarkable memory, and he acquired a sufficient mastery of Latin and Greek at the Newberry academy to enable him to enter the junior class at the South Carolina College, where he graduated in 1812.

He entered the militia, in which he rose to the rank of major-general by the time he was thirty-two. When he was twenty-three he became a representative from Newberry District in the state legislature, but he was defeated for reëlection because of his support of a measure increasing the salaries of judges. In 1822, however, he was again elected to the legislature, where he sat for three consecutive terms and served as speaker during the last two terms. In 1827 he was known to favor a financial measure regarded by his constituents as extravagant, although as speaker he did not vote upon it, and he was not reëlected the next year. His second retirement from the legislature opened for him a wider field, the one in which his greatest reputation was achieved. He had been admitted to the bar in 1814, and the legislature elected him circuit judge in 1828. Two years later he was advanced to the South Carolina court of appeals. Together with David Johnson and William Harper he performed the duties of this court until 1835, when its decision in the cases of *The State ex relatione Ed. McCready* vs. *B. F. Hunt* and of *The State ex relatione James McDaniel* vs. *Thos. McMeekin* (2 Hill, 1), declaring unconstitutional the test oath devised by the nullifiers, incurred the hostility of the dominant party in the state and caused the court to be abolished.

The judges, however, were transferred to the other courts of the state, and he was assigned to the court of law appeals. In this capacity he served for the remainder of his life. Upon the death of John S. Richardson in 1850 he was elected president of the court of law appeals and of the court of errors, and in 1859 he became chief justice of South Carolina.

As a leader in the cause of temperance he exerted a profound influence upon the state. In his early youth, when he sold rum over the counter of his father's grocery to half-pint customers, he acquired an aversion to the traffic in intoxicating liquor, and this was intensified into hatred when indulgence on the part of his father led the latter to bankruptcy and the temporary loss of his mind. In 1832 he took a pledge to abstain from liquor and, in 1833, to abstain from tobacco. He forthwith plunged into the cause of temperance reform. He allied himself with the Head's Spring temperance society, which affiliated with the "Washington movement," a national temperance organization that was then making its appearance in South Carolina, and in 1841 he was appointed president of the South Carolina Temperance Society. In 1849 he joined the Sons of Temperance, in October 1850 was elected president of that body in South Carolina, and at the Richmond meeting in 1852 was elected president of the Sons of Temperance of North America. He delivered numerous addresses for the cause and for a time conducted a column, "The Drunkard's Looking-Glass," in the *South Carolina Temperance Advocate*, a weekly paper published at Columbia.

He was an active and many-sided man; he was president of the Columbia and Greenville railroad, was greatly interested in scientific agriculture and was for many years president of the Newberry agricultural society, one of the earliest of its kind in the state, and served as a trustee of the South Carolina College for forty years. Although of Quaker ancestry he became a member of the Baptist Church and served successively as president of the Newberry Baptist Bible Society, of the Bible board of the state Baptist Convention, and of the South Carolina Baptist Convention. He delivered many addresses on education, Sunday schools, and railroads; among them the two following especially set forth his views on temperance and education, "Address to Lawyers," in *A Course of Lectures on . . . Temperance . . . before the Charleston Total Abstinence Society by Fourteen of its Members . . . 1851* (1852) and *Oration Delivered before the Clariosophic Society . . . 1826* (1827). A writer of ease and facility, he contributed dozens of fugi-

tive essays and letters to the newspapers of the state. His longer works include *The Negro Law of South Carolina* (1848), a paper originally read before a meeting of the state agricultural society; *The Annals of Newberry, Historical, Biographical, and Anecdotal* (1859), that contains a good deal of information about his early life; and *The Biographical Sketches of the Bench and Bar of South Carolina* (2 vols., 1859), a collection still regarded as authoritative. Opposed to both nullification and secession, he was active in the deliberations and conventions of the Union party in 1832, but owing to his advanced age he took no steps against the secession movement in 1860. He was a handsome man. His voice was remarkably clear, and on the bench his charges are said to have been eloquent and impressive. He was married, on June 25, 1818, to Helen Pope of Edgefield. Several years later, upon the death of his grandmother, Hannah (Belton) Kelly, he inherited "Springfield," an estate near Newberry, and resided there until his death.

[Sketch by Mitchell King in *Biog. Sketches of the Bench and Bar*, *ante*, vol. I, copied in U. R. Brooks, *S. C. Bench and Bar*, vol. I (1908) and abridged in *Cyc. of Eminent and Representative Men of the Carolinas* (1892), vol. I; Maximilian Laborde, *A Tribute to Hon. J. B. O'Neall* (1872); *Addresses of J. H. Carlisle*, ed. by J. H. Carlisle, Jr. (1910); *Charleston Daily Courier*, Dec. 30, 1863.] J. W. P—n.

O'NEILL, JAMES (Nov. 15, 1849–Aug. 10, 1920), actor, was one of many foreign-born players whose entire professional life was passed on the American stage. He was born in Kilkenny, Ireland, the son of Edmond and Katherine O'Neill, and was brought by his parents to America when he was five years of age. His schooling, obtained in Buffalo, Cincinnati, and other cities, was meager, and his first appearances on the stage were made in Cincinnati in 1867. In one of these he found himself on the stage carrying a spear as a member of the guard that was to arrest Edwin Forrest in one of his typical robustious characters, and he was so overawed by the reputation and personality of the star that he failed utterly in his task. Undaunted by this failure, he succeeded in securing successive positions in stock companies in Baltimore, Cleveland, Chicago, and other cities.

Finally his great opportunity came, and on Oct. 2, 1876, he became a member of the Union Square Theatre Company in New York, sharing for a time leading rôles with Charles R. Thorne, Jr. His début there was made as the cripple Pierre in *The Two Orphans*, one of the most sympathetic rôles in that lachrymose melodrama, and among the other characters he acted there during that and later seasons were Vladimir in *The Danicheffs*, Mons. Florion in *The Mother's Secret*, Maurice in *Miss Multon*, George Lovell in *The Man of Success*, Mons. de Montaiglin in *Raymonde*, and Julian Gray in *The New Magdalen*. Unlike some actors who have only the one quality to help them advance in their profession, he possessed both the advantage of physical attraction and the distinction of intellectual attainments. He has been described in his early days as "of faultless figure, as erect in carriage as a major, with dark hair and deep brown eyes, darker and deeper for the clearness and whiteness of his complexion, his manner easy and bearing graceful, his voice rich-toned and musical." In 1877 he went to San Francisco and remained there three years, his most notable appearance in that city being as Christ in Salmi Morse's production of the Passion Play at the Grand Opera House which aroused so much discussion and opposition that it was withdrawn by legal process and caused the arrest and fining of members of the company.

With his first appearance in 1882 as Edmond Dantes in a stage version of *Monte Cristo* began a new era in his career. Heretofore he had been known as a versatile actor. Henceforth for practically the rest of his life he was condemned to be identified with one play and one character. Season after season his reappearance as Edmond Dantes was an annual event in many cities throughout the country. He made again and again ineffectual attempts to abandon it, and while he failed to attract the public in one new part after another, in *Monte Cristo* he was always successful. Remembering his earlier triumphs in a wide range of parts, he naturally had no ambition to be famous in one character, but the public would not allow him to be anyone but Edmond Dantes. In time, therefore, he inevitably came to act it by rote, and the interminable repetition of "The world is mine," and the successive "One," "Two," and "Three," became bywords of the stage. Among the other plays he produced from time to time were *Fontenelle*, by Harrison Grey Fiske and Minnie Maddern Fiske, and *Don Carlos de Seville*, a poetic drama by Eugene Fellner. The public did not care to see him in any of them. He was no more fortunate with revivals of *The Three Musketeers*, *The Dead Heart*, and *Virginius*.

In his last active years on the stage he helped in the making of a motion picture version of *Monte Cristo*, and his last real acting was done as Jesse, the Jewish patrician in *The Wanderer*, during the season of 1916–17. William Winter describes him (*New York Tribune*, Oct. 24,

1900, p. 9), while he was still in the full flight of his *Monte Cristo* career, as a "thorough actor, powerful when power is required, very versatile, and in his demeanor, gesture, vocalism, and spirit, honest and sincere," and creating and sustaining "romantic illusion." For some two years before his death, which occurred at New London, Conn., where he had made his home for many years, he had been in failing health, the result of an automobile accident. He had played the part of Edmond Dantes more than six thousand times. He was married to Ellen Quinlan in July 1875, and she accompanied him on many of his tours, although he once remarked that she had somewhat of an aversion for the atmosphere of the stage. Eugene O'Neill, the American dramatist, is their son.

[See: H. G. Fiske, "James O'Neill," in *Famous Am. Actors of Today* (1896), ed. by F. E. McKay and C. E. L. Wingate; A. D. Storms, *The Players Blue Book* (1901); J. B. Clapp and E. F. Edgett, *Players of the Present*, pt. 2 (1901); T. A. Brown, *A Hist. of the N. Y. Stage* (3 vols., 1903); Arthur Hornblow, *A Hist. of the Theatre in America* (1919); A. H. Quinn, *A Hist. of the Am. Drama from the Civil War to the Present Day* (2 vols., 1927); Interview in *N. Y. Dramatic Mirror*, Feb. 2, 1895; the *Inter Ocean* (Chicago), Mar. 8, 1903; "Recalling the Romantic Drama," *Lit. Digest*, Aug. 28, 1920; the *Sun* (N. Y.), *N. Y. Herald*, *N. Y. Tribune*, and *Springfield Republican*, Aug. 11, 1920.]

E. F. E.

O'NEILL, JOHN (Mar. 8, 1834–Jan. 7, 1878), soldier and Fenian leader, was born at Drumgallon in the parish of Clontibret, County Monaghan, Ireland. His father died before the boy's birth. John remained in his native parish, obtaining the elements of an education, until 1848, when he emigrated to America to join his mother and her elder children, who had settled in Elizabeth, N. J., some years before. He attended school for another year, and afterward worked successively as a shop clerk, a traveling book-agent, and proprietor of a Catholic bookshop in Richmond. In 1857 he joined the 2nd United States Dragoons for the "Mormon War." In Utah, it appears, he deserted, and made his way to California, where he joined the 1st Cavalry, with which he was serving as a sergeant when the Civil War broke out. With this regiment he returned to the East to join the Union army and fought in the Peninsular campaign. In December 1862 he was appointed second lieutenant in the 5th Indiana Cavalry, and was promoted first lieutenant in the following April.

He soon acquired the reputation of being an unusually active and daring officer. He distinguished himself near Glasgow, Ky., in June 1863, and again shortly afterward at Buffington Bar, in the course of Morgan's Ohio raid. On Dec. 2 he was severely wounded at Walker's

Ford. Feeling that he was being passed over for promotion, in the spring of 1864 he resigned from his regiment and was appointed captain in the 17th United States Colored Infantry, only to leave the service in November. About this time he married Mary Crow. While working successfully as a claims agent in Tennessee, he became interested in the plans for an invasion of Canada proposed by the party headed by W. R. Roberts [q.v.] in the Fenian Brotherhood. He acted as a Fenian organizer in his district and in May 1866 led a detachment from Nashville to take part in the attack. Finding himself in command of the raiding party at Buffalo he led a force of 600 men, by his account, across the Niagara and occupied the Canadian village of Fort Erie. The next day he defeated a small column of Canadian volunteers near Ridgeway, and that night escaped from Canada with his men by boat before British troops closed in on his position. The raiders were arrested by a United States gunboat but released a few days later, and a charge of breach of the neutrality laws brought against O'Neill was dropped.

A few months later he was appointed "inspector-general of the Irish Republican Army," and at the end of 1867 he replaced Roberts as president of his branch of the Brotherhood and proceeded to prepare for another attack on Canada. There were obstructionists within his own organization, but his threats caused much alarm in Canada. In 1870 he quarreled with his "senate," and only a fraction of the Fenian organization supported him when on May 25 he attempted a raid at Eccles Hill on the Vermont border. His men fled when the Canadians opened fire, and he himself was arrested by a United States marshal and sentenced to two years' imprisonment, but he was released by presidential pardon after three months. He declared he would not again trouble Canada but was persuaded by W. B. O'Donoghue, formerly a member of Louis Riel's rebel government at Fort Garry, to attack Manitoba. The Fenian council, now mistrusting O'Neill, rejected the scheme, but he made the attempt with a few adherents on Oct. 5, 1871. He seized the Hudson's Bay post at Pembina (on territory then disputed between Canada and the United States) but was immediately arrested by United States troops. He was released by the American courts. Later he became agent for a firm of land speculators who desired Irish settlers for a tract in Holt County, Nebr. While thus engaged he died at Omaha. The chief town of Holt County bears his name.

The idea of invading Canada as a means of gaining Irish freedom can hardly be accounted

other than singularly foolish, but friends and foes credited O'Neill with sincerity and courage in his pursuit of his object. He rejected assassination as an Irish weapon, insisting on "fair and honorable fight"; and though Fenianism was condemned by the church, he claimed to be a devout Catholic. His egotism made it hard for him to work with others.

[See O'Neill's own publications: *Address . . . to the Officers and Members of the Fenian Brotherhood, on the State of the Organization* (1868); *Message . . . to the Seventh Nat. Cong.* (1868); *Official Report . . . on the Attempt to Invade Canada . . . 1870 . . . also a Report of the Battle of Ridgeway* (1870); letter in the *Irish American* (N. Y.), Sept. 28, 1867. See also: "Fenians" and "McMicken Reports" series in the Macdonald Papers, Pub. Archives of Canada; Henri Le Caron (Thomas Beach), *Twenty-five Years in the Secret Service* (1892); John Savage, *Fenian Heroes and Martyrs* (1868); G. McMicken, *The Abortive Fenian Raid on Manitoba* (1888), reprinted in *Trans. and Proc. Hist. and Sci. Soc. of Manitoba*, vol. I (1889); *War of the Rebellion: Official Records (Army)*, I ser. XXIII (pt. 1), XXXI (pt. 1); III ser. IV; *Official Army Reg. of the Volunteer Force of the U. S. Army* (Civil War), pts. VI, VIII; *Report of the Adj. Gen. of . . . Ind.*, vol. III (1866); *Irish American*, Jan. 19 and Feb. 2, 1878.]   C. P. S.

O'NEILL, MARGARET L. [See O'Neale, Margaret, 1796–1879].

OPDYKE, GEORGE (Dec. 7, 1805–June 12, 1880), merchant, municipal reformer, publicist, was born in Kingwood Township, Hunterdon County, N. J. He was a son of George and Mary (Stout) Opdycke and a descendant of Louris Jansen Opdycke, who emigrated from Holland to New Netherland prior to 1653. He attended a country school, became a teacher at the age of sixteen, and clerk in a store at Baptistown, N. J., at the age of eighteen. In 1825 he borrowed $500 and in company with another youth went to Cleveland, Ohio, where they established a store. The venture proved only moderately profitable, and the next year they sold their business and sought a more promising location. At New Orleans, learning that clothing was being sold at a profit of one hundred per cent., they set up a store and began manufacturing their own stock. The demand for clothing soon outran the capacity of the plant. Opdyke, seeking a greater source of merchandise, went to New York in 1832 and established probably the first important clothing factory in the city. He also engaged in the retail business there and later opened branch stores at Memphis, Tenn., and at Charleston, S. C. He made and sold principally rough clothing for plantation hands. In 1846 he placed the business in charge of his brother-in-law, John D. Scott, and turned his attention to importing and selling drygoods at wholesale. Both enterprises prospered, and by 1853 Opdyke was a millionaire. During the Civil

War he manufactured uniforms and arms for the Federal government. In 1869, having retired from merchandising, he established the banking house of George Opdyke & Company, which successfully withstood the panic of 1873, though with considerable loss to the fortune of the founder.

Opdyke's Southern experiences convinced him that slavery was an economic evil, not to be extended under any circumstances. In 1848 he began an active political career as a delegate to the convention of the Free-Soil party at Buffalo, and as an unsuccessful candidate for Congress. In 1854 he became a Republican. He was a member of the New York Assembly, 1859; mayor of New York, 1862–63; member of the state constitutional convention, 1867–68; and of the constitutional commission, 1872–73. In politics he was independent, acting always on the principle that the people should have strong, honest, and efficient government. In the Assembly he effectively opposed attempts to grant franchises against the interests of New York City. He attended the Republican National Convention, 1860, and opposed the nomination of Seward because he thought him too closely associated with the Republican boss, Thurlow Weed. As mayor, he vetoed a great number of ordinances designed to grant special favors. His annual message, 1863, contained proposals of many reforms, some of which have been adopted, while others still remain on the program of the municipal reformer. He recommended an increase in the powers of the mayor, and the abolition of state commissions and of county governments which overlapped city governments. He looked forward to a greater city of "Manhattan" which would include New York, Brooklyn, and their environs.

The most severe test of his administration occurred during the draft riots in July 1863. The city had been stripped of troops to repel Lee's invasion of Pennsylvania. The police were under the control of a state commission. Under the laws and the charter the mayor's powers were moral rather than legal. Opdyke obtained the cooperation of the police commission and the soldiers and marines in the harbor forts, issued proclamations calling citizens to arms, and exerted efforts to restore order without compromising with the rioters. In the midst of the disorders the common council passed an ordinance appropriating $2,500,000 to pay the commutation of the men drafted. Opdyke vetoed it because it tended to nullify a federal law, and to put a price upon the rioters' abstaining from further violence. His own claim against the city for heavy property losses during the riots led

Weed to assert that Opdyke had overcharged the city, and also the federal government, in connection with clothing contracts. An unfortunate and indecisive libel suit resulted.

Opdyke also gained some prominence as an economist. His *Treatise on Political Economy* (1851) was designed as an American reply to John Stuart Mill's *Principles of Political Economy*. In it Opdyke expressed his opinion that fiat money was desirable if issued in limited amounts. In a later *Report on the Currency* (1858) he proposed taxing bank notes of small denominations out of existence and advocated the issuance by the national government of gold certificates. These recommendations were subsequently adopted, though not in the form desired by Opdyke. He protested against the overissuance of greenbacks during the war but afterward recommended that the volume of currency be not reduced too quickly. In appearance Opdyke was tall and slender; in manner, gracious. He was a confidant of many leaders in national affairs and a friend of many distinguished scholars and authors. He was married, on Sept. 26, 1829, to Elizabeth Hall Stryker of New Jersey. She with their six children survived him.

[*Official Documents, Addresses, Etc., of Geo. Opdyke, . . . during the Years 1862 and 1863* (1866); C. W. Opdyke, *The op Dyck Geneal.* (1889); C. M. Depew, *1795–1895: One Hundred Years of Am. Commerce* (1895), vol. II; *The Great Libel Case: Geo. Opdyke agt. Thurlow Weed* (1865); the *N. Y. Herald* and *N. Y. Tribune*, June 13, 1880.]   E. C. S.

OPPENHEIM, JAMES (May 24, 1882–Aug. 4, 1932), poet and novelist, was born in St. Paul, Minn., the eldest son of Matilda (Schloss) and Joseph Oppenheim, comfortably situated American Jews. James was a baby when they moved to New York City, where he received his education, chiefly in the public schools. His father's death, when he was six, brought him, too early, a sense of responsibility, and his contacts with Dr. Felix Adler encouraged him in a strenuous ethical discipline, from which the eager sensuous boy sought refuge in the reading and writing of poetry. For a few years he took extension courses at Columbia University, supporting himself by social and secretarial work, and later, by teaching. At twenty-three, June 1, 1905, he married Lucy Seckel, and his unequal struggle with the world began in earnest. Those who recall Oppenheim as he was then, the dark brilliant eyes set in a brooding, full-lipped, sensitive face, remember him as looking the poet's part, but he could not yet accept the coveted rôle. He spent about a year as superintendent of the Hebrew Technical School for Girls (1905–07), but proving too radical, had to resign. Resolving to live by his pen, he wrote popular sentimental short stories and mediocre novels, which expressed his passion for social justice. He believed that his writing was warped by the necessity for making it pay—he had a wife and two sons to support. The fault probably lay as much in the fact that his moral fervor exceeded his ability to convey it.

His first book of verse, *Monday Morning and Other Poems,* appeared in 1909, but it was almost half a dozen years later, when he broke sharply with the middle-class world in which he had been living, that he began to find himself as a poet. In the free rhythms and clear emotions of *Songs for the New Age* (1914) there were signs that he was coming into his own. The happiest period of his career began with the establishment, in November 1916, of *The Seven Arts,* a monthly of which he was the editor and which included among its contributors men who have since become the most distinguished of American writers. When it took a bold stand against the World War, its subsidy was withdrawn, and Oppenheim was ostracized as a traitor. Spiritually and physically sick, he found salvation in the psychoanalytic doctrines of Jung. For a time he was a practising psychoanalyst and also tried to popularize Jung's theories through the press. Unfortunately, he allowed this interest to obtrude itself into his poetry, becoming less self-critical than ever. This is obvious in *The Sea* (1924), a volume containing all of his verse that he wished to preserve. He sinks to prosy banality in the part of the book which reprints *The Mystic Warrior* (1921) and rises to the height of his attainment in the *Golden Bird* (first published separately, 1923), which contains melodious love lyrics and poems successfully fusing the themes of Whitman and the Psalmist.

He was divorced from his first wife in 1914. When his companion, Gertrude Smith, was taken from him by illness, he married Linda Gray, who cherished him in the last years of his life. These were darkened by sickness, poverty, and the clouding of his early fame. He died of tuberculosis at the age of fifty. There was warmth, candor, and sweetness in the man, but his poetic gift was inadequate fully to express his sensitive and insurgent nature. Besides the works mentioned above, he published the following books of prose: *Doctor Rast* (1909), *Wild Oats* (1910), *Pay-Envelopes* (1911), *The Nine-Tenths* (1911), *The Olympian* (1912), *Idle Wives* (1914), *The Psychology of Jung* (1925); and these volumes of verse: *The Pioneers* (1910), *War and Laughter* (1916), *The Book of Self* (1917). Parts of *The Beloved* (1915). a novel, were reprinted as free verse.

[File of *The Seven Arts;* Louis Untermeyer, *The New Era in American Poetry* (1919); Paul Rosenfeld, *Men Seen* (1925); H. W. Cook, *Our Poets of Today* (1923); *N. Y. Times,* Aug. 5 and 31, 1932; information from Arthur B. Spingarn of New York City.]

B. D.

OPTIC, OLIVER [See ADAMS, WILLIAM TAYLOR, 1822–1897].

ORCUTT, HIRAM (Feb. 3, 1815–Apr. 17, 1899), educator, was the youngest son of ten children born to John Snell and Hannah (Currier) Orcutt, of Acworth, N. H. His father, a farmer, was barely able to provide for his large family, and Hiram was obliged to work on the farm, attending the district school but three months in each year. By the time he was eighteen, he had had one term in the academy at Chester, Vt. Inspired by his instructors, he decided to prepare himself for college, and attended school at Cavendish, Vt., Unity, N. H., and Meriden, N. H. At twenty-one, he entered Phillips Academy, Andover, Mass., and two years later matriculated at Dartmouth College, graduating in 1842. Throughout this period he supported himself by teaching school during the winter terms, and on Aug. 15, 1842, he married Sarah Ames Cummings, daughter of Daniel and Hannah (Ames) Cummings, of Haverhill, Mass. After her death, he married Ellen Lazette Dana, Apr. 8, 1865, daughter of Ranson Stephen and Laura Lazette (Moulton) Dana, of Poughkeepsie, N. Y. Immediately after graduating from college, be became principal of Hebron (N. H.) Academy.

In 1843, he was elected principal of Thetford (Vt.) Academy, in which position he achieved a noteworthy reputation among the headmasters of New England. After twelve conspicuously successful years of service there, he accepted an appointment as principal of the Ladies' Seminary at North Granville, N. Y. Here, too, he distinguished himself as teacher and administrator. Having fulfilled the terms of his contract in 1860, he resigned and established the Glenwood Ladies' Seminary at West Brattleboro, Vt., as a private venture. Four years later he was appointed principal of the Tilden Ladies' Seminary at West Lebanon, N. H., and conducted both institutions successfully until 1868, when he sold his interest in the school at West Brattleboro. During these years, he found time to serve also as superintendent of schools in Brattleboro, Vt., and Lebanon, N. H. (1860–66), and as editor of the *Vermont School Journal* (1861–65). He established various educational associations, and gave many lectures before teachers' institutes in both New Hampshire and Vermont. Fo⁻ two years, 1870–72, he represented the town of Lebanon in the New Hampshire General Court. Here he drafted the measures which established the State Normal School at Plymouth, made public school attendance compulsory, and authorized towns to change from the district to the town system of school administration. For six years after its establishment in 1870 he assisted the Normal School as secretary of the board of trustees. In 1880, he resigned from the principalship of the Tilden Ladies' Seminary, and removed to Boston, where he spent the remainder of his life. As early as 1876, he had been a member of the advisory board of the *New England Journal of Education,* and in 1881 he was appointed associate editor and manager of the subscription department. From 1875 to 1898, when he retired, he was manager of the New England Bureau of Education, which, under his direction, became the leading teacher's agency in Massachusetts.

Orcutt was a prolific and influential contributor of educational articles to New England periodicals and newspapers. In addition, he collaborated with Truman Rickard in the preparation of *Class Book of Prose and Poetry* (1847), a book that went through many editions. He published, also, *Gleanings from School-Life Experience or, Hints to Common School Teachers, Parents and Pupils* (1858); *Methods of School Discipline* (1871); *Teachers' Manual* (1871); *Parents' Manual* (1874); *Home and School Training* (1874); *School Keeping; How to Do It* (1885), and *Among the Theologies* (1888).

[*Am. Jour. of Educ.,* Dec. 1865; Paul Monroe, *A Cyc. of Educ.,* IV (1913), 554–55; *Vital Records of Haverhill, Mass.* (1911), II, 80; J. L. Merrill, *Hist. of Acworth* (1869), pp. 90, 251–53; *New England Jour. of Educ.,* June 17, 1876; *Boston Transcript,* Apr. 18, 1899; Orcutt's autobiography (MS.) in the possession of his son, Wm. Dana Orcutt, Boston, Mass.]

R. F. S.

ORD, EDWARD OTHO CRESAP (Oct. 18, 1818–July 22, 1883), soldier, was born in Cumberland, Md., the third son of James Ord, an officer in the United States Navy for a short time, and afterwards a lieutenant in the army during the War of 1812. His mother was a daughter of Col. Daniel Cresap, who had been a lieutenant of Maryland Volunteers. His grandfather had commanded one of the regiments which Washington sent to Pennsylvania to quell the whiskey insurrection. In 1819, the Ords moved to Washington, D. C., where Edward received his early schooling mostly from his father, a thorough scholar. When but seven years old, he showed marked aptitude as a calculator. At sixteen he entered the United States Military

Academy, and graduated in 1839, seventeenth in a class of thirty-one. On July 1, 1839, he was appointed second lieutenant and assigned to the 3rd Artillery. His first service was against the Seminole Indians in the Florida Everglades in 1840. He was promoted first lieutenant for gallant conduct on this expedition. In 1847 he was sent on the *Lexington* from New York, around Cape Horn, to California. Shortly after his arrival, he was dispatched with two men to capture three murderers. He caught up with them at Santa Barbara, shot one who attempted to escape, brought the other two to jury trial before an alcade court, secured their conviction, and promptly executed them. Ord had to take matters in his own hands, for the alcade would neither assume responsibility nor take any action without Ord's direction. Ord received his captaincy on Sept. 7, 1850. At San Francisco, Oct. 14, 1854, he married Mary Mercer Thompson; they had two sons and a daughter.

During 1856, in Oregon, he campaigned successfully against the Rogue River Indians and later against the Spokane Indians in Washington Territory. In 1859, he was in the Artillery School at Fort Monroe, Va., and served in the expedition that suppressed John Brown's raid at Harpers Ferry. At the outbreak of the Civil War, he was stationed at the Presidio, San Francisco, where he was appointed brigadier-general of volunteers on Sept. 14, 1861. He was ordered East and from November 1861 to May 1862 commanded a brigade in the army defending Washington, D. C. During this period, at Dranesville, Va., Dec. 20, 1861, he led the attack against the Confederate forces under Gen. J. E. B. Stuart. The morale of his men was low; but through his brilliant leadership, success was attained and the drooping spirits of the men revived. For his conduct in this action he was brevetted lieutenant-colonel.

He was appointed major-general of volunteers, May 2, 1862. In the Army of the Tennessee he commanded the left wing from August to September 1862, and on Sept. 19, was brevetted colonel for gallant and meritorious service during the advance upon Iuka, Miss. After the battle of Corinth, in October, he joined the Federal army in pursuit of the retreating Confederates at Hatchie, assumed command, and drove back the head of the Confederate column. After this engagement, in which he was severely wounded, he was brevetted brigadier-general. From June 18 to Oct. 28, 1863, he commanded the XIII Army Corps in the Army of the Tennessee in the Vicksburg campaign. During the siege of Vicksburg, he served on Grant's staff and later, July 16,

1863, took part in the capture of Jackson, Miss. From August to October 1863, he served with the Army of Western Louisiana. In March 1864 he joined Gen. Franz Sigel at Cumberland and, with Gen. George Crook, directed the campaign against Staunton, Va. On July 9, 1864, he was given command of the VIII and later, of the XVIII Army Corps, in the operations before Richmond. In the assault and capture of Fort Harrison, Sept. 29, he was severely wounded. After his recovery he assumed command, Jan. 8, 1865, of the Army of the James and the Department of North Carolina. He engaged in the various operations about Petersburg, Va., and in the pursuit of General Lee until the surrender at Appomattox Court House, Apr. 9, 1865. On Mar. 13, 1865, he had been brevetted major-general. His aide-de-camp, the Rev. S. S. Seward, said: "I never saw him under any circumstances lose his self-control or forfeit for an instant his character as a courteous gentleman. . . . Before battle . . . he was exceedingly cautious . . . but as soon as the first bullet whistled over his head he seemed to lose all sense of fear, all hesitation, all thought, except to go forward and win the victory" (*New York Tribune*, July 26, 1883).

Following the war he commanded several military departments in turn until he was retired, Dec. 6, 1880. By Act of Congress, approved Jan. 28, 1881, he was made a major-general on the retired list. Subsequently he became identified with various civilian enterprises and remained so engaged until stricken with yellow fever en route from New York to Vera Cruz. He was taken ashore at Havana, Cuba, where he died. His remains were interred in the National Cemetery at Arlington, Va.

[P. T. Tyson, *Geology and Industrial Resources of California* (1851); *Asso. Grads. U. S. Mil. Acad., Ann. Reunion*, 1884; *War of the Rebellion: Official Records (Army)*; F. B. Heitman, *Hist. Reg. and Dict. U. S. Army* (1903); G. W. Cullum, *Biog. Reg. Officers and Grads. U. S. Mil. Acad.* (3rd ed., 1891), vol. II; records of the U. S. Pension Office.]   C. C. B.

ORD, GEORGE (Mar. 4, 1781–Jan. 24, 1866), naturalist and philologist, was born probably in Philadelphia, where his father, George Ord, formerly a sea-captain, had established himself in 1798 as a ship-chandler and rope-maker. His mother was Rebecca Lindemeyer, daughter of George and Judith Lindemeyer, said to be descended from early Swedish settlers on the Delaware. George entered his father's firm in 1800 and continued the business for some years after his father's death in 1806, eventually retiring, probably in 1829, to live thereafter the life of a gentleman of leisure. He was married in 1815 and had a daughter who died in infancy and a son, Joseph Benjamin Ord, who became an artist and portrait painter.

Of George Ord's early education there is no record, but he acquired somehow a broad and varied knowledge of both literature and science. At twenty-four he was the close friend and companion of Alexander Wilson [*q.v.*], fifteen years his senior, who was then beginning his great work on American birds: *American Ornithology; or, the Natural History of the Birds of the United States* (9 vols., 1808–14). Ord accompanied him on various excursions in the neighborhood of Philadelphia and his name not infrequently occurs on the pages of the *Ornithology*. Upon Wilson's premature death, Ord, who was one of his executors, took upon himself the completion of the work, editing Volume VIII, then ready for the press, and writing all of the text for Volume IX, which covered the birds depicted in Wilson's remaining drawings. Several years later, in 1824–25, he published another edition of the work with much additional material. Because of the excessive modesty which was one of his marked characteristics and his earnest desire not to detract from Wilson's credit, he concealed his participation whenever possible, and it is difficult in some instances to determine which paragraphs are his contributions. In the ninth volume (1814) of the *Ornithology*, he published a life of Wilson, in which he paid full tribute to his lamented friend, the perpetuation of whose memory and the defense of whose work became the great purpose of his life. The appearance of Audubon's beautiful plates about the time that Ord was preparing his later edition excited Ord's jealousy to a high pitch, and with the aid of his friend Charles Waterton he did all in his power to discredit Audubon. The attacks were vigorously met by Audubon's friends and thus arose what has often been termed the Wilson-Audubon controversy, although Wilson had died long before the controversy began.

In 1818 Ord accompanied Thomas Say, Titian Peale, and William Maclure [*qq.v.*] on what was perhaps his only extensive field trip, an expedition to Georgia and Florida resulting in the acquisition of many interesting collections. Besides the biography of Wilson he prepared memoirs of Say and C. A. Lesueur, an anonymous account of the zoölogy of North America for the second American edition (1815) of William Guthrie's *New Geographical and Commercial Grammar*, and a dozen papers on various subjects published in the proceedings of several societies. In later life he disposed of his manuscripts on philology, the results of forty years research, to Latham of London who used them with full credit in the compilation of his new edition of Johnson's *Dictionary*. Ord's profound learning received ample recognition in the honors conferred upon him by the scientific societies of Philadelphia. Personally he is described by Malvina Lawson, daughter of the engraver of Wilson's plates, as "a very singular person, very excitable, almost of pure nervous temperament. Proud, shy and reserved toward strangers; but expansive and brilliant with his friends." He would sometimes get into a temper of rage if opposed in argument but his anger was soon forgotten. He attained the age of eighty-five, outliving most of his old friends and making no new ones. In his last years he was a recluse, withdrawn from the world, living among his books.

[Samuel Rhoads, "George Ord," *Cassinia, a Bird Annual, 1908* (1909); Walter Faxon, "Early Editions of Wilson's Ornithology," *Auk*, Apr. 1901; F. L. Burns, "Miss Lawson's Recollections of Ornithologists," *Ibid.*, July 1917; *Public Ledger* (Phila.), Jan. 26, 1866.]

W. S.

ORDRONAUX, JOHN (Aug. 3, 1830–Jan. 20, 1908), lawyer and physician, son of John and Elizabeth (Charreton) Ordronaux, was born in New York City. His father, a Frenchman, commanded a privateer in the War of 1812 and died in 1841, whereupon John, the only child, was adopted by John Moulton of Roslyn, L. I. He graduated from Dartmouth College in 1850 and from the Harvard Law School in 1852. He practised law at Taunton, Mass., for two years, then removed to New York, utilizing his leisure in the study of medicine. He received an honorary degree of M.D. from the National Medical College, Washington, D. C. (Medical Department of Columbian, now George Washington University), in 1859, where in the following year he lectured on medical jurisprudence. His teaching record was remarkable. For forty-eight years he was lecturer, professor, or professor *emeritus* of medical jurisprudence in various schools of law and medicine: Columbia University Law School, 1860–1908; Dartmouth College Medical School, 1864–1903; National Medical College, Washington, D. C., and Columbian University Law School, 1863–73; University of Vermont, 1865–1908; Boston University Law School, 1872–1902.

On the outbreak of the Civil War he became examining surgeon for volunteers and in 1864 was appointed assistant surgeon of the New York National Guard. His *Hints on the Preservation of Health in Armies for the Use of Volunteer Officers and Soldiers* (1861) and his *Manual of Instructions for Military Surgeons, on the Examination of Recruits and Discharge of Soldiers* (1863) were the fruit of this military service.

In 1869 he published *Jurisprudence of Medicine.* He was the first New York state commissioner in lunacy (1874–82) and revised and codified the lunacy laws of the state. He was the author of *Commentaries on the Lunacy Law of New York and on the Judicial Aspects of Insanity at Common Law and in Equity, including Procedure as Expounded in England and the United States* (1878); *The Plea of Insanity as an Answer to Indictment* (1880); *Judicial Problems Relating to the Disposal of Insane Criminals* (1881); and *Constitutional Legislation in the United States* (1891). The last-named work was an attempt "to expound those administrative powers which, in our dual form of representative government, are sovereign within their several spheres of action," a theory by which "we have secured union without fusion of States and State sovereignty without disintegration of the Union." His contributions to the literature of mental diseases were many and always learned. In the field of letters he discovered scholarship of a high grade. Notable was his poetic translation, *Regimen Sanitatis Salernitanum: Code of Health of the School of Salernum* (1870), a book long out of print and keenly sought by collectors. He was also a contributor of several original translations to *Horace . . . Presented to Modern Readers* (1908), edited by C. L. and J. C. Dana, as to which Dr. Charles L. Dana commented: "It is rather strange that America has contributed so little to the translation or appreciation of our poet. Dr. John Ordronaux has been by far the most successful" (Introduction, p. xiii).

Although of ample means, Ordronaux was the least self-indulgent of men and denied himself much by reason of an innate, almost morbid, prudence in expenditure. For years he restricted himself to a luncheon that should not exceed twenty-five cents in cost. He would even scruple to add a desired book to his shelves. But this trait was not disclosed, or even guessed, in ordinary intercourse with men, to whom he was always a genial and charming companion, except when in the mood of depression that sometimes beset him. The writer remembers vividly Ordronaux's official visits to the State Asylum at Utica in the early eighties, occasions that were always welcomed by members of the medical staff. For there was in those periodic inspections no trace of "snooping" but only an obvious interest in the professional activities and welfare of young ministers to sick wards of the state. His eccentricities of conduct did not escape observation or amused comment. As instances, he would sometimes sleep with his head in a bandbox to outwit the bats, disinfect his bills with camphor, carry a bit of tarred rope in his purse for like protective purposes, and in winter, when putting on his overcoat and muffler, be most careful to "button up the caloric." If his visit fell in hot weather he would prescribe a refreshing drink which he called "psychological lemonade," composed, among other ingredients, of ice-water, dilute phosphoric acid, tincture of gentian, and sugar. He was reputed the real inventor of a "glycerine tonic," since exploited commercially under the name of a well-known early superintendent of the Utica institution in which it was extensively prescribed. On arriving at his next official post he would often send a kind message to the young friends from whom he had just separated himself, sometimes in Latin, on a well-filled postcard, the phrase, *Sparge multa amicitiae verba apud omnes fratres,* being a favorite greeting. He was deeply religious, and occasionally acted as lay reader in the Episcopal Church. He never married, but compensated for that celibacy by becoming beloved father to the community in which for long years he dwelt. He died of cerebral apoplexy, at Glen Head, L. I.

[*The Institutional Care of the Insane in the U. S. and Canada,* ed. by H. M. Hurd, IV (1917), 467–69; T. H. Shastid, in H. A. Kelly and W. L. Burrage, *Am. Medic. Biogs.,* (1920); *Long Island Medic. Jour.,* Apr. 1908; *Nation* (N. Y.), Jan. 23, 1908; L. W. Kingman, *The Kingman and Ordronaux Families* (1911); *N. Y. Times,* Jan. 21, 1908; recollections of Dr. E. N. Brush, Baltimore; personal acquaintance.]   G. A. B—r.

ORDWAY, JOHN (*c.* 1775–*c.* 1817), explorer, was one of ten children of John and Hannah (Morse) Ordway, who lived at Amesbury, Mass., until about 1774 and subsequently at Bow, N. H., where John was born. Ruins of the parental home at Bow show that the father was a substantial farmer. His elder son Stephen lived in later life at Hebron, N. H., and became a prominent citizen there. About 1800 the younger John enlisted in the United States army and in 1803 was sergeant in Capt. Russell Bissell's company of the 1st Infantry, stationed at Kaskaskia, Ill.

Thither in that year came Capt. Meriwether Lewis [*q.v.*], enlisting recruits for his expedition across the continent. Ordway joined the expedition, was continued as sergeant, and appointed to keep the rosters and orderly books. During the first winter of preparation, when the men of the party were encamped at Dubois River, opposite St. Louis, he was frequently in charge of the detachment during the absence of the captains, Lewis and Clark. With the expedition he spent the first winter at the village of the Mandan Indians, leaving there Apr. 7, 1805, for the western journey. The next winter was spent on the shores of the Pacific, where Ordway endured his full share of the hardships and dangers of the situation. On the return journey the two leaders separated, Lewis undertaking a northern route, while Clark with Ordway sought the headwaters of the Missouri. From this point Ordway was dispatched with nine men to join Lewis; his journal covering the period July 13–19, 1806, is the sole record of that portion of the expedition. Ordway's party, augmented by some of Lewis' men, overtook Lewis on July 28, and continued with him to St. Louis, where the united expedition arrived in safety on Sept. 23.

After his return Ordway paid a visit to his home and family in New Hampshire. In 1807 he went back to Missouri, where he bought considerable land and established a plantation in the New Madrid district. His home suffered severely in the earthquake of 1811, when as his sister described the scene, it was "a dreadful sight to see the ground burst and throw out water as high as the trees." Practically nothing is known of Ordway's further career, except that in 1818 his widow, Elizabeth, applied for lands appropriated for the relief of the earthquake sufferers. The journal that John Ordway kept on the expedition was secured by Captain Clark for his records, but then it disappeared for many years. In 1913 it was found among the Biddle papers, and three years later was published in the *Wisconsin Historical Collections* (vol. XXII, 1916). It is a straightforward, clear narrative of the day by day happenings on the journey. Both the commanders trusted Ordway and he appears to have been next to them in both ability and authority.

[Records of the Ordway family are in the Vital Records of Amesbury, Mass.; those of Bow, N. H., are lost, and consequently the date of birth is lacking. See family letters in *Mo. Hist. Rev.,* July 1908; J. H. Morse and E. W. Leavitt, *Morse Geneal.* (1903); O. D. Wheeler, *The Trail of Lewis and Clark* (2 vols., 1904); sketch in preface to the journal, *Wis. Hist. Soc. Colls.,* vol. XXII (1916); *Miss. Valley Hist. Rev.,* June 1915.]   L. P. K.

O'REILLY, ALEXANDER (1722–Mar. 23, 1794), officer in the Spanish army, was born at Baltrasna, County Meath, Ireland, the son of Thomas Reilly. He was taken by his parents to Spain, where at the age of ten he became a cadet in the Hibernia Regiment. Though crippled for life by a wound received in Italy in the War of the Austrian Succession, he won rapid promotion, thanks to native ability and to the patronage of various magnates, one of whom was the Irishman, Richard Wall, then an influential Spanish minister. A rare knowledge of modern warfare, acquired through a mission to Austria and France during the Seven Years' War, made O'Reilly a leader in the reform of the Spanish army. His services in the war with Portugal and in the reorganization of the defenses of Cuba and Puerto Rico won him the rank of major-general (1763) and lieutenant-general (1767).

After the uprising of 1768 against Ulloa, the first Spanish governor of Louisiana, O'Reilly was sent with a force of some three thousand men to take formal possession of the province, punish the rebels, and assimilate the government of the province to that of the other Spanish dominions in America. He carried out his orders with vigor and success. The power of the King he demonstrated by executing five of the ringleaders; his clemency, by pardoning the rest. This is the episode that won him the sobriquet, "Bloody O'Reilly." The comprehensive regulations which he drew up for the administration of Louisiana remained in effect with little change to the end of the Spanish period. His conduct was highly praised by the King and the council of the Indies, and in October 1770 the French ambassador reported that O'Reilly was regarded as the leader of the military party in Spain. Honors were heaped upon him: in 1770 he was made inspector-general of infantry and placed in charge of a school for officers, and in 1771 he was given the title of count. Even the utter failure of his expedition against Algiers in 1775 did not deprive him of the King's favor; but he was demoted from the military governorship of Madrid to that of Cadiz, and his intrigues against Floridablanca later led to his banishment to the province of Galicia. Recalled in 1794 to take command of the army in Catalonia, he died at Bonete, near Chinchilla (Murcia), on the way to his post. His wife was Rosa de las Casas, a member of an influential family. His eldest son inherited the title and took up his residence in Cuba.

[Sources include: Jacobo de la Pezuela y Lobo, *Diccionario ... de la Isla de Cuba* (Madrid), IV (1866), 164; Antonio Ballesteros y Beretta, *Historia de España* (Barcelona, 1923–29), V, 193, 258, 389; Manuel Serrano y Sanz, ed., *Documentos Históricos de la Florida y la Luisiana* (Madrid, 1912), pp. 295–312; Chas. Gayarré, *Hist. of La.* (4th ed., 1903), II, 283–354, III, 1–41; B. F. French, *Hist. Memoirs of La.*, V (1853), 240–91; Marc de Villiers du Terrage, *Les Dernières Années de la Louisiane Française* (Paris, n.d.), pp. 291–326; H. E. Bolton, *Athanase de Mézières* (2 vols., 1914), see Index; J. E. Winston, "The Cause and Results of the Revolution of 1768 in Louisiana," *La. Hist. Quart.*, Apr. 1932; David K. Bjork, "Alexander O'Reilly and the Spanish Occupation of La., 1769–70," in *New Spain and the Anglo-Am. West* (1932), I, 165–82; A. S. Aiton, "Spanish Colonial Reorganization under the Family Compact," *Hispanic-Am. Hist. Rev.*, Aug. 1932; and John O'Hart, *Irish Pedigrees* (ed. 1915), I, 743, 747. O'Reilly adopted the earlier form of the family name.]   A. P. W.

O'REILLY, HENRY (Feb. 6, 1806–Aug. 17, 1886), editor, author, pioneer in the erection of telegraph lines, was born in Carrickmacross, Province of Ulster, Ireland. His father was a merchant who met with reverses in business. His mother was Alicia Ledbetter, the daughter of a physician. The family of three emigrated to America in 1816 and settled in New York, where the boy was apprenticed to Baptiste Irvine, editor and owner of the New York *Columbian,* a newspaper which was a stanch advocate of the Erie Canal project. Owing to a change in the ownership of the paper, the apprenticeship terminated in a year, and O'Reilly's new employers were Clayton & Kingsland, publishers, in whose office he received valuable training. At the age of seventeen he became assistant editor of the *New York Patriot,* the organ of the People's party, which elected DeWitt Clinton governor of New York in 1824. Two years later Henry C. Sleight and Luther Tucker established the *Rochester Daily Advertiser* at Rochester, N. Y. Tucker became its business manager and selected as its editor young O'Reilly, with whom he had been associated on the *Patriot.* The *Advertiser* was immediately successful, and its youthful and vigorous editor soon gained notice as the chief opponent of Thurlow Weed, in the great anti-Masonic excitement which broke out owing to the abduction of William Morgan [*q.v.*]. Weed was chairman of an indignation meeting held in Rochester in December 1826 and became one of the national leaders of the anti-Masonic political party. In an editorial published Mar. 16, 1827, O'Reilly objected to the "harsh words, denunciation and proscription" which were "visited alike upon the innocent and the guilty," and this led to a war of words with Weed, who established an opposition paper in Rochester and, in 1828, had both the editor and the owner of the *Advertiser* indicted for libel. The issue never came to trial.

O'Reilly was constantly advancing a cause. In 1833 he began the agitation for the rebuilding and enlargement of the Erie Canal, and in 1859, when the railroad interests were hostile to the canal, he appealed to the people of the state to protect the interests of the waterway. In 1845 he entered into a contract with S. F. B. Morse and Amos Kendall to raise the capital for the construction of telegraph lines from Eastern Pennsylvania to St. Louis and the Great Lakes. He erected some eight thousand miles of line, but in the course of the venture he broke the terms of his contract. The resulting litigation and added financial difficulties led him to abandon his connection with the telegraph. Aside from innumerable pamphlets on the questions of the day, O'Reilly published in 1838 *Sketches of Rochester,*

with Incidental Notices of Western New York.
In 1859 he gave a collection of historical manuscripts to the New York Historical Society, and
subsequently he gave a smaller collection of documents to the Rochester Historical Society. He
was married to Marcia Brooks, a daughter of
Gen. Micah Brooks. They had one son, Henry
Brooks O'Reilly, who was killed at the battle of
Williamsburg, May 5, 1862. Although O'Reilly
was in many respects a remarkable man, he
lacked prudence in money matters, and old age
found him a poor man.

[See: *The Rochester Hist. Soc. Pub. Fund Ser.,* vol.
V (1926), and vol. IX (1930); Alexander Jones, *Hist.
Sketch of the Electric Telegraph* (1852); J. D. Reid,
The Telegraph in America (1879); Edward L. Morse,
Samuel F. B. Morse: His Letters and Journals (1914),
vol. II; R. H. Gillet, *First Telegraph Case before the
U. S. Supreme Court* (1853); and the *N. Y. Daily Tribune,* Aug. 18, 1886. O'Reilly changed the spelling of
his name to O'Rielly, and that form is on his tombstone, but the name appears more commonly in the usual
spelling.]   W. M. B.

O'REILLY, JOHN BOYLE (June 28, 1844–
Aug. 10, 1890), poet, editor and patriot, son of
William David and Eliza (Boyle) O'Reilly, descended from ancient Irish families, was born at
Castle Dowth, near Drogheda, on the south bank
of the Boyne, where his father kept a school. He
spent four years as an apprentice on the Drogheda
Argus and three in England on the Preston
Guardian, returning to Ireland in 1863 to enlist
in the Tenth Hussars. Like most other young
Irishmen he joined the Fenian Order. Almost a
third of the English army were Irish. Utterly
sincere, young O'Reilly obtained many "recruits,"
but his Fenian connection was discovered in
1866. He was tried by court martial, charged
with "not giving information" of "an intended
mutiny." Sentence of death as a conspirator to
levy war against the Queen was passed on July
9, commuted the same day to life imprisonment,
and subsequently to twenty years of penal servitude. After several years of solitary confinement
at Millbank and a period of hard labor in the
brickyards at Chatham, he was removed to Dartmoor.

O'Reilly was one of the sixty-three political
prisoners deported to Australia in the first company sent there since the uprising of 1848. On
Jan. 10, 1868, the *Hougoumont* dropped anchor
before Fremantle near Perth. He was "Convict No. 9843." Sustained by an ever-buoyant
spirit, he never gave up the idea of escape. Father Patrick McCabe befriended him. The priest
called devoted friends to his aid, and obtained
the assistance of an American whaling vessel.
The prisoner made his start on Feb. 18, 1869.
After weary days of peril and suspense he was
rowed out to sea and taken aboard the whaler
Gazelle, of New Bedford, Captain David R. Gifford. During the ensuing cruise the courage of
the second mate, Henry C. Hathaway, saved
O'Reilly from death, and his ingenuity saved the
fugitive from capture at Roderique. For many
years subsequently in America they were close
friends. Off the Cape of Good Hope he was
transferred to the American barque *Sapphire,*
and at Liverpool he became "third mate" of the
Bombay which landed him in safety at Philadelphia on Nov. 23, 1869. That same day he took
out his first naturalization papers.

He knew nobody in the United States. But
the story of his escape had preceded him and his
personality procured him friends. Already he
was called "the poet." He went on to Boston
and obtained employment on the *Pilot,* the most
influential "Irish paper" in America. As "war
correspondent" he covered the Fenian raid into
Canada from St. Albans. The frank criticisms
of that ill-judged foray by such a writer produced a marked impression. Speedily he rose to
fame. In 1876 the Catholic Archbishop of Boston and O'Reilly bought the *Pilot.* For fifteen
years its influence now was nation-wide. As a
Democrat he wrote vigorously of politics but refused to seek any office. He was a devout Catholic but tolerant and magnanimous. He became
an ardent advocate of Home Rule and the Irish
leader in New England, but he always emphasized the duties of American citizenship. He
lectured throughout the country. His *Songs from
Southern Seas* appeared in 1873; *Songs, Legends
and Ballads* in 1878; *The Statues in the Block*
in 1881; *In Bohemia* in 1886. He published a
novel, *Moondyne,* in 1879, and a work on athletics, *Ethics of Boxing and Manly Sport,* in
1888. With Robert Grant, Frederic J. Stimson
("J. S. of Dale"), and John T. Wheelwright, he
wrote a composite "novel of tomorrow," *The
King's Men* (1884). O'Reilly was the poet for
the O'Connell centenary, for the dedication of
the Crispus Attucks monument on Boston Common, and he read a notable poem at the dedication of the Pilgrim Monument at Plymouth in
1889. He died before reaching his full stature
as a poet. Born with the gift, he began to sing
as a boy. Throughout his life most of his verse-
writing had to be done almost without leisure.
He disdained "the carving of cherry-stones," the
elaboration of trifles. There are good lines in his
poems, the sentiment is kindly, the themes widely varied. He seems most at home in a swinging
ballad measure. Widely popular in his time, he
is now best remembered by a group of short
poems which express his love of the spiritual

things in human life. His genius for friendship gained him the affection of men of all faiths and all grades of culture. He was a founder of clubs, a canoe enthusiast, an excellent athlete, and a social favorite. On Aug. 15, 1872, he married Mary Murphy, the daughter of John and Jane (Smiley) Murphy, of Charlestown. His death at the summer home in Hull was occasioned by overwork and insomnia. A memorial in the Boston Fenway was erected by popular subscription. There are busts in the Boston Public Library and the Catholic University in Washington.

[Sources include: J. J. Roche, *Life of John Boyle O'Reilly* (1891); *Memorials* published by the City of Boston (1890, 1897); files of the *Pilot* and other Boston newspapers; Justin McCarthy, *Reminiscences* (1899), vol. I; Wemyss Reid, *Memoirs and Correspondence of Lyon Playfair* (1899); E. P. Mitchell, *Memoirs of an Editor* (1924); *Boston Transcript*, Aug. 11, 1890; information as to certain facts from O'Reilly's daughter, Miss Mary Boyle O'Reilly.]   F. L. B.

O'REILLY, ROBERT MAITLAND (Jan. 14, 1845–Nov. 3, 1912), surgeon general, United States Army, was descended from an old Irish family, one branch of which, emigrating to Spain, produced Gen. Alexander O'Reilly [*q.v.*], who was captain general of Cuba and one of the Spanish governors of Louisiana. The American branch settled in Pennsylvania before the Revolution and it was in Philadelphia that, to John and Ellen (Maitland) O'Reilly, Robert was born. He was educated in the public schools of his native city and had begun the study of medicine when the Civil War commenced. In August 1862 he was appointed an acting medical cadet and assigned to the Cuyler General Hospital in Philadelphia; later he served as a medical cadet in a hospital at Chattanooga and in the office of the medical director of the Army of the Cumberland.

With the close of the Civil War he resumed his medical studies at the University of Pennsylvania and was graduated in 1866. In May 1867 he was appointed assistant surgeon in the army and was sent out to California by way of Panama with a detachment of recruits. From 1868 to 1869 he was in Arizona with troops operating against hostile Indians. In 1874 he participated in the Sioux campaign in Wyoming and Montana. While on duty incident to labor disturbances in Pennsylvania in 1877, he sustained an injury which incapacitated him for two years. Soon after his return from sick leave, he was assigned to duty as attending surgeon in Washington. In this capacity his attractive personality and his professional skill made him a prominent figure in the capital. He was the White House physician during the two admin-

istrations of President Cleveland, with whom he was on terms of intimate friendship.

Following the outbreak of the Spanish-American War, O'Reilly, then a major, was chief surgeon of Gen. John J. Coppinger's division at Mobile, Ala., and later was transferred to the staff of Gen. J. F. Wade in Havana. The medical department ship *Bay State* was placed at his disposal and he was sent to Jamaica for the purpose of acquiring information relative to the experience of the British army in tropical hygiene. He made a study of the housing, food, and care of troops, and submitted recommendations in relation to these subjects which were of material value. Returning from Cuba in November 1899, he commanded the Josiah Simpson Hospital at Fort Monroe, Va., and later was transferred to San Francisco as chief surgeon of the department of California. On Sept. 7, 1902, he succeeded William H. Forwood [*q.v.*] as surgeon-general of the army. General O'Reilly brought into his office a group of highly intelligent young officers and organized it into divisions, each with a responsible head. Unsatisfactory conditions in the army disclosed by the Spanish War caused the appointment of the Dodge Commission by President McKinley. The findings of the commission relating to the medical department took the form of a number of recommendations, which it devolved upon General O'Reilly to carry out. Among other reforms which resulted was a reorganization of the medical corps and the creation of the medical reserve corps. He was president of the board which recommended the adoption of typhoid prophylaxis for the army. In 1906 he represented the United States at the international conference at Geneva, Switzerland, for the revision of the Geneva Convention. He was retired for age on Sept. 14, 1909, and continued his residence in Washington until his death three years later from uremic poisoning. The only notable contribution to medical literature made by him was in the monograph on military surgery, which appeared in the fourth edition of W. W. Keen's *American Textbook of Surgery* (1903), in which he collaborated with Maj. William C. Borden.

O'Reilly was a man who won affection and loyalty from all who came into intimate contact with him. Though of a sensitive and retiring disposition he had an unfailing fund of courtesy and good nature. He was a devotee of chamber music and an accomplished performer upon the violin. Some of his deepest friendships were with those to whom he was bound by the ties of music. On Aug. 16, 1877, he married Frances L. Pardee of Oswego, N. Y., who, with one daughter, survived him. The death of a son just grown to manhood saddened his later years.

[J. E. Pilcher, *Surgeon Generals of the Army* (1905); F. H. Garrison, "In Memoriam: General Robert Maitland O'Reilly," *N. Y. Medic. Jour.*, Nov. 30, 1912; H. A. Kelly and W. L. Burrage, *Am. Medic. Biogs.* (1920); *Who's Who in America*, 1912–13; *Public Ledger* (Phila.), and *Evening Star* (Washington), Nov. 4, 1912.]   J. M. P—n.

O'RIELLY, HENRY [See O'REILLY, HENRY, 1806–1886].

ORMSBY, WATERMAN LILLY (1809–Nov. 1, 1883), engraver, was born in Hampton, Conn. He received a public-school education and at an early age became an apprentice in an engraving establishment. In 1829 he was a student in the National Academy of Design in New York City, and during his early life he lived at various times in Rochester, in Albany, where he engraved over his own name, and in Lancaster, Mass., where he worked for the firm of Carter, Andrews & Company. Finally he settled in New York City, where he became the proprietor of the New York Bank Note Company and one of the founders of the Continental Bank Note Company. He died in Brooklyn, N. Y., at the age of seventy-four.

During the first quarter of the nineteenth century the process of bank-note engraving was cheapened and facilitated by the introduction of machinery, and by the end of the century handcraftsmanship had been almost entirely superseded. Ormsby represented a curious combination of the two techniques. He was a versatile and accomplished inventor of machinery to facilitate the processes of engraving, but he was bitterly opposed to the complete replacement of the artist-craftsman. He held that notes should be engraved as a unit upon a single plate, with careful craftsmanship exerted on the design and interdependence of the composition. The counterfeiter would thus be foiled "not because he does not know how the work is done, but because he can not do it" (*Cycloidal Configurations*, p. 37). Ormsby was particularly bitter about the claims set forth for "Patent Green Tint" as a safeguard against spurious imitation. "Indeed," he wrote, "unless there is some interposition of Divine Providence, the prospect seems to be, that passports to Heaven will, eventually, be printed in 'Patent Tint.' But unless they are more secure against counterfeiting the 'narrow way' will be terribly crowded" (*Ibid.*, p. 43).

Ormsby was not frequently so urbane about what he considered charlatanry. He displays himself in his writings as a disgruntled eccentric, sensitive about his craftsmanship and childish

about his enmities. He considered himself discriminated against in business, but the forces of industrial change and reorganization were against him. He was an excellent line engraver, however, and was called upon for a great deal of work despite his conviction of persecution. His designs for notes were in wide use by the government at the time of the Civil War. He was the author of several pamphlets, among them *Cycloidal Configurations, or the Harvest of Counterfeiters* (n.d.), and of a volume on paper-money engraving entitled *A Description of the Present System of Bank Note Engraving* (1852).

[D. M. Stauffer, *Am. Engravers upon Copper and Steel* (1907); *Subject Matter Index of Patents for Inventions, 1790–1873* (1874); Frank Weitenkampf, *Am. Graphic Art* (1924); the *Sun* (N. Y.), Nov. 2, 1883.]   E. T.

ORNE, JOHN (Apr. 29, 1834–Nov. 29, 1911), Orientalist, was born in Newburyport, Mass., the son of John and Sarah Ingalls (Morse) Orne. The Orne family was well known and respected in Newburyport, and the name appears more than once in the early town records. John Orne, Jr., after completing the regular course in the Newburyport high school, studied by himself and was able to enter the sophomore class at Amherst College in 1852. Graduating there in 1855 with the degree of A.B., and a member of Phi Beta Kappa, he chose the teaching profession and taught with success in a number of secondary schools, chiefly in Newburyport, Lawrence, and Salem, from 1856 until 1867. In the latter year, Nov. 28, he married Louisa Fisk, daughter of Richard Lindsay, of Salem. They had no children. In this year also he accepted the appointment as sub-master and teacher of physics in the Cambridge High School; and at this post he remained for about twenty years, after which he retired from teaching.

While in Cambridge, Orne became interested in the Semitic languages. Under the guidance of Crawford H. Toy, who went to Harvard as Hancock Professor of Hebrew and Oriental Languages in 1880, he began the study of Arabic, and was introduced by him to the most important working tools of research in this field. He also made considerable progress in Hebrew and was a member of the Harvard Biblical Club. The most of his spare time, however, he devoted to Arabic and Mohammedan studies, pursuing them with remarkable energy and enthusiasm, gradually collecting a considerable library of texts and translations, and ultimately reaching a degree of proficiency in Arabic rarely attained by one who is mainly self-taught. In 1889 he was made curator of the Arabic manuscripts in the Semitic Museum of Harvard University, and he held this office during the remainder of his life. He was a corporate member of the American Oriental Society for twenty-one years, having joined in 1890. He contributed to the *Proceedings* of the society in 1892 (vol. XV) two papers which gave evidence of his scholarship: the one dealing with an important medical treatise which he analyzed and in part translated from one of the manuscripts in the Harvard collection; the other describing, with specimen translations, a highly interesting collection of Arabic mortuary tablets from Egypt, dated in the ninth century A.D., acquired for the Harvard Semitic Museum in 1890. Orne received the degree of Ph.D. from Amherst College in 1896, "for eminent attainments in the Arabic language and literature."

[*Who's Who in America*, 1910–11; obituary notice in the *Amherst Grads.' Quart.*, Jan. 1912; *Biog. Record of the Alumni of Amherst College, 1821–71*; J. J. Currier, *Hist. of Newburyport*, vol. I (1906) and *"Ould Newbury"* (1898); *Boston Transcript*, Dec. 1, 1911; *Boston Daily Advertiser*, Dec. 2, 1911.]   C. C. T.

ORR, ALEXANDER ECTOR (Mar. 2, 1831– June 3, 1914), merchant, was the son of William and Mary (Moore) Orr. He was born in Strabane, County Tyrone, Ireland, whither his father's family had migrated in the seventeenth century from Scotland. Alexander, while traveling in the United States in 1850, was so favorably impressed that he returned the next year to New York City to live. He worked as a clerk in several commission houses before forming, in 1858, a connection with David Dows & Company, at that time possibly the largest grain dealers in the United States. He became a partner in 1861 and the firm's representative on the floor of the Produce Exchange in 1863. Intense interest in the business and a remarkable energy soon made him the dominant member of the firm, a force in the Exchange, and a recognized authority in his field. He helped reorganize the Produce Exchange, 1871–72, was long chairman of its important arbitration committee, a leading organizer of its Benefit Assurance Society and its Gratuity Association, secretary of the building committee which erected the Exchange's three-million-dollar home, and served as president, 1887–88. He gave similar service to the Chamber of Commerce of the State of New York, aided in the erection of its new building, and served as vice-president, 1889–94, and as president, 1894–99.

In 1894 Orr was appointed a member of the Rapid Transit Commission, created by the state legislature to draw up plans for a comprehensive transit system in New York City and to contract for its construction and operation. At the first meeting he was elected president, and he served in this capacity until 1907 when the Commission's duties were transferred to the Public Service Commission. After four years of study, plans were completed for a subway as the central feature of the system. The contracts were let in 1900 and the first trains were operated in 1904, Orr making the chief address at the opening of service. "It is a cheerful fact," commented the *World's Work* editorially (March 1904, p. 4512), "that the costliest municipal convenience ever constructed has been free from corruption and free from political management . . . has been built—in New York, too—without scandal; and very much of the credit for this historic achievement belongs to Mr. Alexander E. Orr."

In 1875–76 Orr served, by Governor Tilden's appointment, as one of the four members of the commission which, in investigating the management of New York's state canals, exposed the operations of the notorious "canal ring." He was frequently called before the state legislature to advise on transportation and marketing problems. He served as chairman of the "citizen's movement" which elected Seth Low mayor of Brooklyn in 1881, and he took a leading part in other reform movements in local New York politics. When president of the Chamber of Commerce during Cleveland's second term, he gave encouragement and powerful support to the president's sound money policies. Orr's knowledge and ability were sought for by many banks, insurance companies, and railways; and, though at one time he was a member of no less than twenty-nine boards of directors, he gave conscientious service to each. When the Hughes Investigation shattered public faith in the New York Life Insurance Company, he was persuaded to become its president, and in eighteen months he had the company completely reorganized and restored to its former standing. In addition, he found time to serve in official capacities for the Brooklyn Academy of Music, the Long Island State Hospital, the Long Island Historical Society, and the Society for the Reformation of Juvenile Delinquents, and he was a trustee of many similar institutions. He was treasurer for nearly fifty years of the Long Island Diocese of the Protestant Episcopal Church, managing its many complicated funds, and contributing large amounts to them. He was survived by three daughters, born to his first wife, Juliet Buckingham Dows, whom he married in 1857 and who died in 1872. His second wife was

Margaret Shippen Luquer, whom he married in 1873.

[The chief source is a privately printed memorial: *In Memory of A. E. Orr* (1917). See also: *Letters and Lit. Memorials of Samuel J. Tilden* (2 vols., 1908), ed. by John Bigelow; annual reports and monthly *Bulletin* of the Chamber of Commerce of the State of N. Y., especially the *Bulletin* for June 1914; *Rapid Transit in N. Y. City and in Other Great Cities* (1905), prepared by the Chamber of Commerce; *Cat. of Portraits in the Chamber of Commerce* (1924), containing a sketch and a copy of the portrait painted by A. H. Munsell, Orr's son-in-law; *N. Y. Times*, June 4, 1914; *Brooklyn Daily Eagle*, June 3, 4, 1914.]   O. W. H.

ORR, GUSTAVUS JOHN (Aug. 9, 1819–Dec. 11, 1887), educator, was born in Orrville, Anderson County, S. C., the son of James and Anne (Anderson) Orr. In 1821 the family moved to Jackson County, Ga., and there young Orr grew into manhood, working on the farm, and attending such schools as there were. In 1835 his father put him in a store at Jefferson, the county seat, but the boy had other plans revolving in his mind. In 1839 he set out for East Tennessee to attend the Maryville academy and then entered the University of Georgia but, owing to a high if not exaggerated sense of honor, left the university at the end of his junior year rather than help the faculty in a matter of discipline. He entered Emory College, Oxford, Ga., and was graduated in 1844. He then resolved to study law, but his record at Emory had been so good that he was offered a position as a teacher in the preparatory department and as a tutor in the college. He returned to Jefferson after two years, however, and began the study of law with one of the resident attorneys, but by the end of the year he gave up the idea of becoming a lawyer. In 1847 he was married to Eliza Caroline Anderson, who bore him ten children, and he accepted a position in a girls' school at Covington, Ga. The next year Emory College offered him the professorship of mathematics. His ability as a mathematician was recognized in 1859, when Gov. Joseph E. Brown appointed him Georgia's commissioner to settle by survey a troublesome boundary dispute with Florida. By 1867 the Civil War and Reconstruction had reduced the college to the vanishing point, and he accepted the presidency of the Southern Masonic Female College at Covington. There he remained until 1870, when he became professor of mathematics at Oglethorpe College, which was removed from Midway to Atlanta that year.

However, the work on which his fame was to rest was yet to be done. In January 1872 the Democrats took control of the state from the Carpet-baggers, and among the first acts of the new governor was the appointment of Orr as state school commissioner. The law for the establishment of a common-school system, passed in 1870, was based on a report he had made in 1869 to the Georgia teachers' association. Thoroughly revised and rewritten in 1872, this new act became the basis of the state's common-school system and served admirably the purpose for many years. He was reappointed successively by the succeeding governors and remained school commissioner until his death. Owing to a school debt caused by his predecessor, he did not open the schools until 1873, and in his work of setting up an educational system he met and overcame many prejudices that had grown up under Carpet-bag management. He wrote many articles for the newspapers and many letters to individuals, and he made hundreds of speeches throughout the state. He early reached the conviction that the federal government might find ways to help education in the states, and in the advocacy of this program he spoke widely over the United States and appeared at various times before congressional committees. In 1881 he was made vice-president of the National Education Association, and the following year he became its president. He had a high sense of justice and a broad outlook in a day when sectional narrowness was too common. He plead for justice to the negro and lost no popularity in his state in doing so. He became the agent for the Peabody Fund in Georgia and directed the use of much of this money for normal institutes and free scholarships.

[*Georgia*, ed. by A. D. Candler and C. A. Evans (1906), vol. III; C. E. Jones, *Education in Ga.* (1889); I. W. Avery, *The Hist. of the State of Ga.* (copr. 1881); L. L. Knight, *A Standard Hist. of Ga.* (1917), vol. II; C. M. Thompson, *Reconstruction in Ga.* (1915); *Atlanta Constitution*, Dec. 12, 1887; S. A. Echols, *Georgia's Gen. Assembly of 1878. Biog. Sketches* (1878).]   E. M. C.

ORR, HUGH (Jan. 2, 1715–Dec. 6, 1798), inventor, patriot, the son of Robert Orr, was born in Lochwinnoch, Renfrewshire, Scotland. He received a common-school education in his native town and then learned the trade of whitesmith, becoming especially skilled in the making of edged tools. When he was twenty-five years old, having mastered also the gunsmith and locksmith trades, he sailed for America, and landed at Boston on June 7, 1740. He spent a year in Easton, Bristol County, Mass., and then removed to East Bridgewater, where he applied for work to a man named Keith, a maker of scythes. The story is told that he was quickly hired when he demonstrated his skill by making a keen razor out of an old iron skillet handle.

Not content merely to fashion scythes in the established way, Orr made constant experiments in an effort to improve the manufacturing methods, not only of scythes but of axes and edged tools generally. Thus he devised and built for the shop a trip-hammer said to have been the first in the colonies. His reputation as a maker of edged tools quickly spread and in a few years when his employer retired, Orr became owner of the shop. House and ship carpenters, millwrights and wheelwrights for twenty miles around came to him for new tools or to have old ones reconditioned. Thus he busied himself for upwards of thirty years, from time to time enlarging his establishment, and training his sons and other workmen in his craft.

Meanwhile, aware of the growing discord between the colonies and the mother country, he prepared his shop for the manufacture of firearms. As early as 1748, for the Province of Massachusetts Bay, he made 500 muskets which were deposited in Castle William, but nearly all of them were carried off by the British when they evacuated Boston. These muskets are believed to be the first ever made in the colonies. At the outbreak of the Revolution, being an ardent supporter of the Patriot cause, Orr again began producing muskets and in addition, "in concert with a French gentleman," built a foundry at Bridgewater, Mass., for casting cannon. At that time the usual practice in making iron or brass ordnance was to cast the piece with a cylindrical cavity somewhat smaller than the caliber desired, but Orr and his partner employed an improved method just then introduced in Europe. This consisted in making a solid casting and boring it to the proper caliber with a boring bar-iron and cutter. Though a difficult method, it yielded a far superior cannon both in strength and accuracy. During the war, Orr successfully produced a great number of iron and some brass cannon, from 3- to 42-pounders, besides a vast quantity of cannon-shot.

When peace was declared he resumed the manufacture of edged tools, but also turned his attention toward helping in the establishment of industries in the new states. A strong advocate of the machine as a substitute for hand labor, he had for years kept himself posted on all new developments taking place abroad in the application of machinery to textile manufacture, and as early as 1753 had invented a machine to clean flaxseed. Through his correspondents abroad he learned of the carding and spinning machines being made and used in England and about 1785 he successfully induced two skilled Scotch mechanics, Robert and Alexander Barr,

who were acquainted with the new machines, to come to America and construct textile machinery in his shop and at his expense. The following year Orr was elected to the Massachusetts Senate and persuaded that body to encourage by practical means the establishment of textile manufactories in the state. State grants were made to enable the Barr brothers to construct a roving machine and "several other machines as might be necessary for carding, roping, and spinning cotton and wool" (Walton, *post*, p. 151) and to enable Thomas Somers, another Scotch mechanic under Orr's direction, to build other textile machinery. About the same time Orr employed at his own expense a man named McClure who knew how to weave by hand with the fly shuttle. This was probably the first use of the fly shuttle in America. The next year, Mar. 8, 1787, the legislature placed the machines made by Somers and the Barrs in the charge of Orr, with the proviso that he should "explain to such citizens as may apply for the same the principles on which said machines are constructed and the advantages arising from their use, and also . . . allow them to see the machines at work" (*Ibid.*). Advertisements to this effect were inserted in the Massachusetts newspapers and the machines soon came to be known as "The State Models." While they were imperfect and of little practical use, it was from them that the early American textile-machinery manufacturers obtained many of their ideas. Although permitted to use them, Orr never attempted to employ the machines for the creation of a manufacturing business of his own.

His interest in metals led directly to his one hobby, namely, the collecting of minerals and ores. This hobby was quite widely known and as a result, from every newly discovered ore deposit throughout the colonies Orr was immediately furnished samples of the rocks and minerals so that at the time of his death he was in possession of a very valuable mineral collection. He was married on Aug. 4, 1742, to Mary Bass of East Bridgewater, and of this union ten children were born. His son Robert Orr followed closely in his footsteps and became a skilled metal craftsman. He introduced the manufacture of iron shovels into Massachusetts and in 1804 became master armorer of the government arsenal at Springfield.

[Seth Bryant, *The Mitchell, Bryant and Orr Families* (1894); Perry Walton, *The Story of Textiles* (1912); *Mass. Hist. Soc. Colls.*, vol. IX (1804); W. B. Weeden, *Economic and Social Hist. of New England* (1891), vol. II; J. L. Bishop, *A Hist. of Am. Manufactures from 1608 to 1860* (3 vols., 1861–68).]
C. W. M—n.

ORR, JAMES LAWRENCE (May 12, 1822–May 5, 1873), speaker of the House of Representatives, governor of South Carolina, Confederate States senator, was born in Craytonville, Pendleton District (now Anderson County), S. C., the great-grandson of Robert Orr who emigrated from Ireland to Bucks County, Pa., about 1730 and later removed to Wake County, N. C., and the son of Martha (McCann) Orr, a daughter of Irish emigrants, and Christopher Orr, a prosperous merchant. He was the brother of Jehu Amaziah Orr [*q.v.*]. His early years were spent in schools near his home and as a clerk in his father's store. In 1839 he entered the University of Virginia, where he began the study of law. Returning to South Carolina he completed his law studies in the office of Joseph N. Whitner and was admitted to the bar when he became of age. In the fall of the following year he married Mary Jane, the daughter of Samuel Marshall of Abbeville District, and began to edit the *Anderson Gazette,* a weekly newspaper. Within two years he abandoned journalism to devote himself to politics and to become the law partner of J. P. Reed. The court records of Anderson for the period show that this firm enjoyed nearly half the law business of that district. In 1844, at the age of twenty-two, he became a member of the state legislature, where he served until 1848. In that body he distinguished himself as the opponent of the parish system and as the champion of the popular election of presidential electors, internal improvements, and the reform of the public schools. Although a believer in the right of secession, he opposed the Bluffton movement, which would have committed the state to another nullification experiment. In 1848, after an exciting canvass, he was elected to Congress, where he served until 1859. In Congress he was largely instrumental in stifling the secessionist tendencies of his state. Although he had voted against the compromise measures of 1850, the following year he canvassed the state against the advocates of immediate secession and won a signal victory. This gave him opportunity to organize the South Carolina branch of the National Democratic party. He was able to bring about the defeat of R. B. Rhett for reëlection to the United States Senate and to get himself chosen head of the state's delegation to the National Democratic Convention of 1856, where he supported the policies of Stephen A. Douglas. These actions, coupled with his opposition to Know-Nothingism, made him very popular in the North, and he was elected speaker of the federal House of Representatives in 1857. He was

mentioned as a possibility for the Democratic presidential nomination in 1860 and was president of the state convention of April 1860, in which he stressed the value of the Union and prevented the delegates to the national convention from being instructed for secession.

Nevertheless, he changed his views to meet the changing sentiment of his state. Already he had overstepped himself, having been defeated for the United States Senate in 1858 for quoting a famous phrase of Webster on nullification. He withdrew from the National Democratic Convention of 1860 with the other South Carolina delegates and ardently championed the withdrawal of the state from the Union. He signed the ordinance of secession, was one of the three commissioners sent to Washington to negotiate for the possession of the Charleston forts, organized Orr's Regiment of Rifles for service under the Confederacy, and, after a brief and undistinguished military career, was elected a Confederate States senator in December 1861. In this capacity he served until the fall of the Richmond government. Realizing that the defeat of the Confederacy was inevitable, he was among the first who prepared for the problems of Reconstruction. He quarreled with President Davis and in 1864 advocated a negotiated peace. Espousing the Reconstruction policies of President Johnson, he played a prominent part in the state constitutional convention of 1865 and was elected governor by a small majority. As governor he pursued a compromising policy. He advocated modification of the notorious "black code" and provision for restricted negro suffrage, and he headed the state's delegation to the Union National Convention of 1866. Yet when Congress refused to accept these overtures, in a defiant mood he advised the state legislature to reject the Fourteenth Amendment. Changing his course again when he saw that congressional Reconstruction would be applied to the South, he shrewdly attempted to accommodate the state to the inevitable. He cooperated with the military officers, advised the whites to accept the Reconstruction acts, and made a statesmanlike address before that Radical state constitutional convention of 1868. Losing the confidence of the whites, he joined the Radical party. He was elected to the circuit bench in 1868 and served until 1870. He supported Grant's Ku-Klux policy before the Republican National Convention of 1872, and the president appointed him minister to Russia. After a few months at his new post, he died of pneumonia at St. Petersburg.

His phenomenal success as a politician was largely due to unusual personal qualities. Although he was neither elegant in manners nor learned, his powerful physique, ringing voice, and intelligent face gave him an air of distinction. Genial and generous, he was liked even by his political enemies. Unlike most South Carolinians of his day, he accurately understood Northern public opinion and knew when it was expedient to accommodate his views to it. Had his advice been followed, South Carolina would have escaped many of its misfortunes. Yet his faults were patent. He changed his views too frequently to inspire popular confidence. His enemies were correct in ascribing this to ulterior motives, for every move he made redounded to his personal advantage in the form of some new public office.

[*Cyc. of Eminent and Representative Men of the Carolinas* (1892), I; B. F. Perry, *Reminiscences of Public Men* (1883); F. B. Simkins and R. H. Woody, *S. C. during Reconstruction* (1932); J. S. Reynolds, *Reconstruction in S. C.* (1905); C. S. Boucher, "The Secession and Cooperative Movement in S. C.," *Washington Univ. Studies,* Humanistic Series, Apr. 1918; L. A. White, "The National Democrats of S. C.," *South Atlantic Quart.,* Oct. 1929; *Charleston Daily Courier,* Dec. 4, 1865, Aug. 26, 1872; *News and Courier* (Charleston), May 7, 1873.]   F. B. S.

ORR, JEHU AMAZIAH (Apr. 10, 1828–Mar. 9, 1921), legislator and lawyer, was born in Anderson County, S. C., the son of Christopher and Martha (McCann) Orr and a brother of James Lawrence Orr [*q.v.*]. About 1843 the family moved to the eastern section of Mississippi. He studied at Erskine College in South Carolina and at the College of New Jersey (Princeton). In 1849 he entered the practice of law at Houston, Miss., and shortly afterward was chosen secretary of the state Senate. In 1852 he became a member of the lower house, and there he actively opposed the immediate sale of the Chickasaw school lands. Unfortunately, the land was sold two years later, after he had completed his term in the legislature and had been appointed United States attorney for the northern district of Mississippi. He was a member of the Democratic convention that nominated Buchanan. Originally opposed to secession, he deplored the split in the Charleston convention and voted for Stephen A. Douglas; but the results of the election of 1860 and the rising tide of war feeling convinced him that the conflict was inevitable, and from that time he supported the Confederacy. He was a member of the Mississippi convention of 1861 that voted for secession and then served in the provisional Congress of the Confederacy. He raised a regiment of 1400 men, the 31st Mississippi Volunteers, and served in the 1862 and 1863 campaigns in Mississippi. In April of the following year

he resigned to enter the Second Confederate Congress. After he was convinced that the establishment of a separate republic in the South was impossible, he maintained that terms, advantageous to the South, ought to be obtained before exhaustion placed it at the mercy of the enemy, and he was disappointed that the Richmond administration, by insisting on Confederate independence as a *sine qua non,* rendered futile the Hampton Roads conference. In a subsequent speech before the legislature of Mississippi, he advocated a change in the executive policy of the Confederacy and blamed President Davis for the failure of the peace negotiations. The criticism was not welcomed at the time (F. A. Montgomery, *Reminiscences of a Mississippian in Peace and War* (1901, pp. 229–30).

At the close of hostilities he was again ahead of his constituency, when he advised the partial enfranchisement of the negroes. In 1870 he became a judge of the 6th judicial circuit and served for six years. He took part in the movement that returned the Democrats to power in Mississippi in 1876. From 1872 until his resignation in 1904 he was an active member of the board of trustees of the University of Mississippi. For fifty years he was an elder in the Presbyterian Church. While he was less in the public eye after the close of Reconstruction, his life was none the less active, for he devoted himself with great success to the practice of law, in which his powers seemed to increase with age. The latter part of his life was spent at Columbus, Miss. He was married twice, first to Elizabeth Ramsay Gates of Chickasaw County, S. C., in 1852, and, second, to Cornelia Ewing Van de Graaff of Sumter County, Ala., in 1857.

[Dunbar Rowland, *Mississippi* (1907), vol. III; *Biog. and Hist. Memoirs of Miss.* (1891), vol. II; *Who's Who in Miss.* (1914); *Pubs. Miss. Hist. Soc.,* vols. II, VIII, IX (1899–1906); *Columbus Dispatch,* Mar. 13, 1921; newspaper clippings in possession of his daughter, Mrs. Franklin Harris, Signal Mountain, Tenn.; date of death from tombstone, Columbus.]
                                                    C. S. S.

ORTH, GODLOVE STEIN (Apr. 22, 1817–Dec. 16, 1882), politician, congressman, was born near Lebanon, Pa., a descendant of Balthazel Orth who is said to have emigrated to Pennsylvania with the Moravian leader Zinzendorf in 1742. After attending the local schools and Pennsylvania College, Gettysburg, he entered the law office of James Cooper. In 1839 he moved to Lafayette, Ind., and was admitted to the bar. The following year, in October, he married Sarah Elizabeth Miller of Gettysburg. In the campaign of 1840 he made his début as a political speaker, stumping Indiana for Harrison. This activity brought him prominence, and in 1843 the Whigs elected him to the state Senate, where he served until 1848. In 1845, as a result of discord in the Loco Foco ranks, he was elected president of the Senate. His name was presented as a candidate for the gubernatorial nomination in 1846, but he withdrew in favor of Joseph Marshall. Although he thought the nomination of Taylor on the Whig ticket a mistaken political move, he served as a presidential elector for Taylor and stumped northern Indiana. His wife died in 1849 and on Aug. 28, 1850, he married Mary A. Ayers of Lafayette. After the enactment of the Compromise Measures of 1850, like many anti-slavery Whigs, he joined the Know-Nothings, but in 1852 campaigned for Scott. He was president of the Indiana Know-Nothing Council for 1854–55, subsequently joined the People's party of Indiana, and out of this helped organize the Republican party in the state.

In 1861, Gov. O. P. Morton [q.v.] appointed him one of the five Indiana representatives to the Peace Conference in Washington. Prejudiced before going, he returned convinced that conflict was inevitable and advised preparation for war. When Governor Morton called for volunteers in July 1862, Orth reported in Indianapolis twenty-four hours later as elected captain of some two hundred men. The danger of invasion over, the company was mustered out, Aug. 20, 1862. In this year Orth was elected to the Thirty-eighth Congress. He served continuously through the Forty-first, but was not a candidate for reëlection in 1870. In Congress he urged vigorous prosecution of the war and later, stringent reconstruction measures. He voted for the Thirteenth and Fourteenth Amendments, opposing the later anti-Chinese legislation as contrary to the latter. Holding at first a position halfway between the Radicals and Johnson, he slowly gravitated toward the extreme Radicals when he became convinced that Johnson was as unwilling to compromise as they.

Following the war, his interest turned to foreign affairs. In 1866 he began a fight for recognition of the right of expatriation. Two years later he undertook the management of the House legislation looking toward the annexation of Santo Domingo, but opposed the recognition of Cuban belligerency as unprofitable. In 1868, also, he framed the Orth Bill which made certain changes in the diplomatic and consular services. In the Forty-first Congress he was one of the small group who brought about the election of James G. Blaine to the speakership. He was recommended in 1871 for appointment as United States minister at Berlin, but it was decided to continue George Bancroft in that post, and Orth was offered, but refused, the commissionership of internal revenue. He was returned to the Forty-third Congress but was not a candidate in 1874. In March 1875, after declining the mission to Brazil, he was appointed minister to Austria-Hungary, but resigned in May 1876 to accept the Republican nomination for the governorship of Indiana. Party discord, however, caused him to withdraw in favor of Benjamin Harrison. In 1878 he reëntered politics and was elected to the Forty-sixth Congress. Reëlected two years later, he died, at Lafayette, Ind., before the expiration of his term. Orth recognized the necessity of machinery in politics, and never hesitated to sacrifice principle for party solidarity. No unpopular legislation ever received his vote.

[W. H. Barnes, *Hist. of the Thirty-ninth Cong. of the U. S.* (1867), and *The Fortieth Cong. of the U. S.,* vol. II (1870); *Biog. Dir. Am. Cong.* (1928); S. M. Cullom, *Fifty Years of Public Service* (1911); *Memorial Addresses on the Life and Character of Godlove S. Orth,* 47 Cong., 2 Sess. (1883); C. B. Stover and C. W. Beachem, *The Alumni Record of Gettysburg Coll.* (1932); *Indianapolis Sentinel,* Dec. 17, 1882; manuscript letters of Orth in the Ind. State Lib.; records in the Adjt.-General's Office, Indianapolis; papers in the William H. English Collection, Univ. of Chicago Lib.]

J. L. N.

ORTHWEIN, CHARLES F. (Jan. 28, 1839–Dec. 28, 1898), grain merchant, was born near Stuttgart, in Württemberg, Germany. His mother died when he was quite young. His father, Charles C. Orthwein, made provision for his schooling and the boy was given the best education which the state schools of southern Germany could afford. In 1854 he came to the United States with his father, brothers, and sisters. After a brief stop in St. Louis the family settled for a time in Logan County, Ill., but the father soon became dissatisfied with his new home, and with the other children, returned to Germany, leaving young Charles behind. His first business experience was in a store in his Illinois home, but he saw larger opportunities in St. Louis, and accordingly obtained employment in the wholesale grocery and commission house of Ed. Eggers & Company. In a short time this concern was dissolved; whereupon he formed a partnership with Gustave Haenschen, under the name of Haenschen & Orthwein, and established a grain commission business. This venture was launched during the Civil War, and the partners' warehouses became a base of supplies for the Union armies. Since trade with the South was cut off, Orthwein turned his attention to the grain markets of other parts of the country and eventually made St. Louis the dominant grain center of the Mississippi Valley.

After the war he dispatched the first grain shipment to Europe by way of the Mississippi River, sending a cargo of 12,000 bushels in 1866. This venture was at first financially unprofitable, but the benefits to St. Louis were important. He frequently addressed business meetings and spoke in private to urge that St. Louis engage in the export trade by way of the Mississippi and the Gulf of Mexico. In furtherance of this project he was instrumental in laying a petition before Congress for river and harbor improvements. He prevailed upon the Illinois Central Railroad and other lines to build more adequate grain terminal facilities in New Orleans and other cities. Making St. Louis the center of his organization, he established branches in many cities in the United States and Europe. He owned the Victoria elevator and mill in St. Louis, several elevators in Kansas City, New Orleans, Galveston, Seneca, Mo., and New York City. He also owned a large tract of land in St. Claire County, Mo. He was interested in the Southern Electric Railway Company of which he was president, and at one time held a very large interest in the National Railway Company. He was president of the Merchants Exchange and a director in the German Savings Bank of St. Louis. He early affiliated himself with the Democratic party, and later became what was known as a "Sound Money Democrat." He was a member of the Church of the United Brethren in Christ. He married Caroline Nulsen, daughter of John C. Nulsen, in 1866, and they had six sons and three daughters. He died at his home in St. Louis at the close of his sixtieth year.

[*St. Louis Post-Dispatch*, Dec. 28, 29, 1898; *St. Louis Globe-Democrat*, Dec. 29, 1898; *St. Louis Republic*, Dec. 29, 1898; Wm. Hyde and H. L. Conard, *Encyc. of the Hist. of St. Louis* (1899), III, 1678.]

O.B.

ORTON, EDWARD FRANCIS BAXTER (Mar. 9, 1829–Oct. 16, 1899), geologist, educator, son of Samuel Gibbs and Clara (Gregory) Orton, was born in Deposit, Delaware County, N. Y. After early manhood he was known simply as Edward Orton. His father was a Presbyterian clergyman, a descendant of Thomas Orton, one of the early settlers of Windsor, Conn. Edward's boyhood was passed mostly in Ripley, N. Y., where his father was then settled. He was fitted for college under his father's tuition and in the academies of Westfield and Fredonia. Entering Hamilton College as a sophomore in 1845, he graduated with high standing in 1848. The year following he served as assistant prin-

cipal in an academy at Erie, Pa., and during 1849–50 studied in Lane Theological Seminary, Cincinnati, Ohio, supporting himself meanwhile by tutoring. At the end of that time, owing to eye troubles and other causes, he withdrew and spent several months in outdoor life on a farm. Later, he made a sea voyage in a coasting vessel. In the spring of 1851 he became a teacher in the Delaware Literary Institute, Franklin, N. Y., but passed the year 1852–53 at the Lawrence Scientific School of Harvard University. The years 1853–54 found him again teaching in the Delaware Institute, but, still intent upon the ministry as a profession, he then entered the Andover (Mass.) Theological Seminary. Without graduating, he was ordained at Delhi, on Jan. 1, 1856, by the Delaware Presbytery.

So far as is recorded he had manifested no marked liking for the natural sciences prior to his entering the Lawrence Scientific School, where he was interested chiefly in chemistry and botany. In 1856, however, he became professor of natural sciences in the state normal school, Albany, N. Y. Charged with holding heretical views, he resigned at the end of three years, and from 1859 to 1865 was principal of an academy at Chester, Orange County, where his success was such that he was elected professor of natural history in Antioch College, Yellow Springs, Ohio, a position he continued to hold until chosen its president in 1872. Meanwhile, in 1869, he had been appointed an assistant on the Geological Survey of Ohio under John S. Newberry [*q.v.*], and in 1873 was made professor of geology and president of the newly established College of Agriculture and Mechanics, which in 1878 became the state university. In 1881 he voluntarily resigned his presidency, but he retained his professorship to the end of his life. In 1882, on the reorganization of the state survey, he was appointed state geologist, a position he held until his death seventeen years later.

Though his interest in geology developed late in life, yet as state geologist he was markedly successful, notwithstanding the delicate position in which he was placed in being called on to take up and complete the work of his former chief (Newberry). During his administration there were brought out volumes V to VII of the final reports of the survey; these differed in a marked degree from those of his predecessor in the attention given to economic problems, particularly clay, coal, oil, and gas. He was the first to point out in a convincing manner the essential conditions for the accumulation in the earth's crust of the last two substances and their true relations, and to warn of the probability of their exhaustion through a continuance of the wasteful practices then employed. He lived to see his forebodings become actualities.

As an administrator, Orton was a compelling force in the organization of the College of Agriculture and its subsequent development into the state university. He was a likable man; quiet in his manner and of a somewhat retiring nature. Sagacious, kindly, and conservative, he won out where a more aggressive man would have failed. His interest in the public welfare was deep, especially in matters of public health and conservation of resources. In his opposition to the reckless wasting of natural gas, he was a pioneer. In 1855 he married Mary M. Jennings of Franklin, N. Y., by whom he had four children; his wife died in 1873 and two years later he married Anna Davenport Torrey of Millbury, Mass., by whom he had two children. He suffered a stroke of paralysis early in December of 1881, which deprived him of the use of his left arm and caused a slight limp in his walk, but he retained his mental powers unimpaired until 1899 when, on Oct. 16, he died suddenly and painlessly.

[Edward Orton, *An Account of the Descendants of Thomas Orton of Windsor, Conn.* (1896); *In Memoriam, Edward Orton, Ph.D., LL.D.*, (1899); G. K. Gilbert, in *Bull. of the Geol. Soc. of America*, Oct. 31, 1900; I. C. White, in *Am. Geologist*, Apr. 1900; Henry Howe, *Hist. Colls. of Ohio*, vol. I (1890); J. J. Stevenson, in *Jour. of Geology*, Apr.–May 1900; Washington Gladden, in *Ohio Archæol. and Hist. Pubs.*, vol. VIII (1900); *Ohio State Jour.* (Columbus), Oct. 17, 1899.]
G. P. M.

ORTON, HARLOW SOUTH (Nov. 23, 1817–July 4, 1895), lawyer, jurist, was the son of Harlow N. Orton, M.D., and Grace (Marsh) Orton. He came of vigorous pioneer stock and was descended from Thomas Orton, an early settler in Connecticut. Both of his grandfathers were Baptist clergymen and fought in the Revolutionary War. He was born and reared on a farm in Madison County, N. Y., and after attending Hamilton Academy he spent two years (1835–37) at Madison University (now Colgate University). For one year he taught in and had charge of Paris Academy in Bourbon County, Ky. He completed his preparation for the bar in the law office of his brother, Myron H. Orton, in La Porte, Ind., where he was admitted in 1838. On July 5, 1839, he was married to Elizabeth Cheney, daughter of a prosperous Maryland planter. He was keenly interested in politics and was an active member of the Whig party, although after 1854 he was an independent Democrat. In 1840 he made nearly one hundred speeches advocating the election of General Har-

rison. In 1843 the governor of Indiana appointed him probate judge of Porter County. He commenced the practice of law in Milwaukee, Wis., in 1847, and six years later became private secretary to Governor Leonard J. Farwell. He then removed to Madison, Wis., where he continued to reside until the time of his death.

In 1854 he was elected a member of the Assembly. The following year he was retained in the case of *Attorney General ex rel. Bashford* vs. *Barstow* (4 *Wis.*, 567), one of the early important cases establishing the right of the judiciary to determine the legality of the election of officers of a coördinate branch of the government. The fact that he was employed as counsel indicates his standing at the bar. He was associated with and opposed to the ablest lawyers of the Wisconsin of his day and played a leading part in the trial of this novel and celebrated case. He was also retained in the so-called Granger Case, *Attorney General* vs. *Railroad Companies* (35 *Wis.*, 425). With other eminent counsel he represented the state. In 1859 he was elected judge of the ninth judicial circuit, was reëlected without opposition, but resigned the office in 1865 to resume the general practice of his profession. He was again elected to the legislature in 1869 and in 1871. In 1876 he was an unsuccessful candidate of the Democratic party for a seat in Congress and in the same year was appointed one of the committee which compiled the *Revised Statutes of the State of Wisconsin* (1878). From 1869 to 1874 he was dean of the law school of the University of Wisconsin, from which institution he received in 1869 the degree of LL.D. He continued the practice of his profession until April 1878, when he was elected a justice of the supreme court of Wisconsin. He became its chief justice in January 1894 and continued to occupy that position until his death.

Physically Orton was a man of powerful rugged frame and was possessed of tremendous energy and vitality. Intellectually he was keen, alert, and vigorous almost to the point of aggressiveness. He possessed in extraordinary degree the ability to express his thoughts in forcible and striking language. Generous, warm-hearted, somewhat impulsive, he had a strong sense of justice and right. With a firm and positive character he combined open-mindedness and the power of listening sympathetically to the views of others. He was not regarded by his contemporaries or those who followed him as a profound student of the law. It was as an advocate that he excelled, so that he was markedly successful in jury trials and in forensic contests where appeals to public feeling and opinion were involved. It was because of his ability along these lines that he was retained in the Barstow case. His service as a member of the supreme court was marked by great industry and thorough devotion to his work.

[See: memorial exercises of the Wis. supreme court reported in 90 *Wis.*, xxi–xlvii; J. B. Winslow, *The Story of a Great Court* (1912); *Biog. Rev. of Dane County, Wis.* (1893); J. R. Berryman, *Hist. of the Bench and Bar of Wis.* (2 vols., 1898); P. M. Reed, *The Bench and Bar of Wis.* (1882); Edward Orton, *An Account of the Descendants of Thos. Orton of Windsor, Conn., 1641* (1896); the *Green Bag*, Apr. 1897; *Madison Democrat,* July 6, 1895.] M. B. R.

ORTON, JAMES (Apr. 21, 1830–Sept. 25, 1877), zoologist, explorer, educator, was born at Seneca Falls, N. Y., the fifth child of Rev. Azariah Giles and Minerva (Squire) Orton and a descendant of Thomas Orton who settled in Windsor, Conn., about 1641. His father, a graduate of Williams College, was a man of great intellectual attainments but lacked the practical gifts necessary for professional or financial advancement, and his life was spent as pastor of small country parishes where salaries were meager and living conditions hard. Four of his eight sons died in infancy. James early became interested in the natural sciences, and the two passions of his youth were the study of natural history and writing. He made numerous collecting trips in the vicinity of his home and sent a long series of communications to the *Scientific American* and other periodicals. At the age of nineteen he published *The Miner's Guide and Metallurgist's Directory* (1849).

Partly because of ill health and partly because of financial difficulties, he was delayed in entering college, but eventually matriculated at Williams and graduated in 1855. There he became intimate with Henry A. Ward, later curator of the museum of the University of Rochester and founder of Ward's Natural History Establishment. With Ward, Orton made many walking trips, especially for the collection of specimens. During his undergraduate days he accompanied two scientific expeditions to Nova Scotia and Newfoundland, and acquired such a reputation as a naturalist that the president of Williams advised him to make the study of natural history his life work. He adhered, however, to his original purpose of becoming a minister, entered Andover Theological Seminary, graduated in 1858, and was ordained to the Presbyterian ministry, July 11, 1860. In 1859 he married Ellen, daughter of Asahel and Mary Foote. She survived him fifty-three years, dying June 12, 1930. He held various pastorates in New York State and in Maine, during the first few years after his ordination, but definitely decided on the life of a naturalist in 1866, when he went to the University of Rochester as instructor in natural history, acting as a substitute for Ward, who was absent on leave. In 1869 he was appointed professor of natural history at Vassar College, which position he held until his death.

Three expeditions to South America, where he explored the equatorial Andes and the region of the Amazons, yielded Orton's most important contributions to science. The first of these expeditions, in 1867, traversed the region from Guayaquil to Quito, down the Napo River to Pebas on the Maranon, and from there to Para by steamer. This involved climbing from sea level at Guayaquil over the western Cordilleras to a height of 15,000 feet. After his return he published *The Andes and the Amazons* (1870). On the second expedition, 1873, he went from Para up the Amazons to Yurimaguas and from there over the Andes to Peru. Numerous communications which on these two trips had been sent to journals in the United States, dealing with the geology, climate, inhabitants, flora, fauna, and economic resources of the countries visited, were ultimately brought together in *The Andes and the Amazons,* of which a third edition appeared in 1876. The collections were distributed among various museums.

In 1876 Orton organized a third expedition. While the first two had been carried out largely at his own expense, the third was financed by Edward Drinker Cope [*q.v.*] of Philadelphia, who was to receive in return whatever fossils were collected. One object of the trip was to explore the Beni River for the commercial advantage of the Bolivian government. Accompanied by Dr. E. R. Heath, whom he had met on an earlier expedition, Orton started out with a guard of soldiers which the government officials strongly advised taking as protection against wild animals and savage men. At the junction of the Beni and Mamore rivers this guard deserted, taking with them most of the other men. The leaders were thus forced to return to the coast. After many hardships they finally reached Lake Titicaca and started to sail across it to Puno in Peru. On this short trip Orton was taken with a hemorrhage and died. Because he was a non-Catholic, permission to bury his body in consecrated ground was refused, but Señor Estaves, owner of a small island in the lake, offered a plot there, which offer was accepted. In 1921 a monument presented by Vassar alumnae was erected at his grave and unveiled with elaborate ceremonies. The collections of this third expedition were taken over by the Peruvian government to be sent to the United States, but they were never received.

An important publication for its time was Orton's *Comparative Zoology, Structural and Systematic* (1876), which was in advance of its contemporaries in stressing function as much as structure, most zoological textbooks of that date being mainly anatomical or taxonomic. He published also *Underground Treasures, How and Where to Find Them* (1872), which a generation after his death was in sufficient demand to warrant a new edition; *The Proverbialist and the Poet: Proverbs Illustrated by Parallel or Relative Passages from the Poets* (1852); and *The Liberal Education of Women, the Demand and the Method* (1873).

[Susan R. Orton, "A Sketch of James Orton," *Vassar Quart.*, Feb. 1916; James Orton, *The Andes and the Amazons* (3rd ed., 1876); E. Albes, "An Early American Explorer," *Bull. of the Pan-American Union*, July 1914; I. K. Macdermott, "An International Dedication Ceremony," *Ibid.*, Aug. 1922; Edward Orton, *An Account of the Descendants of Thomas Orton of Windsor, Conn.* (1896); *N. Y. Tribune*, Oct. 31, 1877.]

A. L. T.

ORTON, WILLIAM (June 14, 1826–Apr. 22, 1878), telegraph executive, came of an old English family. The first of the family in America was Thomas Orton who was living in Windsor, Conn., in 1641 and later was one of the original settlers of Farmington, Conn. The father of William Orton, Horatio Woodruff Orton, a teacher, moved from Connecticut to a farm near Cuba, Allegany County, N. Y. He married Sarah Carson in 1825 and the following year William was born. His father taught him to study and to concentrate his energies. He attended the district schools and the Albany Normal School, from which he graduated in 1846. Meanwhile he worked in a printing shop, and later in the Geneva bookstore of George H. Derby. He also taught school several years. In 1850 he married Agnes Johnston Gillespie; they had eight children. In 1852 he became a partner in the publishing firm of Derby, Orton & Mulligan in Buffalo but in 1856 moved to New York, where he was well known in the publishing business until the failure of his firm two years later. In 1860 he became interested in New York City politics and threw himself into the local affairs of his ward. In 1861 he was elected to the New York Common Council, and there made his mark as a convincing debater and as a leader of the Republican minority. He also took up the study of law and was admitted to the bar in the spring of 1867.

In 1862 President Lincoln appointed him collector of internal revenue at New York. So successful was his conduct of this office during the war that in 1865 President Johnson appointed him commissioner of internal revenue at Washington. Meanwhile, the telegraph had been spreading through the country. By 1864 two companies dominated the industry, the Western Union and the American Telegraph. To compete with these, in that year a third company was formed, the United States Telegraph Company. Its preliminary development was not sufficiently wise for it to stand the struggle, and its president resigned. Well-meaning friends secured the election of William Orton to the presidency in October 1865 and he resigned his commissionership to accept the new task. Becoming acquainted with the actual condition of the company and realizing more and more the importance to the public of a single service in communications, he set to work with Jeptha H. Wade, president of the Western Union, to merge the United States Telegraph Company into the older organization. This was accomplished in April 1866. Wade continued as president of the enlarged Western Union Telegraph Company and Orton became vice-president. At the same time the headquarters of the Western Union were moved from Rochester to New York. Wade and Orton then initiated negotiations with E. S. Sanford, president of the American Telegraph Company, for the merger of that company into the Western Union, and this was completed in June 1866. A year later Wade resigned, and on July 10, 1867, Orton became president.

At this time he was a man of tall, commanding figure, of large frame and dignified bearing. He was built to be a strong man, but the unremitting strain to which he subjected his nervous energies impaired his health and weakened his constitution. As president, he found that the merging of the three companies into one entailed serious problems of financial adjustment, rendered more difficult by the disturbed financial conditions that prevailed during and after the Civil War. To justify the inflated capital of $41,000,000 that the Western Union took over with the mergers the new president had to increase greatly the real assets of the company. Further, the Western Union had now become truly national in scope and in responsibility. The vast railroad and highway development of the time necessitated an enormous amount of new construction. No less did efficient service to the public require expensive replacement.

Orton started out by suspending dividends. He also at once began to encourage invention and to stimulate scientific standards in telegraphic engineering. Once his program got under way, the business and public service of the company increased rapidly. Before 1871 only one telegraphic message could be transmitted over a wire at a time. In that year the Western Union adopted the Stearns duplex system (patented in 1868), and in 1874 the Edison quadruplex system. The result was that the number of telegrams passing daily through the main office of the Western Union in New York City increased from 3,500 in 1871 to 75,000 in 1875.

With unification came also opposition. In 1869 three bills were introduced into Congress to provide that the Government should take over the ownership and operation of the telegraph companies. Orton probably rendered his greatest service to the development of American industry by his fight against these and similar proposals. Appearing repeatedly before the United States Senate and House Committees, by formal address and informal debate he contended for the principles on which he was transforming the telegraphic service of his day. He brought to bear his exhaustive knowledge of the facts of both American and European telegraphy. He opposed any legislation of the kind as impractical and contrary to the best development of telegraphic communications, and he denounced it as confiscatory and unconstitutional. Ever ready to meet attack, and always throwing himself with all his high-strung energy into the struggle, he won. But the long fight, added to the heavy strain of his regular executive and constructive labors, sapped his strength. His tense nervous physique, buoyant though it was, broke, and he died suddenly of apoplexy on Apr. 22, 1878.

[*Ann. Reports of the President of the Western Union Telegraph Company*, 1867–78; *Jour. of the Telegraph*, 1867–78, esp. the Memorial Number, May 1, 1878; *The Telegrapher*, 1864–77; J. D. Reid, *The Telegraph in America* (1879); Edward Orton, *An Account of the Descendants of Thomas Orton of Windsor, Conn.* (1896); *N. Y. Tribune*, *N. Y. Times*, *N. Y. Herald*, Apr. 23, 1878.]   W. C. L.

ORTYNSKY, STEPHEN SOTER (Jan. 29, 1866–Mar. 24, 1916), Catholic prelate, son of John and Mary (Kulczycka) Ortynsky, was born at Ortynyczi, Galicia, Austria, of old Ruthenian stock. Educated in the public school and gymnasium at Drohobycz and in the University of Krakow, from which he received the doctorate in divinity, he was ordained, July 18, 1891, a monk of the Order of St. Basil the Great. As an eloquent preacher in the Slavic tongues and in German, as a writer, as a professor of philosophy in the university at Lawrow, Galicia, as a nationalist patriot, and as hegumenos of the monastery of St. Paul, Michaelovka, Ortynsky attained fame throughout Galicia, Bukovina, Hungary, and the Ukraine. Because of the in-

creased immigration of people of these lands and of adherents of the Roman Catholic Church who followed the Greek rite, it was held desirable in Rome that a bishop be sent to the United States who would have special care of the priests and congregations of Greek Catholics as a safeguard against the religious and political proselyting activities of Greek Orthodox and Pan-Slavic agents. Hence, Dr. Ortynsky was appointed an auxiliary to the Latin bishops with the title of bishop of Daulia and with headquarters at Philadelphia. On May 12, 1907, he was consecrated by Archbishop Szeptycky of Lemberg.

In the rather difficult position which he occupied he displayed wisdom and ability. He was tactful in dealing with the various bishops and in preventing any feeling of conflicting jurisdiction. His work among the Ruthenians and Ukrainians was marked with a high degree of success. He established parishes, built schools, counteracted Greek Orthodox propaganda, fostered Americanization, fought radicalism, and introduced the Sisters of the Order of St. Basil the Great. These achievements led to the establishment of a Ukrainian Greek Catholic diocese and Ortynsky's appointment as Greek Catholic bishop for the United States with St. Mary of the Immaculate Conception Church in Philadelphia (which he established in 1909) as his cathedral (May 28, 1913). He founded St. Basil's Orphanage for dependent children and established for his countrymen the fraternal order "Providence," with its organ *Ameryka*, to which he was an active contributor. During the war he was deeply concerned over Russian atrocities in Galicia and the imprisonment of his patron, Metropolitan Szeptycky. He published an appeal in the form of two courageous pastoral letters (1915), which condemned the Czar's Pan-Slavic crusade of "liberation of Slavic peoples" while he trampled on their churches and undermined their nationalism. At the time of his death he had charge of a half million Greek Catholics, 152 churches, and 150 parish schools.

[*Am. Cath. Who's Who* (1911); *Cath. Encyc.*, VI, 748 f.; P. J. Kenedy, *The Official Cath. Directory* (1907 ff.); *Ameryka*, Mar. 26, 1916; *Evening Bulletin* (Phila.), and the *North American* (Phila.), Mar. 25, 1916; materials from the chancery of the Ukrainian Greek Catholic diocese.]   R. J. P.

OSBORN, CHARLES (Aug. 21, 1775–Dec. 29, 1850), abolitionist, the grandson of Matthew Osborn who emigrated from England probably to Delaware, and the son of David and Margaret (Stout) Osborn, was born in Guilford County, N. C. About 1794 he removed to Knox County, Tenn., where he became a Quaker preacher. As an active minister from 1806 to 1840 he traveled thousands of miles visiting and preaching in nearly every Quaker meeting throughout the United States, Canada, and Great Britain. He lived in Jefferson County, Tenn., Mount Pleasant, Ohio, and from 1819 to 1842 in Wayne County, Ind., excepting the years from 1827 to 1830 that he spent in Warren and Clinton counties, Ohio. In 1842 he removed to Cass County, Mich., and in 1848 to Porter County, Ind., where he died. On Jan. 11, 1798, he married Sarah Newman, who died on Aug. 10, 1812, leaving seven children, and on Sept. 26, 1813, he married Hannah Swain, who bore him nine children.

Endowed by his Quaker environment with a reforming spirit and influenced by the privations of a semi-pioneer life, he maintained with courage and ability his moral, religious, and anti-slavery convictions. In December 1814, at the house of his father-in-law, Elihu Swain, he began his career as an anti-slavery leader by laying the foundations for the Tennessee Manumission Society, whose organization he did not, however, complete until the next February at Lostcreek Meeting House. In 1816 he founded similar societies in Guilford County, N. C. While at Mount Pleasant, Ohio, he published the *Philanthropist*, from Aug. 29, 1817, to Oct. 8, 1818, a paper partially devoted to anti-slavery agitation. It has been asserted that he himself, and, through him, the manumission societies and *Philanthropist* were the earliest advocates of immediate emancipation. This assertion cannot be substantiated. The societies definitely advocated gradual emancipation. His own strong moral and religious convictions did not include demands for immediate emancipation until his affiliation with Garrisonian abolition about 1832. Through the *Philanthropist* he denounced the American Society for Colonizing the Free People of Colour of the United States, afterward the American Colonization Society, as a specious device of slaveholders to protect slavery, expatriate free negroes, and thwart other emancipation schemes. Following Quaker tradition he long opposed the use of products of slave labor, considering them stolen goods because slaves' labor was stolen by their masters. His exhortations resulted in the formation on Jan. 22, 1842, of the Free Produce Association of Wayne County, Ind., and the establishment of a propagandist newspaper, the *Free Labor Advocate and Anti-Slavery Chronicle*. When the conservatives, who, only mildly abolitionist, believed in confining anti-slavery activity to their own religious organization, gained control over the Indiana Yearly Meeting, which before 1842 was dominated by the active abolitionist radicals, they removed

him and others from the Meeting for Sufferings, a governing committee of the Church, on which he had served for years. This was a severe and unexpected blow to him. Bitterly lamenting the conservatives' position, he participated prominently in the secession of 2,000 radicals who formed the Indiana Yearly Meeting of Anti-Slavery Friends in February 1843. He continued his interest in the later activities of the seceders and died condemning the Fugitive-slave Law. After his death, in 1854 the Church published *The Journal of that Faithful Servant of Christ, Charles Osborn*.

[Minutes of the Manumission Soc. of N. C., in the Guilford College Lib.; minutes of Ind. Yearly Meeting of Anti-Slavery Friends in Earlham College Lib.; *Emancipator*, pub. by Elihu Embree, Apr. 30, May 31, 1820; Walter Edgerton, *A Hist. of the Separation in Ind. Yearly Meeting* (1856); Levi Coffin, *Reminiscences* (1876); *Hist. of Wayne County, Ind.* (1884), vol. II; G. W. Julian, "The Rank of Charles Osborn as an Anti-Slavery Pioneer," *Ind. Hist. Soc. Pubs.*, vol. II, no. 6 (1891); S. B. Weeks, *Southern Quakers and Slavery* (1896); P. M. Sherrill, "Quakers and N. C. Manumission Soc.," *Trinity Coll. Hist. Soc. Papers*, X (1914); A. E. Martin, "Anti-Slavery Soc. in Tenn.," *Tenn. Hist. Mag.*, Dec. 1915.]   R. A. K.

OSBORN, HENRY STAFFORD (Aug. 17, 1823–Feb. 2, 1894), Presbyterian clergyman, author, map-maker, was born in Philadelphia, the son of the Rev. Truman Osborn, of New England stock, and Eliza (Paget) Osborn, of a South Carolina family. Henry received the degree of A.B. from the University of Pennsylvania in 1841, entered Union Theological Seminary, where he graduated in 1845, and on Apr. 9, 1848, was ordained a minister in the Presbyterian Church. Meantime he had been stated supply at Coventry, R. I., 1845–46, and in 1846 had gone to Hanover, Va., where he was in charge of a church till 1849. He served pastorates at Richmond, Va., 1849–53; Liberty, Va., 1853–58; and Belvidere, N. J., 1859–65. In 1860, while at Belvidere, he married Pauline Courson, to which union was born one daughter. He had a strong bent toward science, and during his early years in the ministry served for some time as professor of natural science in Roanoke College, Virginia. In 1866 he accepted the professorship of chemistry and mining engineering in Lafayette College, resigning to assume in 1870 that of the natural sciences in Miami University, Oxford, Ohio. Although in 1873 Miami University closed temporarily, he continued his residence in Oxford until his death, devoting his time to the ministry, lecturing, writing, and publishing.

He went abroad for travel and study in 1850–

51 and again in 1858–59. During the second trip he made special studies in the geography and plants of Palestine, as a result of which he published *Palestine, Past and Present* (London, 1859) and *Plants of the Holy Land with Their Fruits and Flowers* (1860), illustrated by original drawings which exhibit accuracy of observation and striking artistic skill. His chief interests from 1873 to the time of his death were the extension of his studies and publication in his two fields of original inquiry, the Holy Land and metallurgy. In connection with his later works on the Holy Land, he established in Oxford a "Map Shop" from which, with the assistance of one employee, for twenty years he published for churches and Sunday schools in England and America his attractive hand-made maps, illustrating the geography of Palestine and the ancient world for the benefit of ministers and Sunday-school teachers. His *New Descriptive Geography of Palestine* was issued in 1877. His publications in the field of mineralogy included *Metallurgy, Iron and Steel* (1869); *A Practical Manual of Minerals, Mines and Mining* (1888); and *The Prospector's Field-book and Guide* (1892). He was a member of a number of scientific societies both at home and abroad. He was a man of versatile talents and striking personality—tall, thin to gauntness, talkative, notably genial among friends, lover of harmless gossip. Like a true philosopher he was indifferent to economic considerations and social conventions. To and from his map shop, in his research laboratory, on field trips, on business errands, he wore his familiar "tile" hat and morning clothes. While much abstracted in his daily contacts, when engaged in conversation or address his mind exhibited a many-sided interest and a keen discrimination that marked him as distinctly intellectual.

[*Gen. Cat. of the Grads. and Former Students of Miami University* (1909); H. C. Baird, biog. sketch, in *Prospector's Field-book and Guide* (2nd ed., 1896); *N. Y. Tribune*, Feb. 4, 1894.]   H. C. M.

OSBORN, LAUGHTON (*c.* 1809–Dec. 13, 1878), poet, dramatist, was a man whose peculiar temperament, antagonistic disposition, erratic outlook on life, and desire to be something different and to live apart from his fellow men, are occasionally found among those in the minor ranks of the literary profession. He was born in New York City, where his father was a well-known and wealthy physician, and during his course of study at Columbia, from which he was graduated in 1827, he is said by at least one classmate to have been studious and popular. That he was studious there can be no doubt. If he was popular, a change must have come over him after he left college, perhaps owing to the death of a favorite sister, and aggravated by the unfavorable reception accorded to his books. After he returned from a year of foreign travel, he lived for nearly half a century in retirement in New York, although he was surrounded by many who might have become his friends and associates in society and the world of letters. In 1831 his *Sixty Years of the Life of Jeremy Levis* was published in two volumes, its rambling style and varied material revealing beyond doubt that he had been a faithful student of Laurence Sterne and *Tristram Shandy*. The harsh and antagonistic comment of the press upon this book set him against the critics and reviewers, and thereafter he waged continuous verbal warfare with them. Many of his books were issued at his own expense and without his name, among his successive publications being *The Dream of Alla-Ad-Deen; The Confessions of a Poet* (1835); *The Vision of Rubeta, an Epic Story of the Island of Manhattan: with Illustrations Done on Stone* (1838), aimed particularly at William Leete Stone, 1792–1844 [*q.v.*], but which also contained a fierce attack on Wordsworth and replies to his critics, and *Arthur Carryl* (1841), a volume of miscellaneous poems and a "novel" in two cantos which gave the name to the volume. These were followed by numerous tragedies and comedies with such titles as *The Heart's Sacrifice, Matilda of Denmark, Bianco Capello*, and *Mariamne, a Tragedy of Jewish History*. He also wrote a *Handbook of Young Artists and Amateurs in Oil Painting*, published in 1845.

In addition to his literary gifts, he was a painter and musician of some skill, and a master of several languages. According to James Grant Wilson, he was at least six feet tall, of fine physique and carriage, while Poe, writing of him when he was about the age of thirty-five, says that he was "probably five feet ten or eleven, muscular and active." Poe also described him as "undoubtedly one of 'Nature's own noblemen,' full of generosity, courage, honor—chivalrous in every respect, but unhappily, carrying his ideas of chivalry, or rather of independence, to the point of Quixotism, if not of absolute insanity. He has no doubt been misapprehended, and therefore wronged, by the world; but he should not fail to remember that the source of the wrong lay in his own idiosyncracy—one altogether unintelligible and unappreciable by the mass of mankind" (*post*, p. 56). His plays were obviously for the library, and not for the footlights, and a search of dramatic records fails to disclose any mention of their production in New York or elsewhere.

[E. A. Poe, *The Literati* (1850); S. A. Allibone, *A Critical Dict. of English Lit. and British and Am. Authors,* vol. II (1870); J. G. Wilson, *Bryant and His Friends* (1886); the *World* (N. Y.), Dec. 14, 1878.]

E. F. E.

OSBORN, NORRIS GALPIN (Apr. 17, 1858–May 6, 1932), editor, long a leader in the public affairs of Connecticut, was born in New Haven, the son of Minott Augur and Catharine Sophia (Gilbert) Osborn. He prepared for college in the Hopkins Grammar School and in 1880 graduated from Yale. His father was owner of the *New Haven Evening Register* and his home, a rendezvous for men of influence in the state and nation. Young Osborn grew up, therefore, in an atmosphere conducive to interest in political matters and acquired high ideals of public service. Upon leaving college he became a reporter on the *Register,* and in 1884, its editor. In 1907 he was made editor-in-chief of the *New Haven Journal-Courier,* which position he held till his death. Under the name "Trumbull," in 1890 he began contributing to the Sunday edition of the *New York Herald* piquant articles on political happenings in Connecticut, which are an invaluable source of historical information. In addition to his newspaper work, he published *A Glance Backward: Editorial Reminiscences* (1905), and delivered the Bromley Lectures on Journalism, Literature, and Public Affairs at Yale in 1920, published the following year under the title *Isaac H. Bromley.* He also edited *Men of Mark in Connecticut* (5 vols., 1906–10) and *History of Connecticut in Monograph Form* (5 vols., 1925), and was a contributor to the *Dictionary of American Biography.*

Both a lucid, forceful writer, and a brilliant speaker, he did as much to mould public opinion in Connecticut during his lifetime as any other one man, while by his contemporaries in newspaper circles his abilities were widely recognized. On every important issue of the day, local and national, he took a decided stand, and maintained it with courageous independence. No one who tried to influence him by base appeals ever remained long in his office. He fought hard but goodnaturedly and with the generosity and gallantry of a born gentleman. Politically, he was an old-time Democrat, and his advice in party councils carried weight. He was on the staff of Gov. Thomas M. Waller in 1883 and thereafter was always known as "Colonel." He was a delegate to the National Democratic Convention of 1892 and enjoyed the confidence of President Cleveland during both his administrations. A

member of the state constitutional convention of 1902, he led a notable but unsuccessful fight to change the antiquated system of representation in the legislature. For some thirty-five years he was active in the Connecticut Civil Service Reform Association; in the presidential campaign of 1896 he broke with his party and was an official of the Connecticut Sound Money League; in the local activities created by the World War, he took a leading part. Prohibition he assailed in season and out of season, attacking it as vicious in principle and deplorable in results. Perhaps his most valuable service, certainly the one that gave him greatest satisfaction, was in connection with the state prison. From 1895 till his death he was on the board of directors and after 1912 its president, acting also as chairman of the parole board. He practically determined the policy of the institution, took a personal interest in the inmates, and was their friend and adviser after their parole. He was both an idealist and a realist. He had implicit faith that the people, sufficiently informed, would do the right thing, and that the world was getting better; but he faced facts with both eyes open.

Tall and debonair, quick at repartee, a spirited raconteur with a rich resonant voice, he at once became the center of any group he joined. Significant of the confidence and regard he inspired is the fact that among his warmest friends were persons widely apart socially and of diverse political and religious views. In 1922 an infection necessitated the amputation of one of his legs. He bore its loss with his customary buoyant cheerfulness, and was soon back at his work, remaining active until shortly before his death. Married Dec. 27, 1881, to Kate Louise Gardner of New York, he was survived by three sons and two daughters.

[*A Hist. of the Class of Eighty, Yale College* (1910); *Who's Who in America,* 1930–31; *N. Y. Times,* May 7, 1932; *New Haven Journal-Courier,* May 7 ff.; personal acquaintance.]

H. E. S.

OSBORN, SELLECK (*c.* 1782–*c.* October 1826), journalist, poet, was born in Trumbull, Conn., the son of Nathaniel Osborn. At an early age he was apprenticed as a printer. From June 19, 1802, to Jan. 3, 1803, he edited the *Suffolk County Herald* at Sag Harbor, N. Y. In 1805 he joined Timothy Ashley in editing *The Witness,* at Litchfield, Conn. The town was at that time strongly Federalist and contained several outspoken critics of President Jefferson and his policies. Democrats encouraged the publishers to expose Federalist fallacies and uphold the President in their columns. Osborn penned editorials with youthful zeal and indiscretion. The prominent Federalists were decorated with opprobious and malodorous nicknames until one, "Crowbar Justice" (Julius) Deming, sued the editors for libel. At the session of the county court in April 1806, they were found guilty, fined each $100 and costs, and ordered under bonds to "keep the peace & be of good behaviour . . . till the next Term of this Court" and "to stand committed within the Gaol of s'd County untill this Judgment be complied with" (Litchfield County Court Records, XVI, 304–05). Ashley exhibited compliance, but Osborn chose to "stand committed" and from his cell, as sole editor, continued *The Witness*. This made him a veritable John Wilkes in the eyes of John C. Calhoun [*q.v.*], then a law student in Litchfield (*New York Patriot*, Nov. 27, 1823), and of the Republican newspapers throughout the country and much political capital was made of his imprisonment. On Aug. 6, 1806, a demonstration was staged in his honor; there was a procession followed by "spread-eagle exercises in the meeting house" and a collation on the Green opposite the jail; the first toast offered was: "Selleck Osborn! the Later Daniel in the lion's den. He is teaching his persecutors that the beasts cannot devour him!" (White, *post*, p. 165). Reporting the incident, a Washington paper said that the "persecution of federalism" had raised Osborn "high in the esteem of dispassionate men" (*National Intelligencer*, Aug. 20, 1806).

It is more than possible that the presence in that Litchfield parade of a squad of cavalry militia from Massachusetts induced Osborn some time after his release to become a cavalryman. He was commissioned first lieutenant of light dragoons in the United States army July 8, 1808, was promoted to captain Feb. 20, 1811, became attached to the first regiment of light dragoons July 6, 1812 (a second regiment having been organized that year), served in the War of 1812 on the Canadian frontier, and was honorably discharged June 1, 1814. He soon returned to newspaper work, associating himself, after a brief interval, with the *American Watchman*, Wilmington, Del., of which, for about three years beginning July 19, 1817, he was the owner and editor (*American Watchman*, July 16, 1817). In 1823–24, zealous to gain the Republican presidential nomination for his friend Calhoun, he collaborated in editing and printing the *New York Patriot*. Later he moved to Philadelphia, where he died.

A regular feature in any newspaper edited by Osborn was a poet's corner, to which he contributed. In *The Witness*, Mar. 4, 1807, appeared a poem called "The Contrast—or War and Peace," containing these lines:

"Heaven hasten the time when the battle shall cease
    And dread terror be banish'd afar;
            When Love
            Like a dove
    With the EMBLEM OF PEACE
Shall return to the Ark, and that wretchedness cease,
    Which embitters the horrors of War."

As these verses indicate, Osborn was an outspoken advocate of peace, despite the apparent contradiction of his career as a cavalryman. A volume of his verse entitled simply *Poems* was published in Boston in 1823. In 1810, at New Bedford, Mass., he married Mary, daughter of Barnabas Hammond. They had two children, a son and a daughter.

[*American Watchman*, July 16, 1817; F. B. Heitman, *Hist. Reg. and Dict. U. S. Army* (1903), containing some inaccuracies; A. C. White, *The Hist. of the Town of Litchfield, Conn.* (1920); E. A. and G. L. Duyckinck, *Cyc. of Am. Lit.* (1875), vol. II; Samuel Kettell, *Specimens of Am. Poetry* (1829), vol. II; Roland Hammond, *A Hist. and Geneal. of the Descendants of Wm. Hammond* (1894); *Litchfield Monitor*, Aug. 13, 1806; Litchfield County Court records; Trumbull (Conn.) Cong. Church records; *Nat. Intelligencer* (Washington, D. C.), Oct. 30, 1826.]
A. E. P.

OSBORN, THOMAS ANDREW (Oct. 26, 1836–Feb. 4, 1898), lawyer, statesman, diplomat, was born in Meadville, Pa., the son of Carpenter and Elizabeth (Morris) Osborn. He was apprenticed to a Meadville printer and earned enough money to attend the preparatory department of Allegheny College (1855–57). He also had a few months of legal study in the office of Judge Derickson of Meadville in 1856. In 1857 he traveled westward to Pontiac, Mich., where his career was officially launched by his admission to the bar just after his twenty-first birthday. In November of the same year he turned westward again and settled in Kansas. He first found work as a compositor in the office of the *Kansas Herald of Freedom* in Lawrence, and as acting editor during the absence of the owner. In the spring of 1858 he opened a law office in Elwood and in the same year was elected attorney of Doniphan County. His winning personality, energy, and ability had by this time been demonstrated to such a degree that in 1859 he took his seat as senator from Doniphan County in the first legislature of the new state of Kansas. He was a Republican and a Free-Stater. In 1862 he was elected president *pro tempore* of the Senate, though one of its youngest members, and presided with conspicuous ability at the impeachment of Gov. Charles Robinson. In the same year, 1862, he was elected lieutenant-governor of Kansas. In 1864 President Lincoln appointed him United States marshal, but political differences caused his removal by President Johnson in 1867.

In the election of 1872 Osborn was made governor of Kansas, and the following year he began his two eventful terms in that office. Three major crises arose, each of which he met with characteristic ability. His efficient relief measures during the "Grasshopper Year" of 1874 earned him the admiration and gratitude of the people of Kansas. The threat of a serious Indian uprising on the southern border of the state was successfully overcome by moderate but determined action. The discovery in 1875 of misconduct in the use of funds by the state treasurer was followed by prompt measures which averted what might have become a serious financial crisis. Under his administration the settlement of Kansas made great progress and many new counties were organized. In 1877, after having unsuccessfully campaigned for a seat in the United States Senate, Osborn was appointed minister to Chile by President Hayes. During his residence at Santiago, Chile became involved in war with Peru and Bolivia. Osborn's attempts to effect a peaceful settlement between the countries were appreciated but futile. With the help of Thomas Ogden Osborn [q.v.], American minister to Argentina, however, he was instrumental in settling the long-standing Patagonian boundary dispute, for which he received the public thanks of the government of Chile. In 1881 he was appointed minister to Brazil by President Garfield. While no sensational event marked his residence at Rio de Janeiro, the Brazilian government showed its appreciation of his four years of service by bestowing upon him the highest honor that could be given a foreigner, the Grand Cross of the Order of the Rose.

Returning to Kansas Osborn resumed his business and political interests. In 1888 he headed the Kansas delegation at the Republican National Convention. The same year he was elected state senator from Shawnee County and held office for two terms. He engaged in extensive business activities, including banking, real-estate, mining, investments, and railroads. He was a director of the Atchison, Topeka & Santa Fé Railroad from 1894 until his death. In 1870 he married Julia Delahay, daughter of Judge Mark W. Delahay of Leavenworth, Kan. They had one son. Osborn died suddenly in 1898, while on a visit to his old home in Meadville.

[Charles S. Gleed, "Thomas A. Osborn," *Trans. Kan. State Hist. Soc.*, vol. VI (1900); W. E. Connelley, ed., *A Standard Hist. of Kan. and Kansans* (1918), vol. II; C. R. Tuttle, *A New Centennial Hist. of the State of Kan.* (1876); *Papers Relating to the Foreign Relations of the U·S.*, 1878–82; *Message of the President of the U. S., Transmitting Papers Relating to the War in South America and Attempts to Bring About a Peace* (1882); D. W. Wilder, *The Annals of Kan., 1541–1885* (1886); the *Topeka Daily Capital*, Feb. 5, 1898.]
I. L. T.

OSBORN, THOMAS OGDEN (Aug. 11, 1832–Mar. 27, 1904), lawyer, soldier, diplomat, was born in Jersey, Ohio, the son of Samuel and Hannah (Meeker) Osborn. He graduated in 1854 from Ohio University at Athens and after reading law for two years in the office of Gen. Lew Wallace at Crawfordsville, Ind., was admitted to the bar. In 1858 he began the practice of law in Chicago. With the opening of the Civil War, however, he threw all his energies into recruiting a regiment of volunteers, the 39th Illinois Infantry, christened the Yates Phalanx in honor of the governor of the state. He was elected lieutenant-colonel of the regiment, which was attached to the Army of the Potomac, and was shortly promoted to colonel. He was wounded in the attack on Fort Wagner and later more seriously in the battle of Drewry's Bluff, when a bullet shattered his right elbow. For gallantry in action he was brevetted brigadier-general. After more than four months he was discharged from Chesapeake Hospital, but, too weak to return to the field, was given a furlough. He spent his period of convalescence delivering a vigorous series of speeches in Michigan, Illinois, and Indiana in Lincoln's second presidential campaign. Returning to active service in December 1864, he remained with his command on the north side of Richmond all winter, and on Apr. 2, 1865, in a dangerous and gallant charge captured Fort Gregg. This resulted in the fall of Petersburg and Richmond. Osborn was made full brigadier-general of volunteers, and the Yates Phalanx was presented with a brazen eagle by the Secretary of War.

After the war Osborn returned to his law practice in Chicago. He was treasurer of Cook County, Ill., in the years 1867–69; served on the board of managers of the National Home for Disabled Volunteer Soldiers; and on Jan. 7, 1873, was appointed a member of the Commission to Inquire into the Depredations Committed on the Texas Frontier, and spent the winter investigating conditions in the Rio Grande Valley. On Feb. 10, 1874, President Grant appointed him minister resident in the Argentine Republic. Never content to fill a passive rôle, he was not only careful to protect American interests, but tried to make himself a valued counselor and trusted friend of the Argentines. On July 6, 1880, his good offices were effective in terminating the civil war between the national government and the province of Buenos Aires. For many years the relations between Argentina and Chile had been disturbed by a misunderstanding over the Patagonian boundary between the two countries. Osborn and his colleague, Thomas Andrew Osborn [*q.v.*], American minister to Chile, took the initiative in bringing about a settlement. The snowy Andes blocked travel between the two capitals, but a treaty was successfully negotiated and ratified (Oct. 22, 1881) by telegraph. Osborn commented that it might well be called "the Wire Treaty." Others suggested "the Osborn Treaty" as an appropriate name. Osborn was publicly thanked by the Argentine government and commended by his own. The Argentine Republic afterward presented him with a shield, "very handsome, artistic, and costly," bearing figures representing Chile and Argentina with hands joined, and the United States extending an olive branch. This shield, said to be the last finished work of Gustave Doré, was hung in the Art Institute of Chicago.

Osborn resigned in 1885 but remained in South America, engaging in railway projects. One link of the Pan-American Railway, from Asunción, Paraguay, to Sucre, Bolivia, was known as the Osborn Concession. He returned to Chicago in 1890 and retired from active business. He died suddenly in Washington, D. C., in 1904, and was buried in Arlington National Cemetery. He never married.

[*Biog. Sketches of the Leading Men of Chicago* (1868); *Chicago Record-Herald*, Mar. 28, 1904; "Hist. of the Thirty-ninth Infantry," in *Report of the Adj.- Gen. of the State of Ill.* (1867), vol. I; "Report and Accompanying Documents . . . on the Relations of the U. S. with Mexico," *House Report 701*, 45 Cong., 2 Sess.; *Papers Relating to the Foreign Relations of the U. S.*, 1874–85; *War of the Rebellion: Official Records (Army)*; *Buenos Ayres Herald*, Nov. 14, 1880; *Who's Who in America*, 1903–05; the *Washington Post*, Mar. 28, 1904.]   I. L. T.

OSBORN, WILLIAM HENRY (Dec. 21, 1820–Mar. 2, 1894), railroad promoter and president, philanthropist, was born at Salem, Mass., the son of William and Anna Henfield (Bowditch) Osborn. He came of old New England stock. His earliest-known direct ancestor was a sea-captain, whom he resembled in his adventurous nature and independence. After attending the rural and high school of his community, he abandoned the routine of formal education at the age of thirteen to enter the East India House of Peele, Hubbell & Company of Boston. Within a few years his aptitude for business won him an appointment as their representative in Manila, where he later established himself in his own interest. Returning to the United States after about ten years, on Dec. 14, 1853, he married Virginia Reed Sturges, daughter of Jonathan

Sturges, a New York merchant and one of the incorporators of the Illinois Central Railroad. Of this road, still incomplete, Osborn was made president in 1855. The company was then in a critical financial position. The "Schuyler frauds" (overissue of the stock of the New York & New Haven road, under the presidency of Robert Schuyler who was at the same time president of the Illinois Central) had made it virtually impossible to negotiate railroad securities, but Osborn reorganized the Illinois Central and placed it on a firm financial basis. When the panic of 1857 with its disastrous accompaniment swept the country, he again brought order into the chaos of the railroad's affairs by negotiating a personal loan, and reëstablished the company's credit by assessments upon stockholders and a new bond issue, thereby giving to the company permanent financial stability. The use of this road by the government during the Civil War for the transportation of troops and war materials and of grain and supplies, the rapid development of the natural resources of the country, and the consequent settlement of the company's lands so contributed to its material success that soon after 1861 it began to pay dividends to shareholders. Its credit continued to rise, and before severing his connection with the company, Osborn was able to negotiate its bonds at 3½%, an unprecedented accomplishment. For about thirty years he controlled the destinies of the Illinois Central, serving for ten years as president (1855–65), twenty-two as director (1854–76), and six as president of the Chicago, St. Louis & New Orleans (1877–82). During the last period he exercised his customary energy and ability in working out plans and policies whereby the Illinois Central acquired this line as an extension to New Orleans and became one of the world's most important railroad properties.

His retirement from business in 1882 meant only a transfer of activity; thereafter he devoted himself to philanthropy and the art of living. His private beneficence had a very wide range; while resident in Chicago he and his wife had actively promoted the welfare of the railroad workers by means of an employees' relief association and a library; in New York he was closely identified with the Society for the Relief of the Ruptured and Crippled, the Bellevue Training School for Nurses, and the New York Hospital. He rounded his career and enriched his personal life by a fine discrimination in literature and art, his library and art collection both being considerable. Among those whose warm friendship he enjoyed were the poet E. P. Whipple, whom he knew from childhood; Frederick

E. Church, the artist; and Samuel J. Tilden. His prominent traits were sincerity, hatred of affectation in people and of sham in men or in measures, and a pronounced tenacity of conviction. Much of his time toward the close of his life was spent quietly on his estate "Castle Rock," at Garrison, N. Y. He died in New York City, survived by two of his four children.

[Family records supplied by a son, Prof. Henry Fairfield Osborn; tributes of friends; recollections of President Stuyvesant Fish, L. V. F. Randolph, E. T. Jeffery; Emerson Hough, "The Settlement of the West: A Study in Transportation," *Century*, Jan. 1902; H. G. Brownson, *History of the Illinois Central Railroad to 1870* (1915); *N. Y. Tribune*, Mar. 4, 1894.]   F. M.

OSBORNE, JAMES WALKER (Jan. 5, 1859–Sept. 7, 1919), lawyer, was born in Charlotte, N. C., the son of James W. Osborne and Mary (Irwin) Osborne. His ancestors on both sides of the house came of North-of-Ireland stock. His father was a judge of the superior court of North Carolina, highly respected and esteemed in his community; his mother was a woman of strong and vigorous mind, deeply read in literature, profoundly interested in public affairs, and a devoted companion to her children. He was graduated in 1879 from Davidson College, North Carolina. He stood high in his classes and showed even then the enormous energy, mental and physical, which characterized him throughout his life. In 1883 he sought a wider field for his ambitions in New York, where he studied in the Columbia University Law School, graduated in 1885, and was immediately admitted to the bar.

He was by principle and by heredity an ardent Democrat and his legal and political activities soon brought him into public notice. In 1891 De Lancey Nicoll [*q.v.*], who was then district attorney of New York County, appointed him as a member of his staff of young men remarkable for their character and ability. In this good company Osborne soon made his mark. During his eleven years of service, he conducted many of the most important criminal prosecutions in the County of New York. Of these, perhaps, the best known were the cases of Roland Burnham Molineux and Albert T. Patrick. In the former, upon the first trial, the defendant was convicted, but the judgment was reversed by the court of appeals, and upon the second trial he was acquitted (*The Molineux Case*, 1929, edited by Samuel Klaus). Albert T. Patrick was convicted, and the conviction was affirmed (182 *N. Y. Reports*, 131), but the sentence of death was commuted by Governor Higgins to life imprisonment, and Patrick was afterwards pardoned by Governor Dix. Osborne was thorough and careful in preparation, logical and forceful in the presentation of his evidence, and searching in his cross-examinations. In his addresses to the jury, he was eloquent and persuasive. In 1902 he resigned and entered into private practice, resuming after an interval membership in the firm of Osborne, Lamb & Petty, with which he had been connected before his public service. In 1905 he was nominated by the Democratic party as district attorney for New York County but was defeated by William Travers Jerome, an independent Democrat, nominated upon a fusion ticket, who won by a small majority.

Osborne continued in private practice during the rest of his life, but accepted a number of public retainers in which he rendered notable service. In 1909, he was appointed a special attorney general of the state of New York for the purpose of investigating and prosecuting the American Ice Company for violation of the anti-trust statutes. After a long and bitterly contested litigation, he was successful in securing the conviction of the Ice Company and the imposition of the maximum penalty. In 1910 he appeared as counsel for State Senator Benn Conger in the prosecution of State Senator Jotham Allds before the New York Senate upon the charge of taking a bribe to influence his action as a legislator. Although Allds had at his back very powerful influence, both political and financial, and counted many devoted friends, Osborne conclusively proved his guilt and his conviction followed (*Documents of the Senate of the State of New York*, 1910, no. 28). In the following year Osborne was counsel for the committee of the New York Senate which investigated political and social conditions in the City of Albany, uncovering many gross evils. In 1913, as special attorney general, he conducted a vigorous investigation of conditions and treatment of prisoners in the state prison at Ossining, which disclosed many abuses and led to the appointment of Thomas Mott Osborne [*q.v.*] as warden of Sing Sing prison.

Along with his professional activities, Osborne was a constant and devoted student of literature and history. He was passionately fond of chess and was an excellent amateur player. To the end of his life, in spite of failing health, he continued his love for and his exercise in athletic sports. On Jan. 8, 1896, he married Lelia Van Wyck, the daughter of Judge Augustus Van Wyck. He was survived by his wife and by their son. In his family life, he showed the same warm feeling and the same kindly sympathy that marked all the other phases of his intense nature. He died in New York at the age of sixty.

[*The Asso. of the Bar of the City of N. Y., Year Book,* 1920; *N. Y. County Lawyers' Asso., Year Book,* 1920; *N. Y. Herald,* Sept. 8, 1919; personal acquaintance.]   G. G. B.

OSBORNE, THOMAS BURR (Aug. 5, 1859–Jan. 29, 1929), biochemist, was born in New Haven, Conn., of old New England stock, the grandson of Eli Whitney Blake [*q.v.*]. His parents were Frances Louisa (Blake) Osborne and Arthur Dimon Osborne, the latter educated as a lawyer and subsequently engaged in banking. From Yale College Osborne received the degree of B.A. in 1881 and that of Ph.D. in 1885. During his boyhood and youth he was greatly interested in the study of plants, insects, and birds, of which he collected hundreds of specimens prior to 1880 when he began to be engrossed in the pursuit of chemistry. A biographer has said: "Osborne had no taste for poetry, the drama or noble prose. He was a realist. . . . A love of nature was music and poetry to him" (E. H. Jenkins, in *Thomas B. Osborne—a Memorial, post,* pp. 281–82). From Prof. Samuel W. Johnson [*q.v.*] of the Sheffield Scientific School he received much early inspiration and encouragement toward a career of research. For a time he served as Johnson's assistant, and on June 23, 1886, married his daughter, Elizabeth Annah Johnson. Two children were born to them. In May 1886 Osborne became a member of the staff of the Connecticut Agricultural Experiment Station, where he labored until his retirement in 1928.

The first of the contributions that were destined to bring him recognition as the foremost expert on the proteins of plants was a paper on the oat-kernel published (1891) in the *Report* of the Experiment Station for 1890. This was followed in the next decade by descriptions of the proteins of no less than thirty-two different seeds. Such proteins were demonstrated to be well-characterized substances worthy of the intensive study of biochemists. This fact was further emphasized when Osborne succeeded in crystallizing many of the seed globulins, thereby rendering carefully purified proteins of definite individuality available for further investigation. Through his own researches on crystalline vegetable globulins, notably the edestin of hempseed, he demonstrated that proteins in general behave towards acids like bases, that they form salts both with acids and with alkalis, and show many evidences of a capacity to undergo electrolytic dissociation and enter into ionic reactions.

Beginning in 1906, with the aid of a number of younger collaborators, he began a series of laborious, carefully executed hydrolytic decompositions of purified proteins that have added greatly to the understanding of their amino acid components. These analyses helped to pave the way for the extensive researches on the nutritive properties or biological value of various proteins which he began in collaboration with Prof. Lafayette B. Mendel of Yale University in 1909. During a period of twenty years of fruitful cooperation in research they published more than a hundred papers in scientific journals. In these were recorded the development of technique for feeding individual small animals with mixtures of somewhat purified foodstuffs—the so-called "synthetic" diets. Among the outstanding contributions were the demonstrations of the unlike "biological value" of different proteins in nutrition and growth. In the course of these studies came the discovery that butter-fat, egg yolk, cod-liver oil, many green leaves, and other parts of plants and animals contain a substance, soluble in fats, that is an indispensable dietary requisite and has since been designated as vitamin A. Lack of this food factor may lead to the appearance of the eye disorder (xerophthalmia), to the genesis of urinary calculi, and to other pathological manifestations. What was subsequently termed vitamin B was also soon brought into the picture of adequate nutrition. Extensive reports were made of the distribution of various vitamins in natural food products. The phenomena of growth, its suppression and acceleration under various regimens, and the effect of the individual inorganic constituents of the diet received attention.

A detailed catalogue of Osborne's further contributions (see *Thomas B. Osborne—a Memorial*) includes investigations of the wheat plant for which he was the first to receive the Thomas Burr Osborne gold medal founded by the American Association of Cereal Chemists in recognition of his outstanding contributions to cereal chemistry. Appreciation of the fundamental character of his protein investigations came early from Germany, where his paper on the oat-kernel was translated and published by V. Griessmayer in 1897. Osborne's own monograph *The Vegetable Proteins,* which first appeared in 1909 and was extensively revised in 1924, is a classic in biochemical literature. Somewhat related to the demonstrations of the unlike biological values of the proteins are the investigations of their immunological or anaphylactogenic properties conducted with great success in collaboration with Prof. H. Gideon Wells of the University of Chicago.

Honors came to Osborne from various sources;

he was elected a member of many learned societies at home and abroad, including the National Academy of Sciences. During the last seven years of his life he was a research associate in biochemistry in Yale University, a designation of distinction that conferred full professorial rank. The breadth of his knowledge and interest is revealed by the fact that in addition to his intense scientific activities, recorded in more than 250 papers and monographs, he served for years as a director of the Second National Bank of New Haven, his acumen in financial matters as well as his lively interest in the political questions and economic problems of the day making him well qualified and most acceptable to the directorate. One of his scientific associates has pointed out (*Thomas B. Osborne—a Memorial*, p. 371) that "few chemists have been privileged to follow the dictates of their interest so long and successfully without the interruptions or distractions that may retard the progress of the devotees of science." Another intimate colleague (*Ibid.*, p. 282) described him as "a wholesome clean-minded man, quick, impulsive, generous and broadminded and in all ways companionable."

[Outlines of Osborne's career will be found in *Who's Who in America*, 1928–29; and in J. M. and Jaques Cattell, *Am. Men of Sci.*, vol. IV (1927). In *Thomas B. Osborne—a Memorial* (Feb. 1930), Bull. 312, Conn. Agric. Experiment Station, are collected a number of biographical sketches (with a photograph), a complete bibliography of his publications, a paper on "The Work of Thomas Burr Osborne" by his associates L. B. Mendel and H. B. Vickery, first published in *Science*, Apr. 12, 1929, and appreciations by Vickery in *Yale Jour. of Biology and Medicine*, Mar. 1929, by Mendel in *Am. Jour. Sci.*, Apr. 1929, by H. D. D. in *Jour. of the Chem. Soc.* (London), 1929, pt. II, p. 2974, and by H. L. Knight in *Experiment Station Record* (U. S. Dept. of Agric.), June 1929. See also obituary in *New Haven Journal Courier*, Jan. 30, 1929.]   L. B. M.

OSBORNE, THOMAS MOTT (Sept. 23, 1859–Oct. 20, 1926), prison reformer, was born at Auburn, N. Y. His father, David Munson Osborne, a manufacturer of agricultural implements, was descended from Richard Osborn of London, England, who, in 1634, settled in Hingham, Mass.; his mother, Eliza (Wright), came of old Pennsylvania Quaker stock. The wealth of his family gave him an opportunity to travel and to receive the cultural education of the privileged few. Upon his graduation from Harvard *cum laude* in 1884 he began an apprenticeship in his father's manufacturing establishment, and on Oct. 27, 1886, married Agnes Devens of Cambridge. After his father's death, he was head of the firm until 1903, when it was absorbed by the International Harvester Company.

Politics interested him early. As member of the Auburn school board, 1885–91 and 1893–95, and as mayor, 1903–06, he proved himself efficient and honest. He soon became recognized as a leader of the upstate Democrats, for short periods held appointive state offices, and served as delegate to the state and national conventions of his party. His avocational interests centered largely around music and dramatics, and he organized and directed in his home city both a symphony orchestra and a dramatic club. His talent as a pianist was particularly a source of enjoyment to himself and to his friends.

Osborne's untiring work for prison reform was his outstanding achievement. Soon after his wife's death in 1896 he became interested in the George Junior Republic, and served for many years as a member and, later, as chairman of its governing board. To this work may be traced his interest in prison administration. In 1906 he concluded an address to the National Prison Association with these words, "The prison must be an institution where every inmate must have the largest practical amount of individual freedom, because 'it is liberty alone that fits men for liberty'" (*Proceedings . . .*, 1906, p. 38). These words of Gladstone thus became for him the guide to a better system of prison treatment. His opportunity to test their validity came in 1913 with his appointment to the chairmanship of the newly created state commission for prison reform. He began his duties in a most unorthodox manner by "serving" a week's term in the Auburn prison; the graphic account of this experience may be found in *Within Prison Walls* (1914). As "Tom Brown" he sought to know how life in prison affected those subjected to it, and he emerged convinced that the conventional treatment crushed the individuality and destroyed the manhood and self-respect of the prisoners, the very foundation on which reformation must rest. During his confinement a prisoner had suggested to him a plan which took form in the famous Mutual Welfare League, through which Auburn prisoners, under sympathetic guidance, achieved a sense of corporate responsibility, which became a powerful force in refittting them for social life. From 1914 to 1916, as warden of Sing Sing, and from 1917 to 1920, as commanding officer of the Portsmouth Naval Prison, Osborne used the Mutual Welfare League plan with conspicuous success. A splendid educational tool was in this way strikingly adapted to prison conditions, and even though the idea of self-government was by no means new, Osborne will probably be remembered as one of its conspicuous exponents, so far as its use in prison administration is concerned. In his two books, *Society and Prisons*

(1916) and *Prisons and Common Sense* (1924), his penal philosophy is well presented, particularly in the former.

Osborne was a man of a singularly fine and upright character. Tall and athletic, he gave the impression of rugged physical strength, and equally strong was his passion for justice and fair dealing. His public life was consequently turbulent, for while he called forth a keen loyalty in most of those who learned to know him intimately, his intransigency and his intolerance of opposition also created for him vigorous enmities. During his prison administration in Sing Sing, particularly, his unsparing criticism of political interference subjected him to the vilest abuse, which culminated in an indictment by the Westchester County grand jury, December 1915, on charges of mismanagement and immorality; the case never came to trial. After his resignation from Portsmouth in 1920, he spent the remaining years of his life lecturing and writing on prison reform. The finest monument to his memory is the "Tom Brown" house in New York City, headquarters of two organizations which he founded and which have recently been merged under the title "The Osborne Association." One of these was the Welfare League Association, an aid society for discharged prisoners, and the other, the National Society of Penal Information, which on the basis of field studies of actual prison conditions, conducts an intelligent propaganda for prison reform. He died in Auburn, N. Y., survived by four sons.

[W. R. Cutter, *Geneal. and Family Hist. of the State of Conn.* (1911), vol. III; *N. Y. Times*, Oct. 21, 1926; J. J. Chapman, "Thomas Mott Osborne" and "Osborne's Place in Hist. Criminology," *Harvard Graduates' Mag.*, March, June 1927; *Thomas Mott Osborne*, pamphlet of memorial addresses published by the Nat. Soc. of Penal Information (n.d.); Frank Tannenbaum in *The Survey*, Oct. 1930–Mar. 1931, and *Osborne of Sing Sing* (1933); F. H. Wines, *Punishment and Reformation* (1919), ed. by W. I. Lane; F. E. Haynes, *Criminology* (1930); C. M. Liepmann, *Die Selbstverwaltung der Gefangenen* (1926); *Who's Who in America, 1926–27*; genealogical information from a son, Charles D. Osborne.]

T. S—n.

OSCEOLA (c. 1800–Jan. 30, 1838), leader in the Second Seminole War, was born probably on the Tallapoosa River among the Creek Indians in what is now the state of Georgia. He was also known as Powell, a name that is explained variously as being that of a Scots father, grandfather, or step-father. Yet in spite of widespread opinion to the contrary it seems probable that he was of pure Indian blood and was a remarkably handsome example of a typical "full-blood and wild Indian" (Catlin's notes in Donaldson, *post*, p. 217; Welch, *post*, pp. 23–24). He is said to have fought against Jackson during the War of 1812 and again in 1818. About 1832 he was living near Fort King, visited the fort frequently, and was from time to time employed to restrain predatory Indians or to arrest deserters from the army. Gradually he began to assume a position of consequence among the Indians, although he had not been born to high rank nor is there any record that he was ever formally chosen a chief. He opposed the treaty of 1832 at Payne's Landing, in which some of the lesser chiefs agreed to removal across the Mississippi within three years, and he rejected the treaty of the next year at Fort Gibson, where some of the Seminoles were tricked into seeming to agree to immediate removal. He was present on Apr. 22, 1835, at the meeting called by Wiley Thompson [*q.v.*] in an effort to persuade the chiefs to acknowledge the treaty of Payne's Landing. Although most of the chiefs contented themselves with a silent refusal to touch the pen to such an instrument, Osceola is reported to have plunged his great knife into the paper in a dramatic gesture of defiance. He was arrested and imprisoned until, feigning a change of heart, he was released with the understanding that he would use his influence in favor of immediate emigratiton.

Instead, he gathered the forces of opposition, accomplished the murder of Wiley Thompson and Charley Emathla, a chief who had signed the treaty of Fort Gibson, and precipitated the Second Seminole War, in which his skill and ruthless daring carried him to a position of authentic leadership. He hid the women and children of the tribe in the great swamps of the region and led the warriors in the perilous work of harassing the white army. He was so successful in his guerrilla tactics as to arouse public criticism of the army and, especially, of its leader, Gen. Thomas S. Jesup [*q.v.*], who, goaded by failure and actuated by the kind of ruthlessness common to both soldiers and civilians on the frontier, ordered Osceola to be seized when he came for an interview in October 1837. In spite of the revulsion of public opinion caused by such a violation of the flag of truce, Osceola was taken to Fort Marion at Saint Augustine and later removed to Fort Moultrie near Charleston, S. C., where he died.

[Files of the Office of Indian Affairs; C. H. Coe, *Red Patriots* (1898), according to a statement by the Indian Office never suppressed by it; Grant Foreman, *Indian Removal* (1932); Andrew Welch, *A Narrative of . . . Oceola Nikkanochee . . . with . . . Hist. of Oceola* (1841); J. T. Sprague, *The Origin . . . of the Florida War* (1848); Thomas Donaldson, "The George Catlin Indian Gallery in the U. S. National Museum," in *Annual Report of the Board of Regents of the Smithsonian Institution*, 1885; *Army and Navy*

Chronicle, Jan. 21, Feb. 18, Mar. 31, Apr. 7, 1836, Dec. 14, 1837; Niles' Weekly Register, Jan. 30, Feb. 6, 20, 1836, Nov. 4, 1837; Niles' National Register, Feb. 3, 17, 1838.]   K. E. C.

OSGOOD, FRANCES SARGENT LOCKE

(June 18, 1811–May 12, 1850), poet, was descended from William Locke who emigrated from England to Massachusetts in 1635. The daughter of Joseph Locke, merchant, and Mary (Ingersoll) Foster Locke, she was born at Boston but lived in childhood in Hingham, Mass. A brother, sister, and half-sister (Anna Maria Foster Locke) wrote verse, and her parents encouraged Fanny to do likewise. Under the pseudonym "Florence," she contributed to the *Juvenile Miscellany* edited by Mrs. Child. In 1834 while preparing verses on the paintings at the Boston Athenæum, she met one of the exhibitors, Samuel Stillman Osgood, a painter of some talent. She sat to him for a portrait and on Oct. 7, 1835, married him. With her husband she soon sailed for London, where Osgood had studied at the Royal Academy. He now gave his time to painting portraits, while she continued to write. The attractive young matron was taken up by Mrs. Norton, mingled in literary circles, contributed to magazines, and published a miniature volume, *The Casket of Fate* (2nd ed., Boston, 1840). A daughter, Ellen Frances, was born July 15, 1836. In 1838 appeared a volume of poems, *A Wreath of Wild Flowers from New England* (reissued, N. Y., 1842), which was well received, though her English fame was slight enough to make Elizabeth Barrett ask Browning in 1845 if he had ever heard of her. The collection contained a drama, *Elfrida*, with some good scenes and one mighty line. Sheridan Knowles asked her to write a play for him, and the result was *The Happy Release, or the Triumphs of Love*, which reached neither the boards nor (apparently) the printer. Her father's death in 1839 called the Osgoods to Boston, where on July 21 a second daughter, May Vincent, was born. The family moved to New York, and Mrs. Osgood contributed to most of the better literary periodicals of the day. Her output included many poems and occasional prose tales, usually including verses. She sometimes used the pen name, Kate Carol. She had an editorial connection with *Snowden's Ladies Companion*, which was merely nominal, but she wrote or prepared for the press several volumes, including *The Poetry of Flowers and the Flowers of Poetry* (1841, often reprinted); *The Snowdrop, a New Year Gift for Children*, and *The Rose, Sketches in Verse* (both Providence, 1842); *Puss in Boots* (1844); *The Cries of New York* (1846); *The Flower Alphabet* (Boston, n.d.). In March 1845, she met Edgar Allan Poe [*q.v.*], with whom her romantic story "Ida Grey" (*Graham's Magazine*, August 1845) and contemporary comment indicate she fell in love. Poe and she were much together at literary gatherings—where Rufus W. Griswold [*q.v.*] was another admirer—they wrote verses to each other, and the critic, willingly blind, gave unmeasured praise in "The Literati" and elsewhere to her mild poetry. When his inspiration failed, he asked her to write a poem for him to deliver in November 1845, in Boston, but her "Lulin" proved unsuitable. Her friendship with Poe was one cause of the quarrels that led to Poe's libel suit against Thomas Dunn English [*q.v.*]. Poe and Frances Osgood probably ceased to meet about 1847, but were not embittered. A selection, *Poems*, was issued in 1846 and a larger selection under the same title appeared with illustrations in 1850; both were occasionally reprinted, the smaller as late as 1861. A daughter, Fanny Fay, born in 1846, died early; the mother was consumptive, but continued to write voluminously. A little pamphlet, *A Letter about the Lions* (1849), was her last separate work—a gentle satire. Her husband went off to California in 1849 without her and returned to find her very ill. They moved into a new home at 112 West 22nd St., New York, where she died on May 12, 1850. She was buried in Mount Auburn Cemetery, Cambridge, Mass. In 1851 her friends published *The Memorial, Written by Friends of the late Mrs. . . . Osgood*, edited by Mary E. Hewitt; it was reissued as *Laurel Leaves* in 1854. A little faded charm still clings to a few of her poems, the lines on Fanny Ellsler, the hymn "Labor," the requiem for Poe, and the songs "Call me pet names" and "My heart is a Music-Box," but she is remembered chiefly as a friend of Poe.

[Biographical sketches of Frances Osgood include one by Griswold in *The Memorial* named above (reprinted in the *International Magazine*, Dec. 1, 1850) and a very good one in J. G. Locke, *Book of the Lockes* (1853). See also the works of Poe; biographies of Poe; and W. M. Griswold's *Passages from the Correspondence of and Other Papers of Rufus W. Griswold* (1898); obituaries in the *N. Y. Daily Tribune*, May 13, 14, 1850, and the *N. Y. Herald*, May 13, 1850; and an article by H. F. Harrington in the *Critic*, Oct. 3, 1880. Many of her papers are preserved with those of Griswold, her literary executor, in the Boston Public Library. A charming portrait by her husband, together with his pictures of Griswold and Poe, are in the N. Y. Hist. Soc. Some of her minor volumes are very rare, no copies of the London *Casket of Fate*, or *The Rose* (mentioned by Griswold) were located by the writer; her *Lines to Mr. Dodson* (Brooklyn, 1885) was issued in an edition of only ten copies. For discussion of some disputed dates of her children's births, etc., see article by T. O. Mabbott in *Notes and Queries*, Jan. 10, 1931.

A book on Frances Osgood is in preparation by Annie Barcus Minga.]
                         T. O. M.

OSGOOD, GEORGE LAURIE (Apr. 3, 1844–Dec. 12, 1922), singer, composer, conductor, and teacher, was born in Chelsea, Mass., the son of John Hamilton Osgood and Adeline (Stevens) Osgood, and a descendant of John Osgood who emigrated to Massachusetts in 1638. As a child he showed an acute sense of pitch, and was given every musical advantage from his earliest years. At Harvard, where he was graduated in 1866, after studying composition and the organ under John Knowles Paine [q.v.], he directed the college glee club and orchestra for three successive years. After graduation he went to Germany, where he remained three years studying singing in Berlin under Ferdinand Sieber and Karl August Haupt, the former famous as an exponent of the old Italian tradition, and German song and choral music with Robert Franz. He then went to Italy for three years of further vocal study at Milan under Francesco Lamperti, after which he made a successful concert tour of Germany. As a result he was engaged in 1872 by Theodore Thomas [q.v.] for a winter tour of the United States with his orchestra as tenor soloist. For some thirty years thereafter Osgood played a leading part in Boston's musical life. He was very popular as a teacher and brought out a number of successful singers. He also directed an annual series of chamber-music concerts of a high quality, and completely transformed the Boylston Club of Boston, of which he was conductor from 1875 to 1893, from a male chorus into a mixed choral organization of two hundred voices. Under the name of the Boston Singers' Society (1890), he established its reputation for brilliant performance of difficult pieces. He translated the texts of many choral works and songs, and published a *Guide in the Art of Singing* (copr. 1874), which by 1917 had gone through eight editions. He also composed a number of part-songs and anthems and fifty songs, besides editing *The Boylston Collection of Choruses.* On Apr. 15, 1868, he married Jeannette Cabot Farley, by whom he had three children; she died Aug. 24, 1888, and on June 27, 1891, he married June Bright. After 1903 he made his home in Europe, first in Geneva, and later, in Godalming, England, where he had a large country estate and where he died.

[Ira Osgood and Eben Putnam, *A Geneal. of the Descendants of John, Christopher, and William Osgood* (1894); *Musical America*, Dec. 23, 1922; *Musical Courier*, Dec. 28, 1922; *Who's Who in America*, 1918–19; death notice in *The Times* (London), Dec. 14, 1922.]
                         F. H. M.

OSGOOD, HERBERT LEVI (Apr. 9, 1855–Sept. 11, 1918), historian, was born on a farm in Canton, Me., in the upper Androscoggin valley, the son of Stephen and Joan (Staples) Osgood. He was descended from John Osgood, who came from Hampshire, England, probably in 1638, lived for a time at Ipswich, Mass., and in 1645 settled in Andover. Intelligently encouraged at home, he passed through the local district school and the Wilton (Me.) Academy to Amherst College. Here he was influenced toward historical scholarship by Professors Julius H. Seelye and Anson D. Morse [qq.v.] and especially by J. W. Burgess, and graduated in 1877, fifth in a class of seventy-nine of which he was president. He taught numerous subjects for two years in Worcester (Mass.) Academy, and then carried on post-graduate study under Morse (taking the M.A. degree in 1880) and at Yale under William Graham Sumner. In 1882–83 he studied in Berlin under Wagner, Schmoller, Gneist, and Treitschke. He saw Ranke several times and in general adopted his view of the province and method of history. Returning to New England he briefly filled in teaching in Amherst and Smith colleges, and in the autumn of 1883 took a position in the Brooklyn (N. Y.) High School, which he held for six years. While teaching there he studied under Burgess and others at Columbia, where the School of Political Science had already reached high development, and in 1889 won his Ph.D. degree with a dissertation on *Socialism and Anarchism* (1889), being a study primarily of the works of Rodbertus and Proudhon.

Upon economic theory, however, he was not to concentrate his interest. He desired a field unworked with the tools of scientific method, marked off by clear boundaries and not too large for the employment of one lifetime; the political history of the English colonies on the American continent he regarded as meeting these specifications. In an article on "England and the Colonies" (*Political Science Quarterly,* Sept. 1887), he urged sympathetic study of the British colonial policy. He was one of the first if not the first university professor in America to question the legal justification of the Revolution, however inevitable it may have been on geographical, economic, and psychological grounds. In 1889–90 he spent fifteen months in the Public Record Office in London carrying on investigations. He was then called to Columbia, advancing to full professor in 1896. Though he taught general European history and the constitutional history of England, he progressively concentrated on the American colonies; from his seminar there began to come a series of more than fifty doctoral dissertations illuminating the early history of every one of the thirteen colonies and Canada as well as phases of British imperial administration in London. He was deeply conscientious in guiding students' researches, sometimes exchanging fifty or sixty letters with a candidate in addition to many personal conferences. He and his students generally confined themselves to legal institutions. "Social and economic forces," he said in 1898 (*Columbia University Bulletin,* June 1898, p. 186), "should be treated as contributing to and conditioning historical development, but the historian must never lose sight of the fact that they operate within a framework of law." A little later in the same year he pronounced his dictum more definitely: "It is only through law and political institutions that social forces become in the large sense operative" (*Annual Report of the American Historical Association for the Year 1898,* 1899, p. 68). Abandoning the customary geographico-economic grouping of the colonies—northern, middle, and southern—he classified them according to their law and polity: royal and chartered, with the latter divided into proprietary and corporate. Three articles in the *Political Science Quarterly* (June–Oct. 1896) on "The Colonial Corporation," and three in the *American Historical Review* (July, Oct. 1897, Jan. 1898) on "The Proprietary Province as a Form of Colonial Government" had contained the elements of the design worked out in the first two volumes of *The American Colonies in the Seventeenth Century* which appeared in 1904. The third volume, published in 1907, traced imperial control throughout the same period. In 1908 he received the Loubat prize for the best work on early American history published during the previous five years.

Realizing that imperial records grew more indispensable as the scholar came forward in the eighteenth century, he went to London again in 1909 and remained there sixteen months; five years later he returned for four months more. By means of grants from Columbia University and the Carnegie Institution he was able to employ copyists during these two visits and similar assistance thereafter in America. At the time of his death in 1918 he had virtually completed his four volumes on *The American Colonies in the Eighteenth Century,* carrying the narrative down to 1763; a fund provided by Dwight W. Morrow made possible their publication in 1924. In these volumes the author felt that he was pioneering, much of the period having had no general scientific treatment before. The whole seven-volume

work is largely the story of the struggle between British executives and colonial assemblies, wherein one may watch the development of the American political spirit which found expression in the Revolution. The posthumous volumes, like their predecessors, were honored with the Loubat prize in 1928.

He was a man of quiet manner, appreciative of music and pictorial art, and given to philosophical reflection. His life work is largely summed up in his seven volumes; he wrote no textbook, his nearest approach to it being the section he contributed on the early history of the United States in the *Encyclopedia Britannica* (11th ed., vol. XXVII, 663–84). He gave comparatively little attention to anything but teaching and writing his chapters, but in 1900 he made a report on the archives of New York for the American Historical Association (*Annual Report ... for the Year 1900,* 1901, vol. II, 67–250) which has remained an unequaled model for such surveys, and after long effort he was chiefly responsible for reforming the archival administration of the state in 1907. In 1905 were published the eight-volume *Minutes of the Common Council of the City of New York, 1675–1776,* which he edited. He was originally strong and athletic, but his severe regimen reduced him to frailty by the age of sixty. On July 22, 1885, he married Caroline Augusta Simonds, daughter of Rev. Alpha Hiram and Sarah (Pettibone) Simonds; she with a daughter and two sons survived him, but the sons died subsequently in early manhood.

[D. R. Fox, *Herbert Levi Osgood, An American Scholar* (1924), with portrait; obituaries in *N. Y. Times,* Sept. 13, 1918; the *Nation* (N. Y.), Sept. 21, 1918; *Columbia Univ. Quart.,* Jan. 1919; Eben Putnam, *A Genealogy of the Descendants of John, Christopher, and William Osgood* (1894), p. 184.]   D.R.F.

OSGOOD, HOWARD (Jan. 4, 1831–Nov. 28, 1911), Baptist clergyman, teacher, and author, was born on "Magnolia Plantation," in Plaquemines Parish, La., the son of Isaac and Jane Rebecca (Hall) Osgood. His father was of New England ancestry, a nephew of Samuel Osgood [*q.v.*]. Although a wealthy planter, he became thoroughly dissatisfied with slavery and moved North, settling near New York City. Born and reared an Episcopalian, Howard Osgood joined the Baptist Church from conviction and at considerable personal cost. Entering Harvard College in 1846, he left in 1849, but nine years later was awarded the degree of A.B. He made an intensive study of the Germany theology. Ordained a Baptist minister, Feb. 12, 1857, he served as pastor at Flushing, L. I., 1856–58, and of the North Baptist Church, New York City,

1860–66. From 1868 to 1874 he was professor of Hebrew at Crozer Theological Seminary, Chester, Pa., acting also as librarian.

It was at the Rochester Theological Seminary, however, that he made his record as a teacher. During 1875–76 he served as acting professor of church history and for the next twenty-five years was librarian and professor of Old Testament interpretation. He was a member of the famous quintet—Strong, Osgood, Stevens, Pattison, and True—which for the last quarter of the nineteenth century was the pride of that seminary. He was a chivalrous Southern gentleman given to hospitality. Master of five languages, devoted to archaeology, rigidly conservative, unwilling to grant any quarter to the historical method of investigation, he spoke and wrote in behalf of a very orthodox interpretation of the Old Testament. His Biblical point of view may be gathered from the following articles and booklets: *The Old Testament, What It Is and What It Teaches* (1879); *Short Sketch of the Christology of the Old Testament* (1880); *Essays in Pentateuchal Criticism* (1888); "Old Wine in New Wine Skins," *Bibliotheca Sacra* (July 1893); contributions to *Anti-higher Criticism* (1894), edited by L. W. Munhall; "President Harper's Lectures," *Bibliotheca Sacra* (April 1895). The arguments now advanced by Fundamentalists were vigorously pressed by him. Because of his union with the Baptist denomination, he wrote on the form and significance of baptism. His *Archaeology of Baptism* (32 pp., plates) contains much first-hand data. Since he regarded the Baptists and Anabaptists as intimately related, he formed at Rochester one of the best American collections of "Anabaptistica." His *Protestant Pedo-baptism and the Doctrine of a Church* (n.d.; Baptist Tracts, vol. II, no. 3) indicates how decisive his break with Anglicanism had been.

Named as a member of the American commission for the revision of the Scriptures, his research in connection with the work of this office resulted in the publication, 1899, of a seventy-four page booklet on *References to the Versions by British Revisers,* a critical study of the accuracy of British scholarship. His most excellent work as translator is found in his "Introduction to the Three Middle Books of the Pentateuch" in the second volume of Philip Schaff's American edition of John E. Lange's *Commentary on the Holy Scriptures.* In addition to the publications referred to, Osgood was also the author of *Grammar of the Hebrew Language for Beginners* (1895); *Old Testament Ethics* (n.d.); "The Oldest Book in the World," *Bibliotheca Sacra*

(October 1888); *Quotations of the Old Testament* (1880) and *Topics in the Psalms* (n.d.).

The last decade of his life although spent in retirement was occupied with diligent research and occasional lectures. On Apr. 14, 1853, he married Caroline Townsend Lawrence, by whom he had three sons and four daughters. He died at Rochester.

[See *Rochester Record,* May 1912 and Nov. 1917; *Who's Who in America,* 1910–11; *Jour. and Messenger,* Dec. 7, 1911; *Democrat and Chronicle* (Rochester, N. Y.), Nov. 29, 1911; Ira Osgood and Eben Putnam, *A Geneal. of the Descendants of John, Christopher, and William Osgood* (1894). The library of the Colgate-Rochester Divinity School contains most of his pamphlets, articles, and books.]   C. H. M.

OSGOOD, JACOB (Mar. 16, 1777–Nov. 29, 1844), religious enthusiast, founder of the Osgooodites, was born at South Hampton, N. H., the son of Philip Osgood, farmer, and a descendant of William Osgood, who emigrated to Salisbury, Mass., in 1638. Philip Osgood was married in succession to Elizabeth, Appia, and Mehitable Flanders, daughters of a South Hampton farmer; Jacob was probably son of Mehitable. In 1790 the family moved to Warner, N. H. Jacob became a farmer; he was also trained as a singer, and taught singing classes. In 1797 he married Miriam Stevens, by whom he had eight children.

In 1802 he was converted, but he rejected both Calvinism and Universalism as inventions of the devil. Although he felt himself ordered of God to preach, timidity prevented, and he became a "pharisee Christian," attending services in the Congregational meeting house. Again awakened religiously in 1805, he began to preach and cause disturbances in the meeting house at Warner and elsewhere. He joined the Freewill Baptists, but refused to acknowledge any theological principles except that one must love God and one's neighbor or be damned. This refusal, together with his unconventional methods of preaching, made him a suspect to the elders of the church. Others embraced his views and in 1812 the Osgooodites became a separate sect. They enjoyed occasional revivals, especially in 1816–17, and won disciples in Warner, Canterbury, Sutton, South Hampton, Newtown, Amesbury Mills, and Newbury-Byfield. As late as 1885 a few still bore the name.

Osgood believed that everything established by law was from the devil. He was particularly opposed to paid ministers, lawcourts, magistrates, town meetings, and military training; he said that it was wicked for Christians to fight. Between 1819 and 1826 a few of the sect were imprisoned and otherwise persecuted for refusing to attend training or pay the fines imposed for absence. Osgood himself had a heifer taken from him, and in 1820 was imprisoned for eleven days; while in prison he preached and sang to his followers through the bars, and also enjoyed much "good beer." When released, he refused to leave the jail, saying that he had been thrust in against his wish and must be carried out; he was, although it took several men to lift his ponderous frame. Members of the sect also suffered some ill treatment from their neighbors, but people soon realized that they were honest and harmless. They were opposed to doctors and practised faith healing. Osgood claims to have healed a consumptive girl by laying his hands on her, after doctors had said her case was hopeless. He is credited with remarkable powers of prayer. According to tradition, God often answered his petitions by sending rain after drought and fine weather after rain; on one occasion, it was said, when a frost in early autumn killed his neighbors' corn, through his prayer to God his own corn was spared. His curses were considered equally efficacious: two or three times persecutors were killed or hurt in accidents after Osgood had threatened them with the wrath of God. Osgoodite meetings were a disorderly mixture of hymns, prayers, and exhortations, in which all the brethren participated. When a lull came Osgood would dismiss them with the words: "If there's no more to be said, meeting's done." When he preached he sat in a chair, closed his eyes, and held the side of his face with one hand. Osgoodite hymns were composed by Osgood and other members of the sect; they consisted mostly of denunciations of clergymen, lawyers, doctors, Calvinists, Methodists, Baptists, Universalists, Millerites, Whig politicians, abolitionists, female reformers, tobacco-smokers, and builders of railroads. Though opposed to tobacco, the Osgoodites attacked the temperance movement because of its clerical origin.

Osgood weighed 345 pounds. He was simple, outspoken, and courageous. "He would talk and weep and laugh almost in the same instant, and his talk never seemed tedious." He was quick in repartee. In spite of his eccentricities he gives the impression of having tried sincerely to be a good Christian.

[*The Life and Christian Experience of Jacob Osgood, with Hymns and Spiritual Songs* (1873), a pamphlet, now rare, printed at Warner, N. H., a copy of which is owned by George H. Sargent, of Warner; Ira Osgood and Eben Putnam, *A Geneal. of the Descendants of John, Christopher, and William Osgood* (1894); Walter Harriman, *The Hist. of Warner, N. H.* (1879); F. M. Colby, "Hist. of Warner," in D. H. Hurd, *Hist. of Merrimack and Belknap Counties, N. H.* (1885); *N. H. Patriot and State Gazette* (Concord), Dec. 5, 1844, for death notice.]   H. B. P.

OSGOOD, SAMUEL (Feb. 3, 1747/48–Aug. 12, 1813), soldier, legislator, politician, was born in Andover, Mass. He was descended in the fifth generation from Capt. John Osgood who came to Massachusetts in 1638 and settled at Andover about 1645. Samuel was the third son of Capt. Peter Osgood and Sarah, daughter of Captain Timothy and Catherine (Sprague) Johnson. Educated at Harvard, he had planned to enter the ministry, but upon his graduation in 1770 he joined his brother Peter in business. Ill health is assigned for this change of purpose. With the outbreak of the Revolution young Osgood joined the army as captain of a company of minute men, became major and aide-de-camp to Gen. Artemas Ward [*q.v.*], and subsequently attained the rank of colonel. His legislative apprenticeship included service in the Essex convention (1774), in the Provincial Congress (1775 and after), in the constitutional convention of 1779, in the state Senate (1780), and in the Philadelphia convention for the limitation of prices (1780). Elected in February 1781, he took his seat in the Continental Congress on June 12, and was reëlected until, by virtue of the three-year limitation prescribed by the Articles of Confederation, his services were terminated, Mar. 1, 1784.

As a member of Congress he was alert and capable, serving on many important committees and having a hand in the preparation of numerous constructive measures, particularly those relating to business and finance. He was, for instance, appointed by Congress a director in the Bank of North America (Dec. 1, 1781) and was a member of the important treasury board throughout his three years of service. Marbois, the secretary of the French legation, himself favorably impressed with Osgood's ability and character, recorded that he was much esteemed for his good sense and integrity (*Affaires Étrangères, États-Unis, Mem. et Doc.*, I). Osgood, for his part, was among those who became decidedly suspicious of the designs of France. He was, in fact, one of that numerous group with whom fear of centralized power and of "aristocratical influence" was becoming an obsession. (See for instance his letters to John Adams and Stephen Higginson, in Burnett, *post*, VII, 378, 414, 430; and letter to John Adams, in *The Works of John Adams*, 1850–56, VIII, 418.) A particular manifestation of this feeling during the latter part of Osgood's career in Congress was directed against the one-man power in finance (Robert Morris) and the outcome was that in 1784 the treasury was put into commission. As Gerry, one of the promoters of the measure, had planned (Gerry to Stephen Higginson, May 13,

1784, Burnett, VII, 522), on Jan. 25, 1785, short-ly after Congress had removed to New York, Osgood was chosen one of the three commission-ers of the treasury. These—Osgood, Walter Liv-ingston, and Arthur Lee—conducted the business of the treasury until the establishment of the new system, with a secretary at the head, in September 1789.

It was altogether in keeping with Osgood's trend of thought in this period that he should oppose the new Constitution. It had cost him, he wrote to Samuel Adams, "many a sleepless night to find out the most obnoxious Part of the pro-posed Plan," and he had finally fixed upon "the exclusive Legislation in the Ten Miles Square" (Jan. 5, 1788, Samuel Adams Papers). Along with numerous others he had favored a "peram-bulatory" Congress (Burnett, VII, 349). Never-theless, he became sufficiently reconciled to the new government to seek an appointment under it, and Washington made him postmaster-general (confirmed Sept. 26, 1789). Osgood's plan for the postal service (*Annals of Congress*, 1 Cong. 2 Sess., cols. 2107–2114; *Am. State Papers: Post Office*, 1834, p. 5) emphasized the importance of connecting the capital with the "extremes," but Congress failed to enact a new measure respect-ing the department until after his retirement. Upon the removal of the government to Phila-delphia he resigned and was succeeded by Tim-othy Pickering [*q.v.*] in August 1791. (For one explanation of his resignation see Octavius Pick-ering and C. W. Upham, *Life of Timothy Pick-ering*, 1873, II, 502.)

No doubt the ties he had established in New York influenced his decision to remain there. His first wife, Martha Brandon, to whom he was married Jan. 4, 1775, had died in 1778 and on May 24, 1786, he had married Maria (Bowne) Franklin, widow of Walter Franklin of New York City. The Franklins were connected with the Clintons by marriage, and this fact doubtless contributed toward bringing about close political relations between Osgood and DeWitt Clinton. In the ten years following 1791 he appears to have taken only minor parts in politics, devoting himself particularly to theological studies. In the campaign of 1800, however, he won election to the New York assembly, and was chosen speak-er. He also won in this campaign a most un-flattering portrait from the vitriolic pen of "Aristides" (William P. Van Ness), who re-ferred to him sarcastically as "that learned and pious expounder of the prophecies" (*An Exami-nation of the Various Charges Exhibited Against Aaron Burr*, new ed., 1804, pp. 31–33). A friend of Jefferson since Congressional days and now a thoroughgoing Republican, Osgood lost no time in offering to the new President his serv-ices (letter to Madison, Apr. 24, 1801, Madison Papers), and was rewarded with the office of supervisor of internal revenue for the district of New York (see his letter to Jefferson, Mar. 30, 1802, Jefferson Papers). A more desirable ap-pointment shortly followed, May 10, 1803, when he was made naval officer of the port of New York. This office he retained until his death. Note-worthy among the acts of his life as a public-spirited citizen of New York was his work as an organizer and incorporator of the Society . . . for the Establishment of a Free School for the Education of Poor Children, later known as the Free School Society, and still later, as the Pub-lic School Society. He was also one of the founders of the American Academy of Fine Arts.

[Letters of Osgood are found in a number of dif-ferent repositories, particularly the N. Y. Pub. Lib. (Samuel Adams Papers and the Emmet Collection), the Mass. Archives, and the Mass. Hist. Soc. (Knox Papers, Heath Papers, Pickering Papers). A body of Osgood Pa-pers is in the N. Y. Hist. Soc. The records of the Board of Treasury, 1784–89, are in the Papers of the Conti-nental Congress, nos. 138–146; to be supplemented by Washington's Letter-Book, no. 8 (Lib. of Cong.). The principal printed sources are: Ira Osgood and Eben Putnam, *A Geneal. of the Descendants of John, Chris-topher, and William Osgood* (1894); *New-England Hist. and Geneal. Reg.*, Jan. 1866; J. G. Wilson, *The Memorial Hist. of the City of N. Y.*, vol. III (1893); M. J. Lamb, *Hist. of the City of N. Y.*, vol. II (copr. 1880); D. S. Alexander, *A Political Hist. of the State of N. Y.*, vol. I (1906); E. C. Burnett, *Letters of Mem-bers of the Continental Congress*, vols. V, VI, VII (1931–34); *Jours. of the Continental Congress*; *N. Y. Gazette & General Advertiser*, Aug. 14, 1813.] E. C. B.

O'SHEA, MICHAEL VINCENT (Sept. 17, 1866–Jan. 14, 1932), educator, author, was the second of the ten children of Michael and Mar-garet (Fitzgerald) O'Shea of LeRoy, N. Y. Michael senior had come to the United States from Valencia, Ireland, at about the close of the Civil War and engaged in farming, of which his son had experience in his youth. Much more important in shaping him, however, were his elder-brother responsibilities for the eight young-er children, since out of these responsibilities seems to have developed his life interest in child-welfare. From the LeRoy Academy he entered Cornell University in 1889 and received the de-gree of bachelor of letters in 1892. Between academy and university he had taught in country schools, and in the university he planned his course with a view to teaching. After his grad-uation he was for three years professor of psy-chology and education at the state normal school, Mankato, Minn. In 1894 he married Harriet Frisbie Eastabrooks of Milledgeville, Ill., who also was a teacher in the normal school at Man-kato. In 1895 he became professor of pedagogy in the Teachers College, Buffalo, N. Y. Two years later President Charles Kendall Adams of the University of Wisconsin, who as president of Cornell had known O'Shea as a student, induced him to come to Wisconsin as professor of education. This position he held to the time of his death.

From 1897 to the end of his life he interspersed his classroom duties with lecturing throughout the United States on subjects concerned with child welfare and education. With a talent for clear and lucid statement, he developed unusual skill in popularizing educational theory, and on the public platform his powers of interpretation were continually in wide demand. For this form of service his intellectual resourcefulness, his native wit, his dynamic vigor, and his charm of personality were invaluable assets. The field of this activity was extended to England and Scotland in 1905, 1906, and 1910, during which years, too, he studied the European schools. In 1905 he was chairman of the American committee at the International Congress of Education at Liège, Belgium, and in 1910 of the International Congress of Home Education at Brussels. His counsel was widely sought by parents, school boards, and both city and state boards of education. In 1925 he made a survey of the all-year schools of Newark, N. J. In 1925–26 he directed an all-state survey of Mississippi's educational system, and in 1927 of Virginia's.

In the field of authorship he was continuously active, his most important productions being *Education as Adjustment* (1903); *Linguistic Development and Education* (1907); *Social Development and Education* (1909); *Mental Development and Education* (1921); *The Child— His Nature and His Needs* (1924); *Newer Ways with Children* (1929). He also contributed to the authorship of various series of elementary school textbooks. At the time of his death he was chairman of the educational board of the Children's Book Club; editor-in-chief of *The World Book Encyclopedia* (19 vols., 1933), of the *Junior Home Magazine,* and of *The Nation's Schools.* He held membership and offices in various scientific and educational associations. The vital imagination and genial curiosity that were his made him welcome and useful among a host of friends. His religious affiliations were with the Congregational Church and he was long officially connected with the Young Men's Christian Association and the Young Women's Christian Association. His wife, two sons, and two daughters survived him.

[*Who's Who in America,* 1930–31; *Wis. State Jour.* (Madison), Jan. 18, 1932; *Jour. of Education,* Jan. 25, 1932; *School and Society,* Feb. 27, 1932; R. G. Thwaites, *The Univ. of Wis., Its Hist. and Its Alumni* (1900).]
W. J. C.

OSLER, WILLIAM (July 12, 1849–Dec. 29, 1919), physician, born at Bond Head, Upper Canada, was the youngest son of the Rev. Featherstone Lake Osler and Ellen Free (Pickton) Osler, who had come from Cornwall in 1837 and were of Anglo-Saxon and Celtic extraction respectively. The father, derived from a family of merchants and ship-owners, was of thick-set build and fair complexion, and was reserved in temperament, though he made himself beloved. The mother, born in London, was slender, short, and of olive complexion; in her girlhood, she was pretty, clever, witty, lively, quick at repartee, wilful but good-tempered, not easily influenced, faithful in friendship, and of strong religious bent. Health and longevity characterized both the Osler and Pickton families. William Osler resembled his mother in mental and emotional traits as well as in personal appearance, though he was also like a paternal uncle, Edward, a navy surgeon and general medical practitioner, of dark complexion and short stature, who was interested in writing and in natural history. As a boy, William Osler was rather undersized, but wiry and well-proportioned, supple in body, with an elastic swinging step; he excelled in cricket, football, and swimming, and was of impulsive but generous temperament. He was full of pranks and practical jokes which were usually harmless but sometimes led to regrets, as when he once killed a pig with a stone, or when he chopped off the tip of his sister's finger, or when he and eight comrades, "fumigated" the house-keeper of a school and in consequence spent a few days in jail and were fined.

After attendance at grammar schools in Dundas and Barrie, Ont., he entered Trinity College School at Weston in 1866, where he came into contact with two strong personalities: first, with the founder of the school and its warden, the Rev. W. A. Johnson, "who knew nature and how to get boys interested in it" (Cushing, *post,* I, 27) and to use books of reference, and, second, with its medical director, Dr. James Bovell, a man of boundless ambition combined with energy and industry but with the "fatal fault of diffuseness," an omnivorous reader, who at this time and during the next few years exerted an extraordinary influence upon the young Osler. While at Weston, he became head prefect, acquired knowledge easily (though he disliked mathematics), won the Chancellor's Prize, and became interested in diatoms and fresh water polyzoa. Through "Father" Johnson's influence, he learned to love the Bible and Sir Thomas Browne's *Religio Medici*.

Though Osler had expected to take holy orders, he decided, apparently under the influence of Bovell and of Johnson, to abandon theology and become a physician. Entering the Toronto Medical School in the autumn of 1868, he worked there and in Bovell's library for two years, after which he went to McGill Medical School, Montreal, because of the better clinical opportunities it afforded. Here he graduated in 1872. In Toronto, at the age of twenty, he had begun what he later called his "ink-pot career" by a brief sketch entitled "Christmas and the Microscope" (published in *Hardwicke's Science-Gossip*, Feb. 1, 1869); and in Montreal, at the age of twenty-two, he began to report cases in medical journals. He had great admiration for one of his McGill teachers, Dr. Robert Palmer Howard, a courtly, scholarly gentleman, who worked hard in the hospital, studied medical literature assiduously, was ever alert to new problems, wrote excellent clinical papers, and, with his colleagues, taught with extraordinary care and accuracy by the methods of the Edinburgh School, introducing the pupils to the writings of Graves, Stokes, and Laennec. Osler, later in life, asserted that to Johnson, Bovell, and Howard he owed his success—"if success means getting what you want and being satisfied with it" (*The Master Word in Medicine*, 1903, quoted by Cushing, I, 69).

After graduation, he spent two years (1872–74) in study in Europe, visiting clinics in Great Britain, in Berlin, and in Vienna. He "walked the hospitals" with Murchison, Jenner, Wilson Fox, Ringer, and Bastian in London, with Traube and Frerichs in Berlin, and with Bamberger, Neumann, and Hebra and other famous specialists in Vienna; but he spent most of his time at work in histology, physiology, and experimental pathology in Burdon Sanderson's laboratory at University College Hospital in London. In this laboratory, he studied the antagonistic action of atropin and physostigmin upon the white blood corpuscles, and observed in the circulating blood, before anyone else, the presence of what later were called the "blood-platelets," describing them so carefully that the results of the studies were presented to the Royal Society (*Proceedings*, vol. XXII, 1874, pp. 391 ff.).

In 1874, he returned to Canada, did a little practice as substitute for another physician in Dundas, where he earned his first professional fee—"speck in cornea...50c" (Cushing, I, 120), served a month as *locum tenens* for the resident physician of the City Hospital in Hamilton "for the consideration of $25.00 and a pair of old-fashioned elastic-sided boots" (*Ibid.*), and then received an offer of a lectureship upon the institutes of medicine in McGill Medical School, which he accepted. In 1875, upon the death of Dr. J. M. Drake, he was officially appointed professor. While at work in histology and physiology, he was industrious also in other pursuits; he performed many autopsies, worked in the smallpox wards (where he contracted the disease himself), read widely and voraciously, helped the library, started a Journal Club, wrote for the medical journals, delivered inspiring addresses, enlivened interest in medical associations, contributed specimens to the museums, saw a few patients in consultation, participated energetically and whole-heartedly in all the medical activities of the city, and infected others with his enthusiasm. In 1876, a new position, pathologist to the Montreal General Hospital, was created for him, and a demonstration course in pathology, modeled upon that of Virchow, which he had observed in Berlin, was immediately undertaken. Three large quarto volumes of records of the autopsies made, written in his own hand, have been preserved. During this period, he held also a professorship in the Veterinary College and maintained an interest in comparative physiology and pathology, making reports upon broncho-pneumonia of parasitic origin in dogs, hog cholera, and bovine tuberculosis. One who knew him at this time commented upon his abounding vitality, his love of work, his promptness, alertness, and cheerfulness, his refusal to think ill of anyone, or to listen to ill-natured gossip or censure, his freedom from self-conceit and boastfulness, his happy knack of friendliness to people of all ages and conditions, and " 'his outgiving, expressing nature, sympathetic and true' " (*Ibid.*, 162).

Along with the laboratory work mentioned, he kept up his interest in clinical medicine, with the result that, in 1878, he was appointed "full physician" to the Montreal General Hospital. He thereupon went to London to take membership in the Royal College of Physicians and to observe clinical work for three months with Murchison, Gee, Roberts, Bastian, Ringer, Sutton, Savage, and Gowers, thus beginning a habit that he strongly recommended to others—that of "quinquennial brain-dusting" (*The Student Life*, 1905, quoted by Cushing, I, 167). At this time he made the acquaintance of Grainger Stewart, Jonathan Hutchinson, Clifford Allbutt, Gairdner, and Broadbent, all of whom he admired for their ideals and their practical clinical methods. While he was attending physician in Montreal, the section of the hospital of which he was given charge underwent a revolution. Though patients were given very little medicine (Osler's treatment has been described as "a mixture of nux vomica and hope"), many recovered readily by virtue of his interest and encouragement; the old patients rapidly disappeared, and new ones stayed but a short time. During this Montreal period, his studies of the anaemias, of aneurysms, and of endocarditis and valvular disease of the heart were notable.

As early as 1884, the year after he was elected a fellow of the Royal College of Physicians of London, he had recognized the possibilities of medical school work on a university basis; he felt sure that greater results would be achieved if there could be better laboratories and a paid staff: "men placed above the worries and vexations of practice, and whose time will be devoted solely to teaching and investigating the subjects they profess" ("On the University Question," editorial in *Canada Medical and Surgical Journal,* January 1884). The summer of that year he spent in Europe (London, Berlin, Leipzig) and while there was offered and accepted appointment as professor of clinical medicine in the University of Pennsylvania. The decision to leave Montreal was difficult, and had to be made, he asserted, by flipping a coin. McGill deplored the loss of a vitalizing influence, exercised by personal contact; Osler, himself, remarked characteristically, that in parting he "felt the chordae tendineae grow tense" (Cushing, I, 229).

His removal to Philadelphia, in 1884, marked the beginning of a twenty-one year period of residence and work in the United States. In his new position, he was startling, at first, with his informal ways and his halting speech, devoid of any attempt at oratorical effect. But his clinical work in the hospital wards, his thorough knowledge of his subject, and his interest in autopsies and in the work of the clinical laboratory, soon gained respect; and, besides, his rare traits of personality made him popular alike as teacher, clinician, and consultant. In addition to regular work in the medical school, he made clinical and pathological studies at Blockley Hospital, and supported and stimulated the medical societies. Many contributions to medical literature, including *The Gulstonian Lectures on Malignant Endocarditis* (1885), the Cartwright Lectures, *On Certain Problems of the Blood Corpuscles* (1886; reprinted from *Medical News,* Philadelphia, Apr. 3, 10, 17, 1886); and his monograph, "The Cerebral Palsies of Children" (*Ibid.,* July 14–Aug. 11, 1888), belong to this period. Now and again his spirit of fun became irrepressible; occasionally he would publish as a practical joke some absurd letter or paper under the pen name "Edgerton Y. Davis of Caughnawauga, P.Q.," that "mischievous half" of his, analogous to M'Connachie, the "fanciful half" of Sir James Barrie.

In September 1888, Osler was appointed physician-in-chief to the new Johns Hopkins Hospital, Baltimore, which was to be opened formally in May 1889. There he remained for sixteen years—probably the most eventful and most influential period of his life. The Johns Hopkins University had appointed William H. Welch as professor of pathology in 1884, and his choice for the professorship of medicine was Osler, a selection that later gained the approval of John Shaw Billings [*q.v.*], adviser of the hospital trustees, and of Daniel Coit Gilman [*q.v.*], president of the University. As the Johns Hopkins Medical School, in which Osler was to be professor of medicine, did not open until four years after the opening of the hospital, the time necessary for the organization of a clinical staff and of the institutional work was available. The hospital was organized upon a unit system comparable to that in use in the great German universities, with a graded resident staff; but the teaching was later conducted more in accordance with the best British and French traditions. The teaching program included instruction of small groups of students who served in the wards as clinical clerks and surgical dressers, practical work in clinical laboratories, amphitheatre clinics, and demonstrations of conditions of "the unwashed" in the out-patient department. Osler selected as his resident physicians, successively, H. A. Lafleur, W. S. Thayer, T. B. Futcher, Thomas McCrae, and R. I. Cole, and he sought, as assistants and internes, what he called "A.A.1. copper-bottomed young graduates" (Cushing, I, 304). He made every effort to infect these men with the spirit of earnestness, the love of thoroughness and of orderliness in work with rigid mastery of one's time, the appreciation of knowledge for its own sake (apart from its value for practice and for pecuniary considerations), the determination to become familiar with the best thought of the world, and the desire to make original contributions to knowledge. Through his pupils he may be said to have created an American school of internal medicine.

In 1891, he published his *Principles and Practice of Medicine,* which became so popular as a text for students and practitioners that, of the first two editions alone, 41,000 copies were sold. By 1930, it had reached its eleventh edition; it has been translated into French, German, Spanish, and Chinese. It was the perusal of this textbook by the Rev. F. T. Gates [*q.v.*], the adviser of Mr. John D. Rockefeller, that led to Mr. Rockefeller's large endowments of work in higher medicine and medical education. Later, with the aid of Thomas McCrae, Osler edited *Modern Medicine* (1907–10), a systematic treatise in seven volumes.

During his Johns Hopkins period, he was an active investigator of typhoid fever, malaria, pneumonia, amoebiasis, tuberculosis (for which he devised the home treatment), cardiovascular disease, the visceral lesions of the erythema group, ball-valve gallstone in the common duct, the relations of gall stones to typhoid, and cyanosis with polycythaemia (Vaquez-Osler disease); but his main contributions to medical research lay in his stimulation and insemination of the minds of others. In the field of public health he was an active propagandist, waging war especially against typhoid, malaria, tuberculosis, anti-vivisectionists, and the conditions responsible for infant mortality. He helped to make the Johns Hopkins Hospital a place of refuge for the sick poor of the city, and he did much for the medical libraries of Baltimore, especially for the library of the Medical and Chirurgical Faculty of Maryland. He was in demand for the making of "occasional addresses," among which *Aequanimitas* (1889), *The Master Word in Medicine* (1903), *Science and Immortality* (1904), and *The Student Life* (1905) may be mentioned as illustrating the charm of his literary style, his love of literary allusions born of his wide reading, his kindly advice and graceful humor, and his practical common sense combined with high ideals of scholarship and of life. One of his addresses, "The Fixed Period" (*Journal of the American Medical Association,* Mar. 4, 1905), in which he referred to Trollope's novel that suggested the chloroforming of men over sixty, caused an unexpected storm of protest. The misinterpretation of his meaning caused him pain, for he had always been especially respectful, tender, and affectionate to older men, and those who knew him were well aware of his especial interest in human beings at the two extremes of life. Moreover, his mission had been to soothe rather than to irritate. He was always composing disputes and bringing together discordant elements in the profession, services that brought him fame as a peace-maker. Throughout this period, as a consulting practitioner he attracted patients from near and far; moreover, he became "the doctor's doctor," and, despite every effort to restrict the number of his patients, was finally overwhelmed by them, a fact that, together with some "sub-

sternal threatenings," had some weight in his decision to accept, in 1905, the call to the Regius Professorship of Medicine in the University of Oxford, which he held until his death nearly fifteen years later.

In Oxford, he soon showed that the opportunities of a Regius professorship are as great as are the qualities of its incumbent. One of his chief interests was the Bodleian Library, of which he was a curator and for which he secured valuable gifts. He was Master of the Almshouse at Ewelme and took a deep interest in the old men there. He participated actively in reforms in public health, in medical education, and in professional organization in England. He was a member of the two committees that advised the Board of Education and the Treasury in the distribution of state grants to the universities. In the development of the Oxford Medical School, the work of the Oxford Press, the formation of the Association of Physicians of Great Britain and Ireland (1906), the launching of the *Quarterly Journal of Medicine* (1906), the amalgamation of the London medical societies into the Royal Society of Medicine (1907), and the formation of its historical section (1912), he took an active part. Throughout life, and especially after fifty, he evinced much interest in the history of medicine and in the collecting of old medical books. He continued to be in demand as an occasional speaker; among his notable addresses after he went to Oxford were *Man's Redemption of Man* (1910); *A Way of Life* (1914), delivered at Yale; *The Old Humanities and the New Science* (1919), a presidential address before the Classical Association. He received many honorary degrees from universities, was elected president of the Ashmolean Natural History Society (1919), the Bibliographical Society (1913–19), and the Classical Association (1919), and in 1911, at the time of the coronation of King George V, was made a baronet, much, he declared, to the embarrassment of his democratic simplicity.

Upon the outbreak of the World War, he was made physician-in-chief of the Queen's Canadian Military Hospital at Shorncliffe, and later shared in the propaganda for disease prevention in the army. Typhoid and paratyphoid, war nephritis, trench fever, the Dardanelles diarrhoea, and the soldiers' heart were among the maladies in which he showed especial interest.

He had married in 1892, when in Baltimore, Grace Linzee (Revere), the widow of Dr. Samuel W. Gross [*q.v.*] of Philadelphia, and the extraordinary hospitality of "the Chief" and Mrs. Osler at 1 W. Monument St., in Baltimore, and later of Sir William and Lady Osler at 13 Norham Gardens in Oxford (which came to be known as "The Open Arms") was noteworthy. Their first child died soon after birth; the second, Edward Revere Osler, was killed in Belgium in 1917 while on active service as an officer in the Royal Field Artillery. In October 1918 his collection of books and an endowment fund were given as a memorial by his parents to The Johns Hopkins University for the encouragement of the study of English literature of the Tudor and Stuart periods. During his later life, Osler suffered from recurrent attacks of bronchitis; he jokingly declared that he sometimes "coughed his Pacchionian bodies loose." At the end of 1919, worn out by war activities and exhausted by grief over the death of his son, he developed an empyema and a pulmonary abscess which, despite operation, proved fatal.

Several portraits of Osler were painted, including paintings by Thomas Corner and by Seymour Thomas, the best known being that by Sargent in a group, "The Four Doctors," which hangs in the Welch Library of the Johns Hopkins Medical School. His appearance in 1903 is reproduced in a plaque made by Vernon in Paris. A well-known sketch made by Max Brödel, showing Osler with halo and wings dominating a cyclone that sweeps away disease, bears the legend: "The Saint—Johns Hopkins Hospital." A part of his personal library, consisting of some 7,600 bound volumes bearing upon the history of medicine and science, was bequeathed to McGill University; it is catalogued in *Bibliotheca Osleriana* (Oxford, 1929), edited by W. W. Francis, R. H. Hill, and Archibald Malloch; his collection of important editions in English literature was given to the Tudor and Stuart Club of The Johns Hopkins University; a third part, consisting chiefly of modern clinical books, was given to the Johns Hopkins Hospital.

His most eminent colleague, Dr. Welch, has stated that, at the time of his death, Osler was "probably the greatest figure in the medical world; the best known, the most influential, the most beloved. . . . His life embodied his precepts, and his students cherished his words" (*Johns Hopkins Alumni Magazine*, 1921, quoted by Cushing, I, 428, n.). "Cultivate peace of mind, serenity, the philosophy of Marcus Aurelius," was his advice; "Think not too much of tomorrow, but of the work of today, the work which is immediately before you." Writing shortly before his death (Cushing, II, 679), he said: "The confounded thing [his illness] drags on in an unpleasant way—and in one's 71st year, the harbour is not far off. And such a happy voyage!

& such dear companions all the way! And the future does not worry."

[The definitive biography is Harvey Cushing, *The Life of Sir William Osler* (2 vols., 1925) ; a shorter work is E. G. Reid, *The Great Physician; A Short Life of Sir William Osler* (1931). A bibliography of his writings (730 items), assembled by M. W. Blogg, appeared in *Bull. Johns Hopkins Hospital*, July 1919. See also a memorial volume of appreciations and reminiscences by various authors with classified bibliography of Osler's writings and a list of writings about him, privately issued as *Bull. No. IX of the Internat. Asso. of Medic. Museums and Jour. of Technical Methods* (Montreal, 1926). Many references are listed in the *Index Catalogue of the Library of the Surgeon-General's Office*, 3 ser. VIII (1929), 469–70.]   L. F. B.

OSSOLI, MARGARET FULLER [See FULLER, SARAH MARGARET, 1810–1850].

OSTENACO [See OUTACITY, fl. 1756–1777].

OSTEN SACKEN, CARL ROBERT ROMANOVICH VON DER (Aug. 21, 1828–May 20, 1906), entomologist, diplomat, was a native of St. Petersburg, and died at Heidelberg, Germany. Although he was a Russian baron, his most productive years were passed in the United States and the bulk of his life work was concerned with the dipterous fauna of America. In 1839, at the age of eleven, he became interested in entomology while on a visit to Baden Baden. He was educated in St. Petersburg, and entered the diplomatic service in 1849. In 1856, when twenty-eight years old, he was appointed secretary to the Russian legation at Washington. Six years later he was made consul general of Russia in New York City, resigning in 1871. After several journeys to Europe he was in the United States unofficially from 1873 to 1877. Before leaving Russia he had written three entomological papers. During his American sojourn he was principally engaged, partly in collaboration with Dr. Hermann Loew of Vienna, in an investigation of the Diptera of America north of the Isthmus of Panama. He published, first, in 1858, through the Smithsonian Institution, a *Catalogue of the Described Diptera of North America*. This was followed by a series of papers, very largely descriptive, and four volumes under the general title *Monographs of the Diptera of North America* (1862–73) by Loew and himself, also published by the Smithsonian Institution. Subsequently, after visiting the principal type collections of Europe, he prepared a second catalogue, of a critical character (Smithsonian Institution, 1878), which, according to an eminent authority, "for clearness, completeness and absolute mastery of the subject, must forever remain an unapproachable model for later workers" (Aldrich, *post*, p. 270). The Loew and Osten Sacken type collection was eventually placed in the Museum of Comparative Zoology at Cambridge, Mass.

In 1877 he went to Heidelberg, where he remained for the rest of his life. He continued to work, carried on a correspondence with entomologists in different parts of the world, and published many papers, mainly rather brief but all of importance. He spoke and wrote many languages, but preferred English, which he used with great clearness and force. In his closing years he jokingly referred to himself as "the grandfather of American Dipterology," a title that he really deserved. Before he died he published at his own expense *Record of My Life Work in Entomology* (three parts; pts. 1-2, including pp. 1-206, Cambridge, Mass., 1903; pt. 3, pp. 207-240, Heidelberg, 1904), which contains his portrait and a critical bibliography of 179 titles in addition to a deal of interesting notes and correspondence.

[J. M. Aldrich and C. W. Johnson, in *Entomological News*, Oct. 1906; G. H. Verrall, in *Entomologist's Monthly Mag.* (London), Oct. 1906; *Illustrirte Zeitung* (Leipzig), June 14, 1906.]   L. O. H.

OSTERHAUS, PETER JOSEPH (Jan. 4, 1823–Jan. 2, 1917), Union soldier, consul, son of Anton A. Osterhaus, was born in Coblenz, Germany. He received his early education in his native city, studied at a military school in Berlin, and served as a volunteer in the 29th Infantry Regiment. In 1846, at Kreuznach in Rhenish Prussia, he married Natilda Born. He became involved in the Revolution of 1848, and when the government triumphed he emigrated to the United States (1849), settling in Belleville, Ill., where he was employed as a drygoods clerk. He later moved to Lebanon, Ill., and operated a general merchandise business. Moving with his family to St. Louis, Mo., in 1851, he became bookkeeper for a wholesale hardware firm.

At the outbreak of the Civil War, he volunteered as a private in the 12th Missouri Volunteers. He was soon commissioned captain, Company A, 2nd Missouri Volunteer Infantry, promoted to major, Apr. 27, 1861, and fought in the battle of Wilson's Creek, Aug. 10, 1861. On Aug. 27 of that year, he was honorably discharged from this commission, and on Dec. 19 following, commissioned colonel, 12th Missouri Volunteer Infantry. Vacating that commission in June 1862, he accepted appointment as brigadier-general, United States Volunteers. He commanded the 1st Division of Gen. S. R. Curtis' corps and, in the Army of the Southwest, a division which took part in the engagement at Pea Ridge, Ark. (Mar. 6-8, 1862). He was in command of the 3rd Division, Army of the Southwest, to Dec. 31, 1862, and of the 9th Division of the same army from Dec. 31, 1862, to Aug. 2, 1863. In this last command he participated in the Vicksburg campaign. In a sharp engagement at Big Black River, Miss., on May 17, 1863, he was wounded by a shell fragment. His next command was the 1st Division, XV Corps of Grant's army at Chattanooga. Under temporary command of Gen. Joseph Hooker, Osterhaus led his troops over Lookout Creek, climbed to the summit of Missionary Ridge, took literally thousands of prisoners, and drove the Confederate southern wing from the crest of the ridge. On July 23, 1864, he was made a major-general of volunteers. He was chief of staff to the commanding general of the military division of West Mississippi to May 27, 1865; commanded the Department of the Mississippi to June 13, 1865; the District of the Mississippi to July 17, 1865; the Northern District of the Mississippi to Sept. 16, 1865; the Department of the Mississippi to Nov. 18, 1865, and the Western District of the Mississippi to Jan. 17, 1866, when he was relieved, having been honorably mustered out Jan. 15, 1866.

General Osterhaus served as United States Consul to France, from June 18, 1866, until Aug. 16, 1877, residing at Lyons. His term included the period of the Franco-Prussian War, and his reports show keen insight into the economic problems involved in French compliance with the conditions of peace imposed by Germany. When relieved by his successor, he returned to the United States and engaged in the manufacture and exporting of hardware. He was again called into public service, however, and acted as vice and deputy consul of the United States at Mannheim, Germany, from Mar. 16, 1898, to Nov. 8, 1900, when he resigned that he might retire and enjoy a rest within the circle of his family and his friends. On June 27, 1902, Congress authorized an additional pension for his services as a major-general of volunteers. This pension was stopped Mar. 20, 1905, for on Mar. 3, 1905, Congress by special act appointed him brigadier-general of the United States Army, and on Mar. 17 he went on the retired list. He lived to the age of ninety-four, his death occurring at Duisburg, Germany, where he was buried. On Nov. 15, 1863, his first wife died in St. Louis, and on July 28, 1864, he married her sister, Amalia Born. By his first marriage he had five children, and by his second, three.

[*War of the Rebellion: Official Records (Army)*; *Battles and Leaders of the Civil War* (4 vols. 1887-88); F. B. Heitman, *Hist. Reg. and Dict. U. S. Army* (1903); T. H. S. Hamersly, *Complete Army and Navy*

Reg. of the U. S. (1882); pension records; consular files, State Department; personnel records, War Department; N. Y. Times, Jan. 6, 1917; family records in possession of Alexander Osterhaus, Hollywood, Cal.]
C. C. B.

O'SULLIVAN, JOHN LOUIS (November 1813–Feb. 24, 1895), journalist, diplomat, was born, according to tradition, on a British man-of-war, in the harbor of Gibraltar. His father, John O'Sullivan, American merchant and sea captain, later consul for the Island of Teneriffe, had served in Miranda's Venezuela expedition in 1806. His grandfather, T. H. O'Sullivan, had been a member of the Irish Brigade in the French army, but during the American Revolution had joined the British army in New York; his great-grandfather, John O'Sullivan, born in County Kerry, Ireland, was adjutant-general in the army of "Bonnie Prince Charlie" in 1745, escaping to France after the defeat at Culloden (*Dictionary of National Biography*, XLII, 318, 319). John Louis O'Sullivan appears to have inherited a family propensity for championing lost causes. He backed Narciso Lopez in his filibustering expeditions against Cuba (1849–51), was twice indicted for violation of the neutrality laws (see *Democratic Review*, April 1852), and though he escaped conviction, lost heavily in those ventures, "having been ruined for Cuba," as he told James Buchanan. During the American Civil War he lived abroad, voicing his Southern sympathy in several pamphlets in which he urged Northern Democrats to end the war, and the British government to recognize the Confederacy. Prior to that time, however, he had won a place of some prominence in American letters and politics.

Educated at a military school in France, at Westminster School, England, and at Columbia College, where he took degrees in 1831 and 1834, he practised law in New York until 1837, when, in collaboration with S. D. Langtree, he established the *United States Magazine and Democratic Review*, first published in Washington, D. C., and in July 1841 moved to New York. The aim of this publication, as O'Sullivan stated it, was "to strike the hitherto silent string of the democratic genius of the age and the country" (*Passages from the Correspondence and Other Papers of Rufus W. Griswold*, 1898, p. 123). The editors succeeded in this aim, for the *Democratic Review* became the mouthpiece for the exuberant nationalism of the period, glorifying all things American and predicting the expansion of the United States till its boundaries should embrace the North American continent and Cuba as well. It was in an article in this magazine (July-August 1845), almost certainly written by O'Sullivan, that the phrase "manifest destiny" first appeared (J. W. Pratt, "The Origin of 'Manifest Destiny,'" *American Historical Review*, July 1927). In the literary field, the *Review* secured contributions from Hawthorne (between whom and O'Sullivan a warm friendship developed), Thoreau, Poe, Bryant, and others. In 1846 O'Sullivan sold the magazine. From August 1844 to 1846 he had also edited the *New York Morning News*, which he had founded jointly with Samuel J. Tilden [q.v.]. In 1841 he was in the New York legislature, where he advocated the abolition of capital punishment. From 1846 to 1854 he was a member of the board of regents of the University of the State of New York. On Feb. 1, 1854 (two years after his trial for filibustering) President Pierce named him chargé d'affaires in Portugal, and on June 19 of the same year he was nominated minister resident. He served in this capacity until 1858, championing American ideals and defending the American conception of "manifest destiny." Thereafter, he resided in Lisbon, London, and Paris until 1871 or later. From 1879 to 1895 he lived obscurely in New York. Julian Hawthorne, who knew him well, has described him as "handsome, charming, affectionate and unlucky, but an optimist to the last." It is noteworthy that at the time of his death "manifest destiny" was again becoming a popular watchword. He was married in 1846 to a daughter of Dr. Kearny Rodgers.

[Numerous personal glimpses of O'Sullivan appear in Julian Hawthorne, *Nathaniel Hawthorne and His Wife* (2 vols., 1885). Consult also F. L. Mott, *A Hist. of Am. Mags., 1741–1850* (1930); Algernon Tassin, *The Mag. in America* (1916); J. W. Pratt, "John L. O'Sullivan and Manifest Destiny," *N. Y. Hist.*, July 1933; files of the *Democratic Rev.* from 1837 to 1846; *N. Y. Tribune*, Mar. 26, 1895.]   J. W. P—t.

OTACITE [See OUTACITY, fl. 1756–1777].

OTERMÍN, ANTONIO de (fl. 1678–1683), is known solely in connection with his administration as governor of New Mexico from 1678 to 1683, during which time occurred the disastrous Pueblo Indian uprising which resulted in the abandonment of New Mexico by the Spaniards for twelve years. When Otermín became governor, Spanish settlers in the upper Río Grande region numbered about 2,900 persons and settlement extended from Isleta in the south, near present Albuquerque, to Taos in the north, a distance of about one hundred and fifty miles, and from Pecos in the east to Jémez in the west, a distance of about seventy-five miles. The most important settlements were Santa Fé, the capital, and also the center of a ranching district known as Río Arriba, and Isleta, which was the center of a flourishing farming community known as

Río Abajo. In the latter district the governor was represented by Lieutenant-Governor García.

In the third year of Otermín's administration a native of the north, Popé, planned a general rebellion, which, because of the discovery of the plot, was begun prematurely on Aug. 10, 1680. The Spaniards in the outlying districts were taken unawares and 380 civilians, including men, women, and children, and twenty-one missionaries lost their lives. One thousand refugees finally assembled at Santa Fé under Otermín and fifteen hundred at Isleta under García, each group being led to believe by the attacking Indians that all other Spaniards in the province had been killed. At Santa Fé Otermín and his group of refugees heroically withstood for nine days a siege during which their position was made unbearable through the diversion of a stream of water by the natives. In a desperate daybreak attack led by Otermín on Aug. 20 the demoralized besiegers were defeated, after which the Spaniards began a retreat to Isleta, from where the southern refugees had retreated toward the south. Overtaking this group, Otermín and the entire body of refugees proceeded to the mission of Guadalupe (at present Juárez, opposite El Paso, Tex.), being accompanied thither by 317 loyal Indians of the Tigua and Piros tribes. By October the Spaniards had been lodged in three temporary settlements in the vicinity of Guadalupe and ultimately the loyal Indians were also lodged in three pueblos, one of them being the historic pueblo of Isleta which at present is situated a few miles below El Paso on the American side of the river.

At Guadalupe the refugees under Otermin were aided by the viceregal government, and, pending the contemplated reconquest of New Mexico, the provincial capital was temporarily designated as El Paso del Río del Norte (present Juárez). In the winter of 1681–82 Otermín led a poorly equipped expedition of 146 soldiers to reconquer New Mexico. Little was accomplished except to ascertain the determination of the rebels and to burn eight pueblos and sack three others located in the heart of the Pueblo region. On returning to El Paso Otermín petitioned for a leave in order to seek medical treatment. The viceregal *fiscal* recommended the disapproval of the request but in August 1683, Don Jironza Petris de Cruzate assumed his duties as successor of Otermín at El Paso. Despite the many available documents of the period 1678–82, nothing is known of Otermín before the former or after the latter year. In a formal complaint filed against him with his successor, the cabildo of Santa Fé stated that Otermín,

"not being able or not wishing to govern," entrusted his authority to his *maestre de campo* Javier, "a man of bad faith, avaricious and cunning," who was charged with having goaded the Indians to rebel in 1680.

[Authoritative accounts of the administration of Otermín are in C. W. Hackett, "The Revolt of the Pueblo Indians of N. Mex. in 1680," in *Quart. Tex. State Hist. Asso.*, Oct. 1911, and "Otermín's Attempt to Reconquer N. Mex., 1681–82," in *Old Santa Fé*, Jan.–Apr. 1916. Consult also Anne E. Hughes, *The Beginnings of Spanish Settlement in the El Paso District* (1914); and Gaspar Perez de Villagrá, *Historia de la Nueva México* (ed. 1900), vol. II, App. III.]

C. W. H.

OTEY, JAMES HERVEY (Jan. 27, 1800– Apr. 23, 1863), first Protestant Episcopal bishop of Tennessee, was born in Bedford County, Va., one of a family of twelve children. His grandfather, Col. John Otey, fought in the Revolution; his father, Isaac, was a farmer and served for thirty years as the representative of his county in the Virginia legislature; his mother was a Matthew, a descendant of Tobias Matthew, Archbishop of York, 1606–1628. At the age of twenty, James Hervey graduated from the University of North Carolina with the degree of bachelor of belles-lettres. Remaining in the university as instructor in Greek and Latin, he had to lead the daily prayers in the chapel. Since he showed evident embarrassment, a friend gave him an Episcopal prayer book, the first he had seen, his parents not being members of any church. On Oct. 13, 1821, he married Eliza D. Pannill of Petersburg, Va., and soon took charge of an academy at Warrenton. Here he was baptized by the village rector, Rev. William Mercer Green, later first bishop of Mississippi. Bishop John S. Ravenscroft [*q.v.*] confirmed him, and on Oct. 10, 1825, ordained him deacon. On June 7, 1827, he was ordained priest by the same bishop.

Settling in Franklin, Tenn., he opened a school, serving also as pastor and missionary for eight years, with only one other Episcopal clergyman in the state. Bishop Ravenscroft visited him in 1829 and the diocese of Tennessee was organized at Nashville. In 1833 there were only five presbyters and one deacon in the diocese, but at the convention held at Franklin in June of that year Otey was elected bishop, and was consecrated in Philadelphia, Jan. 14, 1834. His services by toilsome journeys on horseback extended through Florida, Louisiana, Mississippi, Arkansas, and Indian Territory as well as Tennessee. "Weary, weary, weary," found frequent repetition in his diary. In 1852 he settled in Memphis.

As the originator of the idea, and one of the founders of the University of the South, Bishop

Otey deserves remembrance. The formal meeting for organization was held on Lookout Mountain, Chattanooga, July 4, 1857. Otey made an address, was elected chairman of the meeting and later, chancellor of the institution. Sewanee was selected as the site, and ten thousand acres secured. The legislature granted a charter, Jan. 6, 1858, nearly $500,000 was subscribed, and the corner stone was laid, Oct. 10, 1860. War stopped all further effort and swept away all the subscriptions. Before it was over, Otey had died and Bishop Charles T. Quintard [q.v.] took up the work.

By birth and early training, Otey was an "old-time Whig," a stanch supporter of the Constitution. His letters on the eve of war show the horror it aroused in his soul. The clergy in his diocese were recommended to use the ante-communion office, which did not contain any prayer for the President, in place of the usual services of morning and evening prayer, which included such a petition. He wrote to Secretary of State Seward, begging that hostilities be suspended and imploring him to use his influence with the President in the interest of peace. (See "The Change of Secession Sentiment in Virginia in 1861," in *American Historical Review,* October 1925.) General Sherman treated Bishop Otey with marked respect, did not compel him to take the usual oath of allegiance, and was a frequent attendant at the Bishop's services in Memphis. Notwithstanding the secession of the Southern states, Otey saw no reason for dividing the Church. He felt that at least "the opinions and consent of our northern brethren should be consulted in any such step, and everything avoided as far as possible likely to give offence to any portion of the Church."

The death of his wife in June 1861 was a heavy blow to him, and his own followed in less than two years. They had nine children. His remains lie in the churchyard in Ashwood, where a memorial service is still held every year. He was the author of one book, *Doctrine, Discipline, and Worship of the American Branch of the Catholic Church, Explained and Unfolded in Three Sermons* (1852).

[W. M. Green, *Memoir of Rt. Rev. James Hervey Otey, D.D., LL.D., the first Bishop of Tennessee* (1885), with extracts from his diary, letters, addresses and sermons; A. H. Noll. *Hist. of the Church in the Diocese of Tenn.* (1900); W. S. Perry, *The Hist. of the Am. Episcopal Church, 1857–1883* (1885), vol. II; Daniel McLeod, *The Rebellion in Tenn.: Observations on Bishop Otey's Letter to the Hon. William A. Seward* (1862).]   C. L. W.

OTIS, BASS (July 17, 1784–Nov. 3, 1861), portrait painter, engraver, pioneer in lithography in the United States, was the son of Dr. Josiah and Susanna (Orr) Otis, and a descendant of John Otis who emigrated to Massachusetts in 1630 or 1631 and settled in Hingham. He was born in Bridgewater, Mass. At an early age he is said to have been apprenticed to a scythe-maker in his native town. Dunlap said he was informed that the artist received his first instructions in painting by working for a coach painter, evidently after having completed his apprenticeship in the implement factory. By the time he first appeared in New York, in 1808, he had established a reputation as a painter of portraits. In 1812 he went to Philadelphia and set up a studio. He signalized his arrival in the city by sending eight portraits to the Second Annual Exhibition of the Columbian Society of Artists, in May 1812, which was the first display of his work. To the 1813 Exhibition he contributed among others, a portrait of himself. He painted portraits of Thomas Jefferson, James Madison, Joseph Hopkinson, Commodore Truxtun, Charles Thomson, and Dr. Caspar Wistar for *Delaplaine's Repository of the Lives and Portraits of Distinguished American Characters,* between 1815 and 1818, but only one of these portraits was engraved, that of Jefferson, because the work did not go beyond the first two volumes. The Jefferson portrait was painted from life. For several years Otis appears to have been kept busy copying portraits for Delaplaine, painting many more than those noted above, and annually sending his work to the exhibitions of the Pennsylvania Academy of the Fine Arts.

To the exhibition of 1819, Otis sent the only composition he is known to have painted. This was entitled, "Interior of an Iron Foundry," and is understood to have pictured the place where he served his apprenticeship. The painting was favorably received, and the artist presented it to the Academy. In 1815 he invented the perspective protractor, but this contrivance seems to have attracted little attention, although commended by several artists. He was noted for painting portraits of deceased persons, sketching them in their coffins, and giving them a life-like character on his canvas. One of the distinguished examples of this work was his portrait of Stephen Girard, which he copied at least once, and which is apparently the only likeness of the "mariner and merchant." Dunlap did not think highly of Otis' work, declaring that his portraits were "all of a class; if not so originally, he made them so" (*post,* II, p. 383), although he admitted that Otis had "strong natural talents, and a good perception of character." A year before his death Otis painted a portrait of himself for Ferdinand J. Dreer, of Philadelphia, an antiquary, which was reproduced in the *Pennsylvania Magazine of History and Biography* (October 1913).

Otis' chief claim to fame lies in the fact that he made the first lithograph in America. This has been identified by the writer as the portrait of the Rev. Abner Kneeland, affixed to the volume of his lectures, published in 1818. The plate bears the inscription, "Bass Otis, Sc.," and does not resemble the familiar lithograph, because in Otis' ignorance of the art, he merely etched the stone in a combination of lithotint, stipple, and line, methods not intended to be used in combination. That the plate is a lithograph has been denied by Frank Weitenkampf (*American Graphic Art,* 1924, p. 152), who claims that it was executed on copper. Joseph Pennell, however, who was an expert lithographer, expressed himself to the writer as satisfied that it was a print from a stone. Otis made in precisely the same manner a lithograph which appeared in the *Analectic Magazine,* for July 1819, but he limited his method to expression in line. It was an etching on stone, contrary to the design and purpose of lithography, which is intended for surface and not for intaglio printing. The lithograph in the *Analectic* has always been cited as the first American lithograph, although the magazine that contained it did not claim for it that distinction. Otis was married, in 1819, to Alice Pierie of Philadelphia. In 1845, after her death, he left Philadelphia and opened a studio in New York. Five years later he was painting portraits in Boston but in 1859 he returned to Philadelphia. There he later died and was buried beside his wife and children in Christ Church Burial Ground.

[Jos. Jackson's "Bass Otis, America's First Lithographer," *Pa. Mag. of Hist. and Biog.,* Oct. 1913, contains some errors corrected in this sketch. See also: D. M. Stauffer, *Am. Engravers Upon Copper and Steel* (1907) ; Mantle Fielding, *Am. Engravers Upon Copper and Steel* (1917) ; Wm. Dunlap, *Hist. of the Rise and Progress of the Arts of Design in the U. S.* (rev. ed., 3 vols., 1918) ; E. L. Clark, *A Record of the Inscriptions on the Tablets and Grave-Stones in the Burial Grounds of Christ Church, Phila.* (1864) ; *Vital Records of Bridgewater, Mass.* (2 vols., 1916) ; *Pub. Ledger* (Phila.), Nov. 4, 1861.]   J. J.

OTIS, CHARLES EUGENE (May 11, 1846–Nov. 8, 1917), jurist, was the son of Isaac Otis, a descendant of John Otis who emigrated from England about 1631 and settled in Hingham, Mass., and of Caroline Abigail (Curtiss) Otis. Born on a farm in Prairieville Township, Barry County, Mich., he attended Prairie Seminary at Richland, the Kalamazoo high school, and the University of Michigan, where he received the degree of A.B. in 1869. After teaching school for two years he went to St. Paul and read law with his brother, George L. Otis, a leading member of the Minnesota bar, entering into partnership with him as soon as he was admitted to practice, in 1873. This firm lasted until 1883 when, upon the death of George L. Otis, a younger brother, Arthur G., was associated with the survivor.

An avowed Democrat, Otis was appointed judge of the second district of Minnesota in 1889 by the Republican governor, William R. Merriam, to fill a vacancy. At the general election of 1890 he was nominated by both parties, but in 1896, since he had repudiated the Chicago platform, his own party refused to renominate him. The Republicans supported him, however, and he was elected for another term. Declining a third nomination, in 1903 he resumed the practice of law in partnership with his son, James C. Otis, and these two, a little later, brought into the firm Willis C. Otis, a nephew of the elder member. This organization persisted down to 1917; at that time Willis went into the army, and a new partner, Kenneth G. Brill, was admitted, the firm name becoming Otis & Brill. In 1904 Otis was a candidate for chief justice of the supreme court of the state but, along with the rest of his party, went down to defeat before the Roosevelt landslide.

Always interested in civic matters, he was an alderman of St. Paul from 1880 to 1883 and a member of the library board from 1896 to 1899. As judge, many parties were willing to place their cases in his hands to hear and decide. He sustained the validity of the so-called "Bell Charter" of St. Paul, a new organic law passed in 1891, which did much to secure a more economical and less corrupt government for the city. His principal claim to remembrance, however, comes from his having been appointed, with the consent of all parties, by Judge Walter H. Sanborn of the Eighth United States Circuit Court to take testimony, hear arguments, and report findings of fact and "conclusions of law, together with the forms of decrees which he recommended to be entered, in the nine Minnesota railroad rate cases" (*Proceedings, Minnesota State Bar Association,* 1918, pp. 159–61). The work of taking testimony and hearing arguments lasted from June 2, 1908, to May 26, 1910, and Otis' report as master in chancery was submitted June 29, 1910. His findings and conclusions as to the three roads which were taken for test cases were approved by Judge Sanborn, who rendered a decision in favor of the complainants (the stockholders). These had sought by injunction to prevent the railroad officials from complying with the Minnesota law, on the grounds that the law operated to interfere with interstate commerce, over which Congress and not the state has jurisdiction, and that the prescribed rates were confiscatory, hence in violation of the Fourteenth Amendment. When the case was taken to the Supreme Court of the United States on appeal, that court, speaking through Justice Hughes, reversed the decision on the first point, holding that since Congress had not dealt with this phase of intrastate commerce, the field was open to state action. As to the second point, that the rates were confiscatory, the lower court was sustained as to one railroad, the Minneapolis & St. Louis, but not in the case of the more important ones, the Northern Pacific and the Great Northern. The testimony of his associates both during his lifetime and after his death supports the statement indorsed by the bar association that Otis "was a man of the highest character and ability, a patriotic citizen and an honest, able and fearless judge." On Sept. 3, 1874, he married Elizabeth Noyes Ransom; they had three children, two of whom survived him. His death occurred in St. Paul.

[W. A. Otis, *A Geneal. and Hist. Memoir of the Otis Family in America* (1924); A. N. Marquis, *The Book of Minnesotans* (1907); *Proc. Minn. State Bar Asso., 18th Ann. Session* (1918); 230 *U. S. Reports*, 352; 184 *Fed. Reporter*, 765; *Daily News* (St. Paul), Nov. 8, 1917.]   L. B. S.

OTIS, CHARLES ROLLIN (Apr. 29, 1835– May 24, 1927), inventor, manufacturer, was born in Troy, N. Y., the son of Elisha Graves Otis [*q.v.*] and Susan A. (Houghton). After obtaining a grade-school education at Halifax, Vt., and Albany, N. Y., he entered his father's machine shop at the age of thirteen, and learned his trade. He became especially familiar with steam engines, and when his father moved to Bergen, N. J., to become master mechanic of a bedstead factory there, young Otis, although but fifteen, was made engineer. The following year when his father moved to Yonkers, N. Y., he went with him and assisted in the erection of a new factory there. He worked side by side with his father in the construction of an elevator, and was so impressed by the safety appliance devised by the elder Otis that he urged the latter to establish a shop for the building of elevators. Close association with his father developed in the son the same integrity and genius for invention possessed by the former, and upon his death in 1861 Charles was in a position successfully to carry on the elevator business, which his father had established in Yonkers.

As the demand for elevators increased during the sixties, Otis and his younger brother supplied it, and at the same time continued to make improvements in the machinery. On Oct. 18, 1864, Charles Otis obtained a patent for elevator brakes (No. 44,740); in 1865 he secured three patents for improvements on his father's steam hoisting engine; on Sept. 10, 1867, he patented an improved valve for the steam engine (No. 68,783); and the following year, still other improvements. He succeeded, too, Feb. 21, 1871, in securing a reissue of his father's original patent of 1861, which was assigned to the new firm known as Otis Brothers & Company, organized in 1864. By 1872 the firm was doing a business of $393,000. After the company was incorporated a few years later and the business continued to grow, Otis and his brother retired (1882), selling their holdings to a syndicate of capitalists. Several years later, however, the brothers regained control and Charles was again elected president. He continued in this capacity until 1890, when he retired and spent the balance of his life in travel.

He was appointed a member of the board of education of Yonkers in 1886 and served continuously in that capacity for a great many years. A member of the committee on teachers and instruction, he devoted much time to visiting and inspecting schools. He was an extensive reader and owned a valuable library, including both classical and scientific works. On Aug. 28, 1861, he married Caroline F. Boyd of New York, who died in 1925. Otis' death occurred at Summerville, S. C. His second cousin and nurse, Margaret Otis Nesbit, claimed that he had married her in December 1926 and contested his will, in which he had left her $10,000 out of an estate of $1,250,000. After seven months of litigation, and the payment of gifts, annuities, and legal expenses, the estate amounted to $461,000, of which the widow received $130,000.

[W. A. Otis, *A Geneal. and Hist. Memoir of the Otis Family in America* (1924); C. E. Allison, *The Hist. of Yonkers* (1896); *New York Times,* July 3, Sept. 19, 1927, Jan. 18, 1928; information as to certain facts from the Otis Elevator Co.; Patent Office records.]
                                        C. W. M—n.

OTIS, ELISHA GRAVES (Aug. 3, 1811– Apr. 8, 1861), manufacturer, inventor, the son of Stephen and Phoebe (Glynn) Otis, was born on his father's farm at Halifax, Windham County, Vt. He was a descendant of John Otis who emigrated from England as early as 1631 and settled in Hingham, Mass. Stephen was for many years a justice of the peace in Halifax and also served four terms as a member of the state legislature. Young Otis received his education in his native town, where he remained until the age of nineteen, when he went to Troy, N. Y. Here for five years he carried on building operations. Forced by illness to give up this strenuous work, he secured a trucking business and engaged in hauling goods between Troy and Brattleboro, Vt. After three years, having accumulated a little capital, he purchased some land on the Green River in Vermont, where he built a house and gristmill. The latter was not a success, however, and converting it into a sawmill, he began the manufacture of carriages and wagons, which business he continued rather successfully until about 1845.

Failing health again compelling him to change his occupation, he moved with his family to Albany, N. Y., where he found employment as master mechanic in a bedstead manufactory. In the course of his three years' employment there, he acquired a little capital and with this established a small machine shop, where he did general jobbing work and also constructed a turbine waterwheel of his own invention. The source of power for his shop was Patroon's Creek, and when in 1851 the city of Albany took over the creek as part of its water supply, Otis was forced out of business. Meanwhile, one of his former employers had established a bedstead factory at Bergen, N. J., and Otis moved there late in 1851 to become master mechanic in this factory. The following year his employers began the construction of a new factory at Yonkers, N. Y., and Otis was put in charge of its erection and the installation of the machinery. In the course of this work it became necessary to construct an elevator, and during its building Otis devised and incorporated a number of unique features. The most important of these was a safety appliance that operated automatically and prevented the elevator from falling in case the lifting chain or rope broke.

This elevator, the first with safety appliances, attracted the attention of a number of New York manufacturers with the result that in a short time Otis was given orders for three elevators. He thereupon gave up his position with the bedstead factory and established a shop of his own in Yonkers. The three elevators which he built and installed may be said to be the beginning of the elevator business. In 1854 he demonstrated his safety elevator at the American Institute Fair in New York by standing on a full-size model and deliberately cutting the rope after it had ascended to some height. From this time on, his business gradually expanded until at the time of his premature death he had a plant valued at $5,000 and employed from eight to ten men. Orders for elevators were, of course, not numerous and in addition to carrying on the work of improving them, he devised a number of other mechanical contrivances. On May 25, 1852, he received a patent for railroad car trucks and brakes (No. 8,973), and on Oct. 20, 1857, one for a steam plow (No. 18,468). He also invented a bake oven, patented Aug. 24, 1858 (No. 21,271), but with the invention of his steam elevator, for which he received a patent (No. 124) on Jan. 15, 1861, he established the firm foundation for the elevator business upon which his sons so successfully built. Otis was twice married: first, on June 2, 1834, to Susan A. Houghton of Halifax, who died Feb. 25, 1842; and second, about 1845, to Mrs. Elizabeth A. Boyd. At the time of his death in Yonkers he was survived by his widow and two sons of his former marriage, one of whom was Charles R. Otis [q.v.].

[W. A. Otis, *A Geneal. and Hist. Memoir of the Otis Family in America* (1924); C. E. Allison, *The Hist. of Yonkers* (1896); data from Otis Elevator Company, N. Y.; E. W. Byrn, *The Progress of Invention in the Nineteenth Century* (1900); Patent Office records.]

C. W. M—n.

OTIS, ELWELL STEPHEN (Mar. 25, 1838–Oct. 21, 1909), soldier, was born at Frederick, Md., the son of William and Mary Ann Catherine (Late) Otis, and a descendant of Richard Otis who was in Massachusetts as early as 1655. Elwell graduated at the University of Rochester in 1858 and at the Harvard Law School in 1861, and then began the practice of law in New York. On Sept. 13, 1862, however, he entered the military service as captain in the 140th New York Infantry. With this regiment he served in all the subsequent operations of the V (Warren's) Corps, Army of the Potomac. He became lieutenant-colonel Dec. 23, 1863, and after the battle of Spotsylvania commanded his regiment, replacing the colonel, who had been killed in action. On Oct. 1, 1864, during the operations about Petersburg, he was wounded in the head by a rifle bullet—a wound which occasioned him inconvenience for the rest of his life. He was given sick leave, but being still unfit for duty at its termination he was honorably mustered out on Jan. 24, 1865. For gallant conduct in action he received the brevet ranks of colonel and brigadier-general of volunteers.

In the reorganization of the regular army after the war, he was appointed lieutenant-colonel in the 22nd Infantry, with rank from July 28, 1866. He accepted the appointment on Feb. 7, 1867, and joined his regiment in Dakota. As additional recognition of his services at Spotsylvania, he received the brevet rank of colonel in the regular service. He remained with his regiment in the northwest until 1880, serving in various Indian campaigns, the most important of which was that of Little Big Horn in 1876 and 1877. In 1874 and 1875 he was assistant inspector-general of the Department of Dakota. The ideas which he formed during these years of frontier service are contained in his thoughtful book *The Indian Question*, published in New York in 1878.

On Feb. 8, 1880, he was promoted colonel of the 20th Infantry, and joined his new command on Mar. 31. In the autumn of the next year he moved with headquarters and two companies of his regiment to Fort Leavenworth, having been designated by General Sherman, commanding the army, to establish a school of application for young officers. Three companies from other infantry regiments, four troops of cavalry, and a light battery were added to his command. He organized the school, and remained as its commandant until June 1885. It rapidly established itself as the center of military education in the army. Under various official names, but always colloquially as "Leavenworth," it has had continuous existence, and, among the numerous special schools which have grown up in the army, it has retained its hegemony. In the fall of 1890 he left his regiment to become chief of the recruiting service. He never rejoined it, for on Nov. 28, 1893, he was promoted brigadier-general. He commanded the department of the Columbia until the spring of 1897, then went to the Department of Colorado.

On May 4, 1898, he was made major-general of volunteers, and ordered to San Francisco for duty with the force outfitting for the Philippines. The first expedition sailed on May 25; General Otis went in July, with the fourth. Upon arrival in Manila on Aug. 21 he was placed in command of the VIII Army Corps, comprising all the troops present, and on the 29th he relieved General Wesley Merritt [*q.v.*] in command of the Department of the Pacific and as military governor of the Philippines. The situation was complicated and delicate. The first necessity was to relieve the Spanish officials, both military and civil, throughout the islands, and to establish American government with the least possible confusion. The Spanish officials could not always be found; and when found, their affairs were often in confusion and an orderly transfer impossible. Meanwhile, Aguinaldo and his insurgent government were maneuvering for recognition and for military position in the outskirts of Manila. The American government was established, and, by the exercise of great diplomacy and self-restraint, peace with the insurgents was maintained until Feb. 4, 1899. On that night a Filipino soldier approached the American outposts, refusing to halt or to answer challenges. The American sentinel finally fired, and the fire

was instantly and actively taken up by the insurgent troops. The situation was tense in Manila for a few days, but the city was promptly cleared of insurgents, and American columns took the offensive in all directions. The operations thus begun continued until the insurgent forces were completely scattered, then gradually passed into occupation of the country, suppression of brigandage, and the establishment of civil government. General Otis continued in command until May 5, 1900, when he was relieved by Gen. Arthur MacArthur and returned to the United States. For his services in the Islands he received the brevet rank of major-general in the regular service, and on June 16, 1900, was promoted substantively to that grade. Until his retirement, Mar. 25, 1902, he commanded the Department of the Lakes; he then took up his residence in Rochester, where he remained until his death.

Otis was twice married: first, Oct. 5, 1870, to Louise, daughter of Judge Henry R. Seldon of Rochester, who died Apr. 24, 1875; second, Apr. 13, 1878, to Louise, daughter of Col. Alexander Hamilton Bowman and widow of Col. Miles McAlester. She, with three daughters, survived him. He was a man of medium height, stoutly built, erect, soldierly and distinguished in appearance. He was quiet in his tastes and manner, but forceful and never afraid of responsibility. His command in the Philippines was one continuous series of decisions which had to be made with no precedents to guide; Otis made them, as a rule, without reference to Washington. His legal instincts and training stood him in good stead, and the adaptations of Spanish law to the new conditions, worked out under his direction, still stand as the basis of Philippine administration.

[W. A. Otis, *A Geneal. and Hist. Memoir of the Otis Family in America* (1924); *Official Army Reg.*, 1909; *Hist. Sketch . . . of the U. S. Infantry and Cavalry School, Fort Leavenworth, Kan.* (1895); *Report of Maj.-Gen. E. S. Otis, U. S. Volunteers, on Military Operations and Civil Affairs in the Philippine Islands* (1899); *Army and Navy Jour.*, Oct. 23, 1909; *Democrat and Chronicle* (Rochester, N. Y.), Oct. 21, 1909; information furnished by Mrs. Harry Knight Elston, Otis' eldest daughter, and by Maj.-Gen. Fred W. Sladen, formerly his aide-de-camp.]   O. L. S., Jr.

OTIS, FESSENDEN NOTT (Mar. 6, 1825– May 24, 1900), physician, was born at Ballston Springs, Saratoga County, N. Y., the son of Oran Gray and Lucy (Kingman) Otis, and a descendant of John Otis, born in England, who settled in Hingham, Mass., about 1631. In 1843 Fessenden met with an accident because of which he was unable to continue systematic study. He took up landscape drawing and perspective, which he taught successfully, publishing several textbooks on the subject. One of these, *Easy Lessons in Landscape,* had reached a fifth edition in 1856. Because of his attainments in this field Union College gave him the honorary degree of A.M. in 1851 and the following year he was elected to Phi Beta Kappa. In the meantime he had entered the medical department of the University of the City of New York (now New York University), taking as his preceptor Dr. John Whittaker, demonstrator of anatomy. In 1850 he transferred with Dr. Whittaker to the New York Medical College and graduated therefrom in 1852, receiving the gold medal for his graduation thesis. After an internship at the Charity Hospital, which terminated in 1853, he served as ship surgeon in the Panama, and, later, in the Pacific service, and in 1861 published *Illustrated History of the Panama Railroad,* reissued in 1867 under the title, *History of the Panama Railroad.* He married, in 1859, Frances Helen Cooke of Catskill, N. Y.

In 1860 he began private practice in New York, where he served as police surgeon from 1861 to 1871 and president of the medical board of the police department from 1869 to 1871. He was lecturer (1862–71) and professor of genito-urinary and venereal diseases (1871–90) at the College of Physicians and Surgeons, surgeon to the Charity Hospital for ten years, and consultant to the Manhattan Eye and Ear Hospital and to the New York Skin and Cancer Hospital. He was a fellow of the New York Academy of Medicine, the New York State Medical Society, the British Medical Association, the American Association of Genito-Urinary Surgeons, and the New York Medical and Surgical Society.

His interest came to be concentrated chiefly in genito-urinary diseases. In 1878 he published *Stricture of the Male Urethra; Its Radical Cure* and from that time he was largely concerned with establishing the curability of urethral stricture, and in advocating certain principles which he regarded as fundamental to that cure. The state of medical science in his day confined the surgical attack upon the urinary organs to the urethra. Diseases of other organs were diagnosed as urethral and attacked as such. The doctrines of Otis were at first received unfavorably, but later won acceptance in the United States and had influence in England. The 1889 edition of *Stricture of the Male Urethra* is memorable for its audacious inclusion of a perfectly sound attack by Dr. H. B. Sands upon many items of the Otis theory and the brilliant discussion of this by the author. The theory is recognized today as fantastic yet in practice it provided a basis for attacking strictures of the male urethra more radically and more successfully than they had ever been attacked before. Today Otis is recognized as the first man to have cured stricture. His urethrotome and urethrameter are widely used. His theories are of historic interest and his memory still lives as that of a charming, enthusiastic, and honest gentleman. Among his publications, in addition to numerous contributions to medical journals, are *Classroom Lectures on Syphilis and the Genito-Urinary Diseases* (1878); *Contagion of Syphilis* (1878); *Clinical Lectures on the Physiological Pathology of Syphilis and Treatment of Syphilis . . .* (1881); *Practical Clinical Lessons on Syphilis and the Genito-Urinary Diseases* (1883). He died in New Orleans of a carbuncle during convalescence from double pneumonia.

[W. A. Otis, *A Geneal. and Hist. Memoir of the Otis Family in America* (1924); John Shrady, *The Coll. of Physicians and Surgeons, N. Y., and Its Founders, Officers, Instructors, Benefactors, and Alumni, a Hist.* (n.d.), vol. I; H. A. Kelly and W. L. Burrage, *Am. Medic. Biogs.* (1920); Bransford Lewis, *Hist. of Urology* (1933), I, 74–75; *Medic. Record,* June 2, 23, 1900; *Daily Picayune* (New Orleans), May 25, 1900; alumni records of Union College.]   E. L. K.

OTIS, GEORGE ALEXANDER (Nov. 12, 1830–Feb. 23, 1881), military surgeon, editor of the surgical volumes of the *Medical and Surgical History of the War of the Rebellion,* was a descendant of John Otis of England, who settled in Hingham, Mass., about 1631. His great-grandfather was a physician of Scituate, Mass.; his grandfather was a Boston merchant with an interest in literature; his father, also named George Alexander Otis, was a lawyer, who in 1830 married Anna Maria Hickman, daughter of a Virginian. In 1831 the elder Otis died of tuberculosis, leaving an infant son of the same name. The boy attended the Boston Latin School, and later Fairfax Institute in Alexandria, Va., where he was prepared for college. Entering Princeton in 1846 as a sophomore, he received his bachelor's degree in 1849 and in 1851, that of M.A. At college he displayed a special fondness for literature.

He studied medicine under the preceptorship of Dr. F. H. Deane of Richmond, Va., where his mother resided. In the fall of 1849 he matriculated in the medical department of the University of Pennsylvania, from which school he received the degree of M.D. in 1851. While still an undergraduate in medicine, Sept. 19, 1850, he married Pauline Clark Baury, the daughter of Alfred Louis Baury, an Episcopal clergyman of Newton Lower Falls., Mass.; they had two daughters. After his graduation, he went to Paris, expecting to specialize in ophthalmic surgery, but he found general surgery more attractive. The rioting that marked Louis Napoleon's *coup d'état* in 1851 gave him opportunities to see military surgery and the work of such masters as Velpeau, Roux, and Jobert. He returned to the United States in 1852 and settled in Richmond. In April of the following year, he founded the *Virginia Medical and Surgical Journal,* and made it an excellent periodical, notable for its translations and abstracts from the French. Meanwhile he was not prospering, and in 1854 he removed to Springfield, Mass., from which place he acted as a corresponding editor of the *Journal* until the close of 1859. In Springfield he attended more closely to private practice, and was more successful.

Upon the outbreak of the Civil War he was appointed surgeon of the 27th Massachusetts Volunteers, and was mustered into the Federal service on Sept. 14, 1861. He accompanied the regiment South and served with it in Maryland, Virginia, and North Carolina. For a few months, early in 1863, he was on detached service in the Department of the South. Here he attracted the notice of Surgeon Charles H. Crane, medical director, which notice later led to his assignment to the duty which proved to be his great work for the last sixteen years of his life. On July 28, 1863, he was granted twenty days' leave of absence because of his wife's serious illness. Reaching home on Aug. 1, he learned that she had died on July 24. Having no near relatives to whom to entrust the care of his small daughters, he placed them in a convent. Returning to his regiment, he served with it and on detached duty, including duty as a division surgeon, until May 1864, when he was granted sick leave. In June 1864 he resigned his commission as surgeon of the 27th Massachusetts and accepted an appointment as assistant surgeon, United States Volunteers. While in Washington he again met Surgeon Crane, at this time on duty in the surgeon-general's office, who secured his detail as assistant to Surgeon John H. Brinton, United States Volunteers, then curator of the Army Medical Museum and engaged in collecting materials for a surgical history of the war. In August Otis was promoted to the grade of surgeon of volunteers, and in the following October he was ordered to relieve Surgeon Brinton of his duties. These duties Otis continued to perform until his death. Immediately after the close of the war, under direction of Surgeon-General Barnes, Otis and Surgeon Woodward prepared *Reports on the Extent and Nature of the Materials Available for the Preparation of a Medical and Surgical History of the War* (1866). It presented an impressive array of data and attracted widespread and favorable notice.

In 1866 Otis accepted an appointment as assistant surgeon in the regular army. Meanwhile, he had devoted himself to the study and arrangement of the materials for the surgical history. His *Report on Amputations at the Hipjoint in Military Surgery* was published in 1867, his *Report on Excisions of the Head of the Femur for Gunshot Injury,* in 1869. These monographs met with general favor from the profession and exalted his reputation as a writer. The first surgical volume of *The Medical and Surgical History of the War of the Rebellion* appeared in 1870. It treated of the special wounds and injuries of the head, face, neck, spine, and chest. It was richly illustrated and contained interesting discussions of the vast amount of material dealt with. The second surgical volume was issued in 1876, and treated of the wounds and injuries of the abdomen, pelvis, back, and upper extremities. It was quite as interesting as the first volume and even larger. Both met with a most favorable reception at home and abroad. During the interval between the appearance of these volumes, and later, Otis wrote many articles, the most important being *A Report of Surgical Cases Treated in the Army of the United States from 1865 to 1871* (1871), *A Report on a Plan for Transporting Wounded Soldiers by Railway in Time of War* (1875); and *A Report on the Transport of Sick and Wounded by Pack Animals* (1877). These were all issued as circulars of the surgeon-general's office.

In 1877 he suffered a stroke of paralysis, and was an invalid thereafter until his death. He continued work, however, and at the time of his death, which his friend, Woodward, says came "as a welcome release from suffering" (*American Journal of the Medical Sciences,* July 1881, p. 293), was engaged on the third surgical volume, which was later completed under the editorship of Surgeon D. L. Huntington. Concerning Otis' methods of work, one of his assistants made the following comment: "It must be remembered that in order to achieve these various stupendous successes, the work was not all done by Dr. Otis alone. He had under his direct command at the time, in the old Ford's theater on 10th Street in Washington, a great body of skilled clerks, who did nothing beyond collecting, classifying, and arranging the records of the field and post hospitals of the Civil War; so this great mass of material was ever ready for the use of the medical officer in command of that division of the Museum" (*Medical Life,* May 1924, p. 192).

[W. A. Otis, *A Geneal. and Hist. Memoir of the Otis Family in America* (1924); circulars and circular orders, surgeon general's office, 1881; *Trans. Am. Medic. Ascoc.,* vol. XXXII (1881); *Medic. Life,* May 1924; *Am. Jour. of the Medic. Sciences,* July 1881; *British Medic. Jour.,* Aug. 13, 1881; *Evening Star* (Washington, D. C.), Feb. 23, 1881.]   P. M. A.

OTIS, HARRISON GRAY (Oct. 8, 1765–Oct. 28, 1848), statesman, was born in Boston, the eldest child of Samuel Allyne and Elizabeth (Gray) Otis. His father was brother to James Otis and Mercy Otis Warren [*qq.v.*], and the youngest child of Col. James Otis of Barnstable, Mass. His mother was the daughter of Harrison Gray (1711–94), treasurer of the province of Massachusetts Bay, and a refugee Loyalist in the Revolution. "Harry" Otis, as he was always called by his friends, inherited the winning personality, charming manners, and full-blooded enjoyment of life that have characterized the Otis family for two hundred years, and which marked him off from the somewhat austere and inflexible type of New England political leader. He also developed a brilliant if somewhat facile intellect. His education at the Boston Latin School was interrupted by the siege of Boston. Entering Harvard College in 1779, he graduated first in the class of 1783 and in later years received the usual appointment to the Harvard corporation and board of overseers that are awarded to successful alumni. His father, a merchant who had speculated heavily during the war, went bankrupt after its close. Harry read law with Judge John Lowell [*q.v.*] and was admitted to the Boston bar in 1786. The same year he commanded a volunteer infantry company during Shays's Rebellion, but did not see action; and made a reputation as an orator when taking his master's degree at Harvard.

Otis quickly rose to a leading place at the Boston bar, earned a large income for the period, and acquired within ten years considerable property, largely by investments and speculations in Boston real estate, and Maine and Yazoo lands. On May 31, 1790, he married the daughter of a Boston merchant, Sally Foster (1770–1836), who bore him eleven children. A liberal in social and religious matters, he was a member of the Brattle Square Church (Unitarian). A Federalist, like almost all of his class in New England, Otis first served his party in 1794 by dissuading the Boston town meeting from supporting Madison's anti-British resolutions. The same year, and in 1795, he was elected a Boston representative to the General Court of Massachusetts. Another burst of eloquence in Boston town meeting on April 25, 1796, routed the local Jeffersonians who were attacking Jay's Treaty, and helped to make Boston the "headquarters of

good principles" from the Federalist point of view. President Washington immediately appointed him United States district attorney for Massachusetts, an office which he resigned the same year in order to enter Congress, as the successor to Fisher Ames [*q.v.*].

In Congress (1797–1801) Otis established close relations with the South Carolina Federalists, John Rutledge, Jr., and Robert Goodloe Harper [*q.v.*], and supported the measures of President Adams' administration by speech and written word. He was foremost in creating the system of armed neutrality in 1797–98 to meet French aggression, which, like most of the Federalists, he considered a "Jacobin" offensive to undermine the federal government, and destroy the basis of American society. For that reason, he supported the Alien and Sedition Acts. An ardent admirer of Alexander Hamilton, he was preparing to urge a declaration of war against France in 1799, when President Adams accepted the conciliatory advances of the French government. In the factional fight that then broke out in the Federalist party Otis defended and supported the President. He and Mrs. Otis were leading figures in the "Republican Court" at Philadelphia, but found Washington little to their taste, and he refused to stand for reëlection to Congress in 1800.

Otis then settled down in Boston and became a leader in politics, in society, and at the bar. Charles Bulfinch [*q.v.*] was employed to design for him three of the most distinguished dwelling houses that are still standing in Boston. The first (now 141 Cambridge St.) was built in 1795–96 and sold in 1800, when a much larger one (85 Mount Vernon St.) was erected on Beacon Hill, the greater part of which Otis and a small syndicate had purchased, when a pasture, in order to develop as a residential district. The third Otis mansion (45 Beacon St.), built in 1806, became his home for the rest of his life; and he also maintained the country estate of "Oakley" in Watertown. The Otis houses were centers of Boston hospitality. J. Q. Adams wrote in 1816, "In the course of nearly thirty years that I have known him, and throughout the range of experience that I have had in that time, it has not fallen to my lot to meet a man more skilled in the useful art of entertaining his friends than Otis; . . . His Person while in Youth, his graceful Deportment, his sportive wit, his quick intelligence, his eloquent fluency, always made a strong impression upon my Mind; while his warm domestic Affection, his active Friendship, and his Generosity, always commanded my esteem" (Morison, *post,* I, 224).

In politics Otis was an active party manager, and the principal connecting link of the Federalist aristocracy with the Boston democracy; but he was never admitted to the inner councils of the "Essex Junto," who suspected insincerity in his polished manners, and possible defection in his support of President Adams. His few published orations do not justify the high reputation that he enjoyed as a public speaker. He was fluent, classical in language and diction, but ready in wit and allusion, the favorite orator of Boston town meeting in the generation between Samuel Adams and Daniel Webster. Otis served in the Massachusetts House of Representatives in 1802–05 and in 1813–14 (speaker, 1803–05), and in the state Senate 1805–13 and 1814–17 (president, 1805–06, 1808–11). Although not privy to the Federalist secession plot of 1804, he became an active leader of the state-rights movement in his party at the time of Jefferson's Embargo, consistently opposed the War of 1812, and led the Hartford Convention of 1814. Otis proposed a New England convention as early as 1808, but used his influence against a similar movement during the war until the summer of 1814 when, in his opinion, a convention became necessary to control and moderate the exasperated feelings of New England, to concert maneuvers for interstate defence against Great Britain when the federal government was powerless to help, and to procure concessions to New England commercial interests from the other states. He was chairman of the joint committee of the General Court which reported in favor of the Hartford Convention in October 1814, drafted the call to the other New England States, and was chosen by the legislature second of the twelve Massachusetts delegates to Hartford. In the Convention itself (Dec. 15, 1814–Jan. 5, 1815) Otis served on all important committees, and drafted the final report (*The Proceedings of a Convention of Delegates . . . at Hartford*, 1815), which well expressed his caution, moderation, and averseness to force an issue with the federal government. Appointed by the Governor of Massachusetts on Jan. 31, 1815, one of a committee of three to negotiate with the authorities at Washington about using federal revenues for state defense, he proceeded to the capital, but was met on the way by news of the Peace of Ghent, which rendered his mission abortive and himself ridiculous.

Otis supported both the administrations of Monroe, and helped to inaugurate the "era of good feelings" by entertaining the President at Boston in 1817. He was elected that year to the United States Senate, after declining a Federalist nomination to the governorship of Massachusetts. But he effectually shut himself out from becoming a national figure by becoming the public champion of the Hartford Convention. After consulting his friends on the desirability of publishing the journal of the Convention in 1818, he published *Letters Developing the Character and Views of the Hartford Convention* (1820), and *Otis' Letters in Defense of the Hartford Convention . . .* (1824), engaged in an acrid pamphlet controversy on it with J. Q. Adams (*Correspondence between John Quincy Adams . . . and Several Citizens of Massachusetts Concerning the Charge of a Design to Dissolve the Union . . .* 1829), and frequently adverted to the subject in his public speeches. Every such effort stirred up feelings and charges which he was powerless to allay, and which, however unjustified in fact, he would have better allowed the public to forget. In the United States Senate he did not particularly distinguish himself, although he entered with great ardor into the effort to form a northern bloc against the extension of slavery to Missouri in 1820. The atmosphere of Washington seemed so unfriendly, and his efforts to obtain payment of the Massachusetts war claims were so constantly thwarted, that he resigned his seat in 1822 in order to run for mayor of Boston. On that occasion he was defeated. The Federalist nomination for governor of Massachusetts was given to him in 1823, upon the refusal of John Brooks [*q.v.*] to run again. The Republicans put up a strong candidate, Dr. William Eustis [*q.v.*], and as Otis unwisely made the Hartford Convention the principal issue of the campaign, he was badly defeated; that defeat marked the passing of the Federalist party in its last stronghold.

Otis never relinquished his hold of local public affairs. He was thrice elected mayor of Boston (1829–31), and he acquired some notoriety by refusing to interfere with William Lloyd Garrison. He greatly deprecated and publicly denounced the abolitionist movement, which he foretold would bring about a division of the Union, but refused to countenance any suppression of free speech on slavery. In the 1820's Otis became a considerable owner of manufacturing stock, and a convert to protection, although he had been instrumental in defeating the Baldwin tariff of 1820. After flirting with the Jacksonian party he became a stout Whig, and a supporter of Henry Clay. Always an enemy to democracy, he firmly believed that the country was going to the dogs. In 1848, in his eighty-third year, Otis published a pungent letter against the "fifteen-gallon" temperance law, and another (Boston

Atlas, Oct. 2, 1848), in all the verve of his youthful style, in favor of General Taylor. Old age and debility prostrated him, and before the presidential campaign was over, he died at his Boston residence on Oct. 28, 1848.

[S. E. Morison, *The Life and Letters of Harrison Gray Otis, Federalist, 1765–1848* (2 vols., 1913), with portraits and bibliography; *Pubs. Colonial Soc. of Mass.,* XIV (1913), 329–50; *Mass. Hist. Soc. Proc.,* XLVIII (1915), 343–51; LX (1927), 24–31, 324–30; W. A. Otis, *A Geneal. and Hist. Memoir of the Otis Family in America* (1924); *Great Georgian Houses of America* (1933), pub. for the benefit of the Architect's Emergency Committee; obituary in *Boston Daily Advertiser,* Oct. 30, 1848.]   S. E. M.

OTIS, HARRISON GRAY (Feb. 10, 1837–July 30, 1917), soldier, journalist, was born at Marietta, Ohio, the youngest of the children of Stephen Otis and his second wife, Sarah Dyer Otis. He was descended from John Otis, an early colonist in Massachusetts. He received a brief common-school education and at the age of fourteen became a printer's apprentice. In 1856–57 he attended Wetherby's Academy at Lowell, Ohio, for five months, and afterward took a commercial course at Granger's College at Columbus. He resided for a time in Louisville, Ky., where he became an active member of the new Republican party and served as a delegate from that state to the national convention of 1860. He enlisted in the Union army at the beginning of the Civil War and served with the 12th and 23rd Ohio Infantry. He fought in fifteen engagements, was twice wounded, attained the rank of captain, and at the end of the war was brevetted major and lieutenant-colonel. After his discharge he returned to Marietta and for about eighteen months was publisher of a small local newspaper. In 1866–67 he was official reporter of the Ohio House of Representatives, then moved to Washington where he was foreman in the government printing office (1868–69). During this period he acted as Washington correspondent of the *Ohio State Journal,* and had immediate charge of the *Grand Army Journal.* In 1868 he was a delegate from the District of Columbia to the soldiers' and sailors' convention at Chicago which first nominated General Grant for the presidency. For about five years (1871–75) he was chief of a division in the Patent Office.

In 1876 Otis moved to California. He first settled in Santa Barbara and for four years conducted the Santa Barbara *Press.* From 1879 to 1881 he served as special agent of the Treasury Department to enforce the terms of the lease of the Alaska seal fisheries to the Alaska Commercial Company. In 1882 he moved to Los Angeles and purchased a substantial interest in the *Times,* which about this time had absorbed the *Weekly Mirror;* by 1886 he had acquired full control. For the next thirty years, as president and active manager of the Times-Mirror Company, he was one of California's most picturesque, forceful, and noted journalists. Under his wise and aggressive leadership, the *Times* contributed in many ways to the growth and expansion of Southern California. In 1888, he was largely instrumental in organizing the Los Angeles Chamber of Commerce. His journalistic career was temporarily interrupted by the Spanish-American War. At its outbreak, he was appointed brigadier-general of volunteers, and with his command saw active service in the Philippines. At the end of the war he was brevetted major-general "for meritorious conduct in action at Caloocán."

For many years the *Times* was widely known for its zealous championship of the open shop and for its bitter and unrelenting opposition to union labor. In revenge for its unsparing attacks, a group of union men dynamited the *Times* plant Oct. 1, 1910, destroying the building and killing twenty-one employees. The sensational trial (1911) of the McNamara brothers, charged with the crime, attracted nation-wide attention and came to a dramatic end by their confessions. (See *The New International Year Book,* 1911, pp. 138, 692–93). In 1914 Otis transferred his controlling interest to his daughter and son-in-law, Mr. and Mrs. Harry Chandler, but he continued in active direction of the *Times* until the day of his death. A contemporary journalist, speaking of his "most powerful personality" and "overwhelming individuality," says that "he permeated and dominated his entire establishment. He marched his martial way through every department—editorial, news, mechanical and business. He knew every detail of every department better than the men at the head of them."

In addition to his newspaper interests, Otis became identified with a number of business ventures all of which proved highly profitable: he was president of the board of control of the Los Angeles Suburban Homes Company; a director of the California-Mexico Land and Cattle Company, and president of the Colorado River Land Company, its successor. Throughout his long life he retained his early interest in politics, taking an active part in all state campaigns in California. He was an uncompromising Republican and vehement opponent of the Progressive movement in that party. He was interested in international arbitration, and one of his last efforts was developing the details of his peace program, outlined in his *Plan to End Wars* (1915), a synopsis of which had been published in the *Times* only a few days before his death.

On Sept. 11, 1859, Otis was married to Eliza A. Wetherby, who was actively associated with him in journalism until her death in 1904. Five children were born to them, one son and four daughters. He died at the home of his daughter, Mrs. Chandler, in Hollywood. His own city residence, "The Bivouac," had been given, the preceding Christmas, to Los Angeles County for a public art gallery; it is now known as the Otis Art Institute. Two daughters and thirteen grandchildren survived him.

[R. D. Hunt, *Cal. and Californians* (1926), vol. III; *Circular No. 17*, ser. of 1917, Cal. Commandery, Mil. Order of the Loyal Legion; *A Letter from Harrison Gray Otis* (pamphlet, 1917); J. M. Lee, *Hist. of Am. Journalism* (1923); *The Autobiog. of Lincoln Steffens* (1931), vol. II; F. B. Heitman, *Hist. Reg. . . . of the U. S. Army* (1903), vol. I; W. A. Otis, *A Geneal. and Hist. Memoir of the Otis Family in America* (1924); *Who's Who in America*, 1916–17; *Evening Herald* (Los Angeles), July 30, 1917; *Examiner* (Los Angeles), *San Francisco Chronicle* and *Los Angeles Times*, July 31, 1917.]   P. O. R.

OTIS, JAMES (Feb. 5, 1725–May 23, 1783), politician and publicist, came of a Glastonbury yeoman's family that emigrated to Massachusetts about 1631. His grandfather, John Otis (1657–1727), moved to Barnstable, commanded the militia of that county, served as judge for twenty-five years, and as councilor of the province for nineteen years. John's son James (1702–78), generally called Colonel Otis, a self-educated lawyer, married Mary Allyne of Pilgrim stock; James Otis, born in his grandfather's house at the Great Marshes, West Barnstable, was the eldest of their thirteen children. He was prepared for Harvard by the local minister, graduated with the class of 1743, studied law under Jeremiah Gridley [*q.v.*], was admitted in 1748 to the bar of Plymouth County, and two years later moved to Boston. In the Spring of 1755 he married Ruth, the well-dowered daughter of Capt. Nathaniel Cunningham, a Boston merchant. There were three children, a son and two daughters. Blackburn's portrait of Otis painted in 1755 shows a strong but plump and pleasant countenance, with shrewd, narrow-lidded eyes, giving no hint of the inner flame that eventually consumed him.

By painstaking study Otis became learned in the common, civil, and admiralty law; and his interest in the theory of law was coëval with his interest in the law itself. An enthusiastic student of the ancient classics, he published *The Rudiments of Latin Prosody . . . and the Principles of Harmony in Poetic and Prosaic Composition* (1760); another treatise, on Greek prosody, remained in manuscript and was destroyed with his other papers. He was also an avid reader of classical English literature, and of ancient and modern works on political theory. As a barrister his mind was supple, his apprehension quick, his pleading, brilliant and captivating: following the superior court circuit, he became known in all parts of the province. Thomas Hutchinson [*q.v.*] admitted "that he never knew fairer or more noble conduct in a pleader, than in Otis," who disdained technicalities and "defended his causes solely on their broad and substantial foundations" (Tudor, *post,* p. 36). Enemies later described him as a smugglers' attorney; actually, he acted as king's attorney in the absence of the attorney general in 1754 (Josiah Quincy, Jr., *Reports,* I, 402, note); and later, Governor Pownall appointed him king's advocate general of the vice-admiralty court at Boston.

In 1760, Pitt ordered the Sugar Act of 1733 to be strictly enforced. The royal customs collectors applied to the superior court of the province for writs of assistance, in order to help them in search of evidence of violation. Otis, in his official capacity, was expected to argue for the writs. Instead, he resigned his lucrative office and undertook, for Boston merchants, to oppose the issuance. Unfortunately the circumstances were such as to cause his motives to be questioned. Governor Shirley had promised to appoint Colonel Otis to the superior bench, and asked Francis Bernard [*q.v.*], who became governor in August 1760, to make the promise good. The elder Otis was now speaker of the House, and leader of the bar in the three southern counties; he had great influence over the rural members of the House, and both as member from Barnstable and as colonel of the county militia had cooperated loyally with the administration during the war. On Sept. 11, Chief Justice Stephen Sewall died. Colonel Otis at once bespoke Lieutenant-Governor Hutchinson's influence to be appointed junior associate justice, supposing the chief justiceship filled from the court itself. James Otis' account (*Boston Gazette,* Apr. 4, 1763) differs from Hutchinson's, written many years later (*The History of the Province of Massachusetts Bay,* III, 86; P. O. Hutchinson, *The Diary and Letters of . . . Thomas Hutchinson,* I, 1883, pp. 65–66) as to what assurances were given; but Hutchinson was appointed chief justice Nov. 13, 1760. One rumor had it that James Otis then declared "that he would set the province in flames, if he perished by the fire"; another, that he declaimed from the Aeneid, "Flectere si nequeo superos, Acheronta movebo!" Both stories were flatly denied by Otis; and, as John Adams pointed out, he had resigned an office far more lucrative than the one his father wanted; but the Loyalists always believed that his entire political course, and indeed the Revolution in Massachusetts, arose out of frustrated family ambition (Hutchinson, *History*, III, 88). Otis certainly felt that Hutchinson and Bernard had "double-crossed" him, and that they were endeavoring to accumulate the chief offices in the province.

In February 1761, Otis and Oxenbridge Thacher argued the illegality of writs of assistance before the full bench of the superior court, in the Council chamber at the Old State House, Boston. The picturesque scene was vividly described by John Adams in 1817 (*Works*, X, 247) to Otis' biographer: "Otis was a flame of fire! . . . he hurried away every thing before him. American independence was then and there born; the seeds of patriots and heroes were then and there sown . . ." But exactly what Otis said cannot now be recovered with any exactness. John Adams' notes taken on the occasion contain these significant sentences: "An act against the Constitution is void; an act against national equity is void; and if an act of Parliament should be made, in the very words of this petition, it would be void. The executive Courts must pass such acts into disuse. . . . Reason of the common law to control an act of Parliament" (*Works*, II, 522). The phrase, "Taxation without representation is tyranny," which was not germane to the issue, appears only in Adams' final expansion of his notes, made about 1820 (Tudor, *post*, p. 77). Otis and Thacher lost their case. But in 1766, Otis' position was sustained by Attorney General de Grey, who ruled that the act of Parliament in question did not authorize the issuance of writs of assistance in the Colonies (*Massachusetts Historical Society Proceedings*, LVIII, 1925, pp. 22, 71–73). The significance of Otis' speech, however, lies in his harking back to the constitutional doctrines of Coke and Sir Matthew Hale, invoking a fundamental law embodying the principles of natural law, and superior to acts of Parliament; a doctrine upon which colonial publicists leant during the next twenty-five years, which was embodied in the federal and state constitutions, and which in its final form became the American doctrine of judicial supremacy.

In May 1761, two months after this speech, Otis was chosen one of the four representatives of Boston to the General Court, the provincial legislature. His father was the same year reelected speaker of the House. Hutchinson (*History*, III, 166) credits the two with marshalling the old town and country parties into a popular bloc against the crown officials. In the session of 1761–62, they opposed the administration on sundry questions involving privilege, but promoted a grant of Mount Desert Island to Governor Bernard; this last was really a log-rolling device to get royal consent to establishing new townships in that part of Maine (W. O. Sawtelle, *Publications of the Colonial Society of Massachusetts*, XXIV, 1923, pp. 203–04). Otis was moderately interested in other new townships, but not those.

In his first political pamphlet, *A Vindication of the Conduct of the House of Representatives* (1762), Otis made a brief exposition of the rights of Englishmen, and defended his party's policy vigorously. Scurrilously abused as "Bluster" in the *Boston Evening Post*, Feb. 14, 1763, he lashed back savagely in the *Boston Gazette* for Feb. 28, Mar. 28, and Apr. 4, 1763. Yet, in the midst of these altercations, he struck a high note of patriotism in a Faneuil Hall speech as moderator of Boston town meeting. He extolled the British Constitution and the King; declared "Every British Subject in America is, of Common Right, by Acts of Parliament, and by the laws of God and Nature, entitled to all the essential Privileges of Britons"; that attempts to stretch the royal prerogative were responsible for whatever unpleasantness had occurred; that "the true Interests of Great Britain and her Plantations are mutual; and what God in his Providence has united, let no man dare attempt to pull assunder" (*Boston Gazette*, Mar. 21, 1763). On other occasions, the vehemence of Otis' language distressed even his friends (John Adams, *Works*, II, 142–44); and this conduct was the more wondered at because James was normally good-humored and sociable, like all his family. Friends and foes alike agreed that from 1761 to 1769 Otis was the political leader of Massachusetts Bay, although Samuel Adams was probably more popular in Boston. Otis was also active in local organizations like the "Sons of Liberty," and the "Corkass," which met in Tom Dawes' attic and made up a slate of candidates and measures for the town meeting (*Boston Evening Post*, Mar. 14, 21, 1763).

An appearance of coalition between Otis and Hutchinson in 1763–64, as John Adams remembered (*Works* X, 295–96), "well nigh destroyed Otis' popularity and influence forever"; and when on Feb. 1, 1764, Governor Bernard appointed Colonel Otis chief justice of the common pleas and judge of probate in Barnstable County, many assumed that the family had sold out. Adams declares that only the revival of attacks saved Otis from defeat in the spring election; but an examination of the newspaper files proves that he was not opposed in 1764. The next year, when he was scurrilously attacked in the *Evening Post* (especially in Samuel Waterhouse's ditty "Jemmibullero," May 13, 1765, in which he is called, among other things, a "rackoon" and a "filthy scunk") he almost failed of reëlection. In the meantime, to counteract the new Sugar or Revenue Act of 1764, Otis wrote *The Rights of the British Colonies Asserted and Proved*, published at Boston July 23, 1764, and reprinted in London the next year. "One of the earliest and ablest pamphlets written from the natural law point of view" (C. H. McIlwain, *The American Revolution*, 1923, p. 153), the *Rights* is a closely reasoned statement of the constitutional position of the colonies in the single commonwealth that Otis believed the British Empire to be. In it were developed the principles recorded in his writs of assistance argument, principles to which Otis remained faithful while he kept his reason. The "wavering" or "retreat" often referred to in secondary accounts is found neither in his writings nor his recorded speeches.

The House adopted Otis' doctrine as its own, and on June 14, 1764, he was appointed chairman of a committee of the General Court to correspond with other colonial assemblies. The proposed Stamp Act soon overshadowed the Sugar Act. The Stamp Act Congress was summoned by a circular letter of invitation to the other colonies, adopted by the Massachusetts House on motion of Otis, who was appointed one of the three Massachusetts delegates. A few days afterward came the news of Patrick Henry's Virginia resolves, which Otis thought treasonable, but which temporarily took the leadership of public sentiment out of his hands, fomenting riots at Boston that summer. Otis much preferred "dutiful and loyal Addresses to his Majesty and his Parliament, who alone under God can extricate the Colonies from the painful Scenes of Tumult, Confusion, & Distress" (to Henry Sherburne, Nov. 26, 1765, Stamp Act Manuscripts, Library of Congress). The Congress met at New York on Oct. 7. On this, Otis' second and last journey outside New England, he met other colonial leaders such as Thomas McKean [*q.v.*], who later referred to him as "the boldest and best speaker" (John Adams, *Works*, X, 60), and John Dickinson [*q.v.*], who carried on a friendly correspondence with Otis for several years, and through him published the "Letters from a Farmer" and Liberty Song

in Boston (Mercy O. Warren, *History of the Rise, Progress and Termination of the American Revolution*, 1805, vol. I, 412–14; *Warren-Adams Letters*, I, 1917, pp. 3–7). Otis served on one of the three committees of the Congress, which adopted his constitutional doctrine, while rejecting colonial representation in Parliament, which Otis had proposed in his *Rights of the Colonies*. It seems probable that Otis' colleagues persuaded him that representation would not help the colonies, for he did not mention it thereafter (Hutchinson to Franklin, Jan. 6, 1766, Bancroft Manuscripts, New York Public Library).

Having failed to persuade Governor Bernard to let the courts function without stamped paper until the act was repealed, Otis and his lawyer friends had plenty of leisure. In the "Monday Night Club" of politicians, Otis was "fiery and feverous; his imagination flames, his passions blaze" (John Adams, *Works*, II, 162–63). But he also belonged to the "Sodalitas," a law club that met under Gridley's presidency to study and discuss ancient law; and John Rowe notes Otis' presence at sundry private dinners, public banquets, coffee-house reunions, tea parties, and country-house assemblies (Anne R. Cunningham, *Letters and Diary of John Rowe*, 1903). In the same year, he published three pamphlets. One of these, *Considerations on behalf of the Colonists, in a Letter to a Noble Lord*, was a reply to Soame Jenyns' defence of the Stamp Act. *A Vindication of the British Colonies*, and *Brief Remarks on the Defence of the Halifax Libel on the British-American Colonies*, were replies to Martin Howard's *Letter from a Gentleman at Halifax*, and its sequel. The first, dated Sept. 4, 1765, was a lively discussion of "virtual" representation. Otis declared that Jenyns' reasoning could as well prove the whole globe, as America, represented in the House of Commons; if Manchester and Birmingham were not represented, they ought to be. His greatest indignation was reserved for Howard's statement that the admission of colonial representation would defile the "purity" and destroy the "beauty and symmetry" of the House of Commons (*Vindication*, p. 28). He challenged the justice of suppressing colonial manufactures (*Considerations*, p. 22), and pointed out the exploitation inherent in the imperial system (pp. 29–30). But he still stoutly maintained that Parliament had "an undoubted power, authority, and jurisdiction, over the whole" (*Ibid.*, pp. 9, 13, 36). In *Brief Remarks*, he made a furious attack on his critics.

Otis' pamphlets probably had more influence

in America and England, before 1774, than those of any other American except John Dickinson. They laid a broad basis for American political theory on natural law. Otis avoided the two impasses into which several of his contemporaries stepped: the distinction between external and internal taxation, and the sanctity of colonial charters. But in advocating colonial representation, he took a false turning himself. He had not the foresight to perceive a federal solution: an *imperium in imperio* was to him "the greatest of all political solicisms" (*Vindication*, p. 18). Nor did he face the choice between submission and revolution. If Parliament's sovereign authority was not recognized "the colonies would be independent, which none but rebels, fools, or madmen, will contend for . . . Were these colonies left to themselves, to-morrow, America would be a meer shambles of blood and confusion . . ." (*Ibid.*, pp. 21–22). Neither in theory nor in tastes was Otis a democrat; his often vituperative language arose from his own hot passions, not from any catering to popularity.

At the spring election of 1766, Samuel Adams, whose qualities were needed to temper Otis' rashness and turbulence, and the Hampshire Cato, Joseph Hawley [*q.v.*], were elected with him to the General Court. During the next two years, this triumvirate directed the majority in the House of Representatives. Otis generally prepared the rough draft of the state papers that issued from that body, while Adams did the smoothing and revision. When the General Court met, it refused to reëlect Chief Justice Hutchinson and his Oliver associates to the Council, and James Otis was chosen speaker of the House. Governor Bernard negatived both this election and that of six councilors, including Colonel Otis. During the next two years, no opportunity was neglected by the triumvirate to put the Governor and Lieutenant-Governor in a hole; and Otis spent so much time on public affairs that his law practice was almost completely neglected.

When news of the Townshend Act arrived, Otis was prompt to denounce an incitement to violence which had been posted on the Boston "liberty tree." Presiding over a town meeting that very day (Nov. 20, 1767), he declared that "no possible circumstances" could justify "tumults and disorders, either to our consciences before God, or legally before men" (Richard Frothingham, *Life and Times of Joseph Warren*, 1865, pp. 38–39, notes). Otis also presided over the town meeting on Oct. 28 that launched the non-importation movement. The Massachusetts circular letter, adopted by the House on Feb.

11, 1768, was the joint product of Otis and Samuel Adams (John Adams, *Works*, X, 367). They triumphed when the House voted not to rescind 92 to 17, on June 30, 1768. This spirited defiance did more to unite the colonies than any measure since the Stamp Act. The Massachusetts "92" became another such talisman as No. 45 of the *North Briton*.

The sloop *Liberty* case, the news that Otis and Adams were threatened with trial for treason in England, and that troops were being sent to Boston, followed in quick succession. Yet Otis still continued to oppose direct action. He organized and moderated the town meeting of Sept. 12–13, 1768, which quashed proposals of resistance to the landing of troops, and called a convention at Faneuil Hall ten days later. Otis, to the dismay of Adams, refused at first to take his seat in this convention, kept Adams quiet when he did appear, and doubtless showed his hand in the mild resolutions that the convention passed (W. V. Wells, *The Life and Public Services of Samuel Adams*, 1865, vol. I, 216–18; Hutchinson, *History*, III, 205–06). Considering his repeated efforts to prevent violence, it is not surprising that Otis' irritable nature was stirred to a frenzy of resentment when the publication of some intercepted letters showed that Bernard, and the commissioners of the customs, had been writing home that he was a malignant incendiary. On Sept. 4, 1769, he posted these officials in the *Boston Gazette* as liars. The next evening he entered the British Coffee House at the site of 60 State St., where John Robinson and other crown officers were seated. A brawl ensued in which Robinson struck Otis a severe blow on the head with a cutlass or hanger. Otis was finally rescued by outsiders. He sued Robinson and obtained a verdict of £2000 damages; Governor Hutchinson, who was delighted at what he termed "a very decent drubbing," was planning "to steer this whole business" so as to get Robinson off and reward him with promotion, when Otis, on receiving an apology from Robinson's attorney, released all damages beyond court costs, lawyers' fees, and physicians' bills, which amounted to £112 10s 8d (Tudor, *post*, pp. 360–62, 503–06; *Proceedings Massachusetts Historical Society*, XLVII, 1914, p. 209; *Publications of the Colonial Society of Massachusetts*, XI, 1910, pp. 5–7; Massachusetts Archives, XXV, 437–38, XXVI, 375; papers of the case in Suffolk County Court Files, 102, 135).

Robinson's assault finished Otis' career. It is true that for several years his conduct at times had given people cause to doubt his sanity (*Evening Post*, Feb. 14, 1763, p. 2; *Proceedings Mas-*

sachusetts Historical Society, IV, 1870, p. 53), and an offensive garrulity had been growing on him. His family life was unhappy: Mrs. Otis, "beautiful, placid and formal" (Tudor, p. 20) was a high Tory. But the crack on his head permanently unhinged his reason. "He rambles and wanders like a ship without a helm," noted John Adams in January 1770 (*Works*, II, 226); in February he was "raving mad," broke windows in the Old State House, fired guns from his window (John Rowe, *Diary*, pp. 199, 201), called on Governor Hutchinson, and craved his protection on the king's highway. He did not stand for election in 1770, but seemed so completely restored in 1771 as to be chosen once more, and for the last time; his course at that session was conciliatory. But by September he was as distracted as ever, and began to drink heavily (Massachusetts Archives, XXVII, 228, 246–47); and in December 1771 the probate court, on representation that James Otis was *non compos mentis,* appointed his younger brother Samuel A. Otis guardian (*American Law Review,* July 1869, p. 664). He enjoyed several lucid intervals later; but none of his political opinions recorded subsequent to his injury are important.

After 1771 Otis led a quiet life, well cared for by friends and relatives. On June 17, 1775, he borrowed a gun, and rushed among the flying bullets on Bunker Hill, but returned unscathed (*Proceedings Massachusetts Historical Society,* XII, 1873, p. 69). Only fire from heaven could release his fiery soul; death came, as he had always wished it to come, by a stroke of lightning, as he was watching a summer thunderstorm in the Isaac Osgood farmhouse at Andover, on May 23, 1783.

[In addition to the pamphlets mentioned in the text, Otis probably wrote the political introduction to the 1764 edition of William Wood's *New England's Prospect* (see *Proc. Mass. Hist. Soc.,* VI, 1863, p. 250). All the political pamphlets are reprinted with an introduction by C. F. Mullett in *The Univ. of Mo. Studies,* IV, nos. 3, 4, July, Oct. 1929. The best discussion of their doctrine is in B. F. Wright, Jr., *American Interpretations of Natural Law* (1931). For bibliography of various versions of the writs of assistance speech, see Edward Channing, *A Hist. of the U. S.,* III (1912), 5, notes. Many cases in which Otis was an attorney are reported, and the legality of writs of assistance discussed by Horace Gray, with illustrative documents, in Josiah Quincy, Jr., *Reports of Cases . . . in the Superior Court of Judicature of the Province of Mass. Bay,* I (1865), pp. 395–540; but see an opinion by Attorney General de Grey, printed by G. G. Wolkins in *Proc. Mass. Hist. Soc.,* LVIII (1925), 71–73. Otis contributed many articles, signed and unsigned, to the *Boston Gazette* between 1761 and 1769; answers or attacks may be found in the *Boston Evening Post.* He destroyed all his papers before his death, and as he corresponded little, very few of his letters are in existence. The Otis MSS. and Otis Papers at the Mass. Hist. Soc. are mainly law papers of his father, and

contain but a few personal letters. John Adams' "Diary," and his letters to William Tudor about Otis are in C. F. Adams, ed., *The Works of John Adams,* vols. II (1850) and X (1856). Thomas Hutchinson, as he once promised Otis (Mass. Archives, XXVI, 86), was "revenged of him" in *The Hist. of the Province of Mass. Bay,* III (1828); the more vituperative and gossipy "Origin and Progress of the American Rebellion" written by Peter Oliver in 1781 (Egerton MSS., Br. Museum; copies in Mass. Hist. Soc. and Lib. of Cong.) is amusing, but adds little save invective to Hutchinson. Many of the latter's contemporary comments in his correspondence (Mass. Archives, XXV–XXVI; Bancroft MSS., N. Y. Public Lib.), are printed in J. K. Hosmer, *The Life of Thomas Hutchinson* (1896). Other unfavorable comments may be found in the Bernard and Chalmers Papers among the Sparks MSS. in the Harvard College Lib.

William Tudor, *The Life of James Otis* (1823), is the only biography, and J. H. Ellis, "James Otis," *Am. Law Rev.,* July 1869, pp. 641–65, the only article, worth mentioning. Richard Frothingham, *The Rise of the Republic* (1st ed., 1872), and J. G. Palfrey, *Hist. of New England,* vol. V (1890), contain the fullest account of Massachusetts politics in the period when Otis was active. The portraits of Otis and his wife, painted in 1755 by Joseph Blackburn, are owned by Mrs. Charles F. Russell, and usually exhibited in the Boston Museum of Fine Arts. The best reproductions are in the Catalogue entitled *Massachusetts Bay Colony Tercentenary Loan Exhibition of One Hundred Colonial Portraits,* published by that Museum in 1930. See also W. A. Otis, *A Geneal. and Hist. Memoir of the Otis Family in America* (1924); W. H. Whitmore, *A Mass. Civil List for the Colonial and Provincial Periods* (1870).]

S. E. M.

OTT, ISAAC (Nov. 30, 1847–Jan. 1, 1916), physician and writer, was born in Northampton County, Pa., the son of Jacob and Sarah Ann LaBarre Ott. He studied at Lafayette College, Easton, Pa., receiving his degree of A.B. in 1867, and the next year entered as a medical student at the University of Pennsylvania in Philadelphia, where he received the degree of M.D. in 1869. He began the practice of medicine at Easton, Pa., and always considered that place his home although he was frequently called away by the numerous positions that he held. He was resident physician of St. Mary's Hospital in Philadelphia during the year 1871. After a few years of practical experience he went abroad for further study and attended lectures at the Universities of Leipzig, Würzburg, and Berlin. He was for a time lecturer in physiology at the University of Pennsylvania (1878–79) and in 1879 a fellow in the biology department of John Hopkins University in Baltimore. In 1894 he became professor of physiology in the Medico-Chirurgical College in Philadelphia, and during 1895–96 was dean of the College but resigned that office, preferring to devote more time to his practice, teaching, research, and writing. In addition to his practice in Easton and his teaching in Philadelphia, Ott was for many years consulting neurologist to the Pennsylvania Asylum in Norristown. He resigned from the faculty of the Medico-Chirurgical College two years before his death but continued to be director of laboratories. His death, caused by pneumonia, occurred at his home in Easton.

Ott was not only a successful practitioner and teacher but he found time for extensive researches. He studied the actions of medicines on the human body and the effects of certain drugs, particularly the alkaloids which act as depressants or stimulants, such as cocain, veratria, gelsemium, lobelina, lycoctonia, and thebain. Under the general title of "Contributions to the Physiology and Pathology of the Nervous System" he published at different times a series of twenty neurological papers, among them an account of the retrograde and lateral movements with hypnotism; and a report of the effect of section of the spinal cord on the excretion of carbonic acid. His later researches were devoted to the endocrine secretions and the thermogenetic centers of the brain. He is credited with the discovery of the hormone of milk secretion. Also he was the first scientist to demonstrate that injury to the corpus striatum causes a rise in heat production and body temperature. His papers on his thermogenetic researches include: *A New Function of the Optic Thalami* (1879), in collaboration with G. B. W. Field; *The Heat-Centre in the Brain* (1887); *The Four Cerebral Heat-Centres* (1887), in collaboration with W. S. Carter; *The Thermo-Inhibitory Apparatus* (1887), with Charles Colmar; and *Thermogenetic Apparatus: Its Relation to Atropine* (1887), also with Charles Colmar; and *The Heat-Centres of the Cortex Cerebri and Pons Varolii*. His other writings include: *Action of Medicines* (1878); *Modern Antipyretics* (1891); *Textbook of Physiology* (1904); and *Internal Secretions* (1910). He was a member of the American Physiological Society; the American Neurological Society; German Medical Society of New York; Philadelphia Neurological Society; and the American Society of Naturalists. He was survived by his widow, Katherine (Wykoff) Ott, whom he had married on Oct. 14, 1886.

[Joseph McFarland, memoir in the *Jour. of Nervous and Mental Disease*, Mar. 1916; *Who's Who in America*, 1914–15; J. W. Jordan, *Encyc. of Pa. Biog.*, vol. II (1914); *Jour. Am. Medic. Asso.*, Jan. 1916; H. A. Kelly and W. L. Burrage, *Am. Medic. Biogs.* (1920); *Phila. Evening Bull.*, Jan. 1, 1916; *Pub. Ledger* (Phila.), Jan. 2, 1916.]   F. E. W.

OTTASSITE [See OUTACITY, fl. 1756–1777].

OTTENDORFER, ANNA BEHR UHL (Feb. 13, 1815–Apr. 1, 1884), philanthropist and proprietor of the *New-Yorker Staats-Zeitung*, was the daughter of Eduard Behr, a merchant in Würzburg, Germany. She was born in that city. Living in an age when higher education for women was generally frowned upon, she enjoyed only a common-school training, though showing an early aptitude for learning. Of the first years of her life little else is known. In 1836 or 1837, in company with a relative, she left Germany for the United States, determined to make her own way in the growing republic of the West. The first year she spent with a brother in Niagara County, N. Y. In 1838 she made the acquaintance of a young printer, Jacob Uhl, whom she married in New York City the same year. The early years of their married life were marked by struggle and penury. In 1844 they purchased, on the instalment plan, the German job-printing and book-and-newspaper publishing business of Julius Bötticher in New York. The *New-Yorker Staats-Zeitung* was printed in this office. By dint of the hard work and thriftiness of the two owners, the enterprise proved so successful that they were able the next year to purchase the *Staats-Zeitung,* then a small weekly. Anna Uhl did her full share as compositor, secretary, and general manager. The paper developed first into a tri-weekly, then into a daily publication. In 1852 Uhl died, and the widow, displaying remarkable perseverance and executive ability, not only cared for her six small children but also continued to attend to the constantly growing business of her publishing concern and of the *Staats-Zeitung* in particular. From 1852 to 1859 she was the sole manager, declining several flattering offers of purchase. On July 23, 1859, she was married to her assistant, Oswald Ottendorfer [*q.v.*].

After this marriage, which did not cause Mrs. Ottendorfer to discontinue her managerial activities, the newspaper enjoyed even greater success, financially and professionally, than before. Daily she would receive in her private offices a host of visitors, many of whom came to solicit her philanthropic cooperation. In accordance with her means Mrs. Ottendorfer had always engaged in charitable work; in her declining years, when she had amassed a considerable fortune, she did so extensively. Many of her philanthropies, of considerable scope for their day, were privately bestowed and have never been published. In 1875 she founded the Isabella Home for Aged Women in Astoria, Long Island, named in memory of her deceased daughter. In 1881, she gave, in memory of her deceased son, the Hermann Uhl Memorial Fund for German-American educational purposes in New York City and Milwaukee. The next year she donated a large sum for the women's pavilion of the German Hospital in New York City, and soon after another for the German Dispensary on Second Avenue, also in New York City. Institutions in Brooklyn, N. Y., Newark and Elizabeth, N. J., and Meriden, Conn., also benefited by her charities. She gave liberally, too, for providing means for the study of the German language in New York and elsewhere. In 1883 she was decorated by the Empress Augusta of Germany for her charitable endeavors. Further sums for philanthropic purposes were stipulated in her last will. Of her six children, all by her first marriage, a son and three daughters survived her.

[See: *Harper's Bazar*, May 3, 1884; H. A. Rattermann, *Anna Ottendorfer, Eine deutsch-amerikanische Philanthropin* (1885), reprinted from *Der Deutsche Pionier*, Nov. 1884; A. B. Faust, *The German Element in the U. S.* (1927), vol. II; *Zur Erinnerung an Anna Ottendorfer* (1884); *Sonntagsblatt der New-Yorker Staats-Zeitung*, Apr. 6, 1884.]   E. H. Z.

OTTENDORFER, OSWALD (Feb. 26, 1826–Dec. 15, 1900), philanthropist and proprietor of the *New-Yorker Staats-Zeitung*, was the son of Vincenz and Catharine (Neumeister) Ottendorfer. He was born, according to one source, on Feb. 14, but in all likelihood the later date is correct in conformity to the Gregorian calendar, while the earlier date is based upon Old-Style computation. The youngest of six children, he was born in the town of Zwittau in Moravia, then a province of Austria-Hungary, now in Czechoslovakia. His father was a clothmaker in fair circumstances. After attending the school of his native town and the gymnasia of Leitomischl and Brünn, he entered the University of Vienna in 1846 and studied chiefly philosophy. The next year he emigrated to Prague, learning the Czech language and taking up the study of law at the university. When in 1848 liberal uprisings occurred sporadically in various sections of the German-speaking countries, Ottendorfer took an active part, first in the revolt against the Metternich government in Vienna, then in the Schleswig-Holstein war against Denmark, and finally in the revolutions in Saxony and Baden. From 1849 to 1850 he continued his university studies in Heidelberg but, under the constant menace of arrest by the victorious forces of reaction, decided to flee first to Switzerland, then to the United States. He embarked for America late in September 1850 and arrived in New York on Oct. 26. After many bitter struggles he secured employment in the counting-room of the *New-Yorker Staats-Zeitung* in 1851. The next year, when the proprietor of this newspaper, Jacob Uhl, died, Ottendorfer became the assistant of the widow, Anna (Behr) Uhl (see Ottendorfer, Anna Behr

Uhl), in its management. In 1858 he was made editor; the following year, on July 23, he married Mrs. Uhl.

Under his management the *Staats-Zeitung* flourished, developing from an insignificant foreign-language newspaper into an influential, widely read metropolitan organ. A reform Democrat, Ottendorfer was active in anti-Tammany movements in New York and through his editorial and other public utterances became a force even in national politics. He served as alderman and supervisor in New York City from 1872 to 1874 and was a candidate for mayor in 1874. He gave $300,000 for the erection and endowment of an educational institution in his native town (Die Ottendorfer'sche Freie Volks-Bibliothek) and founded a home for aged and indigent men on Long Island. The Ottendorfer Branch of the New York Public Library in New York was also established by him. He was universally respected as a man of substantial character, stanch liberalism, and great social-mindedness. The Ottendorfer Memorial Fellowship awarded annually to an American student of the German language and literature for study abroad was created in his memory.

[See *Who's Who in America*, 1899–1900; *Zur Erinnerung an Oswald Ottendorfer* (1900), published by the *Staats-Zeitung*; and *Sonntagsblatt der New-Yorker Staats-Zeitung*, Dec. 16, 1900.]   E. H. Z.

OTTERBEIN, PHILIP WILLIAM (June 3, 1726–Nov. 17, 1813), German Reformed clergyman, founder of the Church of the United Brethren in Christ, was born at Dillenburg, in what is now the Prussian administrative district of Wiesbaden, the fourth of the ten children of Johann Daniel and Wilhelmina Henrietta (Hoerlen) Otterbein, and the elder of a pair of twins. His father, grandfather, and five brothers were ministers; his one sister to live to maturity became a minister's wife. He was educated at the Reformed seminary at Herborn, where the Calvinistic theological atmosphere was mollified somewhat by pietistic strains in one or two of the professors. On June 13, 1749, he was ordained as vicar of Ockersdorf in succession to his brother. His evangelical zeal and strictness were disliked by his ecclesiastical superiors, so that when Michael Schlatter [*q.v.*] came to Herborn to recruit missionaries for work in Pennsylvania, Otterbein was encouraged to volunteer. He did, and arrived at New York in Schlatter's company July 28, 1752. Till his death sixty-one years later he was the active pastor of various German Reformed congregations: at Lancaster, Pa., 1752–58; Tulpehocken, 1758–60; Frederick, Md., 1760–65; York, Pa., 1765–74; and of the

Otterbein

Second Evangelical Reformed Church, Baltimore, 1774–1813. On Apr. 19, 1762, he married Susan Le Roy of Lancaster, whose sister a few years later married John William Hendel [q.v.]. His wife's death Apr. 22, 1768, was a grievous affliction to him, and he never remarried. In 1770–71 he made a long-deferred visit to his relatives in Germany. To the end of his life he was a member in good standing of the German Reformed Coetus of Pennsylvania and was regarded in fact as one of its noblest supports. In turn he seems to have prized his relation to the Coetus and always considered himself a minister of the Reformed Church. He was, nevertheless, the instigator of a non-sectarian religious movement, to which, shortly before his death, he gave the status of an independent denomination.

At Lancaster, which was a frontier community when he came to it, Otterbein underwent a period of great emotional stress, accompanied by a clarifying and deepening of his religious convictions such as is usually designated by the term "conversion." Thereafter he devoted himself with heroic energy to religious work and tried particularly to minister to the spiritual needs of the unchurched Germans who were scattered everywhere through the backwoods of Pennsylvania and Maryland. At Whitsuntide one year, probably 1768, he had his famous meeting with Martin Boehm [q.v.] at Isaac Long's farm some six miles northeast of Lancaster, and after that the two men worked together cordially. By 1772 he was organizing classes on the Wesleyan model and appointing class leaders. On May 4, 1774, the day he began his duties in Baltimore, he met Francis Asbury [q.v.], who was ever after his friend and admirer. Otterbein took part in Asbury's consecration Dec. 27, 1784, to the office of superintendent of the Methodists in America. In 1789, at a meeting at Otterbein's parsonage, Otterbein, Boehm, and six lay evangelists formed an organization of a sort and adopted a confession of faith, which was evidently the work of Otterbein himself. During all these years he was making frequent trips through Maryland and Pennsylvania and even into Virginia. In 1800 the first annual conference of the United Brethren was held near Frederick, Md. Otterbein was seriously ill in 1805 and thereafter traveled never more than a few miles from Baltimore, and the movement of which he had been the leader began to fall into the hands of younger men. Many of them by this time were administering the sacraments and conducting themselves in general as if they were ordained ministers. Seven weeks before his death Otterbein was persuaded to ordain three of them, Christian Newcomer, Joseph

Otto

Hoffman, and Frederick Schaffer. Why he had declined for so many years to take this step, and what the condition of his mind was when finally he did take it, were for two generations the subject of violent controversy, and to these questions no decisive answer can be given. By conferring ordination upon them, Otterbein established the United Brethren as, according to Protestant views, a branch of the universal church.

He was a man of lofty character, and in personal culture a strange contrast to his rude associates, all of whom were products of their frontier environment. He left almost no letters or papers, and his only known publication is *Die heilbringende Menschwerdung und der herrliche Sieg Jesu Christi* (Germantown, Pa., 1763). He made a temperate use of tobacco and alcohol, and raised money to buy bells for his church by organizing a lottery, but he opposed the use of organs, patronage of the theatre, and membership in the Masonic order.

[Henry Harbaugh, *The Fathers of the German Reformed Church*, vol. II (Lancaster, Pa., 1857); A. W. Drury, *The Life of Rev. Philip Wm. Otterbein* (Dayton, Ohio, 1884), rev. and incorp. in his *Hist. of the Church of the United Brethren in Christ* (Dayton, 1924); W. J. Hinke, "Philip Wm. Otterbein and the Reformed Church," *Presbyt. and Reformed Rev.*, July 1901; *Minutes and Letters . . . of the German Reformed Congregations in Pa., 1747–92* (1903).]   G. H. G.

OTTO, BODO (1711–June 12, 1787), one of the more influential German settlers of Pennsylvania during the first half of the eighteenth century, senior surgeon of the Continental Army, was born in Hanover, Germany. His father was Christopher Otto, controller of the district of Schartzfels, and his mother Maria Magdalena Nienecken. He was named for his baptismal sponsor, Privy Councilor Baron Bodo von Oberg. He received an excellent scholastic education with a view to entering the profession of medicine, served an apprenticeship with physicians and surgeons in Harzburg, Hildesheim, and Hamburg, was intern for a time at the Lazaretto at Hamburg, and served as surgeon in the Duke of Celle's Dragoons. In 1736 he was married to Elizabeth Sanchen and settled in Luneburg where he was accepted as a member of the "College of Surgeons" and became surgeon to the prisoners and invalids in the fortress of Kalkberg. After the death of his first wife he was married in 1742 to Catharina Dorothea Dahncken. Three sons by this marriage became surgeons and later assisted their father in hospital service during the American Revolution. In 1749 he was appointed chief surgeon for the district of Schartzfels. This position he held until 1755, when, with his family, he emigrated to America on the *Neptune* from Rotterdam. He opened an office in Philadelphia late in 1755, but in 1760 he removed to New Jersey, where his practice is said to have extended over Gloucester, Salem, and Cumberland counties. After the death of his second wife he returned in 1766 to Philadelphia, and later in the same year married Maria Margaretha Paris (J. B. Linn, *Record of Pennsylvania Marriages Prior to 1810*, II, 1880, p. 339), who survived him.

Otto was a stanch Lutheran and through the influence of the Patriarch Henry Melchior Mühlenberg, a lifelong friend, removed to Reading, Pa., in 1773. His influence amongst his countrymen of German descent was great and he became a leader in the patriot cause, serving upon the Berks County Committee of Safety and as delegate to the Pennsylvania Provincial Congress of 1776. Later in 1776 he was appointed senior surgeon of the Middle Division of the Continental hospitals and labored in New Jersey with the wounded from the battle of Long Island. On Feb. 17, 1777, Congress ordered him to Trenton to establish a military hospital for the treatment of smallpox. He remained until September 1777 when he was assigned to a hospital in Bethlehem, Pa. In the spring of 1778 he was placed in charge of the hospitals at Yellow Springs where many of the sick from the camp at Valley Forge were treated. Upon the reorganization of the medical and hospital departments by Congress in 1780, Otto was one of the fifteen physicians selected for the hospital department and was among the last to leave the service Feb. 1, 1782. At the time of his retirement from the army Dr. John Cochran, the director-general, wrote a testimonial commenting upon Otto's humanity and the success of his medical practice. After the war he reopened his Philadelphia office but soon returned to Reading. He had been elected a member of the American Philosophical Society in 1769 and had for many years been an active member of the Pennsylvania German Society. He died in 1787 and is buried in the churchyard of Trinity Lutheran Church of Reading, where a shaft has been erected to his memory by the D.A.R. A sword and some of his surgical instruments are in the collection of the Historical Society of Berks County.

[Most of the information about Bodo Otto is contained in unprinted materials: in the archives of the Pa. German Soc., the Hist. Soc. of Berks County, the Hist. Soc. of Pa., the records of the Adj.-Gen. in Washington, and in documents in the possession of a descendant, James E. Gibson of Phila.]   J. B. N.

OTTO, JOHN CONRAD (Mar. 15, 1774–June 26, 1844), physician, was born near Woodbury, N. J., the son of Dr. Bodo and Catherina

(Schweighauser) Otto and the grandson of Bodo Otto [*q.v.*]. His mother was the daughter of a Swiss immigrant. Young Otto was sent to the College of New Jersey (later Princeton) and graduated in 1792 at the age of eighteen. He entered the office of Benjamin Rush the next spring and became Rush's favorite pupil and close friend until the latter's death. In 1796 he was graduated from the University of Pennsylvania; his graduation thesis was a study on epilepsy. He returned to the subject in later life when in 1828 he thought he had found a successful cure for the disease ("Case of Epilepsy, Successfully Treated," *North American Medical and Surgical Journal*, July 1828). Settling as a practitioner in Philadelphia, he quickly had opportunity to study yellow fever, which appeared in epidemic proportions in 1797, 1798, 1799, 1802, 1803 and 1805. In the second of these epidemics, Otto was himself attacked. In the same year, 1798, he was elected a physician to the Philadelphia Dispensary, a position that he held for five years. He was also for many years physician both to the Orphan Asylum and the Magdalen Asylum.

Otto's most important contribution to medical science was his original description of hemophilia in the *Medical Repository* (vol. VI, 1803, p. 3) under the title "An Account of an Hemorrhagic Disposition Existing in certain Families." Although isolated and incomplete accounts of this hereditary disease can be found in the literature since the time of the Talmud, Otto's may fairly be considered the first adequate description, so that the attention of the medical world was fixed upon it as a recognized clinical entity. He noted the essential feature of transmission in one family (Smith-Sheppard) over a period of at least seventy or eighty years, also "that the males only are subject," and "although the females are exempt, they are still capable of transmitting it to their male children." Two years later Otto published another paper on the same subject (*Philadelphia Medical Museum*, vol. I, 1805, no. 3), giving the history of a Maryland family, and in 1808 his original paper was reprinted in the London *Medical and Physical Journal* (July 1808). Soon confirmed by other American observers, the work was recognized and expanded in Germany by Nasse and Schönlein. It was one of the most notable contributions made by an American to medical science up to that time.

When Benjamin Rush died in 1813, Otto was chosen to succeed him as a physician to the Pennsylvania Hospital and served for twenty-two years. On his resignation in 1834 a special resolution acknowledged his "long, faithful and useful" labors, and it is probable that Otto's own generation attached more importance to his bedside labors and lectures than it did to his description of hemophilia. To meet the expected cholera epidemic in 1832 a committee of twelve leading physicians was appointed to take measures necessary to cope with the situation. Otto was unanimously selected chairman of the body. This was the western extension of the first great modern cholera epidemic. In Philadelphia alone during July and August 1832 there were 2,240 cases with 750 deaths. After the epidemic, the city of Philadelphia presented a handsome silver pitcher to Otto in recognition of his services. Elected a member of the College of Physicians in March 1819, he held various offices in that body, being censor for many years and vice-president for the last four years of his life. Some at least of his papers were read before that body, including an article on "Congenital Incontinence of Urine," which though done in 1830, fourteen years before his death, seems to be the last medical article that he wrote. He died in his seventy-first year, of "extensive organic disease of the heart," though he had for years been a sufferer from frequent attacks of severe "general gout." He was interred in the newly opened Woodlands cemetery in West Philadelphia. In 1802 he had married Eliza Tod. They had nine children, one of whom was William Tod Otto [q.v.].

[Isaac Parrish, memoir in *Summary of the Trans. Coll. of Physicians of Phila.*, vol. I (1846) ; Wm. Osler, "Haemophilia," in Wm. Pepper's *System of Practical Medicine*, vol. III (1885) ; E. B. Krumbhaar, "John Conrad Otto and the Recognition of Hemophilia," *Bull. Johns Hopkins Hospital*, Jan. 1930; *Pub. Ledger* (Phila.), June 29, 1844; information as to certain facts from Otto Tod Mallery, Philadelphia, Pa.] E. B. K.

OTTO, WILLIAM TOD (Jan. 19, 1816–Nov. 7, 1905), jurist, assistant secretary of the interior, United States Supreme Court reporter, was born in Philadelphia, Pa., the son of Dr. John Conrad Otto [q.v.] and Eliza Tod. He entered the University of Pennsylvania in 1829, receiving his degree of A.B. in 1833. After completing his study of law in the office of Joseph R. Ingersoll he moved to Brownstown, Ind., in the fall of 1836. In 1844 he was elected president judge of the second judicial circuit. He was the last judge to be elected by the legislature and served until 1852, when he was defeated by George A. Bicknell, Democrat. For five years, 1847–52, he was professor of law at Indiana University. At thirty-six, he had won the reputation of being one of the ablest presiding circuit judges in the state. On the bench he was autocratic and austere, brooking no familiarity, but outside of official life he displayed a sense of

humor and a pleasing personality. At the expiration of his term in 1853, he moved to New Albany and engaged in private practice. His services were at once in demand for cases pending in the Indiana Supreme Court. In 1855 he was employed to test the constitutionality of the state liquor law as counsel for the appellant in *Beebe* vs. *the State* (6 *Ind.*, 501). In the decision a substantial part of the law was adjudged unconstitutional.

In 1858 Otto was defeated as Republican candidate for the state attorney-generalship. In 1860 he was one of the Indiana delegates to the Republican National Convention. From the first he supported Lincoln and in January 1863 Lincoln appointed him assistant secretary of the interior. In this position he took an active interest in Indian affairs and recommended legislation for Indian betterment. His ability gained him the respect of Orville H. Browning and Hugh McCulloch, who urged Grant to appoint him arbitrator for the United States under the convention with Spain for the adjudication of claims for damages sustained by American citizens in Cuba. He resigned as assistant secretary of the interior in 1871 to accept this position and served until 1875 when he was appointed reporter of the United States Supreme Court. Meanwhile he continued with his law practice, and in January 1873 he argued before the United States Supreme Court on the Judiciary Act of Feb. 5, 1867, maintaining that the Supreme Court, under this act, had no more power than under the Act of 1789 even though the express limitation of powers had been omitted. The decision, given two years later, upheld Otto's arguments (87 *U. S.*, 590). In 1883 Otto resigned as Supreme Court Reporter, having completed seventeen volumes (91–107 *U. S.*) of reports. In 1885 he was appointed one of the United States Representatives to the International Postal Congress at Lisbon. Otto never married, but a tombstone erected by him in the cemetery at Brownstown marks the grave of a woman who was to have become his wife. After his retirement from public life he continued to practise law. He died in Philadelphia in his ninetieth year.

[Sources include: L. C. Baird, *Baird's Hist. of Clark County, Ind.* (1909) ; a short autobiographical sketch written by Otto for William H. English which is in the English Collection at the Univ. of Chicago; *Univ. of Pa. Biog. Cat. of the Matriculates of the Coll. . . . 1749–1893* (1894) ; *Evening Bull.* (Phila.), Nov. 9, 1905.] J. L. N.

OUCONNASTOTE [See OCONOSTOTA, d. 1785].

OURAY (c. 1833–Aug. 24, 1880), a head chief of the Uncompahgre Utes, was born probably at Taos, N. Mex. The meaning of his name is uncertain; although to a treaty made in 1863 he signed himself "U-ray, the Arrow," various interpretations have been offered. The date (1820) given for his birth by Thomas, in the *Handbook of American Indians,* is evidently an error, as well as the statement that he was born in Colorado. Frank Hall (*History of the State of Colorado,* vol. II, 1890) says that his father was a Tabeguache (Uncompahgre) Ute and his mother a Jicarilla Apache and that his boyhood was spent among Mexican rancheros of the better class, from whom he learned to speak Spanish correctly. At eighteen he joined his father's band in southwestern Colorado, and, about 1860, on his father's death, became its chief. In 1862 he was appointed an interpreter, at $500 a year, at the Los Piños Agency in southern Colorado, and in the same year visited Washington in behalf of his tribe. At Conejos, the agency headquarters, he signed the treaty of Oct. 7, 1863, when he was designated by the government as "head-chief of the Western Utes." To Christopher Carson [*q.v.*], who, according to General Sherman, "exercised a powerful influence over him" (Ellis, *post,* p. 248), he became closely attached while Carson was in command at Fort Garland in 1867, and in the summer of that year he aided Carson in suppressing the uprising of a Ute sub-chief, Kaniatse. In February 1868, with a delegation of Utes, he again visited Washington, where, with Carson and others, he negotiated the treaty of Mar. 2. In 1872 he strongly resisted the efforts of the government to compel his tribe to relinquish certain lands granted them in perpetuity, but in the following year accepted a compromise. In the same year the government granted him an annuity of $1,000 which continued until his death, and also built for him a comfortable dwelling. Because of his remoteness from the scene he was unable to prevent the Meeker massacre at the White River Agency, in September 1879; he was, however, able to check the spread of the outbreak and to restore peace. He died at his home on the Los Piños reservation.

Like most of the Utes, Ouray was short and stout. His head was strikingly large, with regular features that bore an expression of good will. He spoke a broken English readily, and he was fond of conversation, especially with cultivated men. His manners were courtly and gentle. From his youth he advocated friendliness toward the whites, and, though stiffly defending the interests of his people, always discouraged violence. In his personal life he was something of a Puritan; he avoided obscene and profane language, never used tobacco, and abhorred whiskey,

though occasionally in company he drank a little wine. From an early day he was inclined to Christianity, and two years before his death he joined the Methodist Church. It has been said of him that he was the only outstanding personality developed among the Ute people. His wife Chipeta, whom he married in 1859 and who endeared herself to the whites by many acts of kindness, survived him for more than thirty years.

[Cyrus Thomas, in F. W. Hodge, *Handbook of Am. Indians,* pt. II (1910); J. H. Baker, *Hist. of Colo.,* vol. I (1927); Thos. Sturgis, *The Ute War of 1879* (pamphlet, 1879); H. H. Bancroft, *Hist. of Nev., Colo., and Wyo.* (1890); Sidney Jocknick, *Early Days on the Western Slope of Colo.* (1913); E. L. Sabin, *Kit Carson Days* (1914); E. S. Ellis, *The Life of Kit Carson* (1889); *Weekly Gazette* (Colo. Springs), Sept. 11, 1880; *Rocky Mountain News* (Denver), Aug. 24, 1880.]
W. J. G.

OUTACITY (fl. 1756–1777), Cherokee chief, lived in the Overhill town of Tamali on the Little Tennessee River in what is now Monroe County, Tenn. He was spoken of by several different names—Ostenaco, Austenaco, or Ustenacah, Judd's Friend or Judge Friend, and Mankiller—and that by which he was most commonly known, probably only a title of rank, was spelled variously, as Outacity, Ottassite, and Otacite. He is often identified with the Wrosetasatow who in 1721 signed a treaty with Gov. Francis Nicholson. In 1757 he led a band of warriors down the Valley of Virginia to join Col. George Washington at Fort Loudoun near Winchester, but in the subsequent uprising led by Oconostota [*q.v.*] he took an active part and was present at the surrender of Fort Loudoun in the Cherokee country in 1760. Although a lesser chief among the Cherokee, he was thrust forward by the influence of British and American authority. His chief claim to distinction was due to a visit to England in 1762 under the guidance of Henry Timberlake [*q.v.*], whose hope of advancement seemed to be in advertising an intimacy with Outacity as proof of influence over the Indians. On the night before he sailed for Plymouth, Outacity made a farewell speech with a moving eloquence that was remembered by Thomas Jefferson half a century later. After a short and easy voyage—though he was sick all the way—he arrived in London on June 18. During this visit he and his two companions bore themselves with graceful dignity and were quite the sensation of the town. They had an audience of an hour and a half with King George, were painted by Joshua Reynolds, and kept Oliver Goldsmith waiting three hours for a visit while, as he complained, Outacity dressed and prinked himself with a savage vanity as great as any to be found in civilization. The *Royal Magazine* for July

1762 carried a full-page engraving of a portrait of Outacity and an article describing the little party. In August they sailed for home and Outacity's brief hour of importance was at an end.

His later history continued to be that of a minor leader. His name was signed to various treaties of the period, and there is record of British attempts to strengthen his position in the tribe in the belief that his loyalty might be more dependable than that of some other Indian leaders. Like the rest of his tribe he fought for Great Britain in the Revolution, and he probably died during that struggle or in the period immediately afterward.

[*Lieut. Henry Timberlake's Memoirs* (1927), ed. by S. C. Williams; Lib. of Cong. transcripts from British Public Record Office, esp. CO⁵: 72, pp. 436–37; *The Colonial Records of N. C.*, vols. VII, VIII, X (1890); *The State Records of N. C.*, vols. XI, XVII (1895–99); Alexander Hewat, *An Hist. Account of ... S. C.* (1779), I, 297–98, II, 238; *London Magazine*, June, July, Aug., Sept. 1762, material indexed under Cherokee; *Annual Register ... 1762* (1763), p. 92; P. L. Ford, *The Writings of Thomas Jefferson*, vol. IX (1898); S. M. Hamilton, *Letters to Washington*, vols. I, II (1898–99); W. C. Ford, *The Writings of George Washington*, vol. I (1889); "The Official Records of Robert Dinwiddie," *Va. Hist. Colls.*, n.s. IV (1884); J. W. M. Gibbs, *The Works of Oliver Goldsmith*, V (1886), 202.]
K. E. C.

OUTCAULT, RICHARD FELTON (Jan. 14, 1863–Sept. 25, 1928), comic artist, was born in Lancaster, Ohio, the son of J. P. and Catherine (Davis) Outcault. He was educated at McMicken College (later part of the University of Cincinnati), and went to Paris for further training in art, returning with his status assured by a beret and a velveteen painting jacket. On Christmas Day, 1890, he was married to Mary Jane Martin, in Lancaster, Ohio. With his wife he removed to New York City, where his comic talents were disciplined and persecuted by the minutiae and drawing-to-scale required of him as draftsman on the *Electrical World* and the *Street Railway Journal*. He found time, however, to do some comic pictures for *Truth,* a weekly journal with a none too respectable reputation, and to submit other drawings to *Life* and *Judge.*

Meanwhile the newspapers were experimenting with color presses, and after many ludicrous failures a process was developed by the New York *World* which seemed satisfactory. Morrill Goddard, the Sunday editor, carried the day for comics rather than fashions as the feature of the new colored supplement, and in casting about for comic talent was referred to Outcault, since the men whose reputations were already established were unavailable because of contracts with comic periodicals. Accordingly, on Sunday, Nov. 18, 1894, Outcault inaugurated the

"funny paper." His first drawing—with significance probably undreamed of—was entitled "The Origin of a New Species." Shortly afterward he produced "Hogan's Alley" and its hero, the "Yellow Kid," which boosted to sensational heights the already notable success of the comic supplement. Meanwhile the *New York Journal* had added a colored page to its regular Sunday edition, and in 1896, with the lure of a tremendous salary, enticed Outcault away from the *World*. George Luks, however, was employed to take his place, and with Luks doing yellow kids for the *World* and Outcault continuing the original in the *Journal* a sensational rivalry developed in Park Row. While this struggle was in process the other papers designated the contenders as "Yellow Kid journals," later shortened to "yellow journals," a term destined to have a career of its own in journalism.

Outcault's next connection was with the *New York Herald*, in which his "Pore Li'l Mose" appeared in 1901 and, in 1902, the renowned "Buster Brown." Buster and his dog Tige eclipsed all their inventor's earlier successes and brought him a fortune and countless offers of employment on foreign newspapers. Buster became a fad that spread all over the country and his name was appropriated for cigars, suits, garters, belts, sweaters, and even children. Outcault published several books on Buster Brown and Tige. He returned to the *Journal* in 1905, but he retired from active work about ten years before his death. He was seriously interested in the theater, delighted in taking part in amateur performances, and was co-author of the dramatic version of *Buster Brown*. He died at his home in Flushing, Long Island, after an illness of about ten weeks.

Outcault was the originator of the bad boy type of humor which dominated the comic productions of the country for the first decade of the twentieth century. The fun of the hoodlum is perennial, but he interpreted it with what he himself called a "kind of epigrammatical humor of a strain that I look on peculiarly as my own."

[R. L. McCardell, "Opper, Outcault and Company: the Comic Supplement and the Men who Make It," *Everybody's Mag.*, June 1905; *Who's Who in America,* 1926–27; obituaries in the New York papers for Sept. 26, 1928, and editorials in the papers for the following day; W. G. Bleyer, *Main Currents in the Hist. of Am. Journalism* (1927), pp. 339–40.]
E. T.

OUTERBRIDGE, ALEXANDER EWING (July 31, 1850–Jan. 15, 1928), metallurgist, was born in Philadelphia, the son of Alexander Ewing and Laura C. (Harvey) Outerbridge, and a member of a family prominent in the shipping business in New York, Newfoundland, and the

Bermudas. He was educated at the Episcopal Academy, Philadelphia, and subsequently received private instruction in chemistry and mathematics. In 1867 he became assistant to Henry Morton [q.v.], then secretary of the Franklin Institute, and when Morton, in the absence of Dr. John F. Frazer, became acting professor of chemistry and physics at the University of Pennsylvania, Outerbridge aided him in his teaching. He also taught English at the Episcopal Academy.

He was appointed in 1868 assistant in the assay department of the United States Mint in Philadelphia. During his ten years in this post he made several notable contributions to metallurgy. For eight months in 1873, at the Mint and in laboratories at Stevens Institute, Hoboken, and the University of Pennsylvania, he experimented with the spectrum analysis of gold, silver, and other metals, reporting his results in the *Annual Report of the Director of the Mint* (1874). In 1876 he developed a method of obtaining thin films of gold or other metals for study under the microscope with transmitted as well as reflected light. He deposited the gold electrically on copper foil, then dissolved the copper, leaving the thin gold film to be mounted on a glass slide. Such films were obtained 1/10,000,000 of an inch in thickness. Later series of experiments dealt with the impurities in silver. While at the Mint he also designed apparatus to collect metallic vapors escaping from the crucibles when precious metals were melted in the furnaces.

In 1878 he declined appointment as chief assayer at the United States Mint in Helena, Mont., but the next year accepted a transfer to the Mint at New Orleans where an assay office was to be reëstablished. After organizing the office, he returned in 1880 to the Philadelphia Mint, but shortly resigned to become metallurgist for A. Whitney & Son, Philadelphia, manufacturers of car wheels. In 1888 he resigned this position and became metallurgist for William Sellers & Company, Philadelphia, in which connection he continued until his death. During the year 1886 he invented a process for carbonizing delicate plant leaves, lace, and other organic substances without rendering them brittle. These carbonized materials or patterns were utilized in moulding iron, steel, bronze or other metals to obtain perfect replicas of such delicate objects to use as dies. For this contribution he received the John Scott Medal from the City of Philadelphia (1888). In a paper read before the American Institute of Mining Engineers, Feb. 20, 1896 (*Transactions,* vol. XXVI. 1897), he made pub-

lic his two years' study on the "mobility of molecules" of solid cast-iron; the Franklin Institute appointed a committee to investigate the subject, publishing the report in its *Journal,* July 1898. The year previous, 1897, he had again received the John Scott Medal for these studies. From them it later became evident that iron castings could be made to grow or change in cubical dimensions while in the solid state without destroying their metallic properties or distorting their shapes (*Mobility of Molecules of Cast-iron,* 1904). For this discovery Outerbridge was awarded in 1904 the Elliott Cresson Gold Medal by the Franklin Institute. While investigating the process of hardening tool steel, he perfected a form of permanent color screen for determining the precise temperature of a bath of molten metal.

Outerbridge was an active member of the Franklin Institute, serving on its committee of science and arts for fourteen years and on its board of managers for five; was made professor of metallurgy in 1901 and president of the mining and metallurgical section in 1908. He was an extensive contributor to newspapers and technical publications. Having great personal charm, he made friends easily. He played on the American cricket team in a number of international matches at a time when that gentlemen's game appealed strongly to Philadelphians. In politics he was an adherent of the Republican party; in religion, a member of the Episcopal Church. He married in 1880 Mary Ely Whitney of Philadelphia, who died the following year after the birth of a son. On Jan. 29, 1905, he married Margaret Hall Dunn, who, with his son, survived him.

[*Jour. Franklin Inst.,* Apr. 1928; J. M. and Jacques Cattell, *Am. Men of Science* (4th ed., 1927); *Who's Who in Engineering,* 1925; *Who's Who in America,* 1926–27; *Pub. Ledger* (Phila), Jan. 16, 1928.]
F. L. G.

OVERMAN, FREDERICK (c. 1803–Jan. 7, 1852), metallurgist, was born in Elberfeld, Germany, and baptized Johann Friedrich in the reformed church at Barmen on Mar. 3, 1805. His parents, Johann Caspar Overmann and Maria Catherina (Ruhl), who were people of humble circumstances, could afford to give him only an elementary education. They then apprenticed him to a merchant, but he found this occupation not to his liking and was apprenticed to a cabinet maker. While becoming proficient in his trade, he utilized every opportunity to gain general knowledge. At the completion of his apprenticeship he started on his *wanderjahre* and, making his way to Berlin, there gained admission to the Royal Polytechnic Institute. Beuth, its director, soon discovered the youth's native ability and encouraged him in every way, introducing him to Alexander von Humboldt and to various architects and artists who were prominent in Berlin at the time. Except for his *Über die frischen des roheisens,* which was published at Brünn in 1838, no record now remains of the successive steps by which he rose to be, at an early age, an authority in Europe on the metallurgy of iron, but according to his biographer (Roebling, *post*) he traveled all over Europe introducing his patented improvements in the puddling of iron and in manufacturing processes. He superintended the erection of a number of large plants, and was for a time in charge of engineering works at the royal mines at Chemnitz, Saxony, presumably an establishment where the pumps and other iron equipment were constructed. He also made a study of the mineral and industrial resources of Austria, collecting data for the use of Prince Metternich in negotiating a new commercial treaty with Great Britain. In the meantime, on May 9, 1829, in the church in which he was christened, he married Wilhelmina Friederike Helena Petzholtz.

In 1842, apparently dissatisfied with political and social conditions in Europe, he came to the United States, where he anglicized his name and passed the rest of his life. It is probable that he went very soon to Pennsylvania, the seat of nearly one-third of the whole iron industry of the United States, which owed most of its growth to German technologists. A scientist rather than a business man, he seems to have had a checkered career of success and failure. Turning to the writing of technological works in English, he published in 1850 *The Manufacture of Iron,* a volume of some five hundred pages, followed by *The Manufacture of Steel* (1851), *Practical Mineralogy, Assaying, and Mining* (1851), *The Moulder's and Founder's Pocket Guide* (1851), and *Mechanics for the Millwright, Machinist, Engineer, Civil Engineer, Architect, and Student* (1851). He had nearly completed *A Treatise on Metallurgy* (1852), 700 pages, dealing with mining as well as the metallurgy of the common metals, when he was accidentally killed by inhaling arsene in his Philadelphia laboratory. The work appeared shortly after his death, with a final chapter added by the publishers and a preface containing a biographical sketch of the author. If Overman had lived to a greater age he probably would have been a leading figure in the development of metallurgy in the United States, but he died almost a decade before the discoveries on the Comstock lode gave a great impetus to non-ferrous metallurgy, and two dec-

ades before the introduction of the Bessemer process into America similarly stimulated the metallurgy of iron. His *Treatise on Metallurgy* went through six editions. It exhibits a surprisingly sound understanding of the nature of alloys, and all his works deserve more recognition than has been accorded them for their influence on the development of mineral technology in America.

[Overman's own writings; preface by John A. Roebling [*q.v.*] to Overman's *Treatise on Metallurgy* (1852); *North American and U. S. Gazette* (Phila.), Jan. 9, 1852; information, including data from church records at Barmen, from the Verein deutscher Eisenhüttenleute.]   T. T. R.

OVERMAN, LEE SLATER (Jan. 3, 1854–Dec. 12, 1930), senator from North Carolina, was born in Salisbury, Rowan County, N. C., the son of William and Mary (Slater) Overman. His father belonged to a family long established in eastern North Carolina but in 1835 removed to Rowan County and there became a successful merchant and manufacturer. After a preparatory training in private schools the boy entered Trinity College (now Duke University) and graduated in 1874. He then taught in Winston-Salem, N. C., but his ambition turned to law and politics. He took an active part in the gubernatorial campaign of 1876 that resulted in the election of Zebulon Baird Vance [*q.v.*], became Vance's private secretary, and, when Vance became United States senator in 1879, was for a time secretary to Vance's successor, Thomas J. Jarvis. In 1878 he was admitted to the bar and on Oct. 31 of that year was married to Mary P. Merrimon, the eldest daughter of Augustus S. Merrimon [*q.v.*]. He began the practice of law in Salisbury in 1880. In 1881 he campaigned in the interest of a prohibition amendment to the state constitution, although Salisbury was the stronghold of the liquor interests. In 1883, 1885, 1887, 1893, and 1899 he was a member of the state House of Representatives from Rowan County and was elected speaker in 1893. As a legislator he manifested courage and became a recognized leader of the Democratic party. He also favored leasing the control of state-owned railroads to railway corporations and the establishment of a corporation commission. In 1895 he was the choice of the Democratic caucus of the legislature for the United States Senate, but he was defeated by Jeter C. Pritchard, who had the support of the Republicans and Populists. In 1903 after a long contest he was elected over Pritchard.

His record as a senator was that of a liberal conservative. He had deep reverence for American constitutional government as established and came to be regarded one of the best constitutional lawyers in the Senate. On the other hand his interest in changing national problems led him to support many measures in the interest of various groups and classes of people when he believed such measure lay within the scope of existing powers of government. Thus he obtained an appropriation for the appointment of commercial agents abroad to aid in the extension of foreign trade, supported the formation of a labor department, and led the fight in the Senate for the Clayton Bill that included in its clauses larger protection of labor interests. Meanwhile he was very vigilant for the interests of North Carolina; notable was the prevention, through his efforts, of suits against the state by Cuba for the redemption of bonds that the supreme court of North Carolina had declared invalid. When the Democratic party obtained control of the Senate in 1913, he became chairman of the rules committee and was ranking member of the judiciary and appropriations committees; and during the prolonged absences of the chairman of the latter committee, he guided deliberations. He gave cordial support to the measures favored by President Wilson during his first term, and in 1913 he was also chairman of a Senate committee that investigated the activities of lobbies. During the World War he consistently advocated strengthening the hand of the chief executive and gave final shape to the Senate bill to empower President Wilson to transfer the functions of one department of government to another. This was known as the Overman Law. In 1918 he was chairman of the sub-committee of the judiciary that investigated German propaganda and, in 1919, chairman of a committee that investigated Bolshevist propaganda. To the time of his death he had served almost twenty-eight years, having been reëlected to the Senate in 1909, 1914, 1920, and 1926. He embodied its best traditions—his snow-white hair, his dignity and courtesy, and his occasional bursts of oratory suggesting the image of a Roman.

[Personal scrapbooks of Overman in possession of family; *Lee S. Overman, Memorial Addresses . . . in the Senate and House of Representatives* (1931); *Who's Who in America,* 1930–31; *News and Observer* (Raleigh), Dec. 12, 1930; *N. Y. Times,* Dec. 12–14, 1930.]

W. K. B.

OVERTON, JOHN (Apr. 9, 1766–Apr. 12, 1833), jurist, pioneer, and politician, was born in Louisa County, Va., the son of James and Mary (Waller) Overton (Overton family data, compiled by Edyth Rucker Whitley, Nashville, Tenn.). His family, of English origin, was well connected but poor, and young Overton taught school for several years in order to assist in the education of his brothers and sisters. In 1787

he migrated to Kentucky for the purpose of studying law and took board in the home of a Mrs. Robards, of Mercer County. Completing his studies two years later, he decided to practise law in the frontier town of Nashville, Tenn. Making his way thither, he became a boarder in the home of the widow of Col. John Donelson. Here he was the bed-fellow of Andrew Jackson, another young lawyer who had shortly preceded him to Nashville (Parton, *post*, I, 149). In 1790 the western part of North Carolina became the Southwest Territory, and Overton was made supervisor of the federal excise (Knoxville *Gazette,* June 5, 1795). During this period he also became much interested in land speculations and was Jackson's partner in some of the most important land deals (Bassett, *post*, I, 13–15). In 1794 these two men purchased the Rice tract, upon which, in 1819, they founded the town of Memphis.

In 1804 Jackson resigned his place upon the bench of the superior court of Tennessee and Overton succeeded to the post, holding this position until the old courts were abolished, Jan. 1, 1810. In November 1811 he was appointed a member of the supreme court of the state to succeed George Campbell. In 1816 he resigned. He published two volumes of *Tennessee Reports* (1813–17), which cover cases tried before the court from 1791 to 1816. Being intimately connected with the formulation of the law during the plastic period of a new jurisdiction, he became the recognized authority on all matters relating to land legislation, and in many cases it was his influence which shaped the form it took. He also built up the largest landed estate in Tennessee and was considered the richest citizen of the commonwealth. After his retirement from the bench, he devoted his entire time to the promotion of his private interests and the political fortunes of Andrew Jackson. In 1821 he, William B. Lewis, and John H. Eaton [*qq.v.*] formed an informal committee of close personal friends for the advancement of Jackson's candidacy for the presidency, and from this time until the election of 1828 they were largely engaged in the defense of their hero against his enemies (T. P. Abernethy, "Andrew Jackson and the Rise of Southwestern Democracy," in *American Historical Review,* October 1927, pp. 71–72). Because he had resided with the Robards family in Kentucky, Overton's services were especially valuable in combating the scandal bruited about during the campaign in connection with Jackson's marriage to Rachel Robards, formerly Rachel Donelson. Though Overton kept complete records of all his transactions, before his death he destroyed his correspondence with Jackson. On the election of "Old Hickory" to the presidency, Overton asked for no office and accepted no favors, remaining in Nashville to the end of his life. He must have possessed rare qualities, for he was unique in being able to live on intimate terms with Jackson as an adviser and friend without friction and without becoming a mere follower.

Henry A. Wise, who visited "The Hermitage" in 1828, described Overton as he sat in the family circle with a bandanna handkerchief thrown over his bald head, nose and chin nearly meeting, making ineffectual efforts to enter into the conversation (*Seven Decades of the Union,* 1872, pp. 100–03). His private life was apparently uneventful. His wife, Mary McConnell (White) May, was the widow of Dr. Francis May, the daughter of Gen. James White, and the sister of Hugh Lawson White.

[The best sketches of Overton are in J. W. Caldwell, *Sketches of the Bench and Bar of Tenn.* (1898), and W. W. Clayton, *Hist. of Davidson County, Tenn.* (1880). See also James Parton, *Life of Andrew Jackson* (3 vols., 1860) ; J. S. Bassett, *Correspondence of Andrew Jackson* (6 vols., 1926–33) ; obituary in *Nashville Republican and State Gazette,* Apr. 17, 1833. There is a good collection of Overton's correspondence in the possession of the Tenn. Hist. Soc., Nashville.]

T. P. A.

OWEN, DAVID DALE (June 24, 1807–Nov. 13, 1860), geologist, third son of the social philanthropist Robert Owen [see *Dictionary of National Biography*] and Ann Caroline Dale, his wife, was born at "Braxfield House," near New Lanark, Scotland. Like his elder brother, Robert Dale Owen [*q.v.*], he received his early training from private tutors and at the Lanark Academy, and then proceeded to the educational institution of Philipp Emanuel von Fellenberg, near Berne, Switzerland. Here he took a three-year course, beginning in 1824. In November 1827, with his brother Richard, he sailed for America, where their father had undertaken to plant a socialistic community at New Harmony, Ind. They reached New Harmony early in January 1828. In 1831, in company with Prof. H. D. Rogers [*q.v.*], David Owen sailed for London, where he attended lectures in chemistry and geology at the London University. Returning in 1832, after recovering from an attack of Asiatic cholera, he entered upon a course in medicine at the Ohio Medical College in Cincinnati, meanwhile spending his summers in arranging and classifying the collection of fossils made by the geologist William Maclure [*q.v.*].

After graduating in medicine in 1836, he spent one summer as a volunteer on the geological survey of Tennessee under Gerard Troost [*q.v.*], and in 1837 accepted the proffered position of state geologist of Indiana. Working without assistants, he made his own field observations and his own chemical analyses in a laboratory he had established at New Harmony. At the end of the first year, having rendered but one report, he resigned to accept an appointment from James Whitcomb, federal land commissioner, to make a survey of the Dubuque and Mineral Point districts of Wisconsin and Iowa, an area of about eleven thousand square miles. In carrying out this task he displayed exceptional energy and administrative ability. He received his commission Aug. 17, 1839, engaged and instructed his 139 assistants as to purposes and methods of procedure, and presented his report on Nov. 14 following, a "feat of generalship which has never been equalled in American geological history" (Merrill, *post,* p. 199). The report was published, under date of Apr. 2, 1840, as *House Document 239* (26 Cong., 1 Sess.). In 1847 he was appointed United States geologist to make a survey of the Chippewa Land District, the work being subsequently extended to include a more complete survey of the northwestern territory of Wisconsin, Iowa, and Minnesota, which with field and laboratory work occupied his time and attention until 1852. It was in the course of this survey that Dr. John Evans made under Owen's direction the first survey of the *Mauvaises Terres,* or Bad lands of the Upper Missouri. The complete report, *Report of a Geological Survey of Wisconsin, Iowa and Minnesota, and Incidentally of a Portion of Nebraska Territory* (1852), formed a quarto volume of 628 pages of text, with fifteen plates of fossils, nineteen folding sections, and a geological map. The illustrations of fossil remains were particularly fine for that period.

In 1854 Owen was appointed state geologist of Kentucky and continued to hold the position for five years. In 1857, he accepted also the position of state geologist of Arkansas, but here his limit was reached: he died in the midst of his task in 1860 and his final report was edited by J. P. Lesley [*q.v.*]. In the meanwhile, however, he had accepted a third office, becoming for the second time state geologist of Indiana—an appointment made with the understanding that the actual work of the survey was to be done by his brother, Richard Owen, who had recently resigned the professorship of geology in the university at Nashville, Tenn. The *Report of a Geological Reconnoissance of Indiana Made during the Years 1859 and 1860 under the Direction of the Late D. D. Owen* was published by Richard Owen in 1862.

Viewed in the light of today, much of Owen's work can be regarded as reconnaissance. He was the first to point out the rich mineral nature of the Iowa and Wisconsin lands, and that the ores of lead and zinc were limited to the magnesian limestone, and the first to give the name *subcarboniferous* to beds immediately underlying the coal of Indiana. He was an artist, and his pictured geological sections are unequaled for their artistic beauty. Of the twenty-five plates in his report of 1840, fourteen are from his own drawings. His chief publications, besides those mentioned above, are the four reports of the Geological Survey of Kentucky (4 vols., 1856–61); *First Report of a Geological Reconnoissance of . . . Arkansas* (1858), and *Second Report . . .* (1860). He is said to have been a man of kindly, equitable disposition. Aside from geology he was most fond of chemistry, and at his own expense built a fully equipped laboratory at a cost of $10,000. He was married on Mar. 23, 1837, to Caroline C. Neef, daughter of Francis Joseph Nicholas Neef [*q.v.*], educational leader of the New Harmony community. Four children were born to them. His death at fifty-three, in the midst of his labors, was due to the undermining of his constitution by exposure and malaria and unremitting attention to his strenuous duties.

[Editorial in *Am. Geologist*, Aug. 1889, based, it is said, on information from Richard Owen; *Am. Jour. Sci. and Arts*, Jan. 1861; *First-Fourth Report of the Geol. Survey in Ky. Made during the Years 1854 to 1859*, vol. IV (1861); *Pop. Sci. Mo.*, Dec. 1895; G. F. Merrill, *The First One Hundred Years of Am. Geology* (1924); G. B. Lockwood, *The New Harmony Movement* (1905); Caroline Dale Snedeker, *The Town of the Fearless* (1931).]   G. P. M.

OWEN, EDWARD THOMAS (Mar. 4, 1850–Nov. 9, 1931), educator, was born at Hartford, Conn. His father, Elijah Hunter Owen, a merchant, of Welsh ancestry, and his mother, Susannah Boardman, of English descent, were of old New-England stock. Owen was educated in the Hartford public schools and was graduated from Yale in 1872 with numerous scholastic and athletic honors. He was a member of half a dozen social and musical clubs and always set down as the proudest accomplishment of his life his winning of the Southgate cup in the single-scull race, in which he broke all previous records. He spent a year in graduate study at Yale, and three more in Europe, two at Göttingen and one in Paris. In 1878 he went to the University of Wisconsin as instructor in modern languages and the following year was made professor of French language and literature. He remained on the faculty until his retirement from active teaching in 1914, serving for several years as head of the department of Romance languages.

Owen's specialty as a scholar lay in a pioneer field. He aimed at rationalizing grammar by a radical revision of its method and nomenclature. He rejected its conventions as pseudo-science, akin to astrology or alchemy. He contended that its classification is unstable, overlapping, and contradictory, and the so-called parts of speech an absurdity. Why, for example, speak of "disjunctive conjunctives"? He paved the way for creating a truly logical grammar, based upon an analysis of the antecedent psychological states that prompt expression, by taking these as an abstract or ideal norm for clarifying and classing usage and the deformations that usage entails. These theories he developed in a series of monographs published in the *Transactions of the Wisconsin Academy of Sciences, Arts, and Letters:* "The Meaning and Function of Thought Connectives" (vol. XII, pt. 1, 1898); "A Revision of the Pronouns, with Special Examination of Relatives and Relative Clauses" (vol. XIII, pt. 1, 1901); "Interrogative Thought, and the Means of its Expression" (vol. XIV, pt. 2, 1904); "Hybrid Parts of Speech" (vol. XVI, pt. 1, 1909); "The Relations expressed by the Passive Voice" (vol. XVII, pt. 1, 1911); "Linguistic Aberrations" (vol. XXIII, 1927), and "Syntax of the Adverb, Preposition, and Conjunction" (vol. XXVI, 1931). He also edited various modern French texts.

Of tall, athletic build and great physical strength, Owen was always a devotee of the outdoor life and outdoor sports. He loved the countryside, sailed and fished on the lakes around Madison, and roamed on horseback over the wooded hills. Later in life he turned gardener on his suburban estate. He was long chairman of the University Athletic Committee, and was a founder of the Madison Park and Pleasure-Drive Association. He donated to the city, in commemoration of two daughters who died in childhood, the beautiful Owen Park and Drive. Another lifelong pursuit was the collecting of butterflies. During frequent midwinter trips in tropic lands he gathered a large collection of rare specimens. He loved leisure, cultivated many interests, was well read and at times boldly personal in his judgments, decidedly Anglo-Saxon and Victorian, though idolizing Balzac and girding at Wordsworth. He was a gentleman of the old school, fond of good talk, full of genial wit and shrewd good sense, of indulgence and enthusiasm. He was married, on Apr. 11, 1874, to Emilie Brace Pratt, of Hartford, Conn. She with two daughters survived him.

[Bull. of Yale Univ.; Obit. Record of Grads. Deceased During the Year Ending July 1, 1932 (1932); R. G. Thwaites, The Univ. of Wis. (1900); E. H. Owen, "Some of the Owen Ancestors," a manuscript genealogy; Wis. State Jour. (Madison), Nov. 10, 1931.]
W. F. G.

OWEN, GRIFFITH (c. 1647–Aug. 19, 1717), Colonial leader, Quaker preacher, surgeon, was born in Wales, the son of Robert and Jane (Vaughan) Owen of Dolseredu, near Dolgelly. Before emigrating to America, he studied medicine and moved to Prescott in Lancashire, England, where he practised as a physician for some years. He became a Quaker by conviction, his father having given up his connection with the Society of Friends. He was married before he left England, but the family name of his wife, Sarah, is not recorded. She died in Philadelphia in 1702. The certificate of membership from Hartshaw West Monthly Meeting in England to Philadelphia states that Owen had "for many years phest [profest] ye blessed Truth," and had "been very well esteemed being of great service in his place."

He came to Philadelphia in the ship *Vine* in company with his father and mother and bringing his wife, three children, and seven servants. They landed at Philadelphia Sept. 17, 1684. Owen settled at first in Merion, now Lower Merion Township, in the tract of 40,000 acres assigned by William Penn to the Welsh Quaker immigrants, but soon afterward moved to Philadelphia, where he built one of the most attractive houses in the new colony. William Penn, in his letters (Penn-Logan Correspondence, *post*, I, 297), refers to Griffith Owen's house with a touch of envy, as being finer than he himself could afford. Owen's medical practice was extensive and he had the reputation of being a skilled surgeon. He was elected a member of the Colonial Assembly in 1686 and the three years following. In 1690 he was chosen a member of the Provincial Council, in which he continued to sit until his death, trusted and beloved by the Proprietor, who refers to him in his letters to James Logan as "honest Griffith Owen" (*Ibid.*, I, 172, 206). On one occasion, however, he strongly opposed the Proprietor's policy, when Penn proposed to sell part of the Welsh Tract to other incoming settlers. Griffith Owen led the opposition to this new policy and drafted the vigorous Remonstrance against it to the commissioners of the government, but the Remonstrance failed and the Welsh Tract was divided.

Throughout his life in the Pennsylvania colony, Owen was one of the foremost Friends in public service. He is mentioned a hundred times in the Minutes of Philadelphia Yearly Meeting. He was appointed to membership on the most important committees of the Meeting, and usually served as chairman. He was chosen to settle differences, to solve complexities, to deal with offenders, to raise funds and to select teachers for William Penn's Chartered School, now the William Penn Charter School. He was one of the outstanding Quaker preachers in the Colony. He traveled frequently on religious visits to England, to Maryland, to the Eastern Shore, to Virginia, and twice to New England. He was in the thick of the struggle over what at that time was called "the Apostasy of George Keith" [q.v.], which rent the harmony of the infant colony. Friends in Philadelphia issued a document—*Our Antient Testimony Renewed* (London, 1695)—which was intended to clarify their theological position in this controversy. This document was in the main drafted by Griffith Owen who was chairman of the committee. It is an important paper since it is one of the very earliest confessions of faith of the Pennsylvania Quakers. It is strikingly theological and orthodox, with almost no emphasis on peculiar Quaker lines of thought. With William Penn, Thomas Story and others, Griffith Owen founded in September 1701 the Meeting of Ministers of Philadelphia (later called Meeting of Ministers and Elders).

In 1704 he married, as his second wife, Sarah Saunders, a widow, daughter of John Songhurst. His interest in the Welsh Tract continued unabated throughout his life, and he often visited the three Welsh Meetings "over the Schuylkill," namely, Haverford, Merion, and Radnor. He died in Philadelphia at the age of seventy years.

[Pa. Mag. of Hist. and Biog., Oct. 1884; "Correspondence between William Penn and James Logan," Memoirs of the Hist. Soc. of Pa., vols. IX–X (1870–72); Robert Proud, The Hist. of Pa. (2 vols., 1797–98); T. A. Glenn, Welsh Founders of Pa. (1913), vol. II, and Merion in the Welsh Tract (1896); The Friend (Phila.), Mar. 10–Apr. 7, Apr. 21–28, 1855; Geneal. Soc. of Pa. Pubs., especially vols. III–VII (Jan. 1906–Mar. 1920), IX (Mar. 1924), p. 46; Jacob Painter, Thomas and Margaret Minshall and Their Early Descendants: To Which Are Added Some Accounts of Griffith Owen and Descendants (1867).]
R. M. J.

OWEN, ROBERT DALE (Nov. 9, 1801–June 24, 1877), social reformer, author, elder brother of David Dale Owen [q.v.], was born at Glasgow, Scotland, the eldest son of Robert Owen [see *Dictionary of National Biography*] and Ann Caroline (Dale) Owen. His mother was the daughter of David Dale, proprietor of the cotton-mills at New Lanark, where Robert Owen was beginning to put into practice his theory of social reform. Robert Dale Owen's whole life, most of it spent in the United States, was shaped by his father's influence. Possessed of much of his father's gift for original and liberal thought in social matters, he added to it a practicality and, after a time, a patience of his own. He was instructed in the New Lanark school and by private tutors until the age of eighteen, when he went for four years to the progressive institution of Philipp Emanuel von Fellenberg at Hofwyl, Switzerland. There he gained "a belief which existing abuses cannot shake nor worldly scepticism destroy, an abiding faith in human virtue and in social progress" (*Threading My Way*, p. 175). On his return to his father's cotton-mill community, he took charge of the school, of which he wrote the only comprehensive description (*An Outline of the System of Education at New Lanark*, 1824), and when his father was absent he managed the factories. In November 1825 he came to the United States with his father, the two proceeding early the next year to New Harmony, Ind., where the elder Owen had determined to begin an experiment in social reform through cooperation and rational education. Robert Dale Owen eagerly volunteered for manual work, but finding himself physically unfit for it, was glad to teach the school and edit the *New Harmony Gazette*. His editorial utterances reflected his enthusiasm for the adventure, but later in life he described the colonists as a "heterogeneous collection of radicals, enthusiastic devotees of principle, honest latitudinarians and lazy theorists, with a sprinkling of unprincipled sharpers thrown in" (*Threading My Way*, p. 286).

No sooner had the New Harmony experiment failed, in the spring of 1827, than he was destined for another disappointment. At New Harmony he had come under the influence of Frances Wright [*q.v.*], ten years his senior and a vigorous personality. In 1825 she had founded Nashoba, near Memphis, Tenn., a community devoted to gradual emancipation of slaves. Owen now went with her to the colony, but finding it in a declining way, he accompanied her to Europe, where he met Lafayette, Godwin, Bentham, and Mary Wollstonecraft Shelley. He was much drawn to the last, and in later life wished he had come under her gentle persuasion rather than the driving force of Frances Wright. On his return to America, after an unprofitable visit to Nashoba he went back to New Harmony to continue the *Gazette*, whither Miss Wright soon followed him. He now engaged with her for two years in the work of the "Free Enquirers," a coterie opposed to organized religion (particularly the evangelical sects with their revivals), and advocating liberal divorce laws, widespread industrial education, and a more nearly equal distribution of wealth. In June 1829 he left New Harmony and took up residence with others of the inner circle in New York. Here he devoted most of his time to editing the *Free Enquirer*, which was the old *New Harmony Gazette* rechristened. He was active in the autumn of this year in forming the "Association for the Protection of Industry and for the Promotion of National Education," his creed for which was belief in "a National System of Equal, Republican, Protective, Practical Education, the sole regenerator of a profligate age." This association was successful in 1829-30 in ousting the agrarians under Thomas Skidmore (author of *The Rights of Man to Property*, 1829) from the councils of the New York Working Men's Party and substituting a program of public education for their dream of equal division of property; but the workers finally repudiated the leadership of the Free Enquirers.

The work which Owen did in New York (promoting of lectures, educational and health centers, and free-thinking publications), corresponded closely to the propaganda activities of his father, whom he joined in England in 1832. For six months father and son were co-editors of *The Crisis;* then the son returned to New Harmony and began the most useful part of his career. He served three terms in the Indiana legislature (1836-38) and gave effect to his educational policies by securing for the public schools one-half of the state's allocation of surplus funds of the federal government. He was elected to Congress in 1842 as a Democrat, and served two terms (1843-47), but was defeated for a third. In 1844 he introduced a resolution requesting the President to notify Great Britain of the termination of the joint occupation of Oregon; this measure became the basis for the solution of the Oregon boundary dispute. In 1845 he introduced the bill under which the Smithsonian Institution was constituted, and as a member of the organization committee of the regents he insisted that the work of the Institution should include popular dissemination of scientific knowledge as well as investigation. His versatility was apparent in his service as chairman of the building committee, and he tried to make his experience available to others by publishing *Hints on Public Architecture* (1849). In the Indiana constitutional convention of 1850 and in the legislature the next year, he successfully advocated property rights for married women and liberality in divorce laws; his views on the latter subject involved him later in a debate with Horace Greeley [*q.v.*] in the *New*

York Tribune, afterwards widely circulated in pamphlet form (*Divorce: Being a Correspondence between Horace Greeley and Robert Dale Owen*, 1860). President Pierce appointed him chargé d'affaires at Naples in 1853, and two years later made him minister. In Italy he embraced Spiritualism, and worked to give the cult a scientific basis for its beliefs. His books, *Footfalls on the Boundary of Another World* (1860) and *The Debatable Land between This World and the Next* (1872), show a strange mixture of credulousness and suspicion.

When he returned to America in 1858 he became one of the leading advocates of emancipation. He was commissioned by the governor of Indiana to purchase arms in Europe for the state troops (May 30, 1861–Feb. 6, 1863). His letter to the President, Sept. 17, 1862, published with letters to Chase and Stanton in a pamphlet, *The Policy of Emancipation* (1863), was credited by Secretary Chase with having "had more influence on him [Lincoln] than any other document which reached him on the subject" (Lockwood, *post*, p. 371). In 1863 the Secretary of War appointed Owen chairman of a committee to investigate the condition of the freedmen, out of which study grew his volume, *The Wrong of Slavery* (1864), an understanding treatment of the whole institution. In *The Future of the North-West* (1863) he protested vigorously against the scheme, put forward in Indiana and the Northwest, of reconstructing the Union by leaving out New England. He was opposed to the immediate enfranchisement of the negro, advocating a plan whereby the suffrage should be granted freedmen after a period of ten years. Besides the publications mentioned, he was the author of *Pocahontas: A Historical Drama* (1837); *Beyond the Breakers* (1870), a novel; and many pamphlets on questions of public interest. In 1873–75 he contributed a number of autobiographical articles to the *Atlantic Monthly*. The first of these (January–November 1873), covering his first twenty-seven years, were published in book form under the title, *Threading My Way* (1874). He was twice married: on Apr. 12, 1832, to Mary Jane Robinson, who died in 1871, and on June 23, 1876, to Lottie Walton Kellogg. He died at his summer home on Lake George, New York, following a period of mental derangement.

[Robert Dale Owen, *Threading My Way* (1874), supplemented by articles in the *Atlantic Monthly*, Feb., June, July, Nov., Dec. 1874, Jan., June 1875; G. B. Lockwood, *The New Harmony Movement* (1905); Frank Podmore, *Robert Owen: A Biog.* (2 vols., 1906); A. H. Estabrook, "The Family History of Robert Owen," *Ind. Mag. of Hist.*, Mar. 1923; L. M. Sears, "Robert Dale Owen as a Mystic," *Ibid.*, Mar. 1928;

"Robert Dale Owen and Indiana's Common School Fund," *Ibid.*, Mar. 1929; Caroline Dale Snedeker, *The Town of the Fearless* (1931); W. R. Waterman, *Frances Wright* (1924); *Indianapolis Journal*, June 27, *Indianapolis Sentinel*, June 26, 1877.]   B. M.

OWEN, WILLIAM FLORENCE (1844–May 4, 1906), actor, was of English and Welsh ancestry on his father's side and of Irish on his mother's. He was born in Limerick, Ireland, and after various attempts as a newspaper writer, in business, and as a public reader in Canada, whither he had gone at about the age of twenty, he at last fulfilled a boyish ambition to become an actor, and remained upon the stage for the rest of his life. He frequently remarked to his friends that it was a decision he never regretted, even when his fortunes were not at the highest flood. More than once he said, in substantially the same words: "To be an actor one must be so filled with love for the work that one must be willing to starve, to suffer, to endure almost anything rather than to give up his profession." His first professional engagement was at Salem, Ohio, Dec. 17, 1867, with Catherine Hayes, as Victor Carrington in Watts Phillips' melodrama, *Nobody's Daughter*, and as Sir Matthew Scraggs in *Sketches in India*. An engagement in stock during the next season at Griswold's Opera House in Troy, N. Y., gave him opportunity to appear in support of several stars in such parts as Sir Hugh Evans in *Merry Wives of Windsor*, Old Deschapelles in *The Lady of Lyons*, Gobbo in *The Merchant of Venice*, and the Second Gravedigger in *Hamlet*. Seasons of miscellaneous engagements here and there in all sorts of characters followed, including appearances with Adelaide Neilson as Sir Andrew Aguecheek in *Twelfth Night*, with Joseph Jefferson as Cockles in *Rip Van Winkle*, and with George Rignold as Pistol in *King Henry V*. During the season of 1885–86 he was leading comedian at the Boston Museum while George W. Wilson, the regular occupant of that position, was temporarily on tour with Booth and Salvini. For several seasons he was leading comedian with Madame Modjeska, playing Touchstone, Sir Toby Belch, Cloten in *Cymbeline*, Michonnet in *Adrienne Lecouvreur*, and Brigard in *Frou Frou*. He also supported Marie Wainwright in the fall of 1889, and Julia Marlowe in 1895–96. Of his impersonation of Falstaff in the latter's production of *King Henry IV* it was said that "it seems as if the whole of the witty knight's soul was given by the actor."

Owen was a member of Augustin Daly's company during a part of the nineties, appearing in comedy rôles in support of Ada Rehan, and when in 1899–1900 Mrs. Fiske produced Langdon Elwyn Mitchell's dramatic version of *Vanity Fair* under the title of *Becky Sharp,* he appeared as Joseph Sedley. He repeated the part upon her revival of that play only a short time before his death, being forced to retire from the stage on account of serious illness. In figure he was rotund of body, his features were of comic cast, in manner he was a comedian of the unctuous type, a genuine Sir Toby Belch, an admirable Falstaff, a perfect Touchstone. He was in all respects an actor and not a clown, his resources being in his mind and in his voice, and not the result of either vocal or physical antics.

[J. B. Clapp and E. F. Edgett, *Players of the Present,* pt. II (1900); Wm. Winter, *Shakespeare on the Stage,* ser. 2 (1915), ser. 3 (1916); *N. Y. Dramatic Mirror,* Mar. 21, 1896, May 12, 1906; *Boston Transcript,* May 4, 1906; personal recollections.] E. F. E.

OWENS, JOHN EDMOND (Apr. 2, 1823–Dec. 7, 1886), actor and manager, although of English birth, became famous on the American stage especially as an interpreter of Yankee characters. His birthplace was Liverpool, but he was of Welsh parentage, the son of Owen Griffith Owen and Mary Anderton, the surname having been changed to Owens by his father in early manhood. When the boy was five years old, the family came to America and made their home in Philadelphia, whither they had been preceded by relatives. There John Edmond was educated in the public schools, and while serving as a clerk in a drugstore he made his stage début, at the age of seventeen, in a minor part at Burton's National Theatre. His progress was slow, his first important character not being given him until Sept. 27, 1841, when at the same theatre he acted Peter Poultice in *The Ocean Child.* Within ten years he had acquired wide celebrity as a comedian throughout the United States and during his long career he managed companies in Baltimore, New Orleans, and other cities. He was sometimes a star, sometimes leading low comedian in stock and traveling companies. In his *Autobiography,* Joseph Jefferson refers to Owens as he saw him in New Orleans in 1846 as "the then rising young comedian," and describes him as "the handsomest low comedian I had ever seen," with a "neat dapper little figure, and a face full of lively expression," and an "effective style and great flow of animal spirits" (*post,* p. 81). In 1856 he first played Solon Shingle in *The People's Lawyer,* and when he was at the Adelphi Theatre in London in 1865, Dickens saw him and pronounced his portrayal of the part as one of the most vivid and natural characterizations he had ever seen on the stage.

Through the years Owens' repertory became extensive; among his most popular impersonations were Toodles, Dr. Pangloss in *The Heir at Law,* Dr. Ollapod in *The Poor Gentleman,* Major Wellington de Boots in *Everybody's Friend,* Caleb Plummer, Paul Pry, Aminadab Sleek, and in fact practically all the stereotyped comedy rôles of that era. In 1876 he added Perkyn Middlewick in Henry J. Byron's comedy, *Our Boys,* then at the height of its popularity, to his list of characters, and when in 1882 he joined the Madison Square Theatre Company in New York, he was seen as Elbert Rogers, the old farmer, in *Esmeralda,* with Annie Russell in the title rôle. In 1885 he retired on account of illness to his estate of Aigburth Vale, about six miles from Baltimore, which he had bought in 1853, and increasing its size by the addition of many acres from time to time, he amused himself, during the intermissions between his engagements and tours in the entertainment of his many friends both in and out of the theatrical profession. He would often say: "Every man has his hobby, and mine is harmless. Spending money on my country residence entertains me, and the improvements I make give work to people who need it." On Apr. 19, 1849, he was married to Mary C. Stevens, daughter of John G. Stevens of Baltimore, and she survived him many years, writing a biography of him, and energetically defending him from what she thought was unfair criticism of his acting by those who denied his skill as an expert comedian. When Clara Morris wrote with somewhat bad taste that even his marriage with the "little orthodox Quakeress" seemed "an expression of eccentricity," Mrs. Owens retorted by saying in a letter to the *New York Dramatic Mirror* (June 22, 1901) that she had evidently been inspired "by imagination rather than memory."

The consensus of opinion about Owens is that he was a comedian who relied mainly for his effects upon the resources of a genuine comic personality, that he did frequently indulge in extravagance of action in order to arouse laughter, that in his impersonations of Yankee characters he was truer to the footlights than to real life, but that his "jolly rotund and flexible features, his plump and comical looking figure, his jaunty air and personal peculiarities were almost as familiar off the stage as his lifelike and truly artistic impersonations were on it." Few American comedians have been more popular in their day; few have lingered longer in the memories of those who saw them. The name of Owens is a tradition of the American stage that inevitably suggests comedy and laughter.

[*Memories of the Professional and Social Life of John E. Owens* (1892), written by Owens' wife; Clara Morris, *Life on the Stage* (1901) and *Stage Confidences* (1902); *The Autobiog. of Jos. Jefferson* (1890); Wm. Winter, *The Wallet of Time* (1913), vol. I; *N. Y. Dramatic Mirror*, June 22, 1901; *Boston Herald*, Jan. 9, 1885; *Brooklyn Eagle*, Oct. 20, 1885; *Sun* (Baltimore), and *N. Y. Times*, Dec. 8, 1886; the *World* (N. Y.), Dec. 11, 1886.]   E. F. E.

OWENS, MICHAEL JOSEPH (Jan. 1, 1859–Dec. 27, 1923), inventor, glass manufacturer, son of John and Mary (Chapman) Owens, was born in Mason County, Va. (now W. Va.). His father was a coal miner with unusual mechanical genius but decidedly unpractical. It was his mother who was responsible for the practical qualities that played such a prominent part in his career. Michael had helped his father in the mines, and at the age of ten, recognizing the family's needs, he took employment in a glass factory in Wheeling, W. Va., where he shoveled coal into the "glory hole" or unit employed for resoftening glass during various stages of its manipulation in blowing. At that time glassblowers worked in two five-hour shifts per day. Black with soot and coal dust Michael would return to his home, bathe and clean up, and be ready for another blackening during the afternoon period. By the time he was fifteen he had become a glassblower.

In 1888, he began work in Toledo, Ohio, in the glass factory of Edward Drummond Libbey [*q.v.*]. Three months later he became its superintendent, and then the manager of a branch factory at Findlay, Ohio. In 1893 he had charge of the famous exhibit of the Libbey Glass Company at the World's Columbian Exposition in Chicago. Somewhat before this time he had begun a series of experiments which led to the perfection of a completely automatic bottle-blowing machine. At first he applied an exceedingly simple principle, using a piston pump to suck glass into a mold from the surface of a pot of molten metal, then placing the gathered mass over another mold into which the article was blown by reversing the pump. The first bottles were decidedly crude, but in time this experiment resulted in a machine of over 9000 separate parts which, as recently modified, is capable of blowing four finished bottles per second. Preliminary patents for these machines were taken out in 1895 (patents No. 534,840; 548,587; 548,588). As the machine was developed, other patents were secured, that of Nov. 8, 1904 (No. 774,690) representing it essentially perfected. In 1903 Owens with Libbey and others organized the Owens Bottle Machine Company. Of this concern, later called the Owens Bottle Company, Owens was manager from 1915 to 1919, and vice-

president from 1915 until his death. He was also vice-president of the Owens European Bottle Company, organized in 1905 with a plant at Manchester, England. When Irving W. Colburn [*q.v.*] began his researches in 1900 on a machine for the continuous drawing of flat sheet glass, Owens, together with his partner, Libbey, provided funds for the perfection of the machine. They purchased the patents in 1912, and in 1916 formed the Libbey-Owens Sheet Glass Company, whose first factory was built at Charleston, W. Va. Of this company Owens was vice-president until his death.

Owens possessed unusual mechanical ability but lacked the scientific knowledge required for the perfection of his plans. He displayed wise judgment, however, in consulting others, and a device thus brought to perfection he always considered a joint invention, though the fundamental idea had been his own. In 1919 he retired as general manager of the Owens Bottle Company to devote more time to his inventions. In addition to his bottle and sheet-glass machines, he perfected machines which were used in other factories for the blowing of lamp-chimneys and tumblers. During his lifetime he was granted forty-five United States patents on apparatus for controlling the operation of molds, annealing ovens, blowing glass, fire-finishing glass articles, the formation of special bottle necks, the making of sheet glass, the dumping of raw materials from the bottom of freight cars, the charging and operating of gas producers, the transferring of hot glass from furnaces to the blowing and drawing units. Some of these patents were taken out jointly with others, but the majority were awarded to him independently. After his death a number of patents were granted that had been applied for during his lifetime. He died in Toledo, survived by his wife, Mary (McKelvey) Owens of Bellaire, Ohio, whom he married in 1889, together with a son and a daughter.

[Keene Sumner, "Don't Try to Carry the Whole World On Your Shoulders," *Am. Mag.*, July 1922; *Michael J. Owens* (privately printed, 1923), a series of memorial articles including reprinted editorials from the *Glass Container*, Jan. 1924, and Toledo papers; *Who's Who in America*, 1922–23; *Toledo News-Bee*, Dec. 27, 28, 1923.]   A. S.

OWSLEY, WILLIAM (1782–Dec. 9, 1862), Kentucky jurist and governor, was born in Virginia, but in 1783 his parents, William and Catherine (Bolin) Owsley, removed with him to Lincoln County, Ky. After a common-school education, he held positions as teacher, deputy surveyor, and deputy sheriff. He studied law under John Boyle and practised in Garrard

County. About 1804 he married Elizabeth Gill. They had five children. In 1809 and 1811 he was a member of the state legislature. Appointed to the court of appeals in 1812, he resigned in 1813 but was almost immediately reappointed. One of the most important decisions in which he participated was *Commonwealth* vs. *James Morrison* (*2 Marshall*, 75), in which the court denied the right of the Bank of the United States to establish branches in Kentucky (*2 Marshall*, 75), although it later yielded to the decision of the federal Supreme Court. Another important case was *Blair, &c.* vs. *Williams* (4 *Littell*, 34), wherein the court held unconstitutional the Kentucky replevin act of 1820 giving debtors two years' grace unless creditors would agree to accept notes of the state bank. This decision met with an outburst of popular criticism, but it was reaffirmed by Owsley's opinion in *Lapsley* vs. *Brashears and Barr* (*Ibid.*, 47), which declared that the court need not follow the opinions of the legislature in interpreting the constitution and that previous replevin laws did not affect the issue. After these decisions the court was abolished by the legislature and a new one created. Nevertheless, he, with his colleagues, John Boyle and Benjamin Mills [qq.v.], continued to function as the old court, and after much controversy the new court was abolished. In 1828 he and Mills resigned, were renominated, but failed of confirmation by the Senate. He resumed practice in Garrard County and was again representative of that county in the state House of Representatives in 1831 and in the state Senate from 1832 to 1834. In 1833 he was a Clay presidential elector and from 1834 to 1836 was secretary of state under Gov. James T. Moorehead. He practised in Frankfort until 1843, when he retired from active practice and, having divided his farm in Garrard County among his five children, bought a new farm in Boyle County, near Danville.

In 1844, as the Whig candidate for governor, he defeated William O. Butler, the Democratic candidate, by a majority of about 5,000 votes. He was an able governor from 1844 to 1848 but was not popular on account of his unsociableness and, especially on account of his removal of Benjamin Hardin [q.v.] as secretary of state. The courts upheld him, but under the constitution of 1850 the governor was denied the power of removing this official. He was tall, slender, erect, simple, reserved. His prompt call of the militia in 1845 prevented a popular rescue of a convicted murderer. On the outbreak of the Mexican War, after receiving a letter from Gen. E. P. Gaines at New Orleans but before receiving official

notice from the War Department, he issued a call for volunteers and in a few days, by means of private subscriptions, had the Louisville Legion on its way to New Orleans. Largely owing to his recommendations, the state debt was decreased and the state prison improved. His last years were spent on his farm near Danville.

[Lewis and R. H. Collins, *Hist. of Ky.*, revised ed. (2 vols., 1874); W. E. Connelly and E. M. Coulter, *Hist. of Ky.* (1922), vol. II; H. Levin, *The Lawyers and Lawmakers of Ky.* (1897); *The Biog. Encyc. of Ky.* (1878); L. P. Little, *Ben Hardin* (1887)]. W. C. M.

PACA, WILLIAM (Oct. 31, 1740–Oct. 13, 1799), signer of the Declaration of Independence, third governor of Maryland, jurist, was born near Abingdon, Harford County, Md., the second son of John and Elizabeth (Smith) Paca. The Paca family may have been of Italian origin; they appear in America as well-to-do planters in the latter part of the seventeenth century. At the age of fifteen William was sent to the College of Philadelphia where he received an M.A. degree in 1759. Shortly afterward he went to Annapolis where he studied law in the office of Stephen Bordley and was admitted to practice before the mayor's court in 1761. He completed his legal training at the Inner Temple in London and was admitted to the bar of the provincial court in 1764. On May 26, 1763, he was married to Mary Chew, the daughter of Samuel and Henrietta Maria (Lloyd) Chew of Annapolis, who had "a very considerable fortune" (Annapolis *Maryland Gazette*, June 2, 1763). Only one of their five children reached maturity. His wife died in 1774 and in 1777 he was married to Anne Harrison of Philadelphia who died three years later.

Paca was first elected to the provincial legislature in 1768 and soon became identified with the party opposed to the Proprietor. With Samuel Chase and others he urged that Governor Eden's proclamation regulating the fees of civil officers should be recalled. This was later done. He also led the opposition against the poll tax which had been laid for the support of the clergy. During this controversy Chase, Paca, and Thomas Johnson wrote (1774) an article in reply to Daniel Dulany and James Holliday who had defended the tax (Delaplaine, *post*, pp. 56–57). It was reprinted in London papers and brought the group into considerable prominence. While in the Assembly Paca was on the committee that directed the construction of the State House at Annapolis. In the preliminaries of the Revolution he became a leader of the patriot cause. He served on the Maryland Committee of Correspondence and was elected to the First Continental Congress in June 1774. In October he returned to Annapolis where he was one of the representatives of that city in the Provincial Convention which met from Nov. 21 to 24. As member of the Second Continental Congress almost continuously from 1775 to 1779 he served on many important committees, among them the special Committee of Thirteen for Foreign Affairs. After Maryland removed the restrictions on the actions of her delegates in June 1776, Paca and his colleagues, Chase, Thomas Stone, and Charles Carroll, were free to vote for and sign the Declaration of Independence (C. F. Adams, *The Works of John Adams*, IX, 1854, p. 416).

Soon after the war started Paca became a member of the Maryland Council of Safety and spent several thousand dollars of his own money outfitting troops. He was in the convention that framed a constitution for the state in August 1776 and was elected one of the fifteen members of the first state Senate. In 1778 he was appointed chief judge of the Maryland General Court and two years later was appointed by Congress as the chief justice of the court of appeals in admiralty and prize cases (*Journals of the Continental Congress*, Feb. 9, 1780). In November 1782 he was elected governor of Maryland by the legislature and was reëlected unanimously in 1783 and 1784, his last term ending Nov. 26, 1785. As governor he was greatly interested in the welfare of returning soldiers and in reviving interests which the war exigency had caused to decline. He took an active part in raising subscriptions for Washington College and laid the cornerstone for the first building in 1783. The Society of the Cincinnati elected Paca to honorary membership for his services during the war. From 1784 to 1787 he served as vice-president of the Maryland Society, though the order was only for those who had served as army officers (*Annals of the Society of the Cincinnati of Maryland*, 1897, p. 32).

Paca was a delegate in the Maryland convention which adopted the federal Constitution in 1788. Although he proposed twenty-eight amendments he voted for adoption when the convention decided it had either to accept or reject the Constitution as submitted to it. In 1789 Washington appointed Paca federal district judge. He held this position until his death at "Wye Hall," his country home, in Talbot County. John Adams described Paca as a "deliberator" (Burnett, *post*, I, p. 67). He was identified with all important political movements in his state from his entrance into politics until his death. The numerous committees on which he served and the offices which he filled bear witness to his devotion to duty.

[H. E. Buchholz, *Governors of Md.* (1908), O. Tilghman, *Hist. of Talbot County, Md.*, vol. II (1915), and John Sanderson, *Biog. of the Signers to the Declaration of Independence*, vol. VIII (1827), contain short but rather inaccurate accounts of Paca's life. For periods and events in his career see: K. M. Rowland, *The Life of Chas. Carroll of Carrollton, 1737–1832* (2 vols., 1898); E. S. Delaplaine, *The Life of Thomas Johnson* (1927); E. C. Burnett, *Letters of Members of the Continental Cong.*, vols. I–VI (1921–33); *Archives of Md.*, vols. XI, XII, XLIII, XLV, XLVII, XLVIII (1892–1931); "Official Letter Book of Governor and Council," Maryland Archives (unpublished), vol. LXXVIII; L. W. Barroll, "Washington College, 1783," in *Md. Hist. Mag.*, June 1911; St. Johns Parish Records, Harford County; "Geneal. Record," in the Md. Hist. Soc.; B. C. Steiner, "Maryland's Adoption of the Fed. Constitution," *Am. Hist. Rev.*, Oct. 1899–Jan. 1900; *Baltimore American*, Oct. 17, 1799; *Fed. Gazette*, Oct. 16, 1799.]
M.E.F.

PACHECO, ROMUALDO (Oct. 31, 1831–Jan. 23, 1899), governor of California, congressman, diplomat, was born at Santa Barbara, Cal. He was the second son of Lieutenant of Engineers Romualdo Pacheco, a native of Guanajuato, Mexico, who went to California in 1825 as an aide-de-camp to Governor Echeandía, and of Doña Ramona Carillo, daughter of Don Joaquin Carillo of San Diego. The period of his childhood was one of turbulence. Spanish rule had come to an end in 1822; Mexico was involved in revolutionary difficulties. In the combat at Cahuenga Pass near Los Angeles in December 1831, Lieut. Pacheco was killed, leaving a widow and two sons, Mariano and Romualdo. Doña Ramona subsequently married an English sea captain, John Wilson. In 1840 the two children were sent to Honolulu for schooling. By the age of fifteen Romualdo was back in California, serving as supercargo on vessels in which his stepfather was interested. He was commanding a trading ship in 1846 when California passed under American control. When the state was admitted to the Union, he took the oath of allegiance to the United States and thereafter became one of the most active of its citizens. His family stood high in native California society and his English education and experience had fitted him for immediate political usefulness. He served several terms in the state Senate and also as judge of the superior court of his county. In 1863 he was appointed state treasurer by Gov. Leland Stanford to fill a vacancy. By subsequent election he served in this office for four years. In 1871 he was elected lieutenant-governor of California, and upon Governor Booth's election to the United States Senate, became governor of the state in January 1875.

Pacheco was the Republican candidate for the Forty-fifth Congress in 1876, for the fourth district. He was given the certificate of election and took his seat in 1877, but the House subsequently decided that his Democratic opponent had won the election by a few votes. Pacheco was the Republican candidate again in 1878, was elected, and was reëlected in 1880. His service at Washington was primarily as a member and subsequently as chairman of the committee on private land claims, a subject of much interest and litigation in California. Ending his congressional services in 1889, he was chosen by President Harrison in 1890 as American minister plenipotentiary to the Central American Republics. The next year he was accredited solely to Guatemala and Honduras. He appears to have satisfactorily represented the United States both in the settlement of the *Colima* dispute and in the harmonization of relations between these Republics. Subsequent to his retirement from the diplomatic service, he accepted the management of a cattle ranch in north Coahuila, Mexico, and later returned to San Francisco to engage in stock brokerage business. He died in January 1899 at Oakland, Calif.

As a public official, Pacheco made an excellent record. While lieutenant-governor of the state, he served, *ex officio,* as warden of the San Quentin penitentiary, where he found conditions which he worked to ameliorate. During his brief service as governor he took a strong attitude toward the development of the state university, and he was notably independent in his refusal to exercise executive clemency to wrong-doers. But perhaps his great service was in uniting the Spanish-speaking element of the state with the American settlers who entered in great numbers from 1849 on, in a common effort to build a harmonious California society and inculcate a loyal citizenship within the United States. In 1863 Pacheco married Mary McIntire, the writer of a number of successful comedies. He was a strikingly handsome man, a fine horseman, and was known among all his acquaintances for his personal charm and cultivated manners. It is related in his family that his greatest pleasure was to assemble at San Luis Obispo guests from far and wide for that typical ranch hospitality in which took place the sports and the unaffected social diversions which are a part of the state's heritage from its Spanish origin.

[H. H. Bancroft, *Hist. of Cal.* (1890), vol. VII; T. H. Hittell, *Hist. of Cal.,* vol. IV (1897); C. E. Chapman, *A Hist. of Cal.: The Spanish Period* (1921); Richard H. Dana, *Two Years Before the Mast* (1869 ed.); *Papers Relating to the Foreign Relations of the U. S.,* 1890–91; obituaries in New York and San Francisco papers; information as to certain facts furnished by Mariano Pacheco of San Luis Obispo.]   D. P. B.

PACKARD, ALPHEUS SPRING (Dec. 23, 708–July 13, 1884), college teacher, brother of Joseph Packard [*q.v.*], was born at Chelmsford, Mass., the son of Hezekiah and Mary (Spring) Packard. He was a descendant of Samuel Packard, who emigrated from Norfolk, England, in 1638 and settled in Hingham, Mass. Alpheus was educated at his father's home in Wiscasset, Me., at Phillips Exeter Academy, and at Bowdoin College, where he was graduated second in his class with the Latin salutatory in 1816. After three years spent in teaching at various Maine academies, he was called to be tutor at Bowdoin, beginning an uninterrupted service of sixty-five years which ended only with his death and which in extent, continuity, and variety has rarely been exceeded in American academic life. From 1824 until 1865 he was professor of the Latin and Greek languages; from 1842 until 1845 also professor of rhetoric and oratory; and from 1864 until 1884 Collins Professor of Natural and Revealed Religion. He was also college librarian from 1869 until 1881; and acting president from 1883 until 1884. On May 16, 1850, he was regularly ordained to the Congregational ministry and added preaching and the conduct of the chapel services at the college to his other manifold duties. For forty-five years he was librarian of the Maine Historical Society, and for over thirty years, a member of the Brunswick school committee.

The long years of service which he gave to so many different offices form but one indication of a character marked by unusual stamina and utter fidelity. All his long life he was in perfect health; and he was remarkably industrious and methodical. Although, like so many other teachers of his generation, he gave the greater part of his time and energy to his classes, he was a competent, if not an original, scholar. He edited *Xenophon's Memorabilia of Socrates, with English Notes* (1839) and wrote and published more than thirty essays and addresses, chiefly on educational and historical themes. As a teacher of the classics he did not emphasize unduly philological and grammatical details but always endeavored to unfold and illustrate the thought of the author. He set forth his theory of the art of teaching in these words: "Like faithful guides, we are to show the pupil the most direct path to knowledge, and become the companions of his way, pointing out to him the most favorable points whence he may view all that is grand and beautiful in the extensive field of human knowledge" (quoted in *Memorial, post,* pp. 5, 6). His methods were singularly effective and he was held in high esteem by his students. It was his good fortune to have under his instruction Longfellow, Hawthorne, and many others of later eminence. Longfellow in his poem *Morituri Salutamus* delivered in 1875 at the fiftieth anniversary of his graduation from Bowdoin paid Packard, the only surviving member of the faculty of the twenties, the well-known tribute:

> "Honor and reverence and the good repute
> That follows faithful service as its fruit
> Be unto him whom living we salute."

He had a character of singular sweetness and gentleness combined with strong conviction. His portrait by Vinton, now in the Bowdoin Art Museum, reveals the features of a strong man, indubitably the gentleman. In person he was described as most impressive, very handsome, with a fine figure, and with none of the carelessness of dress and appearance that is not infrequent in academic circles. He was married, first, in 1827, to Frances Elizabeth, daughter of President Jesse Appleton [*q.v.*], who died in 1839 leaving five children, among them Alpheus S. Packard [*q.v.*], zoölogist of Brown University; and second, in 1844, to Mrs. Caroline W. (Bartelles) McLellan of Portland, who bore him one child. He died suddenly of heart failure at Squirrel Island, Me., while on a pleasure excursion with members of his family, and was buried in Brunswick.

[G. T. Little, *Geneal. and Family Hist. of the State of Maine* (1909), vol. II; W. R. Cutter, *New England Families, Geneal. and Memorial* (1913), vol. I; L. C. Hatch, *The Hist. of Bowdoin Coll.* (1927); *Memorial: Alpheus Spring Packard, 1798–1884* (1886), with bibliog.; *Bowdoin Orient*, July 16 and Oct. 1, 1884; *Daily Eastern Argus* (Portland, Me.), July 14, 1884; *Boston Transcript*, July 14, 1884.]   K. C. M. S.

PACKARD, ALPHEUS SPRING (Feb. 19, 1839–Feb. 14, 1905), entomologist, teacher, was born in Brunswick, Me., and died at Providence, R. I. His father was Prof. Alpheus Spring Packard [*q.v.*] of Bowdoin College; his mother, Frances Elizabeth Appleton, daughter of Rev. Jesse Appleton [*q.v.*], president of Bowdoin, and a sister of the wife of President Franklin Pierce [*q.v.*]. The most of his male ancestors on both sides were ministers, and he was the first scientist in the family. A born naturalist, he began to collect minerals and shells when about fourteen or fifteen years old, and to read the natural history books in the library of the college. At sixteen he began to collect insects, and at eighteen commenced the study of comparative anatomy. The next year he entered into correspondence with Samuel H. Scudder [*q.v.*], then living at Williamstown, Mass., thus beginning a friendship which lasted through life. Entering Bowdoin in 1857, he graduated with the degree of A.B. in 1861. In the summer of 1860 he went with Prof. Paul A. Chadbourne [*q.v.*] upon the students' expedition from Williams College to Lab-

rador, and in the spring of 1864 he accompanied the expedition organized by William Bradford, 1823–1892 [*q.v.*], the marine artist. His observations on these trips are recorded in *The Labrador Coast. A Journal of Two Summer Cruises to that Region* (1891). He was assistant on the Maine Geological Survey (1861–62), examining fossils in the Fish River region for the purpose of determining the age of the rocks.

After his graduation from Bowdoin, Packard went to Cambridge to study under Agassiz, and soon became a student assistant. In the meantime he received the degree of A.M. from Bowdoin (1862) and M.D. from the Maine Medical School (1864). In the latter year he was commissioned assistant surgeon in the first Maine Veteran Volunteers and went to the front, serving until the close of the war. For a year thereafter he was connected with the Boston Society of Natural History and then became curator of the Essex Institute. In October 1867 he married Elizabeth Derby, daughter of Samuel Baker Walcott. That same year he was appointed a curator of the Peabody Academy of Science, Salem, Mass., of which he was later director, and with Edward S. Morse, Frederick W. Putnam, and Alpheus Hyatt [*qq.v.*] founded the *American Naturalist*, of which he was editor-in-chief until 1887. He was lecturer on economic entomology at the Maine College of Agriculture and Mechanics (1870) and at the Massachusetts Agricultural College (1870–78), and lecturer on entomology at Bowdoin (1871–74). In 1869 he published his *Guide to the Study of Insects,* an illustrated volume of large size. The influence of this book on the study of entomology in the United States can hardly be overestimated. There was an unexpectedly large sale, and it was adopted by many of the colleges and universities. Some subsequent editions were published. Through this book, Packard became one of the best-known men in scientific circles in America, and in 1872 was elected to the National Academy of Sciences. In the same year he visited Europe for the first time and was warmly greeted by the most prominent naturalists. In 1873 he was one of the teachers in the Anderson School of Natural History at Penikese, established by the elder Agassiz. He was temporarily connected with the Kentucky Geological Survey in 1874, and in 1875, with the United States Geological Survey of the Territories under Ferdinand V. Hayden [*q.v.*]. In 1877 he became a member of the United States Entomological Commission, with Charles V. Riley and Cyrus Thomas [*qq.v.*], to investigate the Rocky Mountain locust. He resigned his position at the Peabody Academy of Science in

1878 to become professor of zoölogy and geology at Brown University, where he remained for the rest of his life. In 1898 he published his well-known *Text-Book of Entomology*, which dealt with the anatomy, physiology, embryology, and metamorphoses of insects.

During his career he worked incessantly. He was an ardent evolutionist and a man of great breadth of mind. Although a sound taxonomist, having described fifty genera and about five hundred and eighty species in many groups, his work was especially strong along biological lines. His last work was his monumental *Monograph of the Bombycine Moths* (3 vols., 1895–1914), the last volume being completed and edited after his death by T. D. A. Cockerell. He did a great work in popularizing science, but did little public lecturing on account of a defective palate. In addition to his scientific pursuits he was greatly interested in music and art. He was an honorary member of the Entomological Society of France and of the Entomological Society of London. His bibliography contains 579 titles. Aside from the important works already mentioned, he was the author of *A Monograph of the Geometrid Moths or Phalaenidae of the United States* (1876), and *Insects Injurious to Forest and Shade Trees* (1881), of which a second edition appeared in 1890. These constituted the first notable contributions to the study of forest entomology in North America. They were profusely illustrated and dealt almost entirely with the biological aspects of the insects treated. At the time of his death he was generally considered by both American and European scientific men as the broadest, the most learned, and the most accomplished entomologist in the United States.

[T. D. A. Cockerell, in *Biog. Memoirs Nat. Acad. Sci.*, vol. IX (1920), with bibliog.; Samuel Henshaw, *The Entomological Writings of Dr. Alpheus Spring Packard* (1887); *Popular Sci. Mo.*, May 1905; *Who's Who in America*, 1903–05; *Providence Daily Jour.*, Feb. 15, 1905.]   L. O. H.

PACKARD, FREDERICK ADOLPHUS (Sept. 26, 1794–Nov. 11, 1867), editor of Sunday-school publications, was born in Marlboro, Mass. His father was the Rev. Asa Packard, a descendant of Samuel Packard, who emigrated from England to Massachusetts in 1638, settling in Hingham; his mother was Nancy Quincy, also of Puritan descent. For many years Asa Packard was pastor of the Congregational Church in Marlboro. Frederick prepared for college under his uncle, Hezekiah Packard, father of Alpheus S. and Joseph Packard [*qq.v.*], at Wiscasset, Me., and graduated from Harvard in 1814 with honors. He then studied law at Northampton, Mass., and practised at Springfield from 1817

until 1829. In 1819 he became editor and proprietor of the *Hampshire Federalist* (later the *Hampden Federalist*), a weekly journal giving the news of the day as well as articles on literary, scientific, and religious subjects; it was a predecessor of the *Springfield Republican*. In 1822 he married Elizabeth Dwight Hooker, daughter of Judge John Hooker. Shortly after, he united with the First Congregational Church of Springfield, and at once became interested in the Sunday school. He was elected its superintendent in 1827, and in 1828 was sent as a delegate to the Fourth Anniversary of the Sunday School Union. During 1828–29, he was a member of the state legislature of Massachusetts.

In the latter part of 1828 he was asked to become editorial secretary of the American Sunday School Union. Upon accepting the office, he moved to Philadelphia and until 1858 edited continuously all of the weekly and monthly periodicals of the Union, as well as all the books issued with its imprint. Certain unpleasant differences among the managers of the Union led to a suspension of his duties for a short time in 1858. Later, this opposition was withdrawn and he resumed his editorial work, continuing therein until the time of his death in 1867. During the period of his editorship more than 2,000 books passed through his hands. Between forty and fifty of these were written by him, though, owing to his unobtrusive disposition, he did not permit his name to appear on them, a fact which makes it difficult to identify them. In 1837 the Sunday School Union prepared a "Select Library" of some 120 volumes for use in public schools. The following year Packard endeavored to get Horace Mann [*q.v.*] and the Massachusetts Board of Education to approve the introduction of these into the Massachusetts schools. Since, in the opinion of Mann, the books were patently sectarian, their admission was not sanctioned. As a result, Packard carried on for years in newspapers and magazines a persistent attack upon Mann and the Board for excluding orthodox religion from the system of public education. (For full discussion of this episode, see R. B. Culver, *Horace Mann and Religion in the Massachusetts Public Schools*, 1929).

Packard was a man of many interests, and a great worker. He was a director of Girard College for Orphans, and in July 1849 was elected to its presidency, which he declined. He was manager of the House of Refuge, and for twenty-one years editor of the *Journal of Prison Discipline*. He also wrote many articles on religious, educational, and other subjects. Among the magazines of the Sunday School Union which he edited was the *Sunday School Journal and Advocate of Christian Religion* and *Youth's Penny Gazette*, which later became the *Child's World;* the society's annual reports were also prepared by him. His own books include *The Union Bible Dictionary* (1837), *The Teacher Taught* (1839), *The Teacher Teaching* (1861), *The Rock* (1861), and *Life of Robert Owen* (1866). He had four children, among whom were Lewis Richard Packard, professor of Greek at Yale, and John Hooker Packard [*q.v.*].

[Charles Hudson, *Hist. of the Town of Marlborough . . . Mass.* (1862); Annual Reports of the Am. Sunday School Union, particularly *The 44th Ann. Report,* May 1868; E. W. Rice, *The Sunday School Movement 1780–1917 and the Am. Sunday-School Union, 1780–1917* (1917); G. H. Griffin, *Frederick A. Packard, A Memorial Discourse* (1890); *Phila. Inquirer,* Nov. 12, 1867.]   H.I.D.

PACKARD, JAMES WARD (Nov. 5, 1863– Mar. 20, 1928), engineer, inventor, manufacturer, son of Warren and Mary E. (Doud) Packard, was born in Warren, Ohio. His father was a successful business man, engaged first in the hardware trade in Warren and later in extensive sawmill operations in Ohio, Pennsylvania, and New York. James spent a normal boy's life at home and developed a particularly keen interest in mechanics and electricity. He prepared for college in his birthplace, and at the age of seventeen entered Lehigh University, Bethlehem, Pa., the youngest in the class, graduating in 1884 with the degree of mechanical engineer. Immediately following his graduation he went to work in a steam power plant in New York City, and a year or so later obtained the job of foreman for the Sawyer-Mann Electric Company, New York, manufacturers of the Sawyer-Mann incandescent electric lamp. This association presumably gave him his first real opportunity to engage in research and experimentation, for in the course of the succeeding five years he acquired a number of valuable patents. These included a new form of incandescent lamp, a lamp socket, and four patents on improvements in vacuum pumps for exhausting the air from incandescent lamp bulbs.

In 1889 the Sawyer-Mann Company was sold to the Westinghouse interests, which sale included the transfer of Packard's patents; and, although he had the opportunity to connect himself with the new owners, Packard returned to his home in Warren and with his brother started an electrical business under the name of the Packard Electric Company. The following year, with the aid of local capital, the brothers reorganized their company as the New York & Ohio Company, and for more than ten years engaged in the manufacture of electrical transformers, fuse boxes, measuring instruments, and cables. At first these products were of the conventional type, but Packard, devoting his time especially to research, devised a number of improvements, which were immediately manufactured by the company. Thus on Oct. 9, 1894, he obtained two patents for a transformer and fuse box; he devised a number of further improvements in transformers in 1897 and 1899, and perfected a new electrical measuring instrument in 1900.

Early in this decade Packard had become interested also in the "horseless carriage" and bought a French De Dion-Bouton motor tricycle which, incidentally, had been constructed in Massachusetts. He also investigated the early European horseless carriages and as a result, between 1891 and 1893, conceived the idea of building such a vehicle himself. Assisted by one of his shopmen, he drew up plans for a vehicle and negotiated for the purchase of a gasoline engine from Charles King of Detroit. The depression of 1893 unfortunately halted for five years the actual building of the automobile. In 1898, however, he purchased one of the first Winton automobiles and shortly afterwards, in company with George Weiss, who had been one of the organizers of the Winton Company, and W. A. Hatcher, the Winton shop superintendent, he designed and built his first automobile, which was given a road test Nov. 6, 1899. Following this successful trial, the Ohio Automobile Company was immediately formed as a department of Packard's electric company, and the manufacture of Packard automobiles was begun early in 1900. After several years of successful operation, in 1903, with the assistance of outside financial help, he reorganized his company as the Packard Motor Car Company and established a new plant at Detroit, Mich., where it has remained ever since. Although president of the new company, Packard continued to live in Warren. The mercantile side of the business had very little appeal for him, however, and after a few years he relinquished the presidency and for the remainder of his life acted as consultant and adviser to the company. As in his earlier electrical work, so in the automobile field his greatest interest was in research, and he contributed many valuable improvements to the automobile. These included gasoline engines; transmission, ignition and carburetion systems; chassis construction; and braking mechanisms. His success, it has been said, was due primarily to his sensitiveness to mechanical crudeness and his talent to see how things that had been done could be done better. His homes were storehouses of useful and experimental devices, including a collection of watches, which, for exquisite beauty and intricate mechanism, was perhaps the finest ever assembled by an individual. It is now in the possession of the Horological Institute of America, Washington, D. C. His philanthropies were many, the outstanding ones being a million-dollar laboratory for electrical and mechanical engineering given to Lehigh University and the sum of a million dollars given to the Seaman's Institute in New York. In August 1904 he married Elizabeth Achsah Gillmer of Warren, Ohio, who survived him at the time of his death in Cleveland.

[J. G. Butler, *Hist. of Youngstown and the Mahoning Valley, Ohio* (1921, vols. I–II); correspondence with Horological Institute of America and the Packard family; J. R. Doolittle, *The Romance of the Automobile Industry* (1916); *Automobile Trade Jour.*, Dec. 1, 1924; *Automobile Industries*, Mar. 24, 1928; *Cleveland Plain Dealer*, Mar. 21, 1928; *Who's Who in America*, 1926–27; Patent Office records.]   C. W. M—n.

PACKARD, JOHN HOOKER (Aug. 15, 1832–May 21, 1907), surgeon, was born in Philadelphia, the son of Frederick A. Packard [*q.v.*], of old New England ancestry. His father's line went back to Samuel Packard who came to America in 1638; through his mother, Elizabeth Dwight (Hooker), he was descended from Rev. Thomas Hooker [*q.v.*], who emigrated to New England in 1633, and founded the town of Hartford, Conn., in 1636. John Hooker Packard received the degree of A.B. from the University of Pennsylvania in 1850, and that of M.D. from the same institution in 1853. He then went abroad and walked the hospitals of the Old World, spending most of his time in London and Paris, in the latter place seeing some of Nélaton's operations. On his return to America he served as resident physician in the Pennsylvania Hospital, with which institution he was to have a long and honorable career. During the Civil War he was acting assistant surgeon in the United States Army, and served as attending surgeon to the Christian Street and to the Satterlee General hospitals in Philadelphia. Though ill at the time, he obeyed at once emergency orders to report at the scene of action during the battle of Gettysburg, where "for three days and nights he labored incessantly, and then, being utterly unable to continue at work, was sent back to Philadelphia, suffering from a nearly fatal attack of typhoid" (Gibbon, *post*, p. lvii).

In 1863, his election as surgeon to the Episcopal Hospital, Philadelphia, introduced him again to major surgery, especially traumatic major surgery. He resigned from the Episcopal Hospital, when, in 1884, he was elected surgeon to the Pennsylvania Hospital, a position which he

held until 1896. He served also for a number of years as surgeon to St. Joseph's Hospital. He was the type of man who took personal interest in the administration of the institutions with which he was connected. Elected a fellow of the College of Physicians of Philadelphia in 1858, he served faithfully as secretary from 1862 to 1877. In 1885 he was elected vice-president of the college. He also served as Mütter Lecturer, being the first to hold this post. His *Lectures on Inflammation Delivered before the College of Physicians of Philadelphia under the Bequest of Dr. Mütter* were published in book form in 1865. He also gave the second series, published under the title *Notes on Fractures of the Upper Extremity* (1867). Packard was a founder of the Philadelphia Academy of Surgery (1879), the Pathological Society of Philadelphia, and the Obstetrical Society of Philadelphia. He was also an original fellow of the American Surgical Association (1880) and its treasurer (1880–83).

His published works include *A Treatise on Fractures* (1859), a translation of J. F. Malgaigne's work; *A Manual of Minor Surgery* (1863); and *A Hand-book of Operative Surgery* (1870). He contributed to John Ashhurst's *International Encyclopaedia of Surgery* the articles entitled "Poisoned Wounds" and "Injuries to Bones" (the latter, a monograph of 260 pages); and to J. M. Keating's *Cyclopaedia of the Diseases of Children* the chapters entitled "Colotomy" and "Fractures and Dislocations." In 1881 he edited an American edition of Timothy Holmes's *System of Surgery*. He was also responsible for three editions of *The Philadelphia Medical Register and Directory* (1868, 1871, 1873). He was recognized as an expert in medico-legal cases, and often served as expert witness. He was an active member of the Pennsylvania Academy of the Fine Arts, and was on its board of directors from 1884, and chairman of its committee on instruction from 1887 to his death. His own artistic skill was considerable and his hospital histories were often adorned by excellent sketches. His last days were saddened by being forced to give up all active surgical work as the result of an infection of his finger, acquired in the course of his professional duties (1896). He was married, June 3, 1858, to Elizabeth Wood; they had six children, two of his five sons becoming physicians.

[J. H. Gibbon, "Memoir of John Hooker Packard, M.D." *Trans. of the Coll. of Physicians of Phila.*, 3 ser. XXXI (1909); R. H. Harte, "Presentation of the Portrait of Dr. John H. Packard," *Ibid.*, 3 ser. XXXIX (1917); H. A. Kelly and W. L. Burrage, *Am. Medic. Biogs.* (1920); *Who's Who in America*, 1906–07; *Public Ledger* (Phila.), May 22, 1907.]   A. P. C. A.

PACKARD, JOSEPH (Dec. 23, 1812–May 3, 1902), Episcopal clergyman, Biblical scholar, was born at Wiscasset, Me., the son of Hezekiah and Mary (Spring) Packard, and a descendant of Samuel Packard who emigrated from England to Hingham, Mass., in 1638, later moving to Bridgewater. His father enlisted in the Revolutionary army at the age of thirteen, later graduated at Harvard, and was a minister and teacher. Joseph's home life was, therefore, that of a New England country minister's household, very simple, but strongly influenced by religion and learning. He began the study of Latin and Greek at an early age with his father; at twelve went to Phillips Academy, Andover; at fourteen taught Greek and Latin in his father's school; and at fifteen entered Bowdoin College, where his brother, Alpheus Spring Packard, 1798–1884 [q.v.] was professor of Latin and Greek and Henry Wadsworth Longfellow was his French professor. He graduated in 1831, salutatorian of his class, delivering the address in Latin. After graduating, he taught for several years and was in charge of Brattleboro Academy, Vermont.

In 1833 he entered Andover Seminary, and while there became a member of the Episcopal Church, to which he had been attracted by "its liturgy and its ways." He valued highly the historic episcopate, the right of the laity to representation in church councils, the custom of common worship, and the sacraments, and remained during his long life a stanch and devoted churchman of the evangelical school. In 1834 he became professor of Latin, Hebrew, and other branches in Bristol College, and two years later was elected professor of sacred literature in the Theological Seminary in Virginia, where he spent the rest of his life. He was ordained deacon by Bishop Griswold, July 17, 1836, and priest by Bishop Meade, Sept. 29, 1837. In January 1838 he married Rosina Jones, daughter of Walter Jones [q.v.] and grand-niece of "Light-Horse Harry" Lee. They had nine children, four sons and five daughters. He served for twelve years on the American Committee for the Revision of the Bible, published several articles in the *Bibliotheca Sacra*, and edited "The Book of Malachi" (1874) in J. P. Lange's *Commentary on the Holy Scriptures*. In 1874 he became dean of the Seminary and held this position until he retired in 1895. He continued to live at the Seminary until his death.

Packard's life covered almost all of the nineteenth century, and in him two civilizations met: the Puritan of New England and the Cavalier and Church of England of Virginia. His father saw General Washington take command of the army under the elm at Cambridge, his father-in-law commanded the militia of the District of Columbia against the British in 1814, while he himself was acquainted with Generals Lee and Jackson, and lost two sons in the Confederate Army. He was remarkable, also, for his great length of service as a professor in one institution, through which he exerted no little influence upon the religious life of America. He was an honest, accurate, and thoroughly trained scholar, with a fine simplicity of character, singleness of purpose, good judgment, practical wisdom, and unfailing sympathy.

[*Who's Who in America*, 1901–02; T. J. Packard, ed., *Recollections of a Long Life, Joseph Packard, D.D.* (1902); W. A. R. Goodwin, *Hist. of the Theological Sem. in Va.* (1923); *Alexandria Gazette*, May 3, 1902.]

T. K. N.

PACKARD, SILAS SADLER (Apr. 28, 1826–Oct. 27, 1898), pioneer in business education, was born at Cummington, Mass., son of Chester and Eunice (Sadler) Packard. His father was a descendant of Samuel Packard who settled in Hingham, Mass., in 1638 and later removed to Bridgewater. In 1833, when Silas was seven years old, his family migrated to Fredonia, Licking County, Ohio, taking a month for the journey and traveling the entire distance from Troy, N. Y., to Newark, Ohio, by water. His account of this trip and of the family's adventures in the new home, *My Recollections of Ohio* (1890), written many years later, gives a typical picture of the pioneer experiences of hundreds of New England families. A few terms in the district schools and a year in Granville Academy, Granville, Ohio, constituted all the formal schooling that the boy was able to acquire, but his native resourcefulness carried him far. At sixteen he was a teacher of penmanship in country schools. Three years later, having become master of a Kentucky school, he exhibited proficiency in portrait painting, for which he had to prepare his own materials. This interest, however, seems to have been temporary. At Cincinnati in 1848 he resumed the teaching of penmanship in a commercial school and later added bookkeeping to the branches in which he offered instruction. After a brief residence in Adrian, Mich. (1850–51), he spent two years in Lockport, N. Y., removing to Tonawanda, N. Y., in 1853, where he started a weekly newspaper, the *Niagara River Pilot*.

In 1856 he became associated with Henry B. Bryant and Henry D. Stratton in promoting a chain of business "colleges." This enterprise took him to Chicago and to Albany, N. Y. In 1858 he founded Packard's Business College in the city of New York. He also assisted in compiling *Byrant and Stratton's National Book-Keeping,* a series of textbooks the first of which was published in 1860, and from May 1868 to March 1870 he published *Packard's Monthly.* Once having decided that his career was to lie in the field of commercial education, he held to that objective for the remaining forty years of his life. The New York school prospered under his direction; in its first twenty-five years it numbered 6,000 pupils. He was eager and measurably successful in promoting the training of young women for office work and in convincing employers of their capability. The introduction of the typewriter, with the increased demand for stenographers, was met by added facilities for training in those branches. Packard was one of the first business-school proprietors to sense the meaning of the changed conditions in business life and to adapt his methods to them. For many years he held a place of accredited leadership in his chosen vocation. He was accounted a good speaker and writer and was active in several organizations, notably the Ohio Society. On Mar. 6, 1850, he was married to Marion Helena Crocker.

[Theophilus Packard, *The Geneals. of Samuel Packard, of Bridgewater, Mass., and of Abel Packard, of Cummington, Mass.* (1871); Moses Cary, *A Geneal. of the Families Who Have Settled in the North Parish of Bridgewater* (1824); *N. Y. Tribune,* Oct. 28, 1898; B. J. Lossing, *Hist. of N. Y. City* (1884); *Nat. Mag.,* Dec. 1891, pp. 205–08.]   W. B. S.

PACKER, ASA (Dec. 29, 1805–May 17, 1879), railroad builder, congressman, philanthropist, was born at Groton, New London County, Conn., the son of Elisha Packer, Jr. It appears that his formal education was limited to the rudiments secured in the local district school. As a youth he entered the tannery of Elias Smith at North Stonington and so conducted himself that his employer planned to take him into partnership but died before the arrangements were completed. As a result, young Asa, after experimenting with farming in Connecticut and finding conditions unsatisfactory, determined at the age of seventeen to seek his fortune in Pennsylvania. Setting out on foot with a knapsack on his back he arrived in 1822 in Brooklyn, Susquehanna County, where he served as an apprentice to a relative who was a carpenter and joiner. He followed this trade for several years and even worked at it for a time in the city of New York while still maintaining a residence at Springville, also in Susquehanna County, where he purchased land in 1823 and built with his own hands a cabin that served as his home for ten years. Mauch Chunk on the Upper Lehigh at this time acquired real importance owing to the completion of the Lehigh

Valley canal, and Packer became the owner and master of a canal boat that carried coal from this place to Philadelphia. Saving his earnings he purchased coal lands on the Upper Susquehanna and in this way laid the foundations of the fortune that he came to possess. In 1831 he also began to operate a store and boatyard in partnership with his younger and only brother, R. W. Packer, and subsequently took a contract for the construction of canal locks on the upper navigation of the Lehigh which he completed in 1837. The year following he was at Pottsville, building boats to transfer coal to New York by way of the New Canal. He engaged in mining and transporting coal for the Lehigh Coal & Navigation Company and also purchased and operated on his own account mines at Hazleton.

In 1843 Packer entered public life upon his election to the state legislature. As a member of that body he was able to secure an act for the creation of the county of Carbon with Mauch Chunk as its county seat. For five years subsequent to the erection of the county he was associate judge of the county court. In politics he was a Democrat and in 1852 he was elected to Congress from the thirteenth district and served for two terms. While fairly constant in his attendance he made no speeches. He was inclined to be regular, usually voting with the majority of his party, and supporting both Pierce and Buchanan. His power within the ranks of the Democratic party cannot be measured by speeches and public appearances. In the National Democratic Convention of 1868 he received the votes of the Pennsylvania delegation for president; in 1869 he was the Democratic nominee for governor. But he was not destined to enter public office again, although he accepted in 1876 a post as commissioner for the Centennial Exhibition and was especially influential in connection with the Centennial Board of Finance. The year preceding his election to a seat in Congress he acquired a controlling interest in a projected railroad incorporated in 1846 under the name of the Delaware, Lehigh, Schuylkill & Susquehanna Railroad Company, which in 1853 became the Lehigh Valley Railroad Company. This he not only financed but built in spite of the unwillingness of the Lehigh Coal & Navigation Company to support a project that seemed doomed to failure. Although he was financially embarrassed at times before the completion of the road he shared largely in the profits of the mining and transportation business that was developed and became before his death the richest man in Pennsylvania.

At the close of the Civil War Packer decided

to establish an institution for the education of the youth of the region that had for over forty years been the scene of his chief business activities. To achieve this end he set aside $500,000 and also donated a considerable body of land. In 1866 the new institution, Lehigh University, was chartered by the Pennsylvania legislature and opened for instruction in temporary buildings. Packer added greatly to his original gift to this foundation during his lifetime and in his will made it a beneficiary to the extent of $1,500,000. In addition, he liberally endowed the university library. He also gave most liberally to various activities of the Episcopal Church of which he was a member and by his will his great wealth was largely distributed. He died at his Philadelphia residence in his seventy-fifth year. He had married, on Jan. 23, 1828, Sarah M. Blakeslee, the daughter of a farmer of Schuylkill township in Susquehanna County. She with two sons and a daughter survived him. Packer possessed an indomitable will, unusual foresight, and business judgment. He knew the value of money and never allowed himself to divert it to channels that would not be generally profitable or beneficial. Accordingly he never indulged in extravagances but always lived with rigid simplicity.

[*Outline of the Career of the Hon. Asa Packer of Pa.* (1867); M. A. DeW. Howe, *The Lehigh Univ.: Asa Packer, Founder* (1879); J. M. Leavitt, *Univ. Sermon: Memorial to A. Packer* (1879); Henry Coppée, *Asa Packer* (n.d.); *The Biog. Encyc. of Pa. of the Nineteenth Century* (1874); J. W. Jordan, *Encyc. of Pa. Biog.*, vol. VI (1916); M. S. Henry, *Hist. of Lehigh Valley* (1860); *Biog. Dir. Am. Cong.* (1928); C. K. Stark, *Groton, Conn., 1705–1905* (1922); Archives of the Hist. Soc. of Pa.; collection of newspaper clippings relating to Packer in the Lehigh Univ. Lib.]
L. H. G.

PACKER, WILLIAM FISHER (Apr. 2, 1807–Sept. 27, 1870), editor and politician, was born in Howard Township, Centre County, Pa., the son of James and Charity (Bye) Packer. He received but little schooling since his father, a farmer, died when William was but seven years old. In January 1820 he apprenticed himself to a relative, Samuel J. Packer, who was editor of the *Public Inquirer* at Sunbury, Pa., to learn the printing trade. Later the paper was discontinued and he entered the office of Henry Petrikin, publisher of the *Bellefonte Patriot* at Bellefonte, Pa. In 1825 he went to Harrisburg and worked as a journeyman printer on the *Pennsylvania Intelligencer*, published by Charles Mowry and Simon Cameron. Two years later he was appointed clerk in the register's office of Lycoming County at Williamsport, Pa., and at the same time commenced the study of law in the office of Joseph B. Anthony of that place. In the fall of 1827 he formed a connection with John Brandon, pub-

lisher of the *Lycoming Gazette,* which at this time was the only newspaper issued in the northern part of Pennsylvania. On Aug. 18, 1829, he became the sole owner of the paper and published it until May 1836, when he sold it to John R. Eck. The *Gazette* was a Democratic paper and as its editor Packer became a leader in the local affairs of that party and was sent as a delegate to the National Democratic Convention at Baltimore, Md., in 1835. Eventually he became known as one of the ablest politicians of Pennsylvania.

In 1831 Packer worked to secure state appropriations for the completion of the West Branch Division of the Pennsylvania Canal, and from June 1832 until 1835, when the canal was completed, he was superintendent of that division. In 1836 he joined with O. Barrett and Benjamin Parke in publishing the *Keystone* at Harrisburg, Pa., which in a short time became a strong influence in Pennsylvania politics. He retained his interest in this paper until 1841. In February 1839 he was appointed a canal commissioner for the state and served until 1841. The following year he was appointed auditor-general of Pennsylvania and held this office until May 1, 1845. In 1847 and again in 1848 he was elected a member of the state House of Representatives and during both terms served as speaker. In 1849 he was elected to the state Senate. Here he carried through, against strong opposition, the bill to incorporate the Susquehanna Railroad Company, and upon the organization of the company on June 10, 1852, he was made its president. He served until 1854, when the road was consolidated with others to form the Northern Central Railway Company, and then was made a member of the board of directors. In 1857 he was elected governor of Pennsylvania. He was essentially a Northern moderate which was revealed by his strong opposition to the Kansas policy of Buchanan, although he had labored for the latter's nomination at the National Democratic Convention in 1856, and by his opposition to secession in 1861. As governor he continued his activities in behalf of improved transportation facilities for the state. He urged state aid to carry on the construction of the Sunbury & Erie Railroad and shortly after he left office the measure was passed. At the close of his term as governor in 1861 he retired from political life and returned to his home at Williamsport, Pa., where he later died. He had married, on Dec. 24, 1829, Mary W. Vanderbelt, by whom he had six children.

[G. P. Donehoo, ed., *Pa.: A Hist.* (1926), vol. III; W. H. Egle, *An Illustrated Hist. of the Commonwealth of Pa.* (1876); T. W. Lloyd, *Hist. of Lycoming County, Pa.* (1929); J. B. Linn, *Hist. of Centre and Clinton Counties, Pa.* (1883); W. B. Wilson, *Hist. of the Pa.*

Railroad Company (1899), vol. I ; *Pub. Ledger* (Phila.), Sept. 28, 1870.]   J. H. F.

PADDOCK, ALGERNON SIDNEY (Nov. 9, 1830–Oct. 17, 1897), secretary and acting governor of the territory of Nebraska, United States senator, was born at Glens Falls, N. Y., the son of Ira A. Paddock, a prominent lawyer, and Lucinda (Wells) Paddock. He attended a local academy, then entered Union College at Schenectady, N. Y., from which, however, owing to financial difficulties, he was never graduated. Later he taught school and read law. In May 1857 he followed his brother, Joseph W. Paddock, to Omaha, Nebr., where he promptly secured admission to the bar, preëmpted a farm nearby, and threw himself actively into the life of the new community. He was married on Dec. 22, 1859, to Emma L. Mack, daughter of Daniel and Lucinda (Perry) Mack, of St. Lawrence County, N. Y.

Most of Paddock's time was soon absorbed in politics. He identified himself with the Republican party, wrote strong anti-slavery editorials for the *Nebraska Republican,* ran for the state legislature in 1858 and lost, sat in the first Republican territorial convention ever to be held in Nebraska, and attended both the national conventions that nominated Lincoln for the presidency. During the campaign of 1860 he stumped the state of New York for the Republican ticket, and perhaps in reward for this service he was appointed by President Lincoln on Seward's nomination to be secretary of Nebraska territory. This office Paddock held continuously from 1861 to 1867, and twice, once in 1862 and again in 1867, he also acted as governor. He did not, therefore, see service in the Civil War, although he worked energetically to fill the Nebraska quotas of volunteers, and to enlist militia for the defense of the Nebraska frontier against the Indians. During the Reconstruction period, at considerable cost to his political advancement, he stood loyally by the Johnson administration. He went down to defeat in 1866 as the Independent Republican candidate for Congress ; he failed of election in 1867 to the United States Senate, and he declined an appointment tendered him by President Johnson in 1868 as governor of Wyoming. He was still at odds with the dominant wing of the Republican party during the campaign of 1872, when he supported Greeley for president. That same year he changed his residence to Beatrice, Gage County, Nebr., and turned his attention to business.

Paddock rendered his principal public service as a member of the United States Senate for two terms, 1875–81, and 1887–93. He was the politician's ideal senator, for he conceived it to be his chief duty in Washington to look after the interests of his constituents. Few senators have ever worked harder or more successfully at this task ; during his second term alone he was said to have introduced or reported 328 bills that eventually passed. He watched jealously the interests of Nebraskans whenever national policies that would touch them intimately were up for consideration. Perhaps his greatest triumph came in 1890, when in response to a resolution he had introduced the Interstate Commerce Commission investigated the charges of excessive freight rates on western railroads and ordered reductions that saved Nebraska producers many thousands of dollars. He was replaced in 1881 by Chas. H. Van Wyck and in 1893 by William V. Allen, both men of radical tendencies who rose to power on waves of agrarian discontent. From 1882 to 1886 he was a member of the famous Utah Commission which sought with some success to induce the Mormons to obey the national laws on polygamy. Paddock had many friends, and deserved to have them. He was even-tempered, unfailingly courteous, optimistic —particularly with regard to the future of Nebraska—and always a man of his word. He died in 1897 survived by his wife and three of his five children.

[J. Sterling Morton and Albert Watkins, *Illustrated Hist. of Neb.,* vol. I (1905) ; T. W. Tipton, *Forty Years of Neb.* (1902) ; A. C. Edmunds, *Pen Sketches of Nebraskans* (1871) ; H. J. Dobbs, *Hist. of Gage County, Neb.* (1918) ; *Neb. State Jour.* (Lincoln) and *Morning World-Herald* (Omaha), Oct. 18, 1897.]
                                                    J. D. H.

PADDOCK, BENJAMIN HENRY (Feb. 29, 1828–Mar. 9, 1891), bishop of the Protestant Episcopal Church, son of Rev. Seth Birdsey and Emily (Flagg) Paddock, was born in Norwich, Conn., where his father was for many years rector of Christ Church. Benjamin was a sedate, serious-minded youth whose natural bent was toward the ministry. He graduated from Trinity College, Hartford, in 1848 and, after a year spent in teaching at the Cheshire Academy, Cheshire, Conn., of which his father was then principal, he entered the General Theological Seminary, New York, completing his course there in 1852. On June 29 of that year he was admitted to deacon's orders at Christ Church, Stratford, Conn., of which his brother, John Adams Paddock [*q.v.*], later also a bishop, was rector. In May 1853 he married Caroline H. Cooke of Wallingford, Conn., and on Sept. 27, at Trinity Church, Norwalk, he was ordained priest. While deacon he served for a time as assistant minister at the Church of the Epiphany, New

York. Following a few months' rectorship in Portland, Me., which place he left in the interest of his health, he took charge of Trinity Church, Norwich. After about seven years here he went to Christ Church, Detroit. His first wife having died in 1860, he married in 1863 Anna D. Sanger of Detroit. He was always greatly interested in missionary activities, and in 1868 was elected missionary bishop of Oregon and Washington, but declined. In May 1869 he became rector of Grace Church, Brooklyn, where he remained until 1873, in which year he was elected bishop of Massachusetts and on Sept. 17 was consecrated to that office in his own church.

Bishop Paddock had just the qualities which the troubled diocese of Massachusetts needed in its spiritual overseer. His election fell in the period when the strife between high church and low church adherents was most intense. The General Convention of 1871 had been a stormy one, and Paddock had delivered a speech there which had made a strong impression both because of its content and its spirit. In Massachusetts there was much bitterness. After the death of Bishop Eastburn, an implacable opponent of high church practices, each party was eager that one favorable to its views should be chosen as his successor. The election finally narrowed down to a contest between Rev. Henry C. Potter and Rev. James De Koven [qq.v.], leader of the high church movement. When it was clear that neither could be elected, Paddock, a compromise candidate, was chosen. Time proved the choice a happy one. His abilities were in no wise extraordinary, but he was a man of sound judgment, transparent goodness, and singleness of purpose. Not given to speculation, he went placidly on his way, the faith he had received from the fathers undisturbed by doubts within or turmoil without. Though firm in his own convictions, he was not contentious or partisan and allowed great latitude to others. Phillips Brooks said of him that he was "not so much a leader as the creator of conditions of advance" (Allen, post, III, 407). In this respect he rendered a great service to his diocese. He showed practical wisdom of a high order, did not dictate to his clergy but so far as was expedient left them alone, avoided taking sides, and devoted himself assiduously to building up the weak places in the diocese. As a result the discord died out, cooperation took its place, and not only was comparative harmony achieved, but through the missionary interest of the bishop the diocese grew and strengthened. At the age of sixty-three he broke down under his labors, and died of cerebral hemorrhage a few months later. Among his published sermons and

addresses are: *The Church's Ceaseless Work and Chiefest Glory* (1859); *Our Cause, Our Confidence, and Our Consequent Duty* (1861); *The Noble Ambition of a Christian College* (1866); *Diocese of Massachusetts: The Bishop's Commemoration Address on the Tenth Anniversary of His Consecration* (1883); *The First Century of the Protestant Episcopal Church in the Diocese of Massachusetts* (1885). The Bishop Paddock Lectureship at the General Theological Seminary is named in his honor.

[T. M. Clark, *A Memorial Sermon on the Life and Character of Rt. Rev. Benjamin Henry Paddock* (1891); A. V. G. Allen, *Life and Letters of Phillips Brooks* (1901), vols. II, III; *The Churchman*, Mar. 14, 1891; *Boston Herald* and *Boston Daily Globe*, Mar. 10, 1891.]

H. E. S.

PADDOCK, JOHN ADAMS (Jan. 19, 1825–Mar. 4, 1894), bishop of the Protestant Episcopal Church, was born in Norwich, Conn., the eldest son of Rev. Seth Birdsey and Emily (Flagg) Paddock, and a brother of Bishop Benjamin H. Paddock [q.v.]. When twenty years old he graduated from Trinity College, Hartford, and in 1849 from the General Theological Seminary, New York. On July 22 of that year he was ordained deacon at Christ Church, Norwich. He served as assistant to Rev. Lot Jones at the Church of the Epiphany, New York, and in June 1850 married Ellen M. Jones, the rector's daughter, who died shortly after their marriage. In 1850 he was ordained priest at Christ Church, Stratford, Conn., of which church he was rector until 1855. For the next twenty-five years he was in charge of St. Peter's Church, Brooklyn, and active in the administrative work of the diocese of Long Island. On Apr. 23, 1856, he married Frances Chester, daughter of Patrick and Susan Alada (Thurston) Fanning. In 1880 he was made missionary bishop of Washington Territory and on Dec. 15, was consecrated at St. Peter's.

In the spring of the following year he began more than a decade of strenuous activity in the Northwest. On the way out his wife contracted pneumonia and died soon after their arrival on the field. Before leaving the East she had collected money to take with her as the nucleus of a fund for establishing a much-needed hospital. More was added, and on the first anniversary of her death, Bishop Paddock dedicated at Tacoma the Fannie C. Paddock Memorial Hospital (later the Tacoma General Hospital). With good sense and unflagging devotion, never sparing himself, he sought to further the religious and educational interests of the Territory. One of his achievements was the raising of $50,000 in the East to insure a conditional gift of land and money for the establishment at Tacoma of the Anna Wright Seminary, and Washington College. His efforts in this cause impaired his health, and he was never entirely well thereafter. By 1892 the comparatively few missions and parishes of which he had taken charge when he was made bishop had so increased in numbers that the field was divided into two jurisdictions, and he became missionary bishop of Olympia, with some fifty-seven missions and parishes in his care. While returning from the General Convention of 1892, he suffered a stroke and later went to Southern California in the interest of his health. Here, near Santa Barbara, he died; his burial was at Vancouver. Among his published writings are: *An Historical Discourse, Delivered in Christ Church, Stratford, Conn., Mar. 28th, 1855* (1855); and *The Modern Manifestations of Superstition and Skepticism* (1870).

[W. F. Brooks, *Hist. of the Fanning Family* (1905), vol. I; Herbert Hunt, *Tacoma, Its Hist. and Its Builders* (1916), vol. I; *Churchman*, Mar. 17, 1894; *Tacoma Daily Ledger* and *Seattle Post-Intelligencer*, Mar. 6, 1894; information from Fannie Paddock Hinsdale, Vancouver, B. C.]   H. E. S.

PADILLA, JUAN DE (*c.* 1500–*c.* 1544), Franciscan missionary, was a native of Andalusia. It was said that he "had been a fighting man in his youth" (Castañeda, in Winship, *post*, 1904, p. 33). He came to New Spain about the year 1528 and was attached to the Order of Friars Minor in the province of Santo Evangelio. In 1529 he became a military chaplain in the expedition of Nuño de Guzman to Nueva Galicia and Culiacán. In this capacity he served for three years, trying to rescue from oppression and slavery the natives who had been captured by the Spanish settlers on the borderland of the unknown wilderness. In the course of the following years he made many missionary journeys among the Mexican Indians. He built monasteries at Zapotlan, Túxpam, and Tulancingo, ruling the friars as superior and guardian until 1540. In that year, hearing of the new lands discovered by Fray Marcos de Niza [*q.v.*], he was fired with apostolic zeal to Christianize the natives there. In company with Fray Marcos and two other religious of the Order of St. Francis he obtained permission to join the expedition of Francisco Vázquez Coronado [*q.v.*]. One may gauge the stamina of the much-traveled Padilla by the fact that he was a pedestrian in all his journeys. After reaching Zuñi with Coronado he trudged on with Pedro de Tovar to Moqui in the vicinity of the Grand Canyon, and after wending his way back to Zuñi, joined Hernando de Alvarado on a trip of several hundred miles over vast deserts and immense rocky

areas; he accompanied Coronado with a well-selected troop of cavaliers in search of the mythical Quivira and returned with the disappointed General to Cicuye (now known as Pecos, N. Mex.).

When Coronado abandoned New Mexico in 1542, Padilla, Fray Juan de la Cruz, and the lay brother Fray Lúis Descalona remained behind in the midst of the savages, with only one mounted Portuguese soldier as a military escort. Two *donados* of the Franciscan Order (tertiaries) and two Mexican Indian boys also cast their hazardous lot with the friars. Slowly they retraced the weary way to Quivira. The little party plodded the long and painful journey to the place where Coronado had planted a cross, and there established the first mission in the North American Southwest. The religious influence exercised by the padre upon the roving children of the prairies soon gained their confidence and affection, but his ardent missionary zeal urged him to attempt also the conversion of the Guas, a hostile tribe near by. This project was bitterly opposed by the Quivirans, but Padilla was determined to go. Only one day after his departure, he was overtaken by a galloping horde of Quivira Indians. His companions were ordered to flee for their lives, while he dropped on his knees offering his soul to his Master, and as he prayed, the Quivirans pierced him from head to foot with arrows. There has been much difference of opinion about the location of Quivira, the place near which he met his martyrdom. It has been placed on the Canadian River in the Texas Panhandle (Donoghue, *post*) and also in what is now Kansas, somewhat north of the present Wichita (C. O. Paullin and J. K. Wright, *Atlas of the Historical Geography of the United States*, 1932, pl. 38). The year of his death is given variously as 1542 and 1544; the day of his commemoration is Nov. 30.

[Original sources are documents of Coronado, Castañeda, and Jaramillo, in *Coleccion de Documentos Ineditos Relativos al Descubrimiento . . . de las Posesiones Españolas . . .*, III (1865), 363–69, 511–13, XIII (1870), 263–68, XIV (1870), 304–29, translated by G. P. Winship in *U. S. Bureau of Ethnology, Fourteenth Ann. Report, 1892–93* (1896) and in Winship, *The Journey of Coronado* (1904). See also P. J. Foik in *Mid-America*, Jan., Oct. 1930; David Donoghue, in *Southwestern Hist. Quart.*, Jan. 1929; A. F. Bandelier, in *Am. Cath. Quart. Rev.*, July 1890; Augustin de Vetancurt, "Menalogio Franciscano," *Teatro Mexicano*, vol. IV (1871).]   P. J. F.

PAGE, CHARLES GRAFTON (Jan. 25, 1812–May 5, 1868), physician, pioneer in electrical experiment, was the son of a sea captain, Jeremiah Lee Page, and his wife Lucy (Lang) Page. He was of English ancestry, descended from John Page who came to New England in

1630, and was a native of Salem, Mass., where both his parents were born. Entering Harvard in 1828 at the age of sixteen, he graduated four years later and then studied medicine in Boston. He began practice in Salem, but at the same time engaged in experimental research in electricity, this he continued with short intermissions throughout his life, publishing the results from time to time in Silliman's *American Journal of Science and Arts*. Starting with Henry's calorimotor for obtaining sparks and shocks, he developed an induction apparatus of greater intensity than Henry's. This he described in the *Journal* of January 1837, and it is recognized to be in principle, with Ruhmkorff's improvements, the induction coil of today. About this time, too, he devised the self-acting circuit breaker and appears to have been the first to apply it to produce the extreme alterations necessary in induction machines. He independently discovered, also, the remarkable effect produced by substituting bundles of iron wires for solid iron bars in induction coils. Early in 1838, under Page's direction, all these discoveries were incorporated in a coil machine by Daniel Davis, Jr., an instrument maker of Boston, Mass., who subsequently made and sold at a considerable profit many more machines similar to this original one. Page, however, did not receive any financial benefit. In this same year he moved with his parents to Fairfax County, Va. Here he practised his profession for a time, and continued his electrical experiments, especially in the field of magneto-electricity, his chief object being to introduce electro-magnetism as a substitute, to a greater or less extent, for steam power. Being a man of moderate means, however, he could ill afford to devote his full time to this work, and in consequence his progress was rather slow.

About 1841 he was made one of the two principal examiners in the United States Patent Office, and in 1844 accepted, in addition, the chair of chemistry in the medical department of Columbian College (now George Washington University). He was compelled, however, to relinquish this position in 1849 on account of the pressure of his duties in the Patent Office. During this period his electrical work had definitely advanced, and by 1846 he had completed a small reciprocating electro-magnetic engine, having as its source of power the force with which the pole of an electro-magnet is drawn into its magnetizing helix. Three years later, as a result of a series of public lectures on electro-magnetism which he gave in Washington, attended by a special committee of the United States Senate,

Page was granted a special Congressional appropriation to continue his work on a large scale. He built several large stationary reciprocating electro-magnetic engines of both the vertical and horizontal types; then, about 1850, began the construction of a locomotive having two of his electric engines. Upon its completion in 1851, it was tried out over a specially constructed track five miles long between Washington and Bladensburg, Md. The trial was not successful even though a speed of nineteen miles an hour was obtained, mainly because the electric batteries were incapable of furnishing the necessary current to operate the locomotive for any appreciable length of time.

In 1852 he resigned from the Patent Office and, in association with J. J. Greenough and Charles L. Fleischmann, established in Washington the *American Polytechnic Journal*, the first number of which appeared early in 1853. During the two years of its existence (1853–54) he contributed many articles on electricity, including his *History of Induction: The American Claim to the Induction Coil and its Electrostatic Developments*, published in book form in 1867. He continued with his electrical experiments in his own laboratory and patented his design of a reciprocating electro-magnetic engine, receiving patent number 10,480 on Jan. 31, 1854. After the discontinuance of the *American Polytechnic Journal*, Page did not appear in any public capacity until 1861, when he again became examiner of patents in the Patent Office, a position he held for the remainder of his life. Outside of his electrical researches his greatest interest, especially in the latter part of his life, lay in rose culture. In this work he produced several new varieties, which he described in print and cuttings of which he furnished to rose growers both in the United States and abroad. On Sept. 23, 1844, he married Priscilla Sewall Webster of Augusta, Me., and at his death was survived by his widow and five children.

[C. N. Page, *Geneal. Chart of the Page Family* (1917); T. C. Martin and Joseph Wetzler, *The Electric Motor and its Applications* (1887); *Am. Jour. of Science and Arts*, July 1869; Waldemar Kaempffert, *A Popular Hist. of Am. Invention* (1924), vol. I; E. W. Byrn, *The Progress of Invention in the Nineteenth Century* (1900); S. P. Thompson, *Dynamo-Electric Machinery* (1893); P. S. W. Page, *Reminiscences, 1883–1886* (privately printed, 1896); *Evening Star* (Washington), May 6, 1868; Patent Office records.]

C. W. M—n.

PAGE, DAVID PERKINS (July 4, 1810– Jan. 1, 1848), educator, was born in Epping, N. H. His father was a well-to-do farmer who refused for years to allow his son to leave the farm to attend an academy. Finally, when David was sixteen, his entreaties prevailed and for a few months he attended Hampton Academy in New Hampshire and for the next winter taught a district school in the neighborhood. Then, after a few more months at the academy, he taught successively in a district school in Epping for a winter and then in Newbury, Mass. By this time he had determined to make teaching his profession and at the age of nineteen opened a private school in Newburyport. He began with five pupils but before the end of the term there were more applicants than he could accommodate. Two years later, in 1831, he was appointed associate principal of the Newburyport High School, in charge of the English department. In this position he remained for twelve years. On Dec. 16, 1832, he was married to Susan Maria Lunt.

During the winter of 1843 the legislature of the state of New York adopted the normal school system then in operation in Massachusetts and made an appropriation to establish a normal school in Albany in 1844. Opposition was determined and unscrupulous, and the success of the plan depended largely upon the choice of the principal. On the recommendation of Horace Mann and other eminent educators in Massachusetts members of the executive committee entered into correspondence with Page and he was appointed to the position. In Albany he found chaos. The rooms were unfinished; there was no apparatus, and nothing was ready for the opening session. By his tact and energy he was able to overcome the obstacles to progress and soon he had won favor. For three years he gave himself no rest. During the vacations he visited the different parts of the state, attended teachers' institutes, and lectured day after day. Everywhere he removed prejudice, won friends, and attracted pupils to the school. Opposition had died down. By 1847 the school was no longer an experiment, but to achieve this success Page had undermined his own strength. After an illness of a few days he died from pneumonia on Jan. 1, 1848.

Page possessed a singular aptitude for teaching. His intense fondness for study had led him to acquire a good knowledge of Latin and a fair amount of Greek. He was an excellent mathematician and had rather more than an ordinary acquaintance with chemistry and the other natural sciences in addition to a thorough knowledge of history and literature. He studied the natures and capacities of his students and won from them a respect which insured a high degree of order and harmony in his school. He was liked as a teacher and his students attended his lectures with interest. Before he left Newburyport he had delivered several addresses before the Essex County Teachers' Association, which Horace Mann praised most highly. Of his lecture, "The Mutual Duties of Parents and Teachers," six thousand copies, a large number for those days, were printed and distributed among the teachers of Massachusetts. Page's contemporaries have described him as a man of great personal charm. His one published book, *The Theory and Practice of Teaching, or the Motives and Methods of Good School-Keeping*, was issued in 1847, the year before his death. It passed through many editions and was considered an invaluable guide for the inexperienced teacher. He also prepared a "Normal Chart of Elementary Sounds" for class-room use. The best edition of his work on teaching is that issued in 1885 by William H. Payne.

[There is a biographical sketch of Page in W. H. Payne's edition of Page's *Theory and Practice of Teaching*. See also: W. F. Phelps, *David P. Page: His Life and Teachings* (1892); J. M. Greenwood, ed., *The Life and Work of David P. Page* (1893), including some of Page's writings; E. A. Huntington, *A Funeral Discourse on David Perkins Page* (1848); the *Common School Jour.*, Apr. 1, 1848; the *Am. Jour. of Educ.*, Dec. 1858; *Daily Albany Argus*, Jan. 4, 1848.]

J. S—n.

PAGE, JOHN (Apr. 17, 1743 o.s.–Oct. 11, 1808), Revolutionary patriot, congressman, governor of Virginia, was born at "Rosewell," the great house built in Gloucester County by his grandfather, Mann Page [q.v.]. He was the son of Mann and Alice (Grymes) Page and thus represented an alliance of two of the dominant families in Tidewater Virginia. He gave to his grandmother, Judith (Carter) Page, the credit for whetting his appetite for reading and stimulating his inquisitive mind. When nine years old he was put in the grammar-school of the Rev. William Yates with some dozen sons of neighboring planters. The arid training he had there was little to his liking, and after a year a private tutor was engaged for him. When he was thirteen he entered the grammar-school at the College of William and Mary and continued there until 1763, when he finished the regular course in the philosophy schools. At William and Mary he and Thomas Jefferson became fast friends, sharing their ideas and their confidences. Their correspondence spanned fifty years with not a discord in its friendly harmony. It was to him that Jefferson wrote the letters that reveal his youthful romance with the "fair Belinda," Rebecca Burwell who was so soon to marry Jacquelin Ambler (Ford, *post*, I, 342, 357). Of his friend, Jefferson declared thirty years later to Albert Gallatin that he loved him as a brother

(*Ibid.*, VIII, 85). About 1765 Page married Frances, the daughter of Robert Carter Burwell of Isle of Wight County. They had twelve children, five of whom were married to sons and daughters of Thomas Nelson [*q.v.*]. In 1789 Page married in New York City, Margaret, the daughter of William Lowther of Scotland, who bore him eight children. For a time he was president of the Society for the Advancement of Useful Knowledge, at Williamsburg, a group that sought to play the rôle of the Royal Society of London in Virginia. With his friend David Jameson he was interested in astronomy and made experiments in measuring the fall of rain and dew. His friends called him "John Partridge" because of his astronomical pursuits, especially in calculating an eclipse of the sun. He confessed in later years that he did not think he had made great proficiency in any study for he was too sociable to shut himself off in solitude for study as did his friend, Jefferson (Autobiography, *post*, p. 151). He followed the fortunes of the Anglican Church with zeal and such devotion that he was suggested by certain of his friends as the first bishop of Virginia. In his religious convictions he was orthodox, and he opposed on many occasions the free thinking of certain of his fellow Virginians. In 1785 he was a lay delegate from Virginia to the convention of his church in New York.

In politics he began his career as a member of the colonial House of Burgesses under the patronage of his kinsmen, the Nelsons, and he had the favor of the governors, Botetourt and Dunmore. When the tide of Revolutionary sentiment rose he helped to direct its flow as a member of the Council and the Committee of Public Safety and then as lieutenant-governor under Patrick Henry. He was a member of the convention that framed the constitution for Virginia in 1776. He served in a military capacity in the Yorktown campaign and contributed of his private means to the Revolutionary funds. In the election for governor of Virginia in 1779 he ran a close second to his friend Jefferson, but this political matching was not allowed to strain the constancy of their friendship (see Ford, *post*, II, 188). After the Revolution he represented Gloucester in most sessions of the Virginia Assembly until 1789 when he went to Congress. He sat in that body until 1797 when, as he said, John Adams and Alexander Hamilton shut him out (Autobiography, *post*, p. 150). With James Madison, 1749–1812 [*q.v.*], and others he represented Virginia in determining the boundary between Pennsylvania and Virginia in 1784. He waged an active campaign for Jefferson in 1800.

In 1802 he succeeded James Monroe as governor of Virginia and served three successive terms in that office. In the closing years of his life he held the office of commissioner of loans, a federal office to which his friend Jefferson appointed him, recognizing his need of an office with a salary but fearing to place him in a position where his too little discriminating trust in his fellowmen might bring woe to him.

The care of a family of twenty children, the maintenance of the princely mansion of "Rosewell" and his sociable rather than business inclinations brought Page in his later years to a decline in fortunes. In 1786 he had been the largest slave owner in Abingdon Parish in Gloucester County, counting his black people to the number of 160. On his death at the age of sixty-four he was buried in the yard of St. John's Church at Richmond, where many of the stirring scenes of the Revolution took place. His own estimate of his life was that it had been a life devoted to liberty.

[Letters and photostats in Archives of Univ. of Va., and Archives of American Philosophical Soc., Philadelphia; brief autobiography in *Va. Hist. Register*, July 1850, and in Meade, *post*, I, p. 147; *The Writings of Thomas Jefferson*, ed. by P. L. Ford, vols. I, II, IV, VII–IX (1892–98); *Executive Jour. of the Council of Colonial Va.*, vols. III, IV (1928–30); *Am. Hist. Rev.*, July 1896; *Va. Mag. of Hist. and Biog.*, July 1893, July 1896, Oct. 1897, Oct. 1902, Oct. 1911; *Wm. and Mary College Quart.*, Jan. 1896, pp. 200–01, Oct. 1896, Apr. 1916; Wm. Meade, *Old Churches . . . of Va.* (2 vols., 1861); R. A. Lancaster, *Historic Va. Homes and Churches* (1915); R. C. M. Page, *Geneal. of the Page Family in Va.* (1883); *Richmond Enquirer*, Oct. 14, 1808.]   M. H. W.

PAGE, MANN (1691–Jan. 24, 1730), Virginia planter and councilor, was born in Virginia, the grandson of John Page, who emigrated from England about 1650, became the progenitor of the Page family in Virginia, and established his house firmly in lands and public regard. Mann Page was the son of Matthew Page who was active in public and private affairs of the colony. He inherited large possessions from his father while his mother, Mary (Mann) Page, the sole heiress of John and Mary Mann of "Timberneck," Gloucester County, had brought to her husband and children broad acres. Both parents died before he was sixteen years old, and the boy was sent abroad in 1706 to Eton College. In 1709 he entered St. John's College, Oxford. On Feb. 6, 1713/14, he became a member of the Council of Virginia on the recommendation of the governor of the colony, who described him as a man of culture and influence. His associates were the important men of the colony.

By inheritance and by patents taken in his own right he became, according to tradition, the second largest land owner in Virginia. His so-cial and economic position was entrenched by his marriage first, in 1712, to Judith, the daugh-ter of Ralph Wormeley, the secretary of Vir-ginia, by whom he had two sons and a daughter, and second, in 1718, to Judith, the daughter of Robert Carter, 1663–1732 [*q.v.*], by whom he had five sons and a daughter. His father-in-law, "King" Carter, associated Page with him in or-ganizing the Frying Pan Company to mine cop-per on the boundary of the present counties of Fairfax and Loudoun, where they held a tract of some 27,000 acres and reopened an old Indian trail from Tidewater to the mine on Frying Pan Run. At his death when he was still a relatively young man, Page owned land in Frederick, Prince William, Spotsylvania, Gloucester, Es-sex, James City, Hanover and King William counties. His most lasting monument was his home, "Rosewell," begun in 1725 on the right bank of Carter's Creek in Gloucester County, near the junction with the York River. It was barely completed before his death. The years have wrapped about this house many traditions. Built of brick, three stories high, with marble casements, carved mahogany finishings, and a lead roof, it was probably the largest home of an eighteenth-century colonial planter in Vir-ginia. With the wings it had a frontage of 232 feet and something like thirty-five rooms. So severe a drain was the financing of such a struc-ture in planter economy that Page's heirs were embarrassed by the debts that devolved upon them and had to sell lands to realize money to discharge the obligation. At the council board, acquiring and administering his huge tracts of land, stretching wide the patrimony for his rap-idly increasing family, he was a typical gentle-man of his age. When his surviving widow came to write his epitaph she declared, "His publick Trust he faithfully Discharged with Can-dour and Discretion Truth and Justice. Nor was he less eminent in his private Behaviour. . . . " (*Virginia Magazine of History and Biography,* Jan. 1924, p. 45.)

[*Va. Mag. of Hist. and Biog.,* Apr. 1897, July 1898, Oct. 1905, Apr. 1913, Jan. 1923, Jan. 1924; Wm. Meade, *Old Churches . . . of Va.* (2 vols.), 1861); R. C. M. Page, *Geneal. of the Page Family in Va.* (1883); R. A. Lancaster, *Historic Va. Homes and Churches* (1915); *Exec. Jour. of the Council of Colonial Va.,* vols. III, IV (1928–30); *Wm. and Mary College Quart.,* Jan. 1898.]   M. H. W.

PAGE, RICHARD LUCIAN (Dec. 20, 1807– Aug. 9, 1901), Confederate naval and army officer, son of William Byrd and Anne (Lee) Page, was born in Clarke County, Va. His fa-ther, a farmer and planter, was of the Page fam-ily of Virginia which descended from John Page, an immigrant from England in early colonial days. His mother was the sister of Henry, "Light-Horse Harry," Lee [*q.v.*]. He attended the common-schools of Clarke County and Alex-andria, Va. He chose the navy for a career, be-came a midshipman in 1824, and did his first cruising on board the *John Adams* with Admiral Porter in the West Indies. In 1825 he was transferred to the *Brandywine* to convey Gen-eral Lafayette to France. He became a passed midshipman in 1830, was promoted to lieuten-ant in 1834, and to commander in 1855, which grade he held at the outbreak of the Civil War. During this period he did sea duty in nearly every part of the globe and served three tours on ordnance duty and one as executive officer at the Norfolk navy yard. His more important assign-ments at sea were as executive officer and com-mander of the *Independence,* flagship of Com-modore Shubrick, during the Mexican War, as commander of the *Perry* from 1852 to 1854, and as commander of the *Germantown* from 1857 to 1859.

Resigning from the Federal service when Vir-ginia seceded, Page became an aide on the staff of Gov. John Letcher of Virginia and was as-signed to duty in connection with the organiza-tion of a state navy. He supervised the construc-tion of fortifications at the mouth of the James River and on the Nansemond River and Pagan Creek. On June 10, 1861, he was commissioned commander in the Confederate States navy and was assigned to duty as ordnance officer at the Norfolk navy yard. While on this duty he vol-unteered to assist in firing an eleven-inch gun at Sewell's Point against Federal vessels. He was soon promoted to captain and assigned the task of establishing an ordnance and construc-tion depot at Charlotte, N. C., which he operated for about two years. He was with Commodore Tattnall on board the *Savannah* at the naval bat-tle off Port Royal. In 1864 he was commissioned brigadier-general in the provisional army and placed in command of the outer defenses of Mo-bile Bay with headquarters at Fort Morgan, Ala, He gallantly defended his fort against the com-bined sea and land attack of Admiral Farragut and General Granger, but after a terrific bom-bardment which made breaches in the walls of the fort and disabled most of his cannon and set fire to the citadel, he was compelled on Aug. 23, 1864, to capitulate. He was held as a prisoner of war until September 1865. After the war he settled at Norfolk, Va., and took an active in-terest in the affairs of the community. He served from 1875 to 1883 as superintendent of public schools. In 1841 he had married Alexina, daughter of Richard and Elizabeth (Calvert) Taylor of Norfolk, Va. He died at Blueridge Summit, Pa., in his ninety-fourth year. He was survived by his wife and three children.

[*War of the Rebellion: Official Records (Army)*; J. T. Scharf, *Hist. of the Confed. States Navy* (1887); C. A. Evans, ed., *Confed. Mil. Hist.* (1899), vol. III; T. H. S. Hamersly, *Gen. Reg. of the U. S. Navy and Marine Corps* (1882); *Special Orders of the Adjutant and Inspector General's Office, Confed. States*, 1861–65; *Battles and Leaders of the Civil War*, vol. IV (1888); R. C. M. Page, *Geneal. of the Page Family in Va.* (1883); *Encyc. of Va. Biog.* (1915), vol. III; *Va.-Pilot* (Norfolk), Aug. 10, 1901.]   S. J. H.

PAGE, THOMAS JEFFERSON (Jan. 4, 1808–Oct. 26, 1899), naval officer, explorer, was born on his father's estate in Matthews County, Va., eighth son of Mann and Elizabeth (Nelson) Page and grandson of Gov. John Page and Gov. Thomas Nelson [*qq.v.*] of Virginia. He was appointed midshipman Oct. 1, 1827, and joined the *Erie* in the West Indies. Then followed several years of coast survey work, 1833–42, during which time he was promoted to lieutenant, 1837, and gained special favor with the director of the survey, Ferdinand Rudolph Hassler (*Memoir and Correspondence of Charles Steedman, Rear Admiral*, 1912, p. 129; portrait of Page, p. 156). After a cruise in the *Columbus* to the Mediterranean and Brazil, 1842–44, he was attached to the Naval Observatory, and then in the Far East commanded the brig *Dolphin*, 1848–51. Here, in association with his friend R. B. Forbes, a Boston merchant, he realized the need of a surveying expedition in the China seas, for the benefit of commerce and whalers, and upon his return proposed it to the department. This expedition was organized, but enlarged to include the Bering Sea and North Pacific, and put under a senior officer, Commander Ringgold. Page was offered second in command but declined and was subsequently assigned to command another expedition, in the small side-wheel steamer *Water Witch*, to "survey and explore the river La Plata and its tributaries," which had just been opened to commerce after the fall of the dictator Rosas in Argentina. The *Water Witch* left Norfolk Feb. 8, 1853, and after considerable delay at Buenos Aires, during treaty negotiations with the new government, sailed in September for the ascent of the Paraná and Paraguay rivers. In the next two years the expedition covered 3600 miles of river navigation and 4400 miles of exploration ashore, accounts of which appear in the commander's report (*Report of the Secretary of the Navy*, 1856, pp. 430–65) and in his book, *La Plata: The Argentine Confederation and Paraguay* (1859),

which went to two editions and was translated into Spanish.

Page appears to have conducted his work with great energy and with adequate diplomacy, though Lieut. (later Rear Admiral) Ammen, who was for a time under him, expresses the view that Page "was entirely a gentleman, but ... not well fitted to command such an expedition" (*The Old Navy and the New*, 1891, p. 269). Page had secured full privileges in their national waters from Brazil and Argentina, but had difficulties on this point with the dictator López of Paraguay, especially after a quarrel between López and an American trading company organized by the United States consul at Asunción, Edward Augustus Hopkins [*q.v.*], in which Page supported the consul. By a decree of Oct. 3, 1854, the *Water Witch* was excluded from Paraguayan waters, and on Feb. 1, 1855, while under the temporary command of Lieut. William N. Jeffers, she was fired upon from the Paraguayan fort Itapúra while ascending the Paraná. Page was greatly incensed, sought vainly for a demonstration from Commodore Salter of the Brazil Squadron, and on returning home in May 1856, called for an expedition to bring Paraguay to account for this action and alleged injuries to the trading company. President Buchanan took up the matter in his first message (1857), and a force of nineteen ships was dispatched under Commodore Shubrick with Page, now commander (1855), as fleet captain. A treaty with Paraguay was quickly arranged, and Page, relieved of fleet duties, resumed explorations from the spring of 1859 to the autumn of 1860, ascending the Paraguay to the head of navigation.

In the Civil War Page joined the Confederacy, was for over a year in command of batteries at Gloucester Point, York River, and was employed here and elsewhere in Virginia river defenses until March 1863, when he went to Europe to command one of the Confederate ironclads building there. After a year of seclusion in Florence, Italy, he was appointed in December 1864 to command the *Stonewall*, formerly the *Sphynx*, a powerful ironclad built in France for the Confederacy, then sold to Denmark, and by Denmark retransferred after the War of 1864. Page took her out of Copenhagen Jan. 7, 1865, received officers and stores off Quiberon, and then put in at Corunna and later Ferrol. Here he was watched by the *Niagara*, Capt. Thomas Tingey Craven [*q.v.*], and the *Sacramento*, but when the *Stonewall* steamed out on Mar. 24 and challenged battle, Craven prudently refused to risk his wooden vessels. After stopping at Lisbon, Mar. 26, the *Stonewall* crossed to Havana, where on news of the downfall of the Confederacy she was turned over to the Spanish authorities. After the war Page went to Argentina and spent some time on a cattle farm in Entre Rios, then superintended the construction of four Argentine ironclads in England, and about 1880 went to Florence. He died in Rome in his ninety-second year. He was survived by his wife Benjamina, daughter of Benjamin Price of Loudoun County, Va., whom he married at Washington in 1838, and by whom he had five sons and two daughters.

[In addition to the references cited see: "Autobiog. Sketch of Thos. Jefferson Page," *Proc. U. S. Naval Inst.*, Oct. 1923 ; *War of the Rebellion: Official Records (Navy)*, especially 3 ser. I–III ; R. C. M. Page, *Geneal. of the Page Family in Va.* (1883) ; J. D. Bullock, *The Secret Service of the Confed. States in Europe* (1884) ; B. F. Sands, *From Reefer to Rear Admiral* (1899) ; T. J. Page, "The Confederate Cruiser Stonewall," *Southern Hist. Soc. Papers*, VII (1879), 263–80 ; biographical sketch (reprinted from the Richmond *Times*, Oct. 29, 1899), *Ibid.*, XXVII (1899), 219–31.]   A. W.

PAGE, THOMAS NELSON (Apr. 23, 1853–Nov. 1, 1922), diplomat and man of letters, was born at "Oakland," a plantation near Beaver Dam, in Hanover County, Va., the son of Maj. John Page, an artillery officer in the Army of Northern Virginia throughout the Civil War, and the great-grandson of Gov. John Page, 1743–1808 [*q.v.*]. His mother before her marriage was Elizabeth Burwell Nelson, and among his kindred he counted Randolphs, Pendletons, Wickhams, Carters, Lees, and members of other distinguished families. His youth was spent amid scenes of war and reconstruction which so impressed him as to color his whole thinking in after life. As a boy he attended schools in the neighborhood of his home, helped with the farm work, listened to accounts of the golden times "before the War," heard the recent battles feelingly discussed, and read the many good books found in the family library. In 1869 he entered Washington College, Lexington, Va., where he came into personal contact with Gen. Robert E. Lee, then president of the institution. Withdrawing from the college in June 1872, he read law under his father for a year; then, in order to secure money for continuing his education, he spent several months as private tutor in a family living near Louisville, Ky. Entering the University of Virginia in October 1873, he applied himself to study with unusual diligence, and on July 2, 1874, received the degree of LL.B. In the fall of 1874 he settled as a lawyer in Richmond, Va., in time built up a practice, became interested in civic affairs, and took an active part in the social life of the city. On July 26, 1886, he

married Anne Seddon Bruce, who died in 1888.

From childhood Page had shown a relish for literature and had written for college magazines and later for newspapers. His real start as an author, however, was made in 1884, when in the *Century Magazine* for April appeared his dialect story "Marse Chan." Thereafter editors were always pleased to consider his manuscripts, and by degrees he was weaned from the law and entered upon a busy life as story writer, novelist, and essayist. He made numerous friendships among literary men, steadily attracted attention by his work, and by 1889, during a stay abroad, had the satisfaction of finding himself known in some quarters even in England. Upon returning from Europe he made an extended lecture tour which further increased his reputation. After his second marriage, June 6, 1893, to Florence Lathrop Field, the widow of Henry Field of Chicago, he abandoned the practice of law entirely, and removing to Washington, D. C., established a home which became a center of hospitality.

The bulk of his literary work was fiction, most of it dealing with life in the South either just before or just after the Civil War. His most popular books were *In Ole Virginia* (1887), a volume of tales largely in the negro dialect; the novel *Red Rock* (1898) ; a story, *The Old Gentleman of the Black Stock* (1897) ; a collection of sketches and stories, *The Burial of the Guns* (1894) ; and two volumes for children, *Two Little Confederates* (1888) and *Among the Camps* (1891). In the same tone as the fiction and closely akin to it in theme are his essays and social studies, in *The Old South* (1892), *Social Life in Old Virginia* (1897), *The Negro, the Southerner's Problem* (1904), and *The Old Dominion* (1908). Besides the books named he wrote a dozen other volumes of fiction; several semihistorical works and eulogistic biographies, the most ambitious of the latter being *Robert E. Lee, Man and Soldier* (1911) ; a series of elementary lectures on Dante; a collection of dialect verse, *Befo' de War* (1888), published in collaboration with Armistead Churchill Gordon; and a volume of poems, *The Coast of Bohemia* (1906).

In 1913 Page was appointed by President Wilson ambassador to Italy, the duties of which office he performed conscientiously and with success. Upon the outbreak of the World War he aided hundreds of Americans in reaching home; and throughout the years of the struggle his tact and helpful labors won for him the esteem of officials in Rome and of many Italian people. During the peace negotiations he made a fruitless trip to Paris in an attempt to explain the Italian position and demands, and later he wrote a sympathetic account of Italy's aims and part in the fighting: *Italy and the World War* (1920). In 1919, resigning his ambassadorship, Page returned to America and resumed his literary career. Bad health, however, handicapped him, and the death of his second wife in 1921 was a misfortune from which he never fully recovered. He died at "Oakland" on Nov. 1, 1922, and was buried in Rock Creek Cemetery, Washington, D. C. He left no children.

By his friends Page was considered a worthy and representative member of the Virginia aristocracy. He was modest in bearing, instinctively polite, considerate of women, cultivated in taste; throughout life he held fast to beliefs and a standard of conduct acquired in boyhood. A pride in the class from which he sprang in part explains his character, as well as certain qualities found in his literary work. Viewing plantation society as a partisan, he overemphasized its attractive side, minimized or neglected its faults, and failed to penetrate far beneath its surface appearance. In practically all he wrote, whether biography or historical essay or fiction, he was at heart a romancer—a romancer who, perhaps more than any other single man of his generation, exploited the conception of the ante-bellum South as a region of feudalistic splendor. His literary method, no less than his material, proved to be what readers of the day wished; and for more than thirty years his books were widely popular. The dialect tales which first brought him into literary prominence represent his best work; upon these and a few other short stories and sketches his reputation as a man of letters must continue to rest.

[A biography by Page's brother, Rosewell Page, *Thos. Nelson Page: A Memoir of a Virginia Gentleman* (1923), contains first-hand information, as does likewise the appreciative article by Page's friend, A. C. Gordon, in *Scribner's Mag.*, Jan. 1923. *Two Little Confederates*, parts of *The Burial of the Guns*, and other of Page's books have autobiographical value. Comments upon him as a literary figure appear in H. A. Toulmin, Jr., *Social Historians* (1911) and M. J. Moses, *The Lit. of the South* (1910). Information as to certain facts was furnished for this sketch by Mr. Rosewell Page.]

J. H. N.

PAGE, WALTER HINES (Aug. 15, 1855–Dec. 21, 1918), journalist and diplomat, was born at Cary, N. C., of pioneer stock. The Pages were of English origin and belonged to the substantial farmer class. Walter's father, Allison Francis Page, although the owner of a few slaves, disapproved of the institution of slavery and of the sectionalism that held sway in the South before the Civil War. From him Walter early imbibed a strong attachment to the Union and to democracy, and subsequent reading merely confirmed him in these loyalties. From his mother, Cathe-

rine Frances Raboteau, who was of Scotch and Huguenot descent, he inherited an abiding love of nature and an appreciation of good books. The rudiments of his education were acquired under her tutelage and it was she who introduced him to Dickens and Scott. These beginnings, together with a few years at local schools and at Bingham Academy at Mebane, N. C., were Page's preparations for his college course.

In 1871 he entered Trinity College, N. C. (now Duke University), but he had little liking for the place and in January 1873 transferred to Randolph-Macon College, Ashland, Va. The change was an important one, for it brought Page in contact with stimulating companions and with Thomas Randolph Price [*q.v.*], who aroused in him a devotion to Greek and English literature that remained with him throughout his life. In addition Price instilled in the impressionable youth a love of England that doubtless helps to explain Page's immense enthusiasm for the old country and her cause during the World War. From the guidance of Price, Page passed to that of Basil L. Gildersleeve [*q.v.*] at The Johns Hopkins University. Price had obtained for his pupil one of the first twenty fellowships when the new institution opened in 1876, and for the next two years Page pursued his studies under America's most distinguished classicist. But his residence at Johns Hopkins satisfied him that he did not wish to devote his life to Greek scholarship and in March 1878 he left the university.

After two or three false starts, Page definitely chose journalism as his profession and in February 1880 became a "cub" reporter on the *St. Joseph Gazette*, St. Joseph, Mo. In five months he was editor of the paper. The experience was valuable to him, but in the summer of 1881 he withdrew in favor of a novel venture of his own. He made an extended tour of the South to study the region and its problems and prepared for syndication in the leading newspapers of the country a series of penetrating articles based upon his observations. Page had already acquired a vivid style and his experiment proved a distinct success. The New York *World* late in 1881 gave him a roving commission and for a year he traveled first in the West and then with the peripatetic tariff commission of 1882 reporting its hearings. Upon his return to New York he served for another year as literary critic and editorial writer, but resigned when Joseph Pulitzer took over the *World* in 1883. Page now went home to take up a cause that had been close to his heart since boyhood, a crusade for the reconstitution of the South, and particularly of his native state. He acquired control of the Raleigh

State Chronicle, completely revised it, and plunged into a startling campaign that was both iconoclastic and vigorously constructive. He demanded the cessation of Confederate hero-worship and a widening of opportunities for the common man; he pleaded for decent educational facilities for whites and negroes, the promotion of scientific agriculture, local industries, and better roads. Page was sound and prophetic in his reforms, but his audacity and impatience aroused considerable hostility to him (H. W. Odum, *Southern Pioneers in Social Interpretation,* 1925). His paper was not a financial success and in 1885 he was obliged to relinquish it and return to New York.

It was not until 1887, however, when he joined the business staff of the *Forum,* a moribund monthly review, that an opportunity commensurate with his talents came to him. His initial efforts to improve its financial condition were not successful, but when in 1891 he acquired the practical direction of the whole publication, it took on new life and in a few years he made it one of the most entertaining and influential reviews in America. This achievement gave Page a reputation and in 1895 brought him an invitation to become literary adviser and associate editor of the *Atlantic Monthly;* three years later he succeeded to the editorship. His record in it justified the opportunity given him and under his brief but stimulating leadership the magazine departed from its rather conventional New England character and became an outspoken, provocative journal. Page was happy in his work, but fresh enterprises beckoned him to New York again and in 1899 he became a partner in the new publishing house of Doubleday, Page & Company, and the following year founded *The World's Work,* of which he served as editor until 1913. This magazine, devoted to politics and practical affairs, was undoubtedly Page's most important contribution to American journalism. As an editor he was ingenious and resourceful in his methods and persuasive in guiding his writers. "He made a friend of almost every contributor and a contributor of almost every friend" (*Outlook,* June 27, 1928, p. 356). He used his periodical freely to encourage educational, agricultural, industrial, and sanitary improvements in the South and gave much of his time to lecturing, correspondence, and committee work to advance these and other beneficent causes. As a member of the Southern Education Board and the General Education Board he did much to promote the idea of popular education as an indispensable complement to political and social democracy. He was also an active worker on the International Health Commission and on Theodore Roosevelt's Country Life Commission. One of the most social, humorous, and kindly of men, he worked easily with others and his services were much in demand for large philanthropic enterprises.

In politics Page had been a Jeffersonian Democrat since his youth, but he never accepted the leadership of William Jennings Bryan. He was among the early and avowed advocates of the candidacy of his old friend, Woodrow Wilson, for the presidency and gladly accepted the ambassadorship to Great Britain in 1913, partly because he anticipated that it would give him an admirable opportunity to promote Anglo-American ascendancy in world affairs. His winsome personality, cultivation, and sympathetic views speedily won for him a hearty welcome in London, and in the fifteen months prior to the outbreak of the war he worked harmoniously with the President in eliminating causes of friction between the United States and Great Britain, notably in connection with the Mexican and Panama tolls questions. His brilliant and illuminating letters on English life and affairs were greatly enjoyed and valued by the President and stamped him as one of the most fascinating letter-writers of his time. So highly did Wilson value Page's services that when the Ambassador suggested resigning in 1914 for financial reasons, the President obtained funds privately in order that Page might remain in London (Baker, *Wilson,* IV, 32–34).

After the war broke out, however, the two men gradually drifted apart because of their quite different conceptions of the course the United States ought to pursue. Page had little sympathy with Wilson's purpose to maintain a strict neutrality in thought and action and to enforce a full observance of American rights by both groups of belligerents. Almost from the beginning he construed the war as a gigantic assault on democratic civilization by Prussian militarism and believed that the United States should give at least limited support to the Allies by temporarily acquiescing in Britain's restrictions upon commerce between the United States and Germany's neutral neighbors (Hendrick, *Page,* vols. I–III, *passim; Intimate Papers of Colonel House,* I, 304–05; II, 304–13). In the autumn of 1914 he thwarted the administration's efforts to prevail upon the British to accept the provisions of the Declaration of London (1909), which they had not ratified, by threatening to resign if the State Department continued its insistence (Hendrick, I, 383); and in January 1915, in a test case involving the *Dacia,* he enabled the British Foreign

Office to avoid serious complications by suggesting to Sir Edward Grey that the vessel, formerly German-owned but now under American registry, be seized by the French, the expectation being that this would arouse less antagonism in the United States (*Ibid.*, 394; III, 222–26, 236). In these and other ways Page manifested his opposition to Wilson's course in the early stages of the war, but generally he adhered to his instructions. His enthusiasm for the Allied cause was ill-concealed from the British ministry (*Ibid.*, II, 237, 400; Grey, *Twenty-Five Years*, II, 110), however, and probably made him less effective in presenting American contentions than he might otherwise have been. His irritation at the President's policy was greatly intensified when the administration carried on an extended paper controversy with Germany over the sinking of the *Lusitania* and other merchant vessels carrying American passengers instead of promptly severing diplomatic relations and making war preparations. He refused to be a party to Colonel House's peace proposals in London early in 1916 and was hostile to those of Germany and the President in December 1916, because he thought the war must continue until Germany was crushed (House, II, 135–36, 177–78, 402–03).

By this time Page had lost all confidence in his chief; he contended that Wilson had failed to grasp the significance of the struggle and had abdicated leadership in foreign affairs. For these as well as for personal reasons in November 1916 he asked to be relieved, but by the time an answer came (Feb. 5, 1917), the whole situation had changed and at the President's request Page consented to remain. Throughout the neutrality period Page expressed himself with much frankness in letters to Wilson and House and constantly pleaded for a close Anglo-American accord, but his views were discounted as being pro-British (*Ibid.*, I, 456; II, 99, 269–70). That Page was greatly influenced by his residence in London in wartime, and that he underestimated the peace sentiment among the American people and in Congress is apparent, but it is equally clear that his sturdy devotion to his own country, its people and its democracy, was never shaken. Since Page believed that "only some sort of active and open identification with the Allies" could put Americans "in effective protest" against the Central Powers (Hendrick, II, 193), he rejoiced when the United States finally entered the war. He interpreted the step as a vindication of his own contentions, the more so since Wilson's war message took much the same ground as he had advocated earlier. Once in the struggle Page was eager for the United States to participate in

"dead earnest." He urged the immediate dispatch to Europe of naval and merchant fleets and a small expeditionary force to be followed by a powerful army; also the granting to the Allies of a large loan at a low rate of interest. His tasks at the embassy became greater than ever, but he was now contented and hopeful that his cherished purpose of drawing the English-speaking nations together for world leadership would be realized. The strain of official work together with nephritis undermined his health, however, and in August 1918 he was obliged to resign. He returned to the United States in October and two months later died in Pinehurst, N. C., a war casualty. His wife, Willia Alice (Wilson) Page, whom he married in 1880, three sons, and a daughter survived him.

In addition to his voluminous correspondence and journalistic writings, Page was the author of three books: *The Rebuilding of Old Commonwealths* (1902), a group of essays looking toward the training of the "forgotten man" in the South; *A Publisher's Confession* (1905, 1923), which expressed Page's business creed; and *The Southerner* (1909), a novel written under the pseudonym "Nicholas Worth," expressing his ideas for Southern development. But it is his letters, so rich in literary and human quality and so full of whimsical humor, that will stand as Page's most enduring contribution to American literature.

[The principal sources are B. J. Hendrick, *The Life and Letters of Walter H. Page* (3 vols., 1922–25); and *The Training of an American* (1928). A brief sketch of Page's services in London, based largely on Hendrick's volumes, is contained in Beckles Willson, *America's Ambassadors to England* (1928). These works together with Viscount Grey, *Twenty-Five Years* (2 vols., 1925), are extremely favorable to Page. An article hostile to him is, C. H. Grattan, "The Walter Hines Page Legend," *American Mercury*, Sept. 1925. Other very useful sources are: *The Intimate Papers of Colonel House*, ed. by Charles Seymour (4 vols., 1926–28); and R. S. Baker, *Woodrow Wilson: Life and Letters* (4 vols., 1927–31). The series of *Papers Relating to the Foreign Relations of the U. S.*, 1913–18 (1920–33) is indispensable for a detailed study of Page's ambassadorship.]   A. H. M.

PAGE, WILLIAM (January 1811–Sept. 30, 1885), portrait painter, born at Albany, N. Y., was the son of Levi and Tamer (Gale) Dunnel Page. In 1819, when the family moved to New York, the boy of eight was already making drawings of heads, and a likeness of his mother was considered "remarkably correct." He entered Joseph Hoxie's classical school and afterward went to a public school. At the age of eleven he won a prize for a sepia drawing from the American Institute. Three years later he was taken out of school and placed in the law office of Frederic de Peyster, who, becoming convinced that the lad was not qualified to distinguish himself in the legal profession, took him to Col. John Trumbull [*q.v.*], who advised him to "stick to the law." Disregarding this advice, in 1825 he began the study of drawing and painting under James Herring [*q.v.*] ; in 1826 he became the pupil of S. F. B. Morse [*q.v.*] and at the National Academy, where he received a silver medal for drawing.

At the age of seventeen he joined the Presbyterian church and determined to prepare himself for the ministry. To this end he studied for a short time at Andover and at Amherst, but after about two years he suddenly changed his mind and made a prompt return to portrait painting in Albany. He was then nineteen. He fell in love with Lavinia Twibill and they married. After three children had been born to them they fell out and were divorced. Page moved to New York and continued painting portraits with success. He was married to Sara A. Dougherty and with her, in 1844, he went to Boston, where they made a stay of three years. Many of his best portraits were painted at this period. His sitters included John Quincy Adams, Josiah Quincy, Charles Sumner, James Russell Lowell, Wendell Phillips, Charles W. Eliot, and Col. R. G. Shaw. Several of these portraits are in Harvard Memorial Hall. In 1849 Page went to Italy and remained there eleven years, for the most part living in Rome, Florence, and Venice. There he was considered the leading American painter of the day and enjoyed the friendship of eminent literary and artistic personages. He made a special study of Titian's works and tried to discover the secret of their color. It is probable that his own later work suffered in respect of originality and spontaneity from his excessive preoccupation with the methods of the Venetian masters. Much of his work was experimental, but at his best he was a remarkable portraitist. His drawing was especially strong. He became intensely interested in an alleged death-mask of Shakespeare and made a trip to Germany in 1874 especially to study it and make several copies in color. One of these is in the Metropolitan Museum, New York.

While he was living in Italy he obtained a divorce from his second wife, and in 1858 he married Sophia S. Hitchcock, by whom he had six children. He was an academician, and from 1871 to 1873 he was president of the National Academy. From 1860 to the time of his death he practised his profession in New York. He lectured to the students of the National Academy; numbered Lowell, Emerson, Hawthorne, and the Brownings among his friends; and was a picturesque as well as important figure in the art world. His portraits of Governors Marcy and Fenton are in the New York City Hall; his "Ruth and Naomi" belongs to the New York Historical Society; a Holy Family is owned by the Boston Athenæum; five of his portraits, including those of John Quincy Adams and William Lloyd Garrison, with a half-length "Ceres," are in the Boston Art Museum; and "The Young Merchants" is in the Pennsylvania Academy of the Fine Arts. One of his most important historical pieces, "Farragut's Triumphal Entry into Mobile Bay," was purchased by a committee and presented to the Grand Duke Alexis of Russia in 1871. During the last years of his life Page had a home at Eagleswood, N. J., where George Inness [*q.v.*] was his neighbor and intimate friend. They were both Swedenborgians. Page died at Tottenville, Staten Island, at the age of seventy-four.

[Wm. Dunlap, *Hist. of the Rise and Progress of the Arts of Design in the U. S.* (rev. ed., 3 vols., 1918) ; H. T. Tuckerman, *Book of the Artists* (1867) ; Samuel Isham, *Hist. of Am. Painting* (1905) ; W. H. Downes, article in *Atlantic Monthly*, Sept. 1888 ; *Art Jour.*, May 1876 ; *Cat. of Paintings, Museum of Fine Arts, Boston* (1921) ; *Illustrated Cat.: Paintings in the Metropolitan Museum of Art* (1905) ; Geo. Gale, *The Gale Family Records in England and the U. S.* (1866) ; *Albany Eve. Jour.*, Oct. 1, 1885 ; *World* (N. Y.), and *N. Y. Times*, Oct. 2, 1885).]   W. H. D.

PAINE, BYRON (Oct. 10, 1827–Jan. 13, 1871), advocate of state rights in Wisconsin, judge, the son of James H. and Marilla (Paine) Paine, was born in Painesville, Ohio, founded by his mother's grandfather, Edward Paine, a Revolutionary officer from Connecticut. An academy at Painesville gave him his formal schooling, which was later supplemented by wide reading, the acquisition of the German language, and the literary training that is afforded by practice in writing for the press. Removing with his father, who was a practising lawyer, to Wisconsin Territory in the year before its admission as a state, he studied law and was admitted to the bar at Milwaukee in 1849. In the early years of his professional career, when clients were few, he did much writing for the *Free Democrat*, a freesoil newspaper at Milwaukee. He and his father both held the anti-slavery views prevalent at the time on the Western Reserve of Ohio and were sympathetic with the flame of angry protest against the enactment of the Fugitive-slave Law in 1850. In 1854 he appeared before the state supreme court as counsel for Sherman M. Booth, the editor of the newspaper to which he had contributed, when the rescue of a negro, Joshua Glover, involved Booth in criminal proceedings. Paine's argument for the granting of a writ of *habeas corpus* was mainly an attack on the constitutionality of the Fugitive-slave Law (*Uncon-*

stitutionality of the Fugitive Act. Argument . . . in the Matter of the Petition of Sherman M. Booth for a Writ of Habeas Corpus, n.d.). The state court granted the writ, but renewed efforts of the federal authorities ended, in 1859, with the decision of the federal Supreme Court upholding the right of the federal authorities to try Booth. Paine expressed in no uncertain terms his own belief in state sovereignty, and the defiance of the federal authorities voiced by the Wisconsin judges and by him was received with acclamation among anti-slavery men everywhere. He reaped a rich harvest of personal popularity in his own state, which culminated in his election, the spring of 1859, as associate justice of the state supreme court on a campaign platform, remarkable in Wisconsin history, of "State Rights and Byron Paine!" Carl Schurz, then a citizen of Wisconsin, came under the spell. Years afterward the figure of young Paine, whose "tall and sturdy frame, and his face, not regular of feature, but beautiful in its expression of absolute sincerity, kindness, and intelligence, made his very appearance a picture of strength ruled by reason, justice, and benevolence," remained a cherished memory in Schurz's recollections (Schurz, *post,* p. 112).

Nevertheless, in 1861, when Lincoln called for men and resources to defend the Union, no state responded more heartily than Wisconsin. In November 1864 Paine resigned from the bench and was appointed lieutenant-colonel of the 43rd Wisconsin Volunteers. The next May he resumed his law practice in Milwaukee. In 1867 he was reappointed to a seat on the state supreme bench, to which he was later elected and on which he served until his death. In two opinions, of 1869 and 1870, he made the effort to analyze and set forth the convictions he continued to hold concerning state rights and to point out wherein he understood they differed from the doctrine of the right of secession (*Knorr* vs. *The Home Insurance Company* and *In re Tarble, 25 Wis. Reports,* 150–66 and 394–413). The close reasoning and keen exposition of these opinions commanded the respect of his fellow judges and lawyers, most of whom had come wholly to disagree with his view of the once dominant issue. It is noteworthy that a man raised to a judicial station by a popular movement, without regard to his professional qualifications, should have won the confidence and respect of the bar so completely. He was survived by his wife Clarissa R. (Wyman) Paine, whom he had married on Oct. 7, 1854, and by their four sons.

[*"Death of Mr. Justice Paine,"* 27 *Wis. Reports,* 23–68; J. R. Berryman, *Hist. of the Bench and Bar in Wis.* (1898), vol. I; P. M. Reed, *The Bench and Bar of Wis.*

(1882); C. W. Butterfield, *Hist. of Dane County, Wis.* (1880); J. B. Winslow, *The Story of a Great Court* (1912); *The Reminiscences of Carl Schurz,* vol. II (1907); E. E. Bryant, "The Supreme Court of Wis.," *Green Bag,* Mar. 1897; *Chart No. 3, Showing Ancestry of Descendants of Gen. Edward Paine,* comp. by J. L. Paine (1902); *Wis. State Jour.* (Madison), Jan. 14, 16, 18, 1871.]

W. B. S.

PAINE, CHARLES (Apr. 15, 1799–July 6, 1853), manufacturer, railroad promoter, governor of Vermont, brother of Martyn Paine [*q.v.*], was born at Williamstown, Vt., fifth of the eight children of Elijah [*q.v.*] and Sarah (Porter) Paine. A high-spirited, adventurous boy, more interested in sport than study, he was nevertheless destined by his father for a professional career. He entered Phillips Exeter Academy in 1813, and in 1816, following the family tradition, Harvard College, from which he graduated in 1820. Four years of college life proved his capacity for gay and joyous companionship rather than for serious study. A century later, if he had survived the sterner scholastic requirements of his alma mater, he would probably have ranked high among the popular athletes of his class. Overcoming parental objections, he settled after graduation at Northfield, Vt., where he soon became the manager of his father's woollen-mills. Business responsibilities and the close contact with the strong personality of his father brought out his more solid qualities. He, too, became a model of punctuality, exactness, and strict honesty in business dealings, but with somewhat less of sternness than the older man displayed. His enterprise and his initiative in the adoption of improved machinery shortly brought increased prosperity to his factory, now organized on a large scale. Like his father, he interested himself in farming and stock breeding. Here also financial success followed.

Meanwhile, he was taking part in state politics. For one term he was a member of the House of Representatives (1828–29). After standing for the governorship as a Whig in 1835, he was elected to that office in 1841 and again in 1842. Like the other Whigs of his region, Paine was a strong protectionist; unlike the majority of them, he was so incensed by President Tyler's failure to follow the party leaders that he urged a constitutional amendment not merely to limit the president to one term but to deprive him of the veto power, "the only monarchical feature in our form of government" (Governor's message in *Journal of the House of Representatives of the State of Vermont,* 1841, p. 33). He failed to secure a geological survey and a reorganization of the school system in the state, but he did introduce a new and more thorough system of accounting by state officers.

After his retirement as governor, he devoted the rest of his life to railway promotion. Efforts, under charters of 1832 and 1835, to build a railroad through the center of the state had failed from lack of financial support. Paine now became the moving spirit in a new endeavor. The Vermont Central Railroad Company was organized in 1845 with Paine as president of the board of directors. It was intended that the road, crossing the state from northwest to southeast, should form a part of a great trunk line connecting Boston with Chicago by way of northern New York and the Lakes. With the aid of capitalists in Boston, where the financial direction was retained, Paine succeeded in completing the road, Dec. 31, 1849. Unfortunately, and partly through Paine's fault, the railroad left Montpelier, the capital, on a side line, as it did Burlington after connection was made with Montreal. It did, however, pass through Paine's hilltop village of Northfield. Despite his determined efforts, the road was not a financial success. In 1852 it passed into the hands of receivers and Paine in the last year of his life turned to the promotion of a railroad to the Pacific over a southern route. During explorations for this purpose he died of dysentery at Waco, Tex. He had become known for his philanthropy in his own village and elsewhere in the state, but his greatest service was the railroad which his persistence had carried to completion. He was never married.

[*Paine Family Records*, Oct. 1882; J. G. Ullery, *Men of Vermont* (1894); John Gregory, *Centennial·Proc. and Hist. Incidents of the Early Settlers of Northfield, Vt.* (1878); A. M. Hemenway, *The Vt. Hist. Gazetteer*, vols. I (1868), IV (1882); E. S. Gannett, *The Useful Man. A Sermon Delivered at the Funeral of Hon. Charles Paine* (1853); *Vermonter*, vol. XXXVII (1932), nos. 11–12.]   P. D. E.

PAINE, CHARLES JACKSON (Aug. 26, 1833–Aug. 12, 1916), soldier, capitalist, yachtsman, was born in Boston, Mass., the eldest of the nine children of Charles Cushing and Fanny Cabot (Jackson) Paine. He was the great-grandson of Robert Treat Paine, signer of the Declaration of Independence, a grandson of Charles Jackson, jurist, and a brother of Robert Treat Paine, 1835–1910 [*qq.v.*]. After attending the Boston Latin School and graduating from Harvard in 1853, he studied in the law office of Rufus Choate and was admitted to the bar on Sept. 15, 1856. He then visited Europe and on his return spent some months in St. Louis, but from 1858 to the outbreak of the Civil War he maintained an office in Boston. On Sept. 5, 1861, he was authorized to recruit a company, and on Oct. 8 he was mustered in as captain and left

with his troops to join the force about Washington. He was commissioned major Jan. 16, 1862 and was made colonel of the 2nd Louisiana Volunteers on Oct. 23 of the same year. On Nov. 7, 1863, he was given command of a brigade, but he relinquished this assignment to join the staff of Gen. B. F. Butler. On July 4, 1864, the Senate confirmed him as brigadier-general; he commanded a division in various operations under Butler, was made major-general of volunteers by brevet on Jan. 15, 1865, and was mustered out of the army Jan. 15, 1866. After the war he devoted his energies to business affairs. He employed the extensive capital he controlled in large enterprises of the period, principally railroad building and development, and he took a prominent part in the management of several systems, including the Atchison, Topeka & Santa Fé; Chicago, Burlington & Quincy; and the Mexican Central Railway. His financial power and acumen were recognized by the well informed, but he gained little public recognition except an appointment as one of three members of a commission on bimetalism accredited by the United States to Great Britain, France, and Germany in 1897.

Paine was best known as a yachtsman. His narrow escapes from drowning as a youth did not reduce his love for this sport, and in the seventies he became prominent by purchasing the *Halcyon*, a slow craft, and making changes that greatly increased her speed. In 1885 he joined a syndicate to build a cup-defender to represent New England, and this boat, the *Puritan*, won the trial races and beat the British challenger *Genesta*. In the two succeeding years he assumed the entire cost of two more defenders: the *Mayflower*, which won in the trials and in the cupraces against the *Galatea*; and the *Volunteer*, which defeated both American competitors and the Scotch challenger *Thistle*. Edward Burgess [*q.v.*], who designed all of Paine's successful defenders, died before the next race in 1893; but Paine had an entry, the *Jubilee*, which was eliminated in the trials. His interest in yachting continued, however, to his last years, and his practical skill and conspicuous fairness were influences on American yacht design and international sport. He was an unpretentious man, avoiding any kind of display. The old straw hat and plain garb in which he sailed his cup-defenders were often contrasted with the elaborate costumes of less famous and less wealthy owners. He was without aloofness and his unobtrusiveness may have contributed to an underestimation of his ability and achievement. On Mar. 26, 1867, he married Julia Bryant, a grand-daughter of

Hannah Farnham Sawyer Lee [*q.v.*]; they had seven children. He died in Weston, Mass.

[Sources include: *Report of the Harvard Class of 1853, . . . Issued on the Sixtieth Anniversary* (1913); Sarah C. Paine, *Paine Ancestry* (1912), ed. by C. H. Pope; F. B. Heitman, *Hist. Reg. and Dict. of the U. S. Army* (1903), vol. I; *A Testimonial to Chas. J. Paine and Edward Burgess from the City of Boston* (1887), printed by order of the City Council; *Boston Transcript*, Aug. 14, 16, 1916; *N. Y. Times*, Aug. 15, 1916.]

S. G.

PAINE, ELIJAH (Jan. 21, 1757–Apr. 28, 1842), farmer, manufacturer, and jurist, was a native of Brooklyn, Conn., the second of eight children born to Seth and Mabel (Tyler) Paine. His ancestors, of English descent on both sides, had long resided in New England. Financial difficulties delayed his preparation for college. He was studying under the direction of his uncle, Rev. John Paine of Sturbridge, Mass., when in September 1776 he decided to join the Revolutionary army. Military life, however, especially garrison duty at Fort Washington, N. Y., proved uninteresting, and the war promised to drag on indefinitely; accordingly young Paine shortly returned to his studies. In the fall of 1777 he entered Harvard College, from which he graduated in 1781. His high standing is indicated by his nomination in 1782 as first orator by the newly founded chapter of Phi Beta Kappa, and his election as its president in 1783. Meanwhile, he had begun to study law in Boston, under Benjamin Lincoln, and in 1784 was admitted to the bar.

Seeking a place to establish himself, he followed the trend of migration northward to Vermont, pushing deep into the backwoods. With a few friends he made the first settlement at Williamstown during the summer of 1784. Here he cleared a large farm. Here, too, and also in the neighboring township of Northfield, he built saw and grist mills. He was by nature a man of affairs, quick to see a profit, hard at a bargain, punctual in fulfilling his obligations, and equally exacting with others. A stern, masterful man, six feet tall and strongly built, with a powerful voice, he had the initiative, energy, and executive ability which on a broader stage would have made him a captain of industry. In early Vermont he became a farmer on a large scale, a breeder of animals of many sorts, leading the way in popularizing merino sheep. By 1812 he had a flock of 1500 head. Then with characteristic energy he built in Northfield a large woollen-mill, where he produced flannels and broadcloths. Already, in 1803, he had constructed a turnpike connecting his district with the capital at Montpelier. In 1825 he became the first president of the Bank of Montpelier.

Meanwhile he was taking an active part in poli-

tics. Only two years after his arrival in Vermont he was a member and secretary of the constitutional convention of 1786. From 1787 to 1790 he was in the lower house of the state legislature. He served thereafter as judge of probate in the Randolph district (1788–91); as justice of the state supreme court (1791–93); as United States senator (1795–1801); as judge of the United States district court for Vermont, under one of Adams' "midnight" appointments (1801–42); and simultaneously as postmaster of his village (1815–42). He early aligned himself with the Federalists. He voted for the ratification of the Jay treaty, though at the cost of some unpopularity at home. In general he seems to have carried out his public duties with ability, but neither in Washington nor on the bench in Vermont did he leave any particular mark. As a judge he was known rather for strict discipline than for deep learnnig.

Throughout his life he was an ardent supporter of education. He endeavored in vain to have the state university located at Williamstown, but that his interest was not merely that of a real-estate promoter is evidenced by his long and active service as trustee of that institution, and of Middlebury and Dartmouth colleges as well. He took a prominent part in the affairs of the last named, being an aggressive leader of the anti-Wheelock faction in 1815 and thereafter (J. K. Lord, *A History of Dartmouth College*, 1913). He was honored by membership in the American Academy of Arts and Sciences and the American Antiquarian Society. For many years he was president of the Vermont Colonization Society, to which, and also to other benefactions, he contributed generously. He married, June 7, 1790, Sarah Porter of Plymouth, N. H. By her he had eight children; two of his sons were Charles and Martyn [*qq.v.*].

[Manuscript sketch of his father by Martyn Paine in the library of the Univ. of Vt.; *Biog. Dir. Am. Cong.* (1928); John Gregory, *Centennial Proc. and Hist. Incidents of the Early Settlers of Northfield, Vt.* (1878); J. M. Comstock, *A List of the Principal Civil Officers of Vt. from 1777 to 1918* (1918); A. M. Hemenway, *Vt. Hist. Gazetteer*, vol. II (1871); *Vt. Watchman and State Jour.* (Montpelier), May 2, 1842.]

P. D. E.

PAINE, HALBERT ELEAZER (Feb. 4, 1826–Apr. 14, 1905), lawyer, Union soldier, congressman, and commissioner of patents, was the son of Eleazer and Caroline (Hoyt) Paine. He was descended from a long line of Puritan ancestry running back to Stephen Paine who migrated to New England in 1638. He was born at Chardon, Geauga County, Ohio, was educated in the schools of that community, and completed his academic training at Western Reserve College, from which he graduated in 1845. After graduation he removed to Mississippi, where he taught school for a time, but soon returned to Ohio and took up the study of law. In 1848 he was admitted to the bar and began practice at Cleveland. On Sept. 10, 1850, he was married to Elizabeth Leaworthy Brigham of Windham, Ohio. Removing to Milwaukee, Wis., in 1857, he opened a law office there, and soon formed a partnership with Carl Schurz [q.v.]. The latter was so constantly engaged in politics, however, that the work of the office fell almost completely upon Paine. Both were idealists and in considerable measure crusaders. When the Civil War broke out, Paine "turned the key in his office and joined the army." He was commissioned colonel of the 4th Wisconsin Cavalry, July 2, 1861, and brigadier-general of volunteers, Mar. 13, 1863. At Harrisburg, Pa., his regiment was offered a stock train for transportation, which he indignantly refused, and, arming his men with pickhandles, he seized the next suitable train that passed through. He refused to return fugitives and also declined to obey General Butler's order to burn Baton Rouge. His military service was distinguished. He lost a leg in the attack upon Port Hudson, La., and thereafter served on a military commission, as commander of forts in the defense of Washington, and finally as commander of the military district of Illinois. He was brevetted major-general of volunteers, Mar. 13, 1865, for conspicuous gallantry on several occasions, especially at Port Hudson. On May 15, 1865, he resigned from the army.

In the Thirty-ninth, Fortieth, and Forty-first congresses, to which Paine was elected as a representative from Wisconsin, he supported the Radical faction. His two speeches on reconstruction subscribe to the "State Suicide Theory" (*Congressional Globe,* 40 Cong., 2 Sess., App., pp. 272–75, 314–16). In the Fortieth Congress, he was chairman of the committee on militia and in the Forty-first, he served as chairman of the committee on elections, of which he had been a member during his first term in Congress. The position was extremely important, because of the question of seating representatives from the Southern states. As a practical politician, from his position as chairman of the committee on contested elections, he was sometimes forced to answer Thaddeus Stevens' question, "Which is *our* rascal?" His reports to the House were brief, direct, and conclusive.

Declining to stand for reëlection in 1870, he took up the practice of law in Washington. His former law partner, Carl Schurz, pressed him to become the assistant secretary in the Department of the Interior. He declined for financial reasons, but later accepted the post of commissioner of patents. During his eighteen months in this office (November 1878–May 1880), he instituted important changes in the bureau. The most important of these were the substitution of scale drawings for models; the provision that errors of the patent office could be rectified without changing the date of the origin of the patentees' rights; the dating of claims for grants from the time of receipt of the application instead of at some time within three months thereafter; and the introduction of the use of typewriters.

After his resignation Paine resumed law practice, which he followed to the end of his life. In 1888 he published *A Treatise on the Law of Elections to Public Offices,* which remains the authoritative work upon the subject. It exhibits the rules and principles applicable to contests before judicial tribunals and parliamentary bodies, and is based upon American, English, Scotch, Irish, and Canadian authorities. It consists of 900 pages of heavily annotated text and a comprehensive list of cases (to 1888) which constitute the precedents from which the rules and principles are derived. Systematically presenting all the aspects of the law upon elections, it stands as a monument to the industry, comprehension, and thoroughness which were dominant attributes of the author's character.

[*Milwaukee Jour.,* and *Milwaukee Sentinel,* Apr. 17, 1905; S. B. Ladd, "Halbert Eleazer Paine," in *Jour. of the Patent Office Society,* Nov. 1920; *Who's Who in America,* 1903–05; *Paine Family Records,* Jan. 1882, *The Reminiscences of Carl Schurz,* vols. II (1907), III (1908); F. B. Heitman, *Hist. Reg. and Dict. U. S. Army* (1903), vol. I; *War of the Rebellion, Official Records (Army)*; *Biog. Dir. Am. Cong.* (1928).]

J. L. S.

PAINE, HENRY WARREN (Aug. 30, 1810– Dec. 26, 1893), lawyer, was born at Winslow, Me., the son of Lemuel and Jane Thomson (Warren) Paine and a descendant of William Paine who emigrated to Massachusetts in 1635. His mother was a niece of Gen. Joseph Warren [q.v.]. In childhood and youth he was noted for his abstention from the usual recreations. "He never rowed a boat, never skated, never played ball, goal, cards, chess, checkers, or any other game" (Mathews, *post,* p. 196). Entering Waterville (now Colby) College, Waterville, Me., in 1826 and graduating there in 1830, he continued for another year as tutor. He never lost his interest in the institution and from 1849 to 1862 he was a member of its board of trustees.

Following his father into the legal profession, he studied first in the office of his uncle, Samuel S. Warren of China, Me., and then took a year's course at the Harvard Law School (1832–33).

In 1834 he was admitted to the bar of Kennebec County, Me., and began practice at Hallowell. The following year he was elected to the state legislature, where he served through the 1837 session and also in 1853. Meanwhile, May 1, 1837, he was married to Lucy E. Coffin of Newburyport, Mass., and one daughter was born to them. From 1834 to 1839 he was the attorney for Kennebec County, and also became conspicuously successful in private practice. His growing reputation led him eventually into a larger field and in 1854 he established himself in Boston, where for over a quarter of a century he was a recognized leader of a distinguished bar. He was particularly effective before juries; but fair and courteous to his opponents. His professional income was large but he was careless in collecting fees and it was estimated that he gave away $100,000. A Democrat, even during the Civil War, he reluctantly consented to become his party's candidate for governor of Massachusetts in 1863 and again in 1864; but, of course, without hope of success. He is said to have been offered a seat in the United States Senate from Maine in 1853, and also one on the supreme judicial court of Massachusetts in 1867. From 1872 to 1885 he lectured on real property law at the Boston University Law School, with the great popularity of which his own personality had much to do. Failing health and hearing, due to overwork and lack of recreation, caused him to give up teaching as well as practice, and his last decade was passed in virtual retirement. During the last two years of his life he was unable to recognize his friends, and he had "discovered at last that, big as were his ancestors' deposits of vigor and vitality to his credit, he had overdrawn his account for years, and must now repay the excess with compound interest" (Mathews, *post*, p. 197). His career well illustrates the ephemeral nature of the advocate's fame. Efforts in forensic oratory, however effective, are rarely preserved, and records of professional triumphs are too often buried forever in the archives of the courts. Paine inherited from his father a taste for literature; he had a remarkable memory, and was noted for his use of literary allusion and his aptness of repartee. His death occurred in Cambridge, Mass.

[The most extensive account of Paine is William Mathews, "A Great New England Lawyer," *New England Magazine*, Apr. 1894; see also, *Paine Family Records*, No. 1, Nov. 1878; *Green Bag*, Feb. 1894; *Albany Law Jour.*, Jan. 6, 1894; *Boston Transcript*, Dec. 26, 1893.]

C. S. L.

PAINE, JOHN ALSOP (Jan. 14, 1840–July 24, 1912), archeologist and botanist, was born at Newark, N. J., the son of Dr. John Alsop Paine and Amanda S. (Kellogg), who had previously lived in Oneida County, N. Y. After graduating from Hamilton College in 1859, he studied theology at Andover, where he was graduated in 1862. He had shown a particular interest in botany, which led to his engagement by the board of regents of the University of the State of New York to report on the flora of Oneida County. The results of his study were published by the regents as *Catalogue of Plants Found in Oneida County and Vicinity* (1865). His interest in scientific research led him to study for a year (1866–67) at the Sheffield Scientific School of Yale and at the Columbia School of Mines. He was then appointed professor of natural science at Robert College, Constantinople, a missionary institution which had been founded only four years previously. In preparation for his work there he was ordained to the ministry at Newark, N. J., on May 29, 1867. After completing his two-year term at Robert College, he spent a year in the universities of Leipzig and Halle, pursuing scientific and philological studies. From 1870 to 1871 he was professor of natural science and German at Lake Forest University, Illinois. He then returned to the East as associate editor of the *Independent*, a post which he held until his appointment in 1872 as archeologist and naturalist on the staff of the American Palestine Exploration Society.

With this appointment, Paine's career may be said to have reached its climax. Unfortunately, his training was too scattered, and his interests too wide to permit him to take advantage of the opportunity which presented itself for a distinguished scholarly career. He seems, also, to have had difficulties with the head of the expedition, Lieut. Edgar Z. Steever, Jr., a recent West Point graduate. After nearly three months of waiting in Beirut, the base of operations, the expedition was finally able to begin its work in Moab (March 1873), where it continued until midsummer. Only part of the results of its work were ever published, the most important being described by Paine in the *Third Statement of the Palestine Exploration Society*, January 1875, consisting of two papers entitled "The Identification of Mount Pisgah," and "A List of Plants Collected between the Two Zarquas, Eastern Palestine." In 1874 Hamilton College gave him the honorary degree of Ph.D., in recognition of his work.

The following years were devoted to somewhat scattered journalistic work and research in various scientific and philological fields. From October 1881 to July 1884 he edited and published an ephemeral periodical known as the

Journal of Christian Philosophy, and in 1887–88 he was on the editorial staff of the *Century Dictionary.* For a time he thought seriously of specializing in ancient oriental studies, and several papers by him appeared in the *Journal of the American Oriental Society* between 1885 and 1889. These papers show much acuteness and critical ability, but a lack of depth. In 1889 he was appointed curator of casts in the Metropolitan Museum, a post which he held until his retirement in February 1906. During this period he spent much of his time at his home in Tarrytown, N. Y., pursuing researches of a miscellaneous character. His favorite subjects, however, appear to have been the history of the unsuccessful attempts made by Spanish and French followers of Columbus to colonize the eastern coast of North America in the sixteenth century, and the chemistry and radio-activity of rare elements. In the field of archeology he published Handbook No. 7 of the Metropolitan Museum, on its collection of plaster casts and bronze reproductions of ancient sculpture.

[*A Hist. of the Class of '59 of Hamilton Coll.* (1899); *Gen. Cat. of the Theological Sem., Andover, Mass. 1808–1908* (1909); *Torreya,* Aug. 1912; *Who's Who in America,* 1912–13; *N. Y. Times,* July 25, 1912.]   W. F. A.

PAINE, JOHN KNOWLES (Jan. 9, 1839–Apr. 25, 1906), American composer, teacher, and organist, was born in Portland, Me., was married, on Sept. 7, 1869, to Mary Elizabeth Greeley, and died in Cambridge, Mass. He was the son of Jacob Small and Rebecca (Beebe) Downes Paine and was descended from Thomas Payne who emigrated to Yarmouth, in Massachusetts, in the seventeenth century. He came of a musical family. His grandfather, John K. H. Paine, built the first organ in Maine. Of Jacob's five children John Knowles was precociously gifted and was soon destined for a musical career. He studied in Portland with an excellent musician, the organist Hermann Kotzschmar. In 1857, at the age of nineteen, he was given the privilege of being sent to Germany for further study in music. Here he became a pupil of Karl August Haupt in Berlin, one of the foremost German organists, and here he gained that power and facility in organ-playing that was his first distinction and that first established his position as a musician. He is said to have studied also theory and composition with Wieprecht and Teschner. He remained in Berlin for three years and there made a name for himself. In 1861 he appeared in the city as an organ virtuoso, when his playing was praised by German critics as showing mastery of the instrument and especially a command of the difficulties of Bach's

music. He also played with success in other German cities and gave an organ recital in London that won for him commendation. In that year, 1861, he returned to America. His first appearance was at a concert in Portland. This was followed by others in Boston of which *Dwight's Journal of Music* declared that "so marked was the freedom, ease, and repose of Mr. Paine's manner of performance on the organ that one was almost led to overlook the exceeding brilliancy of his execution" (Nov. 9, 1861, p. 254). It was not long before he made for himself the reputation of one of the leading organists of the United States. The great Walcker organ in the Music Hall, Boston, one of the most notable organs in the country at that time, had been bought in Germany, brought to Boston, and put into that hall largely through Paine's efforts while he was still a student in Germany. On this he gave frequent recitals, heard by large audiences, in which he introduced many works of Bach not then widely known in America, and a source of much fretful complaint in the press. He also became organist of the West Church in Boston.

In 1862 Paine resigned his church position to take the post of director of music at Harvard College, acting as organist and choir-master. The catalogue of the college had offered musical instruction "with special reference to the devotional services in the Chapel," and extending to the "higher branches of part-singing," as early as 1856. In the year after his appointment as "instructor of music" Paine added two lecture courses, one on musical form and another on counterpoint and fugue. In 1869 Charles W. Eliot became president of the university, and immediately set about carrying out his revolutionary plans for an elective system and a great increase in the number and variety of courses open to undergraduates. In these Paine had a share. In 1872 he announced a comprehensive elective course in musical theory and in 1873, in the face of strong conservative opposition, he was made an assistant professor and offered three new courses in theory, adding the next year a course in the history of music. One of the chief opponents of these plans was Francis Parkman, the historian, a member of the Corporation, who is said to have ended every deliberation of that body with the words *"musica delenda est"*; and who, for many subsequent years, when the college was faced with a need of funds, was always ready with a motion to abolish the musical department. Finally, in 1875, Paine was promoted to a full professorship, occupying one of the first chairs in music to be established in any American university. He continued his activity in his Harvard professorship till his resignation at the end of the academic year 1905, a short time before his death.

He had begun in his youth in Portland to show his ambition to be a composer. One of his early elaborate works was a Mass in D, which he went back to Berlin in 1867 to conduct at a concert of the *Singakademie*. Contemporary reports suggest that it was a highly competent but scarcely inspired composition. In 1873 his oratorio of "St. Peter" was given in Portland, then a year later in Boston by the Handel and Haydn Society. That, too, was found more commendable for its competence than admirable for its depth and beauty. The fact was that Paine had not yet found himself or emancipated himself wholly from the pupillary status. A great progress was noted in his first symphony, in C minor (*opus* 23), played in 1876 by Theodore Thomas, and much more in his second symphony (*opus* 34), entitled "Im Frühling," played in 1880. At its first performance in Boston this symphony aroused great enthusiasm. An account of it is extant relating how ladies waved handkerchiefs, men shouted in approbation, and the highly respected John S. Dwight, arbiter in Boston of criticism, if not of manners, stood in his seat, frantically opening and shutting his umbrella as an expression of uncontrollable enthusiasm. This approbation extended to numerous other performances in Boston and elsewhere. The next year another and still higher point in his career was reached. In 1881 the classical department of Harvard gave a stage performance, in Greek, of Sophocles' *Œdipus Tyrannus,* for which Paine composed the music, consisting of a prelude for orchestra and numerous choruses for male voices. The performance attracted widespread attention as the first of such classical revivals in the United States upon such a scale, and made a deep impression not only upon scholars but also upon music-lovers. At intervals thereafter Paine produced other important works: a symphonic poem, "An Island Fantasy"; an overture, "As You Like It"; a symphonic poem, "The Tempest"; cantatas including "Phoebus, Arise" (to words by William Drummond); "The Realm of Fancy" (Keats); "The Song of Promise" (George E. Woodberry); "The Nativity" (Milton); and music for a stage performance at Harvard of *The Birds* of Aristophanes. After his resignation in 1905 he hoped to devote himself to composition, but the time allotted him was short. At the time of his death he was at work on a symphonic poem, "Lincoln," left unfinished.

Paine's position in American music was recognized by commissions given him to set to music Whittier's hymn for the opening of the Centennial Exposition in 1876; to write a "Columbus March and Hymn" for the World's Columbian Exposition in Chicago; and a setting of Stedman's "Hymn of the West" for the St. Louis Exposition in 1904. In 1903 he was the official delegate of Harvard to the Wagner Festival in Berlin, where he received a gold medal, and his prelude to *Œdipus* was played at an international concert. In his later years he spent much time on an opera, *Azara,* for which he himself wrote the text, and by which he set great store. The subject is that of Aucassin and Nicolette in the time of the Trouvères in Provence. It was finished and published in English and in a German translation, but it was never produced upon the operatic stage. Concert performances of it were given in Boston several times that disclosed many beauties and certain traits of originality; but it is not clear that any great dramatic power or effectiveness was declared in them. Paine's allegiance was given more and more unreservedly in his maturer years to the romantic tendencies of the mid-nineteenth century, and the influence of Schumann is unmistakably to be discerned in many of his works. He yielded also to the influence of Wagner, though he never became as close an imitator of his methods as many were tempted to become in the years of Wagner's most potent spell. Paine's earlier works were found by many somewhat coldly academic, lacking spontaneity of inspiration. None can make that complaint against the "Springtime" symphony, or "An Island Fantasy," or the music to *Œdipus,* particularly the prelude. As he matured, his expression gained greatly in geniality and in poetic beauty. His romantic tendencies were manifested in program music of the more ideal sort, after Beethoven's canon, "more expression of feeling than delineation." In *Azara* the freedom of dramatic form that came from Wagner's example is to be found; the old-time divisions into arias and other set "numbers" are abandoned and the exigencies of the drama mainly condition the form of the music. But it would not be true to call the music "Wagnerian" in the generally accepted meaning of that term. It is wholly characteristic of Paine.

The best of Paine's works show fertility, a genuine warmth and spontaneity of invention, and a fine harmonic feeling, as well as a sure touch in the organization of form, and skill in instrumentation. It cannot be said that in any real sense they disclose "American" characteristics; Paine's musicianship was purely a product of European influences, as indeed was inevitable in his day and for a good while thereafter. His larger compositions gradually lost their place on orchestral or choral programs. With all their individual charm, sometimes power and impressiveness, they have not shown the vitality of great works of genius. Yet there are always the influences of fashion and the narrow prejudices and often the ignorance of foreign conductors of American orchestras to be reckoned with in accounting for neglect. It is possible that the finer works of Paine would be found to have still a power to give delight, if they were given a chance to communicate it. But whatever may be the present vitality of Paine's music, it made history; it held up a high standard—it rather produced and established a high standard—of American art, and served a valuable purpose in keeping American music in the minds and in the affection of American music-lovers.

Perhaps greater, or at least more lasting than his music, was Paine's influence as a teacher. Harvard left him free to shape his teaching as he chose; and he has been called the first in this country to teach music as an art and not as a trade. Nature had not gifted him with inspiring qualities as a lecturer, but in the years of his activity at Harvard he accomplished a great work in inforcing upon a body of undergraduates destined to become music-lovers and supporters of music, the value of music as a component of a liberal education. To those delving more deeply into the technique of musical theory and musical composition, even to those who became composers, he furnished tools which in his day were none too easy to acquire in America, where institutions for imparting a thorough grounding in that technique were neither numerous nor of high standing. Paine's teaching sent forth from Harvard a number of composers of talent and accomplishment who have contributed much of value to American music, as well as others who have handed on the torch of his learning as teachers and as writers of history and criticism.

[G. T. Edwards, *Music and Musicians of Me.* (1928); J. T. Howard, *Our Am. Music* (1930); *The Development of Harvard Univ.* (1930), ed. by S. E. Morison; L. C. Elson, *The Hist. of Am. Music* (1904); Rupert Hughes, *Contemporary Am. Composers* (1900); *Dwight's Jour. of Music,* May 25, Aug. 10, Aug. 24, Nov. 9, 1861, Feb. 1, 1862; the *Harvard Grads.' Mag.,* Sept. 1906; *Boston Transcript,* Apr. 25, 1906.]

R. A.

PAINE, MARTYN (July 8, 1794–Nov. 10, 1877), physician, was born in Williamstown, Vt., son of Elijah [*q.v.*] and Sarah (Porter) Paine and brother of Charles Paine [*q.v.*]. He received his education from private tutors, among them being Francis Brown, subsequent-

ly president of Dartmouth College. After completing his preparatory education at Atkinson, N. H., Paine entered Harvard College in 1809, receiving his degree of A.B. in 1813. In that year he began the study of medicine under the preceptorship of the well-known Doctors Warren, father and son, of Boston. He entered the medical department of Harvard in 1815 and was graduated M.D. in 1816. His graduation thesis treated the subject of inflammation, and all his life he maintained that "most diseases are inflammatory in origin and demand antiphlogistic treatment." For six years (1816–22) he practised in Montreal and then removed to New York, where he lived for fifty-five years. In 1825 he married Mary Ann Weeks, by whom he had a daughter and two sons. His first published work, *Letters on the Cholera Asphyxia,* appeared in 1832.

In the late thirties he was one of the most active promoters of the medical college of the University of the City of New York and when it opened in 1841 he was associated with Valentine Mott, John W. Draper, Granville S. Pattison, Gunning S. Bedford, and John Revere on its first faculty. Here he continued to teach for some twenty-five years, at first as professor of the institutes of medicine, but after 1850 as professor of therapeutics and materia medica. Though he was not an interesting teacher, for he read his lectures, he came to be regarded as the leading professor of therapeutics in the country. His *Institutes of Medicine* (1847), a work of 1100 pages, went through nine editions, and his *Materia Medica and Therapeutics* (1848), through three. He was a bitter opponent of the use of tobacco and alcoholic liquors. Purging and bleeding were his favorite remedies. He was the last of the confirmed phlebotomists. He enjoyed a considerable European reputation and was a member of the Royal Society of Prussia, the Medical Society of Sweden, the Society of Naturalists and Physicians of Dresden, the Medical Society of Leipzig, several Canadian scientific bodies, and many American medical and historical societies. In America he was renowned "for his thorough acquaintance with modern medical literature and for the wide range of his knowledge of contemporaneous authors" (Gross, *post,* II, 388).

In the early fifties he was sent by his faculty colleagues to Albany to use his influence for the passage of legislation permitting dissections in New York state. Up to 1854 there was a stringent law on the statute books forbidding dissection under penalty of imprisonment at hard labor; and the Board of Councilmen of New York City had urged the legislature "to oppose by every means the passage of any bill legalizing the dissection of dead bodies" (Gross, *post,* II, 388). Paine succeeded in securing in 1854, though by the scantiest of margins, the passage of an act abolishing the law prohibiting dissection. A devout Episcopalian, he published a book entitled, *On Theoretical Geology Sustaining the Natural Constitution of the Mosaic Records of Creation and the Flood in Opposition to the Prevailing Geological Theory* (1856). To him is attributed the authorship of a series of editorial articles, "Medical Education in Great Britain According to Documentary Evidence," published in the *New York Medical Press* in 1859, maintaining the superiority of medical education in the United States over that in Great Britain.

[S. W. Francis, *Biog. Sketches of Distinguished Living N. Y. Physicians* (1867), pp. 25–28, sketch repr. from *Medic. and Surgic. Reporter,* July 21, 1866; S. D. Gross, *Autobiography* (2 vols., 1887); J. J. Walsh, *Hist. of Medicine in N. Y. State* (5 vols., 1919); J. L. Chamberlain, *N. Y. Univ.* (1901); *Medic. Record,* Nov. 17, 1877; *N. Y. Tribune,* Nov. 12, 1877.]   J. J. W.

PAINE, RALPH DELAHAYE (Aug. 28, 1871–Apr. 29, 1925), journalist, author, was born in Lemont, Ill. From his father, the Rev. Samuel Delahaye Paine, who fought in the trenches at Inkerman and who commanded a battery of light artillery in the Civil War, he inherited a passion for daring deeds on both land and sea. From his mother, Elizabeth Brown (Philbrook) Paine, came his admiration for New England's history as exemplified in the annals of the seaport towns. While still a boy in Jacksonville, Fla., where his father held a small parish, Paine saved enough from his salary as a twelve-dollar-a-week reporter to enter Yale College in the fall of 1890. He then began to cover the athletic news for a syndicate of over twenty newspapers and thereby pay for the whole of his own education and a part of his sister's schooling. His powerful physique won him a seat in the university crew and a place on the football squad, and his charm of personality brought to him the highest social honors Yale could offer. Immediately after graduation in 1894, he joined the staff of the Philadelphia *Press,* and two years later he was sent to England to cover the Yale-Oxford crew race, serving again in 1904 in a similar capacity for *Collier's Weekly* at the track meet between the Yale-Harvard and Oxford-Cambridge teams. But it was as war correspondent during the Cuban revolution and the Spanish-American War that Paine enjoyed to the full his love of semi-quixotic adventure, for during that period he combined news-gathering with filibustering under the doughty captain "Dynamite Johnny O'Brien." William Randolph Hearst selected Paine as the proper "fool-adventurer" to take a gold sword to Gomez, the Cuban leader, but after Paine had carried the "bauble" over 5,000 miles he had to *send* it to the patriot, only to learn that the swarthy hero had accepted it with scorn—a fact which Paine found highly amusing.

In 1900 Paine was sent to China to cover the Boxer Uprising (see *The Dragon and the Cross,* 1912, and *Roads of Adventure,* 1922). In 1902 the *New York Herald* placed him in charge of its campaign against the beef trust, a campaign which brought him notice because of its notable success. After a brief connection with the *New York Telegraph* as managing editor, Paine gave up journalism and began his career as fiction writer and historian. His researches as a historian led him to Salem, Mass., where he delved into the history of Yankee shipping and published his results in *The Ships and Sailors of Old Salem* (1909), *The Old Merchant Marine* (1919), and *The Fight for a Free Sea* (1920). As the atmosphere of his alma mater is felt in such fine boys' stories as *The Stroke Oar* (1908), *College Years* (1909), *Sandy Sawyer, Sophomore* (1911), and *First Down, Kentucky!* (1921), so the roar of the seven seas is heard in *The Praying Skipper and Other Stories* (1906), *The Wrecking Master* (1911), *The Adventures of Captain O'Shea* (1913), *The Call of the Off-Shore Wind* (1918), and many others of Paine's sea stories. In 1917 Paine was appointed special observer with the Allied fleets, an experience which was unique and thrilling in the extreme (see *Roads of Adventure*). Into his stories went the influence of his friendships with such war correspondents as Stephen Crane, Ernest McCready, and Richard Harding Davis, and his careful study of Joseph Conrad's writings, the result being a literary style marked by genial humor, graphic phrasing, and vivid picturization.

On Apr. 5, 1903, Paine married Mrs. Katharine Lansing Morse of Watertown, N. Y., and in 1908 they moved to Durham, N. H. Paine represented Durham in the state legislature (1919) and served on the state board of education from 1919 to 1921. He was presented a medal by the citizens of Dunkirk, France, in gratitude for his kindness to the citizens of that city during the war. He died in Concord, N. H., and was laid to rest near his literary workshop at "Shankhassick," his Durham residence. He was survived by his widow, and by five children, two of whom were step-children.

[For further biographical data consult the reunion records of Paine's college class (Yale, 1894), especially the *Quindecennial Record* (1909), the *Quarter-Century Record* (1922), and the *Thirty Year Record* (1925); *Who's Who in America*, 1924–25; the *Granite Monthly*, May, 1925; and A. S. Pier, "A Yale Man of the 'Nineties," in the *Harvard Grads.' Mag.*, Dec. 1925. Jacques des Gachons's preface to *La Victoire Imprévue* (1910), a French translation of six short stories by Paine, is a Frenchman's estimate of Paine's position among American short-story writers. For book reviews of Paine's works see the *Book Rev. Digest* for the years 1906 to 1927 inclusive. Certain information was supplied for this sketch by Paine's classmate and intimate friend, the Rev. Wm. S. Beard, New York City.]   A. E. R.

PAINE, ROBERT (Nov. 12, 1799–Oct. 19, 1882), bishop of the Methodist Episcopal Church, South, was the son of James and Nancy (Williams) Paine and a descendant of Dr. James Paine, who emigrated from England in 1699 and settled in Person County, N. C., where Robert was born. In 1814 his parents moved to Giles County, Tenn. He was sent to the best private schools of the region and was ready to enter the sophomore class of Cumberland College, Nashville, Tenn., when, on Oct. 9, 1817, he had a vital religious experience and became convinced of a call to preach. Within a month after conversion he was traveling a circuit, and in October 1818 was admitted on trial to the Tennessee Conference of the Methodist Episcopal Church. On Nov. 11, 1821, he was ordained deacon, and on Nov. 26, 1823, elder. His rise was rapid; at the age of twenty-four he was sent as a delegate to the General Conference, and he attended every session of that body for the next twenty years.

In 1830, when LaGrange College, Franklin County, Ala., was founded under the patronage of the Tennessee and Alabama conferences, Paine was selected to be its first president, although for four years, out of modesty, he refused to accept the title of president, preferring to call himself superintendent. He had a difficult task directing the affairs of a college which lacked endowment and equipment, but he gave sacrificial service to the institution. For a number of years he contributed more than half of his annual salary to the school. He found the work of a college executive irksome and preferred to be in the pastorate, but for sixteen years, out of a sense of duty to his denomination, he remained as president.

Paine was closely connected with the formation of the Methodist Episcopal Church, South. He was a delegate to the General Conference of 1844, which marked the schism in the Methodist Episcopal Church, and was chairman of the committee that prepared the Plan of Separation, providing for a peaceable division of the Church. He attended the convention at Louisville, Ky., May 1845, where the Methodist Episcopal Church, South, was formally organized, and at its first General Conference, May 1846, he was elected bishop, which office he held for thirty-six years. After his elevation to the episcopacy he made his home at Aberdeen, Miss. He was not a participant in partisan politics. For thirty years prior to the Civil War he did not even vote in presidential elections for fear that such action might harm his moral and religious influence. Because of this attitude, President Buchanan invited him to the White House in November 1860, in order to secure, as Buchanan said, an unbiased statement in regard to the Southern states. As his episcopal duties were hampered during the Civil War, Paine preached in the Confederate camps, secured chaplains for the army, and made his home an asylum for wounded soldiers. When at times the Federal troops came into the vicinity of Aberdeen, it was necessary for the bishop to go into temporary exile in order to avoid capture.

He was sixty-five years old when the Civil War ended, but the next seventeen years of his life were as busy as those of his early and middle manhood. He played an important rôle during the reconstruction period. He advised kindly relations between the whites and the freedmen and was instrumental in organizing the negro members of the Methodist Episcopal Church, South, into the Colored Methodist Episcopal Church in America. His biographer (Rivers, *post*) declares that to no man more than to Bishop Paine was due the prosperity of the Church immediately after the Civil War. He favored the passage of progressive legislation at the General Conference of 1866. He was vitally interested in the securing of a great central university for the Church, and he rejoiced over the founding of Vanderbilt and its provision for theological education. He did not retire from active work until he was eighty-one years of age, and then only a few months before his death.

Upon the request of the General Conference of 1854 he wrote a biography of Bishop McKendree, entitled *Life and Times of William McKendree* (1869). He also prepared a series of articles in 1881 for the Nashville *Christian Advocate,* under the title "Notes of Life." In addition to his ability as an orator and administrator, he was a good financier. At one time he possessed considerable property, but as a result of the Civil War he suffered heavy financial losses. He was married three times: first, in 1824, to Susanna Beck of Nashville, Tenn., who died in June 1836; second, in 1837, to Amanda Shaw of Columbia, Tenn., who lived but a few months thereafter; third, in 1839, to Mary Eliza Millwater. There were two sons by the first marriage and four sons and three daughters by the third.

[R. H. Rivers, *Life of Robert Paine* (1884); J. B. McFerrin, *Hist. of Methodism in Tenn.* (3 vols., 1869–73); Anson West, *A Hist. of Methodism in Ala.* (1893); "Bishop Robert Paine," in *Quart. Rev. of M. E. Church, South*, n.s., vol. V (1882); *Aberdeen Examiner* (Aberdeen, Miss.), Oct. 26, 1882.] P. N. G.

PAINE, ROBERT TREAT (Mar. 11, 1731–May 11, 1814), signer of the Declaration of Independence, jurist, the son of Rev. Thomas and Eunice (Treat) Paine, counted among his ancestors several leaders, ecclesiastical and political, of early New England. He was a direct descendant of Maj. Robert Treat [*q.v.*], a colonial governor of Connecticut, and of Rev. Samuel Treat, one of the stalwart pioneers of Cape Cod. Other notable forebears were Stephen Hopkins, a signer of the Mayflower Compact; and Rev. Samuel Willard [*q.v.*], acting president of Harvard College. A great-uncle, Josiah Willard, was for thirty years secretary of the province of Massachusetts Bay. The first of the Paine family known to be in America was Thomas Payne, who was admitted freeman of Plymouth Colony in 1639. Rev. Thomas Paine, Robert's father, left the pulpit to engage in mercantile affairs at Boston and Halifax, Nova Scotia. At the time of Robert's birth the Paine family lived at Boston in School Street on Beacon Hill, at the foot of which stood Old South Church, where the child was duly christened. He was dedicated to the ministry in accordance with family tradition. After taking highest rank at the Latin School, he entered Harvard College with the class of 1749 and was domiciled at the home of Rev. Nathaniel Appleton, college chaplain. After graduating he taught for a while, then turned to the study of theology. His brief career in the ministry is best remembered for his services as chaplain on the Crown Point Expedition of 1755. To repair frail health he took to the sea—sailing first to Carolina, then to the Azores, Spain, and England, and concluding with a whaling voyage to Greenland.

Paine came upon the New England stage during the transition from an ecclesiastico-centric to a politico-centric form of government. As his forebears had upheld the best Puritan traditions under the old régime, he, true to his heritage, assumed similar responsibilities under the new order. By this time anxiety was subsiding in religious minds over the question as to whether or not the law was a holy calling, and in accordance with the trend of the period Paine gravitated quite naturally toward the Court House. Even while pursuing his theological studies he had begun to read law, and after a course with Benjamin Pratt was admitted to the bar in 1757. He first hung out his shingle at Portland, but in 1761 moved his law books to Taunton. His zeal in the rising Patriot cause resulted in his selection as associate prosecuting attorney in the celebrated "Boston Massacre" trial. His argument with regard to the underlying issue—whether Parliament had a right to quarter a standing army in a town without its consent—carried his name throughout the closely attentive colonies.

He was elected to represent Taunton in the provincial assembly (1773, 1774, 1775, 1777, and 1778). When the call came in 1774 for a Continental Congress to meet at Philadelphia, he was chosen one of the five Massachusetts delegates. The fact that his name was known beyond local boundaries because of his part in the "Massacre" case, his ecclesiastical ancestry and classical education, his travels in the Carolinas, Pennsylvania, New York, and England, and his geographical eligibility as a representative of the foremost town of southern Massachusetts, all contributed to his choice. At the first Congress he was appointed to the committees for drafting rules of debate and for fasting and prayer. In the second Congress, after the battle of Bunker Hill, when the creation and support of an army became the chief concern of Congress, he was appointed chairman of a committee charged with providing gunpowder. He was also a member of a committee to reorganize the militia. At first he was favorable toward the choice of Artemas Ward [*q.v.*], a college-mate, for commander-in-chief of the army; but eventually, under the leadership of John Adams, he voted for Washington. In later years he used this vote for Washington as an argument in favor of a desired federal appointment.

The final appeal to the Crown (July 1775) to preserve amity and good will with the Colonies, known as the Second Petition to the King or the "Olive Branch Petition," bears the signature of Paine, who was one of the few to sign both the "Olive Branch Petition" and the Declaration of Independence. He was reëlected to the Congress in 1776 and served throughout that year. In recognition of his services at Crown Point, he was sent with a commission to negotiate a treaty with the Indians of upper New York; he also served on a committee to establish a hospital. Though elected to the Congress of 1777, he did not go to Philadelphia, but remained in Massachusetts, where he served as speaker of the assembly. He continued, however, to experiment in the manufacturing of gunpowder and served on the committee appointed by Congress in December 1777 to inquire into the failure of the Rhode Island Expedition. In this same year he was elected first attorney-general of Massachusetts; in 1775 he had declined appointment to the Massachusetts supreme court. He was a member in 1778 of the committee of the legislature to prepare a draft of a state constitution and in 1779–80 played an important part in drafting that document. He was also concerned with confiscating the estates of departed Loyalists and with suppressing the rebellion led by Daniel Shays [q.v.] of impoverished Revolutionary soldiers.

Gov. John Hancock, a life-long friend, twice appointed Paine to the new supreme court of Massachusetts. The first of these appointments (1783) he declined, preferring to continue as attorney-general because of the larger salary, but the second (1790) he accepted as becoming the dignity of his advancing years. The extensive area of Maine (then a part of Massachusetts) necessitated tedious travels into remote regions for a justice-in-eyre. On one occasion Paine was arrested for traveling upon the Sabbath and roundly fined by a cross-roads court for violating a law he himself had been instrumental in framing. After fourteen years of service, increasing deafness hastened his retirement from the bench in 1804. He had moved his family to Boston in 1780, establishing a residence in the present Post Office Square, where a tablet indicates its site, and here he passed his sunset years, in daily converse with aristocratic fellow Federalists. Contemporary estimates of him usually remark upon his tendency to drollery, and his letters often display a whimsical extravagance of language. His life-long interest in science, especially in astronomy, led him to become a founder (1780) of the American Academy of Arts and Sciences. Participating actively in affairs of the church, he broke away from the old moorings of Calvinism under the rising tide of "Rationalism," and found shelter in the harbor of Unitarianism. His last public appearance was at the installation of Edward Everett as minister to the Brattle Street Church.

On Mar. 15, 1770, Paine married Sally Cobb, sister of Gen. David Cobb, a lieutenant-governor of Massachusetts. Of their eight children, Robert Treat Paine, 1773–1811 [q.v.]—originally christened Thomas—became widely known as a poet. Robert Treat Paine the Signer died May 11, 1814, and was buried, from the Old Brick Church, in the Old Granary Burial Ground, only a few steps from the spot of his birth.

[Ralph Davol, *Two Men of Taunton* (1912); *The Works of John Adams* (10 vols., 1850–56), ed. by C. F. Adams; John Sanderson, *Biog. of the Signers to the Declaration of Independence*, vol. II (1822); Sarah C. Paine and C. H. Pope, *Paine Ancestry* (1912); *New England Palladium*, Mar. 13, 1814; Paine's Journal of Sixty Years (MS.), in the possession of the family.]

R. D.

PAINE, ROBERT TREAT (Dec. 9, 1773– Nov. 13, 1811), poet, christened Thomas, but legally renamed in 1801 after his eldest brother who died of the yellow fever in 1798, was born at Taunton, Mass., the second son of Robert Treat Paine [q.v.], signer of the Declaration of Independence, and his wife, Sally Cobb, the sister of the Revolutionary General Cobb. The family moved to Boston in the boy's seventh year. Robert attended the Boston Latin School, where he led his class, and in 1788 he matriculated at Harvard. Here he neglected routine exercises for "natural philosophy and elegant literature." Though he wrote Greek fluently and his name was often doubly underscored for excellence in composition, he showed a spirit of independence of authority and was rusticated four months in his senior year for opposing a tutor and airing his wit to President Willard. From the moment that he answered in couplet the satirical thrust of a classmate, declares Prentiss, "his blessed ruin was inevitable." In June 1792 he presented a valedictory poem, and on Commencement Day, a poem on Liberty. After graduating he entered the business world as a clerk of James Tisdale, but his contributions to the *Massachusetts Magazine* and his interest in Sarah Wentworth Morton [q.v.] left little room for business. In the winter of 1792–93, he fell in with the theatrical folk of Board Alley, and when the company moved into the new Boston Theatre in 1793, verses by Paine that had won the gold medal offered for a prologue raised the curtain on Sheridan, Otway, and Shakespeare. The poet found Eliza Baker, sixteen-year-old English actress, more attractive than ledgers. He turned to theatrical criticism, and left Tisdale and business in 1794.

In October 1794 Paine founded the *Federal Orrery,* of which his polite circle expected much. But the editor deserted sober Federalist politics for satire of the Jacobin faction. A mob attacked his house. The son of a man he had pilloried ignored his unloaded pistol, and thrashed him. Paine, never robust for such interludes, declared this whipping the turning point of his life. The *beau monde* dropped him; they had long been uncomfortable in his presence. He was married to Miss Baker in February 1795, and his father closed his door on him. The poet became Master of Ceremonies at the Theatre, ran into debt, and began to drink to excess. At the Harvard Commencement, 1795, he defied President Willard and read the censored lines on Jacobinism in "The Invention of Letters." The poem brought him $1,500. Next year he sold the *Orrery,* and the next, delivered a Phi Beta Kappa poem, "The

Ruling Passion," which brought him $1,200. In June 1798 he wrote "Adams and Liberty" for the Massachusetts Charitable Fire Society. When a host refused him a glass of wine till he had added a stanza on Washington, Paine seized a pen and wrote the best stanza of all. The song ran over the country like wildfire. At the break with France in 1798, he delivered an oration praised by Washington and President Adams, and, at Washington's death, he delivered a eulogy.

In 1798 a short-lived reconciliation with his father was effected. Paine was prevailed upon to study and practise law with Theophilus Parsons. Though he quoted Horace in court, attended plays and whist-parties, and made some bets, he paid off debts and became an exemplary Bostonian, being admitted to the bar in 1802. But the next year found him a satellite of the erratic theatrical Venus, Mrs. Jones. He lost two children within four days in 1804, and was very ill in 1805. Though he planned another paper, a pantomime *Bluebeard,* and a play, and tried to make a beginning on an edition of his collected works in 1808, the old fluency was gone. His shingle was taken down from the cobwebs over his door in 1809. He drifted from poor lodgings to poorer, and died in the attic of his father's house. The best Bostonians attended his funeral. Gilbert Stuart did his portrait from a death mask.

Paine's poetry began in imitation of Dryden and Gray; it ended in catch-words for political campaigns. It is the kind of poetry in which Agriculture and Freedom are capitalized. For a Columbia too young for originality, he served as bard. But Paine's life is more noteworthy. He was spokesman of the fine Neo-Roman cult of patriotism, of the age that produced the Society of the Cincinnati, put the key of the Bastile in Mt. Vernon, raised domes above lawyers invoking Virgil; a lover of reason and the theatre, a sort of sacrifice to youth and liberalism on the altar of aristocratic Boston.

[There is a biographical introduction by Chas. Prentiss to *The Works in Verse and Prose of the Late Robt. Treat Paine, Jr.* (1812) and a review of *The Works,* embracing a critical estimate of Paine's poetry, in the *Port Folio,* May 1813. See also: *Song of Jefferson and Liberty* (1874), ed. by J. P. Kirtland; Sarah C. Paine, *Paine Ancestry* (1912), ed. by C. H. Pope; and the *Columbian Centinel* (Boston), Nov. 16, 1811.]

R. P. T. C.

PAINE, ROBERT TREAT (Oct. 28, 1835–Aug. 11, 1910), philanthropist, was the third son of Charles Cushing and Fanny Cabot (Jackson) Paine and a brother of Charles Jackson Paine [*q.v.*]. He was a descendant of Thomas Paine (or Payne) who settled in Yarmouth, Mass., and was admitted freeman of Plymouth Colony

in 1639, and of Gov. Robert Treat [*q.v.*] of Connecticut, and a great-grandson of Robert Treat Paine [*q.v.*], signer of the Declaration of Independence. Born in Boston, he was educated at the Boston Latin School and Harvard College, graduating from the latter in 1855 at the head of his class. After a year at the Harvard Law School, two years spent in study and travel in Europe, and a further year of legal study, he was admitted to the bar in 1859, and practised in Boston with marked and immediate success. On Apr. 24, 1862, he married Lydia Williams Lyman, by whom he had two sons and five daughters. Through his enterprise and wise investment in railroad and mining property he acquired a large fortune at a comparatively early age. He then retired from business and professional life and devoted himself exclusively to charitable and philanthropic work.

As early as 1870 he began a movement for better housing and in twenty years he had built in the vicinity of Boston over a hundred suburban dwellings, which workingmen were encouraged to buy on easy terms. His most successful and original enterprise was the Wells Memorial Institute for Workingmen, organized in 1879, a pioneer among institutions of the kind in the country. Its building, erected in 1881 at Paine's expense, became a center of industrial and trade-school courses, the seat of a cooperative bank, a successful club for working men, and even a meeting place of organized labor. His activities in behalf of better housing culminated in the Workingmen's Building Association and the Workingmen's Loan Association, both formed in 1888, of which he was the president. He was one of the first to appreciate fully that social problems must be scientifically studied, and in 1887 he and his wife founded the Robert Treat Paine Fellowship to enable Harvard graduates to study, at home or abroad, the ethical problems of society and public and private methods of ameliorating the conditions of the masses. In 1890 he established, with an endowment of $200,000, the Robert Treat Paine Association for the Help and Elevation of Working People, the proceeds of the endowment to be devoted to religious, charitable, and educational work.

It was in connection with the Associated Charities of Boston, of which he was the principal founder and the president from 1879 to 1907, that Paine's best work was done. His numerous addresses on the ideals of modern charity, which had wide circulation in pamphlet form, brought him recognition as a leading authority on the subject. The motto of the Boston Associated Charities, "Not Alms but a Friend," invented by Paine, expresses his idea of philanthropy. He was a director of the American Prison Association and of the Boston Children's Aid Society and was influential in raising the prevailing standards of social responsibility and in securing legislation for social projects. He was an active supporter of the peace movement, president of the American Peace Society from 1891 to his death, and prominent at national and international peace conferences and at those held at Lake Mohonk.

Paine's only political office was his membership in the Massachusetts House of Representatives for the session of 1884–85, during which time he carried on investigations in connection with the committee on charitable institutions, of which he was chairman. Loyalty to his convictions drove him, at considerable cost to himself, into the Mugwump movement of 1884, and he was an unsuccessful Democratic candidate for the Forty-ninth Congress that year. Originally a Unitarian, he went with his family to Trinity Church in 1870 and remained thereafter a prominent member of the Episcopal Church, to the General Convention of which he was many times a delegate. He was chairman of the building committee of Trinity Church, and was primarily reponsible for securing the site and raising the funds for its present edifice. He was always either vestryman or warden of Trinity, and between him and its rector, Phillips Brooks, there existed a rich and lifelong friendship. He was president of the board of trustees of the Episcopal Theological School in Cambridge and a founder of the Phillips Brooks House at Harvard, at the dedication of which he made the address. He was large in mind and body, a genuine idealist, an executive of tact and force, with a rare capacity for winning adherents to a cause in which his convictions were enlisted. His death occurred in Waltham, Mass.

[S. C. Paine and C. H. Pope, *Paine Ancestry* (1912), C. H. Paine, ed.; M. C. Crawford, *Famous Families of Mass.*, vol. II (1930); *Who's Who in America*, 1910–11; *Survey*, Aug. 20, 1910; *Outlook*, Aug. 27, 1910; National Conference of Charities and Correction, *In Memoriam* (1911); *Boston Transcript*, Aug. 12, 1910.]
F. T. P.

PAINE, THOMAS (Jan. 29, 1737–June 8, 1809), revolutionary political pamphleteer, agitator, deist author of *The Age of Reason,* was born in Thetford, England, the son of Joseph and Frances (Cocke) Paine. Joseph Paine was a poor Quaker corset maker, rather unhappily married to a lady who, as an Anglican and an attorney's daughter, must have been somewhat his social superior. Young Thomas went to grammar-school until he reached thirteen, when poverty made it necessary to apprentice him at the paternal trade. At nineteen he left home, shipping on the *King of Prussia* for a brief career as a privateer at the outbreak of war in 1756. His formal education can hardly have gone beyond the rudiments; indeed, as his enemies were delighted to point out, he never learned to write faultlessly grammatical English. In after life he referred frequently and proudly to his Quaker antecedents, and no doubt his feeling for the sanctity of the inner citadel of human consciousness had Quaker origins. But Paine had no trace of Quaker humility, no capacity for mystic self-surrender, and, since he fought in two wars, no absolute doctrines of non-resistance. He never, indeed, formally joined the Society of Friends. Nor, in spite of the efforts of a pious aunt, did he become an Anglican. He relates that a sermon on the Redemption, heard at the age of eight, impressed him with the cruelty implicit in Christianity, and made him a precocious rebel (Van der Weyde, ed., *Life and Works,* VIII, 71). Probably the most permanent influence of these twenty years upon him lay in the monotony of his occupation, in the ugliness of his poverty, in the gap—evident to himself at least—between his abilities and his apparent destiny.

For nearly twenty years more those abilities were concealed from the world. From 1757 to 1774 he was successively, and in various towns, corset maker, exciseman, school-teacher, exciseman again, tobacconist, and grocer. These last occupations he was able to carry on while maintaining his place in the excise. He went through two brief, childless marriages. His first wife, Mary Lambert, died within a year of their marriage at Sandwich on Sept. 27, 1759; the second, Elizabeth Ollive, whom he married on Mar. 26, 1771, while he was stationed at Lewes, was legally separated from him in 1774. The separation seems to have been due, not to any scandal, but to temperamental difficulties on both sides. The mere fact of separation, however, proved later a boon to Paine's enemies, and was generously embroidered to discredit him (George Chalmers, *Life of Thomas Paine,* 1791, pp. 33–35; James Cheetham, *Life of Thomas Paine,* 1809, p. 30). He was twice dismissed from the excise: first, in 1765, for having, as he himself admitted, stamped as examined goods he had not examined at all; and finally, after a reinstatement which shows that his first offense was regarded as venial, for overstaying a leave of absence. The real motive for this second dismissal was probably Paine's activity as agent for the excisemen in their attempt to get Parliament to raise their wages, a form of agitation then rather novel, and even revolutionary. He drew up a brief for his fellow excisemen, *The Case of the Officers of Excise*, privately printed in 1772 (published also in 1793). Cut off from his salary as exciseman, he was obliged to go into an ordinary and by no means discreditable bankruptcy. Like many another defeated European, he decided to try the new world. In London as lobbyist for his fellow-excisemen, Paine had had the luck to meet Franklin, and to make a favorable impression upon him. In October 1774, bearing invaluable letters of introduction from Franklin, this "ingenious, worthy young man" left for Philadelphia (A. H. Smyth, *Writings of Benjamin Franklin*, VI, 1906, pp. 248–49). Those years of failure and poverty had given Paine an education. He had not precisely learned from failure; he had, indeed, failed in business partly through too great a devotion to abstract learning. Ever since he had left school he had spent his spare time and money on books, lectures, scientific apparatus. He read widely but always seriously, worked hard at mathematics, experimented with mechanical contrivances. He thus achieved what was rare in Europe at the time, an education strictly confined to contemporaneous matters. No conservative, no evaluating discipline stood between his temperament and his times. Eighteenth-century science taught him to revolt against a society quite unscientifically constructed.

In Philadelphia, where he arrived on Nov. 30, 1774, Paine fell naturally into journalism. He supported himself largely by contributions to Robert Aitken's *Pennsylvania Magazine*. His first year's work covered a wide range, from recent inventions to "Cupid & Hymen." He was a pioneer in the movement for the abolition of negro slavery (*Pennsylvania Journal*, Mar. 8, 1775), but he cannot be numbered among the first defenders of women's rights. An article on that subject in the *Pennsylvania Magazine*, included by Conway in his edition of Paine's works, has been shown to be a translation from the French, a language Paine could not read (Frank Smith, in *American Literature*, Nov. 1930, p. 277). Nor is it likely that Paine had any personal influence in establishing the text of the Declaration of Independence (Albert Matthews, *Proceedings Massachusetts Historical Society*, XLIII, 1910, pp. 241–53). *Common Sense* gives him sufficient title to originality and fame, and his acknowledged writings are extensive enough without uncertain additions based on "internal evidence."

Common Sense was published as an anonymous, two-shilling pamphlet of forty-seven pages in Philadelphia on Jan. 10, 1776. It urged the immediate declaration of independence, not merely as a striking practical gesture that would help unite the colonies and secure French and Spanish aid, but as the fulfillment of America's moral obligation to the world. The colonies must fall away eventually, Paine said; a continent could not remain tied to an island. If now, while their society was still uncorrupt, natural, and democratic, these colonies should free themselves from a vicious monarchy, they could alter human destiny by their example. Paine was the first publicist to discover America's mission. It is curious that, though his political ideology was thoroughly Jeffersonian, he insisted in all his writings of this period on the necessity for a strong federal union, emphasizing the dangers of particularism and state sovereignty. These centralizing doctrines, emphatic in *Common Sense*, were expanded in *Public Good* (1780), a pamphlet directed against Virginia's western land claims. Paine undoubtedly consulted such leaders as Franklin and Rush about *Common Sense*, but the pamphlet itself was entirely his own, and was launched on his own responsibility. Its success was amazing. Paine himself wrote that 120,000 copies had been sold in less than three months, and his best biographer asserts that 500,000 were sold in all (Conway, *Life*, I, 67–69). Even allowing for exaggeration, these are impressive figures.

Paine's authorship soon became known. After defending himself as "Forester" in the *Pennsylvania Journal* from the attacks of the Loyalist William Smith, he enlisted in the army in time to join in the retreat across New Jersey. At Newark he set to work on his first *Crisis*, which appeared in the *Pennsylvania Journal* on Dec. 19, and in pamphlet form on Dec. 23. The famous words with which it begins, "These are the times that try men's souls," probably did not win the battle of Trenton, but its eloquence did hearten many. Cheetham, Paine's bitter enemy, writes that "the number was read in the camp, to every corporal's guard, and in the army and out of it had more than the intended effect" (Cheetham, *Life*, p. 56). Eleven other numbers of the *Crisis*, with four supernumerary ones, appeared in the course of the war. The whole work shows Paine at his best as a political journalist. Characteristic are number three (April 1777) suggesting vigorous measures against American Tories, and *The Crisis Extraordinary* (October 1780) pointing out how an efficient federal and state tax system could readily shoulder the burden of the war.

Paine's services obviously merited some reward. Occasional journalism was not, in his devoted but careless hands, an adequate means of self-support. In April 1777, he was appointed by Congress secretary to its committee on foreign affairs, a position he filled well enough until he was drawn into the extraordinary affair of Beaumarchais. Before France dared risk active alliance with the revolting colonies, supplies had been sent to America through the medium of Beaumarchais. Payment for these supplies was disputed. Silas Deane [q.v.], American agent recalled from France, upheld Beaumarchais' claim. Congress, however, relying largely on Arthur Lee [q.v.], who was still in France, refused payment. Deane, denied what he considered justice, rashly took to the newspapers in his own defense. Paine had the true revolutionist's scent for corruption, and an optimist's trust in the disinterestedness of the French government. He replied to Deane in the *Philadelphia Packet,* notably on Dec. 15, 1778, Jan. 2, and 9, 1779. In these letters he committed a double indiscretion: he supported his contentions by references to documents (reports from Lee), to which his position gave him confidential access; and by his statements he made it appear that the French government had sent supplies to the revolting colonies while it was still at peace with Great Britain. Under pressure from the French minister, Gérard, Paine resigned his position (Jan. 8, 1779). Gérard asserts that he immediately thereafter got Paine to accept a thousand dollars a year to write anonymously in the papers in support of France, but that he proved an unreliable press agent, and had to be released. The statement has only Gérard's authority, and is inconsistent with Paine's character. He had, indeed, as his conduct in the Beaumarchais affair shows, an idealistic devotion to the revolutionary cause quite proof against the limitations of propriety and tact; but he was incapable of financial dishonesty (Conway, *Life,* I, chap. IX).

Paine was soon (November 1779) given an appointment as clerk of the Pennsylvania Assembly. He continued his *Crisis,* and in 1780 showed further his devotion to the revolutionary cause by heading with a subscription of $500 out of a salary installment of $1,699 (paper) a fund for the relief of Washington's army. In 1781 he accompanied John Laurens to France in search of further financial relief, and returned successfully in the same year with money and stores. Beyond his expenses, he got nothing for the trip, and further, he was obliged to give up his position in the Assembly. The successful peace found him honored but poor. New York, however, gave him a confiscated Loyalist farm at New Rochelle, and Pennsylvania £500 in cash. For Paine's modest needs this was enough, and until 1787 he lived in Bordentown, N. J., and in New York, mildly lionized, writing, and working on his most cherished invention, an iron bridge (D. C. Seitz, "Thomas Paine, Bridge Builder," *Virginia Quarterly Review,* Oct. 1927, p. 571). In 1786 he published *Dissertations on Government, The Affairs of the Bank, and Paper-Money,* in which he asserted that paper money involved inevitable inflation and injustice to creditors, and insisted that the state of Pennsylvania could not legally repeal its charter of the Bank of North America.

Because of his bridge (which he despaired of getting erected in America), and no doubt his temperamental restlessness, he went to Europe in 1787. The fall of the Bastille found him in Yorkshire making desperate efforts to get his bridge built. He had passed two pleasant years, partly in France and partly in England, welcomed by liberals like Condorcet, Fox, and even Burke, as the author of *Common Sense* and the friend of Washington. The bridge did get built, and stood up, though Paine lost money in the affair. He went to Paris late in 1789, and for nearly three years alternated between Paris and London, a self-appointed missionary of the world revolution. England, Paine felt, needed his efforts if the revolutionary movement were to continue its spread, and Burke's downright and immediately popular condemnation of the French Revolution late in 1790 provided an excellent opportunity for him to exert them. Paine replied to Burke early in 1791 with the first part of his *Rights of Man.* A second part followed in February 1792.

The *Rights of Man* was first of all a party pamphlet, an excellent piece of special pleading in defense of specific measures taken in revolutionary France. It is also an exposition of the "principles of 1776 and 1789." Government exists, Paine said, to guarantee to the individual that portion of his natural rights of which unaided he could not ensure himself. These rights, with respect to which all men are equal, are liberty, property, security, and resistance to oppression. Only a republican form of government can be trusted to maintain these rights; and the republic must have a written constitution, including a bill of rights, manhood suffrage, executive officers chosen for short terms and subjected to rotation in office, a judiciary not beyond ultimate control by the people, a legislative body popularly elected at regular intervals, and a citizenry undivided by artificial distinctions of birth and rank, by religious intolerance, by shocking economic inequalities. Such a republic will be well and cheaply governed, or rather, little governed, for "government is no farther necessary than to supply the few cases to which society and civilisation are not conveniently competent" (Van der Weyde, VI, 241). Part II contains, rather inconsistently, numerous proposals for social legislation which show that Paine was not unaware of the class struggle. Finally, the *Rights of Man* was an appeal to the English people to overthrow their monarchy and set up a republic. Paine clearly hoped that his pamphlet would do in England what *Common Sense* had done in America. It did indeed become immensely popular with English radicals, and is said to have sold 200,000 copies by 1793 (Conway, *Life*, I, 346). It was suppressed by Pitt's government, and its author, safe for the moment in France, was tried for treason and outlawed in December 1792.

Paine, with Washington, Hamilton, Madison, and certain Europeans of adequate virtue, had been made a French citizen by the Assembly on Aug. 26, 1792. In September the new Frenchman was elected to the Convention from four departments, choosing to sit for the Pas de Calais. As he could not speak French, and had to have his speeches read for him, his rôle in that assembly was inconsiderable. His friends, notably Condorcet, who knew English well, were mostly among the respectable, prosperous, moderate republicans of the Gironde group, and Paine attached himself to their party. He did, however, assert his independence and his humanity at the trial of Louis XVI by urging that the king be imprisoned to the end of the war and then banished for life. After the fall of the Girondins in June 1793 Paine ceased, on his own admission, to attend an assembly which was but a subordinate part of the tyrannical government of the Terror (Van der Weyde, V, 308). With a few congenial friends, he lived peacefully in the semi-rural Faubourg St. Denis until, a vote of the Convention having deprived him of his French citizenship and parliamentary immunity, he was imprisoned on Dec. 28, 1793, under a law providing for the imprisonment of nationals of countries at war with France. Poor Paine, outlawed in England, was now arrested in France as an Englishman. His imprisonment in the Luxembourg was not very harsh, for he was able to compose part of *The Age of Reason* there. He was never brought to trial and, after the fall of Robespierre had ended the Terror, was released in November 1794 at the request of the new American minister, Monroe, who claimed him as an American citizen.

There has grown up an exaggerated account of Paine's tribulations in France. His imprisonment has been seen as a plot devised by his bitter enemy, the American minister, Gouverneur Morris [*q.v.*], and consented to by violent Jacobin politicians anxious to rid themselves of a dangerous opponent. It is much more likely that the simple, official explanation is the true one. Paine was generally regarded by French politicians as a harmless humanitarian. Even his heresy on the execution of Louis XVI was forgiven on the ground that, as a Quaker, he could not vote for the death penalty. The debates in the Convention make it clear that he lost his French citizenship chiefly because patriotism, fanned by military defeat into hysteria, demanded extreme measures against foreigners. The very fact that he was never brought to trial is conclusive proof that the Jacobins did not desire his death. Morris had a conservative's dislike for Paine's ideas and activities, a social conformist's dislike for his Bohemian habits. When Paine formally applied to him for protection, Morris sent the French foreign minister a letter which mildly disclaimed responsibility for Paine's acts since his acceptance of French citizenship, but which did at least request that information be communicated to the American government. The minister's reply denied Paine's claim to American citizenship. Morris did not press the matter, and wrote Jefferson that Paine, even were the French brought to admit him an American citizen, would still be liable under French criminal law for offenses alleged to have been committed in France, and that he was better off unnoticed in jail than publicly on trial before the pitiless revolutionary courts. It seems gratuitous to attribute hypocrisy to Morris in an act displaying such obvious common sense and tact.

On his release from the Luxembourg, Paine, weakened by illness and without means of support, was hospitably cared for by Monroe and nursed back to health. Restored to his seat in the Convention, he appeared before that body in July 1795 and reiterated his faith in the Rights of Man. He next took up residence with Nicolas de Bonneville, a moderate republican journalist whom he had known before the Terror. Until 1802, when the Peace of Amiens made it safe for him to return to America, he lived in Paris, his slender resources eked out by the kindness of friends. He wrote variously, and helped to organize a little group of "Theophilanthropists," a sort of ethical culture society which aimed to supplant Christian superstitions with an orderly faith in humanity. He published a

Dissertation on First-Principles of Government (1795), and an essay, *Agrarian Justice, . . .* (1797). The *Letter to George Washington* (1796), in which he accused the president of bad faith or at least indifference, and Morris of deliberate plotting against him, was the outburst of a disappointed man not wholly free from delusions of persecution, and did much to injure his reputation in America.

The great work of this period was *The Age of Reason* (Part I, 1794; Part II, 1796). This so-called "atheist's bible" begins with the assertion, "I believe in one God, and no more; and I hope for happiness beyond this life." Paine, of course, was not an atheist, but a deist, and *The Age of Reason* was begun as a final justification for the metaphysical ultimates of his belief. He starts out with the familiar proofs of the existence of God, the argument from design and the argument from a first cause. He defines knowledge in the customary way of his century as clear, mathematical, and scientific. He then proceeds to show that man's knowledge of the Christian God is not that sort of knowledge. The second part of the work is an analysis of both testaments, book by book, designed to show that the Bible is inconsistent, and therefore not infallible. Almost everything that Paine brings forward here is today a commonplace of critical scholarship. His attempts at a treatment of comparative religions, such as his reference to "Christian mythology" and his scandalous analogy between the paternity of the first person of the Trinity and the paternities of Zeus, are modern enough in spirit, and today would offend many professing Christians by their manner rather than their matter—a remark which indeed holds true of the whole book. Having demolished Christianity, Paine returns to his God, whose power is apparent "in the immensity of the creation," whose wisdom is seen "in the unchangeable order by which the incomprehensible whole is governed" (*Ibid.*, VIII, 43).

In October 1802 Paine at last returned home to America. Mere physical absence, however, had not prevented his playing his usual contentious part in American politics. The first copy of the *Rights of Man* to arrive in America was lent by its recipient, J. Beckley, to Jefferson, with the request that he pass it on to the printer to get out an American edition. Jefferson [*q.v.*] passed it on, and wishing, as he characteristically explained later, to take off a little of the "dryness" of a formal accompanying note, added some genial remarks about the pamphlet's uses as an antidote to the "political heresies" of the time. The printer proceeded to publish Jefferson's note as a sort of official preface (P. L. Ford, *Writings of Thomas Jefferson*, V, 1895, pp. 328 ff.). The Federalists at once took up the phrase "political heresies" as leveled at John Adams—as indeed it was. J. Q. Adams as "Publicola" attacked Paine's principles and Jefferson's indiscretion in the *Columbian Centinel* (June–July 1791), and Paine found himself vicariously in the midst of the bitterest possible party warfare. *The Age of Reason* and the *Letter to Washington* served to maintain his highly controversial position in America. In 1801, Jefferson involved himself further by offering Paine passage home in a public vessel, the *Maryland*. By this time, as Henry Adams temperately puts it, Paine was "regarded by respectable society, both Federalist and Republican, as a person to be avoided, a character to be feared" (*History of the United States*, vol. I, 1889, p. 317). Paine wisely refused the offer, and returned on a private vessel.

The last seven years of Paine's life were spent partly in Bordentown, partly in New York City and in New Rochelle. They were marked by poverty, declining health, and social ostracism. Paine wrote little of importance in these years. In New York he mixed with radical society, and especially with the rationalists gathered around Elihu Palmer as the "Columbian Illuminati." Madame de Bonneville, wife of his old Parisian friend, had come to America with her three children, one of whom was Benjamin de Bonneville [*q.v.*], of later fame. Paine generously helped to support the family, stranded in America when Napoleon refused to allow the father to leave France. In these final years of Paine's life center many of the tales told to his discredit—that he was a drunkard, a coward, an adulterer, a tavern atheist. Many of these have no basis at all. But one thing is certain; whether deservedly or not, his last years were those of an outcast. He died in New York on June 8, 1809. There is no evidence of a death-bed repentance, though naturally enough such stories were industriously circulated (Conway, *Life*, II, 420). Since consecrated ground was closed to the infidel, he was buried in a corner of his farm in New Rochelle. In 1819 William Cobbett [*q.v.*], to atone for his bitter attacks on Paine in the nineties, had the latter's bones dug up, and took them back to England, intending to raise a great monument to the patriotic author of the *Rights of Man*. The monument was never erected, and on Cobbett's death in 1835 the bones passed into the hands of a receiver in probate. The court refused to regard them as an asset, and, with the coffin, they were acquired by a furniture dealer in 1844, at which point they are lost to history.

Any attempt at a calm appraisal of Paine's character runs the risk of shading hostile black and friendly white into a neutral gray. Men always described him in superlatives, and in anything less than superlatives he seems unreal. He took an extreme, partisan stand on two issues that still divide Americans: in politics, that of the Jeffersonians against the Hamiltonians; in religion, that of the modernists against the fundamentalists. That Paine was a revolutionary by temperament is a statement on which his admirers and his detractors can agree; but it does but form the start for an analysis of his character. The repressed circumstances of his youth taught him that something was wrong with the world. His familiarity with the scientific and sociological writings of his contemporaries gave him a definite idea of a much better world. Experience helped him to fill in the outlines of this picture of a better world, but hardly to alter them. To the end, Paine would put up with nothing less than the Republic of Man. In America, in England, in France, he was serving, not men, but Reason.

This devotion to an abstraction, combined with a temperament naturally rebellious, made Paine extraordinarily sure of himself. His success as a writer sustained his self-confidence, while his failure at everything else supplied him with an abundance of grievances. This quality appeared to his enemies as a colossal vanity. Étienne Dumont wrote that he "was drunk with vanity. . . . It was he who had done everything in America. . . . He fancied that his book upon the *Rights of Man* ought to be substituted for every other book in the world" (*Recollections of Mirabeau,* 1832, p. 271). Even in the pages of his friend Monroe, this vanity comes out, perhaps in a truer light, as an extraordinary conviction of his own rightness, of his superior obligation to follow the light of his own reason (S. M. Hamilton, *Writings of James Monroe,* II, 1899, p. 441). He had also the unworldliness of the true revolutionary. Much has been made of his failure to enrich himself out of the hundreds of thousands of pamphlets he scattered over the western world, of his selling *Common Sense* at a loss, of his gift of the profits from the *Rights of Man* to the radical London Corresponding Society. But he did these things perhaps as much from indifference as from generosity. He simply lacked, as his early failures in business show, the gift of managing his own affairs. One suspects that towards the end he came to nurse this weakness as a virtue. Indeed, it is difficult to

escape the conclusion that in some respects Paine was the professional radical, the persecuted witness against the sins of the mighty. No doubt he was badly treated by respectable people on his return to America. No doubt he really was persecuted for his failures, big and little, to conform to current standards. But he gained an easy if somewhat shabby martyrdom thereby. And, cruel though the remark may seem, a happy, honored Paine is inconceivable in any world short of his own ideal one.

Of many of the aspersions spread by the pious and the conservative against Paine's character, we can make short shrift. Like most hated public men, he was accused of sexual irregularities, but all the evidence makes him out a singularly chaste man. After his death, Cheetham accused him of adultery with Madame de Bonneville, thirty-one years his junior. She brought a libel action against Cheetham and won it triumphantly (Conway, *Life,* II, 399). Nor can Paine be accused of financial dishonesty. He had numerous connections, especially in France, with men who were enriching themselves at public expense, but no one has succeeded in pinning a single job on him. Neither the charge that he beat his first wife nor that of his cowardice during the New Jersey campaign rests on any real evidence. That of drunkenness is a different matter. Too many people, friends and foes alike, have mentioned Paine's fondness for the brandy bottle for the fact of his drinking to be disputed. In his old age, he probably drank rather frequently. But he never was, as fanatics have charged, a dipsomaniac, nor did he die in *delirium tremens.* He seems always to have been careless about his personal appearance, and age and ostracism made him in his last years a trifle unlovely.

This opinionated and temperamental revolutionary never could bear to inflict physical suffering on any creature. He could not, like Robespierre, be cruel to men under the comfortable illusion that he was destroying abstractions. He did at times incline to think the great mass of people fools. He is reported—in a work of fiction, indeed, but with great psychological truth —as having defended the proposition that the minority is, even in a legislative body, more apt to be right than the majority (Royall Tyler, *The Algerine Captive,* 1802, vol. I, chap. XXVIII). But this paradox has become almost a traditional property of modern liberalism. It was one of the beliefs that helped disarm Paine for action, and prevent him from turning persecutor. In the last madness of the French Revolution he appears touchingly sane and modest. He cared too much for his ideal state—for liberty, equality, and fraternity—to risk trying to realize it. His ideals, his sense of martyrdom and election, his softness, all the qualities that made him a good agitator, combined to turn him against the Terror.

Paine seems never to have labored to learn to write, but to have written easily and well from the moment, near middle age, when he decided to make writing his occupation. Now he did not write romantic prose, nor Augustan prose. He has nothing to do with mystery nor with majesty. But his prose is not pedestrian. He wrote neatly, lucidly, argumentatively, with the simplicity that apes artlessness. His sentences are brief, or at least relatively free from inversions and other Latin tricks. All his rhetoric is centred on the epithet, not on the sentence structure. He is full of telling and quotable phrases: "government is for the living, and not for the dead"; "society is produced by our wants and government by our wickedness"; "the ragged relic and the antiquated precedent, the monk and the monarch, will molder together" (Van der Weyde, VI, 26; II, 97; VI, 302). If, as in the last quotation, the epithets are a trifle theatrical, the effect on his audience is all the more telling. Jefferson thought Paine's style resembled Franklin's. Both men, indeed, wrote simply in a century fond of periodic eloquence. But Paine is moving, almost passionate, in a curiously contentious way; his aphorisms lack the sleek touch of common sense. Paine was always pleading a cause; his books are arguments, rather than expositions. Occasionally his pleading seems unnecessarily involved, or descends to endless chicanery. But in general he succeeds admirably in being interesting, understandable, and irritating—necessary virtues of a revolutionary journalist.

Paine belongs rather to the history of opinion than to the history of thought; he is the propagandist, through whom the ideas of great original thinkers are transmitted to the crowd. Yet one cannot in fairness deny him that measure of originality which makes stereotypes of philosophical abstractions. His written work, and in particular his major writings, *Common Sense,* the *Rights of Man,* and *The Age of Reason* can be taken as one of the typical patterns of eighteenth-century thought in Europe and America —in some respects, perhaps, as the most typical of such patterns. At first sight, his surprising ignorance of French may seem to have limited his command over the materials common to his contemporaries. But he mixed with the leading radicals of both continents, learned a great deal by talking, and thus absorbed his Bayle and his

Voltaire, his Rousseau and his Holbach at second hand.

Fundamental to this pattern of Paine's is the notion that mechanical causation in the Newtonian sense is an absolutely universal phenomenon. The laws of Nature, in his opinion, apply to politics as to astronomy, and in both fields men can, by discovering these laws and adapting their conduct to them, make their lives orderly and agreeable. Now in politics the majority of men have, through ignorance, disobeyed these laws and have reaped the consequence in unhappiness. To set up kings and priests to secure political health is as foolish as to set up magical incantations to secure physical health. An enlightened people will abolish old institutions as old superstitions, and in their place put the law of Nature, codified in the Rights of Man. Force as we know it will cease to exist, and all government will be self-government. Paine does not, of course, put things quite as baldly as this. He fills in the pattern with many and sometimes contradictory details. In particular, he hesitated before a dilemma familiar to his contemporaries: are common men to be trusted to manage their own affairs, or must the enlightened central government restrain selfish or ignorant particularism? Though the theoretical bases of his thought are all on the anarchic side, he often proposes practical measures on the authoritarian side (Van der Weyde, VII, 18; IV, 219 ff.). He makes no real attempt to sound the meaning of his favorite abstractions—rights, liberty, equality. His thought lacks subtlety and shading. Like most of his contemporaries, he is a confirmed environmentalist. But Paine is blunter than any one but a propagandist may be. "Man is not the enemy of man," he asserts, "but through the medium of a false system of government" (*Ibid.,* VI, 209). Heredity is a mere political imposition. It has no justification in nature. Wisdom, in particular, is a "seedless plant" (*Ibid.,* 263).

These political ideas, save where they are preserved in such pieces of ritual as the preamble to the Declaration of Independence or the French Declaration of the Rights of Man and the Citizen, seem now outmoded enough. Much in Paine's writings is almost quaint, as when he argues that his deist God created the solar system in order to teach men mathematics (*Ibid.,* VIII, 83). The nineteenth century pointed out adequately enough the weakness of his political philosophy—the abuse of the deductive method, the assumption that men are capable of guiding their conduct wholly by reason, the contempt for history, the faith in written constitutions, the neglect of economic conflicts. The twentieth century is bidding fair to undermine the mechanical concept of causation on which his whole system rests. But of the work of Paine and men like him this much at least remains: the final destruction of the idea of a society hierarchically organized under a pessimistic and static cosmology; and the belief, now apparently rising again in a chastened form after the anti-rationalism of the nineteenth century, that human reason is man's best guide in politics and in ethics.

As to how much influence Paine's writings exerted on the course of history, there can be no final answer. Conceivably the United States of America might have become a free nation had *Common Sense* never been written. But even those who see history determined by economic and other physical, concrete forces can hardly deny that *Common Sense* helped to humanize and to concentrate such forces. Since his death Paine has lived on as a hero to a relatively small band of free-thinkers, of which men like Ingersoll and Bradlaugh were leaders. He has played in both Anglo-Saxon countries a rôle similar to that played by Voltaire on the Continent. To the majority of Englishmen and Americans, his name has been anathema. Not even his services during the Revolution have made him popular in the land which, after the abstract Republic of Man, he held most dear. There are signs, however, that the "atheist" is being forgotten in the patriot. At the celebration of the centenary of his death in New Rochelle in 1909, a Son of the American Revolution, in full Continental uniform, shared the platform with Painite free-thinkers. But there are still many to whom Paine is, as he was to Theodore Roosevelt, a "filthy little atheist" (*Gouverneur Morris*, 1888, p. 289). The discredit into which Paine fell is no doubt explicable partly by the fact that he was temperamentally a rebel, a socially disreputable professional agitator, and that America has done its best to live down this aspect of its origins; partly by the fact that his life was an unheroic sequence of purely literary struggles.

[Paine's unpublished letters and papers were destroyed by fire while in the possession of General Bonneville. Most of his letters to Jefferson and other contemporaries have been used by Conway in his *Life*. Further scholarly research like that of Frank Smith, "New Light on Thomas Paine's First Year in America," *American Literature*, Jan. 1930; "The Authorship of 'An Occasional Letter upon the Fair Sex,'" *Ibid.*, Nov. 1930, can no doubt add somewhat to our knowledge of Paine's minor journalistic writings. The first critical and complete edition of his works is that of M. D. Conway, *The Writings of Thomas Paine* (4 vols., 1894–96). The edition of W. M. Van der Weyde, *The Life and Works of Thomas Paine* (10 vols., 1925), adds nothing of importance to that of Conway. There are numerous separate and inexpensive editions of *Common*

Sense, The Crisis, the *Rights of Man,* and *The Age of Reason.*

Early examples of hostile lives are those of George Chalmers, or "Francis Oldys" (1791); and James Cheetham (1809); of friendly lives, those of T. C. Rickman (1819), and Gilbert Vale (1841). The standard biography is M. D. Conway, *The Life of Thomas Paine* (2 vols., 1892); this was translated by Félix Rabbe, and published, with additional material, as *Thomas Paine (1737–1809) et la Révolution dans les deux Mondes* (1900). Conway is an uncritical admirer, and constantly exaggerates Paine's achievements; he is somewhat careless about giving exact references to his authorities. But he did a thorough piece of research in Europe and in America, and generously publishes his evidence as well as his conclusions. Subsequent lives by Ellery Sedgwick (1899), F. J. Gould (1925), W. M. Van der Weyde (1925, vol. I of the same author's edition of the *Works*), and M. A. Best (1927), have added no important facts, and little critical interpretation.

For Paine's political and theological ideas, see Leslie Stephen, *Hist. of English Thought in the 18th Century* (2 vols., 1876), I, 458–64; II, 260–64; M. C. Tyler, *The Lit. Hist. of the Am. Revolution* (1897), I, 452–74; C. E. Merriam, "Thomas Paine's Political Theories," *Pol. Science Quart.*, Sept. 1899, pp. 389–403; F. J. C. Hearnshaw, ed., *Social and Political Ideas of . . . the Revolutionary Era* (1931), 100–40. A recent article is H. H. Clark, "Toward a Reinterpretation of Thomas Paine," *Am. Literature*, May 1933. An obituary is in *N. Y. Evening Post*, June 10, 1809. There are no critical bibliographies; see the "Brief List of Paine's Works" in Conway, *Life*, II, 482–83; "Selected Reading List" in A. W. Peach, *Selections from the Works of Thomas Paine* (1928), i–iii.]   C. B—n.

PAINTER, GAMALIEL (May 22, 1743–May 21, 1819), Revolutionary soldier and one of the founders of Middlebury College, was born in New Haven, Conn., the third son and the youngest of the six children of Shubael and Elizabeth (Dunbar) Painter. He was a descendant of Thomas Painter who was living in Massachusetts in 1637 and later moved to Rhode Island. Gamaliel received only a common-school education, perhaps at Salisbury, Conn. Here, on Aug. 20, 1767, he married Abigail Chipman. With her brother, John, he purchased land in the township of Middlebury, Vt., possibly from his own brother, Elisha, who was one of the original grantees in 1761. After preliminary explorations he took his wife and two sons to Vermont in 1773. Until the outbreak of the Revolution he was busy with the usual duties of the backwoodsman, clearing and planting his land, making surveys, opening roads, and, like most early settlers in western Vermont, resisting New York claimants to his lands. With the outbreak of hostilities he promptly joined the army, apparently serving with the expedition to Canada in 1775. The next year he became a lieutenant in Warner's Additional Continental Regiment. Later, he held a captain's commission in Baldwin's Artillery Artificer Regiment. He retired from the service in April 1782. Meanwhile, he had represented Middlebury at the two conventions at Dorset, Jan. 16 and Sept. 25, 1776; and in the

Windsor Convention (1777) which formed the state constitution he sat for Cornwall. When, however, British forces that year occupied much of the western part of the state, he withdrew from Vermont, returning with his family in 1784.

Three years later, after buying part of the site of the future village of Middlebury, he moved there and engaged actively in laying out village streets and selling lots. He erected a gristmill to attract settlers and engaged in various enterprises to promote the prosperity of the settlement which he was fathering. A simple, unassuming man, slow and halting in speech, and without any claims to consideration on the score of culture or education, he nevertheless won a position of authority in the new community. His sturdy physique and native mechanical sense fitted him admirably for the manifold tasks of the frontier. Sound judgment and shrewd business acumen, combined with energy and initiative, soon gave him a competence, which in the next thirty years grew into a considerable fortune for that region.

Having won the respect of his neighbors he renewed his political activity. Though without legal training, he served as assistant judge of Addison County from 1785 to 1786 and from 1787 to 1795. In 1786 he was elected from Middlebury for the first of fourteen terms in the lower house of the state legislature, a service which continued with some interruptions until 1810. Thereafter, he was twice (1813 and 1814) a member of the council which shared the executive powers with the governor. Throughout his life he was a firm Federalist. Conscious of the handicaps of a deficient education, he was an eager promoter of public instruction. He was one of the five original trustees of the Addison County grammar school founded at Middlebury in 1797, and when, in 1800, Middlebury College was added to this institution, Painter was one of its fellows. This administrative position he held until his death. His first wife having died in 1790, about 1795 he married Victoria Ball of Salisbury, Conn., by whom he had one daughter. Some time after 1806 he married for a third time, Mrs. Ursula Bull, daughter of Isaac Bull and widow of William Bull, of Litchfield, Conn. His three children having died, he provided that after the death of his third wife his estate should go to the college which he had helped to found and the building of which he had helped to erect.

[D. L. Jacobus, "The Painter Family," *New England Hist. and Geneal. Reg.*, July 1914; Samuel Swift, *Hist. of the Town of Middlebury* (1859); *Records of the Governor and Council of the State of Vt.*, vol. VI (1878); J. M. Comstock, *A List of the Principal Civil Officers of Vt. from 1777 to 1918* (1918); G. C. Woodruff, *A Geneal. Reg. of the Inhabitants of the Town of Litch-*

field, Conn. (1900); *Hist. Colls. Relating to the Town of Salisbury, Litchfield County, Conn.*, vol. II (1916); F. B. Heitman, *Hist. Reg. of the Officers of the Continental Army* (1914); A. M. Hemenway, *The Vt. Hist. Gazetteer*, vol. I (1868); *National Standard* (Middlebury, Vt.), May 26, 1819; *Conn. Courant* (Hartford), June 8, 1819.]

P. D. E.

PAINTER, WILLIAM (Nov. 20, 1838–July 15, 1906), engineer, inventor, was born on his father's farm at Triadelphia, Montgomery County, Md. He was the son of Dr. Edward and Louisa (Gilpin) Painter and was descended from early seventeenth-century Quaker settlers in Pennsylvania. During the first ten years of William's life his father farmed in various places in Maryland, the last being at Fallston, Harford County, and the boy's education was received in Friends' schools there and in Wilmington, Del. In 1855 he became an apprentice in a patent-leather manufacturing plant in Wilmington. Here he remained for four years, during which time he gave the first evidences of inventive ability, patenting a fare box on Aug. 3, 1858, and a railroad car seat and couch on Aug. 31, of the same year. In 1859 he returned to Fallston, Md., where his father had become the proprietor of a general store, and postmaster, and for the succeeding six years he worked as his assistant. During this time he devised and patented two additional inventions, a counterfeit-coin detector, July 8, 1862; and a kerosene lamp burner, June 30, 1863.

Realizing now that his greatest interest lay in the field of mechanics and mechanical engineering, early in 1865 he moved with his family to Baltimore and there obtained the position of foreman of a machine shop. Here, in the succeeding twenty years he engaged in the construction and improvement of pumping and other machinery for his employers. He conducted, too, in their establishment his own inventive and consulting engineering work, devising upwards of thirty-five contrivances, including an automatic magneto-signal for telephones, a seed sower, a soldering tool, and several pump valves. Soon after 1880 he turned his attention to bottle stoppers, and after several years of experiment obtained a patent, Apr. 14, 1885, for a wire-retaining rubber stopper, the feature of which was that it could be removed easily with one hand. To market this invention, the Triumph Bottle Stopper Company was organized in Baltimore by Painter and his friends. Soon afterward, Sept. 29, 1885, he obtained a patent for a so-called bottle seal, which was the first single-use bottle stopper, other than corks, ever offered the bottling trade. As this could be made and sold for ten times less than the "Triumph" stopper, the company organized to market the latter was disbanded and the Bottle Seal Company was organized to market the new invention. It met with ready approval and provided a large and profitable business in the succeeding seven years. About 1891, however, Painter conceived the idea of a single-use cap stopper of metal, and on Feb. 2, 1892, obtained patents for such a sealing device. These are the basic patents of the "Crown Cork" bottle caps used extensively throughout the world today. To market this latest invention, the Bottle Seal Company was reorganized as the Crown Cork and Seal Company, incorporated Mar. 9, 1892, of which Painter was secretary and general manager until he retired in 1903. Besides the administrative work devolving on him he directed the experimental work as well, developing and patenting practically all of the machinery, not only to manufacture the caps but also to apply the caps to bottles. In the course of his career he was granted some eighty-five patents, the last one being issued after his death. On Sept. 9, 1861, he married Harriet Magee Deacon of Philadelphia, Pa.; at the time of his death, in Baltimore, Md., he was survived by his widow and three children.

[O. C. Painter, *Geneal. and Biog. Sketches of the Family of Samuel Painter* (1903), and *William Painter and His Father, Dr. Edward Painter* (1914); *Trans. Am. Soc. Mechanical Engineers,* vol. XXVIII (1907); Patent Office Records; *Sun* (Baltimore), July 16, 1906.]   C. W. M—n.

PALEY, JOHN (Feb. 6, 1871–Dec. 23, 1907), editor, author, was born in Pleshczenitz, government of Minsk (some accounts say Radoszkowitz, government of Wilna), Russia, the son of Hyman Paley and Hayye Chortow. He received a traditional Jewish training at private schools, the Talmudical colleges of Minsk and Volozhin, and the Rabbinical seminary at Libau, under the directorship of Dr. Hillel Klein. At the last-named city he first commenced to acquire a secular education. Leaving Libau, he continued his studies at Kaunas, in the present Lithuania, and from thence proceeded to Moscow, where he engaged in business. In 1888 he left for the United States, where he remained until his death. He married Sophia Amchaintzky.

Almost from the first day of his arrival in America, Paley was engaged in literary work. His first Yiddish novel, "Di Russishe Helden," was written on the steamer bringing him to New York. It was submitted to and accepted by the Yiddish weekly *Der Volksadvokat*, and resulted in an invitation to join the staff of that paper. He later became its editor and publisher (1889–91). In 1891 he became editor of *Di Yiddishe*

Presse in Philadelphia, and a year later editor and publisher of the *Volkswaechter* in New York (1892–93). The success of this paper won for him a reputation as one of the best Yiddish journalists in the country. When the *Volkswaechter* was merged into the *Jewish Daily News*, he remained on the staff, and shortly afterwards was appointed editor-in-chief.

In Paley's hands the *Jewish Daily News* (*Jüdisches Tageblatt*), the oldest Yiddish daily in the country, became a powerful organ of the Yiddish-speaking masses who held orthodox religious views. Its circulation rose rapidly. It was Paley who introduced into Yiddish journalism all the devices which had popularized the Hearst and Pulitzer publications, including shrieking headlines and sensational news stories. In his vigorous publicistic articles, however, he chose to represent the conservative Jewish opinion which was suspicious of the radical and socialist element in Jewish life. His forceful, intensely Jewish articles, signed Ben Amitai, appealed strongly to Orthodox Jewry throughout the country and won him a large personal following. On the other hand, he was singled out by the Yiddish socialist press for bitter invective and attack. His stirring appeals for noteworthy causes, whether political or charitable, never failed to elicit a quick and effective response from his admirers. His journalistic talents and strong hold on the masses were recognized by both political parties, and turned to advantage in times of political campaigns. Paley wielded his sharp pen until his tragic death by suicide.

In addition to his work as journalist and essayist he was the author of numerous novels and short stories, some of which appeared in the columns of his newspaper. He also translated into Yiddish many works of fiction from world literature and wrote vaudeville sketches and plays, some of which were produced on the Yiddish stage. His last work, a popular history of the United States, which appeared serially in the *Jewish Daily News,* remained unfinished.

[*The Am. Jewish Year Book, 5665* (1904); *Jewish Encyc.* (new ed., 1925), vol. IX; *Am. Hebrew,* Dec. 27, 1907; Zalmen Reisen, *Lexicon fun der Yiddisher Literatur* (Wilna, 1927), vol. II; *N. Y. Times,* Dec. 24, 1907.]   I. S.

PALFREY, JOHN CARVER (Dec. 25, 1833–Jan. 29, 1906), soldier, engineer, was born in Cambridge, Mass., the son of John Gorham Palfrey [*q.v.*] and Mary Ann (Hammond) Palfrey. From his father he inherited an active mind and a puritanical sense of obligation and integrity. He attended the Boston Latin School, graduated from Harvard in 1853, and from West Point, first in his class, in 1857. He was appointed brevet second lieutenant and, later in the same year, second lieutenant in the corps of engineers.

Up to the time of the Civil War he served as assistant to the board of engineers for Atlantic seacoast defenses, and was connected with the construction and repair of the fortifications of Portland Harbor, Me., and Portsmouth, N. H. On the outbreak of war he was ordered to Fortress Monroe, Va., as assistant engineer. From December 1861 to January 1863 he was engaged as superintending engineer in the construction of the fort at Ship Island, Miss., and later was in charge of the construction and repair of the fortifications about New Orleans, the field works of the Department of the Gulf, and the defenses of Pensacola, Fla. He participated in the Red River campaign in 1864 and in the operations against Port Hudson, La., Fort Gaines, Fort Morgan and Mobile, Ala., and in the storming of Blakely. Towards the close of the Red River campaign, when the withdrawal of the supporting gunboats was blocked by the rapid fall of water in the river, Palfrey, then a captain of engineers, surveyed the stream and determined the practicability of engineering expedients by which the water level was raised, allowing the vessels to pass over the rapids and escape capture. In the operations against Fort Gaines and Fort Morgan he had immediate charge of the field works. For his services in the war he was brevetted major, lieutenant-colonel, colonel, and brigadier-general. Immediately after the war, he took part in the reconstruction of the San Antonio and Mexican Gulf Railroad of Texas.

On May 1, 1866, he resigned from the army and became agent of the Merrimack Manufacturing Company, Lowell, Mass. From July 1, 1874, until he retired from active business in 1891, he was treasurer of the Manchester Mills of Manchester, N. H. On Oct. 21, 1874, he married Adelaide Eliza Payson of Belmont, Mass. They had three children, two sons and a daughter. For many years he was an overseer of the Thayer School of Civil Engineering of Dartmouth College. He was a member of the Massachusetts Historical Society, and secretary of the Military Historical Society of Massachusetts. To the publications of the latter he contributed a number of narratives of military operations in which he had participated. Among these were "The Siege of Yorktown" (*Proceedings*, vol. I, 1881) and "Port Hudson" (*Ibid.*, vol. VIII, 1910). He died in Boston, and was buried in Mount Auburn Cemetery, Cambridge.

[G. W. Cullum, *Biog. Reg. Officers and Grads. U. S. Mil. Acad.* (1891); F. B. Heitman, *Hist. Reg. and Dict.* *U. S. Army* (1903); *Battles and Leaders of the Civil War* (4 vols., 1887–88); C. F. Adams, "Tribute to John C. Palfrey" in *Proc. Mass. Hist. Soc.*, 2 ser. XX (1907); *Report of the Harvard Class of 1853 ... Sixtieth Anniversary* (1913); information from the adjutant-general of the army and from General Palfrey's son.]   C. E. T. L.

PALFREY, JOHN GORHAM (May 2, 1796– Apr. 26, 1881), Unitarian clergyman, editor, historian, was a grandson of Maj. William Palfrey who was paymaster of the American forces in the Revolution, and the son of John and Mary (Gorham) Palfrey of Boston, where John Gorham was born. He received his earliest education at a private school, and then went to Phillips Academy, Exeter, N. H., where he prepared for Harvard. He graduated from college with the degree of A.B. in 1815, having for a classmate Jared Sparks [q.v.]. After graduation he studied for the Unitarian ministry and in 1818 was ordained as minister of the Church in Brattle Square, Boston. He remained with that church until 1831, when he was appointed Dexter Professor of Sacred Literature in Harvard, a post which he filled until his resignation in 1839.

He had long before begun to write for the press, his earliest articles appearing in the *North American Review*, of which Sparks was editor. In 1825, during Sparks's temporary absence in Europe, Palfrey acted as his substitute. In 1835 he bought the *Review* and conducted it with much success until he sold it to Francis Bowen [q.v.] in 1843. Between 1817 and 1859 he contributed thirty-one important articles to it. In 1842 and 1843 he was a member of the Massachusetts legislature. Meanwhile, he had become known as a lecturer, mainly on the evidences of Christianity, the Jewish Scriptures, and similar topics. He was interested in education, was chairman of the committee on education in the legislature, and cooperated with Horace Mann [q.v.] in his educational work. From 1844 to 1847 he was secretary of the Commonwealth and from 1847 to 1849 a member of Congress. In 1861 he was appointed postmaster at Boston, retaining that position until 1867. In politics he was at first a Whig and held his earlier offices as such; he was also an abolitionist, and himself freed a few slaves that he had inherited from his father, who had lived for a while in Louisiana.

Among his writings may be mentioned: *Sermons on Duties Belonging to Some of the Conditions of Private Life* (1834); *Academical Lectures on the Jewish Scriptures and Antiquities* (4 vols., 1838–52); *Lowell Lectures on the Evidences of Christianity* (2 vols., 1843); "Life of

William Palfrey," in Sparks's *Library of American Biography* (vol. XVII, 1848) ; and the *History of New England* (4 vols., 1858–75). A fifth volume of the *History,* which he had almost finished but had not had time to prepare for the press before his death, was published in 1890. Palfrey's claim to fame rests on this work. He appears to have been esteemed by his contemporaries, but his curious career—minister, professor, politician, postmaster, editor, writer, lecturer, and historian—indicates a certain lack of definite purpose and aim, a weakness of some sort in his character. As a recognition of his historical work, he was twice elected to the Massachusetts Historical Society and twice resigned, and the Society took no notice of his death in the usual form of memoir. The *History of New England* was the result of a vast amount of research, and he was both painstaking and usually accurate in detail. Although there are minor errors, some of which only subsequent research has corrected, the innumerable foot-notes, which are a feature of the volumes, are still a convenient and useful mine of information as to events and characters in the period he treated. (It may be noted that owing to his advancing age, the last two volumes are considerably inferior to the first three.) By frequently alternating his chapters on colonial affairs with chapters on contemporary events in England, thus attempting to provide the reader with a more adequate background, he introduced what at that time was rather an innovation. For this he deserves much praise. He probably tried to be fair in his judgments and when the volumes appeared they were much acclaimed for their impartiality ; but from the standpoint of today, the whole work must be considered as biased in several respects. In the relations between England and the colonies, Palfrey could see little but tyranny on the one side and God-fearing patriotism on the other. Nowhere does he show any real understanding of motives and problems. The work is strongly biased, also, by his inability to admit any flaws in the Puritans. So far as respects them, the volumes are special pleading throughout. Furthermore, the work is called a *History of New England,* although Palfrey writes as a retained advocate for Massachusetts when dealing with any conflict between that colony and the others, a notable example of this being his treatment of the Massachusetts-Rhode Island dispute over the Quakers. It may also be noted that he wrote as a clergyman and his sympathies were all with the ecclesiastical organization rather than with the laymen throughout the early struggles. Although his work has now been superseded for the general reader, it still retains much value for the special student, and for nearly half a century was the one standard work on New England.

He received the degree of LL.D. from St. Andrew's College, Scotland, as well as honorary degrees from Harvard, and was elected a member of the American Antiquarian Society. On Mar. 11, 1823, he married Mary Ann, daughter of Samuel Hammond of Boston; they had six children, among whom were John Carver Palfrey [*q.v.*] and Sarah Hammond Palfrey. The latter, a woman of varied intellectual attainments, shared her father's interest in liberal theology and was prominent in the social and philanthropic movements of her day. Besides contributing to periodicals, she published poems and several novels.

[*Proc. Am. Antiquarian Soc.,* n.s., vol. I (1882) ; *Report of the Proc. of the Numismatic and Antiquarian Soc. of Phila. . . . 1881* (1882) ; *Biog. Dir. Am. Cong.* (1928) ; J. S. Loring, *The Hundred Boston Orators* (1853) ; *Boston Transcript,* Apr. 27, 1881.] J.T.A.

PALLADINO, LAWRENCE BENEDICT (Aug. 15, 1837–Aug. 19, 1927), Roman Catholic missionary, was born in Dilecto, Italy, and trained in the preparatory colleges and seminaries of Genoa and Stazzius. In 1855 he entered the Society of Jesus and continued his study of philosophy and theology in Jesuit colleges in the Tyrol and at Monaco until he was ordained a priest, at Nice, in 1863. Meanwhile, apparently, he had taught for a time in Verona, during which period he witnessed the battle of Solferino (1859).

He volunteered for the California missions, and taught classes for four years at St. Ignatius College in San Francisco and at Santa Clara (see J. W. Riordan, *The First Half Century of St. Ignatius Church and College,* 1905). Assigned to the Indian missions in the Rocky Mountains (1867), he accompanied a party of Jesuits, including Fathers Urban Grassi and Joseph Bandini, to St. Ignatius Mission among the Flatheads of Montana, incidentally acquiring some knowledge of the dialects of the Walla Walla and Coeur d'Alène tribesmen during the tedious overland journey. For several years he was in charge of the mission and its Indian school, which the government assisted to the extent of contributing eight dollars each for fifty boys. Both an industrial and agricultural institution, it became an experimental farm for Indians and pioneer settlers. About 1873 Palladino went to Helena as an assistant to Father Joseph Menetry [*q.v.*], whose missionary parish covered a huge area. For sixteen years this was his station, but he made frequent journeys throughout Montana to serve isolated settlers, camps, and tribesmen. As an example of his activities, after the battle of Big Hole Basin in 1877, where Gen. John Gibbon defeated the Nez Percés, he brought sisters from Helena and Deer River to nurse wounded Indians and soldiers. In 1883 he made a visitation over the whole diocese in preparation for the coming of the first bishop of Helena, J. B. Brondel [q.v.], in whose diocesan synods of 1884 and 1887 he took a leading part as counselor. In 1884 he was ordered back to his old mission, with which he remained until called to the rectorship of Gonzaga College in Spokane (1894). After his term of service here, he was in Seattle for a short time, but was finally assigned to Missoula, where he continued until his death, though he was somewhat inactive after the celebration in 1925 of his seventieth year in the Society of Jesus.

In 1894 Palladino published a substantial volume, *Indian and White in the Northwest; or a History of Catholicity in Montana*, which ranks as a primary source of information concerning the state, since it was written by one who witnessed its transition from a wild Indian country to a civilized community, was intimately acquainted with its missionaries, traders, miners, trappers, soldiers, and builders, and had traversed every part of its mountains and plains. Other than this book, Palladino's career permitted of no writing save reports on Indians, a sketch of one of his associates: *Anthony Ravalli, S.J., Forty Years a Missionary in the Rocky Mountains* (1884), and reminiscent notes on early Montana (*Woodstock Letters*, 1880).

[In addition to his own writings, see *Records Am. Cath. Hist. Soc.*, Mar. 1923, Mar. 1927; annual Catholic directories; *Helena Independent*, Aug. 20, 1927.]
R. J. P.

PALLEN, CONDÉ BENOIST (Dec. 5, 1858–May 26, 1929), editor, author, publicist, was born in St. Louis, Mo., the son of Dr. Montrose Anderson Pallen and Anne Elizabeth Benoist. His paternal grandfather moved from Virginia to St. Louis, where for more than a quarter of a century he taught at St. Louis Medical College. Montrose Anderson Pallen, a native of Vicksburg, Miss., served as medical director, 1861–63, under Gen. Henry A. Wise, Gen. William J. Hardee, and the Department of Mississippi. In 1874 he was called to teach gynecology at the University of the City of New York; in 1883 he became interested in the organization of the medical school of Fordham University. Anne (Benoist) Pallen was a direct descendant of the Chevalier Benoist who came to America as an officer under Montcalm. Her father, Louis A. Benoist, was a banker in St. Louis.

Condé Pallen was graduated from Georgetown University, Washington, D. C., in 1880, and in 1883 received the degree of master of arts from the same institution. He studied also at St. Louis University where, after acquiring the degree of doctor of philosophy (1885), he remained for a short time as teacher. His love of study next carried him to Rome. Here one of his classmates was a youth who later as Pius XI was to confer upon him the Knighthood of St. Gregory (1926). The decoration *Pro Ecclesia et Pontifice* was earlier given him by Leo XIII.

From 1887 to 1897 Pallen was editor of *Church Progress* (St. Louis). As Roman Catholic revisory editor of the *New International Encyclopedia* and of the *Encyclopedia Americana* he became convinced that the time was appropriate for the publication of a work, the need of which had long been felt by Catholic scholars, which would give "full and authoritative information on the entire cycle of Catholic interests, action, and doctrine." The *Catholic Encyclopedia* (16 vols., 1907–14; supplement, 1922) was the result. Pallen was one of its board of editors, and from 1904 to 1920 was its managing editor. From 1912 to 1920 he served as president of the Encyclopedia Press which was organized to continue the publication of the *Encyclopedia* and to sponsor other works in the Catholic field. He was later editor of the Universal Knowledge Foundation, whose program included a general encyclopedia, *Universal Knowledge*, of which two volumes (1927–28) appeared before his death, and the *New Catholic Dictionary* (1929).

Pallen began in 1885 a career in lecturing and literature which brought him considerable fame in Catholic circles. He contributed papers on American Catholic literature to the Catholic Congress held in Baltimore in 1889; in the same year he delivered the "Centennial Ode" at Georgetown College. An essay, *The Meaning of the Idylls of the King* (1904), brought from Tennyson a treasured letter, reading: "You have seen further into the real meaning of the Idylls of the King than any of my commentators." His other works include: *The Philosophy of Literature* (1897), *New Rubaiyat* (1898), *Epochs of Literature* (1898), *The Feast of Thalarchus* (1901), a dramatic poem; *Death of Sir Launcelot and Other Poems* (1902), *Collected Poems* (1915), *Education of Boys* (1916), *Crucible Island* (1919), a romance; *As Man to Man: the Adventures of a Commuter* (1927), a series of popular articles written to answer accusations based upon misunderstanding of the teachings of the Catholic Church; *Ghost House* (1928);

and *The King's Coil* (1928). He was, besides, a constant contributor to the Catholic periodical press, and as chairman of the National Civic Federation's Department of Subversive Movements, was the indignant foe of restricted immigration, feminism, and social radicalism.

In 1886 he married Georgiana McDougal Adams of St. Louis, whose father, Gen. John Adams of Nashville, Tenn., a graduate of West Point, was killed in the battle of Franklin. She and ten children survived him.

[Family papers; *The Cath. Encyc. and Its Makers* (1917); J. S. Easby-Smith, *Georgetown Univ.* (1907), vol. II; *Who's Who in America,* 1928–29; *The New Cath. Dict.* (1929); *Commonweal,* June 12, 1929; *N. Y. Times* and *N. Y. Herald Tribune,* May 27, 29, 1929.]
L. F. S.

PALMER, ALBERT MARSHMAN (July 27, 1838–Mar. 7, 1905), theatrical manager, was born in North Stonington, Conn., the son of a Baptist clergyman, Albert Gallatin Palmer, and Sarah Amelia Langworthy, and a descendant of Walter Palmer who settled in Stonington in 1653. He attended New York City schools and the New York University Law School from which he graduated in 1860. Although he never practised law, his studies stood him in good stead in the management and control of the theatres whose organizations he undertook in a troubled but progressive period of America's theatre history. In 1872 he first entered the theatre as a partner of Sheridan Shook (a theatre owner with no *flair* for the art of the theatre) in the management of the Union Square Theatre which Shook had on his hands after an unsuccessful experiment in management. One of their first productions was Sardou's *Agnes* in line with the current tradition of the American theatre, in which translations of foreign plays or plays adapted or frankly purloined from foreign sources were the most popular material. Although Palmer had not the distinctive theatre talents or training of the other leading managers of his time—like Wallack, himself an actor and a dramatist with a long theatre tradition behind him, or Augustin Daly, a talented director and producer—he had, nevertheless, certain outstanding virtues which were of value to him and his theatres. John Ranken Towse, who saw many of his performances, has described him as "a man of considerable cultivation, suave, shrewd, worldly, somewhat hesitant and timid in judgment, but with a first-rate executive ability, and a remarkable faculty of finding means to serve his ends. . . . All his representations were distinguished by vigor and vitality, and that cooperative smoothness and proportion which can only be attained by actors long accustomed to each other's

methods and characteristics" (*post,* pp. 140, 141). And Arthur Hornblow substantiates this judgment: "He belonged to that school of managers whom we find in control of the leading theatres in Europe—men of culture, refinement and scholarship, . . . when a refined management gave the drama both dignity and form" (*post,* II, p. 261).

As his experience in the theatre grew, Palmer developed his native qualities of foresight, shrewdness, and good taste. Each year, until 1883, when he retired from the Union Square, he improved his company, widened his repertory, and began gradually to turn his attention to the cultivation and appreciation of American playwrights and of plays of American life and character. In 1883 he thought he would give up theatre management and travel abroad, but after a year of absence he joined the Mallory Brothers and took over the Madison Square Theatre, where he remained until 1891. He then went to Wallack's Theatre at Broadway and Thirtieth Street, renaming it Palmer's, and operated it with varying success until 1896, when he retired permanently from New York theatre management. Not the least of his attributes was his ability to select good advisers and associates. His play-reader and adapter, A. R. Cazauran, had an eager and adventurous taste in drama and the fact that he often recommended and pleaded the cause of plays a little out of the conventional line of the day may be the reason for the statement that three of Palmer's most successful productions, *The Two Orphans,* Sir Charles Young's melodrama, *Jim the Penman,* with Agnes Booth, and *Alabama,* by Augustus Thomas, were urged upon him against his own will and judgment (see MacKaye, *post,* I, p. 241). But the choice of Cazauran as play-reader was in itself an indication not only of Palmer's intelligence, but of his willingness to stand by the decisions of his associates in matters they understood, sometimes, better than he did.

Palmer has been said to have done more than any other manager of his day to encourage native dramatic ability (Moses, *post,* p. 77). His own statements (*Forum,* July 1893) give evidence of a forward-looking desire entirely beyond the general thought of his day to get plays not only by American authors but on native American material, especially material which showed the native American as something beyond the clown, the trader, the backwoodsman. It is on his list that such names as Augustus Thomas, Clyde Fitch, Bronson Howard (*The Banker's Daughter*), and William Gillette (*Held by the Enemy*) begin to be seen as the familiar property of the theatre. Although he himself is not credited with the creation of any great actors, his companies were always well chosen, often by the addition of favorites from his rival's houses. In 1882 he made a real contribution to the life of the theatre by the foundation of the Actor's Fund of America, a charitable corporation of which he was the second president. Palmer's second wife was the divorced wife of Sheridan Shook. She had two children who took Palmer's name and she and Palmer had one daughter, Phyllis. After he had retired from New York theatre management, he managed road tours for Richard Mansfield for some years. He died of a stroke of apoplexy in his sixty-seventh year.

[M. J. Moses, *The Am. Dramatist* (1911); Percy MacKaye, *Epoch* (2 vols., 1927); J. R. Towse, *Sixty Years of the Theatre* (1916), pp. 140–45; Arthur Hornblow, *A Hist. of the Theatre in America* (1919), vol. II; *Who's Who in America*, 1903–05; *N. Y. Dram. Mirror*, Mar. 18, 1905; *N. Y. Times*, Mar. 8, 1905.]
E. J. R. I.

PALMER, ALICE ELVIRA FREEMAN (Feb. 21, 1855–Dec. 6, 1902), educator, was the eldest child of James Warren Freeman and Elizabeth Josephine (Higley) Freeman. She was born in the village of Colesville, N. Y., not far from Binghamton, in the valley of the Susquehanna. Her mother, a farmer's daughter and village beauty, had had some experience in teaching and was a woman of intelligence and sympathy. From her came the child's large, appealing eyes, dark hair, lively interest in things of the mind, marked executive and administrative gifts. When Alice was in her seventh year, this competent mother, herself hardly more than a girl, assumed the support of the four young children in order that her farmer husband might fulfil his desire to be a physician by taking the two years' training at the Albany Medical School. Through her father, Alice inherited a Scottish strain and the romantic courage of the pioneer that quickened all her life's adventure; her father's father had walked from Connecticut to become one of the earliest settlers of Central New York, her father's mother was the daughter of James Knox, of Washington's Life Guard.

The child taught herself to read at three years of age, and attended the village school at four. In 1864, the family moved to the nearby village of Windsor, a more convenient center for Dr. Freeman. Here, in 1865, Alice entered Windsor Academy, a preparatory and finishing school for boys and girls, where at fourteen she became engaged to a young teacher who was earning the wherewithal to continue his own education. It was a decorous and dignified engagement, but the experience, awakening her womanhood, revealed her to her clear-sighted self. When, in 1870, her betrothed entered Yale Divinity School, she discovered that a college education meant more to her than marriage, and six months later the engagement was dissolved, with respect and good feeling on both sides.

She would have a college degree, she said, if it took her fifty years to get it. That magnetic persuasiveness which was to prove so effective in her maturer years won its first victory in this youthful struggle to convince her parents that her ambition was practical and unselfish. In 1872, at seventeen, she took the entrance examinations for the University of Michigan and failed. Her personality had made its impression on President Angell, however, and at his request the examiners allowed her to enter on trial, and she remained. There followed seven years of unflagging industry and indomitable courage, despite ill health from overwork. In 1875, she interrupted her junior year to assist the family fortunes by becoming the head of the high school of Ottawa, Ill., for twenty weeks. In 1876, she received the degree of B.A. from Michigan and taught in a girls' seminary at Lake Geneva, Wis. In 1877 came the first invitation to Wellesley. Henry Fowle Durant [*q.v.*], the founder, had heard of her through President Angell, and offered her an instructorship in mathematics, which she declined. From 1877 to 1879 she taught in the high school of Saginaw, Mich. In 1878, came Wellesley's second call—to teach Greek. Her sister Stella was ill, however, the family needed her; and again she declined. In 1879, Stella died, and with characteristic persistence Durant sent her a third invitation. At twenty-four, she became the head of Wellesley's department of history; in her first year Durant is said to have remarked to a trustee: "You see that little dark-eyed girl? She will be the next president of Wellesley" (*Life, post*, p. 97). Shortly after his death, in 1881, the president, Ada L. Howard [*q.v.*], resigned, and Alice Freeman at twenty-six was appointed vice-president of the college and acting president. In 1882 she became president, and her administrative powers and gifts for organization found here their perfect field.

During the six years of her administration the Academic Council, the inner circle of heads of departments, was established; standing committees of the faculty were formed; entrance examinations were made more severe; courses of study were standardized and simplified; the gymnasium was refitted under the supervision of Dr. D. A. Sargent of Harvard; the personnel of the faculty was strengthened; connections were made with a number of first-rate preparatory schools in different parts of the country. It was the day of beginnings, but no dry list of details can adequately describe the quickening impulse of her ardent and devoted personality. Never bookish, never a scholar, she had a bent for people and a genius for solving the concrete problems, and Wellesley at this time needed just what she could give. The institution was changed from a glorified boarding-school to a genuine college in her day, and the impetus gained from her contagious and eminently practical idealism has never been lost. In matters of general education, she also began to play her part. On Nov. 21, 1881, in Boston, she was one of the small group —seventeen women from eight different colleges —called in conference to consider organizing the women college graduates of the United States into an association for the promotion of the educational interests of women. On Jan. 14, 1882, she made the original motion which led to the organization of the Association of Collegiate Alumnae (forerunner of the American Association of University Women). She served two terms as president, 1885–86 and 1889–90. She was chairman of the important committee on Fellowships, 1889–95, and general secretary with power to direct and supervise the Association's policy in 1901–02. In 1884, she was one of three American delegates at the International Conference on Education in London.

On Dec. 23, 1887, she married Prof. George Herbert Palmer [*q.v.*] of the department of philosophy at Harvard. The record of this unclouded marriage is given in her husband's story of her life (*post*), a book which takes high rank among literary biographies. Although she now resigned her presidency, her connection with Wellesley did not cease. In 1888 she was elected a trustee, and held this office till her death. In 1889, Governor Ames appointed her a member of the Massachusetts board of education, and this position also was hers till she died. In 1891, she was one of five members of the board of managers for the Massachusetts exhibit at the World's Columbian Exposition. From 1892 to 1895 she was dean of women at the University of Chicago.

To secure her acceptance of this appointment, President William Rainey Harper [*q.v.*] released her from any obligation to teach, and fixed the period of her yearly residence at twelve weeks, to be distributed through the academic terms at her convenience. She was to select her own subdean, who would act in her absence. The duties of the office included supervision of the housing and food of the women students, their conduct, and the choice of their studies. Her belief in coeducation made this position especially attrac-

tive to her, but at the end of three years, when the women students were well established in the university, she resigned from an office too important to be executed chiefly in absentia. Meanwhile, in 1893 and 1894, she was active in promoting the changes through which Radcliffe College was formally attached to Harvard University. The International Institute for Girls in Spain, Bradford Academy, the Women's Education Association, each had a share in her busy life. She had joined the Presbyterian Church at fourteen, and later was prominent on the American Board of Commissioners for Foreign Missions and in the Woman's Home Missionary Association.

In December 1902, while on a European holiday with her husband, she died in Paris, of heart failure, three days after an operation for intussusception of the intestine. Thirteen years later her husband published a little book of her verse entitled *A Marriage Cycle* (1915). To those who knew her as the woman of committees and affairs, the administrator and practical executive, occupied on the plane of the obvious, these simple, reticent poems, so genuinely and unaffectedly lyrical, reveal an unsuspected depth of nature and delicacy of spiritual reserve. No estimate of her temperament and achievement is just which does not take into consideration this slender volume.

Although Alice Freeman Palmer was no scholar, her academic recognition was early and continuous. She received the degree of Ph.D. from the University of Michigan in 1882, and honorary doctorates from Columbia (1887) and Union (1895). She is commemorated in the University of Chicago by the chimes in Mitchell Tower, dedicated in 1908; fellowships in the gift of Wellesley and the American Association of University Women bear her name, as does an institute for colored boys and girls in Sedalia, N. C. In 1920 she was elected to the Hall of Fame at New York University among the educators; and in May 1921 the commemorative tablet was unveiled there by her husband. Her ashes, with those of her husband, lie in the Wellesley Chapel, beneath the bas relief by Daniel Chester French, dedicated to her memory in 1909.

[The essential source is George Herbert Palmer, *The Life of Alice Freeman Palmer* (1908), supplemented by *The Teacher, Essays and Addresses on Education* by *George Herbert Palmer and Alice Freeman Palmer* (1908) and A. F. Palmer, *A Marriage Cycle* (1915); Florence Converse, *The Story of Wellesley* (1915); F. M. Kingsley, *The Life of Henry Fowle Durant* (1924). See also *Outlook*, Dec. 13, 27, 1902, Jan. 16, 1904, July 28, 1915, Jan. 12, 1916; *Rev. of Revs.* (N. Y.), Feb. 1903; *Wellesley Mag.*, Feb. 1903; *Wellesley College News*, June 1909; *Wellesley Alumnae Quart.*, July 1921; *University Record* (Univ. of Chicago), July 1908; *Univ. of Chicago Mag.*, July 1910; *Sixty-sixth*

Ann. Report of the Board of Education [of Mass.], 1901–02 (1903); A Service in Memory of Alice Freeman Palmer . . . Appleton Chapel, Harvard Univ. (1903); Boston Transcript, Dec. 8, 1902.] F.C.

PALMER, ALONZO BENJAMIN (Oct. 6, 1815–Dec. 23, 1887), physician, teacher, and author of medical works, was the son of Benjamin and Anna (Layton) Palmer, and a descendant of Walter Palmer who emigrated from Nottingham, England, to Massachusetts about 1630 and settled, ultimately, in Stonington, Conn. He was born in Richfield, Otsego County, N. Y. Although he was left fatherless at nine, he received an adequate preliminary schooling in Oswego, Otsego, and Herkimer. Taking up the study of medicine, he graduated in January 1839 from the College of Physicians and Surgeons of the western district of New York, at Fairfield, Herkimer County.

Soon after his graduation, he moved westward to the comparatively new state of Michigan and settled at Tecumseh. The need for doctors in the new country was great and he soon built up a busy practice. His work was beset with the difficulties attending any pioneer enterprise, but in spite of the busy daily routine, he found time to keep abreast of the best available teachings and in the winters of 1847–48 and 1848–49, took postgraduate courses in New York and Philadelphia respectively. In 1850 he moved to Chicago, where he became associated with Dr. Nathan Smith Davis [q.v.] in a general practice. Two years later he was appointed city physician and became the official medical adviser to the health officer of the city. These latter positions he held for three years. During this period (1852) the cholera epidemic swept through Chicago. As city physician, he had charge of the cholera hospital which cared for fifteen hundred patients in the course of the year. His wide experience and careful observation during this epidemic resulted in a paper, *Observations on the Cause, Nature and Treatment of Epidemic Cholera* (1854), which was followed in later years by other valuable contributions to the study of the subject.

In 1852, Palmer was appointed professor of anatomy at the University of Michigan, but because of a limited budget did not assume the chair. In the same institution he became successively professor of materia medica, therapeutics, and diseases of women and children (1854), and professor of pathology and practice of medicine (1860). The latter position he filled until his death. In 1875, he became dean of the medical department and with the exception of one year held that office until he died. In the meantime, from 1864 to 1867 he was professor of pathology and practice of medicine in the Berkshire Medical Institution at Pittsfield, Mass., and from 1869 to 1879 was professor of the practice of medicine at Bowdoin College. Since his courses at the University of Michigan ended in March, he was able to lecture at the eastern institutions from April to June each year. At the beginning of the Civil War he was surgeon in the 2nd Michigan Infantry (May–September 1861), and was present at the first battle of Bull Run and other engagements.

Besides his well-deserved reputation as a teacher, Palmer became well known and respected through his writings. His wide medical experience culminated in the publication of a textbook entitled, *Treatise on the Science and Practice of Medicine, or the Pathology and Treatment of Internal Diseases* (2 vols., 1882). This was followed by *A Treatise on Epidemic Cholera and Allied Diseases*, published in 1885. His *Lectures on Sulphate of Quinine* had appeared in 1858, and *Epidemic Cholera, Its Pathology and Treatment*, in 1866. *The Temperance Teachings of Science* (1886) reflected his rigid belief in total abstinence from alcoholic stimulants and narcotics. From April 1853 to March 1860, Palmer was editor of the *Peninsular Journal of Medicine and the Collateral Sciences* and its successor, the *Peninsular and Independent Medical Journal*, published at Detroit. He was president in 1872 of the Michigan State Medical Society.

Endowed with a robust constitution, he was "a conscientious and skillful practitioner, an able writer, an earnest and successful teacher, and above all a most estimable citizen and Christian" (Davis, *post*). His success as a physician, writer, and teacher could scarcely have been so far-reaching without his kindly, sympathetic view of life. He was married twice: on July 19, 1843, to Caroline Augusta Wright, who died in 1846, and in 1867 to Love M. Root of Pittsfield, Mass., who survived him. There were no children.

[N. S. Davis, in *Jour. Am. Medic. Asso.*, Dec. 31, 1887; memorial address by C. L. Ford, in *Physician and Surgeon*, June–August 1888; *Medic. Record*, Dec. 31, 1887; *Trans. Mich. State Medic. Soc.*, vol. XII (1888); L. M. R. Palmer, *Memorial of Alonzo Benjamin Palmer* (1890); H. A. Kelly and W. L. Burrage, *Am. Medic. Biogs.* (1920); B. A. Hinsdale, *Hist. of the Univ. of Mich.* (1906); *Detroit Free Press*, Dec. 24, 1887.]
G. M. L.

PALMER, BENJAMIN MORGAN (Jan. 25, 1818–May 28, 1902), Presbyterian clergyman, was born at Charleston, S. C., second of the four children of Rev. Edward and Sarah (Bunce) Palmer. Both parents were of New England stock, his father being a descendant of William Palmer who emigrated to America in 1621. Prepared for college by his parents and at a private academy, Benjamin entered Amherst when he was little more than fourteen years old. There he found friends in Henry Ward Beecher and Stuart Robinson [qq.v.]. He led his class at Amherst, but was expelled in his second year for refusing to divulge the secrets of an undergraduate society. Returning to South Carolina, he taught school until, in January 1837, he entered the University of Georgia, from which he graduated eighteen months later. In 1841 he graduated, also, from the Columbia Theological Seminary, and in April of that year was licensed to preach.

The following autumn he was invited to become pastor of the First Presbyterian Church of Savannah, Ga., and on Oct. 7 he married Mary Augusta McConnell; six children were born to them, only two of whom lived to reach maturity. On Mar. 6, 1842, he was ordained. He served the church at Savannah only until January 1843, when he went to the Presbyterian Church at Columbia, S. C. There he and other ministers founded the *Southern Presbyterian Review*, the first number of which appeared in June 1847. He lectured at Columbia Theological Seminary, and in 1854 resigned his pulpit to accept a professorship there. Two years later he relinquished it and became pastor of the First Presbyterian Church of New Orleans, which he served until his death. He was active in founding the Presbyterian Church in the Confederate States, and was the first moderator of its General Assembly. He participated in establishing Southwestern Presbyterian University and a weekly paper, the *Southwestern Presbyterian*. An ardent defender of slavery, he advocated secession (see *Daily Delta*, New Orleans, Nov. 30, 1860). During the Civil War he was for a time commissioner of his denomination to the Army of the Tennessee. His eloquence, power of mind, breadth of human sympathy, and most of all his perfect integrity and devotion won him high esteem. Notable among his achievements were his efforts for the relief of the persecuted Jews of Russia in 1882, and his leadership in the war on the Louisiana Lottery (1890–91).

In addition to six books he published numerous pamphlets, and contributed many articles to the *Southern Presbyterian Review*, the *Southwestern Presbyterian*, and the *Presbyterian Quarterly*. His books are: *The Life and Letters of James Henley Thornwell, D.D., LL.D.* (1875); *The Family in Its Civil and Churchly Aspects* (1876); *Formation of Character* (1890); *The Broken Home, or Lessons in Sorrow* (1890); *The Threefold Fellowship and the Threefold Assurance* (1892); and *Theology of Prayer*

(1894). His death resulted from injuries which he received when struck by a street car.

[T. C. Johnson, *The Life and Letters of Benjamin Morgan Palmer* (copr. 1906); *Daily Picayune* (New Orleans), May 29, 1902; *Presbyt. Quart.*, July 1902; R. Q. Mallard, "Personal Reminiscences of Rev. B. M. Palmer," in *Union Seminary Mag.*, Dec. 1902–Jan. 1903; L. G. Vander Velde, *The Presbyt. Churches and the Federal Union, 1861–1869* (1932).]   C. F. A.

PALMER, BERTHA HONORÉ (May 22, 1849–May 5, 1918), social leader, was born in Louisville, Ky., the daughter of Eliza Dorsey (Carr) and Henry H. Honoré, a leading business man of the city who later removed to Chicago. She was the sister of Ida Honoré who married Frederick Dent Grant [q.v.]. She attended a convent-school near Baltimore, Md., and also studied under private tutors. In 1871 she was married to Potter Palmer [q.v.]. Soon after her marriage her husband lost a large part of his fortune in the great fire that swept the city, and she bent her energies to help him repair his losses. To her aid and to the excellent business judgment she developed he attributed much of his very great success. She had two sons, the elder born in 1874 and the younger in 1875, and she started on a social career that within a generation reached into every modern capital. She became the unquestioned social leader of the city of Chicago and maintained a social position in other cities of her own country and of Europe. In 1891 she was chosen president of the Board of Lady Managers of the World's Columbian Exposition. In this position she had the opportunity to exercise both her social gifts and her business acumen. She went to Europe to represent the fair and was very successful, especially in Italy and Belgium, in arousing interest in the project. The social connections she made at that time remained important to her all her life. It was principally due to her efforts that the women's department of the fair was so important a feature; she urged that the women's exhibits should have space in each state building, persuaded an imposing list of royal women to lend exhibitions, and obtained equal consideration for the activities of women. In 1892 she was chosen a trustee of Northwestern University. Eight years later, in 1900, President McKinley appointed her as a member of the committee to the Paris Exposition.

During her later years she gave attention to the management of the vast estate she had inherited from her husband in 1902. At her death its value had more than doubled under her management. She spent a great deal of her time and money in charitable and philanthropic work. On one occasion she opened her home for a meeting of the national civic federation, at which several hundred representatives of capital and labor were present. Each year she lent her executive ability and her social experience to the management of the charity ball of Chicago, which grew increasingly important as a social event and as a means of collecting funds. She was said to give some $50,000 annually to charity, and by her will she left about half a million dollars for various philanthropic purposes. During her early married life she and her husband held membership in one of the struggling Disciples of Christ churches in Chicago. Later she became a communicant of the St. James Episcopal Church. She died in her home at Osprey, Fla., on Sarasota Bay.

[J. S. Currey, *Chicago* (1912), vol. III; Newton Bateman, Paul Selby, and J. S. Currey, *Hist. Encyc. of Ill.* (2 vols., 1925); *House Beautiful*, Jan. 1920; *Hampton Columbian Mag.*, Oct. 1911, pp. 540–42; *Munsey's Mag.*, Oct. 1900, p. 32; *World To-day*, Mar. 1907, p. 226; *N. Y. Times*, May 7, 18, 1918; *Chicago Daily Tribune*, May 7, 1918.]   C. M. T.

PALMER, DANIEL DAVID (Mar. 7, 1845– Oct. 20, 1913), founder of chiropractic, was born on a farm at Lake Skoogag, near Toronto, Canada, of pioneer Scotch-Irish parentage. Definite knowledge of his early life is scanty. He had little benefit of schooling and was practically self-educated. When he was in his middle thirties he was a small merchant in What Cheer, Iowa. Here his son, Bartlett Joshua, was born in 1881. Shortly after his wife's death in 1883 he moved to Burlington, Iowa, and took up the practice of magnetic healing, then in 1895 he moved to Davenport, Iowa. He had made some study of osteopathy and of spinal adjustments, interest in which he attributed to the influence of Dr. James Atkinson of Davenport. In September 1895 he made the first trial of spinal adjustment upon the colored janitor of the building in which he had his office, for deafness. As originally stated by Palmer his science "consisted in removing the impingement of nerves in any of the three hundred or more articulations of the human skeleton, particularly the fifty-two articulations of the vertebral column, by using processes of the vertebrae as levers to rack the vertebra into position" (quoted in Gallaher, *post*, p. 34). Later in practice and in teaching, the offending nerve impingements were confined to the intervertebral foramina and the resultant effects charged to impairment of function in the corresponding segments of the spinal cord. The name chiropractic was suggested for the new science by the Rev. Samuel H. Weed of Bloomington, Ill., an early patient. The name (Greek *cheir,* hand, and *praktikos,* efficient) was freely translated by Palmer as "done by hand."

In 1898 he started the Palmer School of Chiro-

practic, with a three months' course. He had but fifteen students during its first five years, his son, Bartlett Joshua, being among the graduates of 1902. Leaving the school in his son's care he went in 1903 to Portland, Ore., where he opened the Portland College of Chiropractic. The venture was not successful and he soon returned to Davenport. In 1906 he was arrested for practising medicine without a license and served a sentence of six months in jail. When released he severed his connection with the school which was left to the direction of his son. He went to Oklahoma City where he participated in the establishment of the short-lived Palmer-Gregory Chiropractic College. From here he returned to Portland and became affiliated with the recently organized Pacific College of Chiropractic. Finding conditions at this school uncongenial he retired to private practice and to writing his *Textbook of the Science, Art and Philosophy of Chiropractic,* which appeared in 1910. This voluminous tome is an unrelated mixture of maxims, poetry, satire, invective, and irrelevances. With "allopathy" as his main target, he spares nobody, least of all his colleagues in chiropractic. In 1906 he had published in collaboration with his son, Bartlett Joshua, *The Science of Chiropractic,* and in 1914 there was published a posthumous volume, *The Chiropractor,* at Los Angeles, his later home. In the meantime the Davenport school had prospered under the younger Palmer. In August of 1913 there was held a widely heralded homecoming of former students. An estrangement of some years' standing existed between father and son, but to this school celebration came its founder, an uninvited guest. While acting as self-appointed leader of a street parade of students and graduates he was struck by a passing automobile and taken unconscious to a hospital. He recovered sufficiently to be moved to Los Angeles where he died about two months after the accident.

Physically Palmer was short and heavy set, with a broad round face and long flowing hair and beard. Of a contentious disposition, he was in continuous feud with his colleagues. He maintained a religious element in his conception of chiropractic healing, which was early discarded by his followers. He was thrice married, his third wife surviving him.

[Harry Gallaher, *Hist. of Chiropractic* (Guthrie, Okla., 1930); Chittenden Turner, *The Rise of Chiropractic* (Los Angeles, 1931); *Who's Who in Davenport,* 1929; *Los Angeles Times,* Oct. 21, 1913.]   J. M. P—n.

PALMER, ELIHU (Aug. 7, 1764–Apr. 7, 1806), militant deist, was the eighth child of Elihu and Lois (Foster) Palmer and a descendant of Walter Palmer who was a freeman of Charlestown, Mass., in 1634 and later settled in Stonington, Conn. Elihu was born and brought up on his father's farm at Canterbury, Conn., and graduated from Dartmouth College in 1787. In college he enjoyed a good reputation for integrity and literary proficiency and was elected to Phi Beta Kappa. He received aid from the college's charity fund and taught school during vacations.

After graduation he preached at Pittsfield, Mass., and studied divinity under Rev. John Foster, who later became a Universalist and fellow radical. A few months later, he received a call to the Presbyterian Church of Newtown, Long Island, where his tenure lasted only six months (1788–89) because of his liberalism. He removed to Philadelphia and joined the Universalists, but a proposed sermon against the divinity of Jesus was too much even for them, and Palmer found it necessary to quit the city to escape the wrath of outraged citizens. With his career as a Christian minister behind him, he studied law under the direction of a brother in western Pennsylvania, returned to Philadelphia, and was admitted to the bar in 1793. Three months later, in the plague of yellow fever, he lost his wife and was himself deprived of sight. This calamity unfitted him for the legal profession and he became a free-lance, deistic preacher. He sent his children to his father in Connecticut and removed to Atlanta, Ga.

After about a year, he moved to New York, which henceforth was the center of his activities. Here he founded a deistical society, to which he preached every Sunday evening. This society was known successively as the Philosophical Society, Theistical Society, and Society of the Columbian Illuminati. Sister organizations in Philadelphia and Baltimore, where Palmer occasionally went to preach, called themselves Theophilanthropists. He also preached in Newburgh, N. Y., where the deists had formed a "Society of Druids." The New York society, to further its activities, established a weekly paper, *The Temple of Reason,* under the editorship of Dennis Driscol, a recent immigrant from Ireland and an ex-priest. After only three months, Feb. 7, 1801, this paper was suspended in New York, but was resumed in Philadelphia the following April. Though experiencing some financial difficulties it survived there for nearly two years. In December 1803 Palmer began publishing in New York *The Prospect: or, View of the Moral World.* He was assisted in this undertaking by his second wife, Mary Powell, a widow, whom he had married in 1803. The *Prospect* appeared weekly until March 1805.

Palmer was a political as well as a religious liberal. More dominated by the ideas of the French revolutionists than by his New England background and directly influenced by Paine, Volney, Barlow, Condorcet, and Godwin, whom he regarded as "among the greatest benefactors of the human race," he saw in the American Revolution the beginning of genuine republicanism and a universal age of reason. In the struggle between the Federalists and Republicans, he was an eloquent and ardent opponent of "tyranny." His religious rationalism, however, was quite out of harmony with the trend of the times. He declared that the Bible offered no internal evidence of divine authority, and that any religious system requiring miracles to establish it was neither reasonable nor true. Organized religion was the product of "ambitious, designing, and fanatic men" who had succeeded in taking advantage of human ignorance. Moses, Mahomet, and Jesus "were all of them impostors; two of them notorious murderers in practice, and the other a murderer in principle." These three together, Palmer believed, had perhaps "cost the human race more blood, and produced more substantial misery, than all the other fanatics of the world." With respect for neither the founders of religious systems nor for the Bible, which he characterized as "a book, whose indecency and immorality shock all common sense and common honesty," Palmer preached the religion of unperverted Nature and rational education. "Man has created moral evil and man must destroy it." The American Revolution and the republican movement had accomplished political emancipation. Education and reason were now to bring about freedom from degrading religious superstitions.

The most complete statement of his thought is his *Principles of Nature; or, a Developement of the Moral Causes of Happiness and Misery among the Human Species* (1802), which was the textbook of his deistical societies. An anonymous pamphlet, *The Examiners Examined: being a Defence of the Age of Reason* (1794), is attributed to him. He was a contributor to *The Temple of Reason* and the *Prospect.* One of his best orations was *An Enquiry Relative to the Moral & Political Improvement of the Human Species* (1797).

Boundlessly optimistic, an eloquent speaker with a deep and sonorous voice, honest in the expression of his beliefs to the point of utter tactlessness and disregard for his financial wellbeing, the blind Palmer was both a heroic and a tragic figure. His main contribution to freethought was the organization of deistical societies with constitutions, ritual, secret meetings, public addresses, and newspapers. His efforts to build a Temple of Nature where deist services could be held, scientific lectures given, children taught, and astronomical observations made, were unsuccessful. At forty-one he had grown old, weary, and tired of opposing himself "constantly to the current of public opinion." When he died of pleurisy in Philadelphia, it was as the champion of a cause which had brought him only poverty and opposition.

[M. D. Conway, *The Life of Thomas Paine* (1892), vol. II; C. F. Emerson, *Gen. Cat. of Dartmouth Coll.* (1910–11); *Posthumous Pieces . . . To Which Are Prefixed a Memoir of Mr. Palmer by His Friend Mr. John Fellows, and Mr. Palmer's Principles of the Deistical Soc. of the State of N. Y.* (1824); J. W. Francis, *Old New York* (1866); *The Autobiog. and Ministerial Life of the Rev. John Johnston, D.D.* (1856), ed. by James Carnahan; E. W. Leavitt, *Palmer Groups* (1901–05); James Riker, *The Annals of Newtown* (1852); John Wood, *A Full Exposition of the Clintonian Faction, and the Soc. of the Columbian Illuminati* (1802); G. Adolf Koch, *Republican Religion: The American Revolution and the Cult of Reason* (1933).]

G. A. K.

PALMER, ERASTUS DOW (Apr. 2, 1817–Mar. 9, 1904), sculptor, son of Erastus Dow and Laurinda (Ball) Palmer, was born in humble circumstances at Pompey, a rural village nine miles from Syracuse, N. Y. He had only six months of schooling, but from childhood, he had a sound body, a clear mind, a delight in beauty, and a skill of hand in expressing form. His first business was carpentry. It is recorded that at the age of nine he constructed a little sawmill, which became the marvel of the townfolk, and that at twelve he was an expert in making window sashes. At seventeen, with two other boys, he set forth on foot to seek his fortune in the western part of the state. Of the three he alone reached Dunkirk, on Lake Erie, where for six years he earned good wages. He next moved eastward to Amsterdam, N. Y., where again he found plenty to do, not only in simple carpentry, but also in wood-carving and cabinet making. After his marriage to Mary Jane Seaman, daughter of a farmer in the neighborhood, he went to Utica, and there built his house. Having seen and admired certain shell cameos, he attempted a cameo portrait of his wife. Though he knew nothing of the technique of the craft, and indeed was obliged to devise the necessary tools, his result was excellent. It met the approval of a connoisseur, who gave an order for his own portrait, and before long Palmer turned from carpentry to cameo-cutting as a means of livelihood. His precise eye and delicate skill of hand found such favor that within two years he had carved two hundred cameos, some of them "perfect gems," according to Tuckerman (*post*, p. 363). When the delicate work proved a strain

on his eyes, at the suggestion of his patron he began to express his ideas in the ampler medium of clay. His first effort, the "Infant Ceres," modeled from one of his children, was successful. When carved in marble, the bust attracted attention at the 1850 exhibition of the National Academy of Design, and Palmer was taken into the Academy as an honorary member.

In 1846 he had moved to Albany where his career as a sculptor, already auspiciously begun, was to continue for a quarter-century. Pleasing bas-reliefs of winged heads called "Morning Star" and "Evening Star" were followed by the "Spirit's Flight," "Mercy," and "Faith." The original of "Faith," a large relief modeled in 1852, for St. Peter's Church, Albany, represents a draped female figure, standing with clasped hands before a cross. Photographs of this gentle composition had a wide popularity in American homes. It was not a masterly work, but its sweetness and simplicity appealed to the public. "Few photographic copies of any work of sculpture have had so large a sale" (Tuckerman, *post*, p. 361). Palmer continued to occupy himself with reliefs and with ideal busts such as the "Infant Flora" and the "June," the womanly "Resignation," and the maidenly "Spring." It was not until 1856 that he produced the "Indian Girl," now owned by the Metropolitan Museum. It was his first full-length marble statue and represented an Indian maid meditating upon a little cross found in the forest. Thus he was about thirty-nine years of age before he found the opportunity to model carefully a nude figure. The wonder is that his eye and hand served him so well. Powers' "Greek Slave," at that time a familiar figure in sculpture, was produced in Florence, in an atmosphere of artistic tradition, while Palmer's "Indian Girl" of 1856 and his more beautiful "White Captive" of 1858 sprang up in virgin soil, not far from the edge of the wilderness.

The "White Captive," now in the Metropolitan Museum of New York, surrounded by sculptures of far greater sophistication, remains his finest work. It tells a story of the American Indian wars, just as the "Greek Slave" tells a story of European strife. It is a simple standing nude figure of a young white girl, awaiting her fate from her savage captors. "Nothing so fine," wrote Lorado Taft, "had come over the seas from Italy; nothing so original, so dramatic, so human; nothing that could approach it, even in charm of workmanship" (*post*, p. 137). In 1864, the critic Jarves had expressed a contrary opinion. To him it suggested "meat and immodesty" (*post*, p. 280). In 1857, Palmer, like other sculptors of his time, hoped that he might design a relief for the empty triangle in the gable of the House wing of the Capitol. Taking as his theme the landing of the Pilgrims, he composed an elaborate small-scale model for a large composition which he hoped would match and perhaps excel Crawford's "Past and Future of the Republic," sculptured over the Senate wing. Utterly untrained though he was in such work, his efforts were encouraged by influential citizens, and he believed that the commission was to be his. It was perhaps fortunate that his design was rejected. The government paid him for his model but did not award the commission.

Palmer was an individualist and firmly believed that beauty in art could be captured in his native state of New York as well as in Italy. His Albany studio, sixteen feet by eight feet, with its north light was said to be one of the best in the country. From that studio came a series of portrait busts in which Palmer's genius found triumphant expression, probably beyond anything that might have been attained in his pediment group. A bust of Alexander Hamilton was of necessity studied from various sources—Ceracchi, Trumbull, Stuart, Robertson, Sharpless—but most of the series were made from life. Among his notable sitters were Washington Irving, Moses Taylor, Erastus Corning, Governor Morgan, Dr. James H. Armsby, and Henry Burden. By a sympathetic searching of American traits revealed with the skill of a hand disciplined from his childhood, the sculptor imparted a new vitality to portraiture in this field. Tuckerman devotes an eloquent paragraph to "marvels of plastic skill" such as the portrait of Mrs. McCormick; Taft states that "it is difficult to conceive a finer bust" than that of Henry Burden.

In 1862, moved by the sacrifices of the Civil War, Palmer created his "Peace in Bondage," a three-quarters' length winged female figure in marble, the nude torso, the head, the wings and the fragment of drapery being carved with a charm rare at that time. Three years later came the majestic seated "Angel of the Sepulchre," an Albany Cemetery monument—a draped male figure definitely prefiguring the noble quality to be attained in such work a generation later by Saint-Gaudens, who, like Palmer, had begun his career in art as a cameo-cutter. It was not until 1873 that Palmer went abroad. At the mature age of fifty-four, well prepared by his own experience as a creative artist, he visited European cities and enjoyed their treasures of art. For a few months he took a studio in Paris, there to work on his studies for his bronze statue of Chancellor Robert R. Livingston. This statue, ordered by

the state of New York, was placed in the national Capitol in 1874. "In matter of interpretation, of charm, and of artistic integrity, nothing finer had been done up to this time by an American sculptor," wrote Lorado Taft (*post,* p. 140). It was Palmer's last important work, but it shows no decline in his powers. The folds of the academic gown are skilfully disposed, and the hands beautifully modeled. A replica, shown at the Centennial of 1876, won a medal of the first class. Also among his works are "Pleasures of Memory," "Emigrant Children," "Sleeping Peri," and "Ambush Chief." He continued to create fine portrait busts, and in his Albany studio Jonathan Scott Hartley and Launt Thompson laid the foundations of their careers.

Despite his lack of early schooling, Palmer was by no means an uneducated man. He learned much by systematic reading, as well as through intercourse with persons of culture who were attracted to him by his goodness and charm. In 1873 Union College conferred upon him the honorary degree of A.M. He is rightly accounted a pioneer, because in such works as the "White Captive," he was the first to endow American sculpture with that greatly needed liberating gift, lyric charm. He died in Albany, where, in the Albany Historical and Art Society, there is a collection of his models in plaster. A son, Walter Launt Palmer [*q.v.*], born in Albany in 1854, gained recognition as a painter of winter landscapes.

[Lorado Taft, *The Hist. of Am. Sculpture* (1904 and later editions) ; C. R. Post, *A Hist. of European and Am. Sculpture* (1921), vol. II ; C. E. Fairman, *Art and Artists of the Capitol* (1927) ; H. T. Tuckerman, *Book of the Artists* (1867) ; W. J. Clark, *Great Am. Sculptures* (1878) ; J. J. Jarves, *The Art Idea* (1864) ; *Art Jour.* (London), Oct. 1, 1871 ; *Albany Evening Jour.* and *N. Y. Times,* Mar. 10, 1904.]   A. A.

PALMER, GEORGE HERBERT (Mar. 19, 1842–May 7, 1933), philosopher, teacher, man of letters, was born in Boston, Mass. His father, Julius Auboyneau Palmer, a merchant of modest means, came of an English family which settled at Little Compton, R. I., in 1636. His mother, Lucy Manning Peabody, was descended from John Peabody, who became a freeman of Boxford, Mass., in 1674; his farm became George Herbert Palmer's summer home. The boy, named for the English poet, was physically feeble, hardly expected to live through infancy. To a long struggle with ill health, which affected all his student years, he attributed his longevity, since it compelled him to learn and observe the regimen under which alone he could maintain his working power.

In spite of frequently interrupted schooling, he

entered Phillips Andover Academy at twelve, spending two years there, and after an interval of travel and of experiment in the wholesale dry goods trade, entered Harvard in 1860, graduating in regular course in 1864. He offered a commencement part on Mill's Utilitarianism—Mill having captured his early enthusiasm as none of the regular teachers in the Harvard of his day had been able to do. Graduate study in philosophy was not available in America at that time, except in schools of theology. Palmer accordingly, after a year of teaching at the Salem High School, entered Andover Theological Seminary in 1865. In 1867, he left Andover to go abroad, spent in Germany fragments of two years, visited France and Italy, and returned to Andover to receive the degree of B.D. in 1870. Later, during a series of summers (in 1878 and following years), he pursued studies in Hegel under the personal guidance of Edward Caird, whom he sought out in Glasgow.

Though as a young man Palmer was painfully shy and hesitant both in speech and in writing, there was in him a personal force which made its impression on observant men. In 1870 President Charles William Eliot [q.v.], then in the second year of his administration, offered him a tutorship in Greek. Entering thus upon his service of forty-three years in Harvard, Palmer at once showed his power as a teacher by inaugurating a series of voluntary readings in the Odyssey, out of which came his remarkable English version, *The Odyssey of Homer,* published in 1884.

In 1872 an opening appeared in philosophy, as instructor and assistant to Prof. Francis Bowen [q.v.]; after one year in this post Palmer was made assistant professor of philosophy; he became full professor in 1883. Though at first he offered introductory courses, and indeed continued throughout his career to teach the introductory history of philosophy to fascinated groups of students, his interest turned decisively toward the theory of ethics: in 1889, "Philosophy 4" became the staple course in that subject, and with it his name as a teacher was peculiarly associated until his retirement in 1913. From 1889, he held the Alford Professorship of "natural religion, moral philosophy and civil polity." Becoming professor emeritus in 1913, Palmer relinquished this chair to Josiah Royce [q.v.]; but he served the University as overseer until 1919, and continued to reside within the Harvard Yard until his death at the advanced age of ninety-one.

Palmer was inclined to disown for himself originality in philosophical thought; he considered himself a critic and expositor rather than a creator of new concepts. There was however a

depth and vigor in his thought to which this estimate does less than justice. While he prized true judgment above novelty, there was an element of genuine creation both in his masterly interpretations of the history of thought, and in his systematic expositions of ethical theory. The clarity for which he incessantly labored, his luminous and fluent prose, gave both hearer and reader an illusion of ease and simplicity which concealed not alone the effort, but also the force of the thinker. In Harvard he was the first to break away from textbook and recitation in philosophy and to work out his own system of ideas in lectures.

He belonged by inheritance to the Puritan tradition, and by training to the line of idealism, but he was a keen critic of Puritanism, its "extreme individualism and lack of a community sense," and he was equally dissatisfied with Hegel, on the ground that Hegel had a defective sense of the meaning of moral contrasts, and submerged the individual in the institution. The Puritan in him corrected the defects of Hegel; and the collectivist in him corrected the Puritan. The ethics of self-realization, characteristic of the English idealism of his day, he could not accept unless it were understood that the self in question is not the solitary or "abstract self," but the "conjunct self," the self as related to and tied in with others, through personal and institutional ties. Without these institutions, individual life is thin, unsatisfactory, ineffective. "Ally your labor with an institution" was his precept and his example. But within the institution, individual conscience must remain alert, correcting the institution and keeping it from the rigidity of death. The most perfect pre-arranged casuistry he considered inadequate to personal moral experience, which is infinite and changing; hence he took the Protestant rather than the Catholic view of authority, and aligned himself with Kant rather than with Hegel in his view of duty. Duty, he was accustomed to say, "is the call of the whole to the part," and duty has its one absolute law, a rule which is so final as to admit no deviation and yet so transparent in its texture as to admit every pulse of moral individuality: it is simply "the law that there shall be law," that conduct shall never be capricious.

The content of his course on ethics was never completely published. Parts of it have appeared in *The Field of Ethics* (1901), *The Nature of Goodness* (1903), *The Problem of Freedom* (1911), *Altruism; Its Nature and Varieties* (1919). These works preserve much of the lucidity and compactness of Palmer's lectures. His most memorable and effective works, however, were those in which his philosophic thought gave itself to the interpretation of personality and art. In his own estimate, three of his books are likely to live a half century: *The Odyssey* (1884 and following), *The English Works of George Herbert* (3 vols., 1905), *The Life of Alice Freeman Palmer* (1908). These he calls his "books of affection and gratitude"; in them his powers of characterization reach their height. With them should be associated a series of contributions to letters: *The Antigone of Sophocles* (1899); *Intimations of Immortality in the Sonnets of Shakspere* (1912); introduction to T. C. Williams' translation, *The Georgics and Eclogues of Virgil* (1915); *Formative Types in English Poetry* (1918).

Palmer's greatness as a teacher was due in no small degree to the artist in him, which compelled him to orderliness of thought and presentation, and made shoddy, unclear expression repugnant to him. His speech abounded in expressions so perfect that "they continued to glow in the dark of the mind." But it was due as well to a discerning and persistent interest in persons. This interest was not indiscriminate: the friendship he offered was never genial, easy, intimate, profuse, but, with warm and enduring affection, held its own dignity and reserve. Few have been so gifted in the capacity for reaching objective estimates of personal ability. It was a part of his rigorous self-discipline to maintain an element of realism in these judgments, and in view of his belief that the imperfect has its own peculiar glories (*The Glory of the Imperfect*, 1891) he had no disposition to ignore the defects and paradoxes of the character with which he dealt. As a result, he was widely sought as a counselor in the placing of men, and left an indelible impress on the personnel of his department at Harvard, which included James, Royce, Münsterberg, and Santayana. This department was in no small measure of Palmer's building. Though he was not a lover of debate, he appreciated diversities of judgment, both in the composition of the department and in the minds of his own students.

Toward himself his judgment was equally objective and rigorous: that he knew and respected his limitations is in no small degree a secret of his success. He had early discovered the principle that limitation is a necessary element in achievement—a principle allied in his mind with the doctrine of the Incarnation—and he studied each defect as a possible source of power. Deficient in physical energy, he husbanded it and spent it with the maximum of effect. He was short in stature, quiet in manner and movement, but his voice was firm, capable of wide dramatic

range, and his person impressive; bushy brows over deep-set eyes lent a suggestion of concentrated will, which seemed perpetually on duty. His simplicity of living, aided by a shrewd practical sense, made it possible for him to accumulate largely and to give generously. He gave to Wellesley College a remarkable collection of first editions of English classics; and in 1930 he added to this gift 900 letters of Robert and Elizabeth Browning. To Harvard he gave a library of the philosophical classics and a collection of editions and papers of George Herbert. Where he felt an obligation of honor or gratitude he interpreted it in a large way, as in his monumental edition of Herbert's writings. Externally his life was decorous, dominated by a passion for order, but although order versus oddity meant for him frequently a lack of interest in novelties of discussion, inwardly he inhabited a wide place; his touch with the classics lent steadiness to his outlook, his judgment was rapid, contemporary, pertinent, wise.

Palmer was twice married: first, June 15, 1871, to Ellen Margaret Wellman of Brookline, a Swedenborgian, somewhat his senior, a woman of marked social and intellectual gifts. The eight years of their marriage, until her death in 1879, did much to facilitate his intercourse with his students: to her he dedicated his *Odyssey*. Some eight years after her death, Dec. 23, 1887, he married Alice Freeman, then president of Wellesley [see Alice Freeman Palmer]. Both marriages were childless. He was widely honored as a scholar, receiving numerous honorary doctorates. In addition to the writings previously mentioned he published *The New Education* (1885), *Self-cultivation in English* (1897), *A Study of Self-Sacrifice* (1902), *The Teacher: Essays and Addresses by George Herbert Palmer and Alice Freeman Palmer* (1908), *Ethical and Moral Instruction in Schools* (1909), *The Ideal Teacher* (1910), *A Herbert Bibliography* (privately printed, 1911), *Trades and Professions* (1914), *The Lord's Prayer* (1920). It was fitting that the last of his published works should be a notable achievement in self-portrayal, *The Autobiography of a Philosopher* (1930), which remains the chief original source for his life.

[In addition to *The Autobiog. of a Philosopher*, published also as the "Introduction" to G. P. Adams and W. P. Montague, *Contemporary Am. Philosophy* (1930), vol. I, see S. E. Morison, *The Development of Harvard University Since the Inauguration of President Eliot* (1930), ch. i, "Philosophy, 1870–1929," by George Herbert Palmer and Ralph Barton Perry; Benjamin Rand, "Philosophical Instruction in Harvard University from 1636 to 1906," no. III, *Harvard Graduates' Magazine*, Mar. 1929; Josiah Royce, "In Honor of Professor Palmer," *Ibid.*, June 1911; R. C. Cabot, "George Herbert Palmer," *Boston Transcript*, Jan. 25, 1913; minute on the Faculty Records of Harvard College, meeting of Oct. 3, 1933; W. E. Hocking, "Professor Palmer, Teacher," *Harvard Crimson*, May 10, 1933; *Boston Transcript*, May 8, 1933; *N. Y. Times*, May 8, 1933.]

W. E. H.

PALMER, HENRY WILBUR (July 10, 1839–Feb. 15, 1913), congressman and lawyer, was born in Clifford, Susquehanna County, Pa., the eldest son of Gideon W. and Elizabeth (Burdick) Palmer, both of New England ancestry. His father was a teacher, farmer, and a member of the constitutional convention of 1872–73. The boy received his education in the Wyoming Seminary at Kingston, Pa., the Fort Edward Collegiate Institute at Fort Edward, N. Y., and the law school at Poughkeepsie, N. Y. He was admitted to the bar at Peekskill in 1860 but shortly afterward left that place to enter the office of Garrick M. Harding at Wilkes-Barre, Pa., where he was admitted to the bar in August 1861. A few days later, on Sept. 12, he was married to Ellen M. Webster of Plattsburg, N. Y., who bore him eight children, and who became noted for her social welfare work among the boys of the coal region. He served under his father as a deputy paymaster in the Union army in 1862 and 1863, but he did not see actual military service. Returning to Wilkes-Barre, he entered a lucrative law practice and became interested in politics. In 1872 he stood for an uncontested seat in the constitutional convention, where he became prominent in the debates as a champion of woman's suffrage, prohibition, and the right of railroads to own and operate coal mines, although he declared himself opposed to the extension of corporate power.

In 1878 in the Republican state convention, he nominated his townsman, Henry M. Hoyt [q.v.], for governor. He stumped the state for Hoyt and was appointed attorney-general when Hoyt was elected. Both Hoyt and Palmer became unpopular with the party leaders before the term was over. Palmer conducted his office with independence, bringing suits for taxes against large corporations and against the common carriers for granting rebates to shippers. He antagonized the legislature by declaring unconstitutional a law granting members an increase in salary. In 1883 he resumed the practice of law at Wilkes-Barre and became counsel for a number of large coal and railroad companies. He amassed a considerable fortune and became a capitalist in his own right; his ardor against the extension of corporate power was noticeably lessened thereafter. In 1889 he was selected by the state Prohibition convention to conduct the campaign for an amendment to the state constitution prohibiting intoxicating liquors. In 1898 he endeavored

to gain the nomination for Congress in order to help save the country from "crazy socialists, populists, and silverites" (*Fifty Years, post*, p. 357). Refusing to engage in the usual convention methods, he failed to get the nomination. In 1900, under a new primary system, he was nominated and elected, and he was reëlected in 1902 and in 1904. In 1909 he again entered Congress for a term. During his incumbency he spoke against trusts but did not join conspicuously in the Rooseveltian attacks. As a trial lawyer he had few superiors. He had a gift for genuine eloquence, which was, however, often marred by bitter invective and harsh personalities. Many of his political doggerels, pungent with acrid partisanship and personalities, are still repeated in the locality. Of commanding presence, imperturbable, and somewhat cold, he was at once a thorough individualist, a Puritan reformer, and a devoted follower of the Republican party as the guardian of the established order. A week before he died, he finished his autobiography, *Fifty Years at the Bar and in Politics* (1913), which is in many ways a candid and often blunt memoir.

[Autobiography, *ante*; G. B. Kulp, *Families of the Wyoming Valley*, vol. I (1885); *Wilkes-Barre Record*, Feb. 16, 1913.]

J. P. B.

PALMER, HORATIO RICHMOND (Apr. 26, 1834–Nov. 15, 1907), composer, director of music, author, was born in Sherburne, N. Y., and died in Yonkers. He was the son of Anson B. Palmer and Abbey Maria Knapp. His mother died before he was three years old and he was thrown upon his own resources at an early age. At seven he was singing alto in the church choir which his father led. He was educated at Rushford (N. Y.) Academy, where after his graduation he taught for two years, and then became the director of music there. In 1855 he was married at Rushford to Lucia A. Chapman, a native of Dryden, N. Y., and a daughter of Rockwell M. and Susan Chapman. His wife was an artist, in 1900 a prize winner at the Paris Exposition. She spent three years in travel and study in Europe, putting the results of her observations into two books, *Grecian Days* (1896) and *Oriental Days* (1897).

While in Rushford Palmer directed the choir and organized a cornet band. His first singing school in a neighboring town was so successful that requests came to him from many places to teach singing classes. He then removed to Chicago where he became choir master in the Second Baptist Church and also published a monthly magazine, *Concordia*. He soon began to write music books for his classes and for the conventions which were popular before the days of the modern singing school. He returned to New York in 1873 and in 1881 organized the Church Choral Union. From a membership of two hundred and fifty the first season it increased to forty-two hundred the third, and continued to grow until it had enrolled some twenty thousand singers. At one of his concerts, given in Madison Square Garden, there were nearly four thousand in the choir. Like the singing schools in the country, and the conventions in the larger towns, the idea of the Choral Union became popular and Palmer was called upon to organize similar groups in Brooklyn, Buffalo, Philadelphia, and Washington. A little later the establishment of the Chautauqua Movement offered an opportunity to develop the idea of a few weeks of intensive training in music, and in 1877 the Summer School of Music at Chautauqua was founded, and Palmer served as its dean for fourteen years. For seventeen successive years he conducted a musical festival at Courtland, N. Y., and for eleven years he was choir master of the Broome Street tabernacle in New York City.

Palmer's contributions to church music were extensive. Perhaps his most popular tunes were those written for "Just for today" and "Yield not to Temptation." The latter, for which he wrote both the words and the music, appeared in *The Song King* (1872) under the title "Looking to Jesus." "Just for today," copyrighted 1887, appeared in his *Book of Gems for the Sunday School* (1887) under the name *Oraz*. While he was on one of his visits to Palestine he wrote both words and music of "Galilee, blue Galilee." His "Master, the tempest is raging," is also reminiscent of the Holy Land. He was awarded the degree of Doctor of Music by the University of Chicago in 1880, and by Alfred University in 1881. He gave frequent lectures on astronomy, talks on his visits to the Holy Land and the Orient, and after he had become converted to the Baconian origin of the works of Shakespeare, he prepared a lecture setting forth his views. His writings include *The Song Queen* (1867); *The Elements of Musical Composition* (1867); *Palmer's Sabbath School Songs* (1868); *Palmer's Theory of Music* (1876); *Palmer's Music Catechism* (1881); *Palmer's Piano Primer* (1885); *Palmer's Class Method of Teaching the Rudiments of Music* (1892); *Choral Union* (1884); *Life-Time Hymns* (1896); *Palmer's Book of Classical Choruses* (1898); and *The Song Herald* (1904).

[*Who's Who in America*, 1906–07; J. H. Hall, *Biog. of Gospel Song and Hymn Writers* (1914); Georgia H. Jones, article in the *Musician*, Nov. 1899; H. J. W.
Gilbert, *Rushford and Rushford People* (1910); *N. Y. Daily Tribune*, Nov. 17, 1907.]   F. J. M.

PALMER, INNIS NEWTON (Mar. 30, 1824–Sept. 9, 1900), soldier, was born at Buffalo, N. Y., the son of Innis Bromley and Susan (Candee) Palmer, and a descendant of Lieut. William Palmer who came to America on the *Fortune* in 1621. He received a common-school education and graduated from the United States Military Academy in 1846 as a brevet second lieutenant. His extended service in the Mexican War included the siege of Vera Cruz, the battles of Cerro Gordo, Contreras, Churubusco, Chapultepec, and the assault and capture of the city of Mexico. He was wounded at Chapultepec and was made a brevet captain for gallant conduct during that battle. Following the Mexican War, he served in various western posts almost without a break until the Civil War. His activities included the march to Oregon in 1849 and service in Oregon, Washington, Texas, and Indian Territory, with both the Mounted Rifles and the 2nd Cavalry. During this period he rose to be a major of cavalry (Apr. 25, 1861). In 1853 he married Catharine Jones, daughter of Col. Llewellyn Jones, of the United States Army, and by this marriage there were three daughters and a son.

In the first few months of the Civil War he served in the defenses of Washington, and as the Confederate armies approached the city in June he was placed in command of the Regular cavalry in the Manassas campaign. He was made a brevet lieutenant-colonel for gallantry at the battle of Bull Run, and was promoted to brigadier-general of volunteers on Sept. 23, 1861. He remained on duty in the defenses of Washington until March 1862, when he was given command of a brigade in the IV Corps, Army of the Potomac, and participated in the Virginia Peninsular campaign, taking part in the siege of Yorktown and the battles of Williamsburg, Fair Oaks, Glendale, and Malvern Hill. In the fall of 1862 he organized New Jersey and Delaware volunteers and superintended camps of drafted men at Philadelphia. The remainder of his war service was in North Carolina, where he served from December 1862 until July 1865. In this period he held various department and district commands, and a portion of the time commanded a division in the XVIII Corps. On Mar. 13, 1865, he was made brevet colonel, 2nd Cavalry, and major-general of volunteers, the latter for long and meritorious service. The following January he was mustered out of the volunteer service and as brevet colonel took command of the 2nd Cavalry, which he had joined in 1855 as a captain.

After the war, promotion was very slow, and he did not become a full colonel until June 1868. For the most part the remainder of his service was in command of the 2nd Cavalry in the expanding West. He performed important duties, frequently commanding important frontier posts as well as his regiment. On Mar. 20, 1879, he retired as a colonel, after more than thirty years' service. He died at Chevy Chase, Md.

[*Army and Navy Jour.*, Sept. 15, 1900; *Army and Navy Reg.*, Sept. 15, 1900; G. W. Cullum, *Biog. Reg. Officers and Grads. U. S. Mil. Acad.* (3rd ed., 1891); *Evening Star* (Washington, D. C.), Sept. 10, 1900; information as to certain facts from a son-in-law, Maj.-Gen. Eben Swift.]   D. Y.

PALMER, JAMES CROXALL (June 29, 1811–Apr. 24, 1883), naval surgeon, was born in Baltimore, Md., one of four sons of Edward Palmer, Baltimore merchant and commissioner of insolvency, and Catherine (Croxall) Palmer. He was a grandson of John and Mary (Preston) Palmer and James and Eleanor (Gittings) Croxall, all of Maryland, and a descendant of Edward Palmer, an Oxford scholar and relative of Sir Thomas Overbury, who secured a grant of Palmer's Island at the mouth of the Susquehanna in 1622 and projected there a college and school of arts. James Croxall Palmer graduated from Dickinson College in 1829 and was able to complete the medical course at the University of Maryland in 1833, although he received his diploma with the class of 1834. In March of the latter year he was commissioned assistant surgeon in the navy, standing first among the candidates then appointed.

His initial service was in the *Brandywine* of the Pacific Squadron and then in the *Vincennes* on a cruise around the world. After duty at the Baltimore naval rendezvous, he was in the Wilkes exploring expedition, 1838–42, first in the storeship *Relief* and later in the *Peacock*, being in the wreck of the latter at the mouth of the Columbia River, and subsequently in charge of the shore party at Astoria. The product of this cruise was a small volume of poems, *Thulia: a Tale of the Antarctic* (1843), republished in 1868 as *Antarctic Mariner's Song*, descriptive of the author's experiences in the south polar seas. In 1842 he was promoted to surgeon, and was in charge of the hospital at the Washington Navy Yard when the wounded from the *Princeton* explosion were brought there. He was in the *St. Mary's* in the Gulf during the Mexican War; in the *Vandalia* of the Pacific Squadron, 1850–53; and after service in the receiving ship *Baltimore*, in the steam frigate *Niagara*, 1857, when she was employed in laying the first Atlantic cable. After two years on the Mediterranean

in the *Macedonian*, he was in charge of the medical service of the Naval Academy, then located at Newport, R. I., during the first two years of the Civil War; and from 1863 to 1865 he was fleet surgeon of the West Gulf Blockading Squadron under Farragut. In the battle of Mobile Bay, after the passing of the forts, Palmer, who was using the admiral's launch *Loyall* to visit the wounded in the fleet, was requested to carry orders to the scattered monitors to attack the *Tennessee*, and executed this hazardous duty, in Farragut's words, "with cheerfulness and alacrity" (Loyall Farragut, *The Life of David Glasgow Farragut*, 1879, p. 425). After the battle he went aboard the surrendered *Tennessee*, where he was chiefly instrumental in saving Admiral Franklin Buchanan [*q.v.*] from the amputation of a shattered leg. Through Palmer's efforts at this time an agreement was reached by which naval surgeons were not to be treated as prisoners of war.

He was in charge of the naval hospital at Brooklyn, 1866–69; was promoted to medical director Mar. 3, 1871; and was surgeon general of the navy from June 1872 until his retirement in June 1873. His death, from a complication of malaria and other diseases contracted during the Civil War, occurred ten years later at Washington, D. C. He was survived by his wife, Juliet Gittings, daughter of James Gittings of Long Green, Baltimore County, Md., whom he married May 22, 1837, and by two children. His contemporaries regarded him as an attractive and scholarly man, of notable gifts as a writer, skilled in his profession, and faithful to every obligation during nearly fifty years in the naval service. John Williamson Palmer [*q.v.*], the author, was his brother.

[Charles Wilkes, *Narrative of the U. S. Exploring Expedition, during the Years 1838 . . . . 1842* (5 vols., 1845); L. R. Hamersly, *The Records of Living Officers of the U. S. Navy and Marine Corps* (3rd ed., 1878); *War of the Rebellion: Official Records (Navy)*; W. B. Atkinson, *The Physicians and Surgeons of the U. S.* (1878); *Sun* (Baltimore), Apr. 25, 1883; *Army and Navy Jour.*, Apr. 28, 1883; information from family sources].   A. W.

PALMER, JAMES SHEDDEN (Oct. 13, 1810–Dec. 7, 1867), naval officer, was born in New Jersey, and was the naval officer of highest rank from that state in the Civil War. After becoming a midshipman on Jan. 1, 1825, he served as a lieutenant on the *Columbia* in 1838 during her cruise around the world, and took part in the attack on Quallah Battoo, Sumatra, in retaliation for outrages on American traders. In the Mexican War he commanded the schooner *Flirt* and was engaged in blockade duty. At the outbreak of the Civil War he was in the Mediterranean in command of the steamship *Iroquois* but was soon ordered to the blockade of Savannah. In September his ship was sent to the West Indies to capture the *Sumter,* which under Semmes had escaped from New Orleans and was seizing Union merchantmen.

Palmer found the *Sumter* in the harbor of St. Pierre, Martinique, and blockaded her, but was unable to prevent her escape one moonless night, for the harbor entrance was some fifteen miles wide and had two openings. As a result of the disappointment of the North, Palmer was deprived of his command, though later a court of inquiry exonerated him. By the time he was restored to the command of the *Iroquois,* in May 1862, Farragut had already captured New Orleans. He sent Palmer, however, to take possession of Baton Rouge and Natchez. Palmer also led the Union fleet in the first passage by Vicksburg, and secured the respect of Farragut by remaining under the fire of the batteries to relieve what he thought was a dangerous concentration of fire on the *Hartford.* Farragut, not understanding the move, shouted through his trumpet, "Captain Palmer, what do you mean by disobeying my orders?" An explanation was given and Farragut never forgot the gallant act. Later he made Palmer commander of the *Hartford* and the latter piloted it past Port Hudson when the *Mississippi* grounded and had to be burned. According to Loyall Farragut (*post*),. Palmer was brave and cool under fire, and was accustomed to go into battle dressed with scrupulous neatness and buttoning on his kid gloves as if he were entering a ballroom. Palmer succeeded Farragut in command of the Union forces on the Mississippi and so missed taking part in the battle of Mobile Bay. Even in command of the West Gulf Squadron, where he also followed Farragut in the fall of 1864, he had his usual bad luck, for before the attack on Mobile City could take place he was superseded by Henry K. Thatcher [*q.v.*]. The latter, however, gave official credit to Palmer for the efficiency of the naval forces, and Palmer himself was in command of the ironclads.

In December 1865, Palmer was assigned the command of the West India Squadron in the *Susquehanna,* and was present at St. Thomas, Virgin Islands, when it was devastated by an earthquake and tidal wave. Probably as a result of his exertions for the stricken inhabitants, he contracted yellow fever and died within a few days. His remains were brought to New York, which he had considered his home, and funeral services were held at the navy yard on Dec. 21, 1867. His promotion to rear admiral had come

on July 25, 1866. He died unmarried; his brother, William R. Palmer, who had risen from a lieutenancy in the topographical engineers to a brevet colonelcy, died in 1862. According to Loyall Farragut, Palmer, in spite of a reserve of manner and a dignified bearing which amounted almost to pomposity, possessed a warm and generous nature.

[The only authority for the month and day of birth is a notation in a Navy Register of 1863 in the office of the Bureau of Navigation. Sources include: *Army and Navy Jour.,* Dec. 21, 28, 1867; J. S. Henshaw, *Around the World: A Narrative of a Voyage in the East India Squadron* (1840); *Official Records of the Union and Confederate Navies,* 1 ser. I (1894); Raphael Semmes, *Memoirs of Service Afloat During the War Between the States* (1869); Loyall Farragut, *The Life of David Glasgow Farragut* (1879), pp. 293, 324, 364; *New-Eng. Hist. and Geneal. Reg.,* Oct. 1868; J. T. Headley, *Farragut and Our Naval Commanders* (1867); *N. Y. Times,* Dec. 22, 1867.]   W. B. N.

PALMER, JOEL (Oct. 4, 1810–June 9, 1881), pioneer and author, was born in Ontario, Canada, the son of Quaker parents, Ephraim and Hannah (Phelps) Palmer, who had moved across the line from the state of New York. He was a descendant of Walter Palmer who in 1630 emigrated from Nottingham, England, to Plymouth colony and died in Stonington, Conn., then in the province of Massachusetts Bay. Through his mother he was a descendant of William Phelps, one of the founders of Windsor, Conn. Taken back to New York state with his family at the outbreak of the War of 1812, he lived in Lewis and Jefferson counties until he was about sixteen. Then he went to Bucks County, Pa., where he worked on canals and other public works and where he was married, first in 1830 to Catherine Caffee and second, after her death, to Sarah Ann Derbyshire on Jan. 21, 1836. That year he removed to Indiana, where he was a contractor for the Whitewater canal, settled at Laurel in Franklin County, and bought land. He was a representative in the state legislature for two terms, from 1843 to 1845, and in the spring of 1845 started across the plains to Oregon. On the way he kept a day-to-day journal that was published in 1847 as *Journal of Travels over the Rocky Mountains.* With only such literary charm as inheres in the sincerity and drama of his record, the *Journal* was for a decade an important guidebook to overland immigrants for information concerning equipment for the journey and such details of the route as the location of suitable camping places, springs, and grassy oases. It remains the most complete record of pioneering along the old Oregon trail. The next year he returned to Indiana and in the spring of 1847, with his family, started on his second journey to the Pacific Northwest.

Shortly after his second arrival in Oregon, he served as commissary-general of the volunteer forces in the Cayuse War and was a member of a commission to persuade neighboring tribes not to join the Cayuse. In the autumn of 1848 he went to California. On his return to Oregon he laid out the town of Dayton on his land claim in what is now Yamhill County, built a gristmill, and settled down to improve his holdings. In 1853 he became superintendent of Indian affairs for the Oregon Territory and bent his enormous energy and personal magnetism to the difficult task of obtaining all their lands from the Indians without creating enough dissatisfaction among them to cause a war. He was a negotiator of nine of the fifteen treaties of cession made between Nov. 29, 1854, and Dec. 21, 1855, and he carried on his duties during the Yakima War led by Kamaiakin and Leschi [qq.v.]. In 1857 he was removed from office, not so much because his negotiations had not prevented an Indian uprising as because the settlers resented his restraint and his consideration for the Indians in carrying out his reservation policy. He was active in projects for the development of the community, opened one of the routes to British Columbia gold mines, was a director and, for a time, president of the Oregon City Manufacturing Company, and was one of the promoters of the Clackamas Railroad Company and of the Oregon Central Railroad Company. He was speaker of the state House of Representatives in 1862 and a member of the state Senate from 1864 to 1866. In 1870 he was defeated as the Republican candidate for governor. He died at his home in Dayton, survived by his wife and seven children.

[Information from Palmer's niece, Mrs. Felix Emanuel Schelling, Philadelphia; transcript of Palmer's manuscript narrative in the Bancroft Lib., Univ. of Cal., and other materials from his great-grand-daughter, Mrs. John G. Flynn, Caldwell, Idaho; H. W. Scott, *Hist. of the Oregon Country* (6 vols., 1924), comp. by L. M. Scott; H. H. Bancroft, *Hist. of the Pacific States*, vols. XXIV, XXV (1886–88); R. G. Thwaites, *Early Western Travels*, vol. XXX (1906); *Ore. Hist. Soc. Quart.*, Sept. 1907, Mar. 1922, Sept. 1930, Sept. 1931; *Hist. of the Willamette Valley* (1885), ed. by H. O. Lang; *Morning Oregonian* (Portland), June 10, 1881.]
K. E. C.

PALMER, JOHN McAULEY (Sept. 13, 1817–Sept. 25, 1900), governor of Illinois, senator, was born in Scott County, Ky., the son of Louis D. and Ann Hansford (Tutt) Palmer, and the great-grandson of Thomas Palmer who emigrated to Virginia from England early in the eighteenth century. His father was a farmer and a Jacksonian Democrat with decided antislavery tendencies that led him to leave Kentucky for Illinois in 1831. He settled near Al-

ton, and in 1834 the boy entered Shurtleff College at Upper Alton, Ill., where he stayed for two years, financing himself by doing odd jobs around the college and town. Then he peddled clocks and taught in a country school before moving to Carlinville in 1839, where he began reading law in the office of John S. Greathouse. In December of that year he was admitted to the bar. His political career started in 1840, when he gave ardent support to Van Buren. On Dec. 20, 1842, he was married to Malinda Ann, the daughter of James Neely of Carlinville, who died in 1885. They had ten children. In 1847 he was elected as a delegate to the Illinois constitutional convention and was later elected county judge under the new constitution. He was elected to the state Senate in 1851 and in 1854 opposed Douglas' Kansas-Nebraska Bill. When a resolution was offered to indorse the bill, he offered a substitute resolution condemning the bill and favoring the Missouri Compromise and the compromise measures of 1850. Although his resolution was rejected, he ran for state senator as an independent Democrat on a platform of opposition to the Kansas-Nebraska Bill and was elected.

He played an important part in the formation of the Republican party in Illinois, serving as president of the Bloomington convention in May 1856 and as delegate to the Republican National Convention at Philadelphia in June. In 1859 he was defeated as a Republican candidate for representative to Congress; in 1860 he was a delegate to the Republican National Convention that nominated Lincoln; and in 1861 he was a delegate to the peace convention at Washington. He began his military career in May 1861 as colonel of the 14th Illinois Infantry. He served in Missouri and at the engagements of New Madrid, Point Pleasant, and Island No. 10, and he received the rank of brigadier-general in December 1861. In 1862 he was made commander of the 1st Division in the Army of the Mississippi, fought gallantly at Stone River and Chickamauga, and was rewarded by the rank of major-general. In August 1864 he asked to be relieved of his command, owing to an altercation with General Sherman concerning his refusal to take orders from General Schofield, who, he claimed, was his junior in rank. The request was granted. Later he was given command of the Department of Kentucky but was relieved by request in 1866. The summer of 1867 found him in Springfield practising law with Milton Hay. He reëntered public life, however, in 1868, when he was elected governor of Illinois on the Republican ticket. In his inaugural address he alienated many Republicans and pleased most Democrats by taking a definite stand for state rights, deprecating the extension of power by the federal government. His administration was a difficult one. Monopolists, lobbyists, and various "rings" all sought special legislation. He did all he could to check hasty and unscrupulous legislation by the use of his veto power, but his efforts were largely unavailing. In all, some 1700 bills were passed. When the people of Chicago were left destitute by the disastrous fire of 1871, he quickly sent money and supplies. However, when Mayor Mason asked for federal troops to maintain order in the city, and Grant provided them, Palmer displayed his state-rights position by protesting that state troops could handle the situation and that the use of federal troops was unconstitutional. He was later sustained by the legislature.

In 1872, disgusted with the corruption of the Grant régime, he joined the Liberal Republicans in support of Greeley and soon thereafter rejoined the Democratic party. In 1884 he was a delegate to the National Democratic Convention that nominated Cleveland for president, and in 1888 he was defeated as Democratic candidate for governor. On Apr. 4 of that year he was married to Hannah (Lamb) Kimball, the daughter of James Lamb and the widow of L. R. Kimball. Three years later he entered the United States Senate as a Democrat. As senator he served on the committees of military affairs, pensions, and railroads. He advocated a constitutional amendment to provide for the popular election of senators and urged the repeal of the Sherman Act of 1890. In 1896 he was the presidential candidate of the National or Gold Democrats on a platform denouncing protection and the free coinage of silver. He polled only 130,-000 votes. He returned to his profession in 1897 but spent most of his time in editing *The Bench and Bar of Illinois* (2 vols., 1899) and in writing his memoirs, *Personal Recollections of John M. Palmer: The Story of an Earnest Life* (1901). He died in Springfield, Ill.

[Autobiography, *ante*; *The Biog. Encyc. of Ill.* (1875); Joseph Wallace, *Past and Present of the City of Springfield* (1904), vol. I; John Moses, *Illinois, Hist. and Statistical*, vol. II (1892); A. C. Cole, *The Era of the Civil War* (1919); E. L. Bogart, *The Industrial State* (1920); *Ill. State Register* (Springfield), Sept. 26, 1900.]   E. B.

PALMER, JOHN WILLIAMSON (Apr. 4, 1825–Feb. 26, 1906), author, son of Edward and Catherine (Croxall) Palmer, and a brother of James Croxall Palmer [*q.v.*], was born and educated in Baltimore, Md. He completed a medical course at the University of Maryland in 1846,

and sailed for California in the gold rush, reaching San Francisco, in the summer of 1849. Here he became the first city physician and in this position he wrote later, "between the day when I first entered San Francisco without a dime, and the day I left it, also without a dime, I was introduced to more of the pathos and tragedy . . . than any other person on the spot" (*The New and the Old*, pp. 31, 32). In 1850 he drifted on to Hawaii and thence to the Far East, where he served as surgeon in the small East India steamer *Phlegethon* through the Second Burmese War, 1851–52.

Returning to America, after further travel in China and India, he definitely gave up medicine, and settled in New York as a writer, contributing to *Harper's New Monthly Magazine*, *Putnam's Monthly Magazine*, and the *Atlantic Monthly*, and publishing his travel sketches in two entertaining volumes, *The Golden Dagon; or Up and Down the Irrawaddi* (1856), and *The New and the Old; or, California and India in Romantic Aspects* (1859). In 1856 he published a collection entitled *Folk Songs*. His comedy, *The Queen's Heart* (1858), was acted with some success by James E. Owens, and in 1859–60 he published translations of Jules Michelet's comedies *L'Amour* and *La Femme* and Ernest Legouvé's *Histoire Morale des Femmes*. On the staff of the *New York Times* at the opening of the Civil War, he proposed, as a Southern sympathizer, a series of letters picturing conditions in the South. His first article, from Richmond, the *Times* was unwilling to publish, but he later became a correspondent from the Southern side for the *New York Tribune*. In the latter part of the war he entered the Confederate service and was on the staff of Gen. J. C. Breckinridge [*q.v.*]. His poem "Stonewall Jackson's Way," a spirited war ballad written within sound of the firing at Antietam, attained considerable popularity.

About 1870 he resumed literary work in New York, serving for many years on the editorial staffs of the *Century* and *Standard* dictionaries and as a reviewer for the *Literary Digest*. He wrote a book on *Epidemic Cholera* (1866), edited *The Poetry of Compliment and Courtship* (1868), and prepared two books on art, *Beauties and Curiosities of Engraving* (2 vols., 1878–79) and *A Portfolio of Autograph Etchings* (1882). His only novel, *After His Kind*, appeared under the pseudonym John Coventry in 1886. In later years he showed a special interest in the social life of colonial Maryland and the old South, and published articles on this theme in the *Century Magazine*, 1893–97, and subsequently in the New

York *Home Journal*. A slender verse collection, *For Charlie's Sake, and Other Lyrics and Ballads,* appeared in 1901, notable chiefly for the martial poems "Stonewall Jackson's Way," "Ned Braddock," which he considered his best, and "The Maryland Battalion." From 1904 until his death from the infirmities of age he lived in Baltimore, loved by a wide circle of friends for his genial charm of manner and remarkable gifts of memory, and as a last though minor figure among the writers who voiced the Southern spirit in the Civil War. He was survived by his wife, Henrietta Lee, whom he married in 1855, and by a son, their only child.

[*Who's Who in America*, 1906–07; *Sun* (Baltimore), Feb. 27, 1906; H. A. Kelly and W. L. Burrage, *Am. Medic. Biogs.* (1920); *Old Maryland*, Mar. 1906.]
A. W.

PALMER, JOSEPH (Mar. 31, 1716–Dec. 25, 1788), manufacturer, soldier, was born at Higher Abbotsrow, Shaugh Prior, Devon, the son of John and Joan (Pearse) Palmer. His mother came from Fardle Mill in the Parish of Cornwood, Devon. He was educated in his native county and spent a few years near Liverpool, where it is believed he learned the technique of salt manufacture. In 1746 he emigrated to America in company with his brother-in-law, Richard Cranch, later a judge on the Massachusetts bench. They first engaged in business in Boston as card-makers for wool-carding. In 1752 they erected a glass manufactory in Germantown (now a part of Quincy, Mass.) where there were settled some Germans skilled in the craft. Fragments of glass bottles made at their works have been found, and they are thick, rough, and of a greenish hue. The two also erected chocolate mills and spermaceti and salt factories at Germantown. Palmer was successful in some of his business pursuits and bought large tracts of land at Pomfret, Conn. In 1770 he made a trip to England for his health and the next year he returned to Quincy.

On Sept. 6, 1774, a delegation from nineteen towns and districts on the south shore of Massachusetts Bay met at Milton to discuss the impending crisis between the colony and the mother country. Of this delegation "Deacon Joseph Palmer-of Germantown" was chosen moderator. He was present at the battle of Lexington, and though not wounded, was so exhausted that it took him some days to recover. He served in the Provincial Congress of Massachusetts during 1774–75 and was made a member of the Committee of Safety at Cambridge. On Feb. 7, 1776, he was commissioned colonel in the 5th Suffolk County Regiment in the Massachusetts militia

for the defense of Boston. Three months later he was chosen brigadier for Suffolk County. On Aug. 21, 1777, he and John Taylor were granted the sum of one hundred pounds sterling, "to repair to Bennington in the Grants [Vermont] to obtain the most authentic Intelligence of the Cercumstan[ces] of the American Forces" (*Massachusetts Soldiers and Sailors of the Revolutionary War*, XI, 1903, p. 803). On Sept. 19, 1777, he was appointed brigadier-general to replace Gen. Timothy Danielson, to command the forces on a "secret expedition" to Rhode Island to attack the enemy at Newport. He proceeded to Tiverton on the 22nd, arriving there in about ten days. He took over the command of two regiments from Plymouth and Bristol counties, but the expedition proved to be a failure and Palmer and Brig.-Gen. Solomon Lovell were notified to attend a court of inquiry at Providence on Nov. 12, 1777, to give information regarding the failure (*Ibid.*, p. 803).

In 1783 Palmer returned to his factories at Germantown, but his health was shattered and he was in financial straits brought about by the depreciation of Continental money. He was greatly indebted to John Hancock for reasons not made clear; and after a disastrous quarrel with Hancock, he was forced to quit Germantown in 1784. He started a salt factory at Boston Neck and moved his family to Dorchester. Although his new factories were fairly successful, they failed to bring the old General health and peace. He died on Christmas day in 1788 at his own home. A year or two before his arrival in America, he had married Mary Cranch of Brood in the parish of Ermington, Devon. By her he had three children. One of his grandchildren was Elizabeth Palmer Peabody [*q.v.*].

[The best sketch of Palmer appears in the *New Englander* for Jan. 1845. See also: *Grandmother Tyler's Book: The Recollections of Mary Palmer Tyler* (1925), ed. by Frederick Tupper and H. T. Brown; W. S. Pattee, *A Hist. of Old Braintree and Quincy* (1878); Alden Bradford, *Hist. of Mass.*, vol. II (1825); *The Jours. of Each Provincial Cong. of Mass. in 1774 and 1775 and of the Committee of Safety* (1838); E. A. Barber, *Am. Glassware* (1900); *Mass. Centinel* (Boston), Dec 27, 1788.]
E. L. W. H.

PALMER, NATHANIEL BROWN (Aug. 8, 1799–June 21, 1877), sea captain, explorer, not only received early prominence for discovering the Antarctic continent, where a peninsula and an archipelago still bear his name, but was also in the forefront of the packet and clipper captains. He was born in Stonington, Conn., the son of Nathaniel and Mercy (Brown) Palmer, and was descended from Walter Palmer who had settled in Stonington in 1653. The father was a lawyer and a shipbuilder. Young

Palmer went to sea at fourteen for four years on a coaster plying between Maine and New York. Like many other Stonington mariners, he became involved in the south-sea explorations stimulated by Edmund Fanning [*q.v.*]. The search for fresh seal rookeries, rather than pure geographical curiosity, stimulated the unusually fruitful activity of this little Sound port. Palmer went as second mate in 1819 on the brig *Hersilia,* Capt. James P. Sheffield, which brought back 8,868 sealskins from the re-discovered South Shetland Islands, south of Cape Horn. The next year, five Stonington vessels under Capt. Benjamin Pendleton returned to the South Shetlands. Pendleton sent Palmer in the little sloop *Hero* of about forty tons to search for new seal rookeries. Palmer discovered the mainland of Antarctica at Orleans Channel in November 1820 and subsequently went to Marguerite Bay in 68° south latitude beyond the Antarctic Circle. In February 1821, he encountered the Russian exploring squadron of Bellingshausen who suggested that the region be called Palmer Land, often miscalled Graham Land. A year later, in the *James Monroe,* Palmer explored the new region more thoroughly and, with an Englishman, discovered the South Orkney Islands. He and Pendleton returned to the scene in 1829–31 in the *Seraph, Annawan,* and *Penguin,* with several scientists including James Eights, but their search for new islands to the westward of the Palmer Peninsula was unsuccessful.

In the meantime, Palmer had made several voyages to the Spanish Main in the *Cadet* and *Tampico,* helping, incidentally, to transport troops and supplies for Bolívar; then he made some trips to Europe in the *Francis.* In 1834 he became a packet captain, one of the most desirable maritime posts of that day. His first command was the New York-New Orleans packet *Huntsville,* belonging to Edward Knight Collins [*q.v.*], who soon promoted him to the *Garrick* and then to the *Siddons* of his "Dramatic Line" to Liverpool. Soon clipper commands in the China trade became more desirable than packets, and Palmer again secured some of the best assignments. He became associated with A. A. Low & Brothers, important New York China merchants, who had the celebrated early clippers *Houqua, Samuel Russell,* and *Oriental* built by Jacob Bell [*q.v.*]. Palmer not only commanded these vessels in turn, making several very fast runs between China and New York, but is also said to have given valuable advice concerning their design and construction. Many prominent skippers, including his younger brothers Alexander and Theodore, had their first training under him. He had retired from active sea service by 1850, after taking the steamship *United States* to Bremen.

He apparently divided the rest of his years between New York and Stonington. When Donald McKay's masterpiece, the *Great Republic,* was burned in 1853, Palmer superintended her rebuilding. He was a director of the Fall River Line and took a special interest in the construction of its steamers. He corrected the official survey of Stonington harbor. He was a thorough sportsman, "being a skilful yachtsman, excellent shot, and truthful fisherman." He was one of the earliest members of the New York Yacht Club in 1845, owned some seventeen yachts, and was an energetic duck-hunter until his death. "Captain Nat," as he was universally known, was more than six feet tall and was a man of great physical strength and endurance. "Though rugged in appearance," writes Captain Clark, "his roughness was all on the outside" (*post,* p. 86). On Dec. 7, 1826, he married Eliza Thompson Babcock. They had no children. He died in San Francisco on his return from a vain attempt to restore his nephew's health by a sailing voyage to China.

[Edmund Fanning, *Voyages Round the World* (1833); E. S. Balch, *Antarctica* (1902); J. N. Reynolds, *Address, on the Subject of a Surveying and Exploring Expedition to the Pacific Ocean and South Seas* (1836); A. H. Clark, *The Clipper Ship Era* (1910); Geo. Powell, *Notes on South Shetland* (1822); J. R. Spears, *Capt. Nathaniel Brown Palmer* (1922); R. A. Wheeler, *Hist. of the Town of Stonington, County of New London, Conn.* (1900); R. G. Albion, *Square-Riggers on Schedule* (1938); W. H. Hobbs, *The Discoveries of Antarctica within the American Sector* (1939); Lawrence Martin, *Antarctica Discovered by a Connecticut Yankee* (1940); Russell Owen, *The Antarctic Ocean* (1941); *House Doc.* 61, 22 Cong., 1 Sess.; *Senate Doc. 10,* 23 Cong., 1 Sess.; *House Doc. 105,* 23 Cong., 2 Sess.; *Daily Morning Call* (San Francisco), June 22, 1877.]   R. G. A.

PALMER, POTTER (May 20, 1826–May 4, 1902), Chicago merchant, real-estate promoter, was born in Albany County, N. Y., the fourth son of Benjamin and Rebecca (Potter) Palmer, both Quakers. His formal education was confined to the elementary school. At eighteen years of age he became a clerk in a general store at Durham, N. Y. After three years he opened a dry-goods store for himself in the neighboring community of Oneida, from which, a little later, he removed his business to Lockport. When he looked about for greater merchandising opportunities, Chicago attracted his attention. Assisted by his father, he opened, in 1852, a dry-goods store on Lake Street, which was then the commercial center of the city. His methods of carrying on his business were so out of the ordinary as to surprise his competitors. He permitted customers to inspect merchandise in their own homes before buying and to exchange purchases already made for other merchandise or for the price paid. This method of retailing finally prevailed among the larger stores in Chicago and came to be known as the "Palmer system." He led the way also in other business innovations, especially in laying increased stress on advertising and on attractiveness in displaying goods for sale. In the fifteen years following his arrival in Chicago he amassed a large fortune, as fortunes were measured at the time in the Central West. This he did, however, at the expense of his health. On the advice of his physicians he retired, in 1867, from active participation in business, turning over the management and control of his store to his partners, Marshall Field and Levi Z. Leiter [qq.v.].

After three years of rest and travel abroad he returned to Chicago as an active business man, now directing his interest to real-estate development. His most notable achievement in this respect was the transformation of what is now State Street from little more than a country road into a wide and attractive business thoroughfare. There he built the first Palmer House and some thirty-two other buildings. These improvements caused the removal of the retail business of the city to State Street from Lake Street, where it had been established for years. When the great fire of 1871 swept away a large portion of his fortune, he bravely began to recoup his losses. He built even larger and more permanent buildings than before. On a new site on State Street, at the corner of Monroe, he erected the second Palmer House, a hostelry that was to become internationally famous. During these years of struggle, he enjoyed the active sympathy and support of his brilliant wife, Bertha (Honoré) Palmer [q.v.], the eldest daughter of a prominent capitalist and real estate owner of Chicago, to whom he was married in 1871 just before the great fire. They had two sons. He spent large sums of money in transforming waste lands along the lake shore, north of the Chicago River, into beautiful building sites and drives. There he built a magnificent home, still a monument to the dominant taste of the day.

He was not too much engaged in his own affairs to give attention to the needs of his community; he was a vice-president of the first board of local directors of the World's Columbian Exposition, the first president of the Chicago Baseball Club, a commissioner during the early years of the South Side park system, one of the original incorporators of the Chicago Association of Commerce and of the Chicago Board of Trade, and an early supporter of the Chicago Young Men's Christian Association. During the Civil War he supported the government by buying heavily of bonds and by cooperating with his fellow townsmen in meeting the requirements for soldiers. He believed in young men, and many were the times that he helped them most generously in business and social ventures. He died in his home in Chicago.

[Newton Bateman, Paul Selby, and J. S. Currey, *Hist. Encyc. of Ill.* (2 vols., 1925); D. W. Wood, *Chicago and its Distinguished Citizens* (1881); J. S. Currey, *Chicago* (1912), vols. I, III; *Chicago Daily Tribune*, May 5, 7, 1902.]   C. M. T.

PALMER, MRS. POTTER [See PALMER, BERTHA HONORÉ, 1849–1918].

PALMER, RAY (Nov. 12, 1808–Mar. 29, 1887), Congregational clergyman, hymn-writer, was born in Little Compton, R. I., and died in Newark, N. J. The son of Judge Thomas Palmer and Susanna (Palmer) Palmer, he traced his descent back to William Palmer who came to Plymouth Colony in 1621. When only thirteen years old, he became a clerk in a drygoods store in Boston, and attended Park Street Congregational Church, where he was under the influence of Rev. Sereno E. Dwight [q.v.]. Having decided to enter the ministry, he spent three years preparing for college at Phillips Academy, Andover, and then entered Yale, where he was graduated in the class of 1830. He taught for several hours a day in a select school for girls in New York City (1830–31), and then at a seminary for girls in New Haven. On Oct. 3, 1832, he married Ann Maria, daughter of Marmaduke and Maria (Ogden) Waud of Newark, N. J. Having studied theology privately, he was ordained and installed as pastor of the Congregational Church in Bath, Me., July 22, 1835, where he remained for fifteen years. In 1847 he made a trip to Europe, sending back letters of travel which were published in the *Christian Mirror*, Portland. From 1850 to 1866 he was the first pastor of the First Congregational Church in Albany, N. Y., and for the twelve years following, 1866–78, he was the corresponding secretary of the American Congregational Union, later the Congregational Church Building Society. One of the principal objects of this organization was to give assistance in the building of meeting houses and parsonages, and during Palmer's incumbency more than six hundred of the former were erected. After 1870 he resided in Newark, and from 1881 to 1884 he was one of the associate pastors of the Bellevue Avenue Church.

He was a man of transparent sincerity, simplicity of faith, and the cheerfulness and confidence which are rooted in untroubled religious convictions. Methodical and of tireless industry, he found time in the midst of parish and secretarial duties to do much writing. Among his published prose works are *Spiritual Improvement, or Aids to Growth in Grace* (1839), reprinted as *Closet Hours* (1851); *Doctrinal Text-book* (1839); *Hints on the Formation of Religious Opinions* (1860); *Remember Me* (1865); *Earnest Words on True Success in Life* (1873). He also contributed much to religious periodicals. A long poem, *Home: or the Unlost Paradise,* appeared in 1872. It is as a hymn-writer, however, that he is best known. His compositions in this field were numerous and are rated by hymnologists as superior to most hymns of American origin (John Julian, *A Dictionary of Hymnology,* 1891). "My Faith Looks up to Thee," which has been translated into many languages, was written soon after he graduated from college and included in *Spiritual Songs for Social Worship* by Thomas Hastings and Lowell Mason in 1832. Some of the other popular hymns which he wrote are "Away from Earth my Spirit Turns," "And Is There, Lord, a Rest?", "O Sweetly Breathe the Lyres Above," and "Take Me, O My Father; Take Me." He published *Hymns and Sacred Pieces* (1865), *Hymns of My Holy Hours* (1867), *The Poetical Works of Ray Palmer* (1876), and *Voices of Hope and Gladness* (1881). His death occurred at Newark from cerebral hemorrhage when he was in his seventy-ninth year.

[*Obit. Record Grads. Yale Univ., . . . 1880–90* (1890); *The Congregational Year-Book* (1888); S. W. Duffield, *Eng. Hymns: Their Authors and Hist.* (1886); *The Independent,* Apr. 7, 14, 1887; *Musical Herald,* Apr. 1882; *Choir Herald,* Dec. 1919; E. F. Hatfield, *Poets of the Church* (1884); L. F. Benson, *Studies of Familiar Hymns* (1903); Charles S. Robinson, *Annotations upon Popular Hymns* (copr. 1893); W. F. Tillett and C. S. Nutter, *The Hymns and Hymn Writers of the Church* (copr. 1911); E. S. Ninde, *The Story of the Am. Hymn* (1921); C. M. Fuess, *Men of Andover* (1928).]   F. J. M.

PALMER, THOMAS WITHERELL (Jan. 25, 1830–June 1, 1913), senator, minister to Spain, was born in Detroit, Mich. His father, Thomas Palmer, removed from Connecticut to Detroit, opened a store, acquired a sawmill, and afterward became interested in the mining industry in the upper peninsula. His mother was Mary Amy (Witherell) Palmer, the daughter of James Witherell, a judge of the supreme court and later secretary of Michigan Territory. In memory of this grandfather Palmer changed his middle name from James to Witherell in 1850. He received his early education in Detroit. At the age of twelve he was sent to Palmer (now Saint Clair), where he entered the private school of O. C. Thompson, a Presbyterian minister, and studied for three years. In 1907 he published a description of these school days, *Mr. Thompson's School at St. Clair in 1842.* In 1845 he matriculated at the University of Michigan, but on account of illness and poor eyesight his studies were twice interrupted, and in 1848 he left Ann Arbor. Sailing with five of his college friends for Spain, he arrived at Cadiz on Dec. 1, 1848, and departed for South America four weeks later. In the summer of 1849 he returned to Detroit. Inspired by the phenomenal success of his father as a merchant, he opened a business office and later a store at Appleton, Wis., but a fire destroyed most of his possessions in January 1852. From 1853 to 1860 he was his father's partner in Detroit. Having married on Oct. 16, 1855, Lizzie Pitts Merrill, the daughter of Charles Merrill, he gradually grew more involved in his father-in-law's extensive lumber interests, and in 1863 he became Merrill's partner. The next year he moved to a suburban home, where he maintained a small farm. When his father died in 1868, he took up the management of the estate's larger tract of land, part of which he donated to the city of Detroit in 1895 for Palmer Park.

In 1873 he was elected a member of the first board of estimates of Detroit. Five years later he won the election for state senator, and in 1883 he became federal senator. Noteworthy are his speeches on woman's suffrage, government regulation of the railroads, and the restriction of immigration. He was chairman of the committee on agriculture. As a debater he was surpassed by few, and he was one of the most popular orators in Michigan. When in 1889 he was appointed minister to Spain, prominent citizens in Detroit honored him with many tokens of esteem. After two years, however, he resigned and soon after his return from Spain was chosen by President Harrison to be a commissioner for the World's Columbian Exposition in Chicago. The board elected him president. After the fair he sustained a nervous collapse, which necessitated a long rest. He withdrew from the political arena, although on many occasions he delivered stirring speeches and witty toasts. He also devoted much time to philanthropy, and he was one of the founders of the Detroit Museum of Art. Among the pamphlets and articles written by him may be noted the following: *Detroit Sixty Years Ago: An Address before the Unity Club . . . 1897* (n.d.), "Sketch of Life and Times of James Witherell" in the *Michigan Pioneer and Historical Society Collections* (vol. IV, 1906), and "Detroit in its Relation to the Northwest" in *The Bi-Centenary of the Founding of City of Detroit* (1902). He died in Detroit, survived by his wife. They had no children but had adopted a son and a daughter.

[M. A. Burton, *Thomas W. Palmer* (1914), later published in *Mich. Pioneer and Hist. Soc. Colls.*, vol. XXXIX (1915); Friend Palmer, *Early Days in Detroit* (1906); *The City of Detroit*, ed. by C. M. Burton (1922), vol. IV; C. McElroy, *Souvenir Hist. of Palmer Park and Sketch of Hon. Thomas W. Palmer*, (1908); *Detroit Free Press* and *Detroit News*, June 2, 1913.]   A. H.

PALMER, WALTER LAUNT (Aug. 1, 1854–Apr. 16, 1932), landscape, figure, and still-life painter, born in Albany, N. Y., was the son of Erastus Dow Palmer [*q.v.*], the sculptor, and Mary Jane Seaman. He received his first lessons in drawing from his father; later he studied painting for two years (1870–72) under Frederick E. Church [*q.v.*] at Hudson, N. Y.; and in 1873 he went to Paris, where he was a pupil of Carolus-Duran for a year (1876–77). Upon his return to the United States in 1877 he opened a studio in New York, where he devoted himself to landscape painting. He made his début a year later, sending to the National Academy exhibition "An Interior" and "Montigny-sur-Loing" (1878). He then concentrated upon winter scenes, in the depiction of which he was eminently successful. He was elected an associate of the National Academy in 1887, on the occasion of his taking the second Hallgarten prize, and he became a member of the American Water-Color Society and of the Society of American Artists. In 1891 he moved from New York to Albany, where the greater part of his professional life was passed thereafter. One of his earliest winter landscapes, "January," was bought by Thomas B. Clarke.

Although landscapes were his most popular subjects, he produced from time to time equally excellent figure pieces and interiors. An interior which was at the Academy in 1878, and which was also hung in one of the exhibitions of the Union League Club, New York, was highly praised by a critic for the New York *Evening Post* (Mar. 15, 1878, p. 2). He sent three of his pictures to the Chicago Exposition of 1893—an "Early Snow," "Autumn Morning Mist Clearing Away" (lent by John G. Myers of Albany), and the early "January" which belonged to Clarke's collection. He was awarded a medal at this exhibition. At the St. Louis exhibition of 1904 he was represented by "Evening Lights" and "Across the Fields," and received a bronze medal for his oil paintings and a silver medal for his four water-colors. Among the other honors which came to him may be mentioned the gold medal of the Art Club, Philadelphia, 1894; the Evans prize at the exhibition of the Ameri-

can Water-Color Society, 1895; the first prize at the exhibition of the Boston Art Club, 1895; the second prize at the Nashville exhibition of 1897; silver medals for water-colors at the Buffalo Exposition of 1901 and at the Charleston Exposition of 1902; a silver medal at the Philadelphia exhibition in 1907; a bronze medal at the Buenos Aires Exposition of 1910; the Butler prize, Chicago, 1919; and the DuPont prize, Wilmington, Del., 1926.

Palmer's landscapes are characterized by the keen and luminous effects of the winter season, the forcible contrasts of light and shade which are the results of sharp frosts and unclouded sunlight. He made the winter with its snows his particular province. "It is not," says Isham, "the snow of Europe, damply evaporating into a leaden sky, but the New England article, crisp and dry in the keen cold and shining dazzling white against the blue horizon" (*post*, p. 440). Palmer was twice married: first to Georgianna Myers, and on Dec. 26, 1895, some years after the death of his first wife, to Zoe de V. Wyndham of England. He died at his birthplace, Albany, survived by his widow and a daughter.

[*Who's Who in America*, 1930–31; Samuel Isham, *Hist. of Am. Painting* (1905); *Catalogue Official Illustré, Exposition des Beaux Arts, États-Unis d'Amérique, Exposition Universelle de Paris* (1900); *Cat. of the Thos. B. Clarke Collection of Am. Pictures* (1891); *Illustrations of Selected Works . . . Universal Exposition, St. Louis, 1904* (1904); *Art News*, Apr. 23, 1932; *Am. Art Annual*, 1923–24; *Biog. Sketches of Am. Artists* (1924), pub. by Mich. State Lib.; *N. Y. Times*, Apr. 17, 1932.]   W. H. D.

PALMER, WILLIAM ADAMS (Sept. 12, 1781–Dec. 3, 1860), lawyer, farmer, and politician, was born at Hebron, Conn., the fourth son in the family of eight children of Stephen and Susannah (Sawyer) Palmer. He was descended from Walter Palmer who settled in Stonington, Conn., in 1653. According to tradition an accident to one hand in his youth unfitted him for farm work and turned him toward a professional career. After a public-school education he entered a law office in Hebron, continuing his studies later at Chelsea, Vt. Admitted to the bar in 1802, he practised law during the next few years in one Vermont village after another. He was living in St. Johnsbury when in 1807 he was elected judge of probate for Caledonia County. To perform the duties of this office he moved to the county seat at Danville where he lived on a farm for the rest of his life except for absences on judicial or political service. While serving as probate judge (1807–08, 1811–17) he was also clerk of his county court from 1807 to 1815. In 1811–12, as well as in 1818, 1825–26, and 1829, he was a member of the lower house of the state legislature. In the meantime he sat for one year (1816) as a justice of the supreme court of the state. He became a leader in the Democratic party. In October 1818 he was elected to fill the vacancy in the United States Senate caused by the resignation of James Fisk, 1763–1844 [*q.v.*], and at the same time was elected for the full term beginning in 1819. At Washington he acquired a temporary unpopularity among Vermonters by voting for the admission in 1819 of Missouri with her pro-slavery constitution. He disclaimed any friendship for slavery but insisted stanchly upon the maintenance of state rights.

Palmer was serving in his state legislature when the anti-Masonic storm broke. He needed no new political stalking horse; he joined the growing movement from conviction, for his democratic sentiments had always clashed with secret societies. As the anti-Masonic candidate he therefore stood for the governorship in 1830. In a three-cornered contest he ran second in the popular vote, his Masonic rival winning when the election was thrown into the legislature. The same legislature refused him election to the United States Senate that year (1830). For the next two years as the anti-Masonic candidate, he was elected by the legislature to the governorship; in 1833 he won by popular vote; in 1834 again by legislative action. In 1835 even the legislature failed after sixty-three attempts to elect a governor. Palmer was forced to retire while his running mate, the lieutenant-governor, carried on the state administration. When in 1836 the Whig element won control of the anti-Masonic councils, Palmer consented to become the candidate of the Democratic bolters. He was defeated but was elected in that year and in 1837 to the state Senate. His retirement the following year ended his political career save for service in the constitutional convention of 1850.

In spite of the bitterness of party passions at the time Palmer appears to have commanded the respect of his opponents. His opposition to the Masonic organization was prompted by an honest and sincere conviction rather than by a desire for political preferment. His appointments while governor showed no discrimination against the Masons for he detested the spoils system. His long public career proved him, if not a brilliant man, at least able, honest, and courageous. In private life his simplicity and his generosity won the devoted affection of his neighbors. He had married in September 1813 Sarah Blanchard of Danville. They had seven children of whom five sons grew to maturity.

[J. G. Ullery, *Men of Vt.* (1894); J. M. Comstock, *A List of . . . Civil Officers of Vt. from 1777 to 1918* (1918); A. M. Hemenway, *The Vt. Hist. Gazetteer*, vol. I (1868); *Records of the Gov. and Council of the State of Vt.*, vol. VIII (1880); E. W. Leavitt, *Palmer Groups: John Melvin of Charlestown and Concord, Mass., and his Descendants* (1901–05); R. A. Wheeler, *Hist. of the Town of Stonington, County of New London, Conn.* (1900); *Biog. Dir. Am. Cong.* (1928).]
P. D. E.

PALMER, WILLIAM HENRY (*c.* 1830–Nov. 28, 1878), entertainer, known on the stage as Robert Heller, was born in England. His father was a musician and is said to have served as an organist in Canterbury Cathedral. The boy was given a thorough musical training. In 1848 he saw the French magician, Robert-Houdin, and was fascinated by his performances. When he discovered that his years of practice on the piano had given his fingers a suppleness and dexterity that assisted him in duplicating the tricks of the magician, his interest in music became secondary to an interest in stage magic. Two of the greatest magicians of history played in London in the succeeding period, Compars Herrmann and John Henry Anderson. Studying the performances of these men and imitating their technique he boldly hired the Strand Theatre in London and advertised his program in 1851 or 1852. He hid his youthfulness and English blondness behind a black wig and beard that copied the appearance of Herrmann. He followed the metropolitan performances with a tour of the provinces with some success but competition was strong and he turned to America. His first New York appearance was in the basement of the Chinese Assembly Hall on Broadway near Spring Street. Later he hired the hall above and played for several months. A tour of rural New England and New York state followed.

Palmer was a poor business man and by 1855 he found himself heavily in debt. He reluctantly turned back to music for a living, played the organ for a church in Washington, D. C., and taught music. In 1855 he married Annie Maria Kieckhoefer of Washington. Three children were born to the couple but the marriage was broken in 1862. Freed from family ties Palmer returned to the stage. For a time his show was backed by an enthusiastic young man who wished to have the privilege of appearing with him. Later he hired a handsome young woman to assist him who was billed as Miss Haidee Heller. In 1864 he took as his manager Hingston, the man who had managed the tours of Artemus Ward, and from that time he was most successful. He opened a *Salle Diabolique* at 585 Broadway, New York City; later he went on tour in the United States; and in 1867 he reported that he had taken in $22,400 in fifteen nights in San Francisco. In 1868 he played in England. On a later tour he went to Australia. In 1876 he returned to America, opening at the Globe Theatre in New York City. From the Globe he went to the Fifth Avenue Hall. In 1878 he played in Washington, Baltimore, and Philadelphia. In Philadelphia he developed pneumonia and died within two days.

After his first New York engagement Palmer abandoned the awesome wig and beard and the French accent, but he did not learn to utilize his natural charm until he came under the influence of Hingston. After his earliest performances he varied his programs by the use of puppets and piano numbers. He first offered classical music but the taste of his audiences, as well as his own prankishness, caused him to substitute comedy numbers. His most famous act in the field of magic was in "second-sight." Although the trick was not new he developed it to an unusual degree. He used both the oral and silent codes and particularly mystified his audiences by using electrical devices. Had he chosen to give his mummery a religious cast his following might have been spectacular, but his lack of seriousness kept the impressionable from believing that his performances entailed anything beyond skilful deception. Dion Boucicault considered him a comedian of the first rank.

[Sources include: Harry Houdini, *The Unmasking of Robert-Houdin* (1908), pp. 205–07; David Devant, *My Magic Life* (1931); H. R. Evans, *Hist. of Conjuring and Magic* (1928); *Conjurers' Monthly Mag.*, Dec. 15, 1906; *M.U.M.*, Aug. 1917, May 1919; *N. Y. Daily Tribune*, Nov. 29, 1878; *Times* (London), Dec. 14, 1878. There are a number of Palmer's playbills in the Houdini Collection in the Lib. of Cong. The year of Palmer's birth is variously given. The exact date remains undetermined.]   K. H. A.

PALMER, WILLIAM JACKSON (Sept. 18, 1836–Mar. 13, 1909), Civil War soldier and railroad executive, was born near Leipsic, Kent County, Del., of Quaker parents, John and Matilda (Jackson) Palmer. In 1842 the family moved to Philadelphia where William was sent to a private school and later to the public grammar and high school. He then worked as a rodman on the Hempfield Railroad (1853), traveled and possibly studied in England (1856), acted as secretary and treasurer of the Westmoreland Coal Company, and from then until the Civil War (1858–61) was private secretary to J. Edgar Thomson, president of the Pennsylvania Railroad. With the coming of the war Palmer followed his conscience in foregoing his Quaker principles. He organized and became captain of the 15th Pennsylvania cavalry in

September 1861 and a year later was commissioned colonel. By the end of the war he was a brevet brigadier-general of volunteers. His record was excellent, in spite of a serious defection among his troops while he was a prisoner in 1862–63, and he was cited for conspicuous service several times, receiving in 1894 the Congressional Medal of Honor. His engagements included Antietam, Missionary Ridge, Chickamauga, the Atlanta campaign, and the final pursuit of Jefferson Davis.

After the war Palmer became treasurer of the Eastern Division of the Union Pacific Railroad, which became the Kansas Pacific in 1869 and later merged into the Union Pacific. He helped further the road's transcontinental ambitions by supervising surveys west of the Rio Grande along the 35th and 32nd parallels to the coast (W. J. Palmer, *Report of Surveys across the Continent, in 1867–'68,* 1869). He also took charge of construction between Sheridan and Denver, Colo. With the completion of the road in 1870 he left it for the new and promising Denver & Rio Grande Railroad, designed to give Denver southern and western connections. As first president of the road he prosecuted the work in spite of the depression of the seventies. A long struggle with the Santa Fé resulted in the loss of a southern outlet and the acquisition of a western route through the Royal Gorge of the Arkansas. A through line to Salt Lake City was opened in 1883. Again Palmer thought his work done; in 1883 he resigned the presidency and the next year his directorship. He found it undesirable, however, to dispose of the Denver & Rio Grande Western (the western part of the through line), for its lease in 1882 was stopped by injunction, a mile of track destroyed, and a receiver appointed. Palmer retained control through the reorganization as the Rio Grande Western in 1889, and finally sold his interest to the parent company in 1901.

Palmer was identified during the eighties with Mexican railroads. A trip through Mexico in 1872 laid the basis for the Palmer-Sullivan concession (1880), which provided monetary aid for the Mexican National Railway, of which he was president from 1881 to 1888. One main line was to run from Mexico city to Laredo, Tex., with a branch to Manzanillo, and another main line was to extend from Mexico city to El Salto. A line to El Paso was lost to the Nickerson interests, but work on the other lines was prosecuted by the Mexican National Construction Company, especially between 1880 and 1883. Active work ended by the late eighties, and a financial reorganization was necessary. Palmer sold his Mexican National interests in the late nineties and retired from all business interests in 1901. He died at his home near Colorado Springs, in 1909. He had married, in October 1870, Mary Lincoln ("Queen") Mellen. Their three daughters survived him. Palmer was a cultured, intelligent, likable man, with wide business and philanthropic interests. He was a prime mover in the founding (1871) and development of Colorado Springs. He helped found Colorado College (1874) and was one of the first trustees. His philanthropies extended also to Hampton Institute. He was an organizer and first president of the Colorado Coal and Iron Company (1879) and laid out Bessemer, now part of Pueblo.

[See: Mary G. Slocum, ed., "Tributes to the Late Gen. Wm. J. Palmer," *Colo. Coll. Pub.,* Social Sci. Ser., vol. II, no. 2 (1909); Jeannette Turpin, ed., *Gen. Wm. J. Palmer* (n.d.); W. F. Stone, ed., *Hist. of Colo.,* vol. III (1918); Frank Hall, *Hist. of the State of Colo.,* vol. III (1891); *Who's Who in America,* 1908–09; J. C. Smiley, *Semi-Centennial Hist. of the State of Colo.* (2 vols., 1913); H. H. Bancroft, *Hist. of Nev., Colo., and Wyo., 1540–1888* (1890); I. H. Clothier, ed., *Letters, 1853–68, Gen. Wm. J. Palmer* (1906); *War of the Rebellion: Official Records* (*Army*); "The General's Story," in *Harper's New Monthly Mag.,* June 1867; *Southern Workman,* July 1929; *Letter of John D. Parry, President of the Union Pacific Railway* (*Eastern Division*) (1868); *Rocky Mountain News* (Denver), Mar. 14, 1909.]   R. E. R.

PALMORE, WILLIAM BEVERLY (Feb. 24, 1844–July 5, 1914), clergyman of the Methodist Episcopal Church South, editor, was born in Fayette County, Tenn., the son of William Pledge and Elizabeth Ann (Hobson) Palmore. When William was only six weeks old his father died, and the boy's early years were a struggle with poverty, suffering, and heartache. When he was fourteen his mother, hoping to improve their living conditions, moved the family to a farm near Malta Bend in Saline County, Mo. William's educational advantages were only such as the simple country schools of Missouri offered. When he was seventeen years of age he joined the Confederate army, serving under General Marmaduke until his surrender at Shreveport, La., in 1865. During much of his service he was standard bearer, but though he was exposed to the enemy's fire constantly, he came through the war without wounds or injuries. Upon being mustered out, he returned to Missouri and entered into business at Waverly, a few miles from the farm at Malta Bend. Here he was converted, joined the Methodist Episcopal Church South, and began to teach in the Sunday school. This experience, coupled with his early religious training, convinced him that he ought to give his life to the ministry. Knowing that he must edu-

cate himself for the work, he went in the early seventies to Nashville, Tenn., and entered the new Vanderbilt University. Returning to Missouri upon the completion of his theological education, he was admitted to the Southwest Missouri Conference of the Methodist Episcopal Church South, and after being licensed to preach, served churches in Kansas City, Springfield, Independence, Marshall, Jefferson City, and the Boonville District.

In 1890 he purchased the *St. Louis Christian Advocate* and became the editor and manager. Successful in the pastorate, he was even more successful as an editor, becoming recognized as one of the leaders of his denomination. He was a member of the Ecumenical Methodist Conferences at Washington (1891) and London (1901) and was a member of four General Conferences of his church. In 1908 he was nominated for vice-president of the United States on the Prohibition ticket, but declined to be a candidate. He was for some time president of the board of Central College for Women, Lexington, Mo. He traveled widely, going to every section of the world and bringing back interesting accounts of his experiences. Lands in West Virginia which he inherited, though poor and infertile from the point of view of agriculture, turned out to be rich in coal. This wealth he used for the advancement of his church, establishing the Palmore Institute at Kobe, Japan, and the Collegio Palmore at Chihuahua, Mexico. In addition, he aided many individual boys and girls in securing education. He never married, and when he died, in Richmond, Va., at the home of a niece, he left to the church all the property he possessed.

[*Central Christian Advocate* (Kansas City, Mo.), July 15, 1914; *Christian Advocate* (Nashville), July 10, Aug. 28, 1914; *Who's Who in America,* 1914–15; M. L. Gray, *The Centennial Vol. of Methodism, Meth. Episc. Ch. South* (1907); *Times-Dispatch* (Richmond, Va.), July 6, 1914; *N. Y. Times,* July 6, 1914.]   I. L. H.

PALÓU, FRANCISCO (c. 1722–c. 1789), Franciscan missionary and historian in Mexico and California, was born in Mallorca, entered the monastery of San Francisco at Palma, and in the Lullian University there in 1740 became a pupil of the famous Junípero Serra [*q.v.*]. Palóu studied and taught at Palma till 1749, when he accompanied Serra to Mexico. After living for five months at the College of San Fernando, the two went in 1750 to serve as missionaries in the Sierra Gorda, northeast of Querétaro. Here, at Jalpan, they spent nine years, Serra as president and Palóu as his companion. At the end of this time they were assigned to the mission of San Sabá, in Texas. But the plans were changed, Serra returned to Mexico city, Palóu succeeded him as president for a year, and then followed him to the capital, where he worked for seven years. In 1767, when the Jesuits were expelled from Baja California, Serra was head and Palóu a member of the band of Franciscans who replaced them. Leaving the capital in July, they crossed Mexico to the Gulf, and on Apr. 1, 1768, reached Loreto, the capital of California.

For a year Palóu was missionary at San Xavier. When in 1769 Serra went to Alta California with the Portolá expedition, Palóu succeeded him as president in the Peninsula. Four years he held this office, showing great energy both in spiritual administration and in raising and sending supplies to San Diego and Monterey. Meanwhile the Franciscans were replaced in the Peninsula by Dominicans, and Palóu successfully supervised the transfer. This task finished, in May 1773 he started north for San Diego. On the way he set up a cross marking the boundary between Upper and Lower California, at a point which helped fix the boundary between Mexico and the United States seventy-five years later. When he reached Monterey (November 1773), Serra was absent in Mexico and Palóu served as acting president till his return. The next year he explored the San Francisco peninsula, and in 1776 he founded the mission of San Francisco (Dolores), which still stands in the heart of the city of San Francisco. For nine years he was head of this mission and the leading figure in the community. In 1784 Serra called him to Monterey (Carmel) and ordered him to go to Mexico on an urgent errand, but just as he was about to sail, Serra suddenly died and Palóu a third time succeeded him as president. In the next year he became president of the College of San Fernando, in Mexico, where he died about 1789.

Palóu is best known for his writings. His letters and reports are voluminous. While in California he compiled his monumental chronicle of the Franciscans in Old and New California, still the best authority on the subject. After Serra's death Palóu wrote at San Francisco his more widely known *Relación Historica de la Vida y Apostólicas Tareas del Venerable Padre Fray Junípero Serra* (Mexico, 1787), on which Serra's fame has chiefly rested till recent times.

[Palóu's life of Serra, translated by C. S. Williams and G. W. James, is published as *Francisco Palóu's Life and Apostolic Labors of the Venerable Father Junípero Serra* (1913); his chronicle of California was first printed in *Documentos para la Historia de Mexico*, 4 ser. VI–VII (1857), reprinted as *Noticias de la Nueva*

California (4 vols., 1874), ed. by James T. Doyle, and translated in H. E. Bolton, *Historical Memoirs of New California by Fray Francisco Palóu, O. F. M.* (4 vols., 1926). For biographical accounts of Palóu, see H. H. Bancroft, *Hist. of Cal.*, vol. I (1884); C. A. Engelhardt (Fr. Zephyrin), *The Missions and Missionaries of Cal.* (4 vols., 1908–15), and *San Francisco, or Mission Dolores* (1924); H. E. Bolton, *Palóu and His Writings* (1926) and *Anza's California Expeditions* (5 vols., 1930).]
H. E. B.

PAMMEL, LOUIS HERMANN (Apr. 19, 1862–Mar. 23, 1931), botanist and conservationist, the son of Louis C. and Sophie (Freise) Pammel, natives of Germany, was born in LaCrosse, Wis., and died on board a transcontinental train in eastern Nevada. When a young lad he moved with his parents to a farm near LaCrosse, where he lived in a log house and attended a country school. Later he entered a business college and took private lessons in mathematics, the languages, and other subjects, preparatory to entering the University of Wisconsin, which he did in 1881, graduating in an agricultural course four years later.

Deciding to study medicine, he entered Hahnemann Medical College, Chicago, in October 1885, but in December following went to Cambridge, Mass., to become private assistant to Prof. William Gilson Farlow [q.v.]. There he remained until September 1886, when he went to St. Louis, Mo., to become assistant to Dr. William Trelease in the Shaw School of Botany, Washington University. In February 1889, in which year he received the degree of M.S. from his alma mater, he moved from St. Louis to Ames, Iowa, to become head of the department of botany of the Iowa State College of Agriculture and Mechanic Arts, a position which he held for forty years. In 1898 Washington University, St. Louis, awarded him the doctorate of philosophy.

During the summer of 1888 and 1889 he did special work on the cotton root rot at the Texas Experiment Station, and at various times he served on special commissions for the United States Department of Agriculture and the Iowa Geological Survey. He also was botanist for the Experiment Station at Ames. From his youth he was intensely interested in all forms of plant life, and the herbarium of Iowa State College contains many thousands of specimens collected by him on his numerous vacation trips. As a conservationist he embraced every opportunity to increase public sentiment in favor of wild life preservation and of establishing Iowa's extensive system of state parks, one of which, in Madison County, was in 1930 renamed Pammel State Park in his honor.

As an author his larger works were *The Grasses of Iowa* (2 vols., 1901); *Ecology* (1903); *A Manual of Poisonous Plants* (1910); *Weeds of the Farm and Garden* (1911); *The Weed Flora of Iowa* (1913; revised 1926); "Prominent Men I Have Met," a series of articles published in the *Ames Daily Tribune* over a number of years and reprinted in several pamphlets; and *Honey Plants of Iowa* (1930), with Charlotte M. King. He also wrote numerous Park and Experiment Station bulletins, and a great number of papers published in the proceedings of learned societies, scientific journals, and the daily press. A set—almost complete —of his books and papers, specially bound, fills about six feet of shelf space in the Iowa State College Library. In his later years he gave many talks and lectures on weeds and conservation, also travelogues illustrated with lantern slides.

He was married in Chicago, June 29, 1888, to Augusta Emmel, and to them were born five daughters and one son. In politics he was in early life a Democrat, but later a Republican, and in religion a member of the Episcopal Church, in which he was a lay reader. He was a member of numerous scientific societies, was president of the Iowa State Board of Conservation (1918–27) and was secretary general (1911–23) and president general (1923–27) of Phi Kappa Phi.

[*Who's Who in America*, 1930–31; *Am. Men of Science* (4th ed., 1927); F. C. Pellett, in *Am. Bee Journal*, May 1931; *Des Moines Register*, Mar. 24, 1931; autobiographical notes left with the Department of Botany, Iowa State College.] R. I. C.

PANCOAST, JOSEPH (Nov. 23, 1805–Mar. 7, 1882), anatomist and surgeon, was born near Burlington, N. J., the son of John and Ann (Abbott) Pancoast. His family was English, and had come to America with William Penn. He received his medical education at the University of Pennsylvania, from which he was graduated M.D. in 1828, and began to practise in Philadelphia, specializing in surgery. There was at that time an organization known as the Philadelphia Association for Medical Instruction—a kind of quizzing body—composed of young men of promise, many of whom became distinguished in later life, and with it Pancoast was identified for a short time. Later (1831) he was appointed to conduct the Philadelphia School of Anatomy, founded in 1820 by Dr. Jason Valentine O'Brien Lawrence. In 1835 he was elected physician to the Philadelphia Hospital (Blockley) and in 1838 was made visiting surgeon to the same institution, retaining the connection until 1845. In

1838, also, he retired from the School of Anatomy and succeeded Dr. George McClellan [*q.v.*] in the chair of surgery in the Jefferson Medical College. In 1841 he was transferred from the chair of surgery to that of anatomy, which he held until 1874, when he resigned. Thus for thirty-six years he filled one or another of the most important chairs in the Jefferson Medical College. In 1854 he was elected to the staff of the Pennsylvania Hospital, resigning in 1864.

Among his principal achievements in surgery were an operation for the remediation of exstrophy of the bladder by plastic abdominal flaps with which to replace the missing anterior vesical wall; an operation for soft and mixed cataracts by passing a hook through the front part of the vitreous humor between the margin of the dilated iris and lens without touching the ciliary body, the soft part of the lens being deeply cut and the hardened nucleus withdrawn by a horizontal displacement along the line of entrance of the needle and the fragment being left in the outer border of the vitreous; an operation for empyema in which a semicircular flap of skin over the ribs was raised, the pleura punctured near the base of the flap, a short catheter introduced—fastened with a strong string so as to make a fistula—and then the flap turned down to serve as a valve after the removal of the catheter; an operation for the correction of occlusion of the nasal duct by puncturing the lachrymal sac and introducing a tiny hollow ivory tube that had been previously decalcified, leaving the tube *in situ* to become absorbed; a strabismus operation for the relief of bad cases in which the tendon of the oblique muscle, being surrounded by rigid connective tissue, must be drawn out with a hook before being cut.

His literary work, which was rather voluminous, began with a translation of J. F. Lobstein's *De nervi sympathetici humane fabrica et morbus* (Paris, 1823) published as *Treatise on the Structure, Function and Diseases of the Sympathetic Nerve* (1831). This was followed by his edition of P. J. Manec's *Great Sympathetic Nerves* (n.d.) and *Manec's Cerebro-Spinal Axis of Man* (n.d). He issued three editions (1839, 1843, and 1846) of Caspar Wistar and William Horner's *System of Anatomy* and contributed numerous miscellaneous papers to medical journals. His greatest achievement, however, was his own *Treatise on Operative Surgery,* of which the first edition appeared in 1844 and the third and last in 1852.

On July 2, 1829, he married Rebecca, daughter of Timothy Abbott. He died in Philadelphia, "beloved and honored by all who knew him." A son, William Henry Pancoast, was also a physician.

[W. S. Miller in *Surgery, Gynecology and Obstetrics*, May 1930; T. H. Shastid in the *Am. Encyc. and Dict. of Ophthalmology*, vol. XII (1918); H. A. Kelly and W. L. Burrage, *Am. Medic. Biogs.* (1920); J. W. Croskey, *Hist. of Blockley* (1929); S. D. Gross, *Autobiog.* (1887), vol. II; J. W. Holland, *The Jefferson Medical Coll. of Phila.* (1909); *Boston Medic. and Surgic Jour.*, Mar. 16, 1882; *Medic. News*, Mar. 18, 1882; *Phila. Medic. Times*, Mar. 25, 1882; *Pub. Ledger* (Phila.), Mar. 8, 1882; for data concerning parents and marriage, *The Friend*, Dec. 31, 1831, and *Poulson's Am. Daily Advertiser* (Phila.), July 4, 1829.]   J. McF.

PANCOAST, SETH (July 28, 1823–Dec. 16, 1889), physician, anatomist, and cabalist, descended from one of the settlers who came to America with William Penn, was born in Darby, Pa., the son of Stephen Pancoast, a paper manufacturer, and Anna (Stroud) Pancoast. His preliminary education was gained probably in the local schools. The first few years of his adult life he spent in business, but when he was twenty-seven years of age, in October 1850, he began the study of medicine at the University of Pennsylvania, from which he was graduated M.D. in 1852. The next year he was made professor of anatomy in the Female Medical College of Pennsylvania (now the Woman's Medical College of Pennsylvania). At the end of his first year, however, he resigned to become professor of anatomy in the Pennsylvania Medical College (now nonexistent), in which position he continued until 1859 when he became professor emeritus. In 1855 he wrote *An Original Treatise on the Curability of Consumption by Medical Inhalation and Adjunct Remedies*; in 1858, *Onanism-Spermatorrhoea; Porneio-Kalogynomia-Pathology;* the next year *Ladies' Medical Guide and Marriage Friend* (copr. 1859; subsequent editions, 1864, 1876); and in 1873 *The Cholera: Its History, Cause, Symptoms and Treatment*.

He conducted private practice and continued to teach in the positions mentioned above for only six years; then interested himself in cabalistic literature, in which field he became a noted scholar and built up probably the largest library of books dealing with the occult sciences ever assembled upon the American continents. The ideas gleaned from his cabalistic reading curiously mingled with his medical and scientific knowledge and led to the production of a few extraordinary books. The first of these was *The Kabbala; or the True Science of Light; an Introduction to the Philosophy and Theosophy of the Ancient Sages* (1877), said to be the first book ever written in the English language that attempted to explain the "Ten Sepheroth" and give the mystical interpretation of the Holy Scriptures as contained therein. This was followed by *Blue and Red Light: or, Light and Its Rays as Medicine; Showing that Light is the Original and Sole Source of Life, as It Is the Source of All the Physical and Vital Forces of Nature, and that Light is Nature's Own and Only Remedy for Disease, and Explaining How to Apply the Red and Blue Rays in Curing the Sick and Feeble* (1877). The title of this work is suggestive of some new and dominating therapeutic idea, but upon examination the book proves to be a cabalistic writing in which mystery, science, religion, and medicine are curiously, and to the average modern reader, incomprehensibly confused.

Pancoast was married three times: first, to Sarah Saunders Osborn; second, to Susan George Osborn; third, to Carrie Almena Fernald. His family included children by all three wives. He died in Philadelphia.

[*A Supplement to Allibone's Critical Dict. of English Lit. and British and Am. Authors* (1891), vol. II; H. A. Kelly and W. L. Burrage, *Am. Medic. Biogs.* (1920); *Public Ledger* (Phila.), Dec. 17, 1889.]   J. McF.

PANTON, WILLIAM (1742?–Feb. 26, 1801), Indian trader, the son of John and Barbara (Wemys) Panton, was born in Aberdeenshire, Scotland, and emigrated to Charlestown, now Charleston, S. C. His life after his emigration falls naturally into three periods. During at least a part of the first period, from about 1770 to 1775, he resided in Charlestown, obtained a South Carolina land grant, and was for several years a member of the firm of Moore & Panton of Savannah. From 1775 to 1784 he spent most of his time in East Florida, where he organized, with Thomas Forbes as his chief associate, the firm, Panton, Forbes & Company, and built up trade and influence with the Creek Indians. His consistently Loyalist attitude, which brought him into conflict with the South Carolina and Georgia Revolutionary authorities early in the Revolution, culminated in his permanent outlawry by two acts of the Georgia Provincial Congress, in 1778 and 1782, and the confiscation of his property.

In the third period, from 1784 to 1801, the most important historically, he lived mostly in West Florida. After the British evacuation of East Florida, in July 1784, it became evident that Spain needed the friendship of the southern Indians for protection against the aggressive Anglo-American backwoodsmen to the north. Convinced that a well-conducted trade offered the best way to get and hold that friendship and finding no Spanish house available, the Spanish government temporarily allowed Panton's firm, now Panton, Leslie & Company, to continue their trade without loss of British citizenship or freedom of worship. As no Spanish house ever became available, Panton, Leslie & Company and their successors kept up the Indian trade and allied activities until the close of the Spanish régime. At its greatest extent the business comprised the trade of the Creek, Choctaw, Chickasaw, and Cherokee Indians, conducted by Panton at the Pensacola headquarters through a chain of branches, agencies, and trading posts ranging from Havana and Nassau to New Orleans and from Mobile to the Chickasaw Bluffs, with a "concern" in London to furnish trade goods and to market the peltries and other commodities received from the Indians. He claimed a monopoly under his royal grants; for only a part of the time, however, was he able to make good his claim. To the difficulties common to mercantile undertakings of the time and those that weighed even more heavily in the affairs of the firm after its reorganization by John Forbes, 1769–1823 [*q.v.*], was added the competition of the American trade made possible by the liberal Indian trade policy of the United States, which in Panton's later years almost drove the firm into bankruptcy. None the less, he was able, in spite of his heavy losses in Georgia and in the Florida Indian trade, to keep the business going and to leave his family and friends more than £10,000. He was able, moreover, for the most part to hold his own in the face of international complications.

Seriously ill, he sailed for Havana on the advice of his physician in January 1801. Because of the war then in progress between Great Britain and Spain he, as a British subject, was denied admittance in spite of his passport from the Spanish commandant of Pensacola. Continuing his voyage to Nassau he broke under the strain, died at sea, and was buried at Great Harbours, Berry Islands. Record and tradition agree in ascribing to him a strong personality and an important rôle in American history. He was exceptional in business ability and resourcefulness, hot-tempered and insistent upon his own rights yet diplomatic, careful in money matters yet generous, and loyal to friends and principle. Never married, he showed a fatherly interest in his young relatives and business associates. He influenced, perhaps more than any other one man, the course of Spanish-Indian frontier relations in the Old Southwest in the last years of the eighteenth century.

[Papers in Public Record Office, London, in Lib. of Cong., and privately owned in New Orleans and Wash-ington; *Am. State Papers: Indian Affairs*, vols. I, II (1832–34), *Public Lands*, vols. III–V (1834–60); W. H. Siebert, *Loyalists in East Fla.* (1929), vol. II; *Revolutionary Records of Ga.*, vol. I (1908), ed. by A. D. Candler, pp. 90, 146, 216, 330, 378; *S. C. Hist. Soc. Colls.*, vol. III (1859), pp. 216, 219; A. P. Whitaker, *Documents Relating to the Commercial Policy of Spain in the Floridas* (1931) and *The Spanish-American Frontier* (1927); Lorenzo Sabine, *Biog. Sketches of Loyalists in the Am. Revolution* (1864), vol. II; C. F. Jenkins, *Button Gwinnett* (1926); P. J. Hamilton, *Colonial Mobile* (1897); R. L. Campbell, *Hist. Sketches of Colonial Fla.* (1892); C. M. Brevard, *A Hist. of Fla.*, vol. I (1924); A. J. Pickett, *Hist. of Ala.*, 2 vols. (1851); J. F. H. Claiborne, *Mississippi* (1880); date and circumstances of death from *Papeles de Cuba*, legajo 203, Archivo de Indias, Sevilla, photostatic copy in Lib. of Cong., numbered within the legajo as 67, and also from transcript of letter in possession of Mrs. Marie Taylor Greenslade, Washington, D. C., who also furnished other information.]   E. H. W.

PARDEE, ARIO (Nov. 19, 1810–Mar. 26, 1892), engineer, coal operator, philanthropist, son of Ariovistus Pardee and Eliza (Platt), was born at Chatham, N. Y. The family genealogy (D. L. Jacobus, *post*) gives his name as Ariovistus, but elsewhere it appears as Ario. The Pardees, according to the family tradition, were of Huguenot extraction, but they had lived in England for at least two generations before George Pardee emigrated to New Haven about 1644. Soon after Ario's birth his father moved to a farm in Stephentown, Rensselaer County, N. Y., where the boy grew up. He attended the district school until he reached the age of fifteen, and thereafter continued to study at home under the direction of Rev. Moses Hunter.

In 1830 he began training as an engineer by becoming a rodman for the surveyors who were locating the Delaware & Raritan Canal in New Jersey. He continued work with the engineers in charge of constructing the canal until 1832, when he went with the chief engineer to locate the Beaver Meadow Railroad connecting the coal mines at Beaver Meadow, Pa., with the Lehigh Canal at Mauch Chunk. His employers soon recognized his ability by placing him in charge of the construction of this road. In 1836 the Hazleton Railroad & Coal Company was organized to exploit the rich vein of anthracite at the present Hazleton. An outlet was needed and Pardee was employed as chief engineer to build a railroad from these mines to the Beaver Meadow road. After its completion he continued as chief engineer of the company.

Resigning in 1840, he began business as an independent coal operator, founding the firm of Pardee, Miner & Company, later known as A. Pardee & Company, which in time became the largest shipper of anthracite coal in the state. As the business grew, Pardee extended his interests until they included mines in various anthracite and bituminous fields, locomotive and car works at Hazleton, iron works at Allentown, in New York state, and in Virginia, and lumber holdings in Pennsylvania, West Virginia, the Carolinas, and in Canada. He also became a director of the Lehigh Valley and other railroads. He first became interested in Lafayette College, Easton, Pa., in 1864. This institution was in financial difficulties, and in 1863 the trustees commissioned the newly elected president, William C. Cattell [*q.v.*], to raise $30,000 in a year as the price of saving the college. After eleven months, having raised only a third of that sum, he preached at Hazleton in the Presbyterian church which Pardee attended, and was the rich man's guest. After hearing of the college's financial embarrassments, Pardee said to Cattell: "Why don't you throw it up if it doesn't pay? That's what we do when we strike a vein of coal that doesn't pay us to work." Cattell then ventured to explain his views of the difference between education and coal mining, and asked Pardee for $20,000. To his amazement, Pardee promptly wrote his note for that amount—said to have been the largest single gift from an individual to an educational institution that had then been made in Pennsylvania. The capitalist, now interested, followed up his investment with larger gifts. As an engineer and businessman he was most interested in the practical type of education. He endowed the "Pardee Scientific Course" in 1866, and in 1871 he offered to erect and equip a building to house it, his total gifts amounting to more than half a million dollars. In 1865 he became a trustee and from 1882 to his death was president of the board. In this capacity he was noted for his business-like application to the affairs of the institution, for his regular attendance at commencements, for his quiet modesty, and for his consistent refusal to make a long speech on any public occasion. He was reputed to have bestowed many charities so quietly that they were known only to the recipients. In Hazleton he was known as "the silent man"—a familiar but elusive figure, engaged in grand and far-flung business schemes, driving quietly and persistently toward his objectives, and disclosing little of his purposes or personality to any but a few close friends—a little group of financial magnates—and perhaps to President Cattell. He was a presidential elector in 1876, and chairman of the board of commissioners for the second Pennsylvania Geological Survey. He was married in 1838 to Elizabeth Jacobs of Butler Valley, who died in 1847, and on Aug. 29, 1848, to Anna Maria Robison

of Bloomsburg. He died suddenly at Ormond, Fla., survived by ten of his fourteen children.

[D. L. Jacobus, *The Pardee Genealogy* (1927); W. C. Cattell, *Memorial Address Delivered at Lafayette Coll. . . .* (1892); H. C. Bradsby, *Hist. of Luzerne County, Pa., with Biog. Selections* (1893); W. H. Egle, *An Illustrated Hist. of the Commonwealth of Pa.* (1877); M. S. Henry, *Hist. of the Lehigh Valley* (1860); D. B. Skillman, *The Biog. of a Coll. Being the Hist. of the First Century of the Life of Lafayette Coll.* (2 vols., 1932); *Public Ledger* (Phila.), Mar. 28, 1892.]
D. L. M.

PARDEE, DON ALBERT (Mar. 29, 1837–Sept. 26, 1919), Union soldier, Southern jurist, was born in Wadsworth, Medina County, Ohio. His parents were Aaron Pardee, a native of that part of Marcellus which became Skaneateles, N. Y., and Eveline (Eyles) Pardee, of Kent, Litchfield County, Conn. The boy attended the public schools of Medina County, Ohio, and the United States Naval Academy (1854–57) at Annapolis. Resigning before graduation he entered upon the study of law in his father's office at Wadsworth, Ohio, and was there admitted to the bar of Ohio in 1859. He was married, Feb. 3, 1861, to Julia E. Hard, of Wadsworth, who died some years later. He practised law in his native county from 1859 to 1861, when he volunteered in the 42nd Ohio Volunteers. He was commissioned major on Oct. 27, 1861. In 1862 his regiment was transferred to the Army of the Mississippi, where he won distinction at Vicksburg and Port Gibson. In 1863 he was made provost-marshal of Baton Rouge. He remained with his original unit until it was mustered out in Arkansas late in 1864, and in March 1865 he was brevetted brigadier-general.

In January 1865 Pardee moved to New Orleans to practise law. His success was immediate. In 1867 he was made register in bankruptcy and in 1868 he was elected judge of the second judicial district of Louisiana, which embraced the parishes of Jefferson, St. Bernard, and Plaquemines. He held this judgeship for twelve years, being reëlected in 1872 and 1876. He was a delegate in 1879 to the Louisiana constitutional convention, and was Republican candidate for attorney-general of Louisiana in 1880. On May 3, 1881, President Garfield, under whom he had served in the war, appointed him United States circuit judge of the fifth circuit, and from 1891, when the circuit courts of appeals were created, until his death in 1919, he was senior judge of the circuit court of appeals for the fifth circuit. He removed to Atlanta in 1898 and maintained his residence there for the remainder of his life, spending a good part of each winter in New Orleans and a few weeks each summer on his farm in Medina County, Ohio. On June

14, 1898, he was married to Frances (Cunningham) Wells of Atlanta.

Pardee was tall and of massive proportions. He enjoyed riding and presented a striking figure on horseback. He was an expert at chess and a constant reader. Although always dignified and outwardly austere he gave to a few intimate associates a warm friendship. Many anecdotes survive to illustrate his kindly sympathy, his subtle sense of humor, his modest dislike of the limelight. On one occasion he refused to see a pistol fall to the floor of the courtroom from the pocket of a lawyer addressing the court. The attorney, hitherto hostile to the Judge, was completely won over by the incident.

It is remarkable how quickly Pardee overcame the handicaps attendant upon his going to live in the South at the close of the war. That he was no Carpet-bagger was immediately apparent, and he quickly won the respect of his late enemies as he practised his profession in their midst. Within three years he was elected judge of an important state court, retaining that position for three terms, then for thirty-eight years he graced the bench of the federal circuit court, achieving distinction as an admiralty judge and as a fair and able judicial administrator of railroads. A Union army officer become Southern jurist, he was able, courageous, and just, a stanch Republican who believed in the results of the war as written into the Constitution, and yet so understanding conditions in the South as to be able to give no offense. After his death his wife discovered in his billfold a small piece of paper on which he had written that the thing he prized most highly, in the long span of his judicial career, was the fact that he had never in all those years had to rebuke or punish an attorney for contempt.

[Sources include: *Who's Who in America*, 1918–19; "Memorial of Don A. Pardee," *Report of the Thirty-Seventh Ann. Session of the Ga. Bar Asso.*, 1920; A. D. Candler and C. A. Evans, *Georgia* (1906), vol. III; D. L. Jacobus, *The Pardee Geneal.* (1927); F. B. Heitman, *Hist. Reg. and Dict. of the U. S. Army* (1903), vol. I; the *Atlanta Jour.*, Sept. 26, 1919; a manuscript biography of Pardee by his associate, the Hon. A. G. Brice; and supplementary information from the Hon. Rufus E. Foster, New Orleans, La.; the Rev. C. B. Wilmer, Atlanta, Ga.; the Hon. John M. Slaton; and Mrs. Frances C. Pardee.]   P. E. B.

PARDOW, WILLIAM O'BRIEN (June 13, 1847–Jan. 23, 1909), Jesuit provincial, educator, and preacher, son of Robert and Augusta Garnett (O'Brien) Pardow, was born in New York City. His paternal grandfather, George Pardow, was of an old Lancashire family and came to New York in 1772, where he married Elizabeth Seton, and later, with William Denman, published *The Truth Teller*. His maternal grandfather was William O'Brien, an heir of the Earl of Inchiquin, who as a United Irishman was forced into exile, and coming to New York in 1800 established a successful banking business with his brother John. As good Irish rebels, the O'Briens refused the New York agency of the Bank of England, thus sacrificing financial reward for an impractical ideal. On both sides, there was a deep Catholic tradition which persecution had enlivened.

Trained in a home of refinement, William was educated in St. Peter's school and in the College of St. Francis Xavier, New York, from which he was graduated in 1864 with the expectation of entering the banking house. Refused as a volunteer on account of his youth, he sorrowfully faced separation from his brother, Robert, who joined a New York regiment and who, incidentally, on the death of his wife joined the Society of Jesus, which he served loyally until his death in 1884 from a contagious disease contracted while attending a hospital on Blackwell's Island. William was inspired with a longing for a religious life and finally made up his mind to become a Jesuit. Two sisters, later known as Mother Augusta and Mother Pauline, soon took vows as nuns of the Society of the Sacred Heart, in which they became mothers superior in Manhattanville and Philadelphia. A novice at Sault-au-Recollet, near Montreal, in 1865, William was influenced permanently by his militant master, James Perron, S. J., an aristocrat and ex-officer of the French army. On Sept. 1, 1866, he entered the juniorate in Quebec, from which he was advanced to Fordham, N. Y., for philosophy, and to Woodstock, Md., for theology (1869–71). In the latter year he was assigned as a teacher of Latin and Greek at the College of St. Francis Xavier, New York, prior to a four years' course in theology at Laval, France, where, in the meantime, he was ordained a priest (Sept. 9, 1877). As a result of the law excluding Jesuits from France, his tertianship at Paray-le-Monial was interrupted when the retreat-villa was seized at the point of the bayonet.

Recalled to the United States, he became in 1880 professor at the college of St. Francis Xavier, socius to the provincial (1884), instructor of tertians at Frederick, Md. (1888), and rector of St. Francis Xavier's (1891). In 1893 he was awarded the provincialship of the New York-Maryland province, in which position he served until 1897. Under his administration the spiritual care of Catholics in Jamaica was transferred from England to the United States. Becoming again a humble member of the Society, he was a teacher at Gonzaga College, Washington (1897–1901), pastor of St. Ignatius Church, New York (1901–03), master of tertians at St. Andrew-on-the-Hudson (1903–06). In the latter year he was a delegate to a general congregation in Rome for the election of the general of the order and associated with the Church of Gesù in Philadelphia. In 1907 he became pastor of the Church of St. Ignatius, New York. His request for missionary service in China (1900) and his offer to go to Tokio when the Jesuits opened their Japanese University did not meet with the approval of superiors.

Pardow was widely known from coast to coast as a preacher of fiery eloquence, clear diction, and magnetic presence, despite a frail, undersized body. Constant appeals came to him to preach in numerous cities, to give retreats for religious and diocesan priests, to deliver missions to non-Catholics, and to explain the church's attitude on marriage, education, divorce, and authority. Ill, but struggling on to complete a mission, he fell a victim to pneumonia and was buried in the characteristic pine box—a final lesson in humility to the crowds who viewed his remains and attended his requiem mass. In 1916, appeared *Searchlights of Eternity,* compiled from notes which he left.

[Justine Ward, *William Pardow of the Company of Jesus* (1914, 1915); *Records Am. Cath. Hist. Soc.,* Mar. 1915; *Who's Who in America,* 1908–09; *N. Y. Times,* Jan. 24, 27, 1909.]   R. J. P.

PARIS, WALTER (Feb. 28, 1842–Nov. 26, 1906), painter, was born in London, England, and studied in the Royal Academy there, and under T. L. Robotham, Paul Naftel, and Joseph Nash. From about 1866 to 1870 he was an architect in the service of the British government in India. About 1872 he came to the United States and in 1894 became a naturalized citizen. He was known in this country as a painter of water colors rather than as an architect, and as an amateur violinist. For the first few years after arrival in America he lived in New York, occupying a studio in Union Square, then made his home in Washington, D. C., for the rest of his life. It was in his New York studio that the famous Tile Club was organized. This club, picturesquely described by F. Hopkinson Smith in his novel, *The Fortunes of Oliver Horn* (1902), was fashioned after artist clubs in Germany and Austria and numbered among its members such men of later fame as Edwin A. Abbey, Frank D. Millet, Augustus Saint-Gaudens, Elihu Vedder, and Alden Weir.

Walter Paris was a large man, broad-shouldered, well-built, and wore moustache and full beard squarely cut. He had a dignity which verged on pomposity and was slow and heavy in movement and speech, the latter distinctly British in accent. But his paintings were exquisitely dainty, and although he prided himself on his breadth of style, his work was done painstakingly with minute attention to detail. His subjects to a great extent were rural English scenes painted, doubtless, from his own early sketches and memory, showing picturesque thatched cottages with flowery dooryards or well-kept kitchen gardens, blossoming hedgerows, and neat roadways. Possibly because of popular demand, he painted these over and over again. A notable exception, however, was a picture painted in gouache (which he seldom used) of the great blizzard of 1899, showing the State, War, and Navy Department Building on Pennsylvania Avenue, Washington, in a whirl of snow—a very difficult theme, most skilfully rendered. This painting is now in the permanent collection of the Corcoran Gallery of Art, which also owns Walter Paris' picture of Marcia Burns's cottage, an historical Washington landmark. Perhaps his most important work, however, was a series of flower studies in water color made from nature as aids to design. These were painted with the accuracy of the scientist and the skill and perception of the trained artist.

Walter Paris played on the violin with taste and intelligence, evidencing thorough training and sensitiveness of feeling, the latter again contradicting the impression given by his stiff manner. Of his own work and attainments he held high opinion, not infrequently frankly expressed, and he was intolerant of criticism, but this characteristic also may have been only the armor worn to protect a supersensitive nature. On moving to Washington he purchased land and built an imposing house as a future home, but he did not marry, and the house—never occupied—was eventually sold. He was a member of the Washington Water Color Club and other professional organizations, and exhibited regularly, but he always held himself somewhat aloof from his professional colleagues. He died Nov. 26, 1906, in a hospital in Washington, as the result of a stroke which occurred ten days earlier.

[*Am. Art Annual,* 1907–08; *Am. Art News,* Dec. 1, 1906; Ulrich Thieme and Felix Becker, *Allgemeines Lexikon der Bildenden Künstler,* vol. XXVI (1932); K. M. Roof, *The Life and Art of William Merritt Chase* (1917); *Evening Star* (Washington), Nov. 26, 1906; catalogues of the annual exhibitions of the Washington Water Color Club; personal acquaintance.]   L. M.

PARISH, ELIJAH (Nov. 7, 1762–Oct. 15, 1825), Congregational clergyman, author, was born in Lebanon, Conn., the son of Elijah and Eunice (Foster) Parish, his mother being descended from the Standish family. He prepared for college at Plainfield Academy and entered Dartmouth with the class of 1785, graduating with high honors. Three years later, perhaps upon his return to Hanover for his master of arts degree, he was admitted to the newly organized chapter of Phi Beta Kappa. Having chosen the ministry as a profession, he studied theology under the Rev. Ephraim Judson of Taunton, Mass. On Dec. 20, 1787, he was installed as pastor of the Congregational church at Byfield, Mass., where he remained until his death.

In his theological views Parish was Hopkinsian and therefore of the strictest Congregational orthodoxy. As a pastor, he was unusually successful and at his death there was not a more united parish in the state. Indeed, he appears to have quite dominated the life of his people, for "it is in no respect an exaggeration to say that any opinion expressed in opposition to their pastor, political, religious, or regarding measures of policy, would have had little chance of finding favour among his people" (Sprague, *post*, II, 270). His preaching had vividness and power. His conversational gifts were also exceptional, and he was noted for his quickness in repartee. In person he was somewhat below middle stature, of a piercing eye, and rapid in his motions. In addition to his parish concerns, he took a warm interest in the political affairs of the country, and, like most of the New England clergy, was a Federalist. Asked to preach the annual election sermon of 1810 before the legislature, he attacked the national administration so acrimoniously that the legislature, gravely offended, refused him the usual compliment of requesting a copy of the sermon for publication. It was published, however, by subscription and widely read (*A Sermon, Preached at Boston, Before his Excellency Christopher Gore . . .* May 30, 1810). Equally vigorous were his published sermons denouncing the War of 1812. In later years, however, his interest in politics waned, and he finally remarked to a friend that "Politics is like the variolus contagion, no man catches it a second time" (*Sermons, post,* p. ix). Eighteen of his sermons and three occasional addresses were published. He also assisted the Rev. Jedidiah Morse [*q.v.*] in his geographical and historical works, publishing in collaboration, *A New Gazetteer of the Eastern Continent* (1802) and *A Compendious History of New England* (1804). In 1810 he published his own *New System of Modern Geography* for schools, and three years later, *Sacred Geography; or, A Gazetteer of the Bible.* He

also wrote, with the Rev. David McClure, *Memoirs of the Rev. Eleazar Wheelock, D.D., Founder and President of Dartmouth College and Moor's Charity School* (1811). A posthumous volume of his sermons with a brief sketch of his life appeared in 1826. On Nov. 7, 1796, he married Mary Hale, daughter of Deacon Joseph Hale of Byfield; they had five children.

[The best sketch of Parish is in *Sermons, Practical and Doctrinal, By the Late Elijah Parish, D.D. With a Biographical Sketch of the Author* (1826); see also Roswell Parish, Jr., "John Parish of Groton, Mass., and Some of His Descendants," in *New England Hist. and Geneal. Reg.*, Oct. 1909; W. B. Sprague, *Annals Am. Pulpit*, vol. II (1857); G. T. Chapman, *Sketches of the Alumni of Dartmouth College* (1867); *Boston Daily Advertiser*, Oct. 21, 1825.]   W. R. W.

PARK, EDWARDS AMASA (Dec. 29, 1808–June 4, 1900), theologian, a descendant of Richard Parke who came to America on the *Defence*, in 1635, was the son of Calvin and Abigail (Ware) Park. He was born in Providence, R. I., and brought up in a home of refinement; his father was a professor in Brown University, his mother, distinguished for her character and culture. His education began early at home; he loved sports, was full of vigor, much given to mischief, and blessed with wit and humor. Growing up under strong religious influence, he reached maturity without the customary conversion crisis, though inclined to gloomy thought. He entered Brown University before he was fourteen years of age, the youngest member of his class; ranked high as a scholar; was assigned the Valedictory Oration, which, however, he declined; and was graduated in 1826. He then taught in the classical schools of Braintree and Weymouth Landing. He was undecided for a time as to his profession; once thought he would be a physician, then was inclined to study law, but finally chose the Christian ministry. In 1828 he entered Andover Theological Seminary, where he distinguished himself as a student and was graduated in 1831. His services were sought by Bangor Theological Seminary and by Congregational churches in Boston and Lowell, Mass., but he declined these offers and became pastor of the Braintree church, being ordained Dec. 21, 1831. As minister he studied hard, preached thoughtful and moving sermons, wrote much, mingled with his people, observed world events, and gained a marked influence.

In 1835 he became professor of mental and moral philosophy and instructor in Hebrew in Amherst College. In 1836 he was called to the Bartlet Professorship of Sacred Rhetoric in Andover Theological Seminary and in the same year, Sept. 21, married Ann Maria Edwards, a great-grand-daughter of Jonathan Edwards. As a preacher and teacher of the art of preaching he had few peers; he ranked with the greatest preachers and orators of his time. His instruction was marked for its learning, skill, eloquence, and influence. He was himself the best example of his own teaching in respect to speaking, reading the Bible, prayers, and manner. His sermons were events in the lives of his hearers, and some became historic in the annals of the American pulpit; noteworthy examples are "Judas," "Peter's Denials of His Lord," *The Theology of the Intellect and of the Feelings* (1850), and an election sermon, *The Indebtedness of the State to the Clergy* (1851).

In 1847, he was transferred to the Abbot Chair of Christian Theology which he occupied for thirty-four years. He was in the "Hopkinsian succession" and was the last outstanding exponent and champion of the "New England Theology," the aim of which, in his own words, was "to exalt God as a Sovereign and to glorify the eternal plan on which He governs the universe." He remained an eager student, was aware of new developments of thought, familiar with the work of scholars in Germany and elsewhere—he translated and edited German theological treatises—and was cognizant of but uninfluenced by new scientific thought. He was distinguished as a teacher of theology by his power of analysis and his skill in presentation, but was more concerned to make his students convinced holders of his system than independent thinkers. He published several pamphlets and was editor and translator, with Bela Bates Edwards [q.v.], of *Selections from German Literature* (1839). In 1844 he became co-editor with Edwards of *Bibliotheca Sacra,* founded the year previous by Dr. Edward Robinson [q.v.]. He was editor in chief from 1852 until the removal of the quarterly to Oberlin in 1884, and associate editor thereafter until his death. He wrote several memoirs, including brief biographies prefixed to collected works of his colleague B. B. Edwards, of Samuel Hopkins, and of Nathaniel Emmons [qq.v.]. In 1859 he edited *The Atonement: Discourses and Treatises by Edwards, Smalley, Maxcy, Emmons, Griffin, Burge, and Weeks,* for which he wrote the introductory essay; in 1858 he collaborated with Austin Phelps and Lowell Mason in compiling and editing *The Sabbath Hymn Book*; in 1885 he issued his *Discourses on Some Theological Doctrines,* while after his death a *Memorial Collection of Sermons* (1902) was compiled and published by his daughter.

In 1881 he resigned his professorship. The remainder of his life he spent in Andover, laboring to perfect his system of theology and viewing with alarm the new developments in the Seminary and in the world. His mind was eclectic rather than constructive, dialectical rather than philosophical, apologetic rather than critical, defensive rather than creative, and did not range beyond the narrow confines of the "New England Theology." He lived to see his best students reject his theology and the movement of thought pass beyond him; he recognized that his system of theology upon which he had worked so hard and so long was out of date, and it was never published.

Park was an impressive figure. A former pupil, describing from memory his appearance in the decade of the forties, mentioned "his slight, tall form, his chiselled features, fine, then, as if wrought in marble, his piercing eyes, and his impressive and animating voice" (Storrs, *post*). He was a delightful companion, a great story teller, a remarkable conversationalist, friendly in his personal relations, with some strong prejudices, essentially unworldly, and almost ascetic in personal habits; his mind dwelt on high themes, and his religious life centered on God. He died at Andover in his ninety-second year and was buried in the Chapel Cemetery.

[k. S. Storrs, *Memorial Address* (1900); Alexander Mackenzie, *Memoir of Prof. E. A. Park* (1901); F. H. Foster, *A Genetic Hist. of the New England Theology* (1907), ch. xiii; *Who's Who in America,* 1899–1900; F. L. Mott, *Hist. of Am. Mags.* (1930); F. S. Parks, *Geneal. of the Parke Families of Mass.* (1909); W. H. Edwards, *Timothy and Rhoda Ogden Edwards of Stockbridge, Mass., and Their Descendants* (1903).]

D. E.

PARK, JAMES (Jan. 11, 1820–Apr. 21, 1883), iron and steel manufacturer, was born in Pittsburgh, Pa., of Scotch-Irish parentage. His father, James Park, was a native of Ireland who probably emigrated to the United States in 1812, and his mother, Margaret (McCurdy), was the daughter of a Scotch-Irish physician resident in Pittsburgh at the time of her marriage. Park's early education was obtained in the Pittsburgh elementary schools, and at seventeen he began his business career in his father's china and metal store, rising to partnership in 1840 with a younger brother, David E. Park. The firm, which later achieved national prominence as Park, Brother & Company, became James Park, Jr. & Company on the father's death in 1843, and gradually expanded its personnel and interests under the leadership of the elder brother. John McCurdy and James B. Scott were at different times members of the firm; an interest was acquired in a cotton-goods factory in Allegheny, Pa., and the Lake Superior Copper Works were founded in 1857 for the manufacture of sheathing copper from Lake Superior ore.

Park retained partial control of these and other varied enterprises throughout his life, but it was not until shortly before the Civil War that he entered upon the most significant activity of his career. At that time he became interested in the iron industry and from 1860 to 1883 he had a prominent part in its development. To this he contributed along two distinct lines: he encouraged the introduction of new industrial processes, although not of an inventive type of mind himself; and he was instrumental in increasing the tariff schedules which entrenched steel in its position of special privilege.

The first real impetus to steel-making was due to a political maneuver, for the framers of the Morrill tariff act of 1861, in the hope of making Pennsylvania safe for the Republican party, increased the duties on iron and steel. Before 1860 many attempts had been made on a small scale at Pittsburgh to produce crucible cast steel, but the first to be commercially practicable was that of Hussey, Wells & Company in 1860. Park's firm followed this in 1862 with the establishment of the Black Diamond Steel Works. After preliminary failures, this plant achieved a product of high quality with American iron, and was said in 1883 to have a greater capacity for crucible steel than any other plant in the world. Park was also connected with the development in the United States of the "pneumatic" process of steel making. Although permanently linked with the name of Sir Henry Bessemer, priority of invention of this process has now been generally conceded to William Kelly [q.v.]. E. B. Ward of Detroit and Z. S. Durfee [q.v.] of New Bedford, Mass., bought control of Kelly's process after experiments had convinced them of its practicability, and in May 1863 they, together with Daniel J. Morrell of Johnstown, Pa., William M. Lyon of Detroit, and James Park, Jr., incorporated the Kelly Pneumatic Process Company. Experimental works were established at Wyandotte, Mich., and there, in the autumn of 1864, the first steel made in the United States by the complete Bessemer process was blown. Park's connection with this enterprise (finally abandoned in 1869) ceased with its purchase by E. B. Ward in 1865.

Park was the first to introduce into the United States the Siemens gas furnace for metal conversion. Invented and patented in England by Charles William Siemens and his brother Frederick, this type of furnace became a vital part of the Siemens-Martin open-hearth steel process. The first Siemens furnace, completed by Park, McCurdy & Company at their copper works on Aug. 14, 1863, was operated successfully. A second one, built later in the same year to heat steel, was not a success. Both these furnaces were constructed from published drawings, and without securing a license from the Siemens brothers. The first licensed introduction of the regenerative gas furnace was not until 1867, at Troy, N. Y. Another experiment was undertaken in 1877 by Park, Brother & Company when, in conjunction with Miller, Metcalf & Parkin, they tried out a process invented by C. W. Siemens for making refined iron directly from the ore. The results were not encouraging, and the attempt was abandoned in 1879.

In September 1882 Park, a vice-president of the American Iron and Steel Association from 1873 to 1883, presided over a convention of the trade, and was authorized to lay its views before the tariff commission created that year with a view to tariff reduction. He testified effectively in defence of the policy which had made his fortune, and after the hearings were over spent much time in Washington lobbying for the tariff bill. He is said to have had great influence in securing the final result as embodied in the bill approved Mar. 3, 1883. It was a cleverly contrived victory for the protectionists, increases in steel duties being concealed under ostensible changes in classification. It is possible that Park's tariff activities in 1882 and the early months of 1883 hastened his death, which occurred at his home in Allegheny, Pa., following an apoplectic stroke. He was survived by his widow, Sarah (Gray) Park, and their five sons and two daughters.

Typically the entrepreneur, Park sincerely believed that what benefited the manufacturer must inevitably also benefit the workingman and the consumer. One eulogist said of him: "We wonder if the manufacturers of this country and its workingmen fully realize the sacrifices that a few willing and earnest men like James Park, Jr., have always made to secure to them the benefits and the blessings of a Protective tariff. ... Mr. Park leaves a large estate, estimated at from two to five million dollars" (*The Bulletin of the American Iron and Steel Association,* May 2, 1883, p. 116).

[G. T. Fleming, *Hist. of Pittsburgh and Environs* (1922), vol. IV; J. N. Boucher, *A Century and a Half of Pittsburg and Her People* (1908), vol. II; J. W. Jordan, *Encyc. of Pa. Biog.,* vol. IX (1918); J. M. Swank, *Hist. of the Manufacture of Iron in All Ages* . . . (1884); *Pittsburg: its Industry and Commerce* (1870); F. W. Taussig, *The Tariff Hist. of the U. S.* (8th ed., 1931); *Report of the Tariff Commission Appointed Under Act of Congress Approved May 15, 1882* (1882), II, 2009–2094; *Pittsburg Dispatch,*

Apr. 23, 1883 ; *Bull. Am. Iron and Steel Asso.*, May 2, 1883.]   L. P. B—t.

PARK, ROSWELL (Oct. 1, 1807–July 16, 1869), educator, Episcopal clergyman, was born in Lebanon, New London County, Conn., the son of Avery and Betsey (Meech) Park, and a descendant of Robert Parke, who came to Boston from England in 1630. His early childhood was spent in his native town, but when he was about twelve years of age his parents moved to Burlington, Otsego County, N. Y. After a period of preparatory study at the Oxford and Hamilton academies, he matriculated at Hamilton College as a sophomore in 1826, but withdrew in 1827 upon receiving an appointment to the United States Military Academy at West Point. He graduated as highest ranking man in the class of 1831, and was commissioned brevet second lieutenant in the corps of engineers of the United States army. In the same summer, he passed the senior examinations at Union College, and received the degree of A.B. His first military duty was in connection with the construction of Fort Adams, at Newport, R. I., 1831. Two years later he was transferred to Fort Warren, Boston, Mass. In 1836 he took charge of the Delaware Breakwater. Deciding to seek a larger field for the expression of his ambitions and talents, he resigned from the army, Sept. 30, 1836, and for the next six years served as professor of chemistry and natural philosophy at the University of Pennsylvania. While here he decided to enter the ministry of the Protestant Episcopal Church, and resigned his professorship in July 1842.

Removing to Burlington, Vt., he prepared for holy orders under the guidance of Bishop George W. Doane [q.v.]. Admission to the diaconate was granted Sept. 10, 1843, and he was ordained priest on May 28, 1844. In 1843 he was appointed rector of Christ Church at Pomfret, Conn. From 1845 to 1852, while fulfilling his pastoral duties, he conducted the Christ Church Hall preparatory school, and as its headmaster became well known throughout New England. Norwich University, in 1850, invited him to become president, but he declined. Late in the spring of 1852 he resigned from his charges in Pomfret and traveled in Europe for six months. Upon his return, he accepted an invitation to establish and become the first president of Racine College, at Racine, Wis. He opened the institution in November 1852, with a program which included scientific studies, leading to the B.Sc. degree, for those who did not wish to devote themselves exclusively to the usual classical course. Many innovations in administration and

instruction were introduced by him. He strengthened the college substantially by uniting with it, in 1859, the St. John's School at Delafield, Wis. His title was then changed to that of chancellor, the former headmaster of St. John's becoming warden. In the enlarged college, the scientific course was discontinued and the elective system established. From 1856 to 1863 Park served, also, as rector of St. Luke's Church, in Racine.

In the latter year, he withdrew from the college and the pulpit, and removed to Chicago, Ill. Here he founded Immanuel Hall, a classical and scientific school, which he conducted as a private venture until his death. He was an original member of the American Association for the Advancement of Science, and was affiliated with many other scientific and literary societies. His published writings include *Selections of Juvenile and Miscellaneous Poems* (1836), a second edition of which appeared in 1856 under the title *Jerusalem and Other Poems*; *A Sketch of the History and Topography of West Point and of the United States Military Academy* (1840); *Pantology: or a Systematic Survey of Human Knowledge* (1841); *Handbook for American Travelers in Europe* (1853). He was married, Dec. 28, 1836, to Mary Brewster, daughter of Benjamin Franklin and Mary Carter Brewster (Coolidge) Baldwin, of Woburn, Mass. After her death, he married, Apr. 25, 1860, Eunice Elizabeth, daughter of Gardner and Elizabeth (Ward) Niles of Waukegan, Ill.

[F. S. Parks, *Geneal. of the Parke Families of Conn.* (1906) ; O. F. Adams, *A Dict. of Am. Authors and Others* (1899) ; G. W. Cullum, *Biog. Reg. Officers and Grads. U. S. Military Acad.* (3rd ed., 1891) ; *The Asso. Grads. U. S. Mil. Acad. Ann. Reunion, 1870* ; *Church Reg.*, Aug. 1869; *Chicago Republican*, July 18, 1869.]
R. F. S.

PARK, ROSWELL (May 4, 1852–Feb. 15, 1914), surgeon, was born at Pomfret, Conn., the son of the Rev. Roswell Park [q.v.]. His mother was Mary Brewster Baldwin, a descendant of Elder Brewster of the Plymouth colony. Roswell Park obtained his academic education in Connecticut and in Racine, Wis., where he attended Racine College (founded by his father), receiving the degree of B.A. in 1872, and that of M.A. in 1875; his medical course he pursued at Northwestern University (M.D., 1876). The following year he became demonstrator of anatomy in the Woman's Medical College, Chicago, serving as such until 1879, when he was appointed adjunct professor of anatomy in Northwestern Medical School. In 1882 he was lecturer on surgery at Rush Medical College, Chicago, and in 1883 he became professor of surgery in the School of Medicine of the University of Buffalo, which position he held until his death; he was also surgeon-in-chief at the Buffalo General Hospital. He received various honorary degrees, was president of the Medical Society of the State of New York and of the American Surgical Association (1900), and was a member of various foreign societies.

At a time when skilful operators were not common, Park was a great surgeon. His principal service, however, was in assimilating and then teaching and making popular new discoveries in pathology and bacteriology. The period between the years 1880 and 1890 was marked by amazingly rapid advances in these branches of science. Practitioners in the United States were somewhat slow in understanding and applying the antiseptic technique of Lister for surgical operations, and Park played an important part in making it—and the later modifications of it—known, and in securing its adoption. He devoted himself especially to surgical pathology, in which he pursued studies both in America and Europe. From these studies various lectures and papers resulted, which had a wide influence in making surgeons realize the importance of pathology. In 1890-91 he gave the Mütter lectures at the College of Physicians and Surgeons, Philadelphia, published under the title, *The Mütter Lectures on Surgical Pathology* (1892), a valuable book at that time. Later, he promulgated certain original views with regard to inflammation, that did not meet with general acceptance. He edited, and largely wrote, a text-book, *Surgery by American Authors* (1896), and in 1907 published a large work, *The Principles and Practice of Modern Surgery*. In subsequent years he was greatly interested in tumors, wrote many papers on the subject, and was instrumental in having founded an institution for the study of malignant tumors, first known as the Gratwick Laboratory, which later became the New York State Institute for the Study of Malignant Diseases. In spite of his having come from a long line of Puritan ancestors, Park's interests were broad and the tendencies of his mind liberal. He was attracted by the cultural, as well as by the strictly scientific side of his profession. He wrote *An Epitome of the History of Medicine* (1897), and published a collection of "border line" essays called The *Evil Eye, Thanatology and Other Essays* (1912), the style of which is singularly felicitous. He was a good lecturer, a good story teller, and an accomplished musician, prominently supporting efforts to bring good music to Buffalo. He was one of the surgeons who attended Presi-

dent McKinley after the latter was shot at the Pan-American Exposition in Buffalo in 1901. In 1880 he married Martha Prudence Durkee of Chicago, and of this marriage two sons were born.

[Memoirs by C. G. Stockton, in Roswell Park, *Selected Papers, Surgical and Scientific* (1914), ed. by Julian Park, and in *Buffalo Hist. Soc. Pubs.*, vol. XXII (1918); H. A. Kelly and W. L. Burrage, *Am. Medic. Biogs.* (1920); *Trans. Am. Surgic. Soc.*, vol. XXXII (1914); *N. Y. Times*, Feb. 16, 1914; *Who's Who in America*, 1912-13.]   H. U. W.

PARK, TRENOR WILLIAM (Dec. 8, 1823–Dec. 13, 1882), lawyer, financier, was born at Woodford, Vt., near Bennington, to which city his parents, Luther and Cynthia (Pratt) Park, removed three years later. The Park family was descended from Richard Parke who emigrated from England to Cambridge, Mass., in 1635. William Park, the grandfather of Trenor, was a quartermaster of Massachusetts troops in the Revolutionary army. During the boy's childhood his family lived in poverty, and as a consequence his educational opportunities were meager and irregular. At the age of sixteen he entered the law office of A. P. Lyman, was admitted to the Vermont bar soon after he had attained his majority, and began to practise in Bennington. On Dec. 15, 1846, he married Laura V. S. Hall.

When his wife's father, Gov. Hiland Hall [*q.v.*], was appointed on the federal commission to settle land titles in California, Park and his family followed him, in 1852, to that state. Here he became junior partner in the firm of Halleck, Peachy, Billings & Park, which included Henry W. Halleck and Frederick Billings [*qq.v.*]. Park is credited with doing "a very large share of the business created by the controversies on land titles in California" (*New York Tribune*, Dec. 21, 1882). The close relation of the firm to commissioner Hall is suggested by the fact that after Hall was displaced by President Pierce he remained for a time as its "general adviser." With such connections the firm and its junior partner reaped their full share of the profits accruing to the lawyers in the tortuous land title business of that period. An important chapter in Park's business career, and a considerable factor in the building up of his fortune, was his connection with the famous Mariposa estate of Gen. John C. Frémont [*q.v.*]. Park had advanced large sums on the security of the estate, had a mortgage covering one-eighth interest, and was in possession as local manager. When the estate was offered for sale in 1863, he proposed to give possession if his accounts were cleared for $1,400,000. In 1863 a company was organized and took over the estate at a valuation of $10,000,000, based almost entirely on the showing made by gold mines in operation. Park returned to the East in that year and had a major rôle in forming the company. It was shortly discovered that the output of the mines, which reached $100,000 a month at the maximum, had been achieved by the familiar expedient of exploiting the richest seams to the full and neglecting development and exploration work. The company, not being provided with adequate working capital to meet the actual conditions, shortly collapsed with disastrous loss to its shareholders.

During the remainder of his life Park made his home in Bennington, where he built a handsome residence. He established the First National Bank of Bennington and became interested in Vermont railroads, assisting in the reorganization of the Vermont Central, purchasing the Western Vermont Railroad, and commencing construction of the Lebanon Central. He seems to have had visions of a system of lines centering in Bennington; but the project failed and he lost heavily. He had narrowly failed of election as United States senator from California in 1862, and he now became active in Vermont politics, serving four terms in the legislature (1865–68). He was a delegate to the Republican National Convention in 1868, aiding in the nomination of General Grant, and serving as a member of the national committee.

Going to Utah in April 1871, Park acquired a controlling interest in the famous Emma mine. By his own statement he "worked it vigorously." In early September he went to London, accompanied by Senator William M. Stewart [q.v.], and, succeeding in forming an English company to take over the mine, received as his share half the stock. In connection with the sale he had induced Gen. Robert C. Schenck, then ambassador to the Court of St. James's, to become a director in the new company. Park loaned Schenck $50,000, without interest, to invest in shares of the new corporation, guaranteeing him by written contract one and one half per cent. a month return on his investment. At the time of the sale the mine was producing $75,000 in silver monthly. Park sold out his remaining interests at a large profit in the fall of that year, and returned to the United States in July 1872. It speedily became evident that the Emma mine had been exploited and its possibilities grossly overstated. Park was sued for fraud and after a five months' trial acquitted. The caustic comment of the judge in later litigation correctly characterizes these transactions: "In conclu-

sion, it is proper to say, that the evidence discloses many circumstances connected with the sale of the Emma mine, which strongly impeach the honor and morality of the transaction, but which are to be eliminated from the case, except so far as they bear upon the question of fraud in law" (14 *Blatchford,* 420). Later Park was interested in the Pacific Mail Steamship lines, of which he was a director from 1875 to 1882. He bought a controlling interest in the Panama Railroad, administered its affairs, and held the position of president from 1875 to his death. In 1881 he sold it to the De Lesseps Panama Canal Company at $300 per share, having stimulated the purchaser by judicious firmness in maintaining the extremely high passenger and freight rates on the shipment of canal building machinery, labor force, and supplies.

Park's first wife having died in 1875, he married Ella F. Nichols of San Francisco on May 30, 1882. His death occurred on the steamship *San Blas,* while he was making a voyage to the Pacific. His benefactions to his home city included $5,000 toward the establishment of the Bennington Public Library, to the maintenance of which he made liberal gifts later. He donated an art gallery to the University of Vermont, of which institution he was a trustee. When the Civil War broke out he sent a check for $1,000 from California as his contribution to the outfitting of Vermont troops. He was greatly interested in the *New York Tribune* fresh air fund for city children, entertaining over a hundred children at his country home. He was modest and unobtrusive but thoughtful, an inveterate reader and possessed of great mental power. In his career he made many enemies but had the capacity also of maintaining firm friendships. Three children by his first wife survived him.

[F. S. Parks, *Geneal. of the Parke Families of Mass.* (1909); Hiram Carleton, *Geneal. and Family Hist. of the State of Vt.* (1903), vol. II; *N. Y. Tribune,* Dec. 22, 1864, Feb. 5, Apr. 16, 1875, Dec. 21, 1882; A. M. Hemenway, *Vt. Hist. Gazetteer,* vol. V (1891); *The Mariposa Estate.... Its Mineral Wealth and Resources* (1873); Benjamin Silliman, Jr., *Review of the Nature, Resources and Plan of Development . . . of the Northern Division of the Mariposa Estate* (1873); L. E. Chittenden, *The Emma Mine. A Statement . . . Prepared for . . . The Committee of Foreign Affairs of the House of Representatives* (1876).]   C. E. P.

PARKE, BENJAMIN (Sept. 2, 1777–July 12, 1835), soldier, jurist, was born in New Jersey and grew up there on a farm, acquiring during his youth such education as the common-schools of the time and place afforded. When about twenty years old he migrated to the West, settling first at Lexington, Ky., where he took up the study of law in the office of James Brown [q.v.]. After his admission to the bar he removed, in 1801, to the newly organized territory of Indiana, residing first at Vincennes and then at Salem. Vincennes, the first territorial capital, was the scene of rather violent local politics in which Parke participated as the friend and supporter of the governor, William Henry Harrison [q.v.]. This allegiance to the most powerful personage in the territory may have paved the way to subsequent preferments. At any rate, in 1804 Parke was made attorney general, and throughout the Harrison régime in Indiana he was from time to time appointed to offices of a military character. While serving as attorney general (1804–08) he was elected in 1805 to the first territorial legislature, and in December of the same year was sent as delegate to Congress, where he served for two terms, resigning in 1808 to accept appointment as territorial judge. In 1816, when delegates were elected to frame a state constitution, he was sent to the convention as a Knox County member, and is credited with being instrumental in securing the adoption of certain educational provisions which became the foundation of the state school system.

Meanwhile, his activity in the local militia at a time when that organization was an arm of real importance in frontier defense was something more than the gratification of a passing ambition for glory. For at least ten years he was in this service, and when the troubles with the Indians culminated in 1811 in the Tippecanoe campaign he raised a company of dragoons and joined the expedition. He participated in the bloody battle of Tippecanoe following Harrison's march, and after that engagement was made commander of the cavalry with the rank of major. The knowledge he acquired of the Indian character made him valuable in a civil as well as a military capacity, and he served as an Indian agent and as a commissioner representing the United States in negotiating various land treaties. The most noteworthy of these treaties was that signed at St. Mary's, Ohio, in 1818, by which the whole central part of Indiana was secured to the whites. The representatives of the federal government on this occasion were Jonathan Jennings, then governor of the state, Lewis Cass [qq.v.], and Benjamin Parke.

As a jurist Parke took high rank among the pioneer judges of Indiana. A contemporary said of him: "His honest mind seemed to look through the technicalities of the case, and seize the merits of it almost without an effort.... He made a first-rate judge; patient, courteous and kind" (Smith, post, p. 147). He was on the bench, all told, about twenty-seven years; first

as a territorial judge, to which office he was appointed by President Jefferson in 1808, then as United States district judge, under a commission dated Mar. 6, 1817, soon after Indiana was admitted to the Union. In the latter office he served until his death. This long service was the more notable by reason of the arduous character of his duties in the days of large circuits and hard traveling. A story survives of his riding horseback from Vincennes to Wayne County, across the state, to try a man for stealing a twenty-five cent pocket knife.

Educationally Parke was a self-made man, yet he attained to a reputation for learning and is said to have acquired one of the largest private libraries in Indiana Territory. He was a promoter of the first public library in the territory, established at Vincennes, and of a later one at Corydon which was the forerunner of the Indiana State Library. He was also connected with the territory's first school of higher learning, Vincennes University, being at one time chairman of its board of trustees. Historical and antiquarian interests also claimed his attention and he was one of the organizers of a society of that character at Vincennes, and afterwards first president of the Indiana Historical Society, founded in 1830. Throughout his latter years he made unceasing efforts to repay money losses due to unfortunate business reverses caused by others. Through frugal living and work, made harder by the handicap of partial paralysis, he managed before his death to free himself of debts for which others were to blame. He has been described as tall and spare in person, of rather frail physique, dignified in appearance, but affable. He married Eliza Barton at Lexington, Ky., before moving to Indiana, and they had two children, a son and a daughter, both of whom died before their parents.

[W. W. Woollen, *Biog. and Hist. Sketches of Early Ind.* (1883); C. W. Taylor, *Biog. Sketches and Review of the Bench and Bar of Ind.* (1895); O. H. Smith, *Early Ind. Trials and Sketches* (1858); Charles Dewey, *An Eulogium upon the Life and Character of the Hon. Benjamin Parke* (1836); *Am. State Papers: Indian Affairs*, vol. II (1834); "Executive Journal of Indiana Territory, 1800–1816," *Ind. Hist. Soc. Pubs.*, vol. III (1905); "Governors' Messages and Letters," *Ind. Hist. Colls.*, vols. VII, IX (1922), XII (1924); *Indiana Democrat* (Indianapolis), July 24, 1835.]

G. S. C.

PARKE, JOHN (Apr. 7, 1754–Dec. 11, 1789), soldier and poet, was born at Dover, Del., the son of Thomas and Ann Parke. Records in the court house at Dover indicate that Thomas Parke was a well-to-do citizen of that place, a hat-maker by trade and sheriff of Kent County, 1758–60. He died in 1766, leaving, besides his widow, who apparently did not long survive him, at least three children. John Parke attended Newark Academy and Newark College, which became the University of Delaware, and then was a student at the College of Philadelphia, forerunner of the University of Pennsylvania, where he received the degree of A.B. in 1771 and that of A.M. in 1775. After graduation he studied law with Thomas McKean [*q.v.*] for some four years. In August 1775, recommended by McKean and Caesar Rodney [*q.v.*], he was appointed assistant quartermaster-general of the Continental Army at Cambridge, Mass., and on June 29, 1776, in New York, was appointed lieutenant-colonel of artificers. He resigned from the army, Oct. 29, 1778, and died on his estate, "Poplar Grove," in Kent County, Del., eleven years later.

Parke is remembered chiefly for a work which he published anonymously in Philadelphia in 1786, entitled *The Lyric Works of Horace, Translated into English Verse: to Which Are Added, a Number of Original Poems, by a Native of America.* The printer of this work, Eleazer Oswald, was one of Parke's comrades in the army, also a lieutenant-colonel, who had set up as a bookseller "at the Coffee House" in 1786. In the volume Parke included translations from other classical poets than Horace and both original poems and translations by other hands than his own. Some of the versions of Horace are really paraphrases which adapt the subject matter to the circumstances of American history, substituting George Washington for the Emperor Augustus. Most of the poems are supplied with dedications and notes of the date and place of writing. These notations indicate that some of the translations were made in 1769–70 at college, that in 1772 Parke had made a journey to Hartford, Conn., and that he was at Valley Forge. Together with land records in which he is mentioned they show that his residence after his retirement from the army was Arundel in Murderkill Hundred, a few miles from Dover.

The poet included in his volume, besides a life of Horace, which he addressed to Benjamin Franklin, and his own version of the odes, a pastoral by John Wilcocks, whom he described as "late an officer of the British Army, my most intimate friend and acquaintance," and whose death in 1772 he commemorated in an elegy; poems by Mr. John Pryor, "a young gentleman of Dover"; and translations written between 1720 and 1730 by David French, Esquire, late of the Delaware Counties. The versification is in the manner of Pope, whom Parke greatly admired, and whose translations he sometimes adopted, with acknowledgment, when his own

seemed inadequate. Bound in the same volume is *Virginia: a Pastoral Drama, on the Birthday of an Illustrious Personage and the Return of Peace, February 11, 1784,* addressed to John Dickinson. The illustrious personage is obviously Washington, and the scene of the action Mount Vernon. Parke is said to have written original poems and satires, including a comedy representing the petty administration of justice, but these are not extant. The dedication of an ode "To my German Flute, Dover, 1770" and another "On hearing Miss Kitty Smith play and sing to the guitar, Philadelphia, 1771" would seem to indicate in the poet at least some taste for music; and the range of his dedications testifies to a wide circle of friends. Deeds in which his name occurs imply that he was unmarried and prove that in 1784 he was the only surviving son of Thomas Parke.

[E. D. Neill in *New-Eng. Hist. and Geneal. Reg.,* July 1876; J. T. Scharf, *Hist. of Del.* (2 vols., 1888), pp. 1039, 1046, and 1163; *Mag. of Hist.,* Extra No. 91 (1923); J. F. Fisher, in *Memoirs of the Hist. Soc. of Pa.,* vol. II, pt. II (1830); G. H. Ryden, *Letters to and from Cæsar Rodney* (1933), p. 62; three unpublished letters by Parke in the library of the Hist. Soc. of Pa.; the guardians' account of Bertles and Cecilia Shee, Dover, Del.]   J. C. F.

PARKE, JOHN GRUBB (Sept. 22, 1827–Dec. 16, 1900), soldier, son of Francis and Sarah (Gardner) Parke, was born near Coatesville, Chester County, Pa. In 1835 his family moved to Philadelphia, where he attended Samuel Crawford's preparatory academy and the University of Pennsylvania. He entered West Point in 1845 and graduated in 1849, second in a class of forty-three. Brevetted second lieutenant, corps of topographical engineers, he was sent to determine the boundary between Iowa and Minnesota. In 1852–53 he was secretary of the board for improvement of lake harbors, and Western rivers and surveyed for the Pacific Railroad route. On Apr. 18, 1854, he was promoted second lieutenant, and on July 1, 1856, first lieutenant. In 1857–61 he was chief astronomer and surveyor for the determination of the northwest boundary between the United States and Canada. The outbreak of the Civil War interrupted this work.

Parke was promoted captain of engineers, Sept. 9, 1861, and moved from the Pacific Coast to Washington early in October. He was made brigadier-general of volunteers, Nov. 23, 1861, and assigned to command the 3rd Brigade in Burnside's North Carolina expedition, which sailed from Annapolis on Jan. 9, 1862. Roanoke Island and Fort Forest were captured, Feb. 8, and Parke's brigade next helped to capture New Bern, N. C. It then invested Fort Macon, which, by skilful use of his batteries, Parke forced to surrender. For this achievement he was brevetted lieutenant-colonel, United States Army, Apr. 26, 1862, and major-general of volunteers, July 18, 1862. When the order came from Burnside to join McClellan in Virginia, Parke became Burnside's chief of staff. He fought at South Mountain, at Antietam, at Fredericksburg, and, when Burnside took command of the Ohio Department, Mar. 25, 1863, Parke became commander of the IX Corps at Cincinnati. Early in June he went to reinforce Grant at Vicksburg, his corps holding the extreme right flank until Vicksburg surrendered. The corps next participated in Sherman's capture of Jackson City with its subsequent railway destruction. For meritorious conduct, Parke was brevetted colonel in the Regular Army.

Ill health now incapacitated him until Sept. 15, when the IX Corps marched to reinforce Burnside at Knoxville and operated against General Longstreet until Dec. 4. The Confederates withdrew northward and Parke's command, IX and XXIII Corps, followed. Longstreet turned and forced Parke back to Blain's Crossroads, whereupon both sides went into winter quarters. On Jan. 26, 1864, Parke again took station at Knoxville and was ordered, Mar. 16, 1864, to report to Burnside, who was reorganizing and recruiting the IX Corps at Annapolis. The corps was ordered, Apr. 23, in support of the Army of the Potomac, being constituted a separate unit responsible to Grant until May 24, when it was assigned to Meade. As chief of staff of the IX Corps, Parke fought in the battle of the Wilderness, in battles around Spotsylvania, in the James River campaign, and in the advance against Petersburg. On June 17, 1864, he was promoted major in the engineer corps. From July 4 to Aug. 13, he was prostrated by malaria. Rejoining his command, he engaged in all subsequent operations against Petersburg, fought at Peeble's Farm, Oct. 2, 1864, Hatcher's Run, Oct. 27, 1864, and Fort Steadman, Mar. 25, 1865. For this latter action he was brevetted brigadier-general, United States Army. The IX Corps fought and won its last action at Fort Sedgwick, Apr. 2, 1865, Parke receiving his brevet as major-general. When Meade was absent, Parke commanded the Army of the Potomac.

After hostilities, he commanded the District of Alexandria and, in July 1865, the Southern District of New York. He was mustered out of the volunteers, Jan. 15, 1866, and resumed his duties as major in the engineer corps. From Sept. 28, 1866, to October 1869, he was again

with the Northwest Boundary Commission. In the meantime, June 5, 1867, he married Ellen Blight of Philadelphia; they had one child, a daughter. On June 1, 1868, he was detailed as assistant chief of engineers, serving until his appointment as superintendent of the United States Military Academy in August 1887. He was promoted lieutenant-colonel in the engineer corps Mar. 4, 1879, and colonel, Mar. 17, 1884. Having served forty years, he was retired at his own request on July 2, 1889. Thereafter he engaged in business in Washington, D. C., as director of the Washington & Georgetown Street Railway Company, and of the National Safe Deposit Company. He was secretary of the Protestant Episcopal Cathedral Foundation, manager of the Columbia Hospital, and president of the Society of the Army of the Potomac. He wrote several valuable reports and compilations, of which *Laws of the United States Relating to the Construction of Bridges over Navigable Waters of the United States, from Mar. 2, 1805, to Mar. 3, 1887* (1887), and "Report of Explorations ... Near the 32d Parallel of Latitude, Lying Between Dona Ana, on the Rio Grande, and Pimas Villages, on the Gila" (*House Executive Document 129*, 33 Cong., 1 Sess., 1855) are the most important. Parke died at Washington, and was buried in the cemetery of the Church of St. James the Less in Philadelphia.

[F. B. Heitman, *Hist. Reg. and Dict. U. S. Army* (1903); T. H. S. Hamersly, *Complete Regular Army Reg. of the U. S.* (1880); G. W. Cullum, *Biog. Reg. Officers and Grads. U. S. Mil. Acad.* (1891); *War of the Rebellion: Official Records* (*Army*); *Thirty-Third Ann. Reunion, Asso. Grads. U. S. Mil. Acad.* (1902); *Washington Post*, Dec. 18, 1900.]   C. C. B.

PARKER, ALTON BROOKS (May 14, 1852–May 10, 1926), jurist, was born at Cortland, N. Y., the son of John Brooks and Harriet F. (Straton) Parker. He was of New England descent, his grandfather, John Parker, having moved from Massachusetts to Cortland County about 1800. He received his early schooling at the academy and the normal school at Cortland, and at the age of sixteen began to teach. He then studied law, at first in the office of Schoonmaker and Hardenbergh, Kingston, N. Y., and later at the Albany Law School, from which he was graduated in 1873. He began the practice of law at Kingston, N. Y. In his first important case he represented Ulster County in a controversy over assessments with the City of Kingston and won at every point, incidentally gaining much popularity in the rural districts. He was elected surrogate in 1877, and was reelected by a large plurality in 1883. In both elections he was the only successful Democratic candidate on the county ticket. His success attracted the attention of the state leaders and made him a member of the National Democratic Convention of 1884. The next year President Cleveland offered him the position of first assistant postmaster-general, which he declined for financial reasons. As chairman of the Democratic state committee, shortly afterward he managed the campaign of David B. Hill [q.v.] for governor so successfully that the entire state ticket was elected. He was rewarded by appointment to a vacant justiceship of the supreme court in the third district. He was appointed to the second division of the court of appeals, 1889; to the general term of the first department, 1892; and to the appellate division of the supreme court, 1896. In 1897, a year when Democratic prospects were dark, he was elected chief justice of the court of appeals by the astonishing plurality of more than 60,000 votes.

After 1885 Parker showed a preference for continuing his judicial career by several times refusing to be considered as a candidate for governor. As chief justice, the tendency of his decisions in civil cases was to hold private litigants to the strict letter of their contracts, and in equity cases, to narrow the application of remedies. In labor cases his attitude, expressed in dissenting opinions or in decisions of a closely divided court, was distinctly liberal. For example, he upheld the right of labor unions to obtain a closed shop by threatening to strike (*National Protective Association of Steamfitters and Helpers* vs. *Cumming, 170 N. Y. Reports,* 315); and the constitutionality of an act of 1897 limiting the hours of work in bakeries and confectioneries to sixty a week (*People* vs. *Lochner, 177 N. Y. Reports,* 144). In general his policy was to uphold legislative acts unless they were forbidden by specific constitutional provisions.

After Bryan's second defeat in 1900 most Democratic leaders believed that the next presidential candidate should be chosen from the eastern wing of the party. Parker was regarded as having exceptional qualifications. He was popular in New York; he had voted for Bryan in 1896; and he had not been embroiled in factional struggles within the party. Prior to the convention of 1904 he refused to make any statements on public questions, and when told that his silence might cost him the nomination, he expressed his willingness to do without it rather than compromise his position as a judge or appear to seek the presidency. David B. Hill and others obtained support for him among most of the delegates and apparently controlled the convention; but they were unable to insert in the

platform a resolution expressing satisfaction with the gold standard. Parker was nominated on the first ballot. He immediately sent to a delegate, William F. Sheehan, a telegram declaring that he regarded the gold standard as "firmly and irrevocably established," and offering the convention an opportunity, if his opinion was unsatisfactory to a majority, to choose another candidate before adjournment (*Proceedings,* p. 277). The convention sent a reassuring reply.

During the campaign the party managers, in order to contrast Parker sharply with their idea of Roosevelt, neglected his liberal record and presented him as safe and conservative. Parker's activities seem to have been based upon much the same principle. He remained at home in the early months, speaking only when delegations visited him. His addresses impressed the country as honest and sincere, but inspired little enthusiasm for him. Just before the election he became more aggressive, and in the course of a short speaking tour, declared that corporations were making huge contributions to the Republican campaign fund in expectation of receiving substantial favors from Roosevelt if he should be elected. Challenged to furnish proofs, Parker refused to reveal the source of his information, which had been given him in confidence. Later investigations proved his charges to have been, in general, correct. He was badly defeated, receiving only 140 electoral votes in a total of 476.

After the election Parker began practising law in New York City. Among other clients, he represented the American Federation of Labor, before a subcommittee of the House of Representatives (1915) concerning the Danbury Hatters' judgment; Samuel Gompers and other labor leaders in contempt proceedings in the Buck's Stove and Range case (33 *Appeal Reports D. C.,* 83, 516; 40 *Appeal Reports D. C.,* 293); and the prosecution in the impeachment of Gov. William Sulzer of New York. In 1912 he was temporary chairman of the Democratic National Convention, and is said to have been opposed to the nomination of Wilson. He was twice married: on Oct. 16, 1873, to Mary Louise Schoonmaker of Accord, N. Y., who died in 1917; and on Jan. 16, 1923, to Amelia Day Campbell of New York City (*New York Times,* Jan. 17, 1923). He died in New York City, survived by his widow and a daughter by his first marriage.

[The campaign biography by J. R. Grady, *The Lives and Public Services of Parker and Davis* (1904), has only a few pages devoted to Parker. His judicial decisions are analyzed briefly by M'Cready Sykes, in the *Green Bag,* Mar. 1904. Other sketches of his career may be found in the *World* (N. Y.), Dec. 2, 1902; the *Sun* (N. Y.), Feb. 8, 1903; *Albany Law Journal,* May 1904; *Am. Monthly Review of Reviews,* Aug.

1904; *N. Y. Times*, May 11, 1926; *N. Y. Herald, N. Y. Tribune*, May 11, 1926; memoir by M. J. O'Brien, in *N. Y. County Lawyers' Asso. Year Book, 1926.* See also: *Official Report of the Proc. of the Democratic Nat. Convention . . . 1904* (1904); F. R. Kent, *The Democratic Party, A History* (1928); *Proc. of the Court for the Trial of Impeachments. The People of the State of N. Y. . . . against Wm. Sulzer . . .* (2 vols., 1913); *Danbury Hatters' Judgment. Hearing before Subcommittee of House Committee on Appropriations . . .,* 63 Cong., 3 Sess. (1915).]   E. C. S.

PARKER, ALVIN PIERSON (Aug. 7, 1850–Sept. 10, 1924), missionary to China, was born on a farm near Austin, Tex., the son of Peter and Mary (Boyce) Parker. Both his father and mother were recently from Virginia. When he was still an infant the family moved to Missouri, where on pioneer farms, first near Hannibal and then in Ralls County, he grew up, sharing in the hard physical labor of frontier agriculture. His parents were earnestly religious, his father having a local preacher's license in the Methodist Church. Opportunities for education were meager, but he had, probably through his father, a passion for learning. He attended country schools and Van Rassler Academy. The money he had saved for college expenses was needed by the family. For a time he taught school in Virginia. Then, after a deep religious experience, he decided to enter the ministry and served several charges.

In 1875 he went to China as a missionary of the Methodist Episcopal Church, South. For several years he was stationed at Soochow, where he was largely responsible for the founding of the strong Methodist Church of which he was long the pastor. He also established and was for years at the head of the Buffington School, later the Buffington Institute, one of the forerunners of Soochow University. At least once he was in charge of his mission's hospital in Soochow. He was transferred to Shanghai in 1896 and there became president of the Anglo-Chinese College, serving in that capacity until 1906. For a time he was presiding elder of the Shanghai Conference of his Church. He was a man of scholarly tastes, and, in spite of the deficiencies in his early formal education, he taught himself enough Greek and Hebrew to enable him to use the Bible in the original, and he achieved a remarkable command of the Chinese language. Much of his time was given to the preparation of literature. He assisted in the translation of the Bible into the Soochow and Shanghai dialects, translated into Chinese a course of mathematics from algebra to mechanics, collaborated in the preparation of a hymnal, and translated and prepared notes on the International Sunday-school Lessons. He

had a part in compiling a vocabulary of the Shanghai dialect and in the revision of the translation of the Old Testament into classical Chinese. Among his other translations were the *Methodist Discipline,* several books of *The Expositors' Bible,* The American Statesman Series, and *The Encyclopædia of Religion and Ethics.* He was long editor of the *Chinese Christian Advocate* and prepared material for both the English and Chinese editions of that periodical. He served as editorial secretary of the China Sunday School Union, and he was book editor of the China Conference. For many of his later years he gave his main strength to the Christian Literature Society for China and for a time was chairman of the editorial staff of that organization. His *Southern Methodism in China* (1924) was going through the press at his death.

In addition to all these literary labors he found time to serve on many of the organizations which had to do with local and national policies of Protestant missions in China, among them the (Christian) Educational Association of China and the National Committee of the Young Men's Christian Association. He preached almost every Sunday of his long career. His counsel was sought by diplomats and other officials and he was offered but declined an advisorship to the Emperor of Korea and a high post in the Chinese ministry of education. In 1923 he returned to the United States on what he hoped was to be merely a furlough but while there died, in Oakland, Cal. In accordance with his wish, he was buried in China. He was twice married, first in December 1878, to Alice Scudder Cooley; and in February 1903, to Susan Williams.

[Annual reports of the Board of Foreign Missions of the Methodist Episcopal Church, South; *Chinese Recorder,* Nov. 1924; *Christian Advocate* (Nashville, Tenn.), Oct. 3, 1924; manuscript life prepared by Mrs. Parker; information from his friends.]   K. S. L.

PARKER, AMASA JUNIUS (June 2, 1807– May 13, 1890), lawyer, jurist, educator, was born in Sharon, Litchfield County, Conn. He was a son of Daniel Parker, a Congregational minister, and Anna Fenn, and a descendant of William Parker, one of the first settlers of Connecticut. In 1816 his parents moved to New York. He was educated by private tutors under the supervision of his father. At the age of sixteen he became principal of Hudson Academy in Hudson, N. Y. He never attended college, but in 1825 he took an examination on the entire course of Union College and was granted the degree of B.A. Two years later, having determined upon the law as a profession, he resigned his position and went to Delhi, N. Y., to study in the office of his uncle, Amasa Parker. In 1828 he was admitted to the bar. In August 1834 he was married to Harriet Langdon Roberts of Portsmouth, N. H., the daughter of Edmund Roberts [q.v.]. Their four children survived him.

Shortly after his admission to the bar he engaged actively in politics as a Democrat. He was a representative in the Assembly, 1834; district attorney of Delaware County, 1834–36; regent of the University of the State of New York, 1835–44; and member of Congress, 1837–39. In 1844 he was appointed circuit judge and vice-chancellor of the third circuit and won general approval during the anti-rent episode by disposing of 240 cases against persons accused of rioting within a period of three weeks. In 1847, after the adoption of a new constitution had abolished the circuit judgeships, he was elected justice of the supreme court for the third district for a term of eight years, the last two of which he sat on the court of appeals. Seeking reëlection, he was defeated by a candidate of the Know-Nothing party. In 1856, when his party was weakened by a division between "Hards" and "Softs," he was nominated for the governorship. He was regarded as a strong candidate because he had taken no part in the party dissensions, and he had won a certain degree of popularity through a decision questioning the constitutionality of the state prohibition law. He was defeated by a plurality of 65,000. He was again nominated for the office in 1858 and was defeated by a plurality of 17,000. Early in 1861 he was chairman of the Democratic and Constitutional Unionist convention at Albany which proposed compromise and conciliation as measures to settle the differences between the North and the South. After the firing on Fort Sumter he supported the federal government in prosecuting the war, protesting, however, against arbitrary arrests which appeared to be chiefly for partisan purposes. Though he was an aspirant for the Democratic gubernatorial nomination against Tilden in 1874, and chairman of an anti-Tilden convention in 1880, his political career may be said to have ended with the Civil War. His only later public office was as a member of the constitutional convention of 1867, in which he served on the important committee on the judiciary.

Continuing his early interest in education, Parker became one of the founders of the Albany Law School, 1851, in which he was a lecturer for nineteen years and special lecturer for ten years longer. He was also a member of the board of trustees of the Albany Female Academy and of Union and Cornell universities. As a lawyer, he was highly regarded. He appeared as counsel in cases involving the national bank taxes, the title to the Trinity Church property, and the boundary between New York and New Jersey. He edited *Reports of Decisions in Criminal Cases . . . State of New York, 1823–68* (6 vols., 1855–68) and was one of the editors of the fifth edition of *The Revised Statutes of the State of New York* (1859).

[*Biog. Dir. Am. Cong.* (1928); A. J. Parker, ed., *Landmarks of Albany County, N. Y.* (1897); D. A. Harsha, *Noted Living Albanians and State Officials* (1891); Martha J. Lamb, "Judge Amasa J. Parker," *Mag. of Am. Hist.,* Sept. 1890; "Amasa Junius Parker," *Report of the Thirteenth Ann. Meeting of the Am. Bar Asso.,* 1890; "Amasa Junius Parker," *Proc. N. Y. State Bar Asso.: Fourteenth Ann. Meeting,* 1891; Jay Gould, *Hist. of Delaware County . . . and a Hist. of the Late Anti-Rent Difficulties in Delaware* (1856); D. S. Alexander, *A Pol. Hist. of the State of N. Y.,* vol. II (1906); *N. Y. Herald,* Aug.–Oct. 1856.]

E. C. S.

PARKER, CARLETON HUBBELL (Mar. 31, 1878–Mar. 17, 1918), economist, labor conciliator, was born in Red Bluff, Cal., the son of William Boyd and Frances (Fairchild) Parker. He grew up in Vacaville, Cal., where he attended public school. Between 1896 and 1913 he studied at the universities of California (B.S. 1904), London, Harvard, Leipzig, Berlin, Heidelberg (Ph.D., *summa cum laude,* 1912), and Munich. Early interested in engineering and mining, he later became absorbed in economics, and attended the seminars of Alfred Weber, Eberhard Gothein, and Lujo Brentano. His studies were repeatedly interrupted by the need to earn a living. He worked as miner in California and British Columbia, newspaper reporter in Spokane, Wash., administrative officer in the University of California, and bond salesman in Seattle, Wash. In 1913 he became assistant professor of industrial economics in the University of California, and in 1917 head of the department of economics and dean of the College of Commerce at the University of Washington.

While in Germany, Parker became interested in the problem of conflict between employers and labor and he later specialized in the study of casual or migratory workers. He sought in psychological maladjustment an explanation for the militant tactics of the I. W. W. and migratory labor in general, and in his psychological analysis of the discontented worker borrowed from such diverse sources as the psychoanalytic school, the behaviorists, Dewey, Veblen, McDougall, and Adler. His principal writings were "The California Casual and His Revolt" (*Quarterly Journal of Economics,* November 1915), and "The I. W. W." (*Atlantic Monthly,* November 1917). These papers are included in *The Casual Laborer and Other Essays* (1920). His doctoral dissertation on the labor policy of the American trust, completed in 1914, was not published, owing to the interruption of communications with the Heidelberg authorities.

In November 1913, while retaining his connection with the University of California, Parker became executive secretary of the California State Immigration and Housing Commission. The salary of $4,000 represented his first financial success, but he resigned the post after a year, feeling that political influences were hampering his work. It was while he held this post that he made his report on the Wheatland hopfield riot of Aug. 3, 1913, a report which became a model for many investigators of labor militancy. Late in 1914 he conducted a similar investigation for the United States government in Phoenix, Ariz. During the World War, he served repeatedly as United States government labor conciliator and succeeded in preventing or terminating more than a score of important strikes. In October 1917 his analysis of the rise in living costs was adopted by the Shipbuilding Labor Adjustment Board of the United States Fleet Corporation as the basis of awards in Pacific shipyards.

The main factors in his success as a labor conciliator were an intimate practical knowledge of the migratory worker gained during his youth, conviction of his own disinterestedness, and a rare personal charm which disarmed all but the most uncompromising. He was for a time an outstanding practitioner of a method hailed by many as a contribution toward the definitive allaying of labor "unrest." He dealt with specific cases rather than with general principles and his technique was that of compromise. He tried to teach employers to make concessions (shorter hours, better living quarters, opportunities for recreation, etc.), while teaching workers to abjure militant tactics and to be content with limited gains. He skilfully utilized the stirring appeal lent by the war situation to such phrases as "the public interest," and in effect gave an American translation of the "civil peace" doctrine and practice which his German teachers had developed out of their older policies of social reform. His work was a striking illustration of the rôle of the academic expert in public affairs, a wartime development which excited much interest among younger progressive political thinkers and is part of the background of subsequent developments in personnel management and "welfare capitalism" in general.

During the last months of his life he began to speak in terms of a subordinate and an upper class, and to raise the question of a new economic order as opposed to the patching of "a rotten system." His analysis of the key-problem of the state, however, never transcended condemnation of the thieving, vulgar, stupid, or "standpat" politician, and death prevented a flexible and inquiring mind from pushing its investigations further. At the height of his career he contracted pneumonia and died after a brief illness. He was survived by his wife, Cornelia (Stratton) Parker, whom he had married Sept. 7, 1907, and by three children. His body was cremated and the ashes scattered on the waters of Puget Sound.

[Cornelia Stratton Parker, *An American Idyll: The Life of Carleton H. Parker* (1919); R. W. Bruère, "Carleton Hubbell Parker," *New Republic*, May 18, 1918; H. E. Cory, "Carleton H. Parker," *Univ. of Cal. Chronicle*, Apr. 1918; *Post-Intelligencer* (Seattle, Wash.), Mar. 18, 1918; information from Cornelia Stratton Parker.]

H.S.

PARKER, CORTLANDT [See PARKER, JOHN CORTLANDT, 1818–1907].

PARKER, EDWIN BREWINGTON (Sept. 7, 1868–Oct. 30, 1929), international jurist, was born in Shelbina, Shelby County, Mo. His grandfather, a substantial Maryland physician, had liberated his 200 slaves some years before the Civil War, but his father, George John Parker, a resident of Missouri, fought in the Confederate army until captured and paroled under oath not to take up arms again. His mother, Emrette (Faulkner) Parker, had been a teacher in Virginia and was a member of the faculty of the college at Fayette, Mo., that later became Howard-Payne College. For a time the boy attended Central College, at Fayette, Mo., but did not graduate. Through the influence of his mother's brother, Alsdorf Faulkner, then a prosperous citizen of Texas, he began the study of law at the University of Texas and received the LL.B. degree in June 1889. Being in debt for his education, he entered the employ of the Missouri, Kansas & Texas Railway and at the end of four years had become assistant general passenger agent. He began the practice of the law in 1893 at Houston, Tex., with the firm of Baker, Botts, Baker & Lovett, one of the largest law firms in the Southwest. On Dec. 27, 1894, he was married to Katherine Putman Blunt, the daughter of Gen. James G. Blunt [q.v.]. In ten years he became a member of his firm, the name of which became Baker, Botts, Parker & Garwood. In ten years more he was recognized as a leader not only at the bar but in business as well, serving as director for a number of successful business corporations.

When the United States entered the World War, he became a member of the War Industries Board and was appointed priorities commissioner. In this latter position he did an enormous amount of work, and in thirteen months his office handled 211,000 applications for priority and issued 192,000 orders. When the war closed, he was made chairman of the Liquidation Commission, and either returned to the United States or sold, principally to France, more than $3,000,000,000 worth of munitions and supplies that had been shipped to France for the use of the United States army. This work finished, he returned to his law practice, as general counsel for one of the great oil companies, the Texas Company, but in 1923 he was again called into the service of the government, this time as umpire of the Mixed Claims Commission, United States and Germany, a position he held until his death. Some 12,400 claims, aggregating $1,480,000,000 were filed with this commission, involving many questions entirely new in international law, such as the use of submarines, airplanes, and poison gas. The published reports of his opinions show a grasp of international law that challenged the admiration of statesmen and experts in international affairs (see especially, United States and Germany Mixed Claims Commission, *Consolidated Edition of Decisions and Opinions*, 2 vols., 1925–26). Before this work was finished, the United States, Austria, and Hungary, with Parker in mind, had drawn a treaty providing for a single commissioner to settle the claims of American citizens against these two parts of the old Austro-Hungarian monarchy. He was selected for this work and before his death had completed the task, disposing of claims aggregating about $41,000,000 (Tripartite Claims Commission, United States, Austria, and Hungary, *Final Report of Commissioner and Decisions and Opinions*, 1933). One other service he was called to render to his country. In 1928 he was named arbiter to determine claims against the United States growing out of the seizure of the German and Austrian vessels that were in American harbors when war was declared. This work was well under way but was not completed at the time of his death in Washington. For his services in these various positions, he was decorated by the United States, France, Belgium, Italy, and Poland. In his will he gave the residue of his estate for a school of international affairs and named a board of advisory trustees, who decided to establish the school at Columbia University.

[*"Memorial to Edwin Brewington Parker," Tex. Law Review*, Oct. 1930; Wilhelm Kiesselbach, *Problems of the German-American Claims Commission*, trans. by E. H. Zeydel (1930), esp. p. 2; *Who's Who in America*, 1929–30; *N. Y. Times*, Oct. 31, Nov. 1, Nov. 12, 1929; information from Oswald S. Parker, Beaumont, Tex., and Clarence R. Wharton, Houston, Tex.]

C. S. P.

PARKER, EDWIN POND (Jan. 13, 1836– May 28, 1920), Congregational clergyman, pastor or pastor emeritus of the Second Church of Christ, Hartford, Conn., for sixty years, though born in Castine, Me., was of Connecticut ancestry. He was a descendant in the seventh generation of William Parker who came to Hartford from England in 1636 and in 1649 settled in Saybrook. In entering the ministry he followed the family tradition, for he was the son of the Rev. Wooster Parker whose father, born in Saybrook, was Rev. James Parker, and whose wife, Wealthy Ann, was the daughter of Rev. Enoch Pond [*q.v.*]. Edwin prepared for college in the academy at Foxcroft, Me., graduated from Bowdoin in 1856, and from Bangor Theological Seminary in 1859. While in college he supported himself in part by teaching winters, giving instruction in music in various Maine towns, and in 1856–57 teaching the classics in Auburn Academy. On Nov. 1 of the year he finished his theological course he married Lucy M. Harris, the adopted daughter of one of his professors, Rev. Samuel Harris [*q.v.*]. Called to the Second Church, Hartford, about this time, he was ordained and installed on Jan. 11, 1860. Circumstances connected with this event occasioned a rather acrimonious controversy. The council had ordained him in spite of the fact that his statement of theological belief was not quite satisfactory to a few of the conservative members. In the *New York Observer* for Feb. 23, 1860, appeared an editorial, inspired by a letter to the editor from a Presbyterian minister present at the council, entitled: "New Gospel in New England. False doctrines taught: boldly encouraged: the reformation demanded." A refutation of the charges, by Rev. Joel Hawes and Rev. Samuel Spring, was printed in the issue of Mar. 8, and another by the same clergymen in the *Independent* of Mar. 22. The *Congregationalist* and the *Recorder* also entered the fray. The whole affair was simply a skirmish in the bitter theological warfare which had long been going on in Connecticut, for which Parker had innocently furnished the occasion, but it gave to the opening of his career an unpleasant notoriety.

During his ministry covering more than half a century, Parker became one of the most distinguished citizens of Hartford and one of the leading Protestant clergymen of the state. A friend of Rev. Nathaniel J. Burton, Rev. Joseph H. Twichell, and Samuel L. Clemens [*qq.v.*], he was associated with the coterie which gave to the Hartford of this period its literary reputation. Parker himself frequently lectured on literary subjects. His general influence, quietly exerted, was varied and substantial. He took little active part in political affairs but his sagacious counsel was a positive, if unobtrusive, factor in matters of civic importance. His ministry, while maintaining the best traditions of New England Congregationalism, had a liberating and broadening effect both locally and outside his own city and state. Theologically he was tolerant and reasonable but not radical. Having an inclination for ritual and a considerable knowledge of music, he contributed to the enrichment of worship in Congregational churches. His own church was perhaps the first of its order in New England to celebrate the Christmas season with a religious service. Many other similar innovations followed. With N. J. Burton and J. H. Twichell he prepared *The Christian Hymnal* (1877). A number of hymns written by himself have come into general use, among them the widely known "Master, no offering." His published addresses include *Biographical Sketch of Horace Bushnell* (1885); and *Historical Discourse in Commemoration of the One Hundredth Anniversary of the Missionary Society of Connecticut* (1898). In 1892 he published *History of the Second Church of Christ in Hartford,* a carefully prepared work of more than four hundred pages, which contains much about the life of Hartford from 1670 to 1892. He also prepared *Family Records, Parker-Pond-Peck* (1892). In 1912 he became pastor emeritus. The following year the *Hartford Courant* began to issue a Sunday edition, to which Parker contributed regularly under the title "Optimus." He was long an influential member of the corporation of Yale College. His first wife died in 1894 and on July 19, 1895, he married Mrs. Lucy A. Gilbert.

[*Gen. Cat. Bowdoin Coll., 1794–1912* (1912); *Who's Who in America,* 1918–19; *The Congreg. Year-Book: Statistics for 1920* (1921); *Obit. Record Grads. Bowdoin Coll. for Year Ending 1 June 1920* (1921); *Congregationalist and Advance,* June 17, 1920; *Hartford Courant,* May 29, 1920; *Hartford Times,* May 28, 1920.]   H. E. S.

PARKER, EDWIN WALLACE (Jan. 21, 1833–June 4, 1901), bishop of the Methodist Episcopal Church, for more than forty years a missionary in India, was born in St. Johnsbury, Vt., the son of Quincy B. and Electa (McGaffy) Parker. He was a grandson of Nathan Parker who, near the close of the eighteenth century, moved from Massachusetts to Vermont. Edwin was reared in a Methodist home and declared that as soon as he knew anything, he knew that

there was a heaven and a hell and that he was free to choose whether he would go to one or to the other. He attended school winters, worked on his father's farm, and for two terms was a student in St. Johnsbury Plain Academy. Converted at twenty, he determined to enter the ministry. After preparatory work in the academies at Newbury and St. Johnsbury, during which he supported himself by farm labor and teaching, in March 1856, with his wife, Lois Lee, whom he had recently married, he entered the Methodist Biblical Institute, Concord, N. H. Completing the three years' course there in two, he graduated in 1858. In the meantime, April 1857, he had been admitted to the Vermont Conference on trial, and in April 1858 he was appointed to the church in Lunenburg, Vt.

The Sepoy Mutiny was an impetus to greater missionary activity in India. New workers were called for, and among the first to respond were Parker and his wife. The former was appointed missionary Feb. 22, 1859, and ordained Apr. 10, at Lynn, Mass., where the New England Conference of the Methodist Church was in session. Six days later the Parkers sailed on the merchant vessel *Boston,* which was bound for Calcutta with a cargo of ice. They arrived at that port on Aug. 21, and reached the mission at Lucknow on Sept. 3. For the remainder of his life Parker was a potent agency in the development of Methodist missionary enterprises in Northern India, much of the time with Moradabad as his base. He was active in almost every branch of the service—preaching and evangelistic work, building operations, management of the press, education, and administration. When the India Conference was organized in 1864, he was appointed presiding elder, and officiated as such, with the exception of some three years, until 1900. While in the United States because of ill health in 1868–70, he and his wife were instrumental in organizing the Woman's Foreign Missionary Society in Tremont Street Church, Boston, and in arranging for the formation of coördinate societies in other great centers of the country. After his return to India he raised funds for the building in Moradabad of a structure combining church and school house, which, after his death, was named the Bishop Parker Memorial High School. With J. M. Thoburn [*q.v.*] he took the lead in establishing the Central Conference of India. In 1884 he was a delegate from the North India Conference to the General Conference, held at Philadelphia. He advised with John F. Goucher [*q.v.*] regarding the village schools in India which this philanthropist financed, and for years gave them his attention.

Always deeply interested in Sunday school work and the training of the young, he formed at Moradabad a young people's society which became the model for many others; and after the Epworth League organization was adopted in India, he served as president of the national society. He was a delegate to the General Conferences of 1892, 1896, and 1900. At the last of these he was elected missionary bishop. Soon after his return to India, however, he became ill and on June 4, 1901, he died at Naini Tal.

[J. H. Messmore, *The Life of Edwin Wallace Parker, D.D.* (1903); *Christian Advocate*, June 13, 1901; *Zion's Herald*, June 12, 1901.]   H. E. S.

PARKER, ELY SAMUEL (1828–Aug. 31, 1895), Seneca sachem, engineer and soldier, was born at Indian Falls, Town of Pembroke, Genesee County, N. Y., the son of William and Elizabeth Parker. The English patronymic was adopted from a white friend, but the father, known as Jo-no-es-do-wa to the Seneca, was a Tonawanda Seneca chief and a veteran of the War of 1812. The mother, Ga-ont-gwut-twus, was descended from Skaniadariio, a great Iroquois prophet.

Parker was reared as a reservation Indian, but received liberal schooling at the Baptist mission school of Tonawanda, and at Yates and Cayuga academies. He quit school at eighteen, and for the next twenty years was frequently the representative of his people in prosecuting Indian claims in Washington, where he was received with interest by the most distinguished, becoming the dinner companion of President Polk. In 1852 he became a sachem of his tribe, with the name Do-ne-ho-ga-wa, or Keeper of the Western Door of the Long House of the Iroquois. Throughout his life he was the champion of his people, defending them from dishonest land schemes of the whites. His association with Lewis H. Morgan [q.v.] was of particular interest, for he gave Morgan important aid in preparing what was perhaps the first scientific study of an Indian tribe, published as *League of the Ho-de-no-sau-nee or Iroquois* (1851). Parker read law but was refused admission to the bar on the grounds that he was not a citizen. He then turned to civil engineering, taking a course at Rensselaer Polytechnic Institute. As an engineer he was conspicuously successful, holding various important posts until 1857, when he became superintendent of construction for various government works at Galena, Ill. Here he became the friend of a clerk and ex-soldier, Ulysses S. Grant. During this period he held many high offices in the Masonic order.

When the Civil War broke out he could not, at first, obtain release from his duties in Galena, but in 1862 he resigned, and in accordance with tribal custom returned to the reservation to secure his father's permission to go to war. Neither the governor of New York nor the secretary of war would commission him on account of his race, and Seward even went so far as to tell him that the war would be won by the whites without the aid of the Indians. Finally, in the early summer of 1863, he succeeded in getting commissioned as captain of engineers, and joined Gen. J. E. Smith as division engineer of the 7th Division, XVII Corps. On Sept. 18 he joined his old friend Grant at Vicksburg as a staff officer, and on Aug. 30, 1864, he was appointed lieutenant-colonel and Grant's military secretary. He was present when Lee surrendered at Appomattox Court House, Apr. 9, 1865, and his huge swarthiness was noted by Lee with uplifted brows, but when it came time to draw up the terms of capitulation, the senior adjutant-general, Col. Theodore S. Bowers [q.v.], was so nervous he could not write, and it was the Indian, Parker, who at Grant's orders made interlineations in the penciled original and then transcribed in a fair hand the official copies of the document that ended the Civil War.

Following the war he remained as Grant's military secretary, being commissioned a brigadier-general of volunteers as of the date of Appomattox. He was appointed first and second lieutenant in the cavalry of the Regular Army, but his most signal military distinctions were his brevet appointments in the Regular Army, as captain, major, lieutenant-colonel, colonel, and brigadier-general, all on Mar. 2, 1867, and all for gallant and meritorious services. On Dec. 25, 1867, he married Minnie Sackett of Washington, from which marriage a daughter was born. He resigned from the army on Apr. 26, 1869, for by one of Grant's first appointments as president, Apr. 13, 1869, he had been made commissioner of Indian affairs. His many changes in the existing system, designed to give justice to the Indians, earned him enemies, and in February 1871 he was tried by a committee of the House of Representatives for defrauding the government. Although entirely cleared of the charges, he was heart-broken, and resigned soon after to go into business. He made a small fortune in Wall Street, but lost it by paying the bond of a defaulter. Later business ventures likewise proved unfortunate, and in his latter years he held positions with the police department of New York City. He died at his country home at Fairfield, Conn. In 1897, with impressive ceremonies, his remains were reinterred in the Red Jacket lot of Forest Lawn Cemetery, Buffalo, N. Y., on land that formerly belonged to his tribe.

[A. C. Parker, *The Life of Gen. Ely S. Parker* (1919); biog. data, including an unfinished autobiog. in *Buffalo Hist. Soc. Pubs.*, vol. VIII (1905); *Personal Memoirs of U. S. Grant*, vol. II (1886); *Army and Navy Jour.*, Sept. 7 and Dec. 7, 1895; F. B. Heitman, *Hist. Reg. and Dict. U. S. Army* (1903), vol. I, which gives day of death as Aug. 30; Horace Porter, *Campaigning with Grant* (1897); *Polytechnic* (Rensselaer Polytechnic Institute), Sept. 28, 1895; obituaries, giving Aug. 31 as day of death, in *N. Y. Times* and *N. Y. Tribune*, Sept. 1, 1895, and *Hartford Courant*, Sept. 2, 1895.]   D.Y.

PARKER, FOXHALL ALEXANDER (Aug. 5, 1821-June 10, 1879), naval officer, was born in New York City, the son of Foxhall Alexander and Sara Jay (Bogardus) Parker, and the nephew of Richard Elliot Parker [*q.v.*]. William Harwar Parker [*q.v.*] was a younger brother. His mother was a daughter of Gen. Robert Bogardus, a New York lawyer and infantry officer in the War of 1812. His father, a native Virginian and descendant of George Parker who settled in Accomac County, Va., in 1650, was a distinguished naval officer who served through the War of 1812, rose to command rank, and in 1848 was sent on an important mission to the German Confederation. He died a captain in 1857. The younger Foxhall Alexander was appointed midshipman from Virginia on Mar. 11, 1839. After service in the West Indies and against the Florida Indians, he studied at the naval school in Philadelphia and was made passed midshipman June 29, 1843. He then served in the *Michigan* on the Great Lakes; in coast survey work, 1848; in the *St. Lawrence* on a Mediterranean cruise, 1849-50; in the *Susquehanna* in the East Indies; and again in the coast survey, 1854-55. In the meantime, Sept. 21, 1850, he was commissioned lieutenant. After four years on the reserved list, he was in the Pacific Squadron, 1859-61. As executive officer of the Washington Navy Yard during the first year of the Civil War, he took active part in the naval campaign on the Potomac, and in July 1861, after the battle of Bull Run, manned Fort Ellsworth, Alexandria, with 250 sailors and marines for the defense of Washington. He was promoted to commander July 16, 1862, and in September following took command of the wooden gunboat *Mahaska*, in which he was senior officer in operation against Matthews Court House, Nov. 22, 1862, being commended by Gen. Erasmus D. Keyes for his "admirable manner" of exercising command. During the following winter he was on special duty

in Washington, and at work on tactical problems, first set forth in his *Squadron Tactics under Steam* (1864) and later in his *Fleet Tactics under Steam* (1870); this latter book attracted attention at home and abroad for its advocacy of "obliquing into line" to avoid exposure of broadsides and facilitate use of the ram. He also wrote *The Naval Howitzer Ashore* (1865) and *The Naval Howitzer Afloat* (1866), both of which were used as Naval Academy textbooks. In June 1863 he took command of the *Wabash* in Admiral J. A. B. Dahlgren's squadron off Charleston, but during the bombardment of Fort Sumter, Aug. 17-23, 1863, he had charge of the four-gun naval battery on Morris Island. From Jan. 1, 1864, until the end of the war he commanded the Potomac Flotilla, which was then chiefly engaged in patrol, reduction of shore batteries, and small combined operations with the army.

Following promotion to captain, July 25, 1866, he commanded the *Franklin*, European Squadron, 1870-71; served as chief of staff in the North Atlantic Fleet, 1872; and in September of that year drew up a new code of signals for steam tactics. He was made commodore, Nov. 25, 1872, was chief signal officer, 1873-76, and in December 1874 acted as chief of staff in the fleet assembled under Admiral A. L. Case for practice in Florida waters just after the *Virginius* affair. From 1876 to 1878 he had charge of the Boston Navy Yard. His death occurred suddenly from enlargement of the heart at Annapolis, Md., where for a year he had been superintendent of the Naval Academy. At his death bed were gathered all of his ten children. He was married, first, Feb. 10, 1846, to Mary Eliza Greene of Centerville, R. I., who died in 1849; second, Nov. 2, 1853, to Lydia Anna, daughter of Capt. H. S. Mallory, U. S. A., who died in 1862; and third, Oct. 20, 1863, to Caroline, daughter of Thomas Donaldson, a Baltimore lawyer. Parker was an able and highly respected officer, keenly interested in the science of his profession and a prominent writer on naval themes. He was chairman of the committee which organized the United States Naval Institute in 1873, and was its president in 1878. In addition to books mentioned above, he wrote *The Fleets of the World: The Galley Period* (1876), the first of a projected series of three volumes on naval history, and *The Battle of Mobile Bay* (1878).

["The Parker Family of Essex . . .," in *Va. Mag. of Hist. and Biog.*, Oct. 1898; M. S. B. Gray, *A Geneal. Hist. of the Ancestors and Descendants of Gen. Robert Bogardus* (1927); L. R. Hamersly, *The Records of Living Officers of the U. S. Navy and Marine Corps*

(3rd ed. 1878) ; *War of the Rebellion: Official Records* (Navy) ; *Army and Navy Jour.* (editorial), June 14, 1879 ; *Washington Post,* June 11, 1879.]   A. W.

PARKER, FRANCIS WAYLAND (Oct. 9, 1837–Mar. 2, 1902), educator, son of Robert Parker, a cabinet maker, and Milly (Rand) Parker, a teacher before her marriage, was born in the township of Bedford, N. H. His father died when he was six years of age, and he was bound out by his uncle to a farmer by the name of Moore, who provided him with a home and allowed him to attend district school eight weeks each winter. Parker records in some biographical notes that the best part of his early education was secured from his contacts with nature on the farm and from his reading of the few books available at the Moore house—the Bible, *The Pilgrim's Progress,* Wayland's *Life of Judson,* and some almanacs. At thirteen years of age he went to Mount Vernon, N. H., where he attended a good school. Here he earned his living by working at odd jobs until he was sixteen, when he began teaching.

He taught in New Hampshire until 1859 and was then called to a school in Illinois. Returning to New Hampshire at the beginning of the Civil War, he enlisted in Company E, 4th New Hampshire Volunteers, being commissioned lieutenant, Sept. 20, 1861. He rose to the rank of lieutenant-colonel, and was wounded, Aug. 16, 1864, at the battle of Deep Bottom. During his convalescence he married Phenie E. Hall of Bennington, N. H. After his marriage he returned to his regiment at Port Royal and served to the end of the war. Later, he taught school in several New Hampshire towns and in Dayton, Ohio, where he was put in charge of the normal school. He experimented with new and radical methods of teaching, following the lines suggested by the work of Dr. Edward A. Sheldon [*q.v.*] of Oswego, whose book entitled *Object Lessons* seemed to him to show how to overcome the formalism then common in American schools. His wife and an only child died while he was at Dayton.

In 1872 he went to Europe and studied in Germany, coming into contact with the new methods of teaching geography developed by Ritter and Guyot. He was also inspired by the developments in natural science, by the new methods of the Herbartians, and by what he observed in the kindergartens. Returning to the United States in 1875, he secured an appointment as superintendent of schools at Quincy, Mass. The community and the superintendent were enthusiastic about the introduction of science into the curriculum, the cultivation of freedom and informality in classroom methods, and the complete elimination of the rigid discipline traditional in New England schools. In 1880 he was called to Boston as one of the supervisors of the school system, and in 1883 he was appointed principal of the Cook County Normal School, Chicago, Illinois, which afterwards became a part of the city school system. Here Parker introduced the new ideas and methods which had made him famous in Quincy and Boston. He imported teachers sympathetic with his views and displaced the conservatives whom he found on the faculty. This action brought down a storm of protest, and for years a continuous battle raged between the reformer and his opponents. In the meantime, the Cook County Normal School became a widely recognized center for vigorous, liberal movements in elementary education. In 1883 he married Mrs. Frances Stuart, first assistant in the Boston School of Oratory. She sympathized fully with the reforms which Parker advocated and greatly reinforced him in his work.

In 1899 he was offered the opportunity to establish an independent normal school by Mrs. Emmons Blaine, who gave him a generous endowment for the new Chicago Institute. In 1901 the Institute was transferred to the University of Chicago and Parker became the first director of the School of Education of the University. This transfer was effected in part because of the cordial sympathy between Parker and Prof. John Dewey, and also because of President Harper's conviction that education as a technical field should be cultivated in the University. Parker did not serve long in his new position, however, since he died in 1902. His publications include *How to Study Geography* (1889) ; *Talks on Pedagogics* (1894) ; and in collaboration with Nellie L. Helm, *Uncle Robert's Geography* (4 vols., 1897–1904).

[William M. Griffin, *School Days in the Fifties* (1906) ; "In Memoriam," *Elementary School Teacher,* June 1902 ; W. S. Jackman, "In Memoriam, Col. Francis Wayland Parker," *National Education Association, Jour. of Proc. . . . 1902* (1902) ; F. A. Fitzpatrick, "Francis Wayland Parker," *Educational Rev.,* June 1902 ; I. F. Hall, *In School from Three to Eighty* (copr. 1927) ; *Who's Who in America,* 1901–02 ; *Chicago Daily Tribune,* Mar. 3, 1902.]   C. H. J.

PARKER, HORATIO WILLIAM (Sept. 15, 1863–Dec. 18, 1919), composer, was born in Auburndale, Mass., of American ancestry. Both his parents had artistic tastes. His father, Charles Edward Parker, was an architect of good reputation. The Boston Post-Office building was constructed under his supervision, and several large buildings in Boston and elsewhere in New England were planned by him. He held the office of superintendent of construction of government buildings in New England. Horatio's mother, Isabella Graham (Jennings) Parker, daughter of a Baptist minister, took a lively interest in literary matters and had a good command of Latin and Greek. She supplied several original poems and verse translations as *libretti* for her son's music. There were besides Horatio a brother, Edward, who later became a surgeon in the navy, and two sisters. Until he was sixteen he attended a private school in Newton, not far from Auburndale. Though this was his only schooling apart from the study of music, his home training and later scholastic environment, from which his unusually alert mind absorbed a full measure of culture, more than made up for the absence of class-room drill. His case is not unlike that of many other artists whose bias towards their chosen art tips the scales against the enthusiastic pursuit of ordinary subjects of study. But like the best of the artists of this class, lack of training made little practical difference, for Parker was exceptionally cultivated in his speech and choice of words, both in English and German, and especially in his mature years had a wide knowledge of matters remote from his profession.

There is no record of musical precocity in Parker. Indeed he did not show much interest in music until after his fourteenth year. His mother, whose tastes embraced music as well as literature, gave him lessons on the piano and organ. When the passion for music once sprang up in him he made up for lost time and at the age of sixteen became organist in a small church at Dedham, Mass., and later at St. John's church in Roxbury, now part of Boston. Not having acquired the ability to read music quickly at sight, he was obliged to commit to memory the whole service of music. During his early period he made studies in theoretical music under various teachers, Stephen A. Emery, the author of a well-known textbook on harmony, John Orth, and George W. Chadwick, all of whom stood high among Boston musicians. In 1882 Parker left Auburndale for study abroad. He was intending to study with the famous composer Joachim Raff, but, owing to the death of Raff, the plan had to be abandoned. Instead Parker went to Munich and enrolled himself in the Hochschule für Musik. He remained there until 1885. He was one of the most prominent and successful students in the school and was admired by the distinguished organist and composer Josef Gabriel Rheinberger, under whom he studied composition and organ-playing and who exerted a strong influence on Parker's music.

Rheinberger himself was a natural descendant of the line of classic German composers, and in composition and teaching showed a devotion to contrapuntal and structural perfection that was only slightly weakened by the softer influence of the Romanticism of his time. It is not difficult to account for the peculiar style that Horatio Parker developed during these formative days. Conservatism and a natural feeling for religion, together with the respect for tradition and validity of technique inculcated by Rheinberger's example, tended to crystallize his manner of expression as well as his point of view. In later years, after much experience in conducting choirs, Parker's style received a third element, the simple seriousness of the English choral style.

Parker graduated from the Hochschule in Munich in 1885, his second essay in elaborate composition, *King Trojan* (*opus* 8), being performed by a chorus and orchestra, with soloists, at the graduation exercises. (His first large composition had been a setting of the Twenty-third Psalm, *opus* 3, for women's chorus and organ, written during his Auburndale-Boston period, and later extensively revised.) At this time he became engaged to Anna Plössl, daughter of a bank official at Munich, but he was obliged to teach for a time before he could gather funds enough to return to Munich and marry, and for a year he was at the Cathedral School, Garden City, Long Island. Soon after the marriage, which took place on Aug. 9, 1886, the couple left Germany and settled in New York. Parker resumed his teaching at Garden City and also held a position at the National Conservatory in New York, then enjoying a prestige because of the presence on the faculty of Antonin Dvořák, the Bohemian composer. During this period Parker acted as organist successfully in three churches, St. Luke's in Brooklyn, St. Andrew's in Harlem, and the Church of the Holy Trinity, which stood at the corner of Madison Avenue and Forty-second Street, New York. Most of his smaller compositions for practical use by church choirs date from this time. Many of them are still in current use.

Parker first became known through performances of his *Hora Novissima* (*opus* 30) for chorus, solos, and orchestra, generally regarded as his masterpiece. He made this beautiful musical setting of the Latin poem of Bernard de Morlaix in 1891 and 1892. His mother supplied an English translation. It was first given on May 3, 1893, by the Church Choral Society of New York at the Church of the Holy Trinity. Productions on a larger scale by the Handel and

Haydn Society of Boston and at the Springfield Festival soon followed. This work and the good reports of Parker's record at Munich made him suddenly famous, as fame went in those days. The two most important positions of his career soon fell to him, the post of organist and choir director at Trinity Church, Boston (1893), and the professorship of music at Yale University (1894). The inconvenience of holding positions in two cities geographically so far apart as Boston and New Haven was offset by the pleasure he got from his association with his many friends among the musicians in Boston, notably Arthur Foote, George W. Chadwick, and Arthur Whiting, who with Parker made an interesting and influential group. Even so, the weekly journeys became irksome, and in 1900 Parker resigned from Trinity Church. As Battell Professor of Music at Yale he was virtually organizer of the system of instruction in music that still (1934) is in force in the School of Music. In 1904 he was made dean of the school. But teaching composition and lecturing on music history was far from being his only contribution to music in his community. Soon after his arrival at Yale he was asked to become conductor of the then recently organized New Haven Symphony Orchestra. Through his efforts the orchestra was taken over by the University. With this guarantee of permanence and the building of the fine concert auditorium Woolsey Hall (1901), the orchestra became a useful laboratory for the Department of Music and an important element in the musical life of New Haven.

In addition to his duties at the University, in 1901 he became organist at the Collegiate Church of St. Nicholas, at the corner of Fifth Avenue and Forty-eighth Street, New York. Also, some years later he became conductor of two singing societies in Philadelphia, the Eurydice Club, a chorus of women, and the men's organization, the Orpheus Club. By arranging his various appointments in such a way as to meet the demands of rehearsals and classes he was able to add to his routine the direction of still another out-of-town organization, the Derby (Connecticut) Choral Club. With the conductorship of the Oratorio Society and of the Symphony Orchestra in New Haven itself completing the list, Parker carried a burden of responsibility hardly equaled in the case of any other American composer. In 1902 he received from Cambridge, England, the honorary degree of Doctor of Music. This was the culmination of a series of honors that already had been bestowed upon him by English musical organizations. The program of the Three Choirs Festival for 1899 at Worcester had included *Hora Novissima,* with Parker conducting. The success was so great that the authorities at Hereford invited him to compose a work for their festival. Parker quickly responded, and the beautiful *Wanderer's Psalm* (*opus* 50) was performed. Other large works of this period were *A Star Song* (*opus* 54), given at the Norwich Festival (1902), and *The Legend of St. Christopher* (*opus* 43), given at Bristol. Parker's mother supplied the poetic text for *St. Christopher.* This work is the most elaborate of his oratorios and contains some of his finest pages. Yet it has not caught the imagination of either English or American audiences as has *Hora Novissima,* upon which his reputation mainly rests. On account of its naturalness and the freshness and beauty of its expression, new and attractive in a dull period of transition in the world's music just after the passing of Brahms and Wagner, this oratorio received the impetus of general approval that still carries it forward.

Parker took a year's leave of absence from Yale in 1901–02, and another in 1912–13. With these exceptions his work at the University went on uninterruptedly from 1894 until his death in 1919. They were busy years, for with all his other duties he composed music incessantly. Throughout his professional life he was honored by one invitation after another to write works for special occasions, and he always filled these commissions promptly. His later period of production is marked by the composition of several large works. His mother, to whom he was attached by especially strong ties of affection, died in 1903. He was from that time on obliged to turn to another writer for texts for his choral compositions. In collaboration with the poet Brian Hooker he produced in 1911 the large and imposing opera *Mona* (*opus* 71). This won a prize (April 1911) offered by the Metropolitan Opera Company, New York, and was lavishly presented the following year. Its austerity and complexity were such as to win for it hardly more than a *succès d'estime.* The composer had grafted upon his earlier and normal manner certain new modes of thought, in which the influence of Richard Strauss may be detected, with the result that his style took on a glamour and harmonic richness which were appropriate to opera but which, with equal appropriateness, had been to some extent excluded from his religious compositions. Yet Parker, with his antecedents and classic training, could not suddenly become "operatic." In 1914 he and Hooker completed a second opera, *Fairyland* (*opus* 77) no less subtle and brilliantly colored than *Mona.* This time the

National Federation of Musical Clubs bestowed the prize and sponsored a performance at Los Angeles. Though the operas have not found a permanent place in the repertory of opera they stand as splendid monuments of the genius of Parker. The orchestration is so skilful and effective as to arouse regret that Parker never found time nor occasion to write pure symphonic music. He seems rather to have been destined to be a master of choral composition, and his most enduring work is in this field. It should be said, however, that no small part of the interest of the oratorios lies in the facile and effective orchestral accompaniment.

Parker spent the long college vacations at his summer home at Blue Hill, Me. He could there compose without interruption, and each year he returned to New Haven with a new work. The wear and tear of composing during the summer after an exhausting season at New Haven broke down his health. For many years he suffered from rheumatism and was occasionally actually incapacitated. The end came in 1919. He had composed an exceptionally beautiful ode, again with Brian Hooker's collaboration, *A.D. 1919* (*opus* 84) which was performed at a ceremony in honor of the Yale men who had fallen in the Great War. This was his final composition. Some of his most poignant and spontaneous music is in this score. He died in December 1919 at the home of his daughter Isabel Parker Semler at Cedarhurst, Long Island. His burial place is in the churchyard of Newton Lower Falls, Mass., near his native village of Auburndale. He was survived by his wife and his three daughters. A memorial service was held at Yale University on Feb. 15, 1920, at which several of his works were performed. Parker had led many classes of Yale men into an appreciation of fine music, and had been of service to the University in a tangible way by composing music for special functions. As early as 1895 he wrote an "Ode for Commencement Day" (*opus* 42), the text by Edmund Clarence Stedman, and in 1901 dedicated a fine setting of Professor Thomas Dwight Goodell's Greek ode "Hymnos Andron" (*opus* 53), to the Yale bicentennial celebration. *Cupid and Psyche* (*opus* 80), a masque with text by John Jay Chapman, was performed in the School of the Fine Arts (1916), and, finally, *A.D. 1919*, which may be regarded as his own memorial. Two of Parker's choral works were composed for the Norfolk (Connecticut) Festival, *The Dream of Mary* (*opus* 82), a Morality, with text by John Jay Chapman, and *King Gorm the Grim* (*opus* 64). For the Centenary of the Handel and Haydn Society of Boston in 1915 he composed the oratorio *Morven and the Grail* (*opus* 79), to a poem of Brian Hooker. He wrote also a large amount of music for organ, the most important being the Concerto in F major (*opus* 55) which he as soloist performed with the symphony orchestras of Boston and of Chicago, and the Sonata in E flat (*opus* 65). In these works the influence of his former master Rheinberger is strong.

Parker's work began in the pioneer days of American music. By the time of his death the pioneer days may be said to have come to an end. His influence was especially valuable during his earlier period when America had just started to educate herself in music. In appearance Parker was notably dignified and commanding, and his features were clean-cut and handsome. He was impatient, but devoted to his friends. In 1905 he was elected to the American Academy of Arts and Letters. He was also a fellow of the American Guild of Organists, and a member of many clubs.

[The most complete and accurate list of Parker's works is that compiled by W. O. Strunk and published in the *Musical Quart.*, Apr. 1930. The library of the School of Music, Yale Univ., has a collection including a nearly complete list of the published works, and all of the manuscripts which were in the composer's possession at the time of his death. The Lib. of Cong. also has an extensive collection of published compositions and a few manuscripts, including the full score of *Hora Novissima*. In each of these libraries are a few works not included in the other. The manuscript full scores of some of the works for chorus and orchestra are in the hands of the publishers of the vocal score. The fullest biographical and critical accounts are G. W. Chadwick, *Horatio Parker* (1921), being the address delivered before the Am. Acad. of Arts and Letters, July 25, 1920; and D. S. Smith, "A Study of Horatio Parker," in the *Musical Quart.*, Apr. 1930. An illustrated article in the *Musical Times* (London), Sept. 1, 1902, gives some additional information. The article in *Grove's Dictionary of Music and Musicians* (3rd ed., 1928), vol. IV, gives the facts of Parker's professional life and a list of the works to which *opus* numbers are assigned. Brief notices in various histories of music in America repeat the facts contained in the works listed, adding some critical comment. The library of the Yale School of Music has a collection of memorabilia including newspaper clippings, contemporary notices of the performance of *Hora Novissima*, *Mona*, and *Fairyland*, programs, obituary notices, correspondence, and copies of published and unpublished essays and lectures.]   D. S. S.

PARKER, ISAAC (June 17, 1768–July 25, 1830), jurist, was born in Boston, Mass., the son of Daniel Parker, a goldsmith, and Margaret (Jarvis) Parker. He was descended from John Parker, of Bideford, Devon, who emigrated to America in 1629 and whose children settled in Charlestown, Mass. After preparation at the Latin Grammar School, he entered Harvard at the age of fourteen and graduated in 1786 with high honors. For a short time he taught at the Latin School, then he moved to Castine, in what was later the state of Maine. There he set up his law practice. On June 19, 1794, he married Rebecca Hall, daughter of Joseph Hall of Medford, a descendant of John Hall who settled in Concord in 1658. They had eight children. In 1796, when he was twenty-eight, he was elected to Congress, but after one term of which little record of activity is available he retired voluntarily to become United States marshal for the Maine district. He was displaced upon Jefferson's accession to the presidency and returned to his law practice. He had made his impression, however, and in 1806 he was appointed a judge of the supreme court of Massachusetts. He was shortly called upon to sit in the trial of T. O. Selfridge, charged with shooting the son of Benjamin Austin [q.v.] in a political quarrel. Feeling ran high and Parker won a great reputation for impartiality. In 1814 he was elevated to the chief justiceship, which post he held till his death. In 1816 he was inaugurated as first Royall Professor of Law at Harvard. It was not a teaching chair, and in May 1817 he laid before the Corporation a plan for a law school. The plan was adopted and the school established, with Asahel Stearns as first instructor. Parker continued to lecture until 1827. He was also an overseer of Harvard and a trustee of Bowdoin and served as president of the Massachusetts constitutional convention of 1820. His published works were confined to his judicial decisions and to a few orations, revealing a somewhat less florid style than that which characterized the times.

Parker's decisions illuminate both the man's character and the jurisprudence of the period. They indicate a mind of exceptional clarity and penetration, albeit with a sensitivity to the needs of changing times. In the words of Justice Story: "It was a critical moment in the progress of our jurisprudence. . . . We wanted a mind to do in some good degree what Lord Mansfield had done in England, to breathe into our common law an energy suited to the wants, the commercial interests and the enterprise of the age" (Palfrey, *post*, p. 28). It was a time when equity was more important than law. Parker rendered this kind of service, and many of his decisions came to be recognized as authoritative generally through the state and federal courts. "He felt that the rules, not of evidence merely, but of all substantial law must widen with the wants of society" (*Ibid.*). In addition he rendered no small service by skilfully consolidating the reforms in the Massachusetts judicial system, instituted in the early years of the century. His character was eminently suited to his rôle. Above the pettinesses of party strife, free from affectation, at the same time both patient and gay, he carried into his public life the rectitude of an active and sincere religious conviction.

[See: J. G. Palfrey, *A Sermon Preached . . . After the Decease of the Hon. Isaac Parker* (1830) ; Lemuel Shaw, address in *Am. Jurist*, Jan. 1831 ; G. A. Wheeler, *Hist. of Castine, Penobscot, and Brooksville, Me.* (1875) ; *New-Eng. Hist. and Geneal. Reg.*, Oct. 1852; Charles Warren, *Hist. of the Harvard Law School* (1908), vol. I ; *Jurisprudent*, July 10, 1830 ; *Boston Advertiser*, July 27, 31, 1830. Parker's decisions appear in *2-17 Mass. Reports* and *1-9 Pickering Reports*.]

E. S. G.

PARKER, ISAAC CHARLES (Oct. 15, 1838–Nov. 17, 1896), congressman, judge, was born in Belmont County, Ohio, the son of Joseph and Jane (Shannon) Parker. His mother was a niece of Gov. Wilson Shannon [q.v.], and Isaac attributed his success largely to her. He attended a country school and then taught and attended Barnesville Academy alternately. By the time he was twenty-one he had picked up enough law to begin to practise and had opened an office in St. Joseph, Mo. He served successively as city attorney, 1860–64, presidential elector in 1864 (voting for Lincoln), corporal in the local militia, judge of the twelfth circuit 1868–70, and member of Congress, 1871–75. In Congress he was a member of the committee on territories of which James A. Garfield was chairman. Here he showed a great deal of interest in the Indians and sought to improve their condition. During his first term he introduced a bill designed to give them civil government in a territory to be called Oklahoma (*Congressional Globe*, 42 Cong., 2 Sess., p. 2954) and he continued to urge the adoption of such a measure as long as he was in Washington. He also favored woman's suffrage in the territories (*Ibid.*, 681). He introduced a resolution calling for an amendment to the Constitution making members of Congress ineligible for the presidency while members and for two years thereafter.

In 1875 President Grant appointed him chief justice of Utah and the nomination was confirmed, but at the request of the President he resigned to accept appointment as judge of the western district of Arkansas. Probably no appointment ever gave more satisfaction. His jurisdiction extended over the Indian Territory, a country infested by "criminal intruders," renegades and fugitives from justice in other states and foreign countries. His predecessor was a weak man, who had allowed the court to fall into disrepute. On taking office (May 10, 1875) one of Judge Parker's first acts was to appoint 200 deputy marshals. He was to need many fearless men: sixty-five deputies were slain while he was in office. In his first term he tried eighteen murder cases and fifteen convictions were secured.

This record struck terror to the hearts of evil doers and raised the hopes of law-abiding citizens. It is said that he passed sentence of death upon 162, in the course of twenty-one years, of whom eighty were hanged (Harman, *post*, pp. 170–80). Very few judges have a like record. Because of his great number of executions he won a reputation—outside the state, among those who did not know him or the conditions in his district—for great severity, but he was neither harsh nor cruel; his sympathies went out to the victim and his family rather than to the murderer. He was well versed in the English common law, but treated the law as a growing organism and believed that the safeguards thrown around the accused to protect him from savage judges should not be used to protect murderers. Some of his decisions were reversed because he had brushed technicalities aside; one murderer was convicted three times and, after Parker's death, escaped with a prison sentence.

Parker had a keen sense of humor and sometimes yielded to it in the court room. He gave freely to charity and never accumulated much property. He was intensely interested in education and served as president of the school board at Fort Smith, Ark., for several years. He is said to have drawn up the bill, passage of which was secured by John H. Rogers, representative for the district, providing for the donation of the United States Reservation in Fort Smith to the schools of the city instead of to a railroad. He married Mary O'Toole, in St. Joseph, Mo., Dec. 12, 1861, and they had two sons. He was buried in the National Cemetery in Fort Smith.

[W. S. Speer, *The Encyc. of the New West* (1881); Fay Hempstead, *Hist. Review of Ark.* (2 vols., 1911); S. W. Harman, *Hell on the Border* (1898), an interesting account of criminals and criminal trials, which must be used with caution; *Arkansas Gazette* (Little Rock), Nov. 18, 1896; conversation with Judge J. M. Hill, who knew Parker intimately.] D. Y. T.

PARKER, JAMES (*c.* 1714–July 2, 1770), printer, journalist, born at Woodbridge, N. J., was the grandson of Elisha Parker of Barnstable, Mass., who moved to New Jersey, and Elizabeth Hinckley, sister of Gov. Thomas Hinckley. His father was Samuel Parker, a cooper, who probably married Janet Ford. James married Mary Ballareau and they had two children: Samuel Franklin, who followed his father's business, and Jane Ballareau, who was married to Judge Gunning Bedford, Jr. [*q.v.*], of Delaware. When James was eleven his father died and on Jan. 1, 1727, he was apprenticed for eight years to William Bradford [*q.v.*], prototypographer of New York. In April 1733, when twenty-one months of his indenture remained, Bradford advertised

his time for sale; but on May 17, Parker ran away. His master offered a reward for his apprehension, describing the boy in this advertisement as being "of a fresh Complection, with short yellowish Hair." He probably "wandered to Philadelphia and found employment with Benjamin Franklin" (Nelson, *post*, p. 18). On Feb. 26, 1742, Franklin formed a silent partnership with him for carrying on a printing business in New York City for six years, furnishing a press, type, and other appurtenances. Later, while Franklin was abroad, Parker acted as his financial auditor in the business of Franklin & Hall of Philadelphia. On Dec. 1, 1743, Parker succeeded Bradford as public printer of New York, a post he held till about 1760. He had several difficulties with the government. He was censured in 1747 for printing a remonstrance of the Assembly to the governor's message. He was brought before the grand jury for printing on Apr. 27, 1752, a "Speech of an Indian," for which he apologized in an interesting article on the circumstances of printers (*New York Gazette, Revived in the Weekly Post-Boy*, Aug. 3). For printing an article in March 1756 on affairs in Ulster and Orange counties, he and his partner were put under arrest, but discharged on revealing the writer's name, apologizing, and paying fees. Again, in 1770, he printed a paper by "A Son of Liberty," who proved to be Alexander McDougall, 1732–1786 [*q.v.*], for which Parker was arrested; but he died before the case was settled. During the Stamp Act troubles of 1765, his New York newspaper appeared in mourning.

Besides his several printing businesses, Parker had varied public interests. In Woodbridge he was captain of a troop of horse, a lay reader in Trinity Church (Episcopal), and postmaster in 1754. This year he was also made postmaster at New Haven, operating through John Holt, his partner. In 1756 he became comptroller and secretary of the general post-offices of the British colonies, and in 1765, when the territory was divided, he had charge of the northern district, operating from Woodbridge. He was made librarian of the library of the corporation of the City of New York in the autumn of 1746, instituted a system of circulating and fines, and prepared and printed a catalogue of the books under his care (*New-York Weekly Post-Boy*, Oct. 13, 1746). On June 2, 1764, he became judge of the court of common pleas of Middlesex County, N. J., and in that year he compiled and printed a work setting forth the duties and powers of justices, entitled *Conductor Generalis*, which for many years had a vogue with public officials.

He was identified with printing and journalism in New York, New Jersey, and Connecticut. In the first two he was public printer, and in Connecticut he was printer to Yale College. Besides public documents, newspapers, and magazines, he printed poetry, fiction, history, science, almanacs, chap books, and works on religion and husbandry. In his day he was in eminence and efficiency the equal of any printer in English-America. He was a better printer than Bradford or Franklin. Among his apprentices and journeymen were those who afterward established themselves near and far. In January 1753 Parker took William Weyman into partnership at New York, and their relations continued until dissolved with acrimony in January 1759. Weyman managed the New York office while Parker was busy at Woodbridge. The New York printery was assigned in February 1759 to his nephew, Samuel Parker, and so continued till John Holt [q.v.] took over the plant in the summer of 1760.

On Apr. 12, 1755, Parker established at New Haven the *Connecticut Gazette,* with Holt as manager and silent partner. The New Haven printery had been set up by Franklin for his nephew, Benjamin Mecom [q.v.]. Holt had come to work for Parker at New York in 1754, and when Parker relinquished this office in the summer of 1760, Holt left New Haven to conduct the New York establishment, where he remained a partner till 1762, when he leased the plant for himself, conducting it till Parker resumed control in the autumn of 1766. At Woodbridge, in 1751, Parker set up the first permanent printing office of New Jersey. He gave this plant exclusive attention from 1753. From 1765, when he went to Burlington, it was managed by his son. At Woodbridge he printed more than seventy-five items, consisting of orations, sermons, discourses, and the public documents of the province. His press issued the first newspaper of New Jersey, really a waif, on Sept. 21, 1765, entitled the *Constitutional Courant,* as a protest against the obnoxious Stamp Act. It was in 1765, while business was slack at Woodbridge, that Parker planned to set up a printing office at Burlington, in part to print for Judge Samuel Smith of that city a *History of New Jersey,* and to do the public printing requested by Gov. William Franklin. For this purpose he borrowed from Benjamin Franklin a press and outfit that Mecom had used in Antigua, Boston, and New York. In New York Parker printed four different periodicals, the *Independent Reflector,* edited by William Livingston, from Nov. 20, 1752, to Nov. 22, 1753, fifty-two weekly numbers; the *Occasional Reverberator,* a folio weekly of four

issues, Sept. 7 to Oct. 5, 1753; *John Englishman,* a folio weekly of ten numbers, Apr. 9 to July 5, 1755; and the *Instructor,* a quarto weekly of ten numbers, Mar. 6 to May 8, 1755. But his greatest venture in periodical literature was printed at Woodbridge, the *New American Magazine,* edited by Samuel Nevill, which ran through twenty-seven numbers from January 1758 through March 1760. This monthly was a financial failure, as all ten predecessors in that field in the colonies had been. In December 1768 Parker offered the remainder for sale at bargain prices to "induce the Curious to preserve some of them from Oblivion" (*New York Gazette, or the Weekly Post-Boy,* Dec. 12, 1768). It was probably on Jan. 4, 1743, that he began the third newspaper of New York, first called the *New-York Weekly Post-Boy,* then the *New York Gazette, Revived in the Weekly Post-Boy,* and finally the *New York Gazette, or the Weekly Post-Boy.* It underwent many vicissitudes till it expired in 1773. Parker suffered greatly for several years from the gout, and death came to him at a friend's house at Burlington on July 2, 1770. He was buried beside his parents in the Presbyterian churchyard at Woodbridge, though he was an Episcopalian. His former partner Holt in an obituary stated that he "was eminent in his Profession"; "possessed a sound judgment & extensive Knowledge"; "was industrious in Business, upright in his Dealings, charitable to the Distressed," and that he "left a fair Character" (Holt's *New York Journal,* July 5, 1770). His estate was executed by his wife (*New York Gazette,* Aug. 6, 1770).

[Parker's newspapers are primary sources for his biography. Family data are best given by W. H. Benedict, in *Proc. N. J. Hist. Soc.,* 4 ser. VIII (1923) and extended in his *New Brunswick in Hist.* (1925). See also J. W. Dally, *Woodbridge and Vicinity* (1873). The best account of Parker's career as a New Jersey printer is Wm. Nelson, "Some N. J. Printers and Printing in the Eighteenth Century," *Proc. Am. Antiquarian Soc.,* n.s. vol. XXVI (1911) and reprinted separately. Pertinent, though not always correct, are Isaiah Thomas, *Hist. of Printing in America* (2 vols., 1874) and C. R. Hildeburn, *Sketches of Printers and Printing in Colonial N. Y.* (1895). For Parker's relations with Franklin see *Proc. Mass. Hist. Soc.,* 2 ser. XVI (1903) and Wilberforce Eames, "The Antigua Press and Benj. Mecom," *Proc. Am. Antiquarian Soc.,* n.s. vol. XXXVIII (1929), also issued separately. On Parker's newspapers see C. S. Brigham, "Bibliog. of Am. Newspapers," in *Proc. Am. Antiquarian Soc.,* especially n.s. vol. XXVII (1917). The history and bibliography of his magazine ventures are best in L. N. Richardson, *A Hist. of Early Am. Mags.* (1931). The history of his first political trouble is related from records by the present writer in the *Lit. Collector,* Nov. 1903.] V. H. P.

PARKER, JAMES (Mar. 3, 1776–Apr. 1, 1868), legislator, was born in Bethlehem township, Hunterdon County, N. J., the son of James and Gertrude (Skinner) Parker. His father was a member of the Provincial Council and of the Board of Proprietors of the colony. The family had taken refuge in Hunterdon County during the Revolutionary struggle but returned in 1783 to the ancestral home in Perth Amboy. Here James Parker was educated by the Rev. Joseph I. Bend, Rector of St. Peter's Church, before going to a preparatory school at Amwell, Hunterdon County. He entered Columbia College, New York, in 1790 and was graduated second in the class of 1793. He was placed in the counting house of John Murray, then a leading merchant in New York, but the death of his father in 1797 obliged him to return home to take up the management of the family estate. In 1806 he was elected to the New Jersey Assembly from Middlesex County. He was reëlected annually until 1811, and again in 1812, 1813, 1815, 1816, and 1818. During his legislative career he was particularly interested in the act of 1817 establishing free schools in the state, the act authorizing aliens to purchase and hold real estate in New Jersey, and the act passed in 1820 prohibiting, under the severest penalties, the exportation of slaves from the state.

Parker returned to the legislature in 1827 chiefly for the purpose of promoting the construction of a canal between the Delaware and Raritan rivers. Although the bill which he reported did not pass in the legislative session of 1827–28, he had the satisfaction a few years later of witnessing the actual construction of a canal essentially the same as that which he had proposed. When the Delaware and Raritan Canal Company was organized, he became a director and held this post until his death. His interest in the boundary question between New York and New Jersey led him to serve on the different boundary commissions until a settlement was reached in 1829. In 1815 and again in 1850 he was chosen mayor of Perth Amboy. Although he had always been a Federalist, he supported the candidacy of Andrew Jackson for the presidency and served as presidential elector in 1824. When Jackson became president in 1829, Parker was appointed collector of the port at Perth Amboy, which at that time had considerable foreign trade. While serving in this office, he was elected to the House of Representatives in 1832 and was reëlected in 1834. His distrust of Martin Van Buren led him to align himself with the Whig party in 1840 and to support its candidates until the fifties, when he joined the Republican party. He was one of the most influential members of the convention called in 1844 to frame a new constitution for New Jersey and served as chairman of the committee on the bill of rights. His

interest in education was recognized by his election to the boards of trustees of Rutgers College and of the College of New Jersey. He was elected vice-president of the New Jersey Historical Society at its formation and subsequently became its president. For many years he was a vestryman of St. Peter's Church, Perth Amboy, and usually represented that parish in the Protestant Episcopal Convention of New Jersey. Freed from the necessity of earning his own living by a generous patrimony, he was always willing to answer the call to public service. He was twice married: on Jan. 5, 1803, to Penelope Butler, daughter of a once wealthy Philadelphia merchant, who died in 1823, and on Sept. 20, 1827, to Catherine Morris Ogden, sister of David B. Ogden [q.v.]. John Cortlandt Parker [q.v.] was a son by the first marriage.

[R. S. Field, "Address on the Life and Character of the Hon. Jas. Parker," Proc. N. J. Hist. Soc., 2 ser. I (1869); K. M. Beekman, "A Colonial Capital: Perth Amboy and Its Church Warden, Jas. Parker," Ibid., n.s. III (1918); Jas. Parker, The Parker and Kearney Families of N. J. (Perth Amboy, 1925); W. N. Jones, The Hist. of St. Peter's Church in Perth Amboy, N. J. (1923); Daily State Gazette (Trenton), Apr. 3, 1868.]
W. S. C.

PARKER, JAMES CUTLER DUNN (June 2, 1828–Nov. 27, 1916), composer, organist, teacher of music, was a son of Samuel Hale Parker and Sarah Parker of Boston and a nephew of Richard Green Parker [q.v.]. His grandfather was successively rector of Trinity Church and bishop of Massachusetts. His father was long senior warden of Trinity. James attended the Boston Latin School and Harvard College. Graduated in 1848, he studied law for three years, but a taste for music, pronounced in boyhood, led him to become as his friend John S. Dwight phrased it, "the first son of Harvard to forsake a dry profession [the law] and follow the ruling passion of his life" (post, p. 442).

Parker went to Leipzig, Germany, in 1851 to pursue academic musical studies with Plaidy, Hauptmann, Richter, and Moscheles. His organ teacher was Johann Gottlob Schneider, II, whose virtuosity on a stiff old organ, at which "one had almost to sit on the keys," greatly impressed him. In September 1854 Parker returned to Boston for a life-time of playing, composing, and teaching for which his thorough professional training and social standing admirably fitted him. He was always the gentleman, courteous, unassuming, scholarly. In 1864 he was chosen organist of Trinity Church. He held this position at the old edifice, destroyed by fire in 1872, and for many years at the new church in Copley Square under its celebrated rector, Phillips Brooks, at whose funeral he played. His church programs were conservative, as were his own compositions. The latter began with occasional hymns and anthems. His first essay in a large form was the "Redemption Hymn," 1887. In 1890 for the seventy-fifth anniversary of the Handel and Haydn Society Parker wrote a cantata, "St. John." His oratorio, *The Life of Man* (1894) was first sung at the Easter concert of this society in 1895. "The Blind King," his only secular composition of importance, was written for the Apollo Club of Boston. These works were untouched by modernism. One of Parker's younger colleagues wrote of him: "Much . . . that is being done today he had no use for; but his knowledge of the classical composers was something to be envied."

Parker's reputation as a teacher brought him many private pupils, several of whom formed in 1862 the Parker Club, devoted to giving choral and instrumental concerts. Early invited by Dr. Eben Tourjée to teach at the New England Conservatory of Music, Parker was a member of its faculty for thirty-seven years, teaching pianoforte and theory. He gave a notable performance at the school's thousandth concert, May 17, 1882. In his later years at the Conservatory he held the position of examiner, listening with patience to the performances of thousands of pupils whom he regarded with impartiality and discernment. At his death he was the oldest member of the Harvard Musical Association. Resolutions of the New England Conservatory faculty, adopted shortly after his death and signed by Louis C. Elson, Wallace Goodrich, and E. Charlton Black, stressed his honorable share in creating a professional and public regard for the great masters of music. Parker's wife was Maria Derby of Andover, Mass., whom he married on Sept. 6, 1859. He died at his home in Brookline.

[*The New England Conservatory Mag.-Rev.*, Dec. 1916–Jan. 1917, has an extended obituary article. See also: biographical notes by J. S. Dwight in Justin Winsor's *The Memorial Hist. of Boston*, vol. IV (1883); *Who's Who in America*, 1916–17; *Boston Evening Transcript*, Nov. 28, 1916.]   F. W. C.

PARKER, JANE MARSH (June 16, 1836–Mar. 13, 1913), author, was born in Milan, Dutchess County, N. Y., the youngest and third daughter of Joseph and Sarah (Adams) Marsh, who were both descended from native families prominent in the American Revolution. She was christened Permelia Jenny but she later adopted the name Jane. At the time of her birth her father was pastor of the Christian (Campbellite) Church in Milan, and when she was two years old the family moved to Union Mills, Fulton County, N. Y., where Elder Marsh served as pastor of the Campbellite church, editor of the Christian Publishing Association, and of the

Christian Palladium, the weekly paper of the sect, and was also the local postmaster. In 1843 her parents became followers of William Miller [*q.v.*] and early in 1844 the family moved to Rochester, where her father edited the weekly journal and numerous other publications of the Millerite movement. This experience with religious hysteria and fanaticism injured the spirit of the young girl whose childhood was oppressed by a sense of impending doom. When old enough to be liberated from her father's religious vagaries, she swung to ritualism and orthodoxy and even contemplated entering an Episcopalian sisterhood. She remained for many years a devout Episcopalian, devoting much energy to church work and religious writing. She attended several private schools in Rochester, among which were the Collegiate Institute and the Clover Street Seminary.

In 1854 she began to write for the lay periodicals of the day. Her stories and poems appeared in various publications, including the *Waverley* and *Knickerbocker* magazines, and friendly criticism encouraged her literary ambitions. More than twenty-five articles, tales, poems, and stories were produced during her eighteenth year alone. On Aug. 26, 1856, she was married to George Tann Parker, a lawyer of Rochester. Several volumes, including stories for boys and Sunday-school books, appeared in the next decade. The most important in this group is *Barley Wood* (1860), which deals with a girl's conversion from sectarianism and is significant for implied personal attitude and autobiographical incident. For a few years her writing was interrupted by her care of her children, but after this interlude she applied her pen with renewed activity. She wrote several volumes and articles on the history of Rochester and central New York state. A novel, *The Midnight Cry* (1886), which utilized the events of the Millerite delusion, material to which she returned frequently for later articles and stories, is disappointing in its failure to capitalize her own personal experience. It was, however, considerably altered by her publisher.

Her long life was comparatively uneventful. In the fall of 1889 she accompanied Frederick Douglass and his party to Haiti and wrote several articles on its problems. The work produced after the death of her husband in 1895 was almost completely in the essay form. She became associated with the editor of Burrow's *Jesuit Relations* and was a frequent contributor to *Harper's,* the *Outlook,* and the *Atlantic Monthly.* Her papers in the "Contributor's Club" of the *Outlook* and the "Spectator" columns of the *Atlantic,* are among her best work. In the fall of 1905 she moved to Escondido, Cal., to live with her daughter. In 1911 they moved to Los Angeles and there she died on Mar. 13, 1913. She was a woman of great personal energy and in addition to her many religious activities engaged herself in women's clubs, patriotic societies, and civic movements. She was particularly interested in the problem of delinquent children and was hostile to woman's suffrage.

[Sources include: Marcelle LeMénager, "The Life and Work of Jane Marsh Parker, 1836–1913," a monograph in the library of Geo. Washington Univ.; *Who's Who in America*, 1910–11; E. R. Foreman, *Centennial Hist. of Rochester, N. Y.*, vol. II (1932); *Los Angeles Times*, Mar. 14, 1913; information as to certain facts from members of Mrs. Parker's family.]   R. W. B.

PARKER, JOEL (Jan. 25, 1795–Aug. 17, 1875), jurist, was born in Jaffrey, N. H. He was descended from Abraham Parker, a native of Wiltshire, England, who had settled in Woburn, Mass., by 1645. His father, Abel Parker, a Revolutionary soldier, was married in 1777 to Edith Jewett of Pepperell and three years later moved from Massachusetts to New Hampshire and cleared a farm. Joel Parker studied at Groton Academy and at Dartmouth, graduating in 1811. He read law in Keene, N. H., and was admitted to the bar in 1817. In 1821 he went to Ohio with a view to opening an office, but he returned in 1822 to resume his practice at Keene. He followed the law with singleness of purpose and achieved a success which was substantial but not sudden. In 1833 he was appointed to the superior court—the highest court in the state— and five years later was promoted to be chief justice. As a trial judge he inspired juries with courage. Lawyers might call him obstinate, but as a colleague explained, this was excusable in a judge who was almost always right. In deciding cases he reasoned to his own conclusions. Upon declining to follow a multitude of decisions sustaining a certain rule, he said: "they are so many that their very number furnishes cause of suspicion that the rule is not quite sound. ... It would seem, if the rule had a solid foundation, that one fifth, or one tenth, of the number might have settled the question. Its numerical strength, therefore, is weakness" (14 *N. H.*, 215, 228). This independence came to notice through his clash with Justice Story. The New Hampshire court gave one construction to the word *lien* in the Bankruptcy Act of 1841, while Story (who had framed the act) enforced a contrary view in the federal circuit court. Neither would recede, but after Story's death the Supreme Court upheld Parker's construction (14 *N. H.*, 509 and 48 *U. S.*, 612).

In November 1847 Parker was appointed Royall Professor of Law at Harvard. On Jan. 20, 1848, he was married to Mary Morse Parker, of Keene. In June he resigned from the bench after having moved to Cambridge. In his new position he was ill at ease and was tempted to go back to New Hampshire. The moot court was a pleasure, but lecturing required a painful adaptation, and he had to begin with unfamiliar subjects. His method was formal and thorough rather than vivid. The poorer men could not follow. "His law . . . was . . . exasperatingly sound; but he could no more give a comprehensive view of a whole topic than an oyster, busy in perfecting its single pearl, can range over the ocean floor" (Batchelder, *post*, p. 223). Yet such men as Joseph Choate and Henry Billings Brown [*qq.v.*] found him a fountain of knowledge, and Justice Oliver Wendell Holmes, another pupil, referred to him as "one of the greatest of American judges, . . . who showed in the chair the same qualities that made him famous on the bench" (*Speeches by Oliver Wendell Holmes, Jr.*, 1891, p. 35). In 1868 he resigned his professorship. For years the great triumvirate, Parker, Theophilus Parsons, and Emory Washburn, had reported that "there have been no new arrangements in relation to the organization of the School or the course of instruction." Unlike Langdell who presently came to invigorate the school, Parker in his methods had not been ahead of his time.

He served in the New Hampshire legislature for three years (1824, 1825, 1826); as delegate from Cambridge to the constitutional convention of 1853, and as commissioner to revise the statutes of Massachusetts. In politics he was Whig, then Republican. When Sumner was attacked he made a speech of protest which, according to a correspondent to the *Edinburgh Review* (October 1856, p. 595), "for earnestness and solemnity of denunciation has not been anywhere surpassed." He opposed the doctrine that secession was constitutional and criticised Taney's opinion in the Merryman case (J. D. Lawson, *American State Trials*, IV, 1918, p. 880). He defended the capture of Mason and Slidell. But as the drama of war and Reconstruction unfolded, his conservative nature recoiled. The Republicans had "dug the grave of the Constitution" (*To the People of Massachusetts*, 1862, p. 10). When Parker's conduct or opinions were impeached, he retaliated. "A good stand-up fight was meat and drink to him" (Batchelder, p. 225). He was especially irritated by clergymen who argued that the president might abolish slavery, saying that their "impudent assumption" that they had a greater knowledge of constitutional law than men trained to the profession was a "nuisance." "If any of them have D.D. attached to their names, that does not disqualify them from being also ASS, and mischief-makers besides" (*Constitutional Law and Unconstitutional Divinity*, 1863, pp. 6, 10). But he had a more genial side. He read poetry and loved flowers. At home and among friends he was affectionate. Students invited to dine were surprised to find he could regard a glass of wine with real enjoyment, and that he was witty. He published more than a score of articles and pamphlets, among which may be mentioned *Daniel Webster as a Jurist* (1852); *Non-Extension of Slavery, and Constitutional Representation* (1856); *Personal Liberty Laws (Statutes of Massachusetts) and Slavery in the Territories* (1861); *Habeas Corpus and Martial Law* (1862); *International Law* (1862); *The War Powers of Congress, and of the President* (1863); *Revolution and Reconstruction* (1866); and *The Three Powers of Government ... The Origin of the United States, and the Status of Southern States* (1869).

[G. S. Hale, "Joel Parker," *Am. Law Rev.*, Jan. 1876; Emory Washburn, memoir in *Proc. Mass. Hist. Soc.*, vol. XIV (1876), and in *Albany Law Jour.*, Aug. 28, 1875; C. H. Bell, *The Bench and Bar of N. H.* (1894); Charles Warren, *Hist. of the Harvard Law School* (1908), vol. II; *The Centennial Hist. of the Harvard Law School* (1918); S. F. Batchelder, *Bits of Harvard Hist.* (1924); *New Eng. Mag.*, July 1912; F. C. Jewett, *Hist. and Geneal. of the Jewetts of America* (1908), vol. I; *Boston Transcript*, Aug. 19, 1875.]
C.F.

PARKER, JOEL (Aug. 27, 1799–May 2, 1873), Presbyterian clergyman, was born at Bethel, Vt. Before entering Hamilton College, from which he graduated in 1824, he had been a district school teacher at Livonia, N. Y. A member of the Presbyterian church there, he organized, under the name of the Catechetical Society of Livonia, what ultimately became a Sunday school. Following two years of study at Auburn Theological Seminary, late in 1826, at the request of several Presbyterian residents of Brighton, near Rochester, N. Y., he undertook to form a new church. This was organized early in 1827 as the Third Presbyterian Church of Rochester, and Parker was installed as pastor. In 1830 the "free-church movement" drew him to New York City, where he became leader of a group of Christians whose aim was to extend church privileges to the poorer people of the city, particularly to those whom they considered excluded from the Reformed Dutch and Presbyterian churches by high pew rents. The First Free Presbyterian Church of New York was organized that year with sixteen members, and

with Parker as pastor. So marked was the growth of the movement that within six years four other free churches had been formed, including Tabernacle Church. After using the Masonic Hall on Broadway for a time, the First Free Church erected on Dey Street a building, the first floor of which was given over to stores, and the second to an auditorium; all seats were free. Nearly seven hundred members were received during Parker's three-year pastorate.

In 1833 he left New York for New Orleans, where he was pastor of the First Presbyterian Church, but in 1838 he was recalled to New York by Tabernacle Church, with which his Dey Street parishioners had united. For two years, beginning in 1840, Parker was the president of Union Theological Seminary, then in its fifth year, and was also its professor of sacred rhetoric and its financial agent. For a long period the institution's financial condition was precarious, largely owing to the business crisis of 1837, and professors' salaries could be paid only in part and irregularly. Accordingly, when, in 1842, Parker received a call to the pastorate of Clinton Street Presbyterian Church at Philadelphia, he accepted, and the office of president remained vacant until 1873. He retained a deep interest in the institution, however, and was one of its directors from 1857 to 1869. In 1852 he became pastor of Bleecker Street Church, New York. This, his third pastorate in that city, was followed by one of six years at Park Street Church, Newark, N. J., 1862–68. Ill health compelled him to resign and his death occurred five years later in New York.

Three factors seem mainly responsible for Parker's renown—the prominence of his four positions in the country's metropolis, the successes in making converts that marked his pastorates; and his own strong individuality, decided convictions, and aggressive methods. In the famous revivals of his time he was a leader. Particularly in the first half of his ministry he was an unusually vigorous, popular, and effective preacher. During his career he published many pamphlets and several bound volumes, including *Lectures on Universalism* (1830) and *The Pastor's Initiatory Catechism* (1855). He also edited *Sermons on Various Subjects* (1851), by John Watson Adams. On May 9, 1826, he married Harriet Phelps of Lenox, N. Y.

[*Gen. Biog. Cat. of Auburn Theol. Sem.* (1918); F. DeW. Ward, *Churches of Rochester* (1871); *Hist. of Rochester Presbytery* (1889); Jonathan Greenleaf, *A Hist. of the Churches of All Denominations in the City of N. Y.* (1846); E. F. Hatfield, *The Early Annals of Union Theol. Sem. in the City of N. Y.* (1876); G. L. Prentiss, *The Union Theol. Sem. in the City of N. Y.*

(1889); *Alumni Cat. of the Union Theol. Sem.* . . .
(1926); *N. Y. Tribune*, May 6, 1873.]   P.P.F.

PARKER, JOEL (Nov. 24, 1816–Jan. 2, 1888), jurist, statesman, was born near Freehold, N. J., the son of Charles and Sarah (Coward) Parker. His father was state treasurer, 1821–32, 1833–36, and state librarian, 1823–36. The son received his early education at Trenton and at Lawrenceville High School, after which he entered the College of New Jersey (later Princeton), graduating in 1839. He studied law under Henry Woodhull Green [*q.v.*] and was called to the bar in 1842, establishing himself at Freehold. His practice became increasingly lucrative. From the first he played an active part in politics. In 1844 he campaigned for Polk and in 1847 he was elected as Democratic assemblyman for Monmouth County. For one term (1852–57), he was Monmouth County prosecutor and conducted trials of state and semi-national interest. His activity in the local militia which he reorganized, and in which he attained the rank of major general (1861), helped to bring him to the front in state politics at the outbreak of the Civil War.

Parker voted for Douglas in 1860 and was a Democratic presidential elector. In the autumn of 1862 he was elected governor and served for a three-year term, beginning in January 1863. The chief problems of his first administration arose out of the Civil War. He was a free and outspoken critic of the federal government for he believed that the seceding states had been driven to resistance by the agitation of misguided Northern abolitionists. He was hostile to the Emancipation Proclamation, believing that it would make peace more difficult. But while approving the New Jersey legislature's proposal of a peace conference, he agreed with Lincoln that secession could not be permitted and that the Union must be preserved, with force if need be. He was careful not to surrender any of the state's rights and he regarded any encroachment by the federal government upon the state as intolerable, even when under cover of "war power" or "military necessity." He opposed the move in Congress to secure the use of the roadway of the Raritan and Delaware Bay Railroad for the War Department, after the Department had been restrained from such use by an injunction, and for this he was praised in New Jersey but censured outside the state for supporting state rights against the general good.

At the same time Parker gave prompt aid in supplying troops for military service. By propaganda and a system of bounties he was able to secure volunteers for the New Jersey quota for nearly a year after conscripts were being drafted in other states. His action in caring for the wounded, for soldiers' families, and for the military cemeteries made him very popular in the state. In the matter of state administration he advocated the change in the dates of the fiscal year in order to make it coincide with the sessions of the legislature. He also sponsored the establishment of a sinking fund for the redemption of the war loans. Being ineligible for a second term immediately, he resumed his private law practice in 1866. His name was placed in nomination for president by the New Jersey delegations at the Democratic conventions of 1868 and 1876. In 1871 he was reëlected governor for another three-year term. Although faced with a Republican legislature with which he occasionally clashed, he retained his popularity. From January to April 1875 he served as attorney-general of the state but resigned to return to private practice. In 1880 he was appointed to the state supreme court, which office he was holding by a second appointment at the time of his death. He died suddenly in Philadelphia of an apoplectic stroke.

Parker was an impressive man, very tall and dignified, and courteous in bearing. But he was neither quick of wit nor original of thought. As a governor he was openly partisan, though never mischievously so. As a judge his conduct was marked by caution. He was married in 1843 to Maria M. Gummere, the daughter of Samuel R. Gummere of Burlington. She with two sons and one daughter survived him.

[The memorial of Parker by J. S. Yard, "Joel Parker, the War Gov. of N. J.," in *Proc. N. J. Hist. Soc.*, 2 ser. X (1890), is included in the *Memorial of Joel Parker* (1889), containing sketches and tributes. Other sources include: Wm. Nelson, ed., *Nelson's Biog. Cyc. of N. J.* (1913), vol. I; *The Biog. Encyc. of N. J. of the Nineteenth Century* (1877); F. B. Lee, *N. J. as a Colony and as a State* (1902), vol. IV, and *Geneal. and Memorial Hist. of the State of N. J.* (1910), vol. III; W. E. Sackett, *Modern Battles of Trenton*, vol. I (1895); chapters by C. M. Knapp in I. S. Kull, *N. J., A Hist.* (1930), vol. III; Parker's messages as governor in *Docs. of the Legislatures of the State of N. J.*, 1863–66, 1872–75; *Pub. Ledger* (Phila.), Jan. 2, 1888; *Daily True American* (Trenton), Jan. 3, 1888.]

                                    H. M. C.

PARKER, JOHN (July 13, 1729–Sept. 17, 1775), Revolutionary soldier, captain of minutemen, was a native of Lexington, Mass. His parents were Josiah and Anna (Stone) Parker, and he was descended from Thomas Parker who was in New England as early as 1635. He served his military apprenticeship in the French and Indian War, and fought at Louisburg and Quebec. At one period he was probably a member of Roger's noted corps of rangers. On May 25, 1755, he married Lydia Moore, by whom he had seven children. In time of peace he was a farmer and mechanic, and held various town offices. On the eve of the Revolution he was captain of a company of minute-men, and he became one of the foremost figures in the opening event of the war at Lexington, Apr. 19, 1775. As the British detachment under Major John Pitcairn [*q.v.*] approached Lexington on the night of Apr. 18, Parker placed a guard around the house which sheltered John Hancock and Samuel Adams, and collected about 130 men. This force he soon dismissed, but as the British column neared the town, he again assembled his men—from forty to perhaps seventy in number. Apparently he had no definite plans; a suggestion has been offered that he was acting under orders from Samuel Adams (Murdock, *post,* p. 24). Modern historians have cast a doubt on the authenticity of the famous words with which Parker is said to have harangued his men, and which are carved upon the modest stone in the green: "Stand your ground. Don't fire 'unless fired upon. But if they mean to have a war, let it begin here." The events which followed are involved in controversy, but in the skirmish on the green eight Americans were killed and ten were wounded (French, *post,* p. 111). Following the skirmish Parker assembled as many militiamen as possible, marched in the direction of Concord, and had a share in the fighting during the British retreat. As the provincials gathered for the siege of Boston, he conducted a small body to Cambridge, but was too ill to have a part in the battle of Bunker Hill. Nothing further is recorded of his career, and he died in the following autumn.

[A. G. Parker, *Parker in America* (1911), pp. 81, 117; Theodore Parker, *Geneal. and Biog. Notes of John Parker of Lexington and His Descendants* (1893); De Forest Van Slyck, "Who Fired the First Shot?" (MS.); Harold Murdock, *The Nineteenth of April, 1775* (1923); Allen French, *The Day of Concord and Lexington* (1925).]   E. K. A.

PARKER, JOHN CORTLANDT (June 27, 1818–July 29, 1907), lawyer, better known as Cortlandt Parker, was born in Perth Amboy, N. J., the son of James [*q.v.*] and Penelope (Butler) Parker. When he was five years old his mother died, and he was brought up by his step-mother, Catherine Morris Ogden. He attended the Perth Amboy Military Academy, and was expected to go into engineering, which at that time did not involve a college education. But by study he prepared for the college entrance examinations and passed them without the knowledge of his father. He entered Rutgers College with the class of 1836 where he led his class and was valedictorian at graduation. The next three years he spent in reading law, first in the office of Theodore Frelinghuysen of Newark, and, upon the retirement of Frelinghuysen, in the office of Amzi Armstrong. He was admitted to the bar as attorney in September 1839, and as counselor in September 1842, continuing in the practice of law until his death. His first public service was as prosecutor of the pleas in Essex County, which office he held from 1857 to 1867.

Parker entered politics in the campaign of 1840 as a Whig, and the Clay-Frelinghuysen campaign of 1844 brought him out in support of his mentor. Although an opponent of the slave trade and the extension of slave territory, he was in favor of the rigid enforcement of the Fugitive Slave Law. He took a prominent part in the organization of the Republican party in New Jersey. Originally a Seward man, he supported enthusiastically the candidacy of Lincoln in 1860 and not only presided at a Lincoln ratification meeting in Newark but also served on a committee to welcome the president-elect when he stopped at Trenton on his way to the inauguration. Meanwhile, on Sept. 15, 1847, Parker married Elizabeth Wolcott Stites, daughter of Richard W. Stites, of Morristown, N. J., thus uniting two well-known families of the state. His interest in the success of Lincoln's administration led him many times to the White House. As president of the state convention in 1864 he worked for the renomination of Lincoln and used his influence to force reconsideration of the Fourteenth Amendment after its first rejection by the New Jersey legislature. He several times declined appointment to the supreme court of New Jersey but in 1871 served with Chief Justice Mercer Beasley and Justice David A. Depue on a commission to revise the laws of the state and in 1873 served on a commission to settle the boundaries between New Jersey and Delaware. In 1872 he declined Grant's offer of a judgeship on the Court of Claims to determine the proper distribution of the *Alabama* award, but in 1876 he accepted an appointment by the President to investigate the Louisiana vote in the Hayes-Tilden election. President Hayes in 1877 sought to name him as minister to Russia and in 1882 President Arthur requested him to represent the United States as minister to Austria, but both offers were declined. He again declined public office when Gov. Foster M. Voorhees in 1902 offered him the United States senatorship made vacant by the death of William Joyce Sewell.

Throughout his life Parker was a devout member of the Episcopal Church, serving for twenty-five years as junior warden of Trinity Church,

Newark, and many times as deputy from his diocese to its general convention. He was always interested in religious and philanthropic work and became president of the board of trustees of the City Hospital in Newark. He served unselfishly the bar associations of his county and state and was in 1883–84 president of the American Bar Association. It is said that he was ambitious for a place on the United States Supreme Court but relinquished his aspirations in favor of his friend Joseph P. Bradley, upon whose life and services he pronounced a eulogy before the Supreme Court at his death. Parker's influence upon the development of law in New Jersey can hardly be overestimated. His work as advisory master of the court of chancery resulted in opinions which have become landmarks in corporate law of the state. For many years before his death in Newark, he was the acknowledged leader of the bar in New Jersey.

[Sources include: E. M. Colie, "Cortlandt Parker, 1818–1907," *Proc. N. J. Hist. Soc.*, 4 ser. V (1920), with a partial bibliography of Parker's addresses; W. M. Magie, "The Life and Services of the Late Cortlandt Parker," *N. J. State Bar Asso.: Year Book*, 1908–09; "Cortlandt Parker," *Report of the Thirtieth Ann. Meeting of the Am. Bar Asso.*, 1907; *Who's Who in America*, 1906–07; *N. J. Law Jour.*, Jan. 1908; and *Newark Evening News*, July 30, 1907. A memorial volume containing Colie's account of Parker's Life and commemorative addresses was published under the title: *Cortlandt Parker, Citizen, Lawyer and Churchman* (1908).]   W. S. C.

PARKER, JOSIAH (May 11, 1751–Mar. 14, 1810), Revolutionary soldier and politician, was the son of Nicholas and Ann (Copeland) Parker and descended from Thomas Parker, who obtained land grants in Virginia as early as 1647. This ancestor was a member of a landed family of Cheshire, and the family seat in Isle of Wight County, Va., Josiah's birthplace, bore the name "Macclesfield." In 1773 Josiah Parker married Mary (Pierce) Bridger, widow of Col. Joseph Bridger, and they had one daughter. At the beginning of the Revolutionary War, Parker entered the army and also became a member of the local committee of safety and of the Virginia revolutionary convention. He served in Virginia under Lee, and later was attached to the northern army under Washington. He attained the rank of major in 1776 and that of colonel the following year, and at the battle of Trenton he was lieutenant-colonel of the 5th Virginia Regiment. In that battle, as well as at Princeton and Brandywine, he received the commendation of the Commander-in-chief. His figure is included in the group of soldiers in Trumbull's painting, "Capture of the Hessians," and it has been stated that he received the sword of Col. Johann Gottlieb Rall at Trenton. His temper was hasty and impulsive, and in consequence of a controversy he resigned from the army in 1778. Near the close of the war, when his native state became the scene of operations, he was appointed by Governor Jefferson to command the Virginia militia south of the James River, and cooperated with Lafayette. He received large grants of land after the war, was a member of the House of Delegates, and from 1786 to 1788 was naval officer for the port of Norfolk.

Parker was an Anti-Federalist and a strong supporter of Patrick Henry. He presented himself as a candidate for delegate to the Virginia ratifying convention of 1788, but was defeated. He was a member of the First Congress, and with his colleagues he gave his vote for a future capital on the Potomac River. His career in Congress extended from 1789 to 1801, and he was at one time chairman of the naval committee. His death occurred on the family estate in Isle of Wight County.

[A. G. Parker, *Parker in America* (1911), pp. 257–61; W. T. Parker, *Gleanings from Parker Records* (1894), pp. 38–41; F. B. Heitman, *Hist. Reg. of Officers of the Continental Army* (1893); *Biog. Dir. Am. Cong.* (1928); *Norfolk Gazette and Public Ledger*, Mar. 19, 1810, which gives day of death as Wednesday, Mar. 14.]   E. K. A.

PARKER, PETER (June 18, 1804–Jan. 10, 1888), medical missionary and diplomat in China, was born at Framingham, Mass., the son of Nathan and Catherine (Murdock) Parker, and a descendant of Thomas Parker who came to Massachusetts in 1635. Peter's father was a farmer and his mother, a farmer's daughter. On both sides of the house his family, in the language of the time, was "pious," and he was carefully reared in the orthodox Congregational faith. In adolescence he passed through the experience of deep despondency followed by joyous conversion which was regarded as desirable in the religious circles with which he was familiar, and soon afterward he felt that he should prepare for the Christian ministry. His parents needed his help on the farm, and he was delayed in acquiring an education. For a time he both went to school and taught school in Framingham. In 1826–27 he was a student in Day's Academy, Wrentham, and from 1827 to 1830 he was in Amherst College. Dissatisfied with the somewhat meager facilities in that young institution, he went to Yale in 1830, and, graduating from the college in 1831, continued in New Haven the study of medicine and theology, receiving the degree of M.D. in 1834. While in New Haven he devoted much time and energy to assisting in the religious life of the community and the college.

Before entering Yale, Parker had thought seriously of becoming a foreign missionary. In 1831 he formally applied to the American Board of Commissioners for Foreign Missions for an appointment, and in due course was accepted and assigned to China. He was ordained to the Presbyterian ministry in Philadelphia on May 10, 1834, and the followng month sailed for Canton, the first Protestant medical missionary to China. Protestant missionaries there were still greatly restricted in their activities, and could pursue their vocation only in Macao and in foreign "factories" at Canton, and even in these places they had to act with circumspectness. Within a few weeks Parker found it advisable to go to Singapore, where there were Chinese and where missionaries had more freedom; here he spent several months studying the language and maintaining a dispensary. By the autumn of 1835 he was back in Canton, and in November of that year, assisted by British and American merchants, he opened the hospital where he was to conduct the practice which became his chief claim to distinction. He specialized on diseases of the eye, particularly on the removal of cataracts, but also performed other operations, including the removal of tumors, and began giving instruction in medicine to Chinese. In 1837 he accompanied to Japan the well-known *Morrison* expedition which tried unsuccessfully to repatriate seven shipwrecked Japanese sailors. In February 1838 there was organized, largely at the instance of Parker, the Medical Missionary Society in China, an organization supported chiefly by the foreign residents in Canton. This soon gave substantial aid to Parker's hospital in Canton, and aided by it, he also opened, for a few months in 1838, a hospital in Macao.

In July 1840, because of the interruption of his work by the war between Great Britain and China, Parker returned to the United States. Here he interviewed members of the administration about developments in China—but probably with little if any effect upon American policy—and here, Mar. 29, 1841, he married Harriet Colby Webster, a relative of Daniel Webster. He visited Europe and both there and in America sought financial support for his hospital. He also attended medical lectures in Philadelphia.

In June 1842 he sailed again for China, where he resumed his medical practice in the Canton hospital. More and more he was drawn into the diplomatic service of the United States. In 1844 he served as one of the secretaries to Caleb Cushing [*q.v.*] in the negotiation of the first treaty between the United States and China. In 1845

he was appointed secretary to the American legation and in interims between commissioners was *chargé d'affaires*, continuing, at the same time, his medical practice. In 1855, ill, he returned to the United States, but that same year he became American Commissioner and Minister to China and was in China until 1857. His tenure of office fell in the particularly difficult years immediately before and in the early part of the second Anglo-Chinese war. In some respects, notably in his desire to occupy Formosa and to join with England and France in a vigorous assertion of foreign claims, his policy was more aggressive than Washington would sanction. Returning to the United States in 1857, he thenceforward made his home in Washington, interesting himself in such enterprises as the American Evangelical Alliance and the Smithsonian Institution.

[Theodore Parker, *Geneal. and Biog. Notes of John Parker of Lexington and His Descendants* (1893); G. B. Stevens, *The Life, Letters, and Jours. of the Rev. and Hon. Peter Parker, M.D.* (1896); *Chinese Repository,* 1836–44, *passim*; Tyler Dennett, *Americans in Eastern Asia* (1922); *Sen. Exec. Doc. 22,* 35 Cong., 2 Sess.; reports of the American Board of Commissioners for Foreign Missions, 1836–47; letters of Parker in the files of the American Board; S. W. Williams, *The Middle Kingdom* (rev. ed., 1883), vol. II; C. T. Downing, *The Stranger in China* (Phila., 1838), vol. II; Alexander Wylie, *Memorials of Protestant Missionaries to the Chinese* (Shanghai, 1867); *Evening Star* (Washington), Jan. 11, 1888.]　　K. S. L.

PARKER, QUANAH [See QUANAH, 1845?–1911].

PARKER, RICHARD ELLIOT (Dec. 27, 1783–Sept. 10, 1840), soldier, statesman, and jurist, the eldest of five children of Captain William Harwar and Mary (Sturman) Parker, was born at "Rock Spring," Westmoreland County, Va. He received his elementary education in the local schools and in 1800, at the age of seventeen, entered Washington College (now Washington and Lee University) where he remained for three years. In 1803 he began the study of law under his distinguished grandfather, Judge Richard Parker, of "Lawfield," Westmoreland County. He was admitted to the bar shortly after reaching his majority and a few years later was chosen to represent his native county in the Virginia House of Delegates. The outbreak of the War of 1812 found him already an officer in the Virginia militia and on Aug. 1, 1812, he was commissioned lieutenant-colonel of the 111th Regiment, composed of troops from Westmoreland and other counties of the Northern Neck, later serving as colonel. He was aroused by General Hull's surrender of Detroit and in an eloquent appeal to Governor Barbour he requested that he be included in any troops sent from

Virginia to the West in order to contribute his "mite of service to retrieve the national honor." Even after it became apparent that no Virginia forces would be ordered to Western duty he continued his pleas, pointing out that the greatest weakness of the militia was lack of training, and that a few officers at least should be sent to the front for experience so that they might return as military instructors, thus anticipating the method of training employed during the World War. But Parker had to rest content with home service, defending the Potomac and Chesapeake regions against British attacks during 1813 and 1814. With the advent of peace he returned to the law which he had abandoned temporarily for the profession of arms but in which he was to gain his greatest recognition.

In 1817 Parker was made a judge of the General Court of Virginia and was a member of that body until 1836. Meanwhile, in 1831, the legislature established the Court of Law and Chancery for Frederick County and he was chosen as its first judge. This necessitated his removal to the Shenandoah Valley and he established his home at Winchester. In 1833 he was recommended by Martin Van Buren for the post of attorney-general in Jackson's cabinet, and in 1836 was chosen to succeed Benjamin Watkins Leigh as senator from Virginia. His senatorial experience was brief, however, for the next year he resigned to become a member of the Supreme Court of Appeals of Virginia, an office which he held until his death in 1840. Although Parker was not a brilliant jurist he was steady and capable, usually in agreement with the majority of the court but not hesitating to dissent when he deemed that circumstances demanded it. His opinions, clear and in general concise, indicate sound scholarship, humanitarianism, and a high sense of judicial responsibility. A member of a prominent family of the planter aristocracy of the Northern Neck of Virginia, he was an Episcopalian by inheritance and by choice. He married Elizabeth, daughter of Dr. William Foushee, the first mayor of Richmond. Parker died at "Soldier's Retreat" in Clarke County, Va., but the legal heritage of his family lived on in his son, Richard Parker, who, at Charles Town in 1859, presided fairly and courageously over the trial of John Brown.

[Calendar of Va. State Papers, vol. X (1892); T. K. Cartmell, Shenandoah Valley Pioneers and Their Descendants (1909); Jour. of the Senate of the Commonwealth of Va. . . . 1836–37 (1837); J. C. Fitzpatrick, ed., "The Autobiog. of Martin Van Buren," Ann. Report of the Am. Hist. Asso. for the Year 1918, vol. II (1920); S. P. Hardy, Colonial Families of the Southern States of America (1911); Va. Mag. of Hist. and Biog., Oct. 1898, Jan. 1899; Daily Nat. Intelligencer (Washington, D. C.), Sept. 17, 1840; records in the Adj.-General's office of the War Dept.]   T. S. C.

PARKER, RICHARD GREEN (Dec. 25, 1798–Sept. 25, 1869), teacher, writer of textbooks, was the youngest son of the Rev. Samuel Parker, rector of Trinity Church, Boston, and later bishop of Massachusetts, and his wife Anne (Cutler) Parker. He was educated at the Boston Public Latin School and Harvard College, where he was graduated A.B. in 1817. He probably began his long teaching career at once, and by 1825 was established in the Boston public school system. He was grammar master successively of the East Roxbury Grammar School (1825–28), the Boylston School for girls and boys (1828), the Mayhew School (1828–29), the Franklin School (1830–36), the Johnson School, organized in 1836 for girls only (1836–48), and the Northern Department of the Johnson School (1848–53). Records of the School Board show that his schools maintained excellent standing. When in 1836 he was transferred from the Franklin to the Hancock School, his former students petitioned the School Board for his return. When he retired, the School Board accorded him the unusual honor of continuation of salary for six months, in consideration of his "long, faithful, and efficient labors." After his retirement from the public schools, he conducted a private school for girls.

Parker is best known as a writer of textbooks of great popularity in their day, some of which passed through many editions. Like most early school-book writers, he covered many fields. His *The Boston School Compendium of Natural and Experimental Philosophy* (1837) was the first of a series of revisions, abridgments, and elaborations which gave an introductory survey of the sciences; while in the field of English composition he published *Progressive Exercises in English Composition* (1832), which had gone through forty-five editions by the end of 1845, *Progressive Exercises in English Grammar* (1834), in which he collaborated with Charles Fox, and *Progressive Exercises in Rhetorical Reading* (1835). The National Series of readers, published by A. S. Barnes & Company, in which Parker collaborated with James M. Watson [q.v.], were popular for many years, especially *The National Fifth Reader* (copr. 1858). He also published *Questions Adapted to Hedge's Logick* (1823), sets of questions in geography for use with the textbooks of other writers, *A Sketch of the History of the Grammar School in the Easterly Park of Roxbury* (1826), and *A Tribute to the Life and Character of Jonas Chickering* (1854). Despite the general popularity of his books, he had his troubles: the manuscript records of the Boston School Committee reveal a controversy over the use of his textbooks in the Boston schools, and a vituperative pamphlet, *A Review of Parker and Fox's Grammar, Part I, Published by Several Friends of Real Improvement* (1839), attacked the book and charged the exercise of undue influence in its adoption.

Though Parker was indefatigably industrious, his labors never amassed for him a fortune. He was fond of music, and contributed critiques to the Boston newspapers on operas and concerts. He was also of a mechanical turn, and amused himself by constructing or reconstructing hand-organs and like instruments. On Apr. 20, 1820, he married Mary Ann Moore Davis, daughter of Amasa Davis and his wife Sarah Moore. They had three daughters and two sons. After his wife's death (Aug. 22, 1848) he married her cousin, Catherine (Hall) Payson, who survived him several years. He was buried in the crypt of Old Trinity Church.

[Sources include Boston School Committee Records (MS.); J. B. Pratt, *Seventy-five Years of Book Publishing* (A. S. Barnes & Company, 1913); *The Necrology of Harvard College, 1869–72* (1872); *Boston Transcript*, Sept. 27, 1869. The Harvard College Library Textbook Collection possesses most of Parker's textbooks, but not all editions.]　　　E. W. F.

PARKER, SAMUEL (Apr. 23, 1779–Mar. 21, 1866), Congregational clergyman, missionary, explorer, was born at Ashfield, Mass., a son of Elisha Parker, a Revolutionary soldier, and of Thankful (Marchant) Parker. He was graduated from Williams College in 1806, served for a time as principal of an academy in Vermont, entered Andover Theological Seminary, and graduated in 1810. Home missionary work in western New York then occupied him until 1812, when he became pastor of the Congregational Church of Danby, N. Y., being ordained Dec. 23. Here he continued till 1827. Thereafter, he acted as agent for the Auburn Theological Seminary, preached at Apulia, N. Y., 1830–32, and at Middlefield, Mass., 1832–33, and taught a girls' school at Ithaca, N. Y.

The venture which forms his chief claim to remembrance was his exploring trip to Oregon for the purpose of selecting sites for Indian missions. His decision to become a missionary was evoked by an account, published in the *Christian Advocate* of Mar. 1, 1833, of four "wise men from the West" who had come to St. Louis seeking for their people the white man's religion. Illustrated with the picture of a monstrous flat-headed Indian, this story called forth volunteers for the missionary cause, among whom were

Parker and Dr. Marcus Whitman [*q.v.*]. Since Parker was fifty-four years old, and not in robust health, his first offer of his services to the American Board of Commissioners for Foreign Missions proved fruitless, but later, having secured assurances of financial support from a local organization at Ithaca, he succeeded in obtaining a commission. Prepared to start for Oregon as early as Apr. 10, 1833 (see letter to A.B.C.F.M.), he actually went to St. Louis in the early summer of 1834, but arrived after the fur-trade caravan for the Rockies had departed. He thereupon returned to the East and spent the next few months in an attempt to enlist missionaries for Oregon.

In the spring of 1835, the Board gave him Marcus Whitman as an associate and the two set out, joining at Liberty, Mo., the caravan of the American Fur Company, with whom they continued, from May 15 to Aug. 12, when they reached the rendezvous on Green River. Finding the Flatheads and Nez Percés assembled there eager for missionaries, Parker went forward alone, under their escort, while Whitman returned to the East with the trading caravan to organize a missionary party. Parker spent the winter of 1835–36 at Fort Vancouver. He then explored the interior, selecting sites for proposed mission stations, and in September, before the arrival of Whitman's party, sailed to the Hawaiian Islands and thence, on a whaler, around the Horn. He reached New London in May 1837. The following year his book, *Journal of an Exploring Tour Beyond the Rocky Mountains* (1838), was published at Ithaca. Several later editions were brought out in America and it was also published in Great Britain. The Whitman Mission was fitted into the scheme resulting from Parker's survey.

Parker seems to have been vigorous, but dogmatic and somewhat arrogant, ill-fitted to conciliate men's opposition or to gain their eager cooperation. He displayed good judgment of the Indian character, however, and wisdom in the selection of sites for missionary labors among the tribes. His Yankee shrewdness also guided him in estimating the agricultural, commercial, and manufacturing possibilities of the Oregon country. His first wife was a Miss N. Sears of Ashfield, Mass.; in 1815 he married Jerusha Lord, of Salisbury, Conn., a niece of Noah Webster. By her he had a daughter and two sons, the youngest being Henry Webster Parker, clergyman, scientist, and author.

[H. W. Parker, "Rev. Samuel Parker, Missionary to Oregon," *The Church at Home and Abroad*, Mar. 1895; *Gen. Cat. Theol. Sem. Andover, Mass., 1808–*

1908 (n.d.) ; W. H. and M. R. Webster, *Hist. and Geneal. of the Webster Family of Conn.* (1915) ; A. B. Hulbert, "Undeveloped Factors in the Life of Marcus Whitman," in J. F. Willard and C. B. Goodykoontz, *The Trans-Mississippi West* (1930) ; references listed in C. W. Smith, *A Contribution toward a Bibliog. of Marcus Whitman* (1909) ; Myron Eells, *Marcus Whitman, Pathfinder and Patriot* (1909) ; manuscript records, including Parker's tender of his services to the Missionary Board, dated Middlefield, Apr. 10, 1833, and his later correspondence and report, in A.B.C.F.M. collection, Cambridge, Mass.]   J. S—r.

PARKER, SAMUEL CHESTER (May 31, 1880–July 21, 1924), educator, was born in Cincinnati, Ohio, one of the large family of Samuel B. and Elizabeth Helen (Chappell) Parker. His father was an Ohio-River pilot, whose boat had been in several of the engagements of the Civil War. His mother was a woman of exceptional mental qualities and exercised a large influence over him, guiding his training until he reached mature years. His education began in the public schools. He attended the technical high school, where he came in contact with T. L. Feeney, the principal, who became his life-long friend and model as a teacher. Later the two were associated as members of the faculty at Miami University in Oxford, Ohio. After completing high school, the boy went to the University of Cincinnati, where he graduated in 1901. He took an active part in undergraduate life and was president of the senior class. He first specialized in chemistry, but during his senior year he became interested in the theory and practice of teaching, to which he devoted his career. He pursued graduate courses in education at the University of Cincinnati in 1902 and later at the University of Chicago and at Teachers College, Columbia University, where he received the M.A. degree in 1903. He came in contact during his graduate work with John Dewey and Edward L. Thorndike, both of whom exercised very large influence over his thinking. In 1903 he became professor of the history of education at Miami University and, with some interruptions due to absence for graduate work, continued at that institution until 1909. In that year he was called to the University of Chicago, where he became dean of the College of Education in 1911. He served as professor of education until the time of his death, though he relinquished the deanship in 1916. In 1915 he went on a camping trip in the Hudson Bay region, where he contracted a fever from which he never fully recovered. After some years of partial disability he died in Chicago. He was married on June 4, 1904, to Lucile R. Jones, of Cincinnati, whom he had known in college. They had one son.

He was one of the most successful writers of textbooks on methods of teaching in his genera-

tion. He wrote for both elementary teachers and high-school teachers. His books are characterized by lucidity of style and directness of attack. He showed extraordinary ability to assimilate and interpret the results of scientific and historical studies in the field of education. His two most important books are *Methods of Teaching in High Schools* (1915) and *General Methods of Teaching in Elementary Schools* (1919). As an administrator, he was the embodiment of systematic procedure. He organized every detail of the work of his clerical staff and of his associates. The impress of his organizing genius is still strong on the department of education in the University of Chicago and on the National Society for the Study of Education, of which he was secretary from 1911 to 1915. He formulated a program for the activities of this society, which is still followed and which has made it one of the most influential educational organizations in the country. As a teacher, he was exacting in his demands on his students and concrete and vivid in his presentations. As a teacher of teachers, he had no tolerance for mediocrity. He held to the philosophy, which he had learned from Dewey, that education must formulate its methods so as to meet the requirements of a changing civilization. He drew his fundamental psychology from Thorndike. He recognized inherited ability as the chief factor in human life. With him, teaching was a means of bringing to full expression the best powers of an individual.

[*Elementary School Jour.*, Sept. 1924; *Who's Who in America*, 1924–25 ; *Chicago Daily Tribune*, July 22, 1924; *N. Y. Times*, July 23, 1924.]   C. H. J.

PARKER, THEODORE (Aug. 24, 1810–May 10, 1860), theologian, Unitarian clergyman, publicist, born in Lexington, Mass., was a descendant of Thomas Parker of Norton, Derbyshire, England, who settled in Lynn, Mass., in 1635, and in 1640 was one of the founders of the town and church of Reading. A grandson removed to Lexington in 1712 and had for grandchild the Capt. John Parker [*q.v.*] who led the Lexington minute-men, Apr. 19, 1775. John (1761–1836), son of the Revolutionary captain, a farmer and mechanic with a vigorous mind and love of knowledge, married Feb. 17, 1784, Hannah Stearns of Lexington, a woman of sensitive religious feeling without concern for doctrinal disputes. Of their eleven children only Theodore, the youngest, became eminent.

The boy's precocious childhood had marks of independent and varied aptitudes. To the end of his life he recalled the thrill of his first discovery of conscience when, in his fourth year, a childish misdeed was checked by a voice within saying loud and clear, "It is wrong." In advance of all instruction, religious awareness began in a form which in his learned maturity he identified with the unrationalized experience of primitive man. When his New England Primer taught him the doctrine of eternal damnation he wept with terror, but vanquished the distress by trusting the divinations of his own kinder heart. In very early years he had an intense passion for beauty in every form. A child of seven years, he inferred from graduations of lichen, moss, grass, bush, and tree, a hierarchy of ascending forms throughout nature. In growing boyhood his historical lore claimed attention in the political discussions of his elders. These varied propensities, early awakened, prefigured his career.

His schooling was limited to four months of two summers, three months of ten winters in a district school taught by college students, and a few months in Lexington Academy. All other weeks were given to farm work and carpentry, but in leisure hours he read borrowed books with voracious appetite and a phenomenally retentive memory. Discerning teachers taught him Latin and Greek and he undertook modern languages by himself. At ten years he made a botanical catalogue of all vegetables, plants, trees, and shrubs that grew by his home, and when not yet twelve he turned to astronomy and metaphysics. At seventeen he began four years of teaching in neighboring district schools. He walked to Cambridge Aug. 23, 1830, and passed the examination for entrance to Harvard College. Too poor to enroll, he was allowed to take the examinations throughout the course and in 1840 was made an honorary master of arts. In March 1831 he became assistant in a private school in Boston and a year later opened his own school in Watertown. He now gained the friendship of Watertown's learned pastor, Convers Francis [q.v.], steeped in German thought, and won the tender love of Lydia Cabot, daughter of John Cabot of Newton. Long hours of teaching, of studying for Harvard examinations, of acquiring Semitic languages and poring over Cousin and Coleridge made a life without play or exercise; they also deprived him of the give-and-take fellowship with other youths that might have trained him to more sustained good humor and more tolerant indifference to praise and blame.

In April 1834 he entered the Harvard Divinity School, where he lived ascetically on scant savings, meager earnings, and a bursary, but prodigally in the expenditure of mental energy—"an athlete in his studies," said his fellow student Christopher P. Cranch [q.v.]. His journal shows a knowledge of twenty languages, and of the most necessary, the knowledge was exact. In Prof. John Gorham Palfrey's absence, he gave the instruction in Hebrew. Echoing the thought of the faculty, he believed in an inspired Bible, a revelation evidenced by miracles, in Christ as the Son of God supernaturally conceived. Nevertheless, in editing with two classmates The Scriptural Interpreter he made use of mild German criticism that brought protests from the readers, and when he graduated, July 1836, he had some doubt of miracles and the virgin birth. A month later he began to translate De Wette's Einleitung in das Alte Testament, a work for which America was not yet ready.

Half a dozen churches offered him a settlement, but because of its proximity to libraries he chose the modest parish of West Roxbury, a suburb of Boston, and there, after marriage with Lydia Cabot, Apr. 20, he was ordained June 21, 1837. In his sermons he avoided controversial matters and presented religion only in terms of his inward experience, but this habit led him, in his private reflections, away from dependence on miraculous revelation to a main reliance on the direct, intuitive religious functioning of man's spirit, "the felt and perceived presence of Absolute Being infusing itself in me." Furthermore, the friendships now made were with the progressive spirits of the New England renaissance—Dr. William Ellery Channing and his nephew W. H. Channing, Charles Follen, Frederic H. Hedge, Wendell Phillips, George Ripley, Emerson, and Alcott [qq.v.]. He hailed Emerson's Divinity School Address (1838) as "the noblest, the most inspiring strain I ever listened to ... [though] a little exaggerated, with some philosophical untruths" (Frothingham, post, p. 106). To the controversy that followed he contributed a pamphlet under the pseudonym of Levi Blodgett, arguing that an intuitive religious faculty makes external props like miracles unnecessary. Difference of opinion on this question was then creating division in Unitarian circles and rumors of Parker's attitude cost him the customary exchanges with the Boston pastors. From such disfavor, in spite of a militant disposition, he suffered abnormally, and the more keenly since his intense studies were now often interrupted by physical depression and despondent moods. German thought and sympathy with Coleridge, Carlyle, and Emerson, however, were surely developing his native reliance on intuition into a systematic intellectual form. An undesigned rupture came with a sermon on The Transient and Permanent in Christianity, preached at an ordination in South Boston, May 19, 1841. In it he demanded that "we worship, as Jesus did, with no mediator, with nothing between us and the father of all." This was Emerson's lyrical deliverance done with a ruder prose, and a community already irritated by controversy reacted violently. The orthodox denounced him in the press; the liberal clergy withheld all tokens of fellowship; nevertheless, the following winter laymen in Boston arranged for Parker to deliver a series of lectures, which were published under the title *A Discourse of Matters Pertaining to Religion* (1842). In this remarkable work, ill received in America but of large circulation in English editions and German translation, Parker's vast erudition fortifies an eloquent appraisement of Christianity as the highest evolutionary ascent of the universal and direct human experience of divine reality. He demanded a new theology, which should be a science of religion and interpret its data by the immanence of God in nature and human experience.

The Boston Association of Ministers, to which Parker belonged, was disquieted. Its members had relaxed inherited doctrine, but they rested truth on supernatural revelation. Feeling became acute when they read an article by Parker in *The Dial* of October 1842. Some of them had served on a council called to consider the conflict of the Rev. John Pierpont with his church over a sermon on traffic in liquor, and now they found their decision denounced as a Jesuitical document in the interest of the liquor trade. In January 1843 the Association suggested that Parker resign his membership, but he refused on the ground that the right of free inquiry was at stake. Soon after, he published his translation of De Wette's *Einleitung,* and then, to secure needed rest, he spent a year in European travel (September 1843–September 1844). It was a year of rich experience for a mind stored with knowledge of history and literature, and significant in Parker's life since conferences with the scholars of many lands made him confident in his theological position and convinced of a mission to spread enlightened liberalism. Opponents created his opportunity. When Rev. J. T. Sargent invited Parker to speak in his mission chapel the controlling Fraternity of Churches intervened and Sargent resigned (November 1844). The rules for a traditional lecture in the First Church of Boston were revised to exclude Parker from future participation (December 1844). James Freeman Clarke's chivalrous exchange with Parker, January 1845, caused members of his church to secede. A group of men, therefore, resolved "that the Rev. Theodore Parker shall have a chance to be heard in Boston" and secured a hall for Sunday services. Parker was heard,

and in January, definitely resigning the West Roxbury pastorate, he was installed as minister of the new Twenty-Eighth Congregational Society of Boston, which in November 1852 found nobler quarters in the new Music Hall. Parker defined this church as a union to cultivate love of God and man with a common regard for Jesus as the highest known representative of God. It was to be active in all possible ways for human welfare, and Parker's devotion to its enterprises entailed the sacrifice of a cherished plan to elaborate a true science of religion with its own specific scientific method.

While in Rome in 1844, reflecting on America's historic task, he judged that popular ignorance and corrupt leadership required a campaign of intellectual, moral, and religious education. In his new pulpit and on lecture tours over a wide area, as well as in frequent publications, he discussed problems of war, temperance, prisons, divorce, education, human rights, the careers of American statesmen, always with a wealth of knowledge and a sober practical judgment. His faith was that social wrong would be righted as men attained consciousness of the infinite perfection of God, of the eternal right, of immortal life. Inevitably, the national situation involved him in the agitating discussion of slavery and thus of political parties and political leaders. Bold speech and bold courage gave him enthusiastic followers and bitter enemies, his frequent harsh invectives and ascription of rapacious motives intensifying the social division.

The results of his intensive study of the history and economic aspects of slavery were presented in *A Letter to the People of the United States Touching the Matter of Slavery* (1848) and in articles in the *Massachusetts Quarterly Review* (1847–1850). Webster's Seventh of March speech and the Fugitive Slave Law (1850) created a crisis, and Parker made passionate speeches in Faneuil Hall (Mar. 25, Oct. 14) and as leader of a vigilance committee was dramatically active in the escape of the fugitive slaves William and Ellen Craft (November 1850) and in the foiled plot to rescue Thomas Sims (April 1851). On Oct. 31, 1852, a week after Webster's death, Parker preached a sermon on the statesman's career, recognizing his great abilities but reprobating his character and motives. Believing in the right to secede and not averse to a separation of North and South, Parker failed to comprehend Webster's supreme devotion to national union and laid his policy to ambition for the presidency with Southern support and to financial obligations to Boston capitalists. Two days after the arrest of Anthony Burns [*q.v.*], another fugitive slave (May 24, 1854), Parker incited Faneuil Hall hearers to rescue the prisoner by an attack on the court house, but the plan miscarried and Burns was deported. With six others, Parker was indicted by the grand jury, but on Apr. 3, 1855, the indictment was dismissed as ill framed. This fact did not hinder Parker from publishing an elaborate *Defence,* valuable for its accounts of the fugitive slave episodes but marred by invectives against the responsible authorities. The Kansas-Nebraska Bill of 1854 occasioned a fresh outburst of sermons and addresses, some passionately rhetorical, others with forceful economic argument. He now foresaw and predicted civil war. With voice and purse he supported the New England Emigrant Aid Society, the Massachusetts Kansas Committee, and as one of a secret committee abetted John Brown's project of a foray in the mountains of Virginia. At Parker's invitation Brown disclosed his plans at a secret meeting in Boston, Mar. 4, 1858, and though Parker predicted failure, he favored the project as likely to precipitate the now inevitable conflict. His political influence is evidenced by his immense correspondence with Sumner, Seward, Chase, John P. Hale, and Charles Francis Adams. Through the mediation of William H. Herndon [*q.v.*] he influenced Abraham Lincoln, who probably derived from him the formula "government of the people, by the people, for the people" (see Chadwick, *post,* p. 323).

Parker's life was strenuous and exciting; sermons, voluminous correspondence, journeys, lectures—in one year as many as ninety-eight—pastoral labor, and publications crowded full each hour. After exposure on a lecture tour in the spring of 1857 he became ill; an operation for fistula, a laming accident, and symptoms of tuberculosis followed. A violent hemorrhage, Jan. 9, 1859, ended all public activity. With wife and friends he sailed for Vera Cruz, Feb. 3, and, much improved, journeyed in June to London and Paris and then on to the home of his friend Edward Desor in Combes Varin, Switzerland. After a winter in Rome, he died in Florence on May 10, 1860, and was buried in the Protestant cemetery outside the Pinto Gate. At a great memorial meeting in Boston, June 17, he was eulogized by Emerson and Phillips. His rich library of nearly 16,000 volumes, bequeathed to the Boston Public Library, is a noble memorial of his far-ranging mind.

Parker's inability to forget social ostracism measures an affectionate man's craving for love. To humble folk and the unworldly great who were his friends, he abounded in beneficence and delightful discourse. Lacking distinguished presence, ungraceful in bearing, unmusical in voice, with little animation of manner, he yet dominated audiences by reasoning power, by full knowledge of facts, by the thrill of his moral idealism, his poetic joy in the world's ineffable beauty, and the glowing ardor of his disclosures of the mystery of communion with God. The sermons of this religious genius have lost none of their kindling power and claim the attention of students of religious experience. The theological views which disturbed his contemporaries have become characteristic of their descendants. His writings are collected in *Theodore Parker's Works* (14 vols., 1863–70), edited by Frances P. Cobbe and published in London; also in the Centenary Edition (15 vols., 1907–11), published by the American Unitarian Association, which includes a valuable introduction and critical notes. A German edition of his writings, *Theodor Parkers Saemmtliche Werke* (5 vols., 1854–61) was prepared by Johannes Ziethen.

[John Weiss, *Life and Correspondence of Theodore Parker* (1864); O. B. Frothingham, *Theodore Parker, A Biog.* (1874); J. W. Chadwick, *Theodore Parker, Preacher and Reformer* (1900); Albert Réville, *Théodore Parker, Sa Vie et Ses Œuvres* (Paris, 1865; English ed., London, 1865); Alfred Altherr, *Theodor Parker in seinem Leben und Wirken* (St. Gallen, 1894). Detailed bibliogs. are in Chadwick's *Life* and in vol. XV of the Centenary Edition of Parker's works.]

F. A. C.

PARKER, THOMAS (June 8, 1595–Apr. 24, 1677), pioneer minister, was born at Stanton St. Bernard, Wilts., the only son of the Rev. Robert Parker, a leading nonconformist (see *Dictionary of National Biography*) who was forced to take refuge in the Netherlands in 1607, and Dorothy (Stevens) Parker. Thomas matriculated at Trinity College, Dublin, in 1610; he proceeded thence to Magdalen College, Oxford, and in 1614 to the University of Leyden, where he studied theology under William Ames. His formal education was completed under Johannes Maccovius at the University of Franeker, where he received the degree of M.Phil. in 1617. There Parker published seventy theses, supralapsarian in character, which precipitated a violent controversy between his teachers and other continental divines. After the Synod of Dort had acquitted Parker of heresy, he settled in Newbury, Wilts., became assistant master of the Free Grammar School there (*The Victoria History of Berkshire*, II, 1907, p. 274), and assistant to the minister. In 1634, with numerous friends and relatives, he emigrated to Massachusetts. The company, after wintering at Ipswich, where Parker assisted the Rev. Nathaniel Ward [*q.v.*], obtained the grant of a nearby township which they named Newbury, and promptly organized a church of which Parker and his cousin James Noyes were ordained ministers. "So unshaken was their friendship, nothing but death was able to part them. They taught in one school; came over in one ship; were pastor and teacher of one church; and Mr. Parker continuing always in celibacy, they lived in one house, till death separated them for a time..." (*Magnalia*, 1855, I, 485). In New England, Parker was an orthodox Calvinist in doctrine, walking forty miles to vote against Governor Vane in 1637 and later hounding the Quakers (J. J. Currier, *History of Newbury, Mass.*, 1902, pp. 41–42, 149); but in matters of ecclesiastical polity, although the son of an eminent English Congregationalist, and the pupil of another, he persuaded himself that Presbyterianism was necessary to restrain the democratic pretensions of the laity, and keep order in the New England churches. He wrote to the Westminster Assembly showing up the weak points of Congregationalism (*The true Copy of a Letter written by Mr. T. Parker ... declaring his judgement touching the Government practised in the Churches of New England*, London, 1644), and in person argued for Presbyterianism at the New England church synods of 1643 and 1662 (J. G. Palfrey, *History of New England*, II, 1865, pp. 171–72; T. Hutchinson, *History of Massachusetts Bay*, 1795 ed., I, 206 note). Although these decided against him, Parker and his colleagues (Noyes until his death in 1656, and afterward Parker's nephew John Woodbridge) continued to rule the Newbury church in a Presbyterian manner, taking the consent of the congregation "in a silential way." The flock was not always silent: a strong section persistently demanded their rights and privileges under the Congregational dispensation, and frequently appealed to church councils and civil courts; but the Bay authorities consistently declined to discipline Parker, who eventually wore out and outlived his opponents, dying on Apr. 24, 1677. He further departed from majority practice and prejudice in admitting the unconverted to communion (Thomas Lechford, *Plain Dealing*, 1867, p. 56), in denouncing the execution of Charles I, and welcoming the royalist restoration (Dedication and Preface to James Noyes's *Moses and Aaron*, London, 1661). "Mr. Parker excelled . . . in praying, preaching, and singing, having a most delicate sweet voice" (*Magnalia*, 1855, I, 486); he conducted a free school to prepare boys for Harvard (Samuel Sewall was a pupil); and wrote interpretations of Bible prophecies, only one of which, *The Visions and Prophecies of Daniel expounded* (London, 1646), was printed.

[Cotton Mather's *Magnalia Christi Americana* (1855), I, 480–88, including a memoir by Parker's nephew and pupil, Nicholas Noyes; S. E. Morison, "The Education of Thomas Parker of Newbury," *Pubs. Colonial Soc. of Mass.*, Apr. 1932, 261–67; J. B. Felt, *The Ecclesiastical Hist. of New England* (2 vols., 1855–62); "Diary of Samuel Sewall," *Colls. Mass. Hist. Soc.*, 5 ser., vol. V (1878); J. J. Currier, *Hist. of Newbury, Mass.* (1902). The church controversy is related at length in Joshua Coffin, *A Sketch of the Hist. of Newbury* (1845). Parker's *Theses*, originally printed at Franeker in 1617, were reprinted in London in 1657 and at Amsterdam (in Ames's *Disceptatio* and *Opera*) in 1658, calling forth several pamphlets in reply, for titles of which see the Catalogue of the British Museum. *The Copy of a Letter . . . to His Sister, Mrs. Elizabeth Avery*, who had embraced Quakerism, printed in London in 1650, has been reproduced in the American photostat series of the Mass. Hist. Soc. Parker's will is printed in *The Probate Records of Essex County, Mass.*, III (1920), 133–35.]
           S. E. M.

PARKER, WILLARD (Sept. 2, 1800–Apr. 25, 1884), surgeon, was born at Lyndeborough, Hillsborough County, N. H., the son of a farmer, Jonathan Parker (b. June 10, 1764) by his wife, Hannah Clark (b. May 8, 1770). His paternal ancestor, Joseph Parker, had settled in Middlesex County, Mass., in 1640. Willard was named for his grandfather, Willard Parker, a descendant of Maj. Simon Willard. His great-uncle, Col. Moses Parker, was fatally wounded at Bunker Hill, and his maternal grandfather, Rev. Peter Clark, fought in the War of the Revolution.

Willard Parker received his primary education in a rural school, and obtained the degree of A.B. at Harvard in 1826, having supported himself during his years at college. Through a chance contact with John Collins Warren, he was diverted from the ministry and took up the study of medicine. He was apprenticed to Dr. Warren and Dr. S. D. Townsend in Boston, attended medical lectures at Cambridge, and graduated M.D. from Harvard in 1830, presenting an inaugural dissertation entitled "A Thesis on Nervous Respiration" (unpublished). During the next eight years he held a succession of titles in various schools: professor of anatomy and surgery, Clinical School of Medicine, Woodstock, Vt., a part of Waterville College, Me. (1830–33), professor of surgery, Berkshire Medical Institution (1833–36), professor of anatomy, Geneva, N. Y. (1834–36), professor of surgery, Cincinnati (1836–37); and he obtained a second doctorate of medicine from the Berkshire Medical Institution. In 1839 he was appointed professor of principles and practice of surgery in the College of Physicians and Surgeons, New York City, and held this post until 1870.

In 1837 Parker went abroad and had a year at Paris, "walking" the wards of the great hospitals in contact with Chomel, Louis, and other stimulating French clinicians of that period. His excellent diary of this trip has been preserved by his descendants and was published by Ruhräh (*post*) in the *Annals of Medical History,* May–September 1933; it gives an intimate picture of his experiences, and illustrates his personal characteristics. On returning to New York he developed a large practice in the field of general surgery and became influential in public affairs. In surgery he was courageous and successful. He is credited with having performed cystotomy for irritable bladder (1850), with having tied the subclavian artery for aneurysm on five occasions (1864), and with having been the first in America to operate successfully upon an abscessed appendix (three of four cases survived, *Medical Record,* New York, Mar. 1, 1867). Though Hancock had operated for appendicitis in London in 1848, Parker was unaware of the fact; his contribution was bold and original and it received the enthusiastic commendation of Reginald Heber Fitz [*q.v.*] who first established appendicitis as a clinical and pathological entity. Parker was also an inspiring teacher, lecturing for many years before crowded classrooms on the principles of surgery. He was president of the New York Academy of Medicine in 1856, and was affiliated with the New York, St. Luke's, Roosevelt, and Mount Sinai hospitals. In 1870 he resigned from official responsibilities and became emeritus professor of surgery. The Willard Parker Hospital for Infectious Diseases in New York was named in his honor.

In public life Parker was an active promoter of the temperance movement, despite the fact that he drank in moderation himself. He was also active in public health. Personally he had a commanding but kindly presence which won the confidence and sympathy of both students and patients. He married June 21, 1831, Caroline Sarah, daughter of Dr. Luther Allen of Stirling, Mass. There were two children by this marriage. His second wife was Mary Ann (Bissell) Coit, daughter of Josiah and Henrietta Perkins Bissell, whom he married May 25, 1844, and by whom he had one son and two daughters. His large library was left to the Medical Society of the County of Kings in Brooklyn.

[John Ruhräh, "Willard Parker," *Annals Medic. Hist.* (N. Y.), May–Sept. 1933; S. W. Francis, *Biog. Sketches of Distinguished Living New York Surgeons* (1866); W. H. Draper, in *Trans. Medic. Soc., State of N. Y.,* 1885; H. A. Kelly and W. L. Burrage, *Am. Medic. Biogs.* (1920); J. P. Warbasse, "Willard Parker and His Medical Library," *L. I. Medic. Jour.,* Mar. 1907; *New-Eng. Hist. and Geneal. Reg.,* July 1884; *N. Y. Tribune,* Apr. 26, 1884; information about certain facts from a great-grand-daughter.]   J.F.F.

PARKER, WILLIAM HARWAR (Oct. 8, 1826–Dec. 30, 1896), naval officer, author, was born in New York City, the son of Foxhall Alexander and Sara Jay (Bogardus) Parker and the nephew of Richard Elliot Parker [*q.v.*]. On Oct. 19, 1841, he was appointed midshipman, and made his first cruise in the *Columbus* to the Mediterranean and Brazil, 1842–44. In the *Potomac* through the Mexican War, he saw active fighting with the naval battery at Vera Cruz and at the capture of Tabasco. In 1847–48 he was at the Naval Academy, graduating first in his class. Subsequent service included an African cruise in the *Yorktown,* ending in shipwreck off the Cape Verde Islands; an instructorship at Annapolis, 1853–57; and duty on the Pacific station in the *Merrimac.* An excellent student and a clear, facile writer, Parker while returning from this station wrote *Instructions for Naval Light Artillery* (1862) and translated a French work, *Tactique Navale,* both used subsequently at the Naval Academy, where he was again instructor, 1860–61. By the time of the Civil War he had been promoted through the various grades to lieutenant.

Unlike his brother, Foxhall Alexander Parker [*q.v.*], he joined the Southern navy, and in command of the gunboat *Beaufort* fought in Lynch's flotilla at Roanoke Island, Feb. 7, 1862, and below Elizabeth City, Feb. 10. In the latter action Parker was ordered to leave his boat, which escaped to Norfolk, and man a battery on shore. He again commanded the *Beaufort* in the battle of Hampton Roads, Mar. 8, 1862, where his ship's force came under heavy fire from shore while alongside the surrendered *Congress.* Parker was an active participant in the post-bellum controversy over the *Monitor-Merrimac* action, of which a valuable record appears in his *Recollections* (*post*). During the winter of 1862–63 he was executive of the ironclad *Palmetto State* at Charleston, took part in the attack on the Union blockading force Jan. 31, and in April–May had charge of two projected torpedo expeditions which were thwarted, once by the withdrawal of the Federal monitors, and again by a deserter's warning. Made captain in 1863, Parker that autumn organized and became superintendent of the Confederate Naval Academy, which consisted of about fifty midshipmen, quartered aboard the gunboat *Patrick Henry,* the ship still remaining part of the James River defense forces. Though commanding the ironclad *Richmond* during the summer of 1864, he continued superintendent of the academy until the close of the war, taking justifiable pride in the quality of its training. In 1863 he published *Questions on Practical Seamanship: Together with Harbor Routine and Evolutions,* and in 1864, *Elements of Seamanship.* On the evacuation of Richmond, he and his cadets were given charge of the government archives and treasure (about $500,000), and guarded them inviolate during the month's retreat southward.

After the war, Parker was captain of a Pacific Mail steamer between Panama and San Francisco, 1865–74, publishing in 1871, *Remarks on the Navigation of the Coasts Between San Francisco and Panama*; president of the Maryland Agricultural College, 1875–83; and minister to Korea in Cleveland's first administration, 1886. His wide reading, charm as a raconteur, and fair-mindedness appear in his *Recollections of a Naval Officer 1841–1865* (1883), one of the most enjoyable books of its type. He also wrote *Familiar Talks on Astronomy* (1889). He died suddenly in Washington, D. C., and was buried at Norfolk, Va. His wife, Margaret Griffin, daughter of Burwell Mosely of Princess Anne County, Va., whom he married Dec. 14, 1853, survived him; he had no children.

[M. S. B. Gray, *A Geneal. Hist. of the Ancestors and Descendants of Gen. Robert Bogardus* (1927); "The Parker Family of Essex . . .," in *Va. Mag. of Hist. and Biog.*, Oct. 1898; J. T. Scharf, *Hist. of the Confederate States Navy* (1887); *War of the Rebellion: Official Records* (*Navy*); *Army and Navy Jour.*, Jan. 9, 1897; *Washington Post* and *Evening Star* (Washington), Dec. 31, 1896.]   A. W.

PARKHURST, CHARLES (Oct. 29, 1845–Feb. 27, 1921), Methodist Episcopal clergyman, editor, was a native of Sharon, Vt., and was a son of Chester and Sarah Ann (Barnard) Parkhurst. After preliminary education in the country schools he began the study of the law at an early age, was admitted to the bar, and practised for five years at Claremont, N. H. Becoming convinced that his proper vocation was the Methodist ministry, he began his preparation for college at Kimball Union Academy, Meriden, N. H., being at the same time actively engaged in preaching. He received his first preacher's license in 1873, joined the Vermont Conference in 1875, was ordained deacon in 1877, and in 1879, the year after his graduation from Dartmouth College, was advanced to elder's orders. After two years spent in the study of Theology at Andover Seminary he transferred to Boston University and supplied the Methodist Church at Auburndale while a student in the theological department. The next ten years he spent in prominent appointments in the Vermont and New Hampshire conferences. In 1888 he was called from his pastorate in Dover, N. H., to the editorship of *Zion's Herald*, a weekly newspaper owned and controlled by the Wesleyan Association of Boston and devoted to the promotion of the interests of the Methodist Church in New England. Attention to his literary ability had been attracted by his articles in the religious papers, especially by those written during a tour in Europe.

He entered upon his editorship at the age of forty-three, in the prime of his physical and mental maturity, and maintained the paper as one of the foremost religious journals of the entire country for thirty-one years—until April 1919, when he resigned. During the major part of his term of office he had no associate editor and his paper, whose leading articles he always wrote, became largely his personal organ. He took few vacations and set strict limits to his outside appointments, so that *Zion's Herald* was in a peculiar sense his life work. He had the courage of his convictions, marked qualities of religious and intellectual leadership, and a rare discernment of the vital issues of the day. His successor, in an article occasioned by Parkhurst's death, enumerated five outstanding issues of his editorship (*Zion's Herald*, Mar. 9, 1921). These were the vigorous espousal of the temperance cause; social and industrial reforms; the area plan for episcopal supervision within the Methodist Church; the rights of colored members of that communion, with the appointment of colored bishops; and the reunion of Methodism North and South. All these questions, highly controversial in their nature, he handled with such wisdom that much advance was made. To these at least one other issue of great importance should be added. The period of his editorship was a time of theological transition resulting from the advance of science and the application of historical and critical methods to the study of the Bible. Parkhurst presented to his readers the sure results of modern scholarship and interpreted them in such a way that those questions which caused turmoil in other communions were to a considerable degree avoided. With him the essence of religion was moral and spiritual rather than dogmatic. He was fearless in his discussion of Methodist doctrine and discipline, his view of the church was broad, and under his editorial leadership *Zion's Herald* became more cosmopolitan than most denominational journals.

On Jan. 2, 1868, Parkhurst married Lucia A. Tyler of Sharon, Vt., who survived him with one son and one daughter.

[The issues of *Zion's Herald* for Mar. 2 and 9, 1921, contain much biographical material. The former has a portrait and the latter, memorial contributions from many sources. Further material is found in *Who's Who in America*, 1920–21; *Boston Transcript*, Feb. 28 and Mar. 8, 1921; *Congregationalist*, Mar. 10, 1921.]
F. T. P.

PARKHURST, CHARLES HENRY (Apr. 17, 1842–Sept. 8, 1933), Presbyterian clergyman, reformer, was born in Framingham, Mass., the son of Charles F. W. and Mary (Goodale) Parkhurst. "My earlier life," he writes in his autobiography, "was that of the ordinary farmer's boy. A single family living half a mile distant made for us our only society" (*My Forty Years in New York,* p. 11). He was not sent to public school until he was twelve years old, and "was thus saved," he says, "the fundamental disadvantage of having cultivated in me a distaste for knowledge." When he was sixteen, he was placed by his father in a grocery store "to sell sugar, molasses and codfish, an experience that was distasteful." His interests were scholarly; and therefore, after a period of special preparation at a local institute, he went to Amherst College, where he was graduated in 1866. In the early fall of this year, he took charge as principal of the Amherst High School. Three years later he went abroad for a year's travel and theological study at Halle, and on his return in 1870 accepted a position as teacher of Greek and Latin at Williston Seminary, Easthampton, Mass. Another trip to Europe took him to Leipzig for a second period of foreign study (1872–73). In 1874 he was ordained by the South Berkshire Association of Congregational Ministers and installed pastor of the Congregational Church in Lenox, Mass. Six years later he was called to the Madison Square Presbyterian Church, New York, where he preached his first sermon on Feb. 29, 1880.

Parkhurst was at this time a studious, sturdy cleric of the distinctly Puritan type. His interests were predominantly scholarly and pastoral. His sermons, read carefully from manuscript, were terse and forceful, but bore little trace of wide popular appeal. In appearance, manner, and habits, he was inconspicuous. Yet in a sermon preached on Feb. 14, 1892, he threw a bomb the detonation of which was heard to the far borders of the land. An unsparing denunciation of "the polluted harpies that, under the pretense of governing this city, are feeding day and night on its quivering vitals . . . a lying, perjured, rum-soaked, libidinous lot," this sermon must ever rank as one of the most famous and effective pulpit utterances in American history (printed in *Our Fight with Tammany,* pp. 8–25). It sprang from years of growing outrage at the alliance of organized politics with vice in New York, and the public indifference to this situation; and more immediately from Parkhurst's work as president of the Society for the Prevention of Crime, to which office he was elected in 1891. "No one was less suspicious than the preacher himself of the disturbing effect it would produce" (*Ibid.,* p. 8). No notice had been given of

its delivery, and it became public only through the enterprise of a roving reporter, W. E. Carson, who chanced to be in the congregation on the fateful Sunday. Furthermore, when the attack unexpectedly swept the city with excitement, and not only cynical politicians but press and public demanded proof of the charges presented, Parkhurst found himself with nothing that could stand the test of a court of law. Unprepared for what had occurred, he was face to face with the prospect of failure and humiliation. Resourceful and dauntless, however, he promptly set about securing the proof required. In his own person, and with the help of friends and detectives, he hunted out the haunts of vice —the saloons and dance halls, the gambling dens and houses of prostitution—to get his evidence; and on Mar. 13, 1892, he preached a second sermon, this time with affidavits as his text. He now became the center of furious attack. He was ridiculed, insulted, threatened; he became the butt of ribald songs and indecent jests. Many of his parishioners questioned the wisdom of his activities, and not a few of his professional brethren lamented his "sensationalism." He was armed with facts, however, and the courage to use them. Slowly but surely an aroused public swung to his support, and in due course, as so many results from a single cause, there came the Lexow Investigation (1894), the defeat of Tammany at the polls, and the sweeping reforms of the Strong administration.

This conflict marked the climax of Parkhurst's career. It was the peak to which everything before had swiftly climbed, and from which everything after slowly fell away. The momentum of his great fame held him as one of New York's popular and effective preachers for two decades. Never again in the forefront of civic affairs, he remained always a caustic critic of official corruption. In 1918, on the consolidation of his church with the Old First Presbyterian Church, he retired as active pastor, and entered upon a serene and prolonged period of old age. His last public utterance, on his ninetieth birthday, was an appeal to the people to overthrow the "new Tammany" (*New York Times,* Apr. 17, 1932). He died suddenly of injuries sustained when he walked off the roof of the porch of his home in his sleep.

He was the author of *Analysis of the Latin Verb Illustrated by the Forms of the Sanskrit* (1870), *What Would the World be Without Religion?* (copr. 1882), *The Blind Man's Creed and Other Sermons* (1883), *The Pattern in the Mount* (1885), *The Swiss Guide* (copr. 1890), *Three Gates on a Side and Other Sermons* (copr.

1891), *Our Fight with Tammany* (1895), *Talks to Young Men* (1897), *Talks to Young Women* (1897), *The Sunny Side of Christianity* (1901), *A Brief History of the Madison Square Presbyterian Church and Its Activities* (1906), *A Little Lower Than the Angels* (copr. 1908), *The Pulpit and the Pew* (1913), and *My Forty Years in New York* (1923). Parkhurst was twice married: first, Nov. 23, 1870, to Ellen Bodman, of Williamsburg, Mass., who had been a pupil of his in the Amherst High School; and, second, Apr. 19, 1927, to Mrs. Eleanor Marx, of New York. From 1892 to 1902 he was a trustee of Amherst College.

[In addition to *My Forty Years in N. Y.*, and *Our Fight with Tammany*, see his *Brief Hist. of Madison Square Presbyt. Ch.*; also *Who's Who in America*, 1932–33, and *N. Y. Times*, Dec. 15, 1931, Apr. 17, 18, 1932, Sept. 9, 1933.]   J. H. H.

PARKHURST, JOHN ADELBERT (Sept. 24, 1861–Mar. 1, 1925), astronomer, was born at Dixon, Ill. His parents were Sanford Britton and Clarissa J. (Hubbard) Parkhurst. After the death of his mother, when he was five, he was adopted by Dr. and Mrs. Abner Hagar, his uncle and aunt, of Marengo, Ill. He attended the public schools at Marengo and entered Wheaton College in 1880. At the end of his sophomore year he left college and taught in the public school of Lombard, Ill., for a year, then entered the Rose Polytechnic Institute, Terre Haute, Ind., where he graduated in 1886 with the degree of B.S. in mechanical engineering. In 1897 the degree of M.S. was conferred on him by the same institution, and in 1906 Wheaton College gave him the degree of A.B. as of the class of 1885. After graduation he spent two years as instructor of mathematics at Rose. The death of his uncle made it necessary for him to return to Marengo, where he was engaged in business for the next ten years.

His interest in astronomy had been stimulated by reading the works of Thomas Dick, and while in Terre Haute he had bought a small lens and fashioned his own telescope. As soon as possible after returning to Marengo he bought and set up a modern 6-inch reflector by J. A. Brashear [*q.v.*], and during his ten years there contributed some fifty articles to astronomical periodicals, chiefly on variable stars. During a part of this time he acted as a non-resident computer for the Washburn Observatory. The opening in 1897 of the Yerkes Observatory of the University of Chicago at Williams Bay, Wis., within thirty miles of his home, was an important event in his career. He was a frequent visitor there, and during the summer of 1898 he was a volunteer research assistant, assigned to the 12-inch telescope. In 1900 he was appointed assistant and from then on devoted his entire time to astronomy. He was made instructor in 1905, assistant professor in 1912, and associate professor in 1919.

His first piece of work at the Yerkes Observatory was *The Spectra of Stars of Secchi's Fourth Type* (1903; also in *Publications of the Yerkes Observatory*, vol. II, 1904), in collaboration with George E. Hale and Ferdinand Ellerman. His chief work, however, was in photometric research—the measurement of the brightness of stars, both visually and photographically. In 1906 the Carnegie Institution of Washington, which had made special grants toward his salary during his first five years at Yerkes, published his *Researches in Stellar Photometry During the Years 1894 to 1906, Made Chiefly at the Yerkes Observatory*. His "Yerkes Actinometry," published in the *Astrophysical Journal*, October 1912, contained the results of many years of painstaking work in determining the visual and photographic brightness, color indices, and spectral types of all stars not fainter than magnitude 7.5, located within seventeen degrees of the north pole. Parkhurst, for Yerkes, also cooperated with the Harvard, McCormick, and Lick observatories in a campaign to extend the scale of brightness of the bright stars to the faint ones (*Memoirs of the American Academy of Arts and Sciences*, vol. XIV, no. 4, August 1923). He also collaborated with Father J. G. Hagen, of the Vatican Observatory, on the latter's *Atlas Stellarum Variabilium* (ser. 1–5, 1899–1908). Another important piece of work was his posthumously published determination of magnitudes in one of the zones of Kapteyn's "Plan of Selected Areas" (*Publications of the Yerkes Observatory*, vol. IV, pt. VI, 1927). Other photometric researches of importance were carried on by his many graduate students. He took part in three eclipse expeditions with the chief object of measuring the brightness of the corona.

Although exceedingly modest, he had unusual ability in imparting his knowledge to his students. Never physically strong, he adhered to a strict discipline of body and mind which enabled him, in spite of bodily ills, to accomplish a full lifetime of work. His longest vacation was one of six months in Europe with his wife, Anna Greenleaf of Terre Haute, Ind., whom he married Nov. 21, 1888. He was an active member of the Congregational Church and Sunday School of Williams Bay, and was elected the first supervisor of the Village of Williams Bay.

[R. G. Aitken and E. B. Frost, in *Pubs. Astron. Soc. of the Pacific*, Apr. 1925 : E. B. Frost, in *Astronomische*

Nachrichten, Mar. 1925; S. B. Barrett, in *Pop. Astron.,* May 1925; *Astrophysical Jour.,* June 1925; *Observatory,* Apr. 1925; *Who's Who in America,* 1924–25; *N. Y. Times,* Mar. 3, 1925.]   R. S. D.

PARKMAN, FRANCIS (Sept. 16, 1823–Nov. 8, 1893), historian, was born in Boston, Mass. He came of old New England stock; his father, the Rev. Francis Parkman, was descended from Elias Parkman who had settled at Dorchester by 1633; his mother, Caroline (Hall), was descended from the Rev. John Cotton. The family had wealth, social standing, and a long tradition of culture. Parkman's father was for thirty-six years the pastor of the New North Church in Boston. The historian's grandfather, Samuel Parkman, had become one of the richest merchants in Boston, and it was the share of this fortune which came to Francis that enabled him, in spite of years of invalidism, to carry on his historical writing.

At about eight years of age he was sent to live with his maternal grandfather, Nathaniel Hall, at Medford, and there attended the school kept by John Angier. He does not seem to have got much from his early schooling, but he had some six or seven square miles of wild forest in which to play, and in tramping, exploring, and trapping the small wild animals, he developed his outdoor tastes to the full. When about twelve years old he was taken back to Boston to live with his own family and attended a private school kept by Gideon Thayer, where he was fortunate in having particularly good instruction in English literature and composition. He was greatly interested in experimental chemistry and amateur theatricals. In 1840 he entered Harvard, where he became a member of various college societies and president of the Hasty Pudding Club. His scholarship record was excellent in the subjects that appealed to him but he paid little attention to the others, although he succeeded in being made a member of Phi Beta Kappa. His outside reading probably had more permanent influence upon him than his strictly collegiate courses.

His life work was already beginning to take shape in his mind and as one of his classmates wrote long afterward, he "even then showed symptoms of 'Injuns' on the brain" (Wheelwright, *post,* p. 322). During the vacations he made long excursions, partly on foot and partly by canoe, through the White Mountains, up the Magalloway River, about Lakes George and Champlain, and in other directions wherever there were woods and wilderness. He was a sportsman and a good shot. In attempting to train himself for this outdoor life, he overstrained himself in the new Harvard gymnasium,

and, in his senior year, had to leave college for a while. In November 1843 he crossed to Europe in a sailing vessel. He visited Sicily and Italy, and while in Rome spent some days in retreat at a convent of Passionist Fathers, an illuminating episode which he recounted in an article written at the time but not published for many years (*Harper's New Monthly Magazine,* August 1890). From Italy he continued rambling for seven months through Switzerland, France, and Great Britain, returning to Cambridge in June in ample time to take his degree at Commencement in August. Immediately after graduation he entered the Law School—though with no intention of practising—for the sake of the mental training it offered. He continued until January 1846, by which time he had done sufficient work to qualify him for the degree of LL.B. and admittance to the bar, though he never applied for the latter. Meanwhile he had made his first appearance in print by publishing during 1845 in the *Knickerbocker, or New-York Monthly Magazine* five sketches based on his earlier vacation rambles and adventures.

On Apr. 28, 1846, he set out from St. Louis on the one really great physical adventure of his life, his journey along the Oregon Trail. It is certain that by now he had formed a more or less definite idea of what his work in life was to be, although, perhaps from his natural reserve and modesty, he had persistently denied that he had any literary ambitions. The expedition was undertaken with two distinct ends in view, to study the Indians and to improve his health. Not long after leaving St. Louis he fell in with a band of Sioux and lived with them for some weeks, observing their habits, customs, and ways of thought. He also had an opportunity to study the life of the white men on the edge of civilization, which was much like the frontier life of two centuries before. He hobnobbed with hunters, trappers, voyageurs, half-breeds, and all the types with which he was to deal in developing his historical themes. In accomplishing the second object of his journey, however, he was not so successful. His eyesight had begun to trouble him and though his constitution was fundamentally strong, he suffered all his life from having overtaxed it. The strenuous exercise with which he sought to cure his maladies seems to have been the worst method he could have chosen. The physical effort of the trip and especially the poor food, told on him severely, and he returned to Boston in October 1846 much worse in body than he had left, though with invaluable knowledge and experience. He now suffered a complete breakdown, and went to a cure at Brattleboro

Vt. There he dictated to his cousin, Quincy A. Shaw, who had accompanied him on the trip, an account of their adventures. Under the title, "The Oregon Trail" it was published serially in the *Knickerbocker* beginning with the issue of February 1847. The first instalment was signed "A Bostonian," but in those that followed Parkman used his own name. The work was published in book form in 1849 as *The California and Oregon Trail,* and, better known under the shorter title, which was resumed in subsequent editions, has always been one of his most popular writings.

In 1848 he began to write his *History of the Conspiracy of Pontiac,* first of the long series of volumes, on the struggle of French and English for the possession of the continent, that was to be his *magnum opus.* In an autobiographical fragment found among his papers he stated that even in his sophomore year in college he had formed the plan of writing a history of the Old French War. That plan had gradually broadened, and the task which he had now set himself would take, he calculated, about twenty years for its completion. At the very outset, however, an obstacle arose on which he had not counted, and the *Pontiac* was begun under what would seem almost insuperable difficulties. The chief ailment from which Parkman suffered had an obscure origin but it appears to have been some weakness of the nervous system. He was later told by one of the most eminent specialists in Paris that he might go insane. When he began the *Pontiac,* "the light of the sun became insupportable, and a wild whirl possessed his brain, joined to a universal turmoil of the nervous system which put his philosophy to the sharpest test it had hitherto known" (Farnham, *post,* p. 324). The difficulties under which he began "were threefold: an extreme weakness of sight, disabling him even from writing his name except with eyes closed; a condition of the brain prohibiting fixed attention except at occasional and brief intervals; and an exhaustion and total derangement of the nervous system, producing of necessity a mood of mind most unfavorable to effort" (*Ibid.,* p. 325). He felt, however, that it was essential that he should have occupation and a motive in life. He was staying with friends on Staten Island at the time, and there were many other friends, mostly feminine, in the nearby city who willingly helped him. He had a frame built in which parallel wires were stretched across his writing paper, and on this, with eyes closed, he made his notes from the volumes and manuscripts read aloud to him. For a while the readings could last only a half hour, and there were days when he could

do nothing. The average rate of progress of his book during this period was six lines a day. After six months he could do better, and was able to complete the part of the work that could be done in Boston. His research had to be continued among books and manuscripts scattered in libraries in Europe as well as in America, the greater part of the material being in French. Still utterly unable to use his eyes for reading, he had as his regular reader a girl from the public schools who did not understand a word of the language. Nevertheless, almost incredible as it may seem, he completed the *History of the Conspiracy of Pontiac* in less than two and a half years, and it was published, in two volumes, in 1851. Considering the difficulties there had been to overcome, it was a marvelous intellectual achievement. In the same year Parkman developed an effusion on the knee which confined him for two years, permanently weakened the joint, and hindered his exercise for the balance of his life.

Meanwhile, on May 13, 1850, he had married Catherine Scollay Bigelow, daughter of Dr. Jacob Bigelow of Boston. In 1853 he had a crisis in his nervous disorder, and, compelled to lay aside his historical work for a while, wrote his only novel, *Vassall Morton,* which was published in 1856. It was probably written for relaxation and to give him occupation while he was unable to do more serious work. It had no great success and he himself regarded it slightingly. In these years he also wrote a few book reviews, but his real work suffered a severe interruption. It was always necessary for him to have some object on which to fasten his interest, and after the publication of his novel he took up the study of horticulture. He became so deeply interested in raising new varieties of flowers, especially lilies and roses, that he never gave up the hobby afterward. His great success in this new and unexpected field resulted in his election as president of the Massachusetts Horticultural Society and, much later, in his appointment as a professor of horticulture at Harvard (1871).

A renewed nervous crisis in 1858 following the death, within a year of each other, of his only son and of his wife, determined him to go to Paris to consult a specialist there, Brown Séquard. He remained in Paris for some months but without any gain to his health, and at the beginning of 1859 he returned to Boston by way of Nice and Genoa. It was "about four years," he wrote later, "before the power of mental application was in the smallest degree restored" ("Autobiography," in Farnham, p. 329). His two small daughters had gone to live with their mother's sister, and he himself lived with his mother and sisters in Boston in the winters and at his own house at Jamaica Pond, in the summers. Here, in his three acres of garden, he carried on his horticultural studies, often in a wheeled chair. In 1862 he formed a partnership to sell the flowers he raised, but the firm did not prosper and lasted only a year. In 1866 he published *The Book of Roses*.

Meanwhile, determined to go on with his histories, as soon as he was slightly better he began once more by sheer will power. In 1865 he published *Pioneers of France in the New World*. By this time, he had also written parts of other volumes and had gathered notes for more. The *Pioneers* at once established his popularity and also his reputation as a historian. Two years later, *The Jesuits in North America* was published, and in 1869 came *The Discovery of the Great West*, better known by the title of the eleventh edition (1879), *La Salle and the Discovery of the Great West*. In 1874 he published *The Old Régime in Canada* and in 1877 *Count Frontenac and New France under Louis XIV*. It was now twenty-eight years since he had begun the narrative and he had long been anxious to write of the final scene. Fearing that if he delayed further he might not live to do so, he broke the sequence at this point and in 1884 published *Montcalm and Wolfe* (2 vols.). In 1892 he finally completed the series with *A Half-Century of Conflict* (2 vols.). During these years he had also been a fairly frequent contributor to magazines: twenty articles, many of them chapters from his books, had appeared in the *Atlantic Monthly*, eleven in the *North American Review*, and many shorter papers elsewhere. By this time his fame was well established as the leading American historian. Only a few months after he had successfully brought to conclusion his incomparable task of over forty years, he suffered a severe attack of pleurisy and was not expected to recover. He did so but died less than a year later from an attack of peritonitis.

In spite of Parkman's constant suffering and the great difficulties under which his work and the social intercourse which he so greatly enjoyed were carried on, there was never anything morbid about him. He had wide interests, loved out-door life, plants and animals, poetry and people, as well as history. He had a sense of humor, and the verdict of those who knew him was that he was a delightful companion. He possessed a wide circle of friends. Almost isolated from the world as he had to be at intervals, he always maintained his outside contacts. In 1868 he was elected Overseer of Harvard; he resigned in

1871 but was reëlected in 1874 and held the office until his second resignation in 1876. In 1875 he was chosen a fellow of the Corporation and served until 1888, when he resigned. He attended the meetings whenever possible. He dedicated his *La Salle* to his college class, that of 1844, and his *Montcalm and Wolfe* to the College itself. He was one of the founders of the Archeological Institute of America in 1879, and later a member of the executive committee; assisted financially in establishing the American School of Classical Studies at Athens; and was a member or honorary member of a score of societies.

In the conception and execution of his work Parkman was primarily an artist, with the result that his history has an enduring place in literature. He chose to depict the contest of two rival civilizations for the control of a continent, against one of the most picturesque of settings —a background of wilderness and savage man contrasting with the civilization of the nations wrestling for supremacy. Furthermore, he was able to visualize from his own experience the people and scenes he portrayed. When he was preparing himself for his task, the primeval wilderness and the primitive men of the earlier days could still be studied through personal contact, and Parkman, instead of confining himself to books, was wise enough to seize the fast disappearing opportunity. "Faithfulness to the truth of history," he wrote, "involves far more than a research, however patient and scrupulous, into special facts. . . . The narrator must seek to imbue himself with the life and spirit of the time" (*Pioneers of France*, p. xii). By moving geographically westward, he moved historically backward, and his work gained immensely thereby in vividness and authenticity. But he placed his chief reliance upon the study of the original sources as they are to be found in British, French, Canadian, and American depositories. He was one of the first of American historians to insist upon a critical use of original manuscript material, and he brought together an extensive and thoroughly representative collection (now in the possession of the Massachusetts Historical Society) of transcripts of the essential documents. He also was instrumental in bringing about the publication (1876–86) of the monumental series of documents edited by Pierre Margry, *Découvertes et établissements des Français dans l'ouest et dans le sud de l'Amérique septentrionale*. Those who have followed Parkman's trail through the sources have been impressed by the scholarly use that he made of them and by the accuracy of his statements. The long series of systematic archival investigations that have been carried on since the completion of his work have supplemented it and have corrected it at certain points but have not impaired its substantial validity. While his history is pure narrative—inimitable narrative —it is not without philosophical implications. Constantly he contrasts the social and political systems of the contending civilizations and seems to find in that contrast a principal cause of the final outcome. He falls short of complete comprehension of the part that the church and the Jesuits had in the contest; neither does he sufficiently take into account the economic and geographic factors, or the vast discrepancy— nearly twenty to one at the close of the struggle —between the compact population of the English colonies and the widely scattered settlements of the French in North America. Finally, he treats his subject as a series of dramatic episodes, each centering around a different group of characters, rather than as the complete story of the struggle lasting for a century and a half between England and France, for the domination of North America and the Caribbean. Nevertheless, the main design of his work is not likely to be superseded, and his fame is secure among the great American historians.

[Collected editions of Parkman's works are *The Works of Francis Parkman* (20 vols., 1897–98) and *Francis Parkman's Works* (12 vols., 1903). C. H. Farnham, *A Life of Francis Parkman* (1900) contains extracts from Parkman's autobiography and a bibliography of his books and articles. See also H. D. Sedgwick, *Francis Parkman* (1904); Edward Wheelwright, "Memoir of Francis Parkman," in *Col. Soc. Mass., Pubs.*, vol. I (1895); *Letters from Francis Parkman to E. G. Squier* (1911); "Letters of Francis Parkman to Pierre Margry," with introductory note by J. S. Bassett, in *Smith College Studies in History*, vol. VIII (Apr.–July 1923); E. F. Wyatt, in *North Am. Rev.*, Oct. 1923; Joseph Schafer, in *Miss. Valley Hist. Rev.* and *Wis. Mag. of Hist.*, both Mar. 1924; C. W. Alvord, in *Nation* (N. Y.), Oct. 10, 1923; G. M. Wrong, in *Canadian Hist. Rev.*, Dec. 1923; Waldo G. Leland, in *Ex Libris* (American Library in Paris), Feb. 1924; O. B. Frothingham and others, in *Proc. Mass. Hist. Soc.*, 2 ser. VIII (1894); *Boston Transcript*, Nov. 9, 1893.]
                                    J. T. A.

PARKS, WILLIAM (*c.* 1698–Apr. 1, 1750), printer and newspaper publisher, was in all probability a native of Shropshire. He established the first presses of Ludlow, Hereford, and Reading in England, and began his unusual record as a pioneer of newspaper publication by establishing, at Ludlow and Reading respectively, the *Ludlow Post-Man* (1719) and the *Reading Mercury* (1723), the earliest journals to be published in those towns. After six years of printing activity in England, he appeared in Annapolis, Md., in March 1725/26, making proposals to the Assembly for the printing of its laws and journals. By an act of October 1727 he was appointed

public printer, and from then until 1737 he continued to serve the province of Maryland in that capacity. In the year 1730 he enlarged his business by the establishment of a press in Williamsburg, the first printing office to be put in operation in Virginia since the inhibition in 1683 of the Jamestown press of William Nuthead [*q.v.*]. Appointed public printer of Virginia in 1732, he devoted his principal efforts thereafter to his Virginia business, and five years later gave up entirely his Maryland connection. In 1733 appeared from his Williamsburg press *A Collection of All the Acts of Assembly Now in Force in the Colony of Virginia*, a work of historical importance, which ranks also as one of the typographical monuments of colonial America. He maintained his position as public printer of Virginia until his death, which occurred Apr. 1, 1750, in the course of a voyage to England. His widow, Eleanor, and a married daughter, the wife of John Shelton, survived him.

Parks's accomplishment in his two colonial offices places him high in the rank of American printers. In 1727, he established the *Maryland Gazette*, the first newspaper to appear in the country south of Pennsylvania. In 1736, the *Virginia Gazette* began publication under his able editorship. In addition to his government work and his newspapers, he gave attention to the publication of numerous works of historical or political character, and of many handbooks and compilations of daily utility. But the point of special interest is that, consistently, he made definite and successful effort to encourage local men of letters by the publication of works of purely literary intention. Through his publication in Maryland of poems by Richard Lewis and Ebenezer Cooke, and in Virginia of poems by John Markland, a "Gentleman of Virginia," "Several Gentlemen of this Country," and others, he nurtured a native literary product in those colonies at a time when most other American printers were devoting themselves to the production of works of the strictest utility. He published in 1747 William Stith's *The History of the First Discovery and Settlement of Virginia*; he published also in different years original medical works by Dr. John Tennent; political and economic tracts by various writers; the earliest American sporting book, Edward Blackwell's *A Compleat System of Fencing* (1734); and the first American cook book, E. Smith's *The Compleat Housewife* (1742). The typographical quality of his work was superior to that of most of his American contemporaries, and his decorated bookbindings were unsurpassed by those of other binders of colonial America. About the year

1743, he built, with the encouragement and active aid of Benjamin Franklin, the first paper-mill to be established south of Pennsylvania. He was one of the earliest printers to urge, in his "Advertisement, Concerning Advertisements" (*Virginia Gazette*, Oct. 8, 1736), the efficacy of newspaper advertising, and in general his activities indicated the possession of qualities of business enterprise, public spirit, and literary taste unusual among the printers of his time. The printers of Virginia have placed a tablet to his memory in Williamsburg.

[Original sources of information concerning William Parks are: *Archives of Maryland*, vols. XXXIV–XXXVI (1914–16), XL (1921); Land Office Records, Annapolis, Md.; *Jours. of the House of Burgesses of Va.*, 1727–40 (1910), 1742–49 (1909), 1752–58 (1909); Wills and Inventories, XX: 183, Court House, Yorktown, Va. Information is found also in *Wm. and Mary Coll. Quart.*, July 1898, Apr., July 1922; Wm. Clayton-Torrence, *A Trial Bibliog. of Colonial Va.* (1908), pt. 1. His life, and a bibliography of books, newspapers, etc. printed by him, are found in L. C. Wroth, *William Parks, Printer and Journalist of England and Colonial America* (1926), being William Parks Club Pubs., no. 3.]   L. C. W.

PARLEY, PETER [See GOODRICH, SAMUEL GRISWOLD, 1793–1860].

PARMLY, ELEAZAR (Mar. 13, 1797–Dec. 13, 1874), one of the founders of dentistry as an organized profession, was born on a farm in the Town of Braintree, Orange County, Vt., a son of Eleazar and Hannah (Spear) Parmly and a descendant of John Parmelee, an early settler of Guilford, Conn. When he was ten years old, his parents removed to northwestern Vermont. He began his education in the rural schools and from 1810 to 1812 attended a first-class school in Montreal, in which city he became a compositor and reporter for the *Canadian Courant*. In 1814 he taught in his home district; and in the following year, as student assistant to his eldest brother Levi S. Parmly first in Boston and then in Quebec, he began his long dental career. His parents removed to a farm in the town of Perry, Ohio, in 1817, and from that year until 1819, Eleazar practised independently as an itinerant dentist, floating down the Ohio and Mississippi rivers on an "ark" and stopping at the principal settlements. He then proceeded to New York City, and shortly sailed for Europe with a view to perfecting himself in his vocation. He paid for a course of instruction with J. F. C. Maury, a prominent dentist in Paris, and late in 1819 entered a partnership with his brother Levi in London. The latter returned to the United States early in 1820, but Eleazar remained in successful practice in London for a year and a half longer, publishing *An Essay on the Disorders and Treatment of the Teeth* (1821; 3rd ed., 1822).

Late in 1821 he returned to the United States, intending to make only a short visit for the recovery of his health, which had been seriously impaired, but for some forty-five years thereafter, though visiting Europe several times, he practised dentistry in New York City exclusively, rapidly rising to preëminence in his profession. In 1823 he became engaged to marry Eliza, youngest daughter of John Jacob Astor [*q.v.*], but her father opposed the match, and she married Count Vincent Rumpff. After this experience, Parmly kept bachelors' hall for over a year with his brother Samuel W. Parmly and his intimate friend Solyman Brown [*q.v.*]; and on June 17, 1827, married Anna Maria Valk Smith, an heiress whose deceased foster father had been a wealthy broker. Eleazar Parmly then established himself at 11 Park Place, where he was joined in 1829 by his cousins Jahial and Ludolph Parmly as student assistants. Jahial continued his association with Eleazar for the next ten years as prosthetic specialist, while Eleazar devoted himself to operative dentistry. In 1832 Solyman Brown began his dental career with Eleazar and the next year published his *Dentologia* with notes by the latter. In 1834 Eleazar and Jahial were joined by David R. Parmly as student assistant, and several other members of the family subsequently had the benefit of Eleazar's instruction.

Eleazar Parmly was a leader in the early opposition to the use of amalgam for filling teeth—an issue which seems to have precipitated the organization (Dec. 3, 1834) of the first dental association, the Society of Surgeon Dentists of the City and State of New York, with Parmly as its first president and Solyman Brown as its first corresponding secretary. In 1839 both were associated with Chapin A. Harris [*q.v.*] and others in the establishment of the first dental periodical, the *American Journal of Dental Science,* of which Parmly was one of the first nominal editors. In the same year he supplied the notes to a new edition of John Hunter's *Natural History of the Human Teeth.* When the American Society of Dental Surgeons was organized in 1840, he was its second vice-president, and received from it one of the original degrees of D.D.S. The degree of M.D. was conferred upon him by some university medical school at about the same time. He was first vice-president of the society, 1841–44, and president, 1844–53. In 1842 he was one of the first to receive the honorary D.D.S. of the Baltimore College of Dental Surgery, of which he was provost from 1848 to 1852. His son Ehrich (born with a twin sister in 1830) graduated from the Baltimore College and began practice with his father in 1851. Eleazar Parmly's wife died in 1857. They had nine children; four sons (three died in infancy), and five daughters. One of the latter married Frederick Billings [*q.v.*], best known as the president of the Northern Pacific Railroad. For many years Parmly was a lay preacher in the Church of the Disciples in New York, and in 1861 he published *The Babe of Bethlehem*, in free verse, a harmony of the Gospel stories of Christ. In that year he opened a hotel, the Parmly House (still in operation, 1934), which he built at Painesville, Ohio, near the farm where his parents had finally settled. In 1867 he published *Thoughts in Rhyme*, a collection of verses written by him between 1818 and 1862 which contain much autobiographical material. During his declining years he spent a large part of his time at his estate, "Bingham Place," at Rumson, N. J. He retired from active practice in 1866, but in the same year became the first president of the New York College of Dentistry, and held the position of emeritus professor of the institutes of dentistry in that college until 1869. He died of pneumonia at his New York City residence, and was interred in his family vault in the Rumson Burying Ground. With the most successful practice in the United States, a fortune from his wife and many profitable real-estate investments, he had become a millionaire. He was an affable gentleman, a forceful public speaker, an interesting writer, and a skilful practitioner, and stood in the forefront of his profession for some thirty years.

[L. Parmly Brown, *The Greatest Dental Family* (1923), reprinted from *Dental Cosmos.*, Mar.–May 1923, containing numerous references to original sources; *Dental Cosmos*, Jan. 1875; *N. Y. Times*, Dec. 14, 1874.]   L. P. B—n.

PARR, SAMUEL WILSON (Jan. 21, 1857–May 16, 1931), chemist, inventor, and teacher, was born in Granville, Ill., the son of James and Elizabeth Fidelia (Moore) Parr. After preliminary training in the academy at Granville, he entered the University of Illinois. Here he was a leader in both literary and athletic activities and graduated with the degree of B.S. in 1884, valedictorian of his class. The following year he spent at Cornell University, from which he received the degree of M.S. On Dec. 27, 1887, he married Lucie A. Hall of Champaign, Ill.; two children were born to them.

Upon completing his work at Cornell, he went to Illinois College, Jacksonville, where, after serving as instructor for a year, he became professor of general science. In 1891 he was called to the University of Illinois as professor of chemistry, which position he held until 1926, when he became professor emeritus, thereafter devoting his time to research and to a number of business enterprises. During the years 1900–01 he studied in Berlin and Zürich. At the University of Illinois he took a keen interest in the various activities of student life. He furthered outdoor sports, was for some years leader of the university glee club, and was chairman of the board of directors of the university Young Men's Christian Association. An effective teacher, he inspired many students to become diligent investigators and good citizens. He was influential in the organization of the curriculum of chemical engineering and of the chemical club, and in the establishment of the chemical library, the first departmental library of the university. His activities extended outside the institution, and he had a part in organizing the state water survey, of which he was a director (1904–05), and served as consulting chemist for the Illinois geological survey, and as consulting engineer for the United States bureau of mines.

Among his scientific accomplishments was his calorimeter for determining the heat value of coal and other solids, invented in 1900 and used in the scientific laboratories of the world. His peroxide bomb (1912) was also a valuable addition to analytical laboratories. Later, he perfected a third type of calorimeter, by which the heat value of gaseous fuels can be determined continuously and accurately. In carrying out the investigations which led to the perfection of these important inventions he was compelled to take up research in related lines. The tables of constants which he needed to use in calorimetry were inaccurate, so he compiled the data for making better tables. The metals available for use in the bomb calorimeter were easily corroded or expensive; accordingly, he set to work to find an alloy which would resist both acid and alkaline corrosion, and would at the same time possess desirable casting and machining properties. Nearly one hundred mixtures of metals were carefully studied before he found the mixture to which he gave the name "illium" after his native state. This alloy is better than platinum as a lining in the bomb calorimeter, and its use as a general corrosion-resisting metal is increasing daily. He studied boiler waters and their treatment and developed a valuable method for the modification of permanently hard water. His study of the embrittlement of boiler plate is a monument to his patience, perseverance, and skill. For thirty years he investigated the origin, physical and chemical properties, classification, and utilization of coal, and he became an international authority upon all coal and fuel problems. In spite of the general feeling that Illinois coal could not be used for the production of coke, he worked out a method of low temperature coking, which won the admiration of fuel experts at home and abroad.

He was a member of numerous scientific and engineering organizations and served on many of their technical committees. He was president of the American Chemical Society in 1928 and was reëlected for a second term, but was unable to serve. In 1926 he was awarded the Chandler Medal by Columbia University "in recognition of outstanding achievements in science." He was the author of a well-known book, *The Chemical Examination of Water, Fuel, Flue Gases and Lubricants* (1911), and his contributions to scientific magazines were numerous and covered a wide field. His system of classifying coal is used in the International Critical Tables. He wrote seventeen of the bulletins published by the University of Illinois Engineering Experiment Station, and was American editor of *Fuel in Science and Practice.* He died in Urbana, Ill.

[*Industrial and Engineering Chemistry,* Sept. 1925; *Chemical and Metallurgical Engineering,* May 1926, June 1931; *Science,* July 3, 1931; *Chemical Bull.* (Chicago), June 1931; *Who's Who in America,* 1930–31; *Time,* Mar. 3, 1930; *Chicago Sunday Tribune,* May 17, 1931; *Fuel in Science and Practice,* June 1925.]

B. S. H.

PARRINGTON, VERNON LOUIS (Aug. 3, 1871–June 16, 1929), teacher, philologist, historian, was born at Aurora, Ill., of Scotch and English ancestry, the son of John William and Louise (McClellan) Parrington. His father, a native of New Hampshire, graduated from Colby College in 1855, became a principal of public schools in New York and Illinois, was a Union captain in the Civil War, and finally practised law in Kansas and was a judge of probate. Parrington attended the College of Emporia, a Presbyterian institution, for several years, was admitted as a junior to the class of 1893 at Harvard College and, after graduating, returned home to teach. A Westerner not only by birth but by conviction, he had been unhappy at Harvard and did not revisit Cambridge and Boston for thirty years. He was instructor in English and French at the College of Emporia, 1893–97; instructor in English and modern languages, 1897–98, and professor of English, 1898–1908, at the University of Oklahoma, losing his post as the result of what he called a "political cyclone"; assistant professor of English, 1908–12, and professor of English from 1912 until his death at the University of Washington. On July 31, 1901, he married Julia Rochester Williams, of Norman, Okla., who with two daughters and a son sur-

vived him. His esthetic nature was rich and well disciplined. He was an enthusiastic student of architecture; wrote excellent verse, especially in his younger years; and took infinite pains with his prose style, which became a perfect expression of the man himself. He spent fourteen months of 1903–04 in England and France and visited Europe again in 1923 and 1929. He taught in the summer sessions of the University of California in 1922, of Columbia University in 1923, and of the University of Michigan in 1927. As a teacher of literature he was extraordinarily effective. At the University of Washington, where he developed a notable series of courses in the history of American literature and thought, he was worshipped by his pupils, but official recognition of his work came slowly and grudgingly. Outside the University he was little known until the first two volumes of his *Main Currents in American Thought* were published in the spring of 1927. The work was recognized at once as the most scholarly and original study of American literature since Moses Coit Tyler's spacious survey of the Colonial and Revolutionary periods, and for two brief, busy years, Parrington enjoyed his renown. Death overtook him unannounced on a Sunday morning at Winchcomb, Gloucestershire, only a few minutes after he had written a last tribute to his friend, James Allen Smith [*q.v.*], to whose memory he had dedicated the *Main Currents.*

Parrington's publications were: "The Puritan Divines, 1620–1720," *The Cambridge History of American Literature,* vol. I (1917); *The Connecticut Wits* (1926); *Sinclair Lewis, Our Own Diogenes* (1927); *Main Currents in American Thought: An Interpretation of American Literature from the Beginning to 1920* (3 vols., 1927–30), the volumes bearing the subtitles of *The Colonial Mind* (1927), *The Romantic Revolution in America* (1927), and *The Beginnings of Critical Realism in America* (1930), which was published as he left it, incomplete and some of it not in its final form; articles entitled, "American Literature to the End of the Nineteenth Century" and "Nathaniel Hawthorne" in the *Encyclopaedia Britannica* (14th ed., 1929); the article on Brook Farm in the *Encyclopaedia of the Social Sciences;* the chapter, "The Development of Realism," in *The Reinterpretation of American Literature* (1928), edited by Norman Foerster; the introduction to James Allen Smith's *The Growth and Decadence of Constitutional Government* (1930); and a number of book reviews in the *Nation,* the *Saturday Review of Literature, Books,* and other periodicals.

His fame depends on the *Main Currents in*

American Thought. The publication of the first two volumes marked a fresh beginning in the study of American literature in its relation to the life of the nation: every work written since has felt its influence. Yet the book did not pretend to be a history of American literature, and as a history of American thought it confines itself pretty strictly to the rise of the idea of democratic idealism and to the struggle to make that idea prevail in the political and economic order. As a work of scholarship the *Main Currents* has already fulfilled its mission, but it continues to display the inexhaustible suggestiveness and vitality of a classic. As an account—shrewd, well informed, witty, and understanding—of a great procession of significant Americans in their relation to the ideas prevailing in their time, the book will not easily be superseded, but it is the personal, artistic quality of it, rather than its scholarship, that makes it one of the landmarks of American literature.

[*Who's Who in America*, 1928–29; *Gen. Cat. Officers, Grads., and Former Students of Colby Coll.* (1920); *Harvard Coll., Class of 1893, Secretary's Report*, 1899, 1910, 1918, 1923, 1933; *Nation*, July 10, 1929; Russell Blankenship, "Vernon Louis Parrington," *Ibid.*, Aug. 7, 1929; J. B. Harrison, *Vernon Louis Parrington, American Scholar* (1929); *Seattle Daily Times*, June 17, 19, 1929. For illuminating criticism of Parrington's work see Charles A. Beard, "Fresh Air in American Letters," *Nation*, May 18, 1927, and Morris R. Cohen, "Parrington's America," *New Republic*, Jan. 28, 1931.]   G. H. G.

PARRIS, ALBION KEITH (Jan. 19, 1788–Feb. 11, 1857), senator, governor of Maine, the only child of Samuel and Sarah (Pratt) Parris, was born at Hebron, in what is now the state of Maine, where his father, one time judge of the court of common pleas for Oxford County, was one of the first settlers. His ancestor, Thomas Parris, the son of a dissenting minister near Plymouth, England, emigrated to Long Island and later removed to Pembroke, Mass. Albion's boyhood was spent on his father's farm. He entered Dartmouth College in 1803 with advanced standing, was graduated in 1806, and immediately commenced the study of law with Ezekiel Whitman [*q.v.*] of New Gloucester. He was admitted to the Cumberland bar in September 1809 and started practice in Paris. In 1810 he was married to Sarah Whitman, the daughter of Levi Whitman of Wellfleet, Mass., who with their five children survived him.

After entering politics in 1811 as attorney for Oxford County, he represented Paris in the Massachusetts House of Representatives in 1813–14 and Oxford and Somerset counties in the Massachusetts Senate of 1814–15. In November of that year he was elected a representative in the

Fourteenth Congress and reëlected in 1816, serving until Feb. 3, 1818, when he resigned to accept appointment as judge of the federal district court for Maine. He was active in the Maine convention of 1819, serving on the committee that drafted the new constitution and as treasurer of the convention. The following year he succeeded Samuel Freeman as judge of probate for Cumberland County. When William King [*q.v.*] resigned as governor of Maine in 1821, Parris was elected, after an interim, in a triangular contest that almost split the Democratic party in Maine. He was annually reëlected until 1826, when he refused to be a candidate. His terms as governor were uneventful ones, in which the lands held in common with Massachusetts and the northeastern boundary were the most prominent matters for discussion. On his recommendation the legislature authorized him to collect materials on the boundary question, which was rapidly becoming serious. In 1827 he succeeded John Holmes [*q.v.*] as United States senator but resigned on Aug. 26, 1828, to become associate justice of the supreme court of Maine. Although long absence from legal work forced him to intensive study, he filled this office intelligently though not brilliantly. This post he gave up in 1836 to become second comptroller of the federal treasury, a position he held for thirteen years. He returned to private law practice in Portland, but in 1852 he was elected mayor with the support of the faction opposed to the Maine liquor law. His only defeat at the polls and his last venture into politics came in 1854, when he was the Democratic candidate for governor. Distinguished for common sense more than for brilliance, he was a politician rather than a jurist or statesman. Guided largely by expediency he advanced from office to office, each more highly salaried than the one before; he sacrificed a senatorship for the safety of a judgeship. He was not a fighter and could not face abuse. Urbane, courteous, shrewd, he built up a great following. He wrote skilful and well-placed political letters. He avoided responsibility on momentous issues. In life he was a practical success.

[William Willis, *A Hist. of the Law, the Courts, and the Lawyers of Maine* (1863); W. B. Lapham and S. P. Maxim, *Hist. of Paris, Me.* (1884); *Maine Hist. Soc. Colls.*, vol. V (1857), pp. xl–xlv; *Eastern Argus* (Portland), Feb. 12, 1857.]   R. E. M.

PARRIS, ALEXANDER (Nov. 24, 1780–June 16, 1852), architect and builder, was descended from Thomas Parris, who came to New England from Topsham, England, in 1683, and later served as the first schoolmaster of Pembroke, Mass. Alexander's father, Matthew, married Mercy Thompson of Halifax, Mass., in February 1780, and the couple moved at once to Hebron, Me., where Alexander was born. Other families from Pembroke settled in this portion of Maine at about the same time; Paris Hill takes its name from the Parris family, and Alexander's cousin Albion K. Parris [q.v.] in time became a United States senator and governor of Maine. Alexander's father died when his son was only three and apparently the widowed mother returned to Pembroke, for the boy was educated in the school there and there apprenticed to a carpenter and builder. He is said at this time to have studied especially Peter Nicholson's *Principles of Architecture*. He married Silvina (or Sylvina) Stetson, Apr. 19, 1801, and for a time was teacher of a common-school.

Between the time of his marriage and the War of 1812 he worked for a while in Portland; the Richard Hunnewell (Shepley) house in Portland, of which his drawings are preserved, dates from 1805. During the War of 1812 he was captain of a company of artificers (engineers) stationed at Plattsburg, N. Y.; and after its close he settled in Boston. Here his most important work was done. The David Sears House, on Beacon Street, now altered and used as the Somerset Club, is dated by a stone in the basement as 1816; Parris' name appears as architect. In 1819, he was the architect of St. Paul's Church on Tremont Street (still extant), which was built by Solomon Willard, the architect of Bunker Hill Monument; this church, the first large classic-revival church of temple type in Boston, marked the end of the colonial tradition and the beginning of the age of revivalism.

During the next decade, Parris' marked engineering skill found scope in his work with Col. Loammi Baldwin [q.v.] as consulting engineer in building the masonry dry dock at the Charlestown Navy Yard; at the same time he built various sea walls in Boston Harbor. He appears to have served as superintendent for Charles Bulfinch [q.v.] in the construction of the Massachusetts General Hospital (completed in 1823), and in 1825 he was the architect for the market hall and the surrounding buildings of Faneuil Hall Market, a scheme of civic betterment remarkable for its day in its combination of broad practical and esthetic ideals. It was much praised at the time, and its continuing usefulness today bears witness to the soundness of his design and execution. During this period he is also credited with the design of the Marine Hospital in Chelsea, and the arsenal at Watertown; it is possible also that he superintended the erection of the

Boston Customs House, though the plans are known to be the work of Ammi B. Young. Between 1834 and 1836, Richard Upjohn [q.v.] was one of Parris' draftsmen; his diary (in the possession of his grandson, Hobart B. Upjohn) shows that in that period he was working on the Boston Court House (usually attributed to Bulfinch), on a fire-engine house, and on further work at the Massachusetts General Hospital and the navy yard in Charlestown. In 1847 (Fentress, *post*) or 1848 (Preble, *post*), Parris was appointed civil engineer of the navy yard at Portsmouth, N. H., a post which he held until his death. Under his direction much levelling was done, the sea wall was completed, and many buildings were enlarged and repaired.

In 1840 Parris had bought the Elisha Briggs estate in the north part of Pembroke, his childhood home. Taken ill in Washington, in the spring of 1852, he was removed to his estate and died there June 16. He was buried in the Briggs cemetery, North Pembroke. His widow died Oct. 3, 1853. Many of his drawings are preserved in the Boston Athenaeum Library; among them "Plans and Elevations of the Massachusetts General Hospital erected under the superintendance of Alexander Parris, 1823"; plans of the Hunnewell House, of a house for Mr. Preble, and of "Pr'th church" (possibly St. John's, Portsmouth, N. H., still standing). The Massachusetts Historical Society owns his competition designs for the Bunker Hill Monument.

[*Columbian Centinel* (Boston), Apr. 30, 1825; W. E. H. Fentress, *1775–1875: Centennial Hist. of the U. S. Navy Yard at Portsmouth, N. H.* (1876); Justin Winsor, *The Memorial Hist. of Boston*, vol. IV (1881); G. H. Preble, *Hist. of the U. S. Navy-Yard, Portsmouth, N. H.* (1892); A. E. Brown, *Faneuil Hall and Faneuil Hall Market* (1900); S. A. Drake, *Old Landmarks and Historic Personages of Boston* (1873); M. V. Tilson, *The Tilson Geneal.* (1911); *Vital Records of Pembroke, Mass. to the Year 1850* (1911); Fiske Kimball, *Domestic Architecture of the American Colonies and of the Early Republic* (1922); C. A. Place, *Charles Bulfinch, Architect and Citizen* (1925); *Commonwealth* (Boston), June 19, 1852.]   T. F. H.

PARRIS, SAMUEL (1653–Feb. 27, 1719/20), clergyman, prominently identified with the Salem witchcraft delusion, was born in London, the son of a merchant, Thomas Parris, but probably lived for a time in Barbados, where his father and his uncle owned extensive plantations. Although it has been asserted that he attended Harvard College, he was certainly not a graduate. As early as 1674 he was engaged in mercantile business in Boston. In April 1686 he attended a council of Boston clergymen (*Collections of the Massachusetts Historical Society*, 5 ser. VI, 1879, p. 21*) and in November 1688 a committee from Salem Village (now Danvers) interviewed him "about taking ministerial office" with them. Since 1672, when after nearly a decade of wrangling, Salem Village had been separated from Salem, three ministers had left because of parish dissensions. Consequently, Parris insisted on an unusually explicit contract before accepting. On Nov. 19, 1689, he took charge, and trouble soon arose over the execution of the contract.

Less than three years later further trouble came to him. In February 1692 his daughter and his niece became subject to curious attacks which physicians and ministers both attributed to "an evil hand." Parris believed that Satan was attacking his flock and that as a faithful pastor he must fight back. Like Cotton Mather [*q.v.*], he was convinced that his best weapons were fasting and prayer (Hale, *post*, p. 23), but the situation got out of his hands when Mary Sibley, a member of his church, gave his West Indian slaves instructions as to how to discover the "witches" and soon the jails were filled with the accused. In the witch trials Parris, like Judge William Stoughton [*q.v.*], accepted "spectral evidence" contrary to the advice of the Boston ministers (cf. Mather, *post*, I, 211). He often acted as court clerk and sometimes as a witness. His testimony against several condemned members of his parish caused disaffection among their relatives, who refused to attend church and drew up a list of grievances against the minister. Parris replied to the charges in his "Meditations for Peace," read to the congregation in November 1694, in which he acknowledged his error in countenancing "spectral evidence" and begged forgiveness. A church council presided over by Increase Mather [*q.v.*] vindicated him, but advised him to leave the village—advice which he did not follow.

In the meantime, another dispute had arisen. The village had set aside some parsonage land in 1691 which Parris soon claimed as his own in lieu of salary arrears. The resulting dispute was taken to the Ipswich court. Parris found his position unbearable and resigned, June 30, 1696, but held the land until the court effected a settlement, September 1697, requiring him to relinquish it and ordering the parish to pay all arrears in salary. His tactless handling of the chaotic affairs of Salem Village had made him odious to many persons, but the Mathers, Judge Sewall, and others did not renounce his friendship when he left the village. Evidently he returned to business in Boston in 1697 (*Suffolk Deeds*, XIV, 1906, p. 423). He was in Concord in 1704/05, in Dunstable in 1711, and spent his last years in Sudbury, where he died. Twice married, he survived both his wives; the first, Elizabeth, died in 1696 at Danvers; the second, Dorothy, in 1719 at Sudbury. They bore him five children.

[*Essex Inst. Hist. Colls.*, vol. XLIX (1913); H. F. Waters, *Geneal. Gleanings in England* (1901), I, 143–44; J. W. Hanson, *Hist. of the Town of Danvers* (1848); C. W. Upham, *Salem Witchcraft* (2 vols., 1867); *Mass. Hist. Soc. Colls.*, 3 ser. III (1833); *Pubs. Col. Soc. of Mass.*, XXIV (1923), 168; John Hale, *A Modest Enquiry into the Nature of Witchcraft* (1702); Cotton Mather, *Magnalia Christi Americana* (1702; ed. of 1853); Robert Calef, *More Wonders of the Invisible World* (1700; repr. 1823); *Proc. Essex Inst.*, vol. II (1862); *A Report of the Record Commissioners of Boston, Mass.*, IX (1883), 155, 158; *Vital Records of Sudbury, Mass.* (1903).]   R. P. S.

PARRISH, ANNE (Oct. 17, 1760–Dec. 26, 1800), philanthropist, was the eldest of eleven children of Isaac and Sarah (Mitchell) Parrish, of Philadelphia, Pa. As early as 1637 the Parrish name is on record in Maryland, Capt. Edward Parrish of Yorkshire having emigrated to Anne Arundel County. A branch of the family moved to Philadelphia, for John Parrish (1702–1745), grandfather of Anne, married Elizabeth Roberts of that city and is recorded a citizen. The community into which Anne was born was a Quaker group, known for its good works and for a faith which, while lacking the force of the earlier Society of Friends, was steeped in religious and charitable interests. Anne's youngest brother, Joseph Parrish [*q.v.*], became one of Philadelphia's leaders in medical and philanthropic circles, and Anne is remembered chiefly as a pioneer in two important charities.

On an occasion when her parents were ill with yellow fever, she vowed that if they should recover she would devote the remainder of her life to benevolence and charity. Accordingly she founded in 1796 a school for girls in necessitous circumstances (later called the Aimwell School) and held the first sessions at a private house at the corner of Second Street and Pewter Platter Alley (now 17 North Second Street). The numbers grew, and in the first year of the school the founder associated with herself as "teaching trustees" Catharine W. Morris and Mary Wheeler. By 1799 there was a board of eighteen and a school of fifty. The course offered at the school included domestic science in various branches as well as the conventional studies. A sewing teacher was engaged, and by 1808, with sixty pupils, the trustees turned the school over to professional teachers and were compelled to borrow a room in the Corporation School House on Fourth Street. After several other moves, Aimwell was finally established at 869 North Randolph Street and continued in operation as a school until 1923. It is a tribute to the thoroughness and foresight of the founder that the school went on with keener annual impetus, though she herself died after its fourth year of existence.

The second institution founded by Anne Parrish was the House of Industry, for the employment of poor women in Philadelphia. This was established in 1795, incorporated in 1815, carried on for a number of years in Ranstead Court, and is still (1934) in active operation. It was the first charitable organization for women in America. Anne Parrish died in 1800 at the age of forty. The only likeness of her is a family silhouette.

[Susanna P. Wharton, ed., *The Parrish Family* (1925); reports of the Corporation of Aimwell School, Philadelphia, 1874, 1902, 1916; original minutes of the Board; Thomas Woody, *A Hist. of Women's Educ. in the U. S.* (1929); *Report of the Female Soc. of Phila.* (1871); Louise G. Walsh and Matthew J. Walsh, *Hist. and Organization of Educ. in Pa.* (1930); J. T. Scharf and Thompson Westcott, *Hist. of Phila.* (1884), vol. II.]   R. M. G.

PARRISH, CELESTIA SUSANNAH (Sept. 12, 1853–Sept. 7, 1918), educator, was born on her father's plantation near Swansonville, Pittsylvania County, Va., the daughter of William Perkins Parrish, a country gentleman owning a large estate in both land and slaves, and his second wife, Lucinda Jane (Walker) Parrish. She began at the age of five years to attend a private school on her father's plantation. In 1862 her father died and in 1863 her mother also. There were no schools in Pittsylvania County during the Civil War, but the aunts with whom the three children lived had a library in which Celestia read every book, and she memorized much from Byron and Shakespeare. In the autumn of 1865, when a private school was opened at Callands, she enrolled and walked every day two and a half miles back and forth over a rough mountain road. There she memorized textbooks on botany, biology, and chemistry, along with the limited curriculum of the "three r's." When in 1867 her uncle and guardian, William B. Walker, died, it was discovered that there was left only a very small legacy. Therefore, she became a teacher in a private school and later in the public school at Swansonville with a salary of $40 a month. Teaching and studying wherever the possibility opened, she not only supported herself, her brother, and her sister, but, when her half-brother died leaving five dependent children, assumed part of the expense of their maintenance.

In 1885 she entered the State Female Normal School at Farmville, Va., was graduated in 1886, and was appointed to teach mathematics. In 1891–92 she took special work in mathematics and astronomy at the University of Michigan. In the autumn of 1893 she went to the newly established Randolph-Macon Woman's College to teach mathematics, psychology, and pedagogy. There is abundant testimony to her rare gifts as a teacher and to her unusual and striking personality. She was able to obtain meager equipment for the course in psychology, to improve apparatus, devise experiments, and establish laboratory work as an essential part of the required course in psychology. During these years she attended several summer sessions, took correspondence work, and, after a few months of residence, received the Ph.B. degree from Cornell University in 1896. In January 1895 she had published in the *American Journal of Psychology* an article "The Cutaneous Estimation of Open and Filled Space," the result of some of her work in the laboratory at Cornell. A little later she studied with John Dewey at the University of Chicago. In 1902 she became professor of pedagogic psychology at the State Normal School in Athens, Ga. There she obtained, through funds furnished by George Foster Peabody, the establishment of what was probably the first practice school for normal students in the South. In 1903 she was one of the organizers and became the first president of the Southern Association of College Women. She began the agitation for a more practical expression of industrial and agricultural training in connection with the common schools. She was interested in the pre-school child long before the importance of that aspect of education was generally recognized. She touched the educational life of the state of Georgia through her teaching and lecturing, but she also touched the educational life of the entire South through her presidency of the Southern Association of College Women. The last position she held was that of supervisor of rural schools of Georgia. From county to county she went on her visits to schools, giving help and inspiration. Her greatest work in her last years was the establishing of schools for adult illiterates. When she died at Clayton, Ga., the Georgia legislature adjourned for her funeral, and on her monument at Clayton are these words: "Georgia's Greatest Woman."

[A brief autobiographical pamphlet published by J. O. Martin, Atlanta, Ga., *The Early Life Story of Miss Celeste Parrish* (1925); material from Miss Mary A. Bacon, Athens, Ga., and from Miss Gillie Larew, Randolph-Macon Woman's College, Lynchburg, Va.; *Atlanta Journal*, Sept. 9, 23, 1918; date of birth from *Who's Who in America*, 1918–19, and from records of the registrar of the University of Chicago.]

L. K. M. R.

PARRISH, CHARLES (Aug. 27, 1826–Dec. 27, 1896), coal operator, was born in Dundaff, Pa., the son of Archippus and Phebe (Miller) Parrish. Shortly after the birth of the child the family moved to Wilkes-Barre, where the father was proprietor of a hotel. Charles attended the Wilkes-Barre Academy and at fifteen became a clerk in the store of Ziba Bennett of Wilkes-Barre. At twenty-one he became a partner in the firm, but in 1856 he withdrew and began to speculate in coal lands. He founded the Kembleton Coal Company and for years originated and developed important and far-reaching business schemes in the fields of mining and transportation. He was president of the Philadelphia Coal Company, which operated the Empire mine, and was one of the organizers and for twenty years president of the Lehigh & Wilkes-Barre Coal Company. He was also one of the organizers of the Lehigh & Susquehanna Railroad; the Sunbury & Wilkes-Barre Railroad, and the Lehigh Coal and Navigation Company, of which he was a director for thirty years. He was also a director of the Jersey Central Railroad. The Sugar Notch and Pine Ridge mines in the Wyoming Valley coal region were operated by the Parrish & Annora Coal Company. For twenty years Parrish was president of the First National Bank of Wilkes-Barre. He was interested in a number of manufacturing concerns and served as president of the Hazard Manufacturing Company which made wire rope. During the early part of the Civil War he organized troops and made generous contributions of money for the prosecution of the war.

Parrish's name is closely associated with the growth of the Wyoming Valley region of Pennsylvania and with the development of its resources. He had the instinct of the speculator and made and lost large sums of money. He was friendly toward the laboring class and established a system of workingmen's insurance in all his companies. In 1885 he was elected to the Wyoming Historical and Geological Society and in 1889 he became a life member. He was married on June 21, 1864, to Mary Conyngham, the daughter of John Nesbit Conyngham. They had four children, three of whom survived him. He died suddenly at Philadelphia, Pa., although he had been in ill health for some years.

[H. E. Hayden and others, *Geneal. and Family Hist. of the Wyoming and Lackawanna Valleys, Pa.* (1906), vol. I; "Chas. Parrish," *Proc. and Colls. Wyoming Hist. and Geol. Soc.*, vol. IV (1899); *Pub. Ledger* (Phila.), Dec. 28, 1896.]   J. H. F.

PARRISH, EDWARD (May 31, 1822–Sept. 9, 1872), pharmacist, teacher, college president, was born in Philadelphia, Pa., the seventh son of Joseph [q.v.] and Susanna (Cox) Parrish. He attended the Friends' School until he was sixteen years of age, then was apprenticed to his brother

Dillwyn, who conducted a drug store on the southwest corner of Eighth and Arch streets. During the term of his apprenticeship he attended the Philadelphia College of Pharmacy and graduated from that institution in 1842. A year later he purchased a drug store at the northwest corner of Ninth and Chestnut streets adjoining the building which housed the University of Pennsylvania. This close proximity to the University brought him into intimate contact with the medical students in particular, and no doubt gave him his first desire to teach. He concluded that the medical students were not sufficiently versed in the practical work of pharmacy to enable them to practise medicine to the best advantage, especially in rural communities where there were no drug stores. To overcome this deficiency in their education and training, he decided to begin a school in the rear of his store for the teaching of practical pharmacy, and opened this school in 1849.

The following year he entered into partnership with his brother and moved to Eighth and Arch streets, where he continued to conduct his school until 1864. In the latter year, he was elected to fill the chair of materia medica in the Philadelphia College of Pharmacy, which position he gave up in 1867 to take over the professorship of theory and practice of pharmacy, the duties of which were more to his liking. This chair he held until his death. In the same year in which he entered upon his duties at the Philadelphia College of Pharmacy, he secured the passage of the act of incorporation of Swarthmore College, and the subsequent founding of this institution was largely the result of his efforts. He served as secretary of the board of managers from 1864 to 1868 and as president of the college from 1868 to the spring of 1871.

In 1848, he married Margaret Hunt of Philadelphia. Four sons and a daughter were the fruits of this union. His writings were many. In addition to a textbook, *An Introduction to Practical Pharmacy* (copyrighted 1855, revised editions 1859, 1864) and a volume entitled *Summer Medical Teaching in Philadelphia* (1857), he wrote numerous papers on subjects of pharmaceutical interest. More than fifty of these were printed in the *Proceedings* of the American Pharmaceutical Association and the *American Journal of Pharmacy*, others in the *Druggists' Circular* and elsewhere. He was elected a member of the Philadelphia College of Pharmacy in 1843, was elected to the board of trustees in 1845, and served as the secretary of the latter from 1845 to 1852, and as secretary of the College from 1854 to 1864. He became a member of the American Pharmaceutical Association at its first meeting in 1852, was elected recording secretary in 1853, first vice-president in 1866, and president in 1868. He was a delegate to the Pharmacopœal Convention in 1860. He was appointed by the mayor of Philadelphia as one of a commission of five to carry into effect the Pharmacy Act of 1872. In August of the same year, he accepted an appointment from the federal government to visit certain Indian tribes in the present Oklahoma that had been placed under the supervision of the Society of Friends, of which he was a member, and while engaged in performing this service, he contracted malarial fever and died, at Fort Sill, Indian Territory.

[*Am. Jour. Pharmacy*, Oct. 1, 1872, May 1, 1873; *The First Century of the Phila. College of Pharmacy and Science* (1922), ed. by J. W. England; S. P. Wharton, *The Parrish Family* (1925); E. H. Magill, *Sixty-five Years in the Life of a Teacher* (1907); *The Reg. of Swarthmore Coll.* (1914); *Druggists' Circular and Chem. Gazette*, Oct. 1872; *Press* (Phila.), Sept. 16, 1872.]   A. G. D—M.

PARRISH, JOSEPH (Sept. 2, 1779–Mar. 18, 1840), physician, teacher, born in Philadelphia, Pa., was the youngest child of Isaac Parrish and his wife, Sarah Mitchell, and a brother of Anne Parrish [*q.v.*]. The first American ancestor of the Parrish family, Edward, came out from England as surveyor-general of the province of Maryland under Lord Baltimore. He and his immediate descendants became the owners of large tracts of land in Maryland and were regarded as wealthy until John Parrish, Joseph's grandfather, lost practically all he owned as the result of guaranteeing a note for a friend. As a consequence Isaac Parrish, Joseph's father, was apprenticed to a hatter and remained in that business throughout his life. He acquired means and gave his eleven children excellent educations. Joseph went to the Friends' School, gained a knowledge of Latin and French, and in his later years studied Hebrew and Greek. After leaving school he served an apprenticeship with his father but in 1802 commenced studying medicine as a pupil of Caspar Wistar [*q.v.*]. He received the degree of M.D. from the University of Pennsylvania in 1805, submitting a thesis which was published under the title, *On the Influence of the Passions upon the Body in the Production and Cure of Disease* (1805). In the same year yellow fever appeared in epidemic form in Philadelphia, and Parrish was appointed resident physician to the emergency hospital which was established by the Board of Health. In 1808 he gave a course of popular lectures on chemistry. He became one of the staff of the Philadelphia Dispensary, and later served that institution as a manager. From 1807 to 1811 he was physician to the Philadelphia Almshouse; in 1811 he was transferred to the surgical staff on which he served until 1821; and from 1816 to 1829 he was a member of the staff of the Pennsylvania Hospital. He was president of the board of managers of the Wills Eye Hospital, 1833–40, and served as vice-president of the College of Physicians of Philadelphia and the Philadelphia Medical Society. When the professorship of anatomy in the University of Pennsylvania was rendered vacant by the death of John Syng Dorsey in 1818, the trustees are said to have chosen Parrish as his successor, but he declined the honor as he deemed it would interfere with his performance of his religious duties. During the cholera epidemic of 1832 he had charge of a cholera hospital, and in recognition of his services was presented by the city authorities with a suitably inscribed silver pitcher.

An interesting episode in his career was his attendance upon John Randolph of Roanoke, when the latter died in Philadelphia in 1833. Parrish was with the dying man almost continuously for four days before his death, during which time Randolph made a will in which he manumitted his slaves. In order that the will might be validated it was necessary for Parrish to make a deposition concerning his patient's mental and physical condition. Parrish was a strong advocate of abolition—served for a time as president of the Pennsylvania Abolition Society—and it is needless to say was only too glad to further Randolph's last wishes. Another object in which Parrish took a deep interest was the abolition of capital punishment. All his life he was a strictly observant member of the Society of Friends.

Parrish made a number of contributions to medical periodicals, chiefly to the *North American Medical and Surgical Journal* and the *Eclectic Repertory and Analytical Review*, of which he was for some time an editor. He edited an American edition of William Lawrence's work on hernia (*A Treatise on Ruptures*, 1811), and in 1836 published *Practical Observations on Strangulated Hernia, and Some of the Diseases of the Urinary Organs*. On Oct. 20, 1808, he married Susanna Cox, daughter of John and Ann Cox, of Burlington, N. J. They had eleven children, all of whom survived their father. Two of them, Isaac and Joseph, became physicians, while Edward [*q.v.*] was a noted teacher of pharmacy.

[S. P. Wharton and Dillwyn Parrish, *The Parrish Family* (1925); G. B. Wood, *A Memoir of the Life and Character of the Late Joseph Parrish, M.D.* (1840); *The Deposition of Dr. Joseph Parrish in John Randolph's Case* (reprinted from the court records for private circulation); H. A. Kelly and W. L. Burrage,

Am. Medic. Biogs. (1920); Henry Simpson, The Lives of Eminent Philadelphians (1859); W. C. Posey and S. H. Brown, The Wills Hospital, Phila. (copr. 1931); T. G. Morton, The Hist. of the Pa. Hospital, 1751–1895 (1895); North American and Daily Advertiser (Phila.), Mar. 19, 1840.]   F. R. P.

PARROTT, ENOCH GREENLEAFE (Nov. 27, 1815–May 10, 1879), naval officer, was born at Portsmouth, N. H., the son of Susan (Parker) and Enoch Greenleafe Parrott, a prominent merchant and naval agent. He was the cousin of Robert Parker Parrott [q.v.]. He was appointed midshipman on Dec. 10, 1831, went to sea in the Brazil Squadron, and after several years in coast survey work was made lieutenant on Sept. 8, 1841. A cruise in the Saratoga of the African Squadron, from 1841 to 1843, brought experience in punitive expeditions against coast settlements. In the Mexican War, while attached to the Congress of the Pacific Squadron, he was in the naval force accompanying Frémont's march from Monterey to Los Angeles, and he was present at the capture of Guaymas and Mazatlán on the Mexican west coast. In 1852–53 he was in the Mediterranean on the St. Louis, celebrated for her rescue in July 1853 of the Hungarian patriot, Martin Koszta, from an Austrian brig of war at Smyrna. A cruise followed in the St. Mary's of the Pacific Squadron, then duty at the naval observatory in Washington, 1857–58, and subsequent special work in Washington. He was in the expedition that evacuated the Norfolk navy yard on Apr. 20 and 21, 1861, and was promoted to commander in this month. His first wartime distinction came with his capture, while commanding the brig Perry, of the privateer schooner Savannah, on June 3, 1861, sixty miles off Charleston. The Savannah had a pivot-gun and made some slight resistance. For this first capture of a Southern privateer, Secretary Welles officially commended the ability and energy of captain, officers, and crew. Shortly afterward Parrott was transferred to the steamer Augusta, in which he took part in the attack on Port Royal on Nov. 7, 1861, and was later engaged in arduous blockade duty, much of the time as senior officer off Charleston. The Augusta went north in August 1862 but was back on the blockade in December and was one of the ships engaged with Confederate rams off Charleston on Jan. 31, 1863, when she was struck by a nine-inch shell. When Admiral Samuel Francis du Pont [q.v.] left the blockading squadron in July following, he sailed north with Parrott in the Augusta, speaking of her at the time as one of the ships that had seen longest and hardest service. Next year Parrott commanded the ironclad Canonicus in the James River, par-

ticipating in the action on June 21, 1864, with Southern gunboats and battery near Howlett's. Commanding the monitor Monadnock, he was in the two attacks on Fort Fisher in the winter of 1864–65 and in the blockade of Charleston until the surrender. Admiral David D. Porter paid high tribute to the personnel of the monitors in this service, "riding out heavy gales on an open coast," and of their commanders declared, "I hope I shall ever keep them under my command" (Official Records, post, 1 ser., XI, 259). Parrott in particular seems to have liked monitor duty, remarking of his craft that he "did not see any difference between her and anything else" (Ibid., p. 602). After the war he was made captain on July 25, 1866, commodore on Apr. 22, 1870, and rear admiral on Nov. 8, 1873. He had duty as commander of the receiving ship at Boston from 1865 to 1868, at the Portsmouth navy yard in 1869, as commandant at Mare Island yard from 1871 to 1872, and in command of the Asiatic Squadron until his retirement on Apr. 4, 1874. Being unmarried, he spent subsequent summers with relatives in Portsmouth and winters at the Fifth Avenue Hotel in New York. For some years his health and mind were affected by paralytic strokes, which finally caused his death. He was buried in the graveyard of Saint John's Episcopal Church at Portsmouth.

[Spelling of middle name and names of parents from records of Saint John's Episcopal Church, Portsmouth, N. H.; L. R. Hamersly, The Records of Living Officers of the U. S. Navy (3rd ed., 1878); War of the Rebellion: Official Records (Navy), 1 ser., I, II, V, X–XIII; Army and Navy Journal, May 17, 1879; N. Y. Herald, May 11, 1879.]   A. W.

PARROTT, ROBERT PARKER (Oct. 5, 1804–Dec. 24, 1877), ordnance inventor, manufacturer, was born in Lee, N. H. He was of English descent and was the eldest son of a prominent ship-owner of Portsmouth, N. H., who served one term as United States senator, John Fabyan Parrott. His mother, Hannah Skilling (Parker) Parrott, was the daughter of Robert Parker of Kittery, Me., a ship-builder and commander of privateers during the Revolution. Parrott attended the Daniel Austin school in Portsmouth and on July 1, 1820, entered the United States Military Academy at West Point, from which he graduated in 1824, third in a class of thirty-one. He was appointed second lieutenant and assigned to the 3rd Artillery. Ordered immediately to duty at the Military Academy, he served there for five years as assistant professor of natural philosophy. Following two years of garrison duty at Fort Constitution, near Portsmouth, N. H., he was promoted to first lieutenant and transferred to Fort Independence, Boston Harbor, Mass., remaining on duty there until 1834, when he was assigned to ordnance duty. After a short staff service in military operations in the Creek Nation, he was promoted to captain of ordnance Jan. 13, 1836, and ordered to Washington as assistant to the chief of the bureau of ordnance. Not long after beginning the duties of this assignment he was detailed as inspector of ordnance in construction at the West Point Foundry, Cold Spring, N. Y. His ability and expert knowledge attracted the attention of Gouverneur Kemble [q.v.], president of the West Point Foundry Association, who induced Parrott to resign from the army and become superintendent of the foundry. His resignation went into effect Oct. 31, 1836. Three years later he succeeded Kemble as lessee of the foundry. In order to supply it with charcoal pig-iron, he purchased a tract of 7,000 acres in Orange County, N. Y., and the Greenwood iron furnace, which he operated in partnership with his brother Peter. For almost forty years thereafter Parrott directed these enterprises and at the same time continued his studies of ordnance. He kept himself well informed on the world's activities in this field and, in addition, prosecuted a course of research and experiment of his own. This work covered a rather wide range at first, but upon learning of the secret production in 1849 of a serviceable rifled cannon by Krupp in Germany, he concentrated his attention on rifled ordnance. For upwards of ten years he continued his experiments, his aim being to produce an efficient rifled cannon, simple in construction and cheap. Eventually he patented, Oct. 1, 1861, a design for strengthening a cast-iron cannon with a wrought-iron hoop shrunken on the breech. The unique feature of the invention was the hoop, which was formed of a wrought-iron bar of rectangular section coiled into a spiral and welded into a solid ring. He also devised and patented, Aug. 20, 1861, an improved expanding projectile for rifled ordnance. The expanding device was a brass ring cast upon and secured to the projectile but susceptible of being expanded into the cannon grooves by the action of the explosive gases. These inventions Parrott offered to the government at cost price, and with the beginning of the Civil War he received large orders for both guns and projectiles. "Parrott guns" were present in the field at the first battle of Bull Run and thereafter in every important engagement both on land and sea. They were made by the thousands and in many calibers, and threw "Parrott projectiles" of from 10 to 300 pounds. It is recorded that "the 200 and 300 pounder Parrott guns were the

most formidable service guns extant in their time" (Paulding, post). Furthermore, their endurance was far in excess of that required of the contemporary rifled cannon of Europe.

With the termination of hostilities, Parrott ceased gun manufacture at the West Point Foundry and in 1867 withdrew from active connection with it. He and his brother continued, however, the operation of the Greenwood furnaces and property until 1877, when Parrott sold his share to his brother and retired. During this latter period he continued his experimental work and invented several improvements in projectiles and fuses. He and his brother also began in 1875, the first commercial production of slag wool in the United States. Parrott held one public office, that of first judge of the court of common pleas for Putnam County, N. Y. (1844–47), an appointment made, no doubt, because of his widely recognized uprightness and sagacity. In 1839 he married Mary Kemble, sister of Gouverneur Kemble and sister-in-law of James K. Paulding [q.v.]. At the time of his death, in Cold Spring, he was survived by his widow and an adopted son.

[G. W. Cullum, *Biog. Reg. Officers and Grads. U. S. Mil. Acad.* (3rd ed., 1891) ; *Ninth Ann. Reunion Asso. Grads., U. S. Mil. Acad.* (1878) ; J. N. Paulding, *The Cannon and Projectiles Invented by Robert Parker Parrott* (1879) ; E. C. Kreutzberg, "Orange County Iron Making," *Iron Trade Rev.*, July 17, 31, 1924; Frederic De Peyster, *Memoir of Robert Parker Parrott* (1878) ; *N. Y. Times*, Dec. 25, 1877 ; data from family; patent office records.]   C. W. M—n.

PARRY, CHARLES CHRISTOPHER (Aug. 28, 1823–Feb. 20, 1890), botanist, born in Admington, Gloucestershire, the son of Joseph and Eliza (Elliott) Parry, came of a line of clergymen of the Established Church. His family moved from England when he was nine years of age to a farm in Washington County, N. Y. The lad showed promise in the schools and an eager interest in the native plants. He attended Union College (A.B. 1842) and then went as a graduate student to Columbia College, where he came under the influence of the botanist, John Torrey [q.v.], and took the degree of M.D. in 1846. In the same year he settled at Davenport, Iowa, and began practice, but the unspoiled flowering prairies led him year by year further and further from what he considered the vexations of a physician's life to an ever-increasing absorption in botanical work. In 1848 he served under David Dale Owen [q.v.] in the geological survey of Wisconsin, Iowa, and Minnesota, and in the next year was appointed botanist to the United States and Mexican boundary survey. In this connection he gave the greater part of the next three years to geological and botanical field work along the boundary from Texas to San Diego, and consequently was well fitted to furnish the introduction, "Botany of the Boundary," to the Survey's report on botany written by John Torrey (*Report on the United States and Mexican Boundary Survey*, 2 vols. in 3, 1857–59). This first-hand experience with the remarkable vegetation of the southwestern deserts, still largely unknown to botanists, confirmed his natural bent. After 1849, for nearly forty years, he devoted his summers chiefly to botanical exploration of the little-known western states and territories, either on his own initiative or as botanist to some surveying expedition or special mission. He was the first to hold the post of botanist in the United States Department of Agriculture and spent three years (1869–71) in Washington at the Smithsonian Institution, organizing the plant collections brought back by government scientific or surveying expeditions.

The alpine flora of the Rocky Mountains in Colorado attracted him, and in his explorations he discovered the species of spruce which he called *Picea Engelmannii* and named Gray's Peak and Torrey's Peak for Asa Gray and John Torrey who visited him in his cabin. In 1874, he took up the old trail of John C. Frémont [*q.v.*] in southern Utah, making discoveries that brought his name to the notice of plant geographers. As the years passed he visited California more and more frequently in connection with his studies of the chaparral. Thorough, cautious, and conscientious, he journeyed in the winter of 1884–85 to the Royal Botanic Gardens at Kew, England, in order to compare his California specimens with types there before publishing his revisions of California manzanitas (*Bulletin of the California Academy of Sciences*, vol. II, 1887) and the species of Ceanothus (*Proceedings of the Davenport Academy of Natural Sciences*, vol. V, 1893). This region was so new to collectors that he turned up many new species, but, what is more important, he was the first investigator of these groups to study living plants in the field in connection with specimens in the herbarium. His many botanical papers were rather brief and mainly of a special character, but his numerous contributions to the newspaper press of Chicago, St. Louis, Davenport, and San Francisco, continued for many years, covered a wider field, dealing with the natural resources of the new West and the general features of the native vegetation of mountains and valleys.

Genial and unaffected in manner and affectionate in disposition, Parry had a capacity for cultivating warm and enduring friendships that stood the tests of camping trips and hundred- or thousand-mile botanical journeys. In the Rocky Mountains of Colorado he had the company of Edward Lee Greene [*q.v.*], and on a wide circuit through the forests of the Pacific Coast that of George Engelmann [*q.v.*]. John Gill Lemmon [*q.v.*] was his companion in a survey of the untouched San Bernardino Mountains, the western Mohave Desert, and the broad plain of the San Joaquin in California, while for two trips into Lower California he chose as a helper Charles Russell Orcutt, whom he brought up to be a notable collector. The wide and easy range of his personal relations furthered his botanical activities in numberless ways. Through J. D. B. Stillman, "forty-niner" and Leland Stanford's personal physician, who had been a fellow student at the medical school, Parry obtained a railway pass on all the Stanford lines, a favor which greatly facilitated his field work. A zest for scraping acquaintance made the little man with the short quick step and delightful ways a welcome figure along routes of travel. Though generally tolerant, Parry could speak boldly at need, as when he printed a sharp denunciation of Katharine Curran, a botanical free lance possessed of talents for personal abuse. The beautiful *Lilium Parryi* of the Southern California mountains, the Lote Bush (*Zizyphus Parryi*) of the Colorado Desert, the Ensenada Buckeye (*Aesculus Parryi*) are but a few of the hundreds of new plant forms—trees, shrubs, and flowers —discovered by Parry in western America. He did his work chiefly at a time when danger of the Indian was largely past, and before herds, the plow, and industrialism had changed or obliterated the native plant societies. His happy personality is, therefore, associated with the most romantic and fruitful period of botanical exploration in the Far West.

In 1853 he married Sarah M. Dalzell, who died in 1858. In 1859 he married a widow, Emily R. Preston, who survived him. During his frequent and prolonged journeys through four decades, the home at Davenport had been steadily maintained and here he died early in 1890.

[Sources include sketch by C. H. Preston, with portrait and bibliography of Parry's writings comp. by his widow, in *Proc. Davenport Acad. Nat. Sci.*, vol. VI (1897); autobiographical letter on early expeditions, *Ibid.*, vol. II, pt. 2 (1880); *The U. S. Biog. Dict. . . . Iowa Vol.* (1878); *Bull. Phil. Soc. of Wash.*, vol. XII (1895); *Botanical Gazette*, Mar. 1890; *Iowa State Register* (Des Moines), Feb. 21, 1890; W. L. Jepson, "Old-time Western Letters" (MS.). Many of Parry's letters are preserved in the herbaria at St. Louis, Ames, and Notre Dame; his large herbarium belongs to the Iowa State College.]   W.L.J.

PARRY, CHARLES THOMAS (Sept. 15, 1821–July 18, 1887), locomotive builder, **was**

born in Philadelphia, the son of Samuel and Mary (Hoffline) Parry. At the age of fifteen he was employed as an apprentice in the pattern shop of the Baldwin Locomotive Works, and after completing his apprenticeship spent several years in the drawing room. He was then advanced through every grade of mechanical labor until 1855, when he was appointed the company's general superintendent in charge of locomotive construction. In 1867 he became a member of M. Baird & Company, the firm that succeeded Matthias W. Baldwin [*q.v.*] in the ownership of the locomotive works. Upon the retirement of Matthew Baird [*q.v.*] in 1873, the firm became known as Burnham, Parry, Williams & Company, which remained its title until after Parry's death.

Parry grew up with the locomotive industry, for the Baldwin Locomotive Works had scarcely produced fifty locomotives when he commenced his apprenticeship. His abilities attracted the attention of his superior officers and his promotion was rapid. Nineteen years after entering upon his apprenticeship, he had become the plant's chief executive in charge of locomotive construction. His first major problem in this position involved the installation of a system of scientific management to replace the rule-of-thumb production methods that prevailed throughout industry in that period. He installed labor-saving devices, commenced having complete drawings of locomotives prepared in advance of their construction, and in general brought the shop methods under which locomotive production was conducted to a much higher level of efficiency. One of his partners attributed "a good deal of the prosperity of the works" to Parry's individual efforts. He was very successful in adjusting his employees' grievances and always endeavored to better their working conditions. He was primarily responsible for the introduction of the piece-work system which was well established prior to his death and more than fifty years later was still in operation in its original form. This wage-payment method, in the opinion of an official of the company, "has been mainly responsible through all these years for the lack of labor troubles for which The Baldwin Locomotive Works has been noted" (Church, *post*). Parry's labor policies were appreciated by the employees, who joined heartily in celebrating the semi-centennial of his connection with the concern.

Parry had few outside interests. He was one of the original founders of Beach Haven, N. J., and paid certain of the village development costs, such as the construction of the Protestant Epis-

copal Church. He traveled in Europe extensively and about ten years prior to his death was engaged by the Russian government to supervise its locomotive construction program; forty locomotives for Russia were built at the Baldwin Works. Parry was a member of the Franklin Institute and for one year a member of the board of managers, a director of the National Bank of the Republic, and a life subscriber to the publication fund of the Pennsylvania Historical Society. He died at Beach Haven in his sixty-sixth year, survived by his widow, a son, and two daughters.

[*Baldwin Locomotive Works, Illustrated Catalogue* (n.d., 1871?); *Hist. of the Baldwin Locomotive Works, 1831–1923* (n.d.); *Railway Age*, May 16, 1931; *Press* (Phila.), July 19, 1887; *Public Ledger* (Phila.), July 19, 22, 1887; Phila. Register of Wills and Phila. Register of Deaths (MSS.), in Phila. City Hall; correspondence with Arthur L. Church of the Baldwin Locomotive Works and with Mrs. Romer Lee, Parry's granddaughter.]   H. S. P.

PARRY, JOHN STUBBS (Jan. 4, 1843–Mar. 11, 1876), obstetrician and gynecologist, was born on a farm in Drumore Township, Lancaster County, Pa. His parents belonged to the Society of Friends. His father, Seneca Parry, died when John was only six years old, but his mother, Priscilla S., continued successfully the management of the farm and the boy received his primary education in the country schools, then spent a few months at the Gwynedd Boarding School. At seventeen, he commenced the study of medicine in the office of the family doctor, J. M. Deaver, with whom he worked for three years. In 1863, he entered the medical department of the University of Pennsylvania and received his doctorate in medicine two years later. During the next year he held the post of resident physician to the Philadelphia General Hospital. At the completion of this practical internate, he married, Apr. 5, 1866, Rachel P. Sharpless of Philadelphia, and commenced his independent practice. His appointment as district physician to the Philadelphia Dispensary enabled him to make a further study of hospital cases; his first paper, "Vesico-abdominal Fistula," appeared in the *Medical and Surgical Reporter*, Sept. 30, 1865.

In 1867 he became visiting obstetrician to the Philadelphia Hospital, where he reorganized the obstetrical and gynecological departments, presented a wealth of material in this field at Blockley before medical students, and soon earned a considerable reputation as a clinical lecturer. His second paper, "Observations on Relapsing Fever as it Occurred in Philadelphia in the Winter of 1869 and 1870," appeared in the *American Journal of the Medical Sciences*, October 1870.

During the next five years he published twenty-eight papers in various medical journals; these were mainly on obstetrics and children's diseases. His contributions on rachitis (*e.g.*, those in *Proceedings of the Pathological Society of Philadelphia*, 1870, and *American Journal of the Medical Sciences*, January 1872) were especially important and proved the prevalence of this "disease" in Philadelphia, although it had previously been considered rare in the New World. In 1872 he was chosen one of the physicians for diseases peculiar to women at the new Presbyterian Hospital and in the same year assisted in founding the State Hospital for Women and Infants. In the spring of 1873, he suffered a pulmonary hemorrhage and was compelled to spend the subsequent winters in Florida. Always mentally active, he there became interested in conchology and botany and also collected data on the possibilities of a subtropical health-resort. He returned to his work in Philadelphia in the spring of 1874, and once more in 1875, but broke down again each time. Despite his failing health, he finished his additions to the second American edition (1875) of William Leishman's *System of Midwifery*, and his own pioneer work, *Extra-Uterine Pregnancy* (copyrighted 1875; published 1876). He died, when only thirty-three years old, at Jacksonville, Fla. At the time, he was one of the council of the College of Physicians, the president of the Obstetrical Society, and vice-president of the Pathological Society of Philadelphia.

[J. V. Ingham, memoir in *Trans. Coll. of Physicians of Phila.*, 3 ser. II (1876); H. A. Kelly and W. L. Burrage, *Am. Medic. Biogs.* (1920); *Medic. News and Library*, Apr. 1876; *Medic. and Surgic. Reporter*, Apr. 1, 1876; *Phila. Inquirer*, Mar. 16, 1876.]   H. B. B.

PARSONS, ALBERT RICHARD (June 24, 1848–Nov. 11, 1887), anarchist, one of the ten children of Samuel and Elizabeth (Tompkins) Parsons, was born in Montgomery, Ala. His parents, both of whom were born and reared in the North, were of colonial ancestry. The mother died when the boy was two years old, and three years later the father. An elder brother, William Henry Parsons, took Albert to his home in Tyler, Tex. After some schooling, the boy became a "printer's devil" in the composing room of the *Galveston Daily News*. At the outbreak of the Civil War, though small of size and but thirteen years old, he joined a local military company, later serving in the cavalry brigade commanded by his brother. After the war, he studied for six months at Waco (now Baylor) University, and then returned to the printing trade. In 1868 he started a weekly newspaper, the Waco *Spectator*,

which soon expired, and in the following year he became a traveling correspondent for the Houston *Daily Telegraph*. He was for several years in the service of the internal revenue bureau and at one time was the reading secretary of the state Senate. On June 10, 1871, at Austin, he married Lucy Eldine Gonzalez, and in the fall of 1873 he settled in Chicago.

Here he joined the Typographical Union and was soon active in labor and radical circles. He became a Socialist, and in the spring of 1881 was the candidate of a Socialist faction for mayor. Already, however, he had come to reject political action, and by 1883 he considered himself an anarchist. On Oct. 1, 1884, the International Working People's Association founded, in Chicago, a weekly newspaper, *The Alarm*, and Parsons was chosen as editor. While occupying this post he made many speaking tours and became widely known as an exponent of extreme radicalism. The movement for the eight-hour day, in which he took a leading part, came to a dramatic climax in front of the McCormick harvester works on May 3, 1886, when police fired into a crowd of strikers. Parsons, who was absent from the city, returned in time to speak at a protest meeting in front of the Haymarket on the following evening. It was a peaceable gathering; the tone of the speakers, according to Mayor Carter Henry Harrison [*q.v.*], who was present, was temperate; and Parsons, with hundreds of others, had left the place when a force of 200 policemen appeared and ordered the remainder of the crowd to disperse. Some one threw a bomb, which exploded, killing or mortally wounding seven of the police and injuring about fifty others. A round-up of radical agitators followed. Though the thrower of the bomb was never identified, eight persons were brought to trial (June 15), charged with being accessories to the murder of one of the policemen. Parsons, who had been indicted but not apprehended, voluntarily joined his seven comrades as the case was called. On Aug. 20, a verdict of guilty was rendered, and Parsons, with six others, was sentenced to death. On Sept. 14, 1887, the state supreme court affirmed the verdict, and on Nov. 2, the federal Supreme Court denied an application for a writ of error.

From the beginning the case had aroused an excited interest throughout the country. The complicity of the defendants in the bomb-throwing was denied, the methods employed in the trial were hotly denounced, and efforts were made by citizens in all walks of life to save the prisoners from death. Parsons, by reason of his general reputation, his voluntary surrender, his eloquent defense at the trial, and the fact that he was the only native American in the group, won an especial degree of sympathy. Appeals were made to Gov. Richard J. Oglesby to commute the sentences, and it is certain that had Parsons consented to apply for clemency, it would have been granted. On the ground, however, that the act would imperil the lives of his comrades he refused. The Governor finally commuted to life imprisonment the sentences of Samuel Fielden and Michael Schwab; Louis Lingg committed suicide in his cell, and Parsons, August Spies, Adolph Fischer and George Engel were hanged. On June 26, 1893, Gov. John P. Altgeld [q.v.] made public a severely condemnatory review of the trial and at the same time pardoned the three surviving prisoners.

Parsons' social philosophy was unformulated; usually he employed the terms socialism and anarchism interchangeably; his expressed views on the use of violence were contradictory, and he nursed the fantastic notion that the invention of dynamite had rendered armies and police bodies powerless. He is remembered rather for his part as the central figure in a great social tragedy than for the validity of his doctrines. He was brave, upright, truthful, and passionately devoted to the cause of freedom and justice. He was, moreover, a friendly man, greatly beloved by his intimates. He left a wife and two children.

[Names of mother and wife and date of marriage have been supplied by Mrs. Parsons. Criticisms of the trial from the legal standpoint are given in M. M. Trumbull, *The Trial of the Judgment* (1888) and in J. P. Altgeld, *Live Questions* (ed. of 1899); the police view is given in M. J. Schaack, *Anarchy and Anarchists* (1889); see also L. E. Parsons, *Life of Albert R. Parsons* (1889); *Chicago Tribune,* Nov. 11, 12, 1887.]

W. J. G.

PARSONS, ALBERT ROSS (Sept. 16, 1847–June 14, 1933), musician, teacher, was born in Sandusky, Ohio, the son of John Jehiel and Sarah (Averill) Parsons. He was descended from Joseph Parsons who was in Springfield, Mass., in 1636. The boy was unusually musical and in 1860 he was regularly engaged as organist of a church in Indianapolis. His first instruction in piano was received from teachers in Buffalo. In 1863 he went to New York, where he studied with Frédéric Louis Ritter. In 1867 he went abroad and for two years studied in Leipzig with Moscheles, Wenzel, Reinecke, Papperitz, and Richter. From 1870 to 1872 he was in Berlin, acting as secretary to the American minister, George Bancroft, and studying with Tausig, Kullak, and Weitzmann. During his years in Germany he became acquainted with Richard Wagner and as a result of this association

prepared an English translation of Wagner's *Beethoven* which he published in 1872. He later became an ardent advocate of Wagner's music and philosophy in the United States.

In 1872 Parsons returned to the United States, and for the rest of his long life made his home in the environs of New York. He established himself as a piano teacher in Steinway Hall on Fourteenth Street, New York, where he remained until the building was torn down in 1926. Then he moved to the new Steinway Hall on Fifty-seventh Street, where he had a studio until the time of his death. He lived to become the dean of New York piano teachers. From 1885 he was head of the piano department of the Metropolitan Conservatory of Music (from 1891 to 1900 the Metropolitan College of Music), New York, and continued in this capacity when the institution became the American Institute of Applied Music in 1900. During his early years in New York he was also active as an organist— for four years at Holy Trinity and for nine years at the Fifth Avenue Presbyterian Church. In 1890 he was president of the Music Teachers' National Association, and from 1893 to 1914 president of the American College of Musicians of the State of New York.

Parsons' writings touched various subjects. His most important work on music was *The Science of Pianoforte Practice* (1886). He wrote a number of songs and piano compositions and in 1917 published *The Virtuoso Handling of the Pianoforte . . . Exercises in Advanced Technic.* As a student of philosophy he sought to examine the spiritual significance of Wagner's work in *Parsifal; the Finding of Christ through Art* (1890). He added a supplementary genealogy to H. M. Burt's *Cornet Joseph Parsons, A. D. 1636–1655* (1901) and published *The Garrard-Spencers of London, England, and Cambridge, Mass.* (1897). Others of his works included *The Road Map of the Stars* (1911), *Surf Lines* (1912), a volume of verse, and *An Evening Prayer* (1917), a poem. He often lectured on Dante and gave readings of the Italian poet's writings, and also lectured on the Shakespeare-Bacon controversy. He designed the symbolic pyramid mausoleum in Greenwood Cemetery, Brooklyn. His wife was Alice Eva Van Ness of New York, whom he married Apr. 23, 1874. They had five children. His death occurred at Mount Kisco, N. Y.

[Articles on Parsons may be found in *Who's Who in America*, 1928–29, and in the American Supplement to *Grove's Dict. of Music and Musicians* (1930). See also Henry Parsons, *Parsons Family* (1912), vol. I; the *N. Y. Herald Tribune* and *N. Y. Times,* June 15, 1933.]

J. T. H.

PARSONS, FRANK (Nov. 14, 1854–Sept. 26, 1908), political scientist, was born at Mount Holly, N. J., the son of Edward and Alice (Rhees) Parsons. His ancestry on his father's side was English and on his mother's, Scotch and Welsh. After graduating with the degree of B.C.E. from Cornell University in 1873, he went to work on a railroad. From 1874 to 1881 he lived in Southbridge, Mass., where, after the railroad became bankrupt, he taught a variety of subjects in the district schools and in the high school. Meanwhile he studied law and in 1881 was admitted to the Massachusetts bar. In 1885 he became chief clerk in a Boston law firm. These were critical years in his career. He discovered a talent for writing that was not satisfied with the humdrum task of editing legal textbooks and a talent for public speaking that needed a larger audience than the classes he taught in the law school of Boston University. The social and economic unrest then agitating the whole country stirred him profoundly. In 1895 he was nominated for mayor of Boston on a platform of municipal reform by the Prohibition, Populist, and Socialist parties. Two years later he resigned his position in the law firm and took leave of absence from Boston University to accept the professorship of history and political science at the State College of Agriculture and Applied Science at Manhattan, Kan. While in Kansas he formulated a plan for a college to be devoted entirely to economic and social studies. At a convention in Buffalo in June 1899 the plan was launched and funds were obtained to found the Ruskin College of Social Science at Trenton, Mo. He was made dean of the lecture extension department and professor of history and economics. The venture seems not to have been successful, for shortly afterward he returned east and resumed his teaching at Boston University.

His western experience focused his attention on two problems, currency and the railroads. In October and November 1896 he published articles on currency in the *Arena*. These were followed in 1898 by a book, *Rational Money*, in which he advocated abandoning both gold and silver as standard money and establishing a managed currency with a commodity dollar of constant purchasing power. The arguments were set forth with remarkable clearness and thorough acquaintance with the scientific literature of the subject. The publisher was Charles Fremont Taylor, a Philadelphia physician and editor of *The Medical World* who had become deeply interested in economic and social reform. With Taylor's backing, Parsons now plunged into study of municipal ownership of public utilities, both in the United States and abroad, and published the results in a substantial volume, *The City for the People* (1900). A part of the book was devoted to the advocacy of direct legislation, since it was his theory that municipal ownership must be accompanied by reform in city government. *The Story of New Zealand* (1904) treated comprehensively the history and economic origins of the country as a background for the description of its experiments in state socialism. In 1901 he was sent by the National Civic Federation to England as a member of a commission to study municipal trading. His observations are recorded in part in his chapter, "British Tramway History," in *Municipal and Private Operation of Public Utilities: Report of the National Civic Federation Commission on Public Ownership and Operation* (1907, vol. II). In 1905 he resigned his position at Boston University to devote himself entirely to the study of American railroads. After much traveling and interviewing of railway officials and other interested persons, he published *The Heart of the Railroad Problem* (1906), which was criticized as lacking discrimination and constructive suggestions.

He was now suffering from Bright's disease and, although he had undergone a serious operation, refused to modify his habits of strenuous work. He became associated with Meyer Bloomfield in settlement work in Boston, and with his intimate friend, Ralph Albertson, he founded the Bread-winners' College. With the financial aid of Mrs. Quincy A. Shaw, he established the Vocation Bureau, and as its director he did valuable pioneer work in the field of vocational guidance. His posthumous book, *Choosing a Vocation* (1909), summarizes his methods. Another posthumous publication was *Legal Doctrine and Social Progress* (1911). He died in the solitary bachelor quarters in Saint James Street, where most of his work had been done. A friend, Edwin D. Mead, described his career as an "attempt to make the world over . . . into some sort of reflection . . . of the Kingdom of God" (Letter to the *Public*, Oct. 16, 1908, p. 683). He brought to bear on certain political and social problems to which most of his countrymen were indifferent a logical mind and a passion for justice, truth, and fairness. Simple and unassuming in manner he was an inspiring teacher and an effective public speaker. Although in general lacking in humor, he proved on occasion a spirited and entertaining companion. Scholars respected him, and the poor loved him.

[*Arena*, Nov. 1908; *Public* (Chicago), Oct. 2, 16, 1908; *Who's Who in America*, 1908–09; *Boston Herald*, Sept. 27, 1908.]　　　　　　　　P. W. B.

PARSONS, JOHN EDWARD (Oct. 24, 1829–Jan. 16, 1915), lawyer, was born in New York City, the son of Edward Lamb and Matilda (Clark) Parsons. His father was English; his mother a member of a prominent family of Wallingford, Conn. He received his early education at a private school at Rye, N. Y., and at the University of the City of New York (now New York University), from which he was graduated, third in his class, in 1848. His ambition on leaving college was to become a banker, but he was unable to find a suitable position. To employ his time he read law in the office of James W. Gerard and James N. Platt and fulfilled the requirements for the degree of M.A. at New York University. Shortly after reaching his majority he invested nearly all of a considerable inheritance in stock of a Nicaragua canal company, which soon afterward became worthless. Realizing that he must earn his living he obtained admission to the bar in 1852 and began to practise law. At first he intended to devote his attention to abstracting titles and other routine work, but when offered an appointment as assistant district attorney about 1854 he accepted it after some hesitation. In this position, which required that he draw all the indictments and try nearly all the cases which arose in the county, he gained experience of great value in his subsequent career. At the height of the power of the "Tweed ring" he became one of the original members of the city bar association, formed to combat corruption in the courts. He was of counsel for the association in its proceedings against Justices Barnard, Cardozo, and McCunn, and lawyer for the managers of the impeachment of Barnard. His activities in this period established him as a leading member of the New York bar.

Parsons was an ardent champion of the principle of industrial combination. In 1887 he drew up the trustee agreement which formed the Sugar Refineries Company, and after a state court decision had declared the charter of one of the participating companies forfeited, he originated the American Sugar Refining Company, in 1891, which soon controlled ninety-eight per cent. of the refining of sugar in the United States. He successfully defended the company in antitrust proceedings before the Supreme Court of the United States (*United States* vs. *E. C. Knight Company*, 156 *U. S.*, 1) which held that manufacturing is not commerce and hence not within the scope of federal powers. In 1903 the American company acquired a controlling interest in the Pennsylvania Sugar Refining Company. Since it was not dissimilar to earlier acquisitions upheld in the Knight case, successive attorneys-general took no action upon it. But in 1909, during the excitement which followed the exposure of frauds in the industry, Parsons and other directors of the company were indicted by a federal grand jury for having made the contract of 1903. After three years the case was brought to trial. It resulted in a disagreement of the jury and was not retried.

Parsons had an almost unerring memory, keen intelligence which enabled him to seize at once upon the essential facts of every case, and the ability to make almost flawlessly logical presentations of cases in the courtroom; but he was somewhat lacking in imagination. In his relations with others he was cold and formal. He was interested in many philanthropic enterprises, including hospitals, civic reform, and Bible and tract societies. In some years he is said to have given more than half his large income to charity. He was twice married: on Nov. 5, 1856, to Mary Dumesnil McIlvaine, who died in 1896, and on Mar. 12, 1901, to Florence (Field) Bishop. By his first wife he had five daughters and a son, Herbert, who became a member of Congress.

[Jos. H. Choate, *Memorial of John Edward Parsons* (pamphlet, 1916); *Gen. Alumni Cat. of N. Y. Univ., 1833–1905*, vol. I (1906); *Who's Who in America, 1914–15*; *Hearings Held before the Special Committee on the Investigation of the Am. Sugar Refining Company . . . House of Representatives* (1911), vols. II and III; *N. Y. Herald*, July 21–22, 1911; Mar. 12–31, 1912; Jan. 17, 1915; *N. Y. Times*, Jan. 17, 1915.]   E. C. S.

PARSONS, LEWIS BALDWIN (Apr. 5, 1818–Mar. 16, 1907), lawyer, railroad president, Union soldier, was descended from Joseph Parsons, an emigrant from England, who settled in Springfield, Mass., in 1636, and later moved to Northampton. Lewis was born in Perry, Genesee County, N. Y., the son of Lewis Baldwin and Lucina (Hoar) Parsons. Christened simply Lewis, he later assumed the full name of his father at the latter's request. His early boyhood was spent in Homer, N. Y. At the age of ten, he moved with his family to St. Lawrence County, N. Y. He attended local schools, at sixteen began to teach country school, and two years later entered Yale College. After his graduation in 1840, he took charge of a classical school in Noxubee County, Miss., remaining some two years, then returned to the North and began the study of law in Cambridge, Mass. Receiving the degree of LL.B. from the Harvard Law School in 1844, he went West and began to practise at Alton, Ill., first in partnership with Newton D. Strong and then with Henry W. Billings. From 1846 to 1849 he was city attorney of Alton. On Sept. 21, 1847, in St. Louis, Mo., he married Sarah Green Edwards, a niece of Ninian Edwards [*q.v.*], former governor of Illinois. She died May 28, 1850, leaving two children, both of whom died before their father. On July 5, 1852, Parsons married her younger sister, Julia Maria Edwards, who died June 9, 1857. There were two children by this marriage, both of whom survived their parents.

Moving to St. Louis in 1854, Parsons was persuaded by clients who had acquired a controlling interest in the Ohio & Mississippi Railroad to devote himself to its affairs. After a temporary sojourn in Cincinnati, first as attorney and financial agent and subsequently as treasurer, director, and president, he returned to St. Louis and in 1860 retired from active connection with the railroad. In May 1861 he served as volunteer aid to Francis Preston Blair [*q.v.*] at the capture of Camp Jackson. Recognizing the inevitability of war, he wrote to his personal friend, General McClellan, and offered his services. He went to Washington, was commissioned captain and assigned to duty in the quartermaster's department. Despite his ardent desire to join the fighting forces in the field, he was kept throughout the war in non-combatant positions in which because of his previous experience he was able to render exceptional service. He was ordered back to St. Louis and in December 1861 was given charge of all transportation by river and rail pertaining to the Department of the Mississippi, including a territory which extended from the Yellowstone to Pittsburgh and New Orleans. For the first time in history, railroad transportation was a major factor in the prosecution of a great war. Parsons brought a semblance of order out of the existing chaos, drafting a set of regulations for rail transportation that became the basis of the general rules for army transportation adopted later, then turned his attention to systematizing river transportation. Promoted colonel of volunteers in February 1862, he was assigned as aide to General Halleck in April, and continued in charge of transportation in the Department until August 1864, when he was ordered to Washington and given charge of all rail and river transportation of the armies of the United States. In 1865, he was promoted to brigadier-general. One of his most striking achievements as chief of transportation of the armies was the moving of General Schofield's army and all its equipment from Mississippi to the Potomac within a period of seventeen days.

After Lee's surrender, Parsons was retained in charge of the transportation of discharged soldiers. He was made a brevet major-general and mustered out on Apr. 30, 1866. He spent two years abroad in an effort to regain his health,

broken down by overwork, then returned to St. Louis in 1869, and on Dec. 28 of that year married Elizabeth Darrah of New York City, who died in 1887, without issue. In 1875, Parsons settled on a farm in Flora, Ill., which was his home for the rest of his life. He served as director of several railroads and other corporations and for a time was president of a St. Louis bank. In 1880 he was candidate for lieutenant-governor of Illinois on the unsuccessful Democratic ticket. He was active in the affairs of the Presbyterian Church and a trustee and patron of Parsons College, Fairfield, Iowa, the establishment of which had been made possible by a bequest of $37,000 from his father. In 1900 he published *Genealogy of the Family of Lewis B. Parsons (Second)*; *Parsons-Hoar.* He died in Flora, Ill., and was buried in Bellefontaine Cemetery, St. Louis.

[*In Memoriam General Lewis Baldwin Parsons* (privately printed, 1908) ; H. M. Burt and A. R. Parsons, *Cornet Joseph Parsons* (1901) ; Henry Parsons, *Parsons Family* (1912), vol. I ; War Dept. records ; *War of the Rebellion: Official Records (Army)* ; F. B. Heitman, *Hist. Reg. and Dict. U. S. Army* (1903), vol. I ; *Obit. Record Grads. Yale Univ.*, 1907 ; *Who's Who in America*, 1906–07 ; *St. Louis Globe-Democrat,* Mar. 17, 1907.]   R. C. C—n.

PARSONS, LEWIS ELIPHALET (Apr. 28, 1817–June 8, 1895), provisional governor of Alabama, was born at Lisle, N. Y., the eldest son of Erastus Bellamy and Jennett (Hepburn) Parsons. His father was a farmer and was associated with Gov. DeWitt Clinton in the agitation for the building of the Erie Canal. The boy was educated in the public schools of New York and read law in that state and in Pennsylvania. About 1840 he removed to Alabama and settled in Talladega, where he formed a law partnership with Alexander White. On Sept. 16, 1841, he was married to Jane Ann Boyd McCullough Chrisman, who bore him seven children. He was earnest in the practice of his profession and was a methodical, hard-working, but never a brilliant lawyer. The guiding principle of his life during the stormy decade before the Civil War was his ardent belief in the Union. He was much criticized for his political wavering through the period, but every political act seems to have been determined by his hope that some way could be found to preserve the Union. In 1856 he voted for Fillmore. In 1859 he was elected on the American ticket to represent Talladega County in the state legislature, where he attracted attention by his efforts to obtain state aid for internal improvements. In 1860 he was a delegate to the Democratic convention and supported Douglas at Baltimore because he believed that the election of Douglas was the only way to save the country.

While outwardly he submitted to the will of the majority he never gave undivided allegiance to the Confederacy. He was reputed to be the head of the Peace Society during the war, although he had two sons in the Confederate Army. In spite of his Union views he seems to have kept the respect of his neighbors and, when President Johnson appointed him provisional governor of Alabama on June 21, 1865, the appointment was generally approved in the state. He was in hearty sympathy with the president's program of conciliation and made every effort to carry it into effect. He recognized all local and judicial officials who had been in office during the Confederacy and permitted them to perform the duties of their offices if they took the oath of allegiance required by the president. He used his influence in Washington to obtain pardons for those who were exempted from the general amnesty. In spite of the interference of the Freedmen's Bureau and the army officers in the state he was able to reorganize the civil government. Under his supervision a new constitution was framed and on Dec. 20, 1865, he retired from office and handed the government over to a successor chosen by the people. He was elected to the United States Senate in 1865 without opposition but was denied his seat by the Republican majority. He supported Johnson in his fight against Congress and was a delegate to the National Union convention in Philadelphia in 1866. In his own state he was the leader of the movement that resulted in the rejection of the Fourteenth Amendment and was said to have originated "the white man's movement" against the ratification of the constitution of 1867. The constitution failed of adoption by 13,550 votes but was put into effect by an act of Congress. He adapted himself to the situation, and in the session of the Alabama legislature of 1872–73 he was the speaker of the Republican House. That act was political suicide, and he never again held office in the state. He practised his profession in Talladega until his death in 1895.

[T. M. Owen, *Hist. of Ala. and Dict. of Ala. Biog.* (1921), vol. IV; Wm. Garrett, *Reminiscences of Public Men in Ala.* (1872); Willis Brewer, *Alabama* (1872); W. L. Fleming, *Civil War and Reconstruction* (1905).]

H. F.

PARSONS, SAMUEL BOWNE (Feb. 14, 1819–Jan. 4, 1906), horticulturist, nurseryman, and landscape gardener, son of Samuel and Mary (Bowne) Parsons, was born at Flushing, Long Island, in a house which had been the home of his family for 150 years. He was educated in a private school and began his career as a clerk in New York City. In 1839 he became infected with the mulberry craze and set out 25,000 mulberry buds. That same year, in partnership with his brother Robert, he established on the ancestral farm in Flushing the nurseries of Parsons & Company. In 1840 he traveled extensively in the West Indies and in 1845 made a voyage to Europe to study the horticulture of the Old World. The following year he added to his experiences by exploring Florida, at a time when most of the state was still a wilderness. Encouraged by what he saw, he bought 160 acres of land near Palatka for $160 and began a citrus plantation and nursery. In 1859, the United States government commissioned him to investigate the horticulture and agriculture of Sicily and the Ionian Islands. The most important consequence of this trip was his importation in 1860 of ten colonies of Italian honey bees, the first to arrive safely and live throughout the winter in the United States. These were turned over to the Rev. L. L. Langstroth [*q.v.*], the noted bee authority, and to the apiary of W. W. Cary & Sons at Colerain, Mass., where the sale of Italian queens began in 1861 (*Gleanings in Bee Culture,* Jan. 15, 1907, p. 106; E. F. Phillips, *Beekeeping,* 1928, pp. 210–13). On Mar. 20, 1862, the nursery firm of Parsons & Company bought from Dr. George R. Hall of Bristol, R. I., a collection he had made representing most of the interesting trees and plants found in Japan, including the first Japanese maples ever brought into the United States. Parsons & Company announced: "A collection so rich and so varied [has] never been obtained from any country, even by the best English collectors" (*Horticulturist,* April 1862). Japanese maples remained one of the Parsons specialties, together with the Asiatic rhododendrons, which they were the first to propagate. In 1870, Samuel Parsons imported the first Valencia oranges from Thomas Rivers, an English nurseryman. These were sent to his Florida nursery, after a few years in his Flushing greenhouses, and were introduced in the early 1870's, especially by Edmund Hall Hart [*q.v.*] of Florida. In 1871, Samuel succeeded to the whole nursery business of Parsons & Company, which was continued as the Kissena Nurseries until within a short time of his death.

Not only was Parsons prominent as an horticulturist, landscape gardener, and nurseryman, but also as a participant in civic activities in Flushing. He was identified with the Flushing school system for twenty-five years and with library work. "In religion, he was a Quaker and in the troublous times previous to the Civil War, he was a staunch abolitionist and took an active part in assisting slaves to liberty" (*Na-*

tional Nurseryman, Feb. 1906, p. 49). He was a charter member of the American Pomological Society and a member of the Massachusetts Horticultural Society from 1856. He was well known as a writer of essays and as a speaker on landscape gardening and horticulture and was offered but declined the editorship of *The Horticulturist,* which had been left vacant by the death of A. J. Downing [*q.v.*] in 1852. His book, *The Rose: Its History, Poetry, Culture, and Classification* (1847 and subsequent editions), is one of the classics of horticulture. In 1869 a new abridged edition appeared, under the title of *Parsons on the Rose,* with much of the poetry and sentiment cut out at the editor's advice. A number of editions of the abridgment were issued, one appearing as late as 1912. Parsons married Susan R. Howland, Nov. 3, 1842, and four children were born to them, one of whom, Samuel B., Jr., became a well-known landscape gardener, at one time superintendent of parks in New York City. The mother died in 1855, and in 1862 Parsons married Mrs. Clara E. Weyman, by whom he had one child.

[L. H. Bailey, *Cyc. of Am. Agric.* (1909), vol. IV and *The Standard Cyc. of Horticulture* (1915), vol. III; *Portrait and Biog. Record of Queens County, N. Y.* (1896); *Gardeners' Monthly and Horticulturist,* Dec. 1887; *Gardening,* Jan. 15, 1906; *N. Y. Tribune,* Jan. 5, 1906; *Florists' Exchange,* Sept. 1, 1900, Jan. 13, 1906, Jan. 27, 1906; W. M. Emery, *The Howland Heirs* (1919); *Trans. Mass. Hort. Soc.,* 1906, pt. II (1907).]
R. H. S.

PARSONS, SAMUEL HOLDEN (May 14, 1737–Nov. 17, 1789), Revolutionary patriot and soldier, was born in Lyme, Conn. His father, Jonathan Parsons, was a strong-minded and able preacher, a follower and close friend of Whitefield. His mother, Phebe (Griswold) Parsons, was related to the influential Griswold and Wolcott families. When the theology of Whitefield proved unpopular with the Lyme congregation, the family moved in 1746 to Newburyport, Mass. Ten years later, however, Samuel, a Harvard graduate of 1756, returned to Lyme to study law under his uncle, Matthew Griswold [*q.v.*]. In 1759 he received his master's degree from Harvard, was admitted to the bar, and settled in Lyme to practise. There, in September 1761, he married Mehetable Mather. Eight children were born to them, one of whom died young.

When only twenty-five Parsons was elected to the Connecticut General Assembly, where he served until 1774. In that year he moved to New London. Through ability as well as influence he was more than once chosen for important offices and, when the Revolution impended, was active in the Connecticut Committee of Corre-

spondence. He was among the first to favor independence and one of the earliest to suggest a colonial congress (Parsons to Samuel Adams, Mar. 3, 1773, Hall, *post,* pp. 20–21). Meanwhile he had enlisted in the militia and on May 1, 1775, he became colonel of the 6th Connecticut Regiment. Before joining the troops at Boston, he shared in the taking of Fort Ticonderoga. Acting on information from Benedict Arnold, he promoted the northern expedition in Connecticut and with some friends raised funds for sending Ethan Allen and his men. After the siege of Boston he was transferred to New York and on Aug. 9, 1776, was commissioned brigadier-general in the Continental Army. At the battle of Long Island he tasted real fighting and barely escaped capture, but for the remainder of the war skirmishes and foraging expeditions were his lot. Stationed almost continuously on the Hudson River or on the Connecticut shore, with little opportunity for brilliance, he was nevertheless an intelligent and conscientious officer. Washington depended upon him for the defense of Connecticut and the arduous work of raising men, procuring supplies, and maintaining the morale of his troops. Because of his position on the Connecticut shore, he also had charge of an important part of the secret service. In December 1779, when General Putnam was incapacitated, Parsons became commander of the Connecticut division, having been the virtual head for over a year. Not until Oct. 23, 1780, however, did an "ungrateful" Congress commission him major-general, a rank suiting his command.

Parsons' chagrin over the failure of Congress to recognize his services only added to a discontent that had been growing since the early years of the Revolution. On quitting his practice to enter the army he had invested his small fortune in government securities the value of which had rapidly decreased. With protraction of the war and depreciation of the currency, he became alarmed concerning his large family and as early as December 1777 considered returning to civil life. As his fears were increased by a steady decline in his health, he frequently applied for leave to resign. He was outspoken in his discontent and did not conceal his intolerance of Congressional inefficiency. Although Parsons' feelings were no different from those entertained by practically every other Continental officer, William Heron [*q.v.*] made the most of them at British headquarters when he offered to "bring Parsons over." Heron, who found it advantageous to be "loyal" to both sides, was one of Parsons' spies, but there is no evidence to show that Parsons knew anything of his more intricate and lucrative dealings with the enemy. Moreover, despite his dissatisfaction, Parsons' zeal in serving the Revolutionary cause did not slacken, and Congress showed itself not wholly unappreciative of his services by refusing to accept his resignation until hostilities were over (July 22, 1782).

After the war Parsons settled in Middletown, whence he was sent to the legislature more than once. His later years are chiefly notable, however, for his share in the development of the Northwest Territory. He had early seen the advantage of receiving land in exchange for his government pay-certificates. With this in mind he used his influence to secure an appointment that would give him an opportunity to examine government lands to the westward, and on Sept. 22, 1785, Congress named him a commissioner to extinguish Indian claims to the territory northwest of the Ohio. When the Ohio Company was formed to secure lands for the Revolutionary soldiers in exchange for their certificates, Parsons was one of the promoters and on Mar. 8, 1787, was chosen one of three directors. In October of that year he became first judge of the Northwest Territory and the following April left for Adelphia, now Marietta, Ohio. So eager was he to provide for his children that at the age of fifty-one he began the life of a frontiersman, never expecting to return to the East and doubtful whether he would see his family again. Doubts which have been raised as to his honesty when in the Ohio Company, although not substantiated, leave a faint suspicion that he may have been too eager for profits.

Returning from a trip to Connecticut's Western Reserve where he also had an interest, Parsons was drowned when his canoe overturned in the rapids of Big Beaver River. He died too soon to realize the fortune he had anticipated from his lands and left his wife and seven children in needy circumstances.

[MSS. in Wm. L. Clements Library and Conn. State Library; C. S. Hall, *Life and Letters of Samuel Holden Parsons* (1905); G. B. Loring, *A Vindication of Gen. Samuel Holden Parsons* (1888), reprinted with revisions from *Mag. of Am. Hist.*, Oct. 1888; Jonathan Trumbull and J. G. Woodward, *Vindications of Patriots of the Am. Rev.* (1896), containing address of vindication by J. G. Woodward to Conn. Hist. Soc., May 5, 1896; S. P. Hildreth, *Biog. and Hist. Memoirs of the Early Pioneer Settlers of Ohio* (1852), containing letters and sketch by Parsons' grandson, S. H. Parsons; Justin Winsor, *The Westward Movement* (1897); *Am. Hist. Rev.*, July 1904, p. 766; Douglas Brymner, *Report on Canadian Archives, 1890* (1891), p. 100; W. P. and J. P. Cutler, *Life, Journals and Correspondence of Rev. Manasseh Cutler* (2 vols., 1888), esp. I, 196–97.]

J. C.

PARSONS, THEOPHILUS (Feb. 24, 1750–Oct. 30, 1813), jurist, was born in Byfield, Mass., the son of Moses Parsons, the parish min-

ister, and Susan (Davis) Parsons, and a descendant of Jeffrey Parsons who settled in Gloucester, Mass., in 1654. At Dummer Academy he was always playing harder or studying harder than any other boy, and at Harvard he continued an insatiable student. After graduating in 1769 he taught school at Falmouth (now Portland), Me., reading law meanwhile with Theophilus Bradbury. He began practice in July 1774, but in October 1775 the destruction of Falmouth by British warships sent him home to Byfield disheartened. What seemed a calamity proved the beginning of his professional success, for in his father's house he found Judge Edmund Trowbridge [*q.v.*], a learned lawyer who had prudently retired there from Cambridge because of his Loyalist sympathies. Trowbridge sent for his whole law library, then much the largest in New England. Thus Parsons acquired an exhaustive knowledge of important English reports and treatises which were inaccessible to most colonial lawyers. His assiduous studies brought on consumption, but he regained his health by a long horseback trip and began practice afresh in Newburyport.

While others were fighting for independence, he was considering what sort of permanent government should follow victory. At the age of twenty-seven he became the dominant member of the Essex County convention opposed to the proposed Massachusetts constitution of 1778 and wrote the convention report, called *The Essex Result*, a pamphlet which not only exposed the weakness of the executive under the abortive constitution, but also outlined the main principles for a republican government which were later adopted by the Federalists. As Parsons was influenced by the writings of John Adams, so his plan was in turn largely followed by Adams in drafting the Massachusetts constitution of 1780. At the Cambridge convention of 1779 which formulated this constitution, Parsons was equally prominent. He and his associates, called by Hancock the Essex Junto, insisted upon strong powers for the governor, a property basis for the Senate, and the virtual establishment of Congregationalism as a state religion. In 1788 Parsons was a delegate to the state convention which ratified the federal Constitution. Although a majority was at first opposed to ratification, sufficient votes were won over by a conciliatory address of the chairman, Hancock, which Parsons wrote, recommending as a condition of ratification several constitutional amendments, some of which were adopted in the federal bill of rights of 1791. Except for a brief service in the legislature (1787–91, 1805),

271

he held no further political office, published nothing on politics under his own name, and never spoke in public unless required to do so by official duties.

His law practice soon became large, extending to all the New England states and occasionally to New York and the United States Supreme Court. In 1800 he left Newburyport for Boston. In learning and intellect he easily led the bar of his time. He knew all the law and the facts about any case he undertook, particularly the technical details of any trade or business involved. And despite his scholarly attributes, he was very successful before a jury. His law office was crowded with pupils until the jealousy of other lawyers was aroused and a rule was established limiting a lawyer's pupils to three. The volume of precedents, of pleadings and other forms, afterward published by Story and other writers, were largely compiled from forms prepared or adopted by Parsons and copied by his students.

In 1806 Parsons was appointed by Governor Strong to succeed Francis Dana as chief justice of the supreme judicial court of Massachusetts. Parsons was then at the head of his profession in the opinion of all lawyers, and the existing judges wished to have a strong man to clear the dockets, then three years behind. Parsons accepted the office at great pecuniary sacrifice. He immediately insisted upon speedy trials, allowing no delays except for genuine reasons. He required lawyers to state their points before beginning and permitted no argument on points which he thought untenable or which were not based on evidence. Thus the dockets were rapidly cleared. But his most important judicial service lay in forming the law of the new Commonwealth of Massachusetts, and indirectly that of other states. In 1806 there were almost no American reports of judicial decisions, and few copies of the English reports were available to American lawyers. Parsons found the law administered by the Massachusetts courts in a chaotic condition and took the opportunity afforded by each case not only to decide that case but to establish rules of general application. These rules he drew from three sources. The first was the English law, which he had absorbed early in his career. Secondly, he combined the English doctrines with his profound knowledge of the unwritten colonial law, for he believed in establishing a system of law in Massachusetts founded upon the institutions and usages of the state. Finally, he shaped the older English and colonial law to meet the new problems presented by rapidly growing commerce. His decisions were particularly useful in the field

of shipping and insurance, where he had the good sense to follow Lord Mansfield's example in learning from merchants what were their usages and establishing the principles embodied in those usages as rules of law. Thus although his opinions lack a philosophical insight or far-reaching analysis of legal principles which would make them interesting to lawyers of a later generation, their learning and sure-footedness gave them great value for his own time. During this critical period when the hostility to British institutions might have led to a rejection of the English common law, probably no man except Story did more than Parsons to carry on the common law and restate it in intelligible form to suit American needs.

Outside working hours, Parsons put the law completely aside and turned to other activities. From boyhood he dipped into mathematics and astronomy. The only composition he ever published under his own name was an "Astronomical Problem" (*Memoirs of the American Academy of Arts and Sciences*, vol. II, pt. 2, 1793, pp. 12–20). His surviving mathematical papers show much interest in the subject, and his improved method of lunar observations was adopted in Nathaniel Bowditch's *New American Practical Navigator* (1802). He possessed extensive chemical, electrical, and optical equipment, and frightened his servants by his experiments. At thirty he began a lifelong devotion to Greek, reading it for relaxation and insisting that it should be taught before Latin. He wrote a Greek grammar, unpublished only because a similar work was reprinted from England. He was a principal founder of the Boston Athenæum and the Social Law Library. Chosen a fellow of Harvard College in 1806, he was influential in securing the appointment of John Thornton Kirkland, his pastor, as president, and shaped the legislation altering the board of overseers. A political opponent on the faculty wrote: "Our college . . . is under the absolute direction of the Essex Junto, at the head of which stands Chief Justice Parsons, . . . a man as cunning as Lucifer and about half as good. This man is at the head of the Corporation. . . . He is not only the soul of that body, but . . . the evil councellor, the Ahithophel of the high federal party" (S. E. Morison, "The Great Rebellion in Harvard College," *Publications of the Colonial Society of Massachusetts*, vol. XXVII, 1932, p. 59).

Whenever he was thrown by business or accident into the company of any person with special information, Parsons never rested until he had learned all that he could. Blacksmiths, carpenters, and painters, not knowing who he was, were convinced by his conversation that he had learned their trades. He kept a large stock of carpenters' tools near his office, making furniture and toys for his children. He was devoted to his family and never remained a day from home if he could avoid it. Although he rarely dined out, he delighted in entertaining in his own home and built a dining room holding thirty persons, which was often filled to the limit. A large proportion of his guests were usually young men. In appearance he was tall and of a large build, with penetrating eyes. Becoming bald about thirty, he afterward wore a wig which was usually in disorder, and his complete inattention to his dress gave rise to many anecdotes. His wife usually traveled with him on circuit, saying that otherwise he would not be dressed fit to be seen. After a year of failing health, he died in Boston after a short final illness in 1813. His last words were: "Gentlemen of the jury, the case is closed and in your hands. You will please retire and agree upon your verdict." Parsons had married, on Jan. 13, 1780, Elizabeth Greenleaf, a descendant of Charles Chauncy [q.v.]. They had twelve children, one of whom was Theophilus [q.v.].

[The main source is *Memoir of Theophilus Parsons* (1859), by his son, Theophilus Parsons. It contains the portrait of Parsons by Gilbert Stuart, and reprints of *The Essex Result*, two mathematical papers, the obituary address of Chief Justice Isaac Parker (also in 10 *Mass. Reports*, 521), and the obituary notice from *New-England Palladium* (Boston), Nov. 2, 1813 (also reprinted in *Boston Gazette*, Nov. 4, 1813, and Boston *Columbian Centinel*, Nov. 6, 1813). Other sources include: F. G. Cook, "Theophilus Parsons," in *Great Am. Lawyers*, vol. II (1907), ed. by W. D. Lewis; S. E. Morison, *The Life and Letters of Harrison Gray Otis, Federalist, 1765–1848* (2 vols., 1913), *A Hist. of the Constitution of Mass.* (1917), and "The Struggle over the Adoption of the Constitution of Mass., 1780," *Proc. Mass. Hist. Soc.*, vol. L (1917); A. L. Morse, *The Federalist Party in Mass. to the Year 1800* (1909); S. B. Harding, *The Contest over the Ratification of the Federal Constitution in the State of Mass.* (1896). The opinions of Parsons appear in 2–10 *Mass. Reports*; the most important were reprinted in his *Commentaries on Am. Law* (1836).]   Z. C., Jr.

PARSONS, THEOPHILUS (May 17, 1797–Jan. 26, 1882), professor in the Harvard Law School, was born in Newburyport, Mass., whence at the age of three he moved with his family to Boston. He was the son of Theophilus Parsons [q.v.] and Elizabeth Greenleaf. Entering Harvard College in 1811, he graduated four years later and then read law in the office of William Prescott, father of the historian and friend of the Parsons family. On account of ill health he made a trip to Europe in 1817, where he lived for some months in the family of William Pinkney, then minister to Russia. On his return to Massachusetts he took up the practice of law,

from 1822 to 1827 in Taunton, thereafter in Boston. During his earlier years he was also an active journalist, as editor of the *United States Literary Gazette* and joint editor of the Taunton *Free Press* and of the *New-England Galaxy*. During the Jacksonian period he was apprehensive that numbers would rise against property and warned that "the body politic [must be invigorated] with the principle that right is not their creation, and depends not on their will, but on His will who made them free" (*An Address, Delivered before the Phi Beta Kappa Society of Harvard University*, 1835, p. 22).

In July 1848 Parsons was appointed a professor in the Harvard Law School. At the bar he had built up a large practice, especially in admiralty, patent, and insurance law. During his first year as a teacher he had to lecture on contracts and real property, with which he was less familiar. After a short period of adjustment he became the most interesting of the memorable triumvirate which included Professors Joel Parker and Emory Washburn. His pleasing diction, a fund of anecdote, and his social grace made his instruction entertaining if not profound. In addition to their lectures and Socratic discussions the professors on occasion addressed the entire school on subjects of legal and political interest. Parsons' oft-repeated anecdotes at these times became traditional. After going to the law school he became one of the most prolific of legal writers. His work on contracts ran through nine editions. The treatise derived much of its merit from the careful notes prepared by Christopher Columbus Langdell, then an impecunious student whose fees were remitted in exchange for this assistance.

To Parsons, who believed that the work of the constitutional fathers was "near to the perfection of republican government," secession came as a severe shock. Throughout the war he was an ardent supporter of the President's military authority: "In my judgment, [the] Constitution has not yet been violated, in any way or to any extent, greater or less. . . . But, if [the] choice *must* be made [between sacrificing nationality or sacrificing the Constitution], I should still say, our nationality must not be lost, and rebellion must not prevail. . . . I can discern no limits to a nation's right of self-salvation" (*Slavery*, pp. 21–23). Parsons had a son in the army and a daughter who rendered outstanding service as an army nurse. In the Reconstruction period he took the position, notably in presiding at a mass meeting in Faneuil Hall, that "as we are victorious in war, we have a right to impose upon the defeated party any terms necessary for our security" (*Boston Morning Journal*, June 22, 1865, p. 4). This included negro suffrage; and until this innovation was established he believed that the Southern states should be held in military occupation.

The year 1869 saw a sweeping change at the law school. There was a growing feeling, shared by the new president, Eliot, that the method of instruction, stabilized for the past twenty years, should be invigorated. Parsons felt it was time to retire. He was succeeded by Langdell, who promptly introduced the case method of instruction. In private life Parsons was a man of warm friendship and lively conversation. In 1823 he espoused the Swedenborgian faith and was deeply concerned with the study and exposition of its philosophy. He took an interest in natural history and in reconciling a view of the origin of species with his religious creed. After his retirement he continued to live in Cambridge where he occupied himself with the revision of his various textbooks and in writing religious essays. He enjoyed the society of his friends, the philosophical discourse of the Magazine Club, and his speculations of the nature of the heavenly kingdom. He had married in 1823 Catherine Amory Chandler, by whom he had three sons and four daughters. His legal works include: *The Law of Contracts* (2 vols., 1853–55); *The Elements of Mercantile Law* (1856, 1862); *The Laws of Business* (1857); *A Treatise on Maritime Law* (2 vols., 1859); *The Constitution* (1861); *A Treatise on the Law of Promissory Notes and Bills of Exchange* (2 vols., 1863, 1876); *A Treatise on the Law of Partnership* (1867 and later editions); *A Treatise on the Law of Marine Insurance and General Average* (2 vols., 1868); *A Treatise on the Law of Shipping* (2 vols., 1869); *The Political, Personal, and Property Rights of a Citizen* (1874). He also prepared a *Memoir of Theophilus Parsons* (1859), an *Address Commemorative of Rufus Choate* (1859), and memoirs of Charles Folsom and Charles Greely Loring for the Massachusetts Historical Society. His miscellaneous writings include: three series of *Essays* (1845, 1856, 1862), *The Law of Conscience* (1853); *Slavery* (1863); *Deus Homo* (1867); *The Infinite and the Finite* (1872); and *Outlines of the Religion and Philosophy of Swedenborg* (1875).

[Charles Warren, *Hist. of the Harvard Law School* (1908), vol. II; *The Centennial Hist. of the Harvard Law School* (1918); memorials of Parsons in the *New Jerusalem Mag.*, Apr., May 1882; the *Albany Law Jour.*, Apr. 10, 1880; *Boston Transcript*, Jan. 26, 1882.]
C. F.

PARSONS, THOMAS WILLIAM (Aug. 18, 1819–Sept. 3, 1892), dentist, poet, translator

of Dante, was born in Boston, the son of Thomas William and Asenath (Read) Parsons. His father, a native of Bristol, England, received the degree of M.D. from Harvard in 1818 and practised medicine and dentistry in Boston. The son attended the Boston Public Latin School for six years, but did not graduate. In 1836 he made his first trip to Italy and other European countries, and upon returning to Boston in 1837, entered the Harvard Medical School. Although he received no medical degree, he practised dentistry intermittently in Boston and afterwards in London, and was commonly called Dr. Parsons. In 1857 he married Anna (or Hannah) M. Allen (1821–1881) of Boston. The last twenty years of his life were devoted to literary pursuits, chiefly in Boston, Scituate, and Wayland. After a period of failing health, he died while visiting his younger sister in Scituate; his body was found in a well into which he had fallen while suffering, apparently, from a stroke of apoplexy. He was buried in Mount Auburn Cemetery, Cambridge.

By nature reserved, sensitive, and deeply religious, Parsons felt himself out of sympathy with the times, and he seldom appeared in general society. T. B. Aldrich (*post*, p. 323) said of him: "He carried his solitude with him into the street." His original poetry is frequently contemplative in tone, dwelling on religion and death, and at times rising to ecstatic fervor, but at other times he could be humorous, personal, and playful. He wrote verses on the death of prominent men and for public occasions such as the opening of the Boston Theatre in 1854, the opening of the Players' Club in New York in 1888. His style was influenced by his study of Dante, an absorbing pursuit with him for more than fifty years. He shared with Dante a horror of slovenly work, and devoted infinite care to perfecting his verses, often rewriting them after they had appeared in print. Nevertheless, he seemed indifferent to the ultimate fate of his poems, which usually appeared in newspapers or magazines, or in small, privately printed volumes.

During his first stay in Italy Parsons started to commit the *Divina Commedia* to memory and to translate it into English. In 1841 he published in the *Boston Daily Advertiser and Patriot* (Oct. 7) the most frequently quoted of his original poems, "On a Bust of Dante," called by Stedman (*post*, p. 55) "the peer of any modern lyric in our tongue." In revised form these verses appeared in a little volume which Parsons printed anonymously in Boston in 1843: *The First Ten Cantos of the Inferno of Dante Alighieri*:

Newly Translated into English Verse. This was the earliest published American translation of any considerable portion of Dante. In 1865 seventeen translated cantos were privately printed by Parsons, and the entire *Inferno,* with Doré's illustrations, was published in Boston in 1867, the year in which Longfellow's version of the entire *Divine Comedy* appeared. Parsons published about two-thirds of the *Purgatorio* between 1870 and 1883 in the *Catholic World.* In 1893, after his death, the whole *Inferno,* all that could be found of the *Purgatorio,* and fragments of the *Paradiso* were issued in one volume. The translation aims to reproduce the spirit rather than the letter of the original; being in rhymed quatrains which correspond to Dante's tercets, the wording is necessarily sometimes extended, yet on the whole the meaning is reproduced with remarkable fidelity. Among rhymed English renderings of Dante's poem, that of Parsons, incomplete though it is, takes high rank for its nobility of style and its verbal felicity. Only his own fastidiousness and desire for perfection prevented him from completing it. Much of Parsons' original verse was inspired by the picturesqueness of the Italian scene; but he had by nature something of Dante's detachment from the world and dwelt, as Louise Imogen Guiney said of him, "in a joyous cloister of the imagination." Among his most finished lyrics are particularly those of religious feeling, like "Paradisi Gloria," which has been called "one of the few faultless lyrics in the language" (Hovey, *post*). Parsons was taken by Longfellow as the model for "the Poet" in his "Tales of a Wayside Inn"; he has been compared to the English writers Gray, Collins, and Landor, and has been called "a poet for poets" (Stedman, *post*).

The poetry of Parsons was collected in two volumes in 1893: *The Divine Comedy of Dante Alighieri,* with a preface by Charles Eliot Norton and a memorial sketch by Louise Imogen Guiney (cf. *Atlantic Monthly,* June 1894); and *Poems,* containing most of his original verse. Smaller volumes of verse had appeared during his lifetime, including: *Ghetto di Roma* (1854); *Poems* (1854); *The Magnolia* (1866); *The Old House at Sudbury* (1870); *The Shadow of the Obelisk* (London, 1872); *The Willey House, and Sonnets* (1875).

[Sources include *Critic,* Sept. 10, 17, 1892; *Boston Transcript,* Sept. 6, 1892; Richard Hovey, *Seaward: an Elegy on the Death of Thomas William Parsons* (1893), which includes a paper reprinted from the *Atlantic Monthly,* Feb. 1893; T. B. Aldrich, "A Portrait of Thomas William Parsons," *Century Magazine,* July 1894; Maria S. Porter, "Thomas William Parsons; with Unpublished Poems by Dr. Parsons, and Letters by Dr. Holmes," *Ibid.,* Oct. 1901; R. W. Griswold, *The Poets and Poetry of America* (1874); E. C. Stedman, *Poets of America* (1885); T. W. Koch, "Dante in America," *Fifteenth Ann. Report of the Dante Soc.* (1896). The name of Parsons' wife appears in the vital records of Boston and Cambridge both as Hannah and as Anna; the latter name is used on her tombstone in Mount Auburn Cemetery.]　　　　K. McK.

PARSONS, USHER (Aug. 18, 1788–Dec. 19, 1868), physician and surgeon, was born in Alfred, Me., the youngest of nine children. His father was William Parsons, farmer, trader, and lumberman, three of whose brothers were Harvard graduates; his grandfather was the Rev. Joseph Parsons, whose immigrant ancestor of that name was one of the first settlers in Springfield, Mass., in the seventeenth century. His mother, Abigail Frost (Blunt) Parsons, was the daughter of the Rev. John Blunt of New Castle, N. H., and a blood connection of Sir William Pepperell, hero of Louisburg.

Usher Parsons' formal education was meager and desultory, but included one year (1800–01) at Berwick Academy. As a lad he worked in retail stores in Portland and Wells. In 1807 he began the study of medicine under Dr. Abiel Hall of Alfred. In 1809 he attended anatomical lectures at Fryeburg under Dr. Alexander Ramsay and later was in the office of the eminent Dr. John Warren of Boston. He was licensed to practise by the Massachusetts Medical Society, Feb. 7, 1812, when war with England was imminent. He was commissioned surgeon's mate, July 6, 1812. Finding that the *John Adams,* which he had been ordered to join in August, had sailed when he reached New York, he volunteered for service on the Great Lakes. Arriving at Buffalo, he did yeoman service during an epidemic of pleuro-pneumonia, and wrote extensively for the press on the cause and treatment of that disease. In 1812–13 he was in charge of the sick and wounded at Black Rock and, after the arrival upon the scene of Commodore Oliver H. Perry in June 1813, sprang into great prominence for his brilliant surgical work. At the battle of Lake Erie, owing to the disability of his associate surgeons on the *Lawrence,* the whole duty of dressing and attending nearly a hundred wounded, and as many sick, devolved upon young Parsons. In a letter to the Secretary of the Navy, Commodore Perry is said to have written: "It must be pleasant to you, Sir, to reflect that, of the whole number wounded, only three have died. I can only say that, in the event of my having another command, I should consider myself particularly fortunate in having him [Parsons] with me as a surgeon" (Abiel Holmes, *The Annals of America,* 1829, II, 455). On the day of the battle and the following day, the wounded from the entire fleet having been brought to his ship, he performed six thigh amputations. For this extraordinary service a grateful country awarded him not only prize-money but a silver medal.

After the war, he served under Perry on board the *Java,* and on Jan. 22, 1816, in view of the threatening attitude of Algiers, sailed in the *Java* for the Mediterranean. Returning to Narragansett Bay, Mar. 3, 1817, he proceeded to Providence with letters of introduction from Commodore Perry. After practising in that city for four months, he attended lectures in Boston, and in March 1818 received the degree of M.D. from Harvard Medical College. In October of that year he published "Surgical Account of the Naval Battle of Lake Erie," in the *New England Journal of Medicine and Surgery.* In July, he had sailed as surgeon on the frigate *Guerrière.* On this cruise he came into profitable contact with the leading physicians and surgeons of Paris and London, among whom were Dupuytren, Baron Larrey, Louis, Laennec, and Abernethy. In London, too, he made the acquaintance of Sir Richard Owen, naturalist and anatomist, with whom he kept up a lifelong friendship and correspondence.

In August 1820, he was chosen professor of anatomy and surgery in Dartmouth College, lecturing there one year. At this time he published *The Sailor's Physician* (1820), a medical guide for use on merchant vessels, of which a second edition appeared in 1824, and a third and a fourth in 1842 and 1851 under the title, *Physician for Ships.* In 1822 Parsons was appointed professor of anatomy and surgery in Brown University, and in this year began his continued residence in Rhode Island. On Sept. 23, 1822, he married Mary Jackson Holmes of Cambridge, daughter of Abiel and sister of Oliver Wendell Holmes [*qq.v.*]. She died June 14, 1825, leaving one son who became a physician and survived his father. In April 1823 Parsons resigned his commission in the navy. In 1831 he was appointed professor of obstetrics in Jefferson Medical College, Philadelphia, and lectured there the following winter. He was several times president of the Rhode Island Medical Society, was one of the organizers of the American Medical Association, and its vice-president in 1853, and was active in founding the Rhode Island Hospital.

Parsons wrote voluminously, his bibliography (1809–67) embracing fifty-six titles. He won the Boylston Prize four times; the prize-winning papers were collected and published as *Boylston Prize Dissertations* (1839). A second edition (1849) included a paper which won the

Fiske Fund prize in 1842. Another notable publication was Parsons' summary of his larger surgical operations in the *American Journal of the Medical Sciences,* April 1848. Among his lay writings were *Life of Sir William Pepperrell, Bart.* (1855), *Indian Names of Places in Rhode Island* (1861), and "Brief Sketches of the Officers Who Were in the Battle of Lake Erie" (*New-England Historical and Genealogical Register,* January 1863). One of his biographers (Spalding, *post,* p. 893) says of Usher Parsons: "Taking him all in all it would be difficult to find a man of greater merit in American medicine, for he gave of his entire mind for over fifty years to the advance of medical science." Deservedly his memory, as of one who never worshipped medicine as a milch-cow, but always as a goddess, is cherished with pride by the profession of Rhode Island. He died in Providence.

[C. W. Parsons, *Memoir of Usher Parsons* (1870), containing bibliog.; J. A. Spalding, in H. A. Kelly and W. L. Burrage, *Am. Medic. Biogs.* (1920); J. W. Keefe, "Traditions of Medicine in Rhode Island," *Boston Medic. and Surgic. Jour.,* Nov. 12, 1925; F. L. Pleadwell, "Usher Parsons," with complete bibliog., in *U. S. Naval Medic. Bull.,* Sept. 1922; S. G. Arnold, *Greene-Staples-Parsons: An Address Delivered before the R. I. Hist. Soc.* (1869); *Providence Journal,* Dec. 21, 1868.]
G. A. B—r.

PARSONS, WILLIAM BARCLAY (Apr. 15, 1859–May 9, 1932), engineer, the son of William Barclay Parsons and Eliza Glass (Livingston), was born in New York City of old New York stock. He was a great-grandson of Henry Barclay, second rector of Trinity Church. In 1871 he went to school in Torquay, England, and for the four years following studied under private tutors while traveling in France, Germany, and Italy. Returning to the United States in 1875, he entered Columbia College. Graduating in 1879 with the degree of A.B., he continued in the Engineering School, then the School of Mines, and received the degree of C.E. in 1882. During the summer of 1881, he had been engaged as engineer for the Blossburg (Pa.) Coal Company, but upon graduation he turned to railroad work and from 1882 to the end of 1885 he was in the maintenance-of-way department of the New York, Lake Erie & Western Railroad. His first books had to do with railroad problems (*Turnouts; Exact Formulae for Their Determination,* 1884, and *Track; a Complete Manual of Maintenance of Way,* 1886), and this interest in rail transportation continued throughout his life. In 1886 he began practice as a consulting engineer in New York and for the following years devoted much time to studying plans for an underground railway in the city, although he also engaged in other railroad and water-supply work, notably that of building, as chief engineer, the Fort Worth & Rio Grande railroad in Texas.

In 1891 the legislature of New York created a Rapid Transit Commission and Parsons was appointed deputy chief engineer under William E. Worthen. Three years later, upon the appointment of a new commission with broader powers, under the chairmanship of Alexander Ector Orr [q.v.], Parsons became chief engineer, but adverse political pressure and other difficulties caused the commission to suspend its activities in 1898. Thereupon Parsons, acting for an American syndicate, accepted the direction of a survey for some 1000 miles of railway in China, primarily on the line from Hankow to Canton. The party passed through the then "closed province" of Hu-nan, and the success of the entire venture depended not alone on engineering skill but primarily upon the ability of the leader of the expedition to meet the extremely difficult diplomatic problems involved. Nevertheless, the mission was accomplished and the small group of American engineers, to the surprise of many of their friends, returned in safety. Parsons told the story of this adventure in *An American Engineer in China* (1900).

Late in 1899 he was recalled by the Transit Commission, since an opportunity to begin subway construction in New York seemed at last at hand. Construction actually started in March 1900. The first subway, extending from Atlantic Avenue, Brooklyn, to Van Cortlandt Park on the West Side and to Bronx Park on the East, for which Parsons had prepared the plans and which is popularly considered his greatest engineering achievement, was at last under way. Writing of the undertaking later, Parsons said: "Some of my friends spoke pityingly of my wasting time on what they considered a dream. They said I could go ahead making plans, but never could build a practical, underground railroad. This skepticism was so prevalent that it seriously handicapped the work" (Walker, *post*, p. 188). Parsons not only overcame the obstacles involved in this pioneer construction, but in doing so, developed standards of design which have been adopted wherever subways have been built and still remain standard after more than a quarter century of almost continuous subway construction.

After the success of the enterprise had been assured by completion of the first section in 1904, Parsons resigned as chief engineer to devote his energies to his consulting practice. He was appointed to the Isthmian Canal Commission in 1904, and early in 1905 went to Panama as a member of the committee of engineers which sub-sequently reported in favor of a sea-level canal. Later, appointed to the international Board of Consulting Engineers, he joined the majority of the board in advocating this type of construction, although in 1906 President Roosevelt approved a lock canal. In 1904 Parsons was also appointed, together with the famous British engineers, Sir Benjamin Baker and Sir John Wolfe Wolfe-Barry, to membership on a board to pass on the plans of the Royal Commission on London Traffic. He always considered his selection for the post one of the greatest of the many honors which came to him. Among his other engineering activities in these years were work as consulting engineer to the Massachusetts Railroad Commission, advisory engineer on traffic problems to Cambridge, San Francisco, Toronto, Detroit, and other cities, and consultant on large hydraulic works such as the Salmon River, Mac-Call Ferry (now Holtwood), and Mohawk hydroelectric developments. In 1905 he undertook to carry through the construction of the Steinway Tunnel under the East River in New York. In order to hold the franchise this work had to be completed in a very short time and Parsons, by building an artificial island near the south end of Blackwell's Island and working from four headings, accomplished the difficult task. In 1905, he had also been appointed chief engineer of the Cape Cod Canal. Completed in 1914, it joined Massachusetts and Buzzard's bays and demonstrated that a canal without locks could be built between two bodies of water where considerable tidal differences existed.

In 1916 Parsons was acting as chairman of the Chicago Transit Commission, but upon the entry of the United States into the World War, he became senior member of the first group of American officers to go to France—a board of engineers appointed to report on the military engineering problems and requirements for engineer troops there. In July 1917 he joined his regiment, the 11th United States Engineers, in England, and he served with them as major, lieutenant-colonel, and colonel until the end of the war. He participated in the engagement at Cambrai, where, suddenly attacked by the Germans while making railroad repairs, the engineers fought with picks and shovels, also in the Lys defensive, and the Saint-Mihiel and Argonne-Meuse campaigns. His book, *The American Engineers in France* (1920), is a valuable and interesting record of these activities. He was cited for "specially meritorious services" and received decorations not only from the United States but also from Great Britain, France, Belgium, and the State of New York.

After the war, he was transferred to the Engineers Reserve Corps with the rank of brigadier-general, and again took up his engineering practice. One of the last great works of his firm (Parsons, Klapp, Brinkerhoff & Douglas of New York) was the international vehicular tunnel passing under the Detroit River and joining Detroit with Windsor, Ont. Opened in 1930, it was the third great vehicular tube in America. In its design and construction older methods were used in new ways, and a new design for tunnel lining was developed.

In connection with a trip to Yucatan in the early 1900's, Parsons became interested in the Maya ruins, and later, when he was appointed a trustee of the Carnegie Institution, he encouraged the undertaking of archeological exploration and preservation of these remarkable remains. He also found time to make an exhaustive study of engineering history. Although he published a book entitled *Robert Fulton and the Submarine* (1922), his historical interest centered particularly on engineers and engineering of the Renaissance, and he gathered a remarkable collection of early books and prints relating to this period. A loyal alumnus of Columbia, Parsons became a member in 1897 and chairman in 1917 of the board of trustees of his alma mater. He took an active part in establishing the University on Morningside Heights. Holding that "it is not the technical excellence of a design which governs, but the completeness with which it meets the economic and social needs of the day," he insisted that the duties of the engineer demanded a broad, rather than a narrowly technical type of training, and his influence had much to do with placing engineering education at Columbia on a higher professional plane. Parsons naturally received many honors and was a member of many engineering organizations. He was a trustee of the New York Public Library and of the Carnegie Institution of Washington, and chairman of the administrative board of the Columbia-Presbyterian Medical Center in New York, where his sudden death occurred. On May 20, 1884, he had married Anna De Witt Reed, daughter of the Rev. Sylvanus and Caroline (Gallup) Reed of New York. She, with a son and a daughter, survived him.

[*Trans. Am. Soc. Civil Engineers*, vol. LIX (1933); *Proc. Am. Acad. Arts and Sci.*, vol. LXVIII (1933); *Who's Who in America*, 1930–31; J. B. Walker, *Fifty Years of Rapid Transit* (1918); *N. Y. Herald Tribune*, May 10, 12, 1932; data furnished by General Parsons' family and by his office.]   **J. K. F.**

PARTINGTON, MRS. [See SHILLABER, BENJAMIN PENHALLOW, 1814–1890].

PARTON, ARTHUR (Mar. 26, 1842–Mar. 7, 1914), landscape painter, born in Hudson, N. Y., was the fourth of the twelve children of George Parton of Birmingham, England, who settled, quite by chance, in Hudson, and of Elizabeth Woodbridge Parton of Mystic (now Old Mystic), Conn. His father, from whom he undoubtedly inherited his artistic talents, was a cabinet-maker by trade. His mother came from a distinguished Massachusetts and Connecticut family, being a descendant of the eighth generation from Rev. John Woodbridge of Stanton, Wiltshire, whose son, Rev. John Woodbridge of Newbury, Mass., married Mercy Dudley, the daughter of Governor Dudley of Massachusetts Bay Colony. Young Parton began to draw and paint while still a schoolboy. From 1859 to 1861 he studied with William T. Richards of Philadelphia and later at the Pennsylvania Academy of the Fine Arts at that city. His first picture was exhibited there in 1862. Three years later he removed to New York, established a studio, and became a regular exhibitor at the National Academy of Design. In 1869 he left for Europe, studying a short while in Paris, but receiving most of his inspiration direct from English and Scottish scenery and from the contemporary landscape painters of those countries. A year after his return to New York in 1871 he was elected an associate of the National Academy of Design, becoming a full academician in 1884. He was also a member of the American Water Color and the Artists' Fund societies. He was an indefatigable worker and his production of landscapes—all of them easel pictures—correspondingly great. He spent his summers in the Adirondacks and later in the Catskills, where he had a small cottage. Something of the character of his work may be derived from typical titles of his canvases: "November"; "A Mountain Brook"; "Delaware River, near Milford"; "Loch Lomond" (Indianapolis Museum); "Nightfall"; "Evening, Harlem River" and "A Night in the Catskills" (both in the Metropolitan); "Misty Morning," "Coast of Maine" (Brooklyn Museum); "Catskill Pines" ("diploma picture," 1884, National Academy of Design); "Buttonball Trees on the Housatonic"; and "June Day in the Catskills."

Parton followed the traditional English landscape practices as modified by the Hudson River school. His work falls below that of his friends Alexander H. Wyant and J. Francis Murphy. In his more romantic aspects it recalls, at times, that of Blakelock and Innis; but for the most part his work is realistic, objective, and, to a later generation, quite out of fashion. The *Yonkers Statesman* describes it as "wholesome, sane, serene and beautiful," which is just. It is always sound and competent, occasionally genuinely poetic, but sometimes uninspired. He was a typical academic product of his time. His life was devoid of colorful incident. He was extremely modest and hated publicity of any kind. He worked hard and exhibited regularly, being represented in most of the larger exhibitions from the Centennial in Philadelphia of 1876 to that of St. Louis twenty-eight years later. Trout fishing was one of his few recreations. On June 7, 1877, he was married to Anna Taylor of Mystic, Conn. He settled in Yonkers, N. Y., where he lived for some thirty years. He died there, survived by his four children, and was buried at Mystic, Conn. His awards include the following: gold medal, Competitive Prize Fund Exhibition, New York, 1878; gold medal, American Art Association, 1886; Temple silver medal, Pennsylvania Academy of the Fine Arts, Philadelphia, 1889; honorable mention, Exposition Universelle, Paris, 1889; Lotos Club Fund purchase, National Academy, New York, 1896; honorable mention, Paris Exhibition, 1900; and bronze medal, "Louisiana Purchase" Exposition, St. Louis, 1904.

[Sources include: C. E. Clement and Laurence Hutton, *Artists of the Nineteenth Century* (1879); J. D. Champlin and C. C. Perkins, *Cyc. of Painters and Paintings* (ed. 1887), vol. III; Mich. State Lib., *Biog. Sketches of Am. Artists* (1924); Gilbert Cranmer, "An Am. Landscape Painter, Arthur Parton," *Monthly Illustrator*, May 1896; *Paintings in the Metropolitan Museum of Art* (1905); Bryson Burroughs, *The Metropolitan Museum of Art, Cat. of Paintings* (1914); *The Woodbridge Record* (1883), ed. by D. G. and Alfred Mitchell; the *Am. Art Annual*, vol. XI (1914); the *N. Y. Times*, Mar. 8, 1914; *Yonkers Statesman*, Mar. 14, 1914; the *Am. Art News*, Mar. 14, 1914; art exhibition catalogues, records of the Nat. Acad. of Design, the Pa. Acad. of the Fine Arts, the Brooklyn Museum, the John Herron Art Inst., Indianapolis, Ind., and family records in the possession of Parton's son, George F. Parton, Bronxville, N. Y.] T. S—r.

PARTON, JAMES (Feb. 9, 1822–Oct. 17, 1891), biographer, miscellaneous writer, was born at Canterbury, England, the third of the four children of James and Ann (Leach) Parton, and was descended from a Huguenot family of farmers and millers who had settled in Kent after the revocation of the Edict of Nantes. In 1827 his widowed mother emigrated to New York with her children. James attended an academy at White Plains, where he acquired an enthusiasm for Homer and a distaste for orthodox Christianity, and, after graduating, stayed on as an assistant teacher. In 1842 he went to England to collect a legacy, which he invested in a year of travel. For the next four years he taught in a private school in Philadelphia. In 1848 he sent to the New York *Home Journal* an essay demonstrating the feminine authorship of *Jane Eyre*, and Nathaniel Parker Willis, the editor, gave him a place on the staff at ten dollars a week.

He was still drudging for Willis in 1854 when a chance conversation in a restaurant made him a biographer. To Daniel Gregory Mason and Lowell Mason, Jr., who constituted the publishing firm of Mason Brothers, he happened to remark that a life of Horace Greeley would be as interesting and as popular as Franklin's *Autobiography*. Asked why he did not write it, he replied that the job would require a year's time and an outlay of $1000. Two weeks later the Masons advanced the money, and Parton went to the *Tribune* office to meet his subject for the first time. After eleven arduous months in the field and with the files of Greeley's papers, the manuscript was ready. Before publication *The Life of Horace Greeley* (1855) sold 7,000 copies and, within a few months thereafter, 23,000 more. No other living American had been exhibited to the public so realistically, with such an abundance of amusing and intimate detail. Delicate literary palates could detect a Barnum-like flavor in the work, but its vogue was well earned, and it remains a landmark in the history of American biography. Parton, with $2,000 of clear profit from his royalties, and with his reputation established, saw his course straight ahead of him. For the next thirty-five years, he was one of the most industrious, prolific, popular, and well-paid writers in the United States.

His principal separate publications were: *The Humorous Poetry of the English Language from Chaucer to Saxe* (1856); *The Life and Times of Aaron Burr* (copyright 1857; enlarged edition, 2 vols., 1864); *Life of Andrew Jackson* (3 vols., 1859–60); *General Butler in New Orleans* (1863); *Life and Times of Benjamin Franklin* (2 vols., 1864); *Life of John Jacob Astor* (1865); *Manual for the Instruction of "Rings," Railroad and Political* (1866); *How New York Is Governed* (1866); *Famous Americans of Recent Times* (1867); *People's Book of Biography* (1868); *Smoking and Drinking* (1868); *The Danish Islands: Are We Bound in Honor to Pay for Them?* (1869); *Topics of the Time* (1871); *Triumphs of Enterprise, Ingenuity, and Public Spirit* (1871); *Words of Washington* (1872); *Fanny Fern: A Memorial Volume* (1873); *Life of Thomas Jefferson* (1874); *Caricature and Other Comic Art in All Times and Many Lands* (1877); *Le Parnasse Français* (1877); *Life of Voltaire* (2 vols., 1881); *Noted Women of Europe and America* (1883); *Captains of Industry* (2 series, 1884, 1891); and *Some Noted Princes,*

Authors, and Statesmen of Our Time (1885). He was a steady, life-long contributor to Robert Bonner's *New York Ledger* and to Daniel Sharp Ford's *Youth's Companion* and wrote a great deal also for the *North American Review* and the *Atlantic Monthly.*

Until 1875 he continued to live in New York. While writing the life of Greeley he was debating with Willis the literary merits of Willis' sister [see Sara Payson Willis Parton], whose work her brother had no desire to publish or to pay for. As a result, Parton left the *Home Journal* and on Jan. 5, 1856, at Hoboken, he married the woman whom he had championed. She was eleven years his senior and hopelessly neurasthenic, and though outward decorum was kept up till the end, Parton was thoroughly unhappy in his marriage. His pent-up affections were lavished on his wife's grand-daughter, Ethel, who had been left an orphan and was reared in the Parton household. They spent their summers in New England, latterly at Newport. Mrs. Parton died in 1872 after six years of painful illness. The next two summers Parton spent at Newburyport, where in 1875 he bought a house of his own. On Feb. 3, 1876, he was married there to his step-daughter, Ellen Willis Eldredge. Two days after the wedding he discovered that the marriage was void under Massachusetts law, and they were remarried in New York on Feb. 10 by the Rev. Stephen Higginson Tyng. A bill to legalize the marriage was passed by the Massachusetts legislature but was vetoed by Gov. Alexander Hamilton Rice. This second marriage brought him the happiness so long denied him. Besides the adopted daughter, Ethel, he had two children, a daughter and a son. Parton himself was a man of great amiability and good sense. Though robust in appearance he was compelled to guard his health and was something of a crank on the subjects of diet, smoking, and drinking. At Newburyport he took an active interest in civic affairs and enjoyed the local society. In his latter years he was seldom in New York. He died at his home after an illness of several weeks.

Parton was the most successful biographer of his generation and a master of the reconstructional method. Writing for a living, he sometimes worked with a haste that made for error and superficiality; yet his errors, such as they are, are seldom misleading, and the superficiality is not often apparent. His preparation for his major undertakings was thorough and elaborate; he was undeviatingly honest, fair, and charitable in his judgments; and he had a positive genius for imparting order and motion to great masses of fact that, in less skilful hands, would have remained inert and stodgy. His great achievements are the lives of Burr, Jackson, Franklin, Jefferson, and Voltaire. None of these is quite obsolete, in spite of the advances made by recent scholarship, and the lives of Franklin and Jefferson are still the best for the general reader. Parton failed occasionally to understand the thought and intellectual background of his heroes, but in presenting them in their habit as they lived he has had no superior.

[C. E. Norton, "Parton's Biog. Writings," *North Am. Rev.*, Apr. 1867; James Parton, autobiog. essay in *Triumphs of Enterprise, Ingenuity, and Public Spirit* (1871); J. C. Derby, *Fifty Years among Authors, Books, and Publishers* (1884); H. A. Beers, *Nathaniel Parker Willis* (1885); *N. Y. Tribune*, Oct. 18, 1891; Henry Bruce, "Mr. James Parton," *Boston Transcript*, Oct. 20, 1891; C. E. L. Wingate, "Boston Letter," and editorial, *Critic*, Oct. 24, 1891; H. P. Spofford, "James Parton," *Writer*, Nov. 1891; J. H. Ward, "James Parton," *New Eng. Mag.*, Jan. 1893; "James Parton's Rules of Biography," *McClure's Mag.*, June 1893; J. J. Currier, "Ould Newbury" (1896); Ethel Parton, "A Defense of James Parton," *Outlook*, Sept. 16, 1911.]
G. H. G.

PARTON, SARA PAYSON WILLIS (July 9, 1811–Oct. 10, 1872), author, known to the reading public as Fanny Fern, was born in Portland, Me., the daughter of Nathaniel Willis [*q.v.*] and Hannah (Parker) Willis. Her father, the pugnacious editor of an anti-Federalist newspaper, was sixth in descent from an English ancestor who settled in Massachusetts about 1630; her mother was a woman of intellect and personal attraction. They were parishioners of the Rev. Edward Payson [*q.v.*], and, for his mother, they first named their daughter Grata Payson, but the name was later changed to Sara. While she was a small child the family removed to Boston. A robust little girl, she attended Catharine Beecher's school at Hartford, where Harriet Beecher was a pupil-teacher. Her nickname in school was "Sal-Volatile" and her reputation was not for studiousness but for thoughtlessness and a tendency to incur bills at local stores. Though the Willis home was frequented by clergymen, Sara never acquired great piety. She was a "natural Universalist" and her teacher wrote regarding her interests, "I fear the world has first place" (Parton, memoir, *post*, p. 37). After school days were over, she contributed occasionally to the *Youth's Companion*, then published by her father.

In 1837 she was married to Charles H. Eldredge, cashier of a Boston bank, and for nine years led a happy life, except for the death of her first child. Her grief over this loss is reflected in many of her essays. After her husband's death, she was obliged to earn a living for herself and two children and attempted sewing and teaching without success. The editor of a Boston home magazine paid her fifty cents for a paragraph called "The Model Minister," signed "Fanny Fern." The paragraph was copied in several Boston papers and thereafter she found a ready market for her life essays. On Jan. 15, 1849, she was married to Samuel P. Farrington, a Boston merchant. Their marriage was probably terminated by divorce, since both remarried. Her first volume of collected essays, *Fern Leaves from Fanny's Portfolio* (1853), had a sale of 80,000 copies and established her popularity. James Parton [*q.v.*], on the staff of the *Home Journal,* one of whose publishers was Nathaniel P. Willis [*q.v.*], Sara's brother, wrote to her, not knowing her identity, urging her to come to New York. She went and on Jan. 5, 1856, married Parton. At about the same time she began her connection with the *New York Ledger,* which lasted until her death. For the *Ledger* she wrote a weekly article, and this, together with her contributions to other papers, made her work amount to a story or sketch a day. She thought out her articles while engaged in other occupations and then wrote them rapidly; they show neither deep reflection nor intellectual quality. She wrote spontaneously, from experience and observation, on every-day subjects of human appeal, and was popular because her combination of common sense, sentiment, and occasional religious teaching met the demands of her age. She caustically satirized pretentiousness, cant, snobbery, and heartlessness displayed by wealth toward poverty, but never tired of eulogizing family life, children, old homes, gardens, and country beauties. Her published volumes include: *Ruth Hall* (1855), a novel, severely criticized because of its personal character—her brother N. P. Willis figures in it in a most unfavorable light; *Fern Leaves from Fanny's Portfolio* (second series, 1854); *Little Ferns for Fanny's Little Friends* (1854); *Rose Clark* (1856), a novel; *Fresh Leaves* (1857); *The Play-Day Book: New Stories for Little Folks* (1857); *A New Story Book for Children* (1864); *Folly as It Flies* (1868); *Ginger-Snaps* (1870); *Caper-Sauce: a Volume of Chit-Chat about Men, Women, and Things* (1872). During her last six years she fought a fatal disease. She continued her articles by dictation when she could no longer use her hands; her last, written a month before her death, was a farewell to Newport, where she had spent the summer.

[*Fanny Fern: A Memorial Volume: Containing her Select Writings and a Memoir, by James Parton* (1873); F. E. Willard and M. A. Livermore, *Am. Women*

(1897); *New-England Hist. and Geneal. Reg.,* Apr. 1849, p. 195; H. A. Beers, *Nathaniel Parker Willis* (1885); N. Y. *Evening Post,* Oct. 11, 1872; *N. Y. Daily Tribune,* Oct. 11, 1872.]   S. G. B.

PARTRIDGE, ALDEN (Feb. 12, 1785–Jan. 17, 1854), military educator, was born at Norwich, Vt., the son of Samuel, a farmer and soldier of the Revolution, and Elizabeth (Wright) Partridge. He was a descendant of George Partridge who came to America about 1636. After early education in the district schools, he entered Dartmouth College in 1802, but did not graduate, for on Dec. 14, 1805, he was appointed a cadet in the army and sent to West Point. The United States Military Academy had been established there in 1802, for the reception and training of cadets, but it had no definite course of instruction, no requirements for admission or graduation, and no fixed period of residence. Cadets were received whenever appointed, taught as seemed expedient to the faculty, and sent from the academy at any time. On Oct. 30, 1806, Partridge was commissioned first lieutenant of engineers. He did not leave West Point, however, for he was immediately assigned to duty as an instructor, and there he was stationed throughout his service in the army. He was promoted to captain, July 23, 1810; appointed professor of mathematics, Apr. 13, 1813; and of engineering, Sept. 1, 1813. For more than two years he was acting superintendent of the academy. His administration was lax and unsatisfactory, and he was superseded by Maj. Sylvanus Thayer. Returning from leave, he assumed command over Thayer and attempted to regain his quarters. The struggle between the two was ended by an order from Washington for Partridge's arrest, and he was tried by court martial on numerous charges of neglect of duty and insubordination, and sentenced, Nov. 27, 1817, to be cashiered. The punishment was remitted by the President, however, and Partridge's resignation from the army followed, Apr. 15, 1818.

For a time he was engaged on the survey of the northeastern boundary of the United States, but in 1819 he established the "American Literary, Scientific and Military Academy" at Norwich, Vt. It was removed in 1825 to Middletown, Conn., but in 1829 its buildings there were sold to Wesleyan University and it was moved back to Norwich. In 1834 it was chartered as Norwich University, under which name it still operates although now located at Northfield, Vt. In 1827 Partridge opened a military preparatory school at Norwich, which existed until the return of the principal institution to that place; and in 1835 he established a "young ladies' seminary," likewise at Norwich. He had always hoped to spread the military academy idea throughout the country; with the help of graduates of Norwich University, now becoming numerous, he established such schools—more or less short-lived—at Portsmouth, Va., in 1839, Bristol, Pa., in 1842, Harrisburg, Pa., in 1845, Wilmington, Del., in 1846, Reading, Pa., in 1850, Pembroke, N. H., in 1850, and Brandywine Springs, Del., in 1853. Meanwhile, he had severed his connection with Norwich University, though he retained ownership of its property, the university leasing it from him when he surrendered the presidency in 1843. He resumed possession in 1845—forcing the University to move to another site near by—and opened his own "American Literary, Scientific and Military University," which, however, he discontinued the next year, selling the property to the Norwich University corporation.

In the establishment of these schools Partridge's primary interest was in national defense. In the War of 1812 he had witnessed the appalling results of neglect of military training, and was convinced that for a nation relying upon citizen soldiers it is vitally important that some of these citizens should be imbued with discipline and trained for command. The military training given in his schools was rudimentary, it is true, but in his day the military art was comparatively simple, and the forces which the United States had put, or expected to put, in the field, were very small. Under the conditions of the time the training given in his schools was distinctly valuable. Partridge may fairly be regarded as the founder of the system of military academies of elementary and secondary grade which have since become so numerous. The present Reserve Officers' Training Corps has a different ancestry, but even in this, Partridge's influence may be traced. In other respects his educational ideas were in advance of his age. Norwich University was an engineering school from the first, and so continued through a long period when engineering, in the United States, was treated rather as a trade to be picked up casually than as a profession to be studied in an institution of learning. This university, too, was among the first to offer collegiate instruction in agriculture. Aside from his educational work, Partridge's activities were varied. He served as surveyor general of Vermont in 1822–23, was elected to the legislature in 1833, 1834, 1837, and 1839, and was three times an unsuccessful candidate for Congress. He died at Norwich. His wife, whom he married in 1837, was Ann Elizabeth, daughter of John Swasey of Claremont, N. H. She survived him half a century, dying in October 1902. He had two sons.

[G. H. Partridge, *Partridge Geneal.* (1915), inaccurate in some details; G. M. Dodge and W. A. Ellis, *Norwich Univ., 1819–1911* (1911), vol. I; *The Memoirs of Gen. Joseph Gardner Swift, LL.D., U.S.A.* (1890); G. W. Cullum, *Biog. Reg. Officers and Grads. U.S. Mil. Acad.* (3rd ed., 1891); unpublished records in the War Department; A. C. True, *A Hist. of Agric. Education in the U.S., 1785–1925* (1929); M. E. Goddard and H. V. Partridge, *A Hist. of Norwich, Vt.* (1905); *Vt. Patriot* (Montpelier), Jan. 21, 1854; *N.Y. Daily Times*, Jan. 23, 1854.]   T. M. S.

PARTRIDGE, JAMES RUDOLPH (c. 1823–Feb. 24, 1884), diplomat and Maryland politician, was the son of the well-to-do merchant Eaton R. Partridge and of Susan (Crook) Partridge, his wife, who had come from Cecil County, Md., to Baltimore, where James Rudolph was born. He received the degree of A.B. from Harvard in 1841 and that of LL.B. from the Harvard Law School in 1843. He appears to have been a capable lawyer, a man of culture and of some literary ability, and the master of four foreign languages. In Baltimore, which remained his home throughout his life, he entered active politics in 1856, when he was elected to the legislature on the American ticket. Gov. Thomas H Hicks [*q.v.*], in 1858, made Partridge his secretary of state and in 1861, according to Henry Winter Davis [*q.v.*], Secretary Partridge kept Governor Hicks loyal to the Union (undated letter to Lincoln, Department of State). He remained a strong Union man, and his name is to be found upon Governor Bradford's personal list of the prominent Union men of Baltimore in 1861 (*Maryland Historical Magazine*, March 1912, p. 85). Indeed, if his plan for distributing arms from the arsenals and forts within Maryland to loyal men for use against secessionist trouble makers (Andrews, *post*, I, 884, footnote) is any criterion, he ranked with the extremists within the Republican Party.

After declining appointment as consul at Shanghai in 1861, Partridge was appointed in September 1862 commissioner to the Exhibition of the Industries of All Nations to be held in London the next year. Shortly afterwards, Feb. 10, 1862, he received appointment as minister resident to Honduras. In spite of his failure to bring Honduras to ratify a treaty negotiated in 1860 and to prevent the outbreak of war between Salvador and Guatemala, his work in Honduras seems to have won the approval of Secretary Seward. He was commissioned minister resident to Salvador in April 1863, where he served until ill health caused his resignation in March 1866. Meanwhile, the Salvadorean government had been overthrown and a new régime recognized in due course by the United States.

After an interval of three years he was appointed Apr. 21, 1869, minister, not to the Argentine as he had wished, but to Venezuela. Here he was chiefly concerned with persuading Venezuela to meet the payments which had been awarded by a mixed claims commission. His handling of the claims question received the commendation of Secretary Hamilton Fish. After the death of one of his daughters he returned to Baltimore in the fall of 1870. Less than a year later, May 23, 1871, he was appointed minister at Rio de Janeiro, then known as Petropolis. Here he was called upon in his official capacity to act with the Italian minister as arbitrator of the claims of Lord Dundonald against the government of Brazil. The arbitrators' award (1873) of £38,675 to the British claimant was apparently more satisfactory to Brazil than to the British. Partridge returned to the United States in the summer of 1877. His last diplomatic mission was to Peru (appointed Apr. 12, 1882), which had recently faced both civil and foreign war. He was instructed to cooperate with Cornelius A. Logan [q.v.], minister to Chile, in bringing about a peace between Peru and Chile. Partridge seems to have exceeded his instructions in this matter and to have returned to the United States under a cloud. Ill health provided the ostensible reason for his resignation in 1883. His wife, Mary, daughter of Jacob Baltzell, whom he had married Oct. 21, 1847, had died seven years later, and he had lost both his children. These circumstances were perhaps responsible for his suicide at Alicante, Spain, early in 1884 (Baltimore *Sun,* Mar. 1, 1884).

[The account of Partridge's diplomatic career is based upon materials in the archives of the Department of State, especially upon the manuscript volumes of the department's instructions to the Central American States for 1858–65, to Brazil for 1862–75, to Peru for 1863–83, to Salvador for 1865–73, to Venezuela for 1866–76 and to Brazil for 1872–74, and upon the manuscript volumes of dispatches from Partridge to the Department. The department's records and letters relating to the appointment of Partridge contain considerable biographical information. Names of wife and mother were obtained from church records through the courtesy of Louis H. Dielman, librarian, Peabody Inst., Baltimore. See also S. F. Bemis, *The Am. Secretaries of State,* VIII (1928), 13f., for the mission to Peru; James Wingate, *The Md. Reg.,* 1857–60; M. P. Andrews, *Tercentenary Hist. of Md.* (1925); *Sun* (Baltimore), Feb. 26, 1884.]   E. W. S.

PARTRIDGE, RICHARD (Dec. 9, 1681–Mar. 6, 1759), merchant, colonial agent, the eldest child of William and Mary (Brown) Partridge, was born in Portsmouth, N. H. His father, a wealthy merchant and ship-builder, served as council member, treasurer of the province,

and as lieutenant-governor from 1697 to 1703. Quarrels with the representative of the proprietor led him to send his son, Richard, to plead his cause before the Board of Trade. The young man, twenty-one years old, made the voyage across the Atlantic in the summer of 1701 and was destined to marry and remain in England for the rest of his life. Gradually he built up a wide circle of acquaintances. By trade a merchant, by faith a Quaker, and brother-in-law of Jonathan Belcher, who was somewhat of a courtier, Partridge had friends in all walks of life. In 1715 he was appointed agent for Rhode Island, which important post he held for forty-four years. He was also employed at various times as agent for other colonies: for New York in 1731; for the Jerseys in 1733; for Massachusetts in 1737; for the Pennsylvania Assembly in 1740; and for Connecticut from 1750 to 1759. In the course of his work he acted as a clearing house of information for the colonial assemblies, conducted lengthy appeals to the Crown, fought detrimental imperial legislation, and kept in check as far as possible the plans of aggressive neighboring colonies.

For many years he was occupied with boundary controversies which arose from the network of conflicting grants in New England. As a result of his labors, which included formal petitions, hearings before the Board of Trade, and almost daily conferences with men of influence, he succeeded in getting established for Rhode Island boundaries which brought the fertile Narragansett Country and Narragansett Bay with its excellent harbor within her borders. Other controversies which engaged his attention were the Massachusetts-New Hampshire boundary, the Connecticut-Massachusetts line, and Connecticut's litigation over the claims of the Mohegan Indians. From 1730 to 1733 he played an active part in the struggle over the Molasses Act, which, though of much less importance, was not unlike that over the Stamp Act. By interviews, by hearings, and by floods of propaganda, both the West Indian merchants and the agents of the American colonies worked frantically to influence the votes of Parliament. When the Act was finally passed, Partridge was credited by his friends with having been responsible for softening some of the features objectionable to the northern colonies. In addition to his official business, he acted as representative for Governor Belcher, an arduous task because of that gentleman's highly irascible nature, and as Parliamentary agent for the London Meeting for Sufferings the purpose of which was to ameliorate the disabilities of the Quakers. In 1759, while engrossed in negotiations arising from the Seven Years' War, he died after a slight illness. His long and full life was occupied almost entirely with protecting the many-sided interests of American colonies in the mother country. On account of his birth and upbringing he understood thoroughly colonial ideals; on account of his long association with men of affairs he understood equally well English traits of character and English habits of thought. Shrewd, resourceful, and genial, he did much to facilitate colonial administration.

[Biographical material on Partridge is scarce. A brief sketch by Marguerite Appleton, "Richard Partridge— Colonial Agent," appears in the *New Eng. Quart.*, Apr. 1932. See also: Rufus M. Jones, assisted by Isaac Shartleff and Amelia Gummere, *The Quakers in the Am. Colonies* (London, 1911); *The Correspondence of Colonial Governors of R. I.* (2 vols., 1902–03), ed. by Gertrude S. Kimball, containing many of his letters to Rhode Island magistrates, and "The Wolcott Papers," *Conn. Hist. Soc. Colls.*, vol. XVI (1916), including some of his letters to Gov. Wolcott; *Gentleman's Mag.*, Mar. 1759.]   M. A.

PARTRIDGE, WILLIAM ORDWAY (Apr. 11, 1861–May 22, 1930), sculptor and writer, son of George Sidney Partridge, Jr., and Helen Derby (Catlin) Partridge, was of New England colonial ancestry but was born in Paris, France, where his father was at that time foreign representative of A. T. Stewart. The family returned to the United States and the boy studied at Cheshire Military Academy, then at Adelphi Academy, Brooklyn, N. Y., and in 1885 at Columbia College, New York. At the age of twenty-one he was sent abroad for three years and studied art in Florence, Rome, and Paris. When he returned he was interested chiefly in sculpture, but he was always versatile. In youth he appeared for a brief time on the New York stage, playing at Wallack's as Steerforth in *David Copperfield*. At one period, encouraged by Phillips Brooks and Edward Everett Hale, he gave public readings from Shelley and Keats. A studio portrait in his middle years shows him with brush and palette. His pen never rusted, and he published both prose and poetry.

In 1887 Partridge was married to Mrs. Augusta Merriam of Milton, Mass., and took her with him to Rome, where he worked with the Polish sculptor, Pio Welonski. After his return in 1889, his knowledge of art and his ability as a speaker were widely recognized. He gave lectures on esthetics in various places and carried on his work in sculpture in his well-equipped studio at Milton, Mass., and later in New York City. In 1892 he made a character study of an aged woman, a bust called "Nearing Home," now in the Corcoran Gallery, Washington, D.

C. The same year found him in London, immersed in Shakespearian lore, and making a bas-relief of Sir Henry Irving, shown at the Royal Academy Exhibition. His first large work was the standing bronze statue of Alexander Hamilton, erected in Brooklyn by the Hamilton Club in 1893. In this figure he sought to express the orator's passion, balanced by restraint. It won high praise from certain critics, notably William H. Goodyear, who in 1894 (*Renaissance and Modern Art*, pp. 264–66) printed an extravagant tribute but withdrew it from the 1908 edition of the work. Other statues are the seated bronze Shakespeare in Lincoln Park (1894), a work of refinement and dignity, without great force; the equestrian statue of General Grant, presented to the city by the Union League Club of Brooklyn in 1896; the Nathan Hale, St. Paul, Minn.; the Samuel Tilden, Riverside Drive, New York, 1926; the Horace Greeley, Chappaqua, N. Y.; and the Pocahontas, erected on Jamestown Island, Va., in 1921. His statues of Jefferson and of Hamilton, as well as his Schermerhorn Memorial, are at Columbia University. Of these works, the Gen. Grant is probably the most successful, both in characterization and in effect.

Partridge was no *animalier* and rightly supplemented his modeling from the living horse by studies of numerous anatomical casts. His modeling was always fluent. It had a certain impressionistic quality which at its best was vivid and poetic but at its worst was slipshod. In his last statue, the Lyon Gardiner for Saybrook, Conn., about to be erected at the time of his death, he apparently departed from methods which had been criticized as giving too sketchy results. His poetic sensitiveness is revealed in the Kauffmann Memorial, Rock Creek Cemetery, Washington (1897), an exedra with seated figure; in his memorial to Joseph Pulitzer, Woodlawn, N. Y., as well as in many religious sculptures, such as the marble Pietà in St. Patrick's Cathedral, New York; the elaborate baptismal font in the Cathedral of St. Peter and St. Paul, Washington; Christ and St. John, Brooklyn Museum; and heads of the Madonna and of Christ, two versions of each. The Metropolitan Museum has his well-known marble head called "Peace." Among his portrait busts are those of Chief Justice Fuller, United States Supreme Court; Dr. S. Weir Mitchell, Philadelphia, Robert Peary, Bowdoin College, Brunswick, Me., the poet Whittier, Boston Public Library. He modeled also a series of imaginative heads— Tennyson, Milton, Burns, Scott, Keats, Shelley, Bryon, Longfellow, Wagner, Beethoven, Carlyle, Velasquez, and Goya. His magazine articles on sculpture are sound and informative. His longer works include: *Art for America* (1894); *The Song-Life of a Sculptor* (1894); *Technique of Sculpture* (1895); *The Angel of Clay* (1900); and *The Czar's Gift* (1906). He was a member of many clubs and societies, was a frequent exhibitor both in the United States and abroad, and is represented in many collections. His second wife was Margaret R. Schott whom he married on June 14, 1905, in Venice. He spent his later years in New York City, where he died, survived by his widow and two children, one the daughter of his first wife.

[Lorado Taft, *Hist. of Am. Sculpture* (1904, 1924, 1930); Chas. E. Fairman, *Art and Artists of the Capitol* (1927); *New Eng. Mag.*, June 1900; *Internat. Studio*, May 1907; *Munsey's Mag.*, June 1898; *Cat. of the Works of Art Belonging to the City of N.Y.* (1909), vol. I; *The Works in Sculpture of Wm. Ordway Partridge* (1914); *Am. Art Annual*, 1930; *Who's Who in America*, 1928–29; *N.Y. Times*, May 24, 1930.]

A.A.

PARVIN, THEODORE SUTTON (Jan. 15, 1817–June 28, 1901), lawyer, university professor, librarian, was born at Cedarville, Cumberland County, N.J., the eldest of thirteen children. His mother, Lydia Harris, was of Scotch descent; his father was Josiah Parvin, of Scotch-Irish forbears. In 1829 the family moved to Cincinnati, Ohio. Theodore Parvin's formal education, begun at the hands of an elderly widow, was supplemented with independent and extensive reading. He attended the public schools of Cincinnati, and thereafter, with a scholarship from William Woodward, he was admitted to Woodward High School (later Woodward College) in 1831 and remained for two and a half years. In 1835 he was given a teaching position in the public schools of the city. In the same year he began to study law under the Hon. Timothy Walker, and in 1837 he graduated from the law school of Cincinnati College. He then read law in the office of Judge John C. Wright and on Apr. 14, 1838, was admitted to practise as attorney and counselor-at-law in the courts of Ohio. In August of that year he was granted a certificate to practise in the Territory of Iowa. His diary for Nov. 28, 1838, notes his admission to practise before the supreme court of the Territory. His first criminal case was tried on the day after his admission. Though his client was found guilty, Parvin succeeded in reducing the sentence from "ten years' imprisonment and $1,000 fine" to "seven days' imprisonment and $10 fine." In 1839, as district prosecutor for the second judicial district of the Territory, he took part in the first term of court in Johnson County, held in a one-story cabin, with the grand jury assembled upon the prairie. In October he accepted an appointment as United States district attorney. He was probate judge for three terms beginning in 1841, and clerk of the United States district court from 1847 to 1857. He had gone to Iowa in 1838 as private secretary to Gov. Robert Lucas and was soon thereafter appointed by the Governor territorial librarian, acting in that capacity until provision for the office was made by the legislative council. In 1840 he served as secretary of the legislative council, and in 1857 he became register of the state Land Office, serving for two years.

Early in his career Parvin urged the necessity of establishing an adequate system of common schools for Iowa. In 1841 he was offered the position of territorial superintendent of public instruction, which appointment, however, he declined. He was one of the organizers of the Iowa State Teachers' Association and its president in 1867. His connection with the State University of Iowa began at the time of its organization in 1854, when he was made a trustee. He resigned this position in 1859 to become "curator and librarian," which title he exchanged a year later for that of professor of natural history. Upon leaving the University in 1870 he devoted himself wholly to his duties as secretary of the Grand Lodge of Iowa Masons and Grand Recorder of the Grand Encampment Knights Templar of the United States. He instigated the building at Cedar Rapids of "the only great Masonic Library in the world." He was among the first curators of the State Historical Society of Iowa and from his collections he contributed to it as well as to other historical institutions. His meteorological records, the only accurate and available data of their kind in the region of the Territory of Iowa, led to the decision on the part of the federal government to establish the United States arsenal at Rock Island, Ill. His attendance at pioneer reunions and at the meetings of the Old Settlers' Association of Johnson County is indicative of the interest he took in history, especially in the pioneer history of Iowa. From 1864 to 1866 he was secretary of the State Historical Society of Iowa and editor of the *Annals of Iowa*, the first quarterly magazine of history in the United States devoted to state and local history. Parvin was married in 1843 to Agnes McCully. At his death he was survived by four children.

[Joseph E. Morcombe, *The Life and Labors of Theodore Sutton Parvin* (1906); "Old Woodward" (1884); *Iowa Hist. Record*, July 1901; *Annals of Iowa*, especially Apr. 1872 and Oct. 1901; manuscript collection relating to Parvin, State Hist. Soc. of Iowa; *Hist. of Johnson County, Iowa* (1883); John C. Parish, *Robert Lucas* (Iowa Biog. Ser., 1907.]

B.F.S.

PARVIN, THEOPHILUS (Jan. 9, 1829–Jan. 29, 1898), obstetrician and gynecologist, was born in Buenos Aires, Argentine, where his father, of the same name, was a Presbyterian missionary. His mother, Mary Rodney, was a daughter of Cæsar Augustus Rodney [*q.v.*]. The boy was sent to Philadelphia for education at an early age and, when eleven, entered the preparatory department of Lafayette College. In 1847 he graduated from Indiana University; during the next three years he taught in the high school of Lawrenceville, N. J., and also studied Hebrew in the Princeton Theological Seminary. In 1852 he finished the two years' medical course at the University of Pennsylvania and received his doctorate in medicine. For a time he was resident physician at the Wills Eye Hospital in Philadelphia. He then began independent practice in Indianapolis and in 1861 he was elected president of the Indiana Medical Society. Three years later he accepted the professorship in materia medica at the Medical College of Ohio, where he taught five years. In 1869 he became professor of obstetrics at Louisville University but, in 1872, transferred to a similar chair in the Indiana Medical College. In 1879 he was president of the American Medical Association and delivered the presidential address at the meeting in Atlanta, Ga. He returned to Philadelphia in 1883 as professor of obstetrics and gynecology at Jefferson Medical College and was with the institution until his death.

Parvin gained an international reputation as an authority on obstetrics. His knowledge of the science and literature of the subject was prodigious. As a practical obstetrician, however, he was without manual dexterity and had less experience as an operator than many of his contemporaries. His *Science and Art of Obstetrics* appeared in 1886, and the following year he edited *A Handbook of Diseases of Women*, translated under his supervision from the original work of von Winkel. He was coeditor of the *Cincinnati Journal of Medicine*, 1866–67; editor of the *Western Journal of Medicine*, 1867–69; and coeditor of the *American Practitioner*, 1869–83. At various times he served as president of the American Medical Journalists' Association, of the American Academy of Medicine, of the American Gynecological Society, and of the Philadelphia Obstetrical Society. He often spent his summer vacations in Europe and was appointed an honorary president of the obstetrical section of the International Medical Congress at Berlin (1890) and of the Periodic International Congress of Gynæcology and Obstetrics at Brussels (1892). Among other honors, he was a member of the American Philosophical Society, an honorary member of the Washington Obstetrical and Gynecological Society, and honorary fellow of the Edinburgh Obstetrical Society. He died in Philadelphia of cardiac asthma. His wife was Rachel Butler, of Hanover, Ind., whom he married in 1853 and by whom he had two sons and a daughter.

[W. H. Parish, "In Memoriam, Theophilus Parvin, M.D., LL.D.," *Trans. Am. Gynecol. Soc.*, vol. XXIV (1899); J. W. Holland, *The Jefferson Medic. Coll. of Phila., 1825–1908* (1909); *A Biog. Hist. of Eminent and Self-Made Men . . . of Ind.* (1880), vol. II; *Am. Jour. Obstetrics*, Oct. 1918; *Pub. Ledger* (Phila.), Jan. 31, 1898.]   H. B. B.

PASCALIS-OUVRIÈRE, FELIX (*c.* 1750–July 29, 1833), physician, was a native of the South of France. After receiving his degree of M.D. at Montpellier, he practised medicine among the French colonists in Santo Domingo for a number of years, until the slave insurrection in 1793, under Toussaint l'Ouverture, forced him to flee. With many other refugees, he embarked for Philadelphia, where he practised for the next seventeen years. He wrote much on medical subjects. In 1798 he signed his writing Pascalis-Ouvrière, but in 1801 and later called himself Felix Pascalis. He had had experience with yellow fever in the West Indies and was therefore qualified to write on that disease, of which there were several severe outbreaks in Philadelphia during his residence there. In 1796 he published *Medico-Chymical Dissertations on the Causes of the Epidemic Called Yellow Fever, and on the Best Antimonial Preparations for the Use of Medicine, by a Physician, Practitioner in Philadelphia,* and followed this in 1798 by *An Account of the Contagious Epidemic Yellow Fever, Which Prevailed in Philadelphia in the Summer and Autumn of 1797,* to which he signed his name. He was at this time a follower of Benjamin Rush in his belief in the domestic origin of the disease, but later, after a trip to Cadiz and Gibraltar in 1805 to study the diseases of hot climates, he changed his views and held that yellow fever was imported by fomites carried in ships. In 1801 he was vice-president of the Chemical Society of Philadelphia and delivered the annual oration. Two letters by him were published in the first volume (1805) of the *Philadelphia Medical Museum*: "Account of an Abscess of the Liver Terminating Favorably by Evacuation through the Lungs," describing a case in which he himself was the patient, and "On the Nature and Effects of Syphilitic Agonorrhoea."

About 1810 he left Philadelphia and moved to New York, where he lived until his death in

1833. He became a close associate of Dr. Samuel L. Mitchill [*q.v.*] and was one of his co-editors on the staff of the *Medical Repository* from 1813 to 1820. He was greatly interested in botany and was one of the founders and at one time president of the New York Branch of the Linnaean Society of Paris. Another subject which greatly absorbed him was the danger of urban burials; in 1823 he published a book entitled *An Exposition of the Dangers of Interment in Cities,* in which he advocated the construction at a distance from every large city of a "Polyandrum" or general cemetery, where all the dead of the city should be interred in hermetically sealed vaults. The grounds were to be surrounded by high stone walls with deep-laid foundations. As the Polyandrum would be situated at a considerable distance from the city, a series of stations, which Pascalis called "luctuaries," were to be built at suitable intervals to afford opportunities for the mourning cortège to rest. In his book he stated that a company was being organized to carry his ideas into effect.

[Letters (MSS.) in the Coll. of Phys. of Phila.; *Trans. Medic. Soc. of the State of N. Y.,* 1834–35; H. A. Kelly and W. L. Burrage, *Am. Medic. Biogs.* (1920).]   F. R. P.

PASCHAL, GEORGE WASHINGTON (Nov. 23, 1812–Feb. 16, 1878), jurist, author, journalist, was born at Skull Shoals, Greene County, Ga., the son of George Paschal and Agnes Brewer. His father was of French Huguenot descent. Though unsuccessful in business, he had an uncommonly good classical education. Agnes Paschal, a woman of the pioneer type, was a descendant of one of the earliest English families settling in North Carolina. She had a wide reputation in northern Georgia as a sick nurse and practical physician and lived to the age of ninety-four. Paschal was educated at home and in the state academy at Athens, where he earned his way by teaching in the preparatory course and by keeping the books of his landlord. He showed an early taste for the law and in 1832 passed an examination for admission to the bar before the superior court of Walker County. About this time a gold rush had begun in Lumpkin County, which together with the land lottery speculation arising from the seizure of the Cherokee lands, seemed to offer a bonanza to the young and briefless barrister. And so to Lumpkin he went to hang out his shingle. After the treaty of 1835 which was repudiated by the great bulk of the Cherokees, Paschal, who had joined a volunteer company of militia, was ordered to New Echota to serve as aide-de-camp under Gen. John E. Wool in the forcible removal of the Cherokees

to Indian Territory. It was on this expedition that he married Sarah, a full-blooded Cherokee, the daughter of Maj. John Ridge, one of the chiefs of the nation.

In 1837 Paschal emigrated to Arkansas and opened a law office, being later joined by his brother. His legal talents soon placed him at the top of his profession and at the age of thirty he was elected by the legislature a justice of the supreme court of Arkansas, for the term of eight years. It was the only office he ever held. A number of his opinions appear in 5 *Arkansas Reports* which are noteworthy for their conciseness, clarity, and learning. Within less than a year on the bench he resigned and returned to the bar of Van Buren, Benton County, just in time to take charge at a critical moment of the Cherokee claims against the United States. Through the efforts of Paschal and his associate counsel the treaty of amnesty of 1846 was adopted. In 1848 he took up his residence in Galveston, Tex., and shortly thereafter moved to Austin where he soon attained first rank at the Texas bar. He was an intense partisan at all times, believing with the faith of a zealot in the right and capacity of the people to govern themselves, but disunion was abhorrent to his conception of state rights. For several years just prior to the war he edited the semi-weekly *Southern Intelligencer,* at Austin, through which he fulminated brilliantly against the Know-Nothings, Free-Soilism, Black-Republicanism, and the abolition of slavery. The crisis of 1860 found him at the head of the Union party of Texas ardently supporting Douglas for the presidency. When the Union party was crushed in the avalanche of secession he retired to his home and devoted the years of the Civil War to writing. During this period, subjected though he was to ostracism and constant danger, he prepared for publication his *Digest of the Laws of Texas* (1866) and *The Constitution of the United States Defined and Carefully Annotated* (1868) both of which works, for their originality and exhaustiveness, added greatly to his fame. Both were republished and the work on the Constitution was translated into Spanish by Nicolás Antonio Calvo, the Argentine jurist.

Impoverished by the war and saddened by the loss of relatives and friends, he left for New York in 1866 to attempt to retrieve his fortunes. In 1869 he opened a law office with his son, George W. Paschal, Jr., in Washington, where his reputation as a jurist and political writer had already been firmly established. He became identified with the Republican party after the war, but in 1872 he supported Greeley for the presidency. He waged a steady fight in the press in favor of the adoption of the Fourteenth Amendment to the Constitution. During the last few years of his life he edited as reporter 28–31 *Texas Reports* and compiled *A Digest of Decisions Comprising Decisions of the Supreme Courts of Texas and of the United States upon Texas Law* (3 vols., 1872–75). The latter is a notable accomplishment in American jurisprudence by reason of the complexity of Texas law, with its fusion of the civil and the common law. During his remaining years in Washington Paschal also lectured at the law school of Georgetown University. In addition to his legal works he was the author of *Ninety-Four Years, Agnes Paschal* (1871), and many political pamphlets and magazine articles. He died in Washington and was buried in the Rock Creek Cemetery. Brilliant of mind and facile of pen, he used his talents to the advancement of his profession and his country. He was married three times. His second wife was Marcia Duval, by whom he had a daughter, Betty, who became well known in English political and literary life as Mrs. T. P. O'Connor. His third wife, a widow, Mrs. Mary Scoville Harper, was intellectually most congenial and helpful, often assisting him in his indexing and editing.

[J. H. Davenport, *The Hist. of the Supreme Court of the State of Tex.* (1917) ; J. S. Easby-Smith, *Georgetown Univ.* (1907), vol. II ; H. S. Foote, *The Bench and Bar of the South and Southwest* (1876) ; Fay Hempstead, *Hist. Rev. of Ark.* (1911), vol. I ; C. R. Wharton, ed., *Tex. under Many Flags* (1930), vol. II ; *In Memoriam, Hon. Geo. W. Paschal* (n.d.) ; Mrs. T. P. O'Connor, *I Myself* (1910) ; *Legal Gazette*, Feb. 9, 1872 ; *N. Y. Tribune, Washington Post*, Feb. 18, 1878.]   J. T. V.

PASCO, SAMUEL (June 28, 1834–Mar. 13, 1917), senator from Florida, was born in London, England, the son of John and Amelia (Nash) Pasco. In 1842 his parents emigrated to Prince Edward Island and in 1846 settled in Charlestown, Mass. He attended the public schools and then entered Harvard College, from which he received the A.B. degree in 1858. Early the next year he went to Jefferson County, Fla., to take charge of the newly organized academy at Waukeenah. Two years in Florida made him an ardent Southerner, and at the outbreak of the Civil War he enlisted as a private in Company H of the 3rd Florida Infantry. He rose to the rank of sergeant and, although his duties were largely of a clerical nature, saw heavy fighting. He was wounded and taken prisoner at the battle of Missionary Ridge. Released on parole after almost a year and a half of confinement in hospitals and at Camp Morton, Ind., he was a convalescent at his home in Florida at the end of the war.

The fifty years of his life after the Civil War were devoted almost entirely to politics, in which he proved himself an adroit leader of the Democratic party. After the resumption of his teaching at Waukeenah for a year, he served for two years as clerk of the circuit court of Jefferson County, until removed from office by the Carpetbag régime in 1868. He then entered the law office of his old regimental commander, W. S. Dilworth, with whom he shortly afterward formed a partnership. On Oct. 28, 1869, he was married to Jessie, the daughter of William Denham of Monticello. They had five children. He practised law at Monticello, the county seat of Jefferson County, until his election to the United States Senate in 1887. From 1872 to 1878 he was a member of the state Democratic committee, and as its chairman in 1876 he was influential in the compromise that restored home rule to Florida. He was a member of the Democratic national committee from 1880 to 1900 and was elector-at-large in 1880 and in 1908. He was president of the Florida constitutional convention in 1885, was elected a member of the state House of Representatives in 1886, and became speaker of the House when it was organized in 1887. He was an unsuccessful candidate for the Democratic nomination for governor in 1884. He served in the United States Senate from May 20, 1887, to Apr. 19, 1899. A fair estimate of his service in the Senate would seem to be that he was a useful senator but not a distinguished one. During his first term his most important committee assignments were those of claims and of public lands, to the latter of which he was appointed in 1891. With the beginning of his second term in 1893, when his party controlled the Senate, he became chairman of the committee on claims and the next year was appointed to a vacancy on military affairs. His work was chiefly of a routine and local character, and he spoke infrequently on the larger issues then agitating the nation. He was defeated for the nomination for a third term in 1899 but was appointed a member of the Isthmian canal commission, in which capacity he served until 1904. Throughout his life he spoke frequently on various subjects and published occasional pamphlets. He wrote the chapter on Florida in H. A. Herbert's *Why the Solid South?* (1890) and in 1910 wrote "Jefferson County, Fla.," which after his death was published in the *Florida Historical Society Quarterly* (Oct. 1928, Jan. 1929).

[*Harvard Class of 1858. First Triennial Report* (1861) ; *Report of the Class of 1858 of Harvard College . . . Fortieth Anniversary* (1898) ; *Who's Who in America*, 1916–17 ; Samuel Pasco, Jr., "Samuel Pasco," *Fla. Hist. Soc. Quart.*, Oct. 1928 ; *Soldiers of Fla. . . .*

Prepared and Published by the Board of State Institutions (n.d.) ; *N. Y. Times,* Mar. 14, 1917.]

R. S. C.

PASQUIN, ANTHONY [See WILLIAMS, JOHN, 1761–1818].

PASSAVANT, WILLIAM ALFRED (Oct. 9, 1821–June 3, 1894), Lutheran clergyman, editor, philanthropist, was born at Zelienople, Butler County, Pa., of Huguenot and German ancestry, the youngest of the five children of Philip Louis and Zelie (Basse) Passavant. His parents were natives of Frankfurt-am-Main. His grandfather, Detmar Basse, came to the United States in 1802 to retrieve his fortune, bought 10,000 acres of land in the Conoquenessing Valley, but returned to Germany in 1817. On "Bassenheim," his estate at Zelienople, the transplanted comforts and elegance of an older society continued to flourish amidst a primitive environment. Passavant owed much to the wisdom, culture, and unassuming piety of his mother, who drew the reins cautiously on his more rampant enthusiasms, supplied him with money when money was most needed, and taught him to rely on his own judgment and intuitions. After graduating in 1840 from Jefferson College at Canonsburg, he studied for two years under S. S. Schmucker at the Gettysburg Theological Seminary, was licensed by the Maryland Synod in 1842 and ordained in 1843, and was pastor 1842–43 of a small church at Canton, a waterfront suburb of Baltimore. While at Gettysburg he did much missionary work in the adjacent hill country and published a *Lutheran Almanac* for the years 1842 and 1843. He was on the staff of Benjamin Kurtz's *Lutheran Observer,* 1842–48. Early in his career he established friendships, destined to endure for life, with Charles Porterfield Krauth, John Gottlieb Morris, and Joseph Augustus Seiss. He began his ministry as a New Lutheran of Schmucker's school and was a successful practitioner of the revivalistic technique then in vogue, but under Krauth's influence he discarded his old beliefs and methods and became a champion of Old Lutheranism and one of the founders in 1867 of the conservative General Council of the Evangelical Lutheran Church in North America.

For the last fifty years of his life he lived in Pittsburgh and devoted his inexhaustible energies and enthusiasm to the home missionary movement and to the establishment of institutions of mercy. Until 1855 he was pastor of the first English Lutheran Church of Pittsburgh. Through his travels and his extensive correspondence he became the most widely known and influential clergyman of his denomination in the Middle West. Though his primary object was the work among English-speaking Lutherans, he early came in contact with German and Swedish Lutheran missionaries, gave them substantial aid and advice, and communicated to them his own sustaining faith in the work. In January 1848 he issued the first number of a monthly periodical, the *Missionary,* which he established both to strengthen the missionary movement and to counteract the tendencies of the *Lutheran Observer.* For several years it gave Charles Porterfield Krauth a medium for the propagation of his theology. In January 1856 Passavant enlarged the format of his paper and made it a weekly, and in 1861 it was incorporated with the *Lutheran* of Philadelphia. In 1881 he established another paper, the *Workman,* which he edited, in cooperation with his son, until his death. He was the dominant influence in the Pittsburgh Synod, which he helped to found in 1845.

His interest in Christian philanthropy, always strong, was greatly stimulated by his visit in 1846 to Theodor Fliedner's famous deaconess institute at Kaiserswerth. Two years later Passavant opened a small hospital in Pittsburgh, and in August 1849 Fliedner visited Pittsburgh, bringing with him four deaconesses, who thus introduced the order into the United States. Passavant and William Augustus Muhlenberg [*q.v.*] were friends, and it is likely that in establishing the American branch of the Lutheran order of deaconesses and the Episcopal Sisterhood of the Holy Communion they influenced each other. Subsequently Passavant founded hospitals in Milwaukee, Chicago, and Jacksonville, Ill., and orphan asylums at Rochester and Zelienople, Pa. He took an active part also in founding orphanages at Mt. Vernon, N. Y., Germantown, Pa., and Boston (West Roxbury), Mass. During the Civil War his deaconesses worked under the direction of Dorothea Dix in military hospitals. He may also be regarded as the founder of the Chicago Lutheran Theological Seminary and of Thiel College at Greenville, Pa., but neither of these institutions fulfilled his expectations. Though he was generous with his own money and successful in persuading others to give, his institutions all suffered from their restricted income, but his business acumen and personal devotion sustained them on their meager resources until they became permanently established. His own capacity for work was prodigious. He never employed a secretary, and those closest to him often found it difficult to relieve him of minor responsibilities that he insisted on shouldering alone.

On May 1, 1845, he married Eliza Walter, of Baltimore, who bore him five children and survived him. He died in Pittsburgh after a brief illness. The management of his institutions was carried on by his son, William Alfred Passavant, Jr., who outlived his father, however, by only seven years.

[*Workman*, Nov. 22, 1894 (memorial number); G. H. Gerberding, *Life and Letters of W. A. Passavant, D.D.* (Greenville, Pa., 1906); Zelie Jennings, *Some Account of Dettmar Basse and the Passavant Family* (privately printed, n.d.); G. H. Trabert, *English Lutheranism in the Northwest* (1914); G. M. Stephenson, *The Founding of the Augustana Synod, 1850–60* (1927) and *The Religious Aspects of Swedish Immigration* (1932).]

G. H. G.

PASTOR, ANTONIO (May 28, 1837–Aug. 26, 1908), theatre manager, actor, better known as Tony Pastor, was born in a house on Greenwich Street, New York. His father was a violinist in Mitchell's Opera House. His brothers, William and Frank, were acrobats and fancy riders in small circuses, and Tony himself spent his youth in the shadow of public performance. He began at the age of six singing comedy duets with Christian B. Woodruff, afterward state senator, at a temperance meeting at the old Dey Street Church, and was kept busy for two years thereafter singing at such meetings which were a highly popular form of diversion. In 1846 he made his first stage appearance at Barnum's Museum, singing in "blackface" to the accompaniment of a tambourine. In 1847 he joined Raymond & Waring's Menagerie, in a long tour, during which he learned to know at first hand many of the local types he afterward portrayed and in which he had a varied experience as clown, minstrel, ballad singer, low comedian, and general performer. At fifteen he was ringmaster of John J. Nathan's circus and subsequently he was with Mabie's circus as a singing clown. He opened his own Music Hall at 444 Broadway in the early sixties, singing comic songs with great success, and during the Civil War he developed a form of historical topical song, dealing chiefly with the events of the war, which made some one say of him that he "sang history into the theatre." In 1865 he went into partnership with Sam Sharpley, an old minstrel man, and opened at 201 Bowery, Tony Pastor's Opera House. Here he worked to perfect the form of entertainment later known as legitimate vaudeville. In 1875 he moved to 585 Broadway, a house of many names, best known as the Metropolitan Theatre. In 1881 he acquired the Fourteenth Street Theatre, neighbor to Tammany Hall, which became famous as Tony Pastor's and which he operated as a variety house until 1908.

Tony Pastor was not only a shrewd theatre manager and an actor of many talents, but a good producer and an idealist within his understanding of the theatre's ideals. His performances were intended to be "unexceptionable entertainment, where heads of families can bring their ladies and children," in distinct contrast to most of the music halls of the day. In spite of his own great popularity as a performer and as a song writer (he wrote over two thousand songs), he never absorbed the first place on his programs but was proud to develop other players and give them a leading chance. Many of the most important comedians and comic singers in American theatre history had their first, or their best, opportunity in Tony Pastor's theatre and under his direction. Among the names of those who were at some time in their career closely associated with him are: Nat Goodwin, Billy Emerson, Francis Wilson, Gus Williams, Denman Thompson, Weber and Fields, Lillian Russell, Evans and Hoey, Lettie Gilson, May and Flo Irwin, Maggie Cline, and Marie Lloyd. Pastor died in Elmhurst, L. I., at the age of seventy-one. Josephine Foley, his wife, whom he married in 1877, died Oct. 5, 1923. They had no children.

["Tony Pastor, the Father of Vaudeville," *Harper's Weekly*, Sept. 5, 1908; Montrose Moses, article in *Theatre Guild Mag.*, Apr. 1931; T. A. Brown, *Hist. of the Am. Stage* (n.d.) and *A Hist. of the N. Y. Stage* (3 vols., 1903); G. C. D. Odell, *Annals of the N. Y. Stage*, vol. VII (1931); *Who's Who on the Stage*, 1908; *N. Y. Dramatic Mirror*, July 27, 1895; *N. Y. Times*, Aug. 27, 1908.]

E. J. R. I.

PASTORIUS, FRANCIS DANIEL (Sept. 26, 1651–*c*. Jan. 1, 1720), lawyer, author, founder of Germantown, Pa., was born in Germany at Sommerhausen, Franconia, the only child of Melchior Adam Pastorius by his first wife, Magdalena Dietz. The Pastorius family was of Westphalian origin, their surname having been originally Scepers (Low German for Schäfer), and for several generations had been prosperous, cultured, and well connected. Pastorius' father (1624–1702) was himself a man of distinction. Educated at the University of Würzburg and the German College at Rome, he embraced the Lutheran faith in 1649, spent ten years as legal counselor to Count Georg Friedrich von Limpurg at Sommerhausen, and later rose to be burgomaster of the Imperial City of Windsheim. He was a prolific writer both in German and Latin, much of his work remaining unpublished. Profound religious feeling elevates some of his verse above the dead level of mere *Gelehrtenpoesie*. Common tastes and aspirations as well as family affection made the relations of father and son unusually sympathetic.

Frantz attended the Windsheim Gymnasium, then under the rectorship of the Hungarian humanist, Tobias Schumberg, and matriculated July 31, 1668, at the University of Altdorf as a student of law and philosophy. He studied also at the universities of Strassburg, Basel, and Jena; was present at the sessions of the Imperial Diet at Regensburg in 1674–75; and returned to Altdorf to take the degree of J.D. under the celebrated jurist, Heinrich Linck, in 1676. He began the practice of law at Windsheim, but at the instigation of his friend, Dr. Johann Heinrich Horbe, a brother-in-law of Philipp Jacob Spener, he removed in 1679 to Frankfurt-am-Main, where he was at once received into Spener's circle and became intimate also with some friends of William Penn. From June 1680 till November 1682 he traveled, as tutor to a young nobleman, in Holland, England, France, Switzerland, and Upper Germany. Religion had, by this time, become his preoccupation; he was dissatisfied with his profession and apprehensive for the future of European society, and was thinking of Pennsylvania as a refuge from the world. In April 1683 a group of Frankfurt Quakers who proposed to buy land in Penn's domain appointed him their agent, and Pastorius set out for America by way of Rotterdam and London. Crossing the Atlantic on the same ship with Thomas Lloyd [q.v.], he arrived at Philadelphia Aug. 20, 1683; completed negotiation with Penn for some 15,000 acres; and in October laid out the settlement of Germantown.

Until his death thirty-six years later Pastorius was the chief citizen of the town. He was the first mayor (bailiff) and served continuously as mayor, clerk, or keeper of records until 1707, when Germantown lost its charter. He was the agent of the Frankfort Land Company until 1700, being succeeded by Johann Jawert and Daniel Falckner [q.v.]. He was a member of the provincial Assembly in 1687 and 1691. He was in constant demand as a scrivener, taught in the Friends' school at Philadelphia from 1698 to 1700, and was master of a school in Germantown from 1702 till shortly before his death. He allied himself from the beginning with the Quakers, but his Quakerism retained more than a tinge of Lutheranism. In 1688 a protest against the practice of keeping slaves, signed by Pastorius, Garret Hendericks, Dirck Op den Graeff, and Abraham Op den Graeff, was sent to the Monthly Meeting of Friends at Lower Dublin. It was the first protest of the kind ever made in the English colonies, but it had no effect. The Friends at Lower Dublin forwarded it to the Quarterly Meeting at Philadelphia, the Quarterly Meeting at Philadelphia forwarded it to the Yearly Meet-

ing at Burlington, and the Yearly Meeting at Burlington quietly suppressed it. On Nov. 6, 1688, Pastorius married Ennecke Klostermanns (1658–1723) of Mülheim-am-Ruhr, by whom he had two sons. Despite his many activities he led an almost idyllic life, with abundant leisure for his garden, his bees, and his study. His published writings consist of only six books or pamphlets, but he was a diligent writer and left to his descendants an immense quantity of manuscript works. The largest and most famous is his "Beehive," a commonplace-book of encyclopedic proportions and scope. Of the published works the most important was the *Umständige Geographische Beschreibung Der zu Allerletzt erfundenen Provintz Pensylvaniæ* (Frankfurt and Leipzig, 1700). *Four Boasting Disputers of This World Briefly Rebuked* (New York, William Bradford, 1697) was aimed chiefly at Heinrich Bernhard Köster and was Pastorius' contribution to the Keithian controversy; *A New Primmer or Methodical Directions to Attain the True Spelling, Reading & Writing of English* (New York, William Bradford, n.d.) is probably the first schoolbook written in Pennsylvania. Pastorius read and wrote seven languages, owned a considerable library, and was one of the most learned men in the English colonies, his knowledge including not only law and theology but science, medicine, agriculture, and history. He wrote verse in German and Latin, like his father, and also in English. The best of his German verse is direct, sincere, and melodious. He died sometime between Dec. 26, 1719, and Jan. 13, 1720.

[M. D. Learned, *The Life of Francis Daniel Pastorius* (in *Ger.-Am. Annals*, vols. IX–X, 1907–08; sep. pub., 1908) is the fullest biog.; but two earlier treatments are still useful: Oswald Seidensticker, *Die Erste Deutsche Einwanderung in Amerika und die Gründung von Germantown im Jahre 1683* (in *Der Deutsche Pionier*, Cincinnati, July 1870–May 1871; sep. pub., 1883; in *Bilder aus der Deutsch-pennsylvanischen Geschichte*, 1885); and S. W. Pennypacker, *The Settlement of Germantown* (in *Proc. Pa.-Ger. Soc.*, vol. IX, 1899, and sep. pub., 1899). The *Umständige Geographische Beschreibung* is translated, with an introduction by J. F. Jameson, in *Narratives of Early Pa., West N. J., and Del.* (1912), ed. by A. C. Myers; M. D. Learned published extracts from the "Beehive" in *Americana Germanica*, vols. I–II (1897–98). See also Oswald Seidensticker, *The First Century of German Printing in America, 1728–1830* (1893) for his manuscripts and published works.]　　　G. H. G.

PATCH, SAM (c. 1807–Nov. 13, 1829), famous for his spectacular diving feats, was born in Rhode Island, followed the sea for a few years, and then became a cotton-spinner in the Hamilton Mills at Paterson, N. J. There he was the mainstay of his widowed mother and was looked upon as a good workman and likable young man. In the fall of 1827 he announced that he was going to jump into the Passaic River from the

Chasm Bridge, which was then building. The police interfered, but on the day the span was dropped into place Sam appeared on an adjacent precipice, made a short speech—Mr. Crane, the bridge engineer, had done a great feat, and he, Sam Patch, was about to do another—and jumped seventy-five feet into the stream. Later he jumped from the bridge.

Warmed by the notoriety, he then went from town to town diving from cliffs, bridges, and masts. People flocked to witness his performances and contributed satisfactorily when the hat was passed. On his wanderings he picked up a fox and a small bear, and on some of his dives the bear was his forlorn companion. He was generally taciturn but when in his cups would parrot his two apothegms, "There's no mistake in Sam Patch" and "Some things can be done as well as others." To most observers he seemed to be a good-natured automaton. By the time he reached Buffalo in October 1829 and dived into the Niagara River from a shelving rock on Goat Island he was a national celebrity. Returning to Rochester, N. Y., where he had established temporary headquarters, he advertised that "being determined to 'astonish the natives' of the west before he returns to the Jarseys," he would jump 125 feet from a scaffold erected on the brink of the Genesee Falls. For this feat he prepared carefully, taking soundings of the pool below the falls and even making a practice dive without accident. On the scheduled day, Friday, Nov. 13, all western New York lined the banks of the Genesee, and excursionists came by schooner from Oswego and Canada. Sam made his speech and jumped, but in mid-air the arrow-like dive became a fall; he struck the water sidewise and disappeared. For months the newspapers were filled with stories of his last dive and rumors of his reappearance. On Mar. 17, 1830, his body was found broken and frozen in a cake of ice at the mouth of the river and was buried at Charlotte. His mother came to weep at the grave, was kindly received, and provided with transportation home. Sam Patch himself passed into the speech and folklore of the nation. For years Danforth Marble [q.v.] played the title rôle in two Yankee comedies, *Sam Patch* and *Sam Patch in France*. Of various dare-devil jumpers who have carried on the tradition the best remembered is Steve Brody.

[The best account is in J. M. Parker, *Rochester* (1884); typical newspaper stories and advertisements appear in *Mass. Spy* (Worcester), Oct. 17, 1827, Nov. 18, 25, 1829; *Buffalo Republican*, Oct. 24, Nov. 21, 1829; *N. Y. Evening Post for the Country*, Nov. 20, Dec. 1, 1829; *Rochester Daily Advertiser and Telegraph*, Oct. 30, Nov. 2, 12, 1829. For the Sam Patch plays see: Falconbridge (J. F. Kelly), *Dan Marble; A*

Biog. Sketch (1851) and G. C. D. Odell, *Annals of the N. Y. Stage*, vols. IV–VII (1928–31); for literary allusions, Robt. C. Sands, "A Monody made on the late Mr. Samuel Patch," *Writings*, vol. II (1835); Nathaniel Hawthorne, "Rochester" (Autograph ed., 1900, vol. XVII); W. D. Howells, *Their Wedding Journey* (1872).]

G. H. G.

PATERSON, JOHN (1744–July 19, 1808), Revolutionary soldier, public official, was born in Newington Parish, Wethersfield, Conn. (now New Britain), the son of Col. John Paterson and his wife, Ruth Bird, and a grandson of James Paterson who emigrated from Scotland to New England some time prior to 1704. John Paterson's taste for military life was doubtless derived from his father who served in the provincial forces during King George's War and the French and Indian War. He graduated from Yale College in 1762, and after teaching school in New Britain for several seasons began the practice of law. On June 2, 1766, he married Elizabeth Lee of Farmington. In 1774, in company with his family and his wife's father, he moved to Lenox, Mass. His gifts for leadership were at once recognized. He was a member of the Berkshire county convention in July 1774 at which the "Solemn League and Covenant" was adopted, whereby the people promised to refrain from consumption of English goods; and he represented Lenox in the first and second provincial congresses in 1774 and 1775.

In the meantime he was engaged in raising a regiment from the middle and southern parts of the county in anticipation of hostilities with England. When the news of the battles of Lexington and Concord arrived, he marched at once to Cambridge, his men being armed and almost completely uniformed. He was commissioned colonel on May 27, 1775, and his regiment, after being reorganized and enlarged, presently became the 15th Continental Infantry. He built and garrisoned Fort No. 3, near Prospect Hill, and during the battle of Bunker Hill protected the American forces from attack in the rear. During the siege of Boston his men had several brushes with the enemy and were complimented by Washington for their alacrity in meeting the foe. In March 1776 he accompanied the army to New York. He was presently ordered to the relief of the American troops in Canada, and after participating in the battle of "The Cedars," retreated by way of Crown Point to Ticonderoga where for a time he was engaged in fortifying Mount Independence. He rejoined Washington's army on the Delaware and participated in the battles of Trenton and Princeton. On Feb. 21, 1777, he was commissioned brigadier-general and in that capacity took part in the operations which resulted in the capture of Burgoyne. He came near to losing his life when his horse was shot under him by a cannon ball. He wintered at Valley Forge, 1777–78, and was engaged in the operations culminating in the battle of Monmouth. Thereafter till the end of the war he was stationed for the most part in the highlands of the Hudson, commanding West Point at various times, and during these years he formed a close friendship with Kościuszko. He was a member of the court martial appointed to try Major André. On Sept. 30, 1783, he was brevetted major-general, and shortly afterwards retired from the army.

Resuming the practice of law at Lenox, he was elected to various civil offices, including those of moderator, selectman, collector of taxes, member of the school board, and representative in the general court. He helped to organize the Society of the Cincinnati and the Ohio Company. As commander of the Berkshire militia, he assisted in the suppression of Shays's rebellion. He had in the meantime become one of the proprietors of the "Boston Purchase," comprising 230,400 acres in Broome and Tioga counties, New York. In 1791 he emigrated with his family to Broome County. Here, as in Lenox, his talent for public service was soon acknowledged. Besides being chosen to several town offices, he was elected to represent his district in the state legislature (1792–93), in the constitutional convention of 1801, and in Congress (1803–05). In 1798 he was appointed to the bench and served as judge of Broome and Tioga counties. He died at Lisle, N. Y.

Paterson was a man of commanding presence, being over six feet tall and of athletic build. When a county judge, he would often walk eighteen miles to court rather than go to the pasture and catch a horse to ride. His success in both military and civil life was due to the confidence which his probity, ability, and good judgment everywhere inspired.

[*Centennial Celebration at Lenox, Mass.* (1876); E. A. Werner, *Civil List and Constitutional Hist. of N. Y.* (1884); *Hist. of Berkshire County, Mass.* (2 vols., 1885); D. N. Camp, *Hist. of New Britain* (1889); *Mass. Soldiers and Sailors of the Rev. War* (16 vols., 1896–1907); Thomas Egleston, *The Life of John Paterson* (1898); F. B. Heitman, *Hist. Reg. of the Officers of the Continental Army* (1914); *N. Y. Geneal. and Biog. Record,* July 1890; F. B. Dexter, *Biog. Sketches Grads. Yale Coll.,* vol. II (1896); *Biog. Dir. Am. Cong.* (1928).]   E. E. C.

PATERSON, WILLIAM (Dec. 24, 1745– Sept. 9, 1806), jurist, was born in County Antrim, Ireland, the son of Richard and Mary Paterson. The family emigrated to America, landing at New Castle on the Delaware in October 1747.

The father spent some time in travel—perhaps as a peddler of tinware made by his uncles in Berlin, Conn.—before settling in Princeton, N. J., where he engaged in the manufacture of tin plate and general merchandising from May 1750 until his removal to Raritan (now Somerville) in 1779. The family fortunes were augmented through real-estate transactions, and William was enabled to enter the College of New Jersey, where he graduated with the Class of 1763. He began the study of law in the office of Richard Stockton [q.v.] in the following year. In 1766 he received the degree of master of arts from his college, delivering an oration on "Patriotism" at the annual commencement. With others he founded the "Well-Meaning Society," 1765–68, which in 1769 was revived as the Cliosophic Society, one of the literary societies still active at Princeton. Although he passed the bar examinations in 1768, Paterson could not be admitted to practice until February 1769 because of the absence of Governor Franklin from the colony. He began the practice of law at New Bromley, Hunterdon County, but in 1772 returned to Princeton. His view of the life of the time and place is recorded in *Glimpses of Colonial Society and the Life at Princeton College, 1766–1773, by One of the Class of 1763* (1903), edited by W. J. Mills. Within a short time he removed to South Branch in Somerset County but later (1779) purchased a farm on the north bank of the Raritan River. His residence was generally described as "the Raritan," a name bestowed upon the entire region lying immediately west of New Brunswick.

On May 11, 1775, he attended the New Jersey Provincial Congress as a deputy from Somerset County; he was reëlected the following year and was chosen successively assistant secretary and secretary. In 1776 also he was a member of the convention that formed the state constitution. In the same year he was chosen attorney general and in 1776 and 1777 was a member of the legislative council of the state of New Jersey. He was an officer in the Somerset County battalion of minute men and a member of the council of safety in 1777. While attorney general his work required him to attend the criminal courts in the counties, although to do so he had to make long journeys on horseback. "It unavoidably occupies the far greater part of my time," he wrote, declining to serve in the Continental Congress after he had been elected in 1780; "I feel its weight, and have more than once been ready to sink under it" (*Somerset County Historical Quarterly,* July 1912, p. 176). He continued to act as attorney general of New Jersey until 1783, when he resigned to resume the practice of law. At this time he removed to New Brunswick. Meanwhile, he married, Feb. 9, 1779, Cornelia Bell, daughter of John Bell, at Union Farm, Hunterdon County. Three children were born to them. Four days after the birth of the youngest, in November 1783, Mrs. Paterson died. Two years later Paterson married Euphemia White, daughter of Anthony White, in whose house at Union Farm his first marriage had taken place.

Public service again claimed his attention when he was chosen a delegate to the Federal Convention at Philadelphia in May 1787. When the debates on the "Virginia Plan" reached the question of representation, Paterson objected to the preponderance of the large states in the proposed government. "The idea of a national Govt. as contradistinguished from a federal one, never entered into the mind of any of them," he declared, "and to the public mind we must accommodate ourselves. We have no power to go beyond the federal scheme, and if we had the people are not ripe for any other" (Farrand, *post*, I, 178). Pointing to the disadvantages which a scheme of representation on the basis of population gave to the small states, he took the leadership, June 15, 1787, in introducing the "New Jersey Plan," which proposed a federal government consisting of legislature, executive, and judiciary. But the federal legislature, unicameral, was to represent states, and not individuals, and the states were to vote equally, without regard to wealth or population. The result was the compromise whereby the states secured an equal representation in the Senate while the members of the House of Representatives were to be apportioned according to population.

Paterson not only signed the completed Constitution but also advocated its adoption in New Jersey. At the inauguration of the new government he was chosen senator from New Jersey and arrived at New York on Mar. 19, 1789, to await the coming of Washington. He served on the committee to count the returns of the presidential election and was placed on the judiciary committee of the Senate. In the original copy of the Judiciary Act of 1789, the first nine sections are in the handwriting of Paterson and the bulk of the remainder in the hand of Oliver Ellsworth [*q.v.*]. Paterson did not remain long in the Senate. Upon the death of Gov. William Livingston [*q.v.*] in 1790 he was chosen by the New Jersey legislature to succeed him, and became governor and chancellor of the state. In 1792 he was authorized to collect and reduce to proper form all the statutes of England which before the Revolution were in force in the colony

of New Jersey, together with all the public acts before and subsequent to the Revolution which remained in force. For his work in preparing the *Laws of the State of New Jersey* (1800), he received the sum of $2,500. He also remodeled the rules of practice and procedure in the common law and chancery courts, drafting what are known as "Paterson's Practice Laws," adopted by act of the legislature in 1799. About 1790 plans were laid for the founding of an industrial town at the falls of the Passaic, and to that end in 1791 the Society for Establishing Useful Manufactures was chartered. In the supplement to the charter the town is referred to as "Paterson."

In 1793 Paterson was appointed associate justice of the United States Supreme Court and thereafter was absent from home the greater part of the year "riding the circuits." A number of his opinions are contained in the report of Dallas and Cranch. He presided over the trials of several of the individuals indicted for treason in the Whiskey Rebellion (Francis Wharton, *State Trials of the United States*, 1849, pp. 102–84), and notably over that of Matthew Lyon [*q.v.*], accused of violation of the Sedition Law of 1798 (*Ibid.*, pp. 333–44). His last appearance in court was in New York, in the summer of 1806, at the trial of Samuel G. Ogden and William S. Smith for violation of the federal neutrality laws, in giving aid to the South American patriot Miranda (Thomas Lloyd, *The Trials of William Smith and Samuel G. Ogden*, 1807). Paterson's health had begun to decline, and he determined to go to Ballston Springs, N. Y., in September 1806, to seek a cure, but stopped at Albany en route and died there in the home of his daughter Cornelia, second wife of Stephen van Rensselaer [*q.v.*]. He was buried in the vault of the Manor House, at Albany. During the time of the Federal Convention, Paterson's colleague William Pierce wrote of him (Farrand, III, 90) : "M. Patterson [sic] is one of those kind of Men whose powers break in upon you, and create wonder and astonishment. He is a Man of great modesty, with looks that bespeak talents of no great extent, but he is a Classic, a Lawyer, and an Orator,—and of a disposition so favorable to his advancement that every one seemed ready to exalt him with their praises."

[A few Paterson MSS. are in the Lib. of Cong. ; there are copies of some among the Bancroft papers at N. Y. Pub. Lib. ; some have been printed in *Somerset County Hist. Quart.*, Jan., Oct. 1913, Jan., Apr. 1914, in *Am. Hist. Rev.*, Jan. 1904, and in Max Farrand, *The Records of the Federal Convention of 1787* (3 vols., 1911). For biographical material see Gertrude S. Wood, *William Paterson of N. J., 1745–1806* (1933), Ph.D. thesis, Columbia Univ. ; F. R. North, *Life of William Paterson* (1930), first pub. in *Paterson Morning Call*; *Somerset County Hist. Quart.*, July, Oct. 1912 ; *N. Y. Geneal. and*

Biog. Record, Apr. 1892; Joseph Clark, A Sermon on the Death of the Hon. Wm. Paterson (1806). See also H. L. Carson, The Supreme Court of the U. S. (1891); L. Q. C. Elmer, The Constitution and Govt. of the Province and State of N. J. (1872); American Citizen (New York), Sept. 15, 1806.]   W. S. C.

PATILLO, HENRY (1726–1801), Presbyterian clergyman, was born in Scotland. At the age of nine, accompanied by an elder brother, he emigrated to Virginia and found employment as a merchant's clerk. Soon, however, he began to devote himself to teaching and study. Experiencing conversion, he felt called to the ministry, and in 1751 put himself under the instruction of Rev. Samuel Davies [q.v.], who was then at Hanover, Va. On Sept. 28, 1757, he was licensed to preach by the Presbytery of ·Hanover, and on July 12, 1758, he was ordained at Cumberland. Three years earlier he had married Mary Anderson.· Until October 1762 he was in charge of the churches of Willis Creek, Byrd, and Buck Island, and for two years or more, beginning May 1763, he supplied the churches of Cumberland, Harris Creek, and Deep Creek.

In October 1765 he removed to North Carolina, serving first, 1764 to 1774, at Hawkfields, Eno, and Little River, and later as pastor of the congregations at Nutbush and Grassy Creek, made up largely of emigrants from Virginia, who gave him 300 acres of land on condition that he would remain with them for the rest of his life. He was one of the early members of the Orange Presbytery and when the Synod of the Carolinas was organized, acted as presiding officer. He was a good classical scholar—Hampden-Sidney College conferred the degree of A.M. upon him in 1787—and engaged in teaching along with his pastoral duties. He also made the religious guidance of the negroes one of his special concerns. In political as well as ecclesiastical affairs he took a prominent part. When, in 1768, Governor Tryon's forces were called upon to put down the "Regulators" who were causing disorder in the state, Patillo and Rev. George Micklejohn, rector of St. Matthew's Church, Hillsboro, were appointed to preach to the troops. They also joined in a pastoral letter, having as its text the first two verses of the thirteenth chapter of Romans. Patillo was a delegate to the provincial congress of North Carolina in 1775, and when the congress resolved itself into a committee of the whole to consider joining the confederation of united colonies, was unanimously chosen chairman.

He is described by one in whose father's home he was a frequent visitor as "of large frame and considerably more than ordinary flesh . . . his features were rather large and coarse, though his face easily lighted up with a smile of good-will. . . . It seemed natural for him to say droll things; and he would frequently keep a whole company convulsed, apparently without being conscious he was doing it" (Anne E. Rice, in Sprague, post, p. 198). He was, however, an eminently devout man. As a preacher he spoke with a loud voice and much earnestness, the attention of his audience being held by the original matter of his discourse. In 1788 he published Sermons . . . I. On the Divisions among Christians: II. On the Necessity of Regeneration to Future Happiness: III. The Scripture Doctrine of Election: IV. Extract of a Letter from Mr. Whitefield to Mr. Wesley: V. An Address to the Deists. He was also the author of A Geographical Catechism . . . (1796), reprinted in 1909 with a biographical sketch. He died in Dinwiddie County, Va., while on a missionary journey.

[The Colonial Records of N. C., vols. V (1887), VIII (1890), X (1890); S. A. Ashe, Hist. of N. C. (1908); J. W. Moore, Hist. of N. C. (1880); A. J. Morrison, Coll. of Hampden Sidney Dict. of Biog. (n.d.); W. B. Sprague, Annals of the Am. Pulpit, vol. III (1859); Richard Webster, A Hist. of the Presbyt. Church (1857); Alfred Nevin, Encyc. of the Presbyt. Church in the U. S. A. (1884).]   C. L. W.

PATON, LEWIS BAYLES (June 27, 1864–Jan. 24, 1932), Old Testament scholar, and archaeologist, was born in New York City, the son of Robert Leighton Stuart and Henrietta (Bayles) Paton. He was graduated from the University of the City of New York (now New York University) in 1884, ranking high in his class. For one year he was teacher in a boys' school, and for nearly two years traveled widely in Europe, studying German, French, and Italian. From 1887 to 1890 he was a student at Princeton Theological Seminary, winning at his graduation a fellowship in Old Testament. Five semesters were then spent at the University of Berlin. In 1892 he became a member of the faculty of Hartford Theological Seminary, where he remained for the rest of his life, being instructor one year, associate professor seven years, and from 1900 on, professor of Old Testament exegesis and criticism. During the earlier part of his teaching career he completed a thesis, published under the title The Original Form of the Holiness-Code (1897), for which he received the degree of doctor of philosophy from the University of Marburg. On Apr. 13, 1890, he was ordained by the Presbytery of Morris and Orange, but transferred to the Congregational Church in 1892. He was married three times: first, in 1896, to Suvia Davison of Hartford, who died in 1904; second, in 1915, to Mrs.

Loraine Seymour (Brown) Calhoun of Hartford, who died in 1924; and third, in 1925, to Katharine Hazeltine of Vassar College.

Paton's paternal ancestors were Scotch Covenanters, while on his mother's side he was descended from English Puritans and early Dutch settlers. In view of this ancestry, it is not surprising, he once wrote, that he was temperamentally a modernist. Despite his conservative instruction at Princeton, he became convinced of the truth of the critical view of the Old Testament before graduation, largely as a result of preparing a thesis on "The Historical Character of the Book of Chronicles." While many institutions in America suffered grievously from the controversies which raged over the Old Testament, Hartford escaped; for although Paton was frank and straightforward in expressing his critical opinions, his thoroughly Christian spirit and attitude were evident to all. It was characteristic of him that when asked to contribute to a series called "Modern Sermons by World Scholars," he should write upon Jesus Christ rather than upon some Old Testament theme.

The chief characteristics of Paton's work as teacher and writer were his keenly logical mind, his determination to get at all the facts and to arrange his treatment in the most orderly fashion. His class-room lectures, as well as nis more public utterances and his writings, were marvels of comprehensiveness and lucidity. Students and fellow scholars alike saw in his work an object lesson of scholarly method. He served as director of the American School at Jerusalem in 1903–04, and thereafter kept in close touch with all the new discoveries which bore even remotely upon his work, making much use of this material in his teaching and writing. For many years he was connected with the *American Journal of Archaeology* in an editorial capacity. Much of his literary work appeared in scholarly periodicals and in encyclopedias. He dealt with the background of Hebrew life and religion in many articles contributed to James Hastings' *Encyclopaedia of Religion and Ethics* (1908–26), notably in those entitled "Baal" and "Canaanites." In the *New Standard Bible Dictionary* (2nd ed., 1926) his most important articles were "Excavation and Exploration," "Social Development of Israel," and "Jerusalem." He also published numerous articles in the *Journal of Biblical Literature* and *American Journal of Theology*. His books include *The Early History of Syria and Palestine* (1901); *Jerusalem in Bible Times* (1908); *A Critical and Exegetical Commentary on the Book of Esther* (1908) in the International Critical Commentary Series; *The Early Religion*

of Israel (1910); *Spiritism and Cult of the Dead in Antiquity* (1921); and he was the editor of *Recent Christian Progress* (1909).

[Unpublished autobiog. in possession of family; biog. sketch appended to doctor's thesis, Marburg 1897; *Who's Who in America*, 1930–31; memorial addresses in *Hartford Sem. Bull.*, May–June, 1932; *N. Y. Times*, Jan. 25, 1932.]					E. C. L.

PATRICK, MARSENA RUDOLPH (Mar. 11, 1811–July 27, 1888), soldier and agriculturist, was born near Watertown, in Jefferson County, N. Y., of Scotch-Irish and English colonial and revolutionary stock, the tenth and youngest child of John and Miriam (White) Patrick. His father's family, originally Kil Patrick, had dropped the prefix soon after reaching New England early in the eighteenth century. Running away from home, where his mother's excessive Puritanism dominated, Patrick became a driver on the Erie Canal, taught school, and in 1831 was studying medicine. Entering West Point the same year, as the protégé of Gen. Stephen van Rensselaer [q.v.], he graduated in 1835, forty-eighth in a class of fifty-one, and was brevetted second lieutenant of infantry. In 1836, while stationed at Fort Mackinac, he married Mary Madeline McGulpin, niece of an agent employed in the Astor fur trade. The Seminole War, staff duty, General Wool's Mexican expedition, and military routine occupied his life from 1837 to 1850, when (though a captain and brevet major) he resigned and engaged in scientific agriculture at Geneva, N. Y.

In 1859 he became president of the New York State Agricultural College, at Ovid. An antecedent of Cornell University, the institution was chartered in 1853, and the cornerstone of its first building was laid in 1859. The following year, with one wing of the building completed and with a faculty of five, the college opened. At the outbreak of the Civil War, Patrick resigned. Preferring service with volunteers, he declined reappointment in the regular army but was persuaded by Governor Morgan to become inspector general of New York volunteers in May 1861. In March 1862, at McClellan's request, he was commissioned brigadier-general of volunteers. As a part of King's Division, McDowell's Corps (recalled to protect Washington), Patrick's brigade saw no service on the Peninsula but participated in the second Manassas and Antietam campaigns, during which the volunteers learned the value of his stern discipline. His tactical skill was recognized by officers of both armies but, to his regret, staff duty again took him from the line, his capacity for great combat leadership untested. With the Army of the Potomac disorganized by battle and change of leaders, McClellan, in October 1862, appointed him provost marshal-general. Although charged with a host of duties—from maintaining order to securing military information—he was conscientious, vigorous, and capable. Successive commanders in turn found him almost indispensable. In 1864 Grant designated him provost marshal-general of all the armies operating against Richmond, and on Mar. 13, 1865, he was brevetted major-general of volunteers for "faithful and meritorious service," a tardy recognition. The rank and file respected and loved him; the Sanitary and Christian Commissions found him a faithful supporter; while the Southern citizenry counted him a friend albeit a conquering invader. Following Appomattox, he commanded the district of Henrico (including Richmond), but in June 1865 Grant suggested to Halleck that Patrick be relieved lest his kindheartedness "interfere with the proper government of the city." Relieved shortly afterward, at his own request, he resigned from the army, June 12, 1865, and went home.

Disgust for Republican policies now led him momentarily into politics as the unsuccessful Democratic candidate for state treasurer. A few years later, as president of the New York State Agricultural Society (1867–68), he pioneered for conservation and reforestation; to check the migration from country to city, he advocated a cottage system for farm workers. His last years, following his wife's death in 1880, were spent in Ohio as governor of the Central Branch, National Home for Disabled Volunteer Soldiers, Dayton. Ever the disciplinarian, he was denounced as a tyrant but, swayed neither by politics nor expediency, gradually gained the respect and love of veterans and townspeople alike. Of commanding presence, with patriarchal beard and thunderous voice, a self-disciplined Presbyterian fearing God only, he had the air of an Old Testament prophet with a dash of the Pharisee.

[Copy of Gen. Patrick's private journal, 1862–65, together with fragments for other years and genealogical and biographical notes by his son, I. N. Patrick, in the writer's possession; G. W. Cullum, *Biog. Reg. Officers and Grads., U. S. Mil. Acad.* (1891); Diedrich Willers, *The N. Y. State Agricultural Coll., at Ovid* (1907); J. H. Mills, *Chronicles of the Twenty-first Regiment, N. Y. State Volunteers* (1887); W. P. Maxson, *Campfires of the Twenty-third* (1863); Lemuel Moss, *Annals of the U. S. Christian Commission* (1868); C. W. Bardeen, *A Little Fifer's War Diary* (1910); D. B. Parker, *A Chautauqua Boy in '61 and Afterward* (1912); M. R. Patrick, *Address Delivered at the Ann. Meeting of the N. Y. State Agricultural Soc.*, Albany, Feb. 12, 1868 (1868); *Twentieth Ann. Reunion, Asso. Grads. U. S. Mil. Acad.* (1889); *N. Y. Times*, July 28, 1888.]   T. S. C.

PATTEN, JAMES A. (May 8, 1852–Dec. 8, 1928), grain merchant, capitalist, and philanthropist, a first cousin of Simon Nelson Patten [*q.v.*], was born on a farm at Freeland Corners, De Kalb County, Ill. He had no middle name, but used the initial "A" for purpose of euphony. His father, Alexander Robertson Patten, a descendant of William Patten who emigrated to the United States in 1794, was one of a group of hardy Scotch-Irish Presbyterians who moved from Washington County, N. Y., to Illinois in the 1840's; his mother, Agnes (Beveridge), belonged to this same pioneer community, having come to Illinois in 1842, at the age of thirteen, with her father. Abandoning farming, Alexander Patten took charge of a general store at Sandwich, Ill., which he ran successfully until his death in 1863. His widow, left to care for a family of five boys of whom James was the eldest, shortly removed to her father's farm. Here James lived until he was seventeen. During the next two years he attended the preparatory department of Northwestern University at Evanston.

Returning to Sandwich, he worked for a time as clerk in the country store which had been his father's, and then spent a year on the farm of an uncle, John L. Beveridge, at that time governor of Illinois. In 1874 he received an appointment as clerk in the state grain inspection department at Chicago. Here he remained until 1878, when, not wanting to continue longer as a political office holder, he went to work for G. P. Comstock & Company, Chicago grain brokers. He speedily won the confidence of his employers by his ability and his probity, but within two years the firm failed. Patten now went into the cash grain business for himself, taking as partners his brother George and Hiram J. Coon. Soon, however, he joined with his brother in establishing the firm of Patten Brothers. The association of the two in the grain commission business remained unbroken until George Patten's death in 1910. In 1903 both brothers became members of the firm of Bartlett, Frazier & Carrington, grain brokers, later Bartlett, Patten & Company.

As a member of the Chicago board of trade Patten became widely known. He joined the board in 1882, was elected a director in 1897, president in 1918, and remained a member until his death. His early experience as a cash grain dealer laid the foundation of his success as a speculator in the grain futures market. On several occasions, notably in 1908 and 1909, he succeeded in anticipating crop conditions in corn, oats, and wheat so surely that he held virtual "corners" in all three grains successively. Later he was successful in cornering the cotton market. In connection with this venture he and three others were indicted in 1912 by the federal government for conspiracy. Patten elected to pay a fine of $4,000, but the other three fought the case and were acquitted. He always maintained that he did not speculate and that his "corners" were not responsible for unusual increases in the price of grain. He never took a position in the market without first having made a thorough study of supply and demand conditions. In addition to his other responsibilities, he was a director of the Continental and Commercial National Bank, the Chicago Title & Trust Company, Chicago, Rock Island & Pacific Railway, Peoples Gas, and Commonwealth Edison companies.

Patten had a keen sense of the responsibility that goes with wealth. Impressed by the fact that both his father and his brother had died prematurely because of tuberculosis, he gave $500,000 to promote the work of the Tuberculosis Institute and founded the Chicago Fresh Air Hospital. He made numerous gifts to small colleges in the middle West, was a generous benefactor of Northwestern University at Evanston, where he made his home, and provided that half of his estate, estimated at fifteen million, should go to charitable institutions upon the death of his widow. He was a Republican and took a keen interest in local and national politics. From 1901 to 1903 he was mayor of Evanston. Always clean-living and essentially religious, he enjoyed a reputation for integrity and good citizenship in his business and social life. His sound judgment, courage, and common sense made him one of the most capable and successful speculators of his time. On Apr. 9, 1885, he married Amanda Buchanan of Chicago; three children were born to them.

[J. M. Patten and Andrew Graham, *Hist. of the Somonauk United Presbyt. Church Near Sandwich, De Kalb County, Ill., with Ancestral Lives of the Early Members* (Chicago, 1928); J. A. Patten and Boyden Sparkes, "In the Wheat Pit," *Saturday Evening Post*, Sept. 3, 17, Oct. 1, 15, Nov. 5, 19, 1927; *Chicago Sunday Tribune*, Dec. 9, 1928; *Chicago Daily News*, Dec. 9, 1928; *Who's Who in Chicago*, 1926; *Who's Who in America*, 1928–29.]   E. A. D.

PATTEN, SIMON NELSON (May 1, 1852–July 24, 1922), economist, was of English and Scotch-Irish stock, the son of William and Elizabeth Nelson (Pratt) Patten, a first cousin of James A. Patten [q.v.], and a descendant of William and Martha (Nesbitt) Patten, who came to Argyle, Washington County, N. Y., in June 1794, from Stonebridge, County Monaghan, Ireland. Two years after their marriage, Simon's parents settled on a homestead in what is now Sandwich township, De Kalb County, Ill., and here the boy was born. The father was an elder in the United Presbyterian church, twice a member of the Illi-

nois legislature, and during the Civil War was captain in the 156th Illinois Volunteers. When four years old, Simon had typhoid fever; his mother contracted the disease and died. Soon afterwards his father married Jane Somes, who was an excellent step-mother.

The boy grew up on the Illinois prairie farm, which in the decades of the fifties and sixties typified in itself the bounteousness of nature when directed by man's intelligence. In his teens he had a ruminative turn of mind which detracted from his father's satisfaction in him as a farm hand. Those who knew Patten best, most of them years later, after he had been transplanted to Philadelphia, have been unanimous in attributing much of the optimism which marked his mature thought to his boyish observations of bursting nature. As will appear later, this view omits other and very different influences which helped direct his mind. He passed through the district school; grew rapidly, being six feet, two inches tall by the time he was fourteen; and at seventeen, as preliminary preparation for the law, he entered the nearby Jennings Seminary at Aurora. Here he formed a lasting friendship with Joseph French Johnson [q.v.], whose social gifts he (an awkward and ungainly countryman) admired and envied. He graduated in the spring of 1874 and spent the next year on the farm, during which time his desire to study the law receded.

In the autumn of 1875 he entered Northwestern University as a freshman, but his heart was not in his work here, and within a few months, drawn by Johnson's letters telling of study in Germany, he followed his friend to the University of Halle. Besides Johnson, he was in intimate association at Halle with Edmund J. James [q.v.] and, most important, with Professor Johannes Conrad (1839–1915), the national economist, statistician, and official counselor who had so large a hand in bringing Germany to industrial maturity. Patten was impressed by the economy of the German people quite as much as by anything he learned in the university. With natural resources far less ample in proportion to population than those of the United States, superior intelligence was employed in their use. Instead of exploitation, there was conservation. Power machinery was a major reliance. Consumption was nicely articulated with production. The mature society of Germany found delight in social amenities, whereas the younger American population derived less pleasure from its wasteful consumption of material things. These lessons were afterwards to be reflected in Patten's teaching and writing, particularly in his emphasis upon the theory of consumption. He received the degree of Ph.D. at Halle in 1878 and came home by way of England.

His American friends at Halle, on returning to America, realized the expectations which their education raised, but only disappointment and dejection awaited Patten. He could find nothing to turn his hand to except the plow, and this he did for a year, to his disparagement in the eyes of his father. It was concluded finally that he must make another try at the law; in the fall of 1879 he went to Chicago for study, but in a few weeks developed eye trouble which compelled his withdrawal, and for the next two and a half years he was inactive, misunderstood, and miserable. Successful treatment by an eye specialist while he was visiting his friend James in Philadelphia gave him renewed interest in life. He cheerfully undertook to teach the same little district school where he had learned his own letters; the next year he received a better position at Homewood, Ill., and in 1888 was superintendent of schools at Rhodes, Iowa. During these years he had been working on a manuscript which, shorn of its worst crudities by his friends Johnson and James, was published in 1885 as *The Premises of Political Economy*. This was a correction of the work of John Stuart Mill in the light of American conditions, with added dissent from the efficacy of *laissez-faire* to discover and promote social interest.

The book secured Patten's appointment as professor of political economy in the University of Pennsylvania in 1888. His work in Philadelphia may be considered under the heads of his effect upon institutions, his teaching, and his writing. In all three capacities he was teleological; to his farthest speculations he sought to give issue in social betterment. He gave form and spirit to the Wharton School of Commerce and Finance, which was the first effort to supply business training in an academic institution. He invigorated and dignified "social work" not only locally but throughout the country. He was no organizer in the accepted sense, and hated administrative detail. He was a singularly gifted teacher, his informal method being peculiarly his own. At once imaginative and profound, he omitted many steps of conventional reasoning, and pounced upon the problems which invited exploration and answer. He revealed most of himself in small groups where a serious discussion excited his interest. His students were so attached to him by admiration and personal loyalty that the designation "Patten men" has come to be perfectly understood. Each of them captured and perpetuated in himself a measure of his teacher's spirit to a degree quite extraordinary in American

scholarship. Scott Nearing has said that "students went from his classes as from a refreshing bath" (*post*, p. 16), and that "one standard was set up in these classes—the public welfare" (*Ibid.*, p. 17). Patten wrote with difficulty, though he published a considerable amount in the aggregate. He was an economic optimist. He sought to banish the gloomy forebodings which had been inherited from the English classical writers. In his eyes, it was not nature which was limited in its capacities, but man who was wasteful and bungling. Thus the necessity of resort to poorer and poorer soils, which was an axiom of the Ricardian school, seemed to Patten a fallacy growing out of a wrong emphasis. If the land were intelligently cultivated, if consumption habits were so altered as to set up demand for a great variety of food products, landlords would not be enriched at the expense of capitalists and laborers. The very increase of population which had been viewed as the prime cause of rent, might give rise to new techniques and new standards of consumption which would counteract the crude tendency toward diminishing returns. Abandoning the older view of an unchanging man under differing environments, and not satisfied with the conception, brought forward by the psychological school, of a changing man in an unchanging environment, he preferred to think of "a solid economics, where the problems of a changing man can be treated in connection with changes in the physical world in which the man lives and through which he is conditioned." His thought equations were filled with variables. He showed how the pessimism of the English classical school sprang from an exploitative economic environment, and in contrast set forth the limitless social improvement which must follow economic conservation. This economic conservation involved the releasing of normal human impulses, the notable raising of the standard of living, and so the increase of man's power over nature. He was fond of showing that society had passed from the older deficit economy into the newer surplus economy, or from a pain economy to a pleasure economy. He thought that the saving which was dictated by the former condition of insufficiency should be replaced by spending in an era of growing abundance. Generous and wise consumption, he believed, would do more to reduce economic inequalities than would a more direct redistribution of wealth. At the same time, he was alive to the advantages of cooperative economic action as opposed to competitive practice.

Patten's mind was mainly deductive. His use of observed fact was often unsystematic, and generally for the purpose of illustration rather than of induction. His thinking process was a compound of gropings and brilliant flashes of recognition. He was apt to be either very inconclusive, or to arrive at an accurate and original judgment as by a stroke of genius. He raised many more economic queries than he ever attempted to solve. The writings of Henry C. Carey [q.v.] and others of the "Philadelphia school" were at least of equal influence on his thought with his farm background and his observation of German economy. Carey—nationalist, protectionist, optimist, revolter from the classical tradition—had been dead only a decade when Patten came to Philadelphia; the similarity of Patten's beliefs to those of Carey and of George Friedrich List [q.v.], not only in favor of protection, but generally, is obvious. Patten's writing in the field of political economy as such may be said to have closed in 1899 with *The Development of English Thought.* Thereafter his interests expanded, and his speculations showed infusions of sociology, psychology, anthropology, and biology. Of his works in this later period, *The New Basis of Civilization* (1907) has had widest reading. His attempts at verse (for example, *Folk Love,* 1919) and a novel (*Mud Hollow,* 1922, partly autobiographical) were revealing but unsuccessful. After his death a number of his papers were collected and published under the title *Essays in Economic Theory* (1924), edited by R. G. Tugwell.

Patten has not been adequately appraised. One may hazard the guess that time will say he was most of all an appealing and stimulating personality. His books are not a satisfactory record of the man. Except here and there in eloquent passages, they do not reveal the secret of his power, which was communicated rather in personal contacts. He was one of the distinguished company of young Americans who came back in the seventies and eighties after study in Germany. The field of economic teaching, investigation, and application in America invited development and organization. Patten with his friend James proposed a "society for the Study of National Economy," which could "combat the widespread view that our economic problems will solve themselves, and that our laws and institutions, which at present favour individual instead of collective action, can promote the best utilization of our national resources, and secure to each individual the highest development of all his faculties." This project gave way before the less declarative American Economic Association, which, however, owed much in its inception to Patten's influence, and of which, two decades later (1908-09), he was president.

Craving society, Patten utterly lacked social graces, and lived much to himself. He looked not unlike Lincoln; he was even more angular, to the last he retained his country accent, and his clothes were always ill-fitting. When he was fifty-one, Sept. 2, 1903, he married, at Canton, N. Y., Charlotte Kimball, much younger than himself, and six years later they were divorced. In 1917, precisely at the entrance of the United States into the World War, Patten was notified by the University of Pennsylvania that he would be retired on account of having reached the age-limit. He claimed that the real reason was to be found in his liberal views, as just then illustrated in pacifist advocacy. He died five years later at Brown's-Mills-in-the-Pines, N. J., after two paralytic strokes, his last days being marked by extraordinary fortitude.

[Scott Nearing, *Educational Frontiers. A Book About Simon Nelson Patten and Other Teachers* (1925); R. G. Tugwell, "Notes on the Life and Work of Simon Nelson Patten," in *Jour. of Pol. Economy,* Apr. 1923; "Memorial Addresses on the Life and Services of Simon N. Patten," in *Annals Am. Acad. of Pol. and Social Sci.,* May 1923, Supplement, containing a full Patten bibliog.; "Memorial to Former President Simon N. Patten," in *Am. Econ. Rev.,* Mar. 1923, Supplement; J. M. Patten and Andrew Graham, *Hist. of the Somonauk United Presbyt. Church near Sandwich, De Kalb County, Ill.* (privately printed, Chicago, 1928); *Public Ledger* (Phila.), Apr. 6, 1917; *Ibid.,* July 25, 1922; *Phila. Record,* July 25, 1922; Ugo Rabbeno, *The Am. Commercial Policy* (2nd ed., 1895), pp. 384–411; H. R. Seager, "Professor Patten's Theory of Prosperity," in *Annals of the Am. Acad. of Pol. and Social Sci.,* Mar. 1902; introduction by Seager to S. N. Patten, *Essays in Economic Theory* (1924), ed. by R. G. Tugwell; R. H. I. Palgrave, *Dict. of Pol. Economy,* ed. by Henry Higgs, vol. III (1923); *Who's Who in America,* 1922-23.]
B. M.

PATTEN, WILLIAM (Mar. 15, 1861–Oct. 27, 1932), zoölogist and paleontologist, was born at Watertown, Mass., the youngest but one of the fourteen children of Thomas and Mary Low (Bradley) Patten. His father was a harness-maker, in whose shop the son worked with little satisfaction to himself. He acquired however a keen interest in birds and aspired to become, like Audubon, an artist-naturalist. Entering Lawrence Scientific School of Harvard University, he paid his own way, in part by taxidermy and by illustrating scientific books. As a freshman he won the Walker prize of the Boston Society of Natural History by a paper, "Myology and Osteology of the Cat," based on work done for the most part before he had entered college. Under Professor Edward L. Mark he studied zoölogy, specializing in insect embryology; he was also an enthusiastic disciple of the geologist Nathaniel S. Shaler. In 1883 he received the degree of B.S. and a Parker traveling fellowship. After a year with Professor Rudolf Leuckart at the University of Leipzig he received the degree of Ph.D. in 1884. He spent the next two years at the zoölogical stations at Trieste and at Naples, then returned to America and for three years was assistant to Dr. C. O. Whitman at the Allis Lake Laboratory at Milwaukee. He was professor of biology at the University of North Dakota for four years (1889–93) before his appointment to the faculty of Dartmouth College, where for twenty-five years he taught comparative anatomy, embryology, and a course centering about organic evolution. He also organized (1920–21) an orientation course for freshmen, called "Evolution," of which he was director until his retirement in June 1931.

Patten's earlier papers (1884–89) on the embryology of caddice flies and of the limpet (*Patella*) were followed by others upon the eyes of molluscs and arthropods, illustrated by drawings since widely copied by textbook writers. From this earlier research he developed a theory of color vision. His paper "On the origin of Vertebrates from the Arachnids" (*Quarterly Journal of Microscopical Science,* August 1890) was followed by a series of brilliant studies (1893–1900) on the anatomy and embryology of the king-crab (*Limulus*), which with scorpions and other arachnids he regarded as closely related to a group of primitive fossil vertebrates (Ostracoderms) about which he published several papers (1902–03). He elaborated the theory further in a book, *The Evolution of the Vertebrates and their Kin* (1912). In 1914 his attention was directed to social philosophy by the idea that harmonious cooperation is necessary for evolutionary progress; this became the theme of *The Grand Strategy of Evolution; the Social Philosophy of a Biologist* (1920).

In search of fossil fishes (Ostracoderms), Patten spent seven summers between 1902 and 1914 in field work in northern New Brunswick, Newfoundland, and Labrador. For scorpions and similar arachnids he traveled to Java, New Guinea, Australia, and Japan (1912), to Costa Rica and Cuba (1921). After reconnoitering for fossil fishes in Sweden, Norway, and Spitzbergen (1925), he made three expeditions to the Island of Oesel, Esthonia (1928, 1930, 1932), where he supervised the excavation of large collections of Ostracoderms. His native talent for drawing and plastic art gave distinction to all his illustrations. His research was always stimulated by his vigorous imagination and his vision of ideal links between great branches of the animal kingdom. Proceeding not by slow processes of induction toward a theory lightly held, he was animated by his theory and pursued it indefatigably. He was skilful at technique, and a keen observer of structural details. The need of harmonious co-operative action in nature and human affairs was to him not a tradition but a new discovery. He was very sociable, an interesting comrade, fond of outdoor and indoor sports, vigorous, robust, and perennially young. He died at seventy-one, the victim of coronary thrombosis. He married on June 28, 1883, Mary Elizabeth Merrill of Bradford, Mass. Their son Bradley Merrill Patten survived him.

[*Who's Who in America,* 1930–31; *Science,* Nov. 25, 1932; T. W. Baldwin, *Patten Geneal.* (1908); *N. Y. Times,* Oct. 28, 1932; data from the Alumni Record Office, Dartmouth Coll.; information as to certain facts from Mrs. William Patten.]   J. H. G.

PATTERSON, DANIEL TODD (Mar. 6, 1786–Aug. 25, 1839), naval officer, was born on Long Island, N. Y., the son of John Patterson, former collector of customs at Philadelphia, and Catharine (Livingston) Patterson, great-granddaughter of Robert Livingston [*q.v.*]. On June 11, 1799, he joined the sloop *Delaware* as acting midshipman and sailed in her on two West Indian cruises during the naval war with France. He was warranted midshipman in August 1800, after his first cruise, and was one of the 159 midshipmen out of 352 retained in the peace establishment of May 1801. He carried on nautical studies till December. Until March 1803 he was in the *Constellation* of the second squadron sent against Tripoli. In May following he sailed again for the Mediterranean in the *Philadelphia* and was a prisoner for more than nineteen months after she was stranded and captured by the Tripolitans on Oct. 31, 1803. Under the excellent tutelage of Capt. William Bainbridge and Lieut. David Porter [*qq.v.*], he was, however, enabled "to profit by the seeming misfortune" (manuscript memoir of his services, November 1813, in Navy Department Library). Upon his return he was stationed at New Orleans from January 1806 to June 1807. He was married in 1807 to George Ann Pollock, the daughter of George Pollock of New Orleans. They had two sons, Carlile Pollock and Thomas Harman [*q.v.*], and three daughters, one of whom, George Ann, was married in 1839 to David D. Porter [*q.v.*].

In March 1808, after a visit to the North, and promotion to the rank of lieutenant, he returned to New Orleans where his friend Porter was in charge. From January 1810 to February 1811 he had a semi-independent command of twelve gunboats, that operated from a base at Natchez and transported most of the troops for the occupation of Baton Rouge in 1810. He was made master commandant on July 24, 1813, and from December following commanded the New Orleans station. Against the Gulf buccaneers his most effective stroke was delivered on Sept. 16,

1814, when, raiding the base of the pirate Jean Laffite [*q.v.*] at Barataria Bay, La., with the schooner *Carolina* and six light gun vessels, he captured six schooners and other small craft. Although it was supported by twenty guns mounted on shore, Laffite's band, about 1,000 strong, fled without resistance, much to Patterson's disappointment (C. F. Goodrich, "Our Navy and the West Indian Pirates," *Naval Institute Proceedings,* Sept.–Oct., 1916, p. 1471). He foresaw clearly the designs of the British against New Orleans in 1814 and indicated the best lines of defense. On Sept. 2, 1814, he refused Jackson's request to send his naval forces to Mobile, and maintained his position at New Orleans where the delay he caused the enemy by the gunboat action on Lake Borgne on Dec. 15 greatly facilitated Jackson's final victory. He was aboard the *Carolina* during her very effective two-hour bombardment of the British camp on the evening of Dec. 23, shouting at the first discharge, "Give them this for the honor of America" (*Niles' National Register,* Sept. 28, 1839, p. 71). The *Carolina* was destroyed by enemy fire on Dec. 27, but with his remaining vessel, the *Louisiana,* he continued to render valuable artillery service, and in the battle of Jan. 8 he commanded a battery of naval guns on the west bank of the river. These had to be spiked and abandoned on the retreat of Morgan's militia but were repaired and ready for action next day. His excellent cooperation throughout the campaign has perhaps not been fully recognized, though he was highly commended by Jackson, received a vote of thanks from Congress, and was made captain on Feb. 28, 1815. Patterson is described at this time as a "stout, compact, gallant-bearing man . . . his manner . . . slightly marked by hauteur" (J. Parton, *Life of Andrew Jackson,* 1860, vol. II, p. 28).

A welcome change from the isolated southern station came finally in 1824 when he was appointed fleet captain and commander of the flagship *Constitution* in Commodore Rodgers' Mediterranean Squadron. Upon his return in 1828, partly no doubt as a warm friend and supporter of Jackson, he was given the important office of one of the three navy commissioners. Afterward he commanded the Mediterranean Squadron from 1832 to 1836. In negotiations to enforce claims against Naples for commercial injuries during the Napoleonic wars, his squadron gave effective support by entering the harbor at Naples one ship after another, until all six were assembled. His death occurred at the Washington navy yard, of which he was commandant, 1836–39, and he was buried in the Congressional Cemetery.

[Master Commandants' Letters, 1813, and Captains' Letters, 1814–24, in Navy Dept. Lib.; E. N. McClellan, "The Navy at the Battle of New Orleans," *U. S. Naval Inst. Proc.,* Dec. 1924; *Daily National Intelligencer,* Jan. 30, Feb. 3, 22, 23, Mar. 6, Dec. 2, 1815, Aug. 26, Sept. 23, 1839; E. B. Livingston, *The Livingstons of Livingston Manor* (1910); information from family sources.]

A.W.

PATTERSON, JAMES KENNEDY (Mar. 26, 1833–Aug. 15, 1922), educator, was the first child of Andrew and Janet (Kennedy) Patterson, of Glasgow, Scotland. The father was a calico printer of limited earnings. At the age of four Patterson injured his left knee in such a way as to be lame ever after, a circumstance which doubtless influenced his later choice of career. In 1842 the family emigrated to America, settling eventually in Madison County, Ind. There as a result of his mother's contrivances he received enough preliminary education to enable him to teach a district school. Realizing that a degree was indispensable to advancement, he matriculated at Hanover College in 1851. He was obliged to interrupt his studies and teach again, but he returned to Hanover College and graduated as valedictorian in 1856. In the same year he became principal of the Presbyterian Academy in Greenville, Ky.; in 1859, principal of the preparatory department of Stewart College, Clarksville, Tenn. The closing of the college following the attack upon Fort Sumter left him and his wife, Lucelia W. Wing, whom he had married Dec. 25, 1859, without income, a situation improved by his election as principal of Transylvania Academy in Lexington, Ky., which managed to keep open throughout the conflict. When Kentucky University was organized under John Bryan Bowman [*q.v.*] in 1865 Patterson was made professor of Latin, history, and metaphysics, and in 1869 he became president of the Agricultural and Mechanical College of Kentucky which had been established in 1865 as an adjunct of the University.

After a visit to England, Scotland, and France in 1875 he returned to find the affairs of the university so discordant as to make inevitable a separation of the units representing respectively denominational and state interests. After the division Patterson remained in control of the fortunes of the Agricultural and Mechanical College, an institution left by the separation without buildings or a site for them, with an annual income of only $9,900, and with a faculty of but five members. Vigorously setting about organization he succeeded in having the campus established in Lexington and in having the legislature vote a yearly appropriation toward its support. This move, however, united most of the other colleges of Kentucky in opposition to the State

College and in a bitter campaign against the principle of a state-supported institution. To add to the seriousness of the situation the building funds gave out before the completion of the projected dormitories and classrooms. In this crisis Patterson contributed his greatest services to the cause of education in Kentucky. He addressed the General Assembly and a legislative committee in behalf of state aid to higher education and pleaded his case so effectively as to win a full triumph for the College and the law intended to support it. To meet the financial emergency he hypothecated enough of his own securities to assure the continuance of the building program. From that time, despite the fact that Patterson had a predilection for cultural schooling, the evolution of the State College into the University of Kentucky was steady. After forty years as head of the institution he retired, Jan. 15, 1910, upon conditions which revealed his almost possessive interest in the university; the partial nullification of these conditions gave rise to quarrels which darkened his closing years. By his will he left to the University a sum of money to found a school for the training of American diplomats.

[Sources include: Mabel H. Pollitt, *A Biog. of Jas. Kennedy Patterson* (1925); a typewritten biography by W. B. Smith (1925) in the library of the Univ. of Ky.; *Memorial Exercises and Addresses in Honor of Jas. Kennedy Patterson* (1924); the *Courier-Jour.* (Louisville), Aug. 16, 1922; information as to certain facts from friends and relatives of Patterson.] G. C. K.

PATTERSON, JAMES WILLIS (July 2, 1823–May 4, 1893), educator, politician, the second child of William and Frances (Shepard) Patterson, was born at Henniker, N. H. His boyhood was spent for the most part in hard work on his father's farm and in the mills at Lowell, Mass., where the family resided for several years. About 1838 he completed his early schooling, which had been somewhat meager, at the local academy in Henniker. After two years' employment in Lowell, and four years as a teacher, he was able to complete his preparation for college. He graduated from Dartmouth in 1848 with high honors. Planning a legal career, he served as principal of Woodstock Academy in Connecticut (1848–51), studying law in the meantime. For a time he considered the ministry as a career and spent a year in the study of theology at New Haven, but he had already made a reputation as a successful teacher, and in 1852 he received and accepted the offer of a tutorship at Dartmouth. In 1854 he was appointed professor of mathematics and on Dec. 24 of the same year married Sarah Parker Wilder of Laconia,

N. H. Five years later he was appointed professor of astronomy and meteorology and held this chair until 1865.

From 1858 to 1862 Patterson was school commissioner of Grafton County. In the latter year he served a term in the New Hampshire legislature and in 1863 he was elected, a Republican, to the national House of Representatives. His House service covered the years 1863–67 and in 1866 he was elected to the United States Senate. Throughout his ten years in Washington he was especially interested in the District of Columbia for which he drafted several education laws, emancipation having created many new problems. As chairman of the joint select committee on retrenchment he submitted notable reports on the consular service (*Senate Report 154,* 40 Cong., 2 Sess.) and on the excessive costs and abuses in the collection of customs revenue (*Senate Report 380,* 41 Cong., 3 Sess.). His career in Washington closed under a cloud created by the Crédit Mobilier scandal, but historians have been puzzled to understand why he was recommended for expulsion when no drastic action was taken in the cases of other more serious offenders. That his conduct had been indiscreet is unquestionable; and his apparent attempt to conceal relevant facts created a bad impression; but many believed the truth of his own statement that he had supposed the stock purchased for him was Union Pacific rather than Crédit Mobilier. His term ended within a few days after the Senate investigating committee had submitted a report recommending his expulsion, and without opportunity for discussion on the floor, a fact which led many to believe that he had been unjustly dealt with. His defense subsequently published, and reprinted in a public document (*Senate Report 519,* 42 Cong., 3 Sess.), is somewhat naïve but strengthens the impression that he was innocent of corrupt motives.

He had been defeated for renomination in 1872 and spent the years following his retirement in Hanover. He traveled extensively and was in frequent demand as a public speaker and lecturer. He again represented Hanover in the legislature for two terms, 1877–78. From 1881 to 1893 he was state superintendent of public instruction. He was largely instrumental in securing the passage of the Act of 1885 substituting the town for the local district as the unit of public-school organization. He resigned in 1893 when again appointed to the Dartmouth faculty, this time as professor of rhetoric and oratory. His reappointment was considered a measure of vindication which he did not live to enjoy fully, his death occurring unexpectedly a few weeks later.

[Sources include: G. W. Patterson, *Jas. W. Patterson as an Educator* (1893), reprinted from *Ann. Report of Supt. of Pub. Instruction ... of N. H.,* 1893; L. W. Cogswell, *Hist. of the Town of Henniker* (1880); J. O. Lyford, *Life of Edw. H. Rollins* (1906), containing references to Patterson's political career; *Biog. Dir. Am. Cong.* (1928); *Granite Monthly,* Oct. 1892, June 1893; J. K. Lord, *A Hist. of Dartmouth Coll.* (1913); obituary notices in New Hampshire newspapers. There is manuscript material on Patterson in the archives of Dartmouth Coll. and the Dartmouth Coll. Lib. has a large collection of Patterson's printed addresses and miscellaneous pamphlets.]   W. A. R.

PATTERSON, JOHN HENRY (Dec. 13, 1844–May 7, 1922), promoter and manufacturer of cash registers, was born near Dayton, Ohio, the seventh of eleven children of Jefferson Patterson and Julia Johnston, and a descendant of John Patterson, of Scotch-Irish stock, who emigrated to Pennsylvania about 1700. Born on a farm of well-to-do parents, and reared in rural surroundings in the neighborhood of the then small town of Dayton, Ohio, he attended the local schools and the Central High School of Dayton, Ohio, then spent a year, 1862–63, at Miami University. In 1864 he enlisted in the 131st Ohio but his regiment got only as far as Baltimore and he saw no active service. Continuing his education, he entered Dartmouth College and graduated with the degree of B.A. in 1867. What he regarded as an acquisition of much useless knowledge at college was the foundation of a lifelong suspicion and dislike of college methods and college men. Upon returning from Dartmouth as a college graduate and veteran of the war, he found nothing to do. He remained upon the family farm for a time, then took a position in 1868 as a canal toll-gate keeper in Dayton. Later he became a coal merchant with his brothers. In 1884, at the age of forty, casting about for a more profitable business than the coal business, he acquired a controlling interest in the National Manufacturing Company at Dayton which manufactured cash registers. The next day after its purchase he was so greatly ridiculed for investing in such a failure that he offered $2,000 to the seller to release him from his bargain, but his offer was refused. The factory of the company, which in December 1884 became the National Cash Register Company, was situated in a dismal slum section of the town of Dayton. There were thirteen employees on the payroll. At an age when most men are consolidating their successes, Patterson started into business with a product that nobody wanted, few knew how to use, and one that met the violent opposition of all those who had to employ it. From this beginning he established eventually a plant whose product became practically indispensable to the commercial world and in a sense revolutionized commercial transactions.

In the first four years of his control of the company Patterson suggested many improvements in the construction of the cash register and took out several patents in his own name. He was not a mechanic, however, and after 1888 left the development of the machine to experts. He devoted his main efforts to the sale of his product and in this field he developed advertising practices which were new and unusual. Sales conventions, sales schools for the education of salesmen and customers, service to customers to maintain the mechanism in operating condition, the establishment of the closed quota territory guaranteeing to salesmen their territory as theirs exclusively, generous payments of large commissions for performance, were all evidences of the new salesmanship that he introduced. At the outset he began to use advertising circulars and always stressed direct mail advertising.

In the factory, he converted the grime and gloom of his original plant into pleasant surroundings. He established an industrial welfare organization to take care of the education, health, and working conditions of his employees and their families, he established a schoolhouse for their education and entertainment, and he converted his factory ground into an industrial garden spot. But his lavish provisions for the health and comfort of his employees were prompted as much by materialistic as humanitarian motives, for he often said: "It pays." His competitive methods were so aggressive that he was left supreme in his field, but he was repeatedly subject to the attacks of government agencies and of other business men. He demanded a maximum of efficiency from his employees and was often merciless in his treatment of them. Physically he was wiry and energetic, and he possessed a highly erratic temperament. He had a genius for management and a mind that retained every detail of his business. Easily obsessed by an idea, he was unhappy until he had converted it into action. After he had been placed on a regimen which included callisthenics in the morning he demanded that the executives in his factory assemble at five o'clock every morning for similar exercises. Good government, aviation, diet, horticulture, horses, education, and invention were but a few of his hobbies. Patterson died on May 7, 1922, at seventy-eight, while he was on his way to Atlantic City. He had retired from the presidency of the company in 1921, but was chairman of the board of directors at the time of his death. He was survived by two children. His wife, Katherine Dudley Beck, of Brookline,

Mass., whom he married on Dec. 18, 1888, died in 1894.

[Sources include: Samuel Crowther, *John H. Patterson, Pioneer in Industrial Welfare* (1923); C. R. Conover, *Concerning our Forefathers . . . Col. Robert Patterson and Col. John Johnston* (1902); R. W. Johnson and R. W. Lynch, *The Sales Strategy of John H. Patterson* (1932); *Fortune,* Aug. 1930; *Who's Who in America,* 1920–21; *N. Y. Times,* May 8, 1922.]
H. A. T., Jr.

PATTERSON, MORRIS (Oct. 26, 1809–Oct. 23, 1878), merchant, philanthropist, was born in Philadelphia, Pa., the eldest son of John and Rachel (Cauffman) Patterson. The father died in 1819, leaving a family of seven children, and the mother opened a grocery store in order to support herself and the family. Morris worked in the store until 1830, when he went into the grocery business for himself. Shortly before this time he had begun to operate a retail coal wharf and in time he decided to engage in coal mining on his own account. He became a pioneer in the development of the anthracite coal trade of Pennsylvania. His coal was brought to Philadelphia in his own boats on the Schuylkill Canal and from there was shipped to other Eastern cities. In Schuylkill County he built up a large trade in groceries with Pottsville and the mining region, shipping the goods in his canal boats when they returned to the mines. He also engaged in transalleghany trade, sending his goods across the mountains in wagon trains. When the Pennsylvania Railroad was first projected he was one of the canvassers for stock subscriptions and was himself an original stockholder. On Jan. 1, 1840, he turned his retail grocery business over to his younger brothers and formed a partnership with Benjamin S. Janney, Jr., under the firm name of Morris Patterson & Company, to conduct a wholesale grocery business. This partnership continued until Jan. 1, 1857, when it was dissolved. In 1845 he had become associated with Joseph Bailey in the manufacture of plate iron at the Pine Rolling Mill near Douglassville, Pa. A few years later he also became associated with Charles L. Bailey in the construction of the Central Rolling Mill at Harrisburg, Pa., which was completed in 1852. He was connected with this concern as a silent partner until it was sold in 1866, at which time he retired from all business activities.

Patterson was very active in church affairs and was ruling elder of the West Spruce Street Presbyterian Church in Philadelphia, the erection of which he largely financed, from 1856 until his death. He also served as a member of the Presbytery of Philadelphia. He was one of the founders and a member of the board of managers of the Pennsylvania Working Home for Blind Men and was connected with many other charitable and philanthropic institutions. In a quiet and unostentatious way he did a great deal of good with the fortune which he had accumulated. In addition to his other business activities he served as one of the directors of the Western National Bank and of the Montgomery Iron Company. He was also a member of the Presbyterian Board of Education and a trustee of Lafayette College to which he was a generous contributor. On Apr. 8, 1846, he was married to Mary Storm and they had three children. He died suddenly in Philadelphia.

[There is a privately printed memorial of Patterson entitled: *Morris Patterson, Born Oct. 26, 1809, Died Oct. 23, 1878* (n.d.). See also: the *Presbyterian* (Phila.), Nov. 2, 1878; *Phila. Inquirer,* Oct. 24, 1878; *Pub. Ledger* (Phila.), Oct. 25, 1878.]
J. H. F.

PATTERSON, ROBERT (May 30, 1743–July 22, 1824), mathematician, was born near Hillsborough in the north of Ireland, the son of Robert and Jane Patterson. His great-grandfather had emigrated from Scotland to escape the persecution of the Presbyterians by the Stuarts. He was sent to school at an early age and distinguished himself for his progress in mathematics. During the wave of martial spirit that spread over Ireland when the French descended upon the coast, Patterson enlisted in a militia company. He was offered a commission in the British army but this he declined. After finishing his education, he emigrated to America in October 1768 and landed in Philadelphia practically penniless. He secured a position as schoolmaster in Buckingham, Bucks County, but left this position to return to Philadelphia, where he taught many of the leading navigators the computation of longitude by means of lunar observations. In 1772, having accumulated the sum of approximately five or six hundred pounds, he opened a country store in New Jersey. He was unfitted for business, however, and seized the first opportunity to close out the enterprise, resuming his former vocation as principal of the academy at Wilmington, Del. His early experiences in Ireland put him in a position to render valuable services as a military instructor upon the outbreak of the Revolution. Three companies were put under his charge. Later he entered the army with the rank of brigade major and served until the British evacuated Philadelphia.

Upon the reorganization of the College and Academy of Philadelphia as the University of Pennsylvania, Patterson was appointed professor of mathematics. He entered the services of the University in December 1779 and served continuously until 1814 when he resigned and was succeeded by his son, Robert M. Patterson. For a period he was vice-provost of the University. He contributed several scientific papers to the *Transactions* of the American Philosophical Society and was a frequent contributor of problems and solutions to mathematical journals. He also published *Lectures on Select Subjects in Mechanics* (2 vols., 1806), and *Astronomy Explained upon Sir Isaac Newton's Principles* (1806, 1809), revised editions of the works of James Ferguson, the Scotch scientist. In 1808 he published a small book entitled the *Newtonian System of Philosophy* and in 1818 he published *A Treatise of Practical Arithmetic,* elaborated from his lectures on the same subject at the University of Pennsylvania. Though the exposition was clear, the book never reached the circulation it deserved because it was difficult for beginners. In the second volume of Robert Adrain's *Analyst* he set as the prize problem the question as to how to correct the measurements of a polygon whose sides are given in size and direction but which when plotted do not close up. The problem was renewed in Volume III and was finally solved by Nathaniel Bowditch in Volume IV.

In addition to his services at the University Patterson found time for public service. He was a member of Select Council of Philadelphia and was elected its president in 1799. In 1805 he received from President Jefferson the unsolicited appointment as director of the mint. He filled this office with distinction and resigned only at the time of his last illness. He was elected a member of the American Philosophical Society in 1783 and became its president in 1819. He was richly endowed both in mind and body. His especial mental inclination was for exact science. He was not alone interested in the discovery of a mathematical or physical truth but was never satisfied until he could see its application in the world of every-day life. Patterson was married, on May 9, 1774, to Amy Hunter Ewing of Greenwich, N. J. They had eight children.

[Memoir of Patterson in *Trans. Am. Phil. Soc.*, n.s. vol. II (1825); F. Cajori, *The Teaching and Hist. of Mathematics in the U. S.* (1890); J. L. Chamberlain, *Universities and Their Sons: Univ. of Pa.*, vol. I (1901); G. B. Wood, *The Hist. of the Univ. of Pa.* (1834); W. E. Du Bois, *A Record of the Families of Robt. Patterson* (1847); *Poulson's Am. Daily Advertiser,* July 24, 1824.]   J.R.K.

PATTERSON, ROBERT (Jan. 12, 1792–Aug. 7, 1881), soldier, industrialist, was born in County Tyrone, Ireland, the eldest son of Francis and Ann (Graham) Patterson. His father took part in the Irish Rebellion in 1798, was sen-

tenced to banishment, and came to America, settling on a farm in Delaware County, Pa. Robert received his early education in the public schools and at fifteen entered the counting house of Edward Thompson in Philadelphia. In the War of 1812, he served successively as captain, lieutenant-colonel, and colonel of Pennsylvania militia; lieutenant, 22nd United States Infantry; captain and deputy quartermaster-general, 32nd Infantry; and captain, 32nd Infantry, being mustered out in June 1815. He returned to Philadelphia and established himself as a grocer, becoming in time a commission merchant with connections in the South. He was married in 1817 to Sarah Ann Engle of Germantown, Pa., who died in 1875. They had eleven children, of whom five died in infancy. In 1835 he visited the upper Mississippi and Iowa, keeping a diary describing the country he saw. Excerpts from this diary were published under the title "Observations of an Early American Capitalist" in the *Journal of American History,* October-December 1907. At first a disciple of Thomas Jefferson, he was one of the five Colonel Pattersons (*North American,* Philadelphia, Dec. 8, 1912) who sat in the state convention of Democratic-Republicans that met at Harrisburg, Mar. 4, 1824, and by acclamation nominated Andrew Jackson for the presidency. He was commissioner of internal improvements in Pennsylvania in 1827; was twice a presidential elector; continued to be a Democrat in politics, but was opposed to free trade.

At the beginning of the Mexican War, he became a major-general of volunteers (July 7, 1846), commanded his division at Cerro Gordo, led the cavalry and advance brigades in the pursuit, and took Jalapa, for which he was honorably mentioned by General Scott. Upon his discharge from the federal service in July 1848, he returned to his business affairs, became prominent in the development of the sugar industry in Louisiana, acquired interests in sugar and cotton plantations, and eventually the ownership of some thirty cotton-mills in Pennsylvania. He was a promoter of the Pennsylvania Railroad and of steamship transportation between Philadelphia and other ports. From 1833 to 1867 he commanded a division of Pennsylvania militia. He was one of the original trustees of Lafayette College from 1825 to 1835 and again from 1874 to 1881, being president of the board from 1876 until his death.

At the beginning of the Civil War he was mustered into federal service, for three months, as a major-general of volunteers, and assigned to command the military department composed of Pennsylvania, Delaware, Maryland, and the

District of Columbia. He crossed the Potomac on June 15, 1861, at Williamsport, Md. Again, on July 2, he crossed the river, pursuing General "Stonewall" Jackson, and on July 3, advanced to Martinsburg, W. Va. In the middle of July he was ordered to hold in check the forces under Gen. Joseph E. Johnston in the neighborhood of Winchester while General McDowell advanced in Virginia. The reason he gave for his failure to give battle to Johnston and to cooperate with McDowell in the battle of Bull Run was that General Scott did not send him the order to attack (*Narrative,* pp. 74–75). At the expiration of his commission, July 27, 1861, he was mustered out of federal service and returned to his business concerns in Philadelphia. After the war he published *A Narrative of the Campaign in the Valley of the Shenandoah in 1861* (1865). His son, Francis Engle Patterson, a brigadier-general of Pennsylvania volunteers, participated in the Peninsular campaign and was killed by the accidental discharge of his own pistol at Fairfax Court-House, Nov. 22, 1862. Robert Patterson died in Philadelphia and was buried in Laurel Hill Cemetery.

[M. V. Agnew, *The Book of the Agnews* (1926); *Niles' Weekly Reg.,* Mar.–Sept. 1824; *Phila. Inquirer,* Aug. 8–12, 1881; F. B. Heitman, *Hist. Reg. and Dict. U. S. Army* (1903); War Department records; "Report of Joint Committee on Conduct of the War," *Sen. Report No. 108* (vol. 3), 37 Cong., 3 Sess.; *North American* (Phila.), Dec. 8, 1912.]   R. C. C—n.

PATTERSON, ROBERT MAYNE (July 17, 1832–Apr. 5, 1911), Presbyterian clergyman, editor, author, was born in Philadelphia and spent practically all his life in or near that city. His parents, John and Margaret (Mayne) Patterson, were natives of the north of Ireland who had come to America early in the eighteenth century. Robert graduated from the Central High School of Philadelphia in 1849, served as official reporter for the United States Senate, 1850–55, and for a time studied law. Turned to the ministry largely by the desire of his parents, he attended Princeton Theological Seminary, graduating in 1859. The same year he was ordained to the ministry by the Presbytery of Philadelphia. In the next forty-seven years he served only two churches as pastor—Great Valley Presbyterian Church, Chester County, Pa., 1859–67 and 1881–1906; and South Presbyterian Church, Philadelphia, 1867–81. His ministry was marked by acceptable preaching and faithful pastoral work. While he was in charge of South Church the membership greatly increased, a burdensome debt was paid, and the building was remodeled. During his second pastorate in Great Valley the church erected a new edifice.

When, in 1906, ill health caused his retirement, he was made pastor emeritus, a distinction which he held until his death after a long illness, five years later.

The activity which made him most widely known was his editorship of two religious weeklies, *The Presbyterian,* as associate editor, 1870–80, and *The Presbyterian Journal,* as editor, 1880–93, each published at Philadelphia. His increasing familiarity with church laws and doctrines, which his articles and editorials disclosed, and the character of his many books led to his being called to take a prominent part in the deliberations of the Church throughout the country. In presbyteries and synods and in the General Assembly, his knowledge of ecclesiastical law was continually in demand. He was sent by his presbytery to thirteen sessions of the General Assembly. In 1880 he was a member of a special committee appointed to prepare a plan for consolidation of the synods and for enlargement of their powers; at different times he also served on six other special committees and commissions of the Assembly. He was a member of the Pan-Presbyterian Council at London in 1875; at Philadelphia in 1880; and at Belfast in 1884. For many years, also, he was one of the members of the Presbyterian Board of Publication and Sabbath School Work.

Of his books, which totaled nearly thirty, several were biographical, including *The Character of Abraham Lincoln* (1865), *Elijah, the Favored Man* (1880), and *William Blackwood* (1894); four were local or general church histories, culminating in *American Presbyterianism* (1896); a number were polemic; and most of the remainder dealt with Christian instruction and church methods, of which *Church Extension in Large Cities* appeared in 1880 and *The Angels and Their Ministrations* in 1900. He also edited Withrow's *Which Is the Apostolic Church?* (1874) and *The Second General Council of the Presbyterian Alliance* (1880). In 1861 he married Margaret Maclay Nourse, daughter of Rev. James Nourse, of Washington, Pa.; she died in 1863. His second wife was Rebecca Thomas Malin, daughter of Joseph Malin of Chester Valley, Pa., whom he married in 1867.

[*Necrological Reports and Ann. Proc. of the Alumni Asso. of Princeton Theological Sem.,* vol. IV (1919); W. S. Garner, *Biog. and Portrait Cyc. of Chester County, Pa.* (1893); *Who's Who in America,* 1912–13; *Public Ledger* (Phila.), Apr. 6, 1911; two manuscripts in lib. of the hist. dept. of the Presbyterian Church, Phila., recording the actions of the Presbytery of Chester on Patterson's retirement (1906) and death (1911).]
P. P. F.

PATTERSON, THOMAS HARMAN (May 10, 1820–Apr. 9, 1889), naval officer, was born in New Orleans, La., the son of Daniel Todd Patterson [*q.v.*] and George Ann (Pollock) Patterson. He was appointed midshipman Apr. 5, 1836, and served first for seven months in the *Porpoise*, participating in coast survey work, and from 1837 to 1840 in the *Falmouth*, Pacific Squadron. Following a year at the naval school in Philadelphia he was made passed midshipman July 1, 1842, standing sixth in his class of thirty-six. He was at the Naval Observatory in 1843, and then spent a year in the West Indies on board the *Lawrence*. He served again in the coast survey from 1844 to 1848. Promotion to the rank of lieutenant came on June 23, 1849, just before a long Pacific cruise in the *Vandalia*. After his return in October 1852 he was assigned to special duty in Washington. Then followed a cruise in the *Jamestown*, African Squadron, from 1854 to 1857; two years at the Washington navy yard; and another African cruise in the *Mohican*. His Civil War service began in October 1861 when he sailed from Boston for Virginia waters in command of the gunboat *Chocura*. The *Chocura* was in the naval force which cooperated with McClellan during the Peninsular Campaign in the spring of 1862. It was the first gunboat to ascend the Pamunkey River to Whitehouse after the evacuation of Yorktown on May 4, and supported Gen. George Stoneman's advance at that point. Patterson was made commander July 16, 1862, and from June to October of that year he was senior officer in the York and Pamunkey rivers. From November 1862 to June 1865 he commanded the sidewheel gunboat *James Adger* on the southeast coast blockade. His ship assisted in cutting out the blockade-runner *Kate* under the Confederate batteries at New Inlet, N. C., on Aug. 1, 1863, and on Aug. 23 came under heavy fire near this point while destroying the beached vessel *Hebe* (D. D. Porter, *The Naval History of the Civil War*, 1886, p. 427). His captures of blockade-runners in this year included the *Cornubia*, on Nov. 8, the steamer *Robert E. Lee* with valuable arms and stores, on Nov. 9, and the schooner *Ella* on Nov. 26. He was senior officer of the offshore blockade at Charleston from September 1864 to February 1865, and a month later operated with the convoy fleet in the Mariguana Passage in the West Indies. He was made captain July 22, 1866, commodore in 1871, and rear admiral in 1877. He commanded the *Brooklyn*, flagship of the Brazil Squadron from 1865 to 1867, and during the next ten years was assigned to various shore duties, being commandant of the Washington navy yard from 1873 to 1876. From 1878 to October 1880, he command-

ed the Asiatic Squadron, and was subsequently engaged in revising the naval regulations. Following his retirement on May 10. 1882, he made his home in Washington where his death occurred after more than three years of ill health. A classmate, Rear Admiral T. H. Stevens, described him as a man "of great dignity of manner and reticent . . . but to those who knew the warm heart beneath the cold exterior . . . of lovable nature, a constant, unswerving friend." He was married in Washington on Jan. 5, 1847, to Maria Montrésor Wainwright, daughter of Col. R. D. Wainwright, U. S. M. C., and had one daughter and four sons.

[L. R. Hamersly, *Records of Living Officers of the U. S. Navy and Marine Corps* (4th ed., 1890) ; *War of the Rebellion: Official Records (Navy)*, 1 ser. VI–XVI ; *Washington Post*, Apr. 11, 1889 ; other material from family sources.]   A. W.

PATTERSON, THOMAS MacDONALD (Nov. 4, 1839–July 23, 1916), lawyer, editor, senator, the third child and second son of James and Margaret (Mountjoy) Patterson, was born in County Carlow, Ireland. After the removal of the family to America when the boy was about ten years of age, he attended school in New York City and Astoria, L. I. In 1853 he went with his family to Crawfordsville, Ind., where he worked first in a printing office and then in his father's jewelry store. After a short term of service in the Civil War with the 11th Indiana Infantry, he enrolled, in 1862, in Indiana Asbury University (now De Pauw University), but transferred in the following year to Wabash College at Crawfordsville. Leaving in his junior year he began to study law in the office of M. D. White of Crawfordsville and was admitted to the bar in 1867. In 1872 he moved to Denver and soon won the reputation of being one of the best trial lawyers in the West. In 1874 he was made city attorney of Denver and later in the same year was elected, as a Democrat, territorial delegate from Colorado to the Forty-fourth Congress. Although his term of office did not begin until Mar. 4, 1875, he went to Washington in time to use his influence, especially with the Democratic members of Congress, to help secure the passage of the Colorado Enabling Act in the closing hours of the Forty-third Congress. At an election held in October 1876, after Colorado had been admitted to the Union, he was defeated by James B. Belford, Republican, for the unexpired term as representative in the Forty-fourth Congress, and also for the full term of the succeeding Congress. Denying the validity of the latter vote, Patterson ran again, but without opposition, at the regular time for Congressional elections in November. The certificate of election was given to Belford, but Patterson challenged his seat and after a contest that attracted wide attention was seated by the House of Representatives (*Congressional Record,* 45 Cong., 2 Sess., pt. I, pp. 145 ff.).

Patterson was active in state and national councils of the Democratic party and was a delegate to the Democratic National conventions in 1876, 1888, and 1892. As a member of the Committee on Resolutions in the last of those conventions he brought in, singly, a minority report in favor of free silver. Voted down, he bolted the party and helped carry Colorado for the Populist candidate, James B. Weaver. He was a delegate to the Populist National Convention in 1896, and its permanent chairman in 1900. In 1901 he was elected to the United States Senate from Colorado by a combination of Democratic, Populist, and Silver-Republican votes. Although he affiliated with the Democratic party while in the Senate (1901–07), he refused to be bound by the instructions of the party caucus and vigorously asserted his right to independence of action as when, for example, he supported President Roosevelt's policies in the Morocco conference and the Santo Dominican treaty (*Congressional Record,* 59 Cong., 1 Sess., pt. II, pp. 1801–06; *Ibid.,* pt. III, pp. 2207 ff.). He was twice the unsuccessful Democratic candidate for governor of Colorado; in 1888 he was defeated by Job A. Cooper, and in 1914 by George A. Carlson. An important element in his political influence in Colorado was the *Rocky Mountain News,* in which he acquired an interest in 1890, and over which he assumed full control in 1892. Until he sold this newspaper in 1913 it was the principal means through which he carried on his crusades for such governmental reforms as the initiative, the referendum, and the direct primary, and against the corporations that, in his judgment, sought to exploit the public. Although rated a millionaire on account of the fees earned in a lucrative law practice and his shrewd purchases of Denver real estate, he was one of Labor's most outspoken champions in the West. He was versatile, dynamic, aggressive, militant, and domineering. He had strong convictions and expressed himself freely without regard to the consequences or effects on friends and associates. He had warm friends, ardent supporters, and bitter enemies. He was not always sound in his judgments or fair in his criticisms, but he was honest and sincere. He did much to free Colorado from corporate control and to put into the hands of the people the means of direct political action. His wife was Katherine Grafton of Watertown, N. Y., to whom he was married in 1863. He was survived by one daughter.

[*Who's Who in America,* 1916–17; *Biog. Dir. Am. Cong.* (1928); J. C. Smiley, *Semi-Centennial Hist. of the State of Colo.* (1913), vol. II; W. F. Stone, *Hist. of Colo.,* vol. II (1918); *Cong. Record,* 65 Cong., 1 Sess., App., pp. 582–85; *Rocky Mountain News* and *Denver Post,* July 24, 1916.]   C. B. G.

PATTERSON, WILLIAM (Nov. 1, 1752– July 7, 1835), merchant, was born at Fanad, County Donegal, Ireland, of Scotch-Irish farmer parents, William and Elizabeth (Peoples) Patterson. At the age of fourteen (1766) he was sent to Philadelphia to enter the counting-house of Samuel Jackson, an Irish shipping merchant. "This gave me," said Patterson sixty years later, "an early knowledge and attachment to that business, a passion that has followed me through life" (Scharf, *post,* pp. 482–83). In 1775, foreseeing an excellent sale for munitions in the rebellious colonies, he embarked all of his property in two vessels which went to France for these supplies, Patterson himself sailing in one of them. A single vessel returned, and, according to tradition, when it reached Philadelphia, the army of Washington, then before Boston, had not powder enough to fire one salute. On his way home Patterson tarried two years in the Dutch and French West Indies, which were the principal places of purchase and sale for the colonies. He was eighteen months at St. Eustatius, but finding the governor, Johannes de Graaff, unable to protect American interests, he moved to Martinique. He accumulated a fortune of more than $60,000, half of which he lost by British captures in a month; the remainder he brought to Baltimore (July 1778) in goods and gold.

He prospered from his first settlement in that city. It was his invariable rule to put half of his fortune into real estate, for he regarded "commerce in the shipping line as a hazardous and desperate game of chance" (Scharf, p. 483). If he lost in his shipping ventures his family (he had thirteen children, several of whom died in infancy) would thus have something to fall back upon, and heirs, furthermore, were not so apt to part with land as with securities. He was typical of the Baltimore merchant princes who increasingly in the next fifty years, as the business of American ports flourished, made the clipper schooner and brig, and later the clipper ship, famous around the world. He was one of the Baltimore merchants who supplied Lafayette with 10,000 guineas which were invested in supplies for the Yorktown campaign, and himself, as a member of the 1st Baltimore Cavalry, went to the peninsula. He was the first president of the Bank of Maryland, established in 1790. In 1799 he was active in raising money to complete the fortification of Whetstone Point (Fort McHenry), gathered supplies for the defense of the place in 1814, and welcomed Lafayette there on his visit in 1824. On Christmas Eve, 1803, his daughter Elizabeth ("Betsey"), eighteen years of age, was married to the nineteen-year-old Jerome Bonaparte, young brother of the Firs Consul of France [see Elizabeth Patterson Bonaparte]. Her parents gave consent most reluctantly, and were prepared for the adamant opposition of Napoleon, which resulted in Betsey's abandonment by her husband at Lisbon in 1805, the annulment of the marriage by the French Senate, and a divorce by Maryland statute in 1812. Patterson said of his daughter that "she has caused me more anxiety . . . than all my other children put together, and her folly and misconduct has occasioned me a train of expense that first and last has cost me much money" (*Ibid.*, p. 488).

Patterson was one of the organizers of the Merchants' Exchange in Baltimore in 1815, gave two acres of land to the city for a park in 1827, and was one of the incorporators and first directors of the Baltimore & Ohio Railroad in the same year. He took delight in riding on the first cars of the railroad, and was given the honor of being the first to cross the Patapsco viaduct, which was named for him. In 1828 he was one of the incorporators of the Canton Company, which has for a century been important in the commercial and industrial life of the city. One of his last public acts was to serve as vice-president of a meeting of Baltimore citizens which condemned the nullification ordinance of South Carolina in 1832. His wife, who died in 1814, was Dorcas Spear, a sister of the wife of Gen. Samuel Smith.

[Autobiographical introduction to Patterson's will in J. T. Scharf, *The Chronicles of Baltimore* (1874); F. A. Richardson and W. A. Bennett, *Baltimore: Past and Present* (1871); *Baltimore American and Daily Advertiser*, July 9, 1835; original receipt book of Patterson, most of the entries being for the decade 1780–90, in lib. of Peabody Institute, Baltimore; E. L. Didier, *The Life and Letters of Madame Bonaparte* (1879); D. M. Henderson, *The Golden Bees* (1928).]
B. M.

PATTIE, JAMES OHIO (1804–1850?), trapper, author, was born in Bracken County, Ky., the son of Sylvester Pattie. The main source of information regarding his father and himself is his dubious *Personal Narrative* (1831), edited (and perhaps largely written) by Timothy Flint. From Kentucky, he says, the family moved to Missouri in 1812. In July 1824, near the present Omaha, father and son joined Sil-

vestre Pratte's Santa Fé expedition, which reached its destination Nov. 5. During the next three years the son, sometimes in company with his father, took part in a number of hazardous trapping journeys. Early in 1828, with his father and six others, he reached Santa Catalina Mission, in Lower California. All were arrested and taken to San Diego, where, according to Pattie, they were subjected to extreme brutalities by Governor Echeandía. Here, on Apr. 24, the elder Pattie died in prison. The son, with his companions, was released early in the following year, and in August 1830, by way of Mexico city, he arrived in Cincinnati. He is assumed to have filed a claim for damages in the Mexican capital, but a recent search (1933) of the papers in the United States Embassy there, as well as in the State Department in Washington, reveals no record of even a complaint by him.

The *Personal Narrative* appeared in the following year, though most of the copies extant bear the date of 1833. A plagiarized version, with the title, *The Hunters of Kentucky,* and purporting to record the adventures of one B. Bilson, was published in New York in 1847. The original text was reprinted as the eighteenth volume (1905) of *Early Western Travels*, with sparse and unsatisfactory annotations by R. G. Thwaites. It was again reprinted, with scanty annotations, by M. M. Quaife, in 1930.

From such knowledge as is available, the elder Pattie appears an estimable person. It is not unlikely, on the other hand, that the son was, as Bancroft characterized him, a conceited and quick-tempered boy with an exceptional capacity for making himself disagreeable. His book, an entertaining narrative of thrilling and painful adventures, has an assured place in frontier literature. It is, however, to be classed as semifiction rather than as history. On matters that can be tested by authentic records it usually proves inaccurate as to dates, names, and localities, and it is frequently erroneous, if not untruthful, as to events. Nathaniel M. Pryor, one of Pattie's companions, pronounced it mostly false. Of the later life of Pattie little is known. He is said to have attended Augusta College and to have made his home for many years in the nearby town of Dover. In 1849 he joined the gold rush and appears to have visited San Diego. At some time in the following winter he was at William Waldo's camp in the Sierra, and left there during a spell of tempestuous weather. He was never heard of again.

[See William Waldo, "Recollections of a Septuagenarian," *Mo. Hist. Colls.,* vols. II, III (1880); S. C. Foster, "A Sketch of Some of the Earliest Ky. Pioneers of Los Angeles," *Pubs. Hist. Soc. of Southern Cal.*, vol. I, pt. 3 (1887) ; H. R. Wagner, *The Plains and the Rockies* (1921). The parts of the *Personal Narrative* relating to California are summarized by H. H. Bancroft, *Hist. of Cal.*, vol. III (1885), with critical comment based on Mexican records. Fresh light on the unveracity of Pattie is given by C. L. Camp, "The Chronicles of Geo. C. Yount," *Cal. Hist. Soc. Quart.*, Apr. 1923 ; and by J. J. Hill, "Ewing Young in the Fur Trade of the Southwest," *Ore. Hist. Soc. Quart.*, Mar. 1923. A more favorable view of Pattie appears in R. G. Cleland, *A Hist. of Cal.: The American Period* (1922).]

W. J. G.

PATTISON, GRANVILLE SHARP (*c.* 1791–Nov. 12, 1851), anatomist, was the youngest son of John Pattison of Kelvin Grove, Glasgow. He was probably educated at the University of Glasgow. At the age of eighteen he was chosen assistant to Allan Burns, the well-known Scotch anatomist, and later succeeded him in the chair of anatomy, physiology, and surgery in the Andersonian Institution. Here he made for himself a reputation as an interesting lecturer and successful teacher. In 1819, on a hint of the possibility of his being called to the chair of anatomy in the medical department of the University of Pennsylvania, he came to the United States. Before sailing he was made a member of the Medico-Chirurgical Society of London and a fellow of the Royal College of Surgeons. Disappointed in his hope of obtaining the professorship at the University of Pennsylvania, he gave a series of private lectures on anatomy in Philadelphia which attracted wide attention. He also published, in 1820, *Experimental Observations on the Operation of Lithotomy*. This brought him notoriety, arousing one of the bitter controversies so often waged by anatomists at that time. In the midst of the controversy he challenged his opponent, Dr. Nathaniel Chapman, professor of the theory and practice of medicine at the University of Pennsylvania, to a duel. Chapman refused the challenge in a famous note. Pattison then posted him "as a liar, a coward, and a scoundrel." Chapman's brother-in-law, Gen. Thomas Cadwalader, accepted the challenge and received a ball in his "pistol arm," which was disabled for the rest of his life. A ball passed through the skirt of Pattison's coat near the waistline. In 1821 he published *A Refutation of Certain Calumnies Published in a Pamphlet Entitled, "Correspondence between Mr. Granville Sharp Pattison and Dr. Nathaniel Chapman."*

In the midst of the controversy, 1820, Pattison was invited to the chair of anatomy, physiology, and surgery at the University of Maryland in Baltimore. While here, 1824, he edited the second edition of Allan Burns's *Observations on the Surgical Anatomy of the Head and*

Neck. In 1826 he resigned his professorship at Baltimore and returned to England, where he was appointed professor of anatomy in the newly organized University of London, now University College. There was serious lack of discipline in the institution, and Pattison made the attempt to control his class. The students rebelled and Wakeley, the editor of the *Lancet* (London), intervened. As a result, Pattison was dismissed from the chair on July 23, 1831. The following year he was invited to the professorship of anatomy at the Jefferson Medical College, Philadelphia, where he acquired the reputation of being the most successful teacher in his subject in the country. He brought great prestige to the new school. Nine years later, on the reorganization of the medical department of the University of the City of New York, he was invited to the chair of anatomy and continued to occupy this position until his death. Gross, in his biographical sketch of him, remarks: "It is no exaggeration to say that no anatomical teacher of his day, either in Europe or in this country, enjoyed a higher reputation" (*post*, II, 257). He devoted himself faithfully to the demonstration of visceral and surgical anatomy and gave very practical lessons in applying knowledge of the subject to the diagnosis and treatment of diseases, accidents, and operations. He was a very popular teacher, for the students felt that they were always securing knowledge that could be applied in the practice of medicine. He spared no pains to arrange clever demonstrations and his teaching produced a deep and lasting impression. He was an editor of the *Register and Library of Medical and Surgical Science* (Washington, 1833–36) and co-editor of the *American Medical Library and Intelligencer* (Philadelphia, 1836).

In addition to his professional work, he was much interested in music and was a leader in the group of music lovers who arranged the production of grand opera in New York City. He was very fond of hunting and fishing, and is said to have been somewhat indolent, for which reason, perhaps, he did not leave more definite remains of his work behind him. He died in New York, survived by his wife.

[S. D. Gross, *Autobiog.* (2 vols., 1887) ; F. P. Henry, *Hist. of Medicine in Phila.* (1897) ; Bardeen, *Encyc. of Am. Medic. Biog.* (1912) ; J. J. Walsh, *Hist. of Medicine in N. Y.* (5 vols., 1919) ; autobiographical material in *Refutation . . .* (1821), mentioned above ; *N. Y. Jour. of Medicine and the Collateral Sciences*, Jan. 1852 ; *Dict. of Nat. Biog.* ; *Gentleman's Mag.*, London, Jan. 1852 ; *N. Y. Herald*, Nov. 13, 1851.]

J. J. W.

PATTISON, JAMES WILLIAM (July 14, 1844–May 29, 1915), painter, writer, lecturer, was born in Boston, Mass. His father was the

Rev. Robert Everett Pattison, who taught in various places and twice (1836–39, 1854–57) held the presidency of Colby College at Waterville, Me. His mother was Frances Wilson, of a well-known New England family. At nineteen he enlisted in the 57th Massachusetts Volunteers and served until August 1865. He was at Petersburg during the siege and sent from there and elsewhere letters and illustrative drawings to *Harper's Weekly,* thus beginning his artistic career. After the war he studied art in New York City under James M. Hart, R. Swain Gifford, and George Inness, then he joined his brother, Everett W. Pattison, in St. Louis, where he opened a studio. He also taught drawing (1868–69, 1872–73), at Mary Institute, a school for girls at Washington University. Here he met and married, in 1871, Elizabeth Abbott Pennell, the daughter of the president of the Institute, Calvin S. Pennell. For a time he shared his studio with William M. Chase [*q.v.*], who became his lifelong friend.

In St. Louis, Pattison began lecturing on art, and the interest he aroused in this way and through other channels bore fruit in the establishment of the City Museum of Art. From 1873 to 1879 he was in Europe, first at Düsseldorf, where he studied with Albert Flamm, then in Paris, where he worked under Luigi Chialiva. In Düsseldorf his wife died, and in 1876 he married Helen Searle, a well-known painter of Rochester, N. Y. He and his artist wife both exhibited in the Paris Salons of 1879, 1880, and 1881, and their home at Ecouen became a rendezvous for painters, writers, and other interesting persons. On account of the ill health of his wife, Pattison returned to America and after a brief sojourn in New York took up residence in the flat country of Illinois. From 1884 to 1896 he was director of the School of Fine Arts at Jacksonville, Ill. In the latter year he became faculty lecturer at the Art Institute of Chicago and removed his home and studio to Park Ridge. He was president of the Chicago Society of Artists, and for many years secretary of the Municipal Art League, and a member of the Society of Western Artists, Cliff Dwellers, and National Arts Club. From 1910 to 1914 he edited the *Fine Arts Journal* of Chicago and for a much longer time contributed weekly "Art Talks" to the *Chicago Journal.* He was also the author of a book, *Painters Since Leonardo* (1904). For several years he lectured on the history of art at Rockford College.

His activities as secretary of the Municipal Art League were not only widespread but beneficent. Through his writings in the newspaper, his lectures in schools and clubs in Chicago and other cities of the Middle West, through competitions and the coördination of effort, he was influential in awakening the consciousness of the public to beauty and civic improvement. Believing that the best way to educate people was to show them good things, he used extensively stereopticon slides, made from photographs he himself had taken or collected in Europe and America for the purpose. He was a member of the Chicago Plan Commission. His efforts were appreciated keenly by his fellow workers. His colleague, Walter Marshall Clute, said of him: "The part he is playing in the cultivation of a better art appreciation and civic pride, in making Chicago a more beautiful place to live in, is no small one," adding, "Mr. Pattison in the development and exercise of his art has worked in a great variety of mediums, handling with equal facility water color or oils, pencil or crayon or charcoal—even the witchery of the etching needle has not escaped him."

At the same time that Pattison was teaching, writing, and lecturing, he was also a productive artist. His paintings were shown at the National Academy of Design and in the annual exhibitions of the American Water Color Society, New York; in the Pennsylvania Academy, Philadelphia, and in the Art Institute of Chicago. His awards included a medal from the Massachusetts Charitable Mechanics' Association, Boston, 1881; and a bronze medal, St. Louis Exposition, 1904. One of his best works, a painting entitled "Tranquility," is owned by the Municipal Art League of Chicago, which includes also in its permanent collection a portrait of him by Louis Betts. Pattison as remembered by his friends was tall, slender, and distinguished in appearance, a charming conversationalist, and an able speaker. In 1905 (his second wife having died) he married Hortense Roberts of Columbia, Tenn. Two daughters were born of this marriage. In 1914 because of his failing health the family went to North Carolina to live. He died at Asheville in 1915.

[W. M. Clute, "Jas. Wm. Pattison," *Sketch Book,* May 1906; *Biog. Record of the Alumni of Amherst Coll., 1821–71* (1883); *Who's Who in America,* 1914–15; *Am. Art Annual,* vol. XII (1915); *Proc. First Ann. Convention of the Am. Federation of Arts* (1910); *Am. Art News,* June 12, 1915; *N. Y. Times,* May 30, 1915; *Charlotte Daily Observer,* May 31, 1915; information from Miss Lena McCauley of the *Chicago Herald* and from members of Pattison's family.]

L. M.

PATTISON, JOHN M. (June 13, 1847–June 18, 1906), congressman, governor of Ohio, was born near Owensville, Clermont County, Ohio, the son of Mary (Duckwall) and William Pattison, a country merchant. His middle initial, which represented no name, was added by himself some time early in life. As a boy he became a clerk in his father's store, and he worked on neighboring farms. In 1864 he joined the 153rd Ohio Volunteer Infantry. At the close of the Civil War he entered Ohio Wesleyan University, from which he graduated in 1869. In order to maintain himself while attending college he taught school and worked in the harvest fields in the summer. Upon graduation he took an agency in Bloomington, Ill., for the Union Central Life Insurance Company, of which he afterward became the head. As the insurance business did not appeal to him at that time he returned to Ohio and studied law in the office of Alfred Yaple of Cincinnati. After his admission to the bar in 1872 he became a member of the law firm of Yaple, Moos & Pattison. For a while he was attorney for the Cincinnati & Marietta Railroad but severed his connection with that corporation from a sense of duty to his constituency, when he was elected in 1873 to the state legislature. He declined renomination and returned to the practice of his profession. From 1874 to 1876 he was attorney for the committee of safety of Cincinnati, a non-partisan organization for civic welfare. On Dec. 10, 1879, he was married to Aletheia Williams of Delaware, Ohio. In 1881 he was elected vice-president and manager of the Union Central Life Insurance Company and in 1891 became president of the company. Under his able management the business of the company was greatly increased owing to his compelling personality, executive capacity, and ability as an organizer.

In 1890, against his personal wishes, he was nominated to fill a vacancy in the state Senate for the Clermont-Brown district. As the redistribution of the congressional districts that was about to be made would determine the complexion of Ohio representation in Congress, his campaign attracted national attention. He was elected and received the largest vote ever given to a candidate for state office in his own county of Clermont. From 1891 to 1893 he was a member of Congress but was an unsuccessful candidate for reëlection. In Congress he helped to obtain one of the first appropriations for rural free delivery. In 1905 he was nominated on the Democratic ticket for governor and after a spirited campaign against Gov. Myron T. Herrick was elected by a majority of 40,000, while the Republican associates of the retiring governor were elected by similar majorities. His victory was a personal achievement, but the strain of the campaign was too great for his health. He lived for five months after his inauguration but was so ill

the whole time that practically his only political act was his inaugural address. He died at his home in Milford, survived by his second wife, Anna (Williams) Pattison, the sister of his first wife.

[*Biog. Directory Am. Cong.* (1928); *Who's Who in America,* 1906–07; *Biog. Cyc. and Portrait Gallery of . . . Ohio,* vol. V (1895); T. E. Powell, *The Democratic Party in . . . Ohio* (2 vols. 1913); *Cincinnati Enquirer,* June 19, 1906; information concerning his middle initial from his daughter, Aletheia Eliza Pattison, Cincinnati.]
R. C. McG.

PATTISON, ROBERT EMORY (Dec. 8, 1850–Aug. 1, 1904), lawyer, statesman, was born at Quantico, Md., the son of the Rev. Robert H. Pattison and Catherine (Woolford) Pattison. Before 1860 the family moved to Philadelphia as the elder Pattison had been appointed to the Asbury Methodist Episcopal Church. The son received his education in the public schools of that city, graduating from the Central High School as valedictorian of his class in 1870. He immediately registered as a law student in the office of Lewis C. Cassidy and on Sept. 28, 1872, was admitted to the Philadelphia bar. After two unsuccessful attempts to obtain office he was on the point of surrendering his political ambitions when Cassidy, who was the leader of a Democratic faction in Philadelphia, suggested that he become the Democratic candidate for city controller on a reform platform. He was elected to this office on Nov. 7, 1877, and three years later was reëlected. On his record in this office he was made Democratic nominee for governor of Pennsylvania in 1882 and was elected by a plurality of 40,202 over his Republican opponent, Gen. James A. Beaver. He was inaugurated on Jan. 16, 1883. His administration was committed to economy and reform and to strong executive action in reducing the state debt and in holding corporations, particularly railroads and canal companies, to a strict obedience to the constitution and the law. Upon the expiration of his term as governor he was ineligible for reëlection and returned to Philadelphia to resume his law practice. In July 1887 he was elected president of the Chestnut Street National Bank and devoted a considerable part of his time to the management of this institution.

In March 1887 President Cleveland tendered Pattison the auditorship of the United States Treasury but he declined the office. Shortly afterward, however, he accepted an appointment as a member of the United States Pacific Railway Commission, authorized by Congress to investigate the "books, accounts and methods of railroads which have received aid from the United States." He was made chairman of the commission and entered upon his active duties on Apr. 15, 1887. He wrote the minority report of the commission which stands today as one of the most valuable contributions to the financial history of the land-grant railroads (*Report of the Commission... of the United States Pacific Railway Commission*, 10 vols. in 5, 1887). In 1890, after an aggressive campaign, he was again elected governor of Pennsylvania by a majority of 16,554 over his Republican opponent, George W. Delamater, for the term extending from Jan. 20, 1891, to Jan. 15, 1895. In his second administration he stressed the policies which had characterized his first tenure of the office and urged the reduction of taxation and reforms in municipal government. On retiring from office he resumed the practice of law in Philadelphia and shortly afterward was elected president of the Security Trust and Life Insurance Company, which position he held until his death. In 1902 he was again Democratic nominee for governor but was defeated. He took an active interest in church work, being a lay delegate to the General Conference of the Methodist Episcopal Church in 1884 and in 1888; fraternal delegate to the General Conference of the Methodist Episcopal Church South in 1890; and delegate to the Second Methodist Ecumenical Council in 1891. He was a member of the board of trustees of American University and of Dickinson College. On Dec. 28, 1872, he married Anna Barney Smith and they had three children. He died in Philadelphia, Pa.

[H. M. Jenkins, ed., *Pa. Colonial and Federal* (1903), vol. II; G. P. Donehoo, *Pa., A Hist.* (1926), vol. III; A. K. McClure, *Old Time Notes of Pa.* (1905), vol. II; J. H. Martin, *Martin's Bench and Bar of Phila.* (1883); the *Press* (Phila.), and *Pub. Ledger* (Phila.), Aug. 2, 1904.]   J. H. F.

PATTISON, THOMAS (Feb. 8, 1822–Dec. 17, 1891), naval officer, was born in Troy, N. Y., the son of Elias Pattison, who owned a large line of freight steamers on the Hudson, and Olivia (Gardiner) Pattison. On his father's side he was descended from Robert Pattison, who came from Ireland to Colerain, Mass., before the Revolution, and on his mother's side from George Gardiner, who settled in Rhode Island in 1638. He was appointed midshipman Mar. 2, 1839, and shortly thereafter sailed in the *St. Louis* on a Pacific cruise which lasted until December 1842. After taking short leave at home, he was assigned to a rigging loft in Boston, and then to the naval school at Philadelphia where he remained until he was promoted to passed midshipman in July 1845. During the Mexican War he served in the steamers *Scorpion* and *Princeton*, the frigates *Raritan* and *Cumberland*, the ordnance ship *Elec-*

tra, and the gunboat *Reefer*. He was on coast survey duty from 1850 to 1851, and then went to the China station as sailing master in the sloop *Portsmouth*, being promoted during the cruise to the rank of lieutenant. From 1855 to 1857 he was stationed at Boston on shore duty. While doing service in the Far East on the side-wheeler *Mississippi*, Pattison witnessed the bombardment of the Pei-ho River forts by the French and British in May 1858. A few months later he had occasion to escort from Simoda to Tokio the first American minister to Japan, Townsend Harris [*q.v.*]. It is presumably on the basis of this visit or some slightly earlier official entry that Pattison is said to have been the first American naval officer to enter Tokio.

After duty at the Sacketts Harbor naval station, N. Y., he began his service in the Civil War as executive of the sloop *Perry*, which captured the privateer *Savannah* off Charleston on June 3, 1861. As this was the first privateer taken, the capture drew from Secretary Welles a commendatory letter to officers and crew (*War of the Rebellion: Official Records, Navy*, 1 ser. I, 30). During the next autumn he commanded the steamer *Philadelphia* of the Potomac flotilla and twice in October was engaged with Confederate batteries along the river. From Dec. 17, 1861, he commanded the steamer *Sumter* on the southeast coast blockade, and was senior officer at Fernandina, Fla., during the summer and autumn of 1862. Early in 1863 he was ordered to the *Clara Dolson* of Porter's Mississippi Squadron, and from Mar. 12, 1863, until July 1, 1865, he was commandant of the naval station established in the former Confederate base at Memphis, Tenn. He had been made lieutenant commander July 16, 1862, was advanced to commander Mar. 3, 1865, and received subsequent promotions to the rank of captain in 1870, commodore in 1877, and rear admiral Nov. 1, 1883, three months before his retirement. His sea commands after the war were the *Muscota* of the Atlantic Squadron from 1866 to 1867, the *Richmond*, which he commanded in the West Indies and then took to the Pacific coast in 1872, and the *Saranac* of the Pacific Squadron in 1874. He commanded the receiving ship *Independence* at San Francisco from 1874 to 1877, the naval station at Port Royal, S. C., 1878–80, and the Washington navy yard, 1880–83. He died at New Brighton, Staten Island, N. Y., where he had made his home after retirement. His wife was Serafina Catalina Webster of Cuba, whom he married in Washington, D. C., July 1, 1850. His only child, Maria Webster, married John Randle of New York.

[*War of the Rebellion: Official Records (Navy)*, 1 ser., vols. XXIV–XXVII; L. R. Hamersly, *Records of Living Officers of the U. S. Navy and Marine Corps* (4th ed. 1890); W. F. Gragg, *A Cruise in the U. S. Steam Frigate Mississippi* (1860); H. F. Andrews, *The Hamlin Family* (1900); W. H. Webster and M. R. Webster, *Hist. and Geneal. of the Gov. John Webster Family of Conn.* (1915); *N. Y. Times*, Dec. 19, 1891.]

A. W.

PATTON, FRANCIS LANDEY (Jan. 22, 1843–Nov. 25, 1932), president of Princeton University, Presbyterian clergyman and theologian, was born at "Carberry Hill," Warwick, Bermuda, the son of George John Bascombe and Mary Jane (Steele) Patton. He learned to read when he was three years old and commenced Latin at the age of seven. After attending Warwick Academy and a grammar school in Toronto he continued his education at Knox College and at the University of Toronto, and then entered Princeton Theological Seminary, from which he graduated in 1865. That same year he was ordained to the Presbyterian ministry, and on Oct. 10, married Rosa Antoinette, daughter of the Rev. J. M. Stevenson, of New York.

During the next sixteen years he obtained a wide experience as preacher, lecturer, and writer for the religious press, and an acquaintance with several chief centers of population in the United States. He was pastor of the Eighty-fourth Street Presbyterian Church in New York, 1865 to 1867; of a church in Nyack, N. Y., 1867 to 1870; of South Church, Brooklyn, 1871; he was Cyrus H. McCormick Professor of Didactic and Polemical Theology at the Presbyterian Theological Seminary of the Northwest (now McCormick Seminary), in Chicago, 1872 to 1881; was pastor of the Jefferson Park Church, Chicago, 1874 to 1881; and edited *The Interior,* a Presbyterian paper, from 1873 to 1876. In 1878 he was chosen to represent America at the Pan-Presbyterian Council in Edinburgh, and was moderator of the General Assembly which met at Saratoga. A year later he was offered a professorship at the Presbyterian Theological College in London, but declined it. In 1881 he returned to Princeton Theological Seminary to occupy a chair founded specially for him by Robert L. Stuart [*q.v.*], which bore the comprehensive name, Professorship of the Relations of Philosophy and Science to the Christian Religion. He was also lecturer on ethics in the College of New Jersey (1883–84), and gave a course on theism to undergraduates. In 1884 he was elected to a college professorship of ethics, and in 1886 was appointed professor of ethics in the seminary also.

When, in 1888, Patton was chosen to follow James McCosh [*q.v.*] as president of the college, he was widely known as a witty and eloquent speaker, a distinguished exponent of theism, and an expert defender of Christian ethics. Whether, in addition to these qualifications and his general character as a man of delightful personal charm, broad classical culture, extensive reading, and humane sympathies, he possessed, or could acquire, the business ability and the specific insight into educational problems which were expected of a college president was uncertain. In the opinion of many of the alumni and friends of the college, moreover, he was handicapped by the fact that in his Chicago days he had been active as prosecutor in the heresy trial which resulted in the withdrawal of the Rev. David Swing [*q.v.*] from the Presbyterian ministry. The college at Princeton was not a sectarian institution, and many felt that the long succession of ministerial presidents should now be broken. Patton was not, at that time, either by training or by reputation the business man whom some desired, nor the man of science or of political experience whom others wished to see made president. He soon demonstrated, however, that, as he declared a college president ought, he knew "an interest-coupon from a railway-ticket" and was "able to understand a balance-sheet as well as to grade an examination-paper" (*Speech, post,* p. 6). From the start his administration was marked by financial success. On the other hand he did not give up for a moment his interest in theology and his belief that education should include religious instruction. "Princeton is too big to be sectarian," he said, ". . . but we mean that . . . he [the student] who comes to us shall have the universe opened to his view and that he shall deal with its facts and the problems of life under theistic conceptions" (*Ibid.,* p. 5).

In no respect did Patton show more tact and foresight than in the important and delicate task of selecting teachers for appointment or promotion. He acted upon the principle that a teacher's personality is more important than the length of his specific preparation and his possession of degrees. With the able assistance of Dean James O. Murray [*q.v.*], Dean Samuel R. Winans, and a faculty devoted to the college's advancement, he managed its internal affairs successfully, but in a manner that would seem amazingly unsystematic to the head of a great institution today. He had no office except his private library; he employed no secretary or stenographer. His dealing with members of the faculty was direct and personal, yet without secrecy or caballing. He continued to lecture on ethics to the senior class and preached in chapel on many Sundays of the academic year, his sermons being of that original and vital kind which exhaust the speaker while refreshing the hearer. He also conducted daily morning prayers when his other engagements permitted. Thus were the fears of the alumni allayed, and it was not long before he had their enthusiastic support and affectionate regard. His extraordinary felicity as an after-dinner speaker and as Princeton's representative on public occasions awakened their pride and won their loyalty. His figure was graceful, his countenance refined, his manner courteous and gentle, characteristics which made the keenness of his wit and his extraordinary command of legal terms and logical distinctions to appear the more remarkable. It was soon realized that he was a worthy successor of those other British subjects, John Witherspoon and James McCosh, who had brought strength and honor to Princeton.

From the beginning of his administration the requirements for admission to the faculty were altered. Up to that time a large proportion of the appointees had been ministers, without much special training for the teaching profession; thereafter, appointments were normally given to men who had done graduate work in specific fields, abroad or in America. To make room for the teaching of new subjects and the activities of new men, the curriculum of undergraduate studies was expanded by the introduction of elective courses at the expense of those previously required. At Princeton, as at other colleges, the evils inherent in the new system were experienced, but before the end of Patton's term of office these were in some measure corrected, and a plan of coördination of courses and of reasonable restriction in the choice of electives was formed.

In 1896, the 150th anniversary of its founding, the College of New Jersey changed its name to Princeton University and marked the event by a sesquicentennial celebration. One of the delegates whispered, a little maliciously, that from being the strongest American college, Princeton had become the weakest university. During the remaining years of Patton's administration much was done to remove the sting of this remark. He made it clear to trustees, faculty, and alumni that the essential functions of the university were to give instruction in the liberal arts and sciences and to provide facilities for the increase of knowledge, and with their cooperation he strengthened and reorganized the graduate school and vastly increased the instruments of research. Six new dormitories, an auditorium, a new library building, and new houses for the literary societies were erected in his administration. "From this period," writes Mr. V. L. Collins, "may be dated the modern development of the campus, the intro-

duction of the English collegiate gothic into American university architecture, the opening of the School of Electrical Engineering, the introduction of new entrance requirements, and the revision of the course of study along lines which were to be perfected in the next administration, the stiffening of the requirements for the higher degrees, the adoption of the honor system in the conduct of examinations . . . and the grant of alumni representation on the board of trustees" (*post*, p. 252). The number of undergraduates rose from 603 to 1354, and of the faculty from 40 to 100.

Although so eminently successful, Patton was not fond of administrative work, and in June 1902, he surprised even his intimate friends by resigning the presidency and nominating Woodrow Wilson to take his place, retaining, however, for twelve years longer the professorship of ethics and the philosophy of religion. Almost immediately after his resignation, in 1902, he was made president of Princeton Theological Seminary, which for nearly a century had had no formal head. This position he held till 1913, when, after a short interval, he withdrew to his old home in Bermuda. He returned every year, however, until near the end of his life, to lecture in Princeton and elsewhere. In his last years he was blind.

He published in 1869 a book entitled *The Inspiration of the Scriptures*, and in 1898 *A Summary of Christian Doctrine*. His chief literary production is *Fundamental Christianity*, dedicated to his wife and published in 1926, soon after the sixtieth anniversary of their marriage. In this volume can be found the substance of many of his lectures, though one misses much of the imaginative gleam and witty sword-play that accompanied their delivery. He died in Bermuda in his ninetieth year. His wife and three of their seven children survived him.

[V. L. Collins, *Princeton* (1914); *Proc. N. J. Hist. Soc.*, Jan. 1936; *Biog Cat. Princeton Theol. Sem.* (1933); *Speech of Prof. Francis L. Patton . . . at the Ann. Dinner of the Princeton Club of N. Y., on Mar. 15, 1888* (1888); *Who's Who in America, 1932–33*; *N. Y. Times*, Nov. 27, 1932; *Princeton Alumni Weekly*, Apr. 25, 1930, Feb. 13, 1931, Dec. 2, 1932.]

G. M. H.

PATTON, JOHN MERCER (Aug. 10, 1797–Oct. 29, 1858), lawyer and statesman, was born at Fredericksburg, Va., the third of eight children of Robert and Anne Gordon (Mercer) Patton. His father, a Scotsman who had emigrated to Virginia prior to the Revolution, made a competent fortune in business. His maternal grandfather, also Scotch, was Gen. Hugh Mercer [*q.v.*]. After studying a year at Princeton, Patton entered the medical school of the University

of Pennsylvania from which he graduated in
1818. He did not practise, however, but returned
to Fredericksburg and studied law. Admitted to
the bar he began the practice of his second profession in which he soon achieved recognition.
On Jan. 8, 1824, he married Margaret French
Williams, daughter of Isaac Hite and Lucy Coleman (Slaughter) Williams of Frederick County.
Six years later he was sent to Congress to fill the
vacancy caused by the resignation of Philip P.
Barbour and was returned in 1831. Although
elected as a Democrat he pursued an independent
course. But in the controversy which raged over
Jackson's withdrawal of deposits from the Bank,
he vigorously supported the President. When a
copy of the resolutions of the Virginia Assembly
disapproving Jackson's action was transmitted
by Gov. John Floyd to Patton, he was unyielding
and rebuked the Governor for officially intimat-
ing the desirability of a different course.

Although successively reëlected to Congress
without opposition, Patton resigned in 1838. Removing to Richmond he resumed the practice of
law, but public service still claimed him and with
both Whig and Democratic support he was elected to the Executive Council or Council of State
of Virginia. Unopposed, he was reëlected to this
office four times and in 1841, as senior councilor,
became acting governor for a brief period following the resignation of Gov. Thomas Walker
Gilmer. But the law proved a jealous mistress
and Patton's interest in politics waned. On several occasions he declined to be a candidate for
public office, but in 1855 he allowed his name to
be presented to the electorate for the office of
attorney-general of Virginia on the American
or Know-Nothing ticket, not because he was
eager for the place but because of its relation to
his profession. Always independent politically he
was attracted strongly by the Know-Nothing
movement and in the campaign he declared his
firm opposition to the slightest control over
Americans by any foreign power, religious or
temporal. Defeated in the election he devoted his
remaining years to his work at the Richmond
bar, of which he was the acknowledged leader.
In 1854 he was appointed to the Board of Visitors
of the Medical College of Virginia, in Richmond,
on which he served as president until his death
in 1858. Patton's greatest achievement, perhaps,
was the revision of the Virginia code. With Conway Robinson he was appointed in 1846 to revise and digest the civil code of Virginia; the
next year revision of the criminal code also was
placed in their hands. Systematically and thoroughly prepared, their *Code of Virginia* (1849)
was far superior to all previous revisions and,

modified only by constitutional and statutory
changes, it remained the code of Virginia until
1873. Although Patton died before the Civil War
he left six sons who served in the Confederate
army.

[H. W. Flournoy, ed., *Calendar of Va. State Papers*, vol. X (1892); *Biog. Dir. Am. Cong.* (1928); R. A. Brock, *Va. and Virginians* (1888), vol. I; T. K. Cartmell, *Shenandoah Valley Pioneers and Their Descendants* (1909); W. A. Christian, *Richmond: Her Past and Present* (1912); J. T. Goolrick, *The Life of Gen. Hugh Mercer* (1906); W. E. Ross, "Hist. of Va. Codification," *Va. Law Reg.*, June 1905; J. M. Patton, *Speech of Hon. John Mercer Patton at the African Ch. Tuesday Night Apr. 3* (1855); *Daily Richmond Enquirer*, Nov. 1, 1858; *Daily Nat. Intelligencer* (Wash., D. C.), Nov. 3, 1858.]   T. S. C.

PATTON, WILLIAM (Aug. 23, 1798–Sept.
9, 1879), clergyman and author, was the third son
of Col. Robert Patton, who was of Scotch-Irish
ancestry, and had come to America when a young
man. He had served under Lafayette in the
American Revolution, and for more than twenty
years, until his death in 1814, was postmaster of
Philadelphia. William's mother was Cornelia
(Bridges) Patton, who traced her ancestry to the
Culpeper and Fairfax families of Virginia and
England. She died when William was eight
years old. He united at the age of eighteen with
the First Presbyterian Church of Philadelphia,
his native city, graduated at Middlebury College
in 1818, and studied several months in Princeton Theological Seminary (1819–20). In 1819
he married Mary Weston. After being ordained
to the ministry in 1820 by the Congregational
Association of Vermont, he removed to New
York City, the home of his wife. Impelled by a
missionary spirit, he gathered together the members who constituted his first church, the Central
Presbyterian, and served it several years without
salary.

His pulpit and business ability led to his being
called in 1833 to the secretaryship of the Central
American Education Society. During the next
four years he recruited the ministry and raised
money for educational purposes, but in 1837 returned to the pastorate. At Spring Street Presbyterian Church he won much success in revival
work, in persuading young men to enter the ministry, and particularly in influencing children.
Apparently the first to propose that a Presbyterian theological seminary be established in New
York City, Patton in 1836 became one of the
four ministerial founders of Union Seminary,
and served as a director from the beginning until 1849, and as instructor or "professor extraordinary" for three years. His last pastorate,
begun in 1848, was at Hammond Street Congregational Church, New York, a new enterprise
initiated by some of his close friends. Financial

difficulties compelled the organization, in spite of increasing membership, to surrender its property in 1852.

During the remaining twenty-seven years of his life his home was in or near New Haven, Conn., and his time was devoted largely to supplying pulpits and to the literary work begun early in his career. In 1834 he had recast a British commentary, Thomas Williams' *Cottage Bible and Family Expositor*, making it substantially a new work. More than 170,000 copies of it were sold in America. In collaboration with Thomas Hastings, he published *The Christian Psalmist* (1839), a hymn book which for a time had a wide circulation, and he prepared British editions of *Edwards on Revivals* (1839) and of C. G. Finney's *Lectures on Revivals of Religion* (1835). Between 1825 and 1879 he made fourteen voyages to Europe, partly on account of his health, which until middle age was precarious. Ambitious to inform Britain of the true spirit of America, in 1861 he wrote articles for English dailies explaining the anti-slavery background of the Civil War, and published in London a pamphlet, *The American Crisis; or, The True Issue, Slavery or Liberty*. In England, as in the United States, he constantly attacked slavery and the alcoholic traffic. He proposed and attended the meeting at London in 1846 which organized the Evangelical Alliance for promoting Christian union and religious liberty throughout the world. During his New Haven days he published additional books, including *The Judgment of Jerusalem Predicted in Scripture, Fulfilled in History* (1877) and *Bible Principles Illustrated by Bible Characters* (1879).

From 1830 to 1870 he was a member of the executive committee of the American Home Missionary Society, and at his death, in New Haven, he left legacies to the American Board of Commissioners for Foreign Missions, to the American Missionary Association in Aid of the Freedmen, and to Howard University, whose president was his son, Rev. William Weston Patton. Of his ten children, five died early, the survivors being two sons and three daughters. The mother of them all was Mary (Weston) Patton, who died in 1857. In 1860 he married Mrs. Mary (Shaw) Bird of Philadelphia, whose death occurred in 1863. His third wife, whom he married in 1864, was Mrs. Emily (Trowbridge) Hayes.

[W. W. Patton, *A Filial Tribute* (1880); Jonathan Greenleaf, *A Hist. of the Churches of All Denominations in the City of N. Y.* (1850); G. L. Prentiss, *The Union Theol. Sem. in the City of N. Y.* (1889); *Gen. Cat. of the Union Theol. Sem.* (1926); and *Necrological Reports and Ann. Proc. of the Alumni Asso. of Princeton Theol. Sem.*, vol. I (1891); *New Haven Evening Register*, Sept. 10, 1879.]   P. P. F.

PAUGER, ADRIEN de (d. June 9, 1726), engineer of the French colony of Louisiana and the first surveyor of the original town of New Orleans, was a native of France. About all that can be said definitely about him prior to his coming to Louisiana is that he was appointed engineer in 1707 and Chevalier of St. Louis in 1720 and had been captain of the Navarre regiment. He was appointed assistant engineer of Louisiana under Le Blond de la Tour [*q.v.*] in 1720, and arrived in Biloxi, the capital of the colony, on Nov. 24 (*Lettres Edificantes Inedits*, V, October 1818). La Tour arrived in the following month. At the time the council of the colony was undecided as to whether they would rebuild Biloxi, which had been almost completely destroyed by fire in 1719, or transfer the capital to some other place. Bienville, the governor of the colony, wished to move the capital to New Orleans, but the council, under the advice of La Tour, decided to reëstablish it a short distance to the west of Biloxi and give it the name of New Biloxi, and in September 1721 the transfer was made.

In the meantime La Tour had been ordered to send Pauger to New Orleans to make a thorough examination of the site to determine whether the settlement should remain there or be moved to some other spot to avoid the dangers of inundation. Pauger went to New Orleans in March 1721, and deeming the site safe, he began at once to lay out the town. He found that the settlers had built their cabins here and there "among the bushes and the clumps of trees" as they pleased without any regard to alignments. (Dumont de Montigny's drawing of the original settlement has been reproduced in Villiers du Terrage, *Histoire de la Fondation de la Nouvelle Orleans*.) The situation was therefore very difficult for Pauger, but he resolutely set to work and with the assistance of about ten soldiers, whom the commandant of the post had put at his service, he was able to clear enough land within twelve days to make possible the tracing of all the streets on the river front. He drew up a plan for a town of about one mile square, which constitutes the French Quarter of the present city of New Orleans, and sent it to La Tour at Biloxi on Apr. 14. Instead of forwarding the plan on to Paris, La Tour is said to have pigeonholed it for fear the capital of the colony would be moved. Bienville, who was eager for that very thing, procured a copy of the plan and sent it to Paris. Shortly thereafter the capital was ordered moved to New Orleans, and La Tour then officially approved of Pauger's plan. (For a refutation of La Tour's claim that he had drawn up the plan originally, see the sketch of La Tour.)

In plotting the town of New Orleans, Pauger aroused a great deal of opposition on the part of some of the inhabitants, for he had to disarrange existing property divisions. He also incurred the enmity of De Lorme, the chief clerk of the colony. In drawing up his plan of the town, he had indicated on it "grants of a few plots to the oldest inhabitants and those most capable of building along the river bank." De Lorme claimed that he had the exclusive right to make concessions and ordered all of Pauger's grants annulled. The matter was finally adjusted after La Tour had recalled Pauger to Biloxi, and with only a few exceptions all of Pauger's concessions were confirmed. One of the few exceptions was the concession that Pauger had conferred upon himself.

In June 1722 La Tour and Pauger left New Biloxi for New Orleans, and after their arrival in July, La Tour began to carry out Pauger's plan for the development of the town. Pauger was, however, soon replaced by Boispinel and sent down the river to the Balize in January 1723. The death of Boispinel in the following September and of La Tour in October advanced Pauger to the position of chief engineer of the colony. His troubles, however, continued. He asked to sit on the colonial board, and though the company granted his request in November 1724, his enemies long prevented him from taking his seat save for matters directly concerning his work. He was, moreover, not able to get the concession which he had made to himself confirmed until September 1725, and in his disgust he began to think of returning to France. He was not permitted, however, to do so. He was stricken with fever and died in his house in New Orleans on June 9, 1726, four days after he made his will, disposing of his property to his friends in the colony. In the founding of New Orleans, Pauger had a very important part, second only to that of Bienville.

[The chief source of information concerning Pauger is Baron Marc de Villiers du Terrage, *Histoire de la Fondation de la Nouvelle-Orleans (1717–22)* (Paris, 1917). A translation of this monograph appeared in the *La. Hist. Quart.*, Apr. 1920. Scattered references to him are to be found in the *Journal Historique de l'Établissement des Français à la Louisiane* (New Orleans and Paris, 1831), and Pierre Heinrich, *La Louisiane sous la Compagnie des Indies, 1717–31* (n.d.). Pierre Margry's *Découvertes et Établissements des Français dans l'Ouest et dans le Sud de L'Amérique Septentrionale . . . Mémoires et Documents Originaux*, vol. V (Paris, 1883), contains a number of official letters to and from Pauger.]
E. M. V.

PAUL, HENRY MARTYN (June 25, 1851–Mar. 15, 1931), astronomer, engineer, and teacher, the eldest of six children of Ebenezer and Susan (Dresser) Paul, was born at Dedham, Mass. His ancestry may be traced directly to Richard Paul (1636), one of the first settlers of Cohannet, now Taunton, Mass. By 1664 Richard's son, Samuel, had moved to Dorchester where his son, another Samuel, acquired a large estate including what was later known as the "Paul Homestead." This was located near Paul's Bridge on the Neponset River in what later became the town of Dedham and still more recently Hyde Park. Here Henry Martyn Paul spent his boyhood in work on his father's farm. He attended the local public schools and after four years at the Dedham High School entered Dartmouth College, from which he received the degree of A.B. in 1873. He won the sophomore prize in mathematics, acted as assistant to his instructors in engineering courses, and during the winter of his sophomore year taught a district school at Waterford, Vt. His extra-curricular activities included editorship, rowing, and music.

In the fall of 1873 he entered the Thayer School of Engineering at Dartmouth and two years later received the degrees of C.E. and A.M. During this period he assisted in teaching astronomy and meteorology in the New Hampshire College of Agriculture and Mechanic Arts. Immediately following his graduation from the Thayer School he was for a few weeks assistant to Prof. Elihu T. Quimby, then triangulating the state of New Hampshire for the United States Coast Survey. He was appointed junior assistant at the Naval Observatory at Washington in August 1875 and assigned to work with the transit circle under Prof. John R. Eastman [*q.v.*]. The telegram ordering him to Washington was relayed by heliotrope from Hanover to the triangulation station on Croydon Mountain. In 1878 he declined the professorship of astronomy at Dartmouth, but two years later (1880) resigned his position at the Naval Observatory to become the first professor of astronomy at the University of Tokio, returning to the Naval Observatory in 1883. At Washington he was chiefly occupied with the time-consuming routine of the transit instrument, the equatorial, the care of the library, the publications, and the time service, but he also took part in observing and discussing observations of the transit of Mercury of May 1878, the total solar eclipse of 1878, the longitude of Princeton, the semi-diameter of the moon, and observations of variable stars, while occasionally contributing to scientific journals. In 1897 he became professor of mathematics in the United States Navy and in 1899 was transferred to the Bureau of Yards and Docks with duties of engineer. In this capacity he served until 1905, when he was assigned to the Naval Academy at Annapolis as teacher of mathematics. Here he remained until 1912, and in the following year he retired from the navy with the rank of captain.

He married, Aug. 27, 1878, Augusta Anna Gray, daughter of Rev. Edgar H. Gray of Washington, and to them was born an only son, who also became an engineer. Paul was a fellow of the American Association for the Advancement of Science, a member of the American Astronomical Society, the Washington Academy of the Sciences, and the Philosophical Society of Washington. His interest in music was lifelong and for many years he was precentor in a Washington church and an officer of the Washington choral society.

[Reports and publications of the United States Naval Observatory, 1876–97; *Gen. Cat. Dartmouth College* (1910–11); *Dartmouth Alumni Mag.*, May 1931; *N. Y. Times*, Mar. 17, 1931; J. M. and Jaques Cattell, *Am. Men of Science* (4th ed., 1927); E. C. Paul, "The Paul Homestead in Dedham," *Dedham Hist. Reg.*, Oct. 1899; D. L. Paul, Fulton Paul, and M. C. Crane, *Family Register of Richard Paul* (n.d.); personal letters and genealogical material in the hands of Mrs. Oliver H. Howe of Cohasset, Mass., Henry M. Paul's sister, who kindly supplied certain information concerning family affairs; information from acquaintances.]

J. M. P—r.

PAUL, JOHN [See WEBB, CHARLES HENRY, 1834–1905].

PAULDING, HIRAM (Dec. 11, 1797–Oct. 20, 1878), naval officer, was born on his father's farm in Westchester County, N. Y. He was a descendant of Joost Pauldinck who came from Holland to New York before 1683, the seventh child of John Paulding, celebrated as a captor of Major André in the Revolution, and his second wife, Esther Ward. Country schooling ended with his appointment as midshipman Sept. 1, 1811, after which he studied mathematics and navigation in New York. In 1813 he was ordered to Lake Ontario but was transferred soon afterward to the Champlain Squadron. In recognition of his gallant services in the battle of Lake Champlain as acting lieutenant in the *Ticonderoga*, he received $1500 prize-money and a sword from Congress. He served in the *Constellation* against the Barbary powers, was promoted in 1816 to the rank of lieutenant, and spent the next three years in cruising in the *Macedonian* of the Pacific Squadron. He then took advantage of an opportunity to study at Capt. Alden Partridge's military academy at Norwich, Vermont, graduating with the class of 1823. While on duty again in the Pacific in the *United States*, he carried Admiral Hull's dispatches from Callao to General Bolivar's headquarters in the Andes—a commission which entailed a journey of 1500 miles on horseback. He volunteered the following year, 1825,

for a long cruise in the South Seas as first lieutenant of the *Dolphin*, pursuing mutineers from the whaleship *Globe*. This voyage brought novel and exciting experiences one of which was described by Charles Henry Davis, 1807–1877 [*q.v.*], as "the boldest act he ever witnessed" (C. H. Davis, *Life of Charles Henry Davis*, 1899, p. 32). In the face of several hundred infuriated savages, Paulding seized one mutineer and marched him to a boat, using the body of his captive as a shield. Descriptions of these activities appear in Paulding's *Bolivar in his Camp* (1834) and his *Journal of a Cruise of the United States Schooner Dolphin* (1831). Both narratives reveal a gift for writing and a fondness for poetry and reading.

In 1828 he married Ann Maria, the daughter of Jonathan W. Kellogg of Flatbush, L. I., and in 1837 purchased a farm on the Sound near Huntington, L. I., where with his family of four daughters and two sons, he enjoyed brief intervals of home life. His sea duty, meanwhile, included two Mediterranean cruises in the *Constellation*, 1830–32, in the *Shark*, 1834–37, and, after his promotion to the rank of captain, a China cruise in the *Vincennes* from 1844 to 1847. His sound judgment, conciliatory temper, and fine presence made appropriate his next assignment to command the new frigate *St. Lawrence*, the first American warship to visit Bremen, and, according to her captain, also the first to venture the "experiment of social intercourse with the people of any part of England" (R. P. Meade, *post*, p. 111). Paulding visited Frankfort during the parliament of 1848, and was earnestly consulted on the subject of building up a German navy, in which, it appears, he was offered a high command. In December 1848 his ship went to Southampton, England, where for a month there ensued cordial exchange of hospitalities. Four years in charge of the Washington navy yard were followed by the command of the Home Squadron, 1855–58, operating mainly in the Caribbean. The chief episode of this command was Paulding's seizure of Gen. William Walker [*q.v.*] and about 150 filibusters who had landed in defiance of the United States sloop *Saratoga*, at Grey Town, Nicaragua. Upon his arrival Paulding threw a force of 350 men ashore, compelled Walker's surrender without bloodshed on Dec. 8, 1857, and sent him and his followers home. This bold action met with approval in the North, but the Buchanan administration set Walker free and soon relieved the commodore of his command. The Nicaraguan government demonstrated its gratitude by presenting Paulding with a jewelled sword.

Though above the age for active command, he was appointed head of the Bureau of Detail in March 1861, with the responsibility of selecting dependable officers for wartime duties. Other duties were added, notably that of leading the expedition which on Apr. 21, 1861, evacuated the Norfolk navy yard. In the complete demoralization there—ships already scuttled and lifting shears cut away, Paulding can hardly be blamed for executing his orders, which were to evacuate after removing or destroying whatever possible; but it meant leaving nearly 3,000 cannon in Confederate hands and subjecting himself to severe criticism. On the board for the construction of new ironclads, Paulding, along with Commander Davis and Commodore Joseph Smith [*q.v.*] met his responsibilities creditably by the selection of the *Monitor* and *New Ironsides* models for immediate completion. John Ericsson [*q.v.*], the designer, wrote to Paulding, Nov. 26, 1862, "Without your firm support the *Monitor* would not have been built" (R. P. Meade, *post*, p. 291). He referred chiefly to his advocacy of the design, but commended also his energy in pushing its construction and equipment while head of the New York navy yard, to which he had been appointed in the autumn of 1861. He remained at this post until April 1865, carrying out the important work of supply and repair for the blockading fleets. During the Draft Riots of July 1863, naval forces under his direction aided effectively in protecting lives and government property. Though retired in December 1861 with promotion to rear admiral (retired) the following July, Paulding was thus actively employed throughout the war. Afterwards, he served as governor of the United States Naval Asylum at Philadelphia, 1866–69, and as port admiral at Boston, 1869–70. Death from heart trouble at his Long Island home ended a long and honorable career, at the close of which he was senior on the retired list and the last officer survivor of the engagement on Lake Champlain.

[Rebecca Paulding Meade, *Life of Hiram Paulding, Rear Admiral, U. S. N.* (1910); Commander R. W. Meade, "Admiral Paulding," *Harper's Mag.*, Feb. 1879; J. T. Headley, in *Farragut and Our Naval Leaders* (1880); L. N. Feipel, "The Navy and Filibustering in the Fifties," *U. S. Naval Inst. Proc.*, Aug. 1918; *Army and Navy Jour.*, Oct. 26, 1878; *N. Y. Times*, Oct. 21, 1878.]
A. W.

PAULDING, JAMES KIRKE (Aug. 22, 1778–Apr. 6, 1860), author and naval official, the youngest son of William and Catharine (Ogden) Paulding, was born at Great Nine Partners, now Putnam County, N. Y., where the family had taken refuge during the Revolution. After commanding several ships, his father be-came a merchant at Tarrytown, an influential patriot, and commissary of the New York militia. To provide food for the soldiers, he assumed an obligation of nearly $10,000, which through a miscarriage of justice bankrupted and temporarily jailed him in 1785. In meeting this disaster, the mother by her thrift and magic needle supported and schooled the children so well that Julia married William Irving and a son William became congressman and mayor of New York City. At Tarrytown, a quiet Dutch village overlooking the Hudson, James, like Wordsworth, acquired an early and enduring love for nature and homespun people. There he received scanty schooling, became dreamy and melancholy, hunted, fished, admired Goldsmith's prose, and met Washington Irving. When about eighteen, he joined his brother in New York and worked in a public office. Living with the versatile William Irving and forming pleasant associations, Paulding became happy, read literature, and observed politics. His acquaintance with Washington Irving ripened into a lasting friendship. The city of New York with its varied cultural and commercial activities was his training school, and in due time the shy boy, like Franklin, working out his own scholastic salvation, became a well-bred man, capable official, and popular writer.

In 1807–08 Paulding and Irving collaborated in a whimsical periodical, *Salmagundi*, which entertained the town and attracted widespread interest. Stimulated by the popularity of this venture and Irving's success in comic history, Paulding next wrote *The Diverting History of John Bull and Brother Jonathan* (1812), which comically depicted the settlement, growth, and revolt of the thirteen colonies. The next year he parodied Scott's verse stories in *The Lay of the Scottish Fiddle*, and, after five years, published his ambitious poem, *The Backwoodsman* (1818). Neither poem enhanced the author's reputation appreciably. Meanwhile, for the *Analectic Magazine* he composed popular sketches of the naval commanders in the War of 1812. Continued British censure of America and a savage review of his poetic parody in English magazines precipitated his impressive defense, *The United States and England*, which was published in 1815. It brought Paulding an appointment by President Madison as secretary of the newly created Board of Navy Commissioners, and to fill this position, he lived from 1815 to 1823 in Washington. On Nov. 15, 1818, he was married to Gertrude Kemble, the sister of Gouverneur Kemble [*q.v.*].

After the Revolution, scores of English travelers visited the United States and returned to

England with gossipy, prejudiced accounts of the new nation. These critics provoked the so-called literary war, to which Paulding contributed five works. His environment explains in part his excusable antipathy to England. Born in exile, he grew up in a region devastated by the British; nine of the Pauldings served in the American army; two of his relatives knew the horrors of British prison ships; his maternal grandfather was cruelly cut across the head by British soldiers, because he had refused to cry, "God save the king!" Besides the two controversial books already mentioned, Paulding wrote *Letters from the South* (1817), which aimed to depict one section truthfully; *A Sketch of Old England* (1822), an unfavorable account based wholly upon his reading; and *John Bull in America* (1825), an effective burlesque. These replies made him famous, and in 1824 President Monroe appointed him navy agent for New York, where with his wife and children he resided till 1838.

Paulding now had adequate income and leisure for writing. Purging his mind of the Anglo-American controversy, he composed realistic tales and novels in consonance with his theory of "rational fiction" based upon Fielding's practice and expounded in 1820. He disliked the inflated English then in fashion, and by his own literary work won Poe's praise and a master's degree from Columbia. Altogether, he published more than seventy tales, six of which were included in Mary Russell Mitford's English collections of 1830 and 1832. Though frequently marred by haste and loose construction, they have distinct merits. They are satiric or witty, wholesome, natural, and national. The best depict Dutch characters and customs; "The Dumb Girl" (1830) resembles and may have influenced *The Scarlet Letter*. Free from romantic extravagance, Hawthorne's gloom, and Poe's melancholy, they exhibit Paulding's fine sense of human values and his love of humor and of life.

In a romantic and sentimental age, he wrote five realistic novels, which appeared in European translations. *Koningsmarke* (1823), an imitative effort, satirizing Scott's romances and internal improvements, depicted the Indians and colonial Swedes of Delaware. After composing a score of tales and a prize-winning comedy, he published his best novel, *The Dutchman's Fireside* (1831), a veracious account of the New York Dutch before the Revolution, admirable for style, description, and characterization. Next came *Westward Ho!* (1832), recounting the adventures of a Virginia family in Kentucky. *The Old Continental* (1846) is a domestic pic-

ture of the Revolution in New York, more convincing than Cooper's *The Spy*. *The Puritan and His Daughter* (1849) is a story of Cromwell's England and Virginia.

In *Letters from the South, A Sketch of Old England, Salmagundi* (Second Series, 1819–20), *A Life of Washington* (1835), *Slavery in the United States* (1836), and in magazine articles, Paulding treated nearly every phase of American life, theorized on prose and poetry, and commented on contemporary authors. He shared Carlyle's adverse opinion of Byron, bewailed American imitation of foreign literature, and denounced our want of confidence and self-respect. His liberal Americanism recognized no sectional bounds. While he sincerely revered God and true religion, he was impatient of servility to a narrow ecclesiastical system. "High rents and heavy taxes," he observed, "will spoil even paradise."

Paulding, feeling like "a gentleman of leisure metamorphosed into a pack horse," was secretary of the navy in Van Buren's cabinet. Strife and intemperance in the service he tried to eradicate by rigid discipline, and he sent the South Sea Exploring Expedition on its four-year cruise to the Oregon coast and the Antarctic Continent. In 1841 his wife died, and the next year he accompanied Van Buren on a long western tour. In 1846 he retired to a country estate near Hyde Park, N. Y., where, surrounded by his children and the beauties of the Hudson, he grew old gracefully. Here he died at eighty-two, and was buried in Greenwood Cemetery, Brooklyn, leaving considerable property to his children. His son William described him as above medium height, strongly built, with fine black hair in youth and brown eyes, and a profile resembling an ancient philosopher.

From 1807 to 1850 Paulding was a prominent political and literary figure in American life, but he has faded into the past. His once useful political and satirical writings are almost forgotten. Much of his fiction may be discarded, for, like his contemporaries, he wrote too much and revised too little. He was, however, distinguished for his versatility and independence, and for his contribution to the short story, and, because of his tales and novels, he deserves to be remembered as the chief Dutch interpreter of the New York Dutch.

[E. A. and G. L. Duyckinck, *Cyc. of Am. Lit.* (1856), vol. II, contains a valuable sketch authorized by Paulding. See also: W. I. Paulding, *Lit. Life of Jas. K. Paulding* (1867) ; P. M. Irving, *The Life and Letters of Washington Irving* (4 vols., 1862–64) ; *The Letters of Washington Irving to Henry Brevoort* (2 vols., 1915), ed. by G. S. Hellman; J. G. Wilson, *Bryant and His Friends* (1886) ; Amos L. Herold, *Jas. Kirke*

Paulding, Versatile American (1926), a critical estimate with bibliography; Oscar Wegelin, "A Bibliog. of the Separate Publications of Jas. Kirke Paulding," *The Papers of the Bibliog. Soc. of America*, vol. XII (1918); V. L. Parrington, *Main Currents in Am. Thought*, vol. II (1927).]
                                            A. L. H.

PAVY, OCTAVE (June 22, 1844–June 6, 1884), Arctic explorer, physician, naturalist, was born in New Orleans, La., but was educated in France, studying science, art, and medicine at the University of Paris, and giving considerable time to travel on the continent of Europe. In his later twenties he was appointed associate commander with Gustave Lambert in an Arctic expedition projected by the French government. The outbreak of the Franco-Prussian war prevented the departure of this expedition, and Pavy, together with Lieutenant Beauregard, a nephew of Gen. Pierre G. T. Beauregard of the Confederate army, organized and equipped at their own expense an independent Zouave corps composed of veteran soldiers and sailors of French parentage who had been residents of North or South America. After the war, Pavy returned to the United States and began preparations for a north-polar expedition by way of Bering Strait. In 1872, just before the expedition was to leave, the sudden death of a financial supporter compelled the abandonment of the project. Pavy then took a course of lectures at the Missouri Medical College, to familiarize himself with English medical phraseology. In 1878 he married Lilla May Stone of Lebanon, Ill. For two and a half years he lived in St. Louis, serving as physician at the Meyer Iron Works and lecturing on the Arctic regions.

In June 1880 he joined H. W. Howgate's expedition to Greenland as surgeon and naturalist, sailing on the *Gulnare*. When the ship, proving unfit for polar navigation, returned to the United States, he remained in Greenland and for a year explored the coast, studying the fauna and flora of the country and becoming familiar with the technique of Arctic exploration. In July 1881 the Lady Franklin Bay expedition under the command of Lieut. A. W. Greely of the United States Army arrived in Greenland, with a commission for Pavy as surgeon of the expedition. Until his death three years later he served in that capacity and for a time acted also as naturalist. He took part in a number of sledge journeys by which this expedition extended the geographic and meteorological knowledge of the region, and in particular brought to light the fact that the polar region is not the sea of solid immovable ice which until then it had been considered. Under the hardships which the party had to endure it was but natural that friction should develop between Pavy—cognizant of his own abilities and with experience as physician, army officer, and Arctic explorer—and Greely. Pavy questioned some of Greely's decisions, and Greely considered Pavy insubordinate, at one time placing him under arrest (Greely, *Three Years of Arctic Service*, II, 62, 66, 320; for Pavy's side of the case, see *North American Review*, April 1886, pp. 371–80). The expedition comprised twenty-five members and had been provisioned for two years. A relief ship had been expected in 1882, but neither that year nor the following year did it appear, and in August 1883 Greely led his party toward Smith Sound. Here they were forced to winter on short rations, the last ration being issued on May 24. The only food remaining was sealskin thongs. One by one, members of the party died of slow starvation, and on June 6, 1884—sixteen days before the rescue of the six survivors—Pavy died at Cape Sabine. In large part, the health of the party during the three years of exposure and the prolonging of the life of a number of its members at Cape Sabine may be ascribed to his services.

[The best biographical material is found in *St. Louis Courier of Medicine*, Feb. 1886, and "Dr. Pavy and the Polar Expedition" and "An Arctic Journal" published by Pavy's widow, L. M. Pavy, in *North Am. Rev.*, Mar.–Apr. 1886. See also, A. W. Greely, *Three Years of Arctic Service* (2 vols., 1886) and *International Polar Expedition: Report on the Proc. of the U. S. Expedition to Lady Franklin Bay* (1888), being *House Doc. 393*, 49 Cong., 1 Sess. The *St. Louis Globe-Democrat*, July 18, 20, 1884, contains some information, not altogether accurate.]
                                            H. A. M.

PAYNE, CHRISTOPHER HARRISON (Sept. 7, 1848–Dec. 4, 1925), negro Baptist clergyman, lawyer, United States official, was born of free parents near Red Sulphur Springs, Monroe County, Va. (now West Virginia). His very intelligent mother was the daughter and had been the slave of James Ellison, who taught her to read and write. She in turn imparted the rudiments of education to her son, who was her only child. Her husband was Thomas Payne, a cattle drover, who died when the boy was two years old. From 1861 until 1864 Christopher was compelled to serve as a body servant in the Confederate army. During the next two years he worked as a farm hand near Hinton, W. Va. He next engaged in steamboating on the Ohio River but soon moved to Charleston, W. Va. Here he attended night school until 1868, when he succeeded in passing the examination for a teacher's certificate in Summers County. He then returned to his old home near Hinton and for a number of years taught school in the winter and did farm work in the summer time.

In 1875 he became a convert to the Baptist

faith, was granted a license to preach in the following year, and in 1877 was ordained. The better to equip himself for his new calling he spent the academic year 1877–78 at Richmond Institute (now Virginia Union University). Lack of means then obliged him to return to West Virginia, where he engaged in missionary work. In 1880, however, he was called to the pastorate of the Moore Street Baptist Church in Richmond, and was able to complete his theological course, supporting his family and mother in the meantime. Graduating in 1883, he was appointed missionary for the eastern division of Virginia. In April of the following year he became pastor of the First Baptist Church of Montgomery, W. Va., and subsequently had charge of Baptist churches in Norfolk, Va., and Huntington, W. Va.

For the purpose of disseminating correct information about the achievements of the colored people he founded the *West Virginia Enterprise*. Later on he started *The Pioneer* at Montgomery, W. Va. His third and last weekly he called the *Mountain Eagle*. His ventures in journalism led to his dabbling in politics. He became an active worker for the Republican party and was rewarded with the position of deputy collector of internal revenue at Charleston, W. Va. During his incumbency of this post, 1889 to 1893, he studied law and was admitted to practice in West Virginia. In 1896 he was elected a member of the state legislature, being the first negro to be so honored. From 1898 till 1899 he was a United States internal revenue agent, and on May 1, 1903, was made United States consul at St. Thomas in the Danish West Indies. This position he continued to fill until the purchase of the islands by the United States in 1917. Thereafter he continued to reside in St. Thomas and served first as prosecuting attorney and then, until his death, as police judge.

He was twice married and was survived by six children. His first wife, whom he married in 1866, was Delilah Ann Hargrove, and his second, A. G. Viney of Gallipolis, Ohio. Payne availed himself of every opportunity to improve his mind and was an eloquent preacher and speaker with a fine flow of language. He had a broad forehead and a straight nose and would easily have passed for a white man with dark complexion.

[W. J. Simmons' *Men of Mark* (1887), *The Crisis*, June 1917; *Jour. of Negro Hist.*, Jan. 1926; Byrd Prillerman, in *Bapt. Sunday School Bull.*, Jan., Feb., Mar. 1926; *Who's Who in America*, 1916–17; information from Payne's daughter, Mrs. Martha Adeline Trent, through the courtesy of the Rev. J. J. Turner, Montgomery, W. Va.]
H. G. V.

PAYNE, DANIEL ALEXANDER (Feb. 24, 1811–Nov. 29, 1893), bishop of the African Methodist Episcopal Church, president of Wilberforce University, was born in Charleston, S. C., the son of London and Martha Payne, who were free persons of color. His parents having died before he was ten years old, he was cared for by relatives. For two years he attended a local Minor's Moralist Society School established by free colored men. He next studied under Thomas Bonneau, a private tutor, and not only mastered English and mathematics but made himself conversant with Greek, Latin, and French. Apprenticed first to a shoemaker and later to a tailor, Payne also worked for four years in a carpenter's shop, of which his brother-in-law was foreman. In 1826 he joined the Methodist Episcopal Church and three years later opened a school for colored children, which in a short while became the most successful institution of its kind in Charleston. It flourished until the South Carolina legislature passed a law, on Dec. 17, 1834, imposing a fine and whipping on free persons of color who kept schools to teach slaves or free negroes to read or write. Obliged to discontinue his school, Payne on May 9, 1835, left Charleston for Pennsylvania, where he entered the Lutheran Theological Seminary at Gettysburg. There he supported himself by blacking boots, waiting at table, and doing other menial tasks. In 1837 he was licensed to preach and in 1839 was ordained by the Franckean Synod of the Lutheran Church. He accepted a call to a Presbyterian church in East Troy, N. Y., but in 1840 moved to Philadelphia, where he opened a school. In 1841 he joined the African Methodist Episcopal Church and in 1842 was received as a preacher at the Philadelphia Conference of that denomination. After serving as a traveling preacher he was appointed to the Israel Church in Washington, D. C. In 1845 he was transferred to Baltimore, Md., where was pastor of Bethel Church.

Chosen historiographer of the African Methodist Episcopal Church in 1848, he traveled extensively in the United States searching for materials. In May 1852 he was elected bishop. As such he exerted himself to raise the cultural standard of the communicants of the denomination by promoting the formation of church literary societies and debating lyceums. During the Civil War he pleaded with Lincoln and other prominent men for the emancipation of the slaves. Without a dollar in hand, on Mar. 10, 1863, he had the temerity to purchase Wilberforce University, an Ohio institution established by the Methodist Episcopal Church in 1856 for the education of colored youths, to which many natural children of slave holders had been sent prior to the War. He was its president for thirteen years. On the day Lincoln was assassinated the main building of the institution was burned. This loss increased the financial burden he had to assume, but during his administration he was instrumental in securing more than $92,000. The enrollment of students also increased greatly. In 1867 he visited Europe for the first time. A delegate to the first Ecumenical Conference of the Methodist Episcopal Church, held in London, England, Payne on Sept. 13, 1881, read a paper on Methodism and Temperance, impressing all by his dignified manners. He also took part in the Parliament of Religions, held in 1893 during the World's Columbian Exposition at Chicago.

After his retirement from Wilberforce he devoted himself to writing and to a continuance of his unrelenting fight against the illiteracy of the colored Methodist ministers. He was of a light brown complexion and below the average height. Very thin and emaciated and weighing only one hundred pounds, he looked like a consumptive. He had sharp features, an intellectual forehead, keen, penetrating eyes, and a shrill voice. Among his publications were *The Semi-Centenary . . . of the African Methodist Episcopal Church in the U. S. of America* (1866), *A Treatise on Domestic Education* (1885), *Recollections of Seventy Years* (1888), *The History of the A. M. E. Church from 1816 to 1856* (1891). Payne was married in 1847 to Mrs. Julia A. Ferris, daughter of William Becraft of Georgetown, D. C.; she died within a year thereafter, and in 1853 he married Mrs. Eliza J. Clark.

[C. S. Smith, *The Life of Daniel Alexander Payne* (1894); J. W. Cromwell, *The Negro in Am. Hist.* (1914); G. F. Bragg, *Men of Maryland* (1925); W. J. Simmons, *Men of Mark* (1887); Wm. W. Brown, *The Rising Son* (1874); A. R. Wentz, *Hist. of Gettysburg Theological Sem. . . . 1826–1926* (n.d.).] H. G. V.

PAYNE, HENRY B. (Nov. 30, 1810–Sept. 9, 1896), representative and senator from Ohio, was the son of Elisha and Esther (Douglass) Payne and the descendant of Thomas Paine (or Payne) who settled in Yarmouth, Mass., and was admitted freeman of Plymouth Colony in 1639. Both parents were natives of Connecticut. In 1795 his father removed to Hamilton, N. Y., where Henry was born. His education was carefully directed, and in 1832 he was graduated from Hamilton College at Clinton. Sometime after he graduated from college he added the middle initial "B" to his name to give what he considered a more pleasing effect. For a period

he studied law under John C. Spencer [*q.v.*] of Canandaigua, N. Y., at that time forming an acquaintance with Stephen A. Douglas that deepened into intimate friendship. In 1833 he settled in Cleveland, Ohio, then a village of 3,000 people, continuing his law studies and, after his admission to the bar in 1834, entering a law partnership with his old classmate, Hiram V. Willson, later a federal district judge. In 1836 he was married to Mary, the daughter of Nathan Perry, a merchant of Cleveland. They had five children, among them, Flora, who married W. C. Whitney [*q.v.*], and Oliver H. Payne [*q.v.*]. Sereno Elisha Payne [*q.v.*] was his nephew. His success in the practice of law was phenomenal, but in 1846 he began to have hemorrhages from his lungs, which necessitated his retirement from active practice. During these early years he held various municipal offices; later, he was a member of Cleveland's first waterworks commission; and as a sinking fund commissioner from 1862 to 1896 he rendered noteworthy service in reforming the city's finances. One of the founders of the Cleveland and Columbus railroad in 1849, he served as its president from 1851 to 1854, when he resigned and became interested in the Cleveland, Painesville, and Ashtabula railroad.

Serving in the Ohio Senate from 1849 to 1851, he displayed such skill as a parliamentarian and party leader that he became the Democratic choice for United States senator in 1851. Protracted balloting resulted in a few Free-Soilers eventually turning the balance in favor of Benjamin Wade. In 1857 as Democratic candidate for governor he lost the contest to the incumbent, Salmon P. Chase, by a narrow margin. He helped nominate Buchanan in 1856 and at the Democratic convention of 1860 reported the platform which, when adopted, prompted the withdrawal of delegates from the lower South. During the war he was an ardent Unionist. In 1872 a Greeley supporter, he was chairman of the Ohio delegation to the Democratic convention at Baltimore. Elected to Congress in a normally Republican district two years later, he served on the committees on banking and currency and on civil service reform, and he was instrumental in preventing legislation to regulate interstate commerce. In 1876–77 he was chairman of the House committee on the electoral count at Tilden's request and was influential in the passage of legislation providing for the electoral commission, of which he became a member. Affable and courteous, with kindly eyes, smooth-shaven face, gentle voice, and a clerical-cut coat he appeared more like a minister than the shrewd, active man of affairs that he was, a director in twenty corporations and a politician devoted to the interests of business. Although a leading presidential candidate at the Democratic convention of 1880, progress in his behalf was thwarted by the commitment of the Ohio delegation to Allen G. Thurman.

Three years later a Payne movement for the senatorship suddenly developed; he received a majority vote in the Democratic legislative caucus and was promptly elected. He served from Mar. 4, 1885, to Mar. 3, 1891. It was asserted that his son, Oliver H. Payne, treasurer of the Standard Oil Company, had spent $100,000 to obtain the election. The Republican lower house of the next state legislature ordered an investigation; fifty-five witnesses were examined, and the evidence was turned over to the federal Senate, which ultimately refused to act. While the charges were never absolutely proved, the absence of satisfactory denials in the face of reiterated accusations, convinced a large portion of the country that Payne's promoters had practically bought his seat (see I. M. Tarbell, *The History of the Standard Oil Company*, 1904, II, 111–19). In the Senate his principal work was as a committee member. Over eighty at the end of his term, he retired to the Euclid Avenue mansion in Cleveland that was his home for sixty years and died of paralysis five years later.

[A few letters in *Ohio Arch. and Hist. Quart.*, Oct. 1913; reference to existence of a valuable diary probably destroyed before Payne's death in J. F. Rhodes, *Hist. of the U. S.*, vol. VII (1906), p. 269; G. I. Reed, *Bench and Bar of Ohio* (1897), vol. II; A. F. P. White, *The Paynes of Hamilton* (1912); *Sen. Misc. Doc. 106*, 49 Cong., 1 Sess. (1886); A. H. Walker, *The Payne Bribery Case* (1886); *John Sherman's Recollections* (1895), vol. II; J. G. Blaine, *Twenty Years*, vol. II (1886); Murat Halstead, *Caucuses of 1860* (1860); *Cleveland Plain Dealer, Cleveland Leader*, and *Cincinnati Commercial Tribune*, Sept. 10, 1896; information concerning his middle initial from his granddaughter, Mrs. Chester C. Bolton.]　　　F. P. W.

PAYNE, HENRY CLAY (Nov. 23, 1843– Oct. 4, 1904), railroad executive and postmaster-general, son of Orrin and Eliza (Ames) Payne, was born at Ashfield, Mass. He was educated in the schools there and at the Shelburne Falls academy from which he graduated in 1859. After a short business experience in Northampton, Mass., and after being rejected as a soldier, he moved to Milwaukee, Wis., in 1863. Here he entered the dry-goods house of Sherwin, Nowell & Pratt, and served as cashier until 1867. He then entered the insurance business in which he achieved considerable success. His first appearance in politics was in 1872, in the Grant-Greeley campaign, when he organized the Young Men's Republican Club, serving as its first sec-

retary and later as chairman. In 1876 he was appointed postmaster of Milwaukee by President Grant and held that position for ten years, during which time he brought the office to a high state of efficiency, paying especial attention to the money-order branch through which he was able to serve the large foreign-born population of the city. When the Democrats assumed control of the national government in 1885 Payne left the post office and engaged in a number of business enterprises, being especially interested in the development of local public utilities. He was made vice-president of the Wisconsin Telephone Company in 1886 and president three years later. In the same year, 1889, he became interested in the possibility of consolidating the street railways of Milwaukee. In 1890, when the Cream City Railroad Company and the Milwaukee City Railroad were merged, becoming the Milwaukee Street Railway Company, Henry Villard of New York was made president and Payne vice-president and general manager. From 1892 to 1895 Payne acted as president of the company. By the latter year the consolidation of the city lines was complete and the company had also absorbed the electric lighting companies of the city. In 1896, however, the company was in financial straits. Payne was named receiver and then was made vice-president of the reorganized Milwaukee Electric Railway & Light Company. Shortly after the reorganization, a serious strike broke out among the employees of the company. Payne was criticized for his unyielding attitude toward the workmen, and although the strike was broken, public sympathy was with the strikers.

Payne also organized the Milwaukee Light, Heat and Traction Company, which built and operated the suburban electric lines running out of Milwaukee, and was president of the Fox River Electric Railway Company, an interurban electric system. In 1890 he was elected president of the Milwaukee & Northern Railroad Company but resigned in 1893 when the road was consolidated with the Chicago, Milwaukee & St. Paul. When the Northern Pacific Railroad failed he was appointed one of the receivers and served from 1893 to 1895. From 1894 to 1896 he was president of the Chicago & Calumet Terminal Railway. Meantime he had continued his services in the Republican party organization. He was secretary and chairman of the Republican county committee of Milwaukee County and of the Republican State Central Committee after 1872, and a member of the Republican National Committee from 1880 until his death in 1904. In 1888 and 1892 he served as delegate to the Republican National Convention, and during the McKinley-Bryan campaign of 1896 he was in charge of the western headquarters in Chicago. Four years later he worked successfully to have Roosevelt nominated as vice-president of the ticket with McKinley. When Roosevelt became president the following year he repaid his political debt by appointing Payne postmaster-general in January 1902. Before he had been in office three years Payne died suddenly in Washington. He had married, on Oct. 15, 1869, Lydia W. Van Dyke, daughter of Richard and Mary (Thomas) Van Dyke of Mount Holly, N. J. He died childless.

[See W. W. Wight, *Henry Clay Payne, A Life* (1907); *Who's Who in America*, 1903–05; *Ann. Reports of the Post-Office Dept.*, 1902–03; the *Railway Age*, Oct. 7, 1904; *Milwaukee Jour.*, Oct. 5, 1904.]
E. L. B.

PAYNE, JOHN HOWARD (June 9, 1791–Apr. 9, 1852), actor, dramatist, editor, diplomat, was born in New York City, the sixth child of William and Sarah Isaacs Payne and a descendant of Thomas Paine (or Payne) who settled in Yarmouth, Mass., and was admitted freeman of Plymouth Colony in 1639. At the age of thirteen he had already prefigured in his imaginative mind his long association with the stage. Though disciplined by the counsel of his family and by hard toil in the New York counting house of Grant and Bennet Forbes, the precocious boy clung to his desire, and from Dec. 28, 1805, to May 31, 1806, published anonymously the first numbers of his *Thespian Mirror*, an eight-page critical review of the New York theatre, which aroused the interest of William Coleman [q.v.], editor of the *Evening Post*. He followed this adventure a few weeks later by his first play, *Julia, or The Wanderer*, acted at the Park Theatre on Feb. 7, 1806. Such talents, coupled with his personal charm, had already launched him upon his career in New York society, in which he was to know intimately Henry Brevoort, James K. Paulding, Charles Brockden Brown, and Washington Irving, when he was snatched by friends from the temptations of the stage to enroll in Union College. His father's bankruptcy, two years later, offered him an excuse to go on the stage and on Feb. 24, 1809, he made his début as an actor on the New York stage as Young Norval in John Home's tragedy of *Douglas*.

Young Payne's triumph was instantaneous, and during the first six months of this year he was a theatrical sensation in both New York and Boston, acting not only in standard popular plays but in *Romeo and Juliet, Hamlet,* and *King Lear*, and as Frederick, perhaps in his own version, in *Lovers' Vows*. But if Payne as an actor rose with meteor-like speed, he fell almost as swiftly, and though he played at the close of the year 1809 with enormous success in Baltimore and Philadelphia, and with a total profit of about $3,200, he found himself unbooked for engagements for the season of 1810–11. The reasons for the dwindling of his fame are obvious. His beautiful face, his eyes, glowing with animation and intelligence, and his melodious voice could not counterbalance the hard facts that, after all, he was on the stage a transient novelty, that he lacked the depth of study which distinguished the older favorites, that patriotic appreciation of a local prodigy could not last forever, and that he had quarreled with the powerful manager, Stephen Price. Nevertheless, Payne's essential talent on the stage cannot be challenged. By 1811 he had overcome some of the defects of his youth; in its issue of December 1811 the *Mirror of Taste* declared: "That genius, which he unquestionably possesses in a degree superior to any tragic actor on the American stage but Cooke, is now more controlled by judgment and at the same time rendered more active and efficient by study."

Payne, sensitive, petulant, and not yet aware of his gifts as a playwright, suffered keenly from these disappointments, and, as other misfortunes thickened about him, displayed that instability of spirits which was to handicap him throughout his life. His plan to turn bookseller and found in New York a literary exchange failed; he was, in spite of great profits from his acting, heavily in debt; and in 1812 his father died. Yet he still cherished his dream of success on the London boards, and when his friends, including Alexander Hanson, William Gwynn, and Jonathan Meredith, collected a fund of $2,000 to encourage him in an English career, he was confident that he would conquer Drury Lane and Covent Garden and return to America as a renowned tragedian. With such hopes and with numerous letters of introduction he sailed, on Jan. 17, 1813, for Liverpool. He was to remain in Europe for twenty years, a period in his fortunes strangely interwoven with fame and poverty. His friends in England, among them Peter Irving and Benjamin West, conspired for a repetition of his early success. Billed as a "Young Gentleman," he again essayed the part of Young Norval. His English audiences acknowledged his gifts, but what Genest said of the decline of "Master Betty" was also true of Payne, the American Roscius: "the Public had by this time recovered their senses." The applause was audible but not overwhelming, and after a tour of the provinces in the spring and summer of 1814 he was back in London, penniless and without prospects. He had gained little save his friendship with Charles Kemble, and the knowledge that to earn a living he must return to authorship. He realized apparently that he was never to duplicate as an actor his early attainments of 1809. He now began a long career of dramatic hackwork, interrupted by attempts to act, by quarrels with managers (notably with Douglass Kinnaird, of Drury Lane), and even by imprisonment for debt.

The story of these years reveals all the erratic brilliance of Payne's mind and also his lovable nature, for the sake of which his devoted friend Washington Irving allowed himself to be tormented in Paris and London by Payne's creditors. In these two cities he now lived, writing and adapting plays for the London and New York theatres. In 1814 he sold to Henry Harris, manager of Covent Garden, where it was acted twenty-seven times, *The Maid and the Magpie,* an adaptation of *La Pie Voleuse* by Caigniez and Baudouin, and in the next year he composed various musical pieces and plays which with one exception never quite reached the footlights. For two seasons (1818, 1819) he conducted the correspondence for Harris' theatre, read manuscripts, wrote press notices, distributed orders on the house, and in other ways helped to promote the fortunes of plays and actors. Occasionally, in the midst of this drudgery, he struck fire, as in the popular success, *Brutus, or the Fall of Tarquin,* an historical tragedy in five acts (Drury Lane, Dec. 3, 1818), with Kean as Brutus and Julia Glover as Tullia. Although by Payne's own admission *Brutus* was in debt to seven other dramatists, among them Hugh Downman and Richard Cumberland, it was acted fifty-two times in this season and passed through six editions. The play showed Payne's skill in handling dramatic scenes, though Genest lamented that it "met with success *vastly* beyond its merits" (John Genest, *Some Account of the English Stage,* vol. VIII, 1832, p. 679).

This curious admixture of achievement and failure continued to characterize Payne's career. In 1820 he leased Sadler's Wells Theatre, but the collapse here of his own melodramas landed him at the end of the year in Fleet Street Prison, for debt. From this predicament he obtained release by his *Thérèse, the Orphan of Geneva,* a profitable adaptation of a French melodrama, which had its first English performance at Drury Lane, Feb. 2, 1821. Fleeing to Paris to escape duns, he sent over to London numerous plays for which Irving and possibly Haz-

litt served as intermediaries. It seems ironic that while all these ambitious dramas were doomed to oblivion, he was to gain a slender immortality from a single song. *Clari, or, The Maid of Milan* (Covent Garden, May 8, 1823), metamorphosed into an opera at the request of Charles Kemble, contained the lyric "Home, Sweet Home!," which was to be sung throughout the English-speaking world during the remainder of the century. For the play, which was acted only twelve times, Payne received fifty pounds, but for the song not a single penny. About the lyric legends cluster, for example, that Payne heard the air from an Italian peasant girl, or that it symbolized his sad, wandering life. Actually, knowing no music, he wrote the words to the measure of the "Ranz des Vaches," and at the time of its composition he was comfortably established in Paris. Eager for fame as actor and dramatist, he won it paradoxically as the author of a sentimental ballad in a relatively prosperous period of his life.

In the summer of 1823, Irving, who had long been fascinated by Payne's theatrical ventures, returned from Dresden with some unfinished operas and was persuaded to collaborate with his friend. Out of this association resulted at least ten plays, seven of which were produced, and two of which were acted with some success. The three-act comedy, *Charles the Second; or, The Merry Monarch* (Covent Garden, May 27, 1824), with Charles Kemble as the King and Fawcett as Captain Copp, was distinguished for unity of structure, rapidity of action, brilliance of dialogue, and very nearly achieved the quality of high comedy. *Richelieu, A Domestic Tragedy* (Covent Garden, Feb. 11, 1826) was less fortunate, in spite of the efforts of Kemble and Mrs. Glover in the leading rôles; it ran for only six nights. The play revealed for the first time, by its dedication to Irving, the collaboration of the dramatist and the essayist.

Although the meager proceeds from these plays discouraged Irving from further sustained collaboration with Payne, he continued to aid his friend by criticizing his manuscripts and by protecting him from his hordes of creditors. From the fall of 1823 to the summer of 1825 Payne was in London, sometimes under the name of "J. Hayward" in order to escape the attentions of these gentlemen. In the intervals of his troubled dealings with managers, he contrived to fall in love with Mary Wollstonecraft Shelley, who told him frankly that she preferred Washington Irving, news which the latter, when Payne later showed him the lady's correspondence, received calmly, if we may judge from an entry in his journal. No proof exists that in this curious triangle any real passion existed, unless it were the temperamental Payne's for Mrs. Shelley. Certainly it caused no rift in the friendship of Payne and Irving, for at this very time Irving secured for Payne a contract with Stephen Price. Between Oct. 2, 1826, and Mar. 24, 1827, Payne, again in London, brought out the twenty-six numbers of his *Opera Glass,* a weekly paper "for peeping into the microcosm of the fine arts, and more especially of the drama," and for five years more, a period which remains somewhat obscure, he lingered in England. On June 16, 1832, with passage money provided by friends in America, he sailed for home, a disillusioned man of forty-one, rich in experience but as poor as ever in purse.

Yet he found himself an eminent citizen. On Nov. 29 a benefit was arranged for him, offering a program which included *Brutus,* with Edwin Forrest, and *Katherine and Petruchio,* with Charles and Fanny Kemble, both now for the first time in America. The benefit's conclusion was *Charles II,* with James W. Wallack as Captain Copp. Between the plays Payne heard an address of welcome, a rendition of "Home, Sweet Home!," and the finale of *Clari.* This and the public dinner were soothing tributes not only to Payne but also to the army of creditors, who at once swarmed down upon the unlucky dramatist and devoured the slight income from the benefit. Undaunted, Payne at once resumed his magnificent schemes, including one for a magazine to be published in London for the advancement of art, science, and belles-lettres in the United States. Not one issue of the magazine ever went to press.

Payne's make-shift way of life now led him into an adventure which almost caused his death, and which elicited from him the most unselfish act of his career. In Georgia, in September 1835, in search of material for his magazine, he became interested in original material owned by John Ross, head of the Cherokee nation, whose affairs with the United States government were then a subject of stormy controversy. Ross turned over to Payne material which was to furnish a series of articles for the magazine. In the midst of these labors the Georgia Guards arrested Ross and Payne and accused the latter of being an abolitionist and in league with the French. Ultimately released, Payne was advised by his captors never to return to Georgia. On his way home, however, he had the courage to publish, in the *Knoxville* (Tennessee) *Register* two articles: "John Howard Payne to his Countrymen" and "The Cher-

okee Nation to the People of the United States." Both essays were lively, forceful accounts not only of his own mishaps, which he was always inclined to view with a humorous eye, but of the wrongs of the Indians. Back in New York he began a history of the Cherokee nation. This is still in manuscript, as is a play of this period, *Romulus the Shepherd King* (1839).

In spite of his misdemeanors Payne was now widely known in America, and when Tyler became president, his advocates secured for him in 1842 through the aid of Daniel Webster an appointment as American consul at Tunis. Recalled by President Polk in 1845, he returned by way of Rome, Paris, and London, reaching New York in the summer of 1847. Once again his creditors made his life wretched. After a struggle against the opposition of Thomas H. Benton, he again obtained in March 1851 the post at Tunis. It was the last act in the drama of his feverish life. During the winter of 1851–52 his health failed rapidly, and he died on Apr. 9, 1852, still beset by unfinished plans and unpaid debts. Thirty-one years later his body was brought to America and interred at Oak Hill Cemetery in Washington.

[A detailed biography of John Howard Payne is in process of composition by E. Allison Grant. The following books throw light upon his career and personality: Gabriel Harrison, *The Life and Writings of John Howard Payne* (1875, 1885); W. T. Hanson, Jr., *The Early Life of John Howard Payne* (1913); Rosa Pendleton Chiles, *John Howard Payne* (1930); *Memoirs of John Howard Payne, the Am. Roscius* (London, 1815); T. S. Fay, "Sketch of the Life of John Howard Payne," *N. Y. Mirror,* Nov. 24, Dec. 1, 1832; A. H. Quinn, *Hist. of the Am. Drama from the Beginning to the Civil War* (1923); P. M. Irving, *Life and Letters of Washington Irving* (4 vols., 1862–64); "Correspondence of Washington Irving and John Howard Payne," *Scribner's Mag.,* Oct., Nov. 1910; *The Romance of Mary W. Shelley, John Howard Payne, and Washington Irving* (Boston, 1907); *Jour. of Washington Irving (1823–24)* (1931), ed. by Stanley Williams; T. T. P. Luquer, "When Payne Wrote 'Home! Sweet Home!,'" *Scribner's Mag.,* Dec. 1915.]

E. A. G.
S. T. W.

PAYNE, LEWIS THORNTON POWELL, 1845–1865 [See BOOTH, JOHN WILKES].

PAYNE, OLIVER HAZARD (July 21, 1839–June 27, 1917), capitalist, was born at Cleveland, Ohio, the son of Henry B. Payne [*q.v.*] and Mary (Perry) Payne. His mother was a daughter of Nathan Perry, honored pioneer merchant of Cleveland, who had been identified with the city's growth since going there as a fur trader in 1804. Soon after his son's birth the father, already successful in the fields of industry and commerce, entered upon a political career. Oliver was educated at Phillips Academy and at Yale University. A member of the class of 1863, he left in 1861 to enter the Union army, his father having procured for him a lieutenant's commission in an Illinois regiment. Soon he was advanced to captain and his company took part in the engagements at New Madrid, Corinth, and Booneville, Miss. On Sept. 11, 1862, he became lieutenant-colonel of the 124th Ohio Volunteers and on Jan. 1, 1863, he was promoted colonel. He was seriously wounded at Chickamauga, suffered a long convalescence, and rejoined his regiment to take a gallant part in the battles of Resaca and Pickett's Mill, his conduct winning him the brevet of brigadier-general for "faithful and meritorious services." In depressed mood after the arduous Atlanta campaign, he resigned on Nov. 2, 1864. Apparently his men held their very young colonel in high regard.

Returning to Cleveland and entering business, Payne rapidly gained a place for himself in the iron industry and also in the pioneer field of oil refining. Until the formation of the Standard Oil Company in 1870, Clark, Payne & Company were the largest refiners in Cleveland and the chief of Rockefeller's competitors. Payne, however, became a shareholder in the notorious South Improvement Company (1872), and a few years later allied his oil interests completely with the Standard Oil Company. He was almost immediately made treasurer, which office he held until his removal to New York City in 1884. His holdings in Standard Oil were at one time exceeded only by those of John D. Rockefeller, the Charles Pratt estate, and the Harkness family. While in Ohio he was a heavy contributor to Democratic campaign funds, and through his father was influential in party matters. He also used his wealth to further his father's career and was charged with securing Henry B. Payne's seat in the Senate in 1884 by bribing the Ohio legislature. The charge, though never proved, was the subject of acrimonious dispute for years. In 1886 the Ohio legislature asked the Senate for an investigation and submitted evidence, but the Senate refused to act. During the debates in the Senate over combinations in trade and industry it was frequently charged that Henry B. Payne was there as a representative of Standard Oil. It was also hinted that Payne's support of Cleveland was a factor in the appointment of William C. Whitney, Payne's brother-in-law, as secretary of the navy.

After going to New York Payne gradually divested himself of his oil holdings and invested in other fields, becoming a director in various banking firms and industrial corporations. He was a dominant figure in the affairs of the American Tobacco Company and its subsidiaries (A. Pound and S. T. Moore, *They Told Barron,* 1930, pp. 49–50) and was influential in the affairs of the Tennessee Coal and Iron Company at the time of its absorption by the United States Steel Corporation. Yachting was his chief recreation, and every summer between 1898 and 1914 he visited Europe in his *Aphrodite,* which when built was the largest, fastest, and most luxuriously appointed steam yacht in the country. At one time it carried him around the world. He lived a bachelor at his Fifth Avenue mansion in winter, but spent other seasons of the year on estates in Ulster County, N. Y., or in Georgia. During his lifetime he was a quiet giver to many causes, his most notable philanthropy being a gift of $500,000 to found Cornell Medical College and further gifts to it totaling over $8,000,000 which enabled it to take front rank among institutions of its kind. In his will he bequeathed $1,000,000 to the New York Public Library, $1,000,000 to Yale University, $1,000,000 to Lakeside Hospital, Cleveland, and smaller amounts to many other medical and educational institutions. The greater part of the remainder of his large estate passed to his favorite nephews, Harry Payne Bingham and Payne Whitney.

[G. W. Lewis, *The Campaigns of the 124th Regiment* (1894); F. B. Heitman, *Hist. Reg. and Dict. of the U. S. Army* (1903), vol. I; Ida M. Tarbell, *The Hist. of the Standard Oil Company* (2 vols., 1904); H. D. Lloyd, *Wealth against Commonwealth* (1894); *Who's Who in America,* 1914–15; A. F. Payne White, *The Paynes of Hamilton* (1912); the *Sun* (N. Y.), *N. Y. Herald* and *N. Y. Times,* June 28, 1917, and *N. Y. Times,* July 7, 1917.]   O. W. H.

PAYNE, SERENO ELISHA (June 26, 1843–Dec. 10, 1914), politician, was born at Hamilton, N. Y., the son of Betsy (Sears) and William Wallace Payne, a farmer and one-time assemblyman, and the nephew of Henry B. Payne [*q.v.*]. The family, soon after his birth, removed to Auburn, where the boy attended the academy. After graduation at the University of Rochester in 1864, he entered the law office of Cox & Avery in Auburn and in 1866 was admitted to the bar. He immediately opened a law office in Auburn, which he maintained to the end of his life, gradually acquiring a large practice. On Apr. 23, 1873, he married Gertrude Knapp of Auburn, who bore him one son. From the first he was interested in politics, became an active Republican worker, and held a succession of local offices: city clerk of Auburn, 1867–68, supervisor of Cayuga County, 1871–72, district attorney for that county, 1873–79, and member of the Auburn board of education, 1879–82. In the fall of 1882 he was elected to the Forty-eighth Congress, and two years later was reëlected, but after the Democrats gerrymandered the district he was defeated for the Fiftieth Congress. He was chosen to a vacancy in the Fifty-first Congress caused by the death of Newton W. Nutting and thereafter served continuously until his death. He was proud of his long tenure and achieved a reputation as one of the most faithful, conscientious, and hardworking representatives in Washington.

Though a plodding member, without brilliance or dash, a slow, heavy speaker, and handicapped in later years by partial deafness, he gradually advanced to the position of a leader. In the Fifty-first Congress he became a member of the ways and means committee and thereafter devoted his chief attention to the tariff. He helped draft the McKinley Tariff of 1890 and made his first important speech to the House in its behalf. Four years later he was one of the principal opponents of the Wilson Tariff. When the Dingley Bill was written in 1897 he stood second in rank on the ways and means committee and had served there longer than any other Republican. He prepared whole schedules of this bill and had the distinction of closing the House debate upon it. In 1899 he served as a member of the American-British joint high commission. When Dingley died that year, he succeeded to the chairmanship of the ways and means committee, and he became one of the so-called "Big Five," a controlling group that included Cannon, Tawney, Dalzell, and James Sherman.

His two principal ambitions were to be speaker and to attach his name to some law of lasting importance. He was denied the first when in 1903 Cannon was chosen presiding officer of the House, the New York Republicans splitting their vote between James Sherman and Payne, either of whom might have succeeded had the other withdrawn. Payne was an effective lieutenant of Cannon, often taking charge of floor strategy. His second ambition was realized, when in 1909 he gave his name to the Payne-Aldrich Tariff. His work in connection with this much-denounced measure was far more palatable to the country at large than Senator Aldrich's (F. W. Taussig, *The Tariff History of the United States*, 5th ed., copr. 1910, 368–408). He conducted long and honest hearings before the ways and means committee, with a close critical comparison of foreign and domestic costs. In introducing the bill he made a detailed explanatory speech, the fullness and conscientiousness of which were in striking contrast with the speeches of McKinley and Dingley in 1890 and 1897 and with Aldrich's speeches in the Senate. The House

made no important changes in the bill; the Senate made 847, half of them of substantial importance and generally upward in trend. Payne showed some resentment, for he had said that duties should be fixed strictly at the difference between the cost in the United States and the cost abroad, and that the best friends of protection were those who tried to keep the rates reasonably protective. He frankly asserted, for example, that the Senate had gone too far in almost doubling the House rates on shingles. In the conference hearings on the Payne-Aldrich Bill he was distinctly more moderate than Tawney and Dalzell. Yet of the bill as finally passed he was a warm defender. In spite of failing health he remained active in the House, and on the day of his death he not only occupied his usual seat but made a short speech on an appropriation bill.

[*Sereno Elisha Payne . . . Memorial Addresses . . . in the House of Representatives* (1916); N. W. Stephenson, *N. W. Aldrich* (1930); D. S. Alexander, *A Political Hist. of . . . N. Y.*, vol. III (1909); A. F. Payne, *The Paynes of Hamilton* (1912); *N. Y. Tribune* and *Evening Post* (N. Y.), Dec. 11, 1914.]

A. N.

PAYNE, WILLIAM HAROLD (May 12, 1836–June 18, 1907), educator, was born in Ontario County, N. Y., near the village of Farmington, the son of Gideon Riley Payne and Mary Brown (Smith). He attended country school during the winter months and by the time he was thirteen had mastered textbooks on algebra and grammar. Since he was of frail constitution, he found farm work heavy as well as irksome, and accordingly his mother, who recognized his bent for study, encouraged him to enter the Macedon Academy in 1852. Here he studied for two years, teaching in country schools part of the time. During the summer of 1854 he attended the New York Conference Seminary at Charlottesville, then gave eighteen months to teaching country schools. On Oct. 2, 1856, he married Sara Evaline Fort, and with her conducted the school at Victor, N. Y., for the next two years. He was then appointed principal of the Union School at Three Rivers, Mich., where his wife's family had settled. Under his administration the school grew from two to six departments in six years, and he won a local reputation. In 1864, he became principal of the union school at Niles, Mich., and from 1866 to 1869 was in charge of Ypsilanti Seminary, resigning that position to become superintendent of public schools at Adrian. He was president of the Michigan Teachers Association in 1866 and editor of its organ, the *Michigan Teacher*, from its first issue, January 1866, to 1870.

During his first year at Adrian he delivered an address, *The Relation between the University and Our High Schools* (published 1871), by which he first attracted attention as an advocate of a coordinated state school system which would permit the pupil to pass by regular steps from the primary grades to the University. He also urged the training of prospective teachers in the technique of teaching. His views met with some opposition, but won the favorable notice of James B. Angell [*q.v.*], president of the University of Michigan, who succeeded, in 1878, in securing the establishment of a chair of education in the University, the first chair of pedagogy in the United States. The following year Payne became its first incumbent. To supply textbooks for his new courses he wrote *Syllabus of a Course of Lectures on the Science and Art of Teaching* (1879); *Outlines of Educational Doctrine* (1882); *Contributions to the Science of Education* (1886); edited D. P. Page's *Theory and Practice of Teaching* (1885), and translated *The History of Pedagogy* (1886) from the French of Gabriel Compayre. He had previously published *Chapters On School Supervision* (1875). The department of education developed under his professorship until it included seven courses offered by the professor himself and four courses in special methods by members of other departments.

In 1887 Payne accepted the dual position of chancellor of the University of Nashville and president of Peabody Normal School, Nashville, Tenn. He reorganized the library; raised the standards of the normal school, which in 1889 was renamed Peabody Normal College; and by 1901 had more than trebled the enrollment. In that year he resigned to resume his old professorship at the University of Michigan, vacated by the death of his successor, Burke A. Hinsdale [*q.v.*]. During the Nashville period he translated *The Elements of Psychology* (1890) and *Psychology Applied to Education* (1893) from the French of Compayre, and *Émile* (1893) from the French of J. J. Rousseau. In 1901 he published *The Education of Teachers*. His first wife had died in 1899, and on July 6, 1901, he married Elizabeth Rebecca Clark. Ill health compelled him to retire from teaching in 1904 and he died in Ann Arbor three years later. He had five children by his first marriage. A colleague (I. N. Demmon, in *Michigan Alumnus*, July 1907) characterized Payne as a perfect disciplinarian, combining gentleness and firmness in a singular degree.

[G. C. Poret, *The Contributions of William Harold Payne to Public Education* (1930), with a bibliog. of printed and manuscript sources: *Report of the Pioneer and Hist. Soc. of Mich.*, vol. IX (1886); *Jour. of Proc. and Addresses . . . Nat. Educ. Asso.*, 1907; *Mich. Alumnus*, Nov. 1901, July 1907; L. C. Aldrich, *Hist. of Ontario County, N. Y.* (1893); *Am. Biog. Hist. of Eminent and Self Made Men, Mich. Vol.* (1878); *Who's Who in America*, 1906–07; *Detroit Free Press*, June 19, 1907.]   R. H. E.

PAYNE, WILLIAM MORTON (Feb. 14, 1858–July 11, 1919), teacher, translator, and literary critic, was born at Newburyport, Mass., the son of Henry Morton and Emma Merrill (Tilton) Payne, and the descendant of William Payne, who emigrated from England in 1635 and settled at Watertown. In 1868 his family removed to Chicago, where the remainder of his life was passed. The boy was educated in the public schools of Newburyport and Chicago. Financial reverses of his family made it impossible for him to proceed to Harvard, as had been designed. Instead, he found employment in the Chicago Public Library (1874–76), and then as a teacher of literature in the high schools of Chicago (1876–1919). At the same time, not accepting misfortune supinely, he undertook a course of self-education which involved severe discipline. And his efforts were eminently successful. He became an accomplished linguist, speaking Norwegian, German, and Italian fluently, and French so perfectly that he deceived Frenchmen as to his origin; and attaining besides a competent knowledge of Swedish, Danish, and Spanish. In later years he traveled repeatedly in Europe. By 1883 he was entering upon his career as a critic and man of letters, and had established a connection with the Chicago *Dial*. He presently became literary editor of the *Chicago Daily News* (1884–88), and then of the *Chicago Evening Journal* (1888–92), and thereafter acted as associate editor of the *Dial* until 1915. In addition, he contributed frequently to periodicals, wrote editorials for the *Chicago Journal* (1917–18), edited *English in American Universities* (1895), *American Literary Criticism* (1904), and two volumes of selections from Swinburne (*Selected Poems*, 1905, *Mary Stuart*, 1906), and wrote sixteen essays and made many translations in prose and verse for C. D. Warner's *Library of the World's Best Literature*. His principal translations, however, were careful and felicitous renderings of Björnstjerne Björnson's dramatic trilogy, *Sigurd Slembe* (1888), and of the same author's epic cycle, *Arnljot Gelline* (1917).

His remarkable activity did not render Payne a drudge. Inevitably the usefulness of much of his journalistic work was exhausted when the immediate occasion for it had passed; but, taken together, this work represents a consistent force through many years in support of the humanities —in support of liberal culture based upon the classical tradition of literature. Payne's criticism was judicial, was concerned more with ideas than with literary form, and was well calculated to maintain tried standards of taste while communicating the significant influences, old and new, which were powerful in the nineteenth century. Though he was less forceful and less individual than Matthew Arnold, he still aimed at the ends which his older English contemporary set before himself; and in so doing he attained a position of more than local influence. For it was he, more than anybody else, who made the *Dial* what it was in its best days. Ninety of his essays for the *Dial* were reprinted in three small volumes—*Little Leaders* (1895), *Editorial Echoes* (1902), and *Various Views* (1902)— which exhibit his critical talent more happily than his two larger, more formal volumes of essays, *The Greater English Poets of the Nineteenth Century* (1907) and *Leading American Essayists* (1910). The former volume was based upon a course of lectures which Payne delivered at the Universities of Wisconsin (1900), Kansas (1904), and Chicago (1904). His work was too quietly performed to gain for him the recognition he deserved in his own day; but the University of Wisconsin made him an honorary LL.D. in 1903, and he became a member of the National Institute of Arts and Letters. At his death after a short illness, he was buried from the home of his lifelong friend, Professor Paul Shorey. He was never married.

[*Who's Who in America*, 1916–17; H. D. Paine, ed., *Paine Family Records*, Nov. 1878–Oct. 1883; *Chicago Herald and Examiner* and *Chicago Tribune*, July 12, 1919; information from Mrs. Herbert E. Bradley (in whose possession Payne's library, scrap-books, and correspondence remain), and from Prof. Paul Shorey.]
R. S.

PAYSON, EDWARD (July 25, 1783–Oct. 22, 1827), Congregational clergyman, was a native of Rindge, N. H. His grandfather, Phillips Payson, his father, Seth [*q.v.*], and two uncles, Phillips and John Payson, were all Congregational ministers. Seth Payson was long pastor at Rindge, and although an epileptic, was able intellectually and active in public affairs. He married a relative, Grata Payson, of Pomfret, Conn. Edward, one of seven children, was educated at home and at the academy in New Ipswich. He was ready for college at sixteen, but although he was extremely susceptible to religious influences from early childhood, his father held him back, since he had not made confession of faith, saying, "To give you a liberal education while destitute of religion, would be like putting a sword into the hands of a madman." Edward, nevertheless, entered the sophomore class of Harvard College in 1800, and graduated in 1803. For the next three years he was principal of an academy in Portland, Me.

While here his thought became increasingly concerned with religion. In September 1805 he joined his father's church, and in August of the following year retired to Rindge to study theology. Licensed to preach on May 20, 1807, he supplied the church at Marlboro, N. H., for about three months, and later became colleague of Rev. Elijah Kellogg at the Second Congregational Church, Portland, Me., where he was ordained Dec. 16, 1807. From December 1811 until his death he was sole pastor. On May 8, 1811, he married Ann Louisa Shipman of New Haven, Conn. They had eight children, one of whom, Elizabeth Payson Prentiss [*q.v.*], was a popular writer of religious fiction.

From about his twenty-first year, Payson was a votary of religion in no ordinary degree. His own spiritual experience and the spiritual welfare of others engrossed his every thought and all his energies. The revival spirit was always burning within him. Twelve hours of each day he gave to study, never less than two to devotions, and at least one day a week he spent in fasting and prayer. He was unhealthily introspective, subject to periods of highest elevation and deepest despair. Doubtless his physical inheritance, and the fact that from the beginning of his pastorate he was a victim of what was probably tuberculosis, had much to do with his mental processes. Although his preaching was frequently dark and menacing, and painted human nature in such colors that unregenerate hearers would address each other on a Monday morning as "Brother Devil," his complete abandon in his faith and calling, his genuine spirituality, and his vivid preaching and oratorical ability inspired reverence for him as a man and gave him great effectiveness in the pulpit. Calls came to him from Boston and New York, but he was not persuaded that they emanated from God, and he stayed in Portland, until, after a long period of failing strength, with extreme suffering at the end, he died in his forty-fourth year. Those who came to view his body saw attached to his breast, as he had directed, the admonition, "Remember the words which I spoke unto you while I was yet present with you." They were also engraved on the plate of his coffin.

After his death, both in the United States and in England Payson became one of the most read of American divines. Previously only a few of his sermons were printed, but *The Bible Above*

All Price (1814) had wide circulation and *An Address to Seamen* (1821), still greater, being translated into several foreign languages. A collection, *Sermons by the Late Rev. E. Payson, D.D.*, was published in 1828, and *A Memoir of the Rev. Edward Payson, D.D.*, containing many letters and extracts from his diary, by Asa Cummings, appeared in 1830. Other volumes of selections were issued, and in 1846 there appeared under the editorship of Cummings *The Complete Works of Edward Payson, D.D.* (3 vols.), the first volume of which contains the *Memoir*.

[W. B. Sprague, *Annals Am. Pulpit*, vol. II (1857); *Our Pastor; or Reminiscences of Rev. Edward Payson, D.D.* (1855); E. L. Janes, *Mementos of Rev. E. Payson, D.D.* (1873); Wm. Willis, *Journals of the Rev. Thomas Smith and the Rev. Samuel Deane, . . . with . . . a Summary Hist. of Portland* (1849); *Christian Observer* (London), Apr., May, June, 1833; *Christian Examiner*, July 1847; *Quart. Reg. and Jour.*, Apr. 1828, Feb. 1831; *Biblical Repertory and Theological Rev.*, Apr. 1831; *Spirit of the Pilgrims*, Nov. 1829, Jan. 1831; *Meth. Mag. and Quart. Rev.*, Oct. 1838; *American Patriot* (Portland), Oct. 26, 1827.]   H. E. S.

PAYSON, SETH (Sept. 30, 1758–Feb. 26, 1820), Congregational clergyman, was born in Walpole, Mass., the son of the Rev. Phillips Payson by his second wife, Kezia (Bullen), widow of Seth Morse. As a child he had a feeble constitution with a tendency to epilepsy. Later he enjoyed vigorous health until within a year of his death. He entered Harvard College in 1773, where he had been preceded by his father, and by an elder brother, Phillips, and was followed by another brother, John, all of whom entered the Congregational ministry. Seth graduated from Harvard in 1777, receiving one of the highest honors in his class. Although in his early religious opinions he inclined toward Arminianism, he became eventually a decided Calvinist.

On Dec. 4, 1782, he was ordained pastor of the Congregational church in Rindge, N. H. Here "he laboured with exemplary fidelity and zeal" until his death thirty-eight years later. As a preacher his reputation was excellent, for his "intellect was sharp and vigorous, his imagination lively," and his ideas "admirably arranged in his own mind." Furthermore, "he was able to communicate them to others with great clearness and force." In the discharge of his other parish duties "his unceasing solicitude was to promote the highest interests of the people of his charge." Throughout his long ministry he "possessed, in a high degree, the esteem and affection of his flock" (Sprague, *post*). He also interested himself in religious affairs outside his parish. Early in the nineteenth century his interest in missions led him to undertake a missionary tour of several

months to the new settlements in the Province of Maine. He also served for several years as vice-president of the New Hampshire Bible Society, and was a member of the American Board of Commissioners for Foreign Missions. In 1815 he represented the General Association of New Hampshire in the General Assembly of the Presbyterian Church in Philadelphia. That his activities outside of his parish were not altogether religious, however, is evident from the fact that from 1802 to 1806 he sat in the New Hampshire Senate, and was recognized as one of its ablest members. In June 1799 he preached the annual sermon before the legislature, which was so powerful as to influence the General Court to strengthen the Sunday laws. In 1813 he was made a trustee of Dartmouth College, a position which he held until his death, taking the side of the college in the events that ultimately precipitated the famous Dartmouth College case.

In addition to the publication of a number of occasional sermons he put forth in 1802 his *Proofs of the Real Existence and Dangerous Tendency of Illuminism*, inspired, without doubt, by the appearance in the United States of the works of Robison and Barruel, as well as by the published sermons of the Rev. Jedidiah Morse [*q.v.*] on the same subject. In his *Proofs,* Payson again called attention to the danger to church and state occasioned by the rise of the Illuminati societies in Europe, and to their probable existence in America. Although a somewhat belated exposition of the subject, the work seems to have attracted considerable attention, particularly among the clergy.

In 1819, after a severe attack of epilepsy, his mind gradually failed and he died in February of the following year. His wife, whom he married in 1782, was his cousin Grata Payson of Pomfret, Conn. They had two daughters and five sons, two of the latter entering the ministry, Edward [*q.v.*] settling in Portland, Me., and Phillips in Leominster, Mass.

[W. B. Sprague, *Annals Am. Pulpit*, vol. II (1857); Isaac Robinson, *The Christian's Knowledge of Christ . . . Sermon Delivered at Rindge, N. H., Mar. 1, 1820, At the Funeral of Rev. Seth Payson, D.D.* (1820); E. S. Stearns, *Hist. of the Town of Rindge* (1875); *Vital Records of Walpole, Mass.* (1902).]   W. R. W.

PEABODY, ANDREW PRESTON (Mar. 19, 1811–Mar. 10, 1893), Unitarian clergyman, college professor, author, was born in Beverly, Mass. He was the son of Andrew and Mary (Rantoul) Peabody, and a descendant of Francis Peabody who emigrated from England to Massachusetts as early as 1635. Andrew Peabody desired that his son be educated for the Christian ministry. "He died." writes the latter. "before I was three years old, and on his death-bed he charged my mother to fulfil his wish, . . . should I be fit for such a calling" (Normandie, *post*, p. 290). The younger Andrew was something of an infant prodigy. He could read at the age of three. He was only twelve when he passed with distinction the entrance examinations of Harvard College. Being "regarded as somewhat immature," he continued for a year under private instruction, with the result that, instead of being retarded, his scholastic advancement was accelerated, "for in this one year's study he anticipated two years of college work" (Peabody, *post*, p. 32). Thus he was only thirteen when he entered college as a member of the junior class. He was graduated at the age of fifteen being "with the exception of Paul Dudley of the class of 1690, the youngest boy . . . that ever received the Harvard degree" (*Ibid.*, p. 32). His scholarship, though excellent, was not exceptional.

Too young to take any steps toward fulfilling his father's dying wish and not old enough to undertake any task commensurable with his scholastic attainments, he ventured upon the work of teaching. At the age of seventeen he was principal of the academy at Portsmouth, N. H. He was hardly successful. In 1829 he entered the Harvard Divinity School, graduating therefrom in 1832, and tutoring during the ensuing year at Harvard College. In October 1833 he was ordained and installed as assistant to Dr. Nathan Parker, minister of the South Parish Unitarian church, Portsmouth, N. H. Two or three weeks later Parker died and young Peabody became pastor of this important church and continued in that position for twenty-seven years. Through a combination of unusual erudition and fineness of character he won an influential following in Portsmouth, while his astonishing literary activities kept his name before an ever widening public. He wrote extensively for the *Whig Review* and in 1853 became editor and proprietor of the *North American Review,* in which relationship he remained for ten years.

In 1860 he was invited to succeed Frederic Dan Huntington [*q.v.*] as Plummer Professor of Christian Morals at Harvard. He served in 1862 and again in 1868–69 as acting president of the college. As Plummer professor it was his duty to conduct daily prayers, to preach two sermons on Sunday, and to exercise pastoral care over the students. He was easily the most beloved of all the professors at Harvard, and in some ways undoubtedly the most influential. It may fairly be said that he made no contribution to scholarship for all his vast learning.

"He was not eloquent as a preacher or inspir-

ing as a teacher; . . . his instruction in ethics was little more than a hearing of stumbling recitations from a memorized text yet, if any one who was in those remote days a student at Harvard College were now asked to name the personal influence which he still recalls as most beneficent, he would almost inevitably single out . . . the friend and counsellor who, by common consent of that generation, was given the title of the College Saint" (F. G. Peabody, *post*, pp. 28, 29).

In temper and outlook, Peabody is best described by the word "conservative." He was a Unitarian partly because of family ties and partly because he valued the wide freedom which that fellowship gave him. Though he prized his Unitarian fellowship very highly and never thought of surrendering it, he had no sympathy with the tendency among his Unitarian associates to depart from the modestly heretical theological position of Unitarian beginnings. It may, quite correctly, be said that he was in closer sympathy with the orthodox Congregationalism of his time than with the prevailing Unitarian thought. He was a prodigious worker. His contributions to the *North American Review* fill 1,600 pages. In the last twenty years of his life, in addition to his college duties, he published 120 books and pamphlets, all of which were written out by his own hand. In the Harvard Library he is credited with 190 titles. His volumes *Conversation; Its Faults and Graces* (1856); *Reminiscences of European Travel* (1868); *A Manual of Moral Philosophy* (1873); *Christian Belief and Life* (1875), and *Building a Character* (1886) suggest the variety of themes he wrote upon. In 1881 he was made professor emeritus, and from 1883 to 1893 was an overseer of the college. On Sept. 12, 1836, he married, in Portsmouth, Catherine Whipple Roberts.

[James de Normandie, in *Heralds of a Liberal Faith,* ed. by S. A. Eliot, vol. III (1910); E. J. Young, *Andrew P. Peabody* (1896), reprinted from *Mass. Hist. Soc. Proc.,* 2 ser., vol. XI (1897); *New World,* June 1893; *Unitarian,* Apr. 1893; *Christian Reg.,* Mar. 16, 1893; C. L. Slattery, *Certain American Faces* (1918); F. G. Peabody, *Reminiscences of Present-Day Saints* (1927); *Harvard Univ. Quinquennial Cat. Officers and Grads.* (1925).]   C.G.

PEABODY, ELIZABETH PALMER (May 16, 1804–Jan. 3, 1894), educator and author, the eldest child of Nathaniel and Elizabeth (Palmer) Peabody, was born at Billerica, Mass. Her father at the time of her birth was practising medicine and dentistry. Her mother, a daughter of Joseph Palmer [*q.v.*], conducted a private school in which her children were trained and was an early American editor of the poetry of Edmund Spenser. As early as 1820, after a childhood in Salem, the sixteen-year-old Elizabeth had opened a private school at Lancaster and had begun a life of teaching. Two years later she began a more ambitious project, a private school in Boston, where she herself studied Greek as a pupil of Ralph Waldo Emerson, then teaching in his brother's school during his first year out of college. In 1823 she went to Maine as a governess; but, attracted by the opportunities of Boston, she returned in 1825 to open another school. While conducting this, she became a friend of the William Ellery Channing family and for nine years she acted as Channing's secretary and amanuensis, a relationship which resulted in her becoming familiar with the writings of Coleridge and other European transcendental writers, and which, nearly fifty years later, resulted in her book, *Reminiscences of Rev. William Ellery Channing, D.D.* (1880). Except for a six months' rest in Salem, she continued the double duty of being secretary and teacher until September 1834, when she relinquished both and became Bronson Alcott's assistant in his Temple School in Boston. The journal of her experiences there and of Alcott's unconventional method of teaching was published anonymously in 1835 under the title *Record of a School.* In 1836 she returned to live with her parents at Salem. Keeping her contacts with Boston, she became one of the first members of the so-called Transcendental Club and visited often in the Emerson home in Concord. Meanwhile, in 1837, she discovered that the author of certain stories which had attracted her attention in the *New England Magazine* was the playmate of her Salem childhood, Nathaniel Hawthorne. She introduced Hawthorne to her Boston literary friends and to her youngest sister, Sophia, whom Hawthorne married in 1842. Another sister, Mary, married Horace Mann in 1843.

In 1839 Miss Peabody returned to Boston and opened a bookshop in West Street. Herself responsive to all current social enthusiasms, and her shop the only one in Boston carrying a stock of foreign books, she found herself in the midst of the transcendental ferment of the time. Groups of reformers met in the shop to plan the Brook Farm community, liberal clergymen and Harvard professors came there for their European books, and in the back room she set up a press and published three of Hawthorne's books, several of Margaret Fuller's translations from the German, and for two years, 1842–43, the organ of transcendentalism, the *Dial,* to which she contributed two articles on Brook Farm. After 1845 she began in earnest her career in education. Before she was thirty she had published elementary textbooks of grammar and history. From 1850 to

1860 she turned her entire attention to the advancement of the study of history in the public schools and in 1856 issued her *Chronological History of the United States.* The reading of one of Friedrich Froebel's books and a conversation in 1859 with his former pupil, Mrs. Carl Schurz, inspired Miss Peabody to establish the first American kindergarten, opened in Boston in 1860. Though the experiment was successful in the eyes of her patrons, she herself feared it was not in full accord with Froebel's theories and, closing the school in 1867, she spent a year in Hamburg studying methods and theory. Returning, she published a magazine, the *Kindergarten Messenger,* from 1873 to 1875, and lectured in various parts of the country.

Indian education attracted her attention about 1880 and her enthusiasm culminated in the discovery of Sarah Winnemucca, founder of a school for Piute Indians, who preyed upon Miss Peabody's credulity and for ten years absorbed whatever money Miss Peabody would send or could persuade her friends to send. After this expensive bit of sentimentality, she retired to Jamaica Plain and to Concord, where from 1879 to 1884 she was a member and lecturer at Alcott's Concord School of Philosophy. The vivacious woman had become one who, in Moses Coit Tyler's words, had a "bulky form, puffy face, and watery eyes," but whose charm of personality, especially in reminiscence, did not desert her. Her final book, *A Last Evening with Allston* (1886), recorded some of her reminiscences and reprinted some of her essays from the *Dial.* She died at Jamaica Plain and was buried in Concord near Emerson and Hawthorne.

[There are type-written copies of "Elizabeth Peabody: A Biog. Study" (1918) by Doris Louise McCart in the Chicago Univ. Lib. and in the N. Y. Pub. Lib. Biographical information can be found in Miss Peabody's books and in her magazine article, "The Origin and Growth of the Kindergarten," *Education,* May–June 1882. See also: G. W. Cooke, *An Hist. and Biog. Introduction to Accompany the Dial* (1902); S. H. Peabody, *Peabody (Paybody, Pabody, Paybodie) Geneal.* (1909); and obituaries in the *Academy* (London), Feb. 3, 1894, *Boston Transcript,* Jan. 4, 1894, and *N.-Y. Daily Tribune,* Jan. 5, 1894.]   R. W. A.

PEABODY, GEORGE (Feb. 18, 1795–Nov. 4, 1869), merchant, financier, philanthropist, was born in South Danvers, now Peabody, Mass., the son of Thomas and Judith (Dodge) Peabody. His first ancestor in America was Francis Peabody, who emigrated from England in 1635 and settled at Topsfield, Mass. The poverty of his parents prevented George from receiving more than a rudimentary education, and at the age of eleven he was apprenticed to a grocer in Danvers. He subsequently held positions of increasing responsibility in Newburyport. Mass., and

Georgetown, D. C. Here, in 1814, he assumed the management of Elisha Riggs's wholesale dry-goods warehouse and was soon admitted to partnership. The next year Riggs & Peabody moved to Baltimore, and in 1829, upon the retirement of Riggs, Peabody became senior partner. He made various trips to England on the firm's business, and in 1835, while in London, performed the first of his great public services, negotiating a loan of $8,000,000 for the state of Maryland, then on the verge of bankruptcy. For his generous act in refusing a commission he received a vote of thanks from the state legislature.

Peabody was an incorporator and the president of the Eastern Railroad, built in 1836, and his experience in railroad financing showed him the profitable character of capital importation. Hence, in 1837 he settled permanently in London, where he had previously established the firm of George Peabody & Company, specializing in foreign exchange and American securities. So powerful did he become that he competed successfully for American business with the Barings and the Rothschilds; while in the panic of 1857, though in a weakened financial position, he challenged the hostile Bank of England to cause his failure. In 1854 he took Junius Spencer Morgan [q.v.] into partnership.

As his business prospered and his wealth assumed large proportions, he added to his intuitive gift of shrewd trading a growing sense of international and social obligation. He became in a way an unofficial ambassador and his great influence was exerted towards preserving Anglo-American friendship. In the years when American credit was much shaken abroad (in 1837 three American houses in London were compelled to suspend payments, and in 1841 nine states suspended interest payments and three repudiated their debts), he used his name and funds to restore confidence. When in 1851 America was humiliated by the failure of Congress to appropriate money for a display at the Crystal Palace exhibition, his gift of $15,000 made it possible to show American products and inventions beside those of other nations. When money was required to fit out a ship to search for Sir John Franklin, the Arctic explorer, Peabody's $10,000 equipped the *Advance*, in 1852, for Elisha Kent Kane [q.v.]. His large and elaborate Fourth-of-July dinners, at which the English nobility met American visitors to London, became a feature of the London season.

Peabody's altruistic activities were not limited to international affairs, however. He retained an abiding love for his native land, which he manifested in a succession of munificent gifts.

Notable among these were $1,500,000 to found the Peabody Institute at Baltimore, Md., which provides a free library, an endowment for lectures, an academy of music, and an art gallery; $250,000 to found the Peabody Institute, Peabody, Mass., which contains a library and some important memorabilia of George Peabody, and affords an endowment for lectures; $150,000 to establish the Peabody Museum of natural history and natural science at Yale; $150,000 to establish the Peabody Museum of archeology and ethnology at Harvard; $140,000 to found the Peabody Academy of Science in connection with the Essex Institute, at Salem, Mass.; and $3,500,000 (The Peabody Education Fund) for the promotion of education in the South. His bequest to his nephew, Othniel C. Marsh [q.v.], enabled the latter to make the collections which established him as one of the leading American paleontologists of his time. Most of Peabody's large fortune was spent in philanthropy, a generosity which was unusual and startling in that age. His most considerable benefaction in England was the donation to the City of London of a sum of $2,500,000 for the erection of working-men's tenements, which still provide clean, comfortable, and airy quarters for hundreds of poor families at a rent less than they would have to pay for inferior rooms elsewhere.

Peabody's liberality won him love and honor in England as well as in his own country. In 1867 Oxford granted him the honorary degree of D.C.L. In 1869 he was given the freedom of the City of London, and in the same year a statue of him was unveiled by the Prince of Wales on the east side of the Royal Exchange. When he refused to accept either a baronetcy or the Grand Cross of the Bath, Queen Victoria sent him an autograph letter of appreciation and a large miniature of herself. He died in London upon his return from a visit to America in 1869. After a funeral service in Westminster Abbey, his body was placed on board H. M. S. *Monarch* and, escorted by a French and an American naval vessel, was brought to America where, after elaborate ceremonies, it was buried in Danvers, Feb. 8, 1870.

Although he was a shrewd merchant, and for the most part made a point of ignoring all direct requests for charity, Peabody had qualities which made him highly attractive to both men and women and especially to young people. His deeply lined face and snow-white hair seemed an index to his character—acute, strong, yet benevolent. He was kindly, generous both to his numerous relatives (he never married) and to the objects of his great benefactions, and, though simple in his personal tastes, moved urbanely in London society. Moreover, in his business dealings there was no trace of the dishonorable practices to which the great American financiers of the next generation sometimes stooped.

[Peabody Papers at Phillips Academy, Andover, Mass., consisting of Peabody's correspondence as he left it, newspaper clippings, and miscellaneous data; Phebe A. Hanaford, *The Life of George Peabody* (1870), excessively laudatory; Lewis Corey, *The House of Morgan* (1930); J. L. M. Curry, *A Brief Sketch of George Peabody* (1898); *Md. Hist. Soc. Fund Pub. No. 3*, Jan. 1870; S. H. Peabody, *Peabody . . . Geneal.* (1909); *N. Y. Daily Times*, June 1, 1853; *Evening Gazette* (Boston), Oct. 11, 1856; *Times* (London), Nov. 5, 1869; *Dict. Nat. Biog.*]
S. H. P.

PEABODY, JOSEPH (Dec. 12, 1757–Jan. 5, 1844), privateersman, mariner, merchant shipowner, was descended from Francis Peabody who emigrated from England to Massachusetts in 1635 and settled at Topsfield, about ten miles from Salem. Joseph was born in Middleton nearby, ninth of the twelve children of Francis Peabody, a farmer, and Margaret (Knight) Peabody. A youth at the time of the outbreak of the Revolution, the boy marched toward Lexington with the Boxford minute-men but they arrived too late for the battle. He then served aboard the Salem privateers *Bunker Hill* and *Pilgrim.* Determined to follow the sea, he realized that education was necessary for advancement, so he spent a year ashore studying at Middleton with his future father-in-law, the Rev. Elias Smith. He served for a brief period in the militia without seeing action, and then went to sea again on the privateer *Fishhawk,* which was captured. Exchanged after being imprisoned at St. John's, Newfoundland, he became second officer on the letter-of-marque *Ranger.* One night as the ship lay in the Potomac laden with Alexandria flour, she was attacked by a band of Loyalists who outnumbered the crew three to one. Peabody, in his nightshirt, led so spirited a defense that they were beaten off, though he was severely wounded. At the close of the war he was captain of a Salem merchantman and before long purchased the schooner *Three Friends* which he commanded for several years in the West Indian and European trade.

By 1791 Peabody had amassed enough money to come ashore and engage as a merchant shipowner. From small beginnings he built up a tremendous business under his single control. He owned a large number of vessels, some of which were built to his order and all of which he freighted and operated. He did considerable business with the Baltic, Mediterranean, and West Indies, but his richest ventures were with India, China, and what Morison terms the "Salem East Indies," dealing in indigo, opium, tea, pepper, and similar products of that region. His little *Sumatra* of 287 tons paid more than $400,000 in duties in three years. His favorite ship, the 328-ton *George* had been built in 1814 for privateering, with unusually fast lines. He bought her at a bargain for $5,250. Between 1816 and 1837 she made twenty voyages to Calcutta and one to Gibraltar, the total duties amounting to $651,743.32. It is likely that the profits were fully equal to the duties. She brought more than half of the 1,500,000 pounds of indigo which Peabody imported from Calcutta between 1807 and 1840. It is said that Peabody employed altogether between 6,500 and 7,000 seamen. He was a generous employer, always ready to reward merit, and thirty-five who entered his service as boys rose to be masters of ships. Practically his only ship to come to grief was the *Friendship,* the crew of which were massacred by the natives at Quallah Battoo in the East Indies, leading to punitive measures by the U.S.S. *Potomac.* He was loyal to Salem even at the expense of profit, building his ships in Salem yards instead of to the eastward, and bringing his cargoes to Salem to be distributed along the coast instead of sending them to the larger markets at Boston or New York. He was a director of the Salem Iron Works but confined himself chiefly to shipping. His wealth was immense for the day, and he paid annual taxes of some $200,000.

Peabody's reputation was such that his credit, it is said, was equal to the government's; he was so fair in his dealings that he never resorted to litigation. In charity, he was generous but unostentatious. In spite of a hasty temper, he generally maintained the dignified reserve reflected in his portrait. He was a devout member of the Unitarian Church. He took no part in politics. In 1812 he helped to frame Salem's petition against war, but once war was declared, supported the government. He married Catherine Smith, daughter of his old tutor, on Aug. 28, 1791, and after her death two years later, married her sister Elizabeth on Oct. 24, 1795, living very happily with her for nearly a half century. He had six sons, two of whom survived him, and one daughter. His death at Salem practically marked the end of Salem's greatness on the sea.

[The sketch of Peabody in Freeman Hunt, *Lives of Am. Merchants* (1858), vol. I, is reprinted from *Hunt's Merchants' Mag.*, Aug. 1845. See also: *Mass. Soldiers and Sailors of the Revolutionary War*, vol. XII (1904); E. S. Maclay, *A Hist. of Am. Privateers* (1899); S. E. Morison, *The Maritime Hist. of Mass., 1783–1860* (1921); C. S. Osgood and H. M. Bachelder, *Hist. Sketch of Salem* (1879); R. D. Payne, *The Ships and Sailors of Old Salem* (1909); G. G. Putnam, "The Ship 'George,'" *Essex Inst. Hist. Colls.*, Jan., Apr. 1923;

C. M. Endicott, "The Peabody Family," *New-Eng. Hist. and Geneal. Reg.*, Apr., Oct. 1848; S. H. Peabody, *Peabody (Paybody, Pabody, Pabodie) Geneal.* (1909).]

R. G. A.

PEABODY, JOSEPHINE PRESTON (May 30, 1874–Dec. 4, 1922), poet, dramatist, was the second child of Charles Kilham and Susan Josephine Morrill Peabody and a descendant of Francis Peabody who emigrated from England to Massachusetts in 1635. She was born in Brooklyn, N. Y., and spent her first ten years there and in New York City. A younger sister died; an older by five years was her close companion. The parents gave unusual attention to their children's education. The father, of artistic tastes and interests, implanted in them his keen delight in the theatre, especially in Shakespeare, and trained them in the appreciation of music and poetry. The mother laid stress, in daily details, upon beauty. These early years surrounded her sensitive nature with nobility of feeling, with harmony and with joy. But the lack of these was also to share in her growth. At Charles Peabody's death in 1884 the saddened widow took the children to live in Dorchester, Mass. Lack of means severely limited their enjoyment of the theatre and of music. Josephine found few friends who shared her tastes. Thrown upon her own resources, she read omnivorously. A note book records six hundred books read between 1888 and 1893. These are poetry, novels, essays, history, philosophy and drama. But her's was a creative mind, not content alone with reading. "Expression is my habitual instinct," she wrote in the diary that gave her one channel of expression. For another channel she wrote poetry, experimenting with form.

In 1894–95 and 1895–96, she was aided to study at Radcliffe College. Here she was stimulated by instruction by Harvard University professors. She was especially influenced by study of Dante, by the Miracle and Morality plays, and by the Elizabethan drama. She now found congenial friends. These were years of rapid artistic growth. In 1894 a poem was accepted by the *Atlantic Monthly,* and a helpful friendship began with Horace Scudder, its editor. His advice, critical yet encouraging, influenced her to prune her work, to demand of herself lucidity and exactitude. Her first volume of poetry was published in 1898—*The Wayfarers.* Her poems now appeared frequently in the leading magazines. Evidence of such gift in one so young brought much publicity and many new friends. Her loveliness of form and face—slender, child-like, with beauty of feature and radiance in expression—increased the admiration for her achievement.

Few guessed the depression, the physical weakness, and the family anxieties, that weighed her down. Only in her diary are these evident, as are the power of her spiritual life and her urge for poetic expression. In the next eight years, under these difficult conditions and with the addition of a lectureship in poetry and English literature at Wellesley College (1901–03), she wrote and published the following poems and plays: *Fortune and Men's Eyes* (1900); *Marlowe* (1901); *The Singing Leaves* (1903); and *Pan, A Choric Idyl* (1904), a "Novello," with musical setting, produced at a state farewell concert to Lord and Lady Minto at Ottawa, Canada.

In 1906 Miss Peabody married Lionel Simeon Marks, of the engineering department at Harvard University. Her artistic self-expression came to its full development in this happy marriage and in motherhood. In 1908 she published *The Book of the Little Past* and in 1909 *The Piper.* In 1910 *The Piper* won the Stratford Play Competition against three hundred and fifteen competitors and was produced at the Memorial Theatre in Stratford-upon-Avon, England, on July 26, 1910. It was played in London and over England, and was produced at the New Theatre, in New York, on Jan. 30, 1911, Contemporaneous with these was her growing concern for conditions of labor, expressed in *The Singing Man.* She shared in that aroused sense of social responsibility and warmth of feeling characteristic of this period in the United States. She also began to take active part in the movement for woman's suffrage, finally joining the Woman's party. In 1912 *The Wings* was produced at the Toy Theatre, Boston. In 1913, *The Wolf of Gubbio* was published. In 1914, she was elected an honorary member of Phi Beta Kappa and gave the Phi Beta Kappa poem at Tufts College. In 1916 *Harvest Moon* was published. Through these and the following years, her gallant spirit and her urge for expression of beauty in poetic form were increasingly engaged in a losing fight with pain and with the insidious and unrecognized hardening of the minute arteries that feed the brain, which brought her death. In 1921 she contributed a *Song for the Pilgrim Women* for the Plymouth Pageant. *Portrait of Mrs. W.,* a play in prose, was published in 1922, a few months before her death on Dec. 4, 1922.

Her artistic development was from lyrical to dramatic poetry. Her keen interest in metrical design and in symbolism was increasingly subjected to the desire for limpid expression, clear to the general reader, and for dramatic form. With a few companions in her art, she kept alive a passing tradition—the poetic drama. Probably, however, her reputation is assured not by her dramatic, but by her lyrical achievement. Here she attained a phrasing of beauty that has, at times, inevitability, and that gives her a permanent place among American poets.

[*The Diary and Letters of Josephine Preston Peabody* (1925), edited by Christina H. Baker, gives biographical material and selections from her diary from her sixteenth year to her death. *The Collected Poems of Josephine Preston Peabody*, with a foreword by Katherine Lee Bates, and *The Collected Plays of Josephine Preston Peabody*, with a foreword by George P. Baker, were published in 1927. See also: A. H. Quinn, *A Hist. of the Am. Drama from the Civil War to the Present Day* (1927), vol. II; S. H. Peabody, *Peabody (Paybody, Pabody, Pabodie) Geneal.* (1909); *Who's Who in America*, 1922–23; *N. Y. Times*, Dec. 5, 1922.]

C. H. B.

PEABODY, NATHANIEL (Mar. 1, 1741–June 27, 1823), physician and Revolutionary patriot, was born at Topsfield, Mass. He was the son of Jacob and Susanna (Rogers) Peabody and a descendant of Francis Peabody who emigrated to New England in 1635 and later settled at Topsfield. He was educated at home and studied medicine with his father, a popular and successful physician. When about twenty years of age he began practice in that part of Plaistow, N. H., afterward made the town of Atkinson, where he resided most of his life. On Mar. 1, 1763, he married Abigail Little. His public career began in 1771 when he was commissioned justice of the peace and of the quorum of Rockingham County by Governor Wentworth. He was from the beginning, however, a supporter of the Revolutionary movement and is reported to have been the first in the colony to resign his royal commission when the final break impended. In December 1774 he participated, with John Langdon and other prominent patriots, in the capture of the magazines at Fort William and Mary, one of the first overt acts of Revolution. For the next twenty years he was a leader in New Hampshire affairs both in the movement for independence and in the difficult task of reorganizing the government and institutions of the colony to meet the responsibilities of the new commonwealth. In 1776 he served his first term in the legislature, being repeatedly elected, with occasional intermissions, until his withdrawal from public affairs in 1795.

His status among the New Hampshire leaders is apparent in the fact that he served on the Committee on Safety which at times exercised almost dictatorial power in local affairs. He repeatedly represented New Hampshire in conferences held to promote the Revolutionary cause and to seek relief from the economic embarrassments caused by the depreciation of the currency and the dislocation of commerce. In addition to his civil activities he was for a time adjutant-general of the militia and accompanied the New Hampshire contingent on the Rhode Island expedition of 1778. In 1779 he was elected delegate to the Continental Congress, serving until Nov. 9, 1780. He was a member of the medical committee and was active in the various affairs of that body. In 1780 he served on a select committee with Philip Schuyler and John Mathews to consult with General Washington and to report on the dangerous conditions then existing. A long letter which he wrote Josiah Bartlett, from Morristown, N. J., on Aug. 6, 1780, is an interesting memorial of this service and shows that he possessed both a keen mind and the ability to express his ideas. His scathing criticism of the feeble, blundering, military policy of the Revolutionary authorities is worthy of the commander-in-chief himself (*New Hampshire State Papers*, XVII, 1889, pp. 399–403).

On the establishment of peace he continued his activity in New Hampshire affairs, served in the legislature, being speaker of the House in 1793, was a member of the constitutional conventions of 1781–83 and 1791–92, assisted in compiling the laws of the state and adjusting them to the new restrictions of the Federal Constitution, declined an appointment to the Continental Congress in 1785, and was defeated in the first election of United States senators in 1788. In 1795 he returned to private life. He is said to have been a successful physician and in 1791 was one of the organizers of the New Hampshire Medical Society. Suffering heavy property losses, he was obliged to spend his last years in constant struggles with creditors, and at the time of his death he was—technically at least—undergoing imprisonment for debt at Exeter. He is described as a man of fine presence, witty and self-confident, unscrupulous at times, a skeptic in religion, extravagant and lacking in some essential qualities of leadership, but able and patriotic.

[The best sketch of Peabody is in Wm. C. Todd, *Biog. and other Articles* (1901); an earlier one appears in J. Farmer and J. B. Moore, *Collections, Hist. and Miscellaneous*, vol. III (1824). See also C. H. Bell, *Hist. of the Town of Exeter, N. H.* (1888); *N. H. State Papers*, vol. XVII (1889), pp. 386–414, containing interesting correspondence between Peabody and various leaders of the period; J. F. Colby, *Manual of the Constitution of the State of N. H.* (rev. ed., 1912); and C. E. Potter, *The Mil. Hist. of the State of N. H.* (1866). The N. H. Hist. Soc. has Peabody letters and miscellaneous papers, and a sketch of Peabody is included in the William Plumer manuscript collections of the Society.]

W. A. R.

PEABODY, OLIVER WILLIAM BOURN (July 9, 1799–July 5, 1848), lawyer, man of letters, Unitarian clergyman, twin brother of William Bourn Oliver Peabody [*q.v.*], was born in Exeter, N. H., the seventh of the ten children of Oliver and Frances (Bourn) Peabody, and the fifth in descent from Francis Peabody—or Frances Pabody, as he sometimes signed himself—who emigrated from England in 1635 and lived nearly half a century in Topsfield, Mass. His father, a graduate of Harvard College and the first student of law under Theophilus Parsons, was a jurist and politician of some note and for thirty-four years a trustee of Phillips Exeter Academy.

Peabody graduated from Harvard College in 1816 in the same class with his twin brother, to whom he bore a strong resemblance in appearance, manner, and endowments, and in the purity and delicacy of his taste. His own desire was to enter the ministry, but he took up the study of law to gratify his father, received the degree of LL.B. from the Harvard Law School and was admitted to the bar in 1822, opened an office in Exeter, sat as a representative in the legislature, 1824–31, edited at different times the *Rockingham Gazette* and the *Exeter News-Letter,* and delivered poems before the Harvard chapter of Phi Beta Kappa and on various occasions of state. The one recited at Portsmouth May 21, 1823, at the centennial celebration of the first settlement in New Hampshire (published in *Collections of the New Hampshire Historical Society,* vol. VI, 1850, pp. 269–77) was his most applauded performance and is a striking example of the persistence in America of the eighteenth-century poetic style. The personal collisions and asperities of the practice of law were repugnant to him, and in 1830 he moved to Boston to assist his brother-in-law, Alexander Hill Everett [*q.v.*], with the *North American Review,* to which he contributed a number of able articles. For Hilliard, Gray & Company he supervised the preparation of the *Dramatic Works of William Shakespeare* (7 vols., 1836; several times reprinted). Though this edition was little more than an intelligent reworking of Samuel Weller Singer's, Peabody did compare his text with that of the First Folio and adopted some of the Folio readings, showing thereby a certain awareness of critical principles and making himself in a sense the first American editor of Shakespeare. For Jared Sparks's *Library of American Biography* he wrote lives of Israel Putnam (vol. VII, 1837) and John Sullivan (2 ser., vol. III, 1844). He was a member of the Massachusetts legislature, 1834–36, and register of probate for Suffolk County, 1836–42. In the latter year he accompanied Everett to the College of Jefferson at Convent, La., as professor of English literature,

but finding the climate enervating he soon returned to Massachusetts.

After studying with his brother at Springfield, he was licensed in 1844 by the Boston Association of Congregational Ministers and was settled in August 1845 as pastor of the Unitarian Church of Burlington, Vt. His saintly life and polished scholarship made a deep impression on his congregation, but his health, never robust, soon began to decline. His last work was the preparation of a memoir of his beloved brother. He died, unmarried, after a short illness and was buried in Burlington.

[E. E. Hale, obituary in *Christian Examiner,* Sept. 1848, reprinted in *Sermons by the Late William B. O. Peabody, D.D.* (1849); C. H. Bell, *The Bench and Bar of N. H.* (1894); S. H. Peabody, *Peabody . . . Geneal.* (1909); *The N. H. Reg. and U. S. Calendar,* 1824–31; *The Mass. Reg. and U. S. Calendar,* 1834–42; Jane Sherzer, "Am. Editions of Shakespeare: 1753–1866," *Pubs. Modern Language Asso.,* vol. XXII (1907).]

G. H. G.

PEABODY, ROBERT SWAIN (Feb. 22, 1845–Sept. 23, 1917), architect, was born in New Bedford, Mass., the son of Ephraim Peabody, minister of King's Chapel, Boston, from 1845 to 1856, and of Mary Jane (Derby) Peabody. His father (Bowdoin College, A.B. 1827), son of a blacksmith at Wilton, N. H., and a descendant of Francis Peabody who settled in New England in 1635, was "a man of keen insight, lofty character and much poetic feeling" (Eliot, *post,* p. 1), while his mother was "a Salem Derby, at a time when that family had acquired in world-wide commerce a wealth considerable in those days" (*Ibid.*). Robert Peabody spent his boyhood in Boston and prepared for college at Mr. Dixwell's school, entering Harvard with the class of 1866. In college he ranked well in scholarship, rowed on a victorious crew, and was chosen chief marshal on Class Day. He went from Harvard to Paris, soon passed the entrance examinations to the École des Beaux Arts and entered the Atelier Daumet. When he was not working at the school, he was sketching architecture in France, England, and Italy. His chief friends of the Paris student years were Frank W. Chandler and Charles Follen McKim [*q.v.*]. In 1870 he came back to Boston to earn his own living. Entirely untrained in office practice, but with a background of Paris study, a skill at sketching, and many influential friends, he formed a partnership with John G. Stearns (Harvard, B.S. 1863), who possessed a marked ability for building superintendence and construction.

The firm of Peabody and Stearns lasted with great success for forty-five years, Stearns dying shortly before his partner. Among the many buildings designed by them are Matthews Hall and the Hemenway Gymnasium at Harvard, the old Providence Railroad Station; the Exchange Building and other downtown office buildings, the Telephone Building, Simmons College, the Wentworth Institute and the Custom House Tower, all in Boston; the Groton School at Groton; the City Hall and State Mutual Life Building in Worcester; the State House at Concord, N. H.; the Union League Club in New York City; The Antlers at Colorado Springs; the Tip Top House at Pike's Peak; Machinery Hall at the World's Columbian Exposition in Chicago; buildings at the Buffalo and San Francisco expositions; and numerous private houses at Newport, Lenox, Boston, Philadelphia, New York, and elsewhere. In designing his larger work Peabody tended more and more to a free interpretation of the style of the Italian Renaissance. In domestic architecture his instinctive feeling for the picturesque stood him in good stead. Through his office passed a stream of young draftsmen who later, going out to all parts of the country, were to make names for themselves and to remember his good influence and generosity. The architectural schools at the Massachusetts Institute of Technology and at Harvard owed much to his care and wisdom. He was an Overseer of Harvard from 1888 to 1899.

For many years he served as president of the Boston Society of Architects. In 1906 he led his fellow architects in the preparation of a *Report Made to the Boston Society of Architects by Its Committee on Municipal Improvement* (1907). In 1908, the Society published *A Holiday Study of Cities and Ports,* from Peabody's pen, a valuable contribution to the Boston problem. His "holiday" had comprised a searching visit to the great ports of Europe. For many years as director and then as president (1900–01), he loyally served the American Institute of Architects, the national organization of his profession. He placed public service as the first duty of the Institute, and joined enthusiastically in promoting the crusade for the artistic development of Washington, begun during his term as president.

Like his ancestors, the "Merchant Venturers of Old Salem," Peabody loved the sea, which he followed as an able yachtsman. Among his many sketches there are marine scenes with all kinds of craft as well as stately buildings and picturesque villages. He wrote fluently and published a number of articles and books on travel and architecture, all illustrated by himself. These included *Note Book Sketches* (1873); *A Holiday Study of Cities and Ports* (1908); *An Architect's Sketch Book* (1912). Even in his final years of illness he produced a charming little

book of imaginary foreign scenes accompanied by appropriate passages in prose and poetry, *Hospital Sketches* (1916). He died at his summer home at Marblehead, Mass., in 1917. In 1871 he had married Annie, daughter of John P. Putnam of Boston, who died in 1911. Three children of this marriage survived him. In 1913 he married Helen Lee, daughter of Charles Carroll Lee of Washington, D. C. His monument is in King's Chapel, Boston, of which he was warden.

[C. W. Eliot, *Charles Eliot, Landscape Architect* (1902); F. G. and R. S. Peabody, *A New England Romance: The Story of Ephraim and Mary Jane Peabody, Told by Their Sons* (1920); Moorfield Storey, in *Later Years of the Saturday Club* (1927), ed. by M. A. DeWolfe Howe; Charles Moore, *The Life and Times of Charles Follen McKim* (1929); Glenn Brown, *1860–1930: Memories* (1931); C. E. Stratton, in *Harvard Graduates' Mag.*, Dec. 1917; R. E. Peabody, *Merchant Venturers of Old Salem* (1912); *Who's Who in America,* 1916–17; S. H. Peabody, *Peabody . . . Geneal.* (1909); *N. Y. Times,* Sept. 24, 1917.]　　R. P. B.

PEABODY, SELIM HOBART (Aug. 20, 1829–May 26, 1903), educator, was born in Rockingham, Vt., the son of Charles Hobart and Grace (Ide) Peabody, and a descendant of Francis Peabody, who emigrated from England to Massachusetts in 1635. While Selim was still a child, his parents moved to Randolph, Mass. His father, a clergyman, desirous of preparing him for the ministry, supplemented his public school tuition by giving him lessons in Greek and Hebrew. When he was twelve years old, his father died, and a well-to-do friend of the family sent the boy to the Public Latin School in Boston for a year (1841–42). Returning to his home, he was placed upon a farm to work for his board and clothes. At fifteen, he was apprenticed to a carpenter, with whom he remained for two years. During this time, he purchased books and read much in anticipation of entering college; for one term he taught school. In 1848 he matriculated at the University of Vermont, receiving the degree of A.B. in 1852, having met his expenses by teaching during winter vacations. On Aug. 9, 1862, he married Mary Elizabeth, daughter of David Knight and Betsey (Farrington) Pangborn. A month later, he was appointed principal of the Burlington High School, where he served one year, resigning to accept the professorship of mathematics and physics at New Hampton Seminary, Fairfax, Vt.

In 1854 he removed to Philadelphia to become professor of mathematics and civil engineering at the Polytechnic College of the State of Pennsylvania. When the financial panic of 1857 forced the college to suspend payments, Peabody secured an appointment as clerk in a United States land office at Eau Claire, Wis. He remained here two years and then became principal of the high school in Fond du Lac, Wis. In 1862 he went to Racine, Wis., to serve as principal of the high school and superintendent of schools. The position of director of the Dearborn Observatory, which had just been established in Chicago, was offered him in that year, but he declined it. His success at Racine was recognized by the Wisconsin State Teachers' Association, which elected him president in 1863. As spokesman for this organization, he advocated a state-supported normal school, and the establishment of teachers' institutes. He also recommended a graded system of state schools, including the high school, the normal school and the state university, a scheme that was later adopted. From 1865 to 1871 he was professor of physics at the Central High School, Chicago, and then for a period of three years, professor of physics at the Massachusetts Agricultural College, Amherst, Mass. While here, he conducted a noteworthy series of experiments on the cause of the ascent of sap in trees. Disagreement with the president of the institution, William Smith Clark [q.v.], with respect to credit for the results of this work led to Peabody's resignation in 1874 (Girling, post, p. 110).

His efforts to reëstablish himself led him to return to Chicago, where he was appointed to his former position at the Central High School, in which he remained until 1878, when he accepted a professorship of mechanical engineering and physics at the Illinois Industrial University. Resigning in February 1880 to serve as editor of *The International Cyclopedia,* he returned in August, as regent (president) *pro tempore.* In March of the following year he was appointed regent. The university was in debt; its endowment from a land grant was small; and its income from tuition meager. Peabody secured the first support which the institution received from the legislature, and increased its endowment by the sale of public lands. In 1885 its name was changed to University of Illinois. He established the agricultural experiment station, in 1887, thereby strengthening his position with the legislature. Meanwhile, he declined the presidency of the Rose Polytechnic Institute and the position of assistant secretary of agriculture under President Harrison.

Resigning in September 1891, he went to Chicago as chief of the department of liberal arts in the World's Columbian Exposition. He was appointed official editor and statistician of the American exhibits at the World's Fair at Paris in 1899; was in charge of the educational exhibits at the Pan-American Exposition, Buffalo, in 1901; and of the South Carolina Interstate and West Indies Exposition at Charleston in 1902. On Aug. 1, 1902, he went to St. Louis as assistant to the director general of the Louisiana Purchase Exposition, and remained there until his death in the following year.

[S. H. Peabody, *Peabody (Paybody, Pabody, Pabodie) Geneal.* (1909), ed. by C. H. Pope; *The Alumni Record of the Univ. of Ill.* (1913); Paul Monroe, *A Cyc. of Educ.,* vol. IV (1913); Katherine Peabody Girling, *Selim Hobart Peabody* (1923); *Who's Who in America,* 1899–1900; *St. Louis Globe-Democrat,* May 27, 1903; Peabody MSS. in the Univ. of Ill. lib.]
R. F. S.

PEABODY, WILLIAM BOURN OLIVER (July 9, 1799–May 28, 1847), Unitarian clergyman, twin brother of Oliver William Bourn Peabody [q.v.], was born in Exeter, N. H., the eighth of ten children of Oliver and Frances (Bourn) Peabody, and fifth in descent from Francis Peabody who emigrated from England in 1635 and settled first at Ipswich and later in Topsfield, Mass. His father, a graduate of Harvard College, was a lawyer and politician, president of the state Senate in 1813 and associate justice of the court of common pleas, 1813–16. Peabody attended Phillips Exeter Academy under Benjamin Abbot [q.v.] from 1808 to 1813, graduated from Harvard College in 1816, taught at Phillips Exeter for a year, returned to Cambridge to complete his theological course with the younger Henry Ware [q.v.], and was ordained Oct. 12, 1820, as pastor of the Third Congregational (Unitarian) Society of Springfield, Mass., to which he ministered until his death some twenty-seven years later. On Sept. 8, 1824, he married Elizabeth Amelia White, by whom he had a daughter and four sons. Despite a frail constitution and much positive ill health he performed the duties of his office with exemplary tact and devotion and was held in veneration by his parishioners and fellow citizens. Early in life he had resolved to shun dogmatism and the sectarian spirit, but he was a close student of the Bible, and his sermons, painstakingly wrought out with both a religious and a literary conscience, were sermons and not mere essays. His literary work was by no means negligible. To Jared Sparks's *Library of American Biography* he contributed lives of Alexander Wilson (vol. II, 1834), Cotton Mather (vol. VI, 1836), David Brainerd (vol. VIII, 1837), and James Oglethorpe (2 ser., vol. II, 1844). For over twenty years he was a frequent contributor to the *North American Review.* He also wrote a great deal for the *Christian Examiner,* contributed occasionally to annuals, and published nine sermons and addresses. As a commissioner appointed by Gov. Edward Everett he prepared *A Report on the Ornithology of Massachusetts*

(1839) which is notable chiefly for its observations on the economic value of birds and its plea for their preservation. It lists 286 species but is less an independent treatise than an appendix to Thomas Nuttall's *Manual of the Ornithology of the United States and of Canada* (1832–34). Peabody was, incidentally, a friend of John James Audubon. He was also something of a poet, author of a *Poetical Catechism* (1823) and of several occasional poems and hymns. He edited the *Springfield Collection of Hymns for Sacred Worship* (1835). The whole range of his literary work is well displayed in two posthumous volumes, *Sermons by the Late William B. O. Peabody* (1849; 2 ed.) and *The Literary Remains of the Late William B. O. Peabody* (1850). The death of his wife, Oct. 4, 1843, and of his daughter, Jan. 28, 1844, were severe trials to him, and thereafter his health declined steadily. His last sermon, preached twelve days before his death, was on the text, "To be spiritually minded is life and peace." He died at Springfield and was buried in the Springfield Cemetery.

[O. W. B. Peabody, memoir prefixed to *Sermons by the Late William B. O. Peabody* (1849); W. B. Sprague, *Annals of the Am. Unitarian Pulpit* (1865); *Heralds of a Liberal Faith*, vol. II (1910), ed. by S. A. Eliot; Henry Ware, *Sermon Delivered Oct. 12, 1820, at the Ordination of the Rev. W. B. O. Peabody* (1820); E. S. Gannett, *Discourse Delivered at the Funeral of Rev. W. B. O. Peabody, D.D.* (1847); Geo. Walker, *Address at the Dedication of a Monument to Rev. W. B. O. Peabody, D. D.* (1861); S. H. Peabody, *Peabody . . . Geneal.* (1909).]   G. H. G.

PEALE, ANNA CLAYPOOLE (Mar. 6, 1791–Dec. 25, 1878), miniature painter, sister of Sarah Miriam Peale [*q.v.*], was born in Philadelphia, the daughter of Mary Claypoole and James Peale [*q.v.*]. Her grandfather, James Claypoole, was said to be the first native Pennsylvania artist. Her uncle, Charles Willson Peale [*q.v.*], her cousins, and her father provided an artistic family background, and she was reared in one of the most cultivated cities of the early republic at a time when miniature painting was practised and appreciated. She studied with her father the technique of oil painting and also of water color on ivory. Her first picture to be exhibited was a still life of fruit shown in Philadelphia in 1811 when she was twenty years old. Soon afterward she achieved some success as a miniaturist and painted portraits of many persons of social and political eminence. The most active period of her work extended from 1820 to 1840. She was twice married: in 1829 to Dr. William Staughton [*q.v.*], an able minister and educator, who died in the same year, and in 1841 to Gen. William Duncan, whom she also survived. She had no children by either marriage.

Most of her miniatures were painted in Philadelphia and Baltimore, although she also worked in Boston and Washington. A Baltimore paper of 1822 in announcing that she was prepared to paint portraits in miniature stated that examples of her work were on exhibition at the Museum. She exhibited at the Pennsylvania Academy of the Fine Arts and was represented in the early exhibitions of the Boston Athenæum.

Anna Peale painted miniatures of Andrew Jackson and his wife in 1819, two of her earliest known portraits; of Commodore Bainbridge, President James Monroe, Dr. Oliver Hubbard, Mr. and Mrs. Henry Rodenwald (1825), Mr. and Mrs. C. P. Dexler, General and Madame Lallemand; and of such attractive young women as Eleanor Britton, Jane Brown, and Margaret Hart Simmons. Only about thirty miniatures by her are known, but she must have painted several times that number. Most of her work is owned by descendants of her subjects, although a few examples may be seen in museums. Among these are the portraits of Madame Lallemand in the Pennsylvania Academy of the Fine Arts and of Mrs. Nathan Endicott in the Boston Museum of Fine Arts. The miniatures are signed with any of her names. On the back of one portrait she wrote: "Miniature of Angelica Vallaye by Anna Peale, widow of Dr. Staughton, also widow of General Duncan." Frequently she signed her miniatures on the front in very small letters "Anna Claypoole Peale" with the date. Sometimes the signature and date are scratched in with a needle. Her technique is detailed and careful. She usually painted flesh surfaces in high colors with great complexity of stroke, a technique which gives somewhat the effect of oil painting. Frequently there are brilliant contrasts of light and shade and the backgrounds are usually dark. Her miniatures are always sprightly and pleasing, though less important artistically than those of her father or of her uncle Charles Willson Peale.

[Sources include: Anne H. Wharton, *Heirlooms in Miniatures* (1898); Harry B. Wehle, *Am. Miniatures* (1927); Theodore Bolton, *Early Am. Portrait Painters in Miniature* (1921); J. T. Scharf and Thompson Westcott, *Hist. of Phila.* (3 vols., 1884); R. I. Graff, *Geneal. of the Claypoole Family* (1893); *Phila. Inquirer*, Dec. 26, 1878.]   J. L. B.

PEALE, CHARLES WILLSON (Apr. 15, 1741–Feb. 22, 1827), portrait painter, naturalist, patriot, was born in St. Paul's Parish, Queen Anne County, Md., the eldest of five children of Charles Peale (1709–1750), a native of Rutlandshire, England, whose progenitors for several generations were in turn rectors of the parish church at Edith Weston. The elder Peale's classical education qualified him as master of the public school at Annapolis after coming to Maryland, and following his marriage in 1740 to Margaret (Triggs) Mathews he removed to Queen Anne County as master of the Free School near Centerville. Two years later he was called to Chestertown as master of the Kent County School. Upon his death in 1750 his widow returned to Annapolis. Charles Willson Peale received the common rudiments of schooling until his thirteenth year when he was apprenticed to Nathan Waters, a saddler. He was released from his indenture at twenty and on Jan. 12, 1762, was married to Rachel, the daughter of the late John Brewer of West River. With means advanced by Judge James Tilghman he was established at his trade with materials supplied by his former master on credit. These obligations and his attempts to meet them by diversifying his pursuits soon involved him in difficulties. Having joined the Sons of Freedom during the Stamp Act agitation, in 1764 he was forced by his creditors, who were Loyalists, to abandon his trade. In his memoirs he recalls the incident as the fortunate turning point in his career since the circumstances resulted in his following the art which thereafter was his sole vocation. His attempts at portraits of himself, his wife, and others brought him a commission to execute portraits on terms which offered more congenial and remunerative occupation than his other pursuits and he thereupon sought instruction from John Hesselius [q.v.], the painter.

In 1765 he accompanied his brother-in-law, Capt. Robert Polk, on a voyage to New England, where after painting several portraits at Newburyport he made the acquaintance at Boston of John Singleton Copley. Proceeding homeward he met with patronage in Virginia which detained him until the following year, and upon his return to Annapolis in 1766 he was awarded recognition which prompted several gentlemen to advance funds to enable him to visit England. Among letters of introduction he carried one to Benjamin West through which he was accepted as a pupil upon his arrival in London in February 1767. His studies under West, supplemented by modeling, miniature painting, and mezzotint engraving, he pursued with characteristic zeal and diligence. He contributed to his support by painting portraits, chiefly in miniature. Other commissions included that for the full-length portrait of Lord Chatham, sent to Virginia in 1768, from which he made his first known engravings. He was represented in two exhibitions of the Society of Artists prior to the founding of the Royal Academy, and while in

London he twice posed for West. Returning to Annapolis in June 1769 he was soon in full employment in Maryland and adjacent provinces with frequent and prolonged engagements at Philadelphia. When Copley left Boston to make his home in England Peale's activities extended farther northward and in the spring of 1776 he established his household at Philadelphia. Congress was then in session and Peale's patrons included delegates and other visitors to the city.

He had joined in patriotic activities incident to the Revolution before leaving Maryland, and when settled in Philadelphia enlisted as a private in the city militia. He was elected first lieutenant and was active in recruiting volunteers when the militia was called out in December 1776. He was in action during the engagements at Trenton and Princeton, and in 1777 was commissioned captain of the 4th Battalion or Regiment of Foot. He continued in active service during the campaign ending with the evacuation of Philadelphia by the British. He also served on important military and civil committees, was chairman of the Constitutional Society, and in 1779 was elected one of the Philadelphia representatives in the General Assembly of Pennsylvania. On the expiration of his term he retired from office although he continued to render public service as occasion offered until the close of the war. During the several encampments he was called upon to paint portraits in miniature of his fellow officers, replicas of which in head size were the nucleus of the portrait collection subsequently formed as his record of the war. In the interval at the close of the war when economic conditions were unfavorable to his profession, he undertook to engrave mezzotint plates from his portrait collection. At this time, while he was making drawings of recently discovered bones of the mammoth, it was suggested to him that his gallery be made the repository also of natural curiosities. His interest in the project was thus aroused and he conceived the idea of founding an institution. He wished to make it public rather than private in character and accordingly, when the museum was established, it was governed by a Society of Visitors. It was removed to the hall of the American Philosophical Society in 1794 and in 1802 by act of the Pennsylvania Assembly it was granted the free use of the State House (Independence Hall) recently vacated by the legislature. It was subsequently incorporated as the Philadelphia Museum under the direction of a board of trustees. In scope and character it ranked with the notable museums of the time.

Peale retired from his profession in the seventeen nineties although he continued to paint at intervals in order to enlarge his portrait gallery and to acquire means for improving the museum, which was largely dependent upon his resources. After he retired to his country place, "Belfield," in 1810, his sons who were naturalists relieved him of active supervision of the museum. His varied hobbies, his interest in applied science and the arts, and his youthful ventures in trade have created misleading impressions of him and have tended to obscure his career as a painter. In 1791 and again in 1795 he attempted to establish academies of the fine arts. These failed through inadequate encouragement, but he was largely responsible for the successful establishment of the Pennsylvania Academy of the Fine Arts in 1805. He was thrice married. Of his six children by his first wife who survived infancy, his sons Raphael and Rembrandt [qq.v.] were painters, and Titian and Rubens, naturalists. By his second marriage with Elizabeth DePeyster of New York in 1791 he had six children of whom Franklin and Titian Ramsay [q.v.] were best known as naturalists. His third marriage (1805) to Hannah Moore, who died in 1821, was without issue. Peale died at Philadelphia and was buried in St. Peter's churchyard. Besides his manuscript memoirs and unpublished writings, he was author of *An Essay on Building Wooden Bridges* (1797); *Discourse Introductory to a Course of Lectures on the Science of Nature* (1800); *Introduction to a Course of Lectures on Natural History* (1800), delivered at the University of Pennsylvania; *An Epistle to a Friend on the Means of Preserving Health* (1803); *An Essay to Promote Domestic Happiness* (1812); and *Address to the Corporation and Citizens of Philadelphia* (1816).

Peale returned to Annapolis in 1769 after two years study under Benjamin West, trained in and accustomed to that school of English painting which often placed the figure in an open-air background beside an altar, a fountain, vase, or statue as required by the classic tradition. His early canvases were usually large, many displaying a full-length figure, and some even whole family groups. For the most part he painted into his backgrounds landscapes, or some incident having a connection with the sitter, and some personal belonging added local color. His figures are somewhat formally placed; the faces solidly and tightly painted; the lips almost uniformly thin, and the hands, while moderately well drawn, are frequently ungraceful. The jabot, shirt-ruffle, the fabric and lace on the women's gowns are painted with scrupulous care, but the eyes, usually oversmall, are the least satisfactory

feature. His later portraits, painted after his art had become an avocation, are so distinct in style and technique that a presumption is raised that he received some instruction from his son, Rembrandt, after the latter's return from study in Paris. While Peale was never a great painter, his work shows sincerity and trained craftsmanship, and he did for Pennsylvania, Maryland, and Virginia what Copley did for Massachusetts: he left scores of pleasing and highly decorative canvases portraying the distinguished men and gracious women from the representative families of the day; he preserved the flavor and dignity of colonial life at its apogee. Peale will always be known as the painter of Washington, as he not only painted the first portrait of him, but during twenty-three years—1772-95—painted him seven times from life, and his son states that Washington sat on seven other occasions for his father to further the painting of a replica of some one of his originals. There is some uncertainty as to which are Peale's life portraits of Washington, but the better authority is as follows: Three-quarter length in the uniform of a colonel of Virginia militia, painted at "Mount Vernon" in 1772; three-quarter length in Continental uniform painted for John Hancock in Philadelphia in 1776; miniature on ivory, probably painted late in 1777; a bust portrait, claimed to have been begun from life at Valley Forge in 1777 (Many authorities consider this canvas to have been cut down from a full-length portrait. Whether Peale could have had the opportunity to paint so large a canvas while on active service and encamped at Valley Forge is an open question); full length, Continental type portrait, ordered by the Supreme Executive Council of Pennsylvania on Jan. 18, 1779 (This is the familiar portrait of Washington standing, with his left hand resting upon a cannon, Nassau Hall and marching Hessian prisoners being in the background.); a bust portrait painted during the sittings of the Constitutional Convention in Philadelphia in 1787; and a bust portrait of Washington when president, painted in Philadelphia in 1795.

Peale painted about sixty portraits of Washington in all. Lacking that insight which enables a great artist to indicate strongly individual character, Peale conscientiously transferred to canvas what he saw before him, and in the portrait of 1779 he uncompromisingly portrayed Washington's small eyes, his high cheekbones, and his rather ungainly figure—the sloping shoulders, the slightly protruding abdomen, the long arms and thin legs. Yet, when this is compared with Houdon's standing statue in Richmond, the similarity is at once apparent. Houdon, the greatest sculptor of his day, had life sittings from Washington, and, therefore, his statue should be accepted as the canon for comparison. Peale's conception of Washington's face was perhaps uninspired, but this portrait of 1779 represents Washington of the Revolution more truthfully than do later portraits by others, even by so great a master as Stuart, who never saw Washington until four years before his death, when, old before his time, care worn and disillusioned, his appearance had much altered, and the loss of his teeth had entirely changed his expression and the shape of his face.

[The biographical details of this sketch were drawn chiefly from Peale's manuscript memoirs, journals, and correspondence, from 1765 to 1827, in the possession of Horace Wells Sellers at the time the sketch was written. Many biographical references to Peale in published sources have been based upon Wm. Dunlap's biography in the *Hist. of the Rise and Progress of the Arts of Design in the U. S.* (2 vols., 1834), which is inaccurate and somewhat bad-tempered. For printed sources, see especially, Cuthbert Lee, *Early Am. Portrait Painters* (1929); A. C. Peale, *Chas. Willson Peale and His Services During the American Revolution* (n.d.); C. W. Peale and A. M. F. J. Beauvois, *A Sci. and Descriptive Cat. of Peale's Museum* (1796); The Pa. Acad. of the Fine Arts, *Cat. of an Exhibition of Portraits by Chas. Willson Peale and Jas. Peale and Rembrandt Peale* (ed. 1923); "Extracts from the Correspondence of Chas. Wilson [*sic*] Peale Relative to the Establishment of the Acad. of the Fine Arts, Phila.," *Pa. Mag. of Hist. and Biog.*, July 1885; Walter Faxon, "Relics of Peale's Museum," *Bull. of the Museum of Comparative Zoöl.*, July 1915; H. W. Sellers, *Engravings by Chas. Willson Peale, Limner* (1933), reprinted from the *Pa. Mag. of Hist. and Biog.*, Apr. 1933, and "Chas. Willson Peale, Artist-Soldier," *Pa. Mag. of Hist. and Biog.*, July 1914; C. W. Janson, *The Stranger in America* (1807); H. S. Colton, "Peale's Museum," *Popular Sci. Monthly*, Sept. 1909; J. H. Morgan, *Two Early Portraits of Geo. Washington* (1927); J. H. Morgan and Mantle Fielding, *The Life Portraits of Washington and Their Replicas* (1931); Theodore Bolton and H. L. Binsse, "The Peale Portraits of Washington," the *Antiquarian*, Feb. 1931; C. H. Hart, "Peale's Original Whole-Length Portrait of Washington," *Ann. Report of the Am. Hist. Asso. for the Year 1896* (1897), and "Life Portraits of Geo. Washington," *McClure's Mag.*, Feb. 1897; *Poulson's Am. Daily Advertiser*, Feb. 23, 1827. The estimate of Peale's work, comprising the last part of the biography, was written at the request of the editor by John Hill Morgan, who, owing to the inability of the author to make a final revision of the article before his death, kindly consented to add an appraisal of the artist.]

H. W. S.

PEALE, JAMES (1749–May 24, 1831), portrait painter in miniature and oils, was born in Chestertown, Md., the fifth and youngest son of Margaret (Triggs) Mathews and Charles Peale and the brother of Charles Willson Peale [*q.v.*]. His father, the eldest son of a Rutlandshire family, had come to the colonies, taught school in Maryland, married, and then kept the Free School in Chestertown. There he died in 1750. The family moved to Annapolis and several years later Charles Willson, who was apprenticed to a sad-

dler, took James under his care to learn the saddlery trade. About 1770, following Charles' example and under his guidance, James Peale gave up his trade to become a painter. His brother taught him the technique of water-color and oil painting and the principles of portraiture. During the Revolution James rendered active service until June 3, 1779, when he resigned. He was first with Smallwood's Maryland Regiment (ensign, Jan. 14, 1776) and later with the 1st Maryland, in which he was commissioned captain Mar. 1, 1778.

After the war he went to Philadelphia to reside with his brother Charles. About 1785 he married Mary Claypoole (1753–1829), daughter of James Claypoole, the artist. Apart from occasional painting trips to the Southern cities he lived most of his life in Philadelphia. He had one son, James, Jr., who became a banker but who in his leisure painted marines and landscapes. Of his five daughters two were Sarah Miriam and Anna Claypoole Peale [*qq.v.*]. He left an abundant pictorial record of himself and of his family. In the Pennsylvania Academy of the Fine Arts may be seen "James Peale and his Family," painted in 1795; "Mary Claypoole Peale," his wife, and a "Portrait of the Artist." He has also left several portraits and miniatures of himself and of his family. His achievement in oil painting is uneven; in general the later work is much finer than the early pieces. Portrait groups painted around 1795 are stiff and awkward, both in arrangement and treatment. Ten years later he had mastered technical difficulties and had developed his own style. Such a picture as that of his two daughters, Anna and Margaretta, in the Pennsylvania Academy, shows him at his best. Naturalness of pose, good drawing, and a sympathetic understanding of both his subject and his medium distinguish the work.

James Peale copied the head of Charles Willson Peale's 1787 life portrait of Washington to make a half-length figure with a sword. This he did several times, varying the background. Examples may be seen in the New York Public Library and in Independence Hall, Philadelphia. There is evidence that he was interested in painting still life, landscapes, and even historical subjects. Several of his paintings of fruit are in New York. He sometimes painted landscape detail in the background of his portraits as for instance in the "Ramsay-Polk family." The "View of the Battle of Princeton," "A View of Belfield Farm, near Germantown" (1811), and "A Rencontre between Col. Allen McLane and two British Horsemen" (1814) are attributed to him. But it is as a miniature painter that he is justly best known. He began by closely following the style of his brother and the miniatures of his first period to about 1795 are on similar small oval or circular pieces of ivory. He was most active in miniature painting between 1782 and 1812. In the former year he painted miniatures of Martha and of George Washington, and again in 1788 he painted another miniature of Washington. Probably both are from life. In the autumn of 1795 when his brother and two nephews were painting portraits of Washington, he also made a small water-color portrait on paper.

From about 1795 his prolific brush produced miniatures which are the work of a finished artist. The drawing is surer, the portraits are developed in fewer and broader strokes, though his lines are always delicate. "Mollie Callahan" (1799) is typical of this period. The size of the ivory is somewhat larger, the color diversified and harmonious, the effect delicate and beautiful. His technique and talent were particularly suited to portrayal of feminine subjects. A mannerism of tucking in the corners of the mouth and drawing the lips in a definite cupid's bow pattern is so common in his miniatures as to become a point of identification. The signature is usually I. P. or J. P. in very small letters with the date.

[For printed sources see: C. W. Bowen, *The Hist. of the Centennial Celebration of the Inauguration of Geo. Washington* (1892); The Pa. Acad. of the Fine Arts, *Cat. of an Exhibition of Portraits by Chas. Willson Peale and Jas. Peale and Rembrandt Peale* (ed. 1923); Theodore Bolton, *Early Am. Portrait Painters in Miniature* (1921); "Life Portraits of Washington by Members of the Peale Family," *Antiquarian*, Feb. 1931; Harry B. Wehle, *Am. Miniatures* (1927); Cuthbert Lee, *Early Am. Portrait Painters* (1929); R. I. Graff, *Geneal. of the Claypoole Family* (1893); *Poulson's Am. Daily Advertiser*, May 26, 1831.]   J. L. B.

PEALE, RAPHAEL (Feb. 17, 1774–Mar. 4, 1825), painter, brother of Rembrandt and Titian Ramsay Peale [*qq.v.*], was born at Annapolis, Md., the eldest child of Charles Willson Peale [*q.v.*] and his first wife, Rachel Brewer of Annapolis. He preferred to spell his name Raphaelle. When he was two years old the family settled in Philadelphia where the boy was to have many advantages. He became his father's pupil and when he was twenty-one painted a water-color profile of Washington. Although not so talented as his younger brother Rembrandt he achieved some success as a miniature painter and after 1815 was favorably known for his still-life pieces. He worked in several mediums: oils and water color on ivory, paper, and vellum. He also used the physionotrace. On May 25, 1797, he was married to Martha McGlathery in Philadelphia. He always made his home there, although he painted in many of the

chief cities of the country. By 1799 he had established himself as a professional miniature painter. At several times during his career he cooperated with his brother Rembrandt in various undertakings. From 1790 to 1799 they were working together in Baltimore attempting to establish a portrait gallery of distinguished persons. In 1803 Raphael painted in Norfolk and the following year with Rembrandt visited Savannah, Charleston, Baltimore, and Boston.

Between 1804 and 1811 Raphael Peale's prices for portraits are said to have declined from fifty to fifteen dollars. For miniatures on ivory and vellum and for profiles his charges also decreased materially. After 1815 when his health began to fail he devoted himself almost entirely to still-life subjects such as fruit, game, and fish. He sometimes signed his miniatures "R. P.," which perhaps accounts for the one-time confusion of his work with that of Rembrandt Peale. He also signed himself "Rap. Peale," "Raph^e. Peale," or in full, "Raphael Peale." Occasionally there was no signature. Representative examples of his miniature portraits are those of Doyle Sweeney, Abiah Brown, and Maj.-Gen. Thomas Acheson, all privately owned. Not more than a dozen miniatures by him are known. Several examples of his still-life paintings are owned by the Pennsylvania Academy of the Fine Arts. His style in miniature painting faintly resembles that of James Peale. He has, however, several distinguishing characteristics of technique such as modeling the features in blue hatching with very little flesh color added. Usually he painted the costume in solid gouache, displaying little variety or interest in color. The backgrounds are light and clear, sometimes painted in delicate cloudlike forms. The drawing is not uniformly skilful but his style was sufficiently personal to permit identification of unsigned pieces. He is said to have been successful in obtaining likenesses. After a lingering illness he died in his fifty-third year, survived by his wife and their seven children.

[For printed sources see Rembrandt Peale's "Reminiscences," in the *Crayon*, Aug. 29, Sept. 19, Oct. 3, 1855, Jan., Apr., June 1856, Feb., Sept., Oct., Nov., Dec. 1857, Nov. 1860; C. H. Hart, "Life Portraits of Geo. Washington," *McClure's Mag.*, Feb. 1897; Harry B. Wehle, *Am. Miniatures* (1927); J. T. Scharf and Thompson Westcott, *Hist. of Phila.* (3 vols., 1884); *The Cat. of the Exhibition of Am. Miniatures at the Metropolitan* (1927); Theodore Bolton, *Early Am. Portrait Painters in Miniature* (1921). There is a manuscript Peale genealogy in the possession of the Geneal. Soc. of Pa.]   J. L. B.

PEALE, REMBRANDT (Feb. 22, 1778–Oct. 3, 1860), portrait and historical painter, son of Charles Willson [*q.v.*] and Rachel (Brewer) Peale, was born at the Vanarsdalen Farm near

Richboro, Bucks County, Pa., where his father, then with the army at Valley Forge, had found refuge for his family during the British occupation of Philadelphia. According to his memoirs Rembrandt Peale completed his studies at private schools in Philadelphia in advance of students of his own age and showed a special interest in literature and a gift for verse-making. He was likewise precocious in the study of drawing and in his thirteenth year painted a creditable self-portrait—his first attempt in oil colors. Besides studying under his father and copying the paintings in his father's gallery he had the opportunity, when he was seventeen, to practise in the school of design which his father and other artists attempted to form in 1795. In the same year at the exhibition of the Academy, Rembrandt was represented by five portraits and a landscape. In September 1795, when the elder Peale painted the last of his numerous life portraits of Washington, Rembrandt was accorded the same opportunity. He carried his portrait to Charleston, S. C., where he claimed to have made ten copies besides painting the portraits of Generals Gadsden and Sumter and Dr. David Ramsay, the historian, for his father's gallery. In 1796 he joined with his brother Raphael in establishing in Baltimore a gallery in which to exhibit their paintings, including copies they had made of their father's portraits of distinguished persons. To this they added a cabinet of natural history objects, chiefly duplicates from the elder Peale's collection. Three years later this venture was abandoned.

After painting portraits in Maryland Rembrandt Peale returned to Philadelphia and publicly announced in 1800 that to avoid confusion with others of his family he would paint under the name of Rembrandt, an ostentation which he speedily abandoned. At about this time he attended a course of lectures on chemistry at the University of Pennsylvania to perfect his knowledge of pigments. He had married in 1798, when barely twenty, Eleanora Mary Short. Being then largely dependent upon his father's support, he sought other means of employment until his reputation as a painter was established. His father had successfully recovered two skeletons of the mammoth or mastodon and Rembrandt assisted in mounting them and carving the replicas of such bones as were missing. The wide interest in this discovery among naturalists prompted the elder Peale to send one skeleton to Europe in charge of Rembrandt, who was assisted by his younger brother Rubens Peale, then in training as a naturalist. Arriving in England in the autumn of 1802 Rembrandt placed himself under

the guidance of Benjamin West and while pursuing his studies painted portraits of Robert Bloomfield, the poet, and Sir Joseph Banks, president of the Royal Society, for his father's collection. In the Royal Academy's exhibition of 1803 he was represented by two portraits. While in London he published his *Account of the Skeleton of the Mammoth* (London, 1802), followed in 1803 by *An Historical Disquisition on the Mammoth*. As the war with France prevented exhibiting the skeleton in Paris as contemplated, the brothers returned to America in November 1803.

In 1804 Peale established a painting room in the State House at Philadelphia, the building having been granted by the legislature as a repository for the elder Peale's gallery and museum. Employed by his father to paint portraits for his collection, he visited Washington where he executed a likeness of President Jefferson and portraits of other prominent characters. In 1805 he assisted in the establishment of the Pennsylvania Academy of the Fine Arts. In that year he exhibited thirty portraits. His reputation was further extended by visits to New York and Boston. Commissioned by his father he visited Paris in the spring of 1808 and painted for the latter's collection the portraits of Houdon, Cuvier, Bernardin de St. Pierre, Abbe Huay, Count Rumford, David, and Denon. Denon, the director-general of museums, offered Peale the government patronage if he would remain in France. Fearing that the disturbed situation in Europe would separate him from his family, he returned to America in October 1808, but to complete his father's commission, again visited Paris in 1809 and remained throughout the following year. He painted largely in encaustic and his work during this and the following decade is generally considered the high point of his art. Upon his return to Philadelphia in November 1810 he painted a large equestrian picture of Napoleon, which was exhibited first at Baltimore in 1811 and later at Philadelphia. He also painted a number of classical subjects.

Although urged by his father to confine his talents to portrait painting, and his exhibitions to Philadelphia, Peale determined to establish a gallery and museum in Baltimore with possibly an academy for teaching the fine arts. Securing support for this venture he erected a building and opened his exhibition in 1814. He aimed to emulate his father by maintaining his museum on a strictly scientific and educational basis, but popular support was insufficient to justify the investment and finally his brother Rubens Peale who had managed the Philadelphia Museum came to his assistance and relieved him of the establishment. In the meantime he had executed his large canvas, 24' x 13', "The Court of Death," which was placed on view in his gallery at Baltimore in 1820 and subsequently exhibited in other cities for a number of years. After leaving Baltimore he practised his art in New York until 1823 when he reopened his gallery and painting room in Philadelphia. During this interval he labored to perfect an ideal likeness of Washington based upon his own and his father's portraits and he then painted a large equestrian picture using his composite studies for the likeness. In 1825 he was again called to New York and during his residence there was elected to succeed John Trumbull as president of the American Academy of Fine Arts. Subsequently his patronage extended to Boston where he resided for a time. While there he became interested in lithography. He executed, among other works, a large head of Washington for which he received the silver medal of the Franklin Institute.

In 1828 Peale again went abroad and for two years traveled, chiefly in Italy, copying the works of notable masters, besides painting original studies and some portraits. During his nine months' residence in Florence he exhibited at the Royal Academy his portrait of Washington, which on his return was purchased by the United States government. Returning to America in September 1830 he published his *Notes on Italy* (1831) and after residing in New York until 1832 he crossed the ocean for the fifth time, having engaged to paint portraits in England. On his return to America in 1834 he resumed his painting at Philadelphia and in his leisure hours perfected a system for teaching drawing and writing described in his *Graphics: A Manual of Drawing and Writing* (1835). In 1839 he published his *Portfolio of an Artist* which contains a number of his original verses. In his last years he devoted much time to his lectures on the portraits of Washington and contributed to magazines articles relating to art and his "Reminiscences." He continued these activities until shortly before his death at Philadelphia in his eighty-third year. He was survived by his second wife, Harriet Caney. By his first wife he had seven daughters and two sons.

It was Rembrandt Peale's misfortune to paint during that half-century when the artistic sense of the English-speaking peoples, at least, almost entirely disappeared. The ugliness of this era was nowhere more manifest than in clothes and household furnishings, and these, perforce, had to appear in Peale's portraits. Technically,

Rembrandt Peale may have been a better painter than his father, but not one of his canvases exhibits the charm and decorative qualities of those of the elder Peale. After his study in Paris, his portraits were painted with that thoroughness then in fashion and in encaustic, so that many almost resemble work in enamel. When in the second decade of the nineteenth century Peale turned to allegorical and historical subjects, and especially after he became obsessed with the idea of exploiting his portrait of Washington, painted in 1823 (known as the "Port Hole" type), as the "ideal" Washington, general portraiture seems to have become a means to an end, and as a result his portraits, while good likenesses, are perfunctory.

[This sketch is based upon the Peale family papers. For printed sources see Rembrandt Peale's "Reminiscences" in the *Crayon*, Aug. 29, Sept. 19, Oct. 3, 1855, Jan., Apr., June 1856, Feb., Sept., Oct., Nov., Dec., 1857, Nov. 1860; C. E. Lester, *The Artists of America* (1846); Wm. Dunlap, *A Hist. of the Rise and Progress of the Arts of Design in the U. S.* (1918), vol. II; The Pa. Acad. of the Fine Arts, *Cat. of an Exhibition of Portraits by Chas. Willson Peale and Jas. Peale and Rembrandt Peale* (ed. 1923); *Description of the Court of Death, an Original Painting by Rembrandt Peale* (n.d.); and "Original Letters from Paris," the *Portfolio*, Sept. 1830. There are manuscripts in the possession of the Pa. Hist. Soc. relating to Peale. His lectures on portraits of Washington are in the library of Haverford Coll. Suggestions for this sketch have been supplied by John Hill Morgan.]   H. W. S.

PEALE, SARAH MIRIAM (May 19, 1800–Feb. 4, 1885), portrait painter, was born in Philadelphia, Pa., the youngest of six children of James [*q.v.*] and Mary (Claypoole) Peale. Of her sisters, Anna Claypoole [*q.v.*] attained distinction as a miniature painter, and Margaretta was a professed painter of still life. Reared in an artistic environment, Sarah Miriam Peale began to study and practise painting during early girlhood. She is said to have assisted her father in his pictures by painting details such as lace and flowers. At eighteen she executed her first portrait, a self-likeness which her uncle, Charles Willson Peale, praised at the time as being "wonderfully like." In the annual exhibition of the Pennsylvania Academy of the Fine Arts in 1818 she was represented for the first time by a portrait of "a lady," described as her "second attempt," and in the following year she exhibited two portraits and four still-life pictures. In subsequent exhibitions her entries included portraits of men in public life, the first being Commodore Bainbridge, U. S. N. Congressman Caleb Cushing, Dixon H. Lewis of Alabama, L. F. Linn of Missouri, H. A. Wise, W. R. D. King (later vice-president), and Senator Benton were also among her patrons.

In 1824 Miss Peale was elected an academician of the Pennsylvania Academy of the Fine Arts, her sister Anna being likewise honored. In 1825 the Marquis de Lafayette gave her four sittings during his second visit to the United States and her portrait of him was highly praised as a faithful likeness. In 1826 she exhibited at the Pennsylvania Academy two miniatures—the first of her work in that medium recorded. Following the death of her father in 1831 she removed with her sister, Jane (Peale) Simes, to Baltimore. She painted there and in Washington until about 1847, when she went to St. Louis. In 1877 she returned to Philadelphia to rejoin her sisters, Margaretta and Anna. During her residence in the West she pursued her art, though her pictures rarely, if ever, found their way to exhibitions in the East where Anna Claypoole Peale continued to paint, thus overshadowing the accomplishments of her younger sister. Her paintings displayed greater virility in style than her sister Anna's miniatures, a quality which gave character to her more numerous portraits of men. She died in Philadelphia in the eighty-fifth year of her age. She had never married.

[Sources include: Anne H. Wharton, *Heirlooms in Miniatures* (1898); J. F. Watson, *Annals of Phila.*, enlarged and republished by W. P. Hazard (3 vols., 1898); Theodore Bolton, *Early Am. Portrait Painters in Miniature* (1921); C. E. Clement and Laurence Hutton, *Artists of the Nineteenth Century* (2 vols., 1885); the *Phila. Record*, Feb. 6, 1885; Peale family papers; exhibition catalogues, Pa. Acad. of the Fine Arts.]

H. W. S.

PEALE, TITIAN RAMSAY (Nov. 17, 1799–Mar. 13, 1885), naturalist, artist, mechanician, born in Philadelphia, Pa., was the youngest son of Charles Willson Peale [q.v.] and his second wife, Elizabeth DePeyster of New York. He was given the name of his half-brother Titian (1780–1798) whose death during the yellow fever epidemic of 1798 was a heavy blow to his father. When convinced of Titian's talent for mechanics the elder Peale placed him with a manufacturer of spinning machines, intending to establish him with his brother Franklin in the cotton-spinning business. Titian however turned from this to study natural history and in his seventeenth year was placed with his brother Rubens Peale, then curator of the museum founded by their father. He attended lectures on anatomy at the University of Pennsylvania and developed skill in the preservation of specimens for the museum and in making drawings of subjects for its records. In 1818 he joined an expedition to the coast of Georgia and eastern Florida with William Maclure, Thomas Say, and George Ord to study the fauna and collect specimens. In the following year he was appointed as assistant naturalist and painter with the United States Expedition under Maj. Stephen H. Long to the Upper Missouri, and he made many of the sketches used in illustrating the papers by members of the party. In 1821 he was appointed assistant manager of the Philadelphia Museum.

Peale was represented in the exhibition of 1822 at the Pennsylvania Academy of the Fine Arts by four water-color paintings of animals. In 1824 he was sent to Florida by Charles Lucien Bonaparte to collect specimens and make drawings for his *American Ornithology* (4 vols., 1825–33), of which the colored plates in volumes I and IV were Peale's work. He also drew some of the plates for Thomas Say's *American Entomology* (3 vols., 1824–28). In 1826 he was again represented by water-color drawings of animals in the Pennsylvania Academy exhibition. While engaged as curator of the Philadelphia Museum he visited the interior of Colombia in 1832 to collect specimens and the following year published *Lepidoptera Americana*. In 1833 he was elected manager of the museum and continued to deliver lectures on natural history in that institution. From 1838 to 1842 he was a member of the civil staff of the United States Exploring Expedition to the South Sea under Charles Wilkes, and it was through Peale's activities that the Academy of Natural Sciences of Philadelphia was enriched by its notable collection of Polynesian ethnica. He also made drawings for a number of the plates which appear in the published accounts of the expedition. He was the author of "Mammalia and Ornithology," published in 1848 as Volume VIII of the *Reports of the United States Exploring Expedition, 1838–42,* but the work was later suppressed. After his return to Philadelphia he resumed the managership of the museum. The financial difficulties which finally led to the sale of the institution ended his connection with its affairs and in 1849 he was appointed an examiner in the United States Patent Office at Washington, an office which he held until 1872.

Peale was one of the founders of the club known as the United Bowmen of Philadelphia which was composed originally of six young men of scientific and social proclivities who practised archery. The organization, uniformed, is shown in Sully's engraving, "The United Bowmen." After retiring from office at Washington Peale devoted his remaining years chiefly to the Academy of Natural Sciences of Philadelphia where his collection of Lepidoptera is preserved. He was married first in 1822 to Eliza Cecilia Laforgue by whom he had six children and second to Lucy Mullen. He died in Philadelphia.

[The author of this sketch used chiefly the Peale manuscripts. For printed sources see: "Titian Ramsey [*sic*] Peale," *Entomol. News*, Jan. 1913; Wm. Churchill, "The Earliest Samoan Prints," *Proc. Acad. Natural Sci. of Phila.*, vol. LXVII (1915); H. B. Weiss and G. M. Ziegler, *Thos. Say, Early Am. Naturalist* (1931); R. B. Davidson, *Hist. of the United Bowmen* (1888); Chas. Wilkes, *Narrative of the U. S. Exploring Expedition* (1845); Edwin James, *Account of an Expedition from Pittsburgh to the Rocky Mountains* (2 vols., 1823); the *Phila. Record*, Mar. 15, 1885. The minutes of Philadelphia Museum are in the manuscript collections of the Pa. Hist. Soc.]   H. W. S.

PEARCE, CHARLES SPRAGUE (Oct. 13, 1851–May 18, 1914), painter, born at Boston, Mass., was the son of Shadrach Houghton and Mary Anna (Sprague) Pearce. His father, a native of Ashford, Kent, England, was brought to the United States when he was six years old, and became a China merchant in Boston. His mother was the daughter of Charles Sprague [*q.v.*], the poet, and a descendant of one of the members of the "Boston Tea Party." Young Pearce was educated at the Brimmer School and the Boston Latin School, Boston; worked in his father's office for five years; and met with some success as an amateur painter in his nonage. In 1873 he went to Paris and for three years studied painting under Léon Bonnat. Owing to delicate health, he spent his winters in Italy, Southern France, Egypt, Algiers, or Nubia. He began to exhibit his paintings in the Paris Salon in 1876, and continued to send work there for many years. The greater part of his life was passed in France. He bought a house at Auvers-sur-Oise in 1885 where, with his wife, Louise Catherine Bonjean, whom he married in 1888, he lived for more than thirty years.

Pearce's specialty was the pictorial representation of the peasant life of Northern France with its background of rustic landscape or quaint villages; but he also painted some Oriental scenes, Bible subjects, and a few portraits. His "Beheading of St. John the Baptist," shown at the Salon of 1881 and later at the Panama-Pacific International Exposition at San Francisco, 1915, is now in the Art Institute of Chicago. "*Peines de Cœur*," exhibited at the Salon of 1885, was awarded the Temple gold medal at the Pennsylvania Academy exhibition of the same year. "*Un Enterrement Civil*" (a village funeral in Brittany), shown at the Salon of 1891, was especially interesting for its rendering of types of Breton character. Pearce's peasant girls, however, generally look more like professional studio models than real peasants. He was one of the American painters called upon to contribute mural paintings for the Library of Congress in Washington, and made a series of six lunettes for the north corridor, symbolizing the Family, Religion, Labor, Study, Recreation, and Rest. These works are well drawn and composed, though the conceptions do not rise above the average level of creative imagination as exemplified in other decorations in the building. Considering the inexperience of the artist in mural work, he acquitted himself creditably in this difficult field. Honors came to him from many sources and in many forms—medals, diplomas, election to high academic distinction in France, Belgium, Denmark, Germany, and the United States. His colleagues showed their esteem for him by making him chairman of the Paris juries for two important international expositions, those at Chicago and St. Louis, 1893 and 1904, and member of the juries of awards for the Paris Exposition of 1889 and the Antwerp Exposition of 1904. His death occurred at his home in Auvers-sur-Oise in his sixty-third year. His work in general is typical of the academic productions of the numerous talented Americans trained in Paris and living in France in the late nineteenth century. It is accomplished school work, well constructed and having many technical merits, but on the other hand it is quite without imagination, poetry, or the "flame of sensibility."

[H. L. Earle, *Biog. Sketches of Am. Artists* (1924); *Art Amateur*, Dec. 1883; *Who's Who in America*, 1910–11; Cat. of T. B. Clarke coll., 1899; *Cat. of the Thomas B. Clarke Coll. of Am. Pictures* (Pa. Acad. of the Fine Arts, 1891); C. B. Reynolds, *Washington, the Nation's Capital* (1912); Rand McNally *Washington Guide* (1915); *Boston Transcript*, May 18, 1914.]   W. H. D.

PEARCE, JAMES ALFRED (Dec. 14, 1805–Dec. 20, 1862), representative and senator from Maryland, was descended in the fifth generation from William Pearce who emigrated from Scotland to the Eastern Shore of Maryland about 1670. The eldest child of Gideon and Julia (Dick) Pearce, he was born at the home of his maternal grandfather, Elisha Dick [*q.v.*], in Alexandria, Va., then in the District of Columbia. The death of his mother when he was only three years old left his early education under the direction of his grandfather, who is best known as Washington's physician. From a private academy at Alexandria he entered the College of New Jersey (Princeton) at the age of fourteen and was graduated in 1822 with high rank. Then applying himself to the study of law in the office of Judge John Glenn in Baltimore, he gained admission to the bar in 1824. He soon commenced the practice of his profession at Cambridge, Md., but his career was interrupted within a year by his removal to his father's plantation on the Red River in Louisiana, where for three years he engaged in sugar planting. When he returned to Maryland, it was to resume the practice of law at Chestertown, though he at the same time found expression for his agricultural tastes by cultivating a farm successfully. On Oct. 6, 1829, he was married to Martha J. Laird, who died in 1845.

His legal career was again interrupted in 1831, when he was elected to the legislature of Maryland, from which he passed in 1835 to Congress. With the exception of a single term, that of 1839–41 when he lost his seat by a small majority in the only defeat of his experience, he sat as a Whig member in the House of Representatives from 1835 to 1843. In the latter year he was transferred to the Senate, where he continued through three successive elections to hold his seat until his death. He was reëlected as a Democrat the last time in 1859 after the disruption of the Whig party. It was probably in the committee rooms that his influence as a senator was most felt, for there his analytical mind, the extent of his information, his industry, and his patience for details gave his opinions authority. A man of broad cultural interests, his natural inclinations caused him to give especial attention on matters of education and science. During this long period of service he interested himself in the welfare of the Library of Congress, the Smithsonian Institution, and the Coast Survey. In the decoration of public buildings, sculptors found in him an ever-ready friend. For years he served on the board of visitors and governors of Washington College at Chestertown, Md., where he also lectured on law from 1850 to 1862.

After careful thought he opposed the concessions to Texas concerning the New Mexico territory proposed in the compromise measures of 1850 and succeeded in having the bill amended, an action that resulted in bitter feeling between him and Clay. He was in advance of his time in the firm stand he took against the spoils system and in favor of arbitration of the Oregon boundary dispute with England. Convinced that he was more useful in the Senate, he declined two positions offered him by President Fillmore: a seat on the federal bench of the district court of Maryland and a position as secretary of the interior. The fact that his name was repeatedly mentioned for the presidency, though probably not seriously, indicates a man who rose above the regular senatorial group. During the heated debates of the last slavery years he constantly opposed agitation as calculated to increase the discords that were dividing the country. Confronted with the actual fact of disunion, he deplored secession as ill-advised but equally deplored a union preserved by force. He soon found himself one of a small group which were futile against a dominant majority. Owing to failing health, he did not enter the Senate after Mar. 24, 1862, though he lingered nine months. He was survived by his second wife, Mathilda Cox (Ringgold) Pearce, whom he had married on Mar. 22, 1847. Social, genial, even playful with his intimates, he enjoyed warm and deep friendships. A brilliant conversationalist, he was at his best in a small circle. He was no politician in the ordinary sense of the word, yet he was one of the most successful public men of his period.

[A few letters in *Md. Hist. Mag.*, June 1921; B. C. Steiner, "James Alfred Pearce," *Ibid.*, Dec. 1921–June 1924; *Cong. Globe*, 37 Cong., 3 Sess., pp. 292–94, 298–302; A. B. Bache, "Eulogy," *Ann. Report of . . . the Smithsonian Institution . . . 1862* (1863); G. A. Hanson, *Old Kent* (1876); C. W. Sams and E. S. Riley, *The Bench and Bar of Md.* (1901).]
E. L.

PEARCE, RICHARD (June 29, 1837–May 18, 1927), metallurgist, was born near Camborne in Cornwall, England, the son of Richard Donald Pearce and his wife, Jenifer Bennett. He inherited an early interest in mining from his father who was one of the superintendents of Dolcoath, the premier tin mine of Cornwall. A common-school education was terminated at the age of fourteen when he went to work in the tin-dressing plant of Dolcoath. In 1855, when only eighteen years of age, he was appointed assistant in chemistry at the Truro mining school where he taught while continuing his own studies. The school was poorly supported, however, and had to close, and three years later he joined his father at Dolcoath as assayer. After a short interval he was called upon again to start local classes in mining instruction, performing the task so well that he was given the opportunity of entering the Royal School of Mines in London. He equipped himself for further teaching under such distinguished professors as Percy and Hoffman, then went to Freiberg, Saxony, in 1865, for further study at the mining academy where he became interested in metallurgical silver processes, particularly those of Ziervogel and Augustin. On his return he built a copper-smelting plant at Swansea in south Wales, directing the operations himself, but he found it difficult to introduce there any practice that was not Welsh. The business, moreover, was conducted on such unsound principles that he was glad to accept the invitation of a London firm to visit Colorado in 1871 to inspect silver mines. He had to render an unfavorable report on this occasion, but he was subsequently asked by the same company to take charge of a smelter to be built in Colorado. Since his health had suffered from the damp climate of Swansea, he welcomed the opportunity to enjoy the clear air and the cheerful atmosphere of the Rocky Mountain region.

He sailed from Liverpool with his wife and three children in 1872. The little smelter near Empire in Clear Creek County, Colo., was soon built and ready for business. Its technical operaations were successful but the supply of pyritic ores was inadequate and the shipments of matte to Swansea entailed a cost which was excessive. Meanwhile, he had made the acquaintance of Nathaniel Peter Hill [q.v.], formerly professor of chemistry at Brown University and at that time manager of a smelter at Blackhawk in the adjoining county of Gilpin. The two metallurgists joined forces in building a reduction works in which Pearce's plan for treating the matte and extracting the precious metals was to be given a fair trial. The new plant was in action at Blackhawk by the end of November 1873. Pearce recognized the great responsibility placed upon him by this new position. In commenting upon the difficulties involved in inaugurating a process hitherto untried in America where many things that he needed were not obtainable, he said, "I found myself obliged from the first to introduce what might be termed makeshifts." Such is the history of technical operations in remote places. Richard Pearce was successful because he was able to adapt his methods to local conditions and to the exigencies of circumstances, and because his experience at Swansea in devising and superintending metallurgic operations performed by comparatively ignorant men taught him how to train unskilled labor to manipulate the intricate devices of a furnace. He was essentially a practical man, that is, a man of educated common sense. During the next thirty years no less than 52 tons of gold (equivalent to $31,200,000) were separated and refined for the Boston & Colorado Smelting Company, first at Blackhawk and later at Argo, near Denver, by the process devised and conducted by Richard Pearce. The larger smelter at Argo was built in 1878, and in the following year a branch smelter was built at Butte to provide matte from the ores of Montana. At this time Pearce lived at Denver, a wealthy man and an honored citizen. In 1885 he was appointed British vice-consul; in 1889 he was elected president of the American Institute of Mining Engineers; and he was twice president of the Colorado Scientific Society,

with which he was closely identified as a charter member and to the *Proceedings* of which he contributed a number of valuable papers on geology and mineralogy. The mineral, pearceite, a sulphide of silver and arsenic, is named for him.

In 1902 he retired from the management of the Argo smelter and returned to Cornwall where, in 1908, he associated himself with Williams, Harvey & Company in building a tin smelter at Bootle, near Liverpool. He was engaged in this pleasant professional activity until 1919 when he left the works in charge of his son and changed his residence to London. There he remained, near to the museums and schools of science, both of which continued to command his lively interest. In 1925, at the age of eighty-eight, he received the gold medal of the Institution of Mining and Metallurgy "in recognition of the services which he had so long rendered to the advancement of metallurgical science and practice." He died on May 18, 1927, within a few weeks of his ninetieth birthday. He was twice married, first to Carolina Maria Lean and, second, to Amelia Elisabeth Hawken.

[T. T. Read, "Richard Pearce," *Mining and Metallurgy,* Feb. 1928; H. V. Pearce, "The Pearce Gold-Separation Process," *Trans. Am. Inst. Mining Eng.,* vol. XXXIX (1909); *Times* (London), May 19, Sept. 12, 1927; information from family sources.]

T. A. R.

PEARCE, RICHARD MILLS (Mar. 3, 1874-Feb. 16, 1930), pathologist and authority on medical education, was born in Montreal, Canada. His father, Richard Mills Pearce, and his mother, Sarah Smith, were both from the United States and moved back to New England soon after their son was born. Pearce received his education at Hillhouse High School in New Haven, Conn. (1889-90), the Boston Latin School (1890-91), the Boston College of Physicians and Surgeons (1891-93), Tufts College Medical School (1893-94; M.D., 1894), and finally at the Harvard Medical School (M.D. 1897). His interest was directed toward pathology by F. C. Mallory, and by W. T. Councilman in whose department at Harvard he served as instructor (1899-1900). From 1896 to 1899 he had acted as resident pathologist to the Boston City Hospital, and during 1899 he was pathologist to three other Boston hospitals.

In 1900 he accepted a post in the department of pathology at the University of Pennsylvania under Simon Flexner, and the following year went to Leipzig to work with Marchand. In 1903 he became director of the Bender Hygienic Laboratory at Albany and professor of pathology at Albany Medical College. He was called in 1908 to the chair of pathology at the Bellevue

Hospital Medical College, New York, and in 1910 he went to the University of Pennsylvania to occupy the first chair of research medicine to be created in the United States, which had been endowed by John Herr Musser. This post Pearce held until his appointment as director of the division of medical education of the Rockefeller Foundation (1920). During the War, as major in the medical corps, he helped organize the laboratory section of the army medical department and served as chairman of the division of medicine and related sciences of the Council of National Defense.

His appointment as a research professor of medicine marked the turning point in his career, and he worked unremittingly throughout the rest of his life to improve scientific medicine. In 1912 he delivered the Hitchcock lectures at California, choosing as his subject "Research in Medicine" and giving a vivid and farseeing portrayal of the history of medical experimentation and of present and future problems of medical education. Since he was a modest man of great alertness, tact, and broad human sympathies, it was scarcely surprising that he should have been selected to direct the great program of medical education inaugurated after the World War by the Rockefeller Foundation. His approach to the gigantic problem of improving world medicine was simple and logical, and it reflected his extraordinary combination of aptitudes for administration, teaching, and scientific investigation. His first years were spent largely as an administrator collecting data about the conditions of medicine in every civilized country; his surveys were models of detailed accuracy and clarity, and they form an incomparable body of source material concerning the history of contemporary medicine. On the basis of information thus secured the Foundation devoted considerable attention to medical education, and in administering the large capital funds expended in influential medical centers during the next seven years (1922–29) Pearce's unusual gifts as a teacher were allowed full expression. He concentrated upon the improvement of the preclinical sciences, giving funds for buildings and endowment, and fellowships for the training of promising teachers and investigators. To facilitate the exchange of information and opinion between countries, he established in 1924 an annual publication entitled *Methods and Problems of Medical Education*. With his keen interest in fostering medical research, he welcomed the important change of policy reflected by the fact that on Jan. 1, 1929, the division of medical education became known as the division of medical sciences of the Rocke-

feller Foundation. "The new undertakings [of the Foundation] differed from earlier programs in being directly aimed at the advancement of knowledge through improvement of clinical facilities or routine teaching laboratories or more fully trained teaching personnel instead of the development of institutions as teaching organizations" (Gregg, *post*).

In addition to many early contributions to pathology and to addresses on medical education (collected in *Medical Research and Education*, 1913) Pearce published a monograph, *The Spleen and Anaemia* (1918). On Nov. 6, 1902, he married May Harper Musser; there were two children, a son and a daughter.

[*Richard Mills Pearce, Jr., M.D. 1874–1930, Addresses Delivered at a Memorial Meeting at the Rockefeller Institute, Apr. 15, 1930* (privately printed); Simon Flexner, in *Science*, Mar. 28, 1930; *Who's Who in America*, 1928–29; Alan Gregg, in *Rockefeller Foundation Quart. Bull.*, Oct. 1931, pp. 538–79; H. T. Karsner, in *Archives of Pathology*, Mar. 1930; G. M. Pierson, in *Am. Jour. Medic. Sci.*, June 1919, May 1930; *N. Y. Times*, Feb. 17, 1930.]   J. F. F.

PEARCE, STEPHEN AUSTEN (Nov. 7, 1836–Apr. 8, 1900), musician, was born in Brompton, Kent, England, the son of Stephen and Elizabeth (Austen) Pearce. The father, a postmaster, gave his six children the best educational opportunities. Two sons, Stephen and James, received special training as organists and choirmasters and were so similarly trained that a biography of one to a certain degree involves also the other. Stephen, the elder brother, was the more learned and his influence was therefore more far-reaching. Both boys sang in the Rochester Cathedral and the nearby Chatham Cathedral choirs (Episcopalian), thus taking part daily in two services and spending the remaining time in the cathedral school. Both received their most important organ training under the eminent organist, John Larkin Hopkins, and were therefore fitted for any organ position. Both entered Oxford and took their degrees of B.Mus., Stephen in 1859, and James in 1860. Stephen continued his study and received the degree of D.Mus. in 1864. In that year he visited the United States and Canada. His brother had preceded him and was organist of the Quebec Cathedral. Stephen had held important positions in London churches and returned to give organ recitals at the Hanover Square Rooms and elsewhere, but in 1872 he came to America to reside. Settling in New York, he became an important factor as organist, theorist, and writer. He held church positions at St. George's, St. Stephen's, Zion, Ascension, the Fifth Avenue Collegiate (Dutch Reformed), all in New York City, and at the First Presbyterian in Jersey

City. For one year (1878–79) he was instructor in vocal music at Columbia College. He also taught harmony and composition at the New York College of Music and was lecturer on harmony at the General Theological Seminary, and at the Peabody Institute and The Johns Hopkins University, Baltimore. Besides these many activities he gave numerous lectures and recitals in other cities. He had a brilliant technique and was doubtless one of the best organists of his time.

With a tremendous capacity for work, in 1874 he became musical editor of the New York *Evening Post* and on occasion contributed articles to the *Musical Courier* and to various other periodicals. He edited a *Pocket Dictionary of Musical Terms* (1889) in twenty-one languages, including Arabic, Chaldaic, French, German, and Greek. He wrote much church and piano music and made many transcriptions of symphonies and oratorios for organ. Among his more important compositions are the following: a three-act children's opera, *La Belle Américaine*; a dramatic oratorio, *Celestial Visions*; a church cantata, *The Psalm of Praise* (in fugal style for solos, eight-part chorus, full orchestra and organ), performed at Oxford University; an Overture in E minor; an orchestral "Allegro Agitato"; several pieces for piano, and a vocal trio in canon form, "Bright Be Thy Dreams." Pearce died on Apr. 8, 1900, in the Jersey Heights Presbyterian Church. He had begun to play the morning service, but feeling ill, he was obliged to lie down and died almost at once of a stroke of paralysis. In appearance he was dignified and fine-looking. Dr. Waldo Selden Pratt, who frequently heard him play, writes of him: "My impression of him was that he was a most competent and accomplished musician, probably too much so to secure full recognition at the time when he came here."

[Sources include: Theodore Baker, *A Biog. Dict. of Musicians* (1900); *Grove's Dict. of Music and Musicians: Am. Supp.* (1930); *Musical Courier*, Apr. 11, 1900; *Evening Post* (N. Y.), Apr. 9, 10, 1900; information as to certain facts from Pearce's niece, Miss Ella Gilmore Pearce, Yonkers, N. Y.]   F. L. G. C.

PEARSE, JOHN BARNARD SWETT (Apr. 19, 1842–Aug. 24, 1914), metallurgist, was born in Philadelphia, Pa. His father, Oliver Peabody Pearse, a merchant sea-captain, was drowned at Cape May, N. J., while saving a bather, when John was six years of age. His mother, Adelia Coffin (Swett), later married Dr. Edward Hartshorne, a metallurgical expert, whose experiences and influence determined the boy's active business career. His early education was obtained under Prof. Charles Short,

who was connected subsequently with Columbia University. By working as a machinist he also gained a certain amount of information concerning metals. Later he entered Yale University, from which he graduated in 1861, with the degree of B.A.

Returning to Philadelphia, he became connected with Booth and Garrett's chemical laboratory, but in June 1863 assumed complete charge of the chemical division of the United States army's laboratory at Philadelphia, where pharmaceutical products for the hospital service were manufactured. At the conclusion of the Civil War he studied metallurgy for more than a year in the School of Mines at Freiberg, Saxony. He then spent a similar period of time at Neuberg and Leoben, Styria, and other places in Europe, visiting mines and observing methods of metal manufacturing. He returned to the United States in December 1867, and two months later was engaged as chemist by the Pennsylvania Steel Works, near Harrisburg. In 1870 he was promoted to the position of general manager, and this advancement enabled him to build up an enviable reputation as a metal expert, particularly in designing and improving Bessemer steel plants and their products. In addition to other achievements, he was instrumental in developing for the first time the process of manufacturing Bessemer pig-iron from native New Jersey and Pennsylvania ores.

In June 1874 he resigned his position to accept appointment as commissioner and secretary of the second Pennsylvania geological survey, which positions he held until 1881. He was also active on the committee in charge of metallurgical and mining exhibits displayed at the Centennial Exhibition, Philadelphia. In 1876 he became general manager of the South Boston Iron Company, a concern engaged in general machine and foundry work, and particularly in the manufacturing of ordnance and projectiles for the United States government. During the next seven years his keen mind and tireless efforts enabled the company to produce new and better products. In 1883, however, his health broke down and he retired from active participation in metallurgical enterprises. The remainder of his life was spent in cultural vocations and in travel. Until 1889 he lived in England studying music, particularly the violin. During the latter part of his life his home was in Boston. He died at his summer residence in Georgeville, Quebec.

He was the author of several publications prepared during the earlier years of his career. In 1869 he completed a translation of *A Treatise on Roll Turning for the Manufacture of Iron* from the German of Peter Tunner. He contributed a paper "On the Use of Natural Gas in Iron Work," to *Reports on the Second Geological Survey of Pennsylvania* (1875). His largest single published work was an historical essay entitled *A Concise History of the Iron Manufacture of the American Colonies up to the Revolution and of Pennsylvania until the Present Time* (1876). Three of his papers were printed in the *Transactions of the American Institute of Mining Engineers,* entitled, "The Manufacture of Iron and Steel Rails" (vol. I, 1874), "The Improved Bessemer Plant" (vol. IV, 1877), and "Iron and Carbon, Mechanically and Chemically Considered" (*Ibid.*).

He was married in Arlington, Mass., Nov. 1, 1876, to Mary Langdon Williams, daughter of David W. Williams of Roxbury (part of Boston), Mass. A son and a daughter were born to them.

[*Monthly Bull. Am. Inst. Mining Engineers,* Dec. 1914; *Directory of Living Grads. of Yale Univ.* (1904); *The Fiftieth Anniversary of the Class of 1861, Yale Coll.* (1912); *Obit. Record Grads. Yale Univ.* (1915); *Boston Transcript,* Aug. 27, 1914; information from Pearse's son, Langdon Pearse.]   H. S. P.

PEARSON, EDWARD JONES (Oct. 4, 1863–Dec. 7, 1928), railroad engineer, best known as chief executive of the New York, New Haven & Hartford Railroad, was born in Rockville, Ind., the son of Leonard and Lucy Small (Jones) Pearson and a brother of Leonard Pearson [*q.v.*]. After preliminary schooling in the West, he entered Cornell University, where he received the degree of B.S. in engineering in 1883. On June 7, 1899, he married Gertrude S. Simmons of Evanston, Ill.; one son was born to them.

Pearson's first railroad experience was with the Missouri Pacific in 1881 as a rodman on the extension from Atchison, Kan., to Omaha, Nebr. The following year he was engaged in construction work in Indian Territory on the line of the Atlantic & Pacific Railroad. In 1883 he was engaged as assistant engineer for the Northern Pacific, to work on the terminal at Portland, Ore., and subsequently was made supervisor of the St. Paul division (1884), supervisor of bridges, buildings, and water supply of the Minnesota and St. Paul divisions (1885), and engineer in charge of construction train service (1890). In the years 1892–94 he was principal assistant engineer of the Chicago terminal lines in which the Northern Pacific was interested. Returning to the exclusive service of the Northern Pacific, he continued to rise in rank, becoming superintendent of the Yellowstone division (1894), superintendent of the Rocky Mountain division (1895), superintendent of the Pacific division (1898), assistant general superintendent of the eastern division (1902), acting chief engineer (1903), and chief engineer (1904).

The transcontinental extension of the Chicago, Milwaukee & St. Paul attracted Pearson in 1905, and he became chief engineer of the Chicago, Milwaukee & Puget Sound Railway, which constructed the Pacific extension for the parent company. During his period of service that road was completed. On June 1, 1911, he became vice-president of the Missouri Pacific and of the St. Louis, Iron Mountain & Southern, having charge of maintenance, operation, and construction. He took a similar vice-presidency of the Texas & Pacific, in March 1915, primarily to direct the construction of a terminal at New Orleans. The following year he accepted still another position of like nature, the vice-presidency of the New York, New Haven & Hartford, with the duty of acting as assistant to the president and of controlling construction, operation, and maintenance. Upon the death of President Howard Elliott, Pearson on May 1, 1917, succeeded him. During the administration of former president Charles S. Mellen [*q.v.*] the "New Haven" had fallen into bad physical and financial condition. The buildings, equipment, and roadbed needed extensive repairs, provision had to be made for a considerable floating debt, rates had to be readjusted, and disposition had to be made of numerous "outside properties." No dividends had been paid on the common stock since December 1913. The task of meeting these and other difficulties had undoubtedly hastened the death of former President Elliott. During Pearson's presidency, which included the war period in which he acted as federal manager, considerable progress was made in restoring the road. Obviously the boom of the 1920's played a part. By 1924 the road showed an operating profit, and the following year Pearson was able to float a bond issue in New England, thus bringing to a successful culmination a long fight to obtain local support. Dividends on the common stock were resumed in 1928. This same year, however, Pearson's health gave way, due in part, no doubt, to his tireless and unsparing efforts on behalf of the road. On Oct. 23 he entered the Johns Hopkins Hospital, Baltimore; on Nov. 26 he tendered his resignation as president, to take effect at the end of the year; and the following month he died.

[*The Biog. Directory of the Railway Officers of America* (1913); *Railroad Gazette,* May 9, 1902; *Railway Age Gazette,* Mar. 26, Apr. 2, 1915, Mar. 17, 1916; *Railway Age,* Dec. 1, 15, 1928; *Who's Who in America,* 1928–29; *N. Y. Times,* Dec. 8, 1928.]   R. E. R.

PEARSON, ELIPHALET (June 11, 1752–
Sept. 12, 1826), first principal of Phillips Academy, Andover, was born in Newbury, Mass., the
eldest son of David Pearson, a thrifty farmer
and miller, and his wife, Sarah (Danforth) Pearson. At Dummer Academy, in Byfield, where he
studied under the famous Master William Moody,
Pearson first met Samuel Phillips [q.v.], with
whom he formed an enduring friendship. He
graduated from Harvard College in the class of
1773, his Commencement part, a disputation with
Theodore Parsons, being considered so excellent
that it was published as a pamphlet (*A Forensic
Dispute on the Legality of Enslaving the Afri-
cans*, 1773). He remained at Cambridge for
further study, and was later licensed to preach
but was never a candidate for a pastorate.

At the outbreak of the Revolution he withdrew
to Andover, escorting the widow of President
Holyoke of Harvard and her daughter Priscilla.
At Andover, he taught in the grammar school,
joined his friend Phillips in various projects, and
especially aided him in drawing up the constitution of Phillips Academy, of which, at the
unanimous request of the trustees, he became the
first principal when it was opened in 1778. Described by Oliver Wendell Holmes as having a
"big name, big frame, big voice, and beetling
brow" (*The Complete Poetical Works*, Cambridge edition, 1895, p. 257), he was a strict
disciplinarian, who, through his masterful personality and careful supervision of his students,
established confidence in the new institution.
But he chafed under the irritating restraints of
his position and, when he received in 1786 a call
to become Hancock Professor of Hebrew and
Oriental Languages at Harvard, he was glad to
escape to Cambridge. On July 17, 1780, he married Priscilla Holyoke, twelve years older than
he, who brought him a dowry of $8,000; by her
he had a daughter. After his wife's death in 1782,
he married, Sept. 29, 1785, Sarah Bromfield, by
whom he had four children.

At Harvard, Pearson was an influential figure,
who, after the death of President Willard in
1804, assumed the duties of president and, but
for his orthodox and conservative Calvinistic
views, might have been elected as Willard's successor. The growing spirit of Unitarianism being distasteful to him, he resigned in 1806 and
returned to Andover, where he was instrumental
through his perseverance and tireless energy in
founding Andover Theological Seminary, destined to become a citadel of Congregational theology in New England. For one year (1808–09)
he was professor of sacred theology in the Seminary, but then retired in favor of Moses Stuart

[q.v.]. He remained in Andover, however, until
1820, as president of the board of trustees of both
the academy and the seminary, an office to which
he had been elected on Aug. 17, 1802, and which
he did not resign until Aug. 20, 1821. In 1820
he moved to Harvard, Worcester County, Mass.
He died in Greenland, N. H., while on a visit to
a daughter, and was buried in the local cemetery.
He was extraordinarily versatile, being both
business man and scholar, musician and agriculturist, preacher and mechanic. Several of his
sermons, preached on special occasions, were
published. His austerity, intolerance, and ex-
plosiveness made him many enemies, but his
rugged personality and brilliant, restless intellect played an important part in American educational history. His students called him "Elephant," "because of his ponderous name and
figure." A recitation building on Andover Hill
is named Pearson Hall in his memory.

[C. C. Carpenter, *Biog. Cat. of . . . Phillips Acad.,
Andover* (1903); *Phillips Bull.*, Jan. 1914; C. M. Fuess,
An Old New England School (1917); W. B. Sprague,
Annals Am. Pulpit, vol. II (1857).]   C. M. F.

PEARSON, FRED STARK (July 3, 1861–
May 7, 1915), engineer, the son of Ambrose and
Hannah (Edgerly) Pearson, was born in Lowell,
Mass. He entered Tufts College in 1879, studied
during the following year at the Massachusetts
Institute of Technology, and then returned to
Tufts where he graduated in 1883. For three
years thereafter, while he served at Tufts as instructor in mathematics and applied mechanics,
he pursued further studies and conducted investigations for various commercial interests. From
1889 to 1893 he was engaged in the electrification
of the West End Street Railway of Boston, Mass.
Cars had been run by electricity before, but this
was the first system of electric traction to be
operated on a great scale and for many years it
was the model for all who sought to equip electric
railways. The generators at the main power plant
were increased at his direction from 120 to 500
horse power—a step so unprecedented that the
Westinghouse Company refused to bid on the
work. The late George Westinghouse considered
this project as epoch-making in the development
of the dynamo. Throughout his life Pearson led
his profession in making demands upon manufacturers for increasing the size of machinery to
the highest practical efficiency.

He was responsible for the introduction of
electric street cars in Brooklyn, in connection
with which project he designed and erected what
was then the largest and most modern electric
power station. For the Metropolitan Street Railway Company of New York City with which he

was associated from 1894 to 1899, he devised and put into successful operation the underground conduit or trolley. It still remains practically as he left it. For this company he designed and erected the 96th Street Power House, at the time (1896) the largest in the country with a total generating capacity of 70,000 horse power. During this period he was in great demand as consulting engineer for electric railways and power transmission lines in the United States, in Canada, Cuba, Jamaica, and England. Pearson also served as chief engineer for the Dominion Coal Company, refusing at one time the presidency of that concern.

Pearson's interests were largely transferred to foreign countries after 1899. In Brazil, he undertook the task of furnishing power to the city of São Paulo by developing the Rio Tieté. At the Falls of Necaxa in Mexico, he built a plant transmitting between 100,000 and 200,000 horse power to the city of Mexico ninety-five miles away. Later he constructed a plant of about the same magnitude at Niagara Falls for supplying electric light and power to Toronto 100 miles distant. At Lac de Bonnet, on the Winnipeg River, he built a 25,000 horse power plant for the city of Winnipeg, Canada. The development of a power plant of about 40,000 horse power for the city of Rio de Janeiro, Brazil, was his next great enterprise, and this was followed by his last important work, the development of the Ebro River for the general use of the city of Barcelona, Spain. The World War, however, interrupted this work when it was near completion.

In addition to his achievements in electrical engineering, Pearson directed many enterprises in other fields, mining, railroading, lumbering, and irrigation. To indulge his love of nature he developed and managed a beautiful estate of thousands of acres in the hill country of western Massachusetts. He was married on Jan. 5, 1887, to Mabel Ward, of Lowell, Mass. Both lost their lives when the *Lusitania* was sunk on May 7, 1915. They were survived by two sons and one daughter. "Pearson was a man of tireless energy. . . . Every subject that he touched he seemed to absorb and master as though he had a special aptitude for every science. His versatility of intellect was marked by all who knew him. He possessed a constructive and creative imagination without which he could never have achieved the enormous works he left, involving, as they did, great originality and prompt comprehension of complicated situations" (*Transactions of the American Society of Civil Engineers*, vol. LXXXVII, 1914, p. 1404).

[*Who's Who in America,* 1914–15; *Gen. Electric Rev.,* vol. XVIII, 1915; Frederic I. Winslow, *Trans. Am. Soc. Civil Eng.,* vol. LXXXVII, 1924; *Proc. Am. Inst. Electrical Eng.,* June 1915; C. Martyn, *The William Ward Genealogy* (1925); *N. Y. Times,* May 8, 1915.]
B. A. R.

PEARSON, LEONARD (Aug. 17, 1868– Sept. 20, 1909), veterinarian, was born in Evansville, Ind., the brother of Edward Jones Pearson [*q.v.*] and the son of Leonard and Lucy Small (Jones) Pearson, natives of New England. His preliminary education was obtained mostly from his mother. From early boyhood he was interested in animals and when he went to Cornell University at sixteen, he elected all the courses offered in veterinary science. Graduating (B.S.) in 1888, he worked for the federal bureau of animal industry during the summer and in the fall entered the Veterinary School at the University of Pennsylvania. When he received his degree of Doctor of Veterinary Medicine (1890) he accepted a position on the teaching staff, with permission to spend the first year in graduate study abroad. In the course of his studies in Germany, he discovered the thermal reaction produced by mallein in horses infected with glanders, and he became deeply interested in tuberculin (just then discovered by Koch) when, in January 1891, Professor Gutmann, of the Veterinary Institute at Dorpat, Russia, demonstrated that it could be used to discover the presence of tuberculosis in cattle before any physical signs were apparent.

In the fall of 1891, he returned to Philadelphia and began his work in the University of Pennsylvania as assistant professor of veterinary medicine, being promoted to a full professorship three years later. He also engaged in practice, and within a few months, in March 1892, made the first tuberculin test of cattle in the western hemisphere. In the years immediately following, through his addresses and writings, he was one of the chief factors in bringing about the general acceptance of this test. When the State Livestock Sanitary Board was established in 1895, he was appointed state veterinarian, becoming a member of the board *ex officio*. He took office Jan. 1, 1896. His organization of the work of the board, the laws he devised and induced the legislature to pass, and his system of suppressing bovine tuberculosis operated so satisfactorily that they were regarded as models and were copied by other states (see his "The Pennsylvania Plan for Controlling Tuberculosis," *Proceedings of the American Veterinary Medical Association,* 1899). Almost at the beginning of the work, he prevailed upon the board to establish a laboratory for research, the University of Pennsylvania providing the space at the Veterinary School. Here, in collaboration with M. P. Ravenel and S. H. Gilliland, he did work that attracted world-wide attention on the relation of bovine to human tuberculosis and on the vaccination of cattle against tuberculosis (Ravenel, "Comparative Virulence of the Tubercle Bacillus from Human and Bovine Sources," *Transactions of the British Congress on Tuberculosis, 1901,* vol. III, 1902; Gilliland, *The Production of Artificial Immunity against Tuberculosis in Cattle,* Pennsylvania State Livestock Sanitary Board, Circular 32, 1915). In 1908, in recognition of his researches, the University of Pennsylvania conferred on him an honorary doctorate of medicine.

While developing and directing the work of the State Livestock Sanitary Board, he continued his connection with the Veterinary School. His conception of the relation of veterinary medicine to the public health on the one hand and to the economics of agriculture on the other and his revelation of the great opportunities for research inspired his students. In 1897, he was appointed dean of the faculty. Through his efforts the endowment funds of the school were considerably increased, the support of the livestock industry was enlisted, and in the course of eight years a total of $450,000 was appropriated to the University of Pennsylvania to erect and equip buildings for the Veterinary School. Additional funds were secured which made it possible to reorganize and enlarge the teaching staff, providing facilities for instruction and research which were unequaled in the United States.

Pearson was of a robust, vigorous constitution and there seemed to be no limit to his capacity for work but eventually, under the intense strain, his health began to fail. In the summer of 1908, his friends advised him to take a rest, but he continued at work until the following June, when he went away, too late, to rest and recuperate. He died, unmarried, at Spruce Brook, Newfoundland, in September 1909, aged forty-one. During his professional career he held many positions of honor and trust. In 1903, he became a member of the Philadelphia board of health and, in 1905, of the advisory board of the state department of health. He was a member of numerous professional, scientific, and agricultural societies, and was honored with the presidency of all the professional organizations in which he held membership.

[*Leonard Pearson* (1909), repr. from *Am. Veterinary Rev.,* Oct. 1909; *In Memoriam—Leonard Pearson* (n.d.); L. A. Klein, "Pioneer Work in Tuberculosis Control," *Jour. Am. Veterinary Medic. Asso.,* Jan. 1021; *Who's Who in America,* 1908–09; *N. Y. Medic.*

Jour., Oct. 2, 1909; *Pub. Ledger* (Phila.), Sept. 21, 1909; personal acquaintance.]   L. A. K.

PEARSON, RICHMOND MUMFORD (June 28, 1805–Jan. 5, 1878), jurist, was born in Rowan County, N. C. His father, Richmond Pearson, who moved from Virginia to North Carolina after service in the Revolution, was a planter and merchant; his mother, Elizabeth, was the daughter of Robinson Mumford, of Connecticut parentage, a descendant of Elder William Brewster [*q.v.*] who had settled in North Carolina after a period in Jamaica (J. R. Totten, *Christophers Genealogy,* 1921, p. 143 and *passim*). Young Pearson was prepared for college in Washington, D. C., and at Salisbury, N. C., and was graduated from the University of North Carolina in 1823. Studying law, he was admitted to the bar in 1826 and began practice at Salisbury. He was a good lawyer, not eloquent, but painstaking in preparation of cases. His presentation of them was simple, logical, and, as he would have phrased it, "full of meat." He began in 1829 four successive terms in the House of Commons. In 1835 he was defeated for Congress, and in 1836 was elected a judge of the superior court. During the next twelve years he gained reputation as an unusually able and efficient trial judge. In 1848, although a Whig, he was elected associate justice of the supreme court by a Democratic legislature. Ten years later he became chief justice. In 1865 he was defeated for the "Johnson" convention, by which all offices were vacated, but he was at once reëlected chief justice, and in 1868, the existing government having been overthrown by congressional reconstruction, he was the choice of both parties for the same position, which he held until his death from apoplexy in Winston while on his way to a session of the court. He was twice married: on June 12, 1831, to Margaret McClung Williams, daughter of Senator John Williams of Knoxville, Tenn., and, after her death, in 1859 to Mary (McDowell), widow of John Gray Bynum.

In 1836 Pearson established a law school at Mocksville. He moved to Richmond Hill in Surry County in 1848 and continued the school there. He proved himself a really great teacher, and more than a thousand students read law under him, whom he filled with enthusiasm for the subject and with lasting personal affection for himself. Three of them were later on the supreme bench with him. He was plain and simple in manner, with a touch of the rough and uncouth, which many thought he cultivated. He had no high degree of culture, was cold and stern in temperament, inclined to be unforgiving in disposition, and was relentless in his determined ambition. For many years he drank to excess. Cold in temper though he was, in intellect he was blazing. He had strong native powers of mind, and, never a wide reader, achieved his intellectual development through reasoning. As a judge, while a master of the common law, he cared little for precedents. He grasped principles firmly and recognized the most delicate distinctions. A striking characteristic was his ability to cut through the artificial and irrelevant matter in a case and reach directly the matter at issue. His style was terse and pithy, baldly unadorned, clear and strong, and his opinions abounded in homely illustrations drawn from every-day life. All his opinions reflect the clarity of his thinking, his grasp of his subject and the law applicable to it, his power of logical analysis and deduction, and his strong personality. They are more, says one commentator, "than repeated precedents, abstract statements, and tedious details. They glow with life, abound with reason, and clothe the law in rich apparel and endow its precepts with soul and spirit" (Lewis, *post*, p. 254). Comparison of Pearson with Thomas Ruffin [*q.v.*], his great predecessor, is almost inevitable. In equity Pearson did not approach him, but in the common law he was certainly Ruffin's equal, if not his superior. "If Ruffin had more *scope*, Pearson had more *point*. If Ruffin had more *learning*, Pearson had more *accuracy*. If Ruffin was larger, Pearson was finer" (Edwin G. Reade, in 78 *N. C.*, 501). Certainly, too, Pearson was more original.

During the Civil War, Pearson incurred great unpopularity throughout the South by his decisions in *habeas corpus* proceedings growing out of the conscription laws, which his critics declared were designed to injure the Confederate cause. His whole conduct in the matter shows his disregard for precedents and for the opinion of others, but his rulings were in accordance with law and were upheld by his colleagues until in *Gatlin* vs. *Walton* (60 *N. C.*, 325), a case involving the power of Congress to change the terms of exemption, he was overruled. His dissenting opinion is notably weak. He opposed secession on constitutional and moral grounds, and he had no love for the Confederacy, but there was about him no taint of disloyalty toward his state. More open to criticism, however, was his conduct during reconstruction. In 1868 he identified himself with the Republican party, published an appeal for Grant's election, and in other ways was active politically. When the bar under the lead of B. F. Moore signed a protest against the political activity of the judges, he was the

prime mover for disabling the signers from practice (*In the Matter of B. F. Moore and Others*, 63 *N. C.*, 389) and did not thereby add to his legal reputation. In 1870 when the Kirk-Holden war occurred, he issued the writ of *habeas corpus* for those illegally held, but, forgetting his favorite legal maxim, *fiat justitia, ruat coelum*, which he had uttered so often in 1863 and 1864, he sustained the governor—William Woods Holden [*q.v.*]—to the extent of refusing to summon a *posse comitatus* to enforce the writs, but, instead, declared the power of the judiciary exhausted (*Ex parte Adolphus G. Moore and Others*, 64 *N. C.*, 802). When the collapse of the movement came, he was pathetically fearful of impeachment. He engaged counsel and prepared a defense which he submitted to the Senate only to have it rejected. He was not impeached, however; largely, it is supposed, because of the influence of his former students. He presided with outward impartiality in the impeachment trial of Holden, but his sympathies were naturally with the Governor and he privately advised his counsel as to their conduct of the case.

[S. A. Ashe, *Biog. Hist. of N. C.*, vol. V (1906); W. D. Lewis, *Great Am. Lawyers*, vol. V (1908); J. G. deR. Hamilton, *Reconstruction in N. C.* (1914), and "The N. C. Courts and the Confederacy," in *N. C. Hist. Rev.*, Oct. 1927; 31–35 and 40–77 *N. C. Reports*; "Proceedings in Memory of Richmond M. Pearson," 78 *N. C.*, 493–509; *Morning Star* (Wilmington), Jan. 8, 1878.]   J. G. deR. H.

PEARSONS, DANIEL KIMBALL (Apr. 14, 1820–Apr. 27, 1912), physician, financier, philanthropist, was born at Bradford, Vt., beside the Connecticut River, in a farmhouse that served also as a wayside inn. His father, John Pearsons, was of Scotch ancestry; his mother, whom he resembled in physical and mental qualities, was Hannah (Putnam) Pearsons, a distant relation of Gen. Israel Putnam. He studied in academies at Bradford and Newbury, and attended Dartmouth College during the freshman year, boarding himself and living on less than one dollar a week, a part of which expense he met by sawing wood at twenty-five cents a cord. Graduating in 1841 from the Vermont Medical College, Woodstock, he entered his profession in Chicopee, Mass., and was promptly successful. In August 1847 he married Marrietta Chapin, daughter of Deacon Giles Chapin of Chicopee; to her at the end of his career he emphatically ascribed much of the credit for his philanthropies.

At her suggestion he sold both their home and his practice in 1851, with a view to entering business, for which she thought he possessed special aptitude. They spent six months in Europe, and then for a few years Pearsons introduced textbooks on physiology, lecturing on the subject in the colleges of several Southern states, in the East, and in the interior. Being asked by acquaintances in Massachusetts to undertake the sale of their farm lands in Illinois, he went to Chicago in 1860 and later became agent for the sale of many thousands of acres held by private owners and by the Illinois Central Railroad Company. An eastern life insurance company also entrusted funds to him for loaning on farm mortgages. Hay was selling at one dollar and a half per ton and corn at ten cents a bushel, but Pearsons inspired possible buyers and despondent farmers with his courage and foresight of future values. In a few years he had sold 200,000 acres. He became a director of Chicago banks and other enterprises, and against the advice of friends invested largely in Michigan pine lands which became very valuable. He served on the Chicago city council, 1873–76, and as chairman of its finance committee gave important assistance in rehabilitating the city's finances which had been demoralized by the devastating fire of 1871. He was one of the founders of the Presbyterian Hospital, 1883, and president of its board for about five years.

In 1885 he removed to Hinsdale, Ill., and in 1889 retired from business to devote himself to giving away his fortune. After making a few preliminary gifts, he sailed with his wife for a year in Europe and the Near East. Returning in 1890 he set himself with characteristic thoroughness and zest to the work he had projected for the next twenty years—for he fully expected to live to the age of ninety. Keenly interested in education from his youth, he was convinced that the colleges of the West and South were of utmost importance to the future of America. At that time they were meagerly endowed and ill able to meet growing educational requirements. Pearsons decided to devote to selected colleges the bulk of his fortune, about five million dollars, by making gifts conditioned upon the securing by the colleges of larger total amounts from others, thus stimulating the institutions to increased exertions and multiplying the number of their supporters. In this way he imparted a powerful stimulus to some forty colleges and several secondary schools. The colleges specially singled out by him for repeated gifts were Whitman (Washington), Pomona (California), Lake Forest (Illinois), Knox (Illinois), Yankton (South Dakota), Berea (Kentucky), Mount Holyoke (Massachusetts), and, for the largest amount of all, Beloit (Wisconsin). He also gave liberally to the Chicago Young Men's Christian Association, Chicago Theological Seminary,

Chicago City Missionary Society, and to the American Board of Commissioners for Foreign Missions.

Pearsons was as unusual in characteristics as in career. Tall, erect, with piercing black eyes, abrupt and unconventional in speech, caustic in criticisms, adamant in refusals, an iconoclast yet a reverent idealist, a rigid economist and a princely giver, severe in manner but profound in his affections, he was regarded by those who knew him but slightly as an interesting eccentric; those who understood him honored and loved him. He died at ninety-two, having divested himself of all his possessions excepting a small annuity and regarding himself as one of the happiest men in the world.

[E. F. Williams, *The Life of Dr. D. K. Pearsons* . . . (1911); D. K. Pearsons, *Daniel K. Pearsons, His Life and Works* (1912), of much less value; E. D. Eaton, *Historical Sketches of Beloit College* (1928); *Who's Who in America*, 1912–13; *Congregationalist*, May 4, 11, 1912; *Literary Digest*, May 11, 1912; *Chicago Evening Post*, Apr. 27, 1912.]   E. D. E.

PEARY, ROBERT EDWIN (May 6, 1856– Feb. 20, 1920), Arctic explorer, the only son of Charles Peary and Mary (Wiley) Peary, came of French and British stock long settled in New England. He was born at Cresson, Pa., whither his family had moved from Maine to engage in the manufacture of barrel heads and staves. On the death of the father, when Robert was not quite three years old, mother and son returned to Maine, settling at Cape Elizabeth, not far from Portland. In the rugged surroundings of this region he spent his childhood and youth, developing the splendid constitution which was to stand him in such good stead in his arduous work later. His education he received in the local public schools and in the Portland High School, and in 1873 he entered Bowdoin College. Here he chose the civil engineering course, did well in his studies, and also took a prominent part in athletics.

On graduation, in 1877, he became a country surveyor in Fryeburg, Me. Two years later he entered the United States Coast and Geodetic Survey at Washington, D. C., as a cartographic draftsman, and after two years' service here, he joined the corps of civil engineers of the navy with the rank of lieutenant (Oct. 26, 1881). In 1884 he went to Nicaragua as assistant engineer of the expedition sent to survey a route for the proposed Nicaragua ship canal. He returned to the United States the following summer. That autumn, in the course of casual reading, he came upon a paper describing the inland ice of Greenland. It captured his interest and he began reading all he could find on the subject. The vast interior of Greenland was at this time still unexplored, and Peary became fired with the ambition to cross the inland ice. Securing six months' leave in the summer of 1886, he embarked as a supercargo aboard a steam whaler, which dropped him off at Godhavn on the west coast of Greenland.

His aim on this expedition was, in his own words, "to gain a practical knowledge of the obstacles and ice conditions of the interior; to put to the test of actual use certain methods and details of equipment; to make such scientific observations as might be practicable" ("A Reconnaissance," *post*, p. 261). He enlisted the interest of a young Danish official at Godhavn, and the two young men with a party of eight natives carried equipment, provisions, and two sledges up to the foot of the ice cap, 1,100 feet above sea level. Here the two explorers started off alone, dragging their sledges. The steep slope was traversed by ridges and gullies with nearly vertical walls and by cracks and crevasses of all widths. They had to contend further with heavy head winds, sleet, and snow. After three weeks they had come about 100 miles from the ice foot, reaching an elevation 7,500 feet above sea level. Another storm now set in and by this time they had rations for but six days, so that return was imperative.

As a result of this reconnaissance, Peary became confirmed in his desire to make Arctic research his life work. On returning to the United States he published an account of his experiences in the *Bulletin of the American Geographical Society* (Sept. 30, 1887) under the title, "A Reconnaissance of the Greenland Inland Ice." The following year his official duties again took him to Nicaragua, this time as engineer in chief of the Nicaragua Canal Survey. On his return he was married, Aug. 11, 1888, to Josephine Diebitsch of Washington, and for the three years following was engaged on naval engineering duties along the Atlantic seaboard, chiefly in New York and Philadelphia. All his spare time was spent in studies dealing with the Arctic and he took advantage of every opportunity to lay before various scientific societies his plans for the crossing of Greenland. He was confident that by starting at the right time of year and following the route of his reconnaissance, he could cover the distance across and back in a single season. To secure financial help for his proposed expedition he stressed the fact that if successful it would give America priority in the crossing of Greenland.

His efforts to enlist help in financing an expedition appeared ready to bear fruit when, early in 1889, came the news of the crossing of Greenland by the young Norwegian explorer, Fridtjof Nansen. This was a serious blow to Peary's hopes, for now the mere crossing of the inland ice could no longer be urged to secure help for an expedition. He therefore began stressing the importance of solving the mystery of Greenland and of determining its northern extent. So earnestly did he labor that he received the support of various American scientific and geographical societies, and early in 1891 he secured eighteen months' leave for the purpose of reaching the northern terminus of Greenland by way of the inland ice. On June 6 of that year the party, consisting of six men and Mrs. Peary, left New York aboard the *Kite,* a Newfoundland sealer which had been chartered for the purpose.

On July 11, the *Kite* was ramming a passage through some heavy ice off the west coast of Greenland when a blow from the iron tiller broke both bones of Peary's right leg just above the ankle. Despite the accident he determined to carry on, and two weeks later the party landed, the leader being carried ashore. The *Kite* then left, to return the following summer to bring the explorers home. Scientific observations were begun at once and a house built before the end of August, when the snow began to fall. Peary by this time was able to hobble about on crutches. On Oct. 19, the sun was seen for the last time, and the six men together with Mrs. Peary—the first white woman to winter with an Arctic expedition—settled down for the long polar night. A number of Eskimos, too, had by this time joined the expedition. Under Peary's leadership the party kept constantly occupied so that when the sun returned in the middle of February they were all in good condition. By the middle of May the supplies had been transported to the edge of the inland ice and by May 24 Peary and three of his men had reached a point about 130 miles from their winter camp. From this place, with one companion and sixteen dogs, Peary continued northeastward for a month, when the northernmost limit of the ice cap was passed and one of the objects of the expedition was achieved. Several days later they came to the Greenland shore of the Arctic ocean, pretty well establishing the insularity of Greenland. On his return to base, which took a month, Peary found the *Kite* at anchor and in September the party reached New York.

This expedition established a brilliant record of achievement. By itself, the sledge journey to the northeast coast of Greenland and back—1,300 miles—was an accomplishment of the first magnitude. Furthermore, in addition to determining the northernmost extension of the ice cap and the insularity of Greenland, this small party had made tidal and meteorological observations, brought back detailed knowledge of hitherto unknown territory, and carried out a careful ethnological study of a little known tribe of Eskimos. On his return Peary received generous recognition, and a lecture tour he made that winter proved successful. The public interest aroused by his achievement as well as the funds from the lecture tour he turned to account in the interest of another expedition to follow up his discoveries, and the month of August 1893 found him again on the west coast of Greenland near his former base. Besides Peary, the party consisted of Mrs. Peary, a nurse, and twelve men. In September the number was increased by the birth of the Pearys' first child, Marie Ahnighito, born farther north than any other white child in the world.

One aim of this expedition was to follow up the land north of Greenland discovered on the previous expedition and reach the Pole if possible. The winter of 1893–94 proved to be a hard one, several of the men broke down, and when in March the trip across the ice cap was begun, a succession of violent storms so crippled the party that after making 120 miles it was necessary to return. By the time they had recuperated, after six weeks, a trip across the ice cap was out of question. In August the steamer appeared to take the explorers home, and all but Peary and two of his men returned. The following spring (1895) the three succeeded in crossing the inland ice, but lack of food and supplies prevented any further exploration on the east coast of Greenland. After considerable hardship they returned to the base camp the latter part of June. In August the steamer arrived and Peary took the opportunity to bring back to the United States two of three large meteorites he had discovered the year before. One of these weighed half a ton and the other three tons. While there was recognition that the expedition had to cope with unusual hardships, the public verdict was that it had met defeat, even if undeserved. The defeat, however, did not lessen Peary's determination to continue in Arctic exploration. While the public mood in the United States was at the moment not favorable to any ambitious Arctic undertaking, he kept interest in the region alive by organizing a party for scientific work along the west coast of Greenland during the summer of 1896. One of the aims of this expedition was to bring back the largest of the meteorites he had discovered, which weighed ninety tons. In this he was unsuccessful and it was only in the following year, on a

similar expedition, that he succeeded in bringing it back.

As a result of his experiences Peary had come to the conclusion that the only practicable means for reaching the North Pole consisted in pushing a ship as far northward as possible to a winter harbor on the Greenland coast, and then early in spring traveling with dogs and sledges due north until the Pole was attained. In the winter of 1896–97 he went to London, and in a lecture before the Royal Geographical Society outlined his plan for reaching the Pole. It won the interest of Lord Northcliffe, who thereupon presented Peary with the *Windward,* the ship that had recently been used in Arctic exploration by a British expedition. Peary now judged the time ripe for an American Arctic expedition. Interest in polar exploration had become world-wide. The famous Norwegian explorer, Fridtjof Nansen, had just returned from his daring expedition in the *Fram,* during which he made a new record for "farthest north," wresting this record from the American, James Booth Lockwood [*q.v.*], who had held it for twenty years. Peary now took the opportunity to write his *Northward over the "Great Ice,"* which was to appear in 1898 in two volumes, and which gave a record of all his expeditions up to this time. The Navy Department did not look favorably on further Arctic exploration, however, and in April 1897 ordered him to report for duty at San Francisco. Immediately he put in a request for five years' leave of absence, but the efforts of prominent scientists to have the Department rescind its order and grant the leave proved ineffectual. It was only a chance meeting with an influential Republican, Charles A. Moore, a day or two before Peary's scheduled departure for San Francisco, that saved the situation. Moore took the case to President McKinley personally, and it was on the latter's order that the five years' leave was granted.

In the midst of preparations for this ambitious expedition the Spanish-American War broke out. Peary was now forty-two years old, with a number of years of Arctic experience and with preparations for his expedition nearly complete. To drop his enterprise at this juncture would in all probability mean the end of Arctic work for him. Under the circumstances, he felt that his polar task could justly be put ahead of any war service he might render. He therefore continued his preparations, and in July 1898, on board the *Windward,* steamed out of New York Harbor for the north. By August he had pushed the ship across Smith Sound, a little above 79°N., where she became icebound. This was nearly 700 miles from the Pole—200 miles farther south than he had planned.

The next few months were spent in advancing food and fuel by sledge to a base on the shores of the Polar Sea, from which a dash for the Pole might be made in the spring. The sledging was over difficult ice, and as the season advanced the temperature fell considerably below zero. In January 1899, after a particularly difficult sledge journey, Peary found himself with both feet badly frozen, necessitating the amputation of eight toes. In a few weeks, however, he was in the field again. During this winter his sledge journeys, which extended over 1,500 miles, clarified the geography of the region about Smith Sound. Not until the fall of 1902, after four years in the Arctic, did Peary return to the United States. During these four years he carried out an extensive series of explorations, and in the spring of 1902 he attained 84° 17′ N., the nearest approach to the Pole in the American Arctic.

The year following his return he was engaged in various duties with the Bureau of Yards and Docks in the Navy Department, but his spare time was still given to his Arctic projects, and in September 1903 he secured three years' leave for an expedition whose main purpose was the attainment of the North Pole. Heretofore he had been handicapped by the lack of a suitable ship to take him to a base in high latitude. This expedition, therefore, was to make use of a ship capable of forcing its way to winter quarters on the north shore of Grant Land. The plan then contemplated a dash for the Pole with the returning light of February. The distinctive features of the plan were the use of individual sledges drawn by dogs, which gave a traveling unit of high speed, the adoption of Eskimo methods and costume, and the fullest utilization of the Eskimos themselves. Financial difficulties at first appeared insuperable, in spite of the help of the Peary Arctic Club—a group of friends and supporters who had financed his previous expedition. In the summer of 1904, however, two members of this club, Morris K. Jesup and Thomas H. Hubbard [qq.v.], each agreed to give $50,000 on condition that the club itself raise not less than $50,000. The sum was finally accumulated and in October the keel of the new ship, the Roosevelt, was laid. The vessel was designed by Peary for the specific purpose of forcing its way through the ice fields of the Arctic waters.

In July 1905 the Roosevelt left New York with a small party, and early in September had reached the north coast of Grant Land. Here the ship wintered, and by February 1906 Peary had gathered his party at Cape Hecla, the point from which the dash to the Pole was to be made. Early in March he started, and for two weeks the journey continued over the broken ice of the Polar Sea, until a region of leads was reached. These were wide cracks in the ice—wide lanes of open water—which checked advance until they closed or were frozen over. By Apr. 21, 1906, Peary had reached latitude 87° 6′ N., only 174 miles from his goal and the nearest approach to the Pole made up to that time. The condition of his dogs and the declining food supply prevented further progress, however, and it was only after a hazardous trip and in an exhausted condition that the party regained the ship. In December of that year the Roosevelt returned to New York; and in the following year Peary published the narrative of this journey under the title, Nearest the Pole (1907).

In July 1908 Peary left for his final polar expedition. He was now fifty-two years old, but he rightly felt that the disadvantage of his age was more than counterbalanced by nearly a quarter century of Arctic experience during which his skill, endurance, and leadership had been thoroughly tested. He had the further advantage of being able to enlist the services of capable and enthusiastic assistants and well-equipped and well-trained Eskimos who were devoted to him. By September the Roosevelt had been pushed to latitude 82° 30′ N., a world's record for a ship under its own steam. The dark months were utilized for making scientific observations, for hunting, and for sledging supplies to Cape Columbia, ninety miles to the northwestward, from which point the attack on the Pole was to be made. On Mar. 1, 1909, the party of six white men, one negro, seventeen Eskimos, 133 dogs, and nineteen sledges set out from Cape Columbia over the sea ice for the Pole. As the main party advanced, the sections which had borne the brunt of trail breaking were turned back, leaving the best dogs and extra supplies with the leader. On the whole the sledging conditions were not very unfavorable, though fourteen days were lost because of leads or open lanes of water. Towards the end of March the previous record of "farthest north"—87° 6′—was broken, and near the 88th parallel of latitude the last supporting party, that under Capt. Robert Bartlett, turned back. From this point Peary, with his negro servant, four Eskimos, and forty dogs, set out for the final dash. On the morning of Apr. 6, although his observations showed him to be in latitude 89° 57′ —only three miles from the Pole—he was so nearly exhausted that with the prize actually in sight he could go no further. After a few hours' sleep, however, he covered the remaining miles, reaching latitude 90° N., and the North Pole was attained.

On his march Peary took three soundings, the last one within five miles of the Pole. Here after paying out all his line—9,000 feet in length—he failed to touch bottom. The North Pole was thus definitely proved to be located in the center of a vast sea of ice. After remaining at the Pole thirty hours, during which astronomic observations were made, the party began the return trip. Forced marches were made by reducing the hours of sleep, and further time was saved by occupying the igloos built during the northern advance. The weather proved favorable, and with the light loads the dogs made rapid progress. The distance from the Pole to the base camp at Cape Columbia was covered in the wonderfully quick time of sixteen days.

By the middle of July 1909 the *Roosevelt* had left her winter quarters with the party aboard and headed south. On Sept. 5 she steamed into Indian Harbor, Labrador, and from this place Peary cabled the news of his attainment of the North Pole. This news, however, came five days after the world had been electrified by the dramatic announcement that Dr. Frederick A. Cook, who had served as surgeon on Peary's expedition of 1891, had reached the Pole on Apr. 21, 1908, or a year earlier than Peary. In the controversy which ensued the large American public was inclined to side with Cook. Peary had won only after many years' striving and planning, and at considerable financial outlay. Cook's sudden appearance from an unheralded expedition, undertaken practically singlehanded, made a much more dramatic appeal to the public at large. Moreover, the press found the latter more amiable in the controversy than Peary, who was certain that the alleged attainment of the Pole by Cook with a small party of Eskimos was an impossibility.

This controversy was a bitter experience to Peary. Instead of receiving the well-merited approbation of his fellow countrymen upon the completion of a heroic task in which he had spent the best years of his life, he was forced to become party to a petty squabble and face the humiliation of having his claims questioned. For it was only natural that after the rejection of Cook's claims on the part of the scientific world, there should arise those who in turn would question Peary's claims. Sinister meaning was read into the fact that on the final dash to the Pole he had taken none of his white assistants, only his negro servant and four Eskimos. Bitter criticism was leveled against him for not having given Capt. "Bob" Bartlett the opportunity to accompany

him clear to the Pole. The rapid sledging to the Pole after the return of Bartlett's supporting party, and the even more rapid progress from the Pole—the result of years of experience, of painstaking preparation, and favorable weather and ice conditions—were pointed to with suspicion. In the trying situation, however, Peary had the whole-hearted support of a host of friends and of the greater part of the scientific world. In October 1909 a committee of experts appointed by the National Geographic Society examined his records and reported that they were unanimously of the opinion that he had reached the North Pole (*National Geographic Magazine*, November 1909). His friends also worked actively to induce Congress to give adequate recognition to his achievements, and early in 1910 a bill was introduced to promote him to the rank of rear admiral and place him on the retired list. His status in the navy was technically that of civil engineer with the rank of commander, and a number of the regular officers opposed the bill on the ground that it would promote Peary over the heads of line officers who were his seniors; opposition was also registered by those who had taken Cook's part in the North Pole controversy. In March 1911, however, a bill was passed tendering him the thanks of Congress and placing him on the retired list of the corps of civil engineers with the rank and retired pay of rear admiral.

This period of controversy was not without its compensations. While the fight for recognition was going on in Congress, Peary brought out his book, *The North Pole* (1910). The leading American geographic societies invested him with their highest honors. Early in 1910 he went abroad for five weeks, visiting various countries, and the great European geographic societies took this occasion to bestow on him their highest awards. In large part these honors recognized his attainment of the North Pole; but in part, too, they were a recognition of the value of his Arctic work as a whole. As a result of his labors, a highly efficient method of polar exploration had been developed—large parties being discarded in favor of the small party, and Eskimo modes of dress and travel being utilized. His Greenland traverses and his later travels had completely revised the map of a large region. His expeditions had made available to enthnology valuable studies of a little known tribe of Eskimos. The sciences of meteorology and hydrography had been enriched by careful observations in regions from which information had hitherto been wanting. Peary's tidal observations include the most northerly observations ever made and constitute an important addition to the knowledge of the tides of the Arctic Ocean.

Peary now retired to his home on Eagle Island, in Casco Bay. Here with his wife, daughter, and son, the latter born in 1903, he enjoyed the pleasures of home life to which he had so long looked forward. In 1913 he became interested in aviation and was made chairman of the committee on aeronautic maps and landing places of the Aero Club of America, an office he retained until his death. On the outbreak of the World War he foresaw the importance of aviation in warfare and labored in organizing the National Aerial Coast Patrol Commission which worked out a comprehensive plan for the protection of the coast. With the entry of the United States into the war, he was made chairman of the National Committee on Coast Defense by Air. At this time, too, he accepted the presidency of the Aero League of America. In May 1919 the hardships he had undergone began to tell on his health, and at Washington, D. C., on Feb. 20, 1920, in his sixty-fourth year, he died. The motives which prompted him in his Arctic work he expressed in a simple statement uttered in 1895 (*Bulletin of the American Geographical Society*, vol. XXVII, 1895, p. 375); "To say that my motives were entirely unselfish, or that I was actuated solely by love of science, would be incorrect, but I can say that the desire to win an honorable and lasting reputation went hand in hand with the desire to add to the sum total of human knowledge."

[Fitzhugh Green, *Peary: The Man Who Refused to Fail* (1926), is the only complete biography; the record of his explorations is found in his books mentioned above and in the *Bull. Am. Geog. Soc.*, 1887–1911 (see A. A. Brooks, *Index to the Bull. of the Am. Geog. Soc., 1852–1915,* 1918); a brief appreciation of the man and his accomplishments is found in the *Geog. Rev.*, Mar. 1920; the question of the rapidity of his marches on the North Pole expedition is discussed in the *Geog. Rev.*, Jan. 1929; J. Gordon Hayes, *Robert Edwin Peary* (1929), written with manifest animus, gives a complete summary of the unfavorable views, especially with regard to his attainment of the North Pole.]   H. A. M.

PEASE, ALFRED HUMPHREYS (May 6, 1838–July 13, 1882), pianist and composer, was born in Cleveland, Ohio, the second of three children of Sheldon and Marianne (Humphreys) Pease, both natives of Connecticut. He manifested very early his devotion to music and drawing, but in order to prevent his development into a professional musician his parents put him through a rigid course of classical study which fitted him to enter Kenyon College at Gambier, Ohio, at the age of sixteen, where they hoped he would have the wisdom to choose another profession. His painting and drawing, however, attracted the attention of a young Ger-

man artist, who persuaded the parents to permit Pease to go to Germany. On arriving in Berlin, he began an intensive study of German and then took up other languages. Once having tasted the freedom of self-direction, he began the study of piano under Theodor Kullak but for some time did not reveal the fact in his letters. At length he persuaded his parents to sanction the pursuit of the art for which nature had endowed him. Besides studying piano with Kullak for three years, he studied composition with Wüerst and orchestration with Wieprecht. For a short time he returned to America but immediately returned to Europe and studied three years with von Bülow. Upon his return he began touring in the principal cities of the United States and was immediately acclaimed as a remarkable performer. He had a brilliant technique, combined with a beautiful quality of tone and delicacy of expression, and he played with ease and grace. His tendency was to favor somewhat popular compositions, especially operatic transcriptions. During the last twelve years of his life he resided in New York City, where he moved in a select group.

Pease achieved considerable success as a composer. Nearly a hundred of his songs became great favorites during his lifetime and of those "Hush Thee, My Baby" was one of the most popular. Indeed it is as a song writer that he is remembered, for most of his piano pieces (largely transcriptions of themes from *Lohengrin, Aïda* and other operas) are forgotten. William Treat Upton (*post,* p. 61) gives him credit for surpassing all his contemporaries "in the lavish use of a vividly tinted palette" and adds: "There is no one of his time in America whose harmonic fabric is so sensuously colored." His first songs were published in 1864—"When Sparrows Build," and "Blow, Bugle, Blow"—and each subsequent year brought new ones. Among his best are "Stars of the Summer Night," "Tender and True, Adieu," and "A Year's Spinning." During his life time his orchestral works were considered important, and his "Reverie and Andante," "Andante and Scherzo," and "Romanza" for brass and reed instruments were performed by Theodore Thomas in New York and elsewhere. His best work was undoubtedly his Concerto in E flat, written in 1875 and performed at an all-American concert at the Centennial Exhibition in Philadelphia, with the composer at the piano, on July 19, 1876. Pease toured with Ole Bull in 1879 and was engaged to tour with Christine Nilsson, but that was prevented by his untimely death which occurred in St. Louis in July 1882. He died of alcoholism—

a habit contracted during a period of sorrow over the tragic death of his brother, who with his wife perished in a railroad disaster near New Hamburg, N. Y., in 1871. Pease never married.

[Frederick Humphreys, *The Humphreys Family in America* (1883); W. T. Upton, *Art-Song in America* (1930); *Appletons' Ann. Cyc.,* 1882; *St. Louis Globe-Democrat,* July 15, 1882; *Chicago Daily Tribune,* July 16, 1882.]   F. L. G. C.

PEASE, CALVIN (Sept. 9, 1776–Sept. 17, 1839), Ohio jurist, was one of the many Ohio pioneers of Connecticut birth. Samuel Huntington, George Tod, and Benjamin Tappan [*qq.v.*] had been his neighbors in the East and were his associates in frontier Ohio. He was born in Suffield, Conn., the eleventh child of Joseph and Mindwell (King) Pease and the descendant of Robert Pease who emigrated from England in 1634 and settled at Salem, Mass. He studied law in the office of his brother-in-law, Gideon Granger [*q.v.*], and was admitted to the bar in 1798. He practised for a short time in New Hartford, but in 1800 he removed to Youngstown, Ohio, and in 1803 he settled permanently in the neighboring town of Warren. In June 1804 he was married to Laura Grant Risley, the daughter of Benjamin Risley of Washington, D. C. They had four sons and three daughters.

He was made clerk of the common-pleas court and served also as the first postmaster of Youngstown. In the bitter contest waged between the advocates of statehood and Gov. Arthur St. Clair, he opposed the governor. Upon the organization of the judiciary of the new state he was appointed presiding judge of one of the three circuits of the court of common pleas. For the next seven years, until March 1810, he traveled over the difficult roads of eastern Ohio dispensing justice according to schedule. In 1806 he rendered a decision that brought him to the attention of the whole state. The Ohio legislature had passed an act granting jurisdiction in civil suits to the justices of the peace to the limit of fifty dollars. He held this act to be unconstitutional because it impaired the constitutional right of jury trial. Ohio Jeffersonians were fully alive to the threat of legislative supremacy that was involved in this application of John Marshall's formula within their state. Their alarm increased when the state supreme court upheld the decision of Pease in a parallel case. The contest between the legislature and the courts dominated state politics during the years 1808 to 1811 (W. T. Utter, "Judicial Review in Early Ohio," *Mississippi Valley Historical Review,* June 1927). George Tod of the supreme court and Pease were impeached by the legislature and barely escaped removal from office.

When his term expired in 1810 Pease was not reappointed because of legislative opposition. He engaged in private practice and served a term in the state Senate, 1812–13. He also aided the postmaster-general, Gideon Granger, in establishing western postal routes. In 1815 a more conservative Assembly elected him to the state supreme court, where his activity from 1816 to 1830 indicated a mind well-balanced rather than brilliant. He read Sterne and Swift in preference to the legal classics. His written opinions, which are comparatively few, may be found in the first four volumes of *Ohio Reports.* His conduct on the bench was so stern that young attorneys trembled before him, yet when his robes were laid aside he was a jovial companion, for he could tell a story or sing a ballad as well as any other. After his retirement from the bench he led a quiet life in Warren. He served one term in the state House of Representatives, 1831–32, where he sponsored bills for the improvement of the treatment of prisoners in the state penitentiary.

[Letters in Western Reserve Hist. Soc. Lib. at Cleveland and in correspondence of Ohio governors in Ohio State Lib. at Columbus; *Green Bag,* Mar., Apr. 1895; *Western Law Monthly,* Jan. 1863; David and A. S. Pease, *A Geneal. and Hist. Record of the Descendants of John Pease* (1869), p. 61; *New-England Hist. and Geneal. Register,* Apr. 1849, pp. 174, 390.]   W. T. U.

PEASE, ELISHA MARSHALL (Jan. 3, 1812–Aug. 26, 1883), governor of Texas, was for nearly fifty years, from the eve of the Texas Revolution to the day of his death, an outstanding figure in the history of the republic and the state. He was born in Enfield, Conn. His father, Lorrain Thompson Pease, was a descendant of Robert Pease who emigrated from England to Salem, Mass., in 1634 and of John Pease, one of the founders of the town of Enfield. His mother was Sarah (Marshall) Pease, of Windsor, Conn. His education was obtained in the public schools of Enfield and in an academy at Westfield, Mass. From his fourteenth year to his twenty-first he was a clerk in a country store and in the post-office at Hartford, where he acquired an elementary knowledge of business and of accounting. He spent the summer of 1834 in the West and in the late fall was in New Orleans on business. There he heard so much of Texas that in January 1835 he removed to Texas and settled at Mina, now Bastrop, and began the study of the law with D. C. Barrett. However, his studies were soon interrupted by the outbreak of the war for Texan independence. He fought in the first skirmish at Gonzales and was then made secretary of the provisional government established by the consultation held at

San Felipe in November 1835. Though not a member of the convention that declared independence in March 1836, he was of great help in drafting the constitution for the new republic. During the struggle for independence he served as chief clerk of the navy and treasury departments and, for a short time, as secretary of the treasury after the death of Hardeman. In November 1836 he became clerk of the judiciary committee of the Congress and drafted the laws to organize the judiciary and define the duties of county officers. Late in 1836 he resumed the study of the law, this time with John A. Wharton of Brazoria. Admitted to the bar in 1837, he formed a partnership with Wharton and, later, with John W. Harris [q.v.]. For a short time, during the days of the republic, he served as district attorney. After Texas entered the Union, he served two terms in the House and one in the Senate of the state legislature. In August 1850 he was married to Lucadia Christinia Niles, the daughter of Richard Niles of Windsor, Conn. They had three daughters.

In 1853 he was elected governor and in 1855 was reëlected on a platform opposed to the doctrines of the Know-Nothing party. The period of his two administrations was one of great prosperity to the state. Under his leadership the public debt was paid; a school fund of $2,000,000 was created; railroad building was encouraged; state institutions were established for the care of the insane, the deaf, and the blind; $100,000 was set apart as an endowment for a state university; and steps were taken to put the university in operation. However, the approach of the Civil War put a stop to this development. Like Houston, he opposed secession, but he remained in Texas during the war, taking no part in it. Before the war he had affiliated with the Democratic party, but he now became a Republican. In 1866 he was a delegate and a vice-president of the Philadelphia convention of Southern Unionists, and later in the year he was a candidate for governor but was defeated by J. W. Throckmorton. In the following year, when the latter was removed by the military authorities as an "obstruction to reconstruction," he was appointed provisional governor by General Sheridan, but he resigned in 1869 because of a difference of opinion between the commanding general, J. J. Reynolds, and himself in regard to the reorganization of the state government. In 1872 he represented Texas in the Liberal Republican convention at Cincinnati that nominated Horace Greeley for the presidency. In 1874, he was offered the collectorship of the port of Galveston, but he declined it. When a second tender of the same office was made by President Hayes in 1879, he accepted it. This was his last public service. He died in the town of Lampasas, where he had gone for his health. While he did not escape the animosities of the Civil War and Reconstruction, he was respected by his foes as well as by his friends. His appointment as military governor, although it arrayed a majority of the people of the state against him, was a fortunate thing for Texas, for no other member of the "radical party," with the possible exception of Andrew J. Hamilton [q.v.], was so sane, so moderate, and so devoted to the welfare of the state.

[J. H. Brown, *Indian Wars and Pioneers of Texas* (n.d.); J. D. Lynch, *The Bench and Bar of Texas* (1885); F. W. Johnson and E. C. Barker, *A Hist. of Texas and Texans* (1914), vols. I, IV; C. W. Ramsdell, *Reconstruction in Texas* (1910); L. E. Daniell, *Personnel of Texas State Government with Sketches of Representative Men* (1892); David and A. S. Pease, *A Geneal. and Hist. Record of the Descendants of John Pease* (1869), p. 143; *New-England Hist. and Geneal. Register*, July 1849, p. 237; *Galveston Daily News*, Aug. 28, 1883.]
C. S. P.

PEASE, JOSEPH IVES (Aug. 9, 1809–July 2, 1883), line-engraver, was born in Norfolk, Conn., the son of Earl P. and Mary (Ives) Pease, and a descendant of Robert Pease who emigrated from England in 1634 and settled at Salem, Mass. Joseph's determination to become an engraver was expressed at a very early age, and when, at fourteen, he was placed in a dry-goods store in Hartford, Conn., he began to imitate the labels and other designs he found attached to pieces of fabric, copying them in pencil. His ambition to be an engraver soon became irresistible; he left the dry-goods business and began to practise, in an untrained, amateurish way, his chosen art. He is said, at first, to have used an awl for a graver and a piece of brass from an old thermometer for a plate; and to have produced his impressions on a roll press of his own construction (Baker, *post*, p. 126). He had a strong mechanical bent and showed great ingenuity in making a turning lathe and building a small power loom, with which he succeeded in weaving cloth six inches in width. It is said that he erected this loom before he was aware that similar pieces of machinery had been constructed by others. Since his crude attempts at engraving revealed undeniable talent, he was apprenticed to Oliver Pelton, a prominent line-engraver of Hartford, and remained with him until he became of age, when he set up for himself. His younger brother, Richard H. Pease, who had also become an engraver, had settled in Philadelphia, and in 1835 Joseph followed him thither.

His pure and somewhat intimate style of engraving in line recommended him to Carey & Hart, who published *The Gift* and several other annuals, and for these publications Pease did his most charming work. All his plates that have been seen are small ones, but none the less delightful on that account. For ten years his work appeared regularly in the annuals, and his plates, despite their diminutive size, were much prized for the artistic and technical skill they displayed, as well as for their good taste. Among the best of these little plates are "Mumble the Peg," from the painting by Inman; "Young Traders," after Page; and "Tough Story," after Mount. Pease also engraved an illustration for *The Spy* —a picture of Washington meeting with Harvey Birch—which has been admired. From 1848 to 1850, he adapted the foreign fashions and engraved the fashion plates for *Godey's Lady's Book*. About 1850 he left Philadelphia and went to Stockbridge, Mass., where he devoted himself to banknote engraving. A little later he bought a farm at Twin Lakes, near Salisbury, Conn., where he continued to engrave vignettes for banknotes. He died on this farm, in the summer of 1883. Pease was married to Mary Spencer of Baltimore, Md., Dec. 8, 1841. He was represented in the exhibition of One Hundred Notable American Engravers at the New York Public Library in 1928.

[David and A. S. Pease, *A Geneal. and Hist. Record of the Descendants of John Pease* (1869); *New Eng. Hist. and Geneal. Reg.*, Oct. 1849; W. S. Baker, *Am. Engravers* (1875); D. M. Stauffer, *Am. Engravers upon Copper and Steel* (1907), vol. I; *One Hundred Notable Engravers* (N. Y. Pub. Lib., 1928); Frank Weitenkampf, *Am. Graphic Art* (1924).]   J. J.

PEASLEE, EDMUND RANDOLPH (Jan. 22, 1814–Jan. 21, 1878), physician, was born in Newton, Rockingham County, N. H., eldest of the four children of James and Abigail (Chase) Peaslee. He entered Dartmouth at the age of eighteen years and graduated with honors in 1836. After teaching school for a brief period in Lebanon, N. H., he tutored at Dartmouth from 1837 to 1839 and utilized this time for the study of medicine at Dartmouth Medical School. Following the custom of the older generation of medical men, he became the private pupil of a practitioner, Dr. Noah Worcester of Hanover, N. H., later transferring to the preceptorship of Dr. Dixi Crosby of the same town, and still later to that of Dr. Jonathan Knight [*q.v.*] of New Haven, Conn. In 1839 he entered Yale Medical School, where he received his medical degree in 1840. After a year's study abroad, he returned to Dartmouth to become lecturer in anatomy and physiology. In 1842 he was made professor. He retained the chair of anatomy and physiology until 1869 and thereafter served as lecturer on diseases of women, 1868–70; professor of obstetrics and diseases of women, 1870–73; and professor of gynecology from 1873 until his death. He was evidently in demand as a teacher, for he held concurrent lectureships or professorships in no less than four other medical institutions. From 1843 to 1860 he was connected as lecturer or professor with the departments of surgery and anatomy at the Medical School of Maine, affiliated with Bowdoin College. From 1852 to 1856 he was professor of pathology and physiology and from 1856 to 1860 professor of obstetrics in New York Medical College. In 1872–74 he taught obstetrics and from 1874 to 1878 was professor of gynecology at the Albany Medical College, while during the latter period he was professor of gynecology at Bellevue Hospital Medical College also. To this work he gave much time and it was his pride that he never permitted other activities to interfere with his scholastic duties. It is no slight indication of a scientific mind that Peaslee, at this early period in the science, was regarded an an authority on microscopy. To the academic field of medicine he made two noteworthy contributions: *Necroscopic Tables for Postmortem Examinations* (1851) and *Human Histology in Its Relations to Descriptive Anatomy, Physiology, and Pathology* (1857).

In 1858 he removed to New York City where he devoted himself to a large and lucrative private practice. His interests now turned largely to gynecology. In 1872 he published his most important work, *Ovarian Tumors; Their Pathology, Diagnosis and Treatment, Especially by Ovariotomy*. This is a comprehensive treatise in which he compiled all the then known facts concerning the anatomy, pathology, diagnosis, and treatment of ovarian cysts. It was especially concerned with the operation of ovariotomy which Peaslee had advocated in New York City in 1864. He made no notable additions to the technique of the operation but compiled carefully and critically practically everything that was known of it, producing a book which was for many years a standard text. It undoubtedly removed many of the objections against ovariotomy which were entertained at that time by the profession, and, although long since displaced by more modern books, retains some historical value, for in it Peaslee established the priority of Ephraim McDowell [*q.v.*] in the methodical and successful removal by surgery of an ovarian cyst. Peaslee was one of the first to advocate and institute the procedure of peritoneal lavage as a prophylaxis against infection.

He was something of a linguist, speaking no less than four foreign languages. In 1860 he was appointed a trustee of Dartmouth College. His clinical duties were confined to his private practice and service (1858–65) as attending physician to the Demilt Dispensary, New York City. During the Civil War he was surgeon to the New England Hospital and the New York State Hospital. The gynecologist T. A. Emmet (*post*) regarded him as an excellent diagnostician and student but less highly as an operator, a judgment which is probably correct. Peaslee married Martha Kendrick of Lebanon, N. H., in 1841, and they had two children, a son and a daughter. He died in New York City.

[B. M. Emmett, in *Am. Jour. of Obstetrics*, May 1913; T. A. Emmet, *Ibid.*, Apr. 1878; *Medic. Record*, Jan. 26, 1878; F. S. Dennis, in H. A. Kelly and W. L. Burrage, *Am. Medic. Biogs.* (1920); Fordyce Barker, in *Trans. Am. Gynecol. Soc.*, vol. III (1879); *N. Y. Tribune*, Jan. 23, 1878.]   H. S. R.

PEAVEY, FRANK HUTCHINSON (Jan. 18, 1850–Dec. 30, 1901), industrialist, was born in Eastport, Me., the son of Albert D. and Mary (Drew) Peavey. His father, who died when Frank was nine years old, and his grandfather were engaged in the lumber trade and ran a line of coasting vessels. They were considered wealthy, but as a boy Peavey determined to make his own way. At the age of fifteen, on money which he had earned, he went to Chicago, where an uncle found him a job as messenger for a grain firm. The next year he worked in a bank, broke down physically, visited his home in Eastport, and in the spring of 1867 was back in Chicago where, in the post-war depression, jobs were scarce. Hearing of an opening in a bank at Sioux City, Iowa, he went to that frontier town, one hundred miles from the nearest railroad. In 1870 he became a partner in an implement firm, Booge, Smith & Peavey, which suffered severe loss by fire the next year. Reorganized as Evans & Peavey, the concern added the buying and selling of grain to its dealings in agricultural implements, and built a small elevator. When, in 1875, the Dakota Southern Railroad reached Sioux City, Peavey, having bought out his partner, extended his grain business and his elevators, obtaining from Minneapolis millers the agency to purchase grain for them. As railroad communications extended, Peavey's elevators increased. Taking Edgar C. Michener as a partner in 1881, and operating as F. H. Peavey & Company, he established the headquarters of the firm in Minneapolis, but did not remove thither himself until 1884.

In the next sixteen years he built up a line of elevators, including one of five million bushels' capacity at Duluth, along the railroad lines of that section. In 1899 he organized the Peavey Steamship Company which, by the summer of 1901, was operating four of the largest freighters on the Great Lakes. He made it a rule "never to embark in an enterprise unless he could control it," and at the time of his death he was the dominating influence in nineteen different concerns—elevator, grain, steamship, land, and piano companies; he was also a director on the boards of two railroads and one large bank. It was his idea that his firm, into which he took his son, George W. Peavey, and his sons-in-law, Frank T. Heffelfinger and F. B. Wells, should survive him; to this end he insured his life for a million dollars, payable to his estate, so that his death might cause no embarrassment to the business. "His mentality was so strong, his energy and business acumen so great, that he insensibly dwarfed his associates. ... He was the Elevator King, and undoubtedly controlled larger interests in this line than any other man in the world" (*Northwestern Miller*, Jan. 1, 1902, p. 19). In a time when consolidation was the order of the day, he saw and grasped the opportunity to build up in the Northwest a powerful combination of elevators and their appurtenances. He took little active part in civic affairs, although he was a member of the Minneapolis board of education for two years and for a time stood back of a Newsboys' Fund, which was calculated to inculcate thrift. In 1872 he married Mary, daughter of Senator George G. Wright of Des Moines, by whom he had three children. He died in Chicago.

[C. E. Flandrau, *Encyc. of Biog. of Minn.* (1900); *Northwestern Miller*, Jan. 1, 1902; *Minneapolis Jour.*, Dec. 30, 1901.]   L. B. S.

PEAY, AUSTIN (June 1, 1876–Oct. 2, 1927), governor of Tennessee, was born near Hopkinsville, Ky., the son of Austin and Cornelia Frances (Leavell) Peay. He was given the middle name, Leavell, but he stopped using it about 1900. He went to Centre College at Danville, Ky. On Sept. 19, 1895, he married Sallie Hurst of Clarksville, Tenn. The following year he began the practice of law in this town, where he made his home for the remainder of his life. Soon he entered politics as a Democrat. In 1900 and 1902 he was elected to membership in the Tennessee House of Representatives. He became chairman of the Democratic state executive committee in 1905. Three years later he was campaign manager for Malcolm R. Patterson, the successful candidate of the anti-Prohibitionists for the governorship. For the next decade he devoted himself to his legal practice, becoming increasingly popular and prosperous. In 1918 he was defeated by Albert H. Roberts for the Democratic gubernatorial nomination. Four years later, however, he won the nomination against three opponents and easily defeated the Republican candidate, Gov. Alfred A. Taylor. In 1924 he was reëlected with negligible opposition, and in 1926 he broke a tradition of many years by winning election to a third consecutive term.

In his campaigns he attacked the political machine that then dominated the state, and he advocated administrative reforms, the reduction of taxes on land, and the improvement of the state's educational system. His speeches were serious and thoughtful discussions of the state's needs, which appealed to the intelligence of the voters. The legislature was unusually responsive to his wishes, and his administrations were notable for the enactment of a number of laws of progressive character. He procured the enactment of an administrative reorganization bill that centralized responsibility and power by regrouping twenty-seven departments and thirty-seven boards into eight departments, headed by commissioners who were directly responsible to the governor. He obtained a considerable shifting of the burden of taxation from the land owner, but he was unable to obtain an amendment to the state constitution that would have made possible an efficient and equitable system of taxation. He effected a reorganization of the highway department that resulted in the efficient construction of many miles of paved roads, financed largely from the proceeds of a tax on gasoline. He advocated successfully much-needed appropriations for the state university and the enactment of a general education bill that established an eight months' term for schools, higher salaries for teachers, and other improvements in the state's educational system. He obtained also the creation of a park in the Great Smokies and a game preserve at Reelfoot Lake. The most notorious piece of legislation of his administrations, however, was an act, in 1925, which made it "unlawful for any teacher in any of the Universities, Normals and all other public schools of the State . . . to teach any theory that denies the story of the Divine Creation of man as taught in the Bible, and to teach instead that man has descended from a lower order of animals" (*Public Acts of . . . Tennessee*, 1925, pp. 50–51). He had not advocated the passage of this measure, and there are private reports that he was greatly angered when the legislature forced him to commit him-

self by sending it to his desk. The labored message he sent to the legislature, and through it to an interested world, in justification of his signature, seems to have been dictated by political expediency and by the conventional opinion that religious and moral safety lie in an "old-fashioned faith and belief" rather than along the new ways of exploration and experiment. "Nobody believes that it is going to be an active statute," he added (*Austin Peay . . . A Collection of . . . Papers and . . . Addresses*, comp. by S. H. Peay, 1929, p. 363). Yet, John T. Scopes, a young teacher in Dayton, was soon prosecuted and convicted under it. Peay had no part in the trial, and the anti-evolution law played an insignificant part in his successful campaign in 1926 for a third term. He died at the executive mansion in Nashville, survived by his wife and their two children.

[Biog. by T. H. Alexander, in *Austin Peay, ante*; *Who's Who in America*, 1926–27; J. T. Moore and A. P. Foster, *Tenn.: the Volunteer State* (1923), vols. I, IV; *Nashville Banner*, Oct. 3, 1927; information concerning name from Mrs. Austin Peay, Clarksville, Tenn.]
P. M. H.

PECK, CHARLES HORTON (Mar. 30, 1833–July 11, 1917), mycologist, was born at Sand Lake (now called Averill Park), Rensselaer County, N. Y., the son of Joel B. and Pamelia (Horton) Peck. He was of English descent, the first member of the family to come to America being Henry Peck, who settled at New Haven, Conn., in 1638. As a boy, Peck helped in his father's sawmill and attended the proverbial log schoolhouse of the settlement. His interest in plants was kindled by fortunate circumstances during the period of his studies at the State Normal School in Albany, where he pursued the special study of botany before it was included in the curriculum. Upon graduation in 1852 he returned to the home farm, devoting all of his spare time to the collecting and analyzing of plants. He prepared for college at Sand Lake Collegiate Institute, and in 1855 entered Union College, from which he was graduated with high honors in 1859. From 1859 to 1861 he taught the classics, mathematics, and botany at the Collegiate Institute and then taught for the following three years at the Albany Classical Institute. On Apr. 10, 1861, he married Mary C. Sliter, also of Rensselaer County, N. Y. A year later he received the A.M. degree from Union College. His interests centered in moss study at this time and through the friendship of George W. Clinton, himself a distinguished botanist, he was appointed in 1867 to the staff of the New York State Cabinet of Natural History. His report of Jan. 1, 1868, to the regents of the University of the State of New York is the first of a notable series which, appearing annually and dealing with many phases of botanical study, came to be known as "Peck's Reports," and ended only with his physical disability in 1912. In 1883, immediately following the passage of a law establishing the office of state botanist, he was appointed formally to that position. The death of his wife in February 1912, and his own serious illness within a year thereafter, prompted him to resign in 1913, but not until January 1915 was his resignation accepted. He died at Menands, N. Y., in his eighty-fifth year.

As state botanist for nearly half a century, Peck naturally gave much attention to botanical exploration, the building up of a state herbarium, and the publication of taxonomic and distributional studies of nearly all groups of plants as represented in the state of New York. He is chiefly celebrated, however, for his long-continued and acute investigations upon the fungus flora of the United States and Canada, in the course of which he described about 2,500 species as new to science. His work was essentially that of a pioneer, only a very few having preceded him in the field of American mycology. The forty-six annual reports are thus devoted largely to the description of new fungi in many different groups, but they are of equal importance, at least, for the series of synoptical studies of most of the large and important genera of fleshy fungi known as agarics, in which the species are described, keyed, and freely illustrated, largely on the basis of specimens collected through Peck's own indefatigable field-work. Other groups than agarics (*e.g.* Boletaceae, Hydnaceae, Clavariaceae) were similarly treated. A self-trained scientist, Peck brought to these studies a highly analytical mind and keen powers of clear description, and, undaunted by lack of proper support and facilities he succeeded in producing an enormous amount of discriminating work. In the absence of any comprehensive general treatise upon the fungi of North America, his contributions were of incalculable value to younger American students, with whom he stood in peculiarly friendly relation through long correspondence and exchange of specimens. His studies in mycology, which are exceeded in importance by those of no other American student, are regarded as basic. As a memorial to his life and services, an exhibit of fifty-seven exquisite models of edible and poisonous mushrooms has been installed in the State Museum at Albany, N. Y.

[*Who's Who in America*, 1914–15; G. F. Atkinson, in *Botanical Gazette*, Jan. 1918; C. E. Bessey, "A Notable Botanical Career," *Science*, July 10, 1914; C. G.

Lloyd, *Mycological Notes*, No. 38, Nov. 1912; *Jour. of the N. Y. Botanical Garden*, Oct. 1917; *Albany Evening Journal*, July 12, 1917.]   W. R. M.

PECK, CHARLES HOWARD (June 18, 1870–Mar. 28, 1927), surgeon, was born at Newtown, Conn., the son of Albert W. and Louise W. (Booth) Peck, and a descendant of William Peck who emigrated to Boston in 1637 and was one of the founders of New Haven, Conn. Charles Howard received his preparatory education at Newtown Academy, studied medicine at the College of Physicians and Surgeons of Columbia University, and received the degree of M.D. from that institution in 1893. He entered upon the private practice of surgery in New York City in 1895, and on Sept. 2, 1896, married Betsy F. Chaffee of Montreal, Canada, who bore him three sons. In 1900 he was made an assistant instructor in operative surgery at the College of Physicians and Surgeons, subsequently advancing through the intervening grades to full professorship in 1909. He also became surgeon to the Roosevelt Hospital, and consulting surgeon to the French and Memorial hospitals, the Hospital for Ruptured and Crippled, the Stamford (Conn.) Hospital, and Vassar Brothers Hospital, Poughkeepsie, N. Y.

When the United States entered the World War, he offered his services to the government and was commissioned a major in the medical reserve. He organized Base Hospital 15, at Chaumont, France, and expanded it to a capacity of 3,000 beds. In April 1918 he was appointed senior consultant in general surgery in the American Expeditionary Forces and in June he was commissioned lieutenant-colonel. He served in France until 1918, when he returned to America. Thereafter, until February 1919, he acted in rotation with Colonels W. J. and Charles H. Mayo, as chief of the department of surgery in the office of the surgeon general of the army. In August 1918 he was commissioned a colonel. After the war he was awarded the distinguished service medal, and was made Officier de l'Instruction Publique by France, and was accorded honorary membership in the 68th Battalion of Alpine Chasseurs "for services rendered to the French Army" during the battle of Chemin des Dames, Oct. 17, 1917. In France he lost a son who was serving in his father's unit.

After the war Peck continued his career of surgical teaching and practice until he died of pernicious anaemia. His friend, Dr. Charles H. Mayo, wrote of him that "as a surgeon, he was resourceful, meticulous, noted for kindliness to tissue and scrupulous haemostatis, skillful in operative maneuvers, and possessed of a mature judgment, the fruit of long and ripe experience" (Mayo, *post*, p. 119). A general surgeon, interested in the whole broad field, he was perhaps best known for his work in gastro-intestinal surgery. While he was not a prolific writer, nearly a hundred articles on medicine and surgery were published by him; the majority of them, however, are case reports and are brief, while none is very long. He was a member of many surgical societies and served as president of the Society of Clinical Surgery, and as treasurer of the American Surgical Association and member of its council from 1915 to the time of his death. He was also fellow of the American College of Surgeons and a member of its board of regents, president of the New York Surgical Society, and vice-president of the New York Academy of Medicine.

[Darius Peck, *A Geneal. Account of the Descendants ... of William Peck, One of the Founders in 1638 of the Colony of New Haven, Conn.* (1877); John Shrady, *The Coll. of Physicians and Surgeons, N. Y.* (n.d.); C. H. Mayo, in *Surgery, Gynecology and Obstetrics*, July 1927; *Am. Jour. of Surgery*, May 1927; *Who's Who in America*, 1926–27; *N. Y. Times*, Mar. 30, 1927.]   P. M. A.

PECK, GEORGE (Aug. 8, 1797–May 20, 1876), Methodist Episcopal clergyman, editor, was a descendant of Henry Peck who came from England, probably in 1637, and was one of the first settlers of New Haven, Conn. George's parents, Luther and Annis (Collar) Peck, migrated from Danbury, Conn., to Otsego County, N. Y., in 1794, and bought land in what is now Middlefield. Here in a log cabin George was born. At the time of his birth there were four other children, three girls and a boy; later three more girls and three boys were born. All the boys became Methodist ministers, one of them, Jesse Truesdell [*q.v.*], a bishop. As a youngster George attended rebelliously a school where the teaching could hardly have been worse, and common forms of punishment, in addition to the whip, were a gag put between the culprit's teeth, and a split stick stuck upon his nose. He also helped an uncle make shoes, "blew and struck" in his father's blacksmith shop, and worked on the farm. Half-Way Covenant Congregationalists in Connecticut, his parents became Methodists in New York, and when about fifteen years old George was converted. In 1814 the family moved to Hamilton Township, Madison County, and the Peck house became a place where Methodists met regularly for conference and worship. George developed into a class-leader and exhorter, and in July 1816 was admitted to the Genesee Conference on trial. In 1818 he was ordained deacon, and the following year,

June 10, he married Mary Myers, daughter of Philip and Martha Myers of Forty Fort, Pa. In 1820 he was ordained elder.

His active service in the Methodist Church covered a period of some fifty-seven years. It began with arduous circuit riding, which was followed by pastorates and numerous terms as presiding elder. From the start he worked diligently to equip himself with the knowledge which others had secured in the schools, and when he was appointed principal of Cazenovia Academy in 1835, a position which he held until 1838, he was able to teach Hebrew, intellectual and moral philosophy, and rhetoric. He had the unusual distinction of being a delegate to thirteen consecutive General Conferences (1824–1872), and through almost a half century of the Church's history he had an important part in shaping its legislation. In 1840 he was elected editor of the *Methodist Quarterly Review* and after conducting it successfully for eight years became editor of the *Christian Advocate*, New York. He was a delegate to the world convention held in London in 1846 at which the Evangelical Alliance was organized. After retiring from the editorship of the *Christian Advocate* in 1852, he was pastor and presiding elder in the Wyoming Conference, Pa., until 1873, when upon his own request a superannuated relation was accorded him. The following year he published *The Life and Times of Rev. George Peck, D.D.*, written by himself. He had previously published numerous books, chiefly controversial or historical, some of which were widely read. Among them are *The Scripture Doctrine of Christian Perfection, Stated and Defended* (1842, 1845, 1848, 1851); *An Answer to the Question, Why are You a Wesleyan Methodist* (1847); *Appeal from Tradition to Scripture and Common Sense; or, An Answer to the Question, What Constitutes the Divine Rule of Faith and Practice* (1844, 1852); *Slavery and the Episcopacy, Being an Examination of Dr. Bascom's Review of the Reply of the Majority to the Protest of the Minority of the Late General Conference of the Methodist Episcopal Church in the Case of Bishop Andrew* (1845); *Formation of a Manly Character* (1853), a series of lectures; *Lives of the Apostles and Evangelists* (3rd edition, 1851); *Early Methodism Within the Bounds of the Old Genesee Conference from 1788 to 1828* (1860); *Our Country: Its Trial and Its Triumph* (1865); *Wyoming: Its History, Stirring Incidents, and Romantic Adventures* (1858, 1868, 1872). Peck died in Scranton in his seventy-ninth year and was buried at Forty Fort, Pa. His daughter Mary Helen married Jonathan Townley Crane [*q.v.*] and became the mother of Stephen Crane [*q.v.*].

[I. B. Peck, *A Geneal. Hist. of the Descendants of Joseph Peck . . . also an Appendix Giving an Account of . . . Deacon William and Henry of New Haven* (1868); J. K. Peck, *Luther Peck and His Five Sons* (1897); F. W. Conable, *Hist. of the Genesee Ann. Conference of the M. E. Ch.* (1876); *First Fifty Years of Cazenovia Sem. 1825-1875* (n.d.); *Ann. Minutes of the Wyoming Conference* (1877); *Christian Advocate* (N. Y.), May 25, June 8, 1876.]   H. E. S.

PECK, GEORGE RECORD (May 15, 1843–Feb. 22, 1923), railroad attorney, was born on a farm near Cameron, Steuben County, N. Y., youngest of the ten children of Joel Munger and Amanda (Purdy) Peck and a direct descendant of William Peck, one of the founders of the New Haven Colony. When he was about six years old, George moved with his family to a farm near Palmyra, Jefferson County, Wis., where he worked on the farm and attended the common schools until, at the age of sixteen, he became a district school teacher. He spent two terms, 1861–62, in Milton Academy, and on Aug. 21, 1862, enlisted as a private in the 1st Wisconsin Heavy Artillery. He was commissioned first lieutenant Dec. 12, 1862, and captain, July 6, 1864, of Company K, 31st Wisconsin Infantry, and participated in Sherman's march to the sea. From 1865 to 1871 he studied law in the office of Charles G. Williams at Janesville, Wis., and attended lecture courses in the law school of the state university at Madison. He was admitted to the bar in 1866, served as clerk of the circuit court of Rock County from Jan. 1, 1867, to Jan. 1, 1869, then engaged in general practice in partnership with J. M. Kimball.

In December 1871 he removed to Independence, Kan., and entered the office of W. H. Watkins, probate judge of Montgomery County. He studied Kansas law, and in time became a member of the firm of Peck & Chandler. Appointed United States attorney for the district of Kansas in 1874, he moved to Topeka. One of his most notable achievements in this office was the winning of the Osage Ceded Land Case (12 *Kan.*, 124; 1 *McCrary's 8th Circuit Reports*, 610; 92 *U. S.*, 733; 16 *Kan.*, 510). He was reappointed in 1878, but resigned in March 1879, to devote himself to general practice. While in Topeka he was a member of the firm of Peck, Ryan & Johnson and head of the firm of Peck, Rossington, Smith, & Dallas. On Feb. 9, 1882, he became general solicitor of the Atchison, Topeka, & Santa Fé Railroad, which position he held until Jan. 1, 1884, and again from Apr. 15, 1886, until Sept. 16, 1895. In 1891 when the Santa Fé attempted to secure control of St. Louis & San Francisco Railway, a stock-holder of the latter

sought to enjoin the sale on the ground that the roads were "parallel and competing lines" and the sale therefore illegal (*Kimball* vs. *Atchison, Topeka & Santa Fé Railroad Co.*, 46 *Fed. Reporter*, 888). Peck's successful handling of the consequent litigation in the circuit court and the Supreme Court gave him a place of first rank among railroad attorneys. When the Santa Fé was forced into receivership in December 1893, he directed the legal proceedings so well that the railroad was successfully reorganized in two years, a notable feat of efficiency. Although a leader of the Republican party in Kansas, Peck did not desire political office, and in 1891 declined Governor Humphrey's offer of a seat in the United States Senate vacated by the death of Senator Preston B. Plumb.

In 1893 when the Santa Fé established general offices in Chicago, Peck moved to that city, becoming a member of the distinguished law firm of Peck, Miller & Starr. After his resignation as general solicitor of the Santa Fé in September 1895, he served as general counsel for the Chicago, Milwaukee & St. Paul Railway until his retirement, Jan. 1, 1911. He was engaged in the foreclosure of the mortgage on the Jacksonville & Southwestern Railroad, was retained in connection with the reorganization of the Northern Pacific, and drafted the articles of incorporation of the Civic Federation of Chicago upon which was modeled the National Civic Federation. In 1896 he was considered by many newspapers as a possible candidate for the Republican presidential nomination.

He was a speaker of unusual ability, much in demand by patriotic societies, private clubs, universities, and colleges. In 1905–06 he was president of the American Bar Association. A lover of literature, history, and biography, he possessed a library of over twelve thousand volumes. He was married, Oct. 24, 1866, to Arabella Burdick of Janesville, Wis., who died Mar. 5, 1896. They had four children. Peck died in Chicago in his eightieth year.

[Darius Peck, *A Geneal. Account of the Descendants in the Male Line of William Peck* (1877); E. A. Bancroft, in *Green Bag*, Sept. 1905, repr. in *Chicago Legal News*, Nov. 18, 1905; J. M. Palmer, *The Bench and Bar of Ill.* (1899), vol. I; *Trans. Kan. State Hist. Soc.*, vol. IX (1906); *Hist. of Montgomery County, Kan.* (1903), ed. by L. W. Duncan; *Mil. Order of the Loyal Legion of the U. S. Commandery of the State of Kan., Circular No. 2, Series of 1923; Santa Fé Employes' Mag.*, Apr. 1923; *Chicago Bar Asso. Record*, Oct. 1924; *Who's Who in America*, 1918–19; *Chicago Daily Tribune*, Feb. 23, 1923; clippings concerning Peck in Kan. State Hist. Soc. Lib.]   J. K. W.

PECK, GEORGE WASHINGTON (Dec. 4, 1817–June 6, 1859), author, journalist, music critic, was born in Rehoboth, Mass., the son of

George Washington Peck and his second wife, Hannah Bliss (Carpenter), and a descendant of Joseph Peck who came to Massachusetts in 1638. The first George Washington Peck is described as having "settled, lived, and died on the homestead" (Ira B. Peck, *post*, p. 66); but his son saw much more of the world. He attended Brown University, graduating in 1837, taught for a time in Indiana and Ohio, engaged in journalism in Cincinnati, and returned east to study law in Boston under Richard Henry Dana [*q.v.*]. It may have been literary as much as legal ambition that led him to seek this association with the author of *Two Years Before the Mast*, but he was admitted to the Massachusetts bar on May 19, 1843, and for the next four years is recorded in the Boston Directory as a "counselor." Yet even during this period he seems to have been most active as a journalist and music critic. He contributed articles on music and the drama to the *Boston Post*, and in 1845 he founded the *Boston Musical Review*, a monthly publication of which only four numbers appear to have been issued. In 1847 he gave up whatever connection he may have had with the law and removed to New York, where he joined the staff of the *Morning Courier and New York Enquirer* and established a rather close connection with the *American Review*, later the *American Whig Review*, which had a brief but rather conspicuous career. In February and May 1847 he published articles on "Music in New York" in this periodical, and from February 1848 to January 1849 was represented by at least one article a month. He was an occasional contributor up to 1850, his subjects including reviews of Longfellow's *Evangeline* and Emily Brontë's *Wuthering Heights*, discussions of Cooper, Dana, Poe, and of Charles Lamb's letters, besides speculations entitled "On the Use of Chloroform in Hanging," fiction, and forty sonnets in two instalments of twenty each. In 1849, under the transparent pseudonym Cantell A. Bigly, he published a volume called *Aurifodina*, describing adventures in California among a strange people whose commonest possession was gold. Obviously modeled on *Gulliver's Travels*, it also suggests Poe's influence and in some ways is like Mark Twain's *A Connecticut Yankee in King Arthur's Court*.

The ravages of consumption, of which he died, reduced the output of his last years; but he made a trip to Australia in 1853, writing letters to the *New York Times*, and published an account of the journey in his *Melbourne and the Chincha Islands; with Sketches of Lima, and a Voyage Round the World* (1854). After the publication of this book there is little certain trace of him till the official record of his death in Boston. Although his literary product is not impressive in quantity nor marked by any high degree of creative power, it displays a broad culture and an enthusiastic appreciation of literature and music. He died unmarried.

[*"Necrology of Brown University," Providence Journal*, Sept. 7, 1859; *Hist. Cat. Brown Univ., 1764–1904* (1905); autobiographical material in Peck's own writings, especially *Melbourne and the Chincha Islands*; Ira B. Peck, *A Geneal. Hist. of the Descendants of Joseph Peck* (1868).]   S. G.

PECK, GEORGE WILBUR (Sept. 28, 1840– Apr. 16, 1916), humorist, journalist, and governor of Wisconsin, was born at Henderson, N. Y., the son of David B. and Alzina Peck. When he was about three years old, his parents removed to Wisconsin and settled on a farm at Cold Spring, Jefferson County. Later they moved to the town of Whitewater, where he attended school. Before he was fifteen, he became a "printer's dèvil" on the weekly *Register* at Whitewater and thus began a connection with newspaper work that continued throughout the most of his life. In 1860 he was married to Francena Rowley of Delavan, Wis. Shortly after this he purchased a half-interest in the *Jefferson County Republican*, a weekly paper with which he continued until 1863, when he enlisted as a private in the 4th Wisconsin Cavalry. He served with this unit as sergeant and later as second lieutenant until it was disbanded in 1866. He went to Ripon and began the publication of a weekly paper, the *Representative*, to which he contributed the first of his humorous articles. In 1868 one of these skits, a letter in Irish dialect signed "Terence McGrant" that satirized the nepotism at the beginning of President Grant's first term, attracted the attention of Marcus M. Pomeroy [*q.v.*]. As Pomeroy was about to launch a daily paper in New York City, he offered Peck a place on the staff in order to continue the "Terence McGrant" letters. These proved sufficiently popular to be brought together in a volume with illustrations, published in New York in 1871 under the title *Adventures of One Terence McGrant*. In 1871 Peck returned to La Crosse and, with a partner, edited Pomeroy's former paper, the *La Crosse Democrat*, in which he supported the candidacy of Horace Greeley for president in 1872. When he withdrew from the *Democrat* in 1874, he began a new paper, the *Sun*, but after four years' struggle he abandoned La Crosse and moved his paper to Milwaukee. With the motto, "It Shines for All," which had been used earlier by Benjamin H. Day [*q.v.*] for the New York *Sun,* Peck's new venture immediately proved a success.

It was in Peck's *Sun* that the "Bad Boy" stories first appeared that were to make Peck's reputation as a humorist throughout the country. In 1883 appeared *Peck's Bad Boy and His Pa,* his best-known book, in which were told stories of the practical jokes played on his father by a mischievous youngster. Within a year another collection of these stories entitled *The Grocery Man and Peck's Bad Boy* (1883) came from the press to add to his popularity. The success of these books augmented that of the weekly *Sun,* which attained a nation-wide circulation of 80,-000 copies. Humorous sketches of his Civil War experiences, *How Private Geo. W. Peck Put Down the Rebellion,* published in 1887, was his last book for several years.

In the spring of 1890 he was elected mayor of Milwaukee on the Democratic ticket. The enactment of the so-called Bennett Law to compel some teaching of English in all schools in the state aroused the fears of Roman Catholics and Lutherans, whose parochial schools were accustomed to give all instruction in foreign languages. As the Republican party, long dominant in Wisconsin, had been responsible for this legislation, the Democrats took up the issue and nominated Peck for governor. His reputation as a humorist and his success in the Milwaukee mayorality campaign made him a promising candidate. He was elected in November 1890. With his genial personality and humorous speeches, his popularity continued after the law was repealed, and he was reëlected again in 1892 against John C. Spooner. Two years afterward, however, he was defeated in the gubernatorial contest and retired to his home in Milwaukee. He ran again for governor in 1904 against Robert M. LaFollette but was defeated. He continued to be a familiar figure in Milwaukee with his gray moustache and goatee, eye-glasses, and a red carnation as a boutonnière. He also appeared occasionally on the lecture platform. Upon taking office in 1890 he turned over the *Sun* to George W. Peck, Jr., his eldest son, who continued it for four years; but its popularity had waned, and in 1894 it was merged with another weekly paper. In 1899 appeared *Peck's Uncle Ike and the Red Headed Boy,* which was followed by *Sunbeams—Humor, Sarcasm and Sense* (1900), *Peck's Bad Boy with the Circus* (1906), and *Peck's Bad Boy with the Cowboys* (1907); but these books did not attain the success that the original Bad Boy Series enjoyed. The latter furnished material for a popular comedy, *Peck's Bad Boy,* and the original stories

were reprinted in paper covers to be sold on trains and at news stands for many years.

[Autobiographical sketch in *Soldiers' and Citizens' Album . . . of Wis.,* vol. II (1890); *Who's Who in America,* 1916–17; A. J. Aikens and L. A. Proctor, *Men of Progress, Wis.* (1897); W. A. Titus, *Wis. Writers* (1930); *Evening Wisconsin* (Milwaukee), Apr. 17, 1916.]

W. G. B—r.

PECK, HARRY THURSTON (Nov. 24, 1856–Mar. 23, 1914), classical philologist, editor, literary critic, was born at Stamford, Conn., of English colonial stock, the son of Harry and Harriet Elizabeth (Thurston) Peck. From his father, a well-known schoolmaster, he acquired his skill as a teacher and the beginnings, at least, of his passion for literature and learning. Excessive reading by candlelight while he was still a mere boy did irreparable damage to his eyes and, by preventing his participation in games and athletics, intensified his bookishness. As a student at Columbia College he won a local renown for intellectual brilliance and wrote prose and verse remarkable for their maturity and polish. Under his editorship *Acta Columbiana* became the most famous undergraduate periodical in the United States. After his graduation in 1881 he studied classical philology in Paris, Berlin, and Rome; was married Apr. 26, 1882, to Cornelia M. Dawbarn, of Stamford, by whom he had two daughters; went in 1883, for some obscure reason, to Cumberland University, Lebanon, Tenn., to obtain the degree of Ph.D.; and in 1884 received the degree of L.H.D. in course at Columbia. He remained in the service of the University for twenty-six years: as tutor in Latin, 1882–86, and in Latin and Semitic languages, 1886–88; as professor of the Latin language and literature, 1888–1904; and as Anthon professor of the Latin language and literature, 1904–10. He was one of the most prominent and useful officers of Columbia during the period of its transformation from a small college into a university of world-wide reputation.

In any society he would have been a man of distinction. A brilliant, versatile, and independent intellect; learning encyclopedic in its range and detail; an astoundingly capacious memory and instant power of association and recall; a ready command of a clear, sparkling prose style; and a faculty for gracious, witty conversation— all these gifts were his, and, though seldom guilty of overt showmanship, he took great delight in their exercise. In professional knowledge, though not in minute accuracy, he was the equal of such Columbia Latinists as Anthon, Drisler, and Short, and he was their superior as a teacher. Like them he insisted that his pupils master their grammar and translate their text into exact, effective English, but he never forgot the purpose behind the discipline. He was saturated with the very spirit of Latin literature, and he brought his whole mind with him to the classroom. In his hands the great Roman classics became an introduction to the literature, ideas, and manners of the western world. To graduate students he offered courses, also, in Latin metrics, the history of the language, and the literature of the Silver Age. His feeling for the nuances of Latin style was precise and delicate, the product of innate aptitude reënforced by close study. Among his philological publications were a students' edition of Suetonius' *De Vita Caesarum Libri Duo* (1889); *Latin Pronunciation* (1890); a translation of *Trimalchio's Dinner* (1898) from the *Satyricon* of Petronius Arbiter; and a textbook, *A History of Classical Philology* (1911). He was the editor, also, of *Harper's Dictionary of Classical Literature and Antiquities* (1897), which is still the most compendious handbook of its class in English. None of these productions gives any adequate indication of Peck's real powers. For many years he looked forward to the time when he would have leisure to write a history of Latin literature and edit a major edition of Juvenal, undertakings for which he was admirably and in some ways uniquely equipped, but fate cheated him of his masterpieces.

He began his long connection with the publishing house of Dodd, Mead & Company by editing their *International Encyclopædia* (1892). He and Daniel Coit Gilman served jointly as editors of the *New International Encyclopædia* (1900–03), but the brunt of the responsibility was borne by Frank Moore Colby [*q.v.*] as managing editor. Peck also edited several compilations and reference books; contributed articles to various magazines; was literary editor of the New York *Commercial Advertiser*, 1897–1901; and was on the staff of *Munsey's Magazine*, 1907–11. His best vehicle, however, was the *Bookman*, a literary monthly launched by Dodd, Mead & Company in February 1895, of which Peck was editor-in-chief until 1902 and a contributing editor until 1907. For some issues he wrote a good part of the contents himself, and his taste, knowledge, and lightness of touch set the tone of the whole magazine. His "Bookman's Letter-Box" was famous, for he answered his readers' questions both authoritatively and wittily. His criticism for the most part was shrewd and good tempered, impressionistic in method, but founded on a keen appreciation of literary technique and a receptiveness to ideas.

He was relatively free from the provincialism

and colonialism that still dominated American criticism. His actual influence on the culture of the period cannot be estimated; but whatever its extent, it was wholly beneficial. His separate publications included: *The Personal Equation* (1897); *What is Good English? and Other Essays* (1899); *Greystone and Porphyry* (1899), a volume of verse, displaying excellent technique but little original poetic insight; *William Hickling Prescott* (1905), a contribution to the English Men of Letters Series; *Literature* (1908), an academic lecture and a characteristic example of his more florid manner; *Studies in Several Literatures* (1909); and *The New Baedeker* (1910), an amusing volume of travel sketches. He also wrote two charming volumes for children, *The Adventures of Mabel* (1896) and *Hilda and the Wishes* (1907). His *Twenty Years of the Republic* (1906), a vivid, pungent history of the United States during the administrations of Cleveland, Harrison, and McKinley, has only recently been displaced as the best summary account of the period. It was an extraordinary feat of literary virtuosity and has become a minor classic. It was characteristic of Peck that he should write his best work in a field so far removed from his professional concerns.

Despite his many activities and incessant reading, he had time to travel extensively and to lead a gracious social life. He bestowed great pains on his more promising pupils, cultivating their personal friendship; wrote sprightly letters to his distant friends; and was an inveterate theatre-goer. His taste in waistcoats and cravats ran to the colorful; his friends attributed his choice of wearing apparel to his defective eyesight. By 1905 or 1906 he began to show signs of mental deterioration and aberration; in September 1908 his wife obtained a divorce from him in South Dakota, and on Aug. 26, 1909, he married Elizabeth Hickman Du Bois, of Philadelphia, a teacher in a New York high school.

In the summer of 1910 the foundations of his security crumbled under him, overwhelming him with disgrace, poverty, and illness. In June of that year Esther Quinn, a former stenographer, brought suit against him for breach of promise, and several sensational newspapers printed as a serial the letters that he had written to the woman. It was his innocence rather than culpability that ruined him. At worst the letters showed that he was an inexpert philanderer, but the obloquy and ridicule excited by their publication brought on a mental collapse. He was dismissed from his professorship and expelled from his clubs; his wife left him; his friends deserted him almost in a body; and magazines refused to print his articles. In January 1913 he declared himself bankrupt. A few months later he was in a hospital at Ithaca, N. Y., desperately ill in body and mind. His first wife, at this juncture, came to his rescue, took him to her home at Stamford, and nursed him back to a semblance of his former health and spirits. It was only a semblance, however. Her efforts to convert him to Christian Science irked him, and finally, with money that she supplied, he rented a cheap room in a lodging house, ate his meals—gourmet that he had been—in a Greek restaurant, and endeavored to earn his living by revising articles for a new edition of the encyclopedia that he had once edited. But his distraught mind was unequal even to such chores, and on Mar. 23, 1914, he committed suicide.

[*Who's Who in America*, 1906–13; *Publishers' Weekly*, Mar. 28, 1914; Robert Arrowsmith, in *Columbia Alumni News*, Mar. 27, 1914; N. G. McCrea, in *Columbia Univ. Quart.*, June 1914; G. S. Hellman, "Men of Letters at Columbia," *Critic*, Oct. 1903; Brown Thurston, *Thurston Geneals., 1635–1880* (1880), p. 203; Thomas Beer, *The Mauve Decade* (1926), pp. 180–99; W. G. Kellogg, "Harry Thurston Peck," *Am. Mercury*, Sept. 1933; *N. Y. Times*, numerous references, 1908–14; J. E. Spingarn, "The Fate of a Scholar," *Poems* (1924); letter from M. H. Thomas, concerning material in the Columbiana collection, Columbia Univ. Lib., *Am. Mercury*, Jan. 1934.]

G. H. G.

PECK, JAMES HAWKINS (c. 1790–Apr. 29, 1836), jurist, one of twelve children of Adam and Elizabeth (Sharkey) Peck, was born in what was then North Carolina, now Jefferson County, Tenn. His father was a Revolutionary soldier and a member of the legislature of Tennessee. He was educated for the bar in Tennessee, served in the state militia during the War of 1812, and settled in St. Louis, Mo., in 1818. When Congress created the federal district court of Missouri he was appointed judge of that court by President Monroe, upon the recommendation of David Barton, senator from Missouri, and Richard M. Johnson, representative from Kentucky. In this capacity he served for fourteen years, during which time he was impeached and acquitted. He was a painstaking, scholarly, and upright jurist. The arduous task of organizing and maintaining the district court in a new state among a people of diverse race and language required and received his best effort.

His impeachment grew out of the numerous pending cases involving land grants. Many land grants in upper Louisiana were made during the Spanish and the French occupancy, and when Missouri was admitted to the Union the titles to more than three-fourths of the land in the state was in dispute. The task of passing upon their validity was placed upon the district court. A test case was heard in 1825, and, as judge of that court, he rendered an oral opinion finding against the claimant. The decision was of such importance that there was a public demand for the publication of the opinion, and it was published in the *Missouri Republican* on Mar. 30, 1826. Luke Lawless, the attorney for the defeated claimant, published an article in the *Missouri Advocate and St. Louis Enquirer* on Apr. 8, 1826, criticising the opinion of the court. Lawless was cited, convicted, and punished for contempt. This induced the lawyer to file a complaint against the judge before the House of Representatives. The House at two separate sessions failed to impeach, but after the charges had been under consideration for more than three years Peck was impeached in April 1830. The status of the land grants had become a political issue, and from 1822 to 1832 there was a prolonged debate in Congress, during which the federal courts were repeatedly attacked. These circumstances made the impeachment possible. The sole charge was that the court oppressively convicted a lawyer of contempt. The trial before the Senate lasted from Dec. 13, 1830, to Jan. 31, 1831, when the vote for acquittal was obtained. James Buchanan, then a member of the House and afterward president, had charge of the prosecution and William Wirt, formerly attorney-general, represented the defense. The proceedings of the trial probably constitute the most thorough commentary available on the law of contempt. As one result of the trial Congress passed a statute, still in force, to define more clearly the circumstances under which courts may punish for contempt.

Although he was never married, Peck's last years were pleasantly spent in the warmth of the friendship of his associates, the closest of whom was David Barton, also a bachelor. In addition to his judicial labors he took an active interest in the civic and cultural movements in Missouri. He died at St. Charles, Mo.

[C. B. Davis, "Judge James Hawkins Peck," *Mo. Hist. Rev.*, Oct. 1932; J. F. Darby, *Personal Recollections* (1880); Wm. Van Ness Bay, *Reminiscences of the Bench and Bar of Mo.* (1878); E. H. Shepard, *The Early Hist. of St. Louis* (1870), pp. 96, 127; *Report of the Trial of James H. Peck . . . before the Senate*, rept. by A. S. Stansbury (1833); *Missouri Argus* (St. Louis), May 6, 1836.]

C. B. D.

PECK, JESSE TRUESDELL (Apr. 4, 1811–May 17, 1883), bishop of the Methodist Episcopal Church, was born at Middlefield, Otsego County, N. Y., son of Luther and Annis (Collar) Peck, brother of George Peck [*q.v.*], and a descendant of Henry Peck, one of the founders of New Haven, Conn. Jesse was the youngest of five brothers, all of whom became ministers; he also had six sisters. His schooling, which was limited, included a period at Cazenovia Seminary. Early disposed to enter the ministry, he was admitted on trial to the Oneida Conference of the Methodist Episcopal Church, June 12, 1832, was ordained deacon in 1834, and elder, in the Black River Conference, on Sept. 1, 1836. In the meantime he served churches at Dryden, Newark Valley, Skaneateles, and Potsdam. From 1837 to 1840 he was principal of the Gouverneur, N. Y., high school, which later became Gouverneur Wesleyan Seminary; and from 1841 to 1848 he was principal of the Troy Conference Academy, Poultney, Vt.

Although only thirty-three years old at the time, he was elected a delegate from the Troy Conference to the General Conference of 1844, at which session action was taken which resulted in a division of the Church over the slavery question. A speech which Peck made on this occasion brought him into wide and favorable notice in the North. In 1848 he was appointed to succeed John P. Durbin [q.v.] as president of Dickinson College, Carlisle, Pa., which position he held until 1852, when he became pastor of Foundry Church, Washington. Two years later, however, he was chosen to fill out the unexpired term of Abel Stevens [q.v.] as secretary of the Tract Society of the Methodist Church. In 1856 he took charge of Green Street Church, New York, but in 1858, on account of his wife's health, he went to California, where for the next eight years he served as pastor in San Francisco and Sacramento and as a presiding elder. Returning to the East, he supplied St. Paul's Church, Peekskill, N. Y., for a time; was pastor of Hudson Street Church (now First Church), Albany, from 1867 to 1870; and from 1870 to 1872, of the Methodist church in Syracuse, being prominent among those who were instrumental in the founding of Syracuse University.

At the General Conference of 1872 he was elected bishop. During the remaining eleven years of his life he presided at eighty-three annual conferences, including those in Germany, Switzerland, Denmark, Sweden, and Norway. He also attended the First Ecumenical Methodist Conference, held in London in 1881. In his busy and varied career he found time to write several books which circulated widely. Among them are *The Central Idea of Christianity* (1856, revised edition, 1876), and *The History of the Great Republic Considered from a Christian Standpoint* (1868), an edition of which under the title of *The Great Republic from the Discovery of America to the Centennial, July 4, 1876,*

appeared in 1876. He also wrote tracts and pamphlets and contributed to Methodist periodicals and holiness magazines. He was a huge man, weighing over 300 pounds, and possessed great physical strength. His body was seldom at rest and his mind was always on the alert. While not bigoted, he was a great lover and defender of his own church. He preached with much force, and as a presiding officer at ecclesiastical gatherings he displayed marked ability. His wife, whom he married on Oct. 13, 1831, was Persis Wing of Cortland, N. Y.; they had no children.

[I. B. Peck, *A Geneal. Hist. of the Descendants of Joseph Peck* (1868); J. K. Peck, *Luther Peck and His Five Sons* (1897); *Life and Times of Rev. George Peck* (1874), written by himself; Wm. S. Smyth, *The First Fifty Years of Cazenovia Sem.* (1877); T. L. Flood and J. W. Hamilton, *Lives of the Methodist Bishops* (1882); *Minutes Ann. Conferences of the M. E. Church* (1883); John M'Clintock and James Strong, *Cyc. of Biblical, Theological and Ecclesiastical Literature,* vol. XII (1891); J. E. King, "Personal Reminiscences of Bishop Jesse T. Peck," in *Christian Advocate* (N. Y.), Sept. 21, 1911; *Christian Advocate* (N. Y.), May 24, June 7, July 26, 1883; *N. Y. Tribune,* May 19, 1883.]   S.G.A.

PECK, JOHN JAMES (Jan. 4, 1821–Apr. 21, 1878), soldier and man of affairs, was born at Manlius, N. Y., the son of John Wells and Phoebe (Raynor) Peck. He received liberal schooling and graduated from the United States Military Academy in the same class as Grant in 1843. He was commissioned brevet 2nd lieutenant of the 2nd Artillery and performed garrison duty until the outbreak of the war with Mexico, serving, with distinction, in every battle save one. He engaged in frontier duty in the West and was present at the skirmish with the Navajo Indians at Tuni Cha, N. Mex., on Aug. 31, 1849, afterward being assigned to recruiting and garrison duty. He resigned from the army on Mar. 31, 1853, bearing the high commendation of his superior officers. Peck married Robie Harris Loomis of Syracuse, N. Y., on Nov. 20, 1850, and six children, three boys and three girls, were born to them. Following his resignation he entered upon a very busy and successful life in Syracuse. He was treasurer of the New York, Newburgh & Syracuse Rail Road Company during this period, as well as cashier and manager of the Burnet Bank. From 1859 to 1861 he was president of the Board of Education and for some years was vice-president of the Franklin Institute of Syracuse. He was a delegate to the National Democratic Convention of 1856 and of 1860, was twice nominated for Congress, and once refused a foreign mission.

At the outbreak of the Civil War he offered his services to the Federal government and refused to aid his friends who were endeavoring to secure for him a high command in the state forces. By virtue of his past services he was commissioned brigadier-general of volunteers Aug. 9, 1861, and served in the defenses of Washington until March 1862. He accompanied McClellan in the Peninsular campaign, serving with such distinction that he was commissioned a major-general of volunteers July 4, 1862. Until September he was in command of all the Federal troops in Virginia south of the James. He rendered his most distinguished military service in the spring of 1863 when he beat off Longstreet's attack at Suffolk, Va. His skill in the disposition of his forces and his personal courage were such that he outwitted Longstreet's attempts to outflank him, beat off his assaults, raised the siege of Suffolk, and ended the campaign by personally leading a small force to capture at Hill's Point five heavy guns which the gunboats of a light flotilla had not been able to silence. For his actions in this area he was highly commended by Dix and Meade. He was seriously injured, however, and was given leave of absence until August 1863, when he assumed command in North Carolina until the end of April 1864. During the following winter he was engaged only in small skirmishes, but his health suffered to such an extent that he was ordered to Washington in the spring and placed on duty in the Department of the East. On Nov. 5 he was given command on the Canadian frontier, remaining at this port until he was mustered out of service on Aug. 24, 1865.

After the war he resumed his civilian interests at Syracuse. He organized the New York State Life Insurance Company in 1867 and acted as president of that organization until his death.

[G. W. Cullum, *Biog. Reg. . . . U. S. Mil. Acad.* (3rd ed., 1891); *Ann. Reunion, Asso. Grads. U. S. Mil. Acad.*, 1901; Elias Loomis, *Descendants of Joseph Loomis in America* (1909), revised by Elisha S. Loomis; *N. Y. Tribune*, Apr. 23, 1878.]   D. Y.

PECK, JOHN MASON (Oct. 31, 1789–Mar. 14, 1858), Baptist preacher and author, was born in Litchfield, Conn., the son of Asa and Hannah (Farnum) Peck. He was the descendant of Paul Peck who probably emigrated to Massachusetts in 1634 and removed to Hartford, Conn., in 1636. His father's poverty and lack of health kept him busy on the farm, and he attended school only a few winter terms. On May 8, 1809, he married Sarah Paine of Greene County, N. Y. With the birth of the first of their ten children both became doubtful of paedobaptism, and soon afterward they left the Congregational for the Baptist Church. Peck was licensed to preach at Windham, N. Y., in 1811 and was ordained in 1813. After about five years in New York pas-

torates his interest in missions led him to preparatory study for the service under William Staughton [q.v.] of Philadelphia. In 1817 with James Welch he established the western mission at Saint Louis; when this was closed in 1820 he remained in the West. In 1822 as missionary of the Massachusetts Baptist Missionary Society he moved to Rock Spring, Ill., where he acquired and cultivated a half-section of land to supplement his appropriation of five dollars a week. Reading as he rode his horse, enduring hunger and cold as part of his routine, he traveled constantly through Illinois, Indiana, and Missouri. To undermine the opposition to missions that he encountered everywhere, he established Bible societies and Sunday schools and by frequent visits kept them alive. Wherever possible he examined schools, the majority of which he considered worse than useless, and he placed good teachers where he could. In 1827 he helped to establish Rock Spring Seminary, the main purpose of which was the training of teachers and ministers. It was soon moved to Upper Alton. In 1835 he raised $20,000 in the East for the institution, half being obtained from Benjamin Shurtleff of Boston, for whom the seminary was renamed Shurtleff College. Peck remained a trustee until his death. A religious periodical, the *Pioneer*, was established at Rock Spring under his editorship in 1829, continuing there or at Upper Alton until 1839, when it was merged with the *Baptist Banner* at Louisville, Ky. He became editor of the *Western Watchman* in 1849. In the meantime his reports and articles were making him known as an authority on the West, and he was led to compile his *Guide for Emigrants,* which appeared in 1831 and again in 1836 and 1837. The first edition of his *Gazetteer of Illinois* (1834) ran to 4,200 copies; it was revised in 1837. In collaboration with John Messinger he prepared a sectional map of Illinois, published in 1835. *The Traveler's Directory for Illinois* appeared in 1840. He wrote a *Life of Daniel Boone* (1847), in 1850 edited a revised and enlarged edition of the *Annals of the West* that had been published in 1846 by James H. Perkins [q.v.], and wrote *Father Clark or the Pioneer Preacher* (1855). His large library burned in 1852, but his first sources were his own observations, noted copiously in his diary while he traveled and amplified by a large correspondence and by interviews.

He took little part in Illinois politics except an unsuccessful candidacy for the constitutional convention of 1847–48. He was active in the colonization society (*Pioneer*, Oct. 27, 1837) but deplored the efforts of the extreme abolitionists. His criticism of Lovejoy and the abolitionists compelled him to defend his attitude toward the tragedy of Lovejoy's murder (*Pioneer*, June 1, 8, 1838). He favored the enforcement of the Fugitive Slave Law and in January 1851 preached a sermon on the subject in the State House at Springfield, *The Duties of American Citizens* (1851). In 1841 and 1842 he acted as agent for the Western Baptist Publication Society and from 1843 to 1846 as secretary of the American Baptist Publication Society. He held a pastorate in Saint Louis in 1849 and in Covington, Ky., in 1854, after which the failure of his health made necessary his return home. He died at Rock Spring.

[Rufus Babcock, *Forty Years of Pioneer Life, Memoir of John Mason Peck . . . from his Journals and Correspondence* (1864); Coe Hayne, *Vanguard of the Caravans* (1931); A. K. de Blois, *The Pioneer School. A Hist. of Shurtleff College* (1900); I. B. Peck, *A Geneal. Hist. of the Descendants of Joseph Peck* (1868), p. 380.]   T. C. P.

PECK, THOMAS EPHRAIM (Jan. 29, 1822–Oct. 2, 1893), Presbyterian clergyman, teacher, was born in Columbia, S. C., the son of Ephraim Peck, a native of Connecticut who had moved South on account of his health and opened a small mercantile establishment in Columbia, and Sarah Bannister (Parke), a daughter of Thomas Parke, professor of the classic languages in the College of South Carolina. The father died when Thomas was ten years of age, after which event the mother lived with her father till his death in 1840. Prepared for college by his mother, and afterwards by John Daniel in the Male Academy of Columbia, Thomas graduated from the College of South Carolina, with distinguished honors, in his eighteenth year. Feeling that he was called to the ministry, he studied, while acting as College librarian, not in the Presbyterian Seminary in the town, but under the personal direction of James Henley Thornwell [*q.v.*], a Presbyterian minister, then professor of metaphysics in the college, who exercised a controlling influence over Peck's mental and spiritual development.

He was licensed by the Charleston Presbytery in 1844, preached for several months to the Salem and Jackson churches in Fairfield County, S. C., then for a year as temporary supply in the Second Presbyterian Church of Baltimore. In 1846 he became pastor of the Broadway Street Church, an offshoot of the Second Church, and in 1857, pastor of the Central Presbyterian Church of Baltimore. On Oct. 28, 1852, he married Ellen Church Richardson, the daughter of Scotch parents, herself a stanch Presbyterian. She bore him seven daughters, three of whom died in infancy and one in early

womanhood. In 1855–56 he collaborated with Rev. Stuart Robinson in publishing the *Presbyterian Critic and Monthly Review*, a paper designed to maintain strict Presbyterian views in polity and doctrine, in which are found many of his characteristic views.

In 1859 he was elected professor of ecclesiastical history and church government in Union Theological Seminary in Virginia. He declined the call, but when it was tendered him again in 1860 he accepted it, feeling that impaired health was unfitting him for the pastorate. Upon the resignation in 1883 of Dr. Robert L. Dabney [*q.v.*], professor of theology, Peck was promptly and unanimously chosen to fill his place, a position which he continued to hold till his death. In 1878 he was elected moderator of the General Assembly of the Presbyterian Church in the United States. He suffered a marked decline of health in 1892, and in October of the following year died of Bright's disease and attendant complications, survived by three of his daughters, all of whom married clergymen.

He published one small book, *Notes on Ecclesiology* (1892), and a number of articles which, with unpublished sketches and notes, were edited by T. C. Johnson and printed under the title, *Miscellanies of Rev. Thomas E. Peck* (3 vols., 1895–97). He rendered his greatest service to the Church as a teacher at Union Theological Seminary. He held that the Bible was the inerrant Word of God, an absolute rule of faith and practice, to which nothing should be added except by good and necessary inference. He believed that Presbyterian doctrine and polity were clearly set forth in the Scriptures, and that the traditional beliefs and practices of the Church, being Scriptural, should be maintained. Many who did not know him well thought that he was severe and cold; friends who pierced his reserve, however, found him warmhearted and affectionate, albeit possessed of strong and unyielding convictions.

[C. R. Vaughan, in *Union Sem. Mag.*, Mar.-Apr. 1894, and in *Miscellanies* (vol. III); T. C. Johnson, in *Christian Observer*, July 4, 1894; R. F. Campbell, in *Union Sem. Mag.*, Mar.-Apr. 1898; *The State* (Richmond), Oct. 5, 1893.]   E. T. T.

PECK, TRACY (May 24, 1838–Nov. 24, 1921), classicist, teacher, was born at Bristol, Conn., the son of Tracy and Sally (Adams) Peck. Through his father he was descended from Paul Peck who came to Hartford with Thomas Hooker in 1636. His mother was descended from Henry Adams who emigrated in 1636 from Devonshire, England, to Massachusetts. By virtue of his own culture and wide experiences abroad in later life, he became thoroughly cosmopolitan in his point of view, but he reflected always in his native integrity, intellectual clarity, and personal simplicity, the force of his colonial New England ancestry. Having prepared for college at Williston Academy, Easthampton, Mass., he entered Yale College, from which he graduated as valedictorian in 1861. During the two years following he studied at Berlin, Jena, and Bonn, traveling also in Italy. Returning to Yale, he received the degree of M.A. in 1864 and was a tutor in Latin for the next three years. From 1867 to 1869 he studied in Rome and Berlin, returning again to a tutorship for the following year. On Dec. 22, 1870, he was married in Brooklyn, N. Y., to Elizabeth Harriet Hall of Hadleigh, England; they had two children, a son and a daughter. During the year 1870–71 he taught Latin and mathematics at the Chickering Classical Institute in Cincinnati. From there he was called to be professor of the Latin language and literature in Cornell University, where he served until he was called to Yale in the same capacity in 1880. He was professor in Yale College for twenty-eight years, retiring in 1908. During the year 1885–86 he was president of the American Philological Association and in 1898–99 director of the American School for Classical Studies in Rome. After retiring from active service he spent most of his time in Rome, where he died and was buried in the English and American Cemetery.

He represented the Connecticut Academy of Arts and Sciences at the Darwin Centennial in Cambridge and London in June 1909. With Prof. Clement L. Smith of Harvard he edited a series of Latin authors, preparing personally with Prof. James B. Greenough [q.v.] one of the volumes of Livy, published in 1893. He also published essays in the *Nation*, the *New Englander*, the *Cornell Review*, the *American Journal of Archæology*, and the *Transactions of the American Philological Association*. He was councilor of the British and American Archæological Society in Rome. A polished and brilliant speaker, he delivered various addresses, the more memorable of which include one at the centennial celebration of the incorporation of Bristol, Conn., in 1885 (see *Centennial Celebration of the Incorporation of the Town of Bristol*, 1885), one at the semi-centennial of Williston Seminary in 1891 (*Baccalaureate Sermon, Oration, and Addresses Delivered at the Semi-Centennial Celebration of Williston Seminary . . . 1891*), and a Latin address before the Phi Beta Kappa Society at Yale in March 1907. His Latin style in both verse and prose was, in the finest sense of the word, elegant; and this Phi Beta Kappa speech was particularly noteworthy for its suggestion of the nomination and election of William Howard Taft as president of the United States.

It is more true of Tracy Peck than of most men that the outline of his life work gives very slight intimation of the real worth of the man. He had an extraordinarily ripe scholarship in the field of Roman life and manners. This resulted from a thorough acquaintance with the more intimate types of Latin literature and with the whole range of Latin inscriptions. Probably no man of modern times has ever known better the ancient city of Rome, especially its peculiar spirit. He also knew all of its material remains: topographical, architectural, and inscriptional. It was his keen understanding of Rome and the Romans and his fine appreciation of their human contributions to civilization that made his classes the delight of all humanistic students. He was intolerant of careless work but his own courtly and chivalrous character made him one of the best-loved and most respected of the scholars of a peculiarly rich period in American classical scholarship. His interest was always in passing on what he had absorbed and his method was that of the teacher rather than the writer. In his latter years in Rome he gave unreservedly of his abundant store of knowledge to all those who came seriously to learn something of that capital of the world. He became deservedly one of the best-known Americans in Rome without ever losing touch with America or ceasing to exert a benign influence on American classical scholarship.

[I. B. Peck, *A Geneal. Hist. of the Descendants of Joseph Peck* (1868), p. 386; *1861–1911: The Fiftieth Anniv. of the Class of 1861, Yale Coll.* (1912); *Yale Univ. Obit. Record*, 1922; *Thirty Year Record: Class of 1890, Yale Coll.* (1922); *Am. Acad. in Rome, Ann. Report*, 1921–22; *Report of the Dean of Yale Coll. to the President*, 1921–22; *Yale Alumni Weekly*, Dec. 2, 1921; *New Haven Journal-Courier*, Nov. 26, 1921; *New Haven Evening Register*, Dec. 11, 1921.]

C. W. M—l.

PECK, WILLIAM DANDRIDGE (May 8, 1763–Oct. 3, 1822), naturalist, was born in Boston. His father was John Peck; his mother, who died when he was seven, was Hannah (Jackson). At the commencement of the siege of Boston in 1776, the family removed to Braintree, Mass., and later to Lancaster. William soon afterwards enrolled at Harvard College, and in 1782 received the degree of bachelor of arts. He then entered the accounting house of a prominent merchant and was destined for commercial pursuits. His father, a naval architect of talent and the designer of ships of war for the government, felt that he was not adequately paid and retired in disgust to a small farm at Kittery, Me. His son speedily followed him there, and for nearly twenty years led a secluded life, busily engaged, however, in making observations in zoölogy and collecting insects, aquatic plants, and fishes. He made rare trips to Boston and to Portsmouth, but his fame grew, although in a restricted circle.

His friends raised a subscription to establish a professorship in natural history in Harvard College and in 1805 Peck was elected thereto. Though at first strongly resisting all solicitations, he eventually accepted the position. He was then sent to Europe to visit the different scientific establishments in England, France, and the North European countries, largely to gain information which would be helpful in the establishment of a botanic garden in Cambridge. During this trip he purchased many books for the library of the new department, and brought back many specimens of natural history. He was a man of great ability in a number of directions: he constructed his first microscope; he was an artist and made exquisite drawings; he was a classical scholar. In 1812 he was one of the incorporators of the American Antiquarian Society.

Peck was probably the first teacher of entomology in the United States and probably the first writer of scientific attainment to enter the field of economic entomology. He wrote "The Description and History of the Canker-Worm" (*Massachusetts Magazine; or Monthly Museum*, September-October 1795), for which he received a gold medal from the Massachusetts Agricultural Society. In 1799 he published *Natural History of the Slug-Worm*, for which he also received a gold medal, and a premium of fifty dollars. In this paper he described the first egg-parasite noticed in the United States. He wrote about the bark-beetles of the pear and of the pine (*Massachusetts Agricultural Repository and Journal*, January 1817) and about the lepidopterous borers in locust trees (*Ibid.*, January 1818). His last paper dealt with insects that affect the oaks and cherries (*Ibid.*, January 1819). In 1818 he published a catalogue of the foreign and American plants in the Botanic Garden, Cambridge.

[Josiah Quincy, *The Hist. of Harvard Univ.* (1860); *Coll. Mass. Hist. Soc.*, 2 ser., vol. X (1823); H. A. Kelly and W. L. Burrage, *Am. Medic. Biog.* (1920); *Boston Daily Advertiser*, Oct 8, 1822.]   L. O. H.

PECKHAM, GEORGE WILLIAMS (Mar. 23, 1845–Jan. 10, 1914), teacher, librarian, entomologist, was born at Albany, N. Y., the son of George Williams Peckham, a lawyer, and of Mary Perry (Watson) Peckham. He was a descendant of John Peckham who was in Rhode Island as early as 1638. In 1853 the family removed to Milwaukee, Wis. Here George was placed in the Milwaukee Academy, but he never cared for Latin, Greek, and mathematics; in fact, he was not interested in any study until, in the early days of the Civil War, he came upon a book of tactics. He and his friend Arthur MacArthur (afterwards a lieutenant-general) worked over this book and determined to enter the army and become great soldiers. His parents, however, did not allow him to enlist until 1863, when he was assigned to Company B, First Regiment, Wisconsin Heavy Artillery. He was mustered out with the rank of first lieutenant at the age of nineteen.

At the earnest wish of his father, he entered the Albany (N. Y.) Law School, living in the family of his uncle, Judge Rufus Wheeler Peckham. After graduation he entered the law office of James T. Brown of Milwaukee. Not caring for the law, he became a student in the medical college of the University of Michigan at Ann Arbor. In 1873 he was called home by his father's death; the college granted him the degree of M.D. in 1881. Asked to take a temporary position as teacher of biology in what at that time was the only high school in Milwaukee—afterwards known as the Eastern High School—he proved an inspiring teacher, and immediately introduced laboratory methods. It is said that he was the first to employ such methods in biological work in any high school in the United States. He immediately engaged in research and was the leading supporter of the so-called Darwinian theory in his community. Elizabeth Maria Gifford, recently graduated from Vassar (1876), came to work in his laboratory, and in 1880 they were married. It was a most fortunate union, and together they carried on investigations almost until his death, publishing very many papers under a joint authorship. In 1888 he was made principal of the high school, and in 1891 was appointed superintendent of public instruction for the city of Milwaukee. He held this post until 1897, when he was made director of the great public library, for which a beautiful building had just been erected. In this position he served until his retirement in 1910. He was a prominent publishing member of the Wisconsin Academy of Sciences, Arts and Letters, and was its president from 1890 to 1893. He had already been president of the Wisconsin Natural History Society.

The Peckhams' scientific work (it is practically impossible to write of them individually in this connection) was largely confined to spiders and wasps. When Mrs. Peckham first joined the high school laboratory, they began a study of the jumping spiders. Commencing with taxonomic studies, they devoted evenings and holidays to the work and published a number of papers. For a time these were limited to descriptions of species and genera, but long vacations spent in the country gave opportunity for field work, and in December 1887 they published in the *Journal of Morphology* the results of a very interesting investigation of the mental powers of spiders. In 1889 and 1890 they published papers on sexual selection and protective resemblances in spiders (*Occasional Papers of the Natural History Society of Wisconsin*, vol. I).

In the meantime they had been watching a ground nest of *Vespa germanica* close to their country cottage, and from this came their very important study of wasps, culminating in their great work entitled *On the Instincts and Habits of Solitary Wasps* (1898). It is a volume of 249 pages, with fifteen plates, and is not only a sound scientific treatise but an altogether charming book. It was based on years of patient, highly intelligent, and very laborious investigations, and ranks today as one of the most valuable books in that field. The somewhat earlier work of the Frenchmen, Fabre and Ferton, and the later work of Phil and Nellie Rau in the United States, together with that of the Peckhams, explored a fascinating field in comparative animal psychology. In Bouvier's *La Vie Psychique des Insectes* (1918) the work of the Peckhams is considered as authoritative. Moreover, their book is a masterpiece of English writing in its clearness, aptness and simplicity. Three children were born to them, a son and two daughters.

[S. F. Peckham and others, *Peckham Geneal.* (n.d.); *Entomological News*, Apr. 1914; *Trans. Wis. Acad. of Sci., Arts and Letters*, vol. XX (1921); *Military Order of the Loyal Legion of the U. S., State of Wis., Circular 6*, ser. of 1914, Mar. 21; *Milwaukee Sentinel*, Jan. 11, 1914.]   L. O. H.

PECKHAM, RUFUS WHEELER (Nov. 8, 1838–Oct. 24, 1909), judge, was the son of the jurist of the same name and Isabella Lacey, and younger brother of Wheeler Hazard Peckham [*q.v.*]. He was born in Albany, N. Y., attended the Albany Boys' Academy, and continued his education in Philadelphia. After traveling with his brother in Europe he returned in 1857 and began to study law. In the year of his admission to the bar (1859) his father was elected a justice of the supreme court of New York, and to the vacancy caused by his retirement from the firm of Peckham & Tremain young Rufus succeeded. He continued as a member thereof for nearly two decades. On Nov. 14, 1866, he was married to Harriette M. Arnold, daughter of a leading New York City merchant. Two sons were born of the union who predeceased their parents.

From 1869 to 1872 Peckham was district attorney of Albany County, in which capacity he won distinction by his successful prosecution of certain express-car robbers. He was later called to assist the state attorney-general in other prosecutions, meanwhile representing important clients as a private practitioner. In 1876 he was a district delegate to the National Democratic Convention where he strongly espoused the interest of Samuel J. Tilden. He became corporation counsel for the city of Albany in 1881 and two years later was elected a justice of the state supreme court. In 1886 he was elected to the court of appeals of New York and is said to have "shown by his opinions in 1891, in the election controversies of that year . . . his independence of political affiliations by ranging himself with the Republican Judges" (*Proceedings, New York State Bar Association, post*, p. 651). At other times during his preceding career he seems to have taken a stand adverse to that of his local party organization and in favor of good government; but evidently he did not antagonize party leaders as his brother Wheeler had in New York City, for when, in 1895, President Cleveland nominated him for a vacancy on the Supreme Court of the United States, Senator Hill, who had successfully opposed his brother's appointment to a similar position the preceding year hastened to let it be known that this nominee was one toward whom he maintained a different attitude, and the nomination was quickly confirmed.

Peckham assumed his new duties on Jan. 6, 1896, and served for more than thirteen years as a member of the nation's tribunal. "His opinions," observed Chief Justice Fuller, "from the first in Volume 160 of our reports to the last in Volume 214, are all lucid expositions of the matter in hand, and many of them of peculiar gravity and importance in the establishment of governing principles" (*Proceedings, New York State Bar Association*, p. 707). Opinions in the following cases have been especially mentioned as revealing Peckham's "great learning and industry": *United States* vs. *Trans-Missouri Freight Association* (166 *U. S.*, 290); *United States* vs. *Joint Traffic Association* (171 *U. S.*, 505); *Hopkins* vs. *United States* (171 *U. S.*, 578); *Addyston Pipe & Steel Company* vs.

United States (175 *U. S.*, 211) ; *Maxwell* vs. *Dow* (176 *U. S.*, 581) ; *Montague & Company* vs. *Lowry* (193 *U. S.*, 38) ; and *Lochner* vs. *New York* (198 *U. S.*, 45). Peckham died at Altamont, near Albany, N. Y., in the fall of 1909. His memory was honored by special services on the part of the New York State Bar Association, Dec. 9, 1909, and the bar of the federal Supreme Court on Dec. 18, of the same year. Addresses were made on these occasions by Elihu Root, Alton B. Parker, and other distinguished members of the legal profession. The resolutions of the New York State Bar Association describe him as "our ideal of a Judge in ability, character and conduct, . . . always courteous yet dignified. . . . He never seemed conscious of his honor, nor did he feel it necessary to maintain an attitude of judicial reserve."

[See: "Proc. on the Death of Mr. Justice Peckham," 215 *U. S. Reports*, v–xiii ; "In Memory of Rufus W. Peckham," *Proc. N. Y. State Bar Asso., 1910* (1910) ; S. F. Peckham, *Peckham Geneal.* (1922) ; *Who's Who in America*, 1908–09 ; *N. Y. Times*, Oct. 25, 1909. In some sources Peckham's middle name is given as Williams.]

C. S. L.

PECKHAM, STEPHEN FARNUM (Mar. 26, 1839–July 11, 1918), chemist, son of Charles and Hannah Lapham (Farnum) Peckham, and a descendant of John Peckham, who had come to Rhode Island as early as 1638, was born at Fruit Hill near Providence, R. I., and spent his early years on his father's farm. He prepared for college at the Friends' (now Moses Brown) School, Providence, and after two years as a clerk in a drug store, entered Brown University in 1859, taking a special course in chemistry. Two years later, in association with Nathaniel P. Hill [*q.v.*] and others, he began to manufacture illuminating oils from petroleum in a plant at Providence planned and constructed largely by himself. The project did not prove immediately remunerative, however, and was abandoned shortly after the outbreak of the Civil War. Together with many others, Peckham enlisted in the army (Aug. 15, 1862), serving first as a hospital steward of the 7th Rhode Island Regiment and subsequently as chief of the chemical department of the United States laboratory at Philadelphia. He remained in the army until the close of the war, being honorably discharged May 26, 1865. In 1865–66, as an expert for the California Petroleum Company, he spent most of his time studying the occurrence of petroleum in the southern part of that state. This work naturally led him into geology, and during the next year or so he made a geological survey of parts of California with special reference to petroleum and allied materials. He made several reports, including one on

the oil interests of Southern California and subsequently an elaborate one on the technological examination of bitumen (prepared in 1867 and published in *California Geological Survey, Geology*, vol. II, 1882), a subject which interested him for many years.

For a number of years, beginning in 1867, he taught chemistry in various institutions: Brown University (1867–68), Washington and Jefferson College, Washington, Pa. (1868–69), State College of Agriculture and the Mechanic Arts, Orono, Me. (1869–71), Buchtel College, Akron, Ohio (1871–72), and the University of Minnesota (1872–80). While teaching in the last-named place he was also chemist of the state geological survey and of the board of health. He had been state assayer of Maine (1869–71), of Minnesota (1873–80), and in 1887 was state assayer of Rhode Island. From 1880 to 1885 he was a special agent of the United States census office and prepared many articles on chemistry, including a *Report on the Production, Technology, and Uses of Petroleum and its Products* (1885), with a bibliography. For the next five years or so he was engaged in various business, scientific, and literary occupations, including the preparation of a long article on petroleum for the *Encyclopædia Britannica* (9th ed., 1875–86). He went to California again in 1893 to serve for a year as chemist of the Union Oil Company. His interest in bitumen led him to visit Trinidad to examine the famous pitch lake. Upon his return he served for four years as an expert on petroleum and asphaltum at Ann Arbor, Mich. In 1898 he entered the service of New York City as chemist, first to the commissioners of accounts and subsequently to the finance department. He held the latter position until January 1911, when ill health compelled him to resign. His scientific work ceased at this time.

In addition to nearly one hundred reports, including those mentioned above, and articles in technical journals, non-technical magazines, and encyclopædias, he wrote *Elementary Treatise on Chemistry* (1876), *Asphalt Paving; Report of the Commissioners of Accounts of the City of New York* (1904) ; and *Solid Bitumens* (1909). He was interested in New England history, was the chief author of a *Peckham Genealogy* (n.d.) and from 1912 to 1915 was associate editor of the *Journal of American History*. His extended services and fundamental contributions to the petroleum and allied industries were recognized by his election to membership in many scientific societies. On June 13, 1865, he married Mary Chace Peck (died Mar. 20, 1892) and on Aug. 1, 1902, Harriet C. Waite Van Buren, a physician. There were two sons and two daughters by the former marriage.

[*Hist. Cat. of Brown Univ., 1764–1904* (1905); *Providence Journal*, July 16, 1918; S. F. Peckham and others, *Peckham Geneal.* (n.d.); *N. Y. Times*, July 13, 1918.]   L. C. N.

PECKHAM, WHEELER HAZARD (Jan. 1, 1833–Sept. 27, 1905), lawyer, was born in Albany, N. Y., the eldest son of Rufus Wheeler Peckham, and Isabella Lacey, and a brother of Rufus Wheeler Peckham [*q.v.*]. He was descended from John Peckham who was in Rhode Island in 1638. He attended the Albany Boys' Academy, a French boarding-school at Utica, where he learned French, and is said to have spent a year at Union College. Being delicate, he did not complete his college course. Instead he traveled for a year in Europe and returned in 1853 to study law at the Albany Law School, of which he was one of the first students, and with his father's firm, Peckham & Tremain, with which he practised after being admitted to the bar in 1854. On Apr. 30, 1855, he was married to Anne A. Keasbey, whom he had met while traveling in Europe. A hemorrhage of the lungs in 1856 caused him such alarm that he left his business for another tour in Europe, and upon his return, fourteen months later, took up his residence for a couple of years at Dubuque, Iowa, removing to St. Paul, Minn., in 1859 and remaining there until 1864. He then returned to the East with health restored and, in the fall of that year, entered into a law partnership with George M. Miller and John A. Stoutenburgh of New York City. The firm had a large general practice, and Peckham proved amply able to handle the very considerable share of it which fell to him. As early as 1868 he appeared in the federal Supreme Court in cases involving the power of a state to tax "greenbacks" (*The Banks* vs. *The Mayor*, 7 *Wallace* 16; *Bank* vs. *Supervisors*, 7 *Wallace* 26). Peckham contended, and was upheld by the Supreme Court, which reversed the holding of the New York court of appeals, that the power did not exist. Among the opposing counsel was Charles O'Conor, who, it is said, was so impressed with Peckham's presentation of the case that he called Peckham to assist him in the prosecution of William M. Tweed and his associates in 1873. There were two trials, the first resulting in a "hung jury," but in the second Tweed was convicted and the heavy work had been done by Peckham.

Like his father before him, he was a vigorous opponent of Tammany Hall, but he never was "in politics" in the sense of seeking office. When appointed district attorney by Governor Cleveland in 1884 he held office less than a year. He was one of the founders of the Association of the Bar of the City of New York in 1869 and served as its president from 1892 to 1894, inclusive. He was also a member of the New York State Bar Association and took a practical interest in law reform. In January 1894 he was nominated by President Cleveland to fill a vacancy on the United States Supreme Court. Senators Hill and Murphy of his own state, both organization Democrats, opposed him because of his independent course, and by invoking the custom known as "senatorial courtesy," prevented his confirmation. But they could not impair the professional standing and reputation which he built up during a half-century at the bar, nor the innumerable friendships which he formed in various parts of the country and in all circles in which he moved. He died suddenly, in September 1905, in his office in New York City.

[The best appreciation of Peckham is Edward Patterson's "Memorial of Wheeler H. Peckham," in *Asso. of the Bar of the City of N. Y.*, 1907. See also: *Proc. of the Twenty-Ninth Ann. Meeting of the N. Y. State Bar Asso.*, 1906; S. F. Peckham, *Peckham Geneal.* (1922); *Who's Who in America*, 1903–05; *N. Y. Tribune*, Jan. 23, 24, 25, and Feb. 17, 1894; *N. Y. Times*, Sept. 28, 1905.]   C. S. L.

PEDDER, JAMES (July 29, 1775–Aug. 27, 1859), agriculturist, editor, and author, was born in Newport, Isle of Wight, England. He was the youngest of a family of ten children. Little is known of his childhood or of his formal education, but that he was well trained seems certain from his later accomplishments. In the early years of his married life he lived at "Buckberry Farm" on the Isle of Wight. About 1809 he went to London and became an assistant of the celebrated chemist and writer, Dr. Samuel Parks, remaining with him for nearly ten years. During this period he published a little book for children, *The Yellow Shoestrings, or, The Good Effects of Obedience to Parents* (1814), which is said to have gone through seventeen London editions and at least two in the United States. About 1819 Pedder was obliged to give up his position with Dr. Parks on account of his health. He went to the Isle of Jersey where, after his recovery, he took charge of Trinity Manor House near St. Heliers for three years, during the absence of the lord of the manor. During the next two years he was engaged in supervising the erection of the chemical works of Amireux and Le Breton. This position he left to take charge of the vast estate of John Christy, the indigo merchant, who from the extent of his possessions in Brecknockshire, Wales, was familiarly known as "The Prince of Wales." For about seven years Pedder remained in his employ.

Believing that America would furnish better opportunities for his labors, he emigrated to Philadelphia in 1832 and was soon appointed by the Philadelphia Beet Sugar Society to make an investigation of the methods employed by the French in the culture of the sugar beet and the manufacture of beet sugar. After spending six months in France, he laid before the Society his findings, published later in a volume entitled *Report Made to the Beet Sugar Society on the Culture in France of the Beet Root* (1836). Subsequently he was employed for several years by Joseph Lovering, the well-known sugar manufacturer of Philadelphia. From Apr. 15, 1840, to July 1843 he edited the *Farmers' Cabinet,* an agricultural journal of merit and very considerable influence, published in Philadelphia from 1836 to 1848. He was a member of the Philadelphia Society for Promoting Agriculture and was elected librarian on Feb. 2, 1842. About 1844 he became corresponding editor of the *Boston Cultivator,* and in 1848 resident editor, which position he continued to hold until his death.

While he was associated with the *Farmers' Cabinet,* he began the publication in its columns of "Frank; or Dialogues between a Father and Son on the Subjects of Agriculture, Husbandry, and Rural Affairs," intended especially for the children of farmers. This popular series of articles was reprinted in part in other agricultural periodicals of the period, namely, the *American Farmer,* the *Cultivator,* and the *New Genesee Farmer,* was published in book form in 1840, and passed through several editions. A work of a technical character which also enjoyed a considerable popularity for several years was his book entitled *The Farmers' Land Measurer, or Pocket Companion* (1842), reprinted as late as 1890. His last days were spent in comparative retirement, but he continued his editorial work up to a few months before his death, which occurred in his eighty-fifth year, at Roxbury (now part of Boston), Mass. He was buried in Forest Hills Cemetery, Jamaica Plain, by the side of his wife, Eliza, who died July 25, 1854.

[*Boston Cultivator,* Sept. 3, 1859; *Hist. Mag.,* Oct. 1859; *Boston Transcript,* Aug. 30, 1859.]   C. R. B.

PEEK, FRANK WILLIAM (Aug. 20, 1881– July 26, 1933), electrical engineer, the son of Frank William and May (Stedman) Peek, was born in Mokelumne Hill, Calaveras County, Cal. He prepared for college in his native town and was graduated in 1905 from Leland Stanford University with the A.B. degree. During his vacations he acquired practical experience with the Standard Electric Company of California and the California Gas & Electric Company. For a

year following his graduation he was employed as test man at the Schenectady, N. Y., plant of the General Electric Company and then he assumed direction of a special test in engineering research, joining the power and mining engineering department of the company in 1907. It was in this capacity that he began the research which first drew attention to him as an investigator of high voltage phenomena. In connection with this project he spent the summers of 1907 and 1908 in the mountains of Colorado studying lightning and the protection of electric transmission lines and in 1910 was amongst the first to join the newly formed consulting engineering department of the General Electric Company organized by Charles Proteus Steinmetz [*q.v.*] in Schenectady. During his first two years here he was engaged in studying the problems of electric transmission at 250,000 volts and in the course of this work he established the laws of corona and investigated electric line insulators. At the same time he took graduate work at Union College, receiving the degree of M.E.E. from that institution in 1911. He continued his research in Schenectady until 1916 when he was transferred to the Pittsfield, Mass., works of the company and placed in charge of the general transformer engineering department. He was later made chief engineer, which position he held at the time of his death.

High voltage and power transmission with related developments were subjects of special research for Peek after 1916. He became increasingly active in the investigation of lightning, designing and building several lightning generators one of which was capable of producing a 5,000,000 volt lightning flash. In 1931 he built a machine which produced 10,000,000 volts, the highest voltage ever controlled by man. During his long career in this special field he was a frequent contributor to technical literature, his articles on the laws of corona, high voltage phenomena, transmission lines calculations and allied problems exceeding two hundred in number. He was the author of *Dielectric Phenomena in High Voltage Engineering* (1915), also published in French (1924). For his paper "High Voltage Power Transmission," published in the *Proceedings of the American Society of Civil Engineers,* vol. XLVIII, no. 9, and read in 1922 before the society, he was awarded the Thomas Fitch Rowland prize of that organization. For his paper "Lightning," delivered as an address before The Franklin Institute in 1924, and published in the *Journal* for February 1925, he was awarded the Levy Gold Medal of that society. He was a member of the American Physical Society, the

American Association for the Advancement of Science, and the American Society of Electrical Engineers of which he was also a director, representing the society on the National Research Council for a number of years. Peek married Merle A. Bell of Oswego, N. Y., on Aug. 9, 1913. She survived him at the time of his death when his automobile was struck by a train at Port Daniels, Quebec, Canada.

[*Who's Who in America*, 1930–31; *Stanford University Alumni Directory, 1891–1931* (1932); *Jour. of The Franklin Inst.*, Jan. 1924; *Electrical Engineering*, Sept. 1933; *N. Y. Times*, July 28, 29, 1933.]

C. W. M—n.

PEERS, BENJAMIN ORRS (Apr. 20, 1800– Aug. 20, 1842), educator, was born in Loudoun County, Va., but at the age of three was taken to Kentucky by his father, Valentine Peers, a Revolutionary soldier. First settling in Nicholas County, the Peers family soon removed to Paris, Ky. In 1817 Peers entered Transylvania University, was in 1819 appointed tutor in Latin and Greek there, graduated in 1821, and remained to teach for a year more. Thinking to become a Presbyterian minister he entered the Princeton Theological Seminary but for some unknown reason left at the end of the academic year in 1823. For an equally unknown reason he then withdrew from membership in the Presbyterian church and became an Episcopalian. In 1826 he graduated from the Theological Seminary of the Protestant Episcopal Church in Virginia at Alexandria and that year was ordained a deacon. Attracted by the educational possibilities in connection with religious observances, he established in June 1829 a Mechanics' Institute at Lexington, Ky. In the same year he visited certain eastern states to examine systems of public education and collected data, which he afterward used perhaps too energetically. The result of this survey was his founding in the same city an Eclectic Institute in October 1830, in which he applied Pestalozzi's principles (Lewis, *post*, p. 68). In November 1833 he proposed unsuccessfully that this school be consolidated with Transylvania University.

However, in the next month he became professor of moral philosophy, proctor of Morrison College, and acting-president of the Transylvania University. He entered at once upon an active prosecution of his duties. His published *Inaugural Address Delivered at the Opening of Morrison College* (1833) shows that he looked forward to making of the university something resembling a state normal school. Some of his pronouncements in this speech are surprisingly modern; he held that "the study of no subject, the dead languages, or the more abstruse parts

of mathematics for example, need be pursued *solely* on account of the valuable discipline it affords the mind" and declared that so far as liberal education was concerned "the argument from utility is daily acquiring greater strength" (p. 10). He insisted that it should be the object of a teacher not to impose upon a youth a fixed and arbitrary curriculum but to stimulate his intellect to voluntary effort. The local newspapers, reporting the November ceremonies, paid less attention to this address than to the fact that Morrison College was opened for the first time. He likewise was active in a convention of state teachers called to discuss educational programs. However, he soon came into collision with the trustees of Transylvania University, and their differences focused in a quarrel over the power of appointing members of the faculty, on which he insisted that at least he be consulted. Still acting-president, on Feb. 14, 1834, he was informed that his "services ... are no longer useful" and that he was "removed from said office" (Minutes of the board of trustees). After vainly trying to get the trustees to make open charges against him, he brought suit against them, asserting that his dismissal in an equivocal manner had given rise to doubts regarding his character. In 1837 he was obliged through a legal maneuver to abandon this effort at justification. Meantime he had opened a boys' school in Louisville and had become rector of St. Paul's Episcopal Church there in 1835. He was later called to New York City to be editor of *The Journal of Christian Education* in 1838 and to assume charge of the Sunday-school publications of his denomination. He continued his interest in training the young; one of his favorite projects was that which contemplated bringing up the children of each parish through constant catechetical instruction, family worship, and right example. Failing health forced him to travel to a milder climate in the hope of recovery but, returning from Cuba to Louisville, he died there. His portrait, painted by Peale, now in the Ehrich Galleries in New York, exhibits a sensitive face and slight body. His scheme of Christian education, published in the *Journal of Christian Education* (Nov.–Dec. 1841), was given earnest contemporary attention; it was the outgrowth of an earlier book, *Christian Education* (1836).

[Letters and minutes of the board of trustees of Transylvania Univ. in the lib. of Transylvania Univ.; *Obituary Notice of Rev. Benjamin Orrs Peers* (1842), reprinted from *Jour. of Christian Education*, Oct. 1842; *The Biog. Encyc. of Ky.* (1878); Lewis and R. H. Collins, *Hist. of Ky.* (2 vols., 1874); A. F. Lewis, *Hist. of Higher Education in Ky.* (1899); *American Jour. of Education*, Mar. 1866; Robert Peter, *Transylvania Univ.* (1896).]

G. C. K.

PEERSON, CLENG (1783–Dec. 16, 1865), immigrant leader and colonizer, served as the promoter and pathfinder for the first group of nineteenth-century Norwegian immigrants to the United States. He was born on the farm "Hesthammer," in southwestern Norway, Tysvær parish, Stavanger *amt,* the son of Peder Hesthammer, his name originally being Kleng (or Klein) Pedersen Hesthammer. He is said to have traveled as a youth in England, France, and Germany. In 1821 he journeyed to New York in company with Knud Olsen Eide, probably as the agent of a group of Quakers and others in the Stavanger region who were interested in emigration as a way of escape from religious and economic difficulties. He returned to Norway in 1824, made a short visit to his home community, and then hastened back to America to make arrangements in western New York for the purchase of land and the erection of houses for the prospective immigrants. When they arrived at New York on Oct. 9, 1825, on the sloop *Restaurationen,* sometimes called the "Norwegian *Mayflower,*" they were met by Cleng Peerson, and most of them followed him to the Kendall settlement near Rochester. For eight years Peerson remained with this colony, but in 1833 he journeyed westward in search of a new site for settlement. This pedestrian reconnaissance took him into Ohio, Michigan, Indiana, Illinois, and probably Wisconsin. His preference for the Fox River Valley in Illinois determined the location of the first Norwegian settlement in the West. He trudged back to New York and the next year, 1834, led the first contingent of Norwegian pioneers to Illinois. The Fox River colony became a center from which radiated many other immigrant settlements in the West.

Ever restless and ever attracted by new frontiers, he founded a Norwegian colony in Shelby County, Missouri, in 1837. Three years later he resided in the first Norwegian settlement in Iowa at Sugar Creek, Lee County, where the federal census of 1840 recorded him as "Klank Pierson." In 1842 he went once more to Norway, where an influential newspaper berated him as an infectious agent in the spread of "America fever." A contemporary account pictures him sitting in a Norwegian tavern on a spring evening in 1843, clad in a long coat, wearing a fur cap, and expatiating in broken "English-Norwegian" on the glories of America to a group of eager listeners (*Bergens Stiftstidende,* Apr. 27, 1843). Later in the year he returned to the United States and guided an immigrant party to the West. In 1847 he joined the Bishop Hill colony in Henry County, Ill., and, his first wife, Catherine, having died

in Norway some years before, he married a young woman called Charlotte Marie, beionging to this Swedish communistic settlement. He soon left, however, both the colony and his wife to rejoin the Fox River settlement. A long-standing interest in Texas prompted him to visit that state in 1849. On his return to Illinois he urged Norwegians to turn toward the Southwest, where they could spread out "so as to have greater freedom in their sphere of action" (*Democraten,* Sept. 7, 1850). Under his guidance a group of Norwegians left Illinois in the fall of 1850 for Dallas County, Texas. In 1854 he removed to Bosque County, and there, in the heart of a Norwegian community, he died on Dec. 16, 1865.

Peerson was a droll and entertaining story teller whose visits were welcomed in frontier homes. He had been attracted by Quakerism in his earlier years, but as an old man he was a pronounced freethinker. He was eccentric, restless, a lover of adventure, in some respects a Peer Gynt, but he was motivated by a genuine interest in the welfare of his countrymen. His claim to historical significance has long been disputed and he has even been characterized as a mere vagabond, but he led the vanguard of Norwegian settlers to the upper Mississippi Valley, and his influence was deeply marked upon the early immigration from his homeland. When he turned to the Southwest, the bulk of the immigrants arriving from northern Europe ignored his counsels but this circumstance does not affect the significance of his earlier efforts.

[T. C. Blegen, *Norwegian Migration to America, 1825–1860* (1931), and "Cleng Peerson and Norwegian Immigration," in *Miss. Valley Hist. Rev.,* Mar., 1921; R. B. Anderson, *The First Chapter of Norwegian Immigration (1821–1840): Its Causes and Results* (1895), and *Cleng Peerson og Sluppen "Restaurationen"* (1925); G. T. Flom, *A History of Norwegian Immigration to the United States from the Earliest Beginning Down to the Year 1848* (1909); A. R. Brækhus, "Cleng Peersons Norgesbesøk i 1843," in *Nordmandsforbundet,* Apr. 1925; manuscript letter of Thormod Madland to Mauritz Halvarsen, June 28, 1825, in the possession of the Minn. Hist. Soc., St. Paul.]

T. C. B.

PEET, HARVEY PRINDLE (Nov. 19, 1794–Jan. 1, 1873), educator of the deaf, was a descendant of John Peet who emigrated from England to America in 1635. The son of Richard Peet, a minute-man in 1776, and of Johannah (Prindle) Peet, widow of Zachariah Brinsmade, he was born and spent his early years on a farm among the rough and beautiful hills of northwestern Connecticut, in Bethlehem, Litchfield County. Though his first educational opportunities were limited to the country school, he learned rapidly and became a teacher in the district schools at the age of sixteen. Later he taught at the private school of Dr. Azel Backus [q.v.] in Bethlehem and then in that of Dr. Daniel Parker in Sharon, Conn. Saving his scanty means and adding to them by farm work during the summer, he entered Phillips Academy, Andover, Mass., in 1816, and Yale College in 1818, graduating from the latter in 1822 among the first ten in his class. In the fall of that year he was invited by Thomas Hopkins Gallaudet [q.v.] to become a teacher in the American School for the Deaf at Hartford, Conn. Here he spent over eight years, in association with Laurent Clerc [q.v.], Lewis Weld, and other brilliant educators of deaf children. Such was his success and energy that he was soon put in charge of the entire business affairs of the institution and, with his wife, was given the care of all the children outside of school hours.

In 1831 he moved to New York, accepting a call to take charge of the New York Institution for the Instruction of the Deaf and Dumb. Here he labored practically all the rest of his life with the greatest success, building up the school from an enrollment of eighty-five to 439 in his thirty-six years of active management. With great foresight he brought about the advantageous sale of the old school site in the city, arranged the purchase of a beautiful new site on the Hudson River at 162nd Street, and erected a then model establishment to accommodate 500 pupils, which was occupied in 1856. He soon sold a small part of the new site at an advanced price, and thus was able to pay off the whole building debt of the new school within a few years. He studied, at first hand, methods of instructing the deaf followed in European schools as well as in American institutions and was a regular attendant and forceful speaker at educational gatherings for instructors of the deaf wherever they were held. He was a man of great vigor, strong convictions, and deep religious feeling. He felt that his pupils were unfitted for life unless they were equipped as Christian workmen to take their places in the world. He was a strict disciplinarian but took a father's interest in all the children under his care. He was a prolific writer on the subject of the deaf, their condition, legal status, number, and education. His *Course of Instruction for the Deaf and Dumb* (3 vols., 1844–49) was used with much success throughout the country. He also wrote a school history of the United States to be used by deaf children. His literary contributions appeared mainly, however, in the *American Annals of the Deaf and Dumb*, in the management of which he assisted for many years.

Peet was married three times: first to Margaret Maria Lewis, Nov. 27, 1823, who died Sept. 23, 1832, leaving three sons, all of whom became teachers of the deaf; second in 1835, to Sarah Ann Smith, who died Dec. 30, 1864; and third, Jan. 15, 1868, to Mrs. Louisa P. Hotchkiss. During his declining years he became blind, but recovered his sight through a skilful operation. He retired from active charge of the New York Institution in 1867, having built it up from a small and poorly equipped school to the largest and best equipped establishment for deaf children in the United States. He continued to reside on the grounds of the school and to give advice to his son and successor, Isaac Lewis Peet [q.v.], until his death.

["Memoir of Harvey Prindle Peet," *Am. Annals of the Deaf and Dumb*, Apr. 1873; H. W. Syle, "A Summary of the Recorded Researches and Opinions of Harvey Prindle Peet," with bibliog., *Ibid.*, July, Oct. 1873; J. B. Burnet, "Memoir of Harvey Prindle Peet," *Am. Jour. Educ.*, June 1857; *Obit. Record Grads. Yale Coll.*, 1873; *N. Y. Tribune*, Jan. 2, 1873; records in the possession of a grand-daughter, Miss Elizabeth Peet, Gallaudet College, Washington, D. C.]   P. H.

PEET, ISAAC LEWIS (Dec. 4, 1824–Dec. 27, 1898), educator of the deaf, the eldest son of Harvey Prindle Peet [q.v.] and Margaret Maria (Lewis) Peet, was born at the American School for the Deaf, Hartford, Conn. His father was an instructor and business manager of the school, and his mother became the matron in charge of domestic affairs. When he was seven years of age his parents moved to New York, where his father took charge of the New York Institution for the Instruction of the Deaf and Dumb, of which he remained active head until 1867. Isaac Lewis Peet was brought up, therefore, in close contact with deaf children and in the midst of work for their education. He attended private schools in New York City, was graduated with honor from Yale College at the age of twenty-one, and immediately thereafter became a teacher under his father in the New York Institution. Here he served successively as instructor, vice-principal, principal, and principal-emeritus until his death. In 1849 he graduated from Union Theological Seminary, but he was never ordained. He succeeded his father as head of the school in 1867 and was its chief executive until 1892, when he retired. He spent the remainder of his life in a beautiful residence adjoining the New York Institution.

Peet was a member of the Conference of Superintendents and Principals of American Schools for the Deaf and its president in 1896. From 1868 to 1895 he served continuously as a member of the executive committee of the Convention of American Instructors of the Deaf. He was president of the Medico-Legal Society of New York City, and was interested in other

welfare work. He wrote numerous articles on
the instruction of the deaf, mostly published in
the *American Annals of the Deaf* or read before
meetings of members of his profession. Notable
among these essays were "The History of Deaf
Mute Instruction during One Hundred Years,
1776–1876" (*Fifty-eighth Annual Report ... of
the New York Institution for the Instruction of
the Deaf and Dumb ... 1876, 1877*) ; and "The
Psychical Status and Criminal Responsibility of
the Totally Uneducated Deaf and Dumb" (*Journal of Psychological Medicine,* January 1872).
He also published *Monograph on Decimal Frac-
tions* (1866) and *Language Lessons, Designed
to Introduce Young Learners, Deaf Mutes and
Foreigners to a Correct Understanding of the
English Language on the Principle of Object
Teaching* (1875).

Peet was married in 1854 to Mary Toles,
daughter of Alvah and Mercy (Fuller) Toles,
of Chautauqua County, N. Y., a brilliant young
deaf woman who had formerly been his pupil.
To them were born a daughter and three sons.

[E. A. Fay and Warring Wilkinson, "Isaac Lewis
Peet," *American Annals of the Deaf,* Feb. 1899 ; *Obit.
Record Grads. Yale Univ.,* 1899 ; *N. Y. Tribune,* Dec.
29, 1898; information furnished by Peet's daughter,
Miss Elizabeth Peet, a professor at Gallaudet College
for the Deaf, Washington, D. C.; personal recollections of the writer.]   P. H.

PEET, STEPHEN DENISON (Dec. 2, 1831–
May 24, 1914), Congregational clergyman,
archaeologist, was born at Euclid, Ohio, the son
of Stephen and Martha (Denison) Peet. His
father was a distinguished clergyman, a man
of great energy, who established some thirty
churches in the Middle West and was one of the
founders of Beloit College and Chicago Theological Seminary. Stephen Denison Peet was
graduated at Beloit in 1851, studied for two years
in the Yale Divinity School, and completed his
theological course at Andover Theological Seminary in 1854. He was married in that year to
his first wife, Katherine Moseley. In February
1855 he was ordained to the ministry and became
pastor of the Congregational Church, Genesee,
Wis. Before he entered upon his first pastorate,
he had traveled for a year or two as a field missionary, establishing small churches in rural
communities. Until 1866 he ministered to various churches in Wisconsin. In that year, at
Elkhorn, Wis., he married Olive Walworth Cutler, who bore him five daughters and two sons.
Accepting a call to New Oregon, Iowa, he left
Wisconsin for thirteen years, returning in 1879.
At various times he was in charge of Congregational churches in New London, Conn.; Ashtabula, Ohio· Clinton, Wis., and Mendon, Ill.

During his college and seminary days he had
been keenly interested in Egyptian, Babylonian
and Grecian antiquities and in the course of his
travels through the northern Middle West he
developed a similar interest in the archaeology
of that section. He liked to inspect, externally,
the ancient earthworks and mound groups of
Wisconsin and Ohio. He attempted no explorations but, walking over the squares, octagons,
circles, and effigies, he speculated upon their
origin, imagining that he perceived in some
small measure the real purpose of their builders.

Throughout his long career he sought to interpret the mysticism not only of the mound
builders but also of the ancient peoples occupying
a higher cultural plane in Mexico and Central
America. In 1875, with Isaac Smucker and Roe-
liff Brinkerhoff [*q.v.*] he took a leading part in
organizing the Ohio Archaeological Association,
forerunner of the Ohio State Archaeological and
Historical Society, founded in 1885. As a member of the earlier organization he attended in
1877 a meeting of the newly founded American
Anthropological Association, and in April of the
following year began to issue the *American Antiquarian and Oriental Journal,* antedating by ten
years the foundation of the *American Anthropologist.* Notwithstanding limited means, he
maintained this publication for thirty-two years.
To it he contributed many papers on his favorite
themes. His chief works published elsewhere
are "Emblematic Mounds in Wisconsin: the
Forms which They Present" (*Wisconsin State
Historical Society, Report and Collections,* vol.
IX, 1882) ; and *Prehistoric America* (5 vols.,
1890–1905). In the light of modern archaeological science, much that he wrote appears visionary and conjectural; yet in this connection it is
proper to record that later studies with reference to mound-builder symbolism indicate the
correctness of some of Peet's views. His real
contribution to anthropology was that of a pioneer. In 1878 when he began to issue his *American Antiquarian* the Peabody Museum had barely been established at Harvard and no other
institution, with the exception of the Smithsonian, was interested in American Indian studies. Unquestionably, Peet's journal stimulated
research, and while the trail he blazed was faint
and irregular, it nevertheless tended in the right
direction and encouraged others to follow.

During the latter part of his life Peet lived
for some time in Chicago, but in 1908 removed
to Salem, Mass., where in 1914 he died. Publication of his *American Antiquarian* ceased the
following year.

[*Ohio Archaeol. and Hist. Soc. Quart.*, Apr. 1917; G. Van R. Wickham, *The Pioneer Families of Cleveland* (1914), vol. II; *Who's Who in America*, 1903–05; *Wis. Hist. Soc. Colls.*, vol. I–XX, *passim* (see Index, vol. XXI, 1915); *Boston Transcript*, May 26, 1914.]

W. K. M.

PEFFER, WILLIAM ALFRED (Sept. 10, 1831–Oct. 6, 1912), journalist, senator from Kansas, was born in Cumberland County, Pa., the son of Elizabeth (Souder) and John Peffer, a farmer. Both parents were of Dutch descent. Although he had slight educational advantages, by the age of fifteen he himself was a teacher. During the gold rush he went to California but returned to Pennsylvania where, on Dec. 28, 1852, he married Sarah Jane Barber, a teacher. The next year the young couple moved to a farm in Saint Joseph County, Ind., and in 1859 to Morgan County, Mo., but during the Civil War, in 1862, they returned to Warren County, Ill. In August 1862 he enlisted as a private in Company F of the 83rd Illinois Infantry. The next year he was commissioned second lieutenant. Most of his service was spent in detached duty. Using the spare time available he read law, and, soon after he was mustered out of the army at Nashville, Tenn., in June 1865, he was admitted to the Tennessee bar. He practised at Clarksville until the close of 1869. Early the following year he removed to Kansas, took up a claim in Wilson County, and combined with its management the practice of law in Fredonia, the county seat. It was not long until he added a third duty, when he purchased a newspaper plant and became editor of the *Fredonia Journal*. In 1875 he removed to Coffeyville, Montgomery County, and there edited the *Coffeyville Journal*. In 1874 he was elected to the Kansas state Senate and in 1880 was a Republican presidential elector.

In 1881 he became editor of the *Kansas Farmer,* at the same time doing some work for the *Topeka Daily Capital.* He transferred his family to Topeka and made that his home. The *Kansas Farmer* became the most powerful farm journal in the state, with non-partisan political interests though with a general tone friendly to the dominant Republican party. When the agricultural distress became acute in 1888 and 1889, Peffer's voice was insistent for rural organization; when the Farmer's Alliance entered the state, he welcomed it, and the *Farmer* became the official paper for one branch. In 1888 he published *Peffer's Tariff Manual,* a pocket-size volume for popular reading. He labored for farmer solidarity and urged remedial legislation, but toward third party activity he was at first hostile. When the creation of the People's party made the alternative unavoidable, he left the Republican party, but he stood as a conservative in the radical party. In 1890 his reputation as a farm leader, his Republican past, and his conservative position combined to win for him election to the United States Senate against more consistent and more radical third party men. In the Senate he was not in either major party organization and so played no important part in legislation. He introduced numerous bills and was a persistent, somewhat tedious speaker on a wide variety of subjects. His tall, well-rounded figure, his unusually long and wavy beard, which he combed constantly with his fingers as he talked, his heavy, dry, excessively statistical speeches, his absence of humor, and his deadly earnestness made him a conspicuous figure in the Senate, and one which in caricature came to typify Populism. For Populism that was unfortunate, since his position was frequently unorthodox and inconsistent. His confusion of thought on financial problems is obvious in his speeches; and his writings, especially his volume *The Farmer's Side* (1891), are undigested summaries of the arguments of various reforming groups, some of them self-contradictory.

He was out of sympathy with the tendency of Populism to unite with the anti-administration Democrats during Cleveland's second term. In 1896 he was not renominated by his own party. He took advantage of the new issue of imperialism to slip back to his first allegiance and published a book on the Philippines to prove his Republicanism, *Americanism and the Philippines* (1900). After the term in the Senate he undertook to prepare an index of discussions of the United States Congress. In 1902 Congress made provision for the purchase of the work as it should be completed but apparently it was never finished. He was the father of ten children, of whom eight lived to maturity. He died at the home of a daughter at Grenola, Kan.

[Brief manuscript autobiographical sketch, dated 1899, in Lib. of Kan. Hist. Soc.; *Hist. of Montgomery County, Kan.* (1903); *Who's Who in America*, 1912–13; *Kan. State Hist. Soc. Colls.*, vol. XVI (1925); *Topeka State Jour.*, Oct. 7, 1912.]   R. C. M—r.

PEIRCE, BENJAMIN (Apr. 4, 1809–Oct. 6, 1880), mathematician and astronomer, was the third child and second son of Benjamin Peirce (1778–1831), for several years a member of the Massachusetts legislature, librarian of Harvard from 1826 to his death, who prepared the last printed catalogue of the Harvard library (3 vols. in 4, 1830–31) and left a manuscript history of the university to the period of the Revolution, subsequently edited by John Pickering and published in 1833 (A. C. Potter and C. K. Bolton,

The Librarians of Harvard College, 1667–1877,
1897, pp. 38–39). His mother was Lydia Ropes
(Nichols) Peirce, first cousin of her husband
and sister of the Rev. Ichabod Nichols, himself
versed in mathematics. He was born at Salem,
Mass., and was of the purest Puritan stock; on
his father's side he was descended from John
Pers or Peirce, a weaver of Norwich, Norfolk
County, England, who had come to Watertown,
Mass., by 1637, and the latter's son Robert who
emigrated to America probably in 1634. While
in his teens at the Salem Private Grammar
School, through a classmate, Henry I. Bowditch
[*q.v.*], young Peirce was brought into contact
with the latter's father, Nathaniel Bowditch
[*q.v.*]. Peirce's estimate of the importance of
the acquaintance thus begun may be judged from
the dedication of his great work on analytic
mechanics, published more than thirty years
later: "To the cherished and revered memory of
my master in science, Nathaniel Bowditch, the
father of American geometry." Peirce entered
Harvard in 1825 and graduated in 1829; Oliver
Wendell Holmes, James Freeman Clarke, and
Benjamin R. Curtis were classmates. For the
two years immediately after graduation Peirce
was associated with George Bancroft at his noted
Round Hill School, Northampton, Mass. Then
for forty-nine years he was a member of the
faculty at Harvard University, first as a tutor
in mathematics in the college, in full charge of
the mathematical work; for the nine years (1833–
42) as university professor of astronomy and
mathematics; and from 1842 till his death as
Perkins professor of mathematics and astronomy.

Peirce's earliest mathematical work was in the
solution of problems proposed in the *Mathematical Diary* (New York, 1825–32), and in revising
and correcting Bowditch's translation, with commentary, of the first four volumes of Laplace's
Traité de Mécanique Céleste (1829–39). In a
paper of the last number of the *Mathematical
Diary* he proved the important result that there
is no odd perfect number with fewer than four
distinct prime factors. During the next few years
he published a series of textbooks which, while
distinctly inferior to the best current in his time,
were certainly stimulating. The plane and spherical trigonometries of 1835–36 were afterward
elaborated into *An Elementary Treatise on
Plane and Spherical Trigonometry, . . . particularly adapted to explaining the construction
of Bowditch's Navigator and the Nautical Almanac* (1840; 3rd ed., with additions, 1845; other
eds. or reprints, 1852, 1861). He compiled *An
Elementary Treatise on Sound* (1836) based on

J. F. W. Herschel's treatise in a volume (1830)
of *Encyclopaedia Metropolitana,* and the original
bibliography at the beginning was interesting
and valuable. *An Elementary Treatise on Algebra* (1837) and *An Elementary Treatise on Plane
and Solid Geometry* (1837), of both of which
there were many later editions or reprints, were
followed by a more advanced work, *An Elementary Treatise on Curves, Functions, and Forces,*
vol. I (1841, new ed., 1852) *containing analytical
geometry and differential calculus*; vol. II (1846)
*containing calculus of imaginary quantities, re-
sidual calculus, and integral calculus,* noteworthy
for conciseness of style and free use of operative
symbols. The projected third volume of this work
dealing with applications to analytical mechanics
was never published, being doubtless superseded
by his characteristic, very notable, and most extensive work, *A System of Analytic Mechanics*
(1855), suitably expounded for those who had
already achieved a good grounding in the subject. A "masterly" discussion of determinants
and functional determinants (Thomas Muir,
The Theory of Determinants, II, 1911, p. 251),
in chapter ten, and numerous other features,
were at the time new in English treatises. The
general title-page of the work suggests that a
much larger scheme of four volumes was in the
author's mind. Along with his textbooks may
be mentioned the periodical which Peirce started and edited, the *Cambridge Miscellany of
Mathematics, Physics, and Astronomy* (April
1842–January 1843), his colleague, Joseph Lovering [*q.v.*], being associated with him as editor
of three numbers. About half of the material
consisted of problems and solutions, and half of
brief articles.

He took an active part in the foundation of the
Harvard Observatory, the occasion being afforded by the great comet of 1843. The work
which first extended Peirce's reputation was his
remarkably accurate computation of the general perturbations of Uranus and Neptune. "In
his views of the discrepancy between the mean
distance of Neptune as predicted by Leverrier,
and as deduced from observation, he was less
fortunate, although, when due consideration is
given to Leverrier's conclusions, there was much
plausibility in the position taken by Peirce" (Simon Newcomb, in *Proceedings of the Royal Society of Edinburgh,* June 5, 1882, vol. XI, 1882,
p. 740; see also H. H. Turner, *Astronomical
Discovery,* 1904; J. M. Peirce, in Benjamin
Peirce's *Ideality in the Physical Sciences,* 1881,
pp. 200–11; W. G. Adams, *The Scientific Papers
of John Couch Adams,* I, 1896, pp. xxxiii, 57,
64). In 1849 the *American Nautical Almanac*

office was established by a congressional appropriation at Cambridge, where it could have the benefit of the technical knowledge of experts, and "especially of Professor Benjamin Peirce, who was recognized as the leading mathematician of America" (Simon Newcomb, *The Reminiscences of an Astronomer*, 1903, p. 63). Until 1867 he was consulting astronomer for the *Almanac* (after 1860, *Astronomical Almanac for the Use of Navigators*). By this time Europe had joined with America in taking cognizance of his achievements. In 1842 he became a member of the American Philosophical Society, in 1850 an associate of the Royal Astronomical Society, London, in 1858 a fellow of the American Academy of Arts and Sciences, in 1860 an honorary fellow of the University of St. Vladimir at Kiev, Russia, in 1861 a corresponding member of the British Association for the Advancement of Science, in 1867 an honorary fellow of the Royal Society of Edinburgh, and a correspondent in the mathematics class of the Royal Society of Sciences at Göttingen. In 1847 he was one of a committee of five appointed by the American Academy of Arts and Sciences to draw up a "program for the organization of the Smithsonian Institution." He was director of the longitude determinations of the United States Coast Survey 1852–67, and superintendent of this Survey 1867–74, while continuing to serve as professor at Harvard. With reference to his appointment as superintendent, Charles W. Eliot wrote: "Those of us who had long known Professor Peirce heard of this action with amazement. We had never supposed that he had any business faculty whatever, or any liking for administration work. . . . Within a few months it appeared that Benjamin Peirce persuaded Congressmen and Congressional Committees to vote much more money to the Coast Survey than they had ever voted before" (*American Mathematical Monthly*, Jan. 1925, pp. 3–4). Although "the extension of the survey of the coast to a great geodetic system, stretching from ocean to ocean, . . . had been remotely contemplated by his predecessor," it was "first actually commenced by Professor Peirce, thus laying the foundation for a general map of the country entirely independent of detached local surveys" (J. E. Hilgard, *Report of the Superintendent of the U. S. Coast and Geodetic Survey . . . June 1881*, 1883, p. 8). While superintendent, Peirce took personal charge of the American expedition to Sicily to observe the eclipse of the sun in December 1870; and for the transit of Venus in 1874 he is often said to have organized the two American expeditions (but see

Simon Newcomb, *Reminiscences of an Astronomer*, pp. 160–70). Peirce continued as consulting geometer of the Survey from 1874 until his death. It was doubtless in connection with problems such as those of the Survey that he was led to formulate in 1852 and elaborate in 1878 what is widely known as "Peirce's criterion" (William Chauvenet, *A Manual of Spherical and Practical Astronomy*, 1863, II, 558; W. S. Jevons, *The Principles of Science*, 2 ed., 1877; H. M. Wilson, *Topographic, Trigonometric and Geodetic Surveying*, 1912). The object of the criterion was to solve a delicate and practically important problem of probabilities in connection with a series of observations. From the first there were critics of the criterion, and its fundamental fallacy was finally proved in 1920 (R. M. Stewart, in *Popular Astronomy*, Jan. 1920, pp. 2–3; see also J. L. Coolidge, *An Introduction to Mathematical Probability*, 1925, pp. 126–27).

In 1863 Peirce was one of the fifty incorporators of the National Academy of Sciences, one of the nine members of the committee of organization, and chairman of the mathematics and physics class. During the early years of the Academy's existence, Peirce presented a number of papers in a new field which developed into his *Linear Associative Algebra* (1870), of which one hundred "lithographed" copies were prepared through "labors of love" by persons engaged at the Coast Survey; a new edition, with addenda and notes by C. S. Peirce, in the *American Journal of Mathematics*, IV, 1881, was reprinted in 1882. The oft-quoted first sentence of the work is as follows: "Mathematics is the science which draws necessary conclusions." This was the most original and able mathematical contribution which Peirce made; it was "really epoch-making" (J. B. Shaw, *Synopsis of Linear Associative Algebra*, 1907, pp. 52–55, 101–06). He himself held it in high esteem. In the introduction he wrote: "This work has been the pleasantest mathematical effort of my life. In no other have I seemed to myself to have received so full a reward for my mental labor in the novelty and breadth of results." Charles S. Peirce [*q.v.*], who got out the second edition of his father's work, declared, "I had first put my father up to that investigation by persistent hammering upon the desirability of it" (*American Mathematical Monthly*, Dec. 1927, p. 526). A careful restudy of Peirce's monograph by H. E. Hawkes (*American Journal of Mathematics*, Jan. 1902, pp. 87–95; *Transactions of the American Mathematical Society*, July 1902, pp. 312–30) showed that in a very able manner Peirce had long anticipated work of the prominent German mathematicians, Study and Scheffers. This was Peirce's last piece of notably creative work. His other volumes were *Tables of the Moon* (1853), *Tables of the Moon's Parallax* (1856), and the posthumous volume of lectures given at the Lowell and Peabody Institutes, *Ideality in the Physical Sciences* (1881). He was an associate editor of the first volume (1878) of the *American Journal of Mathematics,* founded by the Johns Hopkins University under the direction of J. J. Sylvester [*q.v.*]. About one quarter of the titles of Peirce's publications relate to topics of pure mathematics and three quarters to questions mainly in the fields of astronomy, geodesy, and mechanics. While he read before scientific societies many papers concerning his investigations, the printed reports of them are often mere abstracts. "His mind moved with great rapidity, and it was with difficulty that he brought himself to write out even the briefest record of its excursions" (*Nation,* Oct. 14, 1880, p. 268). The nature of parts of some papers fully printed, may be illustrated by a quotation of the concluding sentences from one of them, a paper of 1851, on Saturn's rings, read before the American Association for the Advancement of Science (of which he was president in 1853): "But in approaching the forbidden limits of human knowledge, it is becoming to tread with caution and circumspection. Man's speculations should be subdued from all rashness and extravagance in the immediate presence of the Creator. And a wise philosophy will beware lest it strengthen the arms of atheism, by venturing too boldly into so remote and obscure a field of speculation as that of the mode of creation which was adopted by the Divine Geometer" (*Astronomical Journal,* II, 1851, p. 19).

Though Peirce was the leading mathematician of America, almost up to the time of his death, he was probably in no wise comparable in scientific ability with many contemporary Europeans. But he was exceptional among American mathematicians, at universities of his time, in that the publications of Europeans were the basis of much of his teaching. In 1848, for example, various works he discussed included certain ones of Cauchy, Poisson, Laplace, Monge, Bessel, Gauss, Neumann, and Hamilton. It is interesting to speculate as to the possible publication harvest of Peirce if throughout his career he could constantly have met his mathematical peers, and if he had always had at hand a capable disciple to put his ideas in a form suitable for publication. Professor Coolidge was probably near the truth in writing, "Much more permanently important papers have been written by

men who had only a fraction of his ability" (personal letter, 1933).

Peirce exerted a great influence on the progress of mathematical science in his own country. He was an ardent and enthusiastic friend, ever ready to encourage young men and to promote their work. He had an especial fondness for seeking out comparatively unknown men whose ability had been overlooked, as Newcomb has well remarked. As a teacher he has been termed "a failure," while he was at the same time "very inspiring and stimulating," and profoundly impressive. There was also a delightful abstraction about this absorbed mathematician which endeared him to his students, by whom he was affectionately known as "Benny." President Abbott Lawrence Lowell wrote in 1924: "I have never admired the intellect of any man as much as that of Benjamin Peirce. I took every course that he gave when I was in College, and whatever I have been able to do intellectually has been due to his teaching more than to anything else" (Archibald, *post,* p. 8). Among his pupils were Benjamin A. Gould, Asaph Hall (at the observatory), Simon Newcomb, G. W. Hill (in the *Nautical Almanac* office), William Watson, Charles W. Eliot, and W. E. Byerly. The fascination and magnetism of his personality were alike potent in the lecture-hall, or in a vast seething mass of people at a Jenny Lind concert, when he averted a panic (E. W. Emerson, *post,* p. 100).

He loved children and children loved him "because he was full of humor, with an abounding love of nonsense" (H. C. Lodge, *Early Memories,* 1913, p. 55). In his younger days he enjoyed participating in private theatricals. "As an actor he was apt to be too violent and impetuous; but he was always interesting. He had, indeed, a gift for dramatic expression which served him well in many incidents, both comical and tragical, of his maturer life" (Eliot in *American Mathematical Monthly,* Jan. 1925, p. 4). He was married, July 23, 1833, to Sarah Hunt Mills, daughter of Elijah Hunt Mills [*q.v.*], and had four sons and a daughter. His eldest son, James Mills Peirce [*q.v.*], was a mathematician and administrator at Harvard for half a century. His next son, Charles S. [*q.v.*], was a noted scientist and philosopher. His youngest son, Herbert Henry Davis (1849–1916), was a diplomat. A passport of 1860 describes Benjamin Peirce as of height 5 feet 7¾ inches, and with high forehead, hazel eyes, straight nose, regular mouth, round chin, brown hair, light complexion, and oval face. He was thick set, and wore a full beard and long hair. Two of his portraits are owned by Harvard University; one was painted by J. A. Ames, and the other by Daniel Huntington.

[Besides references given above, the chief sources of printed information are: H. A. Newton, in *Proc. Am. Acad. Arts and Sciences*, vol. XVI, May 1880–June 1881 (1881), and, in slightly different form, in *Am. Jour. of Science*, Sept. 1881; *Benjamin Peirce, A Memorial Collection*, ed. by Moses King (1881); R. C. Archibald, *Benjamin Peirce, 1809–1880* (1925), with a full list of sources, a complete bibliography of Peirce's writings, and reminiscences by C. W. Eliot, A. L. Lowell, W. E. Byerly, and A. B. Chace; *A Hist. of the First Half-Century of the Nat. Acad. of Sciences 1863–1913* (1913); J. Ginsburg, "A Hitherto Unpublished Letter of Benjamin Peirce," in *Scripta Mathematica*, May 1934; T. J. J. See, in *Popular Astronomy*, Oct. 1895; E. W. Emerson, *The Early Years of the Saturday Club 1855–1870* (1918); Florian Cajori, *The Teaching and Hist. of Mathematics in the U. S.* (1890), pp. 133–147; A. P. Peabody, *Harvard Reminiscences* (1888), pp. 180–86; J. L. Coolidge, *Harvard Alumni Bull.*, Jan. 3, 1924, p. 374, and "Mathematics, 1870–1928," in S. E. Morison, Ed., *The Development of Harvard Univ. . . . 1869–1929* (1930); R. S. Rantoul and Henry Wheatland, in *Essex Inst. Hist. Colls.*, vol. XVIII (1881); F. C. Peirce, *Peirce Genealogy* (1880); *Centennial Celebration of the U. S. Coast and Geodetic Survey, Apr. 5, 6, 1916* (1916); H. C. Lodge, *Early Memories* (1913); *The Harvard Book* (1875), I, 172–73. A considerable quantity of Peirce's manuscripts and correspondence was presented to the Am. Academy of Arts and Sciences in 1913. Many other letters of great value, and many unpublished photographs, are owned by his grandson, Benjamin P. Ellis of Cambridge, Mass.]   R. C. A.

PEIRCE, BENJAMIN OSGOOD (Feb. 11, 1854–Jan. 14, 1914), mathematician and physicist, born in Beverly, Mass., was the only son of Benjamin Osgood and Mehitable Osgood (Seccomb) Peirce and a descendant of John Pers, a weaver of Norwich, Norfolk County, England, who emigrated to New England in 1637. For a time his father was professor of chemistry and natural philosophy in Mercer University at Macon, Ga. After an excellent preliminary training including Latin, Greek, and mathematics, young Peirce entered Harvard and graduated in the class of 1876 with highest honors in physics. During the years 1877–80 he was a Parker Fellow in Germany, and in 1879, after two years in Wiedemann's laboratory in Leipzig, he obtained the Ph.D. degree. During the following year he was at Berlin with Helmholtz, from whom he drew much inspiration. Returning to America he taught for a year at the Boston Latin School and was then made an instructor in mathematics at Harvard. In 1884 he was appointed an assistant professor of mathematics and physics, and in 1888 he became Hollis Professor of Mathematics and Natural Philosophy. The course on the Newtonian potential function and Fourier series which he and Professor W. E. Byerly developed marked a new era in mathematical physics in American universi-

ties. The first edition of his *Elements of the Theory of the Newtonian Potential Function* was published in 1886, but the third edition, appearing in 1902, was more than trebled in size. His thirty-two-page *Short Table of Integrals* was issued as a pamphlet in 1889 and also bound in with the 1889 edition of Byerly's *Elements of the Integral Calculus* but after prodigious labor this was expanded to a book of 144 pages (1910). Again enlarged, it became the most valuable work of its kind for ordinary use.

Besides graduate courses in pure mathematics and mathematical physics, particularly the theory of electricity and magnetism and hydrodynamics, Peirce developed laboratory courses in electricity and magnetism, and threw himself vigorously into the prosecution of research which he kept up with unabated assiduity to the end of his life. The list of his fifty-six papers published during the years 1875–1915 is appended to the *Mathematical and Physical Papers, 1903–13, by Benjamin Osgood Peirce* (Cambridge, 1926). Apart from those on various parts of mathematical physics the experimental papers nearly all called for an unusual amount of mathematical theory. Perhaps the most notable are the researches on the thermal conductivity of stone and its variation of temperature, and his researches on magnetism, subjects of extreme difficulty. He was an editor of the *Physical Review*. Among the 150 leading physicists of the country in 1903 he was rated by his colleagues as nineteenth (*American Men of Science*, 5th ed., 1933, p. 1270). His affiliations with scientific groups were numerous. He was elected a fellow of the American Academy of Arts and Sciences in 1884, of the American Association for the Advancement of Science in 1900, of the National Academy of Sciences in 1906, and of the American Philosophical Society in 1910. He was one of the founders of the American Physical Society and its president just before he died. Harvard conferred on him the degree of D.S. in 1912, at which time President Eliot cited him as a "man of science ignorant only of his own deserts." He was also a member of the American Mathematical Society, of the Circolo Matematico di Palermo, of the Astronomical and Astrophysical Society of America, and of the Société Française de Physique. Absolute self-effacement and devotion to duty were fundamentals of his character. His charm of personality and brilliant intellect drew to him a host of friends among students and colleagues. He was married in Edinburgh, Scotland, July 27, 1882, to Isabella Turnbull Landreth, daughter of the Rev. P. Landreth of Montrose and

Brechin, by whom he had two daughters. He died in Cambridge, Mass.

[Sources include: E. E. Hall, "Biog. Memoir of Benj. Osgood Peirce," *Nat. Acad. Sci. . . . Biog. Memoirs*, vol. VIII (1919); John Trowbridge, "Benj. Osgood Peirce, '76," *Harvard Grads.' Mag.*, Mar. 1914; A. G. Webster, "Benj. Osgood Peirce," *Science*, Feb. 20, 1914, reprinted in the *Nation*, Apr. 23, 1914; J. M. Cattell, ed., *Am. Men of Sci.* (2nd ed., 1910); F. C. Peirce, *Peirce Geneal.* (1880); *Who's Who in America*, 1912–13; *Boston Transcript*, Jan. 14, 1914.]

R. C. A.

PEIRCE, BRADFORD KINNEY (Feb. 3, 1819–Apr. 19, 1889), Methodist Episcopal clergyman, social worker, editor, was born in Royalton, Vt., the son of Rev. Thomas C. Peirce and Sally, daughter of Bradford Kinne [*sic*]. The mother was a native of Preston, Conn. Bradford prepared for college at Wesleyan Academy, Wilbraham, Mass., and graduated from Wesleyan University in 1841. The following year he was admitted on trial to the New England Conference of the Methodist Episcopal Church, was ordained deacon in 1844, and elder in 1846. In the meantime, he had held brief pastorates in eastern Massachusetts. In 1847, however, he assumed editorship of the *Sunday School Teacher* and of the *Sunday School Messenger,* both publications of the Massachusetts Sunday School Union. He also wrote several question books for use in promoting knowledge of the Bible. In 1850 he became agent for the American Sunday School Union. Although he passed on to other fields of activity, he never lost his interest in the religious education of the young and found time to write a few books for children which found a place in the Sunday school libraries of the period.

Turning to politics for a time, he was a member of the Massachusetts Senate in 1855 and 1856, and in the latter year he edited with Charles Hale *Debates and Proceedings in the Convention of the Commonwealth of Massachusetts Held in the Year 1788.* His interest in children led him to propose the establishment of the state industrial school at Lancaster, Mass., and he was appointed by the governor a member of the first board of trustees. Soon afterward he was made superintendent and chaplain, serving in these capacities from 1856 to 1862. After a brief pastorate at Watertown, Mass., he was appointed in 1863 chaplain of the House of Refuge, Randall's Island, N. Y., which position he held until 1872. During this period he wrote a valuable history of the institution, containing source material in the form of original documents, under the title *A Half Century with Juvenile Delinquents* (1869).

In 1872 Peirce succeeded Gilbert Haven [*q.v.*]

as editor of *Zion's Herald,* a semi-official Methodist weekly, published in Boston, and one of the most influential papers of its kind in New England. For sixteen years he ably occupied the editorial chair, avoiding controversy whenever possible, but defending with vigor any good cause needing his support. He also became a preacher of wide repute, in great demand at dedications, conferences, preachers' meetings, and Sunday school assemblies. His home life was a happy one. On Aug. 5, 1841, he married Harriet W. Thompson of Middletown, Conn., and three of their four children survived him. He had a pleasing and attractive presence and was courtly and genial in manner. For fifteen years he was a member of the board of trustees of Boston University and for a time financial agent of the institution; for fourteen years he was a member of the Wellesley College board. He lived at Newton Center, Mass., and was actively interested in its schools and public library. Among his books not already cited, the following are worthy of mention: *The Eminent Dead, or the Triumphs of Faith in the Dying Hour* (1846), often reprinted; *Notes on the Acts of the Apostles* (1848), edited by D. P. Kidder; *Life in the Woods, or the Adventures of Audubon* (copr. 1863); *Trials of an Inventor; Life and Discoveries of Charles Goodyear* (1866); *The Word of God Opened* (1868).

[A. M. Hemenway, *Vt. Hist. Gazetteer,* vol. IV (1882), pp. 727–28; *Alumni Record of Wesleyan Univ.* (1883); *Minutes of the Annual Conferences of the M. E. Church: Spring Conferences of 1890* (n.d.); *Official Minutes . . . New England Conference,* 1890; *Christian Advocate* (N. Y.), Apr. 25, 1889; *Zion's Herald,* Feb. 6, Apr. 24, 1889; *Boston Transcript,* Apr. 20, 1889.]

S. G. A.

PEIRCE, CHARLES SANDERS (Sept. 10, 1839–Apr. 19, 1914), philosopher, logician, scientist, the founder of pragmatism, was born in Cambridge, Mass., the second son of Benjamin Peirce [*q.v.*] and Sarah Hunt (Mills) Peirce, daughter of Elijah Hunt Mills [*q.v.*]. He was a brother of James Mills Peirce [*q.v.*]. His father, the foremost American mathematician of his time, an inspiring and unconventional teacher, and a man of forceful character and wide interests, supervised the boy's education to such an extent that Charles could later say, "he educated me, and if I do anything it will be his work." However, Charles had learned to read and to write without the usual course of instruction. He had had independent recourse to encyclopedias and other works for information on out-of-the-way subjects. He showed an intense interest in puzzles, complicated and mathematical card tricks, chess problems, and code languages, some of which he invented for the amusement of his playmates. At eight he began to study chemistry of his own accord, and at twelve set up his own chemical laboratory, experimenting with Liebig's bottles of quantitative analysis. At thirteen he had read and more or less mastered Whately's *Elements of Logic* (1826). His father trained him in the art of concentration. From time to time they would play rapid games of double dummy together, from ten in the evening until sunrise, the father sharply criticizing every error. In later years this training perhaps helped Charles, though ill and in pain, to write with undiminished power far into the night. His father also encouraged him to develop his power of sensuous discrimination, and later, having put himself under the tutelage of a *sommelier* at his own expense, Charles became a connoisseur of wines. The father's main efforts, however, were directed towards Charles's mathematical education. Rarely was any general principle or theorem disclosed to the son. Instead, the father would present him with problems, tables, or examples, and encouraged him to work out the principles for himself. Charles was also sent to local private schools and then to the Cambridge High School, where he was conspicuous for his declamations. After a term at E. S. Dixwell's school, where he was prepared for college, he entered Harvard in 1855. At college he again had the benefit of his father's instruction. About that time, they also began to have frequent discussions together, in which, pacing up and down the room, they would deal with problems in mathematics beyond even the purview of the elder brother, himself destined to become a mathematician. Charles was graduated from Harvard in 1859, one of the youngest in his class. But his scholastic record was poor. He was seventy-first out of ninety-one for the four years, and in the senior year ranked seventy-ninth. He was apparently too young and of too independent a mind to distinguish himself under the rigid Harvard system of those days.

His father wanted him to be a scientist. Peirce hesitated. Not only was he doubtful whether he should devote himself to a life with so few material benefits, but he was drawn to philosophy as well. At college he had already read Schiller's *Aesthetische Briefe,* and had been led to a study of Kant's *Kritik der Reinen Vernunft* which he knew "almost by heart." In July 1861, however, he joined the United States Coast Survey, with which he remained for thirty years, living wherever his investigations led him. About that time he also spent six months studying the technique of classification with Agassiz. In 1862 he

received an M.A. degree from Harvard and the next year the degree of Sc.B. in chemistry, *summa cum laude,* the first of its kind. But the interest in philosophy persisted. In 1864–65 he lectured at Harvard on the philosophy of science, and as one of a select group which included Ralph Waldo Emerson, George Park Fisher, James Elliott Cabot, and John Fiske he gave the university lectures in philosophy, for 1869–70. The next year he was the university lecturer on logic. Meanwhile, from 1869 to 1872, he worked as an assistant at the Harvard Observatory and, from 1872 to 1875, there made the astronomical observations contained in *Photometric Researches* (1878), the only book of his published in his lifetime. It contains material still of value. In 1871 he was in temporary charge of the Coast Survey and the following year became an assistant there, holding the latter position until 1884. In 1873 he was made assistant computor for the nautical almanac and placed in charge of gravity investigations. Two years later, in 1875, he was sent abroad to make pendulum investigations, and to attend, as the first American delegate, the international geodetic conference. His report there that pendulum experiments were subject to a hitherto undetected inaccuracy aroused great discussion and much opposition. But he returned two years later, after the other delegates had had the opportunity to investigate his results, to receive a vote of approval of the congress. Plantamour and Cellérier have acknowledged their indebtedness to him, and his originality in pendulum work has been signalized by Helmert. In that year (1877) he was elected fellow of the American Academy of Arts and Sciences and a member of the National Academy of Science. He had charge of the weights and measures of the United States Coast and Geodetic Survey in 1884–85; was a member of the assay commission of 1888, sat on the international commission of weights and measures, and from 1884 to 1891 was retained as a special assistant in gravity research. But in 1891, either because his experiments had proved too costly or his operations too leisurely, or because of his dissatisfaction with the conduct of the Survey, he ceased to work for the government, and terminated his active scientific career. It was he who first attempted to use the wave length of a light ray as a standard unit of measure, a procedure which has since played an important rôle in modern metrology. Though inaccuracies have been reported, his scientific work has, for the most part, been lauded by competent men for its precision.

Peirce said that he had been brought up in a

laboratory, but he always called himself a logician. Originally led to a study of logic by his philosophic problems, he soon saw philosophy and other subjects almost entirely from a logical perspective. In 1847 George Boole, the founder of modern logic, published *The Mathematical Analysis of Logic,* to be followed in 1854 by his definitive work, *An Investigation of the Laws of Thought.* These works, destined to revolutionize the entire science of logic and free it from the thrall of the Aristotelian syllogism, were practically unnoticed in America until Peirce, in 1867, in a short but important paper read before the American Academy of Arts and Sciences (*Proceedings,* Mar. 12, 1867, vol. VII, 250–61; *Collected Papers,* vol. III), referred to Boole's work and made a number of vital and permanent improvements in the Boolean system. He proposed at that time to publish an original logical paper every month, but soon gave up the attempt because insufficient interest was shown in his published work. Nevertheless, for almost fifty years, from 1866 until the end of his life, while with the Survey and after he left it, he occupied himself with logic in all its branches. His technical papers of 1867 to 1885 established him as the greatest formal logician of his time, and the most important single force in the period from Boole to Ernst Schröder. These papers are difficult, inaccessible, scattered, and fragmentary, and their value might never have been known if it had not been that Schröder based a large portion of his *Vorlesungen über die Algebra der Logik* (3 vols., in 4, 1890–1905) on them, and called attention to the high character of Peirce's contributions. He radically modified, extended, and transformed the Boolean algebra, making it applicable to propositions, relations, probability, and arithmetic. Practically single-handed, following De Morgan, Peirce laid the foundations of the logic of relations, the instrument for the logical analysis of mathematics. He invented the copula of inclusion, the most important symbol in the logic of classes, two new logical algebras, two new systems of logical graphs, discovered the link between the logic of classes and the logic of propositions, was the first to give the fundamental principle for the logical development of mathematics, and made exceedingly important contributions to probability theory, induction, and the logic of scientific methodology. He completed an elaborate work on logic but could not get it published. It was too specialized for the publishers, who preferred elementary textbooks and perhaps the writings of a man in an academic chair. Many of his more important writings on logic, among which are his detailed papers on his new science of semiotics, he never published, and the final appreciation of his full strength and importance as a logician awaits the assimilation of the posthumous papers.

Benjamin Peirce, in a public address in the late sixties, said that he expected Charles to go beyond him in mathematics. In the early eighties, J. J. Sylvester, the great mathematician of the day, is reported to have said of Charles that he was "a far greater mathematician than his father." However, Charles published only a few papers on pure mathematics. His concern was with the more difficult and fascinating problem of its foundations. In 1867 in his paper, "Upon the Logic of Mathematics" (*Proceedings of the American Academy of Arts and Sciences,* Sept. 10, 1867, vol. VII, 402–12; Collected Papers, vol. III), he clearly anticipated the method for the derivation and definition of number employed in the epochal *Principia Mathematica* (3 vols., 1910–13) of A. N. Whitehead and Bertrand Russell. He edited with important notes and addenda (*Collected Papers,* vol. III) his father's *Linear Associative Algebra* (in *American Journal of Mathematics,* July, Sept. 1881), having originally, in the sixties, interested his father in that work. He showed, among other things, that every associative algebra can be represented by one whose elements are matrices. He also made a number of contributions, over a period of years, to the theory of aggregates and transfinite arithmetic, his work often anticipating or running parallel with the heralded work of Richard Dedekind and Georg Cantor. Many of his unpublished studies in such subjects as analysis situs were subsequently repeated by other and independent investigators. Had all his mathematical papers been published in his lifetime, he would have been a more important factor in the history of mathematics than he is today. His work on the logical and philosophical problems of mathematics remains, however, among the foremost in the field.

Pragmatism, Peirce's creation, had its origin in the discussions, in Cambridge, of a fortnightly "metaphysical club" founded in the seventies. Oliver Wendell Holmes, the jurist, John Fiske, and Francis E. Abbot were members. But more important for the history of pragmatism were Chauncey Wright [*q.v.*], a philosopher of power with whom Peirce had frequent heated but profitable discussions; William James [*q.v.*], Peirce's lifelong friend and benefactor, in whose honor he seems later to have adopted the middle name "Santiago" ("St. James" in Spanish);

and Nicholas St. John Green, a lawyer and follower of Bentham who had a tendency to interpret doctrines in terms of their effect upon social life. It had been Kant's emphasis on formal logic which drove Peirce to take up that subject, the history of which he studied with characteristic thoroughness. His interest in the history of logic, in turn, was largely responsible for his contact with the schoolmen. By 1871 he was converted to Duns Scotus' version of realism, a position which he held throughout his life. In the very paper in which Peirce first expounded his Scotistic realism and criticized the nominalism of Berkeley, he roughly outlined the pragmatic position (*North American Review,* Oct. 1871, pp. 449–72). The first definite statement of Peirce's or the pragmatic principle, as it is alternatively called, was not given, however, until 1878. It is contained in a paper, originally written in French in 1877 while he was on his way to the international geodetic conference, later translated by him into English, and published in the *Popular Science Monthly* in January 1878, under the title "How to Make Our Ideas Clear." It was the second of a series of six articles dealing mainly with problems in logic (Nov. 1877, Jan., Mar., Apr., June, Aug. 1878; *Collected Papers,* vol. V, book II; vol. II, book III, B; vol. VI, book I). Together with the first paper of that series which he translated into French, it was published in the *Revue Philosophique* (Dec. 1878, Jan. 1879). In that article he formulated, as the most important device for making ideas clear, the principle that we are to "Consider what effects, which might conceivably have practical bearings, we conceive the object of our conception to have. Then, our conception of these effects is the whole of our conception of the object" (*Popular Science Monthly,* Jan. 1878, p. 293; *Collected Papers,* vol. V, par. 402). This formula has been ridiculed for its awkward and somewhat bewildering repetition, but Peirce contended that he chose each word deliberately, wishing to emphasize that it was concerned with concepts and not with things and was a principle of method rather than a proposition in metaphysics. As usual, he was to receive no recognition for his work until another man called attention to it much later. In 1898 William James first publicly used the term "pragmatism" and acknowledged Peirce's priority in the creation of the doctrine and the name it bears. Peirce's pragmatism, however, is not the same as James's; it has more in common with the somewhat independently developed idealism of Josiah Royce and the later views of John Dewey. In fact, when James heard Peirce lecture on prag-

matism in 1903 he confessed that he could not understand him. On the other hand, Peirce soon rebelled against the characteristic twists which James and others gave to pragmatism. In 1905 he coined the term "pragmaticism," which was "ugly enough to be safe from kidnappers" (*Monist,* Apr. 1905, p. 166; *Collected Papers,* V, par. 414), to characterize his own views; these included much (such as the idea of an Absolute and a belief in universals) that the other pragmatists were disposed to discard. For his version of the doctrine he had but few supporters, and most of these were not in America.

Peirce did share, though, many of the views characteristic of the pragmatic school, developing them in his own, independent fashion. He was a firm believer in the dependence of logic on ethics, argued as early as 1868 against individualism and egoism, and developed social theories of reality and logic. His most important published philosophical contributions, however, are those that embody his cosmology. They are contained in a series of five articles written for the *Monist* (Jan. 1891–Jan. 1893; *Collected Papers,* vol. VI). There he vigorously opposed the mechanical philosophy, defended the reality of absolute chance and the principle of continuity, attempting to solve the hallowed problem of the relation of mind and body, to explain the origin of law, to account for the impossibility of exactly verifying the laws of nature, and to develop his theory of an evolutionary universe. Dewey, James, and Paul Carus, among others, were quick to recognize their importance. The latter, who was the editor of the *Monist,* engaged Peirce in controversy, providing him with some of the space necessary for the further clarification of his position. Though Peirce's tychism, or theory of absolute chance, received more consideration and favorable attention, it was his synechism, or doctrine of continuity, which he considered his real contribution to philosophy, holding it to be, however, a regulative principle rather than an ultimate absolute metaphysical doctrine. His characteristic metaphysical views do not seem to have been wholeheartedly accepted by any established philosopher during his lifetime, though James, Royce, and Dewey have unmistakably acknowledged his influence.

Peirce was not given the opportunity to teach for more than eight years during his entire life. His longest academic connection was with the Johns Hopkins University where he was a lecturer on logic from 1879 to 1884. Apart from his early Harvard University lectures of 1864, 1869, and 1870, he lectured three times before the Lowell Institute: in 1866 on logic, in 1892 on the history of science, and in 1903 on logic. The only other official or semi-official contact he seems to have had with students was through a lecture on number at Bryn Mawr in 1896, three or four lectures on "detached topics" delivered at Mrs. Ole Bull's in Cambridge in 1898, his seven lectures on pragmatism at Harvard in 1903, and two lectures on scientific method before the philosophy club at Harvard in 1907. Yet he was an inspiring teacher. Too advanced perhaps for the ordinary student, he was a vital formative factor in the lives of the more progressive ones, who remembered him later with affection and reverence. He treated them as intellectual equals and impressed them as having a profound knowledge of his subject. Of his small class in logic at Johns Hopkins, four, one of whom was Christine Ladd-Franklin [q.v.], made lasting contributions to the subject in a book which he edited and to which he contributed (*Studies in Logic. By Members of the Johns Hopkins University*, 1883). His love of precision made it impossible for him to make a popular appeal, and he had no capacity for making himself clear to large numbers. This failing would perhaps have been considerably overcome if he had had the opportunity to come into more contact with students who challenged his statements and demanded explications. There is some justice in James's remark that Peirce's lectures were "flashes of brilliant light relieved against Cimmerian darkness" (*Pragmatism*, 1907, p. 5), though the lectures on pragmatism, which this phrase was supposed to characterize, are lucid when placed against the background of his entire system. He would buttress his ideas with a technical vocabulary, creating odd new terms in his attempt to articulate new ideas, trying to cover vast fields in limited space. He did at times show a sudden gift for clear expression, but he lacked the ability to know where further explanation was necessary.

He was eager to teach, but personal difficulties barred his way. He had described himself when a senior at college as being vain, snobbish, uncivil, reckless, lazy, and ill-tempered. He certainly was not lazy out of college. But he was always somewhat proud of his ancestry and connections, overbearing towards those who stood in his way, indifferent to the consequences of his acts, quick to take affront, highly emotional, easily duped, and with, as he puts it, "a reputation for not finding things." He was irregular in his hours, forgetful of his appointments, and, later, careless of his personal appearance. This dark-bearded man of stocky build and medium height with a short neck and bright dark eyes

could, however, be charming at social gatherings, recite with skill and converse delightfully; he was singularly free from academic jealousy, and he could work twenty hours at a stretch on a subject for which he had for years failed to find a publisher. A "queer being" James called him. Peirce himself felt there was something peculiar in his inheritance and put emphasis on the fact that he was left-handed. He could, however, write with both hands—in fact, he was capable of writing a question with one hand and the answer simultaneously with the other. In his years of early promise his peculiar traits were certainly no serious handicap to an academic career. But not only, as he regretted, had his father neglected to teach him moral self-control, so that he later "suffered unspeakably," but he had domestic difficulties as well. On Oct. 16, 1862, when twenty-three years old, he had married Harriet Melusina Fay, three years his senior, a grand-daughter of Bishop John Henry Hopkins [q.v.]. She joined him in his early scientific work, was respected in Cambridge circles, and afterward distinguished herself as an organizer and writer. He divorced her on Apr. 24, 1883, in Baltimore, alleging she had deserted him in October 1876. Shortly afterward, he writes that he married Juliette Froissy of Nancy, France, with whom he lived for the rest of his life and who survived him. His difficulties with his first wife seem to have been an important factor in his loss of academic standing and the partial estrangement of his friends and relatives.

Having inherited some money, he retired in 1887, when only forty-eight years old, to "the wildest county of the Northern States" near Milford, Pa. There he secured a house and tract of land, and fortressed by his large and select library of scientific and philosophic works, many of which were of considerable value, he devoted himself to his writings on logic and philosophy. At the same time he wrote all the definitions on logic, metaphysics, mathematics, mechanics, astronomy, astrology, weights, measures, and universities for the *Century Dictionary* (6 vols., 1889–91), and a gradually increasing number of book reviews on a wide range of topics for the *Nation*. He records that he wrote about 2,000 words a day. This was done with care and in a clear hand. Having a remarkable capacity for self-criticism, on which he prided himself, he would work over his copy, rewriting it as often as a dozen times, until it was as accurate and as precisely worded as he could make it. More often than not, the final manuscript, which might have involved weeks of work, would not be published, but together with all the preceding drafts and miscellaneous scraps incidental to its writing would be allowed to remain on his tables. Immediately, with the same enthusiasm, he would begin another formulation or start on a new topic, to be subjected to the same treatment. He has characterized himself as having the persistency of a wasp in a bottle.

As a young man he had little control over his money; he always remained extravagant. By his retirement from the Survey, he had cut off his government salary of $3,000, and had to live on what he could glean from his occasional lectures, sales of his books, translations, private tutoring, collaboration on dictionaries, work as a consultant, and from private donations. In his home he built an attic where he could work undisturbed or, by pulling up the ladder, escape from his creditors. Though he had been employed by J. M. Baldwin in 1901 to write most of the articles on logic for the *Dictionary of Philosophy and Psychology* (3 vols. in 4, 1901–05), by 1902 he was in debt and on the verge of poverty, doing his own chores and dissipating his energies in small tasks in order to obtain immediate funds. He then applied to the Carnegie Fund for aid in getting his works published. Nine years before he had planned a twelve-volume work on philosophy, which he had to give up, despite many indorsements from leading persons, for lack of subscribers. Now he proposed to submit thirty-six memoirs, "each complete in itself, forming a unitary system of logic in all its parts." These memoirs were to be submitted one at a time and to be paid for when and as approved. Though his proposed memoirs would have dealt with vital issues, and though his application was accompanied by eulogistic letters from the greatest men of the time, his application was rejected, the official reason being that logic was outside the scope of the fund, not being a "natural science." By 1906 he had ceased to review for the *Nation* and had lost most of his other sources of income; the next year he was practically penniless. Under James a small fund, barely enough to keep Peirce and his wife alive, was secured for him through appeals to old friends and appreciative students. He published for three years—papers on logic, pragmatism, epistemology, and religion which are among the best he ever wrote. By 1909 he was a very ill man of seventy, compelled to take a grain of morphine daily to stave off the pain. With undiminished persistency, forming his letters to judge from the tremulous, painstaking script with great difficulty, he kept on writing— or rather rewriting, for by that time he had finally ceased to be original. Five years later he died

of cancer, a frustrated, isolated man, still working on his logic, without a publisher, with scarcely a disciple, unknown to the public at large.

After his death his manuscripts were bought from his wife by the Harvard philosophy department (for their publication, see bibliography). There are hundreds of them, without dates, with leaves missing, unpaginated and disordered; there are duplicates and fragments, repetitions and restatements. His interests were not restricted to logic, pragmatism, metaphysics, mathematics, geodesy, religion, astronomy, and chemistry. He also wrote on psychology, early English and classical Greek pronunciation, psychical research, criminology, the history of science, ancient history, Egyptology, and Napoleon, prepared a thesaurus and an editor's manual, and did translations from Latin and German. James called Peirce the most original thinker of their generation; Peirce placed himself somewhere near the rank of Leibniz. This much is now certain; he is the most original and versatile of America's philosophers and America's greatest logician.

[For years futile attempts were made to organize Peirce's papers; he had himself said that he could not have put them together. In 1927, however, Charles Hartshorne and Paul Weiss thought they saw a systematic connection between most of them, and prepared a ten-volume selection, now in process of publication as *Collected Papers of Charles Sanders Peirce* (5 vols., 1931–34). The foregoing sketch is based mainly on these papers, autobiographical notes, and letters and reminiscences of his relatives, friends, and pupils. See also R. S. Rantoul, *Essex Institute Hist. Colls.*, XVIII (1881), 161–76; articles in *Jour. of Philosophy, Psychology and Scientific Methods*, Dec. 21, 1916, by Josiah Royce, Fergus Kernan, John Dewey, Christine Ladd-Franklin, Joseph Jastrow, and M. R. Cohen; *Chance, Love and Logic* (1923), ed. by M. R. Cohen, containing some of Peirce's published philosophical papers, an introduction, and an almost complete bibliography; F. C. Russell, "In Memoriam Charles S. Peirce," *Monist*, July 1914; E. W. Davis, "Charles Peirce at Johns Hopkins," *Mid-West Quart.*, Oct. 1914; *Harvard College. Records of the Class of 1859* (1896); F. C. Peirce, *Peirce Genealogy* (1880); obituary in *Boston Evening Transcript*, Apr. 21, 1914.]   P. W.

PEIRCE, CYRUS (Aug. 15, 1790–Apr. 5, 1860), educator, was born in Waltham, Mass., the son of Isaac and Hannah (Mason) Peirce and a descendant of John Pers who was in Watertown in 1637. His father, one of the Waltham minute-men, took part in the engagements at Concord, Lexington, and Bunker Hill. During his early days in the district school, Peirce was a student of exceptional promise. His parents, inspired by his ambition and accomplishments, sent him to the Framingham Academy to prepare for college. Later he was placed with Dr. Stearns, the scholarly pastor of Lincoln, for a term of private instruction. At sixteen he entered Harvard College, graduating with honors in 1810. His winter-term vacations from college were spent as teacher in the district school at West Newton. Immediately after graduation he took charge of a private school at Nantucket. After completing two years he resigned and entered the Harvard Divinity School, from which he graduated in 1815. He was persuaded, however, to return to his former place of teaching in Nantucket. On Apr. 1, 1816, he married one of his students, Harriet, daughter of William and Deborah (Pinkham) Coffin. He resigned in 1818 to enter the ministry and was ordained on May 19, 1819, becoming pastor of the Congregational Church in North Reading, Mass.

As a teacher he had been eminently successful; in the pulpit he preached a strict conformity in matters of belief and personal conduct that made him rather unpopular. While in Reading, he espoused the cause of temperance and attracted favorable attention by his sermons and occasional discourses on the subject. After eight years of faithful service he resigned from his church, May 19, 1827, and withdrew from the ministry, finally convinced that his talents could find more effective expression in the schoolroom. In the summer of 1827 he removed to North Andover, where he conducted a school for four years in partnership with Simeon Putnam. Then, after repeated invitations from former friends and patrons, he returned to Nantucket. While engaged here in the management of his private school, he became interested in the condition of the local public schools. At the request of the school committee, he outlined a system which provided for a properly related series of public schools, including the primary, intermediate, grammar, and high school. In 1837, when the new scheme was ready to be launched, Peirce was prevailed upon to relinquish his private school and accept the position of principal of the Nantucket High School. His success there attracted the attention of Horace Mann, secretary of the Massachusetts state board of education, who visited Nantucket for the purpose of observing the results of his reforms.

When the first state normal school was established at Lexington, Mass., in 1839, the state board unanimously elected Peirce principal. He entered upon his new duties, July 3, 1839. The institution opened with three pupils, but within three years the enrolment had increased to a satisfactory number. Peirce realized that it devolved upon him to prove the value of the normal school and gave himself unsparingly to his pioneer task. From the beginning he strove to make his pupils masters of the subjects taught in the schools, insisting that this was fundamen-

tal to all good teaching. In the "model department," a school composed of children of the neighborhood, his normal pupils engaged in practice teaching under his supervision, thereby testing for themselves the principles in which he had instructed them. As a result of his labors he was obliged to resign, in 1842, to seek recuperation. After spending two years at his former residence in Nantucket, he was persuaded to resume his position. The school, meantime, had been moved to West Newton. Here he remained until April 1849, when ill health again forced him to resign. Fortunately, at this time, he was offered an opportunity to travel: the American Peace Society appointed him delegate to the World's Peace Congress, which convened at Paris, Aug. 22, 1849. Upon his return, in 1850, he became an instructor in an academy conducted by Nathaniel T. Allan, in West Newton. He continued in this position until his death.

[S. J. May, *Memoir of Cyrus Peirce* (1857), reprinted in the *Am. Jour. Educ.*, Dec. 1857; *New-Eng. Hist. and Geneal. Reg.*, Oct. 1860; the *Mass. Teacher*, May 1860; M. S. Lamson, *Records of the First Class of the First State Normal School in America* (1903); A. O. Norton, ed., *The First State Normal School in America: The Jours. of Cyrus Peirce and Mary Swift* (1926); F. C. Peirce, *Peirce Geneal.* (1880); *Vital Records of Waltham, Mass.* (1904); *Boston Transcript*, Apr. 7, 1860.]

R. F. S.

PEIRCE, HENRY AUGUSTUS (Dec. 15, 1808–July 29, 1885), merchant and diplomat, son of Joseph Hardy and Frances Temple (Cordis) Peirce was born in Dorchester, Mass., the eleventh child in a family of thirteen. A descendant of Thomas Peirce who settled at Charlestown in 1634, he numbered among his ancestors Gen. Joseph Warren. After a childhood marked by delicate health, he left school at the age of fourteen to assist in the office of his father, who was clerk of the Boston municipal court. There he learned the rudiments of business, but a desire for travel, nourished by wide reading, grew so strong that in 1824 he shipped before the mast for a voyage to the North-West Coast on the brig *Griffon*, of which his brother was captain. They reached Honolulu after five months, and there Henry was promoted to ship's clerk, in charge of stores and trade goods. For more than three years they cruised between Alaska and Mexico, trading for hides and furs with Indians and Spaniards. Returning to Honolulu in 1828, Henry became a clerk in the employ of James Hunnewell [q.v.], a prosperous merchant, whose confidence he so completely gained that two years later the youth of twenty-two was taken into partnership and left with a capital of $20,000 to manage the local business of bartering New-England goods for sandalwood and furs when the senior member went to Boston. In 1833 Hunnewell withdrew from the firm. During the next two years Peirce opened a triangular trade with China and Siberia, and in 1836 took as partner Charles Brewer [q.v.], whom he left in charge at Honolulu when he set sail for Boston in February of that year. Early in the autumn of 1837 he was again in the Pacific with an armed brig which he finally sold at Valparaiso, whence he crossed the continent to Buenos Aires, traveling mostly on horseback. Sailing thence to Boston, he married Susan, daughter of Joseph Thompson, on July 3, 1838. In the following April he sailed for Hawaii as part-owner and master of a schooner and spent the next two years in trading along the Mexican and Californian coasts. In 1842 he sold a vessel and cargo at Mazatlan in Mexico, went overland to Vera Cruz, and sailed thence to the United States.

Retiring from the firm in 1843 with $100,000, Peirce remained in Boston and engaged extensively in the shipping business. At the height of the gold rush in 1849 he took a vessel to San Francisco, where the crew deserted to a man, but he managed to return by way of Hawaii and Canton, arriving in April 1850. For a number of years he was a prominent merchant and shipowner, as well as Hawaiian consul for New England. On the outbreak of the Civil War he contributed $50,000 to equip Massachusetts volunteers and was active in recruiting, but during the war he lost most of his large merchant fleet through the depredations of Confederate privateers. Relatively poor, he invested in 1866 in a Mississippi cotton plantation, which failed badly as a result of floods and bad weather. By selling his Beacon Street mansion he paid all his debts and lived in retirement until appointed in 1869 as minister to the Hawaiian Kingdom. He was responsible for calling in American marines when riots occurred on the election of King Kalakaua in February 1874, and accompanied the latter during the following winter to the United States on a visit which facilitated the conclusion of the reciprocity treaty of 1876. On resigning from his post in October 1877, he was given the order of Grand Commander of Kamehameha in recognition of his services to Hawaii. Illness brought him back to Honolulu in a few months, and on Mar. 1, 1878, he was appointed Hawaiian minister for foreign affairs, a portfolio he held until July, when a quarrel between king and legislature forced his resignation. After a brief visit to Boston he settled in San Francisco, where he died. Enterprising and honorable in business, he lost a considerable fortune through speculation and war. As merchant and diplomat, he believed in American expansion not only to California but also to Hawaii and did all in his power to aid it.

[See: *Biog. of Henry Augustus Peirce* (1880), prepared from a manuscript autobiography; Josephine Sullivan, *A Hist. of C. Brewer and Company, Ltd.* (1926); E. W. West, *The Peirce Family Record* (1894); the *Morning Call* (San Francisco), July 31, 1885. Many of Peirce's dispatches as minister are printed in *House Executive Document 1*, 53 Cong., 3 Sess., pt. 1, App. II.]   W. L. W., Jr.

PEIRCE, JAMES MILLS (May 1, 1834–Mar. 21, 1906), educator and mathematician, born at Cambridge, Mass., was the eldest son of Benjamin Peirce [q.v.] and Sarah Hunt (Mills) Peirce, brother of Charles S. Peirce [q.v.], and grandson of Harvard's librarian and historian Benjamin Peirce. He received the degree of B.A. from Harvard in 1853. After a year in the law school, he was a tutor in mathematics in Harvard College, 1854–58. In 1857, while still a tutor, he entered the Divinity School where he graduated in 1859. During the next two years he preached in Unitarian churches in New Bedford, Mass., and in Charleston, S. C., but he then gave up the ministry and returned as an assistant professor of mathematics to Harvard where he remained in the service of the university until his death. In 1869 he became university professor of mathematics and in 1885 the Perkins Professor of Mathematics and Astronomy. He served as secretary of the Academic Council from its establishment in 1872 until 1889, as dean of the graduate school from its foundation in 1890 until 1895, and as dean of the faculty of arts and sciences from 1895 until 1898. He was one of the pioneers in introducing and expanding the elective system in the College, and during the long administration of his classmate President Eliot he worked shoulder to shoulder with him in fostering graduate study in the university.

In mathematics his chief fields of interest were quaternions, linear associative algebra, and higher plane curves, and for many years he gave popular courses in these subjects. His lectures were exceptionally polished and clear. He was deeply interested in his students, "patient and helpful, . . . understanding and sympathizing with their tastes, their aspirations, and their struggles, as if he were still one of them." His slight published output included: *A Text Book of Analytic Geometry on the Basis of Professor Peirce's Treatise* (Cambridge, 1857), on which Charles William Eliot was an active collaborator; *Introduction to Analytic Geometry* (Cambridge, 1869); *Three and Four Place Tables of Logarithmic and Trigonometric Functions* (Boston, 1871); an article on "Quaternions," in *Johnson's New Universal Cyclopædia* (New

York, vol. III, 1877) ; a memoir in the *Transactions of the American Mathematical Society* (October 1904) ; articles in the *Monthly Religious Magazine* (1856), *Harvard University Library Bulletin* (1878–79), *Harvard Register* (1881), and various reports to the President as an administrative officer. He edited with notes his father's Lowell Lectures under the title : *Ideality in the Physical Sciences* (Boston, 1881). He was a fellow of the American Academy of Arts and Sciences.

His interests and gifts were varied. Widely read in literature, he was in particular a lifelong student of the plays of Shakespeare and an enthusiastic admirer of the work of Shelley. He was fond of travel, a lover of the best in art, and a devotee of music ; but the stage and whist were his passions. He saw most of the best actors and plays for half a century, and he himself was no ordinary dramatic reader. He was never married. His colleague and intimate friend, Professor Byerly, has made the following characterization : "Careful in dress, dignified in bearing, scrupulously polite to everyone, courteous and kindly, he will be remembered ... for his friendly greeting, his earnest speech, at once measured and impetuous, his quick indignation at any suggestion of injustice, and his scorn of everything narrow or crooked or mean. . . . His ready interest in everything human, and his keen enjoyment of life made him the most charming of companions." As in the case of his father he died in the seventy-second year of his life and in the fiftieth of his service to the university.

[The chief sources of information concerning Professor Peirce are the following : J. K. Whittemore, *Science*, July 13, 1906 ; *Report of the Harvard Class of 1853, 1849–1913* (1913) ; W. E. Byerly and T. S. Perry, *Harvard Grads.' Mag.*, June 1906, excellent portrait ; A. S. Hill, *Colonial Soc. of Mass. Pubs.*, vol. X (1907) ; W. E. Byerly, *Proc. Am. Acad. Arts and Sci.*, vol. LIX (1925) ; C. S. Peirce, *Am. Math. Monthly*, Dec. 1927.]

R. C. A.

PEIRCE, WILLIAM (*c.* 1590–1641), shipmaster and compiler of the first almanac in English America, was probably born in England about the year 1590. His name first appears in the colonial records in 1623, his ship, the *Paragon*, having been wrecked in February of that year. In the summer of 1623 he was given command of the *Anne*. Bradford mentions his coming to Plymouth in 1625 in company with Edward Winslow on one of the latter's return trips to America. During the next four years Peirce made constant trips between New England, Virginia, and England conveying emigrants and earning the reputation of having made the largest number of such voyages of his day. He was "for a long period the most noted sail-master

that came into the New England waters" (Roden, *post*, p. 16). In May 1629 he took over the command of the *Mayflower*, described as "of Yarmouth," which was possibly the *Mayflower* of earlier fame.

Peirce was in Virginia at Christmas 1632 on which date he wrote to Boston describing conditions in the southern colony (Bradford, *post*, p. 365). It appears that a short time before that date he was shipwrecked near Feake Isle off the Virginia shore, where presumably he lost the ship *Lyon*. Early in 1633 we find him in command of the *Desire*. During 1634 he explored the island of Nantucket and the shores of Narragansett Bay. On Sept. 3, 1635, he was chosen by the General Court commissioner of military affairs of Massachusetts Bay Colony but served only six months, when he was replaced by Henry Vane. In May 1637 he was chosen, with others, to start a fishery at Cape Ann and the same year was granted two hundred acres of land. At the close of the Pequot War he was sent to the West Indies with a group of Indians, who were sold as slaves. He returned with "cotton, tobacco, and negroes." These were probably the first negroes brought to New England. In 1641 he set out from New England with a party of colonists for Providence in the Caribbean. He found the colony in the possession of the Spanish, who fired upon the ship. Peirce was struck by a bullet and died shortly afterward.

Peirce compiled the first almanac in English America, *An Almanac for the year of our Lord, 1639. Calculated for New England, By Mr. William Pierce, Mariner*. It was a small broadside, printed at Cambridge by Stephen Day. Winthrop describes Peirce as "a godly man and most expert mariner." He also gives a graphic account of his death. By his wife, Jane, Peirce had three children.

[Sources include : *Winthrop's Jour.* (2 vols., 1908), ed. by J. K. Hosmer ; *Bradford's Hist. "Of Plimoth Plantation"* (Boston, 1899), printed by order of the General Court of Mass. ; R. F. Roden, *The Cambridge Press, 1638–92* (1905) ; Chas. Evans, *Am. Bibliog.*, vol. I (1903) ; *Records of the Gov. and Company of the Mass. Bay*, vol. I (1853) ; E. E. Hale, Jr., ed., "Note-Book Kept by Thos. Lechford, Esq., Lawyer in Boston . . . June 27, 1638, to July 29, 1641," *Trans. and Colls. of the Am. Antiquarian Soc.*, vol. VII (1885) ; A. P. Newton, *The Colonizing Activities of the English Puritans* (1914) ; F. C. Pierce, *Pierce Geneal. No. IV* (1889). The date of Peirce's death is uncertain. Winthrop records the event under date of June 21, 1641.]

E. L. W. H.

PEIXOTTO, BENJAMIN FRANKLIN (Nov. 13, 1834–Sept. 18, 1890), diplomat, publicist, journalist, lawyer, was born in New York City, a son of Daniel L. M. Peixotto and Rachel Seixas. His father was a physician, for some time president of the New York Medical Society.

After the death of his father, the thirteen-year-old boy went to Cleveland, Ohio, where the elder Peixotto had at one time served as president of Willoughby Medical College. He eventually became one of the editors of the *Cleveland Plain Dealer,* and a strong supporter of Stephen A. Douglas. At an early age he became deeply interested in the Independent Order B'nai B'rith, a national Jewish fraternal organization. He was elected grand master of the order in 1863, serving till 1866, and was active in founding the Cleveland Orphan Home connected with it. During the Civil War he served for a time with the de Villiers Zouaves in an Ohio infantry regiment. In 1867 he moved to San Francisco. He was gaining recognition there as a lawyer, when in June 1870 he was appointed by President Grant United States consul to Bucharest. The appointment was made in the hope that the alarming persecutions of the Jews in Rumania might be abated. Thus Peixotto's rôle was described in a personal letter handed to him by President Grant just before his departure for his post, which concluded with the words: "Mr. Peixotto has undertaken the duties of his present office more as a missionary work for the benefit of the people he represents, than for any benefit to accrue to himself. . . . The United States, knowing no distinction of her own citizens on account of religion or nativity, naturally believes in a civilization the world over which will secure the same universal laws." (See Kohler and Wolf, *post,* p. 13.)

Both through official channels and in a German newspaper which he founded at Bucharest, Peixotto denounced Rumanian anti-Semitism and aroused public opinion against Rumanian persecution of the Jews. He induced the Rumanian Jews to undertake the important innovation of organizing modern schools for instruction in the Rumanian language and in other modern, as well as Jewish, subjects. During the six years of his consulship, the anti-Semitic movement there was greatly weakened. Largely as a result of his efforts, followed up by denouncements of Rumanian atrocities in Congress and in the parliaments of Great Britain, France, Germany, and Austria-Hungary, important religious minority protective clauses were inserted in the Treaty of Berlin of 1878. Returning to the United States in 1876, Peixotto took an active part in the presidential campaign of that year. In 1877 he was appointed United States consul to Lyons, France, where he rendered valuable service to American commerce. After his return to the United States, he founded in 1886 *The Menorah, A Monthly Magazine,* an important Jewish periodical, which he edited up to the time of his death. It was the only English Jewish monthly in existence for many years. Peixotto was married, in 1858, to Hannah Strauss of Louisville, Ky.

[Sources include: *Jewish Encyc.*; M. J. Kohler and Simon Wolf, *Jewish Disabilities in the Balkan States: Am. Contributions toward Their Removal* (1916); Isaac Markens, *The Hebrews in America* (1888); M. J. Kohler, "Educ. Reforms in Europe in Their Relation to Jewish Emancipation," *Am. Jewish Hist. Soc. Pubs.,* vol. XXVIII (1922); Luigi Luzzatti, *God in Freedom* (1930); I. S. Isaacs, "Benj. F. Peixotto," in A. C. Rogers, *Our Representatives Abroad* (2nd ed., 1876); Adolf Stern, *Denkrede über Benj. F. Peixotto* (Bucharest, 1891). Peixotto's story of the Rumanian mission begins in the first volume of *The Menorah* and ends abruptly in May 1888. Obituaries of him appear in *The Menorah,* Oct. 1890, and in the *N. Y. Tribune,* Sept. 19, 1890. Information as to certain facts was supplied for this sketch by Peixotto's son, George Peixotto.]

                             M. J. K.

PELHAM, HENRY (Feb. 14, 1748/49–1806), painter, engraver, cartographer, was born at Boston where his father, Peter Pelham [*q.v.*], limner, engraver, and schoolmaster, had married Mary (Singleton) Copley, widow of Richard Copley and mother of John Singleton Copley [*q.v.*]. His father died in 1751, and Henry witnessed in childhood the efforts of his mother at her little tobacco shop to keep the family together until her gifted son Copley brought prosperity to them all through his portrait painting. The home was in Lindall Street, where Exchange Place and Congress Street now meet. Thence Henry attended the Boston Latin School. Drawing and painting he is assumed to have studied with his half-brother. It was a likeness of Henry Pelham, then aged ten or eleven, which with the title "The Boy with the Squirrel" was exhibited at London in 1766 and brought Copley his first fame abroad.

Henry Pelham's many letters reveal a naïve, boyish young man, devoted to his mother and half-brother, an efficient assistant to the latter in practical affairs. He himself painted miniatures at this time, several of which are preserved. They reveal admirable workmanship. A much more violent Loyalist than Copley, he expressed himself vigorously against his neighbors whom he held misguided and rebellious. In the winter of 1775, while making a journey on horseback to Philadelphia, he was mobbed at Springfield, Mass., as one of "a damn'd pack of Torys." His sketch of the redoubts on Bunker Hill is reproduced with the Copley-Pelham letters (*post,* p. 327). His "Plan of Boston" was engraved in aquatint at London in 1777. No historian of the American Revolution can ignore his illuminating letters.

With other Loyalists Pelham left Boston in

August 1776. Arrived at London, where the Copleys were settled, he supported himself by teaching drawing, perspective, geography, and astronomy. In 1777 he contributed to the Royal Academy "The Finding of Moses," which was engraved by W. Ward in 1787 (*Bryan's Dictionary of Painters and Engravers*, IV, 1904, p. 87). In the following year he exhibited some enamels and miniatures. Having married Catherine Butler, daughter of William Butler of Castle Crine, County Clare, Ireland, Pelham went to Ireland. His wife, however, died while bearing twin sons, Peter and William, and the father returned with them to London. He and Copley shared in the estate of their mother, who died at Boston Apr. 29, 1789. Soon after this Pelham was named agent for Lord Lansdowne's Irish estates, a work which he followed with energy and ability. He was a civil engineer and cartographer, and his county and baronial maps are important documents of Irish history. He was drowned from a boat while superintending the erection of a martello tower in the River Kenmare.

[For the best account of Pelham see D. R. Slade, "Henry Pelham, the Half-Brother of John Singleton Copley," *Colonial Soc. of Mass. Pubs.*, vol. V (1902). Pelham's letters make up a large part of "Letters & Papers of John Singleton Copley and Henry Pelham," pub. in *Mass. Hist. Soc. Colls.*, vol. LXXI (1914). A letter descriptive of Pelham's life in Ireland, written by John Singleton, is in Martha Babcock Amory's *The Domestic and Artistic Life of John Singleton Copley* (1882).]

F. W. C.

PELHAM, JOHN (Sept. 14, 1838–Mar. 17, 1863), called the "boy major," was one of the bravest and most capable young officers in Lee's army. Largely because of the glamorous descriptions of him in John Esten Cooke's *Surry of Eagle's Nest* (1894), he became to many Southerners almost as romantic a hero as Rob Roy or Ivanhoe. His family was of good English stock. Peter Pelham [*q.v.*], was the first to emigrate to America, his descendants living successively in Boston, Virginia, Kentucky, and, after 1836, in Alabama. John's great-grandfather, Peter, son of the immigrant, was for nearly fifty years organist of Bruton Church in Williamsburg, Va., and his grandfather, Charles, was a major in the Continental Army. His parents were Atkinson Pelham, a large planter and a country doctor, and Martha McGehee, a native of Person County, N. C. Dr. Pelham was opposed to secession but loyally supported the Southern cause, all six of his sons joining the Confederate army.

John Pelham was born on his grandfather's plantation in Benton (later Calhoun) County,

Ala. He entered West Point in July 1856, and resigned Apr. 22, 1861, in order to enter the Confederate army. He was commissioned lieutenant and sent to Virginia. In November Gen. J. E. B. Stuart [*q.v.*] recommended that he organize and be made captain of a battery of horse artillery. This battery formed the nucleus of the famous Stuart Horse Artillery. Under the command of Pelham it soon acquired the ideal qualities of this military branch: quickness and unexpectedness of movement and accuracy of execution. The slender, boyish-looking, modest captain displayed remarkable courage and enterprise at every point, and in posting and firing artillery he showed real genius. Soon he was almost idolized by his men, the fame of the Stuart Horse Artillery attracting to its ranks not only volunteers from his home state, including French creoles from Mobile, but also Virginians, Marylanders, and even foreign adventurers.

In the Seven Days' battles from June 25 to July 1, 1862, he displayed exceptional ability. Though reluctant to lose him, Stuart recommended his promotion with the words, "In either cavalry or artillery no field grade is too high for his merit and capacity" (*War of the Rebellion: Official Records, Army*, 1 ser., XI, part II, 552). On Aug. 16, 1862, he was appointed major. At the second battle of Manassas he rushed up with his horse artillery to protect Jackson's rear from a surprise attack, and at Antietam, while in command of several batteries, he held a point essential to the Confederate position. He continued his brilliant achievements in Stuart's Loudoun County raid, in the fall of 1862, and exercised his unusual ability to keep up with the cavalry in the successful assault on the gunboats at Port Royal and at Fredericksburg. After he had held his position there for about two hours against overwhelming odds, Stuart is said to have sent him the following message: "Get back from destruction, you infernal, gallant fool, John Pelham" (Mercer, *post*, p. 138). Lee recommended him for a promotion to the rank of lieutenant-colonel of horse artillery, but he was mortally wounded at Kelly's Ford, Va., Mar. 17, 1863. He had not only great military ability but a lovable and winning personality as well, and there was wide-spread grief in the South at his death. Stuart named his daughter, born not long afterwards, Virginia Pelham.

[Philip Mercer, *The Life of the Gallant Pelham* (copr. 1929); Heros von Borcke, *Memoirs of the Confederate War for Independence* (2 vols., 1866); H. B. McClellan, *The Life and Campaigns of Major-General J. E. B. Stuart* (1885); John W. Thomason, *Jeb Stuart* (1930); *Daily Richmond Examiner*, Mar. 19, 1863.]

R. D. M.

PELHAM, PETER (*c.* 1695–December 1751), limner and engraver, was born in England, a son of Peter Pelham, named "gentleman" in his will. Many reference books give the artist's birth year as 1684, but passages in the Copley-Pelham letters (*post,* especially p. 8), make it certain that Peter Pelham, Sr., was born later than 1671. *The Registers of St. Paul's Church, Covent Garden, London* (vol. I, 1906) show that Peter Pelham, Jr., and his wife Martha had children beginning with the christening of George Pelham, Jan. 20, 1720. It is fairly inferred from these dates that the future artist was born about 1695, when his father would have been in his early twenties. His portrait, painted by his stepson, Copley, presumably from life or from records of his appearance about 1750, is not that of a man of sixty-six years. (See Charles Pelham Curtis, *Loan Exhibition of One Hundred Colonial Portraits,* 1930.) The senior Pelham is revealed in letters to his son in America as a man of some property. He died at Chichester, Sussex, in 1756. He may have been a kinsman of the distinguished Pelhams of Sussex described in Mark Antony Lower's *Historical and Genealogical Notices of the Pelham Family* (1873), but the relationship has not been proved.

The younger Pelham was one of several artists of London who learned the then new technique of the mezzotint engraving. Of his use of the medium one writer has said: "Pelham handled the rocker heavily, and so gave to his prints a darker appearance than usual" (Alfred Whitman, *The Masters of Mezzotint,* 1898, p. 26). He obviously was well trained as a portrait painter, and he must have had influential connections, for between 1720 and 1726 he produced portrait plates of Queen Anne, George I, the Earl of Derby, Lord Wilmington, Lord Carteret, Lord Molesworth, Dr. Gibson, the Bishop of London, and others. Why, amidst such engagements, Pelham should have emigrated is mysterious, if, as seems not to have been doubted, the impecunious schoolmaster, limner and engraver of Boston, Mass., is identical with the well-employed mezzotinter of London. It is possible that he left in disgrace. (See letter of Peter Pelham, Sr., Sept. 12, 1739, in Copley-Pelham letters.) His portrait of Gov. Samuel Shute, of Massachusetts, painted at London, 1724, was brought, according to plausible family tradition, to Boston to serve as introduction to local celebrities.

Though the actual date of his emigration has been given variously, the record of Peter Pelham's activities at Boston is well established. His portrait of the Rev. Cotton Mather, now at the American Antiquarian Society, Worcester, was painted as copy for the very familiar mezzotint engraving, reproduced frequently. "Proposals" for printing this engraving were published in the *Boston News-Letter,* Feb. 27, 1728. Portraits of several other New England clergymen followed. Pelham was seemingly intimate with John Smibert, the Scottish painter, who settled in Boston in 1730, for he painted Smibert's portrait and made several engravings after Smibert's works. Such professional labors did not produce a sufficient living for an ever-growing family, and Pelham opened a school at which he taught dancing, arithmetic, and other subjects. His first wife dying in Boston, he married on Oct. 15, 1734, Margaret Lowrey, and after her death he married, May 22, 1748, Mary (Singleton) Copley, widow of Richard Copley, tobacconist, late of Limerick, Ireland. Their home, school, studio, and tobacco shop were on Lindall Street (*A Report of the Record Commissioners of the City of Boston,* XV, 1886, p. 367). In this household were reared the future artists, John Singleton Copley and Henry Pelham [*qq.v.*]. Peter Pelham died intestate.

[In the "Letters & Papers of John Singleton Copley and Henry Pelham," pub. in *Mass. Hist. Soc. Colls.,* vol. LXXI (1914), there are nine quite important letters addressed to Peter Pelham in answer to unpreserved letters of his. Pelham's first accurate and painstaking biographer, who, however, did not know of the existence of the correspondence just mentioned, was Wm. H. Whitmore, whose *Notes concerning Peter Pelham, the Earliest Artist Resident in New England* (1867), contains a few inaccuracies, as in its title. Indexes of *Notes and Queries* during the sixties disclose the persistence with which Whitmore sought British aid in his Pelham quest. George Francis Dow's *The Arts & Crafts in New England, 1704–75* (1927) reproduces advertisements inserted by Pelham in Boston newspapers, some of which had not previously been noted. The accounts of Pelham in English works on painters and engravers, from Walpole and Strutt to date, are generally incomplete and inaccurate. For the administration of his estate see the Suffolk County Probate Records, No. 10085.]   F. W. C.

PELLEW, HENRY EDWARD (Apr. 26, 1828–Feb. 4, 1923), philanthropist, was born at Canterbury, England, the son of George Pellew, canon in Canterbury Cathedral and later dean of Norwich, and of Frances (Addington) Pellew, the daughter of Henry Addington, first Viscount Sidmouth. He was educated at Eton and at Trinity College, Cambridge, where he took his B.A. degree in 1850. At Cambridge he was stroke and captain of his college crew and in his last year was stroke and captain of the varsity crew. In 1854 he was commissioned by Baring's, the London bankers, to visit their agencies in the Americas preparatory to accepting a position in New York. Although the post never materialized, he spent two years in travel over a large part of the United States as well as Central and South America. In 1858 he returned to the United States and on Oct. 5 was married at Bedford, N. Y., to Eliza, a daughter of William Jay [*q.v.*]. Returning to England he took up his residence in London, where he was magistrate (J. P.), member of the school board, on the governing boards of such institutions as Hanwell lunatic asylum, Bridewell, Westminster, and other hospitals, and of the Feltenham industrial school. He became secretary of the Keble memorial fund and was instrumental in raising a large amount for the establishment of Keble College, Oxford. During this period three of his children were born, two of whom predeceased him but one of whom became seventh Viscount Exmouth. On Dec. 22, 1869, his wife died and four years later on May 14, 1873, he was married to Augusta Jay, her sister, at the American legation in Vienna, Austria, where her brother John Jay, 1817–1894 [*q.v.*], was at the time United States minister. The issue of this marriage was one daughter.

Since the marriage of a deceased wife's sister was at that time against English law, subsequent to his second marriage he removed with his family to the United States and settled in New York. He later acquired a country place at Bedford, N. Y., which had been part of the Jay estate. Shortly after his arrival he took an active part in coördinating the work of the various charitable organizations then operating in New York City and helped organize the Charity Organization Society, serving on the original central council from 1882 to 1885, on various committees, and as vice-president from 1887 to 1890. He was on the board of managers of the Association for Improving the Condition of the Poor from 1875 to 1887 and was president, 1884–85. He was a commissioner of education in New York, 1880–81, and was helpful in the tenement house reform movement as well as in the establishment of free civic libraries and night refuges. During this period he was also active in Bedford, where his summer home was. He was a member of the vestry of St. Matthew's Church, 1876–77 and 1885–92, and at one time taught a class of boys in the Sunday school. He joined the Bedford farmers' club, an old established institution, in which he took an active interest and of which he was president from 1878 to 1890.

Since the climate of New York did not agree with his health, he moved to Washington in 1885, where he made his home until his death. Selling his country place at Bedford in 1892, he later bought a house at Sharon, Conn., and thereafter spent his summers there. In Washington he served as vestryman of St. John's

Church from 1891 to 1908 and as a delegate to the General Convention of the Episcopal Church in 1891 and 1900. He was one of the incorporators of the national cathedral foundation in 1893 and a delegate to the convention of the diocese of Washington in 1895. He was helpful in establishing King Hall, a theological school for negroes, serving on the board of trustees from 1891 to 1903, was a member and for several years secretary of the commission for work among the colored people, and also a member of St. Monica's league for work among the colored people. The year before his death he fell heir to the title of Viscount Exmouth, but because of his advanced age he made no attempt officially to assume the title, and he died as he had lived for over fifty years, a citizen of his adopted country.

[Personal acquaintance; *Who's Who in America,* 1922–23; *Reports, Constitution, By-Laws and List of Members of the Century Asso. for . . . 1924* (1924); Bernard Burke, *A Geneal. and Heraldic Hist. of the Peerage* (1934); *N. Y. Times,* Feb. 5, 1923.]

T. T. P. L.

PELOUBET, FRANCIS NATHAN (Dec. 2, 1831–Mar. 27, 1920), Congregational clergyman, editor, author, was the eldest son of Louis Michel François Chabrier and Harriet (Hanks) Peloubet. His grandfather and first American ancestor was Joseph Alexander de Chabrier de Peloubet, a French royalist officer who was exiled during the Revolution. Francis was born in New York City, but the family moved to Bloomfield, N. J., where most of his boyhood was spent. Having prepared for college at the Bloomfield Academy, he entered the sophomore class at Williams, where he graduated with honors in 1853. After teaching a year in Bloomfield, he entered Bangor Theological Seminary and graduated in 1857. It had been his purpose to enter the foreign mission field, in preparation for which he had spent much time in the study of the Tamil language. He was actually appointed to India, in fact; but for a variety of reasons he finally decided to enter the home ministry instead, and was ordained at Lanesville, Mass., on Dec. 2, 1857. His pastorates, all in Massachusetts, were at Lanesville on Cape Ann, 1857–60; Oakham, 1860–66; Attleboro, First Church, 1866–71; Natick, 1872–83. In all these communities he labored successfully to lift the social, civic, and educational ideals; during the Civil War he twice visited the front in the service of the Christian Commission.

Peloubet will always rank as a pioneer in the American Sunday school movement. During his Attleboro pastorate he prepared two question books, but was unable to secure a publisher. In

1874, however, after the International Lessons had become almost universally adopted in the Protestant churches, he began a series of question books based on these lessons, which achieved immediate success and soon reached a circulation as high as 116,000 copies a year. In 1880 this publication became a quarterly, with an annual circulation of 150,000 copies. After the wide-spread adoption of the International Lessons, a need arose for a practical commentary for teachers and advanced pupils on the portions of the Bible covered year by year. Accordingly, with a volume for 1875 Peloubet began his *Select Notes on the International Sabbath School Lessons* (*Sunday* was later substituted for *Sabbath*), which ably met that need and achieved immediate success. This publication was issued annually for forty-five years, the veteran editor bidding farewell to his public in the volume for 1921, which appeared in 1920, a few months before his death. Widely used among the Protestant churches of all names and by preachers and teachers on the mission fields, the work is estimated to have had during Peloubet's lifetime a circulation of over a million volumes.

In 1883 he resigned his Natick pastorate and in 1890 established his home in Auburndale, where he spent the remainder of his life in incessant literary activity. He was a prolific contributor to the religious press, and published popular commentaries on the Gospels of Matthew and John and the Acts of the Apostles, *Loom of Life, and If Christ Were a Guest in Your Home* (1900), *The Front Line of the Sunday School Movement* (1904), *Studies in the Book of Job* (1906). In addition he edited *Select Songs for the Singing Service in the Prayer Meeting and Sunday School* (2 vols., 1884, 1893), a revision (1903) of the Oxford University Bible Helps and a revised edition (1912) of William Smith's *International Bible Dictionary,* as well as *Treasury of Biblical Information* (1913) and *Oriental Light Illuminating Bible Texts and Bible Truth* (1914). Peloubet had many interests; he was an enthusiastic devotee of outdoor sports, and his Auburndale home was the center of a large circle of friends. On Apr. 28, 1859, he married Mary Abby Thaxter of Bangor, Me., who with four of their five daughters survived him, one of whom was Mary Alice Peloubet Norton [*q.v.*].

[*Congregationalist and Advance,* Apr. 8, 1920; *Continent,* Nov. 20, 1919; A. R. Wells, in *Select Notes on the International Sunday School Lessons for 1921* (1922); J. Peloubet, *Family Records of Joseph Alexander de Chabrier de Peloubet* (1892); *The Congregational Year-Book, Statistics for 1920* (1921); *Boston Transcript,* Mar. 27, 1920; *Who's Who in America,* 1920–21; information from members of the family.]
F. T. P.

PELZ, PAUL JOHANNES (Nov. 18, 1841– Mar. 30, 1918), architect, the son of Eduard L. and Henriette (Helfensreiter) Pelz, was born in Seitendorf, Waldenburg, Silesia. His father was a historian and writer, and in the revolutionary movement of 1848 was a member of the Frankfort parliament. He found it, therefore, advisable to leave Germany in 1849, and two years later settled in New York, where he wrote copiously on subjects interesting to German immigrants, publishing his work in Chicago, New York, and Germany. Paul remained behind in Germany, receiving his academic education at the colleges of St. Elizabeth and of the Holy Spirit in Breslau. In 1858 he came to New York to join his family. The next year he became an apprentice in the architectural office of Detlef Lienau. Here he stayed until 1866, becoming chief draftsman in 1864. After leaving Lienau, he was briefly employed by an architect named Fernbach; but within a few months left New York and went to Washington, where he entered the service of the United States Lighthouse Board. As its chief draftsman from 1872 until 1877, he was concerned in the designing of a great number of lighthouses, including such beautiful towers as those at Body's Island, N. C., in brick and stone, and Spectacle Reef, Lake Huron, all in stone, with a fine stone balcony cornice. In 1873 he was sent with Maj. George H. Elliot on a tour of inspection to study the lighthouse services of the European powers and contributed many illustrations to Elliot's report (*Senate Executive Document 54,* 43 Cong., 1 Sess.).

Meanwhile, outside of his lighthouse work, he was making designs in association with various other architects. In 1873, with John L. Smithmeyer, he entered the competition for a plan for the Library of Congress, and their design received the first prize. For more than a dozen years thereafter there was vacillation on the part of Congress with regard to the Library, and the plan was studied and restudied; twelve entirely different designs are said to have been prepared. In 1886, the building was authorized and Smithmeyer was appointed architect, but in 1888 the Library Commission was legislated out of existence and the work placed in the hands of Brig.-Gen. Thomas L. Casey, chief of engineers of the army. Smithmeyer was removed but Pelz was retained and directed to prepare a new design, which was followed. In it Pelz returned to the basic ideas of the first competitive scheme. On the completion of the drawings (May 1, 1892) his connection with the building ceased, and it was executed under the supervision of E. P. Casey, of New York, the General's son. The exterior and interior design of the building are far inferior in dignity to the plan, which was epoch-making in its day; at the time of the competition, when the general lines were determined, there was not a contemporary building to compare with it in monumental conception, clarity of thinking, and functional directness. The arrangements for architectural fees on the work were vague, and Smithmeyer and Pelz brought suit in the Court of Claims for $210,000 (or 3% of the alleged cost of the building—a standard architect's fee). On appeal, the Supreme Court, Jan. 23, 1893, upheld the decision of the Court of Claims, awarding Smithmeyer and Pelz six years' combined salary at $8,000 a year over and above their office and drafting costs.

Besides the lighthouses and the Library, Pelz's work (mainly in association with Smithmeyer) included the Academic Building of Georgetown University; Carnegie Library and Music Hall, Allegheny, Pa.; the federal army and navy hospital, Hot Springs, Ark.; the Chamberlain Hotel, Fortress Monroe, Va.; the Aula Christi, Chautauqua, N. Y.; and the Administration Building of the Clinical Hospital of the University of Virginia. He was married on Feb. 23, 1895, to Mary Eastbourne (Ritter) Meem, daughter of Gen. Horatio Gates Ritter, and they had a son and a daughter. He died in Washington, D. C.

[Sketch of Eduard L. Pelz in *Der Hausfreund* (Leipzig), XIX (1876), 37, 40; *Ann. Report of the Lighthouse Board*, 1872–78; *Smithmeyer* vs. *U. S.*, 147 *U. S. Reports*, 342; *Eminent and Representative Men of Va. and the District of Columbia* (1893); *Who's Who in America*, 1916–17; Herbert Small, *Handbook of the New Library of Congress* (1897); Russell Sturgis, "The New Library of Congress," *Arch. Record*, Jan.-Mar. 1898; *Evening Star* (Washington, D. C.), Feb. 25, 1895, Mar. 31, 1918.]   T.F.H.

PEMBERTON, ISRAEL (May 10, 1715–Apr. 22, 1779), Quaker merchant and philanthropist, born in Philadelphia, Pa., was the third of the ten children of Israel and Rachel (Read) Pemberton and a descendant of Ralph Pemberton who emigrated to Pennsylvania from Lancashire, England, in 1682. James and John Pemberton [*qq.v.*] were his brothers. His father was a successful merchant and a member of the Pennsylvania Assembly. Israel received a thorough education in Friends' schools. At that of Thomas Makin, where Pastorius was a master, trouble arose between Pastorius and the boy, which resulted in Israel's being so severely punished that he was placed in another school. His education completed, he entered the mercantile business with his father, James Logan, and John Reynell, and became one of the wealthiest merchants of his time. He was able to keep up a home in the city, two country homes on the Schuylkill, and one in New Jersey. He was interested in various benevolent organizations. When the Pennsylvania Hospital was incorporated in February 1751 he was elected a manager, a position which he filled for twenty-eight years, and he contributed generously to its support. He was also a member of the American Philosophical Society, elected in January 1768. The largest share of his time and money, however, went to the Friendly Association for Regaining and Preserving Peace with the Indians by Pacific Measures, sponsored by the Philadelphia Meeting to keep the Delawares and Shawnees from joining the French in 1756. Pemberton was a trustee and an active member.

At an early age he took an interest in public affairs and in 1739 he was arrested for criticizing Thomas Penn, the lieutenant-governor of the province. He was released on bail and eventually the case was dropped. In 1750 he was elected to his father's seat in the Assembly for the county of Philadelphia. The following year he was appointed member of the board of managers for the State House and grounds. He was active in the movement to force the Proprietors to pay a fair share of taxes and signed the non-importation agreement at the time of the Stamp Act, though in general he strongly urged a policy of peace. In 1756 he resigned from the Assembly because of his opposition to the Indian War, but he was returned ten years later. During the first Continental Congress the Massachusetts delegation were invited by the Friends to attend a meeting at Carpenter's Hall. Pemberton addressed them, urging them to grant liberty of conscience to the Friends and Baptists in their province. This incident is said to be one of the chief reasons for John Adams' animosity toward the Quakers. Holding to his religious convictions, Pemberton was opposed to the Revolution. With others of his faith he refused to take the oath of allegiance to the Commonwealth of Pennsylvania or to promise not to give aid to the enemy. Consequently he and nineteen others were arrested early in September 1777 and imprisoned in the Free Masons' Lodge without trial. Their homes were searched and their papers seized. On the eleventh of September they were taken by wagon to Winchester, Va., where they were held until April of the next year. Pemberton's health was undermined during his imprisonment, causing his death one year later. He married, Mar. 30, 1737, Sarah, daughter of Joseph and Sarah (Stacy) Kirkbride. She died in 1746 and on Dec. 10, 1747, he married Mary, the daughter of Nathan and Mary (Ewer) Stanbury and the widow of Robert Jordan and Capt. Richard Hill.

[F. W. Leach, "Old Phila. Families," Phila. *North American*, July 28, 1907; J. W. Jordan, ed., *Colonial Families of Phila.* (1911), vol. I; *Friends' Miscellany*, Apr. 1835; J. P. Parke, *Geneal. Notes Relating to the Families of Lloyd, Pemberton, Hutchinson, Hudson and Parke* (1898), ed. by T. A. Glenn; C. P. Keith, *Chronicles of Pa. . . . 1688–1748* (1917), vol. II; R. M. Smith, *The Burlington Smiths* (1877); Isaac Sharpless, *A Hist. of Quaker Government in Pa.* (2 vols., 1900); Thos. Gilpin, *Exiles in Va.* (1848); E. P. Oberholtzer, *Phila., a Hist.* (1912), vol. I; G. B. Wood, *An Address on the Occasion of the Centennial Celebration of the Founding of the Pa. Hospital* (1851); *Pa. Mag. of Hist. and Biog.*, Apr. 1886, Jan.–Oct. 1913; *Minutes of the Provincial Council of Pa.*, vols. IV and VII (1851).]   E. M. B—n.

PEMBERTON, JAMES (Aug. 26, 1723–Feb. 9, 1809), Quaker merchant and philanthropist, the eighth of the ten children of Israel and Rachel (Read) Pemberton, and brother of Israel and John Pemberton [*qq.v.*], was born in Philadelphia, Pa. He was educated in Friends' School. In 1745 he traveled in the Carolinas and in 1748 he went to Europe, primarily for business purposes, as he was associated with his father and brother in the shipping trade. His main interest was in the Society of Friends and in the various religious organizations. An active member of Meeting, he sat at the head of the preacher's gallery for many years. When the Meeting for Sufferings, the executive body of the Friends, was established in 1756 he was appointed a member, a position which he held until 1808. With his brother Israel he was one of the trustees of the Friendly Association for Regaining and Preserving Peace with the Indians by Pacific Measures, and was a liberal contributor to its support. He was one of the founders of the Society for the Relief of Free Negroes, established in 1775. In 1787, when it became the Pennsylvania Society for Promoting the Abolition of Slavery, he became vice-president, and in 1790 he succeeded Franklin as president, holding this office for thirteen years. He was a member of the Board of Overseers of the public schools of Philadelphia, for both the city and the county, and took an active part in establishing secondary education in the Friends' schools. A member of the first board of managers of the Pennsylvania Hospital, he served for twenty-two years on the board and acted as secretary from 1759 to 1772. He was elected a member of the American Philosophical Society in January 1768.

Pemberton was elected to the Assembly for the County of Philadelphia but he resigned in June 1756 with five colleagues because of his opposition to a war with the Delawares. In 1757, as clerk of the Meeting, he signed a petition to the governor protesting against forcing the Friends of the Lower Counties to bear arms. He was reëlected to the Assembly in 1765 and held office for four years. At the time of the Stamp Act, he signed the non-importation agreement. He opposed armed resistance to Great Britain and was arrested, imprisoned in the Free Masons' Lodge, and deported with nineteen other Quakers to Virginia. Since they were not permitted to attend meeting, Pemberton helped to set up one of their own. On his return to Philadelphia he gave up all active interest in politics. As early as 1756 he wrote *An Apology for the People called Quakers, containing some Reasons for their not complying with Human Injunctions and Institutions in matters relative to the Worship of God*. In his capacity as clerk of the meeting he wrote, as well, many documents of a religious nature, one of which was a "Remonstrance vs. Erecting a Theatre and Theatrical Performances in Philadelphia." (See *Votes and Proceedings of the House of Representatives . . . of Pennsylvania*, 1775, vol. V, p. 524.) During the exile in Virginia he kept a journal, but more interesting are his letters, which are descriptive, concise, and filled with comments upon the life in the city and country. He died in 1809, in his eighty-sixth year. He had married, on Oct. 15, 1751, Hannah, daughter of Mordecai and Hannah (Fishbourne) Lloyd. After her death in 1764, he married, on Mar. 22, 1768, Sarah, daughter of Daniel and Mary (Hoedt) Smith of Burlington, N. J. Two years after her death he married, on July 12, 1775, Phoebe (Lewis) Morton, daughter of Robert and Mary Lewis.

[See: F. W. Leach, "Old Phila. Families," Phila. *North American*, July 28, 1907; J. W. Jordan, ed., *Colonial Families of Phila.* (1911), vol. I; Isaac Sharpless, *A Hist. of Quaker Government in Pa.* (2 vols., 1900) and *Pol. Leaders of Provincial Pa.* (1919); R. M. Smith, *The Burlington Smiths* (1877); Thos. Gilpin, *Exiles in Va.* (1848); Edward Needles, *An Hist. Memoir of the Pa. Soc. for Promoting the Abolition of Slavery* (1848); G. B. Wood, *An Address on the Occasion of the Centennial Celebration of the Founding of the Pa. Hospital* (1851); J. F. Watson, *Annals of Phila.* (1844), vol. I; *Friends' Miscellany*, May 1835; *Pa. Mag. of Hist. and Biog.*, Jan. 1889, July 1899, July 1914; *Pa. Archives*, 2 ser. IX (1880); *Minutes of the Provincial Council of Pa.*, vol. VII (1851), vol. IX (1852). There are Pemberton manuscripts in the library of the Pa. Hist. Soc.]

E.M.B—n.

PEMBERTON, JOHN (Nov. 27, 1727–Jan. 31, 1795), Quaker preacher, ninth of the ten children of Israel and Rachel (Read) Pemberton and younger brother of Israel and James Pemberton [*qq.v.*], was born in Philadelphia, Pa., where he attended Friends' schools. He entered business with his father and brothers, but soon gave this up so that he might devote his full time to religious work. In 1750, while traveling abroad for his health, he came into contact with John Churchman, a Quaker minister who was on his way to Great Britain on a religious tour. He persuaded Pemberton to accompany him, and for three years they journeyed through the west counties of England, in Ireland, Scotland, and Holland. During the trip Pemberton was persuaded to preach and on his return to Philadelphia he devoted his time to preaching and to missionary work, visiting in Pennsylvania, New Jersey, Delaware, and Virginia. A member of the Friendly Association for Regaining and Preserving Peace with the Indians by Pacific Measures, he attended the Easton conference in 1756. Ten years later he was chosen with John Penn to present the remonstrance against stage plays, prepared by his brother James, to the governor. Further revealing his religious convictions is the provisional lease which Pemberton granted in 1780 for a Coffee House, in which the tenant promised to "preserve decency," keep the house closed on Sunday, and prohibit swearing and card playing, with a penalty of £100 for the first offense.

Opposed to the war against the Delawares in 1756, he was equally hostile to armed resistance to Great Britain in 1777. Early in September 1777 he was notified that orders had been received to take him prisoner. When he refused to leave the house or give up his keys a guard of ten men took him by force. His desk was broken open and the contents seized. With his brothers he was sent to Winchester, Va., a journey of nineteen days by wagon. The year before he had begun to keep a journal, commenting upon the arrest of Friends for refusing to bear arms, and deploring the loss of life caused by war and sickness. He kept this journal throughout his exile, giving a clear picture of his arrest and imprisonment. His chief complaint throughout his imprisonment was of the cold and rain. On Apr. 21, 1778, he left Winchester, arriving in Philadelphia nine days later, the day after he received his official pardon from Washington. He continued to keep up his journal after his return, but the majority of the entries refer only to the Meeting and to various Friends. At the Quarterly Meeting, Feb. 5, 1781, Pemberton was given a certificate to visit the Friends in England. Despite the fact that it was now against the law to leave the country without a passport, he notified the council that he intended to dispense with the formality. Permitted to leave, he went to England, Ireland, and Scotland, visiting and preaching for five years. He returned to Philadelphia but set out again on

May 30, 1794, for Holland and Germany. He held meetings on shipboard, in Amsterdam, and in several towns in Prussia. Early in September he became ill, but he continued to Pyrmont, Westphalia. Thereafter he referred constantly in his journal and letters to his illness, though he commented also upon his surroundings, the scenery, and the people. His condition rapidly grew worse and he died at Pyrmont on the last day of January 1795. Pemberton's wife was Hannah, the daughter of Isaac and Sarah Zane, whom he married in Philadelphia on May 8, 1766.

[F. W. Leach, "Old Phila. Families," Phila. *North American*, July 28, 1907; J. W. Jordan, ed., *Colonial Families of Phila.* (1911), vol. I; Isaac Sharpless, *A Hist. of Quaker Government in Pa.* (2 vols., 1900); J. F. Watson, *Annals of Phila.* (1844), vol. I; Thos. Gilpin, *Exiles in Va.* (1848); G. B. Wood, *An Address on the Occasion of the Centennial Celebration of the Founding of the Pa. Hospital* (1851); *Friends' Miscellany*, Jan., Feb., Mar. 1836; *The Diary of John Pemberton for the Years 1777 and 1778* (1867), ed. by E. K. Price; Thos. Wilkinson, *Some Account of the Last Journey of John Pemberton to the Highlands, and Other Parts of Scotland* (1811); *Pa. Mag. of Hist. and Biog.*, Oct. 1885, Apr.–Oct. 1917.]   E. M. B—n.

PEMBERTON, JOHN CLIFFORD (Aug. 10, 1814–July 13, 1881), soldier, second son of John and Rebecca (Clifford) Pemberton, was born in Philadelphia. He was of Quaker ancestry, great-grandson of Israel Pemberton [q.v.], and a descendant of Ralph Pemberton, of Wigan, Lancashire, who came with his son Phineas to Pennsylvania in 1682. John received his early education in the schools of his native city, and was privately tutored in Hebrew, Greek, and Latin. Entering West Point on July 1, 1833, he graduated four years later, twenty-seventh in a class of fifty. As second lieutenant in the 4th Artillery Regiment, he fought in the Florida Indian Wars from 1837 to 1839, and from 1840 to 1842 served on the Canadian border. On Mar. 19, 1842, he was promoted to first lieutenant. In the War with Mexico, as aide-de-camp of Gen. William J. Worth [q.v.], he participated in the battles of Palo Alto, Resaca de la Palma, Vera Cruz, Monterey, Cerro Gordo, Churubusco, Molino del Rey, Chapultepec, and Mexico city. For bravery throughout these actions, he was brevetted captain, Sept. 23, 1846, and major, Sept. 8, 1847. In recognition of his Mexican services the citizens of Philadelphia presented him with a handsome sword. On Jan. 18, 1848, he married Martha Thompson, daughter of William Henry Thompson of Norfolk, Va.; five children were born to them. Pemberton received his regular captaincy on Sept. 16, 1850. In 1858, under Gen. Albert Sidney Johnston, he took part in the operations against the Mormons in Utah, while the following three years he was occupied with Indian affairs in the northwest.

When the Civil War threatened, he was ordered with troops at Fort Ridgely, Minn., to Washington, D. C. Arrived there, he resigned his commission in the United States Army on Apr. 24, 1861. Gen. Winfield Scott tried to persuade him to accept a commission as colonel in the Federal army, but he refused the offer and proceeded to Richmond. There he was commissioned lieutenant-colonel, Apr. 28, 1861, and assigned the duty of organizing the cavalry and artillery of Virginia. On May 8, 1861, he was named colonel, Provisional Army of Virginia; on June 15, major, corps of artillery, Confederate States Army; on June 17, brigadier-general, Provisional Army, Confederate States; and on Feb. 13, 1862, major-general, Provisional Army, commanding the department which included South Carolina, Georgia, and Florida. He early counseled the abandonment of Fort Sumter as having no protective value for the city of Charleston, and built Fort Wagner and Battery "B," which protected the city even after Union fire had levelled Sumter. Many in the South could not forget that Pemberton was a Northerner, and the Confederate secretary of war was even petitioned to remove him from command. There is no question, however, of his complete loyalty to the Southern cause, or that he had the full confidence of his superiors. On Oct. 13, 1862, he was promoted lieutenant-general and given command of the department embracing Mississippi, Tennessee, and eastern Louisiana. He thus became responsible for the defense of the Confederate stronghold of Vicksburg.

Jefferson Davis instructed him to hold Vicksburg at all costs; Gen. Joseph E. Johnston advised cutting loose from Vicksburg and avoiding a general engagement until sufficient concentration could be effected against Grant. Hampered by these conflicting orders and opposed by the ablest soldier of the North, Pemberton had to work out his own salvation. Besieged by land and water, heavily outnumbered, and short of ammunition, he conducted a stubborn defense. Finally the garrison was reduced to eating rats, cane shoots, and bark; men were so exhausted that they could scarcely stand in the firing trenches, and those still capable of resisting were all too few to man the defenses. On the night of July 2, 1863, when the Federals had closed in to assaulting distance, Pemberton knew that defeat was inevitable. On July 4, he accepted the "unconditional surrender" terms imposed by General Grant. When the exchange

of prisoners had been effected, Pemberton resigned his commission as lieutenant-general and served until the end of the war as inspector of ordnance with the rank of colonel.

Through the foresight and generosity of his mother, he was provided a farm near Warrenton, Va., whither he retired after the war. In 1876 he moved to Philadelphia, and there lived with his brothers and sisters until his death at Penllyn on July 13, 1881. He was buried in Laurel Hill Cemetery, Philadelphia.

[J. W. Jordan, *Colonial Families of Phila.* (1911); *War of the Rebellion: Official Records (Army)*; *Battles and Leaders of the Civil War* (4 vols., 1887–88); *Thirteenth Ann. Reunion Asso. of Grads., U. S. Military Acad. . . . 1882*; G. W. Cullum, *Biog. Reg. Officers and Grads., U. S. Military Acad.*, vol. I (1891); C. A. Evans, *Confed. Military Hist.* (1899), esp. vols. I, V, VII; *Army and Navy Jour.*, July 16, 1881; *Public Ledger* (Phila.), July 14, 1881.]   C. C. B.

PEÑALOSA BRICEÑO, DIEGO DIONISO de (*c.* 1622–*c.* 1687), governor of New Mexico, soldier of fortune, the son of Alonso de Peñalosa, was a native of Lima, Peru. He went to New Spain about 1654, where, according to his later sworn statements, he was employed "in the higher positions, political and military." In 1661, by appointment of the viceroy of New Spain, he assumed the office of governor and captain-general of New Mexico. Obligated to conduct the *residencia,* or official investigation of the administration of his deposed predecessor, Mendizabal, he sacked the latter's home and threw him into prison, thus patronizingly defying the Tribunal of the Inquisition in Mexico, which had issued a writ for the arrest of Mendizabal and the attachment of his property. The breach thus made between Peñalosa and Father Posadas, *comisario* of the Inquisition in New Mexico, soon widened, and during the spirited contest that ensued, Peñalosa in 1663 imprisoned and threatened to kill Posadas. This rash act brought forth a threat to place the province under an interdict. Peñalosa made frantic efforts to effect a reconciliation, but the entire power of the Inquisition was directed against him, and in June 1665, after he had left New Mexico, a formal complaint was made by the Inquisition against him "as a usurper of the jurisdiction" of that Tribunal. Furthermore, he was charged with rape, incest, robbery, and the enslavement of Indian girls, and with having attempted first to bribe and then to blackmail Mendizabal. In his defense Peñalosa admitted rashness, complained of having been governor "of the off-scourings of the earth," cited alleged services in behalf of his king and his religion, and threw himself on the mercy of the court. His pleas were vain, however; and on Feb. 3, 1668, he was reprimanded, fined 500 pesos, deprived of the right to hold political and military office, and exiled forever from New Spain and the West Indies.

Embittered, he went to England where he maintained himself by selling to British officials information concerning the defenses of the Indies. He enjoyed the favor of the king, who prevented his arrest when it was requested by the Spanish ambassador. After some time he went to France, where he assumed various fictitious titles of nobility. Between the years 1678 and 1684, he presented three proposals to Louis XIV to attack New Spain in the name of France, capitalizing, in this connection, his personal knowledge of the regions mentioned. On presenting in 1684 his proposal to attack Pánuco, he also submitted a manuscript "Relación" purporting to be an account of an alleged expedition from Santa Fé to Quivira in 1662. This "Relación," published in 1882 by J. G. Shea (post), has recently been proved fictitious (Miller and Hackett, post). Peñalosa submitted his third proposal just as La Salle arrived from Canada with news of his exploration of the Mississippi River and plans for a settlement near its mouth. The plan of the renowned French explorer superseded that of the exiled Spanish renegade, and the expedition which left France that same year was led by La Salle. After this time nothing more is known of Peñalosa, though, according to Margry (III, 44), he died in 1687, at Paris.

[MSS. in the Archivo General, Mexico City, Sección de Inquisición; transcripts in Univ. of Tex. Lib.; Cesareo Fernández Duro, *Don Diego de Peñalosa* (Madrid, 1882); C. W. Hackett, "New Light on Don Diego de Peñalosa," *Miss. Valley Hist. Rev.*, Dec. 1919; Pierre Margry, *Découvertes et Établissements des Français dans l'Ouest et dans le Sud de l'Amérique Septentrionale*, vol. III (1878); J. G. Shea, *The Expedition of Don Diego Dionisio de Peñalosa* (1882), which accepts the authenticity of the fictitious "Relación"; E. T. Miller, "The Connection of Peñalosa with the La Salle Expedition," *Tex. State Hist. Asso. Quart.*, Oct. 1901; W. E. Dunn, *Spanish and French Rivalry in the Gulf Region of the U. S., 1678–1702* (1917).]

C. W. H.

PENDER, WILLIAM DORSEY (Feb. 6, 1834–July 18, 1863), Confederate soldier, was born in Edgecombe County, N. C. His father, James Pender, was a descendant of Edwin Pender who came from England and settled near Norfolk, Va., during the reign of Charles II. His mother was Sarah Routh, daughter of William Routh also of Virginia. He received his preliminary education in the common schools of his county and at the age of fifteen worked as a clerk in his brother's store. At sixteen he was appointed a cadet to the United States Military Academy from which he graduated in 1854, standing nineteenth in a class of forty-six. Upon graduation he was commissioned brevet second lieutenant in the 1st Artillery and during the same year he was made a second lieutenant in the 2nd Artillery. In 1855 he transferred to the 1st Dragoons and in 1858 was promoted to the rank of first lieutenant in that regiment. From 1856 to 1860 he saw active service on the frontier in New Mexico, California, Oregon, and Washington, participating in numerous lively skirmishes with the Indians. He married Mary Frances, daughter of the Hon. Augustine H. Shepperd of North Carolina, on Mar. 3, 1859. Three sons were born of this union, Samuel Turner, William D., and Stephen Lee. In 1860 he was appointed adjutant of the 1st Dragoons with a station at San Francisco, Cal., but the year following he was ordered to return to the East on recruiting duty.

At the outbreak of the Civil War he resigned his commission and threw in his lot with the Confederacy. He was commissioned a captain of artillery in the provisional army and placed in charge of Confederate recruiting in Baltimore, Md. In May 1861, he returned to his native state and acted as an instructor for new regiments formed at Raleigh and Garysburg. He was elected colonel of the 3rd North Carolina Volunteers on May 16, 1861, and on Aug. 15 was transferred to command the 6th North Carolina Regiment. His regiment served in Whiting's brigade of Smith's division under Gen. Joseph E. Johnston in the Peninsular campaign. For brilliant leadership at the battle of Seven Pines (Fair Oaks) he was promoted to the rank of brigadier-general and assigned to command a brigade of North Carolina troops in Gen. Ambrose P. Hill's division. Pender led his brigade ably in the battle of the Seven Days in front of Richmond and again under Jackson at the second battle of Bull Run, in the Maryland campaign, at Fredericksburg, and at Chancellorsville. He was wounded three times during these battles but never relinquished his command. On May 27, 1863, he was promoted to the rank of major-general, being then only twenty-nine years of age but considered one of the ablest officers of the Confederacy. He was placed in command of a division and demonstrated his fitness for his new command at Gettysburg on July 1, 1863, when he drove the Union troops from Seminary Ridge. The second day of the battle he was severely wounded in the leg by a fragment of shell. He was evacuated to Staunton, Va., where he died on July 18, 1863, following an operation for the amputation of his wounded leg. The loss to the Confederacy of this gallant young officer can be estimated from one of Lee's official reports: "His promise and usefulness as an officer were only equaled by the purity and excellence of his private life" (*War of the Rebellion: Official Records, Army*, 1 ser. XXVII, Part II, p. 325).

[G. W. Cullum, *Biog. Reg. . . . U. S. Mil. Acad.*; *Confederate Military History* (1899), vol. IV; *Battles and Leaders of the Civil War* (1884–1888), vols. II, III; sketch by W. A. Montgomery in W. J. Peele, *Lives of Distinguished North Carolinians* (1898); *Cyclopedia of Eminent and Representative Men of the Carolinas of the Nineteenth Century* (1892), vol. II; *Richmond Daily Whig*, July 20, 1863.]　　S. J. H.

PENDLETON, EDMUND (Sept. 9, 1721– Oct. 26, 1803), Virginia jurist, Revolutionary patriot, was born in Caroline County, Va. His grandfather, Philip, a schoolmaster of Norwich, England, had emigrated in 1682, and the family became established in Caroline at an early date. One of Philip's daughters, Catherine, married John Taylor, grandfather of the well-known John Taylor of Caroline, while his son Henry married Mary Taylor, sister to John. Edmund was their youngest son. His father and grandfather both died in the year that he was born (*Southern Literary Messenger*, June 1857, pp. 422–24), and his mother married again. Left without paternal care, and apparently without property, he was apprenticed at the age of fourteen to Col. Benjamin Robinson, clerk of the court of Caroline and a kinsman of the powerful "Speaker" Robinson (Caroline County Order Books, volume for 1732–40, p. 282). When the lad was sixteen years of age, he became clerk to the vestry of St. Mary's Parish, and at nineteen was made clerk of the Caroline court martial. During these years he worked diligently to educate himself and at twenty was admitted to practise at the local bar. In 1742 he married Elizabeth Roy, but the bride died in childbirth within the year and the infant son never breathed. On June 20, 1743, Pendleton married Sarah Pollard, with whom he lived happily until her death in 1794.

In 1745 he was admitted to practice before the general court. In 1751 he became a justice of the peace of Caroline County, and the next year was elected to the House of Burgesses. Judging by the number of his committee appointments, he was an active member of this body. In 1765 the financial affairs of Speaker John Robinson [*q.v.*], who was also treasurer of the colony, became involved, and his friends made an effort to relieve him by establishing a state loan office. Pendleton was active in this movement, but it failed. When the Speaker died

within the following year, an effort was made by the reforming party to separate the office of speaker from that of treasurer. Pendleton strenuously opposed this move, and again was unsuccessful. It has been said that his stand with the conservative interests on these questions made him leader of the "Cavalier" party in Virginia, to which he was alien by birth. The Stamp Act was passed while these questions were being debated. Pendleton, always conservative and opposed to violent measures, did not favor Patrick Henry's stand on this issue. Nevertheless, he stated it as his view that the House of Commons lacked constitutional authority to pass the offending act, and, as justice of Caroline, he kept the court open and went as far as he could legally to nullify the effect of the legislation (*Proceedings of the Massachusetts Historical Society*, 2 ser. XIX, 1905, pp. 109–12). Though his name does not appear prominently again until the beginning of the Revolutionary struggle, his stand in 1765 clearly indicated what his policy would be when the storm broke.

Immediately upon the approach of the crisis, Pendleton emerged as one of the foremost men in Virginia. His qualifications for leadership were considerable, yet his strategic position doubtless had much to do with his preferment. His place as a leader in the conservative group made his support of the Revolutionary movement highly important. Accordingly, he was selected for membership on the Committee of Correspondence when it was organized in 1773. In 1774 he was sent to represent Virginia in the first Continental Congress. He was a member of all the Virginia Revolutionary conventions, and was president of the two which met in 1775. In that year he was made president of the Committee of Safety, which placed him at the head of the temporary government of the colony. In this position his policy was firm, though not aggressive, since it was his ardent hope that the struggle might be settled by a redress of grievances rather than by war (Lee Papers, University of Virginia Library, Pendleton to R. H. Lee, Apr. 20, 1776; also to delegates in Congress, Oct. 28, 1775). He opposed Patrick Henry's proposal to arm the militia at this time, but when the measure was carried, he, as county lieutenant of Caroline, helped to carry it into effect. When Henry was made commander-in-chief of the Virginia troops, Pendleton was instrumental in giving to Col. William Woodford the active command in the field, thereby bringing down upon himself the enmity of the popular hero of the day. His judgment of the military qualifications of the two men seems to have been just, although there is no question but that Pendleton looked upon Henry as a demagogue, and they were never on the same side of any question. The friction caused by this incident hurt Pendleton's popularity, and though he was reëlected president of the Committee of Safety in December 1775, it was by a reduced majority (H. J. Eckenrode, *The Revolution in Virginia,* 1916, p. 131). It was doubtless on this account, too, that he had to contest with Philip Ludwell Lee election to the presidency of the famous Virginia convention of 1776 (William Wirt Henry, *Patrick Henry,* 1891, I, 333 ff., 356, 389, 445–46). His inaugural speech on assuming the chair foreshadowed a declaration of independence (Rives, *post,* I, 122), and it was he who drew up the resolves instructing Virginia's delegates in Congress to propose the measure. This convention also drew up Virginia's first constitution, and provided for a revision of the laws. Pendleton was placed on the committee charged with the latter function, and the work was completed in 1779 by Jefferson, Wythe, and himself. In the framing of the constitution and in the revision of the laws, Pendleton stood for conservative measures, opposing Jefferson's program of disestablishment of the church and abolition of primogeniture and entail.

On the organization of the new state government, Pendleton became speaker of the House of Delegates. He was returned to that body in 1777, but his attendance was delayed by a fall from his horse, which crippled him for the rest of his life. He returned to the autumn session of the House, and was made presiding judge of the newly organized court of chancery. When the supreme court of appeals was organized in 1779, he became its president and retained this post until his death. From this time forward, his interest in politics was keen but not active. He spent most of his time on his estate, "Edmundsbury," in Caroline, making the journey to Richmond twice each year to attend the sessions of the court (Lee Papers, University of Virginia Library, Pendleton to R. H. Lee, Feb. 21, 1785). Meanwhile he kept up a regular correspondence with his friends in Congress, particularly with James Madison (*Proceedings of the Massachusetts Historical Society,* 2 ser. XIX, 107–67). This semi-retirement was interrupted in 1788 when a convention was assembled in Virginia to decide upon the adoption of the Federal Constitution. Pendleton was known to favor adoption, but was elected president of the convention without opposition. Despite his lameness and his official position, he took the floor on several occasions to defend the new instrument of government, and his political philosophy is revealed in these speeches as well as in his letters to Madison. Here he maintains his belief in the equality of man before the law, denies that he thinks government should be controlled by the well born, and advocates a liberal suffrage (Jonathan Elliot, *The Debates on the Adoption of the Federal Constitution,* 2nd ed., 1836, III, 293–305).

No one familiar with his character could doubt the sincerity of this defender of established institutions. Upon the formation of the new federal government, Washington offered him a district judgeship, which he declined. The long-standing friendship between the two was maintained, but Pendleton dissented from the foreign policy and the financial measures of Washington's administration (Jared Sparks, *The Writings of George Washington,* vol. X, 1836, pp. 27, 369–72). This attitude brought him into the Republican camp, and in 1799, at the request of Jefferson, he published a campaign document in support of the principles of his party (*An Address . . . on the Present State of Our Country,* Boston, 1799; *Writings of Thomas Jefferson,* Memorial Edition, 1903, X, 86–89, 104–110). The conservative colonist and reluctant revolutionist ended his career as a supporter of the liberals, but his principles had hardly changed. Whatever else he was, he was first a Virginian, and the interests of Virginia as he saw them actuated his every move. He was an individualist, never a partisan, and his decisions were made in the light of his personal judgment.

Edmund Pendleton was a typical gentleman of his generation; tall, graceful, suave (see portrait in L. Pecquet du Bellet, *Some Prominent Virginia Families,* 1907, IV, 226). He was methodical, assiduous, and a close rather than a broad legal student. He wrote as he spoke—clearly and convincingly. Jefferson said he was the most able man whom he had ever met in debate, not bearing his opponent down with words, but forcing him to cover with his tenacious strategy (*Writings,* I, 54–56). As a judge, he was cautious, conservative, and sound. The only decision of his which was ever reversed was reversed by himself (Mays, *post*). There was hardly a greater man in Virginia than was Pendleton, but he was lacking in all qualities of showmanship and aggressiveness, and his fame has suffered because he confined his activities so largely to his native state. He died in 1803, leaving no issue.

[Pendleton's papers are scattered. David J. Mays, of Richmond, to whom the writer is indebted for valuable assistance, has collected all those available, and is preparing a biography. Considerable material is scattered through the published and manuscript writings of Washington, Jefferson, Madison, and the other Revolutionary Virginians. The more complète biographies of such characters—particularly William Wirt, *Sketches of the Life and Character of Patrick Henry* (1817); H. S. Randall, *The Life of Thomas Jefferson* (3 vols., 1858); and W. C. Rives, *Hist. of the Life and Times of James Madison* (3 vols., 1859–68)—furnish some information. The best accounts available are by H. B. Grigsby, *The Va. Conv. of 1776* (1855), pp. 45–55, which refers to an autobiographical sketch by Pendleton printed in the *Norfolk Beacon*, Oct. 3, 1834; and D. J. Mays, *Edmund Pendleton* (1926), repr. from *Proc. . . . Va. State Bar Asso.*, 1925. See also H. B. Grigsby, *The Hist. of the Va. Conv. of 1788* (2 vols., 1890–91), being *Va. Hist. Soc. Colls.*, vols. IX, X; Pendleton genealogy in *Va. Mag. of Hist. and Biog.*, beginning in July 1931; *Examiner* and *Va. Argus*, both of Richmond, Oct. 29, 1803.]   T. P. A.

PENDLETON, EDMUND MONROE (Mar. 19, 1815–Jan. 26, 1884), physician, chemist, was the great-grandson of James Pendleton, the brother of Edmund Pendleton [*q.v.*]. He was the third son of Coleman and Martha (Gilbert) Pendleton, who moved to Eatonton, Ga., from Culpeper, Va., in 1800. He was born at Eatonton and his early education was obtained in the private schools there. Owing to financial stress he was, while quite young, forced to discontinue his education and from time to time was engaged in several business undertakings. At one time he became part owner of a jewelry business in Columbus, Ga., and later was engaged in this business in Macon, Ga. While he was working in Macon a copy of Brand's textbook of chemistry gave him his first enthusiasm for this science, and he employed his spare moments in the very careful study of this book, which really laid the foundation for much of his life work. Thus becoming interested in science, he soon decided upon the study of medicine, and obtained a position in a drug store in Macon, Ga. While working as an apprentice, he devoted much time to the reading of medicine under a local physician. He entered the Medical College of South Carolina at Charleston, from which institution he was graduated in 1837. While attending lectures here, he read medicine in the office of Samuel Dickson [*q.v.*]. He also gave much time to a further study of chemistry under the instruction of Charles Upham Shepard [*q.v.*]. While still a student he contributed bits of verse to the Charleston *News and Courier*. He practised medicine in the city of Warrenton, Ga., and there married on Nov. 27, 1838, Sarah Jane Thomas, the sister of James R. Thomas, president of Emory College. They had eleven children. Soon after their marriage they removed to Sparta, Ga., where he practised medicine for thirty years.

During this time he became a slave holder and successfully operated a large plantation. He applied his scientific knowledge to his plantation as well as to his practice. As a pioneer in this field he manufactured fertilizer not only for his own use but for the public market. In 1849 he published an interesting discussion of "The Climate and Diseases of Middle Georgia" (*Southern Medical Reprints*, vol. I, 1849, pp. 314–42). About 1867 he organized the firm of Pendleton & Dozier in Augusta, Ga., for the purpose of manufacturing commercial fertilizer on a large scale. In 1872 he was called to teach agriculture at the University of Georgia, where he remained for four years until he resigned on account of the failure of his health. He did much to organize his department of the university. As a result of his carefully prepared lectures, he published a *Text Book of Scientific Agriculture* (1875) followed by a second edition the next year. He moved to Atlanta in 1877 and founded a corporation for the manufacture of commercial fertilizer, devising and improving formulae in this field. He was one of the first to use cotton seed in the manufacture of fertilizers and to recognize the effect of grain and cotton culture on the phosphoric acid and nitrogen content of the soil.

[Personal papers in possession of grand-daughter, Mrs. G. H. Phillips, Atlanta, Ga.; information from Medical College of S. C. and Univ. of Ga.; *The South in the Building of the Nation*, vol. XII (1909); *Va. Mag. of Hist. and Biog.*, Apr. 1932, p. 181.] J. S. G.

PENDLETON, GEORGE HUNT (July 29, 1825–Nov. 24, 1889), representative and senator from Ohio, minister to Germany, the eldest child of Nathaniel Greene and Jane Frances (Hunt) Pendleton, was born in Cincinnati, Ohio. He was the great-grandson of Nathaniel Greene Pendleton, a brother of Edmund Pendleton [*q.v.*], and through all the rough and tumble of political life in the Middle West, he bore the nickname "Gentleman George" on account of the dignity and manner he inherited from a great Virginia family. He attended the local schools, where he was taught by Ormsby M. Mitchel [*q.v.*], and he was a student in Cincinnati College until 1841. The next three years he studied under private tutors. In 1844 he went abroad and for two years traveled in the principal countries of Europe, studied for a time at the University of Heidelberg, and, making portions of the tour on foot, went to the Holy Land and Egypt. In 1846, upon his return from Europe, he married Alice Key, the daughter of Francis Scott Key and niece of Roger B. Taney [*qq.v.*]. They had two daughters and a son. He studied law in the office of Stephen Fales in Cincinnati, was admitted to the bar in 1847, and until 1852 was a partner of George E. Pugh [*q.v.*]. In 1853 he wa., nominated and elected by a large majority to the state Senate on the Democratic ticket. The energy and ability he displayed in the work of adapting the state laws to the new constitution caused his friends to nominate him for Congress in 1854 before his term in the state legislature was finished. Unsuccessful in that year he was again nominated in 1856 and was elected.

He was a member of Congress from Mar. 4, 1857, to Mar. 3, 1865. He supported Stephen A. Douglas in his attack upon President Buchanan over the question of the admission of Kansas under the Lecompton constitution. He was a Douglas supporter in 1860 and during the Civil War was recognized as one of the leaders of the peace wing of the Democratic party. He believed the war could have been averted and favored the Crittenden Compromise. If secession were necessary, he insisted that it should be peaceable; but if the North insisted on war he warned the House to "prepare to wage it to the last extremity" (*Cincinnati Commercial Gazette,* Nov. 26, 1889). He differed widely, however, from the policy of the Lincoln administration during the conflict. He opposed the suspension of the *habeas corpus* and every attempt to make the military arm of the government superior to the civil. He opposed the passage of the legal tender act upon constitutional grounds and quoted with approval Webster's statement that "gold and silver currency is the law of the land at home, the law of the land abroad: there can, in the present condition of the world, be no other currency" (J. G. Blaine, *Twenty Years of Congress,* Vol. I, 1886, p. 413). Nevertheless, his tact and ability earned for him the respect of his political opponents. He was a member of the judiciary committee, of the ways and means committee, and was one of the committee of managers in the impeachment of Judge West H. Humphreys [*q.v.*]. He was nominated for vice-president on the National Democratic ticket with McClellan in 1864. The year following his retirement from Congress he was again nominated for membership in that body but was defeated.

After the war he was a Greenbacker. If he did not originate the "Ohio idea" of paying the 5–20 bonds in Greenbacks instead of coin, he, at all events, early in 1867 sponsored the proposal. This made his name anathema to the eastern Democracy; and in the Democratic convention of 1868, although the platform adopted committed the party unreservedly to his doctrines, he was deprived of the nomination for the presidency owing to the opposition of the New York delegation and the existence of the two-thirds rule. The following year the Democrats nomi-

nated him for governor of Ohio, but he was defeated by Rutherford B. Hayes. The same year he was chosen president of the Kentucky Central Railroad, which office he held for ten years. In 1878 he was elected by the Ohio legislature to the United States Senate and served in that body from Mar. 4, 1879, to Mar. 3, 1885. He will be remembered best for his connection with civil service reform. In 1883, as chairman of the Senate committee on civil service, he obtained the passage of a bill drafted by Dorman B. Eaton [*q.v.*], providing for the creation of a federal civil service commission and the introduction of competitive examinations. Nevertheless, he was severely abused by the spoilsmen in his party for advocating such a measure as the Democrats had been victorious in the congressional elections of 1882. In 1884 he was defeated for renomination to the Senate. President Cleveland appointed him minister to Germany on Mar. 23, 1885, and he served in this capacity until his death in Brussels.

[G. M. D. Bloss, *Life and Speeches of George H. Pendleton* (1868); *Biog. Cyc. and Portrait Gallery . . . of Ohio,* vol. I (1883); C. R. Fish, *The Civil Service and the Patronage* (1905); W. C. Mitchell, *A Hist. of the Greenbacks* (1903); T. E. Powell, *The Democratic Party of . . . Ohio* (2 vols., 1913); L. P. du Bellet, *Some Prominent Va. Families* (1907), vol. IV, p. 251; *Cincinnati Enquirer,* Nov. 26, 1889; *Cincinnati Times-Star,* Nov. 25, 1889.]

R. C. McG.

PENDLETON, JAMES MADISON (Nov. 20, 1811–Mar. 4, 1891), Baptist minister and educator, was born in Spotsylvania County, Va., the son of John and Frances J. (Thompson) Pendleton. He could not trace his ancestry beyond his grandfather, Henry Pendleton, Jr., of Culpeper County, who served in the Revolution. When James was about a year old, the family moved to Christian County, Ky., where, on a farm near Pembroke, he lived until he was twenty. He attended the local schools, and from 1833 to 1836 an academy at Hopkinsville. At seventeen he had joined the church; he began to preach at nineteen, and was licensed by the Bethel Baptist Church in 1831. For the next two years he preached, taught school, and studied, and on Nov. 2, 1833, he was ordained at Hopkinsville. After some local preaching during the continuation of his studies, he became in 1837 pastor of the Baptist Church at Bowling Green, and the following year, Mar. 13, 1838, he married Catherine Stockton Garnett of Glasgow, Ky. To them four children were born. His twenty-year pastorate at Bowling Green fell during a period when no one could exert an influence in the spiritual and moral life of the community without showing his political proclivities, and Pendleton's development was increasingly adverse to slavery and concerned for the preservation of the Union. He thus supported the proposals of Henry Clay, including that for gradual emancipation of the slaves, a project which did not meet with general approval in Kentucky.

In 1857 Pendleton accepted the chair of theology in Union University at Murfreesboro, Tenn. Here he studied and taught church history as well as Biblical and historical theology, and also served as pastor of the local Baptist Church. At the outbreak of the Civil War his attachment to the Union cause virtually forced him to leave Tennessee, and from 1862 to 1865 he served as pastor at Hamilton, Ohio. A son who had enlisted in the Confederate army was soon killed by accident; but the grief of the father was assuaged by the thought that his son "had never fired a gun at a Union soldier." In 1865 he accepted a call to the Baptist Church at Upland, Pa., where he became one of the original trustees of Crozer Theological Seminary, established three years later. He resigned the Upland pastorate in 1883 and spent the following years with one or another of his children, in Kentucky, Tennessee, and Texas. He died at Bowling Green.

Pendleton won a reputation as a preacher and writer of superior intellectual power, especially during his career at Murfreesboro, when from 1855 to 1861 he was one of the editors of the *Southern Baptist Review Eclectic*. His articles and reviews show a wide range of reading and acute logical powers, based upon certain presuppositions which he never questioned. His later revisions of his early works show little change from his fundamental position (strictly orthodox and essentially "Landmarker"), although in the later works some of his conclusions were not so obtrusively asserted. Among his published works are *Three Reasons Why I am a Baptist* (1853), revised as *Distinctive Principles of Baptists* (1882); *Church Manual* (copyright 1867); *A Treatise on the Atonement of Christ* (1869, revised in 1885); and *Christian Doctrines* (1878), the last two being revisions of articles first published in the *Review and Eclectic*. His autobiography, *Reminiscences of a Long Life* (1891), was published after his death.

[J. M. Pendleton, *Reminiscences* (1891); Wm. Cathcart, *The Bapt. Encyc.* (1881); *Semi-Centennial of Upland Baptist Church, 1852–1902* (n.d.), containing an interpretation by a son, Garnett Pendleton; J. H. Spencer, *A Hist. of Ky. Baptists* (1886), II, 523–25; *Courier-Journal* (Louisville, Ky.), Mar. 5, 1891.]

W. H. A.

PENDLETON, JOHN B. (1798–Mar. 10, 1866), pioneer in commercial lithography in the United States, was the youngest son of Capt. William Pendleton, a native of Liverpool, England, and the commander of a New York and Liverpool packet, who came to America about 1789 and resided in New York City, where he married a widow, and where John and his brother, William S. Pendleton, were born. The father was lost at sea the year John was born, and both boys were early sent to work. William was apprenticed to a copper-plate engraver, and in 1819 went to Washington, D. C., where he practised his craft and the following year was joined by his brother John. Both young men then set out to seek their fortunes in the West, but proceeded no further than Pittsburgh, Pa. Before they had been long in that city, John was invited by Rembrandt Peale [*q.v.*] to exhibit his large painting, "The Court of Death," which was shown in many cities of the country for more than a year. In 1824 William returned to New York but soon went to Boston, where he resumed his business of engraving. About this time John was sent to Europe in the interests of John Doggett, a bookseller, and while he was in Paris, his brother wrote him that he had purchased some lithographic materials and equipment from a merchant named Thaxter, who had imported it, but was unable to use the process successfully. The younger brother's response was to study lithography in Paris, where he purchased abundant supplies which he brought with him upon his return to the United States in 1825. With him he brought also two workmen, Bischbou and Dubois, the latter said to have been the first real lithographic printer in the United States. The firm of W. S. & J. B. Pendleton, Boston, began to print lithographs that same year. Their first work was evidently for the *Boston Monthly Magazine,* December 1825. John continued a member of this firm for five years. In 1826 Rembrandt Peale went to Boston, apparently at the suggestion of John Pendleton, to study lithography, and there drew upon the stone a portrait of Washington which gained a medal in the Franklin Institute exhibition in 1827. In 1829 John Pendleton with Francis Kearny and Cephas Grier Childs [*qq.v.*] founded a lithographing firm in Philadelphia under the style of Pendleton, Kearny & Childs, from which the senior partner withdrew in the same year to found a lithograph house in New York City. Thenceforth until his death, he was a resident of New York. In 1832 he was engaged as a lithographer, and also, in partnership with a man named Hill, as a bookseller and publisher. He was twice married: in 1830 to Eliza Matilda Blydenburgh, who died in 1842; and in 1846 to Hester Travis, who survived him. He died in New York City.

[E. H. Pendleton, *Brian Pendleton and His Descendants . . . and Notices of Other Pendletons of Later Origin in the U. S.* (1910); E. T. Freedley, *Leading Pursuits and Leading Men* (copr. 1856); "Diary of Christopher Columbus Baldwin," *Trans. and Colls., Am. Antiq. Soc.*, vol. VIII (1901); C. H. Taylor, "Some Notes on Early American Lithography," *Proc. Am. Antiq. Soc.*, n.s., XXXII (1923); H. T. Peters, *America on Stone* (1931); Joseph Jackson, "History of Lithography in Phila." (MS.).]

J. J.

PENDLETON, JOHN STROTHER (Mar. 1, 1802–Nov. 19, 1868), legislator and diplomat, was born in Culpeper County, Va., long the home of his branch of the Pendleton family. He was of the sixth generation in America, a descendant of Philip, who settled in Virginia in 1682, and the eldest son of William and Nancy (Strother) Pendleton. After the usual preparatory education he studied law, was admitted to the bar in 1824, and achieved prominence in his practice in Culpeper County. His wife, whom he married in 1824, was Lucy Ann Williams.

Several terms in the Virginia House of Delegates (1831–33 and 1836–39) were followed by his appointment in the summer of 1841 to be chargé d'affaires in Chile. There he accomplished the principal object of his mission by inducing the Chilean government to make payments upon the American claims which it had already recognized. He returned to Virginia in time to secure election as Whig representative of his district in the Twenty-ninth Congress and was reëlected to the Thirtieth, serving from 1845 to 1849. In 1848 he was one of those Virginia Whigs who believed it not expedient to present Clay again as the candidate of the Whig party for the presidency. He and three other Whigs signed a pamphlet entitled *To the Whig Party of Virginia* (Washington, 1848) urging the nomination of Zachary Taylor.

The last phase of his diplomatic career began with his appointment Feb. 27, 1851, to be chargé d'affaires to the Argentine Confederation. He was instructed to secure recognition by that somewhat unstable government of the claims of American citizens and to negotiate with it a commercial treaty. Robert C. Schenck [*q.v.*], United States minister to Brazil, was to act with Pendleton in the negotiation of the Argentine treaty, and the two were also to conclude treaties with Paraguay and Uruguay. Late in 1852 Secretary Everett was able to congratulate Pendleton and Schenck upon their "successful and satisfactory" treaty (of Aug. 28, 1852) with "the Oriental Republic of the Uruguay." The treaty with Paraguay was concluded Mar. 4, 1853, but neither of these treaties was ever proclaimed. The "Treaty of Friendship, Commerce and Navigation" with the Argentine Confederation was signed July 27, 1853, and a treaty for the free navigation of the Paraná and Uruguay rivers, with the same power, was concluded July 10, 1853. The negotiation of the latter treaty, for which Pendleton received the commendation of Marcy, was in keeping with the contemporary American policy of establishing the principle of the free use of international waterways. Both the treaties with the Argentine Confederation were proclaimed in 1855 (W. M. Malloy, *Treaties . . . between the United States and Other Powers*, vol. I, 1910, pp. 18, 20). After his retirement from diplomacy in 1854 Pendleton apparently resumed his law practice (see John S. Pendleton, attorney, *Notes in Relation to the Supply of Water Proposed to be Drawn from the Great Falls of Potomac River for the Use of the National Aqueduct*, 1858). He died in Culpeper County in 1868, without issue.

[*Archives of the Dept. of State*; R. T. Green, *Geneal. and Hist. Notes on Culpeper County, Va.* (1900); E. G. Swem and J. W. Williams, *A Reg. of the Gen. Assembly of Va., 1776–1918* (1918); L. Pecquet du Bellet, *Some Prominent Va. Families*, vol. IV (1907); *Biog. Dir. Am. Cong.* (1928); *The Am. Ann. Cyc., 1868* (1869).]

E. W. S.

PENDLETON, WILLIAM KIMBROUGH (Sept. 8, 1817–Sept. 1, 1899), minister of the Disciples of Christ, college president, editor, was born at Yanceyville, Louisa County, Va., the son of Edmund and Unity Yancey (Kimbrough) Pendleton. His ancestors had been prominent in Virginia for several generations, the earliest of them in America, on his father's side, being Philip, a schoolmaster, who emigrated from Norwich, England, in 1674, returned in 1680, and came over again in 1682 to stay. His father's grandfather, John, was a brother of Edmund Pendleton [*q.v.*]; and his father's grandmother, Sarah Madison, was the sister of President James Madison. On the maternal side, William was of Welsh descent. In his infancy his parents moved to "Cuckoo House," Cuckoo, Louisa County, which an ancestor had built. Here he spent his early days, receiving instruction in nearby schools, and in 1836 entering the University of Virginia. He finished his course there in 1840, and, having spent the last part of it in the study of law, was that year admitted to the Virginia bar.

In the meantime the elder Pendletons had joined the Campbellite movement and had been among the charter members of Gilboa Church, near Cuckoo. In June 1840 William was baptized by Alexander Campbell [*q.v.*]. From that time until Campbell's death the two were intimately associated. In October 1840 Pendleton married Campbell's daughter, Lavinia, who died in 1846, and in July 1848 he married her sister, Clarinda. In 1840 Campbell's plans for an institution of learning embodying ideas of his own bore fruit in the establishment of Bethany College, and he persuaded Pendleton to become in 1842 its first professor of natural philosophy. For the remainder of his active career the interests of the college were his chief concern. In 1845, he was appointed vice-president, and, since the president, Campbell, had many extraneous duties, much of the administrative work fell to Pendleton, and no little of the success of the institution during its formative period is attributable to him. After the death of Campbell in 1866, Pendleton was elected president and served as such until 1886.

During the forty-five years he was connected with Bethany, he took part in the cooperative enterprises of the Disciples, being one of the leading members in their first national convention, October 1849, at which the foundations of their organized missionary work were laid. He also exerted a wide influence through his writings. In January 1846 he became an associate of Campbell in editing the *Millennial Harbinger*, and in 1865, its editor-in-chief, continuing as such until the paper was discontinued at the close of 1870. For years many of the leading articles were written by him. From 1869 to 1876 he was associated with William T. Moore [q.v.] in the editorial management of the *Christian Quarterly*, and in December 1873 he became a member of the staff of the *Christian Standard*, of which Isaac Errett [q.v.] was editor. To both these publications he contributed regularly.

Pendleton also took an active part in the civic affairs of the region in which he lived. He worked energetically for improvement in roads and schools. In 1855 he was the Whig candidate for congressman from his district, opposing the Democratic representative, Zedekiah Kidwell, but was defeated in a spirited campaign. After 1861 he supported the Democratic party. He was a member of the West Virginia constitutional convention of 1872 and was prominent in its proceedings. In 1873 Gov. John J. Jacob appointed him state superintendent of public schools to fill out the unexpired term of Charles S. Lewis, and during his incumbency he framed a school law, which was adopted by the legislature; in 1876 he was elected superintendent and served until 1880. Relinquishing the presidency of Bethany in 1886, he retired to Eustis, Fla., where he had purchased property, and found employment in overseeing his orange groves. Here he was instrumental in establishing a church of the Disciples. He died at Beth-

any, where he had gone to attend the Commencement exercises. A Virginia gentleman of the old school, neither demonstrative nor aggressive, well and variously informed though not technically a scholar, possessed of marked literary ability, fond of music and a good judge of art, he was perhaps the leading representative of the more intellectual of the Disciples. His second wife died in 1851, and on Sept. 19, 1855, he married Catherine Huntington King of Warren, Ohio. He was survived by seven children.

[L. P. du Bellet, *Some Prominent Va. Families* (1907); F. D. Power, *Life of William Kimbrough Pendleton, LL.D.* (1902); W. T. Moore, *A Comprehensive Hist. of the Disciples of Christ* (1909); *Christian Standard*, Sept. 9, 1899.]   H. E. S.

PENDLETON, WILLIAM NELSON (Dec. 26, 1809–Jan. 15, 1883), Episcopal clergyman, Confederate soldier, was born in Richmond, Va., the son of Edmund Pendleton of "Edmundton," Caroline County, Va., and Lucy (Nelson) Pendleton. His father was a grandson of John, brother of Edmund Pendleton [q.v.], member of the Continental Congress and president of the Virginia court of appeals, and his mother was a niece of Gen. Thomas Nelson [q.v.], signer of the Declaration of Independence and governor of Virginia in 1781. After instruction by tutors and at a private school in Richmond he was appointed to the United States Military Academy. Graduating July 4, 1830, fifth in his class, he was appointed second lieutenant in the 4th Regiment of Artillery. He served three years in the army, including one as assistant professor of mathematics at West Point, and resigned in 1833 to become professor of mathematics in Bristol College, Pennsylvania. He occupied a similar chair at Delaware College, Newark, Del., from 1837 to 1839. Meantime, having determined to enter the ministry of the Protestant Episcopal Church, he had been made deacon by Bishop Meade of Virginia in 1837 and ordained priest by Bishop Onderdonk of Pennsylvania in 1838.

Recalled to his native state in 1839 to become principal of the newly established Episcopal High School of Virginia at Alexandria, he held that position for five years and brought the school to a high degree of efficiency and success. He removed to Baltimore in 1844 and conducted a private school for three years, during which time he was also in charge of two small congregations. In 1847 he closed his school to devote himself to pastoral work. He served as rector of All Saints Church, Frederick, Md., until 1853, when he accepted a call to Grace Church, Lexington, Va., which charge he held, with the exception of four years of active service in the Army of Northern Virginia until his death in

1883. At Lexington he ministered not only to the community but to the students of the Virginia Military Institute and Washington College (later Washington and Lee University). He was notably successful in strengthening and building his parish and was a prominent figure in the larger work of the Diocese of Virginia. In 1856 he was elected deputy to the General Convention of the Protestant Episcopal Church. He made many missionary preaching tours in the counties west of Lexington and delivered a series of lectures published in 1860 under the title *Science a Witness for the Bible.*

The outbreak of the Civil War brought insistent demand from the citizens of Lexington and Rockbridge County that he place his military training at the service of his state. Consenting, he was elected, May 1, 1861, captain of the Rockbridge Artillery, and was rapidly promoted, being appointed colonel and chief of artillery on the staff of Gen. Joseph E. Johnston, July 13, 1861, and brigadier-general in April 1862. He served later under Robert E. Lee as chief of artillery in the Army of Northern Virginia until its surrender at Appomattox in 1865. He took part in all the major engagements of the army from First Manassas (Bull Run) to the siege of Petersburg. He was an exceedingly able and efficient master of artillery but at the same time never lost sight of his calling as a minister of the Gospel. He preached to the soldiers as opportunities offered on Sundays and at weekday prayer-meetings and was prominent in the remarkable religious movement among the Confederate soldiers which sent so many of the ablest of them into the ministry of their respective churches after the war was over.

Upon his return to Lexington in April 1865 he was asked to resume the rectorship of his parish, though in their utter poverty his people could pay no salary. His rank in the Confederate army excluded him from the relief accorded by the first amnesty proclamation and he was subjected to many indignities, not being permitted for nearly a year to hold a public service in his church. Nevertheless, he continued as rector, earning his own living as best he could through the difficult days of collapse of civil government, and relinquished his pastoral work in Lexington only with his sudden death on Jan. 15, 1883.

Pendleton was of commanding appearance, in his later years bearing a striking resemblance to General Lee, for whom he was frequently mistaken. He married, July 15, 1831, Anzolette Elizabeth, daughter of Capt. Francis Page, of "Rugswamp," Hanover County, an aunt of Thomas Nelson Page [*q.v.*]. They had one son,

Alexander, who became a colonel in the Confederate army and was killed in battle in 1864, and several daughters, one of whom, Susan, became the wife of Gen. Edwin G. Lee of the Confederate army.

[Susan Pendleton Lee, *Memoirs of William Nelson Pendleton, D.D.* (1893); A. B. Kinsolving, *The Story of a Southern School: The Episcopal High School of Virginia* (1922); *14th Ann. Reunion Asso. Grads. U. S. Mil. Acad.* (1883); G. W. Cullum, *Biog. Reg. Officers and Grads. U. S. Mil. Acad.* (3rd ed., 1891), vol. I; *Living Church,* Jan. 27, 1883; records of the Diocese of Va.]
G. M. B.

PENFIELD, EDWARD (June 2, 1866–Feb. 8, 1925), illustrator, painter, author, was born in Brooklyn, N. Y. His father, Josiah, and his grandfather, Henry L. Penfield, came from Rye, N. Y., their forebears from Fairfield, Conn.; his mother, Ellen Locke (Moore) Penfield, was born in England. Edward Penfield received his elementary education in Brooklyn, but soon left school to become a pupil at the Art Students' League in New York. After several years of study he became, at the age of twenty-four, the art editor of *Harper's Magazine,* and shortly, art editor of *Harper's Weekly* and *Harper's Bazar* also. He served these magazines for more than a decade with great distinction and intelligence, both as editor and as artist, in the former capacity seeking out and encouraging the best talent in the country and directing it into new and interesting channels. He discovered and befriended many a young and struggling artist and did much to raise the standards of magazine illustration. In 1901 he resigned his editorships, however, to devote his entire time to art. He executed a series of mural decorations of outdoor sports in Randolph Hall, Cambridge, Mass., now the property of Harvard University, and in 1903 painted ten panels depicting a fox hunt for the Rochester Country Club. Commercial work, however, absorbed more and more of his interest and time. He made a large number of poster designs, by which he is best remembered, and may be cited as the inaugurator of the brief but golden age of poster art in America.

His work was bold, precise, full of character, and always decorative. His flat tones of solid color bounded by strongly accented black lines are reminiscent of the work of Nicholson, Beardsley, Steinlen, and Toulouse-Lautrec; there is the same forcefulness, directness, and extreme simplicity of means as in a typical Japanese print. He was the pioneer in America of this influence. He retained, however, his individuality; his drawing and even his lettering bear the unmistakable mark of his personality. His knowledge of old forms of dress and uniforms was accurate to the last buckle; his interest in horses, coaches, and carriages led him into collecting ancient conveyances; his love of felines was as strong as Steinlen's. His work compels attention by its pleasant pattern and easy readability and sustains interest by its quality of draftsmanship and accuracy of detail. That his output was "commercial" and not "artistic" was largely due to the spirit of the times.

Percival Pollard's *Posters in Miniature* (1896), for which Penfield wrote an introduction, contains fourteen examples of his work, including a self-portrait. Other designs were collected in *Country Carts* (1900) and *The Big Book of Horses & Goats* (1901). Several illustrated articles contributed to *Scribner's Magazine* were reprinted in *Holland Sketches* (1907) and *Spanish Sketches* (1911). Other notable magazine contributions include "The Ancestry of the Coach" (*Outing*, July 1901) and illustrations for Caspar Whitney's article, "The Country-Cart of To-day" (*Ibid.*, June 1900). Much of his work was done for the Beck Engraving Company of Philadelphia (*e.g.*, an *Almanack for the Year of Our Lord 1919, redrawn from Old Farmers' Almanacks*, 1918); typical of his book illustrations are those for *The Dreamers* (1899) by John Kendrick Bangs; his best posters were made for *Harper's Magazine*; he designed covers for *Collier's* and *Harper's Magazine*, and advertising matter issued by the Franklin Press and by the clothing firm of Hart, Schaffner & Marx.

Penfield was married on Apr. 27, 1897, to Jennie Judd Walker, daughter of Maj. Charles A. Walker. They had two sons, one of whom died in childhood. He lived most of his married life in Pelham Manor, N. Y. He was quiet, modest, unassuming, and retiring to the point of secretiveness. In matters of dress he was as precise as in his work. His health was not strong, though, paradoxically, his art was always robust. He died in Beacon, N. Y.

[A small collection of Penfield's work is preserved at the Memorial High School, Pelham, N. Y. Reproductions appear in *Am. Art by Am. Artists, One Hundred Masterpieces* (1914); *The Pageant of America* (1927), vol. XII; F. C. Brown, *Letters & Lettering* (1902). For comment and biographical material see *Am. Art Annual*, vols. XX (1923–24), XXII (1925); C. B. Davis, "Edward Penfield and His Art," *Critic*, Mar. 1899; *Internat. Studio*, XXV (1905), xxvi–xxvii, XXVI (1905), lv–lx; C. M. Price, "The Cat and the Poster," *Arts and Decoration*, Sept. 1912; Frank Weitenkampf, *Am. Graphic Art* (1924); *Who's Who in America*, 1924–25; S. R. Jones, in *Studio* (London), July 15, 1925; *N. Y. Times*, Feb. 9, 10, 1925; *Art News*, Feb. 14, 1925. Information for the foregoing sketch was also derived from his family and friends, and from the editors of *Harper's Magazine*.]   T. S—r.

PENFIELD, FREDERIC COURTLAND (Apr. 23, 1855–June 19, 1922), journalist, diplomat, author, son of Daniel and Sophia (Young) Penfield, was born at East Haddam, Conn. He graduated from Russell's Military School, New Haven, and after a period of travel and study in England and Germany, he entered newspaper work, joining the editorial staff of the *Hartford Courant* in 1880. He was appointed vice-consul general at London in 1885, and on May 13, 1893, diplomatic agent and consul general at Cairo, where he remained throughout Cleveland's second administration. For the next sixteen years he was engaged in travel and writing. In addition to numerous articles in periodicals on economic and political subjects of international interest, he published *Present Day Egypt* (1899) and *East of Suez* (1907). He received decorations from several European and Oriental governments and from the Pope. His first wife, Katharine Alberta (Welles), widow of Edward B. McMurdy, whom he had married in 1892, died in 1905, and in 1908 he married Mrs. Anne (Weightman) Walker of Philadelphia, one of the richest women of the country.

His service under the previous Democratic administration, his wealth, and his Catholic faith qualified him for appointment by President Wilson as ambassador to Austria-Hungary, July 28, 1913. Within a year he was attending, as special ambassador, the funeral of the murdered Archduke Francis Ferdinand. His reports during the critical days of June 1914 threw little light on the situation; but, as soon as the task of helping fellow citizens out of difficulties brought on by the war had been cleared up, he began transmitting useful information on conditions in the country. He contributed suggestions for the reply to the Austro-Hungarian government's protests of 1915 against American exports of munitions to the Allies (*Papers Relating to the Foreign Relations of the United States*, 1915 Supplement, pp. 788–99). He managed to remain on friendly terms with the ministry of foreign affairs despite the feeling engendered by this correspondence, by the enforced recall of the Austro-Hungarian ambassador at Washington, and by the necessity of satisfactions for the sinking of the *Ancona*. Further embarrassment was occasioned by the labors imposed on him as custodian of British, French, Italian, Japanese, and Rumanian interests (*Ibid.*, 1916 Supplement, pp. 816–18). During the period of strained relations between the United States and Germany in the spring of 1916, due to the sinking of the *Sussex*, he contrived, in a conversation with Baron Burian, on Apr. 25, to enlist his government's influence in behalf of a peaceable solution (*Ibid.*, pp. 269–70). Three weeks later he induced the minister of foreign affairs to take steps ameliorating the tone of the press regarding America, a course repeated in February, 1917 (*Ibid.*, 273–76).

His last weeks in Vienna were occupied in the endeavor to break down the unity of the Central Powers by dissociating Austria-Hungary from Germany's renewal of unrestricted submarine warfare and by engaging her in separate peace negotiations. Messages from Count Czernin transmitted by Penfield, followed by his own report of desperate internal conditions, inspired the President to obtain British approval of a suggestion to the Austro-Hungarian government that, if it would make tangible proposals for peace, the integrity of the monarchy would be substantially assured. In pursuance of instructions dated Feb. 22, the ambassador held half a dozen conversations with Czernin without being able to shake his repudiation of all idea of a separate peace (*Ibid.*, 1917 Supplement, I, 38–44, 55–58, 62–65, 113). Upon the failure of these efforts Penfield was ordered, on Mar. 28, to return to Washington "to consult" with the Department of State. He left Vienna on the day of the declaration of a state of war with Germany. His health never recovered from the strain of the final struggles, and he lived quietly in New York until his death.

[*Who's Who in America*, 1920–21; Albert Welles, *Hist. of the Welles Family* (1876); *N. Y. Times*, Apr. 18, June 6, 26, July 8, 29, 1913, June 20, 1922; *Papers Relating to the Foreign Relations of the United States*, 1914–17 Supplements.]   J. V. F.

PENFIELD, WILLIAM LAWRENCE (Apr. 2, 1846–May 9, 1909), jurist, was born in Dover, Lenawee County, Mich., the fourth of eight children of William and Lucinda (Felton) Penfield, of Connecticut and Vermont families respectively, who had migrated westward in 1835. His boyhood was spent on his father's farm. He attended neighboring schools and earned his way to a course in Adrian College, whence he entered the University of Michigan, graduating with honors in the class of 1870. At this time, according to the catalogues of the University, his middle name was Lorenzo; later he used the form Lawrence. A classmate was William R. Day [*q.v.*], who later became secretary of state and was instrumental in having him called to Washington. After his graduation Penfield taught Latin and German at Adrian College for two years, during which time he studied law and was admitted to the bar. In 1873 he settled in Auburn, Ind., forming a law partnership with H. H. Moody. He was married there on June 28, 1875, to Luna Walter, and they had four children, of whom two, a son and a daughter, survived. Penfield practised law in Auburn for over twenty years, building up a statewide reputation for skill and rectitude. He discharged various public functions, official and unofficial, such as those of city attorney, member of the Republican State Committee, presidential elector and electoral messenger, and delegate (in 1892) to the Republican National Convention. In 1894 he was elected judge of the 35th judicial circuit of Indiana, by the largest majority ever given in that circuit.

Called by President McKinley in 1897 to the solicitorship of the Department of State, he was plunged at once into delicate and important public questions. Within a year came the war with Spain; in 1900 the Boxer troubles in China broke; in 1904 came the war between Russia and Japan; and in the same year, the prostration of governmental authority in Santo Domingo. The brunt of the political and legal problems arising out of these difficulties fell upon Penfield's shoulders. He was the trusted adviser of Presidents McKinley and Roosevelt and Secretaries Sherman, Day, Hay, and Root. To the promotion of international arbitration he made significant contributions. He represented the United States in 1902 at the first arbitration before the Permanent Court of Arbitration at The Hague, in the celebrated "Pious Fund" claim against Mexico, winning for the United States an award of over one and a half million dollars (*Senate Document 28, 57 Cong., 2 Sess.*). The same year, he represented the United States in the so-called "Preferential Claims" arbitration, arising from the blockade of Venezuelan ports by Great Britain, Germany, and Italy to enforce long-standing grievances against Castro (*Senate Document 119, 58 Cong., 3 Sess.*). It is said that he drafted in one evening the complete protocol of this arbitration, which was accepted by all the Powers. In all, he prepared and argued for the United States before international arbitral tribunals fifteen important cases, including, besides those already mentioned, arbitrations with Santo Domingo, Peru, Haiti, Nicaragua, Guatemala, Salvador, and Mexico. In 1904 he was an unsuccessful candidate for nomination for the governorship of Indiana. In 1905 he was appointed special commissioner to Brazil. Late in that year he retired from the Department of State, entering into law partnership in Washington with his son. He was retained in important international cases, and in this period was also appointed professor of international law and of the foreign relations of the United States in the postgraduate course of the Law School of Georgetown University. He died in Washington.

Penfield was the author of several notable magazine articles, including: "International Piracy in Time of War" (*North American Review,* July 1898); "British Purchases of War Supplies in the United States" (*Ibid.,* May 1902); "The 'Pious Fund' Arbitration" (*Ibid.,* December 1902); "The Anglo-German Intervention in Venezuela" (*Ibid.,* July 1903); "The First Session of the Hague Tribunal" (*Independent,* Nov. 27, 1902); "The Venezuelan Case at The Hague" (*Ibid.,* Oct. 29, 1903); "The Hague Tribunal" (*Ibid.,* Dec. 17, 1903); and "International Arbitration" (*American Journal of International Law,* April 1907). His opinions and arguments as solicitor of the Department of State have to a considerable extent become source materials and precedents in international law.

[*Extracts from Addresses and a Sketch of the Life of William L. Penfield* (1904); *Am. Jour. International Law,* July 1910; C. S. Carter, *Hist. of the Class of '70 . . . Univ. of Mich.* (1903); *Who's Who in America,* 1908–09; C. W. Taylor, *The Bench and Bar of Ind.* (1895); *Memorial Record of Northeastern Ind.* (1896); *Washington Post, Indianapolis News,* and *Evening Dispatch* (Auburn, Ind.), May 10, 1909.] E. M. B—d.

PENHALLOW, SAMUEL (July 2, 1665– Dec. 2, 1726), merchant, judge, historian, was born at St. Mabyn, County of Cornwall, England, the son of Chamond and Ann (Tamlyn) Penhallow. His father was friendly with the Rev. Charles Morton [*q.v.*], an active dissenter, who removed to Newington-Green, near London, and founded a school for young men which soon became famous. In 1683 Samuel Penhallow was sent to this school for instruction. Since Morton's educational methods and principles were not in harmony with those of the bishops, his school was closed in 1685 and he invited several of his pupils to follow him to America. Penhallow accepted the invitation and in July 1686 landed with his master at Charlestown, Mass.

He was a sober, godly young man and a student of promise. Aware of his intention to enter the ministry and preach the gospel to the Indians, the Society for Propagating the Gospel in Foreign Parts had promised him twenty pounds a year for three years in order that he might study the language of the Narragansetts, and sixty pounds thereafter as long as he followed the ministry and preached to the Indians. Upon his arrival in Charlestown, however, he found the political future of New England so uncertain that he gave up the idea of becoming a minister. He joined the church at Charles-

town, the pastorate of which Charles Morton had accepted soon after his arrival, but shortly moved to Portsmouth and on July 1, 1687, married Mary, daughter of John Cutt, president of the Province of New Hampshire. This marriage gave Penhallow entry to the governing class of the colony and opened to him many opportunities for lucrative trading ventures.

On Aug. 25, 1699, he took oath as a justice of the peace, in September was chosen speaker of the general assembly, and in December was appointed treasurer of the province, an office which, except during a year's absence in England, he held until his death. Other offices held by him in the provincial government in 1702 were recorder and privy councillor. In 1714 he became a justice in the superior court, and in 1717, chief justice. When Governor Shute was in Massachusetts in September 1717, Lieutenant-Governor Vaughan pronounced himself in authority, and, in spite of Governor Shute's contrary orders, dissolved the general court. Judge Penhallow, having taken the side of Governor Shute, was suspended from the council by Vaughan, but promptly reinstated by Shute. These proceedings being laid before the King, were found sufficient cause to remove Vaughan from office. In 1719 Penhallow was again elected recorder, and held the office for three years. During the Indian wars from 1702 to 1725 he kept a very careful record of events and in 1726 published *The History of the Wars of New-England with the Eastern Indians, or a Narrative of Their Continued Perfidy and Cruelty from the 10th of August 1703 to the Peace Renewed the 13th of July 1713, and from the 25th of July 1722 to Their Submission 15 December 1725.* It is a volume faithfully stating harrowing facts with no attempt made to soften the ghastly deeds of the savage.

Penhallow left a large estate accumulated by his trading ventures and through the inheritance of his first wife, who died in 1713, having borne him thirteen children. His second wife, whom he married Sept. 8, 1714, was the twice-widowed Abigail (Atkinson); by her he had one son. In his will he ordered the usual scarf and gloves given each of the bearers and ministers, and a pair of gloves to each of the watchers; but no further expense. Instead of authorizing the "wine gloves Tobacco & pipes which are usually expended" he stipulated that five pounds be added to the five already left his church for its poor.

[A brief extract from Penhallow's diary is in *Mass. Hist. Soc. Colls.,* 2 ser. I (1814), 161; and a short memoir by Nathaniel Adams, in *N. H. Hist. Soc. Colls.,* 1 ser., vol. I (1824); his will is given in H. H. Metcalf, *Probate Records of the Province of N. H.,* vol.

II (1914); an account of a trading expedition to the Penobscot Indians is printed in *New-England Hist. and Geneal. Reg.*, Jan. 1880; see also Nathaniel Bouton, *Provincial Papers, Documents, and Records Relating to the Province of N. H.*, vols. II–IV (1868–70); P. W. Penhallow, *Penhallow Family* (1885).]

H. R. B.

PENICK, CHARLES CLIFTON (Dec. 9, 1843–Apr. 13, 1914), Protestant Episcopal clergyman, missionary bishop of Cape Palmas, Liberia, was born in Charlotte County, Va., the eldest son of Edwin Anderson and Mary (Hamner) Penick. His early education was received in local schools, in Hampden-Sydney College and Danville Military Academy, and was terminated by the outbreak of the Civil War. He enlisted as a private soldier in the 38th Virginia Regiment, which became part of General Armistead's brigade and General Pickett's division, and was appointed quartermaster sergeant of Company A of his regiment. He was once wounded, but continued in service until the end of the war. He then entered the Theological Seminary of the Protestant Episcopal Church in Virginia, at Alexandria, graduating in 1869. He was ordered deacon June 25, 1869, and advanced to the priesthood June 24, 1870. He was assigned as deacon to Emmanuel Church, Bristol, Va., and shortly after his ordination accepted a call to the rectorship of St. George's Parish, Mount Savage, Md. After a brief ministry here, he became rector of the Church of the Messiah in Baltimore, where he won notable success in reviving and reorganizing the work of a church in the business section of a large city. He was a strong and forceful preacher and writer and an able leader and executive.

On Oct. 30, 1876, he was elected by the House of Bishops of the Protestant Episcopal Church to be missionary bishop of Cape Palmas in Africa, and was consecrated to that office on Feb. 13, 1877. The Missionary District of Cape Palmas had suffered the disorganization of being without a bishop for over three years when Penick undertook his duties. Under his leadership the work was greatly strengthened and extended. The chief effort of his administration was to establish mission stations around Cape Mount. He established there among the Vai people St. John's School, which in its fifty years of existence has trained many of the leaders of Liberian life, both civil and religious, and is today (1934) the outstanding institution in the Missionary District. Penick was a tireless worker. The "confusion worse confounded" which he wrote was the condition when he first landed soon gave place to order, but after five years of service it became apparent that the Bishop could not continue to live in the tropical climate.

While delirious with African fever, he was placed aboard a passing ship and brought to the United States. Upon his return to America he resigned his jurisdiction, his resignation becoming effective in October 1883.

After the recovery of his health, he became rector, successively of St. Andrew's Church, Louisville, Ky. (1883–93); St. Mark's Church, Richmond, Va. (1894–99); Christ Church, Fairmont, West Va. (1899–1904); and the Church of the Ascension, Frankfort, Ky. He served also for a number of years as a representative of the Domestic and Foreign Missionary Society attempting to arouse interest in work among the negroes of the Southern States. Resigning his charge in Frankfort in 1912 on account of advancing years and declining health, he lived in retirement until his death, at Baltimore, in 1914.

Penick married, Apr. 28, 1881, Mary Hoge, daughter of Isaac Hoge of Wheeling, W. Va. One daughter was born of this union.

[E. B. Rice, "Historical Sketch of the African Mission," among records of the National Council of the Protestant Episcopal Church, New York; files of the *Southern Churchman* and the *Liberian Churchman*; War Records, Va. State Lib., Richmond; *Who's Who in America*, 1914–15; *Southern Churchman*, Apr. 18, 25, 1914; *Sun* (Baltimore), Apr. 15, 1914.]

G. M. B.

PENINGTON, EDWARD (Sept. 3, 1667–Nov. 11, 1701), Quaker pamphleteer, surveyor-general of Pennsylvania, youngest son of Isaac and Mary (Proude) Springett Penington, was born in Amersham, Bucks County, England. The family was one of comparative wealth. His grandfather, a London merchant, held several responsible city offices, among them that of lord mayor. As a member of the High Court of Justice which sentenced Charles I, he was sent to the Tower and his property was confiscated at the time of the Restoration. "Chalfont Grange," the home of his son, was seized, but the family was not dispossesed until the year before Edward's birth. Following this loss, Mary Penington began to build a new home at Amersham. As the sole heir of Sir John Proude, she was able to take care of her family comfortably.

Nine years before Edward was born his parents had joined the Society of Friends and meetings were held in their home. Persecutions followed. Isaac Penington served four jail sentences, the last, at Reading, when his youngest son was five years old. He was a prolific pamphleteer, and the list of his writings filled twenty-six pages in the catalogue of Friends' books. Until he was thirteen, a year after his father's death, Edward studied at home under tutors, one of whom was Thomas Ellwood, a recent convert to the Society of Friends. He continued his education at Edmonton. When he was fifteen his mother died, leaving him "£100 to bind him to some handsome trade that hath not much of labor," and four hundred pounds to be given to him when he had reached the age of twenty-two. Like his father he was a devout Friend. Entering into the religious controversies of his sect, he published in 1695 three pamphlets: *The Discoverer Discovered*, and *Rabshakeh Rebuked, and His Railing Accusations Refuted*, and, bound with the latter, *A Reply to Thomas Crisp*, all of which were answers to the attacks of Thomas Crisp upon George Fox and the Quakers. The next year two more pamphlets appeared: *Some Brief Observations upon George Keith's Earnest Expostulation*, and *A Modest Detection of George Keith's (miscalled) Just Vindication of His Earnest Expostulation Published by him as a pretended answer to a Late Book of mine Entituled, Some Brief Observations, &c.* His writings were argumentative, without unusual literary merit.

On April 26, 1698, Penington was appointed surveyor-general of the province of Pennsylvania, an office which he held until his death. He accompanied William Penn to Philadelphia when the latter made his second trip, arriving Nov. 30, 1698. Penington assumed his duties at once. In 1701 he was appointed with James Logan attorney for the disposition of the property of Letitia Penn, the daughter of William Penn and Gulielma Springett, Penington's half-sister. When Letitia Penn returned to England in the early part of November, Penington's duties began. About one week later he died in Philadelphia. At the Friends' Meeting House in Burlington, N. J., he married on Nov. 16, 1699, Sarah, the daughter of Samuel and Sarah (Olive) Jennings (or Jenings). Their only child, Isaac, was born Nov. 22, 1700.

[F. W. Leach, "Old Phila. Families," in the Phila. *North American*, Apr. 26, 1908; Jos. Foster, *Pedigree of Sir Josslyn Pennington* (1878); J. W. Jordan, ed., *Colonial Families of Phila.* (1911), vol. I; Phila. Soc. of Friends, *Quaker Biogs.*, 1 ser. II (1909); J. H. Lea, "Geneal. Gleanings Contributory to a Hist. of the Family of Penn," *Pa. Mag. of Hist. and Biog.*, Apr. 1893; Samuel Needles, "The Governor's Mill and the Globe Mills, Phila.," *Ibid.*, Oct. 1884; Maria Webb, *The Penns and Peningtons of the Seventeenth Century* (1867); J. G. Bevan, *Memoirs of the Life of Isaac Pennington* (1807); Thomas Ellwood, *The Hist. of the Life of Thos. Ellwood, Written by His Own Hand* (1714).]
E. M. B—n.

PENINGTON, EDWARD (Dec. 4, 1726– Sept. 30, 1796), Quaker merchant, the son of Isaac and Ann (Biles) Penington and grandson of Edward Penington [*q.v.*], was born in Bucks County, Pa. His father, justice of the county court, sheriff of the county, and one of the founders of the Philadelphia Public Library Company, was a well-educated man and a large property holder in the county. The son was educated in Friends' schools and then went to Philadelphia, where he became a successful merchant. In 1755 and 1757 he was signing provincial paper money. Four years later, 1761, he was elected a member of the Pennsylvania Assembly and in the same year he became one of the judges of the court of common pleas. He was appointed one of the trustees of the State House and grounds, and in 1762 he was made a member of Sir William Johnson's committee to treat with the Indians. When the Committee of Correspondence was named in Philadelphia in June 1774 Penington was chosen a member and was nominated for the presidency. The following month, July 15, he was elected a deputy for the city and the county of Philadelphia to the first Continental Congress. Opposed to armed resistance, he found himself out of sympathy with the government after the signing of the Declaration of Independence. He has even been considered the author of a piece of Tory poetry, the "Poetical Proclamation," which satirized the committee charged with enforcing the ordinances of the Congress. The poem did appear in his handwriting, but beyond that there is no proof that it was of his composition.

Penington was twice arrested, in 1776 for a few hours, and again in September 1777, when he was sent with a group of nineteen others to the Free Masons' Lodge and later exiled to Winchester, Va., where he remained until April 1778. On his return to Philadelphia he took little active interest in politics until 1790 when he became a member of the city council. The following year he was appointed by the legislature as one of the trustees to distribute money among French refugees living in Philadelphia. He was a manager of the Pennsylvania Hospital from 1773 until his resignation in 1779. He was also a member of the American Philosophical Society, elected on Nov. 25, 1768, and chosen a member of the committee to draft its laws the following January. With the formation of the Society for the Cultivation of Silk, sponsored by the Society, Penington was elected treasurer. He married Sarah, daughter of Benjamin and Sarah (Coates) Shoemaker at Bank Meeting House on Nov. 26, 1754. He died in Philadelphia.

[F. W. Leach, "Old Philadelphia Families," Phila. *North American*, Apr. 26, 1908; J. W. Jordan, ed., *Colonial Families of Phila.* (1911), vol. I; C. P. Keith, *The Provincial Councillors of Pa.* (1883); J. F. Watson, *Annals of Phila.* (1844), vol. I; T. G. Morton, *The Hist. of the Pa. Hospital* (1895); *A Hist. of the Schuylkill Fishing Company*, vol. I (1889); G. B.

Wood, *An Address on the Occasion of the Centennial Celebration of the Founding of the Pa. Hospital* (1851); *Pa. Mag. of Hist. and Biog.*, vol. V. no. 1 (1881), vol. VI, no. 3 (1882), Dec. 1884, and Apr. 1908; *Pa. Archives*, vols. I and III (1875).]

E. M. B—n.

PENN, JOHN (July 14, 1729–Feb. 9, 1795), lieutenant governor of Pennsylvania, was the grandson of William Penn [*q.v.*] and the eldest son of Richard (1706–1771) and Hannah (Lardner) Penn. From his father he inherited in 1771 the life use of a quarter of the proprietary rights in Pennsylvania. As prospective heir and later as governor he was largely subject to his uncle, Thomas Penn [*q.v.*], long the principal proprietor and still longer the chief spokesman of the proprietors of the province. He incurred the displeasure of his elders on account of a youthful marriage to a daughter of one James Cox of London, whom he was compelled to repudiate. He was then sent with a tutor to Geneva to study at the University (1747–51) and from 1752 to 1755 was in Pennsylvania, where he was made a member of the provincial council. He attended as commissioner the Congress on Indian affairs at Albany in 1754. Little is known of his life in England in the years that followed, but in 1763 he returned to America commissioned by his father and uncle as lieutenant governor. Upon the death of his father in 1771 he returned to England for about two years, during which time his brother Richard [*q.v.*] held office, but in 1773 he returned in his former capacity and so continued until the revolutionary movement displaced proprietary control and his authority was superseded by the Supreme Executive Council. The end of proprietary government in Pennsylvania may be dated Sept. 26, 1776, with the last adjournment of the provincial assembly. The governor's acts and meetings of the council closed nearly a year earlier.

Penn's official tasks were extremely difficult. There were new boundary disputes with Connecticut and Virginia, while the long-standing controversy with the Lords Baltimore of Maryland was not settled until the running of the Mason and Dixon line in 1767. Indian affairs, though distinctly better after the treaty of Fort Stanwix in 1768, were always troublesome. Penn had to deal with both disgruntled Indians and rabidly vengeful frontiersmen, like the famous "Paxton Boys." Hostility between people and proprietors represented by assembly and council respectively developed as a result of demands of quit rents by the proprietors and claims by the assembly of their right to tax proprietary land. The conflict came to a climax in 1764 when the assembly petitioned the king for the transfer of the colony from the Penns to the Crown. Besides the Anti-Proprietary party, which had the leadership of Benjamin Franklin and the support of the Quakers, there was a strong group in favor of the Penns' control, including Justice William Allen [*q.v.*], whose daughter became John Penn's second wife, and other influential citizens. The Stamp Act soon diverted animosity against the proprietary into hostility against the royal government, but John Penn's position remained difficult. Naturally the proprietors were, like many of the upper class in Pennsylvania, Loyalists in sympathy at the time of the Revolution. In fact, for a few months in 1777, John Penn was held a prisoner on parole, though he was never found guilty of any overt act against the American cause.

Open hostility to the British Crown would have jeopardized their powers of government, yet the Penns were not wholly averse to the more orderly and moderate ambitions of independence. John Penn seems to have yielded gracefully to the course of events. He received his share in the settlement made upon the former proprietors in the divestment act of 1779, which granted to the descendants of Thomas and Richard Penn the retention of all their private estates and proprietary manors and a compensation of £130,000. Except for some years spent abroad, he continued to reside in Philadelphia or at his country estate, "Lansdowne," on the Schuylkill, until his death. On May 31, 1766, he had married Ann, eldest daughter of Chief Justice William Allen of Philadelphia, and grand-daughter of Andrew Hamilton [*q.v.*]. She survived him, dying July 4, 1830. Apparently he left no children. His marriage brought him in touch with the local society and he enjoyed the personal respect of the Philadelphians. He was a member of the Church of England and was buried in Christ Church, Philadelphia. (That he lived in Bucks County in later life and died there and that his remains were subsequently transferred to England was stated in Watson's *Annals*, but the statements are unconfirmed.)

[Besides the general histories of Pennsylvania see H. M. Jenkins, *The Family of William Penn* (1899), with portraits; Arthur Pound, *The Penns of Pa.* (1932), weak in regard to the later Penns; W. R. Shepherd, *Hist. of Proprietary Govt. in Pa.* (1896); C. P. Keith, *The Provincial Councillors of Pa.* (1883); W. C. Armor, *Lives of the Governors of Pa.* (1873); J. F. Watson, *Annals of Phila.* (2 vols., 1830–44). Original records of the proprietary government have been published in part in *Pa. Archives*, in *Pa. Mag. of Hist. and Biog.*, and in the *Memoirs of the Hist. Soc. of Pa.*; a large quantity, unpublished, are preserved in the custody of the Hist. Soc. of Pa., Philadelphia.]

H. J. C.

PENN, JOHN (May 6, 1740–Sept. 14, 1788), signer of the Declaration of Independence, was born in Caroline County, Va., the son of Moses and Catherine (Taylor) Penn. His father was well to do, but made no effort to secure any education for his son beyond the little he could obtain in a country school of that day. After the death of his father, Penn's kinsman, Edmund Pendleton [q.v.], gave him the use of a fine library in which he studied and read law to such profit that he was licensed at twenty-one. Two years later, July 28, 1763, he married Susannah Lyme.

He practised law with success for some twelve years in Virginia, and in 1774 moved to the neighborhood of Williamsboro in Granville County, N. C., where many of his relatives lived. There, having an attractive personality and ability as a speaker, he became a leader and in 1775 was sent to the provincial congress, where he served on numerous committees and won a reputation for tireless industry. Within a month he was elected to the Continental Congress. He soon lost hope of any adjustment with England and declared: "My first wish is that America may be free; the second that she may be restored to Great Britain in peace and harmony and upon Just terms" (*Colonial Records, post,* X, 456). His service in Congress was performed at great personal sacrifice. Others retired but he held on, writing to his friend, Thomas Person, "For God's sake, my Good Sir, encourage our People, animate them to dare even to die for their country" (*Ibid.,* X, 450). As a member of the provincial congress at Halifax in April 1776, he favored the instruction to vote for independence, and returned to Philadelphia in time to vote for and sign the Declaration. He was a member of Congress until 1777, was elected again in 1778, and served until 1780. The task of the North Carolina delegates was by no means purely legislative; "they combined the functions of financial and purchasing agents, of commissary generals, reporters of all great rumors or events, and in general bore the relation to the remote colony of ministers resident at a foreign court" (E. A. Alderman, *Address . . . on the Life of William Hooper,* 1894, p. 33, quoted by Ashe, *post*). They had to buy military supplies, arrange shipment, and conduct intricate financial operations. All these things Penn did besides attending regularly the sessions of Congress. One contemporary allusion suggests that he found some relaxation from labor in Philadelphia society. Some light is thrown upon his character by his conduct in a certain affair of honor. Henry Laurens, presi-

dent of Congress, challenged him to a duel, but since they boarded at the same place, they took breakfast together on the morning of the day set for the meeting and then started out together for the meeting place. After Penn had assisted his elderly opponent across an almost impassable street, he suggested that they abandon their foolish proceeding, to which proposal Laurens agreed.

In 1780 Penn became a member of the North Carolina board of war. Upon him fell the major part of the work of that body, and he rendered able service, although the board was unpopular with the army and opposed by the governor, whose constitutional powers it curtailed. It was abolished in 1781 at the insistence of Gov. Thomas Burke. Penn had declined a judgeship in 1777, and in July 1781, on the plea of ill health, he refused to serve on the council of state. Robert Morris appointed him receiver of taxes in North Carolina for the Confederation, but he retained the place only a few weeks. He returned to the practice of law, and little is known of the remainder of his life.

[S. A. Ashe and others, *Biog. Hist. of N. C.,* vol. VIII (1917); *The Colonial Records of N. C.,* vols. X–XI (1890–95); *The State Records of N. C.,* vols. XIII–XVI (1896–98), XIX (1901), XXII (1907); John Sanderson, *Biog. of the Signers to the Declaration of Independence,* vol. VI (1825); *Wm. and Mary Quart.,* Oct. 1903, p. 130; E. C. Burnett, *Letters of Members of the Continental Cong.,* vols. I–V (1921–31).]
J. G. deR. H.

PENN, RICHARD (1735–May 27, 1811), lieutenant governor of Pennsylvania, was the second son of the proprietor of the same name (1706–1771) and his wife, Hannah Lardner, and was a grandson of William Penn [q.v.], founder of the province. He was a student for a time, though not a graduate, of St. Johns College, Cambridge. For many years he drifted about without settling down to any profession. Coming to Pennsylvania with his brother John [1729–1795, q.v.] upon the latter's appointment as governor in 1763, he took some part in public affairs until his return to England in 1769. Two years later, when his father's death called his brother home, he was appointed as lieutenant governor by his brother and his uncle, Thomas [q.v.], who were then sole proprietors. In August 1773 he was abruptly superseded by his brother, John. He evidently felt himself wronged either by his removal from office or by the settlement of his father's estate, and was not reconciled to his brother for some months. During his residence with the people of Pennsylvania Richard Penn had secured their confidence, and when he returned to England in 1775 the Continental Congress, then sitting in Philadelphia, entrusted to him the delivery of the "Olive Branch," their final address to the King. This petition he presented, and when it was being considered in the House of Lords he was questioned as to the American colonies, for whose claims he had much sympathy and understanding.

For the rest of his life, except for a brief residence in Philadelphia near its close, Richard Penn lived in England. He was returned four times to Parliament, sitting once for Appleby (1784–90), twice for Haslemere (1790, 1806), and once for Lancaster (1796–1802). His financial situation was apparently straitened during the Revolution, when there was little income from sources in Pennsylvania. From 1787 on he began to receive a share in the funds voted by the newly formed state to descendants of its former proprietors, an interest that was at least trebled at the death of his brother John in 1795. The usual view of his character is that he "possessed a fine person, elegant manners, was of a social disposition, and a *bon vivant*. He was the most popular member of his family who visited Pennsylvania after the death of the Founder" (Thompson Westcott, *The Historic Mansions and Buildings of Philadelphia*, 1877, p. 253). On May 21, 1772, while governor of Pennsylvania, Richard Penn married Mary (1756–1829), daughter of William and Mary Masters and grand-daughter of Thomas Lawrence [*q.v.*]. Of their five children, two sons named William and Richard had some distinction of mind, but none left any children.

[See bibliography under John Penn, 1729–1795.]

H.J.C.

PENN, THOMAS (Mar. 9, 1702–Mar. 21, 1775), proprietor of Pennsylvania, son of William Penn [*q.v.*], the Quaker statesman, and of Hannah Callowhill, his second wife, was born in Bristol, England, in the house of his grandfather, Thomas Callowhill, for whom he was named. About 1715 or 1716 he was sent from the home of his parents in Ruscombe, Berkshire, to London to enter a business career, apparently first in the employ of Michael Russell, mercer, and later as partner in a commercial establishment whose name is unknown. In 1718 his father died, leaving the proprietary interests in Pennsylvania to his widow as executrix for their four sons; but her rights were contested and not established until 1727, after she herself and the youngest son, Dennis, had died. The mortgages on the estate made in the founder's lifetime were not extinguished until some years later. The three surviving sons of William and Hannah Penn divided the proprietor-

ship, half going to the oldest, John, and a quarter each to Thomas and Richard. John died in 1746, bequeathing his half share to Thomas. In 1732 Thomas came to Philadelphia, where he managed the proprietary affairs of the province for nine years. In 1741 he went back to England expecting to return to Pennsylvania, but he never did so, and his further dealings with the officials of the province and his own representatives there were carried on by correspondence.

From his correspondence (preserved in great abundance in the Historical Society of Pennsylvania) and from other evidence, Thomas Penn appears to have been a man of energy and ability. The financial difficulties that had overshadowed the last years of his father's life and the widowhood of his mother were gradually relieved by an increased income to the proprietary from sales of land to immigrants. On Aug. 22, 1751, Thomas Penn married Lady Juliana Fermor (1729–1801), fourth daughter of Thomas, first Earl of Pomfret. In 1760 he purchased the well-known estate of Stoke Poges, in Buckinghamshire, England, which remained in the family for eighty years. Of his eight children, four died in infancy. The others were Juliana, John, Granville, and Sophia Margaretta. To heirs of the last named the Penn property in Pennsylvania so far as it was not already lost to the family at last reverted, all other lines descended from William Penn's marriage to Hannah Callowhill having become extinct in 1869.

Thomas Penn's Quaker origin did not determine his religious allegiance in later life. In 1743 he wrote of the Quakers that he "did not hold their opinions concerning defence," adding, "I no longer continue the little distinction of dress" (H. M. Jenkins, *The Family of William Penn*, 1899, p. 145); and after his marriage he accounted himself a member of the Church of England. Yet he did not wish to be estranged from the Friends, and it was because he was a dissenter from the Church of England that he was prevented by the Test Act and the requirement of an oath from assuming, even when on the spot, the actual governorship of Pennsylvania when such office seemed to him both natural and desirable (see unpublished letters from John Penn in 1733, Historical Society of Pennsylvania). But the descendants of William Penn were very early contrasted unfavorably with their ancestor and failed to command the regard in which he was held by whites as well as by Indians. The Indians, particularly, resented what appeared to some of them a fraudulent purchase, in 1737, of the Forks of the Delaware, made under the terms of the "Walking Purchase." Whatever opprobrium this famous transaction deserves belongs to Thomas Penn, who must have authorized it directly. He was unsuccessful in conciliating even the white colonists, either by personal graciousness during his presence or by effective skill and sympathy in dealing with them through his agents. Nevertheless, as the first Penn to visit the colony after 1704, and as the holder for nearly thirty years of three-fourths of the proprietary and family land in Pennsylvania and Delaware, he was an important figure in the public affairs of Pennsylvania and, except for his father, more influential in its history than any other member of the family. The proprietary form of government was one that could not last, however, and the colony became increasingly intransigent and covetous of complete liberty. It is significant that ten years before Thomas Penn's death and the beginning of the American Revolution the Pennsylvanians were petitioning that jurisdiction over the province be transferred from the proprietors to the Crown.

[See bibliography under John Penn, 1729–1795.]

H. J. C.

PENN, WILLIAM (Oct. 14, 1644–July 30, 1718), founder of Pennsylvania, born near the Tower of London, was the son of Admiral Sir William Penn (1621–1670) and Margaret Jasper, whose father was John Jasper, a merchant of Rotterdam, later of Ireland. Even in childhood Penn was religiously inclined and, although his father adhered to the Anglican faith, the son early came under occasional Puritan influences. After completing about two years at Christ Church College, Oxford, he was expelled in 1662 on account of his non-conformist scruples and activities. This was much to the chagrin and anger of his father, who next sent him on a continental tour to turn him from his extreme religious inclinations. In Paris young Penn seemed for a time to be influenced by court society, as his father desired. Later, however, attending for a time a Huguenot Academy at Saumur, he seems to have received impressions favorable to his later peace principles and to inward spiritual religion (Brailsford, *post*, pp. 120–24). Recalled home by his father at the outbreak of the Dutch War (1665), he had a glimpse of naval activities, sailing with the fleet and returning with dispatches for the King. In this year his mind was again turned to serious contemplation by the horrors of the Great Plague. At this period also he attended Lincoln's Inn for about a year, learning enough law to help him later in business affairs and in meeting the legal issues of religious persecutions. Early in 1666 he went to Ireland, where he took charge of some estates near Cork owned by his father. At this time he again tasted worldly pleasures at the brilliant court of the Duke of Ormonde, Lord Lieutenant of Ireland. He also showed some military prowess in helping to quell a mutiny—and at this time his well known portrait in armor was made.

The great turning point of his life was, however, at hand. He heard again the powerful preaching of Thomas Loe, an early Quaker apostle, who had influenced him some years before. Continuing to attend the meetings of Friends, he was soon in trouble with the authorities and was for a time in prison—where he composed his first appeal for liberty of conscience (*Works*, 1726, I, 2–3; Janney, *post*, 1 ed., pp. 24–25). Released from prison and summoned sharply to England by his father, he soon became an avowed and active Friend. With tongue and pen he vigorously advocated the doctrines of Friends and of political liberalism. Thus the great convictions of his life were definitely shaped and settled. In 1669, while imprisoned in the Tower of London for publishing his unorthodox work, *The Sandy Foundation Shaken* (1668), he composed the first draft of his famous *No Cross, No Crown* (1669; see also edition 1930, p. X), directed against luxury, frivolity, vicious amusements, and economic oppression. Near this time also, besides many religious tracts, he wrote several on political subjects, which together formed a noble and convincing plea for religious toleration, security of person and property, and other rights of free Englishmen. In 1670, after he and William Meade had been arrested for preaching in Gracechurch Street, the liberties of Englishmen were so ably pleaded by Penn himself that the case (the noted "Bushell's Case") resulted first in an acquittal for the defendants, and later in an outstanding victory for the freedom of English juries from the dictation of judges (Braithwaite, *post*, pp, 70–73, with references). In 1670 Admiral Penn died, with a blessing on his lips for the son who came from prison to his bedside. Soon after this the son made a missionary journey through Holland and parts of Germany, spreading the Quaker faith. Returning to England he married, on Apr. 4, 1672, the beautiful and devoted Gulielma Maria Springett, daughter of Mary (Proude) Penington by her first husband, Sir William Springett.

The next half-decade of Penn's life, 1675–1680, saw a continuation of his activities in religion and politics, and the beginning of his connection with America. He made a second missionary journey to the Continent in 1677, in the company of prominent Friends, including George Fox. He visited many towns of Holland and western Germany, winning the interest and affection of various groups of Protestant mystics who were later to settle in his American province. He and some of his fellow apostles formed a notable friendship with the learned and pious Elizabeth, Princess Palatine, upon whom the Quaker teachings made a lasting impression. Returning to England, Penn threw himself with renewed zeal into the political struggles of the last troubled years of the Stuart régime. In these labors he received little support and some opposition from the Quakers, who suffered periodic persecutions and tended to withdraw from "worldly" activities. Penn urged them to take their proper part in the struggle for liberal government. He threw himself actively into two political campaigns for the election to Parliament of his Whig friend, Algernon Sidney. Some of his finest political pamphlets are of this period. In spite of the friendly connections at Court, inherited from his father, he was a forthright champion of toleration for dissenters, frequent elections, and uncontrolled Parliaments (see especially "England's Great Interest in the Choice of this New Parliament," *Works*, 1726, II, 678-82).

His first connection with America was with New Jersey. By a series of transactions West Jersey came into the hands of Friends, and Penn became one of the trustees to manage the property. In 1677 the ship *Kent* arrived in the Delaware River with two hundred settlers to found the town of Burlington. The colonists brought with them the famous Concessions and Agreements for their government (W. A. Whitehead, ed., *Archives of the State of New Jersey*, 1 ser., I, 1880, pp. 241 ff.). Historians are in general agreement that this great charter of liberties came largely from the hand of William Penn. It was the first fruit of his hard schooling in English politics, and his first gift to American government. The charter guaranteed to the settlers the right of petition and of trial by jury. It provided against arbitrary imprisonment for debt, and made no provision for capital punishment even for treason. It guaranteed religious freedom, stating that "no Men, nor number of Men upon Earth, hath Power or Authority to rule over Men's Consciences in religious Matters" (*Ibid.*, I, 253). It provided friendly methods for the purchase of Indian lands. In jury trials in which Indians were concerned the jury was to be composed of six Indians and six whites. These guarantees of personal rights and

of justice formed a rather complete bill of rights, and they were reinforced by the first clear statement in American history of the supremacy of the fundamental law (in the Concessions) over any statutes that might be enacted (*Ibid.*, I, 266). The Assembly was to dominate the government of the province. It was to be freely elected by the settlers and was to serve for one year only —a gesture against the long and controlled Parliaments of the Stuart régime in England. There was to be complete freedom of speech in the Assembly, and the public was to be admitted freely "to hear and be witnesses of the votes." There was no clear and definite provision for an executive, and the Assembly later conceded to the proprietors the appointment of governors. Yet the Assembly was to be "free and supream" and there was no provision for an executive veto. Thus it was not without justification that Penn and his friends said of these Concessions and Agreements: "There we lay a foundation for after ages to understand their liberty as men and Christians ... for we put the power in the people" (Samuel Smith, *History of the Colony of ... New Jersey*, 1765, pp. 80-81). Penn later became a member of a large group of proprietaries, a majority of whom were Quakers, who secured title to East Jersey. However, the rights of government held by this proprietorship were soon brought into question, and by another chain of events Penn transferred his chief interest to his great province west of the Delaware River. His greatest gift to the Jerseys was his part in the Concessions and Agreements of 1677, which have been called "the broadest, sanest, and most equitable charter draughted for any body of colonists up to this time" (C. M. Andrews, *Colonial Self-Government*, 1904, p. 121).

Penn's next and greatest venture into the realm of practical politics was in Pennsylvania. He had inherited from his father, besides a considerable fortune immediately available, a large claim for funds loaned by the Admiral to Charles II. On petition of Penn, the King granted him in 1681, as payment for this debt, a great tract of land north of Maryland. Penn wished to call his province New Wales, or Sylvania, but the King insisted that it be named, in honor of the late Admiral, "Pennsylvania." In 1682 Penn secured from his friend the Duke of York the territory of Delaware, which was at first joined to the government of Pennsylvania but later became a separate province. Penn called his new project a "Holy Experiment" and threw himself with enthusiasm into his plans for it. In 1681 he sent over his cousin, William Markham [*q.v.*], to act as his deputy, and himself followed the next year. He spread broadcast his proposals to settlers, not forgetting his converts on the continent of Europe. His terms for the purchase or rental of land were very liberal and soon attracted large numbers of settlers.

Penn's first Frame of Government for his province was dated Apr. 25, 1682, and appended to it a few days later (May 5) were the Laws Agreed upon in England (Original copy of the Frame of Government in State Library, Harrisburg, Pa.). The government thus provided for was not so strikingly democratic as that of West Jersey described above, the Proprietor being influenced perhaps by the prospective large landholders whom he consulted (W. R. Shepherd, *History of Proprietary Government in Pennsylvania*, 1896, p. 237, note 1). Thus very large powers were given to the Council, as compared with the Assembly. Yet both Council and Assembly were elective, and the governor was given a rather minor place. The fundamental liberties of the individual were guaranteed. Murder and treason were the only crimes made punishable by death. All believers in God "shall in no ways be molested or prejudiced for their religious Persuasion or Practice in Matters of Faith and Worship, nor shall they be compelled at any Time to frequent or maintain any religious Worship, Place or Ministry whatever." Penn's basic belief in a democratic system was tersely expressed in the preface to his great Frame of Government: "Any Government is free to the People under it (whatever be the Frame) where the Laws rule, and the People are a Party to those Laws." Many details of Penn's plan of government were changed upon his arrival in America. The Assembly was self-assertive from the start and the Proprietor was disposed to grant all reasonable requests. He soon learned, however, that he could not please all of the people all of the time, and that the perennial demand of democracy is for more democracy. It was not long before he was driven to write to a group of his contending provincials: "I am sorry at heart for your animosities. . . . For the love of God, me, and the poor country, be not so governmentish, so noisy, and open, in your dissatisfactions" (Robert Proud, *History of Pennsylvania*, 1798, I, 297, note).

The brightest page in Penn's political record is the story of his dealing with the American Indians. Even before his own arrival in Pennsylvania he sent them his message of friendship: "I have great Love and Regard towards you, and I desire to win and gain your Love and Friendship by a kind, Just and Peaceable Life" (*Works*, 1726, I, 122). Perhaps the tradition of the Pro-

prietor's jovial fraternizing with the Indians in their feasts and games has been overemphasized. No doubt the glorification of his Quaker peace policy by uncritical historians has been overdone. Yet the residue of plain truth is a worthy testimonial to William Penn. He did take measures to protect the Indians from the ravages of rum and the rapacity of white traders. He did make every effort to satisfy them in his negotiations for their lands. His best testimonial is that the Indians themselves were deeply loyal to him and always held his name in loving respect (R. W. Kelsey, *Friends and the Indians, 1655–1917*, 1917, pp. 62 ff., *et passim*). Not until his descendants, who forsook his faith and his just policy, had betrayed and defrauded the natives, did the frontiers of Pennsylvania know the terrors of savage warfare. Thus the Indians were faithful on their side to the promises made to William Penn at various treaties with him, "that the Indians and English must live in Love as long as the Sun gave Light." Tradition has fused these treaties into one great treaty "under the elm tree at Shackamaxon," made famous by the brush of Benjamin West, and aptly idealized by Voltaire as the only treaty "between those people and the Christians that was not ratified by an oath, and was never infringed" (*Letters Concerning the English Nation*, 1926 reprint, p. 22).

Penn's first stay in his colony lasted only a year and ten months, but he crowded much into that time. Aside from his cares of government he superintended the laying out of Philadelphia and began the building of his own mansion-house at Pennsbury, some miles up the Delaware River. He made a tour of inspection into the interior of Pennsylvania. He visited New York, Long Island, and the Jerseys. He went to Maryland and later to New Castle to discuss his unhappy boundary dispute with Lord Baltimore. He attended Friends' meetings, and preached when he felt "called." He composed his long and well-known letter (Aug. 16, 1683) to the Free Society of Traders in England, describing with great fulness the woods, waters, animals, men, produce, and all the various possibilities of his great province (*Works*, 1726, II, 699–706). Then, in the midst of his arduous but happy tasks, conditions compelled his return to England, where the Quakers were suffering renewed and bitter persecution and needed his influence at Court. Lord Baltimore, moreover, had already gone to urge his boundary claims in London. Wisdom required Penn to follow, and on Aug. 12, 1684, he sailed for England.

On his arrival there he entered another period

of strenuous activity. His old friend the Duke of York succeeding to the throne in 1685 as James II, Penn was able by his enhanced influence at Court to secure the release from prison of about 1,300 Friends. In 1685 he made his third missionary journey to Holland and Germany, and soon afterward was engaged in a preaching tour of England. As a close friend of the King and a constant advocate of toleration, he was now charged, not for the first time, with being a Jesuit in disguise. Nor was this accusation forgotten by his enemies when King James, in 1687, issued on his own royal authority, his famous Declaration of Indulgence. Penn naturally applauded the new policy, although his political liberalism compelled him to urge the King to buttress the Declaration with the sanction of Parliament. As a loyal friend of James he was greatly compromised by the Revolution of 1688 and the accession of William and Mary. More than once he had to answer accusations of disloyalty before the Privy Council and for a time he went into partial retirement in London until the storm of charges and suspicions abated. For nearly two years (1692–94) his governorship of Pennsylvania was forfeited, but was restored after his full and final vindication of all treasonable activities. Yet during these troublous times he wrote his charming maxims of faith and life, *Some Fruits of Solitude* (1693). Also, in 1693, during a war of alliances in Europe, came his famous *Essay towards the Present and Future Peace of Europe, by the Establishment of an European Dyet, Parliament, or Estates,* a significant early plan for confederation, arbitration, and peace. In 1694 died his devoted and beloved wife Gulielma, and on Mar. 5, 1695/96, he married Hannah Callowhill, who proved to be a loyal and efficient helpmeet. In this period he continued his writing and speaking on religious subjects, influencing among others by his ministry Peter the Great, of Russia, who was visiting England. In 1698 he made a business and preaching journey to Ireland. The effectiveness of his public ministry at this time is indicated by a remark of the Dean of Derry, who heard him preach and afterward said that "he heard no blasphemy nor nonsense, but the everlasting truth . . . [and] his heart said Amen to what he had heard" (Graham, *William Penn,* p. 241).

During these busy and troublous years in England the Proprietor of Pennsylvania was not forgetful of his interests in the New World. In 1697 he drew up and presented to the Board of Trade in London the first thorough-going plan for a union of all the American colonies. In this plan he proposed a central Congress to fix quotas of men and money in time of war, and to deal with common problems in time of peace (Copy in E. B. O'Callaghan, *Documents Relating to the Colonial History of the State of New York,* IV, 1854, pp. 296–97). He secured a partial settlement of his boundary dispute with Lord Baltimore, although the main issue remained unsettled during his lifetime and long after his death. He gave orders in 1689 for the establishment of a public grammar school in Philadelphia, which was opened in that year and still exists as the William Penn Charter School. Yet his own presence was called for in Pennsylvania and he had long desired to answer the call. There were religious troubles, including the schism of George Keith [*q.v.*]. There were administrative problems and political disputes that had long demanded his presence. Finally "the way opened" and he embarked, this time with his family, arriving at Chester, Pa., Dec. 1, 1699, after an absence of fifteen years from his beloved "woodlands" and his "fine greene Country Towne" of Philadelphia. On his second visit he showed his continued interest in the Indians by various meetings with them, making new agreements and renewing old covenants of friendship. He did what he could to mitigate the evils of slavery in Pennsylvania and made a will providing for the later emancipation of his own slaves. He continued his religious activities and, on a visit to Tredhaven (Easton), Md., preached in the presence of Lord and Lady Baltimore. He took measures for the suppression of piracy, granted a charter to Philadelphia, and most important of all, granted the Charter of 1701 to Pennsylvania. In this he renewed his old guarantee of religious liberty, but changed the form of government as established, 1682–83, and modified under Governor Markham in 1696. The new charter made possible the early establishment of separate legislatures for the province and the territories (Pennsylvania and Delaware). The Council ceased to be an elective body and became practically an advisory board to the governor. The Assembly became a single-chamber legislature, elected yearly by the people, on a wide suffrage. Although the governor retained the veto power, the Assembly could usually find means to coerce him. Its existence did not depend upon his call, and it could "sit upon its own Adjournments." Thus it continued practically supreme in the legislative field until the Revolution. The Charter of Privileges of 1701 came to be revered by the people of Pennsylvania as the palladium of their liberties (printed in *Votes and Proceedings of House of Representatives of Pennsylvania,* I, 1752, part II, pp. 1–111).

Penn

Penn had hoped to remain a resident of Pennsylvania but this hope was not realized. On the outbreak of the War of the Spanish Succession a proposal was made in the English Parliament to annex all proprietary colonies to the Crown. Penn's presence in England thus became essential and late in 1701 he again said farewell to his province, this time not to return. Indeed it appears that the constructive work of his life had now been largely accomplished. He was able to retain his proprietorship but his last years were full of trouble and disappointment. He was harassed by almost endless disputes between his governors and the Pennsylvania Assembly. His own choice of deputies and helpers was not always happy. He had serious pecuniary embarrassments and for a time languished in a debtor's prison. He suffered great humiliation and sorrow because of the dissolute life of his son, William Penn, Jr. Yet he continued to some degree his activities of writing and speaking. In 1709, at sixty-five years of age, he traveled "in the ministry" through several counties of England. In 1712 he had almost arranged for a sale of his proprietary government to the Crown when he suffered an attack of apoplexy which soon destroyed his memory and rendered him incapable of further administering his affairs. His faithful wife, Hannah Penn, ably supervised his business interests until his death in 1718 at the age of seventy-four years. In 1727, after her death and that of their youngest son, the proprietorship of Pennsylvania passed into the hands of the surviving sons, John, Thomas [q.v.], and Richard Penn.

As a youth Penn was described as well-built, handsome, athletic, and of courtly manners. In later life he became somewhat corpulent but "using much exercise, retained his activity." The portrait as a youth in armor and the Bevan bust show the strength of his facial features. He was an unusual combination of mystic, courtier, and statesman. Apart from his important religious labors, he founded or helped to found three American commonwealths (New Jersey, Pennsylvania, and Delaware), and made a worthy contribution to the political thought of England and Europe. The Quaker "testimony" concerning him (photostat at Haverford College) drawn up after his death by Reading Monthly Meeting of Friends, England, was no doubt a deserved tribute: "He was a Man of great Abilities, of an Excellent sweetness of Disposition, quick of thought, & ready utterance; full of the Quallification of true Discipleship, even Love without dissimulation . . . he may without straining his Character be ranked among the Learned good & great."

[There are two authentic portraits of Penn: the one of him as a youth in armor, of which an original, or an authentic contemporary copy, is in the Hall of the Hist. Soc. of Pa., Philadelphia; and an ivory medallion bust of him in old age, made from memory after his death by his friend, Sylvanus Bevan. Possibly the portrait by Francis Place is also authentic (Graham, *post*, p. 330). There are biographies as follows: "Journal of His Life," prefixed to Joseph Besse, *A Collection of the Works of William Penn* (2 vols., 1726); Thomas Clarkson, *Memoirs of the Private and Public Life of William Penn* (2nd ed., 2 vols., 1814); W. H. Dixon, *William Penn: An Historical Biography* (2nd ed., 1852); S. M. Janney, *The Life of William Penn* (1852); S. G. Fisher, *The True William Penn* (1900), reprinted as *William Penn* (1932); J. W. Graham, *William Penn, Founder of Pa.* (1917), containing a summary, pp. 310-13, of the various refutations of Macaulay's aspersions upon Penn; M. R. Brailsford, *The Making of William Penn* (1930); Bonamy Dobrée, *William Penn, Quaker and Pioneer* (1932); C. E. Vulliamy, *William Penn* (1934). On his relation to Stuart politics, see P. S. Belasco, *Authority in Church and State* (1928). For the family see H. M. Jenkins, *The Family of William Penn* (1899); and Arthur Pound, *The Penns of Pennsylvania and England* (1932). For the setting of his life work see W. C. Braithwaite, *The Second Period of Quakerism* (1919); and R. M. Jones, *The Quakers in the Am. Colonies* (1911). The *Dictionary of National Biography* emphasizes the European side of Penn's life, as the above account does the American side. A small but important contribution by A. C. Myers, "William Penn, His Own Account of the Delaware Indians, 1683," announced for early publication, contains a brief sketch of Penn's life.

The writings of Penn are largely listed in Joseph Smith, *A Descriptive Catalogue of Friends' Books* (2 vols., 1867), and *Supplement* (1893); also M. K. Spence, *William Penn: A Bibliography* (1932). Besides the collection of Joseph Besse (above), may be cited *Select Works of William Penn* (1771); *The Select Works of William Penn* (5 vols., 1782); Deborah Logan and Edward Armstrong, *Correspondence between William Penn and James Logan* (2 vols., 1870-72; Pubs. of Hist. Soc. of Pa., vols., IX, X). The largest collection of Penn materials, printed and manuscript, in England, is in Friends' Library, Euston Road, London. For this and other collections in England see C. M. Andrews and F. G. Davenport, *Guide to the Manuscript Materials for the Hist. of the U. S. to 1783, in the British Museum* (1908). The largest collections in America, including the important private collection of A. C. Myers, are at 1300 Locust St., Phila., Hall of the Hist. Soc. of Pa. The libraries of Haverford and Swarthmore colleges should also be consulted. Some biographers have been at odds as to whether Penn's mother was actually Dutch, as stated by Pepys, or Anglo-Irish. A. C. Myers stands with Pepys and thus holds that William Penn was "half a Dutchman."] R. W. K.

PENNELL, JOSEPH (July 4, 1857–Apr. 23, 1926), etcher, sprang from an unbroken line of Quakers. His ancestors left Nottinghamshire, England, in 1684, for Pennsylvania, and for generations were husbandmen, until Larkin Pennell, Joseph's father, broke the family tradition by becoming a teacher and later a shipping clerk. He married Rebecca A. Barton. Joseph, born in their quiet house on South Ninth Street, Philadelphia, was their only child. He attended Quaker schools in Philadelphia and later in Germantown, to which place his family moved in 1870. He was a nervous, moody child and preferred to be alone to draw pictures. Often ill, he had frequent accidents, becoming left-handed after he broke his right arm.

In 1876 he graduated from the Germantown Friends' Select School and, in spite of the opposition of his parents, tried to enter the school of the Pennsylvania Academy of the Fine Arts, but was rejected and became a clerk for a coal company at seven dollars a week. It was probably some "perversity" of the romantic, impractical Welsh-Irish blood in his veins that made him, from the first, worship beauty with the same veneration which his sober Quaker relatives accorded to their God, and determined him to become an artist. He joined the night classes of the Pennsylvania School of Industrial Art and soon met Stephen Ferris, who taught him the technique of etching and showed him the work of the Spanish artists Fortuny, Rico, Casanova, and Fabres. Pennell was inspired to imitate the chaste clarity of their pen-and-ink drawings and their brilliant effects of warm, glittering sunshine.

With the Friends' habit of speaking his mind, he severely criticized his school for teaching too much mechanical drawing, and cut so many classes that he was dismissed. One of his instructors, Charles M. Burns, the architect, discerned his promise and persuaded the Pennsylvania Academy School to reconsider and admit him as a pupil; so Pennell abandoned his clerkship and, devoting all his time to art, began to work with the extraordinary industry which never slackened during the rest of his life. Too sensitive to stand the unsympathetic criticisms of Thomas Eakins [q.v.], he left the school and about 1880 hired a studio of his own. Almost immediately he became self supporting, for he had not only a good journalistic sense, but also a gift for salesmanship. This was proved when he took his drawings of a picturesque marsh in South Philadelphia to New York and sold them to Alexander Wilson Drake [q.v.], then art editor of Scribner's Monthly. They appeared in July 1881, and Drake, very much pleased, ordered eight etchings of historical buildings in Philadelphia. Charles Godfrey Leland [q.v.] was invited to write the text, but suggested that his niece, Elizabeth Robins, do it instead. This collaboration led to the meeting of Pennell and his future wife. Their first article, "A Ramble in Old Philadelphia," was published in March 1882 in the Century, which had succeeded Scribner's.

The same year Pennell was commissioned to go to New Orleans to illustrate a series of articles by George W. Cable [q.v.], later published in book form as The Creoles of Louisiana (1884). Pennell reveled in the insanitary picturesqueness,

the good wine, and beguiling cuisine of the old Latin city, and worked with an ecstatic energy, taking time only to write rhapsodic letters to Elizabeth Robins with graphic little sketches on their margins. The New Orleans etchings and drawings made such a stir that Pennell, at twenty-five, had achieved success, and the Century asked him to go to Italy to illustrate articles by William Dean Howells [q.v.] on Tuscan cities. Early in 1883 he joined Howells in Florence, and in a month had finished all the necessary drawings. Then he wandered over Italy, thrilled by its beauty, and his enthusiasm gave birth to a series of Italian plates that were remarkable for so young an artist. He returned by way of England and Ireland, executing various commissions for magazine articles on the way, and was back in Philadelphia by October, ready to plunge into a mass of hack drawings for the Century.

He swept Elizabeth Robins into his welter of work by marrying her in June 1884, and they sailed immediately for Europe. He was to make more illustrations for Tuscan Cities, but an outbreak of cholera in Italy decided the pair to go to London. In the beginning of August they set out on a tandem bicycle to ride to Canterbury, stopping often for Pennell to sketch while Mrs. Pennell took copious notes. The result was a small illustrated book, A Canterbury Pilgrimage (1885), described by Andrew Lang in a leader in the London Daily News as "the most wonderful shilling's worth modern literature has to offer" (Life and Letters, I, 149). In October they finally started for Italy and rode a tricycle from Florence to Rome. He sketched and she wrote and they never missed an art museum. This was the pattern of all their "holidays." In succeeding summers they quartered Europe on wheels, and on one trip rode ten in succession of the highest passes over the Alps. They became the most articulate couple alive, for all their reactions to art, life, and beauty were given expression in the wife's poised and cultivated prose and the husband's eloquent graphic illustrations. The record of these "holidays" fills some twelve volumes.

In 1884, in spite of his ardent Americanism, Pennell decided to live in London because most of his commissions, though from America, were for European drawings, and he could not afford either the time or the money for long ocean voyages. His picturesque, earnest personality, his strong, outspoken convictions and his instant willingness to defend them, soon made him a distinctive figure; and Mrs. Pennell's charm and tact drew around them the few Pre-Raphaelites still living and a group of many of the best known literary men, artists, publishers, and journalists of the day; among them Henley, "Bob" Stevenson, Edmund Gosse, Bernard Shaw, Heinemann, and of course, Whistler.

Pennell's etchings made an immediate impression and were first shown at the Exhibition of the Society of Painter-Etchers in 1885. He had struck his stride and was producing an amazing amount of work, but so great was his artistic integrity that he never slighted a single line. Most of his product was reproduced in the *Century* but some appeared in *Harper's* and in many of the best English magazines. In addition, he illustrated books by P. G. Hamerton, Mrs. Schuyler Van Rensselaer, Justin McCarthy, Washington Irving, Henry James, George W. Cable, F. Marion Crawford, Maurice Hewlett, and many besides. In 1888 he accepted the position of art critic on the *Star,* a London ha'penny daily, but after launching a few attacks—which made London gasp—against the Royal Academy for its pompous shows of huge anecdotal canvases, he was bored by the work and it was Mrs. Pennell who continued it, as she did later on the *Daily Chronicle,* for years conducting both columns.

Pennell believed there was as much art in printing from the plates as there was in making them and that both processes were equally the business of the etcher. In 1892, therefore, he bought a press and from then on, with a few rare exceptions, pulled his own proofs. Always an explorer in new techniques, he experimented with pen, pencil, wash, Russian charcoal, etching, and even mezzotint. When photo-engraving began to replace woodblocks for reproducing illustrations, Pennell, ignoring the contention of William Morris and his disciples that the new process would only vulgarize art, felt it his duty to study the invention to see how it could best be made to serve the cause of illustration, which he felt should be kept alive and contemporaneous.

His close association with Whistler made it only natural that lithography would eventually attract him; but it was not until the approaching centennial of the art had focussed the attention of such artists as Toulouse-Lautrec, Willette, Steinlen, Louis Legrand, and Odilon Redon, and he had seen their lithographs in Paris at the spring Salon of 1895, that Pennell really became enthusiastic over the process. As a result, he persuaded Fisher Unwin to agree to bring out a book on *Lithography and Lithographers* (published in 1898), as a companion to his *Pen Drawing and Pen Draughtsmen,* which had been published in 1889. When he went to Spain in 1896

to illustrate *The Alhambra,* transfer paper and lithographic chalk went with him. These first lithographs were delicate and charming but a trifle anæmic and gray in comparison with the bold ones he was to make later.

Pennell refused to regard illustration as a minor art and fought valiantly to raise it in the public esteem; so when the organization of the Society of Illustrators was suggested in 1895, he threw himself into the project with all his usual steam-engine vigor; but it soon died of inanition and Pennell became a member of the council of the newly formed International Society of Sculptors, Painters and Gravers, and hung the water colors and prints of its first exhibition in 1898. This was so successfully accomplished that he was often invited to serve on committees and juries of international art exhibitions on the Continent, where he worked hard to make the best work of his countrymen known in Europe. He was a devastating critic of anything he considered slipshod, but petty personal jealousy never kept him from extolling the excellent work of others. He searched out Vierge in Paris, made Fisher Unwin arrange a show of his work in London and bring out an English edition of *Pablo de Segovia* with his illustrations, for which Pennell wrote an appreciative preface. For Charles Keene, who contributed subtly humorous illustrations to *Punch,* he did the same thing; and he was the first to praise in print the work of Aubrey Beardsley.

It was during these years that the Pennells' intimacy with Whistler ripened and culminated in his request that they write his biography. To this end he gave them many notes and suggestions before he died in 1903. Three years later, Rosalind Birnie Philip, Whistler's executrix, brought suit to enjoin the Pennells and Heinemann from publishing the *Life.* The trial resulted in their favor, however, and their "authorized edition" of *The Life of James McNeill Whistler* appeared in 1908 and was followed by *The Whistler Journal* in 1921.

Together with other artists Pennell founded the Senefelder Club in London in 1909, to bring lithographers together and hold exhibitions of their prints. The art seemed to him a medium peculiarly well adapted to the portrayal of black masses of factories with their belching smoke, which were beginning to fascinate him as subjects. He described these industrial transcriptions as "The Wonder of Work" (*Joseph Pennell's Pictures of the Wonder of Work,* 1916), and after doing some of them at Birmingham and Sheffield, he sailed in 1912 for Panama to draw the Canal. He never surpassed this series of lithographs for richness of color and virile strength. From Panama he went to San Francisco where he etched a set of plates, and stopped on his way across the continent to do lithographs of the Yosemite and the Grand Canyon, and a series of Washington, which rivaled those of Panama. Mrs. Pennell joined him in their native city and they devoted some months to the preparation of *Our Philadelphia,* published in 1914.

From 1884 to 1912 Pennell was primarily engaged in familiarizing America with the picturesqueness of Europe through the medium of his illustrations in magazines and books. After his journey across the United States, however, he became progressively obsessed with interpreting the beauty of his own land. Nevertheless he continued for a while to live in London and to do European subjects. In 1913 he made a series of lithographs in Greece, later reproduced in *Joseph Pennell's Pictures in the Land of Temples* (1915). When the World War broke out in 1914 he was in Berlin doing more lithographs, but he returned to England immediately and spent the balance of that year helping stranded Belgian artists and organizing picture sales to aid the refugees. After the Panama-Pacific International Exposition in San Francisco in 1915, where he served on the art jury, he made lithographs and drawings of British plants engaged in war work. The War Ministry, realizing their value as propaganda, arranged to show them in London and they were later published as *Joseph Pennell's Pictures of War Work in England* (1917). He sold his lease of the Adelphi Terrace studio to Sir James Barrie, with the intention of returning to the United States, but before he could leave, the French government invited him to make war drawings, so he crossed the Channel in May 1917, but returned almost immediately, unable to stand at such close range the horrors of war. A little later he tried again, managed to do a few unimportant drawings at Verdun, and, on the verge of a nervous breakdown, took ship for the United States. There he recovered his poise and threw himself into making drawings of the industrial war activities of America and volunteer work for the government as a vice-chairman of the division of pictorial publicity, Committee on Public Information.

In 1921 he went with his wife to Washington to make arrangements for exhibiting the valuable collection of Whistleriana they had presented to the Library of Congress. When the exhibition was over they moved to the Hotel Margaret in Brooklyn, where Pennell was enthralled by the gorgeous panorama of New York and its harbor, visible from their window. On an earlier visit in 1904 to serve on the jury of the Louisiana Purchase Exposition at St. Louis, Pennell had etched his first New York sky-scraper. Now he became even more enthusiastic and spent his time suggesting on paper their overpowering mass and the grandeur of their groupings. By way of relaxation he did water colors of the view from his window in all its different atmospheric changes.

In 1922 he was invited to teach etching at the Art Students' League in New York, and threw himself into the work with the keenest gusto. He shared with his pupils all the secrets of his craft, and, during the four years he served, made an eminently successful teacher, for he had rare ability and fired his students with the ambition to work and to experiment. This success was all the more remarkable because he had earned a reputation for being querulous and fault-finding. He resented and was disheartened by the spirit and manner of the polyglot New York which he found upon his return after thirty-three years abroad. Prohibition, too, increased his pessimism, and his fulminations against it became increasingly lurid, picturesque, and frequent, for he believed that "there can be no art in a Dry Desert filled with drunken Hypocrites which we are become" (*Life and Letters,* II, 303). This railing arose partly from his convictions but more from the fact that he was overworked. Making plates, working at his press, teaching, writing *The Adventures of an Illustrator* (1925) and superintending its typography, serving as art critic on the *Brooklyn Eagle* until his outspokenness was more than the journal could stand, helping run the New Society of Sculptors, Painters and Engravers, fulminating against billboards, and lecturing overtaxed his strength, and in 1923 he had a serious illness. As soon as he recovered he was off again at the same pace, and consequently, when in the spring of 1926 he contracted pneumonia, he had no reserve. He died in the Hotel Margaret in Brooklyn, and was buried in the graveyard of the Friends' Germantown Meeting House. By the terms of his will, at the death of his wife their whole estate was to revert to the Library of Congress to found a Chalcographic Museum, complete the Whistler and Pennell collections, and acquire the prints of etchers living or less than a hundred years dead.

Pennell did more than any other one artist of his time to improve the quality of illustration both in the United States and abroad and to raise its status as an art. His incessant industry produced over nine hundred etched and mezzotint plates, some six hundred and twenty-one lithographs, and innumerable drawings and water colors. He was the first to make the varied aspects of industry recognized subjects for the artist. Aside from their artistic value, his prints and drawings will have an ever-increasing historic interest. Not only has he left his graphic portrayals of war work in America and England, but his pictures of ever-changing American cities, and even of London, will soon be records of a reality that has passed. He was a member of numerous societies both in the United States and Europe, was awarded medals at many expositions, and his work is represented in museums and galleries in various parts of the world, including the Luxembourg, Paris; Uffizi, Florence; British Museum and South Kensington Museum, London; Library of Congress, Washington; Art Institute of Chicago; Brooklyn Museum; Metropolitan Museum of Art, New York; Cleveland Museum of Art; and The Prado, Madrid.

[Pennell said he was born in 1860 and believed his birth records had been destroyed by fire, but after his death they were discovered and proved he had been born in 1857. The sources for his life are his own *Adventures of an Illustrator* (1925), and three books by his wife, Elizabeth Robins Pennell: *The Life & Letters of Joseph Pennell* (1929), *Our House and London out of Our Windows* (1912), and *Nights* (1916). See also L. A. Wuerth, *Catalogue of the Etchings of Joseph Pennell* (1928) and *Catalogue of the Lithographs of Joseph Pennell* (1931); Arthur Tomson, "Joseph Pennell," *Art Journal* (London), Aug. 1900; H. W. Singer, "On Some of Mr. Joseph Pennell's Recent Etchings," *International Studio* (N. Y.), Feb. 1907; Frank Weitenkampf, "Joseph Pennell," *Die Graphischen Künste* (Vienna), Jan. 1910; Grace Irwin, *Trail-Blazers of American Art* (1930); *N. Y. Times*, Apr. 24, 1926. *The Lib. of Cong., Joseph Pennell Memorial Exhibition Catalogue* (1927) has the best bibliography so far printed, but it cannot be entirely relied upon.]   E. L. T.

PENNIMAN, JAMES HOSMER (Nov. 8, 1860–Apr. 6, 1931), educator, author, and bibliophile, was born in Alexandria, Va., the son of James Lanman and Maria Davis (Hosmer) Penniman. Both parents were of distinguished colonial ancestry. His father was a graduate of Yale College, as were also a number of relatives. Among his ancestors on his father's side were Roger Wolcott and Matthew Griswold [*qq.v.*], both governors of Connecticut, Judge Charles Church Chandler, a member of the Continental Congress, and Judge James Lanman, senator from Connecticut. On his mother's side were the Rev. Peter Bulkeley [*q.v.*] and James Hosmer, founders of Concord, Mass., and Dr. Jonathan Prescott and his son, Col. Charles Prescott, distinguished colonial gentlemen. His mother grew up in Concord at the time when it was an intellectual center. Thus, through inheritance and environment, she developed ability, character, and charm of personality that undoubtedly exercised a strong influence upon her son. James

prepared for college at the Free Academy of Norwich, Conn., and graduated from Yale College in 1884. After a year spent as a private tutor in Glyndon, Md., he began teaching in DeLancey School, Philadelphia, and became head of the Lower School in 1900, a position which he held until his retirement in 1913. In connection with his teaching he wrote a number of articles and books, including *A Graded List of Common Words Difficult to Spell* (1891); *Prose Dictation Exercises from the English Classics* (1893); *The School Poetry Book* (1894); *Practical Suggestions in School Government* (1899); *New Practical Speller* (1900); *Books, and How to Make the Most of Them* (1911); and *Children and Their Books* (1921).

Meanwhile he became a collector of Washingtoniana and an authority on the history of America in the eighteenth century, writing *George Washington as Commander-in-Chief* (1917); *George Washington as Man of Letters* (1918); *George Washington at Mount Vernon* (1921); *Our Debt to France* (1921); *What Lafayette Did for America* (1921); and *Philadelphia in the Early Eighteen Hundreds* (1923). He had planned and largely completed at the time of his death a two-volume work on George Washington that was to have been published in 1932, and had proposed as a part of the celebration of the bi-centennial of Washington's birth the building of the "Highway of the Thirteen Original States" from Washington to "Mount Vernon." His mother having died in 1914, he founded in her honor in 1915 the Maria Hosmer Penniman Memorial Library of Education at the University of Pennsylvania. In 1920 he established the Penniman Memorial Library of Education at Yale University, which contains more than 80,000 volumes and has become one of the largest libraries of education in the world, and in 1921 he founded the Penniman Memorial Library of Education at Brown University. A man of varied interests, he had a keen relish for sport, especially professional baseball, and a fondness for animals that found expression in a delightful book, *The Alley Rabbit* (1920). He died suddenly at his home in Philadelphia and was buried in Sleepy Hollow Cemetery, Concord, Mass.

[*A Hist. of the Class of Eighty-Four, Yale Coll., 1880–1914* (1914); *Bull. of Yale Univ.: Obit. Record of Grads. Deceased During the Year Ending July 1, 1931*; *Who's Who in America*, 1930–31; *Colonial Families of the U. S.*, vol. VII (1920); *Pub. Ledger* (Phila.), Apr. 7, 1931; *Pa. Gazette*, May 1, 1931.]   A. L. L.

PENNINGTON, JAMES W. C. (1809–October 1870), teacher, preacher, and author, was born in slavery on the Eastern Shore of Maryland. While he was a slave he was known as Jim Pembroke. In his own story of his early life he recalls the desolate, terrifying days of his childhood, deprived of parental care, lacking education, and shrinking from the tyranny of his master's children and the brutality of the overseers. When he was four years old he was given, with his mother, to his first master's son, Frisbie Tilghman of Hagerstown, and was taken to live in Washington County. At nine he was hired out to a stone mason. Returning two years later to the home plantation, he was trained as a blacksmith and followed that trade until he was about twenty-one, when he decided to run away. After experiencing hunger, exhaustion, and escape from capture, he was welcomed one morning by a Pennsylvania Quaker with the friendly greeting, "Come in and take thy breakfast, and get warm" (*The Fugitive Blacksmith, post,* p. 41). He spent six months in this home, and under the guidance of his Quaker teacher, laid the foundation of an extensive education. Some months later he found work on western Long Island, near New York City; he attended evening school, and was privately tutored. Five years after his escape he qualified to teach in colored schools, first at Newtown, L. I., then at New Haven, Conn. While at New Haven he studied theology, and pastorates in African Congregational churches at Newtown, L. I. (1838–40) and at Hartford, Conn. (1840–47) followed. His scholarship and pulpit eloquence attracted favorable attention in Hartford, and he served twice as president of the Hartford Central Association of Congregational Ministers, the membership being all white except himself. During this time he examined two candidates (one a Kentuckian) for their licenses to preach. Closely identified with measures to help his race, he was five times elected a member of the General Convention for the Improvement of Free People of Colour, and in 1843 was sent to represent Connecticut at the World's Anti-Slavery Convention at London. He was also the delegate of the American Peace Convention to the World's Peace Society meeting in London the same year. While in Europe he lectured or preached in London, Paris, and Brussels.

Until a short time before the passage of the "Fugitive Slave Law" (1850) he kept secret, even from his wife, the fact that he was a runaway slave. Fearing recapture, he appealed to John Hooker, of Hartford, to negotiate for his freedom and went abroad until his status should be determined. After many discouragements, a payment of $150 to the estate of his one-time master brought a bill of sale, and a deed of manumission was recorded in the town records

of Hartford, June 5, 1851. In the meantime Pennington had become the first pastor of the First (Shiloh) Presbyterian Church on Prince Street in New York City. This pulpit he occupied for eight years (1847–55). During this time his story of his early life, *The Fugitive Blacksmith* (preface dated 1849; 3rd ed., 1850) was published in London, the proceeds of the sale of the same being intended to aid in financing the new church. He had previously published *Text Book of the Origin and History, &c, &c of the Colored People* (1841). A few of his sermons and addresses survive, including *Covenants Involving Moral Wrong Are Not Obligatory upon Man: A Sermon* (1842), and *The Reasonableness of the Abolition of Slavery* (1856). In 1859 he contributed to the *Anglo-African Magazine* several articles on the capabilities of his race. After 1855 he is listed in the *Minutes* of the Presbyterian General Assembly as a member of the Third New York Presbytery, without a pastorate, his address appearing as New York, Hartford, occasionally Maine. During his last years his usefulness was much impaired by the excessive use of intoxicants (Brown, *post*). In 1869 or early in 1870 he went to Florida, hoping to benefit his health, and at Jacksonville he gathered together a colored Presbyterian church, but he died there soon after.

[In addition to *The Fugitive Blacksmith*, see John Hooker, *Reminiscences of a Long Life* (1899) ; Wilson Armistead, *A Tribute for the Negro* (1848), containing an autographed portrait ; W. W. Brown, *The Rising Son ; or, The Antecedents and Advancement of the Colored Race* (1874) ; W. J. Simmons, *Men of Mark* (1887) ; Hartford (1843–49) and New York City (1848–68) directories ; Hartford Town Records ; references in the Tappan Papers, *Jour. of Negro Hist.*, Apr.-July 1927 ; *Minutes of the Gen. Assem., Presbyt. Ch. in the U. S. A.*, 1871, p. 601, which gives date of death as Oct. 20 ; *N. Y. Observer*, Nov. 10, 1870, which gives date of death as Oct. 22.]   A. E. P.

PENNINGTON, WILLIAM (May 4, 1796–Feb. 16, 1862), governor of New Jersey, congressman, was the son of Phoebe (Wheeler) and William Sandford Pennington [*q.v.*]. He was born in Newark, N. J., received an elementary education in the local schools, and was graduated from the College of New Jersey (Princeton) in 1813. After studying law with Theodore Frelinghuysen [*q.v.*] he was licensed as attorney in 1817, as counselor in 1820, and as sergeant-at-law in 1834. While his father was district judge in New Jersey he acted as clerk of the district and circuit courts from 1817 to 1826. Meanwhile his geniality, candor, and oratorical powers were bringing him an ever-enlarging and remunerative practice as well as making numerous political friends for him. In 1828 he was a member of the state Assembly from Essex County as an Adams Democrat. Later the Penningtons became Whigs, and when in 1837 the Whigs controlled the state legislature he was elected governor and chancellor of New Jersey. He was reëlected annually five times. An imposing man of six feet two, he was known as a genial companion, somewhat of a "character" but possessing, nevertheless, a good deal of common sense. Contemporaries testify that both juries and assemblies fell an easy prey to his eloquence. His decisions as chancellor (1, 3 *Green Chancery Reports*) are brief but clear and pointed. He was not a learned jurist and is said to have bragged in early life that he would get along with as little study as possible. Yet his good judgment preserved him from grave mistakes; only one of his decisions as chancellor was reversed.

Out of the fact that New Jersey had been a doubtful state from the very beginning of the century there developed the chief political excitement of his tenure as governor, namely the "Broad Seal" War. He had been elected governor in 1837 over the Democratic incumbent, Philemon Dickerson [*q.v.*]. The following year Dickerson and four other Democrats claimed to have been elected in five of six congressional districts. One seat was not challenged; it was admittedly Whig. The county clerks certified all six Whigs as elected. In spite of the accusations of corruption Pennington held that he had no authority to go behind the returns and placed the great seal of New Jersey upon the certificates of the six Whigs. In the federal House of Representatives the parties stood so nearly equally divided that the admission of one or the other group of claimants would determine its organization. After ten days of acrimonious debate, it organized with a compromise speaker and three months later admitted the Democratic claimants. Pennington was bitterly attacked for his partisanship in not investigating the questionable returns, and, on the other hand, he was defended loyally by those who resented the refusal of Congress to accept without question the official certificates bearing the state seal.

When in 1843 a Democrat replaced him as governor he withdrew from politics to practise before the higher courts of the state. His ambitions to be chancellor, which had become an appointive office under the new constitution, or to be a minister in Europe were not realized, and he refused posts as governor of Minnesota Territory and as claims judge under the Mexican treaty. His last venture in politics led to another exciting episode in congressional history. He was elected to Congress in 1858, when the House was again deadlocked over its organization, and

it was only after eight weeks of debate, balloting, and negotiation that the moderates of both parties were able to agree upon him as a compromise speaker. As a newcomer he was totally unfamiliar with the procedure, and many were the stories told of his ignorance. He died in Newark, survived by his wife, Caroline (Burnet) Pennington, the daughter of Dr. William Burnet, 1730–1791 [*q.v.*].

[L. Q. C. Elmer, "The Constitution and Government of . . . New Jersey," *N. J. Hist. Soc. Colls.*, vol. VII (1872); *N. J. Law Jour.*, July, Aug. 1897; F. B. Lee, *N. J. as a Colony and as a State* (1902), vol. III; J. T. Nixon, "The Circumstances Attending the Election of Wm. Pennington . . . as Speaker," *N. J. Hist. Soc. Proc.*, 2 Ser., vol. II (1872); A. C. M. Pennington, *The Pennington Family* (1871), reprinted with additions from *New-Eng. Hist. and Geneal. Reg.*, July 1871. *Newark Daily Advertiser*, Feb. 17, 1862.] H. M. C.

PENNINGTON, WILLIAM SANDFORD (1757–Sept. 17, 1826), governor of New Jersey and jurist, was the son of Mary (Sandford) and Samuel Pennington. He was the descendant of Ephraim Pennington who emigrated from England to New Haven, Conn., before 1643 and whose son, also named Ephraim, was one of the early settlers of Newark, N. J., where William Sandford Pennington was born three generations later. His Revolutionary War diary, 1780–81, written while he was an officer of artillery stationed at and near West Point and now preserved in the library of the New Jersey Historical Society at Newark, shows a facility of language that bears witness to a good education. There is reason to believe that he learned the trade of a hatter. On the breaking out of Revolutionary hostilities he joined the Continental Army. He became a sergeant in the 2nd Regiment of Artillery on Mar. 7, 1777, second lieutenant in 1780 to rank from Sept. 12, 1778, and at the end of the war was mustered out as a captain by brevet. He entered business at Newark, and he was elected to the state Assembly in 1797 and reëlected in 1798 and 1799. He read law in the office of Elias Boudinot [*q.v.*].

In 1801, while still serving his clerkship, he was elected a member of the council, which, in addition to its legislative functions, acted with the governor as a final court of appeals and court of pardons. In 1802 he was licensed as an attorney-at-law, in the same year was reëlected to the council, and in 1803 was appointed county clerk of Essex County. In February 1804, before he had completed the three years of practice as an attorney necessary to qualify him for license as a counselor-at-law, he was elected by joint meeting of the Council and Assembly to fill a vacancy in the supreme court, the chief justice of which was Andrew Kirkpatrick [*q.v.*]. Notwithstanding Pennington's short experience as a practitioner, his mature age, natural abilities, and strong common sense supplemented by diligent study enabled him from the beginning to perform the duties of the office to the entire satisfaction of the bar and public. In 1806 he published a *Treatise on the Courts for the Trial of Small Causes*, which he revised and published in a second edition in 1824. In 1806, under a new statute, he was appointed reporter to the supreme court and served as both justice and reporter until 1813. The two volumes of his reports (2, 3 *N. J. Reports*) contain the opinions of the supreme court, including his own, from 1806 to 1813 and are still essential to any New Jersey law library. In 1812 he was put forward by the Republican party for the office of governor but was defeated by a vote of twenty-two to thirty. In 1813 he defeated his former opponent by a vote of thirty to twenty, and he was reëlected in 1814. As governor he was also chancellor and presided in the court of chancery. In 1815 he was appointed by President Madison as judge of the federal district court for New Jersey and held that office until his death. He was married twice: first, about 1786, to Phoebe, the daughter of James Wheeler, an officer of the Revolution, and second, after her death, to Elizabeth Pierson.

[L. Q. C. Elmer, "The Constitution and Government of N. J.," *N. J. Hist. Soc. Colls.*, vol. VII (1872); F. B. Lee, *N. J. as a Colony and as a State* (1902), vols. III, IV; W. S. Stryker, *Official Register of the Officers and Men of N. J. in the Rev. War* (1872); A. C. M. Pennington, *The Pennington Family* (1871), reprinted with additions from *New-Eng. Hist. & Geneal. Register*, July 1871; *N. J. Law Jour.*, July, Aug. 1897; *Fredonian* (New Brunswick), Sept. 20, 1826; *True American* (Trenton), Sept. 23, 1826.]

C. W. P.

PENNOCK, ALEXANDER MOSELY (Oct. 1, 1814–Sept. 20, 1876), naval officer, was born in Norfolk, Va., the son of a prominent Norfolk shipping merchant and naval agent, William Pennock, of the firm of Pennock and Myers. Though left an orphan early in life, he received a good education, and on the recommendation of Capt. James P. Preston and others, was appointed midshipman to fill a Tennessee vacancy Apr. 1, 1828. His promotion to passed midshipman came in June 1834, after he had made cruises in the *Guerrière* of the Pacific Squadron and the *Natchez* of the Brazil Squadron. He then served in the *Potomac* in the Mediterranean and in the *Columbia* in the East Indies, where he led a ship's division in an expedition against the pirates of Quallah Battoo, Sumatra, on New Year's day, 1839. He was advanced to the rank of lieutenant the following March, and in this capacity served in the *Deca-*

tur of the Brazil Squadron from 1843 to 1846, and in the store-ship *Supply* during the Mexican War. Following a second eastern cruise in the *Marion*, 1850–52, he had his first extended shore duty as lighthouse inspector, 1853–56, and again, after commanding the steamer *Southern Star* in the Paraguay Expedition, he was lighthouse inspector at New York.

In spite of his Southern family connections and property interests, he remained loyal to the Union in the Civil War, and on Sept. 20, 1861, was among the senior officers detailed under Capt. A. H. Foote [q.v.] to take over the building of gunboats at St. Louis for the Mississippi flotilla. The following October Foote made him fleet captain in special charge of flotilla equipment, and from the beginning of 1862 until the end of 1864, he commanded the naval base established at Cairo, Ill., where he gained a reputation as one of the best wartime executives of the navy. In estimating his work Charles Henry Davis, 1807–1877 [q.v.], Foote's successor, wrote, "I cannot use any language too strong to convey a just idea of Capt. Pennock's private and official merit. He is devoted to all his duties, with a simple, honest, straightforward zeal, which gives to the performance of them the zest of pleasure" (*Confidential Correspondence of Gustavus Vasa Fox*, II, 1919, 67). David Dexter Porter [q.v.], who followed Davis, declared him "a trump . . . and worth his weight in gold" (*Ibid.*, 140). His command was "literally afloat in wharf boats, old steamers, flatboats, or even rafts, as the government owned no land at that point . . ." (D. D. Porter, *The Naval History of the Civil War*, 1886, p. 135). In addition to the multifarious duties of supply and repair for the distant flotilla, the scope of which is revealed in the mass of his correspondence in the official records of the Civil War, he had immediate command of boats operating in the Tennessee and Cumberland rivers. He was made captain on Jan. 2, 1863, and when Porter left the flotilla in September of the following year, Pennock exercised general command for two months.

After the war he was stationed at the Brooklyn navy yard and then sailed on June 28, 1867, in command of the *Franklin*, flagship of Admiral Farragut's European Squadron, to visit French, Russian, Scandinavian, English, and Mediterranean ports. Both Mrs. Farragut and Mrs. Pennock, who were cousins, accompanied their husbands on this cruise, which proved a constant round of celebrations and entertainments for the distinguished admiral (J. E. Montgomery, *Our Admiral's Flag Abroad*, 1869). Pennock was made commodore on May 6, 1868, and succeeded Farragut in command of the European Squadron from October 1868 to February 1869. He was commandant of the Portsmouth navy yard, 1870–72, and, after promotion to the rank of rear admiral in 1872, was in command of the Pacific Squadron from May 1874 to June 1875. He died suddenly of heart trouble at the Rockingham Hotel, Portsmouth, N. H. Pennock's wife was Margaret, daughter of George Loyall of Norfolk, Va., and he was buried in the Loyall family plot in that city.

[The birth-date accepted in this sketch has been taken from Pennock's tombstone in Norfolk, though Nov. 1, 1813, appears in naval records. For additional biographical data, see: L. R. Hamersly, *The Records of Living Officers of the U. S. Navy and Marine Corps* (1870); Henry Walke, *Naval Scenes and Reminiscences of the Civil War* (1877); *N. Y. Daily Tribune*, Sept. 21, 1876.]
A. W.

PENNOYER, SYLVESTER (July 6, 1831–May 31, 1902), governor of Oregon, was born at Groton, N. Y., the son of Justus P. and Elizabeth (Howland) Pennoyer, both natives of New York. His father was a well-to-do farmer, a community leader, and at one time member of the state legislature. The son went to Homer Academy and at intervals taught several short terms in rural schools. He graduated from the Harvard Law School in 1854. The next year he went by way of Nicaragua to San Francisco and then to Puget Sound, where for a brief period he attempted the practice of law, but he soon removed to Portland, Ore. In 1856 he married Mrs. Mary A. Allen. After six years of teaching he entered the lumber business in 1862, which, together with shrewd investments in Portland real estate, in a few years made him a wealthy man. In 1868 he purchased the *Oregon Herald,* a Democratic newspaper that he continued to edit until 1871. His political career began in 1885, when he suffered a severe defeat as a candidate for mayor of Portland. In that same year he gained a state-wide reputation as a leader in a movement against Chinese laborers, which brought him the Democratic nomination for governor in 1886. He was elected and was reëlected for a second term in 1890. In 1896 he was elected for a two-year term as mayor of Portland.

During his long career he did and said many things that made him seem "peculiar, eccentric, and demagogic" to his more conservative contemporaries (*Morning Oregonian*, May 19, 1890). During the Civil War he had openly sympathized with the Confederacy and afterward advocated the payment of government bonds with federal notes and the issuance of "fiat money." While he was governor he made many recommendations for what seemed to him the necessary liberalization of government. However, throughout his two terms he was confronted by legislative assemblies controlled by his Republican opponents, and in consequence few of his recommendations received legislative approval. He was also severely criticized for too liberal use of his pardoning power. He recommended compulsory arbitration for labor disputes. In 1888 in a threatened conflict between railroad workers and their employers over arrears of wages he intervened to effect a settlement satisfactory to both sides. This experience led him to advocate "a most stringent law" to compel all contractors to make weekly payment to their employees. In his messages to the legislature he asserted that the practice of courts in nullifying legislative enactments was a usurpation of power. He asked for strong legislation against monopoly; he protested against the growing practice of delegating the governor's authority to commissions; and he advocated abolishing the numerous commissions and boards, such as the fish and railroad commissions and the immigration board. He vigorously urged appropriations for the common schools, while at the same time opposing further state support for the state university and agricultural college since that was a tax on all the people for the benefit of the few. He advocated the removal of debt exemptions in tax assessments that had been approved by the legislature in 1891, the taxing of all incomes in excess of $1,000 on a graduated scale, a poll tax of two dollars on every male over twenty-one, a tax upon the gross receipts of express, telegraph, and insurance companies, and anticipated the establishment of a state tax commission in asking for state control of the county tax assessors. He repeatedly vetoed a Portland water bill, finally passed over his veto in 1891, because it provided for the sale of tax-exempt bonds. This action gained him such popularity as to be accounted, by the opposition press, the principal cause of his reëlection as governor in 1890. By 1892 he had passed over to the Populist party. He wrote an article for the *North American Review* (Oct. 1892) on "The Paramount Questions of the Campaign." By this time he had become bitterly hostile to President Cleveland. In his Thanksgiving message of 1893 he recommended to the people that they pray that the President and Congress be guided to restore silver to the position of full legal-tender money, and at Christmas 1893 he addressed a long letter to President Cleveland on this same theme. In 1894 he proclaimed a Thanksgiving day a week later than the one set by Cleveland.

[H. W. Scott, *Hist. of the Ore. Country* (1924), vols. I, III–V, comp. by L. M. Scott; H. K. Hines, *An Illustrated Hist. of Ore.* (1893); Joseph Gaston, *Portland, Ore.* (1911), vol. I; *Oregon State Jour.* (Eugene), May 22, 1886, May 17, 1889, May 3, June 7, 1890, May 2, Oct. 24, 1891, Mar. 11, June 17, 1893; *Morning Oregonian* (Portland), May 31, 1902.]   R. C. C—k.

PENNYPACKER, ELIJAH FUNK (Nov. 29, 1804–Jan. 4, 1888), reformer, was born in Schuylkill Township, Chester County, Pa. He was the son of Joseph and Elizabeth (Funk) Pennypacker and the descendant of Heinrich (or Hendrick) Pannebäcker, a Mennonite who came from the Low Countries to Pennsylvania before 1699. He was the uncle of Galusha Pennypacker [q.v.]. The family was prosperous, and he was educated at the boarding school of John Gummere [q.v.] of Burlington, N. J., where he followed the bent of his master toward mathematics, surveying, and such practical studies. He married, first, Sarah W. Coates in 1831 who had no children and who died ten years later. In 1843 he married Hannah Adamson, who bore him nine children. Both wives were members of the Society of Friends, which he too joined in 1841, being drawn not only by such family ties but also by the anti-slavery sentiment that was a ruling factor in his life. In his early life he taught for a few years, practised surveying, and devoted himself to farming. Between 1831 and 1836 he served several sessions in the state legislature, where his reputation for uprightness and ability attracted the attention of such men as Thaddeus Stevens and Joseph Ritner. His loyalty to what he thought right must have become irksome at times in legislative halls, for Stevens was once minded to tell him not "to be so damned honest" (Still, *post*, p. 689). While in the legislature he served ably in many ways: as secretary to the board of canal commissioners in 1836 and 1837 and a member of that board in 1838, as chairman of the committee on banks, as sponsor for the bill for incorporation of the Philadelphia Reading Railroad, and as collaborator with Thaddeus Stevens in the establishment of the common-school system of Pennsylvania. A career in politics was undoubtedly open to him, but he declined to continue in this path, being unwilling, as one has said, "to hold office under a government that sanctioned human slavery" (Jordan, *post*, p. 492).

After his retirement from public affairs, in 1839, he joined heartily in the abolition movement, serving from time to time as president of the local society and also as head of the Chester

County and the Pennsylvania state anti-slavery societies. His house near Phoenixville, Pa., became one of the stations on the Underground Railroad, and his two-horse wagon was a frequent carrier of black-skinned human freight that sought its way toward the North Star and to freedom. Of the "Railroad" he said, whimsically, when the work was done, that its "stock was never reported in money circles, nor dividends declared, but means were ready as long as necessity required. The Emancipation Proclamation of Abraham Lincoln dissolved the Corporation" (Jordan, *post*, p. 492). He was also prominent in the temperance movement and its candidate for state treasurer in 1875. Woman's emancipation and her equal education also found in him a hearty supporter. His character did not fail to impress his fellow citizens. Whittier said of him, "In mind, body, and brave championship of the cause of freedom he was one of the most remarkable men I ever knew" (statement of Isaac R. Pennypacker in letter Jan. 27, 1931); and another declared, "If that is not a good man, there is no use in the Lord writing His signature on human countenances" (Still, *post*, p. 688).

[Wm. Still, *The Underground Rail Road* (1872); J. W. Jordan, *Colonial Families of Philadelphia* (1911), vol. I; J. S. Futhey and Gilbert Cope, *Hist. of Chester County, Pa.* (1881); S. W. Pennypacker, *Annals of Phoenixville* (1872); *Village Record* and *Local News* of West Chester, Pa., both of Jan. 5, 1888; date of birth from Pennypacker's daughter.]   T. W.

PENNYPACKER, GALUSHA (June 1, 1844–Oct. 1, 1916), soldier, was born in Schuylkill Township, Chester County, Pa., the son of Joseph J. and Tamson Amelia (Workizer) Pennypacker and the nephew of Elijah Funk Pennypacker [q.v.]. His first American ancestor was Heinrich (or Hendrick) Pannebäcker who emigrated to Pennsylvania before 1699. His grandfather had fought in the Revolution, and his father was an officer in the War with Mexico. When Galusha was still in his fourth year, his mother, a French Canadian, died, and his father went to California leaving the boy in care of his grandmother, Elizabeth Funk Pennypacker. He was educated in the private schools of Phoenixville and Schuylkill Township. At the outbreak of the Civil War, he enlisted for three months in the 9th Regiment of the Pennsylvania Volunteers serving as quartermaster-sergeant. On the expiration of his term of enlistment, he returned home and recruited Company A, 97th Pennsylvania Volunteers, of which he was elected captain on Aug. 22, 1861. He was promoted rapidly and attained the rank of colonel by Aug. 15, 1864. On Feb. 18, 1865, he was appointed brigadier-general of Volunteers, the youngest officer of that rank in the war, and less than a month later was made major-general. He served with distinction at Fort Wagner, Drewry's Bluff, Cold Harbor, Petersburg, Green Plains, and Fort Fisher, being wounded seven times in eight months. At Fort Fisher, on Jan. 15, 1865, he led his brigade in a charge across a traverse of the work and planted the colors of one of his regiments on the parapet where he fell seriously wounded. For this act of gallantry he was awarded the Congressional Medal of Honor in 1891.

He resigned from the service on Apr. 30, 1866, but the following July he was appointed colonel in the regular army and assigned to the 34th Infantry. He was again brevetted brigadier and major-general for his conduct at Fort Fisher and for his services during the war, and on Mar. 15, 1869, he was transferred to the 16th Infantry which he commanded until his retirement in 1883. From 1869 to 1877 his regiment was established in the South with headquarters at Nashville, Tenn., and was engaged in assisting the civil authorities in carrying out the Reconstruction Act of Congress. Pennypacker exercised endless patience and tact in executing this very delicate mission and, without departing from his duty, he won the respect and affection of the Southern people and did much to reconcile them to the Federal government. After 1877 he did frontier duty in the Indian country of the West. He was finally retired for disability as the result of his wounds. Urged to be a candidate for governor of Pennsylvania in 1872 he declined on the ground that he had no taste for politics. He never married but spent the last years of his life in lonely retirement at his home in Philadelphia. He died on Oct. 1, 1916, and was buried with the simple rites of the Society of Friends in the Philadelphia National Cemetery.

[*Who's Who in America*, 1914–15; F. B. Heitman, *Hist. Reg. and Dict. of the U. S. Army* (1903); Hamilton H. Gilkyson, "The Life and Services of General Galusha Pennypacker," in G. M. Philips, *An Account of Twenty-One Citizens of West Chester, Penn.* (1919), vol. I; J. S. Futhey and G. Cope, *Hist. of Chester County, Penn.* (1881); *Press* (Phila.), Oct. 2, 1916.]
C. E. T. L.

PENNYPACKER, SAMUEL WHITAKER (Apr. 9, 1843–Sept. 2, 1916), lawyer, judge, governor of Pennsylvania, bibliophile, historian, was born at Phoenixville, Pa. the son of Anna Maria Whitaker and Isaac Anderson Pennypacker and a descendant of Heinrich (or Hendrick) Pannebäcker, who emigrated to Pennsylvania before 1699. The father was a practitioner and university teacher of medicine. Unable to

go to college, Samuel left school in 1859. After working in a country store, teaching in a country school, and serving for a few weeks in the army of 1863, he studied law and was admitted to the bar on May 19, 1866. The following July he graduated in law from the University of Pennsylvania. Prompt election to successive offices in the Law Academy (of which he became president at the age of twenty-four) attested the respect he commanded among his young fellow practitioners. For many years his practice was small; but sound judgment, and learning acquired by exceeding industry and evidenced in professional publications, eventually brought him important clients. He was appointed judge in Common Pleas No. 2 of Philadelphia in 1889 (qualified, Jan. 12), to which office he was elected in November for a ten-year term and reëlected in 1899, after having become president judge of the court two years previously. Patient attention to counsel, ample learning, sound sense, and promptitude in disposal of his cases made his judicial service very satisfactory to the bar. Especially as a *nisi prius* judge he was highly praised. On the bench he was no innovator, nor did his many convictions and strong prejudices deflect his legal judgments, but as governor he later sought to curb what he regarded as particular abuses in the administration of the law. From 1885 to 1889 he served on the Board of Public Education of Philadelphia.

Nominated in June 1902 for governor, he was immediately attacked for "Quayism." Matthew S. Quay [*q.v.*] was a relative; they had common literary interests; they were friends. Pennypacker was always loyal in friendship, nor would he deny every virtue to political bosses. After talking with complete frankness with the people, he was elected by an unprecedented vote. He immediately declared publicly his purpose to consult with all persons, but "especially with . . . politicians," believing this both unavoidable and desirable for popular government. His record, however, was marked by entirely reasonable independence in appointments and measures, and by many excellent accomplishments. Nevertheless, his administration (Jan. 20, 1903–Jan. 14, 1907) was stormy. From judicial life he had derived strong convictions that legislation was excessive, that many statutes were absurd, and that there was an inordinate disposition to multiply statutory crimes. By pressure, vetoes (63 in 1903, 123 in 1905), and threats to veto, he cut by half the legislative output and improved its quality. Every attempt to create a new crime was blocked. He had other convictions: that corporations should not be chartered with

447

nominal capital as mere trial-balloons, or with capitalization too small to protect the public; that water companies should not be delegated powers of eminent domain; nor coal companies (or other corporations) select and pay state-commissioned police utilizable in labor disputes. He corrected all these abuses. He forced a long-delayed reapportionment of representation in the legislature, as required by the constitution; established a department of health; sponsored direct primaries and improved the election laws, curbing corrupt 'practices; advanced conservation of forest land and historic sites; paid the state debt, and left a large balance in the treasury, without new taxation and despite the cost of a state capitol.

This last caused one of the two great political turmoils of his gubernatorial term. The furnishings of the capitol involved corruption on a great scale, but nobody ever hinted or believed that he was corrupt, though many thought he should have detected "jokers" in the contracts. The second turmoil arose from his conviction that a sensational press hampered the administration of justice. His "libel bill" of 1903 and his supporting message roused tremendous opposition. The statute merely authorized actions for damages against newspapers for publication of untruths as facts when there was negligent failure to discover their falsity, and required newspapers to publish the names of their editors and publishers. It was repealed in 1907, but the last-mentioned requirement was reënacted. His only public service after his gubernatorial term was as a member of the railroad, and later the public service commission.

Pennypacker's serious historical studies began before 1872, when he became an active member of the Pennsylvania Historical Society. He formed an unrivaled collection of some 10,000 items on Pennsylvania history. He served as president of the Philobiblon Club (1898–1916), as trustee of the University of Pennsylvania (1886–1916), and as president of the Pennsylvania Historical Society (1900–16). To this last position, particularly, he gave unstinted and devoted service. His reading, of which he kept records, was varied in character and vast in quantity and not a little was in foreign languages. In appearance and voice he was decidedly rural. His language, however, immediately showed the scholar. His conversation combined wide information, humor, practical philosophy, and charm. Perfectly simple in his personal tastes and life, by nature informal and unconventional, he maintained well official dignity when occasion required it. He had abundant self-confidence where it was justified, and this doubt-

less contributed to his successes, but he was modest otherwise, nor did his many strong opinions, or even prejudices, alienate associates. Great vigor, intense interest and endeavor, and extreme conscientiousness were characteristic of him in every undertaking and office. His numerous published writings touch upon his interests in local history and the law. His work as reporter-in-chief of Common Pleas No. 3, 1876–88, is in the *Weekly Notes of Cases* (vols. II–XXIII, 1876–88), but he did work for all the forty-five volumes thereof. His decisions are in the *Pennsylvania County Court Reports* and *Pennsylvania District Courts*, 1889–1902. He died at Pennypacker's Mills, near Schwenksville, Pa., survived by his wife, Virginia Earl Broomall, whom he had married on Oct. 20, 1870, and by their four children.

[See Pennypacker's *Autobiog. of a Pennsylvanian* (1918); H. L. Carson, *An Address Upon the Life and Services of Samuel Whitaker Pennypacker . . . Jan. 8th, 1917* (1917), with bibliography, not complete, of 94 items, and *Samuel W. Pennypacker, An Address Delivered before the Philobiblon Club, Oct. 26, 1916* (1917); *The Pedigree of Samuel Whitaker Pennypacker, Henry Clay Pennypacker* (1892); the *Legal Intelligencer* (Phila.), Dec. 15, 1916; *Report of the Twenty-third Ann. Meeting of the Pa. Bar Asso.* (1917); C. R. Woodruff, "The Paradox of Gov. Pennypacker," *Yale Rev.*, Aug. 1907; *Who's Who in America*, 1916–17; T. M. F., "Hon. Samuel W. Pennypacker," *Searchlight Mag.*, Aug. 1912; *Pub. Ledger* (Phila.), Sept. 3, 1916.] F.S.P.

PENROSE, BOIES (Nov. 1, 1860–Dec. 31, 1921), lawyer, political leader, senator, was born in Philadelphia, the son of Richard A. F. and Sarah Hannah (Boies) Penrose. His father, the son of Charles Bingham Penrose [*q.v.*], was a prominent physician, the descendant of a Pennsylvania family long noted for wealth and culture; his mother, who came from a Delaware family of the same type, formed the character of her son along Spartan lines. Boies was prepared for college by private tutors, also at the Episcopal Academy and in the public schools of Philadelphia; he graduated, *magna cum laude* and with honorable mention in political economy, from Harvard in 1881. For two years thereafter he read law under Wayne MacVeagh and George Tucker Bispham, becoming upon admission to the bar a member of the law firm of Page, Allinson and Penrose. Even as student, however, his interest was in public administration rather than in private practice; from this period dates a scholarly treatise, *The City Government of Philadelphia*, published in 1887 in the Johns Hopkins University Studies in Historical and Political Science, written by Penrose in collaboration with his law partner, Edward P. Allinson, the later chapters of which contained a sympathetic appraisal of the Bullitt reform charter of Philadelphia. Such promise as he may then have given of becoming a reformer soon vanished; instead he neglected clients in order to make the acquaintance of the very practical Republican politicians of his own district, the eighth, becoming in 1884 its representative in the lower house of the state legislature, whence after one term he was advanced to the state Senate, serving continuously in the latter from 1887 to 1897. In 1895 he was defeated by Charles F. Warwick for the Republican nomination for the mayoralty of Philadelphia; but two years later with the support of Matthew Quay, the state leader, he defeated John Wanamaker for the nomination to the United States Senate, in which he served from 1897 until his death, being elected three times by the legislature and twice by direct popular vote. As senator his interest was chiefly in higher tariff rates; membership on the finance committee and, after the retirement in 1911 of Nelson W. Aldrich [q.v.], its chairmanship, greatly enhanced his influence. He became known also as an opponent of prohibition, woman's suffrage, and Progressive policies generally, yet upon occasion he befriended the direct primary in Pennsylvania. After Quay's death in 1904 Penrose succeeded to the leadership of the Republican organization in the state, retaining it, with the exception of the Progressive interregnum of 1912, to the end of his career. He was a member of the Republican National Committee and played a prominent part in the national conventions of that party in 1900, 1904, 1908, and 1916. During 1912 Penrose became involved in a bitter controversy over campaign contributions which was instigated by William R. Hearst and participated in vigorously by Former-President Roosevelt. At this time attacks upon him as a cynical boss of the lowest type, which were more or less current during his whole political life, reached a climax.

In his prime Penrose was a giant physically, six feet, four inches in height, powerfully built, and a lover of vigorous outdoor sports, particularly big-game hunting. He was not an orator, never speaking when it could be avoided and then only on subjects which he had mastered thoroughly. However, he was extremely effective in private conferences and committee work; he stumped Pennsylvania successfully in his own behalf after senatorial elections were transferred to the people; and in the course of legislative debates was capable of brief but powerful rejoinder, not infrequently lighted up by sardonic humor and a devastating frankness. Personally, Penrose was inclined to be aloof and dignified; he was at ease in converse with gentlemen but when with his political cronies capable of conduct and utterances which caused the judicious to grieve and moved the pious to indignation. Like most leaders of his type he could be depended upon to keep his word absolutely; unlike them he cared only for power, not for pelf. Through inheritance and fortunate mining investments he was provided with a sufficiency for his moderate needs early in his career; he is said never to have gained a dollar from politics. Master of the Republican machine in his state for eighteen years, in reality Penrose was dominated by it; absorbed as he was by the minutiae of an organization with nearly 5,000 election divisions and from twenty to twenty-five thousand active and hungry workers, it was impossible for him to devote himself to broad national questions and to leave an imprint upon the policy of the country. Thus although qualified by education and ambition, if not by ideals, he failed to achieve statesmanship; nevertheless he was considerably more intelligent and less grasping than his associates and, at times, his opponents, the local Republican leaders, particularly those known as "contractor bosses." He died in Washington, D. C. He had never married. Richard A. F. Penrose, 1863–1931 [q.v.] was a younger brother.

[The numerous public and party offices held by Penrose are listed in the *Cong. Directory* and in *Smull's Legislative Hand-Book of Pa.* for 1921 and earlier years. Character sketches are presented by C. W. Gilbert in *The Mirrors of Washington* (1921), pp. 228–41; in articles by C. W. Thompson on "The Senate's Last Leader," *Am. Mercury*, June 1924; and by Talcott Williams on "After Penrose, What?" *Century*, Nov. 1922. The Philadelphia *Public Ledger*, Jan. 1, 1922, contains an obituary article; a number of memorial addresses delivered in the Senate and House, 67th Cong., are reprinted in a government publication entitled *Senators from Pennsylvania . . .* (1924). Walter Davenport, *Power and Glory; The Life of Boies Penrose* (1931), a popular biography, is in reality little more than a *chronique scandaleuse*. For genealogy, see J. G. Leach, *Hist. of the Penrose Family of Philadelphia* (1903).]

R. C. B.

PENROSE, CHARLES BINGHAM (Oct. 6, 1798–Apr. 6, 1857), lawyer and political leader, was born at Philadelphia, the son of Clement Biddle and Anne Howard (Bingham) Penrose, and a descendant of Bartholomew Penrose who emigrated from Bristol, England, to Pennsylvania about 1700. Charles received his education in his native city, where, after studying in the office of Samuel Ewing, he was admitted to the bar on May 9, 1821. Establishing himself in Carlisle, Pa., he practised for a score of years and became prominent in local politics. On Mar. 16, 1824, he was married to Valeria Fullerton Biddle.

In collaboration with Frederick Watts (William Rawle's name also appears on the title page of the first volume) he published *Reports of Cases Adjudged in the Supreme Court of Pennsylvania* (3 vols., 1831–33) covering the period from 1829 to 1832, which became widely known to the legal profession. In 1833 Penrose was elected a member of the state Senate, and continued as such until 1841, serving for a time as speaker. His term thus coincided with the rise of the anti-Masonic movement in Pennsylvania, which figured prominently in the state and county elections in 1838. It was charged that the anti-Masonic Whigs, of whom Penrose was one, were bent on seating senatorial candidates from Philadelphia who had not been elected, and when the session opened on Dec. 4, Speaker Penrose found himself confronted with a crowd in the galleries which included some who were determined to thwart that attempt. When he tried to silence one who, on the face of the returns appeared to have been elected, Penrose and his associates were threatened with violence from the crowd, and were obliged to escape, the speaker, according to a Harrisburg paper, having "jumped out of the window, twelve feet high, through three thorn bushes and over a seven-foot picket fence" (quoted by Egle, *post*, p. 146). By way of defense to the opposition's criticism, he issued an *Address to the Freemen of Pennsylvania* (1839), also included in *Address of the Hon. Charles B. Penrose, Speaker of the Senate; and the Speeches of Messrs. Fraley (City), Williams, Pearson, and Penrose, Delivered . . . December 1838* (1839). When the first national Whig administration came into power in 1841, Penrose was appointed solicitor of the United States treasury, and he served until the close of the Tyler régime in 1845. He then opened an office in Lancaster, Pa., where he practised until 1847, removing thence to Philadelphia. In 1856 he was again elected to the state Senate, this time as a "Reform" nominee, and it was while serving there that he died at Harrisburg. Two days later a meeting of the Philadelphia bar was held at which resolutions were adopted deploring the loss of one "whose sudden death, in the midst of honorable labors, has ended a career of distinction and usefulness" (*Legal Intelligencer, post*, p. 117). He had six children, among whom were Richard Alexander Fullerton Penrose, father of Boies and Richard A. F. Penrose [*qq.v.*]; and Clement Biddle Penrose, for many years associate judge of the Philadelphia orphans' court.

[J. G. Leach, *Hist. of the Penrose Family of Phila.* (1903); Alfred Nevin, *Centennial Biog.: Men of Mark of Cumberland Valley, Pa. 1776–1876* (1876); J. H. Martin, *Martin's Bench and Bar of Phila.* (1883); W. H. Egle, "The Buckshot War," *Pa. Mag. of Hist. and Biog.*, July 1899; *Legal Intelligencer* (Phila.), Apr. 10, 1857; *Daily Pennsylvanian* (Phila.), Apr. 7–11, 1857.]   C.S.L.

PENROSE, RICHARD ALEXANDER FULLERTON (Dec. 17, 1863–July 31, 1931), geologist, was born in Philadelphia. He was the fourth of seven sons of Richard Alexander Fullerton Penrose (1827–1908) and Sarah Hannah (Boies) and was a younger brother of Boies Penrose [*q.v.*]. Entering Harvard University in 1880, he graduated in 1884, remaining for further work and receiving the degree of Ph.D. in 1886. In 1885–86 he accompanied Professor N. S. Shaler [*q.v.*] on a geological exploration. His years at Harvard were noteworthy not only for high scholarship but for an active interest in athletics; in 1885 and 1886 he was stroke on the University crew.

His serious work in his chosen field, applied geology, began with the preparation of his thesis, "The Nature and Origin of Deposits of Phosphate of Lime" (published in 1888 as *Bulletin of the United States Geological Survey*, no. 46). From 1886 to 1888 he was manager of mines for the Anglo-Canadian Phosphate Company and was subsequently appointed to undertake surveys of mineral deposits for the states of Texas (1888–89) and Arkansas (1889–92). The results of this work appeared in eight published reports, the most significant of which were "A Preliminary Report on the Geology of the Gulf Tertiary of Texas from Red River to the Rio Grande," *First Annual Report of the Geological Survey of Texas, 1889* (1890), vol. I; "Manganese, its Uses, Ores and Deposits," *Annual Report of the Geological Survey of Arkansas, for 1890* (1891), vol. I; "The Iron Deposits of Arkansas," *Ibid., 1892*, vol. I (1892). In 1892, with the founding of the University of Chicago, he was offered and accepted an associate professorship of economic geology. Promoted to full professor in 1895, he held the position until 1911, when the pressure of growing responsibilities in his mining enterprises made it impossible for him longer to devote any of his time to teaching. From 1893 to 1911 he was an associate editor of the *Journal of Geology*. Noteworthy papers not previously mentioned include: "The Superficial Alteration of Ore Deposits" (*Journal of Geology*, April–May 1894) and "Some Causes of Ore Shoots" (*Economic Geology*, March 1910). Meanwhile, in 1894 he was appointed a special geologist of the United States Geological Survey to examine the gold district of Cripple Creek, Colo., then in its active period of development. The results of this study were published by the government ("Mining Geology of the Cripple Creek District, Colorado," in *Sixteenth Annual Report of the United States Geological Survey . . . 1894–95*, pt. 2, 1895). In 1895 he became one of the founders of the Commonwealth Mining & Milling Company at what is now Pearce, Ariz., of which he was president from 1896 to 1903. In the latter year he was associated with his brother Spencer Penrose, D. C. Jackling, and others in the founding of the Utah Copper Company at Bingham, Utah, which was eventually to develop into the largest copper producing property in North America.

Clear and constructive but not profuse as a scientific author, shunning publicity, modest to the point of diffidence, Penrose was nevertheless an active member of most of the learned societies that were related to his chosen interests. He was a founder and first president (1920–21) of the Society of Economic Geologists and the year before his death was chosen president of the Geological Society of America. His loyalties to his scientific associates were shown during his lifetime by many gifts, always unostentatious, for the support of scientific work—he established the Penrose Gold Medal of the Geological Society of America and of the Society of Economic Geologists—and were evidenced at his death by munificent bequests to the Geological Society of America and to the leading American journals of pure and applied geology by virtue of which he became the foremost patron of his science.

In his native city he served as trustee of the University of Pennsylvania (1911–27), president (1922–26) of the Academy of Natural Sciences of Philadelphia, member of the Fairmount Park Commission (1927–31), and trustee of the Free Public Library of Philadelphia. He never married. He died in Philadelphia of chronic nephritis and arteriosclerosis.

[J. G. Leach, *Hist. of the Penrose Family of Phila.* (1903); manuscript sketch furnished by Miss Marion L. Ives, Penrose's secretary for many years; H. Foster Bain, in *Mining and Metallurgy*, Sept. 1931; Joseph Stanley-Brown in *Science*, Nov. 13, 1931, and *Bull. Geol. Soc. of America*, Mar. 1932, with bibliog.; R. T. Chamberlin, in *Jour. of Geol.*, Nov.–Dec. 1931; *Who's Who in America*, 1930–31; *Phila. Inquirer*, Aug. 1, 1931.]   E. S. B—n.

PENTECOST, GEORGE FREDERICK (Sept. 23, 1842–Aug. 7, 1920), clergyman and author, was born in Albion, Ill., the son of Hugh L. and Emma (Flower) Pentecost. In 1856 he went to Kansas Territory where he became secretary to the governor and clerk of the United States district court. He was a student at Georgetown College in Kentucky from 1860 to 1862, when he was converted and enlisted in the

army to serve for two years as chaplain of the 8th Kentucky Cavalry, United States Volunteers. He entered the Baptist ministry in 1864 and served congregations at Greencastle and at Evansville, Ind., for three years. He was then called to Covington, Ky., where he preached for another year. On leaving Covington he entered upon the first of the two important Baptist pastorates of his career, Hanson Place church, Brooklyn, 1869–1872, and Warren Avenue church, Boston, 1872–1878. His ability as a pulpit orator and his persuasiveness in making converts attracted the attention of Dwight Lyman Moody [*q.v.*] with whom he occasionally joined in evangelistic work during the following two years. He returned to Brooklyn to become pastor of Tompkins Avenue Congregational church in 1880 and remained in this charge until 1887. By this time he had become well known because of his preaching, his evangelism, and his writings. In 1875 he had published *The Angel in the Marble*; in 1879, *In the Volume of the Book*; and, in 1884, *Out of Egypt*. These religious books were written in the prevailing style of the day and were second only to his twelve volumes of *Bible Studies* (1880–89) in popularity. He was now sought as a religious leader in other countries. He conducted evangelistic campaigns in several of the large cities of Scotland in 1887 and 1888; he traveled in India from 1888 to 1891, delivering special lectures to English-speaking Brahmans; and for six years, beginning in 1891, he was minister of Marylebone church, London. In 1897 he published *The Birth and Boyhood of Christ* and *Forgiveness of Sins*. He was pastor of First Presbyterian church in Yonkers, N. Y., during the next five years and published in 1898 *Systematic Beneficence* and *Precious Truths*.

In 1902 he visited Japan, China, and the Philippine Islands, as a special commissioner of the Presbyterian and Congregational Boards of Foreign Missions, to study Christian work in the Orient. For eleven years after his return from Asia he lived in retirement, but in 1914, at the age of seventy-two, he was persuaded by his lifelong friend, John Wanamaker, to become the stated supply of Bethany Presbyterian church of Philadelphia in which Wanamaker was the senior elder. Two years later the aged minister was formally installed as pastor and continued his evangelistic preaching with vigor and fire. During the World War he conducted many patriotic services and meetings and spoke vehemently against all pacifist propaganda. He remained actively at work until his sudden death in 1920. He was survived by two children and his wife,

Ada (Webber) Pentecost, whom he had married in Hopkinsville, Ky., on Oct. 6, 1863. Though his fame as a preacher and writer was greater before 1900 than afterward, he was held in high esteem by many church leaders. He was recognized as a stalwart supporter of Biblical authority, as a pulpit orator whose preaching was marked by deep feeling and unusual breadth of treatment, and as a man of great physical vigor, tireless energy, and sensitive spirit.

[*Who's Who in America,* 1916–17 ; P. C. Headley, *George F. Pentecost: Life, Labors, and Bible Studies* (1880) ; *In Affectionate Memorial of George F. Pentecost* (pub. by Bethany church, Phila., 1920) ; *Presbyterian,* Aug. 12, 1920 ; *N. Y. Times,* Aug. 9, 1920.]

P. P. F.

PEPPER, GEORGE SECKEL (June 11, 1808–May 2, 1890), philanthropist, was born in Philadelphia, the son of George and Mary Catharine (Seckel) Pepper; William Pepper, 1810–1864 [*q.v.*], was a brother. Their grandfather, Henry Pepper (Heinrich Pfeffer), born near Strasburg, Germany, had come to America with his wife Catharine about 1769 and settled in Lebanon County, Pa. In 1774 he moved to Philadelphia, where he made a fortune and died in 1808. His extensive business interests were taken over by his second son, George, who became one of the richest men in the city. In business ability he was probably equaled by no other Philadelphian of the time except Stephen Girard [*q.v.*]. He is said to have had the first greenhouse in Philadelphia and was one of the founders of the Pennsylvania Horticultural Society. Thus George S. Pepper, in the third generation, inherited wealth that gave him ample opportunity to promote the cultural development of his native city, especially since he never married.

He was admitted to the bar Oct. 23, 1830, but gave much of his time to civic interests. For thirty-four years, from 1850 to 1884, he served on the board of directors of the Pennsylvania Academy of the Fine Arts and was its president from 1884 until his death, when the Academy became one of the beneficiaries under his will. In 1853 he was one of a group of public-spirited citizens who decided to erect a building where music could be suitably heard; several of their early meetings were held in his office. The American Academy of Music (now simply the Academy of Music), seating nearly 3,000 and with unusually fine acoustic properties, was opened Jan. 26, 1857, and at once became the center in Philadelphia for musical performances and important public gatherings. Pepper did much to insure the success of the undertaking, not only as a generous subscriber, but also as chairman of the building committee, for a time of the

finance committee, and from 1857 to 1870 ot tne executive committee. Among the many philanthropies that he fostered was the Henry Seybert Fund, for the care of indigent children, of which he was a trustee.

At his death in 1890 the greater part of his estate of about $2,000,000 went to public benefactions, including legacies to ten hospitals, the Franklin Institute, the Zoölogical Society, the Pennsylvania Museum and School of Industrial Art, the Rittenhouse Club, for the purchase of a library, and the Philadelphia, Commercial, and Apprentice libraries. To the University of Pennsylvania he gave $60,000 which was used to endow the George S. Pepper Professorship of Hygiene. In addition to $150,000, a share in the residuary estate was set aside to found a free city library; for although Philadelphia had led in the eighteenth century in the establishment of lending libraries, these had remained close corporations. Pepper realized the inadequacy of his legacy for the purpose intended, but his hope that this might serve as a nucleus was soon realized, largely through the enthusiastic support of the project by his nephew, Provost William Pepper [*q.v.*], and other members of his family. By 1927, when its handsome new building was opened on the Parkway, the Free Library of Philadelphia had twenty-nine branches in the city and about 750,000 books.

[J. W. Jordan, *Colonial Families of Phila.* (1911) ; F. N. Thorpe, *William Pepper, M.D., LL.D.* (1904) ; *The Free Library of Philadelphia, First Annual Report,* Oct. 1896 ; *Exercises at the Opening of the Main Building of the Free Library of Phila. . . . June 2, 1927* (1927) ; *Public Ledger* (Phila.), May 3, 1890 ; *North American* (Phila.), May 7, 1890 ; records of the Pa. Acad. of the Fine Arts, and of the Acad. of Music.]

A. L. L.

PEPPER, WILLIAM (Jan. 21, 1810–Oct. 15, 1864), physician, teacher, was born in Philadelphia, the son of George and Mary Catharine (Seckel) Pepper, and a brother of George Seckel Pepper [*q.v.*]. He received his early education in a school at Holmesburg, from which he went to the College of New Jersey, graduating in 1828. He then began the study of medicine with Dr. Thomas T. Hewson, and in 1829 entered the medical department of the University of Pennsylvania, where he was graduated in 1832, the title of his thesis being "Apoplexy." Soon after his graduation there was an outbreak of Asiatic cholera in Philadelphia, during which he rendered good service as a resident in the Bush Hill Hospital. In the autumn of 1832 he went abroad for further study, working in Paris, particularly with Pierre Louis and Guillaume Dupuytren. At this time Paris attracted the most brilliant of the young American physicians, and he was one of a celebrated group which included Oliver Wendell Holmes [*q.v.*].

Returning to Philadelphia, he took up the practice of medicine. His first professional position was with the Philadelphia Dispensary, and, given charge of a district, he soon attracted attention by the character of his work. In 1839 he was appointed to the staff of the Wills Eye Hospital and in 1841, to the Institute for Instruction of the Blind. In 1842 he was elected a physician to the Pennsylvania Hospital, a position which he held until 1858, and took a prominent part in the teaching carried on there. He was known as a keen diagnostician and was celebrated for his clear and practical instruction, especially in his clinical lectures. In 1860 he was appointed professor of medicine in the University of Pennsylvania, succeeding George B. Wood [*q.v.*], which position he held for four years, ill health compelling his resignation. He is described as of delicate frame and quick and active in his movements. His portrait, in the Medical School of the University of Pennsylvania, suggests a keen, kindly personality. During his stay in Paris he suffered from illness and spent part of a winter in the south of Europe. His health apparently was not robust; he suffered from hemoptysis from which he died.

In 1840 he married Sarah Platt of Philadelphia. There were seven children, of whom two became physicians, George and William [*q.v.*]. He was a member of many medical societies and the American Philosophical Society. He contributed a considerable number of articles to medical journals, but his influence seems to have been exerted more through his knowledge of disease and his excellent teaching than through his writings.

[T. S. Kirkbride, "Biog. Memoir of William Pepper," in *Quart. Summary, Trans. Coll. Physicians and Surgeons, Phila.*, 1865–66 (1867), reprinted separately (1866); F. P. Henry, *Standard Hist. of the Medic. Profession of Phila.* (1897); T. G. Morton, *The Hist. of the Pa. Hospital* (1895); H. A. Kelly and W. L. Burrage, *Am. Medic. Biogs.* (1920); *Phila. Inquirer*, Oct. 18, 1864.]　　　　　　　　　　　　T. M.

PEPPER, WILLIAM (Aug. 21, 1843–July 28, 1898), physician, educator, and public benefactor, was born in Philadelphia, the son of William [*q.v.*] and Sarah (Platt) Pepper, and a nephew of George Seckel Pepper [*q.v.*]. He was a great-grandson of Heinrich Pfeffer who came to America in 1769, and a grandson of George Pepper, Philadelphia merchant, who laid the foundation of the extensive family fortune. The elder William Pepper was one of the foremost physicians of Philadelphia. His frail health and his extensive practice and teaching responsibili-

ties relegated the care and training of the children to their mother, who came of a New Jersey Quaker family. Her calm influence on her son William probably contributed an element of repose to an individuality characterized by mental vigor and tireless energy. His early education was obtained in the school conducted by the Rev. Ormes B. Keith, later in that of Dr. John W. Faries. In September 1858, although as he says his knowledge at the time "consisted largely of Latin and Greek with a small fluency in expression and English composition," he entered the University of Pennsylvania, where four years later he graduated, second in his class. In 1862 he entered the Medical Department, the faculty of which included besides his father, Dr. Joseph Leidy [*q.v.*], and Dr. Richard A. F. Penrose, professor of obstetrics. Following his graduation in 1864, he devoted some months to the care of his father who had been forced to resign his chair in the Medical School and who died in October of the same year. Subsequently, he served one year as resident physician to the Pennsylvania Hospital, and soon afterward was appointed pathologist and visiting physician to the same institution. He later received similar posts at the Philadelphia Hospital, Blockley. Because of his sound pathological training and his growing clinical ability, he was appointed in 1868, lecturer on morbid anatomy at the Medical School of the University of Pennsylvania, and two years later was named to a similar post in clinical medicine. These early teaching appointments were followed by thirty years of service to the University.

In order to enlarge the scope of his knowledge, he spent several months in Europe in 1871, studying methods in medical education and institutional administration and incidentally laying the foundation for his future development as an executive and broad-visioned educator. Upon his return, he threw himself at once into the novel project of establishing a teaching hospital in connection with the University Medical School. A committee was formed of which this young man of twenty-seven was the most active member. The ingenious methods by which he awakened the support of conservative Philadelphia merchants and exploited the city council and the state legislature marked an epoch in the development of the Medical School, the University, the city and the man. Largely through his efforts there was founded in 1874 the first hospital in America intimately associated with a university medical school in which the faculty acted as the staff. Throughout his life he continued to labor for the development of the University Hospital. In 1887 he founded the nurses' training school, placing it under the guidance of a trained director and arranging for a definite course of instruction, and in 1894, as a memorial to his father, he established and endowed the William Pepper Laboratory of Clinical Medicine, the first laboratory in America for the prosecution of advanced clinical studies into the causation of disease.

In 1875 he was made medical director of the Centennial Exhibition to be held in Philadelphia the following year. Under his supervision a model hospital was erected, problems of hygiene and sanitation were solved, and the bureau of medical service displayed such efficiency that he was personally honored by the English and Norwegian governments. During this same period, his professional reputation increased greatly and consequently, in 1876, he was elected to the chair of clinical medicine, newly created. On Oct. 1, 1877, as an introduction to his course of clinical lectures, he delivered a notable address, *Higher Medical Education, the True Interest of the Public and the Profession,* which was published by the trustees. His position as medical director of the Centennial had offered him additional opportunities to acquaint himself with the methods of medical instruction used abroad, and this address dealt with the evils prevalent in American medical education, reviewed the sounder European systems, and suggested correction and new concepts for the American schools. Together with the efforts of President Eliot at Harvard, it paved the way for drastic reforms in American medical education.

In 1884, although in 1880 Pepper had become provost of the University, he was called upon to accept in addition to that office the professorship of the theory and practice of medicine, succeeding to a chair vacated by his father twenty years before. The latter position he filled with distinction until his death. Numerous professional honors came to him. He was a founder (1884) and president (1886) of the American Climatological Society, president (1886) of the American Clinical Association and (1891) of the Association of American Physicians, and a member of the executive committee of the American Medical Association. In 1893, as president of the first Pan-American Medical Congress, he did much to promote international relationships and to endear himself to his Latin-American colleagues.

During his active professional life, he published several hundred papers on medical topics, most of them being transcriptions of his clinical lectures and reports of unusual cases. Some of his contributions are of extreme interest: in one early paper, *The Morphological Changes of the Blood in Malarial Fever* (1867), prepared in collaboration with Edward Rhoads and J. F. Meigs, the pigmented bodies in the erythrocytes, later shown to be the malarial parasites, were accurately described. In a contribution on pernicious anemia (*American Journal of the Medical Sciences,* October 1875), he was the first to call attention to the involvement of the bone marrow. At various times he published observations on the treatment of pulmonary cavities incident to phthisis and on the climatological treatment of that disease (notably in *The Climatological Study of Phthisis in Pennsylvania,* 1887). His shrewd conclusions paved the way for the modern therapeutics of tuberculosis. His better known contributions to medical literature, however, were *A Practical Treatise on the Diseases of Children* (1870), which was a fourth, revised, edition of a work by John F. Meigs [*q.v.*]; *A System of Practical Medicine* (5 vols., 1885–86), issued under his editorship; and a more condensed *Text-Book of the Theory and Practice of Medicine* (2 vols., 1893–94). His fame could rest securely, however, upon two addresses on medical education, that delivered in 1877, mentioned above, and another bearing the same title, delivered in 1893 (*Higher Medical Education, the True Interest of the Public and the Profession; Two Addresses,* 1894). The one formulated fundamental principles, the other described their fruition and offered still loftier conceptions for future accomplishment.

Soon after the resignation of Provost Charles J. Stillé [*q.v.*] in 1880, William Pepper was called upon to undertake the administrative burden of the entire University, in addition to his professorship of medicine and his private practice. Inaugurated as provost Feb. 22, 1881, he made his first report to the trustees in 1883. In the next three years he obtained additional land from the city by arranging for the award of certain scholarships to local high school graduates and reorganized the faculties and curricula of the College, the Dental School, the Law School, and the Towne Scientific School. During this time also he was concerned in the founding of the Wharton School of Finance, the Veterinary School and additions to the University Hospital. By the end of a decade of his provostship, the University had grown greatly; most of the departments were self-supporting or had insignificant deficits, and the funded debt had been reduced through numerous gifts and bequests inspired by Pepper. On land previously acquired, a library and a school of hygiene had been erected and additional property had been secured for future developments. A biological school and a department of physical education had been started, many scholarships and fellowships had been founded, and the College and the Graduate School of Philosophy had been further developed. Partly as the result of the Provost's vigorous example the annual bibliography of the faculties totaled hundreds of publications. In addition, he had introduced the University Extension Lectures by the faculty and other famous scholars and had supported the acquisition of archeological treasures by sponsoring an expedition to Babylonia under the direction of John Punnett Peters [*q.v.*]. Aside from his University duties, he had founded (1886) the College Association of Pennsylvania, forerunner of the Association of Colleges and Secondary Schools of the Middle States and Maryland.

During the last four years of his tenure as provost, a School of Architecture was founded, and on newly acquired land were built the Wistar Institute of Anatomy and Biology, a gymnasium, a chemistry building, an engineering building, and a central heating and lighting station. The medical course was increased to four years, the College curriculum was modified by the adoption of the group elective system, and in 1892 the Bennett School for the graduate instruction of women was opened, marking a radical departure from the traditional policy of the University. Pepper's teaching in the Medical School, his enormous consulting practice, his duties as provost, and the multitudinous outside demands made upon him by virtue of this office made serious inroads on his health and vitality, and in April 1894 he presented his resignation to the trustees, accompanying it with a large gift to the Hospital. In fourteen years, from a loosely organized group of schools, he had raised the University to eminence in academic circles. Some conception of this accomplishment can be obtained by reading the gloomy reminiscences of his predecessor and then turning to his own final report and the tributes paid to him when he retired.

Aside from his professional and University interests, Pepper advanced the welfare of the community by his zealous promotion of any cause directed toward civic betterment or the elevation of the cultural ideals of the public. The University Extension Lectures grew in popularity, and in 1892 the scope of the experiment was enlarged by the founding of the American Society for the Extension of University Teaching. Pepper lived to see this pioneer effort in adult education spread into 343 cities of the Eastern states. The death of his uncle, George S. Pepper, in 1890 revealed a bequest of $250,000 to found a Free Library in Philadelphia, and the nephew directed the utilization of the money in developing an institution capable of unlimited expansion. From a temporary central library at City Hall and two small branches, grew during his lifetime the Philadelphia Free Library.

The resources of his waning strength Pepper devoted to promoting the cause of the Philadelphia museums. The Commercial Museum is a monument to his organizing ability expended in spite of bodily suffering and the press of other exhausting duties. Once recognizing the relation of archeological discoveries to education, he gave his powerful support to the excavations near ancient Nippur and organized the Archeological Association of the University which subsequently (1892) developed into a University department. Vast treasures of unique interest poured into the limited space at the disposal of the University and after his resignation from the office of provost, he was induced to throw the weight of his influence into the creation of an adequate museum, with the result that the University Museum, an edifice of noble proportions, was erected on what had been a smoke-swept dump heap overlooking the Schuylkill.

It was eminently fitting that this nineteenth century citizen and benefactor of Philadelphia should associate himself in marriage with a great-grand-daughter of Benjamin Franklin. On June 25, 1873, he married Frances Sergeant Perry, sister of Thomas Sergeant Perry [*q.v.*], whose mother was a grand-daughter of Sarah (Franklin) and Richard Bache [*q.v.*]. To Pepper and his wife were born four sons, three of whom lived to maturity. To few men has it been given to accomplish so much in so many fields of effort in so short a lifetime. Pepper attained the pinnacle of success in his chosen profession, whether that success be judged by scientific ability or by personal emoluments. The latter were merely a means to an end; he dared not curtail his enormous practice, for by its returns he promoted his larger projects at the University. His personality was magnetic, his enthusiasm contagious. He had the true physician's tenderness and sympathy for his fellow mortal. The demands made upon his time by his practice, his consultation work—which took him all over the Eastern states—his teaching and administrative duties, called forth the utmost reserves of bodily and mental vigor for their accomplishment. For years he slept only for short intervals and enjoyed only momentary relaxation. Even during the last five years of his life, his body racked by the torture of recurring attacks of angina pectoris, he never relaxed his exhausting mode of living, but at length his physical resources were completely spent and he died, in Pleasanton, Cal., in his fifty-fifth year.

[F. N. Thorpe, *William Pepper, M.D., LL.D.,* (1904); *Trans. Coll. of Physicians of Phila.,* 3 ser. XXIII (1901); C. J. Stillé, *Reminiscences of a Provost, 1866–1880* (n.d.); *Annual Reports of the Provost and Treasurer of the Univ. of Pa.,* 1883–94; *Addresses Made at the Meeting Held in Memory of William Pepper . . . in the Chapel of the Univ. of Pa.* (1899); *The Free Lib. of Phila. . . . Ann. Report,* 1896, 1897; *Pub. Ledger* (Phila.), July 30, 1898; MSS. and clippings in the possession of Pepper's son, Dean William Pepper, School of Medicine, Univ. of Pa.]   J. H. P—n.
E. S. T.

PEPPERRELL, Sir WILLIAM (June 27, 1696–July 6, 1759), colonial merchant and soldier, was born in the Pepperrell house at Kittery Point, Me. His father, also William Pepperrell, was a native of Tavistock, near Plymouth, England. As a penniless lad, he had been apprenticed to the captain of a fishing vessel sailing to the New England coast. At the age of twenty-two he had settled on the Isle of Shoals as a merchant. He prospered, married Margery Bray, and ultimately moved to the home of his wife's family, Kittery Point on the mainland. Here he became a justice of the peace and, in time, one of the most prosperous of the New England merchants of his day. Young William's education consisted of the three R's, knowledge picked up while helping in his father's store, and the frontier lore naturally acquired by a boy growing up on the edge of civilization. Indian outrages in the neighborhood were not infrequent, and he was a member of the militia at sixteen. When his only brother died, his father took him into partnership and the firm became known as the William Pepperrells. They dealt in lumber and fish; built ships which they dispatched with cargoes to the southern colonies, the West Indies, the Mediterranean countries, and England, selling vessels as well as cargoes; and imported European products which they sold in Boston. Their constantly increasing profits were invested in real estate, rapidly advancing in value. By 1729 young William had acquired, among other holdings, almost the entire townships of Saco and Scarboro. The firm's large business made it an important factor in foreign exchange, and the younger William spent much of his time in Boston managing affairs there. His business brought him into contact with the leading public men and the good society of town. On Mar. 16, 1723, he married Mary Hirst, grand-daughter of Samuel Sewall [*q.v.*].

At home, advancement in the militia was rapid and at thirty he had become colonel in command of all the militia in the Province of Maine. In 1726 he was elected representative to the Massa-chusetts General Court from Kittery, and the next year became an assistant, or member of the Council, an office to which he was annually re-appointed until his death. For eighteen years he was chosen president of the Council. In 1730 Gov. Jonathan Belcher [*q.v.*], for political reasons, removed the incumbents of the judicial bench and appointed Pepperrell as the new chief justice. The latter at once ordered some books from London and started to study law. It is typical of the happy star which shone over him throughout his career that he could reverse the usual order, becoming chief justice first and reading law afterwards. Upon the death of his father in 1734, he inherited the bulk of the estate. He was now a power in New England, head of the militia of Maine, president of the Massachusetts Council, his ability as a "captain of industry" recognized, connected by marriage with the socially elect, and possessed of one of the largest fortunes in the colony. He had had four children, of whom only two, Elizabeth and Andrew, survived infancy. The young heiress married Nathaniel Sparhawk, and Andrew, after graduating from Harvard with high honors, became his father's business partner in 1744.

Pepperrell's close friend, Governor Belcher, whom he had steadily supported in the continuous salary controversy, was succeeded by William Shirley [*q.v.*], and in the year that Andrew entered business, Great Britain declared war on France. The colonies were at once involved, and Shirley conceived the scheme of capturing Louisbourg, the French stronghold on Cape Breton. A descent by the commander of Louisbourg on a British outpost at Canso Island enraged the English; Shirley pushed his plans rapidly; the help of other colonies was enlisted; and Commodore Sir Peter Warren [*q.v.*], cruising in the West Indies, received orders from England to cooperate with the provincial forces. Between three and four thousand men were dispatched from the colonies, about a third of them from Maine, and Pepperrell was chosen commander of the expedition.

The flotilla bearing the American troops arrived Apr. 30 and found the British fleet waiting at the rendezvous. The troops were disembarked with skill. Pepperrell's experience in the militia had given him no knowledge of Continental methods of attacking fortresses; nevertheless, the siege began. The French garrison, inefficient and corrupt, observing the uncouth movements of the invaders, became suddenly panic-stricken and abandoned the grand battery without striking a blow. The Americans took possession of the enemy's cannon and, with great difficulty, brought up more. It was said by some of the survivors of the siege that it resembled a "Cambridge Commencement," being only half a siege and half an uproarious holiday (Jeremy Belknap, *The History of New Hampshire*, 1812, II, 170). The American supplies ran short, though by the capture of a French frigate sent to relieve the fortress the navy replenished the powder and ammunition; and at times half the attacking force was on the sick list. To the relief of everybody, including the French, the garrison surrendered on June 17.

Though it cannot be claimed that Pepperrell displayed much military skill, he had qualities which greatly helped the enterprise to its successful conclusion. He held the undisciplined colonial troops at their posts by his personal popularity. The cooperation of the British fleet was essential and British and colonials rarely got on well together, but Pepperrell was patient and tactful and for the successful cooperation that was achieved deserves a good share of the credit.

The capture of the fortress was warmly welcomed in England and the leading participants were all honored. Pepperrell was commissioned colonel (Sept. 1, 1745), with authority to raise and command a regiment in the regular British line and in November 1746 was created a baronet, an honor never before conferred on a native American. After the capture he acted jointly with Warren as governor of the conquered territory, raised his regiment, and remained at Louisbourg until late in the spring of 1746. He sat in the Council at Boston in June and then returned to his affairs at Kittery. In September 1749 he went to London, where he was received by the King, and was made something of a social lion. The City of London presented him with a service of plate as a token of respect for his military exploit. He remained there nearly a year, then returned to Kittery. Soon afterward his only son died, unmarried.

His landed property had become very great and he now gradually wound up his mercantile affairs. In 1753 he was one of the commissioners, as he had frequently been before, to negotiate a treaty with the Maine Indians. When the French and Indian War broke out, he was ordered by the King to raise a regiment of 1000 men. Shortly afterward he went to New York on the concerns of his regiment, which was employed in the Oswego expedition with Shirley's. Pepperrell, who had been made a major-general, Feb. 27, 1755, did not accompany them but at Shirley's order took command of the eastern frontier. Early in February 1755 Shirley suggested that Pepperrell lead an expedition against

Crown Point but later changed his mind, and a coolness developed between them. After Shirley went to London in 1756, and the lieutenant-governor died, the Massachusetts government was administered by the Council, and Pepperrell as president of that body was *de facto* governor. He was appointed commander of Castle William and of all the military forces of the colony. On the arrival of the new governor, Thomas Pownall [*q.v.*], in August 1757, Pepperrell was ordered to proceed to Springfield or other parts of the frontier and raise troops for the defense of the province. On Feb. 20, 1759, he was commissioned lieutenant-general in the royal army, but his health was failing, he did not take part in the remaining operations of the war, and on July 6, 1759, he died.

With his death, his baronetcy became extinct. The bulk of his estate was left to his grandson, William Pepperrell Sparhawk, on condition that he take the name Pepperrell, and in 1774 this William Pepperrell was created baronet. He was a Loyalist and fled to England on the outbreak of the Revolution; his property was confiscated, and his only son died unmarried.

[Usher Parsons, *The Life of Sir William Pepperrell, Bart.* (rev. ed., 1856); J. F. Sprague, *Three Men from Maine* (1924); C. A. Harris, in *Dict. Nat. Biog.*; C. H. C. Howard, "The Pepperrell Portraits," *Essex Inst. Hist. Colls.*, vol. XXXI (1894–95); C. H. C. Howard, *The Pepperrells in America* (1906), repr. from *Essex. Inst. Hist. Colls.*, article on William Pepperrell appearing in vol. XXXVII (1901); "The Pepperrell Papers," *Mass. Hist. Soc. Colls.*, 6 ser. X (1899); "The Journal of Sir William Pepperrell Kept during the Expedition against Louisbourg, Mar. 24–Aug. 22, 1745," *Proc. Am. Antiq. Soc.*, n.s., vol. XX (1911); *An Accurate Jour. and Account of the Proceedings of the New-England Land Forces during the Late Expedition* (1746), official journals, pub. in London; *Louisbourg Journals, 1745* (1932), ed. by L. E. deForest; *Correspondence of Wm. Shirley* (2 vols., 1912), ed. by C. H. Lincoln; instructions and letters relating to the Cape Breton expedition, *Mass. Hist. Soc. Colls.*, vol. I (1792); G. E. Cokayne, *Complete Baronetage*, vol. V (1906); *Gentleman's Mag.* (London), Sept. 1759; Benjamin Stevens, *A Sermon Occasioned by the Death of the Hon. Sir Wm. Pepperrell* (1759).]   J. T. A.

PERABO, JOHANN ERNST (Nov. 14, 1845–Oct. 29, 1920), pianist, teacher, and composer, was born in Wiesbaden, Germany, the son of Michael and Christine (Hübner) Perabo. The father was a school teacher and, according to German requirements, also an organist, pianist, and violinist, hence he was well qualified to train his nine children, all of whom became musicians. Ernst, the only child by Michael Perabo's second wife, proved to be the most gifted, and he began the study of piano with his father when he was five years old. In 1852 the family emigrated to America, settling first in New York, where they remained for two years. Ernst received instruction in violin and piano from several teachers and during his second year in New York appeared at a concert given by a teacher named Heinrich. A great future was predicted for him. His parents removed to Dover, N. H., and then to Boston, where they remained for only one year. In Boston he took violin lessons from William Schultze, of the Mendelssohn Quintet Club, and played at a concert under the direction of Carl Zerrahn. The next move took the family to Chicago. Soon thereafter they went to Washington, D. C., solely to obtain an interview with President Buchanan, in the hope that through him they could secure assistance from the government to send the talented child to Europe. They were granted an interview but were not successful in securing funds. They did, however, win the ear of William Scharfenberg, a prominent musician in New York, who formed a committee to defray the expenses of the boy's education in Europe. He sailed for Hamburg in 1858 and spent four years there, but he had to struggle against ill health, which prevented serious music study.

In 1862 he entered the Leipzig Conservatory where he studied piano with Moscheles and Wenzel, harmony with Papperitz, Hauptmann, and Richter, and later composition with Reinecke. In 1865 he won the Helbig prize, and, at the public examination of the Conservatory, he played two movements of the Burgmüller concerto in F# minor, which had just been published. He returned to the United States the same year (1865). He established himself first in New York, as teacher and pianist, and gave a number of concerts that were so successful that he decided to give a series of matinées, at which he performed the sonatas of Schubert. His parents, meantime, had gone to Sandusky, Ohio, to live. He gave several successful concerts there and also at Lafayette, Cleveland, and Chicago. In 1866 he transferred his residence to Boston and remained there until his death. He never gave concerts on a large scale but devoted himself more particularly to teaching, in which he was most successful. For many years he played annually at the Harvard concerts at which he gave many works unknown at that time in America. He was especially commended for his playing of Beethoven, and for his interpretation of the Schubert pianoforte works. Besides having a fluent technique, he was a remarkable sight-reader. He was a zealous conservative, but he approached new works in a spirit of open-mindedness. He married Louise Schmidt of Boston from whom he soon separated. His death occurred at West Roxbury, Mass., in the homestead in which his parents had lived. He wrote

numerous compositions, for the most part forgotten, and many transcriptions, including the first movement of Rubinstein's "Ocean Symphony," parts of Beethoven's *Fidelio,* the first movement of Schubert's "Unfinished Symphony," and several of the Loewe ballads. Of his own compositions, the following are probably the most important: "Moment Musical" (*opus* 1); Scherzo (*opus* 2); Prelude (*opus* 3); Waltz (*opus* 4); "Pensées" (*opus* 11); Prelude, Romance and Toccatina (*opus* 19).

[W. S. B. Mathews, *A Hundred Years of Music in America* (1889); *Who's Who in America,* 1918–19; *Grove's Dict. of Music and Musicians: Am. Supp.* (1930); *Boston Transcript,* Oct. 29, 1920; information as to certain facts from Mr. George A. Burdett of Newton Center, Mass., and from Miss Clementine Miller, Alton, N. H.]   F. L. G. C.

PERALTA, PEDRO de (*c.* 1584–1666), third governor of New Mexico, founder of Santa Fé, was connected with a noble family which originated in Navarre during the middle ages. There is some evidence that he was a university graduate and trained in canon law; also that he had seen military service. He is believed to have been unmarried and about twenty-five years of age in the winter of 1608–09 when he arrived in the city of Mexico. On Mar. 5, 1609, the viceroy appointed him governor of New Mexico, to supersede Juan de Oñate [*q.v.*] and his son Cristóbal, and instructed him "before all else" to see to the founding of a new *villa* with a view to order and permanence. From April to October 1609, Peralta was at Zacatecas, assembling building supplies, foodstuffs, weapons, clothing, carts and livestock, missionaries, soldiers, Indian servants. Probably, therefore, he did not reach Oñate's colony at San Gabriel until March 1610; at least, Oñate and his son did not depart before May.

The name selected by Peralta for the new *villa,* Santa Fé, would suggest a strong piety in his character, yet, as governor, it was his duty to maintain the king's authority as superior to that of the Church, and he was soon crossing swords with the Franciscan missionaries. In the spring of 1612, the *comisario,* Fray Isidro de Ordoñez, was in Mexico city getting the next three years' supplies for the missionaries; and upon his return, late that year, he represented that he had been made *comisario* of the Holy Inquisition also—a false claim for which he was later rebuked by the king and disciplined by his own order. Apparently Peralta required him to show his credentials; Ordoñez refused, called the governor a "schismatic heretic," and posted an excommunication of him. When Peralta disregarded the excommunication, he was seized by Fray Ordoñez with the help of some of the soldiers and colonists and was held prisoner for nearly a year in the convent at Sandía pueblo. Early in December 1612 he managed to escape, "in the dead of winter, and half naked, covered with a buffalo skin like an Indian." His jailer, Fray Estévan de Perea, pursued him with a large force of Indians to a ranch five miles away, but he had escaped to Santa Fé. There he was again seized and brought back "in irons and seated on a beast like a woman." But from Santa Fé, Dec. 13, 1612, he had managed to send a report of his situation to Mexico city; and nearly a year later peremptory orders arrived which effected his release.

Official approval of Peralta's defense of crown prerogatives appeared in his passing a satisfactory *residencia*. Also he was next appointed lieutenant-commander at the port of Acapulco; and in 1621–22 he was alcalde of the royal warehouse in Mexico city. In 1637 he arrived in Caracas, Venezuela; and the following year he married a widow of means, sister of Pedro de Paredes, and bought a half-interest in a trading vessel. From 1644 to 1645 he was auditor of the royal treasury at Caracas; later, he was acting treasurer; and from February 1651 to August 1652, was treasurer, having purchased that office. Late in the latter year he arrived in Madrid, "old and infirm and almost blind, maimed in the right hand and totally incapacitated" through injuries inflicted by enemies in Caracas from whom he had required moneys due the king. He petitioned and was granted (1654) leave to resign, and that his wife and two children be shielded from his enemies and allowed to join him in Spain. Until his death, which occurred in Madrid in 1666, his lot may have been happier, yet his estate was attached by the Jesuit order, and in 1671 the Alférez Pedro de Paredes was striving to salvage something for his widowed sister and her two children.

[Data supplied by France V. Scholes from Staatsbibliothek, Munich: *Codex Monacensis, Hisp. 79*; and data gathered by the writer in Madrid, Seville, and Mexico city; "Instructions for Don Pedro de Peralta," *El Palacio,* June 16, 1928; another translation in *N. Mex. Hist. Rev.,* Apr. 1929; "When Was Santa Fé Founded?" *Ibid.,* Apr. 1929; "Fray Estevan de Perea's Relacion," *Ibid.,* July 1933; L. B. Bloom and T. C. Donnelly, *N. Mex. Hist. and Civics* (1933).]

L. B. B.

PERCHÉ, NAPOLEON JOSEPH (Jan. 10, 1805–Dec. 27, 1883), Roman Catholic prelate and editor, was born at Angers, France. A precocious child, he could read at four; at eighteen he was a professor of philosophy; and at twenty-four he was ordained a priest, after graduating from the Seminary of Beaupréau. He served in various pastorates in France until 1837, when he went to America to assist Benedict J. Flaget [*q.v.*], bishop of Bardstown, Ky., in his missionary work at Portland.

Wishing to raise money to build a church for his parishioners, who were poor, he secured permission to go to New Orleans. There, in the St. Louis Cathedral, he preached such eloquent sermons in French that the Creoles soon subscribed the money he needed, and the Archbishop, Antoine Blanc [*q.v.*], offered him an appointment. Perché, however, asked to be allowed first to go back to Kentucky and finish his church. This work accomplished, he returned to New Orleans, and, in 1842, became almoner of the Ursuline Convent, a post he filled for twenty-eight years. In 1842 began the long drawn-out controversy between Blanc and the wardens of the St. Louis Cathedral over the right to appoint the curate. It became so bitter that it was taken to the courts and the wardens retained the three leading lawyers of the city—Soulé, Roselius, and Mazureau—to represent their side. In order to mobilize public opinion in favor of his church's stand, Perché founded a French weekly called *Le Propagateur Catholique,* which made its initial appearance on Nov. 12, 1842. Although it contained an announcement that it was "published by a society of literary men," Perché himself did most of the writing and struck some doughty blows in defense of his ecclesiastical superior, Archbishop Blanc, whose cause was eventually sustained in the supreme court. The good Abbé was a fearless fighter, and his editorials were so vehemently partizan and pugnacious that they lacked the calm judicial quality which might have been expected of his cloth. He continued, nevertheless, to edit the paper successfully until, in 1857, he resigned on account of his health.

Pope Leo XIII called him the "Bossuet of the American church" on account of his services as a propagandist; and in 1870 Pope Pius IX appointed him coadjutor to Archbishop John Mary Odin [*q.v.*]. At Odin's death in 1870 Perché became the third archbishop of New Orleans. He introduced the Carmelite Order of nuns into the diocese, and in 1872 inaugurated an annual service of thanksgiving for victory at the battle of New Orleans on Jan. 8, 1815. Some of his articles from the *Propagateur Catholique* were reprinted in a small pamphlet entitled *De l'Importance du Marriage sous le rapport social et religieux* (1846). This and a few pastoral letters constitute his literary remains.

[E. L. Tinker, *Les Écrits de Langue Française en Louisiane au XIXe Siècle* (Paris, 1932); Charles Testut, *Portraits Littéraires de la Nouvelle-Orléans* (1850); L. J. Loewenstein, *Hist. of the St. Louis Cathedral of*

New Orleans (1882); J. M. Augustin and T. H. Ryan, *Sketch of the Cath. Church in La. on the Occasion of the Centenary of the Erection of the See of New Orleans in 1793* (1893); R. H. Clarke, *Lives of the Deceased Bishops of the Cath. Church in the U.S.* (1888), vol. III; J. G. Shea, *The Hierarchy of the Cath. Church in the U.S.* (1886); *Times-Democrat* (New Orleans), Dec. 28, 1883.]

E. L. T.

PERCIVAL, JAMES GATES (Sept. 15, 1795–May 2, 1856), poet, geologist, was born in Kensington, Hartford County, Conn., the son of Dr. James and Elizabeth (Hart) Percival. On the paternal side he was descended from James Percival, who settled in Sandwich, Mass., in 1670. His mother, descended from Stephen Hart, one of the Hartford proprietors, had a sensitive, nervous temperament and was inclined to melancholy, a trait transmitted to her sons, Edwin, a painter, and James. An attack of typhoid in 1807 permanently impaired the latter's voice. On the death of his father in the same year, the shy, sickly, studious boy was sent to private school. In later life he complained of "a neglected orphanage" (manuscript letter, dated New Haven, Feb. 16, 1823, unaddressed). An omnivorous reader, he was in childhood exceptionally well informed in geography, and his youthful epic, "The Commerciad," written in 1809, was a versified gazetteer. His career at Yale, interrupted for a year in 1812, was brilliant scholastically; he delved into chemistry and mineralogy under the elder Benjamin Silliman [*q.v.*] and into botany under Eli Ives [*q.v.*], and attained a reputation as a poet. For the graduation exercises in 1815 he wrote and took part in a tragedy, later published under the title "Zamor." During the next three years he vacillated between teaching and the professions of law and medicine, finally entering the medical department of the University of Pennsylvania in 1818. The following year he transferred to the Medical Institution of Yale College and graduated with distinction in 1820. After a brief interval of practice in his native village, he closed his office. Rejection of a marriage proffer and failure to win a lucrative clientele drove him to attempt suicide; but in the same year the publication of several of his poems in *The Microscope*, a New Haven magazine, prompted him to attempt a career as a poet. Into *Poems* (1821) he emptied his portfolio, with the result that his long, Spenserian "Prometheus" was acclaimed the equal of Byron's *Childe Harold*, and his poetic gifts hailed as the most classical in America. The appearance of *Clio I* and *II* (1822), collections of weak lyrics, and of *Prometheus Part II with Other Poems* (1822) did not alter his reputation. The darkly sententious and auto-biographic "Prometheus," though suffering the weakness of improvization, is a meritorious work. Many of his poems were pleas for Greek freedom. A selection from these four volumes appeared as *Poems* (New York, 1823; London, 1824).

For brief periods he edited the *Connecticut Herald*, a New Haven newspaper, taught chemistry at West Point, and served as surgeon in the Boston recruiting office. These positions he resigned because of fancied unjust treatment. His sudden withdrawal as the Harvard Phi Beta Kappa poet in 1824, his petulance as Phi Beta Kappa orator at Yale in 1825, and his resignation as editor of George Bond's *American Athenæum* (New York) in August 1825 aroused a storm of newspaper disapproval, in consequence of which he withdrew from his literary career, publishing only *Clio No. III* (1827), dream-haunted soliloquies, and *The Dream of a Day, and Other Poems* (1843), metrical experiments and translations. Although Percival remained the ranking American poet until the appearance of Bryant's *Poems* (1832), his work is now read only in anthologies, and he was soon forgotten.

While editing Vicesimus Knox's *Elegant Extracts* (6 vols., 1825) and Malte-Brun's *System of Universal Geography* (1827–34), he began a systematic study of languages, translating from a dozen poetic literatures. By reason of his linguistic attainments, he was employed in 1827–28 to assist Noah Webster [*q.v.*] in revising the manuscript and reading the proof of *An American Dictionary of the English Language* (1828).

In 1835 he was appointed state geologist of Connecticut. After presenting two reports (1836 and 1838), which he stipulated must not be published, he planned a comprehensive natural history survey of the state. Gov. William W. Ellsworth [*q.v.*] refused to credit his seriousness and in 1838 blocked a further grant of funds. After vainly attempting to have appropriations renewed, Percival presented "a hasty outline" of his bulky materials in the *Report on the Geology of the State of Connecticut* (1842). This volume is almost unreadable because of its mass of details and the failure to differentiate between important and unimportant matters. It is mainly lithological description, remarkable for the accurate discrimination of crystalline rocks, but in it Percival made a noteworthy contribution to geology in demonstrating the crescent shape of trap dikes, and gave "the best and fullest exemplification" of the laws governing the subterranean forces by which mountains were formed.

During the geological survey, Percival composed many original German poems; translated from Russian, Serbian, and Hungarian; wrote political songs in support of Harrison (*The New Haven Whig Song Book*, 1840); and developed a theory of music, now lost. Poverty-stricken as a result of his unpaid work as geologist and his lavish purchase of books, he took quarters in the State Hospital, New Haven, where he lived as a recluse, engaged occasionally during the next ten years as a railroad surveyor and geologist. For the American Mining Company, between 1851 and 1854 he surveyed the lead-mining district of Illinois and Wisconsin, and in the latter year he was appointed state geologist of Wisconsin but died at Hazel Green, Wis., after the publication of one annual report.

Percival was "an inexhaustible, undemonstrative, noiseless, passionless man . . . impressing you, for the most part, as a creature of pure intellect" (*Atlantic Monthly*, July 1859, p. 59). Unyielding and eccentric, utterly impractical and living alone with his ten thousand books, he was one of the most learned men of his time.

[H. R. Warfel, "James Gates Percival, a Biographical Study" (unpublished dissertation in Yale Univ.); J. H. Ward, *The Life and Letters of James Gates Percival* (1866), somewhat inaccurate and incomplete; W. N. Rice and H. E. Gregory, *Manual of the Geology of Conn.* (1906); James Russell Lowell, in *North Am. Rev.*, Jan. 1867 (1871), an essentially unfair caricature; Timothy Dwight, in the *New Englander*, Apr. 1867, the best characterization of the man; *Cambridge Hist. of Am. Lit.*, I (1917), 279, 523; H. E. Legler, *James Gates Percival: An Anecdotal Sketch and a Bibliog.* (1901); G. P. Merrill, *The First One Hundred Years of Am. Geology* (1924); Alfred Andrews, *Geneal. Hist. of Deacon Stephen Hart and His Descendants* (1875).]   H. R. W.

PERCIVAL, JOHN (Apr. 5, 1779–Sept. 17, 1862), naval officer, was born at West Barnstable, Mass., the son of Capt. John and Mary (Snow) Percival, and a descendant of John Percival who was born in France in 1658 and who settled at Barnstable in 1685. At the age of thirteen he went to sea, and at twenty, commanded vessels in the West Indian and transatlantic trade. He was impressed into the British navy at Lisbon on Feb. 24, 1797, and served in H. M. S. *Victory* and then in a naval brig, but about two years later escaped at Madeira to the American ship *Washington*. During the naval conflict between the United States and France, he served a year as master's mate in the U. S. S. *Delaware* (Recommendation of Capt. Thomas Baker, Navy Library *Misc. Letters*, Feb. 24, 1809), was warranted midshipman on May 13, 1800, and was discharged at the peace establishment in July 1801. He reëntered the merchant service as mate and master, and according to his own statement as reported by B. F. Stevens who later became his ship's secretary, was imprisoned for several months and robbed of his ship at Santa Cruz, Teneriffe, "about 1805" (*United Service*, May 1905, p. 595). Many legends accumulated about these early years before he rejoined the United States navy as sailing master in 1809. "Mad" or "Roaring Jack," as he was called, became a celebrated character in the old navy, humorous, irascible, a superb seaman, the half-fictitious, heroic figure created by Harry Gringo (H. A. Wise) in his *Tales for the Marines* (1855). It is said that he once navigated his ship from the African coast to Pernambuco with his entire crew sick or dead of fever.

In the War of 1812 his first exploit was at New York on July 5, 1813, when he loaded the fishing smack *Yankee* with vegetables and livestock, hid thirty-two volunteers under hatches, and surprised and captured the British tender *Eagle*, overpowering her crew of thirteen, killing her two officers, and towing her into the Battery "amidst the plaudits of thousands . . . " (*The Naval Monument*, rev. ed. 1840, p. 230). As sailing master of the sloop *Peacock* in her victory over the *Epervier* on Apr. 29, 1813, he handled his craft, according to her commander Lewis Warrington [*q.v.*], "as if he had been working her into a roadstead" (*Ibid.*, 132). For his constant attention to duty and for his professional knowledge, Warrington recommended his promotion to the rank of lieutenant in 1814.

After cruises in the *Porpoise* against West Indian pirates he sailed to the Pacific in 1823 as first lieutenant in Hull's flagship *United States*, and in 1825–26, he commanded the schooner *Dolphin* in the South Seas, pursuing mutineers from the whaleship *Globe*. The *Dolphin* was the first American warship to visit Hawaii, and here Percival fell afoul of the missionaries over anti-prostitution ordinances, but during the difficulties which ensued, he curbed a sailors' riot against the restrictions, and was cleared later by a court of inquiry at Charlestown (Navy Library, *Court Martials*, vol. XXIII, no. 531). Made commander in 1831, and captain in 1841, he commanded the *Cyane* in the Mediterranean, 1838–39, supervised repairs to the *Constitution* at Norfolk, 1841–43, and then commanded her in a cruise round Africa to China and back by Hawaii and California from 1844 to 1846. On this memorable voyage he carried in his cabin a stout oak coffin which he later converted into a watering trough at his home in Dorchester. A jeweled sword, given him on the cruise by the Imam of Muscat figured in subsequent litigation for its ownership (*Boston Transcript*, May 20, 1911; Dec. 23, 24, 1912;

Jan. 8, 9, 1913). He was put on the reserved list in 1855. In later years he presented to friends several silver cups, one of which bore the legend: "This Cup, with the Donor, has made three cruises to the Pacific, one to the Mediterranean, one to the Brazils, two to the West Indies, and once around the world, a distance of about 150,000 miles. Has been 37 years in service and never refused duty." He was married in 1823 to Maria, daughter of a Dr. Pinkerton of Trenton, N. J., but they had no children.

[Hiram Paulding, *Jour. of a Cruise of the U. S. Schooner Dolphin* (1831); C. O. Paullin, *Diplomatic Negotiations of Am. Naval Officers, 1778–1883* (1912); I. N. Hollis, *The Frigate Constitution* (1900); B. F. Stevens, "Around the World in the U. S. Frigate Constitution," *United Service*, May 1905; G. W. Allen, ed., *Commodore Hull: Papers of Isaac Hull* (1929); W. D. Orcutt, *Good Old Dorchester* (1893); *Saturday Evening Gazette* (Boston), Aug. 24, 31, 1861; *Boston Evening Transcript*, May 20, 1911.]   A.W.

PERCY, GEORGE (Sept. 4, 1580–*c*. March 1632), governor of Virginia, author, was the eighth son of Henry Percy, eighth earl of Northumberland, by his wife Catherine, daughter of John Neville, Lord Latimer. After some service in the Dutch wars he joined the Virginia expedition which sailed Dec. 20, 1606, his lack of office under the first charter being due perhaps to the cloud under which his brother, Northumberland, then lay. His "Discourse of the Plantation of the Southern Colonie in Virginia," presenting the fullest account of the voyage and the events of the settlement down to Newport's departure, was subsequently abridged and printed by Purchas (*post*, XVIII, 403–19). A resolute and honorable descendant of Hotspur, he soon won the good opinion of his fellows through his industry, courage, and character, while Newport, Smith, and other officers early learned to rely implicitly upon him (Edwin Arber, *Capt. John Smith . . . Works*, 1884, pp. xl, 127, 131–45, 434, 438, 468, 476).

In September 1609, he succeeded Smith as governor, the urgency of Ratcliffe, Archer, and Martin—who may have fixed upon him as their catspaw—and the importunity of the soldiers having prevailed upon him to relinquish his intention of returning to England for his health. For his fame's sake, the decision to remain was unfortunate. Granted that he was a fighting man rather than a skilled executive and disciplinarian, it is unjust to assume, as his detractors have done, that the destitution which befell the colony during "the starving time" was attributable chiefly to Percy's maladministration. He erected a new fort at Point Comfort and otherwise planned for the general welfare, but his illness—he was

"so sicke he could not goe nor stand" (Arber, p. 170)—hampered his authority and curtailed his activity. The successive blundering or dereliction of Martin, Sicklemore-Ratcliffe, and Francis West destroyed the morale of the settlers and antagonized the Indians; famine and fever completed the work; and when Gates reached Virginia in May he found only three score of the population of five hundred. The London Company's "varnished reports" inevitably pointed to incompetence on Percy's part, and, indeed, years afterward Sir Thomas Smythe was reproved "for stating the fact that the trouble was really 'the sickness' and not 'misgovernment'" (Alexander Brown, *The Genesis of the United States*, 1890, II, 617), but the confidence of his associates was unshaken. Delaware, upon arriving at Jamestown, appointed him councilor and commandant, and a month later, during a temporary absence, left him in charge. When Delaware returned to England, Mar. 28, 1611, he designated Percy deputy governor, to preside until the arrival of Dale (May 19); and that stern worthy likewise made Percy his representative while he himself was at Henrico.

In April 1612 Percy left Virginia, and, although retaining landed interests there for several years, apparently never returned. Some time after 1622 he wrote for his generous brother, Northumberland, "A Trewe Relacyon of the ℔ cedeinges and Ocurrentes of Momente wch have Hapnd in Virginie . . ." to justify himself against an account by an unnamed author, presumably Smith. First printed entire in *Tyler's Quarterly Historical and Genealogical Magazine* (April 1922, pp. 259–82), it is valuable for its new light on certain phases of events in Virginia between 1609 and 1612. Of his later life little is known, save that about 1625 he was fighting again in the Netherlands, where in 1627 he commanded a company, and that he died, unmarried, in England.

[Alexander Brown, *The First Republic in America* (1898); Samuel Purchas, *Hakluytus Posthumus, or Purchas, His Pilgrimes* (Glasgow ed., 1906), vols. XVIII, XIX; William Stith, *Hist. of the First Discovery and Settlement of Va.* (1747); E. D. Neill, *Virginia Vetusta* (1885); P. A. Bruce, *Virginia*, I (1924); A. W. Weddell, *A Memorial Vol. of Va. Hist. Portraiture* (1930), reproducing the painting of Percy now at Syon House, Middlesex, England, dated 1615, which supports the assertion that he lost a finger in the Indian Wars, and not in his later Dutch campaign as often stated.]   A. C. G., Jr.

PERHAM, JOSIAH (Jan. 31, 1803–Oct. 4, 1868), showman, originator of the railroad excursion system, first president of the Northern Pacific Railroad, was the son of Josiah Perham and Elizabeth (Gould). He was born in Wilton, Franklin County, Me., where he was educated and spent his early life; he married Esther Sewell. By successive stages he made a considerable fortune as a store-keeper and woollen manufacturer, but this he soon lost through a bad investment; and only by moving to Boston in 1842 was he able to accumulate enough to pay off his creditors.

Forced for a second time into bankruptcy in 1849, he was saved from despair by an idea which only a man of his character could have turned to profit. What he did was, in effect, to anticipate the cinema. He bought in 1850 a panorama of the Great Lakes, established it in Melodeon Hall, Boston, and by an ingenious device which caused the pictures to move across an illuminated screen, he managed to arouse popular curiosity. The surrounding countryside flocked into Boston to see the performance, while the railroads did a roaring business. Perham was a shrewd man, and it occurred to him that if he could induce the railroads to grant a cheap round-trip fare to people coming from neighboring towns to Melodeon Hall, his profits, as well as those of the railroads, would be increased. His plans met with such approval that for years after the Panorama had ceased to exist he was an active agent for cheap fares and the organization of round-trip tours. During the Civil War he published a pamphlet entitled *Gen. Perham's Platform: The Most Feasible Plan Yet Offered for Suppressing the Rebellion* (1862), in which he recommended that the Northern soldiers make conquest of Southern territory and settle permanently there, volunteering, himself, to "arrange with the railroads for tickets at excursion prices for all who emigrate to settle in the conquered territory." To the Army of the Potomac, encamped near Washington, he sold excursion tickets to the capital.

In the course of his work with the New England railroads he became convinced of the need for a transcontinental line; and with commendable energy he formulated plans for a People's Pacific Railroad, "to be owned," as he put it, "by the people in small sums" (Smalley, *post,* p. 103). After an abortive attempt to secure a charter for his company in Massachusetts, he turned to his native state of Maine, where, on Mar. 20, 1860, he was successful. Then, hurrying to Washington, he sought the cooperation of Thaddeus Stevens [*q.v.*] for the purpose of obtaining the passage of a bill giving recognition to his company and granting land to meet the construction expenses of the line. Strong opposition from the Union and Central Pacific railroads was sufficient, however, to crowd Perham's efforts out of existence, and until Stevens prevailed upon him to obviate all danger of competition with the southern railroads by changing to a northern route, the bill had no chance of success. Even then, as amended, it was defeated by opposition to the Maine charter. But Stevens was not discouraged. He assured Perham that if the Maine charter were relinquished, the bill would pass. On May 23 a new draft was introduced, creating the company by direct charter, and this time it was successful. President Lincoln's signature was affixed to it on July 2, 1864.

Perham's charter provided for a capital stock of $100,000,000, and though no mention of a government subsidy had been made, a munificent land grant was bestowed upon the company. The corporators formed a board of commissioners who, after collecting $2,000,000 as security, chose directors and elected Josiah Perham the first president of the Northern Pacific Railroad. He held the post for a year—just long enough to see the failure of his scheme for popular subscriptions. Illness overtook him and he was forced to make settlement of his debts by transferring, in December 1865, the presidency and the franchise of the company to John Gregory Smith [*q.v.*] of Vermont.

Perham died in extreme poverty in East Boston on Oct. 4, 1868. With his ideas for cheap fares and his labors for the Northern Pacific he conferred two great benefits on future railroad expansion. His fight for a charter had not been in vain; his courage and steadfastness were qualities which his successors were not slow to emulate. He and his friends had given the company an organization; it remained for others to make the railroad a reality.

[E. V. Smalley, *Hist. of the Northern Pacific Railroad* (1883); G. J. Varney, *A Gazetteer of the State of Me.* (1886); *Maine Genealogist and Biographer,* Dec. 1875; H. H. Tyndale Collection of Northern Pacific Pamphlets 1860–1870, in the Baker Library, Harvard University; files of the *Boston Traveller, Boston Transcript, Boston Courier,* and *Railway Times,* for the years 1850–68; *Cong. Globe,* 1862–66.] F. E. H—e.

PERIAM, JONATHAN (Feb. 17, 1823–Dec. 9, 1911), horticulturist, agricultural writer, born in Newark, N. J., was one of the ten children of Joseph and Phoebe O. (Meeker) Periam. His father, an officer during the War of 1812, conducted an academy for boys and girls and undertook his son's education. In 1838 the family moved to a large farm on the Calumet River, fourteen miles south of Chicago, where the father started a small nursery from seeds, and set out the first orchard of grafted fruit in Cook County. In the autumn of 1839 the father died and the management of the family's holdings devolved on Jonathan.

At this time he was interested in commercial dairying, but his success in marketing watermelons in Chicago turned him to a long career of gardening and gave him claim to the distinction of being the first professional market gardener in northern Illinois. Eventually his gardens occupied 100 acres. He also specialized in blooded road horses, Devon cattle, and Berkshire hogs. (See his articles in *Transactions of the Illinois State Horticultural Society*, n.s., vols. XI, 1878, XIV, 1881, XXXIX, 1905; and the Chicago *Inter Ocean*, Jan. 24, 1909.) In 1849 he went overland to California on a gold-seeking expedition, returning by sea in 1853 (see his "The Argonaut's Trail," in the *Prairie Farmer*, Feb. 1–Apr. 15, 1912). Some time afterward he married Mary Wadhams, daughter of Carlton Wadhams, and they had four children. During the Civil War he served on the staff of the provost marshal at Chicago. In 1868 he became head farmer, superintendent of practical agriculture, and first recording secretary of the board of trustees at the newly organized Illinois Industrial University, now the University of Illinois. About two years later he became manager of the sugar beet farm and factory at Chatsworth, Ill. From 1873 to 1878 he was a member of the Illinois State Board of Agriculture, serving as its vice-president during that period. When the Chicago Veterinary College was organized he joined its staff and remained a member of it for two years.

As early as 1842 Periam began to correspond with western agricultural periodicals. During the early seventies he served the *Western Rural,* the *Interior,* and *Farm, Field and Fireside* in various editorial capacities. His chief work in this field, however, was his editorship of the *Prairie Farmer* from 1876 to 1884 and from 1887 to 1893. He also edited or wrote a number of compendiums, chief of which are *The American Encyclopaedia of Agriculture* (1881), *The Farmers' Stock Book* (1885); *Pictorial Home and Farm Manual* (1885), adapted to the Australasian colonies by R. W. Emerson MacIvor; *The Prairie Farmer Horse Book* (1891); *The American Farmer's Pictorial Cyclopedia of Live Stock* (1882); *The New American Farmer's Pictorial Cyclopedia of Live Stock* (1900); and *Live Stock; A Complete Compendium for the American Farmer and Stock Owner* (1906), the last three prepared in collaboration with A. H. Baker. He wrote many essays for various agricultural publications and the Chicago dailies, two novels, and a pastoral poem. Notable among his publications is *The Groundswell* (1874). In this book, designed to be sold by subscription to farmers, he attempted to present the farmers' side of the various questions which were prominent during the decade of the Granger movement. Considerable documentary material, especially with reference to the movement in Illinois, is included. His interest in horticulture resulted in his being a life member of the Illinois Horticultural Society, the Horticultural Society of Northern Illinois, the American Pomological Society, and the Wisconsin Horticultural Society, and a frequent contributor to their proceedings; he was the first president of the Chicago Agricultural and Horticultural Society. As a speaker he was effective and pleasing. His last years were spent in cultivating flowers.

[*Ill. Farm and Fireside,* Dec. 1, 1895; *Orange Judd Farmer,* May 23, 1896; *Farmers' Rev.,* May 5, 1906; *Ann. Report of the Wis. State Horticultural Soc. for the Year 1901; Trans. Ill. State Horticultural Soc. for the Year 1911; Chicago Tribune,* Dec. 10, 1911; *Prairie Farmer,* Jan. 1, 1912.]

E. E. E.

PERKINS, CHARLES CALLAHAN (Mar. 1, 1823–Aug. 25, 1886), art critic, organizer of cultural activities, had from his parents, James Perkins and Eliza Greene (Callahan) Perkins, both the material inheritance and the temperament that naturally made him an influential friend of the arts of design and of music in Boston, his native city. The father, descended from Edmund Perkins who emigrated to New England in 1650, was a wealthy and philanthropic merchant; the mother was a gracious, cultivated woman. From the family home in Pearl Street Charles attended several schools before entering Harvard College. The prescribed academic course he found irksome, but he was graduated in 1843. He had previously drawn and painted and, declining chances to enter business, he went abroad soon after graduation, determined to study art. At Rome he became friendly with the sculptor Thomas Crawford [*q.v.*], then struggling against poverty, and gave him encouragement. In 1846 he took a studio at Paris, where he had instruction from Ary Scheffer. Later he was at Leipzig, pursuing studies in the history of Christian art. During a second residence at Paris he took up etching with Bracquemond and Lalanne. He made many etchings to illustrate his own books.

Circumstances led Perkins, a wealthy man, to devote his life to interpreting the art of others rather than to creative art. His love of music competed with his enthusiasm for painting and sculpture. In 1850–51 and from 1875 until his death he was president of the Handel and Haydn Society, Boston, whose concerts he sometimes conducted and for which he wrote meritorious music. He married, June 12, 1855, Frances D.

Bruen, daughter of the Rev. Matthias Bruen, of New York. At their home many concerts and recitals were given. Perkins was the largest subscriber toward the Boston Music Hall, to which he also contributed the great bronze statue of Beethoven, modeled by his friend Crawford—the work which since 1902 has stood in the entrance hall of the New England Conservatory of Music, Boston. An invitation extended to Perkins in 1857 to give some lectures at Trinity College, Hartford, on "The Rise and Progress of Painting," started him as a lecturer. He possessed charm and magnetism on the platform. After a second period of European residence, ending in 1869, he lectured frequently on Greek and Roman art before Boston school teachers, and at the Lowell Institute on sculpture and painting. Thirteen years' service on the Boston school committee amplified his educational work. He brought to Boston the South Kensington methods of teaching drawing and design to children, and he was instrumental in founding the Massachusetts Normal Art School, now the Massachusetts School of Art. As a committeeman he was also assigned the third division of the school system, comprising the North and West Ends. He took pains to know personally all teachers of his division, often entertaining them at his home.

Prior to 1850 Perkins had proposed an art museum for Boston but had found the plan premature. When others twenty years later revived this project he supported it gladly. He was second among the incorporators of the present Museum of Fine Arts, securing for its opening a gift of Egyptian antiquities and making valuable suggestions as to arrangement of exhibits. Among the directors he advocated showing contemporary work as well as the arts of antiquity. He had, meantime, been elected to the presidency of the Boston Art Club, which he held for ten years, and to which he gave much time. He systematically devoted part of each day to writing. *Tuscan Sculptors,* published in London in 1864, brought him a European reputation. It was followed in 1868 by *Italian Sculptors,* with illustrations drawn and etched by the author. He edited, with notes, Charles Locke Eastlake's *Hints on Household Taste* (1872), and *Art in the House* (1879) from the original of Jakob von Falke. In 1878 he brought out, with illustrative woodcuts which he had designed, *Raphael and Michaelangelo,* dedicated to Henry W. Longfellow, whose previously unpublished translations of the sculptor's sonnets were included in the book. His *Historical Handbook of Italian Sculpture* appeared in 1883, and in 1886, in French, *Ghiberti et Son École.* At the time of his death

he had nearly finished his closely documented *History of the Handel and Haydn Society of Boston, Massachusetts,* which other hands completed. He liked society and good fellowship. These he particularly enjoyed at his summer home at Newport, R. I. He was killed instantly by the overturning of a carriage in which he was riding near Windsor, Vt., on Aug. 25, 1886.

[There are tributes to Perkins by Robert C. Winthrop, Thos. W. Higginson, and Samuel Eliot, with a biography by the last-named, in the *Proc. Mass. Hist. Soc.,* 2 ser. III (1888). See also: Justin Winsor, *The Memorial Hist. of Boston,* vol. IV (1881); A. F. Perkins, *Perkins Family* (1890); *Dwight's Jour. of Music,* Mar. 1, 1856; and *Boston Transcript,* Aug. 26, 1886.]

F. W. C.

PERKINS, CHARLES ELLIOTT (Nov. 24, 1840–Nov. 8, 1907), railroad executive, son of James Handasyd Perkins [*q.v.*] and Sarah Hart (Elliott), was born in Cincinnati, Ohio. He was educated in the public schools of Cincinnati and at Milton, Mass. After a short time as clerk in a store, he was advised by his cousin, John Murray Forbes [*q.v.*] of Boston, who was financially interested in railroad developments in the Mississippi Valley, to enter this field. He therefore moved to Burlington, Iowa, and in 1859 became clerk at thirty dollars a month in the office of the Burlington & Missouri River Railroad. This road had received a federal land grant in 1856 and after the panic of 1857 had been purchased by the Chicago, Burlington & Quincy, of which James F. Joy [*q.v.*] of Detroit was president. Together the two roads eventually gave a through route between Chicago and Omaha, but at the moment the Burlington & Missouri River of Iowa was built only seventy-five miles west from Burlington. Perkins was soon made cashier of the road and within a year was promoted to the position of assistant treasurer and secretary, and in 1865 was appointed acting superintendent and later general superintendent, thus serving a valuable apprenticeship for larger tasks in the future.

By 1869 this line had been completed, and immediately the Burlington & Missouri River Railroad in Nebraska was chartered to extend the road west from Omaha. Aided by a federal land grant, the company was able by 1873 to build to Fort Kearny, where a junction with the Union Pacific was formed. In the promotion and construction of this road Perkins was active, being an incorporator and director from the beginning. In 1872 he was elected vice-president of the Iowa line and when this was consolidated with the Chicago, Burlington & Quincy in 1873 he continued in the employ of the combined lines as vice-president and general manager of the roads west of the Missouri River. He was also made director (1875) and vice-president (1876) of the Chicago, Burlington & Quincy. With its 1,343 miles of trackage, its valuation of $50,000,000, and its strong financial and physical condition, the road was one of the longest and best in the country at this time. In 1880 the Burlington & Missouri River Railroad in Nebraska was consolidated with the Chicago, Burlington & Quincy, and the following year Perkins was chosen president of the whole system, succeeding his cousin John M. Forbes, with whom he had worked closely for five years.

Because of his thorough knowledge of the conditions of Western railroading, and of the confidence reposed in him by the Eastern directors and stockholders, Perkins was able to organize the road on a sounder basis and to develop it in conformity with the complex needs of expanding markets and areas of production. The unique position which it held on the railway map of the country was well expressed by Charles Francis Adams [q.v.] in a letter which he wrote in 1882: "The Chicago, Burlington and Quincy and the Union Pacific together constitute the Broadway or Washington street of this continent. They will always be the chief commercial thoroughfare between Chicago and San Francisco." Some of the less profitable enterprises into which the previous management had been drawn, like the so-called River roads to the north of Burlington, were disposed of, and other lines more necessary to the logical expansion westward were built or purchased. Thus, during the next twenty years, to the Chicago, Burlington & Quincy were added, among others, the Republican Valley, the Grand Island & Wyoming Central, the Grand Island & Northern Wyoming, the Big Horn Southern, and the Chicago, Burlington & Northern railroads. By Feb. 21, 1901, when Perkins resigned the presidency, the system contained 7,661 miles and was financially one of the strongest of the major railroads. Of him F. A. Delano, president of the Wabash, wrote: "As a railroad builder he was perhaps as great a strategist as any man this country has produced" (post). He remained, until his death, a director of the Chicago, Burlington & Quincy, his work being primarily in the financial department. In his business dealings he was guided by the highest principles of personal integrity and of careful administration of other people's property. He was a big man physically and was untiringly active, but was uniformly courteous and inspired affection in those with whom he worked. On Sept. 22, 1864, he married his cousin Edith, daughter of Capt. Robert Bennet Forbes [q.v.] of Milton, Mass. Three or four years after his

retirement from the presidency of the Chicago, Burlington & Quincy, he established his home in Westwood, Mass., where he died. He left three sons and four daughters.

[*Geneal. of the Descendants of John Eliot* (1905); F. A. Delano, "Perkins of the Burlington," *Appleton's Mag.*, Mar. 1908; W. W. Baldwin, *Story of the Burlington* (1925), reprinted from *Shipper and Carrier*, May 1925; H. G. Pearson, *An Am. Railroad Builder: John Murray Forbes* (1911); R. E. Riegel, *The Story of the Western Railroads* (1926); *Who's Who in America*, 1906–07; *Boston Transcript*, Nov. 9, 1907.]

E. L. B.

PERKINS, ELI [See LANDON, MELVILLE DE LANCEY, 1839–1910].

PERKINS, ELISHA (Jan. 16, 1741–Sept. 6, 1799), physician, called by one of his biographers a "celebrity par excellence in the quack line," was born in Norwich, Conn., a descendant of John Perkins who came to New England in 1631 and in 1633 settled in Ipswich. His father was Dr. Joseph Perkins, an eminent practitioner in Norwich; his mother, Mary (Bushnell) Perkins. Elisha is said to have studied at Yale, and it is certain that he was given the necessary education for medical practice by his father. He first settled in Plainfield, Conn., where he achieved a considerable reputation. He established an academy there and, according to report, because of the lack of adequate boarding accommodations took many pupils into his own home; he also received patients there for treatment—a common practice in that day. In 1792 he became one of the incorporators of the Connecticut Medical Society and he served as chairman of the Windham County Medical Association for several terms. On Sept. 23, 1762, he married Sarah Douglass of Plainfield, and had by her ten children—five sons and five daughters.

Today his name is known only through his so-called "metallic tractors." These instruments were devised by him in an attempt to apply to medical practice the principles of the discovery of Galvani. They were called "tractors" because of the method of application, being alternately drawn or stroked over the affected part. They consisted of two pieces of metal about three inches long, seemingly of brass and iron, and were quite similar to the modern horse-shoe nail, being rounded at one end and pointed at the other. One side was half round, while the other was flat, with the name "Perkins' Patent Tractors" stamped thereon. Perkins made these magic instruments at his home, in a small furnace concealed in the wall of his house, and sold them for five guineas a pair. In the year 1795 he reported his discovery to the Connecticut Medical Society, but gained little encouragement there from his professional brethren. A short time after, he went to Philadelphia, where he met with a most enthusiastic reception. Here he is said to have made extensive tests in the public hospitals, infirmaries, and other institutions. Congress was then in session, and some of the most distinguished men in the country, as well as physicians, were witnesses. On Feb. 19, 1796, he took out a patent for his tractors, receiving the exclusive right of making them for a period of fourteen years. The following year he was expelled from membership in the Connecticut Medical Society, on the ground that he was "a patentee and user of nostrums" (*Medical Repository*, vol. I, no. 1, 1798).

Besides the invention of the celebrated tractors, Perkins also introduced a remedy which was a combination of common vinegar saturated with muriate of soda. In 1799, during an outbreak of yellow fever in New York, he visited that city for the purpose of using this remedy. After four weeks of assiduous effort, during which time the remedy proved of no avail, Perkins himself contracted the fever and died in his fifty-ninth year.

"Perkinism," as the application of the tractors came to be known, did not, however, succumb with its originator. In 1795 his son, Benjamin Douglas Perkins, a Yale graduate in the class of 1794, went to England to exploit the sale of the tractors. He opened an office at 18 Leicester Square—a house formerly occupied by John Hunter—and immediately established a thriving trade. Three years later, he published a treatise, entitled *The Influence of Metallic Tractors on the Human Body* (1798). In 1803 he established the Perkinean Institution in London, with the Right Honorable Lord Rivers as president, and Sir William Barker as vice-president. It is said that 5,000 cases were treated here. In Copenhagen, where the tractors were extensively used, eleven well-known physicians reported so favorably that the records were printed in an octavo volume. An English translation by Benjamin D. Perkins, *Experiments with the Metallic Tractors,* from a German version of the Danish, was published in 1798. In 1800, however, the doom of Perkinism was sounded by Dr. John Haygarth, of Bath, England, who in that year published *On the Imagination as a Cause and as a Cure of Disorders of the Body,* and declared that he had effected as many cures with tractors made of painted wood.

[G. A. Perkins, *The Family of John Perkins of Ipswich* (1889); James Thacher, *Am. Medic. Biogs.* (1828); H. A. Kelly and W. L. Burrage, *Am. Medic. Biogs.* (1920); W. R. Steiner, "Dr. Elisha Perkins of Plainfield, Conn., and His Metallic Tractors," in *Bull. Medic. Hist. Soc., Chicago,* vol. III (1923); P. G. Perrin, *The Life and Works of Thomas Green Fessenden* (1925), pp. 50–71.] H. T.

PERKINS, FREDERIC BEECHER (Sept. 27, 1828–Jan. 27, 1899), editor, author, librarian, son of Thomas Clap Perkins and Mary Foote (Beecher) Perkins, was born in Hartford, Conn. On his father's side he was a descendant of John Perkins who emigrated to Boston in 1631 and settled in Ipswich in 1633; his maternal grandfather was the distinguished theologian, Lyman Beecher [*q.v.*]; his sister Emily became the wife of Edward Everett Hale [*q.v.*]. Frederic entered Yale with the class of 1850, but left college in the autumn of 1848 and began the study of law in his father's office in Hartford. He did not return to college but in 1860 Yale conferred on him the degree of master of arts.

During 1849 and 1850 he taught school in New York City and Newark, N. J., at the same time continuing the study of law. He was admitted to the bar in Hartford in 1851, but seems to have practised little, if any. He taught school, did editorial work in Hartford, and from 1854 to 1857 was one of the editors of the *New York Tribune.* Returning to Hartford, he became assistant editor of Barnard's *American Journal of Education,* and from 1857 to 1861 was librarian of the Connecticut Historical Society. For more than a decade thereafter he steadily engaged in literary and editorial work. He was editor of the early volumes of the *Galaxy,* was on the staff of the *Independent,* assisted his uncle, Henry Ward Beecher, in editing the *Christian Union,* and from 1870 to 1873 helped his brother-in-law, Edward Everett Hale, edit the magazine *Old and New.* In May 1874 he became assistant in the Boston Public Library, working as bibliographer and special cataloguer there until December 1879. In the summer of the following year he became chief librarian of the San Francisco Public Library, holding that position until November 1887. For seven years thereafter he was engaged in editorial work in San Francisco, returning East in 1894. He died five years later in Morristown, N. J., after a lingering illness.

Perkins was one of the earliest and most energetic workers in the field of library organization and his contributions to library literature were many and varied. He contributed to *Public Libraries in the United States of America, Their History, Condition and Management* (1876), issued by the Bureau of Education, and was an associate editor of the *Library Journal* from 1877 to 1880. Much of his literary work is anonymous and buried in the files of the periodicals with which he was connected. His more important books were, *Charles Dickens* (1870), a biography; *Scrope; or, the Lost Library* (1874), a novel; *Check List for American Local History*

(1876); *Devil-Puzzlers and Other Studies* (1877); and *The Best Reading* (1872), a classified bibliography which went through several editions and was long a standard reference book in public libraries. Brander Matthews ranked "Devil-Puzzlers" among the ten best American short stories. Perkins had an encyclopedic mind. Edward Everett Hale once said that he had never asked him a question without being told the answer or where the answer was to be found. He had a roving disposition, changed positions often, was restless if long in a place, and dissipated his undoubtedly brilliant mentality by not concentrating on one particular vocation. He was tall, straight, imposing looking, outspoken, proud, sternly honest, and a hard worker. In Civil War days, during the New York riots, he once courageously faced a mob to protect a negro. He was married twice; first, on May 21, 1857, to Mary Anne, daughter of Henry and Clarissa (Perkins) Westcott of Providence, R. I.; she died in 1893 and in May 1894, he married Frances, daughter of Samuel C. Johnson of Guilford, Conn., and widow of his uncle, the Rev. James C. Beecher. By his first wife he had two sons and two daughters.

[*Biog. Record of the Class of 1850 of Yale Coll.,* 1861, 1877, and 1901; *Obit. Record Grads. Yale Univ.,* 1899; G. A. Perkins, *Family of John Perkins of Ipswich, Mass.* (1889); *Lib. Jour.,* Feb. 1899; *N. Y. Tribune,* Feb. 4, 1899; data from the librarians of the Conn. Hist. Soc., Boston Pub. Lib., and San Francisco Pub. Lib., and from Perkins' daughter, Charlotte Perkins Gilman.]   G. B. U.

PERKINS, GEORGE CLEMENT (Aug. 23, 1839–Feb. 26, 1923), ship-owner, banker, governor of California, United States senator, was born in Kennebunkport, Me., the son of Clement and Lucinda (Fairchild) Perkins. His father owned a small farm but was chiefly employed as a sailor and officer on vessels trading with the West Indies and the New-England coast. The son's early childhood was spent in cheerless work on the unproductive farm, varied with a few months each year in the district school. Inheriting his father's fondness for the sea, he became, at the age of twelve, cabin-boy on a vessel bound for New Orleans, and followed a seafaring life for the next four years, making several voyages to Europe interrupted only by six months more of schooling at home. When not yet sixteen, he sailed for San Francisco, where he arrived in the autumn of 1855. In a few days he went by boat to Sacramento and tramped from there to Oroville (then called Ophir). For the next two years he worked at placer-mining in Butte and adjoining counties. Meeting with indifferent success, he returned to Oroville and soon became clerk in a country store. By practising the most rigid economy for over two years, he was able to save $800. This, with $1200 borrowed capital, he invested in a ferry at Long Bar on the Feather River, and a year later sold the ferry at a profit of $1000. Returning to the Oroville store, he gradually saved enough to purchase the business, which was now becoming highly remunerative. During this period he built the Ophir flourmill, invested in mining and sheep-raising, and constructed sawmills, most of which investments proved profitable. He also assisted in the establishment of the Bank of Butte County in Chico, and was one of its directors.

In 1860 Perkins cast his first presidential vote for Abraham Lincoln, and throughout the Civil War he was a stanch supporter of the Union cause, as a member of the Oroville National Guards and an aide-de-camp to Gen. John Bidwell. When barely thirty years of age he was elected to the state Senate (1869) as a Republican from a strongly Democratic district (Butte County), and served in that body until 1876. While in the legislature he met Charles Goodall, and in 1872 became a member of the San Francisco firm of Goodall & Nelson. Transferring his Oroville interests to his brother, he moved to San Francisco about 1876 and shortly afterward purchased the interest of his partner Nelson. Thereupon the firm became Goodall, Perkins & Company, and soon was incorporated as the Pacific Coast Steamship Company. The Company acquired most of the coast-line steamers plying between Alaska and Central America; also the Oregon Railway & Navigation Company, the Pacific Steam Whaling Company, and the Arctic Oil Company.

Although an outspoken opponent of the California constitution of 1879, Perkins was elected (September 1879) the first governor under it by a plurality of more than 20,000. As governor from Jan. 8, 1880, to Jan. 10, 1883, he took most pride in the fact that during his administration the state prisons had become practically self-supporting through the establishment, at his recommendation, of the jute-mill at San Quentin and the quarry at Folsom. After careful investigation in each case, he pardoned and commuted the sentences of more prisoners than any other governor of California prior to 1918, and only one of those pardoned was ever returned to prison. In 1886 he was a candidate for the United States Senate but was defeated by Leland Stanford. He reached the Senate, however, through appointment by the governor (July 1893) immediately after Stanford's death. By successive reëlections he remained a senator for nearly twenty-two years. Upon the expiration of his term (March 1915), he returned to his home in Oakland and lived in retirement until his sudden death in 1923. His knowledge of maritime affairs made him prominent in connection with legislation dealing with the navy and ocean traffic, and for four years (1909-13) he was chairman of the Senate committee on naval affairs. He opposed Japanese immigration, had a warm controversy with President Roosevelt over the latter's message proposing naturalization of the Japanese, supported the Panama Canal project, and advocated a protective tariff.

Perkins' interests in California embraced banking institutions as well as railroad and land companies. He was the owner of a large cattle-ranch in southern California, and a heavy investor in quartz and gravel mines throughout the mining sections of California, and in iron mines near Puget Sound. He had a conspicuous part in the preparations for the Panama Pacific International Exposition of 1915; was president of the San Francisco Art Association; a trustee of the California Academy of Sciences, the State Mining Bureau, and of the State Institution for the Dumb and Blind at Berkeley; and for thirty years was the acting president of the Boys and Girls Aid Society. He held high office in the Masonic order and was a member of the Loyal Legion. In 1864 he married Ruth A. Parker of Marysville, who died in 1921. To them were born three sons and four daughters.

[H. H. Bancroft, *Chronicles of the Builders* (1892), vol. II; T. H. Hittell, *Hist. of Cal.*, vol. IV (1897); G. C. Mansfield, *Hist. of Butte County, Cal.* (1918); J. E. Baker, *Past and Present of Alameda County, Cal.*, vol. II (1914); J. M. Guinn, *Hist. of the State of Cal. and Biog. Record of Oakland and Environs* (copyright 1907), vol. I; *Who's Who in America*, 1922–23; *San Francisco Bull.*, Feb. 26, 1923; *San Francisco Chronicle*, Feb. 27, 1923.]   P. O. R.

PERKINS, GEORGE DOUGLAS (Feb. 29, 1840–Feb. 3, 1914), Iowa congressman and editor, was born in Holley, Orleans County, N. Y. His father, John D. Perkins, a lawyer, was a native of Connecticut; his mother, Lucy Forsyth Perkins, was born in Albany, N. Y. The family moved to Indiana and later to Wisconsin, where the father died in 1852, leaving his wife with four children, two sons and two daughters. The elder son, Henry A. Perkins, became a printer, and George followed his example. In 1860 the brothers founded the *Cedar Falls* (Iowa) *Gazette* and published it until 1866, when they sold it, and engaged in business in Chicago for a few years. In 1869 they purchased the *Sioux City Journal* and converted it into a daily newspaper. After the death of his brother Henry in Novem-

ber 1884, George D. Perkins remained as editor and publisher until his death in 1914. For many years also he took part in politics. In 1873 he was chosen state senator. He was state commissioner of immigration from 1880 to 1882, United States marshal from 1882 to 1885, and a member of Congress from 1891 to 1899. He was also delegate to the Republican National conventions in 1876, 1880, 1888, 1908, and 1912. In 1906 he was a candidate for nomination as governor of Iowa against Gov. Albert B. Cummins [*q.v.*] who was seeking a third term. A strenuous preconvention campaign resulted in his defeat by the manipulation of party leaders on the pretext of party necessity. At the convention, according to custom, the nominee was called upon for a speech. Governor Cummins, extremely hoarse from the effect of campaign speaking, responded. Perkins, the defeated candidate, followed Cummins. His opening sentence was: "I thank God that although defeated I am still in possession of my voice and my conscience."

His public service and office-holding Perkins regarded as incidental to his work as a journalist. Probably no feature of the *Sioux City Journal* under his management was more characteristic than the "lay sermons" that appeared every Sunday morning for many years. His humor, his mastery of idiomatic English, and his religious convictions were freely expressed. The familiar Bible stories were explained by reference to modern conditions and the old Biblical figures were made real. Once in 1912 he tried to give them up, but there was so much protest that he continued them. He was a public speaker of great force as well as a trained and effective writer. A solemnly serious face only made his whimsical humor more irresistible. His most expressive features were the eyes which were "large, keen and deep" and met everyone with absolute directness. Perkins was married to Louise E. Julian of Chicago on July 2, 1869. Five children were born to them, two daughters and three sons. His portrait painted by Nicholas R. Brewer hangs in the building which houses the Historical Department of the state government in Des Moines. He was one of the last of the pioneer editors in Iowa and was known throughout the state as "Uncle George."

[See: *Annals of Iowa*, July 1914; the *Sioux City Jour.*, Feb. 4, 1914; the *Reg. and Leader* (Des Moines), Feb. 4, 1914; the *Palimpsest* (Iowa City, Iowa), Aug. 1924; the *Register* (Des Moines), Jan. 4, 1931; *Who's Who in America*, 1912–13.]   F. E. H—s.

PERKINS, GEORGE HAMILTON (Oct. 20, 1836–Oct. 28, 1899), naval officer, was through his father, Hamilton Eliot Perkins, descended from an old Warwickshire family, the Rev. William Perkins coming to Boston in 1632. His mother, Clara Bartlett (George) Perkins, was also of English stock. He was born in Hopkinton, N. H., had his schooling at Hopkinton and Gilmanton academies, and when he was nearly fifteen entered the United States Naval Academy at Annapolis. He had already shown a greater liking for outdoor life and adventure than for books, and at the Academy he but narrowly escaped "bilging" because of scholastic difficulties. He lengthened the four-year course to five, showing superiority only in target practice with the big guns on the summer cruises. After graduation his first duty was in the sloop *Cyane*, dispatched to Nicaragua and Panama, and in the bark *Release*, sent to Paraguay. As acting master of the *Sumter* he was ordered to the dreaded West African coast in 1859 to suppress the slave trade—a duty which lasted for two years and which provided him many an adventure. On Feb. 2, 1861, he was promoted to the rank of lieutenant.

When he returned to the United States the Civil War had already begun, and he was ordered as first lieutenant to the gunboat *Cayuga* assigned to the West Gulf Blockading Squadron under Farragut. As the attack on New Orleans developed, the *Cayuga* was made the flagship of Capt. Theodorus Bailey [*q.v.*], the second in command, and on the morning of Apr. 24, 1862, it led the entire fleet in the passage of the forts. When the fleet reached New Orleans, Captain Bailey asked Lieutenant Perkins to go ashore with him under a flag of truce. Surrounded by a hostile and threatening mob, the two officers made their way to the mayor's office to demand the surrender of the city. Perkins took part in the subsequent operations between New Orleans and Vicksburg, and then as commanding officer of the *Sciota* served seven months of blockade duty on the Texas coast. He was then granted a leave of absence, but when he learned that Farragut was preparing to attack the forts defending Mobile, he volunteered his services again and was promptly assigned to the command of the new river monitor *Chickasaw*. In passing the forts and in his engagement with the Confederate ironclad ram *Tennessee*, he handled the monitor with consummate skill, receiving highest praise from his superiors. He was employed in further operations against the forts and became so valuable that he was continued in command until after the close of the war.

His subsequent service afloat was almost entirely in the Pacific. He had command of the *Ashuelot* on the Asiatic Station, 1877–79, and of the *Hartford* off South America, 1884–85. He was promoted to the rank of commander in 1871, and to the rank of captain in 1882, being retired in 1891 only because of ill health. Five years later he was promoted commodore on the retired list. Farragut said of him, only a month before his own death, "Perkins was young and handsome, and . . . no braver man ever trod a ship's deck; . . . his work in the *Chickasaw* did more to capture the *Tennessee* than all the guns of the fleet put together" (Alden, *post*, p. 205). He was married to Anna Minot Weld, daughter of William Fletcher Weld of Boston, on July 25, 1870. They had one child, Isabel, who later became Mrs. Larz Anderson. The last years of his life were spent largely in Webster, N. H., where he purchased several farms, bred fine cattle and race horses, and indulged the whims of a gentleman farmer. He spent the winters at his home in Boston, where he died a few days after his sixty-third birthday.

[Personal letters in the possession of Mrs. Larz Anderson of Brookline, Mass.; C. S. Alden, *George Hamilton Perkins* (1914); *Letters of Capt. Geo. H. Perkins*, edited by Susan G. Perkins, with biog. sketch by G. E. Belknap (3d ed. 1908); *Official Proceedings at the Dedication of the Statue of Commodore G. H. Perkins at Concord, N. H.* (1903); Isabel Anderson, *Under the Black Horse Flag, Annals of the Weld Family* (1926); *Boston Globe*, Oct. 29, 1899.]   C. S. A.

PERKINS, GEORGE HENRY (Sept. 25, 1844–Sept. 12, 1933), geologist, educator, administrator, was born at Cambridge, Mass., the son of Frederick Trenck Perkins, a Congregational minister and a graduate of Yale in both College and Seminary. Through his father he was descended from John Perkins who emigrated to New England in 1631 and settled in Ipswich. His mother was Harriet T. Olmsted, a niece of Denison Olmsted [*q.v.*], through whom he was descended from Joseph Olmsted who died in Connecticut in 1644. George Henry Perkins had two years of college study in Knox College at Galesburg, Ill., then entered Yale College and graduated with honors in 1867. For post-graduate work in geology he received the Ph.D. degree in 1869. In the autumn of that year he became a member of the faculty of the University of Vermont at Burlington and was continuously active as teacher and administrator to the day of his death, sixty-four years later. He first taught "animal and vegetable physiology," then representing botany and zoölogy. In 1881 he became Howard Professor of Natural History. In 1898 his chair was changed to geology, and he was given added duties as dean of the newly created department of natural sciences. In 1907 he became vice-president and dean of the College of Arts and Sciences, positions which he occupied until near the close of his life. He was acting-president during the years 1917–19. For fifty-six years he was the curator of the university museum. Because of physical disability he relinquished most of his work of teaching, but classes in anthropology met at his residence until three months before his death. For more than thirty years he was the academic balance-wheel of the institution. Combined with a kindly disposition and understanding, he possessed the ability to make prompt and wise decisions. With these gifts he held the confidence and affection of faculty, students, and alumni for many years.

In 1880 Perkins entered public service as state entomologist, which position he held to 1895. He was made state geologist in 1898 and retained the position until his death. The state survey dated from 1845, and seven men had preceded him in the office. The only important survey publication by his predecessors is the inclusive two-volume report by Edward Hitchcock. Perkins' work for the state survey is on record in eighteen biennial volumes of state reports, which contain, besides geological data, much information of varied scientific interest. Perkins was a fellow of the American Anthropological Association, of the American Ethnological Society, and of the Geological Society of America. He had been active in the American Association for the Advancement of Science, as fellow, honorary life member, secretary of the section on anthropology (1883), and as vice-president and chairman of the section on geology (1917). He was a naturalist, in the proper sense of the term, and his wide and lively interest in nature is evidenced by his non-geologic writings, which classify as follows: botany, twenty-one papers; zoölogy, sixteen; archeology, ten; and entomology, nine. Several of his geological papers were published in scientific journals, and about fifty articles in the biennial reports of the Vermont Geological Survey. Perkins was married, in 1870, to Mary Judd Farnham, of Galesburg, Ill. A son, Henry Farnham Perkins, survived him.

[The *Vt. Alumni Weekly*, Oct. 4, 1933, is devoted to the memory of Perkins. See also: G. A. Perkins, *The Family of John Perkins of Ipswich, Mass.* (1889); *Burlington Free Press*, Sept. 13, 1933. A memoir, with bibliography, is to be printed in the *Bull. of the Geol. Soc. of America.*]   H. L. F.

PERKINS, GEORGE WALBRIDGE (Jan. 31, 1862–June 18, 1920), banker, was born in Chicago, a descendant of John Perkins, who emigrated to New England in 1631, and the son of George Walbridge and Sarah Louise (Mills) Perkins. His father had been in business in Buffalo before moving to Chicago, where he entered the life insurance field and became dis-tinguished for his public spirit and philanthropy. The boy did not attend the Chicago public schools until he was ten years old. At fifteen he left school and became an office boy for the New York Life Insurance Company. Rapidly advanced, he became first vice-president by the time he was forty-one. Among other reforms he revolutionized the company's agency system. The practice had been to farm out territory to middle-men or general agents, who appointed those that did the actual soliciting for policies. These so-licitors were often underpaid and improvident, frequently made misrepresentations in order to get initial premiums, and transferred their allegiance as the general agent did his. To end this shifting of personnel Perkins, in 1892, began to dispense with the general agents as fast as their contracts expired. He made the local agents and solicitors a loyal and permanently attached force by employing them directly and by introducing on Jan. 1, 1896, the so-called "Nylic" system of benefits based on length of service and amount of policies written. He also made various trips abroad and obtained permission for his company to do business in Russia and other leading European countries. When he, after repeated solicitations, joined the banking house of J. P. Morgan & Company on Jan. 1, 1901, he relinquished most of his duties with the New York Life but remained connected with it until 1905. In the field of finance he proved himself a skilful business organizer, taking a leading part in the formation of the International Harvester Corporation, International Mercantile Marine Company, and Northern Securities Company. He further devised a working organization for the United States Steel Corporation and the scheme, in force since 1903, of annual offerings of preferred stock to employees on advantageous terms.

At the close of 1910 he withdrew from Morgan & Company to devote himself to work of a public nature and to the dissemination of his views on the correct solution of the business problems of the day. He believed that competition should be replaced by cooperation in the business world; that great corporations properly supervised were more efficient than small competing units; and that workers should receive retirement pensions and share in corporate profits. He made numerous addresses, many of which were later published. Of these perhaps the most important were "The Modern Corporation" in *The Currency Problem. . . . Addresses Delivered at Columbia University* (1908), *National Action and Industrial Growth* (1914); *The Sherman Law* (1915), and *Profit Sharing* (1919). He had an original mind and expressed himself concisely, forcibly, and convincingly in his writings, although he was an ineffective speaker. He had already done notable public service by serving as chairman from 1900 of the Palisades Interstate Park Commission, which under his able direction developed the park from a few hundred acres to fifty square miles of playground. In 1912 he became nationally prominent by joining the Progressive party. He was chairman of its national executive committee and furthered its cause with all his dynamic energy. During the World War he was chairman of a joint state and municipal food supply commission for which he drew up an admirable report on marketing conditions in New York City (*Joint Report on Foods and Markets of Governor Whitman's Market Commission,* 1917). As chairman of a finance committee of the Young Men's Christian Association, he raised $200,000,000 for welfare work among American soldiers abroad. He belonged to some forty societies devoted to various causes. He had an engaging presence and in Andrew Carnegie's words, sweetened "sordid business dealings by the amiability of his manners" (*New York Times, post*). A rare executive, who could inspire his subordinates with enthusiasm, he had no recreations but worked incessantly with tireless activity, not even taking time to read books. He died at Stamford, Conn., survived by his wife Evelyn (Ball) Perkins, to whom he was married in 1889, and by their two children.

[*Who's Who in America,* 1920–21; B. C. Forbes, *Men Who Are Making America* (1917); G. A. Perkins, *The Family of John Perkins of Ipswich* (1889); *Pearson's Mag.,* July 1907; *Current Literature,* Apr. 1911; *Century Mag.,* Apr. 1915, pp. 944–53; *Sun* (N. Y.), June 18, 1920; *Printers' Ink,* June 24, 1920; *Natural Hist.,* May–June 1920; *N. Y. Times* and *N. Y. Tribune,* June 19, 1920.]   H. G. V.

PERKINS, JACOB (July 9, 1766–July 30, 1849), inventor, was born in Newburyport, Mass. He was the son of Matthew and Jane (Noyes) Dole Perkins, and a descendant of John Perkins, who came from England in 1631 and later settled in Ipswich, Mass. Little is known of the first ten years of Perkins' life except that he had meager schooling but showed unusual inventive talent. When he was thirteen years old he became a goldsmith's apprentice and when his master died two years later, Perkins carried on the business. He continued to follow this calling until 1787, producing many novel designs in gold beads and inventing a method of silver-plating shoe buckles. He was then employed for a short time by the State of Massachusetts to make dies for the copper coins struck at the Massachusetts mint. About 1790 he devised a machine to cut and head nails and tacks in a single operation. He organized a manufacturing company, but after patenting the machine, Jan. 16, 1795, he was involved in a lawsuit respecting the invention which continued for seven years and brought about his financial ruin. During the subsequent years of hardship, he turned his attention to bank-note engraving, and devised a steel check plate for printing bank notes which made counterfeiting extremely difficult. In 1809 the State of Massachusetts passed a law compelling banks in that state to adopt the form of note invented by Perkins.

About 1808 or 1810, in partnership with the bank-note engraver Gideon Fairman, he is said to have published a series of school copybooks entitled *Perkins and Fairman's Running Hand,* possibly the first books using steel plates to be printed in America (Stauffer, *post,* I, 209). After spending several years working for engravers in Boston and New York, Perkins rejoined Fairman in Philadelphia in 1814 and with him worked for several years endeavoring to improve Perkins' method of bank-note engraving. Failing to have their process adopted in the United States, they sailed for England in 1818 with many cases of their machinery to compete for the contract for the Bank of England notes then about to be awarded. They were supported by the country banks, but were unsuccessful in the competition. Nevertheless, with capital and influence furnished by the Heath family Perkins proceeded to establish a factory in England for making plates and printing bank notes. The firm of Perkins, Fairman & Heath began business in 1819, and two years later published an account of their process ("Prevention of Forgery," *Transactions of the Society for the Encouragement of Arts,* vol. XXXVIII, London, 1821). In 1840 they were entrusted with the production of the first penny postage stamps, and during the following forty years produced many millions of British postage stamps by the process invented by Perkins.

Shortly after getting his firm definitely established, Perkins began, about 1823, a series of unique experiments with high-pressure steam boilers and engines, which work he continued for the balance of his life. His experiments in this field were numerous and varied and revealed his fearless spirit. In 1827 he had attained working steam pressures of from 800 to 1400 pounds per square inch. He perfected a boiler and single-cylinder engine using steam at 800 pounds pressure and devised a special alloy to be used in conjunction with the engine pistons which became so highly polished as to require no lubricant. That same year he built a compound steam engine of the Woolf type using steam at 1400 pounds pressure and expanding it eight times. In 1829 he patented an improved paddle wheel and in 1831 invented a method of securing free circulation of water in boilers which led the way to the modern water-tube boiler. About 1836 he patented a high-pressure boiler and engine for a steam vessel using steam at two thousand pounds pressure, and while he had difficulties when salt water was used in the boiler, he overcame them by using distilled or rain water. As early as 1820 he had been elected to membership in the Institution of Civil Engineers (London) and in subsequent years he read many papers descriptive of his experimental work not only in high pressure steam but in other fields. These included a plenometer for measuring the speed of vessels, a ship's pump, a method of warming and ventilating rooms and a method of ventilating the holds of ships. For this last invention he was awarded a medal by the Society for the Encouragement of Arts and for the pump invention he received the Vulcan gold medal. He received recognition in various countries, particularly in England, but he was a hundred years ahead of his time. On Nov. 11, 1790, he married Hannah Greenleaf of Newburyport. He died and was buried in London, survived by six children.

[G. A. Perkins, *The Family of John Perkins of Ipswich, Mass.* (1889); R. D. Spear, "High Pressure Steam," in *Wheeler News* (house organ of the Wheeler Condenser & Engineering Company, N. Y. City), Dec. 1926; H. P. Vowles and M. W. Vowles, "Jacob Perkins, 1766 to 1849," *Mechanical Engineering*, Nov. 1931; R. H. Thurston, *A Hist. of the Growth of the Steam Engine* (1878); J. T. Scharf and Thompson Westcott, *Hist. of Phila.* (1884), vol. III; Henry Howe, *Memoirs of the Most Eminent American Mechanics* (1844); J. J. Currier, *Hist. of Newburyport, Mass.*, vol. II (1909); Wm. Dunlap, *A Hist. of the Rise and Progress of the Arts of Design in the U. S.* (rev. ed., 3 vols., 1918), ed. by F. W. Bayley and C. E. Goodspeed; D. M. Stauffer, *Am. Engravers upon Copper and Steel*, vol. I (1907); *Minutes of Proc. of the Inst. of Civil Engineers* (London), vol. XXV (1866); *The Times* (London), July 31, 1849.]   C. W. M—n.

PERKINS, JAMES BRECK (Nov. 4, 1847–Mar. 11, 1910), lawyer, congressman, and historian, was of seventeenth-century Massachusetts stock. His parents, Hamlet Houghton and Margaret Ann (Breck) Perkins, joined the westward movement soon after their marriage in 1836 and left Concord, N. H., for Tremont, Ill. They eventually settled, with other New Englanders, at a Rock River (Illinois) colony called Como. In 1847, with two daughters, the family migrated again, moving on to St. Croix Falls, Wis., where James Breck Perkins was born. After her husband's death in 1851, Mrs. Perkins took her children back to Como, where the childhood of her son was spent in roaming

the woods and fields and acquiring a devotion to nature which he never forsook. Without formal schooling, he was taught to read by his family; he reveled in Scott, Dickens, and stories from Roman and English history. In 1856 his mother returned to the East, settling near her parents, at Rochester, N. Y. Her son now had his first experience of systematic education; his record in high school won him a scholarship at the University of Rochester. Entering in 1863, he became a student of marked excellence. While a freshman he endeavored to enlist in the Union army but was rejected because of his youth. He won first honors in Greek and Latin, and as a junior, upon the advice of President Martin Brewer Anderson, borrowed money to finance a European tour. He traveled, often on foot, through England, France, and Italy. His intellectual tastes were broadened and deepened and his interests aroused in French history and institutions. Returning to Rochester, he graduated as the ranking member of his class (1867).

Following a brief period of study in a law office, Perkins was admitted to the bar and to a partnership. He quickly acquired an excellent practice and the respect of his Monroe County colleagues. He continued to study, and wrote articles for the *American Law Review* on legal and political subjects. He also wrote book reviews for New York newspapers. His entrance to public service began with two terms as city attorney for Rochester (1874–78). He married, in 1878, Mary, youngest daughter of Gen. John H. Martindale [*q.v.*]. Stimulated by his reading in French history and by an ambition to write, he determined to study and interpret an important but, in America, little-known period of French history, the seventeenth and eighteenth centuries. He went again to Paris in 1885 and there completed his first book, *France Under Mazarin With a Review of the Administration of Richelieu* (2 vols., 1886). The favorable reception of this effort led him to continue his studies. He sold his law practice and with his wife left for Europe where they resided, chiefly in France, from 1890 to 1895. He there completed *France Under the Regency With a Review of the Administration of Louis XIV* (1892), and began *France Under Louis XV* (2 vols., 1897). For the Heroes of the Nations Series he later wrote *Richelieu and the Growth of French Power* (1900). His last book, *France in the American Revolution* (published posthumously, 1911), completed a well-rounded survey of two significant centuries in the history of France.

In 1898 Perkins joined a group of distinguished Americans in founding the National Institute of

Arts and Letters, occupying at different times the offices of secretary and treasurer. Political life once more opened to him with a seat in the New York Assembly (1898). His term at Albany was followed, in 1900, by election to Congress from the thirty-second New York district (Monroe County). He was a member of the House of Representatives for five terms, from the Fifty-seventh to the Sixty-first congresses, until his death at Washington, Mar. 11, 1910. He did not live to accept the office of ambassador to Brazil for which he had been designated by President Taft. As a congressman he won the affection, confidence, and admiration of the House. He advanced gradually, but steadily, to one of the principal chairmanships, that of the committee on foreign affairs. With industry and an analytical, painstaking thoroughness he informed himself on the matter of legislative projects. His speeches, therefore, although he was not an orator, commanded the attention of his fellow members. He spoke with care and precision rather than with force and emotion. A Republican, he was from conviction a party man but, withal, fearless and independent in his opinions.

As a historian Perkins began to write at a moment inauspicious for scholars not of the professional guild. Emphasis upon scientific methods of investigation was in the ascendant and the production of monographs based upon intensive research in limited subjects was professionally the most approved form of scholarship. A work of such breadth and scope as that of Perkins was regarded by many of the "scientific historians" as superficial and popular. Historical journals, especially those of France and England, reviewed his books indifferently and none too charitably. More thoughtful and careful reviews in American journals pointed out that Perkins was doing a pioneer service in presenting, in English, a fresh, original, and interesting synthesis of an obscure and much neglected period. Without attempting research in the complete sense of the term, without pursuing a limited subject exhaustively, or seeking hitherto unknown evidence, he nevertheless worked extensively in archive material and with printed sources, avoiding second-hand or standardized opinions. He endeavored to maintain a strict fidelity to documentary evidence and for this reason was, perhaps, prone to confine his investigations to the more formal, official material. His analysis was unbiased, reasonable, and free from sentimentality; and his judgments, particularly of men and policies, were generally sound. His style is lucid and sustained, vigorous and somewhat austere.

His books were widely read and if they added little essentially new in evidence, or little which was strikingly different in interpretation, they yet served, for an unusually long period, a very useful purpose. To the general reader and to many generations of college undergraduates they made a contribution unavailable in the more scholarly monographs.

Perkins was described by his contemporaries as a gentleman of the old school. Cultivated and courteous, hating hypocrisy, he was generous with assistance to others, as when he defended Algernon Sidney Crapsey in the celebrated heresy trial of 1906. In thought he was progressive, but not radical. Averse to exaggeration, he also avoided guesses and moralizing. He was quietly humorous, with a genuine sense of fun. Devoid of jealousy and distrust, his life was singularly happy, full, and generously spent.

[*James Breck Perkins,* a brief sketch by his wife, Mary Martindale Perkins (privately printed, Rochester, 1913), contains extracts from his diary and indicates the outstanding points in his career. Further information has been derived from Mrs. Perkins and from manuscript items in the family papers. See J. J. Jusserand's Introduction to *France in the Am. Revolution* and David J. Hill's review of the same in *Am. Hist. Rev.,* Oct. 1911. Political appreciations are to be found in *House Doc. 1508,* 61 Cong., 3 Sess.]

L. B. P.

PERKINS, JAMES HANDASYD (July 31, 1810–Dec. 14, 1849), author and social worker, father of Charles Elliott Perkins [*q.v.*], was born in Boston, the youngest of the six children of Samuel G. and Barbara (Higginson) Perkins and a descendant of Edmund Perkins who emigrated to New England in 1650. He attended boarding schools at Waltham and Lancaster, Mass., the Phillips Academy at Exeter, and the Round Hill School at Northampton. At the latter school he displayed some superiority in modern languages, and his letters of those years show a poetical, slightly cynical, and highly introspective cast of mind. Among his teachers were George Bancroft, Joseph G. Cogswell, and Timothy Walker. At eighteen he entered as a clerk the business founded by his uncles Thomas H. [*q.v.*] and James Perkins, prominent importers and philanthropists. In 1831 he was sent on a trip for his firm to England and the West Indies; but on his return he abandoned a business career as opposed to his tastes, health, and ethical ideals, and removed to Cincinnati with the expectation of following those horticultural pursuits to which his father had long been devoted. The influence of his former teacher, Judge Walker, now prominent in the Cincinnati bar, caused him to read law; he was admitted to the bar in 1834. He became a brilliant extemporaneous speaker; but his health, which was not robust, was unsuited to sedentary occupations, and he was repelled by practices and attitudes of his profession which offended his sensitive ethical apprehensions. He therefore never devoted himself fully to the practice of the law, but drifted into literary pursuits.

Upon his first arrival at Cincinnati he had formed a connection with James Hall's *Western Monthly Magazine,* newly established in that city, which he maintained for about three years, while he was reading law, writing articles, sketches, and poems for the *North American Review,* the *New York Review,* the *Massachusetts Quarterly,* and other periodicals, and delivering lyceum lectures. In 1834 he became editor of the *Saturday Evening Chronicle,* which, later in that year, he purchased and merged with the *Cincinnati Mirror,* edited by William D. Gallagher and Thomas H. Shreve. Perkins shared the editorial work of these men for six months, until the failure of their publisher in 1835. In the meantime he had married, Dec. 17, 1834, Sarah H. Elliott, of Guilford, Conn. In 1836 he tried gardening and grain-milling at Pomeroy, Ohio, but gave that up to establish himself the next year as a gardener in the edge of Cincinnati. Here he continued writing, publishing in 1838 his *Digest of the Constitutional Opinions of Chief Justice John Marshall.* He was connected with the *Western Messenger,* an important Unitarian monthly, from its beginning in 1835, and was one of its editors in 1839. The First Congregational Society of Cincinnati, a Unitarian body, established him in 1838 as minister at large, in which capacity he continued until the end of his life to work with the poor of Cincinnati. He was president of the Cincinnati Relief Union from its organization in 1841 until his death, was active in prison reform, and was sympathetic with Fourierism. He also conducted a small school for girls.

In 1841 Perkins succeeded his cousin William Henry Channing, his childhood companion and later his biographer, as minister of the First Congregational Society of Cincinnati. He was, however, unsympathetic with denominational Unitarianism, and in 1848 he took steps to form a liberal church based upon practical Christianity. In the following year, under the reaction from an emotional stress caused by the supposed loss and the recovery of his two sons, he committed suicide by drowning from an Ohio River ferry-boat. His body was not recovered. Perkins had been interested in historical investigation, having served as the first president of the Cincinnati Historical Society (1844–47) and the first vice-president of the Historical and Philosophical Society of Ohio (1849). His *An-*

nals of the West (1846) went through several editions. Perkins' features were delicate, with aquiline nose, high forehead, and flowing black hair; he affected carelessness in dress. He had wit and imagination, tinged with recurrent melancholia. His sympathies were warm and he enjoyed to an extraordinary degree the respect of those who were acquainted with his character and qualities.

[The chief source is *The Memoir and Writings of James Handasyd Perkins* (Cincinnati, 1851) in two volumes. The *Writings* were edited by Wm. Henry Channing, who also wrote the *Memoir.* It is doubtful if Channing's assumption that Perkins actually edited the *Western Monthly Magazine* is correct. All other sketches are founded on the Channing memoir.]

F. L. M.

PERKINS, JUSTIN (Mar. 5, 1805–Dec. 31, 1869), missionary, "apostle of Persia," was born in the Ireland Parish of West Springfield, now a part of the city of Holyoke, Mass., the son of William and Judith (Clough) Perkins, and a descendant of John Perkins who came to Massachusetts in 1631 and two years later settled in Ipswich. He spent his boyhood on a farm, but after experiencing a religious awakening at the age of eighteen, studied at Westfield Academy and in 1829 was graduated with honors at Amherst. Following a year of teaching at Amherst Academy, two years as a student at Andover Theological Seminary, and one year as tutor in Amherst College, he was ordained in the summer of 1833. In September he sailed as a missionary of the American Board of Commissioners for Foreign Missions, his appointment being to the remnant of the Nestorian Christians in northwestern Persia.

He found the people poor, ignorant, and degraded, living in a state of serfdom under their Mohammedan rulers. In the autumn of 1835 he established his missionary center in Urumiah, the reputed home of Zoroaster, near a lake of the same name. Religious work was begun at once and was carried on for the most part in entire harmony with the Nestorian clergy, in whose churches the missionaries were soon invited to preach. The establishment of a boys' school at Urumiah, the first Lancasterian school in central Asia, was soon followed by the opening of numerous schools for both boys and girls throughout the surrounding villages; later, at the invitation of the government, schools were established for the Persian Mohammedans. Perkins was the first to reduce the Nestorian vernacular, modern Syriac, to writing, and he at once set about producing a literature for the people. A printing press was established at Urumiah in 1840 and from it issued the eighty works of which Perkins was either the author or translator. Under his editorship a periodical, the *Rays of Light*, devoted to "Religion, Education, Science, Missions, Juvenile Matters, Miscellany and Poetry" was issued, which was continued after his death. His translations of portions of the Scriptures appeared at various times; but his principal Bible translations were the New Testament (1846) and the Old Testament (1852), both printed with the ancient and modern Syriac in parallel columns; and the Old Testament with references, in modern Syriac (1858). His other numerous publications include books for day and Sunday-schools, hymn books, and translations of religious classics such as the works of Watts, Bunyan, Doddridge, and Baxter.

Perkins was widely recognized as one of the most eminent of Syriac scholars, and to him is chiefly due the great lexicon of modern Syriac and English left in manuscript at his death. The high esteem in which he was held by Nestorians and Persians alike enabled him to acquire valuable Syriac manuscripts which have enriched European libraries and have greatly aided scholars in linguistic and theological studies. His contributions to the journals of the American Oriental Society, of which he was a member, the *Deutsche Morgenländische Gesellschaft,* and the *Missionary Herald,* were numerous and important. His *Residence of Eight Years in Persia* (1843), *Missionary Life in Persia* (1861), and *Historical Sketch of the Mission to the Nestorians* (1862) are valuable source materials. Perkins was especially acceptable to the Persians on account of his uniformly polished and courtly manners. He had an iron will and a robust constitution and he worked with persistence and clocklike regularity. He died at the home of a nephew in Chicopee, Mass. On July 21, 1833, he married Charlotte Bass of Middlebury, Vt.; of their seven children, one son survived his parents.

[In addition to the above mentioned sources see G. A. Perkins, *The Family of John Perkins of Ipswich, Mass.* (1889); H. M. Perkins, *Life of Rev. Justin Perkins, D.D.* (1887); *Missionary Herald,* Feb. 1870; *Congregationalist,* June 13, 1870; *Obit. Record Grads. Amherst Coll.,* 1870. A copy of Perkins' lexicon of modern Syriac and English is in the Yale Univ. Lib.] F. T. P.

PERKINS, SAMUEL ELLIOTT (Dec. 6, 1811–Dec. 17, 1879), judge, legal writer, was born in Brattleboro, Vt., the son of John T. and Catherine (Willard) Perkins. His father died when he was five years old and the boy was reared in the family of William Baker, near Conway, Mass., receiving such formal education as the common schools of that day imparted. When he came of age he began to study law at Penn Yan, N. Y., but before settling down he turned to the West. He walked from western New York to eastern Indiana and at Richmond finished his law course with Judge Borden. In 1837 he was admitted to the bar. Taking an interest in politics, he affiliated with and helped to build up a languishing Democratic newspaper, the *Jeffersonian.* This enabled him to strengthen his party in a locality where it had been weak. In 1844 he was appointed prosecuting attorney for the sixth district (Wayne County). In the same year he canvassed the state for James K. Polk, which so enhanced his reputation that James Whitcomb, the Democratic governor, three times made the effort to seat him on the bench of the state supreme court. As the governor's appointment required the confirmation of the Senate he failed twice, but in 1847, after the third nomination, his appointment was confirmed. Five years later, under the new constitution, he was elected by popular vote to the same office, which he retained till 1864. From 1872 to 1876 he was judge of the Marion County superior court, and while holding that office was returned to the supreme court. Here he remained till his death, in 1879, his services as judge totaling a period of about twenty-three years.

In 1857 Perkins was appointed professor of law in the Northwestern Christian University (later Butler University) and again, 1870, he took charge of the law school of Indiana University, where he taught for three years. In this time the department expanded and attendance increased. During his judicial service he published two legal works: *A Digest of the Decisions of the Supreme Court of Indiana* (1858) and *Pleading and Practice ... in the Courts of Indiana* (1859). He is credited with being an able man and a capable judge, though most of his biographers make no mention of three of his decisions which at the time called down upon him widespread disapprobation. One of these obstructed educational progress for several years by holding unconstitutional a law under which the state's school system was hopefully developing (*City of Lafayette et al.* vs. *Jenners,* 10 *Ind.,* 70, 1855). The other decisions annulled the Indiana prohibition law of 1855 (*Beebe* vs. *The State,* 6 *Ind.,* 501; *Herman* vs. *The State,* 8 *Ind.,* 545), under which the state had measurably suppressed the liquor traffic and closed the saloons. Perkins' utterances in his public speeches, in his newspaper writings, and in some of his pronouncements as a judge show him to have been strongly prejudiced in favor of views that have since been discarded as opposed to the best interests of society. He was twice married. After the death of his first wife, Amanda Juliet Pyle, he was married to her sister, Levinia M. Pyle. He had thirteen children, nine of whom died in infancy.

[See L. J. Monks, ed., *Courts and Lawyers of Ind.* (3 vols., 1916); J. P. Dunn, *Ind. and Indianans*, vol. III (1919); J. H. B. Nowland, *Sketches of Prominent Citizens of 1876* (1877); "In Memoriam," 68 *Ind. Reports*, 601–05; *Indianapolis Sentinel*, Dec. 18, 1879.]

G. S. C.

PERKINS, THOMAS HANDASYD (Dec. 15, 1764–Jan. 11, 1854), merchant, philanthropist, was born in Boston, Mass., the second son and one of eight children of James and Elizabeth (Peck) Perkins, and a descendant of Edmund Perkins who emigrated to New England in 1650. His father was a vintner, licensed Aug. 13, 1767, to sell wine at his house on King Street, which was near the scene of the Boston Massacre. His father died in 1773, but his mother took charge of her husband's affairs and until her death in 1807, conducted them so well that she became prominent in business and philanthropy. Before his father's death, Thomas was sent to a clergyman in Middleboro for instruction, after which he attended school in Boston. The siege, however, drove the family to Barnstable on Cape Cod, and he was able there to indulge his strong taste for outdoor activities. Following the evacuation of Boston, he was sent to Hingham to prepare for Harvard, but he decided on a commercial career and entered the counting house of the Shattucks, Boston merchants, remaining till 1785. He then visited his elder brother in Santo Domingo and joined him in business there after a sojourn in South Carolina. Finding the climate detrimental to his health, he returned to Boston by 1788 to manage the firm's affairs there, and to marry on Mar. 25, 1788, Sarah, the daughter of Simon Elliot, of Boston. His place in Santo Domingo was taken by a younger brother. A relative of his wife was captain of a ship in the China trade, and this connection led Perkins to make a voyage of investigation to Batavia and Canton as a supercargo of a ship owned by Elias Hasket Derby, of Salem, after which he embarked in the Oriental trade.

In 1792 the insurrection in Santo Domingo ruined the business there. Perkins' brothers returned to Boston and with the elder he formed a partnership as J. & T. H. Perkins, the name under which the business was conducted till James Perkins' death in 1822, when it was reorganized, but T. H. Perkins remained the principal partner till 1838. Its trade was chiefly with China, but speculative ventures were undertaken wherever they seemed likely to be profitable, and

the business he controlled so long made many handsome fortunes besides his own. In 1795 he spent about eight months in Europe, for the most part in France. While he was there, James Monroe, then United States minister to France, asked him to request permission for George Washington Lafayette to go to America. Securing this privilege from the Committee of Safety, he shared with Joseph Russell, a Boston merchant, the expense of the journey, and had the youth entertained at his Boston home on his way to the Washington household. When Perkins visited the projected capital of the United States in 1796, he was presented to Washington and afterward paid a two-day visit to "Mount Vernon," counting it one of the greatest experiences of his life.

Perkins was a prominent member of the Federalist party and was eight times elected to the Senate and three times to the lower house of the Massachusetts legislature between 1805 and 1824, besides being a presidential elector in 1816 and 1832. He was in Europe for a year in 1811–12, and once he acted as bearer of dispatches to France for the United States ministry in London, running considerable risk through being given a loose document openly addressed to the Minister of Russia, with which country Napoleon was on the verge of war. Notwithstanding his detention, on entering France, as a person suspected of hostility to the country, he managed to prevent the discovery of the document and afterward delivered it. He returned to the United States after the outbreak of the War of 1812 and he was active in opposition to the Madison administration. He was one of the three Massachusetts delegates appointed to go to Washington to present the plea of the Hartford Convention that Massachusetts, alone or in association with its neighbors, be allowed to defend its own territories, and to apply for that purpose Federal taxes collected within its borders. Peace came before this resolution was presented.

Perkins was for a long time an officer of the Massachusetts militia and was generally known as colonel. For a time he was president of the Boston branch of the United States Bank, and he had one of the first railways in the United States constructed in 1827 to transport the product of a granite quarry at Quincy, Mass., of which he was president, two miles to the seaboard. But he was best known for his philanthropies. He was active in indorsing and generous in supporting many public institutions and undertakings, including the Massachusetts General Hospital, the Boston Athenæum, and the Bunker Hill and National Monument associations. His benefactions to individuals were so ready and generous that he was sometimes accused of being a poor judge of character. In 1833 he deeded his residence to the New England Asylum for the Blind for the period it should occupy it, but in 1839 he made the gift unconditional, and since then the institution has borne his name. He was himself blind for a time in his last years, but an operation restored the sight of one eye a few months before his death. Perkins died in Boston in 1854, having survived his wife two years. They had seven children.

[See: T. G. Cary, *Memoir of Thos. Handasyd Perkins, Containing Extracts from His Diary and Letters* (1856); A. T. Perkins, *A Private Proof . . . of the Perkins Family* (1890); *Boston Jour.*, Jan. 11, 1854; *Daily Advertiser* (Boston), Jan. 12, 1854.]   S.G.

PERLEY, IRA (Nov. 9, 1799–Feb. 26, 1874), lawyer and jurist, was born at Boxford, Mass., the eldest child of Samuel and Phebe (Dresser) Perley and a descendant of Allan Perley, who settled in Charlestown, Mass., in 1630. He had few advantages in early years, the death of his father in 1807 leaving the family in somewhat straitened circumstances. He worked on the farm and attended school in the winter months. His mother, however, appreciated the boy's ability in his studies and gave him every encouragement possible. He prepared for college at Bradford Academy and graduated from Dartmouth in 1822 with a distinguished scholastic record. He had defrayed the greater part of his college expenses by teaching school. He was a tutor at Dartmouth, 1823–25, but was bent on a legal career, studying law at Hanover and in the office of Daniel M. Christie at Dover, where his famous successor in the chief-justiceship, Charles Doe [*q.v.*], likewise served his apprenticeship. He was admitted to the bar in 1827 and began practice in Hanover.

From 1830 to 1835 he served as treasurer of Dartmouth College, introducing more efficient business methods, modernizing the accounting system, preparing an inventory of the college property, and advising the trustees on sundry complicated legal and business problems involved in certain Vermont land holdings of the institution. He also represented Hanover for one term in the legislature. He became well known at the Grafton County bar but in 1836 moved to Concord where professional opportunities were better and where he resided for the remainder of his life. On June 11, 1840, he married Mary Sewall Nelson. While a successful advocate, he was regarded by his professional associates as possessing the judicial mind in an eminent degree, an impression which was strengthened by his two years' service as associate justice of the superior court, 1850–52. In 1855 he was appointed chief justice of the supreme judicial court, serving until 1859. In 1864 he was reappointed chief justice, retiring five years later under the age limit imposed by the state constitution. During his last years he occasionally acted as a legal consultant but did not engage in practice before the courts. He twice represented Concord in the legislature (1839–40, 1870–71).

Perley was regarded by contemporaries as one of the most scholarly men on the bench. He had acquired a deep interest in general literature in his early years and retained it throughout his life. He read Latin, French, and Italian literature and was always ready with an apt quotation. He was for many years an active member of the New Hampshire Historical and the New-England Historic Genealogical societies and performed valuable services for both organizations. He was a thorough student of both English and American history and law and his judicial qualifications—both in character and training—were generally recognized. His printed decisions set a high standard and have received widespread commendation from the legal profession. He was occasionally invited to deliver public addresses but was not successful as a platform speaker, however well his material may appear in print. His address on trial by jury, delivered to the grand jury of Grafton County at the November term in 1866, and subsequently printed by their request (*Trial by Jury*, 1867), is a model treatment of the subject. In person he was of small stature, and in manner somewhat shy and nervous, but his intellectual qualities made him an impressive figure in the courtroom. He had a laconic manner on the bench and a characteristic shrewdness and humor which occasionally brightened tedious proceedings and furnished anecdotes which were often told at meetings of the New Hampshire bar.

[J. K. Lord, *A Hist. of Dartmouth Coll.* (1913); C. H. Bell, *The Bench and Bar of N. H.* (1894); *Address in Memory of Hon. Ira Perley . . . Pronounced before the Alumni Asso. of Dartmouth Coll., June 23, 1880* (1881); *Proc. Grafton and Coös Bar Asso.*, vol. III (1898); M. V. B. Perley, *Hist. and Geneal. of the Perley Family* (1906); *Independent Statesman* (Concord, N. H.), Mar. 5, 1874; manuscript material in the archives of Dartmouth Coll.]   W. A. R.

PERRIN, BERNADOTTE (Sept. 15, 1847–Aug. 31, 1920), classical scholar, college professor, was born at Goshen, Conn., the son of the Rev. Lavalette Perrin and Ann Eliza (Comstock) Perrin. His father, a graduate of Yale College in the class of 1840, was a Congregational minister and a member of the Yale Corporation from 1882 to 1889. The family was descended from Thomas Perrin, a French Huguenot who came to Massachusetts in 1690. Bernadotte Perrin was prepared for college at the Hartford High School, entered Yale in 1865, and received the degree of B.A. in 1869. He took high rank as a scholar and received distinguished social recognition from his fellow students. As an indication of his intellectual interests it is significant that this future classical scholar took no prizes in classics, but won high honors in English composition. At that time the work in Latin and Greek was almost entirely grammatical, and the scientific study of language never appealed to him as much as did the literature and history. The year after his graduation he taught in the Hartford High School. The next year he spent in the Yale Divinity School; the next two years in graduate study in classics at Yale. At the close of this period (in 1873) he received the degree of Ph.D. During the year 1873–74 he was tutor in Greek at Yale. Two more years at the Hartford High School as assistant principal were followed by two years of study at Tübingen, Leipzig, and Berlin. On his return he was again tutor in Greek at Yale from 1878 to 1879 and assistant principal of the Hartford High School from 1879 to 1881. He was then called to Western Reserve College as professor of Greek, remaining there until 1893. From 1893 to 1909 he was at Yale, first as professor of the Greek language and literature and after 1902 as Lampson Professor of Greek Literature and History. He was public orator of the University from 1898 to 1908, fellow of the American Academy of Arts and Sciences, and president of the American Philological Association in 1896–97. His death occurred at Saratoga, N. Y. Perrin married his second cousin, Luella Perrin of Lafayette, Ind., on Aug. 17, 1881. She died on July 23, 1889, and on Nov. 24, 1892, he married Susan Lester, daughter of Judge C. S. Lester of Saratoga, N. Y. She survived him together with two sons by his first marriage.

Perrin's undergraduate interest in literary expression rather than grammatical analysis was indicative of the fundamental characteristic of his mind—an intuitive appreciation of the beautiful, and an artist's delight in the creation of beauty. In all his writings and public addresses he paid scrupulous attention to literary form. The brief paragraphs in which, as public orator, he introduced the candidates for honorary degrees, are polished gems of expression. In the daily business of teaching there was never any mere routine. "Every recitation," he said, "should be an event." His scholarly publication

was concerned chiefly with the field of ancient history. A dozen or more papers, published in the *American Journal of Philology* and in the *Transactions of the American Philological Association,* deal with the analysis of the sources of ancient historians and biographers. These studies culminated in his three volumes of translations of Plutarch, with historical notes and introductions on the sources. These volumes covered Themistocles and Aristides (1901), Cimon and Pericles (1910) and Nicias and Alcibiades (1912). His plan to extend this series was frustrated by failing eyesight. He was able to carry through, however, the complete translation of *Plutarch's Lives* (published in the Loeb Classical Library in eleven volumes, 1914–26). This work stands as his great monument. It enabled him to utilize at once his profound knowledge of the sources of Greek history, his enthusiasm for the heroes of antiquity, and his mastery of the English language. The result is an artistic and scholarly achievement of a high order.

[The principal sources are the autobiographies contributed to the various records of the Yale College class of 1869; they are collected in the *Seventh Biog. Record of the Class of 'Sixty-Nine, Yale Coll.* (1910). These can be supplemented by the catalogues and alumni records of Yale College, and in particular by the *Obit. Record of Yale Grads., 1920–21* (1921). The address delivered by his colleague, Prof. E. P. Morris, before the Yale Classical Club on Jan. 4, 1921, is an appreciative treatment of the man in his relation to his university. It was privately printed with the title, *Bernadotte Perrin, 1847–1920* (New Haven, 1921).]

H. M. H.

PERRINE, FREDERIC AUTEN COMBS (Aug. 25, 1862–Oct. 21, 1908), electrical engineer, the son of John Anderson and Rebecca Ann (Combs) Perrine, was born at Manalapan, N. J. He was a descendant of Daniel Perrin, a French Huguenot, who came to America in 1665. His early education was received at the Freehold Institute in New Jersey, and in 1879 he entered the College of New Jersey (Princeton), where he was graduated with the degree of A.B. in 1883. He continued his studies in the graduate school until 1885 when he received the degree of Doctor of Science. His broad education in the arts as well as in science developed habits of study which were to contribute much to his strength of character and to his achievements in widely different types of activity. He adopted as his line of special interest the study of electricity and the equipment needed in its application. His first position after leaving college was with the United States Electric Lighting Company of New York, as assistant electrician. In 1889, he was employed by the John A. Roebling's Sons Company as manager of the insulated wire department in connection with which he did special research to develop more scientific methods for manufacturing the wire product. He became manager and treasurer of the Germania Electric Company of Boston in 1892 and the following year was appointed professor of electrical engineering at Leland Stanford University. As head of the department which he organized, he achieved outstanding success as a teacher, both his personality and his fine education admirably fitting him for the position. He emphasized strongly the need for a thorough study of theory, adhering to the tenet that practical work should only develop familiarity with processes. He himself, however, was intensely interested in the practical application of electricity, and while he was still teaching at Stanford he became the chief engineer of the Standard Electric Company of California, now a part of the Pacific Gas and Electric Company. In this position he designed the first long 60 kilovolt transmission line, for which he received a gold medal at the Paris Exposition in 1900.

He resigned from his positions in California in 1900 to become president and general manager of the Stanley Electric Manufacturing Company of Pittsfield, Mass. This office he resigned in 1904 to enter into practice as a consulting engineer in New York City. In addition to his other duties, he served as one of the editors of the *Journal of Electricity* from 1894 to 1896, and as an editor of *Electrical Engineering* from 1896 to 1898. In 1903, he published *Conductors for Electrical Distribution*. He presented a large number of papers before various organizations, was a member of several of the leading engineering societies including the American Society of Civil Engineers, and was especially active in the affairs of the American Institute of Electrical Engineers of which he served as manager and member of council from 1898 to 1900. On June 28, 1893, he married Margaret J. Roebling, the grand-daughter of John Augustus Roebling [*q.v.*]. She, with their two daughters and a son, survived him when he died at Plainfield, N. J., after an illness of several months.

[H. D. Perrine, *Daniel Perrin "The Huguenot" and His Descendants in Am.* (1910); *Proc. of the Am. Inst. of Electrical Engineers*, vol. XXIX, Nov. 1908; *Jour. of Electricity, Power, and Gas*, Oct. 31, 1908; *Electrical World*, Oct. 31, 1908; *Daily True American* (Trenton, N. J.), Oct. 21, 1908.]   H. H. H.

PERRINE, HENRY (Apr. 5, 1797–Aug. 7, 1840), physician and plant explorer, was born at Cranbury, N. J., the son of Peter and Sarah (Rozengrant) Perrine. He was a descendant of Daniel Perrin, a French Huguenot who settled in New Jersey in 1665. As a youth he taught school at Rockyhill, N. J., and later he studied

medicine. In September 1819, he settled at Ripley, Ill., where he practised medicine energetically for five years, earning the local sobriquet "little hard-riding doctor." On Jan. 8, 1822, he married Ann Fuller Townsend, the daughter of the Rev. Jesse Townsend of Denham, N. Y. His health had been very seriously affected by arsenical poisoning sustained accidentally in 1821, and two years later, in an effort to improve his condition, he sought the milder climate of Natchez, Miss., practising there until 1827 when he accepted an appointment as United States Consul at Campeche, Mexico. During ten years of continuous residence here he made botanical collections which are now preserved in the herbarium of the New York Botanical Garden, but of far greater importance was his persistent and enthusiastic effort to introduce useful tropical plants into southern Florida. This project resulted from a circular letter sent out in 1827, at the instance of President John Quincy Adams, calling upon consular officers to procure foreign plants of known or probable utility for cultivation in the United States. Perrine took the request very seriously, and before long he was flooding the Treasury, State, and Navy Departments with detailed reports on officinal and other economic plants, especially those producing durable fibers. Much of this matter is published in government documents which relate to a plan, proposed by Perrine in 1832, of establishing a tropical plant introduction station in extreme southern Florida upon land to be granted him by Congress. Not until 1838, a year after his return to the United States, was the law finally passed by which he and two associates received the provisional grant of a township on Biscayne Bay.

A nursery which he had begun on Indian Key in 1833 contained, at the time of the grant, over 200 species and selected varieties of useful tropical plants. He now removed to this location with his wife and three children to wait until the end of the Seminole War should permit occupying and planting out the mainland tract. He spent almost two years here, tending and extending the nurseries, but the period of happy activity was abruptly cut short by his death at the hands of marauding Indians. His family escaped, but under the most harrowing and remarkable circumstances. With the burning of his house all of his collections, records, and manuscripts were destroyed. Subsequently the grant was ceded outright to his family by Congress, but his long-cherished plans never came to real fruition. Of all the plants introduced by Perrine the sisal (*Agave sisalana*), which he first described, is the most noteworthy. This and a closely related species, the henequen (*Agave fourcroyodes*), he had introduced upon the Florida Keys in 1833. Fifty years later these two fiber plants were recognized as being commercially important to the British colonies, and when attempts to obtain the jealously guarded propagating stock from Yucatan had failed, recourse was had to Florida, where Perrine's plants had meanwhile run wild. Although the demand was mainly for henequen, the sisal plant had spread the more widely and now furnished easily the huge quantity of bulbils needed for extensive tropical planting. Perrine was noted for his quick sympathies and devotion to duty. In Campeche he had practised medicine gratuitously and with great skill during a cholera epidemic, his extreme popularity undoubtedly overcoming local scruples against the exporting of useful plants. He truly deserves to rank as a pioneer of plant introduction in America.

[H. D. Perrine, *Daniel Perrin "The Huguenot" and His Descendants in Am.* (1910); H. E. Perrine, *A True Story of Some Eventful Years in Grandpa's Life* (1885); *Mag. of Horticulture*, Aug. 1840, Jan. 1841; F. C. Preston, "A Hero of Horticulture," *Bull. of The Garden Club of Am.*, Nov. 1931; C. H. Millspaugh, biog. sketch (MS.) in library of N. Y. Botanical Garden; J. H. Barnhart, biog. sketch in *Jour. of The N. Y. Botanical Garden*, Nov.–Dec. 1921; *Pensacola Gazette*, Aug. 29, 1840.]   W. R. M.

PERROT, NICOLAS (1644–c. 1718), explorer, was born in France. While still a youth he emigrated to New France and was in service with the Jesuit missionaries; later, for two years he was with the Sulpicians of Montreal. These services gave him opportunity to become acquainted with the Indian languages. Leaving the missionaries, he embarked in the fur trade, and may have been one of the Frenchmen who in 1663 went to Lake Superior with the Ottawa trading caravan. In 1667 he signed a contract with Toussaint Baudry for a voyage to the Ottawa country, where, the following year, they appeared at Green Bay, the first French traders to the Algonquian tribes, recently settled in that vicinity. Thenceforth they called Perrot their "father," since he brought them iron implements and weapons.

In 1670, after a very successful trade, Perrot and Baudry returned to Montreal. That autumn Governor Frontenac sent an expedition to take possession of the West for France; with the commander he sent Perrot as interpreter since "none better could be found." In the spring of 1671 Perrot visited Green Bay to secure delegates to the pageant—the ceremony of annexation—which took place June 14, at Sault Ste. Marie. That autumn he was again in Canada,

where he married Marie Madeleine Raclot (or Raclos) and lived on a seigniory at Becancour. Little is known of his activities during the next decade. Frontenac in 1674 awarded him a license for the fur trade and in 1681 he was accused of sending peltry out of the country to the English settlements. In 1683 the new governor, La Barre, permitted Perrot to go West on a trading expedition, then, in 1684, summoned him to bring the western tribes to join his expedition against the Iroquois.

By his many trading excursions Perrot had obtained great influence with the western tribesmen, and the year after his disastrous Iroquois raid La Barre sent him West with a commission as commandant of La Baye and its dependencies. Proceeding to the Mississippi, he built Fort St. Nicolas at the mouth of the Wisconsin and wintered in a trading post at Mount Trempealeau. The next year he built Fort St. Antoine on Lake Pepin and opened trade with the Sioux. That year, 1686, was signalized by his gift to the mission of St. Francis of a silver ostensorium, finely chased and engraved. This relic is now in the museum at Green Bay. In 1687 Perrot was called upon to cooperate in another expedition against the Iroquois. This year he assisted in arresting two English fur-trading expeditions on the Great Lakes. Having returned to Fort St. Antoine after adjusting Indian difficulties at Green Bay, on May 8, 1689, he took possession of the region of the upper Mississippi in a ceremony similar to that of 1671 (*Collections of the State Historical Society of Wisconsin*, vol. XI, 1888, pp. 35–36). The next year, 1690, he discovered a lead mine in what is now southwest Wisconsin and built a fort to aid in its exploitation.

For several years more Perrot was employed among the western tribes, adjusting their disputes, preserving their friendship for France; then, in 1696, all licenses for trade were revoked and all commissions canceled. He returned to Canada, badly in debt and without resources. During Denonville's expedition (1687) 40,000 livres worth of furs Perrot had left at Green Bay were burned. In 1699 he requested permission for his sons to go West and collect his credits but was refused. In 1701, at the great peace treaty, he was employed as interpreter and was earnestly requested by the Indians to return with them as their ruler and guide. This request the governor refused; some time thereafter he was given employment in the militia service along the St. Lawrence. His later years were spent in writing his experiences. One memoir has survived, which was published in 1867 at Paris. His journals were also utilized by

Bacqueville de la Potherie in his *Histoire de l'Amérique Septentrionale* (4 vols., 1722). Perrot was one of the ablest Indian diplomats of the seventeenth century. Sulte called him "the greatest Frenchman of the West" (*post*, p. 12), and none ever had more empire over the fickle and treacherous savages than he. He cooperated with Duluth, Tonty, and other explorers and discoverers. His name is perpetuated in the Perrot State Park, on the upper Mississippi, the site of his Mount Trempealeau post.

[Perrot's "Mémoire" was edited with copious notes by R. J. P. Tailhan, *Mémoire sur les Moeurs, Coustumes et Relligion des Sauvages de l'Amérique Septentrionale* (1864); it is translated together with the portions of La Potherie's history in E. H. Blair, *The Indian Tribes of the Upper Miss. Valley and Region of the Great Lakes* (2 vols., 1911); a sketch of Perrot is in Appendix A (ii, 249–252). G. P. Stickney wrote a biog. of Perrot in *Parkman Club Papers* (copr. 1896). L. P. Kellogg, *The French Régime in Wis. and the Northwest* (1925) contains the most complete account of Perrot's career. See also *Pubs. State Hist. Soc. of Wis.... 1915* (1916); Benjamin Sulte, "La Baie Verte et le Lac Superieur," *Proc. and Trans. Royal Soc. of Canada*, 3 ser., vol. VI (1913).]   L. P. K.

PERRY, ARTHUR LATHAM (Feb. 27, 1830–July 9, 1905), economist, was born at Lyme, N. H. His father, the Rev. Baxter Perry, was a descendant of John Perry, a clothworker, who, after the great London fire of 1666, emigrated to Watertown, Mass. His descendants almost a century later moved to Worcester, where Baxter Perry was married to Lydia Gray, whose ancestor, Matthew Gray, had come to Worcester in a large company of Scotch-Irish in 1718. The qualities of the Scotch-Irish—energy, frankness, conviction—were conspicuous in the character of Arthur Latham Perry.

He was a posthumous child, and the mother's material need was relieved by neighbors, particularly Arthur Latham, the principal merchant of Lyme, for whom the boy was named. "Brought up in extreme poverty without being in the least depressed by it," Arthur attended the village school, and between the ages of thirteen and sixteen, for a part of each session the Thetford (Vt.) Academy, just across the Connecticut River from his home. For the next two years he taught village schools in Vershire, Vt., and Bristol, N. H., and in September of 1848, having been encouraged to do so by President Mark Hopkins, he entered Williams College. In his sophomore year he discovered John Stuart Mill's *System of Logic,* upon which he battened, and which became, he said, the subsoil of his intellectual growth. At his graduation in 1852 he was given the honor of making the "metaphysical oration." He spent the next year teaching in an academy in Washington, D. C., but was promptly called back to Williams as tutor in political economy and history, and the next session was appointed professor of these subjects with the German language added. After 1890 he was able to concentrate upon political economy, of which he held the chair until his retirement as emeritus professor in 1891. On Aug. 7, 1856, he married Mary Brown Smedley of Williamstown, and they had seven children.

Perry's service as an economist falls under three heads—teaching, writing, and propaganda. His class-room instruction was clear, original, and spirited, and he was the cordial friend of the individual students in innumerable ways. His textbooks took the leading place in America in his day; the first one, *Elements of Political Economy,* appearing in 1865 when the field was scarcely occupied passed through a score of editions. He also published *An Introduction to Political Economy* (1877) and *Principles of Political Economy* (1891). About 1863, through Amasa Walker [*q.v.*], he discovered Frederic Bastiat's *Harmonies of Political Economy,* and this work determined the direction of his thought. Twenty years later he said, "I had scarcely read a dozen pages in that remarkable book, when the Field of the Science, in all its outlines and landmarks, lay before my mind just as it does to-day" (*Elements of Political Economy,* 18th edition, 1883, Preface, p. ix). The heart of his preachment, ethical as well as economical, was the necessity of unhampered exchanges, which became, in practical application, an unremitting insistence upon free trade. His devotion to free trade inevitably led, as a consequence of his reformer's zeal, to wide popular advocacy. Under auspices of the American Free Trade League he delivered 200 public addresses across the Continent; he smote protection in communications to the *Springfield Republican* and the New York *Evening Post*; he debated against Horace Greeley; and his pamphlet, *The Foes of the Farmers,* had two printings. He was elected to the Cobden Club of Great Britain. In all of his work, his scientific claims gave ground to his practical purpose. As one of his sons has said, he was not so much philosophical as "creative, imaginative, humanistic" (*A Professor of Life, post,* p. 92). His exaggerations, springing from intense belief, were honest on his part, but sometimes prompted hostility in others.

His avocation, the investigation of the local history of western Massachusetts, pursued indefatigably in state archives and country conversations, issued in his *Origins in Williamstown* (1894); continued in *Williamstown and Williams College* (1899); in his rediscovery of the since famous Mohawk Trail; and in his successful resolve that the Bennington battle monument should be simple and impressive. For fourteen years he was president of the Berkshire Historical and Scientific Society. During a long period he supplied two nearby churches, and he took his turn in conducting the chapel exercises of the college. He died at Williamstown.

[Perry's *Miscellanies* (1902); *Biographical Rev. . . . Berkshire County, Mass.* (1899); *Springfield Republican,* July 10, 1905; Carroll Perry, *A Professor of Life* (1923); John Bascom, *Colls. Berkshire Hist. and Scientific Society,* vol. III (1899–1913), pp. 192–206; *Free Trade Broadside,* vol. I, no. 3; *Williams Alumni Rev.,* vol. XV, no. 4, pp. 131–36, containing also a partial Perry bibliog.; *Ibid.,* vol. XIX, no. 4, pp. 166–67; *Williams Coll. Bull.,* Apr. 1906; information from a member of the family.]   B. M.

PERRY, BENJAMIN FRANKLIN (Nov. 20, 1805–Dec. 3, 1886), governor of South Carolina, was born in Pendleton District, S. C. His father, Benjamin Perry, was a native of Massachusetts and a Revolutionary soldier, who had gone South in 1784 and married Anne Foster of Virginia. The boy's early life was spent on the farm with intermittent attendance at school, but when he was sixteen he went to Asheville, N. C., and was prepared to enter college. He began to study law at Greenville, S. C., however, and, admitted to the bar in 1827, continued there in practice.

A nationalist in belief, he opposed vehemently the policy of nullification, and in 1832 was a delegate to the Union party convention and the same year began to edit the *Greenville Mountaineer,* a Union newspaper. As a Unionist, he was elected to the nullification convention in 1832 and voted against the nullification ordinance. In the second session, 1833, which repealed the ordinance, he was active in support of compromise. During this period, he very unwillingly accepted a challenge from Turner Bynum, editor of the *Greenville Sentinel,* resulting from a political disagreement, and mortally wounded him. In 1834, 1835, and 1846, he was a candidate for Congress but in each election was defeated. From 1836 to 1862 he was frequently elected to the legislature, serving in both the House of Representatives and the Senate. In these bodies he was a strong friend of internal improvements and particularly active in behalf of the Louisville, Cincinnati & Charleston and the Greenville & Columbia railroads. He also favored divorcing the banks from the state. In 1848 he was a Democratic elector. He secured the establishment of the *Southern Patriot* in 1850, the only Union paper in the state, and edited it in spite of bitter opposition. In the legislature of 1850 he was a strong advocate of a Southern convention, but he opposed secession as "merely revolution," and voted against the calling of a convention. He was elected to the convention of 1852, which was called to secede but refused to do so, and he was a member of the committee which considered the whole question of secession. The report of the committee, affirming the right and justification of secession, declared that South Carolina forebore for expediency only. Perry voted against the report and offered a substitute opposing the right of secession, affirming the right of revolution, and vehemently defending slavery. He also opposed an ordinance granting the legislature the power to secede by a two-thirds vote. He was a delegate to the Charleston convention of 1860, and, perfectly frank in his Union views, refused to withdraw with the South Carolina delegation. While to him secession was not only "madness and folly" but rebellion, it did not occur to him to do other than follow his state. Answering an inquiry as to his position, he said, "You are all now going to the devil and I will go with you. Honor and patriotism require me to stand by my State, right or wrong (*Reminiscences, post,* p. 16). He became Confederate commissioner in 1862, district attorney in 1863, and district judge in 1864.

In 1865 Andrew Johnson made him provisional governor. He quickly excited criticism in the North by his reappointment of all who held office at the time of the downfall of the state government, but it was a wise and tactful move, enabling him to secure the adoption of popular election of governor and presidential electors, equal representation throughout the state on the basis of property and population, the destruction of the parish system, the popular election of judges for a term of years, and the ratification of the Thirteenth Amendment. He declined to run for governor, but was elected United States senator. He was denied his seat, however, and continued in the practice of his profession. His activity in politics continued and he was an enthusiastic delegate to the National Union Convention of 1866, and was a bitter and unrelenting opponent of congressional reconstruction. He was a delegate to the National Democratic Convention of 1868 and of 1876, and, in 1872, as a forlorn hope, he ran for Congress.

Perry was not a brilliant man, but he had good abilities, judgment, and poise. In spite of his independence, he made many friends and few enemies. He was an excellent and very successful lawyer, a wide reader, and a prolific writer of journalistic sketches of men and events, many of which were published under the titles *Reminiscences of Public Men* (1883, second series,

1889) and *Biographical Sketches of Eminent American Statesmen* (1887). He was married in 1837 to Elizabeth Frances, daughter of Hext McCall of Greenville.

[H. M. Perry, *Letters of My Father to My Mother* (1889), *Letters of Gov. Benjamin Franklin Perry to His Wife, Second Series* (1890), and biog. sketch in B. F. Perry, *Reminiscences of Public Men* (1883); *Jour. of the Convention of the People of S. C., 1832 ... 1833* (1833); *Jour. of the State Convention of S. C.* (1852); *Jour. of the Convention . . . Held in Columbia . . . Sept. 1865* (1865); J. S. Reynolds, *Reconstruction in S. C.* (1905); J. P. Hollis, *The Early Period of Reconstruction in S. C.* (1905); F. B. Simpkins and R. H. Woody, *S. C. During Reconstruction* (1932); *In Memoriam, Benjamin Franklin Perry* ... (revised ed., 1887); *News and Courier* (Charleston), Dec. 4, 1886; Diary of B. F. Perry in library of Univ. of N. C.]
J. G. deR. H.

PERRY, CHRISTOPHER RAYMOND (Dec. 4, 1761–June 1, 1818), naval officer, was a descendant of Edward Perry, a Quaker leader and pamphleteer, who emigrated from Devonshire, England, to Sandwich, Mass., about 1650. Religious persecution caused several children of the emigrant to seek a more tolerant neighborhood at South Kingstown, R. I. His great-grandson (or possibly grandson) Dr. Freeman Perry, a physician, was for many years president of the South Kingstown council, and for eleven years, 1780–1791, chief justice of the court of common pleas of Washington County. Christopher was born at South Kingstown, the third of the seven children of Freeman and Mercy (Hazard) Perry. A youth at the outbreak of the Revolution, he had a varied service with both the land and sea forces. He enlisted with the Kingstown Reds and was with the army of Gen. John Sullivan in the Rhode Island campaign of 1778. He was on board the privateer *General Mifflin* when that vessel captured the *Tartar* and the *Prosper* and he took part in the siege of Charleston, S. C. He was at different times attached to the Continental ships the *Queen of France* and the *Trumbull,* and participated in the hard-fought battle between the last-named vessel and the *Watt.* Four times taken prisoner, he was confined on the *Jersey* at New York, on the *Concord* at Charleston, S. C., and in the prisons at Tortola, W. I., and Kinsale, Ire., from which he escaped only after a long period of confinement.

He became acquainted, during his sojourn at Kinsale, with Sarah Wallace Alexander, and when he made a voyage to Ireland in 1784 as mate of a merchant vessel, Miss Alexander embarked on board his ship for the return voyage to visit friends in Philadelphia. Before the ship reached America the young couple were betrothed and in August 1784, were married at the home of Dr. Benjamin Rush. For fourteen years after the Revolution Perry made voyages as master or supercargo to Europe, South America, and the East Indies. In June 1798, he entered the navy as captain and was placed in command of the *General Greene,* then under construction at Warren, R. I. A year later he was employed suppressing piracy on the north coast of Cuba, convoying merchantmen to the United States, and cruising on the Santo Domingo station. His last voyage in the naval war with France was to the mouth of the Mississippi River, where he took on board James Wilkinson [*q.v.*], whom he conveyed to the United States. He was retired from the navy under the peace establishment of 1801, and returned to the merchant service, making at least one voyage to the East Indies. He offered his services to the secretary of the navy early in the War of 1812 and received a temporary appointment as commandant of the Charlestown navy yard. After the war he held the office of revenue collector at Newport. His five sons, including Oliver Hazard Perry [*q.v.*], and Matthew Calbraith Perry [*q.v.*], were naval officers, and two of his three daughters married naval officers—one, Ann Maria, marrying George Washington Rodgers [*q.v.*]. At one time there were seventeen cousins of the Perry family at the Naval Academy, Annapolis.

[Record of Officers, Bureau of Navigation, 1798–1801; Miscellaneous Letters, Navy Dept. Archives, 1812, vol. V, 1813, vols. I, II; C. E. Robinson, *The Hazard Family of R. I.* (1895); W. E. Griffis, *Matthew Calbraith Perry* (1887); G. W. Allen, *Our Naval War With France* (1909); *Newport Mercury,* June 6, 1818.]
C. O. P.

PERRY, EDWARD AYLESWORTH (Mar. 15, 1831–Oct. 15, 1889), Confederate soldier, governor of Florida, was born in Richmond, Mass., the son of Asa and Philura (Aylesworth) Perry. He received an elementary education at the Richmond academy and entered Yale College in 1850 but withdrew the next year. After a brief sojourn in Alabama, where he taught school and studied law, he removed to Pensacola, Fla., to begin the practice of law in 1857. On Feb. 1, 1859, he was married to Wathen Taylor, who bore him five children. At the coming of the Civil War he abandoned his law practice, raised Company A of the 2nd Florida Infantry, and became the captain. His regiment was a part of Lee's army in Virginia, and upon the death of its commander he was promoted to the rank of colonel in May 1862. He was badly wounded at the battle of Frayser's Farm and was invalided home. He was appointed brigadier-general in August 1862 and, upon his return to active duty, took command of the little brigade of three Florida regiments, which he continued to lead throughout the war. After the battle of Chancellorsville he had typhoid fever and was again forced to retire from active service, thus missing the Gettysburg campaign. He returned to duty and led his brigade in Lee's defensive campaign until May 1864, when he was severely wounded in the Wilderness fighting and again forced to give up the service. During his absence his decimated brigade was condensed into a regiment and consolidated with another brigade. Upon his recovery he was assigned to duty with the reserves in Alabama.

At the end of the war he resumed the practice of his profession at Pensacola and soon acquired a wide reputation as a lawyer. He was an outspoken critic of Carpet-bag rule in the state, and in 1884 he was elected governor of Florida on the Democratic ticket, his selection being due largely to his fame as a soldier. His administration was a successful one but not distinguished for any great achievements; it was rendered memorable in state annals by the yellow fever ravages at Jacksonville and the disastrous St. Augustine fire. At the end of his administration he retired to private life and died as the result of a stroke of paralysis while visiting in Kerrville, Tex. He was buried in Pensacola.

[*Confederate Mil. Hist.*, ed. by C. A. Evans (1899), vol. XI; *Soldiers of Fla. in the Seminole Indian-Civil and Spanish-American Wars*, prepared . . . under . . . Board of State Institutions (1903); R. H. Rerick, *Memoirs of Fla.* (1902), vol. I; H. G. Cutler, *Hist. of Fla.* (1923), vol. I; *War of the Rebellion: Official Records* (*Army*), 1 ser., vols. XXXIX, pt. 2, XL, pt. 2; *Florida Times-Union* (Jacksonville), Oct. 16, 17, 19, 1889; date of birth from H. E. Aylsworth, *Arthur Aylsworth and His Descendants in America* (1887).]   R. S. C.

PERRY, EDWARD BAXTER (Feb. 14, 1855–June 13, 1924), concert pianist, author and lecturer, was born in Haverhill, Mass., the son of Baxter E. and Charlotte (Hough) Perry. He was blind practically all of his life, as he lost his sight through an accident when he was only two years of age, but this handicap in no wise deterred his activities as a student. He was educated in the public schools of Medford, graduating in 1871. In the same year he went to Boston to study piano—first at the Perkins Institute for the Blind, in South Boston, then with J. W. Hill. Besides his music study, he specialized also in English literature. He remained in Boston until 1875, when he went to Europe for further study with Kullak in Berlin and Pruckner in Stuttgart. Later he studied with Clara Schumann and, in the summer of 1878, with Liszt at Weimar. He also took courses at the University of Berlin and at the Polytechnical Institute at Stuttgart (1875–78) in literature, history, and philosophy. He gave occasional concerts and played before the Emperor of Germany. Soon after his return to America he was appointed professor of music at Oberlin College (1881–83), but from 1883 to 1885 he was again in Europe and again at the Polytechnical Institute in Stuttgart. In 1885 he began to give concerts over the entire United States. He was perhaps the first to devote himself almost exclusively to lecture recitals, and in the period from 1885 to 1917 he gave more than three thousand, comprising practically the entire pianoforte literature available at that time. Besides this record activity, he wrote several hundred articles for magazines, principally for the *Etude*. In 1897–98 he toured in Europe and was everywhere greeted with enthusiasm.

Perry had an adequate technique; his playing was refined and facile, and his interpretations were poetic. His loss of sight had made his other senses particularly acute. But his description of his ideas of physical beauty around him sometimes seemed fantastic to less sensitive persons, and this quality was manifest to some degree in his lecture recitals and in his writings. His *Descriptive Analyses of Piano Works* (1902) is interesting but too rhapsodical to be of dependable value to the student, for Perry read into many of the compositions thoughts and emotional qualities that probably never occurred to the composers. The chief value of the work was to stimulate the search for poetic content in music. His *Stories of Standard Teaching Pieces* (1910) possesses the same quality, but both works had a large sale in their day. In November 1921 Perry went to Frederick, Md., as instructor in piano at Hood College, where he remained only one year. From 1922 until his death he occupied a similar position at Lebanon Valley College, Anville, Pa. On June 21, 1882, he married Netta A. Hopkins of Peoria, Ill. In 1898 he was decorated in Paris with the order of *Chevalier de Melusine* by Prince Lusignan in recognition of Perry's unpublished "Melusina Suite," based upon a legend in the family of the Prince. He died suddenly, of heart failure, at his summer home in Camden, Me. Among his published piano compositions are the following: "Why," "Mazurka Caprice," "Æolienne," "Autumn Reverie," "The Portent," and "The Ballad of Last Island."

[*Who's Who in America*, 1918–19, 1924–25; *Internat. Who's Who in Music* (1918); L. C. Elson, *The Hist. of Am. Music* (1904); *Grove's Dict. of Music and Musicians* (1928); *Musical Courier*, June 26, 1924; the *Etude*, Aug. 1924; *N. Y. Times*, June 15, 1924.]
F. L. G. C.

PERRY, ENOCH WOOD (July 31, 1831–Dec. 14, 1915), painter, was born in Boston

Mass., the son of E. Wood Perry of that city and Hannah (Dole) Perry of Newburyport. When he was seventeen he went to New Orleans, where he worked in a grocery store for four years, saving from his meager earnings $1100—no slight achievement in a city presenting so many temptations to prodigality. With his small capital he sailed for Germany, to study art under Emanuel Leutze, N.A., a well-known figure painter, and remained there for more than two years before going to Paris for a season in Couture's studio. In 1856 he was appointed United States consul in Venice, and even though his duties at that post left him sufficient time to carry on his painting, he resigned in three years and returned to the United States, doing some landscapes around Philadelphia before joining his father who had become a furniture dealer in New Orleans. Young Perry hired a studio on St. Charles Street and advertised himself as a portrait painter. He evidently met with success, and one of his best pictures, which now hangs in the Cabildo at New Orleans, is of Senator John Slidell [q.v.].

In January 1861 the Louisiana state legislature in session at Baton Rouge signed the ordinance of secession, and Perry made a preliminary sketch in oil of the proceeding which is now in the Cabildo. It contains likenesses of many of the most important of the legislators. He also painted about this time a large portrait of Jefferson Davis standing before a map of the Confederate States. Sitters became few, however, because men were too occupied with the grim business of fighting; so Perry went to California and for awhile he painted in San Francisco. In 1863 he was in Hawaii where he did portraits of King Kamehameha IV and his successor, Kamehameha V. When he returned to the United States he painted Brigham Young and other apostles of the Mormon Church, staying in Salt Lake City, Utah, until these commissions were finished. He must have had great ability in salesmanship, for he always contrived to have for sitters the most important people in the cities where he happened to be. His portrait of General Grant was done when Grant was at the height of his military glory.

After he settled in New York in 1865, Perry acquired a reputation for his genre subjects. Some of their titles, such as "Grandfather's Slippers," "Too Little to Smoke," "Good Doggie," and "Is Huldy to Home?," give an accurate idea of them. Although as works of art they are quite valueless today, they were painted with such fidelity to detail that they are still interesting as records of contemporary American interiors, manners, utensils, costumes, household customs, and even crafts, for he delighted in painting women at work, spinning, hackling flax, making patchwork quilts, and performing other tasks which have since completely disappeared from domestic life. He was an excellent draftsman and thoroughly trained in the technique of his profession; his weakness lay in following the passing fashions of his day. In 1868 he was elected an associate of the National Academy of Design, and an Academician in the following year. He was most active on the Academy's school committee and served as its recording secretary from 1871 to 1873, a position he also filled for the American Art Union during its entire existence. He died in New York, leaving a widow, Fanny F. Perry (death notice, *New York Times,* Dec. 15, 1915), and was buried at Newburyport, Mass.

[J. D. Champlin and C. C. Perkins, *Cyc. of Painters and Paintings* (4 vols., 1886–87); *Senate Executive Journal, 1855–58* (1887); G. W. Sheldon, *Am. Painters* (1881); C. E. Clement and Laurence Hutton, *Artists of the Nineteenth Century and Their Works* (1884); I. M. Cline, *Art and Artists in New Orleans during the Last Century* (1922); *Am. Art News,* Dec. 18, 1915; *Am. Art Annual,* vol. XIII (1916); *Who's Who in America,* 1914–15; death certificate, Health Dept., N. Y. City.]
                                                    E. L. T.

PERRY, MATTHEW CALBRAITH (Apr. 10, 1794–Mar. 4, 1858), naval officer; fourth child of Christopher Raymond Perry [q.v.] and Sarah Wallace (Alexander) Perry, was born at Newport, R. I. After attending school in his native town, he entered the navy in 1809 as a midshipman. He saw his first active service on the *Revenge,* commanded by his brother, Oliver Hazard Perry [q.v.]. In 1810 he was transferred to the *President* under Commodore John Rodgers [q.v.], a bluff disciplinarian who stamped many of his qualities upon the young subaltern. Perry's journal or logbook kept on board the *President,* more informative than most writings of this kind, records several unusual experiences, including the action with the *Little Belt* in 1811, the fight with the *Belvidera* in 1812, in which he was wounded, and the cruise off the coast of Norway in the following year, during which he was advanced to the grade of lieutenant. His next vessel, the *United States,* was driven into New London and there remained until near the end of the war. His enforced leisure he improved by marrying on Christmas Eve, 1814, Jane Slidell of New York, a sister of John Slidell [q.v.] and of Alexander Slidell Mackenzie [q.v.].

In 1816 Perry, on leave from the navy, made a voyage to Holland as the master of a merchant vessel. His first active duty after his return to the service was performed in 1820 as executive officer of the *Cyane* when that vessel aided in establishing a colony of American negroes on the west coast of Africa. In the following year he returned to Africa in the *Shark,* his first command, conveying thither the United States agent to the colony, later named Liberia. In 1822 he cruised after pirates in the West Indies, capturing five piratical craft. In 1825–26, as executive officer of the *North Carolina,* 74, the flagship of the Mediterranean Squadron, he participated in a visit to the headquarters of the Greek Revolutionists and in an interview with the captain pasha of the Turkish fleet. At Smyrna he aided in the extinguishing of a disastrous fire and by his extraordinary exertions brought on an attack of rheumatism, from which disease he was never henceforth entirely free. His promotion to the grade of master commandant dated from Mar. 21, 1826. In 1830 he conveyed to Russia, on board the *Concord,* John Randolph of Roanoke, American envoy to that country. At St. Petersburg he was received by the Czar, who invited him to enter the Russian naval service, an invitation he declined. He next joined the squadron in the Mediterranean and in 1832, as commander of the *Brandywine,* participated in the naval demonstration made at Naples with the object of compelling payment of spoliation claims.

In 1833 he was appointed second officer of the New York navy yard and began a long and notable service on shore. He now became a resident of New York City, where henceforth he made his home. Much interested in naval education, he had in 1824 drawn up a plan for a naval apprentice system and he continued his agitation until an apprentice system was established by Congress in 1837. He was a member of the board of examiners that in 1845 prepared the first course of instruction for the Naval Academy at Annapolis. In 1833 he took the lead in organizing at the New York navy yard the United States Naval Lyceum, to promote the diffusion of knowledge among naval officers. He was its first curator, in 1836 its vice-president, and later its president. He was much interested in the *Naval Magazine,* an outgrowth of the museum and the first American periodical conducted by naval officers. He served on a committee that advised the secretary of the navy respecting the scientific work of the United States Exploring Expedition, of which he was offered the command.

Perry's interest in the revolution in naval matériel that began in the 1830's exceeded that of any other officer. An early advocate of naval steamships, he is sometimes called the father of the steam navy. Promoted to a captaincy from Feb. 9, 1837, he was in the same year placed in command of the *Fulton,* one of the pioneer naval steamships, and it fell to him to organize the first naval engineer corps. A report made by him in 1837 (*Senate Document No. 375,* 25 Cong., 2 Sess.) as a member of a naval board appointed to study the water approaches to New York City was used in Congress in behalf of an act creating lighthouses. In the following year he was sent on a mission to England and France to examine the lighthouses of those countries and to collect information on the use and construction of naval steamships and ordnance. His reports made after interviewing many officials, including King Louis Philippe, are valuable digests replete with information and suggestions (for Perry's report on lighthouses, see *Senate Document No. 619, 26* Cong., 1 Sess.). In 1839–40 he conducted at Sandy Hook and on board the *Fulton* the first American naval school of gun practice. At Sandy Hook he established an experimental battery for the testing of guns, shells, and shot. One of his papers to the department dealt with the use of naval steamships as rams. In 1841 he was appointed commandant of the New York navy yard, in which office he could readily serve the department as technical expert on steamships and naval inventions.

In 1843 he was chosen to command the African Squadron organized that year to aid in the suppression of the slave trade, under the provisions of the Webster-Ashburton Treaty, and to protect the settlements of American negroes in Africa. Cruising up and down the African coast he held several palavers with the native chiefs, one of which, that of Little Berribee, ended in a fight with bloodshed and in the burning of several towns. His "ball-and-powder policy" was long remembered by the natives. His next important service was performed during the Mexican War, first as commander of the *Mississippi* and second officer in command of the squadron operating on the east coast of Mexico, and later as the commander-in-chief of the squadron. In the latter part of 1846 he commanded the expedition that captured Frontera, Tabasco, and Laguna. From Mar. 21 to Mar. 29, 1847, he commanded the naval forces that cooperated with the army in the siege of Vera Cruz and shared with Gen. Winfield Scott [*q.v.*] credit for the capitulation of that city. Later he captured Túxpan and other fortified posts, and demanded and received from Yucatan a promise of neutrality. His squadron is said to have been the largest that up to that time had flown the American colors.

From 1848 to 1852 Perry was on special duty at New York, chiefly engaged in superintending the construction of ocean mail steamships. In the summer of the latter year he was once more placed in command of the *Mississippi* and ordered to protect American fisheries off the coast of the British provinces in America, since reports were current that Great Britain was seizing American fishing vessels. He visited the fisheries off Cape Breton and Prince Edward Island and, after reassuring and warning his countrymen, returned home.

His part in the fisheries episode was a brief interlude in the activities of a year spent in preparation for what proved to be the supreme work of his life. In January 1852 he was selected to undertake the most important diplomatic mission ever intrusted to an American naval officer, the negotiation of a treaty with Japan, a country at this time sealed against intercourse with the Occidental powers. He wrote to the secretary of the navy that he was willing to undertake the mission provided the East India Squadron was greatly augmented. The suggestion was accepted, and the government decided to send to Japan an imposing fleet, in the belief that a show of naval power might facilitate negotiations. The official documents relating to Perry's mission included a letter of President Fillmore to the Emperor of Japan, and instructions from the State Department. The last named stated that the objects of the expedition were the protection of American seamen and property in Japan and Japanese waters and the opening of one or more ports to American vessels for the procuring of supplies and for conducting trade. Perry was directed to try first the efficacy of argument and persuasion, but if these failed, he was to change his tone and use more vigorous methods, always bearing in mind however that his mission was peaceful and that the President had no power to declare war. No secret was made of the expedition, which aroused the interest of the whole civilized world.

On Nov. 24, 1852, Perry sailed from Norfolk for China on board the *Mississippi*. Late in May of the following year he assembled his fleet at Napa, Great Lu-chu Island, which he decided to make a port of refuge for his vessels. Here he spent several days calling on the prince regent, exploring the island for scientific purposes, and surveying harbors. While awaiting the arrival of a collier, he visited Port Lloyd, Peel Island, surveyed its harbor, explored the island, and purchased a coaling depot. At length, on July 2, 1853, he sailed from Napa for Yedo, the capital of Japan, with the *Susquehanna*, now his flagship, and three other vessels. According to his plan, he proposed to impress the Japanese by magni-

fying his mission, surrounding his person with an air of mystery, and declining to confer personally with subordinate officials. When on the morning of July 8 his ships approached Yedo Bay, their decks were cleared for action, their guns shelled, and their crews called to quarters. In the afternoon they anchored in Yedo Bay, off Uraga, twenty-seven miles from Yedo, and were soon surrounded by Japanese guard boats, one of which came alongside the flagship. A Japanese official inquired for the commander of the squadron, but since the official was only a vice-governor Perry declined to see him, appointing a lieutenant to inform him that the fleet came on a friendly mission with a letter from the President of the United States which the commander-in-chief wished to deliver to a dignitary of the highest rank. When the official replied that the fleet must go to Nagasaki, the only place in Japan where foreign business was transacted, Perry sent word that he expected the letter to be received in Yedo Bay. On the following day a governor came on board the flagship and again ordered the Americans to go to Nagasaki. Perry sent word that the letter would be delivered where he then was, and if a suitable person was not appointed to receive it he would go ashore with a sufficient force and deliver it, whatever the consequences might be. In the end his boldness and threats succeeded, and on July 14 the letter of the President and other documents were delivered with elaborate ceremonies by Perry himself on shore at the village of Kurihama to the princes Idzu and Iwami, representatives of the Emperor. As it seemed best to give the government time for reflection and discussion, Perry, having informed the princes that he would return in the following year, sailed for China, after a stay of nine days in Yedo Bay.

Suspicious movements of French and Russian naval ships caused him to return to Japan sooner than he had intended, and in February 1854 he once more anchored in Yedo Bay. The Japanese were now conciliatory. The Emperor had issued orders to receive the fleet in a friendly manner and had appointed five commissioners to meet Perry and consider the proposals made in the President's letter. The meeting took place at Yokohama, where the Americans made a second landing marked by much pageantry. There, on Mar. 31, 1854, was signed a treaty of peace, amity, and commerce granting the United States trading rights at the two ports of Hakodate and Shimoda. On his return voyage to China Perry stopped at the Lu-chu islands and negotiated with the islanders a treaty similar to that of Yokohama. Acting under his orders, one of his commodores took possession in behalf of the United States of the Coffin Islands.

As one of the chief diplomatic achievements of the nineteenth century, the opening of Japan will long make the name of Perry memorable. His expedition marked a departure in Occidental policy respecting Japan, in American policy respecting the Orient, and in Japanese policy respecting the western world. Perry was an imperialist bent upon extending widely in the Pacific the commercial and naval interests of America. He has been called the first American official, so far as is known, "to view not merely the commercial but also the political problems of Asia and the Pacific as a unity" (Dennett, *post*, p. 270). On his return to Hong Kong from Japan the American merchants in China gave him an elaborate candelabrum as an expression of their appreciation of his diplomatic services. In ill health and worn out by the labors of his mission he sailed for home on the British steamer *Hindostan* and arrived at New York on Jan. 12, 1855. The federal government, whose politics had changed during his absence, took no special notice of its sailor diplomat. The state of Rhode Island, however, presented him with a silver salver, New York City gave him a set of silver plate, and the merchants of Boston had a medal struck in his honor. In June 1855 he was ordered to Washington as a member of the naval efficiency board (see Samuel Francis du Pont), but his chief duty for more than a year was the preparation of a report of his expedition, which was published by the government in 1856 in three large folio volumes under the title, *Narrative of the Expedition of an American Squadron to the China Seas and Japan*. In the preparation of the first volume, consisting of the narrative itself, he was assisted by Francis Lister Hawks [*q.v.*]. He had previously sought the aid of Nathaniel Hawthorne, upon whom he called in Liverpool on his way home from Japan. Hawthorne declined the task, suggesting that he ask Herman Melville instead, a recommendation which did not meet with Perry's approval.

Perry was of a rather heavy build, blunt, something of a martinet; "Old Bruin" the sailors called him. Hawthorne described him as a "brisk, gentlemanly, off-hand but not rough, unaffected and sensible man" (*Our Old Home and English Notebooks*, Riverside Edition, 1883, I, 548). He had ten children. One of his sons retired from the navy as a captain, and his daughter Caroline Slidell Perry married August Belmont [*q.v.*]. He died in New York City, the third officer of the navy, and was buried in the Island Cemetery, Newport. A statue to his memory was erected in 1868 in Touro Park, Newport, by Mr. and Mrs. August Belmont. In 1901 a monument commemorating his first landing was unveiled in Kurihama, a gift of the Japanese American Association of Japan.

[W. E. Griffis, *Matthew Calbraith Perry* (1887) is a friendly account, which, while not without slips and extraneous information, contains most of the essential facts. See also Record of Officers, Bureau of Navigation, 1809–63; Letters to Officers, Ships of War, Navy Dept. Archives, 1809–14, 1837–52; R. W. Neeser, *Statistical and Chronological Hist. of the U. S. Navy* (1909); I. O. Nitobe, *The Intercourse between the U. S. and Japan* (1891); Tyler Dennett, *Americans in Eastern Asia* (1922); C. O. Paullin, *Diplomatic Negotiations of American Naval Officers* (1912); S. W. Williams [*q.v.*], "A Journal of the Perry Expedition to Japan," *Trans. Asiatic Soc. of Japan*, vol. XXXVII, pt. II (1910), the journal of Perry's interpreter; Sen. Ex. Doc. No. 34, 33 Cong., 2 Sess.; *N. Y. Times*, Mar. 4, 1858.]

C. O. P.

PERRY, NORA (1831–May 13, 1896), poet, journalist, author of juvenile stories, was the daughter of Harvey and Sarah (Benson) Perry of Dudley, Mass. In her childhood the family removed to Providence, R. I., where her father was a merchant. There she was educated at home and in private schools. As a child of eight she wrote a hair-raising romance, "The Shipwreck," which she read to her playmates with great effect. Her book favorites were the *Arabian Nights* and boys' stories, and, as she grew older, Emerson's essays and the poetry of the Brownings. She was rather proud of the fact that she never went through the "Byron age." When only eighteen she began to write for magazines, and her first serial, "Rosalind Newcomb," ran in *Harper's Magazine*, 1859–60. She soon went to live in Boston where she became correspondent for the *Chicago Tribune* and the *Providence Journal*, as well as a contributor of stories and poems to many magazines. She was a favorite among New England readers. One of her most popular poems, "Tying Her Bonnet Under Her Chin," was declined by the *Atlantic Monthly* and was then published in the *National Era* at Washington, D. C. It took the public fancy and was sung and parodied throughout the East. The *Atlantic* then made her an offer for a poem equally good, and she wrote "After the Ball," her best-known piece, first published in the *Atlantic* for July 1859 and sometimes printed under the title "Maud and Madge." Although it was excessively sentimental and morbid, Longfellow is said to have given it moderate praise as "a very cleverly versified poem that—a very artistic poem."

Nora Perry later wrote stories for girls almost exclusively. Her volumes include: *After the Ball, and Other Poems* (1875); *Her Lover's Friend, and Other Poems* (1880); *The Tragedy of the Unexpected, and Other Stories* (1880); *A*

Book of Love Stories (1881); *For a Woman, a Novel* (1885); *New Songs and Ballads* (1887); *A Flock of Girls* (1887); *The Youngest Miss Lorton and Other Stories* (1889); *Brave Girls* (1889); *Lyrics and Legends* (1891); *Hope Benham, a Story for Girls* (1894); *Cottage Neighbors* (1899); *That Little Smith Girl* (1899); *May Bartlett's Stepmother* (1900); *Ju Ju's Christmas Party* (1901); and *A New Year's Call* (1903) in the Children's Friend Series. Character portrayal is the chief merit of her stories, which are very simple in plot but show a knowledge of girls. She was never a systematic writer but wrote only when she felt so inclined. For some time before her death she made her home in a hotel at Lexington, Mass. While on a short visit to her old home at Dudley she suffered a stroke of apoplexy and died.

[F. E. Willard and M. A. Livermore, *Am. Women* (1897), vol. II; Arthur Gilman and others, *Poets' Homes*, 2 ser. (1880); *Critic*, May 23, 1896; *Boston Daily Advertiser* and *Boston Post*, May 15, 1896; *Alphabetical Index of Births, Marriages, and Deaths in Providence*, vol. XII (1908); *Vital Records of Dudley, Mass.* (1908); names of parents and year of birth from Am. Antiquarian Soc.]   S. G. B.

PERRY, OLIVER HAZARD (Aug. 20, 1785–Aug. 23, 1819), naval officer, was born in the village of Rocky Brook, South Kingstown, R. I., the eldest child of Christopher Raymond Perry [*q.v.*] and Sarah Wallace (Alexander) Perry. Matthew Calbraith Perry [*q.v.*] was a younger brother. After receiving elementary instruction in his native town, Oliver was placed in school at Newport, where he learned navigation, having exhibited a liking for the sea. The entrance of his father into the navy smoothed his way into that service, and on Apr. 7, 1799, at the age of fourteen, he was appointed midshipman. Joining his father's ship, the *General Greene,* he saw active service in the West Indies during the naval war with France. During the war with Tripoli he was twice stationed in the Mediterranean, first in 1802–03 on board the *Adams,* and again in 1804–06 on board the *Constellation* and other vessels of the squadron. In 1803 he was made an acting lieutenant and four years later received a permanent lieutenancy. From 1807 to 1809 he was employed in building gunboats in Rhode Island and Connecticut and for a time commanded a flotilla of such craft engaged in enforcing the Embargo. In 1809 he was advanced to the command of the schooner *Revenge* and in 1810 cruised off the coast of the southern states where he effected the recovery of the *Diana,* an American ship sailing under English colors, a performance that was regarded as highly creditable. Early in the following year while under orders

to survey the harbors of New London and Newport, the *Revenge* ran aground in a fog and was lost. A court of enquiry acquitted Perry of blame, since the vessel at the time was in charge of a pilot. He next took command of the gunboats at Norwich and Westerly, with headquarters at Newport, where on May 5, 1811, he was married to Elizabeth Champlin Mason.

Perry was now considered an excellent seaman and an efficient deck officer. Physically handsome, with pleasing voice and manners, he was professionally ambitious, quick in decision, and willing to take risks. His stature was slightly above the average; his body compact, active, and muscular. When war with Great Britain appeared inevitable, he wrote to the secretary of the navy earnestly entreating that he be called into active service. Later he went to Washington to urge his claims, and was promised the first vacancy suitable to his rank, that of master commandant, which he attained in August 1812. Restless and dissatisfied with his post at Newport, which gave him the command of a few gunboats, he tendered his services to the department and to Commodore Isaac Chauncey [*q.v.*] for duty on the Great Lakes. Chauncey wrote to him that he was the very person that he wanted for a "particular service," which later proved to be the command of the naval forces on Lake Erie. On Feb. 8, 1813, the department ordered him to proceed to Sacketts Harbor, N. Y., Chauncey's headquarters. He reached his own headquarters, Erie, Pa., on Mar. 23 and spent the spring and summer energetically employed in building, assembling, equipping, officering, and manning a small fleet—a most arduous task because a large part of his supplies had to be procured on the seaboard and transported through the wilderness. In May for a brief period he was on Lake Ontario where he took part in the capture of Fort George. Chauncey in acknowledging his assistance wrote that Perry was "present at every point where he could be useful, under showers of musketry, but fortunately escaped unhurt" (Mackenzie, *post,* I, 147).

By August, Perry was ready for active operations. His fleet at Erie consisted of ten small vessels, the largest of which were the sister-brigs *Lawrence* and *Niagara,* each of 480 tons burden. The fleet of the enemy blockading him was commanded by Commander Robert H. Barclay. Perry could not cross the Erie bar in the presence of the enemy, for the water there was so shallow that the guns and equipment of his heaviest vessels had to be removed before they could pass over. For a reason never fully explained, however, Barclay relaxed his blockade and gave

Perry a chance to reach the open lake. The latter described his task as one of almost incredible labor and fatigue, but most of the ships were over before the enemy arrived. It has been justly said that the battle of Lake Erie was really won at the Erie bar.

Perry was now joined by Master Commandant Jesse Duncan Elliott [q.v.] with one hundred officers and men, and Elliott, as the second officer of the fleet, took command of the *Niagara,* Perry having made the *Lawrence* his flagship. On Aug. 12 the fleet sailed up the lake, unopposed by the enemy, who had retired to his station at Amherstburg on the Detroit River. Perry made Put-in-Bay his headquarters, some twenty miles north of the present city of Sandusky, from which position he could watch Barclay's movements. He was also convenient to Gen. W. H. Harrison [q.v.], commander-in-chief of the western army with headquarters at Seneca-town, thirty miles to the southward. Twice he reconnoitred Amherstburg and observed Barclay's fleet, consisting of the new flagship *Detroit,* the *Queen Charlotte,* and four other small vessels.

The completion of the *Detroit* and the urgent need of supplies led Barclay to the decision to contest with Perry the possession of the lake. On Sept. 9 he weighed anchor and at sunrise on the following day he was sighted by Perry, who at once sailed out of Put-in-Bay to meet him. In the early morning the British had the advantage of the weather-gage, but before the battle was joined the wind shifted and conferred on the Americans the power of initiative. In weight of metal the Americans had a decided superiority, but in the number of effective men the difference was not material. According to Perry's plan of battle, the *Lawrence* was to fight the *Detroit,* the enemy's most formidable vessel; the *Niagara,* the *Queen Charlotte*; and his smaller vessels, the smaller vessels of the enemy. At 10 A.M. the *Lawrence* was cleared for action and a battle flag was hoisted upon which were inscribed the words attributed to the dying Lawrence, "Don't give up the ship."

The battle began a quarter before noon and lasted until 3 P.M. During its major part the brunt was borne by the *Lawrence.* When the vessel had been shot to pieces, all her guns disabled, and of 103 men, eighty-three killed or wounded, Perry transferred his flag to the *Niagara,* which up to this time had taken but a small part in the battle. After he left the *Lawrence* she struck her colors, but as he soon brought the *Niagara* into action the British were unable to take possession of the former flagship. The ensuing minor part of the battle lasted about fif-teen minutes and ended with the surrender of the enemy's fleet. Barclay's loss was forty-one killed and ninety-four wounded including the commander himself. Perry's loss was twenty-seven killed and ninety-six wounded. More than two-thirds of the casualties were suffered by the *Lawrence.* The results of this decisive victory were far-reaching. The Americans gained control of Lake Erie and held it until the end of the war. Harrison crossed the lake and captured a large part of Upper Canada. The American negotiators at Ghent were able to make good their claims to the Northwest.

In few general actions, according to Admiral Mahan (*post,* II, 64), has the personality of the commander after the battle was joined counted for so much. Of Perry's laconic dispatches announcing his victory, the one beginning, "We have met the enemy and they are ours" was addressed to General Harrison; and the one beginning, "It has pleased the Almighty to give to the arms of the United States a signal victory over their enemies on this lake" (reminiscent of Nelson's dispatch after the battle of the Nile), to Secretary of the Navy Jones. Soon after news of the victory was received in Washington President Madison promoted Perry to the rank of captain, his commission bearing the date of the battle, Sept. 10, 1813. Later Congress added $5000 to the $7500 which was his share of the prize money. The capture of a British fleet by the American navy was unprecedented and it at once raised Perry to a position of renown. On Jan. 6, 1814, Congress adopted a resolution thanking him and requesting the President to give him a gold medal. He received the thanks of the legislatures of Pennsylvania and Georgia. Boston and Newport each gave him a service of plate, several other cities voted him swords, and Baltimore, Washington, and Boston, dined and toasted him. His enjoyment of his well-deserved fame was marred only by the acrimonious controversy that arose with Elliott over the latter's part in the battle. (For an account of this controversy, see sketch of Jesse Duncan Elliott.)

After the victory, Perry cooperated with Harrison in taking possession of Detroit, in transporting troops across the lake, and in fighting the battle of the Thames, in which he served as aide-de-camp to the commander-in-chief. He joined Harrison in issuing a proclamation to the people of western Canada. On Oct. 25 he turned the squadron over to Elliott and began his triumphal journey to Newport. In July 1814 he was ordered to Baltimore to take command of the *Java,* 44 guns, but this ship was unable to go to sea, because of the blockade maintained by the enemy. In September he commanded a battery, with a detachment of seamen, and harassed the British fleet in its passage down the Potomac River from Alexandria.

In 1816–17 as commander of the *Java,* Perry cruised in the Mediterranean. A difficulty that he had at this time with Capt. John Heath of the marines resulted in a court martial and a private reprimand for both officers by the commodore of the squadron, and later in a duel on the famous dueling grounds at Weehawken, N. J., in which neither was injured, Perry declining to fire. In May 1819 he was placed in command of a small fleet and sent upon a delicate mission to the republics of Venezuela and Buenos Aires, whose vessels had been preying upon American commerce. When descending the Orinoco River after concluding negotiations at Angostura, the Venezuelan capital, he fell ill of yellow fever and died within a few days. His body was interred at Port of Spain, Trinidad. In 1826 it was transported on the *Lexington* to Newport, where it found its final resting place, later marked by a granite obelisk erected by Rhode Island, a state that has loyally cherished the name of its hero. Perry had five children; one of his sons entered the navy and one the army.

[There is a considerable literature on Perry and the Battle of Lake Erie, most of which is listed in C. O. Paullin, *The Battle of Lake Erie* (1918), pp. 205–12. See also Records of Officers, Bur. of Navigation, 1798–1825; Letters to Officers, Ships of War, X, XIII, and Private letters, 1813–40, Navy Dept. Archives; A. S. Mackenzie, *The Life of Commodore Oliver Hazard Perry* (2 vols., 1840); J. F. Cooper, *Lives of Distinguished Am. Naval Officers* (1846), II, 146–232; A. T. Mahan, *Sea Power in Its Relations to the War of 1812* (1905), II, 62–101; *Niles' Register,* Oct. 2, 1819.]

C. O. P.

PERRY, RUFUS LEWIS (Mar. 11, 1834– June 18, 1895), negro Baptist clergyman, missionary and educator, journalist, was born in Smith County, Tenn. His parents were Lewis and Maria Perry, the slaves of Archibald W. Overton. Perry's father was a Baptist preacher and such an able mechanic and carpenter that he hired his time from his master and was allowed to move to Nashville with his family. Here Rufus was permitted to attend a school for free negroes until his father ran away to Canada. After his flight the other members of the family were deprived of their temporary freedom and forced to return to their master's plantation. In August 1852 Rufus Perry, who was regarded as dangerous on account of his schooling, was sold to a slave dealer who intended to take him to Mississippi. After remaining in this man's custody for three weeks he followed his father's example and likewise fled to Canada. His goal was Windsor, Ont., where he studied diligently and soon qualified as a teacher among the fugitives of his race. Converted to the Baptist faith in 1854, he some years later studied for the ministry at the Kalamazoo Theological Seminary and after graduating from this institution, was ordained as pastor of the Second Baptist Church of Ann Arbor on Oct. 9, 1861. Subsequently he served as pastor of churches at St. Catharines, Ont., and Buffalo, and still later, of the Messiah Baptist Church in Brooklyn, which he organized in 1887.

In 1865 Perry engaged in general missionary work, laboring for the education and evangelization of the members of his race. He superintended schools for freedmen for a time, but ultimately devoted most of his energies to journalism. He served as editor of *Sunbeam* and of the *People's Journal,* was co-editor of the *American Baptist,* 1869–71, and in later years, 1872–95, was joint editor then editor-in-chief of the *National Monitor,* a Baptist organ. For ten years he was corresponding secretary of the Consolidated American Baptist Missionary Convention and he also served as corresponding secretary of the American Educational Association and of the American Baptist Free Mission Society. He was an eloquent preacher, a fluent debater, and an able writer with an entertaining style. On May 16, 1887, he delivered a lecture on "Light" before the State University at Louisville, Ky., which afterwards bestowed upon him the degree of Ph.D. His only literary effort in book form was *The Cushite; or the Descendants of Ham as Seen by Ancient Historians* (1893). He died in Brooklyn, where he had made his home since about 1870. His wife was Charlotte Handy, by whom he had seven children.

[W. W. Brown, *The Rising Son* (1874); W. J. Simmons, *Men of Mark* (1887); Wm. Cathcart, *The Bapt. Encyc.* (1881); *Courier-Journal* (Louisville, Ky.), May 18, 1887; *Appletons' Ann. Cyc., 1895* (1896); *Brooklyn Daily Eagle,* June 19, July 31, 1895.]

H. G. V.

PERRY, STUART (Nov. 2, 1814–Feb. 9, 1890), inventor, was born in Newport, N. Y. Here he obtained his early education, and then entered Union College, where he was graduated in 1837. Three years later he entered the wholesale butter and cheese commission house established by his older brother and brother-in-law in Newport, with which he was associated for upwards of twenty years. Although he prospered in his business, he was primarily interested in mechanics and devoted most of his spare time to study and invention in this field. After his retirement, about 1860, he gave the remaining thirty years of his life to this work. His first invention, now recognized as notable historically, was a gas engine, for which he obtained United States

Patent No. 3,597 on May 25, 1844. It was operated by the expansion of the products of combustion within the engine cylinder. The invention was the first of the class of non-compression gas engines that were so successfully introduced by Lenoir in France about 1860. Perry's engine utilized the explosive vapors obtained from rosin heated by the exhaust gases in a retort which was part of the engine. Again, in 1846, Perry patented an improved gas engine, obtaining patent No. 4,800 on Oct. 7, 1846. This design incorporated a provision for water-cooling the cylinder, an incandescent platinum igniter for the gas, and a receiver for compressed air to be used in starting the engine. In an effort to find a market, Perry exhibited his engine in the New York store of his brother's company in 1847 but without success. He then turned his attention to bank locks, inspired no doubt by the ingenious work of his friend and fellow citizen Linus Yale the elder. He obtained patents in 1857 for a lock, key, and safe bolt, and in 1858, patent No. 20,658 for an improved bank lock. This was a tumbler lock having no keyhole and a key made up of component parts which could be separated and reassembled to change the lock combination. It is said to have been marketed as the "Great American," and was an improvement on the famous Yale "Infallible" and "Magic" bank locks. Between 1860 and 1865 Perry worked on improvements in horse-powers and secured some ten patents which he assigned to a local manufacturer. He also devised during the sixties a milk-cooling apparatus, a stereopticon, sawmill machinery, and a velocipede. About 1870 he turned his attention to the manufacture of agricultural implements, particularly hay tedders of his own invention, and continued in this occupation for the remainder of his life. He married, in 1837, Amy Jane Carter of Newport, and after her death in 1873 he married Jane W. Maxson, who with a daughter by his first wife survived him.

[*Hist. of Herkimer County, N. Y.* (1879); *New York Journal,* XLVII (1847), 511; correspondence with Union College Graduate Council; Patent Office records.]   C. W. M—n.

PERRY, THOMAS SERGEANT (Jan. 23, 1845–May 7, 1928), author, scholar, and educator, was born at Newport, R. I. His father, Christopher Grant Perry, was the son of Oliver Hazard Perry [*q.v.*], of Lake Erie fame, whose brother, Commodore Matthew Calbraith Perry [*q.v.*], became equally famous because of his negotiations with Japan. His mother was Frances Sergeant, of Philadelphia, and on her side he was, by direct descent, the great-great-grandson of Benjamin Franklin, whose facial characteristics he inherited to a degree that was frequently recognized. His early education was at private schools. At the age of sixteen and a half he entered Harvard College, graduating with the class of 1866.

After graduation he went to Europe for further study, with the intention of returning to a position for life at Harvard as a tutor in French and German. After holding this position from 1868 to 1872, however, he relinquished it and became associated for a time with the *North American Review.* Returning to Harvard in 1877 as instructor in English, he remained there for five years. In 1874 he was married to Lilla Cabot, daughter of Dr. Samuel Cabot of Boston, and soon became an adopted Bostonian. As a lecturer he was notably popular. A volume of his lectures, *English Literature of the Eighteenth Century* (1883), is widely known and read. For several years, at home and abroad, he was engaged in an active literary life. In 1882 he published *The Life and Letters of Francis Lieber,* which was issued also in a German translation; in 1885 *From Opitz to Lessing* appeared. In 1887 he published a small volume in a lighter vein, *The Evolution of the Snob,* which is not, however, so trivial as the title sounds. His *History of Greek Literature,* the most voluminous and comprehensive of his works, appeared in 1890. In addition to his original writings he published translations of contemporary foreign authors, including Turgenev, and Saint-Amand. Although Oliver Wendell Holmes called him "the best read man I have ever known," he refused to be ambitious, saying as he grew older that writing was more a task than a pleasure. In spite of his unusual equipment, which was encyclopedic as well as scholarly, his native temper of the student and appreciator overcame by degrees his interest in original work, and with the exception of a brief biography of his old friend, John Fiske, which appeared in 1906, he published in his later years only an occasional short article.

In 1898 he went with his family to Japan, where for three years he was professor of English at the University of Keiogijiku. After his return to Boston he remained to the end of his life an omnivorous student and reader of many languages, including Sanskrit and Russian. By nature a cosmopolite, and perhaps never quite at home in America, he lived to see himself almost the last of "Old Boston," of which he had been for years a distinguished and familiar figure. He represented the perfection of a culture that has passed, and he is remembered for an impressive and engaging personality that was itself a sort of genius. He was by nature what might be called a rationalist, if not quite a materialist, and yet was hospitable enough to say of Emerson, whose optimistic unworldliness could hardly have satisfied him, that he was "the only man I ever knew who seemed to be different from the rest of mankind." Though inclined to be exclusive in his human relations, he was altogether democratic in his appraisal of his fellow man, frowning only on what he felt to be cheap or mean or common. After a short illness he died at his home in Boston.

[C. B. Perry, *The Perrys of R. I. and Silver Creek* (1913); J. T. Morse, Jr., *Thomas Sergeant Perry, A Memoir* (1929); *Selections from the Letters of Thomas Sergeant Perry* (1929), ed. by E. A. Robinson; *Boston Transcript,* May 7, 1928.]   E. A. R.

PERRY, WILLIAM (Dec. 20, 1788–Jan. 11, 1887), physician, manufacturer of starch, was born at Norton, Mass., the son of Nathan and Phebe (Braman) Perry. His youth was passed on the family farm and his preparation for college attained through a private tutor and a short period at an academy at Ballston, N. Y., where his brother, Gardner, was principal. He entered Union College but remained only a year, transferring to Harvard where he was graduated in 1811. During the next three years he continued medical studies at Harvard and under James Thacher [*q.v.*] of Plymouth and John Gorham and John Warren [*qq.v.*] of Boston, all distinguished physicians in their day. In 1814 he received the degree of M.D. at Harvard Medical School and immediately opened an office at Exeter, N. H. There he continued to practise until almost the end of his extraordinarily long life. Sound judgment, careful attention to his patients, and great professional skill quickly brought him a wide practice and made him the most distinguished physician and surgeon of his time in that section of the country. In his late eighties he was still performing difficult operations and at the age of ninety-two operated successfully for strangulated hernia (Watson, *post*). He was one of the first medical men in his state to urge the establishment of an asylum for the insane. Between 1830 and 1835 he was particularly interested in the subject of insanity, and it was mainly through his influence and exertions that an asylum was erected at Concord. His agitation included the delivery of two lectures on insanity before the state legislature. In 1836 he was appointed lecturer at the Bowdoin College Medical School and served one year; in 1837 he was offered a professorship, but declined.

Perry had a keen interest in chemistry, and after a series of experiments became convinced that "British Gum," an expensive imported product employed as a sizing by cotton manufacturers, could be produced by charring starch. Such a substance he succeeded in making from potatoes, and in the latter part of 1824 completed a mill for the manufacture of potato starch which was soon providing the cotton manufacturers of Lowell with a perfect substitute for "British Gum." In 1827 and again in 1830 the mill was burned to the ground, but within a short time was operating again. The secrets of the business were finally discovered, however, keen competition developed, and Perry gave up the manufacture of starch as no longer remunerative.

Original in mind and straightforward in action, he devoted his talents for over half a century to the highest interests of his community. He lived to be ninety-eight, and few men have more completely won the respect and confidence of their neighbors. It is said that at the last two presidential elections during his life his fellow-citizens waited to vote until he had cast the first ballot. He married, Apr. 8, 1818, Abigail Gilman (1789–1860), the daughter of Nathaniel and Abigail (Odlin) Gilman, and had by her five children. His oldest daughter, Caroline Frances, became the mother of Sarah Orne Jewett [*q.v.*].

[C. H. Bell, *Hist. of the Town of Exeter, N. H.* (1888); G. F. Clark, *A Hist. of the Town of Norton, Bristol County, Mass.* (1859); Arthur Gilman, *The Gilman Family* (1869); *Vital Records of Norton, Mass. to the Year 1850* (1906); I. A. Watson, *Physicians and Surgeons of America* (1896).]   H. U. F.

PERRY, WILLIAM FLAKE (1823–Dec. 18, 1901), first state superintendent of public instruction of Alabama, the son of Hiram and Nancy (Flake) Perry, was born in Jackson County, Ga. When he was ten years old the family moved to Chambers County, Ala. This county was a part of the cession of the Creek Indians that had been made only a year earlier, and the boy grew up in the most primitive frontier conditions, with little or no schooling. Poor as his training was it was better than that of most of his neighbors, and he taught school in Talladega County, Ala., from 1848 to 1853, while studying law. He was married in 1851 to Ellen Douglas Brown in Talladega, Ala., the niece of William P. Chilton [*q.v.*]. They had seven children. He was admitted to the bar in 1854, but he never practised his profession, for in the same year he was elected state superintendent of education and, twice reëlected, served until 1858. The office of superintendent of education had been created in 1854 by an act of the Alabama legislature providing for a free public

Perry

Perry

school system, and he was the first to hold the office. Acting under the law of 1854 he laid the foundations for a strong public school system of Alabama, which were, however, a few years later swept away in the Civil War. He entered upon the task with energy and enthusiasm, but the situation he faced was most discouraging. The population was sparse and the available funds were small. The people were indifferent, and he never had adequate popular support. Teachers and administrators were indifferent and incompetent. In the face of these difficulties he accomplished much. He was able to build an organization and to persuade the legislature to revise the law in 1856 in the interest of greater efficiency of administration.

In 1858 he resigned his position as superintendent of education to become president of the East Alabama Female College at Tuskeegee. He remained there until 1862, when he enlisted in the Confederate army as a private in the 44th Alabama Infantry. Within a few weeks he was elected major by the men of the regiment. His promotion was rapid; on Sept. 1, 1862, he was made lieutenant-colonel and upon the death of the colonel of the regiment at Sharpsburg he was advanced to colonel. He led his regiment in the assault on Round Top at Gettysburg and later at Chickamauga, after which he was cited for gallantry by General Longstreet and recommended for promotion. He commanded his brigade during 1864 and 1865, but his commission as brigadier-general was dated Mar. 16, 1865. He was paroled with his regiment at Appomattox. After the war he returned to Alabama and spent two years as a planter. In 1867 he took charge of a military college in Glendale, Ky., and went from there to Ogden College at Bowling Green, where he became professor of English and philosophy. He published his own account of "The Genesis of Public Education in Alabama" in the *Transactions of the Alabama Historical Society* for 1898 (vol. II). He died in Bowling Green.

[T. M. Owen, *Hist. of Ala.* (1921), vol. IV; Willis Brewer, *Alabama* (1872); Wm. Garrett, *Reminiscences of Public Men in Ala.* (1872); J. J. Garrett, "Forty-Fourth Ala. Regiment," *Ala. Hist. Soc. Trans.,* vol. II (1898); S. B. Weeks, *Hist. of Public School Education in Ala.* (1915); W. G. Clark, *Hist. of Education in Ala.* (1889).] H. F.

PERRY, WILLIAM STEVENS (Jan. 22, 1832–May 13, 1898), Protestant Episcopal bishop, church historian, was born in Providence, R. I., the son of Stephen and Katharine Whittemore (Stevens) Perry. He attended the Providence High School and entered Brown University, but later joined as a sophomore the Harvard class of 1854, with which he graduated.

He attended the Theological Seminary in Virginia for a time and continued his studies under the special guidance of the Rev. Alexander H. Vinton, of Boston. While a candidate for orders, he helped found Grace Church, Newton, Mass. He was made deacon in Newton, Mar. 29, 1857, and ordained priest, Apr. 7, 1858. He served as rector of St. Luke's Church, Nashua, N. H., 1858–61; St. Stephen's, Portland, Me., 1861–63; St. Michael's, Litchfield, Conn., 1864–69; Trinity Church, Geneva, N. Y., 1869–76. From 1871 to 1874 he was professor of history in Hobart College, Geneva, and served for a short time as president of the college (April–September 1876). In 1868 he was appointed by the General Convention, historiographer of the Episcopal Church, and from 1865 to 1876 he was assistant secretary or secretary to the General Convention. On Jan. 15, 1862, he married Sara Abbott Woods Smith, daughter of the Rev. Thomas Mather Smith. He was consecrated bishop of Iowa in 1876, and continued until his death to administer the affairs of his growing diocese. He founded two church schools at Davenport, Iowa: St. Katharine's Hall for girls and Kemper Hall for boys.

Perry's most distinctive contribution to his period was as a historical writer. He stimulated the historical consciousness of the Episcopal Church in America, and preserved material which otherwise might have been lost. He was accurate, and in his work showed clear judgment, seizing upon the important facts in relation to the development of the institution. A student and investigator of early colonial sources, he made many visits to England, and in the archives of the Society for the Propagation of the Gospel, Fulham Palace Library, and the Public Record Office in London discovered valuable manuscripts relating to the origin and development of the Episcopal Church in America. These were published in five volumes (1870–78) under the general title: *Historical Collections Relating to the American Colonial Church*. He also published in two volumes *The History of the American Episcopal Church, 1587–1883* (1885), and *The Episcopate in America* (1895), a collection of biographical sketches. He was in demand as a special preacher and speaker on many historical occasions and many of his addresses and sermons were printed in permanent form. His literary activity is indicated by the fact that a list of his separate publications includes 125 titles. A few of these indicate his interests: *The Faith of the Signers of the Declaration of Independence* (1896?); *The Christian Character of George Washington* (1891); *The Men and*

Measures of the Massachusetts Conventions of 1784–85 (1885); *A Discourse Delivered . . . at Faribault, Minn., on the Eve of the Centenary of the Consecration of the Reverend Samuel Seabury to the Episcopate of Connecticut* (1884); *The Alleged "Toryism" of the Clergy of the United States at the Breaking out of the War of the Revolution* (1895?), and *A Missionary Apostle* (1887), a sermon preached in Westminster Abbey.

[The Harvard College Library has a complete collection of Perry's publications. For biographical data see *Harvard College, Report of the Class of 1854* (1894); *The Am. Church Almanac and Year Book for 1899* (1898); W. S. Perry, *The Episcopate in America* (1895); *Churchman,* May 21, 1898; *Dubuque Daily Telegraph,* May 13, 1898.]
            D. D. A.

PERSON, THOMAS (Jan. 19, 1733–Nov. 16, 1800), North Carolina Revolutionary leader, was born probably in Brunswick County, Va., but lived from infancy in Granville (now Vance) County, N. C. His father was William Person, of Virginia, who went to North Carolina about 1740. The maiden name of his mother, Ann Person, is not known. Thomas became a surveyor for Lord Granville and in the course of years acquired a landed estate of more than 82,000 acres lying in Granville, Halifax, Warren, Franklin, Orange, Caswell, Guilford, Rockingham, Anson, and Wake counties in North Carolina, and in Davidson, Sumner, and Green counties in Tennessee. He became a justice of the peace in 1756, sheriff in 1762, and was representative in the Assembly in 1764 and frequently thereafter. In the Regulation movement he was involved somewhat deeply as counselor and adviser. He was tried at the session of 1770 for perjury and for exacting illegal fees but he was triumphantly cleared. He was not present at the battle of Alamance when the Regulation was suppressed, but he was regarded as so important a leader that he was included in Governor Tryon's list of those excepted from the amnesty which was proclaimed. He was arrested and jailed but was released without trial, and his influence in the Assembly and in the colony grew steadily.

When the Revolutionary movement began Person threw himself into it with intense fervor. Ardently democratic, he believed the struggle to be primarily one for popular government. He headed the Granville delegation in all five provincial congresses, and he served on every important committee including the one which proposed the Halifax resolution of Apr. 12, 1776, instructing the delegates to the Continental Congress to vote for a declaration of independence, the one which drafted the bill of rights, and the one which drew up the Constitution of 1776. In the two congresses of 1776 he ranked with Willie Jones as a leader of the liberal party. In 1775 he was elected a member of the provincial council and in 1776 of the Council of Safety. In 1776 he was elected also a general of militia, but there is no record that he saw active service. He was again made a justice of the peace in 1776, and a member of the council of state, and in 1784 was elected to the Continental Congress but never took his seat. He was a member of the House of Commons from 1777 to 1786, 1788 to 1791, 1793 to 1795, and in 1797—seventeen years in all—and a member of the Senate in 1787 and 1791. In 1787 he became chief commissioner to settle the accounts of the state with the United States.

In 1788 Person was one of the most influential of those who opposed immediate ratification of the federal Constitution, and as a delegate to the Hillsboro convention voted against it. He was also a delegate to the Fayetteville convention of 1789 where he again opposed ratification. The legislature of 1789 named him one of the charter trustees of the state university and he held the place until 1795 and was one of the institution's earliest and most generous benefactors. Person in 1760 married Johanna Thomas of Granville County who died without issue. He died in Franklin County and was buried at Personton in Warren. His career in the General Assembly was notable not only for its length, but for the amount of legislative work which he did. He served on almost every important committee. He was a fighter and an able and adroit political leader, but there was about him nothing of the trickster. A zealous party man, he nevertheless had a passion for justice, equality, and honesty in government which was always stronger than party feeling.

[*The Colonial Records of N. C.,* vols. I–X (1886–90), and *The State Records of N. C.,* vols. XI–XXVI (1895–1905); J. S. Bassett, "The Regulators of N. C. (1765–1771)," *Ann. Report of the Am. Hist. Asso. . . . 1894* (1895); S. A. Ashe, ed., *Biog. Hist. of N. C.,* vol. VII (1908); Louise I. Trenholme, *The Ratification of the Fed. Constitution in N. C.* (1932); *Hist. Papers Pub. by the Trinity Coll. Hist. Soc.,* ser. XIV (1922), pp. 79–81.]
           J. G. deR. H.

PETER, HUGH (1598–Oct. 16, 1660), clergyman, was the son of Thomas Dirkwood or Dyckwoode, who subsequently assumed the surname of Peter, and Martha Treffry. He always signed his name Peter but is often called Peters. He was baptized at Fowey in Cornwall in June 1598; entered Trinity College, Cambridge, in 1613; received the bachelor's degree in 1617/18, and the master's, in 1622. He was ordained deacon Dec. 23, 1621, and priest June 18, 1623, by George Montaigne, Bishop of London. After preaching in Essex, he removed to London, where he lectured at St. Sepulchre's, and became associated with the Puritan feoffees who were raising a fund to buy up impropriations in England, and a member of the Massachusetts Bay Company. The appointment of Laud as bishop of London and the rise to power of the high church party caused him to leave England about 1629. After traveling through Germany, he assisted John Forbes in the congregation of English merchants at Delft and preached to an English congregation at Rotterdam. At the latter place he was joined by William Ames, and perhaps under Ames's influence drafted a covenant for the church embodying the principles of congregationalism, and refused communion to all who would not accept it. Hither he invited John Davenport [q.v.] when the latter failed to win installation as co-pastor with John Paget of the English church at Amsterdam, and here he and Davenport engaged Lion Gardiner [q.v.] to go to New England for the Warwick patentees. His movements in Holland were watched by emissaries of Laud, now archbishop of Canterbury, and probably for this reason he placed John Davenport in charge of his congregation in Rotterdam and departed for New England.

On Oct. 6, 1635, Peter arrived in Massachusetts Bay, and on Dec. 21, 1636, succeeded Roger Williams as pastor of the church at Salem. He was a firm supporter of non-separating congregationalism or the "New England way," and at the time of his settlement at Salem, the church adopted a covenant in some of its details resembling the covenant that he had drafted for the church in Rotterdam. On Mar. 3, 1635/36 he was admitted a freeman of the Bay Colony, and took an active part in the affairs of New England. Soon after his arrival in Massachusetts he and Henry Vane called a meeting to heal the breach between John Winthrop and Thomas Dudley. He served on committees appointed May 25, 1636, and Mar. 12, 1637/38, to draft a code of laws for the colony. He concerned himself with the settlement of the Warwick patentees at the mouth of the Connecticut River, and in the summer of 1636 accompanied George Fenwick [q.v.] to Saybrook. He opposed seizing the corn of the defeated Pequot Indians, but asked for "a young woman or girle and a boy" from among the captives for himself and John Endecott. In November 1637 he attended the examination of Anne Hutchinson by the court at Newtown, and in the following March, her trial before the church at Boston. He was a member of the committee appointed Nov. 20, 1637, "to take order for a colledge at Newetowne," was one of those to

whom the building of the college was intrusted, and his name appeared as an overseer of the college on the theses printed in 1642. With others, he was sent by the governor and council of Massachusetts to settle a dispute in the church at Piscataqua and on leaving that place lost his way and wandered for two days and a night in the woods. He encouraged the fisheries, trade, and shipbuilding of New England, and is characterized by Winthrop (*post*, II, 23) as "a man of a very public spirit and singular activity for all occasions." Against the will of his Salem congregation, he was appointed one of three agents to represent Massachusetts Bay and to further the reformation of the churches in England, and on Aug. 3, 1641, sailed from Boston for the mother country.

In England he secured support for the Bay Colony and Harvard College and assisted in arranging a settlement with the creditors of New Plymouth. In negotiations with the Dutch West India Company he failed to settle the boundary between New England and New Netherland for lack of a commission from Connecticut, although one had been sent to him soon after his departure from New England (*Documents Relative to the Colonial History of the State of New York*, ed. by E. B. O'Callaghan, vol. I, 1856, p. 568). He always intended to return to New England, but with the outbreak of civil war in England he became involved in the affairs of the mother country, and made the poor health from which he suffered all his life an excuse for delay. During the summer of 1642 he served as chaplain with the forces of Alexander, Lord Forbes, in Ireland; in 1644, with the forces of the Earl of Warwick; in 1645 and 1646, with the New Model Army; and in 1649, with Cromwell in Ireland. With the duties of chaplain he combined those of war correspondent and reported the activities of the army to the House of Commons. In sermons preached during the trial of Charles I, he denounced the King, and in a letter to Queen Christina of Sweden some years later explained the reasons for the execution of the monarch. He stood in high favor with the Council of State and the Protector. He was one of the ministers appointed to preach before the Council, for which he received an annuity of £200 and lodgings in Whitehall, and so impressed a visiting New Englander with his high station that he was addressed as Archbishop of Canterbury, which "passed very well." With the overthrow of the Protectorate, he fell from power. On Jan. 9, 1659/60, he was turned out of Whitehall; on May 11 the Council of State, and on June 7 the House of Commons ordered his apprehension; on Aug.

20 he was excepted from the Act of Indemnity; on Sept. 2 he was arrested and committed to the Tower; on Oct. 13 he was tried and condemned; and on Oct. 16, 1660, he was executed at Charing Cross. While awaiting execution, he wrote *A Dying Father's Last Legacy to an Onely Child: or, Mr. Hugh Peter's Advice to His Daughter* (1660). During his lifetime and after his death he was cruelly maligned by both Anglicans and Presbyterians, but he enjoyed the respect of such men as the Winthrops of New England, the Earl of Warwick, Fairfax, and Cromwell.

About 1624 Peter married Elizabeth, the daughter of Thomas Cooke of Pebmarsh, Essex, widow of Edmund Reade of Wickford, Essex, and mother of the second wife of John Winthrop, Jr. She did not accompany him to New England and died in 1637 or 1638. Sometime before Sept. 4, 1639, he married Deliverance Sheffield, a widow, who was the mother of his only child, Elizabeth, baptized at Salem Oct. 1, 1640. His later life was clouded by the insanity of this second wife. In 1665 his daughter married Thomas Barker at All Hallows, London Wall, and as a widow in low circumstances, in 1703 laid claim to his Salem estate.

[E. B. Peters, "Hugh Peter," *Hist. Colls. Essex Inst.*, vol. XXXVIII (1902); William Harris, *An Hist. and Critical Account of Hugh Peters* (1751, 1818); J. B. Felt, *A Memoir or Defence of Hugh Peters* (1851); C. H. Firth, in *Dict. Nat. Biog.*; S. E. Morison, "Sir Charles Firth and Master Hugh Peter, with a Hugh Peter Bibliog.," *Harvard Grads. Mag.*, Dec. 1930; G. C. Boase, and Wm. P. Courtney, *Bibliotheca Cornubiensis* (3 vols., 1874–82); John Venn and J. A. Venn, *Alumni Cantabrigienses*, pt. 1, vol. III (1924); Champlin Burrage, *The Early English Dissenters in the Light of Recent Research* (2 vols., 1912); British Museum, Add. MSS. 6394, printed in *Proc. Mass. Hist. Soc.*, vol. XLII (1909); *Records of the Governor and Company of the Massachusetts Bay in New England*, vols. I–II (1853), ed. by N. B. Shurtleff; *Winthrop's Journal* (2 vols., 1908), ed. by J. K. Hosmer; "Winthrop Papers," *Mass. Hist. Soc. Colls.*, 3 ser. IX (1846), X (1849), 4 ser. VI (1863), VII (1865), 5 ser. I (1871), VIII (1882); Thomas Lechford, *Plain Dealing; or, Newes from New-England* (1642), repub. in *Mass. Hist. Soc. Colls.*, 3 ser. III (1833); "Acts of the Commissioners of the United Colonies of New England," *Records of the Colony of New Plymouth in New England*, vols. IX–X (1859); William Bradford, *Hist. of Plymouth Plantation, 1620–1647* (2 vols., 1912), ed. by W. C. Ford; *Calendar of State Papers, Domestic Series; Acts and Ordinances of the Interregnum* (3 vols., 1911), ed. by C. H. Firth and R. S. Rait.]   I. M. C.

PETER, JOHN FREDERICK (May 19, 1746–July 19, 1813), school-master, preacher, and musician, son of John Frederick and Susanna Peter, was born at Hernndyck, Holland, where his father was pastor of the Moravian congregation. On the death of his mother in 1760, his father was sent to America to assist in the Moravian work at Bethlehem, Pa. The boy continued his education in schools at Gros Hennersdorf, Barby, and Niesky. Besides the usual

training for the ministry, he received instruction on the violin and organ, and in harmony and musical composition.

In 1769 he followed his father to America and was for a year a teacher at Nazareth, Pa. Removing to Bethlehem in 1770, he became accountant and secretary of the Brethren's House, teacher in the boys' school, and organist of the church. For fifteen years his was the inspiration that gave activity to the musical life of Bethlehem. The Collegium Musicum, which had been founded in 1749 by Westerman, was expanded in its aims, and works by Bach, Händel, and Graun were rehearsed and performed, while the orchestra, consisting of the full complement of strings, wood, and brass, played symphonies by Haydn, Mozart, and their contemporaries. In 1786 Peter was sent, in succession, to Hope, N. J., Lititz, Pa., Graceham, Md., and Salem, N. C., where his musical activities were continued and where his talents made definite and permanent impression. In 1793 he returned to Bethlehem with his wife, Catharine Leinbach, a singer, whom he had married in Salem, and became accountant for the diocese, resuming, also, control of musical affairs.

During a life busied with many monotonous details, he composed more than thirty anthems for chorus, solo, and orchestra, and copied vocal and instrumental parts of works by the great composers of his day, for church and concert use. His only secular work is a set of six quintettes for two violins, two violas, and cello, written in the traditional sonata style; they show not only mastery of form, but also originality of melodic outline. Peter was well acquainted with the contrapuntal music of Bach, but his own compositions reflect Haydn rather than the father of the moderns. His choruses are usually written in five parts and seldom pass very far into free counterpoint, but his instrumental accompaniments are always independent of the voices, as to form. With respect to harmony, he very often shows a strong tendency toward the modern habit of chromatic alteration. In 1810 he copied all the vocal and instrumental parts of Haydn's *Creation* and in 1811, under his direction, the work was given its first complete performance on the American continent, some years before its production by the Händel and Haydn Society of Boston.

This talented musician, probably unknown outside of his circle, was, undoubtedly, the first composer of serious concerted music in America. Just what the technical quality of the performances of these pioneers of American music may have been we have no means of knowing; but the seed whence sprang the Bethlehem Bach Choir was in their spirit and in that of their self-sacrificing leader. In the music library of the Moravian Church at Bethlehem the perfectly formed notes and the beautiful handwriting of Peter covered many hundreds of pages. Some of his copies of symphonies by Haydn are dated between 1760 and 1770 and reveal quite clearly the nature of his early training, for the much thumbed and marked copies speak eloquently of hard rehearsals. One of the most significant results of Peter's life is seen in the list of names of some six or eight local composers who fell under his influence, though none of them equaled their master. He died suddenly as he stepped down from the organ bench after a rehearsal.

[Authorities include manuscript diaries of the Bethlehem Congregation, 1770–1813, and of the Brethren's House, 1770–86, copies of the musical works of Peter, and accounts of the Collegium Musicum, 1774–1813, all in the Moravian archives, Bethlehem, Pa.; J. M. Levering, *Hist. of Bethlehem* (1903); Raymond Walters, *The Bethlehem Bach Choir* (1923); J. T. Howard, *Our Am. Music* (1930). The statement that Peter directed a complete performance of Haydn's *Creation* in 1811 is supported by the testimony of one of the original performers and by Peter's copy of the score, which bears marks in his handwriting indicating performance of the entire work.]   A. G. R.

PETER, ROBERT (Jan. 21, 1805–Apr. 26, 1894), physician, chemist, was born at Launceston, Cornwall, England, the son of Robert and Johanna (Dawe) Peter. He came to Pittsburgh, Pa., with his parents in 1817, where from necessity he sought employment and secured a position in Charles Avery's wholesale drug store. Here he acquired and diligently cultivated a decided taste for chemistry. Soon after attaining his majority he became a naturalized citizen, and about that time attended the Rensselaer School (now Rensselaer Polytechnic Institute), Troy, N. Y. He was a member of the Hesperian Society and contributed to *The Hesperus* numerous papers—scientific, literary, and poetical. In 1829 he gave a series of lectures on natural sciences before the Pittsburgh Philosophical Society, of which he was a member, and in 1830–31 he lectured on chemistry in the Western University of Pennsylvania.

In 1832 he went to Lexington, Ky., to be associated with Benjamin O. Peers [*q.v.*] in the proprietorship of his "Eclectic Institute" and to give a course of lectures. When Peers was made proctor of Morrison College and acting president of Transylvania University in 1833, young Peter was installed in the chair of chemistry in Morrison College. He studied medicine in Transylvania, receiving his diploma in 1834, but so intent upon his scientific pursuits was he that he soon gave up the practice of medicine. On

Oct. 6, 1835, he was married to Frances Paca Dallam, and to this union were born six sons and five daughters. To the *Transylvania Journal of Medicine and Associate Sciences,* of which he was editor in 1837, he made numerous contributions, among them being articles entitled "Thoughts on Some Application of Chemistry to Medicine" (October–December 1834), "Notice of the Crab Orchard Mineral Springs" (September 1835), and "A Summary of Meteorological Observations Made During 1837 and 1838" (January 1837–July 1838). In 1838 Peter was elected to the chair of chemistry and pharmacy in the medical department of Transylvania University, which position he held until the closing of the school in 1857. During the last ten years he was dean of the medical faculty. He went to London and Paris in 1839 and expended $11,000 in books and apparatus for his department. From 1850 to 1853 he also served as professor of chemistry and toxicology in the Kentucky School of Medicine, Louisville. After his return from Europe he carried on much experimental work along practical lines. He made a study of calculi and published *Chemical Examination of the Urinary Calculi in the Museum of the Medical Department of Transylvania University* (1846). He also experimented with gun-cotton.

A memorial to the Kentucky legislature, which Peter prepared, resulted in the Kentucky geological survey of 1854, the first large state undertaking of its kind in the West. As chemist of the survey, he made a valuable contribution to knowledge of the minerals and soil of the state, the results of his studies being published in the various reports of the survey. He was the first to call attention to the fact that the productivity of the bluegrass soils of Kentucky is due to their high phosphorus content, and to report on the phosphatic limestone which underlies much of the bluegrass country. He was also chemist for the Arkansas and Indiana surveys directed by David Dale Owen [*q.v.*].

During the Civil War he was acting assistant surgeon in charge of military hospitals in Lexington. When, in 1865, Transylvania, Kentucky University, and the state Agricultural and Mechanical College were merged under the name of Kentucky University, Peter declined the presidency of the last-named and filled the chair of chemistry and experimental philosophy in the other two schools of the University. In 1867–68 he was assistant editor of the *Farmer's Home Journal* and afterwards was a frequent contributor. When the Agricultural and Mechanical College separated from the University in 1878, Peter chose to associate himself with the former as professor of chemistry, remaining in that position until he retired as emeritus professor in 1887. He died at Winton, his country home, in his ninetieth year, retaining almost to the end his youthful appearance, mental and physical vigor, and happy outlook upon life. His son, Dr. Alfred M. Peter, was for forty-two years chemist in the Kentucky Agricultural Experiment Station. Father and son together gave nearly a hundred years of service in chemistry to Kentucky.

[Peter wrote *Transylvania Univ., Its Origin, Rise, Decline, and Fall* (1896), Filson Club Pubs., no. 11, and *The Hist. of the Medic. Dept. of Transylvania Univ.* (1905), Filson Club Pub., no. 20, published with biog. sketch by his daughter, Johanna Peter; see also J. N. McCormack, *Some of the Medic. Pioneers of Ky.* (1917); A. H. Barkley, *Kentucky's Pioneer Lithotomists* (1913); *Trans. Ky. State Medic. Soc.*, 1894; H. A. Kelly and W. L. Burrage, *Am. Medic. Biogs.* (1920); *Courier-Jour.* (Louisville), Apr. 27, 1894.]   G. R.

PETER, SARAH WORTHINGTON KING (May 10, 1800–Feb. 6, 1877), philanthropist, was the daughter of Thomas and Eleanor (Van Swearingen) Worthington. Thomas Worthington [*q.v.*] was a member of an old Virginia family who freed his slaves and started life anew in Chillicothe and Adina, Ohio, where he prospered as a lawyer, and became a political leader. Sarah, born in Chillicothe, was schooled in Frankfort, Ky., and in a private institution near Baltimore, receiving instruction chiefly in the social usages becoming a girl of her position and beauty. In 1816, she married Edward King, son of Rufus King [*q.v.*] of New York, who had completed the course at the Litchfield Law School and settled in Chillicothe to practise his profession. She became an ardent worker in the local Episcopal Church, which she helped to found in 1820, and maintained a cultivated salon on the frontier where she entertained among others Karl Bernhard, Duke of Saxe-Weimar-Eisenach, who recorded his impressions of the family in his *Travels through North America during the Years 1825 and 1826* (1828; II, 149–50). In 1825, she accompanied her father to New Orleans, where she was honored as one of Lafayette's hostesses. Moving to Cincinnati in 1831, the Kings became prominent in social life, aided in founding the Cincinnati School of Law, and assisted in the establishment of the Protestant Orphan Aslyum. In 1836, King died and his widow moved to Cambridge, Mass., where her sons were attending Harvard College. Welcomed by social leaders because of her family connections in New York and Maine, she spent her time in the service of Christ Church and in mastering French, German, and Italian.

With her elder son settled in Cincinnati as a lawyer and the younger in the Philadelphia commercial house of his kinsman, Richard Alsop, she felt free to follow her own bent, and in October 1844 she married William Peter, British consul in Philadelphia. He was an Oxford scholar, a translator of German poetry, and an essayist, and had served as a Whig member of Parliament. The Peters became favorites in social and intellectual circles, and their home was noted for its collections of bronzes, prints, and paintings. After the death of Sarah Peter's younger son, she took his widow and three children to Europe (1851–52). She organized the Philadelphia School of Design for Women, promoted an association for the advancement of tailoresses, and materially aided the Quakers in the erection of the Rosina House for Magdalens. On the death of her husband, Feb. 6, 1853, she returned to Cincinnati, where her home became a rendezvous for artists and musicians. She soon brought together a group of women interested in the fine arts with whose assistance she founded a small art museum, for which she collected masterpieces and worthy copies on her frequent European journeys. By 1876, this group had grown into the Woman's Museum Association, which later fostered the Cincinnati Academy of Fine Arts.

As a result of her sympathetic observations in European Catholic countries, especially in 1854 when she met the American prelates who had gone to Rome for the definition of the Immaculate Conception, she developed an interest in Catholicism. In 1855 she was received into the church at Rome by the picturesque Monsignor Bedini. As a Catholic, her interest in magdalens, orphans, and the indigent became more marked, although her early services were given little support by Archbishop Purcell, who in time came to trust her implicitly. In 1857, she brought the Sisters of the Good Shepherd under Mother Mary Ward from Louisville to Cincinnati and later assisted them in establishing houses in Newport, Ky., Cleveland, and Columbus (*Catholic Telegraph*, Aug. 7, 1858, Mar. 12, 1859). She urged successfully that they be given care of a prison exclusively for women such as she had seen in Paris. She secured a colony of Sisters of Mercy from Kinsale, Ireland, who developed into a strong community and during the Civil War rendered able service as nurses under the leadership of nuns who had served with Florence Nightingale in the Crimea. In 1858 she brought out the Franciscan Sisters from Cologne for work among the Germans. To this community she gave her home and much of her substance, founding hospitals in Cincinnati (1859) and Covington, Ky. (1861). During the Civil War, she joined the Sisters of St. Francis at Pittsburg Landing as a nurse, criticized the inefficiency or corruption of the United States Sanitary Commission, and subsequently, despite bitter criticism from Northern partisans, spent herself in the care of prisoners in Cincinnati. As a result of another trip abroad she induced the Sisters of the Poor from France to join the Cincinnati diocese, where in 1869 they established a refuge for impoverished old people. On a journey to Europe in 1869–70, she was well received by Pius IX and the American bishops at the Vatican Council, who through Purcell were conversant with her charities and her self-sacrificing life. Among her manifold interests she was active to the end; her last efforts were in connection with art exhibits at the Centennial Exhibition. On her death, she was eulogized by Archbishop Purcell and her remains were interred in her mortuary chapel at St. Joseph's Cemetery, Cincinnati.

[Margaret R. King, *Memoirs of the Life of Mrs. Sarah Peter* (2 vols., 1889), a biography by her daughter-in-law, containing copious extracts from her European letters; J. G. Shea, *Hist. of the Cath. Ch. in the U. S.*, IV (1892), 544 f.; *Records of the Am. Cath. Hist. Soc.*, Dec. 1923; *N. Y. Freeman's Journal*, Feb. 17, 24, 1877; *Cincinnati Enquirer*, Feb. 6–9, 1877.]
R. J. P.

PETERKIN, GEORGE WILLIAM (Mar. 21, 1841–Sept. 22, 1916), clergyman, first bishop of the Diocese of West Virginia, was born at Clear Spring, Washington County, Md., the son of the Rev. Joshua and Elizabeth Howard (Hanson) Peterkin. During his boyhood he lived in Maryland, New Jersey, and Virginia, and attended private schools, notably the Episcopal High School at Alexandria, Va., where he won high standing in his studies. He attended the University of Virginia in 1858 and 1859, taught for one year, and then began a course of private study in preparation for the ministry of the Protestant Episcopal Church. Upon the outbreak of the Civil War he enlisted as a private in the 21st Virginia Regiment of Infantry, serving first under General Lee and later under General Jackson. In June 1862 he received a commission as first lieutenant, was appointed aide-de-camp to Gen. William Nelson Pendleton [*q.v.*], chief of artillery in the Army of Northern Virginia, and served with that army until its surrender in 1865.

He graduated from the Theological Seminary in Virginia in 1868 and was ordained deacon by Bishop Johns on June 24, 1868, and priest by Bishop Whittle on June 25, 1869. He served his diaconate as assistant to his father in St. James' Church, Richmond, Va. His first rectorate was St. Mark's Parish, Culpeper County, Va., where he labored for four years to rebuild a parish which had been devastated by war. From 1873 to 1878 he was Rector of Memorial Church, Baltimore, Md. In 1878 he was elected the first bishop of the Diocese of West Virginia and was consecrated in St. Matthew's Church, Wheeling, W. Va., on May 30, beginning an episcopate of thirty-eight years. The new diocese, cut off from the mother Diocese of Virginia in 1877, covered about 24,000 square miles of sparsely settled mountainous territory most of which was inaccessible except on horseback over poor roads and trails. The new bishop found fourteen clergy, twenty-five churches, fewer than 1,200 communicants, and a people to whom his church was little known. He was a true pioneer missionary, indefatigably visiting every section of his diocese, making frequent preaching trips on horseback to remote villages in mountain communities, and winning everywhere the loyal affection of his people. An able organizer and administrator, he laid the broad foundations of the present diocese and became in the process an influential leader in the religious life of the state.

He was deeply interested in foreign and domestic missions, serving for twenty-six years as a member of the national Board of Missions. In 1893, shortly after a mission of the Episcopal Church had been established in southern Brazil, he was sent by the Board to direct its development. Much of the success of that missionary district was due to the policies inaugurated and executed during the six years of his supervision. He was called by the presiding bishop to visit Puerto Rico in 1901, and the development of a new missionary enterprise in that field profited by his advice. He was an able preacher and writer and published numerous addresses and pastoral letters. His most important works include *A History and Record of the Protestant Episcopal Church in the Diocese of West Virginia* (1902) and the *Handbook for Members and Friends of the Protestant Episcopal Church* (1908). Until two years before his death, when increasing ill health forced him into seclusion, he was able to maintain an active contact with the work of his church. He was buried in Hollywood Cemetery, Richmond, Va. Peterkin was married on Oct. 29, 1868, to Constance Gardner Lee of Alexandria, Va. She died in 1877 leaving three children. On June 12, 1884, he married Marion McIntosh Stewart of Brook Hill, Henrico County, Va., by whom he had one child.

[*Who's Who in America*, 1916–17; R. E. L. Strider, *The Life and Work of George William Peterkin* (copr. 1929); Susan P. Lee, *Memoirs of William Nelson Pendleton, D.D.* (1893); W. A. R. Goodwin, *Hist. of* the *Theol. Seminary in Va.*, vol. II (1924); *Wheeling Register*, Sept. 23, 1916.]   G. M. B.

PETERS, ABSALOM (Sept. 19, 1793–May 18, 1869), Presbyterian clergyman, editor, author, was born in Wentworth, N. H., the fourth son of Gen. Absalom Peters, a Revolutionary veteran, and his wife Mary (Rogers) Peters. His first American ancestor in the paternal line was Andrew Peters, whose name appears in Boston records as early as 1659, while his mother's family claimed descent from Rev. John Rogers who was burned at Smithfield in 1555. Absalom became a teacher at sixteen and followed this occupation during his own school days and his years at Dartmouth College, where he was graduated in 1816. Soon after his graduation at Princeton Theological Seminary in 1819, he began preaching at the First Congregational Church, Bennington, Vt., and was ordained there by the Troy Presbytery in 1820. His Bennington pastorate continued till Dec. 14, 1825, when he became secretary of the United Missionary Society of New York, an interdenominational agency working mainly in that state. Under his leadership the American Home Missionary Society was established in 1826, with which the New York society was merged. The new organization, likewise interdenominational, was nation-wide in its scope, having a board of trustees representing sixteen different states. During his twelve years as corresponding secretary the income of the society was increased threefold and the number of its missionaries was quadrupled. He traveled about 75,000 miles, largely under difficult frontier conditions, planted many churches, wrote all the society's annual reports, and from 1828 to 1836 edited the *Home Missionary and Pastor's Journal*.

During these years occurred the formation of the Old and New School parties in the Presbyterian Church, leading up to the schism of 1837. Peters was a Calvinist, but of the more liberal, or New England, type and naturally took his place on the New School side. Never seeking controversy, he did not shirk it when it appeared to be his duty, and his skill in debate was an important factor in the defense of Albert Barnes [*q.v.*] before the General Assembly of 1836. It was during this period, also, that the Union Theological Seminary in New York was founded by a group of Presbyterian clergymen and laymen. Peters, who was one of the leading clerical founders, was a member of several important committees and chairman of the one which drew up the constitution. He was also a director of the seminary from its foundation in 1836 to 1842. In 1837 he retired from his secretaryship to engage in literary pursuits. He became editor of the *American Biblical Repository*, a quarterly, in 1838, and in 1841 founded the bi-monthly *American Eclectic*. In 1842 he became financial agent for Union Seminary and the same year was appointed professor extraordinary of homiletics, pastoral theology, and church government.

Relinquishing all his work in New York in 1844, he became pastor of the First Congregational Church in Williamstown, Mass. Though not formally dismissed till 1857, he spent much of his time during the latter years of his pastorate in duties devolving upon him as financial agent for Williams College, of which he was a trustee from 1845 till his death, and the presidency of which he had declined in 1836. From 1856 he lived in New York, edited the *American Journal of Education and College Review*, and did much preaching and writing. Among his published works are: *Sprinkling the only Mode of Baptism and the Scripture Warrant for Infant Baptism* (1848); and *Life and Time, a Birthday Memorial of Seventy Years* (1866). The latter, written in verse, contains notes of much biographical value. He published, also, numerous sermons and other pamphlets, and left in manuscript "Cooperative Christianity; the Kingdom of Christ in Contrast with Denominational Churches," a title suggestive of his position on an important subject. On Oct. 25, 1819, he married Harriet Hinckley Hatch, daughter of Reuben Hatch of Norwich, Vt. Of their seven children, three sons and two daughters survived their parents.

[E. F. and E. B. Peters, *Peters of New England* (1903); G. L. Prentiss, *The Union Theological Sem. in the City of N. Y.*; *Hist. and Biog. Sketches of its First Fifty Years* (1889); G. T. Chapman, *Sketches of the Alumni of Dartmouth Coll.* (1867); Isaac Jennings, *Memorials of a Century; . . . the Early Hist. of Bennington, Vt., and its First Church* (1869); *N. Y. Tribune*, May 18, 1869.]   F. T. P.

PETERS, CHRISTIAN HENRY FREDERICK (Sept. 19, 1813–July 19, 1890), astronomer, was born at Coldenbüttel, Schleswig, the son of Hartwig Peters, a minister. Having studied at the Gymnasium in Flensburg from 1825 to 1832, he matriculated at the University of Berlin, where he studied mathematics and astronomy under Encke. After receiving his doctor's degree in 1836, he went to Göttingen to study under Gauss. From 1838 to 1843 he was engaged in a survey of Mount Etna, as a member of the scientific expedition organized by Sartorius von Waltershausen. He declined an offer of the directorship of the Catania Observatory on account of certain imposed conditions, but accepted the very important governmental post of director of the trigonometrical survey of Sicily. He was deprived of this position and ordered to leave the country when, in 1848, he sided with the Sicilian revolutionists; but he soon returned to Sicily, where he became naturalized and served as captain of engineers and later as major under Mieroslawski. Catania and Messina were fortified under his direction. After the fall of Palermo in 1849 he fled to France and soon after went to Constantinople. The Sultan planned to send him on a scientific expedition to Syria and Palestine but difficulties arose and eventually, with the beginning of the Crimean War, the plan was abandoned. During his stay here Peters acquired a good working knowledge of Arabic and Turkish, which was of great use to him in his later studies on Ptolemy's *Almagest*.

He came to the United States in 1854 with letters of recommendation from Alexander von Humboldt and obtained a position in the United States Coast Survey. He was stationed for a time at Cambridge, Mass., and at the Dudley Observatory in Albany, N. Y. In 1858 he was appointed director of the observatory at Hamilton College and in 1867, Litchfield Professor of Astronomy and director of the Litchfield Observatory. His scientific interests were wide, his ability and industry, marked. His researches on the sun, begun in Naples in 1845, and carried on until about 1865, blazed the way for further studies. Some of his conclusions were published in "Contributions to the Atmospherology of the Sun," in *Proceedings of the American Association for the Advancement of Science* (vol. IX, 1856). He described how sun spots were apparently divided by bridges of luminous gas, and investigated as far as his observational material permitted the motion of sun spots on the solar disk. After his death *Heliographic Positions of Sun-Spots, Observed at Hamilton College from 1860 to 1870* (1907), edited by E. B. Frost, was published. The task which he set himself in 1860, to prepare charts of the Zodiac, to give the positions of all stars in this belt visible in his 13-inch telescope, involved over 100,000 observations. Begun at a time when photography had not yet come into its own, these charts were to be a record of the sky at that time which could be compared, for the detection of changes, with similar charts made by future astronomers. The immediate result, however, was the discovery of forty-eight new asteroids—at that time a relatively large addition to the list of these bodies. He is said to have found recreation in computing their orbits. He also discovered two comets, one in 1846 while he was at Naples and one in

1857 when he was at Albany (*Monthly Notices of the Royal-Astronomical Society*, vol. VII, 1847; *Astronomical Journal*, Aug. 28, 1857). In 1874 he was sent as chief of the United States expedition to New Zealand to observe the transit of Venus. Observations were seriously hampered by clouds but that of the first internal contact with the sun's disk was successful. This transit was observed by many parties in different places, in the attempt to determine a more accurate value of the sun's distance. In 1869 he organized an expedition to observe the solar eclipse at Des Moines.

Peters also did a great deal of valuable work in the critical discussion and comparison of catalogues of star positions. About 1876 he started his attempt to prepare a more trustworthy edition of the star catalogue in the seventh and eighth books of Ptolemy's *Almagest*. This is the oldest catalogue containing positions of sufficient accuracy to be useful in comparison with modern catalogues for the detection of changes. The original is lost and the catalogue survives in a series of copyings and translations. The oldest copy extant was made several centuries after Ptolemy's time. Peters' task, therefore, was to collate as many of the copies as possible, Greek, Arabic, and Latin, decide what errors had been introduced, identify the stars, and try to recover the positions given in the original. He was well qualified for this task, for he was fluent in most of the European languages and had ample knowledge of Greek, Latin, Hebrew, Arabic, Persian, and Turkish. He had, also, high mathematical ability both in theory and computation. His industry and quick perception enabled him to give the problem the scrupulous study which it required. The examination of manuscripts took him to Vienna, Venice, Florence, Rome, and Paris. He was fortunate in having the collaboration of Edward B. Knobel who, equally interested in the problem, collated the British manuscripts, and, after Peters' death, edited the notes and catalogue (*Ptolemy's Catalogue of Stars; a Revision of the Almagest*, 1915). Among other records of Peters' work may be mentioned *Celestial Charts ... Made at the Litchfield Observatory of Hamilton College* (1882) and "Corrigenda in Various Star Catalogues," in *Memoirs of the National Academy of Sciences* (vol. III, pt. 2, 1886). He was a member of the National Academy of Sciences and a foreign associate of the Royal Astronomical Society. On his visit to Paris in 1887 to attend the convention to inaugurate the international photographic survey of the sky, the decoration of the Legion of Honor was conferred on him by the French government.

He was a man of the highest integrity and honor, courteous and kind and rich in friends.

[The *Am. Jour. Sci.*, the *Sidereal Messenger*, and Hamilton College bulletins use the English form of Peters' name, while the German form is frequently used elsewhere. For biographical data see J. G. Porter in *Sidereal Messenger*, Dec. 1890; A. Krueger, in *Astronomische Nachrichten*, Aug. 1890, also in *Bulletin Astronomique*, 1890; *Monthly Notices Royal Astronomical Society*, Feb. 1891; *Observatory*, Sept. 1890; *Christian Heinrich Friedrich Peters, 1813–1890: In Memoriam* (1890). For references to Peters' many articles in astronomical journals, see Royal Soc. of London, *Cat. of Scientific Papers*, vol. IV (1870), vol. X (1894).]   R. S. D.

PETERS, EDWARD DYER (June 1, 1849–Feb. 17, 1917), mining and metallurgical engineer, son of Henry Hunter and Susan Barker (Thaxter) Peters and a first cousin of John Punnett Peters [*q.v.*], was born in Dorchester, Mass., a descendant of Andrew Peters who was in Massachusetts as early as 1659. Upon his mother's side he was descended from several old Massachusetts families. His mother died soon after his birth and his father married a second time in 1854. Edward received his early education in Massachusetts schools and at the Episcopal School for Boys, Cheshire, Conn. Near the latter was an old tin mine, in exploring which he spent many Saturday afternoons. In 1865 his family went abroad to remain for several years and his technical education was obtained at the Royal School of Mines at Freiberg, Saxony, from which he graduated in 1869. Classroom instruction was supplemented by actual work in nearby mines and smelting works, and during vacation trips he visited mines and metallurgical plants, gathering valuable data on prevailing practices. The fall of 1869 found him in Colorado started on his active career, first as millman and assayer, then as superintendent and metallurgist at the Caribou silver mine. In 1872 he was appointed territorial assayer for southern Colorado, the local press congratulating the district upon obtaining the services of "so thorough and correct a metallurgist." During 1872–74 he designed, built, and successfully operated the Mount Lincoln smelting works.

When, in 1874, mining went into a decline, Peters returned East and, giving up hope of following his profession, entered the Harvard Medical School, graduating in 1877 at the head of a class of sixty-two members. He practised medicine in Dorchester, Mass., from 1877 until 1880, when he returned to mining. In the years immediately following he was associated with and originated some of the largest American copper and nickel smelting plants, including those of the Orford Nickel & Copper Company, Bergen Point, N. J., the Parrott Silver & Copper Company, Butte, Mont., and the Canadian Copper Company, Sudbury, Ont., where he "blew in" the first blast furnace in December 1888 for the production of nickel-copper matte. In 1892 he was called to inspect the Mount Lyell mine, a vast pyritic ore-body carrying some copper and gold, in a most inaccessible part of Tasmania. In Melbourne and other cities en route he was feted, made an honorary member of the principal clubs, and otherwise treated as a celebrity. The following year the results of his survey were published in *Report on the Property of the Mount Lyell Mining and Railway Company, Limited*. In 1893 and 1894, in the interests of the Mount Lyell company, he visited the Rio Tinto mines in Spain, the Mansfeld mines in Germany, and various mines in the western United States. Then for several years he was engaged in consulting work in connection with numerous mining enterprises in Mexico and the United States.

He lectured at Columbia School of Mines in 1901 and at Harvard in 1904. In the latter year he was appointed professor of metallurgy at Harvard and in 1909, Gordon McKay Professor of Metallurgy. During his last few years he held a professorship in the combined mining departments of Harvard and the Massachusetts Institute of Technology. As an author he made important contributions to technical literature, his most valuable work being *Modern American Methods of Copper Smelting* (1887), an authentic and comprehensive treatise which ran through fifteen editions, the last of which, 1895, bore the title *Modern Copper Smelting*. This was replaced by a new book, *The Practice of Copper Smelting* (1911). His other notable work was *The Principles of Copper Smelting* (1907). Peters was one of the commission to make the annual assay (1910) of the coin of the United States at the mint in Philadelphia.

On Sept. 28, 1881, he married his cousin, Anna Quincy Cushing; they had no children. He was something of a musician and in 'cello playing he found relaxation and satisfaction. A farm at Shirley, Mass., purchased in 1914, allowed him to indulge in another hobby—poultry raising. He died in Dorchester, Mass.

[E. F. and E. B. Peters, *Peters of New England* (1903); E. B. Peters, *Edward Dyer Peters, 1849–1917* (1918); *Bull. Am. Inst. Mining Engineers*, Aug. 1918; H. L. Smyth, in *Harvard Alumni Bull.*, Mar. 8, 1917; *Who's Who in America*, 1916–17.]   B. A. R.

PETERS, JOHN ANDREW (Oct. 9, 1822–Apr. 2, 1904), was born in Ellsworth, Me., the son of Andrew and Sally (Jordan) Peters. His father was a merchant and shipbuilder and one of the most prominent men of Ellsworth. The boy was educated at Gorham Academy and Yale College, where he graduated in 1842 with an oration on "The Profession of Politics." He then studied law at the Harvard Law School and in the office of Thomas Robinson of Ellsworth, and he was admitted to the bar in Ellsworth in 1844. Moving to Bangor in that year he began the practice of law in the office of Joshua W. Hathaway, whose partner he became. Later he entered into partnership with Franklin Augustus Wilson. On Sept. 2, 1846, he was married to Mary Ann Hathaway, the daughter of his partner, who died the following year, leaving a son who died in infancy. On Sept. 23, 1857, he was married to Fannie E. Roberts, the daughter of Amos M. Roberts of Bangor. They had two daughters.

His first political offices were those of state senator, 1862–63, and representative in 1864. In 1864 he became state attorney-general and served in that capacity until his election to Congress. Reëlected twice he remained in Congress from 1867 to 1873, working on the committee of patents and public expenditures, the committee on the judiciary, and the joint committee on the congressional library. He was much interested in national provision for the defense of the northeastern frontier and introduced bills for that purpose. As a friend of Blaine, then speaker, he several times sponsored measures that Blaine wished passed. Having refused further election to Congress he returned to Maine to be made at once, 1873, associate justice of the supreme judicial court of the state, and he was again chosen when his term expired in 1880. Three years later, 1883, he was elevated by Gov. Frederick Robie to the position of chief justice. His knowledge of the law, remarkable even when he began the practice of his profession, grew to be encyclopedic, and his decisions as chief justice were marked by lucidity and liberality. Because of their concise and untraditional nature they were much quoted in other states. His impartiality and fairness on the bench were famous, as were his imperturbable dignity and never-failing courtesy. A keen wit and overflowing humor, said to have been inherited from his mother, made him a most effective speaker both in campaigns and in the court room. As an after dinner speaker, he was thought to have no equal in his state. In 1900 his failing health caused his withdrawal from active public service. The remainder of his life was spent in Bangor, where he died.

[Biog. Record of the Class of 1842 of Yale College (1878); Obit. Record of Grads. of Yale Univ., 1904; Who's Who in America, 1903–05; Hist. of Penobscot County, Me. (1882); E. F. and E. B. Peters, Peters of New England (1903); T. F. Jordan, The Jordan Memorial (1882); The Peters' Banquet, Tendered the Hon. John A. Peters . . . 1900 (1900); Daily Kennebec Jour. (Augusta), Apr. 4, 1904; J. W. Porter, "Wayfarer Papers," vol. I, a collection of clippings from Bangor newspapers in Lib. of Me. Hist. Soc.]   M. E. L.

PETERS, JOHN CHARLES (July 6, 1819–Oct. 21, 1893), physician, medical writer, was born in New York City. Apparently he was a studious youth, brought up in a comfortable environment. His medical studies were pursued in Berlin, Vienna, and Leipzig. On his return from Europe he was examined by the Comitia Minora of the Medical Society of the County of New York in 1842 and licensed to practise medicine. His associations were such that he soon acquired a large private practice among the élite of New York. In 1844, with a number of others, he founded the New York Pathological Society; later he was one of the founders of the Medical Library and Journal Society, of which he wrote a brief history (see Detroit Review of Medicine and Pharmacy, November 1875). This organization in its turn contributed much to the greatness of the New York Academy of Medicine and its library. He took an early interest in homeopathy and ere long identified himself with that school of medicine and proceeded forthwith to make rich contributions to its literature. Many of these, issued between 1853 and 1856 from the press of William Radde, were treatises based on T. J. Rückert's Klinische Erfahrungen in der Homöopathie. They included discussions of headaches, apoplexy, diseases of women, diseases of the eye, and nervous and mental disorders. Peters was the author of The Science and Art or the Principles and Practice of Medicine (1858–59), of which only four parts, of ninety-six pages each, were issued. He also wrote "A Review of Some of the Late Reforms in Pathology and Therapeutics" (North American Journal of Homœopathy, February 1860), reprinted separately the same year with an appendix on the illnesses of Washington Irving; "Elements of a New Materia Medica and Therapeutics, Based upon an Entirely New Collection of Drug-provings and Clinical Experience," in collaboration with E. E. Marcy and Otto Füllgraff, published as an appendix to the North American Journal of Homœopathy, 1859–60, and never finished. From 1855 to 1861 Peters was a joint editor of the North American Journal of Homœopathy.

In 1861 the medical world was astonished by the publication in the issue for Aug. 17 of the American Medical Times, then the most influential medical journal in the United States, of Peters' renunciation of homeopathy. Although the article was simply a declaration of independence to indicate the writer's belief that no single system of treatment could be entirely adequate in practice, it brought upon Peters most severe criticisms from both sides. Many narrow-minded views were expressed by critics and the initial effect upon Peters was decided loss of prestige and practice, both of which, however, were regained within a few years. In his new environment he soon became an important factor. He was president of the New York County Medical Society, 1866–67, and continued his literary activity, devoting himself especially to investigation of infectious diseases, especially cholera and yellow fever. In collaboration with Ely McClellan he contributed "A History of the Travels of Asiatic Cholera" to *The Cholera Epidemic of 1873 in the United States* (1875), published by the United States Surgeon General's Office. He was a firm believer in the filth origin of the acute infections and was therefore prepared to accept very early the theory of the bacterial origin of disease.

Peters married, May 16, 1849, Georgina, daughter of Andrew Snelling. He died at Williston, L. I.

[T. L. Bradford, "Biographies of Homœopathic Physicians" (unpublished collection), in Library of Hahnemann Medic. Coll., Phila.; T. L. Bradford, *Homœopathic Bibliog.* (1892); Abraham Jacobi, in *Medic. Record* (N. Y.), Jan. 26, 1907; *Am. Physician,* July 1907; *U. S. Medic. Investigator,* Dec. 15, 1877; *Medic. and Surgic. Reporter,* Aug. 24, 1861; *Medic. Record* (N. Y.), Oct. 28, 1893; *N. Y. Tribune,* Oct. 24, 1893.]
C. B—t.

PETERS, JOHN PUNNETT (Dec. 16, 1852–Nov. 10, 1921), Episcopal clergyman, archeologist, was born in New York City the second son of the Rev. Thomas McClure Peters and Alice Clarissa (Richmond) Peters, and a lineal descendant of Andrew Peters, who came to America from Devonshire, England, appearing in Boston records as early as 1659, and became the first treasurer of the town of Andover, Mass. John attended church schools in New York until he was thirteen years old, and though compelled to abandon school for the next three years, occupied his time so well in private reading, with some aid from tutors, that he entered Yale University at the age of sixteen. He was a member of the first Yale football team, and a leader in intercollegiate football contests. After his graduation in 1873 he was a student in the Yale Divinity School, 1873–75, and in the Yale Graduate School, 1874–76, receiving the degree of Ph.D. in the latter year. From 1876 to 1879 he was a tutor in Yale College. In July 1876 he was ordained a deacon in the Protestant Episcopal Church, and in 1877, a priest. From 1879 to 1883 he was in Germany, studying Semitic languages at the University of Berlin, 1879–81; acting as minister-in-charge and then as rector of St. John's (American) Church, Dresden, 1881–82; and studying at the University of Leipzig, 1882–83. While in Dresden he translated Wilhelm Müller's *Politische Geschichte der neuesten Zeit, 1816–1875* (1875), and to his translation, published in 1882 under the title, *A Political History of Recent Times,* he added an appendix which continued the history to the date of publication. On his return to New York he took charge, for ten months, during his father's absence, of St. Michael's Church, of which his father was rector. In 1884 he became professor of the Old Testament language and literature in the Episcopal Divinity School in Philadelphia, and in 1886, professor of Hebrew in the University of Pennsylvania, holding the positions concurrently.

In 1883 he had obtained from Catharine Lorillard Wolfe [q.v.] a gift of $5,000 to finance an expedition of archeological reconnaissance in Babylonia. Its success, under the leadership of William Hayes Ward [q.v.], encouraged Peters to interest certain Philadelphians in raising a fund for archeological excavation in Babylonia under the auspices of the University of Pennsylvania. For two seasons, 1888–90, the mound of Nuffar, the site of the ancient Nippur, was explored under his personal leadership, and although after 1890 the field work was carried on by John Henry Haynes [q.v.], Peters remained scientific director until 1895. The fruit of his personal labors in this field was published in his *Nippur* (2 vols., 1897).

In 1891 he was made assistant rector of St. Michael's Church, New York, and resigned his post at the Philadelphia Divinity School, although he retained his professorship in the University of Pennsylvania until 1893. In that year, upon his father's death, he became rector of St. Michael's Church. When he resigned the position in 1919, he, his father, and his maternal grandfather, the Rev. William Richmond [q.v.], had held the position in unbroken succession for ninety-nine years. During his long service as rector of St. Michael's, Peters exerted a strong influence in behalf of missionary enterprise and a broader outlook in the Episcopal Church, and was a force in promoting social service and laboring for clean politics in the city and state of New York. In 1904, as vice-president of the Riverside and Morningside Heights Association, he began a long struggle against commercialized vice. He was an outstanding leader in the effort to bring about a better understanding between capital and labor. Some of the papers which this endeavor called forth from his pen were published in 1902 under the title, *Labor and Capi-*

tal. On the centenary of St. Michael's Church in 1907 he published a history of the parish entitled, *The Annals of St. Michael's.*

Through all his religious and social activities, Peters pursued his Biblical and Oriental studies, the results of which were embodied in the following books: *The Old Testament and the New Scholarship* (1901); *Early Hebrew Story* (1904); *Religion of the Hebrews* (1914); *The Psalms as Liturgies* (1922), and *Bible and Spade* (1922). In collaboration with a German scholar, Hermann Thiersch, he published *Painted Tombs in the Necropolis of Marissa* (1905), a description of discoveries the two had made while traveling in Palestine in 1902. In addition to these books Peters was a collaborator in *The Bible as Literature* (1896), *The Universal Anthology* (33 vols., 1899), and *The Historians' History of the World* (25 vols., 1905). After retiring from the rectorship of St. Michael's, he traveled for a year, then became professor of New Testament exegesis in the University of the South at Sewanee, Tenn., but in the autumn of 1921 his heart failed and he died. On Aug. 13, 1881, he had married Gabriella Brooke Forman, daughter of Thomas Marsh Forman of Savannah and Helen (Brooke) Forman of Virginia. Six of his seven children survived him. He was a combination of scholar and citizen of a type that is rapidly becoming extinct in these days of specialization. He was quiet in manner, but displayed originality and determination in the way in which he surmounted obstacles, both in his civic work and in his enterprises as an explorer. In his books he always had a fresh point of view to present; his writing was never an echo of the work of other men.

[E. F. and E. B. Peters, *Peters of New England* (1903); *Yale Univ. Obit. Record,* 1922; *Who's Who in America,* 1920–21; *Churchman,* Nov. 19, 1921; *N. Y. Times,* Nov. 11, 1921.]   G. A. B—n.

PETERS, MADISON CLINTON (Nov. 6, 1859–Oct. 12, 1918), clergyman, lecturer, and author, son of Morgan and Maria (Kemmerer) Peters, was born in Lehigh County, Pa. He was of German ancestry, a descendant of Caspar Peter who came to Philadelphia in 1731. His education was obtained under difficulties; he was unable to complete a college course, but studied at Muhlenberg College and at Franklin and Marshall College (1877–78). After graduating from Heidelberg Theological Seminary, Tiffin, Ohio, he was ordained in 1880 to the ministry of the Reformed Church, and during the next four years held a pastorate in Indiana and was minister to the Presbyterian Church at Ottawa, Ill. When only twenty-four years old he was called to the pastorate of the "First Presbyterian Church in the Northern Liberties," less than a mile north of what is now the shopping district of Philadelphia. For five years, as long as he remained, the church building was filled to its capacity every Sunday. In 1890 he left a prosperous church of nearly 500 members at Philadelphia to assume the pastorate of Bloomingdale Reformed Church in New York, where his abilities as a public speaker continued to attract much attention. Having become convinced that infant baptism is unscriptural, in 1900 Peters left the Reformed Church and accepted the pastorate of Sumner Avenue Baptist Church in Brooklyn. The following year he published a small book, *Why I Became a Baptist.* From 1904 to 1905 he served Immanuel Baptist Church in Baltimore, returning then to New York as pastor of the Baptist Church of the Epiphany, on Madison Avenue at Sixty-fourth Street. The organization was compelled to sell its property late in 1906, and within a brief period it went out of existence, after a history of nearly 120 years. Feeling the constraint of what seemed to him unnecessary sectarian intolerance, Peters soon transferred his membership from the Baptist to the Presbyterian Church, though without accepting a regular pastorate, and continued a Presbyterian until his death. For several years previous to 1907 he had been lecturing to large audiences and holding popular services in theaters and public halls. He now devoted himself to these activities, and to preparing syndicated newspaper articles and writing books. Calling himself "the people's preacher," apparently because of a feeling that many of the city churches were failing to reach the masses, he developed through these mediums a considerable influence among the unorganized religious-minded people of America. Some of his books attained a gratifying circulation, and his manuscripts continued to be welcomed by publishers until his death in his fifty-ninth year, a victim of the war-time influenza epidemic.

Of the twenty-five or more volumes issued by Peters, seventeen appeared during the last eighteen years of his life. Among these were *The Birds of the Bible* (1901); *The Man Who Wins* (1905); *Will the Coming Man Marry?* (1905), a discussion of problems of home and marriage; *After Death What?* (1908); *Sermons That Won the Masses* (1908); *How to Make Things Go* (1909); *Abraham Lincoln's Religion* (1909); *Seven Secrets of Success* (1916); and *Americans for America* (1916). Several of his books were written in behalf of the Jews, such as *Justice to the Jew* (1899); *The Jew as a Patriot* (1902); *The Jews in America* (1905); *Haym Salomon*

(1911) ; and *The Jews Who Stood by Washington* (1915). In 1917, the year before his death, he published *All for America* and *The Masons as Makers of America*; he had already published, in 1913, *The Mission of Masonry*. By his contemporaries he was known as a vigorous thinker, a popular and, at times, brilliant preacher, and a sincere, friendly man. In 1890 he married Sara H. Hart, by whom he had a son and two daughters.

[E. T. Corwin, *A Manual of the Reformed Church in America* (1902); Alfred Nevin, *Hist. of the Presbytery of Phila. and of Phila. Central* (1888); W. P. White and W. H. Scott, *The Presbyterian Church in Phila.* (1895); *Minutes of the Southern N. Y. Baptist Asso.* for 1906 and 1907; *Proc. and Addresses. Pa.-German Soc. of Phila.*, vol. XXX (1924); *Examiner,* Aug. 3, 1905; *Watchman-Examiner,* Oct. 17, 1918; *N. Y. Times,* Oct. 13, 1918; *Who's Who in America,* 1916–17; biog. sketch in preface to Peters' *Why I Became a Baptist* (1901).]   P.P.F.

PETERS, PHILLIS WHEATLEY [See WHEATLEY, PHILLIS, *c.* 1754–1784].

PETERS, RICHARD (*c.* 1704–July 10, 1776), clergyman, provincial secretary and councilor, was born in Liverpool, England, the second son of Ralph Peters, a barrister, and Esther Preeson. Richard finished the academic course at Westminster School before he was fifteen. While there he entered into a clandestine marriage with a servant maid. His parents hearing of it thereupon removed him to Leyden to study for three years. On returning to England he spent five years, against his will, at the Inner Temple studying law. A persistent desire to take orders finally conquered him and he became a deacon in the Church of England (1730) and a priest (1731), and in the latter year matriculated at Wadham College, Oxford. But criticism of his early marriage and the discovery that his second marriage, to a Miss Stanley, was bigamous, caused him so much unhappiness that about 1735 he decided to emigrate to Philadelphia. There he became assistant to the Rev. Archibald Cummings at Christ Church (1736) and is said to have "wriggled himself into the affections of the multitudes, who have generally been bred dissenters" (Keith, *post,* p. 236). An open quarrel with Cummings soon led to his withdrawal from the post. Two discourses, *The Two Last Sermons Preached at Christ's-church in Philadelphia, July 3, 1737* (1737), were a defense against Cummings' attacks upon his character and against charges that he was a papist.

Obliged to seek secular employment, Peters accepted in 1737 an appointment as secretary of the provincial land office which he held until 1760. He was also admitted to the Philadelphia bar. When Cummings died (1741), Peters' friends pressed his name as successor, but the conservatives in the congregation, fearing a rector with such strong proprietary sympathies, blocked his appointment. On Feb. 14, 1742/43, he was appointed provincial secretary and private secretary for the proprietaries, and clerk of the council, and on May 19, 1749, provincial councilor. As provincial secretary he superintended Indian affairs and went on frequent missions to the Indians, including the Albany Congress (1754) and the conference at Fort Stanwix (1768). He was suspicious of the Quaker hegemony in Pennsylvania, repeatedly wrote of "Quaker plots" to injure the proprietors with the King, and diligently endeavored to collect quit rents and to prosecute Scotch-Irish and German squatters. He retired as secretary and clerk of the council early in January 1762 with a comfortable fortune acquired from the Indian trade, but remained provincial councilor until 1776.

In 1762 Peters returned to the ministry, as rector of Christ and St. Peter's churches, though not actually receiving his license until he visited England in 1764–65. He was assiduous in building up the churches spiritually and numerically and toward their financial needs contributed generously from his own purse. For a zealous Highchurchman he was exceedingly tolerant, especially in later life. Toward the Quakers, whom he earlier viewed with distrust, he later developed a warm feeling, and he incurred the displeasure of the Archbishop of Canterbury for opening his churches in 1763 to George Whitefield, whose teachings he had actively opposed at an earlier time. Failing health compelled him to resign his rectorship on Sept. 23, 1775. Sincerely pious without ostentation, Peters was a polished and erudite scholar and a sound thinker, though sometimes given to quixotic views. He firmly believed that a thorough classical education was the best means of remedying existing social evils. Oxford conferred on him the degree of D.D. (1770). Loyal to the proprietaries to the last, he could not sanction separation from the mother country, but he accepted the change with a spirit of resignation. He was one of the first trustees of the Philadelphia Academy which later grew into the College of Philadelphia and from 1756 to 1764 was president of the board of trustees. He helped to organize the Library Company of Philadelphia and the Pennsylvania Hospital. Among his publications are *A Sermon on Education* (1751) and *A Sermon Preached in the New Lutheran Church of Zion, in the City of Philadelphia, 1769* (1769).

[The best account of Peters' life, though hardly adequate, is printed in C. P. Keith, *The Provincial Councillors of Pa.* (1883). See also the Peters Papers, 12 vols., and Letter Books of Richard Peters, 1737–1750, in the library of the Hist. Soc. of Pa., Philadelphia;

N. P. Black, *Richard Peters: His Ancestors and Descendants, 1810–1899* (1904); C. P. B. Jefferys, "The Provincial and Revolutionary Hist. of St. Peter's Ch., Phila., 1753–83," *Pa. Mag. of Hist. and Biog.*, Jan. 1924; W. S. Perry, *The Hist. of the Am. Episc. Ch.* (1885), vol. I; *Pa. Archives*, 1 ser. II–IV (1853); *Minutes of the Provincial Council of Pa.*, vols. IV–X (1851–52); *Pa. Mag. of Hist. and Biog.*, Oct. 1886, July 1899, Oct. 1905, Apr., Oct. 1907, Oct. 1914.]

J. H. P—g.

PETERS, RICHARD (June 22, 1744–Aug. 22, 1828), lawyer, Revolutionary patriot, judge, farmer, son of William Peters and his second wife, Mary Breintnall, was born at "Belmont," the family home, in Philadelphia. His father, an elder brother of the Rev. Richard Peters [*q.v.*], was a lawyer, was born in England, and came to Pennsylvania some time prior to 1739. He was register of admiralty (1744–71) and judge of the court of common pleas, quarter sessions and orphans court. In his youth Richard was greatly influenced by his uncle from whom he acquired a thorough knowledge of the classics and of whom he later wrote: "I was his adopted son and constant companion. With no man . . . have I ever enjoyed more pleasure, or solid instruction, or delight" (Octavius Pickering and C. W. Upham, *The Life of Timothy Pickering*, IV, 1873, p. 205). At his uncle's home he met Washington, George Whitefield, and other prominent men. He attended the Philadelphia Academy and graduated from the College of Philadelphia, now the University of Pennsylvania, in 1761. Ambitious to follow the profession of his father, he then studied law, was admitted to the bar in 1763, and soon acquired a successful practice. He was a commissioner to the Indian conference at Fort Stanwix (1768) and from 1771 to 1776 was register of admiralty.

Although previously associated with the proprietaries, at the outbreak of the Revolution Peters aligned himself with the Whigs and in May 1775 was chosen captain of militia. His military career, however, was short-lived. On June 13, 1776, Congress elected him secretary of the board of war of which he became a full-fledged member on Nov. 27, 1777. Much of the drudgery of the board's work fell upon him and after the summer of 1780 he seems to have managed the war office alone (*The Life of Timothy Pickering*, I, 1867, pp. 216, 229). He was particularly diligent in exposing the peculations of Benedict Arnold and in the latter part of the war in raising money and provisions for the army. He resigned from the board in December 1781 when a single-headed department of war was inaugurated. On Nov. 12, 1782, he was elected to Congress for one year. In 1785 he traveled in Europe, and while in England was instrumental in obtaining the ordination of three bishops for the Episcopal Church in America. He was a member of the Pennsylvania Assembly (1787–90), serving as speaker the last two years, and of the state Senate (1791–92), serving as speaker there also. When the new federal government was organized he was tendered the appointment of comptroller of treasury but declined the post.

On Apr. 11, 1792, Peters was commissioned judge of the United States district court of Pennsylvania. He held this office for the remainder of his life. In the controversy between the federal and state judiciaries the former received his ardent support and in the sphere of admiralty law his decisions have served to distinguish between the judicial and political authorities of the government. Justice Joseph Story later declared himself indebted to Peters "for his rich contributions to the maritime jurisprudence of our country" (W. W. Story, *Life and Letters of Joseph Story*, 1851, I, p. 540). His opinion (*United States* vs. *Worrall*, April 1798) that there was a common law of the United States from which the federal courts acquired a jurisdiction over crimes in addition to that bestowed by federal statute was the basis for prosecutions for libel against the federal government by the Federalists prior to the passage of the sedition law (1798). He published *Admiralty Decisions in the District Court of the United States for the Pennsylvania District, 1780–1807* (1807).

Peters was also a practical farmer. The "Memoirs" of the Philadelphia society for the promotion of agriculture, of which he was the first president, contain more than one hundred papers by him on the subject of agriculture. On his estate he experimented with new agricultural methods, with different breeds of sheep and cattle, with dairy products, and continually exchanged ideas with Washington and his other farmer friends. His *Agricultural Enquiries on Plaister of Paris* (1797) exercised a wide influence in introducing the culture of clover and other grasses. *A Discourse on Agriculture; its Antiquity* (1816), an exposition of agricultural development from earliest times, stresses the need for scientific farming, urges the use of plaster of Paris and other fertilizers, the growth of clover, scientific drainage, premiums for excellence in production, and a state-planned system of roads and canals to give a "more elastic spring" to agriculture. Peters was a brilliant conversationalist, noted for his witticisms, and beloved by his friends for his kindliness and sympathetic feeling. Both in public and private matters he was punctual, painstaking, and patient. His estate, "Belmont," inherited from his father, and standing high on the west bank of the Schuylkill, was the scene of frequent visits by his large circle of prominent friends. From 1788 to 1791 he was a trustee of the University of Pennsylvania. His wife was Sarah Robinson, whom he married in August 1776 and by whom he had six children. Richard Peters, 1810–1889 [*q.v.*], was a grandson.

Peters' son Richard (Aug. 4, 1779–May 2, 1848) succeeded Henry Wheaton as reporter for the United States Supreme Court and compiled the *Reports of Cases in the Supreme Court of the United States, 1828 to 1842* (16 vols., 1828–42). His other published works include: *Reports of Cases in the Circuit Court of the United States for the Third Circuit . . . District of New Jersey, 1803 to 1818, and in the District of Pennsylvania, 1815 to 1818* (1819); *Reports of Cases . . . in the Circuit Court of the United States, for the Third Circuit . . . from the Manuscripts of . . . Bushrod Washington* (4 vols., 1826–29); *Condensed Reports of Cases in the Supreme Court of the United States . . . from its Organization to the Commencement of Peters's Reports* (6 vols., 1830–34); *The Public Statutes at Large of the United States . . . 1789 to Mar. 3, 1845* (1848); and *A Practical Treatise on the Criminal Law* (3 vols., 1847), an edition of the work of Joseph Chitty.

[See: Samuel Breck, *Address Delivered . . . on the Death . . . the Hon. Richard Peters* (1828), reprinted in *Reg. of Pa.*, Nov. 1, 1828; N. P. Black, *Richard Peters: His Ancestors and Descendants, 1810–1889* (1904); A. J. Dallas, *Reports of Cases Ruled and Adjudged in the Several Courts of the U. S.* (4 vols., 1790–1807); J. W. Stinson, "Opinions of Richard Peters (1781–1817)," *Univ. of Pa. Law Rev.*, Mar. 1922; H. D. Eberlein and H. M. Lippincott, *The Colonial Homes of Phila.* (1912); J. T. Scharf and Thompson Westcott, *Hist. of Phila.* (1884), vol. I; *Minutes of the Provincial Council of Pa.*, vols. X–XVI (1852–53); *Pa. Archives*, 1 ser. V–XII (1853–56); *Pa. Mag. of Hist. and Biog.*, July 1899, July 1916, Oct. 1920; and *Poulson's Am. Daily Advertiser*, Aug. 23, 25, 1828. There are 12 volumes of Peters Papers in the library of the Pa. Hist. Soc. at Philadelphia.]   J. H. P—g.

PETERS, RICHARD (Nov. 10, 1810–Feb. 6, 1889), civil engineer, railroad superintendent, agriculturist and financier, was born in Germantown, Pa., of English-Irish and Scotch-Irish ancestry. His parents were Ralph and Catherine (Conyngham) Peters; his paternal grandfather was Richard Peters, 1744–1828 [*q.v.*], Revolutionary leader and federal district judge. His formal education began at the age of five and continued until his family, after financial reverses, moved first to Wilkes-Barre (1821) and then to Bradford County (1823 or 24), where Richard worked on a farm and led an outdoor life. With a few dollars which he had made in the maple-sugar business he went to Philadelphia, where for eighteen months he studied mathematics, drawing, and writing, to prepare

himself for work in the office of William Strickland [*q.v.*], the architect; here he spent six months. Being predisposed to a more active life, and, according to his own account, unfitted for architecture, he assisted in the construction of the Delaware Breakwater, and then for a short time became an assistant engineer in the location of the Camden & Amboy Railroad. An old friend, J. Edgar Thomson [*q.v.*], the chief engineer of the newly organized Georgia railroad, made him an assistant engineer. Peters went to Georgia in 1835, having landed at Charleston and continued his journey over the new Charleston & Hamburg Railroad. He was so successful in surveying the Georgia road, carrying on his work as far as Madison, that two years later he was made superintendent. He immediately became intensely interested in this road, and showed his faith in its future by investing his savings in it. He gave full sway to his inventive genius by devising a spark arrester, and he arranged for running trains in the night by improvising sleeping quarters in the coaches and constructing a headlight on the locomotive by burning pine knots on a sand bed, constructed in front of the smokestack.

On the completion of the Georgia Railroad to Marthasville (1846), a name which he soon changed to Atlanta, he resigned the superintendency. In the meantime (1844), he had set up a stage line from Madison, Ga., to Montgomery, Ala., a business which he continued until the competition of the Atlanta & West Point Railroad, completed a few years later, led him to transfer his stages to a route from Montgomery to Mobile. He continued the latter route until the outbreak of the Civil War. His interest in promoting transportation facilities westward was shown further by his election in 1860 to the presidency of the Georgia Western Railroad (Phillips, *post*, pp. 370–72), and after the Civil War by his directorship of the Atlanta & West Point Railroad. Moving to Atlanta soon after the completion of the railroad to that point, he developed an unbounded faith in that growing railway center and he continued as one of its greatest promoters until his death. Here in 1856 he set up the largest flour mill south of Richmond, and for a source of wood supply he bought 400 acres of land, which later became the heart of Atlanta and greatly enhanced his fortune. In 1847 he had bought 1,500 acres of land in Gordon County and with slave labor developed it into a model plantation. Here he experimented with the best strains of live stock and introduced new plant crops to the South. He bought from the Ural Mountains Angora goats, and he brought to the South some of the finest breeds of horses and cattle; he promoted the raising of sorghum in the South, and reëstablished silk culture. He promoted these interests by occasionally contributing articles to various magazines.

In politics he was a conservative Whig, who opposed secession but loyally accepted the new order when Georgia seceded. During the war he responded to all calls for aid, and at the same time greatly increased his wealth by organizing a blockade-running company. When Sherman burned Atlanta he fled to Augusta, but he was among the first to return and help rebuild the city when connections were reopened. He worked for the removal of the capital from Milledgeville to Atlanta in 1868, and three years later he was a chief promoter in the construction of eleven miles of street railway, becoming president of the company the following year. In 1870 he became one of the lessees and directors of the Western & Atlantic Railway, running from Atlanta to Chattanooga. Though he had no political ambitions, he became a member of the city council soon after the war, and in the early eighties he was elected a county commissioner.

With all his wealth, estimated at over a million dollars, and with his varied interests, Peters found time to be extremely kind and considerate in all his business and social dealings. He was an Episcopalian, and, after the Civil War, a Democrat. He had a robust physique and handsome features. On Feb. 18, 1848, he married Mary Jane Thompson of Atlanta, and to them were born nine children, three daughters and six sons. Seven survived him on his death in Atlanta.

[*Atlanta Constitution*, Feb. 6, 1889; W. J. Northen, ed., *Men of Mark in Georgia* (1911), III, 495–97; A. D. Candler and C. A. Evans, eds., *Georgia* (1906), III, 87–89; U. B. Phillips, *A Hist. of Transportation in the Eastern Cotton Belt to 1860* (1908); N. P. Black, *Richard Peters. His Ancestors and Descendants, 1810–1899* (1904); H. W. Grady, *Forty Years All Told Spent in Live Stock Experiments in Ga.: Richard Peters' Experiments in Live Stock Farming* (n.d.), and article in *Atlanta Constitution*, Oct. 12, 1884.]   E.M.C.

PETERS, SAMUEL ANDREW (Nov. 20, 1735–Apr. 19, 1826), Anglican clergyman, Loyalist, son of John and Mary (Marks) Peters, was born at Hebron, Conn., a descendant of Andrew Peters whose name first appears in Massachusetts records in 1659. He was educated at Yale College, receiving the degrees of bachelor of arts in 1757 and master of arts in 1760. King's College conferred the degree of M.A. on him in 1761 and in later life he claimed to have received that of LL.D. from the University of Cortona in Tuscany, although no such institution seems ever to have existed. In 1758 he went to England to receive holy orders in the Anglican church and in

the following year was ordained deacon and priest and appointed missionary by the Society for the Propagation of the Gospel in Foreign Parts. In 1760 he returned to America and for the next fourteen years served as rector of the Anglican church at Hebron and ministered to the surrounding country. On Feb. 14, 1760, he was married to Hannah Owen, who died Oct. 25, 1765; on June 25, 1769, to Abigail Gilbert, who died July 14, 1769; and on Apr. 21, 1773, to Mary Birdseye, who died June 16, 1774.

As the controversy between Great Britain and the colonies approached a crisis, he was suspected of informing the Bishop of London and the Society for the Propagation of the Gospel in Foreign Parts of events in America, and on the morning of Aug. 15, 1774, he was visited by the Sons of Liberty, who examined his papers and forced him to sign a declaration that he had not written and would not write to England. Following a sermon in which he advised his congregation not to contribute aid or supplies for the relief of Boston, he was again visited by a mob, Sept. 6, 1774, and upon the discovery that he had arms in his house, he was carried to the meeting-house green and forced to sign and read a declaration and humble confession. Shortly after this incident he fled to Boston, leaving behind him a twelve-year-old daughter, an infant son, and some twenty slaves, eleven of whom were liberated by the General Assembly of Connecticut in 1789. On Oct. 25, 1774, he sailed from Portsmouth, N. H., for England, where he received a small pension from the Crown.

He took up his residence in London and occasionally preached in the churches of the city. He wrote for British periodicals and in 1781 published *A General History of Connecticut*, containing his famous account of the "blue laws" which, he alleged, were in force then. It is a highly unfavorable description of the colony of his birth but not as false as some of its critics in New England have maintained. In 1785 he published *A Letter to the Rev. John Tyler, A.M.: concerning the Possibility of Eternal Punishments, and the Improbability of Universal Salvation.* He hoped to obtain an American bishopric and in 1794 he was elected bishop of Vermont by a convention of Episcopal clergymen which met at Rutland, and sent John A. Graham to England to secure his consecration at the hands of the Archbishop of Canterbury. Peters accepted the bishopric and prepared to sail for America in the following spring but on the plea that he was limited by the Act of Parliament of January 1786, and could create no more American bishops, the Archbishop of Canterbury refused to consecrate him. About 1804 Peters lost his pension. He had known Jonathan Carver [q.v.], the explorer, in England, and at the request of Carver's American heirs returned to America in 1805 to further their claim to a large tract of land to the east of the Mississippi River at the Falls of St. Anthony, which they claimed Carver had received from the Sioux Indians in 1767. In March 1806 Peters appeared before a committee of the United States Senate in behalf of Carver's heirs, and in November 1806 he bought their claim. He succeeded in interesting a company of New York merchants in a scheme to settle the territory on the Mississippi and in the summer of 1817 he himself set out to visit the region and spent the following winter at Prairie du Chien, but in 1826 Congress disallowed the claim. After Peters' return to America he published *A History of the Reverend Hugh Peters, A.M.* (1807). He claimed Hugh Peter [q.v.] as his great-grand-uncle, but the relationship has been disproved. Peters died at New York in his ninety-first year and was buried at Hebron.

[E. F. Peters and E. B. Peters, *Peters of New England* (1903); F. B. Dexter, *Biog. Sketches Grads. Yale Coll.*, vol. II (1896); Zadock Thompson, *Hist. of Vt.* (1842); W. W. Folwell, *A Hist. of Minn.*, vol. I (1921); W. B. Sprague, *Annals Am. Pulpit*, vol. V (1859); W. S. Perry, *The Hist. of the Am. Episcopal Church* (2 vols., 1885); E. E. Beardsley, *The Hist. of the Episcopal Church in Conn.* (2 vols., 1866–68); I. W. Stuart, *Life of Jonathan Trumbull, Sen., Gov. of Conn.* (1859); *The True-Blue Laws of Conn. and New Haven and the False Blue-Laws Invented by the Rev. Samuel Peters* (1876), ed. by J. H. Trumbull; J. H. Trumbull, *The Reverend Samuel Peters, His Defenders and Apologists* (1877); W. F. Prince, "An Examination of Peters's 'Blue Laws,'" *Ann. Report Am. Hist. Asso. for 1898* (1899); D. S. Durrie, "Captain Jonathan Carver, and 'Carver's Grant,'" *Report and Colls., State Hist. Soc. of Wis.*, vol. VI (1872); Milo M. Quaife, "Jonathan Carver and the Carver Grant," *Miss. Valley Hist. Rev.*, June 1920; *Am. Archives*, ed. by Peter Force, 4 ser. I (1837), II (1839); *Am. State Papers, Public Lands*, vol. IV (1859); *The Correspondence of John A. Graham, with His Grace of Canterbury, When on His Mission as Agent of the Church of Vt., to the Ecclesiastical Courts of Canterbury and York, for the Consecration of Dr. Peters, Bishop Elect of Vt., 1794–95* (1835); S. J. McCormick, "Dr. Samuel Peters," *Churchman*, May 26 and June 2, 1877.] I. M. C.

PETERS, WILLIAM CUMMING (Mar. 10, 1805–Apr. 20, 1866), music publisher, musician, was born in Woodbury, Devonshire, England. Between the years 1820 and 1823 he came to America with his parents and lived for a short time in Texas. During these same years he studied music with his father, although as a musician he was largely self-instructed. From 1825 to 1828 he taught music in Pittsburgh, and in 1829 moved to Louisville, Ky., where he opened a music store. In 1839 he opened a branch house in Cincinnati, and in 1849 another branch in Baltimore. His home during his later years was in Cincinnati, and it was there that he died sud-

denly of heart disease at the age of sixty-one.

Peters was an important factor in the musical life of the cities in which he lived, and he was especially significant because of his connection with Stephen Collins Foster [q.v.]. According to evidence and tradition it was Peters who was among the first to profit by Foster's songs. When Foster lived in Cincinnati during the years 1846 to 1849 he was a song writer by avocation rather than by profession. He had written several songs which were sung by minstrel performers, and they were so successful that Peters asked Foster to let him publish them. Accordingly Foster gave Peters a number of songs, among them "Susanna," "Louisiana Belle," and "Old Uncle Ned." In spite of other, pirated editions of "Susanna," it is said that Peters made over $10,000 from the sale of Foster's songs. It was probably this success that enabled Peters to expand his business, and to become one of the leading music publishers of the Mid-West. Foster received little, if anything, from Peters. According to one tradition he was paid one hundred dollars for "Susanna" and nothing for "Uncle Ned" (R. P. Nevin, "Stephen C. Foster and Negro Minstrelsy," *Atlantic Monthly*, November 1867). Other reports state that Foster made Peters an outright gift of all the songs. For one year in Baltimore Peters edited and published a musical magazine, the *Olio*. In the final issue, December 1850, a statement was made that the magazine would be discontinued, not because of lack of support, but because of the editor's health, and the difficulty of procuring music plates in Baltimore.

Peters was active as a leader of concerts and choirs, and in composing and writing. He wrote music for the Roman Catholic Church, including a Mass in D. He compiled *Peters' Catholic Harmonist* (1848); *Catholic Harp* (1862), and a number of educational works, among them the *Eclectic Piano Instructor* (1855). He was the editor of a revised and enlarged edition of *Burrowes' Piano Forte Primer* (1849, again revised, 1869). Among his original compositions were "Citizens Guards' March" (1841); "Sweet Memories of Thee" (1839), a song, and "Kind, Kind and Gentle is She" (1840), "a favourite Scotch ballad."

[Information regarding Peters is meager. A number of his compositions are available in collections of old music. For biographical material see W. A. Fisher, *One Hundred and Fifty Years of Music Publishing in the U. S.* (1933); E. J. Wohlgemuth, *Within Three Chords* (1928); *Cincinnati Daily Gazette*, *Cincinnati Commercial*, Apr. 21, 1866; *Appletons' Cyc. Am. Biog.* A complete file of the *Olio* for 1850 is in the collection of Foster Hall, Indianapolis, Ind.] J. T. H.

PETERSON, CHARLES JACOBS (July 20, 1819–Mar. 4, 1887), editor, publisher, and anthor, was born in Philadelphia, Pa., the eldest of the five sons of Thomas P. and Elizabeth Snelling (Jacobs) Peterson. Three of his brothers, Theophilus B., Thomas, and George W., later formed the book-publishing house known as T. B. Peterson & Brothers; Henry Peterson [*q.v.*], editor, publisher, and poet, was his cousin. They were descended from Erick Pieterson (a godson of Archbishop Laurence Pieterson of Sweden) who settled with a Swedish colony on the Delaware in 1638. Charles was a non-graduate member of the class of 1838, University of Pennsylvania, studied law, and was admitted to the bar, but never entered upon legal practice.

When George R. Graham [*q.v.*] purchased *Atkinson's Casket* (later *Graham's Magazine*) in May 1839, he associated the twenty-year-old Peterson with him in its editorship—a relation maintained until the founding of Peterson's own magazine. It has been said that a quarrel with Peterson was the reason for Poe's leaving his editorial position on *Graham's* (John Sartain, *Reminiscences of a Very Old Man,* 1899), though different reasons have been assigned for that rupture by other observers. In March 1840 Peterson purchased the interest of John DuSolle in the *Saturday Evening Post,* thereby becoming doubly the partner of Graham, this time in both editing and publishing. After just three years of this latter connection, he sold his interest to Samuel D. Patterson. In 1840, acting upon a hint from Graham, he founded the *Lady's World,* the name of which was changed in 1843 to the *Ladies' National Magazine* and in 1848 to *Peterson's Magazine.* In this venture he took as an associate Ann Sophia Stephens [*q.v.*], who had been connected with *Graham's,* and who remained a leading contributor to *Peterson's* until her death in 1886. Though she was sometimes listed as editor, Peterson himself was *de facto* editor for the forty-seven years from the founding of the magazine until his own death. *Peterson's* was an imitator of the successful *Godey's Lady's Book,* which it underbid in subscription price, and outstripped in circulation and influence shortly after the Civil War. In the seventies it gained a circulation—unusual at that time—of 150,000 copies. Peterson was also actively engaged in daily and weekly journalism at various times, and wrote sketches and verse for periodicals. He was an editor of Joseph C. Neal's *Saturday Gazette* in the middle forties. When the *Philadelphia Bulletin* was begun in 1847, he was one of its editorial writers; he also worked in that capacity for the *Public Ledger.* He wrote *The Military Heroes of the Revolution, with a Narrative of the War of Independence* (1848) and similar treat-

ments of the War of 1812 and the Mexican War. In 1849 *Grace Dudley, or Arnold at Saratoga* appeared. This was followed by several other historical novels, including *Kate Aylesford, a Story of the Refugees* (1855), *Mabel, or Darkness and Dawn* (1857), and *The Old Stone Mansion* (1859). His most important work was a history of the American navy, first published as *The Naval Heroes of the United States* (1850) and later, in more comprehensive form, as *A History of the United States Navy* (1852) and *The American Navy, Being an Authentic History* (1856). Peterson's was an expansive and genial personality, and he had a notable capacity for friendship. He belonged to that group of littérateurs and magazinists who made Philadelphia a literary center in the forties. His friends have eulogized his cultivation, refinement, and studious habits. He died in Philadelphia, his last days shadowed by the accidental death of an only son. His wife was Sarah Powell, daughter of Charles Pitt Howard.

[Univ. of Pa., *Biog. Cat. of Matriculates of the College* (1893); A. H. Smyth, *The Phila. Mags. and Their Contributors* (1892); *Phila. Inquirer* and *Public Ledger,* both Mar. 7, 1887; *Press* (Phila.), Mar. 6, 1887; *Peterson's Mag.,* May 1887.]   F. L. M.

PETERSON, HENRY (Dec. 7, 1818–Oct. 10, 1891), editor-publisher and poet, was born in Philadelphia, Pa., the son of George and Jane (Evans) Peterson. He was a cousin of Charles Jacobs Peterson [*q.v.*]. Henry Peterson was largely self-educated, being compelled to go to work in a hardware store at the age of fourteen. He formed a partnership with Edmund Deacon for the publication of cheap manuals and reprints when he was twenty-one. For a short time he was connected editorially with Joseph C. Neal's *Saturday Gazette,* and in 1846 he succeeded George R. Graham as editor of the *Saturday Evening Post.* In February 1848 Deacon & Peterson bought the *Post* from Samuel D. Patterson & Company and became sole owners and editors. For twenty-five years, with some changes in partners, Peterson remained the controlling personality in the *Post,* reducing its attention to news and increasing its emphasis on fiction and verse. It was an eight-page folio, of newspaper format, and the oldest of the many American weekly story papers. In April 1873 Peterson sold his interest in this periodical to the Saturday Post Publishing Company, but he remained with it in an editorial capacity for another year. Thereafter he devoted himself to the writing of poetry and fiction. He had already published *Poems* (1863), and *The Modern Job* (1869), a dramatic and philosophical poem of three thousand blank-verse lines with its setting in Pennsylvania. *Pemberton* (1873), a historical novel of the Revolution, was reprinted in 1887 and 1900. *Faire-mount* (1874) is a historico-philosophical poem in couplets. *Helen; or, One Hundred Years Ago,* a poetical drama, was produced in Philadelphia in 1876. *Confessions of a Minister* (1874) and *Bessie's Lovers* (1877) are novels. They were followed by *Caesar: A Dramatic Study* (1879), *Poems: Second Series* (1883), including *The Modern Job* and *Faire-mount,* and the posthumously published *Columbus* (1893), a dramatic poem in six acts. On Oct. 28, 1842, Peterson married Sarah Webb, of Wilmington, Del., a poet, who edited from 1864 to 1874 the *Lady's Friend,* a fashion magazine published by Deacon & Peterson and modeled upon *Godey's Lady's Book.* Peterson's verse, while not distinguished, has ease and thoughtfulness; his chief service was that which he rendered to popular literature in connection with the *Saturday Evening Post.* He died at his home in Germantown, Pa.

[There are no complete files of the *Saturday Evening Post,* but the connections of Henry Peterson with it may be noted in the file in possession of the *Post* itself. For biographical details see J. W. Jordan, *Encyc. of Pa. Biog.,* vol. X (1918) and the *Pub. Ledger* (Phila.), Oct. 12, 1891.]   F. L. M.

PETIGRU, JAMES LOUIS (May 10, 1789–Mar. 9, 1863), lawyer, political leader, was born in Abbeville District, S. C. He was the son of William Pettigrew, a native of Virginia, and Louise Guy Gilbert, the daughter of a Huguenot minister. He bore the names of his two grandfathers: James Pettigrew, who came to Pennsylvania in 1740 from County Tyrone, Ireland, and moved successively to Virginia, North Carolina, and South Carolina; and Jean Louis Gibert, who brought a party of Huguenots to South Carolina in 1763. Since the family was large and means were small, he worked from childhood, securing such schooling as he could. In 1804 he entered the famous school of Dr. Moses Waddell at Willington, and two years later South Carolina College, where, supporting himself by teaching in Columbia, he finished the course and received the A.B. degree in 1809. About this time, apparently, he changed the spelling of his name (Carson, *post,* p. 35). He taught in St. Luke's Parish and at Beaufort for the next three years, studying law the while, and was admitted to the bar in 1812. In that year, although as an intense Federalist he opposed the war, he served for a short while in the militia. Settling at Coosawhatchie, in 1816 he was elected solicitor, and, on Aug. 17, he married Jane Amelia Postell, the daughter of a nearby planter. In 1819 James Hamilton, Jr. [q.v.] offered him an attractive

partnership and he moved to Charleston, where he spent the rest of his life. Rapidly gaining reputation, in 1822 he was elected attorney general, a post much to his liking which he unwillingly resigned in 1830 to become a Union candidate for the state Senate. He was defeated, but within a few weeks was elected to fill a vacancy in the lower house. A thorough-going nationalist, he was an intense opponent of nullification, for which he could find no justification in law, logic, or morals. He wrote a friend, "I am devilishly puzzled to know whether my friends are mad, or I beside myself" (Carson, p. 79). He disliked politics but felt compelled to participate in such a crisis, and, making many speeches, writing numerous newspaper articles, and contributing much wise counsel, found himself in 1832 the leader of the Union party. He wrote the address to the people issued by the Union convention in September (*Southern Patriot,* Sept. 15, 1832) and the protest against the nullification ordinance in December. In the period which followed, he naturally opposed the imposition of the test oath and won the decision from the court of appeals which declared it unconstitutional (2 *S. C.,* 1, 113). During the resulting bitter struggle, he and Hamilton, by cooperation, prevented any collision between their excited followers and finally effected a satisfactory compromise.

From the close of the nullification controversy to the end of his life Petigru held no office, save for two years that of United States district attorney, which he accepted as a matter of duty at the earnest request of President Fillmore when no one could be induced to do so. In 1859 he was elected code commissioner and by annual election retained the position until the completion of the work in 1863 (*Portion of the Code of Statute Law of South Carolina,* 1860–62). He opposed secession but was hopeless of checking the movement. Asked by a stranger in Columbia in December 1860 the location of the insane asylum, he pointed to the Baptist church where the secession convention had just assembled and said: "It looks like a church, but it is now a lunatic asylum; go right there and you will find one hundred and sixty-four maniacs within" (Lewis, *post,* IV, 71–72). But he could not always joke about it. Mistaking the bells for a fire alarm and being told that they announced secession, he exclaimed: "I tell you there is a fire; they have this day set a blazing torch to the temple of constitutional liberty, and please God, we shall have no more peace forever" (*Ibid.,* p. 72). Yet coercion surprised and grieved him, and, in spite of his intellectual belief, passionately held, that the cause was bad, his heart was with the Southern rather than the Northern arms. But his heart was not with the Confederate government. He opposed the Confederate sequestration act in the district court, because, he said, he was free born. During the war his home in Charleston was lost by fire and a house on Sullivan's Island was destroyed in the erection of fortifications.

Petigru was known and admired all over the country. Lincoln seriously considered appointing him to the Supreme Court to replace Justice McLean or Justice Campbell but the difficulties in the way, combined with Petigru's age, dissuaded him. Petigru's position as "the greatest private citizen that South Carolina has ever produced," was unique. An admirer thus describes it: "He never occupied high public station, and yet he was a statesman. He never held judicial positions, and yet he was a great jurist. He never wrote books, and yet his life itself is a volume to be studied. He never founded a charity, and yet he was a great-hearted philanthropist" (Lewis, IV, 30–31). A superb advocate, he was the undisputed head of the state bar for nearly forty years. The profound legal learning he displayed in a case was matched by the simplicity of his deductive reasoning. He "turnpiked the legal pathway out of the most complicated labyrinth of law and fact" (*Memorial*, p. 11). In public affairs Petigru was doomed to the minority because of his nationalism. In other things he largely agreed with his neighbors. He opposed protection vigorously, and, while he did not like the institution of slavery, he was no abolitionist and owned slaves and approved of the domestic side of slavery. Politically, he was perhaps more sympathetic with free-soil ideas than his associates. A friend, always, of the lowly and oppressed, having a passion for mercy combined with his love of justice, he was ready in defence of the slave, the poor white, or the free negro who sought his aid. His manner was hearty, even inclined to be hilarious, but scrupulously courteous. He wrote well and had an unusual voice, capable of expressing every shade of feeling, that made him a really great speaker. In the heart of bitter controversy he retained the respect and the affection of his opponents, and the lasting quality of his fame is evidence of the dynamic character of his personality.

[J. P. Carson, *Life, Letters and Speeches of James Louis Petigru . . .* (1920); W. J. Grayson, *James Louis Petigru. A Biog. Sketch* (1866); W. D. Lewis, ed., *Great American Lawyers*, IV (1908), "James Louis Petigru" by J. D. Pope; *Memorial of the Late James L. Petigru. Proc. of the Bar of Charleston, S. C., Mar. 25, 1863* (1866); *Charleston Mercury*, Mar. 11, 1863.]
J. G. deR. H.

PETTIGREW, CHARLES (Mar. 20, 1743–Apr. 7, 1807), Episcopal clergyman, was born in Chambersburg, Pa. His family was of remote French origin with Scotch and Irish branches. Charles Pettigrew's father, James, of the Irish branch, became estranged from his people because of religious differences and emigrated to America with his wife, Mary Cochran, from County Tyrone, Ireland, in 1740. The family later moved to Virginia and in 1768, to North Carolina where Charles studied under the Rev. Henry Patillo [*q.v.*], who was serving the Presbyterians of that state. Five years later, although still a Presbyterian, he was appointed principal of the academy at Edenton, a school which was practically Episcopalian and which had marked influence on the early history of North Carolina. Here he became an Episcopalian and decided to take orders. He sailed for England in 1774, was ordered deacon by the Bishop of London, and advanced to the priesthood by the Bishop of Rochester in 1775. He returned to America in the last ship that sailed before the Revolution, and became rector of St. Paul's Church in Edenton.

In the fall of 1789, when Bishop White of Philadelphia wrote to Governor Samuel Johnston [*q.v.*], of North Carolina to request that the clergy of the Episcopal church in that state meet to take steps to revive the church organization there, the Governor referred the matter to the Rev. Charles Pettigrew, whom he called "his Pastor and Friend." Pettigrew called a meeting of the clergy, each of the six in the state being asked to bring one layman. Only two clergymen and two laymen, both residents of Tarboro, were present at the meeting in that town on June 5, 1790. They proceeded to organize and to elect deputies for the General Convention of 1792. It was a day of small beginnings, no notice of organization or attendance of delegates appearing in the records of the General Convention, and a permanent organization was not effected until 1817. At a state convention held in Tarboro on May 28, 1794, comprising five clergymen and eight laymen, Pettigrew was elected bishop. He expected to be consecrated at the Convention of 1795, which met at Philadelphia, but he was stopped in Norfolk, Va., by an epidemic of yellow fever, and was delayed until the Convention was adjourned. He returned to his home on the family estate, "Bonarva" in Tyrrell County, N. C., where he built a chapel on his own grounds to serve the surrounding countryside and where he died before being consecrated bishop.

He was twice married, first on Oct. 28, 1778, to Mary Blount who died in 1786, leaving him two sons, one of whom was Ebenezer, the father of James Johnston Pettigrew [*q.v.*], and second, on June 12, 1794, to Mary Lockhart. His letters to his sons written while they were students at the University of North Carolina, 1795 to 1797, throw an interesting light on the student life of the period, and are quoted at length in Battle's history of the University. Pettigrew was instrumental in founding the University in 1789, and was one of the trustees from 1790 to 1793.

[M. D. Haywood, biog. sketch in S. A. Ashe, *Biog. Hist. of N. C.*, vol. VI (1907); J. W. Moore, *Hist. of N. C.* (2 vols., 1880); W. M. Clemens, ed., *North and South Carolina Marriage Records* (1927); W. S. Perry, *The Hist. of the Am. Episc. Ch., 1587–1883* (2 vols., 1885); K. P. Battle, *Hist. of the Univ. of N. C.* (2 vols., 1907–1912); *The Early Conventions Held at Tawborough, A. D., 1790, 1793, and 1794 . . . Collected from Original Sources and Now First Published. With Introduction and Brief Notes by Joseph Blount Cheshire, Jr.* (1882); W. B. Sprague, *Annals of the Am. Pulpit*, vol. V (1859).]   C. L. W.

PETTIGREW, JAMES JOHNSTON (July 4, 1828–July 17, 1863), lawyer and soldier, was born at the family estate, "Bonarva," Lake Scuppernong, Tyrrell County, N. C., the son of Ebenezer and Ann B. (Shepard) Pettigrew. He was the great-grandson of James Pettigrew who emigrated to America in 1740, and the grandson of Charles Pettigrew [*q.v.*], the first bishop-elect of the Episcopal Church in North Carolina. His mother died when he was two years old. He often missed periods of schooling on account of ill health, but he rendered such a brilliant account of himself scholastically under the tutelage of William James Bingham of Hillsboro, N. C., that he was ready to enter the University of North Carolina at the age of fifteen. In his four years at the university he showed exceptional talent and upon his graduation in 1847, he was awarded by President Polk an assistant professorship at the Naval Observatory in Washington. He relinquished this position after two years and commenced the study of law, first in Baltimore, then in Charleston, S. C., where he was associated with his father's cousin, James Louis Petigru [*q.v.*]. In 1850 he took a long European tour with the particular object of studying Roman law in Germany for two years. He then resumed the practice of law in Charleston. He was elected to the General Assembly in 1856 and rapidly became an outstanding figure in the controversy over the slave trade. His minority report against a resumption of the traffic reads today as a thoughtful, well-balanced document. In 1861 he published a book, *Notes on Spain and the Spaniards,* based on his observations of manners and customs in that country.

Prior to the Civil War he was colonel of the 1st Regiment of Rifles of Charleston, and when Major Anderson immured himself within Fort Sumter, Pettigrew took over Castle Pinckney and later fortified Morris Island. When his own regiment was not able to enter the army of the Confederate states upon its own terms, he went to Richmond and enlisted in Hampton's Legion. After the secession of North Carolina in May 1861, he was elected colonel of the 12th Regiment. He first saw service at Evansport, Va., where his regiment was engaged in blocking the Potomac. His services were so conspicuous that President Davis himself wanted to make him a brigadier-general, but he refused on the grounds that he had never led troops in action. His officers and friends, however, persuaded him to accept later, and he served under Johnston throughout the Peninsular Campaign, was severely wounded at Seven Pines, bayonetted, and captured. In two months' time he was exchanged, whereupon he took command of the defenses of Petersburg. In the spring of 1863 he displayed at Blount's Creek his capacity for independent command, and his brigade formed part of the division of Henry Heth [*q.v.*] at Gettysburg. After Heth was wounded on the first day of the battle, Pettigrew took over the command of the division, and directed an advance on the left of Pickett in the famous charge. He was again wounded at the head of his troops near the Stone Wall, but was able to display conspicuous ability as a rear-guard commander during the retreat. On the night of July 14, he was wounded by a small raiding party of Federal cavalry. He died three days later, and was buried at Raleigh, N. C., but in 1866 his body was removed to "Bonarva."

[*S. C. Gen. Assembly, House of Rep., Special Committee on Slavery and the Slave Trade, Report of the Minority* (1858); H. C. Graham, biog. sketch in *Ladies Memorial Asso., Confed. Memorial Addresses* (1886); J. W. Clark, memorial address at the unveiling of a tablet and marble pillar in honor of General Pettigrew, Bunker Hill, W. Va., *N. C. Booklet*, Oct. 1920, Jan.–Apr. 1921, pub. by The N. C. Soc. of the D. A. R.; Mrs. C. P. S. Spencer, biog. sketch in W. J. Peele, *Lives of Distinguished North Carolinians* (1898); S. A. Ashe, *Biog. Hist. of N. C.*, vol. VI (1907).]   D. Y.

PETTIGREW, RICHARD FRANKLIN (July 23, 1848–Oct. 5, 1926), delegate from the Territory of Dakota, first senator from South Dakota, was born in Ludlow, Vt., the son of Hannah B. (Sawtell) and Andrew Pettigrew, who was an abolitionist and maintained a station on the Underground Railroad. The boy's youth was spent on his father's farm in Evansville, Wis., where he attended the public schools and local academy. He entered Beloit College but left in 1867. He studied law at the University of Wisconsin and with John C. Spooner [*q.v.*], and he settled in Sioux Falls in 1870, where he became one of the leaders in the development of the town. He was admitted to the bar in 1871, practised law, engaged in government surveying, and was interested in real estate. He was a member of the House of Representatives of the territorial legislature in 1872 and a member of the territorial council in 1877 and 1879. On Feb. 27, 1879, he was married to Elizabeth V. Pittar, the daughter of John Pittar of Chicago, who bore him two sons. Elected a delegate to the Forty-seventh Congress in 1880, he served from March 1881 to March 1883. He was again a member of the territorial council in 1885. He advocated the division of Dakota Territory into two states, and, when North and South Dakota were admitted in 1889, he was chosen one of the first senators from South Dakota, to serve from October 1889 to March 1901. His most important service in the Senate was in the promotion of legislation reserving from sale the forest lands owned by the federal government. He studied carefully the forestry methods used in Europe, and, with the aid of Charles D. Walcott of the United States geological survey, he drafted an amendment to the timber culture act of 1891 authorizing the president by proclamation to reserve public lands covered by forests. As a result of this legislation 150,000,000 acres were reserved.

He was a non-conformist in politics and religion. He was feared in the Senate because of his bitter personal attacks. One senator described him as "pale malice" and another asked him if he "spit lemon juice" (Beer, *post*, pp. 220, 221). On the other hand he was remembered for his charities and for the efforts he made to improve sanitation and to obtain grain elevators in a small town, and he had many friends who were surprised by his public bitterness. He was a believer in the single tax and opposed the private ownership of land. He favored the government ownership of railroads and telegraphs, and he prepared bills for their purchase and operation. He held the opinion that such public utilities should be operated for service rather than for profit. These views alienated him from his Republican associates, and in addition his opinions about monetary problems brought him into conflict with the sound-money members of the party. He was a delegate to the Republican National Convention at St. Louis in 1896 but left the meetings after the rejection of a resolution in favor of free silver. He also opposed the annexation of the Hawaiian Islands and was a leader in the Senate in opposition to the annexation of the Philippine Islands. His position upon the currency and imperialism led to his defeat for re-election in 1900. He joined the Democratic par-

ty for a time and was a delegate to the national convention in 1908. He opposed entrance into the World War and expressed himself bitterly on the subject. He was indicted, but he was never tried. The indictment, engraved and framed, became one of his valued possessions.

After retirement from Congress he practised law in New York for several years and accumulated a comfortable fortune. Later he returned to Sioux Falls, where he built a large house. He traveled widely and gathered a collection of fossils, flints, and similar objects which, with his house, he bequeathed to the city. He published two volumes: one on *The Course of Empire* in 1920 and the other *Triumphant Plutocracy* in 1922, both largely made up of the materials used in his speeches in the Senate. He was survived by his widow Roberta A. (Hallister) Smith Pettigrew to whom he had been married on Feb. 2, 1922.

[*South Dakota*, ed. by G. M. Smith (1915), vols. I–IV; D. R. Bailey, *Hist. of Minnehaha County, S. D.* (1899); *Who's Who in America*, 1926–27; Thomas Beer, *Hanna* (1929); *Rev. of Rev.* (N. Y.), July 1896, p. 10, Apr. 1900, pp. 394–95; *N. Y. Times*, Oct. 6, 1926; *Daily Argus-Leader* (Sioux Falls), Oct. 5, 6, 7, 9; information from his widow, Mrs. Richard F. Pettigrew, Chicago, Ill.]   F. E. H—s.

PETTIT, CHARLES (1736–Sept. 3, 1806), merchant, Revolutionary patriot, son of John Pettit, was born near Amwell, Hunterdon County, N. J., of French Huguenot stock. His father, whose family emigrated to southern New York about 1650, was a Philadelphia importing merchant and an underwriter of marine insurance. Charles received a classical education. His marriage, Apr. 5, 1758, to Sarah, daughter of Andrew Reed, a Trenton merchant and also his father's business associate in Philadelphia, gave him important connections which opened the way to a public career. Through the influence of Joseph Reed [*q.v.*], his wife's half-brother, he held minor public offices in New Jersey and was appointed a provincial surrogate Nov. 19, 1767. On Apr. 3, 1770, he was admitted to the bar as an attorney and on Nov. 17, 1773, as counselor. He succeeded Reed as deputy secretary of the province, clerk of the council and of the supreme court, Oct. 27, 1769, and was appointed aide to Gov. William Franklin in 1771, with the rank of lieutenant-colonel. When Franklin was arrested as a Loyalist in 1776, Pettit cast in his lot with the colonies and continued as secretary under the new state government until 1778. On Oct. 8, 1776, he was appointed aide to Gov. William Livingston with the rank of colonel, and in the following year drafted a plan for oyer and terminer courts for the new state régime.

On Gen. Nathanael Greene's recommendation Pettit was appointed assistant quartermaster-general of the Continental Army, Mar. 2, 1778. His experience with administrative details and his exacting methods well qualified him for the post. In the keeping of accounts and cash, the particular duties assigned to him, he inaugurated many needed reforms. In the face of congressional interference and a treasury "wretchedly poor" he found his duties exceedingly difficult, and in 1780 would have quit the place if he could have done so "without evident impropriety." He was suspicious of congressional schemes for remodeling the quartermaster's department, but did not, like Greene, think the new plan inaugurated in 1780 was impossible of execution. When Greene resigned as quartermaster-general, Pettit was offered the post, but emphatically declined it. He retained his assistantship, however, feeling that the prompt settlement of all accounts in the department would be facilitated by his remaining. He finally resigned June 20, 1781.

After the war he became an importing merchant in Philadelphia. During 1784–85 he was in the Pennsylvania assembly and in the former year was chairman of a committee of merchants appointed to find means for improving national commerce. From 1785 to 1787 he was a member of Congress. Although a Constitutionalist in Pennsylvania politics and opposed to parts of the federal Constitution, he urged the adoption of the instrument and at the Harrisburg convention of 1788 called to discuss measures for securing its revision, he was largely instrumental by his conciliatory conduct in placating the Pennsylvania opposition. He was the author of Pennsylvania's funding system and of a pamphlet, *View of the Principles, Operation and Probable Effects of the Funding System of Pennsylvania* (1788), urging support of the plan. During 1790–91 he was delegated to present to Congress Pennsylvania's Revolutionary claims against the federal government. As a Jeffersonian Republican, he joined with other Philadelphia merchants in opposing the Jay Treaty (1795) and in 1802 headed a committee appointed to secure relief against French spoliation of American commerce. Much of his later life was devoted to the business of the Insurance Company of North America, of which he was an original director and from 1796 to 1798 and from 1799 to his death, president. He was a trustee of the University of Pennsylvania (1791–1802) and a member of the American Philosophical Society. Recognized as an authority on financial questions, Pettit was a shrewd business man and possessed a calm dignity, a genial manner, and sound practical judgment.

He died in Philadelphia. One of his four children, Elizabeth, married Jared Ingersoll [1749–1822; q.v.]; another, Theodosia, married Alexander Graydon [q.v.]. Thomas McKean Pettit [q.v.] was a grandson.

[*Archives of the State of N. J.*, 1 ser., vols. X (1886), XVI (1902); G. W. Greene, *The Life of Nathanael Greene*, vol. II (1871); T. H. Montgomery, *A Hist. of the Insurance Company of North America* (1885); W. C. Ford and Gaillard Hunt, *Jours. Continental Cong., 1774–1789*, vols. X–XXI (1908–12); *Minutes of the Provincial Council of Pa.*, vol. XVI (1853); *Pa. Archives*, 1 ser., vols. X (1854), XI (1855); *Poulson's Am. Daily Advertiser* (Phila.), Sept. 9, 1806; W. B. Reed, *Life and Correspondence of Joseph Reed* (2 vols., 1847).]
J. H. P—g.

PETTIT, THOMAS McKEAN (Dec. 26, 1797–May 30, 1853), jurist, son of Andrew and Elizabeth (McKean) Pettit, was born in Philadelphia of Scotch-Irish and French Huguenot stock. His father was the son of Charles Pettit [q.v.], merchant and Revolutionary patriot, and his mother, the daughter of Gov. Thomas McKean [q.v.]. Andrew Pettit, a Philadelphia merchant and insurance man, was for many years a director of the Insurance Company of North America, and held the post of flour inspector under Governor McKean. Thomas received a classical education and graduated from the University of Pennsylvania in 1815. Upon leaving college he studied law in the office of his uncle, Jared Ingersoll (1749–1822; q.v.), and was admitted to the bar Apr. 13, 1818. In 1819 and again in 1821 he was appointed secretary of the Philadelphia board of public education. He was city solicitor (1820–23) and on Feb. 9, 1824, was appointed deputy attorney-general of Pennsylvania, which post he held until 1830. Although a member of the intellectual aristocracy, he adhered to the traditional party affiliations of his family and became a Jacksonian Democrat. He was an active member of the Hickory Club, which promoted Jackson's election to the presidency in 1824, and soon came to enjoy wide influence in the councils of the Democratic party in Pennsylvania both because of his ability and his family connections. He was elected to the lower house of the legislature in 1830 and in the following year became a member of the select council of Philadelphia.

His chief ambition, however, was a career on the bench, and on Feb. 16, 1833, Gov. George Wolfe appointed him an associate judge of the district court for the city and county of Philadelphia. He held this office until 1835, at which time the term for which the court was constituted expired. When the legislature passed a new law extending the life of the court for ten years more he was recommissioned associate judge, Mar.

30, 1835, and on the following Apr. 22 was appointed presiding judge, serving in this capacity until 1845. He declined reappointment on the expiration of his term and returned to his law practice. During Van Buren's administration, 1839, he was one of the board of visitors to West Point, and, together with Gov. William L. Marcy [*q.v.*] of New York, prepared the report of the board. Under President Polk he was United States district attorney for the eastern Pennsylvania district (1845–49). On Mar. 29, 1853, President Pierce appointed him superintendent of the Philadelphia mint and the appointment was confirmed on Apr. 4, but his duties at this post were cut short by his death a month and a half later.

Pettit's published writings and speeches include *A Discourse before the Historical Society and the Philomathean Society of the University of Pennsylvania* (1830); "Memoir of Roberts Vaux" in the *Memoirs of the Historical Society of Pennsylvania* (vol. IV, pt. 1, 1840); *An Annual Discourse Delivered before the Historical Society of Pennsylvania* (1828); and *The Common Law Reports of England* (1822), the last named having been prepared for publication in collaboration with Thomas Sergeant. Pettit's judicial decisions reflect a high degree of ability and broad legal training. By temperament he was well fitted for the bench. Because of his patience and composure and his willingness to compromise he was not the stormy petrel in state politics that his grandfather, Governor McKean, had been. He entertained broad ideas on popular education and worked earnestly for its advancement as a citizen, while in the legislature, and as a member of the Philadelphia board of education. He manifested a deep interest in the history of Pennsylvania and was one of the most active members of the Historical Society of Pennsylvania. His wife, whom he married Feb. 7, 1828, was Sarah Barry Dale, daughter of Commodore Richard Dale [*q.v.*], distinguished naval officer. She died in 1839. Of their seven children, three survived him.

[Roberdeau Buchanan, *Geneal. of the McKean Family of Pa.* (1890); Samuel Hazard, *Hazard's Reg. of Pa.*, Feb. 23, July 6, Dec. 14, 1833, Apr. 4, May 2, July 4, Oct. 3, 1835; J. H. Martin, *Martin's Bench and Bar of Phila.* (1883); J. T. Scharf and Thompson Westcott, *Hist. of Phila., 1609–1884* (1884), vol. II; *The Pennsylvanian* (Phila.), June 1, 1853.]   J. H. P—g.

PETTUS, EDMUND WINSTON (July 6, 1821–July 27, 1907), soldier, senator from Alabama, was born in Limestone County, Ala., the youngest child of John and Alice (Winston) Pettus. At an early age death deprived him of his father, but his mother was able to educate him at

Clinton College, Smith County, Tenn. After completing his studies there he read law in the office of William Cooper of Tuscumbia, Ala., and in 1842 was licensed to practise his profession. He selected Gainesville, Ala., as the seat of his efforts. In 1844 he was elected solicitor of the 7th judicial circuit. On June 27 of the same year he married Mary, the daughter of Samuel Chapman of Sumter County, Ala. They had six children. During the Mexican War he served as lieutenant in the United States Army and shortly thereafter went to California. Failing to find a fortune in the distant West he returned to Alabama and in 1851 settled at Carrollton in Pickens County. Two years later he was again made solicitor and in 1855 was elected judge of the 7th circuit. Resigning this office in 1858 he removed to Cahaba, Dallas County, and practised law there until the outbreak of the Civil War During the struggle over the question of secession he was sent as commissioner from Alabama to Mississippi, of which state his brother, John J. Pettus, was governor at the time. Shortly afterward he assisted in the organization of the 20th Alabama Infantry and was elected a major in that command. He was soon promoted to the rank of lieutenant-colonel, and in this capacity he served in General Kirby-Smith's Kentucky campaign and later in the defense of Vicksburg. He was taken captive at the fall of Port Gibson but escaped. During the campaign he succeeded to the command of his regiment, and he acquired military distinction by leading a desperate and successful assault upon a part of the works that had been captured by the Federals. He was again made captive when Vicksburg fell, but he was exchanged, promoted to the rank of brigadier-general, and assigned to Stevenson's division at Chattanooga. He took part in the battles of Lookout Mountain and Missionary Ridge. After the retreat upon Atlanta he followed Hood into Tennessee and participated in the battle of Nashville. He later joined Johnston on his retreat through the Carolinas and finally laid down his arms when his commander surrendered to Sherman.

Returning to Alabama at the close of the conflict he took up his residence in Selma and resumed the practice of law. Though he refrained from seeking public office, he represented his state in the National Democratic Convention from 1876 until 1896, and in that year he became a candidate for the United States Senate. He was elected without difficulty on the Democratic ticket and at the end of his term was chosen to succeed himself. He served from Mar. 4, 1897, until his death at Hot Springs, N. C. He was buried in the Live Oak Cemetery at Selma, Ala.

He typified much that was characteristic of his section and generation. He possessed a vigor of character that was more common in the South than is generally supposed. As he sat in the Senate during his old age, he still exhibited a manly independence of spirit, a ready, fervid, and stilted oratory, a somewhat rustic and old-fashioned style of dress, his feet being clad in the only pair of boots then worn in the Senate, and an urbanity and chivalry of bearing that have gone with the passing of the "Confederate Brigadiers."

[An unsigned manuscript and other material in the files of the Alabama Department of Archives and History; Willis Brewer, *Alabama* (1872); *Confederate Mil. Hist.*, ed. by C. A. Evans (1899), vol. VII; *Who's Who in America*, 1906-07; *John Tyler Morgan and Edmund Winston Pettus—Memorial Addresses* (1909); *Ala. Hist. Soc. Trans.*, vol. II (1898); *Montgomery Advertiser*, July 28, 1907.]   T. P. A.

PEYTON, JOHN LEWIS (Sept. 15, 1824–May 21, 1896), Confederate agent, author, was born at "Montgomery Hall" near Staunton, Va., the son of John Howe and Anne Montgomery (Lewis) Peyton. He was descended from Henry Peyton who was born in London and died in Westmoreland County, Va., about 1659. His father was a distinguished lawyer and public servant. His mother was the daughter of John Lewis, a Revolutionary officer and friend of George Washington. At the age of fifteen he entered the Virginia Military Institute but withdrew in his second year on account of his lack of health. In 1844 he received the degree of Bachelor of Law from the University of Virginia and practised his profession at Staunton until 1852, when he was sent on a secret mission to England, France, and Austria for the Fillmore administration. From 1853 to 1856 he lived in Illinois, where he was prominent in local military affairs. He was married on Dec. 17, 1855, to Henrietta E. Washington of Vernon, N. C., and to them was born one son. Refusing the appointment as federal district attorney of Utah, tendered him on the recommendation of Stephen A. Douglas, he returned in 1856 to Staunton and there engaged in many enterprises. A Whig in politics, he supported the Bell-Everett presidential ticket in 1860 and opposed the secession of Virginia in 1861. He did not regard the election of Lincoln as a cause for secession and believed that the inaugural address promised sufficient protection for slavery within the Union. In fact he "opposed Secession as unconstitutional, or, if constitutional, unnecessary, and the worst of remedies for the South" (*American Crisis, post,* I, 110). Upon the secession of his state, however, he helped organize a regiment, mainly at his own expense, but was physically incapacitated from serving with it in the field. Instead, he accepted

an appointment from North Carolina as her state agent abroad. Embarking from Charleston, S. C., in October 1861, he reached England in November 1861 and remained there until 1876. In his reminiscences of his service abroad he was very critical of the foreign policy of the Davis government and accused it of apathy at the beginning of the contest. Recognition, he thought, might have been obtained then if the commissioners Yancey and Mann, who had to a large extent overcome the opinion that the South was fighting for slavery, had been energetically supported by the home government. During the *Trent* crisis he found that "English admiration of the South was a thing separate and apart from anything like kindred love. . . . They patted her on the back as the weaker of the two combatants. . . . It was not because they loved her, but because they disliked the Yankees" (*American Crisis, post,* II, 101). After an unofficial interview with Lord Palmerston in May 1862 he was convinced of Great Britain's determination to maintain strict neutrality and communicated this conviction to his Southern friends.

He retired to the Island of Guernsey in 1866 and resided there, with the exception of his travels on the Continent, until his return to "Steephill" near Staunton, where he devoted himself to literary and agricultural pursuits. He enjoyed membership in several learned societies at home and abroad, among them the Royal Geographical Society, contributed to several periodicals of his period, and was the author of many books, perhaps the most important of which are: *A Statistical View of the State of Illinois* (1855); *The American Crisis; or Pages from the Note-Book of a State Agent during the Civil War in America* (2 vols., 1867); *Over the Alleghanies and Across the Prairies—Personal Recollections of the Far West, One and Twenty Years Ago* (1869), an excellent description of the old Northwest in 1848; *Memoir of William Madison Peyton* (1873); *History of Augusta County, Va.* (1882); *Rambling Reminiscences of a Residence Abroad* (1888), full of charming observations on social England; and *Memoir of John Howe Peyton* (1894), the biography of his father and a record of life in Virginia.

[Autobiog. material in own writings; H. E. Hayden, *Va. Geneal.* (1891); *Men of the Time*, 9th ed., rev. by Thompson Cooper (1875), 14th ed., rev. by V. G. Plarr (1895); Bezer Blundell, *The Contributions of John Lewis Peyton to the Hist. of Va. and of the Civil War* (1868); an estimate of his ability by W. Hepworth Dixon quoted in footnote in *New-Eng. Hist. and Geneal. Reg.*, Jan. 1881, p. 20.]   W. G. B—n.

PHELAN, DAVID SAMUEL (July 16, 1841–Sept. 21, 1915), Catholic priest and journalist, son of Alexander and Margaret (Creedon)

Phelan, was born at Sydney, Nova Scotia, from which place his family removed to St. Louis, Mo., in 1853. Trained in local schools and by wide reading, he studied theology in the diocesan seminary and was ordained a priest by Bishop P. R. Kenrick [*q.v.*] on May 20, 1863. After serving a few months as a curate at the Cathedral and at Indian Creek, he was assigned to a pastorate at Edina, where as editor of the *Edina or Missouri Watchman* he was imprisoned for his refusal to take the test oath prescribed by the Drake constitution, which he attacked in his journal. A horseman, he was also arrested for violating a town ordinance which limited the speed of riding to ten miles an hour. When the case came to trial he was acquitted largely because the petty persecution involved was obvious. In 1868 he was transferred to the Church of the Annunciation in St. Louis and brought with him his paper, which afterwards was known as the *Western Watchman*. In a sense he was fostered by Kenrick, although the Bishop regarded him as somewhat dangerous as an editor. An excellent orthodox priest, beloved by the poor, a good preacher, a fair German scholar, and a pleasant, witty companion, Phelan was a laborious man. He built the Church of Our Lady of Mount Carmel in North St. Louis, 1872, which he served as pastor until his death; he also organized, in 1881, St. James's Church at Ferguson. As a writer, he attracted favorable attention through *The Gospel Applied to Our Times* (1904), *Christ the Preacher* (1905), and translations of three French works on ascetic theology.

While Phelan regarded journalism as merely an avocation, it was for his editorial independence, his somewhat unscrupulous quotation of private conversations, and his caustic criticism of priests and bishops with whom he did not agree, as the fiery editor of the *Western Watchman* for fifty years that he was known and dreaded. His paper is a chronicle of the Church in the West, but it must be read with discrimination. Anti-Catholic papers culled his columns and found good copy for their purposes, especially when he supported priests in trouble with their bishops. He regarded himself as a defender of the clergy against episcopal arbitrariness. He did not hesitate to censure episcopal interference in the affairs of patriotic societies and American Catholic meddling in the Roman question. A Democrat, he advocated free silver and opposed the war with Spain, though he accepted our colonial policy. A liberal, he advocated Catholic schools for Catholics and public schools for all other citizens, while he supported Archbishop Ireland's Faribault School plan. His defense of the tango and the right of girls to use cosmetics aroused some reforming Protestant ministers, and the Christian Endeavor Society at one time urged his unfrocking. Becoming a teetotaler, he condemned drinking. A militant campaigner against intolerance, he destroyed the American Protective Association in St. Louis by printing the denial of membership on the part of a number of merchants and then ruthlessly publishing their activities in the association from its official record, which he obtained irregularly. He was always in ecclesiastical difficulties, but he accepted censure with equanimity, even printing the official letter. In 1893 he was reproved by Archbishop John J. Kain for an imprudent attack upon a recent episcopal appointment as a lowering of the intellectual level of the hierarchy. Phelan thereupon retorted that since Kain was from a slave state he must be taught how to rule freemen. He was answered by an episcopal proscription of his paper, but Archbishop Ireland, an admirer who was known to have inspired some of Phelan's editorials, especially at the time of the Third Council of Baltimore, compromised the difficulty. Phelan joined Ireland in his condemnation of Cahenslyism and said bitter things relative to German lay and clerical leaders. With Bishop Schrembs he came into open dispute; Archbishop Glennon in a friendly way frowned upon his activities. In spite of his failings, however, he accomplished much good. At his death he was the oldest and best-known Catholic editor of the passing school of militant, independent writers. Rev. David Phelan, editor of the *Antigonish Cabinet,* was his cousin.

[J. E. Rothensteiner, *Hist. of the Archdiocese of St. Louis* (1928), vol. II; *Am. Cath. Who's Who* (1911); Cath. *Fortnightly Rev.,* Oct. 15, 1915; *St. Louis Globe Democrat,* Sept. 22, 23, 1915; information from life-long associates.]   R. J. P.

PHELAN, JAMES (Apr. 23, 1824–Dec. 23, 1892), pioneer San Francisco merchant and capitalist, was born in Queen's (now Leix) County, Ireland. In 1827 his father emigrated to America, taking with him James and his two older brothers, John and Michael, and settled in New York. Such formal education as James received was secured in the public schools of that city. After a few years he became clerk in a grocery store, acquiring much practical experience and developing unusual business capacity at an early age. With his savings, he started a general merchandising business of his own, and was successful from the beginning. His trading operations extended to Philadelphia, Cincinnati, and even to New Orleans. By the time he was twenty-four years of age he had accumulated about $50,000, the foundation of his later fortune.

News of the gold discoveries roused his interest in merchandising possibilities in the new communities springing up in California. Accordingly, in 1849, he disposed of his eastern business interests and started for California via Panama. With keen discernment respecting the needs of early California settlers, he shipped, before leaving the East, a large stock of miscellaneous goods on three different ships. One sank at sea, but the other two reached San Francisco about the time when he himself arrived (Aug. 18, 1849). He and his brother Michael, who had come to San Francisco in the preceding June, formed the partnership of J. & M. Phelan, and carried on a thriving and highly profitable trade until Michael's death in 1858. Thereafter, James continued the business, enlarging the scope of the enterprise and planning all his ventures with rare judgment and foresight. During the Civil War he was among the first of California merchants to include in his operations exportations of large quantities of California wool and wheat to New York and even to foreign markets—always at a handsome profit. For some years, success in the wholesale liquor business added to his rapidly accumulating fortune. He was no less shrewd and successful in real-estate investments, not only in San Francisco and other parts of California, but also in Oregon and in New York City. So conservatively were his purchases made that it is said no mortgage was ever recorded or made against any of his property. At the same time he loaned large sums on first and second real-estate mortgages. On land owned by him, he erected (1881–82) the Phelan Building, one of the first of modern buildings in San Francisco. He also erected a number of blocks in San José.

By 1869, his fortune had become so great that he retired from commercial pursuits, spent a year in European travel with his family, and, upon his return, entered the field of banking, which was to be his chief interest during the rest of his life. In November 1870 he made a trip to Washington and obtained the charter for the first national bank in California, the First National Gold Bank, which is now (1934) operating as the Crocker First National Bank. Phelan was its first president and for many years was a director. In 1889, with James G. Fair [q.v.] and others, he helped organize the Mutual Savings Bank in San Francisco, and was its first vice-president. He was also vice-president of the American Contracting & Dredging Company for dredging the French Panama Canal, a project which brought him large returns. He was identified with the organization of the Firemen's Fund Insurance Company, and later with the Western Fire & Marine Insurance Company. By 1890 his financial interests had become so extensive that he formed a partnership with his brother John, who had been his New York agent in earlier years; and later, with his only son, James Duval Phelan [q.v.]. On May 12, 1859, he married Alice Kelly, daughter of Jeremiah Kelly of Brooklyn, N. Y. She, a son, and two daughters survived him. He died at his unpretentious San Francisco home, and was buried in Holy Cross Cemetery, San Mateo County. His will, disposing of an estate valued at nearly $7,500,000, contained generous bequests for churches, schools, orphanages, and asylums both in California and in his native country. He was a Catholic in religion and an independent Democrat in politics.

[S. B. F. Clark, *How Many Miles from St. Jo? The Log of Sterling B. F. Clark a Forty-Niner . . . together with a Brief Autobiography of James Phelan . . .* (1929); *In Memoriam: James Phelan—Read at a Meeting of the Society of California Pioneers, San Francisco, Apr. 3, 1893* (n.d.); W. F. Swasey, *The Early Days and Men of Cal.* (1891); Alonzo Phelps, *Contemporary Biog. of California's Representative Men* (1881); *The Builders of a Great City: San Francisco's Representative Men* (1891); H. H. Bancroft, *Hist. of Cal.*, vol. VII (1890); *San Francisco: Its Builders Past and Present* (1918), vol. I; R. D. Hunt, *Cal. and Californians* (1926), vol. V; I. B. Cross, *Financing an Empire: Hist. of Banking in Cal.* (1927), vols. I, III; *Examiner* (San Francisco), *Evening Bulletin* (San Francisco), and *San Francisco Chronicle*, Dec. 24, 1892; date of birth established by photographic reproduction of autograph MS., at the Soc. of Cal. Pioneers.]

P. O. R.

PHELAN, JAMES (Dec. 7, 1856–Jan. 30, 1891), author, congressman from Tennessee, was born at Aberdeen, Miss., the grandson of John Phelan, an Irish immigrant who settled in Alabama. His parents were Eliza Jones (Moore) and James Phelan, a lawyer, editor, and Confederate States senator from Mississippi. In 1867 he was sent to school in Huntsville, Ala., and after the family removed to Memphis, Tenn., the next year, he was taught by his father and by private teachers there. Later he attended Kentucky Military Institute. In the winter semester of 1874–75 he became a student at the University of Leipzig and in 1878 was granted the degree of Ph.D. In his dissertation of sixty-four pages, printed in 1878, *On Philip Massinger,* the Elizabethan playwright, he wrote that "the author imagines he has possibly discovered a key for that most intricate problem, in what plays Massinger and Fletcher wrote together" (p. 64). With the exception of delightful allusions to the Elizabethans in subsequent political utterances, he forsook the drama and, returning to Memphis, studied law.

In 1881 he purchased the *Memphis Avalanche.* To the promptings of friends that he enter politics, he was unresponsive till in 1886 he consented to enter the race for the Democratic congressional nomination from the district that included the city of Memphis, and he was nominated over Josiah Patterson. With acutely developed ideas of propriety, he refused to permit his own paper to promote his candidacy, and the editor continued to express views divergent from his on the sectional issue and the negro question. Whereas the editor regarded negro suffrage as "the irritating menace to peace and good order" (*Memphis Avalanche*, Aug. 14, 1889) and urged that the South could not "afford to divide on any question" (*Ibid.*, July 13, 1889), Phelan accepted "the citizenship of the negro race" and designated negroes as "our fellow-Americans, our fellow-Tennesseeans" with rights "as sacred as ours," who "can demand . . . all the privileges that flow from a free ballot and a fair count" (*The New South . . . Speech . . . at Covington, Tenn. on . . . 2nd of Oct. 1886*, 1886, p. 4). Not only on the negro question but on the tariff issue, he opposed Southern agricultural interests. He supported not free trade but a revision of the tariff by which protection would be accorded to infant Southern industries. He defeated his Republican opponent, Zachary Taylor, by a large majority. In 1888 he was renominated without opposition and was reëlected. His seat was contested, however, by his Republican opponent, Lucian B. Eaton, "a Carpet-bagger" and the author of a letter, "worthy of a Brownlow" aiming to stir up race trouble and sectional prejudice (*Memphis Avalanche,* Oct. 31, Jan. 25, 1888). Eaton charged the Democrats with the use of fraudulent ballots, the employment of disreputable election officers, the voting of repeaters and, above all, with the intimidation of negroes. Phelan published counter charges that specified the persons bribed by Eaton and the exact amounts of the bribes (*Ibid.*, Jan. 25, 1889). The case was still pending when Phelan died, a victim of tuberculosis in Nassau, New Providence, where he had gone for his health. He was survived by his widow, Mary (Early) Phelan, the niece of Jubal Early [*q.v.*] and by three children. He left as a monument to his training and industry a *History of Tennessee* (1888), in which he "endeavored to be accurate and impartial . . . to show the simple grandeur and homely nobility of the men who shaped the early destinies of the state of Tennessee" (*Memphis Avalanche*, Mar. 27, 1889).

[*Memorial Addresses on the Life and Character of James Phelan . . . in the House of Representatives and . . . Senate* (1891); "Vita" in dissertation, *ante*; J. M. Keating, *Hist. of . . . Memphis* (1888), pt. 3, pp. 232–43; *Contested-Election Case of L. B. Eaton vs. James Phelan* (2 pts., 1889); *Chattanooga Daily Times* and *Memphis Appeal-Avalanche* for Feb. 8, 1891.]   M. B. H.

PHELAN, JAMES DUVAL (Apr. 20, 1861– Aug. 7, 1930), mayor of San Francisco, United States senator, was born in San Francisco, the only son of James [1824–1892, *q.v.*] and Alice (Kelly) Phelan. He was graduated from St. Ignatius College, San Francisco, in 1881, studied law for a year at the University of California, then traveled for two years. Influenced by his father, he abandoned his early ambition to become a lawyer and writer for a business career, first as partner with, later as heir and successor to his father in the banking business. Eventually, he became president of the Mutual Savings Bank, chairman of the board of directors of the United Bank and Trust Company, and a director of the First National Bank and First Federal Trust Company. As vice-president of the California World's Columbian Exposition Commission, in 1893, he personally attended to the details of constructing the California Building at Chicago, and so wisely managed the affair that $20,000 of the original appropriation was returned to the state treasury. The following year, he took an active part in organizing the Midwinter International Exposition in San Francisco.

During the early nineties, San Francisco was one of the most boss-ridden and corruptly governed cities in the country. Without previous political experience, Phelan was in 1897 selected by the reform element as its candidate for mayor. Elected and twice reëlected, he placed San Francisco in the forefront of well-governed cities. From the beginning, he pugnaciously attacked the corrupt board of supervisors, striking at graft wherever it showed its head. He was credited with saving the city over $300,000 a year by vetoing "jobs" in the board of supervisors. His most enduring achievement was his effective leadership in the drafting and adoption of a new charter for the city, which was adopted over the opposition of both old party machines. Other constructive work distinguished his administration—the beautification of the streets, the building of parks and playgrounds, the erection of fountains. Later, he was personally responsible for the "Burnham plan," from which ultimately came the present civic center of San Francisco. The chief criticism of his administration came in its last year (1901), when, during the strike of the teamsters' union, he placed policemen on trucks driven by non-union men. This led to numerous outbreaks of violence and earned for him the bitter hostility of organized labor—a fact which played a part in the election of his successor. In the fight against the notorious Schmitz-Ruef régime which followed, especially during 1906–08, Phelan took a prominent part, aggressively backing Rudolph Spreckels in the campaign which resulted in the prosecution and conviction of Schmitz and Ruef. During his term as mayor, Phelan took important steps at his own expense whereby San Francisco was eventually able to acquire the right to bring its water supply from the Hetch Hetchy Valley. Afterwards, in 1903 and again in 1913, he headed a San Francisco delegation to Washington on behalf of the project. In the earthquake and fire of April 1906, he lost much but gave unstintedly of his time and means to the work of aiding the suffering and rebuilding the city. To him personally, rather than to the untrustworthy city government, President Roosevelt sent a national relief fund of $10,000,-000, which, with a vast amount of supplies, was distributed by the relief organization of which Phelan was president. In 1913 he was appointed commissioner to Europe to support the invitation of the President to foreign countries to participate in the Panama-Pacific International Exposition of 1915.

Apart from serving as delegate to the Democratic National Convention in 1900, Phelan's political activity prior to 1914 had been restricted to the field of municipal government. In that year, however, he was the successful Democratic candidate for the United States Senate, serving from 1915 to 1921. Before commencing his term, he was appointed by Secretary of State, Robert Lansing, commissioner to investigate charges against James M. Sullivan, American minister to the Dominican Republic; and in his report (May 9, 1915) he recommended the minister's recall. Chief among the committees on which he served in the Senate were those on railroads, coast defense, interoceanic canals, public lands, and naval affairs. He participated in debates upon various measures, and vigorously advocated exclusion of Orientals. He gave the Wilson administration his undivided support until the close of the war; but he favored divorcing the Covenant of the League of Nations from the Treaty of Versailles. He was candidate for reëlection in 1920, but was defeated by his Republican rival, Samuel M. Shortridge. At the conclusion of his senatorial term, he retired from politics, though appearing as the head of the California delegation to the Democratic National Convention of 1924, where he made the speech nominating William Gibbs McAdoo for the presidency.

Phelan's was a many-sided career. In 1898 he was appointed regent of the University of California for a sixteen-year term. On important public occasions, he was an exceptionally pleasing speaker. He also contributed to the field of letters, both in prose and verse, although much

that he wrote was never published. He gave discerning and substantial encouragement to many young painters, sculptors, musicians, and poets, and bequeathed his beautiful Spanish-Italian villa, "Montalvo," at Saratoga, Cal., to the San Francisco Art Association. He was a collector of art treasures, and to him San Francisco is indebted for large gifts of statuary and other works of art. He died, unmarried, at "Montalvo."

[R. D. Hunt, *Cal. and Californians* (1926), vol. IV; *Complimentary Banquet Given to Hon. James D. Phelan by the Officials of the City of San Francisco . . . Dec. 28, 1901* (1901) ; *Meetings of the Board of Supervisors of the City and County of San Francisco: Memorial Services in Honor of the Late Senator James D. Phelan* (1930); Fremont Older, *My Own Story* (2nd ed., 1926); *Overland Mo.*, Nov. 1930; *San Francisco Chronicle*, Aug. 8, 14, 1930; *Who's Who in America*, 1928–29; *San Francisco: Its Builders Past and Present* (1918), vol. I.]

P. O. R.

PHELPS, ALMIRA HART LINCOLN (July 15, 1793–July 15, 1884), pioneer educator, author, the daughter of Capt. Samuel and Lydia (Hinsdale) Hart, was born in Berlin, Conn. On her father's side she was a descendant of Thomas Hooker [*q.v.*], one of the original proprietors of Hartford. The education of her early years, under the care of unusually sympathetic and intellectual parents, was supplemented later in more formal fashion at the "select" school of her sister, Emma (Hart) Willard [*q.v.*], at Middlebury, Vt., at Berlin Academy, and in 1812 at the Female Academy of Pittsfield, Mass. Later she acquired a knowledge of Latin, Greek, French, and Spanish, the sciences—including botany, chemistry, and geology—and mathematics. Meantime, at the age of sixteen, she began teaching, first in a district school near Hartford, where she "boarded round," then, in rapid succession, at Berlin and New Britain, Conn., and in an academy at Sandy Hill, N. Y., of which she was principal.

Her career as teacher was interrupted by her marriage in 1817 to Simeon Lincoln, editor of the *Connecticut Mirror* (Hartford). To them were born three children. After the death of her husband in 1823, she began educational work of importance in association with her sister at Troy Female Seminary, 1823–31, where she served as acting principal while her sister was in Europe. In 1831 she became the wife of Judge John Phelps of Vermont, who was a sympathetic and interested associate in her work as author and teacher till his death in 1849. To them were born a son, Charles E. Phelps [*q.v.*], and a daughter. Returning to teaching in 1838, she became principal of the West Chester (Pa.) Young Ladies' Seminary, later accepted a position at Rahway, N. J., and in 1841 began her service at Patapsco

Female Institute, Ellicott City, Md., where she concluded active teaching in 1856. Removing thence to Baltimore, she devoted her energies to occasional writing and speaking till her death.

Early giving proof of a brilliant mind, she entered the field of authorship with an essay, "On the Duties and Responsibilities of the Teacher," which she read as a substitute when, a candidate for a teaching position, she could not tell her examiners the "exact distance of the largest fixed star from the planet Mars." Under the influence of Prof. Amos Eaton [q.v.] of the Rensselaer Institute, she perfected her knowledge of the sciences and published a series of textbooks, which became popular in the schools; they included *Familiar Lectures on Botany* (1829); *Dictionary of Chemistry* (1830), translated from the French of L. N. Vauquelin; *Botany for Beginners* (1833); *Geology for Beginners* (1834); *Chemistry for Beginners* (1834); *Natural Philosophy for Beginners* (1836); *Lectures on Natural Philosophy* (1836); and *Lectures on Chemistry* (1837). Her views on physical education were doubtless much influenced by her collaboration with her sister in the preparation of *Progressive Education* (1835), a translation of the first part of Madame Necker de Saussure's *L'Education progressive*. More general in nature, but providing an insight into her character and educational work, are *Caroline Westerly* (1833); *Lectures to Young Ladies* (1833), republished in 1836 under the title *The Female Student; or Lectures to Young Ladies*; *Ida Norman* (1848); *Christian Households* (1858); *Hours with My Pupils* (1859); and *Our Country in its Relation to the Past, Present and Future* (1864), of which she was editor. She also contributed articles on various phases of education to periodicals and newspapers. In 1838 she addressed the College of Professional Teachers on "Female Education," in 1866 she spoke before the American Association for the Advancement of Science on the "Work of Edward Hitchcock," and, later, on the "Infidel Tendencies of Modern Science." She became the second woman member of this Association, and was also long active in the Maryland Academy of Science.

Her career as educator was noteworthy, for her popularization of the sciences as fit subjects for girls' education; for her championship of the movement for physical education; for her promotion of a school for girls, Patapsco Female Institute, which became to the South what Troy Female Seminary was to the North—the best substitute for college in a day when colleges for women were unknown; and finally, for her emphasis on training young women for teaching,

which carried the renown of her Institute to many parts of the United States. During her lifetime the content of girls' education changed from "polite" folderol to a substantial "mental discipline," based on the sciences, mathematics, modern and ancient languages. Through her books and the institutions she served, she was an influential contributor to this change. In the *Female Student; or Lectures to Young Ladies,* her conception of formal discipline of the mind is best set forth.

[Valuable biographical material may be found in Almira Phelps's numerous books and articles; see also Emma L. Bolzau, "Almira Hart Lincoln Phelps" (MS., Univ. of Pa., soon to be published); Barnard's *Am. Jour. of Education,* Sept. 1868; Thomas Woody, *A Hist. of Women's Education in the U. S.* (2 vols., 1929); Alfred Andrews, *The Geneal. Hist. of Deacon Stephen Hart and His Descendants* (1875); *The Phelps Family of America* (1899); *Sun* (Baltimore), July 16, 1884; manuscript material relating to her work at Patapsco Female Institute is in the Md. Hist. Soc., Baltimore.]

T. W.

PHELPS, ANSON GREENE (Mar. 24, 1781–Nov. 30, 1853), merchant and philanthropist, was born at Simsbury, Conn., the youngest of the four sons of Thomas and Dorothy (Woodbridge) Phelps. He was the descendant in the sixth generation of George Phelps who, with his brother William, emigrated from Gloucestershire, England, to Dorchester, Mass., about 1630 and five years later removed to Windsor, Conn. His father was a part owner in a saw- and gristmill at Simsbury and had served through most of the Revolution. After his parents died, his father in 1789 and his mother in 1795, the orphaned boy spent the next few years in the home of the local minister learning the saddler's trade from his elder brother, who became his guardian. Shortly after the opening of the century he settled in Hartford and there followed his trade. On Oct. 26, 1806, he was married to Olivia Eggleston, who bore him seven daughters and one son. His first successful mercantile operation was in manufacturing a large number of saddles and shipping them south. His business prospered; he established a branch in Charleston, S. C., and soon he was extending his interests in other lines, particularly in the merchandising and importing of tin plate and other metals. About 1812 he removed to New York, where he associated himself in business with Elisha Peck under the firm name of Phelps, Peck & Company. This company soon became one of the leading concerns in the country in the importing and merchandising of various metals and began to extend its operations into metal manufacturing at Haverstraw and elsewhere in New York state. The partnership was dissolved in 1828. The chief setback to a business career of almost uninterrupted success came in 1832. when a large warehouse he had recently constructed at the corner of Cliff and Fulton streets collapsed with the loss of several lives. At this time he invited his two sons-in-law, William Earl Dodge [q.v.] and Daniel James, the father of Daniel Willis James [q.v.], to join him as partners in the firm of Phelps, Dodge & Company. Under the direction of Phelps and Dodge the firm expanded its interests from merchandising into manufacturing, mining, and railroads. In the middle thirties it became interested in copper manufacturing at Birmingham on the Naugatuck River in Connecticut. Prevented from extending north along the Naugatuck, Phelps and his associates purchased a site farther south, erected a dam, a factory, and some dwelling houses. From this grew the city of Ansonia, named in his honor. Later the Birmingham Copper Mills were consolidated with the Ansonia Manufacturing Company as the Ansonia Brass and Copper Company. Phelps, Dodge & Company was important in the development of Lake Superior copper and Pennsylvania iron, and its loans to George W. Scranton [q.v.] and his brother were important to the growth of the city of Scranton (Martyn, post, pp. 146–47).

Phelps was as well known in his lifetime as a philanthropist as he was as a business man. Extracts printed from his diary indicate a man with an intense desire to follow the Christian teaching, and his life did not belie his piety. He spent an hour each morning in prayer and other devout exercises, and he frequently presided at the weekly prayer-meetings of the Presbyterian Church. He generously supported and at some time acted as president of the American Bible Society, the American Board of Commissioners for Foreign Missions, the American Home Missionary Society, the New York Institute for the Education of the Blind, and the Colonization Society of the State of Connecticut. He was particularly interested in the latter as affording the best method of dealing with negro slavery. After an extended European trip in pursuit of health he died in New York leaving almost $600,000 of his large fortune to religious and benevolent purposes (Martyn, post, p. 154).

[G. E. Prentiss, *A Sermon Preached on the Death of Anson G. Phelps with some Extracts from his Diary* (1854); J. L. Rockey, *Hist. of New Haven County, Conn.* (1892), vol. II, 479; Carlos Martyn, *Wm. E. Dodge* (1890); D. S. Dodge, *Memorials of Wm. E. Dodge* (1887), pp. 17–19; O. S. Phelps and A. T. Servin, *Phelps Family* (1899), vol. II.]   H. U. F.

PHELPS, AUSTIN (Jan. 7, 1820–Oct. 13, 1890), Congregational clergyman, homilete, son of Rev. Eliakim and Sarah (Adams) Phelps, and a descendant of William Phelps who came from England to Massachusetts in 1630 and was one of the first settlers of Dorchester, was born in West Brookfield, Mass. His early experiences and schooling were determined largely by the peregrinations of his father, who moved to Pittsfield, Mass., in 1826, where he was principal of a young ladies' high school; and in 1830, to Geneva, N. Y., where he was pastor of the First Presbyterian Church. While the family was in Pittsfield, Austin attended the Berkshire Gymnasium, conducted by Dr. Chester Dewey [q.v.], and spent a year at Wilbraham Academy, Wilbraham, Mass. After the removal to Geneva, he entered Hobart College, being at that time thirteen years old. At the close of his second year there, he transferred to Amherst, and in December 1835, his father having taken up his residence in Philadelphia, he enrolled in the University of Pennsylvania, from which he graduated in 1837. Following a year of historical reading under Professor Henry Reed, he studied at Union Theological Seminary and the Yale Divinity School, but without having completed a regular theological course he was licensed to preach by the Third Presbytery of Philadelphia in 1840, and on Mar. 31, 1842, ordained as pastor of the Pine Street Congregational Church, Boston. In September of this year he married Elizabeth Stuart, daughter of Moses Stuart [q.v.], professor at Andover Theological Seminary, where Phelps was for a short time a resident licentiate. His wife was later a writer of popular stories and sketches under the pseudonym "H. Trusta," and one of their three children, Elizabeth Stuart Phelps Ward [q.v.], also became a writer. After the death of his first wife in 1852, Phelps married, April 1854, her sister Mary, then suffering from tuberculosis, and cared for her until she died some two years later; and in June 1858, he married Mary A., daughter of Samuel Johnson of Boston.

After a successful six years' pastorate, in 1848 he was called to Andover Seminary to be professor of sacred rhetoric and homiletics. This position he held for three decades, during the last of which he was also chairman of the faculty. In 1879 he was made professor emeritus, having resigned because of ill health, and the remainder of his life was spent in semi-invalidism, although he was able to do much writing. In the theological war waged at Andover during the last years of his life he aligned himself prominently with the conservatives. His published works were numerous, and are devotional, homiletical, and theological in character. With E. A. Park and Lowell Mason he prepared *The Sabbath Hymn Book; for the Service of Song in the*

House of the Lord (1858), and with Park and D. L. Furber, *Hymns and Choirs; or the Matter and the Manner of the Service of Song in the House of the Lord* (1860). Another book, *The Still Hour; or Communion with God,* which appeared in 1860, was also issued in London and Edinburgh, and circulated to the extent of 200,-000 copies. In 1867 *The New Birth, or the Work of the Holy Spirit* was published, and *Sabbath Hours* in 1875. In the early eighties came a series of widely read homiletical works: *The Theory of Preaching; Lectures on Homiletics* (1881); *Men and Books; or Studies in Homiletics* (1882); *English Style in Public Discourse; with Special Reference to the Usages of the Pulpit* (1883), reissued in 1895, with alterations and additions, as *Rhetoric; Its Theory and Practice.* Subsequent works were *My Study and Other Essays* (1886) and *My Note-book; Fragmentary Studies in Theology and Subjects Adjacent Thereto* (1891). He also contributed much to the *Congregationalist.* His death occurred at Bar Harbor, Me., in his seventy-first year.

[E. S. Phelps, *Austin Phelps; a Memoir* (1891); O. S. Phelps and A. T. Servin, *The Phelps Family of America* (2 vols., 1899); *Eighth Gen. Cat. of the Yale Divinity School . . . 1822-1922* (1922); *Gen. Cat. of the Theolog. Sem., Andover, Mass., 1808-1908* (n.d.); *Congregationalist,* Oct. 23, 1890; *Boston Transcript,* Oct. 13, 1890.]   H. E. S.

PHELPS, CHARLES EDWARD (May 1, 1833–Dec. 27, 1908), jurist, soldier, congressman, author, was born in Guilford, Windham County, Vt., the son of John and Almira (Hart) Lincoln Phelps [*q.v.*], and a descendant of William Phelps who emigrated from England to Dorchester, Mass., in 1630. His father was a lawyer of reputation in Vermont and his mother was a teacher and the author of a series of popular scientific textbooks. In 1841 she assumed charge of the Patapsco Female Institute at Ellicott City, Md.

Phelps attended school at St. Timothy's Hall, near Catonsville, Md., and graduated from the College of New Jersey in 1852. The following year he spent at the Harvard Law School and then studied in the office of Robert J. Brent of Baltimore, a former attorney general of the state. After traveling abroad, he began the practice of law in Baltimore in 1855 and was admitted to practice in the United States Supreme Court in 1859. He was a major in the Maryland National Guard (1858–61), which he helped to organize to suppress the Know-Nothings; in 1860 he was elected to the city council of Baltimore on a reform ticket. When as a child he visited an elder brother at Fortress Monroe, he had acquired a taste for military life, but he was so out of sympathy with the outbreak of hostilities in 1861 that he disobeyed orders and resigned from the Maryland National Guard. Later, however, Aug. 20, 1862, he accepted a lieutenant-colonelcy in the 7th Maryland Volunteers. Twice when in action horses were shot from under him, one at the battle of the Wilderness and one at Laurel Hill, near Spotsylvania on May 8, 1864, where he was wounded, captured, and then recaptured by Custer's cavalry. He had been promoted to colonel on Apr. 13 of the same year; on Sept. 9, he was honorably discharged and on Mar. 13, 1865, brevetted brigadier-general for "gallant and meritorious service." Thirty-three years later, Mar. 30, 1898, he was awarded the Congressional Medal of Honor.

During four years in Congress (1865–69), being elected the first time as a Union war candidate and the second as a Union conservative, Phelps opposed radical measures, for his position, he said, was "radical in war and conservative in peace." The duty devolved upon him of supporting the claims of Annapolis as the site of the United States Naval Academy which, during the war, had been temporarily removed to Newport, R. I. He voted for issues regardless of party lines, served on the committees on naval affairs, militia, and appropriations, and was conspicuous as an antagonist of James G. Blaine. He declined an executive appointment as judge of the court of appeals of Maryland in 1867. On Dec. 29, 1868, he married Martha Woodward, and at the expiration of his second term in Congress returned to Baltimore, where he resumed practice of the law in association with John V. L. Findlay. In 1876 he served as commissioner of public schools and the following year commanded the 8th Maryland Regiment, which was called out to preserve order during the strike riots. He was president of the Maryland Association of Union Veterans and a member of various scientific, historical, military, and social organizations. In 1872 he read a paper on "Planetary Motion and Solar Heat" before the American Association for the Advancement of Science.

His later years were occupied with work as judge, professor, and author. From 1882 until his retirement, Mar. 1, 1908, he was a judge of the supreme bench of Baltimore, an incumbency which was extended beyond the age limit by an act of the Maryland legislature; for twenty-three years (1884–1907) he filled the chair of equity jurisprudence and pleading and practice in the law school of the University of Maryland. An able and hard-working jurist, he nevertheless found leisure to write two books of considerable merit, *Juridical Equity* (1894), a treatise on equity jurisprudence, and *Falstaff and Equity* (1901), which was first published as a series of articles in *Shakespeariana* (July, October 1892, April 1893), and is an analysis of the meaning of the phrase "An the Prince and Poins be not two arrant cowards, there's no equity stirring" (1 *Henry IV, Act II, scene 2*). Phelps died in Baltimore, and was buried in Woodlawn Cemetery. He had four sons and two daughters.

[Phelps's carefully compiled scrapbooks are in the possession of his son, F. H. Phelps, Baltimore, Md.; for published biog. material, see O. S. Phelps and A. T. Servin, *The Phelps Family of America* (2 vols., 1899); *Biog. Dir. Am. Cong.* (1928); *Proc. of the Memorial Meeting of the Bench and Bar of Baltimore City in Memory of Charles Edward Phelps, Late Judge of the Supreme Bench of Baltimore City, January the Eleventh, Nineteen Hundred and Nine* (n.d.); *Report of the Fourteenth Ann. Meeting of the Md. State Bar Asso.* (1909); J. T. Scharf, *Hist. of Md.* (1879), vol. III; H. E. Shepherd, *The Representative Authors of Md.* (1911); *Sun* (Baltimore), Dec. 27, 1908.]   H. C.

PHELPS, EDWARD JOHN (July 11, 1822–Mar. 9, 1900), lawyer, diplomat, was born in Middlebury, Vt., the son of Samuel S. and Frances (Shurtleff) Phelps and a descendant of William Phelps who emigrated from England in 1630 and was one of the founders of Windsor, Conn. His father graduated from Yale College in 1811 and the following year removed to Middlebury, Vt., where he resided until his death in 1855. He won distinction at the Vermont bar, served from 1831 to 1838 as a judge of the supreme court of Vermont, and for thirteen years as United States senator from Vermont. Edward J. Phelps graduated from Middlebury College in 1840 and attended the Yale Law School in 1841–42. He completed his preparation for the bar in the office of Horatio Seymour of Middlebury, was admitted to the Vermont bar in 1843, and began practice in Middlebury. In 1845 he removed to Burlington, Vt., which was his home thereafter. In politics he was a Whig, like his father, until the disintegration of that party, when he became a Democrat. In 1851 he was appointed by President Fillmore second comptroller of the United States Treasury, holding that office until the close of the Fillmore administration. As a Democrat in a strongly Republican state he naturally enjoyed slight political preferment in Vermont. He served as state's attorney of Chittenden County, and sat in the state constitutional convention of 1870. In 1880 he was the Democratic candidate for the governorship, and in 1890 and again in 1892 the candidate of his party for the United States senatorship.

At the Vermont bar he attained a position of leadership in a group of lawyers which included such distinguished men as Luke P. Poland. Jacob

Collamer, and George F. Edmunds. While in active practice he appeared in most of the important cases before the Vermont courts, including the litigation concerning the Vermont railroads, which at intervals for a quarter of a century engaged the attention of both the state and federal courts. He also appeared in important cases before the United States Supreme Court. His acknowledged strength and success as a lawyer lay in his grasp of fundamental principles rather than in mastery of legal technicalities or factual details. His legal career culminated in his service, under appointment of President Harrison, as counsel for the United States in the fur-seal arbitration of 1893 between the United States and Great Britain, his associate counsel being Frederic R. Coudert and James C. Carter [*qq.v.*]. His closing argument before the arbitral tribunal, extending over a period of ten days, was an elaborate and able digest of the American case. He was the first president of the Vermont Bar Association, and in 1880 he was elected president of the American Bar Association. In 1888 his appointment to the office of chief justice of the United States Supreme Court, made vacant by the death of Morrison R. Waite, was seriously considered by President Cleveland, but political considerations growing out of his diplomatic service in England were successfully urged against him.

In 1881 he became Kent Professor of Law in Yale University, continuing to hold that chair until his death except for the period of his residence in London. From 1880 to 1883 he was professor of medical jurisprudence in the University of Vermont, his lectures on that subject having been published; and in 1882 he lectured on constitutional law at Boston University. His public career culminated in his appointment by President Cleveland, in 1885, as minister to Great Britain as the successor of James Russell Lowell. Although he was without previous diplomatic experience, his mission at the Court of St. James's was eminently successful. By his tact and ability in the discharge of his official duties, his personal charm, broad culture, and felicity as an occasional public speaker, he won for himself an assured place in the official and social life of England, materially strengthening the ties of friendship between the two countries. Among the important diplomatic matters with which he was called upon to deal were the question of American fishery rights in Canadian North-Atlantic waters, the Bering Sea fur-seal question, which later went to arbitration, the boundary dispute between Venezuela and Great Britain, which in Cleveland's second administration occasioned strained relations between the United States and Great Britain, and the negotiation of an extradition treaty. His diplomatic service terminated early in 1889. As a public speaker he appeared on several notable occasions, among his better-known addresses being one on Chief Justice Marshall delivered in 1879 before the American Bar Association; an address on "The Law of the Land" delivered in 1886 before the Edinburgh Philosophical Institution; an address delivered in New York, in 1890, at the centennial celebration of the federal judiciary; and an address on the Monroe Doctrine before the Brooklyn Institute of Arts and Sciences in 1896. He wrote occasional essays dealing chiefly with legal and political subjects. He died at New Haven, Conn., in his seventy-eighth year. He had married, on Aug. 13, 1845, Mary L. Haight, by whom he had four children.

[There is a memoir of Phelps by J. W. Stewart in Phelps's *Orations and Essays* (1901), ed. by J. G. McCullough. See also: M. H. Buckham, "The Life and Pub. Services of Edw. John Phelps," *Proc. Vt. Hist. Soc. . . . 1899–1900* (1901); W. H. Crockett, *Vermont: The Green Mountain State,* vol. IV (1921), and D. L. Cady's biography of Phelps in Crockett's *Vermonters: A Book of Biogs.* (1931); *Papers Relating to the Foreign Relations of the U. S.,* 1886–88; *Cat. of . . . Middlebury Coll. . . . 1800–1915* (1917); *Who's Who in America,* 1899–1900; O. S. Phelps and A. T. Servin, *The Phelps Family of America* (2 vols., 1899); *N. Y. Tribune, Burlington Daily Free Press,* Mar. 10, 1900. Phelps's argument in the fur-seal arbitration is contained in *Senate Executive Document 177,* 53 Cong., 2 Sess.]　　　　　　　　　　　　　　　　E. C. M.

PHELPS, ELIZABETH STUART, 1815–1852, and

PHELPS, ELIZABETH STUART, 1844–1911 [See WARD, ELIZABETH STUART PHELPS, 1844–1911].

PHELPS, GUY ROWLAND (Apr. 1, 1802–Mar. 18, 1869), founder of the Connecticut Mutual Life Insurance Company, was born at Simsbury, Conn., the seventh of eight children of Noah Amherst and Charlotte (Wilcox) Phelps. He was the descendant of William Phelps who, with his brother George, emigrated from England to Dorchester, Mass., about 1630 and later was one of the first settlers of Windsor, Conn. The boy was graduated from the Medical Institution of Yale College in 1825 and taught school for several winters, devoting his summers to the study of medicine. After this training under local doctors he went to New York to study under Valentine Mott [*q.v.*] and Alexander Mott. He opened an office in New York and practised for a time there and later in Simsbury, when the failure of his health forced him to return there. On Mar. 20, 1833, he was married at Simsbury to Hannah, the daughter of Wait Latimer. After returning to New York and again to Simsbury he was convinced that he lacked the physique necessary for the duties of a successful physician. About 1837 he removed to Hartford and opened a drug store. His drug business prospered from the start. One of his formulas, "Phelps's Tomato Pill," had an extended sale, and the returns from this with the profits of his drug store laid the basis for his fortune.

The delicate health that had proved a handicap to his career as a physician early aroused his interest in life insurance. That business was then in its earliest infancy in America and was eyed dubiously by the general population. However, he made a diligent study of life insurance as carried on in England and the United States, became convinced of the soundness of the idea, and determined to found a mutual company to promote it. After interesting a number of friends and relatives in the project, he wrote a charter for the Connecticut Mutual Life Insurance Company and fought through two sessions of the legislature to have it granted in 1846. In the summer of that year the company was organized with him as secretary. Until his death, twenty-three years later, he remained the dominating influence in the organization, acting as secretary of the company until 1866 and as president from 1866 to 1869. Though not the originator of the mutual system of insurance, he did much to popularize it. For its day, the charter was unusual in the care with which it safeguarded the interests of the policy holders, and the business methods of the company were based on the conservative English practice with some slight modifications to meet American conditions. Before business was started, nineteen men, six of whom were his relatives, guaranteed $50,000, and no policies were issued until applications for $100,000 had been received. Shortly after the organization he went to England to make a further study of English insurance practice. Good financial management and rigid economy carried the company successfully through the panic of 1857 and the boom period of the Civil War. The economy of the company is illustrated by the fact that in the early years Phelps swept out his own office, and friends often met him on the street carrying kindling under his arm to light his office fire. He was a man of quiet habits and studious mind, particularly interested in languages and history. Deeply concerned with public affairs, he served his townsmen as a member of the city council, 1846–47, and as alderman, 1856–59. He was survived by his wife and one of their four children.

[*Commemorative Biog. Record of Hartford County, Conn.* (1901); G. L. Clark, *A Hist. of Conn.* (1914);

P. H. Woodward, *Insurance in Conn.* (1897); *The Conn. Mutual Educational Course,* published by Conn. Mutual Life Insurance Co. (1920); O. S. Phelps and A. T. Servin, *The Phelps Family in America* (1899), vol. I.]   H. U. F.

PHELPS, JOHN SMITH (Dec. 22, 1814–Nov. 20, 1886), congressman, governor of Missouri, was born at Simsbury, Conn., the son of Lucy (Smith) and Elisha Phelps, a member of Congress from 1819 to 1821 and from 1825 to 1829. He was the descendant of William Phelps who emigrated from England about 1630 and the cousin of Guy Rowland Phelps [*q.v.*]. He attended common school at Simsbury and then entered Washington College at Hartford, now Trinity College. He left before graduating on account of his refusal to take the part assigned to him on the Commencement program. In 1859 he was given the degree of A.B. as of the class of 1832. He studied law under his father and was admitted to the bar in 1835. On Apr. 30, 1837, he married Mary Whitney of Portland, Me. Later in the same year the bride and groom settled at Springfield, Mo., where their five children were born. In the small frontier town he prospered and quickly became a leading lawyer of southwest Missouri. He was elected to the state legislature in 1840.

Four years later he was elected to Congress as a Democrat and served in that body continuously for eighteen years thereafter. Within a short time he won distinction as an able and influential debater. Among the leading policies and projects that he advocated were the allotment of adequate bounties to soldiers, government aid for railroads, the establishment of an overland mail service to California, and cheaper postage. After a long fight the postage on ordinary letters was reduced to three cents. He was a leading advocate of the early admission of Oregon and California to the Union. For ten years he was a member of the committee on ways and means and from 1858 to 1860 was its chairman. Although he was not counted as extraordinarily brilliant, nevertheless, his contemporaries appreciated his faithfulness and his efficiency as well as his friendliness. During the last six or seven years of his service in Congress his ability as well as his position of seniority made him the logical candidate for the speakership, but his Northern birth and his Union political convictions caused him to be defeated for the place. When the Civil War broke out he went home, organized the Phelps Regiment, and led it in some of the hardest fighting at the battle of Pea Ridge, Ark. In July 1862 he was appointed by Lincoln military governor of Arkansas, but he soon resigned the position on account of the failure of his health. In his wife he had an able helpmate. During the war her home was turned into a hospital, and she took care of the body of Gen. Nathaniel Lyon [*q.v.*] after the battle of Wilson's Creek. For such services Congress voted her the sum of $20,000, which she used to establish an orphans' home at Springfield for the children of both Union and Confederate soldiers.

In 1864 he resumed his law practice in Springfield. He was the Democratic candidate for governor of Missouri in 1868, but owing to the wholesale disfranchisements of the Drake constitution he was defeated. Under the more liberal constitution of 1875 he became an ideal candidate because he could unify the Northern and Southern factions in Missouri Democracy. In 1876 he was easily elected, and he served the full four-year term. During his administration there was much agitation over strikes, chiefly of railway employees, and over the Greenback movement. He suppressed the strikes with vigor. The movement for currency reform, thanks to the steady economic recovery from the panic of 1873, produced no acute problem for him to solve. He was in hearty accord with the strong contemporary movement looking toward a more liberal support of the public schools of the state. Upon his retirement from office the *St. Louis Globe Democrat* said that "it will hardly be disputed that Missouri never had a better governor than John S. Phelps" (Jan. 12, 1881).

[Walter Williams and F. C. Shoemaker, *Missouri* (1930), vols. I, II; *The Bench and Bar of St. Louis . . . and other . . . Cities* (1884); W. B. Stevens, *Centennial Hist. of Mo.* (1921), vol. II; H. L. Conard, *Encyc. of the Hist. of Mo.* (1901), vol. V; F. C. Shoemaker, *A Hist. of Mo.* (1922); O. S. Phelps and A. T. Servin, *The Phelps Family* (1899), vol. I; *Booneville Weekly Advertiser,* Nov. 26, 1886; minutes of trustees of Trinity College through the courtesy of Professor Arthur Adams.]   H. E. N.

PHELPS, OLIVER (Oct. 21, 1749–Feb. 21, 1809), merchant and land promoter, was born on a farm near Poquonock, Conn., the seventeenth child of Thomas Phelps and the ninth of Ann (Brown), Thomas' second wife. He was a descendant of George Phelps who, with his brother William, came to America in 1630, lived in Dorchester, Mass., and in 1635 moved to Windsor, Conn. Oliver's father died when the boy was but three months old, leaving the mother to bring up the large family. At the age of seven he started work in a general store at Suffield. Without formal instruction, the quick-witted lad picked up his education at odd moments, meanwhile reinforcing his natural instincts as a trader. Self-confident and energetic, he went to Granville, Mass., in 1770, and before the outbreak of the Revolution had built up a prosperous mercantile business. After a brief military service, he was appointed by Massachusetts superintendent of purchases of army supplies (1777). This office he filled with energy and success until the end of the war.

Meanwhile he had entered the lower house of the state legislature (1778–80); later he served in the constitutional convention (1779–80), in the Senate (1785), and in the governor's council (1786). A prosperous, if not a rich man now he had already proven himself a bold operator in various speculative fields. The great post-war boom in wild lands was just beginning and Phelps saw his opportunity in the desire of Massachusetts to sell its huge holdings in western New York—all the land in the state west of Seneca Lake. After much bargaining he and Nathaniel Gorham [q.v.] purchased the preëmptive rights to these six million acres (Apr. 1, 1788) for £300,000 in state notes. This sum, equal at the time to about $175,000, was to be paid in three yearly instalments. The following July Phelps bought the Indian rights to the easternmost third of this purchase and arranged for its survey and division into tiers of townships six miles square. In the meantime he and Gorham sought feverishly to sell enough shares in their enterprise to make possible their payments to the state. They failed, however, and by the successful assertion of the federal government's claim to the triangular tract on Lake Erie, they were also disappointed in a sale they had expected to make of this land to Pennsylvania (Massachusetts Archives, House File 3208). Even with an extension of time they were unable to make their first payment as agreed. With the second instalment soon falling due, in March 1790 they turned back to Massachusetts two-thirds of the original purchase, retaining an embarrassed title to that already bought of the Indians. Payment for this remaining third was in fact long drawn out, for by 1791 state notes were worth nearly double their value in 1788 and the debt of Phelps and Gorham was proportionately increased.

Though Phelps thus saw a huge profit slip through his fingers, he retained his buoyancy and his speculative fervor. Within five years he had acquired title to nearly a million acres along the lower Mississippi, to a share in the Western Reserve, and to lands in many other sections. He was operating largely on credit, however, and when the land bubble was pricked in 1796, his affairs became hopelessly involved. Fearful of following William Duer and Robert Morris, fellow land speculators, to the debtors' prison, he went for a time into hiding. Eventually, after sev-

eral extended visits to the Genesee, he took up his residence in 1802 at Canandaigua. Here he passed his last years managing the remnants of his once extensive land holdings and promoting the interests of the Jeffersonian party. He served one term in Congress from 1803 to 1805. By his wife, Mary Seymour of Hartford, Conn., whom he married Dec. 16, 1773, he had a son, Oliver Leicester, and a daughter, Mary.

[O. S. Phelps and A. T. Servin, *The Phelps Family of America*, vol. II (1899); Orsamus Turner, *Hist. of the Pioneer Settlement of Phelps and Gorham's Purchase* (1851); G. S. Conover and L. C. Aldrich, *Hist. of Ontario County* (1893); R. L. Higgins, *Expansion in N. Y.* (1931); Phelps Papers in the N. Y. State Library at Albany.]   P. D. E.

PHELPS, THOMAS STOWELL (Nov. 2, 1822–Jan. 10, 1901), naval officer, was born at Buckfield, Me., the son of Stephen Decatur and Elisabeth Nixon (Stowell) Phelps, and descendant of George Phelps, who came with his brother William from England to America in 1630 and settled at Windsor, Conn., in 1635. He was appointed midshipman on Jan. 17, 1840, served five years chiefly in the Mediterranean and Brazil squadrons, studied further at the Naval Academy, and was then made passed midshipman. He was wrecked in the *Boston* on Eleuthera Island, Bahamas, in the winter of 1846, served in the *Polk* in Mexican waters from February to April 1847, and was then assigned to the coast survey, in which, except for another Mediterranean cruise in the *Independence* and *Constitution*, he remained until the close of 1852. A year in the receiving ship at Philadelphia was followed by extended duty in the *Decatur* of the Pacific Squadron, 1853–57, during which time he was made lieutenant. His experiences in defending the settlements in Washington Territory during the Indian uprising, are told in his "Reminiscences of Seattle . . . and the U. S. Sloop-of-War *Decatur*, 1855–56" (*United Service,* December 1881). After two years' ordnance work in Washington, D. C., and service in the Paraquay Expedition, 1858–59, he commanded the *Vixen* in survey duty till the opening of the Civil War.

His experience and special skill in this field led to his selection, June 1, 1861, to make a careful survey of the Potomac, a task which he completed during the month in the steamers *Philadelphia* and *Anacostia*. He was frequently in range of enemy batteries at Aquia Creek and elsewhere, his river boats apparently not being suspected of hostile activities. During the autumn his surveying was shifted to the approaches of Pamlico Sound where preparations for the Roanoke Island expedition were being made, his plans again being successfully executed despite skirmishes between his steamer, the *Corwin,* and the Confederate "mosquito" flotilla. Thereafter he carried on similar work in Virginia waters until the Peninsular Campaign of April-May, 1862, when the *Corwin* was employed in reconnaissance and in support for the army. The *Corwin* captured several enemy small craft in York River on May 4, after the evacuation of Yorktown, and on May 7 it ran up the Mattapony River during the battle of West Point and thus prevented a considerable Confederate force from joining the main body of troops. He was made lieutenant commander in July 1862, was engaged from then until March 1863, in a more complete survey of the Potomac, and afterward made various surveys in anticipation of military and naval movements. At the close of 1864 he joined Porter's squadron, commanding the steam-sloop *Juanita* in the second attack on Fort Fisher, Jan. 13–15, 1865. He was made commander in 1865, captain in 1871, commodore in 1879, and rear admiral in 1884, eight months before his retirement. His sea commands after the war were the *Saranac* in the North Pacific, 1871–73, and the South Atlantic Squadron, 1883–84. In intervening periods he had duty at the Mare Island navy yard, San Francisco. On Jan. 25, 1848, he married Margaret Riche Levy, daughter of Capt. John B. Levy of Virginia. They had five children, one of the boys, Thomas Stowell, Jr., entering the navy and rising to the rank of rear admiral. After retirement he made his home in Washington, D. C. His death from pneumonia occurred at a hospital in New York City only a month preceding his wife's death from the same cause.

[Phelps's "Reminiscences of the Old Navy" appeared serially in *United Service,* Apr.–Dec. 1882; see also, *Who's Who in America,* 1899–1900, and for family data, O. S. Phelps and A. T. Servin, *The Phelps Family of America and their English Ancestors* (2 vols., 1899); personal narratives of his Civil War service appear in E. S. Maclay, *A Hist. of the U. S. Navy from 1775 to 1893* (2nd ed., 1899), vol. II; the *N. Y. Herald,* Jan. 11, 1901, and the *Army & Navy Jour.,* Jan. 12, 1901, contain obituaries.]
A. W.

PHELPS, WILLIAM FRANKLIN (Feb. 15, 1822–Aug. 15, 1907), educator, was born in Auburn, N. Y., the son of Halsey and Lucinda (Hitchcock) Phelps, and a descendant of William Phelps, who came from England to Massachusetts in 1630 and later settled in Windsor, Conn. While William was still in the district school he was impressed by the absurdity of the methods of education then in use, which fact doubtless influenced his career as an educator. In 1834 he entered the newly established Auburn high school, an excellent institution, where he learned useful lessons in method and the value of kindness as an educational force. In 1838 the master told William's father that his son was fully able to take a school and in the next fall, before he was seventeen, he taught sixty boys and girls of all ages, attainments, and conditions in a primitive one-room schoolhouse. For the next five summers he attended the Auburn Academy and had instruction from efficient teachers. During the winters he taught in various rural schools, acquiring the reputation of being one of the best teachers in that part of the country.

In 1844 he was called to a large public school in the city of Auburn, where in one room he taught 140 pupils of all ages. He was soon appointed state student from Cayuga County to the normal school in Albany, from which he graduated in 1846. In 1845 he organized a model practice school, which was formally opened in 1846, and which he conducted for seven years. His health requiring that he have rest and change, from 1852 to 1855 he engaged in business and travel. In the latter year he organized the state normal school at Trenton, N. J., serving as principal and professor of the science of education. He was also principal of the Farnum Preparatory School at Beverly, N. J., which he organized in 1856. Removing to Minnesota in 1864, he reorganized the state normal school at Winona and was its head until 1876, when he became president of the normal school at Whitewater, Wis., which position he occupied for two years. From 1881 to 1886 he was secretary of the Winona board of trade; from 1886 to 1887, secretary of the St. Paul chamber of commerce; and from 1887 to 1889, of the Duluth chamber of commerce. He then returned to St. Paul, where he was connected successively with a number of business enterprises. He died in St. Paul, in his eighty-sixth year.

Phelps published *The Teacher's Hand-book* (1875), which was translated into Spanish for use in the Argentine Republic. He was editor-in-chief of the *Educational Weekly,* Chicago, 1877–78. In 1879 he published six brochures— *What Is Education?, Socrates, Pestalozzi, Horace Mann, Froebel,* and *Roger Ascham and John Sturm*—all prepared for use as Chautauqua textbooks. He also revised and edited, 1902, H. W. Pearson's *A Nebulo-Meteoric Hypothesis of Creation.* He was one of the organizers of the American Normal School Association, and its first president (1858–63); he also served as president of the National Education Association (1875–76). At the Centennial Exhibition in 1876 he presided at the first international conference of educators. He was awarded a diploma and silver medal at the French exposition in 1878 for his work as an educator. Among his other achievements was the invention of a map-support for the exhibition of maps and charts of different sizes. He was married in 1854 to Carolyn, daughter of William Chapman of Albany, N. Y., and widow of Crawford Livingston.

[*Am. Jour. of Education*, Dec. 1858; *An Hist. Sketch of the State Normal College at Albany, N. Y.* (1894); *Hist. of Winona County* (1883); C. O. Ruggles, *Hist. Sketch and Notes, Winona State Normal School* (1910); *Bull. of the Winona State Normal School*, Oct. 1907; "Minn. Biogs.," *Colls. Minn. Hist. Soc.*, vol. XIV (1912); *Who's Who in America*, 1906–07; *School Jour.*, Aug. 31, 1907; *St. Paul Dispatch*, Aug. 16, 1907.]   J. S—n.

PHELPS, WILLIAM WALTER (Aug. 24, 1839–June 17, 1894), lawyer, business man, congressman, diplomat, was born in Dundaff, Susquehanna County, Pa. He was a descendant of William Phelps, an English emigrant who came with his brother George to America in 1630 and who settled in Connecticut in 1635. John Jay Phelps, his father, left Connecticut to live for a short time in Pennsylvania and then moved to New York City where he built up a great fortune as an importer and railway promoter. His mother was Rachel Badgerly (Phinney). He attended the Mount Washington Institute, New York City, and then a private school at Golden Hill, near Bridgeport, Conn. He entered Yale before he was sixteen years of age and was graduated second in the class of 1860. On Commencement day, July 26, 1860, he was married to Ellen Maria Sheffield, daughter of Joseph Earl Sheffield [*q.v.*], founder of the scientific school bearing his name. After an extended bridal tour of Europe, he entered the law school of Columbia University and received the degree of LL.B. in 1863 as valedictorian of the class. A highly successful career in New York City as legal representative of several large corporations was cut short by the death of his father in 1869, when he retired to devote himself to the management of family properties and his own business interests. He transferred his residence to an estate at Teaneck near Englewood, N. J., from which district he was elected as a Republican to Congress in 1872. In the House of Representatives he distinguished himself by vigorous speeches on financial subjects and denunciations of the White League. Yet his independence of judgment led him to turn against his party in the contest over the Civil Rights Bill, with the result that he was defeated for reëlection by seven votes. He remained an active party worker, however, supporting Blaine, a close personal friend, in his candidacy for the presidency in the conventions of 1880 and 1884. He was appointed minister to Austria-Hungary on May 5, 1881, but resigned the post within the year and returned to reclaim his seat in Congress, holding it thereafter for three terms. In the convention of 1888 he was supported by Blaine for the vice-presidential nomination (Edward Stanwood, *James Gillespie Blaine, American Statesmen*, 2 ser., vol. III, 1908, p. 309).

The interest taken by Phelps in the Samoan question during his service on the Committee on Foreign Affairs qualified him for an appointment by President Harrison on Mar. 18, 1889, as commissioner to the Berlin Conference on that question. His judgment in reconciling the conflicting views of his colleagues, John Adam Kasson and George Handy Bates [*qq.v.*] and in conceding enough minor points to assure fulfillment of the German government's substantial concessions without permitting it to dictate the settlement, was largely responsible for the measure of success attained (Alice F. Tyler, *The Foreign Policy of James G. Blaine*, 1927, p. 241). Although the outcome was not wholly satisfactory to Secretary Blaine, the quality of Phelps's work warranted his appointment as minister to Germany in 1889. His principal task during four years' tenure of that post was, as it had previously been at Vienna, the presentation of arguments in favor of the removal of the prohibition against importation of American pork products. Success crowned his efforts in September 1891. His cultivated and genial personality and his familiarity with the language of the country made him a popular representative not only among the Germans, but also among the rapidly increasing American colony in Berlin.

Upon his return to America, in the summer of 1893, he accepted an appointment on the New Jersey Court of Errors and Appeals. The confining duties of the position hastened his death within a year of pulmonary tuberculosis. He died at Englewood, N. J., and was survived by his wife and three children. His continued interest in his alma mater was most effectively demonstrated when he became a leader in the "Young Yale" movement which reflected the dissatisfaction of the young alumni with the staid policies of the trustees. A thoroughly stimulating, if somewhat bombastic address delivered by Phelps at an alumni dinner during the Commencement exercises in 1870, was largely responsible for the vigor with which the movement was charged from that date (H. E. Starr, *William Graham Sumner*, 1925, pp. 82–90). He was notably a forceful and witty speaker, equally popular in the intimate circle and on the platform. His benefactions from abundant wealth were wisely and gracefully given in many directions.

[H. M. Herrick, *William Walter Phelps, His Life and Public Service* (1904); *Foreign Relations*, 1891, pp. 505–17; *Obit. Record of Grads. of Yale Univ., 1890–1900* (1900); *N. Y. Times*, June 17, 1894; *N. Y. Tribune*, June 18, 1894.] 　　　　　　　J.V.F.

PHILIP (d. Aug. 12, 1676), Sachem of the Wampanoag Indians, was the leader of the most severe Indian war in the history of New England. The son of Massassoit [*q.v.*], his Indian name was Pometacom, Metacom, or Metacomet, but the colonists dubbed him "King Philip." Assuming the position of Sachem of the Wampanoags at the time of his brother Alexander's death in 1662, for which many Indians believed the Plymouth authorities responsible, Philip renewed his father's treaty with the settlers and conducted himself in a generally peaceful manner for the following nine years. The frequent land sales, which were necessitated by the natives' growing dependence upon English guns, ammunition, blankets, and liquor, restricted the Wampanoags, Narragansetts, and Nipmucks to ever narrowing territories and scarcer game, although the lands seem to have been fully paid for by the whites (S. G. Drake, *Old Indian Chronicle*, p. 3). Philip acted in a haughty and arrogant manner and considered himself on terms of equality with his "brother," King Charles II. Suspected of plotting against the settlers, he was summoned to Taunton in 1671, forced to surrender part of the firearms of his tribe, and fined. The execution in 1675 of three of his warriors for the murder of Sassamon, his former secretary, who had revealed his plots to the English, provoked the conflict known as King Philip's War. Starting in June 1675 in the vicinity of Narragansett Bay, the war spread rapidly through the Plymouth and Massachusetts colonies, and extended westward as far as the settlements on the Connecticut River. The Wampanoags with their Nipmuck allies assaulted most of the outlying towns, burned several and slaughtered countless men, women, and children, while the troops of the United Colonies tried in vain to engage them in a decisive conflict. After an unsuccessful attempt to win the Mohawks to his side (Mather, *post*, p. 38), Philip again fell upon the Massachusetts towns in the spring and summer of 1676, but with less success than formerly. The colonial troops now adopted the policy of destroying the Indians' corn, capturing their women and children, and offering immunity to warriors who would desert Philip. Deprived of most of his followers, including his wife, Wootonekanuske, and son, Philip took refuge in a swamp near Mount Hope (Bristol,

R. I.), where he was shot Aug. 12, 1676, by an Indian serving under Capt. Benjamin Church [*q.v.*]. As a traitor to the King, he was beheaded, drawn, and quartered, and his head exhibited at Plymouth for many years. He was an able and crafty leader, according to Indian standards, and not without some elements of human kindness. Much of his success, however, was due to the inefficiency of the colonial officers, and there is little evidence that he planned a wide-spread conspiracy to exterminate the white settlers. New England paid dearly for her victory, with the destruction of twelve towns, several thousand deaths, and a debt estimated at £100,000.

[The outstanding contemporary works dealing with King Philip's War have been edited by Samuel G. Drake. Among these are: William Hubbard, *The Hist. of the Indian Wars in New England* (2 vols., 1865); Increase Mather, *The Hist. of King Philip's War* (1862); *The Old Indian Chronicle* (1867), a collection of contemporary tracts and letters; and *The Book of the Indians* (1841). The last-named contains letters, documents, and a biography of King Philip. Thomas Church's *Entertaining Passages Relating to Philip's War* (1716) is the account of Capt. Benj. Church. John Easton's account of the war was edited by B. F. Hough and published under the title: *A Narrative of the Causes Which Led to Philip's Indian War* (1858). It is also included in *Narratives of the Indian Wars* (1913), ed. by C. H. Lincoln, a volume in Scribner's Original Narrative Series. Relations between the Indians and the New England Confederation will be found in *Records of the Colony of New Plymouth*, vol. V (1856). The introduction to George M. Bodge's *Soldiers in King Philip's War* (1891) gives a good secondary account.] 　　H.P.S.

PHILIP, JOHN WOODWARD (Aug. 26, 1840–June 30, 1900), naval officer, was born at Kinderhook, Columbia County, N. Y., the son of Dr. John Henry and Lucena (Woodward) Philip, and a descendant of the distinguished colonial Dutch family of Philipse. The final letters of the name were dropped by some branches of the family after the Revolution. After attending Kinderhook Academy he was appointed midshipman, and graduated from the Naval Academy on June 1, 1861. Extremely shy in feminine society, he was in academy days and later a very genial soul, overflowing with humor, trenchant in speech, one of the best loved men in the navy. Despite his youth, his Civil War service was entirely as executive, or second in command, first in the sloop *Marion* in the Gulf, and then in the *Sonoma* in the James River. From his promotion to the rank of lieutenant in July 1862, until the close of 1864 he was in the *Chippewa, Pawnee*, and in the monitor *Montauk* on the southeast coast blockade, where he was frequently in action and where he was wounded, July 16, 1863, in an engagement with shore batteries in the Stono River. He was executive of the *Wachusett* during an Oriental cruise, 1865–67, and was transferred from her to be executive of the *Hartford*.

flagship of the China Squadron. After two years in the *Richmond* of the European Squadron he was again in the *Hartford*, 1872–73. He was made commander in December 1874 and was for two years thereafter on leave as captain of the Pacific mail liner *City of New York*, which he took through Magellan to the west coast. He then commanded the *Adams*, 1876–77, and the *Tuscarora* and *Ranger*, 1877–83, in survey work on the west coast of Mexico and Central America.

In 1882 he was married at San Francisco to Mrs. Josepha Francesca (Tate) Cowan. Then followed his first extended shore duty as lighthouse inspector, 12th District, 1884–87, and as commander of the receiving ship *Independence*, Mare Island, 1887–90. He was promoted to the rank of captain on Mar. 31, 1889, spent a year in the *Atlanta*, became construction inspector of the cruiser *New York*, and commanded her until August 1894. In 1894–97 he was captain of the Boston navy yard, and afterward commanded the *Texas* from October 1897, through the Spanish-American War. Early in the hostilities he devoted himself energetically to making much-needed repairs in his ship, especially improvements in the rate of fire of the turret guns, the results of which were demonstrated effectively at Santiago. The *Texas* operated with the Flying Squadron, then joined the Santiago blockade, and was next to the *Brooklyn* at the west end of the blockading line on July 3, 1898, when the Spanish fleet emerged. Collision with the *Brooklyn*, when she made her much-discussed eastward turn at the opening of the battle, was averted by Philip's "quick appreciation and instant seaman-like action," to quote Admiral Mahan (Maclay, *Life, post*, p. 15), in backing and shifting course. When his crew shouted as one of their salvos hit a Spanish ship, Philip uttered his characteristic words, "Don't cheer, men, those poor devils are dying." He was made commodore on Aug. 10, 1898, and rear admiral Mar. 3, 1899. From January 1899, until his death he was commandant of the Brooklyn navy yard, where his warm sympathy and earnest religious feeling led him wholeheartedly into the movement for the construction of a Sailors' Rest building near the yard. His death occurred suddenly from heart failure, and he was buried in the Naval Cemetery at Annapolis, being survived by his wife, a son, John Woodward Philip, and a stepson, Barrett Philip.

[Many tributes and recollections of fellow officers are included in E. S. Maclay, *Life and Adventures of "Jack" Philip, Rear-Admiral* (1903), which was first published in the *Illustrated Navy*, a memorial magazine in four numbers, May–Aug. 1903, ed. by E. S. Maclay and Barrett Philip; a record of his cruise in the *Wachusett* is also printed in this publication. Family data were contributed by J. W. Philip, a son. See also E. H. Hall, *Philipse Manor Hall at Yonkers, N. Y.* (1912), *Who's Who in America, 1899–1900*, and obituaries in the *Army & Navy Jour.*, July 7, 1900, and the *N. Y. Times*, July 1, 1900.]

A. W.

PHILIPP, EMANUEL LORENZ (Mar. 25, 1861–June 15, 1925), governor of Wisconsin, was born in Sauk County, Wis., the son of Swiss emigrants. His parents, Luzi and Sabina (Ludwig) Philipp, were members of an agricultural colony that has contributed a vigorous element to the life of Wisconsin. The boy attended the public school of his district and was licensed to teach without further formal training. He soon learned telegraphy and was train dispatcher and station agent for the Chicago, Milwaukee & Saint Paul Railway at Baraboo, Wis. In this service he obtained a transfer to Milwaukee. He became a contracting freight agent, took charge of the Gould freight interests, and also was traffic manager for the Schlitz brewery. On Oct. 27, 1887, he was married to Bertha Schweke of Reedsburg, Wis. They had three children. In 1893 he became interested in the lumber business and founded the town of Philipp in Tallahatchie County, Miss. During the following decade he devoted his energies and activities largely to this business. It proved profitable, and he rapidly increased his private estate. However, he retained his connection with transportation. In 1897 he became president of the Union Refrigerator Transit Company and six years later became its manager and proprietor. In 1904 he published *The Truth about Wisconsin Freight Rates*. This was followed in 1910 by *Political Reform in Wisconsin*, in which he was assisted by Edgar T. Wheelock, and which deals with the primary election law, the problems of taxation, and of railway regulation. These titles reveal the transition of his interests from business to politics.

He had become actively interested in politics and was a delegate to the Republican conventions of 1904 and 1908. There he formed acquaintances with the leaders of the national administration. The division of the Republican party, especially in Wisconsin, gave opportunity for leadership of a faction that would cooperate with the national administration, and he seized this opening. Meanwhile, he also became fire and police commissioner of Milwaukee. By 1914 he was fully intrenched in the local machine and was able to obtain the nomination for governor. Reëlected in two successive campaigns to this position, he served from 1915 to 1921. His work as governor was distinguished. He entered upon the task with slight experience in politics and served throughout a period of great stress and agitation. He was pledged to economy and

535

to reduction of the costs of the state institutions. However, he permitted no action until investigation of the institutions had been conducted. This procedure was beneficial and in many instances resulted in definite gains for the institutions. As war governor of a state with a large population of foreign origin, he reflected the sentiments of his people and was critical of the national administration. He had favored an embargo on goods to the Allies, opposed conscription, and opposed sending an army to France. In spite of his pronouncement of his views, General Crowder credited him with the most commendable record of any governor for cooperation in enforcement of the draft law (*Milwaukee Sentinel*, Nov. 5, 6, 1918). He gave every assistance in carrying the war to a successful termination. With the coming of peace he had a constructive plan for getting the soldiers back to the soil by assisting them to procure tracts of cut-over land in Wisconsin. He gave his support to a generous educational bonus for soldiers. Although he was not a Progressive but "an out-and-out corporation man" according to LaFollette (*post*, p. 229), the Progressive leaders admitted that no recognized progressive measure was repealed during his administration. Although a man of limited schooling, he was one of broader interests than his mere profession.

He was a regent of Marquette University, active in the work of the humane society, and a promoter of civic activities and progress. He procured and took great pride in the maintenance of a splendid farm. In appearance he was below average stature, broad and powerfully built. His whole appearance radiated strength of body and character. He was not given to great freedom of expression but on occasion could give vent to deep and moving emotions. He had those qualities that make and retain loyal friends.

[*Messages to the Leg. and Proclamations of Emanuel L. Philipp* (1920); E. B. Usher, *Wisconsin* (1914), vol. VII; *Who's Who in America*, 1922–23; *A Standard Hist. of Sauk County* (1918), vol. II, ed. by H. E. Cole; R. M. LaFollette, *LaFollette's Autobiog.* (1913); *Milwaukee Sentinel*, June 16, 1925.]   J. L. S.

PHILIPS, JOHN FINIS (Dec. 31, 1834–Mar. 13, 1919), soldier, congressman, jurist, was born in Boone County, Mo. His parents, John G. and Mary (Copeland) Philips, were Kentuckians who went to Missouri in 1817. Although he spent his boyhood in a simple pioneer community, the educational and religious influences of his home were strong and the discipline severe. After graduating in 1855 from Centre College in Kentucky, he read law in the office of Gen. John B. Clark, a leading lawyer and politician of cen-

tral Missouri. In 1857 he married Fleecie Batterton of Kentucky and commenced practice at Georgetown, Mo., attaining a large and lucrative business and devoting considerable time and attention to politics and to the Whig party. His career was interrupted by the Civil War which shattered the social, professional, and political life of the state, and forced a decision for or against secession. Philips soon decided, and put at the disposal of the Union his ability and his fine eloquence. As an opponent of secession he was elected a member of the state convention which governed Missouri from 1861 to 1863. He consistently supported the provisional state government and the Lincoln administration. Governor Gamble commissioned him colonel of the 7th Regiment of the state militia, a cavalry regiment. He commanded it with courage and skill until the close of the war, seeing service in several western campaigns.

Philips moved to Sedalia in 1865 and formed a law partnership with George G Vest. In common with many former Whig leaders, who opposed the rule of the Radical Republicans in the state and nation, he became a Democrat. The test oath and registration system were responsible for his defeat for Congress in 1868. When the Democracy regained control in 1874, he became one of the "Big Four," sharing with Vest, T. T. Crittenden, and F. M. Cockrell the leadership of the party in Missouri. Nominated for Congress in 1874, after 691 ballots were taken, Philips was elected and served during the critical years 1875–77. A member of the committee to investigate the election of 1876 in South Carolina, he ably exposed the shocking and grotesque character of the government there (*Congressional Record*, 44 Cong., 2 Sess., Appendix, pp. 102–06). Certain that Tilden had been elected, he supported with reluctance the electoral commission bill and was convinced that Hayes's title was "grounded and steeped in fraud and perjury" (*Ibid.*). He was elected in 1880 to the Forty-sixth Congress, to fill an unexpired term. Familiar with conditions in the depressed South and debtor West he urged that the tariff be sharply reduced and that the government "do something for silver."

He became a commissioner of the state supreme court in 1882, three years later being appointed a member of the Kansas City court of appeals. He liked appellate work and won recognition for his thoroughness and discrimination. At the instance of his former law partner, Senator Vest, he was named by Cleveland in 1888 to the federal bench for the western district of Missouri. He occupied this position until his retirement in 1910. As a judge, Philips was essentially conservative in his economic and social point of view. He was a master of the technical side of the law and of judicial detail, being seldom reversed by a higher court. Lawyers and laymen alike admired and respected his ability and sense of justice. He practised law after retirement from the bench until his sudden death. He was a man of striking personal charm, whose wit and eloquence won him a large number of friends. His formal speech was effective and adorned with classical allusions but he was best known as a raconteur of note.

[For the period of 1888, the files of the *Jefferson City Tribune* and the *Mo. Statesman* are valuable. See also: F. C. Shoemaker, "In Memoriam: Judge John F. Philips," *Mo. Hist. Rev.*, Apr. 1919; *Jour. and Proc. of the Mo. State Convention*, 1861–63; *Who's Who in America*, 1918–19; Philips' *Speeches* (1918); *Kansas City Star*, Mar. 13, 14, 1919.]   T. S. B.

PHILIPS, MARTIN WILSON (June 17, 1806–Feb. 26, 1889), Southern planter, agricultural writer, and reformer, was born in Columbia, S. C., of Irish descent, though his father and grandfather were both born in Virginia. He is said to have graduated from the old South Carolina College at Columbia and in 1829 he graduated from the medical department of the University of Pennsylvania. In this same year he settled in Mississippi and married Mary Montgomery, daughter of William Montgomery. After practising medicine for a short time with small success, he turned to farming and in 1836 purchased a tract of land in Hinds County, Miss., removing there with his wife and the family of William Montgomery. Philips' new home was a well-built log house of considerable pretensions, and to his plantation he gave the name of "Log Hall." Here he won fame as the "Sage of Log Hall" and was familiarly known as "Log Hall" Philips. He took great pride in his plantation, making it one of the most attractive places in the state. He raised fruit trees, sold them, and wrote about them, urging the raising of more fruit in the South. In his orchards were to be found the most desirable varieties. He was also a successful cotton planter and a stockbreeder. A believer in good implements, he was largely instrumental in introducing into Mississippi many of an improved type and in having them exhibited at the Natchez fair. He was preëminently an investigator but not a successful farmer in the opinion of his neighbors, who were inclined to make sport of his extravagant expenditures of money on blooded stock and agricultural experiments and regarded him as a man who farmed on paper.

He kept a diary of his farm operations from 1840 to 1863, which has been published under the title "Diary of a Mississippi Planter" (*Publications of the Mississippi Historical Society*, vol. X, 1909). In 1863 he was forced to flee from "Log Hall" before the invading army from the North. His plantation suffered greatly from the ravages of war and he never returned to it after the close of hostilities, settling at Magnolia, where he engaged in the nursery business. In 1872 he was asked to take charge of the newly created department of agriculture in the University of Mississippi with the title of adjunct professor of agriculture and superintendent of the university farm. Although the agricultural department did not succeed, it was due to lack of support rather than to any lack of ability on Philips' part. After its abolition in 1875, he became proctor of the University, in which position he served with ability until 1880. He died and was buried in Oxford, Miss. His first wife died in 1862 and he was later married in Columbia, S. C., to Rebecca Tillinghast Wade who survived him.

Philips was a prolific contributor to the farm press. Among the dozen or more journals, both in the North and in the South, to which he contributed most frequently were the *American Farmer, Cultivator, American Agriculturist, Southern Cultivator, American Cotton Planter,* and *De Bow's Review.* From 1843 to 1845 he was one of the editors of the *South-Western Farmer,* published at Raymond, Miss. After the death of Willis Gaylord [q.v.] of the *Cultivator* (Albany), he acted as editor until a successor was appointed. From 1867 to 1873 he edited *Philips' Southern Farmer,* published at Memphis, Tenn. He was greatly interested in the cause of education and did much philanthropic work. A prominent member of the Baptist denomination, he served as treasurer of the Mississippi Baptist State Convention for twelve years, contributing liberally of his time and means to advance the educational and missionary enterprises of that body. He was one of the founders of the oldest existing college for women in Mississippi, the Central Female Institute, now Hillman College at Clinton, established in 1853, and was a member of its first board of trustees; he was also one of the early members of the board of trustees of Mississippi College after it passed into the possession of the Mississippi Baptists. In politics he was an uncompromising Democrat. Honest, kind, generous, progressive, and scholarly, he was also somewhat irascible, impetuous, selfwilled, and impatient. No man in his day contributed more to the material and educational development of Mississippi.

[*Pubs. Miss. Hist. Soc.*, vol. X (1909); U. B. Phillips, *Life and Labor in the Old South* (1929); *Cultivator and Country Gentleman*, June 6, 1889; L. H. Bailey, *Cyc. Am. Agriculture*, vol. IV (1909).]

C.R.B.

PHILIPSE, FREDERICK (Nov. 6, 1626–1702), landed proprietor in New Netherland, was a native of Friesland, Holland, son of Frederick and Margaret (Dacres) Philipse. His name also appears as Vreedryk or Vrederyck Felypsen. His father removed with his family to New Amsterdam, probably with Stuyvesant in 1647. The son engaged in trade and rose to affluence. When New Netherland became an English province, he accommodated himself to the new régime. Trade with the Five Nations, the East and West Indies, and Madagascar swelled his profits, further increased by importation of slaves. He also engaged in the manufacture of wampum.

During the years from 1664 to 1674, when Dutch and English authority alternated, Philipse preserved his political equilibrium, unaffected by excessive zeal for either cause. From 1675 to 1688 he served in the council of the colony. When the revolt in New York City made Jacob Leisler [*q.v.*] its head, Philipse and Stephen Van Cortlandt were in charge of administration, committed to them by Nicholson, the retiring lieutenant-governor. Yielding to the storm, they withdrew from public responsibility. On the restoration of regular government, Philipse returned to the council, where he voted for the execution of the death penalty against Leisler and Milbourne. He served in this body until 1698, when his close relations with Governor Fletcher and reputed dealing with Madagascar pirates prepared the way for his final retirement. His resignation was ascribed to a discovery that the home government had determined to order his dismissal. The enterprise of Capt. William Kidd [*q.v.*], originally legitimate, had enlisted the coöperation of leading figures in the English government, besides Lord Bellomont, then governor of New York and New England, Robert Livingston of New York, and probably others in the latter colony. The formal charge of complicity in Kidd's lawless acts, leveled at certain men in high places, broke down in the Commons; but the Lords of Trade, reporting on the affairs of the province of New York, thought Philipse's connection with illegal trade sufficiently clear to warrant his removal. One signature to this report was that of the celebrated John Locke.

In 1672 Elias Doughty sold one-third of the former Adriaen Van der Donck estate, known as upper Yonkers or the Yonkers plantation, to each of three men, one of whom was Frederick Philipse, who thus acquired the nucleus of a magnificent property. The remainder of the estate subsequently became his. By an Indian deed in 1680 he acquired title to land on both sides of the Pocantico River, and by a second deed four years later to all that tract between the Yonkers Creek and Bronck's River. Philipse's total acquisitions were consolidated in 1693 in the Royal Patent of Philipsburgh. The history of this manor is interwoven with the chronicles of the American Revolution and with American literature. Philipse's skill in building was much prized during his first years in the colony, and he was commonly styled Stuyvesant's "architect-builder." He was a carpenter by trade. In romantic Sleepy Hollow he erected a church and also the stone mansion, Castle Philipse. The Manor Hall of Yonkers, which he reared, has been purchased by the state for perpetual preservation in the city of his founding. His New York town house, at Whitehall and Stone streets, was confiscated after the War of the Revolution. Philipse married in December 1662, Margaret Hardenbrook (the name is variously spelled), widow of Pieter Rudolphus (de Vries), who was "a very desirable business partner as well as wife" (Hall, *post*, pp. 39, 61); for his second wife, he married Nov. 30, 1692, Catharine Van Cortlandt, widow of John Dervall. His wealth was increased by his marriages.

[I. N. P. Stokes, *The Iconography of Manhattan Island, 1498–1909* (6 vols., 1915–28); E. B. O'Callaghan, *Documents Relative to the Colonial Hist. of the State of N. Y.*, vols. II–IV (1858, 1853, 1854); J. T. Scharf, *Hist. of Westchester County, N. Y.* (1886); Robert Bolton, *A Hist. of the County of Westchester* (1848); *Minutes of the Common Council of the City of N. Y., 1675–1776* (8 vols., 1905), esp. vols. I and II; E. H. Hall, *Philipse Manor Hall at Yonkers, N. Y.* (1912); B. B. James and J. F. Jameson, *Jour. of Jasper Danckaerts* (1913); *Colls. N. Y. Hist. Soc., Pub. Fund Ser.*, XXV, for 1892 (1893), 369–73.]   R. E. D.

PHILLIPS, DAVID GRAHAM (Oct. 31, 1867–Jan. 24, 1911), journalist, novelist, the son of David Graham and Margaret (Lee) Phillips, was born in Madison, Ind., where his father was a banker. Educated at the public schools and privately instructed in languages, he matriculated at Indiana Asbury University (later De Pauw) but after two years transferred to the College of New Jersey, whence he was graduated in 1887. The following July he became a reporter on the *Cincinnati Times-Star* and showed such unusual talents for journalism that within a year he was employed at a higher salary by the *Cincinnati Commercial Gazette*. In the summer of 1890 he went to New York City, where he joined the staff of the *Sun*. Again distinguishing himself, he soon became one of the paper's most valuable reporters. In 1893 he left the *Sun* for the *World,* which he first served as London correspondent. After a few months he returned to the United States to do general reporting until 1895, when he was assigned to feature writing. In 1897 Joseph Pulitzer transferred him to the editorial department, later giving him charge of the editorial page in the absence of W. H. Merrill.

Despite the progress that he had made in journalism, Phillips was not satisfied with newspaper work. In 1901 he published his first novel, *The Great God Success,* under the pseudonym of John Graham, and early in the next year he left the *World* to devote himself to the writing of magazine articles and fiction. He was a diligent worker, and by the time of his death he had published seventeen novels, a play, and a book of non-fiction. He had also written nearly forty articles for the *Saturday Evening Post* and at least as many more for the *Cosmopolitan, Success,* the *Arena,* and other magazines. In addition to all this he had completed six novels that were published posthumously. His death came suddenly. In the later months of 1910 he received a series of threatening notes, to which he paid little attention. On Jan. 23, 1911, as he was on his way from lunch, a young musician named Fitzhugh Coyle Goldsborough suddenly confronted him and fired six shots into his body, immediately thereafter killing himself. Phillips died the next day. Goldsborough's motive, as revealed in the notes to Phillips and in his private papers, was the desire to avenge the insults that he maintained Phillips had directed against the Goldsborough family in his novels. There was no basis for Goldsborough's charge, and his papers pointed to insanity.

Though Phillips wrote many different kinds of novels, his more characteristic work aimed at the exposure of contemporary evils in business and government. In many articles, and especially in the sensational series called "The Treason of the Senate," which he contributed to the *Cosmopolitan* in 1906, he took a direct part in the muckraking movement; but his fiction of the same type was more voluminous and probably more effective. In *The Cost* (1904) and *The Deluge* (1905) he dealt with financial manipulators, and in *Light-Fingered Gentry* (1907) he capitalized the insurance scandals. In *The Plum Tree* (1905), *The Fashionable Adventures of Joshua Craig* (1909), *George Helm* (1912), and *The Conflict* (1911) he treated national, state, and municipal corruption. As his interest in muckraking declined, he began to concern him-

self with such problems as sexual standards for women (*The Worth of a Woman,* a play, 1908), women's social ambitions (*The Husband's Story,* 1910), and feminine independence (*The Price She Paid,* 1912). Even into these stories, however, he often introduced exposure of industrial and political corruption, as in his most ambitious novel, *Susan Lenox: Her Fall and Rise* (1917), though it is primarily concerned with the position of women in society.

In his own day Phillips achieved considerable popularity. There can be no doubt of the sincerity of his attacks on corruption, nor is it possible to deny that he had a comprehensive knowledge of many aspects of American life. His work is seldom, however, more than journalism. Judged by esthetic standards his literary powers were of a low order, especially his powers of characterization, and he made many concessions to popular taste. The crudities even of *Susan Lenox,* which is much his best work, are often distressing, though the book is vigorous, honest, and sometimes impressive. Indeed, it may be said of Phillips' books taken as a whole that, however biased they may be and whatever literary faults they may have, they do constitute a substantial and not wholly inaccurate record of the social movements of his day.

[The only full-length biography is I. F. Marcosson, *David Graham Phillips and His Times* (1932). There is information about him in Don C. Seitz, *Joseph Pulitzer: His Life & Letters* (1924) and in Frank M. O'Brien, *The Story of the Sun* (1918). The New York papers of Jan. 24 and 25, 1911, contain long but not completely accurate accounts of his life, and there is an obituary in the *Princeton Alumni Weekly,* Feb. 1, 1911. Among contemporary magazine articles the most useful are in the *Book News Monthly,* Apr. 1907, the *Arena,* Mar. 1906, and the *Bookman,* Mar. 1911. Critical estimates may be found in Frank Harris, *Latest Contemporary Portraits* (1927) and F. T. Cooper, *Some Am. Story Tellers* (1911). The present article is to some extent based upon letters from or interviews with I. F. Marcosson, C. E. Russell, E. F. Flynn, J. A. Green, G. H. Lorimer, and other friends of Phillips. The author has also published a longer study of the man and his work in the *Bookman* for May 1931. The manuscripts of Phillips' novels are in the Princeton Library.]

G. H.

PHILLIPS, FRANCIS CLIFFORD (Apr. 2, 1850–Feb. 16, 1920), chemist, son of William Smith and Fredericka (Ingersoll) Phillips, was born at Philadelphia, Pa., and died at Ben Avon, a suburb of Pittsburgh, Pa. His early education was received at home from his mother. He completed his preparation for college at the Academy of the Protestant Episcopal Church in Philadelphia, entered the University of Pennsylvania in 1866, but left in his junior year. During a part of 1870 he was instructor in chemistry at Delaware College, Newark, Del. Soon afterward he went to Germany to continue his study of chemistry. From 1871 to 1873 he studied with Karl R. Fresenius in his private laboratory at Wiesbaden and the following year was fortunate in having the opportunity to be an assistant of the famous analytical chemist. He studied the next year with Landolt at the Polytechnic School in Aachen. Owing to the illness of his father he was unable to complete his work in Germany for the doctor's degree. In 1875 he became a member of the chemistry staff of the Western University of Pennsylvania—now the University of Pittsburgh—where he remained until his retirement in 1915. During his forty years of service he not only taught all branches of chemistry but for much of the time also geology and mineralogy. For one year (1878–79) he lectured in chemistry at the Pittsburgh College of Pharmacy.

His contact with the German system of university education stimulated him to continue his studies and as one result he received the degree of A.M. in 1879 and Ph.D. in 1893—both from the University of Pittsburgh. Moreover, the zeal for research which he acquired in Germany led him to undertake investigations which were original, particularly in the fields of natural gas and petroleum. He did not publish many articles, but his notes show that in his early work he anticipated principles which have been patented in commercial processes. The failure to publish was due partly to modesty and partly to interest in the scientific rather than the commercial aspects of investigations. Again, the skill acquired in analytical procedure under the eye of Fresenius was the basis of a lifelong interest in methods of analysis. He worked continuously on the improvement and standardization of methods, and many details which he established are an integral part of the accepted chemical process for the detection and determination of certain elements. In connection with this work he edited the second edition of *Methods for the Analysis of Ores, Pig Iron, and Steel in Use at the Laboratories of Iron and Steel Works in the Region about Pittsburgh, Pa.* (1901). At the time of his death he had nearly completed "Qualitative Gas Reactions." Another result of his studies in Germany was his knowledge of the literature of chemistry. In order to help his students and others in utilizing German journals he wrote a textbook entitled *Chemical German* (1913, 2nd ed., 1915). Besides chemistry, geology, mineralogy, and crystallography, he was well informed in botany and bacteriology. The last-named science he utilized in his extensive work on drinking water, studies which led to fundamental improvements in the water supply of Pittsburgh.

Phillips was deeply interested in Joseph Priestley, had a large collection of Priestleyana, and planned to write a biography of Priestley, for which he had accumulated sufficient material. He was the originator of the movement which resulted in the establishment by the American Chemical Society of the Priestley Gold Medal. The medal is awarded triennially "for distinguished services in chemistry," and although Phillips did not live to see the culmination of his efforts his name will always be associated with this memorial to Priestley. In 1881 he married Sarah Ormsby Phillips, daughter of Ormsby Phillips, a former mayor of Allegheny. There were two children. He was a member of numerous scientific societies including the American Philosophical Society (1894) and the American Chemical Society (1894).

[Sources include: obituary notices by Alexander Silverman in *Jour. Industrial and Engineering Chemistry*, Apr. 1920, and in *Science*, May 7, 1920; *Jour. of Chemical Educ.*, Apr. 1932; the *Pittsburgh Post*, Feb. 17, 1920; autobiographical notes supplied by Frank H. Ramsay, Pittsburgh, Pa., and additional information from Alexander Silverman.]   L. C. N.

PHILLIPS, GEORGE (1593–July 1, 1644), clergyman, was born probably at South Rainham, Norfolk, England, and died at Watertown, Mass. His father was Christopher Phillips. He matriculated at Gonville and Caius College, Cambridge, in April 1610; received the degree of B.A. in 1613, and that of M.A. in 1617. He took orders in the Church of England, and served for some years as vicar at Boxted, Essex, though the length of his incumbency is uncertain, owing to the loss of the parish registers. Among Phillips' parishioners was John Maidstone, a nephew of John Winthrop's second wife, and later an officer in Cromwell's household. On Nov. 4, 1629, Maidstone wrote Winthrop stating that Phillips was resolved to go to Massachusetts, and highly commending him. Phillips sailed on the *Arbella* in April 1630, and there are frequent references to him in Winthrop's *Journal*. He was one of the seven signers of *The Humble Request*, which is dated April 7, on the eve of sailing, and which was printed that same year. This noble statement has been attributed to Rev. John White of Dorchester, but there seems to be much better ground for believing that Phillips drafted it (Foote, *post*, pp. 196–201).

Phillips was accompanied on the voyage by his wife, daughter of Richard Sergeant, and two children. His wife died a few weeks after landing at Salem. Phillips went with Winthrop to Charlestown early in the summer, and thence with Sir Richard Saltonstall to Watertown, where a settlement was begun in the fall of 1630.

He presumably drafted the covenant of the Watertown Church, of which he remained minister until his death. Soon after settling at Watertown he married Elizabeth, probably widow of Capt. Robert Welden, by whom he had seven children. Phillips was the first minister of the Massachusetts Bay Colony to put into practice the congregational form of church polity (Foote, pp. 202–07), doing so before the arrival of the Rev. John Cotton in 1633, to whom the initiation of the congregational polity has been commonly attributed. In 1632 he was one of the leaders in the protest made by Watertown against the action of the governor and assistants in arbitrarily levying a tax on the town. He and Richard Brown were summoned to Boston, where the matter was debated. The tax was not remitted, but within three months an election of representatives to the General Court was agreed upon, with the understanding that in future no taxes should be levied without the consent of the Court. To this Watertown protest is rightly traced the beginning of representative government in Massachusetts. Phillips also had a hand in drafting the compilation of laws published in 1641.

He was a man of learning, and brought an excellent library to Watertown. Although a sturdy independent he was not aggressive, but was notably modest and courteous. He published nothing in his lifetime, but soon after his death a pamphlet by him was printed with a title page beginning *A Reply to a Confutation of Some Grounds for Infants Baptisme* (1645). It contains three short treatises clearly setting forth Phillips' theory of the church, in reply to a pamphlet printed in London by an Anabaptist, in which Phillips was singled out for attack. His eldest son, Samuel, became an eminent minister at Rowley, Mass., and was the progenitor of Samuel and John Phillips [*qq.v.*], the founders of the academies at Andover, Mass., and Exeter, N. H., and of Wendell Phillips [*q.v.*].

[Cotton Mather, *Magnalia Christi Americana* (ed. 1853), vol. I, pp. 375–79, in some statements inaccurate; W. B. Sprague, *Annals Am. Pulpit*, vol. I (1857); H. W. Foote, "George Phillips, First Minister of Watertown," *Proc. Mass. Hist. Soc.*, vol. LXIII (1931).
H. W. F.

PHILLIPS, HENRY (Sept. 6, 1838–June 6, 1895), numismatist, philologist, and translator, was born in Philadelphia, Pa., a member of a cultured Jewish family whose traditions destined him for the study of law. His father, Jonas Altamont Phillips (1806–1862), a graduate of the University of Pennsylvania, was a successful lawyer, and his grandfather, Zalegman Phillips (1779–1839), also a graduate of the University of Pennsylvania, was looked upon as a leading criminal lawyer of the city. His mother was Frances (Cohen) Phillips, of Charleston, S. C. He received his elementary education in a Quaker school conducted by Hannah and Mary Gibbons and prepared for college in the classical academy of Henry D. Gregory, to whom he attributed his devotion to scholarly pursuits. He entered the University in 1853, graduated in 1856, studied law, and was admitted to the bar in 1859. From the first, however, he lacked the interest in the law that was characteristic of his family and began to give his attention to antiquarian scholarship. Becoming interested in numismatics, he undertook studies which resulted in the publication in 1865 of his *Historical Sketches of the Paper Currency of the American Colonies* and in 1866 of his *Continental Paper Money*. These studies were accepted as authoritative. They were followed by many other works on numismatic subjects.

Phillips mastered foreign languages with ease and was widely read. He published various philological papers and was one of the most active of American contributors of readings for the Oxford Dictionary. At the request of L. L. Zamenhof, of Warsaw, inventor of Esperanto, he translated that author's *Attempt towards an International Language* (1889) and supplied an English-Esperanto vocabulary. In 1877 he was one of a committee of three appointed by the American Philosophical Society to examine into the scientific value of Volapük. He was also interested in folk-lore, serving for a time as treasurer of the American Folk-Lore Society, and was the author of a number of papers on the subject. His facility as a linguist was applied to translations of European poetry, including among others the *Faust* of Adalbert von Chamisso (1881), Spanish poems by Fray Luis Ponce de Leon (1883), and selections from the works of Alexander Petöfi and Hermann Rollett. In 1887 he translated Antonio Gazzaletti's *La Patria dell' Italiano* and in 1892 a finely printed volume of German lyrics. He also published articles on American archeology. These scholarly achievements brought him recognition both at home and abroad. In 1862 he was made treasurer and in 1868, secretary, of the Numismatic and Antiquarian Society of Philadelphia. He became a member of the American Philosophical Society in February 1877, was its curator in 1880, one of its secretaries in 1884, and from 1885 until his death, librarian of the society. From 1892 to 1895 he served as Belgian vice-consul for Philadelphia. In Europe he was elected to membership in more than a score of learned societies and received medals and honors. Always frail, he suffered during his last ten years from hereditary gout, which induced arteriosclerosis. In the winter of 1894–95 he was ordered south for his health and on June 6, 1895, died of uremic poisoning. He was never married.

[See: A. H. Smyth, "Obit. Notice of Henry Phillips, Jr.," *Proc. Am. Phil. Soc. . . . Memorial Vol. I* (1900); J. L. Chamberlain, *Universities and Their Sons: Univ. of Pa.*, vol. II (1902); *The Jewish Encyc.*; the *Press* (Phila.), June 8, 1895.]   J.C.F.

PHILLIPS, JOHN (Dec. 27, 1719–Apr. 21, 1795), founder of the Phillips Exeter Academy, was the second son of the Rev. Samuel and Hannah (White) Phillips, of Andover, Mass. Prepared by his father, he entered Harvard College before he was twelve, receiving four years later the degree of M.A. At graduation, in 1735, he delivered the Latin salutatory oration. For some months he taught school, studying theology and medicine, and settling in Exeter as a teacher at least as early as 1740. Although he made some attempts at preaching, he turned ultimately to business and carried on a country store. On Aug. 4, 1743, he married Sarah (Emery) Gilman, a widow some years older than himself, whose first husband, Nathaniel Gilman, of Exeter, had left her more than eight thousand pounds. Enterprising and thrifty, Phillips soon accumulated a large property, chiefly through speculation in real estate and the lending of money at high rates of interest. Mrs. Phillips died, Oct. 9, 1765, and on Nov. 3, 1767, he was married to the widow of Dr. Eliphalet Hale, the local physician. He had no children.

Phillips was interested in town and state affairs and held several offices, among them that of moderator of town meeting in 1778 and 1779. He served for three years in the General Court (1771–73) and was colonel of the Exeter Cadets. His chief claim to distinction, however, rests upon his philanthropies. He made liberal gifts to Dartmouth College, including a professorship of Biblical history and literature, and he became in 1773 a trustee. In 1781, shortly after the founding of Phillips Academy, Andover, he corresponded with his nephew, Samuel Phillips [*q.v.*], regarding the establishment of a similar school in Exeter. The act of incorporation for the new institution, to be called the Phillips Exeter Academy, was dated Apr. 3, 1781, but the school was not opened until 1783. In drafting this constitution, John Phillips, who was the chief contributor to the endowment, followed in general the ideas and phrasing of the Andover "deed of gift," but reserved to himself much power that, in the Andover plan, had been delegated to the trustees. He contributed approximately $30,000 to the establishment and develop-

ment of Phillips Academy, Andover, and gave much of his remaining fortune to the Phillips Exeter Academy. He was the first president of the Exeter board of trustees and was also a member of the Andover board, and its president from 1791 to 1794.

Formal in his manners and austere by temperament, Phillips was thoroughly Puritanical in spirit and was frugal, conscientious, and religious. The epitaph written for him by Principal Pearson, of Andover, said of him: "Without natural issue, he made posterity his heir."

[G. E. Street, *Hist. Sketch of John Phillips* (1895); A. M. Phillips, *Phillips Geneals.* (1885); L. M. Crosbie, *The Phillips Exeter Academy: A Hist.* (1923); J. G. Hoyt, "The Phillips Family and Phillips Exeter Academy," *North Am. Rev.*, July 1858; C. M. Fuess, *An Old New England School* (1917).]   C.M.F.

PHILLIPS, PHILIP (Aug. 13, 1834–June 25, 1895), singing evangelist, composer of sacred music, was born in Cassadaga, N. Y., the son of Sawyer and Jane Parker Phillips. When he was nine his mother died and a few years later he left home to attend a country school, working on a neighbor's farm to pay for his living. His early interest in music was encouraged by his employer who bought him a melodeon, for which Phillips paid in labor. He learned to play the instrument and to sing and before he was twenty he had organized a singing school of his own in Allegany, N. Y. He built up a small trade in music and instruments by taking his melodeon to the house of a prosperous farmer, where he would play and sing to the members of the household. Later he went into business with D. J. Cook of Fredonia, N. Y. On a business trip to Ohio, when he visited various towns, organized singing schools, and sold his goods, he met Ollie M. Clarke, of Marion, whom he married on Sept. 27, 1860. He had been converted to the Baptist faith, but after his marriage he joined the Methodist church. After living in Marion for two years he moved to Cincinnati to join the music firm of William Sumner & Company. Within the next year or two the firm became Philip Phillips & Company. The "singing pilgrim," as he was called, used the same advertising technique in the cities as he had in the country. He would place his melodeon at the most conspicuous corner, play and sing for passersby, and sell them his wares.

About 1860 Phillips published his first sacred-song collection, *Early Blossoms.* It was followed some two years later by *Musical Leaves,* of which several hundred thousand copies were sold. During the Civil War Phillips held song services in the principal Northern cities, in connection with the Christian Commission, the climax of which was a meeting in Washington, D. C., over which Seward presided. In 1866 he published *The Singing Pilgrim, or Pilgrim's Progress Illustrated in Song.* The following year he moved to New York City where he became the musical editor of the Methodist Book Concern. He published his *New Hymn and Tune Book* (1867) and in 1868, as the culmination of a series of song services in England, his *American Sacred Songster,* of which more than a million copies were sold. Many other works followed, including *The Gospel Singer* (1874); *Song Ministry* (1874); *Gem Solos* (1887); *Six Song Services with Connective Readings* (1892); and, in collaboration with his son, Philip Phillips, Jr., *Our New Hymnal* (1894). Although his books represent a large output, they were for the most part compilations of existing hymns. The popularity of his sacred-song books was aided by his song services. Of these he gave more than 4,000 during his life, their returns devoted to charity. His most ambitious song-service tour was that which in 1875 carried him to the Sandwich Islands, Australia, New Zealand, Palestine, Egypt, India, and Continental Europe. Its experiences were embodied in his *Song Pilgrimage Round the World* (1882). Phillips died in Delaware, Ohio, at the age of sixty.

[Alexander Clark, *Philip Phillips: The Story of his Life* (1883); J. H. Hall, *Biog. of Gospel Song and Hymn Writers* (1914); A. M. Phillips, *Phillips Geneals.* (1885); *Appletons' Ann. Cyc.,* 1895; *Cincinnati Enquirer,* June 26, 1895.]

F. H. M.

PHILLIPS, SAMUEL (Feb. 5, 1752–Feb. 10, 1802), founder of Phillips Academy, Andover, was born in North Andover, Mass., the sixth child of Samuel and Elizabeth (Barnard) Phillips, and the sixth in direct descent from the Rev. George Phillips, 1593–1644 [*q.v.*], the first clergyman of Watertown. At thirteen he entered Dummer Academy at South Byfield, Mass., where he studied under the gifted but eccentric Master William Moody. At Harvard College, where he graduated in 1771, he was faithful and painstaking rather than brilliant, with a tendency toward morbid introspection. He was married, on July 6, 1773, to Phoebe Foxcroft, youngest daughter of the Hon. Francis Foxcroft, of Cambridge, by whom he had two children, only one of whom—John Phillips (1776–1820)—survived his father. Phillips Brooks [*q.v.*] was a descendant.

Settling in North Andover, Phillips was elected in 1775 as delegate to the Provincial Congress. At the outbreak of the Revolution he hastily constructed a powder-mill on the Shawsheen River and after some prolonged experimentation was able to supply the American armies with ammu-

nition. In 1777 he moved to the South Parish of Andover, where, in 1782, he erected an imposing mansion, which was his home until his death. He was a delegate to the state constitutional convention in 1779–80 and served in the state Senate, with the exception of one year, from 1780 until 1801. In 1785 he was chosen to succeed Samuel Adams as president of the Senate. He was appointed in 1781 as justice of the court of common pleas for Essex County and was thereafter usually known as Judge Phillips.

At least as early as 1776, Phillips began to plan for a new type of school and induced his father, whose fortune he did not inherit until 1790, and his uncle, John Phillips [*q.v.*], of Exeter, to be his financial backers. In 1777 he purchased in their names a sufficient tract of land and after consultation with his friend, Eliphalet Pearson [*q.v.*], he drafted a "deed of gift," or constitution, which was one of the significant documents in the history of American education. It provided for the establishment of an endowed academy, controlled by a board of trustees, the majority of whom should be laymen. It explicitly stated that the "*first and principal* object" of the institution was to be "the promotion of true Piety and Virtue," and that the teachers should point out to their pupils "the great end and real business of living." In thus emphasizing the importance of character, Phillips was undoubtedly influenced by John Locke and the English nonconformist academies. He himself was strongly Calvinistic in his theology.

Phillips Academy was the earliest of the endowed academies which, until the public high school began to develop about fifty years later, had such great influence on American education. It was opened, Apr. 30, 1778, with thirteen pupils, under Eliphalet Pearson as principal. Phillips was a member of the original board of trustees and later, in 1796, became its president, devoting much of his time to its affairs. He had previously enjoyed the friendship of George Washington, who visited him at Andover in 1789 and who sent to Phillips Academy one nephew and eight grand-nephews. Phillips was tall and dignified, and rather unbending in his manner. Extraordinarily industrious, he begrudged every moment not spent in work and took as his motto, "Be more covetous of your hours than misers are of gold." Although he was even-tempered, he had little sense of humor and permitted himself few diversions. He was a stanch supporter of the church and a liberal donor to benevolent projects. Afflicted with asthma in his later years, he sought to improve his health by travel, but in vain. He was elected in 1801 as lieutenant-governor of Massachusetts on the Federalist ticket but died shortly after his inauguration and was buried, with public ceremonies, in the cemetery of the South Church, in Andover. He left in his will generous bequests, not only to Phillips Academy, but also for other philanthropic purposes; and his name is still perpetuated in various memorial funds and in the chief recitation hall at Phillips Academy.

[*Biog. Cat. of ... Phillips Academy, Andover* (1903); J. L. Taylor, *A Memoir of His Honor, Samuel Phillips, LL.D.* (1856); A. M. Phillips, *Phillips Geneals.* (1885); C. M. Fuess, *An Old New England School* (1917); manuscript collections owned by Phillips Academy, Andover.]   C. M. F.

PHILLIPS, THOMAS WHARTON (Feb. 23, 1835–July 21, 1912), oil producer, congressman, religious writer, and philanthropist, was born on a farm near Mount Jackson, Lawrence County, Pa., the son of Ephraim and Ann (Newton) Phillips. He was a descendant of the Rev. George Phillips [*q.v.*] who came to Massachusetts in 1630 and was one of the founders of Watertown. Ephraim Phillips died when Thomas was less than a year old, leaving the mother to struggle with the problem of rearing her eight children on the one-hundred acre farm. Poverty constrained her to limit Thomas' formal schooling to that provided by the district schools but he supplemented his meager opportunities by earnest study and wide reading. His ambition was to obtain a college education and enter the ministry. He made preliminary preparation to that end and preached frequently in his early manhood, but the uncertainty of his health dictated the adoption of a more active outdoor life.

He was attracted to the new petroleum industry, and after unsuccessful efforts to produce oil in Lawrence County, went in 1861 to Oil Creek, where Col. Edwin L. Drake [*q.v.*] had driven the first successful well two years before. Here, with his three brothers, he engaged in oil production. The firm at first met with great success and the brothers disbursed their profits generously in religious and philanthropic benefactions, but the panic of 1873, together with the discovery of new oil fields and the consequent fall in the price of oil, made a dramatic change from prosperity to adversity in their fortunes. The payment of their indebtedness, with interest, absorbed the next fourteen years of Phillips' life. In 1887 he was made president of the Producers' Protective Association, a secret organization of some two thousand oil men in thirty-six local assemblies organized primarily to combat the Standard Oil combination; he was at this time one of the largest individual producers in the oil country. When in 1888 the Association

made an agreement with the Standard Oil Company to reduce production, Phillips insisted as a prerequisite to his assent that two million barrels of oil be set aside for the benefit of the drillers who would be thrown out of employment by the shutdown. At the time of his death the T. W. Phillips Gas & Oil Company, of which he was president, owned 850 gas and oil wells, 900 miles of gas lines, and valuable leaseholds of gas and oil lands in Pennsylvania.

Phillips' political career began through his association with James A. Garfield as close personal friend, confidant, and political adviser. When Garfield was nominated for the presidency in 1880, Phillips dropped all business and devoted his entire time to the canvass. It was at his suggestion and with his assistance as author and financial backer that during this campaign the first *Republican Campaign Text Book* was published. He was defeated as a candidate for Congress in 1890 but was successful in 1892 and was reëlected in 1894. He voluntarily retired at the close of his second term. While in Congress he had formulated plans for the appointment of an Industrial Commission "to investigate questions pertaining to immigration, to labor, to agriculture, to manufacturing, and to business," but the act authorizing its creation was not passed until 1898. President McKinley appointed him a member of the Commission and he had an important part in the preparation of its nineteen volumes of reports, which appeared in 1900–02. This service entailed four years of the hardest work of his laborious life. The adequacy of the investigation as well as the constructive character of the conclusions and recommendations presented was perhaps due more to his efforts than to those of any other one man. The Bureau of Corporations was a direct result of this investigation, and the federal departments of labor and commerce carry forward the investigations which Phillips' inventive mind conceived and initiated.

In the midst of his business and political activities, Phillips found time to continue his religious study and writing. In 1866 he was instrumental in forming the Christian Publishing Association for the purpose of issuing a weekly journal, the *Christian Standard*. To this paper, which soon made a name for itself under the editorship of Isaac Errett [*q.v.*], he was a friend and contributor during the rest of his life. In 1905, in the seventieth year of his age, he published *The Church of Christ,* an exposition of the principles of the Disciples of Christ. He gave liberal financial support to Bethany and Hiram colleges, and was the virtual founder of Oklahoma Christian University, renamed Phillips University after he died. His name was also given to Phillips Bible Institute, Canton, Ohio, opened after his death. He established ministerial loan funds at Bethany and Hiram colleges and at Drake, Phillips, and Eugene Bible universities. For many years he supported a missionary in the Northwest, and the local, state, and national Y. M. C. A. and Y. W. C. A. had cause to remember him gratefully as a generous friend. Death found him at New Castle, Lawrence County, Pa., busily engaged in writing an article on the Resurrection.

Phillips married, in 1862, Clarinda, daughter of David and Nancy Rebecca (Arter) Hardman. She died in 1866, and in 1870 he married her younger sister, Pamphila, who survived him. To the first marriage two sons were born, and to the second, three sons and a daughter.

[Biog. sketch by T. W. Phillips, Jr., in T. W. Phillips, *The Church of Christ* (15th ed., 1915); *Who's Who in America*, 1910–11; *Biog. Dir. Am. Cong.* (1928); I. M. Tarbell, *The Hist. of the Standard Oil Co.* (1904), II, 158 ff.; "Supplementary Statement of Thomas W. Phillips," in *Final Report of the Industrial Commission, Vol. XIX of the Commission's Reports* (1902), pp. 652–85; *Pittsburg Dispatch*, July 22, 1912.]

C. E. P.

PHILLIPS, WALTER POLK (June 14, 1846–Jan. 31, 1920), telegrapher, journalist, the son of Andrew Smith and Roxena Minerva (Drake) Phillips, was born on a farm near Grafton, Mass., to which town his parents removed when he was eleven years of age. As a boy he became a messenger for the telegraph at Providence and, being permitted to practise at the key, quickly made himself proficient in the art. His rapidity and precision in taking messages by sound won him first place in a speed contest, in recognition of which Samuel F. B. Morse presented him with a testimonial gold pencil. Attracted to journalism, in 1867 he commenced to devote his nights to reporting for the *Providence Journal* and, the following year, became city editor, then managing editor, of the Providence *Herald*. In 1871 he was a reporter on the New York *Sun*. At intervals, however, he returned to telegraphy. For a time he was a fellow operator with Edison in Boston; during the winter of 1872–73 he was in the Western Union office in New York, and later he was one of the eight experts chosen to man the first leased press wire, which was installed in 1875, connecting New York, Philadelphia, Baltimore, and Washington. He devised a code for news transmission, "The Phillips Telegraphic Code" (1879), and a system for facilitating delivery of telegraphic copy more fully punctuated and better edited. Interested in telegraphy and journalism, he contributed regularly to the *Telegrapher* and

became the associate editor of the *Electrician*, then the leading trade journal. His stories, sketches, and paragraphs, which had been signed "John Oakum," were issued as a little book in 1876, *Oakum Pickings*, and were republished in part twenty years later as *Sketches, Old and New*, with some additions, including an essay, "From Franklin to Edison." He also was the author of *My Debut in Journalism* (1892), a volume of newspaper-office tales.

When the original United Press emerged with apparent suddenness into the arena of news-gathering in the early eighties and began to challenge the entrenched Associated Press, Phillips was the managerial head of the former. He had recently scored brilliantly as the Washington representative of the New York Associated Press through the Hayes administration, from which position he had been called to help perfect the opposition association for papers arbitrarily excluded from the long-established news source. Such was his exceptional organizing ability and grasp of the telegraph situation that, within a short time, by utilizing the independent wires and by making alliances with news agencies abroad operating in rivalry to those supplying the Associated Press, he was delivering regular reports to nearly one hundred dailies on a far-flung network of leased lines. A little later he had obtained a secret arrangement for pooling with the Associated Press and was carrying on an extensive and lucrative sale of exclusive franchises to receive the service. In 1892–93, the United Press under Phillips' management absorbed the New York Associated Press and had practically concluded negotiations for a huge merger with the Western Associated Press papers when irreconcilable disagreements arose over division of territory and matters of control. In the great "War of the News Giants" which followed (1893–97), Phillips was the field marshal for the United Press forces. Success seemed near when he annexed the Southern Associated Press and again when he won over the New England Associated Press, but the endurance and persistence of the new Associated Press finally overpowered the United Press. The collapse occurred in the spring of 1897 and Phillips quit the news-gathering field.

After the extinction of his position as general manager of the United Press, Phillips was prominently connected with the Columbia Graphophone Company as an executive officer for fifteen years and with the American Red Cross, in whose Board of Control he was active during the period of the Spanish-American War. He was one of the early members of the Lotos Club of

New York City. Although large and rotund of form, he became an enthusiastic bicycler and his *Songs of the Wheel,* mostly humorous in tone, which he gathered together in his zeal for the sport, was published in 1897. In this volume he inserted some rhymes of his own set to music, notably "The Stout Man's Conquest." Depressed by the loss successively of his wife, Francena Adelaide Capron, and his son, he spent his closing years in Bridgeport, Conn., and at Vineyard Haven, Mass., where he died.

[In addition to Phillips' works see: Jas. D. Reid, *The Telegraph in America* (1879); Victor Rosewater, *Hist. of Coöperative News-Gathering in the U. S.* (1930); A. M. Phillips, *Phillips Geneals.* (1885); *N. Y. Times,* Feb. 1, 1920.]   V. R.

PHILLIPS, WENDELL (Nov. 29, 1811–Feb. 2, 1884), orator and reformer, was the eighth child and fifth son of John and Sarah (Walley) Phillips, and traced his ancestry back to Rev. George Phillips [*q.v.*], who landed at Salem on the *Arbella* in June 1630. He inherited not only a superb physique and family traditions of a high order, but also ample wealth and an excellent social standing in Boston. At the Boston Latin School, to which he was sent in 1822, he won distinction in declamation; and later, at Harvard, where he graduated in the class of 1831, he showed ability as a debater and a student of history. He was obviously a patrician, animated by chivalric ideals and a spirit of *noblesse oblige.* After three years at the Harvard Law School, he was admitted to the Suffolk County bar and at once opened an office in Boston. Although he was never enthusiastic about his profession, he was able during his first two years of practice to pay his expenses, and he later enjoyed a fair clientage. He married, Oct. 12, 1837, Ann Terry Greene, orphan daughter of Benjamin Greene, a wealthy Boston merchant. She soon became a nervous invalid, confined usually to her room and often to her bed, but their domestic life was very happy. They had no children.

Even before his marriage, Phillips had become identified with the anti-slavery movement, and his wife encouraged him in his abolitionist views. On Mar. 26, 1837, at a meeting of the Massachusetts Anti-Slavery Society in Lynn, he spoke for twenty minutes announcing his allegiance to the cause, but he at first took no part in the work of the organization. His real opportunity presented itself on Dec. 8, 1837, at a public meeting held in Faneuil Hall to protest against the murder of Elijah P. Lovejoy [*q.v.*], the abolitionist editor, at Alton, Ill. Phillips listened in the audience while James T. Austin [*q.v.*], attorney general of the commonwealth, compared the as-

sassins of Lovejoy to the Revolutionary patriots; then, urged by friends, he responded with a stirring indictment of the outrage. His personality and passionate eloquence caught the imaginations of the audience, and his impromptu address was received with cheers. Thus, at the age of twenty-six, he took his place in the front rank of the leaders of the anti-slavery protest.

Possessing an adequate private income which made it unnecessary for him to rely on his profession, he now became a lecturer on the lyceum platform, speaking mainly on the slavery question. His relatives thought him fanatical, but his wife's encouragement counteracted their influence. His ability and family prestige, as well as his charm and persuasive power, made him invaluable as a champion. Broadly speaking, he followed William Lloyd Garrison [*q.v.*] in his refusal to link abolitionism with the program of any political party and like Garrison he condemned the Constitution of the United States because of its compromise with the slave power, but he was never a non-resistant, and he and Garrison occasionally differed on this point. Phillips contributed frequently to Garrison's *Liberator* and, in 1840, went to London as a delegate from Massachusetts to the World's Anti-Slavery Convention, where he supported Garrison in the latter's insistence that women should have the same rights on the floor as men. On Oct. 30, 1842, speaking in Faneuil Hall on the fugitive-slave issue, he said, "My *curse* be on the Constitution of these United States" (Sears, *post,* p. 102). As time went on, he became more denunciatory in his language, arousing such hostility that on several occasions he was almost mobbed. He opposed the acquisition of Texas and the war with Mexico; and he condemned Webster bitterly for his "Seventh of March" speech, in 1850. Ultimately Phillips, like Garrison, demanded the division of the Union. During the Civil War, he was frequently a severe critic of the Lincoln administration, but the Emancipation Proclamation met with his approval as marking a victory for freedom. When, in 1865, Garrison urged the dissolution of the American Anti-Slavery Society, Phillips successfully maintained that it should not be disbanded, and was himself chosen president.

Regarding his mission as one of education, he devoted himself after the Civil War to advocating other moral causes, including prohibition, a reform in penal methods, concessions to the Indians, votes for women, and the labor movement. He was nominated in 1870 by the Labor Reform Party and the Prohibitionists for the governorship of Massachusetts and polled 20,000 votes; the following year he presided over the Labor Reform convention at Worcester and drew up its platform, which contained these words: "We affirm . . . that labor, the creator of wealth, is entitled to all it creates . . . we avow ourselves willing to accept . . . the overthrow of the whole profit-making system. . . . We declare war with the wages system . . . with the present system of finance" (*The Labor Question*, 1884, p. 4; Austin, *post*, p. 264). In this same year (1871) he supported Gen. B. F. Butler [*q.v.*] for the governorship. His denunciation of the moneyed corporations and his urging that the laboring class organize to further its own interests were regarded by some of his contemporaries as marking aberrations of a noble mind. Actually he seems to have had an unusually clear perception of national trends, but he was even further ahead of his time in his labor agitation than he had been when he championed abolition in 1837. In his seventieth year, he delivered the Phi Beta Kappa Centennial Oration at Harvard College, and showed himself to be still uncompromising by denouncing the timidity of academic conservatives. His last public address was delivered at the unveiling of a statue of Harriet Martineau on Dec. 26, 1883. He died after a week's suffering from angina pectoris, and after lying in state in Faneuil Hall his body was interred in the Granary Burying Ground.

Phillips was an aristocratic-looking man, with a rich, persuasive voice and a graceful, self-assured manner. Although famous as an orator, he was seldom rhetorical, and he was amazingly free from verbosity and pomposity. His subjects were many, among the most popular being "The Lost Arts," on which he spoke more than two thousand times; "Street Life in Europe"; "Daniel O'Connell"; "The Scholar in a Republic"; and "Toussaint L'Ouverture." He spoke before all kinds of audiences, large and small, sympathetic and hostile, and, in his prime, he seemed untiring. An omnivorous reader and a thorough scholar, he knew how to impart his knowledge in an easy and appealing way. His mission was that of an agitator, aiming to stir his countrymen to eliminate the evils in their midst. Like all extremists, he was frequently sharp of tongue and unfair to his opponents, but he was courageous, self-sacrificing, magnanimous, and lofty in his ideals, and has been rightly called the "Knight-Errant of unfriended Truth."

[Two volumes of Phillips' *Speeches, Lectures, and Letters* were published, the first in 1863 and the second, after his death, in 1891. The best biographies are Lorenzo Sears, *Wendell Phillips* (1909); G. L. Austin, *The Life and Times of Wendell Phillips* (1884); and C. E. Russell, *The Story of Wendell Phillips* (1914). See also T. ↑N. Higginson, *Contemporaries* (1900), reprint-ing a paper first published in the *Nation* (N. Y.), Feb. 7, 1884; G. E. Woodberry, "Wendell Phillips," in his *Heart of Man and Other Papers* (1920); and Carlos Martyn, *Wendell Phillips* (1890).] C. M. F.

PHILLIPS, WILLARD (Dec. 19, 1784–Sept. 9, 1873), lawyer, author, was born in Bridgewater, Mass., and spent his early years in Hampshire County, where he received a common-school education. His father, Joseph, was a descendant of John Phillips who settled in Duxbury, Mass., before 1640; his mother was perhaps the Hannah Egerton whose marriage to a Joseph Phillips in 1784 is recorded in the *Vital Records of Bridgewater, Mass., to the Year 1850* (1916, II, 296). Willard graduated as valedictorian from the Bridgewater Academy and at eighteen became a teacher. Meanwhile, he prepared for college and in 1806 was admitted at Harvard, where he graduated with high rank in 1810. From 1811 to 1815 he was a tutor there and concurrently studied law with William Sullivan. He records in his diary for this period: "I very much regret having lost so much of my life both in regard to improvement and enjoyment. For this I am indebted to my excessive passions and appetites." He resolved to lead an abstemious life and "not to yield to the importunities of my hosts." In politics he believed that "the general spirit and principles" of the Federalists were good, but urged the disbanding of the party as a step toward placating partisan strife and arriving at a condition where individual merit would count for more. He had a taste for writing which led him into an editorial connection with the *General Repository and Review,* the *North American Review,* and the *American Jurist.* In 1818 he began to practise law in Boston. During 1825–26 he was a member of the legislature. Together with Theophilus Parsons [*q.v.*] he bought the *New-England Galaxy* in November 1828, and its publication continued for six years thereafter. He was chairman of a commission to codify the criminal law of Massachusetts (1837–42), but the commission's report was not adopted. In 1839 he was appointed probate judge for Suffolk County, resigning in 1847 to accept the presidency of the New England Mutual Life Insurance Company. This post he held until he had reached an advanced age. He was honored with membership in the American Academy of Arts and Sciences.

From youth Phillips confided to a voluminous set of notebooks his reflections on what he read, from Weems's life of Washington to Coke's commentary on Littleton. He thought Adam Smith's *Wealth of Nations* "remarkably profound and ingenious." Later, he became a zealot for protective tariffs, and defended the faith in his *Manual of Political Economy* (1828) and a catechism of protective orthodoxy entitled *Propositions Concerning Protection and Free Trade* (1850). He also published *A Treatise on the Law of Insurance* in two volumes, which appeared in 1823 and 1834 respectively. This work ran through five editions. In 1837 he published a little book called *The Inventor's Guide,* and also *The Law of Patents for Inventions.* His declining years were spent in the enjoyment of his friends and books at his home in Cambridge, where he died without symptoms of any acute disease. He was married in 1833 to Hannah Brackett Hill, daughter of Aaron Hill of Boston; she died three or four years later, and subsequently he married her sister Harriet.

[A. M. Phillips, *Phillips Geneals.* (1885); *Proc. Am. Acad. Arts and Sciences,* vol. IX (1874); W. T. Davis, *Professional and Industrial Hist. of Suffolk County, Mass.* (1894), vol. I; John Livingston, *Portraits of Eminent Americans,* vol. I (1853); *Boston Daily Globe,* Sept. 11, 1873; collection of Phillips' early MSS. in the Harvard Coll. Lib.] C.F.

PHILLIPS, WILLIAM (Mar. 30, 1750 o.s.– May 26, 1827), merchant and philanthropist, lieutenant-governor of Massachusetts, was the only son of William Phillips (1722–1804), a brother of John Phillips [*q.v.*], and of Abigail (Bromfield) Phillips, of Boston. He was sent to the Boston Latin School, but the feebleness of his constitution, especially a weakness of the eyes, repeatedly interrupted his education. He early entered business with his father, who was a prosperous merchant. In 1773 he made an extended tour of Great Britain, Holland, and France, returning in December of that year on one of the "tea ships." He married, Sept. 13, 1774, Miriam Mason, third daughter of Jonathan Mason of Boston, and they had seven children. At the outbreak of the Revolution, he removed his family to Norwich, Conn., but he himself labored assiduously for the colonial cause. At the death of his father in 1804, he inherited a large fortune. In the same year he became president of the Massachusetts Bank. In 1805, he was elected to the Massachusetts General Court and served until 1812, when he was chosen as lieutenant-governor on the Federalist ticket, with Caleb Strong as governor. To this office he was reëlected for eleven successive terms. In 1816 and 1820, he was a presidential elector at large. At the election of delegates to the state constitutional convention of 1820, he received the largest vote of any of the Boston candidates; and it was he who called the convention to order on Nov. 15, 1820, in the Hall of Representatives. His political career ended in 1823, with a term in the Massachusetts Senate.

Phillips was one of the most generous benefactors of his time. Elected in 1791 a trustee of Phillips Academy, Andover, founded by his cousin Samuel Phillips [*q.v.*], he was made president of the board in 1821, being the fifth of his family to hold that office. From 1812 to 1827 he supplied the sum of $500 annually for the support of needy students in that school, and in 1818 gave more than $5,000 towards the erection of a new brick academy building. It was said that over a period of years he devoted from $8,000 to $11,000 annually to charitable purposes, and his bequests in his will totaled $62,000, including $15,000 to Phillips Academy and $10,000 to Andover Theological Seminary. He was an original incorporator of the American Board of Foreign Missions, and was president of the American Bible Society, the Massachusetts General Hospital, the American Education Society, the Society for Propagating the Gospel, and many other charitable or philanthropic organizations. He was a member of the Old South Church, being one of the deacons from 1794 until his death.

Phillips was a man of domestic tastes, fond of retirement and averse to publicity. He was sound in his judgments, independent in his opinions, and devoted to duty. His conservatism and caution inspired and held the confidence of others. His portrait, by Gilbert Stuart, owned by Phillips Academy, shows a man much resembling George Washington in features and bearing.

[H. A. Hill, *William Phillips and William Phillips, Father and Son, 1722–1827* (repr. from *New-Eng. Hist. and Geneal. Reg.,* Apr. 1885); B. B. Wisner, *A Sermon Occasioned by the Death of the Hon. William Phillips* (1827); *Biog. Cat. of . . . Phillips Academy, Andover, 1778–1830* (1903); C. M. Fuess, *An Old New England School* (1917); *Columbian Centinel* (Boston), May 30, 1827.] C.M.F.

PHILLIPS, WILLIAM ADDISON (Jan. 14, 1824–Nov. 30, 1893), soldier, congressman from Kansas, author, was born at Paisley, Scotland, the son of John Phillips. He emigrated with his parents to the United States about 1838 and settled in Randolph County in southern Illinois, where he was reared in the strictest tenets of Presbyterianism. He went to the local schools and acquired some training in Latin and mathematics. He became editor of a newspaper at Chester, Ill., studied law, and was admitted to the bar. In 1855 he went to Kansas as a special correspondent of the *New York Tribune* and became conspicuous as a radical anti-slavery journalist and politician. He wrote *The Conquest of Kansas by Missouri and her Allies* (1856) in the interest of Frémont's candidacy for president. He was a participant in many of the important political gatherings in Kansas Territory and became a member of the state legislature. In 1858 he and four associates founded the town of Salina. In 1859 he married Carrie Spillman, who died in 1883. They had four children. At the outbreak of the Civil War he became an officer in the Union Army, winning prominence as a commander of Indian troops in Indian Territory and Arkansas. He was mustered out as colonel of the 3rd Indian Regiment on June 10, 1865.

After the Civil War he returned to law and politics. While most of the anti-slavery radicals became conservatives, he merely transferred his radicalism to economic issues. His economic theories were given formal statement in a book called *Labor, Land and Law; a Search for the Missing Wealth of the Working People* (1886). Repudiating Henry George's single tax, he presented a program including: a graduated land tax for the purpose of reducing the size of holdings, preservation of public timber and reforestation of cut-over land, lease of grazing rights on public domain in tracts large enough to support a family, reservation in the public interest of subsoil rights to minerals, postal-savings banks through which the government might borrow from its people in national emergencies, organization of all labor, graduated taxation of large fortunes and inheritances, and regulation of public utilities. He was elected to Congress from Kansas in 1872, 1874, and 1876, and while there he was interested chiefly in land legislation, postal-savings banks, postal telegraphy, greenbacks, and silver. He was a Republican in politics, and, when he found it necessary to choose between his party and his principles, he supported the party. On questions that were not partisan issues he was independent. His Civil War experiences resulted in close association with problems relating to Indians, especially the Cherokee. After his retirement from Congress he became attorney for the Cherokee and engaged in law practice in Washington, D. C. In 1890 he was again nominated for Congress but was defeated by the candidate of the People's party. He wrote voluminously, fiction, verse, and essays, as well as economic and political discussions. From 1885 to 1887 he published several articles in the *North American Review* (Nov. 1885, July, Sept. 1886, Aug. 1887). However, much of his writing was anonymous and can not be identified. He was survived by his second wife, Anna B. (Stapler) Phillips, to whom he was married in 1885 at Tahlequah in the Indian Territory.

[A few letters in the Lib. of Kan. State Hist. Soc., Topeka; papers in possession of nephew, A. M. Campbell, Jr., Salina, Kan.; Cherokee material in the Lib. of the Univ. of Okla.; *Kan. Hist. Soc. Colls.*, vol. V (1896); *Biog. Directory Am. Cong.* (1928); A. H. Abel, *The Am. Indian ... in the Civil War* (1919) and *The Am. Indian under Reconstruction* (1925); Wiley Britton, *Memoirs of the Rebellion on the Border* (1882), *The Civil War on the Border* (2 vols., 1890–99), and *The Union Indian Brigade* (1922); *Daily Republican* (Salina, Kan.), Dec. 1, 1893.]   J. C. M.

PHINIZY, FERDINAND (Jan. 20, 1819–Oct. 20, 1889), cotton merchant, financier, was of Italian ancestry on his father's side, his grandfather, Ferdinand, having come to America during the latter part of the eighteenth century. He was the eldest son of Jacob and Matilda (Stewart) Phinizy and was born at Bowling Green (now Stephens), Oglethorpe County, Ga. After attending the county schools he entered the University of Georgia, at Athens, whither his family had moved. Here he was graduated with honors in 1838. For the next few years he managed the family plantation at Bowling Green, but his business enterprise and sagacity soon led him into a venture of his own. He secured the contract for grading the first eleven miles of the new Georgia Railroad, leading out of Athens to Augusta. With the profits from this work, he entered the cotton trade in Augusta, setting up first with his classmate Edward P. Clayton under the firm name of Phinizy & Clayton. When by mutual agreement this partnership was dissolved, he organized with two of his kinsmen the firm of F. Phinizy & Company. His business ability was evident from the first, and before the outbreak of the Civil War he had amassed a fortune. In the struggle that followed, he did not enlist in the Confederate army, but instead became a fiscal agent of the Confederate government, and in the course of the four years of the war collected vast amounts of cotton which was run through the Federal blockade. He also marketed many Confederate bonds.

The war levied heavily upon his fortune, but he was able to regain his financial position and at his death handed down an estate estimated to be worth $1,300,000. He rehabilitated his fortune largely through wise management of the cotton trade and through sagacious investments. He bought many railway stocks and bonds, and at various times was a director of the Georgia Railroad & Banking Company, the Augusta & Savannah Railroad, the Atlanta & West Point Railroad, the Northeastern Railroad of Georgia, and the Augusta Factory. He was also a director and dominating force in the Southern Mutual Insurance Company, a director of the Bank of the University (Athens), and a trustee of the University of Georgia.

After the war he continued to show an interest in his former slaves, moving one couple to Athens, where he cared for them throughout their lives. Being emphatically a business man, he had no political ambition. Though he did not belong to a church until late in life, when he joined the Methodists, he was always interested in religious affairs and often entertained in his home visiting Methodist bishops and other churchmen. His religious tastes were simple—almost primitive—and in the rural churches he found his greatest delight. He was much opposed to instrumental music in the churches, and his support of certain congregations was based on their agreement to refrain from introducing it. In 1849 he married Harriet H. Bowdre, of Augusta, and to this union were born eight children. His wife died Feb. 7, 1863, and on Aug. 11, 1865, he married Anne S. Barrett, of Augusta; of this union three children were born. He made Athens his home after the Civil War, and there he died.

[F. P. Calhoun, *The Phinizy Family in America* (1925); W. J. Northen, *Men of Mark in Ga.,* vol. III (1911); A. L. Hull, *Annals of Athens, 1801–1901* (1906); *In Memoriam: Ferdinand Phinizy* (Augusta, 1890); *Athens Weekly Banner,* Oct. 29, 1889; *Athens Weekly Chronicle,* Oct. 26, 1889; *Atlanta Constitution,* Oct. 21, 1889.]
                                        E. M. C.

PHIPPS, HENRY (Sept. 27, 1839–Sept. 22, 1930), manufacturer, philanthropist, was born in Philadelphia, the son of Henry and Hannah Phipps, emigrants from England. In 1845 the family moved to Allegheny City, Pa., where they became next-door neighbors of the Carnegie family. In his *Autobiography,* Andrew Carnegie says that his mother often added $4.00 a week to the family income by binding shoes for Henry Phipps's father, who was a master shoemaker. Henry's education in the public school was supplemented by the influence of his mother, who inspired in him a fondness for poetry. His first regular employment, when he was thirteen years old, was in a jewelry store; then for a time he worked for a news and merchandise dealer. At seventeen he obtained work with Dilworth & Bidwell, dealers in iron and spikes, the Pittsburgh agents of the DuPont powder mills. At first he was office boy and clerk, and later bookkeeper, which position he held until 1861.

In 1859 he became a silent partner in the firm of Kloman Brothers, manufacturers of scales, and in 1861, borrowing $800, purchased a one-sixth interest in the firm, which was reorganized in 1863 as Kloman & Phipps; he kept the books and acquired practical experience with iron forgings and the manufacturing of axles. When the demand for their products created by the Civil War had lessened, Kloman & Phipps

found it expedient to join forces with Andrew Carnegie [*q.v.*], and a company, the Union Iron Mills, was formed in 1867. From this time until they both retired in 1901, Phipps was an associate of Carnegie. He was naturally cautious and disliked change of any kind; moreover, he was content with his income from the iron industry; nevertheless, in 1874, when Carnegie, foreseeing the importance of steel, formed the Edgar Thomson Steel Company, Ltd., for the manufacture of steel exclusively, Phipps took an interest. He was a partner in Carnegie Brothers & Company Ltd. (1881), in Carnegie, Phipps & Company (1886), and in the Carnegie Steel Company, Ltd., recorded in Pittsburgh in 1892 with a capital of $25,000,000, which embraced all of the possessions acquired since the days of the Kloman forge. During all this time, Phipps's contribution to the industry was the steering of a discreet financial course. The fact that his firm came safely through the fluctuations of the post-war iron trade, the establishment of the new steel business, and the business depressions and panics of the period is due in no small part to his careful and accomplished management. His one contribution to the technical side of steel manufacture was a measure of economy: recognizing the value of the chemical expert, he was responsible for the discovery of a use for scale, hitherto a waste product.

In 1899 Carnegie, wishing to retire, gave Phipps and Henry C. Frick [*q.v.*] an option on his interest in the Carnegie Steel Company, Ltd., but even with the aid of W. H. Moore [*q.v.*], Phipps and Frick were unable to raise the funds necessary to effect the purchase. In 1900, the Carnegie Steel Company, Ltd., was reorganized as the Carnegie Company, and a year later, with all its subsidiaries, passed into the hands of the United States Steel Corporation.

After his retirement Phipps devoted himself to the utilization of his wealth for humanitarian purposes. Among his early gifts were public baths, reading rooms, playgrounds, and conservatories in the parks of Allegheny and Pittsburgh. His philanthropies of greatest interest, however, were foundations for combating tuberculosis and mental disease. With the caution of the inquiring business man, he first studied at a distance and helped anonymously the tuberculosis work of Dr. Lawrence F. Flick. When he had satisfied himself as to the wisdom of the course, after a trip of investigation in Europe, he established in 1903 at Philadelphia the Henry Phipps Institute for the Study, Treatment, and Prevention of Tuberculosis, which in 1910 passed into the control of the University of Pennsylvania.

In 1905 at Baltimore he founded the Phipps Tuberculosis Dispensary at the Johns Hopkins Hospital, under Dr. William Osler [*q.v.*] and Dr. L. V. Hamman. He also made possible the sixth International Congress on Tuberculosis held in 1908 in Washington. His interest in mental disease was the result of consultation with Dr. William H. Welch of the Johns Hopkins University, and bore fruit in the foundation of the Henry Phipps Psychiatric Clinic of the Johns Hopkins Hospital, opened in 1913. In addition to these foundations Phipps gave $1,000,-000 for the erection of sanitary tenement houses in New York City. He married, on Feb. 6, 1872, Anne Childs Shaffer, the daughter of a Pittsburgh manufacturer, and they had three sons and two daughters. His well-preserved constitution carried him through more than ninety years of life; he died just before his ninety-first birthday at his home, "Bonnie Blink," Great Neck, L. I.

[*Autobiography of Andrew Carnegie* (1920), ed. by J. C. Van Dyke; Harvey Cushing, *The Life of Sir Wm. Osler* (2 vols., 1925); B. J. Hendrick, *The Life of Andrew Carnegie* (2 vols., 1932); manuscript notes on Phipps in the steel industry from B. J. Hendrick, Esq.; *Cosmopolitan*, Dec. 1902; *Who's Who in America*, 1930–31; *N. Y. Times*, Sept. 23, 1930.]   A. M.

PHIPS, Sir WILLIAM (Feb. 2, 1650/51–Feb. 18, 1694/95), first royal governor of Massachusetts, was born on the Maine frontier, of humble parents, James and Mary Phips. At an early age he was apprenticed to a ship's carpenter, and later practised his trade in Boston for many years. Here he married Mary (Spencer) Hull, the daughter of Capt. Roger Spencer and the propertied widow of John Hull. He became a contractor for building ships and, for a time at least, commanded a sailing vessel. Coming into contact with sea rovers who talked of treasure fishing and the fabulous wealth of sunken Spanish vessels, Phips determined to search for one of these ships reported to have sunk near the Bahamas. He succeeded in interesting Charles II, who equipped him with a vessel, H. M. S. *Rose*, and set forth on his quest in September 1683. This venture failed, but a second, backed by a company under the patronage of the Duke of Albemarle, was successful in finding a vessel off the coast of Hispaniola (Haiti) and raised a considerable treasure. For this achievement Phips was knighted in 1687.

With wealth and newly acquired social position Sir William returned to Boston to become provost marshal-general, a post which James II had granted him as a further reward, in the new dominion government under Sir Edmund Andros [*q.v.*]. Because he was ill received he hurried to England to complain, and there came into touch with Increase Mather [*q.v.*], who was seeking governmental changes. After the Revolution of 1688 the two worked together for restoration of the old charter rule. Phips was again in Boston just after the overthrow of Andros, where he found himself in high favor with the Mather faction, which had come into control. Early in 1690 he joined the Second, or North, Church (Congregational), thereby becoming a parishioner of the Mathers, and at the same time was made a freeman of the colony. He was immediately chosen to command the expedition which Massachusetts was raising against Nova Scotia and won a spectacular victory there by surprising the French and capturing Port Royal. Upon his return to Boston, he found he had been elected magistrate in the provincial government of Massachusetts. Soon afterward he was chosen commander of another expedition against the French, this time consisting of forces sent by the northern colonies against Canada. Chagrined by the failure of this ill-starred expedition, he hastened to England to seek aid in another attempt. Decision at court on the matter was delayed until the king should determine whether to establish dominion or charter government in New England, since if dominion government were established, the new governor general would command the military forces in the war. Finally the king determined on a compromise. He agreed to grant a new charter, based largely on the old one, but reserving to himself the appointment of the governor. Increase Mather, quick to seize every advantage for the colony, agreed to the king's plan but asked and was granted the privilege of nominating the first governor. His choice was Sir William.

The task of the new governor was not easy. The policy which the king desired him to uphold was bound to clash with what Mather expected of him, and party conflicts over religious, economic, military, and political affairs were inevitable. He arrived in the colony in May 1692, when the witchcraft delusion was at its height. After a period of bewilderment, he made a sudden decision and brought the persecution to an abrupt end (*Calendar of State Papers, Colonial Series, America and West Indies, 1689–1692*, § 2551; *1693–1696*, §§ 33, 545). He favored legislation requiring universal taxation for support of the Congregational church, but his administration had to face the bitter opposition of those of other faiths who claimed liberty of conscience as their charter right. In commercial matters he stood for the old free-trade policy, thwarted the customs officials at every turn, connived at piracy, and neglected to reserve the king's share in condemnations (*Ibid., 1693–1696*, §§ 214, 826, 838, 879). As for his military policy, he failed to protect his frontiers and to send the aid which neighboring colonies desired. Although he petitioned the Lords of Trade for permission to conduct another campaign against Canada, he refused to cooperate in the expedition under Sir Francis Wheler against the French in America, claiming that his orders did not arrive in time (*Ibid.*, §§ 545, 578). Probably his greatest mistake lay in crushing party opposition instead of attempting conciliation. He was disliked both by the advocates of the old charter régime and by those who favored dominion government. By using every means to keep these men out of the Council and House of Representatives, he was able to control the majority vote in the General Court, but he thereby gave them one more grievance about which to complain to England.

Socially Sir William seems always to have been at a disadvantage. A "self-made" man, he made a display of fraternizing with ship carpenters and former friends of lowly station, a trait as irritating to the aristocracy as his pompous manner or the undignified outbursts of temper with which he met opposition to his will. At times he could not resist resorting to brute force. He publicly caned a captain of the royal navy who refused to obey his orders, and on another occasion dragged the collector of customs around the wharf for attempting to seize a vessel suspected of illegal trading. In 1694 he was ordered to England to answer a number of charges brought against him by his enemies. His sudden death in London before his case was concluded was doubtless the only thing which prevented his recall, for the evidence of maladministration was very strong against him (*Ibid., 1693–1696*, §§ 1298, 1507). His failure was a great blow to the Mathers, who had expected him to unite all factions and by a sympathetic interpretation of his instructions to restore as nearly as possible the conditions existing in 1684, before the revocation of the charter.

[Cotton Mather's biography, *Pietas in Patriam: The Life of His Excellency Sir William Phipps, Knt.* (1697), repr. in *Magnalia Christi Americana* (1702) and as *The Life of Sir William Phips* (1929), ed. by Mark Van Doren, is totally unreliable, written as it was to defend Increase Mather for his responsibility in Sir William's appointment as governor. Francis Bowen's "Life of Sir William Phips," in Jared Sparks, *The Lib. of Am. Biog.*, vol. VII (n.d.), is only partly reliable, depending too greatly on Mather's account. Other lives are, William Goold, "Sir William Phips," *Me. Hist. Soc. Colls.*, vol. IX (1887); H. O. Thayer, *Sir William Phips* (1927); C. H. Karraker, *The Hispaniola Treasure* (1934); and sketch by J. A. Doyle in *Dict. Nat. Biog.* See also the following articles in the *New England Quarterly*: V. F. Barnes, "The Rise of Wil-

liam Phips" and "Phippius Maximus," July and October 1928; C. H. Karraker, "The Treasure Expedition," Oct. 1932; and R. H. George, "Treasure Trove of William Phips," June 1933. For source material, probably the most interesting is the Knepp Journal of 1683–84, in the British Museum, Egerton MSS., 2526, and the log of the *James and Mary* in the British Museum, Sloane MSS., 50 or 1070; but the following material will be found valuable: Journal and Correspondence of the Lords of Trade, in the Public Record Office; Mass. Archives; *Calendar of State Papers, Colonial Series, America and West Indies, 1689–92* (1901), *1693–1696* (1903); "Andros Records," *Proc. Am. Antiq. Soc.*, n.s., vol. XIII (1901); "Diary of Samuel Sewall," *Mass. Hist. Soc. Colls.*, 5 ser. V (1878). For genealogy, see F. L. Weis, *The Ancestors and Descendants of John Phipps of Sherborn* (1924).]

V. F. B.

PHISTERER, FREDERICK (Oct. 11, 1836–July 13, 1909), soldier and author, was born in Stuttgart, Württemberg, Germany, the son of Frederick and Frederiki Hahn Phisterer. He received his early education in the German schools until his nineteenth year, when he came alone to New York City, landing on June 22, 1855. Within a few months he enlisted at Philadelphia in the United States Army. In March 1856, he joined Company A of the 3rd Artillery, was advanced to the rank of corporal on Oct. 12, 1858, and to sergeant on July 10, 1860. He participated in Wright's expedition against the Spokane Indians, in Indian fighting at Four Lakes and at Spokane Plains in September 1858, in the occupation of the San Juan Islands from July to December 1859, and in Stein's expedition in eastern Oregon and Idaho in the summer of 1860. On Dec. 6, 1860, he was honorably discharged at Vancouver and came east to engage in business in Ohio.

After the first battle of Bull Run in the Civil War, he reënlisted and was made sergeant-major, 18th Infantry, on July 31, 1861. He was commissioned 2nd lieutenant, Oct. 30, 1861, promoted 1st lieutenant, Feb. 27, 1862, and captain, Feb. 15, 1866. He fought with the 18th Infantry throughout the Civil War, and at Stone's River on Dec. 31, 1862, he won lasting fame by volunteering to carry a message, under heavy fire, to a battalion commander whose troops faced capture or annihilation unless warned of their danger. In recognition of his valor, he was presented with the Congressional Medal of Honor on Dec. 12, 1894. He later won the commendation of his superior officers for his gallantry in action during the Chattanooga-Ringgold Campaign of 1863, and in the Atlanta Campaign of 1864.

After the Civil War, he served with the 36th and with the 7th Infantry regiments until Aug. 4, 1870, when he resigned his commission to enter civil pursuits in New York, in Brooklyn, in various cities in New Jersey, and in Columbus,

Ohio. He commanded a company of citizens' police in the Columbus railroad riots in 1877 and was commissioned captain of the Governor's Guards, Ohio National Guard, on Aug. 27, 1877, resigning in January 1879. He entered New York State military service on Jan. 1, 1880, as colonel and acting assistant adjutant-general, was made assistant adjutant-general on Nov. 22, 1892, and was reappointed on Jan. 1, 1897. He served in this capacity through the Spanish-American War, being brevetted brigadier-general on Dec. 22, 1898. He became colonel on the staff of the major-general of the New York National Guard on Mar. 5, 1903, and was brevetted major-general, Jan. 2, 1905. He was given original rank as lieutenant-colonel on the National Guard divisional staff on Jan. 30, 1908, and served as adjutant-general of New York until his death at Albany in 1909. His wife, Isabel Riley, whom he had married at Columbus, Ohio, on Nov. 14, 1867, and two sons, survived him. He is buried in Greenlawn Cemetery, at Columbus. He was a member of the Military Order of the Loyal Legion, the Order of Indian Wars of the United States, the Society of the Army of the Cumberland, and the Medal of Honor Legion of the United States. He wrote, *The National Guardsman on Guard and Kindred Duties* (1879), *The National Guardsman as a Non-Commissioned Officer of Infantry* (1885), *Statistical Record of the Armies of the United States* (1883), and *New York in the War of the Rebellion, 1861 to 1865,* the first edition of which was published in 1890.

[*Who's Who in N. Y. City and State* (4th ed., 1909); General Orders No. 48, General Headquarters, N. Y., July 13, 1909, printed in vol. I of *N. Y. in the War of the Rebellion, 1861 to 1865* (3rd ed., 5 vols. and index, 1912); records of the city historian of Albany, N. Y.; personal letter from his son, Col. F. W. Phisterer, U. S. A.; *Albany Evening Journal,* July 13, 1909.]

C. C. B.

PHOENIX, JOHN [See DERBY, GEORGE HORATIO, 1823–1861].

PHYFE, DUNCAN (1768–Aug. 16, 1854), cabinet maker, was a member of a Scotch family named Fife that, in 1783 or 1784, left their home at Loch Fannich, thirty miles northwest of Inverness, and sailed for America. The parents (or possibly only the widowed mother) were accompanied by several children, one or two of whom died during the voyage. They settled in or near Albany, N. Y., and there the second son, Duncan, then sixteen years of age, became an apprentice to a cabinet maker. Upon attaining his majority he moved to New York, and the directory of 1792 shows that he had a joiner's shop at 2 Broad Street. On Feb.

17, 1793, he married Rachel Lowzade, a native of Holland, who bore him four sons and three daughters. At about the time of his marriage he changed the spelling of his name to Phyfe, and so it appears in the 1794 directory. His business apparently prospered, for in 1795 he moved to larger quarters at 35 Partition Street, and between 1802 and 1816 he purchased the houses on each side and one across the street. In 1816 the name of the street was changed to Fulton. Phyfe's shops and warehouse were on the present site of the Hudson Terminal Building. At the height of his prosperity he is said to have employed over one hundred workmen. He took two of his sons, Michael and James D., into business with him and in 1837 the firm became Duncan Phyfe & Sons. On the death of Michael, in 1840, the name was changed again to Duncan Phyfe & Son. In 1847 Phyfe sold his interest and retired, but continued to live at 193 Fulton Street until his death, which occurred in 1854, in the eighty-sixth year of his age. He was buried in Greenwood Cemetery, Brooklyn.

Duncan Phyfe was described by members of his family who remembered him as a man of slight build—"a very plain man, always working and always smoking a short pipe." He was quiet, independent, and a man of strict and methodical habits. He combined the talents of an artist and a business man to a remarkable degree. He apparently had few interests outside his family and his work. He was a member of the Brick Presbyterian Church and a strict Calvinist. His fame rests upon the excellence of his furniture. Competent critics agree that in design and workmanship it is not surpassed by the finest products of the eighteenth-century cabinet makers of England. He was a master of proportion, line, and detail, and probably himself an expert carver. In the handling of mahogany to bring out its highest values of texture and color he never had a superior. His early work shows his indebtedness to Hepplewhite, Adam, and Sheraton, whose design books he undoubtedly possessed, though at no time was he a copyist. The characteristic curves of much of his work appear to have been derived from the French styles of the Directoire and the Consulate, followed by features strongly Empire in character. These elements he combined gracefully and successfully in a style all his own. Gradually, however, he acceded to the popular demand for furniture in the style commonly called American Empire. The first of this was not without merit, but it began to lose its lightness and grace and degenerated finally into heavy, commonplace forms which Phyfe himself called "butcher furniture." His work may be divided for convenience into the following periods: Adam-Sheraton, 1795–1802; Sheraton-Directoire, 1802–18; American Empire, 1818–30; "butcher furniture," 1830–47. His fame rests upon the furniture made prior to 1825, and the best of it was probably produced before 1814. Chairs, sofas, and tables formed the bulk of his output, though he made other pieces also. The lyre form and crossed slats in his chair backs, outward sweeping curves in chair and table legs, parallel rows of beading, and acanthus carving on pedestal tables are among the more familiar features. He worked almost exclusively in mahogany until the later period of rosewood and black walnut.

Duncan Phyfe unquestionably exerted a corrective and restraining influence on American taste, kept alive the classic tradition well into the nineteenth century, and did more than any other man to postpone the decadence of style that was inevitable with the development of the machine age. In a very real sense he was the last of the great Georgians, the artistic heir of Chippendale, Hepplewhite, Adam, and Sheraton.

[Walter A. Dyer, *Early Am. Craftsmen* (1915, 1920) and "Duncan Phyfe Furniture," *House Beautiful*, Mar. 1915; C. O. Cornelius, *Furniture Masterpieces of Duncan Phyfe* (1922) and "The Distinctiveness of Duncan Phyfe," *Antiques*, Nov. 1922; R. T. H. Halsey and C. O. Cornelius, "An Exhibition of Furniture from the Workshop of Duncan Phyfe," *Bull. of the Metropolitan Museum of Art*, Oct. 1922; W. R. Storey, "Duncan Phyfe Enters on New Renown," *N. Y. Times Sunday Mag.*, Dec. 20, 1925; W. M. Hornor, Jr., "A New Estimate of Duncan Phyfe," the *Antiquarian*, Mar. 1930; *N. Y. Tribune*, Aug. 19, 1854; manuscript notebook of Ernest Hagen, a disciple of Phyfe.]
W. A. D.

PHYSICK, PHILIP SYNG (July 7, 1768–Dec. 15, 1837), surgeon, was born in Philadelphia, the son of Edmund and Abigail (Syng) Physick. His father was keeper of the Great Seal and receiver-general of Pennsylvania, and later agent for the Penn estates. He was anxious that his son should study medicine, but the son was not eager to do so, preferring the art of the goldsmith practised by his maternal grandfather, Philip Syng [*q.v.*]. Many of the inventions and improvements that Physick made in surgical procedures and instruments show that he had strong mechanical leanings. He attended a local school and took his college course at the University of Pennsylvania, graduating in arts in 1785. Yielding to his father's desire, he then began the study of medicine under Dr. Adam Kuhn [*q.v.*], who had been a pupil of Linnaeus, and in 1788 went to London, where John Hunter accepted him as a house pupil and later invited him to remain in London as his as-

sistant. The American youth was fortunate in being associated with Hunter, who had one of the most fertile surgical brains the world has ever possessed. Physick studied at the Great Windmill Street School established by William Hunter, and it is probable that he and Jenner were fellow pupils. In 1790 he was appointed a house-surgeon to St. George's Hospital, which position he held for a year. He then went to Edinburgh, where he graduated in medicine in 1792, his thesis, *Dissertatio Medica Inauguralis de Apoplexia* (1792), being dedicated to John Hunter.

On his return to Philadelphia after receiving his degree he began practice, but at first patients came so slowly that he was greatly discouraged. He rendered good service in the yellow-fever epidemics of 1793 and 1798, contracted the disease himself and, it is said, even had a second attack. He gained one powerful friend, Dr. Benjamin Rush [*q.v.*], who did much to advance his fortunes, and came into contact with Stephen Girard [*q.v.*], who gave material aid to the yellow-fever hospital during the epidemic. He subsequently served as Girard's physician. He was elected to the staff of the Pennsylvania Hospital in 1794, holding this position until 1816. His clinical teaching there was renowned and did much to increase his reputation. In 1800 he was appointed surgeon to the Almshouse and about the same time he gave lectures in surgery at the University of Pennsylvania. At that time the subjects of anatomy and surgery were combined in one chair, but in 1801, Physick was asked by the University students to give independent lectures in surgery at the Pennsylvania Hospital, and these were so successful that in 1805 a separate chair of surgery at the University was created for him. He retained this chair until 1819, when failing health compelled his resignation.

Physick has many advances in surgery to his credit. The use of manipulation instead of mechanical methods of traction in the reduction of dislocations, new methods in the treatment of hip-joint disease by immobilization, a modified splint for certain fractures of the femur and of the ankle, were improvements in which he was largely concerned. He is said to have been one of the first in America to use the stomach tube. He invented needle forceps, which enabled deeply placed vessels to be tied, and the guillotine tonsillotome. He also used a form of snare in the removal of tonsils. He had much to do with the introduction of animal ligatures in surgery and with establishing the practice of leaving them in the tissues to become absorbed. His early experiments showed the value of catgut ligatures. In 1804 he reported a successful operation on an arteriovenous aneurism which had followed venesection (*Philadelphia Medical Museum*, vol. I, 1805, pp. 65–67). He did notable work in surgery of the urinary tract; he devised new forms of catheters, especially the bougie-tipped form, and became celebrated for his ability in operating for stone in the bladder. In 1831 he performed lithotomy on Chief Justice Marshall, removing, it is said, nearly a thousand calculi. The patient was seventy-three years of age at the time, but he made a complete recovery and lived four years longer. Physick persistently believed in the virtues of venesection, and is said to have regretted in his later years that he had bled not too much, but too little.

Physick was not a prolific writer; his publications were chiefly reports in medical journals. His mind was evidently disposed more toward the invention and perfection of mechanical devices and the designing of improved methods of mechanical treatment than toward writing. His views are well represented, however, in *The Elements of Surgery* (1813), by his nephew, John Syng Dorsey [*q.v.*], and in *The Institutes and Practice of Surgery* (1824), by his successor, William Gibson [*q.v.*]. He was honored by election to English and French medical societies and to the American Philosophical Society. Controversies over the cause of the yellow-fever epidemic engendered dissension and bitter feeling among the members of the profession in Philadelphia, with the result that Physick did not become a member of the College of Physicians, but was first president of the Academy of Medicine, a short-lived rival institution.

On Sept. 18, 1800, Physick married Elizabeth, daughter of Samuel Emlen of Philadelphia; they had seven children, of whom four survived infancy. Physick had many illnesses throughout his life; after an attack of fever in 1813, possibly typhoid, he never regained robust health and thenceforth suffered from renal calculus and gradually advancing cardiac disease. He took remarkable measures to avoid the possibility that he might be buried alive and to prevent an autopsy being performed on his body, the more surprising because he had been a strong advocate of the value of such examinations. He left particular directions that a guard should be stationed at his grave to prevent his body being carried away.

In estimating Physick's influence on American surgery, much importance should be given to his association with John Hunter. Stimulated by that great activator of surgical thought, he came to an untilled field as one of the few who

were fitted to cultivate it. Throughout his life his talents led him to originate new procedures and improve methods, and "his chief organ of publicity was his class of students" (Horner, *post*). While the accounts of his times speak of him as a conservative surgeon, it is evident that he could be bold when necessary and there is good reason for the title "Father of American Surgery" frequently bestowed upon him.

[W. E. Horner, *Necrological Notice of Dr. Philip Syng Physick* (1838); Jacob Randolph, *A Memoir on the Life and Character of Philip Syng Physick* (1839), abridged in *Am. Jour. Medic. Sci.*, May 1839; S. D. Gross, *Lives of Eminent Am. Physicians and Surgeons* (1861); F. P. Henry, *Standard Hist. of the Medic. Profession of Phila.* (1897); R. H. Harte, "Philip Syng Physick," *Univ. of Pa. Medic. Bull.*, Feb. 1906; H. A. Kelly and W. L. Burrage, *Am. Medic. Biogs.* (1920); W. S. Middleton, "Philip Syng Physick, Father of American Surgery," *Annals of Medic. Hist.*, Sept. 1929; P. S. P. Conner, *Syng of Phila.* (1891); *Poulson's Am. Daily Advertiser*, Dec. 16, 1837.]   T. M.

PIATT, DONN (June 29, 1819–Nov. 12, 1891), journalist, was born in Cincinnati, Ohio, the son of Judge Benjamin M. and Elizabeth (Barnett) Piatt. The former was the grandson of John Piatt, a Huguenot refugee who married Frances (Van Vliet) Wykoff in Holland, emigrated to the West Indies, and finally came to New Jersey. His son, Jacob, moved to Kentucky in 1795 and later settled in Ohio. Benjamin and Elizabeth Piatt possessed the hardy spirit of pioneers, tempered somewhat by an untutored appreciation of literature and the arts. Donn was the ninth of their ten children. In 1827 the family moved to a homestead, "Mac-o-cheek," near West Liberty, Ohio, where at the district school he laid the foundations of his education, which was continued in the public schools of Urbana and at the Athenaeum, now St. Xavier College, Cincinnati. At each of these institutions he gave evidence of brilliant but erratic abilities. Destined by his father for the law, he soon developed an ungovernable distaste for the machinery of legal practice, from which he found a temporary escape in active participation in the political campaign of 1840, during which he not only distinguished himself by his speeches, but also undertook the first of his editorial ventures, the *Democratic Club*, published at West Liberty. In this short-lived paper he first exhibited his talent for broad humor and crushing invective. After his marriage in 1847 to Louise Kirby, he gave up the law and retired from Cincinnati to "Mac-o-chee," whence both he and his wife contributed articles to various newspapers. In 1852 he was appointed judge of the court of common pleas of Hamilton County, a position from which he resigned the following year in order to take his wife to Paris for medical treatment. In France he served with distinction as secretary to the American legation until his return to "Mac-o-chee" in 1855.

At the outbreak of the Civil War he was commissioned captain in the 13th Ohio Infantry, Apr. 30, 1861, and the following year, Nov. 4, was promoted to the rank of major. On Jan. 1, 1863, he was made a lieutenant-colonel and later acted as chief of staff to Gen. Robert C. Schenck [q.v.]. In the absence of General Schenck, he ordered Col. William Birney [q.v.], who was in Maryland recruiting a colored brigade, to enlist slaves only. For this unauthorized action President Lincoln reprimanded and threatened to cashier him, but he was saved by the intercessions of Stanton and Chase. He was active in the campaign of 1863, when he showed his soldierly acumen by ordering Milroy to evacuate Winchester. This order was overruled by Schenck with the result that Milroy was cut off and his regiments almost annihilated by Lee.

After the war he returned to his old pursuits, and in 1865 was elected to the Ohio legislature, where he served one term. His wife having died in 1864, he married in 1866 her sister, Ella Kirby, whose injuries two years later in a railway accident necessitated their removal to New York. There he was involved more extensively in journalism. In 1868 he moved to Washington as correspondent to the *Cincinnati Commercial*; for a few months in 1871 he was also editor of a department in the *Galaxy* known as the "Club Room." In 1871 he became, with George Alfred Townsend, co-editor and founder of the weekly *Capital*, and his work for this paper is the real basis of his reputation. Townsend withdrew a few weeks after the first number was published, but Piatt continued in active editorship for nine years. The *Capital* affiliated itself with neither political party, but attempted to expose the weaknesses and corruptions of the members of both. So vigorous and pointed were many of Piatt's denunciations that while they brought popularity to the paper, they won for its editor the enmity of many politicians. After the Presidential election of 1876 he denounced the formation of the Electoral Commission as robbing the people of the right of self-government and condemned its subsequent actions as defeating the will of the people. On Feb. 18, 1877, he printed an editorial, entitled "The Beginning of the End," in which he declared: "If a man thus returned to power can ride in safety from the executive mansion to the Capitol to be inaugurated, we are fitted for the slavery that will follow the inauguration." This remark was interpreted by President Grant and others as a threat

to assassinate Hayes, and Piatt was indicted, Feb. 21, 1877, on the charge of inciting rebellion, insurrection, and riot. The prosecution was dropped, however, immediately after Hayes's inauguration. Piatt's complete frankness and outspoken honesty made him one of the most formidable and conspicuous editors of his time.

On his withdrawal from Washington in 1880, he devoted himself to literary composition. In 1887 he published *Memories of the Men Who Saved the Union,* a group of essays on Lincoln, Seward, Chase, Thomas, and others. Its sharp criticisms and its unpopular depreciation of Grant and Sherman attracted considerable attention. The following year *The Lone Grave of the Shenandoah and Other Tales* appeared. After his death, *Poems and Plays* (1893), *The Reverend Melancthon Poundex* (1893), a novel, and *General George H. Thomas* (1893), a critical biography with concluding chapters by H. V. Boynton, were issued. Piatt died at his country house, "Mac-o-chee," where his last years had been spent.

[C. G. Miller, *Donn Piatt: His Work and His Ways* (1893), fulsome but accurate; F. B. Heitman, *Hist. Reg. and Dict. U. S. Army,* vol. I (1903) ; *War of the Rebellion: Official Records (Army)* ; S. B. Hedges, in *Catholic World,* Oct. 1893 ; *Cincinnati Enquirer,* Nov. 13, 1891.]

                                  C. D. A.

PIATT, JOHN JAMES (Mar. 1, 1835–Feb. 16, 1917), poet, journalist, was born at James' Mills (later Milton), Ind., the son of John Bear and Emily (Scott) Piatt. The former was a second cousin of Donn Piatt [q.v.]. They were descendants of John Piatt, a French Huguenot who emigrated first to the West Indies and from there, some time prior to 1670, came to New Jersey. When John James was six years old his parents moved to Ohio, establishing themselves near Columbus. The boy attended the high school in that place, and later, Capital University and Kenyon College. Apprenticed to the publisher of the *Ohio State Journal* to learn the printer's trade, he became acquainted with William Dean Howells [q.v.], who was then associated with that paper, and the two formed a lasting friendship. Some of Piatt's verses appeared in the *Louisville Journal* in 1857, and soon afterward he accepted an editorial position on it. In 1859 he began contributing to the *Atlantic Monthly.* His poem "The Morning Street" evoked Howells' praise and the statement that he himself wished he could write something worthy of inclusion in the *Atlantic* (*Life and Letters, post*). The following year (1860) the two published in collaboration *Poems of Two Friends.*

On June 18, 1861, he married Sarah Morgan

Bryan, poet and contributor to the *Louisville Journal* [see Sarah Morgan Bryan Piatt]. They went to live in Washington, where Piatt was a clerk in the United States Treasury Department from 1861 to 1867. During this period he became acquainted with Walt Whitman [*q.v.*], who frequently referred to Piatt's writings (Barrus, *post*). In 1867 Piatt joined the staff of the *Cincinnati Chronicle,* and removed to North Bend, just below Cincinnati, on the Ohio River. From 1869 to 1878 he was literary editor and correspondent of the *Cincinnati Commercial,* but also served as assistant clerk (1870) and as librarian (1871–75) of the United States House of Representatives. From 1882 to 1893 he was United States consul at Cork, Ireland, and for a few months in the latter year at Dublin.

During all these years he was writing and publishing poetry and some prose. Among his books, in addition to several prepared in collaboration with his wife, are *Poems in Sunshine and Firelight* (1866); *Western Windows, and Other Poems* (copyright 1867); *Landmarks, and Other Poems* (1872); *Poems of House and Home* (1879); *Pencilled Fly-Leaves: a Book of Essays in Town and Country* (1880); *Idyls and Lyrics of the Ohio Valley* (1881); *At the Holy Well, with a Handful of New Verses* (1887); *A Book of Gold, and Other Sonnets* (1889); *Little New-World Idyls* (1893); *The Ghost's Entry, and Other Poems* (1895); *Odes in Ohio, and Other Poems* (1897). He also edited several collections of poems, and from 1907 to 1909 *Midland,* first a weekly, then a monthly, publication which was merged into *Uncle Remus's Home Magazine.* Piatt's poetry shows the regular meters of his time, but is original and varied in subject matter and appreciative of natural beauty, literary associations, and human feeling. His best-known poem is "The Morning Street," a bit of good realism; "The Night Train" is of the same type; "The Western Pioneer" reflects the life of his own forebears; "At Kilcolman Castle" (Edmund Spenser's home) shows literary taste and fancy. When political changes caused Piatt's recall from the consulate in Ireland, he settled at North Bend, Ohio. He continued his literary work, contributing to the *Cincinnati Enquirer* as editor of book reviews and to various periodicals, until a few years before his death, when he became an invalid through injuries received in a carriage accident. He died at Cincinnati; his wife, three sons, and one daughter surviving him.

[W. T. Coggeshall, *The Poets and Poetry of the West: With Biog. and Critical Notices* (1860); E. A. and G. L. Duyckinck, *The Cyc. of Am. Lit.* (1875), vol. II; W. D. Howells, "Editor's Easy Chair," *Harper's Mag.,* July 1917; Mildred Howells, *Life and Letters of William Dean Howells* (1928); Clara Barrus, *Whitman and Burroughs Comrades* (1931); *D. A. R. Lineage Books,* vols. III (1893), LIX (1906); *Who's Who in America,* 1916–17; *Cincinnati Enquirer,* Feb. 17, 1917.]

S. G. B.

PIATT, SARAH MORGAN BRYAN (Aug. 11, 1836–Dec. 22, 1919), poet, was born in Lexington, Ky., the daughter of Talbot Nelson and Mary (Spiers) Bryan. Her grandfather, Morgan Bryan, was a relative of Daniel Boone [*q.v.*], and one of a party that went from North Carolina to Kentucky with him, where Bryan settled what was known as Bryan's Station. Before Sarah was eight years old her mother died, and subsequently the girl lived with the maternal grandmother at Lexington, with friends near Versailles, Woodford County, briefly with her stepmother, and finally with an aunt, at New Castle, Ky. There she was graduated from Henry Female College. Always a devoted reader of poetry, she especially loved Shelley, Byron, Coleridge, Moore, and Scott, and early began herself to write verse. Her first productions appeared in the Galveston, Tex., *News.* Some of her work came to the attention of George D. Prentice, editor of the *Louisville Journal,* who published it and prophesied for her the first place among American poets of her sex. On June 18, 1861, she was married to the poet John James Piatt [*q.v.*], whom she had met at New Castle after her own writings had become widely known through the South. They lived in Washington, D. C., until 1867, then in North Bend, Ohio, and for thirteen years, beginning in 1882, in Ireland, where Piatt was United States consul. There she counted among her friends Jean Ingelow, Edward Dowden, Edmund Gosse, Austin Dobson, Alice Meynell, and Philip Bourke Marston.

During these years she published some seventeen volumes of poems. Two of them, *The Nests at Washington and Other Poems* (1864) and *The Children Out-of-Doors, a Book of Verses, by Two in One House* (1885), were prepared in collaboration with her husband. *Selected Poems* appeared in 1886, and later *Child's World Ballads* (1887), a second series of which was issued in 1895; *An Irish Wild-Flower* (1891); *An Enchanted Castle, and Other Poems: Pictures, Portraits and People in Ireland* (1893); and in 1894 *Complete Poems,* in two volumes. All of her later volumes were published both in London or Edinburgh and in the United States. She was perhaps more highly esteemed in Great Britain, where she was likened to Elizabeth Barrett Browning, than in the United States. Her poetry is free from conventionality and introspective. Essentially feminine, it reflects the joys, griefs, and aspirations of the ordinary woman's life. Much of it was inspired by her own children. Howells commended her for not writing like a man. Katharine Tynan said she had "a gift as perfect and spontaneous as the song of a blackbird" (*Irish Monthly*, July 1886, p. 389). Today she ranks as a minor poet of some excellence. On their return to America the Piatts lived in North Bend, Ohio. Sarah survived her husband and after his death lived with her son in Caldwell, N. J., where she died.

[F. E. Willard and M. A. Livermore, *Am. Women* (1897); Emerson Venable, in *Lib. of Southern Lit.*, vol. IX (1909); E. A. and G. L. Duyckinck, *The Cyc. of Am. Lit.* (1875), vol. II; Katharine Tynan, *Twenty-five Years*; *Reminiscences* (1913); *Who's Who in America*, 1912–13; *Woman's Who Who of America*, 1914–15; *N. Y. Times*, Dec. 24, 1919.]   S. G. B.

PICKARD, SAMUEL THOMAS (Mar. 1, 1828–Feb. 12, 1915), printer, editor, biographer, author, son of Samuel and Sarah (Coffin) Pickard, was born in Rowley, Mass. When he was four years old, his family removed to Auburn, Me., where his father became treasurer of the Lewiston Manufacturing Company, a position he held for forty years. The boy spent his youth in Auburn and secured his education in the elementary schools of that city and at Lewiston Falls Academy. In 1844, after he had completed his course of study at the academy, he went to Portland and there learned the printer's trade. When he had finished his apprenticeship, he became associated with Benjamin P. Shillaber [q.v.] in the publication of a humorous paper, the *Carpet Bag*, at Boston, Mass. In 1852 he sold his interest in this paper to Charles G. Halpine [q.v.] and returned to Portland, where in January 1853 he joined E. P. Weston in the publication of the *Eclectic*. In April 1855 this journal was merged with the *Portland Transcript*, and Pickard became one of its editors and joint owner with Weston, whose interest was later purchased by Pickard's brother, Charles W. Pickard, and with Edward H. Elwell. Under the editorship of Elwell and the Pickard brothers, the *Portland Transcript* became one of the most influential papers in New England. Its subscribers exceeded in number by thousands those of any other paper in Maine. It was a clean, sane, interesting, and wholesome family paper. It early espoused the causes of abolition and prohibition. Its weekly advent into the home brought accurate information, interesting stories, bits of good poetry, wise teachings, knowledge of books and men, and withal good cheer. After nearly forty years, Pickard retired from the editorship of the *Transcript* and went to live in Amesbury and Boston, Mass., where during the remainder of his life he was engaged in literary work.

On Apr. 19, 1876, Pickard married Elizabeth Hussey Whittier, a niece of John Greenleaf Whittier [q.v.] and a daughter of Moses F. and Jane E. (Vaughan) Whittier. By this marriage he had one son. His wife died in Boston, Apr. 9, 1902. For many years Samuel Pickard was a close personal friend and great admirer of the Quaker Poet, and on Whittier's death, in accordance with his expressed desire, became his literary executor and biographer. It proved to be a happy choice. Pickard's *Life and Letters of John Greenleaf Whittier*, which was published in 1894 and has passed through several editions, is written with excellent taste and simple sincerity such as the poet would have desired. This was his most important book. In 1897 he published a little volume, *Hawthorne's First Diary*, which purports to contain several authentic excerpts from a journal which Hawthorne was supposed to have kept during his boyhood days in Raymond, Me. Later Pickard became doubtful of the genuineness of this diary and withdrew the book from further sale. In 1900 he published *Whittier as a Politician*, presenting the poet in a somewhat new light, and in 1904, *Whittier-Land, a Handbook of North Essex,* "containing many anecdotes of and poems by John Greenleaf Whittier, never before collected." Besides these he was the author of numerous reviews and monographs, two of which are "Portland," published in 1898 in *The Historic Towns of New England*, and "Edward Henry Elwell," published in the *Collections and Proceedings of the Maine Historical Society* (2 ser. III, 1892, pp. 1–12). After a long life of useful activity, he died in Amesbury, Mass., in Whittier's old home.

[G. T. Little, in *Obit. Record Grads. Bowdoin Coll.*, 1915; *Biog. Record . . . of Leading Citizens of Cumberland County, Me.* (1896); Joseph Griffin, *Hist. of the Press of Me.* (1872); *Boston Transcript*, Feb. 12, 1915.]   W. B. M.

PICKENS, ANDREW (Sept. 19, 1739–Aug. 11, 1817), Revolutionary soldier, was born near Paxtang, Pa., the son of Nancy and Andrew Pickens, who, having emigrated from Ireland, drifted south with the Scotch-Irish, sojourned eight miles west of Staunton, Va., obtained 800 acres in Anson County, N. C., and in 1752 were on Waxhaw Creek, S. C. He volunteered in James Grant's expedition in 1761 against the Cherokee under Oconostota [q.v.]. Two years later he and his brother sold their Waxhaw inheritance and obtained lands on Long Cane Creek in South Carolina. There he married, on

Mar. 19, 1765, Rebecca, daughter of Ezekiel Calhoun who was a brother of John C. Calhoun's father; at the opening of the Revolution, with a wife and four small children, he was a farmer and a justice of the peace. As captain of militia in the first fight at Ninetysix fort in November 1775, he helped to negotiate the treaty with the Loyalists that followed. During the next two years his services on the frontier brought promotion, and, when Williamson became brigadier-general, Pickens became colonel. His defeat of Colonel Boyd at Kettle Creek, he himself considered the severest check the Loyalists ever received in South Carolina or in Georgia. After the capitulation of Charleston in 1780, he surrendered a fort in Ninetysix District and with 300 of his men returned home on parole. When his plantation was plundered, however, he regarded himself as released from his parole, gave notice to that effect, and rejoined the patriots. His part in the victory at Cowpens brought him a sword from Congress and a brigadier's commission from the state. In April 1781 he raised a regiment, in which the men were enlisted as state regulars for ten months' duty and were paid in negroes and plunder taken from the Loyalists. Active in the capture of Augusta, he cooperated with the Continentals in Gen. Nathanael Greene's unsuccessful siege of Ninetysix and in the drawn battle of Eutaw Springs, in which he was wounded. Thereafter he was occupied mainly with Indian warfare.

Elected to represent Ninetysix in the Jacksonboro Assembly in 1782, he continued in the legislature until sent to Congress for the session of 1793–95. The South Carolina legislature voted him thanks and a gold medal in 1783 for his services in the Revolution and later elected him major-general of the militia. In 1785 he was chosen by Congress to treat with Southern Indian tribes that had been at war with the United States and, until he declined further service in 1801, he was repeatedly appointed to deal with Indian relations. His most laborious service was in 1797, when for six months he was engaged in marking treaty boundaries. In 1792 he declined a command in the western army. For a number of years he lived at "Hopewell," his plantation in Oconee, where he had a store. He also carried on business in Charleston under the firm name of Andrew Pickens & Co. Later he settled at Tomassee in Pendleton District, where he lived in retirement except during a brief interval in the War of 1812. There he died suddenly and was buried at the Old Stone Church, of which he was an elder and a founder. Strict in family devotions and church observ-

ances, he was reputed so Presbyterian that he would have suffered martyrdom before he would have sung one of Watts's hymns. Of medium height, lean and healthy, with strongly marked features, he seldom smiled and never laughed, and conversed so guardedly that "he would first take the words out of his mouth, between his fingers, and examine them before he uttered them" (Wm. Martin to L. C. Draper, Jan. 1, 1843).

[Draper MSS. in Wis. Hist. Soc. Lib.; papers, chiefly of "talks" with Indians, not yet calendared in Charleston Lib. Soc.; A. L. Pickens, *The Wizard Owl of the Southern Highlands* (1933), a biog. tracing his career through the battle of Cowpens and *Skyagunsta* (1934) with revisions and biography to his death; *The State Records of N. C.*, vols. XVI–XIX, XXII (1899–1907); J. B. Grimes, *Abstract of N. C. Wills* (1910); A. S. Salley, *Jour. of the House of Representatives of S. C. Jan. 8, 1782–Feb. 26, 1782* (1916); Thomas Cooper, *Statutes at Large of S. C.*, vol. IV (1838); R. W. Gibbes, *Documentary Hist. of the Am. Revolution* (3 vols., 1853–57); R. N. Brackett, *The Old Stone Church, Oconee County, S. C.* (1905).]

A. K. G.

PICKENS, FRANCIS WILKINSON (Apr. 7, 1805–Jan. 25, 1869), congressman, governor of South Carolina, was born in St. Paul's Parish, Colleton District, S. C., the son of Susannah Smith (Wilkinson) and Gov. Andrew Pickens and the grandson of Andrew Pickens [*q.v.*]. He was educated at Franklin College, Ga., now a part of the University of Georgia, and at the South Carolina College, withdrawing from the latter institution in 1827 while a senior because of dissatisfaction with mess hall regulations. He subsequently studied law at Edgefield under Eldred Simkins, was admitted to the bar in 1828, became Simkins' partner, and married the latter's daughter, Margaret Eliza. Through the study of Aristotle, Rollin, the classic orators, and the state-rights doctrines of Thomas Cooper [*q.v.*] he became passionately fond of the type of republicanism most acceptable in his state. He was proud of his ancestors and of his own abilities, dogmatic in beliefs, impressive in speech, but prudent in action. Inheriting wealth from both parents and through his wife, he established near Edgefield Court House "Edgewood," a large estate with several hundred slaves. Surrounded by a large library and the luxuries of a Southern gentleman, he entertained lavishly. John C. Calhoun, a relation, declared that he was the most promising young man in the state.

While still in college he began his public career by writing a series of anonymous letters to the *Charleston Mercury* upholding Thomas Cooper's doctrines of state sovereignty under the pseudonym of "Sydney" (quoted in Hayne, *post*, pp. 4–5). In 1830 in anonymous letters to the *Edgefield Carolinian* under the pseudonym of "Hampden," he declared that the time had come for South Carolina to put its nullification principles in action. "If we do not succeed constitutionally and peaceably," he wrote, "I am free to confess that I am for any extreme, even 'war up to the hilt'" (Boucher, *post,* p. 56). In 1832 he was elected to the state legislature. There he gained distinction by replying to Jackson's nullification proclamation and by defending the right of the state to exact an oath of allegiance from its officers. To defend the state against threats of federal coercion he raised, among his Edgefield constituents, a contingent of 2,158 men. In December 1834 he succeeded George McDuffie in Congress, where he served until March 1843. His speeches on foreign relations, treasury reforms, and in favor of slavery and state rights placed him among the leaders of that body. He bitterly protested against the acceptance of petitions asking the abolition of slavery in the District of Columbia and warned the South of the danger from the growth of abolitionist sentiment in 1844. He became a member of the state Senate. He was a leader of the South Carolina secession movement growing out of dissatisfaction with the compromise measures of 1850. He was a delegate to the Nashville convention of June 1850, where he declared, "Equality now! Equality forever! or Independence!" (Hayne, *post,* p. 23). He was the presiding officer of the state convention of 1852 and drew up its ordinance favoring secession.

When this secession movement proved abortive, he became more conservative, foreseeing the folly of South Carolina's going to extremes without the cooperation of the other Southern states; his enemies said that he was an aspirant for federal office. He cooperated with James L. Orr and the other National Democrats and in 1856 presided over the state convention to send delegates to the convention that nominated Buchanan. In 1857 he was defeated for the United States Senate by the extremist, James H. Hammond, and in 1859 urged that South Carolina fully participate in the National Democratic Convention of 1860. Although he had previously refused missions to France and England, in 1858 he accepted Buchanan's proffer of the Russian mission. He served in St. Petersburg for two years without special distinction. Foreseeing a crisis in South Carolina, he resigned in the fall of 1860 and returned home. At first he was inclined to oppose precipitate action on the part of the state, declaring, in a speech at Edgefield, that secession should not be made effective until the inauguration of Lincoln; but, carried along with the tide, he later, in a speech at Columbia, espoused the cause of immediate secession. He was nominated for governor by the conservative secessionists. The legislature, after three days of balloting, elected him, and on Dec. 17 he began his two-year term.

He showed great ability in guiding the state in the perilous adventure of secession. In his inaugural address he averred that the North in electing Lincoln had committed "the great overt act" and that South Carolina was ready for no compromise short of secession. He clearly foresaw that the safety of South Carolina as an independent government was dependent upon the possession of the Charleston forts and immediately asked Buchanan to surrender Fort Sumter. This demand, however, was withdrawn when the governor was informed from Washington that the status of the forts would not be disturbed. Believing it a breach of the agreement with Buchanan, he was angered when Major Anderson, on Dec. 26, concentrated his garrisons in Fort Sumter. When Anderson refused to reoccupy his former positions, the governor seized the evacuated forts and the federal arsenal and strengthened the harbor batteries so as to put Sumter at their mercy in case of hostilities. He was responsible for the firing of the first guns of the war when, on Jan. 9, Morris Island batteries prevented the passage of the *Star of the West,* a ship sent to relieve Sumter. When pressed by Anderson to deny responsibility for this act, he replied with a justification (*War of the Rebellion: Official Records (Army),* 1 ser., I, 135) and sent a messenger to Washington demanding the surrender of the fort. However, on the suggestion of Southern leaders this demand was not delivered. He then became convinced that the fort should be immediately reduced. To forestall rash action on his part the newly created Confederate government, on Feb. 12, took over the responsibility for all decisions relating to the forts. The only part that Pickens played in the fateful step of opening fire on Sumter was the transmission to the Confederate authorities of Lincoln's repudiation of whatever words or deeds of his confidential agent, Ward H. Lamon [*q.v.*], had conveyed the impression that the fort would be evacuated, and Lincoln's notice that an attempt would be made to relieve the fort.

Alarmed over the capture of Port Royal in November 1861 and the apparent inability of the governor to provide adequately for the defense of the state, the convention that had passed the ordinance of secession erected in December 1861 an executive council composed of the governor and four others. This body virtually usurped the functions of the governor. Pickens perforce submitted, protesting that there would "now be great imbecility in acting as Commander in Chief" (White, *post*, p. 759). Although the executive council was unpopular, it was not abolished until the end of his term of office in 1862. He retired to his Edgefield estate, emerging in the public eye only once more to urge the state constitutional convention of 1865 to accommodate the state to President Johnson's reconstruction plans. His first wife died in 1842. He then married Marion Antoinette Dearing of Georgia. After the death of his second wife he married in 1858 Lucy Petway Holcombe, the daughter of Beverly Lafayette Holcombe, a Virginian who had emigrated to Texas. Her influence was responsible for his acceptance of the Russian mission. Beautiful and accomplished, she made a splendid appearance in the official circles of St. Petersburg and of the Confederacy. A regiment of South Carolina troops was named the Holcombe Legion in her honor, and her picture was engraved on Confederate currency. Pickens died deeply in debt owing to personal extravagance and to the reverses of war. For thirty years afterward his widow, assisted by their only child, made "Edgewood" the center of a lavish hospitality unique in upper South Carolina.

[Some correspondence in the Lib. of Duke Univ.; Hammond Papers and other manuscript material in Lib. of Cong.; information from Mrs. Sarah L. Simkins, Edgefield, S. C.; articles by J. K. Aull in *State* (Columbia), Jan. 1929; P. H. Hayne, *Politics in S. C.*, *F. W. Pickens' Speeches, Reports, etc.* (1864); LeRoy F. Youmans, *A Sketch of the Life and Services of Francis W. Pickens* (1869); C. S. Boucher, *The Nullification Controversy in S. C.* (1916); L. A. White, "The Fate of Calhoun's Sovereign Convention in S. C.," *Am. Hist. Rev.*, July 1929.]   F. B. S.

PICKENS, ISRAEL (Jan. 30, 1780–Apr. 23, 1827), third governor of Alabama, was born near Concord, Mecklenburg County, now in Cabarrus County, N. C., the son of Samuel and Jane (Carrigan) Pickens. His father was a Revolutionary soldier and was a cousin of Andrew Pickens [*q.v.*]. The boy enjoyed unusual educational advantages, at a private school in Iredell County, N. C., and at Jefferson College in Canonsburg, Pa., from which he was graduated in 1802. He studied law, removed to Morganton in Burke County, N. C., and was admitted to the practice of his profession. In 1808 and 1809 he sat in the upper house of the legislature of his state. From there he was sent to Congress, where he served in the House of Representatives from 1811 until 1817. He voted for the war with Great Britain and throughout that struggle favored the measures of the administration. At his retirement from Congress he became register of the land office at St. Stephens in the new Territory of Alabama. On June 9, 1814, he had been married to Martha Orilla, the daughter of William Lenoir of North Carolina, and with her he removed West. In 1818 he was made president of the Tombeckbee Bank of St. Stephens and the next year represented Washington County in the convention that framed the first constitution of Alabama. Shortly thereafter he removed to Greene County, where he resided for the remainder of his life.

In 1821 the anti-Crawford forces elected him governor of the state. At this time Alabama, with the West in general, was in the throes of the financial depression that followed the panic of 1819. Banks were badly needed to ease the credit situation, and the Alabama constitution provided for the creation of a state institution. Pickens' first legislature chartered such a bank with the preëxisting, privately owned banks as the basis of its organization. The governor vetoed this measure, and no further progress was made during his first administration. He was a candidate for reëlection in the campaign of 1823, in which the bank question was the leading issue. He won his race, and during the same year a state-owned, state-directed bank was chartered. In 1824 it went into operation for the relief of impoverished landowners. This was one of the devices of the rising Democracy of the West, but one that its chief, Andrew Jackson, opposed. Pickens was not originally a Jackson supporter, but he was too good a politician to continue to oppose a movement that was irresistible in his state. During his administration the University of Alabama was definitely incorporated, and he became the first *ex-officio* president of its board of trustees (Minute book, University of Alabama archives). He was an efficient administrator, and much of the fundamental work of organizing the governmental machinery of the state is credited to him. Retiring from the gubernatorial chair in 1825, he was appointed to the United States Senate in 1826, but an infection of the lungs forced his withdrawal from office after a brief issue. Declining an appointment as federal district judge for Alabama, he went to Cuba in search of health but died near Matanzas. He was buried near the place of his death, but later his remains were removed to Alabama and buried in the family cemetery near Greensboro.

[Correspondence in Ala. Department of Archives and Hist., and in Lib. of Cong.; Willis Brewer, *Alabama* (1872); J. H. Wheeler, *Reminiscences . . . of N. C.* (1884); A. J. Pickett, *Hist. of Ala.* (1851), vol. II; T.

M. Owen, *Hist. of Ala. and Dict. of Ala. Biog.* (1921), vol. IV; T. P. Abernethy, *The Formative Period in Ala.* (1922); *Biog. and Hist. Cat. of Washington and Jefferson College* (1889); *Southern Advocate* (Huntsville, Ala.), June 1, 1827.]   T. P. A.

PICKERING, CHARLES (Nov. 10, 1805–Mar. 17, 1878), physician and naturalist, was born in Susquehanna County, Pa., near Starucca. His father, Timothy Pickering, Jr., who was a Harvard graduate and for a time a midshipman in the navy, died in 1807, and Charles was brought up on a farm in Salem, Mass., under the guidance of his mother, Lurena (Cole), and his distinguished grandfather, Col. Timothy Pickering [*q.v.*]. From boyhood he had a keen interest in natural sciences and in his youth made botanical excursions into the White Mountains. He entered Harvard College with the class of 1823 but transferred to the medical department without graduating and was graduated M.D. in 1826. In 1849 he was granted the degree of A.B. as of the class of 1823. In 1827 he settled in Philadelphia where, in addition to practising medicine, he began active work with the Academy of Natural Sciences of which he was already a corresponding member. For ten years he diligently used the excellent resources of the Academy to improve his knowledge; he was active on the zoölogical and botanical committees, and held the offices of librarian (1828–33) and curator (1833–37).

Pickering's ability and attainments were recognized in his appointment to the post of chief zoölogist of the United States Exploring Expedition which sailed to the South Seas in 1838 under the command of Lieut. Charles Wilkes [*q.v.*]. During the voyage, Pickering gave special attention to anthropology and to the geographical distribution of plants and animals, subjects which held his interest for the rest of his life. As a result of studies made on the voyage and on a visit to the East in 1843, he published his first important work, *Races of Men and Their Geographical Distribution* (1848), issued as the ninth volume of the report of the United States Exploring Expedition. The fifteenth volume of the same report was a treatise by Pickering entitled *The Geographical Distribution of Animals and Plants* (1854), which was later supplemented by *Plants in Their Wild State* (1876), published by the Naturalist's Agency in Salem. After his voyage to the South Seas, Pickering made his home in Boston. In 1851 he married Sarah Stoddard Hammond, daughter of Daniel Hammond. The last sixteen years of his life he devoted to painstaking research, the results of which are given in his monumental publication, *The Chronological History of Plants: Man's Record of His Own*

Existence Illustrated through Their Names, Uses and Companionship. His death, in 1878, left this work unfinished, but the editing was carried on by his widow and the book was published in 1879. In addition to his books, he wrote a number of papers contributed to scientific publications and to the learned societies of which he was a member. Despite the wide scope of his interests, his work was scrupulously accurate. As a man he was characterized by sincerity, steadiness of purpose, reticence, and evenness of disposition.

[Biog. sketch in Charles Pickering, *The Chronological Hist. of Plants* (1879); W. S. W. Ruschenberger, in *Proc. Acad. Nat. Sci. of Phila.*, 3 ser. VIII (1879); Asa Gray, in *Proc. Am. Acad. Arts and Sci.*, n.s., vol. V (1878); J. W. Harshberger, *The Botanists of Phila. and Their Work* (1899); H. A. Kelly and W. L. Burrage, *Am. Medic. Biogs.* (1920); *Anniversary Memoir of the Boston Soc. of Nat. Hist.* (1880); *Bull. Essex Inst.*, vol. XII (1881); Harrison Ellery and C. P. Bowditch, *The Pickering Geneal.* (3 vols., 1897); *Boston Transcript*, Mar. 19, 1878.]   F. E. W.

PICKERING, EDWARD CHARLES (July 19, 1846–Feb. 3, 1919), astronomer, was born on Beacon Hill, Boston, Mass., the son of Edward and Charlotte (Hammond) Pickering. He was a great-grandson of Col. Timothy Pickering [*q.v.*] of Salem, Mass., who served in the cabinets of Washington and John Adams; his father and grandfather were Harvard graduates; his father held various offices of trust in large business enterprises which he administered with marked ability; and his uncle, Charles Pickering [*q.v.*], was a naturalist of note.

From such men young Pickering acquired a broad outlook, a spirit of initiative, and a keen sense of business. Proceeding from the Boston Latin School to Harvard, he entered the Lawrence Scientific School, where in 1865 he was graduated S.B., *summa cum laude*, at the age of nineteen. After a year of teaching mathematics in that institution he became assistant instructor in physics, and in 1868 Thayer Professor of Physics, at the Massachusetts Institute of Technology. Here he served till 1877, introducing the laboratory method of instruction. He established a physical laboratory in which the students, guided by his excellent manual, *Elements of Physical Manipulations* (2 vols., 1873–76), made experiments for themselves, being encouraged to publish papers on their original researches. In 1869–70 he constructed an apparatus for the electrical transmission of sound which he described before the American Association for the Advancement of Science, but he sought no patent, for he believed that "a scientific man should place no restriction on his work."

In 1874, he married Elizabeth Wadsworth Sparks, daughter of Jared Sparks [*q.v.*], a former president of Harvard, and in 1876 he was called to be director of the Harvard Observatory. On Feb. 1, 1877, he entered upon the duties which were to be his for forty-two years. The appointment by President Eliot of so young a man, a physicist and not an astronomer, to such an important position aroused some criticism from astronomers of the old school, but the wisdom of the choice was soon justified. Astronomical science had learned much from the so-called "old astronomy" of position, but was then on the threshold of the "new astronomy," which seeks a knowledge of stellar structure and its evolution. Physics held the key to these mysteries, and Pickering was the man to use physical methods with the Harvard equipment.

At the Observatory he found two instruments of large size and finest quality. To avoid duplication of work done elsewhere, he selected photometry as his field of observation, a field almost unexplored with large instruments. He gave an immediate demonstration, measuring by an ingenious photometric method the diameters of Phobos and Deimos, the tiny moons of Mars, then just discovered. Among the scientific achievements of his directorate, stellar photometry should be ranked first. At the time he entered the field, even the magnitudes (brightnesses) of the stars were not fixed on any generally accepted scale. Pickering established a satisfactory scale and substituted instrumental accuracy for uncertain eye estimates. To this end he invented the meridian photometer and employed other similar devices. The magnitudes of 80,000 stars were thus catalogued on the basis of over two million photometric settings, of which more than half were made by him personally.

A second important achievement was the compilation of a "photographic library," as Pickering called it, giving a complete history of the stellar universe down to the eleventh magnitude, written by the stars themselves on some 300,000 glass plates, a history duplicated nowhere else in the world. Photographic images of stars had been obtained at Harvard as early as 1850; with the advent of the dry plate, experiments were resumed about 1882; but it was in 1885 that Pickering began his intensive system of charting the heavens. From these plates the past record of the stars may be studied; Pickering himself was able to plot the path of Eros in the sky from photographs taken four years before this asteroid was known to exist.

He was also a leader in stellar spectroscopy. Stellar spectra indicate the composition, temperature, and physical conditions of the stars. With a prism placed over the camera lens he photographed the spectra by wholesale; laid the foundation of spectral classification now universally accepted, and obtained the material for the new Draper Catalogue containing 200,000 stars. Another important accomplishment of his régime was the establishment in 1891 of an observing station at Arequipa, Peru, to extend his surveys to the southern stars. His achievements in photometric magnitudes, in photography and photographic magnitudes, and in the classification of variable stars as well as of spectra, set a world-recognized standard. Eighty volumes of the *Annals of the Astronomical Observatory of Harvard College* (1855–1919) contain the record of this work. Moreover, under his administration, the Observatory's endowment rose to a million dollars. While not a rich man, he was himself always a large donor, and in later life regularly turned in his salary to increase the institution's scientific output. Twice he received the gold medal of the Royal Astronomical Society; scientific honors came to him from all over the world. He was a founder (1898) and was chosen president in 1906 of the American Astronomical Society, and was beloved of all its members. At the time of his death he was recognized as the "dean of astronomical research in America."

Pickering seldom took a vacation, but found relaxation and inspiration in the music his wife played to him on the piano. He liked chess as a pastime. He made local explorations on a bicycle and founded and was first president of the Appalachian Mountain Club. In this connection he devised the micrometer level, by which he plotted mountain topography. He had no children, but was fond of young people, and with his wife dispensed a stately yet cordial hospitality. Of large stature and commanding presence, he was a gentleman of the older school, combining dignity and social grace with a kindly spirit, eager to give time, data, or financial aid to promising and enthusiastic investigators.

[Harrison Ellery and C. P. Bowditch, *The Pickering Geneal.* (3 vols., 1897); S. I. Bailey, in *Astrophysical Jour.*, Nov. 1919; W. W. Campbell, in *Pubs. Astron. Soc. of the Pacific*, Apr. 1919; A. J. Cannon, in *Popular Astronomy*, Mar. 1919; E. S. King, in *Jour. Royal Astron. Soc. of Canada*, Apr. 1919; J. H. Metcalf, in *Proc. Am. Acad. Arts and Sci.*, vol. LVII (1922); H. N. Russell, in *Science*, Feb. 14, 1919; H. H. Turner, in *Monthly Notices of the Royal Astron. Soc.*, Feb. 1920; *Boston Transcript*, Feb. 4, 1919.]   E. S. K.

PICKERING, JOHN (*c.* 1738–Apr. 11, 1805), judge, the son of Joshua and Mary Deborah (Smithson) Pickering, was born at Newington, N. H. He was descended from John Pickering, who settled at Portsmouth about 1633, and was not connected with Timothy Pickering. After graduation at Harvard in 1761, abandoning his plan of entering the ministry, he studied law and became one of the few really learned lawyers in New Hampshire at this period. After a brief period of practice in Greenland he settled in Portsmouth and resided there for the rest of his life. He married Abigail, daughter of Jacob Sheafe of Portsmouth, but the date is a matter of uncertainty. His practice is said to have been large but not particularly remunerative in view of the petty nature of much of the litigation at this time. His name appears in the early records of the Revolutionary contest as a holder of sundry civil posts, but he took no important part in developments until 1781, when he was a member of the constitutional convention. From 1783 to 1787 he served repeated terms in the legislature as the representative of Portsmouth, declined service as a delegate to the Federal Convention at Philadelphia in 1787, and in 1788 was an influential member of the New Hampshire convention that ratified the United States Constitution. He was a presidential elector in 1788 and 1792, served in the New Hampshire Senate and Council, and in the constitutional convention of 1791-92.

He was appointed chief justice of the superior court of judicature on Aug. 7, 1790, serving until February 1795, when appointed judge of the United States district court. William Plumer, who had served with him in the legislature and the constitutional convention of 1791-92, has recorded some of Pickering's peculiarities, his timidity, his dread of crossing rivers, his tendency to seek seclusion at periodic intervals, and other characteristics which show a somewhat abnormal mentality. His failure to perform regularly the duties of chief justice had on at least one occasion attracted the attention of the legislature (*House Journal*, Dec. 22, 1794). For some years his duties on the federal bench were satisfactorily performed, perhaps as Plumer points out, because it was no longer necessary for him to go on circuit, but in 1801 he suffered a mental breakdown and a member of the federal circuit court was obliged to take over his duties in the district court at Portsmouth.

The abolition of the circuit courts soon after the opening of Jefferson's administration necessitated Pickering's resumption of duty and the situation was obviously incompatible with the proper administration of justice. On Feb. 3, 1803, the President in a special message laid the matter before the House of Representatives (*Annals of Congress*, 7 Cong., 2 sess., p. 460). Lacking precedent for dealing with such a matter and apparently influenced by the bitter party animosity of the day, the House promptly voted articles of impeachment, charging "loose morals and intemperate habits" and conduct "disgraceful to his own character as a judge and degrading to the honor and dignity of the United States." He had unquestionably been guilty of intoxication and profanity in the court room, but his friends and associates presented evidence of exemplary character prior to his mental collapse. After a perfunctory trial in which the defendant did not appear, the Senate formally voted his removal on Mar. 12, 1804. He did not long survive his unmerited disgrace.

[William Plumer, Jr., *Life of William Plumer* (1857), ed. by A. P. Peabody; brief sketch by William Plumer, in *N. H. State Papers*, XXII (1893), 839-43; letter of Plumer, with characterization of Pickering, in *Pubs. Colonial Soc. of Mass.*, XI (1910), 389-90; short paper, dealing with Pickering's character and the charges against him, by A. P. Peabody, in *Proc. Mass. Hist. Soc.*, XX (1884), 333-38; C. H. Bell, *The Bench and Bar of N. H.* (1894); C. W. Brewster, *Rambles about Portsmouth*, 2 ser. (1869); R. H. Eddy, *Genealogical Data Respecting John Pickering of Portsmouth, N. H. and His Descendants* (1884), and *Supplement* (1884). Pickering's career in the legislature can be traced in the *N. H. State Papers*. For his impeachment, see *Annals of Congress*, 7 Cong., 2 sess., and 8 Cong., 1 sess.; and *Extracts from the Journal of the U. S. Senate in All Cases of Impeachment . . . 1798-1904* (1912), 62 Cong., 2 sess., Senate Doc. No. 876.]
W. A. R.

PICKERING, JOHN (Feb. 7, 1777–May 5, 1846), lawyer, philologist, was born at Salem, Mass., the eldest of the ten children of Timothy [*q.v.*] and Rebecca (White) Pickering, and the fifth in descent from John Pickering (1615–57), presumably a Yorkshireman, by trade a carpenter, who settled in Salem in 1637. At the time of John's birth his father was colonel of a Massachusetts regiment quartered in New Jersey. John entered Harvard College in 1792 and early gained a reputation for his devotion to the classics and, in lesser degree, to French. His cousin, John Clark (1755-98), William Emerson's predecessor in the First Church in Boston, addressed to him his *Letters to a Student in the University of Cambridge, Massachusetts* (1796), a little book still useful for the light it casts on the literary culture of that period. After his graduation in 1796, Pickering began the study of law in Philadelphia in the office of Edward Tilghman [*q.v.*] but in July 1797 he embarked at New Castle, Del., for Lisbon to become secretary to William Smith of South Carolina, the American minister to Portugal. He spent two happy years in Portugal, with ample leisure to enjoy the social life of the capital and of Cintra, to study the Romance languages, Turkish, and Arabic, and to continue his reading of the law. In November 1799 he went to London, where he was welcomed by Rufus King and, some months later, became his secretary. He spent much time in the law courts and in the House of Parliament, enjoyed the theatres, visited Paris, Brussels, and the Dutch cities, collected a remarkable library —part of which he was compelled to sell on his return to the United States—and made the acquaintance of various scholars. On Oct. 8, 1801, he landed once more in Boston. His *Wanderjahre* were over; thereafter his longest, almost his only, absence from Boston and Salem was a five weeks' trip to New York, Philadelphia, and Washington in 1832. In 1804 he was admitted to the Essex County bar; and on Mar. 3, 1805, he married Sarah White, who was his first cousin once removed through his father's family, and his second cousin through his mother's. His wife, with their two sons and a daughter, survived him. To her wise management and self-effacing devotion he owed the leisure that enabled him to attain eminence both in the law and in philology.

Pickering moved to Boston in 1827 and in 1829 was made city solicitor, an office that he held until a few months before his death. His reputation as a lawyer was higher with his colleagues than with the public at large, but he was much sought after as a counselor, and his articles on legal subjects, most of them contributed to the *American Jurist*, are the work of a scholar. He was one of the few Americans deeply interested in Roman Law. His political horizon lay somewhere in the western suburbs of Boston, but he represented Salem in the General Court in 1812, 1814, and 1826, was a member of the Governor's Council in 1818, was a senator from Suffolk County in 1829, and drafted *Part First: Of the Internal Administration of the Government* (1833) of the *Revised Statutes of Massachusetts*.

His office library contained only law books, but in his study at home he devoted himself to linguistics. His permanent fame in this department has suffered from the fact that his main interest lay more in learning languages than in elaborating theories about them. Like so many American scientists of his generation and the one following, he was overpowered by the wealth of material unexplored. He acquired, with various degrees of thoroughness, all the principal European and Semitic languages, was acquainted with several of the Chinese group, and was the leading authority of his time on the languages of the North American Indians. His two closest correspondents, on linguistic subjects, were Pierre Étienne Du Ponceau [*q.v.*] and Wilhelm von Humboldt; his greatest admiration, in law as well as languages, was Sir William Jones. His chief service to his own time was his *Comprehensive Lexicon of the Greek Language* (1826; 1829; 1846), which was the best Greek-

English dictionary before Liddell and Scott. In collaboration with Daniel Appleton White he prepared the first American edition of Sallust (Salem, 1805), and he is still remembered as the author of the first published collection of Americanisms, real or fancied, his *Vocabulary or Collection of Words and Phrases which have been supposed to be peculiar to the United States of America* (1816). His own style was that of the most eminent British reviewers. Most of his articles and monographs on linguistic subjects are scattered through the volumes of the *North American Review,* the *Memoirs of the American Academy of Arts and Sciences,* and the *Collections of the Massachusetts Historical Society.* It was said of him, with pardonable exaggeration, that he spent his life in declining honors. Both for his personal qualities and his attainments he was one of the most highly regarded Bostonians of his day. He died in Boston, after a year of declining health, and was buried in Salem.

[Mary Orne Pickering, *Life of John Pickering* (privately printed, 1887), reviewed in *Nation* (N. Y.), Sept. 29, 1887; Charles Sumner, "The Late John Pickering," *Law Reporter,* June 1846, and *The Scholar, the Jurist, the Artist, the Philanthropist* (1846); D. A. White, *Eulogy on John Pickering* (1847); W. H. Prescott, memoir, *Colls. Mass. Hist. Soc.*, ser. 3, vol. X (1849), with a useful, though inaccurate, list of his publications; A. P. Peabody, *Harvard Graduates Whom I Have Known* (1890); Harrison Ellery and C. P. Bowditch, *The Pickering Geneal.* (3 vols., 1897); esp. I, 258–62; H. S. Tapley, *Salem Imprints, 1768–1825* (1927).]　　　　　　　　　　　　　　　G. H. G.

PICKERING, TIMOTHY (July 17, 1745– Jan. 29, 1829), soldier, administrator, and politician, was born at Salem, Mass., where the Pickering family had been prominent since the first years of settlement. An ancestor, John Pickering, was living there in 1637. Timothy was the eighth of the nine children of Timothy and Mary (Wingate) Pickering. His father had sufficient means to give him and his only brother a good education. After graduating at Harvard College in 1763, he returned to Salem and became a clerk in the office of the register of deeds for Essex County, where he was employed at intervals for more than ten years. He studied law and was admitted to the bar in 1768, but, although he held several minor judicial posts in the course of his career, he never attained distinction as a lawyer. He was an early supporter of the Revolutionary movement in Massachusetts, and in this, as in sundry local disputes, displayed great ability as a newspaper controversialist and pamphleteer. He served on various committees engaged in Revolutionary agitation and drafted several notable addresses and petitions. In addition he held various Salem offices, including those of selectman, town clerk, and representative in the General Court, until summoned to more important duties after the outbreak of war.

In 1766 he had received a commission as lieutenant in the Essex County militia and he became a devoted student of military history and tactics. Although unsuccessful in his endeavor to place the Massachusetts militia on a really effective war footing, he performed useful service in drilling the local levies and his activity bore fruit in 1775 when he published *An Easy Plan of Discipline for a Militia,* adopted by Massachusetts in 1776 and widely used in the American army until replaced by the famous manual of Baron Steuben. He was elected register of deeds in October 1774 and, in February of the following year, colonel of the 1st Regiment of Essex County militia. He took part in the military operations in April 1775, and performed varied services, civil and military, during the early months of the war. On Apr. 8, 1776, he married Rebecca White, a woman of great ability and strength of character who had been born in Bristol, England. Their married life continued over fifty years and they had ten children, among them John, 1777–1846 [*q.v.*], and Timothy, father of Charles and grandfather of Edward Charles Pickering [*qq.v.*].

After a brief assignment to coast defense duty he led a Massachusetts contingent to join Washington's army and participated in the winter campaign of 1776–77 in New York and New Jersey. His creditable services and military talents led to Washington's offer of the post of adjutant-general of the United States Army. After some delay he resigned his place as register of deeds and, in a letter of May 7, 1777, of which Congress was informed May 24, accepted the military position. He served with distinction and in November was elected to the newly organized board of war, although continuing to serve as adjutant-general until the following January. Selected on Aug. 5, 1780, as quartermaster-general, he held this important post until after the conclusion of peace. While his conduct of the department was frequently criticized, he performed great services in the face of tremendous obstacles and showed himself to be a man of indefatigable industry and iron determination. His letters constitute an invaluable commentary on the course of the Revolution. He had no illusions as to the character of his countrymen and the real causes of much of the suffering and the prolongation of the war. "If we should fail at last," he wrote, Mar. 6, 1778, "the Americans can blame only their own negligence,

avarice, and want of almost every public virtue" (Pickering and Upham, *post,* I, 211).

On the restoration of peace and after winding up the affairs of his department he engaged in mercantile business in Philadelphia, but because of the post-war depression decided to move with his growing family to the Wyoming Valley. At this time he repeatedly, with voice and pen, expressed disapproval of the harsh treatment of the Loyalists, declaring the policy pursued to be a national disgrace, of which *"the vestiges* will remain to the most distant age" (*Ibid.,* II, 132).

After a preliminary visit to the Wyoming region in 1786, he moved there early in 1787, charged by the government of Pennsylvania with the duty of organizing the new county of Luzerne. He was thus involved in the protracted and bitter dispute between the Connecticut settlers and the Pennsylvania authorities. Although he did his best to settle jurisdictional quarrels and quiet disputed land titles, the dilatory tactics and suspected bad faith of Pennsylvania authorities brought upon him the wrath of the settlers and caused him to be subjected to outrageous treatment on several occasions. He realized the grievances of the settlers, however, showed magnanimity toward offenders, and represented Luzerne County in the convention that ratified the Constitution of the United States, and in the state constitutional convention of 1789–90.

His personal finances being badly involved, apparently because of insufficient capital and excessive purchases of land, he determined to seek public office under the newly organized federal government. On Sept. 8, 1790, he applied to Washington for the postmaster generalship but was first sent on a special mission to the Seneca Indians, who were threatening to join the western tribes in the war then in progress. After the successful conclusion of this mission, he was appointed postmaster general, Aug. 12, 1791. He was repeatedly assigned on missions to the Indians during the next few years, his temperament and sympathies making him an admirable negotiator. He endeavored to protect the tribes from outrage and exploitation by the settlers but his suggestions for an enlightened Indian policy, like those for an effective military establishment, were too advanced for the opinion of his times. His recommendation for the establishment of a military academy, however, was at length accepted by the government. The Post Office Department was still in a rudimentary stage and Pickering's work was necessarily of pioneer character. For over three years he wrestled with its administrative problems. On Jan. 2, 1795, he became secretary of war and his capacity for administrative detail was soon severely tested. In addition to military and Indian affairs, the department included the infant navy, and Pickering performed important services in connection with building and equipping several of the famous frigates which afterwards did so much to establish the naval reputation of the Republic.

In August 1795 the secretary of state, Edmund Randolph [q.v.], was forced to resign, owing to the discovery of dubious transactions with the French minister, and Pickering, who had been prominent in bringing the matter to the President's attention, succeeded to that portfolio. He had, naturally enough in view of his personal and official associations, together with his temperament, become a bitter and uncompromising Federalist. The French Revolution filled him with dread and loathing. The foreign complications accompanying the outbreak of war in Europe convinced him, as they did many of his associates, that France had malevolent designs on American independence and that "French influence" meant the subversion of American institutions and mob rule. As a corollary he became convinced that the British navy constituted the chief barrier against French designs. For more than twenty years his views of French influence and policy constituted an obsession which warped his judgment, weakened his political scruples, and involved him in sundry transactions which clouded his reputation and obscured his great services. He continued in the State Department after John Adams' accession to the presidency and took a prominent part in the turbulent foreign policy of that administration. He entered with enthusiasm into the preparations for hostilities with France in 1798, although protesting vigorously against British encroachments on American rights. While he had never held Washington in the exalted estimation of many contemporaries, he had apparently been greatly influenced by the awesome presence, calm judgment, and iron will of the great Virginian. He had no such sentiments towards Adams. For Hamilton, however, he had unbounded admiration, and, like many leading Federalists, regarded the latter as the real leader of the party. Pickering, on intimate terms with Hamilton, followed a course which a man of finer scruples would have shunned. While retaining his place in the Cabinet, he corresponded with the President's party enemies, intrigued against his appointments to the army then being organized, and in the face of the President's desire to settle difficulties with France, endeavored to widen the breach. The effect on Federalist party fortunes was disastrous, and Pickering

was abruptly dismissed from the State Department, May 10, 1800.

He resumed farming operations in western Pennsylvania but his Federalist friends were determined that his talents should not be lost to the party. His lands were purchased by subscription and Pickering, after twenty-four years' absence, returned to his native county in Massachusetts, taking up farming, first in Danvers and later at Wenham. He was defeated as a candidate for the federal House of Representatives in 1802, but served in the Senate from Mar. 4, 1803, to Mar. 3, 1811. His controversial talents, developed in years of partisan activity, had not hitherto been tested in legislative halls, but he soon became a formidable debater. He was a bitter opponent of most of the measures of Jefferson and Madison. Republican opponents regarded him with malevolence equal to his own. He was repeatedly burned in effigy, and was the subject of continual caricature and slander in newspaper and pamphlet. The acquisition of Louisiana and other Jeffersonian policies convinced him that the interests of the commercial states could no longer be properly maintained within the Union. With Hamilton's death, Pickering's position of leadership among the Federalists made his attitude very significant. His correspondence shows that he was urging on many of his colleagues the desirability of a northern Confederacy, and that he considered peaceful separation entirely feasible (Henry Adams, *Documents relating to New England Federalism, passim*).

Defeated for reëlection to the Senate in 1811, he served as a member of the Executive Council of Massachusetts in 1812–13. In the meantime he was reëlected to the House, serving from Mar. 4, 1813, to Mar. 3, 1817, and distinguishing himself by the virulence of his opposition to the War of 1812. His expectation that the Union would dissolve was apparently never wholly abandoned until the restoration of peace. He retired at the close of his second term, but made an unsuccessful contest for election to the Seventeenth Congress. He moved from Wenham to Salem in 1820 and spent the rest of his life in his birthplace, where in 1829 he died. Of powerful physique and sound health, Pickering remained active to the end of his life. He presents a pleasanter side in his work for agricultural improvement, and in his correspondence on crop rotation, soil fertility, and animal husbandry. He deserves an important place in the history of New England agriculture and Timothy Pickering the farmer, winning a ploughing match in his seventy-fifth year, is a more attractive figure than Timothy Pickering the politician, when almost eighty, fanning the dying embers of his controversy with Adams.

He was deeply interested in American history and planned extensive literary work. His correspondence with Governor Sullivan on the Embargo (*Interesting Correspondence between His Excellency Governour Sullivan and Col. Pickering . . .*, 1808), which was widely circulated as a campaign document; his *Political Essays. A Series of Letters Addressed to the People of the United States* (1812); and *A Review of the Correspondence between the Hon. John Adams . . . and the Late Wm. Cunningham, Esq.* (1824), disclose a mastery of English and a high order of polemical ability. His more ambitious literary projects failed to materialize. Throughout his career, however, he had been a prodigious letter writer, and his carefully preserved papers and notes are of unusual interest. Through his letters and journals move the great figures of the early days of the Republic. There are also glimpses of the soldiers shivering in their huts at Valley Forge, the officers cursing the ingratitude of their country at Newburgh, the Indians in council, the sailors crowding the smoky gundecks of the frigates and privateers, the frontiersmen and teamsters struggling to open the roads to the West, the people dying of yellow fever in the great Philadelphia epidemic of 1793. His judgments of contemporaries are frequently prejudiced and worthless, but his keen observations of places, customs, and conditions render his writings in the aggregate extremely valuable to the historian.

He had great administrative ability, industry, and personal integrity. Although an outstanding member of the die-hard school of Federalism, he was democratic in his personal relations and simple and unostentatious in his habits. His interests were broad and varied, but he had too large a share of the Puritan temperament to be an attractive figure. His portrait by Stuart seems to reveal the harshness, narrowness, and intolerance so often noted by contemporaries. Life to him was a serious matter, "a *probationary state, a school of discipline* and instruction, in which we are to be prepared for admission into the assembly of the saints and angels, to spend an eternity in the presence and worship of the Great Source of being and happiness" (Pickering and Upham, IV, 73). It was quite in keeping with such views that Hamilton, Stephen Higginson, George Cabot, and other very human associates became saints and angels in advance of their translation, and that Jefferson, John Adams, and Governor Sullivan seemed destined

to a very different region. He performed great services for his country; his defects of character, and his political mistakes were common to the group of New England Federalists to which he naturally belonged.

[The great collection of Pickering Papers is for the most part in the custody of the Mass. Hist. Soc., which published a valuable index in its *Collections*, 6 ser., vol. VIII (1896); this volume contains information as to other depositaries of Pickering material. *The Life of Timothy Pickering* (4 vols., 1867–73) by his son Octavius Pickering, who completed vol. I, and C. W. Upham, who finished the work, contains copious extracts from the original manuscript collections. It is a useful biography but glosses over or omits certain aspects of his character and career. See also: M. O. Pickering, *Life of John Pickering* (1887); Harrison Ellery and C. P. Bowditch, *The Pickering Genealogy* (3 vols., 1897), containing a sketch, vol. I, 133–159; H. C. Lodge, in *Atlantic Monthly*, June 1878, the best short sketch. Henry Adams, *Documents Relating to New England Federalism* (1877), throws considerable light on certain aspects of Pickering's career neglected by his biographers. George Gibbs, *Memoirs of the Administrations of Washington and John Adams, Edited from the Papers of Oliver Wolcott* (2 vols., 1846), the biographies and published works of his chief contemporaries, and the more important collections of official papers during the period of his public life contain frequent references to him. There is an obituary in (Salem) *Essex Register*, Feb. 2, 1829.]   W. A. R.

PICKET, ALBERT (Apr. 15, 1771–Aug. 3, 1850), teacher and writer, was a pupil of Noah Webster in Connecticut in 1782 and studied from the manuscript sheets of the famous spelling book. He was largely self-educated. He married Esther Rockwell Hull on May 8, 1791, and about 1794 he began to teach in New York City. Preparation for his work as an organizer was obtained in the Incorporated Society of Teachers, of which he was twice elected president. His Manhattan School, at first for girls only, had a reputation extending beyond the city. It was not only large and successful but was also a pioneer in offering advanced instruction to girls. Like Noah Webster he began writing by compiling a spelling book, the *Union Spelling Book* (1804). Its success led him to the preparation of a series of elementary English texts for spelling, reading, and grammar, which were widely adopted in both the East and the West. Their rapid introduction into schools in the West was certainly one of the influences that led to his later removal to Cincinnati. To make a knowledge of progressive educational ideas more widely available, he undertook the establishment of a teachers' magazine. With the aid of John Picket, the eldest of his five children, he edited and published in New York *The Academician*, a semi-monthly paper, one of the first educational periodicals in the United States. Inexperience and the fact that the editors themselves had to write almost all the copy caused delays in publication. It ran from Feb. 7, 1818, to Jan. 29, 1820, and developed a theory of education based upon psychology, introduced the views of Pestalozzi, Fellenberg, and Lancaster, published school news, and gave practical advice on teaching.

Removing to Cincinnati in 1826, he established another school for girls, was elected to the board of education, and became a trustee of Cincinnati College. When the city established a public school system, he united the teachers of the local private and public schools in 1829 to form an association that soon became the Western Literary Institute and College of Professional Teachers. This body, centering in Cincinnati, had members and affiliated societies in eighteen states in the Ohio and Mississippi valleys and remained active until about 1845. His presidential addresses and his reports as chairman of the executive committee, printed in the *Transactions of the ... Western Literary Institute and College of Professional Teachers, 1834–40* (6 vols., 1835–41), are admirable statements of his program for the teaching profession. Influential in many states, the association was in Ohio one of the deciding factors in establishing a state school system and obtaining the passage of the school law of 1838. He also attempted to establish a normal school and with others obtained a charter for one from the Ohio legislature in 1834, but the institution was still-born. Whether as organizer, journalist, or protagonist of professional education, he aimed to raise the status of teaching and to develop a profession that should be able to guarantee the competence of its members. Those who knew him well speak of his clear mind, his ability as a teacher, dignified presence, and "pure, disinterested zeal in the cause of education" (E. D. Mansfield, *Personal Memories*, 1879, p. 269).

[B. A. and M. L. Hinsdale, "The Western Literary Institute and College for Professional Teachers," *Report of the Commissioner of Educ.* (U. S.), 1898–99, vol. I; *Ohio School Jour.* (Columbus), Sept. 1848; *Common School Jour.* (Boston), Dec. 1850; *Cist's Weekly Advertiser* (Cincinnati), Aug. 16, 1850; *N. Y. Herald*, Oct. 18, 1817, N. Y. *Evening Post*, Aug. 25, 1824; *Western Spy* (Cincinnati), June 20, 1817; *Cincinnati Chronicle*, May 10, 1834; *Cincinnati Daily Gazette*, Dec. 19, 1826, Apr. 5, 1832; *Olentangy Gazette* (Delaware, Ohio), Aug. 9, 1850; birthdate and other material from his great-grand-daughter, Mrs. Thomas E. Rardin, Columbus, Ohio.]   H. G. G.

PICKETT, ALBERT JAMES (Aug. 13, 1810–Oct. 28, 1858), historian, was born in Anson County, N. C., the son of Frances (Dickson) and William Raiford Pickett who in 1818 removed to Autauga County, Ala. There his father entered a large tract of land, opened a store, and engaged actively in the Indian trade. Indian traders made the store their headquarters, and Indians, especially the Creeks, came frequently to the store. The boy became familiar with them, often accompanied the traders on their journeys into the wilderness, and visited the Indians in their villages. For formal education there was little opportunity. He attended the schools opened irregularly in communities near his home. He was eighteen years old when his father sent him to Middletown, Conn., to military school. He reached Wadesboro, N. C., in safety after a journey on horseback, exchanged his saddlebags for a trunk, sold his horse, and made the rest of the journey to Connecticut by stage. Finding that the school at Middletown had been reorganized, he went on to Cambridge, Mass. He spent the next two years in school there and in Stafford County, Va. In 1830 he returned to Alabama and studied law with his brother. Law had little attraction for him, however, and he never took the examination for admission to the bar. He was married to Sarah Smith Harris on Mar. 20, 1832. They had twelve children, nine of whom lived to maturity. Until his death he lived the life of a gentleman planter in Autauga County, spending his winters in Montgomery and his summers on his plantation. He was a military aide to Gov. Clement C. Clay and was active in the preparations for war with the Creeks in 1836.

He early became interested in writing and wrote much for the newspapers on historical and economic subjects. He was interested in experiments for improving agriculture and wrote for the *Southern Cultivator* and other agricultural journals. In politics he was an ardent Democrat and an enthusiastic admirer of Andrew Jackson, declaring that he agreed "with that eminent person in every political opinion he ever held—in every military movement he ever made, and in his whole career through life—both civil, religious, military and political" (Woods, *post*, p. 605). Although interested in politics, office had no attraction for him, and, when his friends proposed to nominate him for governor in 1853, he resolutely refused to allow his name to be considered. His chief literary work was his *History of Alabama and Incidentally of Georgia and Mississippi from the Earliest Period* (1851). It carries the history of Alabama through the territorial period, and it remains today an important source for the history of the period. He had a first-hand knowledge of much of the period of which he wrote, and he spared no labor or expense to obtain accurate information. He spent thousands of dollars in the purchase of books and the copying of manuscripts, and he traveled hundreds of miles to interview people who might give him information. The organization of the book is poor, and its literary style is cumbersome and involved, but it contains invaluable material. He expected to follow this book by a history of the Southwest, but he died before this work was completed. The papers he left form one of the most valuable collections in the Alabama State Department of History and Archives.

[M. L. Woods, "Personal Reminiscences of Col. Albert James Pickett," *Trans. Ala. Hist. Soc.*, vol. IV (1904); C. M. Jackson, *A Brief Biog. Sketch of the Late Colonel Albert James Pickett* (1859); B. F. Riley, *Makers and Romance of Ala. Hist.* (n.d.); T. M. Owen, *Hist. of Ala. and Dict. of Ala. Biog.* (1921), vol. IV; *The South in the Building of the Nation*, vol. XII (1909).] H.F.

PICKETT, GEORGE EDWARD (Jan. 25, 1825–July 30, 1875), Confederate soldier, the son of Colonel Robert and Mary (Johnston) Pickett, and a descendant of William Pickett of Fauquier County, Va., was born in Richmond, Va. He received his early education in the Richmond Academy and the law office of his uncle, Andrew Johnston, in Quincy, Ill., from which state he was appointed in 1842 to the United States Military Academy. He graduated in 1846, the last of his class of fifty-nine members, and went directly from school into the Mexican War. He was commissioned second lieutenant, 2nd Infantry, Mar. 3, 1847, and was transferred in July, first to the 7th and then to the 8th Infantry. He served from the siege of Vera Cruz to the capture of Mexico City. For gallantry at Contreras and Churubusco he was brevetted first lieutenant, Aug. 20, 1847. He was first to go over the parapets of Chapultepec on Sept. 13, 1847, and under the menace of enemy fire, he lowered the Aztec emblem and hoisted the flag of his infantry. From 1849 to 1856 he did garrison duty in Texas, receiving the rank of captain on Mar. 3, 1855.

In January 1851, he married Sally Minge of Richmond, who died the following November. He was assigned frontier duty in 1856 in the Northwest and was engaged almost constantly in Indian fighting. In 1859 American settlers on San Juan Island (Puget Sound) complained of Indian outrages and threatened British aggression. Pickett was ordered to take possession of the island, which he did promptly with a force of sixty soldiers. Three British warships anchored broadside to the camp and warned him off the island, and later the British magistrate aboard the flagship summoned him for trial, but he disregarded both messages. The British next proposed landing a force equal to Pickett's for joint military occupation. To this he replied,

"I am here by virtue of an order from my government, and shall remain till recalled by the same authority" (*Ann. Reunion, Asso. Grads. U. S. Mil. Acad.*, 1876, p. 12). He further announced he would fire upon any landing force. This dangerous mission was accepted by Pickett with full knowledge that his orders were inspired by Democratic officials who hoped to weld together the disintegrating bonds of the Union by the threat of a foreign war. Joint occupation by British and American forces was the solution reached, and Pickett remained in command of the American forces there almost continuously until 1861 when he resigned from the Federal forces. He went to Richmond, was commissioned colonel, and assigned to duty on the lower Rappahannock.

He was made a brigadier-general in February 1862, and his command, by the dash and courage displayed at Williamsburg, Seven Pines, and Gaines's Mill, earned the sobriquet, "The Game Cock Brigade." At Gaines's Mill, on June 27, 1862, he was severely wounded in the shoulder and did not rejoin his command until after the first Maryland campaign. He was promoted major-general in October 1862, and given command of a Virginia division. At Fredericksburg he held the center of Lee's line and later served creditably in the campaign against Suffolk. At Gettysburg, on July 3, 1863, with a strength of 4,500 muskets, his command advanced over half a mile of broken ground against withering artillery and musket fire. With the precision of parade drill they descended one slope, ascended the next, and, with unmatched courage of individual gallantry, assaulted the formidable Union line only to be forced back in defeat. Scarcely a fourth of his command returned from this memorable charge. After the Gettysburg campaign, he commanded the Department of Virginia and North Carolina. His advance from Petersburg on Feb. 1, 1864, to free New Bern, N. C., failed of its objective but secured 500 prisoners and valuable stores. Late in April 1864, his troops, with Robert Frederick Hoke [*q.v.*] commanding, recaptured Plymouth, N. C., just as Pickett was ordered to Richmond. Before he could start, however, General Butler's fleet appeared off Citypoint in the James River, and threatened the back door of the Confederate capital. Butler's sluggish action enabled Pickett to turn the command over to Beauregard with Butler's troops still bottled up at Bermuda Hundred. In the final Union offensives near Petersburg, his division bore the brunt of the attack at Five Forks on Apr. 1, 1865, where he made the greatest fight of his career. He joined Longstreet with the remnants of his command and remained with him until the surrender at Appomattox.

On Sept. 15, 1863, he married the young and beautiful La Salle Corbell of Chuckatuck, Va. Two children, one of whom lived to maturity, were born to them. Peace found him in poverty and deprived of his profession. The Khedive of Egypt offered him a commission as brigadier-general, but he refused service which would separate him from his beloved wife. When Grant became president, he offered him the marshalship of Virginia, but he declined. Instead he accepted the Virginia agency of the Washington Life Insurance Company of New York and was so employed at the time of his death. He died at Norfolk, Va., where his body was placed temporarily in a vault. On Oct. 25, 1875, his remains were borne to Hollywood Cemetery, Richmond, Va., and there buried with full military honors.

[Personal papers in the possession of a member of the family; T. L. Broun, "The Pickett Family," in the *Times-Dispatch* (Richmond, Va.), Apr. 11, 1909; La Salle Corbell Pickett, *Pickett and His Men* (1899), including in appendix a biog. sketch by G. B. McClellan; A. C. Inman, ed., *Soldier of the South, Gen. Pickett's War Letters to His Wife* (1928); *Ann. Reunion, Asso. Grads. U. S. Mil. Acad., 1876*; G. O. Haller, *San Juan and Secession* (1896); J. C. Mayo, "Pickett's Charge at Gettysburg," *Southern Hist. Soc. Papers*, vol. XXXIV (1906); *Richmond Enquirer*, Aug. 1, 1875.]
C. C. B.

PICKETT, JAMES CHAMBERLAYNE (Feb. 6, 1793–July 10, 1872), diplomat, was born in Fauquier County, Va., the grandson of William S. Pickett, and the son of John and Elizabeth (Chamberlayne) Pickett. Some three years after his birth the family moved to Mason County, Ky., but it was from Ohio that he was appointed, Aug. 14, 1813, to be third lieutenant in the 2nd United States Artillery. He left the service in 1815 at the end of the war with Great Britain only to reënter it June 16, 1818, as captain and assistant deputy-quartermaster-general. He served until June 1821. Meanwhile he had tried his hand at editing the *Eagle*, at Maysville, Ky., had read law, and on Oct. 6, 1818, had married Ellen Desha, daughter of Gov. Joseph Desha of Kentucky. Two sons were born to this marriage. In 1821 he returned to the practice of the law and the next year sat in the state legislature as his father had done before him. He achieved the reputation of being one of the foremost scholars of his state. After three years as secretary of state of Kentucky (1825–28), he was ready for the first of a series of federal appointments.

His appointment, on June 9, 1829, to be secretary of legation in Colombia, was the beginning of a diplomatic career of some distinction.

He traveled about Colombia, reporting to the American minister at Bogotá his fears of British commercial aggression and his doubts whether even the sway of Spain could have been more tyrannical than the last five years of republican rule. He found the country still suffering from twenty years of civil war. Returning to the United States, he served for three months in 1835 as superintendent of the United States Patent Office and in January 1836 was appointed fourth auditor of the Treasury Department. Two years later (June 1838) he resumed his diplomatic career. As chargé d'affaires of the United States, he was authorized to conclude treaties of commerce with the Peru-Bolivian Confederation and with the Republic of Ecuador, to which he was appointed special diplomatic agent. By June 13 of the next year, a treaty of peace, friendship, navigation, and commerce with Ecuador, with its "most-favored-nation" clause and its definitions of neutral rights in wartime, was ready for signature. It was proclaimed in September 1842 (8 *U. S. Statutes at Large*, 534). With Peru, Pickett was somewhat less successful. After substantial concessions by the United States, a claims convention providing for the adjustment of the claims of citizens of the United States against Peru was signed on Mar. 17, 1841, but it was not proclaimed until Feb. 21, 1844 (*Ibid.*, 570). It called for a total payment by Peru of $300,000, to be met in ten annual instalments. Pickett found the youthful and tumultuous Peruvian republic no easy country with which to deal, for it was constantly on the verge of insurrection or involved in civil war; and when he returned to the United States late in 1844, he left three claimants contending for the presidency of the nation. Pickett appears to have been a warm expansionist who urged the desirability of an isthmian canal and who approved as early as 1842 of the plans of an American naval officer for detaching San Francisco from Mexico (*Memoirs of John Quincy Adams*, vol. XI, 1876, p. 367). After the close of his diplomatic career he settled in Washington where for some years (*c.* 1848–53) he edited the *Daily Globe*. He was also concerned in a short-lived magazine venture, the *National Monument*, suspended in 1851 for lack of funds (W. B. Bryan, *A History of the National Capital*, 1916, II, 422 n.). After this time, however, he lived in relative obscurity until his death, in Washington, in 1872.

[Pickett's dispatches and the Departmental instructions to Pickett in the archives of the Dept. of State; records of Appointment Office, Dept. of State; "The Pickett Family," *Times-Dispatch* (Richmond, Va.), Apr. 11, 1909; W. M. Paxton, *The Marshall Family* (1885); F. B. Heitman, *Hist. Reg. and Dict. U. S.*

Army (1903), vol. I; *The Biog. Encyc. of Ky.* (1878); H. Levin, *The Lawyers and·Law-Makers of Ky.* (1897), p. 432; *Evening Star* (Washington, D. C.), July 10, 1872.]

E. W. S.

PICKNELL, WILLIAM LAMB (Oct. 23, 1853–Aug. 8, 1897), landscape painter, born at Hinesburg, Vt., was the son of the Rev. William Lamb Picknell and Ellen Maria (Upham) Picknell. His father, a Baptist minister, was of Scotch descent. His mother was a descendant of one of the settlers of Weymouth, Mass. Upon the death of his father, Picknell, then about fourteen years old, went to Boston, and, after a brief interval of business, in 1874 traveled to Rome. There he met George Inness [*q.v.*] and under his tutelage did his first experimental work at painting on the Campagna. After two years in Italy he went to Paris and worked under J. L. Gérôme in the École des Beaux-Arts. He then proceeded to the fishing village of Pont-Aven, Brittany, where he came under the influence of Robert Wylie and put in four years of patient and concentrated work. In 1880 he sent to the Paris Salon his "Road to Concarneau," which made a name for him. It was followed in 1881 by another excellent landscape. The artist then went to England and painted for two winters near the south coast and in the New Forest. "Bleak December," now in the Metropolitan Museum, New York, and "Wintry March," belonging to the Walker Gallery, Liverpool, were conspicuously successful works of this period.

After a decade abroad Picknell returned to America and painted at Annisquam, Mass., for several summers, usually going to the Mediterranean shores for his winter work. He spent one winter in Florida and another in California, where he painted his "In California," which brought $2,025 at the executor's sale of his works, in New York, 1900. He married Gertrude Powers in 1889 and a year later went abroad and remained in France until 1897. He worked in Moret in the summer and at Antibes in the winter. The pictures painted there served to increase his reputation in France, especially the "Déclin du Jour." The death of his only child at Antibes in 1897 was a heavy blow. Picknell was himself far from well, but he sailed for America in July and got to Marblehead, Mass., to die there of heart disease in August, at the age of forty-three. A memorial exhibition of forty-four of his paintings was held at the Boston Art Museum in 1898 and at that time Saint-Gaudens' bronze medallion portrait of the artist was shown. At a sale of his works in New York in 1900, fifty-six pictures fetched a total of $16,-520 (*American Art Annual,* vol. III, 1900, p.

46). His "Road to Concarneau" and "En Provence" are in the Corcoran Gallery, Washington; "Morning on the Loing at Moret" and "Sand Dunes of Essex" are in the Boston Museum of Fine Arts; "Morning on the Mediterranean, Antibes," is in the Luxembourg Museum, Paris; and other good examples are to be seen in the Pennsylvania Academy, Philadelphia, the Brooklyn Museum, and the Carnegie Institute, Pittsburgh. His landscapes are virile. Nothing is extenuated. His style is naturalistic and large; the construction is notably firm, and there is an invigorating atmosphere in his canvases of fresh air and strong sunlight.

[E. W. Emerson, "An Am. Landscape Painter," *Century Mag.*, Sept. 1901, and Foreword in the catalogue of the memorial exhibition, Boston, 1898; *New England Mag.*, Apr. 1896; F. K. Upham, *The Descendants of John Upham* (1892); *Boston Transcript*, Aug. 9, 1897, Feb. 12, 1898; catalogues of executor's sale, 1900; T. B. Clarke sale, 1899; G. I. Seney sale, 1891; E. McMillin sale, 1913; exhibition at Avery Gallery, N. Y., 1890.]

W. H. D.

PICTON, THOMAS (May 16, 1822–Feb. 20, 1891), soldier of fortune, journalist, was Thomas Picton Milner, the son of Jane Milner (*General Alumni Catalogue of New York University,* 1906), who, shortly after his birth, was listed in New York City directories as "widow." Nothing is known of his father. He spent his youth in the home of his maternal grandmother, a woman of wealth, who provided him with a good education. Later in life he dropped his last name, becoming known to his contemporaries as Thomas Picton. After graduating in 1840 from New York University he spent several years abroad. While in France he became an officer in the French army under Louis Philippe, who is said to have made him a knight of the "Legion of the Stranger." With the fall of Louis Philippe in 1848 he returned to New York, but an adventurous spirit still dominated him, and probably toward the close of 1850 he joined the force which Narciso Lopez was collecting in the United States to lead against Cuba. Barely escaping capture when Lopez was taken prisoner, Picton sought refuge from his enemies in the steamer *Palmero*, which was pursued by a Spanish man-of-war. He finally succeeded in reaching New York and for a few years busied himself in journalistic pursuits. But the preparations which William Walker was making for the invasion of Nicaragua once more aroused his filibustering instincts, and he attached himself to Walker's force, becoming for a time paymaster in the General's army. After the shooting of Walker he returned to the United States and with the outbreak of the Civil War raised a company of soldiers which was later incorporated in the 38th New York Infantry, but Picton himself seems to have played no part in the war.

Picton's career as a journalist began as early as 1850 when for a short time he edited in conjunction with his teacher and friend, Henry William Herbert ("Frank Forester"), a periodical called the *Era*. He had already become associated with Edward Z. C. Judson ("Ned Buntline"), active in the organization of the Native American movement, and during the early fifties he became an editor of the *Sachem*, and on its discontinuance, the founder of the *True American*, both organs of the new movement. His love of sports also found expression through journalistic channels, and during his later years he contributed to the *Clipper*; *Turf, Field, and Farm*; and the *Spirit of the Times*. For the last-named periodical he wrote a series of articles, beginning with the issue of Feb. 19, 1881, called "Reminiscences of a Sporting Journalist." These articles, which appeared intermittently until a short time before his death, dealt with sporting, social, and historical topics having reference to the New York of Picton's youth and early manhood. During his years as a journalist, he was also connected with the *True National Democrat*, the *Sunday Dispatch*, and the *Sunday Mercury*. He frequently wrote under the pseudonym of "Paul Preston." Among his publications so designated were *Paul Preston's Book of Gymnastics: or Sports for Youth* (n.d.) and *The Fireside Magician* (1870). His interest in the history of old New York led to the publication in 1873 of a small pamphlet called *Rose Street; its Past, Present, and Future*. He also contributed a biographical sketch of Henry Herbert to the *Life and Writings of Frank Forester* (1882). Among his more creative efforts were two light dramas: *A Tempest in a Teapot* (copyright 1871), and *There's No Smoke Without Fire* (copyright 1872). A volume of poems, *Acrostics from Across the Atlantic*, published in London in 1869 and signed "A Gothamite," has also sometimes been ascribed to him.

Picton was familiarly known to his wide circle of New York acquaintance as Col. "Tom" Picton. He was a distinguished Mason and frequently wrote articles of Masonic interest. At one time he was a member of a city engine company and at another was city paymaster. For some years, too, he acted as assistant cashier of the Nassau Bank. About 1860 he married a Miss Gardner, daughter of a Confederate officer of that name, but a few years later the couple separated. At the time of his death in New York City he was without immediate family connec-

tions, and he was buried in the lot of the Press Club in Cypress Hills Cemetery

[Obituaries in the *N. Y. Recorder*, Feb. 25, 1891; *N. Y. Tribune*, Feb. 22, 1891; *Spirit of the Times*, Feb. 28, 1891; *Masonic Chronicle and Official Bulletin*, Mar. 1891.]   N. F. A.

PIDGIN, CHARLES FELTON (Nov. 11, 1844–June 3, 1923), statistician, inventor, author, was born in Roxbury, Mass., the only son and only child surviving infancy of Benjamin Gorham and Mary Elizabeth (Felton) Pidgin. His father is designated at different times as a "turner," "varnisher," or "finisher," and though he may have been of New England origin, he apparently did not have as long an American descent as his wife, who was of the seventh generation of the Felton family in Massachusetts. Charles Felton Pidgin received in boyhood an injury to his hip that paralyzed one of his legs and necessitated the use of artificial support for it throughout his life, but despite this handicap he entered the Boston English High School in 1860 and graduated from it in 1863. He then secured employment as a bookkeeper in Boston, and he also did a certain amount of writing for newspapers in Boston and elsewhere. In 1870 he became junior member of the firm of Young & Pidgin, manufacturers of linen collars and cuffs, but his connection with this business lasted only two years, and he resorted to newspaper writing for a time. In 1873 he was appointed chief clerk of the Massachusetts Bureau of Statistics of Labor, probably as a result of the recommendation of Carroll D. Wright, who had just been made director of the bureau, and was impressed by Pidgin's ability. In this position he found an outlet for his inventive talent, and he showed great ingenuity and resource in devising methods and instruments for the mechanical tabulation of statistics, some of which were intended to meet the special needs of his own department, but others were patented and exploited commercially.

In the report of the 1885 census of Massachusetts, Pidgin is credited with an important part in organizing and directing it, and until after he was fifty his interest in statistics and in machines of his invention for computing and recording. In 1888 he published *Practical Statistics*, but in 1900 he turned to non-technical literature. At this time he suffered from a cataract that rendered him almost blind, and it may have been his inability to use his eyes that led him to dictate *Quincy Adams Sawyer* (1900), a novel dealing with New England life. This book had a very wide sale and was also successfully dramatized. The success of this venture in the field of creative literature spurred him to further efforts, and he published several other works of fiction within the next few years, the best known being *Blennerhasset* (1901), which dealt with a period and characters he found particularly interesting. In 1903 he was made chief of the Bureau of Statistics of Labor but in July 1907 his reappointment by the governor was not confirmed and he was retired on a pension. The rest of his life he devoted to authorship and invention. He wrote two more volumes in which Quincy Adams Sawyer was the hero, one of which was a detective story, and other works of a varied nature.

In 1917 Pidgin perfected what he called "visible speech," a system designed to make possible the photographing of words as if issuing from the mouths of motion-picture actors. There was no form of communicating thought or recording information in which he did not show aptitude, but his main interest was in what was practical and utilitarian. He did not lack esthetic perceptions, but he was more disposed to make his means of expression effective than he was to take delight in what it expressed. He foresaw the need imposed by the increasing complexity of mechanical civilization for rapid means of accumulating, condensing, and displaying involved records, and he played a part in developing the present methods of mechanical computation and graphic presentation of results. He died in Melrose, Mass., in 1923. He was married on July 3, 1867, to Lizzie Abbott Dane, who died in 1868; on Nov. 25, 1873, to Lucy Sturtevant Gardner, M.D., who died in 1896; and on July 21, 1897, to Frances Fern Douglas, who survived him. In 1906 he adopted a daughter, who also survived him.

[There are obituary notices of Pidgin in the *Boston Transcript*, June 4, 1923, and in the *N. Y. Times*, June 5, 1923. See *Who's Who in America*, 1922–23, for the list of his books; Cyrus Felton, *A Geneal. Hist. of the Felton Family* (1886); *Vital Records of Roxbury, Mass.*, vol. I (1925); and *Boston Advertiser*, June 28, 1907.]

S. G.

PIEPER, FRANZ AUGUST OTTO (June 27, 1852–June 3, 1931), Lutheran theologian, was born at Carwitz, Pomerania, Germany, the son of Augustus and Berta (Lohff) Pieper. Augustus Pieper, a town mayor, sent his sons to the junior colleges at Koeslin and Kolberg. In 1870 his widow took the family to America and Franz attended Northwestern University at Watertown, Wis., where he received the A.B. degree in 1872. He then attended Concordia Theological Seminary at St. Louis, and was graduated in 1875, being ordained in July of the same year. After serving a small congregation at Center-

ville, Wis., for a little over a year, he went in November 1876, to Manitowoc, where he remained until he was called to Concordia Seminary to teach dogmatics and to be an understudy of Dr. Carl Ferdinand Wilhelm Walther [*q.v.*]. He arrived in St. Louis on Oct. 2, 1878, and remained there until his death. In 1880 a storm which had been brewing for three years broke about the head of Dr. Walther. Pieper loyally rushed to his assistance and became involved in a controversy on predestination which was to occupy him actively for the next thirty-five years. By a fine-spun scholastic logic, backed by copious quotations from the sixteenth-century Lutheran fathers, the American Lutheran theologians on both sides tried to establish themselves in the eyes of a church rooted in a European culture. That Pieper was successful in his appeal is seen by the prodigious growth of the Missouri Synod at this time. He wrote tirelessly on this and related subjects in the organs of his synod, his last important word being the genial booklet, published in 1913, *Zur Einigung der Amerikanisch-lutherischen Kirche in der Lehre von der Bekehrung und Gnadenwahl* (translated as *Conversion and Election; a Plea for a United Lutheranism in America*), in which he made an eloquent plea for peace. This book heralded a new day, and in spite of the failure of efforts to make peace with the Ohio, Iowa, and Buffalo synods, Pieper lived to see his synod adopt a very irenic attitude towards its former antagonists.

Pieper was an able administrator. When he became a member of the very distinguished faculty of Concordia Seminary there were sixty-nine students enrolled at the institution. At his death there were 534 enrolled, of whom 432 were in attendance, making Concordia the largest Protestant seminary in the United States. Pieper was one of the magnets that attracted this large group of students, just as he was one of the magnets that had drawn into the membership of the Missouri Synod, of which he was president from 1899 to 1911, 1,200,000 souls. This rapid expansion gave rise to many problems, the most important of which were precipitated by overcrowded quarters. In 1882 the Missouri Synod had built a splendid compound of buildings, but Pieper, who was president of the Seminary from 1887 to 1931, found it necessary to erect a new set of fireproof buildings in 1907, and more during a period from 1923 to 1926, the latter project involving an expenditure of about three and a half million dollars. Besides being president of the Seminary and of the Missouri Synod, he served on innumerable committees.

The work of his church among the colored people was his hobby. He traveled in Europe twice, in 1898 and in 1911, seeking both times to restore his impaired health. Of his numerous writings, his *Christliche Dogmatik* (1917–1924), in three large volumes, will probably have the most enduring value. On Jan. 2, 1877, he was married to Minnie Koehn. They had thirteen children, three of whom became pastors, and five, pastors' wives.

[*Who's Who in America*, 1930–31; *The Concordia Cyc.* (1927), ed. by L. Fuerbringer, T. Engelder, and P. E. Kretzmann; Theodore Graebner, *Dr. Francis Pieper, A Biog. Sketch* (1931); P. E. Kretzmann, "Prof. Franz August Otto Pieper, Dr. Theol.," *Concordia Theol. Monthly*, Aug. 1931; L. Fuerbringer, "Dr. F. Pieper Als Theolog.," *Ibid.*, Oct. and Nov. 1931; *St. Louis Globe-Democrat*, June 4, 1931. Comments upon his life and work were made in practically all the religious journals of the Lutheran Church in America and in some periodicals in Europe.]

J. M. R.

PIERCE, BENJAMIN (Dec. 25, 1757–Apr. 1, 1839), governor of New Hampshire, the son of Benjamin and Elizabeth (Merrill) Pierce, was born in Chelmsford, Mass. He was descended from Thomas Pierce, an English emigrant of 1633–34 who settled in Charlestown, Mass. His father died when the boy was six, leaving him to the care of an uncle; his education consisted of a few weeks' schooling and much farm labor. When the news of the battle of Lexington came, Pierce immediately joined the Massachusetts militia as a private. Remaining in the army until February 1784, he participated in the maneuvers around Boston and in the Saratoga campaign, and was stationed at Valley Forge and in the Hudson Valley; during these years he rose to the rank of lieutenant in command of a company, receiving one promotion for bravery in the battle of Saratoga. When he was mustered out he became an agent for Samson Stoddard of Chelmsford, Mass., who had large tracts in New Hampshire and Vermont. He explored much of this land and in the course of his wanderings picked out a frontier farm in Hillsborough, N. H., where he settled in 1786. On May 24, 1787, he married Elizabeth Andrews, who died the following year; and on Feb. 1, 1790, he married Anna Kendrick (1768–1838), who became the mother of Franklin Pierce [*q.v.*].

In 1786 Pierce was appointed to organize the militia of Hillsborough County as brigade-major and served until 1807, when he resigned with the rank of brigadier-general. He began his political career in 1789, when he was elected to the lower house of the legislature; he was chosen annually for thirteen years and, in 1791, served as a member of the state constitutional convention. In 1803 he was elected a member of the governor's council, and in 1809 he was appointed sheriff of his county. During these years he had become an intensely active supporter of Thomas Jefferson and as a plain farmer warred against the aristocratic Federalists. He strongly supported the War of 1812 but New Hampshire returned to the Federalist fold in opposition to that contest. One of the first things the victorious Federalists did was to remove a number of Republican office holders, among them Benjamin Pierce, in 1813, ostensibly because he refused to recognize the new courts established by the Federalists to eliminate Republican judges. The next year his friends elected him to the governor's council as a vindication and when the Republicans regained power he was reappointed sheriff of Hillsborough County, serving from 1818 to 1827.

Party lines were indistinct in New Hampshire as elsewhere in the 'twenties; new groups were forming. Isaac Hill [*q.v.*] was marshaling a farmers' party in the interior of the state, and, recognizing Pierce's vote-getting strength as a Revolutionary veteran and an agrarian leader, brought him forward as a candidate for the governorship in 1827, 1828, and 1829. He was elected in 1827 and 1829 and, since the governor of New Hampshire had little power, he was content with a few recommendations for the improvement of the militia and local education. By this time he was an ardent Jacksonian; his last public service was as a Democratic elector in 1832. During these years of political activity he had been fairly prosperous as a farmer and had become a local magnate in the town of Hillsborough, where he kept a tavern in his large dwelling on the turnpike. He was a rugged, unlettered pioneer, dominating and patriarchal, who bore the hardships of frontier life easily and maintained a constant interest in the growth of the government he had helped to establish.

[A copy of Pierce's autobiography and a number of his letters are in the N. H. Hist. Soc. Biographical sketches appear in the *Farmer's Monthly Visitor*, Apr. 15, 1839, p. 49, and July 1852, p. 193. An obituary appeared in *N. H. Patriot and State Gazette*, Apr. 8, 1839. See also A. S. Batchellor, ed., "Early State Papers of N. H.," *N. H. State Papers*, vols. XXI, XXII (1892–93); G. W. Browne, *The Hist. of Hillsborough, N. H., 1735–1921* (2 vols., 1921–22); F. B. Pierce, *Pierce Genealogy . . . the Posterity of Thomas Pierce* (1882).]

R. F. N.

PIERCE, EDWARD LILLIE (Mar. 29, 1829–Sept. 5, 1897), lawyer and biographer, brother of Henry Lillie Pierce [*q.v.*], was born at Stoughton, Mass., where his father, Jesse, was a farmer, militia colonel, and sometime teacher and legislator. His mother, Elizabeth, was the daughter of Maj. John Lillie of the staff of Gen. Henry Knox. Pierce always took a keen interest in his family history, which on both sides ran back to the earliest days of the Massachusetts Bay Colony. He was educated by his father and in the academies at Bridgewater and Easton. He graduated from Brown University in 1850 and from the Harvard Law School two years later. At both institutions he was a prize essayist. As a boy he heard Charles Sumner deliver his address on "The True Grandeur of Nations," and later paved the way to a personal acquaintance by sending him some college essays. Sumner's friendship became one of the deepest influences in his life. On leaving the law school Pierce spent some time in Salmon P. Chase's law office in Cincinnati and later was his secretary in Washington. In 1855 he returned to Boston. In these years before the war he emerged from his Democratic and Free-Soil background to become active in Republican politics; he attended his first national convention in 1860. In the first week of the war he enlisted for three months as a private in the 3rd Massachusetts Regiment and participated in the destruction of the Norfolk Navy Yard. In July he was placed in charge of General Butler's "contraband" negroes at Fortress Monroe. In 1866 Secretary Chase sent him to Port Royal, S. C., to supervise the raising of cotton by freedmen (*The Negroes at Port Royal: Report of E. L. Pierce*, 1862, and *The Freedmen of Port Royal, S. C., Official Reports*, 1863). He declined the appointment as military governor of South Carolina.

Pierce held many civil offices: collector of internal revenue at Boston, 1864–66; district attorney of Norfolk and Plymouth counties, 1866–70; secretary of the Board of State Charities, 1870–74; member of the legislature in 1875, 1876, and again in 1897. From 1888 to 1897, except for the year 1894, he was annually chosen moderator of the Milton town meeting. During his second term in the legislature he carried through an important act to limit municipal indebtedness. In 1871 he was nominated but not confirmed as judge of the superior court. He declined an offer of an assistant treasurership from President Hayes. He had large capacities for public service and aspired to a seat in Congress, but he lacked the faculty of vote-getting, and when he was nominated for Representative in 1890 he was defeated. For many years he lectured in the Boston Law School. Sumner named Pierce one of his literary executors, and after the other two executors, Henry W. Longfellow and Francis V. Balch, had declined the opportunity to write an official biography, Pierce undertook the task. The first two volumes appeared in 1877; the latter two he was not able to

complete until 1893. The painstaking preparation involved the examination of many thousand letters, and of newspaper files and congressional debates for a quarter-century. In the estimation of James Ford Rhodes, "one of the most truthful of men, was fortunate in having one of the most honest of biographers" (*Proceedings of the Massachusetts Historical Society, 2 ser. XII*, 1899, p. 11).

Pierce was married to Elizabeth H. Kingsbury of Providence, R. I., on Apr. 19, 1865. She died on Mar. 30, 1880, leaving five sons and a daughter. On Mar. 8, 1882, he was married to Maria L. Woodhead of Huddersfield, England. They had a son and a daughter. He died while on a visit to Paris. It was one of his marked characteristics that he sought and was received into the society of famous men. In almost a score of trips to Europe he came to know many notables, most important in his regard being John Bright. In his profession he became an authority on railroad law. His published writings include, besides his *Memoir and Letters of Charles Sumner, A Treatise on American Railroad Law* (1857); *Index of the Special Railroad Laws of Massachusetts* (1874); *A Treatise on the Law of Railroads* (1881); *Major John Lillie, 1755–1801* (1896), and *Enfranchisement and Citizenship: Addresses and Papers* (1896).

[See J. F. Rhodes, "Memoir of Edward L. Pierce," *Proc. Mass. Hist. Soc.*, 2 ser. XVIII (1905); G. F. Hoar, "Edward Lillie Pierce," *Proc. Am. Antiquarian Soc.*, New Ser. vol. XII (1899); Remarks of A. B. Hart in *Proc. Mass. Hist. Soc.*, 2 ser. XIII (1900); *Dinner Commemorative of Chas. Sumner and Complimentary to Edward L. Pierce, Boston, Dec. 29, 1894* (1895); F. C. Peirce, *Peirce Geneal.* (1880); *Boston Transcript*, Sept. 7, 1897.] C. F.

PIERCE, FRANKLIN (Nov. 23, 1804–Oct. 8, 1869), fourteenth president of the United States, was of English ancestry. The son of Benjamin Pierce [*q.v.*] and Anna Kendrick, he was born at Hillsborough, N. H., on the New England frontier. His father not only gave him a good education at Bowdoin College, where he was in the class of 1824, but also thoroughly imbued him with nationalism and military interests and provided him with an excellent start in law and politics. He studied law under Levi Woodbury at Portsmouth, attended the law school of Judge Howe at Northampton, Mass., and was admitted to the bar of Hillsborough County in 1827. Immediately he entered politics, and in 1829 he was elected a member of the New Hampshire General Court at the same time that his father was elected governor of the state for a second term. With this auspicious start he served four years in the legislature and in spite of his youth was speaker in 1831 and 1832. In 1833 he was elected to Congress and after two terms in the House was sent to the Senate (1837–42). During his nine years' service in the two houses of Congress he made few speeches but was diligent in committee. He was a loyal, consistent Jacksonian Democrat who followed his party leaders without question on all issues except internal improvements, to which he was ever opposed. He consistently respected Southern rights and developed a settled antipathy for political abolitionists, whom he considered dangerous trouble makers who might bring about the destruction of the Union. While he was an ardent nationalist, he believed in promoting the public welfare by harmonizing the conflicting ideas of the sections.

The last years of his service in the Senate were very distasteful. His wife, Jane Means Appleton, daughter of Jesse Appleton [q.v.], former president of Bowdoin College, whom he had married Nov. 19, 1834, was not well and disliked congressional life, especially as her husband's convivial nature was on occasion too much stimulated by the gay life of the capital. The needs of his growing family could not be fully met as a politician, so he resigned from the Senate in 1842 and joined his family in Concord, N. H. In the course of the next ten years he became a noted local lawyer, largely because of his success with juries. His clear and simple statement of legal principles, combined with oratorical skill and personal magnetism, made him convincing. Though but of middle height, he cultivated an erect military bearing; he dressed well and was considered handsome; and he was studiously polite in manner. He delighted in approbation and sought to attune himself to the spirit of any gathering in which he participated. As a result he was popular, whether in polite society or at hotel bars and political caucuses.

From 1842 to 1847 he managed most of the local Democratic campaigns, enforcing strict discipline to keep the party united and victorious. His discipline of John P. Hale [q.v.] for opposing the annexation of Texas, however, was a boomerang, for, as a result, a fusion of Whigs and free-soil Democrats defeated Pierce's party in 1846 for the first time since 1828. Polk in the meantime had appointed him district attorney for New Hampshire, and in August 1846 invited him to become attorney general. Pierce declined this offer as well as an appointment to the Senate. He enlisted for the Mexican War as a private but was not called to service until 1847, when he was appointed colonel and then brigadier-general. He led an army from Vera Cruz to join Scott in his attack on Mexico city but because of accident and illness was prevented from effectual participation in the battles that followed. As soon as the war was over he resigned from the army.

Returning to local politics in defense of the compromise measures of 1850, he took the lead (1850–51) in disciplining a gubernatorial candidate, John Atwood, who appeared to repudiate the Fugitive-slave Law, and attracted much Southern attention. When New Hampshire's candidate for the Democratic presidential nomination, Levi Woodbury, died in 1851, some of the local bosses thought of proposing Pierce's name. The active campaigns of Buchanan, Douglas, Marcy, and the friends of Cass seemed to show clearly that none of these rivals could secure the required two-thirds of the convention of 1852. Pierce's friends carefully planned to take advantage of this situation. He himself was not enthusiastic and did little to aid them except write a letter pledging loyalty to the compromise measures. Their plans, however, were successful. After many ballots the national convention was hopelessly deadlocked and at the suggestion of New England delegates the Southern bloc finally agreed to try Pierce's name; Dobbin of North Carolina led a successful stampede in his favor. William R. D. King [q.v.], a friend of Buchanan, was then nominated for the vice-presidency. The platform pledged the party to abide by the compromise measures of 1850.

During the campaign, Pierce made no speeches. No issues were presented either by the opposition candidates, Winfield Scott, Whig, and John P. Hale, Free-Soiler, or by his own party, so pointless personalities were the chief materials for press writers and orators. Pierce carried every state but four although his popular majority over the field was small, less than 50,000 out of 3,100,-000 votes. While he was busy with the perplexing problems of framing his inaugural address and choosing his cabinet, he was in a railroad accident and suffered the unutterable horror of seeing his only remaining son, a lad of eleven, killed before his eyes. This terrible event completely unnerved Pierce and his wife. He was compelled to enter upon the trying duties of the presidency in a state of nervous exhaustion.

Determined to make permanent the party harmony that had been displayed in his triumphant election, Pierce decided to regard all who had voted for him in 1852 as Democrats worthy of patronage. He made up a cabinet representing all sections: William L. Marcy of New York, James Guthrie of Kentucky, Jefferson Davis of Mississippi, Caleb Cushing of Massachusetts, James Campbell of Pennsylvania, James C. Dobbin of North Carolina, Robert McClelland of Michigan [*qq.v.*]. With their aid he endeavored to distribute the patronage equitably among all sections and all factions. The policies of his administration were to be strictly orthodox: a vigorous foreign policy; *laissez-faire* and a respect for state rights in domestic matters; economy and honest administration. His foreign policy was to consist of a vigorous defense of American rights, especially against British or French encroachment, and a wide expansion of American interests, territorial and commercial. He set out to make Great Britain live up to his interpretation of the Clayton-Bulwer treaty by withdrawing from Nicaragua and Honduras. He also was anxious to settle the Newfoundland fisheries dispute which made naval forces necessary at the fishing grounds and might easily lead to trouble. James Buchanan was sent to England to settle the Central American problem, while Secretary of State Marcy concluded in Washington in June 1854 a treaty whereby the United States granted Canada commercial reciprocity and in return obtained favorable fishing rights. James Gadsden was sent to Mexico to purchase land for a right of way for a southern railroad to the Pacific and negotiated in December 1853 the purchase known by his name. The outbreak of the Crimean War and a change in Spanish politics together with the *Black Warrior* incident convinced Pierce and Marcy in April 1854 that the time was ripe for another attempt to purchase Cuba, so Pierre Soulé, minister to Spain, was instructed to make an offer to that country. At the same time, negotiations were begun to acquire Hawaii and a naval base in Santo Domingo, and inquiries were made of Russia about purchasing Alaska.

Pierce sought to reduce the treasury surplus by paying off the debt and urging upon Congress a lower tariff. He recommended a larger army and navy and suggested plans for better organization, better discipline, and better officers. Plans were drawn up for improving the services of the interior and post-office departments, getting rid of the deficit in the latter, and creating a new department of law for the attorney general. Western development and military efficiency were to be promoted by government aid to a railroad to the Pacific. Sectionalism was to be banished from government and politics. Such were Pierce's plans, few of which he was destined to carry out.

In the first place, his policy of recognizing all factions of his party proved disastrous, for when he attempted to make the New York leaders recognize former Free-Soilers he raised so much opposition in the South that it was doubtful whether the Senate would confirm some of his appointees. Worse still was the unexpected revival of the slavery issue. The leading Democratic senators were interested in a bill to organize Kansas and Nebraska as territories and to repeal the Missouri Compromise. They needed executive aid to insure its passage, so through Jefferson Davis they arranged a conference. They convinced Pierce that the measure was indorsed by the platform of 1852 and he, realizing the necessity of Senate approval of his appointments and foreign policies, accepted it. The Kansas-Nebraska bill became law. The Senate ratified the Gadsden and Canadian reciprocity treaties and confirmed his appointees. However, Congress was so distracted by the fight over the Kansas bill that practically none of his legislative policies were adopted. On the negative side, he was successful in his effort to prevent legislative jobbery and the appropriation of government money for subsidy purposes. His vetoes, in this session, of a large land grant for the ultimate benefit of the indigent insane (Nichols, *post,* p. 349) and of a general rivers and harbors bill, and his refusal, in the next, to sign bills satisfying the French spoliation claims and continuing a subsidy to the Collins steamship line, were all sustained by Congress. Finally, in the last session of his first Congress, some proposals looking to the reform and enlargement of the army and navy were acted upon favorably. During the summer of 1854 popular opinion in the North flared up at the repeal of the Missouri Compromise and new political organizations, anti-Nebraska and anti-Catholic, prepared the ground for the germination of the Republican party; in the meantime the Democrats were badly defeated in the congressional elections of that year. His second Congress paid scant heed to Pierce's recommendations.

In this unfortunate period, Pierce's worst disappointments were diplomatic. Negotiations with Great Britain over Central America were hampered when in July 1854 Captain Hollins destroyed a British protectorate, Grey Town, Nicaragua, in retaliation for an insult to the American minister. The hope of acquiring Cuba was blasted by blunders. In August 1854 Marcy authorized Pierre Soulé [*q.v.*], the minister to Spain, to consult about Cuba with the ministers to Great Britain and France, James Buchanan and John Y. Mason [*qq.v.*]. The conference was held in October, at Ostend and Aix-la-Chapelle. It was supposed to be secret, but, unfortunately, news of it leaked out. The tangible results were a somewhat ambiguous report prepared by Buchanan, signed Oct. 18 by the three ministers, and a covering letter from Soulé, in which he intimated that French and British preoccupation with the Crimean War might make this an opportune time to consider acquiring Cuba, if necessary by force. Word of all this in garbled form was featured in the American press in October and November; Northern prejudices were further aroused against acquiring Cuba; and the loss of Congress by the Democrats put the acquisition of the island beyond the realm of possibility. The plans for annexing Hawaii and securing a coaling station in Santo Domingo also failed.

Meanwhile, difficulties were piling up for Pierce in Kansas. Determined to administer the popular-sovereignty law as fairly as possible, he sought a Southern governor for Nebraska and a Northern executive for Kansas and divided the other offices equally between the sections. For governor of Kansas he chose Andrew H. Reeder [*q.v.*], a Pennsylvania lawyer. Reeder, however, entered into some illegal land operations in the Indian reserves which were especially distasteful to the administration, and was already due for discipline of some sort when trouble developed in the territory between the Northern and Southern settlers. Conditions became so bad that in the summer of 1855 Pierce removed the governor and two judges (one a Southerner) and had an army officer courtmartialed, all for land speculating.

By the fall of 1855 Pierce had rallied somewhat from these successive disappointments and was determined to seek renomination. He became more decisive in his actions and prepared his annual message of 1855 as his platform. It consisted of a vigorous condemnation of the new Republicans as sectionalist agitators, and a strong statement of nationalism. When the House of Representatives failed to organize in December he attempted, by means of vigorous messages describing the need for congressional action, to bring the Southern members of the American party to join the Democrats in supporting an anti-Republican candidate for speaker. In the meantime, civil war had broken out in Kansas. The free-soil group had organized a government independent of the president's territorial officers, and Missourians were threatening to invade Kansas in order to disperse this new organization. The situation became so desperate that in February Pierce issued a proclamation, on the one hand ordering the treasonable free-state government to disperse, and on the other commanding the Missourians to stay in Missouri. To back up this proclamation he placed federal troops at the disposal of Wilson Shannon [*q.v.*], his second governor.

During his campaign for renomination he also pursued a vigorous policy toward Great Britain. Late in December 1855, he had requested Great Britain to recall her minister, Crampton, for sponsoring in the United States the illegal recruiting of troops to be used in the Crimea; after a series of unsatisfactory negotiations he dismissed him summarily, meanwhile continuing negotiations in regard to Central America. These decisive acts showed a more vigorous grasp of the problems of administration but they were not sufficient to restore popularity. The Democratic convention of 1856, uncertain as to the strength of the newly organized Republican party, fell back upon the idea that an old, tried, conservative, and safe man alone could save them from defeat; so they nominated James Buchanan who had been abroad during the heated controversies of the preceding years. Pierce was bitterly disappointed at the result but turned himself whole-heartedly to settling up as many of the problems of the nation as he could before March 4. In Kansas more bloodshed was imminent. Pierce still endeavored to be impartial and to give support to the regular and legal (though pro-slavery) territorial government. He maintained troops in Kansas, and removed Shannon, whose successor, John W. Geary [*q.v.*], went vigorously to work and by October could report, "Peace now reigns in Kansas." The difficulty with the British was finally settled as far as Pierce was concerned by the negotiation of the Dallas-Clarendon treaty in which Great Britain, indirectly and without apology, agreed to leave Central America except for British Honduras; the treaty later failed of ratification. Pierce retired, regretting that Congress had failed to carry out most of his recommendations for administrative reform, but rejoicing in the fact that his party was still in power and had regained Congress.

After his release from responsibility he made an extended tour of Europe and then settled down in Concord, N. H. As the Civil War approached he still deplored the "folly" of the Republicans but resented the hasty action of the South in leaving the Union. At first he gave lukewarm support to the government but it was not long before he was bitterly opposing the Lincoln administration because of its usurpations and destruction of personal and property rights. He became very unpopular even at home and died in social and political obscurity. As a national political leader Pierce was an accident. He was honest and tenacious of his views but, as he made up his mind with difficulty and often reversed himself before making a final decision, he gave a general impression of instability. Kind, courteous, generous, he attracted many individuals, but his attempts to satisfy all factions failed and made him many enemies. In carrying out his principles of strict construction he was most in accord with Southerners, who generally had the letter of the law on their side. He failed utterly to realize the depth and the sincerity of Northern feeling against the South and was bewildered at the general flouting of the law and the Constitution, as he described it, by the people of his own New England. At no time did he catch the popular imagination. His inability to cope with the difficult problems that arose early in his administration caused him to lose the respect of great numbers, especially in the North, and his few successes failed to restore public confidence. He was an inexperienced man, suddenly called to assume a tremendous responsibility, who honestly tried to do his best without adequate training or temperamental fitness.

[More complete details are found in R. F. Nichols, *Franklin Pierce. Young Hickory of the Granite Hills* (1931), which contains an extended bibliography. The Pierce MSS. are divided into three parts, one in Lib. of Cong., one in N. H. Hist. Soc., one in possession of the family. A large file of Pierce letters is in the Burke MSS., Lib. of Cong., and a smaller group in the Lawrence MSS., Mass. Hist. Soc. The collections most valuable for a study of Pierce's administration are the Marcy Collection, Lib. of Cong., and the Buchanan Papers, Hist. Soc. of Pa. His ancestry is described in F. B. Pierce, *Pierce Genealogy* (1882), and his early life in the campaign biographies by Hawthorne (1852) and D. W. Bartlett (1852), and in J. R. Irelan, *The Republic,* vol. XIV (1888), "Hist. of the Life, Administration, and Times of Franklin Pierce." The records of his early political life are found in the N. H. local newspapers, especially the *New Hampshire Patriot.* His Mexican War Diary is in the Huntington Library (photostat copy in Lib. of Cong.). His legal career is best summed up in Davis Cross, "Franklin Pierce the Lawyer," *Proc. of the Bar Asso. of the State of N. H.,* vol. I, no. 1 (1900). The situation in his party which produced his nomination is detailed in R. F. Nichols, *The Democratic Machine, 1850–1854* (1923). His diplomacy is best described in S. F. Bemis, ed., *The American Secretaries of State and Their Diplomacy,* vol. VI (1928), article by H. B. Learned on "William Learned Marcy." Materials on the administrative history of his presidential term are in the archives of the various departments and in the attorney general's MSS. in Lib. of Cong. The newspapers most valuable for comment on his policies are the Washington *Star,* the *Washington Union,* the Baltimore *Sun,* and the *New York Herald.*]   R. F. N.

PIERCE, GEORGE FOSTER (Feb. 3, 1811– Sept. 3, 1884), bishop of the Methodist Episcopal Church, South, educator, was born in Greene County, Ga. His parents were Lovick Pierce, a well-known Methodist preacher, and Ann (Foster) Pierce. In 1826 he entered Franklin College, Athens, where he was graduated with honors in 1829. He began the study of law in the

office of his uncle, Thomas Foster, but feeling called to preach, abandoned his legal studies and in January 1831 was admitted on trial to the Georgia Conference of the Methodist Episcopal Church. His ability as a preacher was immediately recognized and within the next five years he served such leading stations as Augusta and Savannah, Ga., and Charleston, S. C. At the age of twenty-five he was presiding elder of the Augusta district. On Feb. 4, 1834, he married Ann Maria Waldron of Savannah, and to this union seven children were born. In 1838 Pierce was elected president of Georgia Female College (now Wesleyan College), at Macon, the first American college for women empowered by charter to confer a degree. Endeavoring to arouse public sentiment in favor of female education, he presented his views in the *Southern Ladies' Book,* which for ten months in 1840 he edited. It cannot be said that he made a success in his initial attempt as a college executive; he refused to discontinue his evangelistic activities even while president, and as a result the work of the college was somewhat neglected. In 1840 he resigned the presidency, although he served for two years thereafter as the financial agent of the institution.

Upon his return to the itinerancy in 1842 Pierce became recognized as the leading preacher of the Georgia Conference. He was a delegate to the General Conferences of 1840 and 1844, and at the latter conference, which marked the division of the Church, Pierce, although only thirty-three years old, was one of the outstanding leaders in the defense of Bishop J. O. Andrew and one of the chief spokesmen of the viewpoint of the Southern clergy on the slavery issue. He was a member of the convention held at Louisville, Ky., in May 1845, which organized the Methodist Episcopal Church, South, and was a delegate to the General Conferences of 1846, 1850, and 1854. In 1848 he returned to the educational field as president of Emory College, Oxford, Ga. Here he remained until 1854, when he was elected bishop. Upon his elevation to the episcopacy he moved to his plantation, "Sunshine," near Sparta, Ga., which with the exception of one year was his home until his death. It was at "Sunshine" during his spare moments that he had opportunity to engage in his hobby of agriculture. Prior to the Civil War he took little part in politics, but at the outbreak of armed hostilities he held that the Southern states were justified in secession and during the war he devoted a large part of his time to the raising of food supplies for the Confederate army.

As a bishop, he was noted for his pulpit oratory

and his kindness to the preachers, but was often in conflict with the progressive groups in his denomination. He believed in retaining the characteristics of early Methodism. He fought against granting lay representation, and opposed the pew system, long pastorates, choirs, and the establishment of a theological seminary for the Southern church. Concerning the latter proposal he wrote in 1872: "It is my opinion that every dollar invested in a theological school will be a damage to Methodism. Had I a million, I would not give a dime for such an object" (Smith, *post*, p. 558). He resisted all moves leading toward the organic union of the two branches of Episcopal Methodism. Pierce's writings consisted mainly of open letters to the religious periodicals of his denomination. Much of his work as bishop was done in the Western conferences, and his experiences on these trips were related in a series of letters published in the *Southern Christian Advocate*. Some of these were collected in 1857 under the title *Incidents of Western Travel*, edited by T. O. Summers, and in 1886, *Bishop Pierce's Sermons and Addresses*, edited by A. G. Haygood, appeared. He kept a diary between the years 1836 and 1866, and left in manuscript an account of the early life of his father.

[G. G. Smith, *The Life and Times of George Foster Pierce* (1888); "Bishop Pierce as a Farmer," *Meth. Quart. Rev.*, Apr. 1921; "Bishop George F. Pierce," in *Quart. Rev. Meth. Episc. Church, South*, Oct. 1884; O. P. Fitzgerald, *Bishop George F. Pierce* (1896); *Obsequies of George Foster Pierce* (1884); *Atlanta Constitution*, Sept. 4, 1884.]   P. N. G.

PIERCE, GILBERT ASHVILLE (Jan. 11, 1839–Feb. 15, 1901), author, governor of Dakota Territory, and first senator from North Dakota, was born in East Otto, Cattaraugus County, N. Y., the son of Sylvester and Mary Olive (Treat) Pierce, both natives of New York. He received a common-school education, and, when the family removed to Indiana in 1854, he became a clerk for his father in a general store ten miles south of Valparaiso. In 1858 he married Anne Maria Bartholomew and removed to Valparaiso, where he began to read law. He studied in the old University of Chicago for two years and was later admitted to practice in Indiana. When the Civil War broke out he enlisted in the 9th Indiana Volunteers and was elected second-lieutenant. At the end of the three months' term of enlistment, Lincoln appointed him captain and assistant quartermaster. He served under General Grant in the West until the capture of Vicksburg. In November 1863 he was promoted to the rank of lieutenant-colonel and served at Matagorda Island, Tex. The following year he was appointed inspector of the quartermaster's department with the rank of colonel. After serving in South Carolina he was ordered to the department of the Gulf, where he remained till the close of the war. After retiring from the army he again took up his residence in Valparaiso and devoted himself to law and journalism. In 1869 he was a member of the Indiana House of Representatives. At the close of his term he became secretary to Oliver P. Morton [*q.v.*]. This brought him into contact with a more influential group of public men, among whom he was soon well and favorably known. He kept up his interest in journalism and was a correspondent on several important dailies. For two years he served as assistant financial clerk in the United States Senate but resigned in 1871. Shortly after this he returned to Valparaiso and in 1872 obtained a place on the editorial staff of the Chicago *Inter Ocean* through the good offices of E. W. Halford, then editor of this paper. He had considerable literary ability and was the author of a number of books. In 1872 he published *The Dickens Dictionary*, which went through several editions and is now issued uniformly with the library edition of Dickens by Houghton Mifflin Company. In 1876 he published *Zachariah, the Congressman* and in 1883 *A Dangerous Woman*. Both novels were on Washington political life, ran through two editions, and were highly praised by the critics of the time. One of his plays, *One Hundred Wives* (1880), was a still greater success and was played for two seasons by De Wolf Hopper, as leading actor, with the Gosche-Hopper Company.

After serving as managing editor of the *Inter Ocean* for a number of years, he became a member of the editorial staff of the *Chicago Daily News*. He took an active part in the Republican campaigns of 1880 and 1884 and was especially prominent in the movement to nominate President Arthur at the Republican convention of 1884. When the need arose for a new governor of the territory of Dakota, he was named as the most available man for the position. He was at this time a national figure of considerable prominence with many friends in the Northwest and at Washington. He accepted the position in 1884 and moved his family to Bismarck, then a frontier city just coming into notice as the political center of the new territory. It was during his administration that the governor's guard was organized, and this group of young business men of Bismarck afterward became Company A of the territorial militia. In November 1886 he resigned his position. During his four years of service he made an important place for himself in the territory. His fine presence and magnetic personality as well as his administrative ability made him the natural leader of his party at this time. When the territory was divided in 1889 he was chosen as one of the senators from North Dakota. The short term fell to him, and he stood for reëlection in 1891. Owing to a misunderstanding over senatorial patronage he found himself opposed by a group of state politicians, chief among whom was Alexander McKenzie. They were able to control the elections for members of the House and the Senate, and he lost the election to his opponent, Henry Clay Hansbrough. His defeat for reëlection closed his political career.

In 1891 he moved his family to Minneapolis and devoted himself, thereafter, to the field of journalism. He was first connected with the *Daily Pioneer Press* as special writer in the Dakota department, but later he became half owner and publisher, with W. J. Murphy, of the *Minneapolis Tribune*. Failure of health, in the fall of 1891, compelled him to give up his editorial work and seek a warmer climate, first in Florida and then in Colorado. On Jan. 6, 1893, he was appointed by President Harrison as minister to Portugal but was compelled to resign on Apr. 26, on account of continued lack of health. On his return to Minneapolis he found himself unable to continue his editorial work. He died at the Lexington Hotel, Chicago.

[A. T. Andreas, *Hist. of Chicago*, vol. III (1886); *The Biog. Encyc. of Ill.* (1875); *Biog. Directory of Am. Cong.* (1928); *Once a Clown, Always a Clown: Reminiscences of De Wolf Hopper*, written in collaboration with W. W. Stout (1927), p. 15; information from son, Paul A. Pierce, N. Y. City; *Minneapolis Tribune*, Feb. 16, 1901.]   O. G. L.

PIERCE, HENRY LILLIE (Aug. 23, 1825–Dec. 17, 1896), manufacturer of cocoa, mayor of Boston, congressman, was born in Stoughton, Mass., the son of Jesse Pierce and Elizabeth Lillie and a descendant of John Pers (or Peirce) who emigrated to New England in 1637. Edward Lillie Pierce [q.v.] was his younger brother. The father was ultra-conscientious and sensitive; the mother was more forceful, plain-spoken, and with strong prejudices. This environment was scarcely cheerful, but it was tempered with fair educational advantages at home and at Bridgewater and Milton academies. At seventeen, Pierce suffered an illness which ended his formal education and from which he never fully recovered. Even as early as this, however, his interest in public affairs showed itself in the form of contributions to the county paper. By 1848 he was serving as a member of the school committee of Stoughton and was working hard

for the Free-Soil party in the national elections. This interest in freeing the slaves was for some time the dominant note in his outlook on public affairs. For a number of years he engaged in light farm work but in 1849 he moved to Dorchester and there worked in the cocoa factory of his uncle, Walter Baker. Save for one short period, this association continued till his death. In 1854, after the death of Baker and his partner, Sidney B. Williams, the trustees leased the plant to Pierce. From that time till his death he worked to make and then to keep his factory the leader in its field, and saw its business grow forty times over. In 1884 he became full owner of the plant. He was progressive in his methods and constantly alert to discover and introduce improved processes. In all the years he never had any trouble with his employees. He took particular pride in the fact that his products were awarded a gold medal at the Paris Exposition of 1867.

Pierce's political career included four years as representative to the General Court, where he served as chairman of its committee on finance in 1862; three years (1869–71) as alderman of Boston; two years (1872, 1877) as mayor of Boston, and two terms, from 1873 to 1877, as a member of Congress. He opposed the Know-Nothing movement at the height of its power. As mayor he set his face against the vested interests in administration which had been acquired by the city council. He was instrumental in furthering the movement, general throughout the country, which resulted in the transfer of administration from committees of the council to boards set up for special purposes. The health and fire departments were so reorganized during his first term and the police department during his second. These boards were made responsible to the mayor, and he restored to that office its former prestige. In Congress his chief service was as a member of the committee on commerce and was directed toward relieving coastal vessels from state pilotage fees. In the Hayes-Tilden controversy, he and one other Massachusetts Representative were the only Republicans to vote to throw out the Louisiana electoral vote which the electoral commission had counted for Hayes. His voluntary retirement from Congress soon followed as he found himself in many ways out of harmony with his party. In the 1884 campaign he refused to support Blaine and from then till 1896, in presidential elections, he voted with the Democrats. In 1887 he became president of the Massachusetts Tariff Reform League, which was formed to secure general reductions in the tariff. His refreshing sincerity and independence made him a more than usually outstanding local personality at a time when public life generally throughout the country was at a low ebb.

Pierce was a man who acted upon impulses, often odd ones. He masked his keen judgment behind a kindly and innocent-appearing exterior. Wendell Phillips said of him that if Diogenes came to Boston he would find his honest man in the mayor's chair. Particularly in his later years, he became a liberal giver, especially to struggling colored schools in the South and to small Western colleges. He never married, and at his death more than half his large estate was carefully apportioned to various charitable, educational, and religious institutions. In the latter group, he left money to Catholic and Unitarian churches alike.

[J. M. Bugbee, "Memoir of Henry Lillie Pierce," *Proc. Mass. Hist. Soc.*, 2 ser. XI (1897); Justin Winsor, ed., *The Memorial Hist. of Boston*, vol. III (1881); T. T. Munger, "An American Citizen: The Late Henry L. Pierce," the *Century*, July 1897; "A Model Citizen," the *Critic*, Jan. 9, 1897; *Boston Transcript*, Dec. 18, 1896; *Boston Herald*, Dec. 18, 19, 1896.]

E. S. G.

PIERCE, JOHN DAVIS (Feb. 18, 1797–Apr. 5, 1882), Congregational clergyman, educator, was born in Chesterfield, N. H., of old New England stock. His father, Gad Pierce, died two years after John's birth, leaving the mother, Sarah (Davis) Pierce, with two small children and no provision for their livelihood. John was sent to his paternal grandfather in Worcester County, Mass., with whom he spent a cheerless childhood. At the grandfather's death when he was ten years old, the boy went to work on his uncle's farm. Only eight weeks a year of schooling were permitted him, but at twenty he determined to seek an education, bought a Latin grammar, and began its study under the kindly tutelage of Rev. Enoch Pond [*q.v.*]. In less than a year, with his grandfather's legacy of $100 which he received upon attaining his majority, he was able to enter Brown University. He spent a portion of each year in teaching, and graduated in 1822. After another year of teaching in an academy at Wrentham, Mass., he studied for a few months in Princeton Theological Seminary. In 1825 he was ordained and became pastor of a Congregational church in Sangerfield, Oneida County, N. Y. He was a Freemason, and in 1830 this pastorate was terminated by the fury of the Anti-Masonic movement. Pierce thereupon accepted a call to service as a missionary in Michigan. In the fall of 1831 he moved his family to the little pioneer settlement of Marshall, Mich., where there were fewer than a dozen houses but the settlers included eight college men. His second day in Marshall

being Sunday, he conducted church services in a log dwelling, and he is said to have been the first Protestant clergyman to solemnize a marriage or conduct a funeral in Western Michigan (Cooley, *post*, p. 318).

When the state government of Michigan was organized in 1836, Pierce was appointed superintendent of public instruction. The first work devolving upon him in this office was to draft plans for the organization of the primary schools and the state university and for the disposal of public-school lands. In preparation for this work he went East to consult eminent educators, Edward Everett [*q.v.*] and others, and after intensive study he presented a plan which was adopted by the legislature with virtually no change. This plan forms the basis of the present school system of Michigan and the foundation of its university. While superintendent of public instruction Pierce began the publication of the *Journal of Education* (1838–40), the first educational paper in the old Northwest Territory.

In 1841 he returned to Marshall to resume the life of a village preacher. In 1847 he was elected to the state legislature and in 1850 served on a committee to frame a new state constitution. This work was the end of his public career. Impaired health forced him soon afterward to retire to a farm near Ypsilanti. He contributed a paper on the "Origin and Progress of the Michigan School System" to the *Pioneer Collections: Report of the Pioneer Society of the State of Michigan* (vol. I, 1877). Though physically feeble, he retained his mental powers, and his interest in education remained alert until his death, which occurred in Medford, Mass. He was buried in Marshall, Mich. Pierce was married three times: on Feb. 1, 1825, to Millicent Estabrook of Holden, Mass.; on Oct. 28, 1829, to Mary Ann Cleveland of Madison, N. Y.; and in 1833 to Harriet, daughter of Calvin and Elizabeth (Barrett) Reed of Waterville, N. Y. She, with two of his four children, survived him.

[*Mich. Biogs.*, vol. II (1924); *Am. Biog. Hist. of Eminent and Self-Made Men, Mich. Vol.* (1878); C. O. Hoyt and R. C. Ford, *John D. Pierce* (1905); T. M. Cooley, *Mich., A Hist. of Govts.* (1885); G. L. Jackson, *The Development of State Control of Public Instruction in Mich.* (1926); A. C. McLaughlin, *Hist. of Higher Educ. in Mich.* (1891); *Hist. of Calhoun County, Mich.* (1877); *The Congreg. Year Book*, 1883; *Boston Daily Advertiser*, Apr. 6, 1882; *Providence Daily Journal*, June 21, 1882.]

R. H. E.

PIERCE, WILLIAM LEIGH (c. 1740–Dec. 10, 1789), Revolutionary soldier, member of the Federal Convention, was born probably in Georgia, although he entered the Continental Army as from Virginia and spoke of himself as a Virginian (*Magazine of American History*, December 1881, p. 439). Nothing is known of his parents and his early life. About 1783 he married Charlotte, daughter of Edward Fenwick, of South Carolina. One of their two sons died as a child and the other was William Leigh Pierce, author of a volume of verse, *The Year*, published in 1813. During the war, William Pierce—as he is known in contemporary documents—served as aide-de-camp to General Greene, and for his conduct at the battle of Eutaw Springs on Sept. 8, 1781, received the thanks of Congress and was presented with a sword. He left the army as a brevet major in 1783, and engaged in business in Savannah, Ga., as the head of the house of William Pierce & Company.

In 1786 he was elected to the Continental Congress, took his seat in January 1787, and attended the sessions until late in May. His chief claim to remembrance, however, is as a member of the Federal Convention at Philadelphia. He was elected one of Georgia's delegates in the early spring of 1787 and took his place on May 31, six days after the opening session. Although he played no conspicuous rôle in the proceedings of the Convention, he was not without influence. He took part in the debates on three different occasions, speaking once in favor of the election of the first branch of a federal legislature by the people and of the second branch by the states; he spoke again favoring a three-year term instead of a seven-year term for the second branch; and finally, he recommended the strengthening of the federal government as against the state governments. In a letter to St. George Tucker, of Virginia, he registered his general impressions of the Convention and his approval of the new Constitution. Parts of this letter appeared in the *Georgia Gazette*, Mar. 20, 1788 (reprinted in *American Historical Review*, January 1898). He left the Convention in the midst of the proceedings and did not return to sign the finished document. Business misfortunes and the subsequent failure of his firm probably account for his absence.

Pierce's notes on the Convention debates add little to the information contained in the notes of Madison, Yates, and King. They were first published in the *Savannah Georgian*, Apr. 19, 21–26, and 28, 1828, and were printed in the *American Historical Review*, January 1898, from a bound volume of personal papers in manuscript known as "Pierce's Reliques." Much more important are the character sketches which he wrote about his fellow members. They are short, pithy, and decidedly readable. Even more valuable than the descriptions of leaders such as Madison and Franklin are his observations on less prominent

delegates, who, without Pierce's comments, would be little more than names. As for his own character, he remarks simply that his readers are left "to consider it in any light that their fancy or imagination may depict."

[The manuscript volume of Pierce's papers is in the possession of a descendant of his widow. For additional data, see: Max Farrand, ed., *The Records of the Federal Convention of 1787* (3 vols., 1911); *Am. Hist. Rev.*, Jan. 1898; *Mag. of Am. Hist.*, Dec. 1881; D. C. Huger Smith, "An Account of the Tattnall and Fenwick Families in S. C.," *S. C. Hist. and Geneal. Mag.*, Jan. 1913; Fairfax Harrison, *The John's Island Stud* (1931); C. C. Jones, *Biog. Sketches of the Delegates from Ga. to the Cont. Cong.* (1891); W. B. Burroughs, sketch in *Men of Mark in Ga.*, vol. I (1907); A. D. Candler and C. A. Evans, ed., *Cyc. of Ga.* (1906); *Georgia Gazette*, Dec. 24, 1789.]   E. K. A.

PIERPONT, FRANCIS HARRISON (Jan. 25, 1814–Mar. 24, 1899), governor of the "restored" state of Virginia, 1861–68, was the son of Francis and Catherine (Weaver) Pierpoint. The name was spelled Pierpoint by the Virginia branch of the family until 1881 when Francis Harrison returned to the older spelling, Pierpont. His grandfather, John Pierpont, removed from New York State in 1770 and established a farm near Morgantown, Monongalia County, in western Virginia. Here young Francis was born in 1814, but during the same year his father removed from the old homestead to the neighborhood of Fairmont, in what is now Marion County, W. Va. As the boy grew up he helped his father on the farm and in his tannery. In 1835 he entered Allegheny College, Meadville, Pa., and was graduated with the bachelor's degree in 1839. For two years he taught school in Virginia and in 1841 went to Mississippi to engage in the same occupation, but his father's poor health necessitated his return home the next year. Having read law in his spare time, he was now admitted to the bar. In 1848 he became local attorney for the Baltimore & Ohio Railroad, and in 1853 engaged in mining and shipping coal.

From 1844 to 1860 Pierpont took an active interest in politics as an adherent of the Whig party, serving as a presidential elector on the Taylor ticket in 1848. Being an ardent anti-slavery and Union man, he supported Lincoln in 1860. When Virginia in 1861 decided in favor of secession, Pierpont organized a mass meeting at Wheeling in May which called a convention to meet in that town during the following month. This convention, holding that the secessionist officials of the state had vacated their offices, elected Pierpont provisional governor of Virginia. He thereupon organized the Unionist members of the legislature from the western counties into a rump legislature; a constitution was framed, and the name West Virginia adopted. Representatives from this government were seated in the Federal Congress, and in 1863 the state was admitted to the Union. A new governor was elected for the new state, but meanwhile Pierpont had been granted a four-year term as governor of the "restored" state of Virginia; that is, governor of the few counties which were in Federal hands and not in West Virginia. He now moved his capital to Alexandria and carried on under military protection. Upon the fall of the Confederate government, he moved his capital to Richmond and became in fact the governor of Virginia. Under the Johnson régime he conducted the affairs of the state until the reconstruction act went into effect and he was replaced by a military commander on Apr. 16, 1868. While at the head of affairs in Richmond he did what he could to alleviate the suffering and the bitterness which oppressed the people during those ghastly years. Upon his retirement from office, he returned to his home in West Virginia and resumed the practice of law. Subsequently he sat for one term in the legislature (1870) and was collector of internal revenue under Garfield. He died in Pittsburgh, Pa., where for two years he had lived in the home of a daughter. He was buried at his home near Fairmont, W. Va.

Pierpont was apparently one of that large class of men who are selected as leaders in troubled times because they possess strength of conviction rather than strength of intellect. In 1910 a statue of him was placed by West Virginia in Statuary Hall at the United States Capitol. In 1854 he married Julia Augusta Robertson, daughter of Samuel and Dorcas (Platt) Robertson of New York.

[The material dealing with the establishment of West Virginia is voluminous and largely of a partisan nature; the best study is J. C. McGregor, *The Disruption of Va.* (1922). There are sketches of Pierpont in T. C. Miller and Hu Maxwell, *W. Va. and Its People* (1913), vol. II; M. V. Smith, *Va., A Hist. of the Executives* (1893); R. A. Brock, *Va. and Virginians* (1888), vol. I; L. G. Tyler, *Encyc. of Va. Biog.* (1915), vol. III; *Encyc. of Contemporary Biog. of W. Va.* (1894); *Statue of Gov. Francis Harrison Pierpont: Proc. in Statuary Hall* (1910), being *Sen. Doc. No. 656*, 61 Cong., 2 Sess.; F. S. Reader, *Hist. of the Fifth W. Va. Cavalry* (1890); *Pittsburgh Post*, Mar. 25, 1899; *Wheeling Register*, Mar. 25, 1899.] T. P. A.

PIERPONT, JAMES (Jan. 4, 1659/60–Nov. 22, 1714), Congregational clergyman, one of the founders of Yale College, was born in Roxbury, Mass., the son of John Pierpont and Thankful Stow, daughter of John Stow of Kent, England. John Pierpont, born at London in 1617, came to Massachusetts in 1640 and in 1656 purchased three hundred acres of land lying in what is now Roxbury and Dorchester. His father, James, was a cousin of Robert Pierrepont, first Earl of Kingston, and owned a considerable estate in Derbyshire. The business in which he was engaged, involving trade with Ireland, was ruined during the Protectorate, and he came to America to visit his sons, Robert and John, where, at Ipswich, he died. His grandson, James, graduated from Harvard College in 1681. Recommended as "a godly man, a good scholar, a man of good parts, and likely to make a good instrument," he was invited in 1684 to preach as a candidate for the pastorate of the First Church, New Haven. He arrived in that town the following August, and his ministrations gave such satisfaction that he was urged to remain and a house was built and furnished for him. On July 2, 1685, he was ordained pastor, which office he held until his death a little more than twenty-nine years later. He married, Oct. 27, 1691, Abigail, daughter of John and Abigail (Pierson) Davenport, a grand-daughter of John Davenport and of the elder Abraham Pierson [qq.v.]. The following February she died, her illness, it is said, having been caused by exposure to cold on the Sunday following her marriage, when she went to meeting attired, according to custom, in her wedding dress. On May 30, 1694, he married Sarah, daughter of Joseph and Sarah (Lord) Haynes, and a grand-daughter of Gov. John Haynes [q.v.]. She, too, died early, Oct. 7, 1696, leaving him a daughter, Abigail. His third wife, whom he married July 26, 1698, was Mary Hooker, daughter of Rev. Samuel Hooker and grand-daughter of Rev. Thomas Hooker [q.v.]. Sarah, a child of this union, married Jonathan Edwards [q.v.].

Not of extraordinary intellectual endowment, but genuinely good and possessing personal charm, force of character, discretion, and sound judgment, Pierpont had a peaceful and successful pastorate and became highly influential in the colony. In the establishment of the Collegiate School of Connecticut, the beginning of Yale College, chartered in 1701, he was the leading spirit, and as one of the original trustees he, more than any other, directed its course through the critical opening years of its existence. He had much to do with shaping its charter and insuring the school against state or church control; he selected its first president; and through Jeremiah Dummer [q.v.] he secured a library for it from English benefactors and probably brought it to the attention of Elihu Yale. His influence in ecclesiastical affairs is attested by the fact that at the famous Saybrook Synod of 1708 he was one of the leading members and is traditionally credited with having drawn up the original draft of the articles for the administration of church discipline, known as the "Saybrook Platform." His death came in his fifty-fifth year when he was at the height of his powers. One sermon, *Sundry False Hopes of Heaven, Discovered and Decryed,* preached at the North Assembly, Boston, on Apr. 3, 1711, was published with a preface by Cotton Mather the following year.

[R. B. Moffat, *Pierrepont Genealogies* (1913); Leonard Bacon, *Thirteen Hist. Discourses* (1839); J. L. Sibley, *Biog. Sketches Grads. Harvard Univ.,* vol. III (1885); W. B. Sprague, *Annals Am. Pulpit,* vol. I (1857); *New Haven Colony Hist. Soc. Papers,* vol. III (1882), vol. VII (1908); F. B. Dexter, *Biog. Sketches Grads. Yale Coll. with Annals of the College Hist.,* vol. I (1885); Edwin Oviatt, *The Beginnings of Yale* (1916).]   H. E. S.

PIERPONT, JOHN (Apr. 6, 1785–Aug. 27, 1866), Unitarian clergyman, poet, reformer, great-grandson of James Pierpont and grandfather of John Pierpont Morgan [*qq.v.*], was born in Litchfield, Conn., the second of the ten children of James Pierpont, a clothier, by his wife, Elizabeth Collins. He graduated from Yale College in 1804, in the same class with John C. Calhoun, and, after assisting Azel Backus [*q.v.*] for a few months in an academy at Bethlehem, went to South Carolina as tutor, 1805–09, in the household of William Alston, father of Joseph Alston [*q.v.*]. On his return he studied in the Litchfield Law School under Tapping Reeve and James Gould [*qq.v.*] and on Sept. 23, 1810, married his fourth cousin, Mary Sheldon Lord, who bore him three sons and three daughters. Their eldest child was named for William Alston. Having been called to the bar in 1812, he opened a law office at Newburyport, Mass., and, in the leisure afforded by a total absence of clients, composed *The Portrait* (1812), a poem surcharged with Federalist sentiment, which he declaimed Oct. 27, 1812, before the Washington Benevolent Society of Newburyport. It brought him renown as a bard but no retainers, and in 1814 he and his brother-in-law, Joseph L. Lord, went into the retail dry-goods business in Boston and soon took John Neal [*q.v.*] into the firm. They started a branch in Baltimore and for a while the venture flourished, but the dizzy fluctuations of wartime prices were more than they could cope with, and in 1815 the business collapsed. Still in Baltimore, Pierpont published the next year his beautifully executed *Airs of Palestine* (Baltimore, 1816), which was reprinted twice in Boston in 1817, and which put him for the time being in the front rank of American poets. Two later volumes, *Airs of Palestine and Other Poems* (1840) and *The Anti-Slavery*

Poems of John Pierpont (1843), comprise the bulk of his verse. He was an accomplished prosodist. In some of the temperance pieces he is unintentionally humorous, but as the expression of a vigorous, witty, noble mind his poetry has character and is continuously interesting.

Having graduated in October 1818 from the Harvard Divinity School, he was ordained Apr. 14, 1819, as minister of the Hollis Street Church in Boston. He edited two school readers, *The American First Class Book* (1823) and *The National Reader* (1827), which went through many editions and were the first American readers to include selections from Shakespeare; visited Europe and Palestine in 1835–36; published various sermons and lectures; and grew steadily in reputation as an eloquent, thoughtful minister. His penchant for reform was also growing steadily. He worked for the abolition of the state militia and of imprisonment for debt; became an enthusiastic propagandist for phrenology and spiritualism; and pressed to the forefront of the peace, the anti-slavery, and the temperance movements. The pew-holders of the Hollis Street Church did not share these enthusiasms; their temper may be deduced from the fact that the church cellar was rented out to a rum merchant for a warehouse. Several rum merchants who did not attend Pierpont's preachings bought pews in the church; and in 1838 there began a concerted movement, known locally as the "Seven Years' War," to oust him. Pierpont resisted with wit, eloquence, pertinacity, and a fixed determination to maintain the freedom of the Unitarian pulpit. As the war proceeded it became an unscrupulous attempt to destroy his character. He was vindicated by an ecclesiastical council before which he was tried in July 1841, but his enemies continued their campaign against him. Finally, with his back salary paid in full and all the honors on his side, he resigned in 1845. Subsequently he was pastor of the newly organized First Unitarian Society of Troy, N. Y., 1845–49, and of the First Congregational (Unitarian) Church of West Medford, Mass., 1849–58. His first wife having died on Aug. 23, 1855, he married, on Dec. 8, 1857, Harriet Louise (Campbell) Fowler of Pawling, N. Y., who survived him. For two weeks of 1861 he was chaplain of the 22nd Regiment of Massachusetts Volunteers, but the post was too strenuous for his seventy-six years. From then until his death, which took place at Medford, he was a clerk in the Treasury Department at Washington. He was known throughout the eastern United States as a lecturer, and by those who came into immediate contact with him he was remembered as a man with more than a touch of genius.

[F. B. Dexter, *Biog. Sketches Grads. Yale Coll.*, vol. V (1911), with list of sources and a bibliog. of Pierpont's writings; C. R. Eliot, sketch in S. A. Eliot, *Heralds of a Liberal Faith*, vol. II (1910), with list of sources; O. B. Frothingham, *Boston Unitarianism 1820–50* (1890), pp. 184–86; A. A. Ford, *John Pierpont, a Biog. Sketch* (1909); Henry Ware, *A Sermon Delivered in Boston, Apr. 14, 1819, at the Ordination of the Rev. John Pierpont* (1819); *Proceedings in the Controversy between a Part of the Proprietors and the Pastor of Hollis Street Church, Boston, 1838 and 1839* (Boston, n.d.); S. K. Lothrop, *Proceedings of an Ecclesiastical Council in the Case of the Proprietors of Hollis-Street Meeting-House and the Rev. John Pierpont* (1841); G. L. Chaney, *Hollis Street Church from Mather Byles to Thomas Starr King* (1877); H. W. Simon, *The Reading of Shakespeare in American Schools and Colleges* (1932), pp. 20–22; J. R. Dix, *Pulpit Portraits* (1854); *Boston Transcript*, Aug. 27, 1866.]

G. H. G.

PIERREPONT, EDWARDS (Mar. 4, 1817–Mar. 6, 1892), lawyer, attorney-general of the United States, foreign minister, was born at North Haven, Conn., the son of Giles and Eunice (Munson) Pierpont and a descendant of James Pierpont [*q.v.*], one of the founders of Yale College. At baptism he was called Munson Edwards Pierpont, but he later dropped his first name and adopted an early spelling of his surname. He was educated in the schools of his native town and at Yale College, being graduated in 1837. After spending some time in the West he returned to study at the New Haven Law School. In 1840 he was admitted to the bar. He was a tutor at Yale, 1840–41, and then went to Columbus, Ohio, where he became a partner of Phineas B. Wilcox, one of the ablest lawyers of the state. In 1846 he moved to New York City and almost immediately established a successful practice. On May 27, 1846, he was married to Margaretta Willoughby of Brooklyn, N. Y.

After moving to New York he became an active participant in the campaigns of the Democratic party, though he never held office until 1857. In that year he was elected judge of the superior court of the city of New York but resigned in 1860 to resume his practice. Early in 1861 he took a determined stand in favor of coercive measures to preserve the Union. He was a member of the Union Defence Committee which, in the early months of the war, raised several regiments, and also helped to finance movements in favor of the Union in the border slave states. In 1864 he publicly expressed his disappointment at the nomination of McClellan and helped to organize the War Democrats in support of the reëlection of Lincoln. After the close of the war he remained for a time an independent Union Democrat. He approved President Johnson's policy of reconstruction and strongly opposed the program of the radical leaders in Congress. In the election of 1866 he cooperated with the regular organization of the Democratic party; but after the nomination of Seymour and Blair in 1868 he announced that he would support Grant because he had been a former Democrat who had stood by the Union. From that time his political fortunes were bound up with Grant's. He served for a year as United States district attorney for the southern district of New York, 1869–70, and was appointed minister to Russia, 1873, but declined to serve. In 1875 he became attorney-general of the United States, an extremely difficult position, since it involved the prosecution of members of the "whiskey ring," some of whom were close personal friends of the President. Pierrepont brought the offenders to trial and, with the exception of his circular letter to the district attorneys of Milwaukee, Chicago, and St. Louis, denying immunity to those who would testify against the ring, his conduct of the prosecutions was satisfactory to the public. In May 1876 he was appointed minister to Great Britain and served until December 1877.

As a lawyer, Pierrepont attained a high position, appearing for clients in many important cases. With John A. Dix [*q.v.*] he was appointed in February 1862 to examine the cases of state prisoners in the custody of the federal military authorities. In 1867 he assisted the United States district attorney in prosecuting John H. Surratt for complicity in the assassination of Lincoln (see sketch of John Wilkes Booth). Among his other public services, he was a member of the state constitutional convention, 1867–68, and one of the Committee of Seventy (1870) which assisted in freeing New York City from the "Tweed ring." In his later years he published numerous pamphlets on financial questions, most of which advocated the adoption of a bimetallic standard of currency. He died in New York City where he had lived and practised law since his return from England in 1878.

[R. Burnham Moffat, *Pierrepont Geneals. from Norman Times to 1913* (1913); *Record of the Class of 1837 in Yale Univ.* (7th ed., 1887); *Obit. Record of Grads. of Yale Univ. Deceased During the Academical Year ending in June 1892* (1892); *Argument of Hon. Edwards Pierrepont to the Jury, on the Trial of John H. Surratt for the Murder of President Lincoln* (1867); *N. Y. Herald*, Apr. 27, 1869; Feb. 7–Apr. 1, 1876; Mar. 7, 1892; *N. Y. Tribune*, Mar. 7, 1892.]

E. C. S.

PIERSON, ABRAHAM (1609–Aug. 9, 1678), clergyman, first pastor of the settlements at Southampton, L. I., Branford, Conn., and Newark, N. J., was born in Yorkshire, England, probably at Bradford, since he was baptized there on Sept. 23, 1609. He matriculated as a pensioner at Trinity College, Cambridge, in 1629 and was graduated A.B. in 1632, his name appearing on the rolls as Pearson or Peirson. On Sept. 23, 1632, he was ordained deacon at the Collegiate Church, Southwell, Nottingham, under the jurisdiction of York (John and J. A. Venn, *Alumni Cantabrigienses*, pt. I, vol. III, 1924, p. 330, and Institutional Act Books of York Cathedral cited by L. H. Patterson, in *The Pageant of Newark-on-Trent*, 1927, p. 4). Strongly Puritan in his convictions, he left England for the more salutary ecclesiastical atmosphere of Massachusetts, and was admitted to the church at Boston, Sept. 5, 1640. Earlier in the year "divers of the inhabitants of Linne, finding themselves straitened, looked out for a new plantation" (J. K. Hosmer, *Winthrop's Journal*, 1908, II, 4), and going to Long Island founded what is now the town of Southampton. Hugh Peter [*q.v.*] records that in November 1640 he attended the formation of a church at Lynn, composed of persons connected with this enterprise and on the same occasion took "part in the ordination of Abraham Pierson as their guide in the spread of Gospel knowledge and influences" (J. B. Felt, "Memoir of Hugh Peters," *New-England Historical and Genealogical Register*, April 1851, p. 233). The following month this "church formed at Lynn under Rev. Abraham Pierson moves to S. Hampton, L. Island" (J. B. Felt, *Annals of Salem From Its First Settlement*, 1827). About this time, or not long afterward, he was married, it is said to a daughter of Rev. John Wheelwright [*q.v.*], though available information regarding Wheelwright's children makes the truth of this tradition doubtful (see James Savage, *A Genealogical Dictionary of the First Settlers of New England*, vols. III, IV, 1861–62).

Pierson was a stern, unbending Puritan whose piety and learning came to be held in high esteem by the early New England clergy. His conviction that church and state should act in harmony, the latter being governed in its procedure by the law of God, and that church members only should be freemen, was unshakable. The town records of Southampton contain an "Abstract of the Lawes of Judgement as given Moses to the Commonwealth of Israel," written it is said, in Pierson's hand, which the inhabitants adopted for their guidance, though none of its drastic provisions were ever put into effect (J. T. Adams, *History of the Town of Southampton*, 1918, p. 55). He was strongly opposed to Southampton's uniting with Connecticut, which union was effected in 1644, because

in Connecticut those not church members might become freemen; and in 1647 he removed to Branford, New Haven Colony, where John Davenport's church-state views prevailed. In this new settlement he organized a church of which he was pastor for about twenty years, and was prominent in the general affairs of the colony. He also engaged in missionary activities among the neighboring Indians, and acquired some knowledge of their language, receiving financial compensation for this work from the Commissioners of the United Colonies. By their order and with the cooperation of the Society for the Propagation of the Gospel in New England, he translated a catechism he had prepared into the Quiripi dialect, assisted by Thomas Stanton, interpreter-general to the United Colonies for the Indian language. It was entitled *Some Helps for the Indians Shewing Them How to Improve their Natural Reason, to Know the True God, and the True Christian Religion*. The first sheet (sixteen pages) was printed late in 1658 and sent to England, where it was reprinted, and the title page bears that date, although the catechism was not published complete until the following year. Pierson also seems to have had aspirations as a poet, for he wrote "Lines on the Death of Theophilus Eaton," a crude composition in thirty-one stanzas, and a ten-line stanza on the death of Robert Coe. Unwilling to remain in Branford after the absorption of New Haven by Connecticut—which he had vigorously opposed—in the summer of 1667, with practically his entire congregation, he again sought a new settlement where his views of church and state could be put into operation, and established himself at Newark, N. J. Here he remained as pastor until his death, assisted during the last nine years of his life by his son Abraham [*q.v.*], to whom he left his library of more than 400 books, one of the most extensive in the colonies.

[*"Some Helps for the Indians"* is reprinted in the *Conn. Hist. Soc. Colls.*, vol. III (1895), and "Lines on the Death of Theophilus Eaton," in the *Mass. Hist. Soc. Colls.*, 4 ser., vol. VII (1865). See also in addition to references above, Benj. Trumbull, *A Complete Hist. of Conn., Civil and Ecclesiastical* (1818); Cotton Mather, *Magnalia Christi Americana* (1820 ed.), I, 359; D. D. Field, *A Statistical Account of the County of Middlesex, Conn.* (1819); Ebenezer Hazard, *Hist. Colls.*, vol. II (1794); Alexander MacWhorter, *A Century Sermon, Preached in Newark, N. J., Jan. 1, 1807* (1807); J. F. Stearns, *Hist. Discourses Relating to the First Presbyt. Ch. in Newark* (1853); W. B. Sprague, *Annals Am. Pulpit*, vol. I (1857); E. E. Atwater, *Hist. of the Colony of New Haven to Its Absorption into Conn.* (1881); J. C. Pilling, *Bibliog. of the Algonquian Languages* (1891); B. F. Thompson and C. J. Werner, *Hist. of Long Island* (1918), vol. II.]

H. E. S.

PIERSON, ABRAHAM (*c.* 1645–Mar. 5, 1707), Congregational clergyman, first rector of the Collegiate School in the Colony of Connecticut, of which Yale College was the outgrowth, was the son of Abraham Pierson [*q.v.*], who in 1640 came from England to Boston, and is said to have married a daughter of Rev. John Wheelwright [*q.v.*], though the tradition seems doubtful. It is commonly stated that Abraham the younger was born at Lynn, Mass., in 1641, but according to his tombstone in the graveyard at Clinton, Conn., he "deceased March ye 5th, 1706/7, aged 61 years." If the inscription there is to be trusted, he must have been born some time between Mar. 5, 1644/5 and Mar. 5, 1645/6. At this period his father, having left Lynn in December 1640, was still pastor of the Church at Southampton, L. I., from which he moved in 1647 to Branford, Conn. In the latter settlement, only recently established, the boy grew up. He received his early instruction, first, from his father and later, it is thought, from Rev. John Davenport and some of the early schoolmasters of New Haven. Graduating from Harvard in 1668, with a classmate, John Prudden, he studied theology for about a year under Rev. Roger Newton of Milford, Conn. In the summer of 1669 he was called to the pastorate of the church at Woodbridge, N. J., but declined, and became assistant to his father, now pastor of the church at Newark. In March 1672 he was made co-pastor. The year following he married Abigail Clark, with whom he had become acquainted in Milford, a daughter of George Clark, one of the first settlers of that town. After the death of the elder Pierson in 1678 his son became sole pastor, remaining in that capacity for nearly fourteen years. Differing convictions with respect to ecclesiastical polity on the part of minister and people severed their relationship early in 1692, Pierson favoring a moderate form of presbyterian government, while a majority of his parishioners were strongly congregational.

Returning to Connecticut, he was immediately called to the church in Greenwich, but declined to be installed there, although he agreed to supply the pulpit. Two years later he accepted an invitation from the people of Killingworth, now Clinton, to become their pastor. Here he brought peace and unity into a disrupted congregation, and had a successful pastorate which lasted until his death. The old church building was torn down and a new one erected in 1700, for which a bell, probably one of the first in Connecticut to summon people to worship, was secured in 1703. According to a description given, it is said, by one who had seen and heard him often, Pierson was "something taller than a middle size, a fleshy, well formed and comely looking man,"

exceeding pious, and an excellent preacher; kind and charitable to the poor and indigent, who in a special manner lamented his death (J. F. Stearns, *Historical Discourses Relating to the First Presbyterian Church, Newark*, 1853, p. 91). He was also reputed to have been a hard student and a good scholar, and was prominent in all the activities of the little group of Connecticut ministers who laid the foundations of Yale College. In the charter establishing a collegiate school, granted by the General Court of Connecticut in October 1701, he was named one of the ten trustees, and at their first meeting, which began on Nov. 11, he was elected rector. The official location of the school was Saybrook, but since the Killingworth people objected to their pastor's removing thither, the students were instructed in the Killingworth parsonage, and the commencements were held in Saybrook. His connection with the school caused serious friction between himself and his parishioners, but before the questions involved could be settled Pierson was seized with a violent illness which resulted in his death. So far as is known he published nothing; although he prepared a textbook on physics which in manuscript was long used in the early days of Yale. A letter to Increase Mather is printed in the *Collections of the Massachusetts Historical Society* (4 ser. VIII, 1868), two letters to Fitz-John Winthrop are printed in the *Proceedings of the Massachusetts Historical Society* (2 ser. XII, 1899) and several of Pierson's manuscripts are in the possession of Yale University.

[In addition to references cited above see Thomas Clap, *The Annals or Hist. of Yale Coll. to the Year 1766* (1766); Alexander MacWhorter, *A Century Sermon Preached in Newark, N. J., Jan. 1, 1807* (1807); D. D. Field, *A Statistical Account of the County of Middlesex, Conn.* (1819); J. L. Sibley, *Biog. Sketches Grads. Harvard Univ.*, vol. II (1881); W. B. Sprague, *Annals Am. Pulpit*, vol. I (1857); D. M. Mead, *A Hist. of the Town of Greenwich* (1857); *Two Hundredth Anniversary of the Clinton Congreg. Church* (1868); F. B. Dexter, *The Literary Diary of Ezra Stiles* (1901), vol. II, and *Biog. Sketches Grads. Yale Coll.*, vol. I (1885); Edwin Oviatt, *The Beginnings of Yale* (1916).]

H. E. S.

PIERSON, ARTHUR TAPPAN (Mar. 6, 1837–June 3, 1911), Presbyterian clergyman, promoter of missionary activities, editor and writer, was born in New York City, the son of Stephen Haines and Sally Ann (Wheeler) Pierson. His father was a descendant of Abraham Pierson the elder [*q.v.*], through his son Thomas. Up to the time of the financial panic of 1837, Stephen Pierson had been the cashier and confidential clerk of Arthur Tappan [*q.v.*]. At the age of eleven young Pierson entered the Mount Washington Collegiate Institute and two years later, the Collegiate Institute at Tarrytown-on-the-Hudson, from which he shortly transferred to the Ossining School, Sing Sing, of which his brother-in-law, Rev. J. P. Lundy, was principal. Completing his course in the winter of 1852–53, he entered Hamilton College the following September. Here he took high stand as a scholar, was active in religious work, and contributed much verse and prose to New York periodicals. He graduated from Hamilton in 1857, and from Union Theological Seminary in 1860. On May 13 of the latter year he was ordained by the Third New York Presbytery and on July 12 married Sarah Frances Benedict. After having supplied a Congregational church in West Winsted, Conn., on Sept. 5, 1860, he was installed as pastor of the First Congregational Church, Binghamton, N. Y. Later he served the Presbyterian Church at Waterford, N. Y. (1863–69), and the Fort Street Church, Detroit (1869–82). During these years he became an effective and popular preacher. In 1876 his church edifice in Detroit burned, and while it was being rebuilt services were held in an opera house. He had already become convinced that his ambition for literary excellence diminished his spiritual power, and from this time on his preaching was extemporaneous, expository, and evangelistic. He also came to feel keenly that the chief work of the Church is "to rescue unsaved souls," and that conventional church buildings with elaborate architecture and rented pews hinder access to the common people. Expecting a greater field of usefulness along lines in harmony with these views, in the fall of 1882 he accepted a call to the Second Presbyterian Church, Indianapolis, but, disappointed in the cooperation he received, he remained but a few months. From 1883 to 1889, however, he had a fruitful pastorate at Bethany Church, Philadelphia.

He was a man of intense zeal, profoundly convinced of the inspired truth of the Bible, of the efficacy of prayer, and of the second coming of Christ; graphic in his preaching; and with a gift for drawing which enabled him by charts and pictures to illustrate his discourses. As time went on, concern for speedy world-wide evangelization possessed him with increasing force, and during his Philadelphia pastorate he became nationally known as an inspiring leader at missionary and Bible conferences. A friend of Dwight L. Moody [q.v.], he was prominent at Northfield gatherings and it was in no small part through the enthusiasm which he aroused that the Student Volunteer Movement for Foreign Missions was started. In 1886 he published The Crisis of Missions, which did much to arouse missionary

activity in the churches. This was followed by The Divine Enterprise of Missions (1891), The Miracles of Missions (4 vols., 1891–1901), The New Acts of the Apostles (1894), Forward Movements of the Last Half Century (1900), and The Modern Mission Century (1901). In 1888 he became associated with James M. Sherwood in the editorship of the Missionary Review, and after Sherwood's death, two years later, he was sole editor for the rest of his life. Under his supervision the periodical became a picturesque and popular organ. After attending the World Missionary Conference at London in 1888, he made a tour of Scotland with Rev. A. J. Gordon in the interest of missions. His success was such that the next year, resigning his pastorate, he again visited Great Britain, and thereafter devoted himself to evangelistic activity, lecturing and preaching both in the United States and abroad. When Charles H. Spurgeon became ill in 1891 he called Pierson to take his place at the Metropolitan Tabernacle, London, and he continued to supply there for two years, Spurgeon having died in the meantime. Finally convinced that the views on baptism held by the Baptists were Biblical, on Feb. 1, 1896, he was immersed. This fact led to his separation from the Philadelphia Presbytery, and he never thereafter had formal ministerial standing in any denomination. In the latter part of his career he adopted and promulgated the views on personal holiness held by the Keswick Convention, and in 1903 published The Keswick Movement in Precept and Practice. He also published Life Power; or, Character, Culture, and Conduct (1895); The Second Coming of Our Lord (1896); Catharine of Siena, an Ancient Lay Preacher (1898); In Christ Jesus; or, the Sphere of the Believer's Life (1898); George Müller of Bristol (1899); James Wright of Bristol (1906); Seven Years in Sierra Leone; the Story of the Work of William A. B. Johnson (1897); The Gordian Knot; or, the Problem Which Baffles Infidelity (1902); God's Living Oracles (1904); The Bible and Spiritual Criticism (1905), and numerous other works of a similar character. In October 1910 he started on a tour of the missions in the Far East, but after visiting Japan and Korea was forced by the condition of his health to return to his home in Brooklyn, where he died. He was buried in Greenwood Cemetery.

[D. L. Pierson, Arthur T. Pierson (1912); J. K. Maclean, Dr. Pierson and His Message (1911); A. G. Wheeler, The Geneal. and Encyc. Hist. of the Wheeler Family in America (1914); L. B. Pierson, Pierson Geneal. Records (1878); Missionary Review, Aug. 1911, memorial number; N. Y. Times and N. Y. Herald, June 4, 1911.]   H. E. S.

PIERSON, HAMILTON WILCOX (Sept. 22, 1817–Sept. 7, 1888), Presbyterian clergyman, author, was born in Bergen, N. Y., the son of Rev. Josiah Pierson, grandson of Samuel and Rebecca (Parmele) Pierson, and a descendant of Abraham Pierson [*q.v.*]. Throughout his life he had to contend with a weakness of the lungs which more or less determined the course of his whole career. After graduating from Union College in 1843, partly for his health he traveled in Virginia for two years as an agent for the American Tract Society. He then entered Union Theological Seminary, New York, from which he graduated in 1848. Impressed, during a visit to the West Indies, with the religious tolerance in the recently established Dominican Republic, he became agent for the American Bible Society, and distributed Bibles in the French language to schools and individuals (*Thirty-fourth Annual Report of the American Bible Society*, 1850). He returned to the United States in 1850, and spent the next three years in travel and literary work. On Nov. 13, 1853, he was ordained by the Presbytery of New York. He had hoped to become a foreign missionary, but physicians had informed him that his physical condition would not permit, and that neither would he be equal to the duties of a permanent pastorate. Accordingly, he went to Kentucky as agent of the American Bible Society. In this capacity, for five years, he traveled through the back country, covering several thousand miles annually on horseback, holding religious services, and distributing Bibles. From the knowledge thus gained he published some time later, *In the Brush; or, Old-Time Social, Political, and Religious Life in the Southwest* (1881), a lively narrative which gives a valuable portrayal of pioneer conditions and habits. In 1858 he became president of Cumberland College, a Presbyterian school at Princeton, Ky. In addition to his administrative duties he traveled extensively "electioneering for students" and collecting funds. During his term of service an additional building was erected. The outbreak of the Civil War compelled the closing of the institution and Pierson returned North. During the war he served as agent of the American Tract Society in Washington, D. C., and as secretary of the Christian Commission at Toledo, Ohio. From 1863 to 1869 he did religious work among the freedmen in Virginia and Georgia. His activities in Andersonville, Ga., caused him to be driven from the city, and in 1870 he published *A Letter to Hon. Charles Sumner, with "Statements" of Outrages upon Freedmen in Georgia and an Account of My Expulsion from Andersonville, Ga., by the Ku-Klux Klan.*

The remainder of his life was made up of periods of illness, travel, and literary work. From 1885 to 1886 he was state librarian of Ohio. He published *American Missionary Memorial, Including Biographical and Historical Sketches* (1853), and in 1862, *Jefferson at Monticello: the Private Life of Thomas Jefferson,* based upon information and unpublished documents furnished by Capt. Edmund Bacon, a former overseer of Jefferson's estate at Monticello. He contributed to periodicals and was a member of the New York Historical Society. The last two years of his life were spent in Bergen, N. Y., the place of his birth.

[Considerable autobiog. material is to be found in his writings; see also *Gen. Cat. of Union Theolog. Sem.* (1919); and the *Thirty-eighth* to the *Forty-third Ann. Report Am. Bible Soc.* (1854–59).]   H. E. S.

PIERZ, FRANZ (Nov. 20, 1785–Jan. 22, 1880), Roman Catholic missionary, was born near Kamnik in the Austrian province of Carniola. The Slovenian form of his family name was Pirc, but in the United States he used the spelling Pierz. Little is known of his parentage and early life. After an education in the gymnasium and the diocesan seminary in Laibach, he was ordained in 1813 and served successively thereafter three local parishes. He took a keen interest in agriculture and horticulture, and in 1830 published *Krajnski vertnar,* a work on gardening which has remained of importance not only among horticulturists but also among philologists because of its early use of a local dialect.

At the solicitation of a missionary among the Chippewa Indians, Pierz set out in 1835 for the United States as a missionary supported mainly by the Leopoldinen-Stiftung, a Viennese board of missions. His work for many years was with the Indians and settlers about the mission at Arbre Croche, now Harbor Springs, Mich. Prior to 1839, however, he served at Sault Ste. Marie and established important stations on Lake Superior. He was particularly successful in inducing the Indians to become an agricultural people. In 1852 he departed for the upper Mississippi, a large field hitherto neglected by his church. Despite his advanced age he traveled hundreds of miles every year to visit bands of Chippewa. His published reports were successful now, as his earlier letters from Michigan had been, in interesting Catholic Europe in the Indians and thus in providing funds for his work. When the Sioux rose against the whites in 1862, his influence helped to keep the Chippewa from rising also. With the aid of assistants whom he secured in Europe in 1863 he continued to labor among the Indians until 1871. In 1873 he returned to his native land, where he died.

He was an immigrant agent as well as a missionary. Perceiving that white men would inevitably settle close to his Indians, he determined to see that they were German Catholics. Accordingly he sent out a prospectus and published many letters describing central Minnesota in terms calculated to attract this class. The prospectus appeared in his *Die Indianer in Nord-Amerika* (1855), and together with his letters, printed in many European and American periodicals, brought great numbers of Germans to central Minnesota. He apparently published nothing in Ottawa or Chippewa, though his letters of 1843 and 1845 mention a life of Christ, a catechism with prayers and hymns, seventy Indian sermons, and a "Way of the Cross," ready or in preparation for printing.

[Sister Grace McDonald, "Father Francis Pierz, Missionary," *Minn. Hist.*, June 1929; unsigned article by John Seliskar, "The Reverend Francis Pireç, Indian Missionary," in *Acta et Dicta*, July 1911; Fr. Chrysostomus Verwyst, *Life and Letters of Rt. Rev. Frederic Baraga* (1900); A. I. Rezek, *Hist. of the Diocese of Sault Ste. Marie and Marquette*, vol. I (1906); Constant von Wurzbach, *Biographisches Lexikon des Kaiserthums Oesterreich*, vol. XXII (Vienna, 1870); many letters by Pierz in *Berichte der Leopoldinen-Stiftung* (Vienna), in *Annalen der Verbreitung des Glaubens* (Freiburg, Baden), and in *Wahrheitsfreund* (Cincinnati); a brief biography and original letters contrib. by the Rev. Hugo Bren, in *Zentralblatt and Social Justice*, Jan. 1934 ff.; miscellaneous items in the possession of the Minn. Hist. Soc.] G. L. N.

PIGGOT, ROBERT (May 20, 1795–July 23, 1887), stipple engraver, Episcopal clergyman, was born in New York City and at the age of seventeen went to Philadelphia, Pa., where he was apprenticed to David Edwin [*q.v.*] to learn the art of stipple engraving. When he became of age, he formed a partnership with his fellow student, Charles Goodman [*q.v.*], and together they engraved many plates for the *Port Folio*, the *Analectic*, and other publications. Virtually all of their works were signed Goodman & Piggot or C. Goodman & R. Piggot, but the former was the better engraver and artist. After a few years in business the firm was dissolved when the senior partner decided to study law. Piggot then opened a bookstore in Philadelphia and acted as agent to the Adult Sunday School of the city. He placed himself under the instruction of the Rev. James Wiltbank, who taught him the classical languages, and he received deacon's orders on Nov. 30, 1823. The same year he associated himself with the newly organized church of St. Matthew's, Francisville, Philadelphia, as lay reader, and in 1824, on the day the church was consecrated, he was elected its first rector, although he was not ordained a priest by Bishop William White until May 11, 1825. Before that

time he had resigned his rectorship and had accepted a call to another Pennsylvania church. He served in various Episcopal parishes in Pennsylvania and in Smyrna, Del., having become a missionary of the Society for the Advancement of Christianity in Pennsylvania. Later he went to Maryland, and after having had charge of several churches in that state, in 1869 became rector of the parish of the Holy Trinity, Sykesville, Md. He retired in 1883 and died in Sykesville, on July 23, 1887, at which time he was the last surviving clergyman of those ordained by the first bishop of Pennsylvania. On the occasion of the fiftieth anniversary of St. Matthew's Church, Francisville, in 1874, Piggot preached the memorial sermon in the church.

[D. M. Stauffer, *Am. Engravers upon Copper and Steel* (2 vols., 1907); W. S. Baker, *Am. Engravers* (1875); Mantle Fielding, *Am. Engravers upon Copper and Steel* (1917); F. S. Edmonds, *Hist. of St. Matthew's Ch., Francisville, Phila.* (1925); the *Churchman*, Aug. 6, 1887; *Baltimore American*, July 25, 1887.] J. J.

PIGGOTT, JAMES (*c.* 1739–Feb. 20, 1799), Illinois pioneer, was born in Connecticut and is said to have been a privateer in the fore part of the Revolution. In April 1776 he appears as a captain from Westmoreland County, Pa., to serve under Gen. Arthur St. Clair until Oct. 22, 1777. According to family tradition, ill health following the Lake Champlain march caused him to resign his commission and as a volunteer to accompany George Rogers Clark to Kaskaskia. Although it has not been substantiated by records ("Cahokia Records," *post*, p. 190), Reynolds says that Piggott was in command of Fort Jefferson, near the mouth of the Ohio, during the siege of the Chickasaws, which occurred in 1780. This was the year, according to Piggott's later testimony, in which he became a resident of Illinois ("Kaskaskia Records," *post*, p. 421). Whether he was the builder, in 1783, of "Piggott's Fort," a stockade for colonists at Grand Ruisseau, near what is now Columbia, Ill. (Reynolds, p. 59), or merely one of the settlers there ("Cahokia Records," p. 191), it is a matter of record that in 1787 he led a movement against the French authority for which he was placed in irons for twenty-four hours (Philbrick, *post*, p. cclxi). On Aug. 27 of that year he was one of the signers of the contract appointing Bartholomew Tardiveau agent to Congress ("Kaskaskia Records," p. 443), and May 23, 1790, he "and forty-five others" at Grand Ruisseau petitioned the government relative to claims for land which they had risked their lives to improve (*American State Papers, Documents . . . in Relation to the Public Lands*, I, 1834, p. 15).

With the arrival of St. Clair in the territory as governor in 1790 Piggott rose to the place of importance which he had yearned for under French control. Forthwith appointed a militia captain and justice of the peace at Cahokia, he was, Sept. 28, 1795, made judge of the common pleas. The next year as justice of the quarter sessions, he proclaimed the opening of the orphans' court. Meanwhile, 1792–95, he had built a bridge across the River Abbe, later Cahokia Creek, opposite St. Louis, opened a road to the Mississippi bank, and erected two log cabins for the convenience of travelers bound for the Louisiana territory, the origin of the present city of East St. Louis. Ferry service was the next step and this Piggott established in 1797, pledging to Zenon Trudeau, governor of Louisiana territory, "timber at lowest rates" and "products" in return for ferriage rights on the St. Louis side. Piggott's enterprise led Trudeau to make him an honorary citizen of St. Louis.

After operating the ferry for two years, Piggott died of "a fever" at his bark, and was buried, according to one belief, at Kaskaskia. His first wife, Reynolds relates, was buried within Fort Jefferson, during the siege; his second wife, Francies James of Virginia, who bore him eight children, survived him and married again. Threefold was Piggott's contribution to the establishment of American life in Illinois—as a wilderness breaker, as a pioneer officer in the territorial government, and as the founder of a business, which as the Wiggins ferry, became a most lucrative monopoly.

[See John Reynolds, *My Own Times* (1855); C. W. Alvord, "Cahokia Records," *Ill. State Hist. Lib. Colls.*, vol. II (1907) and "Kaskaskia Records," *Ibid.*, vol. V (1909); F. S. Philbrick, "The Laws of Indiana Territory, 1801–09," *Ibid.*, vol. XXI (1930); Robert A. Tyson, *Hist. of East St. Louis* (1875); and J. T. Scharf, *Hist. of St. Louis City and County* (2 vols., 1883). The Appendix to L. U. Reavis, *St. Louis: The Future Great City of the World* (1876), contains a historical lecture about the origin of East St. Louis by Dr. Isaac N. Piggott, James Piggott's son. Information for this sketch was supplied by Mrs. Alice Jones Wientge, of St. Louis, Piggott's great-great-granddaughter.]   I. D.

PIKE, ALBERT (Dec. 29, 1809–Apr. 2, 1891), lawyer, soldier, author, and exponent of Freemasonry, was born in Boston, Mass., the son of Benjamin and Sarah (Andrews) Pike. He was a descendant of John Pike, born in Landford, England, who emigrated to America with his wife, Dorothy Daye, and five children in 1635, and died at Salisbury, Mass. Soon after Albert's birth the Pikes returned to the family home in Byfield, and later moved to Newburyport, in the schools of which town and at an academy in Framingham, Mass., he received his early education. From 1824 to 1831 much of his time was spent in teaching and private study; in his spare moments he wrote poetry. He acquired an excellent knowledge of the classics and in his reminiscences he states that he spent a year at Harvard (*New Age Magazine*, August 1929, p. 462), but there is no record of his enrollment there, though in 1859 Harvard conferred upon him the honorary degree of A.M. As a teacher he was connected with schools in Gloucester, Fairhaven, and Newburyport. He had unbounded physical energy, an avid mind, an adventurous disposition, marked independence, and great determination.

The restraints of New England life becoming irksome, in March 1831, with little money and no very definite plans, he started West. Reaching St. Louis by various means of transportation, he then went to Independence, where he joined a party of hunters and traders going to Santa Fé. After some time in that town he accompanied another expedition into the Staked Plains, and finally arrived at Fort Smith, Ark., having passed through many hardships and exciting experiences. In 1833 he was teaching school in Pope County, Ark. During this year, under the *nom-de-plume* of "Casca," he wrote for the *Arkansas Advocate* of Little Rock a series of political articles, entitled "Intercepted Letters," supporting Robert Crittenden, a Whig, who was opposing Ambrose H. Sevier [*q.v.*], a Democrat, for election as delegate to Congress. These articles were of such merit that through Crittenden's influence the editor of the paper, Charles P. Bertrand, invited Pike to become his associate. He accepted the position and was also made an assistant clerk in the territorial legislature, then in session. On Oct. 10, 1834, he married Mary Ann, daughter of James Hamilton. She had some property, which enabled him to purchase an interest in the *Advocate*, and in 1835 he became sole owner and editor. In 1834 there was published in Boston his *Prose Sketches and Poems Written in the Western Country*. It contained a vividly written account of his recent adventures, "Narrative of a Journey in the Prairie," which also appeared as a serial in the *Advocate*, Apr. 17 to 19, 1835 (reprinted in *Publications of the Arkansas Historical Association*, vol. IV, 1917). Although a Massachusetts man, he supported the slavery provision in the Arkansas constitution of 1836, on the ground that since Arkansas bordered on slave states and was settled largely by slaveholders, freedom there would be inexpedient.

In 1837 he sold the *Advocate*, having in the meantime been licensed to practise law. In the years that followed he became one of the best-informed and most capable lawyers of the Southwest. He was the first reporter of the Arkansas supreme court, his work appearing in the first five volumes of *Reports* (1840–45). In 1842 he published *The Arkansas Form Book*, containing legal forms and a summary of ordinary legal principles. That same year he was admitted to practice before the United States Supreme Court. He took an active part in the Mexican War as commanding officer of a cavalry troop which he had recruited. His criticism of the conduct of the regiment commanded by Col. Archibald Yell [*q.v.*], published in the *Arkansas Gazette* in 1848, involved Pike in a duel with Lieutenant-Colonel John Selden Roane [*q.v.*]. Two shots were fired by each participant without either being hit, after which, through intervention of the surgeons, the affair was settled peaceably. (See account in the *Arkansas Gazette*, Apr. 2, 1893.) He was a stanch Whig in a Democratic stronghold, and later one of the prominent promoters of the Know-Nothing party in his section of the country. He believed himself to be the first to suggest a Pacific railroad convention and he vigorously advocated the building of a Southern line. In 1853 he transferred his practice to New Orleans but returned to Little Rock in 1857. Throughout these years his feelings frequently found expression in published verse.

His career during the Civil War was an unfortunate one. Although not friendly to slavery and claiming to be opposed to secession except as a last and necessary resource, he cast in his lot with the Confederacy rather than desert his friends and abandon his property. In the summer of 1861 he was sent as a commissioner to negotiate treaties with the Indian tribes west of Arkansas. In this enterprise he was partially successful. Later he was commissioned brigadier-general, and under orders of Nov. 22, 1861, the Indian country west of Arkansas and north of Texas was constituted the department of Indian Territory and Pike was assigned to command the same (*Official Records*, 1 ser. VIII, 690). It was his understanding, he claimed, that the Indians recruited would be used only in defense of their own territory. They were employed, however, in the battle of Pea Ridge, Ark., Mar. 7–8, 1862, where they played an inglorious part and committed some atrocities for which Pike was unjustly criticized. Feeling that he occupied an independent command and that the safety of the Indians was in his keeping, he resented exercise of authority over his area by Gen. Thomas C. Hindman [*q.v.*], in command of the Trans-Mississippi district. This resentment led to much friction between the two, and on July 3, 1862, Pike issued a printed circular regarding the situation, entitled *Letter to the President of the Confederate States*. President Davis wrote him under date of Aug. 9, that the publication of this circular was a grave military offense, and that if the purpose was to abate an evil "the mode taken was one of the slowest and worst that could have been adopted" (*Ibid.*, 1 ser. LIII, 822). On July 12, 1862, Pike resigned his commission, but his resignation was not accepted until Nov. 5. In the meantime he aired his grievances in letters to various officials, and under date of July 31, 1862, wrote an address to the chiefs and people of the Indian tribes (printed in *Official Records*, 1 ser. XIII, 869–71). The character of this address was such that Col. Douglas H. Cooper ordered his arrest and wrote President Davis that Pike was "either insane or untrue to the South" (*Ibid.*, 1 ser. LIII, 820–21). The arrest was never actually effected, however, and he was granted leave and permitted to return to his home. He was vigorous in denouncing the spirit and acts of his superiors and published *Charges and Specifications Preferred August 23, 1862, by Brigadier General Albert Pike, against Major General Thomas C. Hindman* (1863). In October, at the expiration of his leave, he attempted to resume command of the Indian department. On Nov. 3, General Hindman ordered his arrest, which in this instance was effected, for on Nov. 19 he wrote President Davis from Warren, Tex., that he was there a prisoner (*Ibid.*, 1 ser. XIII, 921–22). His resignation had before this been accepted and he was later released. During much of the remainder of the war he seems to have been in retirement in Arkansas and probably for a time in Texas, though for a brief period toward the close of hostilities he served as associate justice of the Arkansas supreme court.

For several years after the war he was something of a wanderer. His property had been confiscated and he was looked upon with suspicion both in the South and in the North. He went to New York in 1865, but fearing arrest on the charge of inciting the Indians to revolt, he fled to Canada. His friends made persistent efforts to secure his pardon, and on Aug. 30, 1865, President Johnson issued an order permitting him to return to his home on condition that he take the oath of allegiance and give his parole of honor that he would conduct himself as a loyal citizen. While so conducting himself he was not to be molested by civil or military authorities. These conditions he fulfilled. Indicted for treason by the circuit court of the Eastern District of

Arkansas, he pleaded the President's order. Apparently he was ultimately restored to full civil rights (*New Age Magazine*, June 1930, pp. 425–26; September 1930, p. 534). In 1867–68 he was in Memphis, Tenn., where he practised law and for a time was editor of *The Memphis Appeal*. In 1868 he moved to Washington, D. C. Here he continued his practice, was associate editor of *The Patriot* (1868–70), studied much and wrote much, and devoted a large part of his attention to the interests of Freemasonry.

He had been made a Mason in 1850, a Scottish Rite Mason in 1853, and in 1859 he was elected sovereign Grand Commander of the Supreme Grand Council, Southern Jurisdiction of the United States, an office which he held for thirty-two years. As an administrator, a student and interpreter of Masonry, and as an author, he rendered an invaluable service to Scottish Rite Masonry, becoming highly revered in the United States and widely known abroad. While his services were numerous and varied, his greatest achievements, perhaps, were the rewriting of the rituals, a work upon which he was laboriously engaged over a period of many years, and his *Morals and Dogma of the Ancient and Accepted Scottish Rite of Freemasonry* (1872, 1878, 1881, 1905).

More than six feet tall, of large frame and Jovian countenance, with flowing locks reaching to his shoulders, and a long beard, Pike presented an impressive appearance. His genius was many-sided and his mind ranged over a wide field of subjects. He had a working knowledge of Sanskrit, Hebrew, Greek, Latin, and French, and in his later days he spent much time in studying and translating Eastern writings. To periodicals he contributed numerous articles on diverse subjects. In his own profession he was not only an able practitioner but a student of the law. He prepared a work of considerable length, "Maxims of the Roman Law and Some of the Ancient French Law, as Expounded and Applied in Doctrine and Jurisprudence," which "had it been published, would have placed him in the front rank of American writers on Civil Law" (C. S. Lobingier, in *American Bar Association Journal*, April 1927, p. 208). His reputation as a poet was considerable. Early in his Arkansas career he had sent to *Blackwood's Edinburgh Magazine*, "Hymns to the Gods," which the editor, Christopher North (Dr. John Wilson), published in the June 1839 issue of that periodical with the comment: "These fine hymns . . . entitle their author to take his place in the highest order of his country's poets." They appear in *Hymns to the Gods and Other Poems* (1872), privately printed. A collection under the same title, also privately printed, appeared subsequently in two parts (part I, 1873; part II, 1882). He had previously issued *Nugæ* (1854), and after his death three volumes of selections—*Gen. Albert Pike's Poems* (1900), *Hymns to the Gods and Other Poems* (1916), and *Lyrics and Love Songs* (1916)—were published by his daughter, Lilian Pike Roome. Time has not confirmed Christopher North's rating of Pike as a poet. He had imagination and skill in versification, but was endowed with a better sense of rhythm than of euphony. Some of his poems have a lusty vigor, and of the different versions of "Dixie" his is perhaps the best. His work as a whole, however, is uneven, has little originality, and is frequently reminiscent of other writers.

Pike died in the house of the Scottish Rite Temple, Washington, in his eighty-second year. He left a written communication directing that his body be cremated and his ashes be put around the roots of two acacia trees in front of the home of the Supreme Council; but these instructions were not complied with, and he was buried in Oak Hill Cemetery, Washington. The Supreme Council, Southern Jurisdiction, erected a heroic statue of him in Washington on a reservation designated for the purpose by Congress. His wife had died in 1876 and he had lost three children, one son having been killed in the Confederate service and one drowned in the Arkansas; two sons and a daughter survived him.

[Pike's unpublished MSS. are in the library of the Supreme Council, Scottish Rite of Freemasonry, Southern Jurisdiction, Washington, D. C.; W. L. Boyden, *Bibliog. of the Writings of Albert Pike* (1921), lists published and unpublished works; extracts from his manuscript autobiography are published by C. S. Lobingier in *New Age Mag.*, Aug. 1929–Sept. 1930; files of this magazine contain much other biographical material; see also J. L. Elwell, *The Story of Byfield* (1904); W. F. Pope, *Early Days in Ark.* (1895); John Hallum, *Biog. and Pictorial Hist. of Ark.* (1887); Fay Hempstead, *A Pictorial Hist. of Ark.* (1890); D. Y. Thomas, *Ark. in War and Reconstruction* (1926); *Ark. and Its People* (1930), vol. IV; W. S. MacNutt and others, *A Hist. of Ark.* (1932); *War of the Rebellion: Official Records (Army)*; C. A. Evans, *Confederate Military Hist.* (1899), vols. IX, X; F. W. Allsopp, *Albert Pike* (1928); *Evening Star* (Washington, D. C.), Apr. 2, 3, 1891.]   H. E. S.

PIKE, JAMES SHEPHERD (Sept. 8, 1811–Nov. 29, 1882), journalist, author, was born in Calais, Me., the son of William and Hannah (Shepherd) Pike, and died in that town in his seventy-second year while en route from his home at Robbinston, Me., to the South for the winter months. He was a descendant of John Pike and his son Robert [*q.v.*], who came to Massachusetts from England in 1635. His parents were among the early settlers of Calais, where his father was conspicuous in town affairs and was instrumental in establishing the first schools (1810). In these, maintained with difficulty through the War of 1812, young Pike received his only formal education, which he later described as "not worth mentioning." The sudden death of his father in 1818 left the family in straitened circumstances, and, at the age of fourteen, James entered upon a series of business ventures in his native town, first as a clerk, later in a grain and shipping business, and in 1836, as cashier of the short-lived St. Croix Bank.

By 1840 his success in business was such as to permit him to devote himself to the more congenial work of journalism, in which he had already shown an interest by editing the *Boundary Gazette and Calais Advertiser* (Apr. 12, 1835–July 28, 1836), distinguished for its Whig sympathies and its early advocacy of Harrison for the presidency. Despite his limited education, he had acquired literary taste, a vigorous and picturesque diction, and forceful style. After 1840 he lived during the winter months in Boston, New York, and Washington, becoming actively associated with newspaper work. As correspondent for the *Portland Advertiser,* and especially for the *Boston Courier,* he became familiarly known through letters signed "J. S. P." As Washington correspondent for the *Courier* he described with characteristic vigor and effectiveness the persons and events in Washington during the debates on the compromise measures of 1850. Of Henry Clay, on the occasion of the Compromise speech, he said, "he was neither profound, brilliant, nor soul-stirring," and he characterized Robert Toombs as "burly, choleric, and determined," while Foote was described as "the *coltsfoot* of the bed of senatorial eloquence." The embarrassed editor of the *Courier* was moved to explain that "we do not look singly at the dark side, which he presents in his letter" (*Boston Courier,* Apr. 10, 1850, p. 2). In 1850 he was the Whig candidate for Congress from the seventh district of the state of Maine in opposition to T. J. D. Fuller. Although this district had been strongly Democratic, the seat was closely contested and it was not until ten days after the election that Fuller's victory was assured (*Portland Advertiser,* Sept. 11–13, 1850). In April of that year Pike was invited by Horace Greeley to become a regular correspondent of the *New York Tribune,* and in 1852 he was made an associate editor. Most of the time between 1850 and 1860 he was Washington correspondent for the *Tribune.* His letters during that period, together with the earlier letters to the *Boston*

Courier, are the most interesting of his journalistic achievements, a vivid and colorful description of official Washington during the decade preceding the Civil War. Widely quoted, bitterly attacked or enthusiastically praised, they exerted a profound influence upon public opinion and gave to their author national prominence, first as an uncompromising anti-slavery Whig, and later as an ardent Republican.

When Lincoln was elected to the presidency he named Pike as minister resident to The Hague, and on Mar. 28, 1861, the Senate confirmed his appointment. He arrived at The Hague on June 1, 1861. His diplomatic correspondence reveals him chiefly as an observer of the economic effects of the Civil War upon Europe. The relatively quiet life in a country which offered but few diplomatic problems proved uncongenial, and he returned to the United States on May 17, 1866, although his recall was not presented to the King of the Netherlands until Dec. 1. The remaining years of his life were devoted chiefly to writing, to collecting and publishing his earlier correspondence, and to the attractions of his summer home in Robbinston, Me. He was twice married: first, in 1837, to Charlotte Grosvenor of Pomfret, Conn.; second, in 1855, to Elizabeth Ellicott of Avondale, Chester County, Pa. He published successively *The Financial Crisis: Its Evils and Their Remedy* (1867); *The Restoration of the Currency* (1868); and *Horace Greeley in 1872* (1873). All of these works were based upon what he had previously written for the *New York Tribune.* In 1873 he published his *Chief Justice Chase,* and in the following year, *The Prostrate State: South Carolina under Negro Government,* the result of his observation of the working of the reconstruction government in South Carolina, also published in a Dutch translation in 1875. In 1875 his *Contributions to the Financial Discussion, 1874–1875,* appeared, and was followed in 1879 by *The New Puritan,* a study of seventeenth-century New England, based primarily upon the career of Robert Pike, and by *First Blows of the Civil War,* a contemporaneous exposition of the ten years of preliminary conflict in the United States from 1850 to 1860.

[G. F. Talbot, "James Shepherd Pike," *Colls. and Proc. Me. Hist. Soc.,* 2 ser. I (1890); *New-England Hist. and Geneal. Reg.,* Apr. 1883; C. W. Evans, *Biog. and Hist. Accounts of the Fox, Ellicott, and Evans Families* (1882). Joseph Griffin, *Hist. of the Press of Me.* (1872); I. C. Knowlton, *Annals of Calais, Me., and St. Stephen, New Brunswick* (1875); *Papers Relating to Foreign Affairs, 1861–67* (1861–68); *Portland Advertiser,* Apr. 10–20, 1850, Nov. 29, 1882; *Boston Courier,* esp. Apr. 10, 1850, and Nov. 30, 1882; *N. Y. Tribune,* Mar. 29, 1861; *Sun* (N. Y.), Nov. 30, 1882.]   T. C. V–C.

PIKE, MARY HAYDEN GREEN (Nov. 30, 1824–Jan. 15, 1908), novelist, was born in Eastport, Me., the daughter of Deacon Elijah Dix and Hannah Claflin (Hayden) Green, both of early Puritan stock. The family moved to Calais, Me., when she was quite young, and there she attended public school. Her girlhood was marked by strong religious influences. At the age of twelve she formally joined the Baptist Church, the immersion being performed after ice had been cut from the river for the occasion. At the Charlestown (Massachusetts) Female Seminary, from which she graduated in 1843, her religious convictions deepened under the leadership of its president, the Rev. William Phillips. Abolitionism soon became a focus for her spiritual energy. In 1846 she married Frederick Augustus Pike, a lawyer of Calais, who became a member of the Maine state legislature. Her anti-slavery sentiments were further confirmed by her husband's opinions and by the views of Hannibal Hamlin and James G. Blaine, intimate family friends. After a residence in Augusta, she visited in the South where she made direct observations of slavery. She lived in Washington between 1861 and 1869, when her husband was a member of Congress. The loss of her only brother in the war intensified her feeling against slavery.

Mrs. Pike's first book, *Ida May* (1854), which appeared under the name of Mary Langdon, dealt with a child of wealthy parents who was sold into slavery. It was melodramatic in style and episode, and more than sixty thousand copies were sold in America. It probably derived some of its popularity from the turmoil made by Mrs. Stowe's *Uncle Tom's Cabin*. It was widely read abroad and was reprinted in London and Leipzig. The cruelty of race discrimination is the theme of *Caste* (1856), in which a quadroon girl is forbidden to marry her betrothed who is a white man. This novel appeared under the pen-name Sydney A. Story, Jr.; it was not so popular as *Ida May*. Her next book, *Agnes* (1858), "by the author of *Ida May*," attempted a truthful picture of the Indian interwoven with a plot of the American Revolution. These were her best-known works. At the close of her husband's term in Congress she accompanied him on a journey to Europe. They maintained their residence in Calais, Me., until his death in 1886. She was left a considerable estate and lived for the next nine years with her adopted daughter in Plainfield, N. J. She had become interested in painting and did some creditable landscape canvases. The closing years of her life were spent in retirement and poor health. She lived with her sister in Baltimore and occupied herself in various religious works. She died in Baltimore at the home of her niece, Katherine C. Oudesluys, and was interred at Calais, Me., beside her husband.

[There is considerable confusion in accounts of Mrs. Pike concerning her printed works, caused by erroneous identification of her with a niece and others. Information has been derived chiefly from family correspondence. For printed sources see: I. C. Knowlton, *Annals of Calais, Me., and St. Stephen, New Brunswick* (1875); S. A. Allibone, *A Critical Dict. of English Lit.; and British and Am. Authors*, vol. II (1871); *Boston Transcript*, Jan. 12, 1889; and the *Sun* (Baltimore), Jan. 16, 1908.]   R. W. B.
E. P. W.

PIKE, NICOLAS (Oct. 6, 1743–Dec. 9, 1819), teacher, arithmetician, was born at Somersworth, N. H., the son of Rev. James and Sarah (Gilman) Pike, and a descendant of John Pike who emigrated from Landford, England, to Massachusetts in 1635. Nicolas graduated from Harvard College in 1766, and later received the degree of A.M. there. He married in Newburyport, Mass., Hannah Smith, and between Jan. 1, 1769, and Jan. 7, 1778, five sons were born to them. Hannah died July 7, 1778, and on Jan. 9 of the following year Pike married Eunice Smith, by whom he had one son. For many years he was master of the Newburyport grammar school, occupying that position at least as early as 1773. He also conducted a private evening school (1774–86) and for a time, a school for young ladies. He was town clerk of Newburyport from Mar. 14, 1776 to 1780, served as selectman in 1782–83, and for a considerable period was justice of the peace. Testimony concerning the quality of Pike's teaching is given by Gen. Henry Sewall, who stated that in 1769 and several years previously he had studied under Pike at York, in what is now Maine, particularly "arithmetic and trigonometry." Pike, Sewall says, made some improvement in the school there "with the accession of a new spelling-book, but did not make grammar and geography any part of school studies" (letter printed in *New-England Historical and Genealogical Register, post*, p. 310).

Pike's fame rests chiefly upon his treatise, *A New and Complete System of Arithmetick, Composed for the Use of the Citizens of the United States . . .* (1788). In the year 1793 he published a smaller work, *Abridgement of the New and Complete System of Arithmetick, Composed for the Use, and Adapted to the Commerce of the Citizens of the United States . . . For the Use of Schools, and Will be found to be An Easy and Sure Guide to the Scholar.* Both were first printed by John Mycall in

Newburyport, but the second was printed for Isaiah Thomas [*q.v.*], who acted as publisher and distributor. This famous publisher continued to issue the book for many years. Three years elapsed between the recommendation of the original edition written by Benjamin West, a well-known teacher and mathematician, and the book's appearance. Pike was able to secure, also, the hearty recommendations of the work by the presidents of Yale, Harvard, and Dartmouth, several of their professors of mathematics, and Governor Bowdoin of Massachusetts. Even Washington gave a guarded recommendation when a copy was sent to him (quoted in Blake, *post,* pp. 327–28). The author's confidence in the value of his work was evidenced by the fact that he registered as author in Pennsylvania, South Carolina, Massachusetts, and New York, such registration serving as copyright notice. His confidence was fully justified, for the original work went through eight editions, and the *Abridgement* continued to appear until 1830. He also edited, 1794, Daniel Fenning's *The Ready Reckoner or the Trader's Useful Assistant.* On Aug. 20, 1788, he was elected a fellow of the American Academy of Arts and Sciences.

Pike was the first American arithmetician to attain wide popularity in the field of school textbooks. In his arithmetics the orderly presentation of the subject to children is stressed, the Federal money (then new) is given adequate treatment, and the applications of arithmetic to business are well indicated. The larger edition was an admirable effort, furnishing excellent material in geometry and trigonometry; the abridged edition was particularly well suited to instruction in elementary schools. In these textbooks Pike made an enduring contribution to American education.

[*Vital Records of Newburyport, Mass.* (1911); Arthur Gilman, *The Gilman Family* (1869); Joshua Coffin, *A Sketch of the Hist. of Newbury, Newburyport, and West Newbury, from 1635 to 1845* (1845); J. J. Currier, *Hist. of Newburyport, Mass., 1764–1909* (2 vols., 1906–09); E. V. Blake, *Hist. of Newburyport* (1854); *New-England Hist. and Geneal. Reg.,* July 1880; *Boston Daily Advertiser,* Dec. 11, 1819.]

L. C. K.

PIKE, ROBERT (*c.* 1616–Dec. 12, 1708), colonial official, the second son of John Pike and Dorothy Daye, was born in Whiteparish, Wilts, England, probably spent part of his childhood in Landford, and arrived in Boston with his father, his brother John, and three sisters, on June 3, 1635. They went first to Ipswich, but soon afterward moved to the newly settled town of Newbury, Mass., where Robert lived until 1639, when he joined the colony which founded Salisbury. He took the oath as freeman on May 17, 1637,

just before the exciting election at which Winthrop defeated Vane for governor, and is said to have been of the Winthrop faction. On Apr. 3, 1641, he married Sarah Sanders, and they had eight children; she died Nov. 1, 1679, and on Oct. 30, 1684, he married in Salisbury Martha Moyce, widow of George Goldwyer.

Pike deserves a high place among the defenders of civil and religious liberty in colonial Massachusetts. Elected to the General Court in 1648, he criticized it in 1653 because it made preaching by one not a regularly ordained minister a misdemeanor. The law was designed to prevent certain Baptists from exhorting in the absence of a minister. For his action, which was also to the advantage of the Quakers, he was arraigned before the General Court, tried, convicted, fined, and disfranchised. As a result of his protest, however, the General Court at its next session repealed the law. Nevertheless, Pike's disfranchisement remained and fifteen of the numerous petitioners in his behalf were bound over for trial in the county courts. Whether they were actually tried or punished does not appear. Pike's civil disabilities were removed in 1657. He was immediately elected by the people of Salisbury to represent them again in the General Court. In 1675 he was engaged in a controversy with his pastor, John Wheelwright [*q.v.*], who sent him a document containing criticisms of his conduct and a warning that he might be excommunicated. Pike, as magistrate, summoned Wheelwright to appear before him to account for the document. Wheelwright then excommunicated Pike. Appeals to the General Court resulted in the admonition of both parties, the lifting of the excommunication, and the receiving back of Pike into the fellowship of the church. In 1692, at the height of the witchcraft delusion, Pike raised his voice against the character of the legal evidence upon which the convictions were based. The argument is contained in a letter addressed to Magistrate Jonathan Corwin **and signed by the initials, "R. P."** Though attributed by some to Robert Paine, the evidence indicates, according to Upham (*post*), that Robert Pike was the author. The argument was directed not to proving that witchcraft was a delusion, but to stressing the invalidity of spectre testimony. "Is the Devil a competent witness?" Pike asks. Pike's biographer describes this letter as a cool, close, and powerful argumentative appeal to the judges who were trying the witchcraft cases.

In spite of his controversies with the powers of authority, Pike was not fundamentally opposed to the existing régime and was evidently valued as a man of force and character. He served as major in the Indian wars. During a period of fifty years, except for short intervals, he held public office continuously. In 1688–89, after the revolution in England and the deposition of Andros in Massachusetts, Pike was elected near the head of the poll at a popular election of magistrates. Later, when a list of appointees to fill the same offices was decided on by the Crown, Pike's name was on the list though the names of several of his conspicuous colleagues were omitted. From 1689 to 1696 he was a member of the Governor's Council. He was one of a group who bought the island of Nantucket from Thomas Mayhew [q.v.] in 1659 and had pecuniary interests there at the time of his death. He appears to have lived and died in comparative affluence. He headed the list of commoners of Salisbury after the minister, paid the largest tax in 1652, and he and his wife were first in the list of members of the Salisbury church in 1687. He educated his son John, later minister at Dover, N. H., at Harvard, and defrayed the expenses of a medical education for his grandson Robert. After 1696 he retired to private life and was engaged in giving away to his heirs the property which he had accumulated during his lifetime.

[D. W. Hoyt, *The Old Families of Salisbury and Amesbury, Mass.* (3 vols., 1897–1917); Joshua Coffin, *A Sketch of the Hist. of Newbury, Newburyport, and West Newbury from 1635–1845* (1845); J. S. Macy, *Geneal. of the Macy Family from 1635–1868* (1868); J. S. Pike, *The New Puritan . . . : Some Account of the Life of Robert Pike* (1879); *Records of the Pike Family Asso.*, 1900–1901 and 1902; James Savage, *A Geneal. Dict. of the First Settlers of New England*, vol. III (1861), pp. 436–37; C. W. Upham, *Salem Witchcraft* (1867), vol. II.]   H. S. W.
                                        R. M. W.

PIKE, ZEBULON MONTGOMERY (Jan. 5, 1779–Apr. 27, 1813), soldier, explorer, was bred to a military career. His father, Major Zebulon Pike, served in the Revolution and afterward as an officer in the United States Army; an ancestor, Capt. John Pike, had fought in the early colonial wars; he was a founder of Woodbridge, N. J., in 1666, and the son of John Pike, first of the family in America, who emigrated to New England in 1635. Zebulon Montgomery Pike, whose mother was Isabella Brown, was born at Lamberton, now a part of Trenton, N. J. His childhood was spent in New Jersey and Pennsylvania, where he attended country school. While yet a boy he entered his father's company as a cadet, and at twenty was commissioned a first lieutenant. For several years he served with the frontier army, restlessly awaiting an opportunity to distinguish himself. At length it came, when Gen. James Wilkinson [q.v.] directed him to lead an exploring party to the source of the Mississippi. At the head of a company of twenty men Pike set out from St. Louis on Aug. 9, 1805, with four months' provisions stored away in his seventy-foot keelboat. When they were some distance beyond the Falls of St. Anthony, winter weather set in. Leaving some of the men in a rude stockade, Pike and the others continued the journey, dragging their goods on sleds. They reached what Pike mistakenly took for the source of the river, and after visiting some British trading posts and holding councils with the Indians of the region, returned to St. Louis on Apr. 30, 1806.

The young lieutenant was soon dispatched upon a longer and more important expedition, setting out from St. Louis on July 15, 1806. He was instructed to explore the headwaters of the Arkansas and Red rivers and to reconnoitre the Spanish settlements of New Mexico, being warned to "move with great circumspection . . . and to prevent any alarm or offence" (Coues, *post*, II, 563). After visiting the Pawnee villages on the Republican River, Pike (whose promotion to a captaincy occurred by routine on Aug. 12, 1806) moved up the Arkansas to the site of the present Pueblo, Colo. Here, on a side trip, he made an unsuccessful attempt to reach the summit of the peak that bears his name. After exploring South Park and the head of the Arkansas, he turned southward, seeking the source of the Red River. He crossed the Sangre de Cristo Mountains and on the Conejos branch of the Rio Grande constructed a fort of cottonwood logs. The Spaniards of New Mexico, learning of his presence within their territory, sent a body of troops to fetch him to Santa Fé. He acceded without opposition, for he desired to visit the region and study its geography and resources. From Santa Fé he was taken on to Chihuahua, where he was examined by the commandante general. Here he was well treated, except that his papers were taken from him. (These were destined to rest for a hundred years in the Mexican archives and then to be discovered by an American scholar; see H. E. Bolton, in *American Historical Review*, April 1908, especially p. 523, and "Papers of Zebulon M. Pike, 1806–07," *Ibid.*, July 1908. The papers have since been returned to the United States and are now in the Archives Division of the Adjutant-General's Office, in the War Department.)

After returning to the United States, Pike found his name coupled, in some quarters, with the Burr-Wilkinson scheme for empire in the Southwest. There seems little doubt that Wilkinson ordered the tour with the expectation that its findings would be helpful in promoting his designs, but whether or not young Pike was aware of the connection cannot be determined. He protested his innocence and Henry Dearborn, the secretary of war, in a formal statement gave him a clean slate. Nevertheless, historians continue to differ in the conclusions they draw from the circumstantial evidence. The information Pike gathered was of value to his government, his conduct was not incompatible with patriotic motives, and his subsequent career evidences genuine patriotism. He was commissioned major in 1808, colonel in 1812, and, following the outbreak of the second war with Great Britain, brigadier-general in 1813. When the attack on York (now Toronto), Canada, was launched in April of that year the immediate command of the troops was entrusted to Pike. He led his men to victory, but was killed in the assault (Apr. 27) when the enemy's powder magazine exploded. He had married in 1801 Clarissa Brown, daughter of Gen. John Brown of Kentucky. Several children were born to them, only one of whom, a daughter, reached maturity. She married Symmes Harrison, a son of William Henry Harrison [q.v.]. In 1810 Pike published *An Account of Expeditions to the Sources of the Mississippi and through the Western Parts of Louisiana*, which is the principal source for the story of his explorations. A London edition was published in 1811, and the work was translated into French (1812), Dutch (1812), and German (1813).

[Biographies include *Zebulon Pike's Arkansas Jour.* (1932), ed. by S. H. Hart and A. B. Hulbert; Henry Whiting, "Life of Zebulon Montgomery Pike," in Jared Sparks, *The Lib. of Am. Biog.*, 2 ser., vol. V (1845); Elliott Coues, *The Expeditions of Zebulon Montgomery Pike* (3 vols., 1895); article in *Analectic Mag.*, Nov. 1814, copied in the Supplement to vol. VII (1814–15) of *Niles' Weekly Register*, in the appendix to *Naval Biography* (1815), and in J. M. Niles, *The Life of Oliver Hazard Perry* (1820). See also *Niles' Weekly Register*, June 5, 1813, Oct. 28, 1815; I. J. Cox, "Opening the Santa Fé Trail," *Mo. Hist. Rev.*, Oct. 1930; *Records of the Pike Family Asso. of America*, 1900–04. A contemporary Spanish sketch of the Pike expedition, with collateral correspondence, is in the Archivo Histórico Nacional at Madrid, and a transcript of this is in the Library of Congress.] L. R. H.

PILAT, IGNAZ ANTON (June 27, 1820–Sept. 17, 1870), landscape gardener, was born at St. Agatha, Austria. He received a general education of collegiate rank at the University of Vienna, studied at the botanical gardens connected with the university and also at the Imperial Botanical Gardens at Schönbrunn, and for some years subsequently remained connected with the latter garden. His first important commission, and probably his greatest Austrian work, was the laying out of a park for the famous Prince Metternich. Political troubles induced him to come to America in 1848, and the years immediately following he spent largely in the South, where his name is connected with the laying out of the grounds of several estates in Georgia, including the garden of the Cumming-Langdon house at Augusta. During this period he also made a brief visit to Vienna, where he was appointed director of the Botanical Gardens, but he resigned in either 1856 or 1857 at the call of the commissioners of Central Park, New York City.

Pilat's botanical survey of the Central Park site, made in collaboration with Charles Rawolle, resulted in the publication of a *Catalogue of Plants Gathered in August and September 1857 in the Ground of the Central Park* (1857), a thirty-four-page pamphlet. A later survey entitled "Catalogue of Trees, Shrubs, and Herbaceous Plants on the Central Park, Dec. 31, 1861, with the Months of Flowering and Fruiting of such as have Conspicuous Blossoms or Fruits," was published in the *Seventh Annual Report* of the Board of Commissioners of Central Park, covering the year 1863. These surveys and a book on elementary botany, issued in Austria, were his only publications.

His lasting memorial is his work on Central Park, where his experience and knowledge of plant materials, his cultivated taste, and his great zeal resulted in his successful interpretation of the plans of Frederick Law Olmsted and Calvert Vaux [qq.v.]. The landscape architect Samuel Parsons was of the opinion that neither Olmsted's nor Vaux's knowledge of plants was sufficient to enable them to work out the details of the planting without the assistance of a plant expert who was also a landscape gardener (Parsons, *post*). That Pilat, a true artist, was of the greatest assistance to the designers is attested by themselves. Olmsted and Vaux having resigned as landscape architects of Central Park in May 1863 were reappointed to the position in 1865 and at that time wrote to Pilat as follows: ". . . Before going on to the work again, we desire, as artists, to express our thanks to you, a brother artist, for the help you have so freely rendered to the design in our absence" (*Frederick Law Olmsted, Landscape Architect*, ed. by F. L. Olmsted, Jr., and Theodora Kimball, vol. II, 1928, p. 76).

In 1870 the Board of Commissioners of Central Park was dissolved and its work was taken over by the newly organized Department of Public Parks whose first annual report (1870–71) contains Pilat's plans for the improvement of several of the smaller parks and squares of the city, among them the plan for the development of Mount Morris Park. At the time of his death in 1870 preliminary planting sketches of most of the parks under improvement had been completed. During the last years of his life he also engaged in private practice, doing professional work for William Cullen Bryant, the Massachusetts Agricultural College, Cyrus W. Field, and others. He died at his home in New York City of consumption, thought to have resulted from his untiring devotion to the interests of the Central Park and the exposure consequent thereon. He was survived by a widow, Clara L. (Rittler) Pilat, and by five children.

[Unpublished data in possession of Pilat's son, Oliver I. Pilat, and his nephew, Carl F. Pilat; I. N. Phelps Stokes, *Iconography of Manhattan Island*, III, (1918), 723; Mabel Parsons, *Memories of Samuel Parsons* (1926); Alice G. B. Lockwood, *Gardens of Colony and State* (Garden Club of America, 1934), vol. II; E. H. Hall, "Central Park in the City of New York," App. G, in *Sixteenth Ann. Report, 1911, Am. Scenic and Hist. Preservation Soc.* (1911); "New York City, Parks," in *Twentieth Ann. Report . . . Am. Scenic and Hist. Preservation Soc.* (1915); *Bull. Torrey Botanical Club*, Sept. 1870; *N. Y. Times*, Sept. 20, 1870; *N. Y. Herald*, Sept. 20, 1870; *N. Y. Tribune*, Sept. 20 and 21, 1870; *N. Y. Evening Post*, Sept. 19 and 21, 1870.]   K. McN.

PILCHER, JOSHUA (Mar. 15, 1790–June 5, 1843), fur trader, superintendent of Indian affairs, the son of Joshua and Nancy Pilcher, was born in Culpeper County, Va., to which his grandfather is said to have emigrated early in the eighteenth century. The family removed to Fayette County, Ky., where the father died in 1810. The son studied medicine but soon drifted into the mercantile business and the fur trade. He removed to St. Louis from Nashville, Tenn., about 1815. He became senior warden of the Missouri lodge of Masons organized under a Tennessee charter approved on Oct. 8, 1816. With others, by consent of the legislature, he conducted a lottery for the benefit of this lodge and paid prizes aggregating $60,000. In St. Louis he was associated in busines with N. S. Anderson and, after the latter's death, became a partner of Thomas F. Riddick, a relative, under the name of Riddick & Pilcher. He was one of the directors of the Bank of St. Louis.

He joined in the reorganization of the Missouri Fur Company in 1819, and in 1820 he became president after the death of Manuel Lisa [*q.v.*]. In 1823 he was conspicuous in Henry Leavenworth's campaign against the Arikara Indians. He went on yearly expeditions into the Indian country and spent three years, from 1827 to 1830, with an outfit of forty-five men trading and trapping, going up the Platte River to its source, and penetrating the country beyond the Rocky Mountains. On this journey he was indefatigable and obtained information of great

value for subsequent expeditions. Joining the western department of the American Fur Company after the dissolution of the Missouri Fur Company, he took charge of their post near Council Bluffs in 1831. He spent a number of years in the fur trade of the Upper Missouri and acquired a knowledge of the various tribes of that region. In 1837 he became Indian agent for the Upper Missouri tribes, having served several years previously in similar capacity for the Sioux of the Missouri, Cheyenne, and Ponca. When William Clark [*q.v.*] died, Pilcher succeeded him as superintendent of Indian affairs and served from Mar. 4, 1839, until Sept. 6, 1841. He was intelligent, industrious, and liberal. He was very enterprising and gave vitality to all undertakings in which he was engaged. He was never married, though he was once on the verge of a duel over a young lady to whom he was engaged. He was a devoted friend of Thomas H. Benton and consequently drew the opposition of Benton's enemies. In 1817 he was his second in Benton's first duel with Charles Lucas. In his will he left a note of Benton's for $3500 to the senator's daughter and his dueling pistols to Benton's son. He died in St. Louis of lung trouble.

[St. Louis Probate Court Records; John Dougherty and Chouteau collections in Lib. of Mo. Hist. Soc.; H. M. Chittenden, *The Am. Fur Trade of the Far West* (1902), vols. I, II; F. L. Billon, *Annals of St. Louis . . . 1804-1821* (1888); *Mo. Grand Lodge Bulletin*, Nov. 1927, pp. 167–68, Aug. 1928, pp. 132–38; J. H. S. Ardery, *Ky. Records*, vol. I (1926); Doane Robinson, "Official Correspondence of the Leavenworth Expedition . . . in 1823," *S. D. Hist. Colls.*, vol. I (1902); *Am. State Papers: Indian Affairs*, vol. II (1834); M. C. Pilcher, *Hist. Sketches of the Campbell, Pilcher, and Kindred Families* (copr. 1911); *Mo. Gazette and Public Advertiser* (St. Louis), Aug. 24, 1816, Mar. 29, 1817; *Mo. Intelligencer* (Franklin), Nov. 25, Dec. 2, 9, 16, 1823; *Mo. Reporter* (St. Louis), June 8, 1843; *Mo. Republican* (St. Louis), June 7, 1843.]   S. M. D.

PILCHER, PAUL MONROE (Apr. 11, 1876–Jan. 4, 1917), surgeon and urologist, was born in Brooklyn, N. Y., the son of Lewis Stephen Pilcher, himself a distinguished surgeon, and Martha S. (Phillips) Pilcher. After studying at the Brooklyn Polytechnic Institute, he entered the University of Michigan where he graduated with the degree of B.S. in 1898. Two years later he received the degree of M.D. from the College of Physicians and Surgeons in New York. For two years following graduation, he was an intern in the Seney Hospital, Brooklyn, of which institution his father was senior surgeon. He then went abroad and for a year studied in clinics in Göttingen, Vienna, and Berlin, his work being chiefly in pathology and in the diagnostic use of the cystoscope. While in Europe he came under the influence and teachings of Koenig, Orth, Nitze, and Von Fritsch.

Returning to Brooklyn in 1903, he received appointments to the Seney, German, St. John's, and Jewish hospitals. He resigned these positions in 1910, however, to join his father and brothers in the development of a private hospital. With a splendid surgical training as a background, Pilcher worked with enthusiasm and soon became well known and respected for his thoroughness and skill. He introduced methods for the investigation of patients which have been widely adopted by others. His frequent visits to clinics kept him well-informed as to medical progress elsewhere. His *Practical Cystoscopy and the Diagnosis of Surgical Diseases of the Kidneys and Urinary Bladder* (1911) went through two editions and was widely acclaimed. Besides being an exposition on the comparatively new science of cystoscopy, it was written in a clear, lucid style that reflected a highly cultured background. Following a visit to Copenhagen, he published *Abdominal Surgery, Clinical Lectures for Students and Physicians* (1914), a translation of the work of N. T. Rovsing. He also contributed an important chapter, entitled "Prostatic Obstructions," to *Modern Urology* (1918), edited by Hugh Cabot. He was also the author of many scientific contributions to medical publications, and from 1907 to 1911, edited the *Long Island Medical Journal*. He was operating surgeon at Eastern Long Island Hospital, Greenport; chairman of the section in surgery of the New York State Medical Society; and a member of numerous other professional societies.

Although he died of pneumonia at the comparatively early age of forty, he had already won recognition both as a skilful surgeon and by reason of his original researches in urology, which were pioneer work of their kind in the United States. In 1905 he married Mary Finlay of Montclair, N. J. She, with their two sons, survived him.

[*Annals of Surgery*, May 1917; *Long Island Medic. Jour.*, May 1917; H. A. Kelly and W. L. Burrage, *Am. Medic. Biogs.* (1920); *Trans. Am. Surgic. Asso.*, vol. XXXV (1917); *N. Y. Times*, Jan. 5, 1917.]

G. M. L.

PILKINGTON, JAMES (Jan. 4, 1851–Apr. 25, 1929), athlete, was born in Cavendish, Windsor County, Vt., the son of Thomas Pilkington, a farmer, and his wife, Anne Cusack. He never revisited his birthplace, and his earliest recollections were of Hillsboro, Highland County, Ohio, where his parents settled while he was still an infant. He lost no time in growing up. Giving his age as fifteen, he enlisted June 5, 1863, as bugler in the 24th Independent Battery of Ohio Volunteer Light Artillery and spent the next two years guarding prisoners on Johnson's Island near Sandusky and at Camp Douglas, Ill. When his battery was mustered out in 1865, he set forth in search of the adventure that the war had denied him, wandered through the Southwest, tarried awhile in New Orleans, worked his way up the Mississippi, tried life in Chicago, and finally reached New York, which was his home thereafter. For a number of years he was on the police force. Endowed with a superb body and the generous instincts of a great sportsman, he excelled at boxing, wrestling, rowing, bowling, trapshooting, and all track and field sports. With William Muldoon [*q.v.*] he was one of the founders of the Police Athletic Association and the Empire Athletic Association. On Mar. 11, 1882, at the old Madison Square Garden, he won the national amateur heavyweight boxing and wrestling championships, competing in and winning both events on the same night. He was most famous, however, as an oarsman. At a regatta at Greenwood Lake, N. J., in July 1882, he rowed in singles, doubles, six-oared gig, and eight-oared shell on a mile-and-one-half course, his boat winning every race. As the doubles was first declared a dead heat and had to be rowed over, this meant seven and one-half miles at racing speed. With Jack Nagle, then eighteen years old, as his partner in the national championship doubles at Pullman, Ill., Aug. 8, 1889, he set a record that stood over forty years. He was president of the National Association of Amateur Oarsmen from 1900 to 1920 and remained on the executive committee until his death. For a number of years he was a member of the American Olympic Committee. He worked constantly to interest young men in rowing and was especially successful in encouraging the sport in the New York high schools. When he grew too old to row he became a coach. His training rules were of the simplest: "You want to eat good food and do lots of hard work and get lots of good sleep. And when you're fighting, fight; when you're walking, walk; and when you're rowing, row!" The notion that there was such a thing as "athlete's heart" made him jeer. When his fame as an athlete brought him friends and financial backing, he became a contractor. His firm did work in various parts of the country, but chiefly in New York, where "Big Jim" himself did the first actual work for the original New York subway, beginning the excavation in Bleecker Street Mar. 26, 1900. Later he built part of the Broadway subway north of 135th Street and a section of the Catskill Aqueduct. Failing eyesight compelled him to give up his business activities in 1923, and thereafter he seldom left his home on Sedgwick Avenue opposite the Bronx reservoir, but he continued to accompany the Columbia University crews to Poughkeepsie when they were in training. He died after a brief illness in his seventy-ninth year. His first wife, whom he married in 1877, was Constance Burke; his second wife, Kate Lysaght, and a daughter by his first marriage, survived him.

[*N. Y. Times,* Apr. 26, 27, 1929; *N. Y. Herald-Tribune,* Apr. 26, 1929; *Official Roster of the Soldiers of the State of Ohio in the War of the Rebellion,* X (1889), 630, 633; R. F. Kelley, *American Rowing* (1932), pp. 61–64; *James Pilkington* (booklet issued by the Nat. Asso. of Amateur Oarsmen); information from his daughter, Lily L. Pilkington.]   G. H. G.

PILLING, JAMES CONSTANTINE (Nov. 16, 1846–July 26, 1895), ethnologist, was born in Washington, D. C., the son of James and Susan (Collins) Pilling. He received his education in the public schools and Gonzaga College, a Jesuit institution at Washington. He worked in a book store for a time and became proficient in stenography, which qualification, rare at the time, was to lead to important results in his life work. Beginning as stenographer in the courts of the District of Columbia when he was twenty, he later became an employee of congressional committees and commissions. He was asked by John W. Powell [*q.v.*] to join the survey of the Rocky Mountains in 1875. His imagination was stimulated by this field work with Powell, during which he was one of the party to explore the Grand Canyon, and his interest in the diverse languages of the Indians was aroused by contact with the little-known tribes of the Rockies. He began the life work he was henceforth indefatigably to pursue. The next five years, 1875 to 1880, he spent in collecting ethnological material concerning the Indians and acquiring skill in bibliographical method. He was then appointed chief clerk of the geological survey, and he also served as chief clerk of the ethnological bureau.

His preoccupation with the Indian was mainly in the literature on the languages of the various groups. At the inception of the Bureau of American Ethnology this groundwork was especially needed, and in 1892 he began to devote his whole time to bibliographical work. He produced in a few years an unparalleled work on the bibliography of the Indian tribes. As a preliminary he had begun a "Catalogue of the Linguistic Manuscripts in the Library of the Bureau of Ethnology" published in the *United States Bureau of American Ethnology, First Annual Report* (1881). It was followed by *Proof-sheets of a Bibliography of the Languages of the North*

American Indians (1885). This preliminary work was in the nature of a record of the titles he was able to collect from his own research and from other investigators. The first definite work on a single linguistic stock was the "Bibliography of the Eskimo Language" in 1887, followed by the "Bibliography of the Siouan Languages" the same year, the "Bibliography of the Iroquoian Languages" in 1888, and the following year the "Bibliography of the Muskhogean Languages." Bibliographies of the Athapascan Languages in 1892, the Chinookan in 1893, the Salishan in 1893, and the Wakashan in 1894 completed his great works. These were all published in the series of *United States Bureau of Ethnology Bulletins* (numbers 1, 5, 6, 9, 14, 15, 16, 19). The last article from his pen was published in the *American Anthropologist* in January 1895, entitled "The Writings of Padre Andres de Olmos in the Languages of Mexico." Other articles by him had appeared from time to time in journals and magazines. Without his proficiency as a stenographer the task of preparing these bibliographies would have been impossible. This work traced for scholars a vast mass of literature, much of which was difficult of access in the libraries of the world. Incidentally it led, in great measure, to the gathering of the comprehensive library of the Bureau of American Ethnology, which is regarded as unexcelled in rare books and manuscripts on the Indians. In his work he visited most of the important libraries of the United States, and by correspondence he added material from foreign libraries. Although bibliographical accretions are endless, his work of recognizing and recording so much of the source material for the study of Indian culture will remain a permanent contribution to science. Much of his later work was accomplished in a struggle against advancing disease. He died at Olney, Md., survived by his wife, Minnie L. (Harper) Pilling, to whom he was married in 1888, and by their one daughter.

[Marcus Baker, *In Memoriam: James Constantine Pilling* (1895); *Johnson's Universal Cyclop.,* new ed., vol. VI (1896); W. J. McGee, *Am. Anthropologist,* Oct. 1895.]   W. H.

PILLOW, GIDEON JOHNSON (June 8, 1806–Oct. 8, 1878), soldier, son of Gideon and Anne (Payne) Pillow, was born in Williamson County, Tenn. Graduating from the University of Nashville in 1827, he became a shrewd and successful, but not a profoundly learned, criminal lawyer in Columbia, Tenn., with James K. Polk for some time as his partner. He married Mary Martin, and they had ten children. Pillow held no civil office of any importance and took openly no very prominent part in political affairs, but he delighted in under-cover political manipulations, in which he considered himself adept. He claimed for himself the major responsibility for the nomination of Polk for the presidency in 1844, though this claim was disputed by others. In 1852 he took an important part in negotiations that resulted in the nomination of Franklin Pierce, and in this year and four years later he intrigued unsuccessfully to secure his own nomination for the vice-presidency.

Pillow's claim to notoriety, however, is not based on his activities as a politician, but on his career as a vain, ambitious, quarrelsome, and unsuccessful soldier. Despite his lack of military training or experience, President Polk appointed him a brigadier-general of volunteers in 1846, for service in the war with Mexico, and subsequently advanced him to a major-generalship. After a brief and inactive period of service on the Rio Grande under General Taylor, he was transferred to General Scott's army and took part in the campaign that resulted in the capture of Mexico City. He fought at Vera Cruz, Cerro Gordo, Contreras, and Chapultepec, and was twice wounded. He considered himself Polk's special representative and maintained a confidential correspondence with him. He quarreled violently with Gen. Winfield Scott [q.v.], who charged him with the authorship of a letter, signed "Leonidas," in the *New Orleans Daily Delta* of Sept. 10, 1847, in which Pillow's military activities at Contreras were praised and those of Scott belittled. The charges were examined by two successive courts of inquiry who decided that no further proceedings should be taken against Pillow. Polk took pleasure in acquitting his friend "of any censure," considering him "a gallant and highly meritorious officer" who had been "greatly persecuted" by Scott (*Diary, post*, IV, 7, 17).

On the question of secession, Pillow's position was conservative. He took a prominent part in the Southern Convention which met in Nashville in June and November 1850, and opposed the proposals of extremists from the Lower South. In 1860 he was a Douglas Democrat, and he refused to view the election of Lincoln as in itself a justification of disunion, proposing to save the Union by compromise. When war began, however, he gave his support to the cause of the South and was appointed senior major-general of Tennessee's provisional army. When his troops were transferred to Confederate service, he was greatly chagrined that he was not continued in command of them, but he accepted a brigadier-generalship in the Confederate army.

He fought at the battle of Belmont, Mo., Nov. 7, 1861, and was second in command at Fort Donelson. He proposed that the weary and closely beset army holding this important position of defense attempt to cut its way through Grant's superior forces, but other officers counseled surrender. When Gen. John B. Floyd [q.v.] then relinquished command, Pillow passed it to Gen. Simon B. Buckner [q.v.], and he and Floyd made good their escape before the surrender was effected (February 1862). He was suspended from command for some months (March–August 1862) and the Confederate secretary of war, George W. Randolph, held him guilty of "grave errors of judgment in the military operations which resulted in the surrender of the army" but found no reason "to question his courage and loyalty" (*Official Records*, 1 ser. VII, 313). He protested bitterly, threatened to resign; and during the remainder of the war was given no important command. For some years after the war he practised law in Memphis, with Isham G. Harris as his partner. He died in Helena, Ark.

[C. M. Polk, *Some Old Colonial Families of Va.* (1915); J. H. Smith, *The War with Mexico* (2 vols., 1919); E. I. McCormac, *James K. Polk* (1922); R. F. Nichols, *Franklin Pierce* (1931); P. M. Hamer, *Tenn.: a Hist.* (1933), vols. I, II; *The Diary of James K. Polk* (4 vols., 1910), ed. by M. M. Quaife; proceedings of inquiry in *Sen. Ex. Doc. No. 65*, 30 Cong., 1 Sess., *War of the Rebellion: Official Records (Army)*; "Letters of Gideon J. Pillow to James K. Polk, 1844," *Am. Hist. Rev.*, July 1906; unpublished letters by Pillow in Lib. of Cong., N. Y. Pub. Lib., and library of the Hist. Soc. of Pa.; *Daily Arkansas Gazette* (Little Rock), Oct. 10, 1878.]   P. M. H.

PILLSBURY, CHARLES ALFRED (Dec. 3, 1842–Sept. 17, 1899), flour miller, the eldest son of George Alfred Pillsbury (Aug. 29, 1816–July 15, 1898) and Margaret Sprague (Carlton) Pillsbury, was born at Warner, N. H. His father was a grocer in Warner until 1851, when he became purchasing agent for the Concord Railroad, a position he held for twenty-five years. Charles attended the public schools at Warner and at Concord, prepared for college at New London Academy, and then attended Dartmouth, earning at least part of his college expenses by teaching. After his graduation, in 1863, he went to Montreal where he was a clerk in a produce commission store for about three years. He acquired a share in the business but shortly sold it in order to go West, following his uncle, John Sargent Pillsbury [q.v.], who had settled in Minneapolis in territorial days.

Soon after his arrival in Minneapolis in 1869, Charles Pillsbury purchased a share in one of the flour mills utilizing the water power of the Falls of St. Anthony. It was a small and not particularly successful enterprise, and his partners, because of other interests, left the management to him. At first Pillsbury knew nothing of milling, but he was a man of keen mind, great energy, and physical strength, and soon acquired a working knowledge of the business. He entered the industry at the moment when revolutionary changes were about to transform it and had a large share in bringing these changes about. When Edmond La Croix produced his purifier, making possible the manufacture of a high-grade bread flour from Northwestern spring wheat and introducing "New Process" milling, Pillsbury was one of the first to see the possibilities of the machine. He induced George T. Smith, who claimed to be its co-inventor, to become head miller at the Pillsbury Mill and to install the new machines there. A few years later Pillsbury was one of the leaders in the introduction of the roller process. In consequence, his profits were large and his fortune grew rapidly.

In 1872 he organized the firm of C. A. Pillsbury & Company, the other members being his father and uncle; two or three years later his brother, Fred C. Pillsbury, became a member. In the next decade six more mills were purchased or built by the Pillsburys, including the Pillsbury "A" Mill (completed in 1883), which was advertised to be the largest in the world. In 1878 one of their mills was destroyed by fire, in December 1881 three were burned, but by 1889 they had three mills in operation with a total capacity of 10,000 barrels a day. Their flour brands were widely advertised, they were leaders in building up the flour export trade, and leaders also in experiments with wheat and flour testing, out of which modern systems of laboratory control have been developed.

Charles Pillsbury seems also to have taken a prominent part in organizing the grain trade of the Northwest, through the Millers' Association (Minneapolis) and later the chamber of commerce, so as to concentrate this trade at Minneapolis. The growth of the Minneapolis mills was in part due to extremely favorable freight rates, and Pillsbury was instrumental both in securing such rates and in the building of the Minneapolis, Saulte Sainte Marie, & Atlantic Railway, by which the Minneapolis millers sought to free themselves from their dependence on the Chicago lines. The large scale of his operations forced him to strengthen his sources of supply by building up a subsidiary grain elevator company which owned both country and terminal elevators. He was always greatly interested in the wheat market, and his dealings in it were frequently spectacular if not always financially successful. Curiously, he was usually a bull in the market—

was generally boosting the price of wheat and was quite convinced that short selling should be prevented if possible.

In his later years Pillsbury became interested in a number of other enterprises such as railroads, banking, and lumbering, though milling always claimed the major share of his attention. His strong and winning personality, his travels, and his public utterances made him the best known of American millers. He was usually on very friendly terms with his employees. For five years the firm experimented with a profit-sharing plan under which over $150,000 was paid to the employees. Similarly he aided the Minneapolis coopers to start their coöperative shops, which were for years a notably successful example of producers' coöperation. He made large gifts to charitable and philanthropic undertakings. He was also somewhat interested in politics but played a relatively smaller part in that field than his uncle or his father, who after removing to Minneapolis in 1878 held several municipal offices. From 1878 to 1885 Charles A. Pillsbury was a member of the state Senate, but he held no other official position.

In 1889 an English syndicate purchased the Pillsbury mills, together with those of Senator W. D. Washburn and the water power of the Falls of St. Anthony, combining them to form the Pillsbury-Washburn Flour Mills Company, Ltd. Charles A. Pillsbury retained a large interest in the new company and was made managing director. In this position he was not so successful as in his earlier years. A new type of leadership which emphasized small economies as well as bold pioneering was required, and he had little taste for these. On the other hand, his bold speculations in the wheat market were sometimes disastrous. Nevertheless, under his management the Pillsbury-Washburn Company was the largest milling firm in the world, and at the time of his death, in Minneapolis, the *Northwestern Miller* characterized Pillsbury himself as "easily the foremost figure in the American milling trade."

On Sept. 12, 1866, Charles Pillsbury married Mary A. Stinson of Dunbarton, N. H. Of the four children born to them, twin sons, John S. and Charles S. Pillsbury, survived their father, in whose memory they founded the Pillsbury Settlement House in Minneapolis.

[Isaac Atwater, *Hist. of the City of Minneapolis, Minn.* (1893); C. B. Kuhlmann, *The Development of the Flour-Milling Industry in the U. S.* (1929); D. B. Pilsbury and E. A. Getchell, *The Pillsbury Family* (1898); "The Early History of New Process Milling," *Northwestern Miller,* Aug. 24, 1883; obituary and editorial, *Ibid.,* Sept. 20, 1899; *Minneapolis Journal,* Sept. 18, 1899.]   C. B. K.

PILLSBURY, HARRY NELSON (Dec. 5, 1872–June 17, 1906), chess player, was a descendant of William Pillsbury who was living in Dorchester, Mass., as early as 1641. The son of Luther Batchelder and Mary A. (Leathe) Pillsbury, he was born in Somerville, Mass., where his father was a teacher in the high school. His interest in chess began when he was sixteen and for the next five years he was active in Boston chess circles. After two years' attendance at high school and some slight training in commercial subjects, he abandoned his intention to prepare for business and devoted himself to chess, beginning a career which brought him international distinction. In April 1893 he defeated in Boston the Berlin master, C. Walbrodt, 2–0, and later A. Schottländer of Breslau. He was the first American to engage professionally in extended chess exhibitions. At Philadelphia, in 1893, he played four games blindfold, winning three and losing one. He was also an expert in checkers and bridge, and all three games, as well as memory feats, figured in his exhibitions. After reading once a list of fifty numbered words he could give the word corresponding to any number, the number of any word, or repeat the list backwards. In blindfold play he could repeat from memory the game at any board, or, indeed, begin at almost any point in each game a discussion of it. One of his greatest exhibitions of blindfold play took place at the Franklin Chess Club, Philadelphia, on Apr. 28, 1900, when he conducted twenty games simultaneously (*British Chess Magazine*, June 1900). His ability to remember the sequence of moves in such cases he compared (in a personal talk with the writer of this sketch) to the ability to recall the sequence of the discussions in a series of business interviews. At one time he played as "Ajeeb, the Automatic Player" in the Eden Musée, Boston, obtaining some regular income in this way.

In master tournament play, his success in 1893 in finishing in the first half of a group including Emanuel Lasker (later world's champion), A. Albin, F. J. Lee, and J. W. Showalter, was his first notable achievement. He won first place in 1895 in the Hastings Tournament in England, thus establishing himself among the great master-players of the world. At Vienna in 1898 he tied for first with Siegbert Tarrasch, but lost the play-off. He stood among the first three in twelve tournaments between 1894 and 1904, tying for first at Munich in 1900. In match play he defeated Showalter in 1897 and in 1898, thus acquiring the title of United States champion. He was always a serious student, and contributed to the theory of chess in the defense against the

Ruy Lopez, in the Petroff defense, and in introducing the modern aggressive Queen's pawn opening. Both as the greatest native genius since Paul C. Morphy [*q.v.*] and by his personal charm and versatility, he revived American interest in the noble game.

On Jan. 17, 1901, Pillsbury married Mary Ellen Bush, daughter of Judge Albert J. Bush of Monticello, N. Y. He made the effort demanded by his family tradition to maintain a dignified place in life and was constantly distressed by the difficulty of earning a decent living by chess. The blindfold exhibitions from which he principally derived his income required many hours of concentrated mental effort, sometimes twelve at a stretch, and during this time he smoked strong cigars and sometimes took alcoholic stimulants; to his physical condition he gave little thought. His death at thirty-three, in the Friends' Asylum, Frankford, Pa., was due primarily to a disease contracted in Russia, but resulted in part from the lack of resistance due to his irregular habits.

[P. W. Sergeant and W. H. Watts, *Pillsbury's Chess Career* (1923); *Am. Chess Bulletin*, July 1906; *Lasker's Chess Magazine*, May 1906; personal letter from Pillsbury's brother, Dr. G. D. Pillsbury; D. B. Pillsbury and E. A. Getchell, *The Pillsbury Family* (1898); Richard Réti, *Masters of the Chessboard* (1932); *Who's Who in America*, 1906–07; *N. Y. Times*, *N. Y. Tribune*, *Pub. Ledger* (Phila.), June 18, 1906.]   L. C. K.

PILLSBURY, JOHN ELLIOTT (Dec. 15, 1846–Dec. 30, 1919), naval officer and oceanographer, was a native of Lowell, Mass., the son of John Gilman and Elizabeth Wimble (Smith) Pillsbury, and a descendant of William Pillsbury who emigrated to Massachusetts about 1640. At the age of fourteen he was made a page in the United States House of Representatives and served till appointed to the Naval Academy by President Lincoln in 1862. His training took place at Newport and Annapolis, and in the summers of 1863 and 1864 on the *Marion* and *Saco* respectively as they cruised in search of the *Tacony* and other Confederate raiders. He graduated from the Academy in 1867, was made an ensign in 1868, and subsequently advanced through the grades until July 4, 1908, he became rear admiral. After two years at the Boston Navy Yard, he was sent to the Orient on the *Colorado*, participated in a futile attempt to open Korea to the world, and then returned to San Francisco on the *Benicia*. In 1873 he was at the Torpedo Station, Newport, and on Aug. 26 of that year married Florence Greenwood Aitchison, of Portland, Me.

Pillsbury's first contact with the scientific work of the navy was made in 1874–75, when he went on the *Swatara* to Tasmania and New Zealand with a party of scientists to observe the transit of Venus. When he returned he began service with the Coast Survey, which lasted for fifteen years. His chief work was in the Gulf Stream. In 1876 he invented a current meter for determining the flow of ocean currents at various depths—an instrument which was used till his death (see *Encyclopedia Britannica,* 14th edition, V, 305). While in command of the Coast Survey steamer *Blake* (1884–89) he anchored his ship in water two miles deep, and determined the axis of the Gulf Stream and many of the laws governing its flow—work which has been of permanent value. The record of it appeared first in *Report of the Superintendent of the United States Coast and Geodetic Survey . . . 1890,* and was later published separately under the title, *The Gulf Stream* (1891).

Pillsbury returned to active duty in the navy in 1891, attended the Naval War College in 1897, and when the Spanish-American War broke out was already in command of the dynamite cruiser *Vesuvius,* which was engaged in the blockade of Santiago from June 13, 1898, until after the destruction of Cervera's fleet. Armed with three guns operated by compressed air, the *Vesuvius* would stand in close to the shore on dark nights and fire three dynamite shells at the Spanish batteries. The effect was slight, except that this new form of attack shattered the Spanish morale and dug huge holes where the shells landed. In 1905–07 Pillsbury served under Robley D. Evans [*q.v.*] as chief of staff of the North Atlantic Squadron, where he is credited by his superior with keeping the fleet in fine condition. He then served until 1909 as chief of the Bureau of Navigation, although he was retired on Dec. 15, 1908, and he was also on the board which decided against the claims of Dr. Frederick A. Cook that he had reached the North Pole. He became one of the managers of the National Geographic Society and held various offices in that organization till elected president in April 1919, a few months before his death, which occurred in Washington from paralysis of the heart. He was survived by his wife and one daughter. Besides *The Gulf Stream,* he published "Wilkes and D'Urville's Discoveries in Wilkes Land" (*National Geographic Magazine,* February 1910), "The Grandest and Most Mighty Terrestrial Phenomenon: the Gulf Stream" (*Ibid.,* August 1912), and "Charts and Chart Making" (*Proceedings of the United States Naval Institute,* vol. X, no. 2, 1884).

[D. B. Pilsbury and E. A. Getchell, *The Pillsbury Family* (1898); *Who's Who in America,* 1918–19; *National Geographic Mag.,* Apr. 1920; *Army and Navy* *Reg.,* Jan. 3, 1920; *Army and Navy Jour.,* Jan. 3, 1920; *Evening Star* (Washington), Dec. 30, 1919; L. R. Hamersly, *Records of Living Officers of the U. S. Navy* (7th ed., 1902); F. E. Chadwick, *The Relations of the U. S. and Spain: The Spanish-American War* (1911), I, 379–80; Seaton Schroeder, *A Half Century of Naval Service* (1922); R. D. Evans, *An Admiral's Log* (1910).]   W. B. N.

PILLSBURY, JOHN SARGENT (July 29, 1828–Oct. 18, 1901), flour-miller, governor of Minnesota, one of five children of John and Susan (Wadleigh) Pillsbury, was born at Sutton, N. H. On his father's side he was descended from William Pillsbury (or Pilsbury) who came to Massachusetts as early as 1641, settling first in Dorchester and then in Ipswich; on his mother's side he was also of Massachusetts Puritan stock. After a common-school education, he started to learn a trade, but abandoned it to become a clerk in his brother's general store. Soon after reaching his majority he opened a store of his own in partnership with Walter Harriman [*q.v.*]; two years later he was a merchant tailor and cloth dealer in Concord.

In 1855, after a tour of the West, Pillsbury settled at St. Anthony, Minn. (now a part of Minneapolis), as a hardware dealer, in partnership with his brother-in-law, Woodbury Fisk, and George A. Cross. Moderate success was interrupted by a fire which destroyed a season's stock and by financial panic which prevented rehabilitation for some years. In 1875 he sold his hardware interests in order to devote more time to the lumber and real-estate businesses which he had developed, and especially to the milling enterprise in which, in 1872, he had embarked together with his nephew, Charles A. Pillsbury [*q.v.*], and his brother George A. Pillsbury. About 1875 another nephew, Fred C. Pillsbury, joined the firm. Their milling business grew to be the most extensive in the world for a period, and the products of the Pillsbury Mills were known wherever men used wheat. Their energy and ability in realizing the opportunities of a relatively unexploited region built up for each of the partners a considerable fortune. John Sargent Pillsbury's seemed vast, in those days and in that place, although his multifarious benefactions caused him to leave an estate of only about a million and a half.

Pillsbury was far more, however, than a successful exploiter of a new country; he was a public-spirited citizen in the best sense of the word. For six years (1858–64) he was a member of the city council of St. Anthony. He helped organize the first three regiments which Minnesota sent to serve in the Civil War and the battalion recruited in 1862 to deal with the Indian uprising. In 1863 he was elected one of the Hennepin

County state senators, and, reëlected, served 1864–68, 1871, 1874, 1875. With no special effort on his own part he was nominated for governor by the Republican party in 1875 and elected to the office for three successive terms, serving as chief executive from Jan. 7, 1876, to Jan. 10, 1882. As governor, his most significant triumph was his success in persuading the legislature to provide for the redemption of an issue of railroad bonds authorized in 1858 and repudiated in 1860. This bond issue had been a bone of political contention for twenty years (W. W. Folwell, "The Five Million Loan," *Collections of the Minnesota Historical Society,* vol. XV, 1915), but Governor Pillsbury, after persistent urging, had the gratification in 1881 of signing a measure satisfactory to the claimants and, in his eyes, restoring the honor of the state. It was during this period that Minnesota, in common with other states of the Northwest was plagued with the "grasshopper scourge" which destroyed, season after season, all vegetation over wide areas. Pillsbury was energetic in personally investigating the seriousness of the situation and in securing relief, as well as in coördinating the activities of several states. Essentially a business man and not a politician, he did much to eliminate inefficiency and corruption in both state and local governments. From his own means he kept the penitentiary in operation when the legislature had neglected to make the usual appropriation, and advanced money to replace the burned hospital for insane in order to save the state the expense of a special session.

Significant as was his work in these ways, his most lasting public service was one he rendered the state university. In 1851 Congress had granted two townships of public lands for a university; this land was mortgaged to erect a building which, in turn, bore a mortgage when it was completed in 1857. The crash of that year found the embryo university laden with debt and its regents in despair of ever extricating it. In 1862 the legislature was ready to sell the land to satisfy the creditors. It was at this point that Pillsbury, made a regent in 1863, resolved that something should be done to save the institution. As state senator he was instrumental in securing an act (approved Mar. 4, 1864) by which an emergency board of three, with full powers, was created, and as one of these regents he set himself to the task of satisfying the creditors; he was successful to the extent that when all obligations were met the state still held some 30,000 acres of university lands. In 1895 the legislature made Pillsbury regent for life. For nearly forty years, in the midst of his manifold interests, the university engaged the best of his abilities. He took a personal interest in its plant, its faculty, and its students. During the last decade of his life, when he had withdrawn to a considerable degree from active business, he rarely let a day pass without visiting the campus to consult with President Cyrus Northrop [*q.v.*], and he continued to follow in every detail the life of the institution he had rescued. He died in Minneapolis at the age of seventy-three.

On Nov. 3, 1856, Pillsbury married Mahala Fisk of Warner, N. H. They had a son and two daughters. Both Pillsbury and his wife were lavish in their benefactions of private and public character.

[C. W. G. Hyde and William Stoddard, *Hist. of the Great Northwest and Its Men of Progress* (1901); W. W. Folwell, *A Hist. of Minn.,* vols. III, IV (1926, 1930); *Encyc. of Biog. of Minn.* (1900); H. B. Hudson, "A Public Servant of the Northwest," *Rev. of Revs.* (N. Y.), Dec. 1901; D. B. Pilsbury and E. A. Getchell, *The Pillsbury Family* (1898); J. K. Baker, "Lives of the Governors of Minnesota," *Minn. Hist. Soc. Colls.,* vol. XIII (1908); *Who's Who in America,* 1901–02; Isaac Atwater, *Hist. of the City of Minneapolis* (1893); *Dedication of the Pillsbury Memorial Town Hall in Sutton, N. H.* (1893); E. B. Johnson, *Forty Years of the Univ. of Minn.* (1910); *Minneapolis Jour.,* Oct. 18, 19, 1901.]   L. B. S

PILLSBURY, PARKER (Sept. 22, 1809–July 7, 1898), reformer, was born at Hamilton, Mass., the son of Oliver Pillsbury, a blacksmith and farmer, and Anna (Smith) Pillsbury. He was a descendant of William Pillsbury who came to Massachusetts about 1640. Parker's parents moved to Henniker, N. H., in 1814 and the boy's early education was limited to what the district school of that town had to offer. Until he was well past twenty years of age he worked on farms in New Hampshire and as a wagoner in Massachusetts. In 1835 he entered Gilmanton Theological Seminary, graduating in 1838. After studying a year at Andover Theological Seminary, he was engaged to supply the Congregational church at Loudon, N. H.; but in 1840 opposition to his denunciations of slavery from the pulpit led him to give up the ministry and devote himself to social reform. On Jan. 1, 1840, he married Sarah H. Sargent of Concord, N. H., who cooperated ardently in his activities.

He was an abolitionist of the Garrisonian type, and from 1840 until the emancipation of the slaves was lecture agent for the New Hampshire, Massachusetts, and American anti-slavery societies. An admirer of John Brown, he spoke at a demonstration meeting in Rochester, N. Y., following Brown's execution. In 1840 and again in 1845–46 he edited the *Herald of Freedom,* at Concord, N. H., and from January to May 1866, the *National Anti-Slavery Standard,* New York

City. After the Civil War, he labored for negro suffrage, believing that the right to vote was necessary for the negro's protection. He was also interested in temperance, political reform, international peace, and woman's rights. To the last-named cause he gave his longest service, being one of the earliest and most uncompromising nineteenth-century advocates of justice to women. He severed his connection with the *Standard,* because its managers were more favorable to votes for the negro than to votes for women, long served as vice-president of the New Hampshire Woman Suffrage Association and helped draft the constitution of the American Equal Rights Association. For a year and a half (1868–69) he was joint editor with Elizabeth Cady Stanton [*q.v.*] of the *Revolution,* a radical weekly. Though he held no regular pastorate, he preached for free religious societies in Toledo, Ohio, Battle Creek, Mich., Rochester, N. Y., and elsewhere. In addition to contributions to the papers with which he was identified, he wrote and published a large number of tracts on reforms, and was author of the *Acts of the Anti-Slavery Apostles* (1883), a history of the abolition movement in New England. As a public speaker he was fluent, sarcastic, and thunderous in his denunciations. James Russell Lowell in 1846 referred to him ("Letter from Boston," *Complete Poetical Works,* 1896, p. 112) as

"... brown, broad-shouldered Pillsbury,
Who tears up words like trees by the roots,
A Theseus in stout cow-hide boots."

His interest in the work for human betterment continued to the last, and at the age of eighty-eight he wrote a letter to the convention of the National American Woman Suffrage Association. His death occurred at Concord, N. H. He had one daughter.

[D. B. Pilsbury and E. A. Getchell, *The Pillsbury Family* (1898); E. C. Stanton, S. B. Anthony, and M. J. Gage, *The Hist. of Woman Suffrage,* vols. I–IV (1881–1902); I. H. Harper, *The Life and Work of Susan B. Anthony* (3 vols., 1899–1908); *People and Patriot* (Concord, N. H.), July 7, 1898; *Concord Evening Monitor,* July 7, 1898.]   M. W. W.

PILMORE, JOSEPH (Oct. 31, 1739–July 24, 1825), Protestant Episcopal clergyman, was born at Tadmouth, in Yorkshire, England. His name also appears as Pilmoor. At the age of sixteen he was converted under the preaching of John Wesley, who regarded him as a promising recruit and sent him to the school at Kingswood, near Bristol. Here Pilmore acquired a fair English and classical education. At an early age he became one of Wesley's lay assistants, working as an itinerant preacher in various places, but especially in Wales and Cumberland. In 1769

Wesley issued a call for volunteers to go to the American colonies and Pilmore and Richard Boardman offered themselves. They were accepted and at once sent out, arriving in Philadelphia in October of the same year.

Boardman went to New York, where there was a society already organized; Pilmore remained in Philadelphia, where he found about a hundred Methodists. He was not, therefore, the founder of Methodism in that city but was the first Methodist preacher there, though he had never been ordained by Wesley. He was remarkably successful, his willingness to adapt himself to any situation standing him in good stead; his first preaching was from an improvised stand in the race track. He later itinerated from Boston to Georgia, meeting with all sorts of adventures. On Jan. 2, 1774, he returned to England, probably because of the disturbed condition of the colonies and the fact that he was a stanch Loyalist. He was assigned work first at London and subsequently on the Norwich circuit and at Edinburgh, Nottingham, and York. He vigorously opposed Wesley in the matter of the Deed of Declaration of 1784, and as a consequence of the resulting friction he abandoned Methodism and returned to America. Here he joined the Protestant Episcopal Church which was just then in the process of organizing. He was ordered deacon on Nov. 27, 1785, by Bishop Samuel Seabury; his ordination to the priesthood occurred two days later.

Pilmore then returned to Philadelphia where he at once became rector of the United Parish of Trinity (Oxford), All Saints' (Lower Dublin), and St. Thomas's (Whitemarsh), all in the vicinity of Philadelphia. He added to these duties that of assistant minister, or evening preacher, of St. Paul's, Philadelphia. In 1789 he was a delegate from the diocese of Pennsylvania to the General Convention sitting at Philadelphia. Here he served on the committee on the revision of the Book of Common Prayer and on the sub-committee on the Communion Service. From 1793 to 1804 he was rector of the newly organized Christ Church in New York City, formed by seceders from Trinity Church, who were offended by the refusal of the vestry to call Pilmore as assistant minister of Trinity and evening lecturer. In 1804 he returned to Philadelphia as rector of St. Paul's Church and retained this cure until the end of his life, though he did little work after 1821. About 1790 he married Mary (Benezet) Wood, daughter of Daniel Benezet and widow of Joseph Wood; they had one child, a daughter, who died young. Pilmore was a man of massive frame and robust constitution. His bearing was dignified and his voice described as sonorous. He must have been an amiable, kindly man, for there is a tradition in Philadelphia that he was known popularly as "Daddy Pilmore." He retained throughout his life his early evangelical views, which he set forth with much vigor and fervid eloquence, and he did much to give to the Episcopal churches in Philadelphia the evangelical character for which they were long noted.

[Manuscript sermons of Pilmore may be found in the Pa. Hist. Soc. in Phila.; portions of his journal as an itinerant preacher are given in J. P. Lockwood, *Western Pioneers* (London, 1881); personal reminiscences of Pilmore by the Rev. R. D. Hall appear in W. B. Sprague, *Annals Am. Pulpit*, vol. V (1859). See also, Benjamin Allen, *Sketch of the Life of Dr. Pilmore* (1825); *The Jour. of Rev. John Wesley* (1909), ed. by Nehemiah Curnock; W. J. Townsend, H. B. Workman, and George Eayrs, *A New Hist. of Methodism* (London, 1909), vol. II; W. S. Perry, *Hist. of the Am. Episcopal Church* (1885); N. S. Barratt, *Outline of the Hist. of Old St. Paul's Church, Phila.* (1917); Samuel Small, *Geneal. Records of George Small . . . Daniel Benezet . . .* (1905); *Poulson's Am. Daily Advertiser* (Phila.), July 30, 1825.]   J. C. A.

PILSBURY, AMOS (Feb. 8, 1805–July 14, 1873), prison administrator, was born in Londonderry, N. H., the son of Moses Cross and Lois (Cleaveland) Pilsbury. He was a descendant of William Pilsbury, or Pillsbury, who came to Boston late in 1640 or early in 1641, and married Dorothy Crosbey after an unconventional courtship. Amos spent his early years on the home farm, but when his father became warden of the New Hampshire state prison in 1818 and the family moved to Concord, he was sent to the academy there. He was known as a "dull scholar" and his father soon apprenticed him to a tanner and currier. When at the end of his apprenticeship he was unsuccessful in his attempt to find a journeyman's place at a living wage, he returned home and was in 1824 appointed guard in his father's prison and a year later, deputy warden.

His father had already achieved a more than local reputation, having made his prison a financial asset to the state instead of a liability. For this reason, perhaps, he was called to the wardenship of the new Connecticut prison at Wethersfield in 1826, where Amos soon joined him. When his father retired in 1830, because of ill health, Amos succeeded him, his youth causing the board of directors to express some misgivings about his election. Dissension between him and the directors soon ripened into warfare. In 1832 he demanded a legislative investigation of his work, was removed from office by a new board of directors, exonerated by the investigating committee, and reinstated in 1833, the Assembly compensating him both for the loss of his time and the

cost of his defense (*Minutes of the Testimony Taken Before John Q. Wilson, Joseph Eaton, & Morris Woodruff, Committee from the General Assembly, to Inquire into the Condition of Connecticut State Prison, Together with Their Report and Remarks upon the Same,* 1834). He remained in office until 1845 when political fortunes caused his removal (*Memorial of Amos Pilsbury, Late Warden of the State Prison, to the General Assembly, May Session, 1845,* 1845). His abilities and experiences were not to be lost to the prison world, however. He was immediately called to Albany, N. Y., to supervise the construction of the new county penitentiary, of which he later served as warden, except for a brief period, until his last illness prompted his resignation. Urged to accept the superintendency of the New York City institutions on Ward's Island, he was absent from his position from 1855 to 1860, the last eight months of this period being spent as general superintendent of the metropolitan police, from which position he resigned in protest against the efforts of Mayor Fernando Wood to secure political control of the department. At his death in 1873 he was survived by his wife, Emily (Heath) Pilsbury, whom he had married in 1826, and who had borne him five children, three of whom died in infancy.

The Pilsburys, father and son, are said to have been the first professional prison wardens in the United States, Amos' service in three states covering a period of fifty years. In spite of the early accusations which challenged his competency, all commentators upon his life work unite in approval of his humane attitude toward his prisoners, albeit he was a strict disciplinarian. The two institutions which he headed were spoken of as models in their day and were sources of financial profit to the states. In the seventeen years he spent at Wethersfield that prison earned $93,000 above all expenses. His interest in jail reform made him propose to the General Assembly that each county be given a thousand dollars from the prison's surplus earnings on condition that its jail be rebuilt on the plan of the model jail at Hartford, and he was authorized to make such payments. In his 1841 report to the directors he also urged that the surplus be used to erect and maintain a special asylum for the criminal and pauper insane. His advice was widely sought. He shared in the work of launching the National Prison Association of the United States (1870), now the American Prison Association, and he represented the State of New York at the International Penitentiary Congress in London in 1872. At least one of his officers became widely known, Zebulon Reed Brockway [*q.v.*], who began his prison career under Pilsbury as a guard at Wethersfield and Albany.

[D. B. Pilsbury and E. A. Getchell, *The Pillsbury Family* (1898) ; *Tribute to the Memory of Amos Pilsbury* (1873) ; *Trans. of the Third National Prison Reform Congress . . . 1874* (1874), pp. 31–33 ; David Dyer, *Hist. of the Albany Penitentiary* (1867) ; *Biog. Sketch of Amos Pilsbury, and a Brief Account of the Albany County Penitentiary* (1849) ; *Sketch of the Life and Public Services of Amos Pilsbury, Superintendent of the Albany Penitentiary, and Late General Superintendent of the Metropolitan Police* (1860) ; Joel Munsell, *Albany Ann. Reg.*, 1849 ; O. F. Lewis, *The Development of Am. Prisons and Prison Customs, 1776–1845* (1922) ; *N. Y. Times*, July 15, 1873.]

T. S—n.

PINCHBACK, PINCKNEY BENTON STEWART (May 10, 1837–Dec. 21, 1921), politician, was born at Macon, Ga., the son of a white Mississippi planter, said to be William Pinchback, and of Eliza Stewart who had been a slave. He is sometimes referred to by the nickname "Percy Bysshe Shelley Pinchback." He was born free, because his mother had been emancipated by the father of her children and later sent to Ohio to educate them. About 1847 he was sent to high school in Cincinnati and in 1848 became a cabin boy and, later, a steward on riverboats. He was married to Nina Emily Hawthorne probably in 1860. In 1862, running the blockade at Yazoo City, he reached New Orleans, which was already in possession of the Union forces. He enlisted, raised a company of colored volunteers, known as the Corps d'Afrique, but resigned his commission in September 1863 because of difficulties over his race. Subsequently he was authorized to raise a company of colored cavalry.

At the close of the war he threw himself into Louisiana politics. Shrewd, energetic, aggressive, he represented the typical negro politician of the Reconstruction period. In 1867 he organized the fourth-ward Republican club, became a member of the state committee, and was sent to the constitutional convention of 1868. In 1868 he was elected to the state Senate, where he was elected president *pro tempore* in the exciting session of December 1871, and became, by virtue of that office, lieutenant-governor at the death of the mulatto incumbent, O. J. Dunn, in 1871. For the brief period from Dec. 9, 1872, to Jan. 13, 1873, he filled the gubernatorial office, while Henry Clay Warmoth [*q.v.*] was debarred from serving on account of impeachment proceedings. Though he had been originally nominated for governor by his wing of the Republican party in the fall campaign of 1872 he consented, in the interest of party harmony, to accept the place of

congressman-at-large on the Republican ticket. He was declared elected, but he was never seated because his Democratic opponent contested and ultimately won the seat. His experience in the Senate was similar, for, although elected senator by the Louisiana legislature in January 1873, after a contest of three years he was denied the seat by a close vote. He was, however, allowed payment equal to salary and mileage up to the termination of the contest. In 1877 he left the Republican party to support Governor Nicholls and the Democrats. The last office in his public career was that of surveyor of customs in New Orleans, to which he was appointed in 1882. He was, however, later recognized by several honorary posts. When fifty years old, turning from politics to law, he took the law course at Straight University, now Straight College, in New Orleans, and won admission to the bar, though he never practised his profession. In 1890 he removed to Washington, where he lived until his death.

[W. J. Simmons, *Men of Mark* (1887) ; Ella Lonn, *Reconstruction in La.* (1918) ; H. C. Warmoth, *War, Politics, and Reconstruction* (1930) ; *Times-Picayune* (New Orleans), Dec. 22, 1921 ; *Washington Post* (D. C.), Dec. 22, 1921 ; *Afro-American* (Baltimore), Dec. 30, 1921.]

E. L.

PINCKNEY, CHARLES (Oct. 26, 1757–Oct. 29, 1824), author of the "Pinckney draught" of the federal Constitution, governor of South Carolina, senator, minister to Spain, was born in Charlestown (Charleston), S. C. He was the fourth and eldest surviving child of Col. Charles and Frances (Brewton) Pinckney, and a second cousin of Charles Cotesworth and Thomas Pinckney [*qq.v*]. His father (1731–1782), a wealthy lawyer and planter, first opposed the Revolutionary movement, then accepted the cause and labored actively in its behalf, but after the fall of Charlestown (1780) resumed allegiance to the British Crown and suffered two years later the amercement of his estate (Salley, *post*, pp. 135–38). Though his name appears in the list of Americans admitted to the Middle Temple (May 4, 1773, *American Historical Review*, July 1920, p. 687), the younger Charles seems to have been educated wholly in Charlestown, where in due course he was admitted to the bar (Ford Transcripts, *post*, July 8, 1801). At some time prior to October 1779, he enlisted for military service, for he was then participating, as a lieutenant of the Charlestown Regiment of militia, in the siege of Savannah (Charleston *City Gazette*, July 23, 1818). When captured at the capitulation of Charlestown, he refused to accept "protection" and remained a prisoner until June 1781. From 1779 to 1780 he was a member of the state House of Representatives, and on Nov. 1, 1784, he took his seat as a delegate to the Congress of the Confederation, a position which he occupied until Feb. 21, 1787. When it was proposed (1786) to abandon the claims of the United States to navigate the Mississippi in return for commercial concessions from Spain, he led the opposition which eventually defeated the measure (*American Historical Review*, July 1905, pp. 817–27). Having become convinced that to continue its existence the federal authority must be strengthened, he joined in the memorable plea of Feb. 15, 1786, for a more effectual revenue. A month later, in an address by which he persuaded the New Jersey legislature to rescind its resolution refusing to pay the federal quota, he urged the calling of a general convention to revise and amend the Articles of Confederation (*American Museum*, July 1787, pp. 153–60). In May, he moved in Congress the appointment of a grand committee "to take into consideration the affairs of the Nation," and he probably had a large share in preparing the report which, on Aug. 7, recommended a comprehensive series of amendments to the Articles (McLaughlin, *post*, p. 738).

Besides submitting his celebrated plan for a constitution to the Federal Convention of 1787, Pinckney was a member of the committee that prepared the rules of procedure, and he participated frequently and effectively in the debates throughout the session. It is in the first that his main contribution lies, but it is difficult to determine exactly what this document contained and how much influence it had upon the final result. Thirty-one years after the convention, to supply an omission in the records then being prepared for publication, Pinckney, who had kept no copy of his plan (Pinckney to Mathew Carey, Aug. 10, 1788, manuscript in Library of Congress), sent to the editor from "4 or 5 draughts" in his possession the one which he believed to be his (*Nation*, May 23, 1895, pp. 398–99). This was printed in the Journal (Farrand, *Records*, III, 595–601), but it has been proved to be not the Pinckney plan but instead a slightly altered copy of the report of the committee of detail of a later period of the convention's proceedings (Jameson, *post*). From a variety of sources, however, it has been possible to reconstruct in considerable measure the "Pinckney draught" and to show that it contained at least "thirty-one or thirty-two provisions" that were finally accepted (McLaughlin, *post*, p. 741). This text (Farrand, *Records*, III, 604–09), incomplete though it is, together with what is more perfectly known concerning his part in the de-

bates of the convention, makes it appear not improbable that Pinckney had a larger share than any other individual in the determination of the form and content of the finished Constitution.

At home Pinckney labored for ratification, which was finally accomplished in spite of opposition, especially from the back-country section of the state. After a year in the state privy council he was for two successive terms elected governor (January 1789–December 1792). Fittingly enough, it fell to him to guide the first steps in the adjustment of the relations between the South Carolina and the federal Union (Messages to the General Assembly, MS. House Journals, 1790, 1791). His success in this respect is reflected principally in the new state constitution which was evolved (1790) in a convention of which he was president from a plan which he had apparently modeled as far as possible after the federal instrument (Charleston *City Gazette*, May–June 1790; MS. Journal of the Convention . . . for the Purpose of Revising, Altering, or Forming a New Constitution of the State).

By many considerations Pinckney belonged with the Federalists, who could claim at this time most of the men of property and talents in the South Carolina low-country. To his Pinckney kin, who contributed in Charles Cotesworth and Thomas two of the major chieftains of the party, he added the wide-spreading family of the merchant prince, Henry Laurens [*q.v.*], by marrying (Apr. 27, 1788) the latter's twelfth child, Mary Eleanor. Henry Laurens Pinckney [*q.v.*] was their son. Until reduced through the mismanagement of his agents, his estate enabled him to live in lavish style. Disregard in 1791 of his request for a diplomatic post, preferably London (Ford Transcripts, Aug. 6, 1791), and the appointment instead of Thomas Pinckney, may have begun his alienation from the party. But more important was the fact that he was coming to oppose Federalist policies. In 1795, he denounced Jay's Treaty. The next year he was elected governor for the third time, defeating his brother-in-law Henry Laurens. Now vigorously supporting reforms favored by the Republican back-country (Charleston *City Gazette*, Dec. 6, 1798), he won in 1798 the seat in the United States Senate that was commonly allotted to that section. He became at once the leader among the Republican senators in attacks upon the administration, and later assuming the management of Jefferson's campaign in South Carolina he secured the choice of Republican electors. Among other consequences of this activity was estrangement from "many of his relatives," one of whom (Charles Cotesworth) was the Federalist candidate for the vice-presidency (*American Historical Review,* October 1898, p. 122).

Pinckney's reward was the appointment (March 1801) as minister to Spain. After a leisurely journey through the Netherlands and France, he addressed himself in Madrid to the original object of his mission and was able to send home on Aug. 11, 1802, a convention providing for a joint tribunal to settle claims arising from spoliations committed in recent years upon American shipping by Spanish cruisers, and leaving open for future negotiation similar claims for French depredations carried out within Spain's jurisdiction (*American State Papers. Foreign Relations,* vol. II, 1832, pp. 475–76, 482–83). Unfortunately, the administration permitted delays in ratification which allowed this agreement to become entangled with the larger difficulties which were even then developing between the two countries. One cause of ill feeling he successfully removed by securing, with the aid of the Spanish minister to the United States, the restoration of the right of deposit at New Orleans which had been withdrawn by the intendant. When Pinckney was on the point of renewing his efforts to have the French spoliations included in the claims convention, Bonaparte reached the momentous decision to sell Louisiana to the United States. To Pinckney's cares was now added the task of inducing Spain to acquiesce in this transaction (*Ibid.,* II, 570–71). Having been met with an even more stubborn resistance than hitherto in the claims matter and having good reason to believe that the time was ripe to press for the cession of the Floridas to the United States, a subject which had long been included in his instructions but which of late he had been ordered not to urge without the concurrence of Monroe who was at this time in London, Pinckney combined these three points in a positive note to the Spanish government on Jan. 11, 1804 (*Ibid.,* II, 616–17). A month later Spain, acting under French compulsion, acceded to the sale of Louisiana, but the unexpected decision of the United States to accept the claims agreement in its original form and the passage of the Mobile Act authorizing the erection of a part of West Florida into a United States customs district left Pinckney no ground to stand upon in the other two matters. His request for Spain's renewal of the ratification of the convention being met with refusal unless the United States abandon altogether the French spoliations and repeal the Mobile Act, he now threatened to ask for his passports, believ-

ing that his government was prepared to defend its actions with war (*Ibid.,* II, 618–24; Ford Transcripts, July 30, 1804). Thus matters stood until the arrival of Monroe. Together the two ministers renewed the negotiations but accomplished nothing. In October 1805, Pinckney sailed for home. His mission had not been successful. In the Florida matter he had exceeded his instructions, but the main cause of failure lay with the administration.

On his return to Charleston (January 1806) Pinckney resumed his position as head of the state Republican party. His personal affairs had become sadly disordered during his absence, but he returned to his old seat in the General Assembly, and on Dec. 9, 1806, accepted the governorship for the fourth time. Having advanced from liberalism to democracy, he supported the constitutional amendment which in 1808 gave the back-country increased representation in the legislature and urged another which, when ratified two years later, established universal white male suffrage (Charleston *City Gazette,* Dec. 7, 1808). Twice subsequently (1810–12, 1812–14) he sat in the General Assembly and then declined reëlection. In 1818, however, when it appeared that otherwise the Federalists would elect the congressman from the Charleston district, he entered the lists once more and in the face of bitter assaults upon his private and public life defeated two opponents. In opposition to the proposed Missouri compromise he delivered one of his ablest addresses (*Niles' Weekly Register,* July 15, 1820, pp. 349–57). But his ardor could not withstand "the dreadfully rigorous Climate" of Washington, and he decided not to be a candidate again. His death occurred on Oct. 29, 1824.

Handsome, vain, and, doubtless, something of a roué, though capable of the tenderest devotion to his three young children after the death of their mother (1794), Pinckney possessed that iridescent genius which offends some and dazzles others. To his Federalist contemporaries he was "Blackguard Charlie," a demagogue, a spoilsman, and a corruptionist; to his followers he was a demi-god fit for the presidency. His great egoism induced in him a habit of seeing his own deeds in heroic dimensions. He honestly believed that he had virtually written the federal Constitution, and this, together with other extravagant claims that he made for himself, has raised doubts in the minds of historians which have obscured his real achievements.

[Biographical articles appear in J. B. O'Neall, *Biog. Sketches of the Bench and Bar of S. C.* (1859), II, 138–45; W. S. E[lliott], in *DeBow's Review,* July–Aug. 1864, and *Hon. Charles Pinckney of South Carolina* (pamphlet, n.d.); B. F. Perry, *Biog. Sketches of Emi-*

nent American Statesmen (1887); and E. A. Jones, American Members of the Inns of Court (1924). Mabel L. Webber, manuscript notes on the Pinckney family, and A. S. Salley, S. C. Hist. and Geneal. Mag., Apr. 1901, pp. 133–38, 144–48, contain genealogical material. The "Pinckney Draught" has been critically studied by J. F. Jameson, in Annual Report of the Am. Hist. Asso. . . . 1902 (1903), I, 111–32, and Am. Hist. Review, April 1903, pp. 509–11; A. C. McLaughlin, Am. Hist. Review, July 1904, pp. 735–47; C. C. Nott, The Mystery of the Pinckney Draught (1908); Max Farrand, The Records of the Federal Convention of 1787 (1911), III, 595–611; and T. D. Jervey, Charles Pinckney's Constructive Mind (MS.). A selection of private letters is printed in Am. Hist. Review, Oct. 1898, pp. 111–29. Transcripts of other letters to Jefferson, Madison, and Monroe, prepared by W. C. Ford, are in the S. C. Hist. Society. Episodes in Pinckney's career are treated in T. D. Jervey, Robert Y. Hayne and His Times (1909), and U. B. Phillips, "The S. C. Federalists," Am. Hist. Review, April, July 1909. Pinckney wrote copiously for the Charleston newspapers, especially the City Gazette, and not infrequently reprinted his articles in pamphlet form. An obituary article was published in the City Gazette, Nov. 9, 1824.]

J. H. E.

PINCKNEY, CHARLES COTESWORTH (Feb. 25, 1746–Aug. 16, 1825), soldier, statesman, diplomat, was born in Charlestown (Charleston), S. C. His father, Charles Pinckney, was for a short time chief justice of the province. His mother, Elizabeth (Lucas) Pinckney [q.v.], a woman of unusual force of character, is well known for her part in developing and promoting the culture of indigo in South Carolina. In 1753 Charles Pinckney was appointed agent of the colony in London and went thither with his family, planning to educate in England and on the Continent his sons, Charles Cotesworth and Thomas [q.v.]. In 1758 he left the boys there and, returning with his wife to South Carolina, died within a few months. The elder son studied under a tutor, attended a school in Kensington, and then entered the Westminster School in 1761. After making a high record there, he matriculated at Christ Church College, Oxford, Jan. 19, 1764, and on Jan. 24 was admitted to the Middle Temple. While at Oxford he attended the lectures of Sir William Blackstone. Called to the English bar Jan. 27, 1769, he rode one circuit for experience and then traveled widely on the Continent. In France he studied botany under Charles, chemistry under Fourcroy, and military science at the royal military academy at Caen. He returned to America late in 1769 and, admitted to the South Carolina bar Jan. 19, 1770, at once began successful practice. On Sept. 28, 1773, he married Sarah, the third surviving daughter of Henry Middleton, 1717–1784 [q.v.], and sister of Arthur Middleton, 1742–1787 [q.v.]. She died May 8, 1784, and on June 23, 1786, he married Mary, the daughter of Benjamin Stead.

Immediately after his return Pinckney en-

tered upon a career of public service. He was elected a member of the provincial Assembly in 1769; he was made acting attorney general in 1773 for Camden, Georgetown, and the Cheraws; and in January 1775 he became a member of the provincial congress, in which he took an active and prominent part. A devoted member of the Church of England, and all his life zealous in church work, he, nevertheless, strongly advocated disestablishment. He was made a member of the committee of five and of the special committee, both of them charged with the responsibility for local defense. On Feb. 3, 1776, he was elected to the council of safety, and, on Feb. 10, chairman of the committee of eleven to draft a plan for the temporary government of the province. He was a member of the lower house of the legislature in 1778 and of the Senate in 1779, being chosen president of the latter body. In the same year he was again a member of the council of safety.

After his return from England Pinckney had kept up his interest in military affairs and had soon been made a lieutenant in the militia. Upon the organization of the 1st Regiment of South Carolina troops in June 1775 he was chosen the ranking captain, quickly became major, and in September 1776 was promoted colonel. With his regiment he took part in the defense of Fort Sullivan in June 1776, but when hostilities were suspended in the South his eagerness for active service caused him to secure leave from his regiment and to go north where he served for a time as aide to Washington and was present at the battles of Brandywine and Germantown. He was again in command of his regiment in the Florida campaign of 1778 and in the siege of Savannah. During the attack on Charlestown he was in command of Fort Moultrie. In the council of war called by General Lincoln to discuss the surrender of Charlestown, he vehemently but vainly opposed the suggestion. As a prisoner he was treated with great courtesy by the British officers who sought to detach him from the American cause. To one of these he wrote: "The freedom and independence of my Country are the Gods of my Idolatry." To another he said: "If I had a vein that did not beat with the love of my Country, I myself would open it. If I had a drop of blood that could flow dishonourably, I myself would let it out" (Ravenel, post, p. 297). Later he was sent to Philadelphia where he and his brother were together for a time. Exchanged in 1782, he rejoined the army, and on Nov. 3, 1783, just before his discharge, he was commissioned brigadier-general by brevet.

Once more he began the practice of his profession in Charleston, but he was frequently in the public service. In 1782, before he left the army, he was elected to the lower house of the legislature. In 1787 he was a delegate to the Federal Convention and was prominent in its deliberations. He opposed the imposition of any religious test for office; he suggested the year 1808 as the date at which Congress should assume power over the foreign slave trade; he argued strongly for giving the Senate power to ratify treaties as a wholesome check on the president; and he urged without success that senators should serve without pay. In the following year he was a member of the state convention which ratified the Constitution, and was one of the ablest defenders of the new system of government. He was also a member of the constitutional convention of 1790. He was a strong advocate of locating the state capital at Charleston and was a member of the committee, chosen to reconcile the conflicting claims of the low country and up country, which practically established two seats of government. In 1791 he was offered and declined the command of the army afterward conferred on Gen. Arthur St. Clair. On May 24, Washington wrote a remarkable joint letter to Pinckney and Edward Rutledge, his brother-in-law and partner, urging that one of them accept appointment as associate justice of the Supreme Court of the United States to succeed John Rutledge (W. C. Ford, *Writings of Washington*, XII, 43–44). Both declined. Jefferson might well write Rutledge (Aug. 29, 1791, P. L. Ford, *Writings of Thomas Jefferson*, V, 1895, p. 376): "Would to God yourself, Genl Pinkney [Pinckney], Maj. Pinkney [Pinckney] would come forward and aid us. . . . What is to become of us, my dear friend, if the vine & the fig-tree withdraw & leave us to the bramble & thorn?" On Jan. 22, 1794, Washington renewed an offer previously declined to make Pinckney secretary of war. He replied, "Of all the public offices in our country, the one you mention to me is that which I should like best to fill" (W. C. Ford, *ante*, XII, 405, footnote), but he declined it, as he did the secretaryship of state in August 1795. Finally, however, when Washington, in July 1796, offered him the mission to France to succeed Monroe, and urged it upon him in a most complimentary letter, Pinckney at once accepted. He had been friendly to the revolutionary movement in France from 1789 until 1793, but his sympathies had since become considerably alienated.

He arrived in Paris in December and the Directory declined to recognize his official status. He lingered on until February when he was notified by the police that unless he secured a permit he was liable to arrest. Then in a proper rage he left Paris for Amsterdam. In 1797 Adams nominated him to serve on a special mission to France with John Marshall and Elbridge Gerry [*qq.v.*]; in September he left The Hague and in October joined his colleagues in Paris. The X. Y. Z. affair followed in which Hottinguer (X.) approached Pinckney with a statement of the terms upon which negotiations would be undertaken by the French government. When pressed for a reply, Pinckney exclaimed vehemently: "It is No! No! Not a sixpence!" The familiar slogan, "Millions for defence but not one cent for tribute," is ascribed to Robert Goodloe Harper (*South Carolina Historical and Genealogical Magazine*, Jan. 1900, p. 101; July 1900, p. 264). After the failure of the mission, Gerry remained in Paris, Marshall sailed immediately for America, and Pinckney, with an ill daughter, went to the south of France where he remained for several months before returning home. When, under the stress of the feeling excited by the revelation of the affair, preparations for war began, Washington selected Pinckney for major-general, hesitating for a long time, because of his place and influence in the South, about giving him a lower rank than Hamilton. When the appointments were made by President Adams, Pinckney offered no objection, and, when General Knox declined to accept the lower rank, offered to yield him precedence, saying, "Let us first dispose of our enemies, we shall then have time to settle the question of precedence" (Ravenel, *post*, p. 318). Commissioned July 19, 1798, he was placed in command of all the posts and forces south of Maryland and also of those in Kentucky and Tennessee. Later he was given specific direction of all the cavalry. He was discharged from service, June 18, 1800.

In politics Pinckney was a Federalist of the conservative state-rights group and was never partisan. In the election of 1800 he was the choice of his party for vice-president and, like his brother in 1796, was the innocent party in an unsuccessful scheme of Alexander Hamilton to defeat Adams. In 1804 and 1808 he was the Federalist candidate for president. During these years, so far as his public service permitted, he was busily engaged in the practice of law. He was not a brilliant lawyer, but, learned and essentially sound, possessed of sane common sense, he was effective and had an immense practice. Of imposing figure, genial and full of fun and humor, liberal in opinion, independent and penetrating in his judgment of men and movements, universally trusted and admired, he was also constantly engaged in public undertakings. In the legislature of 1801 he was a strong supporter of the movement which led to the establishment of the South Carolina College and was the first elected member of its board of trustees. In 1810 he became the first president of the Charleston Bible Society and held the office until his death. From 1795 until 1798 he was major-general of the state militia. He was president of the Charleston Library Society. Owning a fine plantation, "Belmont," near Charleston, he had a lively and intelligent interest in agriculture and was a member of the South Carolina Agricultural Society. He was the first president of the South Carolina Society of the Cincinnati, resigning in 1805 to become the third president general of the Society, a position which he held until his death. At "Belmont" and at his home on East Bay in Charleston he dispensed a ready, kindly hospitality. He died in Charleston. Two of his three daughters died unmarried; the third had no children.

Charles Cotesworth and Thomas Pinckney well deserved the characterization of them by William H. Trescott (*The Diplomatic History of the Administrations of Washington and Adams*, 1857, p. 170) : "Cultivated in their tastes and simple in their manners, placed by fortune where the exercise of a graceful hospitality was the habit of their daily life, and the assumption of high duties the natural consequence of their position, brave and gentle, free, with all the genuine frankness of the Southern nature, and yet grave as became earnest men in trying times, able, unselfish, active, their success in life was free from all the feverish excitement of political adventure. They sought neither place nor power, but rose gradually from duty to duty, illustrating in the fulness of their lives and services the virtues of the class to which they belonged."

[Pinckney papers in the S. C. Hist. Soc. and in the possession of various members of the Pinckney family; *Am. State Papers. Foreign Relations*, vols. I, II (1832) ; C. C. Pinckney, *Life of Gen. Thomas Pinckney* (1895) ; H. H. Ravenel, *Eliza Pinckney* (1896) ; H. C. Lodge, ed., *The Works of Alexander Hamilton* (8 vols., 1885–86) ; W. C. Ford, ed., *The Writings of George Washington* (14 vols., 1889–93) ; Max Farrand, *The Records of the Federal Convention of 1787* (3 vols., 1911) ; Alexander Garden, *Eulogy of Gen. Chs. Cotesworth Pinckney* (1825) ; C. E. Gadsden, *A Sermon Preached . . . on the Occasion of the Decease of Gen. Charles Cotesworth Pinckney* (1825) ; U. B. Phillips, "The South Carolina Federalists," in *Am. Hist. Review*, Apr., July 1909 ; F. J. Turner, ed., "Correspondence of the French Ministers, 1791–1797" in *Ann. Report of the Am. Hist. Asso. . . . 1903* (1904) ; II ; J. B. O'Neall, *Biog. Sketches of the Bench and Bar of S. C.* (1859), II, 130–37 ; *Cyc. of Eminent and Representative Men of the Carolinas* (1892), I, 117–20 ; obituary in *Charleston Courier*, Aug. 17, 19, 1825.]

J. G. deR. H.

PINCKNEY, ELIZABETH LUCAS (*c.* 1722–May 26, 1793), also known as Eliza Lucas. is identified with the development of indigo as a staple of colonial South Carolina. She was born probably in Antigua, where her father, Lieut.-Col. George Lucas, had been stationed and later became lieutenant governor. She was educated in England and arrived in South Carolina in 1738, when her father brought his wife and daughters to "Wappoo" plantation, near Charlestown (Charleston), inherited from his father, John Lucas. Upon Colonel Lucas' return to Antigua, Elizabeth was left at the age of sixteen to manage the business of three plantations. Popular in Charlestown society, she yet held herself to a systematic schedule of duties, music, and reading, and even studied sufficient law to draft wills for her poorer neighbors. She loved the plant world and soon was enthusiastically setting out live-oaks for future navies. As "Wappoo" and its twenty slaves were mortgaged, her problem was to find a profitable crop. Her father sent her a variety of West Indian seeds for experiment and about 1741 she first tried indigo, which theretofore had never been a success in South Carolina. She persevered to the third season before she ripened seed, and then her father sent a man from Montserrat to teach her the preparation for market. Upon her happy marriage, May 27, 1744, to Charles Pinckney, a prominent lawyer and a widower of more than twice her age, her parents presented him with the indigo then growing at "Wappoo" and wished to give her the plantation as a marriage dower. Creditors absorbed the plantation, but Pinckney distributed some of the indigo seed among his neighbors, and, after learning all he could from the French prisoners in Charlestown, published his information for the benefit of all.

After her marriage, Mrs. Pinckney lived at "Belmont" plantation on Charlestown Neck, where in consultation with her father's overseer she directed experiments with flax and hemp. She also revived silk-culture; dresses made from her silk are still exhibited. In March 1753, her husband having been appointed colonial agent for South Carolina, she and their children accompanied him to London. After considerable travel in England and a brief sojourn in London, they bought a home at Ripley, intending to remain until the children were educated. Five years later she returned with him to Charlestown for a visit, but he was taken with malaria and died in Mt. Pleasant, July 12, 1758. His will, finally probated in London in 1769, named as executors his wife, and their sons Charles Cotesworth and Thomas [*qq.v.*] when of age. The burden of a very large property, therefore, devolved upon the widow of thirty-six years; and, assisted by a competent overseer, she took up once more the round of plantation duties. Although she did not see her sons again until they were grown, she had a strong influence upon their brilliant careers.

After the Revolution, she went to live with her widowed daughter, Mrs. Daniel Horry, at "Hampton" plantation on the Santee, and there welcomed President Washington in 1791. Soon her health failed, and in April 1793 she sailed for Philadelphia in hope of surgical relief. There, on May 26, she died in her seventy-first year. She was buried in St. Peter's churchyard, Washington at his own request serving as a pallbearer. No portrait of her exists, but she is described as a small woman, with an unrivaled talent for conversation. Her extraordinary charm is reflected in her letters, which have both literary and historical value.

[C. C. Pinckney, *Life of Gen. Thomas Pinckney* (1895); H. H. Ravenel, *Eliza Pinckney* (1896); *S. C. Hist. & Geneal. Mag.*, Oct. 1907, pp. 217–19; Jan. 1913, p. 29; July 1916, pp. 101–02; Jan. 1918, pp. 31, 34; July 1918, p. 134; Oct. 1920, pp. 158–59, reprinting obituary in Charleston *City Gazette & Daily Advertiser*, July 17, 1793.]

A. K. G.

PINCKNEY, HENRY LAURENS (Sept. 24, 1794–Feb. 3, 1863), editor of the *Charleston Mercury*, congressman, mayor, was born in Charleston, S. C., a child of Charles Pinckney [*q.v.*] and Mary Eleanor Laurens, who died at the time of her son's birth. His early education was directed by his father and the Rev. George Buist. In 1812 he was graduated from South Carolina College and later had legal training under his brother-in-law Robert Y. Hayne [*q.v.*] but did not follow the law professionally. At the first opportunity (1816) he secured a seat from Charleston in the state House of Representatives to which he was regularly elected for the next seventeen years, serving acceptably a large part of this time as chairman of the ways and means committee and as speaker during the last three years (1830–1832). In June 1823, he became the proprietor and principal editor of the *Charleston Mercury*, established the previous year, and despite the competition of three other dailies he had soon enlarged its size and added a "country" edition. When in October 1832 he severed connections with it, the *Mercury* had probably the largest circulation of any newspaper of the state and was the most uncompromising champion of "Southern rights," having just concluded a successful agitation in favor of nullification of the tariff acts.

Meanwhile, Pinckney had been elected (1829)

intendant, or mayor, of Charleston. The next year he was defeated by a Unionist, but with the increasing acceptance of the policy of nullification, which had become the main issue in the city campaigns, he was returned to this office at the two ensuing elections and then sent successively to the Twenty-third and Twenty-fourth congresses (1833–1837). Throughout his first term he was in complete accord with the Calhoun state-rights faction, defending at every opportunity the doctrine of nullification as recently applied by his state at the obvious sacrifice of his chances of securing the navy yard and other federal works desired by his Charleston constituents. Early in the next Congress, however, in securing the passage of resolutions which ultimately led to the adoption by the House of the policy of laying on the table "without being either printed or referred" all petitions for the abolition of slavery (see his report, May 18, 1836, 24 Cong., 1 sess., *House Report No. 691*), he brought himself into sharp conflict with the Calhounites who were contending for the outright rejection of these offensive memorials. He was unjustly denounced by the latter as a traitor to the South, the suggestion even being made that he was selling his principles for a navy yard (Elizabeth Merritt, *James Henry Hammond, 1807–1864*, 1923, p. 38). Largely in consequence of this, he lost the support of the country parishes of his district and was defeated for reëlection in 1836. Having retained, however, his popularity with the city electorate, especially the plebeian element, he was again chosen mayor in 1837, 1838, and 1839. During this and his former period in this office he accomplished much in the way of civic improvement, notably the conversion of the College of Charleston (1837) into the first municipal college in the United States and the construction of the White Point or Battery Gardens, the most distinctive feature of Charleston's topography. During the remainder of his life he occupied public offices of only minor importance: collector of the port (1840–1841), member of the state House of Representatives (1844–1845), and city tax collector from 1845 to the time of his death.

He was twice married: to Rebecca Pinckney Elliott and Sabina Elliott Ramsay, a first cousin in each instance, and by the first marriage had two sons and a daughter.

[Mabel L. Webber, manuscript notes on the Pinckney family; W. L. King, *The Newspaper Press of Charleston, S. C.* (1872); obituaries in *Charleston Mercury* and *Charleston Daily Courier*, Feb. 4, 1863.]

J. H. E.

PINCKNEY, THOMAS (Oct. 23, 1750–Nov. 2, 1828), soldier, diplomat, governor of South

Carolina, was a native of Charlestown (Charleston), the son of Charles and Elizabeth (Lucas) Pinckney [*q.v.*], and the brother of Charles Cotesworth Pinckney [*q.v.*]. In 1753 he was carried to England and in 1765 entered the Westminster School. There he took a high stand, particularly in Greek, in which he was the first scholar of his year. He matriculated at Christ Church College, Oxford, Nov. 23, 1768, and on Dec. 16 was admitted to the Middle Temple. He was called to the bar Nov. 25, 1774. He spent an intervening year on the Continent in travel and in study at the royal military academy at Caen, France.

Late in 1774 he returned to South Carolina and was immediately admitted to the bar. Early in 1775 he joined a company of rangers as lieutenant, and upon the organization of the 1st South Carolina Regiment he was chosen a captain. On account of his previous military training he was employed in drilling officers and men. Later he was sent out on recruiting service, at which he proved successful. For a year he was stationed at Fort Johnson in Charlestown harbor and was employed as an engineer in constructing fortifications. In August 1776 he was sent to Fort Moultrie where he remained for two years with the exception of some months spent in recruiting in Maryland, Virginia, and North Carolina. On May 17, 1778, he was promoted major, and on account of his proved skill in handling troops he was constantly called upon to organize and drill new detachments. He took part in the ill-fated Florida campaign of 1778, participated in the battle of Stono in 1779, and, on account of his knowledge of French, was sent as a special aide to Count d'Estaing at Savannah and was thus present during the siege of the city and took part in the assault. In the interval between the British attacks on Charlestown, he practised law, served in the legislature of 1778, and on July 22, 1779, married Elizabeth, the daughter of Jacob and Rebecca (Brewton) Motte. He was in command of part of the defenses of Charlestown during the siege of 1780 and with his brother strongly opposed the surrender of the city. Before its fall he was sent out to hasten the troops expected for relief and thus escaped capture. He immediately went north to join Washington's army but soon returned on the staff of General Gates. He was severely wounded at Camden and was captured. He was, however, soon taken to the home of his mother-in-law, where he slowly recovered, though his wound was to trouble him for years to come. He was then sent with his brother to Philadelphia where they were paroled until they

were exchanged. In September 1781 he was recruiting in Virginia where he met Lafayette, for whom he formed a warm attachment and with whom he served at Yorktown. He then returned to South Carolina where he published a defense of Gates.

General Provost, after his repulse from Charlestown in 1779, burned "Auckland," Pinckney's home on the Ashepoo, and took away all the servants and stock, so Pinckney now took up his residence in Charleston where he practised law successfully. On Feb. 20, 1787, he was elected governor and served, according to South Carolina custom, for two terms of a year each; during this time he did much to restore order in the state, which still suffered from the results of foreign invasion and even more from the civil war that had prevailed during the closing years of the Revolution. Severe with criminals, he was inclined to leniency with respect to the Loyalists, and sought to soften the harshness of the laws against them and the asperities of popular feeling towards them. He was president of the convention of 1788 which ratified the Constitution, and in 1789 declined Washington's offer of a federal judgeship. In 1791 he was a member of the lower house of the legislature and drew the bill creating the court of equity.

In November 1791 Washington offered him the appointment as minister to Great Britain, and Pinckney accepted, his nomination being confirmed in January 1792. His instructions, prepared by Jefferson, ordered him to express "that spirit of sincere friendship which we bear to the English nation." He was further instructed to seek the liberation of American commerce from British restrictions and the protection of American seamen from impressment. Thanks to his personal qualifications, English education, and knowledge of English thought, he was *persona grata* in London, but his ministry, viewed in the large, was not highly successful. Foreseeing war in Europe, he labored to secure a prompt settlement of all questions in dispute, bombarding the Foreign Office with protests and demands that were usually, though not always, ignored. The appointment of Jay to negotiate a treaty hurt his feelings, as he frankly admitted, and he doubtless welcomed his appointment in April 1795 as special commissioner and envoy extraordinary to Spain to negotiate a treaty settling all matters in dispute between the two countries.

In Spain, Pinckney carried on his negotiations entirely with Godoy, the Duke de la Alcudia, better known as the Prince of Peace. In the face of the seemingly insuperable difficulties which at first confronted him, due chiefly to the Spanish policy of indefinite delay, Pinckney was bold, persistent, obstinate, and unfailingly tactful. On August 10, 1795, he submitted to the Spanish government an able state paper dealing with the southern boundary of the United States and the navigation of the Mississippi River. Time and international circumstances combined with his able efforts to bring Spain finally to agreement, and on Oct. 27, 1795, the treaty of San Lorenzo el Real was signed. The boundary settlement was in accordance with the treaty of peace between the United States and Great Britain; the right of free navigation of the Mississippi was recognized; and the privilege of a port of entry at New Orleans and the right of deposit for three years were granted. The treaty also provided for the establishment of a court for the settlement of American claims against the Spanish, and obligated both parties to restraint of the Indians. The treaty signed, Pinckney returned to London. Under special instructions from Washington, and with personal interest and zeal, he exhausted every possible device to secure the release of Lafayette, but without success. On Oct. 10, 1795, he had asked for recall; he now resumed the request, and came home in September 1796.

Before his return the Federalist party had chosen him as candidate for vice-president. He was defeated, however, through the machinations of Alexander Hamilton in his attempt by stratagem to defeat Adams and elect Pinckney president. He received fifty-nine electoral votes. In 1794, while they were in England, Mrs. Pinckney died. On Oct. 19, 1797, he married her sister, Frances, the widow of John Middleton. About the same time he was elected to Congress and took his seat Nov. 23, 1797. A Federalist, though strong in state-rights feeling, he in general supported the administration, but he was not always in agreement with it. He was not eager for war with France in 1798 and doubted the wisdom of elaborate military preparations. He also voted against the Sedition Act. He served until March 4, 1801, when he voluntarily retired. Pinckney's only other public service was in the War of 1812 when he was commissioned major-general and placed in command of the district extending from North Carolina to the Mississippi River. He was active and efficient, but won no special distinction, never seeing active service. He joined Jackson, took command of the forces at the end of the Creek War, and negotiated the treaty which concluded peace. For Jackson he conceived a great admiration

and recommended that he be placed in command of a new military district.

Deeply interested in agriculture, Pinckney was a scientific planter. He wrote frequently for the *Southern Agriculturist,* and in October 1828 published there a report to the South Carolina Agricultural Society on diversification of crops in the low country, based upon the results obtained at an experimental farm which he operated. On his plantations on Santee River, first at "Fairfield," and later at "Eldorado," he demonstrated his ability as a practical farmer as well. Owning a vast area of salt marsh, he remembered his observations in Holland, and, with the aid of a Dutch engineer whom he brought over, he constructed a system of dykes and reclaimed the land for immensely productive rice-planting. He also imported improved breeds of cattle. Pinckney was a wide reader and possessed a large private library. In November 1822, after the Denmark Vesey insurrection, he published, over the pseudonym "Achates," a pamphlet, *Reflections Occasioned by the late Disturbances in Charleston*; in this, after attacking the movement for the abolition of slavery, he made a plea for replacing the negro artisans and mechanics in Charleston with white freemen, arguing the advantages which would result from immigration. In 1806 he was elected president of the South Carolina Society of the Cincinnati, succeeding his brother, and held the position until 1826 when he succeeded him as president general of the Society.

Pinckney was tall and spare in figure, poised and self-controlled, with great personal dignity, but with delightfully easy and courteous manners. A contemporary comment (Robert Goodloe Harper, *Annual Report of the American Historical Association for the Year 1913*, 1915, vol. II, 24–25) gives a just appraisal in dwelling on his "prudence, moderation, sound judgment, great coolness and discretion, calm steady firmness of character, and uniformity of conduct." Many of his contemporaries found in him a strong resemblance to Washington. He died in Charleston after a long and painful illness. By his first marriage he had four children: Thomas, who left daughters only; Charles Cotesworth, through whom all of his name and line descended; Elizabeth, who married William Lowndes [*q.v.*]; and Harriott (or Harriotta) Lucas, who married Francis K. Huger [*q.v.*].

[Papers in the S. C. Hist. Soc., in the possession of members of the family, and in the archives of the Dept. of State; C. C. Pinckney, *Life of General Thomas Pinckney* (1895); H. H. Ravenel, *Eliza Pinckney* (1896); A. S. Salley, Jr., *Jour. of the Convention of S. C. . . . 1788* (facsimile, 1928); *Debates . . . in the House of Representatives of S.-C. . . . on the Consti-*

tution Framed for the U.-S. (1831) ; *Am. State Papers. Foreign Relations,* vols. I, II (1832) ; S. F. Bemis, "The London Mission of Thomas Pinckney, 1792–1796," in *Am. Hist. Review,* Jan. 1923, and *Pinckney's Treaty* (1926) ; U. B. Phillips, "The S. C. Federalists," in *Am. Hist. Review,* Apr., July 1909 ; W. H. Trescott, *The Diplomatic Hist. of the Administrations of Washington and Adams* (1857), p. 170 ; *Cyc. of Eminent and Representative Men of the Carolinas* (1892), vol. I ; J. B. O'Neall, *Biog. Sketches of the Bench and Bar of S. C.* (1859), II, 111–14; "The Pinckney Family of S. C.," in *Historical Mag.,* Sept. 1867 ; obituary in *Charleston Courier,* Nov. 4, 1828.]   J. G. deR. H.

PINE, ROBERT EDGE (1730–Nov. 19, 1788), painter, was born in London. He came of an artistic family and was associated from childhood with artists. His father, John Pine [see *Dictionary of National Biography*], a well-known engraver, was stout and jovial, but the son, Robert Edge, is recalled as a small man of sensitive temperament and irritable disposition. His brother, Simon, was a successful miniature painter at Bath. Instructed by his father, Pine early attained recognition in England as a painter of ability. He was always interested in the theatre, and his first paintings were of actors and actresses in well-known characters. One of his earliest works was a painting of Thomas Lowe and Mrs. Chambers as Captain Macheath and Polly, engraved by McArdell. In 1760, to the first exhibition held in London by the Society for the Encouragement of Arts (now Royal Society of Arts), he contributed a full-length portrait of Mrs. Pritchard as Hermione and also a large painting, "The Surrender of Calais," receiving for the latter a prize of one hundred guineas offered for the best historical work; he won the same prize again in 1763 by his painting, "Canute Rebuking His Courtiers." In 1772, because of "an insult from the president," he withdrew from the Society, and thereafter exhibited in the Royal Academy until 1784.

While in England Pine painted four portraits of Garrick, one of which is now in the National Portrait Gallery, London, and another in the New York Public Library. He also did a large subject picture of Garrick reciting an ode to Shakespeare, which was engraved in stipple by Caroline Watson. Among his other well-known works from this period are a full-length portrait from memory of George II (at Audley End) and a full-length portrait of the Duke of Northumberland (at Middlesex Hospital). In 1782 he showed in London a series of paintings illustrating scenes from Shakespeare, which collection in whole or part he brought with him to America two years later and exhibited in the State House in Philadelphia—one of the earliest, if not the earliest, exhibition of paintings ever held in the United States. At the Royal Academy, 1784, he exhibited portraits of Lord Amherst and the Duke of Norfolk, as well as a "Portrait of Lord Rodney in Action, aboard the *Formidable*," which was later hung in the Town Hall at Kingston, Jamaica. His paintings were popular and were engraved by such well-known engravers as J. McArdle, C. Watson, Valentine Green, Aliamet, Lomax, and Dickinson.

After the death of his brother Simon in 1772, Pine resided for five years in Bath, then returned to London. He was a close friend of John Wilkes, whose principles he espoused, and he was deeply in sympathy with the American cause. In 1784 he came to America, intending to produce a series of historical paintings illustrative of the Revolution. The exact time of his arrival is uncertain, but he was in Philadelphia in November. His portrait of Francis Hopkinson, the first he painted after reaching Pennsylvania, bears the date 1785. He spent several weeks at Mount Vernon in April and May of that year, painting portraits of Washington and members of his family—notably Fanny Bassett Washington and young George Washington Parke Custis. A portrait of Washington's mother, Mary Ball Washington, is also attributed to him (see *New York Genealogical and Biographical Record,* April 1918). In 1787 he made some changes in his portrait of Washington, which is now in Independence Hall, Philadelphia.

Pine did not succeed in carrying out his ambitious plan for a series of historical paintings, although he never completely abandoned it. Before he went to Mount Vernon he spent some time at Annapolis painting portraits of prominent men and women which he intended to use in his larger pictures. Washington, in a private letter, said: "Mr. Pine has met a favorable reception in this country, & may, I conceive, command as much business as he pleases" (W. C. Ford, *The Writings of George Washington,* vol. X, 1891, p. 467). There are contemporary records of portraits by him of General Gates, Charles Carroll, Baron Steuben, Mrs. John Jay, Robert Morris, and others, but his only historical picture completed in America was "The Congress Voting Independence," painted in Congress Hall, and this was finished, presumably after his death, by Edward Savage [*q.v.*]. It is now owned by the Historical Society of Pennsylvania. Robert Morris, the financier, was one of his best patrons and built a house for him "suitable to his objects" on Eighth Street, Philadelphia.

When Pine came to America he brought with him his wife and two daughters, all of whom are said to have been diminutive, like himself. He also brought, as an art treasure, one of the earliest casts of the Venus de Medici, but since, in the words of Joseph Hopkinson, "the manners of our country, *at that time,* would not tolerate the public exhibition of such a figure" (Dunlap, *post,* I, 378), it was kept shut up in its case and only shown privately. After Pine's death, in Philadelphia, from a stroke of apoplexy, his widow, who had assisted him in his drawing classes, secured permission to dispose of his works by lottery. A considerable number of them went to the Columbian Museum, Boston, and there Washington Allston saw them and is said to have been strongly influenced by them, but when the Museum burned the entire collection was destroyed. Joseph Hopkinson, second president of the Pennsylvania Academy, wrote in 1833 that Pine's works "were scattered about in Virginia where he went occasionally to paint portraits" (Dunlap, I, 377), and comparatively few can now be located. Portraits of one of the Lees, Benjamin Franklin, Samuel Huntington, and George Reid, all well authenticated, have been exhibited at the Pennsylvania Academy; the Metropolitan Museum, New York, owns Pine's "Mrs. Reid in the Character of a Sultana"; his "General Gates" belongs to the American Scenic and Historic Preservation Society, New York; his portraits of George Washington Parke Custis and Elizabeth Parke Custis are at Washington and Lee University; "Martha Washington" is at the Virginia Historical Society, Richmond; "Francis Hopkinson" and "Robert Morris" are in the collection of the Historical Society of Pennsylvania, and the portraits of Charles Carroll and Polly Carroll (Mrs. Richard Caton) are still in the possession of the Carroll family of Maryland.

[William Dunlap, *A Hist. of the Rise and Progress of the Arts of Design in the U. S.* (3 vols., 1918), ed. by F. W. Bayley and C. E. Goodspeed; Samuel Redgrave, *A Dict. of Artists of the English School* (1874); H. T. Wood, *A Hist. of the Royal Soc. of Arts* (1913); C. H. Hart, "The Congress Voting Independence," *Pa. Mag. of Hist. and Biog.,* Jan. 1905; J. H. Morgan and Mantle Fielding, *The Life Portraits of Washington* (1931); W. S. Baker, *The Engraved Portraits of Washington* (1880); L. A. Hall, *Cat. of the Dramatic Portraits in the Theatre Collection of the Harvard College Library* (4 vols., 1930–34); sketch by L. H. Cust, in *Dict. Nat. Biog.; Fed. Gazette and Phila. Evening Post,* Nov. 22, 1788; Catalogues of Independence Hall, Metropolitan Museum of Art, Lenox Library, Panama-Pacific Exposition, Hist. Soc. of Pa.]   L. M.

PINGREE, HAZEN STUART (Aug. 30, 1840–June 18, 1901), manufacturer, mayor of Detroit, governor of Michigan, was born at Denmark, Me., the fourth child of Jasper and Adeline (Bryant) Pingree. His father, a farmer, was a descendant of an old New England family. At the age of fourteen he left school to work in a cotton mill and later went into a shoe factory.

During the Civil War he enlisted and was mustered into service at Boston on Aug. 2, 1862, as private in Company F, 14th Massachusetts Infantry, subsequently the 1st Massachusetts Heavy Artillery. He served for two years and reënlisted for the balance of the war. In May 1864 he was captured and was paroled the following November. He was mustered out as a private on Aug. 16, 1865. Soon after his discharge he went to Detroit, Mich., where he secured employment in a shoe factory. In December 1866 he entered a partnership in a shoe-manufacturing enterprise, which subsequently became one of the largest in the West, employing about seven hundred men. He married Frances A. Gilbert in February 1872.

In 1889 Pingree was offered the Republican nomination for mayor of Detroit, then normally Democratic, and was elected in a "reform" campaign. His administration was tempestuous. Relatively inexperienced in politics, he was apparently shocked at the situation he found, though the Detroit government was far from notorious in that day of municipal scandals. A group of private vested interests were controlling politics in self-protection. Pingree had voiced only mild objection to the system in his campaign but his utterances rapidly became more radical and specific. He found the city paying a private utility for street lighting at a rate which seemed to him excessive and after a bitter fight established a municipal electric plant. He boasted of the low cost of his new system, but seems not to have advocated extending the benefits to private users of electricity. Perhaps the most bitter controversy was with the local street railway company. The earlier single-line street railways had been consolidated into a monopoly which gave indifferent service at rates which were said to be excessive. The fight at first centered about an extension of a franchise, which yet had years to run. Pingree proposed to grant extension only on concessions. He then tried to introduce competition by securing a franchise for a second company, only to have the two lines combine. He waged an attack on the toll gates which still cumbered every important road to the city and secured their abolishment. He forced price reductions by gas and telephone companies. When the panic of 1893 filled the city with jobless he inaugurated his plan of gardens for the unemployed and "Pingree's Potato Patches" secured national notice.

To national politics Pingree paid slight attention, but in 1896 he accepted the Republican nomination for governor and was elected. Made governor while still mayor of Detroit, he tried to hold both offices, but the state supreme court ruled that the city office had been vacated. As governor his chief attack was on the railroads and on the legal difficulty in collecting just taxes, growing out of early and incautious charters. His chief strength, a direct appeal to the people, was less effective over the larger area, and he had difficulty in securing the cooperation of his legislatures. He made an effort to dramatize his part and Michigan's contribution to the Spanish-American War, but a scandal concerning the supplies for the Michigan militia marred his administration and the war diverted public attention from state politics. He served two terms as governor. Once more a private citizen, he traveled in Europe and Africa. His interest in the Boers and his prejudice against England led him to begin a history of the Boer War, which his death interrupted. He died in England, and was buried in Detroit. His wife and two of their three children survived him.

Pingree's chief contributions were made while mayor of Detroit. Without specific training for the office or clear-cut theory, he was sometimes inconsistent and seldom constructive. He was best when combating special privilege and corruption, though his controversies were marred by invective and personal reflections. He was constantly at odds with the Republican organization under Senator McMillan, yet his personal popularity made him indispensable. Pingree must be listed as one of the important pre-Roosevelt reformers who awakened public conscience. The people of Michigan, by public subscription, erected a statue to his memory in Grand Circus Park, Detroit.

[Pingree's seven messages as mayor of Detroit and his messages as governor are all printed and with his other printed speeches best show his program and attitude. He kept newspaper scrap-books, 1890–1901, 253 volumes, which are in Burton Historical Collection, Detroit Pub. Lib. His one book, *Facts and Opinions, or Dangers That Beset Us* (1895), is a personal reaction to contemporary problems. Some information on his early business career is contained in an advertising booklet, *Detroit, The Beautiful* (n.d.), pub. by the Pingree Company, Shoe Manufacturers. See also: G. B. Catlin, *The Story of Detroit* (1923); *Mich. Biogs.*, vol. II (1924); W. M. Pengry, *A Geneal. Record of the Descendants of Moses Pengry of Ipswich, Mass.* (1881); *Detroit News* and *Detroit Free Press*, June 19, 1901. There is a manuscript thesis by Muriel Bernitt, "The Campaign of 1896 in Mich." (1931), in the Univ. of Chicago Lib.]   R. C. M—r.

PINKERTON, ALLAN (Aug. 25, 1819–July 1, 1884), detective, was born in Glasgow, Scotland, the son of William Pinkerton, a sergeant of the police force. When Allan was ten years old his father, on duty during Chartist riots, was so severely injured that he never walked again.

Four years later he died. Forced to help maintain the family, the boy was apprenticed at the age of twelve to a cooper; at nineteen he became an independent craftsman. His part in the Chartist demonstrations of 1842 led him to fear arrest, and he decided to go to America. On the day before sailing he married Joan Carfrae. They reached Chicago where Pinkerton found temporary employment in a brewery. The next year they moved to the Scotch settlement of Dundee on the Fox River where he established a cooper's shop of his own. One day while cutting hoop poles on an unfrequented island he chanced upon a rendezvous for counterfeiters and he led a party which captured the entire gang. Similar success followed in several local detective commissions, and in 1846 he was made deputy sheriff of Kane County. An ardent Abolitionist he was also a "foreman" of the Underground Railroad and his shop was a station. Wider recognition came with an invitation to become deputy sheriff of Cook County and he sold a prosperous business to move to Chicago. In 1850 he was attached to Chicago's newly organized police force as its first and at that time only detective. The same year, in response to suggestions from several railroad presidents following a series of robberies, he established, in partnership with E. G. Rucker, a lawyer, a private detective agency, one of the first of its kind in the country. Rucker withdrew within a year, and Pinkerton resigned his city connections to give full time to his venture.

The solution of several sensational Adams Express robberies gave the Agency a national reputation and brought it much Eastern business in the years before the Civil War. In January 1861 Pinkerton was employed by the Philadelphia, Wilmington & Baltimore Railroad to investigate threats by Southern sympathizers against its property. While his operatives were working on the case in Baltimore they learned of an intended attempt on Lincoln's life to be made as he passed through the city on the way to his inauguration. With several of Lincoln's advisers, Pinkerton worked out plans for the President's unexpected night trip (Feb. 22, 23) ahead of schedule to the capital. In April 1861 Lincoln invited Pinkerton to a conference on the subject of a secret-service department, but no action was taken. A few weeks later, at the invitation of Gen. George B. McClellan, a close friend and former client, Pinkerton agreed to organize and conduct a secret service for the Ohio Department which McClellan commanded. Agents were immediately sent into Kentucky and West Virginia, and Pinkerton himself, in disguise, toured Tennessee, Georgia, and Mississippi. When in July McClellan was made commander-in-chief Pinkerton accompanied him to Washington and established headquarters at the capital and an office in the field. He now also directed important counter-espionage activities in Washington. During the war he went under the name of Maj. E. J. Allen, and many officers who knew him well did not suspect his real identity. He resigned upon McClellan's removal in November 1862 and thereafter served as an investigator of numerous claims against the government.

At the close of the war he resumed the personal direction of his Agency and established branches in Philadelphia and New York. In 1869 he suffered a slight paralytic stroke, and thereafter left to others the work of actual investigation. More protective work was being done on an annual payment basis, a type of service inaugurated by Pinkerton in 1860. The Agency was building up a voluminous record of its criminal contacts which at the time was the most usefully complete in America. Pinkerton also devoted much time to writing reminiscent detective narratives to the extent of eighteen volumes, based for the most part upon the Agency's experiences. Written in pleasant style, the books sold like novels and did much to advance the fame and prestige of Pinkerton's name. From an autobiographical viewpoint the most valuable were *Criminal Reminiscences and Detective Sketches* (1879); *The Spy of the Rebellion* (1883); and *Thirty Years a Detective* (1884). The policy in labor disputes that was to win the Pinkertons severe criticism in the closing years of the century was forecast during the strikes of 1877 when Allan Pinkerton still directed affairs. He had come into contact with the more vicious side of early labor combinations and apparently sincerely believed that Unions were hurting rather than helping the cause of the workingman. (See the introduction to his *Strikers, Communists, Tramps, and Detectives*, 1878.) His was not a mind for analyzing social problems but rather a genius for detail, organization, and practical results. After his death his two sons took over the direction of the Agency.

[All of Pinkerton's books are to some extent autobiographical and reveal his opinions. R. W. Rowan's *The Pinkertons* (1931) is popularly written. Pinkerton states in *The Spy of the Rebellion*, p. xxxi, that many of his Civil War papers were destroyed in the Chicago fire. See under E. J. Allen in the index to *War of the Rebellion: Official Records (Army)*; McClellan's report, *House Executive Doc. 15*, 38 Cong., 1 Sess.; Pinkerton's *Hist. and Evidence of the Passage of Abraham Lincoln from Harrisburgh, Pa., to Washington, D. C.* (1868); *Chicago Tribune, N.-Y. Tribune*, July 2, 1884.]

O. W. H.

PINKERTON, LEWIS LETIG (Jan. 28, 1812–Jan. 28, 1875), clergyman, editor, prominent in the activities and controversies of the Disciples of Christ in Kentucky, was a native of Baltimore County, Md. His father, William, was of Scotch-Irish ancestry, and his mother, Elizabeth (Letig), of German. Five of their sons became preachers, and six of their grandsons. Soon after Lewis' birth the family moved to Chester County, Pa., and later to West Liberty, not far from Bethany, in what is now West Virginia. Here he encountered Campbellite influences, and in 1830, having already become dissatisfied with Presbyterianism, his father's faith, he ardently embraced the views of the Disciples. Such elementary schooling as necessary work on the farm had permitted him to secure was now completed at Pleasant Hill Seminary, West Middletown, Pa., and in 1831 he went to Trenton, Butler County, Ohio, and for four years studied medicine, supporting himself by teaching. On Mar. 19, 1833, he married Sarah A. Bell. He began practice in 1834 and the following year settled in Carthage, Ohio. Although successful professionally, he felt impelled to preach, and his evangelical work finally led him in December 1839 to remove to Kentucky and abandon medicine for the ministry.

After short pastorates in New Union and Lexington, he accepted a call to the church at Midway, which he served from 1844 to 1860. Here in the church edifice he opened a school for girls, the Baconian Institute, and soon built for it a schoolroom and dormitory. He was also instrumental in having established the Kentucky Female Orphan School, chartered by the legislature in 1847. For a year, 1848, he published a monthly magazine, the *Christian Mirror*; he edited the Kentucky department of the *Christian Age*, 1853–54; and during the latter year conducted a temperance paper, *The New Era*. Under the urgency of John B. Bowman [*q.v.*], founder of Kentucky University, Harrodsburg, Pinkerton became professor of English in that institution in 1860. A pronounced anti-slavery man and supporter of the Union, he was commissioned as surgeon in the 11th Kentucky Cavalry in September 1862, and also took upon himself the duties of chaplain. His service was soon terminated by a sunstroke, from the effects of which he suffered for the rest of his life. When Kentucky University was transferred to Lexington in 1865, he removed to that place.

After the war his career was a troubled and somewhat unhappy one. His aggressive support of the Union was resented by many of his co-religionists. Pulpits were closed to him; in 1866 he thought it best to resign his professorship. For a brief period he was agent of the Freedman's Bureau in Fayette County, but from 1866 to 1873 he had no fixed charge, though he was offered the presidency of Hiram College in 1867. The opposition to him was not due to his politics alone, but also to his liberal theological convictions. He opposed the legalistic view of religion common among the Disciples, laying emphasis on personal righteousness rather than on conformity to prescribed doctrines and rites; rejected the verbal inspiration of the Bible; sanctioned the admission of the unimmersed into the Church; and advocated the Presbyterian form of church government. He set forth his view in the short-lived *Independent Monthly,* begun in January 1869, which he edited with John Shackleford, Jr., and in other periodicals. Branded as a heretic in his day, he is now recognized as perhaps the first to combat a formalism that threatened the vitality of the Churches of Christ and as one who was a liberalizing force in the history of the Disciples. No one ever questioned his piety, his sincerity, his courage, or his unselfishness.

Apparently through the influence of his friend James A. Garfield, he was appointed in 1873 special mail agent. While he was on a trip to investigate irregular mail service in the Kentucky mountains in October 1874, an illness began from which he never recovered. He published *A Discourse Concerning Some of the Effects of the Late Civil War on Ecclesiastical Matters in Kentucky* (1866), and a few of his writings are preserved in *Life, Letters, and Addresses of Dr. L. L. Pinkerton* (1876), by John Shackleford, Jr.

[In addition to the *Life* mentioned above, see J. T. Brown, *Churches of Christ* (1904); W. T. Moore, *A Comprehensive Hist. of the Disciples of Christ* (1909); W. E. Garrison, *Religion Follows the Frontier* (1931); A. W. Fortune, *The Disciples in Ky.* (copr. 1932); Harry Giovannoli, *Ky. Female Orphan School: A History* (1932); *Christian Standard,* Feb. 6, 13, 1875.]

H. E. S.

PINKHAM, LYDIA ESTES (Feb. 9, 1819–May 17, 1883), patent medicine manufacturer, was born in Lynn, Mass., of English colonial stock, the tenth of the twelve children of William Estes, a shoemaker, by his second wife, Rebecca Chase. She spent her entire life, except for a few years of childhood, in her native town. After completing the course in the academy she became a school teacher. She was a member from its beginning of the Female Anti-Slavery Society of Lynn, was made secretary of the Freeman's Society, and was a lifelong friend of Frederick Douglass. Like most reformers she was too magnanimous to specialize: Swedenborgianism, phrenology, temperance, Graham-

ism, woman's rights, and other causes enjoyed her warm approval, and in later years she embraced spiritualism and fiat money. On Sept. 8, 1843, she married a young widower, Isaac Pinkham, and for the next thirty years she was a wife and mother and not much else. She had four sons and a daughter, the second son dying in infancy. The business that made her famous and her heirs rich was not started until eight years before her death. In the financial smash of 1873 her husband, whose principal occupation was speculating in real estate, lost his money, health, and spirits together, and by 1875 the family, which had never been really prosperous, was reduced to actual want. In their need Lydia bethought her of an herb medicine that she had been concocting off and on for about ten years and that was beginning to have a local reputation as a sovereign remedy for "woman's weakness" and allied disorders. With neighborly kindness she had given the nostrum to whoever asked for it, even to a perfect stranger who had driven all the way from Salem to obtain a bottle of it. As Mrs. Lydia E. Pinkham's Vegetable Compound it made its commercial début in Lynn in 1875.

The meager profits, after the family had been fed, were turned back into the business, and while Mrs. Pinkham labored over the kitchen stove her sons distributed handbills from door to door and endeavored to sell the mixture to druggists in Salem, Boston, and Providence. Daniel, the most aggressive of the three, carried the campaign to Brooklyn and New York, where he received moral encouragement and a substantial cash order from Charles Nelson Crittenton. He was the first, also, to discover that the compound might be recommended impartially for the kidneys of both sexes. In 1876 a label was registered at the Patent Office, and sometime later a column advertisement in the Boston *Herald* gave the sales their first big impetus. Thereafter the Pinkhams bought newspaper space in larger and larger quantities until in 1898 the compound was the most widely advertised merchandise in the country. Besides supervising its manufacture, Mrs. Pinkham wrote the advertisements and answered faithfully a voluminous fan mail. In 1879 she authorized the use of her portrait as part of the propaganda. Her advertisements were an adaptation, at times more than a little quaint, of the language and ideology of the humanitarian and medical cults that had flourished in her youth, and with their intimacy of tone and their appeal to the emotions and to mental symptoms they proved to be remarkably effective exercises in what has been called "creative psychiatry." Worthless as a therapeutic agent (*Nostrums and*

Quackery, post, II, pp. 160–63), the compound was popular as a psychic sedative. In 1881 the two younger sons, Daniel and William, died of tuberculosis, which had been aggravated by overwork and the privations of their years of poverty. Shortly before her own death, which occurred within two years, the business was incorporated. She was its guiding spirit till the last. Since her death her fame has been ministered to not only by the art of advertising but by the national sense of humor, the Uplift, the American Medical Association, and the New Biography.

[Chas. Estes, *Estes Geneals.* (1894); C. N. Sinnett, *Richard Pinkham . . . and His Descendants* (1908); *Nostrums and Quackery* (Am. Medic. Asso., vol. II, 1921); Elbert Hubbard, *Lydia E. Pinkham* (1915); R. C. Washburn, "Lydia Pinkham," *Am. Mercury,* Feb. 1931, and *The Life and Times of Lydia E. Pinkham* (1931).]   G. H. G.

PINKNEY, EDWARD COOTE (Oct. 1, 1802–Apr. 11, 1828), poet and editor, was born in London, where his father, William Pinkney [*q.v.*] of Annapolis, Md., had been serving since 1796 as one of the commissioners of the United States to adjust claims under the Jay Treaty. Edward was the seventh of ten children. His mother, Ann Maria (Rodgers) Pinkney, also of Maryland, was a sister of Commodore John Rodgers [*q.v.*] of the United States Navy. The Pinkneys returned to Maryland in 1804 and lived in Baltimore until 1806, when the father was again sent to England on a diplomatic mission. In 1807 he was named minister to the Court of St. James's and held this post until 1811.

Edward's elementary education was begun in London, and continued in Baltimore at St. Mary's College, which had been established by the Sulpicians in 1803. In November 1815 he turned his back on his books for a commission as midshipman in the navy. His active service at sea continued with brief interruptions until the death of his father in 1822. It included duty in the ship of the line *Washington,* which carried his father on a diplomatic errand to Naples in June 1816, and kept him cruising in the Mediterranean, on board the *Washington* and other vessels, for nearly three years. Returning to America in the sloop *Peacock,* he was assigned to the *Constellation,* from which he was dismissed in 1821 in consequence of a protest which he and others made against what they thought an unjust penalty imposed by the commodore. After apologies, he was restored to duty, but was later involved in a disagreement with the captain. In the United States schooner *Porpoise,* he saw active service in the West Indies against pirates and was cited for bravery. He returned to Baltimore in 1822 and resigned his commission in 1824.

Soon after his resignation Pinkney was admitted to the bar, and practised law in Baltimore as a partner of Robert Wilson, Jr. He had already won some repute as a poet, having published with a musical setting in 1823 *Look Out Upon the Stars, My Love: A Serenade Written by a Gentleman of Baltimore,* and a slender volume entitled *Rodolph, A Fragment,* which won favorable comment from the *North American Review* (January 1824). He now, in 1825, issued a small volume, *Poems,* which included a new version of "Rodolph," and about a score of songs and lyrics. "Rodolph," a Byronic tale of lawless passion, may have influenced Poe's "Al Aaraaf." In the judgment of Poe and other mid-century critics, Pinkney was entitled to high rank among American lyric poets. After a journey to Mexico in the vain attempt to secure an appointment in the Mexican navy, from which he returned in ill health, he was chosen by the supporters of John Quincy Adams to be editor of a new paper, *The Marylander,* created as the organ of their cause. This paper appeared twice weekly from Dec. 5, 1827, and was edited by Pinkney until in 1828 failing health compelled him to retire. He died, less than twenty-six years old, and was buried in the Unitarian cemetery. In 1872 his body was moved to the Pinkney lot in Greenmount Cemetery. On Oct. 12, 1824, he married Georgiana McCausland, daughter of a citizen of Baltimore of Irish birth; they had one child. The poet is described by a contemporary as "a very handsome man." He was punctilious in matters of honor and was several times involved in challenges, though there is no record of his having fought a duel. One of these challenges was to John Neal [*q.v.*], who refused to fight, and Pinkney posted him as a coward. Brief and varied as his career was, his lyrics, particularly "A Health" and "Serenade," have won him what seems a secure place in American poetry.

[T. O. Mabbott and F. L. Pleadwell, *The Life and Works of Edward Coote Pinkney* (1926); Esmeralda Boyle, *Biog. Sketches of Distinguished Marylanders* (1877); C. W. Hubner, *Representative Southern Poets* (1906); *Marylander,* Apr. 16, 1828; *Baltimore Patriot,* Apr. 17, 1828; *N. Y. Mirror,* Apr. 26, 1828.]   J. C. F.

PINKNEY, NINIAN (June 7, 1811–Dec. 15, 1877), naval surgeon, was born in Annapolis, Md., the son of Ninian and Amelia (Grason) Hobbs Pinkney. His father held for thirty years the position of clerk of the council of Annapolis. He had served with distinction in the War of 1812 and was the author of *Travels through the South of France* (1809), which Leigh Hunt said "set all the idle world to going to France." Of relatives who achieved distinction perhaps the best known were his uncle, William Pinkney [*q.v.*], the lawyer, diplomatist, and statesman, and the poet, Edward Coote Pinkney [*q.v.*], a cousin. His brother William became Protestant Episcopal Bishop of Maryland. Ninian Pinkney was graduated from St. John's College in Annapolis in 1830, and from Jefferson Medical College, Philadelphia, with the degree of M.D., in 1833. The brilliant teacher of anatomy at Jefferson, Granville Sharp Pattison, is said to have looked upon Pinkney as his successor, but probably the glamour of travel and the certain income led him to the navy in which he was commissioned as assistant surgeon in 1834. After cruises in South American waters and in the Mediterranean, he served at the naval hospital in Philadelphia, 1838–39. In 1840 he was court-martialed on charges of "disrespectful and provoking language to a superior" and "conduct unbecoming to an officer and gentleman." He was found guilty of part of the charge and was suspended for eight months, but he returned to the service and for three years, 1841–44, was on the west coast of South America. This duty was followed by two years, 1844–46, on the receiving ship in Baltimore, blockade duty during the war with Mexico in 1846, and in 1852, by a coveted appointment at the Naval Academy. It was during the duty at Callao, Peru, 1841–44, that he built up a reputation for skill in surgery. This port was the rendezvous for the whaling fleet in the South Pacific, and to Pinkney fell the practice from this source. From Apr. 20, 1841, to Nov. 29 of the same year he reported forty-one operations of a major character, with but one death. After 1852, when he went to Annapolis, he took an active interest in the affairs of the American Medical Association and in improving conditions in his own corps. He rarely missed an annual meeting of the Association and in 1876 was elected a vice-president.

After another cruise in the Mediterranean, and duty at Washington, Pinkney was assigned as surgeon of the fleet to Admiral David D. Porter's squadron operating in the upper Mississippi. He joined the flagship *Black Hawk* in December 1862, but spent his time largely on the hospital ship *Red Rover*. His accomplishments under Admiral Porter, who became his lifelong friend, attest his ability. He had medical supervision over eighty ships, organized in 1863 the hospital at Memphis, named Pinkney Hospital in his honor, and in one letter to his wife he mentions having traveled 8,000 miles in visiting some ninety-five ships and stations, distributing medi-

cal supplies. After the war he took quite an active interest in politics. He had very definite ambitions about becoming the head of his corps, but the fates were to deny him this honor. He retired on June 7, 1873, with the rank of commodore, and settled with his wife and daughter in Easton, Md., in the house, "Londonderry," which he himself had planned and built. Here he died after a short illness, leaving his widow, Mary Sherwood Hambleton, and his only child, Amelia.

[Sources include: J. M. Toner, memoir in *Trans. Am. Medic. Asso.*, vol. XXIX (1878); F. L. Pleadwell, "Ninian Pinkney, M.D. (1811–1877)," *Annals of Medic. Hist.*, Nov. 1929, Jan. 1930; *War of the Rebellion: Official Records (Navy)*, 1 ser. XXIV, XXV, and XXVI; D. D. Porter, *Incidents and Anecdotes of the Civil War* (1885); Orlando Hutton, *Life of the Right Reverend Wm. Pinkney, D.D., LL.D.* (1890); the *Gazette* (Baltimore), Dec. 17, 1877; family papers; and the S. A. Harrison Collection, Md. Hist. Soc.]

F. L. P.

PINKNEY, WILLIAM (Mar. 17, 1764–Feb. 25, 1822), lawyer, statesman, diplomat, was born at Annapolis, Md., one of four children of Jonathan Pinkney, an English immigrant, and Ann Rind, his second wife. The latter, a native of Annapolis, was a sister of Margaret Rind, Jonathan's first wife, by whom he had one child. When the father's property was confiscated by reason of Loyalist sentiment in the Revolution, poverty necessitated the son's withdrawal from the King William School of Annapolis, at the age of thirteen. In overcoming the handicap of deficient education, Pinkney devoted a lifetime to intense study. According to tradition, he favored Maryland's cause in the war and would often elude the paternal vigilance to mount guard with the Continental soldiers. Sometime later, while he was receiving instruction in medicine from a Baltimore physician, a fortuitous occurrence changed the course of his life. Samuel Chase [*q.v.*] heard him debate in a society of medical students and, perceiving his aptitude for the law, offered the use of his library if he would undertake its study. Pinkney accepted; and in February 1783 entered Chase's office to master the obscurities of pleading and tenures from the black-letter learning of the day. He was called to the bar in 1786 and removed to Harford County to practise.

His first efforts attracted public attention and resulted in his election to the state convention that ratified the Federal Constitution, in April 1788, although Pinkney, under the influence of Chase, voted against its ratification; a circumstance worthy of note in view of his later preeminence as a constitutional lawyer. (See B. C. Steiner, "Maryland's Adoption of the Federal Constitution," *American Historical Review*, October 1899 and January 1900; but Rev. William Pinkney, *post*, p. 17, insinuates that he voted for it.) He was a member of the legislature continuously from October 1788 until his retirement in 1792. At the session in 1789 he delivered a florid speech advocating the abolition of slavery which, twenty years later, was published and distributed in Congress by the Quakers to challenge the consistency of his position on the Missouri question. On Mar. 16, 1789, he was married at Havre de Grace to Ann Maria Rodgers, sister of Commodore John Rodgers [*q.v.*] of the United States Navy; ten children—one of them being Edward Coote Pinkney [*q.v.*]—were born of this union, all of whom survived him. A capricious element in his character was exhibited in connection with his election to the Second Congress in 1790, which was disputed because he did not reside in the district from which he was chosen. He stubbornly contested the point and then, when successful, refused to serve. He was appointed a member of the state executive council in 1792 and was chairman of the council board when he resigned in 1795.

Meanwhile his rise at the bar had been sensational and, in 1796, Washington selected him as joint commissioner with Christopher Gore [*q.v.*], under the seventh article of the Jay Treaty, to adjust American claims for maritime losses. Eight strenuous years in London followed, significant years in his development. Speeches heard in Parliament and in the courts were the models of his later efforts. Contact with men of culture revealed, to his discomfort, the dearth of his own. Accordingly, he was tutored in Latin and Greek, read widely in law and literature, declaimed in private, and began a diligent study of dictionaries and lexicons that was never thereafter relaxed. From the work of the commission he also found time successfully to terminate a chancery suit instituted more than a decade before by Samuel Chase, recovering for the State of Maryland a large quantity of stock in the Bank of England. His prestige was great when he returned to practice in Baltimore in 1804, and on Dec. 1, 1805, he became attorney-general of Maryland. He relinquished this office, however, after six months' service.

Following Pinkney's return, British Admiralty courts began to justify the condemnation of American shipping by reviving the so-called "Rule of the War of 1756." In January 1806 a memorial attacking this "Rule" was drafted by Pinkney for the merchants of Baltimore and forwarded to Congress (*Memorial of the Merchants of Baltimore, on the Violation of Our Neutral Rights*, 1806). It induced Jefferson to appoint him, in the following April, as joint commissioner with James Monroe [*q.v.*], then minister resident in London, to treat with the British cabinet on the subjects of reparations and impressments. Wholly abandoning the three conditions that by their instructions were to form the foundation of the agreement, they signed a treaty remarkable for its failure even to bind the British government. Jefferson angrily repudiated it without consulting the Senate, yet when Monroe left England in October 1807, Pinkney was retained as minister. Immediately affairs became further complicated by the attack of the *Leopard* on the *Chesapeake* and the issuance of the British Orders in Council. Throughout the next four years Pinkney sought fruitlessly to obtain reparation for the former and repeal of the latter. No more difficult, futile task has been assigned to an American diplomat. The presence of a strong Anglophile party at home embarrassed his negotiations, while the conciliatory manner he was forced to adopt diminished his effectiveness. His correspondence with Canning, the foreign secretary, was distinguished alike for restraint under irritation and strength of argument. In finesse, however, he was wanting. On one occasion he was cajoled into making a written offer to repeal the Embargo in return for repeal of the Orders and, because the offer violated instructions, was deeply mortified by its prompt rejection. At length his notes to Wellesley, Canning's successor, elicited only vague replies after long delays, and Pinkney broke relations, rather inamicably, Feb. 28, 1811, convinced that matters would lead, as they did, to war. To admirers of Pinkney the lawyer, Pinkney the diplomat was disappointing. Moreover, there were numerous strictures in the press upon various phases of his work. Henry Adams declares, however, that "America never sent an abler representative to the Court of London" (Adams, *post*, VI, 21).

On his return he was appointed attorney-general in Madison's cabinet, Dec. 11, 1811, and in this office assumed undisputed leadership of the American bar, a leadership he maintained until his death. Owing to the introduction of a bill in Congress, requiring the residence of the attorney-general at the seat of government, he resigned abruptly, Feb. 10, 1814, before the bill was even reported out of committee. In pamphlets, under the pseudonym Publius, he vigorously supported the War of 1812, and as a major of Maryland militia he commanded a battalion of riflemen in the battle of Bladensburg, Aug. 24, 1814, being severely wounded in the arm. At the February term of the Supreme Court in 1815, he delivered a speech in the celebrated case of *The Nereide* (9 *Cranch,* 388), that was even extolled in the opinion (p. 430). He served in the Fourteenth Congress from Mar. 4, 1815, until Apr. 18, 1816, when he resigned to accept appointment as minister to Russia with a special mission to Naples en route. The object of the Naples mission was to obtain compensation from the existing government for shipping seized under the Murat régime. Through the strategy of the Marchese di Circello in avoiding an answer to Pinkney's note until after he had been forced to proceed on his way, the mission utterly failed and compensation was never secured. The prospect upon his arrival in Russia in January 1817 was not promising, for the controversy that followed the arrest of Kosloff, a Russian consul in America, had only recently been settled. Notwithstanding, he quickly accomplished one object of his mission by procuring the recall of every Russian diplomatic officer in the United States; and though he failed to negotiate the commercial treaty that was his primary object, he succeeded in establishing more friendly relations with Russia than had ever theretofore existed. His impatience to return to the bar had been daily increasing and, in declining appointment as minister to England, he wrote Monroe, "My desire is to be a mere lawyer" (Wheaton, *Life,* p. 160). In February 1818, he left Russia without awaiting his recall.

It was while serving in the United States Senate from Dec. 21, 1819, until his death that, as an interpreter of the Constitution, Pinkney performed his greatest work. In the Senate debates on the Missouri question, he became the champion of the slave-holding states and his speeches in opposition to Rufus King [*q.v.*] were an important factor in bringing about the Compromise. His most distinguished labors, however, were in the Supreme Court, where his arguments in *McCulloch* vs. *Maryland* (4 *Wheaton,* 316) and in *Cohens* vs. *Virginia* (6 *Wheaton,* 264) were his crowning achievements. Of the former, Justice Story wrote: "I never, in my whole life, heard a greater speech; it was worth a trip from Salem to hear it . . . his eloquence was overwhelming" (*Life and Letters, post,* I, 325).

During these years his foppish dress, his affected, flamboyant manner of delivery, and his extravagant rhetoric made him a vivid, picturesque figure. Women crowded to hear him and Pinkney, excessively vain, sought their approval as much as the Court's. He literally lived for applause. Though he desired to excel in everything, his ruling ambition was to excel at the bar, and to sustain his reputation there he toiled incessantly, feverishly; yet, oddly enough, sought to create the impression that his knowledge resulted from hasty incursions and that his precise citations of cases, made in an offhand manner, were but chance recollections. Toward those who challenged his supremacy his conduct was insolent and ungenerous. Much criticism resulted from insults offered in court to Thomas Addis Emmet (1764–1827) and William Wirt [*qq.v.*], and a duel with the latter was narrowly averted. For frequent discourtesies to Daniel Webster, the latter boasted of having extorted an apology under threat of a beating (Harvey, *post,* pp. 121–23). Conspicuous in Pinkney's physical appearance were his square shoulders, erect carriage, and intense blue eyes, but most conspicuous were the deep furrows in his face and the heavy circles under his eyes, and to conceal them he used cosmetics. He wore corsets to diminish his bulk. Despite apparent robust health, he was a hypochondriac. In society he was haughty and reserved. He had little sense of humor. Though he spent sixteen years in Europe, he was of counsel in seventy-two Supreme Court cases and acquired what has been described as the most extensive and lucrative practice of his time. That he was the most talented, versatile advocate of his time there can be little doubt. Volumes of contemporary eulogy attest his superiority. Chief Justice Marshall proclaimed him "the greatest man I ever saw in a Court of justice" (Tyler, *post,* p. 141). Chief Justice Taney wrote thirty years after his death: "I have heard almost all the great advocates of the United States, both of the past and present generation, but I have seen none equal to Pinkney" (*Ibid.,* p. 71). He never wrote his speeches, however, and no product of his pen that remains would seem a worthy index of his living fame. But fame in life he considered more desirable and strove to preserve it with increasing anxiety until, exhausted by overwork, he died at Washington and was buried there in the Congressional Cemetery.

[The two biographies are: Henry Wheaton, *Some Account of the Life, Writings, and Speeches of William Pinkney* (1826) and Rev. William Pinkney, *The Life of William Pinkney* (1853). Both are inadequate and panegyric; the latter must be read with care. Another sketch by Wheaton appears in Jared Sparks, *The Lib. of Am. Biog.,* vol. VI (1836). For good sketches see H. H. Hagan, *Eight Great Am. Lawyers* (1923) and A. S. Niles in vol. II (1907) of *Great Am. Lawyers,* ed. by W. D. Lewis. The following periodicals are important: *Law Reporter,* Sept. 1846; *Albany Law Jour.,* Aug. 20, 1870, Mar. 18, 1876, Aug. 2, 1879; *N. J. State Bar Asso. Year Book,* 1906–07; *U. S. Law Intelligencer,* Aug. 1830; *Am. Lawyer,* July 1905; *No. Am. Rev.,* Jan. 1827. For amusing anecdote see *Forum* (London), Jan. 1874. On diplomatic career see: *Am. State Papers, Foreign Relations,* vols. III, IV (1832–34); J. C. Hildt, "Early Diplomatic Negotiations of the U. S. with Russia," in *Johns Hopkins Univ. Studies in Hist. and Pol.*

Sci., vol. XXIV (1906); *Letters and Other Writings of James Madison* (4 vols., 1865); Henry Adams, *Hist. of the U. S.* (9 vols., 1889–93); Madison and Monroe Papers (MSS. Div., Lib. of Cong). For contemporaneous estimates see Wm. Sullivan, *Familiar Letters on Public Characters* (1834); W. P. Kennedy, *Memoirs of the Life of William Wirt* (2 vols., 1849); *Life and Letters of Joseph Story* (2 vols., 1851) and *The Miscellaneous Writings of Joseph Story* (1852), both ed. by W. W. Story; Samuel Tyler, *Memoir of Roger Brooke Taney* (1876); *Life, Letters and Journals of George Ticknor* (2 vols., 1876), ed. by A. E. Ticknor and A. E. Hilliard; Peter Harvey, *Reminiscences and Anecdotes of Daniel Webster* (1877); A. J. Beveridge, *The Life of John Marshall*, vol. IV (1919); *Daily National Intelligencer* (Washington), Feb. 26, 1822. The source for date of marriage is "Maryland Marriages, 1777–1804" (typescript in Md. Hist. Soc.); genealogical material has been taken from records in the possession of Mrs. L. Roberts Carton, Towson, Md.]
J. J. D.

PINNEY, NORMAN (Oct. 21, 1804–Oct. 1, 1862), clergyman, educator, was born in Simsbury, Conn., the son of Butler Pinney, whose wife was Eunice (Griswold), widow of Oliver Holcomb. He was a descendant of Humphrey Pinne, who emigrated from England to Dorchester, Mass., in 1630. Norman received a college training at Yale, where he won the Berkleian Premium and was graduated in 1823. On June 14, 1826, he was elected tutor at Washington (now Trinity) College, Hartford, Conn., and two years later was appointed adjunct professor of ancient languages, with an annual salary of $600. He resigned this position on Sept. 5, 1831. Soon afterward he was ordained by Bishop Thomas C. Brownell of the Protestant Episcopal Church, who was also president of Washington College. In 1829 Brownell had traveled through Kentucky, Mississippi, Louisiana, and Alabama, where his visits lent impetus to the growth of the Episcopal Church, and it was probably due to his influence that in 1831 Pinney went to Mobile as rector of Christ Church. He was active both in his parish and in the affairs of the diocese. Judging from his one published discourse, *A Sermon Preached July 5, 1835 in Christ's Church, Mobile* (1835), he took his responsibilities seriously yet cheerfully; the sermon is marked by clear analysis, an enlightened spirit, and a sensible tone. During his rectorship the floor of the church building fell under the weight of the crowd attending a Fourth of July service. Having come to differ with the doctrines of his Church, he withdrew from the ministry, and was formally displaced by Bishop James H. Otey, on Feb. 27, 1836. Later, he became a Unitarian.

In this same year he founded the Mobile Institute, a school for boys. His educational ideas are set forth in his booklet of fifty-six pages, *The Principles of Education as Applied in the Mobile*

Institute (1836). He foresaw that New Orleans was to become the commercial center of a great inland empire, and hoped that Mobile might aspire to be the educational and cultural center of this region. He understood that in a democracy there is peculiar need for proper education, and considered that the education of his time was too theoretical. He opposed the plan on which many colleges and schools were then being founded, which provided that students should spend part of their time in farm work, on the ground that such labor was "incompatible with that neatness of dress and cleanliness of person which befits a student." He stressed the value of unrestricted sport for boys, and thought corporal punishment necessary only in rare and unusual cases. He attached importance to Latin, mathematics, and English composition, but put less emphasis on history, modern languages, and sciences. The last named he thought important, but not "to be taught in all their minute detail." Parents who wanted their children educated in order to make more money "must of course regard money, not merely as the chief good, but as the only good." The Institute prospered, and many men later conspicuous in Mobile history were educated there. Pinney had important qualifications as an educator and was especially noted for the patient firmness with which he succeeded in bringing out whatever capacity there was in his pupils. He lived quietly, and took no active part in public affairs. Shortly before his death he went to New Orleans, intending to found a boys' school there, but died after a brief illness. He published a number of textbooks, the most of which went through several editions. They include *Practical French Teacher* (1847); *First Book in French* (1848); *The Progressive French Reader* (1850); *The Practical Spanish Teacher* (1855); with Juan Barceló; *Easy Lessons in Pronouncing and Speaking French* (1860); *French Grammar* (1861), with Émile Arnoult. Apparently he never married.

[L. Y. Pinney, *Geneal. of the Pinney Family in America* (1924); H. R. Stiles, *The Hist. and Geneals. of Ancient Windsor, Conn.*, vol. II (1892); *Obit. Record Grads. Yale Coll.*, 1863; information from the treasurer's office, Trinity Coll., Hartford, Conn.; records of the dioceses of Miss. and Tenn.; Erwin Craighead, *Mobile, Fact and Tradition* (1930); *Picayune* (New Orleans), Oct. 2, 1862.]
R. P. M.

PINTARD, JOHN (May 18, 1759–June 21, 1844), merchant, philanthropist, was born in New York, the son of John and Mary (Cannon) Pintard, and was descended from Anthony Pintard, a Huguenot from La Rochelle who had settled at Shrewsbury, N. J., in 1695. He lost both parents during his first year, his father, a seagoing merchant, dying on a voyage to Haiti.

John was brought up by his uncle, Lewis Pintard [*q.v.*]. After preparing at the grammar school of the Rev. Leonard Cutting at Hempstead, Long Island, he attended the College of New Jersey where he received the degree of A.B. in 1776 after running away for a brief military service. He served for some time as deputy to his uncle, who was commissioner of prisoners at New York. In 1780 he went to Paramus, N. J., for a while, and then was associated in his uncle's mercantile operations. On Nov. 12, 1784, he married a celebrated beauty, Eliza, daughter of Abraham Brashear of Paramus. They had two daughters. Inheriting a legacy from his maternal grandfather, he was enabled to go into the China and East India business on his own account, and until 1792, when he was dragged down by the crash of the stock speculations of William Duer [*q.v.*], he was rated as one of New York's most successful and prosperous merchants. Pintard, who had indorsed his notes for more than a million, it is said, lost his entire fortune and was even imprisoned for debt. For eight years he resided at Newark and then declared himself bankrupt in New York. For a short while he was book auctioneer and editor of the *Daily Advertiser*. He then went to New Orleans to try his fortune but decided not to settle there, and was soon back in New York where he spent the rest of his life. He never recovered his old fortune, but his positions as secretary of the pioneer New York fire insurance company and later as bank president seem to have enabled him to contribute generously to the various movements which he sponsored.

Pintard's great work was as a promoter. "He could indite a handbill," says Scoville, "that would inflame the minds of the people for any good work. He could call a meeting with the pen of a poet, and before the people met, he would have arranged the doings for a perfect success. He knew the weak points of every man, and he would gratify the vanity of men and get their money." DeWitt Clinton was always ready to allow Pintard to use his name and moral support for any measure. He developed a real passion for the preservation of historical manuscripts. He purchased a valuable collection of material on the Revolution from a Tory clergyman. In 1789, while visiting Jeremy Belknap, he gave the initial impulse which resulted in the establishment of the Massachusetts Historical Society. In 1791 he organized a historical museum under the auspices of the Tammany Society of which he was the first sagamore and later grand sachem. After the museum passed into private hands, Pintard carried out his original idea by taking

the leading part in organizing the New York Historical Society in 1804. It was one of the many organizations which he served for years as secretary. He also developed the systematic municipal recording of vital statistics during his term (1804–10) as clerk of the corporation and city inspector of New York City.

Religious activity also appealed to him. He was for thirty-four years vestryman of the Episcopalian Huguenot church in New York and translated the Prayer-Book into French for its use. He was also a prime mover in founding the General Theological Seminary and was active in raising funds for it. The American Bible Society, which he called his "brat," he served as secretary and vice-president. He had been an alderman in 1788 and 1789, and in 1790 he sat in the state legislature. After the War of 1812 he helped to revive the Chamber of Commerce and was its secretary from 1817 to 1827. In 1815 he promoted a mass meeting in favor of the Erie Canal project. He engineered the organization of New York's first savings bank in 1819 and was its president from 1828 to 1841. He was also interested in the Sailors' Snug Harbor, the House of Refuge, and the Mercantile Library. A Trumbull portrait shows a handsome and kindly face, with a high forehead. Belknap described him as "very loquacious and unreserved." He had been deafened in youth by a Fourth of July explosion and in his last years was nearly blind. He died in New York at the home of a daughter.

[The chief source is J. G. Wilson, *"John Pintard, Founder of the N. Y. Hist. Soc.,"* an Address before the N. Y. Hist. Soc., Dec. 3, 1901 (1902). See also: J. A. Scoville (W. Barrett), *Biog. Sketch of John Pintard* (1863) and *The Old Merchants of N. Y. City* (5 vols., 1863–69); *Proc. Mass. Hist. Soc.*, vol I (1879), p. xi; E. P. Kilroe, *Saint Tammany and the Origin of the Soc. of Tammany* (1913); J. G. Wilson, *The Memorial Hist. of the City of N. Y.* (4 vols., 1892–93); material in the alumni files of Princeton Univ.; *N. Y. Commercial Advertiser*, June 22, 1844.]
R. G. A.

PINTARD, LEWIS (Oct. 1, 1732–Mar. 25, 1818), merchant, commissary of prisoners, was born in New York City, the son of John and Catherine (Carré) Pintard. He was descended from Anthony Pintard who had escaped from his native La Rochelle after the revocation of the Edict of Nantes and in 1695 settled in Shrewsbury, N. J. Lewis received a fair schooling and a good commercial training in his father's prosperous shipping and commission business to which he later succeeded. By his marriage with Susan Stockton of Princeton, N. J., he became the brother-in-law of Richard Stockton, a signer of the Declaration of Independence, and brother-in-law of Elias Boudinot [*qq.v.*]. In 1760, after the death of his brother John, he practically adopted the infant nephew, also named John [*q.v.*]. By the outbreak of the Revolution, Pintard was reckoned as one of the substantial merchants of New York City. He was a member of the Committee of One Hundred, organized in New York in the spring of 1775. Shortly afterward the Provincial Congress appointed Henry Remsen, Jacobus Van Zandt, and Pintard as a committee to procure gunpowder and clothing from Europe. They raised nearly £4000 on subscription and in September chartered the sloop *Nancy,* sending her to Bordeaux for the necessary supplies which arrived the following summer by the way of St. Eustatius and Providence, R. I.

Pintard remained in New York City after the British occupation and was able to carry on a moderate amount of business during the war. He became commissary of prisoners and held the position until relieved late in the war by Abraham Skinner. There were about 5,000 American prisoners in and around New York in the Provost, in various church and sugar houses, and in the hulks in Wallabout Bay, including the notorious *Jersey.* Pintard, with the aid of several deputies, did what he could to relieve their sufferings. He distributed the money and supplies gathered by Gov. George Clinton and others for the relief of the prisoners. He managed to secure easy and regular access to the prisoners and was active in arranging exchanges. Bad as conditions were, they would probably have been considerably worse had it not been for Pintard's work. At the close of the Revolution he was commissioner for liquidating claims in the state of New Jersey against the United States, a responsible task involving large discretionary power.

For some time after the Revolution, Pintard was the chief importer of Madeira wines into the United States and an exporter of flaxseed to Ireland. Then, like his nephew John, he suffered a heavy financial loss through the collapse of another whom he had trusted. Owing to the failure of a Dublin consignee, his cargoes were seized and £20,000 in bills protested. He was able to continue, however, and engaged in the importation of sugar and molasses from the West Indies until the beginning of the War of 1812. During these years he had commuted to New York from his home in the nearby Huguenot town of New Rochelle, where a street now bears his name. In 1797 he was one of the school commissioners of New Rochelle. He spent the last six years of his life at his wife's home in Princeton, "devoting himself principally to the perusal of the sacred scriptures and to the practice of every Christian virtue in domestic life," and he died there at the home of his son-in-law, Samuel Bayard [*q.v.*].

[J. G. Wilson, *"John Pintard, Founder of the N. Y. Hist. Soc.,"* an Address before the N. Y. Hist. Soc., Dec. 3, 1901 (1902); J. A. Scoville (W. Barrett), *Biog. Sketch of John Pintard* (1863) and *The Old Merchants of New York* (5 vols., 1863–69); *Huguenot Soc. of America, Colls.,* I (1886), 195, 254; *N. Y. in the Revolution as Colony and State,* vol. II (1904), pub. by E. C. Knight; F. G. Mather, *The Refugees of 1776 from Long Island to Conn.* (1913); Danske Dandridge, *Am. Prisoners of the Revolution* (1911); *N. Y. Commercial Advertiser,* Apr. 1, 1818.]   R. G. A.

PINTO, ISAAC (June 12, 1720–Jan. 17, 1791), merchant, scholar, and patriot, was a member of a Portuguese family, a branch of which came to North America, probably by way of Jamaica, before the middle of the eighteenth century. Some members of the family settled in Connecticut as early as 1724; others were settled in New York by 1736. Their names are recorded in the earliest Minute Books of the Congregation Shearith Israel. Isaac Pinto's name occurs in the records of 1740–41, 1747, and 1750. Nothing is known of his immediate ancestry or the place of his birth, where he was educated or how he was related to the other members of the Pinto family. From contemporary sources, he appears to have been a merchant of means who lived from time to time in different places. On the ledger of Daniel Gomez, a New York merchant, he is described in 1741 as being "now at Norwalk, now at Strattsburg" (*Publications of the American Jewish Historical Society,* No. 27, 1920; p. 248). In 1760–62, he was in Charlestown, S. C., where he advertised himself in the *South Carolina Gazette* as a wholesale wine merchant. In 1764 his name was attached to a petition against carrying into effect a certain act of the New York legislature passed in December 1761 (D. T. Valentine, *Manual of the Corporation of the City of New York,* 1850, p. 434). In 1768 he advertised for sale "Choice South Carolina Pink Root" in many issues of the *New York Journal.* In the supplement to the *New-York Gazette* of July 23, 1770, his name was subscribed to a list of importers and shopkeepers who were in favor of continuing the Non-Importation Resolutions of 1765. In 1790 Ezra Stiles referred to him in his *Diary* as "a learned Jew at New York" (F. B. Dexter, *The Literary Diary of Ezra Stiles,* 1901, III, 392). From Nov. 15, 1790, until his death he advertised in the *New York Journal* as a teacher of the Spanish language.

Pinto is best known as the translator into English of the first Jewish Prayer Book printed in America. The work appeared in two parts. The first, *Evening Service of Roshashanah and Kippur,* was published anonymously in 1761; the second, *Prayers for Shabbath, Rosh-Hashanah, and Kippur,* appeared under the author's name in 1766. It can hardly be doubted that the two volumes came from the same hand. The translation was a notable performance in its day. Pinto was probably the translator, also, of *The Form of Prayer . . . for a General Thanksgiving . . . for the Reducing of Canada* (1760). Samuel Oppenheim would attribute to him "The Chapters of Isaac the Scribe," six sketches written in Biblical style that appeared in the *New York Journal or General Advertiser* from Sept. 10 to Oct. 8, 1772 (*Publications of the American Jewish Historical Society,* No. 22, 1914, pp. 39–51). It is possible too that many of the letters in the newspapers that appeared between 1750 and 1775 under the pseudonyms "A. B." and "Philalethes" were from his pen. Pinto died unmarried. An obituary notice which appeared in the *New-York Journal & Patriotic Register* of Jan. 20, 1791, described him as "a much respected citizen . . . whose knowledge of mankind was general. Though of the Hebrew nation, his liberality was not circumscribed by the limits of that Church. He was well versed in several of the foreign languages. He was a staunch friend of the liberties of his country. . . . In his death . . . his relations have lost a firm friend and the literary world, an historian and philosopher." His tombstone can still be seen in the Spanish and Portuguese Burial Ground on Twenty-first Street, New York.

[See: *The Jewish Encyc.*; Index to *Am. Jewish Hist. Soc. Pubs.*; B. A. Elzas, *The Jews of S. C.* (1905); Israel Abrahams, *By-Paths in Hebraic Bookland* (1920); *The Lit. Remains of the Rev. Simeon Singer* (1908), ed. by Israel Abrahams; D. de Sola Pool, "The Earliest Jewish Prayer Book Printed in America," the *Jewish Tribune,* Sept. 5, 1924.]   B. A. E.

PIPER, CHARLES VANCOUVER (June 16, 1867–Feb. 11, 1926), agronomist, was born at Victoria, British Columbia, the son of Andrew William and Minna (Hausman) Piper. A few years after his birth his parents removed to the state of Washington, where young Piper obtained his early education. In 1885 he graduated from the University of Washington with the degree of bachelor of science, receiving in 1892 the master's degree. Between these dates he helped his father run his bakery business in Seattle and in spare time pursued his hobby, botanizing in the Puget Sound and Mount Ranier country. In 1893 he began teaching botany and zoölogy in what is now the State College of Washington, at Pullman, remaining head of his department until 1903. He married Laura Maude Hungate on Sept. 15, 1897, and took time enough from his teaching to secure in 1900 the degree of M.S. from Harvard. During the years at Pullman he made very valuable collections for the school, not only of plants, but also of zoölogical specimens and insects. In this work his students and many acquaintances helped him, especially his assistant, R. Kent Beattie. Together the two young men carried on explorations in Washington, Idaho, and Oregon, collecting and classifying botanical specimens and compiling material published later in *The Flora of the Palouse Region* (1901), *Flora of Southeastern Washington and Adjacent Idaho* (1914), and *Flora of the Northwest Coast* (1915). In 1906 *Flora of the State of Washington* appeared, of which Piper was sole author. These books are still the best works for the botany of that region. In this labor Piper acquired the extreme niceness in the use of terms that distinguished all his later writings.

From 1903 until his death he was employed by the United States Department of Agriculture, being in charge of the office of forage crops investigations from its beginning as a separate unit in 1905. While in this position he accomplished a prodigious amount of work and published many articles, both alone and in collaboration with others. He had a passion for doing things and one of his characteristic expressions was: "What's next?" He himself worked at high pressure and inspired his associates with much of his own enthusiasm. With his capacity for seeing all sides of a project he often arrayed himself in opposition to it, and thus forced its advocate to present his case thoroughly; then he would turn his attention to overcoming every obstacle and carry the project through. He was big in all ways, over six feet in height, broadminded, generous, and absolutely without pretense. Scientists all over the world wrote for his help and sent him specimens.

By the request of the War Department Piper was sent in 1911 to make a survey of forage crop possibilities in the Philippines. He carried out this enterprise so successfully that he was asked in 1923 to make a similar study in the Panama Canal district. His work on grasses led to his most brilliant achievement. Conceiving the idea that somewhere there must grow a cousin of the weedy Johnson grass of the Southern states, without the latter's objectionable features, he sent innumerable requests to the old world for samples of grass and actually found in Sudan, mistakenly classified under the name *Sorghum Halepense,* the grass of his dreams, which he named Sudan grass. In 1913 he published *Sudan*

Grass, a New Drought-resistant Hay Plant, as Circular No. 125 of the Bureau of Plant Industry. The value of this grass crop in the United States since 1918 has been estimated at $10,000,-000 a year. The record of his achievements would be incomplete without mention of his work for the improvement of golf courses. In collaboration with R. A. Oakley he wrote *Turf for Golf Courses* (1917) and contributed many valuable articles on this subject. Among his writings not elsewhere mentioned were *The Soybean* (1923), in collaboration with W. J. Morse, and *Forage Plants and Their Culture* (1914, 1924). For two or three years he worked under the impediment of ill health but in this time he completed unfinished manuscripts, and he left a practically empty desk when death overtook him.

[H. N. Vinall, in *Jour. of the Am. Soc. of Agronomy,* Mar. 1926; R. K. Beattie, in *Proc. of the Biological Soc. of Washington,* vol. XLI (1928); R. A. Oakley, in *Bull. of the U. S. Golf Asso., Green Section,* Mar. 16, 1926; *Who's Who in America,* 1924–25; *Science,* Mar. 5, 1926; *Evening Star* (Washington), Feb. 12, 1926; information from friends and associates.]

L. G.

PIRSSON, LOUIS VALENTINE (Nov. 3, 1860–Dec. 8, 1919), geologist, professor at Yale University, was born at Fordham, N. Y., the son of Francis Morris and Louisa (Butt) Pirsson. His great-grandfather, William Pirsson, came from Chelmsford, Essex, England, to the vicinity of New York in 1796. His son William married Emily Morris of New York, and it was in the comfortable home of his paternal grandparents that Louis was born. His mother died when Louis was four years old; his father saw little of the young son, being absent in South America. At nine years of age Louis became the ward of Thomas Lord of New York, who placed him in the family of the Rev. William J. Blain, pastor of a near-by church, who lived on a small farm near Amsterdam, N. Y. Blain was a strict disciplinarian but a good teacher, and from him Louis received much of his primary education. Here also he was trained in the strict and regular performance of small family duties. He delved into his preceptor's excellent library and acquired a taste for literature and for natural history. Another boy taken into Blain's family helped stimulate his scientific leanings. The two organized collecting excursions, had a small museum in the woodshed, and called themselves naturalists. Birds were Pirsson's chief interest. At sixteen he was placed in Amenia Academy, Dutchess County, N. Y. (later in New Marlboro, Mass.), and entered the Sheffield Scientific School of Yale in 1879. His summer vacations spent at the shore with

his wealthy guardian softened an otherwise severe life with luxurious pastimes and social diversions.

Pirsson graduated from Sheffield with honors in 1882; served as assistant in chemistry; became an expert analyst; and laid the chemical foundation for his later geological work. In 1888 he taught chemistry at the Brooklyn Polytechnic Institute, but in 1889 he left to accept an unusual opportunity, procured for him by his kindly adviser, Professor Brush, to become a field assistant of a United States Geological Survey party under Arnold Hague to study Yellowstone Park. An enthusiastic geologist, he returned to Yale and studied under Professor Penfield. Another field season in Montana developed his interest in igneous geology, which became his life work. Subsequently he studied at Heidelberg, the Mecca of petrologists, and in Paris. While abroad, in 1892, he was called by Professor Brush to Yale to become instructor in mineralogy and lithology. In 1893 he gave the first graduate course at Yale in petrology, which later attracted a continuous flow of graduate students, many of whom were to become distinguished geologists. In 1894 he was made assistant professor, and in 1897 professor of physical geology. In 1902 he married Eliza Trumbull Brush, daughter of his early teacher and adviser, Professor George J. Brush.

As a teacher he held his students "not by picturesque or fascinating language, but by his knowledge of the subject and his clear and fluent presentation of it" (Cross, *post,* p. 182). As a member of the governing board of the Sheffield Scientific School, he served as its secretary; was senior class officer and chairman of the discipline committee; was a member of the board of Sheffield trustees and of its executive committee, and for a brief period was acting director of the school. He was elected a member of numerous scientific societies, and from 1899 until his death was associate editor of the *American Journal of Science,* in which some forty of his contributions were published. His most noted contributions were a series of papers dealing with the igneous rocks of Montana, which Whitman Cross states constitute "one of the most important contributions to American petrology." His analyses and microscopic investigations revealed many interesting rocks, some new to science. In 1903 appeared the *Quantitative Classification of Igneous Rocks,* by Cross, Iddings, Pirsson, and Washington, the great four of American petrology, in which was formulated an entirely new system of classification and a new terminology. Pirsson was also the author of a widely used book on

Rocks and Rock Minerals (1908) and of a text-book of physical geology, which is Part I of the *Text Book of Geology* (1915) by Pirsson and Schuchert. By 1929 Pirsson's part had gone through three editions and was the most widely used textbook of geology in the world.

[Sources include: Whitman Cross, "Biog. of Louis Valentine Pirsson," *Am. Jour. Sci.*, Sept. 1920; R. H. Chittenden, *Hist. of the Sheffield Sci. School*, vol. II (1928); *Yale Univ. Obit. Record of Grads. Deceased During the Year Ending July 1, 1920* (1921); *Science*, May 28, 1920; *New Haven Journal-Courier*, Dec. 9, 1919; private diaries; records of the governing board, Sheffield Scientific School, personal acquaintance.]

A. M. B.

PISE, CHARLES CONSTANTINE (Nov. 22, 1801–May 26, 1866), Roman Catholic priest and writer, was born in Annapolis, Md., the son of an educated Italian refugee, Louis Pise, who married Marguerite Gamble, member of an old Philadelphia family. Charles was sent to George-town College, where in 1815 he joined the Jesuits and attracted the notice of Archbishop Ambrose Maréchal [*q.v.*], by Latin verses written for the Commencement of 1819. In 1820 he withdrew and was sent by Maréchal to Rome. Returning a year later, he completed his theological course at Mount St. Mary's, Emmitsburg, Md., where he was associated with three future archbishops, McCloskey, Purcell, and Hughes. Ordained by Maréchal, Mar. 19, 1825, he taught rhetoric at the "Mount," served as a curate in the cathedral at Baltimore, and as an assistant at St. Patrick's Church in Washington, where he gained a reputation as a preacher of polished sermons. During these years, he wrote "Celara," a poem of the fifteenth century; a Latin elegy on Pius VII; and "Montezuma," a drama in three acts, which was presented by the students of Mount St. Mary's in 1824. These remained in manuscript, but in addition, he published an apologetic novel, *Father Rowland* (1829), which was well received in religious circles; *The Indian Cottage, A Unitarian Story* (1829), in defense of the divinity of Christ, which was reprinted serially in the *Catholic Expositor* (1842); and *History of the Church from Its Establishment to the Present Century* (5 vols., 1827–30), which was never completed beyond the beginning of the sixteenth century. While hardly more than a well-written compilation, this study offered the best Catholic account of the church in English and was certainly the most extended literary work achieved by an American Catholic up to that time. Indeed, prior to Pise, Catholic litera-ture in the United States was confined practically to translations and reprints of foreign authors. In 1832 he revisited Europe. At Rome, he re-ceived on examination the doctorate in divinity,

and was dubbed a Knight of the Sacred Palace and Count Palatine by Gregory XVI, an honor not heretofore held by an American. At the same time he was created a Knight of the Holy Roman Empire.

On his return to Washington, he was nom-inated by Henry Clay, who was rather generally supported politically by the old American Cath-olic element, for the chaplaincy of the United States Senate, and was duly elected, Dec. 11, 1832, despite an intense nativist opposition in press and pulpit to his creed and foreign honors. A slight honor, it nevertheless was a marked recognition of Pise, for he was the only Catholic priest ever selected for that office. His social relations, apparently, were highly satisfactory, because of the friendship of Jackson. A tem-porary pastor at Annapolis (1833), he was called by Bishop John Dubois [*q.v.*] to New York in 1834, where he labored in the parish of St. Joseph's, rent at the time by trusteeism, until he was appointed an assistant to Dr. John Power [*q.v.*] at St. Peter's Church in 1840. Two years later he went abroad to collect funds for the orphanage connected with St. Peter's, armed with a letter of introduction from President Tyler to American representatives in Europe. While in Ireland, he came under the influence of Father Theobold Mathew and returned an ar-dent temperance worker and a friend of the Irish immigrant, though in Irish circles he was crit-icized for his observations on Ireland in the *Catholic Expositor* and particularly for his con-demnation of the Irish clergy for their lack of sympathy for the Mathew movement. In 1849 he built the church of St. Charles Borromeo in Brooklyn, of which he was pastor until his death.

His literary labors did not slacken. With Felix Varela [*q.v.*], with whom he was earlier asso-ciated as a founder of the ephemeral *Protestant Abridger and Expositor* (1832), he launched in 1841 *The Catholic Expositor and Literary Magazine*. Among his books were *The Pleasures of Religion and Other Poems* (1833), dedicated to Washington Irving; *Aletheia, or, Letters on the Truth of Catholic Doctrine* (1843, reprinted 1894); a eulogistic biography, *Saint Ignatius and His First Companions* (1845), which in revised form is still in circulation; *Lectures on the Invocation of the Saints, Veneration of Sacred Images and Purgatory* (1845); *Zenosius or the Pilgrim Convert* (1845), an artificial re-minder of Bunyan; *The Catholic Bride* (1847), translated from the Italian; and *Christianity and the Church* (1850), an adaptation of Louis Lahuré's *Le Christianisme et les Philosophes*

(1846). A Southerner to the core, he was saddened by the Civil War, though his loyalty *de jure* could not be questioned. As a brilliant lecturer, Pise had considerable vogue, but as a critic he was too kindly, just as he was less effective as a controversialist because he was gentle and never acrimonious.

[Sister Eulalia T. Moffatt, "Charles Constantine Pise (1801–1866)," U. S. Cath. Hist. Soc., *Hist. Records and Studies*, vol. XX (1931); J. T. Smith, *The Cath. Church in N. Y.* (1905); M. J. Finotti, *Bibliographia Catholica Americana* (1872); U. S. Cath. Hist. Soc., *Hist. Records and Studies*, vol. II (2 parts, 1900–01); *Cath. Encyc.* XII, 116; M. J. Riordan, *Cathedral Records* (1906); F. X. McSweeny, *Story of the Mountain* (1911); James Fitton, *Sketches of the Establishment of the Church in New England* (1872); Peter Ross, *A Hist. of L. I.* (1902), I, 807; *Columbia*, Nov. 1927; *New York Freeman's Jour. and Cath. Reg.*, June 2, 1866; *N. Y. Herald*, May 27, 1866.]   R. J. P.

PITCAIRN, JOHN (1722–June 1775), British officer, was born at Dysart, Scotland, the son of the Rev. David Pitcairn and his wife, Katherine Hamilton. As a young man he sought service in the Royal Marines, being commissioned captain, June 8, 1756, and major, Apr. 19, 1771. He married Elizabeth, daughter of Robert Dalrymple, of Arnsfield, Dumfriesshire, and Dreghorn Castle, in Midlothian. Of their children two obtained eminence, Robert as a naval officer and David as a physician. (Biographies of both are in the *Dictionary of National Biography*.) Pitcairn accompanied the marines sent to garrison Boston in 1774. He went with the troops dispatched by Gen. Gage on the night of Apr. 18, 1775, to destroy the rebel stores at Concord. Directed by the commander of the expedition, Lieut.-Col. Francis Smith, to push ahead of the main body in order to seize the bridges at Concord, he was in command of the regulars who came into conflict with the minute-men on Lexington Common. He always maintained that the Americans fired first and denied having ordered his own men to fire. Although his horse was wounded, he himself escaped without injury. At Concord he labored with Smith to convince the inhabitants that the British meant no injury, but apparently without complete success, since, according to Smith's report, one of the townspeople struck him. There is a persistent tradition—the truth of which is challenged by reliable authority—that he went to Wright's Tavern, and calling for a drink, stirred the brandy in his glass with his finger declaring that he hoped he would stir the Yankee blood so before night. On the march back to Lexington, his horse, frightened by a sudden volley, threw him off and escaped, obliging him to continue on foot. In the battle of Bunker Hill he was mortally wounded while storming the American

redoubt. It is said that the fatal shot was fired by a negro, Peter Salem, who is depicted in Trumbull's picture of the battle, but there have been other claimants. His son, a lieutenant in the marines, bore him to the water's edge, whence he was transferred to a house in the North End where he died not long after, despite the ministration of a physician sent to his bedside at the special request of Gage. His remains were at first interred under Christ Church. Later they were transferred by friends to the church of St. Bartholomew the Less, London. He was perhaps the only British officer in Boston who commanded the trust and liking of the inhabitants. It is reported that whenever the townspeople had a dispute with the military, they would refer it to him, confident of obtaining just and considerate treatment. By his men he was beloved as a father, and among the last acts of his life was the drafting of a letter to Lord Sandwich in behalf of the worthy and unfortunate under his command. The Lexington Historical Society possesses his pistols and a charming miniature of him.

[Chas. Hudson, "The Character of Maj. John Pitcairn," *Proc. Mass. Hist. Soc.*, vol. XVII (1880); F. B. Dexter, ed., *The Lit. Diary of Ezra Stiles* (1901), vol. I; Richard Frothingham, *Hist. of the Siege of Boston* (1849); Constance Pitcairn, *The Hist. of the Fife Pitcairns* (1905); Harold Murdock, *Earl Percy's Dinner-Table* (1907) and *The Nineteenth of April 1775* (1925); Allen French, *The Day of Concord and Lexington* (1925).]   E. E. C.

PITCAIRN, JOHN (Jan. 10, 1841–July 22, 1916), manufacturer, philanthropist, the son of John and Agnes (McEwen) Pitcairn, was born in Scotland, at Johnstone, near Paisley, Renfrewshire. Coming to the United States before 1850, the family settled in Allegheny, Pa. Pitcairn received an elementary education in the public schools of that city, but, following in the footsteps of his elder brother Robert, began his business career about 1855 in the employ of the Pennsylvania Railroad at Altoona, Pa. His connection with railroads lasted practically without interruption until 1872, and during this period he occupied minor executive positions with the Pittsburg, Fort Wayne & Chicago railway and the Philadelphia & Erie Railroad, as well as with the Pennsylvania Railroad. His advancement was steady, but not spectacular, and in 1872 he resigned the general managership of the Oil Creek & Allegheny Valley Railroad to become an active partner in the firm of Vandergrift, Forman & Company (later Vandergrift, Pitcairn & Company), interested in various phases of fuel distribution. The firm built the Imperial Refinery at Oil City, Pa. Engaged also in the distribution of crude petroleum, Pitcairn is said to have been among the first to recognize the possibilities of the use of natural gas as fuel in manufacturing. A natural gas pipe line, perhaps the first in the United States, was laid from Butler County, Pa., to Pittsburgh under the control of Pitcairn and his partner, J. J. Vandergrift.

The most significant part of his business career was his connection with the plate-glass industry. In 1882 it was proposed to pipe natural gas to a glass factory to be built at Creighton, Pa., and Pitcairn's advice was asked. He became interested in the project to manufacture plate glass, which had hitherto never been successful in the United States. With Captain John B. Ford and others, Pitcairn became in 1883 one of the organizers of the Pittsburgh Plate Glass Company, an enormously successful venture. A director of the company from its incorporation, he was from 1897 to 1905 its president, and from 1894 until his death chairman of the board of directors. As president he inaugurated a policy of extensive experimentation with manufacturing methods. Among the successes achieved under this policy the lehr annealing process is worthy of note. This process of slow, controlled cooling of sheet glass, perfected between 1900 and 1904, has become standard in the industry. During the period of Pitcairn's influence, the company's capacity was greatly increased; at the time of his death it had built and was operating eight factories.

From 1905 until 1916 Pitcairn was increasingly absorbed by the religious activities which had been an important part of his life for many years. He was a follower of Emanuel Swedenborg and identified himself with that branch of Swedenborgianism known as the General Church of the New Jerusalem, which became a separate religious entity in 1890. From then on he became increasingly prominent as the most influential layman of that wing of the church, and was the founder of its distinctive community at Bryn Athyn, Pa. He was an enthusiastic supporter of the doctrine of the General Church that education was a proper and necessary function of the religious organization and was one of the twelve original founders of the Academy of the New Church at Philadelphia in June 1876. In 1897 it was moved to Bryn Athyn, and two years later it was generously endowed by Pitcairn. This unique school includes all phases of education from kindergarten through theological school.

It was Pitcairn's desire to give the community a church building, and this was undertaken in 1912, with the firm of Cram & Ferguson as

architects. As plans were discussed, the original conception of a small architecturally perfect church was greatly expanded. Gradually there was developed a cooperative organization for the building of the church, with craftsmen producing everything necessary—lumber, stonework, metal, glass, sculpture, cabinet-work, embroidery—in workshops at Bryn Athyn. It was a kind of neo-medieval guild system. The result is a magnificent group of ecclesiastical buildings, in a perfect natural setting—on a hill with a background of trees for the towers. The central building is the Cathedral, fourteenth-century Gothic in style; it is flanked by a choir building and a council building, both in twelfth-century Romanesque. At the time of Pitcairn's death none of them had been finished. Pitcairn was married on Jan. 8, 1884, to Gertrude Starkey, who died in 1898. Of their six children, three sons survived the father, who died at his country home, "Cairnwood," at Bryn Athyn. Ralph Adams Cram described him as "an old gentleman of small stature, grave, courtly, keenly intelligent, vigorous beyond his years, an acute business man, and withal possessed of imagination and intense idealism" (*American Architect*, May 29, 1918, p. 710).

[R. A. Cram, "A Note on Bryn Athyn Church," *Am. Architect*, May 29, 1918; M. B. Block, *The New Church in the New World: A Study of Swedenborgianism in America* (1932); *A Brief Handbook of Information concerning the Cathedral-Church at Bryn Athyn, Pa.* (5th ed., 1930); *Glass, Paints, Varnishes and Brushes: Their Hist., Manufacture and Use* (1923), pub. by Pittsburgh Plate Glass Company; J. W. Jordan, *Encyc. of Pa. Biog.*, vol. III (1914); editorial in *Jour. of Educ. of the Academy of the New Church*, Jan. 1917; *N. Y. Herald*, July 23, 1916; *Pub. Ledger* (Phila.), July 23, 1916.]   L. P. B—t.

PITCHER, MOLLY [See McCauley, Mary Ludwig Hays, 1754–1832].

PITCHER, ZINA (Apr. 12, 1797–Apr. 5, 1872), physician and naturalist, was born on a farm near Fort Edward, Washington County, N. Y., the son of Nathaniel Pitcher, a captain in the Revolutionary army, and Margaret Stevenson, a native of Scotland. His father died early, leaving to the mother an unproductive farm and the care and education of four sons. A woman of strong personality, she laid the foundation for a highly useful career for each of her boys. Zina was educated in the common schools and in a local academy. He began the study of medicine with the neighborhood practitioners, then attended the medical school at Castleton, Vt., and, according to the practice at the time, received the degree of M.D. from Middlebury College (1822). Shortly after graduation he entered the army as an assistant surgeon and was sent to

Michigan where during the next eight years he served at posts at Detroit, Saginaw, and Sault St. Marie. He was next transferred to Fort Gibson in the Indian Territory and thence to Fortress Monroe, Va. While here in 1836 he tendered his resignation to the War Department and returned to Detroit to take up the private practice of medicine. His military service was mainly in pioneer surroundings and in close association with Indians. Wherever he went he interested himself in the natural history of the locality, particularly in botany, geology, and meteorology. He furnished material for *A Flora of North America* (2 vols., 1838–43), by John Torrey and Asa Gray, and several new botanical species were named after him. In all his contacts with the Indians he sought the acquaintance and the friendship of the tribal medicine men and familiarized himself with their ideas and practices. The result of this study is found in his chapter on Indian medicine in Henry R. Schoolcraft's *Information Respecting the History, Condition, and Prospects of the Indian Tribes of the United States* (vol. IV, 1854).

Pitcher had taken a prominent part in Detroit life and had made strong friendships there during his earlier stay, so that when he returned in 1836 he found himself from the first a leading citizen. In 1837 he was appointed a member of the first state board of regents, a position he held until 1852. He initiated the movement for a medical department at the University of Michigan, was a member of the committee to study the project, and participated in the opening of the school in 1850. He is credited with the selection of the first faculty of the school and with the draft of the rules to govern the department. He was himself designated professor emeritus. Owing to inadequate clinical material at Ann Arbor he instituted a clinical summer course at St. Mary's hospital and the Marine hospital at Detroit, beginning in 1857. He was designated clinical instructor, the only teaching title that he ever held. Faculty opposition caused the suspension of these courses after two sessions. He was elected mayor of Detroit three times, in 1840, 1841, and 1843. In 1844 he sought to assist the presidential campaign of Henry Clay by running for governor on the Whig ticket, but he went down to defeat with his chief. While mayor of Detroit he was responsible for the enactment of a law by the state legislature which eventually provided the city with its first free public schools. From this beginning developed the common-school system of the state. At various times he held the positions of city physician, county physician, member of the city board of

health, and surgeon to the Government Marine Hospital. For the greater part of his career he was on the staff of St. Mary's hospital. He was president of the Territorial Medical Society (1838–51), of the Michigan State Medical Society (1855–56), and at the Detroit meeting of the American Medical Association in 1856 he was elected its president. He was active in the organization of the Detroit Sydenham Society and of the city and county medical societies.

Pitcher was one of the incorporators of the Michigan Historical Society in 1822, and upon his return to Detroit, was appointed librarian of the society. In 1853 he and Dr. Edmund Andrews founded the *Peninsular Journal of Medicine*. Upon the departure of Andrews to Chicago in 1855, he became a co-editor of the journal, continuing until 1858. He was later an associate editor of the *Richmond and Louisville Medical Journal*. His most notable literary contributions are in the form of reports on clinical cases, epidemics, medical education, and the natural sciences. His scholarly addresses to graduating classes and medical societies show deep insight into the professional problems of the day, always with suggestions looking toward their solution. Though always a general practitioner he was a bold and skilful, though conservative, surgeon. He continued practice until 1871 when failing health compelled him to quit. He was a man of fine personal appearance, genial manner, and dignified bearing. Positive in his convictions, he was strong in his likes and aversions. He was married in 1824 to Anne Sheldon of Kalamazoo, Mich. She died in 1864, and in 1867 he married Emily L. (Montgomery) Backus of Detroit.

[F. G. Novy, biography of Pitcher, in *Physician and Surgeon*, Feb. 1908, with bibliography; *Mich. Univ. Medic. Jour.*, Mar. 1872; *Richmond and Louisville Medic. Jour.*, June 1869; *Trans. State Medic. Soc. of Mich.*, 2 ser. VI (1874); B. A. Hinsdale, *Hist. of the Univ. of Mich.* (1906); *Detroit Medic. Jour.*, July 1909; *Detroit Free Press*, Apr. 6, 1872.]

J. M. P—n.

PITCHLYNN, PETER PERKINS (Jan. 30, 1806–Jan. 17, 1881), Choctaw chief, was born in Noxubee County, Miss., the son of John Pitchlynn, a white interpreter for the federal government, and Sophia Folsom, the daughter of a Choctaw woman and a white man. Eager for an education, he traveled two hundred miles, while still only a boy, to enter a school in Tennessee. He later attended the academy at Nashville. Returning to his home in Mississippi, he built a cabin and began farming. He married Rhoda Folsom according to the rites of the Christian Church, and it is said that by his influence and example he caused the Choctaw to abandon the practice of polygamy. He also helped to stop the traffic in liquor among the Choctaw Indians. His interest in education led him to establish a school in Kentucky for Indian children, which was supported for years by funds granted by the Choctaw government.

In 1828 he went to the West with a delegation sent out to select lands for his people. After the Choctaw treaty of 1830 he removed to Indian Territory with his family, and in 1860 he was elected principal chief. At the outbreak of the Civil War he sought to induce the Choctaw to remain neutral, and he himself always remained loyal to the Union, though he owned about a hundred slaves who were set free by the war. He signed the treaty of Dancing Rabbit Creek in 1830 and the treaty of 1855, and he witnessed, as principal chief, the treaty of Washington in 1866. For many years he represented the tribe in Washington. After the death of his first wife, he was married at Washington to Caroline (Eckloff) Lombardy, the daughter of Godfrey Eckloff. He was a friend of both Andrew Jackson and Henry Clay and met Charles Dickens during the latter's American tour. In *American Notes* (1842, II, 96, 99), Dickens described him as a tall, handsome man with raven black hair, high cheek bones, and piercing black eyes, "as stately and complete a gentleman of nature's making, as ever I beheld." He also mentioned that the Indian chief spoke very good English and had read and understood such English literature as Scott's *Lady of the Lake* and *Marmion*. He was a member of the Lutheran Memorial Church at Washington and was also a prominent Mason. Upon his death in Washington his funeral services were conducted by Gen. Albert Pike. He was buried in the Congressional Cemetery, and a monument was erected over his grave by the Choctaw Nation. A gifted orator, an able statesman, he was not only a popular leader of his own people but also possessed many warm friends among the whites.

[Choctaw Archives in the manuscript collections of the Univ. of Okla.; *Memorial of P. P. Pitchlynn, Choctaw Delegate* (n.d.); F. W. Hodge, *Handbook of Am. Indians*, pt. II (1910); J. B. Thoburn, *A Standard Hist. of Okla.* (1916), vol. I; *Evening Star* (Washington), Jan. 18, 1881.]   E. E. D.

PITKIN, FREDERICK WALKER (Aug. 31, 1837–Dec. 18, 1886), lawyer, governor of Colorado, was born in Manchester, Conn., the son of Eli and Hannah M. (Torrey) Pitkin, and a descendant of William Pitkin [*q.v.*] who emigrated from England to Hartford, Conn., in 1659. For generations the Pitkin family had been prominent in the affairs of the state. Although left an orphan at the age of twelve, Fred-

erick was prepared for college and in 1854 entered Wesleyan University, Middletown, Conn., from which he graduated four years later. Shortly after his graduation from the Albany (N. Y.) Law School in 1859, he began the practice of law in Milwaukee, Wis. Following a serious illness in 1872, he became a health-seeker, visiting Minnesota in the autumn of that year, Europe in the spring of 1873, and Florida in the winter of 1873–74. In October 1874, he went to Colorado and took up his residence in the southern part of that territory, first at Ouray and then at Pueblo.

In Colorado he came into contact with prominent political leaders, who were so much impressed with his personality and ability that they urged and secured his nomination for governor by the Republican party in 1878. In the election he defeated his Democratic opponent, W. A. H. Loveland, by a majority of 2,700 votes in a total of 27,000 votes cast. His first term (1879–81) was filled with stirring events which tested fully his judgment and executive ability. Colorado, only three years in the Union, was still a frontier state with hundreds of Indians within its borders. In September 1879 occurred at the White River Agency the uprising of the Ute Indians known as the Meeker massacre. Governor Pitkin used the full power of the state, in cooperation with the federal troops, for the protection of the ranchers and miners on the frontiers; he vigorously voiced to the authorities in Washington the universal cry in Colorado that "the Utes must go." As the result of a treaty with these Indians in 1880 they were moved from the state in 1881, and a large tract of land on the "western slope" was thus thrown open to settlement. Other perplexing problems that involved the maintenance of law and order in frontier communities were the strike of the Leadville miners, and the struggle between the Atchison, Topeka & Santa Fé Railroad and the Denver & Rio Grande Railway for the control of the Royal Gorge in the canyon of the Arkansas River. Governor Pitkin's proclamation of martial law in the Leadville strike (June 13, 1880) was one of the main points of attack upon him in his campaign for reëlection in 1880, but he was victorious over his Democratic rival, John L. Hough, by a majority of about 5,000 in a total of 52,000 ballots. At the expiration of his second term as governor (1883), he was a candidate for the United States Senate, but was defeated in the Republican legislative caucus by Thomas M. Bowen [*q.v.*].

During the three remaining years of his life he engaged in the practice of law in Pueblo.

He is generally regarded as one of the ablest of Colorado's governors. He was indefatigable in guarding the public interest and in his devotion to duty; his honesty and integrity were never questioned. The lack of decisiveness with which he was sometimes charged was due, not to weakness, but to an extreme conscientiousness and to fear that hasty action might work injustice. He was survived by his wife, Fidelia M. (James) of Lockport, N. Y., to whom he was married on June 17, 1862, and by their two children.

[A. P. Pitkin, *Pitkin Family in America* (1887); Frank Hall, *Hist. of the State of Colo.*, vol. II (1890), vol. III (1891); *Hist. of Colo.: Biog.* (1927), vol. V; *Rocky Mountain News* (Denver), and *Denver Tribune-Republican*, Dec. 19, 1886; information regarding certain facts from Robert J. Pitkin of Denver.]

C. B. G.

PITKIN, TIMOTHY (Jan. 21, 1766–Dec. 18, 1847), statesman, historian, economist, was born in Farmington, Conn., the sixth child of the Rev. Timothy Pitkin (Yale, 1747), pastor of the church at Farmington. He came of distinguished ancestry, being descended from William Pitkin, 1635–1694 [*q.v.*], the founder of the family in America, who settled in Hartford in 1659, and a grandson of William Pitkin, 1694–1769 [*q.v.*], colonial governor of Connecticut. His mother, Temperance Clap, was the daughter of the Rev. Thomas Clap [*q.v.*], rector of Yale College. Timothy Pitkin was prepared for college by his father and brother-in-law. Upon graduation in 1785 he had the honor of delivering the Latin salutatory address. After teaching Latin and Greek for a year at Plainfield Academy, he studied law at Windsor with Oliver Ellsworth [*q.v.*]. From him Pitkin received a strong leaning toward political life. Admitted to the bar in 1788, he began his political career two years later in the lower house of the Connecticut General Assembly. There he served until his election to Congress in 1805. As congressman, he devoted himself industriously to the study of economic conditions in the new nation. He collected public documents and state papers and continually made memoranda from confidential communications from the executive. He was a loyal member of a Federalist group led by Josiah Quincy, his lifelong friend, and to the cause, by supplying much of the statistical material used in Quincy's speeches against the Embargo and Non-Intercourse acts. In 1818 Pitkin served as a delegate to the convention which revised the Connecticut constitution. The defeat of the Federalists brought his service in Congress to an end in 1819. He was at once elected to the Connecticut legislature, retaining his seat until 1830, when he retired from politics. Soon afterward

he gave up his legal work and devoted his remaining years to writing on historical and economic subjects.

In 1816 Pitkin had published *A Statistical View of the Commerce of the United States of America,* a work of unusual importance. A second edition had appeared in 1817. This book he now revised and enlarged. In the third edition (1835), he brought together a large amount of valuable data on the foreign trade of the country and on taxation, manufactures, and internal improvements. His industry in collecting his material and his careful habits of writing made this book the outstanding work of its kind. It still remains a valuable reference work on American economic history. In 1828 he published in two volumes *A Political and Civil History of the United States,* which covered the period 1763–97. Compiled from original sources, the work was marked by "accuracy, judicial temper, excellent judgment, and exhaustive research." Although the style is somewhat uninteresting, and although it is now largely superseded by later histories using material inaccessible to Pitkin, his work is still useful. A continuation of the history he left uncompleted at his death. His interests were wide. He was the author of a plan for the progressive emancipation of the slaves in the border states by the use of funds obtained through the sale of public lands. In college he was interested in astronomy and succeeded in calculating and accurately predicting the famous annular eclipse of the sun in 1790. In recognition of his contributions to statistics, he was awarded in 1837 a medal by the Société Française de Statistique Universelle. He died in New Haven. A devout churchman with pronounced religious convictions, for several years before his death he devoted much time to the study of theology. He married, June 6, 1801, Elizabeth Hubbard of New Haven, by whom he had six children.

[T. C. Pitkin, "Hon. Timothy Pitkin, LL.D.," *Memorial Biogs. . . . New-Eng. Hist. Geneal. Soc.,* vol. I (1880); F. B. Dexter, *Biog. Sketches of the Grads. of Yale Coll.,* vol. IV (1907); A. P. Pitkin, *Pitkin Family of America* (1887); *Columbian Reg.* (New Haven), Dec. 25, 1847.]

P. W. B.

PITKIN, WILLIAM (1635–Dec. 15, 1694), Connecticut lawyer and judge, was the son of Roger Pitkin, probably of Marylebone, England. After an excellent training in the law and perhaps some dabbling in theology, for which he had considerable fondness, he migrated to Hartford at the age of twenty-four. Here he was in 1660 granted liberty to teach the town school. Public life and the law soon claimed him, for in 1662 the General Court appointed him to prosecute certain offenders and two years later he became the colony's attorney for the prosecution of all delinquents. A leading lawyer in the colony, he served occasionally upon the bench, as when he was a member of the special court which met at Fairfield in 1692 to try four women for witchcraft. Apparently only one of the four was convicted and she was probably reprieved through the efforts of Pitkin himself and two other assistants. As assistant in the years 1690–94 he sat generally upon the Court of Assistants, when it met at Hartford, and was often its presiding judge.

Pitkin was a stout champion of Connecticut's colonial liberties. He served in 1683 with other commissioners who visited New York to congratulate the new governor, Dongan, and to press Connecticut's claims to a boundary that should not be more than twenty miles east of the Hudson. Three years later he served in a similar capacity, paying his colony's respects to Governor Andros and vainly requesting New York and Mohawk aid against the Indian enemies of Connecticut. In the critical years of the early nineties he championed the colony's right to control its own militia and to maintain its governmental independence of royal control. In 1690 Connecticut had voted to send troops to Albany at the request of Jacob Leisler for the war against the French, but in 1693 the extremely conservative instructions that Pitkin and his fellow commissioner had received helped to make the intercolonial defense conference in New York an abortive one. He had already in 1692 written the General Court's letter to Sir William Phips politely refusing to relinquish control of the local militia (*Connecticut Historical Society Collections,* vol. III, 1895, p. 245), and in 1694 he was joint author of the pamphlet, "Their Majesties Colony of Connecticut in New-England Vindicated" (*Ibid.,* vol. I, 1860, pp. 83–130). This was a defense against those who would have the Crown destroy the colony's self-government for the reason that the General Court was not always wise and just.

Pitkin was a member of the Church of England, but as there was no congregation in the town, he contended successfully for the right to have his children baptized in the First Church of Hartford, and was himself buried in its churchyard. His property interests lay largely on the east side of the Connecticut River where he was probably the largest land-owner and where he had an interest in a saw and grist mill. His wife was Hannah, the daughter of Ozias Goodwin, one of the early settlers of Hartford.

[See: *The Pub. Records of the Colony of Conn.,* vols. I–IV (1850–68); A. P. Pitkin, *Pitkin Family of Amer-ica* (1887); W. D. Love, *The Colonial Hist. of Hartford* (1914); J. H. Trumbull, *The Memorial Hist. of Hartford County* (2 vols., 1886); C. W. Manwaring, *A Digest of the Early Conn. Probate Records,* vol. I (1904); *Commemorative Exercises of the First Church of Christ in Hartford . . . 1883* (1883), pp. 63–64.]
E. W. S.

PITKIN, WILLIAM (Apr. 30, 1694–Oct. 1, 1769), colonial judge and governor of Connecticut, son of William and Elizabeth (Stanley) Pitkin, was born and lived in Hartford. His father was a prosperous manufacturer, cloth merchant, public man, and jurist, who was the son of William Pitkin, 1635–1694 [*q.v.*], the first of the family in America. The third William was of good figure, tall, affable, and reputed to be "an Example of universal Goodness in all Relations." On May 7, 1724, he was married to Mary Woodbridge, the daughter of the Rev. Timothy Woodbridge of the First Church. William himself, a man of evident piety, was probably a member of the Third Church, that in East Hartford where he lived and owned considerable real property. Here also he and his brother Joseph operated the fulling mills bequeathed to them by their father. William alone fell heir to the clothier's shop where much of their cloth was sold. His father intended him to be a merchant, but from the age of twenty-one, when he was chosen rate-collector, to his death at seventy-five, he was almost constantly in the service of his town or colony. A captain of the train band at thirty-six, he later became major and colonel (1739) in the first regiment. When the Connecticut frontier in 1733 feared an Indian war instigated by the French, Pitkin sat on the committee for defense. Again in 1740 he was active in the cause of defense, a member of the council on war, a war financier concerned with the issue of bills of credit, enrolment officer for the volunteers of Hartford County who were to war on Spain in the West Indies, and later (1743) committee-man for war. After service as commissioner to treat with the Iroquois, he was sent in 1754 to the Albany Congress with Roger Wolcott and Elisha Williams [*qq.v.*]. Their instructions were carefully restrictive, discouraging presents for the Indians and advocating generous royal military assistance with a minimum of financial and military aid from the colony. Pitkin was one of the committee of five for drawing up the plan of confederation.

After an apprenticeship as justice of the peace, William Pitkin received appointment as judge of the county court where he presided from 1735 to 1752. The General Court of the colony elected him in 1741 to the bench of the highest court in Connecticut, the superior court. Here he served faithfully until his election to the lieutenant-governorship in 1754 made him, for twelve years, its chief judge. Meanwhile he had been active in politics. After four years in the Assembly as delegate from Hartford, he became its speaker (1732–34). Twice defeated in the election of assistants, he obtained his seat in 1734. In this capacity he served for twenty years, occasionally combining his duties with those of colonial auditor, canvasser of votes, or commissioner on the Massachusetts boundary and on Mohegan affairs (both 1752). By the time he became deputy governor (1754–66) under Governor Fitch, he was known as a champion of colonial rights against the royal government. Consequently, when Governor Fitch in October 1765 took the oath to administer the Stamp Act, Pitkin received the nomination of the colonial rights men, given perhaps through a meeting of the Sons of Liberty (*Connecticut Historical Society Collections,* vol. XIX, 1921, p. xxv), for governor. The election was a landslide, and after being twice reëlected, and having creditably served nearly three terms, Pitkin died in office in October 1769.

[*Conn. Hist. Soc. Colls.,* vol. V (1896), "The Law Papers," vol. XI (1907), XIII (1911), XV (1914), and "The Pitkin Papers," vol. XIX (1921); Eliphalet Williams, *The Ruler's Duty to Honor, . . . A Sermon Occasioned by the . . . Death of the Hon. Wm. Pitkin* (1770); A. P. Pitkin, *Pitkin Family of America* (1887); *The Pub. Records of the Colony of Conn.,* vols. VII–XIII (1873–85).]   E. W. S.

PITKIN, WILLIAM (1725–Dec. 12, 1789), Connecticut jurist and manufacturer, was the fourth in a line of distinguished Hartford magistrates and prosperous manufacturers of the same name. His father was William Pitkin, 1694–1769 [*q.v.*], and his mother, Mary Woodbridge. The fourth William and his wife Abigail, the daughter of James Church, attended faithfully the Third Church of Hartford of which he was for twenty-nine years deacon. Trained for the law and renowned chiefly for his career on the bench, he found time to carry on the family tradition of manufacturing. He owned power sites and mills that had belonged to his father and his uncle, Joseph Pitkin. When, in December 1775, the General Assembly granted to George Pitkin and himself permission to establish a powder-mill three miles east of the Connecticut River, one of these earlier sites was used. This powder-mill, probably the first in Connecticut, supplied the colony during the Revolution. But the price of powder, set in 1776 by the Assembly at 5s.4d., was too low for profit, and Pitkin received additional compensation at the end of the war. The Act of Jan. 8, 1783, gave to him and two others a monopoly for twenty-five years upon the manufacture of glass in Connecticut, and during the

next year he alone received similar rights over snuff manufacturing with exemption from taxation for fourteen years. In addition to these ventures he had an interest in a forging-mill.

Much of his life was given to public service. At thirty-one he was commissioned captain of the third militia company of Hartford, and two years later, still captain of his third company, he became major-commandant of the first regiment of Connecticut forces which was to serve under Abercromby in the campaign against New France. In 1762 he became lieutenant-colonel of the same regiment. In the realm of politics he served for nineteen years (1766–85) as assistant on the governor's council. During the Revolution he sat almost continuously on the Council of Safety and was known as an ardent patriot. Elected to Congress in 1784, he seems not to have taken his seat. He was considered for the lieutenant-governorship in 1787, but he finished a poor seventh among the eight candidates in the field. The next year, however, he and Elisha Pitkin were East Hartford's delegates to the convention that ratified the new federal constitution, and William cast his vote in its favor. East Hartford had been separated from Hartford after the war, and William Pitkin had been moderator of its first town meeting. In the year of his father's death, 1769, he was made a judge of the superior court and remained until the year of his death, the last year as its chief judge. He was the fourth William Pitkin in the direct line to preside over the highest court of Connecticut.

[See: *The Pub. Records of the Colony of Conn.,* vols. XIII–XV (1885–90) and *The Pub. Records of the State of Conn.,* vols. I–III (1894–1922); *Roll of State Officers of Conn., 1776 to 1881* (1881); A. P. Pitkin, *Pitkin Family of America* (1887); J. H. Trumbull, ed., *Memorial Hist. of Hartford County* (1886), vol. II; Mathias Spiess and P. W. Bidwell, *Hist. of Manchester, Conn.* (1924); *Hartford, Conn., as a Manufacturing . . . Center* (1889).]   E. W. S.

PITMAN, BENN (July 24, 1822–Dec. 28, 1910), phonographer, son of Samuel and Mariah (Davis) Pitman, was born in Trowbridge, Wiltshire, England, one of a family of seven boys and four girls. He received a good elementary education under the direction of the rector of the parish, the poet George Crabbe, and through private instruction at home. His father was the manager of a cloth manufactory, a hand-loom weaver by trade. He was a strict disciplinarian, a strong supporter of education in the parish, and a man of liberal views, as witnessed by the fact that while a member of the Church of England and superintendent of the Sunday school, he served in the same capacity in the Baptist chapel which his wife attended, taking his four elder sons with him, where they all taught classes. In Benn Pitman's biography of his brother Isaac, he says that no trivial conversation was allowed in their home. The children under fourteen were expected to be silent at table; those under twelve stood while eating. When he was twenty-one, Benn began to assist his brother Isaac as a lecturer on phonography. Isaac Pitman had invented a new system of shorthand based on the sounds in the English language and Benn had learned it four or five years before and had superintended the correction of the plates of the first edition of Isaac's book on phonetic shorthand. He was profoundly convinced of the importance of the phonetic principle as a factor in education and general progress, and, filled with the enthusiasm born of this conviction, he now went about the country with his brother Joseph and several other young men, lecturing and teaching.

In 1846, he took charge of a publishing house called the Phonographic and Phonotypic Depot. Three years later he married Jane Bragg, of Manchester. By 1852 Isaac felt that the United States should no longer be left in ignorance of phonography and in the middle of the winter sent Benn and his wife with their two children across the ocean as steerage passengers. After living for a time in Philadelphia, Pa., and Canton, Ohio, Pitman moved to Cincinnati, which remained his home until his death. There he founded the Phonographic Institute, for the teaching of shorthand and the publishing of works on that subject. Although in 1858 Isaac Pitman made radical changes in his system, Benn continued to teach the original method, which he felt to be superior to the new, and which came to be one of the most popular in the United States. During the first years of the Civil War Benn served in the ranks. Later he was employed by the government as a shorthand reporter. He reported a number of famous trials, among them the trial of the conspirators in the assassination of President Lincoln, and he compiled and arranged for publication an abridgment of the testimony (*The Assassination of President Lincoln and the Trial of the Conspirators,* 1865).

He was the author and editor of many works on shorthand and phonetic reform, a number of which were elaborately decorated, and in 1902 published *Sir Isaac Pitman, His Life and Labors, Told and Illustrated by Benn Pitman.* In 1855 he invented an electrochemical process of relief engraving and in 1867, with Dr. J. B. Burns, produced relief stereotype plates by a photo-gelatine process. It is said that the interior of his home in Cincinnati was ornately decorated with woodcarving, the work of himself and

his pupils at the Cincinnati Art School where he taught woodcarving and decorative art for many years. His wife died in 1878, and in 1881 he married Adelaide Nourse, by whom he had one daughter. By his first marriage there were two sons and a daughter. He died in Cincinnati after a long illness.

[*Cincinnati Enquirer,* Dec. 29, 1910; *Cincinnati Commercial Tribune,* Dec. 29, 1910; Alfred Baker, *The Life of Sir Isaac Pitman* (1908); *Rev. of Revs.* (N. Y.), Feb. 1911; *Who's Who in America,* 1910–11.] B. R.

PITNEY, MAHLON (Feb. 5, 1858–Dec. 9, 1924), legislator and judge, was the third child of Henry Cooper Pitney, vice-chancellor of New Jersey, and Sarah Louisa (Halsted) Pitney. He was born at Morristown, N. J., where he received his preparatory education. Before he was eighteen he entered the College of New Jersey (now Princeton University), took the full course, and received the degree of A.B. in 1879. After reading law in his father's office at Morristown he was admitted to the bar and began practice at Dover in the same county. In 1885 he was licensed as a counselor and four years later, upon his father's appointment as vice-chancellor, returned to Morristown and took over the latter's practice which he continued with marked success for nearly a dozen years. On Nov. 14, 1891, he was married to Florence T. Shelton, of his native town, and two sons and one daughter were born to them. In 1894 he was elected a Republican member of the National House of Representatives and served on the committee on appropriations. He had now become a recognized party leader in his region and in the following year was temporary chairman of the Republican State Convention. In 1896 he made an active campaign for reëlection to Congress, stressing his party position on the money question, and won the election by an increased plurality. Two years later he was elected to the state Senate from his native county, became his party's floor leader therein, and in 1901, president of that body. On his forty-third birthday he was nominated by Gov. Foster M. Voorhees for a vacancy on the state supreme court, was confirmed and served from Nov. 16, 1901, to Jan. 22, 1908, when he was advanced to the position of chancellor of the state. After a little more than four years of service in that capacity he was nominated by President Taft, on Feb. 19, 1912, to succeed Associate Justice John M. Harlan of the federal Supreme Court. His nomination was confirmed on Mar. 13, and he took office five days later.

Pitney's service on the Supreme Court continued for somewhat less than eleven years. His opinions (in 225–59 *U. S.*), show painstaking care and a labored style. The opinion in *Hitch-man Coal & Coke Company* vs. *Mitchell* (245 *U. S.*, 229) was a blow to organized labor, since it seriously limited the common-law right of workmen to combine. In *Duplex Printing Press Company* vs. *Deering et al.* (254 *U. S.*, 433) the Clayton Act was invoked to restrain a labor union from boycott. In *Eisner* vs. *Macomber* (252 *U. S.*, 189) Congress was denied the right to tax stock dividends, on the ground that they consti-tuted capital increase, not income. Pitney's opin-ion in *Frank* vs. *Mangum* (237 *U. S.*, 309) deal-ing with due process of law, met a vigorous dis-sent from Justices Holmes and Hughes who held that "mob law does not become due process of law by securing the assent of a terrorized jury" (237 *U. S.*, 347). Although most of his opinions were strongly conservative, in *Mountain Timber Company* vs. *Washington* (243 *U. S.*, 219), in which the Workmen's Compensation Act of the state of Washington was upheld, Pitney delivered the opinion of a liberal majority. He resigned, effective Dec. 31, 1922, having served twenty-five years in public office. After leaving the Su-preme Court he continued to reside in Washing-ton. It was apparently his arduous work on the Supreme Court which compelled him to retire at the relatively early age of sixty-four and caused his premature death a few months later.

[See: E. R. Walker, "In Memoriam: Mahlon Pit-ney," *Am. Bar Asso. Jour.*, May 1925; Wm. Nelson, ed., *Nelson's Biog. Cyc. of N. J.* (1913), vol. II; *Biog. Dir. Am. Cong.* (1928); W. O. Wheeler and E. D. Halsey, *Descendants of Rebecca Ogden and Caleb Hal-sted* (n.d.); T. R. Powell, "The Workmen's Compensa-tion Acts," *Pol. Sci. Quart.*, Dec. 1917, and "Collective Bargaining Before the Supreme Court," *Ibid.*, Sept. 1918; *Who's Who in America*, 1924–25; the *Evening Star* (Washington, D. C.), Dec. 9, 1924.]   C. S. L.

PITTOCK, HENRY LEWIS (Mar. 1, 1836–Jan. 28, 1919), newspaper publisher, paper man-ufacturer, was born in London, England, the son of Susanna (Bonner) and Frederick Pit-tock. In 1825 his father and his grandfather had emigrated from England to Pittsburgh, Pa. His father returned to London, married, and went back to Pittsburgh in 1839, where he followed the printer's trade the rest of his life. The boy attended the public schools of Pittsburgh and the preparatory school of the Western Univer-sity of Pennsylvania and learned to be a practi-cal printer. Induced by newspaper narratives of Oregon in the early 1850's he and his brother Robert undertook the six months' journey to the Northwest. In the autumn of 1853 he began work as a compositor for the *Weekly Oregonian* and soon became a journeyman printer. In June 1860 he was married to Georgiana Martin Bur-

ton, the daughter of E. M. Burton, who died in 1918. Later in the year 1860 he became pro-prietor of the paper at a time when outside news was obtained by pony express, stage, and steam-ship, printing methods were primitive and finan-cial problems difficult. He exerted every effort to get news; he watched all night for the arrival of the stage bringing news and, after the tele-graph was established in 1864, spent a large por-tion of his slender resources to pay for this serv-ice. In 1861 he began to publish the *Morning Oregonian*. The first press was a Ramage, hand-operated, that required a separate impression for each page. The paper supported Lincoln, the Union cause, and Reconstruction, and for the twenty years before 1896 he advocated "sound money" and the gold standard. His undertak-ings prospered; he became state printer, in 1877 he added an afternoon edition, the *Evening Tele-gram*, and in 1881 a Sunday edition, the *Sunday Oregonian*, and he built two large buildings for the newspaper. All competitors of his news-papers in Portland failed before 1902.

Throughout his life he lent his interest and abilities to various enterprises in developing the new country. He helped found the Northwestern National Bank, became president of the Portland Trust Company of Oregon, engaged extensively in logging and lumbering, and was a leader in the building of the railroads from Lyle to Golden-dale, Wash., and from Salem to Falls City, Ore. He was a principal owner in the Baldwin Sheep & Land Company that held 35,000 acres in eastern Oregon, also an organizer of the Harkins Transportation Company that operated steamboats on the Columbia and Willamette rivers, and of the Clearwater Irrigation Power & Boom Company at Lewiston, Idaho. With his brother, Thomas R. Pittock, he held extensive interests in Pittsburgh. Beginning in 1866 at Oregon City he was one of the first to engage in paper manufacture in the Pacific Northwest. At first he used rags for raw material and later wood pulp. In 1868 he built another new plant near Oregon City, and in 1883–85 a third at Camas, Wash. He was an organizer and stock-holder in the Columbia Paper Company, later a part of the Crown Zellerbach Corporation. He was a thirty-third degree Scottish Rite Mason and held high places in other Masonic organi-zations. He was a member of many clubs and civic societies. The geography, resources, in-dustries, and people of the Pacific Northwest were familiar to him as to few others. He died at his home in Portland.

[Autobiog. in *Morning Oregonian*, Dec. 4, 1900; *Ibid.*, Jan. 30, 1919; H. W. Scott, *Hist. of the Ore. Country* (1924), vols. I–V, comp. by L. M. Scott;

Am. Biog.: A New Cyclop., vol. XII (1922); Joseph Gaston, *Portland, Ore.* (1911), vol. II.]   L. M. S.

PITTS, HIRAM AVERY (*c.* 1800–Sept. 19, 1860), inventor, was the son of Abial and Abiah Pitts. Soon after he was born his father moved to Winthrop, Kennebec County, Me., where he worked as the village blacksmith for many years. Hiram and his twin brother, John Avery, attended the district school, and in their father's blacksmith shop learned to make shoes for horses and oxen, sleds and oxyokes, hinges and latches for doors, andirons and tongs for fireplaces, and the other wrought-iron work needed to supply the rural community. After their father's death, probably in 1825, the brothers carried on the business in Winthrop in partnership for upwards of two years; then Hiram retired to devote his whole time to invention. He developed an improvement in the chain type of hand pump, and then turned his attention to the horse-power treadmill. With the help of his brother he worked on this problem for a number of years, and on Aug. 15, 1834, they were granted a patent for the chain band for a horse-power. In their device hard maple rollers connected by an endless chain were substituted for the old-fashioned belt. Shortly after obtaining this patent, the Pitts brothers became partners for the purpose of manufacturing their improved power in Winthrop. Hiram took it upon himself to introduce the machines throughout the state of Maine and elsewhere in New England and met with considerable success, and the treadmill came to be widely used in connection with the "Ground Hog Thresher," or open-cylinder threshing machine. Dissatisfied with the work of the "Ground Hog," Pitts gave considerable thought to the designing of a better thresher, and in 1834, with his brother, built a combined threshing and fanning mill in portable form. In this machine, behind a cylinder similar to that of the "Ground Hog" was an endless apron conveyor, and over it a round beater armed with pegs to agitate the straws and a picker or rotary pitchfork to throw them off the end. The grain fell from the cylinder and conveyor into a trough which conducted it to the fanning mill mounted under the machine. A trough was arranged just behind the sieves to catch the heads of grain, allowing the chaff to blow over and away. These bits of grain, known as "tailings," were conveyed to the sieves to be refanned. Patent No. 542, for their thresher and fanning mill, was awarded the brothers on Dec. 29, 1837. Various minor improvements were made on the original Pitts machine, but the principles of the original invention remained unchanged for over

a half century. For the next ten years Pitts engaged in the successful manufacturing and marketing of his machines in Winthrop, the first three years in partnership with his brother and after 1840 alone. In that year John A. Pitts opened a factory in Albany; after several subsequent moves he settled in Buffalo, where he manufactured the "Buffalo-Pitts" thresher until his death. In 1847 Hiram moved to Alton, Ill., where he began the manufacture of threshers in the shops of a brother-in-law, improving and perfecting them from time to time. Four years later he removed to Chicago, and in 1852 there began the manufacture of these improved threshers. They were called the "Chicago-Pitts" threshers and they soon found a ready market wherever grain was extensively raised. Besides these important inventions, Pitts is said to have devised a machine for breaking hemp and separating the stalk from the fiber, and also several corn and cob mills. He married Leonora Hosley of Livermore, Me., and when he died in Chicago at the age of sixty, he was survived by four sons who carried on his business.

[R. L. Ardrey, *Am. Agricultural Implements* (1894); E. S. Stackpole, *Hist. of Winthrop, Me.* (1925); Waldemar Kaempffert, *A Popular Hist. of Am. Invention* (1924), vol. II; *Daily Times and Herald* (Chicago), Sept. 20, 1860; Patent Office records.]   C. W. M—n.

PLACIDE, HENRY (Sept. 8, 1799–Jan. 23, 1870), actor, was the ablest and best-known member of a notable American stage family. His father was Alexander Placide, a popular acrobat, dancer, actor, and manager, of French birth and origin. His mother, Charlotte Sophia (Wrighten), was the daughter of James Wrighten, for many years prompter of the Drury Lane Theatre in London, and of the actress and singer known on the American stage as Mrs. Pownall. Henry Placide was the second of their five children. His brother Thomas (1808–1877) was a popular comedian, and his three sisters all had stage careers: Caroline (1798–1881) was the wife successively of Leigh Waring and William R. Blake, Jane (1804–1835) was both actress and singer, Eliza (d. 1874) appeared successively as Mrs. Asbury and Mrs. Mann. Henry made his first recorded appearance on the stage in Augusta, Ga., Aug. 23, 1808, at the age of nine, and his last in New York at the Winter Garden Theatre, May 13, 1865, his professional career thereby extending over the exceptionally long period of fifty-seven years.

He first acted in New York at the Anthony Street Theatre as early as 1814, but his name then practically disappears from the records until Sept. 2, 1823, when he appeared at the Park

Theatre as Zekiel Homespun in *The Heir at Law* and Dr. Dablancœur in *Budget of Blunders*. During that interval it is certain that he was acting in obscure regions, and there is one reference to his appearance in 1815–16 in the part of a monkey. After his début at the Park Theatre in 1823, except for brief intervals when he acted elsewhere for short periods (he attempted an engagement at the Haymarket Theatre in London in 1841, but it was an immediate failure), he was the centre of attraction in the New York theatrical world. During his career of twenty years at the Park, he played over five hundred characters, being the original representative of more than two hundred of these. His range extended from clowns of broadest Yorkshire dialect to garrulous Frenchmen, from clumsy hobbledehoys and senile old men to high-bred English gentlemen. He also sang buffo rôles in English opera, and he was as successful in the frothiest and most trivial farce as in the highest type of comedy. Among his rôles were David, Bob Acres, and Sir Anthony Absolute in *The Rivals*, Sir Benjamin Backbite, Crabtree, and Sir Peter Teazle in *The School for Scandal*, Dogberry in *Much Ado About Nothing*, Dr. Ollapod in *The Poor Gentleman*, Colonel Hardy in *Paul Pry*, and Captain Cuttle in *Dombey and Son*. He was the Sir Harcourt Courtly to Charlotte Cushman's Lady Gay Spanker at the first performance of *London Assurance* in the United States, Oct. 11, 1841.

After leaving the Park Theatre, of which he had been for a brief period manager as well as leading actor, he joined the company at Burton's Theatre, and gave distinction to its performances by the contribution of his reputation and his art. "He was not broadly funny like Burton or Holland," says W. L. Keese (*post*, p. 49), "but . . . he was the owner of a rich vein of eccentric humor, and . . . worked his possession effectually. He was an expert in the Gallic parts where the speech is a struggle between French and English, and indeed, since his departure they, too, have vanished from the stage." He made extended tours, throughout the entire country. Joseph Jefferson in his *Autobiography* (p. 155) records a performance at the Baltimore Museum in 1853 of *The School for Scandal*, with Henry Placide as Sir Peter, Thomas Placide as Crabtree, and himself as Moses, referring to Henry Placide as "a finished artist, but somewhat cold and hard in his manner." After his last appearance, in 1865, he was compelled to retire because of ill health and failing eyesight. He made his home thenceforth in Babylon, N. Y., where he died.

[Information about Placide is profusely scattered through many sources; see especially William Dunlap, *Hist. of the Am. Theatre* (1833); G. C. D. Odell, *Annals of the N. Y. Stage*, vols. III–VII (1928–31); J. N. Ireland, *Records of the N. Y. Stage* (2 vols., 1866–67); H. P. Phelps, *Players of a Century* (1880); J. N. Ireland, in *Actors and Actresses of Great Britain and the U. S.: Kean and Booth; and Their Contemporaries* (1886), ed. by Brander Matthews and Laurence Hutton; W. L. Keese, *William E. Burton, Actor, Author and Manager* (1885); *The Autobiog. of Joseph Jefferson* (1889); G. O. Seilhamer, *Hist. of the Am. Theatre* (3 vols., 1889–91); T. A. Brown, *A Hist. of the N. Y. Stage* (3 vols., 1903); Eola Willis, *The Charleston Stage in the XVIII Century* (1924); *N. Y. Tribune*, Jan. 24, 25, 1870; newspaper clippings in the files of the Harvard Library Theatre Collection.]

E. F. E.

PLAISTED, HARRIS MERRILL (Nov. 2, 1828–Jan. 31, 1898), soldier, congressman, governor of Maine, seventh of the nine children of Deacon William and Nancy (Merrill) Plaisted, was born at Jefferson, N. H. He was a descendant of Roger Playstead who settled in Kittery (now Berwick), Me., about 1650. Until the age of seventeen, Harris Merrill Plaisted made his home upon the farm where he was born, attending the district school when there was one. His education was obtained largely during the fall and spring terms, first at Lancaster, N. H., and later at academies in St. Johnsbury, Vt., and New Hampton, N. H. Summers he worked on the farm; winters he taught school. He entered Waterville (now Colby) College in September 1849 and was graduated in 1853, meanwhile paying his way by serving as superintendent of schools in Waterville (1850–53) and principal (1853) of the Waterville Liberal Institute. He was graduated with highest honors from the Albany (N. Y.) Law School in 1855, and studied one year in the office of A. W. Paine at Bangor, Me. Admitted to the bar in 1856, he practised in Bangor until 1861. He voted for Lincoln, taking an active part in the campaign and writing assiduously in behalf of the Union. When the war began, he was appointed lieutenant-colonel by Governor Washburn, and raised a company in thirty days. On Oct. 30, 1861, he became lieutenant-colonel of the 11th Maine Regiment and was promoted to a colonelcy May 12, 1862, in the midst of the Peninsular campaign. Transferred to the Southern Department, he commanded a brigade in the vicinity of Charleston, and during the siege of that city had charge of the famous gun, the "Swamp Angel." In April 1864, he was transferred with his so-called "Iron Brigade" to the Richmond sector. His three leaves, July 1862, February and November 1864, he spent in recruiting men for his depleted ranks, turning over the recruiting fees to the men themselves. Suffering with fever and ague, he was mustered out Mar. 25, 1865, and after a month in a hospital returned to Bangor in the latter part of May 1865. For gallant and meritorious service he had been brevetted brigadier-general of volunteers, Feb. 21, 1865, and major-general, Mar. 13.

Resuming his law practice and entering politics, he twice represented Bangor in the legislature (1867, 1868) and was a delegate-at-large to the Republican National Convention of 1868, at Chicago. In competition with several able lawyers, among them Thomas B. Reed, Plaisted was elected attorney-general of Maine in January 1873. During his three years in this office, he secured twelve convictions in fourteen indictments for capital crimes. He resigned Dec. 1, 1875, and took the congressional seat left vacant by the death of Representative-elect Samuel F. Hersey. As one of the two Republican members of the select committee on trials for whiskey frauds under the chairmanship of J. Proctor Knott [q.v.], he assumed the defense of Grant. He was firmly convinced of Grant's honesty and integrity, and, carefully presenting the results of his investigations, in the opinion of many completely vindicated Grant of complicity. Declining reëlection, he returned to Bangor in March 1877. In 1879 he left the Republican party on the money issue, maintaining that "greenbacks" should be substituted for bank bills which, when outstanding in the hands of the people, he held constituted a loan from the people to the banks without interest. In 1880 he was elected governor as the candidate of both Democrats and Greenbackers, but failed of reëlection in 1883. His term in office was marked by a continuous conflict with the Republican council over political appointments. He was the Democratic nominee for senator in 1883, but was defeated. From 1883 to his death he published and edited at Augusta *The New Age,* which under his influence was an able exponent of Bryan and bimetalism and a strong opponent of Blaine. His death, in Bangor, was due to Bright's disease resulting from malarial poisoning contracted in the army. He married first, Sept. 21, 1858, Sarah J. Mason, who died in 1875, and second, Sept. 27, 1881, Mabel True Hill. Three sons were born to the first marriage and one daughter to the second. He was the author of several trial reports; with F. H. Appleton, of *The Maine Digest* (1880), a digest of decisions of the state supreme court from 1820 to 1879; and also of several unpublished genealogical and autobiographical works.

[*Life and Public Services of Gen'l Harris M. Plaisted* (1880); Richard Herndon, *Men of Progress . . . in and of the State of Me.* (1897), with photograph; Henry Chase, *Representative Men of Maine* (1893),

with photograph; *New Age,* Feb. 4, 1898; *The Story of One Regiment: The Eleventh Me. Infantry Vols. in the War of the Rebellion* (1896); M. F. King, *Lieut. Roger Plaisted of Quamphegon (Kittery) and Some of His Descendants* (1904); *Biog. Dir. Am. Cong.* (1928); *Bangor Daily Commercial,* Jan. 31, 1898.]
R. E. M.

PLANT, HENRY BRADLEY (Oct. 27, 1819–June 23, 1899), founder of the Plant system of railroads and steamboats, was born in Branford, Conn., the son of Betsey (Bradley) and Anderson Plant, a farmer in good circumstances. He was the descendant of John Plant who probably emigrated from England and settled at Hartford, Conn., about 1639. When the boy was six, his father died. Several years later his mother married again and took him to live first at Martinsburg, N. Y., and later at New Haven, Conn., where he attended a private school. His grandmother, who hoped to make a clergyman of him, offered him an education at Yale College, but, impatient to begin an active career, he got a job as captain's boy, deck hand, and man-of-all-work on a steamboat plying between New Haven and New York. He was then eighteen. Among his various duties was the care of express parcels. This line of business, hitherto neglected, he organized effectively, and, when it was taken over by the Adams Express Company and later transferred from steamboats to railroads, he went along with it. After a few years he was put in charge of the New York office of the company. In 1853 his wife, Ellen Elizabeth (Blackstone) Plant, to whom he had been married in 1842, was ordered South for her health. Several months spent near Jacksonville, then a tiny hamlet, impressed the shrewd Yankee with the possibilities of the future development of Florida. The next year he became the general superintendent of the Adams Express Company for the territory south of the Potomac and Ohio rivers. In the face of great difficulties he successfully organized and extended express service in this region, where transportation facilities, although rapidly growing, were still deficient and uncoördinated. At the approach of the Civil War the directors of Adams Express, fearing the confiscation of their Southern properties, decided to transfer them to Plant. With the Southern stockholders of the company he organized in 1861 the Southern Express Company, a Georgia corporation, and became president. His company acted as agent for the Confederacy in collecting tariffs and transferring funds. In 1863, following a serious illness, he took an extended vacation in Europe, and he returned by way of Canada.

After the war the railroads of the South were practically ruined and many roads went bankrupt in the depression of 1873. In this situation he found his opportunity. Convinced of the eventual economic revival of the South, he bought at foreclosure sales in 1879 and 1880 the Atlantic & Gulf Railroad and the Charleston & Savannah Railroad. With these as a nucleus he began building along the southern Atlantic seaboard a transportation system that twenty years later included fourteen railway companies with 2,100 miles of track, several steamship lines, and a number of important hotels. In 1882 he organized, with the assistance of Northern capitalists, among whom were H. M. Flagler, M. K. Jesup, and W. T. Walters [qq.v.], the Plant Investment Company, a holding company for the joint management of the various properties under his control. He reconstructed and extended several small railroads so as to provide continuous service across the state, and by providing better connections with through lines to the North he gave Florida orange growers quicker and cheaper access to Northern markets. Tampa, then a village of a few hundred inhabitants, he made the terminus of his southern Florida railroad and also the home port for a new line of steamships to Havana. For the accommodation of winter visitors he built here, in the style of a Moorish palace, an enormous hotel costing $2,500,000. The subsequent growth in wealth and population of Florida and other states tributary to the Plant system made its founder one of the richest anl most powerful men in the South. A good physical inheritance, preserved by temperate habits, made it possible for him to keep at work until almost eighty years of age. His first wife died in February 1861, and in 1873 he married Margaret Josephine Loughman, the daughter of Martin Loughman of New York City, who with one of his two sons survived him. In his will he attempted to prevent the partition of his properties, to the value of about $10,000,000, by forming a trust for the benefit of a great-grandson, but the will was contested by his widow and declared invalid under the laws of the state of New York. This decision made possible the consolidation of his railroads with other properties to form the Atlantic Coast Line Railroad. His son, Morton Freeman Plant (1852–1918), was vice-president of the Plant Investment Company from 1884 to 1902 and attained distinction as a yachtsman, part owner of the Philadelphia baseball club in the National League, and sole owner of the New London club in the Eastern League. Of the younger Plant's many gifts to hospitals and other institutions the most notable were the three dormitories and the unrestricted gift of $1,000,000 to the Connecticut College for Women.

[G. S. Smyth, *Henry Bradley Plant* (1898); H. D. Dozier, *A Hist. of the Atlantic Coast Line Railroad* (1920); *Railroad Gazette*, June 30, 1899; *N. Y. Herald*, June 24, 1899; *N. Y. Times*, Nov. 5, 15, 1918, for son's activities.]   P. W. B.

PLATER, GEORGE (Nov. 8, 1735–Feb. 10, 1792), sixth governor of Maryland, was born on the family estate, "Sotterley," near Leonardtown, St. Mary's County, Md. He was the grandson of George Plater who emigrated from England to Maryland and became locally prominent, and he was the son of a second George Plater, who was conspicuous in the provincial government, and of Rebecca (Addison) Bowles Plater, at the time of her marriage a widow of ample means. He was graduated from the College of William and Mary in 1753. He then adopted the legal profession. From 1767 to 1773 he served as naval officer of the Patuxent district in a position filled earlier by both his father and grandfather. He was also a justice of the peace of St. Mary's County from 1757 to 1771, a delegate in the lower house of the Assembly from 1757 to 1766, and during the last few years before the Revolution, 1771–74, a member of the Executive Council.

Official position did not debar him from early sympathy with the colonists' quarrel, although he became conspicuous as a leader only as matters approached a crisis. In February 1776 he was appointed by the Maryland Council of Safety one of three collectors in his county to obtain gold and silver coin for military operations against Canada, a task well discharged since in about a month he reported a goodly sum collected. In March following, he and George Dent were selected by the Council of Safety to cooperate with Virginia commissioners in the construction of beacons on each bank of the Potomac. The records indicate success in erecting twenty such stations about five miles apart. Events were now moving swiftly, and on May 24 he was constituted one of a committee of five to invite Governor Eden to leave the province. The next day he was seated on the Council of Safety. Scarcely three months later he was serving on a committee charged to draft a declaration and charter of rights and to form a government for the state. In 1778 he was sent by the legislature to represent Maryland in the Continental Congress, where he served until 1780. It fell to his lot to preside over the Maryland convention that ratified the new federal Constitution. In the first electoral college he cast his vote for Washington for president. He represented St. Mary's County several times in the state Senate after the Revolution. In November 1791 he was elected governor by the Maryland Assembly. It was during his brief incumbency of less than a year that negotiations for the location of the federal capital on Maryland soil were conducted. He was married twice: first, on Dec. 5, 1762, to Hannah Lee, who lived only ten months after her marriage, and then on July 19, 1764, to Elizabeth Rousby of Calvert County. One of their six children married Philip Barton Key [*q.v.*]. Though not a man of large creative ability or of marked individuality, Plater's value as a lawyer and lawmaker came to be appreciated by his constituents and colleagues.

[*Tercentenary Hist. of Md.* (1925), vol. IV; H. E. Buchholz, *Governors of Md.* (1908); C. W. Sams and E. S. Riley, *The Bench and Bar of Md.* (1901); *Md. Hist. Mag.*, Dec. 1907, Mar., June 1920; *Md. Gazette*, Feb. 16, 1792; *Md. Jour. and Baltimore Advertiser*, Feb. 14, 1792.]   E. L.

PLATNER, SAMUEL BALL (Dec. 4, 1863–Aug 20, 1921), classical scholar, teacher, was born at Unionville, Conn., the son of William and Emily Childs (Ball) Platner. His mother, a remarkable woman, daughter of Samuel and Experience (Howland) Ball of Lee, Mass., was of New England stock. His father was a business man of Dutch extraction, who died when Samuel was still a boy. After 1865 the family lived at Newark, N. J., and from the Newark Academy Samuel entered Yale College in 1879. He was graduated with distinction in 1883, remained to study the classics and Sanskrit in the Graduate School for two years, and received the degree of Ph.D. in 1885. Thereafter until his death he was associated with Adelbert College of Western Reserve University, Cleveland, being instructor in Latin and French (1885–90), assistant professor of Latin (1890–92), and then professor of Latin. He married, June 29, 1892, Leonora Sayre of Utica, N. Y. In 1889–90 he studied in Berlin and Bonn and visited Rome for the first time. This visit kindled in him a real enthusiasm for the city of Rome, its history, topography, and monuments, and in the years 1897–98 and 1899–1900, which he spent for the most part in Rome, this enthusiasm was strengthened. Thereafter he returned to Rome as often as he could. He was actively interested in the foundation, in 1895, of the American School of Classical Studies in Rome, and he served the School as annual professor in 1899–1900, as member of its managing and executive committees from the beginning, and as secretary of both committees from 1897 to 1911. He was a member of Phi Beta Kappa, acting secretary (1899) and president (1900–1901) of the American Philological Association, and a member of various other learned societies.

Apart from articles and reviews in periodicals his published work comprises: *Greek and Roman Versification* (1892), translated from the German of Lucian Müller; *Selections from the Letters of the Younger Pliny* (1894); *The Topography and Monuments of Ancient Rome* (1904; 2nd edition, 1911); and *A Topographical Dictionary of Ancient Rome* (1929). A translation of the *Noctes Atticae*, which he had begun, was finished by Professor John C. Rolfe. The *Topographical Dictionary* was nearly completed in 1921, but Platner wished to add the finishing touches in Rome. On the voyage to Europe an attack of acute indigestion affected his heart, which was already weak, and caused his death. Thomas Ashby completed the *Dictionary*, which was published eight years later. It is a monument of sound scholarship, industry, and good judgment. The earlier book is an admirable handbook, and the *Dictionary* is indispensable to all who undertake serious work in the field of Roman topography. As a teacher Platner had no patience with slipshod work and chastised it with biting, though genial, sarcasm. He was extremely conservative and would gladly have kept the college curriculum as it was in his youth. Although most of his colleagues disagreed with his opinions, yet they appreciated so highly his ability and thorough culture as to put him in charge of the McBride Lectures, which became under his management an important element in the intellectual life of Cleveland.

[*Who's Who in America*, 1920–21; *Am. Jour. Archæology*, Jan.–Mar. 1922; *Am. Jour. Philology*, Jan.–Mar. 1922; *Classical Philology*, July 1922; *Yale Univ. Obit. Record*, 1922; *Reserve Weekly*, Sept. 28, 1921, and *Western Reserve Alumnus*, Sept. 1921; *Cleveland Plain Dealer*, Aug. 23, 1921; *Cleveland News*, Aug. 23, 1921; "Samuel Ball Platner, a Memorial Adopted by the Faculty of Adelbert College of Western Reserve University, 1921" (MS., in records of Faculty, Adelbert College.)]   H. N. F.